A
REFERENCE GRAMMAR
OF KOREAN

A
REFERENCE GRAMMAR
OF KOREAN

A Complete Guide
to the Grammar and History
of the Korean Language

SAMUEL E. MARTIN
Yale University

CHARLES E. TUTTLE COMPANY
Rutland, Vermont & Tokyo, Japan

Published by the Charles E. Tuttle Company, Inc.
of Rutland, Vermont and Tokyo, Japan,
with editorial offices at
Suido 1-chome, 2-6, Bunkyo-ku, Tokyo 112

© 1992 by Charles E. Tuttle Publishing Co., Inc.

All rights reserved

ISBN: 0-8048-1887-8
LCC Card No.: 92-62395

First edition, 1992

Printed in Japan

CONTENTS

Part I. KOREAN STRUCTURE
0.0. Introduction. ···1
  0.1. Background and acknowledgments. ···1
  0.2. The structure of the book. ··2
  0.3. Orientation. ··3
  0.4. Grammatical terms. ··3
  0.5. Citations. ···4
  0.6. Romanization. ···5
  0.7. Arbitrary conventions. ··5

1.0. Letters. ··6
  1.1. Hankul symbols. ··6
  1.2. Hankul spelling. ··7
  1.3. Yale Romanization. ··8
  1.4. Transliteration rules. ··9
  1.5. Reinforcement (-q). ···12
  1.6. Initial ¹ and ⁿ. ··15
  1.7. Hankul spelling of u after labials. ··18
  1.8. Word division and internal punctuation. ···18
  1.9. External punctuation. ···20
  1.10. Alphabetization. ··21

2.0. Sounds. ··23
  2.1. Phonemes and components. ··23
  2.2. Vowel descriptions. ··24
  2.3. The pseudo-vowel uy. ··26
  2.4. Consonant descriptions. ···27
  2.5. Syllable structure and consonant liaison. ··29
  2.6. Cluster restrictions. ··30
  2.7. Sequence variants. ···32
    2.7.1. Precision variants. ···32
    2.7.2. Vowel length variants. ···32
    2.7.3. Disappearing h. ··35
    2.7.4. Disappearing w. ···36
    2.7.5. Postvocalic u. ···37
    2.7.6. Intercalated semivowels. ··37
    2.7.7. Desyllabification of i, wu, and o. ··37

2.7.8. Reduction of **wie**. ··· 38
2.7.9. Vowel assimilation. ··· 38
2.8. Standardization variants. ··· 39
2.9. Intonations. ··· 41
2.10. The earlier phonology. ··· 42
  2.10.1. The earlier vowels. ··· 42
  2.10.2. The earlier initials. ··· 43
  2.10.3. Palatalization and dispalatalization. ··· 46
  2.10.4. Nasal epenthesis. ··· 48
  2.10.5. The earlier finals. ··· 49
  2.10.6. Intersyllabic strings; assimilations; conflation and compression. ··· 51
2.11. Lenitions and elisions; sources of *G*. ··· 53
  2.11.1. Velar lenition and elision. ··· 54
  2.11.2. Labial lenition and elision. ··· 56
  2.11.3. Apical lenition; elisions of **l** and **n**. ··· 57
  2.11.4. Sibilant lenition and elision. ··· 59
2.12. The accent of earlier forms. ··· 60
  2.12.1. Accentual patterns. ··· 62
  2.12.2. Accentual variants. ··· 64
  2.12.3. Accent suppression before particles. ··· 68
  2.12.4. The accentuation of verb forms. ··· 69
    2.12.4.1. Vowel-final monosyllabic stems that are rising. ··· 73
    2.12.4.2. Vowel-final monosyllabic stems that are low. ··· 75
    2.12.4.3. Vowel-final monosyllabic stems that are high. ··· 76
    2.12.4.4. Vowel-final monosyllabic stems that are high/low. ··· 79
    2.12.4.5. Bound stems. ··· 84
  2.12.5. Accent and spelling in Middle Korean texts. ··· 85
3.0. Words. ··· 86
3.1. Inflected and uninflected words. ··· 86
3.2. Parts of speech. ··· 88
3.3. Free and bound words. ··· 88
3.4. Ionized parts of speech. ··· 88
3.5. Shortened words. ··· 89
Chart: Parts of Speech. ··· 90
3.6. Vocabulary. ··· 94
3.7. Layers of vocabulary in earlier Korean. ··· 95
4.0. Shapes. ··· 98
4.1. Shape types. ··· 99
4.2. Syllable excess. ··· 100
  List of morph-final strings. ··· 101
  Examples of extra-syllabic excess. ··· 103
4.3. Treatment of **yey**. ··· 109
4.4. Alternations of **l** and **n**. ··· 110
4.5. Shape types of Chinese vocabulary. ··· 112
4.6. Chinese characters. ··· 113
Table: Shapes of Chinese morphemes. ··· 114
4.7. Characters with multiple readings. ··· 116
  4.7.1. Multiple readings: list one. ··· 116
  4.7.2. Multiple readings: list two. ··· 120
  4.7.3. Multiple readings: list three. ··· 122

Contents

    4.7.4. Index to the lists of multiple readings. ··123
    4.8. Chinese morphemes with basic l—. ···124
    4.9. Tongkwuk readings. ··126
  5.0. Forms: nouns. ···130
    5.1. One-shape and two-shape elements ··130
    5.2. Nouns. ···130
      5.2.1. Quasi-free nouns. ··131
      5.2.2. Free nouns. ···131
      5.2.3. Proper nouns; names and titles. ··132
      5.2.4. Deictics. ···133
      5.2.5. Adverbs. ··135
      5.2.6. Bound adverbs (preverbs, verb prefixes). ····································140
      5.2.7. Interjections. ···142
      5.2.8. Bound nouns. ···144
      5.2.9. Bound preparticle. ··145
    5.3. Adnouns and pseudo-adnouns. ··146
      5.3.1. Quasi-adnouns. ···150
      5.3.2. Numerals. See §5.5.1.
      5.3.3. Bound adnouns (prefixes). ···151
    5.4. Postnouns. ···156
      5.4.1. Postnoun/postmodifier adjectival noun (= adjectival postnoun/postmodifier). ············ 160
      5.4.2. Postsubstantives. ··160
        5.4.2.1. Postsubstantive adjectival noun. ···160
      5.4.3. Postmodifiers. ··160
        5.4.3.1. Postmodifier verbal noun intransitive (= inseparable
                adjectival postsubstantive). ···161
        5.4.3.2. Postmodifier adjectival nouns inseparable
                (= inseparable adjectival postmodifiers). ····························161
        5.4.3.3. Postmodifier adjectival nouns separable
                (= separable adjectival postmodifiers). ······························161
        5.4.3.4. Pre-inseparable postmodifier. ··161
      5.4.4. Counters. See §5.5.3.
      5.4.5. Bound postnouns (suffixes). ···162
        5.4.5.1. Core suffixes. ··162
        5.4.5.2. Chinese suffixes. ···165
    5.5. Numbers. ···171
      5.5.1. Number constructions. ··171
      5.5.2. Numerals. ··174
      5.5.3. Counters. ··179
      5.5.4. Irregular counting. ··185
      5.5.5. Fractions. ··188
    5.6. Verbal nouns. ···188
      5.6.1. Defective verbal nouns. ··189
      5.6.2. Transitive verbal nouns. ···190
      5.6.3. Intransitive verbal nouns. ··190
      5.6.4. Adjectival nouns. ··190
      5.6.5. Bound adjectival nouns. ···191
      5.6.6. Conversion constraints on verbal nouns. ·····································191
  6.0. Forms: particles. ···192
    6.1. Characteristics of particles. ···192

- 6.2. Quasi-particles. ...193
- 6.3. Extended particle phrases (phrasal postpositions). ...194
- 6.4. Particles proper. ...195
- 6.5. Particle sequences. ...197
  - 6.5.1. List of particle sequences arranged by prior member. ...199
  - 6.5.2. List of particle sequences arranged by latter member. ...206
- 6.6. Sequences of ending + particle. ...213
- 6.7. Some consequences of particle distribution. ...214
- Table of verb endings + particles and quasi-particles. ...215
- 7.0. Forms: verbs. ...216
- 7.1. Kinds of verbs. ...216
- 7.2. Bound verbs. ...219
  - 7.2.1. Defective infinitives. ...219
  - 7.2.2. Bound adjectives. ...220
  - 7.2.3. Bound postverbs. ...220
- 7.3. Defective verbs. ...220
- 7.4. Causative and passive verbs. ...221
- 7.5. Auxiliary verbs. ...226
- 7.6. Postnominal verbs. ...228
- 7.7. Recursiveness of auxiliary conversions. ...229
- Chart of double infinitive-auxiliary conversions. ...230
- 8.0. Stems. ...230
- 8.1. Conjugations. ...230
- 8.2. Consonant stems. ...231
  - 8.2.1. Stems ending in sonants. ...231
  - 8.2.2. Stems ending in h. ...232
  - 8.2.3. Stems ending in w: -w- (= -P/W-). ...233
  - 8.2.4. Stems ending in l: -T/L-. ...234
  - 8.2.5. S-dropping stems: -(s)-. ...236
- 8.3. Vowel stems. ...237
  - 8.3.1. L-doubling vowel stems: -LL-. ...238
  - 8.3.2. L-extending vowel stems: -L-. ...240
  - 8.3.3. L-inserting vowel stems. ...242
  - 8.3.4. Ambivalent stems: -(H)-. ...242
  - 8.3.5. Irregular stems: ha- and derivatives. ...243
  - 8.3.6. Irregular stems: k-inserting and n-inserting. ...243
- 9.0. Endings. ...244
- 9.1. Sequence positions. ...244
  - Table of endings. ...246
- 9.2. Assertive and attentive endings. ...248
- 9.3. Modifier endings. ...249
- 9.4. The infinitive. ...251
- 9.5. Substantives and derived substantives. ...254
- 9.6. Derived adverb-noun forms. ...255
- 9.7. Complex moods. ...257
  - 9.7.1. Complex moods built on the prospective modifier. ...257
  - 9.7.2. Adjunctives. ...258
  - 9.7.3. Complex moods built on the effective formative -˙ke-. ...258
  - 9.7.4. Gerund-related pseudo-moods. ...259
- 9.8. Transferentives. ...260

Contents

9.9. The structure of earlier verb endings. 260
  9.9.1. Middle Korean finite forms: the basic scheme. 261
  9.9.2. The effective. 262
  9.9.3. Emotives. 263
  9.9.4. Sentence types. 263
  9.9.5. Aspect marking of sentence types. 265
  9.9.6. Nonfinite endings. 265
  9.9.7. Nominalizers. 267
  9.9.8. Exaltation; the politeness marker (-ngi-). 268
  9.9.9. The deferential (-¨zop-). 268
  9.9.10. The modulator (-ˋw^{u}ɤo-). 269
  9.9.11. The copula. 273
10.0. Constructions. 274
  10.1. Problems of word division. 274
  10.2. Constructions and pseudo-constructions. 275
  10.3. Compounds and quasi-compounds. 278
  10.4. Phrases. 280
  10.5. Sentences. 281
  10.6. Sentences with multiple subjects and objects. 284
  10.7. Other views of Korean syntax. 286
  10.8. Syntactic constraints. 287
    10.8.1. Subject-object expansion constraints. 287
    10.8.2. Negative constraints. 289
    10.8.3. Active adjectives; resultative verbs. 289
    10.8.4. Constraints on modifiers. 290
    10.8.5. Auxiliary constraints. 290
    10.8.6. Emotive adjectives. 291
    10.8.7. Separability constraints; auxiliary preemphasis. 291
    10.8.8. Animate-inanimate constraints. 291
    10.8.9. Indirect-object intensification. 292
    10.8.10. Locative constraints. 294
    10.8.11. Copula and particle constraints. 295
    10.8.12. Miscellaneous constraints. 295
11.0. Conversions. 296
  11.1. Nuclear sentences and converted sentences. 296
  11.2. Status conversions. 298
  11.3. Style conversions. 299
    11.3.1. Casual sentences. 301
    11.3.2. Exclamatory sentences. 302
    11.3.3. Circumstantial sentences. 303
    11.3.4. Uncertainty sentences. 303
    11.3.5. Afterthought sentences. 303
  11.4. Tense-aspect conversions. 304
  11.5. Mood conversions. 305
    11.5.1. The plain style. 305
    Mood shift table. 306
    11.5.2. The familiar style. 307
    11.5.3. The intimate style. 308
    11.5.4. The casual intimate style. 308
    11.5.5. The casual polite style. 309

Contents

11.5.6. The semiformal (authoritative) style. 309
11.5.7. The polite style. 310
11.5.8. The formal style. 311
11.6. Voice conversions. 312
11.7. Negation conversions. 315
    11.7.1. Negatives and strong negatives. 315
    11.7.2. Negative preemphasis. 316
    11.7.3. Suppletive negatives. 318
    11.7.4. Negative commands and propositions. 320
    11.7.5. Negatives with verbal nouns. 321
    11.7.6. Double negatives. 321
    11.7.7. Other negative expressions. 322
    11.7.8. Negative sentences with positive force. 322
11.8. Nominalizations. 323
11.9. Adnominalizations; epithemes. 324
11.10. Adverbializations. 329
11.11. Quotations; oblique questions; putative structures. 331
11.12. Reflexive requests; favors. 333
11.13. Sentence connectors. 333
11.14. Apposition. 335
11.15. Order and recurrence of conversions. 335
11.16. Sentence generation. 336
12.0. Mimetics. 340
    12.1. Phonetic symbolism. 340
    12.2. Phonomimes and phenomimes. 340
    12.3. Intensives and paraintensives. 343
    12.4. Word isotopes. 343
    12.5. Mimetic constructions. 344
    12.6. Shapes of mimetic adverbs. 346
    12.7. Iteration. 347

Appendix 1. Lists of stem shapes. 348
Appendix 2. Korean surnames. 366
Appendix 3. Korean provinces. 370
Appendix 4. Japanese placenames. 371
Appendix 5. Radical names. 372
Appendix 6. List of Korean grammar terms. 380
Appendix 7. English index to the list of Korean grammar terms. 389
Appendix 8. Chronological list of texts. 397
Appendix 9. Alphabetical list of texts. 401

Bibliography. 407

Table of abbreviations. 414

Part II. Grammatical Lexicon 415

Index 957

PART 1

KOREAN STRUCTURE

PART 1

KOREAN STRUCTURE

A Reference Grammar of Korean

0.0. Introduction.

A Reference Grammar of Korean is a description of the language spoken in both north and south Korea in the second half of the 20th century. This material is given historical perspective by a description of the structure of the language of the Hankul texts of the second half of the fifteenth century and somewhat later, here called Middle Korean (MK); occasional reference is made to still earlier forms of the language, for which we have only very limited materials in the form of Chinese characters used for their sound value (i.e. as phonograms) or inferences that are made from systematic irregularities in the grammar of the earliest Hankul texts. Attention is paid also to dialect variation reported for the modern language and earlier speech. The core of the modern material reflects the pronunciation and usage of speakers who were born in Seoul before 1950, but that has been updated by observations of the speech habits of younger speakers, both in Seoul and elsewhere. In addition to direct elicitation, tape recordings, and written materials, VCR tapes of quite recent Seoul TV programs have provided authentic data of the contemporary usages referred to in various sections of the book. The sentences are presented in a Romanized form which can be readily converted to a Hankul representation, but they are intended to write spoken language, and do not always coincide with the prescribed spellings. The reader should be aware that Romanized forms such as **pat.e** and **iss.ey yo** are not mistakes, but represent the relaxed pronunciation of the Seoul speakers who have provided or checked them, though the speakers would indeed themselves write the words with the usually seen spellings "**pat.a**" and "**iss.e yo**", following the pronunciations heard in other areas and increasingly among younger speakers in Seoul.

Although a good deal is said about the history of sounds and forms, this work does not address questions of prehistory or genetic relationships. When references are made to Japanese, Chinese, or English data the intention is usually to show how the Korean counterparts are similar or different, or to add perspective on the meaning.

0.1. Background and acknowledgments.

This book has been put together over a period of more than forty years. The first version was written in 1960 under the Program in Uralic and Altaic Languages of the American Council of Learned Societies with support from the U.S. Office of Education. That version was later made available for a time through Bell-Howell. Meanwhile, after a trip to Korea in 1960, I set to work making many revisions and additions, resulting in the 1963 version, which I had hoped to turn into publishable form in fairly short order. The project was set aside, however, because of other priorities: publication of the Korean-English Dictionary and of the textbook Beginning Korean. Then I became deeply involved in writing A Reference Grammar of Japanese, which occupied my time and thoughts for eight years. In doing the research for that book I came to realize the inadequacies of the work I had done on Korean, especially in view of new ideas on Korean syntax which had appeared. Despite that, I decided to circulate photocopies of the 1963 version to a few colleagues for their comments and to use in Yale University seminars in the structure of the Korean language. As a result of similar seminars in the history of Korean, I came to feel the necessity of including materials from earlier centuries which provide perspective on the modern language, and that is what led to the dual nature of the book you see, for it attempts to set the synchronic description into its historical background, which often sheds revealing light on vexing problems.

While many of the example sentences are taken from published texts, most of the modern examples were elicited from Korean colleagues and informants, who were generous with their time and knowledge. I am particularly grateful to Sung-Un Chang (Cang Sengen) and Young-Sook Chang Lee ([¹Yi] Cang Yengswuk) who provided perception and insight, as well as many of the best examples; the late scholar Yang Ha Lee (¹Yi Yangha) was helpful during his collaboration with Sung-Un Chang and me while we were compiling our Korean-English Dictionary. In connection with another project I was able to elicit examples from Sek Yen [Kim] Cho ([Co] Kim Sek.yen) which were useful for this book. I have built upon earlier linguistic work published by Fred Lukoff and Elinor Clarke Horne, and I have freely incorporated material from their books. I have culled good examples from teaching materials prepared by Edward W. Wagner and the excellent textbooks of the Myongdo Language Institute prepared by A.V. Vandesande and colleagues. I have also used to advantage materials found in works by linguists in Korea, both the south and the north. In 1961 I enjoyed some excellent discussions with, among others, Woong Huh (He Wung), Hie-seung Lee ([1]Yi Huysung), Nam Tuk Lee ([1]Yi Namtek), Sung Ny(e)ong Lee ([1]Yi Swungnyeng), Chang-Hai Park (Pak Changhay), and Bong Nam Park (Pak Pongnam), whose textbook for the Foreign Service Institute was helpful. I am grateful to Fred Lukoff for introducing me to MaengSung Lee ([1]Yi Mayngseng), whose assistance in checking delicate points of syntax was of great value. I learned much from my students, not only at Yale but at the University of Washington and at the University of Hawaii, many of whom have become eminent scholars and teachers. In particular, I have been much helped by the stimulating ideas through the years of S. Robert Ramsey and, more recently, J. Ross King; both have been excellent critics who shaped my thinking in many ways. Seungja Choi (Choy Sungca) and Sun-Hee Kim (Kim Senhuy) have provided excellent observations and examples. The final manuscript was read by Choi, King, and Ramsey, who suggested many corrections and improvements, most of which I was able to include. I began this final revision of the work in 1989, while on a sabbatical term at the Center for Korean Studies of the University of Hawaii, where both Dong-Jae Lee ([1]Yi Tongcay) and Ho-min Sohn (Son Homin) gave generous consultation and assistance. I am grateful to them and also to other members of the Center and of the Department of East Asian Languages and the Department of Linguistics for the various facilities they provided. Byron Bender, Robert Hsu, G.B. Mathias, Albert Schütz, and J.M. Unger helped make that half year both productive and pleasant. A great many other scholars of the past and the present, including the late Hyon-Pai Choi (Choy Hyenpay), contributed to the ideas in this book through their published writings and private discussions, and their names will be found throughout the book and in the bibliography. I would be remiss not to mention my indebtedness for information on the modern language to Suk-Jin Chang (Cang Sekcin), Choy Hak.kun, Min-Soo Kim (Kim Minswu), Young-Key Kim-Renaud (Kim Yengki), Kim Thaykyun, Ko Yengkun, Ki-Shim Nam (Nam Kisim), Seok-Choong Song [Song Sekcwung], In-Seok Yang ([1]Yang Insek), Joe Jung-No Ree ([1]Yi Cenglo), Ki-dong Lee ([1]Yi Kitong), and many others mentioned in the following pages. For information on the older language I appreciate the fine work of Huh Woong (He Wung), Wan-jin Kim (Kim Wancin), Kim Minswu, Gwang U Nam (Nam Kwangwu), Kōno Rokurō, Ki-Moon Lee ([1]Yi Kimun), and Sung Ny(e)ong Lee ([1]Yi Swungnyeng), among others, and I hold ever deepening respect for the prodigious achievements of the late Chang-Ton Yu ([1]Yu Changton).

In citing personal names here and in the bibliography I have tried to include the Romanized form preferred by the person, when that is known to me, accompanied by a consistent version in the Yale Romanization. When information on personal preference was not available to me, I cite only the Yale version. To insure consistency, the Yale form is generally used in references within the book.

The preparation of the camera-ready copy of this book was much facilitated by the technical expertise and wisdom of my colleague and mentor Rufus S. Hendon, who has been helpful at every step of the way. His willingness to create and share software to answer my needs is deeply appreciated, as is his patient guidance through difficult problems, where his advice has been unfailingly sound.

0.2. The structure of the book.

A Reference Grammar of Korean is divided into two parts. Part I is a systematic survey of the structure, in which we examine problems of orthography and grammar, set up a system of parts of speech, analyze the constituents of sentences, and explore systematic relationships between sentences.

Part II is a grammatical lexicon, an alphabetically arranged list of particles, endings, affixes, auxiliary verbs, and other grammatically interesting elements, along with certain additional words (including ordinary nouns and verbs) to which quick reference may help clarify the other words listed. This part is not a substitute for a dictionary, since it does not contain most of the "content" words of the lexicon. It was my intention to make the list so complete that the user would find sufficient information about each element of a sentence, other than the meaning of nouns and verb stems, to figure out the grammar of any sentence and be able to translate it accurately.

The various appendix lists are intended to help the user find the meaning or shape of terms not easily located elsewhere, as well as other information that is relatively inaccessible in other sources.

0.3. Orientation.

This book is not trying to prove a theory about the nature of language. I do not maintain that the structure of a language is either discoverable or describable in one and only one "correct", or even uniquely "best", way. The criteria for judging a description vary with the purpose for which it is intended. For a reference grammar the most important criterion is balanced completeness. As much useful information as possible must be given in a form that makes it readily accessible to the user. The information that is most often, or most sorely, needed should be the easiest to get at. Lists are not to be scorned; formulas are not to be worshipped. Economy of statement is a technical criterion relevant to the accessibility of the information; elegance of statement is a psychological criterion relevant to the impact of the information.

Just what information is useful and for whom? The foreigner who is decoding (making out the meaning of) messages spoken or written in Korean is concerned, first of all, with the CONSTITUENCY of sentences. Given a sentence, he wants to know what are its pieces and how do they fit together. He needs to be able to take the sentence apart, to "parse" it. The foreigner who is encoding (making up) messages in Korean is interested in the MANIPULATION of sentences. Given known sentences, what new but related sentences can he say that will be understood and accepted by Koreans? Up to the sentence level our presentation is in terms of item and arrangement: the items are morphemes (words or parts of words), and the arrangement is stated in terms of immediate constituents (IC's) or, in a few cases, unordered strings. Beyond the sentence level, the presentation is in terms of item and process: the items are certain types of simplex sentences, and the processes are CONVERSIONS that turn these into more complex structures.

0.4. Grammatical terms.

You may find the terminology unfamiliar and irksome. If so, think of the categories in terms of concrete representations. Should you not feel comfortable referring to a common form of the verb as the "gerund", take that just to mean "the -ko form" of that verb — or, if you prefer, "the hako form". The grammatical categories of Korean are numerous, diverse, and complexly represented. They cannot easily be put into a frame of reference based on the descriptions of other languages. But in practice it is convenient to choose terms that are somewhat familiar, supplemented when necessary by new terms made up by analogy, with the clear understanding that NO DIRECT CORRESPONDENCE is intended with the categories of other languages that are given similar names.

The set of names found in this book has grown out of terms used in earlier books; many of them stem from Elinor Clark Horne and our teacher Bernard Bloch. One that has troubled many people is "infinitive" for the -e ending. Regardless of the merits of the word itself, the name has become so widespread in discussions of the grammar of Japanese (where it refers to the -i form, sometimes called "continuative stem") that it has surely become the standard. For what is here called the "summative" I earlier applied Horne's term "nominative", but that is better used in reference to the case-marking function of the particle ... i/ka, and so I have abandoned its use for any other purpose. The word "substantive" is sometimes used as a general term for "noun", but here it is narrowed in definition to one of the endings (-um) that make the verb into a form that is used like a noun; other such forms are the summative -ki and the "derived noun" -i. For the -key ending I have changed the earlier term "adverbial" to "adverbative" so that "adverbial" can be used to discuss syntactic phenomena only. I adopt Wagner's term "purposive" to refer to the -ule ending, but what he calls the "expository" is here called the "sequential" (the -uni ending), and what he called the "effective" is called the "projective" (the -tolok ending), so that the term "effective" can designate an aspect marker of Middle Korean (-˙$k^{e}a$- or -˙^{e}a-). In speaking of sentence styles I continue to use "authoritative" to refer to verb forms ending in -o/-so (etc.), as a synonym for "semiformal", Wagner's term, which characterizes the style in a broader way.

0.5. Citations.

Examples taken from modern written materials are not always attributed to the source, since they have frequently been edited as the result of elicitation. Examples from earlier texts are cited by date, text, and page. Two lists of these texts are appended: one arranged chronologically, the other alphabetically. Some of the dates are questionable; I have done my best to make practical decisions on the basis of the bibliographical materials available to me, and to add question marks when they seem appropriate. The intention is to give a specific date whenever possible.

The translations of the text sentences are mostly my own, sometimes made in consultation with others. I believe they are adequate to convey the meanings of the grammatical structures, but I have made only a limited effort to check the translation of philosophical concepts involved in Buddhism or references to ancient China. Chinese names, whether modern or ancient, are given in the now standard Pīnyīn Romanization. References to Middle Chinese forms of the 7th century follow the notations used for similar purposes in Martin 1987 and represent rough approximations to the pronunciation of northern China in the 7th century, along the lines of the phonemic analysis in Martin 1953.

Modern Korean forms are printed in boldface; forms of earlier Korean are printed in italics. The handling of vowel distinctions is slightly different in the Romanization as used to represent the premodern spellings and that used for the modern language. In citing pre-1933 spellings which retain obsolete features (such as the low back vowel *o* that mostly became **a-** and **-u-** in Seoul) the notation writes *wu* and *wo* for all cases of the back rounded vowels, *u* and *o* for all cases of the back unrounded. This "expansive" notation is shown in the italic font used for the Middle Korean forms. Forms from Ceycwu island, which retains the low back vowel (pronouncing it as rounded but distinct from *wo*), are cited in the same way. Unless otherwise specified, an italicized word is to be taken as Middle Korean. When a Chinese character in a Middle Korean text is accompanied by a Hankul syllable to show the prescribed readings, that syllable is printed in small italic capitals. When the character fails to carry a notation of the reading (as in 1481 Twusi) we get the reading from the prescriptions in 1447 Tongkwuk cengwun and put brackets around the word; if the reading is unavailable in Tongkwuk, we infer it from other sources and put an asterisk before the string of small capitals used to represent the syllable.

The quotation marks around forms cited from pre-Hankul sources are intended to remind us that the phonograms are interpreted faute de mieux in terms of their mid-15th century Hankul values; the semantograms (characters used for their meanings) are given as small-capital English words. The Yale Romanization is used for Japanese words, which are underlined. Sanskrit and Chinese words are not typographically differentiated from English, but the diacritic marks usually make them obvious.

Examples were chosen purely to illustrate structural patterns, and I have made no effort to alter ideological, religious, or sexist content that may seem quaint or even offensive. Notice that the term "vulgar" as used here does not mean obscene; rather, it refers to quite colloquial forms, including slang, that are generally avoided in writing and in less relaxed speech.

References to North Korean data are mostly taken from Cosen mal sacen (NKd) and Cosen-e munqpep (CM). As Kim Minswu 1985 points out, there were three distinct periods of prescriptive standardization in North Korea, referred to by the names of the authoritative publications: 1945-54 (the Thongil-an period), 1954-66 (the Chelqcaq-pep period) and 1966- (the Kyupem-cip period). In 1954, after using the unified spelling system that dates from the 1933 Thongil-an, North Korea published Cosen chelqcaq-pep, which introduced a number of changes, such as using the apostrophe for the **sai phyo** that is here Romanized as ···q (§1.5). Some of the changes were abandoned, in whole or in part, with publication of the 1966 Cosen mal kyupem cip, which made efforts to create a normalized "munhwa-e" (cultural language) that incorporated a few dialect or outdated elements (Kim Minswu 1985:129), including **iya yo** for the polite copula that is treated as **iey yo** in modern Seoul. And the 1966 rules prescribed the artificial pronunciation of /l/ (as a flap r) rather than /n/ for the initial of words here Romanized as ^{1}n··· which come from Chinese l···, including ^{1}i(···) and ^{1}y···, where the initial is elided in the south and was at one time pronounced with n··· in the north. (See §1.6.)

A Reference Grammar of Korean

0.6. Romanization.

There are a number of systems for writing Korean words in Romanized form, depending on the purposes for doing so. The popular McCune-Reischauer Romanization, which received official sanction from the Ministry of Education in 1988, tries to approximate the way a Korean word sounds to the American ear, disregarding its internal structure and history. It is generally preferred in citing Korean names and in casually mentioning Korean words in English context. The Yale Romanization, like the various systems of Hankul spelling, takes account of more than just the sound. The two given names **Pok.nam** and **Pongnam** are both written "Pongnam" in the McCune-Reischauer system, but they are kept distinct both in Hankul and in the Yale Romanization. The two surnames **Yang** and **¹Yang** are spelled with the Hankul equivalents of "Yang" and "Lyang" in North Korea, but both are written "Yang" in South Korea and in the McCune-Reischauer Romanization. Four names can be shown as different by the Yale Romanization (**Yang Pok.nam, Yang Pongnam, ¹Yang Pok.nam, ¹Yang Pongnam** — and four more if there are people named **Pok.lam** and **Pong.lam**) but will all be treated alike by the McCune-Reischauer spelling "Yang Pongnam" (or "Yang Bongnam" if the space is ignored). Numerous problems of detail have to be handled arbitrarily in each system of spelling, whether it be Hankul or Romanization. The forms cited for the modern language in this book are not merely mechanical transliterations of Hankul spellings in one or another orthographic standard, but offer additional information about the background of the forms, including phonological details often ignored in Hankul. Koreans may be particularly irritated by the generous sprinkling of "⋯q" to mark certain reinforcements that go unmarked in the usual Hankul spellings. In particular, notations reflecting what is sometimes called "n-epenthesis" (see §1.5), such as **mōsq ip.e** and **anq ip.e** or **mōsq yel.e** and **anq yel.e**, may strike the eye as unnecessary nuisances, since the phenomenon they represent is not immediately apparent to the naive ear. The current trend in Hankul orthography (especially for words with Chinese components such as **munqpep** 'grammar') is to ignore most of the cases of reinforcement, including many of those which come from the Middle Korean adnominal particle *s*. Perhaps it would be more congenial if we made the notation smaller or subscript (**mōs$_q$ ip.e, an$_q$ ip.e**) or used a flimsier symbol, such as the apostrophe, here unavailable because it is needed for other purposes. But we will retain the full notation and invite readers to ignore it when that seems appropriate, as this book often does in alphabetizing lists.

0.7. Arbitrary conventions.

The notational devices and the decisions on punctuation, capitalization, and word division will strike you at times as needlessly fussy or cranky, and of less interest to the student than they are to the technical linguist. Feel free to simplify, modify, and adapt the notations to your own needs. I have attempted to present the material in a manner intended to be maximally useful, one that can be readily converted to that of other systems which retain less information. Decisions on the use of hyphens, apostrophes, and spaces may seem arbitrary in particular cases, as when we write "na-ka-, na-o-, na-su-" and "ka-po-" (but "wā po-"); they are intended to make it easier to identify the phrases. The apostrophe shows where a sound or a string of sounds is omitted in an abbreviation, as in **kanta 'yss.ta < kanta (ko) hayss.ta** 'said (that) he was going'.

Sentences of Romanized Korean, like those of English, begin with capitalized letters, as do names. But both the citation and the translation of the Middle Korean and Ceycwu examples begin uncapitalized. In the italic notations, *W* and *G* represent the voiced fricatives [β] and [γ]. (We have chosen not to use lowercase *v* and *g*, in part because of fear that they would be susceptible to misinterpretation, though these letters would be consistent with our use of *z* for the voiced sibilant.) The capital letters "C" and "V" are used in formulas to mean "(any) consonant" and "(any) vowel"; in other contexts "v" or "V" represents "verb (stem/form)". For both varieties of the Yale Romanization we use the conventional digraph "ng" to represent the velar nasal, rather than the single symbol provided by the phonetic notation [ŋ]. Specifically phonetic notations are usually put between brackets. Specifically phonemic notations are in boldface or italic between slashes, as in "**/ng/** and */ng/* are pronounced as the velar nasal [ŋ]". Brackets are also used to demarcate ellipted words, or parts of words, and elisions of a phoneme or a string of phonemes. When the slash is between two words or letters, it has the usual meaning of "or (optionally)". Material within parentheses may be either enlargements or optional replacements; the context should make the intention clear.

When a Korean citation is within an English sentence, the gloss (translation) is set off with single quotation marks, as in "The word **koki** 'meat', for example, ... ", but the marks are omitted for the glosses of examples not embedded in such context, since the demarcations are obvious.

The macron is used to mark long vowels in modern words like **tōn** 'money', **nwūn** 'snow', **ūmsik** 'food', **sīl** 'thread', **sēm** 'island', and **pām** 'chestnut', though the distinction of long and short vowels has been largely lost by younger Seoul speakers. The dots in the Middle Korean words represent the distinctive pitch of the following syllable (one dot for high, two dots for low rise), and unmarked syllables are treated as low, provided the text is one that normally marked the accent. The position of the dots is kept just where it is in the original text, so that *swon* 'guest' + *i* [nominative particle] is written *swo·n i* (1445 ¹Yong 28) and pronounced *swoni*. The spaces and hyphens correspond to nothing overt in the spellings or pronunciations; they are there just to help your eye identify words and parts of words. MK nouns that appear in an environment where a basic final ···*h* after a vowel or a resonant is suppressed (and not shown by the Hankul) are Romanized as ···*V[h]*, ···*l[h]*, ···*n[h]*. But for the other syllable-excess nouns (§4.2) no indication is given of the basic shape before the reduction: the shapes are written according to the spellings in the texts, which most often indicate the syllables heard rather than the underlying forms.

1.0. Letters.

Korean words can be spelled out with foreign letters of various kinds, including the familiar Roman letters used in this book, or with letters created in Korea by King Seycong and promulgated in 1445. Words of Chinese origin are often written with Chinese characters either alone, without letters to represent the pronunciation, or added in parentheses to identify a word difficult to understand from the sound alone. In modern south Korea it is a matter of controversy whether the continued use of Chinese characters should be encouraged or discouraged.

1.1. Hankul symbols.

Koreans usually write in an alphabet known as Hankul. As a result, the word Hankul is also used to mean 'Korean language, especially as written' and 'Korean letters = literature'. In the system of writing there are symbols to represent each of the phonemes of Korean. The term "Hankul" was first used by Cwu Sikyeng in 1910; earlier the symbols were called **ēnmun**. It is possible to use the system as we use Roman letters, writing horizontally across the line letter by letter: that is called **kalo-ssuki** 'horizontal writing'. But usually the symbols are joined into written syllables, which often but not always correspond to spoken syllables. The written syllables are made up of an "initial" consonant (including zero) + a vowel nucleus or "medial", consisting of a vowel or a semivowel (**y** or **w**) + a vowel, written as a unit. The vowel is sometimes followed by a "final" consonant or two-consonant cluster that is called by the Korean grammarians **pat.chim** 'pedestal'. The syllables are written as blocks (called "logotypes" by 1893 Scott) designed to resemble the shape and spacing of Chinese characters, which are still often used to write, or to clarify, Chinese words in the midst of native Korean words. The initial is written at the top, the nucleus either on the right (those containing **a** or **e** or **i**) or below (those containing **u** or **wu** or **o**). A final **pat.chim** is placed below everything — and slightly to the right, if it is but a single consonant. The shapes of the symbols are altered a bit when they appear in different positions. For example, before **a** the **k** swoops back to the left 가 **ka**, but astride the **o** it has a straighter fall 고 **ko**, and the final **k** is longer, flatter, and straighter: 막 **mak**.

Since there are a limited number of Hankul symbols, representing the basic phonemes of Korean, we can substitute our Roman letters for the Hankul letters with no loss of information. If we are consistent, the Roman transcription can be automatically converted into the Hankul version and vice versa. There are several ways in which Korean can be Romanized, and each scheme involves certain difficulties and special rules. The system used in this book takes time to get used to, because it is designed to be typographically simple by avoiding "odd" letters, such as ŏ (= e) and ŭ (= u). But once you are familiar with the system, it is very easy to use; you will find it more flexible than other systems of putting Korean into Roman letters. With this system anything written in Hankul can be typed out on an ordinary English typewriter or computer keyboard with no special tricks.

How many different syllables does Korean have? For the modern language, computer codes allow about 2,500 Hankul syllables to be differentiated. Using all conceivable sequences, including many that do not occur in any word, [1]Yu Huy (1824 Enmun-ci 18) came up with the staggering number of 10,250 possible syllables. And Kim Hyenglyong (1985:31) found a total of 11,172 different orthographic (= morphophonemic) syllables. His study (31-2) found the total number of different two-syllable strings (morphophonemic dissyllables) to be 31,759,684, of these types (V includes yV):

Type	Example	Strings
1. V-V	oi	441
2. V-VC	a.yang	11,907
3. V-CV	oli	7,938
4. V-CVC	yūceng	214,326
5. CV-V	kyŏ.yey	7,938
6. CV-CV	cwuchey	142,884
7. CV-VC	kyōyang	214,326
8. CV-CVC	pītan	3,857,868
9. VC-V	Yenge	11,907
10. VC-CV	ak.ki	214,326
11. VC-VC	ek.yang	321,489
12. VC-CVC	wūntong	5,186,802
13. CVC-V	kak.o	214,326
14. CVC-CV	sokto	3,857,868
15. CVC-VC	cengqyel	5,186,802
16. CVC-CVC	hyek.myeng	12,308,536

1.2. Hankul spelling.

Koreans, like speakers of English, have spelling problems. Although the Hankul system of writing is very simple, it is not easy to devise a consistent system for spelling out the words of the language. That is because the structure of Korean is somewhat complicated, in that words and parts of words often change the way they sound depending on the words around them. The Korean writer has a choice: he can use the Hankul symbols (or their Roman equivalents) to write phrases EXACTLY AS THEY SOUND, or he can write individual words and parts of words ALWAYS THE SAME WAY regardless of changes in sound. The first method, known as a PHONEMIC orthography, has the advantage that even a foreigner beginning his study of Korean can read sentences without learning a lot of special rules; and he can write down everything he hears – provided he hears accurately – without worrying about what words the phrases contain. But the disadvantage to the reader who already knows the language is obvious: the same word appears sometimes in one shape, sometimes in another. For that reason, native speakers of Korean naturally prefer some sort of MORPHOPHONEMIC orthography, as linguists call the second kind of spelling. Morphophonemic spelling tells the reader a lot about the grammar of the phrase he is reading, since it tries to spell each word (or part of a word) always in the same basic shape, with the expectation that the reader will be able to apply a set of rules that will automatically produce the particular phonemic shape needed to pronounce the phrase. We do something similar in English when we write our plural ending as "s" both after "cat", where it is pronounced as an s, and after "dog", where it is pronounced as a z.

The difficulties that arise in using a morphophonemic orthography are of three kinds:

(1) How far should we go in analyzing words into parts? How can we be sure we have the "same" word-part (= morpheme or string of morphemes) in different words? To what extent should we allow our knowledge, or someone's knowledge, of the history of the words to influence the decision?

(2) When there are several spoken variants for a word, should we try to settle on one as the "standard" form and ignore the others when we write? Perhaps we can let two or more forms coexist as MODEL AND SHORTENING, as with the English forms "do not" and "don't"; or as LITERARY AND COLLOQUIAL, like English "unto" and "to"; or as DIALECT AND STANDARD, like English "dreamt" and "dreamed", "dove" and "dived".

(3) What specific spelling devices should we use to handle certain tricky problems, such as reinforcement (the **sai sios** or **-q** phenomena, §1.5) or the complications of initial l and n which lead to the use of the superscript letters [1] and [n] in the Yale Romanization (§1.6)?

Koreans have contended with these problems for many years, and there have been several attempts to prescribe consistent and comprehensive spelling systems. Two spelling systems have come to enjoy wide use in the years since the end of World War II. One is the official system of South Korea (the Republic of Korea), sometimes called the **Thŏngil-an** or Unified System; the other is that of North Korea (the Democratic People's Republic of Korea or DPRK). The two systems are almost identical in the way they treat problems of the first and second types; they differ in their approach to problems of the third type. Since each system has some advantages, and both are widely used and sanctioned, the spellings of this book are designed to convert into either system automatically. Both systems have undergone several minor revisions and the usages reflected in this book may be modified in future revisions of the systems.

1.3. Yale Romanization.

In the system of Yale Romanization used in this book, the dot or period is used within a word for several purposes, some more important than others:

(1) The dot is used to indicate the "zero" (vowel) beginning of a syllable or other ambiguous situations when the preceding Hankul syllable ends in a **pat.chim** (final) consonant: **mek.e, mek.ko, mek.hinta**. Of course, when the boundary is shown by a space or a hyphen, the dot is unnecessary: **Puk Han** 'North Korea', **kak-kak** "each separately".

(2) The dot is also used to distinguish **e.yV** from **eyV**, **ay.V** from **ayV**, **u.yV** from **uyV**, and **o.yV** from **oyV**. We use the digraphs **ey**, **ay**, **uy**, and **oy** as UNITS except when a dot intervenes. The dot is omitted, however, when the y follows yo because there is no string *yoy, so there is no possibility of misinterpreting the syllable division in a word like **kyōyuk** 'education'. In a word like **mu.yek** 'trade' the dot is just a reminder, because in modern Korean **uy** does not occur after a labial. In a word like **kup.wu** 'classmate', the dot is not strictly necessary, since the syllable /pwu/ is simplified to the spelling **pu** (modern Korean lacks the unrounded syllable */pu/), but I retain the dot for clarity.

(3) A third use of the dot is to remind the reader of the automatic morphophonemic rules (sound changes) between two consonants: ···**th.t**··· is pronounced ···**tt**···, ···**ch.s**··· is pronounced ···**ss**···, etc.; ···**p.m**··· is pronounced ···**mm**···, ···**n.l**··· is pronounced ···**ll**···; in verb forms ···**n.t**··· is pronounced as if ···**ntt**···, ···**n.k**··· as if ···**nkk**···, ···**n.c**··· as if ···**ncc**···, ···**n.s**··· as if ···**nss**···. If we were not trying to follow the Hankul spelling systems, which ignore all three kinds of sound changes, we would spell the verb forms ···**mqt**···, ···**nqk**···, ···**nqc**···, ···**nqs**···, etc.

In the third use, the dot can be omitted with no loss of essential information about Hankul spelling or even (given knowledge in the last case that the word is a verb form) the ultimate pronunciation, and that is what we do in using the Romanization in English contexts, such as the Bibliography. In the first two uses the dot is essential to recover all the word-structure information contained in the Hankul spelling; in the second use it is required as a result of choosing digraphs to write some of the vowels.

In later sections the sound system of Korean is discussed in terms of the Romanization, and the several digraphs are treated as single units. The consonants are represented by **p t c k s, pp tt cc kk ss, ph th ch kh h, m n ng l**; the vowel nuclei are represented by **i ey ay u e a wu** (abbreviated to **u** after a labial) **o oy, yey yay ye ya yu** (an abbreviation of **ywu**) **yo, wi wey way we wa**. In addition the letter **q** is used as a special morphophonemic symbol to show reinforcement (see §1.5), and superscript [1]··· and [n]··· show differences between the spelling systems of the two Koreas (see §1.6). In this book

A Reference Grammar of Korean

the length of a long vowel, ignored in the usual Hankul spelling, is shown by a macron (a line above the vowel); see §2.7.2.

1.4. Transliteration rules.

Here are the complete rules for transcribing Hankul into the Yale Romanization, with the exception of the problems of [1]..., [n]..., and ...q, which are covered in the following sections. The Romanization uses 16 of the usual 26 Roman letters, plus the digraph ng, final ...q, and initial superscript [1]... and [n].... You will occasionally find other superscripts used to show divergences between the spellings of the two Koreas: [s] in iss.[s]o and iss.[s]up.nita; [h] in an[h]ay (see §2.8); [y] in ph[y]ēy and m[y]ēy (see §4.3). In the table of rules the word "space" means "space, hyphen, or other punctuation", C means consonant, 0 means initial zero (the syllable starts with a vowel, y, or w).

CONSONANTS

Hankul	Initial	Example	Final	Examples
ㄱ	k	kikwu	k(.) + m n l	sik.mo (or sikmo)
				kyek.nyen (or kyeknyen)
				tok.lip (or toklip)
			k. + k h 0	sik.kwu, kak.ha, mek.e
			k	yak, siktang, [1]yukpun, mekca, [1]yuksip, patak, ...
ㅋ	kh	khal	kh + space	puekh
			kh(.) + C	puekh.teyki (or puekhteyki)
			kh. + 0	puekh.an (but better written as two words)
ㄲ	kk	kkay	kk + space	pakk
			kk + 0 k (kh)	kkakk.un, kkakk.ko
			kk(.)	kkakk.ta (or kkakkta), kkakk.nun (or kkakknun)
ㅂ	p	papo	p(.) + m n l	ip.mun (or ipmun)
				ip.nap (or ipnap)
				sip.lyuk (or siplyuk)
			p. + p h 0	kup.po, ip.hak, ip.e
			p	ip, ipta, ipko, ipsang, ipcang, ...
ㅍ	ph	pha	ph + space	iph
			ph(.) + C	aph.cang (or aphcang)
			ph. + 0	aph.aph-i
ㅃ	pp	ppye	–	–
ㄷ	t	titinta	t + space	kot
			t. + t h 0	tat.ta
				tat.hinta
				tat.un
			t(.)	tat.chinta (or tatchinta), tat.ko (or tatko), tat.nun (or tatnun), ...
ㅌ	th	thal	th + space	path
			th. + 0	puth.e
			th(.) + C	puth.ta (or puthta), puth.ci (or puthci), puth.nun (or puthnun), ...

Hankul	Initial	Example	Final	Examples
ㄸ	tt	ttal	–	–
ㅈ	c	cal	c + space	nac
			c. + c h 0	mac.ci
				mac.hinta
				mac.un
			c(.)	mac.ta (or macta),
				mac.chwunta (or macchwunta),
				mac.nun (or macnun)
ㅊ	ch	cha	ch + space	kkoch
			ch(.) + 0	coch.a
			ch(.)	coch.ko (or cochko), coch.ci (or cochci),
				coch.nun (or cochnun)
ㅉ	cc	ccanta	–	–
ㅅ	s	san	s + space	os
			s. + s 0	wūs.^{s}up.nita
				wus.e
			s(.)	wūs.ko (or wūsko), wūs.ci (or wūsci),
				wūs.nun (or wūsnun)
ㅆ	ss	ssal	ss. + s 0	iss.^{s}o
				iss.e
			ss(.)	iss.ta (or issta), iss.ko (or issko),
				iss.nun (or issnun)
ㅎ	h	hay	h. + 0	noh.a
			h(.)	noh.ko (or nohko), noh.ci (or nohci),
				noh.nun (or nohnun)
ㅁ	m	mal	m. + 0	sim.e
			m(.) + l	chim.lyak (or chimlyak)
			m	nam, simpang, sīmnun, chāmko
			(But CF §8.1.1	sīm.ko, sīm.ta, sīm.ci.)
ㄴ	n	nal	n. + 0	sin.e
			n(.) + l	Sin.la (or Sinla), Cen.la (or Cenla)
			n	an, sinnun, sinmun, cīnpo,
				^{n}yento, ^{n}yenkam, mence, ...
			(But CF §8.1.1	sin.ko, sin.ta, sin.ci.)
ㄹ	l	latio	l. + 0	sil.ep
			l(.) + n	il.nyen (or ilnyen)
			l	kil, silkwa, silqswu, mullon,
				ppalli, kolmu, kīlta, ...
ㅇ	(ZERO)	al, yen, wenca	ng(.) + l	seng.lip (or senglip)
			ng	pang, tong-an, congi,
				cwungang, thōngil
ㄺ	–	–	lk. + k h 0	ilk.ko, ilk.hinta, ilk.e
			lk(.)	ilk.nun (or ilknun), malk.ta (or malkta),
				pulk.ci (or pulkci), ...

A Reference Grammar of Korean

Hankul	Initial	Example	Final	Examples
ㄼ	–		lp. + p h 0	nelp.e, nelp.hinta
			lp(.)	nelp.ko (or nelpko), nelp.ci (or nelpci), nelp.ni (or nelpni)
ㄿ	–		lph. + 0	ulph.e
			lph(.)	ulph.ko (or ulphko), ulph.nun (or ulphnun), ...
ㄻ	–		lm. + m 0	talm.un
			lm(.)	tālm.nun (or tālmnun)
			(But CF §8.1.1	tālm.ko, tālm.ta, tālm.ci.)
ㄾ	–		lth. + 0	halth.e, halth.un
			lth(.)	halth.ko (or halthko), halth.nun (or halthnun)
ㅀ	–		lh. + 0	ilh.e, ilh.un
			lh(.)	ilh.ko (or ilhko), ilh.nun (or ilhnun), ...
ㄹㅅ	–		ls + space	kols, tols, ols
ㅄ	–		ps + space	kaps
			ps. + s 0	ēps.^{s}up.nita
				ēps.e
			ps(.)	ēps.ta (or ēpsta), ēps.nun (or ēpsnun), ...
ㄵ	–		nc. + c 0	anc.ci
				anc.e
			nc(.)	anc.ko (or ancko), anc.nun (or ancnun), ...
ㄶ	–		nh. + 0	mānh.i
			nh(.)	mānh.ta (or mānhta), mānh.ni (or mānhni)

MEDIALS

Hankul	Romanized	Examples
ㅣ	i	pi, īs.ta, oi
ㅟ	wi	twī, chwuwi, wiseng
ㅢ	uy	uyca, cwuuy, ūyuy, huyta
ㅜ	u after p ph pp m	pul, phul, pun, mun
	wu elsewhere	wuli, hwū, nwun, twūl, kkwum
ㅠ	.yu after a e o (u)	ye.yu, ca.yu, sō.yu
	yu elsewhere	yuli, kyul, hyung, wuyu
ㅡ	u	un, kum, khuta; papputa (§1.7)
ㅔ	e	emeni, khe (yo), pappe, tewuk
ㅙ	we	wenca, kwen, il-wel
ㅕ	.ye after a e o (u)	ca.yen, he.yeng, mo.ye
	ye elsewhere	yek, ^{n}yen, ^{l}yen.ay, kyewul
ㅐ	ey	ney, cēy-il, kakey, pheyn
ㅖ	.yey after a e o (u)	a.yey, no.yey = no^{l}yey, ku.yey
	yey elsewhere	yēysan, ^{l}yēypay, kyēysita
ㅞ	.wey after a e o u	[rare]
	wey elsewhere	wēynq il, kwēy
ㅗ	o	oi, hao, mom, tōn, os, kōpta
ㅛ	.yo after a e o (u wu)	hwā.yo(il), he.yong, sō.yong
	yo elsewhere	yōkwu, yōngpi, iyo, phyo

Hankul	Romanized	Examples
ㅚ	oy	ōykwuk, kkoy, sīoy, poynta
ㅏ	a	ama, koa, tong-an, hāyan
ㅘ	wa	wā (se), pwā, towa, cwāsek
ㅑ	.ya after a e o (u)	a.ya, se.yang, co.yak
	ya elsewhere	yācwung, kyawus, iya
ㅐ	ay	ayki, kkay, hāyan, sensayng
ㅒ	.yay after a e o (u wu)	hā.yay, hē.yay, ppō.yay, ppū.yay
	yay elsewhere	yayki (= iyaki)
ㅙ	way	way, kkway, insway, twāyci

The Hankul symbol for **we** can be written ㅞ, but ㅔ is preferred.

1.5. Reinforcement (-q).

The rules for the treatment of what we call "reinforcement" are somewhat complicated. Roughly speaking, the linguistic facts are as follows. When certain words or parts of words are attached to others that begin with **p t c k** or **s**, that consonant is doubled to **pp, tt, cc, kk, ss**. When they are attached to certain other elements that begin with "zero" (a vowel) or **h**, the vowel or **h** is preceded by **t**; when they are attached to certain elements that begin with **m** or **n**, those onsets are preceded by syllable-final **n**; when they are attached to certain elements that begin with **y** or **i**, the pronunciation is /···ny···/ or /···ni···/ after a consonant and /···nny···/ or /···nni···/ after a vowel, but ···lq y··· and ···lq i··· are realized as /···lly···/ and /···lli···/. Reinforcement of ···n i··· → ···nq i··· /···nni···/ and ···n y··· → -nq y··· /···nny···/, sometimes called "n-epenthesis" (not to be confused with the nasal epenthesis of §2.10.4) is so pervasive that it passes largely unnoticed: **musunq iwus** 'what neighbor', **ōnq yātang** 'the entire opposition party', **sinq yētang** 'a new party in power', **sinhonq ¹yehayng** 'honeymoon trip'. But such reinforcement does NOT occur before the noun **i** 'person; fact / act; ... ', the particle **iya / ya**, the particle **(iyo) / yo**, or the copula stem **i-**. The peculiarities of the phoneme string /yey/ (§4.3) are reflected in the pronunciations /sillēysan/ for **silq yēysan** 'real budget', /kallēycengita/ for **kalq yēyceng ita**, and /musunnēyki/ for **musunq yēyki** (← yāyki < iyaki) 'what talk'. As a result of vowel raising **tōnq (iyaki > yāyki >) yēyki** → /tōnneyki/ 'money talk' may sound just like **tōnq (nāyki >) nēyki** 'gambling'. When the juncture after the accusative particle is dropped, **os ul (l) ip.e** 'wears a garment' is usually said as /osulipe/ with a flap [r] but you may sometimes instead hear /osullipe/. When the particle itself drops, **os [ul] ip.e**, you usually hear /onnipe/ = **osq ip.e** rather than /otipe/ = **os ip.e** with [d]. When the particle gets dropped in **mun (ul) yel.e** 'opens the door' the phrase is usually said as **munq yel.e**, pronounced /munnyele/ and not **mu-nye-le**. There are a few lexical exceptions to the n-epenthesis rule, notably ¹**yuk-i** [yugi] rather than (?)¹**yukq-i** [yungni] 'six-two; sixty-two', familiar in the term ¹**yuk-i-o** '6-25' (= ~ sāpyen / tōng.lan 'the North Korean invasion of June 25th, 1950') which is pronounced /yukio/ or contracted to /yukyo/. We list seven types of examples:

(1) Native Korean sequences (usually compounds of noun + noun) in which the first element ends in a vowel.

(2) Native Korean compounds in which the first element ends in a consonant.

(3) Chinese loanwords (originally, in Chinese, compounds — usually of two syllables) in which the first element ends in a vowel.

(4) Chinese loanwords in which the first element ends in a sonant (m n ng l).

(5) Chinese loanwords in which the first element ends in **l** and the second begins with **t, c,** or **s**. If both elements are bound, the reinforcement is obligatory; if one element is free, the reinforcement is usual but there are exceptions.

(6) Korean verb forms consisting of a stem that ends in a nasal **n** or **m** (from a linguistic point of view also those that end in **nc, lm, lp, lph, lth,** and for some speakers **lk**) plus an attached ending that begins with **t, c, l,** or **s**. Before **s** the reductions of final **nh** and **lh** can be added.

(7) A sequence of the prospective modifier (-**ul**) followed by a noun that begins with **p, t, c, k,** or **s**.

Spellings in both the North and the South ignore the reinforcement that occurs automatically in Type 5 (Chinese loanwords with l + s, l + t, l + c). In the Yale Romanization we prefer to write **lqs**, **lqt**, and **lqc** for these words since in the non-Chinese words there are contrasts with unreinforced **ls**, **lt**, and **lc**. Moreover, it is not always easy to know that a particular word is of Chinese origin.

Both of the Hankul spelling systems also ignore the reinforcement that occurs automatically in Type 6 (verb forms), and indeed there are dialects which do not reinforce these forms (see §8.2.1). Instead of here writing -q, as one might prefer, the Yale Romanization uses a dot as a reminder notation: ···m.t···, ···n.c···, ...

Type 7 is ignored by the South Korean spelling but sometimes indicated in the north, and it was often written in early Hankul texts with a "glottal stop" symbol corresponding to the -q with which we mark it. (The symbol is like the Hankul h but without the short stroke at the top: ㆆ)

Types 3 and 4 (the other Chinese loanwords) are treated the same as Types 1 and 2 (the Korean words) by the North Korean system, but in practice there is variation, perhaps owing to an indecision over whether to admit some of the reinforced forms as "standard". The NK dictionary (NKd) often omits the apostrophe in the entry spelling for words of these types, and gives the pronunciation separately: "sāken [kken]", "sānpo [ppo]". Yet for other entries both the apostrophe and the separate pronunciation are given: "ka'pep [ppep]", "mun'ca [cca]". The South Korean system, too, sometimes treats Types 3 and 4 as if they were 1 and 2 respectively, but many people are inconsistent or forgetful and ignore the reinforcement in the Chinese loanwords. [1]Yi Ungpayk (458) advises us to write the postvocalic "-s" for Type 3 only when there is a minimal contrast with another word that does not have the reinforcement: **kaqpep** 'addition', **kapep** [lit] 'family tradition'; **seqca** [obsolescent?] 'letter (epistle; character)', **sēca** 'illegitimate child'; [1]**īqkwa** 'science', **ī-kwa** 'lesson two'; **hōq-swu** 'number of households', **hoswu** 'lake'; **choqcem** 'focal point', **cho-cem** 'vinegar shop' (? − not found in dictionaries); **yoqcem** 'main point', **yo-cem** 'mattress shop' (? − not found in dictionaries).

For Types 1 and 2, the earlier North Korean rule is very simple: at the end of the prior element add an apostrophe, called **sai phyo** 'between-mark' and looking much like the left side of the Hankul letter 人. The Yale Romanization uses a similar device: add **q** at the end of the prior element. (We prefer to avoid the apostrophe because it is useful for other purposes, such as showing abbreviations.) In the South Korean system a final s is added to the prior syllable when it ends in a vowel (Type 1), and the reinforcement is ignored when the prior syllable ends in a consonant (Type 2), except that as the later element the morpheme **i** 'tooth' is spelled **ni** = /···(n) ni/ (2). At one time, following the practice of the early texts, the ···s··· was written as a separate syllable all by itself and called **sai sios** 'in-between s'; at that time (the early 1930s) it was used for both Type 1 and Type 2.

The following table shows examples of all seven types with the different treatments, together with the pronunciation and the phonemic shape as transcribed in Yale Romanization symbols, but the reduction of syllable-excess at the end of nouns is not shown. Space and hyphen are retained from the notation on the left and do not necessarily reflect the practice for the particular phrase in either the south or the north, since compounds and short phrases are usually written without a break in both parts of the country.

TABLE OF REINFORCEMENT TYPES

	Romanization	South Korea	North Korea	Pronunciation
1.	twīq path	twis path	twi' path	/twīppath/
	payq nolay	pays nolay	pay' nolay	/paynnolay/
	peykayq īs	peykays is	peykay' is	/peykaynnis/
	ku-kkaciq īl	ku-kkacis il	ku-kkacis' il	/kukkacinnīl/
2.	wiq iq-mom	wis is-mom	[*wi' i'-mom]	/winnimmom/[1]
	mulq kyel	mul kyel	mul' kyel	/mulkkyel/
	kangq ka	kang ka	kang' ka	/kangkka/
	cip(q) īl	cip il	cip(') il	/cipīl, cimnīl/

	petulq iph	petul iph	petul' iph	/petulliph/
	kas yang(thay)	kas yang(thay)	kas' yang(thay)	/kannyang(thay)/
	mulq yak	mul yak	mul' yak	/mullyak/
	kethq iph	keth iph	keth' iph	/kenniph/
	yēysq iyaki	yēys iyaki	yeys' iyaki	/yēynniyaki/
	kethq yakta	keth yakta	kath' yakta	/kennyaktta/
	kyelmakq yem²	kyelmak yem	kyelmak' yem	/kyelmangnyem/
	sōngkosq (n)i	songkos ni	songkos' i	/sōngkonni/
	tesq (n)i	tes ni	tes' i	/tenni/
	okq-(n)i	ok-ni	ok'-i	/ongni/
	petq-(n)i	pet-ni	pet'-i	/penni/
	ppetulengq (n)i	ppetuleng ni	ppetuleng' i	/ppetulengni/
3.	kaqpep	kaspep	ka'pep	/kappep/
	sāqken	sasken	sa(')ken, saken	/sākken/
4.	munqca³	munca	mun'ca	/muncca/
	sānqpo	sanpo	san'po, sanpo	/sāmppo/⁴
	inqki	inki	in'ki, inki	/ingkki/⁵
5.	cengqyel	cengyel	cengyel	/cengnyel/
	kyelqsan	kyelsan	kyelsan	/kyelssan/
	kyelqtan	kyeltan	kyeltan	/kyelttan/
6.	kyelqceng	kyelceng	kyelceng	/kyelcceng/
	sīm.ta, sīm.ko	simta, simko	simta, simko	/sīmtta/, /sīmkko/
7.	cēlm.ta, cēlm.ko	celmta, celmko	celmta, celmko	/cēmtta/, /cēmkko/
	halq kes	hal kes	hal' kes, hal kes	/halkkes/

See also §4.2 (end); silh(q)-cung in Part II.

¹ ← /winninmom/; CF CM 1:99. For all uses of the morpheme meaning 'up' NK standardizes wu; the adnoun (or prefix) should be wuq but they have standardized it as wus, the spelling that is used in the south for those phrases that have preserved the older vowel nucleus. See §5.3. This word is not carried by NKd.
² Though the parts are Chinese, this second-degree compound is here treated as if Korean.
³ = kulqca 'letters, written characters'.
⁴ ← /sānppo/
⁵ ← /inkki/

For reasons not clearly understood a fair number of Chinese loanmorphs show a marked tendency to induce reinforcement as the final member of a compound: -(q)kwa 'course' or 'section', -(q)kwen 'chit' or 'sphere' or 'privilege', -(q)ken 'case, matter' (CF sāqken, coqken, ānqken), -(q)ka 'price' (CF tāyqka, yūqka, ¹yūqka, ¹yemqka), -(q)kwi 'couplet' (CF ēqkwi, ¹yenqkwi), -(q)ki 'feeling' (CF yūnq-ki), -(q)kyek 'standing, rule, grammatical case' (CF cwuq-kyek, inqkyek), -(q)ca 'written character', -(q)cem 'point', -(q)cang 'document', -(q)cōy 'crime', -(q)cūng 'illness', -(q)pyēng 'illness', -(q)pep 'law, rule', -(q)po 'step' (sānqpo); -(q)swū 'number' (CF chiq-swu 'size, measure' ≠ chi-swu 'number of inches'); ... . See also -(q)seng '-ness' and cek '-ic' in Part II. The syntactic relationship of the two morphemes in Chinese is irrelevant to the reinforcement: silqkwen can mean either 'real power' or 'lose power'; the verbal noun sānqpo 'stroll' comes from a Chinese verb-object phrase ('scatter one's steps').

For certain phrases we find vacillation in whether to reinforce or not: i kkoch ilum /ikkotilum/ 'the name of this flower' and ku ūmsik ilum /kuūmsikilum/ 'the name of that food' (both M 1:1:390) are more commonly said as i kkochq ilum /ikkonnilum/ and ku ūmsikq ilum /kuūmsingnilum/. Similarly san kkochq ilum 'names of mountain flowers', sothq ilum 'names of pots', (yang)kokq ilum 'names of songs', ¹yekaykq ilum 'passenger names'. Yet tāyhak ilum /tāyhakilum/ is preferred to **tāyhakq ilum** /tāyhangnilum/ 'college name'. (On ···**q y**··· and ···**q i**··· see §4.4.) The word for 'carsick(ness)' is usually said as **chaq melmi** /chammelmi/ but dictionaries ignore the reinforcement; similarly ignored is the usual reinforcement of **chiq sōl** 'tooth brush' and **chiq-swu** 'measure'. Certain phrases, however, are always reinforced: **tankolq tapang** 'a favorite teashop', **tankolq son nim** 'a regular customer' (M 1:1:390); **petulq kaci = petu' namuq kaci** 'a willow(tree) branch' (the apostrophe marks an elision); ... . The phrase **chinkwu(q) cip** 'a friend's house' can rime with **iwus cip** 'neighboring house' but **wuli cip** 'our house' is never *****wuliq cip**. And others are never reinforced: **tōl path** 'a field of stones' (not *****tōlq path**). NKd indicates reinforcement in **chongka** 'gun mount' but no other source confirms that, so it may be a mistake. NKd lacks an indication of reinforcement for **cwungqcung** 'grave illness' and **kyengqcung** 'light illness' (as found in LHS and in Kim Minswu and Hong Wungsen), and no dictionary indicates reinforcement in **hwā(?q)cung** 'a flareup of anger'.

1.6. Initial ^{l} and ^{n}.

Words beginning with a morpheme which has a basic and/or historical shape that begins with **l** are pronounced with an initial **n**. Such words are written in South Korea with an initial **n** but in North Korea they are written with an initial **l**; in this book we write ^{1}n··· for these words. But before **i** and **y** neither **n** nor **l** is pronounced. The South Koreans follow the pronunciation and begin the word **y**··· or **i**···, but the North Koreans write **ly**··· and **li**··· or **ny**··· and **ni**··· depending on the basic and/or historical shape of the morpheme; and here we write ^{1}**y**··· and ^{l}**i**··· or ^{n}**y**··· and ^{n}**i**···, with a few cases of "**(n)**" owing to the inconsistencies found in spelling practices. The following examples show the differences:

	Romanization	South Korea	North Korea	Pronunciation	Meaning
1.	^{n}yenkam	yenkam	nyenkam	/yenkam/	'yearbook'
	^{n}ik.myeng	ikmyeng	nikmyeng	/ingmyeng/	'anonymity'
	^{n}itho	itho	nitho	/itho/	'mud'
2.	^{l}yēnsup	yensup	lyensup	/yēnsup/	'drill (study)'
	^{l}yēy	yey	lyey	/yēy/	'ceremony'
3.	^{l}īhay	ihay	lihay	/īhay/	'understanding'
	^{l}nonmun	nonmun	lonmun	/nonmun/	'treatise'
	^{l}naywel	naywel	laywel	/naywel/	'next month'

The family name ^{l}**Yi**, in English variously spelled Lee, Li, Yi, Ree, Ri, Rhee, ... , is particularly troublesome. In South Korea it is spelled **I** and in North Korea **Li**. The Yale Romanization should be ^{l}**I** but that looks awkward, so we make an arbitrary exception and write ^{l}**Yi**, preserving a resemblance to the form that is familiar from references to the "Yi dynasty". (The phoneme /i/ can be deemed to carry a nondistinctive initial y- which we ignore except for this name.) The pronunciation is **i**, but **ni** is (or was) used by northerners, though the Phyengyang authorities have promoted saying /li/ with an initial flap, like that used in recent foreign loanwords. For them, history has reversed itself: /li/ → /ni/ → /i/ → /li/. Even in South Korea 'Miss ^{l}Yi' is always **Misu Li** [ri] and never *****Misu ^{l}Yi** [i]. Other proper names beginning with ^{l}··· (such as ^{l}**Im**, ^{l}**Yang**, and even ^{l}**No**) may be given reading pronunciations with the flap, and these could become the spoken norm for that part of the country. The authenticity of the pronunciation **ni** is quite clear from attestations such as 1881 Ridel 20, who has that version both in Hankul and in his transcription, and (23) writes "Ni ryengkam" for 'the venerable ^{l}Yi'. 1887 Scott writes "*ni*···" for the etymological *ni*··· in a fair number of words, and also has a few examples that go back to *li*···, such as *ninsoyk* (123) < *linsoyk* 'avaricious'; he writes *ryemnye* 'fear' in one place (127) yet *nyemnye* 'anxiety' in another (176). At the same time, he says (149n) "Though spelt *rika* it is read *ika*" with reference to ^{l}**ī ka** 'profit' [nominative] (CF 166). The pronunciation of *li* as *ni* is reported in the first part of the sixteenth century: the surname ^{l}**Yī** < ¨*LI* is attested as ¨*ni* in ?1517- Pak 1:3a and *ni*¨*chyen* 'profit money' < ¨*LI-CHYEN* occurs in the same work (1:34a) and also in ?1517- ^{l}**No** 1:13a, though in the latter the word appears again (2:60a) as *li*¨*chyen* with the *l* intact. The word *nyenskon* (1527 Cahoy 1:8a=14b) 'lotus root' was lexicalized from the phrase *LYEN S KON* 'root of the lotus'.

All of the words involved in this section are of Chinese origin. Other words that were spelled with ny··· and ni··· in Middle Korean are now written y··· and i···, as pronounced, but when the nasal persists in compounds the spelling in South Korea follows that pronunciation: sŏngkosq (n)i 'cuspid' is written as "songkos ni" in the south but "songkos' i" in the north (without our generous spaces, of course). There are inconsistencies in the decisions, as exemplified by the SK treatment of certain words in group 2, for when the nasal is pronounced in (n)i 'tooth' it is favored by an attention neglected in the case of iph 'leaf', īl 'work, event', and iyaki 'tale'.

The word for 'glass' is historically lyuli, but North Korea spells it yuli (as we expect of South Korea). That means that the phrase /sayngnyuli/ 'stained glass' must be treated as saykq yuli, not sayk ¹yuli or sayk-lyuli. A similar case: ssang-pongq yaktay /ssangpongnyakttay/ 'Bactrian camel', historically lyaktay.

The following words begin with an etymological l··· but are written phonemically with n··· in North Korea as well as South Korea: nasa 'screw, spiral' (CF ¹nasa 'woolen cloth'), naphal 'trumpet', nok 'rust' (CF ¹nok 'stipend'), nampho(-tung) 'lamp', no 'oar', nwu 'loft, pavilion', nwūki 'dampness', nwū-nwū-i 'frequently'. CF Mkk 1960:3:25. The morpheme ¹yen is spelled lyen by North Koreans in ¹yenq-ie 'consecutively' but yen in yen-kephe = yen-kephu 'successively' and in yen-hay and yenpang 'continuously' (a point missed by KEd). CF Mkk 1960:4:23.

The word /silyen/ 'disappointment in love' is etymologically sil-lyen; it is spelled sil.yen in the south and sillyen in the north, so we will write it sil¹yen. A similar case is sal¹yuk 'massacre', pronounced /sallyuk/. We would expect to write no¹yey for /no(.y)ey/ 'slave' (CF hālyey 'male slave') but the spelling in both north and south is no.yey. The word ōlyu 'mistake' (< ō-lyu) has a common variant pronunciation without the l and that is standardized in NKd with the spelling ō.yu.

An epenthetic (intrusive) -l- is found before /y/ in a few compounds: cēylyem < cēy-yem 'manufacturing salt', holyem < ho-yem 'Chinese rough salt'; ph^{y}ēylyem < phyēy-yem 'pneumonia' (spelled phyeylyem in the south but pheyyem in the north so we will write it ph^{y}ēy¹yem), thōylyem < thōy-yem 'pouring hot broth over rice or noodles a little at a time to heat them up' — and perhaps (yang-)hwalyo 'carpet' and pōlyo 'large fancy cushion', if these are properly derived from yo 'mattress' < zywoh < *nhyok, a Chinese import that underwent early naturalization.

In a few words an etymological n is commonly pronounced as /l/: tāylo < tāy-nō 'great anger', hūylo < hūy-nō 'joy and anger', ēlwul < ē-nwul 'inarticulate', yālyo < yā-nyo 'annoyance, interruption'.

A small group of morphemes have the basic shapes lyul and lyel. These morphemes follow a special pronunciation rule. After a vowel or n, the l unexpectedly drops. (The l actually surfaces only after some consonant other than n, including l itself, and then it takes the reflex /n/ so that we would have no idea these morphemes begin with a basic l rather than n without additional information from the history or from dialect pronunciations.) The alternation is ignored in the northern spelling but phonemically noted in the south, so we mark it in our Romanization with -¹y···. Examples will be found in §4.8. When these morphemes are attached to a morpheme that ends with n we insert a dot (cīn.¹yel 'exhibition', cēn.¹yul 'trembling') to remind us of the morpheme boundary in the SK spelling ("cīn.yel", "cēn.yul") as contrasted with the NK spelling ("cīn.lyel" = /cīnyel/, "cēn.lyul" = /cēnyul/). When the preceding morpheme ends with i, wu, yu, or a digraph of vowel + y, there is no need for the dot to mark the boundary, so we write pī¹yel '(being) nasty', pī¹yul 'ratio', swū¹yel 'numerical progression', kyu¹yul 'rules'. But after the other vowels, the SK spelling requires us to insert a dot to prevent interpreting the string of vowel + y as a digraph: to.¹yel 'lining up' (NK "tolyel", SK "to.yel"), phā.¹yel 'explosion' (NK "phālyel", SK "phā.yel"). KEd was inconsistent in not writing the dot for those cases. On problems of spelling and interpreting words containing the morpheme lyō 'fee', see the entry in Part II. See also §4.4.

In the non-Chinese vocabulary the initial nasal of words beginning nye or ni was eventually dropped, so that today 'tooth' is pronounced i in both the north and the south. It is difficult to assign this change to a particular time. It may have set in first for verb stems: we find *yey-* in ?1660 Kyeychwuk and (with raised vowel) *i-* in 1876 Kakok for what was earlier ¨*nyey-* and still earlier °*nye-* and °*ni-* 'go'. In Middle Korean the prevalent form for 'put in' was *nyeh-* > dialect **yeh-**, but a dispalatalized *neh-* is attested in 1466 Kup (SEE p.47). Modern **ic-** 'forget' for earlier *nic-* is attested in the middle of the 18th century and perhaps as early as 1660. There may have been dialect doublets with **ny⋯** competing with **y⋯** and dispalatalized as **n⋯** from fairly early; the ancestor of modern **yeki-** 'regard (as)', first so attested in ?1800 Hancwung, was *nye ̇ki-* in 1481 Samkang and Twusi, but the dispalatalized version *ne ̇ki-* was prevalent from 1449 (Kok) right on down (including 1481 Twusi). The adjective *nyeth-* 'shallow' is spelled *yeth-* in ?1517 Pak-cho and later, and *yath-* in 1608 Twuchang cip.yo. On the other hand, there is but a single example of *nel-* (in 1763 Haytong) for ¨*yel-* the ancestor of modern **yē-l-** 'open', and there are no reports of an initial nasal in modern dialects, so that the one example is suspect. In most words that began with *ni⋯* there is no evidence that the *n* dropped until quite late: *nik-* > **ik-** 'ripen', ¨*niz-* > **ī(s)-** 'continue', *nilk-* > **ilk-** 'read', *ni* > **i** 'tooth' or 'flea', ̇*niph* > **iph** 'leaf', *ni ̇mah* > **ima** 'forehead', ¨*nimca[h]* > **īmca** 'owner', *nil ̇kwup* / *nil ̇kwop* > **ilkop** 'seven', … . For many of these words, some of the northern dialects have retained the nasal: Kim Thaykyun cites **ni** 'tooth' and 'flea', **niph** 'leaf', **nilkop** 'seven', **nīmca** 'owner', **nilk-** 'read', **nip(-hi)-** '(cause to) wear', **nī(s)-** 'continue', **nyeth-** / **nyath-** 'shallow'. The earliest texts had both ¨*nil-* 'arise' and ¨*il-* 'come into being'; could they have once been etymologically the same? The only modern words pronounced with initial **ny⋯** seem to be **nyesek** 'rascal (of a man/boy)' and **nyen** 'bitch (of a woman)', of somewhat obscure etymology but both probably involving the Chinese morpheme **nye** 'woman'. The modern **yeph** '(be)side' was *nyeph* in 1617 Sin-sok (¹Yel 3:24) and just *nyep* in earlier texts (*nye ̇p u[̇]lwo* 1459 Wel 2:36a, *nye ̇p i ̇la* 1459 Wel 2:17b), but dispalatalized *nep.hu.lwo* appears in ?1775 Han-Cheng 204d. It should be kept in mind that Korean also has words beginning **i⋯** and **y⋯** which have never had variant versions with a nasal initial, such as **ip** < ̇*ip* 'mouth', **isul** < *i ̇sul* 'dew', **ilang** < *i ̇lang* 'paddy ridge', **ili** < ̇*ilhi* 'wolf', **iki-** < *i ̇ki-* / *i ̇kuy-* 'win', **ilh-** < *ilh-* 'lose'; **yewi-** < *ye ̇wuy-* 'get thin', **yetelp** < *ye ̇tulp* 'eight', **yeses** < *ye ̇sus* 'six'. These words have not been reported with a nasal initial in dialects, with the exception of Hoylyeng **nyessay** 'six days' (Kim Thaykyun 1986:380a), and that form is surprising, if correct, in view of MK *ye ̇ssway* (1462 ¹Nung 6:17a) and *ye ̇sway* (*s pa ̇m oy* 1481 Twusi 10:4a). But nasal versions are reported for the modern words (**yēyki** < **yāyki** <) **iyaki** 'story, tale', which was first attested in 1775 as *niyaki*, and **ieng** '(roofing) thatch', first attested in the 1730 text of Chengkwu yengen as *niyeng*. (Also reported in 20th-century materials: **nikki** for **ikki** < *isk* 'moss', **nisak** for **isak** < *isak* 'ear of grain' and **nyemul** for **yemul** < *ye ̇mulq* 'to open'; see King 1991b:6.) The nasal dispalatalization in the north and the palatal denasalization in the south is part of a more general process of reducing initial strings of apical (dental or alveolar) + palatal, as described in §4.4.

In Hamkyeng the Chinese morphemes that begin with a basic **y⋯** or **i⋯** (and **uy**, which merges with /i/ even initially in these dialects) are often treated if they were from **ny⋯** or **ni⋯** when attached to a Chinese morpheme that ends in a consonant, even if both morphemes are bound. (Choy Iceng 1960.) We can note these pronunciations with the morphophonemic ⋯**q**:

Standard	Hamkyeng	Pronounced	Meaning
mok.yoil	mokq.yoil	/mongnyoil/	'Thursday'
sap.ip	sapq.ip	/samnip/	'insertion'
cen.ya	cenq.ya	/cennya/	'the night before'
tham.yok	thamq.yok	/thamnyok/	'greed'
cung.ye	cungq.ye	/cungnye/	'donation'
cel.yak	celq.yak	/cellyak/	'economizing'

Such pronunciations are not new. 1889 Imbault-Huart 66 has *sik.nyem* for **sik.yem** 'salt', which must have been pronounced /singnyem/ = sikq.yem.

1.7. Hankul spelling of *u* after labials.

The back unrounded high vowel **u** does not occur after a labial (**p ph pp m**). When expected, it is replaced by the rounded vowel **wu**. That is why the Yale Romanization writes **wu** as just **u** after a labial. Our notation of **pu** can be regarded as a convenient abbreviation of **pwu**. But that is true only when we are speaking of modern Korean. Until sometime after 1700 Korean distinguished labial-onset syllables with the unrounded vowel from their counterparts with the rounded vowel, so that when we cite forms from that period (or specific Hankul spellings from even later) we must distinguish **pu** from **pwu** and **mul** from **mwul**, just as we keep distinct the zero-onset syllables that begin with **u** and **wu**. The present-day Hankul spelling systems usually write **wu** after a labial within a morpheme (**mun** is written m + wu + n, **pun** is p + wu + n, **phun** is ph + wu + n, and **ppun** is pp + wu + n), but choose between basic **wu** and **u** after the zero onset of a morpheme occurring after an element that ends in a labial: **kem.un** ··· ' ··· that is black' and **kum-un** 'gold and silver', but **kam.wu** 'a welcome rain'. We know whether to write **wu** or **u** by recalling other words that contain the same morphemes in environments where the two vowels are distinguished: **cak.un** ··· ' ··· that is small' and **un** 'silver', but **wūsan** 'umbrella'.

There are exceptions. Stems that end in the high back vowel after a labial are given the Hankul equivalent of our Romanized abbreviation [w]u, so that the second syllable of **kippu-** 'be happy' is spelled pp + u even though it is pronounced with a rounded vowel, and the second syllable of **kophu-** 'be empty, hungry' is spelled ph + u. Morphophonemically, the spelled "u" behaves like any other case of **u**, in that it drops when the infinitive ending is attached: **kippe**, **kopha**. We also see **u** sometimes in derived forms: **kwucepun hata** 'is untidy' may be spelled with Hankul p + u + n, reflecting its derivation from **kwucep (sulepta)** + -un. But lexical derivations of that sort are largely ignored under the current spelling standards of both parts of Korea, where the word is written with p + wu + n, as it sounds. The spelling with **u** is used in **kumum (nal)** 'last day of the month' because **kumum** is an etymological variant of **kem.um** 'being black' (i.e. 'dark of the moon'); compare **polum** 'middle day of the month', an etymological variant of **polk-** + -um = **palk.um** 'being bright'. And Hankul regularly spells **u** for the "inserted vowel" used to help pronounce certain final consonants and clusters in foreign words, so that the second syllable of **Aphulikha** 'Africa' is written ph + u rather than ph + wu.

Despite the Hankul spelling, **na ppun** 'only me' and **nappun** ··· 'bad' sound the same, and the three expressions **ku mun** 'that door', **kum un** 'as for gold', and **kum-un** 'gold and silver' are homonyms. The lips are rounded (and usually protruded) throughout the last syllable of each of these phrases.

1.8. Word division and internal punctuation.

As in English and many other languages, people vary considerably when deciding questions of spacing and punctuation. One word or two words? Hyphenate or run together? Until the 20th century Hankul texts were commonly written with no space between words, as is the traditional practice in Chinese and Japanese. The modern use of word spaces began with Toklip sinmun 1 (1896) and was continued by Cwu Sikyeng (1907 "Kwuk.e wa kwuk.mun uy phil.yo"). A similar usage in Japan, found in hiragana newspapers of the Meiji period and in elementary textbooks from 1884, never took hold. (There are examples of word spacing in manuscripts of 1272 left by Shinran.) The Korean decision to use spacing may have been independent, or it may have been influenced by the orthographies of European languages. In 1897 [1]Yi Pongmun (Kwukmun cengli) marked the ends of words by putting little circles below and slightly to the right in the vertical line of Hankul.

In writing Korean the most common practice is to run together things that are spoken together in phrases, especially noun + particle (+ particle) and verb + particle (+ particle). People disagree on whether to write sequences such as adnoun (prenoun) + noun and noun + noun (+ noun + ...) as separate words. Writers like to attach very short elements, especially those of one syllable, to longer elements that are contiguous to them. That fact, combined with hazy notions of grammar to begin with, accounts for the writing of particles together with the preceding noun or verb. Considerable indecision prevails in treating noun compounds, numeral + counter, adverb + verb, and those verb compounds in which the prior element is in a "free" form, carrying an ending, such as the infinitive, rather than just the stem alone. If the form becomes very long, people are apt to break it with a space; if the whole sequence is relatively short, it will likely be run together. A sequence of verb modifier + noun poses a problem, for the modifier is always the head of the prior construction, which can be quite long, but in pronunciation a pause is more likely to come before rather than after the modifier. Unmarked object + verb are often run together, especially if the object is short and the expression common, like **pap mek-** 'eat food'.

To a certain extent, spacing decisions reflect the degrees of potential pause between various constructions, and we can summarize that in a table of linkage (juncture in the rough sense of the word), from openmost to tightest, with examples:

1. Topic (noun + un/nun) + verb — ayki nun mek.e; pap un mek.e
2. Subject (noun + i/ka) + verb — ayki ka mek.e
3. Indirect object (noun + hanthey or eykey) + verb — ayki hanthey cwue
4. Object (noun + ul/lul) + verb — pap ul mek.e
5. Unmarked subject + verb — ayki mek.e
6. Unmarked indirect object + verb — ayki cwue
7. Unmarked object + verb — (pipimq) pap mek.e
8. Adverb + verb — mānh.i mek.e; cal mek.e; mōs mek.e
9. Noun + noun — hak.kyo sensayng; kkoch path
10. Adnoun + noun — ku sālam, ku ay
11. Adnoun + quasi-free noun — ku kes
12. Modifier + noun — kulen sālam; halq sālam
13. Modifier + quasi-free noun — kulen kes; halq kes
14. Numeral + noun — twū son
15. Numeral + counter — twū mali
16. Verb (infinitive/gerund) + aux verb — mek.e twue; mek.ko siph.ta
17. Noun + copula — pap ita
18. Quasi-free noun + copula — ⋯ kes ita
19. Noun + particle — ayki nun; pap ul; cip i
20. Verb + particle — mek.e yo; mek.e to; mek.ko nun
21. Particle + particle (+ particle) — ⋯ ey se; ⋯ ey se to
22. Verb stem + ending — mek-e; khu-n; kitali-ci; ka-syess.ess.keyss.[s]up.nikka

This list does not, of course, exhaust the possibilities. Places in the table should probably be found for other constructions. Where real anxiety arises, for the native speaker and the linguist alike, is in conflicting combinations of linkage constructions, as in **Haksayng hanthey phyēnci sse cwulq kes iey yo** '(He) will probably write the letter for the student', which has the following constituency:

```
Haksayng  hanthey   phyēnci  sse  cwulq  kes       iey           yo
NOUN      PARTICLE  NOUN     VERB AUX    NOUN      STEM+ENDING   PARTICLE

nominal – adnominal    adverbial – verbal
adverbial ─────────────────── verbal
          adnominal ───────────────────── nominal
                    nominal ───────────────────── copula (inf)
                              verbal ─────────────────────────── particle
                                          (adverbial) sentence
```

But the phonological bonds, the words most likely to run together in pronunciation, would be in the following order of closeknitness: (1) **iey yo**; (2) **haksayng hanthey**; (3) **kes iey**; (4) **sse cwul**; (5) **cwulq kes**; (6) **phyēnci sse**. This means that if we were to make only one pause it would likely be **Haksayng hanthey | phyēnci sse cwulq kes iey yo**, if we made two pauses it would be **Haksayng hanthey | phyēnci | sse cwulq kes iey yo**, and if we should make a third pause (unnatural for this sentence) it would be **Haksayng hanthey | phyēnci | sse cwul | kes iey yo**. If we were to make four pauses (still more unnatural) the sentence would be **Haksayng hanthey | phyēnci | sse | cwul | kes iey yo**. Any further pauses, as in taking the next step **kes | iey yo** and the final steps **emeni | hanthey** and **ie(y) | yo**, would be artificial.

From this example it is easy to see the all too frequent conflict between the phonological bondage, or closeknitness of pronunciation, and the immediate constituency, or closeness of grammatical ties. Similar problems in English are exemplified by such expressions as "the highest scoring team", "sharp bladed", "three hundred and first", "your nearest store".

In Hankul texts prepared under my supervision, such as the examples in KEd, we have been liberal in word division. For types 1 through 16 above, either space or hyphen is used (hyphen for some of the very frequent or very short combinations of types 7 through 16); for types 17 through 21 a dot is inserted to set a particle off from the preceding word to which it is attached; and only examples of type 22 are regularly spelled with no internal punctuation. Some such rules, perhaps, could eventually be incorporated into normal Hankul writing, at least in school textbooks, where it is important to reduce ambiguity to a minimum. (Notice the unusually generous word division in the North Korean journal Mkk 1961:4:37-40.) Quite a few homophonous phrases can be distinguished by inserting a pause or "open juncture":

/hōysaey( )nakanta/ = hōysa ey na-kanta 'goes off to the office'
/hōysaeyna( )kanta/ = hōysa ey 'na kanta 'goes off to the office or the like'

/na( )kakiceney/ = na kaki cen ey 'before I go'
/nakakiceney/ = na-kaki cen ey 'before going out'

/wuliyekwaney( )kaca/ = wuli ¹yekwan ey kaca 'let's go to our inn'
/wuli yekwaneykaca/ = wuli ¹yekwan ey kaca 'let's go to an inn'
/wuli yekwaneyka ca/ = wuli ¹yekwan ey ka ca 'let's go to an inn to sleep'

/kuchaykina omyen( )cōkheytta/ = ku chayk ina omyen cōh.keyss.ta 'I hope that the book comes, or something'
/kuchayki naomyen( )cōkheytta/ = ku chayk i na-omyen cōh.keyss.ta 'I hope the book comes out'

The following two expressions will both translate as 'the rice tastes good' yet they represent different constructions:

/pap masi( )cōtha/ = pap (un) mas i cōh.ta ('rice – its taste is good')
/pammasi( )cōtha/ = pap (uy) mas i cōh.ta ('the rice taste is good')

In the examples of this book a hyphen is used in the Romanization as an unobtrusive way to show the first layer of internal structure of some of the words. In the citation of separate forms, the hyphen sometimes shows the direction of attachment: **-e** must have a stem in front and **mek-** must have an ending attached, as in the word **mek.e** 'eats'.

1.9. External punctuation.

Koreans borrow English and Japanese punctuation freely. The standard practices accord, more or less, with the current American usage. Parentheses, commas, and quotation marks are seen more frequently than semicolons or colons. Sentences usually end with a period, but question marks and exclamation points are also frequent, though their usage is not consistent. Korean questions are typically marked by something specific in the sentence, such as the final postmodifier **ya** in ··· **(ha)nun**

ya, usually spelled as an unanalyzed ending ··· (ha)nunya, and the interrogative ending -(su)p.nikka in ··· hap.nikka. For questions so marked there is no need for a question mark, though many writers put one in, anyway. When the interrogation is otherwise unmarked in speech, a rising intonation indicates a question, and such questions are appropriately written with a question mark: **Kim sensayng? Pap mek.e?** If the question mark is reserved to mark only those questions that have a rising intonation, we can write the distinction that is heard with indeterminates, i.e. words that have both interrogative and indefinite meanings: Nwu ka wass.ey yo. 'Who is here?'
Nwu ka wass.ey yo? 'Is someone here?'
Koreans now ordinarily write both these sentences with a question mark, just as at one time they would have written them with a period (or no punctuation); the spoken distinction is lost in the writing.

In this book the question mark is used only for sentences with rising intonation. The period is used at the end of statements and questions with falling intonation, but it is usually omitted when the sentence is cited as an example with the English translation immediately following. See §2.8 for other intonations that might be marked.

In some cases, the grammatical analysis used in this book is more detailed than that reflected in the Hankul spelling systems. As a result, there are some word divisions that produce spellings at variance with the prescriptions of Korean grammarians, such as -un ya for Hankul -unya, -um ulo for Hankul -umulo, -um ey for Hankul -umay. The grammatical lexicon of Part II carries most of the usual Hankul forms with cross references to the spellings I prefer: -unya → -un ya.

In one or two other cases I have chosen to regularize forms that differ from those favored by the Korean grammarians. I prefer the colloquial -e as the shape for the infinitive after stems ending in ···aC- (tat.e) rather than the literary/dialect version -a favored by the grammarians, though I realize many younger speakers are tending to model their speech after the spelling. I prefer the colloquial **hay** as the infinitive of **ha-** rather than the literary **ha.ye** favored by grammarians. But the literary forms are discussed and cross-referenced. Another difference of opinion, more controversial: I do not recognize the validity of a distinction between **-te-** and **-tu-** in certain retrospective endings, and accordingly I treat all cases of **-te-** as literary or dialect variants of **-tu-**.

1.10. Alphabetization.

In the alphabetization employed in Part II, all superscript letters ($^{l...}$ $^{n...}$ $^{s...}$ $^{h...}$ $^{y...}$) are ignored except where entries are otherwise identically spelled, and the same is true for ···q. The other letters have their usual English order a c e g h i k l m n o p s t u w y and the digraphs (kk, ng, wu, ey, ...) are alphabetized by their component letters, as if the words were English. Vowel length is ignored except for words that are otherwise spelled identically: the word with the short vowel comes first.

What about the alphabetization of words written in Hankul? There are several different orders in widespread use, and the student may feel that each dictionary maker is plaguing him with new whims. In general, the schemes fall into two types. The first is most widely used in South Korea, with three variations on what to do with the geminates; the second type is official in North Korea.

(1) k (kk) n t (tt) l m p (pp) s (ss) ···/ng c (cc) ch kh th ph h
    a ay ya yay e ey ye yey o wa way oy wu we wey wi yu u uy i

  (1a) Ignore double consonants except where entries are otherwise the same.
  (1b) Ignore INITIAL double consonants except where entries are otherwise
     the same, but keep a difference for final double consonants analogous
     to that of the singlets:
     k kk ks, n ns, l lk lm lp ls lth lph lh, p ps, s ss
  (1c) Recognize double consonants both initially and finally; make separate
     places for the initial geminates (as in parentheses above), and keep
     the final geminates in the order shown in (1b).

(2) n t l m p s -ng c ch kh th ph h kk tt pp ss cc ···
    a ya e ye o yo wu yu u i ay yay ey yey oy wi uy wa we way wey

In the latter system the circle symbol is treated in the consonant order (after s) only when final in a syllable and pronounced ···ng. When initial it is treated as a carrier for the vowels, and all the vowel-initial words come at the end of the dictionary. In the South Korean system the symbol is usually treated as the same, for alphabetizing, whether it is final or initial. (In the 15th century two slightly different symbols were used and in certain instances the velar nasal ng could begin a syllable.) The North Korean **sai phyo** (···'), like our Romanized ···q, is ignored except when alphabetizing words that are otherwise spelled identically. In the south the written **sai sios** is usually treated just the same as an etymologically final s.

The names of the Hankul letters referring to vowels are simply the vowels themselves. The names of the consonants are two-syllable nouns that echo the consonant at the beginning and the end: **ki(y)ek, niun, tikut** = /tikus/, **liul** = /iul/ or /niul/, **sios, iung, ciuc** = /cius/, **chiuch** = /chius/, **khiukh** = /khiuk/, **thiuth** = /thius/, **phiuph** = /phiup/, and **hiuh** = /hius/. These are the traditional names (CF Cen Cayho 1961). In North Korea the traditional names for **k**, **t**, and **s** have been normalized to **kiuk, tiut**, and **sius**, so as to fit better with the others. The geminate letters are named with **ssang** ··· 'pair(ed), double': **ssang ki(y)ek / kiuk, ssang tikut / tiut, ssang sios / sius, ssang ciuc**. There are no special names for consonant clusters at the end of an orthographic syllable: ···**lk** is called **liul kiyek pat.chim**. The traditional names for the first few letters come from the examples of the sounds in initial and final position given by Choy Seycin in the introduction to his 1527 Hwunmong cahoy, a dictionary of Chinese characters, and that accounts for the anomalous "**ki-yek**", "**ti-kut**", and "**si-os**": the latter two terms end with the non-Chinese words for 'end' (→ modern **kkuth**) and 'clothes', for there were no Chinese syllables ending in -t (Middle Chinese -t → Middle Korean -lq). The symbol representing the velar nasal was exemplified as **i-ung**, showing that it was not be pronounced at the beginning of a syllable, and a different symbol (the circle without a tick at the top) was used for zero. But that was written only at the beginning of a syllable in the readings of the dictionary, for the zero final used by the earliest texts to end the vowel-final syllables was omitted, as had become customary. The modern system uses the tick-topped circle, reshaped as a kind of teardrop, for both the zero initial and the nasal-velar final. (The tick is often omitted and the teardrop flattened to a circle or an oval.) Choy Seycin recognized that the letters *kh, th, ph, c, ch, z* [the triangle △], zero [the circle], and *h* (which he put in that order) were not heard as such at the end of a syllable and he cited examples only in initial position, using the high front vowel: *khi, thi, phi, ci, chi, [z]i, i, hi*. There was no syllable for *khi* among the traditional Chinese readings, so he used the word for 'winnow' as a "non-Chinese" word, though it may well be taken from a Chinese reading outside the mainstream of borrowings. The terms **khiukh, thiuth, phiuph, ciuc, chiuch**, and **hiuh** seem to be modern neologisms, and North Korea uses **khu, thu, phu, cu, chu**, and **hu**. The very earliest way to speak of each Hankul symbol was probably to pronounce it, with the minimal vowel *u* supplied if needed. That is indicated by the statements in 1451 Hwunmin cengum enhay of the type *K nun* 'as for K', in which the focus particle appears in its postvocalic shape. Variant names for some of the letters turn up in 1881 Ridel (xviii): *miwom* for **mium**, *piwop* for **piup**, *cyas* for **ciuc**, and *ihwoyng* for **iung**, which Ramstedt (1939:3) gives as *ihong* = **ihung**; the version in 1874 Putsillo is the equivalent of *ihoyng*, while 1874 P'yankov called the symbol *ihyang*. Ridel's Romanization indicates that **liul** was to be pronounced with an initial [r], but 1874 P'yankov gave the name of the letter as the equivalent of *liur* with a final Russian [r] followed by the "hard mark". 1883 Scott has the equivalent of *tikkut* for **tikut** and of *ngiung* for **iung**.

There are also names for the obsolete symbols of Middle Korean. The term **iung** is used to refer to the zero initial (the circle O), and the symbol for the velar nasal Ȯ is called **yēysq iung** 'ancient iung'. The triangle △ that represents MK *z* is called **pān sios** 'half s' or **samkak hyeng** 'triangle'; the symbol for W ㅱ (p with a little circle below) is called **kapyewun piup** 'light p' and the variant with m instead of p (ㅱ) is called **kapyewun mium** 'light m'; the symbol for *q* ō, intended to represent a glottal stop, is called **yelin hiuh** (= /hius/) 'incomplete h'. A double zero ᅇ, called **ssangq iung** was used in writing a few forms with *yGy* and *yGi* from causative and passive verbs made with the formative *-Gi-*, to make sure they were not taken as *yy* and *y.i* (= /yyi/). Attested: ¨hoy˙Gi- 'cause to do' in the forms ¨hoy˙Gye (1451 Hwun-en 3) and ¨hoyGywo˙m ol (1462 ¹Nung 6:87b); moy˙Gi- 'get tied' in the forms moy˙Gywon (1462 ¹Nung 1:43b, 55b), moy˙Gi˙no.n i ˙'la (1447 Sek 13:9b), moy˙Gywu˙m i (1447 Sek 6:29a), moy˙yGwom ˙kwa (1462 ¹Nung 6:28b) and moy˙Gywo˙m ol (1459 Wel 18:52a), moy˙Gye (1459 Wel se:3b), elk-moy˙Gi˙ta (1447 Sek 13:9b); muy˙Gi- 'get hated' in the forms muy˙Gin (?1468- Mong 19b) and, according to LCT, muy˙Gywon ([1467→]1517 Sapep 5b) – but that is ¨muy¨ywon in the version printed by Kwangmun-kak in 1979 (is this the 1543 edition?). This was a clever extension of the device for writing MK G indirectly by not adding y… after …y or …i. The other device was failing to link a preceding l or z with a following syllable y… or certain common cases of i(…). Geminate hh, called ssang hiuh ㆅ, was used to write the voiced-h initial in the prescribed readings of Chinese words and in representing the verb stem °hhye-, an intensive form of °hye- 'pull, drag'.

The letters that are joined to form a Korean syllable are sometimes found isolated, as when ki(y)ek, niun, tikut, … are used to mark items in a list, like English "A.", "B.", "C.", … . As isolated symbols the letters are called ttan … 'separate …' or 'free-standing …'. In Middle Korean texts several of the isolated letters are used for special purposes. The genitive particle s was often attached to the preceding or following syllable, but it also appears as the sai sios ㅅ between two Hankul syllables or, more often, after a Chinese character or its Hankul pronunciation. In addition to s itself, assimilated variants were sometimes written as isolated letters: ttan pān sios 'free-standing z' ㅿ is found in [¨HHWUW] z ˙nal (1445 ¹Yong 26) 'later days', ttan kiyek 'free-standing k' ㄱ shows up in NGWANG k ¨swon-˙toy (1447 Sek 24:6a) 'to the king', and ttan niun 'free-standing n' ㄴ appears in ¨WUY n ¨nim-˙kum (1586 Sohak 6:40a) 'the king of Wèi'. In 1451 Hwun-en a free-standing W (ttan kapyewun piup) ㅸ was written for the genitive after Chinese words that were given prescribed pronunciations with a hypothetical final consonant to represent the labial semivowel of the Middle Chinese versions. The single bar that represents y in the digraphs of modern Korean was the glide of diphthongs (ey, ay, oy, uy) in Middle Korean, and it appears isolated as ttan i ㅣ to write the nominative particle ˙i after a Chinese character or its prescribed pronunciation in Hankul when that ends in a vowel, causing the MK particle to lose its syllabicity and shrink to the glide y. The same reduction took place for forms of the copula ˙i… : ˙THAY ¨CO 'yn ˙kwo˙t ol (1447 Sek 24:52a) ' … that he was the prince', CIN-ZYE 'yn cyen˙cho 'y˙la (1465 Wen 1:1:1:47a) ' … is the reason it is true'; nim-kum kwa [SSIN-¨HHA] 'yl s oy (1632 Twusi-cwung 6:32a) 'it being a matter of king and court … '. But when the Chinese character was pronounced with a final i or y the glide on the reduced forms was unpronounceable, so that the copula stem was totally lost, leaving the modifier forms as 'n and 'l(q), written with ttan niun ㄴ and ttan liul ㄹ, as in ku CIN-˙SSILQ s TI 'n ˙t ye (1464 Kumkang 87b) 'is that the true wisdom?' and hon ¨THYEY 'l ˙s ila (1482 Nam 1:39a) 'they are a single body'. Yet in the same situation, despite the unpronounceability of …I y or …Y y, the nominative particle was often written with ttan i anyway: ¨LI y ˙NGWOK ˙kwa ¨twolkhwa [= ¨twolh kwa] ˙oy tal˙Gwo.m i ¨ep.swu˙toy (1475 Nay se:3a) 'reason does not have the differences of jade and stone'; ku ¨CCWOY y ˙stwo tye 'y ˙sye ne˙mu.l i ˙'la (1463 Pep 4:83a) such sin is greater than that; ZYE-LOY y ˙cukcay SSIN-˙LUK ¨nay˙sya (1463 Pep 6:97a) 'the tathāgata at once displayed his supernatural power and … '.

2.0. Sounds.

The sounds of Korean are described in terms of phonemes and components (§2.1), followed by a more detailed discussion of the phonetic articulations and the acoustic impressions they impart (§2.2-4). Syllable structure and intersyllabic strings (§2.5-6) are restricted by various assimilations and incompatibilities that have arisen through the years. A variety of sequence variants (§2.7) are found, as well as conflicting judgments on the standardization of competing variants (§2.8). The principal intonation patterns are summarized in §2.9.

2.1. Phonemes and components.

For the variety of Korean speech that we take as our point of departure, the phonemes and their components are as shown below.

Simple vowel nuclei

	FRONT		BACK	
	ROUNDED	UNROUNDED	ROUNDED	UNROUNDED
HIGH	–	i	u	wu
MID	oy	ey	e	o
LOW	–	ay	a	–

Complex nuclei

wi	–	–	–	–	yu
wey	yey	we	ye	–	yo
way	yay	wa	ya	–	–

Consonants

	Lax	Reinforced	Aspirate	Nasal	Liquid
Labial stop	p	pp	ph	m	
Dental stop	t	tt	th	n	l
Alveolar affricate	c	cc	ch		
Velar stop	k	kk	kh	ng	
Spirant	s	ss	h		

2.2. Vowel descriptions.

The vowel chart displays a nearly maximal system. In standard Seoul speech **oy** (mid front rounded vowel) is not distinguished from the diphthong **wey**, and there is no need for the front rounded category at all. The distinction between **(pyēng i) tōycinta** (= tōcinta) '(the illness) worsens' and **(ce sālam i) twēycinta** (< twie cinta) '(he) drops dead' is orthographic for Seoul speakers; many pronounce the first syllable of **twāyci** 'ta 'it's a pig' the same way, as /twey/. Moreover, in rapid speech the **w** will often drop, leaving /tey/ as the first syllable of all three phrases. There are very few words with **wey** or **way**, for that matter, and they are often confused in spelling with the many words that contain **oy**. Examples are **kwēy** 'box, case', **kwēyto** 'railroad track', **kkweyk** 'with a shout' (= **kkwayk**), **kkwēynta** 'strings, puts through', **weyn** 'why, what'; **way** 'why', **waykhong** 'peanuts', **kkway** 'extremely', **insway** 'printing', **yukhway hata** 'is delightful', and a few others.

Some linguists would move **wi** from the group of complex nuclei into the high rounded category of simple vowels, since many speakers tend to pronounce **wi** as a long monophthong [ü] rather than the more common diphthong [üi], coming from an earlier *wuy* [ui]. For most speakers, the phoneme /w/ is represented by simple lip rounding, with the tongue position largely determined by the following vowel: **wi** [üi], **wey** [öe], **way** [ɔ̈e], **we** [o̯ë], **wa** [ɔa]. The phoneme /y/ is usually high [i̯] regardless of the following vowel. Some speakers of the Kyengki area have a full range of rounded front vowels, monophthongizing **wi** [ü], **oy** (and probably **wey**?) [ö:], and **way** [ɔ̈:] alike, at least when these are historically long.

The vowel **e** has two markedly different allophones in Seoul speech: higher [ë] when long, and lower [ɛ̈] (= IPA inverted-v) when short. Many southern speakers give the vowel a slight internal rounding, as if scooping the back of the tongue with a spoon, when it is at the end of a syllable and especially before a pause. In Seoul speech there is a strong trend toward a rounded but unprotruded [ɔ]. Other vowels are less noticeably different when long or short, but in general the long HIGH and MID vowels tend to be higher than the short ones, and the long LOW vowels (if anything) somewhat lower than the short ones.

In the noninitial syllables of Seoul colloquial speech, **wu** is widely substituted for short **o** after a consonant, and (much less often) the syllable **yo** gets pronounced as **yu**, though I believe that is not true of consonant + **yo**. In very common words, especially endings and particles such as **-ko** and **to**, the Seoul colloquial forms (**-kwu** and **twu**) can be regarded as standard relaxed speech. But when **wu** is used for **o** in initial syllables it is considered substandard; **twūn** for **tōn** 'money' sounds vulgar. There are situations where that sort of speech can be effective: **Nwūngtam ici!** 'It's a joke = I'm joking!' (< ˈ**nōngtam**). The substitution of **wu** for [w]o can take place for each word independently: **Cōh.ko mālkwu yo**, **Cōh.kwu mālkwu yo**, and even **Cōh.ko mālkwu yu** and **Cōh.kwu mālkwu yu**, as well as **Cōh.kwu mālko yo** and (?) **Cōh.ko mālko yu**.

A similar raising of the back mid vowel **e** to **u** and the front mid vowel **ey** to **i** is also heard in noninitial syllables, and less commonly even in initial position. You may hear **ūps.ta** (and, for some reason, even **wūps.ta**) instead of **ēps.ta**, **cukta** for **cēkta**, **-usi yo** for **-usey yo**, etc. There are speakers who raise **a** to **e** in variant versions of certain words: ··· **henthey** for ··· **hanthey** 'to', **mulle** for **mōlla** 'dunno', etc. (CF the remarks on **-tun/-ten** in Part II.) Some raised vowels are considered standard. But **eti** 'where' probably comes directly from MK *e ˙tuy* rather than from **e[nu] tey** 'what place'.

Throughout much of southern Korea the vowel **ay** is distinguished from **ey** poorly, if at all. In Seoul speech the distinction is seldom maintained in noninitial position, though speakers are aware of it. The two expressions **sēy kay** 'three things' and **sēykyey** 'world' are usually pronounced identically as /seykey/. One young Seoul linguist says of this pair of words "I can make the distinction, but I don't". (The name of a Honolulu restaurant /phainpeylli/ sounds like "Pine Belly", but it turns out to be "Pine Valley"!) Some of the homonymy that results makes it harder to identify morphemes: the string /ettekhey/ may represent either **etteh.key** or **etteh.k' 'ay** (contraction of **etteh.key hay**); and /ēpsseyyo/ may be intended either as **ēps.e(y) yo** 'lacks it' or **ēpsay yo** 'does away with it'. With further raising of /ey/ to /i/ the expressions **elin i** 'young one' and **elin ay** 'young child' converge. In the areas where **ay** and **ey** have merged, confusion is avoided in various ways. To keep **nay kes** 'mine' distinct from **ney kes** 'yours', for example, Taykwu speakers use **na kes** and **ne kes**. Other word pairs that might be expected to cause difficulty, such as **kāy** 'dog' and **kēy** 'crab' are kept distinct by raising the mid vowel; in Taykwu 'dog' is **kēy** and 'crab' is **kī**. And among younger Seoul speakers one hears "**ney kes – ni kes**" = **nay kes – ney kes** 'mine – yours'; raised vowels are also heard in **ni ka** = **ney ka** 'you' and even **ci ka** = **cey ka** 'I [formal]'. Back formations (hyperurbanisms) are sometimes heard from southerners who merge **ey** and **ay**, as when **cāy-il** is said for **cēy-il** 'number one'; one speaker (recorded on KBC 27:6) said **selmayng** = **selmeyng** < **selmyeng** 'explanation'.

The dialect of Kimhay, on the southern coast, has a minimal system of vowel distinctions. There are six vowel phonemes:

	FRONT (UNROUNDED)	BACK UNROUNDED	BACK ROUNDED
HIGH	i	u/e	wu
LOW	ey	a	o

The quality of the **u/e** vowel varies from high to high-mid (depending on what is around it), as does the mid to low-mid quality of **ey** and **o**. The Kimhay vowel **ey** is cognate with standard (written) Korean **ey**, **ay**, **oy**, **way**, and **wey**; the vowel **i** is cognate with both **i** and **wi** in the standard written language.

The dialect of Ceycwu island (LSN 1978) retains certain features of earlier Korean that were lost in other dialects, notably the vowel traditionally called **alay a** (= *a ˙lay o*), which the Ceycwu speakers pronounce as a lower back rounded vowel ("open o"), though the Middle Korean equivalent functioned as a low back unrounded vowel with the closed o (= *wo*) as its rounded counterpart. As in other dialects the earlier diphthongs represented by our spellings *ey* and *ay* are monophthongized as front unrounded vowels, *uy* has merged with *i*, and the usual pronunciation of *wuy* is *i* after a consonant but after a vowel or pause it is a front rounded vowel, like some versions of standard **wi** (which comes from earlier *wuy*), though the more common Seoul pronunciation is a front rounded glide followed by an unrounded high vowel, rather like the sound in French "huis" or "lui" rather than that of French "oui" (English "we") or "Louis". As in many southern dialects, the distinction of historic *ay* (and *oy*) from *ey* is maintained poorly, if at all, though transcriptions may lead you to think otherwise. The unrounded vowels *u* and *e* are kept apart, and *e* is pronounced as a shwa [ə], rather than the currently popular Seoul pronunciation as a low back rounded vowel [ɔ], the value of which is preempted in Ceycwu by the old vowel *o* which in other dialects has merged with **a** in initial syllables and **u** in other syllables, with further assimilations in particular phonetic environments. Ceycwu retains a syllable *yo* which was merged with *ye* or *ya* in the central dialect of the early Hankul texts, though provision was made for the syllable (by a "double low dot") in the scheme of the letters.

The old diphthongs now monophthongized in most dialects are still heard as diphthongs in various parts of Hwanghay (Kim Yengpay 1984:297), where the pronunciation faithfully follows our spellings of **sāy** 'bird', **kāy** 'dog', **key** 'crab', **oy** 'cucumber', and **ōy-** 'memorize'. The 1898 Tayshin dictionary has good examples of **ai** and **ay** for the diphthongs, including **nwukwuy** for 'who' (← nwukwu i) and **sorai** for 'sound (etc.)' = NK solay(ki) < MK *swo loy* (> Seoul soli).

Most speakers devoice (= whisper) high-vowel nuclei (i wi u uy yu wu) in an environment with **h** or **s** (or consonant + h or s) on one flank and a simple obstruent (p t c k s h) on the other: **puchica, khuta, chwupta, sik.kwu, huksayk. kupsa, swita, swipta, swipsita, huyta**. Some speakers devoice the mid and low vowels in the same environment: **haksayng, saykssi, thokki, thepthephata**. But if there is only one vowel in the phrase it is usually voiced: **sip, huk, swuch; hak, thek**.

2.3. The pseudo-vowel *uy*.

The spelling **uy** is preserved from an earlier stage of the language, when **ey** and **ay** were diphthongs and **wi** was pronounced **wuy** [ui]. At that time **uy** was pronounced [ɨi], but with the monophthongization of the other diphthongs **uy**, too, was monophthongized to /u(:)/ or /i(:)/, depending on the dialect. In Seoul the traditional pronunciation of the monophthong is **u** at the beginning of a word and **i** in noninitial position. But when it is initial in a word, some people attempt a reading pronunciation of the diphthong and say **ui** (in two syllables); that pronunciation has been rapidly spreading among younger speakers, partly as a result of schooling. In the traditional Seoul versions, the word **ūykyen** 'opinion' is pronounced **ūkyen** and the word **cwūuy** 'attention' (which has for its last syllable the same Chinese morpheme 'one's will' that is the first syllable of **ūykyen**) is pronounced **cwūi**. In an obvious compound noun like **Sin-Uycwu**, name of the city of "New Uycwu", two versions are heard: **sinicwu**, treating the sequence as one word, and **sinucwu**, treating it as two words (but with no overt juncture separating the two). But **mu-uymi** 'meaningless' is usually pronounced **muimi** though **ūymi** 'meaning' is **ūmi**; **mu-** 'lacking' is bound and functions as a prefix, whereas **sin(-)** 'new' is quasi-free and can function as an adnoun. (There are no reports of the pronunciation ***mu-umi** > [mu:mi] and it has probably never existed.) The odd-looking word **ūyuy** 'meaning' is pronounced **ūi**.

The spelling **uy**, like the spelling **oy**, is left over from a period when Korean had phonetic diphthongs. The diphthongs *ay* and *ey* began to get monophthongized as front vowels from the late 1700s, but *(w)oy*, *wuy*, and *uy* seem to have persisted into the 19th century, at least. Present-day Korean has reduced the back rounded vowel of the older *wuy* to the semivowel **w** and lengthened the palatal glide **y** into the high front vowel **i** to yield **wi**, but some speakers use a front rounded monophthong [ü] at least in certain environments. A similar front rounded monophthong [ö] is used for older *woy* > **oy** by some speakers (in some environments) but the general pronunciation reduces *wo* to **w** and fronts the vowel to **ey**, so that the syllable merges with the articulation of **wey**, which was separate from **(w)oy** earlier. And there are speakers who, at least sometimes, treat (w)oy as **way**, in Seoul as well as (Kim Yengpay 1984:67) in Phyengan. In Phyengan *wuy* developed into **wi** but at the end of a polysyllable it often dropped the ···y to become **wu** (ibid): **Tang-nakwu = Tang-nakwi** 'donkey' (< *la'kwuy*), **ppey-takwu = ppye-takwi** 'bone'; **pakhwu = pakhwi** 'wheel' (< *pakhw^{u}oy*

< pa˙hwoy), **pawu** = **pawi** 'rock' (< *pawuy* < *pa˙hwoy*). There is no monophthong articulation that could replace the diphthong **uy** without merging it with either **u** or **i**, and many dialects have followed the expected course of pronouncing it as **i**. But in Seoul the word-initial **uy** has resisted that development and monophthongized to **u**, instead. It is possible that in the word-initial position the diphthong version **uy** has simply persisted for some Seoul speakers, as certain linguists would prefer, but I believe it is a back formation based on the spelling, as I have said. There are bits of evidence for the traditional Seoul treatment as early as the end of the nineteenth century, when Tayshin in his 1898 Korean-Russian dictionary wrote the equivalent of /usimi/ for **uysim** 'doubt' (with the accretion of the suffix **-i** that is widely attested in North Korea), though he wrote /uisik/ for **uysik** 'clothes'. The Phyengan development for *uy* is **i** but the particle is either **ey** (as in Seoul) or **u** (as in Cincwu, Mkk 1960:3:31). An early doublet: *i˙ki-* (1445 ¹Yong, 1449 Kok) = *i˙kuy-* (1447 Sek etc.) 'win'.

2.4. Consonant descriptions.

The lax obstruents are weakly articulated; in initial position they are released with a slight puff of local breath (in contrast with the heavy breathing of the aspirates) but are less tense than their English counterparts: [b‘] for **p**···. Between typically voiced sounds (vowels or semivowels, nasals, the liquid), the lax consonants are lightly voiced in rapid speech, as [a:nda] for **ānta** 'knows'. Lax consonants do not occur after other lax consonants; our spellings **pk**, **ks**, etc., automatically represent the phoneme strings /pkk/, /kss/, etc. (see §2.6). The lax consonants **p t k** occur in syllable-final position and there they are unvoiced and unreleased [b⁼ d⁼ g⁼]. 1881 Ridel was quite hesitant about the voiced allophones of the lax consonants: "sometimes ··· but not ordinarily" voiced.

The aspirated consonants are begun with a lax articulation (contrary to some descriptions), frequently velarized, and followed with heavy aspiration that is often accompanied by velar friction: [bʰa] or [bˣa]. The aspirated obstruents are never voiced. The phoneme /h/ is frequently "voiced" (murmured) or dropped between voiced sounds. It is more commonly glottal than velar, but a velar variant occurs, as well as a velarized glottal. Initial **hw**, and especially **hwu**, is often pronounced as a bilabial fricative [F] by many speakers. Ridel (1881:xv) transcribed the aspirates as "hk hp ht tch", and Underwood (1914) used "hk hp ht" but "ch" (writing the lax **c** as "j"). This follows the traditional Romanization of Burmese and has certain virtues in handling morphophonemic problems of Korean (see Martin 1982); Starchevskiy (1890) also wrote the aspiration before the consonant (King 1991a). Roth (1936:6) refers to a system like Ridel's as the "French transcription" (with "tj" for the simple /c/ and the geminates "kk pp ss ttj") and he refers to a somewhat similar system except for "htsch" (with "tsch" for the simple /c/ and the geminates "gg dd bb ss dsch") as the "German transcription".

The reinforced consonants are pronounced with great muscular tension, both locally and through the entire vocal tract. The laryngeal tension continues on into the vowel, which can be described as "laryngealized" (somewhat gargled), and the effect of the release is a clearcut popping similar to that of glottalized consonants but with no separately heard glottal release, so that they sound unlike the glottalized consonants of certain languages native to North America. The tense unaspirated stops of French are somewhat similar to these sounds. The reinforced consonants are never voiced.

The aspirated and reinforced consonants occur only as syllable onsets, but the syllable itself need not be word-initial. When they are internal in the phrase there is no distinction between strings like **appha** and **apha**, or **apppa** and **appa**. In rapid speech only the latter occurs, and we take that to be the phonemic norm; in slow speech the stop is anticipated with closure of the preceding open syllable. These two tempo-controlled articulations, which I call compressed and conflated, are variants regardless of the constituency of the phrases in which they occur. The morpheme boundaries may be **a-pha**, **aph-a**, or **ap-pha** (in basic form also **ap-ha** or **ah-pa**), but the compression and conflation will take place automatically for each, as the tempo changes, giving two phonetic realizations for each phoneme string /apha/ and /appa/, regardless of their meaning, if any. (See Martin 1982 and 1986, where mention is made of similar variation in English words like "upper" and "cookie"; also §2.10.6.)

The nasals are fully voiced, and at the end of a syllable somewhat long. Initial **m**, especially before **(w)u** and **o**, often has an oral release [mᵇ] or even [ᵐb]. Initial **n**, especially before **i** or **e** (as in ney 'yes'), sometimes has a similar oral release [n^d] or [^nd]. (CF Lukoff 1954:4, 11; Martin ?1991: n14.) Ramstedt (1939:14) cites NK dialect forms "^ndui ^nlui; duin luin" for 'four' (nēys), perhaps a variant of the [doy] reported by 1900 Matveev (King 1988b:309) and [noi] in 1898 Tayshin; compare the Hamkyeng form cited by Kim Thaykyun as nei. The velar nasal ng does not occur at the beginning of a word, or after pause, but it can occur as the onset of a noninitial syllable as a result of the consonant "liaison" described in §2.5. In the strings ···ngi and ···ngy··· the velar nasal is fronted and weakened, often disappearing into a nasal y [ĩ], or vanishing completely as in the northern dialect of 1902 Azbuka (and sporadically even in Seoul); King (1988:301-2) reports the phenomenon in 1898 Tayshin, with the nasal vowel remaining, and 1900 Matveev, with no nasality written.

The liquid /l/ occurs after pause only in recent loanwords, and at the beginning of a word only in recent loanwords or in words that do not occur at the beginning of a phrase, such as particles. Internally, /l/ occurs both as a syllable onset and as a coda. When the liquid is syllable-initial, and not preceded by another l, the tongue tip is quickly flapped against the very front of the alveolar ridge, so that the articulation sounds like the single-tap Spanish r or (rather) the somewhat more liquid Japanese r. At the end of a syllable, the l is unreleased and the tongue curls up around and beyond the point where it would have been released, producing a sound that English speakers hear as [l]. The string /ll/, syllable-final l + syllable-initial l, sounds like a long l to a speaker of English, but without the velarization that colors the "dark l" of many English speakers. But Lukoff 1954:40-2 seems to feel that /ll/ is phonetically short like /n/ rather than long like /nn/ [n:n], and some native linguists have expressed a similar feeling. Perhaps that perception (or misperception) is due to the existence of an initial [n···] but no initial [l···], for /l···/ is realized as the flap allophone [r]. Yet at the same time Lukoff (1954:9-10) describes the articulation of /l/ after /l/ as a "pre-flapped [l]" which he writes as [^dl]. Often the Korean l (and even more often the ll) is somewhat palatalized, especially before i or y; that is, the center of the tongue is humped at the same time that the tip of the tongue is making the primary articulation. There have been various reports that the flap allophone is used by northern dialects in place of the lateral used in the south before pause or a consonant, e.g. Ramstedt (1939:11) says the allophone of the liquid before a consonant is [l] in South Korea but [r] in North Korea. And there is evidence for that in Russian transcriptions from the 1800s and early 1900s; the Cyrillic spellings of 1902 Azbuka have [r] for the liquid in -lC- clusters. King 1987 says that the North Hamkyeng dialect preserved in the USSR has [r] word-final and before obstruents. He tells me that such speakers pronounce ···ll··· as a short lateral, in contrast with [r] for the simple ···l···. In the expression il.il liphothe 'daily/everyday reporter' you can hear a sequence of lateral + flap [iril( )ri···] but that probably represents a juncture; with totally suppressed juncture the pronunciation is [irilli···].

In rapid speech, owing to the consonant "liaison", the strings mh, nh, ngh, and lh often occur as syllable-initial clusters, instead of as a syllable-final consonant + the onset h-. Here the h is "voiced" (murmured) and pronounced as a breathy release of the somewhat shortened nasal or liquid, which has its "r"-like sound, as noted by Ridel (1881:xiv). More common is a variant version which drops the h completely; see §2.7.3.

The distinction between the two sibilants s and ss is often difficult to hear, and many Koreans, especially in the south, appear to lack the distinction in their local speech. Though minimal pairs can be found, the functional load of the distinction seems to be fairly low, especially in noninitial position. To an American ear, the best description might be this: s is something LESS than what you expect of an "s", and ss is something MORE. There is a fuzzy "lisp"-like quality to the lax s. If you hear a clearcut "s", it is probably the reinforced ss. If you hear an "s" that you can't make up your mind about, an "s" that seems to have something missing, it is probably the lax s. In the Seoul speech of some, the lax s before i and wi is regularly palatalized [ź'yi] or even palatal [ź'i], and that helps distinguish si from ssi. But in the speech of others, the ss is also palatalized before i and wi, so that palatalization is not so reliable a guide as the lag, after the plain s, in voicing the vowel, a lag that is indicated in our phonetic transcription by the inverted apostrophe used to symbolize lightly aspirated release.

The affricates are palatalized throughout the south, and the stop that begins the affricate is sometimes a palatal stop, which identifies the phoneme more perceptibly than the sibilant release, especially the reinforced **cc**, which tends to suppress the sibilant along with any hint of aspiration. For many Seoul speakers the palatalization is weak or absent before back unrounded vowels, and in the north the nonpalatalized affricate is frequently heard before all the vowels. Figulla 1935:103 says /c/ before /a e o wu/ is the dental affricate [ts], elsewhere (i.e. before /i ey ay wi wey way oy/) the palatal affricate. After a vowel and before a back vowel, the voiced version of the nonpalatalized affricate is sometimes weakened to just [z]. Good examples of that can be heard from a female speaker on the tapes accompanying KBC (Pak Pongnam 1969): ize = **ic.e** 'forgot', ezey = **ecey** 'yesterday', kuzekkey = **kucekkey** 'day before yesterday', sazen = **sacen** 'dictionary', paykhwazem = **payk.hwa-cem** 'department store'; ui(d)za = **uyca** 'chair', mo(d)za = **moca** 'hat'. Despite the description implied in several treatises, it is quite rare to hear [z] in any modern dialect as an allophone of /s/; when [z] or [^{d}z] is heard, it almost always represents /c/. But there is evidence for a [z] allophone of /s/ in earlier Hamkyeng speech, as heard by Putsillo, Matveev, and Tayshin. And Lukoff (1954:8) says of /s/ "After /m, n, ng/ and before a vowel, it may have a weak and sometimes slightly voiced variant [z]." On [z] see also §2.11.4. Ridel, who only hesitantly admitted voiced versions of **p t k**, flatly states (1881:xvii) that there was no [z].

2.5. Syllable structure and consonant liaison.

The Korean syllable is a phonetic entity that is automatically predictable in terms of a string of phonemes: it consists of an initial (the onset), a medial (the vowel or diphthong), and a final (the coda). The onset can be zero or p pp ph t tt th k kk kh c cc ch s ss h m n -ng (-)l; -mh, -nh, -ngh, -lh. The final can be zero or p t k m n ng l. The Korean writing system, and our transcription, has other finals in its "orthographic" syllables, but those are basic forms subject to reduction in the spoken syllables. Modern Hankul uses the same symbol for initial "zero" and final ···ng, though distinctive symbols were once used; the final zero is left unmarked, though it was marked in some of the earliest Hankul texts.

Not all possible combinations of initial, medial, and final occur. Medials beginning with **y** (**yey yay ye ya yu yo**) do not occur after s ss c ch cc t th tt except as contractions from **i** + vowel (**iey iay ie ia iwu io**) — see §3.5.(9), or in a few recent loanwords such as **syussu** (also **syaccu** and **syechu**) 'shirt' for which the less Japanese-sounding **sassu** is also heard. The vowel **u** does not occur after a labial (**p ph pp m**) and that is why we can abbreviate the vowel **wu** to **u** after a labial, so that our "**pu**" = p + wu, "**phu**" = ph + wu, "**ppu**" = pp + wu. In a similar way our "**yu**" = y + wu since there is no **y** + **u**. Medials that begin with **w** (**wi wey way we wa**) do not occur after a labial except as abbreviations of **wu** or **o** + vowel (**wui wuey wuay wue wua oa**), as in **mwe(s)** < **mue(s)** 'what'.

Whenever possible, a syllable shuns the "zero" initial. Korean syllables like to begin with a consonant. When a syllable with the zero initial is appended to a syllable with a final consonant, that consonant shifts over to become the onset of the second syllable: **pap** + **i** is pronounced **pa-pi**, **pang** + **ey** is pronounced **pa-ngey**, **pal** + **ul** is pronounced **pa-lul** and sounds just the same as **pa** + **lul**. When the second syllable begins with **h**, the result is what we would expect from our transcription: ···p + h··· → ···ph··· etc. In rapid speech we even find ···m (···n ···ng ···l) + h··· → ···mh··· (etc.), though the **h** frequently drops in this position. When the first syllable ends in **p, t,** or **k** and the second syllable begins with the same consonant, the first syllable loses its final and the initial of the second syllable doubles: ···p + p··· → ···pp···, etc. (For the fact that ···p + k··· → ···pkk···, ···t + k··· → ···kk···, ···t + s··· → ···ss···, etc., see the following section.)

How many distinct syllables does Korean have? It is difficult to answer this question precisely. Suppose we figure that the initials (including zero and **l-**) are 20 (+ 5 in spoken syllables like **-ngi**, **-mha**, etc. = 25), that the medials are 20 (omitting **uy** because of its limited distribution and doubtful status as a phoneme), and that the finals (including zero) are 8. Then we have a minimum (20x20x8=) 3,200 and a maximum of (25x20x8=) 4,000. From these figures we would perhaps want to subtract the syllables that do not occur in spoken words, but many such syllables will in fact turn up in Hankul

30 PART I   A Reference Grammar of Korean

spellings, for one reason or another, and in addition Hankul has a number of orthographic syllables with additional basic finals (such as **ph th kk ps ls** etc.) and some unusual syllables like **sya cye chyess**, etc. There are undoubtedly some accidental gaps that do not occur in normal words. Perhaps we are safe in saying that Korean has between three and four thousand different syllables, some of which are fairly rare, and many of which are limited to certain sections of the vocabulary, such as Chinese loanwords, inflected forms, and mimetic words (onomatopes).

2.6. Cluster restrictions.

When two syllables occur in uninterrupted sequence, fewer strings of consonants are found than we expect. The occurring strings are shown in the following table. The line across the top shows the end of the prior syllable; the column at the left shows the beginning of the following syllable. At a point of intersection, an expected string is shown in lowercase boldface. An automatic replacement of a morphophonemically expected sequence is shown in boldface italic. The notion of "expected" is with respect to the analysis underlying the Romanization: when a syllable ending in **-p** is attached to one beginning with **-p**, the string that results is syllable-initial **pp-**, pronounced as the onset of the second syllable but optionally picking up a parasitic final **-p** (not the original **-p**) when the articulatory process is slowed down. Syllable boundaries are assumed to be automatically determined at a given tempo. The zero onset and coda are noted with the symbol "0".

	-p	-t	-k	-m	-n	-ng	-l	-0
p-	pp	*pp*	*pp*	kpp	mp	*mp*	ngp	lp	p
ph-	*ph*	*ph*	*ph*	kph	mph	*mph*	ngph	lph	ph
pp-	*pp*	*pp*	*pp*	kpp	mpp	*mpp*	ngpp	lpp	pp
t-	*ptt*	tt	ktt	mt	nt	ngt	lt	t
th-	*pth*	*th*	kth	mth	nth	ngth	lth	th
tt-	*ptt*	tt	ktt	mtt	ntt	ngtt	ltt	tt
s-	*pss*	ss	kss	ms	ns	ngs	ls	s
ss-	*pss*	ss	kss	mss	nss	ngss	lss	ss
c-	*pcc*	cc	kcc	mc	nc	ngc	lc	c
ch-	*pch*	*ch*	kch	mch	nch	ngch	lch	ch
cc-	*pcc*	cc	kcc	mcc	ncc	ngcc	lcc	cc
k-	*pkk*	kk	kk	mk	*ngk*	ngk	lk	k
kh-	*pkh*	*kh*	*kh*	mkh	*ngkh*	ngkh	lkh	kh
kk-	*pkk*	kk	kk	mkk	*ngkk*	ngkk	lkk	kk
h-	*ph*	*th*	*kh*	mh	nh	ngh	lh	h
m-	*mm*	*nm*	*ngm*	mm	*mm*	ngm	lm	m
n-	*mn*	*nn*	*ngn*	mn	nn	ngn	*ll*	n
l-	*mn*	(*nn*)	*ngn*	mn	*ll*	ngn	ll	l
0-								

This table can be regarded as a kind of filter, through which the underlying morphophonemic strings that we expect to occur across morpheme boundaries (or orthographic pseudo-boundaries) are converted to the phonemic strings that serve as input to the rules that tell the articulatory organs how to realize the utterances. A native speaker of Korean unconsciously utilizes a filter of this sort, not directly accessible to observation. The filter can, however, be generated by a set of rules that more or less recapitulates the history of changing phonetic habits through the centuries, and it is possible that the speaker creates his filter, or bypasses it, by making use of such a set of rules. Below are the rules that account for the table, with a few notes on the historical developments that brought them into existence. (The rules are a revision of those in the introduction to KEd. The notes are largely based on Martin 1989 and the works cited there.)

Rules to convert morphophonemic/orthographic strings to phonemic strings:

(1) NASAL LATERALIZATION. Change n to l when it is contiguous to l.
(2) LIQUID NASALIZATION. Change l to n when it is after a consonant other than l or is after juncture.
(3) NASAL ASSIMILATION. Convert the oral stops **p t k** to the corresponding nasals **m n ng** when a nasal (**m n**) follows.
(4) CLUSTER REINFORCEMENT. Reinforce simple **p t k c s** to **pp tt kk cc ss** after an obstruent (**p t k**).
(5) ASSIBILATION. Pronounce **t** as **s** before **s** or **ss**.
(6) ASSIMILATION OF APICALS. Make the point of articulation of **t** and **n** be the same as that of a following labial (**p pp ph m**) or velar (**k kk kh**): t → p or k, n → m or ng.
(7) CLUSTER REDUCTION. Unless deliberately slowing the articulations, reduce three like consonants to two (**ttt** → **tt**); before **h** reduce two like consonants to one (**tth** → **th**).

It will be observed that strings of lax obstruents are not permitted: the expected **kp** is automatically replaced by **kpp**, etc. Since most cases of lax obstruent + reinforced obstruent (**kpp**, ...) are the result of juxtaposing two basic lax obstruents (-k + p-, ...), the default Hankul spelling is ···k-p··· (...) for ALL cases of /kpp/ (...) except when the second element is clearly a form that has a basic shape with initial **pp**··· (...). The string /yakpalle/ can represent both **yak palle** 'applies medicine' and **yak-ppalle** 'is shrewd and quick'. We are reminded of the appropriate spelling in each case by the recurrence of the forms in such unambiguous contexts as **yak ul palle** /yakul( )palle/ 'applies medicine' and **yak.ko ppalle** /yakko( )ppalle/ 'is shrewd and is quick'. As in other cases where morphophonemic decisions are called for, Koreans sometimes get confused and misspell words, either in the morphophonemically safer direction (-kp-, ...) or in their phonemic form (-kpp-, ...) as they are heard. (And the decision on where to divide a word into morphemes is sometimes in conflict with the history of the forms; see §2.10.6 for examples.)

An interesting example is provided by the convergence of the two sentences **pap to iss.e** 'there is also (cooked) rice' and **pap tto iss.e** 'there is more rice', which sound the same in rapid speech when no pause is inserted: /papttoisse/. With pauses ("open juncture") to distinguish the two sentences, they sound different: **pap to iss.e** /paptto|isse/, **pap tto iss.e** /pap|ttoisse/. In slow and overdeliberate pronunciations you may hear -tkk- and -tpp- instead of the usual reductions of -kk- and -pp- from -tk(k)- and -tp(p)-. Some speakers feel that they also articulate -tcc- for the -cc- from -t c(c)- but that is questionable. The pronunciation of -tss- from -t s(s)- is highly artificial; a genuine /tss/ is used by many speakers in pronounced the loanword **syaccu** 'shirt' (also **syassu**) as [šattsi], following the articulatory habits of Japanese, from which the word was borrowed.

As earlier observed (§1.5), Chinese loanwords regularly reinforce the sequences ···ls···, ···lc···, and ···lt··· to ···lqs···, ···lqc···, and ···lqt···. For /lc/ and /lt/ it is fairly easy to find non-Chinese words without the -q-, such as the forms made by attaching the endings -ci and -ta to l-extending verb stems (§8.3.2), and compounds such as **thel cangkap** 'wool gloves'. Words made up of Chinese morphemes may appear in compounds without the reinforcement: **sil-cakca** 'a reliable person', **chelmul-cen** 'hardware store'. For /ls/ it is not so easy to find contrasts, and I suspect there may be Koreans who reinforce all cases to ···lqs···. (To be sure, many Koreans simply fail to distinguish /ss/ from /s/ in any environment; we do not speak of them.) Yet certain types of compounds and phrases turn up cases where I have observed /ls/ from at least some speakers. One textbook (M 1:1:70) indicates **kyŏsilq se** for 'in the classroom' but that is pronounced **kyŏsil se** by speakers I have heard (such as [1]Yi Tongcay). Examples:

pyel soli 'unexpected remark', **pyel swu** 'extraordinary good fortune', **pyel sālam** 'an eccentric'; **Sewul se** 'from Seoul', **Sewul si** 'the city of Seoul', **thukpyel si** 'special city [of Seoul]'; **pāl-soy** 'informing on others', **naphal-swu** 'bugler', **sol-song namu** 'hemlock spruce', **sal-son ulo** 'with bare hands'; **mal sōl** 'horse brush', **cil soth** 'earthenware kettle', **māl somssi** 'eloquence', **māl silqswu** 'tongueslip', **congtal say** 'skylark', **chel say** 'seasonal (= migratory) bird', **thel sīl** 'wool yarn', **cil sas-pan** 'small reed tray attached to an A-frame carrier', **Hānkwuk māl sensayng** 'teacher of Korean'; **sīlsil-i** 'thread by thread, every thread'; **hoth-pel sālam** 'shallow-minded person'; **wul sēyta** '(clan is strong =) has a large family', **kkol**

sānapta 'has an ugly face', pul salunta 'commits to the flames', al sunta (← su-l-) 'emits spawn, lays eggs', nal sunta (← su- < se-) 'gets sharp(-edged), takes an edge', nal seywunta 'sharpens, puts an edge on'; twūl sai 'between the two', but twūlq cwung 'of the two' – [1]Yi Mayngseng tells me that he uses twūlq sai more often than twūl sai and that he thinks twūl cwung occurs but is rare.

In certain compounds made up of Chinese elements the reinforcement seems to be optional: [1]ipal(q)-so 'barber shop', [1]ipal(q)-sa 'barber'.

The assimilations and reductions described here take place across words and phrases, when the phonetic cues to their boundaries are omitted, as often happens in normal rapid speech: **Acik moluni?** 'You still don't know?' (/···ngm···/), **Wang sepang to kkamcak nōllan mas!** 'The taste that surprised Mr Wang!' (ad for 3-minute "instant meal") (/···ngn···/), **kot na onta** 'will come right out' (/···nn···/), **tōn ul nāynta** 'pays the money' /tōnullaynta/, **khunq īl nass.ta** 'that's terrible' /khunnīllatta/.

2.7. Sequence variants.

There are certain types of variants which are widely systematic: a given sequence of phonemes for which we always (or always within a morph or a word), find a variant of consistent shape. There are also some which are less predictable, but also widespread, of a similar sort. Nine types of these SEQUENCE VARIANTS are described below. See also the remarks on **oy** (§2.2) and **uy** (§2.3).

2.7.1. Precision variants.

In speech at a normal rapid tempo, n is replaced by m before p or m, and by ng before k:

sānqpo → sāmppo 'stroll, walk', han pen → ham pen 'one time', cwūnpi → cwūmpi 'preparation', sinmun → simmun 'newspaper', (mōs mek.e → mōt mek.e →) mōn mek.e → mōm mek.e 'can't eat'; chinkwu → chingkwu 'friend', pankawe → pangkawe 'is happy', sonq-kalak → song-kkalak 'finger'.

In faster speech, m is replaced by ng before k:

cāmqkan → cāngkkan 'a while', nemkye → nengkye 'across, over', īmkum → īngkum 'king', cikum kkaci → cikung kkaci 'up to now'.

Sometimes, in fast or sloppy speech, pk(k) is replaced by kk:

komapkeyss.ˢup.nita → komakkeyssumnita 'I will be grateful (to you)', poypkeyss.ˢup.nita → poykkeyssumnita 'I will see you'.

In sloppy speech ng often drops between vowels, especially when it is before i or y:

cwungang → cwuang 'central'; congi → coi 'paper'; tongyang → to.yang 'Orient'; the placenames **Phyengyang** → Phye.yang (→ Pheyyang, §2.7.9), Yangyang → Ya.yang; ... .

Sometimes a final ···ng is dropped: the **hapsung** (jitney) boys in 1960 Seoul would call out **sīche!** for **sīcheng** 'City Hall'. In those days when you left a Seoul restaurant you might hear a cordial **A(n)nyē kapsye!** for **Annyeng hi kapsio!** 'Good-bye, sir'.

A casual reduction of m to w can be heard in rapid versions of ku man twue (yo) > kuwantw[u]e(yo) (§2.7.7) > k[u]wante(yo) = kwante(yo) > k[w]ante(yo) (§2.7.4) > kante(yo) 'cut it out (= stop); let it go (at that)'.

2.7.2. Vowel length variants.

Vowel length is distinctive in Korean, and the long vowel can be considered as a string of two identical short vowels. But many speakers do not use long vowels in all the words for which some speakers retain them, so that most words with a long vowel within a morph have short variants. Even for a speaker making maximum use of the length distinctions, the long vowel is usually restricted to the first syllable of a word, so that virtually every morph with a long vowel has a grammatically conditioned alternant with the short counterpart, as can be seen from the pair of synonyms **ūngpo** = **pōung** 'retribution'. But not all short-vowel morphs have long alternants or variants; many are always short. For practical purposes, I indicate a variable long vowel – any long vowel within a morph – by putting a macron above the letter symbol. In some Korean dictionaries, a long mark is put over the entire syllable; in others, the syllable is followed by two dots, like the colon that is used to mark vowel length in the International Phonetic Alphabet. A problem arises as to whether the length should be marked LEXICALLY, and accordingly seldom written on a syllable that is not initial in a word, or MORPHEMICALLY. The synonym pair cited above showed a lexical marking of the length; a morphemic marking would be ūngpō = pōūng. South Korean dictionaries have generally shown the length morphemically (and etymologically) for words of Chinese origin. The North Korean dictionary (NKd), and the Yale dictionary (KEd), mark the length lexically, as is the general practice of this book, though in a number of examples the morphemic marking will be seen. Lexical marking seems to be the safer approach, since lexical units can be readily checked with native speakers, and many problems arise in morpheme identifications and our decisions on "basic" length for both Chinese and non-Chinese morphemes. The Chinese characters are not always a reliable guide: the cities of **Taykwu** and **Taycen** are pronounced with short first syllables that represent the character tāy 'large, great', for which the length may be heard in words like tāy-hak.kyo 'university'.

The words kiil 'fixed date, term' and kīl(q) 'to be long' at times are homonyms for some speakers; at other times for those speakers and at all times, perhaps, for other speakers, they are not. In rapid speech both words may even sound like kil 'road'. The word chwīim 'inauguration' is to be pronounced in two syllables, with the first long, but it is often said as a single long syllable, and in rapid speech even that may be heard shortened. The distinction between e and ē is the easiest to hear, for in Seoul speech the long variety of that vowel is conspicuously higher in quality, and the short variety is not only lower but backer and more rounded. That helps distinguish heen 'falsehood' from hēn ··· 'old, worn(-out)', and tēpta 'is hot' from te epta 'shoulders more' (An Sangchel 1988:120) and te ēps.ta 'lacks more'. For other vowels the length is mainly observed when needed to distinguish particular sound-alikes in certain contexts. For more examples of vowel length, see KM 8-9.

When a one-syllable phrase ends in a vowel, that vowel is automatically lengthened, so that when cited in isolation the words si 'poem' and sī 'city' are identically /sii/. The automatic lengthening disappears when the word is part of a longer phrase: si to 'poem too', sī to 'city too'. This kind of lengthening is ignored by all the orthographies and most of the linguistic descriptions. (A similar phenomenon is common in western Japan and in the Ryūkyūs.)

He Wung (1965:89) points out some length alternations in verb forms. The vowel length found in many of the verbs here called l-extending, s-dropping, and -w- (p-leniting) stems is lost before endings that begin with a vowel — kē-l- → kel.e 'hangs', cī(s)- → cie 'builds', kōw- → kōpta but kowa 'is pretty' — and also in voice-derived forms such as alli- 'informs' ← ā-l-. The stem pē-l- 'earn money' is an exception (pēl.i 'earning money', pēl.e 'earns money'), probably because it is a reduction of peu-l-; similar exceptions are kkū-l- 'pull' (kkūl.e), coming from earlier kuu-l-, and ssē-l- 'chop' (ssēl.e), which goes back to *sehul-* (LCT 449b). With the exception of tut- 'hear', the verbs that end in leniting t (the verbs here treated as modern l-final stems = -T/L- stems) have vowel length before a consonant, where they preserve the original stop unlenited: kēt.ko 'walking', kel.e 'walks'. The length on these stems resulted from the blend of a Middle Korean low tone on the first vowel and a high tone on a lost vowel that must have followed the consonant before the lenition took place: *keˑtuˑ-ˑkwo > ˑket-ˑkwo, then *keˑtuˑ-ˑe > keˑl-e. A similar history accounts for the vowel length of s-dropping and -w- stems (Martin 1973; Ramsey 1975, 1978); see below. On the accentual exception of tut- 'hear' it is interesting that this seems to be the only one of these stems that Phyengan preserves unlenited, with the infinitive tut.e = Seoul tul.e despite Seoul-like sil.e 'load' and kel.e 'walk' (Kim Yengpay 1984:53).

The vowel length of a Chinese morpheme usually drops when it is noninitial in a word; this is part of a general tendency to retain accentual distinctions only in the initial position.

In addition to the sort of lexical length mentioned above, there also occurs an "expressive lengthening" as a voice qualifier, often accompanied by rasp or other voice qualifiers, for certain mimetic words, such as the last syllable of adjectival nouns ending in -us (hata). CF §14.

Younger Seoul speakers have largely lost the old vowel-length distinctions but they have new long vowels based on dropped ···h··· (§2.7.3) or ···u··· (§2.7.5), or in words borrowed from English and other modern languages. The older vowel-length distinctions are ignored in Hankul orthography. The new long vowels in modern loanwords are also ignored in the North Korean orthography but in the south the length is sometimes written with a repeat of the vowel as a separate syllable (with the zero initial), though occasionally you will see instead a dash (–), a usage borrowed from the Japanese treatment of katakana words. You may find khulīm 'cream' spelled "khu-lim", "khu-li-im", or even "khu-li--m".

Decisions on noting vowel length for certain common words can be troublesome. We have followed LHS, KEd, and NKd in writing the stems cīna- 'go past' and cīnay- 'go past it' (and their derivatives) with a long first vowel, and that is historically correct, but Kim Minswu follows contemporary Seoul standards in writing them short, and the student is advised to treat them as short despite our retention of the length. We write the noun sihem 'examination' without vowel length, but dictionaries list it as sīhem (KEd, NKd) or sihēm (LHS), and the usual pronunciation today is /syēm/, with the intervocalic -h- dropped (as usual) and the i losing its syllabicity (reduced to y) but with compensatory lengthening of the following e. The word traditionally spelled iyaki 'talk, tale' is usually pronounced yāyki or (more commonly) yēyki, and all three versions will be found in this book. The first vowel of the stem komaw- 'be grateful' is short, not long, but sometimes "expressive" length is superimposed in saying Ko(:)mapsup.nita, and that is responsible for the misleading remark in KEd 141b "Some pronounce long [kōmapta]". There are probably a few other cases of this sort that have escaped my attention. The student need not worry about vowel length except when he hears it, for younger Koreans pronounce most of the older long vowels as short, maintaining only those long vowels that are the result of contraction, such as mām < maum 'soul', and the newly arrived long vowels that have come in with modern loanwords (sometimes written double, as geminates): khātu = khaatu 'card', aphāthu = aphaathu 'apartment house', sīcun = siicun 'season', ēythosu = eyeythosu 'ethos', phēsuthu = pheesuthu 'first (base)', khōtu = khootu 'cord', khyū = khyuwu 'cue, Q'. Sometimes a bar is written for the second vowel, and sometimes it is simply ignored. The diphthongized English long vowels are usually treated as eyi and owu.

The distinctive length of the central area corresponds to distinctive pitch or a combination of pitch and length in certain other parts of Korea. In the province of South Kyengsang, for which we have He Wung's description of his native dialect of Kimhay, there are three lexically distinct pitch levels HIGH, MID, and LOW. (The high pitch sometimes has a slight fall, especially on a monosyllable in isolation.) In North Kyengsang (e.g. Antong) and also in North Cenla (e.g. Kwunsan), there are only two lexically distinct pitches HIGH and LOW, and part of the distinction is carried by vowel length. The low pitch of Kimhay is cognate with LONG low nuclei in Antong and the mid pitch of Kimhay is cognate with SHORT low nuclei. (Apparently there are no long vowels in Antong with HIGH pitch.) Farther north, in Hamkyeng (e.g. Hamhung and Hoylyeng) HIGH and LOW pitch are distinguished but there is no cognate distinction of length. Moreover, both the mid and low pitches of Kimhay are cognate with the HIGH pitch of Hamhung, and the LOW pitch of Hamhung is cognate with the high pitch of Kimhay. In each of the Korean dialects the situation is complicated by a certain amount of pitch sandhi (partly described by He Wung) that is similar to the length alternations of standard Korean. We refer here to the "basic" accents of words. The distinctive lexical pitch is not to be confused with the SENTENCE INTONATION of standard Korean, described in §2.8. Speakers from Seoul and from most of the north and west do not differentiate words by pitch alone. But many speakers from the south and east retain their native distinctions of pitch even after they have adjusted their pronunciation to the standard language quite well in other respects.

Below is a table that shows a few stock examples to demonstrate the cognate relationship of pitch and length in the dialects. The first column lists the examples in standard forms; the other columns show the pitch and length for each example in the four dialect types known to me.

STANDARD	SEOUL	KIMHAY	ANTONG-KWUNSAN	HAMHUNG-HOYLYENG
mal 'horse'	short	high	high	low
pay 'pear'				
son 'guest'				
mal 'measure'	short	mid	low short	high
pay 'stomach; boat'				
son 'hand'				
māl 'words'	long	low	low long	high
pāy 'double'				
sōn 'loss'				

In Middle Korean the syllables of the second type were preceded by a dot, representing high pitch, and those of the third type by a double dot, which represented a long rise going from low to high. In the Yale Romanization the two accent marks of Middle Korean can be represented with a raised dot and a dieresis (raised double-dot): swon 'guest', ˙swon 'hand', ¨swon 'loss'.

From a typological point of view, it can be said that Korean words have lexical ACCENT, manifested by pitch or length or a combination of pitch and length, depending on the dialect. Somewhat similar remarks can be made about Japanese. But the tones of Chinese are different: they represent a pitch contour that is part of each monosyllable, just like the consonants and vowels. The accent patterns of Korean and of Japanese spread over longer stretches, since these languages have many polysyllabic words and morphemes.

2.7.3. Disappearing *h*.

The phoneme h freely drops between typically voiced phonemes (the vowels and y w m n ng l): a[h]op 'nine', sīm-[h]i 'extremely', mān[h].i 'lots', sin[h]on 'new marriage, honeymoon', un[h]ayng 'bank', cen-[h]ye 'totally', kyel[h]on 'marriage', chel[h]ak-cek ulo 'philosophically', pāng[h]ak 'school vacation', annyeng [h]i 'in good health', kō[h]yang 'hometown', kyo[h]wan 'exchange', sel[h]wa 'story, tale', in[h]yeng 'doll', um[h]yang 'sound, noise'. The h-less version of kō(h)yang i 'home town [as subject]' can sound like ko.yangi 'cat', though in Seoul that word usually contracts to kwāyngi. And ol hay 'this year' can sound like olay 'for a long time' (both /oley/). There can be more than one dropped h in a phrase: ¹īhay hay (yo) 'I understand' is often reduced to /īeyey(yo)/.

For certain words the version with the elided ···h··· is now considered standard: puengi 'owl' (dialect puhengi, puhii) < ˙pwuhwe˙ngi, hwāng'a = hwanghwā 'sundries, variety goods' < HWANG-˙HWA (for the dropped w in these two words, see §2.7.4); pinye 'hairpin' < pinhye (? < ˙PIN 'hair on temple' + ˙hye 'tongue' or °hye- 'pull'); ili 'wolf' < ˙ilhi. From a strictly synchronic point of view, there is no h in words like mān(h).i, despite the spelling, which is morphophonemic; we infer the h from other forms such as mānkho ← mānh.ko, as it is spelled. In unfamiliar Chinese words, the underlying h will emerge as a kind of reading pronunciation, but it usually drops when the word comes to be often said. Inflected forms of h-final stems are pronounced without the h when it is between voiced sounds, but occasionally you will hear the h restored for emphasis in certain forms, as in Cōh.un kyēy[h]oyk ita 'It is a GOOD plan', though never in other forms, such as cō[h].a > /cōwa/, which can be emphasized only by further lengthening the vowel (cō:wa), for the h has been completely absorbed in the infinitive, and an epenthetic glide w has taken its place. How old is the h-elision and, after a rounded vowel, the epenthetic w? 1882 Ross 35 has nwo.wa.la < noh.a la. There are examples of n[h] in the 1500s and 1700s: ¨ma˙ni (?1517- ¹No 2:26a, Pak 1:20a) and man.i (1703 Sam-yek 5:2) = mān(h).i 'much'; skun.e (1736 ⁿYe 3:13 [LCT]) = skunhe (1783 Cahyul 1) = kkun(h).e 'end'.

Sometimes the entire h··· syllable drops: Na [ha]nthey? 'For me?'; Kulena silphay [hay]ss.c[i] yo 'But they failed'. The verb expression in Pusan ey se Kim Sencwu thukpha-[w]en i pōto hap.nita 'From Pusan, correspondent Kim Sencwu reports' is often said as pōto [ha]p.nita = /pōtomnita/ and equally often as pōt[o h]ap.nita = /pōtamnita/ < /pōt[w]amnita/ (o > w, §2.7.7). A similar example: kac[i] an[h].ulye ko hap.nita = /kacanulyekamnita/ < /··· k[w]amnita/ 'I won't go'.

2.7.4. Disappearing w.

Before a mid or low vowel the phoneme w freely drops after p, ph, ps, m, wu, or o: **sam-[w]el** 'March', **sam [w]en** 'three wen [monetary unit]', **kwu [w]en** 'nine wen', **kyŏ[w]en** 'teacher', **ō-[w]el** 'May', **cēm.[w]en** 'shop clerk', **pep.[w]ang** 'pope', **m[w]e** 'what', **cip.h[w]ey = cip.hoy** 'meeting', **cham.[w]ey** (→ chami → chaymi, §2.7.9) = **cham.oy** 'melon', **ip.[w]en** 'entering hospital', **caps[w]e** 'partakes' (< capswue, §2.7.9). The usual way to say **Māl hay pwā** 'Tell me about it' is [mareba] = **Māl [h]ay p[w]ā**. There are diachronic examples of postconsonantal w dropping even from *wo*, which is usually taken to be a monophthong vowel: *pacwo* (1562) > *paco* (1748) > **paca** 'reed fence'.

In sloppy speech (and widely in Seoul) w often disappears after nonlabial sounds, too, when a mid or low vowel follows: **si[w]en hata** 'is cool', **an [w]ass.ta** 'didn't come', **towa c[w]e** 'does the favor of helping' (< cwue, §2.7.7), **n[w]ā t[w]ess.e** 'put it away' (< noa, §2.7.7) < **no[h].a twuess.e**, **tōngmul-[w]en** 'zoo', **chil-[w]el** 'July', **ceng-[w]el** 'January', **pyēng[w]en** 'hospital', **kong[w]en** 'park', **ceng[w]en ey** 'in the garden', **tāy[h]ak-[w]en** 'graduate school', **cik.[w]en** 'staff, personnel', **k[w]ank[w]ang-kayk** 'tourist', **meych [w]el iess.na yo** /meyt[w]eli(y)enna.yo/ 'what month was it?', **kh[w]aysok hata** 'is speedy' (the first syllable is typically devoiced), **h[w]ankap** '60th birthday', ⁿ**yen[hw]ey** = ⁿ**yenhoy** 'annual meeting', **chen [hw]an** 'a thousand hwan (outdated monetary unit = wen)'. As the last two examples show, hw can drop as a string: **pho[hw]an** 'cannonball, shot (put)', **so[hw]al [h]i** 'sloppily, carelessly' (also /sowali/, /swāli/). For many speakers the phrases **cēn[hw]a 'ta** 'it's a phone call' and **cen [h]ata** 'reports' can converge. The string hw, when not dropped internally or when initial, is articulated by many speakers as a bilabial fricative [F], as noted in §2.4.

From the viewpoint of our Romanization there is an interesting case in **tewun** ··· ' ··· that is warm' → **teun** ··· → (§2.7.5) **tēn** ··· . Notice that all cases of -owun, -owul, and -owum freely contract to -ōn, -ōl, and -ōm; and all cases of -wuwun, -wuwul, and -wuwum to -wūn, -wūl, and -wūm.

Because **oy** is generally pronounced as **wey**, words spelled with that diphthong often end up just as [w]ey, so you may hear **an tey** = **an t[w]ey** for **an toy(e)** 'it won't do; too bad'. Other examples: **pēmc[w]ey** = **pēmcoy** 'crime', **sath[w]ey** = **sathoy** 'declining/refusing office', ... When you hear /keyley/ it may escape you that this could be **k[w]eyl[w]ey** and the word can be found in the dictionary as **koyloy** 'puppet'. The h of **hwey** (< hoy) freely drops along with the labial, but only when a voiced sound precedes, as in **wi[w]en[hw]ey** = **wiwen-hoy** 'committee', and in rapid speech that can even be compressed further to /wēney/! On the other hand, **um.ak-hoy** 'concert' can be reduced to **umakhey** but not to *umakwey or *umakey (the latter could only represent **um.ak ey** 'in/to/of the music'), and **kwuk.hoy** = **kwuk.hwey** 'national assembly' can shorten to **kwukh[w]ey** = **kwukhey** but not to *kwukwey or *kwukey. For **thōywen hayss.ta** 'got out of the hospital' you will hear (**thwēywen** > **th[w]ēy[w]en** =) /thēyen[h]etta/ or even just /thēynetta/.

Further compressions may baffle the ear. When **i** or **u** are left directly preceding a vowel by the eliding of h or w (or hw), the high vowel often loses its syllabicity and becomes a semivowel glide: **si[h]em** 'test' > **syēm** with compensatory lengthening of the remaining syllable. And **swuep** > **swēp** (§2.7.7) 'class instruction' may be further reduced to **sēp**. In rapid speech you will hear drastic reductions such as **kyēyhoyk** = **kyēyhweyk** > **kyēy[h]weyk** > **kyēy[w]eyk** > **kyēyk** = /kēyk/ 'plan'. The expression **swīpsseykoki** is from **sw[u]ipss[w]eykoki** = **swuip soy-koki** 'imported beef', and in dialects you may hear **swīpsseykeyki** < ···**k[w]eyki** < ···**koyki** < **-koki** with partial assimilation (fronting or "umlaut") of the next-to-last vowel to the final high front vowel. The form **swīp** does not further reduce to **s[w]īp** because the w drops only before a mid or low vowel, not **i** or **u**. But notice that some instances of hwu reduced to hw (§2.7.7) are followed by nonhigh vowels, and w before a mid or low vowel freely drops, so that in rapid speech **(ku) hwū ey** 'afterwards' > **(ku) hw[u]ēy** = **(ku) hwēy** sounds like **(ku) hwēy** = **(ku) hōy** '(that) meeting' and both can be further compressed to **(ku) h[w]ēy** = /(ku) hēy/. The city of **Swuwen** is often called /swēn/. The word **kan[h]o-[w]en** 'nurse' will drop the h and/or the w, and /kan(h)oen/ can be further compressed to /kanwēn/, which in turn may drop its w leaving the listener with /kanēn/ to puzzle out.

2.7.5. Postvocalic u.

Sequences of vowel + u are often pronounced with vowel length replacing the u: **kium, kīm** 'weed' (whence **kīm** 'seaweed'?); **taum, tām** 'next'; **maum, mām** 'soul, heart, mind'; **cheum, chēm** 'for the first time'; **maul, māl** 'village'; **keyuluta, kēyluta** 'is lazy'; **koul, kōl** 'district, county'. Since h drops readily a sequence of vowel + h + u is often reduced to a long vowel: **noh.una, nōuna, nōna** 'puts it but', **tāh.uni, tāuni, tāni** 'since it arrives', **cōh.umyen, cōumyen, cōmyen** 'if it's good'. CF §8.1.2, §8.2.4.

A similar reduction whereby i (after Vy) behaves as u does above will be heard in **nayl ← nāyl ← ¹nayil** 'tomorrow'. (The suppression of the newly acquired vowel length remains to be explained.)

2.7.6. Intercalated semivowels.

The vowel component FRONT occurs in the phonemes **i ey ay (oy) (wi)** and the component ROUNDED in **wu o (oy) (wi)**. These two features freely overlap a following vowel to spawn an etymologically unmotivated semivowel y or w. From **pi** 'rain' + **os** 'garment' comes **pi os** 'rain-gear', which sounds like /piyot/. The infinitives **chwue** 'dances' and **chwuwe** 'is cold' ordinarily sound the same /chwuwe/, and the infinitives **peyye** 'gets cut' (← **peyi-**, a passive stem) and **pēye** 'cuts' (← **pēy-**, a transitive stem) are often indistinguishable as /peyye/. Some speakers try to differentiate words like **kiyak** 'weakness of spirit' and **cwuwi** 'surroundings' from the quasi-homonyms **kiak** 'instrumental music' and **cwuuy** /cwui/ 'ism' by holding on to the y and w. Other speakers, however, distinguish a y or w which is motivated (morphophonemically expected from our knowledge of other alternants, e.g. in **yakca** 'weakling' and **sāwi** 'all around') from one which is simply the predictable lag in phase of a phoneme feature. Such speakers make a difference in pronunciation between **nāyo** 'puts out [authoritative style]' (< **nay-o**) and **nāy yo** 'puts out [polite style]' (< **nāy-e yo**). An analogous situation occurs in English with words like "prints" and "prince", which are seldom if ever distinguished in speech.

The practice of the Korean Language Society is to write y or w in all cases of semivowel except when there is a clearcut etymological reason NOT to do so. Within a morpheme the semivowel is written: **iyaki** 'story' (contrast **i aki** 'this child'), **kwiyal** 'paint-brush', **swuwel hata** 'is easy, handy'. The two apparent exceptions of **ppay-as-** 'grasp' and **payam** 'snake' either show the influence of their abbreviations **ppāys-** and **pāym** or else reflect an etymological analysis (CF **as-** 'snatch', dialect variants **piam** and **pi-emi** 'snake'). Other apparent exceptions are **kayam** 'hazel nut' and **sayang** (abbreviation **sāyng**) 'ginger' — but **sayyang** also occurs.

The phenomenon extends to cases of **wu** or **o** + the disappearing h of §2.7.3: **no(h.)a** 'puts' and **towa** 'helps' rime for most speakers, and both are sometimes shortened to **nwā** and **twā** (§2.7.7). These phenomena have been attested for some time: *nwowala* (1882 Ross 35) = **noh.a la** 'put it [there]!' The intercalated palatal semivowel can be seen in the Middle Korean spelling of $\cdots i/y$ + particle `ey` as "$\cdots i/y$ `yey`" (in contrast with the "$\cdots i/y ey$" that represents $\cdots i/y Gey$).

2.7.7. Desyllabification of i, wu, and o.

Sequences of i + vowel or of i + y + vowel are often reduced to y + vowel. The vowel is usually lengthened if it is in the first syllable after pause. The most conspicuous examples are of the infinitives of stems that end in i: **kitalie → kitalye, masie → masye** (usually pronounced **mase**, at least by older Seoul speakers), **kacie → kacye** (usually pronounced **kace**), **kaluchie → kaluchye** (usually pronounced **kaluche**), **titie → titye**, … . Since the honorific marker is **-(u)si-**, the sequence **-(u)sye** is especially common — and usually pronounced as if **-se**, at least by older speakers, but among the younger generation the pronunciation with /sy/ [š] is prevalent and it seems to be spreading. Example: **kasie → kasye (→ kase)**. Shortening of longer infinitives in ⋯ie is standard practice in written Korean nowadays. The one-syllable stems are usually not abbreviated in writing but in speech you hear the same sort of shortening, usually with compensatory lengthening of the vowel: **ttyē** for **ttie** 'wears a belt', **phyē** for **phie** 'smokes (= **phiwe**); blooms', **chyē** (pronounced **chē**) for **chie** 'hits', **cyē** (pronounced **cē**) for **cie** from either **cī(s)-** 'build' or **ci-** 'bear on one's back; … '.

The vowels **wu** and **o** are often reduced to **w** before a vowel and to nothing before **w** + vowel, especially when the result is not immediately followed by a pause: **cwe** for **cwue** 'gives', **twe** for **twue** 'puts away', **twa** for **towa** 'helps', **mwe** (further reduced to **me** by §2.7.4) for **mue** 'what'. The phenomenon extends to words in which the **h** disappears (§2.7.3): **nwa** for **noh.a** 'puts', **cwa** for **cōh.a** 'is good'. The vowel sometimes lengthens: **twā yo** (= **towa yo**), **nwā yo** (= **noh.a yo**), **cwā yo** (= **cōh.a yo**). The reduction of longer infinitives in ···**wue** is in written Korean nowadays but the one-syllable stems ending in **wu** are not usually abbreviated in writing, except that **cwue** and **twue** as auxiliaries are often written **cwe** and **twe**. The ···**w**··· then often drops in rapid speech (§2.7.4).

In general the vowel of monosyllabic infinitives reduced from **i-e**, **wu-e**, and **(w)o-a** are basically long (**cyē, cwē, twē, nwā, pwā, wā**) but the length is suppressed in the past forms: compare **wā iss.ta** 'is (come) here' and **wass.ta** 'came, has come'. And the length is often dropped when the infinitive closely follows other another form, as the auxiliaries often do. In this book we follow LHS (and we correct KEd) in writing **chyē 'ta (pota / poita)** and **chyē tulta** despite the seeming irregularity of **chye cwuta / kata / nāyta / pelita**. NKd has **chye 'ta pota** but **chyē 'ta poita** and, I believe, **chyē tulta** (the photoprint is unclear). The long vowel in the infinitive **wā** 'come' is questionable; the contraction was the usual form in Middle Korean and marked with a single dot, not the double dot that would lead to the modern length. If genuine, the length may be new.

The short vowel of the infinitive in **phye cita** owes to the earlier (and dialect?) form **phyeta** = modern Seoul **phita**. The infinitive **khye** < **khyeta** = **khita** is similar. These infinitives, like that of literary (and dialect?) **seta** = **suta** 'stand', simply absorb the infinitive ending **-e** with no compensatory lengthening, just as **ka** < **kata** absorbs the **-a**. A stem that ends in unrounded **u** drops that vowel when it attaches the ending, and there is no lengthening of the resulting syllable: **khe** < **khuta**, **sse** < **ssuta**, **tte** < **ttuta**, **the** < **thuta**. The irregular length of **kkē cita**, **thē cita** (and for LHS and Kim Minswu **thē ttulita**) is anomalous. Also anomalous is the length of **kkē** from **kkuta**, for which no good explanation is apparent; the earlier form was ˙**pske** (1462 [1]Nung 2:43b, 1481 Twusi 25:13a) with but a single dot, and the earlier form of **the** was similar, ˙**pthe** (1481 Twusi 7:24b). (LHS lists **kke** without a long mark, thus short, but all of his compound verbs have **kkē**. NKd has a long mark for **kkē** itself and a number of the compounds, but strangely leaves **kke cita** unmarked.) There are several pairs of expressions that show irregularity with respect to vowel length. We hear, for example, **kkāy cita**, **kkē cita**, and **thē cita** but **kkay ttulita**, **kke ttulita**, and (according to NKd and KEd) **the ttulita**, though LHS and Kim Minswu have **thē ttulita**, as if the geminate **tt** had curtailed the length. NKd strangely has short **ph'e cita** despite **ph'ē ttulita**; both are long in the other sources.

Other cases of vowel reduction are often heard in the casual construction **-ci yo** → **-c[y]o**, in the command form **-usio / -usipsio** → **-us(y)o / -usips(y)o**, and in an occasional noun, such as **kyēk ca** for **kiek ca** 'the letter K'. I have heard /aneyyo/ = **an' ey yo** ← **anyey yo** ← **ani (y)ey yo** 'it isn't' ← **ani + ie(y) yo**. Also: [1]**nayil** → [1]**nāyl** → [1]**nayl** (§2.7.2) 'tomorrow'; (§3.5.[9]) **oylye** ← **oilye** (§2.7.3) < **ohilye** (< ˙**wohi˙lye**) 'rather'; **toylye** ← **tolie** (< **tolihye** < **twolo-˙(h)hye**) 'conversely'.

2.7.8. Reduction of *wie*.

The sequence **wie** is often replaced by **ōy** (as if by way of *****wye**) and **oy** is often further replaced by **wey**, as noted earlier. Examples are **swīe** → **sōy** 'sours', **swīess.e** → **sōysse** 'soured'; **ttwie** → **ttōy** 'jumps', **ttwiess.e** → **tōyss.e** 'jumped'. The standard Hankul spelling writes this reduction as "**wey**", apparently influenced by the many speakers who do not distinguish **oy** from **wey**; compare the spelling of "**way**" for the infinitives of stems ending in **oy**, §9.4. The stem **sakwi-** (**sakwie** → **sakōy**) is an irregular development from **sa˙kwoy-** 'get acquainted'.

2.7.9. Vowel assimilation.

The vowel **ey** is frequently replaced by **i** in rapid speech when the following syllable contains **i** or **y**: **ciil** → **cēy-il** 'number one', **kitali yo** ← **kital(y)ey yo** ← **kitalye yo** 'waits', **kitali ya** ← **kital(y)ey ya** ← **kitalye ya** 'only by waiting', **cikhi ya 'nta** ← **cikh(y)ey ya 'nta** ← **cikhye ya hanta** 'must maintain'; **kasi yo** ← **kasey yo** ← **kasye(y) yo** '(someone esteemed) goes'; ··· **i yo** ← ··· **(y)ey yo** ←

··· ye yo ← ··· ie yo 'it is'; hwuli chinta ← hwuley chinta ← hwulye chinta 'lashes, whips'.

We also find pairs of words in which one member, usually the more common form, has a front vowel either after c(h) or before a syllable that contains i or y. Examples: achim, achum 'morning'; ilccik(-i), ilccuk(-i) 'early'; ayki, aki 'child'; teyli-, tayli-, tali- 'take (someone) along'; kitayli-, kitali- 'wait'; yēyki, yāyki, iyaki 'story, talk'; tay(n)ni-, ta(y)ngki-, ta(n)ni- 'go back and forth regularly'; caymi, cami 'fun'; hayk.kyo, hak.kyo; teyngi, tengi 'lump'; hayngkil (← hangkil §2.7.1) ← han-kil 'street'. Notice also meychil 'how many days' < myech-(h)ul, not to be misinterpreted as containing the Chinese il < ʾǪILǪ 'day'. More complicated explanations are needed to account for taynchu = tanchwu 'button', weynsswu = wensswu 'enemy', mayntunta = mantunta 'makes', oynthong (or weynthong) = ōn-thong 'entirely'. The adjectival noun weyn-man hata 'is fairly good' is a reduction of wuyen-man hata. Where it causes no confusion the assimilated form has been standardized as the spelling for some of the words. One of the vexing problems is with a large group of voice-derived verbs (causatives and passives) in which a vowel of the stem is often assimilated, and there are back formations "correcting" a legitimate /i/ to /u/ (or, after a labial, /wu/). In question are words like cwuk.i- 'kill' (often pronounced cwiki-) from cwuk- 'die', mek.i- (often meyki-) from mek- 'eat', sok.i- 'cheat' (often soyki-) from sok- 'be cheated'. In the appropriate part of Appendix 1 there is a comprehensive list with cross references from the spoken assimilations or back formations to the standard written forms.

The word soycwu ← socwu < ″SYWOW-″CYWUW 'hard liquor' may reflect metathesis of the glide and/or assimilation. But sōy-koki < ″sywoy-kwoʾki 'beef' is contracted from *ʾsywo ʾoy kwoʾki = so uy koki 'meat of the ox' (CF LCT 1971:223; the accentual anomaly is unexplained). For the compound talk 'chicken' + al 'egg' the expected pronunciation would be /takal/, but instead the standard written form is talk yal (spelled phonemically tal-kyal), and that seems to come from talk [u]y al /talk[e]yal/ < tolʾk oy ʾal 'egg of chicken'. Common variants include talk eyl, talk ayl, and talk yayl. (The possibility of a form like *talk yeyl is excluded by §4.3.) Perhaps similar is the pronunciation /silye/ for /sile/ silh.e 'I dislike it', which is popular today among young women in Seoul, but seems to have been around for a while (1936 Roth 185 gives silh.e / silh.ye). Yet no other ···lh- has that sort of variant: /kkulye/ means only kkulh.i-e 'boil it' and kkulh.e 'it boils' is pronounced /kkule/. It might be thought that the intruded palatal glide of /silye/ is due to the i of the preceding syllable, but there is an attestation of sulhye in 1887 Scott 63, apparently made on the earlier version of the stem, which was ʾsulh-: kaki sultha 'I don't care to go' (1887 Scott 80). One explanation might be a shortening of sul ho.ye > sil-h[ ]ye, with the irregular infinitive ho.ya / ho.ye of °ho- > ha- 'do', for which the attestations of sul-ho.ye (1676 Sin.e 9:10b), sul-ʾhuʾye (1586 Sohak 5:9b), and earlier ʾsul-ʾhoʾya (1447 Sek 13:18a) provide support. Compare modern cen-hye 'entirely' < cen + ha.ye and hāyng-ʾye < hāyng-hye 'by chance' < hāyng < HHOYNG + ha.ye.

Less commonly i is substituted for u in attaching endings to stems that end in ···s-, ···ss-, ···c-, or ···ch-: wusina = wus.una 'laughs but', issina = iss.una 'there is but', chacina = chac.una 'finbut', cochina = coch.una 'follows it but'. The popular Seoul pronunciation til.ye ʾta ponta for tul.ye ʾta ponta 'peers into; looks (gazes) at' assimilates the first vowel to the following palatal syllable. A common phenomenon, especially in the north, is the reversal of ye to ey: pey for pye 'rice plant', making it a homonym of pey 'cloth' and also of the pey which is a variant of pay 'boat; stomach' for those who do not make the ay ≠ ey distinction; Phey(ng)yang for Phyengyang (name of city — often spelled "P'yang" in the headlines of English-language newspapers in Korea); peyng(w)en < pyēngwen 'hospital'. The written word myech 'how much' is usually pronounced meych even in Seoul, and it is so written here.

2.8. Standardization variants.

A number of words appear in several shapes, either phonemically or just orthographically, and they reflect different notions of what is "standard" Korean. In some cases, the words are isolated instances, in other cases they reflect more general problems. There is considerable agreement among the Korean grammarians, in both the north and the south, on most of the isolated cases and on many of the general problems. Where my own observations of current standard usage agree with the decisions of the Korean grammarians I simply use their spellings without comment. In other cases, I have spelled out my differences of opinion, as in my preference for **tat.e** (etc.) over **tat.a** as the infinitive of **tat-** and of **hay** over **ha.ye** as the infinitive of **ha-** (§1.9, §9.3) and my preference for **-tuni** over **-teni** as the retrospective sequential (see the entries in Part II). I have been somewhat crankier than the Korean grammarians in insisting on distinctions between **iya** (particle) and **ia** = **ie** (copula infinitive), between **iyo** (particle) and **io** (copula); with most of them, I deplore the writing of intercalated "**y**" within forms of the copula ("**iye**" for **ie** etc.). But I appreciate the difficulty faced in making these decisions and recognize that most people prefer to write the intercalated y within inflected forms without worrying about the internal structure, since the contraction of (···)**ie** is (···)**ye**. In general, I frown upon the widespread writing of words and phrases in abbreviated forms, since that obscures the grammar and often leads to confusion. In this book I have used an apostrophe to indicate omitted letters, as in '··· = **i-** or **ha-**. In some cases, current South Korean orthographic practice is at variance with the North Korean and those differences I have shown by superscript letters, as follows:

	This book	North Korea	South Korea
1.	iss.^{s}up.nita 'is'	iss.sup.nita[1]	iss.up.nita[2]
	iss.^{s}o 'is'	iss.so[3]	iss.o
2.	an^{h}ay 'wife'	anhay	anay
3.	ŏlʰ-paluta 'is upright, … '	olh-paluta[4]	ol-paluta
4.	u^{y}lyey 'usually'	uylyey	ulyey
5.	m^{y}ēy [Chinese morphs]	mey	myey
	ph^{y}ēy [Chinese morphs]	phey	phyey
	(See §4.3; also §§1.5-6.)		

[1] An example appears in Mkk 1960:4:26 [sic].

[2] But the 1988 revised rules of the Ministry of Education abolishes the spelling "**-up.nita**" and writes **-sup.nita** whenever a consonant precedes. Presumably **-^{s}o** is to be treated similarly; the published rules neglect to inform us of that.

[3] CF Mkk 1960:3:26.   [4] Pronounced /ōlpalu-/ according to NKd.

Earlier I had included here "**mop^{s}si**" 'very', a word that has been spelled both **mopssi** and **mopsi** in South Korea but only **mopsi** in North Korea, which disregards the etymology: **mōs** < ¨**mwot** + **-(p)ssi** < ***'psi**, derived adverb < **(-p)ssu-** < **'psu-** 'use'; CF **mopssul** 'useless, no good' from the prospective modifier. But since the South Korean linguistic authorities, too, mostly favor ignoring the etymology, we will write **mopsi** and treat the adverb as opaque. ([1]Yi Ungpayk 1961 gives the first vowel as long for both **mopsi** and **mopssul**, reflecting the etymology, but that length is not reported by other sources.)

The past **-ess-** and future **-keyss-** behave, of course, like **iss-** in group 1; many South Korean grammarians agree with the North Korean spelling reflected in the superscript ^{s}, but in practice the other spelling is more widespread in the south. We assume here that **-sup.nita** and **-so** are being used after ALL consonant stems. If the less standard versions **-up.nita** and **-uo** are being used throughout, then they should also be used after ss. That is, if you say **mek.up.nita** it makes sense to write **iss.up.nita**, but if you say **meksup.nita** it would be more consistent to write **iss.sup.nita**. The important thing is to use one or the other consistently (CF §9.2). Notice also the remarks on superscript ^{1} and ^{n} (§1.6).

There are a few words which, though historically ···nn···, are actually pronounced ···ll··· (as if coming from ···n.l···). In South Korea the spellings have been standardized as ···n.l···, but in North Korea the historical spellings are used, despite the irregular pronunciation. We write ···n.^{1}n··· :

This book	North Korea	South Korea	Pronunciation
kŏn.¹nan 'difficulty'	konnan	konlan	/kŏllan/
han.¹nan-kyēy 'thermometer'	hannankyey	hanlankyey	/hallangkey/ (§4.3)

In parts of the north there are speakers who substitute **ll** for **nn** in various words, such as **allyeng** for **annyeng**. In Anpyen and Tek.wen of South Hamkyeng **tullunta** is used for /**tunnunta**/ < **tut.nunta** 'hears' (Kim Yengpay 1984:53).

There are other spellings that vary from the current spoken usage in Seoul:
1. The noun **iyaki** 'story' is usually said as **yāyki** or **yēyki**.
2. The gerund **-ko** and the particle **to** are usually **-kwu** and **twu**, even in the speech of people who do not substitute **wu** for **o** wholesale. (CF §2.2.)
3. Less generally recognized is the substitution of **e** for **a** in many common words: ··· **henthey** for ··· **hanthey** (particle), **hekwu** for **hakwu** for **hako** (particle), **he(n)ta** for **ha(n)ta** 'does; is'.
4. The verb stem for 'stand' is written **se-** but pronounced **su-** even by Seoul speakers who do not ordinarily substitute **u** for **e** (except in **-tun** for the written **-ten**, noted earlier). The verb stems written **phye-** and **khye-** are pronounced **phi-** and **khi-** in Seoul; the stem written **kenne-** is pronounced **kēnnu-**. The spellings in this book conform to the Seoul pronunciation.
5. An artificial spelling distinction: **olun** 'right (in direction)' ≠ **olh.un** 'correct'. See §5.3.

I have followed the Korean grammarians in assuming only one standard treatment of the **l**-doubling vowel stems (§8.3.1), such as **pulu-** 'call' and **molu-** 'not know' with their infinitives **pulle** and **mōlla**, but many otherwise standard speakers double the **l** everywhere, pronouncing the stems as **pullu-**, **mollu-**, etc. I have also followed the grammarians in the standard version of the intentive **-ulye / -lye**, with a double **ll** only when attached to the extended stem of the l-extending vowel verbs (**wūllye** 'about to cry' from **wū-l-**), but many speakers use a version with a double **ll** everywhere: **-ullye / -llye**. For such speakers we will have to say that the ending attaches, in the shape **-llye**, to the UNextended stem of the l-extending vowel verbs. And many of those speakers use the vowel **a** instead of **e**: **-ullya / -llya**.

There seems to be confusion among Korean grammarians over whether to spell **-ulq ka** as "**-ulka**" or "**-ulkka**". Some would like to treat anything that appears after a verb stem as an unanalyzable ending, to be written phonemically. (Compare the remarks on **-un ya** in §1.9.)

For a fuller discussion of problems of standardization, see Martin 1968.

2.9. Intonations.

The following statements about intonation follow the analysis in Martin 1954 (= KM). Every phrase or utterance of more than one syllable has a gradual nondistinctive rise throughout until the onset of a particular intonation, which occurs near the end of the phrase and in conjunction with a pause. The meaning of statement, question, suggestion, and command are sometimes carried (in whole or in part) by the intonation, but often these meanings are wholly or partly expressed by morphs in the ending of the verb form.

Seven intonations are recognized for Seoul speech:
1. PERIOD intonation (.): a fall, beginning on the third, second, or last syllable from the end of the sentence (if on the last syllable this intonation is homophonous with 4).
2. COMMA intonation (,): a rise on the last syllable of a phrase.
3. QUESTION-MARK intonation (?): a rise on the third, second, or last syllable from the end of the sentence (if on the last syllable the intonation is homophonous with 2).
4. EXCLAMATION-POINT intonation (!): a quick fall on the last syllable of the sentence, often accompanied by a voice qualifier of overloudness.
5. DOUBLE QUESTION-MARK intonation (??): a dip on the third, second, or last syllable from the end of the sentence (homophonous with 7 when on the last syllable).

6. DOUBLE EXCLAMATION-POINT intonation (!!): a dip on the third, second, or (rarely) last syllable followed by a fall on the next (rarely, the same) syllable.

7. TRIPLE-DOT intonation (...): a dip on the last syllable of a phrase or sentence, often accompanied by a voice qualifier of overlength.

Three phonetic features are involved: rise, fall, and dip. The dip can be described as a fall immediately followed by a rise. King tells me children use ··· **hanta** as an exclamation with dip and rise (**ha**ₙ**ta**).

The question-mark intonation primarily means QUESTION; the exclamation-point intonation shows INSISTENCE. The meaning of the double question-mark is RHETORICAL QUESTION or LIVELY, and that of the double exclamation-point is LIVELY AND INSISTENT. The comma intonation signals TEMPORARY SUSPENSION and the triple-dot intonation expresses HESITATION. The period intonation is the sentence-final default when no other intonation is called for. The intonations marked ?? and !! seem to be peculiar to Seoul speech and are largely limited to casual statements of the **-ci (yo)** type, but occasionally occur with other sentences, as in **Ani (yo)!!** 'No'. For examples of the intonations in various types of sentence, see KM 62.

2.10. The earlier phonology.

Korean of the 15th-century Hankul texts, called (Late) Middle Korean and here dubbed "MK", differed from the language of the 20th century in offering a somewhat richer pattern of sounds and strings of sounds. We can explore the earlier system through the Hankul spellings, making inferences about the articulatory values of the written syllables and the environments where the same string of phonemes was written in varying ways or where different strings were written as if they were the same. From the dates of the texts carrying critical examples we deduce the relative timing of changes in the articulatory habits of Korean speakers over a period of four or five centuries. From the patterns found in the earliest Hankul texts we can surmise changes that must have taken place over the preceding hundred years or so, and reconstruct patterns for that period with relative confidence.

Putting the accent patterns aside for separate study (§2.12), we will seek to date the changes in: (1) the vowel system = syllable nuclei, (2) the initials = onsets, (3) the finals = codas, and (4) the intersyllabic strings = interludes.

What clues we have to the pronunciation of Korean earlier than the 15th century, beyond what we can obtain from internal reconstruction, are words written by means of Chinese characters, for the most part intended as phonological representations of the Korean words. Interpreted in terms of the MK pronunciations of the characters, the forms show few surprises, and there is little to suggest that the system of sounds was drastically different from that recorded by the early users of Hankul.

2.10.1. The earlier vowels.

The earlier language had a vowel system similar to the modern system but with the addition of the low back (and functionally unrounded) vowel *o*. In dialects other than that of Ceycwu the extra vowel was lost and merged with other vowels. In noninitial syllables *o* merged with its higher counterpart, the high back unrounded *u*; that merger began in the 15th century and for the central dialect of the texts it was completed during the 16th century (CF LKM 1972a:118). With the exception of a few words such as *holk* (hol˙k o˙lwo 1518 Sohak-cho 10:23b) > *hulk* (hul˙k ulwo 1586 Sohak 6:122a), in word-initial syllables what *o* merged with was *a* but under certain circumstances in certain dialects *o* was replaced by *wo* — in Phyengan (Kim Yengpay 1984:67) before a labial consonant or a syllable with a rounded vowel so that ˙*nom* > **nom** 'other person' (**nam**) and *non˙hwo-* > **nonwu-** 'divide' (**nanwu-**). The standard language includes a few such cases: ˙*so˙may* / ˙*so˙moy* > **swomay** (1617) > **somay** 'sleeve'. And there are also several words where *o* became *e*, such as ··· ˙*pol* 'time(s), layer(s)' > **ay pel** 'first (in time / order)', *pol˙(s)sye* / *pol˙sye* > **pelsse** [dialect **palsse**] 'already', *po˙li-* > **peli-** 'discard', *to˙li-* > **teli-** [dialect] > **teyli-** 'bring a person along'. (The regular development for the verbs is found in the dialect versions **pali-** and **tali-**.) Writing the old vowel, called *a˙lay o* = **alay a**, persisted in conservative spellings long after its distinctive value was lost. As [1]Yu Huy (1824 Enmun-ci 12) observed, "*o* is confused with *a* (as A 'child', SA 'fact') or with *u* (as *hulk* 'earth')". Symbols were created to write the syllables *yo and *yu, though the sounds did not exist in the language of the writers of the early texts. It is surmised that those syllables had existed in a pre-Hankul version of the language and were lost in the central dialect not long before the creation of Hankul in 1445. There is evidence in dialect forms to reconstruct *yo for a number of words.

The created symbols are found in "ㄱㅛ kyo ㄱㅠ kyu" (1446 Hwun 26a); later the letters ᆢ yo and ᆢㅣ yoy were created and exemplified with the syllables ㄱㆍㆍ kyo and ㄱㆍㆍㅣ kyoy (?1750- Hwunmin cengum wunhay 16a), and still other symbols such as ㅘ yw(y)a and ㆌ yw(y)e were used to write Chinese sounds. CF Ledyard 1966:253, LKM 1972a:126.

In the 15th century the vowels *ey ay oy uy* were articulated as diphthongs, and *wey way woy wuy* were treated as triphthongs. For *woy* and *wuy* this statement may be questioned, since we assumed that the Hankul symbols corresponding to the digraphs *wu* and *wo* of our Romanization represent simple rounded vowels, unlike the diphthongs represented by *wa* and *we*. But I am now prepared to revise that assumption and propose that the rounding represents a functional semivowel even in *wu* and *wo*.

Later the diphthongs got monophthongized, but the syllable *uy* itself, which had become **u** when initial and **i** when not, was partially restored at the beginning of a word as the dissyllable **ui** by younger educated speakers following the spelling tradition for the Chinese morphemes it represents. The modern pronunciation of the genitive marker as /ey/ (the same as the locative marker) may reflect a raised version of /ay/ from the MK allomorph ˙*oy* rather than a lowered version of */i/ < ˙*uy* itself. The triphthong *wuy* became the diphthong **wi**, further monophthongized to a high front rounded vowel [ü] by some speakers. The triphthong *way* was reduced to the diphthong **way** [ɰɛ], and that was further monophthongized by some speakers to the relatively rare articulation of a low front rounded vowel [ɶ], just as *wey* > **wey** was monophthongized by some to the mid front rounded vowel [ö]. In modern Seoul **ay** has merged with **ey** except when word-initial, where the distinction is maintained. In much of the south the two are merged in all positions, and so are **u** and **e**. It is hard to say just when the process of monophthongization took place in various parts of the country. The diphthongs can still be heard as such in parts of Hwanghay, as noted in §2.2, and probably elsewhere, too.

The unrounded **u** was distinguished from **wu** even after labials (*p ph pp m*) until about 1748, but then the vowel was assimilated to the labial, so that the modern **mul** (with "u" an abbreviation of /wu/) represents the two distinct MK syllables ˙*mul* 'water' and ˙*mwul* 'crowd' (for which the modern word is **muli**, with the accretion of the suffix -**i**).

It is generally assumed that earlier the modern back vowels **u** and **e** were articulated nearer (if not all the way to) the front of the mouth. The Seoul pronunciation of **u** today, in fact, is fairly far forward (central rather than back), and the sound of **e** has moved lower and toward the back, getting rounded to something like [ɔ], which approximates the sound we assume for the lost MK vowel *o*. Kim Wancin has proposed that the MK vowels were quite different from the modern values (in all dialects) because a Great Vowel Shift took place. He claims that the shift moved to the back of the mouth those vowels that once were front and that it raised an earlier mid-central shwa *[ə] to the value of the modern *u*, while the former *[e] shifted back to the shwa position which is still heard for **e** in many dialects, though Seoul has moved the vowel on toward the back low rounded version, apparently during the past fifty years. Linguists in Korea generally accept the notion of the vowel shift, it seems, but do not agree on its timing. Together with some of them, I favor retaining values for the vowels of the 15th century that are close to the modern values, while I reserve judgment on the validity of the vowel shift at an earlier period.

2.10.2. The earlier initials.

The language of the 15th century had all the initials of modern Korean with the exception of the initial geminates *pp tt kk cc ss*. In addition the scribes wrote several kinds of clusters. There is general agreement that initials spelled "*pC*…" began with a labial stop. And everyone assumes that there was an oral obstruent at the beginning of the odd word *sna˙hoy* (1447 Sek 19:14b) 'man (male)', probably contracted from *sona˙hoy* (not attested until perhaps 1517), the source of modern **sanay**, though some (such as LCT 121a) would interpret this as [tn] rather than [sn]. Yet many scholars (including LKM

1963:19) have doubted the face value of the initial sibilant written in the clusters "*sp*⋯ *st*⋯ *sk*⋯" and claim that these strings had a pronunciation identical to that of later "*pp tt kk*", the tense and crisply unaspirated stops we refer to as "reinforced". The geminate spellings of these initials were used in the earliest texts only to present somewhat artificial readings for Chinese characters, in an attempt to capture Middle Chinese distinctions that were ignored in nativized borrowings. They were sometimes used also for phrase-internal strings that represented the prospective modifier -*(ᵘ/o)lq* + a voiceless obstruent initial in the following word (especially when it was not a free noun), though these strings were also given other treatments: (1) they were simply ignored, as often in 1481 Twusi and in modern Korean; or (2) they were written with a cluster of final *l* + *q*, a symbol which otherwise wrote the glottal-stop initial of traditional Chinese readings. And the digraphs *ss* and *hh* were used not only to maintain traditional Chinese distinctions but also to write the initials of a few native words that had perhaps incorporated an emphatic prefix. The only such examples of *hh*⋯ are the verb stem *(h)hye-* 'pull; ... ' and compounds that incorporate it. I believe that by and large the textual spellings of native Korean words must be taken at face value, and that when the scribes wrote geminates, including the *ss*⋯ and *hh*⋯, they were pronouncing them tense and with the same crisp release into the vowel that is heard today. When they wrote *sC*⋯ (or ⋯*s C*⋯ or ⋯*s*⋯) they heard a sibilant articulation. The initial clusters include not only the groups *pt*⋯ *pth*⋯ *ps*⋯ *pc*⋯ (no **pk*⋯) and *sp*⋯ *st*⋯ *sk*⋯ but also *pst*⋯ *psk*⋯. Those reluctant to allow the sibilant clusters treat these as equivalent to *pt-* and the missing **pk-*. But that makes it hard to explain the spelling contrasts found in ˙*ptoy* 'dirt', ˙*pstay* 'time', and ˙*sta[h]*, to say nothing of the many strings that attach the genitive particle *s* in a phrase *N s N* to either the preceding or the following noun, or run the words together with no junctures, as indicated by variant spellings (see Martin 1982/3 and ?1991). LKM, however, rejects the notion that reinforcement in obstruent clusters was automatic in the 15th century (as it is today) and upholds the view that the orthographic *pt*⋯ contained a lax apical stop in contrast with the tense version in *pst*⋯. I believe that the "*sC*⋯" clusters were pronounced with a sibilant both when initial (as syllable onsets) and when medial (as interludes). The obstruent after the sibilant was unaspirated (as in modern English) and identical with the reinforced obstruents of modern Korean, so that we can think of them as "*spp stt skk*". The tenseness of the obstruent is a feature of the clustering of two obstruents, of which the minimal case is two identical obstruents, the geminate *pp tt kk cc ss*, as indicated by spellings such as ⋯*l* ˙*tta* for -*lq* ˙*ta* 'will you ⋯ ?'. What happened later (in the 16th century) was simply a suppression of the *s* that left the tense allophones of the simple stops newly standing in contrast with the lax allophones that were now the only version of *p t k* and also *c* and *s*. The change was probably gradual and took place as the corresponding interludes became ⋯*tC(C)*⋯ in accordance with the merger of syllable-final ⋯*s* and ⋯*t* which slowly took hold in the course of the 16th century, after a few earlier harbingers. There was occasional dropping of *p* from initial clusters in a few attestations of the 15th century; by the middle of the 16th century that was more prevalent. The dropping of the sibilant in the *sC* (= *sCC*) clusters was probably complete by 1632, but it is unlikely that it started until the internal -*sC*- had become -*tC*- (= -*tCC*-) in the middle of the 16th century; it probably got under way around 1575. Not all of the modern geminate consonants go back to clusters as such; some were created later as emphatic versions of words, such as the sporadic appearance of forms noticed by Kim-Renaud 1977:92 in casual speech accompanying an emotional connotation. There were a few early verb doublets with *(s)C*⋯ that are thought to reflect a similar connotation added by tensing the initial (id.:93, Ramsey 1978b:64), and the emphatic version is preserved as the modern stem: **kkū(s)-** < *skuzu-* (1463 Pep 7:91a) < *kuzG-* (1463 Pep 2:200b) 'pull', **ccih-** < *stih-* (1466 Kup 2:62b) < *tih-* (1459 Wel 17:19a) 'pound', **ssip-** < *ssip-* (1462 ¹Nung 5:46a) < *sip-* (1462 ¹Nung 8:138a) 'chew', **ssu-** < ˙*ssu-* (1447 Sek se:4b) < ˙*su-* (1465 Wen 2:2:2:41a) 'write'. The doublets have been used to buttress the argument that the *sC*⋯ clusters did not contain a sibilant, at least in these words, but it is quite possible that an emphatic prefix may have had the sibilant pronunciation.

With respect to the readings of the Chinese characters, LKM 1963:20 says that up until 1480 the orthography used experimental elements, but then gave them up and simplified the spellings to be more natural. He finds that the natural readings began with 1496 Cin.en kwenkong, since 1481 Twusi gave no readings for the many Chinese characters it uses. Perhaps that is why it is said that orthographic W and Q were last seen in 1467. But that date is a bit too early, for texts from 1475-85 contain examples:

···W ˙KYWOW-ˉ˙SYWUW (1475 Nay 2:2:69b) 'teach', ˙˙TTWOW (1482 Kum-sam 2:3a) 'way', PPEN-ˉ˙NWOW (1482 Nam 2:6ab) 'agony', ˙˙PPWU-ˉ˙MWUW (1485 Kwan 7b) 'parents'

Q··· ˙QILQ-˙POYK (1475 Nay 2:2:72a, 73b) '100', ˙QILQ-SOYNG (1482 Kum-sam 2:1b) 'life', ˙QAK (1482 Nam 1:77a) 'evil', ˙LI-˙QYEK (1485 Kwan 1a) 'gain'

···LQ CIN-˙SSILQ (1475 Nay 1:47b) 'true', ˙QILQ-˙TTI (1482 Kum-sam 5:18a) 'one ground', ˙KAK-˙PPYELQ (1482 Nam 2:63b) 'particular', ˙HWOLQ-ZYEN (1485 Kwan 9a) 'suddenly'

And it should be noted that 1481 Twusi wrote ···lq C··· in at least one passage: ··· ˙se nilGwuylq ˙ta (23:44a) 'will you be able to achieve the writing of ... ?'. But usually the reinforcement after the prospective modifier was simply ignored by this work and later texts, with occasional exceptions: ˙˙kin [KWA-˙KUK] ˙ul ˙˙mal kkwo (1481 Twusi 10:27b) 'will they give up the long spears?'; ˙˙hwol ˙tt i.n i ˙˙la (1588 Mayng 13:1b) 'will do'. There are examples of ···lq C in virtually all of the texts from 1445 to 1462; and also ?1468- Mong, with ···lq t, ···lq c (15b, 24a), ···lq s, ···lq st, and even ···lq h (5b); and one exceptional case in 1475 Nay (puthulq ˙ka 1:2a). But 1463 Pep, 1463/4 Yeng, 1464 Kumkang, and 1482 Kum-sam have only ···l CC for *···lq C, and the reinforcement is totally ignored by 1465 Wen, 1466 Kup, 1482 Nam, and 1485 Kwan. The texts that use ···lq C also have examples of ···l CC to varying degrees, but the admirably morphophonemic spelling of 1449 Kok has only ···l ˙ss oy and ···l ˙ss ye (it lacks an example of *···lq s), and uses ···lq C for all other cases. The glottal was also used by one or more of the texts in ···lq st, ···lq sk, ···lq psk, ···lq pst, ···lq pt, ···lq th, and ···lq kh. Since in a few instances it was used even before a voiced initial such as n or wo, the second symbol of the ···lq string perhaps sometimes reflected nothing about the pronunciation, but just helped identify the ending.

A number of Hankul-written words began with initial l···. Some, such as ˙˙lwongtam 'joke' and lwo˙say 'mule', are known to be of Chinese origin; and others, such as la˙kwuy 'donkey' and le˙ngwul 'raccoon-dog' are probably borrowings from Mongolian and Tungusic languages. The adnoun la˙won (1463 Pep 5:202b) 'joyful' — ˙lawon in 1481 Twusi 7:25 — may be a contraction of ˙LAK ˙hwon˙ ··· that is joyous'. The l··· in these nativized borrowings and the many Chinese words beginning with L··· were probably not distinguished from n··· by most Koreans of the 15th century, just as the two initials were not kept apart later: the Chinese loanword LOY-˙ZILQ (1459 Wel 7:16a) '(to)morrow' was assimilated as noy˙zil (1482 Nam 1:40b). But there may have been speakers who kept initial l··· distinct from n···: 1898 Tayshin has [rasil] for 'tomorrow'.

An initial z··· occurs in a few nativized borrowings from Chinese, such as zywoh 'mattress' (Middle Chinese nhywok), as well as in readings of Chinese characters, always as ZY··· or ZI···, and a couple of mimetics (zel-zel, zem-zem). The origin of ˙zywuch > yuch 'the four-stick game' is unknown, but I suspect that the shape was earlier *nywusk or *niwusk, in view of the Hamkyeng dialect versions (nwus, nyukku, nyukkwu, nyukki, yukku, yukkwu, yukki, yuchi); a variant of ne(yh) 'four' may be the first part of the word. It is unclear whether, or how, initial z- (or z···) was pronounced, but it continued into the 16th century before eventually disappearing. Internal ···z··· resulted from lenition of s (including s from *c), often at the end or the beginning of a morpheme or forming a morpheme in itself. A few nouns seem to have had an intrinsic ···z··· that remains to be explained, though I believe that they too contain lenitions from s or, in the following words, *c: mozom > maum 'heart, mind', kye˙zulh / kye˙zul > kyewul 'winter', kozolh / kozol > kaul 'autumn', ... (The second syllables of these words were written with affricate-initial phonograms in 1400+ Kwan-yek.) As Ramsey has shown, the ···z- verb stems come from underlying ···z^u/o- (see §8.2.5), and that in turn I believe is the result of leniting an s, under conditions as yet unclear. See §2.11.4.

In modern Korean a phonetic syllable can begin with the velar nasal provided it is between vowels, but with a few marginal exceptions the ···ng is final in a morpheme or in a syllable of a polysyllabic morpheme. There are a couple of MK morphemes with the initial ng···: the polite marker

-*ngi* and a bound noun *ngek* 'place', as in *kunge˙kuy* (= **ku ngek ˙uy*) 'there'. But words and phrases did not begin with the velar nasal. The traditional initial NG··· was written for Chinese readings, but when the words were nativized the initial was omitted, as was the glottal initial Q···. There are at least 25 examples of NG··· that are illegitimate from the standpoint of seventh-century Chinese or of Sino-Japanese. Virtually all begin with NGW··· or NGYW···, as in NGWANG 'king', ¨NGWUW 'exist, have', and ¨NGYWENG 'longlasting'. But a glide is uniquely lacking in the perfective particle ¨NGUY (1451 Hwun-en 2a), and while Tung T'ung-Ho reconstructed a voiced velar fricative for the Old Chinese initial of this particle, Karlgren had treated it as z. The Old Chinese reconstruction for all the NGW··· and W··· words, based on shared graphic components in etymological sets, assigns them a voiced velar — a stop in Karlgren's system, a fricative in Tung's. The character meaning 'do; serve' has two readings in the texts: NGWUY and ˙WUY (sometimes ¨WUY), and the nativized version is ¨wuy (1446 Sek 6:7b, 24a). The colloquial pronunciation of the 15th century lacked the means to cope with the prescribed distinction of NGYEN 'polish' : YEN 'extend' : QYEN 'smoke', or of ˙NGWUY 'guard' : ˙WUY 'position' (also ¨WUY) : ˙QWUY 'entrust' (also ¨QWUY), with the resulting homonymy found in today's **yen** and **wi**. Kōno (1968:17) says that in Korea NGA was pronounced like *(Q)A*, presumably as /a/, from very early, since there is a (mis)spelling with the phonograms NGA-TWO for the name of the priest called A-TWO who came to Korea from China in 375. Quite a few nativized fish names end in ···*nge* and that represents a retention of the initial of NGE 'fish' when not at the beginning of a word, as in ¨*linge* (1518 Sohak-cho 9:25a) = ¨LI-NGE (1466 Kup 1:52b) 'carp'; *chyenge* 'herring' (1799 ¹Nap-yak 27b) must go back to *CHYENG-NGE (unattested as such, but see 1527 Cahoy 1:11a=20b), with the two nasals simplified to one. In the 16th century the symbol for the velar nasal came to be written only at the end of a syllable and fell together in graphic shape with the zero initial with which it was in complementary distribution.

2.10.3. Palatalization and dispalatalization.

In the 15th century the phoneme *c* and its aspirated counterpart *ch* were affricates, as they are today, but they were not palatalized. The realization of *c* was as [ts···] or (§2.10.6) [···dz···]. The palatalized articulations of the apicals in syllables such *tye thye cy chye sye nye lye* was an anticipation of the glide and must have been present also in *ti thi ci chi si ni li*, as contrasted with *tuy thuy cuy chuy suy nuy luy*. Because of examples of *hy···* and *hi···* that turn up in various dialects as s(y)··· and **si** we can probably assume that *hye* and *hi* (perhaps also the uncommon *hhye* and *hhi*) were palatalized. Later, all these articulations underwent divergent developments in different parts of the peninsula.

In the south the nonpalatalized affricates were palatalized: *ce* merged with *cye* and *che* with *chye*, so that there are two modern syllables **ce** and **che**, spelled ¨cye¨ and ¨chye¨ only when they are contracted from ¨cie¨ and ¨chie¨. Then the palatalized stops were affricated: *tye* and *ti* merged with *ce* and *ci*. (The modern Seoul **ti** is a monophthongization of *tuy*, a raising of **tey** in specific words, or the result of borrowing foreign words; and **tye** is for the most part a shortening of ti(y)e < tuy(y)e.) The syllable *si* was made or kept palatal (a single frontal articulation, so not to be described as ¨palatalIZED¨); *sye* got dispalatalized and merged with *se*, but was reintroduced to represent the shortening of si(y)e. At the beginning of a word, *ny···* and *ni···* (including *ly···* and *li···* pronounced as *ny···* and *ni···*) dropped the apical articulation and merged with *y···* and *i···*, and they are so written in the standard orthography of the south. Modern Seoul word-initial **ni** is the result of monophthongizing *nuy*, raising the **ney** of specific words, or foreign borrowing. The suspective ending in Phyengan is **-ti** from MK -˙*ti*, though the influence of Seoul has made the palatalized version **-ci** quite popular (Kim Yengpay 1984:100).

In much of the north the affricates stayed apical, with no frontal coarticulation except before *y* or *i*. But in those cases there was an erosion of the palatal quality: *cye* merged with *ce*, and *tye* with *te*. The dispalatalization extended to *nye* and *lye*, which were not differentiated from *ne* and *le*, with the result that [n]**yeca** 'woman' is pronounced **yeca** by southern speakers but **neca** by many in the north, where the spelling is standardized as ¨nyeca¨ instead of the southern ¨yeca¨. Internally, Phyengan has **swulo** for **swulyo** 'completing a course' and **illwu** for **illu** 'topnotch' (Kim Yengpay 1984:69).

We are not sure just when these changes happened, though the affrication of *ti* and *ty* seems to have taken hold around the turn of the 18th century (LKM 1972a:67-8). For the nasal, there are words that have individual histories, and a few doublets existed already in the 15th century. The verb stem ⁿyeki- 'deem' was written *nye˙ki-* in 1481 but earlier the spelling was *ne˙ki-*, a form that persists in 1936 Roth 37, no doubt the result of his hearing of South Hamkyeng speech. The verb *neh-* 'put in' appears as early as 1466 (Kup 1:13a, 2:41b) but the prevalent version was *nyeh-* (as in 1447 Sek 9:21a), which led to modern **yeh-** in Kyengsang (and elsewhere); yet here Seoul uses the glideless version **neh-** heard widely in the north. In the word for 'yes' Seoul also follows the northern form **nēy** rather than the southern **yēy**. 1894 Gale writes (95) *niaki* 'story' (**iyaki** > **yāyki** > **yēyki**) and (165) has the passage "*yeng ila howo* it is called 'nyeng' (mat)" – note the initial "ny" in the gloss – which must be a contraction of **(n)ieng** 'thatching', derived from °*ni-* > ¨*ni-* > **nī-** 'thatch (a roof)'.

1902 Azbuka kept *sy* [š] distinct from *s*, as did 1900 Matveev; and 1898 Tayshin "*tsiui*" < MK ˙*cwuy* 'rat' seems to intrude the glide *y* without palatalizing or deaffricating the *c* [ts]. (Azbuka has *hāysye* ? < *hāy [i]sie* for 'did'.) 1894 Gale 65 gives -*l syeng pwuluta* and -*l syeyta* 'it is likely that' (= **-ulq seng siph.ta**).

Among early signs of palatalization: fronting of the vowel in *a˙cik* (1463 Pep 1:14a, ...) < *an˙cok* (1447 Sek 6:11a, 1463 Pep 1:44a, ...) 'yet' (? < **a˙ni cek* 'not time'), ˙*ho.yem ˙cik* (1518 Mayngca 14:21b) = ˙*ho.yem ˙cuk* (id. 14:16a) 'worthy of doing', *achim* (1736 ⁿYe-sa 3:9; cited from LCT 522b) < *a˙chom* (1447 Sek 6:3b) 'morning'; the doublet *wum˙chi-* (*wum˙chye* 1462 ¹Nung 2:43b) = *wumchu-* (*wum˙che* 1462 ¹Nung 2:40a) 'huddle, shrink'. Notice also, without affrication, *ti˙s ˙'i* (1449 Kok 43) = ˙*to˙s ˙'i* (1459 Wel 10:20b) 'like'; *kile˙ki* (1568 Sohak 2:49a) = ˙*kuy˙lye˙ki* (1527 Cahoy 1:8b=15a) = *kulye˙ki* (1462 ¹Nung 8:121b) = *kulye˙kuy* (1459 Wel 2:40b) 'wild goose'. On the other hand the front vowel of **silh.ta** is not attested until quite late; 1894 Gale (177) has *sulkhwo* 'disliking' < *sulh-* < ˙*sul˙ho-*. Yet (99) he writes *nucin* for **nuc.un** 'late' and offers the option of *hol sti* (= **hal tti**) or *hol ci* (= **hal[q] ci**) 'whether to do'; in ··*ul ci entyeng (to)* (64) he has both affricated *ci* < ˙*ti* and unaffricated *ty*··, if the representations are taken at face value. But there are examples of *t* and *th* in ?1517- ¹No that are affricated in the Kyucang-kak version of 1795 ¹No-cwung though not in the Phyengyang kam.yeng version, which is older in its language: ¨*tywo˙hi* (?1517- ¹No 2:66a) = *tywohi* (1795 ¹No-cwung [P] 2:59b) = *cywohi* (id. [K] 2:61b) 'nicely'. The same stem appears somewhat earlier in *cywoha ˙'yla* (1763 Haytong 103); and the postmodifier ˙*thyey* 'pretense' is written *chyey* as early as 1730 (Chengkwu yengen 92). Examples of *c* written for *ty* and *chy* for *thy* are found in 1632 Twusi-cwung, according to An Pyenghuy 1957.

Palatalization of velars also took place, mostly in Kyengsang and Hamkyeng. King 1988b:291 finds seven examples of velar palatalization [k] > [tš] in 1900 Matveev, including *ciwo* 'long' = **kio** < **kī-l-**, *cilumi* 'butter' = **kilum** 'oil, grease', *ciley* 'on the road' = **kil ey**; also, with simple affrication [k] > [ts] for the /c/, *cili* = **kil** 'road'. The word **kimchi** 'pickled cabbage' is a back formation (by false analogy) from **cimchi**, widely heard in the south (and also in Hamkyeng), the expected palatalization of *tim˙choy* (1527 Cahoy 2:11a=22a) from Chinese *TTIM-*¨*CHOY* 'soaked vegetables' (LCT 1971:46). A similar hypercorrection is responsible for the development of **cēmsim** 'lunch' into the dialect variant **kyemsim**, which appears in 1894 Gale 164 with the gloss 'dinner'. The word goes back to *[¨]tyemsim* (1518 ¹Ye-yak 38a) and comes from Chinese ¨*TYEM-SIM*, which refers to those Dim Sum tidbits that "dot your heart" at lunch time. A similar case: *kyel* (1898 Tayshin) for **cel** < *tyel* 'temple' (King 1988b:295:n18). Dialect **chi** corresponds to standard **khi** for three nouns: 'winnow' (˙*khi*), 'height' (˙*khuy*), and 'rudder', which has only the variant ˙*chi* in the earlier attestations (1527 Cahoy 2:12b=25b "*mis* also *chi*" – of *mis* nothing more is found, perhaps < ¨*mi[l]s* 'pusher'). (1874 Putsillo also attests *chi* 'rudder'.) So the standard version of **khi** for 'rudder' seems to be yet another hypercorrection. Putsillo has *kina-* for **cīna-** < ¨*ti-*°*na-* 'pass by'.

For **Cye**(···) the palatal quality is often shifted from the consonant to the vowel, metathesizing the glide so as to produce the mid front monophthong of the modern language: **selmyeng** > **selmeyng**, **Phyengyang** > **Pheyngyang**, ... (King 1990 has examples that argue for **ye** > **yey** > **ey** with loss of the initial glide after the fronting took place, rather than metathesis of the glide.) In Phyengan (Kim

Yengpay 1984:69-70) c(h)ye > c(h)ey with nonpalatal [ts-], and sye > sey; hy-- dispalatalizes to h--- in general, as well as in hey- 'ignite' < (h)hye- (standard khye- = khi-). The word myech 'how many; a few' is widely pronounced meych and that is the way we write it for the modern language in this book. The dispalatalization of the syllables m^yey and ph^yey is recognized by the NK orthography but not by the standard spelling in South Korea. Both maintain a distinction of kyey from key and hyey from hey that is no longer part of the spoken language.

2.10.4. Nasal epenthesis.

A small number of words have forms with and without a nasal before an affricate. There being nothing obvious about affrication and nasality that would motivate a sporadic insertion of that sort, we wonder whether the form with the nasal is not, in fact, the basic form. But for verb stems such as a(n)c- 'sit' and ye(n)c- 'put on top' several kinds of evidence led LKM 1964 to the conclusion that the versions without the nasal are older.

Ramsey 1978a:54-6 gives a good description of the situation, and points out that for certain words the nasal insertion happened only after a non-affricate had become an affricate. Thus te˙ti- 'throw' picked up the nasal of modern Seoul tenci- only after the syllable ti become ci. And hwon˙ca (1518 Sohak-cho 10:6a) 'alone' did not have a nasal so long as it remained howo˙za < hoWo˙za < *hopo(n)˙za (see honca in Part II). Yet if the etymology is *ho[n] ˙pwun ˙sa 'just one only', that already contains the nasal – and has another that is elided; but if the etymology is *ho[n] ˙po[l] ˙sa 'just one layer', the nasal is not expected. The adverb acik '(not) yet' goes back to a˙cik (1463 Pep 1:14a), which is attested also as an˙cik (?1517- ¹No 2:12a, ?1517- Pak 1:64a) and an˙cok (1447 Sek 6:11a, 1463 Pep 1:44a), a form surviving as the South Hamkyeng an˙cuk cited by Ramsey, and it perhaps has the etymology *a˙ni cek 'not time'. If the nasal were original in all (or most) cases there would be no need to explain why it did not develop for more than a small number of the words with affricates. And the variable elision of the nasal could perhaps be attributed to whatever motivates the liquid elision before apicals, the MK suppression of stem-final l before t n c s. Somehow the nasal elision never happened to mence < mwon˙cye(y) (also mwon˙coy) 'ahead; earlier' in most of Korea, but one dialect in South Cenla has mocye (Choy Hak.kun 139). There was a nasal in an earlier attestation, according to the interpretation by Kim Wancin (1980:155) of the phonograms in hyangka 14:10.

The verb stem a(n)c- appears as az- or as- in the forms as.non (1447 Sek 19:6a) and az˙nwo˙la (1462 ¹Nung 1:3b) but that represents the reduction of the syllable excess (...nc- → ...c- > ...s-, different from the modern ...nc- → ...n-). If the stem had really ended in the lenited sibilant ...z- < ... so- we would expect the rising accent on the first syllable of those forms, as in the similar forms of 'seize': ¨as.non (1481 Twusi 22:49b), ¨as.nwon (1481 Twusi 16:68b), ¨asno˙n i (1459 Wel 7:46b [ni miscarved as na]), ¨asno˙n i ˙'n i (1462 ¹Nung 9:40a). Similar remarks apply to ye(n)c-: the forms without the nasal can be treated as reductions of ...nc-, with no rising pitch for yes.no˙n i ˙'la (?1517- Pak 1:56a) and a surprising initial high for ˙yes.non (1481 Twusi 22:36b). All modern dialects have the nasal; Ceycwu alone is reported to have a doublet aci- / anci-. No modern dialect lacks the nasal for enc- (nor does any show initial y...). Putsillo 1874:572 has three forms with the nasal (ansswo, ansswukuy, ansswukey) and one without (acuwo). LKM observes that 1103 Kyeylim (#317) uses phonograms interpreted as "a-cek-ke-la" (for anc.kela 'sit down!') and 1400+ Kwan-yek (#349) used phonograms taken as "a-ke-la", both without the nasal, which could have been noted with a phonogram "an-", used by Kwan-yek to write "an-ta" (#389) for ¨anta (? = a˙no˙ta or = ¨al˙ta) 'knows' or the one used by Kyeylim to write "an(-h ay kwopoy)" (#229) for ˙an˙h oy kowoy 'undergarment'.

There is an additional mystery. For the well-attested stem mon˙ci- 'stroke' there are examples of a variant without the affricate: mo˙nye (1459 Wel 21:133a), mo˙nisi˙kwo (id. 18:14a), ... Modern dialects all have the affricate.

NOTE: In the first entry of Ramsey 1978a:55 correct the Seoul form to enchi and the gloss to 'saddle blanket', corresponding to the earlier enchi (?1720- Waye 2:17b) < e˙chi (1481 Twusi 20:9b).

2.10.5. The earlier finals.

Koreans of the fifteenth century had syllables that, like the modern syllables, could end in a vowel or in one of the consonants *p t k m n ng l* but there were also syllables ending in an *s* that contrasted with *t* and was surely pronounced as a sibilant. Among the "overstuffed" morphemes were nouns and verb stems that ended in the affricate *c*, in the aspirates *ch kh th ph* and simple *h*, as well as clusters such as *lk lp lph lm nc nh sk* and a few others. The extrasyllabic element spilled over into the following syllable when an ending or particle beginning with a vowel was attached; otherwise (before consonant or juncture) it was reduced to one of the codas permitted to a syllable. In the case of simple *h* that meant it was dropped in the "free" form, so that *nwoh* 'rope' was pronounced (and written) *nwo* unless followed by a vowel-initial particle (*nwo˙h o˙lwo* 'with a rope') or by the copula (*nwo˙h i˙la* 'it is a rope'); but when a particle or ending beginning with *t* or *k* was attached, the basic *h* emerged as heavy aspiration so that *nwoh* + ˙*two* was pronounced (and written) *nwo˙thwo* 'also/even the rope', and *nah-* + -˙*kwo* was *na˙khwo* 'giving birth'. Some texts, such as 1449 Kok, wrote the syllable excess morphophonemically so that *kwoc* 'flower', for example, was always written the same, while other texts wrote the phonemic form *kwos* when no vowel-initial particle was attached. But even the most generous of the morphophonemic spellers wrote the phonemic forms of phrases with those morphemes ending in a basic simple *h* and did so until quite modern times when (apparently around 1933) the "**h-pat.chim**" was invented. But by then the *h*-final nouns, dropping all traces of the *h*, had become ordinary nouns ending in a vowel (so that **no** 'rope' behaved like **no** 'oar') and only the verb stems required the **h** final. There is evidence for final ···*h*, presumably so pronounced, in earlier phonograms (1250 Hyangyak) for ˙*mah* 'yam' and (1103 Kyeylim) for ˙*cah* 'foot(rule)' and *pa[h]* 'straw rope'; there is no later direct evidence of the *h* in *pa[h]*, but King tells me the word is treated like other ···*h* nouns that are exempted from the umlauting rule in Hamkyeng. Cf LKM 1972a:85-6.

The 15th-century distinction of ···*s* from ···*t* was lost during the middle of the 16th century (1576 [1]Yuhap 1:8 spelled "*sis namwo*" for the *sit namwo* 'maple tree' of 1527 Cahoy 1:5b = 10a), so that in modern Korean the syllable-final phoneme ···*t* neutralizes those two final consonants, as well as the morphophonemic finals that were already neutralized in ···*t* (···*th* and for some ···*lth*) and in ···*s* (···*c*, ···*ch*). The affricates (···*c* and ···*ch*) were distinguished in syllables written with phonograms in 1250 Hyang-kup (LKM 1972a:83-5), but they had fallen together before 1400+ Cosen-kwan, which wrote words ending in ···*c* ···*ch* ···*s* alike, with a Chinese character (THOUGHT) that must have represented a sibilant. In transcribing Manchu and Mongol the syllable-final ···*s* was treated as a sibilant (in contrast with the stop ···*t*) as late as 1748 (Martin ?1991:n13).

The Hankul system of initials made provision to distinguish five kinds of "throat" sounds at the beginning of a syllable: (1) simple vowel onset, using the zero initial; (2) sharp onset with the glottal stop *q*···; (3) the nasal velar *ng*···; (4) breathy onset with *h*···; and (5) the reinforced (murmured) breathiness of *hh*···. These were all needed to write the traditional distinctions of reading Chinese characters, but speakers of Korean did not normally distinguish *q*··· or *ng*··· from the smooth onset; 1446 Hwun [25b] explicitly states that the glottal onset was not distinguished from the smooth in native Korean words. And in the Chinese readings, the *q*··· was traditionally distinctive only before *i* or a glide: QI(···) QY··· QYW··· QW··· were supposed to be different from I··· Y··· YW··· W··· but for the other vowels the *q*··· was automatic so that the only versions were QA(···), QE(···), QO(···), QU(···). For the Chinese readings only, the early spellings put a final zero (the circle symbol) below a syllable that ended in a vowel, so that every Chinese syllable carried a **pat.chim** of some sort, but this practice fell into disuse by the early 1500s. The zero (the circle symbol) was distinguished from the final ···*ng*, which had the teardrop shape with a tick at the top. When the open syllables of even the Chinese readings came to be written like the open Korean syllables (with no **pat.chim**) and the differentiation of initial *ng*··· from zero fell into disuse (by the 1490s), the symbols for the zero initial and the final velar nasal were placed in complementary distribution, and they ended up merged into a single symbol with different realizations as onset (nothing) and as coda (velar nasal).

Among the ···*lC* clusters, ···*lq* was written in non-Chinese expressions only for the prospective modifier '(⋯ that is) to do/be', which had the effect of reinforcing the simple obstruents *p t k c s* (but not *h*) when they began a following noun in close juncture. The phenomenon was also written, as later, by using the geminate clusters: ⋯*l CC*⋯ = ⋯*lq C*⋯. And after 1480 it was often left unwritten; realizing that the liquid represents the final of the modifier, the scribe keeps constant the shape of the noun and spells ⋯*l C*⋯. So the coda ⋯*lq* represents a morphophonemic phenomenon rather than a string of two phonemes. The ⋯*q* anticipates the tense component of the reinforced obstruent, recognizing that it is not part of the basic shape of the noun – nor, originally, of any other morpheme of the language, since the modern geminate initials became phonemic only by grace of the initial *p*⋯ and *s*⋯ clusters. It is likely, however, that the source of the morphophonemic peculiarity is an attachment to the modifier of the genitive (= adnominal) particle *s*, as evidenced by the spelling ⋯*ls C*⋯ for a few examples of the structure (see -˙*ul s* in Part II). The coda ⋯*LQ* was also used regularly to represent the reading of Middle Chinese unreleased final ⋯t, the "entering tone" equivalent of ⋯n in the other three tones. There was apparently no difference in pronunciation from an ordinary ⋯*l*, as shown by some of the words written as normal Hankul rather than character readings, but the creators of the system must have realized there was something odd about this group of syllables. They may have been aware that in this millennium some Chinese dialects, such as the language of Canton (Guǎngdōng), retain the 7th-century ⋯p ⋯t ⋯k while others (such as southern Mandarin) use a glottal stop for all syllables with the entering tone, merging the three codas: ⋯p ⋯t ⋯k > ⋯q. (Still others, such as northern Mandarin, lost the stops and merged the syllables into the other tones in various ways.) The creators of the system of spelling out the readings of Chinese characters may have been baffled by the Korean choice of ⋯*l* for the syllable coda when ⋯*t* was available in Korean words; 1446 Hwun [22] explicitly notes that the Chinese coda is properly ⋯*t* but that it is popularly treated as ⋯*l*. A satisfactory explanation of that has yet to be offered. Perhaps at the stage when the Chinese words were coming into the language Korean lacked a syllable-final ⋯*t*; the etyma with the MK final stop could have come about by shortening forms with a final vowel (is the negative ¨*mwot* from *˙*mwo˙ta*?), so that ⋯*l* was the only available coda similar to the Chinese, and then as now it was already a lenition of basic *t* in certain words.

Yet there are at least two facts that suggest the coda ⋯*LQ* may not have been the same as /⋯*l*/. The first fact: in forms of the verb 'do' the contraction of *hok*⋯ to *kh*⋯ (rather than '*k*⋯) and of *hot*⋯ to *th*⋯ (rather than to '*t*⋯) takes place when the preceding phoneme was VOICED (*m n ng l w* V Vy), but ⋯*LQ* was sometimes treated as if voiceless: ˙*KYWELQ* ˙*key* (not *khey*) *ho˙n i* '[he] let them decide it' (1447 Sek 9:20a), just like *na ˙kot ˙˙key* (1447 Sek 6:1b) and *ko˙tok ˙˙ti* (1462 ¹Nung 1:67a). There are counterexamples: *THWONG-˙TTALQ khe˙tun* (1463 Pep 1:9a) 'if they are knowledgable' rather than ˙*ke˙tun* (as in ¨*mwot ˙ke˙tun*), ¨*KAY-˙THWALQ ˙khey* (1459 Wel 21:48a) 'so as to emancipate', rather than ˙˙*key*. And *˙*ho-to˙lwok* > *CYWUNG-˙ZILQ ˙tho˙lwok* (1465 Wen se:5a); *ho˙ti* > ˙*POLQ ˙thi* (1463 Pep 4:93b), ˙*TTAY-˙SSILQ ˙thi* (1464 Kumkang 38a), and even ˙*KYWELQ ˙thi* (1482 Nam 1:50a) contra the earlier example. Other cases of *l* are treated as voiced: ˙*ecul ˙khwo* 'is disturbed and' (1447 Sek 6:3b), ˙*ecul ˙khey ˙ho.ya* (1482 Kum-sam 2:19b) 'making them disturbed', ˙*ecul ˙thi a˙ni ˙ho˙ya is˙nwon˙t oy* (1462 ¹Nung 1:69b) 'when it is not disturbed'; *CIN ˙ol ˙khwo ˙cye ho˙m ye n*' (1462 ¹Nung 7:73b) 'when one wants to be true'. And compare modern **kyel kho** 'absolutely (not)' < ˙*KYWELQ* + *h[o]˙kwo* 'deciding'. The second fact: in Chinese binoms the modern language always reinforces an initial t⋯, c⋯, or s⋯ of a morpheme which follows a morpheme that ends in ⋯l (see §1.5): **palqtal** = /palttal/ 'development' < ˙*PELQ-˙TTALQ*. Since this reinforcement has traditionally been ignored in the Hankul spellings, we presume that it continues the articulatory habits of the earlier language.

The MK voiced fricative *W* was a phoneme that represented the lenited form of *p* (§2.11.2). As a coda the symbol was also to write the labial glide (postvocalic ⋯u or ⋯o) that was traditional to certain Chinese syllables, but in the pronunciation of Koreans the letter was simply ignored.

The lenition of *k* (§2.11.1) was shown by a device that we interpret as the phoneme *G*, which was distinctive only after *l z y i*. (The device blocked the liaison that normally would make the *l* or *z* a syllable onset and would insert a *y* before a vowel following *y* or some cases of *i*.) After the 1400s *G* lost its phonetic effect, as shown by absence of the device in some of the spellings of 1527 Cahoy, such as *ke˙zwuy* (> **kewi**, dialect **kesi**) for earlier *kez˙Gwuy* 'intestinal worm' (CF LKM 1972a:86).

2.10.6. Intersyllabic strings; assimilations; conflation and compression.

The interludes between syllabic nuclei (vowels) of modern Korean comprise all the possible sequences of coda + onset, but with assimilatory adjustments that merge morphophonemically distinct strings, so that **ip man** 'just the mouth', **iph man** 'just the leaf', and **im man** 'just the beloved' are pronounced alike as /imman/. Variant spellings sometimes indicate an understandable confusion about the forms that make up certain words: *ancumpangi* (1894 Gale 183) = **anc.um pangi** is written for **anc.un payngi** 'cripple' and **pipin pap** (1965 Dupont 137) for **pipimq pap** 'rice hash'.

In MK spellings nearly all expected strings are found, so that there are quite a few interludes. To these are to be added the many strings created by the genitive (= adnominal) marker *s*. That particle in the structure *N s N* was handled in three ways: it was written as the coda (or part of the coda) of the preceding N, it was instead attached to the following noun as the onset (or part of the onset), or it was placed all by itself as a graphic syllable in its own right. The extreme case is probably *tolks ˙pstay* (1446 Hwun [25b]) = *tolk s ˙pstay* 'the Hour of the Cock', a phrase that was probably pronounced with one or two junctures, if all consonants were fully articulated. Comparable pronunciation problems in English can be found in "the milk's splatter", "sports credits", and "a barely glimpsed strain".

Whenever possible a syllable of Korean begins with an onset, so that if a morpheme that ends in a closed syllable is put before one that begins with a vowel, its coda becomes the onset of the second syllable and the first syllable becomes open. That is why **ip i** 'the mouth [as subject]' sounds like **i pi** 'this rain (or broom)' when the latter is pronounced without a juncture. This liaison phenomenon seems to have been present in the language as far back in time as we can go. When a spelling retains as coda a movable string and uses the zero circle to write the onset of a vowel-initial second element, we know that the string was written morphophonemically or includes a juncture — or (before *y* or *i*) that it represents /G/ (§2.11.1).

The assimilatory phenomena that affect the interludes quite often lead to the merger of morphophonemic strings, as we have seen in the replacement of voiceless oral + nasal by the corresponding nasal + nasal, but some are at an allophonic level — they are purely phonetic. Voicelessness is a nondistinctive feature in Korean. Obstruents are voiceless after or before juncture or when clustered with another obstruent (including h). Otherwise they are voiced, except that (at least in modern Seoul speech) s and h are intrinsically voiceless and, both alone or clustered, spread the voiceless stretch over most or all of the syllable — the vowel and often a final ···m ···n ···ng ···l, as well. The contrary tendency is for the simple h to get murmured and dropped between intrinsically voiced sounds (vowels, m n ng l). On the possible voicing of s to [z] in dialects and older varieties of the language, see §2.4, §2.11.4. The lenition phenomena of earlier Korean appear to support the notion (Martin ?1991:n2) that the MK simple stops and the affricate *c* were voiced between vowels, as they are today, and that the lenitions taking place were just a matter of the voiced stops weakening to fricatives. Since *s* was already fricative, however, a distinction between the unlenited and the lenited forms must mean it was voiceless when not lenited, assuming that the spelling indicates the situation with reasonable accuracy. What about the allophones of *l*? It is quite possible that the flap version [r] was common as a coda and that the lateral developed as part of the tendency to foreclose the release of consonants in the coda when they could not be moved over to become the onset of a following syllable, but the timing of both matters is uncertain. In any event, recognition that lateral articulations exist is made in 1446 Hwun ([25b]) which says "light and heavy *l* are not distinguished in Korean" and "there is only one initial in Chinese syllables", but suggests making a letter for the light liquid (**kapyewun liul**) by putting a circle below *l* (like that put below *p* or *m* to write W). The symbol was adapted by Korean scholars writing Manchu and Mongol glossaries of the 1700s, who put the little circle to the right of the syllable with the *l*; the circle was used also to mark other peculiar phonemes, so that it functioned as a kind of asterisk or pointer rather than a mark specific to the liquid.

Evidence of the nasal assimilation rules became more common in spellings (or misspellings) of the late 1600s, but there are examples I have seen of -pn- → -mn- from 1586, of -kn- → -ngn- from 1553, and of -tn- → -nn- from as early as 1481 and perhaps one from an unavailable text of 1466 (Mok 1; cited from LCT 406b): punnon ← puth.non 'igniting'. Noun stems ending in -h dropped the coda before a nasal (as before a vowel), so that wuh + ˙ma˙ta → wu ˙ma˙ta (1447 Sek 6:31a) 'atop every one', but that may be because all nasal-initial particles were loosely attached. With verb stems, however, the processive -no- attached tightly, and a stem-final -h- was realized as either t or n: il˙hwum cit.no˙n i ˙'la (1459 Wel 2:49b) 'affixes a name' ← cih-, cet˙nwon ˙t ol (1462 ¹Nung 2:54a) '(the fact) that one fears it' ← ceh-; ˙cwonno˙n i (1463/4 Yeng 1:59b) 'is quite pure' ← ˙cwoh-, nwot˙nwo˙n i (1447 Sek 13:19ab) 'sends one off' ← nwoh-. Some early texts used the unique syllable-initial geminate nn- to write the result of -h- + -n-, as in ˙han ˙swum ti.nnon swo˙li (1447 Sek 19:14b) 'the sound of uttering a deep sigh' and ta.nno˙n i ˙'la (1451 Hwun-en 15a) '(it is that) it touches' ← tah-. When the stem ended in -lh- the result was the unique string -l.nn-, as in il.nno˙n i ˙'la (1462 ¹Nung 2:2a) '(it is that one) loses' ← ilh-. The same text will also write il.no˙n i (1:62b) '(that one) loses', so perhaps the difficult pronunciation iln-no- was simplified to just il-no-, since there was no other need for syllable-final -ln. There are also rare spellings of -lh.n- as in halh.no˙n i (1462 ¹Nung 8:5b) '(it is that one) licks', retaining the basic morphophonemic shape. But the most common spelling is -l.n-, as in tung ˙ul al˙nwo˙n i (1459 Wel 2:9a) ← alh- 'has an aching back' and sul˙nwon ˙pa 'yl ˙s oy (1481 Twusi 8:7b) ← sulh- 'because it is distressing'.

In the modern standard language the liquid dominates the nasal in the morphophonemic strings -ln- and -nl-, both of which merge with -ll-, pronounced as a long lateral with lateral release. Misspellings indicate that this merger began in the 1700s. In the 1800s there was a tendency to write "l.n" for /ll/ regardless of the etymology.

Variant spellings indicate that some of the different consonant strings written between vowels were phonetically equivalent. The difference in spelling is due to (1) considerations of the basic shape of the morphemes juxtaposed, (2) attention to compression or conflation under differing speeds of articulation (tempos), (3) misinterpretations and indecisions stemming from other factors. In the case of simple interludes, the placement of the syllable boundary (as indicated by the dots in the Romanization) was irrelevant to the pronunciation except when it indicated a juncture, usually shown by space or hyphen in the Romanization. The following sets of orthographic strings were phonetically equivalent in Middle Korean (a dot shows the syllable boundary):

s.p	= .sp	p.t	= .pt	ns.k	= n.sk	lp.s	= l.ps
s.k	= .sk	p.th	= .pth	ns.t	= n.st	lp.sk	= l.psk
s.t	= .st	p.s	= .ps	ms.k	= m.sk	lp.psk	= l.psk
s.s	= .ss	p.h	= .ph	ms.t	= m.st	lp.c	= l.pc
s.G	= .zG¹	k.h	= .kh	m.psk	= m.sk	lp.t	= l.pt
		t.h	= .th	m.pst	= m.st	lp.h	= l.ph
		p.sk	= .psk			lk.k	= l.kk = lq.k
						.nn	= n.n
						l.nn	= l.n

¹ As in pos˙Ga (1447 Sek 6:31a) = poz˙Ga (1462 ¹Nung 1:5a) 'crush'.

Through the centuries spellers have been plagued by the fact that when the tempo of speech slows, the reinforced and aspirated consonants are anticipated by closing a preceding open syllable: **appa** and **apha** become **ap-ppa** and **ap-pha**, **kacca** and **kacha** become **kat-cca** and **kat-cha**. (But you will rarely hear the word /isse/ slowed to become *it-sse or /mōsse/ said as *mōt-sse.) Since each of these strings can represent several morphophonemic strings, the speller has to pay attention to the morphemes to know whether to write t.h, t.th, .th, th., or h.t – or even th.h, h.th, th.th (though the morpheme structure makes those particular spellings unlikely). In rapid speech these strings will all be compressed to just /th/ and in slower speech they will all be conflated to /tth/. Texts of the past several hundred years have many examples of misleading conflated forms such as that of 1894 Gale *cip.phoyngi* for **ciphayngi** 'staff', and those cited in Martin 1982, to which can be added an earlier example of perhaps a similar sort (assuming a scribal interpretation of *nyek* as *nyekk*): TWONG *nyek ˙kuy* [= *nye˙k uy*] *chi l'* (1466 Kup 1:21b) 'the ones from the east'; compare *twong nyek ˙kwo˙lwo* [= *nye˙k wo˙lwo*] (1518 Sohak-cho 9:98a) = *twong ˙nyek ˙khu˙lwo* [= ˙*nye˙kh u˙lwo*] (1586 Sohak 6:91a) 'to the east'. Earlier texts also have examples of misguided morpheme divisions such as 1894 Gale *pip.ye* (162) = **pipye** 'mix' and *nyek.yes.ci.wo* (113) = ⁿ**yekyess.ci yo** 'deemed', as well as etymologically motivated examples such as **cip.wung** (1936 Roth 42) 'roof' and *pak.aci* (1881 Ridel 166) 'gourd dipper' (so spelled also in 1632 Kalyey 4:20a).

When the reinforced consonants emerged as phonemes in their own right, the *s* which had so often preceded them was widely used to write *sp st sc sk* where the modern language has chosen to institutionalize a different device, less common earlier, the geminate **pp tt cc kk**. Since the syllable-final -*s* had merged with -*t* in the 16th century, a majority of the morphemes that are heard in certain environments as ···**t** are written ···**s** because in other environments (before a vowel-initial particle, ending, or copula) they have the sibilant pronunciation. These morphemes, too, get conflated in slow speech as shown by such spellings as *wos.si* (1894 Gale 99) = **os i** 'clothes [as subject]' and *stus.sun* id. 109) = **ttus un** 'as for the meaning', in both of which the interlude represents a long sibilant. In *nas.cun* (id. 110) = **nac.un** 'low' and in *is.hun nal* (id. 115) = **ithun nal** ← **ithut nal** 'the next day' the *s* represents an apical stop: /natcun/, /itthunnal/. In the case of *pas.sol* (id. 104) = **path ul** 'the field [as object]' the slow form /passul/ tells us that Gale was hearing a dialect that had simplified some of the overstuffed nouns, **path → pas**.

When foreign words have an interlude spelled "···tt···" Koreans like to use the Hankul final ···**s** to represent the first initial: **Los.ttey** 'Lotte', **Cheyusu Maynhays.then Unhayng** 'Chase Manhattan Bank'. This violates the unstated rule that the conflated form is to be written only if a morpheme boundary is recognized. A corollary to the rule is that /ptt/ (or the like) is to be spelled **p.t** unless the second morpheme begins with **tt**, but in the case of **ipttay** 'up to now' and **cēpttay** 'not long ago' the decision ignores the etymology (< ˙*i* + ˙*pstay,* ˙*tye* + ˙*pstay*), as it does in **copssal** 'millet grain' (< *cwo[h]* ˙*psol*) and similar words, and associates the second syllables directly with modern nouns **ttay** 'time' and **ssal** 'grain'.

2.11. Lenitions and elisions; sources of G.

The fifteenth-century language of the early Hankul texts offers many examples of the weakening or total loss of certain consonants between vowels. Some of the effects can be seen at the end of verb stems or at the beginning of suffixes and particles. Others are internal to words or morphemes. The Hankul system made provisions to write voiced fricatives for labial, velar, and sibilant categories. These functioned as distinct phonemes *W, G,* and *z* in the language of early texts, but we have reason to believe that other varieties of Korean of that day retained the *p, k,* and *s* which had been lenited to create the passing distinction of the voiced fricatives. Many examples of these MK sounds turn up unlenited in modern dialects, especially those of Kyengsang and Hamkyeng (CF Ramsey 1975, Martin 1982/3, Kim Yengpay 1984:168-72): **melkwu** 'mulberry, wild grapes' (melwu) < *melGwuy*, **molkay** 'sand' (molay) < *mwol˙Gay*; **masul** 'village' (maul) < *mozolh*; **saypi** 'shrimp' (saywu) < *sa˙Wi*; ··· . In the case of verb stems, the lasting effects of the lenitions can be seen in the shape alternations of the -W- stems (···w-/···p-), the -(S)- stems (···s-/··· -), and some of the -LL- stems (···lu-/···ll-). The -T/L- stems, earlier as today, showed an alternation of the stop ···**t-** before a consonant and the flap ···**l-** before a vowel; the flap represents a lenition of the stop. Since certain dialects today do not have the lenited forms for -W-, -(S)-, and -T/L- stems, we assume they are preserving paradigms of unwritten forms of the fifteenth-century language that were closer to the original system. (An alternative argument would say that these dialects have restructured the paradigms by analogy.) We believe that the motivating factor for the lenitions was largely accentual, but the detailed circumstances remain to be adequately described. Some of the patterns probably result from accompanying vowel elisions and other factors inducing compression. The susceptible particles and endings mostly have velar initials (-*k*··· → -*G*···), but notice also the bound stem -¨*zoW*- (deferential), source of the modern **-sup-** that marks the formal style, and the particle `za 'precisely, only (if)', still said (i)sa as a dialect version of Seoul (i)ya, which comes from attaching that particle to the nominative marker `i, then eliding all cases of -z- so that `i`za became ia, which inserted the glide heard in iya. Elsewhere it is proposed that the copula forms ila and (?)iley are lenited versions of i-ta and i-tey.

The phoneme G as assumed here neutralized the several kinds of lenition. The 15th-century spelling distinguished the phoneme only after y, i, l, and z, but it seems likely that earlier it may have been present between two vowels, especially when one or the other was the minimal (and often epenthetic) u or o, and especially between y and u or o, where we will write yGu and yGo even though there is no contrasting */yyu/ or */yyo/: keyGulu- / keyGulG- 'be lazy', ¨nwuyGus.pu- 'be remorseful', ... For a number of such words the source of the G can be found in dialect versions that preserve the original consonant: keyGulu- / keyGulG- 'be lazy' is keykulu- in North Kyengsang (Kim Hyengkyu 1974:368) and Hamkyeng (Kim Thaykyun 1986:55), and nwuuy < *nwu[G]uy 'sister' not only has dialect versions nwupay, nwupi, nwupu but was written with the phonograms "nwu-pi" in 1400+ Cosen-kwan. For a verb stem like towoy- 'become', where a missing consonant is suspected, we are tempted to write, for example, "to[G]woy-" with the understanding that the source of the [G] may be a velar (a lenited k) or a labial (a lenited p), and occasionally even a sibilant (z = lenited s). In the case of 'become' we know the missing consonant was labial because of the attested variant toWoy-, so we can presume a history of *topoy- > toWoy- > *toWwoy- > *to[G]woy- > t[o]woy- = modern toy-. But we will forgo writing [G] in these cases and use that notation only for the elision of the velar initial of certain bound elements (`kwa, `kwos, `kwom; `ka, `kwo; `key, `kuy; ... ) which appear with the lenited velar (`Gwa, `Gwos, `Gwom; `Ga, `Gwo; -`Gey, -`Guy) after l, y, and often i. Such notations as `[G]wa and -`[G]wo are offered as helpful reminders of the immediate sources of forms with elision. But we will write 'become' as towoy-, and similarly leave implicit the likely dropped consonant in these words, among others: e`[ ]wul`Gwu- 'join them', ku[ ]wul- 'act', mwu[ ]u- 'shake', no[ ]woy(`ya) 'again', sa`[ ]ol / sa`hol 'three days', te[ ]u- 'increase', ta[ ]o- 'get exhausted'.

Because of the neutralization represented by the phoneme, Kim Cin.wu and To Swuhuy (1980) treat our -G- as a juncture phenomenon rather than a segment holding specific phonetic content. And G may very well have become a purely graphic convention in later stages of the orthography, before it vanished altogether.

In our Romanization of modern Korean we sometimes indicate an elision with an apostrophe, though not in paradigmatic forms. Among the elisions represented by the apostrophe are these: [k] in [1]yu'-wel 'June', [p] in si'-wel 'October', [m] in camca' kho 'quietly', [ng] in su' nim 'monk', [l] in cha'-cita 'is sticky', [i] in kac'-kac(i) = kaci-kaci 'all kinds', [e] in hal-'meni, [wu] in mak'-kelli 'coarse liquor', ... And sometimes the elision is of a syllable: [ci] in ape' nim 'father', [ni] in eme' nim. (The elision in these two expressions is ahistorical, for the etyma are ap^e/a and em^e/a.)

2.11.1. Velar lenition and elision.

Under certain circumstances the MK velar stop k lenited to the sound that we transcribe as G, which was probably articulated as a voiced fricative (velar or laryngeal) or at least a glottal squeeze. The sound was recognized only after y, i, l, and z (zG was often written sG). Hankul used indirect devices to show it, blocking the usual liaison that would (1) make ···l or ···z the onset of the following syllable and (2) accrete a syllable-initial y before a vowel after ···y or ···i.

The circumstances calling for velar lenition (CF LCT 1961) involve the joining of noun + particle or verb + ending. The endings include the gerund -`kwo, the adverbative -`key or its variant -`k$^u$oy, and those complex endings that incorporate the gerund or are built on the effective formative -`ke-; but there are no examples of lenition (to *-`Gi) of the summative -`ki, which was little used at the time. The lenition took place after all stems ending in ···y-, ···l-, or ···z- but not after most of those that ended in ···i-. For an ···i- stem to qualify, it had to be:

(1) the copula `i··· , which predicates nouns. Examples can be found in these entries of Part II: `i`Gen ma`lon, `iGe`na, `iGe`nol = `iGe`nul, `iGen`tyeng, `iGe`n ywo, `iGe`tun, `i`Gey, `i`Ge`za, `i`Gwo, and their shortenings to 'y··· and '···.

(2) the causative ″ti- 'drop it' (< °ti- 'fall').

(3) one of a few polysyllabic stems ending in ‧‧‧li- (such as spu˙li- 'sprinkle', e˙li- 'be stupid', ...) that were probably confused with the structure -u˙l i '‧‧‧ (copula prospective modifier + postmodifier + copula). But most of the ‧‧‧li- stems do not trigger the lenition: po˙li˙kwo 'discarding it', ki˙li˙kwo 'praising', ... And the "confused" stems do not always lenite: e˙li˙Gwo (1462 ¹Nung 7:67a, 1463 Pep 2:242a) but also e˙li˙kwo (?1517- Pak 1:9a) 'being stupid'; no˙li˙Gesi˙nol (1445 ¹Yong 8; for *no˙li˙kesi˙nol = *no˙lisike˙nol) '[the emperor's command] came down, and ... ', yet no˙li[˙]kwo (1481 Twusi 10:35b) 'coming down'.

The peculiar behavior of the stems ˙i- and ″ti- led LKM to the conclusion that the basic forms they represent are ˙iy- and ″tiy-; contrast ti˙kwo (1445 ¹Yong 86) 'falling' with ″ti˙Gwo = ″tiy˙Gwo (1459 Wel 10:24b) 'dropping it'. Independent motivation for that conclusion can be seen in the MK abbreviation of the copula as 'y- after a vowel (where modern Korean usually suppresses i- leaving no trace) and in the derivation of the stem ″ti- from *ti-˙[G]i- (intransitive verb + causative), as confirmed by the accentuation.

Nouns and adverbs that end in ‧‧‧i generally triggered the lenition: ″ne y ˙i˙cey swo˙li˙Ga a˙ni ˙Ga (1462 ¹Nung 4:126b) 'is it now your sound or isn't it?'; ˙i˙Gwa (1451 Hwun-en 1b) 'with / and this'; ku˙li˙Gwos (1459 Wel 8:62b) 'just / precisely that way'; ˙wuli˙Gwos kyeyGwu˙m ye n' (1459 Wel 2:72a) 'if we are the ones defeated'. But after the negative precopular noun a˙ni 'not' and the expression hon ka˙ci 'one kind = the same' the lenition seems to have been optional: ˙tye non hwo˙za ″salom a˙ni˙ka (1475 Nay 2:1:16a) 'isn't he a person alone?'; ˙i ˙SYWELQ-˙PEP ka, ˙i ˙SYWELQ-˙PEP a˙ni˙Ga (1482 Kum-sam 4:37b) 'is this preaching the law or isn't this preaching the law?'

hon ka˙ci˙ka talo˙n i˙ye (1459 Wel 8:31b) 'are they the same or different?'; hon ka˙ci˙Ga a˙ni˙Ga (1462 ¹Nung 1:99a) 'is it the same or not?'

The obligatorily leniting nouns include most prominently the postmodifier ˙i 'the one that ‧‧‧ ; the fact that ‧‧‧ ' in all of its uses. Most examples involve the zero abbreviation of the copula stem, as seen in these entries of Part II: -u˙l i 'Ge˙m ye, -u˙l i 'Ge˙n i (˙Gwa, ˙'ston), -u˙l i 'Gen ma˙lon, -u˙l i 'Ge˙nul, -u˙l i 'Ge˙ta, -u˙l i 'Gwan˙toy. I have been unable to find structures with *-u˙n i 'G‧‧‧. And all of the examples of /-(u)˙li˙Gwo/ or /-(u)˙ni˙Gwo/ are questions (-u˙l i˙Gwo, -u˙n i˙Gwo, see below), for there seem to be no such expressions with the copula gerund (*-u˙l i˙″Gwo or *-u˙n i˙'Gwo). In structures with the postmodifiers ˙ka and ˙kwo 'question', the copula modifier (˙in) is usually suppressed: (-u˙n i˙Ga, -u˙n i˙Gwo; -u˙l i˙Ga, -u˙l i˙Gwo; -ke˙n i˙Gwo) but there are examples that let it surface, as found in the entries a˙ni 'n˙ka (= a˙ni˙Ga = a˙ni˙ka), a˙ni 'n˙kwo (= a˙ni˙Gwo = *a˙ni˙kwo), and ˙in˙kwo of Part II. Also included: the suspective -˙ti (< ˙t i, postmodifier + nominative particle), as found in nwop˙ti˙Gwos (1459 Wel 1:37b) 'the higher they are ... '.

The particles ˙kwa 'with', ˙kwos 'precisely', and ˙kwom 'each' regularly lenite to˙G‧‧‧ after a noun that ends in l (including LQ), y, or i. The velar initial is totally suppressed after other vowels (including vowel + w); we note this by writing the G in brackets, as a reminder to help identify the morphemes. The postmodifier ˙ka 'question', is regularly preceded by a modifier but the copula modifier ˙in is usually omitted, so that ˙ka stands right after the noun, as if a particle, and it lenites just like the other particles. The few exceptions written without lenition may be due to scribal error or later restructuring:

na˙la[h] s˙kul˙i ″ta ″HWO˙uy˙hoy˙Gwon˙pa˙ka (1586 Sohak 6:41b) is a rewrite of na˙la[h] s ˙kul˙Gwel i ″ta CHWOY-″HWO˙uy˙hon kes˙ka (1518 Sohak-cho 9:45b) 'is the writing of the nation's history all by Cuī Hào?';

ha˙nol kwa˙sta.h i˙khu˙kwo (1481 Twusi 21:2a) 'heaven and earth are large' should be ha˙nol ˙Gwa (1462 ¹Nung 8:131b) or ha˙nol khwa = ha˙nolh˙kwa (1462 ¹Nung 2:20b).

The example na kwos (?1800 Hancwung 90; cited from LCT) 'precisely I' is from a late text. The word cey˙kwom (1518 Sohak-cho 8:3a) is a shortening of ceyye˙kwom 'individually', a derivation yet to be explained. The adverb-intensifying suffix -˙kwom (which may or may not be the same etymon as the particle) never lenites: *ta˙si-˙kwom* (1447 Sek 6:6a) 'again', *kwop˙koy-˙kwom* (1459 Wel 1:47b) 'double; twice (the age)'. Perhaps juncture could account for *a˙lwo˙m i a˙ni˙ka* (1462 ¹Nung 3:33a) 'isn't it that one knows?' The postmodifier *˙kwo* 'question', like *˙ka*, occurs after a noun by omitting the copula modifier. It lenites after *l, y,* and *i*: *mu˙sum elkwul˙Gwo* (1462 ¹Nung 3:59a) 'what face is it?', *mu˙sus ¨ccwoy˙Gwo* (1463 Wel 1:7a) 'what sin is it?', *hon ka˙ci a˙ni [˙]Gwo* (1482 Nam 2:42a) 'isn't it the same?'. After other vowels, both elided and unelided velar are found: *¨es.ten cyen˙cho [˙G]wo* (1482 Kum-sam 3:52b) 'what kind of cause is it from?', *˙i mu˙su˙kwo* (1482 Kum-sam 2:41a) what is this?', *mu˙sum yang˙co˙kwo* (1462 ¹Nung 3:84a) 'what are the looks?'; *ne˙'y susu˙ng i˙nwu˙kwo* (1447 Sek 23:41b) 'who is your master?'; *¨es.tyey il˙hwum i˙PALQ-¨ZYA˙[G]wo* (1464 Kumkang se:8b) 'why is the name prajñā (wisdom)?' In Chinese passages the Chinese particle YA is followed by the Hankul *[G]a* (?1468- Mong 53a) or *˙[G]wo* (1482 Kum-sam 3:52a).

When attached to a noun that ends in basic ···*h* a metathesis takes place: ···*h ˙k*··· → ···˙*kh*···. The only example offered for *˙ka* is *hona˙kha* [= *honah˙ka*] *ye˙sus˙ka* 'are they one or are they six', and that is given by LCT 706a as "1462 ¹Nung 106", but both the locus and the citation seem to be in error; it was perhaps taken from *hona˙khwa* [= *honah˙kwa*] *ye˙sus˙kwa* 'one and six' on the preceding page. The form in the example, however, is just what we would expect, parallel to that of *˙kwo* in *ku ¨es˙te˙'n˙sta˙khwo* [= *˙stah˙kwo*] (1463 Pep 5:165a) 'what land is that?'.

The 15th-century lenition of velar-initial particles was indicated orthographically throughout the 16th century. But in texts from the 1540s and later (cited by NKW 54-5) there are a number of random spellings of unlenited *˙kwa* after vowels (including *i*), *y, l,* and ···*[h]*, often in close proximity to a lenited version. The 17th-century texts always write *k* after *l* and often (randomly) after a vowel, as well. For both *˙kwom* and *˙kwos* the velar was written in the few examples found in later texts. The elided form of *˙kwa*, spelled *"wa"*, was always used in 19th-century texts (as in the 20th century), but there was some random variation in the 17th and 18th centuries, as seen in *twos.th oy kwoki wa yes kwa yang uy kwoki kwa* (1799 ¹Nap-yak 18a) 'the meat of the pig and the meat of the fox and the sheep'.

There are examples of lexical lenition, as in *kaci-Gaci (s nay lol)* (1569 Chilqtay 10b) 'all kinds (of smells)', lexicalized from *ka˙ci ka˙ci* (1463 Pep 5:137b). And there are velar elisions in nativized Chinese words:

˙mwo[k]˙ywok (1489 Kup-kan 1:104, 1527 Cahoy 3:11a = 5b) 'bathing' < *˙MWOK-˙YWOK* (1447 Sek 6:27b) and *˙mwo[k]˙ywok˙thang˙co* (?1517- Pak 1:52a) 'bathhouse' < *THANG-¨CO*.

˙lywu[k]-˙we˙l uy (?1517- ¹No 1:27b) = *nywu[k]-wel* (1608 Thay-yo 16a) 'June' < *˙LYWUK-˙NGWELQ*; Cf *˙si-˙Gwe˙l ey n'* (?1517- Pak 1:18a) < *˙SSIP-˙NGWELQ* 'October'.

soyng-[k]ang (1527 Cahoy [Tōkyō] 1:14a, 1489 Kup-kan 6:21 [cited from LCT]) > *soyng-yang* (1562 Cahoy [Hiei] 1:7b, 1583 Kwang-Chen 3b) = *soyngkang* (1583 Sek-Chen 3b) 'ginger' < *SOYNG-KANG*.

Although the MK spelling of final ···*l* unlinked to a following vowel is usually to be treated as *-lG-*, when the vowel begins a particle in those texts (such as 1449 Kok) that treat particles as separate words, no *"G"* is to be written: *˙i˙nal ay˙za* (1449 Kok 109) – Cf *mozom˙ay* (ibid.). In other texts we find *na˙l ay, mozo˙m ay, ...*, syllabified phonetically. But the *-G-* is indicated, as part of the noun, for forms of *azo / azG*··· 'younger brother' such as *az˙G on* (1445 ¹Yong 24), *az˙G i* (1445 ¹Yong 103), *az˙G i˙la* (1462 ¹Nung 1:86a), and *az˙G ilwo˙n i* (1462 ¹Nung 1:76b).

2.11.2. Labial lenition and elision.

Spellings with ···*G*··· do not always derive from a lenited velar; some are from lenited labials. We know this either from variant forms that retain the labial or from modern dialect versions with ···*p*···. Despite that information, we will write the MK sound as *G* except when there are morphophonemic grounds to do otherwise, as there are when other forms of the paradigm of a verb contain a labial. In the case of *e˙lwu sol˙[W]wo˙l i˙'syas˙ta* (1463 Pep 4:70-1) 'it will be possible to tell them' we choose to identify clearly the stem by noting its ellipted W, a lenition of *p*, as *[W]* rather than write the *G* that would be called for by our rules, because of other forms in the paradigm and also the competing version found in sol˙Wwo.l i ʼ˙n i (1449 Kok 2). But because of what happened to the vowel (-Wu- > -Gwu-) we write ˙chiGwun (1481 Twusi 6:43a) = ˙chiWun (1459 Wel 18:51a) 'cold' < *chipu-. The phoneme G when used represents a neutralization, thought to be the result of merging the labialized velar fricative and the velarized labial fricative, articulations that are hard to keep apart.

The lone particle is pu˙the '(starting) from', shortened from (··· ˙ᵘ⁄ol) pu˙the, a verb infinitive. That particle usually keeps its initial, even after i, y, and l: ˙i pu˙the (1447 Sek 13:1a, 1463 Pep 1:65a) 'starting from this', ¨a˙lay pu˙the (1449 Kok 109) 'from earlier', ¨nyey pu˙the (1459 Wel 2:70a) 'from long ago', [no example of ···l?]. There are only two or three examples of a lenited form Gwu˙the < *Wu˙the < pu˙the, such as wo˙nol Gwu˙the (?1517- ¹No 1:35b) 'starting from today' and ¨en˙cey Gwu˙the (?1517- Pak 1:13a) 'since when'. And there are no examples of *···phu˙the with metathesis of noun-final ···h; instead the independent form of the ⁿᵒᵘⁿ ᵃᵖᵖᵉᵃʳˢ, ᵃˢ ⁱⁿ wu pu˙the (1464 Kumkang se:6a) 'from above'. The modern particles **pota** and **poko** are derived from the transferentive and the gerund of the verb **po-** 'look at, see'.

No verb endings begin with p···, but the bound adjective -p- is incorporated in a group of subjective adjectives that end in ···W-, such as ¨swuyW- (> **swiw-**/**swīp-**) 'be easy' from ¨swuy- 'rest'. And the verb stem pat- 'butt' becomes -˙Wat- > -˙Gwat- > -**wat-** to derive a few intensive stems: koli˙Gwat- 'conceal', nilu˙Gwat- 'raise', ta˙Gwat- 'approach; defy', mulli˙Gwat- 'spurn; repel', penguli˙Gwat- 'crack/split it', ˙thiGwat- 'push up against', wuy˙Gwat- 'lift up'.

Lenition of -p··· in compound nouns: tay-¨We˙m ul (1445 ¹Yong 87) 'a mighty tiger' < ¨pem 'tiger'; phwunglywu-Wa˙ci (1459 Wel 24:28b) 'musician' < ··· pa˙ci 'a professional'; kolo-˙Wi (1459 Wel 1:36b) 'a fine rain, a drizzle' < ˙pi 'rain'; mwosi˙Gwoy = mwosi˙pwoy (?1517- Pak 1:51b; in contiguous passages) 'ramie cloth' (> **mosi pey**); ˙pwul˙Gwep (?1517- Pak 1:74b) = ˙pwul˙pep (id. 1:75b) < ˙PWULQ-˙PEP 'Buddha's Law', ˙syel˙Gwep (id. 1:75a) < ˙SYWELQ-˙PEP 'explaining the Law'. There is even one example of pye··· > -Wye···: ˙swoy-Wye˙lo (1445 ¹Yong 3:13b [Chinese text]) 'Iron Cliff' [placename]. Examples that survive in the modern language include **si'-o li** '15 leagues' and **si'-wel** 'October' < ˙si-˙Gwe˙l ey n' (?1517- Pak 1:18a) < ˙SSIP-˙NGWELQ; CF **yu'-wel** 'June' < ˙lywu[k]-˙we˙l uy (?1517- ¹No 1:27b) = nywu[k]-wel (1608 Thay-yo 16a). An elision of noun-final ···p gives us ci[p] s 'of the house' in ku ci[p] s ˙sto˙l i (1447 Sek 6:14a) 'the daughter of that house', na 'y ci[p] s ke[˙]s ul (?1517- ¹No 2:49a) 'things of my house', i˙Gwut ˙ci[p] s nul˙ku˙n i (id.) 'the old man in the house next door', ...

The most common labial lenition is that of the -W- stems, with ···p- before a consonant but ···W- > ···w- before a vowel. Most of the -W- stems are adjectives, but there are a small number of verb stems, too (see §8.2.3). The -W- stems include ···lW-, for which the only modern example is the literary **sēlw-** = **selew-** < ¨syelW- 'be sad'. MK had ¨ptelW- = **ttēlp-** 'be puckery', ¨polW- = **pālp-** 'tread', and ¨yelW- = **yē/ālp-** 'be thin', which do not lenite in the modern language, and also ¨kolW- 'line up; compare', which is obsolete. Other MK ···lW- stems: [*¨]molW- 'be sad', ¨solW- 'humbly say' (modern **saloy-**), ¨skolW- 'be difficult', ¨tulW- 'pierce, bore' (modern **ttwulh-**, Hamkyeng **twulp-**).

For a few words we know from dialect evidence that the ···G··· within an opaque lexical item represents the weakening of a labial stop, rather than a velar. The noun i˙Gwuc 'neighbor' (1462 ¹Nung 3:37a) has the modern dialect versions **ipuci, ipucey, iput, iwuci, iwut**, as well as the standard **iwus**, and it is written with the phonograms ¨i-pun¨ in 1400+ Cosen-kwan. (The Hankul **ipus** in 1569 Chiltay is thought to be one of many dialect influences from Kyengsang, where it was published.)

2.11.3. Apical lenition; elisions of l and n.

The apical stop t weakened to the flap allophone of l. That, we assume, is what accounts for the peculiarities of the -T/L- (or "leniting T") stems as contrasted with the regular ···t- stems. The final ···t- of the leniting stems was replaced by ···l- when a vowel followed.

There are a few etymological examples of lenited t → l (Martin 1983:27): mwolan 'peony' (1576 ¹Yuhap 1:7b) < ¨MWUW-TAN, ˙cho˙lyey (1527 Cahoy 1:34a=18b) 'order' < ˙CHO-˙TTYEY (1447 Sek 19:8b). In certain cases the source of the lenition survives as the modern affricate because of the (southern) merger **ty > c**, as in the doublet **tōlyang/tōcang** 'Buddhist seminary' < (?*)¨twotyang < ¨TTWOW-TTYANG (1447 Sek 24:36a). The MK doublet pa˙lol (1445 ¹Yong 2) = pa˙tah (1459 Wel

1:23b) 'sea' may go back to a hypothetical *pa˙talh. And the adverb ˙tat (1447 Sek 9:16a) suggests that talo-/talG- 'be different' < *talok- (§8.3.1) is a lenition of *tatok-. The noun me˙li < ma˙li 'head' is written with the phonograms "ma-ti" in 1103 Kyeylim. The Ceycwu word iti 'this way' (Seng ¹Nakswu 1984:24) appears to preserve the unlenited source of MK ˙i˙li. The copula forms ila < ˙i˙la and iley are probably lenited from ita < ˙i˙ta and itey.

Before another apical sound (t, c, s, n, and rarely l itself) the phoneme l was often elided. The elision was quite regular in verb forms, so that the word representing ¨al-˙ta 'knows' was pronounced and spelled ¨a˙ta. In listing these -L- verbs we take note of the ellipsis (writing, for example, ¨a[l]ta) but in general we follow the spelling and write the forms as they sound. (The headings of dictionary entries such as "¨alta" in LCT and NKW can be thought of as written morphophonemically or etymologically.) Though we often note elided consonants such as ···[l]··· with an apostrophe, that is not done within a stem or paradigmatic form: ¨sa˙ti < ¨sa[l]-˙ti, ¨sa-˙two < ¨sa[l]-˙two or < ¨sa[˙ti] ˙two, ¨sa˙nwon < ¨sa[l]-˙nwon. Many modern dialects continue to elide the liquid before an apical, and even in Seoul the l is sometimes suppressed before -ca (māca) 'as soon as' (Part II, -ca NOTE 1). In fishing villages of North Kyengsang (Choy Myengok 1979:23) when ···l is stem-final it drops before ALL consonants, not just apicals, and stems ending in ···lm- are reanalyzed as ···mu-. The dropping of stem-final ···l- takes place also when stems are compounded: ¨sa[l]-˙ni- 'go on living'; ¨nwo[l]-[˙]ni- > nōnil- 'stroll'; ¨two[l]-[˙]ni- > tōnil- 'walk around, circle'; ¨wu[l]-˙ni- 'go on crying'.

In specific phrases MK nouns ending in ···l (including the reduction of basic ···lh) sometimes elided the liquid before the genitive particle s (CF He Wung 285, 313-4): pa[l] s pata˙ng ay (1462 ¹Nung 10:79a) 'on the sole of the foot'; ˙ki[lh] s ˙ko˙z ay s namwo mi˙th uy i˙sye ˙sye (?1517- ¹No 1:27b) 'under a tree by the side of the road'. That seems to be the origin of the adnoun mus 'many, all (sorts of)' < mwus < ˙mwu[l] s 'of the crowd' and of the noun tokki 'ax' < ¨twos˙kwuy < *¨two[l] s ˙kwuy '(ear/)edge of stone'. Spellings that leave the ···l s or ···n s intact tell us the particle was probably set off by juncture. For an unusual elision before n··· of the string [l s], see Part II, s NOTE 1. Less often, a noun-final n is elided before the particle s: swo[n] s twop (1462 ¹Nung 1:51b) — preserved by 1874 Putsillo as swotthopi; ˙i ˙ma[n] s ˙kam yang ˙uy (?1517- ¹No 2:22a) 'for no more sheep than this' = i man.skan yang ey (1795 ¹No-cwung [P] 2:20a; by then presumably pronounced /nkk/) = i man yang ey (id. [K] 2:21a). But the several examples of ˙ma[n] ˙two may be simply ˙ma + ˙two: ··· cywungsoyng ˙ma ˙two ¨mwot ˙hwo-ngi ˙˙ta (1447 Sek 6:5a) 'is inferior to [the life of] any living creature'. (It is quite possible that the final n of ˙man developed from a separate morpheme attached to ˙ma.) See Part II.

In compound nouns final l sometimes drops before n, l, s, or c: ˙pso[l]-¨nwun (1527 Cahoy 1:1b=2b) = psol-nwun (1576 ¹Yuhap 1:4a) 'pellets of dry snow' (ssalaki nwūn); ˙chil-˙pha[l] ˙li s ˙kil˙h i (?1517- ¹No 1:60a; < ˙CHILQ-˙PALQ ¨LI) 'a road of seven or eight leagues'. The word phā'-il 'the eighth (of April = Buddha's birthday)' must have elided the l of phal-il < ˙PALQ-˙ZILQ at a time when the Chinese morpheme for 'day' was felt to begin with an apical sibilant.

Etymologies with elision of l before an apical (LKM 1963:87-8) include:

kyeo-sali (1748 Tongmun 2-46; cited from LCT) 'mistletoe' < *kyezu(l) sali ('winter life'); "WINTER-ul-sa-li" (1431 Wellyeng), "WINTER-sa-i" (1250 Hyang-kup);

kwu[l]-cwokay (?1544- Akcang: Cheng-san) 'oysters and clams; oyster (with shell)' = ˙kwul s cywokay (1489 Kup-kan 6:81; cited from LCT); "kwulq-cwo-kay" (1250 Hyang-kup);

minali < *munali < *mul nali 'parsley'; "WATER-nay-lip" (1250 Hyang-kup).

In a maximally informative notation all elisions can be shown with the elided consonant between brackets, as above for [l]. And it is possible, as set forth in Part II, to treat ···[l]-˙two as ···[-ti] ˙two though that is probably not the best historical explanation. When the elision is between two words (or within a noun compound), the apostrophe is used: kau' nāy 'throughout the autumn', kyewu' nāy 'all winter long'; atu' nim, tta' nim; so' namu 'pine tree'; cha'-tōl 'quartz; silicon'; ˙na'-˙tol 'days and months'; ppu'-takw(un)i 'a part or corner sticking up' (< ppul 'horn'); mu'-soy 'cast iron'; **panu' cil** 'needlework, sewing', kantu'-cak kantu'-cak 'swaying gently' (< kantul kantul); cha'-pssal '(hulled) glutinous rice'.

Before **i** and **y** the phoneme **n** is sometimes weakened to just nasality and even dropped. Ramsey (1978:52-3) says that in South Hamkyeng both **n** and **ng** are reduced to nasality on the preceding vowel when **y** or **i** follows, but a trace of the apical articulation of the **n** remains in that the preceding vowel will not be fronted (in the usual assimilation to the following **y** or **i**). Speakers in various places say [ãi] or [ai] for **ani** 'no'. Examples of n-elision from fishing villages of North Kyengsang (Choy Myengok 1979:23): ku key cip i a(y)ila(y) 'that's not a house'; ma:i = mānh.i 'lots'. The MK noun ¨kwoy 'cat' has the earmarks of a missing consonant *kwo˙[ ]i and 1103 Kyeylim writes the word with the phonograms "kwo-ni". Quite a few modern dialects, including that of Ceycwu, attest the word as **konayngi** (Kim Hyengkyu 1974:b-170), retaining the nasal.

2.11.4. Sibilant lenition and elision.

Before a vowel the stem-final consonant of ···(s)- verbs (§8.2.5) like **cīs-/ci-** 'build' and **nās-/na-** 'be/get better' vanishes in modern Seoul, but in MK it was a voiced [-z-], so that the infinitives were spelled ci˙ze and na˙ze, using the obsolete triangle symbol for the MK /z/. Since modern dialects retain forms such as /nasa/ for **naa** 'get/be better' ← nā(s)-, we assume that the MK version was an ephemeral lenition of an earlier -s-, a lenition which took place under conditions absent from the regular s-final consonant stems (see Martin 1973, Ramsey 1975). Most of the modern ···s- stems were leniting in the 15th century, including **as-** 'seize', but **pes-** 'take off (clothes, ...)' and its obsolete variant **pas-** are attested only as regular ···s- stems. And MK **is-** (> modern **iss-**) 'exist', a contraction of MK **isi-**, never lenited, for that allomorph was used only before consonants. The verb **wūs-** 'laugh' was a leniting stem in the 15th century, with the infinitive wu˙ze, but the lenition did not survive to give us modern *wue, and the stem is regular today. Kim Wancin (1973) believes that this stem was restructured because of a clash between the homonyms that developed for such forms as MK wu˙lun > wūn ' ··· that cried' and wu˙zun > wu-un → wūn ' ··· that laughed'; but notice that 1876 Kakok has (122) wu-un and (90) wu-um as forms of 'laugh'. Are there any modern dialects that treat the verb as leniting?

According to the map in LSN 1956:103 the unvoiced [s] is retained for MK z in dialects of the northeast and much of the south but is lost in the middle and the northwest; the area where -z- was lost is somewhat wider than that of the loss of distinctive pitch accent but it covers that territory. LSN concludes that the assimilatory voicing of -s- between voiced sounds (vowels, *l, m, n*) arose in the middle and northwestern areas during the middle ages (1300-1600); it was apparently not present in the Sinla language, he says, and it began to disappear again in the middle of the 16th century. He did not address the question why some MK words have ···z··· but others have ···s···. Unless we can establish prosodic conditions for the lenition, the exceptions will have to be treated as the result of dialect mixture or the failure to maintain or even establish an orthographic tradition in the midst of the collapse of the distinction. Did the modern dialects lacking the distinction of -(s)- stems ever go through a stage when they had the voiced [z]? Probably not, though that would be implied by an explanation that would have their modern paradigms restructured by analogy. As mentioned in §2.4, it is rare to hear [z] as an allophone of /s/ in any modern dialect, but there is evidence for that in earlier Hamkyeng speech as reported by Putsillo in 1874 (see Martin ?1991, King 1990), though it is apparently absent in that area today. There would seem to be no good motivation for a voiced fricative sound to become voiceless precisely in all-voiced environments, so I assume that modern **s** (rather than elided [z]) in areas for which the voiced version was earlier reported must be due to people being overwhelmed by the habits of nearby speakers who never gave into the lenition.

Some of the MK words with ···z··· appear with s in modern dialects: kozolh/kozol 'autumn' > **kasil, kusul, kisil** as well as standard **kaul**; mozolh 'village' > **masul, masil, maswul, ... ,** as well as standard **maul**; *mwuzu / mwuzG-* < **musuk* 'radish' > **musu, musi, muku, mukkwu, mutkwu,** and (Pukcheng) **mukk** as well as standard **mwuwu**. The word for 'kitchen' appears both as *puzep* (1451, 1466, 1481) > *puep* (1632) and as *puzek* (1481, 1527) > *puek* (1632) and has the modern dialect versions **pusep, pusap, pusek, pusik, pucek, pucik,** (Pukcheng) **pēkk** as well as standard **puekh** (usually treated as **puek** in Seoul); it is probably from an old compound with *pu[l] s ··* 'of the fire' attached to a variant of **seph** < **s(y)ep[h]* (the *syep* spelling is in 1632 Kalyey but earlier attestations are all *sep*, and the hypothetical final *h* is not attested before the 20th century), perhaps a variant of *nyeph / nyekh* 'side', which would help account for the doublet forms with *-p* and *-k*. It is unclear how far back the final aspirated velar of the standard version *puekh* can be traced; Scott wrote *pwuek ey* (1887 Scott 196 = 1893 Scott 240). For more on **puekh** see Ramsey 1984. The noun *mozom* 'heart, mind' > **maum** is reported as *moum* or *mosum* in Ceycwu dialects; the MK *z* may have lenited from *c*, since phonograms of 1400+ Kwan-yek (item 405) represent "*mo-com*". It should be kept in mind that a few of the *-z-* words survived with an affricate (instead of **s** or zero): **honca** 'alone' (see the entry in Part II and the discussion in §2.10.4), ... And the particle **kkaci** < *s koc(i)* < *s ko˙c(ang)*, as well as *ko˙cang* 'end' and (> **kacang**) 'most, very', offers evidence for the history of ˙*kos* < *ko˙zo* < **ko˙co* 'brink, edge'. LKM 1972a:38-9 calls attention to the forms ˙*swon˙cwo* (?1517- Pak 1:63a) < ˙*swonzwo* (1447 Sek 6:5a) 'by his / her own hands, personally' and *mwomcywo* (1617 Sin-Sok chwung 1:36) = ˙*mwomswo* (1586 Sohak 6:25a) [= *chin˙hi* 1518 Sohak-cho 9:27b] < ˙*mwomzwo* (1481 Twusi 6:34a) 'with one's own body, personally', and would explain modern **samcil** 'Double Three day (= the third of March)' as continuing a nativized SAM-˙ZILQ 'day three'. He also mentions MK *namcin* 'man, husband', which must be from a nativized NAM-ZIN.

Some of the *-z-* words are lexicalized from phrases: ˙*ilza˙ma* (1462 ¹Nung 6:70b, 1463 Pep 7:159a) 'indulging in' < ˙*il (˙lwo) sa˙ma* 'making it one's business'. And ˙*twu˙zeh* 'a few' is from ˙*twu[lh]* + a variant of ˙*seyh* 'three'. Other examples of lenition of a morpheme-initial sibilant include the deferential -˙*zow-* and the particle ˙*za*.

The stem ˙*wuzW-* 'be laughable', found in ˙*wuzWu˙l i* (1445 ¹Yong 16) and ˙*wuz˙Wi* (1449 Kok 179) has undergone a second lenition (labial) by attaching the leniting bound adjective *-p-*; the source form must have been **wusupu-*. The stem ˙*yez˙Gwo-* (˙*yez˙Gwa* 1462 ¹Nung 10:41a, ˙*yes˙Gwa* 9:87b) derives from **yez-Wwo-* < ˙*yes-˙pwo-* 'spy on' (He Wung 126).

2.12. The accent of earlier forms.

The language spoken in modern Seoul differs from the 15th-century language in lacking accentual distinctions that are still found in northeastern and southern parts of the peninsula in the form of patterns of pitch or combinations of pitch and vowel length. Although some of the southernmost dialects (such as Kimhay) have three pitch levels — high, mid, low — others (such as Antong) have two levels, high and low, but distinguish some of the low syllables by lengthening the vowel. Still other dialects (such as Hamhung) merge those two categories but end up with both pronounced high and the expected high pronounced low. And in older Seoul speech the vowel length of the third category was preserved, but a difference of pitch level got lost, so that there was a merger between the short high and low syllables. In most of the texts of the 15th century a single dot was placed to the left of a high-pitched syllable, a double dot to the left of syllables that were long and rose from low to high, and the low short syllables were left unmarked. When a word is cited in isolation without tone marks we cannot be sure whether it represents all low syllables in a tone-marked text or is taken from a text that did not mark the tones. In words and phrases of more than one syllable the stretches of tones formed accentual patterns, much like those of Japanese pitch accent, and that makes Korean different from a tone language such as Vietnamese or classical Chinese. Scholars of the early Hankul period were acutely aware of the traditional Chinese four tones (sā-seng) and wrote these for the Hankul readings of Chinese characters, equating the low tone with the "even" tone (**phyeng-seng**), the high tone with the "going" tone (kē-seng), and the long low-high with the "rising" tone (sāng-seng).

The "entering" tone (**ip-seng**) was posited by Chinese phonologists to account for the syllables ending in unreleased voiceless stops ‑p, ‑t, and ‑k, still heard in Cantonese but lost in northern Chinese. In borrowing Chinese words, Koreans treated those stops as ‑p, ‑l, ‑k, with the apical version written ‑LQ in Hankul readings of characters, and marked them with the single dot of the "going" tone. But the character readings, with respect to tone as well as other features, were somewhat artificial, constructed to conform to the information that Chinese phonologists had compiled as riming guides for the language of the 7th century. Chinese words that got into popular usage were often treated differently, though the "even" tone (accounting for almost half the Chinese morphemes) was usually equated with the Korean unmarked low tone.

The accentual patterns of native Korean words did not, of course, come from China, but must be considered a distinctive part of the ancestral forms. Because of partial correlations between the accent and the canonical shapes of morphemes, it is suspected that at least some of the patterns were internal developments, so that possibly the ancestral language may have treated pitch as nondistinctive; but that hypothesis remains unproven. The low-high rise marked by the double dot is often the result of collapsing two syllables (low + high) into a single long syllable; and sometimes, especially in verb forms, it indicates retention of the high pitch of a syllable that elided its vowel, typically the nondescript *u* or *o* that represented a minimal vowel quality. Thus for 'walk' the modifier *ke˙lun* < **ke˙tu-n* (1459 Wel 1:27b) has an overt vowel to carry the high tone, but the gerund ˙*ket˙kwo* < **ke˙t[u]-˙kwo* (1449 Kok 130) does not, so the high pitch is added on to the low pitch of the preceding syllable. (See Ramsey 1978a:209-24.)

The MK tone dots have been transcribed as they appear (or do not appear) in the cited passage when that is from a photocopy of the original text or when it is from a secondary source that included the information. The examples from 1445 ¹Yong carry the accents of LKM's 1962 interpretation. I have added in brackets a few tone marks that I think are missing because of broken type, or that are the result of surface processes (such as the frequent loss of a dot from a string of three dotted syllables), where the restoration helps the reader see the structure. I have not, in general, given the basic or reconstructed dots for strings of morphemes in endings. There, as toward the end of long phrases in general, a tendency developed to disregard distinctive accent after the first in a stem (or a noun), either omitting the marks or indicating an automatic "sing-song" tune of alternating pitches. The tendency became quite noticeable in 1481 Twusi, where Kim Chakyun (1979), like Kim Wancin and Ceng Yenchan earlier, observes that many particles and endings that had been marked ˙ (high) in 1445 ¹Yong, 1447 Sek, 1449 Kok, and 1459 Wel are left unmarked (low) or marked ¨ (low-high), and that is even more striking in 1587 Sohak; he characterizes the trend as (38) "neutralization at end of word". We have left unmarked the frequent suppression of a final dot on the infinitive ending when a particle (with dot) is attached, such as *e˙wule ˙za* (1451 Hwun-en 13a) CF *e˙wu˙le* (1463 Pep 2:114b). And for the most part we do not call attention to suppression of the second of three dots on contiguous syllables, as in ˙*pwola˙m ol* (?1468‑ Mong 20a) 'the sign' − CF ˙*pwo˙la.m i˙n i* (1459 Wel 21:217-8), but we make a few exceptions when it helps account for the words in a phrase: ˙*wos ˙kwa ˙pap [˙]kwa ˙ay* (1481 Twusi 16:19a), ˙*swoy [˙]yey ˙sye* (1459 Wel 2:28b), *swo˙li [˙]yey ˙sye* (1447 Sek 24:1b), ˙*hoy [˙]yey ˙za* (1447 Sek 23:13a), ˙*i kak˙si [˙]lwo ˙za* (1459 Wel 7:15b). We leave unmarked the suppression of an accent in ¨*twuy.h ey ˙nun* (1445 ¹Yong 30) = ¨*twuy[˙]h ey ˙nun*, CF ¨*twuy˙h ey n'* (id. 70).

There are numerous examples of the crasis of a final low pitch with the tonal residue of an ellipted high-pitch syllable (CF He Wung 337): ¨*nay˙h ay to¨li ¨eptwo˙ta* (1481 Twusi 25:7a) 'there is no bridge on the river' < *toli ˙[i]*; ¨*CO ˙non mot nwu¨uy ˙˙Gwo ˙MOY ˙non azo nwu¨uy ˙˙la* (1459 Wel 21:162a) '[the Chinese word] ¨*CO* is an older sister, ˙*MOY* is a younger sister' < *nwuuy ˙i˙Gwo ‑ nwuuy ˙i˙la*. That is what accounts for the rising accent in preconsonantal forms of the -L- stems (§8.3.2).

2.12.1. Accentual patterns.

A limited number of patterns were available for words of a given length. The patterns are shown below, with examples, for nouns and adverbs of one, two, and three syllables.

L	H			R
mol 'horse'	˙*mal* 'measure'			¨*mal* 'words'
LL	HL	LH	LR < LLH	RL
pwoli 'barley'	˙*seli* 'midst'	*me˙li* 'head'	*mak¨tay* 'club'	¨*cyepi* 'swallow'
	HH(/·HL)			RH
	˙*mwo˙koy* 'mosquito'			¨*ke˙cus* 'false'
	(HLL/)HLH	LHH	LLH	RHH
	˙*twos.ka˙pi* 'goblin'	*mye˙nu˙li* 'wife'	*kama˙kwoy* 'crow'	¨*a˙mo˙lyey* 'how'
	HLH	LHL	LLR	RLH
	˙*muci˙key* 'rainbow'	*ye˙tolay* '8 days'	(−)	¨*sama˙kwoy* 'mole'
LLL	HHH			RLL
cintolGwuy 'azalea'	˙*kuy˙lye˙ki* 'goose'			(−)
LRL	HRH	HLR	LHR	RHL
(−)	(−)	˙*ema¨nim* 'mother'	*a˙pa¨nim* 'father'	¨*ke˙cu-¨mal* 'lie'
RRL	RRH			RLR
(−)	(−)			(?)

Ramsey, following Ceng Yenchan (1971), assumes that certain patterns freely varied with each other: HH / HL; LHL / LHH; HLL / HLH / HHL. That assumption is made for two reasons: the patterns are merged in the reflexes found in the modern dialects, and for some of the words the early attestations vary. We find three kinds of evidence for a given etymon:

(1) Only one pattern is attested. For these, we have no direct evidence that the pattern was not distinctive.

(2) Two or three patterns are attested and the variants are unmotivated, in that they cannot be explained by their environments. For certain words there may be only one attestation for a variant pattern, while for other words there are several attestations for each pattern.

(3) Certain words accentuated H(H)H are converted to H(H)L when a particle or copula expression is attached. This is a prosodic adjustment, as if to avoid a long string of high syllables, though such plateaus can be found in other phrases.

In the examples that follow, the English gloss is given first.

Type H X X

HHH
'wild goose' ˙*kuy˙lye˙ki* (1527 Cahoy 1:8b=15a)
HLH / HHL
'goblin' ˙*twos.ka˙pi* (LCT; 1447 Sek 9:36b, 1449 Kok 163, 1482 Kum-sam 4:23a); ˙*twos˙kapi '˙n i* (1459 Wel 21:105a).
HHH / HLH (? or HLL, attributing the accent to the particle)
'crane' ˙*twu˙lwu˙mi* (LCT; 1459 Wel 7:66a, 1527 Cahoy 1:9a=16a); ˙*twulwu˙m[i] uy* (?1517- Pak 1:27b)
HLH
'rainbow' ˙*muci˙key* (1445 ¹Yong 50, 1462 ¹Nung 2:87b, 1481 Twusi 16:42b, 1527 Cahoy 1:1b=3a)
'tadpole' ˙*wolchang-˙i* (1527 Cahoy 1:12b=24a) = ˙*wolchang* (1446 Hwun 29a; the dot is strangely missing in the Taycey-kak repro, but it is clear on the photo plate included in ¹Yi Sangpayk 1957)
'rather' ˙*wohi˙lye* (1459 Wel 1:37a, 21:149a; 1462 ¹Nung 2:67a; 1463 Pep 2:77a, 2:158a, 4:192-3; 1475 Nay 2:1:2b)

HLR
'mother' `ema ″nim (1445 ¹Yong 90, 1449 Kok 16, 1459 Wel 2:6b), ~ `i (1459 Wel 8:84b) = `ema ″ni`m i (1459 Wel 21:27b, 21:28a)

HLH / HHH
'grandfather' `hana`pi (= `ha.n a`pi) (1527 Cahoy 1:16a=33a), `hana`pi l' (1445 ¹Yong 125); `ha`na`pi (?1517- ¹No 2:34a)

HHL / HLH / HHH
'peak' `tyeng`paki (1447 Sek 6:43b, 1459 Wel 18:16b); `tyengpa`ki (1465 Wen 2:2:1:38a); `tyeng`pa`ki (1527 Cahoy 1:13a=24b) 'peak'

HLH / HHL
'elephant' `kwokhi`li ' ´Gwo (1459 Wel 1:27b), `kwokhi`li ' `n i (id. 1:28a); `kwo`khili (1527 Cahoy 1:9b=18a) < * `kwoh ki`l[u]- `i 'nose long-one' = 'long-nosed one'

Type L X X

LLH
'ant' kayya`mi (1447 Sek 6:35 [¹Yi Tonglim version], 6:37, 1481 Twusi 15:56a, 1482 Nam 2:32a), kayya`mi l' (1481 Twusi 7:18b) = ka.ya`mi (1459 Wel 18:39b, 1481 Twusi 8:8a, 1482 Kum-sam 5:36a)
'branch' kayya`ci (1481 Twusi 23:23a) = ka.ya`ci (1481 Twusi 10:5b)
'here' inge`kuy (1447 Sek 19:17b; 1459 Wel 13:35b, 14:59a; 1481 Twusi 7:14a; 1482 Nam 1:14a)

LHL
'eight days' ye`tolay (1459 Wel 2:35ab)
'mullet' ka`mwothi (1527 Cahoy 1:11a=20b)

LHR
'acorn' two`thwo-″pa.m ol (1481 Twusi 24:39a) = LHH two`thwol-`Gwam (id. 25:26b)
'father' a`pa ″nim (1449 Kok 23); ~ `ul 1459 Wel 8:84b, ~ `i 10:2a; a`pa ″nim s `kuy (1447 Sek 6:1a)

LHH
'harp' ke`mun-`kwo (1481 Twusi 16:30b; 1586 Sohak 6:94b), ke`mun-`kwo y (1481 Twusi 21:35a)
'nine days' a`ho`lay (1447 Sek 9:31a = 1459 Wel 9:51ab)
'puddle' wung`te`ngi (1527 Cahoy 1:3a=5b)
'sneeze' co`choy`ywom (1475 Nay 1:49b, 1527 Cahoy 1:15b=29b, 1586 Sohak 2:7a)
'wife' mye`nu`li (1447 Sek 6:7a, 1527 Cahoy 1:16a=31b, 2:1a)
'acorn' (1) two`thwo`li ([1517→]1614 Saseng 2:68a [dots obscured in repro], 1527 Cahoy 1:11b)
(2) two`thwol-`Gwam (1481 Twusi 25:26b)= LHR two`thwo-″pa.m ol (id. 24:39a)

LHL / LHH
'aunt' a`comi (1445 ¹Yong 99, 1481 Twusi 8:38a); a`co`mi (1527 Cahoy 1:16b=31b, 1:16b=32a), a`com[y] oy `swon-toy (1475 Nay 2:1:29b)
'midst' ka`won-toy (1482 Kum-sam 2:65a), ka`won-toy s (1482 Kum-sam 2:31b); ka`won-`toy (1447 Sek 6:31a; 1459 Wel 1:4a, 1:30a, 2:51b, 9:22b; 1462 ¹Nung 2:84b, 3:38a; ?1468- Mong 43b, 64b; 1481 Twusi 15:44a; 1518 Sohak-cho 8:32b), ka`won-`toy n' (1449 Kok 70), ka`won-`toy l' (1482 Kum-sam 2:65a), ka`won-`toy s (1527 Cahoy 3:34b=15b)
'a mute' pe`weli (1550 ¹Yenghem 11b); pe`we`li (1447 Sek 19:6b, 1459 Wel 17:52a, 1527 Cahoy 2:16b=34a)
'packsaddle' ki`luma (1481 Twusi 15:1b, 21:22b, 22:8b; 1586 Sohak 5:54a); ki`lu`ma (1527 Cahoy 2:13b=27a)
'seagull' kol`myeki (1481 Twusi 7:37a, 10:2a, 15:53a, 21:38a); kol`mye`ki (1527 Cahoy 1:9a=16b)
'traveler' na`kunay (1481 Twusi 7:2a [LCT is wrong], 7:9a, 7:14b, 7:26b, 10:2b, 15:23a, 15:31b); na`ku`nay ' `n i (?1517- ¹No 1:18b)

At least one noun has variants starting either low or high:

LLH / HLH
'cricket' moyya˙mi (1527 Cahoy 1:12a=22b), moyya˙m[i] oy (1482 Nam 2:40b); ˙moyya˙mi (1481 Twusi 15:27b; LCT "˙moyGa˙mi", but ya is clear in the repro), ˙moyya˙m[i] oy (1481 Twusi 20:8b)

There are a few words with more than one rise. They are reduplications, phrases, or half-assimilated Chinese loans:

RR
'always, ever' ¨nay¨nay (1445 ¹Yong 16, 1447 Sek se:2a, 1463 Pep 2:20b [dots obscured in repro])
'filial devotion' ¨hywo¨yang (1586 Sohak 6:50b = 1518 Sohak-cho 9:55a) < ˙HYWOW-˙YANG
'grudge' ¨wen¨mang (1586 Sohak 6:83b) = ¨wen˙mang (1518 Sohak-cho 9:90a) < QWEN-˙MANG
RRH
'bird beak' ¨say ¨pwu˙li (1527 Cahoy 3:3b=6b)

To the examples of rise patterns we can add various forms of verbs and compound verbs, taken from examples in Part II and here listed without gloss or source:

RRL ¨ti-¨nayGwo
RRH ¨ket-¨nay˙ya
RLR ?
RLL ¨etusil, ¨wulGenul
RLH ¨ayGwa˙thye, ¨azop˙kwo, ¨cyektwo˙ta, ¨cywokwo˙ma, ¨ep.su˙sya, ¨hoyGi˙ta, ¨hoyGwo˙ta, ¨ilGe˙tun, ¨kyesi˙ta, ¨mantha˙la, ¨salGe˙na, ¨samke˙nul, ¨sitcop˙key, ¨twolo˙sya, ¨wulGwe˙le
RHH ¨al˙Gwa˙tye, ¨cwos˙soWa˙n, ¨cye˙ku˙na, ¨nam˙to˙lwok, ¨sa˙ni˙ta, ¨wu˙ni˙ta
RHL ¨a˙losil, ¨a˙losyam, ¨a˙molyey, ¨ep˙kesin, ¨ep˙siGwul, ¨ep˙susil, ¨kye˙siken, ¨mey˙zoWa
LLR kolo¨chywom
LRL cap¨sopke˙n, mas-¨nala, tut¨copkwo, tu¨zopta
LRH tut¨cop˙kuy, nip¨sop˙kwo, tut¨cop˙ti
LHR kol˙hoy-¨nay
HRH ?

Examples of (invariant) LH:
'butterfly' na˙poy (1462 ¹Nung 7:83b; 1481 Twusi 15:11b, 21:6b; 1527 Cahoy 1:11b=21b), napoy ˙lol (1463/4 Yeng 1:22b; dot obscured?), na˙pwoy (1481 Twusi 15:32a, 23:20a) ≠ na˙p oy 'of the monkey' (1465 Wen se:64a, 1482 Kum-sam 2:44b) = nap ˙uy (1481 Twusi 20:21a)
'bug' pel˙Gey (1447 Sek 9:24b, 1449 Kok 28a, 1459 Wel 9:26a, 1462 ¹Nung 7:83b, 1463 Pep 2:107a [dot obscured in repro], 1527 Cahoy 3:2a=3a)
'fault' he˙mul (1459 Wel 2:6a; 1462 ¹Nung 4:53a, 4:122a; 1463 Pep 4:36b; 1527 Cahoy 2:17a=35a, 3:29a); he˙mu˙l (~ ul 1445 ¹Yong 119; ~ i 1447 Sek 9:4b, ~ un 1462 ¹Nung 7:85a)
'fish; flesh, meat' kwo˙ki (1447 Sek 6:10b; 1481 Twusi 7:5a, 7:7b, 10:31b, 16:19b, 22:7b; ?1517- ¹No 1:22a; 1527 Cahoy 2:11a=21b, 3:2a=3a), ~ ˙lol (1447 Sek 9:12a), ~ lol (1481 Twusi 25:14b), ~ non (1481 Twusi 16:19b), ~ ˙la ˙two (1447 Sek 9:13a); kwo˙k[i] oy (1459 Wel 1:14a), ~ lan (1481 Twusi 21:3a)
'root' pwul˙hwuy (1445 ¹Yong 2, 1462 ¹Nung 2:22a, 1463 Pep 2:131a, 1481 Twusi 7:23b, 1527 Cahoy 3:2a=3b), ~ ˙˙la (1459 Wel se:21a), ~ ˙lol (1447 Sek 6:30b, 1449 Kok 99)
'scales (of fish, etc)' pi˙nul (1527 Cahoy 3:2a=3a; ~ ˙ul 1449 Kok 28a, ~ ˙Gwa 1459 Wel 7:35a), pi˙nu˙l ey (1447 Sek 13:8a), pi˙nu.l ol (1482 Nam 1:64a), pi˙nol (1481 Twusi 25:14b)

2.12.2. Accentual variants.

Certain words are attested with two or more accentual patterns. In the most common type, the variant loses all dots but the first, exemplifying the tendency to neutralize pitch distinctions in the later part of a word:

'as if' ˙ma˙chi (1447 Sek 6:25b, ?1517- Pak 1:23a, ?1517- ¹No 2:66a) > ˙machi (1481 Twusi 7:7b, 10:9a; 1482 Kum-sam 2:53a)
'fitting' ˙mas˙tang (1462 ¹Nung 1:89a; error?) > ˙mas.tang (1447 Sek 13:12b, 1462 ¹Nung 10:42b, 1463 Pep 3:196b, ?1468- Mong 20a, 1481 Twusi 8:6b, 1482 Kum-sam 2:37a, 1475 Nay 2:1:49a)

'deliberately' kwu˙thuy˙ye (1459 Wel 9:13b, 1463 Pep 2:203a, 1481 Twusi 20:29a) > kwu˙thuyye (1449 Kok 145; 1481 Twusi 10:12a, 25:29a)
'first' pi˙lu˙se (1463 Pep 1:131a, 1465 Wen 1:2:3:6a) > pi˙luse (1464 Kumkang se:6b; 1465 Wen 1:2:2:140a, 2:3:1:25a, 2:3:1:52a, 2:3:2:68a; 1475 Nay 2:1:16ab; 1482 Kum-sam 2:3a, 4:36b; 1482 Nam 1:33b)
'mirror' ke˙wu˙lwu (1462 ¹Nung 2:17b,b; 1481 Twusi 21:35b) > ke˙wulwu (1447 Sek 24:20b; 1459 Wel 8:20b; 1482 Kum-sam 2:63a, 3:31a)
'obligatorily' mwo˙lwo˙may (1447 Sek 6:2b; 1451 Hwun-en 13a; 1459 Wel se:17a, 7:15b, 14:31b, 23:91b; 1462 ¹Nung 4:77a; 1465 Wen 2:3:2:44a; ?1468⁻ Mong 10b; 1463 Pep 4:148b; ?1517⁻ ¹No 2:44a) > mwo˙lwomay (1475 Nay 1:76b; 1481 Twusi 15:6a, 15:42b, 20:4b; 1482 Nam 1:24a)
'necessarily' pan˙to˙ki (1462 ¹Nung 1:17a, 1:67a) > pan˙toki (1465 Wen 1:1:1:63a, ?1468⁻ Mong 13a)
'king' ¨nim-˙kum (1445 ¹Yong 33, 49, 84, 121; 1459 Wel 1:31b) > ¨nim-kum (1481 Twusi 10:9b, 22:46 [faint]; 1475 Nay 1:9b)
'woman' ¨kye˙cip (1463 Pep 2:28b; 1447 Sek 6:6b) > ¨kyecip (1447 Sek 6:4a, 19:19b, 24:2b; 1459 Wel 7:10b, 8:94b; 1463 Pep 4:176a,b)

The honorific term for '(one's) words' is usually ¨mal-ssom but when it is before the particle ˙o˙lwo it appears as ¨mal-˙ssom, as in 1447 Sek 13:48a (¨mal-˙sso.m o˙lwo) and 1465 Wen se:11a (¨mal-˙so.m o˙lwo); CF He Wung 328. (He Wung misreads 1451 Hwun-en 1a as a similar example with the nominative particle, but the text has ¨mal-sso.m i˙la.)

The word for 'cloud' is ˙kwulwum (1445 ¹Yong 42; 1447 Sek 19:41b; 1449 Kok 81; 1459 Wel 2:51b, 7:35a, 7:31-2; 1462 ¹Nung 4:6a, 8:50b; 1463 Pep 3:35a; 1465 Wen 1:1:10b; 1481 Twusi 7:23b, 8:11b, 15:9a, 15:9b, 21:7b, 21:14b, 21:22b, 21:41b; 1482 Nam 1:34a; 1482 Kum-sam 3:36b; ...) but there is at least one example of ˙kwu˙lwum: ˙kwu˙lwu.m i˙la (1459 Wel se:18a), yet on the next page (18b) ˙kwulwu˙m ulh.

A word for 'branch' is cited as ˙kaci by LCT and as ˙ka˙ci by NKW, and He Wung gives a single example of the latter, ˙ka˙ci ˙lwo˙ta (1481 Twusi 7:1a), but in the only reproduction of the passage I have seen the marking is unclear; in any event, it could be treated as ˙ka˙c' ilwo˙ta with the second dot going with the copula form (˙ilwo˙ta). Other examples (1447 Sek 13:47a, 1449 Kok 19, 1459 Wel 1:43b, 1481 Twusi 8:3b, 15:4a) all seem to be ˙kaci. Compare the LH word ka˙ci 'kind, sort' (as noun 1465 Wen 1:1:2:61a; as counter 1447 Sek 6:4a and 24:2b, 1459 Wel 21:88-9, 1462 ¹Nung 2:17a, 1481 Twusi 8:24b, 1482 Kum-sam 4:40a), whence hon ka˙ci 'same' (1447 Sek 13:29a, 23:4a; 1459 Wel 2:61a, 8:31b, 9:22a; 1462 ¹Nung 1:17a, 1:99a, 2:19a, 6:54a; 1482 Kum-sam 4:20b; ?1517⁻ Pak 1:72).

Ramsey 1978a:109 has a list of forty two-syllable nouns said to be High-Low or High-High in Middle Korean, including the above three. But for these three, at least, the attestations of the High-High versions are very few, as we see above, and perhaps are to be accounted for as a back-shift of the initial accent of the copula forms ˙i˙la and ˙ilwo˙ta and of the particle ˙o˙lwo, which often functions as an adverbialization of the copula ('so as to be, being, as'). Of the other words listed by Ramsey, for 'fly' LCT has ˙pho˙li (1527 Cahoy 1:11b=21b) and NKW ˙pholi (1481 Twusi 10:28b, 20:26a), but the High-High pattern occurs only isolated in the 16th-century dictionary; the word is one of several early examples of the accreted noun/suffix -i and was earlier (1446 Hwun 27b) just ˙phol. The only tone-marked examples of ˙kwuki 'ladle' (1527 Cahoy 2:7a=11a), ˙pak.ha 'mint' (1527 Cahoy 1:8a=15a), and ˙toypha 'plane' (1527 Cahoy 2:8b=16b) are High-Low, as are those of:
'chick' ˙piywuk (1446 Hwun 28a)
'owl' ˙puheng (1446 Hwun 28a) = ˙puhweng-i (1527 Cahoy 1:8b=15b), probably < ˙puhweng (pa˙hwoy) 'Phoenix (Rock)' (1445 ¹Yong text 5:27b) = ¨pwonghwang (1527 Cahoy 1:8a=15a) < ¨PWONG-HWANG
'midst' ˙seli (˙seli ˙yey 1445 ¹Yong 4, 1449 Kok 124; 1459 Wel 9:35f; 1481 Twusi 7:10b, 10:13a, 16:39a; ˙seli ˙'la 1459 Wel 1:19b). If not a mistake, kwulwum se˙li lwo ˙sye (1481 Twusi 22:21b) treats the first two words as a compound; we expect a dot on the first syllable of ˙kwulwum 'cloud'.
'taro' ˙thwolan (1481 Twusi 7:21b, 22:56a; 1527 Cahoy 1:7b=14a)

The only attestations of the following words are High-High:
'jar' ˙tan˙ti (?1517- Pak 1:41a, 1527 Cahoy 2:7a=12b)
'rice wash-water' ˙stu˙mul (1459 Wel 21:110b, 1527 Cahoy 3:5b=11a)
'strawberry' ˙ptal˙ki (1527 Cahoy 1:6b=12a; correct the heading "˙ptalki" in LCT 199a)
'belch' ˙thu˙lim (1527 Cahoy 1:15a=29b)
'helmet' ˙thwu˙kwu (1445 ¹Yong 52, 89; 1527 Cahoy 2:14a=28a)
'goat' ˙yem˙sywo (1527 Cahoy 1:10a=19a)

The word for 'wave' is normally treated as a phrase: ˙mul s ˙kyel (1465 Wen 1:2:3:22b) = ˙mu[l] s ˙kyel (1527 Cahoy 1:2b=4b), ˙mul s ˙kye.l i (1449 Kok 107; 1482 Nam 2:58a, 2:58b), ˙mul s ˙kyel s (1447 Sek 13:9b, 1459 Wel 9:22b, 1462 ¹Nung 8:84a, 1463 Pep 1:51a), ˙mul s ˙kye.l ul (1463 Pep 1:51a, 1465Wen 1:2:1:28a), ˙mul s ˙kye.l uy (1481 Twusi 8:11b), ˙mul s ˙kye.l i˙la (1462 ¹Nung 1:64a). But the second dot is absent in: ˙mul s kye˙l ul (1481 Twusi 10:3b) and ˙mul s kyel TYWUNG ˙ey (?1468- Mong 43a) – yet ˙mul ˙s ˙kye˙l ey (ibid.). CF 'tear' ˙nwun s ˙mul (1449 Kok 45, 1475 Nay 2:2:13b; ~ [˙]Gwos 1481 Twusi 8:30a), ˙nwun s ˙mu.l ey (1481 Twusi 8:45b), ˙nwun s ˙mu.l ul (1481 Twusi 7:10b) = ˙nwun z ˙mu˙l ul (1445 ¹Yong 91). Other words treated as phrases include:

˙pal s tung 'heel' (~ ˙kwa 1463 Pep 2:12a, ~ ˙ul 1463 Pep 1:55a, ~ ˙i˙Gwo 1463 Pep 1:55a), ˙pal s tu˙ng i (1459 Wel 2:40b, 2:57a; 1463 Pep 2:12a); and the lexicalized all-low version pa[l] s tung (1527 Cahoy 1:15a=29a).

˙pal s pa˙tang 'sole of foot' (~ s 1459 Wel 2:37b), ˙pal s pa˙ta˙ng i (1459 Wel 2:40a, 1462 ¹Nung 2:115b), ˙pal s pa˙ta˙ng ay (1466 Kup 1:32b; 1:63b lacks dot on /ng ay/); and the lexicalized pa[l] s pa˙ta˙ng ay (1462 ¹Nung 10:79a), pa[l] s pa˙tang (1527 Cahoy 1:15a=29a).

˙pal s kalak 'toe': ˙pal s kala˙k ol (1482 Nam 1:50a); and the lexicalized pa[l] s kala˙k o˙lwo (1447 Sek 6:39a [¹Yi Tonglim version]).

Ramsey concludes that all cases of High-High or High-Low belong to a single class of words with optional retreat (or spread?) of the high pitch, whether both variants are attested or not. In this book, a noun attested in only one variant is cited in that form; those with two variants are cited as one or the other, depending on the distribution. In effect, we imply that the earlier language had two classes, which eventually fell together, as indicated by the accent classes of the modern dialects described by Ramsey. To the extent we differ with Ramsey, it is perhaps a question of the timing of the merger of patterns, but we end up with at least four accent classes and he has only three: Low-Low (as in toli 'bridge', mozom 'mind', motoy 'joint', polom 'wind', pwuthye 'Buddha', ...), Low-High (as in kwo˙ki 'fish, meat', na˙lah 'nation', se˙li 'frost', a˙tol 'son', a˙chom 'morning', ...), and High with the pitch of the second syllable nondistinctive as in these examples:

HH / HL
'child' ˙a˙ki (1447 Sek 9:25b; 1459 Wel 1:44b, 8:100b, 8:101b, 21:124b; 1463 Pep 6:47a; ?1517- Pak 1:56a, 1:57a, 1:57b), ˙a˙k[i] oy (1459 Wel 8:81b, 8:83a); ˙aki (1447 Sek 6:13b; 1449 Kok 148; 1459 Wel 2:33b, 8:86a, 8:86b, 10:24b, 23:74b, 23:87a; 1475 Nay 2:1:40b; 1485 Kwan 10b)
'drought' ˙ko˙mol (1527 Cahoy 1:3a=2a), ˙ko˙mol s (1447 Sek 9:33b, 1462 ¹Nung 8:115a); ˙komo˙l ay (1445 ¹Yong 2, 1463 Pep 2:28a), ˙komo˙l i (1481 Twusi 7:36b, 25:11b)
'firefly' ˙pantwoy (1446 Hwun 29ab; 1465 Wen 1:2:3:40b, 2:2:1:52a; 1481 Twusi 8:40a, 21:9a, 24:7a; 1482 Nam 2:59b); ˙pantwoy ˙lol (1481 Twusi 6:20b)
 = ˙pan˙two (1527 Cahoy 1:11b=21b); ˙pan˙twoy ˙lwo[˙]ta or ˙pan˙two ˙ylwo[˙]ta (1481 Twusi 8:12b)
'food' (*[TTA-˙PPEN] >) ˙cha˙pan (1447 Sek 6:16a, 1527 Cahoy 2:10a=20a), ˙cha˙pan ˙ol (1449 Kok 122), ˙cha˙pan ˙two (?1517- Pak 1:7a); ˙chapan (1459 Wel 1:32a), ˙chapa˙n on (1459 Wel 2:25b), ˙chapan ˙ul (1481 Twusi 24:63a); [˙]chapa˙n i (1481 Twusi 22:6a)
'granny' ˙hal-'˙mi (1459 Wel 10:17b, 1527 Cahoy 1:16a=31a), ˙hal-'mi ˙lol (1445 ¹Yong 19); ˙hal-'m[i] oy (1482 Kum-sam 3:12a; 1482 Nam 1:8b, 2:4a)
'lightning' ˙pen˙key (1445 ¹Yong 30, 1447 Sek 6:32a, 1449 Kok 161, 1463 Pep 3:35a, 1482 Kum-sam 2:44a, 1527 Cahoy 1:1b=2b); ˙penkey (1465 Wen 2:1:2:19a), ˙penkey s (1482 Kum-sam 2:44b)

'mark' ˙pwo˙lam (1463 Pep 5:14a, 1527 Cahoy 1:18b=35a), ˙pwo˙la˙m i (?1517⁻ ¹No 2:16a), ˙pwola˙m ol (?1468⁻ Mong 20a); ˙pwolam (~ ˙ho˙ya 1462 ¹Nung 1:70b, ~ ˙ho.ya 1482 Nam 1: 70b), ˙pwo˙la.m i˙n i (1459 Wel 21:217-8, 1462 ¹Nung 8:119b)
'mother' ˙e˙mi (1527 Cahoy 1:16a=31a; 1459 Wel 8:86a, 21:22a, 21:27a, 21:53a; 1482 Kum-sam 2:61a; 1481 Twusi 8:67b), ˙e˙mi ˙lul (1518 Sohak-cho 9:55a), ˙e˙mi l' (1462 ¹Nung 5:85b), ˙e˙m[i] uy (1459 Wel 21:21b), [˙]e˙mi i˙sya (1459 Wel 8:83a); ˙emi ˙lol (1447 Sek 6:1b; 1459 Wel 21:20a, 93a), ˙emi ˙two (1447 Sek 6:3b), ˙emi ˙Gwa (1462 ¹Nung 5:85b); ˙emi ˙˙la (1459 Wel se:14a),
'net' ˙ku˙mul (?1517⁻ Pak 1:70b; 1527 Cahoy 2:17a), ˙ku˙mu.l i˙la (1464 Amitha 7a); ˙kumu˙l ey (1447 Sek 9:8a, 1462 ¹Nung 8:93a), ˙kumu˙l i (1459 Wel 8:10b), ˙kumu˙l un (1481 Twusi 7:3a), ˙kumu˙l ul (1463 Pep 2:8b, 2:24b), ˙kumul s (1481 Twusi 21:38a)
'rabbit' ˙thwos˙ki (1465 Wen 1:68a, 1527 Cahoy 1:10b=19b), ˙thwos˙ki l' (1481 Twusi 16:36b); ˙thwos.ki (1481 Twusi 21:38a, 1482 Kum-sam 4:63a), ˙thwos.ki ˙lol (1481 Twusi 10:26a), ˙thwos.k[i] uy (1462 ¹Nung 1:74a, 1466 Kup 1:6a, 1482 Kum-sam 2:66b) = ˙thwos.k[i] oy (1481 Twusi 24:25b, 1482 Kum-sam 4:36b)
'shade' ˙ko˙nol (1462 ¹Nung 8:50b, 1463 Pep 6:165a, 1527 Cahoy 1:1a). ˙ko˙nol˙h i (1462 ¹Nung 8:51a)l ˙ko˙nol˙h ay (1465 Wen 3:1:2:50a); ˙kono˙l i (1463 Pep 5:180a), ˙konol ˙Gwos (1481 Twusi 23:8a), ˙konol˙h ay (1463 Pep 2:103-4, 1481 Twusi 7:24a), ˙konol˙h i (1459 Wel 18:26a, 1463 Pep 3:45b, 1481 Twusi 24:30a), ˙konol.h on (1481 Twusi 15:9b)
'sleeve' (1) ˙so˙may (1527 Cahoy 2:11b=23a); ˙somay (1481 Twusi 8:45b), ˙somay ˙lol (1481 Twusi 20:47a, 22:25a), ˙somay ˙yey (1481 Twusi 6:4a, 23:2a),
(2) ˙so˙moy ˙yey (?1517⁻ Pak 1:72a), ˙so˙moy s (1463 Pep 1:31b)
'snake' ˙poy˙yam (1527 Cahoy 1:1b=22a), ˙poy˙ya.m i˙Gwo (1459 Wel 21:42b); ˙poyya˙m i (1445 ¹Yong 7), ˙poyya˙m oy (1463 Pep 2:165b), ˙poyya˙m on (1481 Twusi 21:38b), ˙poyya˙m ol (1481 Twusi 15:8b), ˙poyyam ˙kwa y (1462 ¹Nung 7:79a, 1481 Twusi 6:4a), ˙poyyam ˙kwa (1550 ¹Yenghem 15b)
'thunder' ˙wul˙Gey (1447 Sek 6:32a, 1463 Pep 3:35a, 1482 Kum-sam 2:2b, 1527 Cahoy 1:2b), ˙wul˙Gey s (1481 Twusi 10:18a); ˙wulGey (1481 Twusi 7:24b, 10:19a; 1482 Nam 34b)
'topknot' ˙syang˙thwu (1527 Cahoy 2:12b=25a) = ˙syangthwo (1586 Sohak 2:2a)
'twenty' ˙su˙mul ˙sal (1445 ¹Yong 32) '20 arrows', ˙su˙mul ˙kwo˙t ile˙la (1447 Sek 6:38a) 'it was 20 places', ˙su˙mul[h] hon ˙hoy s so˙zi ˙yey (1447 Sek 6:47a) 'in the space of 21 years'; ˙su˙mul.h i˙m ye (1462 ¹Nung 2:57b), ˙sumul˙h in SSI-˙CYELQ ˙ey (1462 ¹Nung 2:8b) 'when 20 (years old)', ˙su˙mu˙nal (?1517⁻ Pak 1:8b) '20th day', ˙su˙mu˙na˙mon ˙hoy ˙lol (1447 Sek 24:2a) 'for over 20 years', ˙su˙mu ˙nas (?1517⁻ Pak 1:20a), ˙su˙mu˙lyang ˙two (id. 1:20b); ˙su˙mul˙h ey ˙sye (1462 ¹Nung 2:6b), but ˙sumul˙h ey (ibid., also 1481 Twusi 8:19a)
'wolf' ˙il˙hi (1527 Cahoy 3:10a=18b); ˙ilhi ˙Gwa (1447 Sek 9:24b) 'and wolves'; ˙ilhi towoy˙ye ˙ys.two˙ta (1481 Twusi 10:19b) 'has become a wolf'.

Not in Ramsey's list of HH / HL nouns:
'bowl' ˙swo˙la s (?1517⁻ Pak 1:56a); ˙swola ˙lol (1586 Sohak 2:3b)
'mosquito' ˙mwo˙koy (1447 Sek 9:9b, 1459 Wel 9:26a), ˙mwo˙kuy (1527 Cahoy 1:1:11b=22a); ˙mwokoy swo˙li ?< ˙mwokoy [s] swo˙li (1462 ¹Nung 4:3b); [˙]mwo˙koy (1579 Kwikam 2:60a)
'net-edge guide ropes' ˙pye˙li (1527 Cahoy 2:8a=14b); ˙pyeli ˙lol (1481 Twusi 16:63b)
'now' ˙icey [< ˙i cek 'this time'] (1447 Sek 6:5b, 6:11ab, 24:16a; 1459 Wel se:13b, 2:42b, 2:64a, 8:98a, 8:101a, 9:35f, 10:8b, 13:19ab, 21:21b; 1481 Twusi 7:31b, 8:10b, 8:38a; 1482 Nam 1:30b), ˙icey n' (1463 Pep 2:41a), ˙icey s (1447 Sek se:6b, 1459 Wel 2:9b, 9:35d), ˙icey ˙two (1459 Wel 2:64a), ˙icey ˙za (1449 Kok 115), ˙icey ˙˙la (1459 Wel se:13b); ˙i˙cey (1462 ¹Nung 4:126b, ?1517⁻ ¹No 1:1a), ˙i˙cey l' (1462 ¹Nung 10:19a). Also icey (1459 Wel 23:78a), icey n' (1463 Pep 5:178b).
'pillow' ˙pye˙kay (1527 Cahoy 2:6b=11b); ˙pyekay (1463 Pep 2:73a, 1481 Twusi 15:11b)
'picture' ˙ku˙lim (1527 Cahoy 3:9v=20v); ˙kulim (1481 Twusi 16:25b, ?1517⁻ Pak 1:64b)
Note that kuli˙mey (= kulim˙cey) is a noun meaning 'reflection, image, shadow' and is not to be taken as ˙ku(˙)lim 'picture' + particle ˙ey, for which we lack an example.

'plow' `ko·lay` (1527 Cahoy 1:6a=11r); `kolay` (1481 Twusi 16:39a); *kolay* (1446 Hwun 28a, 1481 Twusi 25:22a)

The noun `hyenma` 'how many / much' has both syllables high in `hyen·ma s` with the genitive particle.

For certain words the accent-marked attestations are really too few for us to draw conclusions:

'thunder' `pye·lak` (1527 Cahoy 1:1b=2b) is also attested (says LCT) in 1481 Twusi 18:19, but that text is not available to me;

'flute' `phi·li` (1527 Cahoy 2:16r=32b) is reported also in 1481 Twusi 9:40, to which I lack access;

'lotus persimmon' `kwo.ywom` (1446 Hwun 28b) appears also with the odd pattern HR `kwo¨ywom` (1527 Cahoy 1:6b=12a) and it is HH `kwo¨ywom` in 1517 Saseng 2:13a (says NKW, but the Taycey-kak repro lacks the dots).

The first-person plural pronoun `wu·li` (1447 Sek 6:5a; 1459 Wel 13:35b, 13:36a; ?1517- Pak 1:54a; ...) suppresses the second accent when followed by a particle: `wuli ·Gwos` (1459 Wel 2:72a), `wuli ·two` (1459 Wel 8:100a), `wuli ·za` (1463 Pep 5:121b), `wuli n'` (1459 Wel 2:69b), `wuli ·tol·h i` (1447 Sek 9:40a, 19:30b; 1459 Wel 10:12b, 10:31a, 18:18b), `wuli ·tol·thwo` [= `tolh ·two`] (1459 Wel 18:3a), `wuli ·uy` (1463 Pep 2:231a). Modifying a noun in the sense 'our' the word is often `wuli` (1445 ¹Yong 3; 1459 Wel 18:42b, 21:193b; 1462 ¹Nung 10:42b; 1463 Pep 2:5b; 1482 Nam 1:54b; ?1517- Pak 1:51a) but there are also examples of `wu·li` (1447 Sek 6:5b; 1451 Hwun-en 1a; 1459 Wel 2:69a, 2:70b) which might be treated as compressions of `wuli ·uy`. Some cases where a single dot occurs for an earlier double dot may be due to broken type (as seen from the placement of the remaining dot), but often these result from historic change, whereby the double-dot (low rising) accent merged with the simple high accent represented by the single dot, so I have generally left these the way the text carries them.

The hypothesis that (at least by a certain time) the high pitch was distinctive only in the first syllable of a word will account for some of the variant accents found for verb forms in §2.12.4: `ho(·)ya` 'do', `ti(·)ye` 'fall', `pwuy(·)ye` 'cut', `psti(·)kwo` 'insert', `psu(·)ti` 'use', `ptu(·)m ye` 'float', ... But the majority of the HH- stems do not exemplify the variation. The hypothesis that there was no distinction between LHL and LHH could account for accent variants in a few verb forms:

pwo·nayya (1481 Twusi 25:27b) = *pwo·nay·ya* (1447 Sek 24:15ab) 'send'

te·pule (1481 Twusi 7:37a, 20:29a) = *te·pu·le* (1447 Sek 6:23a, 13:15a; 1459 Wel 2:6b) 'take along'

i·kuyti (1481 Twusi 8:42a) = *i·kuy·ti* (1481 Twusi 7:7b, 1586 Sohak 2:9b) − CF *i·kuy·ye* (1459 Wel se:9a) 'win'

e·wulGwo (~ ·*two* 1449 Kok 134) = *e·wul·Gwo* (1462 ¹Nung 3:38a) 'join'

ne·kikwo (1481 Twusi 25:23a), *ne·kiti* (1481 Twusi 16:61b, 1482 Kum-sam 5:14a, 1475 Nay se:6a) = *ne·ki·kwo* (1462 ¹Nung 1:34b), *ne·ki·ti* (1447 Sek 24:3ab, 1475 Nay 1:17a) 'deem'

¨*te·leWun* (1447 Sek 13:33b) = ¨*tele·Wun* (1459 Wel 9:24a, 1459 Wel 18:39ab), ¨*tele·wun* (1462 ¹Nung 4:38b) 'dirty'

il·Gwusyan (1447 Sek se:5b); CF *il·Gwu·sya* (1459 Wel 21:218b) 'achieve'

Peculiarities in the accent patterns of certain pronouns and indeterminates are not amenable to generalization (CF Ramsey 1978a:170-4, ¹Yi Sangek 1978:112-6); the attested facts are stated in the individual entries of Part II.

2.12.3. Accent suppression before particles.

A number of nouns suppress the high pitch on a syllable before the locative-allative particle ·*ey* and its variant ·*oy* (He Wung 327). Included are most of the monosyllabic nouns that have the high pitch, and at least one two-syllable noun:

`kalh` 'knife'→ *kal·h ay* (1466 Kup 1:82a)

`kilh` 'road' → *kil·h ey* (1447 Sek 6:3b, 6:15b; 1481 Twusi 7:6a, 8:2b, 10:27b; 1482 Nam 1:49b; ?1517- Pak 1:54a)

`kwoh` 'nose' → *kwo·h ay* (1447 Sek 13:38b, 1459 Wel 1:36b), *kwo·h ay ·sye* (1462 ¹Nung 3:24b)

`kwuy` 'ear' → *kwuy ·yey* (1447 Sek 19:16a, 1449 Kok 2, 1475 Nay 1:37a)

˙mwom 'body' → mwoˑm ay (1447 Sek 19:19b, 1462 ¹Nung 10:18a, 1481 Twusi 8:33-4) and mwoˑm ay s (1447 Sek 9:12a, 1459 Wel 2:53b)
˙moyh 'moor' → moyˑh ay (1463 Pep 6:154b, 1481 Twusi 7:30a), moyˑh ay s (?1468- Mong 27; 1482 Nam 1:4a, 1:49b; 1482 Kum-sam 3:34b), moyˑh ay sye (1481 Twusi 7:39a)
˙nac 'daytime, noon' → naˑc oy (1445 ¹Yong 101)
˙nwun 'eye' → nwuˑn ey (1481 Twusi 25:9b, 25:47a)
˙pich 'light' → piˑch ey s (1447 Sek 19:18a), piˑch ey ˑsye (1481 Twusi 8:9b)
˙ptut 'meaning, mind, intention' → ptuˑt ey n' (1447 Sek 19:34a), ptuˑt ey s (1447 Sek 9:26b)
˙tet 'time' → aˑni han teˑt ey (1463 Pep 4:32a, ?1468- Mong 26b, 1485 Kwan 9a) 'in a short while'
˙pam 'evening, night' → paˑm oy (1447 Sek 6:19b, 1462 ¹Nung 1:16b), paˑm oy ˑtwo (1459 Wel 2:27a), paˑm oy [ˑ]za (1481 Twusi 23:6b)
˙pwom 'spring' → pwo[ˑ]m oy (1482 Kum-sam 2:6b; the repro obscures the dot)
˙stah → staˑh ay (1449 Kok 41; 1459 Wel 1:28b; 1462 ¹Nung 8:123a; 1481 Twusi 7:7b, 15:45a, 21:42b, 25:43a; ?1517- Pak 1:64b)
˙swoˑli 'sound' → swoli ˑyey (1481 Twusi 7:39a)
For at least one word this holds for the genitive uses of the particle ˑ^u⁄oy, too: ˙nom 'another person' → noˑm oy + NOUN PHRASE (1447 Sek se:6a, 1463 Pep 2:28b, ?1517- Pak 1:9b, 1465 Wen 3:3:1:62a, ?1468- Mong 20b, 1518 Sohak-cho 8:15a [noˑm is smudged], 1475 Nay 1:9a); and also as the genitive-marked subject of an adnominalized verb (1465 Wen se:77a). That differs from ˙nwom 'lowly person' where the genitive is ˙nwoˑm oy (1459 Wel 17:76b), later reduced to ˙nwo.m oy (1481 Twusi 7:6b).

Monosyllabic nouns which do not lose their accent before the locative: ˙hye 'tongue', ˙hoy 'sun', ˙poy 'belly', ˙pi 'rain', ˙mul 'water', ˙mwul 'crowd', ˙pul 'fire', ˙pol 'community, village' as in ˑi ˙poˑl ay 'in this village' (1459 Wel 8:94a), ˙skwum 'dream'. Kim Wancin would assign these exceptions an underlying pattern of High-High, rather than just the single High assigned to the other accented monosyllables. Perhaps the high persists from a lost or absorbed second syllable?

The word for 'bosom' is not attested without the locative particle, but we infer that phwuˑm ey is from *˙phwum on the basis of the attested accent of the related verb ˙phwum- 'embrace'.

In the same environment (before the locative marker) the double dot is sometimes reduced to a single dot, i.e. the low-high rise becomes just high:
¨mwoyh 'mountain' → ˙mwo.h ay s (1482 Kum-sam 3:36b) = ¨mwoyˑh ay s (1482 Kum-sam 3:33a); but ¨mwoyˑh ay (1449 Kok 41), ¨mwoyˑh ay s (1481 Twusi 7:30b)
¨swok 'deep inside' → ˙swo.k ay s (1481 Twusi 7:24b) but ¨swoˑk ay (1459 Wel 1:13a)
¨twolh 'beam' → ˙twol.h ay (1481 Twusi 7:5a) 'to the beams'
Usually the double dot is retained: ¨nwuˑn ey s ˑtol (1482 Kum-sam 2:61b) 'moonlight on the snow'; ˙mul s ¨koˑz ay (1459 Wel 8:99a) 'at the water's edge'; (··· s) ¨iˑl ey (1475 Nay 2:2:47b) 'in the event (of ···)'; ¨twuyˑh ey ˑsye (1445 ¹Yong 28), ¨twuyˑh ey n' (id. 70), ¨twuy.h ey ˑnun (id. 30), ¨twuy ˑh ey (s ···) (1459 Wel se:24b) 'in back'.

The modern dialects of Hamkyeng and Kyengsang show a similar cleavage of monosyllabic tonic nouns, and the grouping is probably inherited from the 15th-century accent, but we lack sufficient data to set up a system of correlations that will account for the exceptions. (See Ramsey 1978a:167-9.)

The accent of a monosyllabic noun is sometimes lost before the genitive particle s, perhaps evidence that certain cases of N₁ s N₂ are compound nouns: ¨mwoyh → mwoy[h] s ¨kwoˑl ay (1447 Sek 6:4b, 1449 Kok 141) 'in a mountain valley', ...

2.12.4. The accentuation of verb forms.

There are many complexities in the accentuation of MK verb forms and the corresponding forms in the modern dialects. Studies by He Wung, Kim Wancin, Ceng Yenchan, Kim Chakyun, ¹Yi Sangek, and others shed light on many of the problems, and in particular Ramsey 1978a presents a wide view of the situation and discusses the interpretation of the available data in admirable detail.

We must assume a basic accent for the endings -ˑ^u⁄om, -ˑ^u⁄olq, and -ˑ^u⁄on so as to account for such phrases as paˑtoˑm ye (1462 ¹Nung 8:104b), meˑkulq ˑtet (1459 Wel 8:8b), and twoˑtoˑn i (1445 ¹Yong

101) even though the accent is often or always suppressed in many structures. That is why there are discrepancies between the accent of entry citations and examples for some of the forms in Part II.

Stems fall into two major types, depending on whether they begin high (single dot) or low (no dot or double-dot), but many of the monosyllabic low-accent stems that do not end in a consonant take on high pitch before certain endings – or, put another way, many of the monosyllabic high-accent stems that end in a vowel lose the accent in many of the common paradigmatic forms, such as the gerund -˙kwo, the adverbative -˙key, the indicative assertive -˙ta, the suspective -˙ti, the hortative -˙cye, the substantive -(˙^{u}o)m which appears only in the complex structure -(˙^{u}o)˙m ye, the modifier -(˙^{u}o)n and prospective modifier -(˙^{u}o)l(q) and forms based on these (including the subjunctive attentive -˙la, as in ho˙la 'do it'). But they retain the accent before the infinitive -˙^{e}a, the honorific -(^{u}o)˙si-, the deferential -˙zop-, and the aspect markers -(˙)no-, -˙t^{e}a-, -˙k^{e}a-. This seems to indicate that the infinitive, like the other markers, was originally a bound stem. (And that deepens my suspicion that -˙^{e}a is cognate with Japanese a[r]- 'be'.) The polite marker -ngi is like the bound stems, to judge from (˙˙˙˙^{e}a) ˙ci-ngi ˙˙ta 'wants (to do)' < °ci-, ˙˙˙ ˙i-ngi ˙˙ta (1459 Wel 21:218b) 'it is ˙˙˙ ' < ˙i-, and kwo˙c i ˙phu-˙tos ˙ho-ngi ˙˙ta (1463 Pep 1:85b) 'the flowers seem in bloom' – but also ¨ep-˙tos ho-ngi ˙˙ta (1462 ^{1}Nung 1:105b) 'seems to lack'. If so, the lack of an initial dot on ha-ngi ˙˙ta (1463 Pep 7:68b, 1464 Kumkang 62b) 'are many' < °ha- is puzzling. The high/low stems are basically low before the modulator (-˙w^{u}o- etc.), though after most vowels that is obscured by the usual ellipsis of that morpheme, which leaves behind an accentual trace:

¨na˙toy (1447 Sek 19:7b, 1449 Kok 185) ← na-˙[wo]-˙toy, ¨nalq (1462 ^{1}Nung 3:24b) ← na-˙[wo]lq < °na- 'emerge'

¨ha˙m ol (1482 Kum-sam 3:19a) ← ha-˙[wo]-m < °ha- 'much / many'

¨cwulq (1447 Sek 9:12a) ← cwu-˙[wu]-lq < °cwu- 'give'

¨wo˙m i (1459 Wel 9:10b, 1482 Kum-sam 3:19a), ¨wo˙m ol (1482 Nam 1:50b), ¨wo[˙]m ay (1481 Twusi 21:25b) ← wo-˙[wo]-m < °wo- 'come'

¨pwom (1462 ^{1}Nung 2:84a) ← pwo-˙[wo]-m < °pwo- 'see'

But after ˙˙˙i- the modulator survives intact:

ni˙ywu˙n i (1481 Twusi 7:1a), ni˙ywun (id. 10:18b) ← ni-˙wu-n, ¨niywon (1482 Nam 1:72b; ?= ni˙ywon) ← ni-˙wo-n < °ni- 'roof, thatch (a roof)'

¨cywu˙m un (1462 ^{1}Nung 8:8a) = (?*)ciywu˙m un ← ci-˙wu-m < °ci- 'carry on the back'

¨cywu˙m ey (1481 Twusi 7:6b) = (?*)ciywu˙m ey ← ci-˙wu-m < °ci- 'cut (wood)'

There is something odd about the accent of ˙iywo˙m on (1482 Nam 2:64a) where we expect *i˙ywo˙m on ← i-˙wo-m < ˙i- 'carry on the head'; perhaps the scribe misplaced the dot.

Compare the modulated forms of those stems that are always high:

˙thywo˙toy (?1468- Mong 53a) ← ˙thi-˙wo-˙toy, ˙thywon (id. 10a) ← ˙thi-˙wo-n, ˙thywum (1463 Pep 5:38a) ← ˙thi-˙wu-m < ˙thi- 'hit'

˙skoy˙ywom (1462 ^{1}Nung 10:1b) ← ˙skoy-˙wo-m < ˙skoy- 'wake up'

Before the causative formative -˙i- the high/low stems are basically low, and that accounts for the rising accent of some of the stems of group 1a below: ¨nay- 'make emerge' < *na-˙i- < °na- 'emerge', ¨pwoy- 'show' < *pwo-˙i- < °pwo- 'see', ¨syey- 'erect, let / make stand' < *sye-˙i- < °sye- 'stand', ¨tiy-$_{1}$ 'drop, let / make fall' < *ti-˙i- < *°ti-$_{1}$ 'drop', and ¨tiy-$_{2}$ 'smelt (metal), create (out of metal)' probably < *ti-˙i- < °ti-$_{2}$ 'become'. The basic final y on ¨tiy-$_{1}$ 'drop' and ¨tiy-$_{2}$ 'smelt, create' is needed to account for the velar lenition in such forms as ¨ti˙Gwo$_{1}$ (1459 Wel 10:24b) 'dropping' and the unattested *¨ti˙Gwo$_{2}$ 'smelting, creating'. (The only other case of basic iy- is ˙iy-, the copula, with the gerund form ˙i˙Gwo.) The summative -˙ki is nonleniting, and that accounts for ˙swoy ku˙lus ¨tiki ˙yey s ˙swo.h i˙la (1465 Wen 1:1:2:181a) 'it is a mold for making metal vessels'.

Interestingly, when the summative -˙ki started taking over part of the work of the suspective -˙ti, it was treated not like -˙ti or -˙key, but like the bound stems: ˙ka˙ki (?1517- ^{1}No 1:26b), ˙pwo˙ki (id. 1:37b) – compare ka˙ti (id. 2:7a), pwo˙ti (below). The earliest examples of the summative, however, are what we expect: ho˙ki ˙lol ˙cul˙kye (1447 Sek 6:13a), ho˙ki ˙lol ˙culki˙ti (1459 Wel 10:18b). And that 16th-century text also has *ho˙ki ˙Gwa* (?1517- ¹No 2:43b), so the first two examples above may be scribal errors. Another regular example: ¨*il ho˙ki yey* (1481 Twusi 25:7b).

The transferentive, to my surprise, is treated as if a bound stem: ˙*kata ˙ka* (1445 ¹Yong 25, 1482 Nam 1:36b), ˙*wota ˙ka* (1447 Sek 23:57b), ˙*hyeta ˙ka* (1481 Twusi 16:1b), ˙*hota ˙ka* (1462 ¹Nung 3:84a, 1482 Kum-sam 2:31b), ˙*na˙ta ka ˙'m ye* (1459 Wel 21:215b), ˙*tita ˙ka 'm ye* (1481 Twusi 25:43a), ... That argues in favor of the notion that *-ta˙ka* is a bound infinitive rather than the indicative assertive *-˙ta* + particle ˙*ka*, as it is viewed in this book. The only apparent counterexample, in ˙*na-ka˙kwo cye tha ˙ka* ··· (1481 Twusi 8:29a) 'I want to go out but ··· ', is probably a surface reduction of ˙*na-ka˙kwo ˙cye ˙hota ˙ka*. Also arguing for explaining the transferentive as a bound infinitive is the accentuation of the low-pitched stems that are closed monosyllables:

    makta ˙ka k (1466 Kup 2:66a), and not **mak˙ta ˙ka k*

    cwukta ˙ka (1445 ¹Yong 25) despite *cwuk˙ta* (1459 Wel 17:21a)

    is.ta ˙ka (1482 Kum-sam 2:13b), and not **is˙ta ˙ka* despite *is˙ta* (1462 ¹Nung 2:83a; 1463/4 Yeng 2:62a; 1482 Kum-sam 3:9b; 1482 Nam 1:14a; ?1517- ¹No 1:62b, 2:36a)

There is another set of structures on which the accent sheds light. What I had earlier taken as the indicative assertive *-˙ta* (and ˙*i˙la*) + forms of the emotive bound verb ˙*s[o]-* I now realize must be retrospective emotive forms: *-˙taswo˙la*, *-˙taswo˙n i*, *-˙ta˙songi ˙'ta*, *-u˙l i ˙'la[˙]s-ongi ˙'ta*, *-u˙l i ˙'la[˙]songi ˙'ta*. (See the entries of Part II, where they are so treated.) That is because of the accent of the stem in such forms as ˙*hotaswo˙la* (1481 Twusi 16:18a), ˙*ho˙taswo˙n i* (1446 Sek 13:43b), and ˙*ho˙ta˙s-ongi ˙'ta* (1462 ¹Nung 2:6-7).

In citing a stem or the "naming" form (the indicative assertive) of the high/low verbs we will use a hollow dot (˚), meant to represent zero (the low pitch) except when one of the relevant elements is attached — the infinitive ending or one of the bound stems. With the prominent exception of ˚*ho-* 'do; be' there are no high/low stems ending with the minimal vowel ᵘ⁄o, for those are all high; the stems that end ···*e-* or ···*a-* are all of the high/low type. (There are no low-pitch monosyllabic stems ending ··· ᵘ⁄o-, but there are such stems with the shapes ··· ᵘ⁄oy- and ¨··· ᵘ⁄oy-.) This fact may be used to argue that the vowel of ˚*ho-* must be a reduced form of some other vowel. Elsewhere I use the irregular infinitive to support the claim that the stem was earlier the unique shape **hyo-* (see the entry ˚*ho˙ta* in Part II). It may be questioned whether the semivowel adequately strengthens the minimal vowel, but compare the monosyllabic stems that end in ···*w*ᵘ⁄o-, which all belong to the high/low group with the unexplained exception of ˙*skwu-* 'dream', which may well be contracted from a dissyllabic stem (as suggested by the initial cluster) and ˙*hwo-* 'broad-stitch', for which the modern hō- (and dialect accent corresponding to the long vowel) would suggest an earlier version *˚*hwo-* like ˚*pwo-* 'see'.

We find the following groups of monosyllabic stems that do not end in a consonant:

(1) Stems that are RISING, here marked with a preceding high double dot (¨···-). None end in ··· ᵘ⁄oy- (without preceding *w*) or in ··· ᵘ⁄o-, nor in ···*w*ᵘ⁄o-; the apparent exceptions such as ¨*cwu-* or ¨*pwo-* are modulated forms of non-rising stems (˚*cwu-*, ˚*pwo-*).

(1a) Rising in all forms. These stems end in ···*ay-*; ···*ey-*, ···*yey-*; ···*w*ᵘ⁄oy-. Also ¨*hoy-*, the causative of ˚*ho-* 'do', and two stems ending in basic ···*iy-* that were originally causatives, too: ¨*tiy-₁* 'drop, let/make fall' and ¨*tiy-₂* 'smelt, create (out of metal)'. The modulated versions of simple ˚···*a-*, ˚···*e-*, ˚···*wo-*, and ˚···*wu-* also belong here: ¨*ka-* ← *ka-˙[wo]-* < ˚*ka-* 'go', ¨*sye-* ← *sye-˙[wu]-* < ˚*sye-* 'stand', ¨*pwo-* ← *pwo-˙[wo]-* < ˚*pwo-* 'see', ¨*cwu-* ← *cwu-˙[wu]-* < ˚*cwu-* 'give'.

(1b) Rising in most forms (including the effective forms with *-G*ᵉ⁄a-), but not the infinitive and forms containing the modulator or the short version of the effective aspect marker *-˙(y)*ᵉ⁄a-. These stems end in ···*w*ᵘ⁄oy-, ···*ay-*, ···*ey-*, ···*yey-*. We mark them with two hollow dots (˚˚···-).

(2) Stems that are always LOW, here left unmarked (···-). These stems end in ··· ᵘ⁄oy- or ···*w*ᵘ⁄oy-.

(3) Stems that are always HIGH, here marked with a preceding high dot (˙···-). These stems end in ···*i-*, ···*w*ᵘ⁄oy-, ···*oy-*, or (?) ···*uy-*; also the copula ˙*iy-*. The stems ˙*skwu-* 'dream' and ˙*hwo-* 'broad-stitch' exceptionally belong here, rather than in group 4.

(4) Stems that are HIGH/LOW, here marked with a preceding hollow dot (˚···-). They are low except in

the infinitive and when compounded with other stems, including bound stems such as the honorific (-^{u}o˙si-), the aspect markers (-˙k^{e}a-, -˙t^{e}a-, -˙no-), the deferential (-¨zop-), and the polite (-ngi ⋯). These stems end in ⋯a-, ?⋯e-, ⋯ye-, ⋯w^{u}o-, ⋯i-. (Apparently there are no monosyllabic stems that end in ⋯e- without a y before the vowel.) The stems stay low when -˙two 'even/too' or -˙tos 'like' is attached.

The accent groups to which a stem of a given shape may belong:

	1a ¨⋯-	1b °°⋯-	2 ⋯-	3 ˙⋯-	4 °⋯-
⋯i-				+	+
⋯^{u}o-				+	+
⋯^{u}oy-		¨hoy-		+	°ho-
⋯wu-		( )		˙skwu-	+
⋯wo-		( )		˙hwo-	+
⋯w^{u}oy-	+	+	+	+	+
⋯ye-		( )			+
⋯ey-	+	+			+
⋯yey-	+	+			+
⋯a-		( )			+
⋯ay-	+	+			+
	RISING	RISING/LOW	LOW	HIGH	HIGH/LOW

The parenthesized blanks are modulated stems (stem + modulator) only.

There are stems that end in ⋯i- both in Group 3 and in Group 4. Only the effective forms of °ni- 'go' are attested: ˙nike (1445 ¹Yong 58, 1459 Wel 8:1a), ˙ni˙ke (1459 Wel 8:101b); ˙nike˙la (1459 Wel 8:101a); ˙ni˙kesi˙n i (1459 Wel 8:93ab); ˙ni˙kesi˙tun (1445 ¹Yong 38); ˙nike˙nol (1463 Pep 4:37b). From these ˙ni-ke- forms alone we cannot tell whether the stem belongs with Group 3 (HIGH) or group 4 (HIGH/LOW), but we assign it to Group 4 to accord with °nye- 'go', from which it was likely derived. The somewhat later stem ¨nyey- seems to belong with Group 1a (ALWAYS RISING).

A number of accentually anomalous examples have to be explained individually, as prosodic adjustments or scribal mistakes: ˙wUY [˙]ho˙sya (1463 Pep 7:17a); ˙i˙la [˙]hosya˙l i (1447 Sek 6:17a), ˙kot [˙]hosi˙n i (1463 Pep 2:43b); ho˙n i [˙]Gwo (1481 Twusi 7:40a), ¨mwot ho˙si.l i ˙˙la (1462 ¹Nung 2:50b); ¨ep-˙tos [˙]ho-ngi ˙˙ta (1462 ¹Nung 1:105b); solang [˙]hosi˙nwon pa˙lol (1475 Nay 1:55b); ¨mwot ho˙ya ˙ys.ke˙nul (1462 ¹Nung 8:57a); a˙ni ho.ya is˙ta.n i (1481 Twusi 7:23a), a˙ni ho˙ya ˙ys.ta˙n i (1465 Wen 1:1:1:44b), a˙ni hotwo˙ta (1481 Twusi 8:2a); ˙QILQ-˙TTYENG ho˙sa-ngi ˙˙ta (1459 Wel 8:96b). We would expect the contractions of °ho-k^{e}a- to be ˙kh^{e}a⋯ and that is what we find in ˙kh^{e}an ma˙lon, ˙khesin, ˙khesina, and ˙khesin ma˙lon. But most of the other forms are attested only without the accent: khe˙n i (˙Gwa, ˙˙la), khe˙nol, khe˙nul (˙za), khen˙t i, (a˙ni) khan˙t i ˙.n i ˙˙la, khen˙tyeng (CF ˙hoken˙tyeng), khe˙ta, khe˙tun. And only khe[˙]n ywo despite ˙kha.n ywo (1481 Twusi 16:37b), khe˙n i˙Gwa despite a˙ni˙kha.n i˙Gwa (1481 Twusi 16:61b). These anomalies are probably the result of secondary loss of the accent, though the details are unclear. That must be the case, too, for khe˙za (1475 Nay 2:1:16b) < ˙hoke˙za; compare ˙khe˙za (1463 Pep 2:224b). There are a few similar cases for ˙the⋯ < ˙hote⋯ , such as ku˙le the˙n i a˙ni the˙n i (1459 Wel 9:36d) < ˙hote˙n i, a˙ni tha˙n i (1463 Pep 2:28b) < ˙hota˙n i, a˙ni thwo˙ta (1481 Twusi 8:2a, 16:22b) < ˙hotwo˙ta.

There are two ways to look at the stems of group 4. The usual assumption (He Wung, Kim Wancin, Ramsey 1978a) says that the stems of the first group are historically low and acquired an accent before the infinitive, the bound stems, and so forth. ¹Yi Sangek 1978:119 (and now Ramsey 1992) would treat the stems as high, especially because as the first element in compound verbs they are high regardless of the following stem. (But the form in the compound is often the infinitive.) There are arguments both ways. Suppose we say that all the stems in groups 3 and 4 were basically high, but that those with the sturdier vowels suppressed the accent in the paradigmatic forms mentioned. We would then have to explain why there are examples of ⋯i- in both groups, and there seems to be nothing else that differentiates these two sets of stems. Several causative and passive stems are derived from monosyllabic vowel stems and the derived stems almost all start low, even those from the always-high stems: ˙pto˙i- (1481 Twusi 16:71a) < ˙pto- 'pick, pluck', thoy˙Gwo- (1459 Wel 7:52b) < ˙tho- 'receive, undergo' or 'ride', skoy˙Gwo- (1481 Twusi 15:26a) < ˙skoy- 'awaken' [the first dot of the LCT entry "˙skoy˙Gwo˙ta" is an error], pso˙i- (1459 Wel 14:7b) < ˙pso- 'wrap', pco˙i- (1475 Nay 2:2:51b) < ˙pco- 'weave', psu˙i- (1481 Twusi 23:38a) < ˙psu- 'use', su˙i- (1481 Twusi 10:39b) < ˙su- 'write', ptuy˙Gwo- (1459 Wel 8:99a) / ptuy˙Gwu- (1459 Wel 18:56b, 1481 Twusi 22:39b) < ˙ptu- 'float', phwuy˙Gwu- (1462 ¹Nung 7:16b, …) < ˙phwuy- 'burn (a fire)'. The one exception (LCT 693b) is from a passage poorly reproduced: [?˙]choy˙i- (1466 Kup 2:18a) < ˙cho- 'kick'. Examples derived from the high/low stems of group 4: ¨hoy- < ho˙i- < °ho- 'do', ¨cay- < *ca˙i- < °ca- 'sleep', ¨nay- < *na˙i- < °na- 'emerge', sye˙i- (1518 Sohak-cho 9:19b) [LCT ¨syei˙ta is incorrect] = ¨syey- (1445 ¹Yong 11, 1481 Twusi 15:29b [under wrong entry in LCT]), ¨pwoy- < *pwo˙i- < °pwo- 'see'. Yet ˙cii- (1459 Wel 21:106a; CF LCT 683b) < °ci- 'carry on the back' is inexplicably high.

The entries in the dictionaries are unreliable guides for many of the verbs discussed here: NKW has °sye˙ta 'stand' with an initial dot while LCT lacks the dot; LCT has a dot on °hhye˙ta but not on °hye˙ta 'pull' while NKW omits the dot for both; neither dictionary has a dot on °sa˙ta 'buy'. Of the high group, ˙hoy˙ta 'white' has the dot in NKW but not in LCT.

Further complications of stem behavior are largely the result of compressing syllables. They are taken up in the description of verb conjugations.

2.12.4.1. Vowel-final monosyllabic stems that are rising.

Group 1a. Rising in all forms

¨pwoy- 'show': ¨pwoyGwo ˙cye (1465 Wen se:43b), ¨pwoyGwo ˙za (1447 Sek 6:34ab); ¨pwoy˙m ye (1462 ¹Nung 6:89a); ¨pwoy˙ya (1459 Wel 13:35b, 1463 Pep 4:63a); ¨pwoyye˙ton (1462 ¹Nung 2:23a); ¨pwoy˙Gesi˙nol (1449 Kok 110); ¨pwoyno˙ta (1465 Wen 1:1:2:107a); ¨pwoy˙sya (1462 ¹Nung 2:17a); ¨pwoyywo˙m i (1459 Wel 10:7b), ¨pwoy˙ywo.l i ˙'la (1459 Wel 21:21b)

¨pcwoy- 'shine': ¨pcwoyGwo (1481 Twusi 8:47a); ¨pcwoyl (1463 Pep 3:12b, 1462 ¹Nung 4:72b, 1527 Cahoy 3:6a=13a); ¨pcwoy˙m ye n' (1466 Kup 2:14b); ¨pcwoy˙n i (1459 Wel 2:51a); ¨pcwoy˙ya (1459 Wel 1:48b, 1462 ¹Nung 3:76a); ¨pcwoynon (1482 Kum-sam 3:59a); ¨pcwoyywo˙m ol (1481 Twusi 7:13b), ¨pcwoyywo˙n i (1481 Twusi 10:31-2)

¨nay- 'make emerge, … ': ¨nay˙ti (1463 Pep 2:249b), ¨nayti (?1468- Mong 18b); ¨nay˙Gwo (1481 Twusi 8:30ab); ¨nay˙Gey (1459 Wel 21:20a, 1462 ¹Nung 1:29a); ¨nayl ˙ss oy (1463 Pep 3:180ab), ¨nay.l i ˙'le.n i ˙'la (1464 Kumkang 79b) − nay.l i (1463 Pep 5:196b) = ¨nay˙l i; ¨nay.n i ˙'la (1447 Sek 24:16b); ¨nay˙m ye … (1459 Wel 7:48a); ¨nay˙ya (1447 Sek 6:9b, 1449 Kok 49), ¨nay˙ye (1518 Sohak-cho 10:34b); ¨nayya˙nol (1482 Kum-sam 4:39a); ¨naynwon (1447 Sek 9:12a); ¨nayno˙n i (1459 Wel 1:27b); ¨nay˙ywon (1462 ¹Nung 3:24b); ¨nay˙sya (1463 Pep 6:97a); ¨naysil (1447 Sek 24:37ab, 1459 Wel 1:11a), ¨naysi˙n i '-ngi ˙'ta (1445 ¹Yong 8); ¨nay˙ywol (1481 Twusi 21:42a), ¨nayywo˙m i (1482 Kum-sam 4:39a), ¨nayywo.m i˙la (1462 ¹Nung 4:27b)

¨kay- 'get clear': ¨kay˙Gey (1459 Wel 10:88a); ¨kayl (1527 Cahoy 3:1b=2a); ¨kayn (1462 ¹Nung 10:1b), [¨]kay[˙]n i (1481 Twusi 23:20a); ¨kayGe˙nol (1481 Twusi 16:65a); ¨kaytwo˙ta (1481 Twusi 7:7b)

¨cay- 'put to sleep': ¨cay˙key (?1517- ¹No 1:47b; ˙key = ˙Gey); ¨cayte˙n i (1447 Sek 6:16a). The infinitive should be *¨cay˙y^ea, the effective forms *¨cay˙G^ea…, and the modulated stem *¨cay˙yw^u/o-.

¨pskey- 'pierce': ¨pskey˙Gwo (1459 Wel 1:2a, 2:48b); ¨pskey˙m ye (1459 Wel 8:24b, 1462 ¹Nung 1:28a, 1465 Wen 1:1:2:16b); ¨pskey˙n i (1445 ¹Yong 23, 43), ¨pskey˙n i '-ngi ˙'ta (1445 ¹Yong 50); ¨pskey (1518 Sohak-cho 8:35a, 1463 Pep 5:194b); ¨pskey˙ye (1449 Kok 4), ¨pskey˙ye ti˙n i (1449 Kok 41), ¨pskeyye ˙ys.ke˙tun (1459 Wel 1:27b); ¨pskeyye˙nul (1449 Kok 41); ¨pskeyywo˙m ol (1465 Wen 1:1:1:76a); ¨pskeyGa˙la (1481 Twusi 24:37a); ¨pskey˙Ganwos˙ta (1481 Twusi 24:26b); ¨pskeyzo˙Wa (1459 Wel 1:6b); ¨pskeysi˙n i '-ngi ˙'ta (1449 Kok 14); ¨pskeytwo˙ta (1462 Kum-sam 3:48a)

¨mey- 'shoulder, bear': ¨mey˙ti (1465 Wen 1:1:1:90a); ¨mey˙Gwo (1465 Wen 1:1:1:90a, 1586 Sohak 6:66a); ¨meyl (1527 Cahoy 3:10b=23b); ¨mey[˙]m ye (1963/4 Yeng 2:73b); ¨mey˙syam

(1463 Pep 4:79a); ¨meyte˙n i (1449 Kok 119); ¨mey˙zoWa (1459 Wel 10:10b), ¨mey˙zoWa ˙za (1459 Wel 10:12b), ¨mey˙zoWo˙n i (1459 Wel 10:12b); ¨mey˙zoWwo˙l ye (1459 Wel 10:12a), ¨meyzo˙Wwo.l i '˙la (1459 Wel 10:10b)

¨sey- 'be strong': ¨sey˙m ye (1459 Wel 1:28a); ¨seyn (1459 Wel 2:6b); ¨seyl (1459 Wel 10:30a); ¨seysil (1449 Kok 40). This assignment assumes that the unattested infinitive would be *¨sey˙y^ea, the effective forms *¨sey˙Ge- or *¨sey˙y^ea-, the modulated stem *¨sey˙yw^uo-.

¨hyey- 'reckon, count; think, consider, figure': ¨hyey˙ti (1459 Wel 17:34b; 1463 Pep 3:62b); ¨hyey˙Gwo (1459 Wel 2:63b); ¨hyey˙Gwo k (1481 Twusi 15:4a); ¨hyey˙Gey (1459 Wel 1:19a, 1463 Pep 1:26a); ¨hyeyl (1447 Sek se:1b; 1527 Cahoy 2:1b=2b, 3:9a=21a), ¨hyey˙l i ˙le˙la (1459 Wel 1:21a); ¨hyey˙ye (1447 Sek 6:6a, 13:26a; 1459 Wel 7:31b; 1462 ¹Nung 3:76a) − Is hyey˙ye ˙two (?1517- Pak 1:61b) an error?; ¨hyey˙Gen ˙t ay n' (1459 Wel 21:104a, 1462 ¹Nung 1:101a), ¨hyey[˙]Gen ˙t un (?1517- Pak 1:64a), ¨hyeyGa˙l ye two (1459 Wel 21:14a), ¨hyeyye.l i ˙Ga (1481 Twusi 10:12a); ¨hyeym ¨hyey˙non (1459 Wel 9:13b), ¨hyeynon ˙ta (1447 Sek 6:8a), ¨hyeynwo˙la (1481 Twusi 15:5b) ¨hyey˙sya (1445 ¹Yong 104); ¨hyeyzo˙Wol (1447 Sek se:1b); ¨hyeyywo˙toy (1462 ¹Nung 4:123b); ¨hyey˙ywom (1465 Wen 3:3:1:62a), ¨hyeyywu˙m i (1481 Twusi 21:42a); ¨hyey˙ywon (1447 Sek 19:11b), ¨hyeyywo˙n i (1481 Twusi 14:4b)

¨syey- 'make stand; build': ¨syey˙Gwo (1447 Sek 6:44b); ¨syey˙m ye (1459 Wel 17:37a); ¨syey˙ye (1447 Sek 9:19b, 1462 ¹Nung 4:123b), ¨syey˙ya (1459 Wel 21:213a), ¨syeyya ˙two (1482 Kum-sam 3:48b); ¨syeysi˙n i (1445 ¹Yong 11); ¨syeyno˙n i (1459 Wel 18:82b); ¨syeyzo˙Wa (1449 Kok 65), ¨syey˙zoWo˙n i (1449 Kok 10), ¨syeyzo˙Wosi˙n i (1449 Kok 34), ¨syeyzop˙nwon (1447 Sek 13:14b); ¨syey˙ywolq (1462 ¹Nung 5:8b); ¨syey˙ywo˙m i (1462 ¹Nung 1:19a), ¨syeyywo˙m ol (1475 Nay 2:2:15b), ¨syey˙ywo˙m o˙lawa (1459 Wel 23:76b); ¨syeyywo˙toy (1459 Wel 17:37b)

¨nyey- 'go': ¨nyey.m ye (1481 Twusi 23:19b); ¨nyeyywo˙toy (1482 Kum-sam 5:38a). Some of the unattested forms must have been *¨nyey˙ti, *¨nyey˙Gwo, *¨nyeyn, *¨nyeyl(q), *¨nyey˙m ye, *¨nyey˙y^ea, *¨nyey˙yw^uom.

¨kyey- '(time) pass, exceed': ¨kyeytwo˙lwok (1459 Wel 7:9b); ¨kyeyGe˙tun (1459 Wel 7:31b; broken type looks like "key"). This assignment assumes that the unattested infinitive would be *¨kyey˙y^ea, the modulated stem *¨kyey˙yw^uo-.

¨tiy-₁ 'drop, let / make fall': ¨ti˙Gwo (1459 Wel 10:24b [twice]), ¨tiGwo (1481 Twusi 15:14ab); ¨tiye (1481 Twusi 7:18b); ¨ti˙sya (1449 Kok 45); ¨tiGe˙tun (1481 Twusi 10:32a); ¨tiywo˙m ol (1481 Twusi 8:57b), ti˙ywo˙m ul (?1517- Pak 1:44b)

¨tiy-₂ 'smelt (metal); create (out of metal)': ¨ti[˙]m ye (1482 Kum-sam 2:31a); ¨ti˙ye (1465 Wen 2:2:2:24b) = ¨ti[˙]ye (1482 Kum-sam 2:30a); ¨ti˙zowo˙m ay (1463 Pep 1:220a); ¨ti˙ywun (1465 Wen 1:1:2:181a); ¨ti[˙]ki ˙yey s (1465 Wen 1:1:2:181a)

¨hoy- 'make / let do': ¨hoy˙Gey (1462 ¹Nung 3:115b), ¨hoy˙m ye n' (1449 Kok 99); ¨hoy˙l i '-ngi s ˙kwo (1464 Kumkang 11a); ¨hoyn (1482 Nam 1:68b); ¨hoy˙ye (1447 Sek 9:21a, 1459 Wel 9:39a, 1482 Nam 2:5a), ¨hoyye (1481 Twusi 7:16b, 25:37a); ¨hoy˙non (1463 Pep 1:9b); ¨hoy˙sya (1447 Sek 6:7b); ¨hoysi˙m ye (1465 Wen 1:2:2:92b)

The stem ¨ey- 'turn' is attested only in the suspective ¨ey˙ti (1518 Sohak-cho 8:2b). If the infinitive was *¨ey˙y^ea, it belongs to Group 1a; if it was *ey˙y^ea to 1b.

<u>Group 1b. Rising in all forms except the infinitive, the modulated forms, and the short effective forms</u>

°°pwuy- 'be empty': ¨pwuy˙m ye (1449 Kok 18) = ¨pwuy.m ye (1482 Kum-sam 2:54a); ¨pwuy.l i ˙ye (1459 Wel 1:37a); ¨pwuyn (1481 Twusi 7:4a, 10:32b) ‖ pwuy˙ye (1459 Wel 1:48b); pwuy˙ywu˙toy (1462 ¹Nung 5:59b), pwuy˙ywu˙m ey (1447 Sek 13:10a)

°°mwuy- 'move': ¨mwuyta (1459 Wel 2:14a); ¨mwuy˙ti (1462 ¹Nung 3:9b); ¨mwuyGwo (1481 Twusi 15:52b) = ¨mwuy˙Gwo (1482 Kum-sam 4:39b); ¨mwuy˙m ye (1449 Kok 172, ?1468- Mong 42b) = ¨mwuy.m ye (1481 Twusi 7:23b); ¨mwuyl (1445 ¹Yong 2; 1459 Wel se:2b, 2:14a); ¨mwuyn (1481 Twusi 15:15b, 1482 Kum-sam 2:18a); ¨mwuyno˙n i (1463 Pep 3:35a); ¨mwuyte˙n i (1449 Kok 172), ¨mwuyte˙la (1481 Twusi 8:10a) ‖ mwuy˙ye (1459 Wel se:3a, 1462 ¹Nung 3:117a); mwuy˙ywo.m i˙Gwo (1465 Wen 2:3:2:32a), mwuy˙ywum (id. 1:1:2:106-7), mwuy˙ywu.m ey (1481 Twusi 7:29b)

°°*cwuy*- 'grasp'; ¨*cwuyGwo* (1466 Kup 1:15b), ¨*cwuy˙lak* (1462 ¹Nung 1:108b, 113a) ‖ *cwuy˙ye* (1481 Twusi 25:21a); *cwuy˙ywom* (1462 ¹Nung 1:109b)
°°*swuy*- 'rest': ¨*swuy˙ti* (1462 ¹Nung 8:128a); ¨*swuyGwo* (1481 Twusi 22:10a, one of the dots is faint), ¨*swuy˙Gwo cye* (1463 Pep 3:83a); ¨*swuy˙Gey* (1463 Pep 2:203a); ¨*swuyl* (1459 Wel 1:48a), ¨*swuy˙l i 'lwo˙ta* (1481 Twusi 22:33b); ¨*swuyno˙n i* (1481 Twusi 16:33b). The unattested infinitive should be **swuy˙ye*, the modulated stem **swuy˙yw*ᵘ*/o*-; *swuy˙Gwu˙m un* (1459 Wel 13:18b), though listed by LCT under ¨*swuy*-, ought to be from the causative stem *swuy˙Gwu*- and *mo˙l ol swuy˙Gwola* (1481 Twusi 21:44b) must be from a variant of that stem, *swuy˙Gwo*-.
°°*woy*- 'wrong; left(-hand)': ¨*woy˙ta* (1447 Sek 9:14a), ¨*woyta* (1445 ¹Yong 107; 1482 Nam 1:38a, 38b, 39a); ¨*woy˙ti* (1482 Nam se:2a); *woy˙Gwo* (1481 Twusi 8:10a) — ? repro error for ¨*woy˙Gwo*; ¨*woy˙Gey* (1462 ¹Nung 9:77b); ¨*woy.m ye* (1482 Nam 1:39a); ¨*woyl* (1527 Cahoy 3:12b=29a; 15a=34b); ¨*woyn* (1447 Sek 6:30a, 9:36a; 1482 Kum-sam 2:34a), ¨*woy˙n i* (1459 Wel 1:42b, 1462 ¹Nung 2:59a, 1482 Kum-sam 2:3b), ¨*woy.n i* (1482 Nam 1:39a) ‖ *woy˙ywo.m i* (1482 Nam 1:39a), *woy˙ywo˙m ol* (1462 ¹Nung 9:83b; 1463 Pep 1:6a, 1:10b). The unattested infinitive should be **woy˙y*ᵉ*/a*.
°°*mwoy*- 'accompany, escort' is attested only with -*zoW*- attached: ¨*mwoyzo˙Wa* (1446 Sek 23:31b).
°°*twoy*- 'hard; severe': ¨*twoyn* (?1517⁻ Pak 1:18a); ¨*twoy˙sya* (1459 Wel 10:5a), ¨*twoysya˙m ay* (1475 Nay 2:2:63b) ‖ *twoy˙ywola* (1475 Nay 2:2:15a). The unattested infinitive should be **twoy˙y*ᵉ*/a*, the effective forms **¨*twoy˙G*ᵉ*/a*… or **¨*twoy˙y*ᵉ*/a*-. Other unattested forms: **¨*twoy˙ti* and **¨*twoy˙Gey*.
°°*tey*- 'burn': ¨*tey˙Gwo* (1459 Wel 7:18a); ¨*tey˙n i n'* (1466 Kup 2:7b); ¨*teyGe˙nul* (1475 Nay se:4a), ¨*teyGe˙n ya* (1518 Sohak-cho 10:3a) ‖ *tey˙ye* (1466 Kup 1:9b). The unattested modulated forms would be **tey˙yw*ᵘ*/o*-… , the short effective forms **tey˙ye*… .
°°*pyey*- 'pillow one's head on': ¨*pyeyGwo* (1466 Kup 1:61b); ¨*pyey˙m ye* (1459 Wel 1:17a) ‖ *pyey˙ye* (1481 Twusi 22:19a); *pyey˙ywun* (1459 Wel 1:17b)
*°°*myey*- 'get clogged': *myey˙ye* (1459 Wel 8:84a, 8:98a) 'get clogged', *myey˙ye 'ys.kwo* (1481 Twusi 20:33a), *myey˙ye 'ys.twota* (1481 Twusi 20:35a). Only the infinitive is attested.
°°*syey*- 'get white': ¨*syey˙Gwo* (1459 Wel 17:47b, 1463 Pep 5:120b); ¨*syey˙m ye* (1462 ¹Nung 2:9b), ¨*syeyn* (1445 ¹Yong 19; 1481 Twusi 8:12b, 10:2b, 10:6b, 21:14a), ¨*syey.n i* (1481 Twusi 7:12a); ¨*syeyla 'n˙t oy* (1481 Twusi 21:42b); ¨*syeyto˙lwok* (1481 Twusi 16:18a); ¨*syeytwo˙ta* (1481 Twusi 7:28a) ‖ *syey˙ywom two* (1481 Twusi 15:49b). The unattested infinitive should be **syey˙ye*; the effective forms should be **¨*syey˙G*ᵉ*/a*… or **syey˙y*ᵉ*/a*… .
°°*pay*- 'destroy, exterminate; capsize': ¨*payta* (1481 Twusi 15:34a); ¨*payti* (1481 Twusi 22:37b); ¨*payGwo* (1481 Twusi 20:4b); ¨*pay˙m ye* (1463 Pep 5:43a, 1475 Nay 1:1b) ‖ *pay˙ya* (1462 ¹Nung 10:92a, 1463 Pep 1:109a, 1482 Nam 2:57b); *pay˙yan ma˙lon* (1445 ¹Yong 90); *pay˙ywo.m ol* (1481 Twusi 21:36b), *pay˙ywo.l i '˙la* (1459 Wel 7:46b)
°°*cay*- 'swift; deft': ¨*cay˙Gwo* (?1517⁻ Pak 1:45b); ¨*cayn* (?1517⁻ Pak 1:30a, 1527 Cahoy 2:5a=10a), ¨*cay˙n i '˙la* (?1517⁻ No 1:12b) ‖ *cay˙ya* (1449 Kok 74, 157). The unattested effective forms should be **¨*cay˙G*ᵉ*/a*… or **cay˙y*ᵉ*/a*-, the modulated stem **cay˙yw*ᵘ*/o*-.
°°*say*- 'dawn': ¨*sayl* (1462 ¹Nung 10:45b, 1527 Cahoy 1:1b); ¨*sayno˙n i* (1481 Twusi 15:46a); ¨*sayGe˙tun* (1447 Sek 6:19a); ¨*say˙to˙lwok* (1463/4 Yeng 1:41b) = ¨*say˙two˙lwok* (?1517⁻ Pak 1:21b). The form *sa˙ya two* (1482 Kum-sam 4:52b) is either a mistake for the expected infinitive *say˙ya* or made on an otherwise unattested variant stem **sai*-. The modulated stem: **say˙yw*ᵘ*/o*-.

2.12.4.2. Vowel-final monosyllabic stems that are low.
Group 2. Stems that are low in all forms

chuy- 'make/let eliminate': *chuy˙ywu˙l ye* (1459 Wel 13:21a), *chuy˙ywu.l i '˙n i* (id. 13:20b, 1463 Pep 2:206a), *chuy˙ywu.l i '˙la* (1465 Wen se:47a), *chuy˙ywo˙m on* (1463 Pep 2:207a). Contracted < *chu˙i*- (*chu˙i˙kwo* 1463 Pep 2:241a, *chu˙ike˙tun* 1518 Sohak-cho 9:24b), causative of ˙*chu*-₁.
muy- 'hate': *muy˙ti* (1459 Wel 9:42a); *muy˙m ye* (1447 Sek 13:56b); *muyl* (1462 ¹Nung 8:30a); *muysya.m i* (1463 Pep 2:19b, but part of a longer passage in which all of the dots are absent);

muy˙nwola (1481 Twusi 7:20b, 23:23a); *muy˙ywo˙m i* (1462 ¹Nung 4:27b), *muy˙ywu˙m ul* (1462 ¹Nung 9:109a, 1464 Kumkang 79b)

suy- 'be sour': *suy˙Gwo* (1481 Twusi 15:21b); *suy˙m ye* (1462 ¹Nung 5:37b, 1463 Pep 6:68b); *suyn* (1445 ¹Yong text 5:4b, 1462 ¹Nung 2:115b, 1466 Kup 1:32a); *suyl* (1527 Cahoy 3:6b=14a)

ptuy- 'make / let it float': ˙*ptuy˙Gwo* (1481 Twusi 10:34b); *ptuy˙ywo˙m on* (1462 ¹Nung 6:26b), *ptuy˙ywu˙m i* (1463 Pep 7:50a)

stuy- 'wear (a belt), gird oneself with': *stuy˙Gwo* (1482 Nam 2:18b); *stuy˙m ye* (1586 Sohak 2:2b); *stuy˙ye* (1463 Pep 2:39b [broken type]); *stuy˙sya* (1445 ¹Yong 112); ¨*stuy* < **stuy-˙i* 'belt' (der n)

*poy-*₁ 'get pregnant with (child)': *poy˙Gwo ˙cye* (1462 ¹Nung 7:55b); *poyn* (1463 Pep 6:47a); *poyl* (1527 Cahoy 1:17b=33b); *poy˙ya* (1447 Sek 13:10a, 1462 ¹Nung 4:76a); *poy˙ywon* (1459 Wel 8:81a)

*poy-*₂ 'soak': *poy˙Gwo* (1462 ¹Nung 5:88a); *poy˙n i* (1466 Kup 1:16a)

moy- 'tie / sew (on), attach': *moyl* (1459 Wel se:3a, 1462 ¹Nung 8:106b); *moy˙n i* (1449 Kok 76); *moy˙ya* (1463 Pep 4:37b), *moy˙ye sye* (1481 Twusi 8:53b) − CF *moy˙ye* (1465 Wen 1:1:1:89b) < *moy˙i-* (VP), *moy˙Gye* (1459 Wel se:3b) < *moy˙Gi-* (VP); *moy˙syan* (1462 ¹Nung 5:24a), *moy˙yesi˙na* (1481 Twusi 7:34a); *moy˙ywom* (1465 Wen 1:2:2:161a), *moy˙ywo.m i˙la* (1462 ¹Nung 5:88a), *moy˙ywo˙m ol* (1464 Kumkang 83, 1465 Wen 1:1:1:101b); *moy˙ywolq* (1462 ¹Nung 7:8a), *moy˙ywon* (?1468- Mong 58, 1481 Twusi 8:47b)

ptwuy- 'jump': *ptwuy˙Gwo* (1482 Nam 2:66a); *ptwuy˙m ye* (1482 Kum-sam 2:13a); *ptwuyl* (1459 Wel 9:19b); *ptwuy˙n i* (1482 Kum-sam 4:31b); *ptwuy˙ye* (1481 Twusi 16:2b; 1462 ¹Nung 8:15a, 8:40a, 8:139a); *ptwuy˙ywo˙la* (1462 ¹Nung 8:139a)

pthwuy- 'spring, snap, splash': *pthwuy˙n i* (1481 Twusi 25:53a); *pthwuy˙nwos.ta* (1481 Twusi 25:19a; dot smudged); *pthwuy˙ye* (1481 Twusi 17:13a). VC *pthwuy˙Gwun* (1445 ¹Yong 48).

twoy- < *towoy-* < *toWoy-* 'become': *twoy˙Gwo* (1518 Sohak-cho 8:3b; faint dot), *twoy˙kwo* (1586 Sohak 1:7b); *twoy˙n i ˙la* (1518 Sohak-cho 10:6b); *twoy˙sikwo* (1588 Cwungyong 19b). The unattested infinitive should be **twoy˙ya*; the modulated stem **twoy˙ywo-*.

2.12.4.3. Vowel-final monosyllabic stems that are high.

Group 3. Stems that are high in all forms

˙*skwu-* 'dream': ˙*skwu˙kwo* (1449 Kok 67); ˙*skwum ˙skwulq* (1462 ¹Nung 4:130a); ˙*skwumywo˙m i* (1475 Nay 2:2:73a)

˙*hwo-* 'broad-stitch': ˙*hwol* (1527 Cahoy 3:9a=19b); ˙*hwo˙wa* [= ˙*hwo˙a*] *is˙kwo* (?1517- ¹No 2:52b)

˙*twoy-* 'measure' − noun ˙*twoy* '(measure)' (1459 Wel 9:7b); ˙*twoy˙ti* (?1517- Pak 1:67b); ˙*twoy˙Gey* (?1517- Pak 1:12a); ˙*twoy˙m ye n'* (?1517- Pak 1:12a); ˙*twoy˙non* (1459 Wel 9:7b); ˙*twoyGe˙nul* (1447 Sek 6:35b); ˙*twoyte˙n i* (1447 Sek 6:35a, 1449 Kok 168); ˙*twoyywo˙m i˙lwoswo˙n i* (1481 Twusi 8:10a). The unattested infinitive should be *˙*twoy˙ya*.

˙*pwuy-* 'cut': ˙*pwuyGwo* (1481 Twusi 8:61a) − ¨*pwuyGwo* (id. 7:38b) must be a mistake; ˙*pwuyn.i* (1481 Twusi 7:38b); ˙*pwuyl* (1527 Cahoy 3:3a=5b) = ˙*pwuylq* (1459 Wel 8:98b); ˙*pwuyye* (1481 Twusi 7:32b) = ˙*pwuy˙ye* (1459 Wel 1:45a, 1482 Kum-sam 4:31a); ˙*pwuynon* (1481 Twusi 7:18b, 10:32a); ˙*pwuy˙ye˙tun* (1459 Wel 1:45a). The modulated form in *pwuyywo˙m ol* (1481 Twusi 21:24b) should carry a dot at the beginning; I lack access to the text of ⁽?⁾ ˙*pwuy˙ywul* (1481 Twusi 9:30˙).

˙*phwuy-* 'burn (a fire)': ˙*phwuy˙Gey* (1462 ¹Nung 7:16b, 7:18a); ˙*phwu˙m ye* (1459 Wel 7:35a); ˙*phwuyn* (1462 ¹Nung 7:18a). Presumably the infinitive was *˙*phwuy˙ye*. The causative stem is *phwuy˙Gwu-*.

˙*chu-*₁ 'eliminate, get rid of': ˙*chu˙key* (1463 Pep 2:214b); ˙*chu˙m ye* (1465 Wen 2:1:1:52a); ˙*chul* (1465 Wen se:47a); ˙*chwu˙m* (∼ *on* 1459 Wel 13:21a, ∼ *un* 1463 Pep 2:207a)

˙*chu-*₂ 'sift': ˙*che* (1459 Wel 17:17b, 1462 ¹Nung 7:9a); ˙*chwu˙m on* (1463 Pep 5:155b)

˙*chu-*₃ 'dance': ˙*chukwo* (1481 Twusi 8:41b); ˙*chu˙m ye* (1459 Wel 21:190b)

˙*khu-* 'big': ˙*khu˙kwo* (1447 Sek 6:32b); ˙*khu˙kuy* (1447 Sek 6:34a), ˙*khu˙key* (1462 ¹Nung 1:3a, 1518 Sohak-cho 9:24a); ˙*khu˙m ye* (1462 ¹Nung 2:4ab, 1463/4 Yeng 2:12b), ˙*khu˙m ye n'* (1459 Wel 23:77a); ˙*khul* (1527 Cahoy 3:11a=25b); ˙*khun* (1445 ¹Yong 27; 1462 ¹Nung 4:18b; 1463 Pep

2:190a, 2:231b, 2:232a, 7:141b; ˀ1468⁻ Mong 47b; 1482 Kum-sam 3:25b, 4:22a); ˙khe (1447 Sek 6:12b, 1449 Kok 28, 1459 Wel 2:47b), ˙khe˙za (1463 Pep 2:224b); ˙khu˙kenul˙za (1482 Kum-sam 2:16a); ˙khwu.m u˙lwo (1459 Wel 1:29b)

˙phu- 'bloom': ˙phu˙kwo (1459 Wel 21:2a); ˙phulq (1447 Sek 13:25a); ˙phu˙m ye (1459 Wel 2:31a, 21:6b), ˙phu.m ye (1482 Kum-sam 2:6b), ˙phu˙m ye n' (1459 Wel 2:47a); ˙phun (1447 Sek 13:25a, 1481 Twusi 21:15b), ˙phu.n i ˙˙la (1459 Wel 2:47a); ˙phe (1449 Kok 158, 1459 Wel 2:47a), ˙phe ˙ys.non (1482 Nam 1:37b), ˙phe ˙ys.ke˙tun (1463 Pep 6:47a), ˙phe ˙ys.te˙n i (1447 Sek 6:31a, 1449 Kok 9, 1459 Wel 1:21a, 1481 Twusi 8:34b), ˙phe ˙y˙sywo.m ol (1481 Twusi 23:30b); ˙phuke˙tun (1459 Wel 8:75b); ˙phutwo˙ta (1482 Kum-sam 3:33a, 1482 Nam 1:66a); ˙phu-˙tos (1463 Pep 1:85b); ˙phwu˙m i (1462 ¹Nung 1:19a), ˙phwu.m ol (1482 Kum-sam 3:33b); ˙phwulq˙t i (1462 ¹Nung 1:19ab); [˙]phwu˙toy (1459 Wel 7:57b)

˙ptu-₁ 'float': ˙ptu˙ti (1462 ¹Nung 6:26b), ˙ptun (1462 ¹Nung 1:62b; 1481 Twusi 7:12b, 21:22b); ˙ptu˙lak (1481 Twusi 7:2a); ˙ptu˙m ye (1462 ¹Nung 3:79b) and ˙ptu.m ye (1462 ¹Nung 2:31a); ˙pte (1462 ¹Nung 1:47b); ˙ptwu˙m i (1462 ¹Nung 3:106a)

˙ptu-₂ 'open (eyes)': ˙ptu˙kwo (1449 Kok 65); ˙ptukuy (1482 Kum-sam 2:59b); ˙pte (1462 ¹Nung 1:59a); ˙ptuke˙na (1459 Wel 8:8b) ˙ptwu˙m i (1463 Pep 2:163b)

˙ptu-₃ 'spoil': ˙ptul (1527 Cahoy 3:6a=12a); ˙ptun (1466 Kup 2:61b); ˙ptuno˙n i (1466 Kup 2:61b)

˙pthu- 'burst': ˙pthuti (1463 Pep 2:243a); ˙pthukwo (1481 Twusi 25:26b); ˙pthe (1481 Twusi 7:24b)

˙psku- 'extinguish': ˙pskuti (1482 Kum-sam 5:3a); ˙pskun (1459 Wel 8:38b, 1463 Pep 6:153a); ˙pske (1459 Wel 2:71b, 1462 ¹Nung 2:43b, 1481 Twusi 25:13a); ˙pskuke˙nul (1447 Sek 6:33b); ˙pskunun (1449 Kok 106); ˙psku˙sya (1449 Kok 101); ˙pskwutoy (1482 Kum-sam 5:3a)

˙psu-₁ 'bitter': ˙psuta (1481 Twusi 8:18a); ˙psu˙m ye (1462 ¹Nung 3:9b, 5:37b); ˙psun (1462 ¹Nung 3:9a, 1466 Kup 78b, 1482 Kum-sam 2:50a); ˙pse (1459 Wel 2:25b); ˙pswum (1462 ¹Nung 3:10a). The expected dot is mistakenly omitted in ˙psul (1527 Cahoy 3:6b=14b).

˙psu-₂ 'use': ˙psu˙ti (1447 Sek 19:30b), ˙psuti (1482 Kum-sam 5:8a) – 1518 Sohak-cho 10:1b has psu˙ti ˙non but that may be a mistake, since the preceding line has ˙psul; there seems to be a mistake also in psu˙key (1459 Wel 23:73a) 'so as to use', countered by ˙psukwo ˙˙la a little later in the same passage; ˙pse (1462 ¹Nung 1:81a, 1463 Pep 2:240a, 1481 Twusi 8:17a); ˙psunon (1451 Hwun-en 1b, 1482 Kum-sam 2:17b); ˙psu˙sya (1445 ¹Yong 77); ˙pswu˙toy (1464 Kumkang 87b), ˙pswu.m i (1482 Kum-sam 5:8a); ˙pswul (1462 ¹Nung 1:19a)

˙(s)su-₁ 'write': ˙sun (1482 Kum-sam 3:7b); ˙ssul (1527 Cahoy 3:9a=20b); ˙ssu.m ye (1447 Sek 6:43a, 1463 Pep 2:163a); ˙sse (1447 Sek 9:30a), ˙se (1481 Twusi 23:44a); ˙sswutoy (1463 Pep 4:72b), ˙sswun (1447 Sek se:4b)

˙(s)su-₂ 'wear on head': ˙sukwo (1482 Nam 1:30b, 1481 Twusi 15:6b), ˙ssu˙kwo (1459 Wel 10:95b, 1463 Pep 7:176a)

˙stu-₁ 'cauterize': ˙stukwo (1466 Kup 1:22a); ˙stu˙l i (id. 1:41a); ˙stula (id. 1:36b)= ˙stu˙la (id. 1:3a, 19a, 25a, 26b, 29a, 76a); ˙stu˙m ye n' (id. 1:22a); ˙stum (ˀ1517⁻ Pak 1:38a); ˙stu˙n i (ibid.); ˙ste (1466 Kup 2:72b); ˙stwutoy (1466 Kup 1:20a, 36b) = ˙stwu˙toy (ˀ1517⁻ Pak 1:38b); ˙stuno˙n i (id. 1:57a)

˙stu-₂ 'scoop': ˙stu˙kwo (1481 Twusi 15:54a), ˙ste (1475 Nay 1:3a), ˙stul (1527 Cahoy 2:15a=7a)

˙cho-₁ 'cold': ˙cho˙kwo (1459 Wel 1:26b); ˙chol (1527 Cahoy 1:1b=1a, 3:1b=2a); ˙chon (1449 Kok 102); ˙chwom (1462 ¹Nung 3:12a). The unattested infinitive should be *˙cha.

˙cho-₂ 'get full': ˙cho˙ti (1449 Kok 180); ˙cho˙m ye (1447 Sek 19:7b); ˙chon (ˀ1517⁻ Pak 1:55b, 1518 Sohak-cho 8:27b); ˙cha (1447 Sek 6:4b, 1449 Kok 140), ˙cha˙za (1462 ¹Nung 8:28b); ˙choke˙za (1447 Sek 19:39a); ˙chwo˙m ol (1463 Pep 3:98b); ˙cho˙sya (1459 Wel 2:8b)

˙cho-₃ 'kick': ˙chokwo (1482 Nam 1:50a); ˙thi-˙cho˙m ye (1449 Kok 39); ˙chol (1527 Cahoy 3:4b=8b); pak˙cha (1481 Twusi 15:33a)

˙cho-₄ 'attach, fasten on': ˙cho˙ti (1481 Twusi 8:49b); ˙cha (1465 Wen se:8b); ˙choke˙na (1462 ¹Nung 7:46a); ˙chwon (1481 Twusi 25:8a)

˙pho- 'dig': ˙pho˙kwo (1449 Kok 60); ˙pha (1459 Wel 1:7b, 1462 ¹Nung 7:9a, 1481 Twusi 21:42a); ˙phwom (1463 Pep 4:95b), ˙phwo˙m ol (1462 ¹Nung 3:87b) `pto-` 'pick, pluck': `ptokwo` (1475 Nay 2:2:69b), `pto.l i ' ˙Gwo` (1481 Twusi 10:8b); `pta` (1449 Kok 99, 1459 Wel 2:12b); `ptonon` (1475 Nay 2:2:68b, 1481 Twusi 8:15b); `ptoten` (1481 Twusi 15:21a), `ptwo.m ol`, `ptwotoy` (1475 Nay 2:2:69a)

`ptho-₁` 'pluck (harp strings), play (string music)': `pthokwo` (1481 Twusi 24:38a, 1482 Kum-sam 4:10b); `ptho.m ye` (1482 Kum-sam 2:11b); `pthol` (1459 Wel 8:49a, 1527 Cahoy 2:9a=17a); `pthono˙ta` (1482 Kum-sam 5:8a). The unattested infinitive would be *`ptha`.

`ptho-₂` 'cut open, split': `ptho˙kwo` (1459 Wel 23:73b, 1466 Kup 2:79a); `ptha` (1482 Nam 1:15a)

`pco-₁` 'salty': `pco˙m ye` (1462 ¹Nung 5:37b); `pcol` (1527 Cahoy 3:6b=14a, 3:8a=17b); `pcon` (1459 Wel 1:23a, 1466 Kup 1:32a); `pcwom` (1462 ¹Nung 3:51a). The unattested infinitive: *`pca`.

`pco-₂` 'weave': `pco˙ti` (1462 ¹Nung 9:53b), `pcon` (?1517⁻ Pak 1:29a), `pcol` (1475 Nay 2:2:51b, 1527 Cahoy 3:8b=19a); `pca` (1475 Nay 2:2:51a, 1481 Twusi 20:19a); `pcwon` (1463 Pep 2:140a). The forms `pcoy˙isya` (1475 Nay 2:2:51b) and `pcoy˙ye` (id. 2:52a) are from the causative `pcoy˙i-`.

`psko-` 'peel, husk, shell; hatch': `psko˙kwo` (1481 Twusi 7:32-3); `psko˙m ye` (1463 Pep 2:116a, 2:117a). The unattested infinitive would be *`pska`, the modulated forms *`pskwo-`.

`pso-` 'wrap': `pso˙kwo` (?1517⁻ Pak 1:28a) `pso.m ye n'` (1481 Twusi 16:67b); `pson` (1481 Twusi 8:33-4); `psa` (1481 Twusi 20:39a); `pswon` (1481 Twusi 21:4b)

`(s)so-` 'valuable': `sso˙ta` (?1517⁻ ¹No 2:4b); `sso˙m ye` (1447 Sek 13:22b); `sson` (1459 Wel 18:78b); `ssa` (1463 Pep 2:140a). The unattested modulated forms would be `sswo-⋯` .

`tho-₁` 'ride': `tho˙ti` (?1517⁻ Pak 1:37b); `tho˙kwo` (1459 Wel 10:28a), `thokwo˙cye s` (1481 Twusi 15:55b); `thol` (1459 Wel se:18a); `thon` (1459 Wel 1:27b); `tha` (1482 Nam 1:36b); `tho˙sya` (1459 Wel 1:27b); `thwon` (1445 ¹Yong 34)

`tho-₂` 'receive, undergo': `thoti` (1481 Twusi 8:33a); `tho.m ye` (1475 Nay 1:se:2b); `thon` (1447 Sek 19:2b); `tha` (1481 Twusi 7:2b); `tho˙no.n i ' ˙la` (1462 ¹Nung 1:89a); `thwo.m i` (1475 Nay 3:63a)

`tho-₃` 'burn (a fire):' `tho˙ti` (1462 ¹Nung 9:108b); `thol` (1465 Wen 1:1:2:181a)

`hoy-` 'white': `hoyta` (1482 Kum-sam 4:22b); `hoy˙Gwo` (1459 Wel 1:23a); `hoy˙Gey` (1445 ¹Yong 50); `hoyl` (1459 Wel 1:22b); `hoyn` (1445 ¹Yong 50; 1447 Sek 6:43b; 1481 Twusi 7:1a, 16:60a; 1527 Cahoy 2:14b=29b); `hoyGe˙nol` (1481 Twusi 16:1a). Probably scribal errors: ?[˙]hoy˙Gwo (1463 Pep 1:148b); ?[˙]hoyywo˙m ol ko˙cang muy˙nwola (1481 Twusi 23:23a) – CF `hoyywo˙m ol` (1481 Twusi 7:27a). The unattested infinitive: *`hoy˙ya`. Variant `huy-` (`huyn mo¨toy ⋯` 1481 Twusi 25:2b).

`moy-` 'remove (weeds), weed': `moyl` (1527 Cahoy 3:3a=5a); `moyya` (1481 Twusi 7:34b); `moy˙ywo˙m i` (1462 ¹Nung 1:19a); `moy˙ywolq˙t i` (1462 ¹Nung 1:19a)

`soy-` 'leak': `soy˙ti` (1463 Pep 3:56a); `soy˙m ye n'` (1466 Kup 1:78a) – [˙]`soy˙m ye n'` (1459 Wel 23:77b) omits the dot here and twice above in the line; `soyl` (1463 Pep 1:24b); `soy˙ya` (1463 Pep 6:89b); `soy˙non` (1462 ¹Nung 6:106b, 1465 Wen 1:1:2:107b), `soynon` (1447 Sek 13:10b); `soy˙ywom` (1465 Wen 1:1:2:97b)

`skoy-` 'wake up': `skoyti` (1481 Twusi 10:7a, 1485 Kwan 3a); `skoy˙Gey` (1459 Wel 13:18b); `skoy˙m ye` (1464 Kumkang 38a, ?1468⁻ Mong 42b); `skoylq` (1447 Sek 9:31a); `skoyn` (1465 Wen 1:2:1:47a); `skoy˙ya` (?1468⁻ Mong 59a); `skoy˙yan` (1465 Wen 1:1:2:151a); `skoyGe˙na` (1459 Wel 10:70b); `skoyywo˙n i` (1459 Wel 10:24b), `skoy˙ywom` (1465 Wen 1:1:2:37b), `skoyywo˙m ol` (1481 Twusi 21:20b).

`chuy-` 'slant, lean': `chuyti` (1463/4 Yeng 1:52a), `chuyn` (1459 Wel 1:45b); `chuy˙ye` (1465 Wen 1:1:110a, 1586 Sohak 2:62a)

Critical examples are lacking for `kuy-` 'crawl', `skuy-` 'shun', `spuy-` 'drain', `pco-₃` 'squeeze', and a few others. The only examples of `muy-` 'get cracked' are of the infinitive, as in `muyye˙tye` (1481 Twusi 16:29b). These are put into the always-high group by default.

`iy-` (copula): `i˙Gwo` (1459 Wel 1:31a); `i˙Gey` (1462 ¹Nung 2:27b); `i˙la` (1447 Sek 6:17a; indicative assertive); ⋯ `i˙m ye` (1463 Pep 5:30a), ⋯ `i˙m ye n'` (1459 Wel 2:49a); ⋯ `in` (1462 ¹Nung 2:6b, 2:8b; ?1517⁻ ¹No 2:54b); `i˙sya` (1447 Sek 13:29a), `isi˙na` (1449 Kok 2); `i-ngi ' ˙ta` (1447 Sek 24:46b, 1459 Wel 21:218b); `ila˙n i` (1446 Sek 6:19b; retrospective modifier). Presumably the loss of accent is secondary in `syel˙hu.n in ˙hoy˙yey` (1462 ¹Nung 2:6b), ¨`twul.h i˙m ye` (1447 Sek 13:49b), ˙SYANG `isya-˙s-ongi ' ˙ta` (1447 Sek 23:22b), ⋯ .

`chi-` 'raise': `chi˙kwo` (1463 Pep 7:77b), `chil` (1459 Wel 8:87a); `chinon` (1459 Wel 1:46b)

`pski-` 'insert, ... ': `pskikwo` (1481 Twusi 10:26a) = `pski˙kwo` (?1517- Pak 1:26a); `pskil` (1459 Wel 13:56b), `pski˙m ye` (1463 Pep 5:13a); `pskye` (1459 Wel 2:18b, 1465 Wen 2:3:1:54b, 1475 Nay se:7a) − ¨`pskye` (1466 Kup 1:88a) must be a mistake

`pti-` 'steam': `ptil` (1462 ¹Nung 4:18b, 1527 Cahoy 3:6a=12a); `ptin` (1481 Twusi 7:18a, 1586 Sohak 5:48b); `ptye` (1462 ¹Nung 6:89b, 1481 Twusi 20:38a, 1482 Kum-sam 5:45b); `ptinon` (1481 Twusi 8:9b)

`thi-` 'hit': `thi˙m ye` (1462 ¹Nung 8:88b), `thi˙m ye n'` (1447 Sek 6:28a); `thil` (1527 Cahoy 3:13a=30a); `thye` (1447 Sek 6:28a, 1449 Kok 156); `thike˙tun` (1459 Wel 7:53b); `thino˙ta` (1462 ¹Nung 4:130a); `thywo˙toy` (?1468- Mong 53a), `thywon` (?1468- Mong 10a), `thywum` (1463 Pep 5:38a)

2.12.4.4. Vowel-final monosyllabic stems that are high/low.

Group 4. Stems that are high only before the infinitive ending or one of the bound stems

°`ci-₁` 'want to do' (aux): `ci˙la` (1447 Sek 24:8a, 24:9b; 1459 Wel 1:10b, 1:11b, 7:12a, 8:101b; 1462 Pep 2:28b; 1481 Twusi 8:1b, 22:35a) ‖ ˙`ci˙ye` (1462 ¹Nung 1:16b), ˙`cye` (1447 Sek 6:14b, 6:15a; 1451 Hwun-en 3b; 1459 Wel 18:3a, 21:124-5; 1462 ¹Nung 1:38a, 7:73b; 1465 Wen se:43b, 1:1:2:75b, 2:3:1:47a; 1481 Twusi 7:14a, 8:38b, 15:55b; 1586 Sohak 6:35b), ˙`cye ˙y.n i ˙˙la` (1463 Pep 4:134b); ˙`ci-ngi ˙˙ta` (1445 ¹Yong 58; 1447 Sek 6:22b, 24:8b; 1459 Wel 2:9b, 2:27b, 8:1a, 8:4-5, 10:10b)

°`ci-₂` 'carry on the back': `ci˙kwo` (1463 Pep 2:165a), `cil` (1527 Cahoy 3:10b=24a); ¨`cywum` (1463/4 Yeng 2:73b), ¨`cywu˙m ul` (1481 Twusi 24:32a) ‖ ˙`cye` (?1517- Pak 1:11b; 1481 Twusi 7:28a) < ˙`ci˙ye`

°`ci-₃` 'chop (wood)': ¨`cywu˙m ey` (1481 Twusi 7:6b) ‖ ˙`cinon` (1481 Twusi 7:39a). This assignment assumes such unattested forms as *`ci˙ti`, *`ci˙kwo`, *`cin`, *`cil(q)`, *˙`cye` < *˙`ci˙ye`.

°`(c)ci-` 'get fat': `ci˙ti` (?1517- Pak 1:22b); `ci˙kwo` (1481 Twusi 16:62b); `cin` (1481 Twusi 15:4b, 1466 Kup 1:80a); `cci˙key` (1459 Wel 23:73a) ‖ `sol[h] ˙cye` (1481 Twusi 16:15b) < *˙`ci˙ye`

°`i-` 'carry on the head': `i˙ta` (1482 Nam 2:64a); `i˙kwo` (1482 Kum-sam 2:11a − also 1481 Twusi 18:10, unavailable to me); `il` (1527 Cahoy 2:10b=24b) ‖ ˙`iye` (1449 Kok 34) = ˙`i˙ye` (1462 ¹Nung 8:93b, 1463 Pep 4:174a). The substantive *`i˙m ye` is unattested; ¨`im` (1482 Kum-sam 5:34a) is the modulated substantive (we expect *¨`ywum` < *`i˙ywum`) = ˙`iywo˙m on` (1482 Nam 2:64a), see p. 70.

°`ni-` 'roof, thatch': ¨`nil` = `nil` (1527 Cahoy 3:8r=18r) ‖ `nisi˙kwo` (1475 Nay 2:2:72b). SEE p. 70.

°`ti-₁` 'fall': `ti˙kwo` (1445 ¹Yong 86); `ti˙key` (1459 Wel 1:29a); `til` (1527 Cahoy 3:3a=5a); `tin ˙t ol` (1445 ¹Yong 31) − ¨`tin tol`¨ (LKM 1962:117) must be a misprint (CF Taycey-kak repro) ‖ ˙`ti˙ye` (1447 Sek 9:27b, 1518 Sohak-cho 10:11b), ˙`tiye` (1481 Twusi 15:44a); ˙`tike˙nul` (1447 Sek 6:30-1), ˙`tike˙tun` (1462 ¹Nung 1:19a); ˙`tinwon` (1481 Twusi 21:14b); ¨`tywu.m ul` (1481 Twusi 23:30b), ¨`tywu˙m i` (1482 Kum-sam 2:49b), ¨`tywu.m ay` (1482 Kum-sam 2:6b); ¨`tywulq` (1447 Sek 9:28a)

°`ti-₂` 'become' (aux): `ti˙key` (1447 Sek 6:13a); `ti˙kwo` (1481 Twusi 20:16a); `ti˙m ye` (1459 Wel 2:71b); ‖ ˙`ti˙ye ˙ys.ke˙nol` (1481 Twusi 15:44b)

°`psti-` 'overflow': `psti˙m ye` (1449 Kok 178), `psti˙kwom` (1459 Wel 7:9b). There are no attested examples that would call for ˙`psti···`, but such forms as ˙`psti˙ye` and ˙`psti(˙)ke···` must have existed.

°`ca-` 'sleep': `ca˙ti` (?1517- ¹No 1:47b); `ca˙kwo` (?1517- ¹No 1:10b); `ca˙key` (?1517- ¹No 1:46b); `ca˙m ye` (?1468- Mong 42a); `calq` (1462 ¹Nung 9:88a), `cal` (1459 Wel 1:25b, 1527 Cahoy 1:15b=30b) ‖ ˙`ca za` (1481 Twusi 16:66a); ˙`casya` (1482 Nam 2:76a), ˙`cano˙n i` (1447 Sek 13:10b)

°`ha-` 'many / much': `halk ˙ka` [= `halq ˙ka`] (1465 Wen 1:2:2:136a); `ha˙m ye` (1459 Wel 10:19a), `ha˙m ye n'` (1481 Twusi 22:20a); `han` (1445 ¹Yong 19, 1447 Sek 6:25b, 1459 Wel 17:44a, 1463 Pep 4:84b) − ˙`han ˙pi` (1445 ¹Yong 67) 'heavy rain' must be either a mistake or a variant of the modulated modifier ¨`han` (1447 Sek 6:2b); `ha˙n ye` (1447 Sek 19:4a), `ha˙n i ˙˙la` (1459 Wel 2:31b) ‖ ˙`ha ˙two` (1463 Pep 7:62b), ˙`ha˙a` (1459 Wel 1:24a), ˙`hano˙n i` (1445 ¹Yong 2, Manlyek text); ˙`hasin` (1449 Kok 18); ¨`ha˙m ol` (1482 Kum-sam 3:19a) ← `ha-˙[wo]-m`. SEE p. 70 for `ha-ngi ˙˙ta`.

°`ka-` 'go': `ka˙ti` (?1517- Pak 1:67b, ?1517- ¹No 2:7a); `ka˙kwo` (1462 ¹Nung 7:73b); `ka˙key` (1447 Sek 6:9b); `ka˙m ye` (1459 Wel 8:10b, 1481 Twusi 7:3b), `ka˙mye n'` (1447 Sek 6:22b); `ka-˙tos` (1459 Wel 2:7a) ‖ ˙`ka` (1447 Sek 6:35b; 1459 Wel 2:11a, 10:20b, 18:71b; 1462 ¹Nung 2:50b; 1463 Pep 1:77a;

1481 Twusi 7:2a, 8:37b, 8:40a; ˀ1517⁻ Pak 1:37b, 1:54a, 1:64b); ˙ka˙a (1447 Sek se:6b, 6:1a, 6:6b, 13:10b, 24:37b; 1459 Wel 8:100b, 10:13ab, 18:71b, 23:65a; 1463 Pep 2:138b); ˙ka˙sya (1445 ¹Yong 58; 1447 Sek 6:45b; 1459 Wel 1:5b, 2:11b), ˙ka˙non ˙ta (ˀ1517⁻ ¹No 1:1a), ˙kano˙n i (1445 ¹Yong 2, 1447 Sek 6:9b), ˙kanon ce˙k uy (1447 Sek 6:19a), ˙kata ˙ka (1445 ¹Yong 25, 1482 Nam 1:36b)

°na- 'emerge': na˙ti (1462 ¹Nung 1:8b) — Cғ modulated ¨na˙ti (1447 Sek 6:19a); na˙kwo (1459 Wel 1:46a); na˙key (1463 Pep 1:158b); nan (1459 Wel 1:28b, 21:216a; 1463 Pep se:7b); nal (1527 Cahoy 1:17b=34a); na˙m ye (1447 Sek 23:44a; 1462 ¹Nung 1:51b), na˙m ye n' (1462 ¹Nung 7:74b); ¨na˙toy (1447 Sek 19:7b, 1449 Kok 185) ← na-˙[wo]-˙toy, ¨nalq (1462 ¹Nung 3:24b) ← na-˙[wo]-lq (1459 Wel 21:215b) ‖ ˙na (1481 Twusi 7:39a); ˙na˙a (1449 Kok 41, 1459 Wel 1:5a); ˙na˙ta ka ˙'m ye (1459 Wel 21:215b)

°sa- 'buy': sa˙kwo (1481 Twusi 7:21a); sa˙key (ˀ1517⁻ Pak 1:2a), sal (1527 Cahoy 3:9b=21a) ‖ ˙sa (ˀ1517⁻ ¹No 2:21a); ˙sa˙a (1447 Sek 6:8a, 1459 Wel 1:10b)

°(h)hye- 'pull, drag': hhye˙kwo (1449 Kok 39), hye˙kwo (1463 Pep 4:93b); hye˙ti (ˀ1517⁻ ¹No 2:31a); hhyen (1463 Pep 2:100b) — ¨hhyen (1462 ¹Nung 1:17b) is the modulated modifier; hhyel (1459 Wel se:3a), hyel (1527 Cahoy 1:18b=35b) ‖ ˙hhye (1463 Pep 1:158b, ˀ1468⁻ Mong 58a); ˙hye˙a (1482 Kum-sam 2:64b); ˙hyeta ˙ka (1481 Twusi 16:1b)

°nye- 'go': nye˙ti (ˀ1468⁻ Mong 41b, 1481 Twusi 7:6a); nye˙key (1463 Pep 2:39b, 1481 Twusi 7:6a); nyel (1447 Sek 9:21b, 1482 Nam 1:28b) = nyelq (1459 Wel 21:119a), nye˙l i ˙Gwo (ˀ1517⁻ ¹No 1:30b) > nyey.l i Gwo (1795 ¹No-cwung [P] 1:27b), nye˙cye (ˀ1517⁻ ¹No 1:10b) = nyeycya (1795 ¹No-cwung [P] 1:9b); nye˙m ye ¨nye˙m ay (1482 Kum-sam 4:2a) ‖ ˙nye (1481 Twusi 7:2a, 14:29b, 25:29a, 14:29b; ˀ1517⁻ ¹No 1:1b); ˙nye˙a (1449 Kok 86); ˙nyeke˙tun (1463 Pep 3:155b); ˙nyenun (1459 Wel 7:52b), ˙nyenon (1481 Twusi 21:14a), ˙nyenwon ˙t ol (1482 Kum-sam 4:2a); ˙nyesi˙n i (1482 Kum-sam 4:54a), ˙nyesil (1463 Pep 2:39b)

°phye- 'spread it': phye˙ti (1481 Twusi 8:4b); phye˙kwo (1462 ¹Nung 9:88a); phye˙key (1459 Wel 18:61b); phyel (1459 Wel 21:4a, 1527 Cahoy 3:6a=12b); phye˙m ye (1481 Twusi 16:55a) ‖ ˙phye (1447 Sek 9:21b, 9:29a; 1462 ¹Nung 1:4a), ˙phye˙a (1447 Sek 6:6a, 13:10a), ˙phye˙e ˙ys.ten (1447 Sek 6:2a); ˙phye˙ta˙la (1463 Pep 4:170a); ˙phyesi˙m ye ˙phyesi˙kwo k (1462 ¹Nung 1:108b); ˙phye˙sya (1462 ¹Nung 1:3a); ˙phyesyan ˙t ila (1482 Kum-sam 5:35b); ˙phyesi˙nwon (1482 Nam 1:5a)

°sye- 'stand': sye˙ta (1447 Sek 19:13a); i˙le sye˙ti (1475 Nay 1:34a); sye˙kwo (1463/4 Yengka 2:12a), syel (1527 Cahoy 3:12a=27a), ¨syelq (1462 ¹Nung 3:36a; modulated) ‖ ˙sye˙a (1447 Sek 19:31a, 1459 Wel 2:64b), ˙sye˙e (1459 Wel 10:17b); ˙sye˙sya (1445 ¹Yong 28). The phrase ans.ke˙na [˙]syeke˙na (1447 Sek 19:5b) 'whether sitting or standing' suppresses the stem accent even before the effective aspect -˙ke-, but that is peculiar to this idiom.

°wo- 'come': wo˙ti (1459 Wel 7:29b); wo˙key (1447 Sek 6:43b), wo˙kwo (1481 Twusi 16:65a); wolq ˙t ol (1449 Kok 147), won ˙ta (ˀ1517⁻ Pak 1:51a), wo˙n i (1459 Wel 1:45a); wo˙m ye n' (1586 Sohak 4:33a); ¨wo˙m i (1459 Wel 9:10b, 1482 Kum-sam 3:19a), ¨wo˙m ol (1482 Nam 1:50b), ¨wo[˙]m ay (1481 Twusi 21:25b) ← wo-˙[wo]-m ‖ ˙woke˙na (1459 Wel 9:43a); ˙woke˙nol (1481 Twusi 8:40a); ˙woke˙ton (1482 Kum-sam 3:27b), ˙woke˙tun (1459 Wel 10:25a), ˙wona˙ton (1447 Sek 6:16b, 19:6a), ˙wa˙ton (1463 Pep 3:2b); ˙wo˙sya (1459 Wel 8:55b), ˙wosya ˙two (1447 Sek 6:4b), ˙wosya ˙za (1445 ¹Yong 38); ˙wosi˙n i (1459 Wel 1:5b); ˙wo˙silq (1459 Wel 2:18b), ˙wosil ˙ss ye (1447 Sek 23:29a); ˙wosi˙n i (1459 Wel 1:5b); ˙wosin ˙t i (1463 Pep 5:119b); ˙wona ˙two (1481 Twusi 25:23a); ˙wona ˙two (1481 Twusi 25:23a); ˙wona˙ta (ˀ1517⁻ Pak 1:3a); ˙wo˙nan ˙t i (ˀ1517⁻ ¹No 1:68b); ˙wo˙na˙la (1459 Wel 7:7b, ˀ1517⁻ ¹No 1:57b); ˙wona˙n i (1463/4 Yeng 1:90b); ˙wonan ˙t i (1463 Pep se:21a); ˙wona˙n ywo (1447 Sek 6:19b); ˙wo˙no-ngi ˙'ta (1447 Sek 6:29b); ˙wono˙n ywo (1447 Sek 6:29b); ˙wo˙nwo˙la (ˀ1517⁻ ¹No 1:1b); ˙wonwon ˙t in ˙t ay n' (1459 Wel 10:7b); ˙wota ˙ka (1447 Sek 23:57b); ˙woten ˙t ey n' (1445 ¹Yong 51)

°pwo- 'see': pwo˙ti (1462 ¹Nung 2:37a; 1481 Twusi 7:29a, 8:24a); pwo˙kwo (1447 Sek 6:14a, 6: 19a, 6:30a, 19:10a, 24:20b; 1459 Wel 17:17b; 1482 Kum-sam 2:1b); pwo˙key (1447 Sek 13:10a); pwon ˙ta (1462 ¹Nung 2:8b, ˀ1468⁻ Mong 58a); pwolq (1462 ¹Nung 2:111a); pwo˙m ye (1447 Sek 23: 22a, 13:23b, 19:10a; 1465 Wen 1:2:1:39b); ¨pwom (1462 ¹Nung 2:84a) ← pwo-˙[wo]-m; pwo-˙two (1447 Sek 24:28b) ‖ ˙pwo˙a (1459 Wel 10:4b), ˙pwoa ˙cye (1447 Sek 6:14b); ˙pwoken ˙t ey n' (1447

Sek 6:6a), ῾pwoken ˙t ay n' (1459 Wel 7:12b, 1462 ¹Nung 2:6-7); ῾pwo˙asi˙tun (1459 Wel 2:58b); ῾pwoa˙ton (1447 Sek 6:15b); ῾pwosi˙kwo (1447 Sek 6:17b, 1449 Kok 43); ῾pwosi˙m ye (1475 Nay 1: 9-10); ῾pwosin ˙t ay (1449 Kok 49); ῾pwo˙sya (1463 Pep 5:100a); ῾pwono˙n i (1447 Sek 13:25ab, 1462 ¹Nung 1:108b), ῾pwo˙no.n i '˙la (1459 Wel 21:206a), ῾pwonon ˙ta (1462 ¹Nung 1:83b); ῾pwonwon (1459 Wel 2:53a); ῾pwonwo˙la (1481 Twusi 15:52b, ῾pwonwo[˙]la 7:11a); ῾pwonwon ˙ka (1449 Kok 2), ῾pwonwon ˙t i˙m ye (1459 Wel 17:35a), ῾pwonwon ˙t on (1475 Nay 1:77b)

°(s)swo- 'shoot; sting' (not spelled ῾pswo- before the early 1500s): sswo˙ta (1446 Hwun 24a); sswo˙ti (1481 Twusi 10:26a); swol (1459 Wel 14:61b); the exceptional ῾sswo˙m ye (1462 ¹Nung 8:88b) seems to be a mistaken continuation of the high pitch of the preceding string ca˙pu˙m ye ˙thi˙m ye ‥ , and the dot on ῾pswol 'to shoot' (1527 Cahoy 3:5a=9a) is also a mistake that a few entries later is countered by the expected pswol 'to sting' (id. 3:5a=10a). ‖ ˙swoa (1481 Twusi 7:18a, 1482 Kum-sam 4:52a), ˙swoa ˙za (1465 Wen 1:1:1:113a), ˙swa (1481 Twusi 16:56b); ˙sswo˙sya (1445 ¹Yong 63), ˙sswosi˙n i (1445 ¹Yong 57). Also swo˙ta (1446 Hwun 24a) 'overturn' ?< 'shoot it down'.

°cwu- 'give': cwu˙kwo (1463 Pep 4:37b); cwu˙key (1465 Wen 2:3:1:125a); cwul (1527 Cahoy 3:9b=21b, 3:10a=21b), cwu˙l i 'Ge˙n i (1447 Sek 9:13a), cwu˙l i ˙ye (1447 Sek 9:12b); cwu˙m ye (1447 Sek 9:12a), cwu˙m ye n' (?1517-̆ Pak 1:43a) ‖ ˙cwue (1481 Twusi 7:23b), ˙cwue ˙two (1463 Pep 2:77a); ˙cwusi˙m ye n' (1447 Sek 23:55b); ˙cwue ˙nul (1459 Wel 17:20a); ˙cwu˙esi˙tun (1447 Sek 6:22b), ˙cwu˙esi˙ton (1475 Nay 1:9-10); ˙cwunu˙n i (1464 Kumkang 21b); ˙cwu˙sya (1445 ¹Yong 41). Unexplained: ¨mwut.cye ˙cwukwo ˙za (?1517-̆ ¹No 1:51b) ← *¨mwut˙cye cwu˙kwo ˙za.

°twu- 'put away': twu˙ti (1482 Kum-sam 2:65a); twu˙kwo (1447 Sek 6:23ab, 6:26a, 9:14a; 1459 Wel 1:28a, 21:78b), twu˙kwo n' (?1517-̆ ¹No 1:43b, 1518 Sohak-cho 8:37b), twu˙kwo ˙za (1459 Wel 7:9a); twul ˙tta [= twulq ˙ta] (1459 Wel 2:64a), twu˙l i ˙Ga (1481 Twusi 8:3b) ‖ ˙twu˙e (1447 Sek 6:26a); ˙twuten ˙t ay n' (1463 Pep 2:231b); ˙twusi˙kwo (1445 ¹Yong 58); ˙twu-῾sywo˙sye khe˙nul (1445 ¹Yong 107)

°nwu- 'void (urine/feces)': nwu˙m ye n' (1466 Kup 1:11b) ‖ ˙nwu˙non (1586 Sohak 4:30b)

°ho- 'do': ho˙ti (1475 Nay 1:70b); ho˙kwo (1447 Sek 6:6a, 6:29a, 6:35b, 13:36a, 24:3b; 1451 Hwun-en 3b; 1459 Wel 1:13b, 1:26b, 1:30a, 1:30ab, 2:11a, 2:69a, 7:5b, 7:15b, 7:16a, 8:38b, 9:10b, 9:55ab, 10:9b; 1462 ¹Nung 8:104b; 1475 Nay 1:9-10, 1:34a, 1:84a; 1481 Twusi 8:27b, 23:23a; 1482 Kum-sam 2:6b, 2:21a, 2:55a, 2:65a, 3:55a, 4:48b; ?1517-̆ Pak 1:25a, 1:39b, 1:43a, 1:57a; ?1517-̆ ¹No 2:54b; 1586 Sohak 6:9b), ho˙kwo k (1481 Twusi 8:33-4, 15:5a), ho˙kwo n' (1459 Wel 17:54a; 1463 Pep 6:15b; 1482 Kum-sam 2:37a), ho˙kwo '˙la (1447 Sek 6:46a; 1459 Wel 1:13b, 10:4b); ho˙key (1447 Sek 24:3a, 1459 Wel 21:219b), ho˙kuy (1447 Sek se:6a, 9:5a, 24:2b);

ho˙m ye (1447 Sek 9:12a, 9:17b, 13:22b, 13:23a, 19:7a, 19:7b, 21:68b, 23:34b, 24:28b; 1459 Wel 2:16a, 2:53a, 10:20b, 21:120a, 21:146a; 1462 ¹Nung 1:113a, 2:8b, 2:20b; 1463 Pep 3:178b, 5:212b; 1463/4 Yeng 2:126a; ?1468-̆ Mong 62ab; 1475 Nay 1:76-7; 1482 Kum-sam 2:5b, 2:7b, 3:3b, 5:40b; ?1468-̆ Mong 12a, 62ab, 1481 Twusi 7:31b; 1586 Sohak 2:9b), ho˙m ye n' (1447 Sek 24:6b, 1459 Wel 1:12b, 1:49b, 8:62b, 10:18a; 18:18b; 1462 ¹Nung 1:77b, 3:47b, 5:85b, 7:73b; 1463 Pep 4:75a, 1463/4 Yeng 2:70a, 1464 Kumkang 64b, 1466 Kup 2:64a; 1482 Kum-sam 2:5b, 5:48-9);

hol (1481 Twusi 7:20b, 8:4b, 15:47b; 1459 Wel 1:18a, 18:13b; 1464 Kumkang 81b, 87b; 1475 Nay 1:35b; 1482 Kum-sam 2:20a; 1518 Sohak-cho 8:13b; 1586 Sohak 2:9b), holq (1459 Wel 8:69b); hol ˙tta (1463 Pep 4:176b) = hol ˙ta (?1517-̆ Pak 1:10a, 1586 Sohak 6:50b); ho˙l ye (1463 Pep 3:86a; 1464 Kumkang 69b; 1481 Twusi 21:38a); ho˙l ywo (1447 Sek 6:24a, 1462 ¹Nung 2:81a, ?1517-̆ Pak 1:3a); holq ˙t ol (1462 ¹Nung 3:68b) = hol ˙tt ol (1463/4 Yeng 1:5b); hol s (1475 Nay se:6a, 1:34a, 1:77a, 3:61a; 1482 Kum-sam 5:10b); hol ˙ss ol (1462 ¹Nung 1:29a) = holq ˙s ol (1462 ¹Nung 2:61a); hol ˙s i (1481 Twusi 8:1b) = hol ˙ss i (1463 Pep 2:60a), hol ˙ss i˙Gwo (1447 Sek 9:37a) = hol ˙s iGwo (1482 Kum-sam 2:20b); hol ˙ss i˙la (1447 Sek 6:46a, 1459 Wel 2:66b, 1462 ¹Nung 1:2b) = hol ˙s i˙la (1465 Wen se:8b, se:77a); hol ˙ss i˙m ye (1459 Wel 2:60a); hol ˙ss i˙n i (1459 Wel 2:16a; 1462 ¹Nung 1:2b, 3:12b) = hol ˙s i[˙]n i (1482 Nam 2:6b); hol ˙ss oy (1447 Sek 6:2a, 13:36a, 19:25b, 24:40a; 1459 Wel 2:60a; 1462 ¹Nung 9:22a, 10:18a, 21:142b; 1463 Pep 1:164a) = hol [˙]ss oy (1463 Pep 1:158b) = hol ˙s oy (1481 Twusi 7:5a); ho˙l i (1447 Sek 13:15a; 1459 Wel 9:52a,

14:31b; 1462 ¹Nung 1:8b, 1:75a, 7:18a; 1463 Pep 1:208a, 2:6b, 2:28b; 1464 Kumkang 43a; 1465 Wen 1:2:2:4a; ?1468⁻ Mong 10b; 1481 Twusi 7:7b, 22:7b); *ho'l i ˙za* (1463/4 Yeng 2:111a); *ho'l i ˙Gwo* (1459 Wel 21:49b, 1481 Twusi 7:7b, 8:29a; ?1517⁻ Pak 1:7b, 1:64a, 1:74a) = *ho'l i [˙]Gwo* (1459 Wel 21:49b; 1481 Twusi 22:7b; ?1517⁻ Pak 1:74a); *ho'l i ˙'la* (1447 Sek 6:1b; 1459 Wel 1:17a, 2:36b, 7:15b, 8:7a, 9:35de, 10:14b; 1462 ¹Nung 1:44a; 1463 Pep 3:47a; 1475 Nay se:6a); *ho'l i 'l ˙ss oy* (1447 Sek 6:2b; 1459 Wel 1:28a, 2:61a, 7:15b) = *ho'l i 'l s oy* (1481 Twusi 8:2b); *ho'l i ˙'n i* (1459 Wel 1:49b, 1462 ¹Nung 5:85b, 1465 Wen 1:2:3:6a) = *hol[˙]l i ˙'n i* (1463 Pep 4:86b); *ho'l i 'n t ay n'* (1482 Nam 2:6ab); *ho'l i '-ngi ˙'ta* (1447 Sek 6:4a, 24:28a, 1459 Wel 1:17a, 10:12b); *ho'l i '-ngi s ˙kwo* (1459 Wel 9:24a, 23:91b; 1482 Kum-sam 2:4ab); *ho'l i 'n ˙t ye* (1475 Nay 1:7a); *ho'l ye* (1462 ¹Nung 3:43b; 1463 Pep 3:86a); *ho˙la* (1447 Sek 6:9b, 9:41a; 1459 Wel 7:42a, 8:8b; 1481 Twusi 8:7a, 25:56b; 1482 Kum-sam 5:14a; 1482 Nam 1:50b; ?1517⁻ Pak 1:6a); *ho˙la 'n ˙t oy* (1447 Sek 9:26b; 1459 Wel 13:35b, 1462 ¹Nung 3:24b; 1482 Kum-sam 2:2a);
Unexplained: *coy˙cwo ˙hol ˙˙syeng ˙i* (1518 Sohak-cho 8:37b) 'those who have talent'.

hon (1445 ¹Yong 47, 123; 1447 Sek 6:15b, 6:19a, 6:22a, 9:19-20, 13:33b, 13:39a, 13:47a, 13:39a, 24:2a; 1459 Wel 1:14ab, 1:23b, 1:46a, 2:12a, 7:7b, 7:48a, 8:38b, 10:8b, 10:9a, 10:19a, 17:12v, 18:13b, 21:34ab, 21:129a, 21:216a; 1462 ¹Nung 1:3a, 1:18b, 1:23b, 1:77b, 1:113a, 2:81a, 2:92b, 2:98a, 2:111a; 1463 Pep se:23a, 2:24a, 2:26a, 2:172ab, 3:180ab; 1464 Kumkang 72b; 1465 Wen 2:3:2:68a; ?1468⁻ Mong 20b, 47b; 1475 Nay 1:25b, 2:2:47b; 1481 Twusi 7:23b, 8:13b, 8:42a, 13:13a, 16:61b, 20:29a, 21:3b, 21:20a; 1482 Kum-sam 2:68b, 3:25b, 5:30-1; ?1517⁻ Pak 1:64a; ?1517⁻ ¹No 2:53b; 1586 Sohak 2:9b, 4:13a); *ho˙n ywo* (1459 Wel 8:95a); *hon ˙t ol* (1445 ¹Yong 69; 1459 Wel 17:17b, 17:33b), *hon ˙t on* (1447 Sek 24:18a; 1459 Wel 2:70b; 1481 Twusi 8:7a); *hon ˙t ay* (1447 Sek 24:49b, 1459 Wel 8:101b, 1481 Twusi 24:13a); *hon ˙t oy* (1462 ¹Nung 7:54a); *ho˙n i* (1445 ¹Yong 6, 18; 1447 Sek 6:5ab, 6:6a, 6:17b, 6:22a, 9:19-20; 1459 Wel se:11a, 18:7b, 21:216ab, 23:65b; 1462 ¹Nung 1:53a, 2:17b, 2:40b, 7:27a; 1463 Pep 1:249a, 3:196b, 6:144a; 1465 Wen 1:1:1:45b, 3:3:1:62a; ?1468⁻ Mong 20b; 1475 Nay se:8a, 1:18a; 1481 Twusi 7:13b, 8:9a, 15:42b, 15:47b, 16:70b, 22:50a; 1482 Kum-sam 2:1b, 2:2a, 3:3b, 3:19b, 3:34b; 1518 Sohak-cho 10:3a); *ho˙n i ˙za* (1447 Sek 24:20b; 1482 Kum-sam 2:3a); *ho˙n i ˙'la* (1447 Sek 6:2b; 1459 Wel 7:44b, 7:70a; 1462 ¹Nung 1:113a, 4:11a, 10:42b; 1463 Pep 2:113b, 2:173a; 1464 Kumkang 11a; 1475 Nay 2:1:30b; 1482 Kum-sam 2:3a; 1482 Nam 2:5a) = *ho˙n i ˙'[˙]la* (1465 Wen 2:3:1:38b, 1481 Twusi 16:47b; 1482 Nam 2:5a); *ho˙n i -ngi s ˙kwo* (1445 ¹Yong 28); *ho˙n i ˙Ga* (1481 Twusi 7:14a, 10:42a); *ho˙n i ˙Gwo* (1518 Sohak-cho 10:24b) = *ho˙n i [˙]Gwo* (1481 Twusi 7:40a); *ho˙n i ˙ya* (?1468⁻ Mong 31a, 31b); *ho˙na* (1462 ¹Nung 2:89b); *ho-˙tos* (1447 Sek 13:45a, 1462 ¹Nung 1:53a)

‖ *˙ho˙ya* (1445 ¹Yong 123; 1447 Sek se:2b, 6:1a, 6:3b, 6:4a, 6:8a, 6:8b, 6:9a, 6:11a, 6:13b, 6:15b, 6:16b; 6:23a, 6:27b, 6:34a, 6:35b, 9:4b, 9:14a, 9:24a, 9:40a, 13:19a, 13:36a, 13:43b, 13:49b, 13:57a, 13:57b, 13:58a, 13:59a, 13:61a, 13:58a, 13:59a, 13:61a, 18:26b, 19:6a, 19:8a, 19:29b, 23:11b, 23:29a, 24:6b, 24:29a, 24:37b; 1459 Wel 1:12b, 1:15a, 1:16b, 1:17b, 1:30ab, 1:53a, 2:42b, 2:60a, 2:69a, 7:13b, 7:17b, 7:31-2, 8:7a, 8:104b, 9:52a, 10:31a, 10:31b, 13:35b, 17:35a, 13:43b, 17:54a, 17:85a, 18:3a, 18:7b, 18:26b, 21:20a, 21:120b, 21:129b; 1462 ¹Nung 1:58a, 1:90b, 2:6b, 2:67a, 3:42b, 6:29a, 7:13a, 7:24a, 7:73b, 10:1b, 10:18a; 1463 Pep se:21a, 1:208a, 2:172ab, 2:226a, 3:47a, 3:104b, 3:196b, 3:197a, 4:75a, 4:154b; 1463/4 Yeng 2:62a; 1464 Kumkang 79b, 87b; 1465 Wen se:5a, 1:2:2:136a; ?1468⁻ Mong 22b, 32b, 43a, 62b; 1475 Nay 2:1:16a; 1481 Twusi 8:27b; 1482 Kum-sam 2:1b, 2:2a; 1485 Kwan 3a, 4b; ?1517⁻ Pak 1:3a, 1:6a, 1:18b, 1:54a; ?1517⁻ ¹No 2:19b, 2:36a; 1550 ¹Yenghem 8b; 1586 Sohak 2:9b); *˙ho.ya* (?1468⁻ Mong 13b; 1475 Nay 1:77b, 1:84a, 2:2:17b; 1481 Twusi 6:43a, 7:2b, 7:9b, 7:12a, 8:2b, 8:33b, 8:52a, 16:19a, 16:37b, 20:29a, 22:7b, 22:34-5, 23:44a, 25:18a; 1482 Kum-sam 2:10a, 2:24b, 2:57a, 2:65a, 3:27b, 3:31a, 3:50b, 5:35b, 5:40b; 1482 Nam 1:24a, 2:2b, 2:63a), *˙ho.ya ˙sye* (1481 Twusi 25:56b), *˙ho.ya n'* (1481 Twusi 7:29a), *˙ho.ya two* (1459 Wel 1:13a, 21:20a; 1481 Twusi 22:7b, 24:59b), *˙ho.ya ˙za* (1447 Sek 6:2b; 1459 Wel 1:47a, 10:14b; 1462 ¹Nung 1:44a) = *˙ho˙ya za* (1586 Sohak 4:9b); *˙ho˙ye* (1518 Sohak-cho 8:33b), *˙ho˙ye ˙sye* (?1517⁻ Pak 1:54b; 1518 Sohak-cho 8:38-9);

˙ho.ya˙nol (1447 Sek 6:8b, 23:23b; 1459 Wel 7:15b; ?1468⁻ Mong 32ab; 1481 Twusi 22:35a; 1482

Nam 1:30b); ˙ho.yaˑn ywo (1482 Kum-sam 3:52a); ˙ho.yasiˑnol (1459 Wel 2:64a, 1482 Nam 1:14a); ˙ho.yaˑton (1482 Nam 1:44-5)

˙hokeˑtun (1447 Sek 24:3a, 1459 Wel 21:34ab); ˙hokeˑna (1447 Sek 13:52a, 1462 ¹Nung 8:77a); ˙hokeˑnul (1447 Sek 6:16a, 1475 Nay 2:1:30a); ˙hokanˑt iˑla (1459 Wel 17:36b), ˙hokaˑn ywo (1481 Twusi 16:1b); ˙hoˑkesiˑnol (1459 Wel 2:5a); ˙hoˑkesiˑn i ˑGwa (1459 Wel 1:12b); ˙hokesˑta (1481 Twusi 21:42a); ˙hoˑke.n i ˑGwa (1482 Kum-sam 3:55a)

˙hoteˑla (1447 Sek 6:15b, 6:30a, 24:3ab; 1459 Wel 2:42b; 1586 Sohak 5:48b), ˙hotaˑla (1447 Sek 6:24b, 1459 Wel 7:14b, ?1517- Pak 1:37b); ˙hoten (1447 Sek 6:19a), ˙hoteˑn i (1447 Sek 6:8-9, 6:19a, 19:40b; 1459 Wel 2:42b, 7:24b, 7:29b; 1481 Twusi 7:29a), ˙hoˑte.n i ''la (1459 Wel 1:8ab); ˙hoˑtan (1459 Wel 7:13b); ˙hoˑtan (1459 Wel 1:7-8, 7:13b, 23:65b), ˙hotaˑn i (1447 Sek 13:57b, 24:3a; 1463 Pep 2:5b, ?1517- Pak 1:58b), ˙hoˑta.n i ''la (1463 Pep 1:158b); ˙hoˑte-ngi ''ta (1447 Sek 6:15a), ˙hoˑta-ngi ''ta (1463 Pep 2:4b); ˙hoteˑtun (1447 Sek 19:34ab, 1481 Twusi 15:31b); ˙hoˑtesiˑta (1447 Sek 6:1a, 6:44a; 1459 Wel 1:18b, 2:26-7); ˙hoteˑsin (1447 Sek 13:58a); ˙hoˑtesiˑn i (1449 Kok 41, 1459 Wel 10:18b); ˙hotwoˑta (1481 Twusi 7:12ab, 21:15a; 1482 Kum-sam 2:27b, 2:28b; 1482 Nam 1:36a; ?1517- Pak 1:46b), ˙hoˑtwoˑta (1518 Sohak-cho 10:18b), ˙hotwuˑta (1462 ¹Nung 3:116b), ˙hoˑtwuˑta (1518 Sohak-cho 10:18b)

˙honoˑta (1447 Sek 6:2a, 6:14b; 1481 Twusi 7:2a, 8:1b, 8:52a); ˙honon (1447 Sek se:1a, 9:33a; 1451 Hwun-en 1b), ˙hoˑnon (1459 Wel 21:215b, 1462 ¹Nung 1:77b, 8:104b; 1518 Sohak-cho 9:90a); ˙hononˑkwo (1447 Sek 6:27a); ˙hononˑta (1459 Wel 9:46a, 1462 ¹Nung 1:84a, 1481 Twusi 8:24a, ?1517- Pak 1:31b); ˙hoˑnon t oy (?1517- ¹No 1:35b); ˙honoˑn i (1459 Wel 1:30ab, 5:59b, 9:23-4; 1462 ¹Nung 6:43a; 1481 Twusi 7:24b, 10:42a; 1482 Nam 1:36b); ˙hoˑno.n i ''la (1447 Sek 6:5b, 13:2a; 1459 Wel 1:23b, 2:2a, 10:18b; 1459 Wel 1:11a; 1462 ¹Nung 6:43a; 1481 Twusi 20:34b; 1586 Sohak 2:25a), = ˙hono.n i ''la (1481 Twusi 16:19b) = ˙honoˑn i ˑla (1482 Nam 2:6ab), ˙hoˑno.n i ˑnon (1586 Sohak 4:43a), ?1517- Pak 1:58a); ˙hoˑno.n i s ˑka (1447 Sek 6:18a) = ˙hono.n i s ˑka (1447 Sek 6:16b), ˙honoˑn i n' (1481 Twusi 16:39b); ˙honoˑn ywo (1462 ¹Nung 2:111a, 1586 Sohak 6:58a); ˙hoˑnwon (1459 Wel 13:35b; 1462 ¹Nung 1:90b, 2:17a, 7:74b), ˙honwon (1447 Sek se:6a, 6:36a, 9:40b, 13:18-9; 1459 Wel se:16a; 1463 Pep 5:212b; 1482 Nam 2:30b; 1586 Sohak 6:44a), ˙honwoˑn i (1447 Sek 19:29b; 1459 Wel 1:11b, 13:37a, 21:125b; 1481 Twusi 21:13b), ˙hoˑnwo.n i s ˑka (1447 Sek 6:16b); ˙honwoˑla (1447 Sek 6:8a, 1459 Wel 8:35a, 10:4b, 10:18a; 1462 ¹Nung 1:17b; 1475 Nay se:6a, 1:37a; 1481 Twusi 7:5a, 8:35a, 15:23b, 22:26a, 25:23a); ˙hoˑnwo-ngi ''ta (1447 Sek 6:25b); ˙honwosˑta (1481 Twusi 20:4b, 20:29a)

˙hosiˑkwo (1447 Sek 13:15a, 1459 Wel 10:6a, 21:219a); ˙hoˑsikeˑtun (1459 Wel 8:48b); ˙hosilˑss oy (1459 Wel 2:62b); ˙hosiˑta (1447 Sek 13:30b); ˙hoˑsitan (1459 Wel 23:65a); ˙hoˑsitenˑka (?1517- Pak 1:51a); ˙hoˑsitasˑta (1459 Wel 21:208a); ˙hositeˑla (1447 Sek 13:59a); ˙hosin (1447 Sek 9:29a, 13:35b; 1475 Nay 1:40a); ˙hoˑsitwoˑta (1481 Twusi 8:10b); ˙hosiˑna (1482 Kum-sam 5:10b); ˙hosiˑn i (1445 ¹Yong 107; 1447 Sek 6:9b, 23:53b; 1462 ¹Nung 2:92a; 1464 Kumkang 81b; 1482 Kum-sam 4:45a), ˙hoˑsi.n i ''la (1462 ¹Nung 2:49a, 1463 Pep 4:192-3); ˙hoˑsinoˑn i (1447 Sek 6:5b, 24:9a; 1459 Wel 1:10b, 1:25b); ˙hosiˑm ye (1459 Wel 2:58b), ˙hosiˑm ye ˑn (1449 Kok 36); ˙hosilq (1449 Kok 50; 1447 Sek 23:52b, 53a); ˙hosilˑss oy (1445 ¹Yong 34, 92, 121; 1459 Wel 2:62b), ˙hosilˑs oy (1465 Wen 1:2:1:16b); ˙hoˑsi.l i ''la (1459 Wel 1:7-8); ˙hoˑsi.l i ˑl ˑss oy (1445 ¹Yong 92, 1459 Wel 9:11b), ˙hoˑsi.l i ''la (1459 Wel 1:7-8); ˙hosilaˑn ˑt oy (1481 Twusi 22:7b); ˙hosin (1447 Sek 9:29a, 1459 Wel se:9a, 1475 Nay 1:40a), ˙hosinˑta ˑmaˑta (1459 Wel 1:15a); ˙hosiˑn i (1445 ¹Yong 42, 64; 1447 Sek 6:9b; 1459 Wel 1:52a; 1449 Kok 43; 1465 Wen 1:1:2:125b; 1482 Kum-sam 3:3b, 5:14a), ˙hoˑsi.n i ''la (1447 Sek 23:42a, 1465 Wen se:6a, ?1468- Mong 49b); ˙hoˑsinoˑta (1447 Sek 13:26b); ˙hoˑsinon (1447 Sek 6:5b), ˙hosiˑnon (1447 Sek 23:22b); ˙hoˑsinonˑka (1447 Sek 13:25b); ˙hoˑsinoˑn i (1447 Sek 6:5b; 1459 Wel 1:10b, 2:69a, 9:11b, 9:35de; 1463 Pep 4:117a; 1465 Wen se:6a); ˙hoˑsinoˑn i ''la (1465 Wen se:6a); ˙hoˑsinoˑn ywo (1447 Sek 13:26a); ˙hosiˑnwon (1462 ¹Nung 1:86a, 1463 Pep 5:169b), ˙hoˑsinwonˑt i (1459 Wel 17:42a); ˙hoˑsi-ngi ''ta (1459 Wel 21:218b), ˙hoˑsitwoˑta (1481 Twusi 8:10b);

`ho˙sya (1447 Sek 6:4b, 6:9b, 6:17b, 13:27a; 1459 Wel 2:36b, 2:70b, 8:93b, 9:35de; 1462 ¹Nung 3:68b; 1463 Pep 2:231b; 1482 Kum-sam 2:2b), `hosya (1459 Wel 8:93b, 1463 Pep 2:231b, 1475 Nay 2:1:43a, 1481 Twusi 22:46a), `hosya˙za (1447 Sek 6:12a, 1463 Pep 1:16a); `hosya˙m i (1462 ¹Nung 10:42b, 1463 Pep 5:100a, 1482 Kum-sam 5:14a), `ho˙sya.m i˙la (1459 Wel 14:58a), `hosya˙m ay (1459 Wel 14:59a), `hosya˙m olwo (1482 Nam 1:33b), `hosya˙m on (1462 ¹Nung 3:2a, 4:13ab; 1463 Pep 6:145b, 7:180b); `ho˙sya˙na (1465 Wen se:6a); `ho˙syan (1447 Sek 13:25b, 1463 Pep 6:144a), `hosyan (1447 Sek 6:7b, 1463 Pep 4:167a); `ho˙syal (1465 Wen 1:1:2:75b)

2.12.4.5. Bound stems.

It is difficult to predict the accent of later syllables in verb forms incorporating the common bound stems showing status, respect, and aspect. We will assume a basic and etymological accent for -˙k^e/a- (and variants -˙G^e/a- and -˙$^e/a$-), the effective, and for -˙t^e/a-, the retrospective. That is needed to account for such forms as:

RETROSPECTIVE nilk˙ten (1481 Twusi 21:42b), nilo˙ten (1459 Wel 9:36d), mwot˙te˙n i (1445 ¹Yong 9), is˙ten˙t ay n' (1464 Kumkang 79b), is˙ten˙ta (?1517-˙Pak 1:37b), is˙tesin˙ka (1445 ¹Yong 88, 89), pat˙te˙n ywo (?1517-˙Pak 1:19b), mek˙te˙la (?1517-˙¹No 2:53b); `ho˙tan cyen˙cho˙lwo (1459 Wel 7:13b), ...

EFFECTIVE cephu˙kesi˙n ywo (1449 Kok 123), kap˙kan˙t i.n i ˙'la (1459 Wel 18:18b), kos˙ke˙sin ma˙lon (1447 Sek 13:63a), me˙ke˙ta (?1517-˙¹No 2:39a), me˙ke˙nul (1447 Sek 6:32a), is˙kesi˙ton (1475 Nay 1:40a), na˙ma is˙kesi˙nol (1447 Sek 23:56b), nilo˙kesi˙tun (1482 Kum-sam 4:50b) = nilu˙kesi˙tun (1447 Sek 9:27a), nilo˙kesi˙na (1459 Wel 18:49b), talo˙kesi˙nul (1445 ¹Yong 101),˙ca˙kesi˙nol (1482 Nam 1:28b), `wo˙kesi˙nol (1459 Wel 7:10a) = `wo˙nasi˙nol (1447 Sek 6:44b), ˙khu˙kenul˙za (1482 Kum-sam 2:16a), ...

Quite often the accent of the marker will be suppressed for prosodic or other reasons that are hard to pinpoint. But no word of that sort will lack dots altogether: one or more of the other syllables will be marked as accented.

The situation for the PROCESSIVE is more complicated, so we put its dot in parentheses in citing the morpheme -(˙)no-. A number of the forms are attested as accentual doublets or near-doublets:

`ho˙non (1459 Wel 21:215b; 1462 ¹Nung 1:77b, 8:124b; ?1517-˙¹No 1:35b; 1518 Sohak-cho 9:90a; 1588 Mayng 13:13a) but also `honon (1447 Sek se:1a, 9:33a; 1481 Twusi 7:1b); `ho˙no.n i (1586 Sohak 2:30b, 4:43a) but ['be many'] `hano˙n i (1445 ¹Yong 2, Manlyek text; 1459 Wel 1:30ab; 1482 Nam 1:36b); `ho˙no.n i ˙'la (1447 Sek 6:5b, 13:2a; 1459 Wel 1:11a, 1:23b, 2:2a; 1462 ¹Nung 6:43a, 8: 86b; 1481 Twusi 20:34b;˙?1517-˙Pak 1:58a; 1586 Sohak 2:25a) but also `hono˙n i ˙'la (1482 Nam 2:6ab) and `hono.n i ˙'la (1481 Twusi 16:91b).

˙kanon (1447 Sek 6:19a, 1481 Twusi 7:10b) and `kano˙n i (1445 ¹Yong 2, 1447 Sek 6:9b) but ˙ka˙non˙ta (?1517-˙¹No 1:1a)

`ho˙nwon (1459 Wel 13:35b, 1462 ¹Nung 1:90b) but also `honwon (1447 Sek se:6a)

`hosi˙non (1447 Sek 23:22b) but also `ho˙sinon (1447 Sek 6:5b)

¨a˙no.n i ˙'la (1482 Kum-sam 2:3a) and `pwo˙no.n i ˙'la (1459 Wel 21:206a, 1465 Wen 1:2:1:39b) but also ¨sano˙n i (1447 Sek 13:10a, 1481 Twusi 25:23a)

Processive modifier forms are usually unaccented: ···[˙]non. The common form is.non ··· ' ·· that is/stays' is always unaccented, and that is true also of its contracted versions 'ys.non and 's.non with rare exceptions that imply *is˙non as the model: towoy˙ye 'ys˙no˙n i (1481 Twusi 8:42a), ~ ˙Gwo 7:26b), towoy˙ye 'ys˙no˙n ywo (1481 Twusi 8:42a); ma[˙]ka 's˙non (?1517-˙Pak 1:40a).

Processive indicative assertive forms (···no˙ta) never carry the accent on the aspect marker: ˙hono˙ta (1447 Sek 6:2a, 6:14b; 1481 Twusi 7:2a, 8:1b, 8:52a), ¨ano˙ta (1462 ¹Nung 2:114b), i˙kuyno˙ta (1481 Twusi 15:6a), mwo˙lono˙ta (1462 ¹Nung 1:16b), mekno˙ta (1481 Twusi 25:18a).

When the modulator -˙w^u/o- is attached to the processive, the combined form -˙nwo- (sometimes -˙nwu-) is usually accented: `ho˙nwon (1459 Wel 13:35b, 1462 ¹Nung 1:90b), is˙nwo˙n i (1447 Sek 6:20a), tut˙nwon ka (1449 Kok 2), towoy˙nwo˙n i (1463 Pep 2:28b), cap˙nwola (1481 Twusi 10:7b), ip˙nwola (1481 Twusi 8:42a), `hosi˙nwon (1462 ¹Nung 1:86a), wolm˙ki˙si˙nwo˙swo-ngi ˙'ta (1463 Pep

2:47a). But not in these examples: ˙honwon (1447 Sek se:6a), [˙NGWEN] honwon ˙t un ... (1579 Kwikam 1:24b); ˙honwo˙la (1459 Wel 10:4b); ¨mwutnwo˙la (1481 Twusi 22:39b) = ¨mwunnwo˙la (1481 Twusi 16:39b); ˙po˙lanwo˙la (1447 Sek se:6a); ˙wonwos˙ta (1481 Twusi 7:39a); ˙twu-'ys.nwon (1482 Nam 1:15a); nilu˙sinwon (1447 Sek 9:35b; CF 1459 Wel 55-6).

After the honorific marker, the processive is sometimes accented — ˙hosi˙non (1447 Sek 23:22b), but usually not: ˙ho˙sinon (1447 Sek 6:5b), ˙ho˙sino˙ta (1447 Sek 13:26b); sisu˙sinon˙ka (1449 Kok 124), tas.ko˙sino˙n i (1447 Sek 6:12a), nilu˙sino˙n i (1447 Sek 13:47b, 1462 ¹Nung 1:38a), ˙ka˙sinon (1459 Wel 2:52a), ˙nye˙sino˙n i '-ngi s ˙kwo (1447 Sek 6:23a), ¨alo˙sino˙n i '-ngi s ˙ka (1447 Sek 6:14-5). After the deferential -¨zop- the processive morpheme is normally not accented, but there are a couple of exceptions: cwo¨ccop˙non (1463 Pep 1:24b), ki˙tuli¨zop˙no.n i '˙la (1447 Sek 24:5b).

When the polite marker -ngi is attached the processive morpheme is always accented (-˙no-ngi ...): ˙pho˙no-ngi ''ta (1459 Wel 8:94b), ˙wo˙no-ngi ''ta (1447 Sek 6:29b), ˙wosi˙no-ngi ''ta (1459 Wel 10:8a). And -ngi itself never carries an accent.

The underlying accent of the honorific marker -ᵁ⁄ₒ˙si- often surfaces: ˙ho˙sino˙n (1459 Wel 1:25b), ˙ho˙sino˙n i (1447 Sek 6:5b; 1459 Wel 1:10b, 2:69a), ˙ho˙sino˙n i ''la (1465 Wen se:6a), ˙ho˙sino˙n i '-ngi s ˙kwo (1447 Sek 24:9a, 1459 Wel 9:35de), ˙ho˙sino˙n i ˙si˙n i ''la (1463 Pep 4:117a); ˙ho˙sino˙ta (1447 Sek 13:26b), ˙ho˙siten ˙ka (?1517- Pak 1:51a); kwutu˙si˙ta (1463 Pep 2:173a); nwopho˙si˙kwo (1463 Pep 2:173a); tulu˙si˙kwo (1447 Sek 13:30b); sisu˙sinon ˙ka (1449 Kok 124); nilku˙si˙nwon (1465 Wen se:68a); ceho˙sya (1449 Kok 46), cwocho˙sya (1459 Wel 8:93b, 1463 Pep 3:19b), meku˙sya (1459 Wel 10:9a), anco˙sya (1459 Wel 8:101a); ... . Sometimes the accent appears on the preceding vowel: ¨ep˙susi˙kwo (1462 ¹Nung 1:18b), ¨ep˙susi˙ta (1449 Kok 53), ¨ep˙susya˙m i (1463 Pep 2:15-6) — CF ¨ep.su˙sya (1463 Pep 2:22a); ¨sa˙mosi˙n i (1447 Sek 6:4a); ¨a˙losi˙m ye (1465 Wen 1:2:3:6a); te˙pu˙lusi˙n i (1449 Kok 52); ¨wu˙lusi˙kwo (1459 Wel 8:101a); ˙tu˙lusya˙m i (1447 Sek 23:44a); twuthe˙wusi˙m ye (1462 ¹Nung 10:42b); ... . We can regard this as a prosodic displacement which pushes the accent back a syllable; there are no examples of the dot appearing on both the sibilant syllable AND the epenthetic vowel. When there is a dot on the syllable preceding ...˙si... it is usually part of the accent pattern of the stem: mwo˙lo˙sya (1445 ¹Yong 19, 1459 Wel 21:210b), na˙thwo˙sya.l i ''la (1459 Wel 17:78b), il˙Gwu˙syan (1459 Wel 21:218b), ˙tho˙si˙l i ˙le˙la (?1517- Pak 1:64b), ne˙ki˙sya (1447 Sek 6:17b), a˙ni ''sya (1463 Pep 2:6a), ...

The basic rising accent of the deferential -¨zoW- is the result of contraction from *-zo˙po- (< *-oso˙po-) and it surfaces for some of the forms: cap¨sopke˙n i (1459 Wel 21:203a), mak¨sopke˙nul (1459 Wel 10:1b), ilkhot¨copnwon (1482 Kum-sam 4:11b), pat¨copte˙la (1459 Wel 2:37b), tut¨copkwo ˙za (1449 Kok 106), ... But in many of the forms only the low pitch survives: ˙hozo˙Wa (1447 Sek 24:5b), ¨pwozo˙Wa.n i (1459 Wel 8:17b), ˙kazo˙Wwon (1459 Wel 8:92b), tutco˙Wolq (1447 Sek 9:2a), ¨a˙zoWol ˙kka (1445 ¹Yong 43), ˙hozop˙kwo (1447 Sek 6:1b, 24:5b), ¨sitcop˙key (1447 Sek 24:10b), ˙pwozop˙ta (1459 Wel 8:28a, 18:81a), ˙hozop˙ten (1447 Sek 13:51a), ... Sometimes, instead, a high pitch appears, as the result of a prosodic displacement from the following element: ˙pwo˙zowa ˙two (1462 ¹Nung 1:47a), ˙ka˙zoWa ˙za (1447 Sek 23:40a), ˙ho˙zoWo˙m ye (1447 Sek 6:17a), ˙ho˙zopke˙na (1447 Sek 13:53b), ˙ho˙zopno˙n i (1463 Pep 5:186a), ...

2.12.5. Accent and spelling in Middle Korean texts.

The accent dots of Middle Korean were written to the left of the syllable and therefore vary in where they stand in the stream of phonemes depending on the extent to which morpheme identifications are permitted to override phonetic considerations. The text Wel.in chen-kang ci kok (= 1449 Kok) normally separates particles from a preceding noun that ends in a resonant: ye˙lum ˙ul (99), ˙nom ˙i ... ˙nom ˙ol (11), ˙ema ¨nim ˙i (17), mozom ˙o˙lan (121); nwun ˙ey (2), cey ˙kan ˙ol (40); ˙sal ˙i (41), ˙stol ˙ol ... mye˙nol ˙i (36); ... . But forms of the substantive are excepted: pwus˙kulywo˙m i (120). And the syllabification is phonetic for nouns with a voiceless final: ci˙p ul (45); ˙pa˙p ol (122); kwo˙c i (7), mi˙th uy ˙non ... (70). Noun + copula, like verb stem + ending, was left unanalyzed, and that accounts for the syllabification of /kwo-mil/ in ˙mwom ˙i ... ceyye˙kwo.m il ˙ss oy (134).

Sekpo sangcel (= 1447 Sek) spells noun + particle according to the spoken syllables, but certain nouns ending in ...ng are excepted, probably because they are clearly of Chinese origin: cywungsoyng `i (6:19b), ¨yang ˙o˙lwo (6:24b); CF ¨cywu˙ng uy (6:19a), susu˙ng uy (6:29b), for which the Chinese origin is less apparent. Examples of the usual syllabification: no˙m oy (se:6a); ˙ku˙l ul (se:6a); ˙pu˙l i (6:33a); ˙mwu˙l i (6:28a); ˙sto˙l i (6:13b, 14a), ˙sto˙l ol (6:15a), a˙to˙l i (6:5a, 9b), a˙to˙l ol (6:3b, 5b), a˙to˙l oy (13:19a); ha˙no˙l i (6:35b), ha˙no˙l on (6:36a) ¨i˙l ol (6:8a, 18a, 26a, 27a; 9:5a; 13:33b; 19:40b), ¨i˙l i (6:9a; 9:17b; 19:10b, 20b, 24b) ¨i˙l oy (se:5b); ¨ma˙l ol (6:8b, 13:47b, 24:1b), ¨ma˙l on (6:36a, 9:27a), ¨ma˙l i (6:36a, 25:53b) tuthu˙l i (6:30b); ci˙p uy ˙sye (6:16a), ˙tul cci˙p i (6:35b); ¨hoyngtye˙k ul (1447 Sek 6:2b); nye˙k ul (6:25a), nye˙k uy ˙sye (6:33b), nye˙k o˙lwo n' (1446 Sek 6:3a); ce˙k i ... (6:40a), ce˙k uy (6:19a), ce˙k u˙lan (6:11a).

The text of [1]Yongpi echen ka (= 1445 [1]Yong) follows the spoken syllables: ˙no˙m i (48), ˙no˙m on (77); ˙kwulwu˙m i (42), mozo˙m ol (85), ¨nim-˙ku˙m i (49) ˙hyen pe˙n ul (31); mo˙l i (31), ˙nwun z ˙mu˙l ul (91), ¨mil ˙mu˙l i (67), ˙ku˙l ul (7), ¨pye˙l i (50, 101), palo˙l ay (2); twoco˙k i (33), twoco˙k ol (19, 115); ˙kwo˙t ol (110), ˙kwo˙t ay (26); ˙ptu˙t i (8); na˙c oy (101).

The spellings of Nayhwun (= 1475 Nay) are similar, but exceptions are made for certain morphemes with final resonants, some of which are of obvious Chinese origin (kesang ˙ul 1:70b, ¨cams.kan ˙ina 2:1:2b, si˙cyel ˙ey 3:32a, ˙chapan ˙ul 2:2:73b, kanan ˙i 2:2:59b) though others are not: ¨nim-kum ˙i (10a), swu˙l ul (3:61a). CF ˙mwo.m o˙lwo (2:1:30a), no˙m oy (1:9a), mozo˙m ay (se:6a); ˙swo˙n i (1:18a); ¨ma.l i (2:2:47b), he˙mu.l i (1:84a), ¨i.l ol (1:53a, 1:84a, 2:1:40b).

Twusi enhay (= 1481 Twusi) follows the pronunciation in syllabifying noun + particle, but makes a few exceptions for morphemes with final resonants, both Chinese (¨sya˙wong ˙ol 25:9b) and non-Chinese (swul ˙ol 15:38a, yet for the same word also swu˙l ul 8:34a).

The later version of Sohak enhay (= 1586 Sohak) generally demarcated the particles: ¨kye˙sim ˙ay (6:122a) = ¨kye˙sim ˙ay (SEE p. 267), ancum ˙ul (3:9b), a˙chom ˙uy (4:33a), kunsim ˙ul (4:9b); ¨pyeng ˙i (1586 Sohak 6:27a), ¨syeng ˙i (8:37b); ˙kul ˙ul (6:102b), ¨mal ˙i (5:95b); swon ˙ay ˙choyk ˙ul (6:102b); ... . There were a few lexicalized exceptions: cwuk˙u.m wolwo (2:11a). The adverb ¨man˙il (2:4b) 'if' reflects the Chinese source 'one in ten thousand [chances]'. And 1586 Sohak overanalyzed ¨nwul ˙ul (6:58a) = ¨nwu ˙lul (1449 Kok 52) 'whom'. The earlier version known as Pen.yek Sohak enhay (= 1518 Sohak-cho) syllabified phonetically: ka˙zo˙mye˙lwo˙m on (9:90a) − CF ka˙omyel˙wom ˙un (1586 Sohak 6:83b); ¨sa˙lo˙m uy (8:22a) − CF ¨sa˙lom ˙i (5:48b); no˙m oy (8:15a); il˙hwu˙m i (8:2b); ˙swo˙n i (10:3a) − CF ˙swo˙n ol (6:102b). Occasionally it conflated ···l ˙ul to ···l ˙lul, as in na˙la[h] ta˙soliten ˙il ˙lul [< ¨il ˙ul] (9:39a) = ˙ta˙solim ˙ul (1586 Sohak 6:35b).

None of the texts had a way to write final h or consonant clusters, so they were always syllabified phonetically: ¨nay˙h i (2); sta˙h ay (1449 Kok 41), ˙sta˙h ˙ol (1447 Sek 6:19a); wu˙h u˙lwo (1447 Sek 13:13b); tu˙lu˙h ey (1445 [1]Yong 69); ¨twuy.h ey ˙nun ... al˙ph oy ˙non ... (1445 [1]Yong 30); ˙kil˙h ul (1447 Sek 6:19a, 1449 Kok 86); ha˙nol˙h i (1445 [1]Yong 21, 30, 34); ˙tol˙h i (1449 Kok 11); an˙h ay (1475 Nay 1:4b); nam˙k ol (1449 Kok 86), nam˙k i (1449 Kok 99); nyen˙k ul (1445 [1]Yong 20), nyen˙k i (1447 Sek 6:22b, 24:43b); twos˙k ol (1475 Nay 10a); hon ¨na˙th ay (1445 [1]Yong 47).

3.0. Words.

The description of Korean grammar in this book is based on a division of Korean sentences into WORDS, and an assignment of each word to a PART OF SPEECH. The decisions on word boundaries are based on syntactic criteria, and therefore they are more generous than the decisions that underlie the writing of spaces in Hankul texts, where the criterion is purely phonological, based on the likelihood of pause when a sentence is said. A short word, such as a postpositional particle that marks the grammatical function of a noun phrase, is usually joined to the preceding word as if a suffix, so that you will not hear an overt pause or slowdown between the words; but a silent grammatical juncture lurks just below the surface of the structure, and we find it convenient to reveal that with a space in our Romanized sentences.

3.1. Inflected and uninflected words.

On the basis of internal structure, the words of Korean clearly fall into two classes: inflected and uninflected. Each inflected word consists of a STEM + an ENDING. The stem (sometimes called the

BASE) belongs to a large but limited class of constituents which do not occur except with the attachment of one of a much smaller class of endings; the endings do not occur except when attached to a stem. Apparent exceptions:

(1) Derivationally related nouns and verb stems:

  hemul < he˙mul 'error, misdeed', hemu-l- (< ?) 'tear down'
  īl < ¨il 'event, happening, matter; job, work', ¨il- 'come into being, happen'
  kēm 'black checker' (= hukci), kēm- < ¨kem- 'be black'
  kīl < ¨kil 'fathom', kī-l- < ¨kil-'be long'
  kot < ˙kwot 'straightway', kot.ta < kwot- 'be straight' (or ˙kwot 'place'?)
  kkwumi 'beef shreds', kkwumi- < ˙skwu˙mi- 'decorate'
  mak < mak 'last', mak- < mak- 'block, obstruct; ... ; complete, put an end to, ... '
  phum < *˙phwum (→ phwu˙m ey) 'bosom', phum- < ˙phwum- 'carry in the bosom'
  pis < pis 'comb', pis- < pis- 'comb the hair'
  pophul 'nap', pophu-l- '(cloth) has a nap'
  ppyēm 'span', ppyēm- 'measure by the span'
  sin < ˙sin 'shoe', sin- < ¨sin- 'wear on the feet'
  sōl 'skin pustules', sō-l- 'be itchy and sore'
  tēl 'less', tē-l- < ¨tel- 'lessen'
  tti < ˙stuy 'belt', tti- < stuy- 'wear (a belt)'

In the case of -L- stems we might conclude that the noun is the imperfect adnominal (= prospective modifier), deriving kīl 'fathom' from kīlq 'to be long', but there is little to argue against treating such cases as simply the stem. The noun of the pair kamul < ˙ko˙mol 'drought' and kamu-l- < ˙ko˙mol- 'go without rain' could be a reduction of kamulm, the regular substantive of the verb, in contrast with the irregular derived substantive kamul.um 'drought', which preserves the expected earlier form of the substantive in its uncontracted form (kamulm 'going without rain' < *˙ko˙mo˙lom); unfortunately, we lack attestations until around 1700 for either the verb stem or the noun. Neither as 'year of age' nor as 'flesh' can sal be directly related to sā-l- < ¨sal- 'live' for the nouns earlier had the low-back vowel /o/, MK sol and ˙solh, respectively. Similar: nal < ˙nolh 'warp', na-l- < nol- 'thread the warp (of a loom)'. Nor can we easily relate an 'inside' to ān- < ¨an- 'clasp to one's bosom' because the noun was earlier ˙anh (as attested by the h preserved in anphakk < anh pakk 'inside and outside'), nor cīs 'gesture' to cī(s)- < ¨ciz- 'make, do' because the noun apparently comes from an earlier ¨cus 'appearance'.

We should consider also those cases of derived nouns and adverbs that coincide with a stem having final ···i- or ···y-, such as kalkhwi 'a rake' and kalkhwi- 'to rake', toy < ˙twoy 'a measure' and toy- < ˙twoy- 'to measure', kkoy < ˙skwoy 'ruse' and kkoy- < ˙skwoy- 'cheat out of'. When verb stem and noun coincide in shape it is hard to decide which came first; often all we can say is that the two are derivationally related. In some instances the meaning of one of the pair is clearly secondary: ai lul pāy- < poy- 'conceive a child' must come from pay < ˙poy 'belly', not the other way around.

(2) The last word of Sālam sallye cwū 'Save me!' and Na com cwū 'Give me some!' is a contraction of cwuu < cwuo; compare cwuso contracted (by way of cwusyo) from cwusio 'give!'. Similar are I ke(s) pō 'Look at this!' and Ka-pō 'Go and see!' < poo. CM 1:119 is confused about these forms and those of (4) below.

(3) The stems i- 'it is' and ha- 'does; is' are often abbreviated to zero, leaving the endings standing as if free. In this book the abbreviation is shown by an apostrophe: twū si 'myen 'if it's two o'clock', pata 'ci 'it's the sea'; ka ya 'keyss.ta 'I'll have to go'.

(4) The infinitive (§9.4) has a zero alternant after certain stems, e.g. ka from ka- 'go'. In the intimate style we find commands like Ese ka 'Go on!' and I ke l' sa 'Buy this!'

(5) There are a few odd abbreviations like po' to tut' to mōs hanta = poci to tut.ci to mōs hanta 'can neither see nor hear' (similarly o' to ka' to mōs hanta 'can neither come nor go', olu' to nayli' to mōs hanta 'can neither rise nor fall'), and ...-' tus = ...-nun tus 'seemingly (...-ing)'. In Middle

Korean the *t-* forms could attach directly to the stem, and *-l-* stems elided the liquid. Starchevskiy (1890:668) described that and included the *sa* version of the particle *za*, the source of **(i)ya**, as well as *two* and *tus*; there are MK examples of that in Part II.

Unlike stems, uninflected words occur freely without the requirement that something be attached. There is a class of PARTICLES and they are very similar to the verb endings in some respects, but the nouns occur freely without a particle, in a great variety of environments, and many of the particles are found attached to verb forms (stem + ending) as well as to nouns.

3.2. Parts of speech.

In this book all the inflected words are called VERBS. There are, to be sure, many subclasses, but they share the characteristic of being stems that require the attachment of one of the inflectional endings in order to serve as a free word. The uninflected words divide into two broad categories called NOUNS and PARTICLES. The characteristic of particles, which are typically quite short, is that they occur as the last member of a PHRASE, or as part of a string that can be treated as the last member. In pronunciation they are attached to the last word of the phrase: a noun or a verb form or some other particle. These characteristics they share with forms of the copula (**i-**), a secondary subclass of verb. Typically, particles occur after nouns, but some of them also are attached to verb forms, not only those forms which often serve as the head of a nominal phrase (as does **haki** 'doing') or an adverbial phrase (as does **hakey** 'so as to do') but also forms which often stand as the head of a verbal phrase, such as **hay** 'does'. Particles that are CASE MARKERS specify valences that certain other languages express through affixes or prepositions; CONTEXTUAL particles (delimiters and particles of focus) convey information carried in many other languages by articles, adverbs, prosodic elements, or word order. Many of the particles originated as bound nouns or verb forms.

The verb ending is considered to be in construction only with its stem. The particle, on the other hand, is taken to be in construction with the entire phrase, which may end in a noun, a verb form, or one or more prior-attached particles. In a string of particles, the constituents are assumed to peel off from the right, even when two (such as **ey se**) form a frequent collocation.

3.3. Free and bound words.

The borderline between "free" and "bound" forms is not always easy to delineate and many decisions have to be somewhat arbitrary, but I try to be as consistent as possible. Every word is to some extent "bound" in that there are constraints upon its occurrence: 'eats' can take as its object 'rice' but not 'his high-jumping' though 'likes' can take both phrases as objects. But some words are much more severely bound than others, so that it is easier to list their constraints in general terms. In this book I speak of FREE and QUASI-FREE nouns, of FREE and BOUND verbs. I also speak of certain words as being SEPARABLE or INSEPARABLE, meaning that elements (such as particles) either can or cannot be inserted between those words and the other words with which they are typically in construction. Another kind of word category is that of the BOUND NOUNS, nouns that are restricted in construction to limited sets of partners. The bound ("prenoun" =) adnoun approaches the status of a noun prefix, the bound "postnoun" approaches that of a noun suffix. The bound "preverb" approaches the status of a verb prefix or an adverb, the bound "postverb" approaches that of a verb suffix. Ultimately perhaps all noun prefixes should be called "bound adnouns" and all noun suffixes should be called "bound postnouns", but I have made a division, based on the relative range of occurrence with different sets of nouns.

In the same sort of way, it might be said that those particles which appear only after nominals approach the noun subcategory of "postnouns" and those which appear only after verbals approach the category of verb endings. The difference lies in the constituency of the phrases: I consider that the particle always stands in construction with the entire remainder of the phrase.

3.4. Ionized parts of speech.

The chart labeled PARTS OF SPEECH (pp 90-91) presents a detailed overview of my analysis of Korean word types. We find three "polar" categories: the major groups of NOUN and VERB, the minor group PARTICLE. There are numerous subcategories, some interrelated in complex ways that I have tried to capture in the chart. The categories of VERBAL NOUN and POSTNOMINAL VERB are "ionized" in that they show what seem like chemical bonds (attractions) between the categories of noun and verb. The verbal nouns occur in phrases that are in construction with postnominal verbs. Some of the verbal nouns also turn up in other constructions as ordinary nouns, and some of the postnominal verbs also occur as other subcategories of verb. Certain verbal nouns are SEPARABLE, in that they can form a phrase with additional elements (such as particles) before the appearance of the postnominal verb, while other verbal nouns are INSEPARABLE. And some of the postnominal verbs are separable, in that a particle or the like can intervene between the preceding noun and the postnominal verb, while others are inseparable. Frequently an inseparable verbal noun turns out be also PRE-INSEPARABLE (that is, it combines only with INSEPARABLE postnominal verbs), but some are PRE-SEPARABLE for they occur with postnominal verbs that, with certain other verbal nouns, are separable. Auxiliary verbs are also divided into separable and inseparable.

The class of VERBS divides into TRANSITIVE and INTRANSITIVE, and the intransitive includes the subcategory of ADJECTIVE (= descriptive verb), which in turn has the one-member subcategory of COPULA, a general noun-predicator. In the same sort of way, verbal nouns have properties of transitive (vnt = transitive verbal noun), intransitive (vni = intransitive verbal noun), and adjectival (adj-n = adjectival noun). There are a few verbal nouns that are DEFECTIVE, for they occur with only a few paradigmatic forms of the postnominal verb; there are also a few DEFECTIVE VERBS. In earlier treatments I have restricted the terms "verbal noun" and "adjectival noun" to constructions with the postnominal verb and adjective **ha-** 'do/be', since those are the most common. But the extended treatment offered here is logically more consistent. A list of examples of each of the part-of-speech categories will be found in later sections (§§5-7), and information on the constructions involved should be sought in those sections and in the appropriate entries of Part II.

3.5. Shortened words.

Some words frequently appear in shortened form. We have already (§3.1) called attention to the "zero" abbreviation of **ha-** 'do/say/be' and **i-** 'be'. After a vowel these stems may fail to emerge and that leaves just the endings, standing alone as if free words: ···V **'myen** = **hamyen** 'if it does/is' or = **imyen** 'if it is'. The suppression of **i-** takes place after a vowel unless the stem is itself followed by a vowel (as in the past **iess.ta** or the infinitive **ie**), when **i-** merely reduces to **y-** after a vowel: **kama 'ta** 'it's the oven' but **kama yess.ta** 'it was the oven'. The suppression of **i-** is so common after a vowel as to be considered standard (an alternant of the copula rather than a variant), but the abbreviation of **ha-** is somewhat less predictable and therefore, except in a few complex endings like **-ulye 'myen**, it is usually treated as a shortened variant. The difference in the way that suppressed **ha-** and suppressed **i-** are treated reflects the fact that the phonological bondage of the copula with a preceding word is closer than that of **ha-**. In **ka ya 'keyss.ta** 'I'll have to go' there is no pause, but one can be inserted with the **ha-** restored as **ka ya | hakeyss.ta** 'I will have to go'. On the other hand, it sounds pedantic or bookish to say **wuli nala ita** for **wuli nala 'ta** 'it's our country'.

The shortened forms of the plain and prospective modifiers of these two verbs (**'n** = **han** 'that did; that is' or = **in** 'that is', and **'l(q)** = **hal(q)** 'that is to do/say/be' or = **il(q)** 'that is to be') are homonyms with the shortened forms of the postvocalic shape of the topic and object particles (**n'** = **nun**, **l'** = **lul**). In our Romanization we distinguish them by the location of the apostrophe: **uysa 'n** (**sālam**) '(a person) who is a doctor', **uysa n'** 'as for the doctor'. The "zero" abbreviation of the processive modifier of **ha-** (**'nun** = **hanun**) is distinguished only by our apostrophe from the homophonous full postvocalic shape of the topic particle **nun**: **cangsa 'nun** (**sālam**) '(a person) who is engaging in business', **cangsa nun** 'as for business'. When writing, Koreans do well to avoid abbreviations as much as possible. It makes the content easier to understand if you write out in full the forms of the copula and **ha-** wherever they occur in a Hankul text, and spell particles in their full forms, as well as taking care to specify the grammatical role of phrases by marking them with the appropriate particles more often than is usual in speech, where case markers are casually dropped.

Chart: Parts of speech (left)

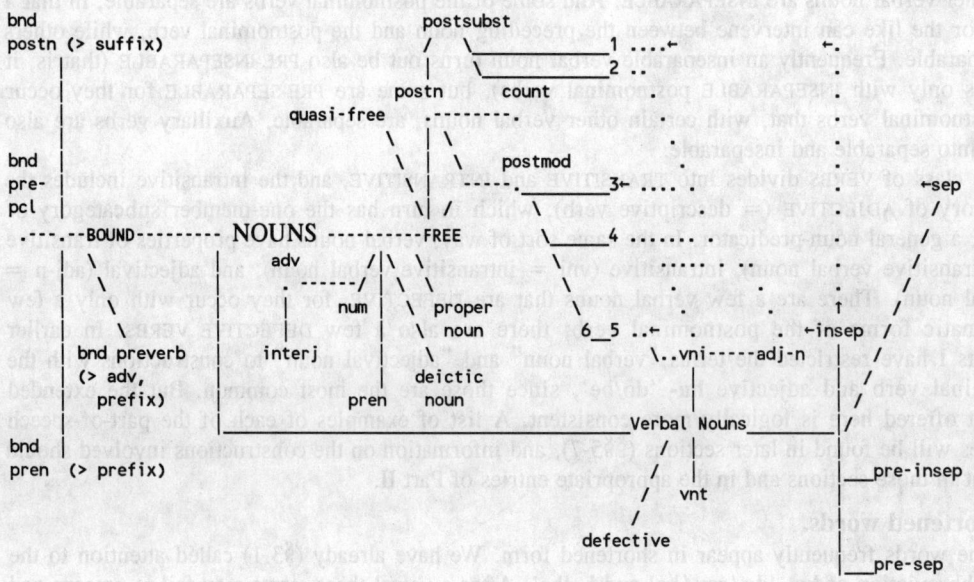

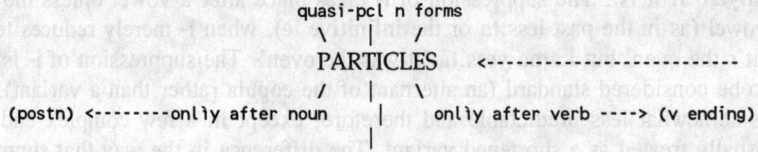

1 postsubst adj-n insep: cik
2 postnom/postmod adj-n insep: man
3 postmod adj-n sep: pep, tus
4 postmod adj-n insep: ak, man, (p)pen, wu
5 postmod vni insep: chek, (s)sa
6 pre-insep postmod: seng/sang

A Reference Grammar of Korean

Chart: Parts of speech (right)

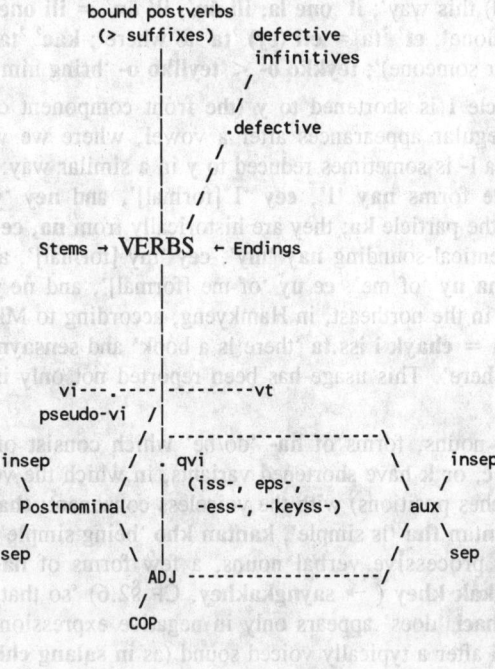

There are various other sorts of common abbreviations:

(1) **ke = kes** 'thing, one, fact'; **mue, mwe, mwes = mues** 'what, something'; **an ··· = ani** 'not'; **key = keki** 'there' or **= (ku) kes i** '(that) one'; **cēy = cēki** 'there'; **yey = yeki** 'here'; **-ulq cey = -ulq cek (ey)** '(at) the time that'; **anh- = an ha- = ani ha-** 'do / say / be not'; **-canh- = haci anh- (= haci ani ha-)** 'do / say / be not'; **mas i 'ss.ta (mas-iss.ta) = mas i iss.ta** 'is tasty'; **caym' iss.ta** or **caymi 'ss.ta**. Notice that /masitta/ is **mas i 'ss.ta** with the particle overtly present because the synonymous phrase **mas iss.ta** (without the particle i) is /matitta/.

(2) **il' lo = ili lo** '(toward) this way'; **il' one la, ili ōn', il' ōn' = ili one la** 'come here!'; **k'an twu- = ku man twu-** 'leave it alone'; **et' 'ta = eti (ey) 'ta** 'to where'; **kac' 'ta cwu- = kacye 'ta cwu- = kacie 'ta cwu-** 'bring it (for someone)'; **teykko o- < teyliko o-** 'bring him along'.

(3) The nominative particle **i** is shortened to **y** (the front component combining with a preceding vowel) in some of its irregular appearances after a vowel, where we would expect the suppletive alternant **ka**, and the copula **i-** is sometimes reduced to **y** in a similar way: (**kes → ke →) key = kes i** or **kes i-**. The nominative forms **nay** 'I', **cey** 'I [formal]', and **ney** 'you' appear either alone or pleonastically followed by the particle **ka**; they are historically from **na, ce,** and **ne +** this reduction of the particle **i** to **y**. The identical-sounding **nay** 'my', **cey** 'my [formal]', and **ney** 'your', on the other hand, are contractions of **na uy** 'of me', **ce uy** 'of me [formal]', and **ne uy** 'of you'. The pleonastic sequence **i ka** is used for **i** in the northeast, in Hamkyeng, according to Mkk 1960:4:26, which has the examples **chayk i ka iss.ta = chayk i iss.ta** 'there is a book' and **sensayng i ka osinta = sensayng i osinta** 'the teacher comes here'. This usage has been reported not only in dialects of Hamkyeng but also of Kyengsang.

(4) After most adjectival nouns, forms of **ha-** 'do/be' which consist of the stem with an attached ending that begins with **t, c,** or **k** have shortened variants, in which the vowel drops and **h** undergoes metathesis (that is, it switches positions) with the voiceless consonant: **tha** for **hata**, **chi** for **haci**, **kho** for **hako**. Examples are **kantan tha** 'is simple', **kantan kho** 'being simple', and **kantan chi** 'is simple, I suppose'. After certain processive verbal nouns, a few forms of **ha-** shorten in the same way: **sayngkak hakey → sayngkak khey** (**→ sayngkakhey**, CF §2.6) 'so that one thinks'. The shortened version of the suspective **haci** 'does' appears only in negative expressions, where it is optional. The variant has two shapes: **chi** after a typically voiced sound (as in **salang chi anh.nunta** 'does not love') and **'ci** after a typically voiceless sound (as in **sayngkak 'ci anh.nunta** 'does not think'). After an adjectival noun the shortening of **haci** 'is' is usually **chi** regardless of the preceding sound, as in **nek.nek chi anh.ta** 'is not enough' and **phyen.an chi anh.ta** 'is not comfortable'. But many people seem to use **'ci** and **chi** in free variation with both descriptive and processive verbal nouns. In the 15th century the short variants enjoyed wider use, including examples of 'do' as a transitive verb: CIN ˙ol ˙khwo ˙cye ho˙m ye n' (1462 [1]Nung 7:73b) 'if one wants to do the true thing'. The aspirated forms (˙tha < ho˙ta, ˙thi < ho˙ti, ˙khwo < ho˙kwo, ˙khey < ho˙key / ˙khuy < ho˙kuy) occur only after voiced sounds, and the unaspirated forms (''ta, ''ti, ''kwo, ''key, ''kuy, ...) appear only after voiceless sounds, but the ···LQ of Chinese loanwords, though probably pronounced just as /l/, was sometimes treated as voiceless (SEE p. 50): pat non˙hwoki ˙lol ˙KYWELQ ˙key ho˙n i (1447 Sek 9:19-20) '[he] let them divide the fields'. (The Middle Chinese source of ···LQ was an unreleased final /t/.)

(5) There are a few examples of dropped **p** (CF §2.11.2): **phul-'ath** [dialect] = **phul path** 'weedy spot, bush, thicket'; **si'-wel ← sip-wel** 'October' (we would expect **sip-'el**, see §2.7.4) and **si'-o li = sip-o li** '15 leagues'; **ka'-o** [dialect?] **kap-o** (a cyclical binom); **ttelum ha-** (< **ttēlp-** + -**um**) 'be a bit astringent'. There are also a few examples of dropped **k**, notably [1]**yu'-wel** ← [1]**yuk-wel** 'June' (but this may have been influenced by the poetic name for June [1]**yuwel** 'flowing month') and **ōnyu'-wel** 'May or June'. But **mokwa < ¨mwo-˙kwa** (1527 Cahoy 1:6a=11a) = **mok.kwa < ˙MWOK-KWA** 'Chinese quince' and **Paychen < Paykchen** (placename) are variant borrowings. The texts provide at least one example of m dropped after p: ˙pap-e˙ki (?1517- [1]No 1:45b; the initial circle is too round to be an m) < ˙pap me˙ki (1481 Twusi 15:4b) 'eating, having one's meal'.

(6) Final l drops in many words when they serve as the first member of a compound that has the next member beginning with an apical articulation:
kyewul 'winter', kyewu' sal.i 'winter garb', kyewu' nay (also kyewul nay with /ll/) 'all through the winter'
kaul 'autumn', kau' nay 'all through the autumn'
hanul 'heaven', hanu' nim 'God'
pul 'fire', pu' napi 'moth (← fire butterfly)', pu'-nemki 'a kind of stove', pu'-ce 'fire tongs (← chopsticks)', pu' son 'fire scoop (← hand)', pu' sap 'fire shovel'
atul 'son', atu' nim 'esteemed son'
ttal 'daughter', tta' nim 'esteemed daughter'
chal 'sticky', cha' co 'glutinous millet', cha' tol 'flint (← sticky stone)', cha' pssal (spelled chap-ssal) 'glutinous rice'
hwal 'bow', hwa' sal 'arrow'
mal 'peck', ma'-toy 'pecks and measurefuls'
mul 'water', mu'-cawi 'pump', mu'-nem.i '(?) overflow', mu' com 'athlete's foot, fungus'
mul 'dye', mu'-sayk 'dyed color'
panul 'needle', panu' cil 'needlework', pan'-cit koli 'sewing box' < *panu'-ci[l] s ˙kwo˙li
kumul 'net', kumu' cil 'netting'
kempul 'dried grass and twigs', kampu' namu 'tinder'
petul 'willow', petu' namu 'willow tree'
sol 'pine', so' namu (also sol namu) 'pinetree'
ssal 'rice', ssa'-cen 'rice store'
ipul 'bedclothes', ipu' cali 'bedclothes and mattress'
cwul 'line', cwu' tay 'fishing line and pole'
nal 'day', na'-nal-i 'day by day'
tal 'month', ta'-tal-i 'month by month'
sī-nay 'streamlet' (from sīl 'thread, ... ' + nay 'stream')
si'-tha(y) 'ox pack' (from sīt- / sil- 'load' + thay / tha = cim 'burden')

Notice also kwutu-ccil 'hypocáust work' and kwutwu-ttay 'hypocaust' from kwutwul 'hypocaust' (by by way of *kwutwu[l] s cil, *kwutwu[l] s tay?); pha'-il from phal-il '8 April = Buddha's birthday'. This dropping of the liquid before an apical consonant was a general phenomenon in Middle Korean (CF §2.11.3), and it regularly occurred in verb forms such as ˙ma˙ti and ˙ma˙ta for modern mālci and mālta. The modern language retains the basic -l- of such stems except before n (mānun) and s (māsinta), or in fossilized forms such as -ca māca. The elision of l before n is no longer productive, however, and newer formations regularly have l.n, pronounced /ll/. See nim in Part II. Some dialects apparently never elided the l, e.g. that of Ceycwu (LSN 1978:18): toltol-i 'monthly', nalnal-i = /nallali/ 'daily', ttol-nim = /ttollim/ 'your daughter'. On the other hand, the [1]Yukcin dialect reflected in the Cyrillic versions of 1902 Azbuka retained the liquid elision of Middle Korean.

(7) When the infinitive ending -e is attached to a stem ending in i, the form is usually shortened by one syllable: ···ie → ···ye. The shortened form is more or less the written standard for polysyllabic stems (kitalye ← kitalie 'waits for') but monosyllabic stems are usually spelled out in full (kie 'crawls') except for the unshortened copula (ye = ie 'it is') and the auxiliary verb ci- 'become' (-e cye = -e cie 'gets to be' as in hulye cye 'gets to be cloudy'). Except in special circumstances the phoneme /y/ does not occur after s, c, cc, or ch, but the recommendation of the orthographers is to regularize the abbreviation ···ie → ···ye in these cases, too, and write kasye (rather than kase) for kasie 'someone esteemed goes', kacye (rather than kace) for kacie 'holds, gets', kaluchye (rather than kaluche) for kaluchie 'teaches', sal-ccye (rather than sal-cce) for sal-ccie 'gets fat'. What is said for the infinitive ending -e also applies to the past-tense forms in (···i- +) -ess-: kasyess.ta (rather than kasess.ta) for kasiess.ta 'someone esteemed went', kacyess.ta (rather than kacess.ta) for kaciess.ta 'has got', kaluchyess.ta (rather than kaluchess.ta) for kaluchiess.ta 'taught', sal-ccyes.ta (rather than sal-

ccess.ta) for **sal-cciess.ta** 'got fat'. The endings **-sye** and **-syess-** are particularly frequent because they contain the honorific marker **-(u)si-**, which can be used to turn almost any verb stem into an honorific. Some speakers pronounced ···**sye** not as /se/ but as /sye/ with the palatal sibilant they have learned to make for foreign loanwords such as **syassu / syaccu** 'shirt', but I have not heard speakers make a distinction of /cye/ from /ce/. The shortening of ···**ie** to ···**ye** is the source of virtually all cases of **ty**, **thy**, and /**tty**/: **titye** = **titie** 'treads', **pethye** = **pethie** 'props', **eph-tye** /epttye/ = **eph-tie** (= **eph-tulie**) 'overturns'. Words which, in the spellings of earlier days, once had **ty-** are now pronounced **c-** in the south and in the standard language, **t-** in the northwest dialects, such as that of Phyengyang, which is famous for the word **tengke-tang** = **cengke-cang** '[railroad] station' (from earlier **tyengke-tyang**) — see §2.10.3. I have tried to follow the recommendation of the Korean Language Society in this book, though I would prefer to have all the forms spelled out in full as ···**ie**, both in the Romanization and in Hankul, so as to avoid possible confusion.

(8) The dropping of **h** or **ng** (§2.7) sometimes leads to further shortening of vowel strings: **ohilye** → (**oilye** →) **oylye** 'rather, contrary to expectation'; **kongyen hi** → **ko'yen 'i** → **kōyni, kwāyni** 'in vain'; **āymay han** → **āymay '(e)n** → **āymen** 'vague'; **siwen hata** → **syēn hata** 'is refreshing'.

(9) ···**' tus hata** = **-nun tus hata** (in literary clichés) 'seems to do'; ···**' mōs hanta** = **-ci mōs hanta** 'cannot do' (in a few expressions).

(10) Final ···**i**, at times itself a morpheme, drops from the first member of a number of compounds, especially those involving diminutive suffixes: **kkoli** + **-ayngi** → **kkolayngi** 'tail', **kaci** + **-angi** → **kacangi** 'branch', **kkochi** + **-ayngi** → **-ayngi** → **kkochayngi** 'skewer, spit', **thokki** + **-ayngi** → **thokkayngi** 'rabbit', **ppuli** + **-eyngi** → **ppuleyngi** 'root'; **taykali** + **-ppali** → **taykal-ppali**, + **-ppayki** → **taykal-ppayki** 'head'.

(11) A phrase with two similar syllables juxtaposed sometimes reduces the first: **ec' cenyek** = **eceyq cenyek** 'last night'.

(12) The auxiliary adjective **siph.ta** appears in a shortened form taken from the southern dialect variant **siphuta**. Although that variant itself is seldom heard in Seoul, the shortening found in **-ko 'phuta** (= **-ko siph.ta**) 'wants to' is quite common: **nay ka poko 'phun sinmun** 'the newspaper I want to see'.

(13) For still other cases of shortening, see the various stems that are called **s**-dropping (§8.1.5), ambivalent (or **h**-dropping, §8.2.4), and — from the viewpoint of the Hankul spelling — the **l**-extending vowel stems (§8.2.2).

3.6. Vocabulary.

By source the bulk of Korean vocabulary falls into three classes, which I will call CORE or (even though it may contain early loanwords) native-Korean, CHINESE (systematically borrowed from China), and ENGLISH, though the class contains modern loanwords from other European languages. Many of the modern loanwords were borrowed through their Japanese renderings, but some of those have been given new versions taken directly from English. There remains considerable controversy over the standardization of current loanwords from English. The trend is to favor close imitation of American pronunciation of the words, rather than to follow Japanese patterns, as was sometimes done in the past. But for words well established over several generations, the now traditional version is usually conceded.

The Chinese vocabulary, which can be referred to as "Sino-Korean" when reference to it might be confused with the language spoken in China, has been well integrated during the past thousand years and it is now a component of the language — in sheer quantity the major component. It is interesting to observe that while the majority of all words in a Korean dictionary are of Chinese origin, only about ten percent of the words in the so-called "basic vocabulary" come from Chinese. Virtually all non-Korean words have been brought into the language as uninflected words, as some kind of noun. When the word clearly carries a verbal meaning, Korean has treated it as a verbal noun, putting the loanword into construction with a postnominal verb, typically **ha-** 'do/be'. But there are also verbal nouns in the core vocabulary, most conspicuously the mimetic words described in §14. I know of only two verb stems of possible Chinese origin: **sangwu-** 'harm' (= **sang ha-**) ? < SYANG ˙hwo- and **pāy-** < *poy-* 'conceive (a child)', if that is from the Chinese morpheme **pay** < PHOY 'fetus' rather than **pay** < ˙*poy* 'belly'. (The non-Chinese etymology is supported by the Japanese derivation of hara˥mu < *para-ma- 'get pregnant' from hara˥ < *para 'belly'; there is no alternative possibility from Chinese.)

Owing to the severe restrictions on syllable types in Chinese, morphemes of the Chinese vocabulary are limited to a rather neat pattern of shapes, roughly those permitted by the chart of Korean syllables spoken in isolation, with the exception of most of those with geminate initials (**pp tt cc ss kk**). A list of all the occurring types of Chinese vocabulary will be found in §4.5; those shapes that end in ···**p** ···**l** ···**k** had final unreleased ···p ···t ···k in Middle Chinese, as they still have in Cantonese. The core vocabulary, on the other hand, includes some shapes which are less than a syllable, such as the -**n** of **chan** ... '... that is cold' from **cha-**, the -**ss-** of **kass.e** 'went' (from **ka-**) or even less than a phoneme, as in the alternant of the infinitive that is represented by the palatal feature (front component) reflected by our spelling -**y** in **hay** 'does' from **ha-**. The core vocabulary includes some shapes which are more than a syllable but less than two syllables: **kiph-** in **kiph.e** 'is deep', **pakk** in **pakk ey** 'outside', **kkoch** in **kkoch ita** 'it's a flower', **kaps** in **kaps i** 'the price [as subject]'. And it includes some shapes which are two or three syllables (**phulu-** in **phuluta** 'is blue', **meli** 'head', **cwumeni** 'pouch', **kitali-** in **kitalinta** 'waits') or something slightly more than two: **muluph** in **muluph i** 'the knee [as subject]'. Words of four syllables or more are usually either borrowings or compounds (as are many words of two or three syllables), but in some cases the origins are obscure.

The alternations in shape of the Chinese vocabulary are fairly easily stated, as are the basic shapes. For the Korean vocabulary the statements are more complicated because: (1) "overstuffed" morphemes (like **pakk** and **kiph-**) must be reduced to permissible syllables when not followed by the copula **i-** or a particle that begins with a vowel; (2) decisions must be made on morpheme boundaries within words, and the decisions are not always so easy as they are for the Chinese vocabulary, where we are helped by the restricted shapes and the morphemic writing system of Chinese; (3) there are several special rules when endings are attached to verb stems.

Two morphemes, core and Chinese respectively, sometimes have shapes that begin with **ng**. These are -**ngaci** 'offspring of' (ultimately perhaps from **aki** 'child', though we find no other cases of affricating palatalization of the velar in a noninitial syllable) in **songaci** 'calf' (**so** 'cow'), **mangaci** 'colt' (**mal** 'horse'), and **kangaci** 'pup' (**kay** 'dog'); and -**nge** 'fish' in fish names taken from the Chinese: **ocinge**, **punge**, ˩**nonge**, ˩īnge, **sange**, **swunge**, **kwānge**, and **paynge** < **payk-(ng)e**.

3.7. Layers of vocabulary in earlier Korean.

By the time Hankul was created Korean had acquired many borrowed words from various other languages, such as Manchu and Mongol. Most of the loans, however, came from classical Chinese, which was the standard written means of communication. The Chinese words were borrowed as logographic characters and pronounced with an approximation to the Middle Chinese sounds. But some of the words were borrowed early and got thoroughly nativized, so that their association with the characters, and the traditional Chinese phonetic values, was forgotten. Most loans, however, retained their association with Chinese even when they became part of the common vocabulary of speech, as when **san** 'mountain' and **kang** 'river' displaced the native words attested as MK ¨mwoyh and ko˙lom.

Scholars set up a system of somewhat artificial readings for the characters and codified this in a dictionary of character readings that was published in 1448 under the title Tongkwuk cengwun (¨TWONG-˙KWUYK ¨CYENG-˙NGWUN — the tone mark on the first syllable is unexplained). The Tongkwuk readings were an attempt to capture in terms of Hankul symbols the traditional phonetic distinctions of Middle Chinese as found in the rime lists written by Chinese philologists. This reconstruction of Chinese phonology took place nearly five centuries before the Sinologist Bernard Karlgren interpreted the distinctions of Middle Chinese in terms of the Swedish Dialect Alphabet. The Tongkwuk readings were written as Hankul syllables immediately following the corresponding Chinese characters in many of the texts of the 15th century. The modern way of pronouncing Chinese characters used in Korea is simpler than the Tongkwuk readings in that certain unrealistic distinctions (such as the initial velar nasal and glottal stop) are abandoned, and the unaspirated voiceless initials of Middle Chinese are equated with the plain series of Korean obstruents, rather than the emerging tense (reinforced) series favored by the prescriptive orthographers of the 15th century.

For certain words the prescriptive readings coexisted with nativized versions, so that a number of doublet forms can be found in the texts. The nativized version often appears in Hankul without the accompanying Chinese characters (CF LCT 1971:78):

cin˙sil lwo (1481 Twusi 20:19b) = CIN-˙SSILQ lwo (1482 Kum-sam 2:16a) = CIN-˙SSILQ ˙lwo (1459 Wel 9:36d) 'truly'

cywongywo (1518 Sohak-cho 8:9a cywong¨ywo y ← cywongywo ˙i; 1586 Sohak 3:8b) 'essence, the essential' = CWONG-˙QYWOW (1482 Kum-sam 2:69a)

cywungsoyng (1447 Sek 6:19b, ...) = ˙CYWUNG-SOYNG (1447 Sek 6:5b, ...) 'creatures'

kanan (1475 Nay 2:2:47b; 1482 Nam 1:30b), kannan (1475 Nay 1:30a) = KAN-NAN (1447 Sek 6:15b, 13:56b; 1465 Wen 3:3:1:62a) 'poverty; poor'

kuypyel (1445 ¹Yong 35, 1459 Wel 2:43a) 'tidings, news, a letter' = KUY-˙PYELQ (1447 Sek 24:16a)

kwong˙so (1447 Sek 9:30b) = KWONG-˙SSO (1459 Wel 9:50b) 'engaging in public affairs'

mi˙hwok (1447 Sek 9:36b) = MYEY-˙HHWOYK (1459 Wel 9:17b) 'bewilderment'

¨naycywong (1462 ¹Nung 1:20a, 1463 Pep 3:161a), ¨nay˙cywong (1518 Sohak-cho 8:19b) = ¨NAY-CYWUNG (1447 Sek 13:29b) 'finally'

si˙cyel (1475 Nay 2:2:47b, 3:32a; 1481 Twusi 7:25b) > si˙cel (1518 Sohak-cho 8:19b, 21b) = SSI-˙CYELQ (1447 Sek 9:2a, 13:47b, 13:60b; 1462 ¹Nung 2:114b, 5:85b; 1459 Wel 18:83a; 1465 Wen 2:3:1:52a; ...) 'time (when)'

syang˙nyey (1447 Sek 6:10a; 1459 Wel 10:7b, 17:35a; 1463 Pep 5:212b, 1464 Kumkang 64b, 1482 Kum-sam 2:25a, ?1517- Pak 1:14b) = SSYANG-˙LYEY (1447 Sek 9:14a) 'always'

twocok (1445 ¹Yong 30; > twocek) = ˙TTWO-˙CCUK (1459 Wel 2:19b) 'thief' (= **totwuk**)

tyangsyang (1466 Kup 2:64a) = TTYANG-SSYANG (1459 Wel 8:8b, [1447→]1562 Sek 3:22b) 'always'

¨wen ˚ho- (?1517- Pak 1:60a) = ¨NGWEN ˚ho- (1586 Sohak 6:44a) = ˙NGWEN ˚ho- (1447 Sek 9:40b, 13:44b, 24:18a; 1459 Wel 13:35b)

wuytwu (1447 Sek 13:6a) = NGWUY-TTWUW (1459 Wel 10:25a) 'forming the head / van'

¨wuy ˚ho- (1447 Sek 6:1a, 6:7b, 6:13b, 6:16a, 13:49b) = ˙WUY ˚ho- (1459 Wel 7:17b, 9:5-6, 13:35b, 13:36a, 17:54a; 1463 Pep 2:172ab, 2:231b, 7:17a; 1465 Wen se:6a; 1482 Kum-sam 5:48-9) 'do for (the sake of)'

LCT 1971:78 finds over thirty words that were usually written without the appropriate Chinese characters, and presumably they were all well assimilated. Additional notes on some of those words:

¨camskan (1459 Wel 7:15b) = ¨cams.kan (1447 Sek 13:53b; 1475 Nay 1:55b, 2:1:2b; 1463 Pep 2:226a; 1465 Wen 1:1:1:44b; 1481 Twusi 7:1b; 1482 Kum-sam 2:13b; 1482 Nam 2:31a) 'a while' < (?*)˙CCAM s KAN "the space of a while"

˙cukcay (1459 Wel 9:35f; 1463 Pep 6:97a; 1466 Kup 2:4b) < ˙cukca˙hi (1447 Sek 6:2a, 6:11a, 9:12b, 24:16a; 1459 Wel 2:6b) 'suddenly' < *˙CUK CA [< *˙CHO] ˙hi

coy˙cwo (1447 Sek 6:7a) 'talent, ability' < *CCOY-CHWOW

¨cwosim (1447 Sek 9:37a, 1459 Wel 1:6a) 'taking care' < *CHWOW-SIM = Beijing cāoxīn

cyang˙cho (1459 Wel 1:18a, 17:78b; 1462 ¹Nung 1:28b, 7:73b; 1463 Pep 1:123a, 3:35a; 1475 Nay 2:1:30a; 1482 Kum-sam 4:22b) 'in future' < *CYANG-˙CHO (> Beijing jiāngcì 'for a while; almost')

¨hoyng˙tyek (1447 Sek 6:2b) 'deeds' < (?*) ˙HOYNG˙TUK "perform virtue" (CF Soothill 221b; LCT and Kim Wancin assign the second syllable to two different characters but both are read ˙CYEK)

in¨so (1459 Wel 2:9a) 'greeting (bow)' < *ZIN-˙SO "people-thing" (> Beijing rénshì 'gift')

kwu˙kyeng (1459 Wel 2:27b, 2:35b, 7:11a) 'viewing' < *˙KWUW-¨KYENG "seek the scene"

kwuy-s kes (1447 Sek 6:19b, 1482 Kum-sam 2:7b, 3:27b, 3:34b) < ¨KWUY s kes "devil('s) thing"

˚lwongtam (1447 Sek 6:24b, 1459 Wel 1:44b) 'joke' < *˙LWONG-TTAM "play talk"
˚moyzyang (1463 Pep 2:189b; 1481 Twusi 7:2b, 22:1b) > ˚moyyang (1481 Twusi 15:20a, 1518 Sohak-cho 10:12b) ?> ˙moy˚yang (id. 9:24b), ˙moyyang (id. 10:1b) 'always' < ˚MOY (S) ˙YANG "each('s) appearance"
phwunglywu (1447 Sek 9:21a, 13:9a) 'music' < *PWONG-LYWU (CF Beijing fēngliu 'elegance')
pwun˙pyel (1447 Sek, 9:29b, 13:36a; 1459 Wel 2:6a) 'thinking, considering, worry' < *PWUN-˙(P)PYELQ (> Beijing fēnbye 'separate, distinguish')
si˙hwok (1462 ¹Nung 9:88a, 1463 Pep 6:145b, 1481 Twusi 8:8a) 'sometimes; perhaps' < *SSI-˙HWOK
syang toWoy- (1459 Wel 1:43a) 'is common, vulgar' < SSYANG 'constant, always'
tangta.ng-i (1447 Sek 19:34a, 1459 Wel 1:7b, 1466 Kup 2:64a, 1481 Twusi 7:4b, 1482 Kum-sam 4:20b) = tangtang-i (1481 Twusi 7:9a, 7:31a, 20:34b) < *TANG-TANG˙hi 'suitably'
˚tyangka (1447 Sek 6:16b, 6:22a) '[marriage into] the husband's family' < *˚TTYANG-KA

For cyen˙hye, ˚hoyng˙hye, and ˙twok˙hye see Part II, hye. LCT's list is representative, but not exhaustive. We can add, among others:
namcin (1459 Wel 1:43b) 'male; husband' < *NAM-ZIN "male person"
nam˙phyen 'husband' < *NAM-PPYEN "male side / direction / party"
˚sya˙wong 'husband' < *˙SYA-WONG "house elder"
kansywu °ho- (1447 Sek 9:36a, 1465 Wen 2:3:2:88b), kanso °ho- (1475 Nay 3:32a) < *(˙)KHAN-˚SYWUW 'guarding' > Beijing kānshǒu
˙tyang˙so 'selling' (1459 Wel 13:8b, 23:64a; 1463 Pep 6:170b) < *TTYANG-˙SO "market event"

Several common elements of modern Korean have Chinese origins that are now largely forgotten: ··· ca 'person' < ˚CYA, ··· cha 'on the verge; (as) an incidental consequence of; (for) the purpose of' < ˙CHO 'next, second(ary)', ...

Certain characters were given more than one reading (§4.7), sometimes reflecting divergent meanings in classical Chinese, and this led to doublet compounds, as well: ˚KAY-˙THWALQ (1459 Wel 14:39b, 1462 ¹Nung 7:27a, 1482 Kum-sam 2:4ab) = ˚HHAY-˙THWALQ (1447 Sek 13:43b) 'emancipation'. Here the character itself represents a triplet, with a third reading ˙HHAY as in ˙MYWOW-˙HHAY (1482 Kum-sam 5:24b) 'the wondrous understanding'. Doublet forms that differ only by accent are virtually unfound in the Chinese part of the vocabulary. Tongkwuk cengwun recognizes more than one tone for certain characters: 'dye' is listed as ZYEM, ˚ZYEM, or ˙ZYEM, but the only example I have found is the last, in the expression ˙ZYEM-˙CCYENG (1465 Wen 2:3:1:43a) 'pure-washed'. The character for 'separate, special' was read both ˙PYELQ and ˙PPYELQ: ˙KAK-˙PYELQ˙hi (1447 Sek 13:10b) = ˙KAK-˙PPYELQ˙hi (1462 ¹Nung 1:89a, 1482 Nam 2:63b) 'especially'.

Indirect evidence that the usual reading of MWON 'gate' was mwun (as made explicit in 1527 Cahoy 2:4a=7a) can be found in the choice of variant forms of particles in these passages: spol˙li MWON˙ul ˚yel˙la ˚ho˙ye ˙ys.te˚n i (1459 Wel 10:25a) 'wanted to open the door quickly' (we expect MWON˙ol); kasoy˙lwo˙hwon [MWON]˙ulan sywokcyel [˚]ep.si [˚]ye[˚]ti [˚]mal[˚]la (1481 Twusi 7:9a) 'do not to your regret open a door made of thorns' (we expect MWON˙olan). Incorporated in the word SA-MWON 'sramaṇa': SA-MWON˙uy˚swon-˙toy (1447 Sek 24:22a) 'to the śramaṇa' (we expect˙oy). In sep [MWON]˙ey (1481 Twusi 7:9b) 'to the twig gate' the writer was probably following the nativized mwun that would have been the normal spoken version, as attested in Hankul somewhat later (?1517- Pak 1:12b), for otherwise we would expect the particle to be˙ay.

Some of the compounds may have been borrowed from Chinese dialects of the day:
˙cokya (1445 ¹Yong 25, 1447 Sek 6:5b, 9:33a; 1459 Wel 13:8b) < *˙CCO-KA = Beijing zìjiā 'self'
phunco (?1517- ¹No 2:23, 26) < *˚PWUN-˚CO = Beijing fěnzi 'starch'
sywu˙lwup (1446 Hwun 29a [the dot is missing in the Taycey-kak repro but clear in the photocopy of ¹Yi Sangpayk 1957]) 'umbrella' ?< *˚SYWUY-˙LIP = (?) dialect equivalents of Beijing shuǐ 'water' + lì (< *lyep) 'umbrella'
yang˙co (1447 Sek se:5a, 6:13b, 23:4a; 1459 Wel se:16a, 8:15b, 8:19b, 23:86b; 1462 ¹Nung 3:84a)

< *˙YANG-¨CO = Beijing yàngzi 'appearance'; CF the postmodifier ¨yang < ˙YANG 'pretense'. But other compounds were possibly made up in Korea and then nativized. That appears to be the explanation for cyen˙cho (1447 Sek 6:2b; 1459 Wel 7:13b, 9:35d; 1462 ¹Nung 1:64b, 1:77b; 1465 Wen 1:1:1:47a; 1463 Pep 5:169b; 1482 Nam 1:5a) 'cause, reason' < CYEN 'effect' + ˙CHO 'next, second(ary)'; perhaps ¨chyen-lyang (1447 Sek 9:13a, 24:47b; 1463 Pep 6:144a; ...) 'money and food' < CCYEN 'money' + LYANG 'provisions' (modern Beijing qiánliang means 'tax; husband's allowance') and (**canchi** <) ˙can˙choy 'banquet' < CHAN 'meal/eat' + ¨CHOY 'vegetable'. The noun hwe (1462 ¹Nung 6:96b, ...) 'boots' is taken from an ancestor of Beijing xuē ('boots', not xié 'shoes') that is more immediate than the form reflected in the reading HWA.

Some of the Buddhist terms are borrowed from Chinese transcriptions of Indic words: MI-˙LUK 'maitreya (the Buddha to come)', ˙NYELQ-PPAN 'nirvāṇa (extinction)', ˙PPI-KHWUW 'bhikṣu, (almsman, mendicant monk)', ˙PPI-KHWUW-NI 'bhikṣuni (nun)', SA-MI 'śrāmaṇera (religious novice)', SAM-MA-˙TI (1462 ¹Nung 5:31b) 'samādhi [a trance-like state of unperturbable meditation]', SAM-˙MOY 'samādhi (meditation)', SA-MWON 'śramaṇa (begging monk, ascetic)'. Others are Chinese calques (loan translations) of Indic expressions: ˙CYENG-˙KAK 'sambodhi (Buddha wisdom)', ˙CYWUNG-SOYNG 'sattva (all living things)', ˙KYELQ-˙CIP = 'saṃgīta (a council to consolidate and collect the Buddha's teachings and to decide orthodoxy)', ˙PEP 'dharma, (Buddha's) law', SYENG-MWUN 'the śrāvaka (= hīnayāna disciple in the first stage)', ¨SYWOW-SSING 'hīnayāna (the Lesser Vehicle)', ˙TTAY-SSING 'mahāyāna (the Greater Vehicle)', ¨TTWOW 'mārga (the Way)', YWEN 'pratyaya (secondary cause)'.

A number of words sound as though they might be from Chinese, but no characters have been associated with them, e.g. **yengmun** 'reason' (no early attestations?), ¨ywumwu (1447 Sek 6:2b, 1449 Kok 61) = ¨ywu˙mwu (1518 Sohak-cho 8:22a) 'a letter', ¨cywong 'slave' (? < CYWONG 'follow, obey'), ... Certain words often suggested as Chinese loans may have other origins. Kang Hengkyu 1988:192 takes soyng˙kak 'thought' to be from Mongol sanaga rather than Chinese ¨SOYNG 'contemplate, recollect' + ˙KAK 'awaken' (LCT 1971:78, with question mark), and solang 'thought > love' to be connected with ˙solh 'flesh' (and/or ¨sal- 'live'? − the vowel is disconcerting) rather than from SO-LYANG (LCT 1971:87) = Beijing sīliáng 'consider', but those etymologies seem less convincing than the Chinese compounds. The noun nungkum 'apple' (first attested ?1834-) is from lingkum (?1517- Pak 1:4b) < LIM-KKUM. Both ¨cywung 'monk' and ˙swung 'nun' seem to be variant forms of SUNG 'Buddhist priest'. The expression ˙sywok˙cyel ¨ep˙si 'in vain, futilely' seems to be from ˙SYWOK-˙CYELQ ¨ep˙s-i 'without (even) a brief religious ceremony'.

Kim Wancin (1971:228-30) lists 36 words that he considers to be prehistoric borrowings from Chinese, which preceded the wholesale borrowings called Sino-Korean, referring to reconstructions of Middle and Old Chinese readings of certain characters. Some of the words are well deserving of such attribution: ˙cah 'measure', sywoh 'vulgar, lay(man)', tyeh 'flute', and zywoh 'mattress' are surely Chinese loanwords, as is ˙mek 'ink stick'. The nouns ˙pwut 'writing brush', pwuthye 'Buddha', and tyel 'temple' are to be considered together with their Japanese counterparts as cognate borrowings. The derivation of cek 'time' from Old Chinese *dyeg (> Beijing shí) is intriguing but must be weighed against the comparison with Japanese toki˥, just as the derivation of ¨kwom < kwo˙ma 'bear' from Old Chinese *gyum must be weighed against Japanese kuma˥, and the derivation of tolk 'chicken' from Old Chinese *tyeg 'bird' must share attention with the putative Japanese cognate tori˥. Other derivations that look good include ˙sal 'arrow' from Old Chinese *šyer and ˙pwoy 'hemp cloth' from Middle Chinese *pwo˙ 'cloth' (Kim Wancin mistakenly labeled this shape as Old Chinese, but that form was *pwag). On the other hand, mol 'horse' is more likely to have been directly borrowed from Mongol mori rather than an early Chinese equivalent of ¨MA, as Kim Wancin proposes.

4.0. Shapes.

Morphemes are abstract entities that take on shape only when they are realized as what are sometimes called MORPHS, just as phonemes take on substance only when they are articulated as PHONES. When a single phoneme is articulated with perceptibly different sounds, often determined by the environment, the phones are said to be ALLOPHONES of that phoneme. When a morpheme is realized in more than one shape, usually depending upon the adjacent sounds or morphemes, the morphs are said to be ALLOMORPHS of that morpheme. Quite often the variation in the shapes can be described in general terms that apply to groups of morphemes or to TYPES of shape. Words and stems often contain more than one morpheme, and they too can also be described in terms of shape types.

4.1. Shape types.

A word, or a morpheme, sometimes occurs in more than one shape. The SHAPE is the way the element is represented in phonemes, as actually pronounced. In general we find a resemblance between the several shapes of a given element. Except for the nominative particle i/ka and a few of the inflectional endings, the different shapes of a given morpheme or word have some stretches of phonetic makeup in common. The differences in shape between the alternants of many morphemes and words can be stated in general terms; such statements are often called MORPHOPHONEMIC rules. Some of these rules were stated in §2.6; a glance at the chart of permitted consonant clusters tells us to expect that a morpheme which sometimes has the shape sip can be expected to show the shape sim (and even the shape si) in certain environments. These alternations are so automatic (every "expected" ···p before a nasal turns out to be pronounced ···m) that for the most part they are disregarded by the Hankul spelling and by the Yale Romanization. When we hear the spoken sequence ···mm··· we cannot be sure that it will be spelled p + m (or ph + m, ps + m) instead of m + m unless we recognize the morphemes or words involved. As a result of convergence, Korean has a fair number of words and phrases that sound the same but are spelled differently because each constituent part is always written according to its "basic" shape, as found in some of its other environments. That is why the string /cimman/ is written cim man when it means 'just the burden' but cip man when it means 'just the house' and ciph man when it means 'just the straw'.

The alternations shown in the cluster table are AUTOMATIc in that you apply them to shapes regardless of the particular words involved; and they are FULLY AUTOMATIC because you need not even know what the grammar of the words may be. A similar kind of fully automatic alternation is found in English when an expected "s" is pronounced /z/ after /g/: we do not have to know the grammar to pronounced "legs" as /legz/, for the rules of our language automatically keep us from saying /legs/. Such rules work for nonsense words as well as real words: the pseudo-word "blegs" can only be pronounced /blegz/.

Notice that the morphophonemic rules apply only if the two syllables are run together, with no pause intervening. In general, that is true for most of our rules for alternations that occur at the point of contact between Korean morphemes or words. Thus, l + n → /ll/ in ku tul ney /kutulley/ 'they', tal nala /tallala/ 'the moon (as a place)', saynghwal-nan /saynghwallan/ 'the hardships of life', tūl-nol.i /tūlloli/ 'picnic', and other expressions where pause virtually never intervenes. In certain other expressions, pause is infrequent: kaul nal /kaullal/ 'autumn day/weather', onul nal /onullal/ 'today' — compare onul nal(-ssi) /onul|nal(ssi)/ 'today the weather ··· '. The expression cal nol.a 'plays nicely' (adverb + verb) is usually pronounced without pause /callola/. Pause is infrequent between short unmarked object and verb, so that atul nah.ko ttal nah.ko 'giving birth to sons and daughters = (lived) happily ever after' is usually said /atullakho|ttallakho/. With a marked object, there are common versions with or without pause: al ul nāynta 'lays eggs' may be heard as /alullāynta/ or as /alul|nāynta/. Since the accusative particle ends in l and the verb nāy- 'puts out, ... ' takes many different nouns as object, that verb is frequently heard in the alternant shape lāy-. There are also cases of unmarked subject + verb that are such common expressions they are usually said without an intervening pause, e.g. pul nanta /pullanta/ 'a fire breaks out' (= pul i nanta). Kyel nanta and kol nanta, both meaning 'gets angry' (from 'temper appears'), are usually pronounced /···ll···/ as are their synonyms kyel nāynta and kol nāynta ('displays temper'). If a pause is inserted, it would be more natural to attach the appropriate particle to mark the subject or object: kyel i | nanta, kyel ul | nāynta. In expressions of modifier + nominal, an intervening pause is usually unnatural in relaxed speech, so that tte-nal nal 'the day to leave' is usually pronounced /ttenallal/. We can know the appropriate spelling for the expressions **-ul nalum ita** 'it depends on' and **-ul nawi (ka) ēps.ta** 'there is not enough to; there is hardly a need to' only from etymology or reading pronunciations, for they are usually pronounced with /···ll···/. To be sure, by inserting a somewhat artificial pause the Korean speaker can distinguish an otherwise homophonous phrase like **salq kos** 'places to buy (them)' from **sal kkoch** 'flowers to buy', both /salkkot/ in normal speech, and **mōs kanta** 'can't go' from **mōs kkanta** 'can't peel', both /mōkkanta/ in normal speech.

The only cases of fully automatic (phonemically determined) alternation other than those from the table of permitted clusters are (in part) the alternations of **l** and **n** (§4.4) when after pause, and of **yey** (§4.3) when not after pause. Other alternations are widely but not fully automatic, because you have to be aware of at least some grammar to decide whether they apply. In the following sections six kinds of alternations are described:

(1) Treatment of syllable excess, §4.2.

(2) Treatment of **yey**, §4.3.

(3) Treatment of **l** and **n**, §4.4.

(4) Occurrence of reinforcement (**-q**) with the prospective modifier **-ul**, §1.5, §9.3.

(5) Occurrence of reinforcement (**-q**) with consonant stems that end in sonants (**m, n,** or an **l** that is reduced from basic **lp, lph, lm, lth, lk**), §8.1.1.

(6) Various alternations of "two-shape" elements, §5.1.

4.2. Syllable excess.

There is a limited group of "overstuffed" morphemes, each of which has a basic form that ends in a consonant that can occur only at the beginning of a Korean syllable or in a string of consonants that can occur only if divided between two syllables, part at the end of one syllable and part beginning the next. The "overstuffing" or SYLLABLE EXCESS is heard only before certain vowels. Before pause or a consonant — and in certain constructions also before a vowel — the excess is replaced by those corresponding consonants which are permitted at the end of a syllable. Before certain consonants the excess replacement then undergoes further replacements, those that are phonemically determined for the consonant (§2.6). For example, **kaps** 'price' is reduced to the shape **kap** before pause or in phrases like **kap to** 'the price too'; the final **p** of this shape **kap** is then subject to the automatic alternations of any final **p**, so we hear /kamman/ for **kaps man** 'just the price'.

Before a vowel which (1) begins a particle, such as the nominative marker **i** or the accusative **ul**, (2) begins the copula **i-**, or (3) begins an inflectional ending, such as the infinitive **-e** or the adversative **-una**, the full basic form is heard with its syllable excess intact: **kaps ul** 'the price [as object]', **kaps i** 'the price [as subject]', **kaps ita** 'it's the price'. (The phonemic shapes are actually /kapssul/ and /kapssi(···)/, because of the automatic rule under which an orthographic **ps** is not distinguished in pronunciation from **pss**, as we earlier observed.)

Before a vowel which does not begin an inflectional ending, the copula, or a particle, the usual treatment reduces the excess: **kaps olumyen** 'when the price rises' is pronounced /kapolumyen/ and **kaps ālki elyewe** 'it's hard to find out the price' is pronounced /kapālkielyewe/. There are exceptions in a few compounds (**yetelp hay** 'eight years' is /yetelphay/), in derived verb forms (**olk.hi-** 'get roped' /olkhi-/), and in iterated noun + the adverb-deriving suffix **-i** (**moks.moks-i** 'in portions, in shares' is /mongmokssi/). In a few combinations both treatments occur: /masisse/ or /matisse/ for **mas iss.e** 'is tasty' but the former is better regarded as **mas i 'ss.e**, a reduction of **mas i iss.e**, as we had occasion to remark earlier. According to one study (Kim Hyenglyong 1985) in modern written Korean there are 1,757 different orthographic syllables that carry a "final" component (**pat.chim**), and 1,384 (= .787) of these carry codas that are allowed at the end of a PHONETIC syllable: **p t k m n ng l**. The remaining 373 (= .213) represent morphemes with syllable excess.

The following list of morph-final strings includes all the occurring types of syllable excess. Some of the types occur with both nouns and verb stems; others only with one or the other. There are also stems ending in **h, lh, nh**, and **w**, for which see §§8.2.2-3. Historically, there are nouns that once ended in **h, lh, nh**, and **mh**, but they have dropped the final **h** in modern Korean. The etyma have left morphophonemic relics in the case of **salh** 'flesh', **anh** 'inside', **amh** 'female', and **swuh** 'male', but the words in which a reflex of the **h** appears are now spelled (with respect to this feature) phonemically: **salkhoki** = **salh-koki** 'red meat', **anphakk** = **anh-pakk** 'inside and outside', **swukhay** = **swuh kāy** 'male dog', **amkhay** = **amh kāy** 'female dog'. (See below for more on this. A list of the MK ···*h* nouns is at the end of this section.) There are also relics of excess at the beginning of certain syllables: **pssi** = **ssi** 'seed' in **pyepssi** = **pye-pssi** 'rice seed', **pssal** = **ssal** 'grain' in **īpssal** = **ī-pssal** 'raw rice', **pttu-** = **ttu-** 'open (one's eyes/ears)' in **chiptte** = **chi-ptte** 'looking with raised eyes', ... For the inflectional stems ending in ···l-, which show different behavior from other elements ending in **l**, see §8.1.4. There are a few archaic examples of excess **mk** in nouns: **namk** = **namu** 'tree' (CF modern **namak-sin** 'wooden shoes'), **kwumk** = **kwumeng** 'hole'. These go back to MK nouns that had two allomorphs which developed from *-$m^u\!/ok$; there were similar types from *-$n^u\!/ok$, *-$s^u\!/ok$, *-$l^u\!/ok$, and *-$l^u\!/ol$. Those nouns are listed in §8.3.1, where we see how the verb stems of this type developed into the peculiar alternation found in the modern -LL- verbs. For all of the nouns with more than one shape, including those with syllable excess, the free shape that occurs before pause is also used before certain particles, such as the MK genitive **s**.

The first column of the list shows the morph-final ending, the second column shows the phoneme to which the excess is reduced; the third column gives a noun example, and the fourth a verb example. The notes immediately follow the list.

LIST OF MORPH-FINAL STRINGS

p		cip 'house'	cap- 'catch'
t[1]		nāt 'grain'	tat- 'close'
k		mok 'throat'	mek- 'eat'
l		mal 'horse'	tul- 'listen'[2]
m		kām 'persimmon'	kām- 'shampoo'
n		an 'inside'	sin- 'wear on feet'
ng		khong 'soy bean'	–
th[3]	t	path 'field'	math- 'take charge of'
s	t	os 'clothes'	pes- 'take off, doff'
ss	t	–	iss- 'exist, stay'
c[4]	t	nac 'daytime'	chac- 'look for'
ch[4]	t	kkoch 'flower'	coch- 'follow'
ph	p	aph 'front'	ciph- 'lean on'
ps	p	kaps 'price'	ēps- 'not exist'
kh	k	puekh 'kitchen'	–
kk	k	pakk 'outside'	kkakk- 'cut, mow'
ks	k	moks 'share'	–
ls	l	tols 'cycle; postnatal year of age'	–
lth	l	–	halth- 'lick, taste'
lk	k, (l)	talk 'chicken'	ilk- 'read'
lm	m, (l)	[sālm 'life']	kwūlm- 'go without food'
lp	p, (l)	(yetelp 'eight')	pālp- 'tread on'
lph	p, (l)	–	ulph- 'intone, chant'
nc	n	–	anc- 'sit down'

[1] Many speakers treat the few nouns ending in a basic **t** as if they ended with an **s**. Even **tikut** 'the letter T' is pronounced with final **s** by most speakers when it is followed by, say, the nominative marker **i**. But the Hankul spelling writes final **t** for this and for a few other nouns. Choice of final **s**

instead of **t** for the basic form of certain words, such as **ches** … 'first', would seem to be arbitrary, or based on the notion "when in doubt treat final /t/ as if from s". The only basis for writing the adverb **mōs** 'not possibly' with a final **s** rather than the **t** used in older spellings is the word **calmos** 'mistake', derived from **cal mōs hanta** 'cannot do it well' /cal(l)mōthanta/, which is treated as having a final **s** (**calmos ul hanta** 'makes a mistake').

² But the consonant-stem **tut-** / **tul-** 'hear' is never pronounced with the syllable-final ···l, in contrast with the l-extending vowel stem **tu-l-**, which has the syllable-final allophone before a consonant, as in **tulko** 'entering' (compare **tut.ko** 'hearing'). The infinitive **tul.e** is said as **tu-le**, with the flap allophone, whether it means 'hear' or 'enter'. SEE §8.3.2.

³ In Seoul **th** + **i**, or **t** + **hi**, is regularly replaced by /chi/: **path ita** is pronounced /pachita/ 'it's a field' though **path ey** is /pathey/ 'in the field', and the passive forms **ket-hi-**, **tat-hi-**, **mut-hi-**, **ppet-hi-** are usually pronounced with /···chi-/. Notice that a morpheme boundary is always involved; there are no cases of /thi/ within a morpheme. In a similar fashion, **t** + **i** is replaced by /ci/: /kwuci/ for **kwut.i** 'firmly' (but **kwut.e** 'is firm' is pronounced /kwute/); /ttampaci/ for **ttam pat.i** 'sweatshirt' (but **ttam ul pat.e** 'receives sweat'), /haytoci/ for **hay tot.i** 'sunrise' (but **hay ka tot.a** 'the sun rises'), /mītaci/ for **mī-tat.i** 'sliding door' (but **mīlko tat.e** 'pushes and closes').

⁴ Many southern speakers treat noun-final **c**, **ch**, and **th** as if **s**: /nasey/ instead of /nacey/ for **nac ey** 'in the daytime', /kkosi/ instead of /kkochi/ for **kkoch i** 'the flower [as subject]', /pasi/ instead of /pachi/ for **path i** 'the field [as subject]' — and the pronunciation /pathi/ is heard in the north.

The reduction of the excess is as follows. A string of more than one consonant simplifies to one, by dropping all consonants in excess of the first, with the exception of certain cases involving the liquid and an obstruent. The strings **ls** and **lth** act like most clusters, dropping all but the **l**. The string **lp** also acts this way for the one noun example: **yetelp** reduces to /yetel/. Noun-final **lk**, however, reduces to **k**, so that **talk** becomes /tak/. For verb stems the strings **lk**, **lm**, **lp**, and **lph** are given both treatments as competing variants. The standard variant seems to treat the liquid as excess, so that **ilk-**, **kwūlm-**, **pālp-**, and **ulph-** are reduced to **ik-**, **kwūm-**, **pāp-**, and **up-** before adding an ending that begins with a consonant, such as **-ta** or **-sup.nita**. But some people retain the liquid, so that the reduction is to **il-**, **kwul-**, **pāl-**, and **ul-**. Those who use the compound adjective **yēlp-pulk-** 'be light red' seem to pronounce it /yēlpulk-/. Stem-final **lk** is most commonly treated in the standard way (with the **l** dropping) except when attached to endings that begin with **k**, where the other treatment seems more common: **ilk.ko** and **ilk.ki** are pronounced /ilkko/ and /ilkki/ rather than the /ikko/ and /ikki/ that (automatically compressed from **ik-kko** and **ik-kki**) we would expect as consistent with /ikcci/ ← **ilk-ci** and /ingnun/ (← **ik-nun**) ← **ilk-nun**. The proper analysis of these forms is **il-** + /kko/ (etc.), the reinforced (-q) allomorph of **-ko**, rather than **ilk-** + **-ko**, since endings regularly reinforce after a liquid reduced from a cluster. Compare the unexpected treatment of **salk** 'leopard cat' + **kwāyngi** 'cat' → **salk kwāyngi** /salkkwāyngi/ 'leopard cat' where we expect /sakkwāyngi/ as consistent with **talk koki** /takkoki/ 'chicken meat'. In overprecise speech, a theoretically dropped liquid sometimes reappears, giving anomalous syllable-final clusters, as in /talktto/ for /taktto/ = **talk to** 'chicken too'. That is somewhat similar to the retention, or reimposition from spelling, of /l/ by certain English speakers in words such as "palm" and "calm".

After dropping any excess, if what remains is not a permissible syllable-final consonant (**p t k l m n ng**), as with **s ss c ch**, or if it is an **l** which is the last phoneme of a consonant stem (§8.1.4), but not an **l** reduced from a cluster, that remaining consonant is treated as the phoneme /t/ with whatever reflex would be appropriate to **t**. (But historically the **l** of the -T/L- stems is a lenited form of *t*.)

Below is a fairly complete list of examples for each extrasyllabic final. But instead of **s**, for which there are a large number of examples (as there are for **p k m n ng l**), those examples ending in a basic **t** are listed, since their number is much smaller. In each list, all the nouns are grouped at the end.

A Reference Grammar of Korean

EXAMPLES OF EXTRASYLLABIC EXCESS

t   et- < ″et- 'obtain', it- 'be good', ket- < ket- 'fold up', kot- < kwot- 'be straight', kwut- < kwut- 'be hard, firm', mit- < mit- 'trust, believe in', mot- [obsolete] < mwot- 'gather up', mut- < mwut- 'bury', mut- < mwut- 'stain, color', nat- / nath- [obsolete] < nat- / nath- = nathana- < na᾿tha °na- 'appear', pat- < pat- 'receive', pet- < pet- 'stretch out (like a road)', ppet- 'extend, stretch out (an arm or a leg)', ssot- < ῾swot- 'pour out', tat- < tat- 'close', tit- (a truncation of titi- < tu᾿tuy-) 'tread, step on', tot- < twot- 'sprout, bloom; (sun / moon) rise', ttut- < ῾ptut- 'bite, snatch, graze';

kot < ῾kwot 'immediate, direct; to wit', ῾kwot > kwos 'place', mat < mot 'senior, eldest', nāt < ″nat 'grain', ″pet > pēs 'friend', ῾tet > tes 'a while'.

th   cith- < tith- 'be saturated, (liquid) thick, (color) dark', ῾heth- 'get disarrayed / scattered', huth- < ῾huth- 'get dispersed, scatter out', kath- < ῾koth- < ῾kot °ho- 'be like; be together', kith- 'remain', math-$_1$ < math- 'smell, sniff (it)', math-$_2$ < mast- 'take charge of', nath- / nat- [obsolete] < nath- / nat- = nathana- < na᾿tha °na- 'appear', path- < path-$_1$ 'sift, drain; (liquid) dry up', payth- < path-$_2$ 'spit out', puluth- (truncation of puluthu- < pulu᾿thu-) 'get swollen', puth- < puth- 'stick, be attached', yath- / yeth- < yath-/yeth- < nyeth- 'be shallow';

hoth < hwoth 'single', keth < kech 'surface, shell', khongphath < khwong᾿phoch 'kidney', koputh (= koputhangi) 'outside fold of a bolt of cloth', kkuth < (··· s) ῾kuth 'end' (but kkuthu in kkuthu-meli 'butt-end'), kyeth < kyeth 'side', melimath < (me᾿li math) 'head (of bed or grave)', mith < mith 'bottom, underside', muth < mwuth 'land, shore', nāth < ″nath 'piece, unit', pakkath < pas[k] kyeth 'outside', path < path 'dry field, garden', phath < ῾phoch 'a kind of red bean', pyeth < pyeth '(sun)light', sath < sath 'crotch', soth < swoth 'pot', swuth < (?*)swusk (CF Kim Thaykyun 323b) 'quantity, bulk (as of hair)', toth [obsolete] < twoth 'boar'.

ss   iss- < is(i)- 'exist, stay', -(ᵉ/a)ss- (past) < - ᵉ/a is(i)-, -keyss- (future) ? < - ῾ke ᾿ys(i)᾿ta. There is also ssāyss- 'be plentiful', contracted from ssah.ye iss- 'be piled up', which lacks the expected modifier form (*ssāss.un), replacing it with ssāyn, contracted from ssah.in. The modifier form of iss- is relatively uncommon but it occurs: see the entry iss.un in Part II.

c   aykkwuc- ? < * ″ay s kwuc- 'be undeservedly misfortunate', cac- '(wind) ease up, calm down', cac- < coc- 'be frequent, incessant', cac- / cec- 'lean back', cec- < cec- 'get wet', cic- < cuc- '(dog) bark, bay', ccic- < ῾pcuc- 'tear it', ccoc- 'twist (a pigtail)', cīs-kwuc- 'be annoying', chac- < choc- 'look for, find', ic- < nic- 'forget', ic- 'wane; get chipped', kac- < ῾koc- 'be prepared' (rare except in the causative kac.chwu- < ko᾿chwo- = koc-῾hwo- 'make ready'), kac- (a truncation of kaci- < ka᾿ci-) 'possess', kkoc- < kwoc- 'insert', kkwucic- < kwu᾿cic- / kwu᾿cit- 'scold (a child)', kwuc- 'be bad, vile; (weather) be threatening', (nwun i) kwuc- 'go blind', mac- < mac- 'be suitable, appropriate', mac- < mac- 'meet; face', mayc- < moyc- 'bind, tie', mec- [dialect?] < mec- = memchwu- < me᾿chwu- = memul(u)- (< me᾿mul-) 'stop', mec- 'be bad', nac- < nac- 'be low', nuc- < nuc- 'be late', peluc- 'scatter, dig out', pic- < pic- 'brew, ferment, make', putic- 'bump into', pulu-cic- 'cry out, shout', seluc- < selec- 'discard' (obsolete), selkec- < selGec- (obsolete) = selkeci ha- 'do dishes', tac- (truncation of taci- ? < [dialect] tati-) 'harden by stamping, press, mince';

cec < ῾cyec 'milk', coc 'penis', i᾿su᾿lac '(wild) cherry' > isulach = isulac(h)i [dialect], kac᾿ (truncation of kacwuk < kach, used as adnoun) 'leather', kalac (truncation of kalaci < kalati ?1834-) 'foxtail (plant)' (= kangaci phul), kic 'coat collar; portion', kwoc$_1$ (> kkoc.i) 'skewer', koc < kwoc$_2$ 'cape, promontory' (postnoun), koc᾿ (truncation of kocang 'place', CF kos < ῾kwot 'place'), mec 'cherry', nac < ῾nac 'daytime', nuc 'late' (adnoun), nuc [obsolete] > nuch 'sign, portent, omen', ōn-kac᾿ < ῾won-῾kas (truncation of ōn kaci < ῾won ka᾿ci 'all kinds'), pām-nuc (= pām-nucengi) 'chestnut blossoms', pec (= pecci) 'cherry', pic < pit 'debt', pon koc᾿ (truncation of pon kocang) 'native place' (= pon kos <

pwon kwot).

ch   **coch-** < *cwoch-* 'follow', **ccoch-** < *pcwoch-* 'pursue', **kech** = **kecwuk** 'surface, exterior', **kich-** (? truncation) = *kichi-* 'cough', **ich-** 'get tired', **mich-** < *mich-* (? truncation of **michi-**) 'attain, reach', **nwiwuch-** < ¨*nwuyGuch-* (truncation of **nwiwuchi-** < ¨*nwuyGuchi-*) 'regret', **sich-** (truncation of **sichi-**) 'sew a quilt', **ssich-** [dialect] = **ssis-** 'wash' < *sis-*, **takuch-** (truncation of **takuchi-**) 'bring nearer';

˙*ach* 'reason', ˙*cich* > **kis** 'feather(s)', **isulach** = **isulac(h)i** (dialect) < *i˙su˙lac* '(wild) cherry', **kach** < *kach* 'skin, hide', **kkoch** < *(··· s) kwoc* 'flower', **meych** (**myech**) < ˙*myech* 'how much / many', **mich** [literary] 'and', **nach** < *noch* 'face', **nuch** < *nuc* [obsolete] 'sign, portent, omen', **pich**$_1$ < *pyeth* 'sunshine', **pich**$_2$ < ˙*pich* 'color; sign, mark; scene(ry)', ˙*such* 'time interval, while', **swuch** < *swusk* 'charcoal', **tach** (**tech**) ˙'anchor', **tech** (dialect **tek**) 'snare; small drum' < **tesk*, **toch** < *twosk* 'sail', **yuch** ?< **nywusk* 'Four Sticks (a Korean game)'. NOTE: The noun **och** 'sumac, lacquer' was attested as *woch* in 1608 Thaysan 53a (*wo.ch ol*) but earlier it appeared as *wos* in 1463 Pep 1:219a (*wo˙s i˙la*).

ph   **ciph-** < *tiph-* 'lean (hands) on, feel (pulse)', **eph-** < *eph-* 'overthrow' (rare except in compounds and **twicipe eph-** 'turn inside out or upside down'), **iph-** = **ulph-** > **ulph-** 'chant', **kaph-** < *kaph-* 'reward, repay', **kiph-** < *kiph-* 'be deep', **noph-** < *nwoph-* 'be high', **siph-** < *sikpu-* 'be inclined toward, be desirous', **teph-** < *teph-* 'cover with, use as a cover', **tunoph-** 'be lofty', **thoph-** 'search everywhere for; soften and spread hemp tufts (to make rope)', ? **puph-** (= **puphu-l-**) in **puph-tāy-** and **puph-tā-l-** (but the aspiration could not be realized here, so this seems to be a purely orthographic or historical example).

aph < *a(l)ph* 'front' (and compounds such as **ocil-aph** 'front of an outer garment'), **ciph** < ˙*tiph* 'straw', **hēngkeph** < *heng˙kes* < ¨*hen* (< **he˙[l-o]n*) *kes* 'piece of cloth' [···**ph** unexplained], **iph** < ˙*niph* 'leaf', ˙*iph* 'gate', **keseph** 'a levee reinforcement; a weed potcover; vegetables for **pipimq pap**', **muluph** < *mwulwuph* 'knee', **nuph** (dialect **nwuph**) 'marsh, swamp', ˙*pwuph* > **puk** 'drum', **seph** < *syeph* 'kindling, firewood; gusset; prop', **swuph** < ˙*swuph* 'forest', **yeph** (/ ··· **nyekh**) < *nyeph* / *nyekh* 'side, flank'.

ps   **ēps-** < ¨*eps-* (?< **e-˙p[i]s[i]-* or **e˙pV is[i]-*) 'be nonexistent' and certain stems derived from it: **kā.yeps-** 'be pitiful', **mayk-ēps-** 'be despondent', **sil-ēps-** 'be frivolous, unsubstantial', **silum-ēps-** 'be absentminded, vacant', **sokcel-ēps-** 'be futile, hopeless', **yel-ēps-** 'be timid, cowardly';

kaps < ˙*kaps* 'price'.

kh   – ;

puekh < *puzek* / *puzep* ?< **˙pu[l] s(y)ep[h]* 'kitchen', ··· **nyekh** 'direction' (see **yeph**).

kk < **sk** **kkakk-** < *kosk-* 'cut, shave, pare', **kkekk-** < *kesk-* 'break off', **kyekk-** < *kyesk-* 'experience, undergo', **mukk-** < *mwusk-* (?< **˙mwu[l] sk···*) 'make into a bundle', **nakk-** 'fish' from **naks-** < *naksk-* (CF **naks-i** spelled **nakk-si** 'fishing'; SEE **-si** in Part II), **pokk-** < *pwosk-* 'roast', **sekk-** < *sesk-* 'mix it', **sokk-** (dialect **sokkwu-**) < *swos˙kwo-* (?= *swos-˙kwo-* 'raise') 'weed out', **takk-** < *task-* 'polish', **tekk-** 'get dirty / rusty', **yekk-** < *yesk-* 'knit, weave';

pakk < *pask* 'outside'; **pusk** (?< **pu[l] sk···*) 'moxacautery', **swusk** > **swuch** 'charcoal', **twosk** > **toch** 'sail', **twosk** > **tos(-cali)** 'mat'.

ks   – ;

moks < *mwok* 'portion' (···s unexplained; blended with *mwus* 'bundle' < *mwusk-*?), **neks** < *neks* 'spirit', **saks** < *saks*$_1$ 'charge, fare', *saks*$_2$ > **ssak** 'sprout', **seks** 'surge of emotion (especially anger); a mooring', ˙*syeks* 'reins', **ches-paks** [dialect] 'first', **mayks** [dialect] = **mayk** 'pulse'; ˙*naks* 'fish hook' (> **nakk.si**).

h   (For MK ···*h* nouns, see p. 109.) ? **ccah-** [dialect] = **cca-** < ˙*pco-* 'weave', **ccih-** < *tih-* 'pound, ram', **ceh-** 'fear' – also (1465 Wen 1:2:3:40a) *cyeh-*, *cih-* 'affix', **cōh-** < ¨*tywoh-* 'be good / liked', ˙*cwoh-* 'be clean', **eh-** < *[p]eh-* 'get cut' (mistakenly treated as "*eth-*" in

LCT 558a, the correct analysis is LCT 1971:22) – CF e˙hi- < [p]e˙hi- 'cut it', nah- < nah- 'be born', neh- < nyeh- 'put in', noh- < nwoh- 'put', peh- 'get cut', pih- 'sprinkle, sow' (? < ˙pi 'rain' + °ho- 'do'), ppāh- 'grind', ssah- < (s)sah- 'pile / heap up, build', spih- / spyeh- = pih-, tah- < tah-₁ 'touch; arrive', ttah- < tah-₂ 'braid'. (SEE §8.2.2.)

mh   (For MK ‥mh nouns, see p. 109.)

nh   (For MK ‥nh nouns, see p. 109.) anh- (< a˙ni ho-) 'not do/be' (negative auxiliary) and compounds that contain it, hunh- < hun ha- < hun °ho- 'be common, plentiful, easily had, cheap', kkonh- 'mark, grade, rate', kkunh- 'break / cut off; stop', mānh- < ¨manh- < ¨man °ho- 'be much / many'. (SEE §8.2.2.)

lh   (For MK ‥lh nouns, see below.) alh- < alh- 'ail', halh- > halth- 'lick, taste', helh- = hel ha- < ˙hel °ho- 'be easy, undemanding', ilh- < ilh- 'lose', kolh- < kwolh- 'be unfilled, half-empty', kolh- < kwolh- 'rot', kkulh- < kulh- 'boil', kkwulh- 'bend knees (to kneel)', olh- < ˙wolh- 'be right', silh- < ˙sulh- 'be disliked', ssulh- < sulh- 'polish (grain)', talh- 'wear away; boil dry', ttwulh- < ¨tulw-(/ tolw-) 'pierce'. (SEE §8.2.2.)

ls   – ;
kols '(water-)course, (fixed) direction', ¨kwols > kol(ay) 'hypocaust flue', ols 'compensation, reparation', tols < twols 'cycle, postnatal year of age'.

lth   halth- < halh- 'lick, taste', hwulth- 'tear off something stuck to the surface, rinse out something stuck inside a bowl; thresh';

– .

lk   elk- < elk- 'wrap, tie up, fasten', kalk- < kolk- 'scratch with a sharp point', kulk- < kulk- 'scratch', kwulk- < kwulk- 'be burly', malk- < molk- 'be clear', mulk- < mulk- 'be thin, watery', nalk- < nolk- '(thing) be old', nulk- < nulk- '(person) get/be old', olk- 'trap, ensnare', palk- < polk- 'dawn; get/be bright', (p)pulk- < pulk- 'be red';
chilk < ˙chulk 'arrowroot; striped', holk (variant of hol) 'a growth', hulk < holk 'earth, soil', katalk (= katak) 'strip, piece, strand', kkatalk 'reason', kisulk (= kisulak) 'edge, border', selk < selk [obsolete] = selki 'wicker trunk', salk < solk 'leopard cat', siwulk (variant siwul) < si˙Gwulk 'edge' [old-fashioned] (= kacang-cali), talk < tolk 'chicken'. [1]Yi Yuncay also gives the pre-separable intransitive verbal noun inseparable wulk (ha- 'get rash / hasty') but I am unable to find evidence that the l is ever pronounced; the spelling may be historical or based on an association, morphemic or dialectal, with the stem olk- or with the stem pulk-. ([1]Yi Yuncay was mistaken in labeling the word adjectival.)

lG / l^U/o < *l^{U}ok SEE §3.3.1.
ll / l^{U}ol < *l^{U}ol SEE §3.3.1.

lm   cēlm- < cyelm- (1775) < ¨cyem- 'be young', cilm- 'bundle up to carry, pack on back', ¨kalm- 'store/hide it', kōlm- < [¨]kwolm- 'fester', kwūlm- < [¨]kwulm- 'go without food', pālm- 'measure off by the arms; guess', sālm- < ¨solm- 'boil', tālm- 'resemble' < ¨talm- 'spread (disease)', ¨telm- 'get dirty / dyed', ōlm- < ¨wolm- 'move' (= olm.ki-) and 'be infected by, catch (a disease)';
sālm 'life', ālm 'knowledge', and all other regular substantives from the l-extending vowel stems (§8.2.2, §9.5)

lp   ccalp- / ccelp- (< cyelp-) < tyalo- / tyel^U/o- < tyelG- < *tyelW- ? < *tyalop- / tyelup- 'be short, fine', ¨kolW- 'line up, array; compete', nelp- < nel^U/o- ? < *nelup- 'be wide', pālp- < ¨polW- 'tread on', sēlp- (= sēlw- [obsolete] = sēlew-) < ¨syelW- 'be sad', ttēlp- < ¨ptelW- 'be astringent', yalp- / yelp- < ¨yelW- 'be thin, faint, light';
˙kolp 'layer; time', ˙salp > sap 'shovel', yetelp (dialect yatul, yatap, yatak) < ye˙tulp / ye˙tolp (< *yotolp) 'eight' (see below).

lph   ulph- < ulph- / iph- 'chant'; aytalph- < ¨ay ˙tolp- 'feel pity', kotalph- [lit.] = kotalphu- 'be tired' (< kwo˙tol˙ph-a 'with great effort');
– , alph = aph > aph 'front'.

nc   anc- < a(n)c- 'sit down', enc- < enc- < yenc- 'place, put up/on', kki-enc- 'shower oneself';

nk / nu < *nuk SEE §8.3.1.
mk / mo < *mok SEE §8.3.1.
mk / mwo < *mwok SEE §8.3.1.
mk / mwu < *mwuk SEE §8.3.1.
zG / z^u/o < *s^u/ok SEE §8.3.1.

Not included in the list are the names for letters of the Korean alphabet. These are rather artificial concoctions, usually pronounced according to a common variant: **tikut / tikus** 'the letter T', **thiuth / thius** 'the letter TH', **chiuch / chius** 'the letter CH', **phiuph / phiup** 'the letter PH', **khiukh / khiuk** 'the letter KH'. There is also **hiuh**, the only known case of noun-final h in the standard orthography. The h is treated as /t/ before pause or consonant, and should be either /h/ or dropped before the copula or a particle beginning with a vowel, but in fact this word nearly always gets the variant treatment represented by the basic shape **hius**. The bound preparticle **pa.yah** (§5.2.9) is written together with its particle **ulo** as an unanalyzed word: **pa-ya-hu-lo**. The verb stems with final ⋯**lph**- carry a literary flavor; they seem to be truncated from vowel stems ending in ⋯**lphu**-, as shown by the third example.

An example of ⋯**nth** is found in Khun sacen, which lists **panth** as a variant of **pān** 'half'. I am told that /panthun/ is South Cenla dialect for **pān un** 'as for half'. [1]Yi Yuncay lists **panth** as Kyengsang dialect. The **th** is etymologically unexpected and its origin is unknown (?< hatun).

When followed by a vowel that is NOT the beginning of an ending, a particle, or the copula, syllable excess is reduced just as before a consonant, so that the common noun-final ⋯**s** is pronounced **t** and articulated as the onset of the vowel-initial syllable to which it is attached. Examples:

s → t: **os an** 'inside the garment' /otan/, **kulus an** 'in the plate' /kulutan/, **ches atul** 'first son' /chetatul/, **ches insang** 'first impression' /chetinsang/, **ches umcel** 'first syllable' /chetumcel/, **kis os** 'a kind of mourning robe' /kitot/, **has os** 'padded garment' /hatot/, **wus os** 'outer garment' /wutot/, **wus akwi** 'crotch between thumb and index finger' /wutakwi/, **ūypus atul (emi, epi)** 'step-son (-mother, -father)' /ūputatul/ (/ūputemi/, /ūputepi/), **yēys wang** 'ancient kings' /yēytwang/, **swus ūmsik** 'fresh food' /swutūmsik/, **hes wus.um** 'empty smile' /hetwusum/, **pelus ēps-** 'lacks manners' /pelutēpss-/, ...

c → t: **cec emeni** 'wet-nurse' /cetemeni/, ... Compare **cec hyeng** 'older nursemate ("milk-brother")' /cethyeng/.

ch → t: **kkoch ahop songi** 'nine flowers' /kkota(h)opssongi/, **kkoch alay** 'under the flower' /kkotalay/, **hayq-pich ani 'myen** 'unless it is sunshine' /hayppitanimyen/, **och olu-** 'get lacquer-poisoned' /otolu-/.

t: **mat atul** 'eldest son' (but **mat ita** 'is the eldest' Seoul /macita/), ... Compare **mat hyeng** 'the eldest brother' /mathyeng/.

th → t: **soth an** 'in the pot' /sotan/, **path alay** 'below the field' /patalay/, **path wi** 'above the field' /patwi/ (compare **path twī** 'behind the field' /pattwī/), **hoth os** 'single-layer garment' /hotot/, **kkuth ani 'ta** 'it is not the end' /kkutanita/, **pith ēps-** 'lack color' /pitepss-/, **puth-an-** 'hug' /putan-/, **sath-sath-i** 'in every corner, exhaustively' /sassachi/.

ps → p: **kaps echi** 'worth' /kapechi/, **kaps ēps-** 'lack value' /kapepss-/ (compare **kaps ci-** 'be of value' /kapcci-/).

ph → p: **aph.aph-i** 'in front of each' /apaphi/, **iph wi** 'on the leaf' /ip(w)i/ (CF §2.7.4), **muluph wi** /mulup(w)i/ 'on the knee'. Compare **noph-tala(h)-** 'be sort of tall' /nopttala(h)-/.

kh → k: **puekh an** 'in the kitchen' /puekan/.

ks → k: **neks ēps.i** 'absentmindedly' /nekepssi/.

ls → l: **tols an ey** 'within the first year of life' /tolaney/.

The following cases involve reinforcement (-q, CF §1.5.): **alayq i** 'lower teeth' /alaynni/, **aphq** ima 'forehead' /amnima/, cipq īmca 'householder' /cimnīmca/, hothq ipul 'single quilt' /honnipul/, kyepq ipul 'double quilt' /kyemnipul/, pamq isul 'evening dew' /pamnisul/, sōkq iph 'the inside leaf' /songnip/, ttekq iph 'seedleaf' /ttengnip/, wiq ip-swul 'upper lip' /winnipsswul/ 'upper lip'. For certain examples the reinforcement may be optional: pathq ilang 'field ridge' /pannilang/ is also reported as path ilang /patilang/. The orthographically identical path ilang 'field and the like' with the colloquial particle ilang / lang is pronounced /pachilang/, and many speakers say /pasilang/.

In a few expressions, contrary to what we expect, the syllable excess persists, as in yetelp hay 'eight years' /yetelphay/ where we would expect (?*)yetel(h)ay. The word for 'eight' has been restructured as yetel(q) for most speakers, who say yetel ita and not yetelp ita for 'they are ten'. In causatives and passives, the derived stems preserve as much of the excess as can be pronounced: palp-hi- 'get trodden on' /palphi-/ is the passive of pālp- 'tread on', but kolm-ki- 'has it fester', the causative of kolm- 'fester', must be reduced to /komki-/. And most derivatives are like compounds and reduce the excess: noph-talah- 'be sort of tall' /nopttala(h)-/, nelp-tala(h)- /nelttala(h)-/ 'be sort of wide', kwulk-tala(h)- 'be sort of burly' /kwukttala(h)-/ or /kwulttala(h)-/.

[1]Yi Ungpayk 454 calls our attention to the rule by which compounds are spelled phonemically rather than morphophonemically if the last consonant of a double-consonant pat.chim is not pronounced:

kolmak / kwulmek ha- 'be almost full' from kolh- / kwulh- 'be not yet full' (but notice kwūlm- 'go without food, starve');

kolpyeng 'deep-seated disease; fatal blow' from kolh- 'rot' + pyēng 'illness';

halccak halccak 'in little licks' from halth- 'lick' + -cak (diminutive suffix < cāk- 'little');

silccwuk / saylccwuk ha- 'be sullen' from silh- + suffix -cwuk;

malsswuk / melsswuk ha- 'be neat' from malk- 'clear' + suffix -swuk;

malccang / melcceng ha- 'be intact, perfect' from malk- 'clear' + suffix -cang/-ceng;

olmu 'snare' from olk- 'bind, lay a snare' + ?; one proposed etymology has olk.a kam- > *olk.a kam-i > olkami 'snare' > *olkamu > *olk'mu > olmu. It is unclear just why silh-cung (= silhq-cung) 'ennui' is not spelled according to its pronunciation /silccung/.

Moreover, there are examples of phonemic spelling even when the syllable excess is pronounced:

yalphak ha- 'be thin-surfaced' from yalph- 'be thin' (with syllable excess retained) + suffix -ak, or (with syllable excess suppressed) + the mimetic phak 'deflated, flat; soft', probably unrelated to Chinese loanmorph pak < 'PPAK 'thin';

silkhum ha- 'be dislikable' from silh- + suffix -kum (CF silh.ko 'disliking' /silkho/).

The structure of malkkum / melkkum ha- 'be clean' can be explained as a reduction of malk- → mal- before attaching the suffix, which then reinforces its initial, as it does in malk-ko and malk-ci when pronounced /malkko/ and /malcci/ rather than the competing version /makko/ ← mak-ko and /makcci/ ← mak-ci.

Some confusion exists over whether there are two versions of 'rather wide': /nepttala(h)-/ = nelp.talah- and /nelttala(h)-/ = nelttala(h)- (spelled nel.tala(h)- in North Korea). NKd lists both versions and suggests that the latter comes from nelu- 'be broad'; most South Korean authorities prefer the second version (nel··· not nep···) but derive it from nelp-. A similar problem: /nepccik/ and /nelccik/. The South Korean authorities seem to prefer the latter and spell it phonemically. NKd lists nelp.cik (presumably to be pronounced /nepcik/) but refers it to the entry nel.cik for which the pronunciation is explicitly stated as /nelccik/; there are entries for /nepccek/ spelled both nelp.cek and nep.cek, and similarly for /nepccwuk/.

Finally, we should keep in mind the ongoing tendency to restructure the basic forms of most nouns bearing syllable excess. Even Seoul speakers often simplify noun-final ···ps to just ···p; the pronunciation /kap/ for kaps 'price' in ūmsik kap[s] ey nun in drill 3.7 of KBC 24 is not a slip of the tape or the tongue, but a variant of what is heard as /kapss/, a more formal version, in mulken kaps ey nun in drill 3.9. In everyday speech people quite often say /kapun/ and /kapulo/ (for kaps un, kaps ulo) instead of /kapssun/ and /kapssulo/, even though they may well say /kapssi, kapssita/ for kaps i, kaps ita. The liquid in talk 'chicken' is widely ignored, so that tak i and tak ul are the commonly heard nominative and accusative forms; the liquid is retained in a derivative talkyal 'egg'. In modern usage moks 'portion' and kols 'course, channel' are generally just mok and kol: Ku ttang un nay mok[s] ip.nita; ney mok[s] un ... 'That land is my share; your share ... '; Kol[s] ul kiph.key pha la 'Dig the channel deep!'. We can treat puekh 'kitchen' as an obsolescent version of the widely used puek (also pēk); but pakk 'outside' persists unsimplified. The noun muluph 'knees' is heard either with the simplified basic form mulup or in a derivative muluphak(-i), which preserved the syllable excess when the diminutive suffix -ak was added. But aph 'front', yeph 'beside', and iph 'leaf' (also iphali, ipsakwi) commonly retain the older basic shapes. Modern Seoul speech is in flux on the question of merging noun-final ···th, ···ch, and ···c with ···s. The four-stick game is generally treated as yus rather than the older yuch; och 'lacquer; sumac' is treated just like os 'garment'; and path is more often heard with final s than with the traditional th or (before i) ch. But both meych and meys are common for the orthographic myech 'how many', and only the affricate is heard in nac ey 'in the daytime / afternoon', though you may notice an allophone of that which is articulated as a voiced sibilant [z]. There are no good examples of noun-final ···t, since nāt of nāt-al 'grain' is no longer a free noun, and earlier cases of noun-final ···t merged with ···s over two centuries ago, so that ˙mwot 'nail' and ˙mwos 'pond' are now both mos. Despite these remarks on colloquial usage, this book follows the traditional spellings and we treat syllable excess as basic to those nouns that began simplifying it relatively late.

Earlier forms of the language had a wider array of extrasyllabic finals, including stems ending in ···sk- (> ···kk-) and ···st- (> ···th-). There were even a few nouns without vowels: see in Part II the entries psk 'time', s 'fact', t 'fact'. The reduction of the excess was similar to what it is today, but in the 15th century there was no need to reduce ···s since it was a syllable-final consonant. Stems ending in ···(n)c- such as a(n)c- 'sit' reduced to ···s-, as did those ending in ···z- (lenited from ···s···) and those ending in ···sk- and ···st-. The doublet wumchu- / wumchi- 'huddle, shrink' contracted to a reduced stem wums- in a few examples. The noun poych 'oar' must be the result of truncating an unattested phrase ˙poy ˙chi 'boat rudder'.

In the modern language final ···h, ···nh, and ···lh occur only for verb stems, but in Middle Korean there were nouns that had these basic codas (and also ···mh), which surface as the aspirating of a voiceless consonant that begins a following particle, though the /h/ was suppressed when the noun was in isolation, i.e. before pause. As mentioned above, there is evidence for some of these noun-final h's in such modern compounds as am-khay < amh kāy 'female dog' and swu-khay 'male dog' < swuh kāy. The spellings of 1898 Tayshin show final h for a number of nouns with the particle i (or incorporated -i) attached: ttahi, tta 'earth'; patahi, pata 'sea', twuihyi 'behind' (= Seoul twī ey); and even one case of final h in isolation, narahi, narah. (1874 Putsillo gives 'behind' as twui, twuhe.) All these nouns had a basic final -h in Middle Korean. The standard noun nai 'age' must have developed like the Tayshin nahi, by incorporating -i to the MK noun that had the basic shape ˙nah and survived in its "free" shape as na in modern dialects (e.g. the South Hamkyeng version used by 1936 Roth 197); CF naq sal 'age, years [often derogatory]' (KEd). 1894 Gale writes (48) hon.a.hun 'as for one' (< MK hona˙h un), and (148) hon.a (< MK hona[h]) with an unexpected syllable break perhaps reflecting the allomorph hon··· but missing in hona.hi (80); also (82) pata.hi and pata.hul for the nominative and accusative of 'sea' (< MK pa˙tah), and (64) chol.ha.li for chalali 'rather' (< MK chol˙hali).

Some of the stems ending in the final aspirate seem to have incorporated the pro-verb °ho- > ha- 'do/be', which was prone to elide its minimal vowel, leaving the h behind to fend for itself. Although ilh- is the only MK version for 'lose', 1898 Tayshin attests both ilhata (with palatalized [l]!) and iltha ("irta" with [r]!). [1]Yi Congchel 1983 clearly writes mān ha- (with the Chinese character MYRIAD) for mānh-; the basic stem in the earliest Hankul texts is sometimes ¨man °ho-, sometimes ¨manh-. The basic form of MK word for 'above' was wuh; the final h was suppressed when the noun preceded juncture (that is, when it was not followed by a closely attached particle or copula form), and it is that form which survives as the standard North Korean wu, while Seoul has standardized wi < wu[h] +

incorporated -i, a development more common as a northern characteristic. (1894 Gale 133 writes *mwul wu.huy* 'in the water'.) NKd lists a dialect form **wuthi**, not in the Hamkyeng dictionary nor in Choy Hak.kun (though he has "uge" = **wukey**), which may reflect the earlier **h**, but the derivation is unclear. There are two examples of ··*ngh*: *stang.h ay* (1617 Sin-Sok [1]Yel 4:64) 'on the land' seems to be a hybrid of earlier *sta ̇h ay* and *stang* (id. Hyo 1:1), but *syang ̇h ay* 'regularly' (1518 Sohak-cho 8:9b) is not so easily explained.

In the following lists of MK nouns ending in ··*h* a few of the examples occur as doublets, with or without the *h* in the basic form. That means there are competing phrases without the *h* where we would expect it. (Of course, all the nouns suppress the *h* when they occur as free forms.) The two versions of the doublets are separated by a slash.

MK nouns with final ··*mh*: ̇*amh* 'female', ̇*wumh* 'cave'.

MK nouns with final ··*nh*: ̇*anh* 'inside'; ̇*enh* 'dike'; ̇*kinh*, ̇*skinh* 'string'; *twuy-anh* (1576 [1]Yuhap 2:28b, 1632 Twusi-cwung 6:50a) = ̇*wuy-̇anh* 'garden'.

MK nouns with final ··*lh*: ̇*alh* 'egg' ̇*cholh* 'source' (CF ̇*stolh*); *ha ̇nolh / ha ̇nol* 'heaven'; ̇*kalh / ̇kal* 'knife' (̇*kal ̇lwo* 1465 Wen 3:2:2:10a = ̇*kal.h of ̇ ̇ Jlwo* 1462 [1]Nung 6:109b; ̇*kal ̇Gwa* 1462 [1]Nung 6:28b = ̇*kal ̇khwa* 1459 Wel 9:43b); ̇*kilh* 'path'; *ko(̇)nolh / ̇ko(̇)nol* 'shade'; *kowolh* 'district' (= *kowolkh, koWol*); *kozolh / kozol* 'autumn'; *kye ̇zulh / kye ̇zul > kye[z]ol(h)* winter; ̇*malh* 'stake'; ̇*milh* 'wheat'; *mozolh* 'village'; ̇*nolh*[1] 'blade'; ̇*nolh*[2] 'warp (threads)'; *nomolh* 'greens'; *polh > pholh > phol* 'arm'; *poyzolh / poyzol* (< *poy solh) 'entrails' (*poyzol ̇tol ̇h ol* 1463 Pep 2:105b); ̇*ptulh / ̇ptul* 'garden' (̇*ptul ̇Gwa* Twusi 25:39a); *pyelh* 'cliff'; ̇*solh* 'flesh'; ̇*stolh* 'origin, source' (CF ̇*cholh*); ̇*sukwulh* 'rural area' (= ̇*sukwol,* ̇*sukowol,* ̇*sukoWol*); ̇*su ̇mulh* 'twenty'; ¨*syewulh /* ¨*syewul,* ¨*syeWul[h]* 'capital' (¨*syewul ̇lwo* 1481 Twusi 24:45b, ¨*sye ̇wul ̇se / ̇two* ?1517- Pak 1:53b [accent unexplained]); ̇*tolh* 'group' (plural); ¨*twolh*[1] 'bridge'; ¨*twolh*[2] 'stone'; ¨*twulh* 'two'; *wolh* 'this year'; ̇*wulh* 'fence'; ̇*yelh* 'ten'; *yelh* 'hemp seed'.

MK nouns with postvocalic final ··*h*: ̇*cah* 'foot'; *cwoh* 'millet'; *honah* 'one'; *kuluh* 'root'; ̇*kwoh* 'nose'; ̇*mah* 'yam'; *mah / ma* 'monsoon' (= *tyang-ma[h]*), 'south, south wind (= *mah polom > **maphalam**); ̇*moyh* 'moor'; ¨*mwoyh* mountain'; ̇*mwoh* 'corner'; *na ̇cwoh* 'evening' = *na ̇cwoy*; ̇*nah* 'age'; *na ̇lah* 'land'; ¨*nayh* 'river'; ¨*neyh* 'four'; *ni ̇mah* 'forehead'; ̇*nimcah /* ¨*nimca* 'master; you'; *nwoh* 'cord'; *pa ̇tah* 'sea'; *pwoh*[1] 'beam'; *pwoh*[2] 'cloth'; ¨*seyh* 'three'; ̇*stah* 'ground'; *tuluh* 'hat brim' (?1517- [1]No 2:52a); *tu ̇luh* 'moor'; ¨*twuyh* 'rear'; *tyeh* 'whistle'; ̇*swoh*[1] 'swamp'; ̇*swoh*[2] 'matrix, mold, die'; ̇*swuh*[1] 'male'; ̇*swuh*[2] 'forest' = ̇*swuph*; *sywoh* 'layman'; ¨*si[l] -* ¨*nayh / -* ¨*nay* (¨*si* -̇ ¨*nay lwo* 1481 Twusi 21:34a) 'stream'; ̇*theh* 'site'; *wuh* 'above'; *ye ̇leh* 'several'; *zywoh* 'mattress'.

4.3. Treatment of yey.

The phoneme string /yey/ occurs only after a pause; in other positions it is automatically replaced by /ey/, so that **pon yēysan** 'the main / original budget' is pronounced either /pon|yēysan/ or /ponēysan/. The string /ey/ itself begins the basic form of very few words (**eywu-** 'surround', **eyi-** 'cut', ... , and recent loanwords) so that it is infrequent after pause.

Among the Chinese morphemes, the South Korean spelling writes **phyey** for /phey/ as in ph[y]ēy 'lungs', and **myey** for /mey/ in the bound noun m[y]ey, which appears in ūym[y]ey 'sleeve', m[y]ēykwu 'sleeve opening', [1]yenm[y]ey '(in) company', and punm[y]ey 'parting (of people)'. Both North and South spell **hyey** for /hey/ in Chinese loans such as **hyēyseng** 'comet'. Certain elements beginning with /key/ are distinguished in Hankul by the spelling **kyey**, such as **kyēysi-** 'stay [honorific]', **kyēysi** 'revelation' (pronounced just the same as **kēysi** 'notice, bulletin'), but there seems to be no good reason for any of these spellings, except perhaps historical. The spelling conventions are that only South Korea writes the unpronounced distinction of **myey : mey** and **phyey : phey**, but both South and North write the unpronounced distinctions of **kyey : key**, **hyey : hey**, and **yey : ey**. (CF Mkk 1960:9:37-8.)

Because of the automatic alternation of **yey** with **ey**, morphemes with the basic shape **lyey** (such as the common one meaning 'rite, ceremony') never actually occur in that shape at all; it is a fictive form based on the occurring alternants /ley/ (as in **sillyey** 'discourtesy' /silley/ and **kōlyey** 'ancient rites'

/kōley/) and /yey/, as in ¹yēypay 'worship'.

In addition to word variants like /⋯ ēysan/ for yēysan, which have to be caught on the fly and can be ignored for most purposes, we also observe the alternation of /ey/ and /yey/ in morphemes with the basic shape yēy, such as the one that means 'esthetic, art' and occurs initially in yēyswul 'esthetic techniques' and finally in mun.yey 'literature and art, humanities' = /muney/, hak.yey 'science and art = arts and sciences' = /hakey/, kongyey 'arts and crafts' = /kongey/, kiyey 'crafts' = /kiey/, swuyey 'handicraft' = /swuey/, etc. The dialect variants nēy (northern and modern-Seoul) and yēy 'yes' can be seen as a somewhat similar case, from a basic *nyēy.

4.4. Alternations of l and n.

Except in recent loanwords (latio 'radio', nyūsu 'news', nikheyl 'nickel'), in a few native oddities (see below), and in the grammarians' neologisms liul 'the letter L' and niun 'the letter N', the phoneme l does not occur after pause, nor do the strings ny and ni. In older loanwords l⋯ → n⋯ : ¹Nwuka pok.um 'the gospel of Luke', nampho(-tung) 'lamp'. After pause, a morpheme whose basic allomorph begins with l appears in an alternant beginning with n. But those morphemes whose basic allomorphs begin with li, ni, ly, or ny appear in allomorphs which begin with i or y:

		BASIC SHAPE	SHAPE AFTER PAUSE
l : n		yōlo 'major road'	¹nōpyen 'roadside'
n : n		sīnay 'city confines'	nāypu 'inside part'
ly : y		nolyek 'effort'	¹yek.hayng 'exertion'
ny : y		swunye 'nun'	ⁿyeca 'woman'
li : i		sāli 'reason'	¹īyu 'reason'
ni ; i		¹nōni 'a kind of clay'	ⁿiyok 'mud bath'

So far as the alternants after pause occur ONLY after pause, they can be called phonemically determined, provided we ignore the recent loanwords and a few native oddities such as nyesek 'rascal of a man', nyen 'rascal of a woman', nyen-nom 'men and women rascals', niun 'the letter N'. But in most words the "altered" allomorph occurs word-initially whether the word is preceded by pause or not: ku ⁿyeca 'that woman', i ¹nōpyen, … . That is sometimes obscured by the "-q" phenomena discussed below.

Certain other cases must be specified in detail. The word for 'league' or 'Korean mile' has the shape /ī/ except after a numeral, where it has the shapes /lī/ or /nī/ (written li): il lī 'one mile', ī li 'two miles', sam lī /samnī/ 'three miles', etc. The Chinese word for 'two' always has the shape /ī/ except after the word il 'one': il-ī 'one or two' is usually pronounced /illī/. The word for 'reason' has the shape /ī/ (written ¹ī) except after the prospective modifier: -ul lī ēps- 'not stand to reason that ⋯ '. The Chinese word for 'six' has the shape /yuk/ (spelled ¹yuk) except after a numeral: sip ¹yuk = sip-lyuk /simnyuk/ '16', ¹yuk-sipq ¹yuk /yukssimnyuk/. See §5.5.

A number of words beginning with i⋯ or y⋯ have alternants beginning with ni⋯ or ny⋯ (or reflexes of those strings) which appear in certain environments; these are best treated as cases of reinforcement (-q): cipq īl /cimnīl/ or cip īl /cipīl/ 'housework', halq īl /hallīl/ 'things to be done'. In the case of the noun īl the MK form had an oral beginning, but certain other nouns that nowadays behave the same way were spelled as ni⋯ or nye⋯-: i 'tooth' was MK ˙ni and iph 'leaf' was ˙niph (in contrast with ˙iph 'gate') but ip 'mouth' was MK ˙ip. We are tempted to write "alayq ni" for 'lower teeth', and that would be historically correct, but we have no way of keeping that situation apart from /alaynnipsswul/ 'lower lip' where "alayq nip-swul" would be historically incorrect. For the modern language we will treat all cases alike and write not only alayq ip-swul but also alayq i, letting a rule interpret "q i" as /nni/ and "q y" as /nny/ in examples such as hanq yeph = /hannyeph/ 'one side'. For Chinese words, the historical ny-, ly-, and li- are in general so written in the North Korean orthography, and the initial nasal is preserved in the spoken dialects, with loss of the -y- (except in ¹Yukcin). The initials of those strings are represented by superscript ⁿ and ¹ in the Yale Romanization:

ettenq ⁿyeca /ettennyeca/ 'what sort of woman', ponq ⁿyento /ponnyento/ 'this year period', musunq ¹īyu lo /musunniyulo/ 'for what reason', kulenq ¹yek.hayng /kulennyekhayng/ 'such exertion'; yang ¹yoli /yangnyoli/ 'western food', Cwungkwukq ¹yoli /cwungkwungnyoli/ 'Chinese food'; sampaykq ¹yuksip-o il /sampayngnyukssipoil/ '365 days'. The behavior of these is not distinguishable from that of the historically correct y··· and i··· : musunq yoil /musunnyoil/ 'what day of the week', nolanq yangmal /nolannyangmal/ 'yellow stockings' (KBC), kulenq ilmyen /kulennilmyen/ 'such a side (to it/him)', Pusanq yek /pusannyek/ 'Pusan station', Sewulq yek /sewullyek/ 'Seoul station', sīcheng-aphq yek /sīchengamnyek/ 'City Hall Station'; sonnimq-yong siktang /sonnimnyong|sikttang/ (KBC 2:24) 'guest dining room', chaykq yenkwu /chayngnyengkwu/ 'book research'. For certain strings the reinforcement is optional: kkoch(q) ilum 'fower name' can be said either /kkotilum/ or /kkonnilum/. The poetic noun im 'beloved' (so spelled in the north as well as the south) was earlier nim and is probably the same morpheme as the honorific postnoun ··· nim < MK ¨nim 'esteemed ···'; the noun īmkum < MK ¨nim-´kum 'king' probably contains the same etymon.

Almost all verbs beginning with i··· or y··· have the reinforced form, but only after prefixes or the negative adverbs mōs and an: mōsq ic.e /mōnnice/ 'can't forget', mōsq il.e na /mōnnilena/ 'can't arise', mōsq ilk.e /mōnnilke/ 'can't read', mōsq ik.e /mōnnike/ 'can't ripen', mōsq ip.e /mōnnipe/ 'can't wear', mōsq yel.e /mōnnyele/ 'can't open'; anq ic.e /annice/ 'doesn't forget', anq il.e na /annilena/ 'doesn't arise', anq ilk.e /annilke/ 'doesn't read', anq ik.e /annike/ 'doesn't ripen', anq ip.e /annipe/ 'doesn't wear', anq yel.e /annyele/ 'doesn't open'. For the stem iss- 'stay, be' the q seems to be optional for mōs but usual for an (because of pervasive n-epenthesis): mōs(q) iss.keyss.e /mōtikkeysse/ or /mōnnikkeysse/ 'can't stay', anq iss.keyss.e /annikkeysse/ 'won't stay'. The Middle Korean source of iss- was spelled without an initial nasal, *isi-*, but almost all the other relevant stems were spelled ni··· or ny···. For those verbs the non-reinforced treatment is sometimes heard (mōs ic.e /mōtice/, mōs yel.e /mōtyele/), but not commonly. An example with a prefix is cisq-iki- /cinniki-/ 'knead; mince'. When the accusative particle is omitted in the phrase os ul ipko 'wearing clothes' the phrase can be pronounced either /otipkko/ = os ipko or /onnipkko/ = osq ipko. If only the juncture after the accusative particle is dropped, you may hear both /osulipkko/ with the flap [r] and /osullipkko/ = os ulq ipko.

There are also words which begin with /y/ but have alternants beginning with /ny/ in certain environments. The word ⁿyen 'year' after a numeral is pronounced /nyen/ (and that is automatically /lyen/ after l); the same pronunciation is common after ku 'that' and similar adnouns. The MORPHEME for 'year' has the shape /yen/ spelled ⁿyen when word-initial, but elsewhere it is nyen (including /lyen/ after l) elsewhere: ¹naynyen 'next year'; mal.nyen 'the later (closing) years'; ⁿyenkam 'yearbook'; ⁿyento 'year period'; ⁿyen-nyen 'year after year', CF ¹yennyen 'successive years' and yennyen 'prolonging one's years (= life)'.

For a few words, such as those cited on p. 41, history has gone awry and confusion is rife. Some Koreans treat ···n-n··· the same as ···n-l··· and ···l-l···, namely as /ll/, and say Allyeng hasimnikka for Annyeng hasip.nikka 'How are you?'. The words kwannyem 'idea' and kōnnan 'difficulty' are often treated as if kwan.lyem /kwallyem/ and kōn.lan /kōllan/, and those spellings are included in some of the dictionaries, and we have taken account of a few of these by writing such Romanized versions as kōn.¹nan. (The word /kwēllyen/ 'cigarette' is usually spelled phonemically, though etymologically it is kwēn.yen.) Somewhat similar cases are kilyem for kinyem 'memory, souvenir' and kīlung for kīnung 'talent, ability'. Double /ll/ sometimes appears for no good reason where a single /l/ is expected; such forms are usually to be regarded as dialect variants. Occasionally, reinforcement (-q) is involved: /mullyak/ 'liquid medicine' is best treated as mulq yak. That is perhaps the best way, too, to treat 'one or two': ilq-ī.

Dialects of the northwest dispalatalized the older initial *ty thy ny*, while the southern dialects affricated *t(h)y* so that they merged with the affricates *c(h)y* and retained the glide but dropped the nasal of *ny*. (Only ¹Yukcin preserves the original situation.) That is why for Seoul ⁿyeca 'woman' and chengke-cang 'station' (< *tyengke-tyang*) northerners are known to say neca [nədza] and tengke-tang.

These phenomena were noticed by [1]Yu Huy in 1824 Enmun-ci (p. 7): "In Korean pronunciation **tya**, **tye** have become **cya**, **cye**; **thya**, **thye** have become **chya**, **chye**. Only in Phyengan province do people not equate **thyen** 'heaven' with **chyen** 'thousand' and **ti** 'earth' with **ci** 'arrival'." There are examples of *c* for *ty* and *ch* for *thy* in the 1632 edition of Twusi enhay (CF An Pyenghuy 1957). Seoul irregularly has **neh-** < *nyeh-* 'put in' where we would have expected **yeh-** (as in various dialects), reflecting the MK variant *neh-* attested in 1466 Kup (see p. 47) and perhaps influenced by the initial of **noh-** 'put'. 1898 Tayshin writes *nyetta* (?= /nyetha/) 'lay, stow'. (Tayshin *nipsiuely* 'lips' must be a back formation, for MK had *ip si˙Gwul* without the nasal initial.) The northern tendency to dispalatalize has weakened in the 20th century, and the southern palatalizations in loanwords such as **latio** > **lacio** 'radio' and **tisuthoma** > **cisuthoma** 'distoma' are now common in the north, as well (Mkk 1960:9:39).

For more on **ny-** and **ni-** see §1.2. For further discussion of alternations involving **l** see §5.1, §8.1.4, §§8.2.1-3; §4.7, §4.8; §1.6; §2.6. CF. Thak Huyswu 1956:160-7.

4.5. Shape types of Chinese vocabulary.

The table on pp. 114-5 shows all the shape types that occur in "normal" basic readings of Chinese characters. With the exception of those queried with question marks, which were included out of deference to Korean dictionaries, I believe examples can be found of real words containing morphemes with shapes to justify the inclusion of each of the entries in the table. Distinctions of vowel length are ignored. Certain shapes (such as **lye**) are always short, regardless of the particular morpheme represented, and certain shapes are always basically long (like **thē**, which represents a single morpheme). But other shapes are distinctively short or long depending on the morpheme. The long vowel in these shapes usually corresponds to the Middle Chinese "rising" and "falling" tones, but there are many exceptions. Parentheses enclose marginal or special shapes.

Although there are characters that are to be read with the syllables **cum**, **cwul**, **nin**, **nwal**, **nyek**, **nyep**, and **phik**, they are not used in loanwords found in modern Korean, so those have been left blank in the table. There are no characters read with the syllables **cwang**, **hi** (as distinct from **huy**), **kul**, **kya**, **mam**, **non**, **nyak**, **nyang**, **nyey**, **op**, **phyu**, or **pik**; these, too, are blank in the table. Among the filled slots in the table, several shapes appear in only a few loanwords and some of the n··· shapes do not appear in environments critical for deciding the initial. For kh··· the only shape is **khway**.

A few of the rarer shapes, with examples:

hyul	kwūhyul 'relief (of the poor)', **hyulkum** 'relief fund'
kyak	**kyak.kum** 'collecting funds'
nīm	ⁿīmkum 'pay', ⁿīmtay 'lease'
nwul	**nwul.en** 'stammering speech', **mok.nwul** 'innocence and lack of eloquence'; but **ēnwul** 'inarticulate' is commonly said as /ēlwul/
nwūn	**nwūn.cho** 'fresh grass', **nwūnhan** 'mild cold', **nwūn.lok** 'light green'
nyel	ⁿYelpan 'Nirvāṇa'
nyuk	ⁿyuk.hyel 'nosebleed'
phyak	**phyak hata** 'is snippy', **koyphyak hata** 'is fussy'
thum	**thum.ip** 'trespassing'

The shapes **kkik**, **ssang**, and **ssi** are anomalous in beginning with reinforced consonants, but the North Koreans standardize **kkik** 'ingest' as **kik**, and **ssi** was spelled **si** in earlier times. The reading **ssang** 'pair' first appeared in 1677, but the reading **ssi** 'clan' seems to be fairly new, and is probably the result of truncation from compounds (···q si 'the clan of ··· '), just as the initial reinforcement of a few nouns such as **kkoch** 'flower' are to be accounted for. The noun **thāl** 'mishap, ... ' is associated with a Chinese character that has the traditionally assigned reading **i**, but both the sound and the meaning are peculiarly Korean, so the word is not to be taken as part of the Chinese vocabulary. The origin seems to be unknown but it is probably the same as the word **thāl** 'karma' attested (¨*tha˙l ol*) in 1462 [1]Nung 8:78b, of unknown etymology. The modern meaning is attested from 1785.

4.6. Chinese characters.

To write most words of the Chinese vocabulary the Koreans have traditionally used Chinese characters, called **Hānqca** or **Hānmunq-ca**. For each syllable of a Chinese word there is an appropriate traditional character, so that knowing the characters is often a help in finding out what morphemes make up the word. The bulk of the Chinese vocabulary consists of binoms – two-morpheme (hence two-syllable) words. You can suspect that you are hearing a Chinese word, and accordingly that the word can be written in Chinese characters, whenever you hear a word that consists of any two syllables listed in the shape-type table. Sometimes, of course, you may be wrong, especially if one of the syllables (such as **ka** or **sa**) is of a very common type anyway. You would be mistaken to think that **salang** 'love' should be written with Chinese characters. And **sayngkak** 'thinking', despite its definitely Chinesey flavor (and perhaps even a Chinese etymology), is not written with characters.

The Chinese characters are listed in dictionaries, and the dictionaries are usually organized according to a somewhat arbitrary system that analyzes the structure of each character so as to find a "radical", traditionally the element that gives the character its category of meaning, and a residual part that is often called the "phonetic" because it hints at the pronunciation. The 214 Radicals are ordered according to the number of strokes originally made in writing them (some are now written with fewer strokes than the order implies), and each of the characters is listed according to its Radical number + the number of residual strokes. For example, the character 梅 **may** 'plum' is listed under Radical 75 (the Tree or Wood Radical), in the subgroup of characters that have a residual-stroke count of 7, so that we can designate its general location as "75.7". The radical, as so often, is on the left and by itself is a character that means 'tree'. The part on the right is the phonetic; by itself it is the character **may** 'every' 每, which is listed under Radical 80, while the bottom part of that character by itself is **mo** 'mother' 母. It sometimes happens that a character has a residual-stroke count of zero; that is, the character is a radical itself, like 木 **mok** 'tree' 75.0. When there are several characters with the same residual-stroke count, the order is usually determined by an arbitrary tradition that follows earlier dictionaries. Most Korean dictionaries of Chinese characters also have an index by "total stroke count", which is useful if the radical is not readily ascertainable, and an index by Korean readings arranged according to the Hankul alphabet, with the order under each reading determined either by the radical or by the total stroke count. A list of the names by which Koreans call the 214 Radicals will be found in Appendix 5. (Some of the names, like the radicals they represent, are rare.)

When we look up a character in a Chinese character dictionary, called **Hānqca sacen** or (after the name of a dictionary famous in ancient China) **okphyen** "Jewel Book", we are given only scanty information, usually just a Korean "reference tag" which tells us the appropriate pronunciation and something of the meaning. If there are several meanings or readings, each is given, usually following the traditional entries of large Chinese dictionaries, so that the information is often archaic and not always relevant to real loanwords that are used in Korean today. The typical form of a reference tag for a noun is the Korean translation (as a noun or noun phrase) + the reading: 人 **sālam in** 'the **in** that means **sālam** "man"'. The reference tag for a verb typically gives the Korean translation in the form of a prospective modifier (or a phrase that ends in one) + the reading: 見 **polq kyēn** 'the **kyēn** that means **pol** "to see"'. The prospective modifier is also used for the adjectives, but a few of the adjectives are tagged with the simple modifier, to differentiate them from processive use of the same stem: 大 **khun tāy** 'the **tāy** that means **khun** "big"' < *khun tay* (1576 [1]Yuhap 2:47b) vs **khulq tāy** (Kim Sepcey 1957:59) 'the **tāy** that means "to grow"'; 長 **kīn cang** 'the **cang** that means "long"' < *[¨]kin tyang* < *TTYANG* (1576 [1]Yuhap 2:48a) vs *[¨]kilq [¨]tyang* < *¨TTYANG* (ibid.) 'to grow' (replaced by **cala-**). Notice that while often a comma sets off the reading from the gloss ("sālam, in", "pol, kyēn", "khun, tāy") it is usual to pronounce the tag without a pause, and the prospective modifier regularly carries the reinforcing **-q**.

The table on the next two pages is a continuation of §4.5. from the preceding page.

[continuation of §4.5]

SHAPES OF CHINESE MORPHEMES

a	ya	wa	e	ye	-	ay	way	ey	-	yey	o	yo	-	oy	wu	yu	-	uy	i	wi
ang	yang	wang	-	yeng	-	ayng	-	-	-	-	ong	yong	-	-	wung	yung	ung	-	ing	-
ak	yak	-	ek	yek	-	ayk	-	-	-	-	ok	yok	-	-	wuk	yuk	-	-	ik	-
am	-	-	em	yem	-	-	-	-	-	-	-	-	-	-	-	-	um	-	im	-
ap	-	-	ep	yep	-	-	-	-	-	-	-	-	-	-	-	-	up	-	ip	-
an	-	wan	en	yen	wen	-	-	-	-	-	on	-	-	-	wun	yun	un	-	in	-
al	-	wal	el	yel	wel	-	-	-	-	-	ol	-	-	-	wul	yul	ul	-	il	-

ka	-	kwa	ke	-	-	kay	kwa	key	kwey	kyey	ko	kyo	koy	-	kwu	kyu	-	-	ki	kwi
kang	-	kwang	-	kyeng	-	-	-	-	-	-	kong	-	koyng	kwung	-	kung	-	-	-	-
kak	kyak	kwak	-	kyek	-	-	-	-	-	-	kok	-	koyk	kwuk	-	kuk	-	(k)kik	-	-
kam	-	-	kem	kyem	-	-	-	-	-	-	-	-	-	-	-	kum	-	(kim)	-	-
kap	-	-	kep	kyep	-	-	-	-	-	-	-	-	-	-	-	kup	-	-	-	-
kan	-	kwan	ken	kyen	kwen	-	-	-	-	-	kon	-	-	kwun	kyun	kun	-	kin	-	-
kal	-	kwal	kel	kyel	kwel	-	-	-	-	-	kol	-	-	kwul	kyul	-	kil	-	-	-
						khway														

ha	-	hwa	he	-	-	hay	hway	-	hwey	hyey	ho	hyo	hoy	-	hwu	hyu	-	-	huy	hwi
hang	hyang	hwang	-	hyeng	-	hayng	-	-	-	-	hong	-	hoyng	hwung	hyung	hung	-	-	-	hwi
hak	-	hwak	-	hyek	-	hayk	-	-	-	-	hok	-	hoyk	-	hyuk	huk	-	-	-	-
ham	-	-	hem	hyem	-	-	-	-	-	-	-	-	-	-	-	hum	-	-	-	-
hap	-	-	-	hyep	-	-	-	-	-	-	(hop)	-	-	-	-	hup	-	-	-	-
han	-	hwan	hen	hyen	hwen	-	-	-	-	-	hon	-	-	hwun	-	hun	-	-	-	-
hal	-	hwal	hel	hyel	-	-	-	-	-	-	hol	-	-	hwul	hyul	hul	-	hil	-	-

ma	-	-	-	-	-	may	-	-	-	-	myey	mo	myo	-	-	mu	-	-	mi	-
mang	-	-	-	myeng	-	mayng	-	-	-	-	mong	-	-	-	-	-	-	-	-	-
mak	-	-	-	myek	-	mayk	-	-	-	-	mok	-	-	-	muk	-	-	-	-	-
man	-	-	-	myen	-	-	-	-	-	-	-	-	-	-	mun	-	-	-	min	-
mal	-	-	-	myel	-	-	-	-	-	-	mol	-	-	-	mul	-	-	-	mil	-

-	-	-	-	-	-	pay	-	-	-	-	po	-	-	-	pu	-	-	-	pi	-
pang	-	-	-	pyeng	-	-	-	-	-	-	pong	-	-	-	pung	-	-	-	ping	-
pak	-	-	-	pyek	-	payk	-	-	-	-	pok	-	-	-	puk	-	-	-	-	-
-	-	-	pem	-	-	-	-	-	-	-	-	-	-	-	-	-	-	-	-	-
-	-	-	pep	-	-	-	-	-	-	-	-	-	-	-	-	-	-	-	-	-
pan	-	-	pen	pyen	-	-	-	-	-	-	pon	-	-	-	pun	-	-	-	pin	-
pal	-	-	pel	pyel	-	-	-	-	-	-	pol	-	-	-	pul	-	-	-	-	-

pha	-	-	-	-	-	phay	-	-	-	-	phyey	pho	phyo	-	-	-	-	-	phi	-
-	-	-	-	phyeng	-	phayng	-	-	-	-	-	-	-	-	phung	-	-	-	-	-
-	phyak	-	-	-	-	phayk	-	-	-	-	phok	-	-	-	phuk	-	-	-	-	-
-	-	-	-	phyem	-	-	-	-	-	-	-	-	-	-	phum	-	-	-	-	-
-	-	-	-	-	-	-	-	-	-	-	-	-	-	-	-	-	-	-	phip	-
phan	-	-	-	phyen	-	-	-	-	-	-	(phun)	-	-	-	-	-	-	-	-	-
phal	-	-	-	-	-	-	-	-	-	-	phil	-	-	-	-	-	-	-	-	-

na	-	-	-	mye	-	nay	-	-	no	nyo	noy	nwu	-	-	ni	-
nang	-	-	-	nyeng	-	-	-	-	nong	-	-	-	nung	-	-	-
nak	-	-	-	-	-	?nyek	-	-	-	-	-	nyuk	-	nik	-
nam	-	-	-	nyem	-	-	-	-	-	-	-	-	-	nim	-
nap	-	-	-	?nyep	-	-	-	-	-	-	-	-	-	-	-
nan	-	-	-	nyen	-	-	-	-	-	-	-	nwun	-	-	-
nal	-	?nwal	-	nyel	-	-	-	-	-	-	-	nwul	-	nil	-

la	-	-	-	lye	-	lay	-	-	lyey	lo	lyo	loy	lwu	lyu	-	li	-
lang	lyang	-	-	lyeng	-	layng	-	-	-	long	lyong	-	-	lyung	lung	-	-
lak	lyak	-	-	lyek	-	-	-	-	-	lok	-	-	lyuk	luk	-	-
lam	-	-	-	lyem	-	-	-	-	-	-	-	-	-	lum	-	lim	-
lap	-	-	-	lyep	-	-	-	-	-	-	-	-	-	-	-	lip	-
lan	-	-	-	lyen	-	-	-	-	-	lon	-	-	lyun	-	-	lin	-
lal	-	-	-	lyel	-	-	-	-	-	-	-	-	lyul	-	-	-	-

ta	-	-	-	-	-	tay	-	-	-	to	-	toy	twu	-	-	-	-
tang	-	-	-	tek	-	-	-	-	-	tong	-	-	-	tung	-	-	-
-	-	-	-	-	-	-	-	-	-	tok	-	-	-	tuk	-	-	-
tam	-	-	-	-	-	-	-	-	-	-	-	-	-	-	-	-	-
tap	-	-	-	-	-	-	-	-	-	-	-	-	-	-	-	-	-
tam	-	-	-	-	-	-	-	-	-	ton	-	-	twun	-	-	-	-
tal	-	-	-	-	-	-	-	-	-	tol	-	-	-	-	-	-	-

tha	-	-	-	the	-	thay	-	-	-	tho	-	thoy	thwu	-	-	-	-
thang	-	-	-	-	-	thayng	-	-	-	thong	-	-	-	-	-	-	-
thak	-	-	-	-	-	thayk	-	-	-	-	-	-	-	thuk	-	-	-
tham	-	-	-	-	-	-	-	-	-	-	-	-	-	thum	-	-	-
thap	-	-	-	-	-	-	-	-	-	-	-	-	-	-	-	-	-
than	-	-	-	-	-	-	-	-	-	thon	-	-	-	-	-	-	-
thal	-	-	-	-	-	-	-	-	-	-	-	-	-	-	-	-	-

ca	-	cwa	-	ce	-	cay	-	cey	-	co	-	coy	cwu	-	-	ci	-
cang	-	-	-	ceng	-	cayng	-	-	-	cong	-	-	cwung	-	cung	-	cing	-
cak	-	-	-	cek	-	-	-	-	-	cok	-	-	cwuk	cuk	-	cik	-
cam	-	-	-	cem	-	-	-	-	-	-	-	-	-	?cum	-	cim	-
cap	-	-	-	cep	-	-	-	-	-	-	-	-	-	cup	-	cip	-
can	-	-	-	cen	-	-	-	-	-	con	-	-	cwun	-	-	cin	-
-	-	-	-	cel	-	-	-	-	-	col	-	-	?cwul	-	-	-	-

cha	-	-	-	che	-	chay	chway	chey	-	cho	-	choy	chwu	-	-	chi	chwi
chang	-	-	-	cheng	-	chayng	-	-	-	chong	-	-	chwung	-	chung	-	ching	-
chak	-	-	-	chek	-	-	-	-	-	chok	-	-	chwuk	-	chuk	-	chik	-
cham	-	-	-	chem	-	-	-	-	-	-	-	-	-	-	-	chim	-
-	-	-	-	chep	-	-	-	-	-	-	-	-	-	-	-	chip	-
chan	-	-	-	chen	-	-	-	-	-	chon	-	-	chwun	-	(chun)	-	chin	-
chal	-	chwal	chel	-	-	-	-	-	-	-	-	-	chwul	-	-	chil	-

sa	-	-	-	se	-	say	sway	sey	-	so	-	soy	swu	-	-	si,ssi	-
sang,ssang	-	-	seng	-	-	sayng	-	-	-	song	-	-	swung	-	sung	-	-	-
sak	-	-	-	sek	-	sayk	-	-	-	sok	-	-	swuk	-	-	sik	-
sam	-	-	-	sem	-	-	-	-	-	-	-	-	-	-	-	sim	-
sap	-	-	-	sep	-	-	-	-	-	-	-	-	-	sup	-	sip	-
san	-	-	-	sen	-	-	-	-	-	son	-	-	swun	-	-	sin	-
sal	-	-	-	sel	-	-	-	-	-	sol	-	-	swul	-	sul	-	sil	-

4.7. Characters with multiple readings.

For each Chinese character there is usually one basic "reading" (= pronunciation). This means that each character represents one loanmorph in the Chinese vocabulary; of course the pronunciation is subject to the same sort of automatic alternations as any other element in Korean (···p becomes ···m before m···, etc.). But some characters have two, and rarely three, readings that cannot be predicted except by knowing the particular words in which they are used. There are two types of multiple readings. In the one type, difference of meaning goes with the difference in shape, and we have two loanmorphs represented by a single Chinese character with usually a single etymological origin. In the other type, there is no difference in meaning; we have variant versions of the same loanmorph. There are a few cases that are simply variants that have been spawned for the whole word, and those we have not listed below: **phyengphung** for **pyengphung** assimilated the first syllable to the aspiration of the second; **¹nachim-phan** for **¹nachim-pan** 'compass', where the aspiration of the last syllable comes from assimilating to the preceding syllable, is the standard form in the North Korean dictionary. Nor have we included **khan**, which seems to be a nonstandard variant of **kan** 'interval'.

In the list of the first type of multiple readings, the reference tag is shown for each reading and critical examples are given. In the second list, the meaning of the character is given on the left; then critical examples are listed and the relevant morph shapes are presented in small capital letters, with the more common shape given first. There follows a third list of a few morphemes with unpredictably varying shapes that begin with basic l··· or n··· (CF §4.4, §4.8).

4.7.1. Multiple readings: list one.

CHARACTER	SHAPES	TAGS	EXAMPLES
1.3 丑	chwuk / chwu	so chwuk 'sign of Ox'	chwuk-si 'Hour of the Ox'
		ilum chwu (in names)	Kong Songchwu (person)
3.3 丹	tan / lan	pulk.ulq tan 'red'	tanswun 'red lips'
			tansim 'sincerity'
		molan (uy) lan 'peony'	molan 'peony'
5.10 乾	ken / kan	hanul ken 'Heaven (as divination symbol)'	ken-kon 'Heaven and Earth'
		malulq kan 'be dry'	kanco = kenco 'drying'[1]
9.7 便	phyen / pyen	phyen-hal phyen 'comfortable'	phyen.li 'comfort'
		tāysopyen (uy) pyen 'easing nature'	tāypyen 'defecating'
			sōpyen 'urinating'
18.7 則	cuk / cik	kot cuk 'id est'	yencuk 'if so'
		pepchik chik 'rule'	pepchik 'rule'
			kyuchik 'regulation'
19.2 分	pun / phun	nanwulq pun 'divide; minute'	punswu 'fraction'
			pun swū 'no. of minutes'
		tōn phun 'farthing'	il-phun 'one farthing'
21.3 北	puk / pay	puk-nyekh puk 'north'	nam-puk 'North and South'
		phāy-halq pay 'suffer defeat'	phaypay 'defeat'
28.9 參	cham / sam	chamka hal cham 'participate'	chamka 'participation'
		pyēlq ilum sam (constellation)	samseng '21st of the 28 Constellations'
30.3 合	hap / hop	hap-hal hap 'join'	haptong 'combination'
		hop hop (measure)	il-hop 'one hop (a third of a pint)'

30.4 否	pū/pī	ani pū 'not' mak.ulq pī 'clog up'	pūkyel 'voting down' pīsayk 'frustrated by fortune'
30.6 咽	in/yel	mok-kwumeng in 'throat' mok-meyilq yel 'choke'	inhwu 'throat' o.yel 'sobbing'
32.10 塞	sayk/say	mak.ulq sayk 'block, stop up' pyenpang say 'fort'	cēnsayk 'obstruction' cilqsayk 'disgust' saykchayk 'sidestepping responsibility' sengsay 'fortress' yosay 'fortress'
37.6 契	kyey/ke	kyēyyak kyēy 'contract' Kelan (uy) ke (phonetic)	kyēyyak 'contract' kyēyki ha- 'reach deadline' Kelan 'Khitan Tatars'
38.8 婆	pha/pa	nulk.un kyēycip pha Sapa-sēykyey pa	¹nōpha 'old woman' Sapa 'Saha; This World'
40.8 宿	swuk/swu	cam-calq swuk 'stay overnight' pyēl swu 'constellation'	swukpak 'lodging' sengswu 'the stars' īsip-phalq swu 'the 28 Constellations'
50.2 布	phō/pō	pellil phō 'spread' tōn pō 'alms'	phōko 'decree, proclamation' pōsi 'Buddhist almsgiving'
53.6 度	to/thak	pep to 'law; degree' heyalil thak 'estimate'	ⁿyento 'year period' cengto 'degree, extent' ¹yōthak 'conjecture' yothak 'mental telepathy' chōnthak ha- 'surmise'
53.11 廓	kwak/hwak	tey-twuli kwak 'enclosure' pīl hwak 'empty'	sengkwak 'castle walls' hwakcheng 'purification'
60.6 率	sol/lyul SEE §4.8 (p. 125).	kenulilq sol 'command' pī¹yul ¹yul 'ratio'	thōngsol 'general command' insol 'leading (people)' kwēnsol 'the family one heads' pī¹yul 'ratio' nung.lyul 'efficiency'
60.9 復	pu/pok	tasi pu 'again' hoypok-halq pok 'recover'	puhwal 'resurrection' puhung 'revival' wangpok 'round trip' pok.kwu 'restoration'
60.12 徵	cing/chi	puluq cing 'recruit' um.ak chi '4th note of pentatonic scale'	sangcing 'symbol' cingpyeng 'conscription'
61.8 惡	ak/o	mōcil ak 'bad' miwe hal o 'hate'	sēn-ak 'good and/or bad' ak.han 'villain' cungo 'hatred' hō-o 'likes and dislikes'

64.8 推	chwu / thōy	kalul chwu 'discriminate'	chwutan 'judgment'
		ssah.ul thōy 'accumulate'	thōycek 'accumulation'
64.9 提	cey / li	pachilq cey 'offer'	ceychwul 'presentation'
		Poli (uy) li (phonetic)	Poli 'Bodhi, Buddhahood'
66.11 數	swū / sak / chok	sēym swū 'number'	swūqca 'numeral'
			...(-q) swū 'number of ...'
		cacwu sak 'frequent'	pinsak ha- 'be frequent'
			saksak 'constantly'
			sakchey 'constant shifting of personnel'
		ppaykppayk hal chok 'dense'	chok.ko 'fine mesh'
72.4 易	yek / i	pakkwulq yek 'change'	mu.yek 'trade'
			Yekse 'the Book of Changes'
		swiwulq i 'easy'	yongi ha- 'be easy'
73.3 更	kāyng / kyēng	tasi kāyng 'again'	kāyngsin 'renovation'
			kāyngsayng 'rebirth'
		kochilq kyēng 'change'	pyēnkyeng 'change'
			kyēngcil 'change (in structure)'
75.11 樂	lak / ak	culkil lak 'rejoice'	¹nak.wen 'paradise'
		um.ak (uy) ak 'music'	um.ak 'music'
79.6 殺	sal / swāy	cwuk.ilq sal 'kill'	sal.in 'murder'
		sangsway (uy) swāy 'attack'	sangsway 'counter-balancing'
			swāyto 'onslaught'
			kāmsway ha- 'impair'
85.4 沈	chim / sim	camkil chim 'sink'	chimmol 'sinking'
		ilum sim (name)	Sim ssi 'Mr Shim'
85.5 沸	pi / pul	kkulh.ulq pi 'boil'	pitung 'boiling'
		sāym sos.ulq pul 'jet'	pul.yen ha- 'be quick-tempered'
85.10 滑	hwal / kol	mikkulewul hwal 'slippery'	hwalqsek 'talcum'
		iksal kol 'humor'	kolkyey 'humor'
94.4 狀	sang / cang	mo.yang sang 'appearance'	sangthay 'state, condition'
			hyengsang 'form'
		kulq-cang cang 'document'	sāng(q-)cang 'citation of merit'
			kongkayq-cang 'open (public) letter'
94.7 狹	hyep / hap	cop.ul hyep 'narrow'	hyepchak 'narrowness'
		ilum hap (in names)	Hapchen (place)
102.7 畫	hwā / hoyk	kūlim hwā 'drawing'	hwāka 'artist'
		kul-ssi hoyk 'brush stroke'	hoyk swū 'stroke count'
106.0 白	payk / pay	huyn payk 'white'	paykpal 'white hair'
		Paychen pay (name)²	Paychen onchen 'Paychen hot springs (spa)'

109.4	省	seng / sayng	salphilq seng 'investigate'	sengchal 'reflection'
				sengmyo 'visiting ancestral tombs'
				kwuk.mu seng 'State Department'
				Santong seng 'Shantung (Shāndōng) Province'
			tēlq sayng 'lessen'	kāmsayng 'curtailment'
				sayng.lyak 'abbreviation'
120.4	索	sayk / sak	chac.ulq sayk 'seek'	swusayk 'search'
				mosayk 'groping'
				sasayk 'speculation'
				sayk.in 'index'
			ssulssul-halq sak 'lonesome'	sak.yen hata 'is lonesome'
			cwul sak / sayk	chelqsa(y)k 'cable'
140.9	著	ce / chak	ciulq ce 'create'	cese 'written works'
				ceca 'author'
			putic.chil chak 'hit'	chak.lyuk 'landing'
				chakswu 'putting one's hand to, beginning'
140.9	葉	yep / sep	iph(-sakwi) yep 'leaf'	ci-yep 'branches and leaves; minor details'
			ilum sep (in names)	Sep ssi 'Celcius'
				Kasep(-wen) 'Kāśapa (plain)'
144.0	行	hayng / hang	tanil hayng 'go; do; market'	¹yehayng 'travel, a trip'
				unhayng 'bank'
				··· hayng 'bound for ··· '
				hayng.lyel³ 'procession'
			hang.lyel hang 'degree of relationship'	hang.lyel³ 'degree of relationship'
145.4	衰	soy / choy	yak-halq soy 'weak'	soyyak 'debilitation'
			sangpok choy 'mourning garb'	chamchoy (a kind of mourning garb)
147.0	見	kyēn / hyen	polq kyēn 'see'	kyēnhay 'opinion, view'
			nathanal hyen 'appear'	alhyen 'royal audience'
149.7	説	sel / sey / yel	māl-halq sel 'speak'	selhwa 'narration; sermon'
			tallaylq sey 'coax'	yusey 'electioneering'
			ilumq yel (in names)	Kim Sam.yel (person)
149.15	讀	tok / twu	ilk.ulq tok 'read'	tokse 'reading (books)'
			kwicel(q) twu 'phrase'	kwutwu 'punctuation'
				¹ītwu 'Idu'⁴
157.5	跛	pha / phī	celttwuk-pal.i pha 'lame'	phahayng 'limping'
			kiwul.ye sul phī 'lean to one side'	phīlip 'standing on one leg'
167.0	金	kum / kim	hwangkum kum 'gold'	(hwang)kum 'gold'
			ilum kim (in names)	Kim ssi 'Mr Kim'
				Kimhay (city)

170.6 降	kāng / hang	naylilq kāng 'descend'	kāngha 'descent'
			sungkang-ki 'elevator'
		hangpok hang 'surrender'	hangpok 'surrender'
213.0 龜	kwi / kyun / kwu	kepuk kwi 'tortoise'	kwisen 'tortoise-shaped boat'
		son thē-cilq kyun 'chapped'	kyun.¹yel 'fissure'
			¹Yi Cengkwu (person)
		ilum kwu (in names)	Kwupho (place)

¹ Popularly **ken** in the meaning 'dry' too, as in **ken-cēnci** 'dry battery' (Ceng Insung 225).
² See also **paynge** < **pay-nge** 'whitebait' (§3.6).
³ Identical morpheme **lyel**; minimal contrast of **hayng** and **hang**.
⁴ Chinese characters once used to write Korean particles, endings, and the like.

4.7.2. Multiple readings: list two.

CHARACTER	SHAPES	MEANING	EXAMPLE 1	EXAMPLE 2
1.4 不	pul / pu¹	not, un-	pulphyen 'discomfort'	putang 'injustice'
			pul-kongphyen 'unfair'	puceng 'uncertainty'
9.2 什	cup / cip	ten, some	cupki 'furniture'	cip.mul 'furniture'
9.5 佐	cwā / cā²	assist	pōcwa 'assistance to superior'	cāpan 'salted fish or caviar'
11.2 內	nāy / nā	inside	nāyoy 'in and out'	nāin 'court lady'
12.0 八	phal / pha³	eight	phal-wel 'August'	(sā-wel) pha-il 'Buddha's birthday'
12.2 六	¹yuk / ¹yu / nyu	six	¹yuk.il '6th day'	¹yu'-wel 'June'
			ōlyuk.il '5th or 6th day'	ōnyu'-wel 'May or June'
18.2 切	cel / chey	cut	celqtan 'amputation'	ilchey 'altogether (< one cut)'
			kāncel 'eagerness'	
18.6 刺	cā / chek	stab	cākuk 'stimulation'	cheksal 'stabbing to death'
			cākayk 'assassin'	
24.0 十	sip / si'	ten	sip-il 'eleven'	si'-wel 'October'
29.2 反	pān / pen	reversal	pāntay 'opposition'	pentap 'turning it into rice land'
				pencen 'converting rice land back'
30.2 句	kwu / kwi	sentence	kwutwuq-cem 'punctuation mark'	kwicel 'couplet'
40.3 宅	thayk / tayk	house	kathayk 'domicile'	tayk 'your house'
			cwūthayk 'residence'	si-tayk 'husband's house'
48.7 差	cha / chi	difference	chai 'difference'	chamchi(-pucey) 'lack of uniformity'
50.5 帖	chep / chey	document	swuchep 'notebook, album'	cheyci, (cheymun) 'document of appointment'
64.8 掣	chel / chey	restrain	chelqcwu 'hindrance'	?cheyli⁴ 'restraint'

68.9	斟	cim / chim	guess	cimcak 'conjecture'	chim.lyang (same)
72.11	暴	phok / phō	violent	phoktong 'riot'	hoyngpho 'tyranny'
				phokphung 'tempest'	phōhak 'tyranny'
				phokto 'rioters'	(phōto 'rioters')
					phōki = capho-(caki) 'despair'
72.15	曝	phok / pho	expose	phok.yang 'burning sun'	phopayk 'bleaching in the sun'
75.0	木	mok / mō	tree, wood	mok.kun 'tree root'	mōkwa 'papaya' (< mok-kwa)
85.6	洞	tong / thōng	alley; clear	tongkwu 'village'	thōngchal, thōngchok 'discernment'
107.0	皮	phi / pi	skin	phipu 'skin'	¹nokpi 'deerskin'
115.5	秤	phyeng / ching	balance	chenphyeng 'balance, scales'	chingchwu 'balance weight'
119.10	糖	tang / thang	sugar	tangpun 'sugar content'	selthang 'granulated sugar'
				photo-tang 'glucose'	sathang 'sugar; sweets'
140.6	茶	ta / cha	tea	tapang 'teahouse'	(hong)cha '(black) tea'
				takalq-sayk 'light brown'	(chaq-pang, chaq cip) → tapang 'tearoom'
149.7	誓	sē / sey	swear	sē.yak 'oath'	mayngsey 'pledge'
149.12	識	sik / ci	knowledge	cisik 'knowledge'	phyoci = phyosik 'mark, signal'
159.0	車	cha / ke	vehicle	cha 'vehicle, car'	cacen-ke 'bicycle'
				kicha 'train'	cengke-cang 'rail station'
				catong-cha 'auto'	
161.0	辰	cin / sin	Sign of the Dragon	cin-si 'Hour of the Dragon'	thānsin 'birthday'
184.0	食	sik / sa	eat	ūmsik 'food'	tansa 'lunch-basket rice'
187.4	駄	thay / tha	stupid; burden; ...	thaycak 'worthless work'	si-tha 'load'⁵

¹ The ···l drops regularly before t or c (CF §3.5).

² CF §2.7.4.

³ CF §3.5.

⁴ ¹Yi Ungpayk 571. I cannot find the word in any dictionary, nor can I find ?cheycen 'lightning-fast', a purported example that comes from an unknown source.

⁵ But usually pronounced si-thay. In fact, does anybody say /sitha/? I assume (perhaps wrongly) an etymology that involves both sīt-/sil- 'load' and the Chinese loanmorph: si[t]-tha(y). The final -y is etymological and not a reduction of the incorporated i that is common for nouns in certain northern dialects. The si-tha version is not found in the major dictionaries; is it a ghost? Kim Minswu and Hong Wungsen treat thaycak as nonstandard for thacak, a version that I have not found in the other dictionaries.

4.7.3. Multiple readings: list three.

CHARACTER	SHAPES	MEANING	EXAMPLE 1	EXAMPLE 2
40.11 寧	nyeng / lyeng < ˙NYENG	calm	annyeng ha-[1] 'be in good health' cengnyeng 'for sure'	milyeng 'illness, indisposition'
61.5 怒	no / lo < ˙˙NWO	anger	no ha- 'get angry' pūnno 'indignation' kyek.no 'wild rage'[2]	tāylo 'great anger'
149.8 論	lon / non / ([1]non) < LWON	discussion	[1]īlon 'logic' īlon 'dissent' en.lon 'discussion' mullon[4] 'of course'	uynon 'discussion'[3] [1]nonmun 'treatise, dissertation'
149.9 諾	?nak / lak < ˙NAK	acquiesce	sungnak[5] 'consent'	helak 'permission' khwaylak 'ready assent'

[1] But those speakers who say /allyeng/ are treating this as a single-reading character **lyeng**. For them **cengnyeng** is properly to be analyzed as **ceng.lyeng**.

[2] From this form alone we would not know whether the appropriate spelling of the second element in /kyengno/ is **lo** or **no**. The practice is to write **lo** only when /l/ is pronounced. Notice that /pūnno/ could not be "**pūn.lo**" for that would be pronounced /pūllo/.

[3] [1]Yi Ungpayk draws a distinction between **uynon** 'discussion' and **uylon** 'argument' and on that both NKd and LHS agree, but KEd puts the two words together as **uy**[1]**non** and gives **uylon** as a variant pronunciation of **uynon**, a shape that is unanticipated, in any event, though attested from at least the late 19th century: *uynwon ho.ye la* (1893 Scott 4) 'consult!'.

[4] This could, of course, be from "**mul.**[1]**non**" but we decide on **lon** for reasons of history and the relative infrequency of [1]**non** in environments where it would be distinguishable.

[5] I see no reason we cannot write **sung.lak** and say the character has only the reading **lak** with /nak/ as an automatic alternant. If some speakers say (?)**khwaynak**, however, that is another matter.

A Reference Grammar of Korean

4.7.4. Index to the lists of multiple readings.

ak / lak	75.11	II		hyen / kyēn	147.0	I
ak / o	62.8	II		hyep / hap	94.7	I
cā / chek	18.6	II		i / yek	72.4	I
cā / cwā	9.5	I		in / yel	30.6	I
cang / sang	94.4	I		kan / ken	5.10	I
ce / chak	140.9	II		kang / hang	170.6	I
cel / chey	18.2	I		kāyng / kyēng	73.3	I
cey / li	64.9	II		ke / cha	159.0	II
cha / chi	48.7	II		ke / kyēy	37.6	I
cha / ke	159.0	II		ken / kan	5.10	I
cha / ta	140.6	I		kim / kum	167.0	I
chak / ce	140.9	I		kol / hwal	85.10	I
cham / sam	28.9	II		kum / kim	167.0	I
chek / cā	18.6	II		kwak / hwak	53.11	I
chel / chey	64.8	II		kwi / kwu	30.2	II
chep / chey	50.5	II		kwi / kyun / kwu	213.0	I
chey / cel	18.2	II		kwu / kwi	30.2	II
chey / chel	64.8	II		kwu / kwi / kyun	213.0	I
chey / chep	50.5	II		kyēn / hyen	147.0	I
chi / cha	48.7	I		kyēng / kāyng	73.3	I
chi / cing	60.12	I		kyēy / ke	37.6	I
chik / cuk	18.7	II		kyun / kwi / kwu	213.0	I
chim / cim	68.9	I		lak / ak	75.11	I
chim / sim	85.4	II		lak / ?nak	149.9	III
ching / phyeng	115.5	I		lan / tan	3.3	I
chok / swū / sak	66.11	I		li / cey	64.9	II
choy / soy	145.4	I		lo / no	61.5	III
chwu / chwuk	1.3	I		lon / ¹non	149.8	III
chwu / thŏy	64.8	I		lyeng / nyeng	40.11	III
chwuk / chwu	1.3	II		mŏ / mok	75.0	II
ci / sik	149.12	II		mok / mŏ	75.0	II
cim / chim	68.9	II		nā / nāy	11.2	II
cin / sin	161.0	I		?nak / lak	149.9	III
cing / chi	60.12	II		nāy / nā	11.2	II
cip / cup	9.2	I		no / lo	61.5	III
cuk / chik	18.7	II		¹non / lon	149.8	III
cup / cip	9.2	I		nyeng / lyeng	40.11	III
cwa / ca	9.5	II		nyu / ¹yuk / ¹yu	12.2	II
hang / hayng	144.0	I		o / ak	61.8	I
hang / kang	170.6	I		pa / pha	38.8	I
hap / hop	30.3	I		pan / pen	29.2	II
hap / hyep	94.7	I		pay / payk	106.0	I
hayng / hang	144.0	I		pay / puk	21.3	I
hop / hap	30.3	I		payk / pay	106.0	I
hoyk / hwā	102.7	I		pen / pan	29.2	II
hwā / hoyk	102.7	I		pha / pa	38.8	I
hwak / kwak	53.11	I		pha / phal	12.0	I
hwal / kol	85.10	I		pha / phī	157.5	I

PART I **123**

phal / pha	12.0	II		sep / yep	140.9	I
phī / pha	157.5	I		sey / sē	149.7	II
phi / pi	107.0	II		sey / sel / yel	149.7	I
phō / phok	72.11	II		si / sip	24.0	II
pho / phok	72.15	II		sik / ci	149.12	II
phō / pō	50.2	I		sik / sa	184.0	II
phok / pho	72.11	II		sim / chim	85.4	I
phok / pho	72.15	II		sin / cin	161.0	II
phun / pun	19.2	I		sip / si	24.0	II
phyen / pyen	9.7	I		sol / ¹yul	60.6	I
phyeng / ching	115.5	II		soy / choy	145.4	I
pi / phi	107.0	II		swāy / sal	79.6	I
pī / pū	30.4	I		swū / sak / chok	66.11	I
pi / pul	85.5	I		swu / swuk	40.8	I
pō / phō	50.2	I		swuk / swu	40.8	I
pok / pu	60.9	I		ta / cha	140.6	II
pū / pī	30.4	I		tan / lan	3.3	I
pu / pok	60.9	I		tang / thang	119.10	II
pu / pul	1.4	II		tayk / thayk	40.3	II
pul / pi	85.5	I		tha / thay	187.4	II
pul / pu	1.4	II		thak / to	53.6	I
pun / phun	19.2	I		thang / tang	119.10	II
puk / pay	21.3	I		thay / tha	187.4	II
pyen / phyen	9.7	I		thayk / tayk	40.3	II
sa / sik	184.0	II		thōng / tong	85.6	II
sak / sayk	120.4	I		thōy / chwu	64.8	I
sak / swū / chok	66.11	I		to / thak	53.6	I
sal / swāy	79.6	I		tok / twu	149.15	I
sam / cham	28.9	I		tong / thōng	85.6	II
sang / cang	94.4	I		twu / tok	149.15	I
say / sayk	32.10	I		yek / i	72.4	I
sayk / sak	120.4	I		yel / in	30.6	I
sayk / say	32.10	I		yel / sel / sey	149.7	I
sayng / seng	109.4	I		yep / sep	140.9	I
sē / sey	149.7	II		¹yu / ¹yuk / nyu	12.2	II
sel / sey / yel	149.7	I		¹yuk / ¹yu / nyu	12.2	II
seng / sayng	109.4	I		¹yul / sol	60.6	I

4.8. Chinese morphemes with basic l···.

A number of problems arise with morphemes which had a basic l··· initial in Middle Chinese. In South Korea the standard practice is to spell these morphemes in two ways: with n··· (or zero before i, y) if they are at the beginning of a word, with l··· elsewhere. In North Korea the morphemes are spelled with initial l··· in all positions. Our Romanization writes ¹n··· (or ¹··· before i, y) for these cases where the two systems diverge. There are a few morphemes which, despite an etymological l···, are standardized to n··· in both Koreas: no = ¹no 'oar', nwu = ¹nwu 'loft, pavilion', nwū = ¹nwū 'frequent' (CF nwūnwūi = ¹nwū¹nwū-i 'frequently'), nwūki = ¹nwūki 'dampness'. In the word sil¹yen 'disappointment in love', we find an unusual shortening of the expected sillyen, ignored in the North Korean spelling, but indicated in South Korea by writing sil.yen. A similar case should be no¹yey /no(.y)ey/ 'slave' (CF hālyey 'male slave', kwan.lyey 'official slave', ¹yēysok 'subordination'), but the North Korean spelling seems to be no.yey, like that of the south.

A Reference Grammar of Korean

A small group of morphemes have the shapes **lyul** and **lyel**. These morphemes follow a special pronunciation rule: after a vowel or **n**, the **l** unexpectedly drops. The liquid actually appears only after **l** or some consonant other than **n** (when it appears in the reflex /n/), so that we would not know that these morphemes begin with a basic **l** (rather than **n**) without additional information from their history or from dialect pronunciations. The alternation is ignored in North Korean spelling, but noted by the South Koreans, so we mark it by ···¹y··· in our Romanization. Examples:

		CHARACTER	AFTER VOWEL	AFTER ···n	AFTER ···l	ELSEWHERE
LYUL < ʾLYWULQ		60.6 律 rule	kyu¹yul /kyuyul/ 'discipline'	sen.¹yul /senyul/ 'rhythm'	illyul /illyul/ 'uniformity'	pep.lyul /pemnyul/ 'law'
		95.6 率 ratio	pī¹yul /pīyul/ 'ratio' ¹ī¹yul /īyul/ 'interest rate'	hwān.¹yul /hwānyul/ 'exchange rate'	kwulqcel-lyul /kwulccellyul/ 'index of refraction'	nung.lyul 'efficiency'
		75.6 栗 chestnut	phi¹yul /phiyul/ 'unshelled chestnut'	san.¹yul /sanyul/ 'Japanese chestnut'	hallyulq-sek /hallyulssek/ 'stones cut to chestnut size'	hwang.lyul /hwangnyul/ 'dried peeled chestnuts'
LYEL < ʾLYELQ		19.4 劣 inferior	wu¹yel /wuyel/ 'superiority and inferiority' pi¹yel /piyel/ 'baseness'	chen.¹yel /chenyel/ 'lowly, humble'	collyel /collyel/ 'clumsiness'	yong.lyel /yongnyel/ 'inferiority'
		18.4 列 rank, order	¹na.¹yel /na.yel/ 'array'	pan.¹yel /panyel/ 'class rank'	illyel /illyel/ 'a line'	hayng.lyel /hayngnyel/ 'procession'
		86.6 烈 fierce	uy¹yel /u.yel/ 'heroism'	sen.¹yel /senyel/ 'veteran patriot'	yellyel ha- /yellyel(h)a-/ 'be ardent'	mayng.lyel /mayngnyel/ 'fury'
		145.6 裂 rip	phā.¹yel /phā.yel/ 'explosion'	kyun.¹yel /kyunyel/ 'fissure' pun.¹yel /punyel/ 'disruption'	kyellyel /kyellyel/ 'rupture'	cak.lyel /cangnyel/ 'explosion'

4.9. Tongkwuk readings.

<u>Tongkwuk Cengwun</u> (¨*TWONG-*˙*KWUYK* ¨*CYENG-*˙*NGWUN*)

	k	kh	kk	ng	t	th	tt	n	p	ph	pp	m	c	ch	cc	s	ss	q	h	hh	-	l	z
vol 1																							
1. -ung	+		+	+	+			+	+	+		+	+		+			+	+	+	+		
¨-ung		+		+																			
˙-ung	+		+	+	+			+				+	+		+			+	+	+	+	+	
˙-uk	+	+	+		+	+		+	+			+	+	+	+	+			+	+	+		+
-ing					+	+		+	+	+	+		+			+			+	+			
¨-ing					+	+										+							+
˙-ing						+				+		+				+	+						+
˙-ik					+	+		+				+				+	+	+	+				
-oyng	+	+			+	+		+	+	+	+	+	+	+	+	+			+		+	+	
¨-oyng	+											+	+		+			+			+		
˙-oyng	+				+	+		+				+	+		+			+			+		
˙-oyk	+	+			+	+		+	+	+	+	+	+		+	+			+				
2. -woyng	+	+																	+	+	+		
¨-woyng	+																			+			
˙-woyng																				+			
˙-woyk	+																		+	+	+		
3. -wuyng	+																			+			
˙-wuyk	+																						
4. -wong	+	+		+	+	+		+	+	+	+	+	+		+	+			+		+		+
¨-wong	+	+				+		+	+	+	+	+	+	+		+			+		+		+
˙-wong	+	+	+			+		+	+	+		+	+			+			+	+	+		
˙-wok	+	+	+	+	+	+		+	+	+	+	+	+	+	+	+			+		+	+	+
-ywong						+						+	+	+	+	+			+		+	+	+
¨-ywong						+		+	+			+	+	+	+				+		+	+	+
˙-ywong						+		+				+				+			+		+		
˙-ywok						+						+			+	+			+		+		+
5. -ang	+	+	+	+	+	+		+	+	+	+	+	+	+	+	+			+	+	+		+
¨-ang	+	+	+	+	+	+		+	+	+	+	+	+	+	+	+		+	+	+	+		
˙-ang	+	+	+	+	+	+		+	+	+	+	+	+	+	+	+		+	+	+	+		
˙-ak	+	+	+		+	+		+	+	+	+	+	+	+	+	+			+		+	+	
-yang					+	+	+		+			+				+	+		+	+	+	+	+
¨-yang					+	+	+		+			+				+	+		+	+	+	+	+
˙-yang					+	+	+					+				+	+		+	+	+	+	+
˙-yak					+	+	+					+				+	+	+	+	+	+	+	+
-wang	+	+		+		+	+									+			+	+	+		+
¨-wang	+	+	+													+			+		+	+	
˙-wang	+	+		+	+											+			+		+	+	
˙-wak	+	+			+	+		+	+							+			+	+	+		+
vol 2																							
6. -wung	+	+	+																+				
¨-wung																							
˙-wung			+																				
˙-wuk	+	+	+																+				
-ywung					+	+	+						+	+		+	+		+		+	+	+
¨-ywung						+							+			+			+				
˙-ywung						+							+			+			+				
˙-ywuk					+	+	+	+					+			+	+		+		+	+	+
	k	kh	kk	ng	t	th	tt	n	p	ph	pp	m	c	ch	cc	s	ss	q	h	hh	-	l	z

A Reference Grammar of Korean

(vol 2)	k	kh	kk	ng	t	th	tt	n	p	ph	pp	m	c	ch	cc	s	ss	q	h	hh	-	l	z
7. -yeng	+	+	+	+	+	+	+	+	+	+	+	+	+	+	+	+	+	+	+	+	+	+	
"-yeng	+	+			+	+	+	+	+	+	+	+	+	+		+		+		+	+	+	
'-yeng	+	+	+	+	+	+	+	+	+	+	+	+	+	+		+	+	+		+	+	+	
'-yek	+	+		+	+	+	+	+	+	+	+	+	+	+		+	+		+	+	+	+	
-yweng	+	+	+	+									+					+	+	+	+		
"-yweng	+	+		+															+	+		+	
'-yweng				+														+	+	+			
'-ywek	+	+																	+	+		+	
8. -on	+				+		+											+					
"-on		+		+																			
'-on	+																						
-un	+		+	+									+		+			+	+	+			
"-un	+		+	+									+					+		+			
'-un	+	+	+	+									+						+	+			
'-ulq	+	+	+	+									+		+			+	+				
-in					+	+	+	+	+	+	+	+	+	+	+	+	+	+		+	+	+	+
"-in	+					+	+					+		+	+	+	+				+	+	+
'-in					+	+	+		+				+	+	+		+	+	+		+	+	+
'-ilq	+	+			+	+	+	+	+	+	+	+	+		+		+	+	+		+	+	+
9. -won	+	+			+	+	+		+	+	+	+	+	+	+		+		+	+	+		+
"-won	+	+				+	+		+		+	+	+	+		+			+		+		
'-won	+	+		+	+	+	+	+	+	+	+	+	+	+	+	+				+	+		+
'-wolq	+	+		+	+		+		+	+	+	+	+	+	+					+	+		+
10. -an	+	+		+	+	+	+	+	+	+	+	+	+	+	+	+	+		+	+	+		+
"-an	+	+		+	+	+	+	+	+	+	+	+	+	+	+	+	+		+	+	+		+
'-an	+	+		+	+	+	+	+	+	+	+	+	+	+	+	+	+		+	+	+		+
'-alq	+	+		+	+	+	+					+	+	+	+		+		+	+	+		+
-wan	+	+			+	+	+	+	+				+	+	+		+		+	+	+		+
"-wan	+				+	+	+	+	+				+	+	+		+		+	+	+		+
'-wan	+	+			+	+	+	+	+				+	+	+		+		+	+	+		+
'-walq	+	+			+	+	+	+	+				+	+			+		+	+	+		+

vol 3

	k	kh	kk	ng	t	th	tt	n	p	ph	pp	m	c	ch	cc	s	ss	q	h	hh	-	l	z
11. -wun	+		+	+				+	+	+	+								+	+			
"-wun	+	+		+				+	+	+	+								+				
'-wun	+		+	+				+	+	+	+								+	+			
'-wulq	+	+		+				+	+	+	+								+	+			
-ywun	+	+		+	+	+	+						+	+		+	+		+		+	+	+
"-ywun		+	+	+									+	+		+	+		+		+		+
'-ywun													+			+	+		+				+
'-ywulq	+		+	+	+	+							+	+		+	+		+		+		+
12. -en	+	+	+	+				+	+	+									+	+			
"-en	+		+	+					+	+	+								+	+			
'-en	+	+	+	+				+	+	+									+	+			
'-elq	+	+	+	+					+	+	+								+	+			
-yen	+	+		+	+	+	+	+	+	+	+	+	+	+	+	+	+		+	+	+	+	+
"-yen	+	+		+		+	+		+	+	+	+	+	+	+	+	+		+	+	+	+	+
'-yen	+	+		+	+	+	+	+	+	+	+	+	+	+	+	+	+		+	+	+	+	+
'-yelq	+	+		+	+	+	+	+	+	+	+	+	+	+	+	+	+		+	+	+	+	+
-wen		+	+	+															+	+		+	
"-wen	+	+	+	+															+	+		+	
'-wen	+	+	+	+															+	+		+	
'-welq	+	+	+	+															+	+			

	k	kh	kk	ng	t	th	tt	n	p	ph	pp	m	c	ch	cc	s	ss	q	h	hh	-	l	z
-ywen	+					+							+	+	+	+	+		+	+	+	+	+
"-ywen	+	+	+			+	+						+	+	+	+		+	+	+	+		+
'-ywen	+					+		+					+	+		+	+	+	+	+	+		+
'-ywelq	+	+				+							+	+	+	+		+	+	+	+	+	+
13. -om													+	+	+	+							
"-om														+									
'-om													+		+								
'-op													+		+								
-um	+	+	+	+															+	+		+	
"-um	+		+	+	+				+	+									+	+			
'-um	+		+	+															+	+			
'-up	+	+	+	+															+	+		+	
-im					+		+	+					+	+		+	+					+	+
"-im					+		+						+	+		+	+					+	+
'-im					+		+	+					+	+		+	+					+	+
'-ip					+		+						+	+	+	+	+					+	+
-am	+	+			+	+	+	+					+	+	+	+			+	+	+		+
"-am	+	+			+	+	+	+					+	+	+	+			+	+	+		+
'-am	+	+			+	+	+						+	+	+	+			+	+	+		+
'-ap	+	+			+	+	+	+					+	+	+	+			+	+	+		+

vol 4

	k	kh	kk	ng	t	th	tt	n	p	ph	pp	m	c	ch	cc	s	ss	q	h	hh	-	l	z
15. -em		+								+						+	+						
"-em	+		+	+						+	+					+	+						
'-em	+	+		+					+	+						+	+						
'-ep	+	+	+	+						+	+					+	+						
-em	+	+			+	+	+	+					+	+	+	+	+		+		+	+	+
"-em		+			+	+	+	+					+		+	+	+		+		+	+	+
'-em		+			+	+	+	+					+	+		+	+		+		+	+	+
'-ep	+	+			+	+	+	+					+	+	+	+	+		+		+	+	+
16. -woW	+	+		+	+	+	+	+	+			+	+	+	+	+	+		+	+			+
"-woW	+	+			+		+	+		+		+	+	+		+			+	+			+
'-woW	+	+		+	+		+	+	+			+		+		+	+		+	+			+
-ywoW	+	+	+	+	+	+	+	+	+			+	+	+	+	+	+		+	+	+	+	+
"-ywoW	+	+		+	+	+	+	+	+			+	+	+		+	+		+	+	+	+	+
'-ywoW	+	+		+	+	+	+	+				+	+	+		+	+		+	+	+	+	+
17. -wuW	+	+	+	+	+	+		+				+	+	+		+	+		+	+			+
"-wuW	+	+	+	+	+	+		+				+	+	+		+			+	+			+
'-wuW	+	+	+	+	+	+		+				+	+	+		+			+	+			+
-ywuW	+		+		+	+	+	+	+			+	+	+		+	+		+	+		+	+
"-ywuW	+				+	+	+	+					+	+		+	+		+	+		+	+
'-ywuW					+	+	+	+					+	+		+	+		+	+		+	+

vol 5

	k	kh	kk	ng	t	th	tt	n	p	ph	pp	m	c	ch	cc	s	ss	q	h	hh	-	l	z
18. -o													+	+		+	+						
"-o													+	+		+	+						
'-o													+	+		+	+						
-i		+			+	+	+	+	+	+			+	+	+	+	+		+	+		+	+
"-i		+			+	+	+	+	+	+			+	+	+	+	+		+			+	+
'-i		+			+	+	+	+	+	+			+	+	+	+	+		+			+	+
-oy					+	+			+	+		+	+	+	+	+			+	+		+	
"-oy						+				+		+	+	+	+				+	+			
'-oy					+	+	+			+		+	+	+	+				+	+		+	+

| k | kh | kk | ng | t | th | tt | n | p | ph | pp | m | c | ch | cc | s | ss | q | h | hh | - | l | z |

	k	kh	kk	ng	t	th	tt	n	p	ph	pp	m	c	ch	cc	s	ss	q	h	hh	-	l	z
(vol 5, 18)																							
-uy	+	+	+	+					+	+									+	+			
"-uy	+	+	+																+	+			
·-uy	+	+	+																+	+			
19. -woy	+	+	+	+	+	+		+	+	+		+	+	+		+	+		+	+			
"-woy	+	+	+		+	+		+	+	+			+	+		+	+		+	+			
·-woy	+	+	+		+	+			+	+			+	+		+	+		+	+			
20. -ay	+	+	+	+	+	+		+	+	+		+	+	+		+	+		+	+			
"-ay	+	+	+		+	+		+	+	+			+	+		+	+		+	+			
·-ay	+	+			+			+	+	+		+	+	+		+	+		+	+			
-way	+	+																					
"-way	+																						
·-way	+																						
21. -wuy	+	+	+		+	+		+	+	+		+	+	+		+	+		+	+			
"-wuy	+	+	+		+	+		+	+	+			+	+		+	+		+	+			
·-wuy	+	+	+		+	+			+	+			+	+		+	+		+	+			
-ywuy	+	+						+															
"-ywuy	+	+																					
·-ywuy	+	+																					
vol 6																							
22. -yey	+	+	+	+	+	+		+	+	+		+	+	+		+	+		+	+			
"-yey	+	+	+		+	+		+	+	+			+	+		+	+		+	+			
·-yey	+	+	+		+	+			+	+			+	+		+	+		+	+			
-ywey	+	+																					
"-ywey	+	+																					
·-ywey	+	+																					
23. -wo	+	+	+	+	+	+		+	+	+		+	+	+		+	+		+	+			
"-wo	+	+	+		+	+		+	+	+			+	+		+	+		+	+			
·-wo	+	+	+		+	+			+	+			+	+		+	+		+	+			
24. -a	+	+	+	+	+	+		+	+	+		+	+	+		+	+		+	+			
"-a	+	+	+		+	+		+	+	+			+	+		+	+		+	+			
·-a	+	+	+		+	+			+	+			+	+		+	+		+	+			
-ya	+	+	+		+								+	+		+	+		+	+			
"-ya													+	+		+	+		+	+			
·-ya													+	+		+	+		+	+			
-wa	+	+	+		+	+		+					+	+		+	+		+	+			
"-wa	+	+			+	+							+	+		+	+		+	+			
·-wa	+	+			+	+							+	+		+	+		+	+			
25. -wu	+	+	+		+	+		+	+	+		+	+	+		+	+		+	+			
"-wu	+	+	+		+	+		+	+	+			+	+		+	+		+	+			
·-wu	+	+	+		+	+			+	+			+	+		+	+		+	+			
-ywu													+	+		+	+		+	+			
"-ywu													+	+		+	+		+	+			
·-ywu													+	+		+	+		+	+			
26. -e	+	+	+	+															+	+			
"-e	+	+	+																+	+			
·-e	+	+	+																+	+			
-ye	+	+	+		+								+	+		+	+		+	+			
"-ye	+	+											+	+		+	+		+	+			
·-ye	+	+	+										+	+		+	+		+	+			
	k	kh	kk	ng	t	th	tt	n	p	ph	pp	m	c	ch	cc	s	ss	q	h	hh	-	l	z

5.0. Forms: nouns.

The noun typically enjoys a certain independence. Unlike verb stems, which require that some ending be attached, a noun may appear unaccompanied by a particle or other marker. In the broadest sense, the noun is a kind of default category comprising many subcategories which are defined by combinatorial restrictions. A pure noun typically can occur as a nominative-marked subject and/or as an accusative-marked object, while a pure adverb does not attach a case marker. But a word that names a time or a place functions sometimes as a pure noun and sometimes as an adverb, and there are other cases where a single word is described as belonging to two or more parts of speech.

5.1. One-shape and two-shape elements.

Certain particles have one shape after a word ending in a consonant and a different shape after a word ending in a vowel. There are certain inflectional endings, too, which have one shape when attached to a stem with a final consonant and a different shape when attached to a stem with a final vowel. (For the purpose of defining vowel-stem and consonant-stem conjugations, the basic ···w- of our analysis, in origin a lenited p, counts as a consonant, and the basic ····-l-, originally part of the stem, is treated as an extension of the vowel.) There are other particles and endings, some of which have but one shape and some of which have more than one but do not select the shape on the basis of the final phoneme of the element to which they are attached. Particles and endings of the first type can be called TWO-SHAPE, and those of the second type can be called ONE-SHAPE, even though elements of either type may surface in additional shapes due to other factors, such as the automatic reinforcement of a voiceless obstruent after a voiceless stop (§2.6). In colloquial Korean the stem of the copula belongs with the two-shape elements, but our Romanization takes the zero shape as an abbreviation: **tangsin ita** 'it's you', **na 'ta** 'it's me'. Examples of one-shape particles are **ey** 'to, at', **uy** 'of' (for which the pronunciation is /ey/, too), **kkaci** 'all the way up to, even', **to** 'even, also', **se** 'at, from', **man** 'just, exactly', **mata** 'each, every', **puthe** '(starting) from', ... Here are examples of two-shape particles, with the postconsonantal shape (as elsewhere in this book) cited first: **i/ka** (nominative), **ul/lul** (accusative), **iya/ya** 'only if it be', **un/nun** (subdued focus), **kwa/wa** 'with, and', **iyo/yo** (polite style). The particle **ulo/lo** (manner, direction, state or change of state, means, reason, ...) is peculiar in that the postvocalic form **lo** is used also after the consonant ···l, as in **yenphil lo sse** 'writes it in pencil'; contrast **yenphil ul sse** 'uses a pencil'. Examples of the one-shape and two-shape endings will be found in §9.

5.2. Nouns.

A noun, in the broad sense, occurs in at least one of four environments:

(1) before a particle: **achim i wass.ta** 'morning has come';

(2) before the copula **i-** as a complement: **achim ita** 'it's morning';

(3) before a noun or noun phrase which it modifies: **achim hayq-pich** 'morning sunlight';

(4) in absolute constructions, which may be interpreted in any appropriate role, including adverbial: **achim wass.ta** 'morning has come' (= **achim i wass.ta**) or 'arrived in the morning' (= **achim ey wass.ta**).

In normal speech, nouns are never followed by pause in environments 1 and 2; in environments 3 and 4, pause is more frequent, especially in 4. The English obligatory categories of singular/plural, definite/indefinite, and general/specific are essentially absent from Korean nouns. Without special marking, as by a numeral or by an element such as ··· **tul** '(as) a group', we are not told whether **chayk** means '(a) book', 'the book', '(some) books', or 'the books'. Specific words are intrinsically singular or plural, notably such pronouns as **na** 'I/me' and **wuli** 'we/us', but the intrinsic meaning may be overridden by semantic extensions, just as the English royal or editorial "we" is often used as a singular. According to Seok-Choong Song (Song Sekcwung) "plural marking in Korean individuates, whereas the unmarked category categorizes its referent"; he notes that plural marking is obligatory for nouns that have "specific reference", and that is borne out by pronouns, proper names, and the like.

5.2.1. Quasi-free nouns.

A quasi-free noun has great freedom of combination but it is always preceded by an element such as **i** 'this', **ku** 'that', or **ce** 'that (yonder)', or by an adnominalized phrase 'which (is/does) ... ' or a modifying noun phrase. (In contrast, the quasi-adnouns, §5.3.1, are always followed by a noun or a noun phrase.)

The following list of quasi-free nouns includes some that are often called "imperfect nouns" (**pul-wancen myengsa**) or "dependent nouns". I refer to some of these as postnouns and postmodifiers. What a given quasi-noun may be preceded by is an individual property of the word. Some of the words are occasionally free under highly restricted circumstances: **thek** need not be modified when it is followed by **ēps.ta** or **ēps.i**. But idiomatic expressions of that sort deserve separate entries in the lexicon.

LIST OF QUASI-FREE NOUNS

- ··· ca 'person'
- ··· ccak (= ccok) 'direction';
- = kkol 'appearance'
- ··· ccok 'direction'
- ··· cek 'time'
- ··· chi 'stuff, thing; guy, one'
- ··· chuk 'side'
- ··· chwuk 'group'
- ··· cīs 'act, motion'
- ··· cuum (cium) 'approximate time'
- ··· hay 'possessed thing, one's'
- ··· i 'person'
- ··· ilsswu 'constant (bad) habit'
- ? ··· keli 'material, ... '
- ··· kes 'thing, one, fact, ... '
- ··· key 'one's place, home'
- ··· kkan (ey) 'by one's own account'
- ··· kos 'place'
- ··· mulyep 'time'
- ··· nolus 'job, role'
- ··· ppal 'manner' (rare)
- ··· pun 'esteemed person'
- ··· tey 'place, ... '
- ··· thas 'fault' (also verbal noun transitive 'blame')
- ··· thek 'reason, limitation; resources; ... '
- ··· ttolay 'of (that) age or size'
- ··· ttan (ey) '(by) one's own kind judgment'
- ? ··· ttawi 'of the sort, and the like'
- ? ··· tūngci 'vicinity'
- ··· tūngtung 'et cetera'

Restrictions on the occurrence of the quasi-free nouns vary. Some are severely limited, as shown by the individual entries in Part II. Certain postmodifiers and postnouns that can perhaps be regarded as quasi-free have not been included here for various reasons. A few words that others have included in this category are omitted because I have found them in sentence-initial position and decided to treat them as free nouns: **ttaymun** 'reason; the sake of ··· ' is omitted only because a sentence can begin **Ttaymun ey** ··· 'Therefore ··· ' and we might well consider that usage an abbreviation of **Kuleh.ki ttaymun ey** ··· 'Because of its being that way ··· '. See also the entries **chwuk, nom, nyen**, and **nyesek** in Part II. And notice the uncommon use of **palo** (3 in the entry of Part II).

In contrast with the quasi-free nouns, BOUND NOUNS (§5.2.8) occur only in very limited types of compound (like the "cran···" of English "cranberry"). Most are here treated as bound adnoun = prenoun (or prefix), bound postnoun (or suffix), and bound preverb (bound adverb or prefix). There appear to be several BOUND PREPARTICLES, as listed in §5.2.9.

5.2.2. Free nouns.

A noun that is further unspecified is simply a free noun. At present I do not break the category down into as many subclasses as might be desirable for various purposes. I fail to distinguish COUNT nouns, MASS nouns, ABSTRACT nouns, etc., though the distinction can surely be drawn on the basis of the selection of counters; nor do I here distinguish between ANIMATE and INANIMATE, but see §10.8.8 for a useful correlation of distribution with the corresponding verb classes, in that there are verbs that have only animate subjects or only animate objects (or both). A more refined classification will emerge from further syntactic analysis. For purely practical convenience, I set up the subclass of PROPER NOUNS and that of DEICTICS, which includes pronouns and indeterminates (interrogative-indefinites). There are also deictic verbs and adjectives (**kule-** 'do that way', **kuleh-** 'be that way'). Verbs of motion can also be described as deictic, since the choice of **o-** 'come [to where I am]' and **ka-** 'go' depends on the position (location or psychological involvement) of the speaker and the hearer: **o-** "move toward me / here / now" is the semantically marked form, and **ka-** is the default. On the subtleties of choosing one or the other of this pair of verbs, see [1]Yi Cenglo 1985. (Standard Japanese uses the corresponding pair of verbs in a similar fashion. There may be dialects in both Japan and Korea that differ from the standard usage.) [1]Yi Kitong 1988 describes the semantic difference between **o-** and **ka-** as moving TOWARD or AWAY FROM the "deictic center", which includes not only "me / us, here, now" but also "the normal / desirable state, proper shape / conditions".

5.2.3. Proper nouns: names and titles.

Personal names are often of two syllables, and one of the syllables is sometimes used as a generation reference, so that brothers may be named **Sengen** and **Cwuen**, or **Cengkil** and **Cengmin**. The Chinese character for the common syllable is called the **tollimq ca** or **hang.lyelq ca**. Female names often take as a second syllable the suffix **-huy** (a Chinese loan meaning 'princess'), and in rapid pronunciation **-huy** sounds like **-i**, the common hypercoristic suffix that is added only to names ending in a consonant and is not to be confused with the nominative marker **i / ka**: **Chwunhyang-i (ka / lul)** 'Little Chwunhyang [as subject/object]', **Chwunhyang (i / lul)** 'Chwunhyang [as subject / object]', **Chwunhuy (ka / lul)** 'Chwunhuy [as subject / object]'. A girl who is called /swuni/ may bear the straightforward name **Swunhuy**, incorporating the suffix **-huy**, but she may write her name with a spelling variant **Swuni**; or, she may write it **Swun-i**, especially when it is a short form for names like **Pokswun(-i)** or **Cengswun(-i)**. Similar short forms are heard for other names, such as **Swuk-i** for **Yengswuk-i**, **Tong-i** for **Poktong-i**, ... Either the family name or the given name may be of one or two syllables — rarely, even three — so that a full name may have as few as two or as many as four syllables: **He Wung, Payk [1]Nakcwun, Sen.wu Wung, Ulqci Muntek, He Nanselhen**. The three-syllable type is the most common in Korea, as it is in China. Given names of three syllables are unusual and typically of non-Chinese origin, though the syllables may sound like Chinese elements, and characters are sometimes assigned to them on a phonetic basis. Korean names are usually said with the family name first, as in Chinese, Japanese, and Vietnamese. When the personal name has two syllables, some people like to Romanize it as two words, with or without a hyphen. A man named **Kim Cen.il**, for example, may want to write his name as Kim Cen Il or Kim Cen-Il and in English call himself C.I. Kim. Some Koreans have "foreign" names, either in addition to Korean names, or in place of them; the name is often Biblical. When the family name is Korean it is probably better to write that first: **Kim Phollin** (= Pauline), **Cen Tawis** (= David). If the name is that of a foreigner (other than Chinese or Japanese), it is best to leave the name in the foreign order even in Hankul, and to let it revert to the foreign spelling when Romanizing: "Samuel E. Martin" not "Martin Samuel-E.". In English texts Koreans usually try to follow the foreign order, so that the late [1]Yi Sungman is referred to by the English spelling he preferred "Syngman Rhee" and the educator **Payk [1]Nakcwun** writes in English under the name "George L. Paik".

A name, either a surname or a full name, is often followed by a TITLE: **sensayng** (or with varying connotations **ssi, kwun, sepang,** ...) 'Mr' (**ssi** can sometimes mean 'Mrs' according to Roth 281), **puin** or stylishly **samo (nim)** or **sensayng (nim) samo** or **sensayng samo nim** 'Mrs', **yang** 'Miss', **sayngwen** 'Mr' or ' ... Esquire', **cwusa** 'director; petty officer', **paksa** 'Dr' (Ph.D.), **uysa** 'Dr' (medical), **moksa** 'Reverend', **sinpu** 'Father', **kyōswu** 'Professor', **kak.ha** 'His / Your Excellency', **cēnha** 'His / Your Royal Highness (Prince ...)', **sēngha** 'His / Your Holiness (the Pope)', **sēngsang** 'His / Your Majesty (the King)', **phyēyha** 'His / Your Imperial Majesty', etc. Most of the titles can be followed by the postnoun **nim** 'esteemed', and **nim** sometimes follows a name directly: **Yēyswu nim** 'Jesus', **Sek.ka-yelay nim** 'Buddha', **Kongca nim** 'Confucius', **Mayngca nim** 'Mencius'. In bookish style contemporary names occur this way, too: **Kim nim** '(Mr) Kim', **Sen.wu nim** '(Mr) Sen.wu'.

There is an adnoun title **Sēng** ··· 'Saint ··· '. In addition, two adnouns are in current use as titles in South Korea: **Misu** 'Miss' (of a young unmarried professional woman or office colleague), **Misuthe** 'Mr' (of a male colleague): **wuli cicem ey se īl hanun Misu Kim hakwu Misuthe Pak un** 'Miss Kim and Mr Pak who work in our branch office'. In North Korea, the postnoun title **tongci** 'comrade' is in vogue: **Kim tongci** 'Comrade Kim'. Placenames have a basic form (like **Phyengyang, Payktwu, ˡNaktong, Cēycwu,** etc.) which can be considered a free noun, even though frequently the more common version includes a following category designator to specify the kind of place: **Phyengyang si** ('city'), **Payktwu san** ('mountain'), **ˡNaktong kang** ('river'), **Cēycwu to** ('island'). Other common designators are **tō** 'province', **kwūn** 'county (prefecture)', **myēn** 'township', and the somewhat less productive **ˡyelqto** 'archipelago', **(-)man** 'bay', **(-)hāy** 'sea', **(-)yang** 'ocean', **(-)hāng** 'port', **(-)lī** 'village', **(-)kwu** 'ward', **(-)kwung** 'palace', **(-)sa** 'temple', **(-)yek** 'station', **(-)sen** 'line', **(-)to** 'ferry'. And to the list we can add **(-)mun** 'gate' as in **Kwanghwa mun** (the main gate of Kyengpok Palace), **(-)cwa** 'constellation' as in **Kolay cwa** 'the constellation Cetus'. As remarked earlier, Koreans show a marked tendency to take any monosyllabic word and tack it on to an adjacent word, so that a name like **Nam san** 'South Mountain' or **Hān kang** 'Han River' is often taken to be a single word. For consistency, it seems better to Romanize the more productive category designators as separate words, even though they are monosyllables and even when they are attached to other monosyllables. Notice that **to** 'island', **to** 'ferry (point)', and often (§2.7.2) **tō** 'province' are homonyms. Some of the provinces are divided into North and South (like the Dakotas): **Phyengan puk to** 'North Phyengan (province)', **Phyengan nam to** 'South Phyengan (province)'. When writing, Koreans often treat **puk-to** and **nam-to** as units. A list of the Korean provinces will be found in Appendix 3. In Appendix 4 you will find lists of Japanese placenames with their Korean readings. It must be kept in mind, however, that Koreans often use phonetic approximations to the Japanese pronunciation for many Japanese names, and especially for those which are not of Chinese origin, such as Nagasaki (**Nakasakhi**). For other foreign names there are sometimes two forms: **Mikwuk** or **Ameylikha** 'America'. In general the "foreign" forms are more modern and sophisticated, but those based on Chinese characters are more succinct and often better known. (They are also easy to abbreviate: **Mi-Han** ··· 'American-Korean ··· '.)

Other proper names are book titles, corporation names, and the like. These are often characterized by abbreviation and ambiguity, sometimes intentional, so that it is not always easy to figure out the appropriate word division for the Romanized form. Such a proper noun will frequently have a final category designator that functions like those for places mentioned above: **(-)sa** 'company', **(-)sā** 'history', **(-)cen** 'tale' or 'biography', etc.

5.2.4. Deictics.

Deictics are those elements which alternate in reference depending on who is speaking. To be consistent we would have to include as deictics the honorific marker **-(u)si-**, which marks the subject of a verb as someone other than the speaker because it is someone toward whom the speaker is showing special esteem; the honorific particle **kkey** 'to someone esteemed'; personal names; and perhaps a few other things that, for various reasons, we will treat separately. Notice that names and titles are very often used as pronominal substitutes. Perhaps the most common polite way to say 'you' is **sensayng nim** or **sensayng**. Without going into all the details of usage, we can assemble the following lists.

PRONOUNS

I / me	na (/ nay)	we / us	wuli
I / me [formal]	ce (/ cey)	we / us [formal]	cē-huy
you	ne (/ ney)	you all	ne-huy
you [familiar]	kutay	you all [familiar]	ku (ney) tul
	caney		caney tul / kkili
	i sālam[1]		i(-i) tul / kkili
you [impersonal]	tangsin	you all [impersonal]	tangsin tul / kkili

you [to inferior]	ce (/ cey)	you all [to inferiors]	ce tul / kkili
		you all [disrespectful]	keyney²
you [formal]	sensayng (nim)	you all [formal]	yele pun
'Sir'	sensayng (nim)		
'Madam, Ma'am'	puin / samo (nim)		
oneself	caki, ce, casin, cachey	themselves	caki tul, cěhuy
itself	cachey		
he / him, she / her	ku ⋯ (i, sālam, pun, nom, ca, …) ce ⋯ (i, sālam, pun, nom, ca, …)	they / them	ku ⋯ tul, ku ⋯ ney (tul) ce ⋯ tul, ce ⋯ ney (tul)
it ('this')	i (kes)	they / them	i (kes) tul
('that')	ku (kes)		ku (kes) tul
('that')	ce (kes)		ce (kes) tul

¹ Also: 'my spouse (he / she)'. ² ?< keki ney; ?< ku ai ney (CF kaytul < ku ay tul)

CORRELATIVES

Indeterminate	Generic	Proximal	Mesial	Distal
enu 'which, some'	āmu '(any)one'	i / yo 'this (one)'	ku / ko 'that (one)'	ce / co 'that (one) yonder'
eti 'what / some place'	(āmu tey) 'any place'	yeki / yoki 'this place'	keki / koki 'that place'	cěki / coki 'that place yonder'
ecci 'what / some way'	āmuli 'any way'	ili / yoli 'this way'	kuli / koli 'that way'	celi / coli 'that way yonder'
ette (ha-) 'how, somehow'	āmule 'anyhow'	ile / yole 'thus'	kule / kole 'so'	cele / cole 'so, yea'

Notice that **eccay** = **ecc' 'ay** is contracted from **ecci hay** 'is / does what way', and **etteh-, āmuleh-, ileh-, kuleh-**, etc., are from **ette ha-, āmule ha-, ile ha-, kule ha-**, etc.

The word **eti** can be regarded as from **etey**, a dialect variant of **enu tey** 'what place' (CF p. 25). And **ěncey** 'what / some time, when' is contracted from **enu cek (ey)** '(at) what time'; it is unclear just how the related words **i(n)cey** 'now', **ecey** 'yesterday', and **kucey / kucekkey** 'day before yesterday' were derived. Other indeterminates are **nwukwu** (but **nwu** before the nominative marker **ka**) 'who / someone', **mue(s)** 'what / something' (obsolete **musum / musam**), **musun** 'which / some ⋯ ', **meych** < **myech** 'how much / many, some amount / number', **elma** 'what / some quantity' (< ˝en˙ma < *e˙nu˙ma), and **way** 'for what / some reason, why', which has the shape **wěyn** when adnominal, as in **wěynq īl in ya** 'what's the matter?' (with falling intonation) or 'is something the matter?' (with rising intonation). The word **etten** ⋯ 'what sort of ⋯ ' is the modifier form of **etteh-**, thus ultimately an abbreviation of **ette han** ⋯ ' ⋯ that is what way'. Although I am unable to offer examples of early sentences that use the indeterminates in a non-interrogative way, I presume that the language of the 15th century did not differ from the modern language in that respect.

There are a few paradigmatic gaps in the use of the deictics. As Cang Sekcin observed, you can say **i ttay** 'this time' and **ku ttay** 'that time' but not *****ce ttay** 'that [distant] time'. The derived forms **ipttay** 'up to now' (= **yethay**) and **cěpttay** 'not long ago' are not paralleled by *****kupttay** 'up till then'.

The proximal and mesial deictics can also be used anaphorically, but not the distal. In that respect, Korean differs from Japanese, where the corresponding (k)a- words can be used to mean 'that obvious

… [known to both you and me or to all]'. For Korean anaphora there is only a two-way distinction of **i** and **ku** (Pak Hwaca 1982). In **i kes ce kes** 'this and that; something or other' the distal deictic is not anaphoric though it is indeed metaphoric, for the 'that' is not visible.

The connotations of personal pronouns are apt to change through time. The anaphoric designator **ku** 'that one' is used as a third-person pronoun only in rather formal writing, for it is impersonal as compared with **ku sālam / i / nom / ...** . When used, it has a masculine orientation, but it can also refer to females. A fairly new (post-1945?) pronoun **ku-nye** (perhaps modeled on Japanese ka⁷no-zyo) is used consistently by some authors for references to 'she / her' while others refer to females by using **ku** and **ku-nye** interchangeably. 1880 Underwood says *i*, *ku*, and *ce* are "disrespectful when referring to people". These days it is quite popular to use terms with the honorific ··· **nim** for pronominal reference. Intimates sometimes use **caki** 'oneself' to refer to either the first or the second person. For the second person, polite usage calls for a title or name + title: **sensayng nim, Kim sensayng** 'you(, Mr Kim)'. Informal words for 'you' include **i sālam**, which can also be used to mean 'this person; he / him, she / her'. And **i phyen** can refer either to 'you (all)' or (= **i ccok**) to 'I / me; we / us', in addition to the basic meaning of 'this side'.

5.2.5. Adverbs.

An adverb is a noun that occurs typically (and a few of them perhaps exclusively) in absolute position, i.e. as an ADVERBIAL PHRASE. There are also unusual cases where the adverbial phrase modifies an entire copula sentence: **Pelsse chwulkun ip.nikka** 'Are you leaving for work already?'; **Pelsse Taycen ita** 'It's already Taycen' (on a train trip); **Tayk i palo Kim Pok.il ssi 'sey yo?** 'Are YOU, then, Kim Pok.il?'; **Enu-tes kaul iess.ta** 'It was autumn before we knew it'; **Acwu yātan tul ita** 'What a fuss!' (CM 2:52); **Kkok machan-kaci 'ta** 'They are exactly the same' (CM 2:52); **I ttang un ōn-thong tōl-path iess.ta** 'This land was all a field of stones' (CM 2:52).

One step removed is the still more unusual case where the adverbial phrase is adnominalized (§11.9) by position only: **kas sumul (ita)** '(he is) just 20', **palo ku chayk** 'that very book'; **tan hana (lul)** 'just one', **kyewu twūl (in ya)** 'only two?' This is especially common with time and place nouns: **te alay** 'farther down', **cokum aph** 'a little ahead', **acwu chōykun (ey)** 'quite recently'. One case is especially interesting: **Kkway yele chayk tul i iss.ta** 'There are quite a lot of books', in which the adverb **kkway** apparently modifies the adnoun **yele** despite **Kkway chayk i iss.ta** '(he) has quite a lot of books', in which **kkway** modifies the sentence **chayk i iss.ta** 'books exist', because we can say **Kkway yeles i iss.ta** 'There are quite a lot of them'. CF (CM 2:56) **kkway say kēnmul** 'quite a new building', **acwu yele sāqken tul** 'very many incidents'. (For a somewhat different interpretation of these structures, see CM 1:453-4.) Adverbs, especially those of degree, can modify other adverbs: **acwu ppalli** 'very quickly'.

Most adverbs can be followed by either the particle **un / nun** or the particle **to**, and the ubiquitous particle **tul** sometimes attaches to an adverb: **Phyen hi tul hasey yo** 'Take it easy (you people)!' The only clear exceptions seem to be **mōs** 'definitely not, cannot' and **an(i)** 'not', and certain conjunctional adverbs (**mich, cuk, ko lo, ...**); KEd carries one example of **an tul V**: **An tul mek.nun ya?** 'Aren't you folks eating?' It has even been suggested that, after all, **to** may just be possible with both **an(i)** and **mōs** as these examples indicate: **Ku nun kongpu lul ani to halye 'n' i wa meli to napputa** 'On top of not studying, he has a poor head, too'; **Ku nun kongpu lul mōs to halye 'n' i wa nung.lyek to ēps.ta** 'In addition to not studying, he is lacking in ability, too'; **Cham mōs to sayngkyess.ta** 'How ugly he is!'. In Middle Korean *a ni* could be followed by *two* and *non* and sometimes an adverb or adverbial phrase intervened before the verb; see Part II. What is more, *a ni* can appear directly before the accusative, locative, and comitative markers as if it were a noun. Such structures are the result of a direct nominalization of a noun predication with the copula form (we expect ˙i˙lwom or ˙i˙ywom) ellipted and the particles attached to *a ni* itself:

¨twul[h] a˙ni ˙lol cwo˙cha ˙ssywun ˙hosya˙m i˙la (1465 Wen 1:1:2:57a) 'it is that he follows pursuing what is not two [but one]'.

̈twul ̇h i ̈twul[h] a ̇ni ̇lol il ̇hwu ̇m i KHWONG- ̇SYANG ̇i ̇la ̇ho ̇si.n i ' ̇la (1464 Simkyeng 38a) 'said the name for two not being two is "unreality"'

swon s kalak ̇kwa swon s kalak a ̇ni ̇yey ̈na ̇mo ̇n i ̇Gwa a ̇ni ̇Gway ̈twul ̇hi ̈ep.su ̇mol nilo ̇si.n i ' ̇la (1462 ¹Nung 2:61b) 'said that to the finger and the non-finger, the remaining and the non-remaining there are no two of them'.

Ani is used alone before the copula (Ani 'ta 'It is not') and as an interjection meaning 'No!'; mōs is sometimes followed by the versatile particle tul. The only other occurrence of the morpheme mōs not directly followed by a verb seems to be in the word calmos 'mistake', derived from cal mōs ··· 'can't ··· very well'; calmos is also used in absolute position, as an adverb, so that calmos hayss.ta can mean either 'made a mistake' (= calmos ul hayss.ta) or 'did it wrong' (= ··· calmos hayss.ta). CF cal (l) mōs hayss.ta 'did (or could) not do it well'

Among the other adverbs those which seldom, if ever, occur with focus particles such as un/nun or to, can usually be followed by the plural marker tul, which is the ultimate test for separability. Examples of adverbs marked by un/nun, to, man, etc., will be found under the entries for individual particles in Part II. Most adverbs of time can also take the ablative puthe '(starting) from' and/or the allative kkaci '(continuing) all the time till': Ilccik puthe al.ess.ta 'I knew it from early on'; Akka puthe kitalyess.ta 'I've been waiting for some time; I started waiting a while ago'. CF pelsse puthe 'for some time now'.

If we were to regard the adverb as a noun that has dropped its marker (a handy but inaccurate concept), the appropriate particle would be ulo/lo or, especially with time words, ey. Sometimes we find parallel or competing expressions, with and without the particle: pōthong (ulo) 'usually', onul (ey) 'today', ili (lo) 'this way', ...

The following lists are not exhaustive, but ample. To make the lists more useful, I have divided the adverbs into rough semantic categories, in lieu of the more rigorous groups that will have to await further study: (1) adverbs of time, (2) adverbs of degree, (3) adverbs of contingency, (4) adverbs of assertion, (5) conjunctional (connective) adverbs, (6) adverbs of manner. There is overlap among the lists and with other lists; way, for example, is also listed as a deictic. Usually the English translations are enough to indicate which items are used frequently in other than absolute position (e.g. onul 'today'). With a few exceptions, I have included neither phrases nor the large number of derived adverbs such as ppalli 'fast' and the phrases with ··· hi (< ha-). Notice also the regular inflectional category -key called adverbative (§9).

(1) ADVERBS OF TIME

Many of these words are pure nouns that are directly adverbialized. We know they are pure nouns because they can be used as subjects and objects: Cikum i palo nala lul wi hay se īl ul hay ya halq ttay 'ta 'Now is the time we should work for the nation'. But some of the words in the list (kot 'immediately', pelsse 'already', ...) are not pure nouns, for they cannot be so used.

ēncey 'when; sometime'
(t)tāyttum 'at once'
mak 'just (at the moment); just now'
pelsse 'already'
pelsse puthe 'for some time now'
imi 'already'
icey, incey 'now; from now on'
cikum 'now'
sipang [? lit] 'now'
pangkum 'just now (= a bit ago)'
kumpang 'just now (= shortly)'

tangkum 'at present'
tangpun-kan 'for the time being'
say lo 'newly'
kas 'just (+ ages by tens), barely, freshly, newly (born)'
onul (nal) 'today'
¹nayil 'tomorrow'
ec(ekk)ey 'yesterday'
kuc(ekk)ey 'day before yesterday' (Kyengsang dialect ālay)
ku-kkuc(ekk)ey, samcak-il 'three days ago'

moley 'day after tomorrow'
kulphi 'three days from now, the day after the day after tomorrow'
ku-kulphi 'four days from now'
kumnyen 'this year'
cak.nyen, cīnan hay 'last year'
kulekkey, cāycak.nyen, ci-cinan hay 'year before last'
ku-kkulekkey, samcak-nyen 'three years ago, the year before the year before last'
¹naynyen, myengnyen 'next year'
¹nay¹nay-nyen, hwūnyen, cāymyeng-nyen 'year after next'
¹nay-hwūnyen, hwū-hwūnyen 'three years from now'
hwūq-nal 'someday (in the future)'
cangcha 'in the future'
aph ulo 'in the future'
ilkan 'in a few days'
taum 'next'
chacha, chachum 'gradually'
cēmcha lo 'gradually'
cēmcem 'more and more, gradually'
tangcho'y = tangcho (ey) 'at first, originally'
ponti, wen.lay, wenak, wenchey, a.ye(y) 'from the beginning'
ponsi 'originally, formerly'
nul, hangsang, hangyong 'always'
nosang 'constantly'
¹yensok 'continually'
cwul-kot 'continually'
yēng(yeng) 'forever'
cina-sayna 'night and day' (< cīna sāyna)
cacwu 'often' (< cac-wu, derived adverb)
māyil 'every day'
māypen, māyyang 'every time'
māywel 'every month' (= tal mata)
māynyen 'every year' (= hay mata)
cāmsi, cāmqkan 'for a little while'
olay '(for) a long time' (< adjective infinitive)
twuko-twuko 'for a long time' (< vt gerund)
tangcang 'then and there, on the spot'
kot 'immediately'; 'id est' → (5)
kot-cang 'right away'
samus 'right away'; 'quite (different)' → (2)
inay 'immediately (after)'
elphᵘ/ᵢs 'at once'

nallay, nayngkhum / nuyngkhum 'promptly, lickety-split'
phettuk 'in a flash'
enu-tes 'before one realizes it, in no time'
enttus 'suddenly (seeing)' (? < enu-tes)
chēnchen hi 'slowly'
ppalli 'quickly' (derived adverb < ppalu-)
ellun 'at once'
ese 'right away'; 'please' → (3)
akka 'a (little) while ago'
coman-kan 'sooner or later'
iss.ta (ka) 'after a while, presently, shortly'
elma an ka (se) 'soon, before long'
mē(l)ci anh.e 'soon, before long'
kumsay = kumsey (< kumsi ey) 'any minute (now)'
mīkwu ey 'shortly, soon'
mence 'first of all'
mili 'in advance'
ciley 'in advance, beforehand'
piloso 'initially'
cheum (ulo) 'for the first time'
ilccik 'early'
ilqtan '(when) once; for the moment'
¹imsi (lo) 'temporarily'
(kkuth-)kkuth-nay 'to the last, to the end'
olay kan man ey 'at long last'
mo chelem 'at long last; with great effort'
tutie, machim-nay 'at last'
nācwung (ey) 'finally'
ttay-ttay lo 'occasionally; now and then'
kakkum 'occasionally'
ittakum 'occasionally, now and then' (< iss.ta + -kum)
tele 'occasionally'; 'somewhat' → (2)
com chelem + NEGATIVE 'seldom'
(ttay) machim 'just in time'
twī-miche 'soon after'
miche '(not) yet' (< michye, vi infinitive)
acik, acik to 'still, yet'
han-kkep(en) ey, tan-swum ey, tan-khal ey 'at one time, at a stretch'
ilkē ey 'at one stroke, at the same time'
hamkkey 'together'
kath.i 'together'; 'like' → (6), derived adverb < adjective kath-
iuk.ko 'in a short while', abbr < iuk (= isuk) hako

(2) ADVERBS OF DEGREE (and QUANTITY)

A few of these words (tā, motwu, ...) also function as pure nouns and can be marked as subject (··· i / ka) or object (··· ul / lul).

phek, phek una 'very'
kkway 'very; relatively; fairly well'
ssek 'very'
ocwuk 'very; indeed'
maywu 'very' (derived adv < adj māyw-)
tāytan hi 'very' (derived adverb)
sīm hi '(does) very much' (derived adverb)
(ci)kuk hi 'very' (derived adverb)
nung hi (··· halq swu iss.ta) 'nicely, easily (able to do)' (derived adverb)
kkumccik 'i 'exceedingly' (derived adverb)
hako 'muchly' (gerund of obsolescent adj ha- 'great; much, many')
ha to 'indeed' (infinitive + particle)
sangtang hi 'relatively, comparatively, rather' (derived adverb)
cham 'real, very'; 'truly' → (4)
yekan 'to (no) usual degree'
cak-cak 'moderately, not too much'
tā 'all'
cōy(-ta) 'all'
motwu(-ta) 'all' < mot-wu, derived adverb < vt mot- (+ adv tā)
mot'-ta 'all' (abbreviation of motwu-ta)
kac.chwu(-kac.chwu) 'all' (derived adverb < vt kac.chwu-)
(ōn-)thong 'totally, completely, all'
mocoli 'entirely'
cen-hye 'totally' (< cen ha.ye)
yēng 'totally, completely, quite' (NKd 4628b); (= yēngyeng) 'forever'
kkang-kuli 'wholly' (derived adverb < vt kkang kuli- 'finish')
nemu 'too, overly, to excess' [+ adj or verb] (< nem-wu, derived adverb < vi nēm-)
humssin, humppek 'thoroughly, to the fullest (measure)'

(3) ADVERBS OF CONTINGENCY
mān.il < ¨man˙il < ˙MEN-˙QILQ 'if' (~ ··· -umyen, -ess.tula 'myen; ~ ··· kyengwu ey nun)
mān.yak < ˙MEN-˙ZYAK 'if (perchance)'
sellyeng, selhok, selqsa 'if (mayhap)'
kālyeng, kāsa 'if (say)'

(4) ADVERBS OF ASSERTION
ama (to) 'perhaps; likely, probably'
kulssey 'maybe; well ... '
ha.ye-kan 'anyway, at any rate'

cinthang 'to one's fill'
tampp^a/$_u$k, tempp^e/$_u$k 'overflowing'
hānsa kho 'to the bitter end'
oloci 'mainly'
haphil 'of all things (persons, places)'
kocak 'at most' (= mānh.e to)
cēng 'very'; 'truly' → (4)
mopsi 'terribly'
acwu 'extremely; quite'
te 'more'
tewuk, tewuk(.)i, tewuk te 'still more'
com te 'a little more'
han-kyel 'much more; especially'
han-chung 'all the more'
tēl 'less'
tele 'somewhat'; 'occasionally' → (1)
ke(ci-)pan 'over half, nearly (all)'
yepuk 'how very much'
hwelssin by far, overwhelmingly'
kacang 'most; very'
camos 'highly, exceedingly'
samus 'completely (different); ? very hard'; 'right away' → (1)
muchek 'exceedingly'
mulye (+ NUMBER) 'no more than ··· '; CF pulkwa (adnoun, p. 148)
mulus (+ NUMBER) ' ··· or so'
taman 'just'
ocik 'only'
tanci 'merely'
cokum, com 'a little'; 'please' → (4)
ceypep 'fairly, tolerably, passably'
yak.kan 'some; somewhat'
keuy, kecin 'almost'
kyewu 'hardly' (derived adverb < ··· kyew-)
kansin hi 'barely'
pyel lo '(not) particularly'

pilok < pi˙lwok 'even if' (~ ···-ci man, -e to, -ulq ci 'la to, -una, -kena, -ko to; ~ ··· ila to)
ām' man 'however (it may be)'
āmuli 'however (much)'
machi 'like, as, if'

hamulmye 'all the more / less (so)'
molumciki 'by all means, necessarily' (< molum cik hi, derived adverb)

ha.ye-thun 'anyway, at any rate' (< ha.ye hatun)
kwā.yen, kwāsi 'sure enough'
ttan un 'now that I come to think of it, as for that, to be sure'
cengnyeng '(for) sure, certain(ly)'
(cin)sil lo, sil un 'truly'
cēng 'truly'; 'indeed, very' → (2)
cham (ulo) 'truly'; 'very' → (2)
cēng-mal 'truly'
cinceng (ulo) 'really'
cham-mal 'truly'
sāsil (lo / un) 'in truth'
ccacang 'for a fact, truly'
mīsangpul 'indeed'
ttok 'exactly'
palo 'right, precisely'
cuk 'precisely'; 'id est' → (5)
an(i) 'not'
mōs 'definitely not; cannot'
toce-hi 'cannot possibly'
selma (< *hyelma* < hyen-ma, CF elma) 'by no means, surely (not)'
ilwu '(cannot) possibly' (derived adverb < ilu- 'reach')
kyel kho 'absolutely (not)' (< ... hako)
cokum to '(not) even a little'

thel-kkuth mankhum to '(not) even a bit (a "hair-end")'
tom(uci) + NEGATIVE 'not at all'
hwaksil hi 'certainly' (derived adverb)
mattang hi 'by rights' (derived adverb)
ttopaki 'without fail; completely'
mullon, mulon 'of course'
pitan + NEGATIVE 'not only'
kwuthay(e) '[not] making a special effort (troubling oneself to do so)' [usually spelled kwuthayye]
cēypal 'please, hopefully, I hope'
pūti 'please'
ese 'please'; 'right away' → (1)
āmu-ccolok 'by all means; please' (? < āmu ecci ha-tolok)
u^{y}lyey (hi / lo) 'as usual; as a matter of course; without fail; for sure'
ungtang 'for sure'
kkok 'for sure'
pantusi 'certainly' (? < pantus 'i 'straight')
kiphil kho 'by any means, at all costs'
kie-(h)i 'by all means'
tāy-kwancel, to-taychey '(wh...) on earth?!'
tāypem 'on the whole, in general'
tāykay 'on the whole, in general'
mulus 'on the whole, in general'

(5) CONJUNCTIONAL (CONNECTIVE) ADVERBS

mich [literary] 'and' (also particle)
nāyci (nun) [literary] 'and'
tto-nun 'and/or'
tto 'and, moreover, further'
tto-han 'too, also, as well; either'
yeksi 'too, also, as well'
hok(-un) 'or else, or again'

tasi 'or, again, further'
kot 'id est'; 'immediately' → (1)
cuk 'id est, namely, to wit'; 'precisely' → (4)
tekwu(nta)na 'moreover, in addition'
tolie 'instead, rather, on the contrary'
ohilye 'rather, preferably, more likely'
ko lo 'therefore, so'

+ various forms of kule (kuli) ha-, etc., such as kulemyen 'then', kuliko 'and', etc.
+ "sentence connectors" (§13)

NOTE: kyem 'and, as well as' is treated as a postnoun.

(6) ADVERBS OF MANNER

ecci 'how; why'
way 'why'
cal 'well, nicely'
tul 'plurally, as a group' (also other parts of speech; see Part II)
kak-kak 'each, every; respectively';
~ ulo 'from moment to moment'
cey-kak.ki, cey-kakkum 'each one, severally'
selo 'mutually; together'

ta-cca ko-cca lo 'without the least warning, unexpectedly, suddenly, directly' (§5.2.9)
mōllay, nam mōllay 'unbeknownst to others, secretly' (< molu- + -ay)
musim kho 'unintentionally, innocently'
naypta 'violently, suddenly'
tul(.)ipta 'forcefully'
hampu (lo) 'recklessly' (§5.2.9)
makwu, mak' 'carelessly, at random; hard, much' (? derived adverb < mak-)

honca 'alone' (also a pure noun: ~ ka)
honca se 'alone, by oneself' (CF twul-i se 'as a pair')
(il)pule 'on purpose, intentionally, deliberately',
cimcis 'on purpose, intentionally, deliberately'
puci-cwung (ey) 'unawares'

cikcep (ulo) 'directly; personally'
kāncep ulo 'indirectly'
sonswu 'with one's own hands' (< son + so, variant of se)
kosulan hi 'intact' (§5.6.1)
kaman hi 'quietly' (§5.6.1)
nalan hi 'in a row' (§5.6.1)
canttuk 'till full, to capacity; fully, intently'

+ impressionistic adverbs of movement and appearance (phonomimes, phenomimes — §14)
+ X hi, XY hi, X-yen hi (see entry hi in Part II)
+ N₁N₁-i (see entry -i in Part II)
+ N₁N₁, in which N₁N₁ = cōsim cōsim 'cautiously', kwuntey kwuntey 'in (various) places', pangwul pangwul 'in drops', ...
+ derived adverbs from inflected stems (see entries -i, -wu / -o in Part II)
+ adverbative forms (see entry -key in Part II)
+ a few infinitives (such as samka 'respectively') and miscellaneous inflected forms
+ deictic adverbs of manner and direction (ili, kuli, celi, ... ; §5.2.4) and derivatives (kulek celek, ... ; see Part II)
+ deictic adverbs of degree (i-taci, ku-taci, ce-taci, ... ; i man, ku man, ce man, ... ; see Part II)
+ many adjectival nouns + ··· cek with ulo: celqtay, mīswul, ...
+ many nouns with ulo: ekci, han kaci, him, īm.uy, kong, maum, macimak, pāntay, yelqsim, ...
+ many nouns with the temporal-locative particle ey: īcen, īhwu, achim, nac, pam, ...

I have not listed a category of adverbs of place. Except for a few adverbs derived from adjectives, such as mēlli 'in the distance' and kakkai 'nearby', and adverbs derived from iterated nouns (kos.kos-i 'everywhere', cipcip-i 'in every house') expressions of place are usually phrases of noun + particle — typically ey, (ey) se, ulo, but also other particles — or place nouns used in absolute position. But this is true also of many of the adverbs of time listed above (though not all of them); the classification obviously needs refinement. The principal criterion to indicate an adverb rather than a pure noun is that the word will not occur as subject (marked by i / ka) or direct object (marked by ul / lul). There are rare exceptions, under unusual circumstances, as in Mence ka te cōh.ass.ci? (Icey n' kulen kihoy ka olq kes kath.ci anh.a) 'Don't you wish you'd done it first? (It's unlikely there'll be another such opportunity now.)' (CM 2:120).

There are also deictic adverbs of direction (ili, kuli, celi, ...) and deictic place nouns (yeki, keki, cēki; eti); see §5.2.4. Compare, too, phrases with the postnouns kkili and kkes (Part II). A few strings of two adverbs are spoken together as a simple phrase, and these are often treated as lexical compounds: com-te 'a little more', tto-tasi 'yet again', tewuk-te 'still more', motwu-ta 'all', cōy-ta 'all'. CF Mkk 1960:7:34.

5.2.6. Bound adverbs (preverbs, verb prefixes).

The few morphemes that are prefixed to inflected stems are here called bound adverbs or PREVERBS, but they are usually treated as verb prefixes. Eleven attach to verbs of the processive type only, but es- and hes- function also as bound nouns with the postnominal adjective toyta:

    cat- 'small, fine' (as adnoun, see p. 150)
    cis- 'hard, severely, roughly'
    es- 'crooked, ... ' (also adnoun)
    hes- 'vain, mistaken; mis-··· ; open' (also adnoun; = heq- < he < HE 'empty')
    hwi- 'round and round; enveloping; thoroughly, completely; recklessly'
    pi-, pis- (just a spelling alternant?) 'crooked, ... ' (also adnoun)
    toy- 'back, again; in reverse'
    twi- 'back(wards); extremely; recklessly; thoroughly, completely'
        (< twī < ¨twuyh 'behind; excrement')

tes- 'additionally' (also adnoun; = **teq-** < **te** 'more')
tey- 'incompletely, partially, unsatisfactorily'
tul- 'hard, violently, thoroughly'
tul.i- 'hard, extremely, recklessly, suddenly; into, inward'

Three preverbs attach to descriptive verbs (adjectives) only:
say(s)-/si(s)- 'vivid, deep, intense'
tu- 'very' (emphatic)
yāl- 'despicably'

The extended forms of **say(s)-/si(s)-** are treated as **sayq-/siq-** by the North Korean spelling system. I suspect that the final -s of **es-**, **pis-**, and perhaps **cis-** are also ⋯q (as that of **tes-** more obviously is), although they are written with ⋯s in the North Korean system, too. The ⋯s of **mōs** 'cannot' could also be from ⋯q (CF **mō-cala-** 'be insufficient'), despite the noun **calmos** 'mistake', which is a later formation (see §4.2, §5.2.5), and the earlier spelling ῟*mwot*. (That is, the earlier final ⋯*t* in some instances may be another form of the same marker of subordination as the ⋯*s* that is ancestral to most cases of ⋯q.)

There are several pseudo-preverbs of transparent derivation:
yes- 'on the sly' (obsolete stem 'spy on')
chi- 'upward' (obsolete stem 'ascend')
che- 'abundantly, thoroughly, extremely, severely, at random, without permission or cause' (< **chye** = **chie**, vt infinitive 'hit, ... ')
ēy- 'surrounding' (< **eywu-**, vt 'surround')
kala-(anc-) 'sinking' (a bound infinitive, perhaps < **kal.e** 'plow [under]'?)
kule- 'pulling; clutching' (variant of **kkul.e**, vt infinitive)
salo 'alive, awake' (derived adverb < **sā-l-** 'live' + suffix **-o** = **-wu**)
elwu 'caressing' (derived adverb < **elu-** 'pamper' + suffix **-wu**), not to be confused with the archaic adverb *e'lwu* 'possibly' (see Part II)

As an adverb **il** 'early' seems to be limited to the expression **il kkay-** 'wake up early' but **il** also occurs as an adnoun, and 'early' is usually expressed by the adjective **ilu-** or the adverb **il-ccik**. Some of the regular monosyllabic adverbs (**cal** 'well', **mōs** 'definitely not, cannot', **tēl** 'less', ...) might be taken to be preverbs, but they are saved from the tag "bound" because of their wide distribution: they freely occur in new formations, and most of them can be separated from the verb by focus particles or the like. Certain compound verb stems (verb + verb) might be misviewed as adverb + verb, especially those with obscure etymologies such as these: **pulu-cic-**, **pulu-cwī-**, **pulu-thu-**, **pulu-pttu-**; **ppom-nāy-** (< **ppop-māy-**); **tha-ilu-**; **ce-peli-** (< **cie peli-**); **momc(y)e-nwuw-** (**mom ul cie nwuw-**). CM 1:421 lists **(p)pet-** as the equivalent of a bound adverb which means 'out(wards), mistakenly, mis-' in **(p)pet-ka-**, **pet-na-**, **pet-noh-**, **ppet-titi-**, **ppet-chi-**, **ppet-su-**; also **sel-** (< **se-l-**) with the meanings 'half-cooked, raw; unfamiliar' in **sel-teychi-**, **sel-salm-**, **sel-ik-**, **sel-talwu-**, **sel-mac-**, **sel-capcoy-**.

A few other bound elements attach to the beginning of verb stems, such as **alo-** in **alo-sayki-** and **ek-** in **ek-nwulu-** and other verbs; each poses special problems. The bound element **ēpsin-** in **ēpsin-yeki-** 'disdain, slight, neglect' obviously comes from **ēps.i** + **yeki-**, thus 'treat as nonexistent'. The Hankul spelling pins the irregularity on the first element, but historically it is properly placed with the second, and I would prefer to write **ēpsi(-)nyeki-**. The LHS dictionary implies that the pronunciation is /⋯nny⋯/; if that were true, we would have to write **ēpsinq yeki-** but no other sources confirm that pronunciation. Some sources (Cosen-e so-sacen, Kwuk.e say sacen, ...) give the initial vowel as short. The first element in **hu-nukki-** 'sob' seems to be a truncation of the phonomime **huk** (**huk**) 'sob (sob)!'. Somewhat obscure elements: **to-** in **to-math-**; **tong-** in **tong-calu-**; **hol-/hwul-** in **hol-kapun ha-** and **hol-potul / hwul-putul ha-** (see entries in Part II). The **cen** in **N ey cen kkam-kkam hata** 'is completely ignorant of N' is a shortening of **cen-hye** < **cen ha.ye**.

For other "prefixes" see the bound adnouns of §5.3.3.

5.2.7. Interjections.

An interjection is a subclass of adverb that typically occurs by itself as a minor sentence, often with the exclamation-point intonation (§2.8) and special voice qualifiers (not treated in this book), sometimes with expressive length (§2.7.2) or abrupt end – the glottal catch, Romanized as final ···q. I have not made a special study of this part of the lexicon, so that the words given below (mostly without translations) are largely taken from the works of others, notably Choy Hyenpay 1959:581-2 and Kim Pyengha 1:266 ff. Among the items are a few words that are transferred bodily from other parts of speech: **cōh.ta** 'it is good' = 'fine!'. The interjections are arrayed in semantic categories; a closer study would probably lead to a rearrangement. Notice that the particle **una/na** is often used to emphasize adverbs and interjections; examples will be found in Part II.

(1) calling people		**yeposipsio!, yeposey yo!, yeposio!, yepo!** (in descending order of politeness)
		i p(w)a!
		i ay!
		ana! 'hey!' (S. Kyengsang dialect)
		i! 'hey look out!'
		ungya! [ūya] (friendly, women to women)
		swi(-swi)!, swis! [swiq] 'psst!', 'hush!'
(2) calling animals		**kwukwu!** (chickens)
		weli! (dogs)
		olay olay! (pigs)
		ile! (< il.e) 'giddyap!' (to horse or ox)
		nēymi! 'here calf!' – also (13)
(3) shooing animals		**i kāy!** 'get, dog!'
		i kwāyngi, i kōy! 'get, cat!'
		swē!, hwei! 'shoo, birds!'
(3a) shooing people		**ya ya!** 'out of the way, you kids!'
		yaytula! pīkhyela! 'get out of the way!'
(4) YES to call		**ney! (yey!), nay!; kulay!, ung!; way!, mue!** (in descending order of politeness)
(5) YES to command		**ney! (yey!), nay!; kulay!, ung!; onya!, o!, ī! [ī̄:]** 'all right! OK!' (in descending order of politeness)
(6) YES to question[1]		**ney! (yey!), nay!; kulay!, ung!**
(7) 'Yes of course'		**ām (mullon ici, kuleh.kwu malkwu)!; āmulyem!**
(8) NO to question[1]		**ani olssita!, ani (ey) yo!, ani!**
(9) 'Not sure'		**kulssey olssita!; kulssey yo!; kulssey!**
		cham 'uh; oh!'
(10) hesitation		**um** 'hmm'
		ce, ca; cēki 'uh'
		ka se (nun / llang / llang un) 'and uh'
		mue ('la ko / 'la 'nun / 'la 'n' / 'la 'lq ka) 'uh'
		māl ita, māl ia, māl ya 'I mean, you see, you know'
(11) urging, inviting		**ca!**
(12) encouraging		**wiye!**
		pethye la! 'hold out!'
		ppop-nay la! 'be proud!'
		i-nom!, ku-nom!, ce-nom!
(13) damning		**nēyncang!, yēyncang!, cēyncang (mac.ul / chil)!**
		nēyki!, cēyki!, nēymi![2]

A Reference Grammar of Korean

PART I 143

(14) disgust,					on!; ey!
    dissatisfaction			chi!; si!; ēysi!
(15) censure					atta!; aytta!; eytta! — also (16)
						aykay(kay)!
						eti l'!
(16) sneer					eytta! — also (15); eyla!
(17) snicker					he(he)!; phi!; phu!; hwu!
(18) rejection					pikhye la! 'out of the way!'
(19) effort					ai(kwu)!; chwi!
						i(y)echa!, i(y)engcha!, iungcha!, yēcha!, e.yecha!,
						   ekiyacha!, iyessa!, e.yessa!
(20) pain					ayko!, aiko!, aykwu!, aikwu!, eykwu!, ei(kwu)!, aywu!
(21) fright					ii!, wuwu!
						eypi(ya)!, eyttukela!
						ikki (na)!, ikhi (na)!
(22) anger					ey!, eys! [eyq], eyik!, eyk(.)ki; wen!
(23) disappointment				e(ng)!
						apulssa!, eppulssa!
						acha!, echa!
(24) pity					aacha (aikwu)!, aikya!, aykay!, eyku!
						celen!; haha! — also (30)
(25) denial					eti!, etten!; wēyn ke l'!
						chenman ey (yo)! '[not] in ten million = not at all'
(26) recall					eyla!; as.a la!
(27) recognition				cham!; cēng-mal!
						kuleh.ci!; kulem!
						āmulyem, ām
(28) surprise					a(a)!; ak! [aq]; ai!; yaa!
						ayko!, aiko!, aykwu!, aikwu!; eykwu!, eikwu!
						ema (na)!, eme na!; eykwumeni!
						ikki (na)!, ikhi (na)!, ikhu!
						atta!, eytta!; wātta!
						celen!; ke!
(29) sigh					he(he)!, ha(ha)!, hwu!, hwuyu!
(30) laughter					he(he)!, ha(ha)!, hi(hi)!, ho(ho)!
(31) delight					aa!; yaa!
						eyla!; eyla cōh.kwun a!; eyla manswu!
						mānsey!
						cōh.ta! — also (32)
(32) approval					cōh.ta! — also (31)
						cal hanta!
						olh.ta!, olh.ci!
						elssa! — also (33); elssikwu (na)!
						ikhi!, ikhwu!, ikhu!
						aykhay!
(33) sarcasm					eyttwu eytta! (dialect?)
						a(c)cwu! 'and how!'
						elssa! — also (32)
						khayssāmey! (Kyengsang; < hakey hay ssamyen se)

	ēlepsyo! (< ēlim ēps.e yo)
	yongyong!
	allangchong!
(34) ingratiation	aii!
(35) other	uak! 'boo!; puke!'
	u(ng)a! 'bawl!' (of baby)
	(kaychiney) sswēy! (said after sneezing)
	koswuley! (kosiley!, kkosiley!, kosiney!)[3]

[1] As in many languages (but not English) the reply to a negative question accords with the surface structure ("Yes, we have no bananas") rather than the underlying meaning, unless the negativization is merely rhetorical, as in an invitation.

[2] Some of these words have vivid etymologies: **nēymi** comes from **ne uy emi** ⋯ 'your mother ⋯ '.

[3] This is said: (1) when performing a shaman rite; (2) when eating in the open country; (3) shortly after leaving a house from which food is taken. Kosi was the legendary teacher of farming.

To the lists can be added mimetic adverbs like **kkaok** 'caw!' and other phonomimes like **swī! swiya!** 'tinkle-tinkle!' (sound of child urinating), and occasionally some of the phenomimes (§12).

5.2.8. Bound nouns.

We will call certain elements bound nouns and bound compound nouns (CF §5.2.1). Of these, many are bound adnouns (§5.3.3) and bound postnouns (§5.4.5). Others are bound as subjects or objects (**pal-petwungi** in **pal-petwungi chi-** 'stamp one's foot'), and some are of doubtful classification (**cheng** 'membrane', **pho** 'quantity' — see Part II). There are also bound adjectival nouns, or "postadjectivals" (§5.6.5); CF the bound postverbs (§7.1.3). The word **mangceng** 'although' occurs as a postmodifier (§5.4.3) and also, probably as a reduction of **-ki ey 'l mangceng**, after the summative form **-ki** + particle **ey**; it, too, is a kind of bound noun. Notice also the quasi-adnouns (§5.3.1) and the bound preparticles (§5.2.9).

Other bound elements of obscure etymology include the "pre-postnominals" **alum** in **alum-tapta** 'is worthy of **alum** = is beautiful' (perhaps from **alam** 'tree ripe' < **al pam** 'shelled chestnut') and **alis** (or **aliq**) in **alittapta** 'is worthy of **ali**(s) = is charming' (< ?); the **-thi** in **kokay-thi** 'a steep twisting road over a mountain ridge' (CF Japanese [mi]-ti 'road' and ti-mata 'crossroads').

The morpheme **tes** 'interval of time' is treated as a bound noun (rather than, say, a quasi-free noun) because it occurs only in the compounds **enu-tes** 'before one knows it' and **tes-ēps.ta** 'is ephemeral' (no particle permitted to intrude). Possibly similar is **nacel** 'half-day', which seems to be limited to the expressions (1) **han nacel** 'one / a half-day', **pān nacel** 'quarter-day'; (2) **achim / cenyek nacel** 'in the course of the morning / afternoon'; (3) **nacel kawus** 'the better part of a day'.

Certain bound nouns (suffixes) are limited to one or just a few nouns, as is true of the many vulgarizers, the constituents of mimetics, and categorizers like ⋯ **cin(i)** 'falcon'. Such elements are often of obscure etymology: **can satali** (= **can sāsel** = **can māl**) 'small talk'; **kācis- / kēcis-puleng(i)**, **-puli** = **kācis / kēcis mal** 'lie, falsehood'; **kho-mayngnyengi / -mayngmayngi** 'one who speaks with a nasal twang'; **pola** in **nwūn pola** 'snowstorm' and **mul pola** 'spray of water'; **sal** in **mom sal** 'general fatigue'; **sali** = **coki** 'yellow corvina' in **polum sali** 'a coki caught at midmonth (high tide)' and **kumum sali** 'a coki caught at the end of the month'. Some nouns are probably the result of lexicalizing a phrase: **pal ssasim** 'fidgeting' perhaps < 'foot (deigning to) be swift'? Probably a variant (or special use) of a Chinese verbal noun: **yak sisi** 'administering medicine'. The noun **kophayngi** has three meanings, and there may be more than one etymology: 'coil; round trip' ? < **ko** 'loop' + **-phayngi**; 'the critical moment, the climax' = **kop(-)i** < **kop-** 'bend, turn' + **-phayngi** or **-h-ayngi**.

Sometimes the second element seems to be an obscure noun that is being explained by the first element: **ip-swul** < **ip siwul** < *ip si Gwul* 'the edges (line) of the lips' (? < 'bowstring'); **nwunq sep** (**nwun-ssep**) 'eyebrow'; **sin-pyena** 'the stitched part of a shoe'; **soy-sulang** 'a forked rake'; **pyen-cwuk** 'rim, brim'; **twī-thongswu** 'the back of the head'; **thopq yang** 'saw blade' (probably a diminutive *ni-ang < ˙ni 'tooth'); mith celmi 'basis, foundation'; ōymyen swusay 'flattering'; ocwum sothay 'diuresis, a weak bladder' (CF sothayk 'swamp'). The expression tamq pyelak = tamq pyek 'wall; blockhead' seems to contain either an expanded variant of pyek < ˙PYEK 'wall' or a variant of pyelang < pyelh 'cliff'; CF sonq pyek "hand wall" = 'the flat of the hand'. Sometimes an obsolete noun is found: nwun-sselmi < nwunq selmi 'a quick eye (for learning things)' < selmuy = sulki < sulkuy 'sagacity, good sense'. The second element of ip sim 'boldness / brazenness of words; eloquence' and payq sim 'impudence, nerve, chutzpah' is a dialect variant of him 'strength, power'.

The second element of cho-sung 'first days of the month; newborn', i-sung 'this world', and ce-sung 'the other world' is a variant of (sayng <) SOYNG 'life, ... '. The second element of ssi-as 'seeds' (not attested before 1775) is probably a lenition — Gas from ka˙c[i] 'variety'. The noun namnye-chwuni 'hermaphrodite' may have a variant of -chwungi = -cwungi or (directly) of cwung < CYWUNG 'middle' + i 'person'. The second element of pic-cisi 'intermediary party to a loan' looks like a derived noun *cis.i (dialect < ci˙zi; the standard version should have been *cii) from cīs.ta 'makes'. But it might be cīs 'act, gesture' (probably the stem of cīs.ta used as a noun) + i 'person'. The noun meyali 'echo' can be traced back to moy-ali < ¨mwoy-˙zali, a compound of ¨mwoy 'mountain' + probably either a variant of swo˙li 'sound' or the particle s + a variant of *wu˙l-i 'sound' (and not sa˙l-i 'living'). The ccim of mokchim ccim 'hitting one with a wooden pillow' and mongtwungi ccim 'clubbing' looks to be a variant of chim, substantive of chita 'hits'. The -tha(y)ki of homtha(y)ki 'crotch' may be a variant of (t)tayki 'stick' attached (presumably) to hom 'groove'. The -han(-i) of wentwu-han(-i) 'melon planter / farmer' seems to be limited to that term alone, and han is usually treated as a Chinese loan. The noun pok-cheli 'an unlucky person' is perhaps better pokchel-i < pokchel '(repeating another's) failure' (< ˙PWOK-˙THYELQ 'rut left by a capsized carriage') + i 'person'. The expression namu cicekwi 'wood chips' is a variant of (dialect) namu kicekwi, according to KEd, but the composition of that is unclear; CF cice-kkaypi 'wood chip', namuq kaypi 'piece of wood, splinter', ccic- 'tear, rip'. The noun humcileki 'stringy ends of meat' probably has a suffix, but just where to cut is a problem: humcilek-i, humcil-eki, hum-cileki? There is no clear source for the first part; the best candidate is hūm ci- 'get scarred, marred, flawed' (< *¨HUM / *¨KEM 'deficiency'). The relationship of kkoli < skwo˙li and kkolang(c)i 'tail' with kkongci 'tail of bird' is unclear; kkongci is probably a contraction of kkolangci, from kkol-ang[i] + ci (bnd n) 'stuff, thing'. The second element of cāng-acci 'dried radish or cucumber slices seasoned with soy sauce' is of unknown origin but may contain ci 'stuff, thing' (CF achi, -aci, chi). Variants of chay-ccik 'whip' have -ccwuk and -ccok, and the last is probably the source, perhaps identical with ccok < (p)cwok 'piece'. How kkun and kkunapul '(piece of) string' are connected is unclear.

In Part II we treat -so of mom-so 'in person' and -swu of son-swu 'with one's own hand' as variants of a bound particle.

5.2.9. Bound preparticles.

The bound preparticle mo occurs in mo chelem 'like mo = taking great pains, with much trouble / effort; at long last'; this appears to be the only preparticle followed by chelem. The etymology is unclear. Perhaps it is the noun mo that refers to a difficult and desirable arrangement of the four sticks in a game of yuch; or perhaps it is somehow related to mōs 'cannot'. But most likely it is an abbreviation from āmo = āmu 'any'; CF mō-ccolok from āmu-ccolok.

Several bound preparticles precede the particle ulo / lo and the resulting structures are treated as unanalyzed adverbs by Korean grammarians:

    sinap in sinap ulo (dialect variant sinam ulo) 'at odd moments' (with the earmarks of a Chinese binom si + nap / nam but the actual etymology is obscure)
    susu lo 'of itself, spontaneously; oneself' < susa < sa-sa < SO SO ('private private')
    kakkas in kakkas ulo 'barely'
    pa.yah (note the rare final h) in pa.yah ulo 'nearly, on the verge of; in full swing'
    no-pak.i (< no(sang) 'constant') in no-pak.i lo (= puth-pak.i lo) 'fixedly'

Here we can include the first element of the following expressions, too:

ol[h] ulo 'to the right' (< adjective olh-; not *ol lo!)
ōy lo 'to the left' (< adjective ōy-)
muth ulo 'in a lump, at one time' (< ?; Cf mus 'all')
thong ulo 'all, wholly' (Cf ōn-thong)
ken ulo = kenseng (ulo) 'in vain' (etymologically identified with the adnoun 'dry, dried')
nal in nal lo 'raw' (also an adnoun, and perhaps etymologically derived from nal 'to be born', the prospective modifier of na-)
hol lo 'alone' (also an adnoun)
pyel lo 'specially' (also adjectival noun, pre-postnominal + na-)
sayng ulo 'raw; unreasonably' (also adverb and adnoun; a bound Chinese morpheme 'birth')
cel lo, ce(y)-cel lo 'automatically, without effort' (apparently from ce 'oneself')
ta-cca ko-cca lo 'unexpectedly, without any warning, suddenly, directly' (< ?)
maynani lo 'empty-handed' (? < adnoun māyn + derived adverb anh.i)

We may wonder whether to include also ka( )lo 'horizontally', sēy( )lo 'vertically', and se( )lo 'mutually'. But kalo may be a derived adverb from kalu- 'cut across', as palo is from palu- 'be straight, right'. And (k)k^{e}akkwu(-)lo 'upside down' is to be connected with (k)k^{e}akkwule (ci-) 'tumble'. (For the purely orthographic distinction of ka ulo 'toward the edge' from kalo, and of se ulo 'toward the west' from selo 'mutually', see the entry ulo in Part II.)

The nouns hoth 'single(-ply)' and mat 'eldest' are limited to occurrences before the particle ulo, before the copula ita, and before the postnominal verb ci-; each is also an adnoun. There are probably other precopular nouns, and perhaps some also occur with ulo, but they have not come to my attention. One interesting case is tahayng, which is usual only with ulo (tahayng ulo 'luckily') and ita (tahayng ita 'is fortunate'). The word does not normally occur with other particles, but the nominative i/ka will be present when the copula is negativized: tahayng i ani 'la pulhayng ita 'it isn't fortunate, it's unfortunate'. Tahayng is mistakenly used for yohayng 'good luck' in tahayng ul palanta = yohayng ul palanta 'gazes on (= receives) good luck'; and tahayng also occurs as an adjectival noun 'be fortunate' but only in the forms tahayng hakey (to) 'fortunately (indeed)', tahayng hi 'fortunately', and tahayng han(q īl) 'a fortunate (matter)' − Cf §5.6.1. We might wish to consider as a precopular noun the ani of the negative copula ani 'ta 'it is not' (ani also occurs as an interjection); see the discussion in §11.7.1.

5.3. Adnouns and pseudo-adnouns.

One of the environments of the noun is before another noun (or noun phrase) which it modifies. Some words occur exclusively or typically only in that position. These we call ADNOUNS; they can also be called PRENOUNS. Often included by Korean grammarians are the PSEUDO-ADNOUNS, some of which are derived from reinforced forms of nouns (hays 'new, of the year; sunny, of the sun' < hayq ··· < hay 'year; sun') and some of which are modifier forms of a verb that have come to emphasize some special meaning a little more than other forms of the verb do. Korean grammarians prefer to spell 'right (in direction)' as olun to distinguish it from 'right (in correctness)', which they spell as olh.un. I am inclined not to call most of these forms adnouns, but they are included in the lists below. In a sense, any modifier can serve as a pseudo-adnoun, but those that are so treated by the Korean grammarians are usually distinguished by some kind of parallelism with single morphemes elsewhere in the vocabulary: hēn 'old' (< hē-l- vi 'get old, wear out') is the antonym of say 'new' and a synonym of the Chinese bound adnoun kwū- 'old'; sēn 'half-done = immature' (< sē-l- 'be half-done') is a synonym in some contexts of the adnoun sayng, a single morpheme of Chinese origin. Certain nouns have special, and usually shorter, shapes in adnominal position (kac' ··· = kacwuk 'leather', 'mak ··· = macimak 'last'); I have not listed these as pseudo-adnouns. Notice also the adjective construction X-una X-un 'that is ever so X', limited to adnominal use (see -una in Part II).

There are three lists of adnouns: (1) those that seem to occur only as adnouns, (2) those that have some other uses (briefly noted in parentheses), and (3) pseudo-adnouns, for which the etymological

A Reference Grammar of Korean

sources are indicated. There are numerous constraints on the occurrence of individual adnouns; these have not yet been explored in any systematic fashion, but hints as to their nature can be found in both the examples and the translations in the entries of Part II. Some adnouns, we will see, can be separated from the following noun by other modifying phrases; others, more like the bound adnouns (or prefixes) in this respect, cannot be separated. In the lists below, those adnouns which are clearly separable are marked "+", those clearly inseparable are marked "−", and the intermediate or questionable cases are marked "(+)".

LIST 1: ADNOUNS (EXCLUSIVE)

- −   ches 'first'
- −   cēy '···th' ordinalizer (with Chinese numerals) (< ˙TTYEY)
- +   ku− / ko-kkacis 'such a ··· as that'
- +   i- / yo-kkacis 'such a ··· as this'
- +   ce- / co-kkacis 'such a ··· as that'
- +   ney-kkacis 'the likes of you'
-     cey-kkacis 'the likes of himself / herself / themselves' (not 'the likes of me'!)
- (+)   yēys 'old, ancient' (< yēyq ··· < ¨nyey s; CF noun yēy < ¨nyey)
- (+)   yenu(y), yeni 'usual; (most) other'
- (+)   ōn 'whole, entire' (CF the Chinese bound adnoun cen-)
- +   ōn kac' 'all'
- +*   han 'one (← hana); the whole; the peak, extreme, most, very; about, approximately'
  - *In the meanings 'one ··· ; a certain ··· '.
- −   han, hal 'large, great; proper' (modifier and prospective modifier < ha- obsolescent adjective 'much, many')
- −   hān 'outdoors, outside'
- +   ku- / ko-man 'that little ··· '
- ?   ku- / ko-mas 'that little ··· '
- −   al 'bare, ... '
- +   swun 'pure; net' (< SSYWUN)
- −   swus 'pure, innocent' (? < swu[n] s)
- −   ūypus, ēpus 'step-(relative)'
- −   itum (nal, tal, hay) 'the ensuing / next (day, month, year)'
- (+)?   kwūn 'extra, uncalled-for, excess'
- −   has 'cotton-padded; with spouse'
- (+)   tan 'only; single' (but usually an adverb) (< TAN)
- +   ttan 'another, different'
- +   yak 'about, approximately' (< ˙QYAK)
- −   yāng (atul, ttal, pumo) 'adoptive / foster (son, daughter, parents)' (< ˙YANG)
- (+)?   kēkum (+ TIME PHRASE) 'ago, earlier, back (from now)' (< ˙KE-KUM)
- −   tol 'wild, rough; untutored; inferior' (? variant of tūl, below)
- (+)?   māy 'quite, much (the same)'
- (+)?   māy 'each' (< ¨MOY)
- (+)?   kak 'each, every' (< ˙KAK)
- (+)?   mō '(a) certain' (= āmo = āmu; but from mo < ¨MWUW)
- +   oman [? dialect] 'whole, all, every, many' (? < ōn + mānh-; ? < ō-man '50,000')
- (+)   mus < ˙mwu[l] s 'many, all sorts of'
- +   musun 'what; some one ··· '
- +   enu 'which; any'
- (+)?   tong 'the same; the said' (< TTWONG)
- (+)   pon 'this; main; real' (< ¨PWON)

(+) hyēn 'the present (existing, actual)' (< ˙HHYEN)
(+) wen 'the original' (< NGWEN)
− cāy 'resident in' (< ˙CCOY)
− tok 'by oneself, alone' (< ˙TTWOK)
− pay-nāy(q) 'newborn' (< noun + vc. 'expel [from] belly')
− si 'one's husband's (relatives)' (< SSI)
− soy 'a small one' (Chinese bound adnoun so- < ¨SYWOW + particle uy)
− sōy 'of cattle' < ¨sywoy < syw[o] ˙oy (§2.12.3) < *˙sywo ˙oy.
− (k)kamak 'black' (< adjective (k)kam- + -ak)
− ōng, ongtal 'small and sunken'
− (p)palkan, (p)pelken 'utter, downright' (< adjective modifier)
− ppetuleng 'out-turned': ppetulengq (n)i = petq-(n)i = tesq (n)i 'buck teeth', ppetuleng i 'person with buck teeth'
− kalang 'fine, tiny, shriveled'; (= kalangi) 'forked'
− yang 'foreign, western, Occidental-style' (abbreviation < se.yang < SYEY-YANG)
− ⁿye 'woman, female' (abbreviation < ⁿyeca < ¨NYE-¨CO)
− nam 'man, male' (abbreviation < namca < NAM-¨CO)
− mok 'wood(en)'; (= mok.myen) 'cotton' (< ˙MWOK)
− ho 'of foreign origin, especially from ancient China' (< HHWO)
− tang 'of Chinese origin' (< noun 'Tang dynasty') (< TTANG)
− pēm 'pan-, all-' (< PPEM)
(+) ¹yāng 'both' (numeral) (< ¨LYANG)
− ¹nāyng 'cold, iced': ¹nāyng khephi 'iced coffee', ¹nāyng saita 'chilled cider', ¹nāyngq kwuk 'cold soup' (< ¨LOYNG / LYENG)

LIST 2: ADNOUNS (NON-EXCLUSIVE)

+ i / yo 'this' (noun + particles)
+ ku / ko 'that' (noun + particles)
+ ce / co 'that' (noun + particles)
(+) say 'new' (noun + lo, + low-)
− oy 'only, single' (noun + lo, + low-; bound adverb + ttē-l-)
(+) āmu 'any' (as noun 'any person')
− mat 'first-born, eldest' (noun + ulo, + ita)
(+) cen 'former' (also noun, postnoun; < CCYEN)
− 'mak-nay 'last-born, youngest' (? noun)
− cho 'of the first ten days of the month; early' (also postnoun; < CHWO)
− ay 'the very young; (= a.yey) the very first' (also noun, abbreviated < ai 'child'; bound noun in ayq toyta)
− tūl 'wild' (as noun 'prairie, moor')
− cin 'deep (in color)' (also adjectival noun 'be deep or thick'; < CIN)
− yēn 'light (in color)' (also adjectival noun 'be light or soft'; < ¨ZYWEN)
− kāy 'wild, ... ' (noun 'dog')
(+) kō 'the late (deceased)' (also noun and postmodifier 'reason'; < ˙KWO)
− phus 'green, unripe, ... ' (also bound noun in elyem-phus; ?< ˙phu[l] s)
− ōl, ō' 'early-ripening' (also noun 'vigor, ... ')
− il 'early' (also adverb; CF ilu- 'be early', ilccik < ilq-cik)
− nuc 'late, belated' (< adjective nuc-; also adverb?)
− tes 'additional' (also bound adverb) (< teq ⋯ < te 'more')
− cap 'mixed; poor; ... ' (also bound noun + toy-; < ˙CCAP)

A Reference Grammar of Korean PART I 149

- pi(s) 'crooked, ... ' (also bound adverb)
- es 'crooked, ... ' (also bound adverb)
- mey 'nonglutinous' (also bound noun in **mey ci-** 'be nonglutinous', **mey-malu-** 'be fallow')
- cha(l) 'glutinous' (also bound noun in **cha' ci-** 'be glutinous'; < **cha-** 'sticky')
- thong 'whole, intact, untouched' (also adverb, bound noun)
- hoth 'single' (also noun + **ulo**)
- mac' 'facing, ... ' (also adverb; abbreviation of derived adverb **macwu** < **mac-wu**)
- sang 'common, ordinary, ... ' (also bound noun; < SSYANG)
+ yele 'numerous' (= numeral **yeles**)
- pān 'half' as in **pān pengeli** 'half-mute' (also numeral 'half', postnoun 'and a half'; < ˙PAN)
- nal 'raw' (also noun + **lo**; ? < **nalq** prospective modifier < **na-** 'be born')
(+)? sayng 'raw; crude; live; real; arbitrary; utter' (also noun + **ulo**, adverb + **mek-**; < SOYNG)
- emci 'main, principal' (also noun = **emci kalak** 'thumb')
- ¹yen (prenumeral) 'continuing through, running' (also noun 'continuation', vnt 'connect, continue'; < LYEN)
- kang 'forced; unadulterated, plain; dry' (also bound adverb + **malu-**; < ˙KKANG)
- ken 'dry, dried' (also bound preparticle, adjectival noun; < KKEN)
- hes 'false' (also bound noun; < **heq** ... < HE S)
- swu(h) 'male' (also bound noun 'convex, external, protruding')
- am(h) 'female' (also bound noun 'concave, internal')
- kayk 'uncalled-for' (also bound noun; noun 'guest' < ˙KHOYK)
(+)? kūn 'about, nearly' (also bound noun?; < ¨KKUN)
- cham 'real, true, genuine' (also adverb, interjection, ? noun)
- pyel 'special' (also bound noun; < ˙(P)PYELQ)
+ pulkwa 'only, merely' (+ QUANTITY) (also adjectival noun; < ˙PWULQ-˙KWA)
- sen 'first, prior' (also noun 'first move'; < SYEN)
? sēng 'Saint' (also noun; < ˙SYENG)
(+) chin 'sharing blood ties': **chin apeci** 'blood father' (also adjectival noun 'intimate'; < CHIN)
- ōy 'maternal': **ōy hal-'meni** 'maternal grandmother' (also bound adnoun 'external', noun = **pakk** 'outside, ... '; < ˙NGWOY)
(+) tang 'the said; the appropriate; (age) at a time' (also postnoun 'for each', vnt 'undergoes, confront; copes', vni 'confronts', adjectival noun 'is reasonable, appropriate'; < TANG)

LIST 3: PSEUDO-ADNOUNS

(+) taum-taum 'next but one' (noun + noun)
+ pyel-pyel, pyel-uy pyel 'special' (bound noun + ...)
- cēy-il 'first, prime', cēy-ī 'second', ... (see Numbers, §5.5)
+ nay 'my' (abbreviation < **na uy**)
+ ney 'your' (abbreviation < **ne uy**)
+ cey 'one's own' (abbreviation < **ce uy**)
? i-nay 'this my ... ; my'
- hay, hays (< **hayq** < ˙hoy s) 'new, of the year; sunny, of the sun'
- wi(q), wis 'upper' (< noun **wi** 'above'). The variant **wu(q)**, found in only a few set phrases nowadays, is treated as an adnoun **wus** in both North and South Korea. The NK dictionary treats **wi** as dialect, **wu** as standard. CF Mkk 8:42 (1960): "**wi** is used as the noun in the central area but **wus/wis** when it is the prefix [or adnoun]". The NK dictionary standardizes the spelling **wus** (as do the South Koreans) where one would expect the apostrophe to write the **-q**, and that spelling indeed turns up in CM 1:226, where **wuq meli** ("wus-me-li") 'upper

head' is cited along with **alayq meli** 'lower head', which is spelled with the apostrophe in NKd, as well. The Middle Korean form was *wu[h] s*.

-      **alay(q), alays** 'lower'
-      **phalang / pheleng** 'blue' (noun)
- (+)?   **(k)kemceng** 'black' (noun)
-      **nolang / nwuleng** 'yellow' (noun)
-      **ppalkang / ppelkeng** 'red' (noun)
-      **com** 'petty' (noun, abbreviation < **cokum**)
- ?   **tāymo han** [rare] 'important, main' (defective adjectival noun)
- ?   **āymen** [uncommon] 'off-the-point, extraneous, devious (remarks), vague' (abbreviation < **āymay hen** = **āymay han** ' ··· that is vague'
- (+)   **ēps.nun** 'impoverished, needy' (< ' ··· that lacks')
- +   **hanta 'nun, hanta ko (ha)nun** 'admitted to be capable (strong)'
-      **sēn** 'half-done = immature' (modifier < **sē-l-** vi)
- +   **hēn** 'old; worn out' (modifier < **hē-l-** vi)
-      **palun** 'right' (modifier < **palu-** adjective)
-      **olun** 'right' (variant of **olh.un**, modifier < **olh-** adjective)
-      **ōyn** 'left' (modifier < **ōy-** adjective)
- (+)?   **can** 'small, fine, thin' (modifier < **ca-l-** adjective)
- (+)   **talun** 'other' (modifier < **talu-** adjective)
- +   **kac.un** 'all' (modifier < **kac-** = **kaci-** 'hold')
- +   **mōtun** 'all' (< **mot.un** = **moin** 'gathered')
-      **ongkun** 'whole; intact, original; untouched' (modifier < **onku-l-** adjective)
- (+)?   **māyn / mīn** [also with short vowel] 'nothing but, unadulterated, bare' (modifier < **mī-**)
-      **māyn** 'all the way, the very, the extreme' (? from preceding entry)
- (+)   **kīn-kin** 'long long ··· ' (iterated modifier < **kī-l-** adjective)
- (+)?   **mak-talun** 'dead-end' (modifier < **mak-talu-** 'come to an impasse', compound vi)
-      **hethun** 'silly' (< **heth.un** modifier < **heth-** = **huth-** 'scatter')
-      **ol** 'this, the present; next, the coming' (prospective modifier < **o-** 'come')
-      **wang** 'big, king-size' (noun 'king'; < NGWANG)
-      **mal** 'big, large-size (animal or plant)' (< noun 'horse')
- ?   **mu'** 'light, watery' (< noun **mul** 'water'; CF **mulk-** 'thin, watery')

Certain morphemes that might be thought to fall in the category of adnouns we will treat as free nouns: **cheng** 'green or blue', **hong** 'red', **huk** 'black', **payk** 'white'; **cēng** 'real, true; center, ... '; ... . See also **omphak / wumphek** in Part II.

CM 1:212 lists **cas** 'small, fine' with two examples: **cas cwulum** 'crease' and **cas cing** 'small shoe-nail'. South Korean dictionaries treat this element as **cat-**, a variant from **ca-l-** 'be fine'. It could also be viewed as a shortening of **cati can** ' ··· that is quite fine indeed'; as < **calq** 'to be fine'; or < **caq** (= **ca-l-**). The spelling with **t** is supported by **cat-talah.ta** 'is rather fine'.

The words **kas** 'just (+ ages by ten)' and **tan** 'only' are usually adverbs; see §5.2.5.

5.3.1. Quasi-adnouns.

Some of the Chinese nouns which have the earmarks of freedom, being of two or more syllables, are nonetheless restricted to positions modifying a noun or noun phrase, and occasional examples in other positions are to be dismissed as awkward at best. Among these "quasi-adnouns" are the defective verbal nouns (§5.6.2) that have only the modifier form: **tāymo han** 'prominent', **mōmo han** 'celebrated', ... For 'unique' we find both **yuil han** and **yuil uy** (as in ~ **mokcek** 'unique goal'); also **yuil mui han** (less commonly **yuil mui uy**) 'unique and unmatched'.

Other quasi-adnouns are listed below in several groups:

(1) Quasi-adnouns with **uy**

pulhwu uy 'undying, immortal'
pulphay uy 'unvanquished, unconquerable'
cisang uy 'supreme, sublime'
celqsey uy 'peerless'

mīcung-yu uy 'unprecedented'
pul.yo pulkwul uy (? **pul.yo uy**,
? **pulkwul uy**) 'indomitable'
pulka-pun uy 'indivisible'

(2) Quasi-adnouns without **uy**

kwukcey (mūncey) 'international (problems)'
wensi (sāhoy) 'primitive (society)'
coki (chilyo) 'early (treatment)'

kanay (kongep) 'domestic (industry)'
ⁿ**yelyu (cak.ka)** 'woman (writer)'
ilqtay (cangkwan) 'grand (sight)'

(3) The bound postnoun **cek** '⋯ic' produces compounds which are somewhat like quasi-adnouns that do not take **uy**, but they can also occur:

before **ulo**, as in **kwahak-cek ulo** 'scientifically';

before forms of the copula especially the modifier, as in **kwahak-cek (in) thāyto** 'a scientific attitude' and **thāyto ka kwahak-cek ita** 'has a scientific attitude';

before the nominative marker **i/ka** when followed by a negativized copula expression: **thāyto ka kwahak-cek i ani 'ta** 'does not have a scientific attitude'.

(4) The bound postnoun **sāng** '⋯-wise, with respect to' (the basic vowel length of the morpheme is usually suppressed when it functions this way) creates compounds that are often used like adnouns, but they may be separated from the modified noun by the copula modifier **in** or (more commonly) by the particle **uy**, as in **I ke n' kyengcey-sāng (uy) mūncey 'la ko polq swu iss.ta** 'This can be looked at as a question relevant to economics'. (Contrast the behavior of **cek** '⋯ic', which never occurs with **uy**.) The compounds also occur before various particles, but usually the particles are present because they are required by later elements of the sentence. The **sāng** compounds, unlike the **cek** compounds, do not occur as predicate complement with ⋯ **ita** 'it is ⋯', nor with most conversions of the copula other than the adnominal **in** (and substitution by **uy** is more common) and such adverbial conversions as **ina** and the negative **ani 'la**. See the entry in Part II for examples.

Why are **sāng** and **cek** treated as "bound" postnouns, rather than free? Mainly because in general they do not attach to non-Chinese elements, though there are numerous contrary examples, and **sāng** may be more versatile than I have allowed, as is its Japanese counterpart (⋯ **zyoo**). The compounds that result from attaching the bound postnoun are special kinds of quasi-adnoun.

5.3.2. Numerals. See §5.5.1.

5.3.3. Bound adnouns (prefixes).

The occurrence of specific adnouns is restricted in various ways. In general, I have treated as free all those adnouns that are not of Chinese origin and in addition those Chinese adnouns which are widely used to modify nouns of non-Chinese origin as well as those that are Chinese. Some of the free adnouns are restricted to a rather small group of partners they can modify, others are quite productive. I have set up only one non-Chinese bound adnoun: **yel-** 'young, new' (of unclear etymology, see the entry in Part II). But there are a lot of Chinese bound adnouns and they are quite productive, though they combine almost exclusively with Chinese vocabulary. When one of them occurs widely also with non-Chinese vocabulary it is included in the list of free adnouns (for example **sayng**). But certain fairly free nouns, such as **cen** 'before', **hwū** 'after', and **cwung** 'midst, middle' will be found included, for in putting the list together I have been more concerned with convenience than with consistency.

The list of Chinese bound adnouns is arranged alphabetically, in order to display homonyms; examples are given to illustrate just why each morpheme deserves the treatment as an adnoun. The examples are all of occurrences with free two-syllable Chinese nouns; when the same morpheme is followed by a bound morpheme I do not treat it as an adnoun. Accordingly **sin-** 'new' is an adnoun in **sin-sēykyey** 'new world' because **sēykyey** 'world' is a free noun, but not in **sinmun** 'newspaper' because **mun** is not a free noun (at least in this meaning). When a one-syllable bound adnoun is combined with a one-syllable free noun of the Chinese vocabulary, it is difficult to decide whether to treat the string as one word or two, for often the two-syllable string is more common and older than the free occurrence of the noun, which is sometimes based on a special meaning or a shortening of a longer equivalent. When in doubt we can always use a hyphen. In fact, I prefer a hyphen for all cases of bound adnouns, at least within texts: **sin-sēykyey** despite say **sēykyey** which means virtually the same thing 'a new world'. The problem of freedom or bondage of Chinese morphemes is quite vexing and requires further study. (See the discussion in §5.4.5.) The bound adnoun **pi-** 'un-, non-', for example, is largely limited to Chinese nouns, but it can be found for a few recent loanwords of English origin, such as **pi-Kaythollik(-)kyēy se nun** 'in non-Catholic circles', where the bondage of **-kyēy** 'world' is also in question. Similar problems of free versus bound occur in **cho-inkan(-)cek** 'superhuman' (CF §5.3.1), **cho-inkan(-)hwa** 'superhumanization', and perhaps **pi-yēyswulq-cek** 'unesthetic'.

List of bound adnouns

SHAPE	CHARACTER	MEANING	EXAMPLES
ak-	惡	bad	~ sencen 'bad propaganda', ~ insang 'bad impression', ~ phyengqka 'bad evaluation'
cak-	昨	preceding; yesterday	~ hōykyey-nyen 'the last fiscal year', ~ swuip-sey 'the last income tax', ~ sipsam-il 'yesterday the 13th'
cāy-	再	again, re-	~ chwulpal 'restart', ~ ipkwuk 'reentry (into a country)', ~ hwal.yak 'reactive, active again'
cang-	長	long	~ kēli 'long distance', ~ hayng.lyel 'long parade (procession)', ~ sikan 'long time'
cē-	低	short; low	~ sokto 'low speed', ~ kiap 'low (air) pressure', ~ cwupha 'low frequency', ~ hyel.ap 'low blood pressure'
cen(-)₁	前	the former, ex-	~ puin / mānwula 'ex-wife', ~ swusang 'ex-premier', ~ nāykak 'former cabinet', ~ namphyen 'former husband', ~ su' nim 'a former priest'
cen(-)₂	全	the entire (CF ōn)	~ (ca.yu) sēykyey 'the entire free world', ~ (Mikwuk) inmin 'the entire (American) people'; ~ Sewulq-Cangan (ul cēnmang hanta) '(has a panoramic view of) the whole city of Seoul'
cēng-	正	regular, full	~ kyōswu 'full professor', ~ kyōwen 'regular teacher', ~ hōywen 'regular member'
cey-	諸	various, several, the [plural]	~ palmyeng 'various inventions', ~ mincok 'the (several) nationalities', ~ mūncey '(the) various problems', ~ pangmyen '(the) several directions'
cēy-	帝	imperial; imperialist	~ cengpu '(the) imperial government', ~ cengchayk 'imperal(ist) policy'
cha-	此	this	~ sāsil 'this fact', ~ sāhoy 'this society', ~ sēykyey 'this world'
chin-	親	1 blood-related 2 pro-	~ hyengcey 'blood brother', ~ pūmo 'the genetic parents' ~ cengpu 'pro-government', ~ Yengkwuk 'pro-Britain', ~ Puk-Han 'pro-North Korea'

A Reference Grammar of Korean

cho-	超	super, ultra	~ **sokto** 'superspeed', ~ **ca.yen** 'supernatural', ~ **umpha** 'ultrasonic(s), supersonic', ~ **inkan** 'super(hu)man' (CF **choin** 'superman')
chōng-	總	overall, general, total	~ **kōngkyek** 'general offensive', ~ **sayk.in** 'general index', ~ **sacik** 'mass resignation', ~ **tōngwen** 'general mobilization', ~ **sānchwul** 'mass production'; ~ **maliq swu** 'total number of animals', ~ **Mikwuk (uy) huk.in inkwu** 'the total black population of the United States'
chōy-	最	most, extreme(ly)	~ **wutung** 'most excellent', ~ **sinsik** 'ultra-modern', ~ **chemtan** 'spearhead'
ci-	支	branch	~ **kongcang** 'branch factory', ~ **sen.lo** 'branch rail line'
cik-	直	direct	~ **swuchwul** 'direct exportation', ~ **kōpayk** 'true confession', ~ **hyēnsang** 'true circumstance'; ~ **kwuk** 'undiluted liquor, sauce, ... ', ~ **kkwul** 'pure honey'
con-	尊	the honored; your	~ **hōysa** 'your firm', ~ **philqcek** 'your handwriting', ~ **ceyan** 'your suggestion'
cōng-	終	final, last	~ ¹**yelcha** 'the last train', ~ **cēncha** 'the last streetcar (or train)', ~ **(p)pesu** 'the last bus'
cwu-	主	main, principal	~ **sānmul** 'the main crop / product', ~ **sān.ep** 'the principal industry', ~ **pēm.in** 'the chief culprit', ~ **sengpun** 'the main ingredient', ~ **umco** 'leitmotif'
cwūn-	準	quasi-, acting	~ **hōywen** 'associate member', ~ **sawen** 'junior employee', ~ **kyōwen** 'teaching assistant'
cwung(-)	中	middle	~ **kīep** 'medium(-size) enterprise', ~ **hak.kyo** 'middle school', ~ **sēyki** 'medieval centuries'
cwūng-	重	heavy	~ **kongep** 'heavy industry', ~ **kumsok** 'heavy metal', ~ **kikwan-chong** 'heavy machine-gun', ~ ¹**notong** 'heavy labor'
ē- *	御	the esteemed; your	~ **kaceng** 'your home', ~ **kwuk.ka** 'your nation', ~ **ceyan** 'your suggestion / proposal', ~ **puin** 'your wife'
			* Japanese usage, sarcastic in Korean.
hā(-)	下	bottom, lower; last, later, ...	SEE Part II, p. 514.
hay-	刻	the said	~ **hak.kyo** 'the said school', ~ **sāqken** 'the incident in question', ~ **inmul** 'the said person'
he-	虛	false; sham (CF **hes**)	~ **phungsel** 'false gossip', ~ **yengsang** = **hesang** 'virtual image (in optics)'
hō-	好	good	~ **hyelqsayk** 'good complexion', ~ **inmul** 'good person', ~ **insang** 'good impression', ~ **kihoy** 'good opportunity'
hwal-	活	living, live	~ **hwāsan** 'live volcano', ~ **mūtay** 'legitimate stage' ~ **sintek** 'active grace'
hwū(-)	後	the later	~ **pānki** 'second term', ~ **sēyki** 'later centuries', ~ **hayng.lyel** 'after-column'
ī-	異	different	~ **punca** 'foreign element', ~ **incong** 'different (alien) race', ~ **pun.ya** 'different field', ~ **mincok** 'alien race'
¹in-	隣	neighboring, nearby	~ **chōnka** 'neighboring cottage', ~ **pulak** 'neighbor community', ~ **wūpang** 'nearby friendly nation'

kā-	假	1 false, pretend, fake	~ **hyengsa** 'fake detective', ~ **munse** 'false document', ~ **cwūso** 'false address', ~ **uysa** 'quack doctor', ~ **sacang** 'phony company-head'
		2 makeshift, temporary, provisional	~ **kēnmul** 'temporary building', ~ **kyōsa** 'temporary instructor', ~ **tōlo** 'temporary road', ~ **sisel** 'makeshift facilities', ~ **cengpu** 'interim government', ~ **ip.hak** 'provisional admission (to a school)'
kang-	強	hard, tough	~ **ōykyo** 'firm diplomacy', ~ **tāychayk** 'strong policy', ~ **cengpu** 'strong government'
ko-	高	high, tall	~ **cwupha** 'high frequency (wave)', ~ **hyel.ap** 'high blood pressure', ~ **kiap** 'high (air) pressure', ~ **sokto** 'high speed'
kong-	公	official; public	~ **saynghwal** 'public life', ~ **māymay** 'public transaction', ~ **hōytang** 'public meeting place'
kwī-	貴	1 the worthy; your	~ **pōko** 'your report', ~ **puin** 'noble lady', ~ **kwuk.ka** 'your nation', ~ **hōysa** 'your firm', ~ **chwulphan-sa** 'your publishing house'
		2 valuable, precious	~ **kumsok** 'valuable minerals', ~ **tongca** 'one's precious son'
kwū-	舊	old	~ **sāhoy** 'old society', ~ **sitay** 'old times', ~ **sēykyey** 'the old world', ~ **cēyto** 'the old system', ~ **hwāph^{y}ey** 'the old currency'
kyeng-	輕	light(weight)	~ **kikwan-chong** 'light machine-gun', ~ **kongep** 'light industry', ~ **kumsok** 'light metals', ~ **mūcang** 'light armaments', ~ **pēm.in** 'minor offender', ~ **phok.kyek** 'light bombardment'
kum-	今	the present; this month's	~ **cwumal** 'this weekend', ~ **hayngsa** 'this event', ~ **sēyki** 'the present century'
kup-	急	abrupt; express	~ **cēnhwan** 'sudden turn', ~ **yōngmu** 'urgent business', ~ **cīnpo** 'rapid progress'
mal-	末	end, last	~ **hak.ki** 'the final term (of three school terms), the last trimester', ~ **kwicel** 'the last verse', ~ **sēytay** 'the last generation', ~ ^{1}**yelcha** 'the last train'
man-	滿	fully, a full	~ **cangsik** 'full decoration', ~ **kihan** 'full time limit, full term', ~ **ō-nyen** 'a full five years'
mang-	亡	the late, deceased	~ **kyōcang** 'the late principal', ~ **puin** 'one's late wife', ~ **swukpu** 'one's late uncle'
mī-	未	not yet, un-, in-	~ **hwūn.lyeng** 'untrained', ~ **kyelqsan** 'unsettled (accounts)', ~ **kyōyuk** 'uneducated', ~ **punmyeng** 'indistinct, unclear', ~ **wānseng** 'incomplete'
mol-	沒	devoid of, ···less, eliminating	~ **chwīmi** 'tastelessness', ~ **inceng** 'inhumanity', ~ **sangsik** 'devoid of common sense'
myeng-$_1$	名	noted, famed	~ **paywu** 'eminent actor', ~ **sōsel** 'well-known novel', ~ **thamceng** 'famous detective'
myeng-$_2$	明	the coming; next year's	~ **hōykyey-nyen** 'the coming fiscal year', ~ **sayngil** 'one's next birthday', ~ ^{1}**yu'-wel** 'June of next year'
mu-	無	lacking, ···less, without	~ **cengpo** 'without information', ~ **kwankyey** 'irrelevance', ~ **uymi** 'meaningless(ness)'

nan-	難	difficult	~ ceymok 'hard topic', ~ sāep 'difficult business', ~ mūncey 'tough problem'
¹nay-	來	the coming; next year's	~ cwumal 'next weekend', ~ hak.ki 'next term', ~ hayngsa 'the coming event, coming events', ~ sēngthan-cel 'the coming Christmas'
nāy-	內	1 internal; secret 2 female	~ chwulhyel 'internal hemorrhage', ~ kwungceng 'inner palace', ~ punpi 'internal secretion' ~ cwucang 'petticoat government'
ōy- *	外	external	~ chwulhyel 'external bleeding', ~ Mongko 'Outer Mongolia', ~ punpi 'external secretion', ~ swuwi 'outer guard', ~ yuseng 'outer planets'
			* As free adnoun 'maternal'; as noun = pakk 'outside, ... '.
pān-	反	anti-; counter-	~ cak.yong 'reaction', ~ hyek.myeng 'counter-revolution', ~ kwahak-cek 'anti-scientific', ~ S(s)olyen 'anti-Soviet'
pay-	背	anti-	~ cengpu 'anti-government', ~ Ilpon 'anti-Japan(ese)', ~ Yengkwuk 'anti-Britain, anti-British'
phi-	彼	that	~ kyēngkwan 'that policeman', ~ kyōsa 'that teacher', ~ sawen 'that employee'
phī-	被	suffering, undergoing	~ ap.pak 'oppression, suffering', ~ sēnke 'undergoing an election'
phyeng-	平	ordinary	~ hōywen 'ordinary member', ~ sawen 'ordinary employee', ~ sīmin 'ordinary citizen'
phʸēy-	弊	unworthy; my	~ hak.kyo 'my school', ~ kaceng 'my home', ~ kwuk.ka 'my country'
pi-	非	not (being); non-, un-	~ cēnthwu-wen 'non-combatant', ~ hōywen 'non-member', ~ hyēnsil 'unreality', ~ kongsik 'unofficial', ~ māyphum 'an article not for sale'
pū-	副	1 assistant, vice- 2 side, by-, subsidiary	~ hōycang 'vice-chairman', ~ kyōcang 'assistant principal', ~ putay-cang 'assistant commander' ~ cak.yong 'side effect', ~ sānmul 'by-product'
pul- / pu-	不	not, un-	PUL-: ~ chincel 'unkind(ness)', ~ hwal.yak 'inactive(ness)', ~ phyengtung 'inequality' PU-: ~ ca.yen 'unnatural(ness)', ~ ca.yu 'discomfort', ~ cektang 'unsuitable(ness)', ~ totek 'lack of virtue'; Cf putong-san 'real estate'
sa-	私	private, personal	~ ¹iik 'private interest', ~ saynga 'bastard', ~ saynghwal 'private life'
sāng-	上	first of 2 or 3; earlier	See Part II.
sin-	新	new	~ kilok 'new record', ~ palmyeng 'new invention', ~ sēykyey 'the new world'
sō-₁	小	small, little	~ cicwu 'small landowner', ~ kwuk.ka 'small nation', ~ kyumo 'small scale'
sō-₂	少	few, scanty	~ inq-swu 'small number of people', ~ pyengqswu 'small number of soldiers', ~ sōmay-cem 'few retail stores'

ta-	多	many	~ **chwīmi** 'many hobbies', ~ **hayngsa** 'many activities', ~ **pangmyen** 'many quarters; versatile', ~ **umcel** 'polysyllable'
tăn-	短	short	~ **kēli** 'short distance', ~ **siil** 'a short length of time', ~ **swumyeng** 'a short span of time'
tāy-₁	大	great, big, major	~ **cengke-cang** 'major rail station(s)', ~ **cēnthwu** 'major battle', ~ **hayngsa** 'big event', ~ **hwal.yak** 'great activity', ~ **kyēngki-cang** 'large stadium'
tāy-₂	對	against, toward, versus	~ **Cwungkwuk** 'against/toward China', ~ **Mikwuk** 'toward America', ~ **ōykwuk** 'toward foreign countries'
tha-	他	other	~ **cwūso** 'other address', ~ **panghyang** '(the) other direction', ~ **pānmyen** 'the other half side'
uy-₁	疑	pseudo-, false	~ **sengtay** 'false vocal cords', ~ **yangphi-ci** 'false parchment'
uy-₂	儀	adopted, foster	~ **camay** 'foster sister', ~ **hyengcey** 'foster brother', ~ **pep.lyul** 'adopted law', ~ **pumo** 'foster parents'
yēn-	軟	soft	~ **ōykyo** 'soft diplomacy', ~ **phipu** 'soft skin', ~ **tāychayk** 'soft policy', ~ **tokse** 'light reading'
¹yeng-	令	the esteemed; your	~ **hyengcey** 'your (or his) brother', ~ **kacok** 'your family', ~ **puin** 'your (or his) wife', ~ **swukpu** 'your uncle'

5.4. Postnouns.

A postnoun occurs exclusively or typically after a noun; in our analysis the noun modifies the postnoun, which functions as the head of the phrase. In a sense, the postnoun is a further restricted type of quasi-free noun (§5.2.1). The quasi-free noun **hay** 'possessed thing, one's' would be considered a postnoun if it were not for the fact that it occurs after **nay** 'my' rather than **na** 'me'. Some of the postnouns are taken from inflected forms; a number are also used as other parts of speech, and those are separately listed below. Some of the items given are much more limited in occurrence than others and they would perhaps be better listed as bound postnouns; it is hard to draw the line. Good cases could be made for including here the following items, treated as Chinese suffixes in §5.4.5.2: **-ce** 'authored by', **-ci** (periodical titles), **-cok** 'tribe', **-hwa** 'flower', **-kyēy** 'world' (see §5.3.3), **-kyo** 'religion', **-phyen** 'compiled by'. Compare these with **hayng** 'bound for', which is included here. The word **ccay** could be set up as a separate subcategory "postnumeral" since it nearly always follows a numeral, just as its Chinese counterpart **cēy-** could be set up as a separate category "bound prenumeral"; but **ccay** also occurs with the adnouns **ches** 'first' and **mal** 'last' (**mal ccay** is entered in LHS 920a), and it can occur after a NUMBER phrase as well as after a numeral: **sēy pen ccay** (or **sēy ccayq pen**) 'third time' (in a more literary form **sam-hoy ccay**); **ttek ul nēy kay ccay mek.nunta** 'I'm eating my fourth rice cake', CF **nēy pen ccay ttek i cēy-il khuta** 'the fourth rice cake is the biggest'. For the postcounter (···q) **swū** 'number of ··· ', see §5.5.1.

(1) Postnouns (exclusive)
 achi₁ 'person'
 achi₂ / echi 'worth'
 awus see **(k)awus**
 ca(y)ngi 'doer, -er, one, ... '
 ccali 'worth; amount; a person wearing'
 ccay '-th' (ordinalizer of non-Chinese numerals and number phrases)
 ceng kkey 'around, about (a certain time)'

chi₁ 'a fixed quantity'
chi₂ 'a general sense, a feel'
chwungi / chongi 'one, person, thing'
ciki 'a guard, a keeper'
cil 'act, behavior' (CF noun cīs 'gesture', cī(s)- 'make, do')
(···q) cwung(-payki) vulgarizer (spelled -ccwung- in South Korea)
echi / achi SEE achi / echi
hayng 'bound for, dispatched to' [semi-literary]
he 'approximately (a certain quantity)' [semi-literary]
kal 'discrimination, division, branch, kind'; [neologism] branch of study, -ology'
kālyang 'approximately (so many), about' (follows number)
kāmali 'a person who is the butt of ··· '
kan 'an interval of ··· ; between, among'
(k)awus 'and a half'
(k)kayngi diminutive
kkal vulgarizer (? < ···q kal)
kkes 'to the full extent of'
kkey '(= ceng kkey) around, about (a certain time); near (a place)'
kkili 'separate group (of people)'
kkol 'at the rate of, ··· each, per unit'
kkwulek = ···q kwulek 'the act of'
kkwuleki 'an overindulger in' (? < ···q kwulek -i)
kkwun 'a man occupied with or noted for' (= ···q kwun; ¹Yi Ungpayk prefers -kkwun)
koc 'the Cape of ··· '
kwuni 'person' (? < ···(q) kwun + i): is pallok ~ 'idler' the only example?
kyēng 'around, about (a certain time)'
may 'shape, form, cast'
nāy 'throughout, all through (a period of time)'
ney 'group (of people)'
ong 'the Venerable Mister ··· '
pachi 'a person with a vocation (dating from feudal days) that deals with ··· '
(···q) pal 'line, streaks, rays; impression'
(···q) palam 'without one's ··· on' (see also below)
panciki 'adulterated with'
pang 'in care of'
p(h)a(y)ki, p(h)e(y)ki 'person, thing, one; child'
pha(y)ngi 'person, thing, one; child' (see also payngi below)
phok 'of the same age group; approximately, about'
ppak vulgarizer
ppel 'the kin-relationship (standing) of ··· '
sang 'Mr, Mrs, Miss, Ms' (suffixed to Japanese names; < Japanese san)
soswu 'plus some (extra), ··· odd, a bit over ··· ' (< sōswu 'a small number, minority')
ssi 'clan; Mr'
ta(k)ci '(this / that) extent, degree'
tepeki 'lots / heaps of'
theym (them, theymi, thek) 'as much as, all of'
thi 'the mark (looks, air, appearance, manner) of' (? < noun 'dirt'; ? Seoul dialect
    variant < thāy 'appearance')
thwungi / thongi 'one, person, thing'
thwuse(y)ngi 'covered or smea red with'

(t)tam 'latent power; wallop'
ttawi 'and the like, of the sort' (< ···q tawi, der noun < taw- 'be worthy of the name of')
ttayki, ttuki, te(y)ki, tek.kwungi 'one, person, thing' [vulgar]
tteli 'thing' [vulgar] — Does this occur only in tung tteli 'back'?
tūng 'and so on; the above several' [semi-literary]
tūngci 'and such places; and vicinity' (also quasi-free noun?)
yang 'Miss'

(2) Rhythmically misanalyzed compound nouns
   nwun-i 'a person with eyes such that ··· '   phal-i 'a person with arms such that ··· '
   pal-i 'a person with feet such that ··· '   son-i 'a person with hands such that ··· '

(3) Derived nouns (§9.6) that are used only as postnouns
   alh.i 'ache, illness'
   cap.i 'taking'
   kal.i 'changing; remodeling'
   keli 'at intervals of, skipping, jumping'
   kel.i 'gait'
   kel.i 'a hanger, a stand (for)'
   ket.i /keci/ 'collection, gathering up, harvest of'
   nah.i 'a weave. a yarn of'
   pak.i 'imprinted with, ... '
   pat.i /paci/ 'receptacle for, ... '
   phal.i 'selling'
   ppop.i 'an extractor (pull, pincer, claw) for'
   puli 'one who works (something); work, doing, act, trick'
   puth.i /puchi/ 'of the class of, made of'
   sal.i 'living, life; garb, clothes'
   ssi < (p)ssi 'the use (state, condition, quality, mode) of'
   tot.i /toci/ 'rising'
   ttut.i /ttuci/ 'thing stripped of ... ' — Are ppye ~ and al ~ the only examples?
See also (cim) sil.i, (sil-kwup) tal.i, (sīpiq) cwup.i.

(4) Inflected forms (occurring also in other environments)
   chiki 'game of hitting ··· ' (kōng chiki 'ball hitting')
   mayc.ki 'concluding it' (kkuth mayc.ki 'final touches')
   naki 'being born in; a person from'
   nayki 'product; display; person displaying (= naki); a person from'
   pat.ki 'receiving; receiver of'
   sswuki 'a boiled dish of' (wen-pap sswuki 'soup with rice and rice cakes in it')
   ttāym 'warding off; mending'
See also -nam(.)un (pp. 164, 174, 704).

(5) Used also as free nouns, sometimes with a different meaning
   cen 'before; Dear ··· [in letter]' (as free noun 'earlier time', as adnoun 'former')
   chey 'style (of writing); body' (as noun, literary)
   cwuuy 'ism, doctrine'
   cwuuy-ca '-ist, ideologist, advocate of'
   ···q keli 'material, stuff for; basis; doing; appearance'
   meli vulgarizes nouns (as free noun 'head')
   nim 'esteemed person' (as obsolete free noun 'you; lover')
   nolus 'job, role'

pang 'shop, shopkeeper's, store' (as free noun 'room')
sik 'style'
taykali vulgarizes nouns (as free noun 'head [vulgar]')
ttakci vulgarizes nouns (as free noun 'crud')
ttaymun 'reason' (quasi-free noun?)

(6) Also particle, adverb
tul 'group' (see detailed entry in Part II)

(7) Also postmodifier
ccay 'and all, as it is'
chay 'intact'
īhwu 'after, from (the time when) ··· on'
īlay 'ever since, after during the past ··· '
nalum 'depending on'
ppun 'only'
tay (lo) 'original state'
thong 'impetus, ... '

(8) Also postmodifier, noun
cwung < TYWUNG 'midst, middle of'
(···q) kīm 'impetus' (as free noun 'steam')
(···q) kyel 'impetus' (as free noun 'wave')
pakk 'outside (of)'
(···q) palam 'impetus' (as free noun 'wind')
CF nyekh (p. 739)

(9) Also postmodifier, postsubstantive
(···q) seng < ˙SYENG 'quality'

(10) Also postmodifier, suffix (bound postnoun)
payngi 'one, person'

(11) Also suffix (bound postnoun)
tali 'one, fellow, guy'

(12) Also counter
pun 'a portion for, enough for' (as counter 'minute')

(13) Also postnominal verbal noun intransitive
chi, cha 'bad weather (around a certain day)'

(14) Also adverb
kang 'strong; a little over ··· , ··· and a fraction'
namcis, nek.nek 'fully, all of, at least' + number
ppa-tus 'just under, a little short of, (falling) short' (ppa'-tus abbr < ppānun tus)
yak 'weak; just under, a fraction less than' (< ˙ZYAK)

(15) Also verbal noun (transitive / intransitive)
pal 'dispatch(ed)' [semi-literary]

(16) Also noun, adnoun, adjectival noun
···q cwūng ("ccwung") 'a weight of (··· nyang, ton, phun); weighty'

(17) Also adnoun, numeral
pān (number +) 'and a half'; 'half'

(18) Pseudo-postnoun
sim (dialect variant of him) in payq sim 'belly strength' = 'endurance' or 'greed' and in
ip sim 'mouth strength' = 'volubility'
-nyang (from ··· in yang) in i- / ku- / ce-nyang 'this / that / that way'

Notice also the place postnouns (§5.2.3). Some of those occur as free nouns: san 'mountain', kang 'river', ... Others are more restricted: yang 'ocean', lī 'village', sil 'valley' (archaic for kōl in Omey-sil). And some are free nouns only as abbreviations: hāng = hāngkwu 'port'.

5.4.1. Postnoun/postmodifier adjectival noun (= adjectival postnoun/postmodifier).

The morpheme **man** plays several grammatical roles. When predicated by **hata** it is an adjectival noun, but **man hata** is always preceded by a noun (**N man hata**) or by the prospective modifier (**-ul man hata**, §5.4.3.2). Elsewhere I have treated **man** and **hata** as inseparable (i.e. nothing can intervene), but for some speakers, at least, that is not quite true, for ··· **man to hata** is possible.

5.4.2. Postsubstantives.

There are four constructions that involve a substantive (**-um**/**-m**) followed by a morpheme. I treat the morphemes that can follow as a subclass of postnoun and call them postsubstantives: **-um a**, **-um sey**, **-um say**, and **-umq seng**. The last word (**seng**) also occurs as a postnoun and as a postmodifier. For the meanings and use of the constructions, see the entries in Part II.

5.4.2.1. Postsubstantive adjectival noun.

This formidably labeled subcategory is set up to account for the peculiar behavior of the morpheme **cik** in the construction **-um cik ha-**, for which the meaning and use will be found in Part II. Elsewhere I treat **cik** and **ha-** as inseparable, but for some speakers the focus particle **to** can intervene.

5.4.3. Postmodifiers.

A postmodifier occurs after the several modifier categories of inflected words (§9.3) typically, exclusively, or exclusively in a clearly distinct meaning. In the list below, the postmodifiers are divided into groups according to privileges of occurrence.

(1) Exclusively after modifiers
   a 'question'
   (**-ulq**) **c^e/aksimyen** 'if'
   ccok-ccok, cok-cok 'every occasion that'
   ci_1 'uncertain fact, ... '
   ci_2 '(the time) since'
   cince [obsolete] 'behoovement'
   cintay [obsolete; colloquial] 'time when'
   cuk(-sun) 'when'
   i 'question'
   ka, ko 'question'
   nawi '(not) enough to, ... '
   (**-ulq**) **say** [obsolete] 'since, while' (< ˙*s oy*)
   swulok 'to the full extent that' (< ˙*s o´lwo k*)
   twung) 'one of two conflicting states'
   tul 'conceded fact' (< ˙*t ol*)
   ya, yo 'question'

(2) Exclusively after modifiers in the relevant shape or meaning
   cwul 'likely fact; way, ability'
   īl 'definite fact; experience'
   kes 'tentative fact, ... '
   lī 'reason' (< ˝*LI*)
   pa 'tentative fact; circumstance'
   phok 'supposition; appearance; seeming'
   phūm 'appearance; behavior'
   tey 'circumstance, event'
   the 'footing, standing, relationship;
      (= **kyengwu**) circumstance'
   the, they 'intention or expectation'
   ttalum 'only, just'

(3) Also postnoun
   ccay 'and all, as it is'
   chay 'intact, the original state'
   nalum 'depending on'
   ppun 'only'
   seng 'quality'
   tay (lo) 'original state, as is / was;
      in accordance with; as soon as'
   thong 'impetus, ... '

(4) Also postnoun, noun
   kīm, kyel, palam 'impetus, ... '

(5) Also postsubstantive
   (**-ulq**) **sey** — see the entry in Part II

(6) Also postnoun, suffix
   payngi 'one, person'

(7) Also bound noun (after summative, p. 685)
   mangceng 'although'

(8) Also inflectional ending, ? particle
   kwu(me)n, kwun a, kwulye 'oh I see ... '

(9) Also noun, adverb
   han phyen 'in addition, and, but, ... '

(10) Also noun
   kkuth 'the final consequence'
   kyem 'at the same time'. (SEE p. 672)
   nameci 'excess, remainder'
   sēym 'calculation, conjecture, speculation'

A Reference Grammar of Korean

(11) Also particle
(-ulq) son = s-un [obsolete] '[as for] the likely fact (that ···)'

A group of pseudo-postmodifiers, regular nouns (free or quasi-free), occur more widely:

cakceng 'intention, resolve'
cek 'time'
(-tun) cha 'the course of'
chām 'the point, the verge'
chēci 'situation, circumstance'
hān 'extent, limit'
hwū 'after'
hyēncang 'the very act / scene'
hyengphyen 'process, circumstance'
i 'person, one; fact, act'
kām 'feeling'
kes 'thing; one'
kil 'way'
kkatalk 'reason'
ko (lo) '(for) the reason'
kyengwu 'circumstance'
¹īyu 'reason'
māl 'words, ... '
matang 'instance, case'
mokcek 'aim, purpose'

mo.yang 'appearance'
mulyep 'time'
nolus 'job, role, part'; (~ i 'but')
nyekh 'direction; toward'
pakk 'outside of, except for'
sai, say 'midst'
sesul 'force'
taum 'next'
tāysin 'substitute; instead of'
tey 'place' (≠ tey 'circumstance')
the 'site' (≠ the, they 'intention, expectation')
thek 'reason, grounds'
(to)cwung 'midst'
tong-an 'while'
ttay 'time'
twī 'after'
yang 'pretense; appearance; intention'
yēyceng 'intention'
¹yolyang 'plan, intention'

5.4.3.1. Postmodifier verbal nouns intransitive inseparable (= inseparable verbal postmodifiers).

This heavily labeled category is needed to account for **chey** (**chek**) 'pretense' and **ssa** 'appearance' in constructions of modifier + **chey** (or **ssa**) + **ha-**. These words are postmodifiers that are at the same time also verbal nouns. For examples, see Part II.

5.4.3.2. Postmodifier adjectival nouns inseparable (= inseparable adjectival postmodifiers).

There are four postmodifiers that are at the same time adjectival nouns inseparable:

ak / lak 'one of two alternating states'
man 'worth ···ing' (also particle, postnoun)
···q pen (or "ppen") 'on the verge of'
wu 'general appearance'

But at least some speakers allow the focus particle **to** between each of these and the following **ha-** (CF §5.4.1); for such speakers these words belong in the next group. (For examples, see Part II.)

5.4.3.3. Postmodifier adjectival nouns separable (= separable adjectival postmodifiers).

Each of two postmodifiers is at the same time an adjectival noun, like those in the preceding section, but differs from them in that it can be separated from the **ha-**, e.g. by the focus particle **to** 'even, also' (for examples, see Part II):

pep 'good reason to be, ... '
tus 'the idea / feel of'

5.4.3.4. Pre-inseparable postmodifier.

The postmodifier s^eang 'appearance' (< ˙SYANG) is unique: in the standard language it is always followed by the postnominal adjective inseparable **siph-**. For examples, see p. 773.

5.4.4. Counters. See §5.5.2.

5.4.5. Bound postnouns (suffixes).

As with the adnouns (§5.3.3), some postnouns have quite stringent occurrence restrictions. Most which are of native Korean origin have been included as "free postnouns" above. Some of those also occur, as do a number of other morphemes, after bound elements such as verb stems, bound nouns of various sorts, etc. For that reason there is some overlap between the earlier list and the following lists. The suffixes in §5.4.5.1 are non-Chinese; they typically attach to native Korean elements. In the following section are the Chinese suffixes, which typically attach to Chinese elements. For the Chinese list, examples are provided to show why they deserve to be treated as suffixes. As with the adnouns we are again vexed by the problem of deciding freedom and bondage of Chinese morphemes; in fact, with the suffixes it becomes even more of a problem. Let's consider some examples. The free noun **hōy** means 'meeting, ... ', the free noun **um.ak** means 'music'. Should we not consider **um.ak hōy** 'concert' as simply a construction of two nouns, like **hak.kyo sensayng** 'school teacher' or **yeki koki-cap.i** 'the fishing in this place'? The noun **yak** 'drug, medicine' is free and **pang** 'shop' is a free postnoun; should we consider **yak pang** 'drugstore' as two words? Since **pyēng** 'illness' is a noun and **phipu** 'skin' is a noun, is **phipuq pyeng** 'skin disease' a noun + noun construction? What about **pyēng cwung** in the midst of illness'? In general, I have conservatively treated one-syllable Chinese elements as essentially bound, with their freedom apparent only when they are in construction with non-Chinese elements. So I have treated **pyēng** as a free noun in expressions such as **kapyewun pyēng** 'a light illness' and **palq pyēng** 'foot-soreness', but as a bound element in **cwūngpyēng** 'serious illness' where **cwūng-** is a bound adnoun, and in **pyēngwen** 'hospital' where **-wen** is a bound postnoun. I am uncertain what to do with **phyēyq pyeng** 'lung disease, TB', where **phyēy** is a Chinese element that is the free noun meaning 'lungs', yet the occurrence of the reinforcement marker **-q-** argues for treating the combination as a construction of noun + noun. But **-q-** shows up within Chinese compounds that I would certainly not want to treat as two words (**sānqpo** 'walk', **munqca** 'written characters', **sāqken** 'incident'), and there are many cases where it would be impossible for **-q-** to surface, e.g. before **-wen**.

Perhaps further studies of frequency and distribution will resolve these problems. Meanwhile, the best we can say is as follows. Many Chinese morphemes sometimes appear, at least weakly, as free nouns; but all Chinese morphemes are at least sometimes bound. In compounds with other Chinese morphemes it is better to regard any one-syllable constituent as bound (bound adnoun, bound noun, bound postnoun) unless it is clearly proven otherwise. Dictionaries of Korean sometimes hyphenate obvious two-syllable compounds, especially when they were made up in Korea and have no counterparts in China.

I am inclined to make a special exception of free Chinese nouns and counters + (···q) **swū** 'the number of ··· ' because of the exceptionally wide range of distribution (CF §5.5.1). So I would write **chwulqsayngq swū** 'the number of births', **sāmangq swū** 'the number of deaths', **haksayngq swū** 'the number of students', **ceycak swū** 'the number of products'; **kwēnq swū** 'the number of volumes', **sālamq swū** 'the number of people' — but **inq-swū** 'the number of people' because **in** 'person' is not normally used as a counter in Korean. I am also tempted to space off ··· **cek** '···ic' and ··· **sāng** '···-wise' for similar, but less compelling, reasons: see pp. 151, 440, 769. I prefer to hyphenate compounds of one-syllable synonyms or antonyms: **pok-tek** 'happiness and prosperity', **cen-hwū** 'before and after'.

5.4.5.1. Core suffixes.

The core suffixes can be divided into twelve groups:

        (1) diminutives
        (2) miscellaneous (pseudo-diminutives, vulgarizers, personalizers, ...)
        (3) deriving both adjectival nouns and impressionistic adverbs
        (4) deriving adjectival nouns
        (5) deriving adverbs
        (6) deriving adverbs from iterated nouns
        (7) deriving adverbs from processive verbs

A Reference Grammar of Korean

      (8) deriving adverbs from adjectives
      (9) deriving nouns from adjectives or processive verbs
      (10) deriving nouns from processive verbs or nouns
      (11) pseudo-suffix -si deriving noun from processive verb
      (12) deriving excess numeral from decimal numerals

Details on the individual items will be found in the entries of Part II.

(1) Diminutives

    -k   -eni (? → 5)
    -ak / -ek   -wuni [dialect]
    -a(y)ki / -e(y)ki   -keypi (in tes-keypi)
    -ang / -eng   -(k)kayngi
    -a(y)ngi / -e(y)ngi   -khe(y)ngi
    -a(y)ci   -che(y)ngi
    -al / -el   -ma(y)ngi
    -al.i / -el.i, (-oli / -ali)   -tayngi (in yeph-tayngi)
    -ul^{e}a(y)ki / -l^{e}a(y)ki   -thayngi
    -ul^{e}a(y)ngi / -l^{e}a(y)ngi   -the(y)ngi
    -amchi (? → 5)   -sakwi, -say (in iph-sakwi/-say)

(2) Miscellaneous

    -ttakci vulgarizes nouns (also postnoun, noun 'crud')
    -ttakseni (?) vulgarizes nouns
    -taykali vulgarizes nouns (also postnoun, noun 'head' [vulgar])
    -meli vulgarizes nouns (also postnoun, noun 'head')
    -pal vulgarizes nouns (? also noun 'foot')
    -akw(un)i vulgarizes nouns
    -ceng 'one' [vulgar]
    -cengi 'stuff' [vulgar]
    -tali 'one, fellow, guy' (also postnoun)
    -takwu, -takw(un)i 'hard thing' (vulgarizes noun)
    -(t)tayki 'thing, one'
    -te(y)ki 'thing, one, guy'
    -tek.kwungi 'thing, one, guy'
    -ttuki 'thing, one, guy
    -(t)twungi 'thing, one, guy'
?   -cwungi 'one'
    -chwungi 'one'
    -chongi 'one' (?)
    -cha(y)ngi 'one, thing, stuff'
    -eci 'stuff'
    -thong 'thing; part of body'
    -(q-)po 'one, thing, person'
    -potwu 'one, thing, person'
    -payngi 'one, thing, person' (also postnoun, postmodifier)
    -pangi, -pe(y)ngi 'one, thing, person'
    -eng-payngi 'person' (diminutive + ...)
    -khengi 'thing, person'
    -kwangi 'person'
    -swungi 'one, thing'

-songi 'person'
-soy 'person', makes informal names for boys
-tol(-i) 'stone', popular in boys' names
-tong(-i) makes names endearing names for children
-i '...y, ...ie' (after consonant only) makes names endearing (children) or jocular / derisive (adults)
-huy₁ makes female names
-huy₂ makes pronouns plural
-a(y)mi / -e(y)mi 'one, thing, person'; makes animal / fish / bird names
-a(y)pi / -e(y)pi makes animal / fish / bird names
-pak.i 'an inlaid one, one with something stuck in or attached'
-pat.i 'receptacle, ... '

(3) Deriving both adjectival nouns and impressionistic adverbs

-(c)cok / -(c)cwuk   -mak / -mek
-(c)cak / -(c)cek, -chak / -chek   -(p)pak
-(c)cang = -(c)cak   -ppuk
-(c)cik   -(s)sek
-(c)cimak   -sil
-cin   -sin
-(c)cum   -sul
-(c)cumak   -(s)swuk
-kkak / -kkek   -swung
-(k)kis   -ttak / -ttek
-(k)kul   -ttuk
-(k)kus   -(t)twuk

(4) Deriving adjectival nouns
-kom, -(k)kum (hata) (CF mankhum, ittakum)

(5) Deriving adverbs
-ccolok in the word āmu-ccolok and its synonym mō-ccolok (? < -tolok, ? < ecci ha-tolok)
-khwung
-ulu, -wulwu

(6) Deriving adverbs from iterated nouns
-i (CF 8, 9)

(7) Deriving nouns from processive verbs
-ay (variant -ey), -kay (variant -key) 'gadget, device, ...er'

(8) Deriving adverbs from adjectives
-i / -li; -chwu, -wu

(9) Deriving nouns from adjectives or processive verbs
-i

(10) Deriving nouns from processive verbs or nouns
-wung

(11) Pseudo-suffix -si- (in nakk-si 'fishing' < naks- + -i = 9)

(12) Deriving excess numeral from decimal numerals
-nam.un (usually spelled -namun)

We might also add the suffix that makes approximate numerals out of numerals: -es / -e (with some irregularities). And there are suffixes like -(u)k, -(u)l, -(u)m, -(u)n, -(u)s, ... , involved in the derivation of impressionistic adverbs (§12).

5.4.5.2. Chinese suffixes.

The Chinese suffixes (or bound postnouns) are arranged alphabetically below. Compare the lists in Choy Hyenpay 651-2, Kim Pyengha 115-6, CM 1:218-31. Some of the morphemes could be said to be free nouns in literary uses or in special meanings, e.g. **hak** = **hak.mun** 'learning'. We might question whether **cung** 症 'ailment' and **sēng** 情 'nature' should not be treated as free nouns. Note that **sāng** 上 '…-wise' and **cek** 的 ' …ic' have particularly wide combinatorial privileges in forming quasi-adnouns (§5.3.1). Good cases could be made for including as free postnouns (§5.4) the following items: **-ci** 誌 'periodical', **-ce** 著 'authored by …', **-cok** 族 'tribe', **-hwa** 花 'flower', **-kyey** = **kyēy** 界 'world', **-kyo** = **kyō** 教 'religion', **-phyen** 編 'compiled by …', **-sen** 選 'selected by …'.

List of Chinese suffixes (bound postnouns)

SHAPE		MEANING	EXAMPLES
-a	兒	child	cēnung ~ 'feeble-minded child', chencay ~ 'child genius, precocious child', hōnhyel ~ 'mixed-blood child, half-breed'; CF koa 'orphan', sōa 'infant, child'
-an	岸	shore, littoral	Sehay ~ 'the West (= Yellow) Sea Coast', Tonghay ~ 'the East (= Japan) Sea Coast'
-ca	者	person, fellow	āytok ~ 'devoted reader', ko.yong ~ 'employee', ¹notong ~ 'laborer'; CF hakca 'scholar', pyēngca 'invalid'
-cang₁	長	head, chief	wiwen ~ 'the head / chairman of a committee', … ; CF sacang 'company president'
-cang₂	場	place	chwuk.kwu ~ 'a football field', kyēngma ~ 'a race track', sakyek ~ 'a shooting ground / gallery, a firing range', wūntong ~ 'a playground, an athletic field'; CF nongcang 'farm', kongcang 'factory'
(q)-cang₃	狀	document, letter	col.ep ~ 'diploma, graduation certificate', hyep.pak ~ 'intimidation letter', sokayq ~ 'letter of introduction', sīn.imq ~ 'credentials', wiimq ~ 'letter of attorney', kongkayq ~ 'open letter', chotayq ~ 'letter of invitation'
-ce	著	authored by …, written by …	Kim paksa ~ 'written by Dr Kim', kwahak-ca ~ 'authored by a scientist', ōykwuk-in ~ 'by a foreigner'
-cek	的	…ic, …ical	SEE Part II, p. 440; CF p. 151.
-cel	節	festival	ātong ~ 'Children's Day', kaychen ~ 'Foundation Day [of Korea]', sēngthan ~ 'Christmas'
(q)-cem	點	point of	chwulpalq ~ 'starting point, point of departure', tōchak ~ 'arrival point', wikiq ~ 'point of danger'
-cey₁	齊	remedy (for …)	sohwa ~ 'a digestant', sotok ~ 'a disinfectant', salkyun ~ 'an antiseptic'
-cey₂	制	system	kyōyuk ~ 'educational system', ¹yāngwen ~ 'bicameral system', ¹yuk-sam-sam ~ '6-3-3 system (of schools)', pōngken ~ 'feudal system'
-chayk	策	policy	pānkong ~ 'anti-communist policy', pān-Mi ~ 'anti-American policy', yunghwa ~ 'a policy of appeasement'; CF cengchayk 'policy'
-che	處	place, office, agency, bureau, large facility	insa ~ 'personnel office', kongpo ~ 'Office of Public Information', kunmu ~ 'place of employment', kwūkup ~ 'relief agency', kwan.li ~ 'administrative office', ¹yen.lak ~ 'liaison office'
-cheng	廳	government office, administrative center	Cwungang ~ 'the Capitol', Ōyca ~ 'Office of Foreign Supply'; CF Sīcheng 'City Hall'

-cho	草	grass, weed, plant	kumcam ~ 'dandelion' (= mintulley), mānpyeng ~ (a rhododendron), kumpul ~ 'elecampane (Inula japonica)', pullo ~ 'a herb of eternal youth'; CF ^{n}nancho 'orchid'
-ci$_1$	地	place, land	kecwu ~ 'place of residence', cem.lyeng ~ 'occupied territory', cwūthayk ~ 'a residential area'; CF koci 'upland', phyengci 'flatland'
-ci$_2$	祇	1 paper	insway ~ 'printing paper', panca ~ 'ceiling paper', hwāsen ~ (? hwā-senci) 'a thin rough paper', pyek ~ = topay ~ 'wallpaper' [toypay (CM 1:225) must be dialect]
		2 newspaper titles	Ppulawuta / Ppulaputa ~ 'Pravda', Icupeycciya ~ 'Izvestia', Thaimucu ~ 'the Times'
-ci$_3$	誌	periodical	cwukan ~ 'a weekly', welkan ~ 'a monthly'; Thaimu ~ 'Time Magazine', Laiphu ~ 'Life Magazine'
-cok	族	tribe, group, people, nationality	Intian ~ 'Indian tribes', Thipeythu ~ 'Tibetans', ^{n}Yecin ~ 'the Ju(r)chen'
-cong	種	variety	kāylyang ~ 'improved variety', cāylay ~ 'native variety', ōylay ~ 'nonnative variety'
(q)-cung$_1$	證	certificate	hapkyek ~ 'certificate of qualification (passing)', itongq ~ 'certificate of moving'
(q)-cung$_2$	症	ailment	hyēnhwunq ~ = ecilq ~ 'vertigo, dizziness', kyelhayk ~ 'tuberculosis', pokchangq ~ 'swollen-belly ailment', sinkyengq ~ 'nerve disorder'; ēmseyq ~ ? 'depression; pessimism'; CF kalqcung 'thirst', hwā($^?$q)cung 'anger, displeasure'. This element also occurs bound in silhq-cung /silccung/ 'displeasure' (< adj silh-) and kapkap-cung 'uneasiness' < adj-n kapkap (ha-).
-cwu	主	master, boss	kongcang ~ 'factory boss', kiep ~ 'boss of the enterprise'
-e	語	language, word(s)	Cwungkwuk ~ 'Chinese', Hānkwuk ~ 'Korean', Ilpon ~ 'Japanese', hōching ~ 'designation(s)', swusik ~ 'a modifier'; CF en.e 'language', Yenge 'English', kwuk.e 'vernacular'; cwue 'subject', swul.e 'predicate'
-ha	下	under	SEE Part II, p. 514.
-hak	學	science, study, ...ology, ...ics	sāhoy ~ 'sociology', kyengcey ~ 'economics', mulli ~ 'physics', en.e ~ 'linguistics'
-han	漢	person, guy, fellow	muloy ~ 'shifty loafer', mun.oy ~ 'layman', putek ~ 'unvirtuous fellow'; CF kōyhan 'suspicious-looking guy'
-ho	號	1 number	cēy sip-sa ~ (sil) '(Room) No. 14'
		2 issue, number	kinyem ~ 'commemorative issue / number'
		3 name, designation	Māsan ~ 'the S.S. Masan', Thōngil ~ 'the Unification Express' (a train); CF kwūho 'slogan'
-hoy	會	gathering, meeting	cwātam ~ 'a roundtable discussion', ^{1}nāngtok ~ 'a (gathering for) reading; a reading group', um.ak ~ 'a concert'; CF myēnhoy 'interview'
-hwa$_1$	化	conversion, ...ization, ...ize	hap.li ~ 'rationalization, streamlining, reordering', kikyey ~ 'mechanization', kwuk.yu ~ 'nationalization', mincwu ~ 'democratization', tōngmul ~ 'brutalization', tosi ~ 'urbanization'
-hwa$_2$	花	flower	hāytang ~ 'sweet briar', mukwung ~ 'the Rose of Sharon', chāysong ~ 'portulaca (rosemoss)', nungso ~ 'trumpet flower'; CF kwuk.hwa 'national flower'

-il	日	day (also counter)	**konghyu** ~ 'a legal holiday', **kwukchi** ~ 'National Humiliation Day', **thānsayng** ~ 'birthday (of a sage)'; CF **sayngil** 'birthday', **kiil** 'fixed date; death anniversary'
-in	人	person	**ca.yen** ~ 'a natural person, natural man', **Hānkwuk** ~ 'a Korean', **munhwa** ~ 'a person of culture'; CF **siin** 'poet'
-ka₁	家	professional	**cengchi** ~ 'politician', **mīswul** ~ 'artist', **sap.hwa** ~ 'illustrator', **thamhem** ~ 'explorer', **yēyswul** ~ 'artist'; CF **cak.ka** 'writer'
-ka₂	歌	song	**āykwuk** ~ 'patriotic song', **cacang** ~ 'lullaby', **nongpu** ~ 'farmer song'; CF **cōka** 'dirge', **sōngka / sēngka** 'hymn'
-ka₃	哥	quasi-title	affixed to surname (humble or pejorative)
-ka₄	街	street	**cwūthayk** ~ 'residential street', **Cong.lo sam** ~ 'Bell Street at Third Street' (an area once notorious for prostitution), **pēnhwa** ~ 'busy street, thoroughfare'
-kam	感	a feeling	**ap.pak** ~ 'oppressive feeling', **kincang** ~ 'tense feeling', **māncok** ~ 'a feeling of satisfaction', **pul.an** ~ 'uneasy feeling'; CF **chok.kam** 'the sense of touch', **yuk.kam** 'sensuality', ¹**yuk.kam** 'sixth sense'
-kayk	客	guest, person	**mangmyeng** ~ 'an exile, a refugee', **mōhem** ~ 'an adventurer', **wūntong** ~ 'a sport spectator, fan'; CF **hayngkayk** 'tourist', **sungkayk** 'passenger'
-ki₁	器	device, instrument	**kyēylyang** ~ 'ga(u)ge, meter', **chuk.lyang** ~ 'surveying instrument', **chuk.wū** ~ 'a rainfall ga(u)ge' **pyēn.ap** ~ 'transformer', **punto** ~ 'protractor'; **sohwa** ~ (1) 'fire-extinguisher', (2) 'digestive organs'; CF **hyungki** 'lethal weapons, arms'
-ki₂	機	1 machine	**apchak** ~ 'press', **cwuco** ~ 'type-caster', **insway** ~ 'printing machine', **palqtong** ~ 'motor'
		2 (air)plane	**phok.kyek** ~ 'bomber', **swusong** ~ 'transport plane'
-ki₃	期	period of time	**chochang** ~ 'pioneer days', **pun.lan** ~ 'chaotic period'; CF **choki** 'early period', **malki** 'later period'
-kong	工	artisan	**kīnung** ~ 'technician', **kumsok** ~ 'metal worker', **mōphi- cēyphum cēyco-** ~ 'furrier', **pangcik** ~ 'textile worker', **pelmok** ~ 'lumberjack', **swuk.lyen** ~ 'skilled craftsman'; CF **mok.kong** 'woodworker', ⁿ**yekong** 'factory girl'
(q)-kwa	科	1 course, class	**kwuk.eq** ~ 'Korean course', **swūhak** ~ 'mathematics course', **Yengeq** ~ 'English course'; CF **hak.kwa** 'course'
		2 taxonomic family	**cangmiq** ~ 'roses', **cīntallayq** ~ 'azalea'
		3 office, bureau, section	**cengpoq** ~ 'intelligence / information bureau (or section)', **hayngcengq** ~ 'administrative office', **insaq** ~ 'personnel division / office', **pōkup** ~ 'supply section'
-kwan₁	官	government official	**cānghak** ~ 'an inspector of schools', **kēmchal** ~ 'public prosecutor', **kēm.yel** ~ 'censor', **sihem** ~ 'examiner'
-kwan₂	館	place, building	**mīswul** ~ 'art gallery', **pak.mul** ~ 'museum', **sīkong** ~ 'public auditorium', **sīmin** ~ 'City Center', **tāysa** ~ 'embassy', **yenghwa** ~ 'movie theater, cinema'; CF **hōykwan** 'meeting hall', ¹**yekwan** 'hotel'
(q)-kwen	權	power, authority, (also noun)	**hayngcengq** ~ 'administrative authority', **myēng.lyengq** ~ 'commanding authority', **sapep** ~ 'judicial power'; CF **silqkwen** 'real power', **phāyqkwen** 'hegemony'

-kwu₁	口	entrance, wicket, hole, opening, window	cepswu ~ 'reception window', chwul.ip ~ 'entrance (and exit)', chwul.nap ~ 'window / wicket for collections and disbursements', kāyphyo ~ 'the ticket (fare) adjustment window', pūnhwa ~ 'a (volcanic) crater'; CF ipkwu 'entrance', chwulkwu 'exit'
-kwu₂	具	tool, implement	munpang ~ 'stationery supplies', pānghan ~ 'cold-weather gear', wūntong ~ 'athletic goods'; CF kikwu 'utensil, appliance', tōkwu 'tool'
-kwuk₁	國	country, state, nation	kōnghwa ~ 'republic', mincwu ~ 'democracy', kwuncwu ~ 'monarchy'; CF ponkwuk 'homeland', cek.kwuk 'enemy country', ākwuk 'our country'
-kwuk₂	局	agency, office	chelqto ~ 'railway station', sam.lim ~ 'bureau of forestry', wuchey ~ 'post office'; CF yak-kwuk 'pharmacy'
-kwun	軍	army	cengpu ~ 'the government forces', hyek.myeng ~ 'revolutionary army', hāypang ~ 'an army of liberation'; CF hāykwun 'navy', kongkwun 'air force'
-kyey₁	界	world, circles, kingdom, -dom, realm	chwulphan ~ 'publishing circles', sasang ~ 'the world of ideas', tōngmul ~ 'the animal kingdom', um.ak ~ 'musical circles'; pi-Kathollik ~ 'non-Catholic circles'
-kyey₂	系	system; lineage; faction	tōngmul ~ 'animalia, the animal kingdom', thāyyang ~ 'solar system'
-kyey₃	計	ga(u)ge, meter; scheme	ap.lyek ~ 'manometer, pressure gauge', cheyon ~ '(body) thermometer', han.lan ~ '(weather) thermometer', kiap ~ = chengwu ~ 'barometer', phungsok ~ = phung.lyek ~ 'anemometer'; miin ~ 'ensnaring with a beautiful woman'; CF sikyey 'timepiece'
-kyey₄	屆	report	chwulqsek ~ 'attendance report', kyelqsek ~ 'report of absences', chwulqsayng ~ 'birth report', kecwu ~ 'report of residence'
-kyo	教	religion, teaching	Isullam ~ 'Islam', Kitok ~ 'Christianity', Molumon ~ 'Mormonism'; CF Pulkyo 'Buddhism'
-lo	路	street	Sēycong ~ 'Sēycong Street', Thayphyeng ~ 'Thayphyeng Street', Ulqci ~ 'Ulqci Street'; CF tōlo 'roadway, street'
-lyo	料	charge, fee; materials	SEE Part II, p. 679.
-lyu	類	kind, sort, species	inkan ~ 'human species', nuktay ~ 'wolf species', phō.yu ~ 'mammalia', tōngmul ~ 'animal species'; CF alyu 'adherent, follower; a second', cong.lyu 'kind, sort'
-mang	網	network	chelqco ~ 'barbed wire', cocik ~ 'organization(al) network', kyōyang ~ 'cultural network', ¹yen.lak ~ 'communications network'
-mul	物	stuff, thing, matter	chwulphan ~ 'publications', insway ~ 'printed matter', paysel ~ 'excrement(s)'
-pay	輩	people, group [pejorative]	cengsang ~ 'petty politicians; politicos', kāngto ~ 'robbers', kansang ~ 'fraudulent merchants', moli ~ 'profiteers', sōnyen ~ 'young people'
-pha	派	group, faction, clique	cēnhwu ~ 'the après-guerre (postwar) group', insang ~ 'the impressionists', ¹nāngman ~ 'the romantics'; CF sinpha / kwūpha 'the new / old school'

-phum	品	goods	cāyko ~ '(goods in) stock', hapkyek ~ 'approved goods', kakong ~ 'processed goods', swuip ~ 'imported goods', wulyang ~ 'superior merchandise'; CF kyēngphum 'a premium (free gift)', sangphum 'merchandise'
-phung	風	style, manner(s)	cangkwun ~ 'proud manner', cāngpu ~ 'manly manner', se.yang ~ 'western (= Occidental) manners', sikol ~ 'country manners', Kwantong ~ 'Kwantong style'
-phyen	編	compiled by ⋯ (abbr < phyen[chan] ham)	Hankul Hak.hoy ~ 'compiled by the Korean Language Society', Mīswul Hak.hoy ~ 'compiled by the Art Institute', Mun Seyyeng ~ 'compiled by Mun Seyyeng'; CF phyenca 'compiler'
-pi	費	expenditures for ⋯	chilyo ~ 'medical expenses', kasel ~ 'construction costs', saynghwal ~ 'living expenses', swusen ~ '(expenditures for) repairs'; CF hōypi 'membership fee / dues'
-pu₁	部	section; office; ministry	cayceng ~ 'ministry of finance', chēyyuk ~ 'department of physical education', wisayng ~ 'ministry of public health'; CF ponpu 'headquarters'
-pu₂	夫	menial; workman	chengso ~ = sōcey ~ 'cleaning man, janitor', chwīsa ~ 'cook', sēythak ~ 'laundryman'; CF hwāpu 'fireman, stoker', kwāngpu 'miner'
-pyel	別	division, separation, classification	chwulqsin ~ 'classification by place of birth', cik.ep ~ 'breakdown by occupation', kyeykup ~ 'class division', namnye ~ 'separation by gender', sengcek ~ 'grouping by grades (achievement)', sengpun ~ 'classification by elements (components or ingredients)', ^{n}yen.lyeng ~ 'division by age'; CF phanpyel 'discrimination'
(q)-pyēng	病	illness	phipuq ~ 'a skin disease', simcangq ~ 'heart trouble', wicangq ~ 'alimentary disorder'; CF phungqpyeng 'palsy, paralysis'
-sa₁	師	person, master	^{l}īpalq ~ 'barber', maswulq ~ 'magician', senkyo ~ 'missionary'; CF kīsa 'technician', kyōsa 'teacher', uysa 'physician'
-sa₂	士	scholar, person	kikwan ~ 'engineer', pihayng ~ 'aviator', pyēnho ~ 'lawyer'; CF paksa 'Ph.D.', haksa 'B.A., A.B.'
-sa₃	社	company, corporation	chwulphan ~ 'a publishing house, a publisher', sinmun ~ 'a newspaper (company)', thongsin ~ 'a news agency'; CF hōysa 'company'
-sa₄	史	history of ⋯	kēnchwuk ~ 'the history of architecture', Mikwuk ~ 'American history', munhak ~ 'history of literature', se.yang ~ 'history of the west'; CF ^{l}yeksa 'history'
-sayng	生	1 student	chonyen ~ 'freshman', kāngsup ~ 'short-course student', silqsup ~ 'trainee', yēnkwu ~ 'research student, student researcher'; CF haksayng 'student'
		2 birth	yūn.welq ~ 'born in a leap-month', īm-cin ~ 'born in the 29th year of the 60-year cycle'; CF chwulqsayng 'birth'
-se	書	writing, document	cungmyeng ~ 'certificate', ^{l}ilyek ~ 'a personal history, one's (career) resumé, vita', incung ~ '(a written) authentication', pocung ~ '(written) guarantee'; CF congse 'vertical writing', hoyngse 'horizontal writing'

-sel	說	theory, view	pāntay ~ 'opposite view', ^{1}yenghon-pulmyel ~ 'the theory of eternal life'; CF haksel 'scholarly theory'
-sen$_1$	線	line	cēhang ~ 'line of resistance', Kyeng-Pu ~ 'Seoul-Pusan line', pāngwi ~ 'defense perimeter', samphalq ~ 'the 38th parallel'; Mayk-Āte ~ 'the MacArthur line (along the ^{1}Naktong River)'; CF congsen 'vertical line', hoyngsen 'horizontal line'
-sen$_2$	撰	selection; selected by ···	Kim Caywen ~ 'selected by Kim Caywen', sīmsa wiwen ~ 'selected by a judging committee'
(q)-seng	性	nature, quality	chēnyeq ~ 'virginity', chwungsilq ~ 'substantiality; loyalty, faithfulness', pyēnthayq ~ 'abnormality', thuk.iq ~ 'peculiarity', wihemq ~ 'dangerousness'; CF phūmseng 'quality of goods'. SEE Part II, p. 773.
-sil	室	room, office, lab, small institution	cokak ~ 'sculptor's studio', mok.yok ~ 'bathroom', silhem ~ 'laboratory', tose ~ 'the library (room)', ungcep ~ 'the drawing-room', yēnkwu ~ 'seminar (room)'; CF kayksil 'guestroom', onsil 'hothouse'
-so	所	place, institution, institute, facility	chilyo ~ 'infirmary', ^{1}īpal(q) ~ 'barber shop', sāmu ~ 'office', yēnkwu ~ 'research institute (facility, laboratory)', ^{1}yoyang ~ 'sanatorium (sanitarium)'; CF cangso 'place', cwūso 'residence'
-swu	手	hand, person	kikwan ~ 'locomotive engineer', kyohwan ~ 'switchboard operator', wūncen ~ 'driver'; CF cōswu 'assistant', kiswu 'assistant engineer', sēnswu 'athlete'
-swul	術	technique, art, trick	insway ~ 'the art of printing', sakyo ~ 'the art of social intercourse'; CF maswul 'magic', swuswul 'operation'
-tam	談	talk(s), tale, report (on ···)	kyenghem ~ 'a story of personal experience', mōhem ~ 'an adventure story', palkyen ~ 'a tale of exploration', ^{1}yehayng ~ 'a travelog'; CF hōyhwa 'conversation'
-tay$_1$	隊	group, outfit	kyēngkwan ~ 'police squad, posse', kyēngpi ~ 'garrison', thamhem ~ 'expedition, exploration party', ūngwen ~ 'cheerers, rooters; reinforcements'; CF putay 'detachment', kwuntay 'troops'
-tay$_2$	帶	belt; zone	hwāsan ~ 'volcanic zone', kwūco ~ 'buoy, life preserver', sam.lim ~ 'forest zone'; CF citay 'zone, belt'
-thong	痛	pain, ache, ···algia	hyungpu ~ 'chest pain', sinkyeng ~ 'neuralgia, nerve pain'; CF chithong 'toothache', twuthong 'headache'
-to$_1$	度	(year) period	cak.nyen ~ 'last year', kumnyen ~ 'this year', 1960-nyen ~ 'the year 1960'; CF ^{n}yento 'year period' We could treat ···nyen-to as a binom ···nyento.
-to$_2$	圖	painting, drawing, view	cokam ~ 'bird's-eye view', miin ~ 'portrait of a beauty', sanswu ~ 'landscape', tānmyen ~ 'cross-sectional view'; CF cito 'map', chwukto 'reduced drawing'
-wen$_1$	院	institution	koa ~ 'orphanage', Haksa ~ 'the Scholars Institute (of Kolye times)', swuto ~ 'monastery', tāyhak ~ 'graduate school'; CF hak.wen 'the academy', pyēngwen 'a hospital', sawen 'a temple'
-wen$_2$	園	garden; park; institute	kwāswu ~ 'an orchard', tōngmul ~ 'a zoo', yuchi ~ 'kindergarten'; CF kongwen 'a (public) park'

A Reference Grammar of Korean PART I 171

-wen₃	員	clerk, member, employee	cēnthwu ~ 'combatant', congep ~ 'employee', swukcik ~ 'night-duty man', tāyuy ~ 'congressman'; CF cēm.wen 'store clerk', hōywen 'member', īm.wen 'staff member', puwen 'a member of the section', sengwen 'a constituent member'
-ye	餘	with excess, ... odd, over	Added to decimal and higher-unit Chinese numerals; see §5.5.2.
(q)-yem	炎	inflammation, ...itis	kwancelq ~ 'arthritis', mayngcangq ~ 'appendicitis', ¹nuk.makq ~ 'peritonitis' On the irregular phʸēy¹yem 'pneumonia', see p. 16.
-yōng	用	for the use of ...	haksayng ~ 'for students', kaceng ~ 'for household use', kyōsa ~ 'for faculty', namca ~ 'for men', philki ~ 'for writing (purposes)', sāmu ~ 'for business (use)'

See also proper names, §5.2.3. Free nouns sometimes occur in compounds as if suffixes. It is not always easy to decide whether a single Chinese morpheme occurs alone as a free noun (other than as an abbreviation of a binom) or not. And some bound postnouns occur only in vocabulary that is highly circumscribed, e.g. -tam 潭 'lake' in Payk.lok-tam 白鹿潭 ("White Deer Lake"), the name of the crater lake on top of Mt Hanla on Ceycwu island.

5.5. Numbers.

Numbers are a way of quantifying things. Languages express quantification in various ways, often as adnominal modification of the noun ("two candies") or of a representative counter ("two pieces of candy"), and sometimes as a noun substitute ("I want two/lots [of them]"). Some languages are more rigid than others in the structures they permit. Korean is fairly flexible, but some of the possible constructions are more common than others, and when two or more structures are allowed each may have specific connotations.

5.5.1. Number constructions.

As in many languages, the number expressions in Korean introduce special problems. We recognize two important classes of words: NUMERALS, a subclass of noun, and COUNTERS, a subclass of postnoun. A counter occurs typically after a numeral, but it can also form a construction with the postcounter (···q) swū 'the number of ··· ': (chayk) kwēnq swū 'the number of books'. (Chayk swū is also said, but less commonly.) Notice that counters, as counters, are not modified by i 'this', ku 'that', kulen 'such', ... In i pen kaul 'this autumn', pen is a noun 'time'.

There are three kinds of counters: UNIT, MEASURE, and NUMERAL. A UNIT counter counts individual instances of a countable noun: chayk han kwēn 'one book', kāy twū mali 'two dogs', pay sēy chek 'three boats', sengnyang-kaypi (= sengnyang) sēy kay 'three matches'. A MEASURE counter registers the amount of a measurable noun (chan han can 'one cup of tea', maykcwu twū pyeng 'two bottles of beer', sengnyang sēy kap 'three boxes of matches') or of units of time (han si 'one o'clock', han sikan 'one hour', han tal or il-kaywel 'one month', sam-nyen 'three years') or of money (chen wen 'a thousand wen'). A NUMERAL counter is a numeral that is itself being counted, and so functions as a counter after another numeral: sam-payk 'three hundred', sā-chen 'four thousand'. Many of the measure counters ('cupful, boxful', ...) and a few unit counters (sālam 'person' in haksayng han salam 'one student') could be labeled "temporary counters" since they occur also as free nouns, often counted by other counters: can han kay 'one cup' — but sālam han salam (or han myeng) 'one person'. Some of the other counters occur also in constructions other than numbers, for example chay (counter for buildings) in salang chay 'detached house', an chay 'main house'.

Among the countable nouns, there are some that have specific unit counters but many others lack specific counters and are counted simply by the numeral alone. The numeral without a counter CAN be used to count any noun. The following sentences, meaning 'One book exists' = 'We've got one/a book', illustrate the constructions that occur with countable nouns that involve the nominative case particle (Pcl), numeral (Num), numeral + counter (Num-Count), and the adnominal particle (**uy**):

    (1) N Pcl Num-Count   Chayk i han kwēn iss.ta.
    (2) N Num-Count Pcl   Chayk han kwēn i iss.ta.
    (3) N Pcl Num-Count Pcl   Chayk i han kwēn i iss.ta.
    (4) Num-Count uy N Pcl   Han kwēn uy chayk i iss.ta
? (4a) Num-Count N Pcl   ? Han kwēn chayk i iss.ta.
    (5) N Num Pcl   Chayk hana ka iss.ta.
    (6) N Pcl Num   Chayk i hana iss.ta.
    (7) N Pcl Num Pcl   Chayk i hana ka iss.ta.
? (8) Num uy N Pcl   ? Hana uy chayk i iss.ta.
    (8a) Num N Pcl   Han chayk i iss.ta.

Some nouns, however, do not occur in constructions of type (8a). You can say **thokki hana** 'a rabbit' and **talk (i) hana** 'a chicken' but not ***han thokki** or ***han talk**. Instead you say **han mali thokki** and **han mali talk**; CF CM 1:139. With a juncture between, it is possible to say **han | thokki** in the meaning 'a certain rabbit'. The juncture may be hard for the ear to catch in that phrase but it should be clear in similar phrases: **han | talk** 'a certain chicken' will have a slightly aspirated (and certainly voiceless) articulation of /t/, while the unacceptable ***han talk** would have the voiced allophone [d]. There is a distinction between **han | sālam** 'a certain person', where the length of the first-syllable vowel is maintained after the juncture, and **han salam** 'one person', where the lack of juncture leads to suppression of the vowel length, though there may be speakers who retain the length (CF **han kwēn**, …). Structure (8a) was quite common in the earlier language: ¨ney a˙to˙l i (1459 Wel 2:6b) 'the four sons'; ¨sey ˙sa˙l i (1445 ¹Yong 89) 'three arrows'; hon the˙li ˙lol (1447 Sek 6:27a) 'one hair'; ¨ney polo˙m ay (1447 Sek 24:20b) 'on the four walls'.

Tsukamoto 1986 seems to disallow (4a), the reduction of (4), but he is thinking of a different source for the surface structure: a preposing of the adverbialized number rather than a reduction of the adnominalized number. There are a few examples of the latter from earlier Korean: ¨twu ¨nas ¨twon ˙i˙Gwo (?1517- Pak 1:52a) 'it is (= costs) two coins, and … '; ˙na y syel˙hun lyang un ˙i˙i˙sye ˙yla (?1517- Pak 1:62a) 'I have thirty taels of silver (= money)'. And an example with an adnoun modifying the noun: na ˙'y ¨twu swang ˙say hwe˙l ul ta˙ka ¨ta ton˙nye ˙hoy˙ya po˙likwa ˙'la (?1517- Pak 1:35a) 'I took my two pairs of new shoes and wore them both out getting about!' Corresponding to the unreduced (4) is the MK structure Num Count s N, as in hon ˙cwul s ˙kul (1481 Twusi 21:25b) 'a single line (of news)' and ¨ney ka˙ci s ¨SSYWUW-¨KHWO ˙lol (1447 Sek 6:4a) 'the Four Miseries'.

The most common structure in modern Korean is that of (2) and (5): N Num(-Count) Pcl. This seems to be an inversion of (4a), the questionable reduction of (4). Since the number word modifies the noun, we expect it to precede the noun, so that (4) is the logical starting point for deriving the other structures. In Japanese when the noun is subject or object the most common and least ¨marked¨ structure is (1), which adverbializes the quantifier. This structure also occurs in Korean, but it may be a modern innovation, perhaps taken from Japanese usage, since there are no Middle Korean examples. Japanese permits the adverbial to be preposed (put before the noun), in what Tsukamoto calls ¨quantifier forward floating¨, but Korean does not permit sentences like *Sēy myeng chinkwu ka wuli cip ey wass.ta ← Chinkwu ka sēy myeng wuli cip ey wass.ta 'Three friends came to my house'. Modern examples of structures (1) and (6), with the adverbialized number:

Sacen ul han kwēn mantulq yang ulo caylyo lul mouko iss.ta 'I am gathering data with a view to compiling a dictionary'.

Namuq kaci lul hana kkekk.ess.ta ko yātan hana namuq kaci ka elma 'na khulq sey māl ici 'He is making such a fuss over the branch I broke, but I ask you, how big a branch is it anyway?!'

¹**Naynyen imyen catong-cha lul hana sakey ccum toylq key 'ta** 'Next year I'll be in a position to buy a car'.

Helum han cip ina-ma nay cip ul hana kacyess.umyen cōh.keyss.ta 'I wish I had a house of my own, however humble it might be'.

The unusual structures of (3) and (7) above mark both the noun and the numeral(-counter) phrase with the nominative particle. The accusative particle, too, permits such structures (**chayk ul hana lul pwass.ta**) but they are not usually compatible with other particles, such as that marking the indirect object: *****chinkwu eykey twūl eykey cwuess.ta** → **chinkwu twūl eykey** (or **twū chinkwu eykey**) **cwuess.ta** 'gave it to two friends'. But when the dative phrase is optionally marked by the accusative particle (**ul / lul**) instead of the dative particle (**eykey** or **hanthey**) the structures are acceptable, at least to some speakers: **Emeni ka ai tul ul motwu lul sēnmul ul cwuess.ta** 'The mother gave a present to each of the children' (LR 24:174:n6). There are advantages to "copying" the nominative or accusative marker instead of letting the quantifier stand as an adverb, in that the reference of the adverbialized number could be either to the subject or to the object, so that (as Gerdts 1985 points out) **A ka B eykey C lul sēys cwuess.ta** is ambiguous as to whether three of the A or three of the C are involved, whereas **A ka B eykey C lul sēys ul cwuess.ta** is unambiguously 'A gave three of C to B' and **A ka B eykey C lul sēys i cwuess.ta** is unambiguously 'Three of A gave C to B'.

Numbers (whether numeral + counter or just numeral) are allowed to "float" away from the nouns they are counting when those nouns are subjects or direct objects. The float is normally not permitted if the noun has some other role in the sentence, unless that role is secondary to an underlying role as subject or object, as in the causative structure of **Nay ka haksayng eykey sēys tte-nakey hayss.ta** 'I let three of the students leave' ← **Haksayng i sēys (i) tte-nass.ta** 'Three of the students left'. A special case is found in **Nay ka haksayng eykey sēys i tte-nakey hayss.ta** 'I let the students leave in groups of three (or as a group of three)', where the nominative-marked quantifier is allowed to float although the underlying subject to which it refers has been converted from nominative to dative (**haksayng i** → **haksayng eykey**) under the causativization. We know that this is the nominative-marked quantifier (and not, say, a variant of **sē-i** 'three persons') because the suppletive alternant of the marker appears in **Nay ka haksayng eykey yel hana ka tte-nakey hayss.ta** 'I let the students leave in groups of eleven (or as a group of eleven)'. The underlying structure seems to be something like: "I let the students do it such that three [of them] leave". In a simpler sentence without the causativization you might get **haksayng i sēys i ...** or **haksayng ul sēys ul ...** 'three of the students [as subject or object]'. Perhaps these are just cases of a kind of pseudo-float using the multiple-case marking that is permitted for genitives, from an underlying structure *****haksayng uy sēys** 'three of the students', but that explanation seems disconfirmed by the fact that, unlike Japanese, Korean does not permit the structure *****N uy Num.** (CF Tsukamoto 1986. I find no examples of *****N s Num** in earlier Korean.)

The floating of the numbers is usually called "quantifier float", since in other languages (such as Japanese) there are quantifiers like 'all' and 'lots' that can behave the same way as the number words. It should be noted that Korean **tā** 'all' and **mānhi** 'much / many' are adverbs, unlike the number words, so that they will occur only in structure (1) as N pcl **tā / mānh.i** 'N entirely / muchly', and only that structure is therefore found for them in earlier Korean, too. Exceptionally the adverb **motwu** 'all; each, every' is also now (and perhaps newly) treated as a noun that can take the nominative and accusative markers. To say 'all N' or 'many / much N' you use the corresponding adnominal forms **mōtun** and **mānh.un**. The word **meych < myech** 'how many; a few', is a numeral, and like the other numerals it can stand as subject or object. The most frequent occurrence is before a noun or a counter: **meych tal(q tong-an)** 'how many months (time)', **meych salam / pun ina** 'about how many people', **meych pen** 'how many times'. But it can also occur alone without a counter: **Swu ka meych ina toysinun ci yo** 'May I know your age?' And, with or without the counter, it can occur in the various structures open to the numerals: **Thokki meych (mali) eykey punpay han sēym in ya** 'How many rabbits do you figure got their rations?'; **Son nim meych pun i osip.nikka** 'How many guests are expected?'; **Chayk** meych kwēn ul ilk.ess.ta 'I read a few books'; Ku ttolay lul meych kay te sa 'ta cwuo 'Buy a few more of that size'; Ko ttolay meych i chac.e wass.ess.ta 'A group (of boys) of that age had been here to call'.

Once the quantifier is floated as an adverbial it has the freedom of other movable adverbs and may move away from the noun to which it refers. According to Gerdts (1985:55) **Ku cik.kong i sonq-kalak i kikyey ey sēys i callyess.ta** can be taken either as 'Three fingers of the workman were cut on [cut off by] the machine' or 'The fingers of three workers were cut on [cut off by] the machine'.

Although the plural particle **tul** can freely occur after just about any phrase, and can be inserted repeatedly to increase the emphasis, it is not quite the same as quantifier float, because the reference is only to the subject, and that may be implied rather than expressed. Notice that **(Wuli ka) chayk tul (ul) tul ilk.ess.ta** 'We read our books' only the second **tul** can be the plural-subject marker, the first must be the postnoun marking a noun as explicitly plural. The sentence **Chayk tul ilk.ess.ta** is ambiguously 'I read the books' or 'We read the book(s)' unless the accusative marker is explicitly located: **Chayk tul ul ilk.ess.ta** 'I (or we) read the books', **Chayk ul tul ilk.ess.ta** 'We read the book(s)'.

5.5.2. Numerals.

We could define a NUMERAL as any noun that answers the question **Meych in ya** 'How many is it?', but we want to include a few additional items. Not only does the numeral freely occur before the copula **ita** ('it is such-and-such a number') and before particles, both in arithmetic statements and as a substitute for constructions of numeral + counter, but it also occurs as an adnoun before a noun or a counter. And it appears in absolute constructions, as an adverbial phrase.

There are subclasses of numerals:

(1) quasi-numerals
    elma 'how much; some amount'
    meych < myech 'how many; some'
    ¹yāng 'both' (adnoun only)
    swū 'a number of; some, several'*

*As an adnoun. In this use **swū** ··· is largely limited to Chinese counters, for the other counters prefer **yele** ··· 'several' (< **yeles** 'about ten'), but **swū** ··· is an option for certain common counters: **kāy swū / yele mali** 'several dogs'. The morpheme is also used as a postcounter 'the number of'.

(2) numerals proper, core
    hana / han < *honah / hon* 'one',
    twūl / twū < ¨*twulh* / ¨*twu* 'two',
    sēys / sēy / sēk / sē < ¨*seyh* / ¨*sek* / ¨*se* 'three', ...

(3) numerals proper, Chinese
    il 'one', ī 'two', sam 'three', ... ;
    ¹yeng, kong 'zero'; pān, celpan 'half'

(4) approximate numerals, core
(based on the bound counter **-es**)
    twues / twue < ¨*twu˙zeh* / ¨*twu˙ze* 'about two'
    ('two or more' 1887 Scott 97), ... ;
    yeles / yele < *ye˙leh / ye˙le* 'ten or so; a number (of), quite a few'

(5) approximate numerals, Chinese
    il(q)-ī 'one or two', ī-sam 'two or three', ...

(6) excess numerals, core
(the tens + suffix **-nam.un** 'left over', often spelled **-namun**)
    ye-nam(.)un / -nam(.)u '10-odd' [dialect variant yelamu(n)], ... , ahu-nam(.)un / -nam(.)u '90-odd'

(7) excess numerals, Chinese
(the tens and higher units + suffix **-ye**)
    sip-ye '10-odd', ... , payk-ye '100-odd', ... ;
    CF **mulye payk** 'no less than 100', **mulus payk** 'a hundred or so'

Note that ··· **(k)awus** and ··· **pān** 'and a half' are postnouns that appear after the construction numeral + counter. CF the numeral **pān** 'half'.

The two sets of numerals proper, core and Chinese, are used with different sets of counters. Typically the core numerals are more "free" than their Chinese counterparts, e.g. in replacing constructions of numeral + counter. But there are no core numerals for hundred, thousand, or ten thousand in modern Korean, so where we would expect a core morpheme the Chinese numeral is used instead:

99 people	ahun ahop salam	kwu-sip kwu-myeng
100 people	payk salam	payk-myeng
101 people	payk han salam	payk il-myeng
199 people	payk ahun ahop salam	payk kwu-sip kwu-myeng / -in
20,002 people	ī-man twū salam	ī-man ī-myeng

The Chinese morpheme **pān** 'half ··· ; ··· and a half' is also used where the core set is appropriate: **pān sikan** 'half an hour', **twū sikan pān** 'two hours and a half', **twū si pān** '2:30 o'clock'.

Some of the core numerals have shortened shapes when they are in modifying position: **chayk twū kwēn** but **chayk twūl** 'two books'. The full shape, however, usually appears before the postnoun (the "postnumeral") **ccay**, so that ordinarily in Seoul 'second' is **twūl ccay**, though less commonly (in dialects) you will hear the shortened shape: **twū ccay = twūl ccay**. There seems to be confusion over whether to use the shortened shape of a numeral before **ccay**. The full shape is more common for 'second' (**twūl ccay**), as we have just said, and the shortened shape is used for 'eleventh' (**yel han ccay** – similarly for '21st', '31st', ...) and for 'twentieth' (**sumu ccay**), but the longer forms are also found: **yel hana ccay** and **sumul ccay**. For 'third' and 'fourth' it is purely a spelling problem, since the pronunciation would be identical in either case, owing to the way the morphophonemic rules work. The prevailing spelling standard in South Korea favors the full forms: **sēys ccay** rather than **sēy ccay**, and **nēys ccay** rather than **nēy ccay**. But the North Korean grammar CM prefers the short forms. And Ceng Insung 1960:190-2 tries to set up a distinction between (1) **ches ccay, twū ccay, sēy ccay**, ... , **yel han ccay**, ... , **sumu ccay** and (2) **hana ccay, twūl ccay, sēys ccay**, ... , **yel hana ccay**, ... , **sumu(l) ccay**. In the meaning equivalent to ··· **pen ccay** '···th' he would use the first group, the shortened forms, and the second group would be used when ··· **ccay** is a synonym of ··· **chay** 'and all, the whole, intact'. But my informants say that it is awkward to make combinations of numeral + **chay** (or the **ccay** that is a synonym of it). Instead, they prefer to insert a counter: **yel han kay ccay** means either 'the eleventh (thing)' or (= **yel han kay chay**) 'all eleven (things)'. Yet you may run across **hana ccay / chay** in the meaning **han kay ccay / chay** 'one whole (thing)'.

This postnumeral element **ccay** makes the expected ordinals for all non-fractional core numerals, but where *****han(a) ccay** would be expected we find instead a unique compound of adnoun + postnoun: **ches ccay** 'first'. However, the string **han ccay** will turn up in **yel han ccay** '11th', **sumul han ccay** '21st', **payk han ccay** '101st', ... We also find **payk ccay** '100th', **chen ccay** '1,000th', ... Moreover **ccay** occurs also with **meych** ('how-manyeth') and with some of the approximate numerals (CF Choy Hyenpay 1959:566).

The Chinese numerals are made ordinal by the adnoun **cēy** ··· '···th': **cēy-il** 'first', **cēy-i** 'second', **cēy-sam** 'third', ... And we find **cēy payk** (etc.) as well as **payk ccay** for '100th'; notice that 'hundred and first' is either **cēy payk-il** or **payk han ccay**.

The core numerals for '3' and '4' have the special shapes **sēk** and **nēk** before certain counters (usually beginning with t··· or c···) and **sē** or **nē** before certain others. For some of the counters there is variation between the several alternants – as, for some, there is a choice between using Chinese or core numerals. The numerals **yel** 'ten' and **yetel(p)** 'eight' are treated as **yelq** and **yetelq** before counters that begin with a plain obstruent (p t c s k): **yelq kay** '10 things', **yelq tay** '10 machines (or vehicles)', **yelq cang** '10 sheets', **yelq pen** '10 times' (CF **il-pen** 'number one'), **yelq pun** '10 people' (CF **phal-pun** 'eight minutes'), **yetel[p]q pam** 'eight nights', **yetel[p]q si** '8 o'clock'. The shape **yelq** also appears in **yelq-twul / -twu** 'twelve'.

Many of the odd forms of the numerals are regularized by younger speakers; sometimes there is a difference of meaning or nuance. Or the irregular form is heard in set phrases: a person who says **sēy tal(q tong-an)** 'three months (long)' – and, being young, counts ten days as **sip-il** – may nonetheless say **sěk-tal yel.hul** '3 months and 10 days = 100 days' but only because that is a lexicalized phrase with special significance.

The following lists are designed for convenient reference. Theoretical problems of inclusion, arrangement, and the like, are passed over in silence. The morphemic structure of the core numerals involves various alternations of shape; the alternants are shown in the right column of the first list as "bound core elements".

(1) LIST OF CARDINAL NUMERALS

Chinese numerals	Core numerals	Bound core elements
0 ¹yeng, kong		
½ pān, celpan	··· (k)awus[1]	
··· pān		
1 il	hana / han	hanak[2], ha
2 ī; ¹yāng 'both'	twūl / twū	it
3 sam	sěys / sēy / sěk / sē	sen, sa, sel
4 sā	něys / něy / něk / ně	net, na, ma
5 ō	tases	tāys, tāy, tas, ta, swī
6 ¹yuk	yeses / yes[3]	yes, yeys, yey
7 chil	ilkop	il, nil, nilkop[4]
8 phal	yetel(p) / yetel[p]q[5]	yetul, yet
9 kwu	ahop	ahu
10 sip	yel / yelq[6]	(un, hun, n, wun)
11 sip-il	yel-hana / -han	
12 sip-i	yelq-twul / -twu	
13 sip-sam	yelq-seys / -sey / -sek / -se	
14 sip-sa	yel-neys / -ney / -nek / -ne	
15 sip-o	yel-tases	
16 sip-lyuk (sipq-¹yuk)	yel(q)-yeses	
17 sip-chil	yel(q)-ilkop	
18 sip-phal	yel(q)-yetel(p)	
19 sip-kwu	yel-ahop	
20 ī-sip	sumul / sumu	
21 ī-sip il	sumul hana / han	
22 ī-sip ī	sumulq twūl / twū	
23 ī-sip sam	sumulq sěys / sēy / sěk / sē	
24 ī-sip sa	sumulq něys / něy / něk / ně	
25 ī-sip ō	sumulq tases	
26 ī-sip(q) ¹yuk*	sumul(q) yeses	*/īsimnyuk, īsip|yuk/
27 ī-sip chil	sumul(q)	
28 ī-sip phal	sumul(q) yetel(p)	
29 ī-sip kwu	sumul ahop	
30 sam-sip	sel(h)un[7]	
33 sam-sip sam	sel(h)un sěys / sēy / sěk / sē	
40 sā-sip	mahun	
44 sā-sip sā	mahun něys / něy / něk / ně	
50 ō-sip	swīn, [dialect] swīhun	
55 ō-sip ō	swīn tases	
60 ¹yuk-sip	yeyswun	
66 ¹yuk-sipq ¹yuk	yeyswunq yeses	
70 chilq-sip	ilhun	
77 chilq-sip chil	ilhunq ilkop	

80 phalq-sip	yetun, [dialect] yatun	
88 phalq-sip phal	yetunq yetel(p) / yetel[p]q	
90 kwu-sip	ahun (but ahu before -nam.un)	
99 kwu-sip kwu	ahun ahop	
100 payk, (il-payk)	— (obsolete on < ˙won)	
101 payk il	payk hana / han	
115 payk sip-o	payk yelq-tases	
144 payk sā-sip sā	payk mahun nēys/nēy/nēk/nē	
200 ī-payk		
300 sam-payk		
306 sam-payk(q) ¹yuk*		*/sampayngnyuk/ or
400 sā-payk		/sampayk|yuk/
500 ō-payk		
600 ¹yuk-payk		
700 chil-payk		
800 phal-payk		
900 kwu-payk		
1000 chen (il-chen)⁸	— (obsolete cumun < ˙cu˙mun)	
2000 ī-chen		
3000 sam-chen		
4000 sā-chen		
5000 ō-chen		
6000 ¹yuk-chen		
7000 chil-chen		
8000 phal-chen		
9000 kwu-chen		
10 000 mān (il-man)	— (? kol, kkol)⁹	
100 000 sip man	— (? cal)	
1 000 000 payk man	— (? wul)	
100 000 000 ek (il-ek)		
1 million million co (ilq-co)		

¹ Fairly limited: **sek ca kawus** 'three and a half **ca**', **twū mal kawus** 'two and a half **mal**', **toy kawus** 'one and a half **toy**'. As the last example shows, **han** ⋯ is usually not expressed when **kawus** is added.

² **Hanak** is an occasional free variant of **hana** before **ssik**.

³ The shape **yes** occurs before **nyang, toy, mal, pāl**.

⁴ The shape is **il** in **iley** '7 days', **nil** in **yey-niley** '6 or 7 days', and **nilkop** in **yey-nilkop** '6 or 7'.

⁵ Dialect **yatal, yatul, yetup**. In Seoul (and widely) the ⋯**p** surfaces only in **yetelp hay** 'eight years'; in dialects it will also be heard in **yetelp-i** 'eight people' (not currently used in Seoul).

⁶ But **ye** ⋯ before **-nam.un**.

⁷ The form without the **h** is preferred.

⁸ The version **il-chen** is used only in arithmetic or meticulous listing. If a counter follows, **il-** is not used: **sēnswu chen-myeng** 'a thousand athletes'.

⁹ SEE CM 1:307. Is this (as suggested by Sin Kichel 1958:117), based only on the set expression **kol payk pen** 'many many times' and the synonymous **(k)kol chen pen**? There are few (if any) examples of the last three numerals, which are said to be archaic.

(2) LIST OF ORDINAL NUMERALS

		Chinese	Core
	1st	cēy-il	ches ccay; uttum ('top'); [dialect] han ccay
	2nd	cēy-i	twūl ccay (less commonly twū ccay; "it-ccay, is-ccay" seem to be artificial)
	3rd	cēy-sam	sēys ccay (also spelled sēy ccay)
	4th	cēy-sa	nēys ccay (also spelled nēy ccay)
	5th	cēy-o	tases ccay
	6th	cēy-¹yuk (/cēyyuk/ only!)	yeses ccay
	7th	cēy-chil	ilkop ccay
	8th	cēy-phal	yetel(p) ccay
	9th	cēy-kwu	ahop ccay
	10th	cēy-sip	yel ccay
	11th	cēy sip-il	yel-han ccay
	12th	cēy sip-i	yelq-twul ccay
	20th	cēy ī-sip	sumu ccay (less commonly sumul ccay)
	100th	cēy-payk	payk ccay
	133rd	cēy-payk sam-sip sam	payk sel(h)un sēys ccay
how-manyeth		–	meych ccay < myech ccay

(3) LIST OF APPROXIMATE CARDINAL NUMERALS

	Chinese	Core
1-2	il(q)-ī /il-ī, il-lī/	han(a)-twul, han-twu han-twues / -twue '1 or 2'
2		twues / twue 'about 2'
2-3	ī-sam	twū(l)-seys / -sey / -sek / -se twū-senes / -sene 'about 2 or 3'
3		senes / sene 'about 3'
3-4	sam-sa	sene-netes / -nete 'about 3 or 4'
4		netes / nete 'about 4'
4-5	sā-o	nete-tays 'about 4 or 5'
5		tāys 'about 5'
5-6	ō-¹yuk /ō.yuk, ōlyuk, ōnyuk/	tāy-yeses 'about 5 or 6'
6-7	¹yuk-chil	ye(y)-nilkop 'about 6 or 7'
7		–
7-8	chil-phal	il(ko)-yetel(p) 'about 7 or 8'
8-9	phal-kwu	yet-ahop 'about 8 or 9'
9-10	–	yeles / yele 'about 10; several, many'
10+	sip-ye	ye-nam(.)un / -nam(.)u '10-odd' [dialect yelamu(n)]
10-20	il(q)-ī sip	–
20+	īsip-ye	sumu-nam(.)un / -nam(.)u '20-odd'
20-30	ī-sam sip	–
30+	samsip-ye	sel(h)un-nam(.)un / -nam(.)u, sel(h)un namcis '30-odd'
30-40	sam-sa sip	–
40+	sāsip-ye	mahun-nam(.)un / -nam(.)u, mahun namcis '40-odd'

A Reference Grammar of Korean

...	...	...
...	...	...
90+	kwusip-ye	ahu-nam(.)un / -nam(.)u, ahun namcis '90-odd'
90-100	–	–
100+	payk-ye	payk namcis '100-odd'
110+	payk sip-ye	–
120+	payk īsip-ye	–
130+	payk samsip-ye	–

Notice also: **swū-sip** 'several tens (of)', **swū-payk** 'several hundred', **swū-chen** 'several thousand', **swū-man** 'tens of thousands (of)', **swū-ek** 'hundreds of millions (of)'.

(4) LIST OF APPROXIMATE ORDINAL NUMERALS

	Chinese	Core
2nd or so	–	twue ccay
2nd or 3rd	cēy ī-sam	twū-sey ccay
		twū-sene ccay 'about 2nd or 3rd'
3rd or so	–	–
3rd or 4th	cēy sam-sa	sene-nete ccay 'about 3rd or 4th'

Other such forms seem awkward, especially **ches-twu ccay** and **yele ccay**. But **yele(s) ccay** can be used as an abbreviation of **yele pen ccay**, as in the following exchange: **I pen ey nah.un Kim ssi ney ai ka ches ayki 'n ka yo? – Kulssey olssita; ama yele(s) ccay toylq ke l' yo** 'Is this the first child for the Kims? – I don't think so, it must be one of several'.

(5) LIST OF EXCESS ORDINAL NUMERALS

	Chinese	Core
10th or so	sip-ye ccay	ye-nam(.)u ccay
20th or so	īsip-ye ccay	sumu-nam(.)u ccay
...	...	...
90th or so	kwusip-ye ccay	ahu-nam(.)u ccay
100th or so	payk-ye ccay	–
1,000th or so	chen-ye ccay	–
10,000th or so	mān-ye ccay	–

5.5.3. Counters.

The following list of counters is not quite exhaustive, but it is fairly representative. There are three columns: the first lists the typical units counted, the second shows an example with core numerals, the third shows an example with Chinese numerals. In general, the examples are given with the numeral '3' in order to show which counters take the shapes **sēk** or **sē** (and for '4' **nēk** or **nē**). If there is a blank in the core or Chinese column, the counter does not normally occur with those numerals. However, the Chinese numeral must be used when there is no core numeral ('100', ...).

LIST OF COUNTERS: GROUP ONE

Units counted	with core numerals	with Chinese numerals
things, items, matches, pencils	(mulken sēy) kay '3 objects'	
units, items, bits, grains, beans	(khong sēy) nath '3 beans'	
books, magazines; 20 sheets of Korean paper	(chayk sēy) kwēn$_1$ '3 books'	
animals, birds, fish	(kāy sēy) mali '3 dogs'	

animals (horse, ox)	(so sēy) phil '3 oxen'	(kwunma sam)-phil '3 army horses'
		(nongwu sam)-twu '3 farm oxen'
honored persons	(son nim sēy) pun '3 guests'	
persons, people	(sālam sēy) salam '3 people'	
persons [formal]	(haksayng sēy) myeng '3 students'	
flat things, sheets, papers, newspapers, letters	(sinmun sēk) cang '3 newspapers'	
sheets, mats	(cali sēy) ttwayki '3 mats'	
buildings	(cip sēy) chay '3 houses'	(cwūthayk sam)-ho / -tong₁ '3 dwellings'
vehicles, machines	(catong-cha sēk) tay₁ '3 automobiles'	(catong-cha sam)-tay '3 automobiles'
long objects with handles (bushes, brooms, guns, scythes); pencils (but kay is more common)	(pus sēk) calwu '3 writing brushes'	
cigarettes; pipefuls	(tāmpay sēy / sēk) tay₂ '3 cigarettes'	
slaps	(ppyam sēk) tay₃ '3 slaps (on cheek)'	
suits of clothes, garments; sets of dishes / tableware; copies of a set of documents	(yangpok sēy) pel '3 suits'	
ten garments / dishes	(cekoli / kulus sēk) cwuk '30 vests/plates'	
(menu) dishes	(Cwungkwukq ¹yoli sēy) cepsi '3 Chinese dishes'	
pairs of footwear or gloves	(sin-pal sēy) khyel(l)ey '3 pairs of shoes'	
cannons, big guns		(tāypho sam)-mun '3 guns'
trees, shrubs	(namu sēy) kulwu '3 trees'	(namu sam)-cwu '3 trees'
places, institutions		(kongcang sam)-kayso '3 factories'
places, locations, spots	(thullin tey sēy) kwuntey '3 errors'	
fields	(non sēy) paymi '3 fields'	
boats	(pay sēy) chek / chay '3 boats'	
small round things (berries, nuts, beads, bullets, lenses)	(photo / pām sēy) al '3 grapes / chestnuts'	
poems	(si sēy) swu '3 poems'	(si sam)-swu '3 poems'
written characters, letters	(kulqca sēk) ca '3 letters'	
chapters (of text)	(kul sēk) cang '3 chapters'	
pieces of sewing thread	(sīl sēy) nim '3 pieces of thread'	
skeins of thread	(sīl sēy) they '3 skeins of thread'	
pairs of chopsticks	(ceq-kal sēy) may '3 pairs of chopsticks' More commonly just **ceq-kal sēys**.	
hung pictures (any kind); scrolls	(kūlim sēy) phok '3 pictures'	
agenda items, assembly bills	(sēy) ken '3 items / bills'	(sam)-ken '3 items / bills'
kinds, sorts	(os sēy) kaci '3 (kinds of) garments'	

A Reference Grammar of Korean

LIST OF COUNTERS: GROUP TWO

Units counted	with core numerals
bunches (of vegetables / firewood)	(namul sēk) tan '3 bunches of greens'
bunches (of flowers, plants)	(kkoch sēy / sēk) tapal '3 bouquets'
bunches, clumps (of false hair, seaweed)	(myēk sēy) kkokci '3 clumps of seaweed'
sheaves, tied bunches; strings of tobacco	(pye sēk) cwul '3 sheaves of rice'
sheaves of straw	(ciph sēy) mus$_1$ '3 sheaves of straw'
bundles of chopped firewood	(cangcak sēy) mus$_2$ '3 bundles of firewood'
loaves	(ppang sēy) tengeli '3 loaves of bread'
pinches, dashes (of spice / herbs)	(yangnyem sēy) capam '3 dashes of spice'
fist(ful)s, handfuls	(molay sēy) moswum '3 handfuls of sand'
mouthfuls, sips	(mul sēy) mokum '3 sips of water'
bottle(fuls)	(maykcwu sēy) pyeng '3 bottles of beer'
cup(ful)s	(cha sēk) can '3 cups of tea'
bowl(ful)s	(pap sēy) kulus '3 bowls of rice'
box(fuls), small	(sengnyang sēy) kap '3 boxes of matches'
box(fuls), large	(kwaca sēy) sangca '3 boxes of cakes'
cratefuls	(sakwa sēy) kwēy-ccak '3 crates of apples'
packet(ful)s	(yak sēy) pong '3 packets of medicine'
packs (of herbal remedies)	(yak sēy / / sēk) chep '3 packs of herbs'
20 packs (of herbal remedies)	(yak sēy / sēk) cey '60 packs of herbs'
bag(fuls)	(ssal sēy) kama$_1$ '3 bags of rice'
cakes, blocks, squares	(twupu sēy) mo '3 cakes (squares) of bean curd'
(human) backloads	(namu sēy) cim '3 (back)loads of wood'
(pack)loads	(koksik sēy) pali '3 (pack)loads of grain'
loads, bundles, packs, pieces of luggage	(cim sēy) ccak '3 pieces of luggage'
bolts of cloth	(philyuk sēy) phil '3 bolts of cloth'
bolts of cloth; heads of cabbage, gourds	(kwāngmok / paychwu sēy) thong '3 bolts of cloth / cabbages'
letters, telegrams	(cēnhwa sēy) thonghwa '3 calls'
24 needles	(panul sēy) ssam '3 dozen needles'
100 raincovers or tobacco-pouches	(kalmo/ssamci sēy) kama '300 raincovers / pouches'
tied bundles of 10 flat dry edibles	(kwulpi sēy) kas '3 bundles of dried corvina'
10 eggs in a straw wrapper	(talkyal sēy) kkwule(y)mi '3 wrappers of eggs'
bundles of 50 cucumbers or eggplants	(oi / kaci sēy) keli '150 cucumbers / eggplants'
reams (500 sheets) of paper	(congi sēy) ^{1}yen '3 reams of paper'
20 sheets of Korean paper	(congi sēy) kwēn$_2$ '60 sheets of paper'
200 sheets of Korean paper; a roll of paper; 20 almanacs	(congi sēy) chwuk '600 sheets of paper'
100 fruits, radishes, cabbages, bulbs of garlic	(kām sēk) cep '300 persimmons'
plants, heads (of cabbage)	(pāychwu sēy) phoki '3 heads of cabbage'

a bundle (of 10 brushes **pus**,
  50 bolts of cloth **pey**,   (... sēk) tong$_2$ '30 (brushes), 150 (bolts),
  200 herring **piwus**)   600 (herring)'
fish (as a commodity)   (mulq-koki sēy) kay '3 fish'
handfuls of fish
  (2 large, 4-5 small fish)   (kotunge / coki sēy) son '6 mackerels / corvinas'
10 fish   (mulq-koki sēy) mus '30 fish'
20 fish   (mulq-koki sēk) tulem '60 fish'
20 cuttlefish   (ocinge sēy) chwuk '60 cuttlefish'
20 pollacks [rare]   (myengthay / puk.e sēy) khway '60 pollacks /
      dried pollacks'

2000 fish   (mulq-koki sēy) pali '6000 fish'
bunches of barley   (poli sēk) tan '3 bunches of barley'
30 bunches of barley   (poli sēy) haci '90 bunches of barley'
1500 bunches of barley   (poli sēk) tong$_3$ '4500 bunches of barley'
2000 tiles   (kiwa sēy) wuli '6000 tiles'

LIST OF COUNTERS: GROUP THREE

Units counted	with core numerals	with Chinese numerals
(hours) o'clock	(sēy) si '3 o'clock'[1]	
hours	(sēy) sikan '3 hours'	
nights	(sēy) pam '3 nights'	
weeks	(sēy) cwukan / cwuil '3 weeks'	(sam)-cwukan / -cwuil
months (See separate list.)	(sēk) tal '3 months'	(sam)-kaywel '3 months'
years	(sēy) hay '3 years'	(sam)-nyen '3 years'
years old	(sēy) sal '3 years old'	(sam)-sēy '3 years old'
spells, periods (of activity)	(sēy) cham '3 spells'	
seconds		(sam)-cho '3 seconds'
minutes		(sam)-pun '3 minutes'
parts, fractions		(sam)-pun '3 parts'
ten-percents		(sam)-hal '30 percent'
degrees		(Sep-ssi sam)-to '3° centigrade'
		(wito / kyengto sam)-to '3° longitude / latitude'
times	(sēy) pen '3 times'	(sam)-hoy '3 times'
moves (in chess / checkers)	(sēy) swu '3 moves'	
(gun)shots	(sēy) pāng '3 shots'	(sam)-pal '3 shots'
rounds (esp. of 5 arrows shot)	(sēy) swun '3 rounds'	
floors, stories	? (sēy) chung '3 floors'	
(...th) floor / story	? (sēy) chung '3rd floor'	(sam)-chung '3rd floor'
wen, yen, yuan, dollar		(sam)-wen '3 wen'
hwan [obsolete = wen]		(sam)-hwan '3 hwan'
cen, sen, cents		(sam)-cen '3 cen'
(old copper coin)	(sēy) niph '3 coppers'	
(old coin) taels	(sēk) nyang '3 taels'	
(old coin) **yepcen**		(yepcen sam)-mun '3 yepcen'

A Reference Grammar of Korean

(old dime = 10 phun)	(sē) ton '3 old dimes'
(old Korean penny)	(sē) phun '3 pennies'
dollars	(sam)-pul '3 dollars'
marks	(sam)-malukhu '3 marks'
rubles	(sam)-lwupul '3 rubles'
pounds	(sam)-phauntu / -pang '3 pounds'
shillings	(sam)-silling '3 shillings'
liras	(sam)-lila '3 lira'
francs	(sam)-phulang '3 francs'

[1] Also (sēk) cem, said to be used by "the uneducated".

LIST OF COUNTERS: GROUP FOUR

Units counted	with core numerals	with Chinese numerals
(1) Linear measure		
.0303 mm		(sam)-mo
.303 mm		(sam)-li
3.03 mm = .119 in	(sēk / sē) phun	(sam)-phun
3.03 cm = 1.193 in	(sēy) chi	(sam)-chon
.303 m = 0.994 ft	(sēy / sēk) ca[1]	(sam)-chek
1.818 m = 1.988 yd	(sēy) kan	(sam)-kan
109 m = .542 furlongs		(sam)-ceng
3.927 km = 2.44 m		(sam)-li[2]

[1] Yeses ca '6 ca' is often said as ye(y) ca.
[2] But this counter is generally used only in multiples of five. Traditionally it refers to several different lengths; the best overall translation is the equally vague English "leagues".

(2) Square measure		
330.7 sq cm = .355 sq ft		(sam)-cak
33.07 sq cm = 3.556 sq ft	(sēy / sē) hop	
3.307 sq m = 3.952 sq yd	(sēy) phyeng	
91.15 sq m = 3.92 sq rods		(sam)-mu
9.915 ares = .245 acres		(sam)-tan
(3) Liquid and dry measures		
.018 liters = .152 gills		(sam)-cak
.18 liters = 1.524 gills	(sēy / sē) hop	
1.805 liters = 3.81 pints	(sēk / sē) toy	(sam)-sung [rare]
18.05 liters = 19.04 qt	(sē) mal	(sam)-twu [rare]
180.5 liters = 47.6 gal	(sēk) sem	(sam)-sek; (sam)-kok [rare]
(4) Weight measures		
.003759 gram		(sam)-mo
.03759 gram		(sam)-li
.3759 grams	(sē) phun	
3.759 grams = 2.117 drams = .13228 ounces	(sē) ton	
.601 kg = 1.323 lb	(sēy / sē) kun	
3.759 kg = 8.27 lb	(sēy) kwan	
1.803 kg = 3.969 lb = 30 kun		(sam)-kyun[1]

[1] Rare, except in chen-kyun pota mukepta 'is ever so heavy'.

The interrelationships of the measure units can be displayed as follows:

(1) 10 mo   = 1 li
    10 li   = 1 phun
    10 phun = 1 chi
    10 chi   = 1 ca
     6 ca   = 1 kan
    10 kan   = 1 cang
     6 cang = 1 ceng
    36 ceng = 1 lī

(2) 10 cak   = 1 hop
    10 hop   = 1 phyeng
    30 phyeng = 1 mu
    10 mu   = 1 tan
    10 tan   = 1 ceng

(3) 10 cak = 1 hop
    10 hop = 1 toy
    10 toy = 1 mal
    10 mal = 1 sem

(4) 10 mo   = 1 li
    10 li   = 1 phun
    10 phun = 1 ton
    160 ton = 1 kun
    1000 ton = 1 kwan

LIST OF COUNTERS: GROUP FIVE

Units counted	with core numerals	with Chinese numerals
fathoms (8 or 10 ca; 5 ca)	(sēy) kil	(sam)-cang
grams	(sēy) kulam	
kilo(gram/watt/meter)s	(sēy) khillo	
spans	(sē) pāl	
(double-)span of rope; 10 handspans of rope	(saykki sēy) pāl '3 pāl of rope'	
handspans of rope	(saykki sēy) ppyem '3 handspans of rope'	
50 pāl of rope	(saykki sēk) tong₄ '150 pāl of rope'	
spans (of thread / string / rope)	(sīl / no-kkun / saykki sēy) palam	
double armspans (around)	(sēy) alum	
inches	(sēy) inchi	
feet	(sēy) phīthu	
yards	(sēy) yātu, mā	
miles		(sam)-mail
"miles, leagues" (? = lī, when less than ten)	(sēy) macang	
ounces		(sam)-aunsu
pounds		(sam)-phauntu
tons	(sēy) thon	(sam)-thon / -ton
generations, the ···th		(Heyn.li sam)-sey 'Henry III'
sizes of rice field (in terms of the yield)	(sēy) ma'-ciki; (sēy) toy-ciki	
meals	(sēy) kki	
wins (at wrestling)	(sēy) heli	
times (as much)	(sēy) kopcel¹ '3 times as much'	
(dawn) cock-crows	(sēy) hway (ccay) '3 cock-crows (3rd cock-crow)'	
shoe-sizes		(sam-)mun 'size 3'

dozens	(sēy / sēk) thā
(male-female) pairs	(sāy sēy) ssang '3 pairs of birds'
(thread weave density)	(mumyeng sēk) say '3-thread cotton cloth'
one of a pair (CF han-ccak 'a set')	(sin-pal sēy) ccak '3 odd (unmatched) shoes'

[1] The word **kapcel** usually means only 'two-fold'; 'double' is **kop** or **kop-cayngi**.

5.5.4. Irregular counting.

A few units are counted in irregular ways: days, years, months; people; cattle and horses (of certain ages).

(1) DAY; DAY OF MONTH	NORMAL	FORMAL
how many days; what day (of the month)	meych nal	meychil (myechil); meychit nal
1 day; 1st of month	halwu; halwuq nal	il-il
2 days; 2nd of month	ithul; ithut nal	ī-il
3 days; 3rd of month	sahul; sahut nal	sam-il
3 or 4 days	sanāl	sam-sa-il
4 days; 4th of month	nahul; nahut nal	sā-il
4 or 5 days	natāl	sā-o-il
5 days; 5th of month	tassa; tassayq nal	ō-il
6 days; 6th of month	yessay; yessayq nal	[1]yuk-il
6 or 7 days	yey-niley	[1]yuk-chil-il
7 days; 7th of month	iley; ileyq nal	chil-il
8 days; 8th of month	yetuley, [dialect] yatuley; yetuleyq nal	phal-il[2]
9 days; 9th of month	ahuley; ahuleyq nal	kwu-il
10 days; 10th of month	yelhul, yelhul nal	sip-il
11 days; 11th of month	yel halwu; yel halwuq nal	sip-il il
12 days; 12th of month	yel ithul; yel ithut nal	sip-i il
13 days; 13th of month	yelq sahul; yelq sahut nal	sip-sam il
14 days; 14th of month	yel nahul; yel nahut nal	sip-sa il
15 days; 15th of month	yelq tassay; yelq tassayq nal	sip-o il
the midmonth (day = the 15th)	polum (nal)	
16 days; 16th of month	yel yessay; yel yessayq nal	sipq-[1]yuk il
17 days; 17th of month	yel iley; yel ileyq nal	sip-chil il
18 days; 18th of month	yel yetuley; yel yetuleyq nal	sip-phal il
19 days; 19th of month	yel ahuley; yel ahuleyq nal	sip-kwu il
20 days; 20th of month	sumu nal	ī-sip il
21 days; 21st of month	sumul halwu	ī-sip il-il
22 days; 22nd of month	sumu ithul	ī-sip ī-il
23 days; 23rd of month	sumu sahul	ī-sip sam-il
24 days; 24th of month	sumu nahul	ī-sip sā-il
25 days; 25th of month	sumulq tassay	ī-sip ō-il
26 days; 26th of month	sumul yessay	ī-sip(q) [1]yuk-il
27 days; 27th of month	sumu iley	ī-sip chil-il
28 days; 28th of month	sumu yetuley	ī-sip phal-il
29 days; 29th of month	sumu ahuley	ī-sip kwu-il
30 days; 30th of month	(? selun nal)	sam-sip il
31 days; 31st of month	(? selun halwu)	sam-sip sip-il
the last day of the month	kumum (nal)	

From 1-31, the terms either count days or name the days of the month; but, unless it is the only form, the term with ··· **nal** usually just names. For **phal-il** the variant **phā'-il** means only the 8th of the month, and it is usually taken to refer to the 8th of April, Buddha's birthday.

For 21-31 the native forms are uncommon. They are usually replaced by the Chinese forms, and that may account for the unexplained choice by my sources of **sumu** or **sumul** in a given expression. In dialects more comfortable with the older forms the choice may be better motivated.

When the first ten days of the month are designated it is customary to attach the adnoun **cho(-)**: **cho halwu, cho ithul, ... , cho yelhul**.

To designate a quantified period of time ···**q tong-an** is often added: **yelhulq tong-an** '10 days' = **sip-ilq tong-an** 'ten days (duration)', **polumq tong-an** = **sip-o il(q) tong-an** 'fifteen days'. The postnoun (or suffix) **kan** 'interval' is often added to the terms for '21-31 days (duration)' (CF M 1:173): **sam-sip il-kan(q tong-an)** '(a period of) 31 days'.

Naming days of the week

what day	musun nal, musunq yoil	
Sunday	il.yo(il (nal))	
Monday	wel.yo(il (nal))	
Tuesday	hwā.yo(il (nal)	
Wednesday	swuyo(il (nal))	
Thursday	mok.yo(il (nal))	
Friday	kum.yo(il (nal))	
Saturday	tho.yo(il (nal))	

(2) YEARS

how many years	meych hay	meych nyen
what (which) year	musun / enu hay (of 60-yr cycle, ...)	meych nyen (of calendar)[1]
1 year	han hay	il-nyen (also Year 1)
2 years	twū hay, ithay	ī-nyen (also Year 2)
3 years	sēy hay	sam-nyen (also Year 3)
4 years	nēy hay	sā-nyen (also Year 4)
5 years	tases hay	ō-nyen (also Year 5)
6 years	yeses hay	[1]yuk-nyen (also Year 6)
7 years	ilkop hay	chil-nyen (also Year 7)
8 years	yetelp hay /yetelphay/	phal-nyen (also Year 8)
9 years	ahop hay	kwu-nyen (also Year 9)
10 years	yel hay	sip-nyen (also Year 10)
20 years	sumu hay[2]	ī-sip nyen (also Year 20)
100 years	payk hay	payk-nyen (also Year 100)

[1] Seki 1992 = Tanki 4325. (The myth says Korea began in 2333 B.C.)
[2] But ´sumul ´hoy (1481 Twusi 16:18a).

(3) MONTHS

how many months	meych tal	meych-kaywel
1 month	han tal	il-kaywel
2 months	twū tal	ī-kaywel
3 months	sēk tal	sam-kaywel
4 months	nēk tal	sā-kaywel
8 months	yetel[p]q tal	phal-kaywel
10 months	yelq tal	sip-kaywel

what month	musun tal	meych wel, musun wel
January		il-wel(q tal); ceng-wel
February		ī-wel(q tal)
March		sam-wel(q tal)
April		sā-wel(q tal)
May		ō-wel(q tal)
June		¹yu'-wel(q tal)
July		chil-wel(q tal)
August		phal-wel(q tal)
September		kwu-wel(q tal)
October		si'-wel(q tal)
November		sip.il-wel(q tal); tōngciq tal
December		sip.i-wel(q tal); sēt tal

(4) PEOPLE

In Seoul, people are usually counted regularly with **han salam, twū salam, ...** , or (more formal) **han myeng, twū myeng, ...** , and in compounds and set expressions also **il-in, ī-in, ...** , as in **il-in (ī-in) yōng pang** 'a room for one (two)'. In certain other areas, people are counted with the bound noun **i** 'one, person' as follows:

1 person	han(a)-i, hanq-i /hanni/
2 people	twūl-i, twū-i
3 people	sē-i
4 people	nē-i
5 people	tases-i, tasesq-i
6 people	yeses-i, yesesq-i
7 people	ilkop-i, ilkopq-i
8 people	yetel-i, yetelp-i
9 people	ahop-i, ahopq-i
10 people	yel-i, yelq-i
20 people	sumul-i

Ko Yengkun (1989 LR 25:102) gives the forms **myech-i** 'how many people' and **yeles-i** 'many people' but I have been unable to confirm them. Perhaps there is confusion with **myech i** = **meych i** and **yeles i**, in which **i** is the nominative marker and there is nothing referring to people, as such. Choy Hak.kun (1978:1048) lists the form **yelesi** as a dialect equivalent to **yeles** and not specifically meaning people; this is an example of the common incorporation of **-i** by nouns that is described in Part II.

(5) HORSES AND OXEN OF A CERTAIN AGE

1-year-old	hansup
2-year-old	twūsup
3-year-old	salup; [dialect] sēysup
4-year-old	nalup
5-year-old	tasup
6-year-old	yesup
7-year-old	ilop
8-year-old	yetup
9-year-old	asup, kwulup
10-year-old	yellup, tam(p)ul

There are also a few variant forms of the numerals with certain of the counters: **tay ca, ta(s) ca = tases ca** (CF **tāys ca** 'about 5 feet'), **yes ca = yeses ca; tas ton = tases ton, yes ton = yeses ton**. In the game of tag (**swullay capki**) the counting goes: 1 **hanalttay**, 2 **twualttay**, 3 **samacwung**, 4 **nalttay**, 5 – (?), 6 ¹**yuk-nangkeci**, 7 – (?), 8 **phalttay**, 9 **cangkwun**, 10 **kotulay-ppyong**.

5.5.5. Fractions.

Examples of numeral fractions and how they are read:

$1/2$	ī-pun uy/ci il; celpan
$1/3$	sam-pun uy/ci il
$2/3$	sam-pun uy/ci ī
$3/4$	sā-pun uy/ci sam
$5/6$	¹yuk-pun uy/ci ō
$7/8$	phal-pun uy/ci chil
1.3	ilq-cem sam ("one-point three")
2.1	ī-cem il
(0).314	(¹yengq-)cem sam il sā

Some grammarians treat **(-)punci** as a unit (suffix or postnoun); the **ci** is a Chinese particle equivalent to the core adnominal marker **uy**.

5.6. Verbal nouns.

A VERBAL NOUN is typically followed by a POSTNOMINAL VERB. Many verbal nouns are PRE-SEPARABLE, in that they are followed by separable postnominal verbs such as **ha-** 'do/be', **toy-** 'get done', **sikhi-** 'cause to do', **ka-** 'go to do', **(na-)o-** 'come (out) to do', **po-** 'see to it, do', ... These verbs are called separable because they are sometimes separated from certain verbal nouns by the insertion of a particle – at least **tul, to, man,** or **un/nun**; and often **ul/lul** or **i/ka**. Those verbal nouns from which a separable postnominal can be separated are called SEPARABLE VERBAL NOUNS; Cf Hankul 108:42 (1955). Most of the two-syllable verbal nouns are separable and most of the one-syllable verbal nouns are inseparable, but there are exceptions. Some of the verbal nouns are PRE-INSEPARABLE: they occur before inseparable postnominal verbs such as **ha-** 'behave, go (boom!, ...)' (a homophone of **ha-** 'do/be' and the same etymon), **keli-** 'behave repeatedly', **tāy-** = **keli-**, **k(h)uli-** 'behave', **sulew-** 'be, give the impression of being', ... These verbs are called inseparable because they do not allow a particle (not even **to** or **un/nun**) to intervene. (But certain speakers allow **sulepta** to be set apart in vivid contexts: **Calang to sulewe haney!** 'How proud he is!'; **salang/iksal/yātan to sulepta** 'is quite lovely / droll / irksome', ...) The inseparable postnominal verbs are sometimes attached to pre-inseparable verbal nouns, sometimes to separable verbal nouns, i.e. to verbal nouns that can occur with particles when in construction with separable postnominal verbs.

Some verbal nouns occur only in constructions of verbal noun (with or without particle) + postnominal verb. (But note that the postnominal verb **hanta** is sometimes dropped, especially when the forms **ham** and **hako** are used in headlines; see §10.2, 11b-d.) Other verbal nouns occur also as free nouns, for example **kongpu** 'study' in **i kongpu ka elyepta** 'this study is difficult'. We are dealing with three independent variables of the grammar:

(1) verbal noun only ≠ free noun also;
(2) pre-separable verbal noun ≠ pre-inseparable verbal noun;
(3) separable verbal noun ≠ inseparable verbal noun.

For each verbal noun in the lexicon, such three-way information should be sought. (See below for two more pieces of information that we require.) Most Korean dictionaries list as free nouns certain items that seem to be limited, in speech at least, to use as verbal nouns.

Just as the class of verbs divides into transitive and intransitive, the class of verbal nouns divides into verbal noun TRANSITIVE (vnt) and verbal noun INTRANSITIVE (vni); some are both, for example **sīcak hanta** can mean either 'begins it' or 'it begins'. A construction of vnt + postnominal verb can take a direct object: **Yenge lul kongpu hanta** 'studies English'. For separable verbal nouns transitive there is sometimes an alternative way to express the object: **Yenge kongpu lul hanta** 'does English study' (**Yenge** adnominal to **kongpu**) or 'studies – English' (**Yenge** adverbial, i.e. absolute, to the predicate **kongpu lul hanta**). The separable verbal noun may take the object marker, especially if no other object is present: **kongpu lul hanta** 'does some studying, studies'. Normally, if the verbal noun is modified (by an adnoun or modifier construction) it cannot take another object and it is usually followed by the accusative particle: **elyewun kongpu lul hanta** 'does some difficult studying', **i kongpu lul hanta** 'does this studying'.

The class of intransitive verbs has a subclass of descriptive verbs (= adjectives), characterized by the lack of processive forms that are present for the processive intransitive (and all transitive) verbs. Similarly, the class of intransitive verbal nouns divides into the processive (vni proper) and the descriptive ones that we call ADJECTIVAL NOUNS (adj-n). (For a few adjectival nouns that appear in unexpected forms, see §7.1, p. 217.) The adjectival nouns form constructions with postnominal verbs that are descriptive; those we call postnominal adjectives. Apparently **ha-** is the only common postnominal adjective that is separable.

The lexicon should seek the following information about each verbal noun, in addition to the three variables mentioned above:

(4) vnt ≠ vni ≠ adj-n;
(5) the specific postnominal verb(s) a given verbal noun occurs with. For example, some but not all vnt that occur with **ha-** also occur in a passivizing conversion with **toy-** (see §5.6.6).

A construction that consists of vni + postnominal verb will not take a direct object. A separable vni is sometimes set apart from **ha-** by the particle **ul/lul** (as well as **to** and **un/nun**) or from **toy-** by the particle **i/ka**: **kyelhon (ul) hanta** 'gets married', **kekceng (i) toynta** 'gets worried'. And between VN **ul/lul** and **ha-** you may hear one of the adverbs **an** 'not', **mōs** 'cannot', or **cal** 'well; lots; often': **kongpu lul an/mōs/cal hanta**.

Among the verbal nouns, some are best treated as a subclass of the impressionistic (mimetic) adverbs, §12. Many of the other verbal nouns are from the Chinese vocabulary, but there are also verbal nouns in the core vocabulary: **kancik** 'keep', **kekceng** 'bother', **kyēnyang** 'aim', **kwi-ttwim** 'hint', **tacim** 'pledge', **melmi** 'feel nauseous', **pasim** 'plane', **pēl.im** 'earn', **son cis** 'gesture', ... And some are from the stock of modern English loans: **nokhu** 'knock, hit', **tulaipu** 'drive', **ssain** 'sign, signal', ...

It is difficult to decide whether to treat many of the verbal nouns borrowed from Chinese as transitive or intransitive. Often an etymological "object" is already incorporated in the Chinese expression (**kwēnnong** 'encouraging agriculture', for example, includes **nong** 'agriculture'), so that it seems pleonastic to add a separate object. Yet many of the verbal nouns listed by dictionaries as being intransitive are used colloquially with pleonastic objects: **nongsa lul kwēnnong hanta** '(farming-) promotes agriculture'.

5.6.1. Defective verbal nouns.

Defective verbal nouns are those which occur with only a few (or just one) of the expected paradigmatic forms of the postnominal verb:

DERIVED ADVERB:
mutan hi 'without reason/leave'
chōng hi 'all, entirely, wholly'
kām hi 'with daring'
kōng hi 'alike'
kuk hi 'extremely'
kunkun hi = **kunkun** (= **kyewu**) 'almost'
kkun hi = 'tenaciously, persistently'
kiyen hi 'for sure'
congsok hi 'without delay'
kupke hi 'suddenly'
kosulan hi 'intact'
kaman hi 'quietly'
kkol-kkol hi 'sorrowfully (weeping)'
nalan hi 'in a row'

MODIFIER (CF §5.3.1):
yuil han 'unique'
mōmo han 'prominent'
tāymo han 'main, important'

CONDITIONAL:
(k)elphis hamyen 'all too often'
tacik hamyen (= **kikkes hamyen**) 'at most'

INFINITIVE + PARTICLE:
tacik hay ya 'at most'

GERUND:
(··· **un/nun**) **kosa hako** 'apart (from ···)'
kyel kho 'definitely (not)' < **kyel(qtan) hako**
cengnyeng kho (< **hako**) = **cengnyeng** 'definitely'
phil.yen kho (< **hako**) = **phil.yen** 'for sure'

Those with ··· **hi** are obviously adjectival nouns, since **hi** comes only from the postnominal adjective **ha-**, but it would be difficult to say for sure whether the other cases should be regarded as processive or descriptive verbal nouns. The cases with ··· **han** have already been treated (in §5.3.1) as quasi-adnouns, so we might do well to treat the others as types of quasi-adverb.

Certain verbal nouns occur in several but not all of the paradigmatic forms: **tangmyen** 'confront' appears only with **han, hakey,** and **hamyen,** as in **tangmyen han mūncey** 'the problem that confronts us', **ilen mūncey ey tangmyen hakey toymyen** 'if we come to confront such a problem', and **ilen mūncey tangmyen hamyen** 'if such a problem confronts us'. And **tahayng** 'fortunate' seems to appear only with **hakey, hi,** and **han;** see also §5.2.9 for its occurrence with **ulo** and **ita.** Most of the verbal nouns that occur in extended particle phrases (§6.3) are limited to infinitive (**ha.ye** or **hay se**) and modifier (**han**) forms, e.g. ··· **ulo in ha-** 'be due to'. But some have a few additional forms (e.g. ··· **ey uy ha-** 'rely upon' occurs at least in **uy hamyen, uy hanta, uy hako,** and **uy hamye**), and some occur only in the infinitive: ··· **ey cuum / cey hay (se)** 'on the occasion of'.

5.6.2. Transitive verbal nouns.

Most two-syllable transitive verbal nouns that occur with the separable verb **ha-** are themselves separable and occur as free nouns: **kongpu** 'study', **sayngkak** 'think', **kwūkyeng** 'view (for pleasure)', **taycwung** 'estimate', **salang** 'love', **mac.i** 'meet', ... But **hetak hanta** 'nibbles on what has been set apart' is an inseparable vnt. The monosyllables **wēn** 'desire', **māl** 'say', and **kum** 'appraise, fix the price of' are also separable and occur as free nouns ('desire', 'worth', and 'price'). Most monosyllabic vnt, however, are inseparable: **cen** 'convey, report' (related noun 'biography'); **tāy** 'face, relate to' (related noun 'pair; versus'); **cheng** 'invite' (as noun 'invitation'); **cey** 'subtract', **hap** 'add', **kam** 'deduct', **kwu** 'get, buy', **sang** 'harm', **tang** 'undergo', **thayk** 'choose', **pong** 'seal', **yo** 'need'.

5.6.3. Intransitive verbal nouns.

Most of the two-syllable intransitive verbal nouns that occur with the separable verb **ha-** are separable: **kyelhon** 'get married', **sānqpo** 'take a walk', ... Of the monosyllabic vni, only **īl** 'work' (of the core vocabulary) appears to be separable; all the others are inseparable: **kwan** 'be relevant, related', **sok** 'belong', **ung** 'agree, consent'.

For the inseparable verbal postmodifiers **chey / chek** and **ssa,** see §5.4.3.1.

5.6.4. Adjectival nouns.

Quite a few adjectival nouns (mostly of two syllables) serve also as free nouns and are separable from **ha-** by the particle **to:**

kanan 'poverty / poor'
kānung 'possibility / possible'
kātang 'appropriateness / appropriate'
kēman 'haughtiness / haughty'
kwung 'destitution / destitute'[1]

phikon 'tiredness / tired'
pulhayng 'misfortune / unfortunate'
sicang 'hunger / hungry'
yēngwen 'eternity / eternal'

[1] As a free noun: **kwung ey ppā cin cip** 'a house fallen into destitution'.

For the separable adjectival postmodifiers **pep** and **tus** see §5.4.3.3, and the entries in Part II.

There are also quite a few two-syllable (or longer) adjectival nouns that do not occur as free nouns but are quasi-inseparable. In colloquial usage they are usually inseparable, but occasionally the constructions can be split by the multivalent word **tul** 'plurally' (here treated as a particle), and in written texts the particles **to** and **un / nun** sometimes intervene: **puncwu tul hata** 'are all busy', **puncwu to hata** = **puncwu haki to hata** 'is busy indeed / also'. A few of these quasi-inseparable adjectival nouns: **emaema** 'elegant', **kkaykkus** 'clean', **puncwu** 'busy', **thunthun** 'strong'.

Most adjectival nouns of one syllable are inseparable, even though a few of them occur also as free nouns or other parts of speech: **chēn** 'lowly', **mōs** 'be inferior' (not to be confused with the etymologically related adverb 'cannot, definitely not'), **sil** 'be substantial, ... ' (also bound noun, bound adnoun), **sok** 'speedy'. There are four inseparable adjectival postmodifiers. They are treated in §5.4.3.2 (p. 161) and in the entries of Part II.

5.6.5. Bound adjectival nouns.

Some adjectival nouns are inseparable (in that they are never separated from the following **ha-**) and are attached to adjective stems:

-tama, -tala (→ -tama(h)-, -tala(h)-) 'rather (of size)'
-(k)kum 'rather'
-(c)cek, -(c)cak, -chek 'rather ⋯ish'
-(c)cek-cikun, -(c)cak-cikun, -chek-cikun 'rather ⋯ish'
-swuk ' ⋯ish'
-swuk(-)uley ' ⋯ish'
-cepcep ' ⋯ish, slightly colored (tinged)'
-(k)kulum SAME
-(u)tay-tay, -(u)tey-tey, -(u)tayng-tayng, -(u)teyng-teyng SAME
-(u)chwung-chwung SAME
-(u)chik-chik SAME
-(u)thoy-thoy, -(u)thwi-thwi SAME
-upsulum ' ⋯ish, slightly colored (tinged); slightly characterized by'
-us(ul)um / -s(ul)um ' ⋯ish, slightly characterized by'
-(u)m(-)uley ' ⋯ish'
-(u)s (see §12 and Part II)
-kkey 'dull and ugly (colored)'

These could be called "adjectival postadjectivals"; compare the bound postverbs of §7.1.3. Examples will be found in Part II under **-usulum**. Shape alternations are discussed in §12.

5.6.6. Conversion constraints on verbal nouns.

In §11.6 we describe special passive conversions for those verbal nouns of more than one syllable: ⋯ **hanta** → ⋯ **toynta**, → ⋯ **tang hanta**, → ⋯ **pat.nunta**. These conversions are limited to specific transitive verbal nouns, which must be listed. Moreover, there are intransitive verbal nouns which also occur with **toynta**, perhaps as an abbreviation of ⋯ **hakey toynta**. Cf **hōn.lan (hakey) toynta** from **hōn.lan hata** 'is disarranged', an adjectival noun. And a few verbal nouns do not occur with **hanta**, but only with **toynta**. We can make representative lists:

(1) ⋯ **hanta** → ⋯ **tang hanta**

    vnt **kēcel** 'refuse'

(2) ⋯ **hanta** → ⋯ **pat.nunta**

    vnt **cwūmok** 'watch'   **yōngse** 'forgive'
        hyep.pak 'threaten' $sokay_1$ 'introduce (people)'

(3) ⋯ **hanta** → ⋯ **toynta**

    vnt **kamkum** 'imprison'   [1]**noncung** 'prove'
        kilok 'record'   **sīcak** 'begin'
        kolye 'consider' $sokay_2$ 'introduce (ideas, culture, knowledge)'
        kyōyang 'educate'   **kwelki** 'be roused to action'
    vni **kāmtong** 'be emotionally moved'   **pensik** 'breed'
        cungtay 'enlarge, grow'   **tankyel** 'unite'
        hapkyek 'qualify'

(4) ··· **toynta** only (and no ← ··· **hanta**)

vni   ¹**īik** 'prove profitable'
     kāchayk 'get scolded'   **mapi** 'get paralyzed'
     kiceng 'be ready-made, established'   **moswun** 'be contradictory'
     koco 'reach a climax'   **sangchi** 'coincide'
     kyel.wen 'become enemies'   **sōtuk** 'be earned'

(5) ··· **hanta** only (and no → ··· **toynta**)

vnt   **kak.o** 'apprehend'
     kāngsup 'assault'   **pāngkwan** 'observe as bystander'
     kansep 'interfere'   **pokcong** 'obey'
     kyēngthan 'admire'   **taywu** 'treat'
     mulqsayk 'search out'   **tokchang** 'create'

vni   **kyekcen** 'battle'   **panghwang** 'wander'
     mūntap 'quiz'   **pihayng** 'fly'
     myēnto 'shave'   **puncayng** 'dispute in factions'
     nampok 'dress as a man'   **tamhwa** 'chat'
     nolyek 'endeavor'   **tapcang** 'answer (in writing)'
     pakswu 'applaud'   ¹**yehayng** 'travel'

Most verbal nouns of more than one syllable can be used in the causative conversion ··· **hanta** → ··· **sikhinta**:

vnt   **chwucin** 'propel'
     hāypang 'liberate'   **hwaksin** 'be convinced of'

vni   **ciyen** 'delay'
     cungka 'increase'   **kyelhap** 'combine'
     hāysan 'disperse'   **mūcang** 'arm for war'
     kāmso 'decrease'   **yak.hwa** 'grow weak'

For the permissible dropping of (··· **hanta** →) **haci** in conversions of verbal-noun sentences, see §11.7.5, and for the stylistic dropping of (··· **hanta** →) **hako**, see p. 277. Dyads of like verbal nouns (vnt + vnt, vni + vni, adj-n + adj-n) occur in construction with the postnominal verb **ha-**; we might regard these as instances of an optionally omitted **hako**: vn₁ [**hako**] vn₂ **ha-**. Apparently both verbal nouns must be of two syllables. For examples, see §10.2.

6.0. Forms: particles.

Particles are words that mark grammatical relationships, focus, emphasis, attitude, and a variety of emotional meanings. A Korean particle follows the word or phrase which it is marking, so that the Korean particles (like those of Japanese and many other languages) may be called POSTPOSITIONS, by analogy with the prepositions of western languages, such as English. It is often difficult to translate a given particle from one language to another, just as it is difficult to translate prepositions, which serve a similar function in English. The translation of a Korean particle will sometimes be a preposition in English, but it may instead involve word order or the placement of sentence stress, the choice of definite or indefinite article, and other subtleties that are difficult to pinpoint.

6.1. Characteristics of particles.

All particles sometimes occur before pause, but it is unusual for a pause to occur before a particle, for the particle is normally attached to the preceding word in close phonological juncture, in spite of the fact that it is in construction with the entire preceding phrase, not just the preceding word. Most particles sometimes occur (1) after a noun; certain particles also / instead occur (2) after various inflectional categories; and some of the particles also occur sometimes (3) after other particles. When particles occur in sequence, as in **wuli apeci EYKEY SE POTA TO** 'also / even than from our father', they peel off from the end, and each forms an immediate constituent with the entire preceding phrase:

> wuli apeci eykey se pota + to 'also / even'
> wuli apeci eykey se + pota 'than'
> wuli apeci eykey + se 'from / at'
> wuli apeci + eykey 'to / at a person'
> (wuli 'we / us' + apeci 'father')

Most of the common particle sequences are included as entries or as subentries in Part II. An attempt was made to elicit all conceivable sequences, including some which are merely "awkward", but not completely rejected. In general the focus particles (**un / nun, to, iya / ya**) come last in a string, but **man** 'just' occurs in several positions, as can be seen from the examples under the entry in Part II. The particles **i / ka** (nominative), **ul / lul** (accusative), **un / nun** (subdued focus), **to** (highlighted focus), and **iya / ya** (highlighted contingency) are mutually exclusive. But the nominative particle can occur after the other particles in certain hypostatic contexts, such as echo questions or denials ('it isn't [a matter of] " ... "'), or expressions such as ··· **i / ka mūncey 'ta** 'the problem is [the matter of] " ... "', into which a fragment is inserted from an assumed echo. These unusual situations are largely ignored here, but mention is made of particle sequences of nominative following other particles (such as **ey, eykey,** and **ulo**) under similarly limited circumstances, because those strings are more likely to be encountered than (*)**ul / lul i,** (*)**un / nun i,** (*)**to ka,** or (*)**iya / ya ka.** Although **Tōn ul [ ] i mūncey 'ta** is barely possible for 'The problem is [that he wants/...] money', there appears to be no comparable context that would permit **Tōn i [ ] lul** ... , except as a forced ellipsis: "**Tōn i**" lul "**tōn ul**" lo **kochyess.ta** 'I corrected [the phrase] "**tōn i**" to "**tōn ul**"'. Such special conditions would even allow an iteration of the same particle: "**Tōn ul**" ul "**tōn ulo**" lo **kochyess.ta** 'I corrected [the phrase] "**tōn ul**" to "**tōn ulo**"'; "**Wuli ka**" ka mūncey 'ta 'The problem is the [phrase] "**wuli ka**"'.

A particle particularizes and limits the grammatical relationship of the phrase to the rest of the sentence, places the word in perspective with respect to the rest of the sentence, or (if at the end of the sentence) shows how the sentence is regarded with respect to the discourse or the speech situation.

6.2. Quasi-particles.

Sometimes it is difficult to decide whether what we have is NOUN + PARTICLE or just NOUN + NOUN. There is one helpful test. The words **na** 'I / me', **ce** 'I / me' [formal], and **ne** 'you' have the alternant shapes **nay, cey,** and **ney** before a noun but not before a particle — with the exception, for special reasons (p. 196, note 1), of the nominative particle **ka**. What follows the pronominal reference in **nay sayngkak** 'my opinion' or 'thoughts of (= about) me' and (**ne wa**) **nay yeph** 'beside (you and) me' is a noun. For that reason we decide to treat **man** in **na man** 'just me' as a particle. And we can set up a class of QUASI-PARTICLE to take care of the extended use of phrases like **pakk ey** 'except for' in **na pakk ey** 'except for me' and **cip pakk ey ēps.ta**, which has two meanings 'there are none outdoors' and 'there's only the house' (= **cip man iss.ta**). The literary synonym **ōy ey** is to be treated the same as **pakk ey**. In a sense, perhaps **man** could be called a quasi-particle, too, since it also serves as an adjectival noun; but because we treat **man** as a particle it follows that **ku** is a noun, not an adnoun, in **ku man** 'just that'. Other quasi-particles are **kawuntey, cwungkan,** and **sai** 'midst': **ne wa na kawuntey / cwungkan / sai** 'between you and me'. In **na ttaymun** 'because of me' **na** is a noun and **ttaymun** a postnoun (not a particle because no "other" particle can be inserted before it — see below, §6.4), but in **nay ttaymun** 'for my sake' **ttaymun** is a noun.

In addition to noun quasi-particles, there are also quasi-particle verb forms which I choose not to call particles, but treat as specialized uses of the verb itself:

(1) **kath.i,** pronounced /kachi/, the derived adverb of **kath-** 'be like or with'. I regard **na kath.i** 'like me' as an abbreviation of **na wa kath.i**. The full form means either 'like me' (= **na chelem** with a particle) or 'with me' (= **na wa hamkkey** with an adverb in reciprocal valence 'together with'); the

abbreviated form means only 'like me'. Notice that the expression is inflected through all categories: **na kath.un ya** 'is it like me?', **na kath.ess.ta** 'it was like me'.

(2) **kaciko** 'with, ... ', the gerund of **kaci-** 'hold'. See the entries **kaciko** and **-e kaciko** in Part II.

(3) all forms of the copula, especially **ila / 'la, ila to / 'la to, in tul / 'n tul, ina / 'na, ita (ka) / 'ta (ka), iko / 'ko, imye / 'mye**.

(4) all forms of the verb **ha-**, notably **hako**. But this word I treat as a particle proper when optionally it substitutes for **wa / kwa** 'with, and'. That is for various reasons, primarily the great frequency of **hako** and its wider distribution than other forms of **ha-**.

(5) the abbreviation **tholok** (< **hatolok**). This functions like a postnoun of very limited distribution. See the entry in Part II.

(6) **mattana** 'according to (something said)' < **mac.ta hana** 'says it fits but'.

(7) **chiko** (vt gerund) 'considering as'.

(8) **mālko**, gerund of **mā-l-** 'refrain, desist'.

Perhaps all these quasi-particles could be regarded as transitional types or "particles in the making". The verbal origin of several of the particles proper is still transparent: **cocha, pota, puthe, mace, mankhum, ...** . Some Korean dictionaries list as a particle the uncommon use of **palo** marked "3" in the entry of Part II, but I prefer to treat it as a quasi-noun.

6.3. Extended particle phrases (phrasal postpositions).

In expository prose some of the verbs and verbal nouns are used as a way of extending and particularizing a particle. Most of these semi-literary clichés form two kinds of phrases: ADVERBIAL, with the infinitive or the infinitive + the particle **se** but occasionally with the gerund, and ADNOMINAL, with the plain modifier. (In the table "**ha.ye / hay se**" means both the literary **ha.ye** and the colloquial **hay se** are used.) The extended particle phrases function much like simple particles, so we call them phrasal postpositions.

	ADVERBIAL	ADNOMINAL	MEANING
(1)	ey kwan ha.ye / hay se	ey kwan han	'respecting, concerning, about'
(2)	ey tāy ha.ye / hay se	ey tāy han	'directed toward; treating, concerning, regarding; against, opposing'
(3)	ey pān ha.ye / hay se	ey pān han	'in opposition to, contrary to'
(4)	ey pī ha.ye / hay se	ey pī han	'compared with. relative to'
(5)	ey in ha.ye / hay se	ey in han	'in accordance with' CF 26
(6)	ey uy ha.ye / hay se	ey uy han	'depending on, based on'
(7)	ey ¹im ha.ye / hay se	ey ¹im han	'facing, confronting, meeting, in the presence of'
(8)	ey hān ha.ye / hay se	ey hān han	'limited / restricted to'
(9)	ey kung ha.ye / hay se	ey kung han	'throughout' (= ey kelchye)
(10)	ey pichwe	–	'in view / light of, according to'
(11)	ey ttal^e/a (se)	–	'consequent to'
(12)	ey iss.e (se)	–	'in, at, for'
(13)	ey cēy ha.ye	–	'on the occasion of'
(14)	ey cuum ha.ye	–	'on the occasion of'
(15)	ul pilos ha.ye / hay se	ul pilos han	'beginning with, (starting) from'
(16)	ul tang ha.ye / hay se	ul tang han	'facing, confronting'
(17)	ul hyang ha.ye / hay se	ul hyang han	'(facing) toward'
(18)	ul thong ha.ye / hay se	ul thong han	'through (= via or throughout)'
(19)	ul kyek ha.ye / ?hay se, ul kyek hako	ul kyek han	'separated by; with ... between; at intervals of'
(20)	ul wi ha.ye / hay se	ul wi han	'for the sake / purpose of, on behalf of'

(21) ul ki ha.ye — 'at the time of'
(22) ul kkiko — 'along(side), parallel to, following'
(23) ul mak.lon hako — 'to say nothing of'
(24) ul pulko / pulkwu hako — 'disregarding'
(25) ulo malmiam.e/a (se)   ulo malmiam.un   'in accord(ance) with; owing to';
(26) ulo in ha.ye / hay se   ulo in han   'in consequence of';
  [with passive] = ey(key) 'by'
(27) ulo ha.ye / hay se — 'on account of' (Part II; CM 1:165)
(28) ulo ha.ye-kum — 'causing / letting' (Part II; CM 1:165)
(29) kwa tepul.e (se) — 'together with, in common with'
(30) kwa awulle (se) — 'in addition to'

An interesting fact about these expressions is that they are used after phrases that would not otherwise take the particle. We can say, for example, that the particle **ey** occurs after the postmodifiers **ka** and **ya** 'question', but only in such expressions as **olunun ka / ya naylinun ka / ya ey ttal^e/a (se)** 'depending on whether it is rising or falling'. In a number of other cases a particle called for by the following expression will occur after phrases that would not otherwise attach the particle:

(31) ⋯ kwa / wa pāntay 'ta 'it is in opposition to'
(32) ⋯ kwa / wa pāntay lo 'in opposition to'
(33) ⋯ kwa / wa ilpan ita 'it is the same as (the case of)'
(34) ⋯ kwa / wa kath.i (kath.ta) '(it is) the same as, like'
(35) ⋯ kwa / wa hupsa hata 'it closely resembles (the case of)'
(36) ⋯ kwa / wa talli (taluta) '(it is) different from'
(37) ⋯ kwa / wa hamkkey 'together with'
(38) ⋯ kwa / wa tongsi ey 'at the same time (together) with'
(39) ⋯ ey to pulkwu hako 'regardless of, despite'; CF (24) above
(40) ⋯ i / ka mūncey 'ta 'it is a question; the question is (one of)'
(41) ⋯ i / ka ani 'ta 'it is not (that), it is not a case of'
(42) ⋯ ul mak.lon hako 'to say nothing of'; = (22) above

Compare CM 1:165, 266-7.

I have not included ⋯ **ey kelchye** 'extending over (a period of time, ...)', for it is just the infinitive of ⋯ **ey kelchi-** 'extend over', which seems to occur freely in all forms. There are, of course, quite a large number of verbs which call for the dative particle **ey** rather than (or as well as) the accusative particle **ul / lul**. See §10.8.

6.4. Particles proper.

The list of particles that follows is partly ordered by semantic groups, but I have omitted tag translations since they would be misleading. The full range of meaning (often extensive) and use (often overlapping) will be found in the entry for each particle in Part II. I have indicated a few strings that are often treated as single particles by Korean grammarians, such as **ey se**. The sequences that have actually been found or elicited, together with further distributional limitations, are given in §6.5-6 and individually in Part II.

1. i / ka[1]
2. ul / lul[2]
3. ulo / lo
   ulo se / lo se
   ulo sse / lo sse
4. ey
   ey 'ta (ka)
5. eykey; [honorific] kkey
6. hanthey
7. poko
8. tele
9. kkaci
10. se
    ey se
    eykey se, hanthey se; kkey se
11. puthe
12. iya / ya
13. man (also adjectival noun)
14. mankhum, manchi
15. khenyeng

16. mata
17. ssik
18. ccum
19. un / nun³
20. to
21. cocha
22. mace (variant maca)
23. pota (also [written-style] adverb)
24. chelem
25. kwa / wa
26. hako
27. sekken
28. ilang / lang (= sekken; = kwa / wa)
29. ullang / llang (= un / nun)
30. ko (after verb forms in indirect quotations)
31. iyo / yo
32. kwulye (after verb forms)
33. kkwuna (as particle, only after -ca)
34. uy
35. ci (= uy in Chinese clichés)
36. a / ya
37. una / na (after interjections, -key, -ulyem)
38. la (only after -e/a)
39. tul (also postnoun, adverb)
40. son (only after -ta; also postmod) [obsolete]
41. ppun (only after -ta; also postnoun, postmod)
42. nāyci (NUMBER$_1$ ~ NUMBER$_2$)
43. (-ulq ci) enceng
44. (-ki nun) sāylo (ey) / sāylye

¹ In the standard language i follows a consonant and the suppletive ka follows a vowel. But in some northern dialects i or its reduction y occurs after vowels, too, and that is the regular pattern found in the early Hankul texts. There are cases, especially in the north, of pleonastic ⋯ i ka (but no *⋯ ka ka or *⋯ ka i) which suggest that the ka may have been added for emphasis; the standard nay ka 'I' for na ka (a common dialect version) probably represents that formation, as do ney ka 'you' (dialect ne ka), cey ka 'I [formal]' (dialect ce ka) and dialect nwi ka for standard nwu ka 'who'. The 15th-century forms of these words were ˙nay (1447 Sek 6:14b, 6:19b, 6:24:29b) < ˙na ˙i, ¨ney < ne ˙i (1447 Sek 6:1a), ¨cey (1447 Sek 9:14a, 9:21a – correcting Martin 1988, which copied a misprint in NKW) < ce ˙i, and ¨nwuy (1449 Kok 36) < nwu ˙i.

² In Cincwu (South Kyengsang) lo is used for lul but ul is never said as ulo (Mkk 1960:3:31). In parts of the north people drop the final liquid and say lu for lul and u for ul. Some of the northern dialects use (u)lwu or (u)lu for (u)lo, so that for certain speakers the form used for the standard ul / lul may converge with that used for ulo / lo after a vowel or the liquid. The shape lul readily abbreviates to just l' and both versions coexisted in the first Hankul texts and apparently also in the language of the 12th century and earlier, if our interpretations of the hyangka orthography are correct. See note 3.

³ The shape nun readily abbreviates to just n' and both versions coexisted in the first Hankul texts and earlier materials, as did l' and lul. For both these particles it is usually assumed that the short form represents the original morpheme and the full form iterates (reduplicates) that. CF Kim Wancin 1975.

The last three cases (42, 43, 44) are somewhat anomalous. Apparently they are always in close juncture with the preceding phrase, so they are treated by most Korean dictionaries as particles rather than, say, as bound nouns or adverbs. Compare the note on kot in Part II.

Nouns of relative location, such as wi 'atop, above', alay 'below', and yeph 'beside', are not treated as particles. In chayk-sang wi ey 'on top of the desk' only the ey is a particle, and the preceding expression is NOUN + NOUN for two reasons:

(1) we can say just wi ey 'on top' without a preceding noun (but of course 'on top' implies 'on top of SOMETHING'), and wi occurs in other positions as a free noun, though not modified by an adnoun or verb modifier (so that in ku wi 'on top of that' ku is a noun, as it is in ku man 'just that');

(2) 'above me' is nay wi ey not *na wi ey. The same is true of yeph (ey) 'beside': nay yeph (ey) 'beside me' shows that yeph is a noun even though tangsinq yeph 'beside you' and wuli yeph 'beside us' might leave one wondering whether it is not a postnoun or particle. There are dialects (such as that of Taykwu) in which na yeph, na wi, etc., are used instead of the forms with nay, but speakers of those dialects say na chayk for 'my book'. For such dialects, the fact that wi and yeph can begin a sentence is sufficient criterion to establish that they are not postnouns or particles. Nouns of relative location can be thought of as distilled from a kind of semantic predication that locates one noun with

respect to another. Other such nouns: **an** 'inside' (something rather empty), **sōk** '(deep) inside' (something rather full), **kawuntey** 'inside; between, among', **sai** 'between, among; midst, during', **cwung** 'midst, among', **cwuwi** 'around (the periphery of)', **kyeth** 'beside, in the vicinity of', **mith** '(at) the base/bottom of; beneath', **aph** 'in front of; (= **cen**) before, ahead of', **twī** 'behind; (= **hwū**) after, later than', ... By their meaning ('between, among') some of these words locate a noun with respect to two or more other nouns.

Moreover each of the particles listed as occurring with nouns is sometimes preceded by at least one other member of the same list. That is the ultimate distributional fact that determines the list.

6.5. Particle sequences.

Particles occur in sequences of two (**eykey se**), three (**eykey se nun**), and even four (**ey se puthe uy**) or, rarely, more (**ccum ey se pota to**, ...). The longer sequences usually end with one of the particles **un/nun, to**, or **uy**. In my analysis the constituency cut is always between the particle on the right and the remainder of the phrase, so that each particle "peels off" in turn from the right. Yet even though this analysis does not treat the particles in sequence as in construction with each other, it is interesting to see what sequences can be found. I have looked for all possible shorter combinations and tried to elicit those which I could not find in texts. Some sequences alleged to exist (e.g. by CM) are rejected because I have been unable to elicit satisfactory examples. Among these are:

?* chelem iya mal lo; (ey) se lul; (ey) se lo, ey wa; ina to,
 pota 'na, pota uy, pota chelem, pota kkaci, pota ya mal lo,
 man iya mal lo, tele 'na-ma to, tele uy, ulo lul, ulo wa.

The sequences that have been found are supplied with substantiating examples in the entries of Part II. Here part of that information is recapitulated in a different form.

Ignoring for the moment certain synonyms, such as the colloquial synonym **hanthey** for **eykey**, and less interesting forms, such as **poko** and **tele** for only some of the uses of **eykey**, we will examine the sequences of particles that have been found to occur after nouns and include the copula forms **ila to, ina(-ma), in tul, itun ci**, and **(i)ta (ka)** as if they were particles. Some of the strings are rare, and some of the examples are extremely colloquial. Certain sequences could be elicited only in sentences that speakers considered "awkward". Undoubtedly there are sequences that have been missed; in particular, I would expect to find more with final **un/nun** and **to**, since I did not try to elicit all possible longer sequences with those two particles. Some of the sequences with **i/ka** as the last member are obtainable only with the copula negative construction ··· **i/ka ani 'ta** (SEE remarks at end of §11.7.2) and these are marked "N". In the lists I have used the designations **eykey, (k)wa**, and **sekken** to include sequences that were actually found with the more common Seoul colloquial forms **hanthey, hako**, and **ilang/lang** (respectively). The more exact information given in Part II suggests that a few of the colloquial versions, because of the relative infrequency of the sequence, are rejected in favor of the less colloquial synonyms; see, for example, the notes on **man kwa** (→ **man hako**), **kwa kkaci** (→ **hako kkaci**). Although **hako** occurs more freely than **kwa/wa**, certain extended particle phrases (§6.3), because of their stiff and literary flavor, take only **kwa/wa**: you do not hear **hako** taking the place of the less colloquial particle in ··· **kwa/wa tongsi ey** 'at the same time (together) with ··· '.

In the two lists that follow, the sequences are given alphabetically: in the first list by the prior member, in the second by the latter member. Each particle is listed by its postconsonantal shape even though the other shape might be appropriate to the particular sequence, so that **eykey + (k)wa = eykey wa, eykey + i/ka = eykey ka**. Space within two-word units is here shown as "_".

It will be seen that virtually no other particle ever follows these markers:

 i/ka (But there are examples of **i/ka tul** in Part II. And see **-ta ka ka** in §6.6; this may be an
  argument against that analysis.)
 ul/lul (But there are examples of **ul tul** in Part II.)

uy
to (But there are examples of **to tul** in Part II.)
iya (mal lo)
ila_to
ina (But there are examples of **ina lul** and **ina tul** in Part II.)
ina-ma
ita_(ka) (But there is an example of **'ta ka tul** in Part II.) Contrast **-ta (ka)**, which can be followed by **(n)un, to, tul, (i)ya**, and even **ka**.
itun_ci

The particle **un / nun** is followed only by **khenyeng** or by **tul**, and **khenyeng** is followed only by **un / nun** or by **tul**. That means it is possible to get ⋯ **un / nun khenyeng un**, as in the following (perhaps somewhat unlikely) sentence: **Cel.yak ulo ey ya māl lo nun khenyeng (un) hana to ēps.ta** 'Far from being a matter of economizing on them, I just haven't got a single one'. The particle **ssik** is preceded only by **ccum**; the particle **mankhum** is preceded only by **chelem, eykey**, and **kkaci**. In older usage, **mata** is preceded only by **ccum** but modern usage prefers the order **eykey mata, (ey) se mata**, and **eykey se mata (kkey se mata)** to the older usage with **mata** first; and rather than **mata ey** the modern usage prefers simply **mata**. That leaves **ssik eykey** and perhaps **ccum eykey** as the only sequences with a particle preceding **eykey**.

Every particle that occurs after a noun is sometimes preceded by at least one other particle. That criterion alone is sufficient to distinguish a particle from a postnoun.

The list of particles excludes the sequence **kkey se** (honorific oblique subject); it has the same following partners as **se** alone, and additionally also **i / ka, mata**, and **sekken**. In Seoul **sekken** is usually replaced by the synonym **ilang**; I have assumed that the distribution is the same in the same meaning. (The particle **ilang** is also used as a synonym of **hako** = **kwa / wa** 'with'.) Like **eykey (se)**, the sequence **kkey se** is preceded only by the particles **ssik** and **mata**, and modern usage refers **kkey se mata**. Not included are strings with **ppun (man)** 'only' such as **ulo se ppun** and **ey se ppun man**, which will be found in Part II. Notice also (in Part II) the unusual sequences **ulo sse (nun)** and **iya mal lo**, as well as the written-style strings **ey iss.e se ('na, nun, uy)**.

There are pairs in contrasting or competing order:

cocha mace	: (mace cocha)
ccum chelem	: chelem ccum
ccum eykey	: eykey ccum
ccum ssik	: ssik ccum
ey cocha	: cocha ey [rare]
ey kkaci	: kkaci ey
ey man	: man ey
eykey ccum	: ccum eykey
se (k)wa	: (k)wa se [rare]
ulo kkaci	: kkaci lo
ulo man	: man ulo
kwa man	: man kwa (→ man hako)

We can add the cases with **mata** mentioned earlier:

eykey mata	: (mata eykey)
ey se mata	: (mata ey se)
eykey se mata	: (mata eykey se)
kkey se mata	: (mata kkey se)

There are longer sequences such as:

kkaci ey se mace : ey se kkaci mace.

A Reference Grammar of Korean

6.5.1. List of particle sequences arranged by prior member.

ccum –	chelem	chelem iya		
	cocha	cocha to		
	ey	ey (i)na		
		ey se	ey se pota	ey se pota to
	eykey			
	i (/ka)			
	ila_to			
	ina			
	ina-ma			
	in_tul			
	iya			
	kkaci	?kkaci (i /) ka		
		kkaci (i)ya		
		kkaci man		
		kkaci (n)un		
		kkaci to		
	mace	mace to		
	man	man ila_to		
		man un		
	mankhum	mankhum ina		
	mata			
	pota	pota (n)un		
		pota to		
	puthe	puthe (i /) ka		
		puthe (n)un		
		puthe se		
	se	se pota	se pota (n)un	
		se puthe	se puthe (i /) ka	
			se puthe (n)un	
	ssik	ssik ila_to		
		ssik ina(-ma)		
		ssik man	ssik man ila_to	
		ssik ulo	ssik ulo to	
		ssik un		
	to			
	ul			
	ulo			
	un			
	uy			
chelem –	ccum	ccum ila_to		
		ccum ina(-ma)		
		ccum in_tul		
		ccum iya		
		ccum man	ccum man un	
		ccum kkaci	ccum kkaci ka	
			ccum kkaci (i)la_to	
			ccum kkaci (i)n_tul	

		ccum kkaci (i)ya	
		ccum kkaci man	ccum kkaci man un
	cocha	ccum kkaci to	
	ila_to		
	ina(-ma)		
	in_tul		
	iya		
	khenyeng		
	kkaci	kkaci (i)ya	
		kkaci (n)un	
	mace	mace to	
	man	man ila_to	
		man to	
		man un	
	mankhum	mankhum ila_to	
		mankhum ina(-ma)	
		mankhum in_tul	
		mankhum iya	
		mankhum man	
		mankhum to	
		mankhum un	
	pota	pota (n)un	
	puthe		
	to		
	un		
cocha —	ey [rare]		
	(i /) ka		
	ila_to		
	(i)na(-ma)		
	(i)ya		
	mace		
		?puthe (i /) ka	
	to		
	(l)ul		
	(u)lo		
	(n)un		
	?uy		
ey —	chelem		
	cocha		
	(i /) ka		
	(i)la_to		
	(i)na(-)ma		
	(i)n_tul		
	(i)ta(_ka)		
	(i)ya		
	khenyeng		
	kkaci		
	(k)wa		

A Reference Grammar of Korean

	mace		
	man		
	pota		
	puthe		
	se	se chelem	
		se cocha	
		se (i /) ka N	
		se (i)na(-ma)	
		se (i)n_tul	
		se (i)ya	
		se khenyeng	
		se kkaci	se kkaci mace
		se (k)wa	
		se mace	se mace puthe
		se man	se man ila_to
		se mankhum	
		se mata	
		se pota	
		se puthe	se puthe (i /)ka
			se puthe to
			se puthe (n)un
			se puthe uy
		se sekken	
		se to	
		se tul	
		se (n)un	se (n)un khenyeng
		se uy	
	sekken		
	to		
	(l)ul		
	(u)lo	(u)lo uy	
	(n)un	(n)un khenyeng	
	uy		
eykey –	ccum	ccum iya	
	chelem		
	cocha		
	(i /) ka N		
	(i)la_to		
	(i)na(-ma)		
	(i)n_tul		
	(i)ta(_ka)		
	(i)ya	(i)ya tul	
	khenyeng		
	kkaci		
	(k)wa		
	mace		
	man	man i(/ka)	
		man ila_to	
		?man to	
		?man un	
	mankhum	mankhum man	mankhum man un

	mata		
	pota	pota to	
	puthe		
	se	se chelem	se chelem man
		se cocha	
		se (i)ka	
		se (i)la_to	
		se (i)na(-ma)	
		se (i)n tul	
		(i)ta(_ka)	
		se (i)ya	
		se (k)wa	
		se mace	
		se man	se man to
			se man un
		se mata	
		se pota	se pota to
		se puthe	se puthe (i /) ka
		se to	
		se tul	
	sekken	se (n)un	
	to		
	tul		
	(l)ul		
	(u)lo	(u)lo puthe	
		(u)lo uy	
	(n)un		
	uy		
kkaci –	ccum	ccum un	
	cocha	cocha to	
	ey	ey se	
		ey (n)un	ey se mace
	(i /) ka		
	(i)la_to		
	(i)na(-ma)		
	?(i)n_tul		
	(i)tun_ci		
	(i)ya	(i)ya mal_lo	
	khenyeng		
	mace		
	man	man ila_to	
	se		
	to		
	tul		
	(l)ul		
	(u)lo		
	(n)un		
	uy		

A Reference Grammar of Korean

```
kwa –       ccum
            chelem      chelem man
            cocha
            ey
            (i /) ka
            (i)la_to
            (i)na
            (i)ya
            kkaci       kkaci (l)ul
            mace        mace to
            man         ?(man ulo)        man ulo (n)un
                        man un
            pota
            puthe
            se [rare]
            to
            tul
            (l)ul
            (u)lo [rare]  (u)lo nun
            (n)un
            uy

mace –      (cocha)
            (i /) ka
            (i)la_to
            (i)na-ma
            (i)n_tul
            ?(i)ya
            man
            puthe       puthe (i /) ka
            to
            (l)ul
            (n)un
            uy

man –       ey
            i (/ ka)
            ila_to
            ina(-ma)
            in_tul
            iya
            ?kwa→hako
            to
            ul
            ulo         ulo nun
                        ulo uy
            un
            uy
```

204 PART I A Reference Grammar of Korean

```
mankhum  –  (cocha)
             i (/ ka)
             ila_to
             ina(-ma)
             ?in_tul
             iya
             man              man ila_to
             ssik
             to
             ul
             un

mata     –  (ey)             (ey se)
             (eykey)          (eykey se)
             (*)(i /) ka
             (i)na
             (i)ya
             khenyeng
             kkaci
             (k)wa
             man
             pota
             puthe
             se
             (?)to
             (l)ul
             (u)lo
             (n)un            (n)un khenyeng
             uy

pota     –  (i)la_to
             ?(i)na-ma
             (i)ya            (i)ya mal_lo
             khenyeng
             man
             to
             (n)un
             uy

puthe    –  cocha
             (i /) ka
             (i)la_to
             (i)na(-ma)
             (i)ya
             khenyeng
             man
             pota
             se
             to
             tul
```

A Reference Grammar of Korean

	(l)ul	
	(n)un	
	uy	
se –	chelem	
	cocha	
	(i /) ka N	
	(i)la_to	
	(i)na(-ma)	
	(i)n_tul	
	(i)tun_ci	
	(i)ya	
	khenyeng	
	kkaci	
	(k)wa	
	mace	
	man	
	mankhum	
	pota	
	puthe	puthe (n)un
	sekken	
	to	
	tul	
	(n)un	(n)un khenyeng
	uy	

NOTE: Also found are **kkey se ka** and **kkey se sekken**.

sekken –	ccum	ccum iya
	cocha	
	iya	
	khenyeng	
	kkaci	
	mace	
	man	
	pota	pota to
	puthe	
	tul	
	ul	
	un	un khenyeng
ssik –	uy [rare]	
	ccum	
	chelem	
	cocha	
	eykey	
	i (/ ka)	
	ila_to	
	ina(-ma)	
	in_tul	
	iya	
	khenyeng	
	kkaci	kkaci (i)la_to
		kkaci (n)un

	kwa	
	mace	
	pota	
	puthe	
	to	
	ul	
	ulo	
	un	un khenyeng
	uy	
ulo −	(i /) ka N	
	(i)la_to	
	(i)na(-ma)	
	(i)ya	(i)ya mal_lo
	kkaci	
	mace	
	man	
	pota	
	puthe	puthe (i /) ka
	se	se mankhum
		se (i)ya
		se (i /) ka
		se pota se pota to
		se to
		se (n)un
		se uy
	sekken	
	to	
	(n)un	
	uy	

6.5.2. List of particle sequences arranged by latter member.

− ccum	chelem	
	eykey	
	kkaci	
	kwa	
	sekken	
	ssik	
− chelem	ccum	
	ey	
	eykey	
	kwa	
	mankhum	
	se	ey se
		eykey se
	ssik	
− cocha	ccum	
	chelem	

A Reference Grammar of Korean

	ey		
	eykey		
	kkaci		
	kwa		
	(mace)		
	puthe		
	se	ey se	
		eykey se	
	sekken		
	ssik		
	ulo		
– ey			
	ccum		
	cocha [rare]		
	kkaci		
	kwa		
	man		
– eykey	mata		
	(ccum)		
	(mata)		
	ssik		
– i / ka			
	ccum		
	cocha		
	ey		
	eykey N		
	kkaci	?ccum kkaci	
	kwa		
	mace		
	man	eykey man	
	mankhum		
	mata		
	puthe	ccum puthe	
		(cocha puthe)	
		eykey puthe	
		mace puthe	
		se puthe	ey se puthe
			eykey se puthe
		ulo puthe	
	se N	ey se N	
	ssik		
	ulo N		

NOTE: Also found is kkey se ka.

– ila_to	ccum	chelem ccum	
	chelem		
	cocha		
	ey		
	eykey		
	kkaci	?ccum kkaci	chelem ccum kkaci

	kwa		
	mace		
	man	ccum man	
		kkaci man	
		mankhum man	
		ssik man	
	mankhum		
	pota		
	puthe		
	se	ey se	
		eykey se	
	ssik	ccum ssik	
	ulo		
− (i)na	ccum		
	chelem		
	cocha		
	?ey	ccum ey	
	eykey		
	kkaci		
	kwa		
	man		
	mankhum	ccum mankhum	
	mata		
	puthe		
	se		
	ssik		
	ulo		
− (i)na-ma	ccum		
	chelem		
	ey		
	eykey		
	kkaci		
	mace		
	man	eykey man	
	pota		
	puthe		
	se	ey se	
		eykey se	
	ssik		
	ulo		
− (i)n_tul	ccum	chelem ccum	
	chelem		
	ey		
	eykey		
	?kkaci	ccum kkaci	
	mace		
	man		
	?mankhum	chelem mankhum	

A Reference Grammar of Korean

	puthe		
	se	ey se	
		eykey se	
	ssik		
– (i)ta(_ka)	ey		
	eykey		
	ulo		
– (i)tun_ci	kkaci		
	se		
– (i)ya	ccum	chelem ccum	
		eykey ccum	
	chelem		
	cocha		
	ey		
	eykey	ccum eykey	
	kkaci	ccum kkaci	
	kwa		
	mace		
	man		
	mankhum		
	mata		
	pota		
	puthe		
	se	ey se	
		eykey se	
	sekken		
	ssik		
	ulo		
– khenyeng	chelem		
	ey		
	eykey		
	kkaci		
	mata		
	pota		
	puthe		
	se	ey se	
	sekken		
	ssik		
	un	ey (n)un	ey se (n)un
		mata (n)un	
		se (n)un	
		sekken un	
		ssik un	

– kkaci	ccum		
	chelem		
	ey		
	eykey		
	kwa		
	mata		
	se	ey se	
	sekken		
	ssik		
– (k)wa	ey		
	eykey		
	man		
	mata		
	se	ey se	kkaci ey se
		eykey se	
	ssik		
– mace	ccum		
	chelem		
	cocha		
	ey		
	eykey		
	kkaci		
	kwa		
	se		
		ey se	
		eykey se	
	sekken		
	ssik		
	ulo		
– mankhum	ccum		
	chelem		
	se	ey se	
		ulo se	
– mata	ccum		
	ey		
	eykey		
		ey se	
		ulo se	
– pota	ccum		
	ey		
	eykey		
	kwa		
	mata		
	puthe		
	se	ey se	
	sekken		

A Reference Grammar of Korean

	ssik			
	ulo			
— puthe	ccum			
	ey			
	eykey			
	kwa			
	mace		ey se mace	
	mata			
	se	ey se		
	sekken			
	ssik			
	ulo			
— se	ccum			
	ey	ccum ey		
		mata ey		
	eykey			
	kwa [rare]			
	mata			
	puthe			
	ulo			
— sekken	ey			
	eykey			
	se	ey se		
	ulo			
— ssik	ccum			
— to	ccum			
	chelem			
	cocha	ccum cocha		
		kkaci cocha		
		mankhum cocha		
	ey			
	eykey			
	kkaci	ccum kkaci	chelem ccum kkaci	
	kwa			
	mace	ccum mace		
		kwa mace		
	man	eykey man	eykey se man	
	mankhum			
	mata			
	pota	ccum pota		
		se pota	ey se pota	ccum ey se pota
		sekken pota		
	puthe			
	se	ey se		
		eykey se		
		ulo se		

	ssik		
	ulo	ssik ulo	
– (l)ul	ccum		
	cocha		
	ey		
	eykey		
	kkaci	kwa kkaci	
	kwan		
	mace		
	man		
	mankhum		
	mata		
	puthe		
	sekken		
	ssik		
– (u)lo	ccum		
	cocha		
	ey		
	eykey		
	kkaci		
	kwa [rare]		
	man	?(kwa man)	
	mata		
	ssik		
– (n)un	ccum	chelem ccum	
		kkaci ccum	
	chelem		
	cocha		
	ey	kkaci ey	
	eykey		
	kkaci	ccum kkaci	
		ssik kkaci	
	kwa		
	mace		
	man	ccum man	eykey se man
		kwa man	
	mankhum		
	mata		
	pota	se pota	
	puthe	ccum puthe	
		se puthe	ey se puthe
	se	ey se	
		eykey se	
		ulo se	
	sekken		
	ssik	ccum ssik	

	ulo	kwa (u)lo	
	man ulo	kwa man ulo	
– uy	ccum		
	cocha		
	ey		
	eykey		
	kkaci		
	kwa		
	mace		
	man		
	mata		
	pota		
	puthe	se puthe	ey se puthe
	se	ey se	
	sekken [rare]		
	ssik		
	ulo	ey (u)lo	
		eykey (u)lo	
		man ulo	

6.6. Sequences of ending + particle.

Some of the particles listed in §6.4 occur in quite limited environments, and a few are found only after verb forms. For example, una / na is found only after -ulyem, -key, and -sey; ppun and son (as particles) only after -ta; kkwuna only after -ca; kwulye (as particle) only after statement forms -sup.nita and -ney (and ilq sey = iney), suggestion forms -upsita and -sey, command forms -usio and -key; la only after the infinitive -ᵉ/a. The particle that marks indirect quotation ko '(saying / thinking that ...)' is used after plain quotation forms -(nun)ta 'does / is', -tula 'was (doing it), I recall', -ca 'let's', -la 'do!'; after the intentive -ulye 'intending / wanting to do'; after the adjunctives -nula and -ulla; and after the postmodifier ya 'question' that appears in -un ya, -nun ya, -tun ya, ... Only a few verb forms are never followed by a particle, notably the sequential -uni, for the strings /-unipota/ and /-unimankhum/ represent -un i pota / mankhum with the particle attached to a modifier + the postmodifier i 'fact (that ···)'. Certain endings are followed by only a few particles or quasi-particles:

-ule / -le is followed by (un /)nun, to, tul, and (ul /)lul;
-una / -na is followed by tul and awkwardly by (i)la to and (i)tun ci (see also ina tul in Part II);
-una-ma is followed by yo and somewhat awkwardly by to;
-(nun)ta is followed by ko, tul, and man;
-ney is followed by tul, man, and kwulye;
-so / -o is followed by tul and man;
-kwun is followed by a;
-keni is followed by (kwa /)wa.

The particle tul '(acting) severally' can be inserted rather freely in verb phrases, but not even it can be inserted into the fixed sequences -e la, -ta ppun, -ta kwulye, and -ca kkwuna. Where tul goes is after the other particles in those cases, as well as in -e yo (tul) 'do / are severally' [polite] and -ta ko (tul) hanta 'says that they do / are'. Although -(sup)nita tul occurs, it cannot be quoted as such, even directly; there is no *-ta tul hako (or ila ko) hanta. And notice that it is NOUN tul iyo rather than *NOUN iyo tul in fragment sentences such as Nwukwu tul iyo 'Who all?' [polite].

Verb forms have not been found before the particles eykey 'to (a person)', ssik 'each', or sekken 'and the like', nor before the quasi-particle ina-ma 'at least, even'. Of these, sekken is the only one that is likely to turn up, if we keep looking. I was able to elicit the particle mata 'every' only after

-umye, and in an awkward example at that. The particle **uy** 'of' was elicitable only after the summative **-ki**; the particle **(k)wa** 'with' only after **-ki** or in extended particle phrases (§6.3) after the substantive ending **-um**. The poorer distribution of **-um** is unsurprising, for it is less colloquial than **-ki**.

The table on p. 215 shows the sequences found or elicited for most of the particles and quasi-particles after common verb endings. Sequences for which I have only awkward examples are indicated by "x" instead of "+". Sequences with the particle **i / ka** that seem to be available only when followed by the negative copula are noted by "N". The table is so arranged that the particles form a vertical axis, and are arrayed alphabetically by the postconsonantal shape as in earlier lists. The endings form the horizontal axis, and at the appropriate intersection each sequence discovered or elicited is indicated by a "+", those unfound by a "−". Notice that the list is largely limited to sequences of just ONE particle after an ending; there are longer sequences and they are not limited to those here shown in more detail for **se** only. We can find not only **-ki ey** but also **-ki ey to**, **-ki ey nun**, **-ki ey ya**, **-ki ey tul**, **-ki ey pota**, **-ki ey sekken**; not only **-ci yo** but **-ci yo man** and **-ci yo man un**. And many cases of ending + **man** can be followed by **un** or **to**.

6.7. Some consequences of particle distribution.

When we look at the particle sequences found after nouns and after verb forms, certain things come to our attention. The particle **se** is frequently preceded by the particle **ey** after nouns; often the same expression may be said with or without the intervening **ey**, the meaning unchanged. But in some cases, including the summative **-ki** and the substantive **-um**, the expression is awkward (or unheard of) without the intervening **ey**. In other cases, such as the verb forms **-e se**, **-ko se**, and **-umyen se**, it is the intervening **ey** that is unheard of. These facts, I think, are what leads the Korean grammarians (in disregard of **eykey se** and **hanthey se**) to set up a single particle **eyse** and treat **se** (after a noun) as an abbreviation of that particle. The **se** which occurs after verb endings is treated either as a separate particle or as part of an unanalyzed ending that is distinct from the form without the particle. (A case could be made that **-e** is an abbreviation of **-e se**, but no one has claimed that, so far as I know.) We can also see why the Korean grammarians would hesitate to accept **la** in **-e la** as a particle, since nothing can intervene between the infinitive and the particle, and **la** occurs as a particle only after the infinitive, which actually turns up in a variant "pre-la" shape after certain stems: **one la** for **wā la**, **kake la** for **ka la**, **iss.ke la** for **iss.e la**, ... (§8.3.6). In fact, **-e la** developed from MK -ˊ(k)e-ˋla with the imperative ending attached to the bound stem that marked the effective aspect, and **one la** < ˋwo-ˋna-ˋla contains a suppletive form of that aspect marker.

The grammarians' preferred treatment of some of the uses of **-ki ey**, **-ki lo**, **-um ey** (= **-umay**), and **-um ulo** as single unanalyzable endings, distinct from ending + particle, is supported by certain of the particle sequences. And their preference for treating the transferentive **-ta** as an abbreviation of an unanalyzed ending **-taka**, rather than analyzing that as the assertive **-ta** + particle **ka** (as it is here viewed), is perhaps supported by the recurrence of the particle **ka** in the sequence **-ta ka ka**, even though that is a by-product of the negative copula. (There are historical arguments against the analysis of **-ta ka**, too, but the matter remains open. See §9.8 and Part II; for MK accent evidence, see p. 71.)

The treatment of certain forms of the copula as particles is also supported by particle sequences. The "quasi-particles" included in the sequence tables occur freely in positions where other forms of the copula would be unusual or impossible. (We are, of course, here excluding from our discussions of distribution certain kinds of peripheral utterances, such as those that occur when talking ABOUT words.)

It will be noticed that certain "particles" after verb endings (**kwulye**, **kkwuna**, **una / na**, **la**, **son**, **ppun**) differ from particles after nouns in that no other particle is insertible, and that mutual insertibility was our ultimate criterion for being sure that an element after a noun really IS a particle. In a sense, what we do is to establish a class of noun particles on that basis, then we notice that some of these particles (**se**, **iya / ya**, **iyo / yo**, ...) also occur after verb endings, with greater restrictions, and finally we discover that a few other elements, still more restricted, seem to belong in the same class, because they occur after verb endings that are otherwise free.

A Reference Grammar of Korean

TABLE OF VERB ENDINGS + PARTICLES AND QUASI-PARTICLES

	-ca	-ci	-e	-key	-ki	-ko	-ta_ka	-tolok	-tula	-ulye	-umye	-umyen	-um
ccum	–	–	+	+	+	X	–	+	–	+	+	+	–
chelem	–	–	+	–	–	–	+	–	–	+	+	+	+
cocha	X	–	+	+	+	X	+	+	+	+	+	+	+
ey	–	–	–	–	+	–	–	–	–	–	–	–	–
i/ka	N	+	+	+	+	+	N	N	–	+	N	N	+
(i)la_to	–	–	+	+	+	+	–	–	–	+	+	+	+
(i)na	+	+	+	+	+	+	+	+	+	+	+	+	+
(i)n_tul	–	?	+	+	+	+	+	+	+	+	+	+	+
(i)ta_ka	–	–	+	+	–	+	–	+	–	+	+	+	–
(i)tun_ci	–	–	+	+	+	+	+	+	+	+	+	+	–
(i)ya	+	+	+	+	+	+	+	+	+	+	+	+	+
(i)yo	+	+	+	+	+	+	+	–	–	–	–	–	–
khenyeng	+	–	+	+	+	+	+	+	–	+	+	+	–
kkaci	+	+	+	+	+	+	+	+	+	+	+	+	+
kwa/wa	–	–	–	–	+	–	–	–	–	–	–	–	+
mace	–	–	+	+	+	+	+	–	–	+	+	+	+
man	–	+	+	+	+	+	+	+	–	+	+	+	+
mankhum	–	–	+	+	+	+	+	+	–	+	+	+	+
pota	–	–	+	+	+	+	+	+	–	+	+	+	+
puthe	+	+	+	+	+	+	+	+	–	+	+	+	+
se	–	–	+	–	–	–	–	–	–	+	+	+	+¹
se ka	–	N	–	–	–	–	–	–	–	–	–	N	–
se 'la_to	–	–	+	–	+	–	–	–	–	–	–	–	+
se 'na	–	–	+	–	–²	–	–	–	–	–	–	–	+
se 'n_tul	–	–	+	–	–²	?	–	–	–	–	–	N	+
se 'tun_ci	–	–	+	–	–²	–	–	–	–	–	–	–	–
se ya	–	–	+	–	–²	+	–	–	–	–	–	–	–
se man	–	–	+	–	–²	–	–	–	–	–	–	–	–
se puthe	–	–	+	–	–²	+	–	–	–	–	–	–	–
se to	–	–	+	–	–²	–	–	–	–	–	–	–	–
se nun	–	–	+	–	–²	–	–	–	–	–	–	–	+³
to	+	+	+	+	+	+	+	+	–	+	+	+	+
tul	+	+	+	+	+	+	+	+	–	+	+	+	+
ul/lul	+	+	+	+	+	+	+	+	–	+	+	+	+
ulo/lo	–	–	+	+	+	+	+	+	–	+	+	+	+
un/nun	–	+	+	+	+	+	+	+	–	+	+	+	+

¹ But **-um ey se** (···) occurs.

² Less awkward with **ey** inserted, but unlikely even so.

³ Also **-umyen se kkaci**, **-umyen se tul**.

7.0. Forms: verbs.

In the following sections we examine various kinds of verbs (§7.1), bound verbs (§7.2), verbs with defective paradigms (§7.3), derived stems that are causative or passive (§7.4), auxiliary verbs (§7.5), and postnominal verbs (§7.6).

7.1. Kinds of verbs.

Each verb may be classed as transitive (vt) or intransitive (vi), though a few stems serve both functions: **kuchinta** (vi/vt) means either 'ends it' or 'it ends'. A verb that is sometimes preceded by a direct object is transitive. All transitive verbs are also processive so that the opposing category of descriptive is relevant only for intransitive verbs.

A semantic direct object may be marked by the accusative particle **ul/lul**, but that particle is also used to mark other roles. If we use the cooccurrence of an accusative-marked phrase to categorize "transitive" verbs, we will have to recognize what I have called PSEUDO-INTRANSITIVE verbs (pseudo-vi), which function like those intransitive verbs that are seldom, if ever, preceded by an accusative-marked phrase. The accusative phrase could still be treated as an object, but the object is limited to certain kinds:

(1) a noun showing the destination: **hak.kyo lul kanta** = **hak.kyo ey kanta** 'goes to school, attends school'.

(2) a noun showing the purpose: **kwūkyeng ul kanta** = **kwūkyeng ul hale kanta** 'goes to see it';

(3) as an object complement, the substantive form of the same stem (or other semantically and/or etymologically cognate objects): **cam ul canta** = **canta** 'sleeps (one's sleep)', **chwum ul chwunta** = **chwunta** 'dances (a dance)', **kel.um ul kēt.nunta** = **kēt.nunta** 'walks (one's steps)', **kkwum ul kkwunta** 'dreams (a dream)', **wus.um ul wūs.nunta** 'laughs (a laugh)' (CF **sālam uy musik ul wūs.nunta** 'laughs at a person's ignorance', with a transitive use of the verb); *kichom kis.kwo* (1608 Twu-cip 1:10b; < *kich(i)-*) 'coughing (a cough)'. But notice that **kūlim ul kūlinta** 'draws (a drawing), paints (a painting)' and **cim ul cinta** 'bears a burden' are transitive verbs + tangible objects. There are also a few cognate subjects: **noph.i ka noph.ta** 'is high (in height)', **kiph.i ka kiph.ta** 'is deep (in depth)', **nelp.i ka nelp.ta** 'is wide (in width)', **khi ka khuta** 'is big (in bigness) = is tall (in stature)', **kil.i ka kīlta** 'is long (in length)'.

(4) an expression of duration: **sahul ul onta** 'comes for three days'.

(5) an expression of order or number of times: **ches-ccay lul kanta** 'goes first', **sēy pen ul kanta** 'goes three times'.

(6) a place traversed or a path traveled: **kang ul kēnne kanta** 'goes across the river', **kil ul kel.e kanta** 'walks (along) the road', **unhayng ul cīna kanta** 'passes the bank'.

(7) a quantified distance traversed: **chen-li lul ttwinta** 'leaps a thousand leagues'.

(8) an affected part of the body: **tali lul cēnta** 'limps (in a leg)'.

(9) substituting for some other particle in an unusual paraphrase: **swul ul chwī hanta** = **swul ey chwī hanta** 'gets drunk on liquor'. (But many, I am told, reject **ul** and prefer **swul i chwī hanta**).
Quite a few intransitive verbs take accusative-marked objects in specialized figurative senses, such as **su-** 'stand' in **aph-cang ul su-** 'stand in the van (in the lead)' and **Keki l' susye ya toykeyss.nun ya** 'Must you stand there?' Usually we can say that **ul/lul** in these expressions is simply substituting for some other particle, typically **ey**, or for a larger construction.

A verb is INTRANSITIVE if it is never preceded by a (semantic) direct object: **nuc-** 'be late', **cwuk-** 'die', **anc-** 'sit down', **iss-** 'stay'. Each of the intransitive verbs falls into one of the following classes. A PROCESSIVE verb lacks the category of plain indicative assertive **-ta**, replacing it by the processive assertive **-nunta/-nta**, except in literary Korean and in set literary phrases used in the colloquial. All transitive verbs are processive, but some of the intransitives are DESCRIPTIVE verbs — here called ADJECTIVES (adj). The reference is not so broad as suggested by the corresponding English category, which includes not only predicated adjectives but also many attributive terms that are treated as nouns or adnouns in Korean.

An adjective lacks the following paradigmatic forms:

(1) processive forms — the processive modifier **-nun**, the processive assertive **-nunta / -nta**, and the processive adjunctive **-nula**;

(2) the intentive (**-ulye / -lye**) and purposive (**-ule / -le**) forms;

(3) subjunctive forms — the subjunctive attentive (= imperative) **-ula**, the subjunctive assertive (= hortative or propositive) **-ca**, ...

But the subjunctive assertive **-ca** occasionally occurs in the meaning 'as soon as' even with adjectives, as in **nal i ttattus haca** 'as soon as the weather is warm', and in the meaning 'as well as (being)' even with the copula (see **ica** in Part II). And adjective stems sometimes appear in the construction **-e la**, normally expressing a plain command, but here carrying an exclamatory meaning 'is indeed': **Ai komawe la!** 'Heaven be praised! Thank goodness!', **Cham ulo tal.e la!** 'How sweet it is!', **Ai koso hay la!** 'Serves you right!'. Compare the copula form **ila**. It is unclear whether the bound particle **la** in the two meanings of **-e la** is a single etymon or has separate origins, nor do we know whether it comes from a reduction of the copula form in one or both of these usages, to say nothing of the imperative ending **-ula / -la** itself. Moreover, a few adjectival-noun constructions appear as genuine commands (**-e la**) and propositions (**-ca**), and in the intentive **-ulye** and purposive **-ule** forms. Acceptable examples are given by CM (1:425, 428-9, 435) for **chwungsil** 'being faithful', **co'.yong** 'being quiet', **täytam** 'being bold', and **minchep** 'being alert'. Co Sek.yen tells me she will accept **chwungsil hay la**, **chwungsil halye hanta**, etc., but rejects such forms as **chwungsil hale kanta** 'goes for the purpose of being faithful', a situation more processive in nature than 'goes with the intention of being faithful'. These few exceptions can simply be handled as semantic extensions or as abbreviations of some processive structure (with the meaning of 'acting, behaving' rather than 'being').

The COPULA (cop) is a descriptive verb (an adjective) which almost never occurs after pause, for it predicates a noun or noun phrase, with the meaning of 'it is ... ', 'it is a case (instance, kind) of ... ', 'it is identified or specified as ... ', or (after a nominalization) 'it's that ... '. The stem is **i-** (defective literary variant **ilo-**, defective formal variant **iolssi-**) after a consonant. After a vowel the initial /i/ is usually shortened to zero, i.e. dropped, when a consonant follows, as in **pata 'ta** = **pata ita** 'it's the sea'; when a vowel follows, the stem vowel is reduced to **y-**, as in **pata yess.ta** = **pata iess.ta** 'it was the sea', **pata ye (se)** = **pata ie (se)** 'it's the sea (and ...)'. In written Korean the **i-** after a vowel may or may not be reduced or dropped, but a full vowel syllable is usually written in forms that would otherwise leave a single consonant stranded: **im** (substantive), **in** (modifier), **il(q)** (prospective modifier). CF Mkk 1960:5:27. In addition to the various limitations of the adjective with respect to inflectional endings, the copula also lacks the projective and adverbative forms: we find no occurrences of ***itolok** 'to the point where it is ... ' or ***ikey** 'so that it is ... ', though Middle Korean had the expected forms.

At least fourteen stems underlie complete paradigms as both processive and descriptive verbs:

cala- 'reach, grow; be sufficient, enough'	**mac-** 'tally; be correct'
etwuw-[1] 'get dark; be dark'	**mulu-** 'get soft; be soft'
ha- 'do; be'	**nā(s)-** 'get better; be better'
huli- 'get cloudy; be cloudy'	**nuc-** 'get late; be late'
khu- 'get big; be big'	**nulk-**[3] 'get old; be old'
kiph-[2] 'get deep; be deep'	**palk-** 'get bright; be bright'
kwut- 'get hard; be hard'	**pulk-** 'get red; be red'
kyēysi- 'exist; stay' [honorific]	**tēlew-**[1] 'get dirty; be dirty'

[1] Some speakers reject **etwuw-** and **tēlew-** as processive verbs. Examples: **Nal i etwup.nunta — ppallay lul ketwe la** 'It's getting dark — gather the laundry up'; **Keki anc.ci mala — os i tēlep.nunta** 'Don't sit there — you'll get your clothes dirty'.

[2] Apparently **kiph-** is processive only in **pam i kiph.ess.ta** 'the night has deepened', perhaps by analogy with **nuc.ess.ta** 'it has gotten late'.

[3] For some speakers, at least.

With less predictable differences in meaning, certain SHAPES represent both processive verbs and adjectives: **kolu-** 'is even' or 'makes it even', **pet-** '(tooth) is protruding' or 'it stretches out; stretches it out', ... (See Appendix 1.)

The intransitive verbs **iss-** 'stay; exist, be located; have', **ēps-** 'not exist; not have', and tense markers deriving from **iss-** (the past **-ess-** and the future **-keyss-**) have all the processive forms EXCEPT the processive assertive, but **iss.nunta** occurs in the meaning 'stays' with the negative forms **mōs(q) iss.nunta** and **an iss.nunta** (see §11.7.3). For a plain-style statement 'exist, is (at); has' you use **iss.ta** not (*)**iss.nunta** and **ēps.ta** not *****ēps.nunta**. Yet in all meanings the processive modifier forms **iss.nun** and **ēps.nun** are more common than the simple modifiers **iss.un** and **ēps.un**, which they have largely replaced in standard speech. (But the simple modifiers are found in Phyengan; see Part II.) The preceding description is inadequate for modern Seoul speech (^{1}Yi Tongcay 1990), which differentiates **iss-$_1$** 'stay' from **iss-$_2$** (the other meanings) and treats it as a regular intransitive verb that shares most but not all of its paradigmatic forms with the quasi-processive verb. To reconcile the two descriptions, we might suggest that there are speakers, or at least writers, who replace **iss.nunta** 'stays' with the shorter **iss.ta** (which also has the other meanings), perhaps obligatorily in certain situations, such as quotations, and optionally in others, such as negatives. For ῭*eps-* the MK texts attest both the modifier ῭*ep˙sun* and (more often) the processive modifier ῭*ep˙non*; the predication can be negativized as ῭*ep˙ti a˙ni* ˚*ho-*, but I have not found **a˙ni* ῭*eps-*. For the stem *is(i)-* the modifier is *isin*, the prospective modifier is *isil(q)*; the processive modifier is *is.non* and its modulated form is *is˙nwon*. The predication can be negativized as *is˙ti a˙ni* ˚*ho-*, but I have not found (?*)*a˙ni is(i)-*. Examples of the Middle Korean forms will be found under their entries in Part II.

The past is simply **-ess.ta** and the future **-keyss.ta**, irrespective of whether the stem is processive or descriptive. These stems and markers seem to lack any use of the subjunctive forms, the intentive, or the purposive, except for **iss-** itself in the meaning 'stay', and they are not common even for it. These verbs and bound auxiliaries (the tense markers) can be called quasi-processive in their behavior; we will label them quasi-verbs intransitive (qvi). Ceng Insung 1960:262-3 neatly describes **iss-** as "a verb that lacks the form ***iss.nunta**" (but that is not true of modern Seoul speech) and **ēps-** as "an adjective that has the extra form **ēps.nun**". He says that the honorific **kyēysi-** is like **iss-**, yet I find that both **kyēysita** and **kyēysinta** are used for the plain present. The stem **ēps-** occurs in the construction **-e cinta** 'gets to be', normally limited to adjective stems though there are a few cases with intransitive processive verbs (see the entry in Part II); *****iss.e cinta** does not occur. Notice that **ēps-** has the derived adverb form **ēps.i** (< ῭*ep˙si*) 'without', but (*)**iss.i** (**i˙si*) 'with' occurs only in dialects (p. 584).

The stem **iss-** is particularly tricky; see p. 319 for evidence that it should be treated as three homonyms 'stays', 'is', and 'has'. In the meaning 'is' and 'has', the appropriate auxiliary for such nuclear focus conversions as V_1-**ki nun ha-** = V_1-**ki nun** V_1- is the descriptive **hata** (with the modifier **han** and not **hanun**), but in the meaning 'stays' the processive **hanta** (with the modifier **hanun**) is called for: **Cip ey iss.ula 'ni-kka iss.ki nun hanta man un ku sālam i olq ka?** 'Told to stay home, I do stay home but will he come?'; **Ku palam-cayngi ka cip ey kakkum iss.ki to hanun kes ul kkwum ey to mōllass.ta** 'I didn't even dream that playboy would stay home every now and then, too'. Japanese, on the other hand, uses the auxiliary <u>suru</u> (its counterpart of **hanta**) for **a˙r-** 'be' and 'have' as well as for [w]o˙r- or [w]i- 'stay': **a˙ri / [w]o˙ri wa suru**.

A CAUSATIVE verb (vc) is a transitive verb which is a member of a pair of stems that are related in shape. The other member of the pair is active: either transitive or intransitive, and if intransitive either processive or descriptive. The causative stem differs from the active stem by the suffixing of a causative formative, which has several different shapes (§7.4). Such verbs are LEXICAL causatives that must be listed in the dictionary; they are not freely derived. But most verbs can freely participate in a syntactic structure we will call the PERIPHRASTIC causative (**-key hanta**, etc.). On similarities and differences between these two kinds of causative, see §11.6.

A PASSIVE verb (vp) is a member of a shape-related pair, of which the active member is transitive and the passive member is usually an intransitive processive verb, but some passives take objects (see

§7.4, §11.6). The passive member is marked by a suffixed formative (§7.4). A CAUSATIVE verb is made by attaching a similar formative to the stem of an active verb, which may be intransitive or transitive. Reference here is to LEXICAL passive and causative verbs; they are listed in dictionaries, but you do not make up new ones. On the other hand, the periphrastic causative and passive structures are freely created as needed. See §11.6 for the voice conversions.

An AUXILIARY verb (aux) is used in close juxtaposition with some other verb, which is usually in the infinitive (-e/a) or gerund (-ko) form. The auxiliary conveys a somewhat different meaning from what its stem carries when it stands as an independent verb, if the stem can so be used. There are processive auxiliaries (= auxiliary verbs proper) and descriptive auxiliaries (= auxiliary adjectives). Some of the auxiliaries are SEPARABLE: a particle may intervene between the auxiliary and the verb form with which it is used. If nothing can intervene, the auxiliary is INSEPARABLE.

A POSTNOMINAL verb is a verb that is used in close juxtaposition with a verbal noun. SEPARABLE postnominal verbs (**ha-** 'be'; **ha-** 'do', **ka-** 'go', **sikhi-** 'cause', **toy-** 'become') are sometimes set apart from the verbal noun by a particle; INSEPARABLE postnominal verbs (**low-** 'be characterized by', **sulew-** 'be, give the impression of being', **taw-** 'be like'; **keli-** or **tāy-** 'behave so as to give the impression of') occur only right after the noun.

7.2. Bound verbs.

Certain verbs are always attached to some other verb, or to a noun. Among these BOUND VERBS, we can single out defective infinitives, bound adjectives, and bound postverbs (or verb suffixes).

7.2.1. Defective infinitives.

Most of the defective infinitives, recognizable by the characteristic infinitive ending **-e/-a** (§9.4), often preceded by **-(u)l-** (which seems to be some sort of formative), are inseparably attached to the auxiliary verbs **ci-** (vi) and **ttuli-** (vt):

ekule 'dislocate, go against'	**pekule** 'split, separate'
hay(e) 'wear (out)'	**pule** 'break'
hune 'demolish; collapse'	**pulke** 'bulge out'
kasule 'bristle'	**sakule/a** 'collapse, wither'
(k)kopule/a 'bend'	**sosule/a** 'frighten, startle'
okule, wukule 'curl up, warp; break'	**ssule** 'topple'
pasule, pusule 'break'	**thute/ttut.e** 'tear' [dialect] (= the < thu-)

But **(k)kiwul.e (ci-/ttuli-)** 'tilt' is the infinitive of an adjective **(k)kiwu-l-** 'tilted, aslant', and **mune (ci-/ttuli-)** 'demolish' is the infinitive of the transitive verb **mun(u)-** 'demolish'.

Five defective infinitives serve as verbal or adjectival nouns predicated by the postnominal verb/adjective stem **ha-**:

ile 'being/doing like this, so'	**ette** 'being/doing what way, how'
kule 'being/doing like that, so'	**āmule** 'being/?doing any way'
cele 'being/doing like that, so'	

The verbal use ('doing') for the first four was not present for the corresponding MK forms *i'le, ku'le, 'tye'le, "es'te*, and *"a'mo'la* (which is attested in very few forms), and it largely went unnoticed until quite recently.

Only two defective infinitives seem to have other (also inseparable) attachments: **kule** 'dragging, pulling' — apparently from an unattested variant of **kkul.e** 'pulling' (coming from a formation made on the prospective modifier *ku[z]ul(q)* of MK *kuz-*), in **kule mou-** 'rake up', **kule tangki-** 'gather and pull', **kule cap-** 'grasp, clutch', ... ; and **wule** 'coming off and/or up', which is probably an abbreviation of **wulele** ← **wulelu-** 'lift one's head up', in **wule na-** 'soak out', and **wule na-o-** 'spring/well up'. We might want to include here certain elements of obscure or aberrant etymology such as **kala-(anc-** 'sink'); **kalma-(tu-l-** 'alternate'); **kelme-(ci-** 'shoulder, bear'); **kelthe-(anc-** 'sit astride', **tha-** 'mount astride', **tul.i-** 'bring it all in', **mek-** 'gobble it all up'); **pe/alke-(pes-** 'strip naked'); **cwuce-(anc-** 'slump, fall, cease').

The Hankul orthography treats none of these bound elements as infinitives, so it fails to set off the -e/a ending in any of them, and our Romanization neglects the boundaries, too.

7.2.2. Bound adjectives.

Certain elements, usually treated by Korean grammarians as suffixes, derive adjectives from inflected stems (and, in some cases, bound nouns). They are described in these entries of Part II:

- **-ta(h)-, -tala(h)-** 'be rather ... '
- **-a(h)- / -e(h)-** 'be rather ... '
- **-tama(h)-**, abbreviation of **-tama ha-** (bound adjectival noun, §5.6.5)
- **-ep-** (variants **-up-, -ap-**) / **-p-** = **-ew- (-uw-, -aw-) / -w-**
- **-pu-** (derives adjectives from adjectives, verbs, bound nouns)

7.2.3. Bound postverbs.

By bound postverb we refer to certain formatives that are suffixed to verb stems to form new stems, usually intensive, causative, or passive:

INTENSIVE	-chi-	-li-
	-chwu-	-lu-
	-khi-	
CAUSATIVE, PASSIVE	-chwu-	-li-
	-hwu- (spelled -chwu-)	-(i)wu-
	-chi-	-wu-
	-i-	-kwu-
	-hi-	-ay-
	-ki-	-y-
	-ukhi-	-u-
	-ikhi-	

For details and examples, see Part II and also §7.4, §11.6.

We might wish to consider as "bound postverbs", too, the past and future markers (-ess- etc. and -keyss-) that I have chosen to include with the endings for the following reason. These elements occur only before some, but not all, of the final "mood" endings, unlike the other elements we are calling bound postverbs. Moreover, the tense markers attach freely to ALL stems, unlike the bound postverbs, for which the stems must be individually specified. It is this last criterion alone which excludes from the bound postverbs the honorific marker -usi-, for it occurs freely before all the mood endings, as well as before the tense markers. A final criterion would be simply one of sequence: whatever the decision, we will see that the bound postverbs making intensives, causatives, and passives occur in a position BEFORE the series of positions described for the verb endings in §9.1.

7.3. Defective verbs.

Several verbs occur in only a few of the paradigmatic forms:

tā-l- 'request' → tao, tāko (tākwu), tālla (notice that tālla 'nta is an abbreviation of tālla ko hanta); on the irregularity of the forms, see Part II

tepu-l- 'accompany' → tepulko, tepul.e (se)

kalo- 'say' → kalotoy

(... ulo) malmiam- (§6.3) → malmiam.e/a (se), malmiam.un

chamq ta(la)h- 'be gentle' → chamq ta(la)h.key

Choy Hyenpay 1959:338-9 also includes a bound infinitive **taka** '(drawing) near' from a supposed *tak-, but there is no reason not to consider this to be just the expected literary or dialect variant infinitive of **taku-** 'bring (draw) close', for which the normal colloquial infinitive in Seoul is **take**. To be sure, **taku-** itself probably comes from *tak- (> tah- 'touch, arrive, ... ') + the causative postverb -u-, but we can ignore the etymology in our synchronic description. To the contrary, Choy Hyenpay 1960 (Hankul 127:7-27). See also the note on **-ta (ka)** in Part II.

Certain intransitive verbs or phrases with the meaning 'gets to be' occur only in the past or in the simple modifier form, and these are sometimes mistaken for adjectives, since the usual translation of 'has gotten to be' is 'is'. Proof that they are not adjectives is that the past is necessary to give the present resultative meaning: **cal nass.ta** 'is nicely formed', **mōs nass.ta** 'is ugly', **sēylyen toyess.ta** 'is refined'. A few expressions are treated, apparently in free variation, as either intransitive processive verbs or as adjectives: **pāla cyess.ta** or **pāla cita** 'is shallow'; perhaps **pyel nass.ta** (? — rejected by Co Sek.yen) or **pyel nata** 'is odd'. On the other hand, there are some cases which appear only as adjectives: **emcheng nata** 'is enormous', **mo nata** 'is angular = is difficult in personality', **ttwukpyel nata** 'is quick-tempered'. KEd treats **hoth ci-** and **hwumi ci-** as the intransitive 'become simple' and 'form a bend; get deep / secluded', but both NKd and LHS cite them as adjectives.

The variant copula stems **ilo-** and **iolssi-** are also defective; see Part II. I am not quite sure why LHS lists **māta-** 'reject, abhor' as a defective transitive verb. The entry in Kim Minswu and Hong Wungsen's dictionary has **māta-** simply "transitive". NKd does not list the verb, which might be thought to come from a contraction of *mā ha-ta with the infinitive of the MK adjective ¨*ma-* 'dislikable, disliked', a structure equivalent to modern **silh.e hanta** 'dislikes'. But the lone MK example is CAY-¨MYEY `lol ¨mata `khesi`nol 'though he treats the alms rice as despised' (1459 Wel 8:78a). If the structure is parallel to the **-e hanta** of modern Korean, then LCT was wrong in his citation form "¨ma`ta" for he should have used "¨mata`ta". If he took the structure to be ← ¨ma-[`]ta ho-`kesi`nol 'though he says / feels it is despicable', the entry citation is correct (but there is something odd about the accent). In that case, the transitive stem **māta-** derives from a contraction of the quotative structure **-ta (ha)-**. It is not clear just when the use of **hanta** to transitivize the adjective infinitive developed; it may be not be all that old. The only other use of ¨*ma-* cited by LCT is *ku lol mata kwos nekisimyen* 'if you regard it precisely as despicable' (1676 Sin.e 4:15a). Perhaps all these uses are semantic extensions of the verb ¨*ma[l]`ta* 'desists', i.e. "rejects".

7.4. Causative and passive verbs.

There are related pairs of Korean verbs which differ in what is called VOICE. We find two major types: PASSIVE related to ACTIVE, and CAUSATIVE related to ACTIVE. The relationship is both semantic and formal. The underlying stem is usually the same, but the passive or causative includes a bound postverb (§7.2.3). Causative verbs (vc) are always transitive, and passive verbs (vp) are typically intransitive (= vpi) but some take a few objects so we will label them transitive passive (= vpt). The types of derivation can be seen from the following scheme:

vc ← vt
← vi
← adj
vp(i) ← vt
vpt ← vt

One unusual case looks like a vp from a vi: **menci ka palam ey pullinta** 'the dust gets blown by the wind', CF **palam i pūnta** 'the wind blows' and the lack of a *****palam i menci lul pūnta** 'the wind blows the dust'. But the most appropriate derivation appears to be something like this: **(sālam i) menci lul pūnta** '(a person [etc.]) blows the dust' → **menci ka (sālam eykey) pullinta** 'the dust gets blown (by the person)' → [**palam ey (iss.ta)** '(it is) in the wind' →] **menci ka palam ey pullinta** 'the dust gets blown in the wind = it blows in the wind'. A couple of similar cases are **kāmki (ey) tullinta** 'catches a cold' (= **kāmki ka tunta**), **tali lul tachinta** 'gets injured on the leg' from **tah.chi-** from **tah-** 'touch' (vi). (Most of the examples given by CM 1:273, however, seem to be in error.)

The transitive passives all seem to refer to unsought suffering:
cap.hi- 'have someone take (from one)' < **cap-** 'take': **pal ul cap.hinta** 'gets caught by the leg', **kyelqcem ul cap.hinta** 'has fault found with one'.
ccalli- 'get it cut' < **ccalu-** 'cut': **mok ul ccallinta** 'gets one's throat cut = gets fired'.
ccilli- 'get it pierced (stabbed, pricked)' < **ccilu-** 'stab'.

chayi- 'get kicked on/in' < **chay-** 'kick': **kasum ul chayinta** 'gets kicked in the chest' (compare **kōng i cal chayinta** 'the ball kicks well').

cilli- 'get kicked in the ‥ ' < **cilu-** 'kick'.

halth.i- /halchi-/ 'get it licked or swiped' < **halth-** 'lick'.

kkayi- 'get hit on' [dialect? − CF NKd 4231a] < **kkay-** 'hit': **cengkangi lul kkayinta** 'gets hit in the shin'.

kka(y)kk.i- 'get it scraped' < **kkakk-** 'scrape': **sālam i nach ul kka(y)kk.inta** 'a person gets his face scraped = loses face' − and that can also be said as **sālam i nach i kka(y)kk.inta** 'a person, his face gets scraped'.

mek.hi- 'have it eaten up': **talun sālam hanthey tōn ul mek.hinta** 'has one's money "eaten up" = gets swindled by another person'.

peyi- 'get cut on' < **pēy-** 'cut': **sonq-kalak ul khal ey peyyess.ta** 'got one's finger cut on a knife'.

ppāys.ki- 'have someone grab, suffer the loss of' < **ppāys-** < **ppay-as-** 'grab': **kōngsan kwun hanthey Sānghay lul ppāys.kyess.ta** 'suffered the loss of Shanghai to the Communist troops'.

ttelli- 'get stripped (= robbed) of' < **ttē-l-** 'shake off': **tōn ul ttellinta** 'is stripped of one's money'.

According to Song Sekcwung 1967:177, the transitive passive will occur only when there is a WHOLE-PART relationship between the two nouns. Occasionally a causative is used with unexpected meanings similar to those of the transitive passive: **sēykan ul mocoli thaywunta** '(burns up =) loses all one's furniture in a fire'.

The basic meaning of most causative verbs is something like 'makes it so that something happens or is'. There is no good general translation in English, which offers a choice of 'makes someone do it', suggesting force and coercion, or 'lets someone do it', suggesting permission to do something the other person wants to do. The expressions 'has someone do it' and 'gets someone to do it' are ambiguous, for they can translate causatives, passives, or simple favors. The Korean causative implies neither force nor permission. Only from the context can you tell whether the act someone is caused to perform is something he wants to do, or something he is forced to do.

The basic meaning of most passive verbs is something like 'gets so that something happens to it or might happen to it'. Often the meaning of a Korean passive verb has some extra flavor of AVAILABLE or POTENTIAL undergoing of an action. Compare **san i pointa** 'the mountains can be (are available to be) seen − whether anyone is looking or not' with **san ul ponta** 'the mountains are seen; someone sees the mountains'. Similar examples (CM 1:328) are **yeki se nun koki ka cal cap.hinta** 'a lot of fish are caught here' and **i mun un swīpkey yellinta** 'this door opens easily (is easily opened)'. In English we often use passives to avoid committing ourselves to the identification of the subject. In Korean the device is unnecessary for that purpose, since an overt subject is not required by Korean sentences.

For more on the syntax of causatives and passives, see §11.6.

The morpheme for the causative bound postverb has several shapes which are identical with the shapes of the passive. As a result, convergence sometimes produces homonymous causative and passive forms from the same active stem:

anki- vp 'get embraced', vc 'embrace' ← **ān-** vt 'embrace'
cap.hi- vp 'get caught', vc 'cause to catch' ← **cap-** vt 'catch'
ep.hi- vp 'get carried', vc 'cause to carry' ← **ep-** vt 'carry (on back)'
halth.i- /halchi-/ vp 'get licked', vc 'cause to lick' ← vt **halth-** 'lick'
ilk.hi- vp 'get read', vc 'cause to read' ← **ilk-** vt 'read'
kkakk.i- vp 'be cut', vc 'cause to cut' ← **kkakk-** vt 'cut'
kwup.hi- vp 'get broiled', vc 'make someone broil' ← vt **kwūw-** 'broil'
mulli- vp 'get bitten', vc 'cause to bite' ← **mu-l-** vt 'bite'
palp.hi- vp 'get stepped on', vc 'cause to step on' ← **pālp-** 'step on'
poi- (pōy-) vp 'be seen', vc 'cause to see, show' ← vt **po-** 'see'

silli- vp 'get loaded', vc 'cause to load' ← sīt- / sil- vt 'load, carry'
simki- vp 'get planted', vc 'cause to plant' ← sīm- vt 'plant'
ssip.hi- vp 'get chewed', vc 'cause to chew' ← ssip- vt 'chew'
ssui- vp 'get used; get written', vc 'cause to use; cause to write' ← ssu- 'use; write'
ttut.ki- vp 'get bitten', vc 'cause to graze' ← ttut- 'bite, graze'
tulli- vp 'get heard', vc 'cause to hear' ← tut- / tul- 'hear'

These homonymous pairs of causatives and passives are not differentiated by accent or vowel length in standard speech, despite what is said in CM 1:275-6. CF Ceng Insung 1960:92-3.

In certain stems we find a string that could be representing one of these two formatives, but either there is no underlying active counterpart to justify an analysis like sik-hi- for sikhi- 'cause' (can we perhaps analyze the stem as s-ikhi- and take s- to be an allomorph of ha-?); or, if there is an underlying form (tul-li- = tul-lu- 'drop in', tu-l- 'enter') the syntactic relationship between the two does not correspond to that expected for voice-related pairs. Verbs of this sort lead us to recognize another derivative bound postverb that happens to be of the same shape as the causative. It might be appropriate to treat some of the odd cases of passives formed on intransitives in the same way. There is also tuli- 'give to a superior', which is historically a causative formed on tu-l- 'hold up'.

The passive and causative bound postverbs have so many shapes in common that we will consider them together. The shapes divide into two thematic groups: (1) those which include the PHONEME i, and (2) those which include the phoneme wu (but not the phoneme i); there is also (3) an athematic group, in which we will include the reductions of i to y. Formatives with the wu theme (and, apparently, the athematic formatives) all form only causatives, with the possible exception of one questionable stem, puliwu- vp 'be employed' < puli- vt 'employ'. Formatives with the i-theme form both causatives and passives.

The shapes are listed below with critical examples given for each shape. C = causative, P = passive; T = transitive, I = intransitive, A = adjective (descriptive stem). The down arrow (↓) means the preceding string from the stem is omitted (deleted) when the formative is added, and the right arrow (→) means the stem string on the left is replaced by the string on the right; these are synchronic statements, not necessarily recapitulating the history of the formations. Notice that the two distinct origins of the modern ···lu- / ···ll- stems (§8.3.1) are reflected in the derived stems: hulu-/hull- 'flow' makes the causative hulli- < hul˙l-i- 'make flow', and olu- / oll- 'rise' makes the causative olli- < wol˙G-i- 'raise'.

1. i theme (causative, passive)
    -i-   cwuk.i- 'kill' (C) ← cwuk- 'die' (I)
                  mek.i- 'feed' (C) ← mek- 'eat' (T)
                  kiwul.i- 'tilt' (C) ← kiwu-l- 'be tilted' (A)
                  noph.i- 'heighten' (C) ← noph- 'be high' (A)
                  noh.i- 'get put' (P) ← noh- 'put' (T)
                  nanw(u)i- = nanwe ci- 'be divided' (P) ← nanwu- 'divide' (T)
                  hulli- 'make flow' (C) ← hulu- / hull- 'flow' (I)
    -hi-   anc.hi- 'seat' (C) ← anc- 'sit down' (I)
                  kkulh.i- 'makes it boil' (C) ← kkulh- 'boil' (I)
                  kwup.hi- 'bend' (C) ← kwup- 'be bent' (A)
                  ip.hi- 'cause to wear' (C) ← ip- 'wear' (T)
                  mek.hi- 'get eaten' (P) ← mek- 'eat' (T)
    (aw↓)-i-   akki- 'spare; value' (C) ← akkaw- 'is regretful; is precious' (A)
    (wu↓)-hi- kat.hi- 'be confined' (P) ← katwu- 'confine' (T)
    -ki-   swumki- 'conceal' (C) ← swum- 'be hidden' (I)
                  olm.ki- 'move it' (C) ← olm- 'move' (I)
                  pes.ki- 'unclothe' (C) ← pes- 'take off, remove' (T)
                  ccic.ki- 'get torn' (P) ← ccic- 'tear it' (T)

-chi-	kuluchi- 'ruin' (C) ← kulu- 'be wrong' (A)	
	sos.chi- 'raise; exasperate' (C) ← sos- 'tower up, rise' (I)	
	— But /sochi-/ could be treated as **sos-hi-**.	
-ukhi-	il.ukhi- 'raise' (C) ← i-l- 'rise' (I)	
-ikhi-	tol.ikhi- 'turn (head)' (C) ← tō-l- 'turn' (I)	
···l-li- < -Gi-	alli- 'inform' (C) ← ā-l- 'know' (T)	
	salli- 'let live' (C) ← sā-l- 'live' (I)	
	mongkulli- 'make (grain) awnless' (C) ← mongku-l- 'be awnless' (A)	
	phalli- 'get sold' (P) ← pha-l- 'sell' (T)	
	olli- 'raise' (C) ← olu- / oll- 'rise' (I)	

Almost unique: **pemulli-** 'be mixed' (P) and 'cause to mix' (C) **pemuli-** 'mix' (T). The form **pemuli-** was earlier *pe˙muli-*, a causative ← *pe˙mul-* 'whirl it (around)' (T) and 'tie it up' (T), surviving figuratively in **pemu-l-** 'be involved, mixed up in'. Apparently similar: **holli-** 'get infatuated' (P) ← **holi-** 'infatuate' (T). And **killi-** 'get raised' (< *kil˙Gi-* < *ki˙l[u]-G-i-*) is a late development.

2. **wu** theme (causative only)

-wu-	kkaywu- 'wake someone' (C) ← kkāy- 'come awake' (I)	
	kel.wu- = 'fertilize' (C) ← kē-l- 'be fertile'	
	tot.wu- 'raise it' (C) ← tot- 'rise' (I)	
(u↓)-wu-	palwu- 'straighten' (C) [usually replaced by **palo cap-**] ← palu- 'be right' (A)	
-chwu-	kot.chwu- 'straighten' (C) ← kot- 'be straight'	
-(c)hwu-	nac.chwu- 'abase, make low' (C) ← nac- 'be low' (A)	
	nuc.chwu- 'loosen; delay' (C) ← nuc- 'be slack; be late' (A),	
	mac.chwu- 'spell' (C) ← mac- 'be correct' (A)	
	cac.chwu- 'quicken' (C) ← cac- 'be incessant' (A)	
	kac.chwu- 'prepare' (C) ← kac- = kaci- 'have' (T)	
(u→ey)-wu-	seywu- 'make stand, establish' (C) ← su- 'stand' (I)	
(ew→ey)-wu-	teywu- 'heat' (C) ← tew- 'be hot' (A)	
-ywu- < -i-wu-	caywu- 'put to sleep' (C) ← ca- 'sleep' (I)	
-kwu-	sos.kwu- 'make rise' (C) ← sos- 'spring up' (I)	
	tot.kwu- 'make it higher', (= tot.wu-) 'raise it' (C) ← tot- 'rise' (I)	

3. athematic (causative, passive)

-ay-	ēps.ay- 'eliminate; use up' (C) ← ēps- 'be nonexistent' (I) — but see p. 429!	
-y-	nāy- 'put out' (C) ← na- 'emerge' (I)	
	cāy- = caywu- 'put to sleep' (C) ← ca- 'sleep' (I)	
	pōy- = poi- 'show, let see' (C), 'get seen' (P) ← po- 'see' (T)	
(u↓)-ey-	kēnney- 'carry over' (C) ← kēnnu- 'cross over' (T)	
(h↓)-y-	tāy- 'bring in contact' (C) ← tāh- 'come in contact' (I)	
-u-	kilu- 'raise' (C) ← kī-l- 'get big' (I) — see below	

The voice-deriving bound postverbs should not be confused with the intensive bound postverb **-chi-**, which is morphemically related to the auxiliary verb **chi-** that is used after the infinitive as an intensifier. See Part II for examples of the postverbs, and compare Choy Hyenpay 1959:351. The intensive postverb seems to have the shape **-chwu-** in **tulchwu-** 'raise, expose, ... ' (← **tu-l-** 'hold up; lift; cite'), but there is a dialect variant with the expected shape **tulchi-**, and there may be some connection with the obsolete verb **chi-** 'raise' (CF the bound preverb **tul-**); there is also **tulkhi-** 'get discovered, caught', a specialized use of a passive from the same **tu-l-**. I have not included **-chwu-** among the shapes of the intensive, but the **-li- / -lu-** of **tulli- / tullu-** 'drop in' (← **tu-l-** 'enter') is there. The **-khi-** of **tulkhi-** is not listed, only the causative **-ikhi-** (probably < **-i-khi-**) and **-ukhi-**.

Some of the complications of shape are the result of phonological changes from earlier forms. The Middle Korean causatives and passives were made with these formatives:

A Reference Grammar of Korean   PART I 225

-`i-	cwu`ki- 'kill' (C) ← cwuk- 'die' (I)
	me`ki- 'feed' (C) ← mek- 'eat' (T)
	non`hwoi- 'get divided' (P) ← non`hwo- 'divide' (T)
	na`hi- 'cause to give birth to' (C) ← nah- 'bear' (T)
	il`hi- 'cause to lose' (C) ← ilh- 'lose' (T)
	hul`li- 'make flow' (C) ← hulu- / hull- 'flow' (I)
	wol`Gi- 'raise' (C) ← wolo- / wolG- 'rise' (I)
-(`)y-	¨cay- 'cause to sleep' (C) ← °ca- 'sleep' (I)
	¨nay- 'cause to emerge' (C) ← °na- 'emerge' (I)
	¨ken`ney- 'carry it over' (C) ← ¨ken`ne- 'cross over' (I)
	˙pwoy- 'cause to see' (C), 'gets seen' (P) ← °pwo- 'see' (T)
	¨syey- 'cause to stand' (C) ← °sye- 'stand' (I)
-`ki-	swum`ki- 'conceal' (C) ← `swum- 'lie in hiding' (I)
	wolm`ki- 'move it' (C) ← ¨wolm- 'move' (I)
	pes`ki- 'unclothe' (C) ← pes- 'remove, strip off' (T)
-`hi-	an`chi- 'cause to sit' (C) ← anc- 'sit' (I)
	ca`phi- 'cause to catch' (C), 'get caught' (P) < cap- 'catch' (T)
	el`khi-, elk`khi-, elq`khi- = el`khi- 'get tied' (P) < elk- 'tie' (I)
	me`khi-, mek`hi-, mek`khi- 'get eaten' (P) < mek- 'eat' (T)
	ni`phi-, nip`hi- 'cause to wear' (C) < nip- 'wear' (T)
	pa`khi-, pak`hi- 'get stuck / printed' (P) < pak- 'stick in / on, print' (T)
	pat`hi- 'cause to get' (C) < pat- 'get' (T)
	twot`hi- 'cause to rise, raise' (C) < twot- (I)
-`Gi-	moyngkol`Gi- 'cause to make' (C) ← moyng`kol- 'make' (T)
	mul`Gi- 'get bitten' (P) ← mul- 'bite' (T)
	nol`Gi- 'cause to fly' (C) ← nol- 'fly' (I)
	sal`Gi- 'cause to live' (C) ← ¨sal- 'live' (I)
	skol`Gi- 'get spread' (P) ← `skol- 'spread' (T)
	tul`Gi- 'cause: to hear, to enter, to lift' (C)
	kil`Gi- 'increase it' (C) ← ¨kil- 'get big' (I)
	twol`Gi- 'cause to turn' (C) = twolo- ← ¨twol- 'turn' (I)
-`Gw^{u}o-	el`Gwu- 'cause to freeze' (C) ← ¨el- 'freeze' (I)
	me`mulGwu-, me`mulGwo- 'cause to stay' (C) ← me`mul- 'stay' (I)
	mey`Gwu- 'cause to shoulder' (C) ← ¨mey- 'shoulder' (T)
	sul`Gwu- 'cause to vanish' (C) ← `sul- 'vanish' (I)
	tu`li`Gwu-, tu`li`Gwo- 'cause to hang down' (C) = tu`li- (T)
	twol`Gwo- 'cause to turn' (C) = twolo- / twolG- ← ¨twol- 'turn' (I)
	kil`Gwu-, kil`Gwo-, kil`Gwuy- 'raise' (C) = kil^{u}o- ← ¨kil- 'get big' (I)
-`Gw^{u}oy-	¨nilGwuy- 'cause to reach' (C) ← ni`lu- = ni`lul- 'reach' (I)
	al`Gwoy- 'inform' (C) ← ¨al- 'know' (T)
-^{u}o- < *-G-	kil^{u}o- / kilG- < *kil^{u}o-G- 'raise' (C) ← ¨kil- 'get big' (I)
	twolo- / twolG- < *twolo-G- 'cause to turn' (C) ← ¨twol- 'turn' (I)

The vowel of -`Gw$^u$o- may represent an incorporation of the modulator -`w^{u}o-; if so, the etymon of the formative was simply -G-, as indicated also by -^{u}o- < *-G-. The infinitives of the last two examples are kil`Ge (1465 Wen 1:1:1:111a) and tol`Ga (1447 Sek 6:4b); Cf kil`Gwe (1447 Sek 9:17a) and twol`Gwa (1632 Twusi-cwung 16:56b) = twol`Ga (1481 Twusi 16:55b), twol`Gye (?1517- Pak 1:21b) – from twol-`Gi- (> **tolli**-). But ¨ep.si`Wa (1449 Kok 155), ¨ep.si`Wozo`Wa (1459 Wel 17:77a), and ¨ep`siWo`n i (1459 Wel 23:65b) indicate a labial *-i-p^{u}o- (echoing the p of ¨eps-?).

7.5. Auxiliary verbs.

Auxiliary verbs are used in construction with preceding verb forms, most often the infinitive **-e** or the gerund **-ko**; less often the suspective **-ci**, the adverbative **-key**, the transferentive **-ta**, and the unusual cases of 34, 45, and 46 in the lists below. In these lists all the auxiliary descriptive verbs (= auxiliary adjectives) are segregated from the auxiliary processive verbs (= auxiliary verbs proper), and each auxiliary is preceded by an indication of the category of verb form with which it enters into a construction: the letters A (adjective), C (copula), and V (processive verb) represent the stem before the "-..." that designates the ending. With some misgivings I offer tag translations for the auxiliaries, but the reader is urged to look up the separate entries in Part II for more detailed descriptions and examples. The separable auxiliaries are marked by the symbol # placed after the number; they can be set apart from the preceding verb form by at least the particles **un/nun** or **tul**. Since we distinguish auxiliary constructions from simple compounds or sequences in which both verbs retain their usual meanings and functions, not included are such forms as **-e neh-** 'do and put in'. And idiomatic formations such as **ka(-)tah-** 'arrive (there)' and **wa(-)tah-** 'arrive (here)', **tāy(-)ka-** 'arrive (there) in time' and **tāy(-)o-** 'arrive (here) in time' are best put in the dictionary as lexical entries, since you will seldom if ever separate the infinitive from the following stem, even by the particle **se**. At the left of each item in the lists below there is information on attaching the honorific marker to the main verb (α), to the auxiliary (β), or to both ($\alpha\beta$). A plus (+) means it is possible to attach **-usi-**, a minus means that it is not possible. When the plus is italicized (+) the honorific marker is attached only under special circumstances of one kind or another; even in some of the cases marked with the minus it is possible to get the honorific verbs **capswusi-** 'eat', **cwumusi-** 'sleep', and **kyēysi-** 'stay' (also **tol.a kasi-** when it means 'die'), though not the regularly derived forms such as **hasi-** 'deign to do', **kasi-** 'deign to go', and **pat.usi-** 'deign to receive'.

LISTS OF AUXILIARY VERBS

Auxiliary processive verbs (aux v)

+-usi-						
α	β	$\alpha\beta$				
−	+	−	1.	#	V-e tāy-	[intensive] 'do hard / continuously'
−	+	−	2.		V-e chi-	[intensive] 'do hard / continuously'
+	−	−	3.		V/A-e ssah-	'do/be more than an ample extent'
−	−	−	4.		V/A-e ppā ci-	'(get old, rotten, musty) through and through'
−	+	−	5.		V-e (p)peli-	[exhaustive] 'do completely'
−	+	−	6.	#	V-e twu-	[completive] 'get it done'
−	+	−	7.	#	V/A-e noh-	[anticipatory] 'do for now/later' / 'be all ... '
+	−	−	8.	#	V-ko na-	[transitional] 'just did, come from doing'
+	+	+̸	9.	#	V-e na-	[continuative] 'keep doing, do and do again' − CF **-e na-** as regular compound (**kkāy na-** 'recover one's senses, come to')
+	+	+̸	10.	#	V-ko mā-l-	[terminative] 'finish(ed) doing'
?	?	?			V-ko ya mā-l-	'end in doing, end up doing'
+	−	+			V/A/C-ko mālko	'of course do/be'
+	+̸	+	11.	#	V-ta (ka) mā-l-	'do a while and then stop'
+	+	+	11a.	#	V-ta (ka) mōs ha-	'fail to do, try but cannot'
+	+	+	12.	#	V-ko tani-	'go around doing' (Treat as regular compounds?)
−	+̸	−	13.		V-e mek-	[vulgar and pejorative] − CF 44.
−	+	−	14.		V-e nāy-	[perseverative] 'do all the way'
−	+	−	15.	#	V/A-e ka-	[out-directive, exo-developmental] 'away, ongoing' − CF regular **-ko ka-** 'go ... doing'

−	+	−	16.	# V/A-e o-	[in-directive, endo-developmental] 'this way, upcoming' − CF regular -ko o- 'do and come'
+	+	+	17.	# V-e po-	[exploratory] 'try doing' (NOT 'try to do' = -ulye ko ha- or -ki ey him ssu-)
?	+	?	18.	# A-e/-key poi- (pōy-)	[semblative] 'look like (it is)'
−	+	−	19.	# V-e cwu-	[favor] 'do for' − separable by 'ta
+	−	−	19a.	# V-e tālla; V-e tao (tāko)	[reflexive request, §11.2] 'ask someone to do for for one' − separable by 'ta
−	+	−	20.	# V-e tuli-	[honorific favor] 'do for (an esteemed person)'
−	+	−	21.	# V-e pachi-	[honorific favor] 'do for (an esteemed person)'
+	+	+	22.	# V-ci anh-, V-ci an(i) ha-	[negative] 'not do' − CF 43.
+	+	+	23.	# V-ci mā-l-	[prohibitive] 'refrain from doing' − usually in a subjunctive form (imperative, hortative)
			24.	# (V) ha-	'do' − dummy verb (general auxiliary) in such structures as V-ki to ha- 'indeed / also do'
+	+	+	25.	# V/A-key ha-	[causative] 'make it so that' − see §7.4
+	+	+	26.	# V/A-key toy-	[externally conditioned gradual inceptive] 'get so that, come to do/be'
−	+	−	27.	# A/V-key kwū-l-, A-i kwū-l-	[behavioral] 'act in a manner that is' − usually A-key, but mōs kyentikey 'unbearably' ← vt
−	+	−	28.	# A-e ha-	[catheticizer, emotion transitivizer] 'project an emotion (toward something / someone)'
			29.	V-e cilu-	= 30.
−	+	−	30.	V-e ttuli-	(1) turns vi into vt (2) intensifies transitivity of vt and defective infinitives
−	+	−	31.	V-e ci-	(1) [inceptive] 'get to be, become, grow' − usually A-e ci- but sometimes V-e ci-, e.g. pel.e ci- 'split' ← pē-l- vi (2) 'get/be done': turns vt or defective inf into vi (3) intensifies vi
+	+	+	32.	# V/A-e (se) cwuk.keyss.ta	'so much one could die; very much'
+	+	+	32a.	# V-e (se) mōs sālkeyss.ta	'so much one will not live; extremely'
+	+	+	32b.	# V-e (se) hon nass.ta	'so much it frightened one witless; extremely'
+	−	−	33.	# V/A-e kaciko	'with (the accomplishment or resultant fact)'
+	−	−	34.	# V-ulye ko tu-l-	'threaten (try, be about) to do'
−	+	−	35.	V-e tu-l- / tul.i-	'do into, upon, at' (Treat as regular compounds?)
+	+	+	36.	# V-ko iss-	[progressive] 'be doing, be ···ing'
−	+	−	37.	# V-e iss-	[resultative] 'be done, be ···ed'

Auxiliary adjectives (aux adj)

+	+	+	38.	# V-ko siph-	[desiderative] 'want to do'
−	−	−	39.	V-ko ci-	[literary] = 38.
−	−	−		V-ko ca / ce / cie	'wanting / intending to do' (= -ulye)
−	−	−	40.	V-e cii-	[literary] = 38.

−	−	−	41.	#	V-e ci-	in **mes-tul.e ci-** 'be nice'; and in free variation with 31 (aux. v.) in **pāla ci-** 'be (or get) shallow'[1]
+	−	−	42.	#	(A) ha-	'be' — dummy adjective (general auxiliary) in such structures as **A-ki to ha-** 'indeed / also be'
+	+	+	43.	#	A-ci anh-, A-ci an(i) ha-	[negative] 'not be' — CF 22
+	−	−	44.		A-e mek-	[vulgar and derogatory] — CF 13
+	−	−	45.		V-na po-,	
				#	V-nun ka po- A-un ka po-	[semblative] look as though, seem
+	−	−	46.	#	V/A/C-na siph- -ta siph- -ulila siph- -ess.umyen siph-	[semblative] feel as if — also postnominal verb with **tus, sang / seng, ka, ya, -ulq kes man**

[1] The critical examples are **ku kes cham mes-tul.e cita** (not *cyess.ta) 'that is real nice' and **ku kes i pāla cita / cyess.ta** 'that is shallow'.

7.6. Postnominal verbs.

Postnominal verbs occur in construction with preceding nouns, typically verbal nouns (§5.6). Some of the postnominal verbs are separable, at least by the particles **un / nun, to,** or **tul,** and they are marked with "#".

LISTS OF POSTNOMINAL VERBS

Postnominal processive verbs (postnom v)

1.		keli-	'behave in a way that creates the impression of'; XX ha- = X keli- 'repeatedly / continuously do'
2.		tāy-	[colloquial] = 1.
3.		k(h)uli-	'do'
4.		ha-	'behave, go (boom!, ...)': X ha-, XX ha- = X keli-
5.		i-	'behave, go' — as in **wumcik i-** 'move, budge'
5a.		na-	'behave, feel' (in **kamcil na-** 'feel impatient')
6.	#	ha-	'do'
7.	#	ttē-l-	'do'
8.	#	puli-	'do'
9.	#	phi(wu)-	'do'
10.	#	ppāy-	'do'
11.	#	po-	'do; see to'
12.	#	(na-)ka-	'go (out) to do'
13.	#	(na-)o-	'come (out) to do'
14.	#	sikhi-	'cause to do' [causative] — see §7.4
15.	#	toy-	'get/be done' [passive] — see §7.4
16.	#	pat-	'incur the doing of, have done to one' [passive] — see §7.4
?17.	#	ssu-	'use, do; [? causative]'
18.		ci-	'get / become characterized by'
19.	#	chi-	'do'
?20.	#	cī(s)-	(= 6) in **kyelqceng cī(s)- / ha-** 'decide'
21.		ēps-	'lack' — can be treated as regular compounds

Postnominal adjectives (postnom adj)

?22.		ēps-	'be lacking / deficient in; be bad with respect to': SEE Part II.
22a.	(#)	kwuc-	'be bad with respect to' (simswul kwuc- rarely is simswul i kwuc-)
23.		na-	'be' — pyel nata or pyel nass.ta [defective vi] 'is special'; mas nata / nanta [A/V] 'is tasty'
24.	#	ha-	'be'
25.		ha-	'be, give the impression of being': X ha-, XX ha-
26.		mac-	= 25
27.		sulew-	= 25
28.		(h)ow-	[obsolete] = 27 = 25
29.		low-	'be characterized by' [occurs only after vowel]
30.		(···q) toy-	'be'
30a.		kath-	'be ...-like' — inseparable in engtheli kath-, ...
30b.		cha-	'be full of / in' — inseparable in an cha-, ...
31.		taw-	'be like, be worthy of being'
32.		ci-, chi-	'be, be characterized by'
32a.		cew-	'be characterized by' — Are the only examples swus cew- 'be simple-hearted' and pich cew- 'be dignified'?
33.	#	ccek-	'feel, give / have a feeling of'
34.	#	(tus) siph-	'feel / look (like)' — separable by to
35.		(s^e/ang) siph-	'seem to be' — separable by to
36.		(ka, ya, -ulq kes man) siph-	'feel / look (like)'
37.		(sēng) p^a/$_u$lu-	[dialect] = 35

We can add to the list of postnominal verbs **lop.hi-** 'makes it be characterized by' (occurring only after a vowel), a causative from the postnominal adjective **low-** (item 29 above). I have excluded from the list **cōh-** 'be good with respect to, have a nice ··· ', **sānaw-** 'be bad with respect to, have a bad ··· ', and other such words carried in the lists of CM 1:447-9, because these adjectives seem quite freely separable by the particle **i / ka** and therefore do not differ in kind from other adjectives that are preceded by a noun (+ particle).

The stem **ha-** 'do / say / be', which has so many uses (see the entries in Part II), is both processive and descriptive. The two uses contrast nicely in **te hata** (adj-n) 'be more, be worse' and **te hanta** (vni) 'get worse (exaggerated)' or (vnt.) 'add, gain, increase'.

7.7. Recursiveness of auxiliary conversions.

What, if anything, constrains the application of an auxiliary conversion to a sentence that had already undergone an auxiliary conversion? Apparently the only restrictions are those of semantic incompatibility (the result does not make sense), or unwieldiness (the sentence is too heavily burdened for easy processing). If it were not for these constraints, an infinite number of longer and longer sentences could be created just by reapplying auxiliary conversions. There are a fair number of sentence types with a sequence of no more than two auxiliary conversions. The table below, compiled by [1]Yi Tongcay in 1962, shows those sequences of two infinitive-auxiliary conversions that are acceptable (+) and those that are not (−). The auxiliaries are assigned letters (A to X) arbitrarily and these are used as references at the left (the first conversion) and at the top (the second conversion). The key to the letters is on the extreme left. If you want to know whether it is permissible to reapply **-e noh-** to a sentence which has already had it, you look for the "G-G" intersection and find a "−" that means there are no such sentences as *hay noh.a noh.ass.ta 'did it for later for later', though it is possible to apply the conversion to a main verb **noh-** 'put' as in **phyēnci lul chayk-sang wi ey noh.a noh.ass.ta** 'I put the letter on the desk for the time being'. An examination of the table will reveal that in general a conversion cannot be reapplied. There seems to be an exception in **Ce sālam hanthey mul.e pwā ('na) poca** 'Let's try asking that fellow' and similar expressions, so you will find a " + " at the intersection "M-M" in the chart. A more involved sentence such as ?**Ce sacen ul pwā pwā poca**, if possible, is better taken as a conjoined sentence with two main verbs **po-** and translated 'Let's try looking in that dictionary to see'.

CHART OF DOUBLE INFINITIVE-AUXILIARY CONVERSIONS

-e +		A	B	C	D	E	F	G	H	I	J	K	L	M	N	O	P	Q	R	S	T	U	V	W	X
tāy-	A	−	+	+	+	+	+	+	+	+	+	+	−	+	−	+	+	+	+	+	+	+	−	−	+
chi-	B	−	+	−	−	−	−	−	−	+	−	+	−	−	−	−	−	−	−	−	−	−	−	−	−
ssah-	C	+	+	−	+	+	+	+	+	+	+	+	+	+	+	+	+	+	+	+	+	+	+	−	+
ppā ci-	D	−	−	−	−	−	−	−	−	−	−	−	−	−	−	−	−	−	−	−	+	−	−	−	−
peli-	E	+	+	+	+	−	+	+	+	+	+	+	+	+	+	+	+	+	+	+	+	+	+	−	+
twu-	F	+	+	+	−	+	+	+	−	+	+	+	+	+	+	+	+	+	+	+	+	+	+	−	+
noh-	G	+	+	+	+	+	+	+	−	+	+	+	+	+	+	+	+	+	+	+	+	+	+	−	+
na-	H	+	−	−	+	−	+	+	−	+	+	−	+	+	−	−	+	+	−	+	+	+	−	+	+
mek-	I	+	−	−	−	−	−	−	−	−	−	−	−	−	−	−	−	−	−	−	−	−	−	−	−
nāy-	J	+	+	+	−	+	+	+	+	−	+	+	−	+	+	−	+	+	+	−	+	+	−	−	+
ka-	K	+	+	−	+	+	+	+	+	−	+	−	+	+	−	+	+	+	+	+	+	+	−	−	−
o-	L	+	−	−	+	−	+	+	+	+	−	+	−	+	+	+	+	+	+	+	+	−	−	−	−
po-	M	+	+	+	+	+	+	+	+	+	+	+	+	+	+	+	+	+	+	+	+	+	−	−	+
pōy- (poi-)	N	−	−	+	−	+	−	−	−	−	−	−	−	−	−	−	−	−	−	−	−	−	−	−	+
cwu-	O	+	+	+	+	+	+	+	−	+	+	+	+	+	+	+	+	+	+	+	+	+	+	−	+
tuli-	P	+	−	+	−	+	+	−	+	+	+	+	+	+	+	+	+	+	+	+	+	+	−	−	+
pachi-	Q	−	+	−	−	−	+	−	−	−	−	−	−	−	+	−	−	+	+	−	−	−	−	−	+
tālla/tao/tāko	R	+	+	+	+	+	+	+	+	+	+	+	+	+	+	+	+	+	−	+	+	+	−	+	+
ha-	S	−	−	−	−	−	−	−	−	−	−	−	−	−	−	−	−	−	−	−	−	−	−	+	−
ttuli-	T	−	+	−	−	−	−	−	+	−	−	−	−	−	−	−	−	−	−	−	−	−	−	−	−
ci-	U	+	+	+	+	+	+	+	+	+	+	+	+	+	+	−	+	+	+	+	+	+	+	−	+
cwuk.keyss.ta	V	+	−	−	−	−	−	−	−	−	−	−	+	+	+	+	+	+	+	+	+	+	+	−	+
kaciko	W	+	+	+	+	+	+	+	+	+	+	+	+	+	+	+	+	+	+	+	+	+	+	+	+
iss-	X	−	+	−	+	+	+	+	+	−	+	+	−	+	+	−	−	+	+	−	−	+	+	−	−
		A	B	C	D	E	F	G	H	I	J	K	L	M	N	O	P	Q	R	S	T	U	V	W	X

8.0. Stems.

We describe the verb stems of Korean in terms of conjugations, sets of stems that differ from each other in shape when attached to various groups of endings. Behind the complications of the modern conjugations you will see a simpler system at work in earlier forms of the language.

8.1. Conjugations.

Each inflected form consists of a stem + an ending. It is possible to classify stems and endings into groups according to the ways in which alternant shapes are attached to each other. We find two kinds of ending: in rough terms, ONE-SHAPE endings (-ko, -ta, -ci, -sey, -nun, -keyss-, -ess-, -kka, -^{e}a, ...) and TWO-SHAPE endings (-sup.nita/-p.nita, -so/-o, -una/-na, -umyen/-myen, -nunta/-nta, -un/-n, -ul/-l, -um/-m, -usi-/-si-, ...). The two-shape endings have one shape which is attached to a stem that ends, in its basic form, with a CONSONANT and another shape which is attached to a stem that ends with a VOWEL in its basic form, but some of the vowel stems have an l-extension before certain of the endings. The one-shape endings may actually have more than one shape — the infinitive has several shapes (-e, -a, zero, ...) – but the choice of alternants is not correlated with the kind of sound at the end of the stem.

With this in mind we can set up CONJUGATIONS, or classes of verb stems. Those stems which attach the shapes **-sup.nita, -so, -una, -umyen, -un, -ul, -um, -usi-**, etc., are CONSONANT stems. Those which attach the shapes **-p.nita, -o, -na, -myen, -nta, -n, -l, -m, -si-**, ... , are VOWEL stems. Vowel stems and consonant stems attach one-shape endings, such as **-ko, -ta, -ci, -nun, -e/a**, ... , in the same way.

In addition to the major dichotomy of consonant stems and vowel stems, we also find a few h-dropping stems that we will call AMBIVALENT, and several verbs with minor irregularities that we can lump together as IRREGULAR stems. Among consonant verbs we distinguish:

(1) stems ending in /h/ which are regular in the Hankul orthography (and if ···ah- take the infinitive ending as -a) but ambivalent in colloquial speech except for the infinitive, which is regular -e (but -a after ···ah- or ···oh-) – CF the infinitive ····ay of the truly ambivalent stems, such as **kuleh-** 'be so'.

(2) stems ending in /w/ and /l/ which are quite regular in our Romanization – though they show automatic alternations unusual outside the inflectional system (/w/ → /p/ before a consonant, and /l/ → /t/) – but which must be treated as the special classes of "irregular P, irregular T" in the analysis underlying the Hankul spelling, reflecting the fact that the alternation is the result of a pre-Hankul lenition of p and t before a stem-final *^{u}/o- which was later elided.

(3) s-dropping stems, which involve a special type of alternation that is the result of a pre-Hankul lenition of s before a stem-final *^{u}/o- which was later elided. Among the vowel verbs we distinguish the subclasses of l-extending vowel stems, l-doubling vowel stems, and l-inserting vowel stems.

8.2. Consonant stems.

Below are examples of all occurring types of consonant-final stems.

ip- 'wear'	**pālp-** 'tread on'
noph- 'be high'	**ulph-** 'intone, chant'
ēps- 'be nonexistent'	**tālm-** 'resemble'
tat- 'close'	**kām-** 'shampoo'
kath- 'be alike'	**ān-** 'embrace'
wūs- 'laugh'	**anc-** 'sit down'
iss- 'exist; stay; have'	**noh-** 'put'
chac- 'look for, find'	**ilh-** 'lose'
coch- 'follow'	**kkunh-** 'cut'
mek- 'eat'	**kakkaw-** 'be near'
takk- 'polish'	**tut- / tul-** 'hear'
ilk- 'read'	**cī(s)-** 'build'
halth- 'lick, taste'	

One anomalous adjective stem ends in ···**lw-**: **sēlw-**, a contracted form of **sēlew-** 'sad'. And a truncation of **ilu-** 'be early' creates the anomalous stem **īlq-** that is found in what seems to be a dialect form, **īlqkena mālkena** = **ilukena nuc.kena** 'early or late, sooner or later'. A comprehensive list of the shapes of shorter stems is arranged by conjugation in Appendix 1. Some of the consonant-final stems turn up in dialect versions with a final ···**u-**: **simu-** for **sim-** 'plant' (see the remarks at the end of §8.3.1), **siphu-** for **siph-** 'desirous', **kathu-** for **kath-** 'like, same'.

8.2.1. Stems ending in sonants.

A typically voiceless obstruent (p t s c k) is reinforced (→ pp tt ss cc kk) after a stem-final **m, n,** or **l** (reduced from syllable excess, since a basic l is treated as /t/ in this environment, §8.2.4). That reinforcement, not present in certain dialects and fairly recent in the central area (see Martin ?1991), is ignored by the Hankul spelling, but we note it in our Romanization by a dot. To be consistent, we would like to use "···q" in place of the dot, but that would be misleading in terms of the Hankul spelling. The reinforcement is completely automatic only within the inflectional system, though it is widespread in other parts of the structure (especially after /l/), where we write it with q; see §1.5. Examples:

	-ko	-ta	-ci	-sup.nita	-nun
halth-	halth.ko	halth.ta	halth.ci	halth.sup.nita	halth.nun
'lick'	/halkko/	/haltta/	/halcci/	/halssumnita/	/hallun/
nām-	nām.ko	nām.ta	nām.ci	nām.sup.nita	nāmnun
'remain'	/nāmkko/	/nāmtta/	/nāmcci/	/nāmssumnita/	/nāmnun/
tālm-	tālm.ko	tālm.ta	tālm.ci	tālm.sup.nita	tālm.nun
'resemble'	/tāmkko/	/tāmtta/	/tāmcci/	/tāmssumnita/	/tāmnun/
ān-	ān.ko	ān.ta	ān.ci	ān.sup.nita	ānnun
'hug'	/ānkko/	/āntta/	/āncci/	/ānssumnita/	/ānnun/
anc-	anc.ko	anc.ta	anc.ci	anc.sup.nita	anc.nun
'sit'	/ankko/	/antta/	/ancci/	/anssumnita/	/annun/

In 15th-century Korean one-syllable stems that ended in ···*m*- (including ···*lm*-) and ···*n*-, like the counterparts of the modern -(s)-, -w-, and -T/L- stems, began with the rising tone marked by the double dot (¨) when attached to endings that began with a vowel — specifically, the infinitive -˙^{e}/a, the modulator -˙w^u/o-, and (interestingly) the honorific -^{u}/o˙si-. But before other endings, the stem began with the low tone that is left unmarked, and a high pitch (the single dot ˙) appears at the beginning of the ending. From that we conclude that these stems were originally dissyllabic ··· ˙m^u/o-, ··· ˙n^u/o-, and (before the lenition) ··· ˙s^u/o-, ··· ˙p^u/o-, and ···t^u/o-. The rising tone results from blending the basic initial low with the high tone left stranded when the vowel was elided. Accordingly, a form like ¨sa˙mosi˙m ye (1482 Kum-sam 2:3b) contains ¨sam- < *sa˙m[o]- 'make' + -o˙si- (honorific) but a form like sa˙mo.n i ˙'la (1459 Wel 2:27b) contains the original stem sa˙mo- + -n, the modifier ending — here entering into an extended predicate with the postmodifier ˙i and the abbreviated form of the copula indicative attentive ˙i˙la, which is ˙y˙la but automatically suppresses the glide after /i/. Forms for 'hug' include the infinitive an˙a (1449 Kok 57, 1459 Wel 8:85b) and the honorific modifier found in ¨an˙osi˙n i '-ngi ˙'ta (1459 Wel 8:86a; sic, ¨an-˙o-) 'hugs', which has a rising accent like the gerund ¨an˙kwo (1459 Wel 8:100-1) and the deferential infinitive ¨anzo˙Wa (1449 Kok 23), among other forms. An explanation similar to that for ···*m*- and ···*n*- stems accounts for some of the peculiarities of the -l- verbs (§8.3.2), which were originally ···*l*- stems.

8.2.2. Stems ending in *h*.

When attaching an ending that starts with a consonant, a stem that ends in a vowel + h treats the h as /t/ — which is then subject to automatic alternations (§2.6) — unless the ending-initial consonant is t, c, or k, with which the h undergoes metathesis. A stem that ends in a sonant + h (namely lh and nh) drops the h unless the ending-initial consonant is t, c, or k, with which the h undergoes metathesis. But stems which end in vowel + ph, th, or ch reduce the syllable-excess to p or t before attaching a consonant-initial ending of any kind, and show the aspiration only when the ending begins with a vowel and so can accommodate the syllable excess. (There are no endings that begin with p; there are no verb stems ···kh-.)

	-ko	-ta	-ci	-sup.nita	-nun
noh-	noh.ko	noh.ta	noh.ci	noh.sup.nita	noh.nun
'put'	/nokho/	/notha/	/nochi/	/nossumnita/	/nonnun/
ilh-	ilh.ko	ilh.ta	ilh.ci	ilh.sup.nita	ilh.nun
'lose'	/ilkho/	/iltha/	/ilchi/	/ilssumnita/	/illun/
kkunh-	kkunh.ko	kkunh.ta	kkunh.ci	kkunh.sup.nita	kkunh.nun
'sever'	/kkunkho/	/kkuntha/	/kkunchi/	/kkunssumnita/	/kkunnun/

Before a vowel, the stem-final **h** goes unpronounced but it is sometimes restored for emphasis, as described in §2.7.3, or as a reading pronunciation. In Middle Korean a noun, as well as verbs and adjectives, could end in a basic *h* (*nwo˙h on* 'the cord'), which metathesized when a particle such as ˙*two* or ˙*kwa* was attached, and the resulting strings were written phonemically: *nwo˙khwa* ← *nwoh ˙kwa* 'with the cord'. Before a voiced consonant or as a free form, such nouns suppressed the final **h** and it went unwritten in Hankul: *nwo* ← *nwoh* 'cord'. For a list of these nouns, see §4.2. There are a few compound nouns that may show the metathesis, such as *pol˙thwok* (1459 Wel 21:7b; 1466 Kup 1:36a; 1481 Twusi 22:13a, 16:24a) 'elbow' ?< *polh ˙twok*, treated by LCT as *pol[h] ˙thwok* but the second noun appears only in this compound.

According to the rules in KEd a stem that ends ···**lh**- is treated like ···**l**-, but that will not account for the fortition that is found in **ilh.sup.nita** /ilssumnita/ and **ilh.so** /ilsso/. Kim-Renaud (1986:24-5, 22:n7) would derive such forms by three rules: **ilh-so** → *ilt-so ("h-unreleasing") → *ilt-sso ("post-unrelease fortition") → **ilsso** ("coronal [= apical] deletion"). I wonder, however, if the fortition may not be simply a part of the almost automatic rule **ls** → **lss** (§2.6), which applies generally to most strings, with a few exceptions (in Seoul) such as ···**l se**, in which the particle can be treated as an abbreviation of **ey se**. Notice that the KEd rule implies that the reductions ···**lh** → ···**l**, together with reductions from ···**lth**-, form a new category, not to be confused with either the -T/L- stems (**kēt-/kel-** 'walk') or the -L- stems (**kē-l-** 'hang'), for the modifier forms differ:

ilh- 'lose'	ilh.sup.nita /ilssumnita/	ilh.nun /illun/
kēt-/kel- 'walk'	kēt.sup.nita /kēssumnita/	kēt.nun /kēnnun/
kē-l- 'hang'	kēp.nita/kēmnita/	kēnun < ˙˙ke˙non

8.2.3. Stems ending in w: -W- (= -P/W-).

Stem-final **w** alternates with **p** before a consonant and coalesces with a following **u** in the vowel phoneme **wu**; and that is one reason we write what is traditionally regarded as a single phoneme with a digraph that consists of **w** + **u**. The basic **w** is heard only before the infinitive ending -^{e}/a and the past-tense element derived from the infinitive (-^{e}/ass-), yet also sometimes before the derived adverb/noun ending -**i**: **tewi** 'warmth' but **kakkai** 'vicinity, nearby'. The following examples show the contrast between a vowel stem ending in ···**wu** ('give'), a -p/w- stem ('help'), and a p-final stem ('wear'):

	-ko	-sup.nita	-nun	-^{e}/a	-una
cwu-	cwuko	cwup.nita	cwunun	cwue[1]	cwuna
tōw-	tōpko	tōpsup.nita	tōp.nun	towa	towuna
ip-	ipko	ipsup.nita	ip.nun	ip.e	ipuna

[1] Usually not distinguished in pronunciation from /cwuwe/ 'pick up' (§2.7.6).

The modern Hankul writing system has no way to show a **w** at the end of a syllable, since /w/ is written as part of the vowel medial, and so the infinitive **towa** has to be written **to** + **wa** and the adversative **towuna** must be written **to** + **wu** + **na**, even though the endings are clearly -**a** and -**una**. Since morph-final **w** occurs only for inflected stems, the alternations of **w** are completely automatic — phonemically determined. (See also the remarks on -W- stems in §9.5-6.) In some of the provinces the -W- stems are treated as regular ···**p**- stems: Hwanghay and Phyengan (Pak Wensik 25); Kyengsang, Cenla, and Hamkyeng (Choy Hyenpay 1959:332-3); Mkk 1960:3:33 cites Cincwu in South Kyengsang. The **w** is thought to have been a voiced fricative in the 15th century (/W/), and the stems were probably lenited from an original *-*p*(^{u}/o)- under conditions that kept them apart from the ···**p**- stems, where the labial stop did not lenite (see Martin 1973, Ramsey 1975).

There are many adjective stems that end in **w**, but only a few processive verbs: **kīw-** 'mend, darn', **kwūw-** 'cook, broil', **nwuw-** 'lie down', **nwuw-** 'bleach' [rare except in the passive **nwui-** = **nwī-** 'get bleached'], **pōyw-** '(I) humbly see', **tōw-** 'help', **yeccwuw-** 'tell (a superior)', **cesswuw-** [obsolete?] 'bow to a divinity' = **cesswu(s)-** [dialect?], **cwūw-** 'pick up', **tut-caw-** [literary, archaic] '(I) humbly hear / listen'.

The anomalous adjective sēlw- is contracted from sēlew- 'be sad'; compare the noun sēlwum 'sadness' < sēlw- + -um (substantive).

Middle Korean treated these -P/W- stems in much the same way. The w was also written as W (the voiced bilabial fricative) or as Ww. The stem ¨twoW- 'help' seems to be unique in that it is often spelled ¨two[W]-, with the labial consonant/semivowel elided but the endings attached as if it were still there. That is similar to what happens for the -(s)- stems, once the MK -z- is totally lost, as in modern ciun < ci˙zun ' ··· that has built'. Examples of 'help': two˙[ ]a (1463 Pep 1:14b, 1481 Twusi 8:50b); ¨two[Jo˙sya (1462 ¹Nung 1:37b); two˙[Jol (1462 ¹Nung 8:57a), two[ ]˙o.1 i ˙ye (1465 Nay 3:62a), two˙[Jon (1482 Nam 1:65b). If a -w- were inserted before the epenthetic o of all but the first example, the forms would be taken as two˙wo-, the modulated stem. Compare this stem with ¨kwoW- 'pretty': kwo˙wa (1481 Twusi 22:43a), ¨kwoWo˙sya (1459 Wel 21:211b). The stems with other vowels have either W or w in the forms that do not have p: ¨swuyW-, ¨kiW-, mu˙zuyyeW-, sa˙wonaW-, ... ; also ··· lwoW- and ··· loW-. When the adverb-deriving suffix -i is attached, however, any -W- stem normally drops the final labial: ¨swuy˙i 'easily' < ¨swuyW-, ¨kwo˙i 'nicely' < ¨kwoW-, ... Interestingly, King 1991b:7 reports that Soviet materials on Korean from the 1920s consistently preserve the unlenited p for the -P/W- stems, treating them as regular ···p- stems, but tōp- 'help' is given exceptional forms with the labial consonant eroded: toa for the infinitive (= towa) and towum for the substantive.

Roth (1936:163) gives as the "extended" stem for kwūp- 'bake', cwūp- and cip- 'pick up' the forms kwu-u-, cwu-u-, ci-u- without the labial glide, but (173-4) he has tōp- 'help', kōp- 'be pretty', nwūp- 'lie down', and etwup- 'be dark' with the extension (p →) ···wu, as expected, except that cip- is nonleniting in the standard language. His data may reflect dialect divergences.

The MK stems began with the rising pitch (¨) except when attaching endings that began with a basic vowel. We explain that by assuming that they were originally low-initial dissyllables which had retained the high pitch of an elided vowel ··· ˙p[ᵘ/o]- (before lenition of the p to W) and blended it with the initial low to produce the rise. For more on this, see the discussion in §8.2.1.

8.2.4. Stems ending in l: -T/L-.

When attaching an ending that starts with a consonant, a stem that ends in a basic l treats that final consonant as if it were /t/. Korean dictionaries cite verbs in the indicative assertive form -ta, and that form has an orthographic -t- instead of -l- for these stems; Korean grammarians treat the stems as "irregular T stems", just as they treat the -w- stems as "irregular P stems". Pak Wensik (24) says the stems are treated as regular t-final consonant stems in Hwanghay and Phyengan. (Kim Yengpay 1984:53 says tut- 'hear' is the only stem of this type that is regular in Phyengan; sīt-/sil- 'load' and the others all lenite the t to l as in Seoul.) Mkk 1960:3:33 says there are two variant treatments in Cincwu in South Kyengsang: the local mūl.ko /mūlkko/ and the standard mūt.ko /mū[t]kko/ 'asking'. The Cincwu version, which may be regarded as ···lq-, is also reported from Hamkyeng. The existence of the lq may lend support to Cook's speculation that these stems have an underlying form ···lt-, though I believe that to be historically inaccurate. An alternative theory has the -T/L- verbs continuing a lost distinction between two kinds of liquid: earlier *r as well as l. The most likely historical explanation, however, is that these stems have lenited a final t (underarticulating the stop as a flap) under conditions that kept them apart from the ···t- stems that did not lenite (see Martin 1973, Ramsey 1975), so that the -T/L- stems are quite parallel to the -W- ("p-leniting") stems. Dialects which do not differentiate these two types of stems from their nonleniting counterparts, the ···p- and ···t- stems, just never underwent the lenition. Those dialects which lack the ···t- version altogether have generalized the lenited forms, and that accounts for the data reported by ¹Yi Iksep from Myengcwu county of Kanglung, where kēlkkwu means 'walking' (standard kēt.ko) and kēlkwu means 'hanging it' (standard kēlko), kelumwun means 'if one walks' (standard kel.umyen) and kēlmun means 'if one hangs it'.

The consonant stems ending in l (lenited from t) are to be kept distinct from l-extending vowel stems (§8.3.2), for these are treated as "regular", i.e. l-dropping, stems by the Korean grammarians, who fail to draw the major dichotomy between consonant-final and vowel-final stems that we rely upon here. The grammarians are historically correct, in that etymologically the extension is part of the stem.

Interestingly, the 1930 grammar of the Soviet Koreanist O Changhwan treated the -L- stems much as Martin 1954 and this book do (King 1991d). The following examples illustrate the differences between an l-extending vowel stem (kë-l- 'hang'), a consonant stem that ends in l (kël- 'walk'), and a regular consonant stem that ends in t (ket- 'gather up, fold / roll up').

	-ko	-sup.nita	-nun	-e/a	-una
kë-l-	këlko	këp.nita	kënun	kel.e	këna
kël-	kët.ko /kë[t]kko/	kët.sup.nita /këssumnita/	kët.nun /kënnun/	kel.e /kele/	kel.una /keluna/
ket-	ket.ko /ke[t]kko/	ket.sup.nita /kessumnita/	ket.nun /kennun/	ket.e /kete/	ket.una /ketuna/

The only form in which the l-extending vowel stems fall together with the l-final consonant stems is the infinitive and the past-tense forms that are built on it: kel.ess.ta 'hung' or 'walked'.

Variations of /l/ with /t/ turn up spottily in other parts of the vocabulary, as in these words:
 ithul 'two days', ithut nal /ithunnal/ 'the next day'
 meychil, meychit nal /meychinnal/ 'what day of the month'
 puchwul 'squatting board in toilet', puchwut tol 'squatting stones'
 phul 'grass', phut so /phusso/ 'cow on summer diet of grass'
 sël (nal) 'New Year('s day)', sët tal 'December'
 sahul 'third day', sahut nal /sa(h)unnal/ 'third day of the month'
 swul 'spoon', swut kalak /swukkalak/ 'spoon'
 ca-l- 'be fine, small', cat-talah- 'be quite fine (small)'
 së-l- 'be unfamiliar', sët-pulu- /seppulu-/ 'be awkward, clumsy'

He Wung (313:n35) explains sët tal, swut kalak, and mus ··· = /mut/ (1722 Sipkwu) = mwul(-i) 'the (whole) group, all' < ˙mwul as a /t/ that comes from the /s/ of së[l] s tal < ¨se[l] s ˙tol (1466 Kup), swu[l] s kalak, and mu[l] s ··· , used to represent the adnominal (genitive) particle (CF Part II, s NOTE 1). That leaves sël < ¨sel (1481 Samkang) and swul < ˙swul (1481 Twusi) as the original forms. In KEd I treated swul as a further contraction of swut kal(ak) and did not try to explain sël, though it would have been possible to suggest the contraction së[t ta]l. Those explanations, however, must be rejected in favor of He Wung's, despite my remarks in KM 54:n32, and his explanation will apply to the other nouns above, as well. That is, all noun-final alternations of ···l and ···t··· are from ···[l] s ··· , with the liquid elided (for more on that, see §2.11.3 and the entry for the particle s in Part II). Notice that ¨sel also meant 'years of age' (modern sal) and therefore may be connected in some way with ¨sal- 'live, be alive'.

See Martin 1983:27 for etymological examples of lenited $t \to l$. In some cases the source of the lenition survives as the modern affricate because of the (southern) merger ty > c: tolyang or tōcang 'Buddhist seminary' < MK ¨twotyang < ¨TWO-¨TYANG. The lenited form of the plain copula ila ← i-ta is used in quotations.

A note on notation. Contrary to the historical development, we are not considering the -l- of the l-extending bases as elided (dropped) in the several paradigmatic forms where it fails to appear, and therefore do not use an apostrophe to mark its absence. We write sānta for 'lives' rather than "sā'nta". Accordingly, we will not consider as abbreviation the unextended form of the stem in verb compounds such as ë-nok- (< ë[l]-) 'freeze and then thaw' and tu-nallinta (< tu[l]-) 'lifts it and makes it fly'. If we modify our description to match the history, we could still omit the notational reminder of the elision, which goes unmarked in the Hankul orthography, saving our apostrophes for more meaningful cases of optional contractions, such as l' for lul, and elision of the final consonant of a noun in compounds (pu' son 'fire scoop', mu'-tepta 'is sultry', na'-nal-i 'day after day, daily'), rather than let them clutter up the verb paradigms.

The stem tut- / tul- 'listen, hear' is the only -T/L- stem with the vowel /u/, and in MK it was unique in having the same low initial accent in all forms. The *t*-leniting stems of Middle Korean that did not have the minimal high vowels *u* or *o* began with the rising pitch (¨) except when attaching endings that began with a basic vowel. (The expected rising pitch automatically lost its high component in closed syllables like C^uoC, leaving only the low pitch: $[¨]C^uoC- < *C^uo\,C[^uo]-$.) We explain that by assuming that they were originally low-initial dissyllables which had retained the high pitch of an elided vowel … $'t[^uo]-$ (before lenition of the t to l) and blended it with the initial low to produce the rise. For more on this, see the discussion in §8.2.1.

8.2.5. S-dropping stems: -(s)-.

A few stems end in basic s when a consonant-initial ending is attached but drop the s when the ending starts with a vowel. The SELECTION of the vowel-initial alternant of a two-shape ending is just like that for any other stem so that shapes beginning -u… will often follow the vowel that remains when the s drops. In ordinary speech, however, the minimal vowel u is often dropped after a vowel (§2.7.5) and that leaves the stem shape much like that of the h-dropping ambivalent stems and the regular h-final stems that drop the h between vowels (§8.2.2, §2.7.3). It will prove helpful to compare a simple vowel stem (na- 'emerge'), an h-final consonant stem (nah- 'give birth to'), an s-dropping stem (nā(s)- 'get / be better'), and a regular s-final stem (as- 'seize'). The table below shows the pronunciations heard for each spelling.

	na-	nah-	nā(s)-	as-
-ko	nako	nah.ko	nās.ko	as.ko
	/nako/	/nakho/	/nā[t]kko/	/a[t]kko/[1]
-ta	nata	nah.ta	nās.ta	as.ta
	/nata/	/natha/	/nātta/	/atta/
-ci	naci	nah.ci	nās.ci	as.ci
	/naci/	/nachi/	/nācci/	/acci/
-sup.nita	nap.nita	nah.sup.nita	naup.nita	as.sup.nita
	/namnita/	/nassumnita/	/naumnita/ →	/assumnita/
		nah.up.nita	/nāmnita/	
[dialect]		/naumnita →/		
		/nāmnita/		
-nun	nanun	nah.nun	nās.nun	as.nun
	/nanun/	/nānnun/	/nānnun/	/annun/
-e/a	na	nah.a	naa	as.e(, asa)[2]
	/na/	/naha/ →	/naa/ = /nā/	/ase(, asa)/
		/naa/ = /nā/		
-una	nana	nah.una	nauna	as.una
	/nana/	/nahuna/ →	/nauna/ →	
		/nauna/ →	/nāna/	
		/nāna/		

[1] The bracketed t is normally suppressed (§2.6): -tk- → -tkko → -kko.

[2] The Hankul orthography standardizes the historical spelling **as.a**, and in certain dialects only that form is heard, but we have chosen as standard the Seoul **as.e** (see §9.4), though the verb is uncolloquial.

The pronunciation /nassumnita/ corresponds to both **nass.ˢup.nita** 'emerged' (← na-, past formal) and **nah.sup.nita** 'gives birth to' (← nah-, nonpast formal). The plain past of na- is /natta/ (nass.ta) with short vowels; the long first-syllable vowel in /nātta/ signals 'gave birth to' (nah.ass.ta) or 'got better' (naass.ta). Notice that the shape of the infinitive after …a(s)- and …a(h)- is -a, even though Seoul speakers use the shape -e after …aC-, including as- and the more colloquial **ppay-as-**. Despite the Hankul orthographic prescription we treat **as.e** as the standard colloquial infinitive and speak of **as.a** as a literary or dialect version of that. Under the influence of schoolroom and dialect pronunciations the Seoul colloquial standard may be reverting to the older form, but it would be premature to say now (1991) that the historical change in Seoul has been reversed.

With the suppression of postvocalic **h** and **u**, the h-final consonant stems fall together with the s-dropping stems when the infinitive or a two-shape ending is attached, and together they differ from a simple vowel stem (such as **na-**) only by the length of the vowel left behind. But the forms are kept distinct in Hankul spelling, at least by those who spell correctly, since the spelling is based on the uncontracted forms.

It will be recalled that long vowels in the l-extending, s-dropping, and -w- stems are shortened BEFORE ENDINGS BEGINNING WITH A VOWEL (§2.7.2). In general, that is not true of the h-final consonant stems: **cōh.a** 'is good' = /cōa/ or, with epenthetic glide (§2.7.6), /cōwa/. But occasionally the shortened forms are heard: /co(w)a/ or even /cwa/ and (§2.7.4) in rapid speech /ca/. In /cōna/ ← /cō(h)una/ for **cōh.una** 'is good but' we could attribute the length to the dropped -u- but we might just as well say it is retained from the basic shape. The shortening of the long vowels reflects their origin as the MK low-high rising tone which resulted from contraction of the high-pitched syllable following the basic low with which the stems began (see below).

According to Mkk 1960:3:33, speakers of Cincwu in South Kyengsang treat only the stem **cī(s)-** 'build' as s-dropping; the other s-dropping stems are regular s-final consonant stems like **as-** 'seize' and **wus-** 'laugh'. Horne 1950-1 came across only the one stem **cī(s)-** and decided on a clever analysis that treated the stem as basic **ciy-**, perhaps misled by the y-epenthesis (§2.7.6; §2.11) that makes the infinitive **cie** sound like /ciye/. Finding cases with other vowels, I amended her analysis and treated these stems as ending in a basic **q**, to account for the reinforcement reflexes that are the only evidence in Seoul speech that the stem has a basic final consonant. In the 15th century the stem-final consonant was a voiced [z] before a vowel, so that the infinitive was spelled *ci ze*, using the obsolete triangle symbol for the MK /z/. Since modern dialects retain forms such as /nasa/ for **naa** 'get/be better' ← **nā(s)-** and lack the distinction from regular ···s- stems, we assume that the MK version was an ephemeral lenition of an earlier -s-, a lenition which took place under conditions (a later-elided minimal vowel) absent from the regular s-final consonant stems (see Martin 1973, Ramsey 1975). For more on the history of the stems with ···(s)- < ···z- see §2.11.4.

The MK verb **kuz-** 'pull' is the only *s*-leniting stem with the vowel /u/ and it continues its initial low pitch through a following /u/, as in *kuzu˙m ye* (1481 Twusi 23:10a), but that is a reduction of **kuzGu-*, as we can see from forms with other vowels, such as the infinitive *kuz˙Ge* (1463 Pep 2:200b), and the earlier shape of the stem is reconstructed as **kusuk-* (see §8.3.1). On the other hand, the MK verb **toz-** 'love', with the other minimal vowel *o*, is from **to˙s[o]-*, and has such forms as *to˙zo˙m ye* (1462 ¹Nung 4:31a), *to˙zon* (1462 ¹Nung 9:96a), and *to˙za* (ibid.). The other stems began with the rising pitch (˙) except when attaching endings that began with a basic vowel (whether ᵘ/o or ᵉ/a). We explain that by assuming that they were originally low-initial dissyllables which had retained the high pitch of an elided vowel ··· ˙s[ᵘ/o]- (before lenition of the *s* to *z*) and blended it with the initial low to produce the rise. For more on this, see the discussion in §8.2.1. Presumably **koz-** 'cut' is like **toz-** 'love' and accordingly is from **ko˙s[o]-*, but only the infinitive *ko˙za* is attested. Similarly only the infinitive *puz˙Ge* is attested for **puzG-** < **pusuk-* = **pozG-** < **posok-* 'crush'.

8.3. Vowel stems.

There are groups of stems which end in every vowel but one: **swī-** 'rest', **sēy-** 'count', **toy-** 'become', **nāy-** 'put out', **ssu-** 'use; write', **sa-** 'buy', **cwu-** 'give', **po-** 'see'. The exception is the vowel **e**, for the only examples of ···**e-** in Seoul speech are the abbreviations **ile-**, **kule-**, **cele-**, and **ette-**, and these are irregular stems (§8.3.5) because the infinitives (**ilay**, **kulay**, **celay**, **ettay**) are like **hay**, the irregular infinitive of **ha-** 'do/say/be'. The Hankul spelling writes the stem **su-** 'stand' as **se-** (thereby clarifying to some extent the causative stem **seywu-** 'make stand'), and that is what it must once have been (for MK had °*sye-*), but in Seoul speech the verb is regularly **su-**. There are, however, a few clichés which retain **sen** for the modifier (used as an adnoun) instead of the more usual **sun**. Two stems end in ···**ye-** in the Hankul spelling (and in non-Seoul speech), as they did in Middle Korean: **phye-** 'smooth out, ... ' and **khye-** 'turn on (lights), ... '. I treat these as back formations from the Seoul stems **phi-** and **khi-**, based on the contracted infinitives **phye** ← **phie** and **khye** ← **khie**, despite the earlier versions and the variant pronunciation **phey-** and **khey-**, which is apparently confined to northern speakers. A similar case is **kēnnu-**, spelled **kēnne-** by the Korean grammarians, thereby clarifying the causative **kēnney-**. The Hankul spellings are historically correct: **phi-** was °*phye-* in the 15th century, and **khi-** was first attested in the early 16th century as *khye-*; **kēnnu-** was MK ¨*ken ̇ne-* < ¨*ket ̇na-* (the second vowel assimilated to the first) from a compound verb ¨*ket-°na-* ('walk' + 'emerge').

Most of the endings attach to the vowel stems in a simple and expected fashion, but there are various complexities involving both the ending and the stem for the infinitive form; they are set forth in §9.4.

8.3.1. L-doubling vowel stems: -LL-.

The l-doubling vowel stem has a shape which ends in vowel + **lu-**. When the infinitive (**-e / -a**) or the past tense (**-ess- / -ass-**) is attached, the vowel **u** drops, as expected, and the remaining **l** geminates — as not expected: **pulu- → pulle** 'calls', **molu- → mōlla** 'does not know' (the long **ō** in the infinitive and forms derived from it is an irregularity). Many Koreans regularize these verbs by doubling the **l** everywhere; they treat the stems as **pullu-**, **mollu-**, etc. Since the modern Hankul system makes no provision for two l's at the end of a syllable block, the second **l** is perforce written as the initial of the second syllable (**pul + le, mol + la**) even though the infinitive ending itself is just the final vowel.

The odd behavior of these stems goes back to the earliest Hankul texts, so we must reconstruct a still earlier history to account for them. The basic forms were probably pre-MK **pulul-* and **¨mwolol-*. When a consonant was attached, the final liquid dropped, *pulu- ̇ta* < **pulul- ̇ta* and *pulu- ̇kwo* < **pulul- ̇kwo*; but when a vowel was attached, the minimal vowel MK $^u\!/\!o$ (> **u**) itself dropped: *pull-e* < **pulul-e*. Yet among the modern **-ll-** verbs there are some, such as **talu-** 'be different', for which the 15th-century infinitive was given a spelling (with "*···l·-*") that we interpret as /*···lG-*/ with the liquid followed by a consonant (probably a voiced velar fricative): **talle** = **talla** < *tal ̇Ga*. These stems we reconstruct as pre-Hankul **···l$^u\!/\!o$G-*, probably lenited from **···l$^u\!/\!o$k-*, so that the MK stem *talo- / talG-* was earlier **taloG-* < **talok-* and the **G* dropped before a consonant (**taloG-ta* → MK *talo ̇ta* > modern **taluta**) but before a vowel the cluster *···lG···* assimilated the fricative to the liquid and produced the modern *···ll···* : **taloG-a* > MK *tal ̇Ga* > **talla** > (Seoul) **talle**. The Taycen version of **taluta** is **taltha**, with a stem **talh-** that may reflect the *G* (see also the Phyengan version, p. 240); another Cenla version **talpu-** (Choy Hak.kun 1978:1191) either carries a suffix or implies that the reconstruction **talok-* should be corrected to **talop-*. (LHS gives a Kyengsang version as **talp-**.) There is other evidence pointing to an original shape like **···l$^u\!/\!o$p-* for the doublets that lie behind **ccalp- / ccelp-** (< *cyelp-*) < *tyalo- / tyel$^u\!/\!o$-* < *tyelG-* < **tyelW-* 'be short, fine' ? < **tyalop- / tyelup-*, **nelp-** and **nelu-** < *nel$^u\!/\!o$-* 'be wide' ? < **nelup-*.

Certain peculiarities of dialect versions of stems are also to be accounted for in terms of stem alternants in the Hankul texts for which an earlier single form is to be reconstructed. Most of the types are represented both in verb stems and in nouns, as shown below. (This table is adapted from Martin 1982/3:8-9, with corrections. The Middle Korean alternants are followed by the modern Seoul forms.)

(1)   **···mok-*   **simok-* 'plant'
                             simo- / simk- > **sīm(q)-**
                        *tomok- 'soak'
                             tomk- / tomo- > **tamku-**

     *···mwok   **namwok* 'tree'
                             namwo / namwok··· > **namu**

     *-mwuk   **kwumwuk* 'hole'
                             kwumwu / kwumk··· > (**kwumeng**)
                        *pwulmwuk 'bellows'
                             pwulmwu / pwulmk··· > (**phulmu**)

(2) *-n^u/ok   *nyen^u/ok 'other' ? < *nyonok[1]
                                                         nyen^u/o / nyenk··· > **yenu**

*···s^u/ok(-)   *posok- 'crush'   *asok 'younger sibling'
                pozo- / pozG- > **pa(s)-**   azo / azG··· > **awu**
                = **paswu-**
                                                 *yes^u/ok 'fox' ? < *yosok[1]
                                                   yez^u/o / yezG··· > **yewu**
                     *kusuk- 'pull'   musuk 'radish'
                kuzu- / kuzG- > **kkū(s)-**   muzu / muzG··· > **muwu, mū**

(3) *···l^u/ok(-)   *talok-[2] 'differ'   *calok 'gunnysack'
                talo- / talG- > **talu- / tall-**   calo / calG··· > **calwu$_1$**
                                                   *colok 'handle'
                                                  colo / colG··· > **calwu$_2$**
                                                  *nolok 'ferry'
                                                  nolo / nolG··· > **nalwu**
                                                  *nwolok 'roe deer'
                                                  nwolo / nwolG··· > **nolwu**
                                                  *siluk 'steamer'
                                                  silu / silG··· > **silwu**

(4) *···l^u/ol(-)   *molol- 'dry up'   *molol 'ridge'
                molo- / moll- > **malu- / mall-**   molo / moll··· > **malwu**
                *hulul- 'flow'   *holol 'one day'
                hulu- / hull- > **hulu- / hull-**   *holo / holl··· > **halwu**

(5) *···lok, ···lol   *kolok, *kolol 'powder'
                                                  kolo / kolG··· , / koll··· > **kalwu**

[1] When the vowel of the first syllable is *e*, the reduced vowel of the second syllable appears both as *u* and as *o*, so we reconstruct an undecided *^{u}/o. The situation probably points to original *yo··· for such morphemes, even in the absence of other evidence.

[2] Or perhaps *talop- (see above). What evidence we have for the nouns points to a velar, not a labial: in many dialects (Choy Hak.kun 1978) 'roe deer' is **nolki** or **nolkay(ngi)**, and 'steamer' is **silki** in Kangwen (Tokyey) and also (Kim Yengpay 1984) in Phyengan.

For the last example the evidence may indicate competing versions, one of Type 2 and the other of Type 4, the two types represented by the modern l-doubling stems. Dialect forms (**kalgi, kalgu**) confirm the velar, while forms such as **kallu** and **kalli** may be the result of *lG* > *ll*, and that is the source of the doublet, as confirmed by the dating of *kol.l oy* (1795 [1]No-cwung 1:20b [K]) < *kol˙G oy* ([?]1517- [1]No 1:23a) and *kol˙G ul* ([?]1517- [1]No 1:23b), where the later version of the passage has *kol.l i* (1795 [1]No-cwung 1:20b [K]) though LCT 9b has that as "*kol.l ol*". But Ramsey 1975:40 thinks we should reconstruct the doublet on the basis of Ceycwu **kolol** (Hyen Phyenghyo 1961:116a). I wonder if all the forms may come from a unique shape *kolGol < *kol(o)kol, conceivably a reduplication.

Of the nouns with two alternants, the shape on the left of the slash is the "free" form, used alone or before certain peripheral particles such as ˙*two* (highlighted focus), ˙*kwa* (comitative / reciprocal), ˙*lwo* (instrumental), *s* (genitive), and sometimes ˙*non* (subdued focus). The shape on the right is required to attach the primary particles ˙*i* (nominative), ˙*ul* (accusative), ˙^{u}/oy (genitive or locative / allative), ˙^{e}/ay (locative / allative), and sometimes ˙^{u}/on (subdued focus), as well as the copula ˙*i*··· .

Some of the modern dialects retain features that more clearly point to the earlier forms. In Phyengan, for example (Kim Yengpay 1984:88, 90, 104, 168-71), the following nouns have /lk/ for earlier *l^u/ok: **calk(i) = calwu** 'bag' or 'handle', **kalk(i) = kalwu** 'flour', **malk(i)** also **mall(i) = malwu** 'ridgebeam' **nangk(i) = namu** 'tree', **nolk(i) = nolwu** 'roe deer' (attested as [norogi] = **noloki** in 1898 Tayshin), **silk(i) = silwu** 'steamer'. And the following nouns have /lk/ for MK *lG*: **elkey-pit = elley-pis** 'coarse wooden comb', **kelk(w)um = kelum** 'fertilizer', **kwulk^e/ay = kwulley** 'bridle', **melkwu** = **melwu** 'mulberry', **molkay** = **molay** 'sand', **nilkwey** = **iley** 'seven days', **pelkeci** = **peleci** 'worm', **swulkwu** = **swuley** 'wagon', **sⁱ/ᵤlkeng** = **sileng** 'shelf', **tolkaci** = **tolaci** 'bellflower'. An earlier velar is also indicated by Phyengan **alkwuy-** = **alli-** 'let know, inform' and probably **taluh-** / **talu-** 'be different' (with such forms as **taluh.key** and **talun**). Perhaps also (Kim Yengpay 1984:103) the Phyengan stem **kilk-** = **kīl-** 'be long'; notice *kil˙li* (1586 Sohak 4:53b) ?< **kil˙Gi* 'for a long time' (= *ki˙li* > **kil.i**), also MK ˙*kilh* 'path' (? < 'length') and the peculiar spelling ˙*kilq˙h ol* for one occurrence of its accusative (1462 ¹Nung 6:80a).

The noun *mi˙lu* 'dragon' looks as if it should have the forms *milG⋯* < **miluk* or *mill⋯* < **milul* but the only examples are of the free form in glossaries. In other texts the Chinese word *LYWONG* is used for dragon. The following words, probably nativized Chinese nouns containing the diminutive suffix -*zo* (= ˙˙*co*), have only one shape, unlike the words in (2) above:

co˙zo > *couy* > **cawi** 'kernel' or (˙*nwun s* ~) 'pupil (of eye)'
pwo˙zo > *pwo[z]o* > **po** 'small bowl'
swu˙zo, swu˙zu > *swu[z]o* 'a seal-ribbon' ?< *˙˙SYWUY-˙˙CO*
sway˙zo > *sa[z]o* > **(cwu)-sawi** 'dice'

8.3.2. L-extending vowel stems: -L-.

The l-extending vowel stem selects the appropriate alternant of a two-shape ending in the same way as an ordinary vowel stem, but it adds an **l** to the stem before certain endings:

before all ONE-shape endings that begin with a vowel or with a voiceless consonant other than **s** – and ¹Yi Ungpayk 1961:499 prefers the extension before **s** (of a one-shape ending), too, treating **nōlsey** as standard and **nōsey** as variant;

before only those TWO-shape endings that begin with **l** or **m** + vowel or **y**, such as -**lye**, -**la**, -**myen** – and -**m** when it is followed by a vowel-initial particle shape such as **ulo**, **ey**, or **a**.

Perhaps the rule can be more clearly stated: the -**l**- extension is present except before **p, s, n, mC, m|** and except before the ending -**o**. Accordingly the stem **tu-l-** 'enter' makes the forms **tulko, tulta, tulci, tulkeyss.ta, tul.e, tul.ess.ta, tullye, tulla, tulmyen, tulm ulo**; but **tuo, tunun, tunta, tuna, tun, tul(q)**, and /**tum**/ (spelled **tulm**) + pause or consonant. A long vowel in a one-syllable l-extending stem is shortened in the infinitive and past forms: **kē-l-** 'hang' becomes **kel.e, kel.ess.ta**. (The length in the stem reflects the monosyllabification of a pre-MK dissyllable: **ke˙lu-* > ˙˙*kel-* / *ke˙lu-*.) There is a substandard variety of speech that inserts /**u**/ between the liquid and a following **m** or **l** (also **n**? – see below): **pulumyen** = **pūlmyen** 'if it blows' (CF An Sangchel 1988:153), **wulul(q)** = **wūl(q)** 'to cry' (Kim-Renaud 1986:112, who says these forms are the more common type in Chwungcheng). According to ¹Yi Tongcay 1989:147 forms like **sal.umyen** for **sālmyen**, **salu.lye** for **sāllye**, and **sal.ul(q)** for **sāl(q)** (to live'), which are ˙˙less commonly used and less readily accepted˙˙ occur (for Seoul) ˙˙only in the speech of some, mostly young, speakers˙˙. There may also be speakers who drop the liquid and say **wūmyen** for **wūlmyen** 'if one cries' (Kim-Renaud 1986:113:n8). In Taycen it is usual to say **mel.un** for **mēn** '(that is) distant' and **kel.un** for **kēn** '(that has) hung'. In describing the variants in conjugation of stems such as **kī-l-** ('be long') one suggestion (1936 Roth 141) is to think of a ˙˙shortened stem˙˙ **kī-** and an ˙˙extended stem˙˙ **kilu-** as supplementary to the normal stem. That may be helpful in considering dialect variants such as **āci** = **ālci** and **alusio** = **āsio** ('know').

It is unclear whether all of the several nonstandard treatments are analogical innovations or whether some are simply preserving uncontracted forms from the earlier language. The Middle Korean treatment of the modifiers (the elided *[ᵘ/o]* is explained below):

⋯*l[ᵘ/o]-n* → ⋯*n*, as in ˙˙*an cyen˙co ˙lwo* (1462 ¹Nung 9:13a) 'since he knew' = **ān kkatalk ulo**; ˙˙*an ti˙s 'i* (1449 Kok 43) 'as if he knew' = **ān tus 'i**, ˙*a˙n i* (1482 Kum-sam 2:2b) 'knew' = **ān kes ita**; ˙˙*men ˙tuy s HHWO-˙KYWOW ˙lol* (1459 Wel 2:69a) 'alien teachings from distant places' = **mēn tey**

⋯*l[ᵘ/o]-no-n* → ⋯*non*, as in ˙˙*a˙no.n i ˙'la* (1482 Kum-sam 2:3a) 'knows' = **ānun kes ita**

⋯*l[ᵘ/o]-l(q)* → ⋯*ll* before *i* or *y*, as in ˙˙*al˙l ye* (˙*mwot ho˙l ye*) (1463 Pep 3:86a) 'can you tell me (or not)?' and ˙*NYELQ-PPAN ay ˙tull i ˙Gwo* (1482 Kum-sam 2:13b) 'how will they possibly enter nirvāṇa?' = **tulq kes in ko**

···l[ᵁ/o]-l(q) → ···l(q) (except before i or y), as in ˙tul ˙tt ol (1463 Pep 1:55b) 'that you can enter' = **tulq kes ul**
There is a puzzling form *annon* for ¨a˙non in 1887 Scott 122; perhaps it is a mistake, or a secondary doubling of the *n* for emphasis.

Before the honorific, modern Seoul uses the "shortened stem" but the earlier language had the "extended stem":
¨a˙losi˙m ye (1465 Wen 1:2:3:6a) = āsimye 'knows and'
¨wu˙lusi˙n i (1449 Kok 57) = wūsini 'cried (and)'

Three situations placed a sibilant directly after a stem, and in these forms the "shortened stem" was used, with the *l* elided: ˙tuson ˙ta (1462 ¹Nung 5:31b) 'does one enter?' (emotive *-so-*), ¨azop˙kwo (1449 Kok 109) 'humbly knowing' (deferential -¨zoW-), ˙tu-˙sa (1447 Sek 13:58a) 'only entering' (= ˙tule ˙za). The basic form of the -L- verbs must have been ···lᵁ/o- but the surface forms are often reduced to ···l- (with loss of the vowel) or ··· (with total loss of the syllable). For those stems beginning with a low pitch (the unmarked tone), the reducing syllable had a high pitch (···˙lo-) and that was kept and blended with the initial low so that, for example, *a˙lo-* became ¨al··· and ¨a-, but the basic accent survived in the infinitive a˙l-a, the modulated forms a˙l-wo-, and the forms with the elided-initial version of the effective forms a˙l-a··· (but not in ¨al-˙Ga··· with the lenited-initial version). The critical factor for the low initial accent is that the surface form of the attached element begins with a basic vowel. That means we must treat the honorific as basically vowel-initial: ¨a˙l-osi-, ¨wu˙l-usi-. One further point: the initial low of a stem with the vowel *u* (but not *wu*) or the vowel *o* (but not *wo*) stayed low in all forms, so that *tul-* 'lift' has such forms as *tun* (1481 Twusi 8:35a), *tunon* (1463 Pep 4:19a), *tul(q)* (1527 Cahoy 3:10b=23b), *tu˙ti* (1463 Pep 2:173b), and *tu¨zopke˙na* (1447 Sek 13:53b), as well as *tu˙le* (1449 Kok 73), *tu˙lwum* (1482 Kum-sam 3:22a), and *tul˙Gwo* (1459 Wel 7:8a). Likewise *mul-* 'bite', *nul-* 'be better', and *pul-* 'envy' (but not ¨*pwul-* 'blow'). There is a counterpart in the initial high pitch of the stems ˙*tul-* 'enter' and ˙*sul-* 'vanish', which is retained in all forms. But the two phenomena may have come about in different ways. Middle Korean had no word-initial syllables *¨Cul or *¨Col except for stems with final consonant clusters as found in ¨kolp˙kwo (1481 Twusi 20:22a) 'lining them up', ¨solp˙kwo (1459 Wel 1:15b) 'telling a superior', and ¨tulp˙kwo (1463 Pep 6:154b) 'piercing'. The few attestations to the contrary are scribal errors: ¨pol˙sye (?1512- Pak 1:37b) must be a mistake for *pol¨sye* (id. 1:5b), a variant (1462 ¹Nung 1:37a, 1518 Sohak-cho 8:7a) of *pol˙sye* (1465 Wen se:68a, 1481 Twusi 7:8a, 1483 Kum-sam 2:2b) = *pol˙ssye* (1447 Sek 6:35b; 1459 Wel 9:36a; 1462 ¹Nung 3:25ab, 9:117a, 1463 Pep 4:63b) 'already'. Therefore the accent of forms such as *kol˙Gwo* (1466 Kup 1:10a) 'changes and' or *tul˙Gwo* (1459 Wel 7:8a) 'lifts and' are functionally equivalent to that of ¨mel˙Gwo (1459 Wel 10:23b) 'is far and'. Even without the accentual clue we will still account for the choice of regular, extended, or shortened stem by assuming that the original stem had two syllables, the second of which bore a basic high pitch. Stems with the higher of the minimal vowels:
*˙tu˙lu- > ˙tul- 'enter', *˙su˙lu- > ˙sul- 'vanish';
*tu˙lu- > [¨]tul- 'lift', *mu˙lu- > [¨]mul- 'bite', *nu˙lu- > [¨]nul- 'be better', *pu˙lu- > [¨]pul- 'envy'. This notation presumes a stage when the low-rise was actually pronounced, but such a stage may not have existed: the reduction of the expected low-rise to just low may have been simultaneous with the truncation. In any event, in Part II we leave the initial syllable of these stems unmarked (i.e. low), following the Hankul spellings. Stems with the lower of the minimal vowels:
*˙ko˙lo- > ˙kol- 'grind', *˙pho˙lo- > ˙phol- 'sell', *˙so˙lo- > ˙sol- 'burn it', *˙sko˙lo- > ˙skol- 'spread it out', *˙spo˙lo- > ˙spol- 'be sharp-pointed; launder; sip', *˙to˙lo- > ˙tol- 'hang';
*ko˙lo- > [¨]kol- 'change', *mo˙lo- > [¨]mol- 'roll it up', *no˙lo- > *[¨]nol- 'fly', *to˙lo- > [¨]tol- 'be sweet; weigh it'.

In citing the l-extending stems of modern Korean, it is handy to mark them off from those consonant stems that end in l (lenited from a pre-MK *t*) by inserting a hyphen before the extension, for when we write **tu-l-** 'enter' that way not only are we reminded that it belongs with the vowel-stem conjugation but that it is different from **tut-** / **tul-** 'hear' (§8.2.4), though the two stems have in common the shape of the infinitive **tul.e** 'enters' or 'hears', and the past-tense forms based on that.

In Hankul the **-l-** extension should always be written with the final syllable of the stem, so that 'enters' and 'hears' are both spelled **tul.e**, but many Koreans violate this rule by beginning the first syllable of the ending with the letter l when possible, especially in the infinitive, and such spellings were common in all but a few of the early texts. The best way to state the Hankul spelling rule is perhaps as follows. For the l-extending vowel stems such as **tu-l-** 'enter', write the l − at the end of the last syllable of the stem − only when it is heard, but always write the substantive as ···**lm**. For the l-final consonant stems such as **tul-** 'hear' (the -T/L- stems), write a stem-final l whenever the l is actually heard, but in all other forms write a stem-final t.

Some of the l-extending stems are confused by many Koreans with regular or l-doubling stems in their paradigmatic forms: we find both **ecilun** and the standard **ecin** for the modifier of **eci-l-** 'be kind, good' and **situlun** alongside **situn** for the modifier of **situ-l-** 'wither, wilt' (as in ∼ **chāyso** 'wilted vegetables' and ··· **son** 'withered hand'). We find also **āl.um** for **ālm** 'knowledge', and **al.un** for **ān**, the modifier of **ā-l-** 'know'. I have also heard /**alumnita**/ = **al.up.nita** for **āp.nita**. Common variants, usually considered nonstandard in the modern language, drop the l before t, l, and especially c: **āci** (= **ālci**) **mōs hanta** 'can't know', **āta** (= **ālta**) **siph.i** 'as we know'. For the negative auxiliary in **haca māca** (= **mālca**) '(no sooner than =) as soon as one does', the shorter form seems to be the norm. All these variants were the usual forms in earlier Hankul texts (§2.11.2), so that the modern standard usage shows either a restoration or a preservation of spoken versions of the language that never did suppress the l.

8.3.3. L-inserting vowel stems.

The l-inserting stem ends in a vowel + **lu**, like the l-doubling stem, but instead of dropping the **u** and doubling the l it adds an l before the infinitive or the past-tense element: **nwulu-** 'be yellow' → **nwulule**. (The orthography, of course, spells the l with the ending: **nwu-lu-le**.) There are only a few such stems: **nwulu-** / **nolu-** 'be yellow', **phulu-** 'be blue', (**kām**)-**phalu-** 'be blue', and **ilu-** 'reach'. Compare **ilule** 'reaches' with **ille** (< *nil˙Ge*) 'says' or (< *il˙Ge*) 'is early' from l-doubling stems **ilu-** < *nil^{u}o-* / *nilG-* < **nil^{u}oG-* and *il^{u}o-* / *ilG-* < **il^{u}oG-*. And compare **nwulule** 'is yellow' with **nwūlle** 'presses down' < MK *nwu˙lu-* / *nwull-* < **nwu˙lul-*. The l-inserting stems must be < *···l^{u}ol-*, but that is clearly attested only for **ilu-** < *ni˙lul-* 'reach'. Taycen regularizes the verb **ilu-** to **ilulu-**, so that **ilulun kos** is said for **ilun kos** 'place reached'.

Aside from the few l-inserting stems, all stems that end in ···**lu-** seem to be the l-doubling type, with the following exceptions, which are simply among the regular vowel stems that happen to end in ···**u-**: **ttalu-** (→ **ttale** or **ttala**) 'conform, obey; pour', **chilu-** (→ **chile**) 'pay, disburse', **tatalu-** (→ **tatale** or **tatala**) 'arrive' from a consonant stem **tatal-** (**tatat.ta**), **mak-talu-** (→ **mak-tale** or **mak-tala**) '(an alley) be closed at one end', and **wulelu-** (→ **wulele**) 'lift one's head, look up, respect'.

South Korean dictionaries also list **salu-** 'winnow' as regular, with the infinitive **sale** (or **sala**), but North Korean dictionaries list it as l-doubling, like the verb **salu-** 'set afire' with the infinitive **salle** (or **salla**). I have been unable to confirm either version, for the common way all my informants say 'winnow' is **khi cil ha-**.

8.3.4. Ambivalent stems: -(H)-.

Ambivalent stems are treated as consonant stems that end in h (§8.2.2) before **-sup.nita** and before one-shape endings not beginning with a vowel (i.e. those other than the infinitive and the past-tense element, which are like the forms of irregular stems, §8.3.5), but as vowel stems, with the h dropped, before two-shape endings other than **-sup.nita** / **-p.nita**. These stems are all derived from an infinitive (**-e**/**-a** etc.) + a reduced form of the irregular adjective **ha-** 'be', so their infinitives and past-tense forms are similar to **hay** and **hayss-** (§8.3.5). Stems derived from the processive verb **ha-** 'do, say' are not ambivalent (despite mistaken spellings by some writers), they are just irregular vowel stems like **ha-**. Compare the following examples:

	ADJECTIVE		VERB INTRANSITIVE
stem	kule(h)- 'be like that'		kule- 'do/say like that'
gerund	kuleh.ko /kulekho/		kuleko
suspective	kuleh.ci /kulechi/		kuleci
formal statement	kuleh.sup.nita		kulep.nita
	/kulessumnita/		/kulemnita/
adversative		kulena	
substantive		kulem	
infinitive		kulay	

In the spoken language all ···h- stems (§8.2.2) are usually treated as if ambivalent, but they have regular infinitives: neh.e (often pronounced /nē/), noh.a (often pronounced /noa/ or even /nwa/, §2.7.7). And they always have the alternant -a (rather than -e) after ···ah-, as in tah.a (often /tā/) from tah- 'touch; reach'. Roth (1936:158) gives the infinitive of cokomah- 'small' as cokoma and of twungkuleh- 'round' as twungkule but has ···ay for the infinitive of the other ambivalent stems.

8.3.5. Irregular stems: ha- and derivatives.

The infinitives are irregular for the stem ha- < °ho- both as the processive verb 'do / say' and as the adjective 'be' (but not the obsolete ha- < °ha- 'big, much, many'), and for certain processive stems derived from it. The infinitives of ha-, ile-, kule-, cele-, ette-, and āmule- are hay, ilay, kulay, celay, ettay, and āmulay. The infinitive of ha- has the literary variant ha.ye (also ha.ya). The past-tense forms follow the pattern of the infinitive: hayss- or ha.yess-, ilayss-, kulayss-, ... There are no literary variants for the derived verbs because they are abbreviations and in formal writing they are expanded to their models: ile hay or ile ha.ye (= ilay), kule hayss- or kule ha.yess- (= kulayss-). Ette 'what way' has a variant ecce, and from that comes a derived adverb (§9.6) ecci with about the same meaning. Notice that /eccay/ 'how' is an abbreviation from ecci hay (→ ecc' 'ay). There is also a derived adverb from the adjective ha- 'be', with the shape hi < ˙hi (§9.6). And we might want to consider sikhi- 'cause to do' as an irregular alternant s- of the stem ha- + the bound postverb -ikhi- (found also in tol.ikhi-); see §7.4.

8.3.6. Irregular stems: k-inserting and n-inserting.

A few stems have two infinitive forms: the normal one is formed as expected, the special one is used only before the command particle la. Do not confuse this word with the subjunctive attentive ending -ula / -la, which is attached directly to the stem and produces a plain command used only in quotative constructions or literary forms. The two are indeed etymologically related, though not quite not as directly as the shapes seem to suggest. Notice the exclamatory use of adjective infinitive + la and see the historical remarks in the entries of Part II. For vowel stems that end in ey, oy, ay, or a the two command structures will sound identical: sēy(e) la, sēyla 'count!'; oy(e) la (spelled "wayla" in the Hankul orthography, CF §9.4), ōyla 'memorize!'; nāy la, nāyla 'pay!'; sa la, sala 'buy!'. But for the other stems a difference is heard: mek.e la, mek.ula 'eat!'; nol.a la, nōlla 'play!'; kie la, kila 'crawl!'; ttwie la, ttwila 'jump!'; cwue la, cwula 'give!'; sse la, ssula 'write!'. In Seoul the forms for 'stand!' are different (se la, sula) but they are identical in the literary / dialect forms (se la, sela).

The vowel stems ca- 'sleep', na- 'emerge, ... ', ka- 'go', and toy- 'become', together with the consonant stem iss- 'stay', insert a k before attaching this secondary infinitive ending: cake la, cala 'sleep!'; nake la, nala 'emerge!'; kake la, kala 'go!'; iss.ke la, iss.ula 'stay!'. The vowel stem o- 'come' uniquely inserts n: one la, ola. In Hankul spelling the inserted phoneme is written as the onset of the infinitive syllable, and the string with the particle is considered by the grammarians to be an unanalyzed ending (ka-ke-la, o-ne-la, iss-ke-la). There may be other stems that belong to this class. According to Choy Hyenpay 1959:334-5, competing variants of the type iss.e la and iss.ke la occur for that verb and also tul- 'hear' (tul.e la and tut.ke la), cwuk- 'die' (cwuk.e la and cwuk.ke la), anc- 'sit' (anc.e la and anc.ke la), and su- 'stand' (se la and suke la). Choy treats the -ke version as "dialect" for all these stems, but that may not be entirely accurate. I have heard **ka la** for **kake la** and for **one la** we can expect to hear **wā la** (which I am told is a "Seoul-ipsism"). In the expression **toylq tay lo toy(ke) la** 'let what may happen happen!' either treatment is accepted. Some people insert **-k-** for all one-syllable stems ending in ···a-. The **-k-** and the **-n-** come from morphemes marking the "effective" aspect of Middle Korean.

9.0. Endings.

We describe the verb endings in terms of sequence positions (§9.1): where each ending fits when put into a long string of endings. More detailed information is given for the specific categories in separate sections (§§9.2–8). The modern verb system developed from an earlier scheme, which is described in a similar fashion in §9.9. The description focuses on form and shape, but both here and in later parts of the book attention is paid also to function and meaning.

9.1. Sequence positions.

The total number of paradigmatic endings for modern Korean is well over 400. And that number does not include structures that are here treated as inflected form + particle (such as **-e se, -e to, -e ya, -e la; -ki ey, -ki lo; -ko nun; -ci man; -um ulo,** ...) or cases of modifier form + postmodifier (such as **-tun ci, -nun ya, -ulq ka, -nun tey,** ...), or abbreviated quotative constructions (such as **-ta 'nta ← -ta hanta, -ulye 'nta ← -ulye hanta, ila 'nun ← ila hanun,** ...). Korean grammarians often lump these constructions together with the inflected forms, and in those cases where the syllable division could show a difference (as with **-nun ya**) the Hankul spelling system leaves them unanalyzed.

We can class the ingredients of the various endings into rough semantic categories: STATUS, TENSE, ASPECT, STYLE, and MOOD. None of these terms are to be taken as identical in reference to the way they are used in descriptions of other languages, though there are obvious similarities. See §11 for some of the ways the categories are used in Korean.

There are two morphemes of TENSE. The PAST marker is historically a contraction of the infinitive mood (typically **-e**) + the stem **iss-** 'exist', and it has the typical shape **-ess-**, with the vowel **e** subject to most of the same variations as those of the infinitive mood ending **-e**, including the shape **-ass-**. We say the contraction is historical because today **anc.e iss.ta** 'is seated' means something slightly different from **anc.ess.ta** 'sat down'. The FUTURE marker has the typical shape **-keyss-**. While it could be regarded as an abbreviation of the shortened variant **ke** of the word **kes** here meaning '[tentative or probable] fact' + **iss-**, the historical origin seems to be the effective infinitive -˙ke + **iss-**, so that the difference between **-ess-** and **-keyss-** comes from the difference between -˙e and -˙ke. The meaning of the past marker is a definite and completed action or state (and so, usually past); the future marker shows an incompleted action and it is used both for a definite future and a probable present (or past). The probable future is expressed by the periphrastic expression **-ulq kes ita** 'it is the probable fact that it will happen/be', with the subject usually limited to the second and third person, since the first person is someone the speaker can make more definite statements about. On this structure is built a probable-past construction **-ess.ulq kes ita** 'it is the probable fact that it will have happened/been'. The action or state of PAST-PAST (**-ess-ess-**) is more remote or more definitely completed than that of PAST, but it is not necessarily related to some other past action, and therefore it does not always correspond to the English pluperfect 'it had happened/been'. Typical cases and their implications are **kass.ess.ta** 'he went (but is back)' as against **kass.ta** 'he went – and is still away' = 'he's gone', **wass.ess.ta** 'he came (but left again)' = 'he was here' as against **wass.ta** 'he came – and is still here' = 'he's here', and **mek.ess.ess.ta** 'I ate – but I'm hungry again' as against **mek.ess.ta** 'I've eaten – so I'm full'. The action or state of PAST FUTURE is either future perfect ('will have happened/been, would have happened/been') or probable past ('probably happened/was, likely has happened/been'). There are PAST-PAST FUTURE forms (**kass.ess.keyss.ta**), but they are rarely heard.

The STATUS morpheme is the honorific marker, which shows a special deference toward the subject of the inflected form – or, in a few constructions, toward an indirect or implied subject. See §11.2. There are five ASPECT morphemes: INDICATIVE, SUBJUNCTIVE, RETROSPECTIVE, and

PROSPECTIVE. The exact range of meaning for each is hard to put into words except in a list of the meanings of all the endings which include the morpheme. The SUBJUNCTIVE aspect underlies, when combined with the assertive mood, the ending which expresses suggestion, proposition, or immediate sequence ("as soon as"), and has the plain-style form **-ca**. When combined with the attentive mood, the subjunctive is realized as the imperative ending that is used to express commands, plain-style **-ula**. The RETROSPECTIVE aspect means something like 'it has been observed that ... '. The observation can be that of the speaker, that of someone else, or a purely grammatical device, used to express a recent past. The PROSPECTIVE shows an action which is to be (by wish, obligation, or just expectation) or a state which is yet to be. The PROCESSIVE focuses attention on an action under way, in process.

The number of what we are calling MOOD morphemes is much larger, and it is at times difficult to decide whether to add to that number by counting as a separate mood an element which can perhaps be broken into smaller parts. I have preferred a rather atomistic analysis. The term "mood" is used very loosely to cover the grammatical meaning of the final morpheme in each inflectional ending. Four of the moods are particularly troublesome because of their frequency and the complexity of alternations in shape when they are combined with other morphemes (see also §11.3, §11.5): the assertive, attentive, apperceptive, and modifier (or adnominal).

The ASSERTIVE mood when attached to indicative, retrospective, or processive aspects gives us forms which can be called "statement" or "declarative", for they assert some fact. When attached to the subjunctive aspect, the assertive mood gives us a form which can be called "suggestion" or "propositive" or "hortative", for it asserts a proposition or suggestion — or, in the plain form **-ca** only, it shows an immediate sequence ("no sooner ... than"). Sometimes the suggestion or proposition is addressed primarily to oneself, the speaker, and translates as 'let me' or 'I will' or 'I must'. More commonly it is inclusive 'let us, let's'. Occasionally, it urges the addressee (in place of a direct command), as in **Ca, phyo lul ppalli sapsita** 'Well (let's you just) hurry up and buy the tickets!'.

The ATTENTIVE mood when attached to indicative, retrospective, or processive aspects gives us forms which can be called "question" or "interrogative": they await a verbal response on the part of the listener. When attached to the subjunctive aspect, the attentive mood gives us a form which can be called "command" or "imperative": it is an order which awaits an action response on the part of the addressee.

The APPERCEPTIVE mood indicates a sudden realization on the part of the speaker, 'Oh, I see that ... !' Certain expected occurrences of this mood are replaced by periphrastic constructions; see §11.5. There are retrospective apperceptive forms, **-tu-kwu(me)n**, but they are interchangeable with the retrospective modifier + postmodifier **-tun kwu(me)n**, and probably they can be regarded as abbreviations of that structure, which is seldom heard in full.

The MODIFIER mood indicates that the form modifies (partially describes) the following noun or noun expression. The resulting forms are adnominal endings; they have sometimes been referred to as "participles".

If we examine all the endings and divide them up into constituent elements, we find seven SEQUENCE POSITIONS, provided we ignore the complex moods discussed in §9.7. The maximum seven-slot possibility can be shown by the ending **-usyess.ess.keyss.^{s}up.nita** /-us(y)essekkeyssumnita/, the honorific past-past future formal indicative assertive, with a meaning something like 'probably deigned to do it at an earlier time, sir'. When we separate the parts of the string by hyphens and write each part according to its basic shape, the ending looks like this: **-usi-ess-ess-keyss-sup-ni-ta**.

The various shapes of the ending morphemes are displayed, in accordance with their sequence positions, in the following table and in the list of mood morphemes that follows it. The assertive and attentive moods have been split into two subsections to facilitate discussion; as a result, the shapes **-ta** and **-ey** are repeated. A slant bar separates forms which alternate depending on whether the attaching stem ends in a consonant or a vowel in its basic shape. Parentheses enclose dialect versions of the standard forms: **(-up-)** for **-sup-**, **(-uo)** for **-so**. A zero alternant is shown as "**[ ]**".

TABLE OF ENDINGS

1. STATUS
Honorific
-usi / -si-
-us(y)- / -s(y)-

2. TENSE
Past
-ess-
-ass-
-ss-
-yess-
-yass-

3. TENSE
Past
-ess-

4a. TENSE
Future
-keyss-

4b. ASPECT
Prospective
-ul- / -l-

5. STYLE
Formal
-sup- (-up-) / -p-
-u-
-[ ]-

6. ASPECT
1. Indicative
-ni-
-n-
-[ ]-
2. Subjunctive
-si-
-sy-
-[ ]-
3. Retrospective
-ti-
-tu-
-t-
-l-
4. Processive
-nun- / -n-

7. MOOD
1. Assertive (§9.2)
   1a. Declarative
   -ta ; -la
   -ey
   -so (-uo) / -o, [adj variant] -ui / -i
   1b. Propositive
   -ta
   -ca
   -ey
2. Attentive (§9.2)
   2a. Interrogative
   -kka
   -i
   -a
   2b. Imperative
   -o
   -ula / -la
3. Apperceptive (§11.5)
   -kwumen, -kwun, -kwulye
   3a. Extended apperceptive -kwun a
4. Modifier (§9.3)
   -un / -n
   -[ ]q (after prospective)
5. Infinitive (§9.4)
   -e, -ey, -ye, -yey
   -a, -ya
   -y, -[ ]
6. Adversative 'but' -una / -na
   6a. Extended adversative 'but anyway'
   -una-ma / -na-ma

7. Sequential 'as' (< adverbialization of modifier + postmodifier)
   -uni / -ni < *-u˙n i* '[its being] the fact that ... '
   7a. Extended sequential 'therefore' **-uni-kka / -ni-kka**
8. Suspective 'questioned / denied fact; supposed / presumed fact' **-ci**
9. Projective 'to the point where, so that' **-tolok**
   9a. Extended projective 'so that indeed' [dialect] **-tolok-i**
10. Adverbative 'so that' **-key**
    10a. Extended adverbative 'so that indeed' [dialect]
        -key-kkum (= **-key to**), **-key-sili**
11. Gerund 'and also' **-ko**
12. Summative 'fact, act' **-ki**
    12a. Extended summative 'since, because' [dialect] **-killey** (= **-ki ey**)
13. Substantive 'fact, doing' (§9.5) **-um / -m**
    13a–d. Complex moods built on the substantive
    13a. Conjunctive 'and' **-umye / -mye** (< **-um** + **ie** copula infinitive)
    13b. Extended conjunctive = conditional 'if, when'
        -umyen / -myen (< **-umye n'** = **-umye nun**)
    13c. Contingent 'upon, as a result of (doing)'
        -um ey / -m ey (treated as **-umay / -may** by the grammarians)
    13d. Assumptive 'I'm willing to, I will/promise'
        -um a / -m a (see below); **-um sey / -m sey**
14. (= 4b + 7.4 =) prospective modifier **-ulq / -lq**
14a–i. Complex moods built on the prospective modifier (§9.7.1)
    14a. Intentive **-ulye / -lye**
    14b. Purposive **-ule / -le**
    14c. Frustrated intentive **-ulyes-man (un) / -lyes-man (un)**
    14d. Prospective assertive **-ulita / -lita; -ulila / -lila**
    14e. Prospective attentive **-ulikka / -likka**
    14f. Prospective sequential **-ulini / -lini**
    14g. Prospective literary indicative assertive
        -ulinit/ɹa / -linit/ɹa
    14h. Intentive assertive [old-fashioned]
        -ulyetta / -lyetta (usually spelled **-ulyes.ta**)
    14i. Cajolative **-ulyem (una) / -lyem (una)**
15a–j. Complex moods built on the effective formative -˙*ke*- (§9.7.3).
    15a. Tentative adversative **-kena**
    15b. Tentative sequential **-keni**
    15c. Semi-literary sequential **-kwantey**
    15d. Provisional **-ketun**
    15e. Tentative conditional **-ketumyen**
    15f. Literary conditional **-kentay**
    15g. Semi-literary concessive **-ken man (un)** (= **-kes man**)
    15h. Literary concessive **-kenul**
    15i. Tentative assertive **-kes.ta**
    15j. Tentative suspective **-kes.ci**
    15k. Immediate future **-ukkey / -kkey** (= **-u'q key / -'q key** < **-[u]lq key**)
16. Transferentive (§9.8) **-ta (ka)**
17. Concessive (p. 823) **-toy**
18. Derived adverb-noun (§9.6) **-i, -li ; -o, -wu**

Our spacing of **-um a** (14d) indicates a rather casual juxtaposition of **-um** and **a**, but the form is actually quite old, possibly even cognate with the Old Japanese future ending ‑‑‑(a)-mu, and the fact that it can be put into an indirect quotation (**chayk ul sa cwum a ko yaksok hayss.ta** 'promised to buy me a book'), like some of the assertive and attentive forms, casts doubt on our analysis. But notice that questions are normally put into indirect quotations by way of adnominalization to the (bound) postmodifier **ya** or **ka** 'question': the spacing of **cwum a ko** may be as defensible as that in **cwuess.nun ya ko** (with obligatory processive marker) or **cōh.un ya ko**. Treating these and similar endings as opaque entities, as the Hankul orthography does, skirts the issue of morphological identity.

9.2. Assertive and attentive endings.

Below are listed the principal endings which combine the assertive and attentive moods with the morphemes of aspect and style. The list is not a style paradigm, such as that found in §11.3; for different styles, the same semantic category is sometimes represented by periphrastic constructions or simply does not occur. The first column shows the spelling of the ending, the second shows the morph division, and the third gives a label for the category.

-ta	-[ ]-ta	PLAIN indicative assertive (= declarative): in the colloquial attached only to adjective stems, or to adjective + honorific marker, and to past and future elements (attached to any stem), or to the quasi-processive stems **iss-** and **ēps-**. But see §9.8.
ila / 'la	i-[ ]-la	indicative assertive of the copula when it is used in QUOTATIVE constructions
-ney	-n-ey	FAMILIAR indicative assertive
-so / -o[1]	-[ ]-so / -[ ]-o	AUTHORITATIVE indicative assertive
-ui / -i	-[ ]-ui / -[ ]-i	AUTHORITATIVE indicative assertive [variant with adjective (and also **iss-, ēps-, -ess-, -keyss-**?)]
-sup.nita / -p.nita[1]	-sup-ni-ta / -p-ni-ta	FORMAL indicative assertive
-ca	-[ ]-ca	PLAIN subjunctive assertive (= propositive)
-sey	-s-ey	FAMILIAR subjunctive assertive (= propositive)
-upsita / -psita[2]	-up-si-ta / -p-si-ta	FORMAL subjunctive assertive (= propositive)
-tula	-tu-la	PLAIN retrospective assertive
-ti	-t-i	PLAIN retrospective attentive (= interrogative)
-tey	-t-ey	FAMILIAR retrospective assertive
(iley =) itey	(i-l-ey =) i-t-ey	FAMILIAR retrospective assertive of the copula
-suptita / -ptita[1]	-sup-ti-ta / -p-ti-ta	FORMAL retrospective assertive
-ni	-n-i	PLAIN indicative attentive (= interrogative)
-na	-n-a	FAMILIAR indicative attentive (= interrogative)[3]
-sup.nikka / -p.nikka[1]	-sup-ni-kka / -p-ni-kka	FORMAL indicative attentive (= interrogative)
-ula / -la	-[ ]-ula / -[ ]-la	PLAIN subjunctive attentive (= imperative)
-usio / -sio / -psio[3]	-u-si-o / -[ ]-si-o / -p-si-o	FORMAL subjunctive attentive (the last shape is attached to the honorific marker). A popular misspelling: "-usiyo / -siyo / -psiyo".
-suptikka / -ptikka[1]	-sup-ti-kka / -p-ti-kka	FORMAL retrospective attentive (= interrogative)
-ni^t/la	-ni-^{t}/la	LITERARY indicative assertive

[1] South Koreans often write the alternant **-o** for **-so** and the variant **-up-** for **-sup-** after the sequence ss (of **iss-, -ess-, -keyss-**) and after **ēps-**. The automatic alternations (§2.6) are such that both ss + so and ss + o correspond to /sso/, and both **ēps-** + **-o** and **ēp-** (← **ēps-**) + **-so** correspond to /ēpsso/. The variant forms seem to be older, and also occur as nonstandard versions after any consonant; that may account for the tendency to write them whenever they are not in actual conflict

with the pronunciation, but **-o** is expanded to **-uo**: **mekuo** = **mekso** 'eats', **wusuo** = **wus.so** 'laughs'. We could follow the South Korean habit of writing **iss.up.nita**, **-ess.uptikka**, **-keyss.o** (even though we analyze the endings as **-sup.nita**, **-suptikka**, **-so**, etc.), but in this book we indicate both spellings with the notations **-ˢup.nita**, **-ˢuptikka**, **-ˢo**, etc. A number of South Korean authorities, too, favor writing the forms with s unless one is using the variant forms **-up.nita** and **-o** throughout the text, with ALL consonant stems. And, in fact, the always-s versions became the new standard in South Korea in 1988.

2 The shapes **-psita** and **-psio** are used after the honorific **-si-**. The shape **-psita** is used after all vowels (**kapsita** 'let's go!') but **-psio** normally appears only after the honorific **-si-**, so that **ka-psio** is treated as a nonstandard variant of **ka-sio**. The shape **-upsita** occurs regularly after a consonant, so that **ilk.supsita** is treated as a nonstandard version of **ilk.upsita** 'let's read it!' You will sometimes hear **-upsio** for **-usio** after a consonant (**ilk.upsio** = **ilkusio** 'read it!'), and **-sio** sounds the same as **-usi yo**, variant of **-usey yo** ← **-usye yo** used for polite-style commands and propositions as well as statements and questions. You may also hear **-supsio** after a consonant (**ilk.supsio** = **ilk.usio**); such forms are nonstandard. [1]Yi Ungpayk 1961:565 draws an artificial distinction between "**-sio**" for questions, commands, or exclamations and "**-siyo**" for statements or conjoinings. Yet (566) he completely rejects "**io**" in favor of "**iyo**", whatever the meaning; CF §11.5.7.

3 CF the adversative **-una/-na**, with which there is some overlap in usage, e.g. with the meaning 'or' in the construction **-una ... -un** for adjectives. The familiar indicative attentive **-na** is used also for **-nun ka/ya**; CF **pi ka ona pota** = **pi ka onun ka pota** 'It seems to be raining'. But adjective + **-na pota** is rejected in favor of **-un ka pota**, as in **cōh.un ka pota** 'it seems to be all right'.

See also **-ulita/-lita**, **-ulikka/-likka**, **-ulyetta/-lyetta**, **-kes.ta**. Notice also the unusual colloquial forms **-(su)pci yo** and **-(u)psey** among the entries of Part II.

9.3. Modifier endings.

The modifier mood marks a form as the head of a construction that modifies (= is adnominal to) a following noun or noun phrase. If the stem is that of a processive verb, the English translation of the plain modifier form (**-un/-n**) is usually in the past or perfect: **on sālam** 'a person who came, a person who has come', **ilk.un chayk** 'a book one has read'. When the stem is that of a descriptive verb, the English translational equivalent is usually in the present tense: **khun cip** 'a house that is big, a big house', **hak.kyo sensayng in Kim sensayng** 'Mr Kim who is a school teacher'. To say 'a house which was (observed to be) big' you have to use a retrospective modifier **khess.tun cip**, and for 'Mr Kim who was (at the time recalled) a school teacher' you can say **hak.kyo sensayng itun Kim sensayng**. See §11.8. Forms without the explicit past or future markers are either present by default, as it were, or are timeless. They are often used to refer to past happenings and even more often to future events.

The various modifier forms are listed below. In the first column is the spelling of the occurring alternants, with the typical shape (the one that occurs after a consonant) given first. Shape alternants are separated by a slant bar when they alternate according to whether the last phoneme of the stem is a consonant or a vowel. Other alternants (such as those involving the past element, which varies in the same ways as the infinitive, §9.4) are indented beneath the typical shape.

-un / -n	-un / -n	modifier
-ess.un	-ess-un	past modifier
-tun	-t-un	retrospective modifier
-ess.tun	-ess-t-un	past retrospective modifier
-ass.tun	-ass-t-un	
-ss.tun	-ss-t-un	
-yss.tun	-yss-t-un	
-yess.tun	-yess-t-un	

-ess.ess.tun	-ess-ess-t-un	past-past retrospective modifier
-ass.ess.tun	-ass-ess-t-un	
-ss.ess.tun	-ss-ess-t-un	
-yss.ess.tun	-yss-ess-t-un	
-yess.ess.tun	-yess-ess-t-un	
-keyss.tun	-keyss-t-un	future retrospective modifier
-ess.keyss.tun	-ess-keyss-t-un	past future retrospective modifier
-ass.keyss.tun	-ass-keyss-t-un	
-ss.keyss.tun	-ss-keyss-t-un	
-yss.keyss.tun	-yss-keyss-t-un	
-yess.keyss.tun	-yess-keyss-t-un	
-nun	-n-un	processive modifier
-keyss.nun	-keyss-n-un	future processive modifier
-ul.nun / -l.nun	-ul-n-un / -l-nun	prospective processive modifier
-ess.keyss.nun	-ess-keyss-n-un	past future processive modifier
-ass.keyss.nun	-ass-keyss-n-un	
-ss.keyss.nun	-ss-keyss-n-un	
-yss.keyss.nun	-yss-keyss-n-un	
-yess.keyss.nun	-yess-keyss-n-un	
-ess.ess.keyss.nun	-ess-ess-keyss-n-un	past-past future processive modifier
-ass.ess.keyss.nun	-ass-ess-keyss-n-un	
-ss.ess.keyss.nun	-ss-ess-keyss-n-un	
-yss.ess.keyss.nun	-yss-ess-keyss-n-un	
-yess.ess.keyss.nun	-yess-ess-keyss-n-un	
-ess.nun	-ess-nun	past processive modifier
-ass.nun	-ass-nun	
-ss.nun	-ss-nun	
-yss.nun	-yss-nun	
-yess.nun	-yess-nun	
-ess.ess.nun	-ess-ess-n-un	past-past processive modifier
-ulq / -lq	-ul-[ ] / -l-[ ]]q	prospective modifier
-ess.ulq	-ess-ul-[ ]q	past prospective modifier
-ass.ulq	-ass-ul-[ ]q	
-ss.ulq	-ss-ul-[ ]q	
-yss.ulq	-yss-ul-[ ]q	
-yess.ulq	-yess-ul-[ ]q	
-ess.ess.ulq	-ess-ess-ul-[ ]q	past-past prospective modifier
-ass.ess.ulq	-ass-ess-ul-[ ]q	
-ss.ess.ulq	-ss-ess-ul-[ ]q	
-yss.ess.ulq	-yss-ess-ul-[ ]q	
-yess.ess.ulq	-yess-ess-ul-[ ]q	

The reinforcing **q**, usually ignored in Hankul spelling, will surface whenever the prospective modifiers are in the proper environment (see §1.5)

The complex forms of the processive modifier occur only before:
(1) the postmodifiers **ci** 'uncertain fact (whether)', **ka** 'question', **tey** 'circumstance', **ya** 'question';
(2) the postmodifier adjectival noun **pep** (hata); also ?-**ess.nun tus** (hata / siph.ta);
(3) sentence-final **ke l'** in exclamations.

The prospective processive modifier **-ul.nun** apparently occurs only before the one postmodifier **ci** 'uncertain fact (whether)' and there it is semantically interchangeable with **-keyss.nun** or **-ulq**. The past modifier **-ess.un** occurs only before the somewhat literary postmodifier **cuk** 'if, when, ... '; the listing in CM 1:379 of **-ess.un tul** is rejected. Forms also rejected are the future modifier **-keyss.un** and future prospective modifier **-keyss.ul** included in the overly tidy table in CM 1:378; the past-past modifier **-ess.ess.un** in the same list is tentatively accepted, though no example is given. Despite the presence of the processive morpheme **-n-** (here semantically empty), the modifiers **-ess.nun**, **-keyss.nun**, and **-ul.nun** can be attached to adjective stems and even to the copula. In that, they differ from the simple processive modifier **-nun**: you can say **chwupkeyss.nun ci** or **chwuwul.nun ci (to mōlla)** 'perhaps it will be cold' but not *****chwup.nun ci** → **chwuwun ci** 'perhaps it is cold'.

9.4. The infinitive.

The name "infinitive" is here applied to the ending typically shaped **-e**, and the forms made by attaching the appropriate shape to verb stems. The reference should not be confused with the use of that term in talking about the grammar of other languages, though it has been applied to a very similar form in Japanese. English speakers name verbs by the translation of the Latin infinitive "to ... " but Koreans name a verb by the indicative assertive **···ta** even when that form is not otherwise in use, as is true when **mekta** is replaced by **mek.nunta** 'eats', with obligatory marking as a processive verb.

The Korean infinitive is used in the following ways:

(1) by itself at the end of a nonfinal clause to mean 'and so' or 'and then';

(2) as a connecting form used with an auxiliary verb (§7.5) or to link two ordinary verbs in a kind of "regular compound", such as **il.e na-** 'get up', **na o-** → **na-o-** 'come out', **al.e tut-** 'understand', ... ;

(3) followed by the particle **se** with about the same meaning as (1), but more colloquial;

(4) followed by the particle **ya** with the meaning 'only if ... ' in such expressions as **-e ya ha-** and **-e ya toy-** 'only if we ... will it do' = 'we have to (do it)';

(5) followed by the particle **to** with the meaning 'even though ... ' in such expressions as **-e to cōh-** 'be all right even if (one does)' = 'may (do), it is all right (to do)';

(6) followed by the particle **la** to make a command in the unquoted plain style;

(7) by itself at the end of a sentence to present a statement, question, command, or suggestion in the INTIMATE style (§11.3);

(8) followed by the particle **yo** at the end of a sentence to present a statement, question, command, or suggestion in the POLITE style (§11.3).

The typical shape of the infinitive ending is **-e**, but the shape is **-a** when the last vowel of the stem is **o** or a **w** which is reduced from a basic **o**, such as **wā** < **o-** + **-a** 'comes'. For stems ending in **···ah-** the usual infinitive is **···ah.a** pronounced /aa/, as in **tāh.a** 'arrives' — but **tāh.e** (pronounced /taae/) is sometimes heard. For ambivalent stems the infinitive is **-ay**, coming from **hay**, the infinitive of **ha-**, as in **āmulay** ← **āmule(h)-**, but **(p)pū.yay** ← **(p)pū.ye(h)-** 'be misty' is usually treated as **(p)pū.yey** and pronounced /(p)puey/ (§4.3). The infinitive of the inseparable postnominal adjective **low-** 'be (characterized by)' is regularly **lowa**, but there is a common colloquial variant **lowe**; it is perhaps to be explained by the older form of **low-** which is said to have been **lowup-** (or perhaps **lowuw-**?). In the literary language, in literary clichés in the colloquial, in dialects, and in the standardizing prescriptions of the Korean Language Society the ending is **-a** if the last vowel of the stem is /a/, as well as if it is /o/, and occasionally in texts we find **-a** used after other vowels (CF the colloquial variant **ia** = **ie** 'it is'). We can treat **pat.a** as a variant for the Seoul **pat.e**, but from the point of view of the Korean Language Society, **pat.e** is a colloquial variant of **pat.a**. The Seoul form has been around a while: 1887 Scott 107 has *patela* 'receive [it]!' despite the first form in (id. 160) *pas.kwua* (= /pakkwa/) *wonela* = **pakkwe one la** (< ˙wo˙na˙la).

There are eleven special comments to be made regarding alternations of stem and infinitive ending. The first six of these apply correspondingly to the attachment of the past marker (typically **-ess-**) as well as to the infinitive (typically **-e**). Statements 7 through 11 do not apply to the past marker.

(1) Stems of more than one syllable which end in ⋯i- reduce that vowel to y before attaching -e: **kitali-e → kitalye** (spelled "ki-ta-lye") 'waits for'. When the result is ⋯**cye**, ⋯**chye**, ⋯**sye** — or a combination producing ⋯**chye**, such as ⋯**t.hye** ← ⋯**t.hi-e** or ⋯**th.ye** from ⋯**th.ie**, by the Seoul rule which pronounces **th + i** or **t + hi** as /chi/ — the actual pronunciation is /ce, che, se/ but we follow the Hankul spelling in retaining the written **y** as an indication of the reduced **i**. Stems of one syllable which end in **i** simply add **-e** and that is the way the Hankul spelling treats them: **ttie, chie, cwie, phie, ie, …** . But in pronouncing these words speakers often shorten **ie** to **yē** (§2.7.7, §2.7.8). And many Koreans, hearing the intercalated semivowel in the unshortened forms (§2.7.6) write the last syllable of these infinitives as ⋯**ye**. That is harmless, for there is no possibility of confusion, and it continues the Middle Korean tradition of writing the intercalated palatal glide whenever it occurs. (Our practice of writing **ie** for the copula infinitive could lead to confusion with the infinitive of **ī(s)-** 'continue', so that is a point in favor of keeping the old spelling **iye**, though this book has not done so.) On the other hand, we must deplore the mistake of writing ⋯**wu-we** for the infinitives of stems ending in ⋯**wu-**, since these should be kept distinct from the infinitives of stems ending in ⋯**wuw-** (§8.2.3). The opposite mistake **wue** for **wuwe** also occurs: **nwu˙e** (?1517⁻ Pak 1:42b) = **nwu˙we** 'lies'. On the irregularities of the MK verb ˙**two[W]-** 'help' see §8.2.3.

(2) The separable auxiliary verb **ci-** 'become, … ' has the infinitive form /ce/, as expected from desyllabification (§2.7.7) and reduction of **cy** to /c/ (§2.6), but it is about the only one-syllable stem regularly given a shortened infinitive in the Hankul spelling, which usually writes **cye** as we do, though **chie** 'hit (etc.)' is often spelled **chye**, pronounced /che/ or /chē/.

(3) Stems that end in ⋯**u-** drop that minimal vowel before adding **-e**: **ssu- → sse** 'writes', **ttu- → tte** 'floats', **pappu- → pappe** 'is busy', **ippu- → ippe** 'is pretty'. Notice that in the last two cases the orthographic **u**, both in our Romanization and in Hankul, represents the phoneme /wu/. Actually we can say that the **u** of our Romanization behaves the same way in the combination of letters we write for the single unit /wu/: **pakkwu- → pakkwe** 'exchanges', **nanwu- → nanwe** 'divides'. But the infinitives of one-syllable /wu/ stems are normally spelled out in full: **cwu- → cwue** 'gives' — in speech often shortened to **cwe**, especially as the auxiliary for favors. An exceptional case is **phu-** 'dip, ladle', which is spelled **ph + wu** (not **ph + u**) in Hankul and has an infinitive spelled **phe**. In Romanized form that infinitive looks regular enough, but from the Hankul point of view it is best described as a shortening of the expected **phue** (ph+wu+-e) by way of a **phwe** which drops its **w** after a labial (§2.7.4). The l-doubling stems (§8.3.1) drop **u** but double the **l**: **pulu- → pulle** 'calls'. The choice of **-e** or **-a** for the shape of the ending depends on the vowel of the ACTUAL preceding syllable: **molu- → mōlla** 'not know', **kophu- → kopha** '(stomach) is empty, hungry'.

(4) Stems that end in ⋯**a-** or ⋯**ay-** add zero (nothing) to make the infinitive, for they have absorbed the ending: **ka- → ka** 'goes', **nāy- → nāy** 'puts out, pays'. The stem **ha-** 'do/say/be' has the irregular infinitive **hay**, with literary variants **ha.ye** and **ha.ya**; see §8.3.5. The only stems that end in ⋯**e-** are **ile-/yole-** 'do or say this (way)', **kule-/kole-** 'do or say that (way)', **cele-/cole-** 'do or say that (way)', **ette-** 'do or say what (way)', and **āmule-** 'do or say any thing/way'. These have the infinitives **ilay/yolay, kulay/kolay, celay/colay, ettay** and **āmulay**. As a result of the merger by many dialects of /ay/ and /ey/, especially in noninitial syllables, the infinitive **hay** is sometimes said as **hey**, and even in Seoul you will usually hear **iley, kuley, celey, ettey**, and **āmuley** for what is written as **ilay, kulay, celay, ettay**, and **āmulay**.

(5) Stems that end in ⋯**ey-** or ⋯**oy-** (usually pronounced like ⋯**wey-**) absorb the ending so that they add zero (nothing) to make the colloquial infinitive: **sēy- → sēy** 'counts', **kkwēy- → kkwēy** 'pierces', **tōy- → tōy** 'is thick'. But a trace of the ending is found in the infinitives of stems with originally short vowels, for the infinitives are long: **toy- → tōy** 'becomes'. Bear in mind that all one-syllable phrases are automatically long, so you will hear the difference between the vowels of the infinitives **hay** 'do/say/be' and **nāy** 'put out, pay' only when immediately followed by another syllable: **hay to** 'even doing/saying/being' and **nāy to** 'even paying'. And the past forms are similar: **hayss.ta** 'did; said; was' and **nāyss.ta** 'paid'. (But the 1988 Ministry of Education guidelines treat **hay** as a colloquial

contraction of **ha.ye** that has a long vowel, **hāy**. See the entry **hay** in Part II.) The literary variant infinitive of stems that end in ···**ey**- or ···**oy**- adds **-e** (often miswritten as "**ye**" because of the automatic glide, §2.7.6): **sēye, kkwēye, tōye**, popularly spelled "**seyye, kkweyye, toyye**". Moreover, He Wung (9) and others say that ···**oy**- + **-e** should have the infinitive **tway**, and that seems to be common in modern writing. He Wung also says that ···**wi**- + **-e** → ···**wey**, so that the infinitive for **ttwi-** 'jump' would be **ttwēy**, and **kkwi-e** → **kkwēy** 'flatulates' would rime with **kkwēy** 'pierces'. I am a bit unhappy with both these claims. I suspect that the former is due to the modern confusion, first of **oy** with **wey** and then of **(w)ey** with **(w)ay**, for you will hear overcorrected (or Phyengan dialect) pronunciations of **ōykwuk** 'foreign lands' as **wāykwuk**. The second claim is to be accounted for by the reduction of /**wie**/ to /**ōy**/ as described in §2.7.8. There is more at stake here, however: we must account for such historical changes as **twāyci** 'pig' < **to.yaci** < *two(y)yaci* (1819) < *twos-aci* (1819) = *twotaci* (?1660-) < *twoth* (1445 ¹Yong 43) and **ttwāyki** < *stwoyyaki* (?1800-) < ˙*ptwo˙yaki* '[one] patch (of field)' (1586 Sohak 5:83a; paraphrase of *kun* '[not even one] catty' 1518 Sohak-cho 8:2b).

(6) The few l-inserting stems (§8.3.3) insert an **-l-** before adding the infinitive ending: **ilu-** → **ilule** 'reaches'. The **l** is usually written as the initial of the ending syllable: **i-lu-le**. Compare the l-doubling **ilu-** → **ille** 'tells' or 'is early' and the l-extending **i-l-** → **il.e** 'rises'. The inserted **l** (like the doubled **l**) is part of the earlier basic shape of the stem.

(7) The k-inserting and n-inserting stems (§8.3.6) have regular infinitives and in addition a special version, with the shape **-k-e** or (**o-** 'come' only) **-n-e**, used only before the particle **la** to make a command. Historically the **-k-** is a separate morpheme but we treat it as an extension of the stem. In any event, it is not part of the infinitive morpheme, though written as the initial of that syllable: **ka-ke-la** 'go!', **o-ne-la** 'come'.

(8) When the infinitive is followed by the polite-style particle **yo**, in relaxed speech the final **-e** is usually pronounced **-ey** if preceded by **ss, ps, i, y**, or the **s(y)** of the reduced honorific marker (but not the final **s** of a consonant stem like **wūs-**, nor the ···**sy-** that is a reduction of stem-final ···**si-**):

iss.ey yo = iss.e yo 'there exists'
mek.ess.ey yo = mek.ess.e yo 'we've eaten'
hakeyss.ey yo = hakeyss.e yo 'I'll do it'
ēps.ey yo = ēps.e yo 'there isn't any'
nay chayk iey yo = nay chayk ie/ia yo 'it's my book', nay moca (y)ey yo (§4.3) = nay moca ye/ya yo = nay moca ie/ia yo 'it's my hat'
kas[y]ey yo = kasye yo = kasie yo 'deigns to go'
wūs[y]ey yo = wūsye yo = wūsie yo 'deigns to cry' < wū-l-; CF wus.e yo 'laughs' and wus.us[y]ey yo = wus.usye yo = wus.usie yo 'deigns to laugh'
māsey yo = māsye yo = māsie yo 'deigns to desist' < mā-l-; CF masye yo = masie yo 'drinks' and masis[y]ey yo = masisye yo 'deigns to drink'

In addition there is the anomalous **kath.ey yo = kath.e yo** 'is the same', but there are no other examples for stems ending in **th**; CF **puth.e yo** 'adheres to', **yeth.e yo** 'is shallow', **math.e yo** 'smells it' ... . The adjective **kath-** derives from a contraction of the obsolete adjectival noun (*)**kat ha-** < MK ˙*kot ˚ho-*; that may account for its odd behavior. Gale wrote *kos.ta* and *kos-hota* (*kos-ha, kos-hun*).

Because the relaxed forms are seldom written, many Koreans will want to correct textbook examples to the "standard" written versions, i.e. leave off the final **y**. That is particularly true if they are not from Seoul, for the polite stylization with **-e yo** itself seems to have originated in the Seoul area. (A Kyengsang speaker will often use the formal style instead.)

In the intimate style of speech (§11.3), which places an infinitive at the end of the sentence without the particle **yo**, some Koreans (especially women in Seoul) often use the variant infinitives as if the **yo** were still there: **iss.ey** for **iss.e, mek.ess.ey** for **mek.ess.e, hakeyss.ey** for **hakeyss.e, ēps.ey** for **ēps.e, kasyey /kasey/** for **kasye, kath.ey** for **kath.e**, ... In rapid speech ···**ye yo** may sound like ···**ey yo**, as in **kitaley yo** for **kitalye yo** 'waits for'. And /**ey**/ may be raised to /**i**/ (§2.7.9), especially when it is not initial, so that we sometimes hear **kitali yo = kitaley yo = kitalye yo**. From the pronunciation /kasi(y)o/ we cannot be sure whether we are hearing **kasio** 'go!' (or 'deigns to go' in the AUTHORITATIVE style) or **kasi yo = kasey yo = kasye yo = kasie yo** 'deigns to go' (in the POLITE style).

(9) In the intimate style, the copula infinitive **ie/ye** or **iey/yey** (··· **yey** = /ey/, §4.3) is more often pronounced **ia/ya**, at least among Seoul speakers: **nay chayk ia = nay chayk ie** 'it's my book', **nay moca ya = nay moca ye** (= **nay moca ie**) 'it's my hat'. The variant **ia/ya** is not be confused with the homonymous particle ··· **iya/ya** 'only if it be ··· '. That particle was MK ··· *(i)˙za*; when the medial /z/ dropped, an epenthetic glide was inserted, leading to the standard spelling **iya/ya** for the particle, and that spelling is widely used in Hankul also for the variant of the copula infinitive, following the practice of the earlier writers. We will use only the morphophonemic spelling **ia/ya** for the variant of the copula infinitive; despite the popular use of **iya/ya** as the written form of that, we will save this spelling for the particle. On **i[y]a** vs **i[y]e** for the copula infinitive, see p. 273.

(10) The variant polite copula **iey yo** is often shortened to **(y)ey yo** even after a consonant: **chayk (y)ey yo = chayk ie(y) yo** 'it's a book'. In the abbreviated probable future construction which consists of the prospective modifier **-ulq** + **ke** (the shortened version of **kes**, here 'probable/likely fact') + copula, the copula may take the variant subphonemic shape of just the palatal feature **y**, as in expressing 'will likely do':

halq ke y = halq ke (y)ey = halq kes ie/ia [intimate style];
halq ke y yo = halq ke (y)ey yo = halq kes (y)ey yo = halq kes ie(y) yo [polite style];
halq ke yta = halq ke 'ta = halq kes ita [plain style];
halq ke yp.nita = halq ke 'p.nita = halq kes ip.nita 'will probably do' [formal style].

The subphonemic **y** is, of course, written as a component of the preceding vowel in Hankul, which runs all the words of these phrases together. More commonly we hear the versions **halq ke yo** [polite, with the copula infinitive absorbed or simply unexpressed] and **halq ke ya** [intimate].

(11) A literary variant infinitive for the copula is **ila**; the same shape is regularly used in quoting the indicative assertive of the copula (**chayk ila ko hanta** 'says it is a book', **moca 'la ko hanta** 'says it is a hat'). The literary variant is heard in colloquial expressions such as ··· **ila to** = ··· **ie to** 'even being ···' and **Sensayng ila (se) cemccanh.ta = Sensayng ie se cemccanh.ta** 'Being a teacher, he is well-mannered'. The origin of this usage may be a quotative structure. Compare the use of **iyo/yo** as a variant of the copula gerund **iko** (see the entry in Part II), which preserves an earlier form that came from the dropping of a lenited velar (MK ··· *˙i ˙Gwo*) and the insertion of the palatal glide.

9.5. Substantives and derived substantives.

The substantive mood **-um/-m** is a nominalization that is used in the following ways:

(1) with a small number of verbs, as the complementary object of the verb itself, as in **cam ul ca-** 'sleep a sleep' and **chwum ul chwu-** 'dance (a dance)';

(2) with the particle **ulo** to mean 'because', as in **kongpu cal hayss.um ulo cal ālci** 'I studied hard so I knew it well, you see';

(3) occasionally with other particles (**-um ey, -um a, ...**), and before the copula, e.g. **sēym** 'calculation' as a postmodifier in sentences like **Kwīsin ul pon sēym in ya** 'Do you figure you were seeing a ghost?';

(4) sentence-final in the DOCUMENTARY style of written Korean, as in the shop sign **Tāmpay ēps.um** 'No cigarettes available';

(5) with the adjectival postsubstantive inseparable **cik** in **-um cik ha-** 'likely/acceptable to do; worth doing'.

Some of the ···**w**- stems have variant shortened substantives in **-m** instead of **-wum** (= ···**w-um**): **musem = musewum** 'fear', **etwum = etwuwum** 'darkness', **kwiyem = kwiyewum** 'cuteness', **ppukkulem = pukkulewum** 'shame', **pulem = pulewum** 'envy'. Not all ···**w**- stems have the shortened variant: there is only **miwum** for 'hatred'. (In general, one-syllable stems lack the shortening, but polysyllabic stems permit it.)

In addition to the shortened variants, which are freely interchangeable with the longer forms in all environments, there are a few irregularly formed DERIVED SUBSTANTIVES which are limited in that they do not occur in the uses (2), (4), and (5), nor usually in use (1) — there is the apparent exception of swūm ul swīm ulo 'because one breathes a breath', but notice the expected derived substantive swiem below. (The noun in mokum ul mek.um ulo 'because someone takes a puff' is not from mek-, it is from a variant of mekum- 'swallow'.) Some derived substantives:

    cwukem 'corpse' ← cwuk- 'die' → regular substantive cwuk.um 'death';
    mutem 'tomb, grave' ← mut- 'bury' → regular substantive mut.um;
    sālam 'person' ← sā-l- 'live' → regular substantive sālm 'life';
    cokom, cokum, com 'a little' ← cēk- 'be few / little' → regular cek.um;
    makam 'terminal date, deadline' ← mak- 'block, obstruct; complete, put an end to; ... ' →
        regular mak.um (but makam is sometimes mistaken to be a Chinese loanword);
    heyem 'swimming' ← hēy- 'swim' → regular hēym;
    col.um 'sleepiness' ← cō-l- 'doze' → regular cōlm;
    wul.um 'crying, weeping' ← wū-l- 'cry, weep' → regular wūlm;
    al.um 'knowledge' ← ā-l- 'know' → regular ālm — see §8.3.2;
    sayam, sāym 'jealousy' ← saywu- 'envy' → regular saywum;
    wumkhum / ongkhum 'handful' ← wumkhi- / omkhi- 'grasp' → regular wumkhim / omkhim;
    kiem kiem 'crawling along' ← ki- 'crawl' → regular kim;
    swiem swiem 'with frequent rests' ← swī- 'rest' → regular swīm;
    iem(q) iem 'continuously' ← ī(s)- 'continue, join' → regular ium.

It may be argued that the last three examples should be derived from the infinitive (-e) rather than directly from the stem. But the source of these and most of the other derived substantives ending in -em or -am is in the Middle Korean form we are calling the "effective substantive", i.e. a substantive made on the effective stem, which otherwise appeared only before ˙cik °ho˙ta. In the 15th century the regular substantives of the ···l- stems had an uncontracted ···l^uom, but the only attestations of that are derived substantives such as wu˙lum 'crying' < ¨wul- 'cry' and e˙lum 'ice' < ¨el- 'freeze', for the modulator was obligatorily inserted when the substantive was used as subject or object (wu˙l-wu-m + ˙i or ˙ul), etc., and in the extended structures with ··· ˙ye (n') the unmodulated form was contracted to ···lm: ¨al˙m ye > ālmye 'knows and', ¨wul˙m ye n' > wūlmyen 'if / when one cries'. In the modern language the unmodulated substantives survive in the contracted version regardless of the structure they are in. They are pronounced with the liquid suppressed ···[l]m and the m treated as syllable-final unless there is a following vowel to carry the nasal and allow the full cluster to appear: ā[l]m (to) 'the knowing (too)' but ālm ulo 'with (because of) knowing'.

9.6. Derived adverb-noun forms.

The adverbative mood ends in -key and means 'so that; so as to (do/be)'; it is attached to any stem but the modern copula i-, and the form that results is syntactically used as an adverbial. In addition, many stems have a form we can call the DERIVED ADVERB-NOUN; it is made by attaching to the stem either a suffix with the shapes -i and -li or a suffix with the shapes -o and -wu. The suffix -o or -wu seems to make only adverbs, but perhaps nalwu 'ferry' ← nalu- 'transport' is an example of -wu deriving a noun; see also -wung in Part II. The suffix -i or -li makes both adverbs and nouns, sometimes from the same stem, so that kiph.i means both 'deeply' (MK ki˙phi) and 'depth' (MK ki˙phuy). Notice that the derived adverb nelli 'widely' is best derived from the adjective nelu- 'be wide' (+ -li) and the derived noun nelp.i 'width' is derived from nelp- 'be wide' (+ -i). Not every stem has such a form today, so we cannot make up expected forms without knowing in advance whether they are actually used. For that reason, we call this a derived form, rather than a part of the inflectional paradigm, though we list it at the end of the table of mood endings. The usual mood suffixes attach to any stem, so that we can make up quite acceptable forms without having heard them before. The suffix -i is also used to make adverbs out of iterated nouns: cip-cip-i 'every house' (= cip mata), na'-nal-i 'daily', ta'-tal-i 'monthly', nam-nam-i 'between unrelated persons'. You will notice certain peculiarities in attaching the suffixes:

(1) Final ···u- of a vowel stem drops: **pappi** 'busily' ← **pappu-** 'be busy', **puphi** 'bulk' ← **puphu-** 'be bulky', **khi** 'height' ← **khu-** 'be big', **āy-pali** 'skinflint' from **āy-palu-** 'be money-mad'; **palo** or **palwu** 'right, directly' ← **palu-** 'be right'.

(2) The final ···w- of certain consonant stems drops: **kakkai** 'nearby' or 'vicinity' ← **kakkaw-** 'be near', **pankai** 'gladly' ← **pankaw-** 'be glad', **elyei** 'with difficulty' ← **elyew-** 'be difficult', **swii** (also **swui**) 'easily' ← **swīw-** 'be easy'. In **kyewu** 'hardly, barely' ← **kyew-** 'be too much for one' the appropriate division of forms is **kye-wu**. But not all stems drop the **w**: **tewi** 'warmth' ← **tēw-** 'be warm'. The inseparable postnominal adjective **sulew-** 'be, give the impression of' drops not only the **w** but usually the preceding vowel as well: **kapcak sulew-** 'be sudden', **kapcak suli** 'suddenly'; but there is a variant **kapcak suley** in which **w** drops and the **i** suffix is reduced to **y**. CF **swus cey** 'sincerely' ← **swus cei** ← **swus cew-** 'be pure, sincere'. And the derived adverb from the inseparable postnominal adjective **low-** 'be' is typically **loi**: **swūnco low-** 'be smooth, orderly', **swūnco loi** 'smoothly'.

(3) The adjective stem **mukew-** 'be heavy' has the derived noun form **mukey** 'weight', in which the **w** drops and the suffix is reduced to the phoneme component **y**, as in **suley** ← **sulew-** above. A shortened variant of **elyei** 'with difficulty' (← **elyew-** 'be difficult') is **el[y]ey**.

(4) The suffix **-i** is attached in the alternant **-li** to the EXTENDED shape of some **l**-extending stems: **mēlli** 'afar' ← **mē-l-** 'be far'. But others attach the shape **-i**: **kil.i** 'length' or 'lengthily' ← **kī-l-** 'be long', **nol.i** 'game' ← **nō-l-** 'play'. The suffix is usually attached in the alternant **-li** to the single-l shape of l-doubling stems, though we could equally well say it is attached in the alternant **-i** to the double-l shape: **talli** 'differently' ← **talu-** 'be different', **ppalli** 'fast' ← **ppalu-** 'be fast' — but CF **yak-ppali** 'shrewd one' from **yak-ppalu-** 'be shrewd and quick'.

(5) The suffix **-wu** has the shape /chwu/ after **yath-** 'shallow' → **yath.chwu** 'shallowly' and after **kot-** 'straight' → **kot.chwu** 'straight', which is usually spelled just **kochwu** in Hankul.

(6) An s-dropping stem, as expected, drops the **s** before adding the vowel-initial suffix: **ii** 'joining' ← **ī(s)-** 'join, continue, ... ', as in **way-ii** 'a technique of joining small pieces of wood'.

(7) Some derived nouns, mostly from stems ending in **i** or **y**, can be said to have a zero form of the suffix; see the note in the entry for **-i** in Part II.

(8) The adjective **ha-** 'be' has the irregular form **hi**. Since the **h**, and even the entire syllable **ha-**, is so often dropped in ordinary speech, the word **hi** frequently sounds like **i**, and some people write it this way, confusing it with the suffix **-i**. Because many Koreans seem to confuse the ENDING **-i** with the WORD **hi** we run across anomalous (and mistaken) forms like "**kohi**" = **koi** 'nicely' from **kōw-** 'be nice, pretty' with the **w** dropped.

We can perhaps look at **ili** 'this way', **kuli** 'that way', and **celi** 'that way' (§5.2.4) as contractions of **ile hi**, **kule hi**, and **cele hi**. And, similarly, **ecci** 'what way' as a contraction of **ette hi** → **ett[e h]i**, the palatalization and affrication taking place after the **tt** was put in contact with the **i**. But the simple adverbs are attested from early Hankul texts as ˙i˙li, ku˙li, ˙tyeli, and ¨es˙ti, and may have been made as derived adverbs from the defective stems *˙i-l-, *ku-l-, *˙tye-l-, and *¨est- that produced the infinitives ˙i˙le, ku˙le, ˙tye˙le, and ¨es˙te, which serve as bound adverbs before the postnominal adjective °ho- > **ha-** 'be', forming adjectival nouns. A similar defective stem *¨am˙o-l- '(be) any way' produced the derived adverb ¨a˙moli (> **āmuli**) 'however much' and the infinitive ¨a˙mola that is attested in the Middle Korean texts only by the contracted forms ¨amo˙lan < *¨amo˙la [ho]n and ¨a˙mola˙tha < *¨a˙mo[˙]la ho˙ta) but produces a full paradigm in modern **āmule ha-** as well as its contraction **āmuleh-**.

In combinations of an adjectival noun which ends in a basic ···s + the word **hi**, there are three possible treatments, here exemplified by **kkaykkus hi** 'cleanly':

The excess **s** is, as expected, treated as **t** and **t** + **hi** (like **th** + **i**) becomes **chi**, so we hear /kkaykkuchi/ from some speakers, mostly northerners.

The **h** is dropped but the ···s is treated as ···t, so the form is said as /kkaykkuti/, but in Seoul **t** + **i** → **ci** so that it is /kkaykkuci/. This treatment seems to be rare; I have never heard it, but others have.

The **h** is dropped and the remaining **i** is linked as if it were a particle or suffix, so that the **s** remains a sibilant: **kkaykkus 'i /kkaykkusi/**.

For bound adjectival nouns, only the latter treatment has been observed (··· **tus 'i** 'as if' ← ··· **tus ha-** 'give the idea / impression of') and it seems to be the common version for the others, as well.

[1]Yi Ungpayk 1961:456 advises writing phonemically any ···i adverb that lacks a ··· **hata** partner: **pantusi, kapcaki, ilcciki, ...** . But (472) **kos.kos-i, cip.cip-i, ...** . When there is a **hata** form, the adverb might be pronounced three ways. His advice on Hankul spellings:

If the adverb is always pronounced without the aspiration, write "**-i**" (equivalent to our **'i**), as in **ttwulyes 'i** 'clearly' ("**ttwulyes-i**"), **khum cik 'i** 'greatly; generously' ("**khumcik-i**").

If the adverb is pronounced both ways (**hi** or **'i**), write it as "**hi**", as in **nek.nek hi** 'amply', **sepsep hi** 'unfortunately'; **tantan hi** 'solidly, firmly', where the **h** would be elided in normal speech, anyway.

If it is always pronounced with the aspiration, write "**-hi**", as in **kup hi** 'hastily', **kuk hi** 'extremely', **cok hi** 'sufficiently, fully'. These rules apply to adverbs that lack the **hata**, too, so that the spelling is **cēk-i** (= **cēk.i**) 'somewhat' but **cak-hi** 'very' (< 'little' used ironically).

In addition to those fairly active suffixes, there are also two suffixes **-ay** and **-kay** which make nouns and, in the case of **-ay** an occasional adverb such as **mōllay** 'in secret' ← **molu-** 'not know' and **killay** 'for a long time' ← **kī-l-** 'be long'; examples will be found in Part II. For some of the resultant forms dictionaries prefer variant versions with **-key**, as in **cipkey** 'tweezers' and **cikey** 'A-frame carrier'. Many Koreans do not maintain the distinction of the vowel **ay** from the vowel **ey**, in any event, especially when it is not in the initial syllable of a word.

9.7. Complex moods.

We should say something about the derivation of the "complex" moods listed as categories 13, 14, and 15 in the mood table of §9.1. For some purposes it is better to treat these endings as unanalyzed units; for other purposes it will be revealing if we consider their component parts. Some of the forms are rather literary in character.

9.7.1. Complex moods built on the prospective modifier.

The INTENTIVE mood **-ulye / -lye** 'with the thought in mind to (do), with the intention of (doing)', often used in the construction **-ulye (ko) hanta** 'intends / wants / tries to (do)', consists of the prospective modifier **-ul** + an element **ye**, which is a variant of the postmodifier **ya** 'question'; CF **-ulq ka hanta** 'thinks about doing, considers doing'. The PURPOSIVE mood **-ule / -le** seems to be a shortening of the intentive. It is used only in conjunction with verbs of motion, typically **ka-** 'go' and **o-** 'come', with the meaning 'for the purpose of', though other words may intervene between the statement of purpose and the verb expressing movement. The intentive also can be followed by a verb of movement: ··· **halye (ko) kanta / onta** 'goes / comes with it in mind to do ··· '.

The FRUSTRATED INTENTIVE **-ulyes-man (un) / -lyes-man (un)** is a semi-literary expression with the meaning 'I had hoped that ··· (would do) but' or 'should have (done) but'. The ending appears to be from the intentive (**-ulye**) + **-q** + the particle **man** 'just, but', which can be followed by the particle **un** to subdue the clause and thereby focus attention on what follows, just as happens in **-ci man (un)**.

The PROSPECTIVE ASSERTIVE **-ulita / -lita** and PROSPECTIVE ATTENTIVE **-ulikka / -likka** mean either '(I) will be glad to (do)' or 'will probably (do)' and interrogative versions of those: **Nwu ka halikka – Nay ka halita** 'Who wants (= is willing) to do it? – I'll be glad to do it'. These endings consist of the prospective modifier **-ul** + the copula stem **i-** + the assertive ending **-ta** or the attentive ending **-kka**. Notice that **ita** occurs also as the plain indicative assertive 'it is' but **(-)ikka** does not occur elsewhere, for the plain indicative attentive of the copula is **ini**, and **kka** turns up only in the formal **ip.nikka**. Historically, these forms are contracted from the MK polite structures -*u ̇l i ̇'-ngi ̇'ta* and -*u ̇l i ̇'-ngi s ̇ka*. There is also the PROSPECTIVE SEQUENTIAL **-ulini** < **-ul i 'ni** 'since (it is that) it will happen' (= **-keyss.uni**) – normally followed by a command, proposition, or statement of volition – and the PROSPECTIVE LITERARY INDICATIVE ASSERTIVE **-ulini^t/ta** 'is sure to do, will surely be' [old-fashioned] < **-ul i 'n i 'ta** 'it is that it is that it will happen / be'.

The old-fashioned INTENTIVE ASSERTIVE **-ulyetta / -lyetta**, in Hankul usually written **-(u)lyes.ta**, is a semi-literary form sometimes used to express a probable future, like **-ulq kes ita**. The ending consists of **-ul + yeq = ye** (a variant of the postmodifier **ya**, as found in **-ulye**, with **-q**) + **-ta**.

The CAJOLATIVE **-ulyem (una) / -lyem (una)** is an endearing command used by mothers to children: **Mek.ulyem (una)** 'Do let's be a good boy and eat now!'. The ending consists of the intentive **-ulye** + the substantive **-um / -m** — or, more likely, **'m** the shortened form of **ham**, substantive of **ha-** 'do / say' and here 'feel', often followed by the softening particle **una / na** ("We feel we want to, don't we)"; the particle is also used in **Anc.key na** 'Won't you have a seat?'

9.7.2. Adjunctives.

There are two forms we call ADJUNCTIVES. The PROSPECTIVE adjunctive **-ulla / -lla** is a two-shape ending which consists of the prospective morpheme **-ul- / -l-** + the attentive ending **-ula / -la**. The PROCESSIVE adjunctive **-nula** is usually treated as a one-shape ending and consists of the processive morpheme **-nun- / -n-** + the attentive ending **-ula / -la**. But a substandard variant treats the processive adjunctive as a two-shape ending **-unula / -nula** as if it were from the plain modifier **-un / -n**. The processive adjunctive occurs, with or without a following particle **ko**, in two meanings: 'what with doing, as a result of doing' and 'with the idea to do, with the intention of doing'; the particle **ko** is more common with the second meaning. There are a few occurrences with abbreviated forms of **ha-**, such as **-nula 'myen** and **-nula 'ni**, for which see p. 722. A variant: **-nola < - ˙nwo ˙la** (p. 272, p. 734) with the modulated processive **-n[o]- ˙wo-**. The prospective adjunctive **-ulla / -lla** sometimes has the same meaning as the processive 'what with doing' (perhaps the flavor is more 'what with having to do' or 'what with being faced with the prospect of doing'). Another meaning is 'lest, for fear that it will happen', and there it may be an abbreviation of **-ulila / -lila**, the prospective assertive. Notice that the same shape **-ulla / -lla** is a widely used dialect variant also of the intentive **-ulye / -lye**, and that is often the best guess when you come across the form.

9.7.3. Complex moods built on the effective formative - ˙ke-.

Because the postmodifier **ke(s)** can be taken as 'probable, likely, or tentative fact' when it follows the prospective modifier, I once presumed that it was incorporated in certain complex moods, which are attached as one-shape endings directly to a stem or to the past or future markers, mostly carrying a meaning that can be described as "tentative". But that meaning for the structure with **ke(s)** is carried by the prospective modifier **-ulq** itself and need not be treated as inherent to **ke(s)**. The true source of most of the complex "tentative" forms seems to be the MK aspect formative - ˙ke-, which was attached to stems to make what we are calling the EFFECTIVE stems. Forms made on the effective stem are interpreted as sometimes a presumed future and sometimes as a definite past, depending on the form and the context. The effective and the retrospective were mutually exclusive aspects in Middle Korean and they seem to have functioned as opposites. Both have become less common in modern Korean and their earlier meanings are not so apparent.

The TENTATIVE ADVERSATIVE **-kena** continues the MK effective adversative - ˙ke ˙na. This form is often used in contradictory pairs with the meaning 'whether ⋯ or ⋯ ' in much the same way as the ordinary adversatives. The phrase can become an object: **hyen.yek ey iss.kena pi-hyen.yek ey iss.kena lul mak.lon hako** 'regardless of whether we are in active service or not.

The TENTATIVE SEQUENTIAL **-keni** comes from - ˙ke ˙n i, which is the MK effective modifier + the postmodifier ˙i (factual nominalizer). The general meaning of **-keni** is something like 'with the likely fact / reason that ⋯ ', often marking contradictory pairs (**cwukeni pat.keni** 'giving or taking'). See Part II for examples.

The PROVISIONAL **-ketun**, with a variant **-ketullang**, means 'if, provided that ⋯ , given that ⋯ ; surely, indeed'. The MK form was - ˙ke ˙tun (also - ˙ke ˙ton) and that apparently consists of the effective formative + an element - ˙tun (or - ˙ton), which is the postmodifier *t* 'fact' + the subdued-focus particle ˙*u̯on* ("given that ⋯ "). The element attaches to the retrospective formative - ˙te- to make the retrospective conditional form *-te ˙tun* (= *-te- ˙t un*) 'but, and; if, when'. (The particle **ullang / llang** is a variant, obsolete or vulgar, for **un / nun**.) See Part II for examples.

The TENTATIVE CONDITIONAL **-ketumyen** is a nonstandard dialect form, equivalent in meaning to the ordinary conditional **-umyen/-myen** 'if, when'. It is probably a blend of **-ketun** and **-umyen**; no earlier forms are found.

The LITERARY CONDITIONAL, in the colloquial limited to a few clichés, has the shape **-kentay**. It preserves the heart of a MK structure *-ken ˙t ᵉ/ay n'*, made up of the effective modifier + the postmodifier *t* 'fact' + the locative marker *ᵉ/ay* 'at/in; to' subdued with the focus particle *n(ᵁ/on)*: "given in the fact that ... " → 'if, when'.

The SEMI-LITERARY SEQUENTIAL **-kwantey** 'such that, so that', followed by a question doubting the adequacy of the reason, is MK *-kwan˙toy* and it may be related to **-kentay**. The *-kwa-* seems to be a variant of the effective *-ke-*.

The SEMI-LITERARY CONCESSIVE **-ken man (un)** means the same thing as **-ci man (un)** 'even though, although, but'. The earlier form was *-˙ken ma˙non/ma˙lon* with the effective modifier and a postmodifier of uncertain origin, perhaps *˙ma* 'extent' + particle *˙non* (> *˙lon* by dissimilation?).

The obsolete LITERARY CONCESSIVE **-kenul** < *-˙ke˙nᵁ/ol* is used in two meanings, 'although, while' (= **-ci man**) and 'as, since, when, upon' (= **-um ey**). The source is *-˙ken [ ] ˙ᵁ/ol*, with the accusative particle applied to a direct nominalization of the tentative modifier. The direct nominalization is probably to be taken as the result of reducing the postmodifier *˙i* 'fact' to the glide *y* which is lost before the minimal vowel ᵁ/o; compare a similar elision before the genitive marker (adnominalizer) that is discussed in NOTE 2 of the entry *˙uy* in Part II (p. 923).

The TENTATIVE ASSERTIVE **-kes.ta** or its equivalent casual form the TENTATIVE SUSPECTIVE **-kes.ci** has three meanings: 'does/is I assume (suppose, think)', 'surely (certainly) does/is', and 'given this and that' (enumerating a series of reasons that argue a conclusion). Choy Hyenpay 1959:350 gives an obsolete meaning of "past tense" to the form **-kes.ta**, which seems odd. On p. 351 he gives the modern meanings of (1) definite assertion, as in **Ne nun kakes.ta** 'You ARE going!' and **Ne kuli hayss.kes.ta** 'You certainly did so!', and (2) habitual, for which I lack good examples, unless the sentence **Tto sok.ass.kes.ta** 'Deceived again!' will do. Notice that the ending is sometimes pronounced /-keytta/ and is then homonymous with the plain future **-keyss.ta**. Both **-kes.ta** and the future **-keyss.ta** probably contain the MK effective formative *-˙ke-* and reductions of the verb **iss-** < *is(i)-* 'exist', rather than directly continuing the MK *-ke˙ta* (effective indicative assertive). But **-kes.ta** could instead be a continuation of a barely attested *-kes˙ta* that seems to contain the emotive bound verb *s-*.

The IMMEDIATE FUTURE **-ukkey/-kkey** = **-u'q key / -'q key**, contrary to the opinion expressed in KM, is nothing more than an abbreviation of the probable future **-ulq key**. (The critical example in KM 47 was a mistake; only **Nay ka cip.u'q key** occurs for 'I've got it!'.)

9.7.4. Gerund-related pseudo-moods.

The gerund occurs (1) linking two clauses with the meaning 'and also', (2) as a connecting form linked directly with an auxiliary verb (§7.5), (3) occasionally before a particle, as in **hako ya mal.e** 'must do it'. The gerund also occurs in a couple of constructions that are often regarded as separate endings, so we might call them pseudo-moods.

The HABITUAL consists of the gerund + the particle **(un/)nun**, often in the shortened form **n'**, and is followed by the auxiliary **hanta** 'does': **sānqpo lul kako n(un) hayss.ta** 'I used to go for walks'.

The LITERARY DESIDERATIVE consists of the gerund + **ca**, a variant of **ce = cye < cie**, the infinitive of the auxiliary adjective **ci-** 'want to (do)', so that **-ko c(y)e hata** would seem to be the literary analog of **-ko siph.e hanta** 'is desirous of (doing)', but semantically it is closer to the colloquial intentive **-ulye ko hanta** 'has it in mind to (do)'. Choy Hyenpay 1959:312 gives a different etymology for **-ko ca**, but it is unconvincing in view of his remarks on p. 516 about **-ko cita** and **-ko ciko**. In North Korea the spelling is **-koce**.

Historically, the various apperceptive elements **kwumen, kwulye**, ... , are shapes of a complex pseudo-mood based on the gerund **-ko** (in its Seoul dialect form **-kwu**) + the particle **man** 'just, but' (in a variant **men**) – or again, in the case of **kwulye**, + an abbreviated shape of the intentive **halye**.

9.8. Transferentives.

The transferentive mood **-ta**, frequently followed by the particle **ka**, indicates a CHANGE or SHIFT of action — a reversal, a nullification, or an unanticipated and unrelated consequence if attached to the past marker, usually an interruption otherwise. When two past transferentives are followed by a form of **hanta** 'behaves', the meaning is that of alternation, doing first one thing and then the other. The transferentive of the copula, which usually appears in the postvocalic shape **'ta (ka)** — though there are examples of **ita (ka)** in Part II, is often used after particles of location to show a shift in location: ··· **ey 'ta** 'into, onto' and notice also **mues ey 'ta sse** 'what's it used for?'. The form can be inserted between an infinitive and a verb of giving to emphasize a shift of physical space in the performance of the favor reported: **-e ('ta) cwunta** '(goes and) does for someone', **-e ('ta) tulinta** '(goes and) does for someone superior'. Occasionally it is inserted in other constructions of infinitive + verb, e.g. **tte 'ta mī-l-** 'push aside; shift blame onto another'. And it shows a shift of direction after infinitives such as **naylye** 'descends' (**naylye 'ta** 'downward'), **tul.ye** 'puts in' (**tul.ye 'ta** 'inward'), ... Notice also the expressions **-ta mōs hay** 'being more than one can bear to (do)', as in **hata mōs hay (nācwung ey nun totwuk cil hayss.ta)** 'at wit's end (finally committed theft)'.

You will observe that the ending of the transferentive is the same shape as one of the assertive endings **-ta** and all of the forms are the same, with the exception of the processive stem + transferentive **-ta** as in **tat.ta** ··· 'closes and / but ··· ; interrupts closing and ··· ', a form that has no assertive homonym for the colloquial speaker, who says **tat.nunta** (processive assertive) for 'closes'. The two moods transferentive and assertive contrast in the example **kass.ta wass.ta hay**, which can mean either 'they are going and coming (alternately)' or (= **kass.ta wass.ta ko hay**) 'he says he is back (= has gone and then come back)'. It might be said that the transferentive is simply the assertive (or indicative assertive) + the particle **ka** and that the occurrences without the particle are just abbreviations of this more complex expression. In that case, we should know that **kass.ta wass.ta hay** means 'they are going and coming' when we can substitute **kass.ta ka wass.ta ka hay** with no relevant difference of meaning, and it would have the other meaning ('he says that ··· ') when we cannot insert the second **ka**. (The first **ka** is appropriate in either sense.) But notice that **kass.ta ka wass.ta hay** with just the first **ka** is ambiguous as to whether it represents **kass.ta ka wass.ta ka hay** or **kass.ta ka wass.ta ko hay**. See the entry for **-ta ka** in Part II.

For a different interpretation of the transferentive, as derived from **tak.a**, the infinitive of **tak-** = **taku-** 'approach', see Choy Hyenpay 1960 (Hankul 127:7-17); CF Ceng Insung 1960:161-3. That may be the right explanation of the etymology, but I believe that the synchronic view taken here can stand independent of the history of how the form came into being, which is still rather unclear, and may well be along lines not too different from this description, though serious questions are raised by the observations made on p. 71, p. 273, and p. 588; also pp. 423-4 (*a ̇ni 'la ̇ka*).

9.9. The structure of earlier verb endings.

Each Korean verb confronts us with a daunting number of bewildering forms, but many of the seemingly disparate shapes can be analyzed as complex structures made up of a reasonably small inventory of basic parts. In §9.1 we explored the positional order of such basic parts for the modern verb forms. In §9.9.1 we present a similar, but richer, scheme for the Middle Korean verb. Several important elements did not survive into modern Korean except as peripheral nuisances. In particular, the effective aspect (§9.9.2) and the modulator (§9.9.10) are important categories of the earlier language that are difficult for us to appreciate today. The emotive structures of §9.9.3 were used where the modern language has developed other means of showing the speaker's attitude toward what he is saying, such as the apperceptive, circumstantial, and exclamatory sentences described in §11.3.

In both the earlier language and its later development matters are complicated by various surface adhesions of formerly loose elements, with the immediate history often obscured by compression. We must resist the tendency to simply list the surface strings as unanalyzed entities, for that puts an unnecessary strain on learning and making use of the possible ways something can be said. Instead, we will attempt to achieve a maximally generous apportionment of word boundaries, based more on combinatorial factors than on prosodic evidence. At the same time, our notation attempts to capture unobtrusively the syllable divisions of the original spelling, which varied considerably from text to text, or even within a single text. The spaces we write represent grammatical information that is not directly supplied by the texts, for they recognized graphic syllables and morphemes but no unit between those chunks and longer strings, such as sentences. Modern writers usually insert spaces that break up the Hankul text into phrases, basing the boundaries on likely surface junctures – pauses, or momentary slowdowns in the articulatory process. The main principles followed are to attach particles at the end of the phrase, just like verb endings, and to keep many complex ending structures as unbroken strings. At the levels of phrase and morpheme alike people vary in deciding just which complex structures are to be left unanalyzed. With respect to compound nouns, the situation is much like that faced by writers of English ("solid, space, or hyphen?") but usually without the benefit of the hyphen.

9.9.1. Middle Korean finite forms: the basic scheme.

The following chart presents a synopsis of the elements that comprise the basic structures of the earlier verb endings, ordered under eleven sequence positions. That is followed by a brief list of the categories included in each position. Further descriptions of the forms produced will be found in later sections, and in Part II. Variable vowels are shown as $^e a$ and $^u o$; the criteria for choosing between variants are described in the individual entries of Part II. The lenited and elided forms of velar-initial morphemes are given separately (k, G, $[G]$). In this chart and those that follow the basic accent is often left unindicated, but it is marked in the surface strings of the endings when they are cited.

Middle Korean finite forms: the basic scheme

1	2	3	4	5	6	7	8	9	10	11
-zop-	-($^u o$)si-	-no-	-w$^u o$-	-two-	-$t^e a$-	-($^u o$)n	i	-ngi	s	ka
				-swo-	-$k^e a$-	-($^u o$)l(q)				Ga
				-nwo-	-$G^e a$-					kwo
					-$[G]^e a$-					Gwo
					-$^e a$-					ta
					-kwa					-ta, -la
					-Gwa					-a, -ya

1 deferential, humble; object-exaltation. SEE §9.9.9.
2 honorific = subject-exaltation. Also FOLLOWS the retrospective: -ˑ$t^e a$-ˑsi- = -($^u o$)ˑsi-ˑ$t^e a$-. And the effective: -ˑke-ˑsi- = -($^u o$)ˑsi-ˑGe-. SEE §9.9.8.
3 processive. Mutually exclusive with the retrospective and the effective (6).
4 modulator. SEE §9.9.10.
5 emotive; emotive-emotive (double emotive): -ˑnwo-ˑswo-, -ˑtwo-ˑs(wo)-, -ˑnwo-s-ˑtwo-. Before -ngi (at least) -ˑswo- < -s-ˑwo- and -ˑnwo- < -(ˑ)n[o]-ˑwo- (LCT 1973:296). SEE §9.9.3.
6 aspect: the retrospective; the effective (§9.9.2).
7 aspect: the perfect (= realized); the imperfect (= unrealized).
8 summational epitheme ('fact').
9 polite marker. SEE §9.9.8.
10 adnominal particle. SEE s in Part II (p. 764).
11 mood: postmodifiers ('question') above the line; suffixes below.

9.9.2. The effective.

The effective aspect is marked with nonfinal suffixes (here loosely called "infixes") as shown across the top of the chart below. The particular strings of morphemes that attach at the end of each suffix are listed beneath it. I am treating /-kwala/ as a final suffix -kwa which incorporates the infix and is followed by the exclamatory elements 'la or swo'la (see the end of this section).

Markers of the effective aspect

-ᵉ/a-	-kᵉ/a-, -Gᵉ/a-	-tᵉ/a- (cop i-lᵉ/a-)	-kwa, -Gwa
+	+	+ -n	
		-lq	
		-n i [rare]	

-m	-m	
-n i ('la)	-n i ('la)	-ta → -la
-n i Gwa	-n i Gwa	
-nᵘol	-nul	
-n ywo	-n ywo	
	-n ye	
	-n ya	
-ten		
-l(q) [-al(q)]		
-la		
-l i Ga		
-n ti	-n ti	
-ta	-ta	
	-s-ta [rare]	
-sin i		

The -ᵉ/a- links ···l, as in me˙len ··· (1463 Pep 2:41a) ' ··· who have grown distant' — CF ¨melGe˙nul (1463 Pep 6:5b) 'become distant and then'; it inserts y after ···i or ···y, as in pi˙chwuyye˙nul (1445 ¹Yong 42) 'shone and then'; and °ho- 'do' → ˙ho.ya-. We might think of this as -˙[G]ᵉ/a- with elided G, but that would be implausible for forms like ni˙c-e- 'forget' or me˙k-e- 'eat', though the latter can be treated as me[k]-˙ke-, an explanation that fits also the adverbative in me[k]˙key ˙za (1518 Sohak-cho 18b). Such forms are found for only a few ···k- stems: aside from forms for mek- 'eat' I have found only se˙kenol (1473 Pep 2:56b) < sek- 'rot'. Contrast pak.ke˙nul (1449 Kok 41) < pak- 'embed', sol˙ma nik-ke˙ta (?1517- ¹No 2:35a) < nik- 'get well cooked', sik.ke˙ton (1481 Samkang chwung 27a, 1489 Kup-kan 6:50; cited from LCT) < sik- 'get cool'; cwuk.kesinol (1447[→1562] Sek 11:20; cited from LCT), cwuk.ken ˙t i (1481 Samkang chwung 6b), cwuk.ke-ngi ˙'ta (1481 Samkang chwung 22a) < cwuk- 'die'. The variant with no trace of the velar is not common, and I have not found examples for stems that end in ···p(h)- or ···t(h)-. An additional problem: ˙th[o]-a- 'ride' → ˙tha- in ˙tham cik (1481 Twusi 7:2a). Forms such as -˙Gᵉ/a- and -˙Gwa are the result of leniting k to G after ···l, ···y, and ···i (copula stem); the G is shown indirectly, by writing the zero initial. It has been suggested that the copula ends with an underlying y (˙iy- in contrast with ˙i- 'cover', which does not take lenition), and that is also thought to account for the lenitions after the stem ¨ti- 'drop' = ¨tiy- < *ti-˙i-, a causative derived from °ti- 'fall' (which is followed by the unlenited forms). The few exceptions of lenition after ···li- stems, such as no˙li˙Gesi˙nol (1445 ¹Yong 8) and ko˙liGe˙nul (1482 Nam 1:54b), are apparently due to confusion (= false analogy) with the structures ··· ˙l i '-. (SEE Martin 1982/3:n11.) Most of the effective forms of °wo- 'come' become ˙wo˙na-, whence modern **one la** [dialect **ona la** 'come!'] and **Ili on**' 'C'mere [Come here]!', but there are a few forms with ˙wo˙ke-, too. The unique behavior of the stem °wo- may be explained as an incorporation of the stem °na- 'emerge', substituting for the stem °ka- 'go', the likely source of the effective -˙k⁽ᵉ⁾a-, which would have been incompatible with 'come', if a feeling for those meanings was there when the earlier forms were created. The exceptions with ˙wo-˙ke- (˙woke˙na, ˙woke˙nol, ˙woke˙tun) must have been created by analogy at some later time, when the meaning 'go' had been forgotten and the endings were more opaque; we would have expected *˙wo-˙ka-. The effective substantive -˙⁽ᵉ⁾am is used only before ˙cik °ho˙ta; the copula effective substantive ˙i ˙Gem (lenited from -˙kem) appears only as the truncation ··· ˙[y]˙Gem in -u˙l i ˙˙Ge˙m ye. Although -˙⁽ᵉ⁾a- is usually treated as an unexplained variant of the effective -˙k⁽ᵉ⁾a-, King 1991c refines the hypothesis of Ko Yengkun 1980 that the two forms are distributed according to the transitivity of the stem. For more on this, see the entry -e- in Part II (p. 466).

The distinction of -˙ta- and -˙ka- as first-person 'I, we', versus -˙te- and -˙ke- for the other persons, is clearly stated by LCT 1973:317-8, but (as he says) many examples seem to be in conflict and the distinction was perhaps pre-Hankul — if, indeed, it really existed.

The form -˙kwa (-˙Gwa) appears before ˙˙la and swo˙la to make an exclamatory first-person statement; see also -˙kwa˙tye < -˙kwatoy˙ye < *-˙kwa to[wo]y˙ye. There are but few examples in the texts. It might be the modulated infinitive of the effective, a contraction of *-˙k[e]-˙wo-˙a; if so it contradicts the otherwise valid rule (given below) that the modulator never precedes the infinitive ending. Another difficulty with that explanation: the accent of pwo˙kwa ˙˙la (1481 Twusi 7:13a, 16:52b) is like that of the gerund (pwo˙kwo) rather than that of the effective (˙pwoke···).

9.9.3. Emotives.

The emotive bound stems express a subjective statement, often poetic or exclamatory. They are incorporated in the predication structures displayed below.

Emotive statements

-two-ta[1]	-two-s-te-la	-two-swo-n i	-two-swo-ngi 'ta
i-lwo-ta[2]			i-lwo-swo-ngi 'ta[2]
-two-s-ta			-two-s-te-ngi 'ta
-nwo-s-ta			-nwo-swo-ngi 'ta
-ta-s-ta / (i)la-s-ta[3]	-ta-swola	-ta-swo-n i	-ta-so-ngi 'ta
-⁽ᵉ⁾a-so-la			
-sya-s-ta[4]			

[1] Also a few examples of -twu-ta.
[2] Or -u˙l i ˙lwo-˙ta, -u˙l i ˙˙lwo-˙swo-ngi 'ta. We treat ˙ilwo˙ta as a variant of the copula (see §9.9.11).
[3] Retrospective + emotive -˙s[o]- + indicative assertive -˙ta.
[4] Modulated honorific -(ᵘ/o)˙sya- + emotive -˙s[o]- + indicative assertive -˙ta.

The emotives are mostly built on the bound verb stems *-˙t[o]- and -˙s[o]-, usually in their modulated versions -˙two- and -˙swo-. A double emotive can be made by joining the two stems: -˙two-˙swo-, etc. Another kind of exclamatory sentence is made with -˙⁽ᵉ⁾a ˙y˙la, equivalent to modern -e ˙la; see the entries in Part II.

There are also emotive questions, phrased with the emotive modifier -s-on or the processive emotive modifier -˙no-s-on followed by the postmodifier ˙ta. See Part II for examples.

9.9.4. Sentence types.

Below are listed the various structures that are used to express different types of sentence. Many of the structures are based on nominalizations made with the postmodifier ˙i 'fact' (= kes) used as a summational epitheme after the perfect and imperfect adnominal forms: in rough translation '[it is] the fact that ⋯ does/did (is/was)'. Such nominalizations are followed by overt forms of the copula to make extended predicates — 'it's [the case] that ⋯ ', and the other forms can be treated as elliptical versions of that common type of predication, which usually had little function except to make the statement somewhat indirect or poetic. Stronger versions of the extended predicate were made with the postmodifiers *s* (after imperfect -*lq* only) and *t* 'fact' (after -*lq* or -*n*), and these nominalizations were also used in other structures of some importance, such as -*lq ˙s oy* 'since, because'. The *˙i* had other uses as an extruded epitheme 'the one that ⋯ '. The extrusion was usually from the subject of the adnominalized sentence 'one who ⋯ ' but occasionally from the object 'one whom ⋯ ': *ne ˙[G]wa kol˙Wo˙l i ˙˙ep.su˙n i ˙˙la* (1459 Wel 18:57b) 'there is no one to compare with you'.

Sentence types

COMMAND	-$(^u\!o)$˙*la*; -˙$^e\!a$˙*la*, -˙$k^e\!a$˙*la*
	-˙*kwo* ˙'*la*, -˙*Gwo* ˙'*la*
	-˙$^e\!a$ ˙*ssye*
	-$(^u\!o)$˙*sywo*˙*sye*
SUGGESTION/DESIRE	-˙*cye* (˙'*la*) [incorporated aux adj inf]
	-˙*sa-ngi* ˙'*ta* [to a superior]
PROMISE	-$(^u\!o)$˙*m a*
EXCLAMATION (apperceptive)	-$(^u\!o)l$˙*ssy*$^e\!a$ = -$(^u\!o)lq$ ˙*sy*$^e\!a$ < -$(^u\!o)lq$ *s* ˙*y*$^e\!a$
	-*i*-˙*kwan*˙*tye*
STATEMENT/QUESTION	-$(^u\!o)$˙*n i*
	-$(^u\!o)$˙*l i*
STATEMENT	-˙*ta*; -˙*la* after -˙*w*$^u\!o$-, -˙*nwo*-, -˙*t*$^e\!a$- (and ˙*ile*-), (-)˙*swo*-, ? ˙*ci*- (desire), cop ˙*i*- (but honorific ˙*isi*˙*ta*) and var cop ˙*i*˙*lwo*-, but not after -˙$k^e\!a$- (-*ke*˙*ta*) or -˙*two*- (-*two*˙*ta*).
QUESTION	-$(^u\!o)n$ + ˙*ta*, ˙*ka*, ˙*kwo*
	-$(^u\!o)lq$ + ˙*ta*, ˙*ka*, ˙*kwo*; ˙*t* (⋯)
	-$(^u\!o)$˙*n i* + ˙*Ga*, ˙*Gwo*, ˙*ya*;
	-$(^u\!o)$˙*l i* + ˙*Ga*, ˙*Gwo*, ˙*ya*;
	-$(^u\!o)$˙*n [i]* + ˙*ye*, ˙*ywo*
	-$(^u\!o)$˙*l [i]* + ˙*ye*, ˙*ywo*
	-$(^u\!o)$˙*n i* '-*ngi s* ˙*ka*/˙*kwo*
	-$(^u\!o)$˙*l i* '-*ngi s* ˙*ka*/˙*kwo*
(negative)	*a*˙*ni* ˙*Ga*/˙*Gwo*
Extended predicates:	-$(^u\!o)$˙*n i* '⋯
	-$(^u\!o)n$ ˙*t i*⋯ , -$(^u\!o)n$ ˙*t i*˙*n i* ('⋯)
	-$(^u\!o)lq$ ˙*t i*⋯ , -$(^u\!o)lq$ ˙*t i*˙*n i* ('⋯)
	-$(^u\!o)lq$ ˙*s i*⋯ , -$(^u\!o)lq$ ˙*s i*˙*n i* ('⋯)

The extended predicates are used to make FACTUAL sentences by predicating a summational epitheme (˙*i, s, t* 'the fact that ⋯ ') with some copula form or, as if directly, with the copula elipted.

9.9.5. Aspect marking of sentence types.

Sentences are marked for the aspects of perfect, imperfect, processive, and retrospective by various morphemes, most commonly incorporated in the modifier endings.

Aspect marking of sentence types

	PERFECT	IMPERFECT	PROCESSIVE	RETROSPECTIVE
STATEMENT			-ˈno ˈta -ˈnwoˈla[1]	-(^{u}/o)ˈl i ˈleˈla
	-(^{u}/o)ˈn i ˈˈla -(^{u}/o)ˈn i ˈ-ngi ˈˈta	-(^{u}/o)ˈl i ˈˈla -(^{u}/o)ˈl i ˈ-ngi ˈˈta	-ˈno.n i ˈˈla -ˈnoˈn i ˈ-ngi ˈˈta -ˈnwo-ngi ˈˈta[2]	
QUESTION	-(^{u}/o)n ˈkaˈ ˈkwoˈ ˈta -(^{u}/o)ˈn i ˈ-ngi s ˈkaˈ ˈkwo	-(^{u}/o)lq ˈkaˈ ˈkwoˈ ˈta -(^{u}/o)ˈl i ˈ-ngi s ˈkaˈ ˈkwo	-non ˈkaˈ ˈkwoˈ ˈta -ˈnoˈn i ˈ-ngi s ˈkaˈ ˈkwo	?
FACTUAL₁	-(^{u}/o)ˈl i ˈˈn i -(^{u}/o)ˈl i ˈˈn i ˈˈla	?		

FACTUAL₂		-(^{u}/o)lssila =
		  -(^{u}/o)lq ˈs iˈla
		-(^{u}/o)lssiGwo =
		  -(^{u}/o)lq ˈs i-ˈGwo		

EXCLAMATORY STATEMENT ('I / we ... !')		-ˈkwa ˈˈla, -ˈGwa ˈˈla -ˈkwa-ngi ˈˈta, -ˈGwa-ngi ˈˈta -kwa swoˈla		

1 = -ˈno-ˈwo-ˈta with the modulator
2 = -ˈno-ˈwo-ngi ˈ[y-]ˈta with the modulator

9.9.6. Nonfinite endings.

Various structures can be attached to a stem to make a nonfinal clause, coordinate with or (more often) subordinate to the final clause that follows. A few structures of stem + ending incorporate relatively free elements, and they can perhaps be treated as abbreviations of analytic phrases. These elements begin with an apical, and before them an ·-l- stem elides its final liquid. The pertinent morphemes are the bound adjectival noun ˈtos, the postmodifier t 'fact', which adds the nominative particle to make -ˈti, the suspective, but also attaches the accusative (ˈt ol) and other particles, and the particles ˈtwo = -ˈti ˈtwo and (rarely) ˈsa = -ˈe ˈza. The elements -ˈtoy, -ti ˈWi, -toy.ye, and -ˈtoˈlwok were more definitively absorbed, but -ˈtoy may have been compressed from -(no)n ˈtoy. Some of the forms listed below are so important that we give them paradigmatic labels (INFINITIVE, GERUND, ...), as well as tag translations.

Nonfinite endings

-ˈᵉa, -ˈyᵉa, ˈhoˈya   and, ... INFINITIVE[1]
   + k, ˈsye, ˈtwo, ˈza, ...   (various kinds of emphasis)
-ˈᵉa-[si-]ˈnol   when, since, as; although CONCESSIVE
-ˈke-[si-]ˈnol, -ˈGe-[si-]ˈnol   when, since, as; although CONCESSIVE

-ˈkwo, -ˈGwo + k, ˈsye, ˈtwo, ˈza, ... + n'	and, ... GERUND (various kinds of emphasis) and, but, when (much more/less ...)
-ˈkwom °ˈho-	do repeatedly (CF -ko nun ha-)
-ˈke-/-ˈGe-(si-, ...-)ˈtun	if, when PROVISIONAL [= EFFECTIVE CONDITIONAL] (after ˈwo- 'come')
-na-ˈton	
-ˈa-(si-, ...-)ˈton	if, when EFFECTIVE CONDITIONAL
-ton	if, when CONDITIONAL (< t + ˈᵘ/ₒn)
-(ᵘ/ₒ)ˈna	but ADVERSATIVE
-ke-/-Ge-ˈna	but; whether ... or ... EFFECTIVE ADVERSATIVE
-ˈkᵉa.n/-ˈGᵉa.n/-ˈᵉa.n i ˈGwa	but/and (even more)
-ˈno.n i ˈGwa	but/and (even more)
-ˈkᵉan/-ˈGᵉan/-ˈᵉan maˈlon	but
-ˈken maˈnon	but
-ken/-Gen ˈtyeng	although
-kwanˈtoy, -Gwanˈtoy	since, as
-ˈtoy	and ACCESSIVE → -ˈwo-ˈtoy; cop ˈilwoˈtoy, honorific -(ˈᵘ/ₒ)syaˈtoy
-(ᵘ/ₒ)n ˈt oy/ay (n')	and, but
-ˈte-/-ˈke-n ˈt ᵉay/oy n'	and then; if, when
-ˈwᵘ/ₒ-l ˈtyeyn	if, when
-(ᵘ/ₒ)ˈn i	(its being that ...) EXTENDED PREDICATE
-(ᵘ/ₒ)lssoy = -(ᵘ/ₒ)lq ˈso y	as, since, so; because
-(ᵘ/ₒ)ˈla 'n ˈt oy	and therefore; because
-(ᵘ/ₒ)ˈla	if, when; since
-wᵘ/ₒ-ˈl ye	for the purpose of, in order to
-(ᵘ/ₒ)ˈlak	with the intention of; + °ˈho- intend to do
-ˈta ka, ˈila ˈka	and/but then (changing to ...) TRANSFERENTIVE
-ˈkey/-ˈGey, -ˈkuy/-ˈGuy²	so as to be/do; (in a manner) such that
-te-ˈtun	but, and; if, when RETR CONDITIONAL (hon. -ˈtesiˈtun)
-ˈtoˈlwok	all the way to where, until
-ˈtos °ˈho-; -ˈtoˈs 'i	be as if ... ; as if
-ˈᵉam ˈcik °ˈho-	be likely/possible, be somewhat/quite ...
-(ᵘ/ₒ)l ˈsolwok	the more ... (the more ...)
-ˈt i →	
-ˈti	(1) = -ki ka; (2) = -ci [ka] (+ neg aux)
-ˈti maˈla (k)	= -ci mālko 'not ...ing but (instead)'
-ˈti ˈGwos	the more ... (the more ...)
-ˈt ol	= -ci lul
-two = -ˈti ˈtwo	(+ neg aux 'not ... even/either')
-tiˈWi, -tiˈGwuy, -tiˈGwey, -tiˈGwoy	but (= -ci man)
-ˈsa = -ˈe ˈza	only/precisely if
-ˈkwo/-ˈGwo ˈcye	wanting to: + °ˈho-, + ˈˈwen °ˈho-
-ˈkwaˈtye, -ˈGwaˈtya	wanting to
-ˈkwatoyˈye, -ˈGwatoyˈye	wanting to
*-ˈkey 'sˈkwo, -ˈGey 'sˈkwo	wanting it to happen
-ˈkuy 'sˈkwo	wanting it to happen
*-ˈkwo s, -ˈGwo s	wanting it to happen
-toy.ye	I hope/desire that ...
-ˈkᵉa, -ˈGᵉa + ciˈla, ˈci-ngi ˈˈta	I hope/desire that ...

¹ When the infinitive is attached, stems ending in ···*i*- or ···*wu*- usually reduce those vowels to semivowels (···*i*-˙*e* > ···˙*ye*, ···*wu*-˙*e* > ···*we*) and stems ending in ···*u*- drop that vowel (···*u*-˙*e* > ···˙*e*). Stems ending in ···*wo*- often reduce that vowel to a semivowel (···*wo*-˙*a* > ···˙*wa*) but the unreduced version is also found, as in *to˙thwoa* (1475 Nay 3:41a) = *to˙thwa* (1463 Pep 2:113b) 'fight'. The only stem with ···*o*- is °*ho*- 'do', and its infinitive is irregular: ˙*ho˙ya*. (Stems such as *mwo˙lo-* / ¨*mwoll*- attach the infinitive to the ···*ll*- shape: ¨*mwol˙la* 'not know'.) For stems with ···*a*- the infinitive ending is absorbed by the stem: ˙*ka*-˙*a* > ˙*ka* 'go', ˙*sa*-˙*a* > ˙*sa* 'buy'. Forms with ···*a*-˙*a* and ···*e*-˙*e* represent the effective infinitive, as in ˙*sa˙a ci˙la* (1459 Wel 1:10b) 'I want to buy' and ˙*phye˙e ˙ys.ten* (1447 Sek 6:2a) ' ··· that one has stretched'. But *te˙e* (1459 Wel 1:47b, 23:76b; 1462 ¹Nung 76:2; 1463 Pep 6:10b) < *te[u]*-˙*e* 'increase' is the simple infinitive; the unattested effective infinitive would be **teu˙ke*. And *ta˙a* (1445 ¹Yong 84, 1447 Sek 9:16b; 1462 ¹Nung 9:114b, 10:9a) < *ta[o]*-˙*a* 'exhaust' is also a simple infinitive.

² And uncommonly -˙*koy* / -˙*Goy* (He Wung 602-5).

9.9.7. Nominalizers.

Nominalizations are usually made with the substantive (= literary summative) suffix -(˙*ᵁ/o*)*m*, but the modulator is normally obligatory, so the ending is -˙*wᵁ/om*, attached to the stem under the rules for the modulator stated in §9.9.10. The copula is (?˙*i˙lwom* /) ˙*(y)˙lwom* = ?˙*i˙ywom* / ¨*(y)wom*. The honorific of the substantive is -(ᵁ/o)˙*syam*, and the honorific substantive of the copula ought to be ?*˙i˙syam* / ˙*(y)˙syam*, or ?*˙i˙lwo˙syam* / ˙*(y)˙lwo˙syam*, but examples of those copula forms have not been found. In extended structures based on the substantive (such as -˙ᵁ/o˙*m ye*) the modulator is absent: ˙*i˙m ye* [< ˙*i-m ˙i-˙e*], ˙*i˙m ye n'*, ... ; ˙*isi˙m ye (n')*, ... Compare the two substantives in *te˙tuy˙m ye spol˙lwo˙m i* (1462 ¹Nung 6:54a) 'the tardiness or promptness'. Examples: ¨*twul[h] a˙ni* ˙'*m ye* (1459 Wel 8:31b) 'are not two, nor ... ', ¨*ne ˙y˙m ye* (1459 Wel 8:5b) 'it is you and ... ', ··· *towoy˙m ye* (1447 Sek 6:34a) 'it becomes ··· and ... ', ¨*nay˙m ye* (1459 Wel 7:48a) 'we impart it and ... ', *mwoncye* ¨*mal ˙hosi˙m ye* (1459 Wel 2:58b) 'he speaks first and ... ', *mwoncye* ˙*mas ˙pwosi˙m ye* (1475 Nay 1:9-10) 'first tries the taste and ... '.

Notice that either *i˙sywom* / ˙*(y)˙sywom* or *i˙sywum* / ˙*(y)˙sywum* is the modulated substantive of *is(i)*- 'exist', and ˙*sywom* or ˙*sywum* (when not optionally representing ˙*y˙sywom* or ˙*y˙sywum* after a Chinese word ending in ···*ɪ* or ···*ʏ*) is the modulated substantive of its shortened form ˙*si*-. The honorific is ¨*kyesi˙m ye n'* ([1447→]1562 Sek 3:1a), modulated as ¨*kyesya˙m ay* (1445 ¹Yong 26); in ¨*kye˙sim ˙ay* (1586 Sohak 6:122a) the ˙*sim* must be broken type for ˙*syam*. The substantive of °*sye*- 'stand' is *syem* (*sye˙m ye n'* 1462 ¹Nung 6:29a), with honorific (?*) ˙*sye˙sim*; and the modulated substantive is ¨*syem* = *sye˙wum*, honorific (?*) ˙*sye˙syam*. The modulated substantive of ˙*psu*- 'use' is ˙*pswum* (1447 Sek 9:12a, 1462 ¹Nung 10:42b); for ˙*ptu*- 'float' the form is ˙*ptwum* (˙*ptwu˙m i* 1462 ¹Nung 3:106a, ˙*ptwu˙m ey* 1459 Wel 8:6a); for ˙*khu*- 'big' it is ˙*khwum* (˙*khwu.m u˙lwo* 1459 Wel 1:29b). The modulated substantive of °*hye*- 'pull' is ¨*hyem* (¨*hyem ˙kot* [broken type lost the upper dot], ¨*hye˙m on* 1465 Wen 2:1:1:16a), of ¨*hyey*- 'reckon' it is ¨*hyey˙ywum* (¨*hyey[˙]ywu˙m i* 1481 Twusi 8:36a). The form for °*ho*- 'do' is ˙*hwom* and for ˙*ho˙si*- 'deign to do' it is ˙*ho˙syam*: ˙*hosya˙m olwo* (1482 Nam 1:33b), ˙*hosya˙m on* (1459 Wel 14:58a; 1463 Pep 6:145b; 1462 ¹Nung 1:17b, 4:13a; 1465 Wen se:12a), ˙*hosya˙m i* (1462 ¹Nung 4:13b, 10:42b; 1463 Pep 5:100a), ˙*ho˙sya.m i˙la* (1459 Wel 14:58a). But in extended structures the substantive appears unmodulated: ˙*hosi˙m ye* (1459 Wel 2:58b).

There are a few examples of the nominalizing -˙*ki* (the summative): -˙*ki l'* ¨*al*- 'know to do'; -˙*ki ˙lol ˙cul˙ki*- 'be glad to do, delight in doing'; -˙*ki ˙lol* ˙ᴋʏᴡᴇʟǫ °*ho*- 'decide to do'; -˙*ki ˙yey* 'in doing'. (Examples in Part II.) Wider use of the summative took hold in the 17th century. In the modern language, the MK nominalizations with the substantive have largely been replaced by analytic structures that consist of modifier + **kes** 'fact; thing; one'.

Notice also the summational nominalizations made up of modifier + the postmodifier ˙*i* 'fact'. These are used to express a favorite MK sentence type of 'it is [the fact] that ··· ', referred to as "factual predication" or "the extended predicate".

9.9.8. Exaltation; the politeness marker (-ngi).

As in the modern language, earlier speakers of Korean used various devices to show their respect for the subject and toward the listener. To exalt or show honor to the subject the verb stem attaches a bound auxiliary (usually referred to as a suffix or an infix). The morpheme is combined with other elements to make paradigmatic forms parallel to the unmarked (nonhonorific) forms.

The honorific stem can be modulated (§9.9.10):

-(^{u}/o)˙si- + -˙w^u/o- modulator → -(^{u}/o)˙sya-
  + -˙^{e}/a infinitive → -(^{u}/o)˙sya
  + -s- emotive → -(˙^{u}/o)syas-˙ta

Both the effective honorific and the honorific effective occur:

-˙^{e}/asi-, (…y, …i) -˙y^e/asi- = -˙k^e/asi-, -˙G^e/asi- = -(^{u}/o)˙si˙ke-

Do not confuse this with:

-˙^{e}/a ˙s(i)…, (…y, …i), -˙y^e/a ˙s(i)… inf + aux is(i)…
-˙k^e/a ˙s(i)…, (…y, …l), -˙G^e/a ˙s(i)… effective inf + aux is(i)…

Optional order of the honorific is possible also for the provisional, which consists of the effective + incorporated *t* 'fact' + pcl ˙(n)^u/on:

-˙esi˙t^u/on, (…y, …i) -˙yesi˙t^u/on = -˙kesi˙tun = -^{u}/o˙sike˙tun

And it is possible, as well, for the concessive, which consists of the effective modifier + the accusative marker ˙(l)^u/ol:

-˙^{e}/asi˙n^u/ol, (…y, …i) -˙y^e/asi˙n^u/ol = -˙k^e/asi˙n^u/ol = -(^{u}/o)˙sike˙nul

The bound stem -¨zop- (-¨sop-, -¨cop-), with its morphophonemic peculiarities (§9.9.9), was attached to make forms that are deferential toward the listener or that exalt the direct or indirect object. Before a vowel the *p* often becomes *W* or *w*: -zowa ← -zoW-a; -zowo… ← -zoW-o… , ← -zoW-wo-.

When both exaltations are present, the deferential (object exaltation) comes first: -zo˙W-osi- ← *-(o)so˙po-si- as in -zo˙wosya˙m ol, -zo˙wosi˙kwo, -zo˙wo˙site˙n i. Such forms are used to show respect to the listener when referring to his acts toward a superior, as when I ask whether "you" will humbly offer something to Buddha. Not every example of …si- represents the honorific. The morpheme is not present in ˙TTAY-SSIN ˙tol˙h i ¨mwoy˙sizo˙Wo˙n i (1449 Kok 23) '[twenty-seven] great gods served to guard round him', for the verb ¨mwoy˙si- is a contraction of * ¨mwoy˙ye isi-.

The polite marker -ngi shows respect toward the addressee, like modern -(su)p-ni-. It is sometimes reduced to -ng', and the copula polite form … '-ngi = [i]-ngi is occasionally ellipted altogether (CF He Wung 1970:118-9):

˙ho˙nwo.n i s ˙ka (1447 Sek 6:16b) = ˙ho-no-˙wo-n ˙i [˙i-ngi] s ˙ka
is.no˙n i s ˙ka (1447 Sek 6:14b) = is-n-on ˙i [˙i-ngi] s ˙ka
a˙ni tutco˙Wa 'ys˙tesi˙n i s ˙ka (1447 Sek 17a) = … is-˙te-si-n ˙i [˙i-ngi] s ˙ka

Compare the unellipted structures in e˙nu y ˙za ˙mos ¨tywoho˙n i '-ngi s ˙ka (1447 Sek 6:35b) 'which one is best?', ˙SYENG-ZIN ˙i ¨kyesi.n i ˙'n i '-ngi s ˙ka (1465 Wen se:68a) 'is there a holy man here?'

9.9.9. The deferential (-¨zop-).

The bound stem used to make the deferential is -¨zop- < *-so˙po- or *-oso˙po-. For Middle Korean we take the synchronically basic shape to be -¨zoW- and account for the -s… forms as assimilations; that is just opposite from the viewpoint taken in Martin 1982/3, where the basic form was taken to begin with -s…, like the reconstruction of the earlier stem. I believe the immediate ancestor of ALL cases of z was s, even for particular morphemes that do not preserve evidence of the conditioning factors, such as the accentual residue of a lost vowel. Similarly in all cases, I believe the ancestor of -W- was p, and that of the last consonant of the -T/L- stems was t. The revised reconstruction of *-so˙po- as *-oso˙po- follows from taking -¨zoW- as the basic synchronic shape for Middle Korean. The initial vowel of the reconstruction is not to be confused with the epenthetic …^{u}/o…, for it did not function to separate the ending from a preceding vowel. Instead, it accounts for rules of attachment that are unique to this stem.

A Reference Grammar of Korean

How -ʺzop- attaches:

⋯s-ʺzop-	→	⋯sʺsop-, ⋯ʺssop- (including ʺ⋯z- < *⋯soˑpo-)
⋯sk-ʺzop-	→	⋯sʺsop-
⋯h-ʺzop-	→	⋯ʺssop-
⋯lh-ʺzop-	→	⋯lʺssop-
⋯c-ʺzop-	→	⋯ʺccop-; also ⋯sʺcop-, ⋯tʺcop-
⋯ch-ʺzop-	→	⋯ʺccop-; also ⋯sʺcop-, ⋯tʺcop-
⋯nc-ʺzop-	→	⋯nʺccop-; also ⋯ntʺcop-, ? ⋯sʺcop-
⋯t-ʺzop-	→	⋯tʺcop- (including ⋯t-/⋯l- < *⋯ˑto-)
⋯th-ʺzop-	→	⋯tʺcop-
⋯p-ʺzop-	→	⋯pʺsop-
⋯ph-ʺzop-	→	⋯pʺsop-
⋯ps-ʺzop-	→	⋯pʺsop-
⋯lp- (⋯lW- < *⋯lˑpo-) →		⋯lpʺsop-
⋯k-ʺzop-	→	⋯kʺsop-
⋯lk-ʺzop-	→	⋯lkʺsop-
⋯l-ʺzop-	→	⋯ʺzop-
⋯m-ʺzop-	=	⋯mʺzop-
⋯n-ʺzop-	=	⋯nʺzop-
⋯-ʺzop-	=	-ʺzop- (stems that end in vowels or diphthongs)

Source of strings in the attached forms:

⋯pʺsop-	←	⋯p-ʺzop-, ⋯ph-ʺzop-, ⋯ps-ʺzop-
⋯kʺsop-	←	⋯k-ʺzop-
⋯ʺssop-	←	⋯s-ʺzop-, ⋯h-ʺzop-
⋯sʺsop-	←	⋯s-ʺzop-, ⋯sk-ʺzop-
⋯sʺcop-	←	⋯c-ʺzop-, ⋯ch-ʺzop-
⋯tʺcop-	←	⋯t-ʺzop-, ⋯th-ʺzop-; ⋯c-ʺzop-, ⋯ch-ʺzop-
⋯ʺccop-	←	⋯c-ʺzop-, ⋯ch-ʺzop-
⋯mʺzop-	=	⋯m-ʺzop-
⋯nʺzop-	=	⋯n-ʺzop-
⋯ʺzop-	=	⋯-ʺzop-, ⋯l-ʺzop-

A scribal error must be responsible for kiˑtulicopˑti (1463 Pep 2:7a) < kiˑtuˑli- 'wait for'; it should be corrected to kiˑtulizopˑti.

9.9.10. The modulator (-ˑw^u/o-).

The modulator is a bound stem that attaches to other stems and modulates the meaning, in varying ways and to varying degrees depending upon the ending(s) that follow. Below we describe: how the morpheme is attached; what meaning it imparts; the restrictions that apply in making up forms. The modulator gradually fell into disuse starting from the early 1600s (LCT 1973:346).

The modulator attaches as follows:

(0) After a consonant the morpheme is attached with no special peculiarities, whether the stems are short or long: meˑkwumwoˑm i (1482 Kum-sam 3:3b) ← meˑkwum- 'swallow; harbor', tatoˑlwom (1482 Kum-sam 3:28b) ← tatot- 'reach', ˑmukeˑwuˑm i (1462 ¹Nung 7:86b; = ˑmuke[W]-ˑwu-m) ← ˑmukeW- 'heavy'.

(1) As they do before ALL vowels, o and u drop before -ˑw^u/o-: ˑkhwu.m uˑlwo (1459 Wel 1:29b) ← ˑkhu-ˑwu-m 'being big', ˑpcwoˑm on (1463 Pep 7:120b) ← ˑpco-ˑwo-m 'being salty', ˑthwo.m i (1475 Nay 3:63a) ← ˑthoˑwo-m 'receiving', ˑphwom (1463 Pep 4:95b) ← ˑpho-ˑwo-m 'digging'. The form ˑphaˑm ol (1462 ¹Nung 3:87a) is unexplained and tacitly corrected by LCT to the expected ʺphwoˑm ol. In the phrase teˑwoˑm ol (1481 Twusi 23:23a) ← teu-ˑwo-m 'becoming more (so)' the choice of

-ˊwo- rather than of -ˊwu- seems ill-motivated; CF teˊwuˊm un (1451 Hwun-en 14a) 'adding [a tone dot]'. Another violation of harmony: ˊtuˊlwolq (1462 ¹Nung 2:111a) = ?*ˊtuˊlwulq 'to enter'.

(2) ...i + -ˊw^u/o- → ...iˊyw^u/o-: ˊculkywoˊm ol (1463 Pep 2:249b, 1481 Twusi 22:7b) < ˊculki- 'delight'; meˊkywom (1482 Nam 2:63b) < meˊki- 'feed'; namwo ¨cywu.m ey (1481 Twusi 7:6b) < namwo °ci- 'chop wood'.

(3) ...y + -ˊw^u/o-- → ...yˊyw^u/o-: ¨hyeyˊywom (1465 Wen 3:3:1:62a), ¨hyeyywuˊm i (1481 Twusi 21:42a) < ¨hyey- 'reckon'; muyˊywo.m ol (1481 Twusi 25:23a) = muyˊywuˊm ul (1464 Kumkang 79b) < muy- 'hate'; towoyˊywoˊm i (1463 Pep 4:75a) < towoy- 'become'.

(4) The copula usually appears as ˊiˊlwo- but occasionally as ˊiˊywo-/ˊywo-: ˊiˊlwom/ˊlwom = iˊywom/ˊywom; aˊniˊlwoˊm i (1459 Wel 2:55b, 1482 Kum-sam 2:27b), hon kaˊciˊlwoˊm ol (1468- Mongsan 19a); aˊniˊlwon (1482 Kum-sam 2:27b), keˊwuˊlwuˊylwonˊt i (1462 ¹Nung 2:17b); ˊilwoˊtoy (1463 Pep 2:28b, 1462 ¹Nung 1:87b), ˊylwoˊtoy (1462 ¹Nung 7:24a, 1464 Kumkang se:5b – after Chinese words); aˊn[i]ˊywoˊm i (1459 Wel 1:36a); are there examples of unabbreviated ˊiˊywom? See also -ulˊswongiˊta = -ulqˊsˊ[y]wo-ngiˊta.

(5) The verb °ho- 'do, say' has the modulated substantive ˊhwom but also ¨hwom, as if the stem vowel were more open (see 7 below), but probably the accent is a residue from contracting ˊhoˊywom (see just below). Examples: ¨hwoˊm i (aux, 1459 Wel 21:22a); ˊhwom ('saying', 1459 Wel 1:31b), ˊhwoˊm i (after verbal noun, 1463 Pep 5:148b) = ˊhwo[ˊ]m i (1482 Kum-sam 2:16a), ˊhwoˊm ol (aux, 1462 Nung 1:108b), ˊhwo[ˊ]m ol/on (1481 Twusi 7:31b). Instead of attaching to °ho- the modulator can attach to ˊho.y-: ˊho.y-ˊwo-m → ˊho.ywom (1482 Nam 1:3a, 1463 Pep 3:63a), ˊho.ywoˊm ol (1481 Twusi 8:24b); ˊho.y-ˊwo-n → ˊho.ywon (1459 Wel 9:6b, 1482 Kum-sam 2:25a), ˊho.y-ˊwo-lq → ˊho.ywolq (1459 Wel se:10b); ˊho.y-ˊwo-ˊla → [ˊ]ho.ywoˊla (1481 Twusi 21:25b); ˊho.y-ˊwo-ˊtoy → ˊho.ywoˊtoy (1447 Sek 13:57b). These forms look as if they were made on the effective stem ˊhoˊya- with the final vowel ellipted, but perhaps they are telling us something about the prehistory of the stem: °ho-/ho.y- < *hyo-, see the note on °hoˊta in Part II.

(6) The honorific modulates as -(ᵁ/o)ˊsi-ˊw^u/o- → -(ᵁ/o)ˊsya-. Examples: ... ˊhosyaˊm on (1462 ¹Nung 1:17b) 'his saying that ... '; patcoˊwosyaˊm ol (1459 Wel 18:62b) '[seeing] that you are giving it to him'; heˊmu.l i ¨epˊsusyaˊm i (1463 Pep 2:15-6) 'that he has no blemishes'; ¨cyeˊkusyaˊm i ¨kyeˊsiken ˊtyeng (1463 Pep 3:189b) 'though there are those who have little'; [ˊTUK-NGWEN] ¨wolˊmosyamˊtwo (1445 ¹Yong 4) 'that he moved to Tek.wen'; kuˊcasiˊm ye ¨kyesyaˊm ol (1475 Nay 1:44a) 'that he is there asleep'; ˊhoˊsya.m iˊla (1459 Wel 14:58a); towoyˊsyaˊm i (1459 Wel 1:21a) 'it is deigning to do'; cwochoˊsyaˊm i (1475 Nay 2:1:49a) 'that you follow'; teuˊsya.m ol (1463 Pep 4:192-3) '[he seeks] to enhance'.

(7) After e a wu wo the -ˊw^u/o- automatically drops, but it can be retained for clarity. Examples with the morpheme suppressed but assumed because the ending requires the modulator: ˊpolaˊm ol (1481 Twusi 7:7a), ˊpolaˊm ay (?1517- Pak 1:68a) ← 'look; hope', iˊGemˊkwaˊlol (1462 ¹Nung 4:21b) ← iˊGe- 'shake'. But most vowel-final polysyllabic stems are compounds with the same behavior as the final monosyllabic stem: ¨ket-¨naˊtoy (1459 Wel 2:19a) < ¨ket-°na- 'walk across; cross'. When the modulator is suppressed, the accent of a monosyllabic stem changes to rising:
¨pwoˊm on (1459 Wel 8:9b), ¨pwoˊm iˊn i (1482 Kum-sam 2:63a) ← pwo-ˊ[wo]-m < °pwo- 'see'; ¨woˊm ol (1482 Nam 1:50b), ¨woˊm i (1482 Kum-sam 3:19a) ← wo-ˊ[wo]-m < °wo- 'come'
¨twuˊm i (1459 Wel se:22b) ← twu-ˊwu-m < °twu- 'put away'; ¨cwulˊptu.t i (1481 Twusi 7:40a) 'the idea to give it' ← ˊcwuˊwu-m < °cwu- 'give', ¨cwuˊtoy (1447 Sek 19:3a) 'give it and' ← cwu-ˊ[wu]- toy < °cwu- 'give', ˊcwulqˊt iˊla (1447 Sek 9:12a) 'is to give it' ← cwu-ˊ[wu]-lq < °cwu- 'give'
¨nyeˊm i (1481 Twusi 20:11b) < °nye- 'go'; ¨hyem (1465 Wen 2:1:1:16a [broken type lost the upper dot]) < °hye- 'draw [a needle]'; ¨hhye.m oˊlwo (1462 ¹Nung 7:90a) 'by pulling', ¨hhyeˊtoy 'leads to ... and' (1462 ¹Nung 1:69a) < hhye-ˊ[wu]- < °hhye- 'pull, lead'

¨nam ˙kwa (1447 Sek 6:19a), ¨na˙m ol (1447 Sek 9:16b) ← na-˙[wo]-m and ¨na˙toy (1447 Sek 19:7b, 1449 Kok 185) ← na-˙[wo]-˙toy < °na- 'emerge'
¨ca˙m ay (1462 ¹Nung 10:82a), ¨ca[˙]m ol (1481 Twusi 8:27b) ← ca-˙wo-m < °ca- 'sleep'
¨ha˙m ol (1463 Pep 5:100a, 1482 Kum-sam 3:19a) ← ha-˙wo-m < °ha- 'be many'; ¨ha˙toy (1445 ¹Yong 13); ˙ptu˙t i ¨han cyen˙cho lwo (1447 Sek 6:2b) 'because the desires are great'
˙e˙m[i] uy ¨kan ˙sta˙h ol (1459 Wel 21:21b) 'the land where your mother went' ← ka-˙wo-n < °ka- 'go'; CF ka˙n i ˙˙la (1447 Sek 6:20b) 'went'

A peculiarity is that the accent change apparently can take place before attaching the modulated honorific: ˙i ˙SYANG ˙on ˙YWOK-˙QOY ˙uy ¨na˙syan ˙t i a˙ni ˙si˙n i (1462 ¹Nung 1:42a) 'this aspect is not what desire is born from' ← ˙na-˙si-˙wo-n. But also, without the change: ˙ka˙sya (1447 Sek 6:45b, 1459 Wel 2:11b), ˙hosya (1447 Sek 6:12a) = ˙ho˙sya (1482 Kum-sam 2:2b), ˙ho˙syan (1463 Pep 6:144a), ˙ho˙syam (1482 Nam 1:33b), ... The modulated honorific may well be the EFFECTIVE with the modulator absorbed (i.e. suppressed, as with ··· a- stems in general, p. 270): -^{u}/o ˙si-˙(G)a-[˙w^u/o-].

A compound verb may be treated like the final stem: (mac-°na- >) mas-°na- 'meet' → mas-¨na- in mas-¨nala (1481 Twusi 8:13b).

(8) ···l- + -˙w^u/o- = ···˙lw^u/o-, as in a˙lwo˙m i (1462 ¹Nung 1:55a) < ¨al- 'know'.
···l^u/o- + -˙w^u/o- = ···l˙lw^u/o-, as in ¨mwol˙lwol (1447 Sek 13:37b) < mwo˙lo- 'not know', mol˙lwom (1459 Wel 2:42a) < molo- 'get dry', hul˙lwo˙m ol (1462 ¹Nung 10:18a) and hul˙lwu˙m oy (1463 Pep 6:86b) < hulu- 'flow'.

(9) In general, strings like -zowo- are treated as modulated (= -zoWwo-) and strings like -zoWo- as unmodulated. But for those endings that do not permit the modulator to intrude, strings like -zowo- are equivalent to the unmodulated -zoWo-. The relevant cases are -¨zowo˙m ye = -¨zoWo˙m ye, -¨zowo˙m ye n' = -¨zoWo˙m ye n', and the infinitive -¨zo˙wa = -¨zo˙Wa. Before the honorific -(^{u}/o)˙si- and its modulated form -(^{u}/o)˙sya- strings like -zowo- are also equivalent to -zoWo-. Thus there is only one modulation in -zo˙wosya˙m ol.

The modulator has three meanings:
        (1) nothing (vacuous use, obligatory or optional)
        (2) the subject is first-person
        (3) the sentence is adnominalized to an epitheme extruded from the object
This description follows the theory of He Wung. An alternative theory, maintained by LSN and toward which LCT is also inclined, treats the basic or original meaning as volitive. An argument can be made that the volitive meaning in the obvious cases is carried by the attached prospective modifier ending -˙^{u}/olq. But a similar argument would attribute the cases that strongly imply first-person subject to other elements, and LCT is concerned about the many examples where a modulated form refers to the second or third person as the subject. Whatever the original meaning, it was attenuated by the time the texts were written and eventually disappeared, though traces of the morpheme lingered on. Both theories on the meanings of the modulator must make allowance for the various restrictions that require or preclude its presence, as described below.

Restrictions

1. The modulator is never used before: -˙kwo, -˙Gwo
                                                -˙kuy, -˙Guy
                                                -˙to˙lwok
                                                -(^{u}/o)˙m ye (n')
                                                -°^{e}/a

For a possible exception, see the etymology of -˙kwa suggested in §9.9.2 (p. 263).

2. The modulator is obligatory before the accessive -˙toy → -˙w^u/o˙toy and before most uses of the substantive -(^{u}/o)m → -˙w^u/om. But -(^{u}/o)˙m ye (n') never takes modulation. Simplex nouns are derived

from either the modulated or the unmodulated substantive: *e˙lum* 'ice' < ¨*el*- 'freeze', *kelum* 'gait, pace' < ¨*ket*- / *kel*- < **ke˙lu*- 'walk' (but *ke˙lwu˙m ey* in 1481 Twusi 16:70b); *wu˙lwum* (1459 Wel 1:27b) = *wulwum* (···) (1775 Han-Cheng 5:47a [on p. 145a]; LCT 592b "*wulum*" is a mistake) = **wul.um** 'crying' < ¨*wul*- 'cry' (also *wul˙Gwum* < ˙*wulu*- / ˙*wulG*- < * ˙*wuluG*-), *ki˙chwum* (1447 Sek 19:39a) = *ki˙chum* (1463 Pep 6:102b) < *kich*- 'cough'.

3. The modulator expresses first-person subject:
 before -˙*ta* (→ -˙*la*)   -*w*^u/o-˙*la* 'I/we ... ', CF -˙*ta* 'you/he ... '
 before -*(*^u/o*)˙n i*   -*w*^u/o-˙*n i* 'I/we ... ', CF -˙*n i* 'you/he ... '
It can be preceded by -*(˙)no*-, and -˙*no*-˙*wo*- → -˙*nwo*-:
 -˙*nwo*-˙*la* 'I/we ... ', CF -*no*-˙*ta* 'you/he ... '
 -˙*nwo*-˙*n i* 'I/we ... ', CF -*no*-˙*n i* 'you/he ... '

4. The subject-exalting -*(*^u/o*)˙sya*- ← -*(*^u/o*)˙si*-*w*^u/o- will not occur when the modulator expresses a first-person subject, for "I" never exalt myself: *-*(*^u/o*)˙sya*-˙*la*, *-˙*sya*-˙*n i*

5. Sometimes the modulator as a marker of first-person subject will occur with -*(*^u/o*)˙l i ˙˙la*, -*(*^u/o*)˙l i ˙˙n i*, or -*(*^u/o*)˙l i ˙-ngi ˙˙ta*:
 -˙*w*^u/o-˙*l i ˙˙la* 'I/we will' ...
 -˙*w*^u/o-˙*l i ˙˙n i*
 -˙*w*^u/o-˙*l i ˙-ngi ˙˙ta*

6. The modulator is optional (and vacuous) with -˙*no-ngi ˙˙ta*:
 -˙*nwo-ngi ˙˙ta* = -˙*no-ngi ˙˙ta*

7. In adnominalized sentences, including -*(*^u/o*)˙n i ˙˙la* and -*(*^u/o*)˙l i ˙˙la*, the modulator is obligatory when the epitheme has been extruded from the OBJECT:
 -˙*w*^u/o-*l(q)* 'that one is to do it to'
 -˙*w*^u/o-*n* 'that one did it to'
 -˙*nwo-n* 'that one is doing it to'
And with subject exaltation:
 -*(*^u/o*)˙syalq*   ← -*(*^u/o*)˙si*-˙*w*^u/o-*lq*
 -*(*^u/o*)˙syan*   ← -*(*^u/o*)˙si*-˙*w*^u/o-*n*
 -*(*^u/o*)˙si˙nwon* ← -*(*^u/o*)˙si*-˙*no*-˙*w*^u/o-*n*
But there are occasional slips from careless authors who omit the modulator even though the epitheme is extruded from the object; CF He Wung 1970:139.

8. When the epitheme has been extruded from the SUBJECT, the modulator will not be found. If it has been extruded from some other adjunct (TIME, PLACE, INSTRUMENT, REASON, etc.) or is an intruded epitheme (such as the summational ˙*i*, *s*, *t*, and ˙*cwul* 'fact that'), the modulator is vacuously optional.

-˙*(*^u/o*)lq*	[I/you/he] who (will) do it	that [I/you/he] (will) do it
-*w*^u/o*lq*	[you/he] who (will) do it	that [you/he] (will) do it
-˙*(*^u/o*)n*	[I/you/he] who did it	that [I/you/he] did it
-*w*^u/o*n*	[you/he] who did it	that [you/he] did it
-˙*non*	[I/you/he] who am/are/is doing it	that [I/you/he] is doing it
-˙*nwon*	[you/he] who are/is doing it	that [you/he] are/is doing it
-*(*^u/o*)˙silq*	[you/he] who (will) do it	that [you/he] (will) do it
-*(*^u/o*)˙sin*	[you/he] who did it	that [you/he] did it
-*(*^u/o*)˙si˙non*	[you/he] who are doing it	that [you/he] are doing it

Cen Cenglyey 1990 observes that the MK words corresponding to what are here called quasi-free nouns or postmodifiers vary in the degree to which the preceding modifier can be modulated. He notes that the structures they form change function through time from nominal phrase > adverbial phrase >

"verbal ending". The less noun-like (the more adverbial or predicative) the function, the less likely will the word be preceded by the modulated forms. But he notes that *t(o)* and *s(o)* are exceptional because the structures they form were already in the process of becoming verbal endings. By that he mainly refers to the structures sometimes called extended predicates: modifier form (of a predication) + *t* or *s* + a form of the copula ˙*i*‧‧‧ , with the meaning 'it is (the fact) that ‧‧‧ '.

9.9.11. The copula.

The copula ‧‧‧ ˙*i*- has an extended version ‧‧‧ ˙*i˙lwo*- that incorporates a lenited shape of the emotive morpheme -˙*two*- and perhaps implies a more subjective judgment than that expressed by the unextended copula. Most of the forms occur for each version, but some are more common as one or the other. Both ˙*ilwo˙ta* and ˙*ilwo˙la* are used, the latter being required in quotations. But *˙*i˙ta* seems to be replaced by ˙*i˙la* in all cases, except for the structures -*ngi* '˙*ta* and (infinitive -˙*e*, particle ˙*ey*, or adverb +) ˙*ta ˙ka*. (The lack of *-*ngi* '˙*la* and *-˙*e* ˙*la* ˙*ka* casts doubt on the historical accuracy of this analysis. See the note on **ita** in Part II, p. 588.) The form ˙*i˙la* also functions for the infinitive before a particle (˙*sye*, ˙*two*, ˙*za*), and that is the only situation where we can expect the copula infinitive to appear, since the copula does not take auxiliaries, unlike the verb and the adjective. We expect the infinitive to be *˙*i˙ya* if the copula stem is ˙*i*- but (*) ˙*i˙ye* if the stem is taken as ˙*iy*-, for which there is evidence in the leniting of suffix-initial *k* to *G* (as in the gerund ˙*i˙Gwo*). We believe that the form ˙*i˙ye* and its postvocalic reduction '˙*ye* can be found serving as a quasi-particle meaning 'whether, or; and; or/and the like' after a noun or the (unmodulated) substantive -˙*ᵘom*, for which the resulting structure -˙*ᵘo˙m ye* functions to conjoin predicates and is usually treated as a simple ending like the gerund -˙*kwo* (of similar function). There are also examples of *a˙n*' '˙*ye* = (?*)*a˙ni* '˙*ye* for the negative copula infinitive, and an 1887 example of *an*' '*ya*. In modern Korean **i(y)a** is found as a variant of the regular **i(y)e**; in Seoul that is now limited to the end of a sentence. In dialects **iya se/to/ya** can be found and it may be that Seoul **iey/[y]ey yo** came about by raising **iya(y) yo** < **i(y)a + yo** rather than from **i(y)e yo** as is usually (and here) assumed; CF ¹Yi Unceng, Hankul say sosik 201:10 (1989).

Both ˙*ilwo-ngi* '˙*ta* and ˙*i-ngi* '˙*ta* occur, but only ˙*i˙lwo˙swo-ngi* '˙*ta* and not *˙*i-˙*swo-ngi* '˙*ta*; similarly ˙*i˙lwoswo˙n i* and not *˙*iswo˙n i*. (Neither *˙*i-˙*two˙swo*- nor *˙*ilwo-˙*two˙swo*- is found.) The honorific is ˙*isi*- (infinitive ˙*i˙sya*) and there is no *˙*i˙lwosi*-; compare ¨*ilu˙sya* (1459 Wel 18:33b), the honorific infinitive of 'become'. The copula deferential is ˙*izoW*- and there is no *˙*ilwozoW*-; I lack examples of the deferential honorific (?)*˙*izow˙o˙si*-. The initial vowel of both ˙*i*- and ˙*i˙lwo*- normally reduces to '*y*‧‧‧ or is elided ('‧‧‧) after a vowel. The negative copula appears in both versions: *a˙ni* '˙*la*, *a˙ni* '*lwo˙la*. I have found no examples of ?**a˙ni* '*ta* or ?**a˙ni* '*lwo˙ta* and perhaps they never existed. Notice that MK *a˙ni* '˙*ta* (LCT 513b) is an abbreviation of *a˙ni [ho]˙ta*, as is *a˙ni˙tha* (p. 425).

The extension can be explained as a lenition of the emotive -˙*two*- (as LCT views it, at least for some of the forms). We might, however, consider taking ˙*i˙lwo*- as the modulated form of ¨*il*-, a MK stem roughly synonymous with *towoy*- 'become, come into being' (see Part II and LCT 622b for forms and examples), but if that were true the accent should be **i˙lwo*- with initial low pitch (§8.3.2). The form ˙*i˙lusyas˙ta* (1445 ¹Yong 100) is the copula retrospective honorific emotive, with the -*l*- a unique variant of -*te*- (see the argument in the entry ˙*i˙lusyas˙ta* of Part II, p. 572). We would have expected *˙*i˙lesyas˙ta* as the lenited version of *˙*i˙tesyas˙ta*; compare ˙*i˙lesi˙ta* (1447 Sek 13:35b) for the copula retrospective honorific indicative assertive. The indicative assertive ¨*i˙ta* (1459 Wel 7:44b, 1462 ¹Nung 8:33b) 'becomes' is identical with that of the copula (*˙*i˙ta* →) ˙*i˙la* except for accent and lack of lenition (˙*i˙le* is the infinitive of ¨*i[l]˙ta*). The MK copula apparently did not make use of the suspective (*˙*i-˙*ti*), but the verb ¨*il*- had the form ¨*i˙ti*. Modern Korean uses **ici** (and **ani 'ci**) at the end of a sentence (followed by **yo** in polite style) to make casual sentences, and also in structures such as **Ney kes i ani 'ci nay kes ita** 'It isn't yours, it's mine' or its counterpart **Nay kes ici ney kes i ani 'ta** 'It's mine, it isn't yours'. Not only is there no MK copula suspective (*˙*i˙ti*), neither are there examples of the summative *˙*i˙Gi* (*'*y˙Gi*, *'˙*Gi*), despite modern **iki**. (MK used the summative very little, in any event; some of the modern uses take the place of MK nominalizations with *t* 'fact'.) On the other hand, there are examples of ˙*i˙Gey*, the copula adverbative 'so as to be', despite the lack of modern *ikey, as well as examples of ˝il˙Gey (and variant ˝il˙Guy) 'so as to become' (see Part II).

Accent differentiates the modifiers ˝in ' ⋯ that has become' (1462 ¹Nung 9:85a) from ˙in ' ⋯ that is' (?1517- ¹No 2:54b), and ˝il(q) (1462 ¹Nung 4:38b) / ˝ill(q) (+ ˙i ⋯ → ˝il˙li⋯ 1445 ¹Yong 123) '[it is] that it will become' from ˙il(q) ' ⋯ that is to be', as in ... [˙]il ˙ss oy (1447 Sek 6:45b) and e˙nu ˝hoy 'l[q] ˙kwo 1481 Twusi 7:4b 'what year was it?'. There is no processive modifier for the copula (*˙i˙non) but ˝il- 'become' has ˝i˙non as in swo˙li ˝ino˙n i (1451 Hwun-en 13a) 'sounds [= syllables] are formed'.

The verb infinitive i˙le 'become' (1445 ¹Yong 2, ~ ˙za 1462 ¹Nung 8:40a) has a higher vowel than the copula form ˙i˙la, the source of which but for accent could be a variant of i˙le, rather than the lenition of *˙i˙ta that I suggest elsewhere. The intransitive stem ˝il- underlies a derived causative stem ilG- / il^{U}o- < *il^{U}oG- 'accomplish, make', for which the modulated stem is il˙Gw^{U}o-. LCT assumes that the ˙i˙lwo- variant copula is the modulated retrospective *˙i-˙t(e)-˙wo-, so that the -l- allomorph of the retrospective is not then unique to the form ˙i˙lusyas˙ta. And the emotive -˙two- appears to be a similar formation -˙t[o]-˙wo- with the vowel reduced and elided, perhaps ultimately to be identified with the retrospective, if not with the postmodifier t 'the fact (that)'.

After a vowel (including vowel + y or w) the copula ˙i- is abbreviated to ˙y- but even that is automatically suppressed after i or y, so that ˙[y]- is written just ˙-. As a result, after i or y certain of the copula forms merge with abbreviations of forms of °ho- 'do/be', and only context tells you when ⋯y ˙˙m ye is to be taken as ˙i˙m ye rather than ho˙m ye. But the copula lenites endings that start with the voiceless stops (⋯y ˙˙la = ˙[y]˙la < ˙i˙la ← *˙i˙ta) so that ⋯y ˙˙ta can only be from ho˙ta. And ˙˙kwo is from ho˙kwo, for the abbreviation of the copula gerund is ˙˙Gwo = ˙[y]˙Gwo < ˙i˙Gwo.

10.0. Constructions.

The words of Korean enter into a variety of constructions which form phrases that serve as constituents of sentences. Below we discuss the problem of dividing a phrase into words, to begin with, and then describe the formation of sentences in terms of predicates and adjuncts, with observations on features that constrain the acceptable combinations of syntactic components.

10.1. Problems of word division.

One of the most perplexing of the basic problems in describing Korean syntax is that of deciding whether a given stretch of morphemes is one word or a phrase of several words. For some languages such decisions can largely be based on phonological cues: is there a pause, or could there be a pause? In Korean that is not the most useful criterion, for adjacent elements are apt to stick to each other even if they are not closely tied grammatically. Instead, we base our decisions on freedom of combination. Can the individual elements occur in other and widely varying environments? Is the unit, though restricted in occurrence, grammatically parallel to similar units that occur more widely? It is this relative freedom of combination that enables us to decide the phrase structure of sentences. Typically, a free word is always an immediate constituent of some larger sequence. No "IC cuts" separate some part of the word and put it with an adjacent element.

A number of the Korean constructions often described as compounds I prefer to call "pseudo-compounds" because they can be analyzed as phrases that consist of free words. For example, the string /pammeke/ representing the phrase **pap mek.e** 'eats rice = eats (one's meal)' is sometimes treated as a compound that consists of noun + vt, but I think of **pap** here simply as a noun in its absolute, unmarked, use — for which the "object" role is inferred from the context. The accusative particle can be inserted, making the role of the noun explicit: **pap ul mek.e**. And virtually any object — or subject — can drop its role-specifying particle, especially when (as here) the role is obvious from the meanings of the words themselves, so that the number of such would-be "compounds" is almost infinitely large by any logical principle of inclusion or exclusion. Korean grammarians choose to include in their dictionaries some but not other lexical items of this sort when either (1) the phrase has acquired a special idiomatic flavor, or (2) the phrase corresponds to a single-word translation in English (or Japanese or Chinese), or to a single-word synonym in the core vocabulary.

I prefer to retain the term "compound" to refer strictly to a word that includes at least one bound constituent, such as a verb stem (with no ending attached) or an affix. As far as affixes go, I follow different tendencies with respect to the core and the Chinese vocabulary, giving the benefit of the doubt to any core element in question as a "word", even when its distribution is severely limited, but regarding one-syllable Chinese elements as typically bound even when they are very productive. To some extent these judgments are influenced by historical considerations, but I believe they correspond to something in the structure of the vocabulary that is unconsciously felt by the native speaker. And not all elements of Chinese origin are considered part of the "Chinese" vocabulary in our description. The word **chayk** is simply the Korean word for 'book', despite its origin as a monosyllable of Chinese. (The synonym for **chayk** in the Chinese vocabulary consists of two quite different morphemes: **secek**.) A single etymon may serve in both vocabularies: **san** is the Korean noun for 'mountain' but in **tungsan** 'mountain climbing' it is a bound Chinese morpheme.

10.2. Constructions and pseudo-constructions.

Not only does Korean enjoy a variety of constructions, it also offers pseudo-constructions. A pseudo-construction is a sequence of one or more words that is often wrongly taken as a unit. For example, the particle sequences (especially the arguable case of **ey se**) are often taken as single unanalyzed elements, but as I interpret the constituency each particle is in construction with the entire phrase that precedes it, so that the first cut is between the two particles, not between the string of particles and the rest of the phrase, as the other treatment would suggest. Shown below are examples of some, but undoubtedly not all, types of construction. (Cf LHS 1955:256 ff.)

List of constructions with examples

1.	noun + noun	**onul nal** 'today', **ip mas** 'taste (to the mouth)', **Kim sensayng** 'Mr Kim', **Kim Poktong-i** 'dear little Kim Poktong', **Kim Poktong(-i) emeni** '(dear little) Poktong's mother', **wuli nala** 'our nation; Korea', **Ilponq sālam** 'a Japanese', **Yenge chayk** 'an English book', **kotung hak.kyo** 'high school', **mulqcil munhwa** 'material culture', **Kwukcey ¹Yenhap** 'the United Nations', **siksa cwūnpi** 'meal preparation', ...
1a.	noun phrase + noun	**Mikwuk tāysa-kwan aph** '(the area in) front of the American Embassy', **Yēnhuy Tāy-hak.kyo pū-kyosu** 'an associate professor at Yenhuy University', **i tal welkup** 'this month's salary', **ku kkoch pongoli pich** 'the color of those flower buds' or 'the bud-color of those flowers', ...
1b.	pseudo-compound noun + noun	**pal-mok mul** 'ankle-deep water', **pan'-cit koli** (= **panu'-cilq koli**) 'embroidery ring', ... (The meaning is different from the components; or, at least one of the components is bound.)
1c.	noun + noun phrase	**Mikwuk saynghwalq pep** 'the American way of life', **wuli cak.un cip** 'our little house', ...
1d.	noun + pseudo-compound noun	**pataq mulq-koki** 'saltwater fish', **patak ches-ccay** 'first from the bottom'
1e.	noun phrase + noun phrase (see below)	**Hankul Hak.hoy Khun Sacen** 'the Unabridged Dictionary of the Korean Language Society', **kotung hak.kyo ip.hak sihem** 'the high school entrance examination', ...
1f.	pseudo-compound noun + compound n	**pal-mok mulq-kyel** 'ankle-deep waves' (?), ...
1g.	noun + vi subst	**palq kel.um** 'pace; gait'
1h.	vc substantive + (noun + noun)	

		pat.him swulq cip '(a kind of liquor package store)', ...
1i.	adverb + noun (phrase)	(1) **palo ku (chayk)** 'that very one (book)', **cokum aph** 'a little ahead', ... (see §5.2.5)
		(2) **toy thucip** 'carping (back) at one's superiors', **olay(q) tong-an** 'a long time', **mence sikan (ey)** '(in) the previous / preceding hour', ...
1j.	adverb + number	**kkway yeles** 'quite a lot', **kas sumul** 'just twenty years old', ... (see §5.2.5)
1k.	noun + derived noun	(1) < **vi hay tot.i** 'sunrise', ...
		(2) < **vt koki cap.i** 'fishing; fisher(man)', **aph cap.i** 'guide; catspaw', **son cap.i** 'handle', ...
1kk.	der n (← adj) + noun (← summative)	**noph.i / nelp.i ttwiki** 'the high / broad jump', ...
2.	noun + postnoun	**panu' cil** 'embroidering', **pangmangi cil** 'paddling (laundry)'; **sensayng nim** 'esteemed teacher / sir', ...
2a.	vt subst + postnoun	**pakkwum cil** 'exchanging', ...
2b.	n phrase + postnoun	**Yensey tāy-hak.kyo kyōswu tul** 'the professors at / of Yensey University', ...
2c.	... postnoun phrase + postnoun	**Yensey tāy-hak.kyo kyōswu tul ney** 'the professors at / of Yensey University' [the first cut is before **ney**], ...
2d.	pseudo-compound noun + postnoun	**palq-kil cil** 'kicking', ...
2e.	bound compound noun + postnoun	**pal-petwung cil** 'stamping one's feet', ...
2f.	adnoun + postnoun	**ches ccay** 'first'; **sayngq kwun** 'greenhand, novice', ...
2g.	number + postnoun	**twūl ccay** 'second', ...
2h.	iterated postnoun or counter → adverb	**kkili kkili** 'group by group', **kwuntey kwuntey** 'here and there'
3.	adnoun + noun	**ches insang** 'first impression', **i nom** 'this rascal', **yēys nal** 'ancient days', **ōn sēykyey** 'the whole world', ...
3a.	compound adnoun + noun	**ney-kkacis nom** 'a rascal like you', ...
3b.	adnoun + noun phrase	**ku cak.un cip** 'that little house', ...
4.	numeral + noun	**pān tal** 'half a month', **twū sensayng** 'the two teachers / gentlemen', **ahop chayk-sang** 'nine desks', ...
4a.	numeral + counter	**twū si** 'two o'clock', **payk wen** '100 wen', **han kwēn** 'one (book)', **swū kwēn** 'several (books)', ...
4b.	counter + noun	**kwēnq swu** (← **swū**) 'the number of books', ...
4c.	noun + counter	**el.umq cang** 'a sheet of ice', ...
5.	noun + particle	**cip ey** 'to the house', **kicha lo** 'by train', **chinkwu hanthey** 'to a friend', **sensayng kkey** 'to the teacher', **Mikwuk se** 'from / in America', **cēki kkaci** 'up to there', ...
6.	noun phrase + particle	**wuli cip ey** 'to our house', **wuli cak.un cip ul** 'our little house [as direct object]', ...
6a.	number + particle	**hana ka** 'one [subject]', **payk ul** 'a hundred [object]', ...
6b.	counter phrase + particle	**chayk han kwēn to** '(not) even one book', **ahop si puthe** 'from nine o'clock, starting at nine', **(sālam) han salam i** 'one person [as subject]', ...
7.	particle phrase + particle	**achim ey nun** 'as for in the morning', **yeki (ey) se to** 'even at / from this place; here too', **sensayng khenyeng un** 'far

8.	noun + copula	**yenphil ita** 'it's a pencil', **achim imyen** 'if it's morning', ...
8a.	noun phrase + copula	**wuli emeni 'ci!** 'it's our mother!', **kotung hak.kyo 'p.nikka?** 'is it a high school?', **ilk.ko siph.un chayk ia** 'it is a book I want to read', **achimq pap imyen** 'if it is breakfast', **Yenge chayk ina** 'an English book or something', ...
8b.	counter phrase + copula	**chayk han kwēn ita** 'it's a book', **payk wen ina** 'a hundred wen or so', **twū si 'myen** 'if it's two o'clock', ...
9.	particle phrase + copula	**Mikwuk se 'ta** 'it's from/in America', **ahop si puthe 'myen** 'if it starts at nine o'clock', ...
10.	adverb + copula	**ani 'ta** 'it's not'; **(yeki se) palo 'ta** 'it's straight ahead', ...
11.	noun (phrase) + verb	(1) vi **ayki iss.ta** 'there is (one has) a baby', **ayki nanta** 'the baby is born', ... (2) adj **ayki cōh.ta** 'the baby is nice; the baby likes it; I like the baby', ... (3) vt **ayki ponta** 'the baby sees' (= **ayki ka ponta**) or 'sees the baby' (= **ayki lul ponta**); **pap mek.nunta** 'eats (a meal)'; **na cwue!** 'gimme!'; ...
11a.	verbal noun + postnominal verb	— see entries for postnominal verbs (§7.6) in Part II
11b.	verbal noun + ellipted ham = ha(n)ta	[in headlines, telegrams, stage directions] **tungcang [hanta]** 'enters (stage)', **phok.kyek [ham]** 'bombards', ...
11c.	verbal noun + ellipted hako	**Pusan ul chwulpal [hako] Mikwuk ulo kanta** 'departs Pusan and goes to America', ...
11d.	adjectival noun + ellipted hakey	**hōn.lan [hakey] toynta** 'gets disordered', ...
12.	counter phrase + verb	**twū pen hayss.ta** 'did it two times', **(chayk i) han kwēn iss.ta** 'there is a book', **(chayk ul) han kwēn cwunta** 'gives a book', ...
13.	adverb + verb (phrase)	**cal hanta** 'does (it) well', **cal (l) mōs hanta** 'does not do well', **kkok (l) cal mōs hanta** 'does not do well for sure', ...
14.	verbal noun + verbal noun	vni + vni **ipsin yangmyeng (hanta)** 'rising in life and making a name', **phāyka mangsin (hanta)** 'going to rack and ruin' adj-n + vni **cici-pucin (hanta)** '(makes but) slow progress' adj-n + adj-n **īsang yalus (hata)** '(is) odd and queer', **ttattus micikun (hata)** 'is warm but not warm enough', ... vnt + vnt **phōwi kōngkyek (hanta)** 'surrounding and then attacking', ...
15.	verb + auxiliary	— see the entries for auxiliary verbs (§7.5) in Part II
16.	verb infinitive + verb (auxiliary)	**kacye o-** 'bring'; **ka-po-** 'go see'; **na-ka-** 'go out'
17.	verb gerund + verb	**(mal ul) thako tani-** 'go around riding (a horse = on horseback)', **nōlko mek.nunta** '(plays and eats) = leads a life of ease/indolence', ...

Some of the verb forms, notably **-ki** and **-um**, regularly enter into constructions like nouns; others (the modifier forms **-un, -nun, -ulq,** ...), like adnouns. But bear in mind that the entire verb phrase (including such adjuncts as the subject and the object) goes with the verb as a constituent of any wider structure. CF §11.7, §11.8.

The constituency of long noun phrases can be puzzling: **haksayng mīswul cēn.lam hōy** 'student art exhibition' could have its first IC cut at any of the three spaces, and even lexicalizing the last two words to make the compound **cēn.lam-hoy** does not help decide whether we are talking about an art exhibition by/for the students or an exhibition of student(-made) art. There are also problems of "collapsing" constituents as in **kwuk.mun + munqpep → kwuk.munqpep** 'vernacular grammar', **uyhak + haksayng → uyhaksayng** 'medical student', **cān swul + swulq cip → cānswulqcip** 'draft liquor shop'. Notice the ambiguity, at least in writing, of **I cip īmca ka nwukwu 'n ya** 'Who is this house-owner?' (→ **i cipq īmca**) or 'Who is the owner of this house?' (= **i cip cipq-īmca** or **i cip uy īmca**), where the ambiguity can be resolved if juncture is inserted either before **cip** or before **īmca**. See below (§10.3) for further thoughts.

10.3. Compounds and quasi-compounds

In addition to the quasi-compounds that have been covered as constructions (such as noun + noun), there are others that I include here with the list of full-fledged compounds: those that involve some bound element, especially a verb stem. The quasi-compounds are marked below with a "Q". I have arranged the items according to the grammar of the resulting construction. This list can be thought of as a continuation of the list of §10.2, even though it is arranged differently. Notice that I do not generally treat Chinese binoms like **hak.kyo** 'school' as compound nouns, since both elements are often bound, and so many cases are on the borderline between morphology and etymology that only clearcut cases will be treated as compounds, e.g. **chayk-sang** '(book table →) desk' is a compound because both elements are free nouns that just happen to come from Chinese. The constituency of certain compounds is obscured by the simultaneous occurrence of the same morpheme in two words that are combined: ¹**inkunche** 'neighborhood' could be treated as a shortening of ¹**inkun kūnche** 'neighboring vicinity'. But there are difficulties. While **uyhaksayng** 'medical student' could be treated as a shortening of **uyhak haksayng** 'student of medicine' (see the "collapsing" IC's at the end of §10.2), the noun **sōhaksayng** 'primary-school student' is not so simple, because the normal word for 'primary school' is **sō-hak.kyo** rather than **sōhak**, so we will have to say that **sōhak-sayng** consists of a bound shortening of **sō-hak.kyo** + a shortening of **haksayng** or, probably better, a suffix (bound postnoun) **-sayng** 'student'.

List of compounds with examples

1.	n + vt (vc) → n	**ip-nay (lul nāy-)** '(do) mimicry' (CF **hyungnay** 'mimicry' ← **hyung ul nāy-** 'bring out the defects')
2.	iterated subst → n; ... → adv	**sayngkim-sayngkim** 'appearance, looks'; **hullim-hullim** 'in little driblets'
3.	iterated subst + suf → n; ... → adv	**ssum-ssum-i** 'use', **toym-toym-i** 'makeup, character'; **kel.um-kel.um-i** 'at each step'
4.	subst + same-stem der n → n	**kel.um-kel.i** 'gait, manner of walking', **mek.um-mek.i** 'way of eating, appetite'
5.	vt + n → n	**kkekk-soy** 'clamp', **ppalq-tay** 'straw' (← "suck stem")
5a.	cpd vt + n → n	**nāymi-son** 'a pushover' (← **nāy-mi-l-**)
6.	vt + vt der n → n	**palp-tatum.i** 'smoothing by trampling'
7.	vi + n → n	**kwulq-tay** 'axis' (← "roll stick"), **puth-cāng** 'built-in cupboard', **ik-pancwuk** 'hot-water dough; kneading' (← "half-cooked")
8.	vt + bound postn → n	**mek-sim** 'hunger'
9.	adj + n → n	**petq-(n)i** 'protruding teeth', **okq-(n)i** 'in-turned tooth'
9a.	cpd adj + n → n	**kkekciq-son** 'heroic measure'
Q10.	vt inf + vt → vt	**pat.e ssu-** 'write down (from dictation)' (← "get and write")
Q11.	n (ey/ulo) + vt → vt	**twī ī(s)-** 'follow after' = **twī ey ī(s)-**; **pic cwu-** 'lend' = **pic ulo cwu-**; **kewul sām-** 'model on, use as mirror' = **kewul lo sām-**; **saks nāy-/noh-** 'hire (out)' = **saks ey/ulo sām.ta**
Q12.	(··· uy) n (ul) vt → vt	**mas po-** 'sample (the flavor of)' = ··· **uy mas ul po-**; **pal poi-** 'show a part ("foot") of' = ··· **uy pal ul poi-**
13.	vi + vi → vi	**kwulm-cwuli-** 'starve', **o-ka-** 'come and go'

A Reference Grammar of Korean   PART I   279

Q14.	bound adv + vt → vt	pī tatum- 'smooth (down/out), preen'
15.	vt + vi → vi	īs-tah- 'continue in contact', īs-ta-l-$_1$ 'continue', tāy-cilu- 'stand up to, defy'
16.	vt + vt → vi	?
17.	vt + vt → vt	pat-tul- 'lift, hold up', yē-tat- 'open and shut' ← yē-l-, with t dropped before t (§3.5), īs-ta-l-$_2$ 'connect it', īs-tay- 'connect/continue it', puth-coch- 'follow; revere'
Q18.	bound inf + aux v inseparable → vi	ppā ci- 'fall'
19.	n (i/ka) + vi → vi	pal mac- 'fall into step' = pal i mac-; pal ppā ci- 'fall out of step' = pal i ppā ci-; sēng na- 'get angry' = sēng i na-; palam na-ka- 'lose one's vigor' = palam i na-ka-
Q19a.	n (ey) + vi → vi	twī ttel.e ci- 'fall behind, lag' = twī ey ttel.e ci-
19b.	bnd n + qvi → qvi	tes-ēps- 'be ephemeral'
19c.	n (i/ka) + adj → adj	him sēy-/cha- 'be strong', nachq ik- 'be familiar (in face)', kethq yak- 'be superficially shrewd', kway kulu- 'go amiss' ← "divination sign is wrong" — or is this from an obsolete variant of kkulu- (vi) "divination sign comes undone"?
19d.	n (ey) + adj → adj	son-swīw- 'be easy', nwun-pusi- 'be dazzling (to the eyes)', nam-pukkulew- 'be ashamed before others'
19e.	n (kwa) + adj → adj	nam-talu- 'be different from others; be uncommon'
19f.	n (ul) + vt → vi	pal ppay- 'evade' = pal ul ppay-; palam cap- 'take to frivolous ways' = palam ul cap-; īl po- 'work' = īl ul po-; pal mac.chwu- 'get in step' = pal ul mac.chwu-; sēng nāy- 'get angry' = sēng ul nāy-
Q20.[1]	vi subst (ul) + same vi → vi	chwum (ul) chwu- 'dance', kkwum (ul) kkwu- 'dream', ttwim ul ttwi- 'jump', cam (ul) ca- 'sleep', wus.um (ul) wūs- 'laugh, smile', kel.um (ul) kēt-/kel- 'walk (a gait)'
Q21.	bound compound n + postnominal v → vi	pal-petwungi chi- 'stamp one's feet'
Q22.	bound adv + vi → vi	il kkay- 'wake up early'
23.	adj + adj → adj	mayp-cca- 'peppery and salty', cay-ppalu- 'swift and fast', sēy-cha- 'strong (and full)', kēl-cha- 'richly fertile', kem-phulu- 'a blackish blue', ōlʰ-palu- (← olh- + palu-) '(just and) right = upright, honest'; *noph-nac- in noph-nac-i (derived noun) 'undulations, ups and downs' — or is this a compound of der n + der n (noph.i 'a high' + *nac.i 'a low')?
24.	adj + adj-n → adj n	tal-poltuley (hata) '(is) sweet and soft'; tongkul-napcak/twungkul-nepcek (hata) '(is) round and squat'
25.	iterated adj → adj-n	ttel-ttel (hata) '(is) inferior; (is) disinclined, leery' (← ttēlp- 'astringent')
Q26.	adj der n + (i/ka) + same adj → adj	khi (ka) khu- 'be tall, big', noph.i (ka) noph- 'be tall, high', nelp.i (ka) nelp- 'be wide', kiph.i (ka) kiph- 'be deep' — CF kwulk.ki (ka) kwulk- 'be bulky, thick' with adj summative

[1] Because the verbs are transitive (and can take other objects) kūlim ul kūli- 'draw a picture' and cim ul ci- 'bear a burden' do not belong here. Of course, the real criterion may be semantic: kūlim and cim are tangible, the others are abstract. In noph.i ttwiki lul ttwinta 'jumps the high jump' we also

have a cognate object, but in **chen-li lul ttwinta** 'jumps a thousand leagues' the object is one of extent. In **kil ul kēt.nunta** 'walks the road' we find a traversal object. None of these special types of object are diagnostic of transitivity in a deep sense, but dictionaries often have difficulty in deciding where to draw the line between a surface transitivity and deep transitivity, so that **chwu-** 'dance' is usually listed as transitive but **kēl-** 'walk' as intransitive.

See also:
27.   noun + bound postnoun (suffix) → noun — §5.4.5
28.   bound adnoun (prefix) + noun → noun — §5.3.3
29-32. bound adverb + verb (vi, vt, adj) → verb (vi, vt, adj) — §5.2.6
33.   bound verb + bound postverb → verb — §7.1.3
34.   bound preparticle + particle — §5.2.6

There is a type of pleonastic compound, or phrase, that consists of words containing synonymous morphemes. Typically one of the morphemes is Chinese and the other not: **sam-wel(q tal)** '(the month of) March', **mok.yoil (nal)** '(the day of) Thursday', **chello(q kil)** 'railway (way)' **chipun(q kalwu)** 'toothpowder (powder)', **cheka(q cip)** 'home of wife's parents', **myēnto (khal)** 'razor'; ? **sonq swuken** 'handkerchief'; **Cangan-sa (cel)** 'Cangan(-sa) Temple', **Tāytong-kyo (tali)** 'Taytong(-kyo) Bridge', ... In the case of **yekcen (aph)** '(in front of) the station[-front]', the noun **yekcen** is now simply a synonym of **yek** 'station' and has lost the etymological meaning of the ···**cen**.

10.4. Phrases.

Phrases end in a noun (in the broadest sense), a particle, or a verb form. Phrases that end in a verb may be VERBAL (if the verb ends in a sentence-final mood), NOMINAL (if the verb ends in such nominalizing moods as the summative **-ki** or the substantive **-um**), ADNOMINAL (if the verb ends in a modifier mood such as **-un, -ul, -nun,** ...), or ADVERBIAL (if the verb ends in nonfinal **-e, -ko, -umyen, -ulye,** ...).

A phrase that ends in (or simply is) a noun is NOMINAL when in construction with a particle (and the particle is in adnominal relationship to noun); the resulting phrase is ADVERBIAL unless the particle is **uy**, which makes the phrase ADNOMINAL, but it is NOMINAL if the phrase itself is in construction with a further particle. It will be noted that the term "adverbial" as used here includes all cases of the absolute (unmarked) use of nouns, regardless of the apparent meaning: **ecey wass.ta** is treated as one and the same construction whether it means '[I] came yesterday' or 'yesterday came', for the ambiguity is inherent in the syntax. A phrase that ends in a noun is ADNOMINAL when in construction with (that is, when modifying) a following noun or noun phrase. Some sentences are ambiguous in that a phrase may be construed as either adnominal or adverbial, depending on the constituency: **ilq-cwuilq tong-an ip.wen chilyo lul pat.ess.ta** can mean either (1) 'underwent one week's hospital treatment' (= ··· **tong-an uy ··· chilyo**) or (2) 'underwent hospital treatment for one week' (= ··· **tong-an ulo ··· pat.ess.ta**).

A particle turns a nominal phrase into an adverbial or (if **uy**) adnominal phrase. It turns an adverbial phrase (nominal + particle; or ····**e,** ····**ko,** ...) into another adverbial phrase or (if **uy**) into an adnominal phrase. A sentence-final particle (**yo**) turns the entire sentence into an adverbial (absolute) phrase, whereas a final postmodifier (····**nun ya,** ...) turns the sentence into a nominal phrase. These "sentence phrases" have special uses, equivalent to a verbal sentence, for which see §11. The particle itself is considered adnominal or adverbial depending on the other partner of the construction. The illustrations below will make this analysis clear. The symbols used are N (nominal), D (adnominal), V (Verbal), A (adverbial). The same English sentence 'Where has that newspaper gone that I was reading?' is translated by (1) a nominal sentence (in the plain style); (2) an adverbial sentence (in the polite style); (3) a verbal sentence in the formal style.

(1) nay ka poko iss.tun sinmun i eti kass.nun ya
```
    N-----D  A--------V
       A--------------V
            D----------------------N
                N---------------D  A---------V
                      A-------------------V
                           D----------------------N
                                     N
```

(2) nay ka poko iss.tun sinmun i eti kass.e(y) yo
```
    N-----D  A--------V
       A--------------V
            D----------------------N
                N---------------D  A---------V
                      A-------------------V
                           D----------------------N
                                V------------------
                                     A
```

(3) nay ka poko iss.tun sinmun i eti kass.ˢup.nikka
```
    N-----D  A--------V
       A--------------V
            D----------------------N
                N---------------D  A---------V
                      A-------------------V
                           V
```

There is (at least in dialect) even a kind of adnominal sentence, as a variant of the plain style, with the postmodifier **ya** or **ka** dropped (p. 306, p. 307):

(4) **nay ka poko iss.tun sinmun i eti kass.nun**
```
    N-----D  A--------V
       A--------------V
            D----------------------N
                N---------------D  A---------V
                      A-------------------V
                           D (--------------------[ya])
```

You will find several kinds of adverbial sentences; see, for example, the entries **kes ul (ke l')** and **'myen se** in Part II.

10.5. Sentences.

If we leave aside the question forms and the particle-colored sentences (such as the polite ··· **yo** or the apperceptive ··· **kwun**), the typical sentence ends in a verbal. A sentence is quite complete, and even quite usual, with nothing but a verb: **Ponta** '[Someone] looks at [something / someone]'.

To the verb we can add almost any number of adverbial phrases with additional information:

        Ayki ponta ' ··· ; the baby is involved'.
        Emeni ponta ' ··· ; the mother is involved'.
        Cikum ponta ' ··· ; now is involved'.
        Ayki emeni ponta ' ··· ; the baby, the mother are involved'.
        Cikum ayki emeni ponta ' ··· ; now, the baby, and the mother are involved'.

The order in which we add the additional information is determined by the relative importance we attach to it: the more important, novel information, the more startling things less likely to be already known, come later. All the following sentences are possible:

Cikum ayki emeni ponta.	Cikum emeni ayki ponta.
Ayki cikum emeni ponta.	Emeni cikum ayki ponta.
Ayki emeni cikum ponta.	Emeni ayki cikum ponta.

None of them tells you anything explicit about who does the looking or who gets looked at, and only by knowing the meaning of the word **cikum** do you realize that it could not have those roles. The words **cikum, ayki,** and **emeni** are simply adverbial phrases. Only their individual meanings are helpful in deciding which two could be subject and object: under normal circumstances **ponta** takes a personal subject and either a personal or an impersonal object, so that if **kōng** 'ball' were to replace either 'baby' or 'mother' it would pretty well resolve for the hearer the question of subject and object — though there would still be the outside chance that a whimsical speaker meant 'the ball looks at the baby' whether that makes strict sense or not. The word **cikum** is an adverb of time, unable to take the role of personal subject or object nor of impersonal object, so it does not lead to ambiguity. Both of the sentences **Emeni ayki ponta** and **Ayki emeni ponta** are ambiguous as to subject and object. Or, rather, they are DISINTERESTED in the subject/object relationship; all sentences are ambiguous in that they are disinterested in some of the possible information that could be supplied about a situation. There is, however, a normal expectation about what the speaker or hearer will likely treat as novel information; the object is more likely to be the element close to the verb, so that it is a good guess that **Ayki emeni ponta** is intended to mean 'The baby looks at the mother' — such a good guess, in fact, that many speakers may not be happy with the notion that the other interpretation ('The MOTHER looks at the baby') is possible.

Both of the sentences **Emeni ayki ponta** and **Ayki emeni ponta** are ambiguous not only with respect to subject and object, for the two nouns could be taken as a constituent, with the first adnominal to the second, and that could be made explicit by inserting the particle **uy** after the first. So there are several possible translations, depending on how each of the sentences is construed:

(1) 'The baby looks at the mother'	Ayki (ka) emeni (lul) ponta.
	Emeni (lul) ayki (ka) ponta.
(2) 'The mother looks at the baby'	Emeni (ka) ayki (lul) ponta.
	Ayki (lul) emeni (ka) ponta.
(3a) 'The mother's baby looks [at it / someone]'	Emeni (uy) ayki (ka) ponta.
(3b) 'The baby's mother looks [at it / someone]'	Ayki (uy) emeni (ka) ponta.
(4a) '[Someone] looks at the mother's baby'	Emeni (uy) ayki (lul) ponta.
(4b) '[Someone] looks at the baby's mother'	Ayki (uy) emeni (lul) ponta.

Korean sentences perhaps tend to be interested in fewer of the details than English sentences, which require more of the several participants in a scene to be explicitly stated. In Korean the subject/object relationship is often left unclear, even when the meanings of the words themselves do not make the role players obvious. The ambiguity of the subject/object relationship can be resolved by inserting one or both of the appropriate case-marking particles as SPECIFICATION: in **Emeni ka ayki ponta** or **Ayki lul emeni ponta** the mother is looking at the child, and in **Emeni lul ayki ponta** or **Ayki ka emeni ponta** the child is looking at the mother. But if the two nouns are next to each other the possibility of the genitive relationship remains: **Emeni ayki lul ponta** could mean someone looks at the mother's child, and **Emeni ayki ka ponta** could mean the mother's child looks at someone. With the explicit marking of roles for all nouns mentioned, including **Emeni uy ayki (⋯) ponta**, the situation is clear.

The particles most useful for clearing up syntactic ambiguity are **i/ka** (nominative: often the subject), **ul/lul** (accusative: often the direct object), **ey** (dative: to mark an impersonal indirect object), **eykey** and its synonyms (dative: to mark a personal indirect object), and **uy** (adnominal or genitive: to mark the possessor, among other roles). There are also oblique forms for an impersonal subject (⋯ **ey se**, more commonly meaning 'at' or 'from') and a personal subject: **eykey se** usually means 'from a person' but it can mark an oblique subject (p. 501, p. 504), especially in the honorific form **kkey se**

(p. 637). An adverbial role is often cleared up syntactically with the particles **ulo/lo** and **ey** (each having a variety of meanings): **pam-nac ulo** 'night and day = always', **achim ey** 'in the morning', **Pusan ulo** 'to Pusan', **hak.kyo ey** 'to/in school', ...

The particles can, of course, be used even when the sentence is unambiguous: **Achim ey ayki ka kōng ul ponta** 'The child looks at the ball in the morning' (or any order of the three noun-particle strings, with differences of emphasis). When the sentence would be ambiguous with no particle, one alone (subject or object) is sufficient to clear up the ambiguity, but both may be used. In fact, there is a feeling that sentences with explicit particles are better and clearer Korean, fully edited. Ambiguous sentences, and those that escape ambiguity only by the particular choices for nouns and verbs, are often felt to have the particles "missing" and to be sloppy ways of expressing oneself. A very popular way of looking at the sentence is to assume that the noun roles are first marked in the immediately underlying structure and then "deleted" (suppressed or omitted) at the point of articulating the output.

Yet even with particles, ambiguity often continues to be present. That is because in ordinary speech the common focus particles, such as the subduing ··· **un/nun** ('as for ··· , guess what: ... ') and the highlighting ··· **to** ('even/also ··· '), are mutually exclusive not only with each other but also with the nominative and accusative particles, so that the following fully edited sentences are still ambiguous:

Emeni nun ayki ponta.   **Emeni to ayki ponta.**
Emeni nun ayki to ponta.   **Emeni to ayki nun ponta.**

And **Emeni to ayki to ponta** (or **Ayki to emeni to ponta**) is ambiguous in many ways, for when taken as a single constituent the structure **X to Y to** means 'both X and Y (as subject/object)' and it is not possible to insert particles that would show whether you mean 'both mother and baby look at [it/someone]' or '[someone] looks at both mother and baby'. The sentences can be disambiguated only by specifying the missing role-player: **apeci ka** 'the father (looks at both)' or **apeci lul** '(both look at) the father'. The structure **X to Y to hanta** 'both X and Y do' or 'does both X and Y' is a reduction of **X to [ ] Y to hanta**, with ellipsis of the gerund **hako** or the conjunctive **hamye**.

More details on the use of the individual particles will be found in the entries of Part II. Notice that a phrase with **un/nun** naturally tends to come toward or at the beginning of a sentence because, as implied earlier, the position farthest back from the verb is the natural place to put information that is assumed to be lacking in novelty. The Korean sentence snowballs, as it were, gaining in vitality and interest as it builds up to the verb. That is in marked contrast with the English sentence, which usually sets up a subject, spits the verb out very quickly, and then slowly unwinds, like a clock running down. The English speaker gets his punch in at the beginning, and then relaxes — or adds hedges and reservations, or indulges in afterplay. The Korean builds the tension up, then explodes with his verb and almost immediately subsides.

From what we have said above, it sounds as though Korean has free word order for the arguments taken by the predicate, and that is largely true for many common simplex sentences. But certain kinds of sentences require the arguments to follow a certain order, such as those with multiple subjects or objects that come from underlying adnominal (genitive) relationships, as described in §10.6. (Martin 1975 refers to the multiple-subject sentences of Japanese as "multiparous", claiming that they originate in multiple underlying predications that have undergone genitivization.) In addition to those, a few other sentence types have fixed word order and do not permit scrambling (Choy Yengsek 1988):

A ka B ka toynta 'A becomes B'
A ka B ka cōh.ta 'A finds B nice, A likes B'
A ka B lo pointa 'A looks (seems) to be B'
(C ka) A lul B lo yekinta '(C) considers A to be B' (the order of **C ka** is irrelevant; it can appear after **A lul** or **B lo**)

To this list we can add sentences with the negative copula:

A ka B ka ani 'ta 'A is not B'

Notice that while **B ka A ka ani 'ta** 'B is not A' has the same truth value, it is not saying the same thing, for the perspective is different.

10.6. Sentences with multiple subjects and objects.

A Korean sentence can have more than one subject but ordinarily only one direct object, though there may be more than one accusative-marked noun when the accusative is used for marking something other than the direct object and in certain special cases we will describe. Compare **Nwu ka meli ka aph.un ya** 'Who has a headache?' (both the sufferer and the body part are subjects of the adjective, in somewhat different ways) and **Nwu ka meli lul alh.nun ya** 'Who is sick in the head?' (with a transitive verb). Korean is much like Japanese with respect to multiple subjects, but Japanese seldom permits the kind of multiple accusatives that we find in Korean. Conjoined subjects or objects ('X and Y') are, of course, treated as a single constituent and therefore one syntactic subject or object in the surface sentence, which in such cases could be regarded as derived from a conjoining of two or more sentences that have the same verb − or as including a stripped-down copular sentence that packages the multiple nouns before assigning roles.

The process by which subjects proliferate leads to a fixed word order, for it is a kind of genitivization, whereby each of the subjects successively narrows the specification: **Ku puin i meli ka kawuntey ka il-pupun i pich-kal i nōlah.ta** 'The color of a part of the middle of that woman's hair is yellow'; **Mul-thong i ⋯ patak i han kwi-thwungi ka kwumeng i nass.ta** 'The water bucket sprang a leak in one corner of the bottom' (CM 2:109). That also accounts for certain constructions with quantification (see §5.5.1): **Chayk-sang un selap i tases i iss.ta** 'The desk has five drawers (to/in it)', **Wuli ka motwu ka ⋯** 'All of us' (CM 2:109). Certain combinations of subject + verb form close-knit idioms, and that will account for **sakwa ka pelley (ka) mek.nunta** 'an apple gets wormy' and **i ka pelley (ka) mek.nunta** 'a tooth decays'. Examples of multiple subjects:

Na nun ku ka kapyepki ka ccak i ēps.ess.ta 'I found him incredibly frivolous'.
Ku nun sēngmi ka sinkyeng-cil i ani 'ta 'He has nothing nervous to/in/about his temperament'.
Ku nun him i cangsa ka toyess.ta 'His strength paid off'.
Emeni nun twumey saynghwal i acwu nentel-meli ka nass.ta 'His mother came to hate the backwoods life'.

Although we speak of the multiple-subject structure as a kind of cumulative genitivization it should be noted that the relationship between the two nouns in N₁ i/ka N₂ i/ka ⋯ is more narrowly defined than that of the nouns in N₁ uy N₂ with the adnominal particle, which neutralizes all sorts of relationships. **Ku uy kūlim i cōh.ta** 'His picture is good' can refer to a picture he painted or owns; or, it can refer to a picture that portrays him. But **Ku ka kūlim i cōh.ta** must be subject-oriented so that it cannot mean a picture that is 'of him' as the object of the portrayal.

There are colloquialisms that offer two direct objects, of which one is replaceable by **ulo/lo** or by **eykey** (or **ey**) in more formal speech: **īl ul muk-cwumeni lul (or lo) mayntul.e noh.a** 'makes a mess of things', **latio lul (or ey) pyēng ul nāynta** 'gets a radio out of order', **nwui ka elin awu lul (or eykey) os ul ip.hinta** 'the sister dresses her little brother'. With causative constructions, as in the preceding example, colloquial usage sometimes replaces A ka B eykey C lul CAUSATIVE with A ka B lul C lul CAUSATIVE; CF Choy Hyenpay 1959:409. These double-accusative usages are considered sloppy by many careful speakers, but there are examples from the earliest texts: *[˙SO-ˀHOY] ˙lol nyen˙k ul ˀcwu.l i ˙ye* (1445 ¹Yong 20) 'would the four seas be given to anyone else?!' One way to avoid double accusatives with a minimum of fuss is just to drop one of the particles, usually the one nearest the verb: **latio lul pyēng nāynta** 'gets the radio out of order'.

Korean grammarians offer examples of multiple objects similar to the multiple subjects, which come from a genitive-marked relationship of whole to part, but such examples as the following (from CM 1:151-2) are rejected by some speakers:

Sakwa lul kkepcil ul pes.kinta '[I] remove the peel of the apple' − usually said as **Sakwa lul kkakk.nunta** '[I] peel the apple'.
I yangpok kām ul chima cekoli lul mantulmyen ettelq ka 'How about making a skirt and jacket out of this material?' − better said as ⋯ **kām ul** (or ⋯ **kām ulo**) **kaciko** ⋯ .
Kkoch ul mul ul cwunta '[I] water the flowers' − better as **Kkoch ey** ⋯ .

Yet other examples are not rejected: **mulq-koki lul pay lul ttanta** 'opens the belly of the fish' or 'cleans the fish', ... A few acceptable examples that are highly colloquial (CM 2:109):

Ku lul nwun ul twūl ul tā swuswul ul hayss.ta 'They operated (on him) on both of his eyes'.

Ku lul sakwa lul twū kay lul cwuess.ta 'I gave him two of the apples'.

I tongi lul patak ul kwumeng ul nāy se khong namul ul kilunta 'I make holes in the bottom of this pot to grow bean sprouts'.

It has been observed that the relationship between the two nouns in a structure N_1 **ul/lul** N_2 **ul/lul** is usually restricted to the inalienable possession of N_2 by N_1 as a body part, a topographical feature, a relational location, or the like.

For more examples, see the entry **ul** in Part II. See also the remarks (in §11.6) on the replacement of **ey**, **eykey**, and **ulo** by the particle **ul**. It is possible to obtain similar specification-narrowing structures with multiple phrases marked by the locative **ey** or **ey se**, by juxtaposing the phrases (with or without adding focus to one or more of them):

I tōl-mayngi ey nun thum-sayki ey swupun i mānh.ta (CM 2:109) 'There is a lot of water content in the fissures of this stone'.

Hak.kyo ey se wūntong-cang ey se wuli tul i pon sāsil ip.nita (Mkk 1961:4:11) 'It is a fact that we have seen in the gym at school'.

Such sentences differ from the simple conjoining of sentences with a shared predicate: **Tosi ey se, nongchon ey se, kuliko pata ey se wuli uy sayngsan uy pulq kil un tewuk sēy-chakey tha oluko iss.ta** (ibid.) 'The flame of our production is rising more vigorously in the cities, in the farm villages, and on the sea'. A given predicate can take more than one instrumental phrase, provided that each refers to a separate kind of instrumentality that can be differentiated by paraphrase: **In.lyek ulo [= ul sse se nun] thop ulo onul an ulo [= ey] ku mānh.un namu lul tā khyelq swu nun tōce hi ēps.ess.keyss.ta** (ibid.) 'We would never have been able to saw that much wood within a day with manpower and saws'.

There are Middle Korean examples similar to some of the modern structures:

HE-KHWONG ˙ol mwolwoki ˙cokyay s ˙mwo.m ol ¨sa˙mosi˙m ye (1482 Kum-sam 2:3b) 'he instantly creates his own form out of empty space, and ... ' (← *HE-KHWONG ˙o˙lwo*).

pwoksyanghwa namwo ˙[G]wa pe˙tu' namwo s ˙kaci ˙lol TWONG nyek ˙kuy [= nye˙k uy] chi l' ˙KAK-˙KAK ¨sey nil˙kwup ˙CHWON ˙ol ka˙cye 'ta ˙ka (1466 Kup 1:21-2) 'take a branch of peach tree and willow tree, the ones from the east, three and seven inches [long] respectively, and ... '.

But it is more common to have a different verb for each accusative phrase, and some strings are complex in their derivation. In the passage *kwot [KUN-¨KUY] lol wolm˙kye ¨wo.m ol ci˙ze k kozol s ˙poy s twos˙k ol [¨]nay ¨hen ci˙p ulwo ˙sye ˙na ka˙la* (1481 Twusi 20:52a) 'straightway convert a canvas [to use] as the sail for an autumn boat and set off from my shabby home [on your mission]' the second *˙ol* marks a phrase that includes everything from the beginning ('that which you have converted the canvas to be') as the object of the infinitive *ci˙ze* 'make it', and the third *˙ol* marks the object of the infinitive *¨nay* 'put it out'.

With certain intransitive verbs and verbal nouns, it is possible to have two or more indirect objects that reflect a genitive (whole-part) relationship: **Nay ka Yenghuy eykey ima ey ōyn ccok ey khisu hayss.ta** 'I kissed Yenghuy on the left side of the forehead' (CF Kim Yengcwu 1989:462).

On double nominatives and accusatives see also negative conversions (§11.7) and nominalizations (§11.8). And compare §10.8.1. There are some good examples and pertinent comments in Kim Payklyen 1960, who characterizes five kinds of multiple adjunct:

(1) The second subject or object forms a construction to which the first stands in a larger relationship (= our whole-part "genitivization").

(2) The first object is indirect, only the second is direct (for the first ··· **ul/lul** is substituting for ··· **ey**, ··· **ulo/lo**, ...).

(3) The second subject or object is a complement for certain verbs: (··· i / ka) toy- 'become ... ', (··· ul / lul) mantu-l- / sām- 'make it into ··· ', ...

(4) The second subject forms a predicate with ani 'ta 'is not ··· '.

(5) Only the first subject or object is really marked for "case", the other(s) are mainly providing emphasis, by repetition or apposition.

Examples of double objects from Hong Kimun 1947 illustrate four of these:
(1) **Poli lul ssi lul ppulinta = Poli ssi lul ppulinta** 'We plant the barley seed'.
  Pesen ul kho lul mancinta = Pesen kho lul mancinta 'I touch the toe of the sock'.
(2) **Cokha lul pang ul ssullinta = Cokha eykey pang ul ssullinta** 'I have my nephew sweep the room'.
  So lul phul ul ttut.kinta = So eykey phul ul ttut.kinta 'I let the ox graze the grass'.
  Kay lul pap ul mek.inta = Kāy eykey pap ul mek.inta 'I feed the dog'.
Notice that **Kāy lul kwāyngi lul mek.inta** will only be taken as 'I let the dog eat the cat' and not the other way around; the order is fixed despite the permutability of the underlying sentence **Kāy eykey kwāyngi lul mek.inta = Kwāyngi lul kāy eykey mek.inta**. That leads to multiple ambiguities for **Kāy to kwāyngi to mek.inta**; one of the meanings could be 'I let the dog, too, eat even the cat' but none could be *'I let the cat, too, eat even the dog'.
(3) **Mul ul elum ul ma(y)ntunta = Mul lo elum ul ma(y)ntunta** 'We turn water into ice'.
  Cokha lul atul ul sāmnunta = (but better than) **Cokha lul atul lo sāmnunta** 'I adopt my nephew as my son'.
(5) **So lul hana lul** (or **han mali lul**) **santa** 'I buy an ox'.

Although in general it is possible to "scramble" the phrases that serve as adjuncts to the predicate, so that the object can be emphasized by putting it before the subject, the order of the like-marked case phrases (especially objects) is restricted by the semantic relations which allowed the structures to be formed. The sentence **(Ku namca ka) emeni lul pol ul ttaylyess.ta** '(He) hit the mother on the cheek' cannot easily be said as ***(Ku namca ka) pol ul emeni lul ttaylyess.ta** though the subject can be moved to other positions: **Emeni lul ku namca ka pol ul ttaylyess.ta** 'The mother he hit on the cheek', **Emeni lul pol ul ku namca ka ttaylyess.ta** 'HE hit the mother on the cheek'. The order of 'mother' and 'cheek' is fixed even when thematization and focus are applied: **emeni nun (ku namca ka) pol ul ttaylyess.ta** 'As for the mother, he hit her on the cheek' but not ***pol un (ku namca ka) emeni lul ttaylyess.ta** 'As for the cheek, it was the mother's that he hit', which could be expressed as **Pol un emeni uy pol / kes ul ttaylyess.ta**, using an overt genitive structure.

Certain idiomatic expressions with a built-in case marker function as if simplex verbs, so that we need not concern ourselves unduly with sentences like **Ku sayngkak i te ki ka mak.hyess.ta** (Dupont 193) 'That thought was still more extraordinary'.

10.7. Other views of Korean syntax.

The view of Korean sentences offered here differs in one important way from the view held, I believe, by several other linguists. Their view, in brief, is that Korean nominals occur in various "cases", somewhat like the cases taken by the nouns of Latin or Greek or Russian. Each of the particles, or of a subset of what are here called particles, is a marker for a "case": nominative, accusative, dative, instrumental — the exact terminology is of no great importance. When nominals occur, as so often they do in Korean, with no overt marker, they are said to be either (1) in an unmarked "absolute" case, or (2) in one of the marked cases with the particle "deleted" (dropped). In Lukoff 1947 "zero" allomorphs are given for both the subject and the object markers; the deletion of other particles is left unexamined.

That theory, at least in one version, would not admit that GRAMMATICAL ambiguity is present in sentences that are, when heard, ambiguous: **Koki mek.e** can mean either '[I] eat fish / meat' = **Koki lul mek.e**, or 'The fish eats [it]' = **Koki ka mek.e**. My view is that the expansions which precede the verbal heart of the sentence are basically ABSOLUTE in type — in my terms "adverbial" to the verb; the particles are added, as a kind of adnominal modification of the noun, when the speaker desires to specify in greater detail the nature of the adverbial relationship. CM (1:169-73) offers examples of deletion for ALL the particles, though a few are restricted in that they cannot drop in all their "meanings" — notably some of the dative, comitative, and instrumental types. I would call this REQUIRED SPECIFICATION and attribute it to other elements in the sentence, such as certain verbs that demand a particularly specified adverbial. CM notes that "dropping the vocative" is "more polite", but isn't that just another way of saying that the vocative particle, like English 'hey!', includes some flavor of brusqueness?

The omission of case markers seems to be more common in Korean than it is in Japanese. Examples of omitted **i/ka** (nominative):
    Kep na yo? /kemna.yo/ 'Are you afraid?'
    Sayngkak ēps.e 'I don't think so (= I don't want any)'.
Examples of omitted **ul/lul** (accusative):
    Kkwum kkey [= **kkāy**] 'Stop dreaming'.
    Pul kkē yo 'Turn off the light!'
    Os pes.e /o[t]ppese/ 'Take your clothes off!'
And of **eykey** or **hanthey** (dative):
    Nam pukkulepta 'I am ashamed before others'.
    Cey pelus kāy mōs cwunta 'You can't get rid of a bad habit even by giving it to your dog'.
    mol pwoli manh.i mek.imyen sol cinta if you give the pony plenty of barley he will grow fat' (1887 Scott 172).

Compare the remarks of 1881 Ridel 169 (Observations générales sur les cas):
    Les terminaisons ou signes des cas servent à rendre plus clair le sens de la phrase. Lorsque ce sens est assez clair par lui-même leur emploi est facultatif; on peut les mettre ou les omettre à volonté, ce qui a lieu, non-seulement dans le langage ordinaire, mais aussi bien souvent dans les livres. On s'exposerait au ridicule si l'on voulait toujours et partout faire usage des cas, et, au lieu de passer pour un *précieux* bien instruit, on serait regardé comme un *ignorant* qui ne connaît ni le langage ni les coutumes du pays.

10.8. Syntactic constraints.

Not every verb can occur in all the verb constructions we have listed (in §7.5 and elsewhere); not every simple verb sentence can take the same adjunct expansions (as found in §10.5, §11.1); not every specification is possible for every expansion. There are various constraints imposed upon the possible sentences of the language. Though these are primarily semantic in nature, to some extent they can be described in terms of classes of verbs, as we have already done in a preliminary sort of way with such labels as "verb : adjective : copula" and "transitive : intransitive"; and in terms of classes of nouns, such as "animate : inanimate" and the like. Such classes, while usually labeled with semantic notions in mind, are made up of members that adhere to certain constraints that can be described as part of the syntax. This section is an attempt to explore some of these constraints, but it is far from complete, and much further research is needed.

10.8.1. Subject-object expansion constraints.

The most obvious constraints are those involving subjects specified by the nominative particle **i/ka**, direct objects specified by **ul/lul**, and indirect objects specified by the personal particle **eykey** (or its more colloquial synonym **hanthey**) or by the impersonal **ey**.

We will divide the verbs into those which can take no subject, those taking one subject, and those taking more than one. I have yet to find a verb that cannot, under the proper circumstances, take a subject. The quasi-processive verbs **iss-** 'have' and **ēps-** 'lack' can take two subjects, in the sense of nominative-marked noun phrases, as can many (perhaps all) adjectives in the special sense of X ka Y ka ··· 'A has a ··· B', as in **Nwu ka meli ka khun ya** 'Who's got a big head?'. The first subject marks the possessor and the second marks the possessed, but a scrambled order is possible: **Meli ka nwu ka khun ya** 'Just WHO has got a big head?' Such sentences are particularly common with adjectives of quantity or size, such as **mānh-** 'have lots of', **cēk-** 'have few', **tumu-l-** 'have few', **khu-** 'have a big ⋯ ', **cāk-** 'have a small ⋯ '. The copula affirmative takes one nominative-marked phrase **A ka X ita** 'A is X' or 'For A it is a matter of X' but the negativized form takes two such phrases, **A ka X ka ani 'ta** 'A is not X' or 'For A it is not a matter of X', and permits the occurrence of the nominative particle **i / ka** after phrases that otherwise do not occur with it (§6.5 − CF §10.8.7, §11.7.2).

Object constraints put verbs into the following classes:
(1) no object:
   (a) **anc-** 'sit down', **cwuk-** 'die', **...-e ci-** 'get to be ⋯ ', **huli-** 'get cloudy', ... (vi)
   (b) **khu-** 'be / get big', **kwut-** 'be / get hard', **mulu-** 'be / get soft', **nā(s)-** 'be / get better', **palk-** 'be/get bright', **pulk-** 'be / get red', ... (adj/vi)
   (c) **cāk-** 'be small', **nwūle(h)- / nōla(h)-** 'be yellow', **tumu-l-** 'be rare', **cēk-** 'be few', **mānh-** 'be many', **cōh-** 'be good', ... (adj)
(2) one object, direct:
   (a) **mek-** 'eat', **po-** 'look at', **chac-** 'look for; visit', ... (vt)
   (b) **anc.hi-** 'seat', **cwuk.i-**, ... (vc ← vi)
   (c) **teywu-** 'heat', ... (vc ← adj)
(3) one object, pseudo-direct:
   (a) **ka-** 'go', **o-** 'come', ... (⋯ ul = ey 'to')
   (b) **ka-** 'go', **o-** 'come', ... (vn ul = vn halye 'intending to')
   (c) **ca-** 'sleep', **chwu-** 'dance', **ttwi-** 'jump', **wūs-** 'smile', **kēt- / kel-** 'walk', ... (**V-um ul V- = V-**)
   (d) **ka-** 'go', **o-** 'come', **po-** 'look at', ... , ... (⋯ ul = tong-an ' ⋯ for (a while)')
   (e) **ka-** 'go', ? ... (⋯ ul = ulo 'in the sequence order of ⋯ ')
   (f) **kēnnu-** 'cross', **cīna-** 'pass by' (a place as traversal object)
   (g) **su-** 'stand', **chwī ha-** 'get drunk', ... (⋯ ul = ey 'at' or ulo / lo 'toward; due to')
   (a-g) are pseudo-intransitive verbs (§7.1)
   (h) **mek.hi-** 'have something eaten', ... (transitive passives, §7.4, §11.6)
(4) one object, indirect:
   (a) **ka-** 'go', **o-** 'come', **tullu- / tulli-** 'drop in on', ...
   (b) **tulli-** 'be heard', **nwulli-** 'be pressed down', and all passives except the transitive passives
(5) two objects, direct and indirect (or direct substituting for indirect, §10.6):
   (a) **cwu-** 'give (it to)', **pha-l-** 'sell (it to)', **ponay-** 'send (it to)', **ha-** 'say (it to)', **ssu-** 'write (it to)', **kaluchi-** 'teach (it to)', **kalikhi-** 'indicate (it to)'; [for most speakers] **paywu-** 'learn (it from)'; ...
   (b) − the indirect object adds **se** 'from' to its specification:
      tul- 'hear (it from)', **kkwu-** 'borrow (it from)', **et-** 'obtain (it from)', **sa-** 'buy (it from)'; [for some speakers] **paywu-** 'learn (it from)', ...
   (c) (vt)**-e cwu-** 'do (it) for (⋯)', ...
   (d) (vc ← vt) 'have him do it': **mek.i-** 'feed', **poi-** 'show', ...
   (e) (**A ka B hanthey se C lul) sokay pat-** '(A) get introduced (by B to C)', ...
(6) two objects, both indirect
   (vi)**-e cwu-** 'do for' (the vi carries an inherent indirect object with it)

To the extent that we can categorize nouns as animate / personal (those taking the semantically marked indirect-object particle **eykey** or colloquial **hanthey**) and inanimate / impersonal (those taking the semantically unmarked indirect-object particle **ey**), we can categorize subjects and objects as being animate / personal or inanimate / impersonal. That permits us to find further constraints on verbs:
   (1) subject restricted to animate: **nō-l-** 'play', **cwuk-** 'die', **sā-l-** 'live', **po-** 'look at', ... ; all honorifics (if they are made from double-subject adjectives, **iss-**, or **ēps-** the possessor must be animate)
   (2) subject restricted to inanimate: **huli-** 'get cloudy', **palk-** 'get bright', **chwuw-** '(weather) be cold', **cha-** 'be cold (to the touch)', **kala-anc-** 'sink', ...

(3) direct object restricted to animate: **cwuk.i-** 'kill', **manna-** 'meet', ...
(4) direct object restricted to inanimate: **ssu-** 'write', **ip-** 'wear', **kaluchi-** 'teach', ...
(5) indirect object restricted to animate: **kaluchi-** 'teach', **paywu-** 'learn from', ? **cwu-** 'give', ...
(6) indirect object restricted to inanimate: ?

For many verbs there are no animate-inanimate constraints. In some cases the constraint applies to the subject but not the object (or the other way round); in some cases opposite constraints apply to the subject and the object: **kaluchi-** 'teach' requires an inanimate direct object but both the subject and indirect object are animate. The constraints are not so hard and fast that exceptional sentences do not occur. In particular, animation and disanimation (§10.8.8) can temporarily suspend the system.

10.8.2. Negative constraints.

The constraints that obtain in negative constructions are treated in a general way in §11.7. You will find that **mōs ponta** 'can't see' occurs, but there is no *__mōs cōh.ta__ despite the occurrence of **cōh.ci mōs hata** 'isn't good at all', and there is only one type of negative possible for the copula (**ani 'ta** but no *__mōs ita__). In §11.7.2 there is mention of a class of processive verbs that, like adjectives, when focused can be preemphasized with the particle **i/ka** as well as with the particle **ul/lul**. If we set up a class of **ka**-preemphasizables, we will want to include in it:
(1) all adjectives;
(2) virtually all passives (with occasional problems of awkwardness);
(3) the intransitive verb **toy-** 'become' in all its uses;
(4) virtually all intransitive processive verbs pronounced **ci-**, including the auxiliary in **-e ci-** 'get to be, become';
(5) a few miscellaneous intransitive verbs, including **cwuk-** 'die', **phi-** 'bloom', and **kāmki tulli-** 'catches a cold'.

Most verbs and adjectives can occur with the long version of the strong negative ····**ci mōs ha-**, and the verbs can occur also with the short version **mōs** ··· . But most of the processive verbs (not adjectives) that are **ka**-preemphasizable cannot occur with **mōs**; the exceptions, and the individual ways in which they are exceptional, are listed in §11.7.2. Some adjectives cannot take the strong negative, notably those referring to weather conditions: **chwuw-** 'be cold', **tēw-** 'be warm' — but **tēw-** also occurs in the meaning 'be warm to the touch' and can be negativized as **tēpci mōs hata** in this meaning, for which an appropriate subject would be **mul** 'water' but never **nal** 'day, weather'.

Other negative constraints are found in §11.7.3 (Suppletive negatives).

10.8.3. Active adjectives; resultative verbs.

Ordinarily we find that only verbs enter into the construction **-nun cwung ey** 'in the midst of ···ing', but the adjective **pappu-** 'be busy' occurs with **-un cwung ey**: **pappusin cwung ey** 'in the midst of your being busy'. There seem to be other adjectives of this sort, e.g. **koy lowusin cwung ey** 'in the midst of your being ill'. Perhaps **cwung** here takes on an extended, nontemporal meaning, as in these examples:

Kānguy sokto ppalun cwung ey pal.um mace napputa 'Not only is his lecture speed too fast, but even his pronunciation is bad'.

Chwulkun sikan nuc.un cwung ey cha-sāko kkaci naney 'I'm late for work and on top of that there's a car accident' — or is **nuc-** an intransitive verb here?

Kattuk ina mōs-nan cwung ey tali to cēnta 'He's not only awfully ugly, he's lame as well'.

Most verbs of action can occur with **-nun sai/tong-an (ey)** 'while ···ing', but there is also a group which can appear with **-un sai/tong-an (ey)** 'while in the state resulting from having done': **ka-** 'go', **o-** 'come', **tul.e ka-/o-** 'enter', **na-ka-/-o-** 'exit', ... Are the only cases those which include **ka-** or **o-**, or are there other verbs that are similar? Compare the occurrence of past and past-past with different meanings: **kass.ta** 'went (and is gone)', **kass.ess.ta** 'went (and is back)'. Since there are other verbs that imply such reversible results, e.g. **mek.ess.ta** 'ate (and is still full)' and **mek.ess.ess.ta** 'ate (but is hungry again)', we might wonder whether these could occur with **-un sai/tong-an (ey)**, but my informants reject such attempts as *mek.un sai 'while still full from eating', *ssis.un sai 'while still clean from being washed', and *ssun sai 'while still written and not yet erased'. (These meanings could be conveyed by the ··· tay lo construction; see the entry in Part II.)

10.8.4. Constraints on modifiers.

The occurrence of modifier forms of verbs is constrained by various restrictions on the possible uses of adnominalized sentences, not only in terms of the categories of tense and aspect but also in terms of the three-way classification of verb, adjective, and copula. These constraints have not been studied in a systematic way, but information on each postmodifier will be found in the appropriate entry of Part II. Although adnominalized sentences cannot modify nouns of relative location such as **wi** 'above' and **yeph** 'beside' according to what we have said in §6.4, but that statement should be reexamined since the restraint does not hold for the corresponding situation in Japanese ('above where ··· , beside where ··· ').

10.8.5. Auxiliary constraints.

Many of the auxiliary constructions (§7.5) occur quite freely or are restricted only in that, say, they reject adjectives — or, conversely, processive verbs. But others are quite limited. For example, I have not been able to find more than a few stems for most of the following constructions:

-e chinta	mek-, wūs-; kkamule-chi- 'swoon'; ? tō-l- (CM)
-e mek.nunta	ha-, ic-, kaluchi-, noh-, sok.i-, (cal to) toy-
(→ mek.ess.ta, mek.keyss.ta)	
-e mekta	keyulu-
-e nāynta	chac-, iki-, kyenti-, mak-, ssawu-, ssu-l-, (īl ul kiil ey) tāy(e) ha- 'finish a job on time', ... ; ilk-, pha-
-e ppā cinta	kolh-, ssek-; hē-l-, keyulu-, malu-, nulk-, talh-, yak-
-e ssah.nunta	mek-, nō-l-, ssawu-, tte-tu-l-; hun ha-, mānh-
-e tāynta	kkapu-l-, masi-, mek-, mō-l-, mūt- / mul-, ssawu-, tte-tu-l-, twulu-, wuki-, wū-l-, wūs-; (soli lul) cilu-, (kēcis mal ul) kkwumi-, (ocwum) ssa-

Of perhaps greater interest are the aspect-tinged classes that occur with **-ko iss-** (in four different meanings) and with **-e iss-**:

(1) **-ko iss.ta** 'is in the act of doing': **mek.ko iss.ta** 'is eating', **wūs.ko iss.ta** 'is laughing', **poko iss.ess.ta** 'was looking at it' (compare **pwass.ta** 'saw it'), **chac.ko iss.ess.ta** 'was looking for it' (compare **chac.ess.ta** 'found it'), ...

(2) **-ko iss.ta** 'habitually / regularly / routinely does': **taniko iss.ta** 'goes (around), commutes', **phalko iss.ta** 'sells (regularly, as a business)', **sako iss.ta** 'buys (as a professional buyer)', **kaluchiko iss.ta** 'teaches (as one's job)', ...

There seems to be considerable overlap between (1) and (2). If it is total, the difference may be semantic only.

(3) **-ko iss.ta** 'is in the state of doing': **kitaliko iss.ta** 'is waiting', **ssuko iss.ta** 'is using', **memchwuko iss.ta** 'is stopping', **pethiko iss.ta** 'is supporting', **kyenti(e nāy)ko iss.ta** 'is bearing up'; **mek.una māna hako iss.ta** 'is uncertain whether to eat or not'.

Expressions with auxiliaries may be constrained by the aspectual nature of the verb: **math.e cwuko iss.ta** 'is favoring us by taking care of it' and **poa cwuko iss.ta** 'is favoring us by looking at / after it' are acceptable, but *****mek.e cwuko iss.ta** 'is favoring us by eating it' is rejected.

(4) **-ko iss.ta** 'is in the continuing state resulting from doing': **os ul ipko iss.ta** 'is wearing clothes', **moca lul ssuko iss.ta** 'is wearing a hat', **neykthai lul māyko iss.ta** 'is wearing a necktie'; **cako iss.ta** 'is sleeping'; **mōs hako iss.ta** 'has been unable to do it (and is still unable)'.

(5) **-e iss.ta** 'is in the continuing state resulting from doing': **anc.e iss.ta** 'is seated', **nwuwe iss.ta** 'is recumbent (lying down)'; **allye cye iss.ta** 'is known', ? other cases of **-e iss.ta**: **cha iss.ta** 'is full', (··· **ulo) toye iss.ta** 'is made up (of ···)', **nam.e iss.ta** 'is left over'; **tul.e iss.ta** 'is inside/within', **ka iss.ta** 'is gone', **wā iss.ta** 'is come, is here'; **ip.wen hay iss.ta** 'is in the hospital, is hospitalized'; **cwuk.e iss.ta** 'is dead'; ... . In **(kil) kēnne iss.ta** 'is across (the way)' the infinitive serves as a postnoun.

10.8.6. Emotive adjectives.

Certain subjective adjectives of evaluation and emotion ('it is ··· according to my reactions, it is such as to produce such-and-such a reaction; I feel such-and-such a reaction toward it') can be transitivized and also externalized so that 'HE' finds it reaction-producing, by following the infinitive **-e** with the auxiliary verb **hanta**. These include: **cōh-** 'be liked, be found likable' with the antonym **silh-** or **miw-** 'be disliked, be found dislikable' (notice that the antonym of **cōh-** meaning 'good' is **nappu-** 'bad'), **musew-** 'be frightening, feel frightened', **komaw-** 'be obliging, feel grateful', **culkew-** 'be enjoyable, feel enjoyment', ... At least one intransitive verb behaves in a similar way, but apparently only when the result is adnominalized: **kamcil na-** '(I) feel impatient' → *kamcil na hanta 'he is impatient; I am impatient of it' → **kamcil na hanun mosup** 'the appearance of being impatient'.

These adjectives are not constrained from appearing in the construction **-e cinta** 'becomes ··· ': **cōh.a cinta, miwe cinta, musewe cinta; komawe cinta** (of limited distribution); and some accept **kamcil na cinta** 'grows impatient'.

10.8.7. Separability constraints; auxiliary preemphasis.

In the lists of §7.5 the auxiliaries are marked for "separability". There are several elements which can separate the preceding verb form (e.g. the infinitive **-e**) from the following auxiliary (e.g. **cwu-**): the particles **un/nun, to,** and **tul** are the most common, but for some of the auxiliaries the verb form is set off also by **man, se, iya/ya, ina/'na,** and **ita/'ta (ka)**. The ubiquitous particle **tul** 'acting severally' is the best diagnostic for separability: if **tul** cannot intervene, usually nothing can. The constraints seem to be specific to each auxiliary rather than general in nature. Certain close-knit combinations of **V-e V-** are separable even though they may be treated as lexical compounds in the dictionaries: **pala (to/'ta) po-** 'gaze at', **tol.a (tul) ka-** 'return', ...

Of particular interest are cases of auxiliary preemphasis with the particles **i/ka** or **ul/lul**, of which the negative preemphasis described in §11.7.2 is a special case. Some structures found:

(1) **-ko siph.ta** → **-ko ka/lul siph.ta** 'want to do'
(2) **-e iss.ta, -e ponta, -e kanta, ...** → **-e lul iss.ta (ponta, kanta, ...)** [jocular]
(3) **-key an toynta** 'doesn't get to (do)' → **-key ka/lul an toynta**.

Limitations on further applying conversions to auxiliary structures are probably individual to the particular auxiliary. Often a conversion such as negativization can be separately applied to the main verb or to the auxiliary, or again both may be negativized.

10.8.8. Animate-inanimate constraints.

An indirect object is marked by **eykey** (or **hanthey**) when animate, by **ey** when inanimate. Using this criterion we can clearly characterize most nouns as either animate or inanimate, but there are a few difficulties caused by the following factors (CM 1:140-1):

(1) animation (or personification):
   Tal nim un inkong wiseng eykey taceng hakey iyaki lul kel.ess.ta 'The (man in the) moon engaged the man-made satellite in friendly conversation'.

(2) disanimation (or depersonification):
   Ku uy yēnkwu nun tōngmul ey kwuk.han toyess.ess.ul ppun man ani 'la thuk hi konchwung ey māy-tallye se ku pēm.wi lul te nem.e suci anh.ess.ta 'His research was not only restricted to animals, but was especially involved with insects and did not go beyond that area'.

(3) treating a group to be animate as a whole, but inanimate (impersonalized) as made up of individual members:
> Kwuntay eykey kōngkup hanta 'They supply the army' — Kwuntay ey tul.e kanta 'He enters (the ranks of) the army'. (But Co Sek.yen prefers ey for the first sentence, too.)
> Sam-hak.nyen eykey wusung-ki lul cwuess.ta 'They gave the Excellence Banner to the third grade (class)' — Sam-hak.nyen ey taninta 'He attends the third grade'.

Concepts such as **unhayng** 'the bank', **hōysa** 'the company', **hak.kyo** 'the school', **kwuk.min** 'the populace', **wuli nala** 'our nation', ... , can be taken as animate and given the dative ··· **hanthey** or ··· **eykey**, though they are more commonly treated as inanimate with the dative ··· **ey**. There may be a question whether the sentences with **ey** involve an "indirect object", strictly speaking; it is hard to draw the line between the directional meaning of **ey** and the more abstract meaning.

On the basis of the animate-inanimate distinction in nouns we can mark subject-object constraints for certain verbs (§10.8.1).

Certain expressions use either **ey** or **eykey** for an animate indirect object: **Ōykwuk sālam ey / eykey hūngmi lul kacinta** 'He takes an interest in foreigners', **I yak un wiq-pyēng hwānca eykey / ey cēy-il ita** 'This medicine is the best thing for stomach sufferers'. Certain extended particle phrases (§6.3) are usually constructed with **ey** only, regardless of the noun: (··· **ey) uy hay se, ttal^e/a se, kwan hay se, tāy hay se** (at least in the meaning 'about, in reference to'), ...

10.8.9. Indirect-object intensification.

For certain verbs that call for an indirect object it is possible to intensify that valence by following the particle with **'ta (ka)**. Here, in disagreement with the Korean grammarians, we treat /ta(ka)/ as the copula transferentive, optionally + particle **ka**; see §9.8. But for other verbs, the transferentive intensification is most unlikely or impossible. Contrast the particle **to**, which can be used after any phrase of noun + **ey** to highlight the phrase as a whole (or the noun itself) rather than apply just to the meaning of the particle **ey**.

The examples that follow, partly taken from a list in CM 1:155 that was designed to illustrate the animate-inanimate distinction of §10.8.8, has been checked with native speakers for the insertibility of 'ta (ka). The examples are accordingly arranged in six groups. (Examples preceded by a question mark are doubted or rejected by Co Sek.yen, who is reluctant to accept the insertion with adjectives and many intransitive verbs, but speakers I had checked with earlier were more tolerant of the structures. She offered a few additional examples, however, which are marked with "+" below.)

(1) ey, ey 'ta, ey 'ta ka
   pyek ey ('ta, 'ta ka) kī-taynta 'leans against the wall'
   chilphan ey ('ta, 'ta ka) kul ul ssunta 'writes on the blackboard'
   tāy-hak.kyo ey ('ta, 'ta ka) phyēnci lul ssunta 'writes a letter to he university'
   tose-kwan ey ('ta, 'ta ka) chayk ul kicung hanta 'donates a book to the library'
   unhayng ey ('ta, 'ta ka) ponaynta 'sends it to the bank'
   ttang ey ('ta, 'ta ka) ttel.e ttulinta 'drops it on the ground'
   tāmpayq-tay ey ('ta, 'ta ka) pul ul puth.inta 'lights a pipe'
   cilmun ey ('ta, 'ta ka) tāytap hanta 'answers the question'
   ettenq īl ey ('ta, 'ta ka) 'na kwankyey hanta 'has relevance to a certain matter'
   saynghwal ey ('ta, 'ta ka) hūngmi lul kacinta 'takes interest in life'
   kkoch ey ('ta, 'ta ka) mul ul cwunta 'waters the flowers'
   kwanyek ey ('ta, 'ta ka) chong ul kyenwunta 'aims a gun at a target'
   congi ey ('ta, 'ta ka) kilum ul mek.inta 'oils paper'
   huyn pathang ey ('ta, 'ta ka) kum munuy 'a gold pattern on a white background'
   Yeksi ku api ey ('ta, 'ta ka) ku atul ikwun! 'Like father like son!'
   Kath.ci-anh.unq īl ey ('ta, 'ta ka) hwā lul nāyl phil.yo ka eti iss.e yo 'Is there any need to lose your temper at the least little thing?'

A Reference Grammar of Korean

    Swul ey ('ta, 'ta ka) koki ey ('ta, 'ta ka) cal mek.ess.ta 'We ate well – wine, and meat, and so forth'.
(?) ip ey ('ta, 'ta ka) tāmpayq-tay lul munta 'puts a pipe in one's mouth'
(?) uyca ey ('ta, 'ta ka) anc.nunta 'sits down on a chair'
 ? kēnkang ey ('ta, 'ta ka) cōh.ta 'is good for one's health'
(?) kongpu haki ey ('ta, 'ta ka) papputa 'is busy with one's studies'
 ? swul ey ('ta, 'ta ka) chwī hanta 'gets drunk on liquor'
 ? I pi ey ('ta, 'ta ka) eti kasip.nikka! 'Where ever are you going in such a rain?!'
 ? Selthang un han kun ey ('ta, 'ta ka) elma 'p.nikka 'How much is sugar a pound?'
 ? Ku uy pak.hak ey ('ta, ta ka) nōllass.ta 'I was surprised at his wide learning'.
 ? Pulunun soli ey ('ta, 'ta ka) cam i kkayyess.ta 'I awoke at the sound of someone calling'.
(?) Kulenq īl ey ('ta, 'ta ka) mue l' nōpal-tāypal ia 'Why get mad at such a thing?'
 + kongpu ey ('ta, 'ta ka) yel.uy lul tā hanta 'devotes oneself to one's studies'
 + Sewul ey ('ta, 'ta ka) sālq kos ul malyen hayss.ta 'I set up a place to live in Seoul'.
 + Piq mul ey ('ta, 'ta ka) ppallay lul hamyen ttay ka cal kanta / cinta 'Washing clothes in rain water gets rid of the dirt easier'.
(2) ey, (?) ey 'ta, (??) ey 'ta ka
    Sewul ey tōchak hanta 'arrives in Seoul' – in rather colloquial contexts 'ta (less likely 'ta ka) may occur, but both are better avoided.
    kongpu ey ('ta, 'ta ka) yel.uy ka cikuk hata 'is devoted to one's son's studies' – and both are unlikely
    pi ey ('ta very awkward, *'ta ka rejected) cec.nunta 'gets wet in the rain'
    chong-al ey ('ta perhaps, *'ta ka rejected) mac.nunta 'gets hit by a bullet'
    Kwuncwung i hwanhuy ey ('ta awkward, *'ta ka rejected) nēmchiko iss.ta 'The crowds are overflowing with joy'.
    I yak un wiq-pyēng ey ('ta may be acceptable, but *'ta ka is rejected) cēy-il ita 'This medicine is the best thing for stomach troubles'.
(3) probably ey only
    Phyengyang ey tol.a wass.ta 'came back to Phyengyang'
    kacca cungmyeng-se ey sok.nunta 'is deceived by a false identity card'
    tewi ey cici anh.nunta 'is not bested by the heat'
    mul ey millinta 'is pushed by the water'
(4) ey only
    kongcwung ey nanta 'flies in(to) the air'
    cēncayng ey na-kanta 'goes off to war'
    halwu ey twū pen 'two times a day'
    sip-nyen ey han pen 'once every ten years'
    kāmki ey kellinta / tullinta 'catches a cold'
    chwīmi ey mac.ta 'is to one's taste'
    elkwul ey pan hanta 'falls in love with a face'
    ku sālam ey kwan hay se 'with respect to him, about him'
    Chwuwi ey etteh.key cīnaysey yo 'How are you getting along in all this cold?'
    Cekcin ey tolkyek ita! '(It's) charge the enemy lines!'
 ? payk wen ey phanta 'sells it for a hundred wen' (Co Sek.yen OK's payk wen ey 'ta ka phanta)
(5) eykey / hanthey, eykey / hanthey 'ta, eykey / hanthey 'ta ka
    sacang eykey ('ta, 'ta ka) kuleh.key māl hanta 'says that to the boss'
    haksayng eykey ('ta, 'ta ka) chayk ul pointa 'shows the book to the student'
    nam eykey ('ta, 'ta ka) īl ul hakey hanta 'has someone else do the job'
    ai eykey ('ta, 'ta ka) pap ul mek.inta 'feeds the child'
    nam eykey ('ta, 'ta ka) tōn ul mek.hinta 'gets one's money swindled by someone'

ⁿyeca eykey ('ta, 'ta ka) chwī hanta 'is intoxicated with a woman'
haksayng eykey ('ta, 'ta ka) congi lul cwunta 'gives the student some paper'
cek eykey ('ta, 'ta ka) chong ul kyenwunta 'aims a gun at the enemy'
Son nim i tongsayng eykey ('ta, 'ta ka) cēnhwa lul kel.ess.ta 'The guest phoned his younger brother'.
? Son i tongsayng eykey ('ta, 'ta ka) tah.ass.ta 'His hand touched (his) younger brother'.

(6) probably eykey / hanthey only
emeni eykey tol.a wass.ta 'came back to his mother'
ku nom tul eykey sok.nunta 'are deceived by those rascals'
nam eykey cici anh.nunta 'does not give in (yield) to others'
kwancwung tul eykey millinta 'is pushed by the spectators'

10.9.10. Locative constraints.

For expansions that indicate location ('in, at') Koreans use the particle **ey** 'being at' or **(ey) se** 'happening at'. (We are not here concerned with the fact that **se** also means 'from'; that meaning correlates with a small class of verbs that includes **o-** 'come', **ka-** 'go', **nayli-** 'get off / down', **ppāy-** 'remove', ...) In general, **ey** is used with certain adjectives (of quantity / frequency) and a few verbs of stative meaning, such as **su-** 'stand', **nām-** 'remain', **anc.ko iss-** 'be sitting' or **anc.e iss-** 'be seated', ... ; **ey se** is used in other cases, notably with verbs of activity. But certain verbs and adjectives are used with either **ey** or **(ey) se**:

¹yekwan ey (ey se) memunun / swīnun son nim 'a guest staying / resting at an inn'
san kwa tūl ey (ey se) phinun kkoch 'the flowers blooming in the mountains and fields'
photay wi ey (ey se) nallinun kiq-pal 'the flag flying over the gun battery'
? cēnthwu ey (ey se) sūng.li hanta 'are victorious in war' — with **ey se** Co Sek.yen prefers **sūng.li lul ketwunta** 'garners victory'
I maul ey (ey se) sāsip.nikka? 'Do you live in this village?'
Kosan sik.mul cwung ey (ey se) etten kes i yūmyeng han ya 'Among Alpine plants which ones are well known?' — apparently provoked also by **cwung**, since only **ey** is accepted in **Kosan sik.mul ey ...** 'Of Alpine plants ...'.

In these cases there seems to be no difference of meaning, and most speakers have a preference for one or the other. Cang Sengen (Sung-Un Chang), for example, says that he prefers ··· **ey se sānta** 'lives in ···'. A difference of meaning obtains between **Cēki ey pointa** 'It is visible there (= you can see that it is there)' and **Cēki ey se pointa** 'It is visible from there (= you go there and you can see it)'.

For **iss.ta** 'exists; has' and **ēps.ta** 'is lacking, lacks', and the adjectives the choice of **ey** or **ey se** depends on whether the subject of the verb is a THING or an EVENT (CF CM 1:154):
kāngtang ey iss.tun phiano 'the piano (that was) in the lecture room' ← Phiano ka kāngtang ey iss.tula 'The piano was in the lecture room (I noticed)'.
kāngtang ey se iss.tunq īl 'the event (that was happening) in the lecture room' ← Īl i kāngtang ey se iss.tula 'The event was in the lecture room (I observed)'.
That gives us a diagnostic for setting up a class of EVENT NOUNS. Perhaps all processive verbal nouns would fall in this category; does it include any nouns that are not, in fact, verbal nouns?

The following quantifying adjectives seem to be similar to **iss.ta**: **mānh.ta** 'is / has much, are many', **cēkta** 'is / has little, are few', **tumulta** 'is rare, are few', and the adjectival nouns **hun hata** 'is frequent, are common / many' and **katuk hata** 'is filling / ample, are many indeed'. Yet it is possible to say either **Hānkwuk ey se (nun) san i mānh.ta** 'In Korea there are lots of mountains' or **Hānkwuk ey (nun) san i mānh.ta**; perhaps the latter means something more like 'Korea has lots of mountains'.

For copula sentences, **(ey) se** seems to be the normal particle: **Sewul ey se pec kkoch i hanchang ita** 'The cherry blossoms are in full bloom in Seoul', **Ilpon ey se yākwu ka tāy-inqki 'ta** 'In Japan baseball is very popular'. Such sentences express a judgment, and so do most adjective sentences, so we expect them to take locatives with **ey se**.

Elsewhere (Martin 1975) I have taken the position that the Japanese counterpart of **ey se** (the Japanese particle de) is the RESIDUAL (default) locative marker, and the counterpart of **ey** (the Japanese particle ni) is specifically in valence with a few particular verbs of stative meaning, notably the Japanese verbs expressing existence and possession. There are extenuating circumstances: ni will mark a place where something is found, i.e. discovered to BE, or the site where something is bought or sold that cannot be moved, such as land or a house. I believe Korean is similar to Japanese in this respect, but may differ in rejected **ey se** for certain adjective sentences that take de in Japanese. That means if you start a sentence with 'In Korea ··· ' before deciding on a predicate, you say **Hānkwuk ey se** ··· and then correct that to **Hānkwuk ey** ··· if and only if you select a specific predicate that calls for it (··· **san i mānh.ta** 'there are lots of mountains ··· ', ··· **chinkwu ka iss.ta** 'I have a friend ··· ') but not otherwise. There are delicate problems and unexpected exceptions to this generalization; these need to be explored, as Martin 1975 tried to do for most of the similar Japanese problems. Notice, for example that of a tenant it can be said **cip ey hāswuk hako iss.ta** 'is lodging at the house' (and some speakers reject *****cip ey se** ···), yet of a landlady one says **cip ey se hāswuk chinta** 'provides lodging at the house', also **cip ey se son nim ul chinta** 'entertains guests at the house'. See pp. 496, 503-4.

In pursuing this subject, care must be taken not to mistake an occurrence of the subordinating particle **uy** 'of' for **ey** just because the two particles are pronounced alike. Notice too that the particle **ey** can carry also the allative meaning '(going) to', and that will perhaps (by semantic extension) account for **San ey tanphung i cinta** 'The mountains take on autumn tints' and **Pakk ey nwūn i wā yo** 'It's snowing outside'.

10.8.11. Copula and particle constraints.

There are individual constraints on what particles and forms of the copula can occur after certain quasi-free nouns, postnouns, postmodifiers, and the like. (The lists in CM 1:174-5 are suggestive but far from complete; a more rigorous table is called for.) There are similar constraints on certain words of the Chinese vocabulary (CM 1:176-7), such as **cāylay** 'being (as) usual', **kāmang** 'possibility', **kākwan** 'being worth seeing; being ridiculous', **mucin-cang** 'being inexhaustible'. And a group of words from the core vocabulary are similar in their constraints: **engmang** 'mess', **machan-kaci** 'being the same'.

The particle **tele** is used as a substitute for the dative marker **hanthey**, or its less colloquial synonym **eykey**, when the indirect object is socially inferior (or, at most, equal) to the subject and the verb is one of telling, ordering, asking, showing, instructing or the like: (**māl**) **ha-** 'tell', **mūt-/mul-** 'ask', **cheng ha-** 'request; invite', **yōkwu ha-** 'demand', **cilmun ha-** 'inquire', **āykel ha-** 'appeal', **kaluchi-** 'teach', **kalikhi-** 'point out', **poi-** 'show', ... The particle **poko** can be used with (all?) the same verbs without any social connotation; it is derived from the gerund of the verb **po-** 'look at' but the particle does not require the visible presence of the person being told (etc.) and there is potential ambiguity in **na poko māl hayss.ta** 'said it to me' or 'looked at me and said it' in that only the former meaning would apply if the subject were **cāng-nim i** 'a blind person'.

10.8.12. Miscellaneous constraints.

Our attention is called by CM to several minor constraints. The pronouns **cē-huy** 'we / us' and **ne-huy** 'you (people)' never take the particle **uy** when used adnominally (CM 1:258). The directional adverbs **ili** 'this way', **kuli** 'that way', and **celi** 'that way (over there)' lack the "predicate" (pre-copular) and adnominal uses and never occur with the particle **uy**; they do not occur with the particle **ey** (instead **ulo/lo** is used); and they are rarely found with the particle **kwa/wa** (or its colloquial synonym **hako**), so that the example **Ili wa celi wa twū kil i iss.ta** 'There are two roads, one this way and one over that way' (CM 1:260) is unusual. There are, of course, constraints between pronouns and styles of speech (CM 1:261), depending upon attitudes toward the referents of a sentence and of the deictic situation. A rough guide to the correlation between sentence stylization and ways of referring to the first and second person:

'I / me'	'you'	style
na	ne	-ta; -e, -ci
	caney	-ney
	tangsin, kutay	-o
ce	tangsin, kutay; TITLE	-e yo, -ci yo
	TITLE	-sup.nita

Other things to be noted:

(1) The word **āmu** 'any' requires its sentence to include some such form as ··· **to**, ··· **ina / 'na**, ····**una / -na**, ··· **itun / 'tun ci**, ····**tun ci**, ...

(2) Some adverbs are severely limited in use, and the limitations need to be explored.

(3) There is no way to predict the acceptability of noun compounds: **onul nal** 'today' is common but speakers reject *[1]**nayil nal** 'tomorrow' and (despite CM 1:357) *****ecey(q) nal** 'yesterday'.

The verb **kaci-** 'hold, have' has several peculiarities that relate to aspect. For example, it does not occur with the plain transferentive **-ta (ka)**; there is no *****kacita (ka)**. The expression **kac'ta** is a contraction of **kacye 'ta**, the infinitive + the copula transferentive in its use as a quasi-particle. (Other examples of **-e 'ta** will be found in Part II.) Are there other verbs that lack the transferentive? Notice that both **iss.ta (ka)** and **ēps.ta (ka)** are used:

Ecey kkaci iss.ta ka onul un eti lo kass.nun ya 'He was here till yesterday, but where's he gone now?'

Tōn ila n' iss.ta ka (to) ēps.ko ēps.ta ka (to) iss.nun kes ita 'Money is something that now you have it now you don't'.

Tōn i ēps.ta ka sayngkini acwu heyphuta 'New money is carelessly spent'.

The expression **iss.ta (ka)** 'exists / stays and then' is often used in the sense 'after a while', and in that meaning it is sometimes treated as an unanalyzed adverb and spelled phonemically as **i-tta(-ka)**.

11.0. Conversions.

Simple sentences are easy to process and understand, but a speaker finds it economical to package as much information as possible in a single complex sentence, made by expanding or converting one or more simple sentences through systematic processes of various types. These processes are described in the following sections and referred to by the general term of sentence CONVERSIONS.

11.1. Nuclear sentences and sentence conversions.

It is possible to think of all the sentences of a language as derivable by various systematic processes from a small number of quite simple basic sentence types. If we leave aside a few odds and ends in the way of minor sentences, such as **Nwuku** 'Who?', we are tempted to say that Korean has only one nuclear sentence type. But instead we will say that there are three such types, which can be represented by somewhat arbitrarily chosen samples:

(1) verbal sentence   **Ponta.**   'Someone looks at (sees) it / one.'
(2) adjectival sentence   **Cōh.ta.**   'It is good.'
(3) copular sentence   **Cip ita.**   'It is [a matter of] a house.'

In literary, rhetorical, or poetic contexts certain forms of the copula may go unexpressed: **Wuli nun mincwu chengnyen (imye), inmin uy atul-ttal (ita)** 'We are the youth of the masses, the sons and daughters of the people' (CM 1:180). All the copula does, after all, is predicate the noun.

Our three sample sentences can be taken and turned into other sentences – ultimately, we would like to think, all the sentences – by processes such as the following.

(1) We can SUBSTITUTE other verbs, adjectives, or nouns:

     Cwuk.nunta.   'Someone dies.'
     Khuta.   'It is big.'
     Kim sensayng ita.   'It is Mr Kim.'

The choice of particular classes of nouns to precede the copula **ita** and of particular classes of adjectives and verbs will impose constraints upon the choice of words elsewhere in the sentence. We do not say *Kāy ka Kim sensayng ul cwuk.nunta 'The dog dies Mr Kim' nor, except by a special dispensation called "personification", **Kōng i ayki lul ponta** 'The ball looks at the baby'. But in our choice of a particular one of the three nuclear sentence types, we impose much broader constraints upon the kinds of operations possible, and that is why we need all three types, even though the predicates of the second and third type may be regarded as restricted subclasses of the first.

(2) We can EXPAND the sentence, by prefacing the predicate with one or more adverbial phrases and/or, in the case of the copular sentence, by prefacing the noun with an adnominal phrase:

(Cikum) (emeni ka) ayki lul PONTA 'Now the mother looks at the baby'.
(Yeki se) cip i KHUTA 'The houses are large (here)'.
(Ku kes i) wuli CIP ITA 'That (thing), it is our house'.

We do not look at the structure of the phrases themselves as converted; we do not set up "kernel phrases" from which the others are derived by a series of operations, since the operation would consist merely of addition. However, parts of phrases that are themselves derived from sentences, such as modifier phrases, will include conversions listed below. It would be possible, of course, to assign — somewhat arbitrarily — a kind of kernel sentence that would derive each phrase so that noun + subject marker could be obtained from the kernel sentence **Ayki ka ponta** 'The baby looks at it', but that procedure seems both unnatural and unnecessary.

(3) We can CONVERT or transform the sentence by applying somewhat interdependent processes:

1. status elevation: normal → honorific.
2. style shift: plain → formal, → semiformal (authoritative), → familiar, → intimate (including intimate casual and circumstantial), → polite (including polite casual and circumstantial).
3. tense-aspect shift: present (or timeless) → past, → future, → tentative, → retrospective; and combinations of these.
4. finite-mood shift: statement → question, → command, → proposition, → apperception.
5. voice shift: active → causative, → passive.
6. negation: affirmative → negative, → strong negative.
7. condensation: sentence → nominalization, → adnominalization, → adverbialization.
8. quotation: sentence → quoted sentence.

A basic form is postulated for each category and labeled above as "normal, plain, present, statement, active, affirmative sentence", to which all three of our nuclear sentences correspond. The other forms mentioned are considered as produced by some process of derivation from the basic form.

(4) We can transform the EXPANSIONS of expanded sentences by means of the following processes:

9. switching emphasis (order of the expansions). We are assuming no "normal" order, but that may be untenable, since there is usually a least marked version, such as TIME - PLACE - SUBJECT - OBLIQUE OBJECTS - DIRECT OBJECT - VERB.
10. subdual of focus (with the particle **un/nun**).
11. highlighting of focus (with the particle **to**).
12. restriction (with the particle **man**) and other focus settings.
13. grammatical specification by assigning particles to roles, such as marking the subject, object, and indirect object; or the instrumentality, location, time, and so forth.

Substitution and expansion have been discussed in earlier sections; no more will be said about them here. Material on specification and focus will be found in Part II under each of the relevant particles (see the list in §6), and in the discussion of phrase order in §10.5. The remaining categories are taken up in the following sections: §11.2. Status conversions; §11.3. Style conversions; §11.4. Tense-aspect conversions; §11.5. Mood conversions; §11.6. Voice conversions; §11.7. Negation conversions; §11.8. Nominalizations; §11.9. Adnominalizations; §11.10. Adverbializations; and §11.11. Quotations. Certain special problems of reflexive requests and quoted favors are described in §11.12. And in §11.13 there is a discussion of sentence connectors derived from adverbializations.

11.2. Status conversions.

The honorific marker **-usi-/-si-** can be attached to a stem in order to show a special deference toward the subject of that stem, usually the direct subject: **posinta** '[someone exalted] deigns to look at', **cōh.usita** '[someone honored] is good', **Kim sensayng isita** '[someone esteemed] is Mr Kim'. But sometimes, especially with adjectives, the copula, **iss-**, **ēps-**, and idiomatic expressions of various kinds, the deference is toward the less direct subject (expressed or implied), such as the possessor or beneficiary, or toward the psychological subject (the one who feels or reacts):

Kim sensayng i kāy ka iss.usip.nikka 'Does Mr Kim have a dog?' (The dog is the direct subject – here the possessed, and Mr Kim the indirect subject – here the possessor.)

Pak sensayng eykey phyēnci lul ssunun tey, musun pūthak hal māl-ssum i ēps.usip.nikka? 'I am writing to Mr Park – is there anything you want me to tell him?' (The implied indirect subject is 'you', the source of the request.)

Ku pun un hwullyung han hakca (i)sina sangsik i ēps.usita 'He is a fine scholar but he lacks common sense'. (The implied subject, who is the [non-]possessor of common sense, is extruded and thematized, and subdued as 'that esteemed person'.)

Khi ka khusip.nita 'You are tall'.
Son i kowusip.nita 'You have nice hands'.
Sayngkak i cōh.usip.nita 'Your idea is good'.
Cōh.usin sayngkak ip.nita / Cōh.un sayngkak isip.nita / Cōh.usin sayngkak isip.nita 'That's a good idea you have there'.
Chayk i mānh.usikwun yo 'I see you have a lot of books!'
Emeni son un cham cal to wumcik isinta 'Mother's hands work quite deftly'.
Pyēng i tā nausyess.ˢup.nikka? 'Are you all over your illness?'
Sensayng nim to os i tā cec.usyess.ˢup.nita kwulye 'I see you got your clothes wet, too, sir'.
Sensayng nim un i pang i maum ey tusip.nikka? 'Does this room please you?'
Sāep i cal toysip.nikka? 'Is your work going well?'
Cip i cham khusikwun yo 'My what a big house you have!'
Cōh.usin cip ilokwun yo 'My what a nice house you have!'

The following cases are frowned upon but often said:

Ileh.key palam i pūsinun tey wā cwusye se komapsup.nita 'I appreciate your coming with the wind blowing [at you] this way'.

Nappun nal-ssi 'sin tey (Nappusin nal-ssi ey) wā cwusye se komapsup.nita 'I appreciate your kindly coming to us in such bad weather'.

On the subtleties of reference, see Lukoff 1978. On multiple subjects, see §10.6.

Since the purpose of the honorific marker is to elevate the status of the subject, that phrase must be personal and other than the first person. You never use honorific forms of yourself. There is one type of exception to the requirement for a personal subject: 'it rains (snows)' is often said as **pi ka (nwūn i) osinta** or **pi ka (nwūn i) naylisinta**. But no other statements of weather phenomena are treated as intrinsically deferential, and some speakers reject **nwūn** 'snow'.

Some verbs are commonly replaced by euphemisms in place of the expected regular honorific formations: **capswusi-** (abbreviated often to **capswus-**) or **cāsi-** < ¨c(w)asi- is used for (*)**mek.usi-** 'deign to eat', **cwumusi-** for ***casi-** 'deign to sleep', **tol.a kasi-** 'deign to go back' for (*)**cwuk.usi-** '[an honored person] dies' (but **wuli lul wi hay cwuk.usin Yēyswu nim** 'Jesus who died for us'). For the honorific forms of the stem **iss-** (strictly speaking the three homonymous stems meaning 'be', 'stay', and 'have') see the discussion under suppletive negatives (§11.7.3). The euphemistic replacements are much like simple nonhonorific stems in freely entering into larger structures, for they are not subject to the combinatorial restrictions of **-usi-**.

In complex conversions involving more than one verb, it is often possible to put the honorific marker on each of the stems or on both:

    V-(usi)ki ka swiw(usi)- / elyew(usi)- 'be easy / hard for one to do'
    V-(usi)ki ka cōh(.usi)- / silh(.usi)- 'like / dislike to do'

V-(usi)ki lul cōh.a / silh.e ha(si)- 'like / dislike to do'
V-(usi)ki lul sīcak ha(si)- 'begin to do'
V-(usi)ki ey him ssu(si)- 'try to do'

On the acceptability of marking as honorific a verb with an auxiliary, see the chart in §7.5 (p. 226).

An obsolete variant of the honorific marker has the shapes **-usiop-/-siop-** (also **-usiap-/-siap-**) before one-shape endings and the shapes **-usio-/-sio-** (also **-usia-/-sia-**?) before two-shape endings. The obsolete imperative ending **-usiopsose/-siopsose**, as in the form **cwusiopsose** 'please give us' used in prayers, consists of this element **-siop-** + an obsolete ending **-sose**, which sometimes drops and leaves just **cwusiop** (also **cwusiap**).

Parallel to the honorific marker there is an obsolete element with the shape **-sa(o)w-/-ow-**, which is described by Korean grammarians as "humble", but since the humility often seems to refer to the object or indirect object rather than the subject (**Ak ey se kwū haopsose** 'Deliver us from evil') it can be equivalent in force to the honorific. On the other hand, a derived version **-caow-** (abbreviation **-caw-**) or **-caow-/-cao-**, usually attached only to stems that end in **t c ch nc**, seems to have only the meaning 'I / we humbly do': **Tut.caopkentay ...** or **Tut.cao(wu)ni ...** 'From what has reached my humble ears, ... ', **Mut.caopkentay ...** or **Mut.cao(wu)ni ...** 'May I venture to ask ... '. This too is obsolete. About the only modern humble stem is **pōyw-** 'I have the honor of seeing', and we might say that this verb is the converse of **posi-** 'deign to look at' in that it elevates the status of the OBJECT (explicit or implied) rather than the SUBJECT: **Tto pōypkeyss.ˢup.nikka** 'I'll be (having the honor of) seeing you again' — and 'you', of course, are worthy of deference.

There are other devices to exalt the status of phrases in the expansion of the nuclear sentence. The indirect object can be exalted by using the honorific particle **kkey** 'to someone esteemed' in place of **eykey** or its synonyms such as **hanthey**, and to say 'from someone esteemed' you replace **eykey se** with **kkey se**. One way of exalting a personal subject is to turn it into an indirect subject with the particle sequence **ey se** 'from; at' — as in **hōysa ey se cwunta** 'the company gives it', the usual way to state an impersonal subject — but replacing the indirect-object particle **ey** with its honorific form **kkey**, as in **sensayng nim kkey se cwusip.nita** 'you deign to give it'. Another way to make any personal title honorific is to add the postnoun **nim**, as in **sensayng nim** 'the esteemed teacher / maestro / gentleman' (often 'you, sir'), **paksa nim** 'the esteemed Doctor', **samo nim** 'Madam', **Kim sensayng nim** 'the esteemed Mr Kim', **Kim sensayng (nim) samo nim** 'Madame Kim, Mrs Kim'. The postnoun is also used with kin terms, both male and female: **ape' nim** 'honored father' ← **apeci** 'father', **eme' nim** 'honored mother' ← **emeni** 'mother', **atu' nim** 'esteemed son' ← **atul** 'son', **tta' nim** 'esteemed daughter' ← **ttal** 'daughter', **hyeng nim** 'esteemed elder brother' ← **hyeng** 'elder brother' (also 'you' in a letter to a male colleague of any age). There are both honorific and humble terms for kinship roles. In general, the honorific version is used in addressing one's own elder kin and in speaking of someone else's kin of any age. Younger kin are usually addressed by name or nickname. In speaking of one's own kin, less honorific forms are in order, but honorifics are often heard even so, perhaps as a carryover from childhood inculcation, especially with reference to grandparents and parents.

11.3. Style conversions.

Koreans speak in different STYLES depending on the person with whom they are talking. The style chosen shows something about the social rapport which the speaker feels to exist between himself and the person he is addressing. The stylization of a sentence differs, of course, from the insertion of the honorific marker **-usi-/-si-**, in that the verbs containing the honorific show a special deference toward the SUBJECT of the verb form, and that subject may or may not be the same as the person to whom one is speaking. Honorific forms occur in ALL styles of speech. If you are talking to a child about his teacher, you might use the PLAIN style, but at the same time insert the honorific marker for each verb which has the teacher for a subject.

Each style is marked by the choice of the final verb expression in the sentence. Each of our three sentence types can be altered from the basic, plain-style forms by doing something to the inflected word (**Ponta; Cōh.ta; ··· ita**). The possible sentence-final types are realized through the finite-mood shifts of §11.5, where all of the shapes are presented. The full range possible for kinds of ending expression — statement, question, command, proposition, or apperception — is specifically marked only for the plain and formal styles. The other styles have certain gaps, and those are filled either by using a basic form (the statement) from the same style or by "borrowing" a form from some other style — in a sense, changing one's style in order to make certain types of sentences. A command, for example, is often made in a more polite style than a statement, even though both are said to the same person. The FORMS that correspond to the ending-expression types, which will be found in §11.5, differ for the three nuclear sentences in the different styles, and the command and proposition forms are lacking for adjectival and copular sentences in all styles, except that a form equivalent to the plain command is used to make adjectival exclamations such as **komawe la** 'heaven be praised!'. Statements can be made by using the assertive endings (for the polite, formal, semiformal, and familiar styles); the infinitive (for the intimate style); or the infinitive + particle **yo** (for the polite style). In the plain style, questions are sometimes asked by a nominal sentence that is made by adnominalizing the nuclear sentence and adding a postmodifier meaning 'question' as in **Ponun ya** 'Does (one) look at it?'.

There are six styles: plain, formal, semiformal (or authoritative), familiar, intimate, and polite. There is one additional style that is unspoken, the DOCUMENTARY, which typically uses the substantive to make a nominalization of the sentence (**Ponta → Pom; Cŏh.ta → Cŏh.um; Cip ita → Cip im**). After two-syllable verbal nouns **ham** 'does' is often omitted at the end of a documentary sentence, especially in newspaper headlines. Within the intimate and (+ the particle **yo**) the polite styles, there are two special types of sentence: the CASUAL, which uses the suspective **-ci** (**Ponta → Poci; Cŏh.ta → Cŏh.ci; Cip ita → Cip ici**); and the EXCLAMATORY, which uses an adnominalization (§11.9) + the postmodifier **tey** 'circumstance' to make a nominal sentence or, with **yo**, an adverbial sentence. We could treat these as two substyles of the intimate and polite. There are also three kinds of SUSPENDED sentences in the intimate and polite styles: the CIRCUMSTANTIAL type, made just like the exclamatory sentence (adnominalization + **tey**); the UNCERTAINTY type, consisting of an adnominalization + the postmodifier **ci**, an abbreviation of ⋯ **ci to molunta** 'maybe'; and the AFTERTHOUGHT type, an adverbialization (§11.10) with the gerund **-ko**.

We will summarize the uses of the various styles as follows:

1. PLAIN style (in Korean labeled **hāy-la**). Plain forms are used by adults to children, by children (and sometimes older friends of about the same age) among themselves. The forms are also found in impersonal writings and quotations, but in these cases, the questions and commands have special characteristics that set the substyle apart as QUOTATIVE PLAIN, further discussed in §11.11. The plain style is regarded as a sort of "basic" style for the purpose of giving grammatical examples, citing forms, and the like.

2. FORMAL style (in Korean labeled **contay** or **hasipsio**). The formal style is used when addressing someone toward whom a certain reserve is in order: a high official, a professor, one's employer, a famous person one does not know well, a foreigner, a doctor, a preacher, a scholar, ... The style is also common in certain set greetings, such as **Annyeng hasip.nikka?** 'How are you?', and other clichés even when the style of the rest of one's conversation may be more relaxed. (The greeting can actually be given in several styles. The polite **Annyeng has(y)ey yo?** is especially common, and to babies Koreans sometimes say **Cal iss.ni?** with the same meaning.) The formal style is mixed with the polite. You put most of your sentences in the polite, a few of them every now and then in the formal, somewhat the way some Americans insert "sir" or "ma'am" into every third or fourth sentence. Upon first meeting a stranger, it is good practice to begin in the formal style, especially if you are a foreigner, and then lapse into the polite style after the ice has thawed a bit. The polite style seems to be a Seoul development that has spread. In parts of Kyengsang and other areas you may notice the formal style being used for situations where the Seoul speaker would choose the polite style.

3. SEMIFORMAL style (in Korean labeled **hao**). The semiformal or authoritative style is used mostly by people in AUTHORITY in some situation, such as a policeman talking to a traffic offender, a man speaking to a personal servant or menial (who replies in formal or polite speech), or an older man

giving advice to a younger relative. There is a variant of this style in Seoul speech, **-swu** / **-wu** ← **-so** / **-o**, that is used to seniors, including servants, within the family circle. (To family juniors the intimate and plain forms are appropriate, and to friends the familiar style is used.) The semiformal style seems to be used less and less, and younger people regard it as old-fashioned. Roth (1936) says that **-so** / **-o** is often called the "middle" (= middlingly respectful) form, as contrasted with the high (respectful = formal, polite) and the low (plain). According to [1]Yi Hyosang (1991:154), who calls it the "formal lateral style", this style is "particularly preferred when there is a conflict among politeness factors: a husband speaking to his wife, a younger supervisor to an older supervisee, or a superior officer to an older inferior"; letters written in this style "are perceived as very stylish, literary, and courteous".

4. FAMILIAR style (in Korean labeled **hakey**). This is a friendly style somewhere between the intimate and the polite. It is widely used among adult male friends who are not quite close enough to use the intimate style, and less widely by (or to) women. In most cases of friendship that are like that shown by the male use of the familiar (or "buddy-buddy") style, women seem to use the polite style, but sometimes the intimate. There are indications that the familiar style, though still heard, is on the way out in the Seoul area. [1]Yi Hyosang (1991:156) says this style is "used only among grownups, e.g. by a senior addressing a grownup junior or between grownup social equals" and is "typically used by parents-in-law addressing their sons-in-law, or by a supervisor to a male supervisee", noting that it is "never used among biological family members". He also observes that this style is used in letters between male friends of about the same age who would usually use the **-e** or **-ta** styles in speaking to each other.

5. INTIMATE style (together with the polite labeled **pān-mal** in Korean). The intimate style, which is the polite style minus the particle **yo**, is the most common way adults who are close friends or relatives talk to one another. Often sentences in the plain style are freely mixed with those in the intimate, especially by younger people.

6. POLITE style (together with the intimate labeled **pān-mal** in Korean). The polite or "**-e yo**" style, which is the intimate + the particle **yo**, is perhaps the most widely heard way to end a sentence, and the most generally useful style for the foreigner. Adult Koreans who are not close friends or relatives use this style among themselves. Children use it in speaking to adults, who usually address them in the plain style. When a Korean approaches a stranger for information, he most often speaks in the polite style. If he felt sufficiently in awe of the stranger's appearance to find the formal style called for, he would probably hesitate to approach the person with his question.

11.3.1. Casual sentences.

The CASUAL sentence may be either intimate (**-ci**) or polite (**-ci yo**, often reduced to **-c[y]o**) and it has several uses which we can sum up in the tag translation 'suppose':

(1) A casual statement anticipating agreement. With the double question-mark intonation we get a meaning something like 'I suppose it is, isn't it; don't you agree with me; n'est-ce pas' as in **Kongwen ey kaci (yo)??** 'I suppose we are going to the park, aren't we.'

(2) A casual suggestion or proposition. With the period intonation or the double exclamation-point intonation there is often the meaning 'let's (us); I suggest that we; how about; suppose we' as in **Kongwen ey kaci (yo)!!** 'Suppose we go to the park!'

(3) A casual reminder question. Sometimes with either of the exclamation-point intonations the meaning is that of an accusing sort of reminder: 'Didn't you say ... ? But you said ... !', as in **Tekswu kwung ey to yūmyeng han pak.mul-kwan i iss.ta (ha)ci!!** 'Didn't you say there's a famous museum in Tekswu Palace too?'

(4) A casual informative statement. With the period intonation the casual style is often used to impart information. From the basic meaning of the morpheme **ci** 'uncertain fact', a flavor of uncertainty — largely feigned — colors the information given, and that has the effect of softening the statement much like English 'you know, I think, it seems to me, I guess, I suppose':

Poktong-i to kaci (yo). 'Poktong-i is going too, you know.'
Kuleh.key hamyen cōh.keyss.ci (yo). 'I guess that will do.'

Though you may make statements about yourself in this way, you seldom answer questions about yourself with casual statements, for it would seem evasive not be more definite with information about your own activities and intentions when directly queried on them.

(5) A casual command. With the period or the exclamation-point intonation, the casual style can be used as a soft command 'suppose you just ··· ':

Tāyhap-sil ey anc.e se kitalisici yo(!) 'Suppose you girls sit down and wait in the lounge'.

(6) A casual question. With the question-mark intonation, the casual style indicates a yes-or-no question 'I suppose that ··· ?':

Kongwen ey kaci (yo)? 'I suppose we're going to the park?'

Eti kaci (yo)? 'I suppose you're going somewhere?' — CF Eti ka (yo). or Eti kana yo. 'Where are you going?'

Questions which contain a content-interrogative (such as **mues** meaning 'what' rather than 'something') often seem too specific for such a casual inquiry; but they sometimes occur, with the period intonation:

Phullathuphom un meych pen ici yo. 'What (number) platform do you suppose it is?'

To sum up the uses of the casual -ci (yo) with the various intonations:

-ci yo.	(1) 'I suppose ··· '; 'I guess ··· '; ' ··· ; you know'
	(2) 'Suppose we ··· '; 'Let's (us) ··· '
	(3) 'Suppose you ··· '; 'Please ··· '; 'Do ··· , willya'
	(4) 'I suppose ··· ?'; 'Wh··· do you suppose ··· ?'
-ci yo?	(1) 'I suppose ··· ?'
-ci yo??	(2) 'I suppose ··· , don't you agree'; ' ··· n'est-ce pas'
-ci yo!!	(1) 'Suppose we ··· ', 'Let's (us) ··· '
	(2) 'But I thought ··· ', 'Didn't you say ··· ?!'

According to [1]Yi Hyosang (1991:454) the **-ci** forms are COMMITTAL: they "express the speaker's commitment to the truth of the information conveyed with varying degree of certainty", ranging from probable to certain. Apt translations for **-ci** statements include 'obviously', 'definitely', 'for sure', and 'of course', or 'you know' and 'you see', pointing to the obviousness of the information. "In interrogative contexts, the suffix expresses asking confirmation on information the speaker is committed to. In imperative or propositive contexts, the suffix expresses suggestion for an action which the speaker believes to be proper in a given context."

See also the entry **-pci yo** in Part II. Notice that **-ci yo** is usually reduced to a single syllable **-cyo** and pronounced /co/.

11.3.2. Exclamatory sentences.

Exclamatory sentences occur in the intimate and (+ **yo**) polite styles. They are made by adnominalization (§11.9) + the postmodifier **tey** 'circumstance' and the exclamation-point intonation, though sometimes the simple period intonation is used. When the suspensive or triple-dot intonation is heard the same expression is CIRCUMSTANTIAL, §11.3.3. The meaning is something like 'my what ··· !' or 'oh isn't it ··· ', and sometimes in English a final low-pitched 'though' (or an initial 'But') catches the feel of the Korean:

Chwuwun tey (yo)! 'Gee but it's cold!'
Cōh.un tey (yo)! 'How nice!'
Cōh.un kos in tey (yo)! 'But what a nice place!'
Phyen.li han tey (yo)! 'Isn't it convenient, though!'

Such expressions differ from the meaning of the apperceptive sentence (§11.5) primarily in the focus of emphasis. The apperceptive sentence stresses the suddenness of realization, or the novelty of the situation produced by the realization. The exclamatory sentence stresses the genuineness or intensity of the state described, much as the simple exclamation point does in English prose. When the exclamatory sentence is accompanied by the "??" intonation, as it occasionally is, it means about the same thing as the casual 'isn't it':

Nemu yātan sulen tey yo?? 'Isn't it too noisy, though?'

Exclamatory sentences are more often built on adjectival and copular sentences, but there are verbal examples, too:
> **Nwun ey ttuynun tey!** 'It's striking (to the eye)!'
> **Wuli sāchwun tul i ku hak.kyo ey tanyess.nun tey** 'Why, my cousins went to that school!'

A few adjectives can make exclamatory sentences by using the colloquial **-ulq si ko** and the literary **-un ci ko**; see the entries for those expressions in Part II.

11.3.3. Circumstantial sentences.

One type of suspended sentence is made with a modifier form + the postmodifier **tey** 'circumstance', usually accompanied by the suspensive or triple-dot intonation: **Ponta** → **Ponun tey** ... ; **Cōh.ta** → **Cōh.un tey** ... ; **Cip ita** → **Cip in tey** ... . The meaning is something like 'it is this way, so ... ', 'and uh ... ', 'but uh ... ', '(but) you know ... ', ' – you know? – '. A circumstance is mentioned with some unstated conclusion to be drawn from it, perhaps a conclusion one hesitates to put into words. For any such utterance, the speaker can always go ahead and supply the implied conclusion, and he may very well do so if prompted:
> Kim: **Cey ka onul pappun tey yo** ... 'I'm sorta busy today, you know, ... '
> Pak: **Kulay se yo** ... 'And so ... ?'
> Kim: **Sāmu sikan ey mōs okeyss.ey yo.** 'I won't be able to come for office hours'.

The circumstantial sentences are sometimes used to ask questions in the intimate and polite styles, as well as to make comments. Notice the difference of meaning that accompanies a difference in intonation when an indeterminate (a content-interrogative) is present:
> **Ce ke n' musun chayk in tey??** 'What sort of book is it(, anyway)?'
> **Ce ke n' musun chayk in tey!** 'Gee, I guess it must be some sort of book!'

Compare:
> **Ce ke n' musun chayk ia.** 'What sort of book is it?'
> **Ce ke n' musun chayk ia!** 'It must be some sort of book!'

Further examples:
> **Chima nun musun pich in tey??** 'What color is the skirt(, anyway)?'
> **Musun tāykwel kath.un tey??** 'Is it like some sort of palace?' – This could also be taken as a fragment, 'You mean the place [**tey** = **kos**] that looks like some sort of palace?'

11.3.4. Uncertainty sentences.

Sentences can be adnominalized (§11.9) and followed by the postmodifier **ci** + the particle **to**, as an expansion of the verbal sentence **Molunta** 'I don't know' to express the meaning 'perhaps, maybe'.
> **Ponta.** → **Ponun ci to molunta.** 'Maybe someone is looking at it.'
> **Cōh.ta.** → **Cōh.un ci to molunta.** 'Maybe it is good.'
> **Cip ita.** → **Cip in ci to molunta.** 'Maybe it is a house.'

These sentences can then be abbreviated by dropping **to molunta**, and the result is an UNCERTAINTY sentence in the intimate or (+ **yo**) polite styles, usually accompanied by the period intonation:
> **Cip ey iss.nun ci (yo).** 'Maybe she is at home.'
> **Kuleh.key hamyen cōh.keyss.nun ci (yo).** 'Maybe we should do it that way.'
> **Tol.a wass.nun ci (yo).** 'Perhaps he's back.'

11.3.5. Afterthought sentences.

Afterthought sentences are made in the intimate and (+ **yo**) polite styles by an adverbialization (§11.10) with the gerund **-ko**, which is commonly pronounced **-kwu**, especially before **yo** in this colloquial structure. According to Pak Sengwen (108-9) the sentence-final gerund can be used either to express an afterthought, as here described, or in answer to a question. Ordinarily the gerund does not occur at the end of a sentence, but it can be used to finalize a kind of afterthought in much the same way that an English sentence sometimes begins with 'And also, ... ':
> **Phyo nun eti se sa yo. Tto kaps un elma 'ko yo.** 'Where do we buy tickets? And how much are they?'

I kes un mues iko, ce kes un mues in ka yo. – **I kes un tangsin uy moca 'ko, ce kes un tangsin uy chayk iko yo.** 'What is this, and what is that? – This is your hat, and that is your book.'

Pipimq pap un ili cwusey yo. – ¹**Nāyngmyen un ili cwusiko yo.** 'Serve the mixed rice here. – And the chilled noodles, here.'

Ka (se) cwumusey yo; na ttaymun ey caci anh.ko kitalici māsiko yo. 'Go off to bed; don't wait up for me.'

There are many other ways of stating an impromptu afterthought, of course, including common inversions such as **Pappi kwūlci mala, sikan i nek.nek hani** 'Don't rush, (for) there's plenty of time'. The use of a syntactic inversion that puts the subject or object at the end, after the verb, is an effective stylistic device in poetry, popular both in Korea and in Japan.

A special use of afterthought structure is seen in the expressions **-ko mālko (yo)!** 'of course ···!': **Ponta → Poko** (§11.10) → **Poko mālko (yo)!** or **Pokwu mālkwu (yo)!** 'Of course I'm looking at it!'.

11.4. Tense-aspect conversions.

We have referred (§9.1) to two tense markers (**-ess-** past, **-keyss-** future), and to five aspect markers: indicative and subjunctive (which combine with the assertive and attentive moods to form some of the endings treated as mood conversions in §11.5), retrospective (**-tu-**, ...), prospective (**-ul-**, ...), and processive (**-n-**, **-nun-**, ...). But by tense-aspect conversions we do not refer directly to the specific morphemes that go to make up what we are calling the verb-final "moods", but rather to categories of sentence relationship such that our nuclear sentences can be transformed in these ways:

(1) Present → Past. **Ponta** → **Pwass.ta** 'I looked at it'; **Cōh.ta** → **Cōh.ass.ta** 'It was good'; **Cip ita** → **Cip iess.ta** 'It was a house'.

(2) Past → Past-Past. (**Ponta** →) **Pwass.ta** → **Pwass.ess.ta** 'I looked at it (but I have forgotten what it looked like)'; (**Cōh.ta** →) **Cōh.ass.ta** → **Cōh.ass.ess.ta** 'It was good (and then something went wrong)'; (**Cip ita** →) **Cip iess.ta** → **Cip iess.ess.ta** 'It was a house (or so I thought, but later it turned out to be something else)'. It is difficult to set up situations adequate to call for the past-past without a bit of artificiality, and the verbs of going and coming seem to work best: **Onta** 'He comes' → **Wass.ta** 'He has come = He is here' → **Wass.ess.ta** 'He came (but left) = He was here'; **Kanta** 'He goes' → **Kass.ta** 'He has gone = He is away' → **Kass.ess.ta** 'He went (but came back) = He is back'. Other situations are set up with verbs that imply a result likely to be reversed or changed such as eating (and getting full but later feeling hunger again), borrowing (but later repaying), getting tired (but renewing one's energy with rest), getting cloudy (but then clearing up later), ...

(3) Present → Future. **Ponta** → **Pokeyss.ta** 'I will look at it' (or, below, 'He probably looks at it'); **Cōh.ta** → **Cōh.keyss.ta** 'It will be good' (or 'It probably is good'); **Cip ita** → **Cip ikeyss.ta** 'It will be a house' (or 'It probably is a house').

(4) Present → Tentative. Same as (3); often preceded by **ama** 'likely'.

(5) Future → Future tentative. (**Ponta** →) **Pokeyss.ta** → **Polq kes ita** (abbreviation **Polq ke yta** or more often **Polq ke 'ta**); (**Cōh.ta** →) **Cōh.keyss.ta** → **Cōh.ulq kes ita** 'It will probably be good'.

(6) Past → Past Future. (**Ponta** →) **Pwass.ta** → **Pwass.keyss.ta** 'I will have looked at it' (or, below, 'He probably looked at it'); (**Cōh.ta** →) **Cōh.ass.ta** → **Cōh.ass.keyss.ta** 'It will have been good' (or, below – and more likely, 'It must have been good'); (**Cip ita** →) **Cip iess.ta** → **Cip iess.keyss.ta** 'It will have been a house' (or – and more likely, 'It probably was a house').

(7) Past → Past Tentative. Same as (6); often preceded by **ama** 'likely'.

(8) Past-Past → Past-Past Future. (**Ponta** → **Pwass.ta** → **Pwass.ess.ta** →) **Pwass.ess.keyss.ta** 'I will have looked at it (but will have forgotten it)' (or, below, 'He probably looked at it – but forgot what it looked like'); (**Cōh.ta** → **Cōh.ass.ta** →) **Cōh.ass.ess.ta** → **Cōh.ass.ess.keyss.ta** 'It will have been good (but then something will have gone wrong)' (or, below and more likely, 'It probably was good – but then something went wrong'); (**Cip ita** → **Cip iess.ta**) → **Cip iess.ess.ta** → **Cip iess.ess.keyss.ta** 'It will have been a house (but then will have turned into something else)' (or – and more likely, 'It probably was a house – but then turned into something else').

(9) Past-Past → Past-Past Tentative. Same as (8); often preceded by **ama** 'likely'.
(10) Present → Retrospective. **Ponta** → **Potula** '(When observed) he was looking at it'; **Cōh.ta** → **Cōh.tula** '(According to my observations) it was good, it was found to be good'; **Cip ita** → **Cip itula** '(I noticed) it was a house'. The one who did the observing must be the speaker of the statement.
(11) Past → Past Retrospective. (**Ponta** →) **Pwass.ta** → **Pwass.tula** 'I found that he had been looking at it'; (**Cōh.ta** →) **Cōh.ass.ta** → **Cōh.ass.tula** 'I noticed it had once been good'; **Cip ita** → **Cip iess.ta** → **Cip iess.tula** 'I remembered that it had been a house'.
(12) Past-Past → Past-Past Retrospective. (**Ponta** →) **Pwass.ta** → **Pwass.ess.ta** → **Pwass.ess.tula**; .... The forms are rare in speech; when written they are sometimes used just as emphatic forms of (11).
(13) Past Future → Past Future Retrospective. (**Ponta** → **Pwass.ta** →) **Pwass.keyss.ta** → **Pwass.keyss.tula** '(From what I observed) he will have looked at it' or 'He likely looked at it'; ... . Not too common; see the entry **-ess.keyss.tula** in Part II.

The meanings of present, past, and future conversions are sometimes at variance with what the label seems to call for; see the entries **-keyss.ta** and **-ess-** in Part II. Examples given by CM 1:316-7 show the present used for (1) permanent or habitual; (2) future, especially definite expectation with verbs of departure and arrival; (3) historical present; (4) command-like instructions, such as recipes or stage directions; (5) citing a series of actions. For more on the retrospective, see p. 325.

Korean resembles English rather than Japanese in expressions of the type **acik an / mōs V-ess.ta** 'has not yet V-ed'. In Japanese the nonpast negative will appear in such sentences (ma'da sinai).

11.5. Mood conversions.

In speaking of mood conversions we use the term "mood" in a somewhat narrower sense than before, to refer to the finite moods. Specifically, we treat the STATEMENT as basic and regard each of the other moods – question, command, proposition, and apperception – as a conversion from that. Because of the complexities of form taken in the various styles (§11.3), I have prepared a table to display the forms used for each category and it includes also the retrospective forms (§11.4) because of their interrelated complexities. In the table an arrow pointing up means "use the simple statement form, perhaps with a different intonation". An arrow pointing to the left means "use a form from a less polite style", one pointing to the right means "use a form from a more polite style". An arrow pointing both left and right means "use either a less or a more polite style". The difference between the styles is not entirely a gradation of politeness as such, to be sure, but for the purposes of this table we will so consider it. Some categories offer several possibilities, for which there is generally a slight difference in usage; the options are cited here in the order of the relative frequency with which they are chosen. The table on p. 306 summarizes the facts that are discussed in detail, style by style, in later sections. In the table **(-)kwun** represents also **(-)kwumen** and **kulye** represents also **kwulye**.

There are several colloquial and dialect forms that do not appear in the table, such as **-(su)pci yo**, **-(u)psey**, **-la kwu**, **-ca kwu**, ... They will be found as individual entries in Part II.

11.5.1. The plain style.

PLAIN STYLE: Statement.
The indicative assertive **-ta** is attached to adjectives, to the copula, to **iss-** and **ēps-**, and to all cases of the tense markers **-ess-** and **-keyss-** (regardless of what kind of stem they may be attached to): **Cōh.ta** 'It's good'; **Nay kes ita** 'It's mine'; **Cip i iss.ta** 'I have a home', **Tōn i ēps.ta** 'I have no money'; **Pwass.ta** 'I looked at it'; **Pokeyss.ta** 'I will look at it'. But verbs attach the PROCESSIVE assertive **-nunta / -nta**: **Ponta** 'He looks at it'. The copula has a special alternant when used in quotative constructions (§11.11): instead of **ita / 'ta** we hear **ila / 'la** in **Cip ila ko hayss.ta** 'They said it's a house', **Pusan ila 'nun tosi** 'the city called (= of) Pusan', and **na 'la to** 'even though / if it be me'.

PLAIN STYLE: Question.
(1) The indicative attentive, in the form of the one-shape ending **-ni**, is attached to any stem: **Cōh.ni?** (/cōnni/) 'Is it good?'; **Cip ini?** 'Is it a house?'; **Poni?** 'Do you see it?'; **Pwass.ni?** 'Did you see it?'; **Iss.keyss.ni?** 'Will there be any?' Do not confuse this with the two-shape ending called the sequential,

Mood shift table

	PLAIN	FAMILIAR	INTIMATE	CASUAL	CAS.POL.	SEMIFORM.	POLITE	FORMAL
STATE-MENT	-ta, i-la -nunta	-ney	-e	-ci	-ci yo	-so	-e(y) yo	-sup.nita
QUESTION	-ni -n(un) ya -nun ka, ... -nun -un ka	-na	← ↑ -nun tey	-ci 'ni	← ↑	↑	-un ka yo -na yo	-sup.nikka
APPER-CEPTION	-kwun -nun kwun	← -ney kulye	←	←	→	← →	-kwun yo -nun kwun yo	-sup.nita kulye
RETRO. STATE-MENT	-tula	-tey, ?i-ley	←	←	→	→	-tey yo -tun tey yo -tula ko yo	-suptita
RETRO. QUES-TION	-tun ya -tun	-ti	←	←	←	← →	-tey yo -tun ka yo	-suptikka
RETRO. APPER-CEPTION	-tukwun	←	←	←	→	← →	-tukwun yo, -tun kwun yo	-suptita kulye
SUGGES-TION	-ca	-sey	-ulq ka -ulye	←	↑ →	← ↑ →	-ulq ka yo	-upsita
COMMAND (quoted)	-e la, ... -ula	-key (na)	← ↑	↑	↑ →	← ↑ →		-usio, ...

-uni / -ni. The forms are alike after a vowel, so that **poni** ⋯ can mean 'since you see it', but they contrast after a consonant: **Mek.ni?** 'Does he eat?', **mek.uni** ⋯ 'since he eats'; **Pwass.ni?** 'Did you see it?', **pwass.uni** ⋯ 'since you saw it'; **Pokeyss.ni?** 'Will we look at it?', **pokeyss.uni** ⋯ 'since we will look at it'. However, [1]Yi Tongcay tells me that older Seoul speakers prefer **-un i** for consonant-final adjective stems: **Cōh.un i?** /cō(u)ni/ 'Is it good?', **Cak.un i?** 'Is it little?' (instead of **Cāk.ni?** /cāngni/).

(2) Processive verbs, **iss-** and **ēps-**, **-ess-** and **-keyss-** (attached to any stem) may use the PROCESSIVE MODIFIER **-nun** + the postmodifier **ya**: **Ponun ya?** 'Are you looking at it?'; **Pwass.nun ya?** 'Did you see it?'; **Pokeyss.nun ya?** 'Will we see it?'; **Cōh.ass.nun ya?** 'Was it good?'; **Cōh.keyss.nun ya?** 'Will it be good?'; **Iss.nun ya?** 'Is there any?' The postmodifier is sometimes pronounced **i** or **a** (**Ponun i? Ponun a?**), and the processive modifier **-nun** is sometimes abbreviated to **-n'**, so that you will hear **Pon' ya**, **Pwass.n' ya**; **Pokeyss.n' ya?**; **Iss.n' ya?** The forms like **Poni?** in (1) above may very well be simply **Pon' i?** ← **Ponun i?** = **Ponun ya?** You may also hear **Ponun ya?** as **Ponun a?** and **Pon' a?**

(3) A modifier form + the postmodifier **ka** is a structure attached mostly to adjectives and the copula, but occasionally to verbs, too: **Cōh.un ka?** 'Is it good?'; **Cōh.ulq ka?** 'Will it be good?'; **Cip in ka?** 'Is it a house?'; **Ponun ka?** = **Ponun ya?** 'Do you see it?' CF **Polq ka?** 'Shall we look at it?' = 'Let's look at it!' (FAMILIAR suggestion).

(4) The same as (2) but with the postmodifier **ya** omitted: **Ponun?** 'Do you see it?'; **Pwass.nun?** 'Did you see it?'; **Pokeyss.nun?** 'Will we see it?'; ... . This usage seems largely confined to the dialect of Phyengan province, where **-kān** is also used for **-keyss.nun (ya)**.

How do we choose among these several patterns? Follow the most common practice (leaving aside for the moment quotations, §11.11):
Use **-ni** for verbs, **iss-**, **ēps-**, **-ess-**, and **-keyss-**.
Use **-un ka** or **-ni** for adjectives and the copula.

PLAIN STYLE: Apperception.

The apperceptive endings **-kwun (a)**, **kwumen**, **-kwulye** are attached to adjectives, to **iss-** and **ēps-**, and to **-ess-** and **-keyss-**, as in: **Cōh.kwun!** (or **Cōh.kwun a!** or **Cōh.kwumen!** or **Cōh.kwulye!**) 'Oh, it's nice!'; **Iss.kwumen!** 'So there is some!'; **Ēps.kwulye!** 'Why, there isn't any!'; **Pwass.kwun a!** 'Why, they've seen it!'; **Pokeyss.kwun a!** 'We're going to see it!' But verb stems use the processive modifier + the apperceptive postmodifier **kwun** (**kwun a**, **kwumen**, **kwulye**), as in **Ponun kwun (a)!** 'Why, you're looking at it!'. And the copula stem is often replaced by a variant **ilo-**: **Cip ilokwun a!** or **Cip ikwun a!** 'Why, it's a house!' [1]Yi Hyosang 1991 says these forms represent sudden perception of unassimilated information or evidence, said to express oneself rather than inform the listener.

PLAIN STYLE: Retrospective statement.

The retrospective assertive **-tula** attaches to any stem: **Potula** 'He was looking at it (I noticed)'. CF §11.4.

PLAIN STYLE: Retrospective question.

(1) The retrospective modifier **-tun** + the postmodifier **ya**, as in **Potun ya?** '(Did you notice) was he looking at it?' and **Pwass.tun ya?** '(Could you tell) had he been looking at it?'

(2) The same construction omitting the **ya**: **Potun? Pwass.tun?** Largely confined to Phyengan.

PLAIN STYLE: Retrospective apperception.

The retrospective apperceptive **-tu-kwun** (**-tu-kwun a**, **-tu-kwumen**, **-tu-kwulye**) attaches to any stem; or, you can use the full form from which that is probably abbreviated, the retrospective modifier + the postmodifier **kwun** (**kwun a**) and variants **kwumen** and **kwulye**: **Potun kwun** = **Potukwun** 'Why, I see he's been (found to be) looking at it!'

PLAIN STYLE: Suggestion or proposition.

The subjunctive assertive **-ca** is used to express the meaning 'let's do it': **Poca** 'Let's look at it!'. The mood does not occur for adjective, copula, **-ess-** or **-keyss-**; nor for **ēps-**, but **iss-** can make a proposition in one of its meanings, **Iss.ca** 'Let's stay!' (The negative is **Iss.ci mālca** 'Let's not stay!')

PLAIN STYLE: Command.

When final in an unquoted verbal sentence, a command is expressed with the infinitive **-e** + the particle **la**, as in **Pwā la!** 'Look at it!' (Certain verbs have an alternant infinitive form in this construction; see §8.3.6.) The formally corresponding conversion of an adjectival sentence produces an exclamation: **Cōh.a la!** 'How nice!' In a quoted sentence (§11.11) the command is expressed by the subjunctive attentive **-ula / -la** as in **Pola ko hayss.ta** 'He told me to look'.

11.5.2. The familiar style.

FAMILIAR STYLE: Statement.

The familiar indicative assertive form **-ney** is used: **Poney** 'I see it'; **Pwass.ney** 'I saw it'; **Pokeyss.ney** 'I will look at it'; **Cōh.ney** /cōnney/ 'It is good'; **Cip iney** 'It is a house'. But adjectives and the copula often take the prospective modifier **-ul(q)** + the postmodifier **sey**, instead: **Cōh.ulq sey** 'It's good!'; **Cip ilq sey** 'It's a house'.

FAMILIAR STYLE: Question.

The familiar indicative attentive form **-na** is used: **Pona?** 'Do you see it?'; **Pwass.na?** 'Did you see it?'; **Cip ina?** 'Is it a house?'; **Cōh.na?** /cōnna/ 'Is it good?' — CF. the /cōna/ variant of **Cōh.un a?** = **Cōh.un ya?** (PLAIN style) and of **cōh.una** 'is good but'.

FAMILIAR STYLE: Apperception.

Shift to the plain style. But some people will add the particle **k(w)ulye** after **-ney**.

FAMILIAR STYLE: Retrospective statement.

The familiar retrospective assertive **-tey** attaches to a verb or adjective: **Potey** '(I noticed) he was looking at it'; **Cōh.tey** 'I found it was nice'. The copula form is **itey** or **?iley** (presumably a lenition from **itey**, CF **ila** for the copula **ita** in a quotation): **Cip itey** 'I noticed it was a house'. Do not confuse this with **-ta 'y** = **-ta hay** and ⋯ **ila 'y** = ⋯ **ila hay**; see entries in Part II.

FAMILIAR STYLE: Retrospective question.

The familiar retrospective assertive **-ti** attaches to any stem: **Poti?** '(Did you notice) was he looking at it?'; **Cōh.ti?** 'Did you find it nice?'; **Cip iti?** '(Could you tell,) was it a house?'

FAMILIAR STYLE: Retrospective apperception.

Shift to plain style.

FAMILIAR STYLE: Suggestion or proposition.

The familiar subjunctive assertive **-sey** is attached to a verb: **Posey** 'Let's look at it'.

FAMILIAR STYLE: Command.

The adverbative **-key** 'so that it be/do ⋯ ' is attached to a verb, and may be followed by the particle **una / na** to soften the effect: **Pokey (na)!** 'Look at it! (Have a look!)'

11.5.3. The intimate style.

INTIMATE STYLE: Statement.

The infinitive **-e** attaches to any stem: **Pwā** 'I see it'; **Pwass.e** 'I saw it'; **Pokeyss.e** 'I'll look at it'; **Cōh.a** 'It's good'. The copula infinitive **ie** is often pronounced **ia** (and misspelled **iya**) with the shortened form **ya** after a vowel and in fast speech sometimes even after a consonant: **Cip ia** 'It's a house'; **Na ya** 'It's me'. Ending a statement the infinitive ending **-e** is sometimes pronounced **-ey** after **-(u)si-**, **iss-**, **ēps-**, **-ess-**, **-keyss-**, and **kath-**, especially in the speech of women. (CF §9.4.)

INTIMATE STYLE: Question.

(1) Use the statement form with the appropriate intonation: **Pwā?** 'Do you see it?'; **Cōh.a?** 'Is it nice?'; **Cip ia (ie)?** 'Is it a house?'; **Pwass.e?** (or **Pwass.ey?**) 'Did you see it?'; **Pokeyss.e?** (or **Pokeyss.ey?**) 'Will we see it?'

(2) Shift to the familiar or plain styles.

(3) For verbal sentences, **iss-** and **ēps-**, **-ess-** and **-keyss-**, you can use the processive modifier **-nun** + the postmodifier **tey**: **Ponun tey?** 'Do you see it?'; **Pwass.nun tey?** 'Did you see it?'; **Pokeyss.nun tey?** 'Will we see it?' Sometimes, too, the modifier **-un** + **tey** can be used for adjectival and copular sentences: **Chima nun musun pich in tey** 'What color's the skirt?'; **Musun tāykwel kath.un tey?** 'Isn't it like some sort of palace?'

INTIMATE STYLE: Apperception. Shift to plain style.

INTIMATE STYLE: Retrospective statement. Shift to familiar or plain style.

INTIMATE STYLE: Retrospective question. Shift to plain style.

INTIMATE STYLE: Retrospective apperception. Shift to plain style.

INTIMATE STYLE: Suggestion or proposition.

(1) The prospective modifier **-ul(q)** + the postmodifier **ka**, often with the lively "??" intonation: **Polq ka?(?)** 'Shall we have a look?'

(2) Shift to familiar or plain style.

(3) Use the Statement form (the infinitive) with the appropriate intonation: **Pwā!** 'Let's look!'

(4) [old-fashioned, literary] Use the intentive **-ulye / -lye**: **Polye** 'Let's have a look at it'; **Com te mek.ulye** 'I'd like us to eat a little more'; **Cikum halye** 'Let's do it now'. CF the cajolative **-ulyem / -lyem** (§9.7.1). In northern dialects the intentive is often pronounced **-uley / -ley**; do not confuse that with a vowel-raised variant of **-ula / -la 'y** as in **Na com poley** (= **pola 'y)!** 'Look at me!'

INTIMATE STYLE: Command.

(1) Shift to familiar or plain style.

(2) Use the Statement form (the infinitive) with the appropriate intonation: **Pwā!** 'Look!'

11.5.4. The casual intimate style.

CASUAL INTIMATE STYLE: Statement.

The suspective **-ci** attaches to any stem: **Poci** 'I see it'; **Pwass.ci** 'I saw it'; **Pokeyss.ci** 'I think I'll see it'; **Cōh.ci** 'I think it's nice'; **Cip ici** 'It is a house, you see'.

CASUAL INTIMATE STYLE: Question.
(1) Follow the suspective with the indicative attentive of the copula **ini**/**'ni**: **Poci 'ni?** 'Do you suppose he sees it?'; **Pwass.ci 'ni?** 'Do you suppose he saw it?'; **Pokeyss.ci 'ni?** 'Do you suppose we'll see it?' (This seems to be a dialect usage. See p. 458.)
(2) Use the Statement form with the appropriate intonation: **Poci?(?)**; **Pwass.ci?**; **Pokeyss.ci?**; **Cōh.ci?**; **Cip ici?**
(3) Shift to plain style.
CASUAL INTIMATE STYLE: Apperception. Shift to plain style.
CASUAL INTIMATE STYLE: Retrospective statement. Shift to familiar or plain style.
CASUAL INTIMATE STYLE: Retrospective question. Shift to plain style.
CASUAL INTIMATE STYLE: Retrospective apperception. Shift to plain style.
CASUAL INTIMATE STYLE: Suggestion or proposition.
(1) Use the Statement form, usually with the "!" or "!!" intonation, but sometimes just the ".": **Poci!(!)** 'Suppose we have a look at it!'
(2) Shift to intimate, familiar, or plain style.
CASUAL INTIMATE STYLE: Command.
(1) Use the Statement form, with "!" or "." intonation: **Poci!** 'Suppose you look at it'.
(2) Shift to intimate, familiar, or plain style.

11.5.5. The casual polite style.
CASUAL POLITE STYLE: Statement.
This is the same as the casual intimate with the addition of the particle **yo** after the suspective **-ci**, and the resulting **-ci yo** is often shortened in pronunciation to **-c[y]o**: **Poci yo = Poc[y]o**; **Pwass.ci yo = Pwass.c[y]o**; **Pokeyss.ci yo = Pokeyss.c[y]o**; **Cōh.ci yo = Cōh.c[y]o /cōcho/**; **Cip ici yo = Cip ic[y]o**.
CASUAL POLITE STYLE: Question.
(1) Use the Statement form with the appropriate intonation: **Poci yo?(?) = Poc[y]o**; **Pwass.ci yo? = Pwass.c[y]o?**; **Pokeyss.ci? = Pokeyss.c[y]o**; **Cōh.ci yo? = Cōh.keyss.c[y]o?**; **Cip ici yo? = Cip ic[y]o?**
(2) Shift to plain style.
CASUAL POLITE STYLE: Apperception. Shift to polite style.
CASUAL POLITE STYLE: Retrospective statement. Shift to polite or formal style.
CASUAL POLITE STYLE: Retrospective question. Shift to polite or formal style.
CASUAL POLITE STYLE: Retrospective apperception. Shift to polite style.
CASUAL POLITE STYLE: Suggestion or proposition.
(1) Use the Statement form, usually with the "!" or "!!" intonation, but sometimes just the ".": **Poci yo!(!) = Poc[y]o!(!)** 'Suppose we have a look!'
(2) Shift to polite or formal style.
CASUAL POLITE STYLE: Command.
(1) Use the Statement form, with "!" or "." intonation: **Poci yo!** 'Suppose you look at it'.
(2) Shift to polite or formal style.

11.5.6. The semiformal (authoritative) style.
SEMIFORMAL (AUTHORITATIVE) STYLE: Statement.
The semiformal indicative assertive **-so/-o** (dialect **-uo/-o**) attaches to any stem: **Poo** 'I see it'; **Pwass.^{s}o** 'I saw it'; **Pokeyss.^{s}o** 'I will see it'; **Cōh.so** 'It is good'; **Cip io** 'It is a house' — CF two other utterances that sound identical: the polite fragment **Cip iyo** 'A house.' and the variant polite copular sentence **Cip i yo = Cip (y)ey yo = Cip iey yo** 'It is a house'.
For adjective stems there is a variant **-ui**/**-i**, as in **Cōh.ui = Cōh.so** 'It is good' and **Chai = Chao** 'It is cold to touch' (← **Chata**). CF LHS 2266b, 2289a.

SEMIFORMAL (AUTHORITATIVE) STYLE: Question.
Use the Statement form, with the appropriate intonation: **Poo?** 'Do you see it?'; **Pwass.ˢo?** 'Did you see it?'; **Pokeyss.ˢo?** 'Will we see it?'; **Cōh.so?** or **Cōh.ui?** 'Is it good?'; **Cip io?** 'Is it a house?'
SEMIFORMAL (AUTHORITATIVE) STYLE: Apperception. Shift to plain or polite style.
SEMIFORMAL (AUTHORITATIVE) STYLE: Retrospective statement. Shift to plain or polite style.
SEMIFORMAL (AUTHORITATIVE) STYLE: Retrospective question. Shift to plain or polite style.
SEMIFORMAL (AUTHORITATIVE) STYLE: Retrospective apperception. Shift to plain or polite style.
SEMIFORMAL (AUTHORITATIVE) STYLE: Suggestion or proposition.
(1) Use the Statement form with the appropriate intonation: **Poo!** 'Let's have a look at it!'
(2) Shift to familiar or plain style.
SEMIFORMAL (AUTHORITATIVE) STYLE: Command.
(1) Use the Statement form with an appropriate intonation: **Poo!** 'Look at it!'
(2) Shift to familiar or plain style.

11.5.7. The polite style.
POLITE STYLE: Statement.
The infinitive **-e** + the particle **yo** attaches to any stem: **Pwā yo** 'I see it'; **Pwass.e(y) yo** 'I saw it'; **Pokeyss.e(y) yo** 'I will see it'; **Cōh.a yo** 'It is good'; **Cip ie(y) yo** 'It is a house'. The copula is often shortened to **ye(y) yo**, which usually sounds like **ey yo** (§4.3): **Cip (y)ey yo** 'It is a house'. The mid vowel is sometimes raised to high: **Cip i yo** = **Cip (y)ey yo**. CF **Cip io** 'It is a house' [semiformal], **Cip iyo** 'A house' [polite fragment]. All three sound alike: /**cipi(y)o**/.
POLITE STYLE: Question.
(1) Use the Statement form with the appropriate intonation: **Pwā yo?** 'Does he see it?'; **Pwass.e(y) yo?** 'Did he see it?'; **Pokess.e(y) yo?** 'Will we see it?'; **Cōh.a yo?** 'Is it good?'; **Cip ie(y) yo?** or **Cip (y)ey yo?** or **Cip i yo?** 'Is it a house?'
(2) The familiar indicative attentive **-na** + the particle **yo** attaches to any stem: **Pona yo?** 'Does he see it?'; **Pwass.na yo?** 'Did he see it?'; **Pokeyss.na yo?** 'Will we see it?'; **Iss.na yo?** 'Is there any?'; **Ēps.na yo?** 'Isn't there any?' This is more common with verbal sentences, including **Iss.ta** and **Ēps.ta**, but it is also heard with adjectives when they are past or future (**Cōh.ass.na yo?** 'Was it good?'; **Cōh.keyss.na yo?** 'Will it be good?'), and sometimes when they are in the present tense: **Cōh.na yo?** 'Is it good?'
(3) A modifier + the postmodifier **ka** + the particle **yo** will attach to any stem, and is common with present-tense adjectival and copular sentences (**Cōh.un ka yo?** 'Is it good?'; **Cip in ka yo?** 'Is it a house?'), but it occasionally occurs also with past, future, and verbal sentences.
As a rule of thumb: use **-na yo** with a verb stem, the past **-ess-** or future **-keyss-**, **iss-** and **ēps-**; and use **-un ka yo** with an adjective stem or the copula.
POLITE STYLE: Apperception.
(1) Adjective stems, **iss-** and **ēps-**, **-ess-** and **-keyss-**, attach the apperceptive ending **-kwun** (or **-kwumen**) + the particle **yo**: **Cōh.kwu(me)n yo!** 'Oh, it's nice!'; **Iss.kwu(me)n yo!** 'Why, so there is!'; **Ēps.kwu(me)n yo!** 'But there aren't any (of them)!'; **Pwass.kwu(me)n yo!** 'Oh, he's seen it!'; **Pokeyss.kwu(me)n yo!** 'Why, we'll see it!'
(2) Verb stems attach the processive modifier **-nun** + the postmodifier **kwu(me)n** + the particle **yo**: **Ponun kwu(me)n yo!** 'Oh, he sees it!'
POLITE STYLE: Retrospective statement.
(1) Use intimate (**-tey**) + the particle **yo** = **-tey yo**.
(2) Use polite retrospective apperceptive or polite retrospective circumstantial (**-tun tey yo**).
(3) Use plain retrospective statement + **ko yo** = **-tula ko yo**.
POLITE STYLE: Retrospective question.
(1) The retrospective modifier **-tun** + the postmodifier **ka** + the particle **yo** attached to any stem: **Potun ka yo?** 'Were they looking at it?'; **Pwass.tun ka yo?** 'Had they been looking at it (or could you tell)?'

(2) Shift to the formal style.
POLITE STYLE: Retrospective apperceptive.
(1) The retrospective apperceptive ending **-tukwu(me)n** + the particle **yo** attaches to any stem: **Potukwu(me)n yo!** 'Why, I see he's been looking at it!'. This seems to be a contraction of the next option.
(2) The retrospective modifier **-tun** + the postmodifier **kwu(me)n** + the particle **yo** attaches to any stem: **Potun kwu(me)n yo!** 'Why, I see he's been looking at it!'.
POLITE STYLE: Suggestion or proposition.
(1) The prospective modifier **-ul(q)** + the postmodifier **ka** + the particle **yo** with "??" intonation: **Polq ka yo??** 'Shall we look at it?'
(2) Use the Statement form, with "!" or "." intonation: **Pwā yo!** 'Let's look at it!'
(3) Shift to the formal style.
POLITE STYLE: Command.
(1) Shift to the formal style.
(2) Use the Statement form, with "!" or "." intonation: **Pwā yo!** 'Look at it!'

11.5.8. The formal style.

FORMAL STYLE: Statement.
All stems attach the formal indicative assertive **-sup.nita / -p.nita** (with the dialect or spelling variant **-up.nita** after a consonant): **Pop.nita** 'I see it'; **Pwass.ˢup.nita** 'I saw it'; **Pokeyss.ˢup.nita** 'We will see it'; **Meksup.nita** (dialect **Mek.up.nita**) 'I eat it'; **Cōh.sup.nita** (dialect **Cōh.up.nita**) 'It is good'; **Cip ip.nita** 'It is a house'.

FORMAL STYLE: Question.
All stems attach the formal indicative attentive **-sup.nikka / -p.nikka** (with the dialect or spelling variant **-up.nikka** after a consonant): **Pop.nikka** 'Does he see it?'; **Pwass.ˢup.nikka** 'Did he see it?'; **Pokeyss.ˢup.nikka** 'Will we see it?'; **Meksup.nikka** (dialect **Mek.up.nikka**) 'Does he eat it?'; **Cōh.sup.nikka** (dialect **Cōh.up.nikka**) 'Is it good?'; **Cip ip.nikka** 'Is it a house?'.

FORMAL STYLE: Apperception.
(1) Shift to the polite style.
(2) All stems attach the formal indicative assertive **-sup.nita / -p.nita** (with the dialect or spelling variant **-up.nita** after a consonant) + the particle **kwulye** (usually, however, pronounced **kulye**): **Pop.nita k(w)ulye!** 'Oh, I see he's looking at it'.

FORMAL STYLE: Retrospective statement.
All stems attach the formal retrospective assertive ending **-suptita / -ptita** (with the dialect or spelling variant **-uptita** after a consonant): **Poptita** '(I noticed) he was looking at it'; **Cōh.suptita** (dialect **Cōh.uptita**) 'I found it nice'; **Cip iptita** '(I recall) it was a house'.

This form is little used in Seoul; people prefer the polite apperceptive **-tu-ku(me)n yo** or circumstantial **-tun tey yo**.

FORMAL STYLE: Retrospective question.
All stems attach the formal retrospective attentive ending **-suptikka / -ptikka** (with the dialect or spelling variant **-uptikka** after a consonant): **Poptikka** '(Did you notice) was he looking at it?'; **Cōh.suptikka** (dialect **Cōh.uptikka**) 'Did you find it nice?'; **Cip iptikka** 'Was it a house?'.

FORMAL STYLE: Retrospective apperception.
(1) Shift to polite style.
(2) All stems attach the formal retrospective assertive ending **-suptita / -ptita** (with the dialect or spelling variant **-uptita** after a consonant) + the particle **k(w)ulye**: **Poptita k(w)ulye** 'Oh, (I remember noticing) he was looking at it!'

FORMAL STYLE: Suggestion or proposition.
Verbal stems attach the formal subjunctive assertive **-upsita / -psita** (with a variant **-supsita** after a consonant): **Popsita** 'Let's have a look at it'; **Ilk.upsita** (or **Ilk.supsita**) 'Let's read'. Since we are

using the formal style it is often appropriate to show respect to the other person included in the action, the addressee, by making the form honorific: **Kasipsita** 'Let's go'; **Capswusipsita** 'Let's eat'; **Tusipsita** 'Let's have a drink'.

FORMAL STYLE: Command.

Verbal stems attach the formal subjunctive attentive ending **-usio / -sio**, with the alternant **-psio** after the honorific **-usi- / -si-**: **Posio** (with honorific **Posipsio**) 'Look at it!' — CF **Posi yo ← Pos(y)ey yo = Posye yo** 'You see it' (polite honorific statement). Since we are using the formal style, it is natural to make the stem honorific to show respect to the subject of the action, who is the person addressed ('you'): **Posipsio** 'Please look at it'; **Kasipsio** 'Please go'; **Capswusipsio** 'Please eat'. It should be noted that the prevailing practice in South Korea is to spell final **/…io/** as "**…iyo**" in all instances, without regard to the basic form of the components of the endings.

Commands can be turned into requests, in any style, by using the auxiliary verb **cwunta** 'gives (the favor of doing), does for (someone)': **Pwā cwusipsio** or **Pwā cwus(y)ey yo** or **Pwā cw(u)e** or **Pwā cw(u)o** or **Pwā cwukey** or even occasionally **Pwā cw(u)e la** 'Look at it for us / him'.

11.6. Voice conversions.

In §7.4 we found related pairs of Korean verbs that differ in voice: passive built on active, causative built on active. The derived verbs are often spoken of as "morphological" passives and causatives (like English "feed them cake"), in contrast with the periphrastic structures (like English "let them eat cake") that play a similar role. We observed that causative verbs (vc) are always transitive and that passive verbs (vp) are typically intransitive (vpi) but some of these take a few nouns as direct objects so we decided to call them transitive passives (vpt). Looking at these verbs we can see the following conversion schemes:

(1) A ka X lul vt → B ka A eykey X lul vc
(2) A ka vi (or adj) → B ka A lul vc
(3) A ka B lul vt → B ka A eykey vpi
(4) A ka B uy [or B eykey (se)] X lul vt → B ka A eykey X lul vpt

Examples:

(1) **Ai ka pap ul mek.nunta** 'The child eats the food' → **Emeni ka ai eykey pap ul mek.inta** 'The mother has / makes / lets the child eat the food'.

(2) **Ai ka uyca ey anc.nunta** 'The child sits down on the chair' → **Emeni ka ai lul uyca ey anc.hinta** 'The mother seats the child on the chair'.

Cengto ka noph.ta 'The level is high' → **Wuli ka cengto lul nop.hinta** 'We raise the level'.

(3) **Kāy ka sālam ul munta** 'The dog bites the man' → **Sālam i kāy eykey mullinta** 'The man is bitten by the dog'.

Wuli ka san ul ponta 'We see the mountain' → **Wuli eykey san i pointa** (or **San i wuli eykey pointa**) 'The mountain is visible to us'. Notice that the order of sentence expansions is determined by the sentence profile (the relative importance of the adjuncts) and is of no relevance to the voice conversion, which is manifest only in the particular specification of the expansions by particles.

(4) **Sensayng i haksayng eykey (se) yakcem ul cap.nunta** [better with … **eykey se**] 'The teacher catches the student on a weak point' (or, **Sensayng i haksayng uy yakcem ul cap.nunta** 'The teacher catches a weak point of the student') → **Haksayng i sensayng eykey yakcem ul cap.hinta** 'The student gets caught on a weak point (or, gets his weak point caught) by the teacher'.

Not all verbs have derived causative and passive stems. If a verb lacks such a derived stem, or even if it has one, it can be turned into the causative or the passive by using periphrastic conversions:

(1) A ka X lul vt → B ka A eykey X lul vt -key hanta
→ B ka A lul sikhye (se) X lul vt -key hanta
(2) A ka vi (or adj) → B ka A lul vi(/ adj) -key hanta

            → B ka A lul adj -key mantunta
(3) A ka B lul vt   → B ka A eykey vt -um ul pat.nunta
                         tang hanta

But **tang hanta** seems to be limited to VN **[ham] ul tang hanta**, and **eykey** is often replaced by **eykey se**: **Mōtun sālam eykey / hanthey se phi ham ul tang hanta** 'He is shunned by all'.
Examples:

(1) **Ai ka wuyu lul masinta** 'The child drinks the milk' → **Emeni ka ai eykey wuyu lul masikey hanta** 'The mother gets the child to drink the milk'.

Sik.mo ka pap ul cīs.nunta 'The cook prepares the rice' → **Emeni ka sik.mo eykey [or, sik.mo lul sikhye (se)] pap ul cīs.key hanta** 'Mother has the cook prepare the rice'.

(2) **Haksayng i anc.nunta** 'The student sits down' → **Sensayng i haksayng ul anc.key hanta** 'The teacher has the student sit down'.

Cip i khuta 'The house is big' → **Wuli ka cip ul khukey hanta** 'We make the house big(ger)'.

Ku i ka ttok-ttok hata 'He is bright (intelligent)' → **Hak.kyo kyōyuk i ku i lul ttok-ttok hakey mantul.ess.ta** 'Schooling made him bright'.

Sālam tul i ku i lul ki hanta 'People shun him' → **Ku i ka sālam tul eykey phi ham ul pat.nunta** 'He is shunned by people'.

When a derived causative verb exists, its meaning is usually narrower than that of the periphrastic construction: the meaning of **anc.hinta** 'seats one' is included in the broader meaning of **anc.key hanta** 'has / lets one sit down'.

Verbal nouns of one syllable that are not free get only the periphrastic treatment: **pong hanta** 'seals it' → **pong hakey hanta** 'has one seal it', **cheng hanta** 'invites' → **cheng hakey hanta** 'has / lets one invite', **hap hanta** 'adds' → **hap hakey hanta** 'has / lets one add'. I have been unable to find any good cases of a one-syllable adjectival noun; for **mōs hata** 'is inferior' the conversion is rejected, and there are only questionable examples for **sok hata** 'is speedy', **chēn hata** 'is lowly', and **sil hata** 'is substantial':

? **palq kel.um ul sok hakey hanta** 'quickens (speeds up) one's steps'
(?)**cey mom ul cey ka susu lo chēn hakey hanta** 'cheapens one's body oneself'
(?)**achim mata wūntong ul hay se mom ul sil hakey hanta** 'builds up one's body with exercise every morning'

Some of the intransitive verbal nouns are a bit awkward in this conversion, too:
(?)**Ku sālam ul munhwaq kwa ey sok hakey hanta** 'They attach him to the cultural section'.

Verbal nouns and adjectival nouns of more than one syllable, and also free verbal nouns of only one syllable such as **īl** 'work' and **māl** 'talk', are subject to the conversions in the following ways:

(1) A ka X lul vnt hanta   → B ka A eykey X lul vnt sikhinta
                                          hakey hanta

(2) A ka vni hanta   → B ka A lul / eykey vni sikhinta
                                          hakey hanta

    A ka adj-n hata   → B ka A lul adj-n mantunta
                                          hakey hanta

(3) limited to certain transitive verbal nouns, which should be marked in the lexicon (for further constraints, see §5.6.6):

A ka B lul vnt hanta   → B ka A eykey X lul vnt (lul) pat.nunta
                                          tang hanta

A ka X lul vnt hanta   → B ka A eykey X lul vnt pat.nunta
                                          tang hanta

A ka X lul vnt hanta   → X ka vnt (i) toynta

Examples:

(1) **Sāmu-wen i congi lul cwūmun hanta** 'The clerk orders paper' → **Nay ka sāmu-wen eykey congi lul cwūmun sikhinta** (or, **cwūmun hakey hanta**) 'I have the clerk order paper'.

Nay ka (ku sālam ul) sayngkak hanta 'I think (of him)' → **Kulenq īl i na eykey (ku sālam ul) sayngkak hakey hanta** 'Such events make me think (of him)'.

(2) **Ku sālam i kyelhon hanta** 'He gets married' → **Apeci ka ku sālam ul kyelhon sikhinta** (or, **hakey hanta**) 'His father makes him get married'.

Ku sālam i īl hanta 'He works' → **Apeci ka ku sālam eykey īl hakey hanta** (or, **īl sikhinta** – but ?*īl hakey sikhinta is unacceptable to some speakers) 'His father makes him work'. I do not know why **eykey** is accepted in this sentence but rejected (in favor of **ul**) for the preceding sentence.

Wuli saynghwal i nek.nek hata 'Our life is rich' → **I kes i wuli saynghwal ul nek.nek hakey hanta** 'This enriches our life'.

(3) **Wuli ka totwuk nom ul kwutha hanta** 'We attack the thief (with our fists)' → **Totwuk nom i wuli eykey kwutha (lul) tang hanta** 'The thief is attacked by us'.

ⁿYeca ka kyelhon ul kēcel hanta 'The woman refuses the marriage' → **Namca ka ⁿyeca eykey kyelhon ul kēcel tang hanta** 'The man is refused marriage by the woman'.

Ku i ka wuli lul hyep.pak hanta 'He threatens us' → **Wuli ka ku i eykey hyep.pak (ul) pat.nunta** 'We are threatened by him'.

Wuli ka ku lul cwūmok hanta 'We pay attention to him' → **Ku i ka wuli eykey cwūmok (ul) pat.nunta** (or, ··· **wuli uy cwūmok ul** ···) 'He has attention paid to him by us' (or, 'He is subject to our attention').

Sālam tul i ku māl ul cwūn māl ila ko selmyeng hanta 'People explain that word as an abbreviation' → **Ku māl i cwūn māl ila ko selmyeng toynta** 'That word can be explained as an abbreviation'.

More difficult to explain:

Nay ka ku īl i kuleh.ta ko sayngkak hanta 'I think it is that way' → **Kuleh.ta ko sayngkak toynta** 'That's the way it is thought to be'. (We would have expected the source to contain **ku īl ul** ···.)

We must bear in mind several things about these voice conversions. The particle **eykey** can be replaced by a more colloquial synonym, **hanthey**. If the indirect object is impersonal, the particle will be **ey**: **kōngpho ey salo cap.hinta** 'is seized with fear'. These particles are separately called for, on their own, by certain verbs (giving/writing/telling TO ···) and sometimes that results in ambiguity: **Ku ay hanthey i kes ul selmyeng hakey hasio** can mean either 'Have him explain this' or (less likely) 'Have someone explain this to him'. If we clear the ambiguity up a bit we can say **Ku ay hanthey ne hanthey i kes ul selmyeng hakey hasio** 'Have him explain this to you'. Or, to avoid the juxtaposition of two **hanthey** phrases, **Ku ay hanthey i kes ul ne hanthey selmyeng hakey hasio**. You could also substitute **eykey** for the first **hanthey** or rephrase the beginning: **Ku ay hanthey (lo) ka se** ··· 'Go to him and ··· '. When there are two **hanthey** phrases the one nearest the verb that calls for an indirect object goes with that verb. When there is only one **hanthey** phrase, you cannot tell for sure whether it goes with the verb or with the conversion. The farther from the verb it is placed, the more likely it goes with the voice conversion.

The particles **ey, eykey,** and **ulo** are sometimes replaced in colloquial or sloppy speech by **ul/lul**. (That caused us some difficulties in defining transitivity, §7.2.) As a result, occasionally we hear a causative sentence with two **ul** phrases. The one nearest the verb is usually the direct object of the verb, the one further removed is a replacement for the indirect-object particle: **ai lul os ul ip.hinta** = **ai eykey os ul ip.hinta** 'gets the child dressed'. It is possible to make a kind of causative on a causative conversion: **A ka B eykey X lul vt -key hanta** → **C ka A eykey B lul sikhye (se) X lul vt -key hanta** 'C gets A to get B to do X'. An example: **Na nun sāmu-wen eykey sāhwan ul sikhye se congi lul cwūmun hakey hayss.ta** 'I had the clerk make the office boy order paper'.

A literary variant of **eykey** in causative sentences is the expression **ulo ha.ye-kum** (obsolete **ulo ha.ye**). The colloquial variant, as we have noted, is **hanthey**. In passive sentences the literary variants of **ey(key)** are **ulo, ulo malmiam.ᵉ/a, ulo in ha.ye**, and **ey uy ha.ye**.

The passive conversions are not to be confused with the construction **-key toy-** 'gradually get to be, get so that' as in the following sentences:

Ai ka payq nol.i lul cōh.a hakey tōyss.ta 'The child came to enjoy boat rides'.
Tōn i ēps.e to kongpu hakey tōyss.ta '(It came about that) even with no money I got to study'.
Kim sensayng to māl hakey tōyss.ta 'Mr Kim happened (or, got) to talk, too'.
Sāwel i toymyen nongpu tul un puncwu hakey toynta 'When it becomes April, farmers get busy'.

As an optional abbreviation of **hakey toynta**, the verb **toynta** will sometimes appear after an adjectival noun, as in **hōn.lan (hakey) toynta** 'gets disordered'. Notice that all uses of **toynta** 'becomes' fall together with all passives in the constraints associated with negative preemphasis (§11.7.2).

Koreans prefer a simple intransitive to a passive, whenever possible: **Ce uy atul i mācek eykey cwuk.ess.ta** (Roth 353) 'His son died at the hands of bandits' = 'His son was killed by bandits'.

The auxiliary structure **-e ci-** means 'gets to be, becomes' and is applied to adjectives and intransitive verbs. But it can also be used with certain transitive stems to make a kind of periphrastic passive: **ccic.e cinta** 'it tears = it gets torn', **allye cinta** 'it gets known', ... [1]Yi Kitong 1988 says that the derived stems express spontaneous acts (not wished or controlled) but the periphrastic conversions are made on controlled, voluntary acts. Thus an agent is implied for the latter, but not the former:

Mun i yellyess.ta 'The door opened (came open)'.
Mun i yel.e cyess.ta 'The door got opened [by someone]'.

Yet it is difficult to include specification of the agent without choosing the simpler active sentence: ?***Mun i/un ku namca eykey yel.e cyess.ta** 'The door got opened by the man' → **Mun ul/un ku namca ka yel.ess.ta** (= 'The door, the man opened it'). SEE **-e cita** in Part II.

11.7. Negative conversions.

Korean sentences are negated in more than one way. Short predicates can be denied by preposing a negative adverb. Longer predicates use the periphrastic (or "sentential") negativization, by attaching the suspective ending **-ci** to the stem and following that with a negative auxiliary. That option is available for the short predicates, too. There are a number of special features in negative sentences, and some of them are covered in the following sections. (See also §10.8.2).

11.7.1. Negatives and strong negatives.

An affirmative sentence can be turned into a negative ("**ani**") or a strong negative ("**mōs**") in two ways: the short (or simple) negative and the long (or complex) negative.

Short Negative

	a n i			m ō s
1. Ponta.	→	An(i) ponta.	Ponta. →	Mōs ponta.
2. Cōh.ta.	→	An(i) cōh.ta.		
3. Cip ita.	→	Cip i ani 'ta.		

Long Negative

	a n i			m ō s
1. Ponta.	→	Poci ani hanta. anh.nunta.	Ponta. →	Poci mōs hanta.
2. Cōh.ta.	→	Cōh.ci ani hata. anh.ta.	Cōh.ta. →	Cōh.ci mōs hata.
3. —		—		—

The translation of the **ani** negative is '(does/is) not', of the **mōs** 'definitely not; not possibly, cannot, (absolutely) will not'. In the sense of mere possibility the word 'can' usually translates as **-ulq swu iss.ta** and 'cannot' is **-ulq swu ēps.ta**. In the sense of knowhow (ability) the Korean is **-ulq cwul ānta (ā-l-)**. When 'can' is used to mean permission 'may, be permitted to', the appropriate Korean is **-e to cōh.ta** (or **kwaynchanh.ta**); permission is denied with **-umyen an toynta**.

For adjectival sentences, the **ani** negative has both the short form and the long form, but only the long occurs for the **mōs** negative. And there are some adjectives which never take the strong negative, notably those describing weather. There is no *****Chwupci mōs hata** from **chwūw-**, and **Tēpci mōs hata** from **tēw-** 'be warm' can have as its subject only **mul** 'water' or the like, but never **nal(-ssi)** 'the weather'. (For water, or anything you can touch, 'cold' is **cha-**.) The intransitive verb **mō-cala-** 'becomes deficient' will not take the **mōs** negative, perhaps because a shortened form of **mōs** is incorporated in the stem itself; there is no *****mōs mō-calanta** or *****mō-calaci mōs hanta**.

As remarked in §5.2.9, we might wish to consider **ani** in **ani 'ta** 'it is not' as a precopular noun. Korean grammarians usually treat **anita** as an unanalyzed stem, the "negative copula" as against the affirmative copula **ita**, and that is certainly a convenient way to look at it. The one critical context that could help point toward a preference for one treatment or the other on morphophonemic grounds is indecisive: the past is either /**anietta**/ = **ani 'ess.ta** or /**anyetta**/ = **an' yess.ta**. So we have no clearcut reason to choose to write **anita, aninya,** ... (following the usual Hankul spelling – "when in doubt do not analyze") rather than **ani 'ta, ani 'n ya,** ... , as we have done in this book. Notice that the grammar of **ani 'ta** and **ita** is different, in that the negative marks the predicate complement (the B of "is B"), as well as the subject, with the nominative particle; but in the affirmative, with **ani** absent, the copula is attached to the complement with no marking particle: **A ka B ka ani 'ta** 'A is not B' ← **A ka B (i)ta** 'A is B'. But sometimes the nominative particle **i/ka** is omitted after the complement in a negative copula sentence, too, and that was true of the language in the early Hankul texts, as well; see the entry for the particle **i** in Part II. The particle is sometimes omitted also after the complement of **toynta** 'becomes'. And **i/ka** is obligatorily suppressed when a focus particle or delimiter (such as **un/nun, to**) is attached; it is usually omitted, too, when the complement is delimited by **man** or **ppun** 'only'. The expression **A ka ani 'la B 'ta** 'It's not A, it's B' has roughly the same meaning as **B 'ci A ka ani 'ta** 'It's B, not A'. To say 'it is neither A nor (is it) B' you highlight the complements and conjoin the sentences with **-ko**, as in **Ku kes un kaykwuli to ani 'ko, olchangi to ani 'ta** 'That is neither a frog nor a tadpole'. With the affirmative, since nothing can intervene between the complement and the copula, you highlight the copula itself (in its summative form **i-ki to ha-** 'it is indeed/also'): **Ku i nun uysa (i)ki to hako um.ak-ka (i)ki to hata** 'He is both a physician and a musician' = **Ku nun uysa 'mye (tto) um.ak-ka 'ta** 'He is a physician and (also) a musician'. Or, the sentence can be rephrased as 'not only ... but also ...': **Ku i nun uysa (i)ki man (or (i)l ppun man) ani 'la um.ak-ka (i)ki to hata** 'He is not only a physician but also a musician'.

Both the short negatives and the long negatives are found in the earliest Hankul texts. In colloquial passages, such as those of 1447 Sekpo, the shorter forms are somewhat more frequent than the longer ones. The long negative is a sentential negation, and implies a greater scope than the short negative, which basically negates just the verb phrase. But you will sometimes find a short negative doing the work of the longer form (i.e. negating the whole sentence) when the stem itself is short; conversely, the long form will sometimes be preferred for longer stems (especially of adjectives) even when the scope does not extend beyond the verbal phrase itself. The short negative is quite direct; in certain situations, the long negative may be perceived as less brusque and therefore more polite.

11.7.2. Negative preemphasis.

In order to emphasize the verb being negated it is possible to take the long negative and insert a particle after the suspective **-ci**. For processive verbs the particle is normally **ul/lul**:

anc.ci anh.nunta 'does not sit' → **anc.ci lul anh.nunta** 'does not SIT'

ku kes ul poci anh.nunta 'does not LOOK at that' → **ku kes ul poci lul anh.nunta** 'does not LOOK at that' (smoother with **ku kes ul** → **ku kes un**)

With adjectives either the particle **ul/lul** or the particle **i/ka** can be inserted in the longer negatives to emphasize the adjective being negated: **Tolie kyelkwa ka cōh.ci ka (or lul) mōs hayss.ta** 'On the contrary, the results were no good at all'; **coqken ey mac.ci ka (or lul) anh.ko** 'without meeting the qualifications at all, lacking the least qualification'.

Certain classes of verbs can undergo negative preemphasis with **i/ka** as well as with **ul/lul**:

(1) Passives, apparently all of them. But **ka** is awkward (ungrammatical?) when the passive can take an object (vpt) and that object is expressed, so that while **tachici** (< **tah.chici**) **ka anh.nunta** 'doesn't get INJURED' is acceptable, (*)**tali lul tachici ka anh.nunta** 'doesn't get INJURED ON THE LEG' is awkward at best, and one speaker suggests amending it to ··· **tachye cici ka anh.nunta**. Certain idiomatic cases seem to be exceptions. Some speakers accept **Yakcem ul cap.hici ka anh.nunta** 'does not have one's weak points SEIZED UPON', **mok ul callici ka anh.nunta** 'does not get one's throat CUT = doesn't get FIRED', and **nach ul kka(y)kk.ici ka anh.nunta** 'does not have one's face SCRAPED = doesn't LOSE FACE'. Yet (?)**tōn ul mek.hici ka anh.nunta** 'does not get one's money EATEN = doesn't get SWINDLED out of one's money' is found awkward, and speakers prefer to say **tōn i mek.hici ka anh.nunta** 'one's money does not get eaten (= taken by deceit)'. Perhaps we could make an argument for a different order of applying the conversions (and accordingly a different constituency analysis) in the two situations. The "idiomatic" examples could be taken as adding the object AFTER the passive conversion (**cap.nunta** → **cap.hinta** → **yakcem ul cap.hinta**), the others as adding the object BEFORE the conversion (**mek.nunta** → **tōn ul mek.nunta** → **tōn ul mek.hinta**). And at least one speaker rejects almost all the examples with derived passives.

(2) All cases of **toy-** 'become', including **-key toy-** 'get so that' and VN + (**i/ka** +) **toy-**, as well as N + **ulo/lo** (as well as **i/ka**) + **toy-**.

(3) All cases of almost all intransitive processive stems pronounced **ci-**, including **kkoch i cinta** 'flowers fade', **ttay ka cinta** 'dirt comes off', **cangma ka cinta** 'the rainy season sets in', **pel.e cinta** 'it opens up', **nul.e cinta** 'it dangles', **ssot.a cinta** 'it pours down', **ssule cinta** 'it topples over', **ttel.e cinta** 'it falls (out); it separates', **ppā cinta** 'it falls', **khye cinta** 'it ignites; (light, ...) goes on', **kkē cinta** '(light, ...) goes out'. But for the transitive **ci-** (as in **pic ul cinta** 'owes a debt') the pre-emphasis with the particle **ka** is awkward (ungrammatical?); it is also difficult (impossible?) for the intransitive **cinta** 'is defeated, loses', **sala cinta** 'vanishes', and **swūm (i) cinta** 'breath expires = dies'.

(4) The intransitive verbs **cwuk-** 'die' (**Cwukci ka/lul anh.nunta** 'He just won't die!'), **phi-** 'bloom' in **kkoch i phi-** 'flowers bloom', **tulli-** in **kāmki ey tullinta** 'catches a cold'; and perhaps a few others.

(5) Periphrastic passives (§11.6) with VN (+ **ul**) + **tang hanta** are slightly awkward with **ka** as pre-emphasis, but apparently not ungrammatical. Those with **pat-**, on the other hand, are all rejected.

In interesting contrast with the behavior of adjectives and of the other verbs, most of the processive verbs that allow either **ka** or **lul** for preemphasis cannot have the **mōs hanta** form, even without pre-emphasis. There is no ***mek.hici (lul/ka) mōs hanta** 'can't/won't get eaten', ***kakey toyci (lul/ka) mōs hanta** 'can't/won't get to go', ... But we can do this: **mōs kanta** 'can't/won't go' → **mōs kakey toynta** 'gets so one can't/won't go' → **mōs kakey toyci lul/ka anh.nunta** 'doesn't get so one can't/won't GO'. And **poici (lul/ka) mōs hanta** occurs, but only as the causative 'can't show', not as the passive 'can't get seen'; the passive and causative stems derived from **po-** 'see' converge in shape. Exceptions:

(1) **phinta**: **Pi ka an wā se kkoch i phici (ka/lul) mōs hanta** 'The flowers are unable to bloom because of the lack of rain'.

(2) **ttel.e cinta** 'be separated' (but not 'fall'): **Ttel.e cici (ka/lul) mōs hanta** 'It can't be SEPARATED'.

(3) **kunul (i) cinta**: **Kunul (i) cici lul mōs hanta** 'It won't get SHADY' — but preemphasis with **ka** is somewhat awkward.

(4) **swūm (i) cinta**: **Ku ¹nōin un cāngnam ul mōs pwass.ta ko tomuci swūm i cici lul mōs hako iss.ta** 'The old man just won't die, saying he has not seen his eldest son'.

(5) **cwuk.nunta**: **Cwukci lul mōs hanta** 'I can't DIE = I just won't die' (but not ***cwukci ka mōs hanta**).

(6) **sala/sule cinta**: **I sēysang ey ēps.e to cōh.ulq pyēngsin in tey, yōngki ka ēps.e sala cici lul mōs hako iss.ta** 'While an invalid the world might be as well without, I lack the courage to slip away'.

(7) **ppā cinta**: **Ppā cici lul mōs hanta** 'I can't get rid of it' — but **Ppā cye na-oci lul mōs hanta** is more common.

(8) **ippe cinta**: **te ippe cici (lul) mōs hanta** 'can't get any prettier' occurs, but *****ippe cici ka mōs hanta** does not.

(9) **kēnkang hay cinta**: **Com chelem kēnkang hay cici (ka/lul) mōs hanta** 'can't get the least bit healthier'.

We might expect that these verbs of "becoming" would lack the command and suggestion forms, but the only limitations seem to be semantic: **Com te ippe cye la** 'Get a little prettier!'; **Te ippe cici mal.e la** 'Don't get any prettier' (by way of **ippe cici mōs hanta** 'can't get any prettier'); **(Com te) kēnkang hay cye la** 'Get better!'; **Ppalli kkē cye la** 'Get lost!'; **Puth-tulliki cen ey kkē cica** 'Let's vanish (= escape) before they catch us!'

Notice that **iss.ta** (§11.7.3) in the meaning 'stays' has only the **lul** preemphasis: **iss.ci lul anh.nunta** 'doesn't STAY' (***iss.ci ka anh.nunta**). In the meanings 'is (at)' and 'has (got)' both kinds of preemphasis are possible, but with 'has (got)' they are apparently limited to certain forms of the auxiliary, such as **anh.e**.

Though negative preemphasis might be expected with the double negative (§11.7.6), instead we usually find the focus subdued (i.e. deemphasized) with the particle **un/nun**, as in **ai tul i ēps.ci nun anh.e to** 'although he does NOT lack children = although he DOES have children'. (You will also find focus highlighting with **-ci to anh-** and **-ci to mōs ha-** 'not even/either', and restriction with **-ci man anh-** 'not just'. I lack an example of **-ci man mōs ha-** 'not just' but I see no reason not to expect it, too: Part II has **-ci pakk ey mōs ha-**.) We also find, however, **Kulenq īl i ēps.ci lul anh.e iss.ta** 'There ARE some such cases' (not accepted by all speakers), apparently an infinitive-adverbialization from (*)**ēps.ci lul anh.ta**. There seems to be no ***Cōh.ci ka anh.ci anh.ta**, except perhaps as a joke, but **Cōh.ci anh.ci ka anh.ta** sometimes occurs, in contexts appropriate to **Cōh.ci anh.ci anh.ta**.

The copula lacks a long negative (except in rhetorical questions), so there can be no preemphasis. But notice the normal marking of the complement noun with **i/ka** before **ani 'ta** in contrast with its obligatory absence before **ita**. The fact that the copula negative will allow particle sequences otherwise unobtainable (see §6.5) suggests the somewhat special function that the particle is playing here.

Negative preemphasis can be treated as a special case of AUXILIARY PREEMPHASIS, discussed in §10.8.7. Compare the extended adversative **-uni-kka**, the extension of which looks as if it might be **-q-** + the particle **ka**, but here similar to the ⋯**unikka** (< ⋯-$^u\!/_o\,\hat{n}\,i\,s\,\hat{\;}ka$ 'question of the fact that ⋯ ') of the formal question ending **-sup.nikka**, so probably from the bound noun **ka** 'question', at least etymologically. (Perhaps the late-blooming nominative **ka** has the same origin as the bound noun.)

11.7.3. Suppletive negatives.

The negative of **ā-l-** 'know' is usually **molu-** 'not know'. We find **ānta** 'knows' → **molunta** 'does not know' rather than → **an ānta** or → **ālci anh.nunta**. But a rhetorical question can be built on the latter form: **Ku sālam ālci anh.nun ka** 'You surely don't know him?' to be contrasted with ⋯ **molunun ka?** 'Don't you know him?' and ⋯ **moluci anh.nun ka** 'Of course you are not unacquainted with him?' (see the discussion in §11.15). And **an ānta** is accepted in some contexts. Co Sek.yen offers these examples:

Kongpu man ālci mālko nōnun kes to com al.e la! – **Silh.e yo, na n' kulen ke n' an āllay yo** [= **āllye ko hay yo**] 'Don't confine your knowledge to work alone, get acquainted with a bit of fun! – No, I have no desire to acquaint myself with that sort of thing.'

Nay mom ey hāy lowuni-kka ilpule an āllye ko haci 'As it is harmful to my body (= health), I deliberately choose not to get acquainted with it!'

Ne ilen kes āni? – **An ānta (ko) halq swu nun ēps.ci** 'You know such things? – How could I not?!'

The strong negative is either **mōs ā-l-** (short) or **ālci mōs ha-** (long) as expected: **Ku kes ul ālci mōs hayss.ta** 'I didn't know that' – or **mōllass.ta**, but **mōs al.ess.ta** is rejected as awkward, if not ungrammatical. For more on the negative of 'know' see **moluta** in Part II.

The verb **iss-** 'exists' is especially tricky, for in some of its uses the expected negative form is replaced by **ēps-** 'be lacking'. Because of what happens in the negative and honorific conversions, it

A Reference Grammar of Korean

seems wise to recognize at least three homonymous verbs: (1) 'stays'; (2) 'is located' = 'is at'; (3) 'is possessed' = 'has'. The following paradigms display the occurring forms. The notations at the left: A = **ani** negative, M = **mōs** negative, C = longer negative with **-ci**, L = preemphasis with **lul**, K = preemphasis with **ka**; S = the honorific (**-usi-**/**-si-**) for the numbered verb.

	1. iss.ta 'stays'	2. iss.ta 'is (at)'	3. iss.ta 'has'
A	anq iss.nunta, anq iss.ta	anq iss.ta, ēps.ta	ēps.ta
A C	iss.ci anh.nunta, iss.ci anh.ta	iss.ci anh.ta	(iss.ci anh.ta)[1]
A C L	iss.ci lul anh.nunta	iss.ci lul anh.ta	iss.ci lul anh.ta[1]
A C K	–	iss.ci ka anh.ta	iss.ci ka anh.ta[1]
M	mōs(q) iss.nunta	–	
M C	iss.ci mōs hanta	iss.ci mōs hata	iss.ci mōs hata
M C L	iss.ci lul mōs hanta	iss.ci lul mōs hata	iss.ci lul mōs hata
M C K	–	iss.ci ka mōs hata	iss.ci ka mōs hata
	↓	↓	
	S 1., S 2. kyēysinta, kyēysita		S 3. iss.usita[2]
A	an kyēysinta, an kyēysita		ēps.usita[2]
A C	kyēysici anh.nunta, kyēysici anh.ta		(iss.usici anh.ta)[3]
A C L	kyēysici lul anh.nunta, kyēysici lul anh.ta		–
A C K	kyēysici ka anh.ta		
M	(mōs kyēysinta)[4], mōs(q) iss.usinta		
M C L	(kyēysici mōs hanta)[4], iss.usici lul mōs hanta, iss.ci lul mōs hasinta		

[1] Apparently this occurs only as the basis for interrogative conversions: **iss.ci (ka) anh.un ya**. The pronunciation is also /annunya/ as well as /anunya/, but that version is not be interpreted as **anh.nun ya**, for it is **anh.un ya** + a morpheme of emphasis that geminates the first nasal.

[2] The question forms are **iss.usin ya** and **ēps.usin ya**, as expected from descriptive (adjective) stems; contrast **iss.ta** → **iss.nun ya**, **ēps.nun ya**. There is also **iss.ci anh.usin ya** with the interrogative made on an honorific **iss.ci anh.usita** (does that occur?) that is made on the negative (*)**iss.ci anh.ta**, which apparently does not occur.

[3] Apparently this does not occur except as the basis for the interrogative conversion **iss.usici anh.un ya** and the infinitive-adverbialization **iss.usici anh.e**.

[4] Less common than the following forms. There is also **kyēysici mōs hasinta**, honorific made on negative from honorific, so that the honorification is pleonastically repeated. **Iss.usici mōs hanta** is a negative made on the honorific and **iss.ci mōs hasinta** is an honorific made on the negative.

The auxiliary **iss-** in **-ko iss.ta** and **-e iss.ta** is much like the first **iss.ta** ('stays') except that there are no **an**/**mōs** ⋯ **iss.nunta** forms. Using the examples **ipko iss-** 'is wearing' and **anc.e iss-** 'is seated':

anq ipko iss.ta   an anc.e iss.ta
ipko iss.ci (lul) anh.nunta   anc.e iss.ci (lul) anh.nunta
mōsq ipko iss.ta   mōs anc.e iss.ta
ipko iss.ci (lul) mōs hanta   anc.e iss.ci (lul) mōs hanta

The particle **tul** 'severally' can always be inserted after **-ko** and **-e**, regardless of the other conversions.

The form **-ko iss.usi(n)ta** occurs but **-ko kyēysinta** (or **kyēysita**) is to be preferred. The honorific can, of course, be applied twice (**-usiko kyēysinta**), and when the negative is included even three applications are possible (**-usiko iss.usici mōs hasinta**), but simpler forms are usually preferred: **-ko iss.usici mōs hanta** or **-ko iss.ci mōs hasinta**.

Some of the forms are hard to elicit in isolation. They are more readily produced when put into quotations, questions (especially if ironic or rhetorical), and the like: **mōs(q) iss.nunta 'y; iss.ci anh.nunta 'myen; ...** .

Both **mōs(q) iss.nunta** and **iss.ci mōs hanta** sometimes occur, but there seems to be no ***mōs iss.ta**, ***iss.ci mōs hata**, ***mōs ēps.ta**, or ***ēps.ci mōs hata**. (We are excluding here the literary style, often used in diaries, which regularly replaces the processive forms by unmarked forms without the processive morpheme, so that **mōs(q) iss.nunta** → **mōs iss.ta**, **iss.ci mōs hanta** → **iss.ci mōs hata**.) That raises the question whether **mōs taniko iss.ta** is to be regarded as **mōs taniko + iss.ta** (**taninta** → **mōs taninta** → **mōs taniko** → **mōs taniko iss.ta**) rather than **mōs + taniko iss.ta** (**taninta** → **taniko iss.ta** → **mōs taniko iss.ta**).

Examples to illustrate some of the forms listed:

1 A **Yo say cip ey anq iss.ta / iss.nunta** 'He doesn't stay home lately'.
2 A **Cikum cip ey anq iss.ta** 'He is not at home now'.
2 S A **Cikum cip ey an kyēysinta / kyēysita** (but not **iss.usita**) 'He is not at home now'.
2 A C **Ku nal cip ey iss.ci anh.ess.ta** = (A) ··· **cip ey ēps.ess.ta** 'He wasn't home that day'.
  Ce alay ey se poni-kka, ney ka iss.ci anh.e! 'I looked from down there and who was it but you!'
2 A C (L/K) **Āmuli chac.e pwā to pang an ey iss.ci (lul / ka) anh.ta** 'Search as you will, it just isn't in the room'.
  Cip ey chayk i mānh.i iss.ci (lul / ka) anh.nun ya 'Aren't there lots of books in the house?'
3 A C (L/K) **Tōn i iss.ci (lul / ka) anh.na, cip iss.ci (lul / ka) anh.na – musun kekceng i iss.keyss.e** 'Haven't you got money, haven't you got a house – what's your worry?' NOTE: Choice of **lul**, **ka**, or neither must be the same in both phrases.
1 M **Ku nal cip ey mōs(q) iss.ess.ta** 'He couldn't stay home that day'.
1 M C **Ne kuleta ka n' hōysa ey iss.ci mōs hanta** = (1 M) **Ne kuleta ka n' hōysa ey mōs(q) iss.nunta** 'You keep on like that and you won't be able to stay on at the office'.
1 S M C **Ku pun kuleta ka n' hōysa ey mōs(q) iss.usinta (mōs kyēysinta, iss.ci mōs hasinta) ko hay la** 'Tell him if he keeps on like that he won't be able to stay on at the office'.
1aux M **Kuleta ka n' yeki mōs puth.e (tul) iss.nunta** 'You (guys) keep on like that and you won't be able to hold on here (you'll get fired)'.
1aux M C **Kuleta ka n' yeki mōs puth.e (tul) iss.ci (lul) mōs hanta** 'You (guys) keep on like that and you won't be able to "stick" here (you'll get fired)'.
3 M C (L/K) **Tōn i mānh.i iss.ci (lul / ka) mōs hata** 'He can't have much money (despite appearances or hopes)' – CF **Tōn i mānh.i ēps.ta** 'He hasn't got much money'.
  Silhem kikyey nun wuli hak.kyo ey to ēps.ci n' anh.ta (/? **anh.nunta**) **haci man ...** 'They say it isn't that our school completely lacks laboratory equipment, but ... '.

11.7.4. Negative commands and propositions.

The negatives of commands and propositions are made with the auxiliary **mā-l-** 'desist; end':

  Ponta. → (**Poci mōs hanta.** →) **Poci mal.e la!** 'Don't look!'
  Ponta. → (**Poci mōs hanta.** →) **Poci mālca!** 'Let's not look!'
  Iss.ta. → (**Mōs(q) iss.nunta.** →) **Iss.ci mal.e la!** 'Don't stay!'
  Iss.ta. → (**Mōs(q) iss.nunta.** →) **Iss.ci mālca!** 'Let's not stay!'

There seems to be no negative from the pseudo-command form of the adjectival sentence used as an exclamation: **Cōh.a la!** 'How nice!' But above we have suggested that the order of application of the conversions is statement → strong negative → command (rather than, say, statement → command → negative), so that we would not expect such a form.

Negative preemphasis (§11.7.2) can occur with commands and propositions:

Ponta. → Poci mōs hanta. → Poci lul mōs hanta. → Poci lul mal.e la!
Ponta. → Poci mōs hanta. → Poci lul mōs hanta. → Poci lul mālca!

To say 'Don't V_1; do V_2 (instead)' or '(Please) V_2 instead of V_1' Korean has the expression V_1-ulq kes ēps.i V_2-sey yo (or V_2-e la etc.). Examples will be found in Pak Sengwen 297.

From the above remarks you would conclude that the imperative forms **-ci mōs hay la** and **-ci mōs hala** are ungrammatical, but they can appear when the speaker is putting a hex, as it were, on the listener: "May you be unable to do it! (= I pray that you not succeed!)". **Ikici mālla** means 'Don't win!' (pleading or commanding) but **Ikici mōs hay la** means 'I want you to be unable to win = I pray for your defeat'. That accounts for the otherwise perplexing sentence ([1]Yi Kitong 1988:61) **Nwu ka mōs kala ko hayss.na?** 'Did anyone tell you not to go?' meaning "Do you think I don't want you to go?!" or "Has anyone kept you from going?!" (= **Nwu ka mōs kakey hayss.na?**).

11.7.5. Negatives with verbal nouns.

Constructions of verbal noun + postnominal verb behave like ordinary simple verbs, except in the following cases. When the short version of the strong negative is applied, the **mōs** usually occurs BETWEEN the verbal noun and the postnominal verb in the case of most two-syllable verbal nouns and the one-syllable verbal noun **īl** 'work'. But in further conversions, the **mōs** may come before the verbal noun: despite the lack of *mōs sayngkak hanta as such, we hear **Kulen kes to mōs sayngkak hamyen, etteh.key!** 'You should think of things like that, at least'. For the one-syllable verbal nouns other than **īl** (including free and separable ones) the **mōs** MUST precede the verbal noun. Examples:

Group 1　　īl mōs hanta (*mōs īl hanta) 'can't work'
　　　　　　sayngkak mōs hanta (*mōs sayngkak hanta) 'can't think'
　　　　　　salang mōs hanta (*mōs salang hanta) 'can't love'
　　　　　　taycwung mōs hanta (*mōs taycwung hanta) 'can't estimate'
Also note:　yenghwa kwūkyeng ul mōs hanta =
　　　　　　　　ul haci mōs hanta =
　　　　　　　　haci mōs hanta =
　　　　　　yenghwa lul kwūkyeng mōs hanta =
　　　　　　　　haci mōs hanta 'can't see the movie'
Group 2　　mōs cēn hanta (*cēn mōs hanta) 'can't transmit'
　　　　　　mōs cheng hanta (*cheng mōs hanta) 'can't invite'
　　　　　　mōs kūm hanta (*kūm mōs hanta) 'can't prohibit'
　　　　　　mōs wēn hanta [rare] (*wēn mōs hanta) 'can't request'

The simple form is difficult to elicit in some cases, such as **mac.i mōs hanta** 'can't welcome' from **mac.i hanta**, but it turns up in the adverbialization **mac.i mōs hay se** 'unwillingly'.

According to my observations, **an(i)** does not appear before a free verbal noun (*an(i) VN hanta → VN an(i) hanta = VN haci anh.nunta) and the short negative does not appear at all with adjectival nouns: *an(i) AN hata, *AN an(i) hata. The Hamkyeng dialect is said to allow the local reflex of **ani**, pronounced [aĩ], to precede verbal nouns and to invade the V-e V structures more freely than Seoul.

Verbal-noun sentences often optionally drop the word **haci** before a negative auxiliary: **Kuleh.key māl (haci) anh.keyss.ta** 'I won't speak that way', [n]**Yēm.lye (haci) māsey yo** 'Don't worry'. Compare the dropping of **ham, hako,** and **hakey** in the documentary style (p. 277, p. 300; Part II).

11.7.6. Double negatives.

The double negative (negative → negative) can have the meaning of a strong positive ('of course') or a reaffirmation ('to be sure'), but in Korean it is used primarily to make a positive statement less direct, not unlike the expression "not unlike" = "rather like" in English. As far as truth value goes, ēps.ci anh.ta 'does not lack' = iss.ta 'has (got)', just as iss.ci anh.ta 'has not (got)' = ēps.ta 'lacks'. The sentence ēps.ci anh.ta apparently occurs only in further conversions such as ēps.ci anh.e iss.ta 'has (got) it without a doubt'. A stronger form can be made: ēps.ulq swu ēps.ta 'lacks the possibility of not having it' = iss.ta 'has (got) it' — CF iss.ulq swu ēps.ta 'lacks the possibility of having it' = ēps.ta 'lacks it'.

Double negatives are more common, perhaps, for adjectives. Cōh.ci anh.ci anh.ta or An cōh.ci anh.ta means 'It isn't that it isn't good; you can't say it isn't good'. Stronger: Cōh.ci mōs haci anh.ta or Cōh.ci anh.ci mōs hata. Still stronger: Cōh.ci mōs haci mōs hata.

The double negatives permitted by verbs are more limited, and usually have the focus of the suspective -ci subdued by the particle un/nun: Acwu mekci anh.ci nun anh.nunta 'It isn't that I don't eat at all (it's just that I eat so little)'; Acwu mekci mōs haci n(un) anh.nunta 'It isn't that I completely CAN'T eat (but I can only eat a little)'. The forms (?*)V-ci nun mōs haci mōs hanta and (?*)V-ci nun anh.ci mōs hanta seem not to occur, but there are examples of V-ci anh.ci mōs hanun such as kaci anh.ci mōs hanun ipcang ey iss.ta 'is in a position where one cannot afford not to go (= is obliged to go)'. For double negatives with 'know' see the entry moluta in Part II.

Negative preemphasis (§11.7.2) is rare with the double negative and it is only made with the particle ul/lul, never with i/ka.

A kind of periphrastic double negative is made with ··· key ani 'ta 'it is not the case that ··· ', in which key < kes i. An example: Kup haci anh.un key ani 'ci man son i mō-cala se eccelq swu ēps.ta 'Of course it is an urgent matter, but there's nothing we can do, being short of hands'. This is the only way a copular sentence can be rendered doubly negative: Khunq īl i ani 'n key ani 'ci man eccelq tōli ka ēps.ta 'Of course it is a serious matter, but there is nothing we can do about it'.

An amusing incident is told of old Dr Underwood and a Korean merchant who advertised Ēps.nun kes ēps.ta 'There is nothing we have not got' (= Ēps.nun kes i ēps.ta). When called to account for an item not carried, the merchant explained Ēps.nun kes un ēps.ta 'What we haven't got, we haven't got'. More examples of double negatives:

Kulenq īl i ēps.ci nun anh.ta 'Such things DO (sometimes) happen'.

Haci anh.umyen an toykeyss.ta 'It won't do if you don't do it' = Hay ya toykeyss.ta 'You'll have to do it'.

Kuleh.ci anh.umyen an toynta 'It's no good unless it is that way' = Kulay ya toynta 'Only if it is that way is it all right = it has to be that way'.

11.7.7. Other negative expressions.

In addition to the particles ul/lul and i/ka, there are other elements which can intervene between the suspective -ci and the negative element. Aside from -ci nun anh-, -ci nun mōs ha-, and -ci to anh-, the only ones that have come to my attention are those listed in CM 1:284:

-ci man mōs hanta: Mannale kaci man mōs haci, phyēnci 'na cēnhwa nun halq swu iss.ta 'You can't just go see him (e.g. in jail, hospital, ...), but you can write him a letter or telephone him' — CF ··· kaci mōs haci man, ··· .

-ci to mōs hanta: Ilum ul ssuci to mōs hanta 'He can't even write his name' — CF Ilum to ssuci (lul) mōs hanta; Musewe se chac.e kaci to mōs hanun tey yo 'He's so scared he dares not visit him!'

-ci ya mōs hal ya: Tāy-hak.kyo lul na-wass.nun tey Yenge ccum ul haci ya mōs hal ya?? 'He is a college graduate — of course he can talk English!'

-ci 'na mālci: Mili khun soli lul haci 'na mālci; (i key musun changphi ya) 'He shouldn't have boasted beforehand; (what a shameful thing)!'

11.7.8. Negative sentences with positive force.

In negative questions used rhetorically the intended force is positive: Kaci anh.e?! 'Isn't he going?' or 'He's going, isn't he?' = 'Surely he is going'. Such sentences allow the suspective form of the past and the future and even the copula: **Kass.ci anh.e?!** 'Surely he went', **Kakeyss.ci anh.e?!** 'Surely he will go', **Haksayng ici (iess.ci) anh.e?!** 'Surely he is (was) a student'. As statements (or nonrhetorical negative questions), these sentences must be **Kaci anh.ess.e, Kaci anh.keyss.e**, and **Haksayng i an' ye(ss.e)**. (With the proper question intonation, those sentences can function rhetorically, too.) The **-ci anh-** structure is commonly shortened to **-c' anh-**. The rhetorical use of negative questions extends to expressions of doubt, fear, or anxiety: **Kass.ci anh.ulq ka kekceng sulepta** 'I am afraid / worried that he may have gone'. For more on this, see Kim Tongsik 1981.

11.8. Nominalizations.

Nominalization is the process of taking a sentence and turning it into a nominal phrase that can be used in some larger sentence as a single noun might be used:

Ponta 'He looks at it' → **Poki (ka cōh.ta)** 'Looking (is nice = is nice-looking)'.
Paywunta 'He learns it' → **Paywuki (ka elyepta)** 'To léarn it (is hard)'.
Onta 'He is coming' → **Oki (lul palanta)** '(We hope) that he is coming'.
Chamka hanta 'He participates' → **Chamka haki (lul kēcel hanta)** '(He refuses) to participate'.

As these examples show, one common nominalization uses the SUMMATIVE form (stem + **-ki**): **ponta** → **poki**; **cōh.ta** → **cōh.ki**; **cip ita** → **cip iki**. Another common nominalization uses an ADNOMINALIZATION (§11.9) + **kes** 'thing, one, fact, act, ...': **Cwunta** 'He gives it' → **Cwunun kes ul** (= **cwuki lul**) **cwuce hanta** 'He hesitates to give it'. (Earlier Korean used the substantive form **-um** for that kind of nominalization. See below.)

The nominalized sentence can be treated much like any noun. It can be followed by a particle, by another nominal which it modifies (**na-kaki cen** 'before going out', **ēps.ki ttaymun** 'because there were none'), by various particles, and occasionally by the copula: **ileh.key haki 'ta** 'Let's decide to do it this way'. Nominalizations with **kes** are especially flexible in use, and they occur freely predicated by the copula, sometimes with special meanings: **Yeki se n' tāmpay lul an phinun kes ita** 'It's a matter of not smoking here = It's No Smoking here'. For further examples, see **kes** and **-ki** in Part II.

The nominalized sentence may already contain adjuncts of its own (subjects, objects, etc.), so that when it is turned into a nominal that is used itself as an adjunct of the matrix sentence into which it is embedded you will sometimes find a sequence of phrases each marked with the same particle. In such cases the particle after the nominalization often drops: **Chayk ul ilk.ki (lul) cōh.a hanun ya?** 'Do you enjoy reading books?'; **Phyēnci lul ssuki (lul) sīcak hanta** 'He starts to write the letter'.

A less common nominalization is made with the SUBSTANTIVE form (stem + **-um/-m**). Aside from the sentence-final use in the DOCUMENTARY style (§11.3), and certain somewhat literary idioms (see **-um ey** and **-um ulo** in Part II), most cases of **-um** are single verbs or adjectives turned into nouns. But sometimes a larger source sentence is involved:

Māl i ani 'ta 'It is not language' → **Sayngkak i kot māl i ani 'm kwa kath.i ...** 'Just as thought is not language, ... '.

Yelq pen tut.nunta 'We hear it ten times', **Han pen ponta** 'We see it one time' → **Yelq pen tul.um i han pen pom man kath.ci mōs hata** 'Seeing once is better than hearing ten times'.

Ne uy sinpun i haksayng ita 'Your status is (that of) a student' → **Ne uy sinpun i haksayng im ul ic.ci mal.e la** 'Don't forget that you are (in the status of) a student'.

Kim Yengcwu 1985 explores the choice of **-um** vs. **-ki** and finds three semantic factors at work:
(1) influence — affecting the realization of the complement proposition;
(2) modified factivity — the truth value is presupposed for the complement proposition; or, if that precedes the time of the matrix act, the truth value is implied by the speaker;
(3) forward implication — the truth value is implied by the speaker for a complement proposition that follows the time of the matrix act.

Verbs of perception and discovery are found to occur with **-um** but not **-ki**; verbs of beginning, continuing, or stopping occur with **-ki** but not **-um**; verbs of helping occur with either, but with differing connotations. Kim Yengcwu (177) also notes that when the nominalizations with **kes** and with **-ki** are contrasted, **kes** tends to refer to concrete events and **-ki** to more abstract events.

Middle Korean made extensive use of the substantive, and the nominalizations it produced correspond in some cases to the modern structure of adnominalization + **kes** and in other cases to the modern use of the summative **-ki**. Other cases of **-ki** are equivalent to uses of -˙**ti**, the immediate ancestor of the suspective **-ci**, and there are a few examples of -˙**ki**, as well (see Part II).

Nominalizations can be made on the past (**-ess.ki, -ess.um**) and the future (**-keyss.ki, -keyss.um**), but these are used less freely than the constructions built on the postmodifier **kes** 'fact' following the various adnominalizations of tense-aspect conversions: **hayss.ta → han kes, hatula → hatun kes**, ...

To qualify as a sentential "nominalization" the construction must involve (or be able to involve) more than just a verb form shorn of adjuncts, for we treat cases of that sort as lexical derivations, nouns derived from the **-ki** summative form or made by the derived-noun suffix **-i** or the like. In the case of **-um** and **-ki** the nominalizations apparently do not enter into construction with the particle **uy**, as the lexically derived nouns would do; instead, they proceed directly to the adnominal function by simple juxtaposition. CF CM 1:384.

Among the special uses of nominalized conversions, attention should be directed to **-ki to (ha-)** and **-ki nun (ha-)** as a technique for highlighting or subduing the focus on the sentential nucleus, the verb or adjective itself, much as the particles **to** and **un/nun** are used to mark the focus on a noun or noun phrase (§10.5, §11.1). Special types of nominalization worthy of attention are adnominalizations + postmodifiers, especially those (**ci, ka, tey, ya**) which call for the complex **-nun** modifiers; some of these are used as full sentences, e.g. in the question conversions of §11.5.

There is a peculiar construction that we will call a POSTAPPOSITIONAL nominalization. It consists of a sentence adnominalized to a generalizing epitheme, typically **kes** 'thing/one' or Middle Korean ˙**i** 'one that ··· ', which semantically echoes the subject or object in the adnominalized sentence. An example: ... **yeki cēki so ka han mali twū mali iss.nun kes i po.yess.ta** 'one or two cows were visible here and there' (Wagner 39). MK examples: ¨*salom pwo˙n i* ¨*mata* (1447 Sek 24:13b) 'everyone he saw', *ne y nay oy ... ˙TTWO-˙THWALQ honwo.n i lol pwono.n i* ([1447→]1562 Sek 11:7-8, cited in He Wung 1975:356) 'you have seen me achieve salvation and deliverance'; ˙*kil[h] maka ˙s˙non* [= *ma˙ka ˙s˙non*] *hon ˙phe˙ki s ˙sa˙m i ˙pi ˙wona˙tun kwos ˙phwuy˙Gwo polom ˙kol˙kye˙tun ye˙lum moys.non ke˙s ˙ye* (?1517- Pak 1:40a; *moys.non ← moyc-non*) 'a hemp plant blocking the road blossoms when it rains and bears fruit when the wind blows'. Similar examples in Japanese are discussed in Martin 1975:860-2 and in Kuroda 1974-7.

11.9. Adnominalizations; epithemes.

Any Korean sentence can be made adnominal to modify a nominal in some larger sentence (the matrix into which it is embedded) by replacing the final inflected form with the appropriate MODIFIER. See §9.3 for the forms. The patterns can be summarized for our nuclear sentences as follows:

(1) **Ponta. → Ponun** ··· ' ··· that one sees' or ' ··· that/who sees it' or ' ... that one sees it'.
 Cōh.ta. → Cōh.un ··· ' ··· that is good' or ' ··· that it is good'
 Cip ita. → Cip in ··· ' ··· that is a house' or ' ··· that it is a house'

(2) **Ponta. → Pwass.ta. → Pon** ··· ' ··· that one saw' or 'that/who saw it' or 'that one saw it'
   → Pwass.nun (ci, ka, tey, ya) ···
 Cōh.ta. → Cōh.ass.ta. → − (Use **Cōh.un** ··· ↑ ; or **Cōh.tun** ··· ↓)
   → Cōh.ass.nun (ci, ka, tey, ya) ···
 Cip ita. → Cip iess.ta. → − (Use **Cip in** ··· ↑ ; or **Cip itun** ··· ↓)
   → Cip iess.nun (ci, ka, tey, ya) ···

Co Sek.yen has suggested that we regard the simple modifier **-un**, when it is used to express the past for the verb, as an obligatory reduction of **-ess.nun**, so that: **pwass.ta → *pwass.nun (sālam) → pon (sālam)**. Before **ci, ka, tey,** and **ya** it is obligatory NOT to reduce the form.

(3) **Ponta. → Potula. → Potun** ··· ' ··· that one saw(, it has been observed)' or ' ··· that/who was seeing it(, it has been observed)' or ' ··· that one saw(, it has been observed)'.
 Cōh.ta. → Cōh.tula → Cōh.tun ··· ' ··· that was good(, it has been observed)' or ' ··· that it was

good(, it has been observed)'.

Cip ita. → Cip itula. → Cip itun ··· ' ··· that was a house(, it has been observed)' or ' ··· that it was a house(, it has been observed)'.

(4) Ponta. → Pwass.ta. → Pwass.tula. → Pwass.tun ··· ' ··· that one saw(, it has been observed)' or ' ··· that / who saw it(, it has been observed)' or ' ··· that one saw it(, it has been observed)'.

Cōh.ta. → Cōh.ass.ta → Cōh.ass.tula. → Cōh.ass.tun ··· ' ··· that was [or had been] good(, it has been observed)'.

Cip ita. → Cip iess.ta. → Cip iess.tula. → Cip iess.tun ··· ' ··· that was [or had been] a house(, it has been observed)' or ' ··· that it was [or had been] a house(, it has been observed)'.

(5) Ponta. → Pokeyss.ta. → Pol(q) ··· ' ··· that one will see' or ' ··· that / who will see it' or ' ··· that one will see it'.
→ Pokeyss.nun (ci, ka, tey, ya) ···
→ Pol.nun ci ···

Cōh.ta. → Cōh.keyss.ta. → Cōh.ul(q) ··· ' ··· that will be good' or ' ··· that it will be good'.
→ Cōh.keyss.nun (ci, ka, tey, ya) ···
→ Cōh.ul.nun ci ···

Cip ita. → Cip ikeyss.ta. → Cip il(q) ··· ' ··· that will be a house' or ' ··· that it will be a house'.
→ Cip ikeyss.nun (ci, ka, tey, ya) ···
→ Cip il.nun ci ···

(6) Ponta. → Pwass.ta. → Pwass.keyss.ta. → Pwass.ul(q) ··· ' ··· that one probably saw' or ' ··· that / who probably saw it' or ' ··· that one probably saw it'.
→ Pwass.keyss.nun (ci, ka, tey, ya) ···
→ Pwass.ul.nun ci ···

Cōh.ta. → Cōh.ass.ta → Cōh.ass.keyss.ta → Cōh.ass.ul(q) ··· ' ··· that probably was good' or ' ··· that it probably was good'.
→ Cōh.ass.keyss.nun (ci, ka, tey, ya) ···
→ Cōh.ass.ul.nun ci ···

Cip ita. → Cip iess.ta → Cip iess.keyss.ta. → Cip iess.ul(q) ··· ' ··· that probably was a house' or ' ··· that it probably was a house'.
→ Cip iess.keyss.nun (ci, ka, tey, ya) ···
→ Cip iess.ul.nun ci ···

But the forms in -ess.ul(q) seem to be infrequent except when the prospective modifier is conventional with a particular noun (or postmodifier) such as **ttay** 'time (when ···)': **elyess.ulq ttay** 'when (one was) young' can be regarded as a conversion of **(ku ttay) elyess.ta** '(at that time) one was young' more easily than of **(ku ttay) elyess.keyss.ta** '(at that time) one probably was young'.

There are also past-future retrospective modifiers **-ess.keyss.tun**, presumably from something like **Ponta. → Pwass.ta. → Pwass.keyss.ta. → Pwass.keyss.tula. → Pwass.keyss.tun** ··· ' ··· that, according to observation, one probably saw' or ' ··· that / who, according to observation, probably saw it' or ' ··· that, according to observation, one probably saw it'. But, like the past-future retrospective, occurrences are rare, and I have been unable to find examples that native speakers feel happy with. (Choy Hyenpay lists examples, but they sound unnatural.)

The modern retrospective carries a restriction when it is predicative (rather than adnominal): the subject cannot be first person, because **-tula** is reporting the speaker's perceptual experience as evidence for his statement. This narrowing of the retrospective to 'I observed that ··· ' was not present in Middle Korean, which used the retrospective to report recent past events in general; the requirement of perceptual observation by the speaker seems to have come in with the development of the past-tense marker **-ess-**. (That marker was made by contracting the infinitive-auxiliary conversion **-e iss-**, which also survived uncontracted as the modern perfect-resultative structure.) The MK sentence ˙na y ˙˙lwongtam ˙hota˙la (1447 Sek 6:24b) 'I was joking' cannot be translated into modern *Nay ka

¹nōngtam hatula; instead, it must be rendered as **Nay ka ¹nōngtam hayss.ta** (or **hako iss.ess.ta**). But the adnominalization carries no such restriction, so that you can say **nay ka hatun ¹nōngtam** 'the joke I was making' for the (unattested) MK ˙na y ˙ho˙tan ¨lwongtam. On these interesting points, see Cang Sekcin 1973, Cang Kyenghuy 1985, Choy Tongcwu 1988, ¹Yi Hyosang 1991.

The quasi-processive verbs **iss.ta** and **ēps.ta** adnominalize in the same way as **ponta**, but their "past" adnominalizations **iss.un** and **ēps.un** are fairly rare. Where they are expected, we more often hear the "present" (**iss.nun, ēps.nun**) or the retrospective (**iss.tun, ēps.tun**).

Several characteristics of Korean adnominalizations should be pointed out. One is that the relationship between the adnominalized sentence and the nominal that it modifies is intrinsically ambiguous: **ponun ayki** can mean either 'the baby that is looking at it' (← **Ayki ka ponta** 'The baby looks at it') or 'the baby one is looking at' (← **Ayki lul ponta** 'One looks at the baby'). Expanding the adnominalized sentence sometimes clarifies the meaning: **kōng ponun ayki** is certainly more likely to mean 'the baby that looks at the ball' than to mean 'the ball that looks at the baby'. But that is because the listener knows a lot about babies and balls. From what he knows about babies and dogs, **kāy ponun ayki** could mean either 'the baby that looks at the dog' or 'the baby that the dog looks at'. Adding grammatical specification to the adjuncts expressed in the expansion helps considerably: **kāy ka ponun ayki** could only mean 'the baby that the dog looks at', because direct object is the only role left available, and **kāy lul ponun ayki** could only mean 'the baby that looks at the dog' because it is the subject role that is now available and the object role is not. The relationship need not be subject or object: **ku i ka kongpu hatun hak.kyo** 'the school he has been studying at' is a conversion of **Ku hak.kyo ey se ku i ka kongpu hatula** 'He was studying at that school (as I recall)', and **emeni ka tōn ul cwun ai** 'the child the mother gave the money to' is a conversion of **Ku ai eykey emeni ka tōn ul cwuess.ta** 'Mother gave money to that child'. The noun that serves as the head of the structure (the target of the adnominalization) is an EPITHEME and epithemes are of several kinds:

(1) extruded from a constituent of the adnominalized sentence (and in the process losing any case particle that may have marked the source phrase)

(1a) from the subject (or other nominative-marked phrase): **sinmun ul ponun namca** 'the man (who is) looking at the newspaper' ← **Ku namca ka sinmun ul ponta** 'That man looks at the newspaper'; and, from the possessor in a possessive sentence: **tōn i ēps.nun haksayng** 'a student (who is) without money' ← **Ku haksayng i tōn i ēps.ta** 'That student lacks money'.

(1b) from the direct object (or other accusative-marked phrase): **ku namca ka ponun sinmun** 'the paper the man is looking at' ← **Ku namca ka ku sinmun ul ponta** 'That man looks at the newspaper'.

(1c) from the indirect object: **nay ka sēnmul ul ponayl chinkwu** 'the friend whom I'm sending a gift to' ← **Nay ka ku chinkwu hanthey sēnmul ul ponaykeyss.ta** 'I am going to send a gift to a friend'.

(1d) from an adverbialized phrase, or a phrase with oblique-case marking:

(TIME WHEN) **Haksayng iess.tun yēys nal (ul sayngkak hanta)** '(I think of) the old days when I was a student' ← **(Nay ka) yēys nal ey haksayng iess.ta** 'I was a student in the old days'.

(PLACE WHERE) **wuli ka pap ul mek.un cip** 'the house where we ate our meal' ← **Wuli ka ku cip ey se pap ul mek.ess.ta** 'We ate our meal in that house'.

(PLACE TO WHERE) **um.ak-ka tul i kanun tapang** 'a teashop that musicians go to' ← **Um.ak-ka tul i ku tapang ey kanta** 'Musicians go to that teashop'.

(INSTRUMENT WITH WHICH) **nay ka yenphil man kkakk.nun khal** 'the knife that I use only to sharpen pencils with' ← **nay ka ku khal lo yenphil man kkakk.nunta** 'I sharpen only pencils with that knife'.

(2) with a transitional epitheme

(2a) of time: **Ku ka tte-nan ithut-nal (ey ku emeni ka cwuk.ess.ta)** 'The day after he left (his mother died)'.

(2b) of place: **mānh.un kawuntey se hana (lul kacinta)** '(I take) one of many'.

(2c) of circumstance: **Pi ka onun tey (com te kyēysita kasipsio)** '(Stay a little longer); it's raining'.

(3) with a resultative epitheme: **pi ka onun soli (lul tut.nunta)** '(I hear) the sound of it raining'.

(4) with a summational epitheme – in various functions, including factual (or "extended") predication 'it's that ... ': **Il-nyen cen ey pon kes i ku lul macimak pon kes iess.ta** 'The last I saw of him was a year ago'.

In an identificational sentence, the Identified is the subject and the Identifier is the complement of the copula, unmarked in the affirmative but marked by the nominative particle in the negative: **Wuli ka Hānkwuk sālam ita** 'We are Koreans', **Wuli ka Ilponq sālam i ani 'ta** 'We are not Japanese'. The Identifier is not epithematized, but the Identified is freely extruded as an epitheme: **Hānkwuk sālam in wuli** 'we who are Koreans', **Ilponq sālam i ani 'n wuli** 'we who are not Japanese'. The epitheme can serve any role in a matrix sentence, including that of Identified. A sentence such as **Hānkwuk sālam in wuli 'ta** would seem to mean 'It is we who are Koreans', but it serves as a stylistic variant of the simple identificational sentence (**Wuli ka Hānkwuk sālam ita**) and it is to be translated as 'We are Koreans'. This phenomenon of EPITHEMATIC IDENTIFICATION, representing a stylistic inversion of the underlying subject (the Identified), can be found in Middle Korean texts:

KYWOW-KYWOW ˙ho.ya ¨pyel s kawon-toy s twu˙lyewun ˙to.l isyas˙ta (1482 Kum-sam 2:24b) 'brightly shining it is a round moon in the midst of clouds' = 'a round moon is shining in the midst of clouds'.

¨alay ˙PALQ "CHOY-"NYE matco˙Wa ˙PPEM-MA-LA ˙KWUYK LIM ˙CCYENG ˙SSO ˙lwo ˙kazo˙Wwon ˙na 'ylwo˙n i (1459 Wel 8:92b) 'having met the eight comely maidens I went [with them] to Woods-Calm Temple in the land of the brahmans'.

cyens˙kos ¨cywung i tu˙le ¨nay˙Gey hol ˙ss ol nil˙Gwon ˙CCO-˙CO 'yla (1462 ¹Nung 1:29a) '[the word] ˙CCO-˙CO (pravārana = end of restraint) means letting the monks express themselves as they will'.

e˙nu ˙lol nil˙Gwon ˙CYENG ˙PEP-"NGAN ˙kwo (1482 Kum-sam 2:69a) 'what does "the true Dharma Eye" mean?' [the copula modifier ˙in is ellipted before ˙kwo 'question'].

Similar epithematic identification is found in both modern and classical Japanese.

The particles in the adnominalized sentence (or what is left when a constituent is extruded as an epitheme) remain much the same as in the source sentence. In general, focus subdual of the subject or object of a modifying phrase is avoided, since the particle **un/nun** would usually set the word off as the subdued adjunct (subject, object, or whatnot) of the entire larger sentence, the matrix in which the adnominalized sentence is embedded. Compare **Ilk.e se nun an toynta** 'You mustn't read it' → **ilk.e se an toynun (chayk)** '(a book) that you mustn't read'. Instead of taking **i/ka**, the subject of an adnominalized sentence is sometimes marked by the particle **uy**. At first I thought this was due to the influence of Japanese, where the corresponding particle no is sometimes used in place of ga to mark the subject of an adnominalized sentence (see Martin 1975:659-64 for the details). But the Korean usage goes back to the earliest Hankul texts and is true not only for the particle **uy** (and its MK ancestors) but also for the now obsolete particle *s* of Middle Korean. The Middle Korean particles *ᵘ⁄oy* and *s* can substitute for ˙i in adnominalized sentences, both when the epitheme (head noun) is extruded from one of the noun arguments and when it is a summational epitheme, including *t* and *s*:

˙i ˙SYANG ˙on ˙YWOK-˙QOY ˙uy ¨na˙syan ˙t i a˙ni ˙si˙n i (1462 ¹Nung 1:42a) 'this aspect is not what desire is born from'.

ku ˙psk uy CYE-¨CO y api ˙uy PPYEN-QAN ˙hi ancon˙t ol ¨al˙Gwo ¨ta a˙p[i] oy key ˙ka a˙p[i] oy key nilGwo˙toy (1463 Pep 2:138b) 'at that time the masters, finding that the father was seated comfortably, all went to the father and said to the father as follows ... '.

˙HHOYNG on ˙HHAK-ZIN ˙oy HHOYNG hol ˙s iGwo (1482 Kum-sam 2:20b) '[the word] ˙HHOYNG means that the scholar performs, and ... '.

I have not found an example of this phenomenon with ˙i as the epitheme, either as extruded ('the one that ... ') or summational ('the fact that ... '); it probably does not occur, though adnominal modification is possible, as in the passage *˙SSYWOK ˙oy CAY-˙KAY ˙yey ˙two mek˙ti a˙ni ˙khwo n' ˙homol˙mye CIN-˙SSILQ s tas.no˙n i 'sto˙n ye* (1462 ¹Nung 8:4-5) 'when even in the fasts of commoners they refrain from eating them [the five forbidden roots], how much more so the true student (of the discipline)?' Nominalizations made with the substantive ... *(ᵘ⁄o)m*, corresponding to modern ····**-(u)n (-(u)lq, -nun,**

-tun) kes 'the fact that ... ' permitted the option: LWO-ˇLWOW y kutuy s ˇwoˑm ol kituˑliˑtela hoˑla (1482 Nam 1:50b) 'he has been long waiting for you to come'; ˇtwu ˇsaloˑm oy ˑPWOK ˑTUK ˇetwuˑm i hon kaˑci ʼˑn i ˇesˑtyey ʼGeˑn ywo [< ˑhokeˑn ˑywo] (1447 Sek 23:4a) 'how did it happen that two people's obtaining happiness and virtue was the same?'.

Middle Korean *kes* usually served as a generalized replacement for an extruded epitheme 'thing' or 'the one', as in KWONG ˑoy nilkuˑsiˑnwon keˑs un ˇesˑte ʼn ˇmaˑl i-ngi s ˑkwo (1465 Wen se:68a) 'what words are you reading, my Lord?', but like *t* or *s* it could also be used as a summational epitheme 'the fact that ... ':

KON ˑoy ˇnin keˑs i aˑni ʼʼGen maˑlon (1462 ¹Nung 2:81b) 'it is not that a root arose, but ... .'
ˑmwoˑm ol ˇmwot miˑtulq keˑs iˑn i (1447 Sek 6:11b) 'the body is not to be trusted'.
ˇsyenghyen tiˑGwuy ˑyey ˇmwot kal ˑka pwunˑpyel aˑni hol keˑs iˑl i (1518 Sohak-cho 8:13b) 'will not worry over whether one might be unable to go to the position of a sage'.
Examples in the role of extruded epitheme (replacing a more specific noun):
nonun keˑs iˑm ye (1459 Wel 1:11a) 'things that fly and ... '.
poyˑhwoˑnon keˑs i muˑsu ˇiˑl in ˑkwo (1518 Sohak-cho 8:33b) 'what is it we learn?'.
SSIN-ˑLUK [ˑ]uy ˑHWA ˑhoˑsyan keˑs un pas[k] ˇchyenlyang ˑay ˇnamˑti ˇmwot hoˑn i (1463 Pep 6:144a) 'what the supernatural power has brought into being is no more than external property'.

In contemporary Japanese the no option is largely stylistic, but earlier it appears to have involved focus and emphasis (the ga option being more emphatic), and that may be true of the Korean situation, too: marking the subject of the adnominalized sentence with **uy** rather than **i/ka** deemphasizes it much as the particle **un/nun** subdues the focus on the theme of the matrix sentence.

NOTE: Despite our translation, the ˑuy in ˇta QWUY-NGWANG ˑuy naˑmon KWONG aˑni ˑka (1463 Pep se:13a) 'is it not all the achievement left by the mighty king?' is not marking the underlying subject, for the verb ˇnam- is normally intransitive, and the structure in question is probably to be treated as ... naˑmon KWONG 'the achievement that remained' with an epitheme extruded from the subject of [unattested] QWUY-NGWANG ˑuy KWONG i naˑma ʼ(y)sˑta 'the mighty king's achievement has remained' leaving the adnominal phrase behind, perhaps to avoid the construal 'the achievement of the king who remained' that would be suggested by naˑmon QWUY-NGWANG ˑuy KWONG.

We naturally expect an adnominalization to be followed by a noun or noun phrase as its head, but occasionally the structure will occur at the end of a sentence, usually with an implied nominal or an obviously ellipted noun, as in some of the question conversions (§11.5) and in certain set exclamations such as ¹**nāncang mac.ul** (or **chil**)! 'dammit!' where the implied nominal is probably **nom** 'rascal − to be beaten mercilessly!'. There are also constructions of modifier + postnoun and the like, perhaps to be treated as quasi-compounds (§10.3), since they usually involve verbs unaccompanied by adjuncts. An example: **nan cil** 'unchaste behavior (by women)' from the modifier of **na-** 'go out' (and not from LAN 'disorder').

The copula adnominalizations (... **in**, ... **ilq**, ...) are often replaced by adnominalizations based on quotations (§11.11) even when no actual quoting is intended. This is especially common in stating names of people or things: **Kim Poktong ila ʼnun sālam** 'a man (they call) Kim Poktong', **wenca-than ila ʼn kes** '(the thing called) the atom bomb'. Copula sentences can be adnominalized, in a sense, also by dropping the copula and letting the noun stand alone in adnominal position (or specifying the adnominal role with the particle **uy**). Compare the stylistic dropping of the copula mentioned in §11.1.

Adnominalization can be applied to quite complex sentences that are the result of prior conversions of various kinds, including other adnominalizations already embedded in the complex sentence to be adnominalized. When one confronts an unheralded epitheme in structures where English often uses a clarifying adnominalizer in the form of a relative pronoun or adverb, minimally "... that", problems of interpretation arise as one tries to decide both the scope and the role(s) of the epitheme, which may be extruded from more than one underlying role in a complex adnominalization. The grammar of Korean adnominalization is very similar to that of Japanese adnominalization, as described in Martin 1975.

11.10. Adverbializations.

An adverbialization turns a sentence into an adverbial phrase for a larger sentence by changing the final inflected form into some other form. Some of the adverbializations are often used to end a sentence that is not necessarily a truncation of a larger sentence, though that is probably the origin of such usages as sentence-final **-e (yo), -ko (yo), -nun ke l' (yo), -nun tey (yo), -uni-kka (yo),** ... . Representative semantic types of adverbialization are listed below.

"and" forms

gerund **-ko** 'and also; and then' < ˙*kwo*
conjunctive **-umye / -mye** 'and also; and then' < -˙$^u/o$˙*m ye*
sequential **-uni / -ni** (in some uses) 'and thereupon' < -˙$^u/o$˙*n i*
infinitive **-^{e}/a** (or **-^{e}/a** + particle **se**) 'and then; and so' < -˙^{e}/a ˙*sye*
modifier **-un / -n** (etc.) + postmodifier **kes** + particle **i** 'and so (I infer)' (see Part II for examples)

"but" forms[1]

adversative **-una / -na** < -˙$^u/o$˙*na* (and extended adversative **-una-ma**,
   tentative adversative **-kena** < -˙*ke˙na*)
concessive **-toy** < accessive -˙*toy*; **-(u)toy** (SEE p. 823)
literary concessive **-kenul** < -˙*ke˙n$^u/o$l*
semi-literary concessive **-ken man** < -˙*ken ma˙non / ma˙lon*
frustrated intentive **-ulyenman / -lyenman**
suspective **-ci** + particle **man**
infinitive **-e** + particle **to** 'even if ... ; though ... ' < -˙*e ˙two*
conditional **-umyen / -myen** + particle **se** + particle **to**
modifier **-un, -(ess-/keyss-)nun, -(ess-/keyss-)tun, -ulq / -lq** + postmodifier
   ke(s) + particle **ul / l(ul)**[2]
modifier **-un / -n, -(ess-/keyss-)nun, -(ess-/keyss-)tun** + postmodifier **tey**
   + particle **to** 'even though (given the circumstance that) ... '
modifier **-un / -n** + postmodifier **tul** 'granted that ... , even though ... ' [literary] < -˙$^u/on$ ˙*t ol*

[1] Concessive conversions suggested by CM: **hanta** → **hatula to, hayss.ta** → **hay to, hakeyss.ta** → **halq ci 'la to** (or **hal mangceng**). Notice also **halq ci enceng**.

[2] Sometimes the particle **i**: **Ilenq īl i iss.ulq ka pwā se ilccik-i onta ko han kes i ... (nemu pappe se mōs wass.ta)** 'I was afraid this kind of thing would happen, so I meant to come earlier, but ... (I was too busy to get here)'. See also **-ta (ka)** 'and/but then'. The **-ulq ke l'** forms are common in various extensions of meaning; see the entry in Part II.

"when / if" forms

sequential **-uni / -ni** < -˙$^u/o$˙*n i*
   (and tentative sequential **-keni** < -˙*ke˙n i*, prospective sequential **-ulini** < -˙$^u/o$˙*l i ˙'n i*)
conditional **-umyen / -myen** < -˙$^u/o$˙*m ye n'*
conditional **-umyen / -myen** + particle **se** 'while'
contingent **-um / -m ey (-umay / -may)** < -˙(w)$^u/o$˙*m ^{e}/ay*
provisional **-ketun** < -˙*ke˙tun*
tentative conditional **-ketumyen**
literary conditional **-kentay**
subjunctive assertive **-ca** 'as soon as', often + **māca** ← **mālca** 'no sooner ... than'
infinitive **-e** + particle **se** 'and then' < -˙*e ˙sye*
infinitive **-e** + particle **ya** 'only if' < -˙*e ˙za*
transferentive **-ta** (+ **ka**) 'and / but then' < -˙*ta (˙ka)*
infinitive **-e** + **pwā (la)** or **posey (yo)** 'suppose ... ' = 'if'

"since / therefore" forms

sequential **-uni / -ni** — especially the extended sequential **-uni-kka / -ni-kka (n')**
infinitive **-e** + particle **se** 'and so' < -˙e ˙sye
substantive **-(ess-/keyss-)um/-m** + particle **ulo / lo** < -˙ᵘ⁄₀˙m ᵘ⁄₀˙lwo
modifier **-un / -n** etc. + postmodifier **kes** + particle **i / ka**
modifier **-un / -n, -(ess-/keyss-)nun, -(ess-/keyss-)tun** + postmodifier **ke(s)** + particle **ul / l(ul)**
? modifier **-un / -n** etc. + postmodifier **kes** + particle **ulo / lo**
modifier **-un / -n** etc. + postmodifier **kkatalk** + particle **ulo / lo**
summative **-(ess-/-keyss-)ki** + particle **ey** or particle **ulo / lo**
summative **-(ess-/-keyss-)ki** + noun **ttaymun** + particle **ey; -killey (-killay)**
modifier **-un / -n, -(ess-/keyss-)nun, -(ess-/keyss-)tun** + postmodifier **tey** — see also §11.3.3

"so that, so as to" forms

adverbative **-key** (CF the uses in causative conversions) < -˙key
derived adverb **-i** (for those adjectives that have the form)[1] < -˙i
projective **-tolok** 'to the point that ··· ' < -˙to˙lwok
intentive **-ulye / -lye** < -˙ᵘ⁄₀˙l ye; purposive **-ule / -le**
processive adjunctive (+ particle) **-nula (ko)**

[1] Since the derived adverb can retain the syntactic properties of the underlying adjective, carrying its own adjuncts, such as a subject.

The above lists are by no means exhaustive. They could be considerably enlarged if we take into account all the adverbializations built on other conversions, such as the "when" form made by first adnominalizing the sentence with the prospective modifier **-ul(q)** and then adding the noun **ttay** 'time (when ···)', with or without the particle **ey** 'at'. Nor have we gone into all the various uses of these adverbializations, e.g. the use of the gerund **-ko** and the infinitive **-e** with auxiliaries (§7.5). See also the use of the summative **-ki** with the particle **to** or the particle **un / nun** to highlight or subdue the focus on the nominalization (mentioned in §11.8, §11.16).

More information on each adverbialization will be found in the individual entries of Part II. A great deal more needs to be said, in particular for the foreign student of Korean. One vexing question: how do we know when 'because' is to be expressed with **-uni(-kka)** and when with **-e (se)**? According to Lukoff and Nam (1982), **-uni-ikka** represents logical ARGUMENTATION derived from DISCOVERY and **-e se** represents a logical ASSERTION OF CAUSE derived from RELATED SEQUENCE. For more on this problem, see [1]Yi Cenglo 1975 and 1978, [1]Yi Cengmin 1979, and [1]Yang Insek 1972. The Korean situation is similar to the difference between the Japanese constructions ··· **no de** and ··· **kara**, which Mikami attributed to a difference between objective versus subjective reason (Martin 1975:857). The argumentation (objective) construction permits the insertion of the past tense, **-ess-uni(-kka)**, but that is difficult or impossible with the causal-assertion (subjective) construction: [1]Yi Cenglo rejects *-ess.e se and others say it sounds artificial and suggest replacement with just **-e se**, using the past only for the final verb of the sentence. In the meaning of causal assertion **-e se** cannot be followed by a command or a proposition (i.e. by another subjective form), a restriction similar to that for Japanese ··· **kara**. If not asserting causality, **-e se** can be followed by a command or proposition: **Yeki anc.e se kitalisipsio** 'Please sit here and wait'. We can think of **-uni-kka** as a strengthened form of **-uni**, emphasizing the argument or discovery, and we can think of **-e** as a relaxed form of **-e (se)**, perhaps weakening the assertion or maybe just a contraction; but the longer and the shorter forms are not interchangeable in all situations.

A related problem is when to use **-e (se)** for the 'and (then)' meaning and when to use **-ko** or the emphasized version **-ko se**; see the entries in Part II. As with the adnominalizations, adverbializations of the copula are often built on the quotation conversion, so we sometimes find **ila 'myen**, ··· **ila 'ni**, etc., where we might expect just **imyen, ini**, etc., with an added touch of the hypothetical.

11.11. Quotations; oblique questions; putative structures.

Quotations are frequent in Korean. Quoted is not only what people have said, but also what the speaker thinks or intends (**-ulye ko hanta**), and sometimes the "quotation" is merely a grammatical device that is used to lengthen, soften, or emphasize a sentence. Direct quotation — reporting the exact words — is not common in conversation, and in books it is usually introduced by the formula **A ka māl haki lul** ··· 'A's saying [as direct object]' and ended by the formula **hako (māl) hayss.ta** 'said' or just **hako** 'saying' as an afterthought sentence (§11.3.5). Another way to state a direct quotation is to append to the quoted sentence the expression ··· **(i)la ko (māl) hayss.ta** 'said ["that it is"]' or just ··· **hayss.ta** 'said' (King 1988a). This treats the quoted sentence (or fragment) as if it were a noun, and seems to be a fairly recent innovation. Since virtually all finite verb forms end in a vowel, the pseudo particle **ila ko** is nearly always heard in the postvocalic shape **'la ko**, and some speakers feel uncomfortable identifying it with **ila ko**. When a juncture is inserted between the quoted sentence and the quoting verb phrase, the abbreviation **'la ko** remains and is not restored to **ila ko**: "Ēps.ᵘup.nita" | **'la ko hayss.ta** 'said, "There are none"'. But that just shows that the juncture is inserted late in the process of phonetic realization and is somewhat artificial. When the quoted sentence ends in a consonant, only the full form **ila ko** can be pronounced: "Son nim i osyess.kwumen" **ila ko hayss.ta** or "Son nim i osyess.kwun" **ila ko hayss.ta** 'said, "Why, a guest has arrived!"'; "Cāmqkan man kitalilyem" **ila ko hayss.ta** 'said, "Why don't you just wait a little bit?"'.

Indirect quotations — reporting the gist — have the expected shift of specification, pronominal reference, honorifics, etc. A person will not use honorifics about himself, but in quoting what he has said I may well want to use honorifics about his acts and intentions, and I will remove any honorific references to me. The sentence is left in the PLAIN style — or reduced back to the plain style from whatever stylization it may have undergone. But in quotations the plain style copula changes from **ita** to **ila** and the command changes from **-e la** to the subjunctive attentive **-ula / -la**, as in these examples:

Cip ita. 'It is a house.'   Cip ila ko hayss.ta 'He said it is/was a house' or 'He called it a house'.
Mek.e la! 'Eat!'   Mek.ula ko hayss.ta 'He told me to eat'.

Notice that the English translation of **-ula ko hanta** is often 'tells one to do it' and the translation of **-ca ko hanta** is often 'suggests doing it'.

Quoted questions are always in the **-nun ya** version of the plain forms (**-nun ya**, **-keyss.nun ya**, **-ess.nun ya**) and **-un ya** is used only for the present adjectives and copula, so that **cōh.ta** → **cōh.un ya (ko)** but **cōh.keyss.ta** → **cōh.keyss.nun ya (ko)**. The form **-ul ya** is used only in literary questions, usually rhetorical. A somewhat bookish variant for quoting adjective and copula questions uses **-un ka** instead of **-un ya**: Musun māl in ka (ko) mul.ess.ta = Musun māl in ya (ko) mul.ess.ta 'He asked which word it was (or: what the talk was all about)'.

What is quoted is followed by a verb of saying (telling, inquiring) or of thinking (opinion, intention): **māl hanta** or just **hanta** 'says', **mūt.nunta (mul.e)** 'asks, inquires', **cwucang hanta** 'claims', **myēng.lyeng hanta** 'orders, commands', **sayngkak hanta** 'thinks', … . Optionally the particle **ko** can be attached to show the end of the quoted content. If the quoting verb is omitted the quotation is left as a fragment, or "afterthought", and the particle **ko** is used to end the sentence.

In addition to the sentence-final forms (statement, question, command, suggestion — but not the apperceptive), the intentive is also indirectly quoted: **-ulye (ko) hanta** 'feels that one would like to do; has it in mind (has the intention) to do; tries/starts to do; will do'. Common variants, often regarded as nonstandard, are **-ulya / -lya** and **-ulla / -lla** + **hanta** or an abbreviation of that structure which leads to the contracted forms **-ulla 'nta**, **-ulla 'y**, … . The familiar question form **-ulq ka** is quoted with the meaning 'is thinking of doing, is wondering whether to do', as in **Kalq ka hanta** 'I am thinking of going'. The intentive **-ulye / -lye**, it should be noted, probably comes from the prospective modifier **-ul** + a variant of **ya** 'question'. Quotation also underlies **-nula ko** and **-ulla ko**.

Since the quotation may, but need not, include the particle **ko**, we can speak of a SIMPLE quotation (**-ta hanta** etc.) and an EXPANDED quotation (**-ta ko hanta** etc.). In addition, there is an ABBREVIATED quotation made with contracted forms of **ha-**: **-ta 'nta, -la 'nta, -ca 'nta, -nun ya 'nta,** ... . The form **-ulye 'nta** is an abbreviated version of **-ulye hanta** and the expanded version is **-ulye ko hanta**.

These remarks refer to indirect quotation. In addition to the three kinds of indirect quotation – simple, expanded, and abbreviated – there is also direct quotation with the particle **hako** or the pseudoparticle **ila ko**. A direct quotation can be reported as SAID by anyone, including the speaker, but it can be reported as THOUGHT only by the speaker. An indirect quotation, on the other hand, can be reported as thought or said by anyone. In Middle Korean both direct and indirect quotations were made in the same several ways and could be differentiated only by the words within the quoted sentence, such as the pronouns, deictics, and verbal endings. The quotation was optionally marked by *ho˙ya*, the infinitive of °*ho-* 'do; be; say', here functioning like modern **hako**, and followed by a verb of saying; if the verb of saying was the minimal °*ho-* itself, the quotation stood unmarked; like modern **hako**, *ho˙ya* could not be used when immediately followed by a form of the same stem, and it was optional only before the other verbs of saying. Middle Korean also had a naming construction NAME *i˙la* °*ho-* 'say it is, say it to be' = 'call it NAME'. And there was a pattern - *toy* " ... " *(°ho-)*, with the accessive form of a verb of saying (*nil˙Gwo˙toy* 'says', *mwu˙lwo˙toy* 'asks', *solang hwo˙toy* 'thinks'), like modern **haki lul** " ... " **ha-** (or **hako māl ha-**) 'says / said as follows: " ... ". For more on the history of reported speech see the excellent survey in King 1988a and the works cited in his bibliography. The quotative particle **ko** (probably from an abbreviation of **hako**) is first attested in the 20th century (Kim Sungkon 1978:199), except for one case of **halya ko** in 1890 Starchevskiy (King 1991a:191).

The abbreviated quotations of statements are used with a special meaning in the following styles: plain (**-ta 'nta**), formal (**-ta 'p.nita**), semiformal (**-ta 'o**), familiar (**ta 'ney**). The special meaning is one of emphasis or insistence, something like 'I TELL you it is / does = it really is / does; mind you it is / does'. Sometimes the translation 'you see' or 'you know' or 'don't you know / see' is appropriate; and sometimes irony is implied. The common and rather vacuous Japanese expression ... (to iu) wa⌉ke desu 'I mean' has been suggested as a good translation.

Somewhat similar to quotation is the citing of OBLIQUE QUESTIONS. These are stated by changing the postmodifier **ya** to **ci**: **Kanun ya?** 'Is he going?' → **kanun ci** ... ' ... whether he is going (or not)', **Eti kass.nun ya** 'where did he go?' → **eti kass.nun ci** ... ' ... where he went', **Mues i pissan ya** 'What is expensive?' → **mues i pissan ci** ... ' ... what is expensive'. In addition to the future processive modifier **-keyss.nun** that we expect, there is an optional and more common form: the prospective processive modifier **-ul.nun**, and that form is restricted to use with the postmodifier **ci**. The pattern: **Mues ul pat.keyss.nun ya** 'What will we get?' → **mues ul pat.keyss.nun / pat.ul.nun ci** ... ' ... what we will get'. The oblique question is to be followed by an information verb such as **ā-l-** 'know', **molu-** 'not know', **ic-** 'forget', **kiek na-** 'remember', **sayngkak na-** 'recall', **kaluchi-** 'tell, teach', etc. These oblique questions – used in such sentences as 'I don't know whether he is coming', 'I forgot what I got', 'Do you recall how much it was?' – are the source of UNCERTAINTY sentences, which can be regarded as elliptical: **----nun ci (to molunta)** 'maybe ... ' (§11.3.4).

In Japanese an adnominalized quotation (... to iu/itta ...) is sometimes used as a substitute for the adnominalized copula, identifying the following noun by the word or phrase that precedes the quotative particle, but such use in Korean is more limited, so that **Chelqswu ka ssess.ta 'nun chayk** means only 'the book that [someone] says Chelsswu wrote' and not *'the book that Chelsswu wrote' → **Chelqswu ka ssun chayk** (Whitman 1989:350); moreover, the quoting verb can be marked for exaltation, as in **Chelqswu ka ssess.ta 'sinun chayk** 'the book that [someone esteemed] says Chelsswu wrote'.

The term "putative structure" refers to ways of imputing to a noun a state (usually expressed by an adjective, but perhaps sometimes by an intransitive verb or a copula-predicated noun) through the use of a quotational sentence, which can take as a direct object the optionally raised subject of the putativized sentence: **elkwul i kopta ko hanta** 'says that the face is pretty' → **elkwul ul kopta ko hanta** 'says the face to be pretty'. If there are two nominative phrases only the first can be raised: (**na nun) ku ⁿyeca ka elkwul i kopta ko sayngkak hanta** 'I think she has a pretty face' → **ku ⁿyeca lul elkwul i kopta ko sayngkak hanta** 'I think her pretty of face (in the face)' but not *... ⁿyeca lul elkwul ul ⋯ . CF Choy Yengsek 1988:178:n8. We reject as unnatural the sentences offered by Yun Cengmi 1989 to justify the claim that adverbial elements can be similarly raised (*eykey lul).

11.12. Reflexive requests; favors.

Requests are ordinarily made with an honorific command form of the verb cwu- (→ cwu-si-) 'give' in one of the more polite styles: **I kes com cwusipsio (cwusey yo)** 'Please give this to me/him'; **I kes com hay cwusipsio (cwusey yo)** 'Please do this (for me/him)'. But in the plain and semiformal styles there is a special conversion used to make the request reflexive '(I ask you to) give it to me [rather than someone else] – or: to do it for me': **cwula → tālla** [plain], → **tao/tawu** [semiformal]. An emphatic synonym for **tālla** is **tāko/tākwu**. (On the irregular forms of this auxiliary verb, see Part II.) Requests are quoted in the expected way, (cwusipsio ←) cwue la → cwula (ko ha-), only if the request is for someone else's benefit. To say 'he requests it for himself' – that is, he says "do it for me" or "give it to me" – you apply the reflexive request conversion **cwula → tālla**. For examples, see the entries **tālla** and **tālla 'nta** in Part II.

Notice that FAVORS, not treated here as one of the conversions, are stated by using the infinitive -e + the auxiliary verb **cwu-** 'give' or **tuli-** 'give to a superior (hence never me)'; **A ka B eykey X lul hay cwunta/tulinta** 'A does X for B'. And favors can be requested: **B eykey X ul hay cwusey/tulisey yo** 'Please do X for B'. So the requested favor can be quoted: **(A eykey nun) B eykey X lul hay cwula /tulila ko hanta** 'asks A to do X for B'.

Some Korean dictionaries list a verb **tāllanta** 'requests', but that is misleading, for the form in question is an abbreviation of **tālla (ko) hanta**, as clearly shown by the past **tālla 'yss.ta**. (If there were such a verb as *tāllanta, the past would be *tāllass.ta.)

11.13. Sentence connectors.

There are a lot of phrases, mostly derived from adverbializations, that are frequently used to introduce and connect sentences. Below is a partial list of such "prologs" and "insertions" (CF Kim Pyengha 2:127-9) or "conjunctors" (CF ¹Yi Tongcay 1978), arranged very roughly by meaning.

Kuliko ⋯ 'And ⋯ '
Kulay se ⋯ 'And so ⋯ ' or 'And then ⋯ '
Kulemyen ⋯ 'Then ⋯ '
Kuleca ⋯ 'Thereupon ⋯ '
Kulemyen se ⋯ 'Meanwhile ⋯ '
Tongsi ey ⋯ 'At the same time ⋯ ', 'Also, ⋯ '
Han phyen ⋯ 'And (at the same time) ⋯ ',
'But ⋯ (on the other hand)', (**Han phyen** ulo nun ⋯) 'But perhaps ⋯ '
Kuleni ⋯ , Hani ⋯ 'Then ⋯ ' or 'So ⋯ '
Kuleni-kka (n') ⋯ 'Then ⋯ ' or 'So ⋯ '
Kulem ulo ⋯ 'So ⋯ '
Kulem ⋯ 'Well ⋯ ' or (= **Kulem ulo**)
'So ⋯ ' or (= **Kulemyen**) 'Then ⋯ '
Kuleki ey ⋯ , Kuleki ttaymun ey ⋯ 'So ⋯ ',
'Therefore ⋯ '
Way 'n ya hamyen ⋯ 'The reason is that ⋯ ;
If I may explain why, ⋯ '
Kulen cuk ⋯ 'Then ⋯ ', 'Thereupon ⋯ '
Ttal%a se ⋯ 'Consequently ⋯ '
Ili ha.ye ⋯ , Ili hay se ⋯ 'Thus ⋯ '
Yeki lo puthe ⋯ 'From here (this) ⋯ '
Ku/I wa hamkkey ⋯ 'Together with (on top of) that/this ⋯ '

Nay sayngkak kath.umyen (kath.e se nun) ⋯
'If it were me ⋯ ', 'If you want my advice ⋯ '
Kath.un kaps imyen ⋯ 'If it's all the same ⋯ ',
'If you don't mind ⋯ ', 'If possible ⋯ ', 'If one or the other ⋯ ', 'If anything ⋯ '
Mupang hasimyen ⋯ 'If you don't mind ⋯ '
Nōllapkey to ⋯ 'To my amazement ⋯ '
Yath-kwuc.key to ⋯ 'Strange to tell ⋯ '
Caymi sulepkey to ⋯ 'Delightful to say ⋯ '
Tahayng hi to ⋯ 'Happily enough ⋯ '
Hayngpok sulepkey to ⋯ 'Luckily enough ⋯ '
Pulhayng hakey to ⋯ 'Unfortunately ⋯ '
Yukam sulepkey to ⋯ , Yukam sulepci man ⋯ 'Sad to tell ⋯ '
Sepsep hakey to ⋯ 'To my regret ⋯ ' or 'To my disappointment ⋯ '
Kwayssim hakey to ⋯ 'Outrageously enough ⋯ '
Sayngkak hakentay ⋯ , Sayngkak hay poni-kka ⋯ 'Come to think of it ⋯ '
Cimcak hakentay ⋯ 'Presumably ⋯ ', 'I presume that ⋯ '
Pokentay ⋯ 'Now that I look at it ⋯ '
Cāmsi tol.a pokentay ⋯ 'Looking back for a moment ⋯ '

Ppun (man) ani 'la ⋯ , Ppun (man) tele ⋯ 'What's more ⋯ ', 'Not only that but ⋯ ', 'Moreover ⋯ '
Tekwuntana ⋯ 'What's more ⋯ ', 'Moreover ⋯ ', 'Besides ⋯ '
X, keki ¹yen han Y "Y or X"; X, keki ¹yen ha.ye, Y ⋯ 'X, together with Y, ⋯ '
Hok un ⋯ 'Or else ⋯ '
Tto nun ⋯ 'Or (else) ⋯ ; Nor ⋯ (either)'
Ku cwung ey to ⋯ 'Especially ⋯ '
Hamulmye ⋯ 'Much more / less ⋯ '
Kulelq swulok ⋯ 'All the more ⋯ '
Saysam sulepkey ⋯ 'Now ⋯ ', 'Again (newly) ⋯ ', 'All the more ⋯ ', 'Specially ⋯ '
Ani na talulq ka ⋯ 'Sure enough, ⋯ ', 'Just as I suspected, ⋯ '
Ani 'n key ani 'la ⋯ or Pipul ila ⋯ 'Sure enough ⋯ ', 'To be sure ⋯ ', 'Of course ⋯ ', 'Not but what ⋯ ' (CF. §11.7.6)
Thullim ēps.i ⋯ , Uysim ēps.i ⋯ 'Surely ⋯ ', 'Doubtless ⋯ , No doubt ⋯ '
Te twū mal ēps.i ⋯ , Twū mal halq kes ēps.i ⋯ 'It goes without saying (repeating) ⋯ '
Molumciki ⋯ 'Preferably ⋯ ; Necessarily ⋯ ' (< molum cik 'i)
Māl hana māna ⋯ 'Needless to say ⋯ '
Payksa pulkyey hako ⋯ 'Regardless ⋯ '
Āmuli sayngkak hay to ⋯ 'In any case ⋯ '
Etteh.key hatun ci ⋯ 'In any event ⋯ '
Ama to ⋯ 'Maybe ⋯ ', 'Likely ⋯ '
Āmulye 'na (mān.il ey) ⋯ 'Maybe ⋯ '
Kulelq cintay ⋯ 'If that should happen ⋯ ', 'If that be true ⋯ '
Molumyen molutoy ⋯ 'I may be wrong but ⋯ ', 'If my guess is right ⋯ ', 'Perhaps ⋯ '
(...) molulq ka ⋯ '(...) unless perhaps (⋯)'
Kuleta ka ⋯ 'But / And then ⋯ '
Kulena ⋯ , Hana ⋯ , Hena ⋯ 'But ⋯ ', 'Still ⋯ '
Kuleh.ci man ⋯ 'But ⋯ '
Kulay to ⋯ 'Even so ⋯ '
Kulelq ci 'la to ⋯ 'Be that as it may ⋯ '
Kuleh.ta (ha)tula 'y to ⋯ 'Be that as it may ⋯ '
Kulem ey to pulkwu hako ⋯ 'Nonetheless ⋯ ', 'Nevertheless ⋯ '
Kulel mangceng ⋯ 'Nevertheless ⋯ '
Way kulen ya (ha)myen ⋯ , Way 'n ya hamyen ⋯ 'The reason is that ⋯ '; 'If I may explain (why) ⋯ '

Ches ccay lo ⋯ 'In the first place ⋯ ', 'First of all ⋯ '
Twū ccay lo ⋯ 'In the second place ⋯ '
Kkuth ulo ⋯ , Macimak ulo ⋯ 'Finally ⋯ '
¹Yēy / I lul tulmyen / hamyen ⋯ (also tulca 'myen, tul.e se) 'For example ⋯ '
¹Yēy khentay ⋯ 'For example ⋯ '
(⋯) ilul they 'myen ⋯ 'so to speak', 'as it were', 'if we give it a name / label ⋯ '
Cuk ⋯ = Kot ⋯ 'To wit ⋯ '
I wa kath.i ⋯ 'In this / like manner ⋯ '
Ile han kwankyey ey se ⋯ 'In this respect ⋯ '
(Wuli ka) ponun pa wa kath.i ⋯ 'As we see ⋯ '
Tut.kentay ⋯ 'From what I hear ⋯ '
Sōmun ey uy hamyen ⋯ 'According to rumor (to what they say) ⋯ '
Sālam tul i māl haki lul ⋯ (ila hap.nita) 'As people say ⋯ '
Sinmun ey pōko han pa ey uy hamyen ⋯ 'According to what was reported in the newspaper ⋯ '
Yō nun ⋯ 'The point is ⋯ ', 'To summarize ⋯ '
Yō khentay ⋯ 'In outline ⋯ ', 'In summary ⋯ ', 'In brief ⋯ ', 'To be concise (succinct) ⋯ '
Yōyak hamyen ⋯ 'In sum ⋯ '
Kantan hi māl hamyen (māl hay se) ⋯ 'To put it simply (briefly) ⋯ '
Han mati lo māl hay se ⋯ 'To put it in a word (in a nutshell) ⋯ '
Tāychwung māl hamyen ⋯ 'Speaking roughly ⋯ ', 'In short ⋯ '
Khukey nun ⋯ 'More broadly (speaking) ⋯ '
Khukey cap.e se ⋯ 'At the largest / most ⋯ '
Te cenghwak hi māl hamyen ⋯ 'To put it more precisely ⋯ '
Talli māl hamyen ⋯ , Hwan.en hamyen ⋯ 'To put it another way ⋯ '
Tasi māl hamyen (or hay se) ⋯ 'To repeat ⋯ ' or 'To put it another way ⋯ '
Pakkwe sayngkak hamyen ⋯ , Tol.ikhye sayngkak hako / hamyen ⋯ 'On second thought ⋯ '
Māl ul pakkwe se ⋯ 'To change the subject ⋯ '
Yetam ici man ⋯ 'In this connection I may add that ⋯ '
Yetam un ku man hako ⋯ 'To return to the subject ⋯ '
⋯ iyo / yo?, ⋯ iyo / yo!, ⋯ ullang / llang ' ⋯ uh ⋯ ', 'you know, you see' (like Japanese ne)
Talum ani 'ko / 'la 'It's just that ⋯ ; just'

A Reference Grammar of Korean PART I 335

Māl haca 'myen ··· 'If you ask me ··· '
Nay sayngkak ulo (se) nun ··· , Nay
sayngkak ey nun ··· 'In my opinion ··· '
Na poki ey nun ··· 'As I view the matter ··· '

··· māl ia (iya), ··· māl iey yo, ··· māl io (iyo), ··· māl ici (yo), ··· māl ita, ··· māl iney 'I mean', 'you know', 'you see', 'don't you know', 'don't you see?', 'uh ··· '

See also the use of **-e pwā (la)** and **-e posey (yo)** within a sentence (under the entry **-e pota** in Part II).

11.14. Apposition.

Apposition is the juxtaposition of two expressions (usually but not necessarily noun phrases) having the same reference ("A which is X"): **nay salang hanun atul [in] ne lul** 'you [who are] my beloved son' (Roth 279). This is the common type, the specifying apposition, in which the second expression gives a more detailed specification of the first expression, as clearly seen in **Kimchi ssel.un kes iss.e?** 'Do you have any ready-sliced kimchi?'. A distinction has been drawn between a summarizing apposition, in which the second noun phrase sums up a set of nouns, and a detailing apposition, in which the second phrase gives further information about the first (CM 2:167-9):

Sap, kwayngi, homi, kok-kwayngi, nas tul − cak.ep ey phil.yo han tōkwu tul ul kaciko chengnyen tul un tte-nass.ta 'The youths set out taking the tools necessary for the operation − spade, hoe, weeding hoe, pick-ax, sickle'.

Cak.ep ey phil.yo han tōkwu lul − sap, kwayngi, homi, kok-kwayngi, nas tul ul kaciko chengnyen tul un tte-nass.ta 'The youths set out taking spade, hoe, weeding hoe, pick-ax, sickle − the tools needed for the operation'.

11.15. Order and recurrence of conversions.

Since an infinite number of sentences can be made by applying a finite number of operations to our nuclear sentences, it follows that some of the operations can be applied repeatedly. Substitution alone, even with expansion, would give us a large number of sentences, but not an infinite number.

There can, of course, be increasing expansion of a nuclear sentence, supplying more and more of the possible kinds of adjuncts (**Ponta, Ayki ponta, Ayki emeni ponta, Ayki emeni cikum ponta, ...**), but there will be a limited number of slots available for a given verb. Each expansion can itself be expanded, by adnominal or adverbial modification of some sort: **ayki, wuli ayki** 'our baby', **kāy hako nōnun ayki** 'the baby playing with the dog', **kāy hako nōnun wuli ayki** 'our baby playing with the dog', and so on, to no easily discernible limit. An expansion can be grammatically specified with one of a small group of particles, and repeated specification is possible up to at least three (**ayki eykey** 'to the baby', **ayki eykey se** 'from the baby', **ayki eykey se pota** 'than from the baby'). The specified expansion can have its focus subdued with the particle **un/nun** or highlighted with **to: ayki eykey nun/to, ayki eykey se nun/to, ayki eykey se pota nun/to**. There are many gaps in the actual sequences that occur, as indicated in §6.5. In a very limited way the tense-aspect shift can be regarded as recurrent, for there is a past built on a past (**-ess-ess-**) and a future built on that (**-ess-ess-keyss-**), as well as a future built on a simple past (**-ess-keyss-**).

To some extent, an order lurks behind the sentences that result from applying the conversion processes. We can make a negative out of an honorific (**ponta → posinta → posici anh.nunta**) or an honorific out of a negative (**ponta → poci anh.nunta → poci anh.usinta**) or an honorific out of a negative-made-on-an-honorific (**ponta → posinta → posici anh.nunta → posici anh.usinta**). The first possibility is preferred, but the others are also heard.

It is possible to make a negative out of a periphrastic causative (**kanta → kakey hanta → kakey haci mōs hanta** 'can't let him go') or a causative out of a negative (**kanta → kaci mōs hanta → kaci mōs hakey hanta** 'makes it so he can't go'). A negative can be made out of a causative-made-on-a-negative (**kaci mōs hakey haci mōs hanta** 'can't make it so he can't go'), and a causative can be made out of a negative-made-on-a-causative (**kakey haci mōs hakey hanta** 'makes it so he can't let him go').

Negation can be applied to desiderative expressions (**-ko siph.ta**) in several ways. **Kako siph.ci anh.ta** (and **Kako siph.e haci anh.nunta**) is preferable to **An kako siph.ta** (and **An kako siph.e hanta**) for 'I do not want to go'; you can also say **Kaci anh.ko siph.ta** 'I want not to go' with a slightly different implication. In Seoul you will not hear *Kako an siph.ta or *Kako siph.ci an hanta, but such structures are said to be used in Hamkyeng dialects. For the double negative **Kaci anh.ko siph.ci anh.ta** 'I do not want not to go' is possible and moreover better than (?*)**An kako siph.ci anh.ta**.

Some of the ambiguous sentences that show divergent constituency (IC cuts) result from the application of certain conversions before others: **an hwumchye mek.nunta** can be either **an + hwumchye mek.nunta** 'doesn't steal and eat' (= **hwumchye mekci anh.nunta**) or **an hwumchye + mek.nunta** 'eats without stealing' (= **hwumchici anh.e mek.nunta**).

Certain sentences seem to be derived by way of nonoccurring sentences: **Ānta** 'You know him' → *__Ālci anh.nunta__ 'You don't know him' → **Ālci anh.nun ka** 'Don't you know him?! = Surely you know him?'. To make the statement 'You don't know him' Korean uses a suppletive negative (§11.7.3), yet we cannot say that the negative question derives from that, because we find both **Molunun ka** 'Don't you know him?' and **Moluci anh.nun ka** 'Of course you don't know him?'. It may well be argued that these facts indicate there are two kinds of negative questions: one in which the negativization is applied before the interrogativization (**Ānta → Molunta → Molunun ka**), producing a literal question, and the other in which the interrogativization is applied before the negativization (**Ānta → Ānun ka → Ālci anh.nun ka**), producing a rhetorical question. In the overwhelming majority of cases the result is formally the same for both types; the verb for 'know' is unusual. And there are other cases in which "along-the-way" sentences are rare or unelicitable, if not totally nonexistent. Since some of the verb paradigms are defective, we expect certain types of gap in sentence paradigms as well.

11.16. Sentence generation.

There would be several possible ways to convert the analysis of syntax made here into what is optimistically called a "generative" grammar. Since native speakers are more interested in the CONTENT of their remarks than in the form taken by the remarks, and they are concerned less with grammatical issues than with making sense, it is doubtful that any construct of a grammarian can seriously pretend to show how a given speaker actually goes about creating and producing a given sentence. On the other hand, the restatement of a syntactic description as an algorithm for the automatic production of sentences can sometimes reveal interesting things about the linguist's view of the language — and indirectly perhaps about the language itself.

One such ordering of the description into a "do it yourself" set of instructions, or decision procedures, can be presented in sketchy fashion as follows. Six groups of instructions are marked with Roman numerals; they embrace 19 general instructions, with further subgroups indicated within each.

I. 1. Choose a nuclear sentence:
    Ponta = VERBAL sentence
    Cōh.ta = ADJECTIVAL sentence
    Cip ita = COPULAR sentence
2. Substitute:
    Ponta → Kanta, → Mek.nunta, → ... (pick a verb)
    Cōh.ta → Khuta, → Mānh.ta, → ... (pick an adjective)
    Cip ita → Sālam ita, → Onul ita, → ... (pick a noun)
3. If the choice was copular, expand the noun with adnominal(s):
    sālam → ku sālam 'that person', → ...
    → **nay ka (cal) ānun sālam** 'a person I know (well)', → ...
    → **nay ka cal ānun ku sālam**, → ...
    → ...
4. Expand the sentence with adverbial adjunct(s):
    Ponta. → Ayki ponta, → Emeni ponta, → Cikum ponta, → ...
    → **Ayki emeni ponta, → Emeni ayki ponta, →**

→ Ayki emeni cikum ponta, → Emeni ayki cikum ponta,
→ Cikum ayki emeni ponta, → Cikum emeni ayki ponta,
→ Ayki cikum emeni ponta, → Emeni cikum ayki ponta
→ ...
5. Expand each sentence expansion with adnominal(s):
ayki → wuli ayki, → (kāy hako) nōnun ayki, → ...
→ kāy hako nōnun wuli ayki, → ...
(There are constraints: the expansion must be capable of 6; it must not be an adverb.)
6. Specify each expansion (with the role-appropriate particle):
ayki → ayki ka, → ayki lul, ayki eykey, ...
→ ayki eykey se, → ...
→ ayki eykey se pota, → ...
(The occurring sequences are restricted in various ways.)
7. Subdue (un / nun) or highlight (to) the focus of each expansion:
ayki → ayki nun / to; cikum → cikum un / to; ...
ayki eykey → ayki eykey nun / to; ...
ayki eykey se → ayki eykey se nun / to; ...
ayki eykey se pota → ayki eykey se pota nun / to

II. 8. Shift voice –
if VERBAL, to causative:
(A ka B lul) ponta → (C ka A eykey B lul) pointa
pokey hanta
or to passive:
(A ka B lul) ponta → (B ka A eykey) pointa
if ADJECTIVAL, to causative:
(A ka) cōh.ta → (C ka A lul) cōh.key hanta
if COPULAR, to nothing.

III. 9. Elevate the status of the subject:
ponta → posinta; mek.nunta → capswusinta
cōh.ta → cōh.usita
sālam ita → sālam (or ... pun) isita

IV. 10. Negate:
10a. ponta → an(i) ponta; ānta → (*)an ānta → molunta (§11.7.3)
cōh.ta → an(i) cōh.ta
cip ita → cip i ani 'ta
10b. ponta → poci anh.nunta; ānta → (*)ālci anh.nunta → molunta
cōh.ci → cōh.ci anh.ta
—
10c. ponta → mōs ponta; ānta → mōs ānta
—
—
10d. ponta → poci mōs hanta; ānta → ālci mōs hanta
—
cōh.ta → cōh.ci mōs hata (But some adjectives cannot do this, e.g. chwuw-; p. 316.)
9+10b   ponta → posinta → posici anh.nunta
10b+9   ponta → poci anh.nunta → poci anh.usinta
(9+10b)+9 ponta → posinta → posici anh.nunta → posici anh.usinta
10a+10b (cōh.ta →) chwupta → an chwupci anh.ta
10b+10b cōh.ta → cōh.ci anh.ta → cōh.ci anh.ci anh.ta
10b+10d cōh.ta → cōh.ci anh.ta → cōh.ci anh.ci mōs hata

11. Preemphasize negation:
- 10b+11   ponta → poci anh.nunta → poci lul anh.nunta
  cōh.ci → cōh.ci anh.ta → cōh.ci ka/lul anh.ta
- 10d+11   ponta → poci mōs hanta → poci lul mōs hanta
  cōh.ta → cōh.ci mōs hata → cōh.ci ka/lul mōs hata

But with certain passives, toy-, ci-, ... (p. 317) 10b+11 shows this pattern: pointa → poici anh.nunta → poici ka/lul anh.nunta. And there is no 10d (*poici mōs hanta 'can't be seen').

12. Subdue (un/nun) or highlight (to) the focus on the negation:
- 10b+12   ponta → poci nun/to anh.nunta
  cōh.ta → cōh.ci nun/to anh.nunta
- 10d+12   ponta → poci nun mōs hanta
  cōh.ta → cōh.ci nun/to mōs hata

V. 13. Shift tense-aspect:
- 13a. past   ponta → pwass.ta; mek.nunta → mek.ess.ta
  cōh.ta → cōh.ass.ta
  cip ita → cip iess.ta
- 13a+13a   ponta → pwass.ta → pwass.ess.ta; mek.nunta → mek.ess.ta → mek.ess.ess.ta
  cōh.ta → cōh.ass.ta → cōh.ass.ess.ta
  cip ita → cip iess.ta → cip iess.ess.ta
- 13b. future   ponta → pokeyss.ta
  cōh.ta → cōh.keyss.ta
  cip ita → cip ikeyss.ta
- 13a+13b   ponta → pwass.ta → pwass.keyss.ta
  cōh.ta → cōh.ass.ta → cōh.ass.keyss.ta
  cip ita → cip iess.ta → cip iess.keyss.ta
- (13a+13a)+13b   ponta → pwass.ta → pwass.ess.ta → pwass.ess.keyss.ta
  cōh.ta → cōh.ass.ta → cōh.ass.ess.ta → cōh.ass.ess.keyss.ta

VI. 14. Shift mood:
- 14a. question   Ponta. → Poni?
  Cōh.ta. → Cōh.ni?, → Cōh.un ka?
  Cip ita. → Cip ini?, → Cip in ka?
- 14b. suggestion   Ponta. → Poca.
- 14c. command   Ponta. → Pwā la!
- 14d. apperception   Ponta. → Ponun kwun (a) / kwumen / kwulye!
  Cōh.ta. → Cōh.kwun (a)!, Cōh.kwumen!, Cōh.kwulye!
  Cip ita. → Cip i(lo)kwun (a)!, Cip i(lo)kwumen!, Cip i(lo)kwulye!
- 10d+14b   Ponta. → Poci mōs hanta. → Poci mālca.
- 10d+14c   Ponta. → Poci mal.e la.
- 10d+11   Ponta. → Poci mōs hanta. → Poci lul mōs hanta.
- (10d+11)+14b   Ponta. → Poci mālca. → Poci lul mālca.
- (10d+11)+14c   Ponta. → Poci mal.e la. → Poci lul mal.e la.

15. Adnominalize – 15+3, 15+5:
  Ponta. → ponun ···
  Cōh.ta. → cōh.un ···
  Cip ita. → cip in ···
        → cip uy ···
        → cip ···

A Reference Grammar of Korean

16. Nominalize — 16+2, 16+4(+6):
16a. Summative   Ponta. → poki
                     Cōh.ta. → cōh.ki
                     Cip ita. → cip iki
16b. Substantive Ponta. → pom
                     Cōh.ta. → cōh.um
                     Cip ita. → cip im

17. Adverbialize — 17+4(+6):
17a. Gerund   Ponta. → poko
                     Cōh.ta. → cōh.ko
                     Cip ita. → cip iko
17b. Adverbative Ponta. → pokey
                     Cōh.ta. → cōh.key
                     Cip ita. → cip ikey
17...

18. Quote (+6): Ponta. → ponta (ko)
                     Cōh.ta. → cōh.ta (ko)
                     Cip ita. → Cip ila (ko)
14b+18   Ponta. → Poni? → ponun ya (ko)
                     Cōh.ta. → Cōh.ni? → cōh.un ya (ko)
                     Cip ita. → Cip ini? → cip in ya (ko)
14c+18   Ponta. → Pwā la! → pola (ko)

19. Shift style:
19a. Formal   Ponta. → Pop.nita.
                     Cōh.ta. → Cōh.sup.nita.
                     Cip ita. → Cip ip.nita.
19b. Semiformal ... ...
19...

The instructions (or "rules") must be applied taking into account the constraints that are described in various sections of this book. Points of recursion can be seen in 14 (adnominalize) where the adnominalized sentence can be reapplied at 3 (expand the noun before the copula of a copula sentence) and/or at 5 (expand each sentence expansion):

    Ponta. → ponun (15) → Ponun cip ita. (3) ← Cip ita. (1)

Or again in 16 (nominalize) where the nominalized sentence can be reapplied at 2 (substitute — in the copular sentence) and/or at 4 (expand the sentence — which then can go on to 6 and 7, etc.). Or again in 17 (adverbialize) which can also be reapplied at 4.

To be sure, applying these rules will produce many sentences that do not occur. Further study will perhaps help refine the set of rules to eliminate those sentences whose failure to occur is not due to semantic accident.

Some of the rules could be looked upon as special cases of applying a series of the other rules. For example, 12 (subdue or highlight focus on negation) might be considered 16··· (suspective: **Ponta.** → **poci**) + 7 (subdue or highlight the focus of the expansion: **poci** → **poci nun**) + 2 (substitute — in the verbal sentence: **Ponta.** → **Hanta.**) + 10a (**Hanta.** → **Ani hanta.**, abbreviated → ··· **anh.(nun)ta**). The abbreviation of **ani ha-** to **anh-** is the main reason for giving 11 and 12 as separate rules; notice also that the abbreviated form **anh.(nun)ta** cannot be used as a stand-alone sentence, unlike **Ani hanta**. A somewhat similar case may be seen in the following thinkable rule:

9´. Subdue (**un** / **nun**) or highlight (**to**) the focus on the sentence itself:
   Ponta. → Poki nun / to hanta.
   Cōh.ta. → Cōh.ki nun / to hata.
   Cip ita. → −

This rule of nuclear focus can be broken down into an application of 16a (summative: **Ponta.** → **poki**) + 7 (subdue or highlight the focus of the expansion: **poki** → **poki nun / to**) + 2 (substitute: **Ponta.** → **Hanta.** or **Cōh.ta.** → ··· **hata**). The only difficulty, aside from a vague feeling of unnaturalness, is the rather special nature of the dummy verb / adjective **hanta / hata**, which serves as a carrier for further conversions, much as English "do" serves to carry the inflection (and often the focus) in certain expressions, such as the inverted interrogative. We are also troubled by the parallelism between the expressions **poki nun poci man** 'looks at it, all right, but' and **cōh.ki nun cōh.ci man** 'is good, all right, but' and the synonymous expressions **poki nun haci man** and **cōh.ci nun haci man**, for along the way there seems to be no *poki nun ponta or cōh.ki nun cōh.ta, and even **Poki nun hanta** and **Cōh.ki nun hata** are a bit strange without further conversions.

The appropriate place for the nuclear-focus rule would seem to be between III (9) and IV (10). With 9 (status elevation of the subject) the order can apparently vary: **poki nun hasici man** or **posiki nun haci man** or even (reapplying 9) **posiki nun hasici man** 'DOES design to deign to look but'.

It may well be that all situations calling for the dummy **ha-** should be set up as separate rules: **-ki to ha-**, **-ki man ha-**, **-ko nun ha-**, **-ta mōs ha-**, ... (See the entries in Part II.)

12.0. Mimetics.

Mimetics are strings of phonemes chosen (or thought to be chosen) so as to report immediate reactions to the sounds, the looks, or the feel of a situation. In Korean such strings enter into a set of structures that overlay the normal set and impart connotational meanings in addition to whatever other meanings may be present. Cf G.A. Pak 1958, 1961; Fündling 1985.

12.1. Phonetic symbolism.

Korean makes rich use of a system of phonetic symbolism to create connotational variants of words. Many adjectives and adverbs, as well as some verbs and deictics, appear in several shapes that are systematically related in accordance with this system. In some cases the semantic relationship is weak or lost, so that the ties between the words are etymological rather than morphemic. For example, **nalk-** < *nolk-* 'is old = not new' and **nulk-** < *nulk-* 'is old = not young' would fit one of the patterns for word isotopes (§12.4) but the specialization of meaning, though understandable − the light isotope for "things", the heavy for "people" − is unique. Again, the verb stem **phu-** 'scoop out, dig' would seem to be a heavy isotope of **pha-** < *ˈpho-* 'dig', but the connotational relationship seems lost. The isotopic difference of meaning is practically gone from **yoli** 'this way', **koli** 'that way', **coli** 'that way (yonder)' in the directional meaning, though it is still present in the manner meaning. We can speculate that **kot-** < *kwot-* 'be straight' and **kwut-** < *kwut-* 'be hard' may once have been isotopes of the same etymon; and we can wonder about **nām-** < *ˈnam-* (< *naˈmo-*) 'remain, be left over' and **nēm-** < *ˈnem-* (< *neˈmu-*)'be in excess', and perhaps even **mak-** < *mak-* ' ... ; stop (fill) up' and **mek-** < *mek-* 'eat'.

12.2. Phonomimes and phenomimes.

There are about a thousand "impressionistic adverbs" in Korean. The group is traditionally divided into PHONOMIMES (**uyseng-e**) and PHENOMIMES (**uythay-e**). The reference of the phonomimes is primarily to a subjective impression of sounds, those of phenomimes to subjective impressions of sight, smell, taste, touch, or nonspecific reaction. The impressionistic adverbs are typically of one or two syllables, sometimes expanded into more. Many of them seem to be related, etymologically or morphemically, to more respectable items in the vocabulary (such as ordinary verbs and adjectives), but some appear to be pure creations of mimetic play. Many of the impressionistic adverbs appear in several related shapes. When the difference is one of reinforced rather than plain initial consonant we call the form an INTENSIVE (**sēyn māl**), and when the difference is one of aspirate rather than plain or reinforced consonant we call the form a PARAINTENSIVE (**keseyn māl**). When the difference is a systematic alternation in medial vowels (a kind of "ablaut") we speak of WORD ISOTOPES. There is also a limited amount of phonetic symbolism in the codas of closed syllables, though we cannot find so clearcut a case for setting up a system. There are only a few paradigmatic sets, and they are incomplete. Even so, a case can perhaps be made for the following syllable-final symbolism:

···l smooth-flowing or liquid
  kkol kkol 'bubble-bubble'   **ping-kul(ulu)** 'around smoothly'
  kkwal kkwal 'gushing, gurgling'   **posul** 'in a drizzle, gently'
  kkul kkul 'tsk tsk'   **putul$_1$** 'quivering'
  ppal ppal 'dripping freely'   **putul$_2$** 'soft'
  kantul 'gently swaying'   **sāl sal** 'gently, softly'
  kapul 'moving lightly'   **sōl sol** 'soft-flowing, smoothly, effortlessly'
  pal pal 'trembling, shivering'   **swāl** 'with a great flow, in torrents'
  pancil 'slippery, slick'   **senul** 'cool (like air)' (CF **sen-tul, sen-sen, sen-palam**)

There may be a secondary association with the **-(w)ul** in **mul** 'water', **swul** 'wine', **pul** 'fire', **pangwul** 'bubble, drop', **kay-wul** 'river, stream', **kewul** 'mirror', **kyel** 'wave', … ; **wū-l-** 'weep', **hulu-** 'flow', **kwulu-** 'roll', … .

···ng round, hollow, or open
  ping, pping, phing 'around'   **(p)pong / (p)pung** 'with a poop (of flatulence)'
  kkwung 'with a (hollow) thud'   **p(h)otong** 'chubby, plump'
  kkwūng hata 'is gloomy, glum'   **ssing** 'whistle of the wind'
  ppang 'pop, bang!; with a hole in **kkwang, khwang** 'thump!'
    it, glaring, gaping'
  (p)ang-kul, -sil, … 'smiling'   **kkwāyngkulang kkwāyng kkwāyng kkayng**
  (s)sang-kul, -sil, … 'smiling'   'gong gong gong!'

There may be a secondary association with **twungku-l-** 'be round', **kwungku-l-** 'be hollow, empty', **kwuleng** 'pit', **kwumeng** 'hole', **kwutengi** 'hollow, dent', **kwungtwungi** 'buttocks', … .

···k abrupt, shrill, tight
  ppayk / ppik 'whistling (steam),   **kkayk / kkik** 'with a yell'
    crying (birds, shrill voice)'   **kkwayk / kkweyk** 'yelling, quacking'
  ppayk = ppaykppayk-i 'tightly   **(k)kan(t)tak / (k)ku(n)(t)tek** 'budging; bobbing'
    packed'   **ka(t)tuk** 'full'
  (p)pakak / (p)ekek 'shrill sound as of **kkak** 'tight, firm, fast'
    two dry walnuts scraped together'   **kkaktwuk / kkektwuk** 'slicing unevenly'
  pak 'with a rip'   **kkam(c)cak / kkum(c)cek** 'being startled'
  pak hata 'is tight; is stingy'   **kkam(p)pak / kkum(p)pek** 'winking, blinking'
  ppak ppak / ppek ppek hata 'is dry **kkyalwuk / kkilwuk** 'craning one's neck'
    and hard, tight (like a wheel   **palak / pelek** 'suddenly; insistently'
    turning); narrow-minded'   **palkkak / pelkkek** 'in a sudden outburst of passion'
  pūk / pōk 'with a scratch / rip'   **(p)palttak / (p)pelttek** 'with a jerk, with a gulp'
  (p)pokcak / (p)pukcek 'bustling,   **pasak / pesek** 'rustle, crunch, crinkle'
    thronging'   **(p)paykak / (p)pikek** 'creaking, squeaking'
  sswuk / ssok 'abruptly'   **pokak / pukek** 'bubble, pop (in fermenting)'
  ssik 'with a sudden smile'   **ppyo(c)cok** 'sharp-pointed'
  ssak / ssek 'in one clean stroke / sweep' **pulsswuk / polssok** 'popping/blurting out unexpectedly'
  ssaktok / ssektwuk 'chopping, snip!' **(s)sakak / (s)sekek** 'crisp, crunchy'

For ···**p** it is hard to find good examples, but I suspect it may work like ···**k**. For ···**s** (/**t**/), ···**m**, and ···**n** it is hard to find isolated examples. But in associated relationship with other finals, ···**s** seems to mean something like 'in small, fine, pointed detail', **-n** to suggest 'a light, quick movement', and **-m** to imply 'over a large area' or 'amply, nicely':

SMOOTH **-l**	ROUND **-ng**	ABRUPT **-k**	FINE **-s**	LIGHT **-n**	SPREAD **-m**
(k)kamul 'blurred, hazy; flickery'		**kkamak** 'flickering, blinking, winking'	**(k)kamus** 'speckled, dotted with black'		
(k)kapul 'moving up and down; frivolous'			**(k)kapus** 'rather light'	**(k)kapun** 'light, nimble'	
kephul 'fluttering, flapping'			**kephus** 'flapping, fluttering'	**kephun** 'flapping, fluttering'	
		kkilccik 'rather long'			**kilccum** 'nice and long'
					kyalum / kilum 'nicely oval'
	(k)kiwu- twung 'tilting, rocking'		**(k)kiwus** 'slanting a bit'		**(k)kiwu-tum** 'slanting, sloping'
			kkaykkus 'clean'		**kkaykkum** 'comely'
(k)kopul 'meandering'			**(k)kopus** 'slightly bent'	**kopun** 'submissive, compliant'	
(p)pang-kul[1] 'with a smile'			**(p)pang-kus** 'with a smile'		
			pekus 'loosened; slightly apart'	**pekun** 'loose'	**ppekkum** 'cracked, split'
santul 'blowing cool and gentle'		**san(t)tuk** 'with a sudden chill'	**santtus** 'clean, cool, neat, light'		
(s)soksal 'whispering'		**soksak** **(s)soktak** 'whispering'		**(s)sokon** 'whispering'	
				kalkun 'scratchy to the throat; greedy'	**kkalkkum** 'pricking, irritating'

[1] CF **ping-kul** 'around smoothly'.

The associations of final consonants are complicated by the derivative suffixes that end in various consonants: **-um, -un, -ul, -us, -sulum**, ... The elements **nukus** (XX, XXh = Xk) and **nukul** (Xk) mean much the same thing, 'feeling nauseated'; CF **nukun / nakun** (XX, XXh = Xk) 'flexible, bending'. It is likely that some of the cases of mimetic ···n, ···l, and ···m represent reductions of an old version of han, hal, and ham from ha- 'be/do' (MK °ho-). We are tempted to wonder whether there is a relationship between the postnoun cil 'a process' and the noun cīs 'an act, a gesture' — CF cī(s)- 'make', even knowing that the noun was earlier ῭cus (? < *ci῭z-us). But these are etymological speculations.

12.3. Intensives and paraintensives.

Connotational variants show the following set of relationships of initial consonants:

SIMPLE	p	t	s	c	k	0 [vowel][1]
INTENSIVE	pp	tt	ss	cc	kk	–
PARAINTENSIVE	ph	th	–	ch	kh	h

[1] As in engkhu-l- / hengkhu-l- 'entangle'.

Certain variants are dialect forms of words that have been standardized in one of the shapes and do not admit a connotational variant, such as the common use of thuli- for the postnominal verb with the standard form ttuli-. The intensive and paraintensive forms can be treated as having an infix, -q- and -h- respectively. And the infixes sometimes turn up in unexpected places, e.g. the intensive in -e ppeli- for -e peli- 'get it all done'; the paraintensive in pul i nakhey for pul i nakey 'so that sparks fly' = 'hastily', and kulech'anh.e to for kulec'anh.e to 'nevertheless'. In the KEd etymology I mistakenly assumed that /camcakho/ 'silently' was from cam cako 'sleeping (a sleep)' + -h-, but actually the word is cam-ca' kho < cam-cam hako.

12.4. Word isotopes.

Some Korean words have several shapes that vary in vowel quality. For the meaning 'with a moan or a groan' there are four shapes: kkayng, kking, kkong, and kkwung. Kkayng and kkong are used for light quiet moaning, kking and kkwung for heavy loud groaning; I doubt that kkayng and kkong are perfect synonyms, but I do not know what the difference is. The differences in connotation that we have managed to pin down I refer to in terms of "word isotopes": a given word may have a LIGHT isotope and a HEAVY isotope. Certain vowels (a, ay, o, oy) are typical of the light isotopes, others (e, ey, wu, wi < wuy) are typical of the heavy. The vowels u and i are either heavy or neutral. The isotopic difference of meaning is not always strongly present, and sometimes one isotope is felt to be "neutral" or "basic" (i.e. connotationally unmarked) — frequently the one with the heavy vowel, unless the underlying meaning is in itself strongly suggestive of the light vowel. Usually the more "neutral" isotope is etymologically older, but we cannot always be sure. Thus payng, ppayng and phayng are LIGHT isotopes to ping, pping, and phing, which seem to be more neutral than heavy; and singtwung (XX hata) is a HEAVY isotope to sayngtong 'fresh as a daisy, bright-eyed, hale-and-hearty' which seems to be more neutral than LIGHT. In the meaning 'damp-dry' (p)potok is definitely LIGHT in connotation, and (p)putuk is usually neutral, but occasionally HEAVY. In certain word families it is appropriate to recognize a neutral form in addition to the light and heavy isotopes: for 'limping, hobbling' the light isotope is (c)calttok, the heavy (c)cilttwuk, and (c)celttwuk appears to be neutral (CF cē-l- 'hobble').

The meanings of the isotopes range from 'petite' (good) to 'dinky' (bad) for the LIGHT and from 'ample' (good) to 'bulky, clumsy' (bad) for the HEAVY. Specifically, the LIGHT isotope is used of something light of weight, or tiny, or delicate, or fragile, or bright and airy; or again, it is used by a person who is (or wants to behave as if he were) light, airy, small, delicate, fragile. For this reason, the light isotopes are often used by or of women and children, the heavy by or of men. (Can this be correlated with preferences for -a vs -e to represent the infinitive ending after a stem-final syllable with the vowel /a/?) The weight of the isotope, as it were, may fall either on the referent of the particular word or, perhaps less often, on the person who does the talking. The light isotope is often extended to a pejorative connotation. From the meaning 'small' we move on to the meanings 'petty, paltry, insignificant, dinky' and from the meaning 'fragile' we move on to the meanings 'unsubstantial, flimsy, flighty, frivolous, silly'. So ku nom means just 'that guy' but ko nom means 'that silly guy, that stupid fool, that worthless rascal'. And **kēcis mal** is a 'falsehood', but **kācis mal** is a 'dirty stinking lie'. The HEAVY isotope refers to things which are weighty, ponderous, serious, clumsy, unwieldy, and bulky — or which are dark, gloomy, or somehow inaccessible. We are tempted to link the vowel symbolism with the Chinese philosophical concept of **thaykuk** 'the great ultimate' which divides into **um** 'the dark side' and **yang** 'the bright side', as in the monad symbol on the flag of the Republic of Korea, and indeed the isotopic vowels are referred to by Korean linguists as 'bright' (**yang**) and 'dark' (**um**) sounds. But in Chinese thinking the male element is 'bright' and the female 'dark', so the Korean concept seems askew here, just as in its choice of LOWER vowels for the light isotopes and HIGHER vowels for the heavy isotopes runs counter to the notions of Edward Sapir, Roger Brown, and others, with respect to the non-culturally determined "naturalness" of phonetic symbolism. Moreover, the Chinese idea centers on brightness and energy or vitality, while the Korean seems to focus more on substance.

In some cases we have what look like isotopes, but the meanings are too divergent to class the words together. For example, **ssal ssal** means 'chilly, cold' and **ssul ssul** means 'lonely, dreary'. In some cases the word has both literal and figurative (or abstract) meanings; often the isotopic difference holds just for the literal meaning, and only one of the forms (often the light) occurs in a figurative sense, or else both forms occur, but as pure synonyms with no connotational feelings apparent. For example, **ssaktok ssaktok** is the light isotope and **ssektwuk ssektwuk** is the heavy isotope of a word that means 'chopping, snipping, slicing off', but in the figurative sense 'a choppy sentence' only the light isotope is used.

The isotopes are not limited to impressionistic adverbs. Observe the following pairs, in which the first word is neutral and the second a light isotope: **ek-swu, ak-swu** 'heavy rain'; **ekci, akci** 'stubbornness'; **yewi-, yawi-** 'get emaciated'; **ic.e peli-, yaca peli-** 'forget'; **inceng, yancang(-meli)** 'humaneness'. (There may be a similar etymological relationship between **enc-** 'put on top' and **anc-** 'sit'.) The Chinese vocabulary is not totally immune from the mimetic phenomena: **yamchi** is the light isotope of [1]**yemchi (ēps.ta)** '(has no) sense of shame', pejorative. The isotope is spelled with y⋯ in NKd, not [1]y⋯ .

For the neutral deictics **i** 'this', **ku** 'that', and **ce** 'that (yonder)' we find the light isotopes **yo, ko**, and **co**; for **yeki** 'here', **keki** 'there', and **cēki** 'there (yonder)' we find the light isotopes **yoki, koki**, and **coki**. The verb **(h)opinta** has a light-heavy relationship with **(h)wupinta** 'scoops it out'. The adjective meaning 'small' is **cēkta**, but this form is now mainly used in the meaning 'small in number or quantity, few', and the light isotope **cākta** is used as the common adjective for 'small in size'. (There is also the form /**cok**/ in **cokum / cokom** 'a little', a derived substantive, from which is contracted the adverb **com** 'a little; please'.) The stem meaning 'be large' has a heavy vowel in its neutral form, and we are not surprised that it lacks isotopes: **khuta**. But perhaps the trace of a light isotope can be found in the obsolete adjective **hata** 'is much / great, are many', now limited to the modifiers **han** ⋯ and **hal** ⋯ 'great, grand' (as in **han kil** > **hayngkil** 'highway' and **hal-apeci** 'grandfather'), the gerund **hako (mānh.ta)** 'extremely (many)', **ha (to)** ⋯ 'extremely (indeed), muchly', and the first word in **hachi anh.ta** 'is trivial' — which is either a paraintensive or a variant of the suspective **haci**. The adjective 'heavy' (**mukepta**) has heavy vowels, as does the adjective 'dark' (**etwupta**); these have only the neutral forms. The all-purpose stem **ha-** 'do / be' is sometimes heard in a heavy isotope **he-**, especially in men's speech. This seems to be independent of the general vowel raising thought to be in process in the Seoul area.

A few sets of words show fronting (palatalization) used for mimetic effects independently from the isotopes, as seen in the pair **nōylah.ta / nwīleh.ta** (< *nwoy⋯ / nwuy⋯*) 'is a sickly yellow', derived from **nōlah.ta / nwūleh.ta** 'is yellow'.

12.5. Mimetic constructions.

The impressionistic — or "mimetic" — adverbs occur in constructions that can be symbolized as follows:

X		adverb or interjection (of 1, 2, or 3 syllables)
XX		iterated (repeated) adverb or interjection
X hata		adjectival noun + postnominal adjective
X hanta		verbal noun + postnominal verb
XX hata		iterated adjectival noun + postnominal adjective
XX hanta		iterated verbal noun + postnominal verb (= X kelinta = X täynta)
X inta		verbal noun + postnominal verb (usually = X hanta)[1]
X (h)i		adjectival noun + derived adverb ← postnominal adjective

[1] CM 1:408 implies that **inta** is the same in meaning as **kelinta**, and that **X kelinta** shows greater repetition that **XX hanta**.

We can set up form classes for the various shapes as follows. One group will occur only as adverbs (X, XX); one group only as adverbs and/or adjectival nouns (X, X hata, XX hata); one group only as adverbs and/or verbal nouns (X, X hanta = X kelinta / täynta, X inta). And, finally, one group can occur as either adjectival or verbal nouns. Within each of these four groups there are subgroups:

MAJOR CLASS	SUBCLASS	EXAMPLE (see KEd for meanings)
I. adverb	1. X	kkok
	2. X, XX	ken(t)tus
	3. XX	swung / song; (s)swungteng / (s)songtang
II. adjectival	4. X hata, (X hi, X 'i)	kapus
	5. XX hata, (XX hi, XX 'i)	?
	6. XX, XX hata	kamcak₁
	7. X hata, (X hi, X 'i), XX, XX hata	kapun
	8. X, X hata, (X hi, X 'i), XX, XX hata	colmak
	9. X, X hata, XX	kalssang; kkalkkun
	10. X hata, XX hata	?
	11. X, XX hata	?
III. verbal	12. X kelinta	kkaylkkak
	13. XX, X kelinta	kephun
	14. X hanta, XX, XX hanta = X kelinta	kachis
	15. X inta, XX, X kelinta	kkancak
	16. X, XX, X kelinta	kangcang
	17. X, X inta, XX, X kelinta	katak₁
	18. X, X hanta, XX, XX hanta = X kelinta	kkik
	19. X, X hanta, X inta, XX, XX hanta = X kelinta	kkam(c)cak₃
	20. X, X hanta	picwuk₁
	21. X, X kelinta	picwuk₂
IV. verbal / adjectival	22. X inta, XX, XX hanta = X kelinta; XX hata	kancil
	23. XX, XX hanta = X kelinta; X hata	kangtong
	24. X, XX, XX hanta = X kelinta; X hata, (X hi)	?
	25. X, XX, XX hanta = X kelinta; XX hata	pulsswuk
	26. X, X kelinta; X hata	?

12.6. Shapes of mimetic adverbs.

The mimetic adverbs occur in shapes of one or two syllables, for the most part. With respect to initials, there are three patterns of alternation:

(1) C plain, Cq intensive, Ch paraintensive: **ping, pping, phing** 'around'
(2) Cq intensive (or plain), Ch paraintensive: **kkwal, khwal** (XX, X kelinta) 'gushing, gurgling'
(3) C plain, Ch paraintensive: **wupi-cek, hwupi-cek** (XX, X kelinta) 'scooping out'

When there are two syllables, we find various subtype groupings:

(1) C-C, Cq-C: **kangtong, kkangtong** 'hopping up and down' (XX, X kelinta 'is too short')
    C-Ch, Cq-Ch: **komthul, kkomthul** (X, X hanta, XX, X kelinta) 'wriggling'
    C-Cq, Cq-Cq: **palttak, ppalttak** (X, XX, X kelinta) 'jerking, gulping'
    C-C, Ch-C: **potong, photong** (XX, XX hata) 'chubby, plump'
(2) C-C, C-Cq: **katun, kattun** (X hata, XX, XX hata) 'light, nimble'
    Cq-C, Cq-Cq: **kkampak, kkamppak** (X, X hanta, X inta, XX, X kelinta) 'winking, blinking, flickering'
    C-C, C-Ch: **sikum, sikhum** (X hata, XX hata) 'sourish'
    C-Cq, C-Ch: **palkkak, palkhak** (X = XX) 'in a sudden outburst, topsyturvy, in turmoil'; X kelinta 'it bubbles up; squashes it under foot'
(3) C-C, C-Cq, Cq-C: **pantuk, panttuk, ppantuk** (X, X hanta = X inta, XX, X kelinta) 'shining, glistening'
(4) C-C, Cq-C, Cq-Cq: **ka(n)tak, kka(n)tak, kka(n)ttak** (X, XX, X kelinta, X inta, X ēps.ta) 'budging, nodding, bobbing'
(5) C-C, C-Cq, C-Ch: **sapun, sappun, saphun** (XX, p X kelinta; pp, ph X) 'with soft muffled steps'
(6) C-C, Cq-C, C-Ch: **salkkang, ssalkang, salkhang** (XX, X kelinta) 'hard-chewing, lumpy'
(7) C-C, Cq-Cq, Cq-Ch: **kangcang, kkangccang, kkangchang** (X, XX, X kelinta) 'taking long strides'
(8) C-C, C-Cq, Cq-C, Cq-Cq: **pancak, panccak, ppancak, ppanccak** (X, X hanta = X inta, XX, X kelinta) 'sparkle, glitter, twinkle'

In the last example the intensive becomes more and more emphatic as (1) the reinforcement moves to the beginning, and (2) the reinforcement repeats.

Some of the vowel alternation patterns found in word isotopes are shown below, with the light vowel given first (and only it exemplified):

a/e	kkal (XX, X kelinta) 'laughing loudly'
a-a / e-e	sapak (XX, X kelinta) 'crunching'
a-o / e-wu	(k)kangtong (XX, X kelinta) 'jumping up and down'
a-wu / e-wu	(p)pantwung (XX, X kelinta) 'idling, loafing'
a-u / e-u	kasul (XX hata) 'rough, bristly; stubborn'
a-u-a / e-u-e	kantulang (XX, X kelinta) 'wobbling, swaying'
a-i / e-i	paksin (XX, X kelinta) 'swarming, crowding, thronging'
a-i-a / e-i-e	(k)kachicak (XX, X kelinta) 'getting in the way'
a-ay / e-ey	?
a/u ? < o/u	kkan (XX hata) 'sticky'
a-a / u-e	(k)a(n)(t)tak (X, XX, X kelinta, X inta) 'budging, bobbing'
a-u-a / u-u-e	(k)ka(t)tulak (XX, X kelinta) 'strutting, swaggering'
a-u / u-u	kkalkkum (X hata) 'dashing, smart; sharp, harsh'
a-u / (w)u-u	(p)patuk (XX) 'persistently, obstinately'
a-a / u-u	ssapsal (X hata) 'slightly bitter'
a/i	sam (XX hata) 'slightly flat, tasteless'
a-i-i / u-i-i	pacici(k) (X, X hanta, XX, X kelinta) 'rip; fizz'
a-i-e / u-i-e	pacilen (X hata) 'diligent'

A Reference Grammar of Korean

ya⋯/i⋯	(k)kyawus (X hata) 'aslant'
	yalkus (X hata, XX, XX hanta = X kelinta) 'rickety'
ay/i ? < *oy/uy*	kkayk (X, X hanta, XX, XX hanta = X kelinta) 'cry, yell'
ay-a / i-e	kkaycak (XX, X kelinta) 'scribbling, scratching'
ay-u / i-u	(p)paythul (XX, X kelinta) 'staggering'
ay-wu / i-wu	saylccwuk (XX, X kelinta) 'distorted, out of shape'
ay-i / i-i	kaysin (XX, X kelinta) 'listless, languid'
ay/ey	?
ay-a / ey-e	kkaycak (XX, X kelinta) 'halfheartedly, unenthusiastically'
ay-i / ey-i	kkaycil (XX, X kelinta) 'halfheartedly, unenthusiastically'
ay-i-a / ey-i-e	kkaycilak (XX, X kelinta) 'halfheartedly, unenthusiastically'
o/wu	sōl (XX) 'soft-flowing, effortlessly'
	song (XX) 'minced; perforated'
o-o / wu-wu	(s)sokon (XX, X kelinta) 'whispering'
o-o-o / wu-wu-wu	ppyolothong (X, X hata, XX, XX hata) 'pouty, sulky'
o-a / wu-e	kkolttak (X, X hanta, X kelinta) 'gulping, swallowing'
o-i / wu-i	(k)kom(c)cil (X, XX, X kelinta, X mōs hanta, X ēps.ta, X inta) 'budging'
o-i-a / wu-i-e	(k)kom(c)cilak (X, XX, X kelinta, X mōs hanta, X ēps.ta, X inta) 'budging'
o-wu / wu-wu	(k)komul (XX, X kelinta) 'moving sluggishly'
o-wu-e / wu-wu-e	(k)komulak (XX, X kelinta) 'moving sluggishly'
o-u / wu-u	(k)komthul (X, X hanta, XX, X kelinta) 'w(r)iggle'
o-u-u / wu-u-u	kkoluluk 'rumbling, gurgling, snorting, cackling'
wa/wu	kkwang (X, X hanta) 'boom, rattle, roar'

It will be seen that a heavy isotope never contains a light vowel in its first or second syllable, and only rarely in the third syllable. A light isotope, however, can contain a heavy vowel in any noninitial syllable. Many of the two-syllable impressionistic adverbs have an etymologically recognizable morpheme, such as a verb or adjective stem, as the first syllable, and the second syllable is to be regarded as a derivative suffix. The most popular of the suffixes are the groups -(c)cak / -(c)cek, -chak / -chek; -(c)cok / -(c)cwuk; -(c)cik, -(c)cimak, -(c)cumak. These are probably all related to cāk- / cēk- 'little'. We also find the diminutive suffixes -ak / -ek, -ang / -eng, etc., which have widespread use outside the mimetic system. Other derivative suffixes found are -kkak / -kkek, -mak / -mek, -(p)pak, -ppuk, -(s)sek, -sil, -sin, -sul, -(s)swuk, -swung, -ttak / -ttek, -ttuk, -ttwuk. And -ulu and -wulwu are adverb-deriving suffixes similar in kind. There are undoubtedly other suffixes which should be added to this list. In some cases I have hesitated because of uncertainty about the etymology of the prior syllable, in other cases there are syntactic factors which make the seeming "suffix" better handled as something else.

12.7. Iteration.

Sentences, phrases, and words are often repeated for emphasis or other special effects. When the repeat is partial, that is called (partial) REDUPLICATION. When the entire expression (or its verb) is repeated, that is called ITERATION or (especially when what is repeated is less than a word) total reduplication. When a noun is iterated it is often to be taken as plural or collective: **cip cip mata** '(each and) every house'. Iterated adjectives occur in several structures used to intensify the meaning: **khuti khuta, khuki to khuta** 'is ever so big'; **khuna khun ⋯ , khuko khun ⋯** 'a really big ⋯ '; ⋯ . Iterated processive verbs refer to repeated or habitual happenings: **ilk.ko ilk.un ku phyēnci** 'that letter which I read and read'; **Kitaliko kitalitun nal i wass.ta** 'The long-awaited day has come'; **Ilum molulq sāy tul i nac.un hanul ul nal.e kako nal.e oko hayss.ta** 'Birds of unknown name flew back and forth low in the sky'; **Il.yoil mata na lul chac.e oko chac.e oko (chac.e oko n') hayss.ta** (Dupont 125) 'He was in the habit of coming to see me every Sunday'.

Appendix 1. List of stem shapes.

The following lists attempt to include all shorter stems: those of one or two syllables, and in certain cases of three. Longer stems are usually compounds of more than one stem, as are some of the shorter stems cited here, or of noun + stem. In general, no meanings are given, only shapes; the same shape may correspond to a number of homonyms, and these sometimes differ in etymologies. Those shapes followed by $_A$ are of adjective stems only, those followed by $_{VA}$ are of both adjective and verb stems. When the $_A$ is in parentheses, the adjective is auxiliary or postnominal only. When the $_V$ is in parentheses, the shape is uncommon or questionable as a processive verb. The notation $_{Cop}$ marks the copula stem, and the irregular stem **ha-** is marked with ｜ . The lists are arranged according to the linguistically interesting features that they illustrate; within that frame of reference, the lists are alphabetical. For lists 4-8 (longer i-stems), variant forms are cited that are the result of vowel assimilation (§2.7.9). In most of the cases the "assimilated" form, while quite common in speech, is avoided in writing. In some cases the historically "assimilated" form has acquired independent status and either replaces or contrasts with the historically "unassimilated" form. Bracketed together are the several groups of verbs which are spelled differently but pronounced alike (owing to convergences of morphophonemic sequences). These mostly involve causative and passive stems, but in some cases also the normal verbs. List 7 (longer i-stems with sibilants) displays all the honorific verbs derived from one-syllable stems, with the source stem shown after " < ". Normal stems that are homonyms of honorific verbs are shown in a separate column.

Guide to the lists

1 – 11. Vowel stems and h-stems

1. One-syllable vowel stems and ⋯h- stems
2. Longer vowel stems, except for ⋯wu- and ⋯i-
3. Longer ⋯wu- stems
4. Longer ⋯i- stems (except velar, palatal, sibilant, liquid)
5. Longer ⋯i- stems with velars: ⋯ki-, ⋯kki-, ⋯khi-
6. Longer ⋯i- stems with affricates: ⋯ci-, ⋯cci-, ⋯chi-
7. Longer ⋯i- stems with sibilants: ⋯ssi-, ⋯si-, honorifics in ⋯-si-
8. Longer ⋯i- stems with liquids: ⋯li-, ⋯lli-
9. L-extending vowel stems (CF 1): ⋯a-l-, ⋯e-l-, ⋯o-l-, ⋯wu-l-, ⋯u-l-, ⋯i-l-
10. L-doubling vowel stems (CF 1, 9): ⋯alu-, ⋯elu-, ⋯olu-, ⋯wulu-, ⋯ulu-, ⋯ilu-
11. L-inserting vowel stems (CF 1, 10)

12 – 17. Consonant stems

12. Consonant stems: ⋯p- and ⋯w- (CF 3, 1 ⋯wu-)
13. Consonant stems: ⋯ss-, ⋯ps-, ⋯ph-, ⋯s-, ⋯(s)-, ⋯t-, ⋯t/l- (CF 9), ⋯lq-, ⋯c-
14. Consonant stems: ⋯ch-, ⋯th-, ⋯lth-, ⋯lh-, ⋯lph-, ⋯lp-, ⋯lw-
15. Consonant stems (velars): ⋯k-, ⋯kk-, ⋯lk-, ⋯ks-
16. Consonant stems (nasals): ⋯m-, ⋯lm-, ⋯n-, ⋯nc-, ⋯nh-
17. Ambivalent stems: ⋯a(h)-, ⋯ay(h)-, ⋯e(h)-

A Reference Grammar of Korean

List 1. One-syllable vowel and -h- stems

⋯a-	⋯ay-	⋯e-	⋯ey-	⋯o-	⋯oy-	⋯ah-	⋯eh-	⋯oh-	⋯wu-	⋯wey-	⋯wi-	⋯u-	"⋯uy-"	⋯i-
				o-	ōy-$_{VA}$									i-$_{VCop}$
														ī-
ca-	cāy-$_{VA}$			cōy-		cōh-$_A$			cwu-		cwī-			ci-$_{V(A)}$
														cī-[11]
cca-$_{VA}$	ccāy-$_{VA}$			ccō-	ccōy-	ccah-								cci-
cha-$_{VA}$	chāy-					Dial.			chwu-					chi-
ha-$_{VA}$!		(he-)	hēy-	hō-							hwi-		huy-$_A$	
ka-	kāy-		kēy-[6]	kō-	kōy-									
	khāy-		khe-[1]									khu-$_{VA}$		khi-[12]
			khye-[2]											
kka-	kkāy-			kko-	kkōy-				kkwu-	kkwēy-	kkwi-	kku-		kkī-[13]
mā-	māy-		mēy-	mō-[8]	mōy-									mī-
na-	nāy-				nōy-	nah-	neh-	noh-	nwu-		nwī-[9]			
(pay-$_{VA}$)														
	pāy-		pēy-	po-	pōy-									
pha-			phye-[3]	phyēy-[7]					phu-			(phu-)[10]		phi-
	ppay-					ppah-								ppī-
	ppāy-													
			se-[4]		soy-							su-		si-$_A$
	sāy-		sēy-$_{VA}$		sōy-						swī-			
ssa-$_{VA}$	ssāy-		sse-[5]	sso-	ssoy-	ssah-			sswu-			ssu-		
	tāy-		tēy-$_{V(A)}$		toy-$_V$	tah-			twu-		twi-			
					tōy-$_A$									
tha-	thāy-										thwi-	thu-	thuy-	
tta-	ttāy-		ttēy-		ttoy-	ttah-					ttwi-	ttu-		tti-
												ttuy-		

⋯ih-
ccih-

[1] = khu-   [6] = kēywu-   [8] = mou-   [9] = nwui-   [10] See ⋯wu-.   [11] = ciwu-
[2] = khi-   [7] = phī-, phii-   [12] = khye-
[3] = phi-   [13] = kkī(i)-, kkiwu-
[4] = su-   [14] = pii-, piwu-
[5] = ssu-

List 2. Longer vowel stems, except for ···wu- and ···i-

···a-	···ay-	···e-	···ey-	···o-	···oy-	···wi-	···u-	"···uy-"
				na-o-			mou-	yeuy-
cam ca-								
ancha-_A_	twichay-					pichw(i)i-		
pek cha-_A_	anchay-							
kĕl-cha-_A_								
te-ka-	cc^e/akay-					sakwi-	camku-	
na-ka-	pp^e/akay-					y^e/akwi-_A_	nungku-	
samka-	ccokay-						cingku-	
	kaykay-					halkhwi-	taku-	
	pho-kay-					kalkhwi-		
						pakkw(u)i-		
				ilo-	aloy-		chilu-	
cala-	pokkay-	c^{u}ole-		(kalo-)	saloy-		ttalu-	
pala-	ukkay-	k^{u}ole-						
	kalay-	yole-/ile-						
tālla-	kalkay-							
nŏlla-	palay-							
	kallay-		selley-					
cīna-	tallay-		tulley-				tullu-[4]	
kas-na-	nŏllay-							
tte-na-	olay-_A_							
kyek-na-	heymay-							
kep na-	cīnay-							
|mas na-	ponay-	kĕnne-[2]	kĕnney-			nanw(u)i-	kĕnnu-	
|manna-[1]							tenu-	
nĕm-na-							kkonu-	
sin-na-							nonu-	
							kunu-	
							munu-	
	tē(-)say-	na-se-[3]	ek-sey-_A_			ke-swi-	na-su-	
	ēps.ay-		ke-sey-_A_				tō-su-	
			kwut-sey-_A_				twī su-	
			ppe-sey-_A_					
pissa-_A_	nal-ssay-						āy ssu-	
cay-pssa-_A_								
māta-	chi-tāy-					ho-toy-		
	kī-tay-					kotoy-		
········	········					········	········	
namula-						pācawi-	tatalu-	
nathana-	nathanay-						wulelu-	
VN + ha-!							puluthu-	

[1] < mac-na-   [2] = kĕnnu-   [3] = na-su-   [4] = tulli-. Instead of the unique shape **tullu-** we would expect, if anything, an l-doubling **tulu-**. **Tulli-** is more common and better suited to be treated as "standard", but **tullu-** is also widely used and it is treated as standard by many authorities.

A Reference Grammar of Korean

APPENDIX 1   351

List 3. Longer ⋯wu- stems

(There are no stems that end in ⋯owu-, ⋯wiwu-, ⋯hwu-, ⋯sswu-, ⋯ttwu-, ⋯pu-, ⋯mu-.)

⋯awu-	⋯aywu-	⋯ewu-	⋯eywu-	⋯oywu-	⋯iwu-	("⋯uywu-")
ssawu-	caywu-	kewu-	eywu-	oywu-	iwu-	ttuywu-
	chaywu-		key(wu)-		ciwu-	ssuywu-
	kkaywu-		meywu-		cciwu-	
	paywu-		seywu-		chiwu-	
	saywu-		teywu-		kkiwu-	
	thaywu-				piwu-	
	ttaywu-				phiwu-	
	……				……	
	sisaywu-				kaliwu-	

⋯cwu-	⋯ccwu-	⋯chwu-	⋯kwu-	⋯khwu-	⋯kkwu-	⋯ngwu-
kyencwu-	yēccwu-	chac.chwu-	angkwu-	mulkhwu-	kakkwu-[1]	sangwu-[2]
		|machwu-	engkwu-		pakkwu-	
		|mac.chwu-	heyngkwu-		sos.kwu-	
		kamchwu-	ilkwu-		tot.kwu-	
		nac.chwu-	talkwu-			
		nuc.chwu-				
		memchwu-				
		tulchwu-				

[1] < kac.kwu-   [2] = sang ha- (? < ˙[h]wu- < ˙hwo-, modulated stem of °ho- 'do')

⋯swu-	⋯twu-	⋯thwu-	⋯lwu-	⋯nwu-	⋯ppu-	⋯phu-
naswu-	katwu-	tathwu-	kalwu-	kanwu-	kappu-	aphu-
muswu-	ketwu-	yethwu-	palwu-	(kenwu-)	nappu-	hēyphu-
pa/uswu-	tot.wu-		kel.wu-	kyenwu-	pappu-	kophu-
				kyelwu-		
				sulwu-	(yeyppu-)	puphu-
				ilwu-	ippu-	……
				milwu-	……	kanyalphu-
					mippu-	koktalphu-
					sippu-	kwusulphu-
					kwuppu-	sekulphu-
					……	ēsulphu-
					(e.yeppu-)	nwiwuppu-

List 4. Longer ⋯i- stems (except oral velar, palatal, sibilant, liquid).

(There are no stems that end in ⋯ppi- or ⋯tti-.)

⋯ai-	⋯ayi-	⋯ei-	⋯eyi-	⋯oi-	⋯oyi-	⋯wui-
ccai-	kkayi-	khyei-[1]	eyi-	ccoi-	coyi-	kkwui-
sai-			?peyi-	kkoi-	koyi-	mui-
ssa(h).i-				moi-	kkoyi-	nwui-[2]
				poi-		……
				no(h).i-		nanw(u)i-
						pakkw(u)i-
						pichw(u)i-

···ui-   ···ii-   ···pi-   ···phi-   ···mi-
ssui-   chii-   hᵉ/api- (→ hᵉ/aypi-)   cap.hi- (→ cayphi-)   cemi- (→ ceymi-)
thui-   kii-   hopi-/hwupi- (→ hoypi-   palp.hi- (→ paylphi-)   yemi- (→ yeymi-)
                khii-³   /hwipi-)   salphi- (→ saylphi-)   kkwumi- (→ kkwimi-)
                kkii-   tempi- (→ teympi-)   sᵉ/alphi-_A (→ sᵉ/aylphi-)   sumi- (→ simi-)
                              nwupi- (→ nwipi-)   nelph.hi- (→ neylphi-)
                              pumpi- (→ pimpi-)   cep.hi- (→ ceyphi-)
                                                                  tep.hi- (→ teyphi-)
                                                                  cop.hi- (→ coyphi-)
                                                                  noph.i- (→ noyphi-)
                                                                  kwup.hi- (→ kwiphi-)
                                                                  nwup.hi- (→ nwiphi-)
                                                                  cip.hi-
                                                                  ip.hi-

···ti-   ···thi-   ···ni-   ···ngi-   ···hi-
mati-_A (→ mayti-)   pethi- (→ peythi-)   ani [i]-_Cop   tongi- → toyngi-   ssah.i- (→ ssay[h]i-)
teti-_A (→ teyti-)   tuthi- (→ tithi-)   tani- (→ tayni-,   (cangi- ←) cayngi-   noh.i- (→ noy[h]i-)
kyenti- (→ keynti-)   tayngki-)   pangi- (→ payngi-)   kkulh.i- (→ kkil[h]i-)
eph.ti- (→ eyptti-)   cini-   pacangi-/pecengi- (→
muti-_A (→ miti-)   pacayngi-/peceyngi-)
titi-

¹ = khii-   ² = nwup.hi-   ³ = khyei-

List 5. Longer ···i- stems with oral velars

···ki-   ···khi-   ···kki-
(maki- ←) mayki-   mak.hi- (→ maykhi-)   akki- (→ aykki-)
| (paki- ←) payki-   (nakhi- ←) naykhi-   as.ki- (→ aykki-)
| pak.i- (→ payki-)   pak.hi- (→ paykhi-)   math.ki- (→ maykki-)
| (saki- ←) sayki-   kalk.hi- (→ kaylkhi-)   takk.i- (→ taykki-)
| sak.i- (→ sayki-)   palk.hi- (→ paylkhi-)   (ppakki- ←) ppāys.ki-
kalki- (→ kaylki-)   cek.hi- (→ ceykhi-)   kkekk.i- (→ kkeykki-)
kkalki- (→ kkaylki-)   mek.hi- (→ meykhi-)   (kkekki- ←) kkeykki-
camki- (→ cayngki-)   elk.hi- (→ eylkhi-)   pes.ki- (→ peykki-)
kamki- (→ kayngki-)   engkhi- (→ eyngkhi-)   (pekki- ←) peykki-
namki- (→ nayngki-)   sok.hi- (→ soykhi-)   pokk.i- (→ poykki- →
tamki- (→ tayngki-) | mongkhi-/mungkhi- (→   pekki-)
| tangki- (→ tayngki-)| meyngkhi-/mingkhi-)   (ekki- ←) eykki-
| (tangki- ←) tayngki-| omkhi-/wumkhi- (→   sekk.i- (→ seykki-)
(sangki- ←) sayngki-   oyngkhi-/wingkhi-)   ccoch.ki- (→ ccoykki-)
ppᵉ/aki- (→ ppᵉ/ayki-)   olk.hi- (→ oylkhi-)   kwuc.ki- (→ kwikki-)
pᵉ/alki- (→ pᵉ/aylki-)   muk.hi- (→ mikhi-)   wus.ki- (→ wikki-)
| sᵉ/angki- (→ sᵉ/ayngki-)| kwulk.hi- (→ kwilkhi-)   mukk.i- (→ mikki-)
| (sengki- ←) seyngki- | chwukhi- (→ chwikhi-)   ttut.ki- (→ ttikki-)
semki- (→ seyngki-) | kulk.hi- (→ kilkhi-)   nukki- (→ nikki-)
eki- (→ eyki-)   nulkhi- (→ nilkhi-)   pikki-
mek.i- (→ meyki-)   tulkhi- (→ tilkhi-)   pis.ki-

A Reference Grammar of Korean

yeki- (→ yeyki-)
engki- (→ eyngki-)
kemi- (→ keyngki-)
(ceki- ←) ceyki-
(khengki- ←) kheyngki-
koki- (→ koyki-)
kkoki- (→ kkoyki-)
nok.i- (→ noyki-)
ok.i- (→ oyki-)
sok.i- (→ soyki-)
komki- (→ koyngki-)
olm.ki- (→ oyngki-)
(thoki-/thwuki- ←)
 thoyki-/thwiki-
thongki-/thwungki- (→
 thoyngki-, thwingki-)
|wuki- (→ wiki-) |
|wuk.i- (→ wiki-)|
kwuki- (→ kwiki-)
kkwuki- (→ kkwiki-)
cwuk.i- (→ cwiki-)
|chwuki- (→ chwiki-) |
|chwuk.i- (→ chwiki-)|
nwuk.i- (→ nwiki-)
swuk.i- (→ swiki-)
phungki- (→ phingki-)
swumki- (→ swingki-)
kwulm.ki- (→ kwingki-)
ttwungki- (→ ttwingki-)

cikhi-
|ikhi-
|ik.hi-
ilk.hi-
pīkhi-
|sikhi-
|sik.hi-
......

kalikhi- (→ kaylikhi-)
(nalikhi- ←) naylikhi-
tol.ikhi- (→ toylikhi-)
il.ukhi- (→ ilikhi-)

mungki- (→ mingki-)
culki- (→ cilki-)
(culki- ←) cilki-
kwulm.ki- (→ kwingki-)
ttwungki- (→ ttwingki-)
mungki- (→ mingki-)
|culki- (→ cilki-)|
|(culki- ←) cilki-|
hulki- (→ hilki-)
|(sungki- ←) simki-
|(sungki- ←) sinki-
(ccungki- →) ccingki-
iki-
piki-

ssis.ki-
ccic.ki-
......
napukki- (→ napikki-)
ppay-as.ki- (→
 ppay-aykki-)
kelikki-
kali-kki-

kkoktuki- (→ kkoktiki-)
twutulki- (→ twutilki-)
ttwutulki- (→ ttwutilki-)
(poktaki- ←) poktayki-
helttek i- (→ heltteyki-)
sosak i- (→ sosayki-)
wumcik i-

List 6. Longer ···i- stems with palatals

···ci-
cha-ci-$_A$ (→ chayci-)
(chaci- ←) chay-ci-
hay ci-
kaci- (→ kayci-)
ppā ci- (→ ppāyci-)
taci- (→ tayci-)
taci- (→ ttayci-)
kanci-$_A$ (→ kaynci-)
kkan-ci-$_A$ (→ kkaynci-)
manci- (→ maynci-)
sal-ci-$_A$ (→ saylci-)
sal-cci- (→ saylcci-)
che-ci- (→ cheyci-)
kkē ci- (→ kkēyci-)
peci- (→ peyci-)

penci- (→ peynci-)
tenci- (→ teynci-)
coci- (→ coyci-)
toci-$_A$ (→ toyci-)
tōci- (→ tōyci-)
mo ci-$_A$ (→ moyci-)
ōl-ci-$_A$ (→ ōylci-)
chwuci-$_A$ (→ chwici-)
phuci-$_A$ (→ phici-)
(twuci- ←) twici-
wuci-$_A$ (→ wici-)
ici-
cici-
tung ci-
thul ci-$_A$

ppye ci-$_A$ (→ ppeyci-)
ph'ē ci- (→ phēyci-)
phye ci- (→ pheyci-)
mey-ci-$_A$
teci- (→ teyci-)
thē ci- (→ thēyci-)
kenci- (→ keynci-)

pule ci-
sala ci-
sule ci-
ssule ci-
ha.ye ci-
----^{e}/$_a$ ci-

···cci-
hoth ci-
pic ci-

nwukci- (→ nwikci-)
kyekci- (→ keykci-)
kkekci- (→ kkeykci-)

···chi-
cac.hi- (→ caychi-)
(chachi- ←) chaychi-
hwachi- (→ hwaychi-)
kat.hi- (→ kaychi-)
|machi- (→ maychi-)
|(machi- ←) mayc.hi-
|(machi- ←) maychi-/michi-
|pachi-
|pat.chi-
|pat.hi- (→ paychi-)
|path.i-
|path.chi-
ppachi- (→ ppaychi-)
|tachi-
|tat.chi-
|tat.hi- (→ taychi-)
|tah.chi-
kakchi- (→ kaykchi-)
sak-chi- (→ saykchi-)
kwut.hi- (→ kwichi-)
|puchi-
|puth.chi- (→ pichi-)
|puth.i-
|(puchi- ←) pichi-
(ppuchi- →) ppichi-
|muchi- (→ michi-)
|(muchi- ←) michi-
michi-/maychi-
(mulchi- ←) milchi-
cwuk-chi- (→ cwikchi-)
|hwulchi- (→ hwilchi-) |
|hwulth.i- (→ hwilchi-) |
takchi- (→ taykchi-)

halth.i- (→ haylchi-)
kal(u)chi- (→ kaylchi-)
tālchi- (→ taylchi-)
salchi- (→ saylchi-)
kāmchi- (→ kaymchi-)
|anchi-
|anc.hi- (→ aynchi-)
|an chi-
ānchi- (→ āynchi-)
mangchi- (→ mayngchi-)
capchi- (→ caypchi-)
cec.hi- (→ ceychi-)
(cechi- ←) ceychi-
|kechi- (→ keychi-)
|ket.hi- (→ keychi-)
techi- (→ teychi-)
(hechi- ←) heychi-
|ppechi- (→ ppeychi-)
|ppet.chi- (→ ppeychi-)
wumchi- (→ wimchi-)
nwungchi- (→ nwingchi-)
twungchi- (→ twingchi-)
mongchi-/mungchi- (→
  meyngchi-/mingchi-)
homchi-/hwumchi- (→
  hoymchi-/hwimchi-)
(twuchi- ←) twichi-
kuchi- (→ kichi-)
(kuchi- ←) kichi-
(kkuchi- ←) kkichi-
suchi- (→ sichi-)
tungchi- (→ tingchi-)
kēlchi- (→ kēylchi-)

ttelchi- (→ tteylchi-)
sel-chi- (→ seylchi-)
enc.hi- (→ eynchi-)
kēmchi- (→ kēymchi-)
eph.chi- (→ eypchi-)
yepchi- (→ yeypchi-)
cepchi- (→ ceypchi-)
phyelchi- (→ pheylchi-)
kyeng-chi- (→ keyngchi-)
kochi- (→ koychi-)
noh.chi- (→ noychi-)
tot.chi- (→ toychi-)
cokchi- (→ coykchi-)
holth.i- (→ hoylchi-)
nongchi- (→ noyngchi-)
copchi- (→ coypchi-)
kop-chi- (→ koyp-chi-)
kkop-chi- (→ kkoyp-chi-)
(ōchi- ←) ōychi-
chichi-
|ic.hi-
|ichi-

······
iachi- (→ iaychi-)
ellechi- (→ elleychi-)
chiwu-chi- (→ chiwichi-)
nwiwuchi- (→ nwiwichi-)
samuchi- (→ samichi-)
kal(u)chi- (→ kalichi-)
(pusuchi- ←) pusichi-
|(putuchi- ←) putic.hi- |
|(putuchi- ←) putic.chi-|

A Reference Grammar of Korean

APPENDIX 1   355

List 7. Longer ···i-stems with sibilants

/ss/   olssi-   ceksi- (→ ceyksi-)   kapsi- (→ kaypsi-)

/s/   (There are no front-vowel homonyms in conflict with front-vowel honorifics.)

Homonym	Honorific	From	Front-vowel Honorific	From
	āsi-	ā-l-	(→ āysi-)	
casi-	ca-	ca-	(→ caysi-)	
	(cāsi- ←)		cāysi-	cāy-
	(cāsi- ←) causi-	cā(s)-	(→ cāsyi-)	
	ccasi-	cca-	(→ ccaysi-)	
	(ccāsi-)		ccāysi-	ccāy-
	(ccāsi- ←) cca(h.)usi-	ccah-	(→ ccāysi-)	
	chasi-	cha-	(→ chaysi-)	
	(chāsi- ←)		chāysi-	chāysi-
	hasi-	ha-	(→ haysi-)	
	|kasi-	ka-	(→ kaysi-)	
kasi-	|kasi-	ka-l-	(→ kaysi-)	
	kāsi-	kā-l-	(→ kāysi-)	
	|kkasi-	kka-	(→ kkaysi-)	
	|kkasi-	kka-l-	(→ kkaysi-)	
	(kkāsi- ←)		kkāysi-	kkāy-
	(khāsi- ←)		khāysi-	khāy-
	masi-	ma-l-	(→ maysi-)	
masi-	|māsi-	mā-l-	(→ māysi-)	
	|māsi-	mā-	(→ māysi-)	
	(māsi- ←)		māysi-	māy-
	|nasi-	na-	(→ naysi-)	
	|nasi-	na-l-	(→ naysi-)	
	(nāsi- ←)		nāysi-	nāy-
	(nāsi- ←) nausi-	nā(s)-	(→ nāysi-)	
	(nāsi- ←) na(h.)usi-	nāh-	(→ nāysi-)	
	(pasi- ←)	pay-	paysi-	pay-
	(pāsi- ←)	pāy-	pāysi-	pāy-
	(pāsi- ←) pausi-	pā(s)-	(→ pāysi-)	
	|phasi-	pha-	(→ phaysi-)	
	|phasi-	pha-l-	(← phaysi-)	
	(phasi- ←)		phaysi-	phay-
	(phāsi- ←)		phāysi-	phāy-
	ppasi-	ppa-l-	(→ ppaysi-)	
	(ppasi- ←)		ppaysi-	ppay-
	(ppāsi- ←)	ppah-	ppāysi-	ppāy-
	(ppāsi- ←) ppa(h.)usi-		(→ ppāysi-)	
	sasi-	sa-	(→ saysi-)	
	sāsi-	sā-l-	(→ sāysi-)	
	(sāsi- ←)		sāysi-	sāy-
	ssasi-	ssa-	(→ ssaysi-)	
	(ssāsi- ←) ssa(h.)usi-	ssah-	(→ ssāysi-)	
	(ssāsi- ←)		ssāysi-	ssāy-

tasi-	tasi-	ta-l-	(→ taysi-)	
	tāsi-	tā-l-	(→ tāysi-)	
	(tāsi- ←) ta(h.)usi-	tah-	(→ tāysi-)	
	(tāsi- ←)		tāysi-	tāy-
	thasi-	tha-	(→ thaysi-)	
	(thāsi- ←)		thāysi-	thāy-
	ttasi-	tta-	(→ ttaysi-)	
	(ttāsi- ←) tta(h.)usi-	ttah-	(→ ttāysi-)	
	(ttāsi- ←)		ttāysi-	ttāy-
	(ēsi- ←)		ēysi-	ēy-
	(ēsi- ←)		(ēysi- ←) eyisi-	eyi-
	(ēsi- ←)		(ēysi- ←) eywusi-	eywu-
	ēsi-	ē-l-	(→ ēysi-)	
	cēsi-	cē-l-	(→ cēysi-)	
	(cēsi- ←) ceusi-	cē(s)-	(→ cēysi-)	
	hesi-	he-	(→ heysi-)	
	(hesi- ←)		hēysi-	hēy-
	hēsi-	hē-l-	(→ hēysi-)	
	kēsi-	kē-l-	(→ kēysi-)	
	(kēsi- ←)		kēysi-	kēy-
	mēsi-	mē-l-	(→ mēysi-)	
	(mēsi-)		mēysi-	mēy-
	nēsi-	nē-l-	(→ nēysi-)	
	(nēsi- ←) ne(h.)usi-	neh-	(→ nēysi-)	
	pēsi-	pē-l-	(→ pēysi-)	
	sesi- = susi-	se- = su-	(→ seysi-)	
	(sēsi- ←)		sēysi-	sēy-
	ssēsi-	ssē-l-	(→ ssēysi-)	
k(y)ēysi-				
	tēsi-	tē-l-	(→ tēysi-)	
	thēsi-	thē-l-	(→ thēysi-)	
	ttēsi-	ttē-l-	(→ ttēysi-)	
	yēsi-	yē-l-	(→ yēysi-)	
	osi-	o-	(→ oysi-)	
	(ōsi- ←)		ōysi-	ōy-
	(cosi- ←)		coysi-	coy-
	cōsi-	cō-l-	(→ cōysi-)	
	(cōsi- ←) cō(h.)usi-	cōh-	(→ cōysi-)	
	ccōsi-	ccō-	(→ ccōysi-)	
			ccoysi-	ccoy-
			ccōysi-	ccōy-
	hōsi-	hō-	(→ hōysi-)	
		kō-	(→ kōysi-)	
		kō-l-	(→ kōysi-)	
			(→ kōysi-)	
		kōw-		
			kōysi-	kōy-
		kko-	(→ kkoysi-)	
			kkōysi-	kkōy-

A Reference Grammar of Korean

mōsi-	mōsi- < mousi-	mō- < mou-	(→ mōysi-)	
	mōsi-	mō-l-	(→ mōysi- → mēysi-)	
			mōysi- (→ mēysi-)	mōy-
		nō-l-	(→ nōysi-)	
	nōsi- ← no[h.]usi-	noh-	(→ nōysi-)	
			nōysi-	nōy-
			posi- (→ poysi- → peysi-)	po-
			(*pōysi- → peysi-)[1]	pōy-
			*pōywusi-[1]	pōyw-
	(sosi- ←)		soysi-	soy-
	(sōsi- ←)		sōysi-	sōy-
	sōsi-	sō-l-	(→ sōysi-)	
	ssosi-	sso-	(→ ssoysi-)	
	ssōsi-	ssō-l-	(→ ssōysi-)	
	(ssōsi- ←)		ssōysi-	ssōy-
	(tosi- ←)		toysi-	toy-
	(tōsi- ←)		tōysi-	tōy-
	tōsi-	tō-l-	(→ tōysi-)	
	(tōsi- ←) towusi-	tow-	(→ tōysi-)	
	wūsi-	wū-l-	(→ wīsi-)	
	cwusi-	cwu-	(→ cwisi-)	
	cwūsi-	cwū-l-	(cwīsi-)	
	(cwūsi- ←) cwuwusi-	cwuw-	(→ cwīsi-)	
	(cwūsi- ←) cwuusi-	cwu(s)-	(→ cwīsi-)	
	(cwūsi- ←)		cwīsi-	cwī-
	(ccwūsi- ←) ccwuusi-	ccwu(s)-	(→ cwīsi-)	
	chwusi-	chwu-	(→ chwisi-)	
	(chwūsi- ←) chwuwusi-	chwuw-	(→ chwīsi-)	
	(hwusi- ←)		hwisi-	hwi-
			ǀkīsi-	kī-
			ǀkīsi-	kī-l-
	(kīsi- ←) kiwusi-	kīw-	(→ kīsi-)	
			khisi-	khi-
			khīsi-	khī-
			khiisi-	khii-
			kkīsi-	kkī-
			kkīisi-	kkīi-
	(kkisi- ←) kkiwusi-	kkiwu-	(→ kkisi-)	
	kwūsi-	kwū-l-	(→ kwīsi-)	
	(kwūsi- ←) kwuwusi-	kwūw-	(→ kwīsi-)	
	kkwusi-	kkwu-	(→ kkwisi-)	
	(kkwusi- ←)		kkwisi-	kkwi-
	(kkwēsi- ←)		kkwēysi- (→ kkwīsi-)	kkwēy-
			ǀmīsi-	mī-
			ǀmīsi-	mī-l-
	(mīsi- ←) miwusi-	miw-		
	musi-	mu-l-	(→misi-)	
	mūsi-	mū-l-	(→ mīsi-)	

	nwusi-		nwu-	(→ nwisi-)
	(nwūsi- ←) nwuwusi-		nwuw-	(→ nwīsi-)
pusi-	pūsi-		pū-l-	
	(pūsi- ←) pwuusi-		pū(s)-	(→ pīsi-)
				| pīsi-	pī-
				| pīsi-	pī-l-
	(pīsi- ←) piwusi-		piwu-	
				phisi-	phi-
	(phisi- ←) phusi-		phu-l-	(→ phisi-)
	(phīsi- ←) phiwusi-		phiwu-	
				ppīsi-	ppī-
sswusi-	(sswisi- ←) sswusi-		sswu-	(→ sswisi-)
				swīsi-	swī-
	(swīsi- ←) swiwusi-		swīw-	
	(twisi- ←) twusi-		twu-	(→ twisi-)
				twisi-	twi-
				thwisi-	thwi-
				ttwisi-	ttwi-
				isi-	i-
		(īsi- ←) iusi-		i(s)-
		(īsi- ←) iusi-		ī(s)-
				| īsi-	ī-
				| īsi-	ī-l-
				| cisi-	ci-
				| cisi-	ci-l-
		(cīsi- ←) ciusi-		cī(s)-
				ccisi-	cci-
				ccīsi-	ccī-
				chisi-	chi-
				hisi- = huysi-	huy- = hi-
				sisi-	si-$_A$
				| ttisi-	tti-
				| ttisi- = ttuysi-	tti- = ttuy-
				thisi- = thusi-	thi- = thu-
	ttuysi- = ttisi-		ttuy- = tti-	
	thuysi- = thisi-		thuy- = thi-	
	(kūsi- ←) ku(u)si-		ku(u)-l-	
			kū(s)-	
	khusi-		khu-	
	kkusi-		kku-	
	kkūsi-		kkū-l-	
	nusi-		nu-l-	
	susi- < sesi-		su- < se-	
	ssusi-		ssu-$_{VA}$	
	tusi-		tu-l-	
	| thusi-		thu-l-	
	| thusi-		thu-	
	ttusi-		ttu-	

[1] But *pōysi- and *pōywusi- do not occur because of the passive and humble meanings of the stems.

A Reference Grammar of Korean

List 8. Longer ···i- stems with liquids (···li-, ···lli-)

···li-	···lli-	···li-	···lli-
ali-$_A$ (→ ayli-)	alli- (→ aylli-)	|cwuli- (→ cwili-)	
c^{e}ali-$_A$ (→ c^{e}ayli-)	calli- (→ caylli-)	|cwul.i-/col.i- (→ cwili-/coyli-)	
chali- (→ chayli-)			
|hali- (→ hayli-)		kwuli-$_A$ (→ kwili-)	kwulh.li- (→ kwilli-)
|h^a/$_u$li-$_A$ (→ h^{ay}/$_i$li-)			kwūlli- (→ kwīlli-)
kali- (→ kayli-)	kalli- (→ kaylli-)	kkwuli- (→ kkwili-)	kkwulli- (→ kkwili-)
	kkalli- (→ kkaylli-)		mulli- (→ milli-)
	malli- (→ maylli-)		(mulli- ←) milli-
(nali- ←) nayli-	nalli- (→ naylli-)	nwuli-$_A$ (→ nwili-)	nwulli- (→ nwilli-)
	p^{e}alli- (→ p^{e}alli-)	nwūli- (→ newīli-)	
	phalli- (→ phaylli-)	|puli- (→ pili-)	(pulli- ←) pilli-
	ppalli- (→ ppaylli-)	|(puli- ←) pili-/payli-$_A$	
s^{e}ali- (→ s^{e}ayli-)	salli- (→ saylli-)	ppuli- (→ ppili-)	phulli- (→ philli-)
|talli- (→ tayli-)	|talli- (→ taylli-)		
|tal.i- (→ tayli-)	|talh.li- (→ taylli-)		twulli- (→ twilli-)
(ttali- ←) ttayli-	ttalli- (→ ttaylli-)		ttwulh.li- (→ ttwilli-)
y^{e}ali-$_A$ (→ y^{e}ayli-)		(culi- ←) cili-$_{VA}$	(culli- ←) cilli-
eli-$_{VA}$ (→ eyli-)	elli- (→ eylli-)		(cculli- ←) ccilli-
|c^{e}ali-$_A$ (→ c^{e}ayli-)		|(kuli- ←) kili-	hulli- (→ hilli-)
|cel.i- (→ ceyli-)		|kuli- (→ kili-)	(kulli- ←) killi-
|celi- (→ ceyli-)		|kuli '- (→ kili-)	ku(u)lli- (→ killi-)
|celi '- (→ ceyli-)		(kkuli- ←) kkulh.i- (→ kkili-)	kkulli- (→ kkilli-)
keli- (→ keyli-)	kelli- (→ keylli-)		
kkēli- (→ kkēyli-)	kyelli- (→ keylli-)	|nuli-$_A$ (→ nili-)	nulli- (→ nilli-)
	nelli- (→ neylli-)	|nul.i- (→ nili-)	
pyeli- (→ peyli-)		(suli- ←) sili-$_A$	(sulli- ←) silli-
peli- (→ peyli-)		|tuli- (→ tili-)	ssulli- (→ ssilli-)
pēl.i- (→ pēyli-)		|tul.i- (→ tili-)	tulli- (→ tilli-)
teli-$_A$ (→ teyli-)	thelli- (→ theylli-)	ttuli- (→ ttili-)	thulli- (→ thilli-)
(teli- ←) teyli-	ttelli- (→ tteylli-)	......	......
y^{u}oli-$_A$ (→ y^{e}ali-)	yelli- (→ yeylli-)	pulali-	kkapsalli-
oli- (→ oyli-)	olli- (→ oylli-)	ssulali-$_A$	ikkulli-
|coli- (→ coyli-)	colli- (→ coylli-)	tosali-	mongkulli-
|coli '- (→ coyli-)		tasuli-	tongkulli-
|col.i-/cwul.i- (→ coyli-/cwili-)		kenuli-	twungkulli-
		kēntuli-	kesulli-
holi-/hwuli- (→ hoyli-/hwili-)	holli- (→ holli-)	(t)twutuli-	kwusulli-
		eph-tuli-	ccotulli-
|koli-$_A$ (→ koyli-)	kolh.li- (→ koylli-)	omchuli-/wumchuli-	huntulli-
|koli '- (→ koyli-)	kkolli- (→ kkoylli-)	omuli-/wumuli-	ku(u)lli-
	molli- (→ moylli- → meylli-)	ccakuli-	kongkulli-
		ccikuli-	kwungkwulli-
noli-$_{VA}$	nolli- (→ noylli-)	swukuli-	amulli-
	ssolli- (→ ssoylli-)	twukuli-	pophulli-/puphulli-
toli- (→ toyli-)	tolli- (→ toylli-)	ccayngkuli-/ccingkuli-	awulli-/ewulli-
yoli '- (→ yeyli-)		ccongkuli-/ccwungkuli-	muncilli-
wuli- (→ wili-)	wulli- (→ willi-)	kamuli- *(continues)*	

(List 8 continued)

pemuli-
hwumuli-
(k)kopuli-/(k)kwupuli-
kophuli-/kwuphuli-
ccayphuli-/cciphuli-

List 9. L-extending vowel stems

···a-l-	···e-l-	···o-l-	···wu-l-	···u-l-	···i-l-
ā-l-	ē-l-	cō-l-	wū-l-	kū-l-	ī-l-
ca-l-$_A$	cē-l-	kō-l-	cwū-l-	(= kuu-l-)	ci-l-$_A$
ka-l-	hē-l-$_{VA}$	kko-l-	kwū-l-	kkū-l-	kī-l-$_A$
kā-l-	kē-l-	mō-l-	mu-l-	nu-l-	
kka-l-	mē-l-$_{VA}$	nō-l-$_{VA}$	mū-l-	su-l-	mī-l-
kwā-l-	nē-l-	sō-l-$_{VA}$	pū-l-	ssu-l-	pī-l-
ma-l-	pē-l-$_{VA}$	ssō-l-	phu-l-	tu-l-	......
mā-l-	sē-l-	tō-l-	......	thu-l-	nani-l-
na-l-	ssē-l-	......	(k)kyawu-l-/	......	canci-l-$_A$
		mu' so-l-	(k)kiwu-l-$_A$	ikku-l-	cha-ci-l-$_A$
pha-l-	tē-l-	ey-tō-l-	(kewu-l-)	kanu-l-	eci-l-$_A$
ppa-l-$_{VA}$	thē-l-	kenmō-l-	setwu-l-	mantu-l-	kechi-l-$_A$
sā-l-$_{VA}$	ttē-l-		(p)pittwu-l-$_A$	santu-l-	kēni-l-$_A$
ta-l-$_{VA}$	yē-l-		kkay-mu-l-	ketu-l-	chi-mi-l-
tā-l-	......		ppay-mu-l-	kkē tu-l-	mōci-l-$_A$
......	kāmye-l-		amu-l-	tte-tu-l-	nōni-l-
ay ta-l-			kamu-l-	ttētu-l-	tōni-l-
oy-tta-l-$_A$			tamu-l-	ppye-tu-l-	kwumni-l-
is-ta-l-			emu-l-$_A$	engkhu-l-	(< kwupq-i-l-)
(kāmā-l-)			cemu-l-	hengkhu-l-	
			hemu-l-	ongku-l-	
			memu-l-	tongku-l-$_A$	
			pemu-l-	mongku-l-$_A$	
			tumu-l-$_A$	kwungku-l-$_A$	
			y^e/$_a$mul-$_A$	twungku-l-$_A$	
			kkapu-l-	wuku-l-$_A$	
			tepu-l-	twip(t)tu-l-	
			p^u/$_o$phul-	pī-thu-l-/	
			kkē-twu-l-	pāy-thu-l-	
			(= kkē twulu-)	huntu-l-	
				cc^i/$_a$tu-l-	
				kuu-l-	

The dictionaries list one stem that ends in **ay-l-**, the mining term **kway-l-** 'seem a poor vein, seem low in ore content'. It is an oddity.

A Reference Grammar of Korean

List 10. L-doubling vowel stems

···alu-	···elu-	···olu-	···wulu-	···ulu-	···ilu-
calu-	elu-	olu-	kwulu-	ulu-	ilu-$_{VA}$ [3]
kalu-	kelu-	colu-	mulu-	hulu-	cilu-
malu-	nelu-$_A$	kolu-$_{VA}$	nwūlu-	kulu-	ccilu-
nalu-	pyelu-	molu-	pulu-	kkulu-	kilu-
palu-	pyēlu-	tolu-	twulu-	......	......
ppalu-$_A$			......	k^e/ayulu-$_A$	tacilu-
salu-[1]			^{e}/awulu-	kunulu-	ecilu-
salu-[2]			kewulu-	kesulu-	mucilu-
talu-$_A$			cwumulu-	chwusulu-	mu-ccilu-
......			kkapulu-	twisulu-	muncilu-
kapcalu-			setwulu-		cicilu-
				sethwulu-	sicilu-
				sen-twulu-	
				cac.chwulu-	

[1] 'set afire'   [2] 'winnow' said by NK sources to be l-doubling, but SK sources say it is regular. It is not the common term anywhere.   [3] 'say; early'

There are no stems with -ylu- except k^e/aylu-, contraction of k^e/ayulu-.

CF the regular vowel stems with the infinitive ···le rather than ···lle:
    ttalu-, chilu-, tatalu-, mak-talu-, wulelu-; ? salu- 'winnow'.

List 11. L-inserting voĖwel stems

(kām-)phalu-$_A$	nolu-$_A$	nwulu-$_A$	ilu- 'reach'
		phulu-$_A$	

List 12. Consonant stems: ···p- and ···w-

(For ph and ps and for lp see 13. There is no stem ···pp-.)

···ap-	···aw-	···ayw-	···ep-	···ew-	···op-	···ow-	···oyw-
cap-	taw-$_A$	mayw-$_A$	ep-	kyēw-$_A$	cop-$_A$	kōw-$_A$	pōyw-
......	......	nayw-$_A$	cep-	tēw-$_A$	kop-$_{VA}$	low-$_A$	
tacap-	pat.caw-		......	......	kkop-	tōw-	
ket-cap-	tut.caw-		wucep-	swus cew-$_A$	ppop-	......	
keth-cap-	ttakaw-$_A$			ttukew-$_A$		say low-$_A$	
	akkaw-$_A$			mukew-$_A$		oy low-$_A$	
	kakkaw-$_A$			nukkew-$_A$		koy low-$_A$	
	kokkaw-$_A$			kikkew-$_A$		......	
	halkaw-$_A$			twukkew-$_A$		nalkhalow-$_A$	
	salkaw-$_A$			helkew-$_A$		kkatalow-$_A$	
	talkaw-$_A$			sulkew-$_A$		sasa low-$_A$	
	tālaw-$_A$			sēnkew-$_A$			
	hollaw-$_A$			sēlew-$_A$			
	kkol taw-$_A$			tēlew-$_{(V)A}$			
	kapyaw-$_A$			mulew-$_A$			
	sānaw-$_A$			pulew-$_A$			
	tothaw-$_A$			sulew-$_A$			
	(continues)			*(continues)*			

(List 12
continued) ......
  anthakkaw-$_A$
  cangkulaw-$_A$
  alum-taw-$_A$
  alittaw-$_A$

kelyew-$_A$
malyew-$_A$
elyew-$_A$
twulyew-$_A$
k^e/$_a$pyew-$_A$
maysew-$_A$
musew-$_A$
mu'-tew-$_A$
sinkew-$_A$
ccin-tew-$_A$
huy-ttew-$_A$
twuthew-$_A$
kwīyew-$_A$
......
kaculew-$_A$
ecilew-$_A$
k^a/$_u$ncilew-$_A$
kkancilew-$_A$
tencilew-$_A$
p^e/$_a$kkulew-$_A$
maykkulew-/
 mikkulew-$_A$
sikkulew-$_A$
cayngkulew-/
 cingkulew-$_A$
p^e/$_a$ntulew-$_A$
susulew-$_A$
kwun(ten)-
 cilew-$_A$

...wup-	...wuw-	...wiw-	...uw-	...ip-	...iw-	...lw-
kwup-$_A$	cwūw-	swīw-$_A$	–	ip-	kīw-	sēlw-$_A$
......	chwuw-$_A$	......	......	cip-	miw-$_A$	
ēcwup-$_A$[1]	kwūw-	aswiw-$_A$	(t)t^a/$_u$suw-$_A$	ssip-	......	
mecwup-$_A$	nwuw-		wusuw-$_A$	......	kūliw-	
swucwup-$_A$	nwūw-			heycip-	can-miw-$_A$	
	......			kko-cip-		
	etwuw-$_{(V)A}$			mocip-		
	(cesswuw-)			pho-cip-		
				kkucip-		
				pīcip-		
				wucip-		
				......		
				palkucip-		

[1] The NK dictionary Cosen-e so-sacen lists this as ēcwuw-$_A$, but NKd has it with the unleniting **p**. KEd gives both versions.

A Reference Grammar of Korean

List 13. Consonant stems: ⋯ss-, ⋯ps-, ⋯ph-, ⋯s-, ⋯(s)-, ⋯t-, ⋯t/l-, ⋯lq-, ⋯c-

⋯ss-[1]	⋯s-	⋯(s)-	⋯t-	⋯t/l- (CF 9)	⋯c-
iss-	as-	cā(s)-	pat-	tat-/tal-	cac-$_{VA}$
-ess-	ppāys-	nā(s)-$_{VA}$	tat-	(cēt-/cel-$_{Dial.}$)	chac-
-keyss-	pes-	?pā(s)-[2]	et-	kēt-/kel-	kac-
	(yes-)	cē(s)-	ket-	kyēt-/kyel-	mac-$_{VA}$
	sos-	cwu(s)-	pet-$_{VA}$	mūt-/mul-	nac-$_A$
	wūs-	mu(s)-	ppet-	pūt-/pul-	tac[i]-
	kis-	pū(s)-	kot-$_A$	nwūt-/nwūl-	mayc-
	pis-	kū(s)-	(mot-)	tut-/tul-	cec-
	ssis-	kkū(s)-	ssot-	kīt-/kil-	(mec-$_{VA}$)
	……	ī(s)-	tot-	sīt-/sil-	ccoc-
	pilus-	cī(s)-	kwut-$_{VA}$	……	kkoc-
		……	mut-	kkaytat-/kkaytal-	kwuc-$_A$
		(ceswu(s)-)	ttut-	(tatat-/tatal-)	nuc-$_{VA}$
			mit-		ccic-
			tit[i]-		ic-
					pic- = pici-

⋯ps- = /pss/	⋯ph-		⋯lq- (< lu-)	
ēps-	kaph-		ilq-$_A$	aykkwuc-$_A$
……	eph-			cīs-kwuc-$_A$
kā.yeps-	teph-			kkwucic-
	noph-			peluc-
	thoph-			seluc-
	?puph- =			selkec-
	puphu-			mapic-?$_{Dial.}$
	ciph-			putic-
	kiph-$_A$[3]			……
	siph-$_A$			pulu-cic-
	……			kōm-salkuc-$_A$
	tu-noph-$_A$			

[1] There is also ssāyss-$_A$, a contraction of ssah.ye iss-. It lacks a modifier form, replacing *ssāyss.un by ssāyn, a contraction of ssah.in.   [2] = paswu-.   [3] Also $_V$ in pam i kiph.ess.ta only.

List 14. Consonant stems: ⋯ch-, ⋯th-, ⋯lth-, ⋯lh-, ⋯lph-, ⋯lp-, ⋯lw-

⋯ch-	⋯th-	⋯lth-	⋯lh-	⋯lph-	⋯lp-	⋯lw-
coch-	kath-$_A$	halth-	alh-	ulph-	pālp-	sēlw-$_A$
mich[i]-	(nath-$_{obs}$)	(hulth-)	helh-$_A$ (= hel ha-)	……	cc^{e}alp-$_A$	
(ssich-$_{Dial.}$)	path-	(holth-)	olh-$_A$	?aytalph-$_A$	y^{e}alp-$_A$	
……	yath-$_A$	hwulth-	kolh-		nelp-$_A$	
nwiwuch(i)-	payth-		kkolh-$_{VA}$		ttēlp-$_A$	
	yeth-A		kkwulh-$_{VA}$			
	huth-		ttwulh-			
	puth-		kkulh-			
	cith-A		?kulh-$_A$ (= kulu-)			
	……		ssulh-			
	puluth(u)-		silh-$_A$			
			ilh-			

List 15. Consonant stems: velars (⋯k-, ⋯kk-, ⋯lk-, ⋯ks-)

⋯k-	⋯kk-	⋯lk-	⋯ks-
cāk-$_A$	kkakk-	k^a/$_u$lk-	(naks-$_{obs.}$)
mak-	nakk-	m^a/$_u$lk-$_A$	
pak-	takk-	palk-$_{VA}$	
sak-	yekk-	nalk-$_A$	
y^{e}ak-$_A$	kkekk-	elk-	
cek-	kyekk-	e/alk-	
cēk-$_A$	sekk-	olk-	
-ccek-$_A$	tekk-	*polk-/pulk-$_A$	
mek-$_{V(A)}$	pokk-	wulk-$_A$	
sek-	sokk-	pulk-$_{VA}$	
ssek-	mukk-	nulk-$_{VA}$	
ok-/wuk-		ilk-	
nok-			
sok-			
cwuk-	pik[i]-		
chwuk-	sik-		
muk-	⋯⋯		
nwuk-$_A$	tulmek-$_A$		
ik-	simek-$_A$		
ccik-	heysik-$_A$		

Dictionaries list **sayngkak-** but that is just an abbreviation of **sayngkak ha-** and it lacks a full paradigm of its own: there is no infinitive *sayngkak.^{e}/a, only sayngkak hay (ha.ye).

List 16. Consonant stems: nasals (⋯m-, ⋯lm-, ⋯n-, ⋯nh-, ⋯nc-)

⋯m-	⋯lm-	⋯n-	⋯nh-	⋯nc-
chām-	pālm-	ān-	anh-$_{VA}$ (= ani ha-)	anc-
kām-$_{VA}$	sālm-	non[u]-[1]	mānh-	enc-
kkam-$_A$	tālm-	?mun[u]-	kkonh-	⋯⋯
nām-	cēlm-$_A$	kkun- (= kkunh-)	munh-	kki-enc-
sām-	ōlm-	sin- (< sīn-)	hunh-$_A$ (= hun ha-)	
tām-	kōlm-		kkunh-	
kēm-	kwūlm-	[1] and nan(u-) =	⋯⋯	
nēm-	cilm-	nanwu- < nan hwo-	cemcanh-$_A$	
ppyēm-			enccanh-$_A$	
phum-			hachanh-$_A$	
ppum-			kichanh-$_A$	
swūm-			kwaynchanh-$_A$	
sīm-			kwichanh-$_A$	
⋯⋯			⋯⋯	
tatum-	potum-		ēcwup-canh-$_A$	
tetum-	⋯⋯		katang-chanh-$_A$	
mekum-	katatum-		ansim-chanh-$_A$	
sesum-	malmiam-		....-chanh-$_A$	

A Reference Grammar of Korean

List 17. Ambivalent stems

All are adjectives, so "$_A$" is omitted.

···a(h)-	···ay(h)-[1]	···e(h)-
-ta(h)-[2]	colay(h)-	cele(h)-/cole(h)-
-tala(h)-[3]	kolay(h)-	kule(h)-/kole(h)-
	yolay(h)-	ile(h)-/yole(h)-
		ette(h)-
		āmule(h)-
nōla(h)-		nwūle(h)-
nōyla(h)-		nwīle(h)-
palka(h)-		pelke(h)-
ppalka(h)-		ppelke(h)-
kkama(h)-		kkeme(h)-
phala(h)-		phule(h)-, phele(h)-
pō.ya(h)-		pū.ye(h)-
ppō.ya(h)-		ppū.ye(h)-
ha.ya(h)-		he.ye(h)-
malka(h)-		melke(h)-
myalka(h)-		milke(h)-senule(h)-
sanula(h)-		senule(h)-
ssanula(h)-		ssenule(h)-
ttongkula(h)-		twungkule(h)-
		(teng)tengkule(h)-
		ssangkule(h)-
c^e/akuma(h)-, cokuma(h)-		
say-kkama(h)-		si-kkeme(h)-
say-khama(h)-		si-kheme(h)-
say-ppalka(h)-		si-ppelke(h)-
say-phala(h)-		si-phele(h)-
say(q)-nola(h)-[4]		si(q)-nwule(h)- /si(n)nwu···/
say(q)-ha.ya(h)-[5]		si(q)-he.ye(h)- /si(t)he···/
say(q)-malka(h)-[6]		si(q)-melke(h)-

[1] These three stems are colloquial variants of the more standard forms in the column to the right.

[2] Abbreviation of -tala(h)-: khe-ta(h)-, ? ...

[3] ki-tala(h)- (← kī-l-), khe-tala(h)- (← khu-); kop-tala(h)-, kiph-tala(h)-, noph-tala(h)-, kwulk-tala(h)-, nelp-tala(h)-, nelq-tala(h)- (spelled nel-ttala(h)- in SK but nel-tala(h)- in NK; ?← nelu- rather than nelp-), ? ...

[4] Pronounced /say(n)no···/.

[5] Pronounced /say(t)ha···/.

[6] Pronounced /say(m)mal···/.

Appendix 2. Korean surnames.

The following list of 284 Korean surnames is ordered by frequency, from the most to the least popular. It is followed by an alphabetized list. The data come from Kwuk.e kyoyuk yenkwu-hoy 1960:99-100. An obvious error (left unchanged): 桂 **Kyey** is given both for 81 and for 246.

1 李 ^{1}**Yi**	35 南 **Nam**	69 馬 **Ma**$_1$	103 董 **Tong**
2 金 **Kim**	36 康 **Kang**$_2$	70 愼 **Sin**$_3$	104 琴 **Kum**
3 朴 **Pak**	37 田 **Cen**$_2$	71 明 **Myeng**	105 印 **In**
4 崔 **Choy**	38 任 **Im**	72 蘇 **So**$_1$	106 皇甫 **Hwangpo**
5 鄭 **Ceng**$_1$	39 河 **Ha**$_1$	73 周 **Cwu**$_2$	107 靜 **Chen**$_2$
6 趙 **Co**$_1$	40 郭 **Kwak**$_1$	74 薛 **Sel**$_1$	108 芮 **Yey**
7 尹 **Yun**	41 禹 **Wu**$_1$	75 魏 **Wi**$_1$	109 史 **Sa**$_1$
8 姜 **Kang**$_1$	42 丁 **Ceng**$_2$	76 卓 **Thak**	110 慶 **Kyeng**$_1$
9 張 **Cang**$_1$	43 羅 ^{1}**Na**	77 延 **Yen**$_1$	111 庾 **Yu**$_2$
10 韓 **Han**$_1$	44 池 **Ci**$_1$	78 奇 **Ki**	112 睦 **Mok**
11 吳 **O**$_1$	45 元 **Wen**$_1$	79 表 **Phyo**$_1$	113 昔 **Sek**$_2$
12 林 ^{1}**Im**	46 閔 **Min**	80 宣 **Sen**$_1$	114 程 **Ceng**$_3$
13 安 **An**	47 具 **Kwu**$_1$	81 桂 **Kyey** = 246	115 皮 **Phi**
14 宋 **Song**	48 嚴 **Em**	82 王 **Wang**	116 卜 **Pok**
15 徐 **Se**$_1$	49 方 **Pang**$_1$	83 孟 **Mayng**	117 智 **Ci**$_2$
16 黃 **Hwang**	50 成 **Seng**$_1$	84 玉 **Ok**	118 公 **Kong**$_2$
17 洪 **Hong**	51 辛 **Sin**$_2$	85 秦 **Cin**$_2$	119 獨孤 **Tok.ko**
18 全 **Cen**$_1$	52 兪 **Yu**$_1$	86 余 **Ye**$_1$	120 景 **Kyeng**$_2$
19 權 **Kwen**	53 蔡 **Chay**$_1$	87 太 **Thay**	121 賈 **Ka**
20 柳 ^{1}**Yu**$_1$	54 玄 **Hyen**	88 奉 **Pong**$_1$	122 溫 **On**
21 高 **Ko**	55 陳 **Cin**$_1$	89 承 **Sung**$_1$	123 胡 **Ho**$_1$
22 文 **Mun**$_1$	56 咸 **Ham**	90 片 **Phyen**$_1$	124 晋 **Cin**$_3$
23 白 **Payk**	57 邊 **Pyen**$_1$	91 潘 **Pan**$_1$	125 邢 **Hyeng**
24 梁 ^{1}**Yang**	58 千 **Chen**$_1$	92 蔣 **Cang**$_2$	126 賓 **Pin**$_1$
25 申 **Sin**$_1$	59 廉 ^{1}**Yem**$_1$	93 南宮 **Namkwung**	127 陰 **Um**
26 孫 **Son**	60 楊 **Yang**$_1$	94 陸 ^{1}**Yuk**	128 杜 **Twu**
27 劉 ^{1}**Yu**$_2$	61 孔 **Kong**$_1$	95 諸 **Cey**	129 章 **Cang**$_3$
28 許 **He**	62 吉 **Kil**	96 鮮于 **Sen.wu**	130 弓 **Kwung**
29 裵 **Pay**	63 石 **Sek**$_1$	97 魚 **E**$_1$	131 韋 **Wi**$_2$
30 曹 **Co**$_2$	64 呂 ^{1}**Ye**	98 牟 **Mo**$_1$	132 甘 **Kam**
31 盧 ^{1}**No**$_1$	65 魯 ^{1}**No**$_2$	99 殷 **Un**$_1$	133 簡 **Kan**$_1$
32 朱 **Cwu**$_1$	66 卞 **Pyen**$_2$	100 鞠 **Kwuk**$_1$	134 葛 **Kal**
33 沈 **Sim**	67 秋 **Chwu**$_1$	101 龍 ^{1}**Yong**	135 扈 **Ho**$_2$
34 車 **Cha**	68 都 **To**$_1$	102 房 **Pang**$_2$	136 左 **Cwa**

137 司空 Sakong	174 花 Hwa$_1$	211 汝 Ye$_2$	248 珠 Cwu$_3$
138 錢 Cen$_3$	175 萬 Man	212 謝 Sa$_2$	249 敦 Ton$_2$
139 彭 Phayng	176 馮 Phung	213 介 Kay	250 吞 Tham
140 邵 So$_2$	177 燕 Yen$_2$	214 漢 Han$_2$	251 干 Kan$_2$
141 尙 Sang$_1$	178 頓 Ton$_1$	215 鳳 Pong$_2$	252 竿 Kan$_3$
142 范 Pem$_1$	179 浪 ^{1}Nang	216 舍 Sa$_3$	253 垣 Hwan
143 楔 Sel$_2$	180 阿 A	217 閻 Yem	254 炭 Than
144 諸葛 Ceykal	181 强 Kang$_3$	218 單 Tan$_2$	255 遷 Chen$_3$
145 唐 Tang	182 班 Pan$_2$	219 扁 Phyen$_2$	256 鮮 Sen$_2$
146 夏 Ha$_2$	183 墨 Muk	220 濂 ^{1}Yem$_2$	257 先 Sen$_3$
147 莊 Cang$_4$	184 段 Tan$_1$	221 斤 Kun	258 標 Phyo$_2$
148 西門 Semun	185 及 Nay$_1$	222 星 Seng$_2$	259 召 So$_3$
149 施 Si$_1$	186 袁 Wen$_2$	223 丘 Kwu$_2$	260 則 Chuk
150 柴 Si$_2$	187 包 Pho$_1$	224 襄 Yang$_2$	261 肖 Cho$_2$
151 慈 Ca	188 判 Phan	225 鮑 Pho$_2$	262 何 Ha$_3$
152 陶 To$_2$	189 梅 May	226 旁 Pang$_5$	263 那 ^{1}Na
153 龐 Pang$_3$	190 倉 Chang$_2$	227 恩 Un$_2$	264 和 Hwa$_2$
154 甄 Kyen	191 夫 Pu	228 要 Yo	265 賀 Ha$_4$
155 昇 Sung$_2$	192 麻 Ma$_2$	229 西 Se$_2$	266 瓜 Kwa
156 邦 Pang$_4$	193 大 Tay	230 菜 Chay$_2$	267 甞 Sang$_2$
157 弼 Phil$_1$	194 鳶 ?= 鈌 Kyek	231 應 Ung	268 桑 Sang$_3$
158 邕 Ong$_1$	195 芸 Wun$_1$	232 剛 Kang$_4$	269 仰 Ang
159 東方 Tongpang	196 姚 Co$_3$	233 俊 Cwun	270 廣 Kwang
160 楚 Cho$_1$	197 彬 Pin$_2$	234 凡 Pem$_2$	271 卿 Kyeng$_3$
161 平 Phyeng	198 國 Kwuk$_2$	235 道 To$_3$	272 井 Ceng$_4$
162 荀 Swun$_1$	199 伊 I$_2$	236 端 Tan$_3$	273 勝 Sung$_2$
163 昌 Chang$_1$	200 丕 Pi	237 眞 Cin$_4$	274 敬 Kyeng$_4$
164 毛 Mo$_2$	201 雲 Wun$_2$	238 永 Yeng	275 靈 ^{1}Yeng
165 鍾 Cong$_1$	202 海 Hay	239 鄒 Chwu$_2$	276 守 Swu
166 執 Cip	203 舜 Swun$_2$	240 仇 Kwu$_3$	277 谷 Kok
167 葉 Yep	204 雍 Ong$_2$	241 翁 Ong$_3$	278 畢 Phil$_2$
168 異 I$_1$	205 占 Cem	242 貢 Kong$_3$	279 骨 Kol
169 氷 Ping	206 米 Mi	243 江 Kang$_5$	280 釋 Sek$_3$
170 夜 Ya	207 奈 Nay$_2$	244 於 E$_2$	281 郁 Wuk
171 路 ^{1}No$_3$	208 艾 Ay	245 伍 O$_2$	282 律 ^{1}Yul
172 于 Wu$_2$	209 宗 Cong$_2$	246 桂 Kyey = 81	283 藿 Kwak$_2$
173 雷 ^{1}Noy	210 后 Hwu	247 門 Mun$_2$	284 席 Sek$_4$

Alphabetical list of surnames followed by rank

阿 A	180	陳 Cin_1	55	后 Hwu	210	權 Kwen	19
安 An	13	秦 Cin_2	85	玄 Hyen	54	具 Kwu_1	47
仰 Ang	269	晉 Cin_3	124	邢 Hyeng	125	丘 Kwu_2	223
艾 Ay	208	眞 Cin_4	237	異 I_1	168	仇 Kwu_3	240
慈 Ca	151	執 Cip	166	伊 I_2	199	鞠 $Kwuk_1$	100
張 $Cang_1$	9	趙 Co_1	6	林 ^{1}Im	12	國 $Kwuk_2$	198
蔣 $Cang_2$	92	曹 Co_2	30	任 Im	38	弓 Kwung	130
章 $Cang_3$	129	姚 Co_3	196	印 In	105	鳶?= 鴃 Kyek	194
莊 $Cang_4$	147	鍾 $Cong_1$	165	賈 Ka	121	甄 Kyen	154
占 Cem	205	宗 $Cong_2$	209	葛 Kal	134	慶 $Kyeng_1$	110
全 Cen_1	18	左 Cwa	136	甘 Kam	132	景 $Kyeng_2$	120
田 Cen_2	37	朱 Cwu_1	32	簡 Kan_1	133	卿 $Kyeng_3$	271
錢 Cen_3	138	周 Cwu_2	73	干 Kan_2	251	敬 $Kyeng_4$	274
鄭 $Ceng_1$	5	珠 Cwu_3	248	竿 Kan_3	252	桂 Kyey	81 = 246
丁 $Ceng_2$	42	俊 Cwun	233	姜 $Kang_1$	8	桂 Kyey	246 = 81
程 $Ceng_3$	114	魚 E_1	97	康 $Kang_2$	36	麻 Ma_2	192
井 $Ceng_4$	272	於 E_2	244	强 $Kang_3$	181	馬 Ma_1	69
諸 Cey	95	嚴 Em	48	剛 $Kang_4$	232	萬 Man	175
諸葛 Ceykal	144	河 Ha_1	39	江 $Kang_5$	243	梅 May	189
車 Cha	34	夏 Ha_2	146	介 Kay	213	孟 Mayng	83
昌 $Chang_1$	163	何 Ha_3	262	奇 Ki	78	米 Mi	206
倉 $Chang_2$	190	賀 Ha_4	265	吉 Kil	62	閔 Min	46
蔡 $Chay_1$	53	咸 Ham	56	金 Kim	2	牟 Mo_1	98
菜 $Chay_2$	230	韓 Han_1	10	高 Ko	21	毛 Mo_2	164
千 $Chen_1$	58	漢 Han_2	214	谷 Kok	277	睦 Mok	112
静 $Chen_2$	107	海 Hay	202	骨 Kol	279	墨 Muk	183
遷 $Chen_3$	255	許 He	28	孔 $Kong_1$	61	文 Mun_1	22
楚 Cho_1	160	胡 Ho_1	123	公 $Kong_2$	118	門 Mun_2	247
肖 Cho_2	261	扈 Ho_2	135	貢 $Kong_3$	242	明 Myeng	71
崔 Choy	4	洪 Hong	17	琴 Kum	104	羅 ^{1}Na	43
則 Chuk	260	花 Hwa_1	174	斤 Kun	221	那 Na	263
秋 $Chwu_1$	67	和 Hwa_2	264	瓜 Kwa	266	南 Nam	35
鄒 $Chwu_2$	239	垣 Hwan	253	郭 $Kwak_1$	40	南宮 Namkwung	93
池 Ci_1	44	黃 Hwang	16	藿 $Kwak_2$	283	浪 ^{1}Nang	179
智 Ci_2	117	皇甫 Hwangpo	106	廣 Kwang	270	及 Nay_1	185

奈 Nay$_2$	207	標 Phyo$_2$	258	申 Sin$_1$	25	禹 Wu$_1$	41
盧 ^{1}No$_1$	31	丕 Pi	200	辛 Sin$_2$	51	于 Wu$_2$	172
魯 ^{1}No$_2$	65	賓 Pin$_1$	126	愼 Sin$_3$	70	郁 Wuk	281
路 ^{1}No$_3$	171	彬 Pin$_2$	197	蘇 So$_1$	72	芸 Wun$_1$	195
雷 ^{1}Noy	173	氷 Ping	169	邵 So$_2$	140	雲 Wun$_2$	201
吳 O$_1$	11	卜 Pok	116	召 So$_3$	259	夜 Ya	170
伍 O$_2$	245	奉 Pong$_1$	88	孫 Son	26	梁 ^{1}Yang	24
玉 Ok	84	鳳 Pong$_2$	215	床 Song	14	楊 Yang$_1$	60
温 On	122	夫 Pu	191	承 Sung$_1$	89	襄 Yang$_2$	224
邕 Ong$_1$	158	邊 Pyen$_1$	57	昇 Sung$_2$	155	呂 ^{1}Ye	64
雍 Ong$_2$	204	卞 Pyen$_2$	66	勝 Sung$_3$	273	余 Ye$_1$	86
翁 Ong$_3$	241	史 Sa$_1$	109	守 Swu	276	汝 Ye$_2$	211
朴 Pak	3	謝 Sa$_2$	212	荀 Swun$_1$	162	廉 ^{1}Yem$_1$	59
潘 Pan$_1$	91	舍 Sa$_3$	216	舜 Swun$_2$	203	濂 ^{1}Yem$_2$	220
班 Pan$_2$	182	司空 Sakong	137	段 Tan$_1$	184	閻 Yem	217
方 Pang$_1$	49	尙 Sang$_1$	141	單 Tan$_2$	218	延 Yen$_1$	77
房 Pang$_2$	102	常 Sang$_2$	267	端 Tan$_3$	236	燕 Yen$_2$	177
龐 Pang$_3$	153	桑 Sang$_3$	268	唐 Tang	145	永 Yeng	238
邦 Pang$_4$	156	徐 Se$_1$	15	大 Tay	193	靈 ^{1}Yeng	275
旁 Pang$_5$	226	西 Se$_2$	229	卓 Thak	76	葉 Yep	167
裵 Pay	29	石 Sek$_1$	63	呑 Tham	250	芮 Yey	108
白 Payk	23	昔 Sek$_2$	113	炭 Than	254	李 ^{1}Yi	1
范 Pem$_1$	142	釋 Sek$_3$	280	太 Thay	87	要 Yo	228
凡 Pem$_2$	234	席 Sek$_4$	284	都 To$_1$	68	龍 ^{1}Yong	101
判 Phan	188	薛 Sel$_1$	74	陶 To$_2$	152	柳 ^{1}Yu$_1$	20
彭 Phayng	139	楔 Sel$_2$	143	道 To$_3$	235	劉 ^{1}Yu$_2$	27
皮 Phi	115	西門 Semun	148	獨狐 Tok.ko	119	兪 Yu$_1$	52
弼 Phil$_1$	157	鮮于 Sen.wu	96	頓 Ton$_1$	178	庾 Yu$_2$	111
畢 Phil$_2$	278	宣 Sen$_1$	80	敦 Ton$_2$	249	陸 ^{1}Yuk	94
包 Pho$_1$	187	鮮 Sen$_2$	256	董 Tong	103	律 ^{1}Yul	282
鮑 Pho$_2$	225	先 Sen$_3$	257	東方 Tongpang	159	尹 Yun	7
馮 Phung	176	成 Seng$_1$	50	杜 Twu	128	王 Wang	82
片 Phyen$_1$	90	星 Seng$_2$	222	陰 Um	127	元 Wen$_1$	45
扁 Phyen$_2$	219	施 Si$_1$	149	殷 Un$_1$	99	袁 Wen$_2$	186
平 Phyeng	161	柴 Si$_2$	150	恩 Un$_2$	227	魏 Wi$_1$	75
表 Phyo$_1$	79	沈 Sim	33	應 Ung	231	韋 Wi$_2$	131

Appendix 3. Korean provinces

	Province	Abbreviation	Capital city
North Korea	Hamkyeng puk to 咸鏡北道	Ham-Puk 咸北	Chengcin 青津
	Hamkyeng nam to 咸鏡南道	Ham-Nam 咸南	Hamhung 咸興
	[1]Yāngkang to 兩江道	–	Hyēysan 惠山
	Cakang to 慈江道	–	Kangkyey 江界
	Phyengan puk to 平安北道	Phyeng-Puk 平北	Sin-Uycwu 新義州
	Phyengan nam to 平安南道	Phyeng-Nam 平南	Phyengyang 平壤
	Hwanghay puk to 黃海北道	Hwang-Puk 黃北	Saliwen / Kayseng 沙里院 / 開城
	Hwanghay nam to 黃海南道	Hwang-Nam 黃南	Haycwu 海州
	[puk] Kangwen to [北] 江原道	–	Wensan 原山
South Korea	[nam] Kangwen to [南] 江原道	–	Chwunchen 春川
	Kyengki to 京畿道	–	Sewul –
	Chwungcheng puk to 忠清北道	Chwung-Puk 忠北	Chengcwu 青州
	Chwungcheng nam to 忠清南道	Chwung-Nam 忠南	Taycen 大田
	Kyēngsang puk to 慶尚北道	Kyēng-Puk 慶北	Taykwu 大丘
	Kyēngsang nam to 慶尚南道	Kyēng-Nam 慶南	Pusan 釜山
	Cen.la puk to 全羅北道	Cen-Puk 全北	Cencwu 全州
	Cen.la nam to 全羅南道	Cen-Nam 全南	Kwangcwu 光州
	Cēycwu to 濟州	–	Cēycwu 濟州

A Reference Grammar of Korean

Appendix 4. Japanese placenames

The modern trend is to transliterate Japanese placenames from kana (or Japanese pronunciation) into Hankul: **Took(h)yoo** or **Tokkyo** 'Tōkyō', **Oosak(h)a** 'Ōsaka', **Nakasak(h)i** 'Nagasaki', ... But because the names are usually written with Chinese characters, it is still common to follow the tradition of using the Korean readings of those characters: **Tongkyeng** 'Tōkyō', **Tāyphan** 'Ōsaka', **Puk.hay-to** 'Hokkaidō', ... Below is an alphabetically ordered list of the 42 prefectures (ke^ʔn = hyēn) of Japan with the Korean readings to the right. That is followed by a cross-reference list arranged according to the Korean versions.

Japanese prefectures with the Korean readings of the characters (…ʔ-ken 県 = … hyen 縣):

愛智 Aichi	Āyci	岩手 Iwate	Amswu	岡山 Okayama	Kangsan
秋田 Akita	Chwucen	香川 Kagawa	Hyangchen	佐賀⁵ Saga	Cwaha
青森 Aomori¹	Chengsam	神奈川³ Kanagawa	Sinnaychen	埼玉 Saitama	Kiok
千葉 Chiba	Chen.yep	鹿児島⁴ Kagoshima	¹Nok.ato	滋賀 Shiga	Caha
愛媛 Ehime	Āywen	高知 Kōchi	Koci	島根 Shimane	Tōkun
福井 Fukui	Pokceng	熊本 Kumamoto	Wungpon	静岡⁶ Shizuoka	Cengkang
福岡 Fukuoka	Pok.kang	三重 Mie	Samcwung	栃木 Tochigi	Manmok
福島 Fukushima	Pokto	宮城 Miyagi	Kwungseng	徳島 Tokushima	Tekto
岐阜 Gifu	Kipu	宮崎 Miyazaki	Kwungki	鳥取 Tottori	Cōchwi
群馬 Gumma	Kwunma	長野 Nagano	Cangya	富山 Toyama	Pusan
広島² Hiroshima	Kwāngto	長崎 Nagasaki	Cangki	和歌山 Wakayama	Hwakasan
兵庫 Hyōgo	Pyengko	奈良 Nara	Naylyang	山形 Yamagata	Sanhyeng
茨城 Ibaraki	Chaseng	新潟 Niigata	Sinsek	山梨 Yamanashi	San.li
石川 Ishikawa	Sekchen	大板 Ōita	Tāyphan	山口 Yamaguchi	Sankwu

¹ = 青森　　² = 廣島　　³ = 神奈川　　⁴ = 鹿兒島　　⁵ = 嵯峨　　⁶ = 靜岡

Korean readings of characters used to write Japanese prefectures:

Amswu	Iwate	Hyangchen	Kagawa	Pokto	Fukushima
Āyci	Aichi	Kangsan	Okayama	Pusan	Toyama
Āywen	Ehime	Kiok	Saitama	Pyengko	Hyōgo
Caha	Shiga	Kipu	Gifu	Samcwung	Mie
Cangki	Nagasaki	Koci	Kōchi	San.li	Yamanashi
Cangya	Nagano	Kwungki	Miyazaki	Sanhyeng	Yamagata
Cengkang	Shizuoka	Kwungseng	Miyagi	Sankwu	Yamaguchi
Chaseng	Ibaraki	Kwunma	Gumma	Sekchen	Ishikawa
Chen.yep	Chiba	Kwāngto	Hiroshima	Sinnaychen	Kanagawa
Chengsam	Aomori	Manmok	Tochigi	Sinsek	Niigata
Chwucen	Akita	Naylyang	Nara	Tekto	Tokushima
Cwaha	Saga	¹Nok.ato	Kagoshima	Tōkun	Shimane
Cōchwi	Tottori	Pok.kang	Fukuoka	Tāyphan	Ōita
Hwakasan	Wakayama	Pokceng	Fukui	Wungpon	Kumamoto

Appendix 5. Radical names

Chinese characters are put into dictionaries according to a system of 214 "radicals", which were set up to represent the semantically significant components of characters. The radical may appear as the top, the bottom, or the right part of the character; sometimes it wraps all around the rest of the character, and sometimes it is enclosed inside the character. But most often it appears as the left-side part. What remains is quite often a hint about the pronunciation of the character, and that graphic hint is called the "phonetic" of the character. Whether the non-radical part of the character is a phonetic or not, the traditional number of strokes required to write it is important, for it determines the order of the characters under the radical; that number is known as the "residual stroke count". The radicals themselves are ordered according to the number of strokes it takes to write their traditional shapes, but today some of those shapes are abbreviated, so that not all of the simpler-looking radicals are found toward the beginning of the dictionary, though most of the complicated ones are toward the end.

Foreigners like to refer to the radicals by their number, but East Asians are used to referring to them by a name that reflects the meaning. While our reference to a character is "64,4", meaning one of the characters with four residual strokes under Radical 64, the Korean will think of it as "HAND, 4". The names of the radicals are often given category designators or titles according to where the graphic element is found in the character. The word for 'radical' is **puswu** and this is shortened to ··· **pu** as a designator. The specific category designators are the following nouns, used with specialized meanings:

    pyen 'left-side radical'
    mith ("beneath", also **alay** 'below') or **meli** ("head") 'top-piece radical, roof'
    pat.chim ("prop" or "pedestal") 'bottom-piece radical'
    mom ("body") 'right-side radical; dominant-size radical'
    an ("within") 'a loose wrapper' (such as 104 and 169)
    sōk ("deep inside") 'a tight wrapper' (such as 20 and 30)

Because the **pyen** are so common, the term is sometimes generalized to mean just "radical" (= **pu**). When a radical frequently occurs in more than one position, several designators are given for it in the list below. The list was compiled from several sources; it aims to be comprehensive, but there probably exist other terms that could be added. Among the western names are some common terms from Japanese, prefaced by "[J]"

Shape(s)	Num.	Name(s)	Meaning, western names / mnemonics
一	1	il-hoyk, "han"-il pyen	one
		"han"-il mith	"one" roof
丨	2	"ttwulh.ulq"-sen/-kon mom	rod
		"sēymq-tay seywqulq"-sin pu	"counting stick"
丶	3	"pul-ttong"-cwu pu; cem	spark; dot
		han cem mith	top dot
丿	4	ppichim pyen	slant; [J] kana <u>no</u>
乙, 乚	5	"sāy"-ul pyen / mom	"bird"; fishhook, 2d Stem
亅	6	kalkol(ang)i mom	barb
		"kalkᵒ/wuli"-kwel pu	
二	7	"twū"-ī mom / pyen / pu	two
亠	8	twū mith, mun kas-meli	"two top, gate hat-head"; lid
		"twāyci"-hay mith	"the roof in Sign of the Boar"
亻	9	("sālam"-)in pyen	man (left side)
𠆢		napcak "sālam"-in pyen / alay	"spread-out man" (top / bottom)
儿, ㄦ	10	"ecin sālam"-in pyen / pat.chim / pu	"kindly man"; Legs

入		11	"tulq"-ip mith / pu / pyen	enter(ing)
八, ⺍		12	"yetelph"-phal (mith)	eight (roof)
冂		13	"mālq"-kyeng pyen, "mēlq"-kyeng pu	roll up; upside-down box, 3-sided frame
冖		14	mīn kas-meli (CF 40)	"bald hat-head"; bald roof, [J] kana <u>wa</u>
冫		15	ī-swu pyen	two waters; ice
几, 几		16	"kwey"-kwey mom, ansek-"kwey" mom	table; windy
凵		17	pēllin "ip"-kwu (CF 22, 30)	spread "mouth"; open box
			wi thē-cin "ip"-kwu	top open "mouth"
刀		18	"khal"-to pyen	sword, knife
刂			sen / sun "khal"-to (mom)	"standing sword" (right)
力		19	"him"-lyek pyen / mom	strong, strength
勹		20	"ssal"-pho pyen / sōk	wrap(ping)
匕		21	"piswu"-pi mom	"dagger"; spoon, [J] kana <u>hi</u>
匚		22	thē-cin "ip"-kwu (CF 17, 30)	open "mouth"; box on side
匸		23	"thē-cin eywun tam" pyen (CF 31)	"open enclosure wall"
			"kamchwul"-hyey sōk	hide, hiding
十		24	"yel"-sip pu / mom	ten; cross
卜, ⼘		25	"cem"-pok mom / pu	divination; [J] kana <u>to</u>
卩, ⺋		26	pyeng pūcel pyen	(military) seal; stiff ear
厂		27	ēmho pyen	cliff
			mīn ēmho pyen¹	bald cliff
			kileki an / mith	inside / below goose; trailing goose
厶		28	"manul"-mo (mith)	garlic (roof); [J] kana <u>mu</u>
			sasa mith	private (roof)
又		29	"tto"-wu mith / pyen	again
口		30	"ip"-kwu pyen / sōk	mouth
囗		31	"eywun-tam" pyen / sōk (CF 23)	"enclosure wall"; box
			khunq "ip"-kwu pyen	big mouth
土, ⼟		32	"hulk"-tho pyen / mith / pat.chim	earth
士		33	"senpay"-sa pyen / mith	scholar; warrior, samurai
			"senpi"-sa pyen	scholar
夂		34	"twīcil"-chi mith	lag; winter (roof), summer legs
			"twī-cye ol" chi pyen	
夊		35	"chēnchen-hi kel.ulq"-soy pyen	slow walk; winter variant
夕		36	"cenyek"-sek pyen	evening; [J] kana <u>ta</u>
大		37	"khun / khulq"-tāy mom	big
女		38	"kyēycip"-nye pyen	woman
子		39	"atul"-ca pyen	child
宀		40	kas meli (mith)	"hat head"
寸		41	"mati"-chōn mom / pyen	inch
小		42	"cek.ulq"-sō mom / pu	little
			"cak.ulq"-sō pyen	

尤	43	"tewuk"-wu pyen cellwum-pal.i wang pyen	more; crooked big "lame king radical"
尸	44	"cwukem"-si mith	corpse; flag
屮	45	"ōyn son"-cwa pyen	left hand; old grass
山	46	"moyq"-san pyen, "meyq"-san pu/pyen	mountain
巛, 川	47	kāymi-heli mith "nāy"-chen pyen	"ant waist" (top) river; curving river
工, 工	48	"cangin"-kong mom	artisan; carpenter square, [J] kana e
己, 已, 巳	49	"mom"-ki mom	self; snake
巾	50	"swūken"-ken pyen	towel; cloth, napkin
干	51	"pangphay"-kan mom/pyen	shield; one-ten, dry(ing)
幺	52	"cak.ulq"-yo pyen	little; short thread
广	53	ēmho mith/pyen[1], "pawi cip"-em mith	cliff; dotted cliff, dot-goose roof, MA-roof
廴	54	cem ēps.nun chayk-pat.chim (CF 162) mīn chayk-pat.chim "tangkil"-in pat.chim	"undotted book-prop" "bald book-prop" "go"; stretch(ing), long stride
廾	55	mith-sumul (c)ip/sip	"bottom-twenty"; bottom grass, twenty legs, letter H
弋	56	cwū'-sal uy pu, "cwū'-sal"-ik pyen	"string-attached arrow"; ceremony
弓	57	"hwal"-kwung pyen	(archery) bow
⼹, ⺕, 彑	58	thē-cin "kalo"-wal	open "flat"-wal (Radical 73); pig's head, kana yo
彡	59	"thelek"-sam (pyen) "ppichin sēk"-sam (pyen)	(short) hair; three hairs, slanting three
彳	60	twū in-pyen, cwūng in-pyen	double man; going man
心; 忄	61	"maum"-sim pyen, simpang pyen (left)	heart
⺗		"mith maum" sim (bottom)	bottom heart
戈	62	"chang"-khway mom, "chang"-kwa pyen	tassled spear
戶	63	"cikey"-ho pyen	door(frame)
手	64	"son"-swū pyen	hand
扌		cay-pang pyen (left)	[looks like] side of cay ("talent")
⺘		mith "son"-swū pu (bottom)	bottom hand
支, 辵	65	"cithayng (halq)"-ci pyen "cici"-ci pyen	support branch (12 Earth's Branches)
攴, 攵	66	"tung-kul.wel" mun (mom/pu), tung "ke'l" mun	back(wards) letter; folding chair; [J] to-mata, (right) no-bun
文	67	"kul.wel" mun (pu/pyen)	letters; literary
斗	68	"mal"-twu pu/pyen	peck, bushel; dots-and-cross
斤	69	"nal"-kun pyen; "nās"-kun pyen nāth-kun pyen	blade, ax; scythe (unit of weight)

方	70	"mo"-pang pyen	direction; square
无	71	"imi"-ki mom	already; crooked heaven
日	72	"nal"-il pyen	day; sun
曰	73	"kal(o)"-wal pyen²	flat sun; (Confucius-)say
检	74	"tal"-wel pyen	moon
木	75	"namu"-mok pyen	tree
欠	76	"haphum"-hum pyen	yawn(ing)
止	77	"kuchilq"-ci pyen	stop(ping)
歹	78	"cwuk.ulq"-sa pyen	death; [J] ichi-ta
殳	79	kac.un "tung-kul.wel" mun (CF 67)	the whole back(wards) letter; [J] ru-mata
母, 毋	80	"emi"-mō pyen	mother
		"māl"-mu pu / pyen	desist
比	81	"kyencwulq"-pī mom / pyen	compare, comparing
		"kolulq"-pī pu	?
毛	82	"thelek"-mo pat.chim / pu / pyen	fur
氏	83	"kak"-ssi ssi (pyen)	clan
气	84	"kiwun"-ki mith / pyen	steam
氵	85	samswu pyen (left)	three waters
水		"mul"-swu pyen	water
氺, 米		"alayq mul" swu(/ pyen) (bottom)	bottom water
火	86	"pul"-hwa pyen	fire
灬		¹yenhwa (pyen) (bottom)	row-fire; bottom fire
		nēk-cem (bottom)	four dots
爪, ⺥, ⺤	87	"son-thop"-co pyen / mom	claw
父	88	"api"-pu mith / pyen	father
爻, 爻	89	"sakwil"-hyo pu	socialize; double X
		"cemqkway"-hyo pyen	(divination sign)
爿	90	"cāngswu"-cang pyen	general; bed; left side
		tung "cokak"-phyen pyen (CF 91)	reversed slice
片	91	"cokak"-phyen pyen	slice; right side
牙	92	"ekumq-(n)i"-a pyen	tusk; big tooth
牛, 牜	93	"so"-wu pyen	ox, cow
犬, 犭	94	"kāy sasum"-lok pyen, "kāy"-lok pyen	dog / animal
		"kāy"-kyen pu / pyen	
玄	95	"kᵉ/am.ul"-hyen pyen	dark
玉, 王	96	"īm-kum"-wang pyen	king
		"kwusul"-ok pyen	jewel, jade
瓜	97	"oi"-kwa pyen	melon
瓦	98	"kiwa"-wa mom / pu / pyen	tile
甘	99	"talq"-kam mom / pyen	sweet
生	100	"nalq"-sayng pyen / pu	birth

用	101	"ssul(q)"-yōng mom / pu / pyen	use, using
田	102	"path"-cen pyen	field; rice field
疋	103	"ccal"-phil mom, "phil"-phil pyen	roll of cloth; [J] animal counter
疒	104	pyēngcil an / mith	sick, ill
		?pyēngnyek (= ?pyēngq-yek) an	[Kim Minswu 1961]
癶	105	"philq"-pal mith	develop (roof); dotted tent
		"kel.ulq"-pal (pyen)	north
		"pukpang"-kyey mith	roof of the Tenth Heaven's Stem
白	106	"huyn / huylq"-payk pyen	white
皮	107	"kacwuk"-phi pyen	skin
皿	108	"kulus"-myeng (pat.chim / pu)	dish, saucer, plate
目	109	"nwun"-mok	eye
		"nwun"-mok mith = "nēk"-sa mith	eye roof = top four, net (122)
矛	110	"chang"-mo pyen	spear, bayonet
矢	111	"sal"-si pyen	arrow
石	112	"tōl"-sek pyen	stone
示	113	"poilq"-si pyen	show(ing)
肉	114	"cimsung palq-cakwuk"-yu pyen	(animal) footprint
禾	115	"pye"-hwa pyen	grain; two-branch tree, [J] <u>no-gi</u>
穴	116	"kwumeng"-hyel mith	cave (roof)
立	117	"selq / sulq"-lip pyen	stand(ing)
竹,	118	"tay"-cwuk pyen / meli	bamboo
米	119	"ssal"-mi pyen	rice
糸	120	"sīl"-sa pyen	(long) thread, silk
缶	121	"cangkwun"-pu pyen³	jar
网	122	"kumul"-mang	net; side-eye
		"nēk"-sa mith, napcak "nēk"-sa	top four, squat four
羊	123	"yang"-yang pyen	sheep
羽	124	"kis"-wu pyen / pu	wing
老	125	"nulk.ul"-lō (pyen / mith)	old (man)
而	126	"mati"-ī mom	joint, (conjoiner) word
		"māl i(u)lq"-ī pyen	phrase to continue
		"tto"-ī pyen	and also, furthermore
耒	127	"cayngki"-loy pyen	plow, three-branch tree
		"posup"-loy pyen	plow(share)
耳	128	"kwi"-ī pyen	ear
聿	129	"ōcik"-lyul pyen	merely; brush
		"iyey"-lyul pyen = "i ey"-lyul pyen	whereupon, immediately
肉	130	"koki"-yuk pyen	meat
月		"yuk tal"-wel pyen (left)	meat-moon
臣	131	"sinha"-sin pyen	statesman; subject
自	132	"susulo"-ca pyen / pu	self; dotted eye

A Reference Grammar of Korean

至	133	"ilulq"-ci pyen	arrive, arriving
白	134	"celkwu"-kwu pyen	mortar
舌	135	"hye"-sel pyen	tongue
舛	136	"ekil"-chen pyen	dance, dancing legs
舟	137	"pay"-cwu pyen	ship, boat
艮	138	"kuchilq"-kan pu / pyen	end; (dot-less) good
色	139	"pich"-sayk mom / pyen	color
艸, 艹, ⺿	140	chotwu (mith)	grass-top (roof)
		"phul"-cho mith	grass roof
虎	141	"pēm"-hŏ (mith), pēm meli	tiger (roof)
虫	142	"pelley"-chwung pyen	bug, insect
血	143	"phi"-hyel pyen / pu	blood; dotted dish
行	144	"tanil"-hayng pyen	go(ing)
衣	145	"os"-uy pyen /otipyen/	clothing, clothes
襾, 西, 覀	146	"senyekh"-se mith	west roof
		"teph.ul"-a pu	cover
見	147	"polq"-kyēn mith	see(ing)
角	148	"ppul"-kak pyen	horn
言	149	"māl-ssum"-en pyen	speak(ing), speech
谷	150	"kol"-kok pyen / pu	valley
豆	151	"phath"-twu pyen, "khong"-twu pyen	bean
豕	152	"twāyci"-si pyen	pig, hog
豸	153	kac.un "twāyci"-si pyen	the whole hog; clawed dog
貝	154	"cokay"-phāy pyen	small shell
赤	155	"pulk.ulq"-cek pyen	red
走	156	"tal.a-nalq"-cwū pyen / pat.chim	run(ning)
足, ⻊	157	"pal"-cok pyen	foot
身	158	"mom"-sin pyen	body
車	159	"swuley"-ke pyen	car
辛	160	"maywulq"-sin pyen	bitter
辰	161	"pyēl"-cin mom / pyen	star; small dragon (5th of 12 Earth's Branches)
辶, 辶	162	(kac.un) chayk pat.chim	the whole book-prop (CF 54)
		"swīmye kalq" chak	slowly go; road, [J] <u>shinnyū</u>
邑	163	"koul"-up pyen	big village
阝		wū pupang (mom) (CF 170)	right(-side) village
酉	164	"talk" yu pyen	rooster (10th of 12 Earth's Branches); wine
采	165	"punpyel-hal"-chay pyen	discriminate
		"namul"-chay pyen	vegetables; topped rice, [J] <u>no-gome</u>
里	166	"maul"-lī pyen	village(-mile)
金	167	"soy"-kum pyen	metal

至	168	"kīn/kīlq"-cang pyen	long
門	169	"mun"-mun (an)	gate
阜	170	"entek"-pu pyen	hillock
阝		cwā pupang (CF 163)	left(-side) village; small village
隶	171	"michil(q)"-i pu, "mith"-i pyen	slave
隹	172	"sāy" chwu (pyen)	old bird, short-tailed bird
雨, ⻗	173	"pi"-wū pyen / mith	rain (roof)
青	174	"phulul"-cheng pyen	blue
非	175	"ani 'lq"-pi mith / pyeth	not; negative
		"ani"-pi pu	
面	176	"nach"-myēn pyen, "myēn"-myēn pyen	face
革	177	"kacwuk"-hyek pyen	shoe leather, rawhide
韋	178	"kacwuk"-wi pyen	tanned leather; different
韭	179	"puchwu"-kwu pyen	leek
音	180	"soli"-um pyen / pu	sound, noisy
頁	181	("meli"-hyen →) "meli"-hyel pu / pyen	head; big shell, page (CF 154)
飛	182	"nalq"-pi pyen / pu	fly(ing)
風	183	"palam"-phung pyen / mom / pu	wind
食	184	"pap"-sik pyen	food, eat(ing)
首	185	"meli"-swu	head; neck
香	186	"hyangki"-hyang pyen / pu	perfume
馬	187	"mal"-mā pyen	horse
骨	188	"ppye"-kol pyen	bone
高	189	"noph.ulq"-ko pyen / pu	high
髟	190	"thelek"-pal mith / pyen	long hair
鬥	191	"ssawul"-thwu (mith / sōk)	battle; broken gate
鬯	192	"hwalq"-cip-chang pu	bow case; herb
		"swul"-chang pyen	wine
鬲	193	"tanci"-kyek pyen	jar; tripod (cauldron)
		"oci-pyeng"-kyek pyen	
鬼	194	"kwīsin"-kyek pyen	devil
魚	195	"koki"-ē pyen	fish
脹	196	"sāy"-cō pyen	bird
鹵	197	"sokum-path"-lo pyen	salt
鹿	198	"sasum"-lok pu	deer
麥	199	"poli"-mayk pat.chim / mom / pyen	wheat, barley
麻, 麻	200	"sam"-ma pu / pyen	hemp
黃	201	"nwulᵘ/ₑl"-hwang pyen / pu	yellow
黍	202	"kicang"-se pyen	miller
黑	203	"kem.ul"-huk pyen / pu	black
黹	204	"panu'-cil"-chi pu	sew(ing), embroidery
黽	205	"mayngkkongi"-mayng mom / pu / pyen	frog

A Reference Grammar of Korean

鼎	206	"soth"-ceng pyen / mom / pu	kettle
鼓	207	"pul"-ko pyen / mom	drum
鼠	208	"cwi"-sē pat.chim / mom / pyen	rat
鼻	209	"kho"-pi pyen	nose
齊	210	"kacilen-halq"-cey mom[4]	even, alike; [J] <u>Saitō no sai</u>
齒	211	"i"-chi (pyen)	tooth
龍	212	"yong"-lyong pyen	big dragon
龜, 亀	213	"kepuk"-kwi mom / pu / pyen	turtle
龠	214	"phili"-yak pu / pyen, "ce"-yak pyen	flute

[1] Kim Minswu 1961 uses the dialect variant **umho** = **ēmho** (Radicals 27 and 123).

[2] **Kalo** is an obsolete form of a defective verb **kalu-** 'say' (MK *kolo-* / *kolG-* < **kolok-*) that is found only in the forms **kalotoy** < *kol᛫G-wo-᛫toy* 'as [he] says' and **kalasitay** < *ko᛫lo-᛫sya-᛫toy* 'as he deigns to say', but underlies the stem **kalu-chi-** 'teach' (MK *kolo᛫chi-*).

[3] There is a mistake in KEd ("**cangkwu**") that was copied from a misprint in Kim Minswu 1961 (Radical 121).

[4] Kim Minswu 1961 uses a dialect variant "**kancilen-hal**".

Appendix 6. Korean grammatical terms.

Korean grammarians have created quite a few new terms to refer to phenomena in Korean grammar. Some of the terms are intended to replace Chinese compounds used by grammarians in Japan or China. The following list is intended as an aid to reading works by the grammarians and correlating the various synonyms found in the literature. The list is long but far from exhaustive.

an mayc.um ssi-kkuth nonfinal suffix / ending
an nophim (nonhonorific =) plain style; status-unmarked forms
an wullimq soli = **museng-um** unvoiced sound, surd
cakyek kyek ?qualificative case ("as, in the role / capacity of" = ···ulo)
cali = **kyek** (grammatical) case
cali pakkwum = **cen.wi** transposition, inverted order (of morphemes), inversion, anastrophe
caliq pep case (formation / marking)
cali(q pep) tho-ssi = **kyek cōsa** case marker / particle
calip hyengyong-sa a free adjective
calip hyengsik a free form
calip ilum-ssi = **calip myengsa** a free noun
calip īmca-ssi a free indeclinable
cap.um ssi = **ciceng-sa** = **kyēysa** copula (noun predicator)
catong(sa) = **cey wumcik-ssi** an intransitive verb
caum = **tah-soli** a consonant
caum cep.pyen consonant assimilations (between syllables)
cenchey kwuseng the total structure
cēnhwan hyeng = **cwungtan hyeng** = **kuchim kkol** the transferentive form
cēnhwanq pep the transferentive (mood)
censeng = **phūmsa censeng**
censeng-e a word converted from some other part of speech
censeng ēmi function-converting suffixes (e.g. nominalizers, adnominalizers, adverbializers)
cen.wi = **cali pakkwum** transposition, inverted order (of morphemes), inversion, anastrophe
cep.mi-sa = **cep.mi-e** = **twīq kaci** suffix
cepsa = **cep.e** = **kaci** affix
cepsok-pep conjoining, conjunction
cepsok pūsa = **ium ecci-ssi** a conjunctive (conjunctional) adverb
cepsok-sa = **ium ssi** = **is-ssi** a conjunction, a connective
ceptwu-sa = **ceptwu-e** = **aph kaci** prefix
cep.yo-sa = **sap.yo-e** = **sap.ip-e/-sa** = **sōk kaci** an infix

cēy-i inching second person ("you, you people")
cēy-il inching first person ("I / me, we / us")
ceylo uy pyēn.i hyengthay a zero allomorph
cēy-sam inching third person ("he/him, she/her, they / them")
cey wumcik.im pyēnhyeng the intransitivized or passivized form (**-e ci-**), intransitivization
cey wumcik-ssi = **catong(sa)** an intransitive verb
ceyyak-pep = **kwusok-pep** conditional (mood)
chalyey sēym-ssi an ordinal numeral
chā.yong-e a borrowed word, a borrowing; a loanword
cheq-kyek locative or allative case
chep.e a reduplication, an iterative word
ches ccay cali a primary case
ches ccay cali tho-ssi a primary case marker / particle
chesoq kyek locative or adessive case
ches soli = **choseng** (syllable-)initial sound
chey style
cheyen = **īmca ssi** indeclinables (other than particles); nouns
chium = **iq soli** a sibilant or affricate
choseng = **ches soli** (syllable-)initial sound
chōyso calip hyengsik a minimal free form
chwucengq pep = **mīcengq pep** the presumptive (indefinite) mood
chwuk.lyak /chwungnyak/ → **chwuk.yak**
chwukso toyn mati = **tānphyen-cek in mati** a contracted phrase
chwuk.yak /chwukyak/ [not in the dictionaries] contraction, contracting, contracted: ~ **hata** contracts it, ~ **toyta** it gets contracted; ~ **hyeng** a contracted form, a contraction; ~ **pyēnhyeng** a contracted alternant, a contracting transformation
chwusang myengsa = **kkol ēps.nun ilum-ssi** an abstract noun
ciceng-sa = **kyēysa** = **cap.um ssi** copula (noun predicator)
cikcep īmca māl direct subject
cikcep īn.yong direct quotation
cikcep sengpun an immediate constituent
cokak = **sengpun** part (of a sentence)
coq-kyek the instrumental case

concay-sa quasi-verb of existence (iss-, ēps-, kyēysi-)
congciq-pep = **machimq pep** = **ūyhyangq pep** (sentence-)final form, conclusive, predicative (mood)
congkyel ēmi final / finite suffix
congseng = **kkuth soli** (syllable-)final sound
congsok-cek hapseng-e = **swusik-cek hapseng-e** a subordinate compound
conkyengq pep honorification, exaltation; (use of) honorifics
con-piq pep stylizations, speech styles
contayq māl honorifics, an honorific
contayq pep honorification
cōsa = **tho ssi** particle
coseng mōum = **kolwum holq-soli** an epenthetic vowel
coum harmony; euphony
coum-so = **kolwumq soli** an epenthetic sound / phoneme
cwuchey the subject (of a sentence)
cwuchey kyem.yang subject deference (humilification)
cwuchey noph.im(q pep) subject honorification (exaltation)
cwucheyq pep subject (formation / marking)
cwue = **īmca māl** subject (phrase)
cwuq-kyek cōsa = **īmca cali tho-ssi** a subject marker; a nominative-case particle
cwuq-kyek hyeng = **īmca kkol** the subject form, the nominative
cwul.im contraction, compression, abbreviation, shortening
cwul.im kkol contracted form
cwulki = **ēkan** stem
cwūn-kwulkok pep the declension of a noun, quasi-inflection
cwungching near-distant reference = mesial; second person
cwungseng medial sound = syllable nucleus; (glide and) vowel
cwungtan hyeng = **cēnhwan hyeng** = **kuchim kkol** the transferentive form
cwungum sayng.lyak syncope
cwupu the subject (element / part)
cwu-sengpun = **uttum cokak** a main constituent
cwutong(sa) active (verb), active voice
ecci kkol adverbial form; derived adverb
ecci māl = **pūsa-e** adverbial (phrase)
ecci māl mayin ilum-ssi adverbial bound noun

ecci ssi, ec-ssi = **pūsa** adverb
ēcel = **mati** = **iun māl** = **kwu** a phrase; a clause
ēhyeng (word) form
ēkan = **cwulki** stem
ēkun = **ppuli** root
ēmi = **ssi kkuth** suffix; an (inflectional) ending, a verb ending
ēswun word order
etteh-ssi, et-ssi = **hyengyong-sa** an (inflected) adjective
etten ssi, en-ssi = **kwanhyeng-sa** = **maykim ssi** an adnoun, a prenoun, a determiner
haim = **sā.yek** causative
haim kkol the causative (form) of a verb
haim māl = **sā.yek-e** a causative (verb)
haimq pep causative voice; causativization
hakey chey familiar style
hānceng-e/-sa a determiner, an adnoun, a prenoun
hānceng pyēnhyeng a noun-modifying form; an adnominalization
hānceng-swu the adnominal form of a numeral (han ⋯ , twū ⋯ , sēy ⋯ , ⋯)
han-kinungq pep a single-function mood
hao chey the semiformal (authoritative) style
hapseng-e a compound (word)
hapseng ecci-ssi a compound adverb
hapseng(q) īmca-ssi a compound indeclinable
hapsengq pep compounding
hapseng phul.i-ssi = **hapseng yōngen** a compound predicative (verb)
hapsyo chey the formal style
hap.yong pyēngse combining two or more letters to write initial consonant clusters
hasose chey obsolete literary style
hay-la chey plain style
hēlak pep the permissive mood
hesa a grammatical word, a marker, a particle, an affix (vs **silqsa** a content-word, a stem)
he.yong-cek haim māl a permissive causative
hiathwusu = **holq-soli chwungtol** hiatus
him-cwum māl an emphatic / intensive word
him-cwumq pep the emphatic mood (= -˙*two*; -ᵘ/o˙*na*)
hoq-kyek = **pulumq cali** vocative case; ~ **cōsa** vocative marker / particle
hol-lo ilum-ssi = **ko.yu myengsa** proper noun
hol-lo māl / ssi = **tok.lip-e/-sa** absolutes (such as interjections, vocatives)

holq-soli = mōum vowel
holq-soli chwungtong = hiathwusu hiatus
holq-soli cohwa = mōum cohwa vowel harmony
holq-soli ssi-kkuth an ending that begins with a vowel, a vowel ending
holq-soli tho-ssi a particle that begins with a vowel, a vowel particle
hōnhap-e a hybrid word
hoth holq-soli a simple vowel
hoysangq pep = kyenghemq pep the retrospective mood
hupsaq pep the (re)semblative mood (-tus < -˙tos)
hwakcengq pep = kicengq pep the definitive (definite) mood
hwaktay hyeng = hwaktay toyn hyengthay = nul.e nan hyengthay enlarged / expanded form
hwal.yong = kkuth pakkwum conjugation
hwal.yong hyeng = kkuth pakkwum kkol a conjugational form
hwal.yong (uy) ssi-kkuth a conjugational ending
hwuum laryngeal (glottal) sounds
hyāngcinq kyek the prolative or allative case
hye-kkuth soli an apical (tongue-tip) sound
hyēncay (the) present
hyengsik myengsa a "formal" noun = quasi-free noun, quasi-noun
hyengthay a (morphological) form
hyengthay-cek kwuseng morphological structure
hyengthay-cek pyēn.i hyengthay a morphophonemic alternant
hyengthay-lon morphology
hyengthay-so a morpheme
hyengthay umso a morphophoneme
hyengthay-umso-cek pyēntong / pyēn.i morphophonemic alternation
hyengthay umwun-so a morphophoneme (?); a morpheme (shape), an allomorph
hyengyong-sa = etteh-ssi, et-ssi an (inflected) adjective
hyēnsilq pep the processive mood
hye-yeph soli a lateral sound
hyusik pause
īcwung mōum = twū kyep holq-soli diphthong
ihwa (cak.yong) dissimilation
ilum kkol a noun form, a nominalization
ilumq pep = myengsaq pep nominalization; the substantive and summative forms
ilum ssi, im-ssi = myengsa noun

īmca cali tho-ssi = cwuq-kyek cōsa a subject marker; a nominative-case particle
īmca cokak the subject (constituent / phrase)
īmca kkol = cwuq-kyek hyeng the subject form, the nominative
īmca māl = cwue subject (phrase)
īmcaq pep subject formation, subject marking
īmca ssi = cheyen indeclinables (other than the particles); nouns, pronouns, and numbers
īm.uy pyēntong an optional transformation / variation
īm.uy pyēntong hyeng = īm.uy-cek pyēn.i hyengthay an optional variant (form)
inching(q pep) grammatical person
in tāymyengsa personal pronoun
in.yen affinity, motivation
īn.yong-e = īn.yong māl a quotational phrase, a quotation
ip-seng the "entering" tone = ˙⋯P, ˙⋯LQ, ˙⋯K (treated as kē-seng)
ip-swulq soli a labial sound
ip.um(q pep) = phītong the passive (voice)
ip.um kkol the passive (form) of a verb
ip.um māl = phītong-e/-sa a passive (verb)
ip.um uy kaci the passive affix
iq soli = chium a sibilant or affricate
is-ssi = ium ssi = cepsok-sa a conjunction, a connective
ium ecci-ssi = cepsok pūsa a conjunctive (conjunctional) adverb
iumq pep = cepsok-pep conjunction, the conjunctive mood(s)
ium ssi = is-ssi = cepsok-sa a conjunction, a connective
iun māl = kwu = ēcel = mati a phrase; a clause
kaci = cepsa = cep.e an affix
kachiq pep the evaluative mood (-um cik)
kac.un phul.i ssi a full-paradigm verb (a nondefective verb)
kal.i soli = machal-um a fricative (sound)
kalimq pep = sēnthayk-pep the selective mood (-una, -kena)
kāmthan cōsa an interjectional particle, an exclamatory particle
kāmthanq pep the exclamatory mood
kāmthan-sa = nukkim ssi, nuk-ssi an interjection
kāncep īmca māl indirect subject = topic
kāncep īn.yong indirect quotation

kāncep noph.im indirect honorification (exaltation)

kangco yēngthanq pep ("emphatic exclamatory") the effective aspect (-'ke-)

kangsey stress, emphasis, accent

kangsey-e an emphatic word

kangsey-hyeng an emphatic form

kapyewun soli a "light" (= lenited, weakened) sound

kāsang-cek (hyengthay-so, kaci) hypothetical / fictive (morpheme, affix)

kaykchey an object

kaykchey noph.im object honorification (exaltation); ~ māl an object honorific; ~q pep the object-honorific (-exalting) mood

kellim ssi = kwankyey-sa a relative (pronoun / adverb); a relativizer

kē-seng the "going" tone (high), in MK texts marked with a dot (˙)

keseyn soli = kyek.um = yūki-um an aspirated sound, an (a heavy) aspirate

keth kwuco (outer structure =) surface structure

kicengq pep = hwakcengq pep the definitive (definite) mood

kincang holq-soli = kincang moum a tense (fortis) vowel

kinung = kwusil function

kipon hyeng = uttum kkol the basic (tenseless) form; the dictionary form (of a verb)

kipon hyengthay basic form

kipon-swu cardinal numbers

kipon wel basic sentence

kkol form

kkol ēps.nun ilum-ssi = chwusang myengsa an abstract noun

kkol ēps.nun kaci an ellipted particle, a zero (form of a) particle

kkol ēps.nun pyēn.i hyengthay a zero allomorph

kkol pakkwum morphophonemic alternations, alternations in form

kkoyimq pep the hortative (mood), the propositive

kkuth soli = congseng = (syllable-)final sound

kkuth pakkwum = hwal.yong conjugation

kkuth pakkwum kkol = hwal.yong hyeng a conjugational form

kkuth pakkwum phyo a conjugational paradigm (chart)

kkwumim = swusik modification

kkwumim māl = swusik-e a modifier (phrase)

kkwumim ssi = swusik-sa = kwansa a modifier, a modifying word [adnouns, adverbs, modifier (= adnominal) and adverbative forms of inflected words]

kok.yong declension

kolwum: holq-soli ~ vowel epenthesis

kolwumq soli = coum-so an epenthetic sound / phoneme

kolwum holq-soli = coseng mōum an epenthetic vowel

kōngtay māl honorific words / speech, honorifics

kōngtayq pep = noph.imq pep status marking, respect language, honorifics and humilifics

kōngtongq pep the propositive (= the hortative) mood

kos tāy-ilum-ssi a locative pronoun

ko.yu myengsa = hol-lo ilum-ssi a proper noun

kuchim kkol = cwungtan hyeng = cēnhwan hyeng the transferentive form

kūlim ssi an adjective

kul.wel = wel a sentence

kunce-e = mith māl a root (word)

kūnching near reference = proximal; first person

kwāke past

kwāke-mīwan "past imperfect" = retrospective

kwanhyengq kyek = maykimq cali the adnominal (genitive) case

kwanhyengq kyek cōsa = maykimq cali tho-ssi the adnominal (genitive) particle

kwanhyeng-e = maykim māl an adnominal phrase, a modifier (phrase),

kwanhyengq pep adnominalization, the adnominal mood

kwanhyeng pu an adnominal (phrase)

kwanhyeng-sa = maykim ssi = etten ssi, en-ssi an adnoun, a prenoun, a determiner

kwanhyeng-sa hyeng an adnominal form, a modifier

kwankyey-sa a relative (pronoun / adverb); a relativizer

kwankyey pūsa a relative adverb

kwankyey tāymyengsa a relative pronoun

kwansa = swusik-sa = kkwumim ssi a modifier, a modifying word [adnouns, adverbs, the modifier (= adnominal) and adverbative forms of inflected words]

kwāto-um a glide, a transitional sound

kwu = iun māl = ēcel = mati a phrase; a clause

kwukay-um a palatal sound

kwukayum-hwa palatalization

kwulkok (uy) kaci an inflectional affix
kwulkok pep inflection (= conjugation and declension)
kwulkok uy pēmcwu inflectional category
kwusil = kinung function
kwusok hyengsik a bound form
kwusok myengsa = pul-wancen myengsa = mayin ilum-ssi a bound noun
kwusok-pep = ceyyak-pep the conditional mood [includes sequential, temporal infinitive, etc.]
kyek = cali case
kyek cōsa = cali tho-ssi case marker / particle
kyek.um = yūki-um = keseyn soli an aspirated sound, an (a heavy) aspirate
kyek.um-hwa aspirating, adding aspiration (to a sound)
kyemsa māl humble speech, self-humbling words, humilifics, obsequities
kyemsonq pep humilifics, self-humbling words, obsequities
kyem.yangq pep = sangtay noph.im(q pep) = tul.u.l i noph.im deferential (formal style)
kyencwumq cali tho-ssi = tāypiq kyek cōsa comparison-complementizer, particle marking the complement (= standard) of a comparison
kyencwum māl = tāypi-e the complement of a comparison
kyencwumq pep = pīkyoq pep comparison; the comparison mood
kyenghemq pep = hoysangq pep the retrospective mood
kyengum = toyn soli "hard" (= reinforced, tensed, fortis, crisply unaspirated) sounds
kyengum-hwa fortition, reinforcement, tensification
kyep congseng a syllable-final consonant cluster
kyep hapseng-e a double compound
kyep holq-soli SEE twū ~ , sēy ~
kyep ip.um māl a double passive (phrase / verb)
kyep nam wumcik-ssi a double-transitive verb
kyēysa = cap.um ssi = ciceng-sa copula (noun predicator)
kyuchik tōngsa a regular verb
kyuchik yōngen regularly inflected words
machal-um = kal.i soli a fricative (sound)
machimq pep = congciq-pep = ūyhyangq pep (sentence-)final form, conclusive, predicative (mood)
māl mith a word root
māl pon = munqpep grammar

mati = ēcel = iun māl = kwu a phrase; a clause
mati [1]yenkyel tho-ssi phrase-conjoining particle, a phrase-conjoiner
mayc.um ssi-kkuth a (verb-)final ending
mayin ilum-ssi = kwusok myengsa = pul-wancen myengsa a bound noun
mayin phul.i ssi a bound verb / adjective / copula
maykimq cali = kwanhyengq kyek the adnominal (genitive) case
maykimq cali tho-ssi = kwanhyengq kyek cōsa the adnominal (genitive) particle
maykim kkol (verb-)modifier form, adnominal form, participle
maykim māl = kwanhyeng-e an adnominal phrase, a modifier (phrase)
maykimq pep adnominal modification; adnominalization
maykim pyēnhyeng adnominal transformation, adnominalization; adnominalized form
maykim ssi = kwanhyeng-sa = etten ssi, en-ssi an adnoun, a prenoun, a determiner
mīcengq pep = chwucengq pep the presumptive (indefinite) mood
michimq pep the projective (mood)
minkan ēwen folk etymology
mith māl = kunce-e root (word)
mokcek-e = pulim māl object (phrase)
mokcek kyek = pulimq cali the accusative case
mokcek kyek cōsa = pulimq cali tho-ssi a (direct-)object marker, an accusative particle
mon tāy-ilum-ssi = sāmul tāymyengsa an inanimate pronoun (He Wung 274)
mōum = holq-soli vowel; ~ cohwa vowel harmony
mul.um māl = uymun-sa an interrogative (word); an indeterminate
mul.umq pep = uymunq pep the interrogative (mood); interrogation
mul.um(q pep) tho-ssi an interrogative particle, a question particle
muncheyq pep (grammatical) mood
munqpep = māl pon grammar
munqpep pēmcwu grammatical category
munqpep-so grammatical element
museng-um = an wullimq soli unvoiced sound, a surd
myēng.lyengq pep the imperative (mood)
myengsa = ilum ssi, im-ssi noun
myengsa hyeng a nominalization (made by the substantive / summative), the nominalized form

myengsaq pep = ilumq pep nominalization; the substantive and summative forms
mīci-ching indeterminate (reference), unknown (interrogative)
mīlay future
nam wumcik-ssi = thatong(sa) a transitive verb
¹na¹yelq pep the continuative / coordinative / conjunctional mood; the gerund (as a continuative)
nukkim ssi, nuk-ssi = kāmthan-sa an interjection
nāth mal = tan.e word
nāth mal ¹yenkyel tho-ssi a word-conjoining particle, a (noun-)conjoiner
noph.imq pep = kōngtayq / contayq pep status marking, respect language, honorifics and humilifics
nul.e nan (= hwaktay toyn) hyengthay = hwaktay hyeng an expanded / extended form
nungtong(sa) active (verb), active voice
pān holq-soli = pān moum a semivowel
pangq-cem side dots = tone (accent) marks beside a Hankul syllable of Middle Korean
pangphyenq cali = pangphyenq kyek the instrumental case
pangphyenq cali tho-ssi = pangphyenq kyek cōsa an instrumental marker / particle
pangphyen-e = pangphyen māl an instrumental (phrase)
pangphyenq kyek cōsa = pangphyenq cali tho-ssi an instrumental marker / particle
pangphyen māl = pangphyen-e an instrumental (phrase)
pangwiq kyek locative or adessive case
pān mal intimate (-e) and polite (-e yo) styles
panpok hyeng repetitive form
pat.chim Hankul syllable-final consonant(s)
pēmcwu category; SEE kolkok ~, munqpep ~
pep mood (of a verb); mode, category; marking / formation; device(s)
phachal-um = puth-kal.i soli an affricate
phasayng derivation(al), deriving, derivative
phasayng-cek hapseng-e a derivative compound
phasayng cepsa a derivational affix
phasayng ecci-ssi a derived adverb
phasayng ilum-ssi a derived noun
phasayng īmca-ssi a derived indeclinable
phasayng ium-ssi a derived conjunction
phasayng (uy) kaci a derivational affix
phasayngq pep derivation
phasayng phul.i-ssi a derived inflected word (predicative)

phasayng tho-ssi a derived particle (= a particle derived from a verb form etc.)
phasayng yōngen a derived inflected word (predicative)
phītong = ip.um(q pep) the passive (voice)
phītong-e / -sa = ip.um māl a passive (verb)
phul.e ssuki linearized Hankul
phul.i cokak the predicate (constituent)
phul.i māl = sēswul-e/-pu a predicate
phul.i ssi = yōngen the inflected words [verbs, adjectives, copula], predicatives
phūmsa = ssi a part of speech
phūmsa censeng change of the part of speech, conversion of the grammatical function
phyeng-seng the "even" tone (low), normally unmarked
phyengum plain sounds, the lax obstruents (of Korean: p t c s k)
phyengum-hwa the conversion of an aspirated or reinforced obstruent to its plain counterpart (the corresponding lax obstruent)
phyomyen kwuco surface structure
pīkyoq kyek the comparative case ("than, as much as")
pīkyoq pep = kyencwumq pep comparison; the comparison mood
pīlyeyq pep the proportional (mood) ["the more ... the more ..."]
pi seng-cel.um nonsyllabicity, nonsyllabic
pi-thōnge-cek hapseng-e an asyntactic compound
pōchwung-e a complement
pōchwungq pep (?) suppletion; (?) complementation
pōco cōsa = towum tho-ssi auxiliary/ancillary particle(s); delimiters (and focus particles)
pōco ēkan bound auxiliary, stem formative
pōco yōngen = towum phul.i-ssi auxiliary verb or adjective
pok.hap-e a compound (word)
pok.hap myengsa a compound noun
pok.hap tōngsa a compound verb
pon- basic; (= uttum) main
pon-mun = uttum wel the main clause / sentence
ponti ecci-ssi a basic adverb (i.e. not a derived adverb)
pon-tong(sa) = uttum wumcik-ssi the main verb; CF uttum phul.i-ssi
pōthong myengsa = twulwu ilum-ssi a common noun
ppuli = ēkun a root
puceng-ching indefinite reference

pulimq cali = mokcek kyek the accusative case
pulimq cali tho-ssi = mokcek kyek cōsa = a (direct-)object marker, an accusative particle
pulim māl = mokcek-e object (phrase)
pulimq pep the accusative (formation), object marking
pulkwu(-cek) hyengthay(-so) a defective form (morpheme)
pulkwu(q) kaci an adversative or concessive affix
pulkwuq pep = yāngpoq pep the adversative or concessive (mood)
pulkwu phul.i-ssi a postnominal verb or adjective
pulumq cali = hoq-kyek the vocative case; ~ tho-ssi a vocative marker / particle
pul-wancen myengsa = kwusok myengsa = mayin ilum-ssi a bound noun
pul-wancen tōngsa a defective verb
pūsa = ecci ssi, ec-ssi an adverb
pūsa-e = ecci māl an adverbial (phrase)
pūsa hyeng an adverbialization (made by the infinitive, adverbative, gerund, ...)
puth-kal.i soli = phachal-um an affricate
pyēnchik tōngsa an irregular verb
pyēnchik yōngen irregularly inflected words
pyēnhwa change, shift
pyēnhyeng transformation, conversion
pyēn.i hyengthay a morpheme alternant, an allomorph
pyēn.i umso a morphophonemic alternant (?), a morphophoneme
pyēnsengq kyek the mutative (= factive) case
sālam tāy-ilum-ssi a personal pronoun
samcwung mōum = sēy kyep holq-soli a triphthong [such as yey]
sāmul tāymyengsa = mon tāy-ilum-ssi an inanimate pronoun
sangcing-cek ppuli a symbolic (mimetic) root
sangcing-e a symbolic word; a mimetic
sāng-seng the "rising" tone (low-high and long), in MK texts marked with two dots ":" and transcribed as ¨ in MK examples cited here
sangtayq kyek the confrontational dative case; the reciprocal case
sangtay noph.im(q pep) = tul.u.l i noph.im = kyem.yangq pep deferential (formal style)
sap.ip-e/-sa = sap.yo-e = cep.yo-sa = sōk kaci an infix
sā-seng the four tones (of Middle Chinese): phyeng-seng, sāng-seng, kē-seng, ip-seng
sātong(sa) causative (verb), causative voice

sā.yek = haim causative
sā.yek-e = haim māl a causative (verb)
sayng.lyak pyēnhyeng a deletion transformation; ellipsis
sā.yongq kyek the instrumental case
selmyengq pep the explanatory (mood) = the accessive (- *toy*)
seng-cel.um syllabicity, syllabic
sengco tone, a toneme; accent
sengpun = cokak part (of a sentence)
sēnthayk-pep = kalimq pep the selective mood (-una, -kena)
sēswul-e/-pu = phul.im māl the predicate
sēswulq pep predication
sēy ccay cali a tertiary case
sēy ccay cali tho-ssi a tertiary case marker
sēy kyep holq-soli = samcwung mōum a triphthong [such as yey]
sēym ssi = swūsa a numeral
sicey tense (system)
sikhimq pep the imperative (mood)
silqcil myengsa a real (? substantive) noun
silqsa a content-word (vs hesa a grammatical word, a marker, a particle)
simchung kwuco = sōk kwuco deep structure
sōk kaci = sap.ip-e/-sa = sap.yo-e = cep.yo-sa an infix
sok-kyek genitive (possessive) case
sōk kwuco = simchung kwuco (inner structure =) deep structure
sōk ttus (inner =) deep meaning / structure
soli hyungnay sound mimicry, phonomimesis, onomatopoeia
sō.yuq kyek cōsa a genitive (possessive) particle
ssi = phūmsa a part of speech
ssi kkuth = ēmi suffix; an (inflectional) ending, a verb ending
ssi kkuth pakkwum inflection, conjugation
swūn.[1]yel normal order
swūnse-swu ordinal numbers
swusik-e adnominal (word), (noun) modifier
swū tan.wi mayin ilum-ssi (number unit bound noun =) a counter, a numerary adjunct or auxiliary; a classifier
swū tāymyengsa numerary pronouns = numerals
swūlyang tāymyengsa numerary-quantitative pronouns
swūsa = sēym ssi a numeral
swusik = kkwumim modification
swusik-cek hapseng-e = congsok-cek hapseng-e a subordinate compound; ~ ilum-ssi a sub-

ordinate compound noun, a bahuvrihi
swusik-e = kkwumim māl a modifier (phrase)
swusik-sa = kkwumim ssi = kwansa a modifier, a modifying word [adnouns, adverbs, the modifier (= adnominal) and adverbative forms of inflected words]
swutong = ip.um passive; ~ thay, swutongq pep passive voice
tah-soli = caum a consonant; ~ ie pakkwim sandhi (alternations) = adjustments to consonants at morpheme boundaries; ~ ssi kkuth an ending beginning with a consonant; ~ tho-ssi a particle (shape) beginning with a consonant; ~ ttey a consonant cluster
tan.e = nāth mal word
tānphyen-cek in mati = chwukso toyn mati a contracted phrase
tanswun-e a simple word
tāy-ilum-ssi = tāymyengsa a pronoun
tāy-kwake past-past
tāymyengsa = tāy-ilum-ssi a pronoun
tāypi-e = kyencwum māl the complement of a comparison
tāypiq kyek cōsa = kyencwum cali tho-ssi a comparison-complementizer, a particle marking the complement (= standard) of a comparison
tāysangq pep object (formation / marking)
tāytung-cek hapseng-e a coordinative (dvandva) compound
tāytung-cek hapseng ilum-ssi a coordinative noun compound
thalq-kyek the ablative case
thallak elision; deletion
thatong(sa) = nam wumcik-ssi a transitive verb
thatongq seng transitivity
thōnge syntax, syntactic
thōnge-cek hapseng-e syntactic compound
thōnge-cek kwuseng syntactic structure
thōnge-lon syntax
thōngelon-cek kinung syntactic function
tho ssi = cōsa a particle
thukswu cōsa special particles = particles of emphasis and focus
tok.lip-e/-sa = hol-lo māl / ssi absolutes (such as interjections, vocatives)
tonghwa (cak.yong) assimilation
tong.lyuq kyek the similative case ("like, as")
tōngmyengsa a verbal noun (= a nominal verb)
tōngsa = wumcik-ssi, wum-ssi a verb
tongsiq pep the simultaneous mood

tongum sayng.lyak haplology; simplification of geminates
towum phul.i-ssi = pōco yōngen an auxiliary verb or adjective
towum tho-ssi = pōco cōsa auxiliary / ancillary particle(s); delimiters (and focus particles)
to.[1]yel inverted order, inversion
tōyn soli = kyengum "hard" (= reinforced, tensed, fortis, crisply unaspirated) sounds
toy-phul.iq pep the repetitive / iterative (mood)
ttan i the Hankul letter ㅣ (y or i) standing alone with no initial
ttay maykim(q pep) ? tense / time modification; modifier tense(/ aspect)
ttuye ssuki writing with spaces (to separate the words)
twīq kaci = cep.mi-sa = cep.mi-e a suffix
tul.u.l i noph.im = sangtay noph.im(q pep) = kyem.yangq pep deferential (formal style)
twū-kinungq pep a double-function mood
twū kyep holq-soli = īcwung mōum a diphthong
twūl ccay cali a secondary case
twūl ccay cali tho-ssi a secondary case marker / particle
twulwu ilum-ssi = pōthong myengsa a common noun
umcel a syllable
umseng a Yin (= dark, heavy) vowel (= u, e, wu); CF yangseng
umseng-cek pyēn.i hyeng(thay) a heavy isotope (of a word)
umso a phoneme
umwun phonemes and prosodemes, the phonology (of a language); rime
uttum (···) = pon- main, chief
uttum cokak = cwu-sengpun a main constituent
uttum kkol = kipon hyeng basic form
uttum phul.i-ssi the main predicative; = uttum wumcik-ssi = pon-tong(sa) the main verb
uttum sēym-ssi = [1]yāng-swūsa the cardinal numerals
uttum wel = pon-mun the main clause / sentence
uttum wumcik-ssi = pon-tong(sa) the main verb; CF uttum phul.i-ssi
uycon hyengyong-sa a dependent adjective = an auxiliary adjective
ūyhyangq pep = congciq-pep = machimq pep (sentence-)final form; conclusive, predicative
uymunq pep = mul.umq pep the interrogative (mood); interrogation

uymun-sa = mul.um māl an interrogative (word); an indeterminate
uyseng-e a phonomime, an onomatope
uythay-e a phenomime, a descriptive mimetic
ūytoq pep intention moods: the intentive, purposive, and desiderative
wancen tōngsa a full-paradigm verb, a nondefective verb
wel = kul.wel sentence
wel sengpun sentence constituents
wenhyeng basic (original) form
wen.inq kyek causal (causal ablative) case
wēnching distant reference = distal; third person
wichi cali = wichiq kyek the locative case; ~ tho-ssi a locative marker / particle
wichi-cek cōsa a locational (locative) particle
wichi-e = wichi māl a locative (phrase)
wichiq kyek = wichi cali the locative case; ~ cōsa locative marker / particle
wichi māl = wichi-e a locative (phrase)
wichi māl mayin ilum-ssi a locative bound noun
wichiq pep locative(/allative) marking
wichiq pep tho-ssi a locative(/allative) particle
wullim voicing, being voiced (sonant)
wullimq soli = yūseng-um a voiced sound, a sonant
wumcik-ssi, wum-ssi = tōngsa a verb
wūnso a prosodeme
wūnso pyēntong prosodic morphophonemics; morphotonemics; accent alternations
[1]yak.e = cwūn mal an abbreviation, a contraction, a shortening,
yaksok pep the promissory or cajolative mood (= -ulye 'm)
yāngpoq pep = pulkwuq pep the adversative or concessive (mood)
yangseng a Yang (= light) vowel (= o, a, wo); CF umseng

yangseng-cek pyēn.i hyeng(thay) a light isotope (of a word)
[1]yāng-swūsa = uttum sēym-ssi the cardinal numerals
[1]yāng tāymyengsa counters, numerary adjuncts, (noun) classifiers and quantifiers
yēq-kyek cōsa a dative particle
yelin soli = yēn.um lax (lenis) consonants, plain consonants (p t k s c)
[1]yelkeq kyek the enumerative (= concatenative, "and") case
[1]yencep junction, juncture
[1]yenkyelq pep conjoining; the conjunctive mood; the infinitive (as continuative)
[1]yenkyel(q pep) tho-ssi a conjunctive / conjoining particle
[1]yenkyel ēmi a continuative (nonfinite) suffix
yen.um a prolonged sound; a long vowel or syllable
yēn.um = yelin soli lax (lenis) consonants, plain consonants (p t k s c)
yetelp pat.chim the eight syllable finals in 1446 Hwunmin cengum: k ng t n p m s l
[1]yēysa māl ordinary words / speech
yōngen = phul.i ssi inflected words [verbs, adjectives, copula]
yōngpanq kyek the comitative case
[1]yūchwu analogy
yūki-um = kyek.um = keseyn soli an aspirated sound, an (a heavy) aspirate
yulayq kyek the elative or ablative case
[1]yusa cepsa = pisus han kaci a quasi-affix
yūseng-um = wullimq soli a voiced sound, a sonant
yūyen-hwa motivated: cal ~ toyci anh.nunta is not well motivated
yūyenq-seng motivation; motivated

Appendix 7. English index to the list of Korean grammatical terms.

abbreviation cwul.im; ¹yak.e = cwūn mal
ablative case thalq-kyek; (elative or ~) yulayq kyek
absolutes tok.lip-e/-sa = hol-lo māl/ssi
abstract noun kkol ēps.nun ilum-ssi = chwusang myengsa
accent alternations wūnso pyēntong
accent (= stress) kangsey; (= tone) sengco
accessive (= -῾toy) selmyengq pep
accusative (formation) pulimq pep
accusative case pulimq cali = mokcek kyek
accusative particle mokcek kyek cōsa = pulimq cali tho-ssi
active (verb) cwutong(sa), nungtong(sa)
adessive case chesoq kyek
adjective kūlim ssi; (inflected) hyengyong-sa = etteh-ssi, et-ssi
adjustments to consonants at boundaries tah-soli ie pakkwim
adnominal (word) swusik-e
adnominal case kwanhyengq kyek = maykimq cali
adnominal form kwanhyeng-sa hyeng = maykim kkol; ~ of a numeral hānceng-swu
adnominal marker/particle kwanhyengq kyek cōsa = maykimq cali tho-ssi
adnominal modification maykimq pep
adnominal mood kwanhyengq pep
adnominal phrase kwanhyeng-e = maykim māl; kwanhyeng pu
adnominal transformation maykim pyēnhyeng
adnominalization kwanhyengq pep = maykimq pep; maykim pyēnhyeng; hānceng pyēnhyeng
adnominalized form maykim pyēnhyeng
adnoun kwanhyeng-sa = maykim ssi = etten ssi, en-ssi; hānceng-e/-sa
adverb pūsa = ecci ssi, ec-ssi; derived ~ ecci kkol
adverbial (phrase) pūsa-e = ecci māl
adverbial bound noun ecci māl mayin ilum-ssi
adverbial form ecci kkol
adverbialization (form) pūsa hyeng
adversative or concessive (mood) yāngpoq pep = pulkwuq pep
adversative or concessive affix pulkwu(q) kaci
affinity in.yen
affix cepsa = cep.e = kaci; hesa
affricate (sound) phachal-um = puth-kal.i soli
allative or prolative case hyāngcinq kyek

allomorph: an ~ hyengthay umwun-so; pyēn.i hyengthay
alternations: morphophonemic (form) ~ kkol pakkwum
analogy ¹yūchwu
anastrophe cali pakkwum = cen.wi
ancillary particle = auxiliary particle
apical (tongue-tip) sound hye-kkuth soli
aspirate: an (a heavy) ~ keseyn soli = kyek.um = yūki-um
aspirated sound keseyn soli = kyek.um = yūki-um
aspirating, adding aspiration kyek.um-hwa
assimilation tonghwa (cak.yong)
asyntactic compound pi-thōnge-cek hapseng-e
authoritative (semiformal) style hao chey
auxiliary (verb or adjective) pōco yōngen = towum phul.i-ssi
auxiliary particle pōco cōsa = towum tho-ssi
bahuvrihi swusik-cek hapseng-e ilum-ssi
basic pon-, kipon ··· = uttum ···
basic adverb (= underived adverb) ponti ecci-ssi
basic form kipon hyengthay, (= original form) wenhyeng; (of a verb) kipon hyeng = uttum kkol
basic sentence kipon wel
borrowed word, borrowing chā.yong-e
bound auxiliary (stem formative) pōco ēkan
bound form kwusok hyengsik
bound noun kwusok myengsa = pul-wancen myengsa = mayin ilum-ssi
bound verb(/adjective/copula) mayin phul.i ssi
cajolative or promissory mood yaksok pep
cardinal numbers kipon-swu
cardinal numerals ¹yāng-swūsa = uttum sēym-ssi
case (formation/marking) caliq pep
case (grammatical) cali = kyek
case marker/particle kyek cōsa = cali tho-ssi
category pep; pēmcwu
causal (causal ablative) case wen.inq kyek
causative (verb) sātong(sa); sā.yek-e = haim māl
causative (voice) haim = sā.yek, sātong
causative voice haimq pep
causative: the ~ (form) of a verb haim kkol
causativization haimq pep
change pyēnhwa
change of part-of-speech (phūmsa) censeng
chief uttum (···) = pon-

classifier swū tan.wi mayin ilum-ssi
classifiers, counters, numerary adjuncts, and quantifiers ¹yāng tāymyengsa
clause iun māl = kwu = ēcel = mati
combining two or more letters to write (initial) consonant clusters hap.yong pyēngse
comitative case yōngpanq kyek
common noun pōthong myengsa = twulwu ilum-ssi
comparative case pīkyoq kyek
comparison: ~ mood kyencwumq pep = pīkyoq pep; complement of a ~ tāypi-e = kyencwum māl
comparison-complementizer kyencwumq cali tho-ssi = tāypiq kyek cōsa
complement pōchwung-e; ~ of a comparison kyencwum māl = tāypi-e
complementation (?) pōchwungq pep
compound (word) hapseng-e, pok.hap-e
compound adverb hapseng ecci-ssi
compound indeclinable hapseng(q) īmca-ssi
compound noun pok.hap myengsa
compound predicative (= verb) hapseng phul.i-ssi = hapseng yōngen
compound verb pok.hap tōngsa
compounding hapsengq pep
compression cwul.im
concatenative: the ~ (= enumerative, "and") case ¹yelkeq kyek
concessive or adversative (mood) pulkwuq pep = yāngpoq pep
concessive or adversative affix pulkwu(q) kaci
conclusive (mood) machimq pep = congciq-pep = ūyhyangq pep
conclusive congciq-pep = machimq pep = ūyhyangq pep
conditional (mood) ceyyak-pep = kwusok-pep
confrontational dative case sangtayq kyek
conjoiner: (noun) ~ nāth mal ¹yenkyel tho-ssi
conjoining ¹yenkyelq pep
conjoining, conjunction cepsok-pep
conjugation (of a verb) hwal.yong = kkuth pakkwum
conjugation, inflection ssi kkuth pakkwum
conjugational ending hwal.yong (uy) ssi-kkuth
conjugational form hwal.yong hyeng = kkuth pakkwum kkol
conjugational paradigm (chart) kkuth pakkwum phyo
conjunction cepsok-sa = ium ssi = is-ssi

conjunction iumq pep = cepsok-pep; derived ~ phasayng ium-ssi
conjunctional mood ¹na¹yelq pep
conjunctive (conjunctional) adverb cepsok pūsa = ium ecci-ssi
conjunctive mood ¹yenkyelq pep
conjunctive mood(s) iumq pep = cepsok-pep
conjunctive / conjoining particle ¹yenkyel(q pep) tho-ssi
connective cepsok-sa = ium ssi = is-ssi
consonant caum = tah-soli
consonant assimilations (between syllables) caum cep.pyen
consonant cluster tah-soli ttey; syllable-final ~ kyep congseng
consonant(s): syllable-final in Hankul pat.chim
content-word silqsa
continuative (nonfinite) suffix ¹yenkyel ēmi
continuative mood ¹na¹yelq pep
contracted alternant chwuk.yak pyēnhyeng
contracted form chwuk.yak hyeng = cwul.im kkol
contracted phrase: a ~ chwukso toyn mati = tānphyen-cek in mati
contracting transformation (form) chwuk.yak pyēnhyeng
contraction (contracting, contracted) chwuk.yak = cwul.im
contraction: a ~ ¹yak.e = cwūn mal
conversion pyēnhyeng
conversion of grammatical function (phūmsa) censeng
converted: SEE word converted ...
converting an aspirated or reinforced obstruent to its plain counterpart (the corresponding lax obstruent) phyengum-hwa
coordinative (dvandva) compound tāytung-cek hapseng-e
coordinative mood ¹na¹yelq pep
coordinative noun compound: a ~ tāytung-cek hapseng ilum-ssi
copula (noun predicator) cap.um ssi = ciceng-sa = kyēysa
counter swū tan.wi mayin ilum-ssi
counters, numerary adjuncts, (noun) classifiers and quantifiers ¹yāng tāymyengsa
dative particle yēq-kyek cōsa
declension kok.yong; ~ of a noun (= quasi-inflection) cwūn-kwulkok pep
deep meaning / structure sōk ttus

deep structure sōk kwuco = simchung kwuco
defective: a ~ form (morpheme) pulkwu(-cek) hyengthay(-so)
defective verb pul-wancen tōngsa
deferential (= formal style) kyem.yangq pep = sangtay noph.im(q pep) = tul.u.l i noph.im
definitive (definite) mood hwakcengq pep = kicengq pep
deletion thallak
deletion transformation sayng.lyak pyēnhyeng
delimiters (and focus particles) pōco cōsa = towum tho-ssi
dependent adjective (= an auxiliary adjective) uycon hyengyong-sa
derivation phasayngq pep
derivation(al), deriving, derivative phasayng
derivational affix phasayng cepsa = phasayng (uy) kaci
derivative compound phasayng-cek hapseng-e
derived adverb phasayng ecci-ssi; ecci kkol
derived conjunction phasayng ium-ssi
derived indeclinable phasayng īmca-ssi
derived inflected word (predicative) phasayng phul.i-ssi = phasayng yōngen
derived noun phasayng ilum-ssi
derived particle phasayng tho-ssi
descriptive mimetic uythay-e
determiner maykim ssi = kwanhyeng-sa = etten ssi, en-ssi; hānceng-e/-sa; SEE adnoun
device(s) pep
dictionary form (of a verb): the ~ kipon hyeng = uttum kkol
diphthong twū kyep holq-soli = īcwung mōum
diphthong īcwung mōum = twū kyep holq-soli
direct-object marker/particle mokcek kyek cōsa = pulimq cali tho-ssi
direct quotation cikcep īn.yong
direct subject cikcep īmca māl
dissimilation ihwa (cak.yong)
distal (reference) wēnching
distant reference wēnching
double compound kyep hapseng-e
double passive (phrase/verb) kyep ip.um māl
double-function mood twū-kinungq pep
double-transitive verb kyep nam wumcik-ssi
dvandva tāytung-cek hapseng ilum-ssi
dvandva compound tāytung-cek hapseng-e
effective aspect kangco yēngthanq pep
elative or ablative case yulayq kyek
elision thallak

ellipsis sayng.lyak pyēnhyeng
ellipted particle kkol ēps.nun kaci
emphasis kangsey
"emphatic exclamatory" kangco yēngthanq pep
emphatic form kangsey-hyeng
emphatic mood (= -˙two; -u_o˙na) him-cwumq pep
emphatic word kangsey-e
emphatic/intensive word him-cwum māl
ending: inflectional ~, verb ~ ssi kkuth = ēmi
ending beginning with a consonant tah-soli ssi kkuth
ending beginning with a vowel holq-soli ssi-kkuth
enlarged form hwaktay hyeng = hwaktay toyn hyengthay = nul.e nan hyengthay
"entering" tone ip-seng
enumerative (= concatenative or "and") case ^{1}yelkeq kyek
epenthesis: vowel ~ holq-soli kolwum
epenthetic sound/phoneme kolwumq soli = coum-so
epenthetic vowel kolwum holq-soli = coseng mōum
euphony coum
evaluative mood kachiq pep
"even" tone phyeng-seng
exaltation conkyengq pep; (subject honorification) cwuchey noph.im(q pep)
exclamatory mood kāmthanq pep
exclamatory particle kāmthan cōsa
existence: quasi-verb of ~ concay-sa
expanded form nul.e nan hyengthay = hwaktay toyn hyengthay = hwaktay hyeng
explanatory (mood) selmyengq pep
extended form nul.e nan hyengthay = hwaktay toyn hyengthay = hwaktay hyeng
factive (= mutative) case pyēnsengq kyek
familiar style hakey chey
fictive/hypothetical (morpheme, affix) kāsang-cek (hyengthay-so, kaci)
final ending (of verb) mayc.um ssi-kkuth
final form: (sentence-)~ machimq pep = congciq-pep = ūyhyangq pep
final sound (of a syllable) kkuth soli = congseng
final/finite suffix congkyel ēmi
first person ("I/me, we/us") cēy-il inching; (= proximal) kūnching
folk etymology minkan ēwen
form kkol; (of a word) ēhyeng; (morphological

~) hyengthay
form alternations kkol pakkwum
"formal" noun hyengsik myengsa
formal style hapsyo chey
formation pep
fortis sounds tōyn soli = kyengum
fortition kyengum-hwa
free adjective calip hyengyong-sa
free form calip hyengsik
free indeclinable calip īmca-ssi
free noun calip ilum-ssi = calip myengsa
fricative (sound) kal.i soli = machal-um
full-paradigm verb wancen tōngsa = kac.un phul.i ssi
function kwusil = kinung
function-converting suffixes censeng ēmi
future mīlay
geminates: the simplification of ~ tongum sayng.lyak
genitive (adnominal) case maykimq cali = kwanhyengq kyek; (possessive) sok-kyek
genitive marker/particle kwanhyengq kyek cōsa = maykimq cali tho-ssi
genitive (possessive) particle sō.yuq kyek cōsa
gerund (as continuative) ¹na¹yelq pep
glide kwāto-um; ~ and vowel cwungseng
"going" tone kē-seng
grammar māl pon = munqpep
grammatical category munqpep pēmcwu
grammatical element munqpep-so
grammatical mood muncheyq pep
grammatical person inching(q pep)
grammatical word hesa
Hankul letter ㅣ (y or i) standing alone with no initial ttan i
Hankul syllable-final consonant(s) pat.chim
haplology tongum sayng.lyak
"hard" sounds tōyn soli = kyengum
harmony coum
heavy isotope (of a word) umseng-cek pyēn.i hyeng(thay)
hiatus holq-soli chwungtong = hiathwusu
honorific words/speech kōngtay māl
honorification conkyengq pep, contayq pep
honorifics and humilifics noph.imq pep = kōngtayq pep
honorifics kōngtay māl, contayq māl
honorifics: the use of ~ conkyengq pep
hortative (mood) kkoyimq pep; kōngtongq pep
humble speech kyemsa māl

humilification (= subject deference) cwuchey kyem.yang
humilifics kyemsa māl; kyemsonq pep
hybrid word hōnhap-e
hypothetical/fictive (morpheme, affix) kāsang-cek (hyengthay-so, kaci)
immediate constituent cikcep sengpun
imperative (mood) myēng.lyengq pep = sikhimq pep
impersonal (authoritative) style hao chey
inanimate pronoun sāmul tāymyengsa = mon tāy-ilum-ssi (He Wung 274)
indeclinable: derived ~ phasayng īmca-ssi
indeclinables (other than particles) īmca ssi = cheyen
indefinite (presumptive) mood mīcengq pep = chwucengq pep
indefinite reference puceng-ching
indeterminate uymun-sa = mul.um māl
indeterminate, interrogative (word) mul.um māl = uymun-sa
indeterminate (reference) mīci-ching
indirect honorification (exaltation) kāncep noph.im
indirect quotation kāncep īn.yong
indirect subject = topic kāncep īmca māl
infinitive (as continuative) ¹yenkyelq pep
infix sōk kaci = sap.ip-e/-sa = sap.yo-e = cep.yo-sa
inflected words [= verbs, adjectives, copula] yōngen = phul.i ssi
inflection kwulkok pep; ssi kkuth pakkwum
inflectional affix kwulkok (uy) kaci
inflectional category kwulkok uy pēmcwu
inflectional ending ssi kkuth = ēmi
initial sound (of syllable) ches soli = choseng
instrumental: the ~ case pangphyenq cali = pangphyenq/sā.yongq kyek = cōq-kyek; ~ phrase pangphyen māl = pangphyen-e
instrumental marker/particle pangphyenq cali tho-ssi = pangphyenq kyek cōsa
intensive/emphatic word him-cwum māl
intention moods (the intentive, purposive, and desiderative) ūytoq pep
interjection kāmthan-sa = nukkim ssi, nuk-ssi
interjectional particle kāmthan cōsa
interrogative (mood); interrogation mul.umq pep = uymunq pep
interrogative (word) mul.um māl = uymun-sa
interrogative particle mul.um(q pep) tho-ssi

A Reference Grammar of Korean

intimate style and polite style **pān mal**
intransitive verb **catong(sa) = cey wumcik-ssi**
intransitivization, an intransitivized form **cey wumcik.im pyēnhyeng**
inversion, inverted order **cali pakkwum = cen.wi; to.¹yel**
irregular verb **pyēnchik tōngsa**
irregularly inflected words **pyēnchik yōngen**
iterative (= repetitive) mood **toy-phul.iq pep**
iterative word **chep.e**
junction, juncture **¹yencep**
labial sound **ip-swulq soli**
laryngeal (glottal) sounds **hwuum**
lateral sound **hye-yeph soli**
lax (lenis) consonants **yelin soli = yēn.um**
lax obstruents **phyengum**
lenis (lax) consonants **yelin soli = yēn.um**
lenited sound **kapyewun soli**
light isotope (of a word) **yangseng-cek pyēn.i hyeng(thay)**
"light" (= lenited, weakened) sound **kapyewun soli**
linearized Hankul **phul.e ssuki**
literary style: obsolete ~ **hasose chey**
loanword **chā.yong-e**
locational (locative) particle **wichi-cek cōsa**
locative (phrase) **wichi māl = wichi-e**
locative bound noun **wichi māl mayin ilum-ssi**
locative case **wichi cali = wichiq kyek; chesoq kyek, cheq-kyek, pangqiq kyek**
locative marker / particle **wichi cali tho-ssi = wichiq kyek cōsa**
locative pronoun **kos tāy-ilum-ssi**
locative(/allative) marking **wichiq pep**
locative(/allative) particle (marker) **wichiq pep tho-ssi**
long syllable / vowel **yen.um**
main clause **pon-mun = uttum wel**
main constituent **cwu-sengpun = uttum cokak**
main sentence **pon-mun = uttum wel**
main **pon- = uttum ···**
main predicative / verb **uttum phul.i-ssi = uttum wumcik-ssi = pon-tong(sa)**
marker **hesa**; SEE particle
marking (···) **pep**
medial sound **cwungseng**
mesial = near-distant reference **cwungching**
mimetic (symbolic) root **sangcing-cek ppuli**
mimetic (word) **sangcing-e**
mimicry: sound ~ **soli hyungnay**

APPENDIX 7   393

minimal free form **chōyso calip hyengsik**
mode **pep**
modification **kkwumim = swusik**
modifier (noun ~) **swusik-e**
modifier (phrase) **kkwumim māl = swusik-e; maykim māl = kwanhyeng-e**
modifier **kwansa = swusik-sa = kkwumim ssi; kwanhyeng-sa hyeng**
modifier form (of verb) **maykim kkol**
modifier tense(/aspect) **ttay maykim(q pep)**
modifier = a modifying word **swusik-sa = kkwumim ssi = kwansa**
mood: grammatical ~ **muncheyq pep**; ~ (of a verb) **pep**
morpheme **hyengthay-so**; ~ (shape) **hyengthay umwun-so**
morpheme alternant **pyēn.i hyengthay**
morphological form **hyengthay**
morphological structure **hyengthay-cek kwuseng**
morphology **hyengthay-lon**
morphophoneme **hyengthay umso**; (?) **hyengthay umwun-so**
morphophonemic alternant **hyengthay-cek pyēn.i hyengthay**; (?) **pyēn.i umso**
morphophonemic alternation **hyengthay-umso-cek pyēntong / pyēn.i; kkol pakkwum**
morphotonemics **wūnso pyēntong**
motivated: is not well ~ **cal yūyen-hwa toyci anh.nunta**
motivation **in.yen**
motivation; motivated **yūyenq-seng**
mutative (= factive) case **pyēnsengq kyek**
inanimate pronoun **mon tāy-ilum-ssi = sāmul tāymyengsa**
near reference = proximal **kūnching**
near-distant reference = mesial **cwungching**
nominalization (= noun form) **ilum kkol**
nominalization (made by the substantive or the summative) **myengsa hyeng**
nominalization; the substantive and summative forms **myengsaq pep = ilumq pep**
nominalized form **myengsa hyeng**
nominative (form) **īmca kkol = cwuq-kyek hyeng**
nominative **cwuq-kyek hyeng = īmca kkol**
nominative-case particle **īmca cali tho-ssi = cwuq-kyek cōsa**
nonfinal suffix / ending **an mayc.um ssi-kkuth**
nonsyllabicity, nonsyllabic **pi seng-cel.um**
nondefective verb **kac.un phul.i ssi = wancen tōngsa**

nonhonorific = an nophim
normal order swūn.¹yel
noun myengsa = ilum ssi, im-ssi
noun: derived ~ phasayng ilum-ssi
noun conjoiner nāth mal ¹yenkyel tho-ssi
noun form ilum kkol
noun modifier swusik-e
noun-modifying form hānceng pyēnhyeng
noun predicator: SEE copula
nouns (indeclinables) cheyen = īmca ssi
nouns, pronouns, and numbers īmca ssi = cheyen
nucleus: syllable ~ cwungseng
number unit bound noun (= counter) swū tan.wi mayin ilum-ssi
numbers, nouns, and pronouns īmca ssi = cheyen
numeral swūsa = sēym ssi
numerary adjunct / auxiliary swū tan.wi mayin ilum-ssi
numerary adjuncts, counters, (noun) classifiers and quantifiers ¹yāng tāymyengsa
numerary pronouns = numerals swū tāymyengsa
numerary-quantitative pronouns: the ~ swūlyang tāymyengsa
object kaykchey
object (formation / marking) tāysangq pep
object (phrase) pulim māl = mokcek-e
object exaltation kaykchey noph.im
object honorific kaykchey noph.im māl
object honorification kaykchey noph.im
object marker: SEE direct-object marker
object marking pulimq pep
object-exalting (object-honorific) mood kaykchey noph.imq pep
obsequities kyemsa māl; kyemsonq pep
obsolete literary style hasose chey
onomatope (onomatopoetic word) uyseng-e
onomatopoeia soli hyungnay
optional transformation īm.uy pyēntong
optional variant (form) īm.uy pyēntong hyeng, īm.uy-cek pyēn.i hyengthay
optional variation īm.uy pyēntong
order (of words) ēswun
ordinal numbers swūnse-swu
ordinal numeral chalyey sēym-ssi
ordinary words / speech ¹yēysa māl
palatal sound kwukay-um
palatalization kwukayum-hwa
part (of a sentence) cokak = sengpun
part of speech ssi = phūmsa
participle maykim kkol

particle cōsa = tho ssi, hesa; a derived ~ phasayng tho-ssi
particle beginning with consonant tah-soli tho-ssi
particle beginning with a vowel holq-soli tho-ssi
passive verb ip.um māl = phītong-e/-sa
passive ip.um(q pep) = phītong, swutong; the ~ (form) of a verb ip.um kkol
passive affix ip.um uy kaci
passive voice swutong thay, swutongq pep
passivized form cey wumcik.im pyēnhyeng
past kwāke
"past imperfect" (= retrospective) kwāke-mīwan
past-past tāy-kwake
pause hyusik
permissive causative he.yong-cek haim māl
permissive mood hēlak pep
person: grammatical ~ inching(q pep)
personal pronoun in tāymyengsa = sālam tāy-ilum-ssi
phenomime uythay-e
phoneme umso
phonemes and prosodemes umwun
phonology (of a language) umwun(-lon)
phonomime uyseng-e
phonomimesis soli hyungnay
phrase mati = ēcel = iun māl = kwu
phrase-conjoiner, phrase-conjoining particle mati ¹yenkyel tho-ssi
plain consonants yelin soli = yēn.um
plain sounds phyengum
plain style hay-la chey; (= nonhonorific) an nophim
possessive case sok-kyek
possessive particle sō.yuq kyek cōsa
postnominal verb or adjective pulkwu phul.i-ssi
predicate phul.i māl = sēswul-e, -pu
predicate sēswul-e/-pu = phul.im māl
predicate: the ~ (constituent) phul.i cokak
predication sēswulq pep
predicative (mood) machimq pep = congciq-pep = ūyhyangq pep
predicatives phul.i ssi = yōngen
prefix aph kaci = ceptwu-sa = ceptwu-e
prenoun SEE adnoun
present (time) hyēncay
presumptive (indefinite) mood chwucengq pep = mīcengq pep
primary case ches ccay cali; ~ marker / particle ches ccay cali tho-ssi
processive mood hyēnsilq pep

projective (mood) **michimq pep**
prolative or allative case **hyāngcinq kyek**
prolonged sound **yen.um**
promissory or cajolative mood **yaksok pep**
pronoun **tāymyengsa** = **tāy-ilum-ssi**
pronouns, nouns, and numbers **īmca ssi** = **cheyen**
proper noun **ko.yu myengsa** = **hol-lo ilum-ssi**
proportional (mood) ["the more ... the more ... "] **pīlyeyq pep**
propositive mood **kkoyimq pep** = **kōngtongq pep**
prosodeme **wūnso**
prosodic morphophonemics **wūnso pyēntong**
proximal **kūnching**
qualificative case ("as, in the role / capacity of" = ... **ulo**) **cakyek kyek**
quantifiers, counters, numerary adjuncts, and (noun) classifiers [1]**yāng tāymyengsa**
quasi-affixes [1]**yusa cepsa** = **pisus han kaci**
quasi-free noun **hyengsik myengsa**
quasi-inflection (the declension of a noun) **cwūn-kwulkok pep**
quasi-noun **hyengsik myengsa**
question particle **mul.um(q pep) tho-ssi**
quotation, quotational phrase **īn.yong māl** = **īn.yong-e**
real (? substantive) noun **silqcil myengsa**
reciprocal case **sangtayq kyek**
reduplication **chep.e**
regular verb **kyuchik tōngsa**
regularly inflected words **kyuchik yōngen**
reinforced sounds **tōyn soli** = **kyengum**
reinforcement **kyengum-hwa**
relative: a ~ (pronoun / adverb) **kellim ssi** = **kwankyey-sa**
relative adverb **kwankyey pūsa**
relative pronoun **kwankyey tāymyengsa**
relativizer **kellim ssi** = **kwankyey-sa**
repetitive form **panpok hyeng**
repetitive (= iterative) mood **toy-phul.iq pep**
resemblative (= semblative) mood **hupsaq pep**
respect language **noph.imq pep** = **kōngtayq pep** = **contayq pep**
retrospective mood **hoysangq pep** = **kyenghemq pep**
rime **umwun**
"rising" tone **sāng-seng**
root (word) **mith māl** = **kunce-e**
root **ppuli** = **ēkun**
sandhi (alternations) **tah-soli ie pakkwim**

second person ("you, you people") **cēy-i inching**; (mesial reference) **cwungching**
secondary case **twūl ccay cali**; ~ marker / particle **twūl ccay cali tho-ssi**
selective mood **kalimq pep** = **sēnthayk-pep**
self-humbling words **kyemsa māl**; **kyemsonq pep**
semblative (= resemblative) mood **hupsaq pep**
semiformal (authoritative) style **hao chey**
semivowel **pān holq-soli** = **pān moum**
sentence **kul.wel** = **wel**
sentence constituents **wel sengpun**
sentence-final form **machimq pep** = **congciq-pep** = **ūyhyangq pep**
shift **pyēnhwa**
shortening **cwul.im**; [1]**yak.e** = **cwūn mal**
sibilant: ~ or affricate **iq soli** = **chium**
side dots (beside a MK syllable) **pangq-cem**
similative case **tong.lyuq kyek**
simple vowel **hoth holq-soli**
simple word **tanswun-e**
simplification of geminates **tongum sayng.lyak**
simultaneous mood **tongsiq pep**
single-function mood **han-kinungq pep**
sonant (being ~) **wullim**
sonant (= voiced sound) **wullimq soli** = **yūseng-um**
sound mimicry **soli hyungnay**
special particles (= particles of emphasis and focus) **thukswu cōsa**
speech styles **con-piq pep**
status marking **noph.imq pep** = **kōngtayq / contayq pep**
status-unmarked forms **an nophim**
stem **cwulki** = **ēkan**; (= content-word) **silqsa**
stem formative (bound auxiliary) **pōco ēkan**
stress **kangsey**
style **chey**
stylizations **con-piq pep**
subject (constituent / phrase) **īmca cokak**
subject (element / part) **cwupu**
subject (formation / marking) **cwucheyq pep**
subject (of a sentence) **cwuchey**
subject (phrase) **cwue** = **īmca māl**
subject exaltation **cwuchey noph.im(q pep)**
subject deference **cwuchey kyem.yang**
subject form **īmca kkol** = **cwuq-kyek hyeng**
subject formation **īmcaq pep**
subject humilification **cwuchey kyem.yang**
subject marker **īmca cali tho-ssi** = **cwuq-kyek cōsa**; subject marking **īmcaq pep**

subordinate compound swusik-cek hapseng-e = congsok-cek hapseng-e; ~ noun swusik-cek hapseng-e ilum-ssi
substantive and summative forms ilumq pep = myengsaq pep
suffix twīq kaci = cep.mi-sa = cep.mi-e; ssi kkuth = ēmi
summative and substantive forms ilumq pep = myengsaq pep
suppletion (?) pōchwungq pep
surd an wullimq soli = museng-um
surface structure keth kwuco = phyomyen kwuco
syllabicity, syllabic seng-cel.um
syllable umcel
syllable-final consonant cluster kyep congseng
syllable-final consonant(s) in Hankul pat.chim
syllable-final sound kkuth soli = congseng
syllable-initial sound choseng = ches soli
symbolic (mimetic) root sangcing-cek ppuli
symbolic word sangcing-e
syncope cwungum sayng.lyak
syntactic compound thōnge-cek hapseng-e
syntactic function thōngelon-cek kinung
syntactic structure thōnge-cek kwuseng
syntax thōnge-lon
syntax, syntactic thōnge
tense (fortis) vowel kincang holq-soli = kincang moum
tense (system) sicey
tense / time modification ? ttay maykim(q pep)
tensed sounds tōyn soli = kyengum
tenseless form (of a verb) kipon hyeng = uttum kkol
tensification kyengum-hwa
tertiary case sēy ccay cali; ~ marker / particle sēy ccay cali tho-ssi
third person ("he / him, she / her, they / them") cēy-sam inching; (distal reference) wēnching
tone, toneme sengco
tones: the four ~ (of Middle Chinese) sā-seng
tongue-tip (apical) sound hye-kkuth soli
topic = indirect subject kāncep īmca māl
total structure cenchey kwuseng
transferentive: ~ mood cēnhwanq pep; ~ form cēnhwan hyeng = cwungtan hyeng = kuchim kkol
transformation pyēnhyeng

transitional sound kwāto-um
transitive verb nam wumcik-ssi = thatong(sa)
transitivity thatongq seng
transposition cali pakkwum = cen.wi
triphthong: a ~ sēy kyep holq-soli = samcwung mōum
unaspirated sounds tōyn soli = kyengum
unknown / interrogative mīci-ching
unvoiced sound an wullimq soli = museng-um
verb tōngsa = wumcik-ssi, wum-ssi
verb ending ssi kkuth = ēmi
verb-final ending mayc.um ssi-kkuth
verb modifier form maykim kkol
verbal noun (= nominal verb) tōngmyengsa
vocative case pulumq cali = hoq-kyek
vocative marker / particle pulumq cali tho-ssi = hoq-kyek cōsa
voiced (being ~) wullim
voiced sound wullimq soli = yūseng-um
voicing wullim
vowel ending holq-soli ssi-kkuth
vowel epenthesis holq-soli kolwum
vowel harmony holq-soli(= mōum) cohwa
vowel holq-soli = mōum
vowel particle holq-soli tho-ssi
vowel: (glide and) ~ cwungseng
vowel: ending beginning with a ~ holq-soli ssi-kkuth
vowel: particle beginning with a ~ holq-soli tho-ssi
weakened sound kapyewun soli
word nāth mal = tan.e
word-conjoining particle nāth mal [1]yenkyel tho-ssi
word converted from some other part of speech censeng-e
word form ēhyeng
word order ēswun
word root māl mith (= ēkun = ppuli)
writing (initial) consonant clusters by combining two or more letters hap.yong pyēngse
writing with spaces (between words) ttuye ssuki
Yang (= light) vowel (= o, a, wo) yangseng
Yin (= dark / heavy) vowel (= u, e, wu) umseng
zero (form of a) particle kkol ēps.nun kaci
zero allomorph ceylo uy pyēn.i hyengthay, kkol ēps.nun pyēn.i hyengthay

Appendix 8. Chronological list of texts.

This finder list is based on several sources, primarily the lists in LCT and NKW, edited for practical reference. Some of the dates are best guesses and may be cited differently by other scholars. (The earliest date given is when the work was created or first published, but extant versions may be later.)

Abbreviation	Date	Title. (Author. Notes.)
Kyunye	1075	Kyunye cen
Kyeylim	1103	Kyeylim [1]yusa. Son Mok = Sūn Mù. repro Hankwuk kocen chongse 3
Saki	1145	Samkwuk saki. Kim Pusik
Hyang-kup	1250	Hyangyak kwukup-pang
Yusa	1285	Samkwuk yusa. Il.yen
Taymyeng	1395	Taymyeng-lyul cik.hay. [[1]Itwu]
Kwan-yek	1400+	Cosen-kwan yek.e. repro Hankwuk kocen chongse 3
Yangcam	1415	Yangcam kyenghem chwal.yo. [[1]Itwu]
Wellyeng	1431	Hyangyak chaychwu wellyeng
[1]Yong	1445	[1]Yongpi echen ka: 1-10, songs 1-125. Kwen Cey, Ceng [1]Inci, An Ci; notes by Seng Sammun, Pak Pangnyen, [1]Yi Kay
Hwun	1446	Hwunmin cengum haylyey. Seycong, Ceng [1]Inci
Sek	1447	Sekpo sangcel: 6, 9, 13, 19; 11; 23, 24. Swuyang (> Seyco)
TC	1448	Tongkwuk cengwun: 1-6. Choy Hang et al. [compiled 1447]
Kok	1449	Wel.in chenkang ci kok: songs 1-194. Seycong
Hwun-en	1451	Hwunmin cengum enhay. CF ?1750-
Hong	1455+	Hongmu cengwun sek.hwun: 1-16
Wel	1459	Wel.in sekpo: 1, 2, 7, 8, 9, 10; 11; 13, 14, 17, 18, 21, 23
[1]Nung	1462	[1]Nungem kyeng enhay: 1-10. Seyco. Translation of Śurangama sūtra
Pep	1463	Pep-hwa = Myopep [1]yenhwa-kyeng enhay: 1-7. Yun Salo, Hwang Swusin, et al. Translation of Saddharma pundarīka sūtra
Yeng	1463/4	[Sencong] Yengka-cip enhay: 1-2. Sin Mi et al.
Sim	1464	[Pan.ya paramilta] Simkyeng enhay. Han Kyeyhuy et al. Translation of Prajñā pāramitā hṛdaya sūtra
Kumkang	1464	Kumkang [pan.ya phalamil] kyeng [enhay]. Han Kyeyhuy et al.
Sangwen	1464	Otay-san Sangwen-sa chwungchang kwensen-mun = Sangwen-chep = Taysan echep
Amitha	1464	Amitha kyeng enhay = Pul-sel Amitha kyeng enhay. Seyco. Translation of Sukhavatīvyūha
Wen	1465	Wenkak kyeng enhay: 1-12. Sin Mi, Hyolyeng, Han Kyeyhuy. Translation of Mahā-vaipulya pūrṇa-buddha sūtra prasannārtha sūtru
Mok	1466	Mok.wuca-swusim-kyel [cho-kan]. Sin Mi. CF 1500
Kup	1466	Kwukup-pang enhay: 1-2. CF 1608; 1489
Sapep, Pep.e	1467→1517	Pep.e = Sapep.e. Sin mi. [first edition not extant]
Mong	?1468-	Mongsan hwasang pep.e [1]yaklok enhay. Sin Mi. LKM 1972: "1472"
Nay	1475	Nayhwun: 1, 2:1, 2:2, 3. Nagoya (Ōsa-bunko) text 1522; Kyucang-kak text 1611. CF 1656, 1736
Twusi	1481	Twusi enhay [cho-kan]: 5-10; 11; 12-13; 15-25. Co Wi, Uy Chim. Translation of poems of Dùfǔ. CF 1632
Samkang	1481	Samkang hayngsil-to: 1-3. CF 1511, 1514, 1617
Nam	1482	[Yengka-taysa cungto-ka] Nammyeng-chen [sensa] kyeysong enhay: 1-2. Seycong, Seyco
Kum-sam	1482	Kumkang kyeng samka-hay: 2-5. Han Kyehuy, [1]No Sacin
Kwan	1485	Kwan.um kyeng enhay = Pulceng-sim talani-kyeng enhay: 1-3

Otay	1485	Otay-cin.en (with Hanmun text of ¹Yenghem ¹yakcho, CF 1550). Later editions 1536, 1550. CF 1568 Cin-en-cip
Kup-kan	1489	Kwukup kan.i-pang: 1, 3, 6 (of 8). CF 1466.
Ilopha	1492	Ilopha (= Irofa = Iroha). Hankul pronunciation of Japanese syllabary
Ak-kwey	1493	Ak.hak kweypem: 1-9. Seng Hyen, Pak Kon. Hankul pp 211-35 only
¹Yuk	1496	¹Yukco [taysa] pep po-tan kyeng enhay: 1-3
Kwenkong	1496	Cin.en kwenkong = Kongyang sisik-mun (= Sisik kongyang-mun) enhay = Sisik kwenkong enhay = Pem-um kyeng
Mok-cwung	1500	Mok.wuca-swusim-kyel: cwung-kan. CF 1466
Sam-cwung	1511	Samkang hayngsil-to: cwung-kan. CF 1481; 1514; 1554, 1606, 1729
Sok-Sam	1514	Sok Samkang hayngsil-to. CF 1481, 1511; 1554, 1606, 1729
Sa, Saseng	1517	Saseng thonghay: 1-2. Choy Seycin
Sapep, Pep.e	1517←1467	Pep.e = Sapep.e. Sin Mi. [2d edition; also 1543. 1st edition lost]
Pak	?1517-	Pak thongsa enhay [cho-kan] = Pen.yek Pak thongsa: 1 (of 3). Choy Seycin. CF 1677
¹No	?1517-	¹Nokeltay [cho-kan] = Pen.yek ¹Nokeltay: 1-2. Choy Seycin. CF 1670
¹No-Pak	?1517-	¹No-Pak ciplam [cahay]. Choy Seycin. [Chinese words explained.] SEE ¹Yi Pyengcwu, ¹No-Pak ciplam ko (Cinswu-tang 1966)
Sohak-cho	1518	Pen.yek Sohak: 6, 7; 8, 9, 10. Kim Cen, Choy Swuksayng. CF 1586
¹Ye-yak	1518	¹Ye-ssi hyangyak enhay. Kim Ankwuk
Ilyun	1518	Ilyun hayngsil-to [cho-kan]. CF 1539
Pyek(.on)	1518	Pyek.on-pang enhay
Kan-Pyek	1525	Kan.i Pyek.on-pang. (lacks tone marks)
C, Cahoy	1527	Hwunmong cahoy: 1-3. Choy Seycin. Two versions in 1971 Tankwuk tay-hak.kyo edition with indexes by LKM
Siyong	?1530	Siyong hyangak po
Ilyun-cwung	1539	Ilyun hayngsil-to: cwung-kan. CF 1518; 1606, 1729
Wuma	1541/3	Wuma-yangce yem.yek-pyeng chilyo-pang
Pun-on	1542	Punmun on.yek ihay-pang. Kim Ankwuk
Sapep, Pep.e	1543	Pep.e = Sapep.e. Sin Mi. [2d (3d?) edition; Kwangmun-kak 1979]
Akcang	?1544-	Akcang kasa
¹Yenghem	1550	[Pen.yek] ¹Yenghem ¹yakcho. Hankul transl of 1485 Hanmun text
Uncwung	1553	Uncwung kyeng [enhay] = [Pulsel taypo] Pumo uncwung kyeng [enhay]; CF 1564, 1592, ?1778-1800
Kwuhwang	1554	Kwuhwang chwal.yo
—	1554	later edition of 1511 Samkang hayngsil-to: cwung-kan
Sek 3, 11	1562←1447	Sekpo sangcel, 2d edition.
Uncwung₂	1564	later edition of 1553 (Uncwung kyeng); CF ?1778-1800
Cin.en	1568	Cin.en-cip. (Choy Hyenpay 1961:244-5.) CF 1688, 1689, 1800
Cicang	1569	Cicang kyeng enhay: 1-3. Hakco taysa
Chiltay	1569	Chiltayman-pep: Cin.ye-seykyey, Samsin-yelay, Hwangcek-tungci
Kwang-Chen	1575	Kwangcwu Chenca-mun. CF 1583, 1804
¹Yuhap	1576	Sincung ¹Yuhap: 1-3. CF 1838 (Siebold edition)
Kyeycho	1577	Kyeycho-simhak.in-mun
Palsim	1577	Palsim-swuhayng-cang
Yawun	1577	Yawun cakyeng
Kwikam	1579	Senka Kwikam enhay: 1-2. (Written 1564 in Chinese by Sesan taysa, Hankul translation by Kim Hwa toin 1579, date of printing 1610)
Sek-Chen	1583	Sekpong Chenca-mun. CF 1575, 1804
Sohak	1586	Sohak enhay: 1-6. CF 1517; 1744. (6 of 1586 = 9 and 10 of 1517)

Tayhak	1588	Tayhak enhay
Cwung	1588	Cwungyong enhay
¹Non	1588	¹Non.e enhay: 1-4
Si	1588	Sikyeng enhay: 1-20
Cwuyek	1588	Cwuyek enhay: 1-9
Secen	1588	Secen enhay: 1-5
Mayng	1588	Mayngca enhay: 1-14
Hyo	1588	Hyokyeng enhay. Sonkei-kaku Bunko, Tōkyō (LKM 1972)
Si-mul	1588	Sikyeng mulmyeng enhay
Uncwung₃	1592	later edition of 1553 (Uncwung kyeng); CF ?1778-1800
–	1606	later edition of 1511 Samkang hayngsil-to: cwung-kan
En-Kup	1608	Enhay Kwukup-pang. CF 1466
Twu-cip	1608	Twuchang cip.yo [enhay]: 1-2
Thay	1608	Thaysan cip.yo [enhay]
Twu-hem	?1608+	Twuchang kyenghem pang
Nay-cwung	1611	Nayhwun: ?cwung-kan, Kyucang-kak text. CF 1475; 1656, 1736
¹Yenpyeng	1612	¹Yenpyeng cinam
Tonguy	1613	Tonguy pokam: 1-25
Sin-Sok	1617	Tongkwuk Sinsok Samkang hayngsil-to: hyoca 0, 00, 1-8; chwungsin 0, 00, 1; lyel.nye 0, 00, 1-8. CF 1481, 1511; 1514, 1606, 1729
T-cwung	1632	Twusi enhay: cwung-kan: 1-25. CF 1481
Kalyey	1632	Kalyey enhay: 1-10
Hwapho	1635	Hwapho-sik enhay: 1-2. CF 1685
Kwennyem	1637	Kwennyem yolok. (LKM 1972)
Makyeng	1649⁻	Makyeng chocip enhay: 1-2. CF 1682
Kyeng-hwun	?1650	Kyengsey hwunmin cengum [tosel]. Myeng Kok, Choy Sekceng. repro Hankwuk kocen chongse 3
Elok-chong₁	1652	Elok chonglam. CF. 1669. repro Tayhak-sa
Pyek-sin	1653	Pyek.on sinpang
Nay-cwung	1656	Nayhwun: cwung-kan. (? later edition of 1611) CF 1475, 1611, 1736
Kyengmin	1656	Kyengmin-phyen enhay: se, 1, 2:se
Elok	1657	Elok-hay. About Chinese
Hwang-po	1660	Kwuhwang po.yu-pang
Kyeychwuk	?1660⁻	Kyeychwuk ilki. Includes fictional events of 1623 and earlier.
Elok-chong₂	1669	Elok chonglam. CF. 1652. repro Tayhak-sa
¹No-cwung	1670	[not extant] → 1795; CF 1517⁻, 1795
Swukcong	?1674-1720	Swukcong enkan. Letters of the era; cited by LCT 715a:5.
Sin.e	1676	Chep.hay sin.e: 1-10. CF 1781. About Japanese
Pak-cwung	1677	Pak thongsa enhay: cwung-kan: 1-3. CF 1517⁻. About Chinese
Kyeng-wun	1678	Kyengsey cengwun. Choy Sekceng
Ma-cwung	1682	Makyeng chocip enhay: cwung-kan: 1-2. CF 1649⁻
Hwa-cwung	1685	Hwapho-sik enhay: cwung-kan: 1-2. CF 1635
Cin.en₂	1688	Cin.en-cip: 3 vols of mantras. ¹Nang Kyu. (Pulkyo sacen 832b.) CF 1568, 1689
Cin.en₃	1689	Cin.en-cip. (Choy Hyenpay 1961:244-5.) CF ?1568, 1688. mantras
Yek, Yek.e	1690	Yek.e ¹yuhay: 1-2. Sin Ihayng, Kim Kyengcwun. CF 1775. About Chinese
Cacho	1698	Sincen Cacho-pang enhay. CF 1796
Phal	1703	Phalsey-a. Later edition 1774. About Manchu
Cheng-Lo	1703	Chenge ¹Nokeltay: 1-8. CF 1765. About Manchu

Sam-yek	1703	Sam-yek chonghay: 1-10. Choy Hwuthayk. CF 1774. About Manchu
Soa	?1720-	Soa-lon. Sin Kyeyam. Later edition 1774. About Manchu
Yahwa	?1720-	Yolo-wen yahwa-ki. Pak Twusey. (Published by Ul-yu 1949)
Tongmong	?1720-	Tongmong sensup samhay. Pak Seymu
Way, Waye	?1720-	Waye ^{1}yuhay: 1-2. English translation Medhurst 1835. About Japanese
Thayphyeng	?1720+	Thayphyeng kwangki enhay: 1, 3-5. (Should be dated earlier?)
Payklyen	?1723-	Payklyen-chohay
Kwu-Tay	1728	Chengkwu yengen: Tayhak pon. Chen Thayk, ed. CF 1730
–	1729	later edition of 1511 Samkang hayngsil-to: cwungkan. CF 1539
Kwu-O	1730	Chengkwu yengen: O-ssi pon. CF. 1728
E-Nay	1736	[Nayhwun: cwung-kan =] Ecey Nayhwun. 1974 repro Aseya munhwa-sa. CF 1481; 1611, 1656
^{n}Ye, ^{n}Ye-sa	1736	^{n}Ye-sase enhay: 1-3
Mong-Lo	1741	Monge ^{1}Nokeltay: 1-8. Also 1766, 1790. About Mongolian
E-So	1744	Ecey Sohak enhay: 1-6. CF 1518, 1586
Sanghwun	1745	[Ecey] Sanghwun enhay
Songkang	1747	Songkang kasa: 1-3. Ceng Chel. (Pages numbers run through book.)
Hwatong	1747	Hwatong cengum thongsek-wun ko
Tongmun	1748	Tongmun ^{1}yuhay. Hyeng Munhang. Manchu vocabulary
Hwun-wun	?1750-	Hwunmin cengum wunhay. [^{1}Ye Am] Sin Kyengcwun [Swunmin].
Sam.wun	1751	Sam.wun senghwi
Wanglang	1753	Wanglang panhon cen
Colam	1755	Chen.uy Colam enhay: 1-5
E-Hwun	1756	Ecey Hwunse enhay
Haytong	1763	Haytong ka.yo. ^{1}No Kacay, Kim Swucang
Kokum	1764	Kokum kakok
Iltong	1765	Iltong cangyu-ka. Kim Inkyem
ChL-sin	1765	Chenge ^{1}Nokeltay sinsek
Pak-sin	1765	Pak thongsa sinsek enhay: 1-3. CF 1517-, 1677
Monge	1768	Monge ^{1}yuhay: 1-2. ^{1}Yi Ekseng. CF 1790. Mongolian vocabulary
Sipkwu	1772	Sipkwu-salyak enhay
Sam-yek cwung	1774	Sam.yek chonghay: cwung-kan. CF 1703
Yek-po	1775	Yek.e ^{1}yuhay po. CF 1690
Han-Cheng	?1775	Han-Cheng munkam: 1-15. ^{1}Yi Swu. Chinese-Korean-Manchu glossary
^{n}Yempul	1776	^{n}Yempul pokwen-mun
Myenguy	1777	Myenguy-lok enhay: 1-3. Kim Chiin et al. CF 1778
Pangen	1778	Pangen cipsek: 1-4. Manchu, Mongolian, Japanese
Sok-Myeng	1778	Sok Myenguy-lok enhay: 1-2. CF 1777
Uncwung$_{4,5}$	?1778-1800	later editions of 1553 (Uncwung kyeng); CF 1564, 1592
Mulpo	1780	Mulpo. ^{1}Yi Caywi
Sin.e-cwung	1781	Chep.hay sin.e: cwung-kan: 1-12. CF 1676
Cahyul	1783	Cahyul cenchik
Pyeng-ci	1787	Pyenghak cinam [enhay]: 1-2
Tonghan	1789	Kokum seklim 8: Tonghan yek.e. ^{1}Yi Uypong
Samhak	1789	Samhak yek.e. About Mongolian. (LCT 1972)
Monge-po	1790	Monge ^{1}yuhay pophyen. CF 1768
Chep-Mong	1790	Chep.hay Monge. About Mongolian
Mu.yey	1790	Mu.yey pothong-ci enhay = Mu.yey topho thongci enhay
^{1}In.e	1790	^{1}In.e taypang. Choy Kuylyeng. K version of Ringotaihō, Japanese
Muwen	1792	[Cungswu] Muwen-lok enhay: 1-3. (LCT 1973: "1791")

¹No-cwung [P]	1795←1670	¹Nokeltay enhay: cwung-kan [Phyengan kam.yeng]: 1-2. Cғ ?1517-
¹No-cwung [K]	1795←1670	¹Nokeltay enhay: cwung-kan [Kyucang-kak]: 1-2. Cғ ?1517-
Chengcang	1795	Chengcang-kwan cense
Cacho-cwung	1796	Sincen Cacho-pang enhay: cwung-kan
Olyun	1797	Olyun hayngsil-to: 1-5. Cғ 1859; 1884
¹Nap-ya	1799	[Enhay] ¹Nap-yak cengchi-pang
¹Yun.um	1800-	¹Yun.um enhay
Tongen	1800-	Tongen kolyak: 1-2. Ceng Kyo
Cwu-Chen	1804	Cwuhay Chenca-mun. Cғ 1575, 1583
Cung-sam	1805	[Sin-kan] Cungpo Samlyak cik.hay: 1-3. (LCT 1973: "enhay")
Aen	1819	Aen kakpi: 1-3
Enmun-ci	1824	Enmun-ci. ¹Yu Huy. repro Hankwuk kocen chongse 3
¹Yu-mul	?1834-	[¹Yu-ssi] Mulmyeng-ko: 1-5. (Chōsen gakuhō 15-20)
Medhurst	1835	Translation of a comparative vocabulary of the Chinese, Corean, and Japanese languages. W.H. Medhurst ("Philo Sinensis"). Batavia.
Siebold	1838	Lui-Ho sive Vocabularium Sinense in Kôraïanum conversum. Batavia
Cheksa₁	1839	Cheksa ¹yun.um. (Different book with same name 1881.)
Ocwu	?1840	Ocwu yenmun cangcen sanko
Thaysang	1852	Thaysang kam.ung-phyen tosel enhay: 1-5. (LCT 1973: "1851")
Myengseng	1855	[Kwanseng ceykwun] Myengseng kyeng enhay
Olyun₂	1859	later edition of 1797
Kosan	?1864-	Kosan yuko: 1-6. Yun Sento
Kyuhap	1869	Kyuhap chongse
Kakok	1876	Kakok wenlyu. Pak Hyokwa, An Min.yeng
Han.yang	1880	Han.yang-ka
Hancwung	?1800	Hancwung-[man]lok
Cin.en₄	1800	later edition of 1568
Kyengsin	1880	Kyengsin-lok enhay
Samseng	1880	Samseng-hwun kyeng
Kwahwa	1880	Kwahwa consin
Cokwun	1881	Cokwunlyeng cekci
Cheksa₂	1881	Cheksa ¹yun.um. (Different book with same name 1839.)
E-Chek	1881	[Ecey-yu tayso minlyo kup woyin tung] Cheksa ¹Yun.um
E-Phal	1882	Ecey-yu Phal-to sa-to kilo inmin tung ¹Yun.um
Hwa-en	1883+	Hwaum kyeymong enhay: 1-2. ¹Yi Unghen
Kwan-Olyun	1884	Kwanseng ceykwun Olyun kyeng. Cғ 1797
Camsang	1886	Camsang cip.yo
Chenswu	1889	Chenswu kyeng enhay
Ak-kasa	1893	Ak-kasa
Uy-lok	1893	Uy¹yel-pi chwung-hyo-lok
Hwae	?1895	Hwae ¹yucho
Toklip	1896	Toklip sinmun: 1-150
Nongka	?1900	Nongka wellyeng-ka

Appendix 9. Alphabetical list of texts.

(Alphabetized by the abbreviations.)

Abbreviation	Date	Title. (Author. Notes.)
Aen	1819	Aen kakpi: 1-3
Ak-kasa	1893	Ak-kasa
Ak-kwey	1493	Ak.hak kweypem: 1-9. Seng Hyen, Pak Kon. Hankul pp 211-35 only

Akcang	?1544-	Akcang kasa
Amitha	1464	Amitha kyeng enhay = Pul-sel Amitha kyeng enhay. Seyco. Translation of Sukhavatīvyūha
Cacho	1698	Sincen Cacho-pang enhay. CF 1796
Cacho-cwung	1796	Sincen Cacho-pang enhay: cwung-kan
Cahoy	1527	Hwunmong cahoy: 1-3. Choy Seycin. Two versions in 1971 Tankwuk tay-hak.kyo edition indexed by LKM
Cahyul	1783	Cahyul cenchik
Camsang	1886	Camsang cip.yo
ChL-sin	1765	Chenge ¹Nokeltay sinsek
Cheksa₁	1839	Cheksa ¹yun.um. (Different book with same name 1881.)
Cheksa₂	1881	Cheksa ¹yun.um. (Different book with same name 1839.)
Chengkwu	1730	Chengkwu yengen: O-ssi pon. CF 1728
Chengcang	1795	Chengcang-kwan cense
Cheng-Lo	1703	Chenge ¹Nokeltay: 1-8. CF 1765. About Manchu
Cheng-O	1730	Chengkwu yengen: O-ssi pon. CF 1728
Cheng-tay	1728	Chengkwu yengen: Tayhak pon. Chen Thayk, ed. CF 1730
Chenswu	1889	Chenswu kyeng enhay
Chep-Mong	1790	Chep.hay Monge. About Mongolian
Chiltay	1569	Chiltayman-pep: Cin.ye-seykyey, Samsin-yelay, Hwangcek-tungci
Cicang	1569	Cicang kyeng enhay: 1-3. Hakco taysa
Cin.en	1568	Cin.en-cip. (Choy Hyenpay 1961:244-5.) CF 1688, 1689, 1800
Cin.en₂	1688	Cin.en-cip: 3 vols. ¹Nang Kyu. (Pulkyo sacen 832b.) CF 1568, 1689
Cin.en₃	1689	Cin.en-cip. (Choy Hyenpay 1961:244-5.) CF ?1568, 1688
Cin.en₄	1800	later edition of 1568
Cokwun	1881	Cokwunlyeng cekci
Colam	1755	Chen.uy Colam enhay: 1-5
Cung-sam	1805	[Sin-kan] Cungpo Samlyak cik.hay: 1-3. (LCT 1973: "enhay")
Cwu-Chen	1804	Cwuhay Chenca-mun. CF 1575, 1583
Cwung(yong)	1588	Cwungyong enhay
Cwuyek	1588	Cwuyek enhay: 1-9
E-Chek	1881	[Ecey-yu tayso minlyo kup woyin tung] Cheksa ¹Yun.um
Elok	1657	Elok-hay. About Chinese
Elok-chong	1652	Elok chonglam. CF 1669. repro Tayhak-sa
Elok-chong₂	1669	Elok chonglam. CF 1652. repro Tayhak-sa
E-Hwun	1756	Ecey Hwunse enhay
E-Nay	1736	[Nayhwun: cwung-kan =] Ecey Nayhwun. 1974 repro Aseya munhwa-sa. CF 1481; 1611, 1656
E-Phal	1882	Ecey-yu Phal-to sa-to kilo inmin tung ¹Yun.um
E-So	1744	Ecey Sohak enhay: 1-6. CF 1518, 1586
En-Kup	1608	Enhay Kwukup-pang. CF 1466
Enmun-ci	1824	Enmun-ci. ¹Yu Huy. repro Hankwuk kocen chongse 3
H, H-haylyey		SEE Hwun
H-en		SEE Hwun-en
H-wun		SEE Hwun-wun
Han-Cheng	?1775	Han-Cheng munkam: 1-15. ¹Yi Swu. Chinese-Korean-Manchu glossary
Hancwung	?1800	Hancwung-[man]lok
Han.yang	1880	Han.yang-ka
Haytong	1763	Haytong ka.yo. ¹No Kacay, Kim Swucang

Hong	1455+	Hongmu cengwun sek.hwun: 1-16
Hwa-cwung	1685	Hwapho-sik enhay: cwung-kan: 1-2. CF 1635
Hwae	?1895	Hwae ¹yucho
Hwa-en	1883+	Hwaum kyeymong enhay: 1-2. ¹Yi Unghen
Hwang-po	1660	Kwuhwang po.yu-pang (also: Kwu-po)
Hwapho	1635	Hwapho-sik enhay: 1-2. CF 1685
Hwatong	1747	Hwatong cengum thongsek-wun ko
Hwun	1446	Hwunmin cengum haylyey. Seycong, Ceng ¹Inci
Hwun-en	1451	Hwunmin cengum enhay. Later edition ?1750⁻
Hwunmong		SEE Cahoy
Hwun-wun	?1750⁻	Hwunmin cengum wunhay. [¹Ye Am] Sin Kyengcwun [Swunmin]. CF 1451
Hyang-kup	1250	Hyangyak kwukup-pang
Hyo	1588	Hyokyeng enhay. Sonkei-kaku Bunko, Tōkyō (LKM 1972)
Ilopha	1492	Ilopha (= Irofa = Iroha). Hankul pronunciation of Japanese syllabary; LKM repro 1965 Tose 8: - (Ul-yu munhwa sa)
Iltong	1765	Iltong cangyu-ka. Kim Inkyem
Ilyun	1518	Ilyun hayngsil-to [cho-kan]. CF 1539
Ilyun-cwung	1539	Ilyun hayngsil-to: cwung-kan. CF 1518; 1606, 1729
¹In.e	1790	¹In.e taypang. Choy Kuylyeng. Korean version of Japanese Ringotaihō
Kakok	1876	Kakok wenlyu. Pak Hyokwa, An Min.yeng
Kalyey	1632	Kalyey enhay: 1-10
Kan-Pyek	1525	Kan.i Pyek.on-pang. (lacks tone marks) CF 1518
Kok	1449	Wel.in chenkang ci kok: songs 1-194. Seycong
Kokum	1764	Kokum kakok
Kosan	?1864⁻	Kosan yuko: 1-6. Yun Sento
Kumkang	1464	Kumkang [pan.ya phalamil] kyeng [enhay]. Han Kyeyhuy et al.
Kum-sam	1482	Kumkang kyeng samka-hay: 2-5. Han Kyehuy, ¹No Sacin
Kup	1466	Kwukup-pang enhay: 1-2. CF 1608
Kup-kan	1489	Kwukup kan.i-pang: 1, 3, 6 (of 8)
Kwahwa	1880	Kwahwa consin
Kwan	1485	Kwan.um kyeng enhay = Pulceng-sim talani-kyeng enhay: 1-3
Kwan-Olyun	1884	Kwanseng ceykwun Olyun kyeng. CF 1797
Kwan-yek	1400+	Cosen-kwan yek.e. repro Hankwuk kocen chongse 3
Kwang-Chen	1575	Kwangcwu Chenca-mun. CF 1583, 1804
Kwenkong	1496	Cin.en kwenkong = Kongyang sisik-mun (= Sisik kongyang-mun) enhay = Sisik kwenkong enhay = Pem-um kyeng
Kwennyem	1637	Kwennyem yolok. (LKM 1972)
Kwikam	1579	Senka Kwikam enhay: 1-2. (Written 1564 in Chinese by Sesan taysa, Hankul transl by Kim Hwa toin published 1579, printing date 1610)
Kwuhwang	1554	Kwuhwang chwal.yo
Kwu-po	1660	Kwuhwang po.yu-pang (also: Hwang-po)
Cheng-Tay	1728	Chengkwu yengen: Tayhak pon. Chen Thayk, ed. CF 1730
Kyeng-hwun	?1650	Kyengsey hwunmin cengum [tosel]. Myeng Kok, Choy Sekceng. repro Hankwuk kocen chongse 3
Kyeng-wun	1678	Kyengsey cengwun. Choy Sekceng
Kyengmin	1656	Kyengmin-phyen enhay: se, 1, 2:se
Kyengsin	1880	Kyengsin-lok enhay
Kyeycho	1577	Kyeycho-simhak.in-mun
		Kyeychwuk ilki. Includes fictional events of 1623 and earlier.

Kyeychwuk	?1660-	
Kyeylim	1103	Kyeylim ¹yusa. Son Mok = Sūn Mù. repro Hankwuk kocen chongse 3
Kyunye	1075	Kyunye cen
Kyuhap	1869	Kyuhap chongse
L…		→ ¹N… , → ¹Y… , → ¹I…
Ma, Makyeng	1649-	Makyeng chocip enhay: 1-2. CF 1682
Ma-cwung	1682	Makyeng chocip enhay: cwung-kan: 1-2. CF 1649-
Mayng	1588	Mayngca enhay: 1-14
Medhurst	1835	Translation of a comparative vocabulary of the Chinese, Corean, and Japanese languages. W.H. Medhurst ("Philo Sinensis"). Batavia. CF ?1720- Waye ¹yuhay
Mok	1466	Mok.wuca-swusim-kyel [cho-kan]. Sin Mi. CF 1500
Mok-cwung	1500	Mok.wuca-swusim-kyel: cwung-kan. CF 1466
Mong	?1468-	Mongsan hwasang pep.e ¹yaklok enhay. Sin Mi. LKM 1972: 1472
Monge	1768	Monge ¹yuhay: 1-2. ¹Yi Ekseng. CF 1790. Mongolian vocabulary
Monge-po	1790	Monge ¹yuhay pophyen. CF 1768
Monge-Lo	1741	Monge ¹Nokeltay: 1-8. Also 1766, 1790. About Mongolian
Mulpo	1780	Mulpo. ¹Yi Caywi
Muwen	1790	[Cungswu] Muwen-lok enhay: 1-3. (LCT 1973: "1791")
Mu.yey	1792	Mu.yey pothong-ci enhay = Mu.yey topho thongci enhay
Myengseng	1855	[Kwanseng ceykwun] Myengseng kyeng enhay
Myenguy	1777	Myenguy-lok enhay: 1-3. Kim Chiin et al. CF 1778
Ny…		→ ⁿY…
Nam	1482	[Yengka-taysa cungto-ka] Nammyeng-chen [sensa] kyeysong enhay: 1-2. Seycong, Seyco
¹Nap-yak	1799	[Enhay] ¹Nap-yak cengchi-pang
Nay	1475	Nayhwun: 1, 2:1, 2:2, 3. Nagoya (Ōsa-bunko) text 1573; Kyucang-kak text 1611. CF 1656, 1736.
Nay-cwung	1656	Nayhwun: cwung-kan. (? later edition of 1611) CF 1475, 1611, 1736
Nay-cwung₀	1611	Nayhwun: ?cwung-kan, Kyucang-kak text. CF 1475; 1656, 1736
¹No	?1517-	¹Nokeltay [cho-kan] = Pen.yek ¹Nokeltay: 1-2 [unavailable to LCT]. Choy Seycin. CF 1670
¹No-cwung	1795	¹Nokeltay enhay: cwung-kan: 1-2 [= LCT "No"]. CF ?1517-. Two versions: P = Phyengan kam.yeng and K = Kyucang-kak [in which the language looks newer]
¹Non	1588	¹Non.e enhay: 1-4
Nongka	?1900-	Nongka wellyeng-ka
¹No-Pak	?1517-	¹No-Pak ciplam [cahay]. Choy Seycin. [Chinese words explained.] See ¹Yi Pyengcwu, ¹No-Pak ciplam ko (Cinswu-tang 1966)
¹Nung	1462	¹Nungem kyeng enhay: 1-10. Seyco. Translation of Śurangama sūtra
Ocwu	?1840	Ocwu yenmun cangcen sanko
Olyun	1797	Olyun hayngsil-to: 1-5. CF 1884
Otay	1485	Otay-cin.en (with Hanmun text of ¹Yenghem ¹yakcho, CF 1550). Later editions 1536, 1550. CF 1568 Cin-en-cip
Pak	?1517-	Pak thongsa enhay [cho-kan] = Pen.yek Pak thongsa: 1 (of 3). Choy Seycin. CF 1677
Pak-cwung	1677	Pak thongsa enhay: cwung-kan: 1-3. CF 1517-. About Chinese
Pak-sin	1765	Pak thongsa sinsek enhay: 1-3. CF 1517-, 1677
Palsim	1577	Palsim-swuhayng-cang
Pangen	1778	Pangen cipsek: 1-4. Manchu, Mongolian, Japanese

Payklyen	?1723-	Payklyen-chohay
Pep	1463	Pep-hwa = Myopep ⁿyenhwa-kyeng enhay: 1-7. Yun Salo, Hwang Swusin, et al. Translation of Saddharma puṇḍarīka sūtra
Pep.e = Sapep	1467→1517	Pep.e = Sapep.e. Sin mi. Also 1543
Phal	1703	Phalsey-a. Later edition 1774. About Manchu
Pokwen		SEE ⁿYempul
Pun-on	1542	Punmun on.yek ihay-pang. Kim Ankwuk
Pyek(.on)	1518	Pyek.on-pang enhay. CF 1525
Pyek-sin	1653	Pyek.on sinpang
Pyeng-ci	1787	Pyenghak cinam [enhay]: 1-2
Sek	1447 →1562	Sekpo sangcel: 6, 9, 13, 19; 23, 24. Swuyang > Seyco (2d edition): 3, 11
Saseng	1517	Saseng thonghay: 1-2. Choy Seycin
Saki	1145	Samkwuk saki. Kim Pusik.
Sam-cwung	1511	Samkang hayngsil-to: cwung-kan. CF 1481; 1514; 1554, 1606, 1729
Samhak	1789	Samhak yek.e. About Mongolian. (LCT 1972)
Samkang	1481	Samkang hayngsil-to: 1-3. CF 1511, 1514, 1617
Samkwuk		SEE Saki, Yusa
Samseng	1880	Samseng-hwun kyeng
Sam.wun	1751	Sam.wun senghwi
Sam-yek	1703	Sam-yek chonghay: 1-10. Choy Hwuthayk. CF 1774. About Manchu
Sam-yek cwung	1774	Sam.yek chonghay: cwung-kan. CF 1703
Sanghwun	1745	[Ecey] Sanghwun enhay
Sangwen	1464	Otay-san Sangwen-sa chwungchang kwensen-mun = Sangwen-chep = Taysan echep
Sapep, Pep.e	1467→1517	Pep.e = Sapep.e. Sin Mi. [2d edition; also 1543. 1st edition lost]
Saseng	1517	Saseng thonghay: 1-2. Choy Seycin
Secen	1588	Secen enhay: 1-5
Sek	1447 1447→1562	Sekpo sangcel: 6, 9, 13, 19; 23, 24. Swuyang (> Seyco) (2d edition): 3, 11
Sek-Chen	1583	Sekpong Chenca-mun. CF 1575, 1804
Si	1588	Sikyeng enhay: 1-20
Si-mul	1588	Sikyeng mulmyeng enhay
Siebold	1838	Lui-Ho sive Vocabularium Sinense in Kôraïanum conversum. Batavia. CF 1576 ¹Yuhap
Sim	1464	[Pan.ya paramilta] Simkyeng enhay. Han Kyeyhuy et al. Translation of Prajñā pāramitā hṛdaya sūtra
Sin.e	1676	Chep.hay sin.e: 1-10. CF 1781. About Japanese
Sin.e-cwung	1781	Chep.hay sin.e: cwung-kan: 1-12. CF 1676
Sin-Sok	1617	Tongkwuk Sinsok Samkang hayngsil-to: hyoca 0, 00, 1-8; chwungsin 0, 00, 1; lyel.nye 0, 00, 1-8. CF 1481, 1511; 1514, 1606, 1729
Sipkwu	1772	Sipkwu-salyak enhay
Siyong	?1530	Siyong hyangak po
Soa	?1720-	Soa-lon. Sin Kyeyam. Later edition 1774. About Manchu
Sohak-cho	1518	Pen.yek Sohak (6, 7; 8, 9, 10). Kim Cen, Choy Swuksayng. CF 1586
Sohak	1586	Sohak enhay: 1-6. CF 1518; 1744. (6 of 1586 = 9 and 10 of 1518)
Sok-Myeng	1778	Sok Myenguy-lok enhay: 1-2. CF 1777
Sok-Sam	1514	Sok Samkang hayngsil-to. CF 1481, 1511; 1554, 1606, 1729
Songkang	1747	Songkang kasa: 1-3. Ceng Chel. (Page numbers run through book.)
Swukcong	?1674-1729	Swukcong enkan. Letters of the era; cited by LCT 715a:5

T-cwung	1632	Twusi enhay: cwung-kan: 1-25. CF 1481
Tayhak	1588	Tayhak enhay
Taymyeng	1395	Taymyeng-lyul cik.hay. [¹Itwu]
Thaysan	1608	Thaysan cip.yo [enhay]
Thayphyeng	?1720+	Thayphyeng kwangki enhay: 1, 3-5. (Should be dated earlier?)
Thaysang	1852	Thaysang kam.ung-phyen tosel enhay: 1-5. (LCT 1973: "1851")
Toklip	1896	Toklip sinmun: 1-150
Tongen	1800-	Tongen kolyak: 1-2. Ceng Kyo
Tonghan	1789	Kokum seklim 8: Tonghan yek.e. ¹Yi Uypong
Tongkwuk, TC	1448	Tongkwuk cengwun: 1-6. Choy Hang et al. [compiled 1447]
Tongmong	?1720-	Tongmong sensup samhay. Pak Seymu
Tongmun	1748	Tongmun ¹yuhay. Hyeng Munhang. Manchu vocabulary
Tonguy	1613	Tonguy pokam: 1-25
Twu-cip	1608	Twuchang cip.yo [enhay]: 1-2
Twu-hem	?1608+	Twuchang kyenghem pang
Twusi	1481	Twusi enhay [cho-kan]: 5-10; 11; 12-13; 15-25. Co Wi, Uy Chim. Translation of poems of Dùfù. Cwung-kan (1-25) 1632
Twusi-cwung	1632	Twusi enhay: cwung-kan: 1-25. CF 1481
Uncwung	1553	Uncwung kyeng [enhay] = [Pulsel taypo] Pumo uncwung kyeng
Uncwung₂	1564	Uncwung kyeng [enhay] = [Pulsel taypo] Pumo uncwung kyeng
Uncwung₃	1592	Uncwung kyeng [enhay] = [Pulsel taypo] Pumo uncwung kyeng
Uncwung₄,₅	?1778-1800	Uncwung kyeng [enhay] = [Pulsel taypo] Pumo uncwung kyeng
Uy-lok	1893	Uy¹yel-pi chwung-hyo-lok
Wanglang	1753	Wanglang panhon cen
Way, Waye	?1720-	Waye ¹yuhay: 1-2. English translation Medhurst 1835. About Japanese
Wel	1459	Wel.in sekpo: 1, 2, 7-8, 9-10, 13-14, 17-18, 21, 23; 11-12 found 1987
Wellyeng	1431	Hyangyak chaychwu wellyeng
Wen	1465	Wenkak kyeng enhay: 1-12. Sin Mi, ¹Nonyeng, and Han Kyeyhuy. Translation of Mahā-vaipulya pūrṇa-buddha sūtra prasannārtha sūtru
Wuma	1541/3	Wuma-yangce yem.yek-pyeng chilyo-pang
Yahwa	?1720-	Yolo-wen yahwa-ki. Pak Twusey. (Published by Ul-yu 1949)
Yangcam	1415	Yangcam kyenghem chwal.yo. [¹Itwu]
Yawun	1577	Yawun sakyeng
ⁿYe, ⁿYe-sa	1736	ⁿYe-sase enhay: 1-3
Yek, Yek.e	1690	Yek.e ¹yuhay: 1-2. Sin Ihayng, Kim Kyengcwun. CF 1775
Yek-po	1775	Yek.e ¹yuhay po. CF 1690
ⁿYempul	1776	ⁿYempul pokwen-mun
Yeng, Yengka	1463/4	[Sencong] Yengka-cip enhay: 1-2. Sin Mi et al.
¹Yenghem	1550	[Pen.yek] ¹Yenghem ¹yakcho. Hankul translation of 1485 Hanmun text
¹Yenpyeng	1612	¹Yenpyeng cinam
¹Ye-yak	1518	¹Ye-ssi hyangyak enhay. Kim Ankwuk
¹Yong	1445	¹Yongpi echen ka: 1-10, songs 1-125. Kwen Cey, Ceng ¹Inci, An Ci; notes by Seng Sammon, Pak Pangnyen, ¹Yi Kay
¹Yuhap	1576	[Sincung] ¹Yuhap: 1-3. CF 1838 (Siebold edition)
¹Yuk = ¹Yukco	1496	¹Yukco [taysa] pep po-tan kyeng enhay: 1-3
¹Yu-mul	?1834-	[¹Yu-ssi] Mulmyeng-ko: 1-5. (Chōsen gakuhō 15-20)
¹Yun.um	1800-	¹Yun.um enhay
Yusa	1285	Samkwuk yusa. Il.yen

Bibliography.

An Pyenghuy. 1957a. "Cwung-kan Twu-si enhay ey natha-nan [t] kwukayum-hwa ey tay-ha.ye". LHS festschrift 329-42.
___. 1957b. "Cwungsey kwuk.e uy puceng-e 'ani' ey tay ha.ye". Kwuk.e kwuk.mun hak 20:628-34.
___. 1968. "Cwungsey kwuk.e uy sok-kyek emi '-s' ey tay ha.ye". LSN festschrift 337-45.
___. 1971. "Hankwuk-e palqtal-sa 2: munqpep-sa". Hankwuk munhwa-sa taykyey 5:167-261.
___. 1977. Cwungsey kwuk.e kwukyel uy yenkwu. Ilqci-sa.
An Sangchel [Ahn, Sang-Cheol]. 1985. The interplay of phonology and morphology in Korean. University of Illinois dissertation.
Aoyama Hideo. 1972. "Gendai Chōsen-go no gisei-go". Chōsen gakuhō 49:1-24.
___. 1974. "Chōsen-go no hasei-gitaigo shikō". Chōsen gakuhō 72:1-82 [horizontal].
Azbuka dlya koreytsev. 1902. Kazan': Pravoslavnoe Missionerskoe Obshchestvo.
Cang Cangmyen. 1959. "Cosen-e chelqcaq-pep ey se sai-phyo sa.yong ul ceyhan halq tey tay-ha.ye". Cosen emun 5:55-67.
Cang Kyenghuy. 1985. Hyentay kwuk.e uy yangthay pemcwu yenkwu. Seoul: Thap chwulphan-sa.
Cang Sekcin [Chang, Suk-Jin]. 1973. A generative study of discourse: pragmatic aspects of Korean with reference to English. LR 9:2, suppl.
Cen Cayho. 1961. "Hankwuk camo myengching ko", Kwuk.e-kwuk.mun-hak 24:89-101.
Cen Cenglyey [Chun, Jung-Rae]. 1990. "Cwungsey kwuk.e uycon myengsa kwumun ey tay han il-kochal". En.e-hak 12:147-160 (English summary 161).
Ceng Insung. 1960. [Uymun haysel] Hankul kanghwa. Seoul: Sinkwu munhwa-sa.
Ceng Yenchan [Jeong, Yeon-chan]. 1976. Kwuk.e sengco ey kwan han yenkwu. Seoul: Ilqco-kak.
Choy Hak.kun. 1978. Hankwuk pangen sacen. Seoul: Hyenmun-sa.
Choy Hyenpay [Choi, Hyon-Pai]. 1937; (revised) 1959. Wuli mal pon. Seoul: Cengum-sa.
___. 1960. (Hankul 127:7-27)
Choy Iceng. 1960. "Pal.um ey se cwuuy hal myech kaci". Mkk 1960:9:14-5.
Choy Myengok. 1979. "Tonghay-an pangen uy umwun-lon cek yenkwu — Kyeng-Puk Yengtuk-kwun [n]Yenghay-myen echon ul cwungsim ulo". Pangen 2:1-34.
Choy Sungca [Choi, Seungja]. 1985. "Explanations of negation in Korean". HSIKL 1:124-34.
Choy Tongcwu [Choi, Dong-Ju]. 1988. 15-seyki kwuk.e uy an mayc.um-ssi '-te-' ey kwan han yenkwu. M.A. thesis, Seoul National University.
Choy Yengsek [Choi, Young-Seok]. 1988. "S´ deletion vs. raising: evidence from Korean". LR 24:169-93.
CM = Cosen-e munqpep. Phyengyang: Kwahak-wen en.e munhak yenkwu-so. 2 volumes: 1. Eum-lon hyengthay-lon (1960, repr. Tōkyō 1961); 2. Muncang-lon (1963, repr. Tōkyō 1963)
Co Miceng [Jo, Mi-Jeung]. 1976. "The retrospective suffix and speech level of narration in Korean". Ungyong en.e-hak [Applied Linguistics] 8:1.57-80.
Cook, Eung-Do = Kwuk Ungto
Cosen mal sacen [= NKd]. 6 volumes, 1960-2. Phyengyang: (Cosen mincwu-cwuuy inmin konghwa-kwuk kwahak-wen) En.e munhak yenkwu-so. Repr. in 2 volumes, Tōkyō 1962-3: Hak.wu sepang.
Cosen-e so-sacen = Cosen-e mich Cosen munhak yenkwu-so. 1956. Cosen-e so-sacen. Phyengyang.
Cwu Sikyeng. 1910. Kwuk.e munqpep. Kyengseng [Seoul]: Pak.mun sekwan.
Dupont 1965 = Dupont, René; Millot, Joseph. Grammaire Coréene. Seoul: Thap chwulphan-sa.
En.e-hak [1]nonmun-cip 6. 1985. Phyengyang: Kwahak payk.hwa sacen chwulphan-sa.
Figulla, H.H. 1935. "Prolegomena zu einer grammatik der koreanischen sprache". Berlin-Universität Mitteilung des Seminars für Orientalische Sprachen 38:101-21.
Fündling, Dirk. 1985. Koreanische onomatopöie: ein beitrag zu struktur und semantik der lautmalerei. Seoul: Thap chwulphan-sa.
Gale, J.S. 1894. Korean grammatical forms. Seoul: Trilingual Press.
___. 1897. A Korean-English dictionary. Yokohama: Kelly and Walsh.
___. 1916. Korean grammatical forms: revised edition. Seoul: The Korean Religious Tract Society.

Gerdts, Donna B. 1985. "Surface case and grammatical relations in Korean: the evidence from quantifier float". HSIKL 1:48-61.
Hamkyeng dictionary = Kim Thaykyun 1986
Han Senhuy. 1985. "Puceng-mun ey tay-han yenkwu". En.e-hak [1]nonmun cip 6:216-52 (Phyengyang).
Hattori Shirō et al. (Kim Tongcwung [Dongjun Kim], Umeda Hiroyuki, Watanabe Kil.yong [Kilyong Kim Watanabe]). 1981. "Gendai Souru-hōgen ni oite okori-tsutsu aru boin no tsūji-teki henka". Gengo no kagaku 8.11-56.
He Wung [Huh, Woong]; [undated] = He Wung 1975.
___. 1955. [1]Yongpi echen ka. Seoul: Cengum-sa.
___. 1958. Kwuk.e umwun-lon. Seoul: Cengum-sa.
___. 1964. "Seki 15-seyki kwuk.e uy sa.yek phitong uy cepsa". Tonga Munhwa 2:127-66.
___. 1975. Wuli yeys mal pon: 15-seyki kwuk.e hyengthay-lon. Seoul: Saym munhwa-sa.
___. 1971. [Kayko sinphan] Kwuk.e umwun-hak. Seoul: Cengum-sa.
___. 1987. Kwuk.e ttay-maykimq pep uy pyenchan sa. Seoul: Saym munhwa-sa.
___. 1989. 16-seyki wuli yeys mal pon. Seoul: Saym munhwa-sa.
He Wung; [1]Yi Kangco. 1962. [Cwuhay] Wel.in-chenkang ci kok. Seoul: Sinkwu munhwa-sa.
Hong Kimun. 1947. Cosen munqpep yenkwu. Seoul: Sewul sinmun sa.
Hong Yunphyo. 1975. "Cwuq-kyek emi '-ka' ey tay ha.ye". En.e-hak 3:65-92.
Horne, E.C. 1950-1. Introduction to spoken Korean. 2 volumes. New Haven: IFEL.
Howell, R.W. 1965. "Linguistic status markers in Korean". Kroeber Anthropological Society Papers 33:91-7.
HSIKL = Harvard Studies in Korean Linguistics: 1 (1985), 2 (1987), 3 (1989).
Hyen Phyenghyo. 1961. Ceycwu pangen yenkwu. Seoul: Cengkwu-sa.
I — SEE [1]Yi
Imbault-Huart, M.C. 1889. Manuel de la langue coréenne parlée. Paris: Imprimerie Nationale.
Im Hopin; Hong Kyengpho; Cang Swuk.in. 1987. Oykwuk-in ul wi han Hankwuk-e munqpep. Seoul: Yensey tay-hak.kyo chwulphan-pu.
Kang Cenghuy. 1988. Ceycwu pangen yenkwu. Hannam Tay-hak.kyo.
Kang Henkyu. 1988. Hankwuk-e ewen yenkwu sa. Seoul: Cip.mun-tang.
Katsuki Hatsumi. 1986. "Chōsen-go ni okeru meishi tensei gobi 'gi' [-˙ki] no shutsugen ni tsuite". [Kyōto-daigaku] Gengo-gaku kenkyū [Linguistic Research] 5:41-66.
KBC = Korean Basic Course = Pak Pongnam 1961
KEd = A Korean-English dictionary = Martin; Lee; Chang 1967
Khlynovskiy. 1904. Russko-Yaponsko-Koreyskiy voenniy perevodchik, 2d ed. Irkutsk.
Khun sacen = Hankul Hak.hoy. 1947-5. 6 vols. Seoul: Ul-yu munhwa-sa.
Kim Cinswu. 1987. "'-ko', '-(u)mye', '-(u)myense' uy thongsa-uymi uy sangkwanq-seng". Kwuk.e-hak 16:621-45.
Kim Chakyun. 1979. "Phyengchuk-pep kwa aykseynthu punsek-pep". En.e-hak 4:29-56.
Kim Cin.wu [Kim, Chin-W.]; To Swuhuy [Toh, Soo-Hee]. 1980. "Rule reordering in Middle Korean phonology". LR 16.75-86 (1980).
Kim Hyengkyu. 1954. "Cwuq-kyek tho 'ka' ey tay-han soko. Choy Hyenpay festschrift 93-107. Seoul: Sasang-kyey sa.
___. 1960. "Kyengyeng-sa wa 'ka' cwuq-kyek tho muncey". Hankul 126:7-18.
___. 1962. "'Ka' cwuq-kyek tho ey tay han kochal". Kwuk.e-sa yenkwu 199-211. Seoul: Ilqco-kak.
Kim Hyenglyong. 1965. "Wuli mal munhwa-e uy pat.chim ey tay-han yenkwu". En.e-hak [1]nonmun cip 6:20-78. Phyengyang: Kwahak payk.hwa sacen chwulphan-sa.
Kim Kil.yong = Watanabe Kim Kil.yong
Kim Minswu [Kim, Min-Soo]. 1961. Say cacen. Seoul: Tonga chwulphan-sa.
___. 1985. Puk-Han uy kwuk.e yenkwu. Seoul: Kolye tay-hak.kyo chwulphan-pu
___. 1971. Kwuk.e munqpep-lon. Seoul: Ilqco-kak.
Kim Minswu; Hong Wungsen. 1968. Conghap kwuk.e sacen. Seoul: Emun-kak.

Kim Panghan. 1957. "Kwuk.e cwuq-kyek cep.mi-sa 'i' ko". Seoul University Theses 5.67-108.
___. 1965. "Kwuk.e cwuq-kyek emi 'i' ko caylon". Hakswul-wen ¹nonmun cip 5:32-61, English summary 61.
Kim Payklyen. 1960. [on multiple adjuncts; ? Mkk 1960:1 or 2]
Kim Pyengcey. 1980. Cosen-e pangen sacen. Phyengyang: Kwahak payk.kwa sacen chwulphan-sa.
Kim Pyengha 1 = Kim Pyengha; Hwang Yuncwun. 1954. Cosen-e kyokwa-se, cey-il phyen: eum-lon kwa hyengthay-lon. Moskva. [Grammatika koreyskogo yazyka 1: morfologiya.]
Kim Pyengha 2 = Kim Pyengha 1955. Cosen-e munqpep, ha-phyen: muncang-lon. Moskva, 1955. [Grammatika koreyskogo yazyka 2: sintaksis.]
Kim Sepcey. 1957. [Myengmun] Sin okphyen. Seoul: Myengmun-tang.
Kim Sungkon. 1971. "Tho-ssi '^u/oy' uy palqtal ul salphim: thuk hi ku kyeypo uy mosayk ul wi ha.ye". Hankul Hak.hoy 50-tol kinyem ¹nonmun cip 155-84.
___. 1978. Hankwuk-e cosa uy thongsi-cek yenkwu. Seoul: Taycey-kak.
Kim Thaykyun. 1986. Ham-Puk pangen sacen. Seoul: Kyengki Tay-hak.kyo chwulphan-pu.
Kim Tongsik [Kim, Dong-sik]. 1981. "Puceng ani 'n puceng", En.e 6:2:99-116.
Kim Wancin. 1970. "Muncep sok uy 'wa' wa kwucep sok uy 'wa'". LR 6:2.1-16.
___. 1973. "Kwuk.e ehwi mamyel uy yenkwu". Cintan hakpo 35:35-59, English summary 169-70.
___. 1975. "Um.wun-lon cek yuin ey uy han hyengthay-so cungka ey tay ha.ye". Kwuk.e-hak 3.
___. 1980. Hyangka haytok-pep yenkwu. Sewul tay-hak.kyo chwulphan-pu.
Kim Yengcwu [Kim, Young-Joo]. 1985. "Semantic conditions for the occurrence of sentential nominalizers Um and Ki". HSIKL 1:168-77.
___. 1989. "Inalienable possession as a semantic relationship underlying predication: the case of multiple-accusative constructions". HSIKL 3:445-68.
Kim Yengpay. 1984. Phyengan pangen yenkwu. Seoul: Tongkwuk tay-hak.kyo.
Kim Yengsek [Kim, Young-Seok]. 1985. Aspects of Korean morphology. Pan Korea Book Corp.
Kim Yongkwu. 1986. Cosen-e ¹ilon munqpep: muncang-lon. Phyengyang: Kwahak payk.hwa sacen chwulphan-sa.
Kim-Renaud Young-Key [Kim Yengki]. 1986. Studies in Korean linguistics. Seoul: Hanshin.
King, J.R.P. 1987. "An introduction to Soviet Korean". LR 23:3.233-74.
___. 1988a. "History of reported speech in Korean". Paper read at LSA annual meeting.
___. 1988b. "The Korean dialect materials in Matveev's 1900 *Reference Book to the city of Vladivostok.*" LR 29:281-329.
___. 1989. "A 1902 Cyrillic-script rendition of "Red Riding Hood" in North Hamkyeng dialect". HSIKL 3:39-48.
___. 1991a. Russian Sources on Korean Dialects. Harvard University dissertation.
___. 1991b. "Dialect elements in Soviet Korean publications from the 1920s". Chicago: Seventh Conference on the Non-Slavic Languages of the Soviet Union.
___.?1991c. "Towards a history of transitivity in Korean". Proceedings of the Conference on the Theory and Practice of Historical Linguistics, U of Chicago Special Publications in Linguistics 2.
___.?1991d. "A Soviet Korean grammar from 1930". Hankwuk mal kyoyuk 3:1-18.
KM = Korean Morphophonemics = Martin 1954
Ko Sinswuk. 1987. Cosen-e ¹ilon munqpep: phumsa-lon. Phyengyang: Kwahak payk.hwa sacen chwulphan-sa.
Ko Yengkun. 1981. Cwungsey kwuk.e uy sisang kwa seq-pep. Seoul: Thap chwulphan-sa.
___. 1987. Phyocwun cwungsey kwuk.e munqpep-lon. Seoul: Thap chwulphan-sa.
Kōno Rokurō. 1950. "On the intensive stem of middle Korean". Gengo kenkyū 16:116-25; reprinted in 1959 Kōno Rokurō chosaku-shū 1:499-507.
___. 1968. Chōsen kanji-on no kenkyū. Tōkyō: monograph reprint from Chōsen gakuhō.
Kuno Susumu; Kim Yengcwu [Young-Joo Kim]. 1985. "The honorific forms of compound verbals in Korean". HSIKL 1:178-89.

Kuroda, Shige-Yuki. 1974-7. "Pivot-independent relativization in Japanese". Papers In Japanese Linguistics 3:59-93, 4:85-96, 5:157-79.
Kwuk Ungto [Cook, Eung-Do]. 1973. "Double-consonant base verbs in Korean". LR 9:2.264-73.
Kwuk.e kyoyuk yenkwu-hoy. 1960. [Kwuk.e haksup chamko chalyo.] Seoul: Yenghwa chwulphan-sa.
Kwuk.e kwuk.mun hak.hoy. 1958. Kwuk.e say sacen. Seoul: Tonga chwulphan-sa.
LCT ← ¹Yu Changton; [undated] = LCT 1964.
___. 1961. "$k > 0$ kokwu". Chōsen gakuhō 21/22:46-63 horizontal (= 1051-1034), English summary 41-2 (= 1100-1099).
___. 1964. ¹Yi-co-e sacen. Seoul: Yensey tay-hak.kyo chwulphan-pu.
___. 1971. Ehwi-sa yenkwu. Seoul: Myeng munhwa-sa.
___. 1973. ¹Yi-co kwuk.e sa yenkwu. Seoul: Senmyeng munhwa-sa.
Ledyard, Gari K. 1966. The Korean language reform of 1446: the origin, background, and early history of the Korean alphabet. UC (Berkeley) dissertation. UM 66-8333.
Lee — SEE ¹Yi —
LHS ← ¹Yi Hisung [Lee, Hi-seung]; [undated] = LHS 1961.
___. 1955. Kwuk.e-hak kaysel. Seoul: Mincwung sekwan.
___. 1959. Kwuk.e-hak ¹nonko. Seoul: Mincwung sekwan.
___. 1961. Kwuk.e tay-sacen. Seoul: Mincwung sekwan.
LKM ← ¹Yi Kimun [Lee, Ki-moon]
___. 1959. "Sip.lyuk seyki kwuk.e uy yenkwu". Kolye tay-hak.kyo Mun.li ¹noncip 4:19-70.
___. 1962. "¹Yongpi echen ka kwuk.mun kasa uy cey-muncey". Aseya yenkwu 1:87-113, English summary 129-31.
___. 1963. Kwuk.e phyokiq-pep uy ¹yeksa-cek yenkwu [Historical studies in the Korean writing system]. [English summary]
___. 1964. "Tongsa ekan anc-, yenc-' uy saq-cek kochal". [Tonam] Co Yuncey paksa hoykap kinyem ¹nonmun cip 341-50.
___. 1972a. Kwuk.e umwun sa yenkwu. Seoul: Hankwuk munhwa yenkwu-so.
___. 1972b. Kwuk.e-sa kaysel, rev ed. Seoul: Mincwung sekwan.
___. 1978. "The reconstruction of *yo in Korean". Papers in Korean Linguistics 41-3.
___. 1979. "The vowel system of Middle Korean". Mélanges de Coréanologie offerts à M. Charles Haguenauer, Mémoires du Centre d'Études Coréenes, Collège de France 111-7.
LKM, Kim Cin.wu, ¹Yi Sangek. 1985. Kwuk.e umwun-lon. 2d edition. Seoul: Cengum-sa.
LR = Language Research = En.e yenkwu [a linguistics journal]. Seoul: SNU.
LSN ← ¹Yi Swungnyeng [Lee, Sung-Nyong]
___. 1954. Kwuk.e-hak kaysel. Seoul: Cinmun-sa.
___. 1956. '"z"-um ko (A study of the sound "z" in the 15th-16th century)'. Seoul University theses 3:51-235 (1956); reprinted in (LSN) Kwuk.e-hak ¹nonko 3-175 (Tongyang chwulphan-sa 1960).
___. 1961. Cwungsey kwuk.e munqpep. Seoul: Ul-yu munhwa-sa.
___. 1978. Ceycwu-to pangen uy hyengthay-lon cek yenkwu. Seoul: Thap chwulphan-sa.
Lukoff, Fred. 1947. Spoken Korean, 2 volumes. New York: Holt.
___. 1954. A grammar of Korean. University of Pennsylvania dissertation.
___. 1978. "On honorific reference". Festschrift for [Nwunmoy] He Wung 539-62. Seoul: Kwahak-sa.
___ ; Nam Kisim [Nam, Ki-Shim]. 1982. "Constructions in -nikka and -ŏsŏ". Linguistics in the Morning Calm (¹Yang Insek, ed.) 559-83.
M = Myŏngdo = Vandesande
Martin, Samuel E. 1951. "Korean phonemics". Language 27:519-33.
___. 1953. The phonemes of Ancient Chinese. American Oriental Society.
___. 1954. Korean morphophonemics. Baltimore: Linguistic Society of America.
___. 1962. "Phonetic symbolism in Korean". American Studies in Altaic Linguistics (UA Series 13) 117-89. Bloomington, Indiana: Indiana University.

___. 1964. "Speech levels in Japan and Korea". Language and Culture in Society 407-15.
___. 1968. "Korean standardization: problems, observations, and suggestions". Ural-Altaische Jahrbücher 40:85-114.
___. 1973. "Comments". LR 9:2.282-7. (Lenition in irregular stems.)
___. 1975. A reference grammar of Japanese. New Haven: Yale University Press.
___. 1982. "Features, markedness, and order in Korean phonology". Linguistics in the Morning Calm 601-18. Seoul: Hanshin.
___. 1982/3. "On the consonant distinctions of earlier Korean", Hankul 175:59-172 (1982); corrected and revised version, New Haven 1983.
___. 1986. "Phonetic compression and conflation in English and in Korean". Studies in Korean Language and Linguistics (Nam-Kil Kim [Kim Namkil], ed.) 118-24.
___. 1987. The Japanese language through time. Yale University Press.
___.?1991. "On dating changes in the phonetic rules of Korean". Festschrift für Bruno Lewin, vol. 3. Bochum. [written 1982/1987]
Martin, Samuel E.; Lee, Yang Ha [[1]Yi Yangha]; Chang, Sung-Un [Cang Sengen]. 1967. A Korean-English dictionary. New Haven: Yale University Press.
Mkk = Mal kwa kul
Mun Changtek; [1]Yu Uncong; Pak Sangil. 1985. Cosen mal mac.chwumq-pep sacen. Sim.yang = Shenyang (PRC): [1]Yonyeng mincok chwulphan-sa.
Munkyo-pu kosi 1988. [prescriptive rules from the Ministry of Education]
[1]Na Cinsek. 1977. "Kyeng-Nam pangen mal-pon". Hankul 159:42-82.
Nam Kisim [Nam, Kishim (Ki-Shim / Ki Shim)]. 1978. "'-ess.ess-' uy ssuim ey tay-ha.ye". Hankul 162:95-139.
Nam Kisim; Ko Yengkun, eds. 1982. Kwuk.e uy thongsa-uymilon. Seoul: Thap chwulphan-sa.
Nam Kisim; Ko Yengkun. 1985. Phyocwun kwuk.e munqpep-lon. Seoul: Thap chwulphan-sa.
Nam Kwangwu [Nam, Gwang U] → NKW.
NKd = Cosen mal sacen. Contains 170,000 entries (Mkk 1960:8:33).
Nam Phunghyen. 1976. "Kwuk.e pucengq-pep uy palqtal". Munqpep yenkwu 3:55-81.
Nikol'skiy, L.B. 1974. "K interpretatsii sluchaev otsustviya padezhnykh morfem v koreyskom yazyke". Issledovaniya po vostochniy filologii 180-4.
NKW ← Nam Kwangwu [Nam, Gwang U]; [undated] = Nam Kwangwu 1979
___. 1960. "Cwuq-kyek cosa 'ka' ey tay ha.ye". [NMK:] Kwuk.e-hak [1]nonmun cip 371-8.
___. 1974. "Wencin moum-hwa hyensang ey kwan-han yenkwu: '-pputa, -phuta' cek.ki lul cwungsim ulo". Kwuk.e-hak [Journal of Korean Linguistics] 2:31-8.
___. 1979. Koe sacen, revised and enlarged edition. Seoul: Ilqco-kak.
O'Grady, William. 1987a. "Discontinuous constituents in a free word order language". Syntax and Semantics 20:241-55.12.14.
___. 1987b. "The interpretation of Korean anaphora". Language 63:251-77.
___. 1991. Categories and case: the sentence structure of Korean. Philadelphia: Benjamins.
Okutsu Keiichirō. 1979. "Nihon-go no juju-dōshi kōbun: Eigo Chōsen-go to hikaku shite". Jimbun-gakuhō 132:1-27.
Pak, G.A. 1958. "Morfologicheskie osobennosti izobrazitel'nykh slov v koreyskom yazyke". Voprosy koreyskogo i kitayskogo yazykoznaniya 99-117.
___. "Slovoobrazovanie na baze izobrazitel'nykh slov". Koreyskiy yazyk: sbornik statey. 182-201.
Pak Hwaca [Park, Whaja]. 1982. Aspects contrastifs du japonais et du coréen. University of Stockholm.
Pak Pongnam [Park, Bong Nam]. 1969. Korean basic course, 2 volumes. Washington, D.C.: Foreign Service Institute, Department of State.
Pak Pyengchay. 1974. [1]Non-cwu Wel.in chenkang ci kok (sang). Seoul: Cengum-sa.
Pak Sengwen. 1972. Hyōjun Kankoku-go. Tōkyō: Kōrai shorin.
Pak Swuk.kyeng. 1960. "Sai-phyo (') uy sa.yong ey tay-ha.ye". Mkk 1960:12:12-6.

Pak Yonghwu. 1960. Ceycwu pangen yenkwu. Ceycwu: Tongwen-sa. Revised edition 1988, 2 vols, Seoul: Sengtong munhwa-sa.
Patterson B.S. 1974. A study of Korean causatives. U of Hawaii Working Papers in Linguistics 6:4.
Putsillo, Mikhail. 1874. Opyt Russko-Koreyskogo slovarya. St. Petersburg: Hogenfelden.
P'yankov, V.G. 1874. Koreyskaya azbuka. St Petersburg.
Ramsey, S.R. 1975. "Middle Korean W-, z-, and t/l- verb stems". LR 11:1.59-68.
___. 1978a. Accent and morphology in Korean dialects. Seoul: Thap chwulphan-sa.
___. 1978b. "S-clusters and reinforced consonants". Papers in Korean Linguistics 59-68.
___. 1984. "The origin of the Korean word for 'kitchen'". Yu Chankyun festschrift 843-7. Taegu [= Taykwu]: Kyemyong [= Kyeymyeng] University Press.
___. 1992. "Proto-Korean and the origin of Korean accent", Asian Historical Phonology (W. Boltz, ed.) 215-38.
Ramstedt, G.J. 1939. A Korean grammar. Mémoires de la société finno-ougrienne 82. Helsinki.
Ree SEE ¹Yi
Ridel, Félix-Clair. 1881. Grammaire Coréenne. Yokohama: Levy et Salabelli.
Ross, J. 1877. Corean Primer. Shanghai: American Presbyterian Mission Press.
Roth, Lucius. 1936. Grammatik der koreanischen sprache. Tek.wen: St Benedikt.
Scott, James S. 1887. A Corean manual. Seoul: English Church Mission Press.
___. 1893. A Corean manual. Second edition. Seoul: English Church Mission Press.
___. 1891. English-Corean Dictionary. [Seoul:] Church of England,
Se Thaylyong [Seo, Tae-Lyong]. 1980. "Tongmyeng-sa wa hwuchi-sa /un/ /ul/ uy kice uymi". Cintan hakpo 50:97-120.
Seng Nakswu [= ¹Nakswu]. 1984. Ceycwu-to pangen uy phul.i-ssi uy iumq-pep yenkwu. Seoul: Cengum-sa.
Shibatani Masayoshi. 1973. "Lexical versus periphrastic causatives in Korean". Journal of Linguistics 9:281-97.
Shibu Shōhei. 1975. "Chūki Chōsen-go no ganbō-hō gobi ni tsuite". Tōyō gakuhō 56:01-014.
Sin Changswun [Shin, Chang-Soon]. 1972. "Hyentay Cosen-e uy yongen poco ekan 'keyss' uy uymi wa yongqpep". Chōsen gakuhō 65:119-40.
Sim Cayki [Shim, Jae-Ki]. 1982. Kwuk.e ehwi-lon. Cip.mun-tang.
Sin Kichel; Sin Yongchel. 1958. Phyocwun kwuk.e sacen. Seoul: Ul-yu munhwa-sa.
SNU = Seoul National University
Son Han [Sohn, Han]. 1978. "Tensification in compound boundaries in Korean". Papers in Korean Linguistics 113-20.
Song Namsen [Song, Nam Sun]. 1987. Thematic relation and transitivity in English, Japanese, and Korean. London: SOAS dissertation.
Song Sekcwung [Song, Seok Choong]. 1967. Some transformational rules in Korean. Indiana U diss.
___. 1986. Review of Lukoff: An introductory course in Korean. Korean Lingustics 4:123-6.
___. 1988. Explorations in Korean syntax and semantics. Berkeley: UC Center for Korean Studies.
Soothill, W.E; Hodous, L. 1937. A dictionary of Chinese Buddhist terms. London: Kegan Paul.
Starchevskiy, A.V. 1890. Nashi sosedi. [A multilingual phrasebook.] St Petersburg.
Tayshin, A.I. 1898. Russko-Koreyskiy slovar'. Khabarovsk.
Thak Huyswu. 1956. Cosen eum kaylon. Tōkyō: Hak.wu sepang.
Tsukamoto Hideki. 1986a. "On the interaction of morphology and syntax of agglutinative languages". [Kyōto-daigaku gengo-gaku kenkyū-kai] Gengo-gaku kenkyū 5:25-40.
___. 1986b. "Sūryō-shi no yūri ni tsuite − Nihon-go to Chōsen-go no taishō kenkyū". Chōsen gakuhō 119/120:33-70 [English summary 28-9 horizontal].
Underwood, H.G. 1890a; 2d ed. (Seoul) 1914. An introduction to the Korean spoken language. In two parts: Part 1. Grammatical notes. Part 2. English into Korean. New York: A.D.F. Randolph.
___. 1890b. A concise dictionary of the Korean language. Yokohama: Kelly and Walsh.

Vandesande, A.V. 1968. Myŏngdo's Korean. Seoul: Myŏngdo Language Institute.
Wagner, E.W.; Kim Cengswun [Kim, Chongsoon]. 1963. Elementary written Korean, Han'gŭl text, Part II. Harvard-Yenching Institute.
Watanabe Kim Kil.yong. 1978. "Causative constructions in Korean". ICU Summer Institute of Linguistics Bulletin 11:171-88.
Whitman, J. 1989. "Topic, modality, and IP structure". HSIKL 3:341-56.
[Wunhe] ¹Yong Ha. 1961. Pulkyo sacen. Seoul: Pepthong-sa.
¹Yang Insek (Yang, In-seok/-Seok). 1972. Korean syntax: case markers, delimiters, complementation, and relativization. Seoul: Payk.hap sa.
___. 1974. "Two causative forms in Korean". LR 10:1.83-117.
¹Yi Cenglo [Ree, Joe J(ungno)]. 1975a. "A semantic analysis of (u)ni and (e)se". LR 11:1.69-76.
___. 1975. "Demonstratives and number in Korean". The Korean language: its structure and social projection (Ho-min Sohn, ed.) 33-46.
___. 1978. "A re-analysis of (u)ni and (e)se". Papers in Korean Linguistics 177-84.
___. 1985. "Pragmatics of deictic verbs". HSIKL 2:226-33.
¹Yi Congchel. 1983. Hyangka wa Man.yepcip-ka uy phyokiq-pep pikyo yenkwu. Seoul: Cip.mun-tang. [English abstract 203-8.]
¹Yi Hisung [Lee, Hi(e)-seung] → LHS
¹Yi Hyosang. 1991. Tense, aspect and modality: a discourse-pragmatic analysis of verbal affixes in Korean from a typological perspective. UCLA diss.
¹Yi Iksep. 1972. "Kang.lung pangen uy hyengthay-umso-lon cek kochal", Cintan hakpo 33. Reprinted 1977: Pangen yenkwu (Kwuk.e-hak ¹nonmun sen 6) 275-301.
¹Yi Kanghwun [Rhee, Kang-Hoon]. 1982. "Kwuk.e uy pok.hap myengsa ey se uy kyengum-hwa hyensang". Linguistic Journal of Korea 7:299-321.
¹Yi Kikap [Lee, Kee-Kap]. 1981. "Ssi-kkuth '-a' wa '-ko' uy ¹yeksa-cek kyochey". LR 17:2.227-36.
¹Yi Kimun [Lee, Ki-moon] → LKM
¹Yi Kitong [Lee, Keedong (Kee-dong, Ki-dong/-Dong)]. 1987. "The meanings of the two passives in Korean". LR 23:185-202.
___. 1988. A Korean grammar. Mimeo typescript.
¹Yi Kiyong. 1979. "Twu kaci puceng-mun uy tonguyq-seng ye-pu ey tay ha.ye". Kwuk.e-hak 8:60-93.
¹Yi Kun.yeng 1961. "Myengsa kyek sa.yong ey se uy myech kaci muncey". Mkk 1961:4:8-11.
___. 1985. Cosen-e ¹ilon munqpep: hyengthay-lon. Phyengyang: Kwahak payk.hwa sacen chwulphan-sa.
¹Yi Mayngseng [Lee, Maeng-Sung]. 1968. Nominalizations in Korean. LR 4:1, suppl.
¹Yi Sangek [Lee, Sang Oak]. 1978. Middle Korean tonology. University of Illinois dissertation.
¹Yi Sangpayk [Lee, Sang-Beck]. 1957. Hankul uy kiwen [The origin of the Korean alphabet HANGUL according to new sources]. Seoul: Thongmun-kwan.
¹Yi Sek.lin. 1955. "Kyep-swu lul natha-naynun 'tul' uy yenkwu". Hankul 108:41-2.
¹Yi Sungwuk. 1981. "Pok-tongsa uy hesa-hwa — cwuq-kyek emi-sa 'ka' uy palqtal ey tay ha.ye". Cintan hakpo 51:183-202.
¹Yi Swungnyeng [Lee, Sung-Nyong] → LSN
¹Yi Tongcay [Lee, Dong-Jae]. 1987. "Kuliko: an adverb or a conjunctor?". Korean Linguistics 1:61-81.
___. 1989. "Classification of verb suffixes and suffixal phrases". LR 25:329-59.
¹Yi Tong.lim. 1959. [Cwuhay] Sekpo sangcel. Seoul: Tongkwuk tay-hak.kyo.
¹Yi Ungpayk. 1961. Hankul mac.chwumq-pep sacen. Seoul: Munho-sa.
¹Yi Uyto [Lee, Ui-do]. 1990. Wuli mal ium-ssi kkuth uy thongsi-cek yenkwu. Seoul: Emun-kak.
¹Yi Yuncay; Kim Pyengcey. 1947. Phyocwun Cosen mal sacen. Seoul: Amun-kak.
¹Yu Changton → LCT
Yun Cengmi [Yoon, Jeong-Me]. 1989. "ECM and multiple subject construction in Korean", HSIKL 3:369-81.
Yutani Yukitoshi. 1978. "Hyentay Hankwuk-e tongsa punlyu". Chōsen gakuhō 87:1-35 (horizontal).

Table of abbreviations

A adjective
abbr, ABBR abbreviation; abbreviated
adj adjective
adj-n adjectival noun
adn adnoun
adv adverb
advers adversative
alt, ALT alternant
AN adjectival noun
ANT antonym
assert assertive
attent attentive
AUTH authoritative (style)
aux auxiliary
bnd, BND bound
C consonant; copula
CM Cosen-e munqpep 1, 2
colloq colloquial
cop copula
count, Count counter
cpd compound
decl declarative
der derived
der adv derived adverb
der n derived noun
dial, DIAL dialect
dimin diminutive
esp especially
fut future
ger gerund
H high (pitch)
HEAVY heavy isotope
hon, HON honorific
IC(s) immediate constituent(s)
indic indicative
intent intentive
insep inseparable
interj interjection
irreg irregular
KBC Korean Basic Course
KEd A Korean-English dictionary
L low (pitch)
LIGHT light isotope
lit, LIT literary
LCT ¹Yu Changton (1964)
LHS ¹Yi Hisung (1961) [Lee, Hi-seung]
LKM ¹Yi Kimun [Lee, Ki-moon]

LR Language Research; low-rise (pitch)
LSN ¹Yi Swungnyeng [Lee, Sung-Nyong]
M Myŏngdo; Myŏngdo's Korean
MK Middle Korean
Mkk Māl kwa kul
mod modifier
n, N noun
N noun; North
N/S North and South
neg, NEG negative
NK North Korea
NKd North Korean dictionary
NKW Nam Kwangwu (1979) [Nam, Gwang U]
num numeral
obs, OBS obsolete
pcl particle
polite
postadnom postadnominal
postn postnoun
postnom postnominal
postsubst postsubstantive
pref prefix
prepcl preparticle
proc processive
prosp prospective
qvi quasi-intransitive verb
R rise, rising (pitch)
retr retrospective
semi-lit semi-literary
sep separable
S South
SK South Korea
SNU Seoul National University
subj subjunctive
subst substantive
suf suffix
SYN synonym
v, V verb
V verb; vowel
var, VAR variant
vc, VC causative verb
vi intransitive verb
vn, VN verbal noun
vni intransitive verbal noun
vnt transitive verbal noun
vp, VP passive verb
vpt transitive passive verb
vt transitive verb

PART 2

GRAMMATICAL LEXICON

GRAMMATICAL LEXICON

a, 1. postmodifier = **ya** (question). SEE **-un ~, -nun ~, -ul ~, -tun ~**.
 2. postsubstantive ("shall I") = **sey**.
a, particle. [**ya** after vowel]
 1. (vocative) hey! o(h)! say! ¶**Pokswun a ili one la** Come here, Pokswun. **Palk.un tal a O** shining moon! **Ak a** Hey baby! HEAVY **iye/ye**. HON [lit] **isiye/siye**.
 NOTE 1: In speech the vocative particle is used only to inferiors (or, occasionally, to equals); superiors are called by name or title.
 NOTE 2: When two or more people are called, each is separately marked as vocative, rather than conjoined before the marking: **Yengswuk a Pokswun a ili one la** Yengswuk and Pokswun, come here.
 2. (exclamatory) SEE **-keyss.ta ya; -kwun a; ? -nya (-n' ya = -ni a); -Geˑnˑiˑ'sto.n a**.
 3. (postsubstantive) SEE **-um a**.
-a < -ˑa, alt of inf (**-e < -ˑe**) after a syllable that contains /o/ or [literary, DIAL; the standard spelling] /a/. **ota (→ oa) → wā, pota → poa → pwā, noph.ta → noph.a, tōpta → towa, nōlta → nol.a; moluta → mōlla, nāmˑta → nam.ᵉ/a, kālta → kal.ᵉ/a, maluta → mallᵉ/a**. Some of the dialects use only **-a**, regardless of the preceding vowel (CF Choy Myengok 1979).
 NOTE: Sometimes **-ˑa** turns up unexpectedly in early texts where we would expect **-ˑe**: ¨**epˑsa** (1445 ¹Yong 111, 1449 Kok 124) = ¨**epˑse** (1447 Sek 9:12b) 'not exist', ¨**eˑta** (1459 Wel 8:80b) = ¨**eˑte** (1449 Kok 88) 'get', **mwuˑla** (1449 Kok 153) = **mwuˑle** (1445 ¹Yong 62) 'inquire', **wuˑza** (1449 Kok 168) = **wuˑze** (1518 Sohak-cho 10:12b) 'laugh', ˑ**tuˑla** (1449 Kok 157) and ˑ**tula** (1459 Wel 7:26a) = ˑ**tuˑle** (1449 Kok 101) 'enter'. Such forms point to **-ˑa** as the basic shape of the infinitive.
-a- 1. → -ˑ**Ga-** (after *l, y, i*) = -ˑ**ka-** = -ˑ**ke-** (effective). 2. = -ˑ**ka-** (effective).
-ˑa 1. → -ˑ**Ga** (after *l, y, i*) = -ˑ**ka** = -ˑ**ke** (effective infinitive). 2. = -ˑ**ka** (effective inf).
ˑ**a** = ˑ[**z**]**a**, particle. SEE -ˑ**key**ˑ**a**.
ˑ**ach,** postmod. the reason that ... . ¶*pwu¨thye y ˑili niloˑsyan ˑa.ch on* (1482 Kum-sam 4:27a) the reason Buddha said this ... .
achi, postnoun. 1. designates persons from the object of their occupation or labor; CF **echi, chi, pachi, kwun**. ¶**cangsa ~** a peddler, a trader. **caycwu ~ = caycwuq kwun** a person of talent. **kwusil ~** [obs] a person in public office. **pyesul ~, pis ~ /pitachi/** a petty official. **sīcang ~** a market merchant. **tōngca ~** a cook. **tongnyang ~** a beggar.
 2. (< ˑ**achi**) = **echi** (worth). ¶*tas mal achi 'na syacya* (1728 Cheng-tay 141; from LCT) I'll buy five pecks worth. CF ¨**cywokwoˑm** *achi*; **elma-chi < elma [a]chi**.
-aci, suffix (diminutive; vulgarizer). CF **-aki, -angi, -langi**. [? < **-aki**]
 1. ¶**pokaci = pok** blowfish. **mokaci = mok** neck. **myek/myekaci** throat. **pomulaci = pomul** lint, scraps, bits. **kkolaci = kkolakseni = kkol** appearance, shape.
 2. ¶**pakaci** gourd dipper < **pak** gourd; spelled *pak.aci* in Gale 1894:126. **sōkaci** nature, disposition < **sōk** the insides.
 3. ¶**kangaci** pup(py) < **kāy** dog. **songaci <** **so** ox. **mangaci** colt < **mal** horse.
-ˑ**a ciˑla,** infinitive (or effective infinitive) + aux indic assertive. wants to do. ¶*taˑsos cwulˑki ˑlul ˑsaˑa ciˑla* (1459 Wel 1:10b) I want to buy five blossoms.
-ˑ**a ˑci-ngi** ¨**ta,** infinitive (or effective inf) + aux polite + copula indic assertive. wants to do. ¶¨**mal tuˑle ilozoˑWa ˑci-ngi** ¨**ta** (1447 Sek 6: 22b) I want to create them [= the monasteries] according to what I hear him say.
-ˑ**a ˑcye,** infinitive (or effective inf) + aux inf. ¶*na yˑpwoa ˑcye ˑhonoˑta solˑWaˑssye* (1447 Sek 6:14b) tell him that I would like to see him. CF -ˑ**kwo ˑcye**.
-ah.ta, bnd adj -(H)- (inf **-ay**); LIGHT ↔ **-eh.ta**. gives the impression of being, looks/feels (to be). [abbr < **-a** inf + **hata**]
 1. attaches to adjective, with irregularities. ¶**hā.yah.ta** is (pure/snow) white, is quite pale. **(k)kāmah.ta** is jet-black. **mālkah.ta** is clear, clean. **(p)palkah.ta** is red, crimson. **phalah.ta** is blue/green. **(p)pō.yah.ta** is a milky white; is pearly, misty. **say-phalah.ta** is deep blue. **say-ppalkah.ta** is a vivid red; is brazen. **say(s)-nolah.ta** is a vivid yellow. **(t)tongkulah.ta** is round, circular.
 2. attaches to an adverb, an adjectival noun, or a mimetic. ¶**(s)sanulah.ta** is chilly.
ai, adverb [DIAL] = **ani** not. 1. [Hamkyeng] (pronounced [ãi] with nasality). 2. SEE **a(y)i**.

ak, n = aki (baby etc.) in compounds and with the vocative particle. ¶Ak a! Hey baby!
ak, postmod. (one of two alternating states): SEE -ul ~. The shape is (-l) lak when the prosp modifier is from an -L- stem; colloquially, from any vowel stem. ¶Tul lak nal lak [colloquial] = tul lak nal ak entering and exiting.
-ˊa k, inf + emphatic particle. ¶ ˊhotaˊka PWUN-ˊPYELQ ˊSYENG ˊi tuthuˊl ul yeˊhuyˊya k "THYEY ¨epˊswolqˊt inˊt ay n'ˊi ˊnon alˊph oy s tuthuˊl ey s PWUN-ˊPYELQ ˊhoˊnwon kuliˊmey s ˊiˊl i.n i ˊ'la (1462 ¹Nung 1:90b) if the characteristic of differentiation is removed from the dust so that it has no form this is a matter of the image that one distinguishes in the dust ahead. SEE maˊla k.
-ak, suf (dimin), LIGHT ↔ -ek; CF -(c)cumak, -aki, -aci, -angi, -langi. ¶i cumak < i cum lately. mul(u)phak < muluph knee. naylimak (kil) downhill (road) < naylim (vi substantive) descending. ttumak hata are few and far between < ttum gap, interval < subst of ttuta (adj) is separated; CF ttūm (= ttuum) hata is infrequent. yᵉathumak hata < yᵉathum hata is a bit shallow / light(-hued) < yᵉathum (adj subst) being shallow. yo cumak < yo cum lately, of late. (k)komcilak / (k)kwumcilek < (k)komcil / (k)kwumcil sluggish, feeble. pasak with a crunch / rustle < pās.ta = paswuta breaks. (k)komulak / (k)kumulek < (k)komul / (k)kumul moving sluggishly. (k)kamak (adn) black, dark < (k)kām.ta is black.
-a kaciko SEE -e kaciko
? -a kacwuko [N Kyengsang DIAL] = -a se, -e se, inf + pcl. SEE Choy Myengok 1979.
-aki, suffix (? < -ak.i cpd suffix); LIGHT ↔ -eki. ¶kancilaki an irritating person < kancil tickling. ōla(y)ki bits of thread, cloth, or paper < ōl strand, ply, warp. ssalaki broken bits of rice < ssal rice. VAR -ayki. CF -ak, -aci, -angi, -langi, -ali; -(u)laki, -(u)leki.
-a kkaci SEE -e kkaci
-akseni, suf (vulgarizes nouns). ¶kkolakseni < kkol (appearance etc.). CF -ak, -eni, -ttakseni.
-akw(un)i, suf (vulgarizes nouns). ¶sathakw(un)i crotch < sath. CF kkamakwi crow ? < kka-kka caw-caw (sound), ? < kkām- black; thum-pakw(un)i; -ekw(un)i; akwu, akw(ul)i, ekwu]
al, 1. n. egg; bead, small round object; grain (nāt ~), berry; sore knot in muscle. CF al-mayngi kernel, substance.

2. counter. (small round objects)
3. adn. small and round. ¶ ~ hangali a small jar. alq yak a pill.
4. bare, naked, stripped (down to essentials), out-and-out, bald; essential, important, core; net; real, true-to-life, sure-enough; down-to-earth; thorough, complete, whole. ¶ ~ cwul bare wire. ~ kkakcengi mean boy; miser. ~ kok hulled or grit-free (pure) grain. ~ pam cracked / shelled chestnut; ripe-fallen (= alam < al [p]am). ~ panul needle without thread. ~ pul unprotected live charcoal. ~ puphi net volume (bulk). ~ ttang [rare?] unsheltered or naked land. ~ (-q) sēm an uninhabited island. ~-q sok core; substance; secret information. ~-q sim sympathy; hidden strength. ~ (-q) kwungtwungi bare buttocks/bottom. CF alccam essence, alcca best thing.
-al, suffix (< 'egg'); LIGHT ↔ -el (diminutive). iphal(i) = iph leaf. CF -ali; -ak, -aki; al (counter), nwun-al eyeball.
'al(q) = [h]al(q). CF 'l(q) = [ha]l(q).
āl(q) < ¨al(q) < *alˊ[o]l(q), prosp mod < ālta < ¨a[l]ˊta. ¶¨alq SSI-ˊCYELQ ˊi (1447 Sek 9:2a) when one knows. CF ¨all ···; aˊlwol(q).
-ˊal(q), effective prosp mod. ¶ ˊNGEP-¨KWA ˊSOYK ¨ep.swuˊm ul aˊlalqˊt ilwoˊta (1459 Wel 1:36b) it is to know that there is no form (rūpa) to the fruit (phala) of karma. mwoˊlwomay [PWONG-ˊHWA] ˊay s wuytwu hoˊn i lol aˊlalˊt ilwoˊta (1481 Twusi 15:42b) it is by all means to recognize those who lead in moral reform by example.
-ˊaˊla, effective subj attentive (command); alt of -ˊeˊla = -ˊkeˊla. ¶¨ta ZYE-LOY S QWUY-ˊLUK ˊilwonˊkwoˊt ol aˊlala (1447 Sek 9:28a) know that all are parts of the tathāgata's authority.
-a la, infinitive + particle. SEE -e la.
-a 'la, inf + abbr < ila (cop). SEE -e 'la. CF - aˊyˊla.
-a 'la to SEE -e 'la to
alh.i, postnoun (der n < alh.ta). ache, sickness. ¶kasum ~ a pain in the chest, chest trouble. nwun ~ an eye ailment, eye trouble. pay ~ a stomachache. i ~ a toothache. CF pyēng.
-ali, suffix (< -al.i, cpd suf); LIGHT ↔ -eli (dimin). ¶ccokali odd ends (scraps) of paper or cloth. hangali jar < hang. iphali = iph leaf. kyeng-ali "a shifty Seoulite". songali/swungeli = songi / swungi cluster. tongali part; gang,

A Reference Grammar of Korean

group. ? **ttoali** (ttwāli) a head-pad (when carrying things on the head). CF **-aki, -ak**.
-aˑl i ··· , effective prosp mod + postmod ('fact').
 ~ ˑGa. ¶[ˑSO-ˑCCWA] y [ˑˑKAM] hi [HWEN-ˑSWO] ˑhwo.m ol maˑla.l i ˑGa (1481 Twusi 8:25b) will the four thrones dare put an end to the uproar?
 ~ '-ngi s ˑka. ¶ku ˑnal s CANG-NGEM ˑul ˑˑta solˑWaˑl i '-ngi s ˑka (1449 Kok 127) am I to report all that day's majesty?
 ~ ˑye. ¶NUNG ˑhi ˑNGWOK ˑkot hon mozoˑm ay s myeˑnuli ˑlol ˑpwoa.l i ˑye (1475 Nay se:8a) will I be able to find a girl [for my son] with a heart like a jewel?
ˑˑall ··· (+ ˑˑi, ˑye postmod) < alˑ[o]l(q), prosp mod < ˑˑa[l]ˑta (knows).
ˑˑall i ··· = ˑˑal[o]l i ··· < *aˑlo-l ˑi ··· , prosp mod < ˑˑa[l]ˑta (knows) + postmod.
 ~ 'Geˑm ye (1482 Kum-sam 5:37b).
 ~ 'Geˑn i ˑston (1462 ¹Nung 2:114b).
 ~ ˑGwo (1449 Kok 52, 1481 Twusi 15:37b, 15:47b).
 ~ ˑˑla (1462 ¹Nung 7:26a).
 ~ 'lasˑta (?1468- Mong 32ab).
 ~ 'leˑn i (1518 Sohak-cho 8:41a).
 ~ ˑˑlwoˑswo-ngi ˑˑta (1459 Wel 21:14a).
 ~ ˑˑlwoswoˑn ye (?1517- Pak 1:14b, 1586 Sohak 4:29b).
 ~ 'lwoˑta (1481 Twusi 7:13b, ?1517- Pak 1:14b).
 ~ ˑn i (1464 Kumkang se:6b, 1465 Wen 2:3:1:110a).
 ~ ye (?1517- Pak 1:14b).
ˑˑalˑl ye = ˑˑal[o]ˑl ye < *aˑlo-l ˑye, prosp mod ('to know') + postmod. ˑˑalˑl ye ˑˑmwot hoˑl ye (1463 Pep 3:86a) can you tell me (or not)?
ālm < ˑˑalm < alˑ[o]m, substantive < **ālta** < ˑˑa[l]ˑta (knows). ¶ˑˑalˑm ye (1482 Kum-sam 2:3a, 5:14a) knows and ... . CF **aˑlwom**.
ālta < ˑˑa[l]ˑta, vt -L-. (The negative is often replaced by **moluta**; see §11.7.3.)
 1. knows, has knowledge of; finds out, gets knowledge of. ····ulq / -un / -nun / -tun + cwul (lo) **ālta** thinks (supposes, assumes, expects, believes) that ...; ····un / -nun / -tun + cwul (ul) **ālta** = mod + kes ul ~ knows (recognizes, acknowledges) that ..., -ulq cwul (ul) **ālta** knows how to do (also: knows that it or one will be / do).

 2. understands, comprehends, appreciates, knows; realizes, recognizes, is convinced of. ¶**Ku hyengphyen ul cal ālko iss.ess.ta** I well understood his situation.
 3. assents, complies. ¶**Nēy, al.ess.e(y) yo** = **Nēy, ālkeyss.e(y) yo** Yes, I will (see to the situation or the request that you mention).
 4. is acquainted with, knows. ¶**Ku cen puthe ku i lul ālko iss.ta** I have known him a long time.
 5. notices (perceives, finds) that ··· .
 6. infers (surmises, tells, guesses) that ··· .
 7. is aware / conscious of, is sensitive to, feels (shame, indebtedness).
 8. has experience of (exposure to), knows.
 9. is concerned with, has to do with. ¶**Ne uy ālq pa ka ani 'ta** It is no concern of yours.
 10. (X lul Y ulo ~) considers (X to be Y), regards, takes. ¶**han sālam ul talun sālam ulo cal-mos** ~ mistakes one person for another. **Na lul mues ulo al.ᵉ/a** What do you take me for?
aˑlwol(q), modulated prosp modifier < ˑˑa[l]ˑta (knows). ¶**aˑlwo.l i ˑˑla** (?1468- Mong 13a). **aˑlwolq ˑt ilwoˑta** (1462 ¹Nung 1:67a). **aˑlwolq ˑt i.n i ˑˑla** (1447 Sek 19:10b). **aˑlwol ˑtt iˑn i '-ngi ˑˑta** (1463 Pep 7:175a). **aˑlwolq ˑtoy ˑˑepˑse-ngi ˑˑta** (1459 Wel 21:21b).
aˑlwom, modulated subst < ˑˑa[l]ˑta (knows). **aˑlwoˑm i** (1462 ¹Nung 1:55a; ?1468- Mong 39a). **aˑlwoˑm ol** (1463 Pep 4:148b; ?1468- Mong 5a, 30b).
aˑlwon, modulated modifier < ˑˑa[l]ˑta (knows). ¶**aˑlwon ˑˑyang hoˑkwo** (?1517- Pak 1:25a) pretend to know and ... . **woˑnol za aˑlwoˑn i** (1463 Pep 4:36a) that I just today found out ... .
-aˑl ye, effective prosp modifier + postmod (= intentive). ¶ˑˑcams.kan ˑina mozom nwoˑha ˑphyeaˑl ye ˑmwom ˑtwo ˑwohiˑlye isˑti aˑni kheˑn i (1475 Nay 2:1:2b) for a little while I have wanted to set forth [what I have in] my heart and my body itself has been more or less absent.
am < ˑamh, adn, bnd n.
 1. female. [Often reflects the basic shape **amh**.] ¶ ~ **khes** < **amh kes** a female, a she-animal. ~ **khāy** < **amh kāy** a bitch (she-dog). ~ **kho.yangi / khwāyngi** < **amh ko.yangi / -kwāyngi** a female cat. ~ **khom** < **amh kōm** a female bear. ~ **thalk** < **amh talk** a hen.

~ thot / thwāyci < amh tot / twāyci a sow.
~ phitwulki < amh pitwulki a she-dove. ~
phēm < amh pēm a tigress. ~ phyengali <
amh pyengali a hen-chick. ~ khweng < amh
[k]kweng a pheasant hen.
2. concave, internal. ¶ ~ chicil internal
hemorrhoids. ~ khiwa < amh kiwa) concave
tile. ~ thōlccekwi < amh tōlccekwi female
hinge, gudgeon. ~ tanchwu (NOT /th/!)
buttonhole or snap-fastener. ANT swu [swuh].
CF an, an^{h}ay; eme.
ām, interj (abbr < āmulye 'myen) of course,
certainly, sure. ¶Ām kuleh.ci Yes, of course.
Definitely.
'am = [h]am. CF 'm = [ha]m.
ā'm = ālm, substantive < ālta. knowledge.
-am / -em (der substantive) < -˙^{e}/am (effective
substantive). SEE -um (cik hata).
ama < (*) ¨a˙ma (SEE ¨ama˙two, ¨a˙ma-
khe˙na), adverb. perhaps; likely.
-a mace SEE -e mace
¨a˙ma-khe˙na, bnd adverb + abbr < ˙hoke˙na.
anyhow, in any case.
-a man SEE -e man
ama to < ¨ama˙two, adverb + pcl. perhaps
indeed, like as not.
-amchi, suffix (derives adv from adj-n, adv).
¶ilccikamchi [< ilccik-amchi] a bit earlier.
nucikamchi [< nucik-amchi] rather late;
CF nucikeni < nucik [h]eni (= hani) SAME.
melccikamchi [< melccik-amchi] [DIAL] a bit
far(ther). [? < ham haci]
-am cik < -˙am ˙cik (effective substantive +
postsubst adj-n insep) SEE -um cik.
ameyng, adverb [Ceycwu DIAL (Seng ^{1}Nakswu
1984:39)] = āmuli
amh SEE am
-ami, suffix; LIGHT ↔ -emi; VAR -aymi.
1. one, thing, person. ¶olkami a noose, a
snare; a trap, a trick (< olk.ta lays a snare).
omulami a toothless old man / woman (<
omul / wumul mumbling). ? pikaymi [DIAL] =
puthi (wooden back support for loom worker)
< ?. tongkulami a circle (< tongkulta is
round).
2. (forms names of creatures); CF -api.
kwittwulami a cricket (< kwittwul chirping).
olppaymi an owl (< ?). philami a dace (< ?).
3. -am 'i = -am hi. melccikam 'i [DIAL] =
melccik 'i rather far. CF melccik-amchi.

ām' māl, abbr < āmu māl, adn + n. any word.
ām' man = āmuli however much: ~ hay to
whatever one may do, any way you look at it;
~ pwā to whatever one may see, however
much one may look; ~ mānh.^{e}/a to at the very
most.
¨amo = ¨amwo > āmo = āmu
¨amo˙lan, mod < ¨a˙mola˙tha (= ¨a˙mwolah˙ta).
any / what sort of.
¨a˙mola˙tha (= ¨a˙molah˙ta, abbr < *¨amo˙la
˚ho˙ta), adj -(H)-. is any / what sort of.
¨a˙mola˙thwo (= ¨a˙molah-˙two). no matter
what, anyway.
¨a˙moli, ¨amo˙lyey (1447 Sek 6:46a), adv. how
(= etteh.key), in some / any way.
¨a˙molyey ˙'na (1447 Sek 6:13b, 24:28a), adv +
pcl. anyhow, anyway.
amoli SEE amwoli
āmu < ¨amwo (noun, adnoun, postnoun).
1. n. any person, anybody; so-and-so. ¶ ~
kay SAME (less polite). ~ ~ various people.
Āmu(q) soli to an tul.ul they 'ni ku īl ul hay
to cōh.ta You are unlikely to get scolded by
anybody, so you can go ahead do it. SYN mō.
CF nwukwu ('tun ci, 'na).
2. postnoun. (after family name) so-and-so,
something-or-other. ¶Kim ~ (kay) 'la 'nun
sālam a man called Something-or-other Kim.
3. adn. any, "any old"; what(···). ¶ ~ kes (to)
anything (at all). ~ māl (abbr < ām' māl)
any word. ~ īl any incident. ~ sālam (to)
anybody (at all). ~ tey ('na, to) any place (at
all). ~ ttay (wā to) any time (you come).
CF musun (··· ina, itun ci), ām' man.
āmu-ccolok, adv. by all means, if at all possible.
CF -tolok. [? < āmu ecci ha-tolok]
āmu'h.ci (to) = āmuleh.ci (to) anyway.
āmu'h.kena = āmuleh.kena
āmu'h.tun (ci) = āmuleh.tun (ci)
āmu 'la to anybody at all. ¶Āmu 'la to one la
Somebody — anybody, come here!
āmulay, 1. inf < āmuleh.ta. ¶ ~ to anyhow,
anyway, (not) in any way.
2. abbr < āmuli hay to say what you will,
anyway.
āmule, adj-n. ~ hata = āmuleh.ta is any way,
is any-which-way. CF ile, kule, cele, ette.
āmuleh.ci, suspective < āmuleh.ta.
~ to anyway. ABBR āmu'h.ci.
āmuleh.kena, tent advers < āmuleh.ta. any

way at all; as one pleases.

āmuleh.key, adverbative < **āmuleh.ta**. in any way.

~ **'na** (in) any which way, carelessly, in a slovenly manner: ~ **īl hata** does a slapdash job; ~ **kul ul ssuta** writes carelessly. CF **etteh.key 'na**; SEE **'na**.

~ **to** any (which) way at all, quite carelessly.

āmuleh.ta, adj-n -(H)- (inf **āmulay**), abbr < **āmule hata**. is any way.

āmuleh.tun (ci), retr modifier (+ postmodifier). anyhow, in any event, one way or another.

āmulemyen (conditional < **āmuleh.ta**) = **āmulye 'myen**, abbr < **āmulye hamyen**. (Examples: KEd, M 3:3:117.)

1. (not) in any way, in any case, by any means, under any circumstances.

2. ~ **etteh.ni** (or **etten ya**) (no matter) whatever it may be, whatever one says.

āmulen, mod < **āmuleh.ta**. any (such). ~ **tul** however it might be.

āmuli, adv. however much, even though; surely (not). ¶ ~ **kath.i** SAME. ~ **hay to** however much one may do. ~ **tōn i iss.e to** however much money one may have. **Āmuli nuc.e to tases si kkaci nun cip ey tol.a ka ya hanta** I have got to be home by five o'clock at the latest. **Wuli nun āmuli elyewunq īl ey se 'la to twulyewe haci anh.nunta** We are not afraid in any situation, however difficult it may be for us. **Āmuli puluna tāytap hanun sālam un ēps.ess.ta** However hard I shouted there was no one who answered. CF **ce(y)-, i-, ku-, nay-, ney-amuli**.

āmuli 'na, adv + cop advers. [mostly female] surely, ever (so much). ¶ **Āmuli 'na "KAL"-ki chwulak ulo ō-payk myeng īsang i cwuk.ess.ta 'y** Goodness gracious, to think that over five hundred people died in the crash of the KAL plane! SEE **una / na** (NOTE).

āmulye 'm(yen), abbr < **āmuli halye hamyen**. of course; surely (not). CF **āmulemyen**.

āmulye 'na, abbr < **āmuli halye hana**. any way you like.

āmulye 'ni, abbr < **āmu halye hani**. whatever one may think / say, anyway, even so; surely [not]. ¶ **Āmulye 'ni kulelq swu ka iss.na** Even so, how can it be that way?! **Āmulye 'ni ku ay ka kulen cīs ul hayss.ulla kwu** Surely he wouldn't have done such a thing?!

The following KEd examples are rejected, at least for standard speech: (?*)**Hako siph.ketun āmulye 'ni halyem** If you want it done, I'll go ahead and do it. (?*)**Āmulye 'ni ku ya kuleh.ci** Anyway, that's the way things are. Also: (?*)**Āmulye 'ni kuleh.ci anh.ci** Surely it can't be that way.

¨**amwo (···)**, 1. = **āmu (···)** any; what(···).

2. = **e'nu** [not know] which / what. ¶ ¨**amwo ke'kuy 'two ce 'y 'mwu'l ey wuytwu hon ke's ul** NGWANG **i'la 'ho'no.n i ''la** (1459 Wel 1:23b) whoever is superior in his group is called king. ¨**a'mwo 'man 'two ¨mwot ''ti a'ni ho'kwo ce 'lol ¨cye'ku'na cwu'm ye n' 'kwot ho'l i ''la** (?1517- Pak 1:43a) without its being very much if you give him a little he will do it right away. ¨**a'mwo s ¨i'l iGe'na** (1447 Sek 13:41a) whatever event it may be. ¨**amwo 'to 'la 'sye won 'twong mwo'lo'tesi'n i** (1459 Wel 2:25b) she didn't know just what place it had come from (**'la** = [i]la). ¨**amwo toy 'sye won 't i 'mwollwo.l i** ([1447→]1562 Sek 3:18a) I don't know where they have come from. ¨**amwo 'toy 'two ma'kon 'toy ¨ep'si** (1459 Wel se:8ab) with no hindrance at all anywhere. **na 'y 'e'mi** ¨**amwo 'toy 'na 'ys.non 't i ¨mwol'lay-ngi ''ta** (1459 Wel 21:53a) I do not know what place my mother has been reborn into. ¨**a'mwo 'yGe'na 'wa ··· 'twola 'ho.ya 'two** (1459 Wel 1:13a) whoever might come and ask you to give him ··· ; CF ¨**amwo 'y'na** (1447 Sek 9:17a, 21a).

¨**amwo 'y'Gwo** SEE **'y'Gwo**

¨**amwo 'y'na** SEE **'y'na**

amwoli (1894 Gale 64, 69) = **āmuli**

an, adv (abbr) = **ani** (not). CF **mōs**. Do not confuse with **anh.ta** = **an(i) hata**, **anh.nunta** = **an(i) hanta**. This shortening of **ani** before a verb is not attested before the late 1800s: **katen ci an katen ci nay alwon thyey ani honta** (1887 Scott 204) I don't care whether he goes or not. 1874 Putsillo has **ani** but lacks **an**.

NOTE: For 'doesn't begin' you can say either **sīcak an hanta** or **an sīcak hanta**, but it is uncommon to find **an** before other verbal nouns. For 'doesn't try doing it' you can say either **hay an ponta** or (better) **an hay ponta**. For 'doesn't come to an end' you may hear either **an kkuth nanta** or **kkuth an nanta**. Similar remarks apply to **mōs**.

'an = [h]an. CF **'n** = [ha]n.

ān < ¨an < *a·[lo]n, mod < ālta < ¨a[l]·ta (knows). ¶ *CCANG kozom ¨an SSIN-¨HHA 'y·n i (1459 Wel 1:27a; epithematic identification) the courtier knew the content of the vaults. ¨an cyen·cho ·lwo (1462 ¹Nung 9:13a) because one knew. CF a·lwon.

-an [Ceycwu DIAL (Seng ¹Nakswu 1984:79-80)] = -a (se) infinitive, = -ko gerund. [< -·a n'] ·an, 1. → -·Gan (after l, y, i) = -·kan (var) = -·ken (effective mod).

2. = -·kan (var) = -·ken (effective mod).

-a n', abbr < -a nun

-a 'na SEE -e 'na

aney yo = anyey yo = ani 'ey yo it is not [POLITE style].

-ang, suffix; LIGHT ↔ -eng.

1. dimin. ¶ kolang < kōl furrow; (?) hollow; (?) valley. tolang < tol ditch. matang (< obsolete mat) a threshing-ground; a place; a situation, case. pang strap < pa rope: "kēl-ppang" = kēlq pang, "meyl-ppang" = mēylq pang, and "cil-ppang" = cilq pang.

2. makes noun from adj. ¶ nolang yellow < noluta is yellow. phalang blue < *phaluta, SEE phalah.ta is blue. (p)palkang red < *(p)palk.ta, SEE (p)palkah.ta is red.

3. makes adverb from adverb, mimetic. kantul(ang) / kentul(eng) (XX, XXh = Xk) wobbling, swaying. kosilang / kwusileng (XX, XXh = Xk) grumbling, nagging. CF ttokkang ttokkang clearly < ttok-ttok (-kk- = -qk- ?).

-ang [Ceycwu DIAL (Seng ¹Nakswu 1984:79-80)] = -a (se) infinitive, = -ko gerund

angi = ai (pronounced [ãi] with nasality), adv [Hamkyeng DIAL] = ani not.

-angi, suffix; LIGHT ↔ -engi.

1. diminutive. ¶ kacangi a branch < kaci. kwāyngi < ko.yangi < koy-angi cat (= obsolete koy). kkolangi < kkol-angi < kkoli tail.

2. makes n from adj, v. ¶ ciphangi a walking stick < ciph- lean on. But the constituency differs in: (k)kopulang-i a bent / crooked one, napulang-i bits (scraps, pieces), nolang-i a "Yellow" = miser, ppalkang-i a red one, a "Red" = Communist. Also this is probably in ccokulang-i 'one that is crushed / withered' < ccokulang < *ccokul- (CF ccokula ci- / ttuli-, ccokuli-).

CF -aki, -aci; -kayngi, -tayngi, -layngi, -mayngi, -payngi, -cayngi.

-·a-ngi ·'ta, effective polite + cop indic assert. ¶ nek·s i e·nu ·CHYWU ·yey kan ·twong ¨mwol·la-ngi ·'ta (1459 Wel 21:27a) I do not know to which hell her spirit went. ·TTAY-NGWANG ·ha na ·two ZYE-LOY ¨kyesin ·toy ·lol mwo·lozo·Wa-ngi ·'ta (1459 Wel 21:192a) oh mighty king, I do not myself know where the tathāgata is! VAR -·ay-ngi ·'ta.

anh.i, derived adverb < anh.ta (aux adj); SYN anh.key. so (such) that it is not. ¶ cēkci anh.i mek.ess.ta ate quite a lot. cōh.ci anh.i yekita takes it poorly. mōs-'ci anh.i cal hanta does as well as (no less well than) the others. CF ani.

anh.ko, 1. aux ger. not being / doing; without (or: instead of) being / doing. SEE -ci anh.ko.

2. = haci anh.ko. ¶ Āmu māl to anh.ko kuce kass.ta He went away without saying a word. (k)kom(c)cak anh.ko se iss.ta stands motionless.

anh.ta, auxiliary; abbr < an hata < ani hata; (inf anh.e or anh.a).

1. aux adj. is not. ¶ Cip i khuci anh.ta The house is not large.

2. aux v. does not. ¶ Ku sālam i moca lul ssuci anh.nunta He does not wear a hat.

ani < a·ni, negative. DIAL ai, a(y)i.

1. precopular n. (is) not. ¶ I kes i nay kes i ani 'ta This is not mine. NOTE: There is no other negative structure for the copula. The MK copula modifier ·in is usually (but not always) dropped before the postmodifiers ·ka and ·kwo (question), and that accounts for examples like SYEN-SOYNG ·on ·PPYENG a·ni ka (1482 Nam 1:30b) 'aren't you ill?' and the examples with velar lenition (SEE a·ni ·Ga, a·ni ·Gwo). On the optional omission of the nominative particle marking the complement, see pp. 549-50.

2. adverb. not. ABBR an. CF mōs; ēps.ta, moluta. ¶ ~ kata (mekta) does not go (eat). Ani ttayn kwulttwuk ey yenki nalq ka ¨Does smoke rise from a chimney where a fire has not been lit?¨ = Where there is smoke, there is fire. Sālam toyko ani toynun kes un ney nolyek ey tallyess.ta It depends upon your own endeavor whether you become a success or a failure. ne 'y susu·ng uy ¨TTYEY-¨CO y ¨es·tyey a·ni ·wono·n ywo (1447 Sek 6:29b) how come the disciple of your master is not coming?

˙NGWOY-῾῾TTWOW 'yn ˙t ol a˙ni cwocco˙Wo˙l i (1449 Kok 99) will not follow any false doctrines. CF **anh.i**. DIAL **a(ng)i**.

NOTE 1: Makes the short negative for verb and adjective stems. Some speakers find this awkward for polysyllabic adjectives, preferring **mikkulepci anh.ta** to **an mikkulepta** 'is not slippery', but other speakers have no such reservations and freely say **an napputa** (= **nappuci anh.ta**) 'is not bad', as well as the generally accepted **an cōh.ta** (= **cōh.ci anh.ta**) 'is not good'. Apparently some speakers avoid the short negative for all adjectives (M 1:1:215 says "normally used only with action verbs"). Notice that the adverb **mōs** can occur only before verb stems; the strong negative of adjectives must be the long form: **cōh.ci mōs hata** 'can't possibly be good, isn't good at all' (not *****mōs cōh.ta**).

NOTE 2: Usually precedes the stem directly. In older texts there are exceptional cases with an adverb or even a longer phrase between: CYE-THYEN ˙ul a˙ni ῾῾ta nilul ῾῾spwun ˙tyeng (1447 Sek 13:7a) 'I will not say [the names of] all the heavens, but ... '; hon NGUY-SIM ˙on pwu˙῾῾thye y a˙ni ta˙si ˙nasin˙ka ho˙kwo ... (1447 Sek 24:3b) 'one doubt: asking whether Buddha has not been born again and ... '; pan˙toki ingey is.no˙n i a˙ni muten ˙hi ne˙kye ˙SSO-˙SYANG ˙ol ka˙poyya˙i ne˙kino˙n ye (1465 Wen 3:2:2:42ab) 'are those who are here necessarily not treating [things] indifferently and treating affairs (phenomena) lightly?' Yes-or-no copula sentences can be conjoined with the particle ˙kwa and ellipted copula: ˙HHAP ˙kwa ˙HHAP a˙ni ˙Gwa s ῾῾LI ῾῾ta nilo˙syan ˙ptut tuthul s ˙HHWAN-˙SYANG ˙i.n i (1462 [1]Nung 2:107a) 'the meaning of all he has said about the principle of what is meet and what is not meet is [that it is] the illusion of [floating] dust'; CYE-˙PEP ῾῾NGWUW-MWU ˙[G]wa ˙i ˙SSILQ i˙m ye a˙ni ˙Gwa ˙i SOYNG i˙m ye SOYNG a˙ni ˙lol kol˙hoyno[˙]n i (1463 Pep 5:30a) 'discriminates the existence (or lack) of the laws and [that] this is real or not real and [that] this is life or not life' — The object is a direct nominalization of the conjoining of the Chinese noun with the copula sentences; and the structure would be clearer with another ˙Gwa before the accusative marker at the end.

NOTE 3: Can precede particles ˙Gwos, ˙non, ˙two, but there are no examples of *a˙ni ˙za.

3. interj. 3a. no; nope; huh-uh. ¶**Phyēnci lul ssess.ni?** – **Ani, nācwung ey ssul they 'ta** Have you written the letter? – No, I am going to write it later. **Ani yo** No. (I don't think so.) **Ku kes un han salam i wumcik ilq swu ēps.ta; ani, yelq salam ila to wumcik ilq swu ēps.ta** One man could not move it – nor ten.

3b. [sometimes **āni** with expressive length] what, why, dear me, good heavens (shows surprise, doubt, disbelief, etc.). ¶**Ani i key wēynq īl in ya** Why, what happened?

˙a˙n i, mod < ῾῾a[l]˙ta + postmod. SEE ~ 'la.

-˙a˙n i = -˙[G]a˙n i = -˙ka˙n i, effective mod + postmodifier. ¶[˙TTAY-CYEN] hon ῾῾na˙th ay [˙TTWOLQ-˙KWELQ] ˙i ˙nwol˙lazo˙Wa˙n i (1445 [1]Yong 47) with a single shot of his mighty arrow the Turks took fright. ῾῾ne y ho˙ma mas-˙nazo˙Wa˙n i CCYEN-SOYNG ῾῾CCWOY-˙NGEP ˙ul e˙lwu pe˙su.l i ˙'la ˙hosil ˙ss oy (1459 Wel 2:62b) you have already faced it; because he says you are to rid yourself well of the sinful deeds of an earlier life ... . ῾῾nyey [˙LWOK-SAN] ˙oy [˙LWAN] hol kwo[˙]t ol ῾῾mwolla˙n i wo˙nol selu ῾῾pwol˙cwu.l ol ῾῾es.ti ῾῾all i ˙Gwo ho˙n i (1481 Twusi 15:47b) (?) in the old days they did not know rebellion by the mountain feof-doms; today we wonder how to discover a way to look at each other.

ani cham, cpd interj. oh, uh; that reminds me; I just thought of something.

ani 'ci, neg cop suspective.

~ **yo.** ¶**Ku ⁿyeca uy tānqcem ul molunun pa ka ani 'ci yo** I am not blind to her faults.

ani 'e = ani ye (neg cop inf)

ani 'ess··· = ani yess··· (neg cop past)

ani 'ey yo, (precopular n + cop inf + pcl =) neg cop polite. it is not.

a˙ni˙Ga = a˙ni ka (= a˙ni 'n˙ka) is it not? ¶˙i˙SYWELQ-˙PEP ka, ˙i˙SYWELQ-˙PEP a˙ni˙Ga (1482 Kum-sam 4:37b) is this preaching the law or isn't this preaching the law? a˙ni˙i ῾῾HOYNG-˙CYA [< *˙῾HHOYNG-῾῾CYA] a˙ni Ga (1496 [1]Yuk 1:41-2) no, is it not this pilgrim?

a˙ni˙Ge˙n i˙'ston = a˙ni˙'[y]Ge˙n i˙'ston, neg cop effective mod + postmod + pcl. ¶˙῾῾a˙ti ῾῾mwot ho˙m ye n' ˙SIK ˙i a˙ni˙'Ge˙n i˙'ston (1462 [1]Nung 3:47b) if you do not recognize it [the scent] you just must lack awareness!

aʹni ʹGeʹn i ʹsto.n a (+ exclamatory pcl). ¶ʹna y ˈstwo ˙say tatay hwuyhwuy aˈni ʹGeˈn i ʹsto.n a (?1517- Pak 1:73a) I am not a crude Tatar Muslim, after all!

aˈni ˙ˈGen maˈlon = aˈni ʹ[y]ˈGen maˈlon, neg copula effective modifier + postmodifier. ¶KON ˙oy ˙˙nin keˈs i aˈni ˙ˈGen maˈlon (1462 ¹Nung 2:81b) it is not that a root arose but ... . THYEN ˙kwa ˙NGWOK ˙kwa ˙˙spwun aˈni ˙ˈGen maˈlon (1465 Wen 2:1:2:43b) it is not just heaven and hell, but ... .

aˈni ʹGeˈnul ˙za = aˈni ʹ[y]ˈGeˈnul ˙za, neg cop lit concessive + pcl. ¶penˈtuˈki ˙PEP-HHWA y aˈni ʹGeˈnul ˙za ... (1462 ¹Nung 1:17a) though they cannot be the Lotus sūtra exactly, ...

aˈni ˙ˈGey = aˈni ʹ[y]ˈGey, neg cop adverbative. ¶ ˙˙twulˈh i aˈni ˙ˈGey holˈss i (1462 ¹Nung 8:34a) to make it so that they are not two.

?aˈni ˙Gwo = aˈni ˈn ˙kwo. ¶? eˈtuy s ˙˙saloˈm i ˙ani ˙Gwo (1481 Twusi 8:14b; displaced accent dot) is there no place I belong?

?*aˈni ˙ˈGwo = *aˈni ʹ[y]ˈGwo, neg cop ger. Where we expect this form we find instead aˈni ˙ˈm ye or aˈni ˙ˈla.

aˈni ˙Gwos, adverb + pcl. precisely / just if not. ¶aˈni ˙Gwos ˙cwusiˈm ye nˈ ˙hi.m uˈlwo eˈlwu ˙hwoˈl i ˙ˈta (1447 Sek 23:55b) if you just won't give him to us we may use force. aˈni ˙Gwos mekuˈm ye nˈ ne ˈy meˈli lol peˈhywo.l i ˙ˈla (1459 Wel 10:25ab) if you do NOT eat it I will cut your head off.

ani hata₁ < aˈni ˚haˈta, adverb + v / adj = neg v / adj. ABBR an hata, anh.ta; CF mōs hata.

1. does not do.

2. aux (follows suspective -ci < -ˈti).

2a. aux adj. is not. ¶Ku ⁿyeca ka ippuci ani hata She is not pretty.

2b. aux v. does not. ¶Kongpu haci ani hanta He does not study.

ani hata₂ < aˈni ˙haˈta, adv + adj. is not much; are not many. ¶aˈni han ˙toy (1447 Sek 6:25b) a place not very big [that it would not cover all of]. aˈni han ˙tet (1459 Wel 17:44a, 1463 Pep 4:84b) a short while. aˈni han teˈt ey (1463 Pep 4:32a, ?1468- Mong 26b, 1485 Kwan 9a) in a short while.

aˈni ˙hoˈke.n i ˙Gwa SEE ˙hoˈke.n i ˙Gwa

aˈni ˙hoken ˙tyeng SEE ˙hoken ˙tyeng

aˈni ˙hoˈkesiˈn i ˙Gwa SEE -ˈkesiˈn i ˙Gwa

aˈni hoˈkwo, neg v/adj ger. ¶ ˙khuy ˙˙cek[ˈti] ˙two ˙khu[ˈti] ˙two aˈni hoˈkwo (1459 Wel 1:26b) was neither tall nor short. ˙homa polˈko.m ye eˈtuwun ˙˙twu kuˈth ey putˈti a[ˈ]ni hoˈkwo (1482 Kum-sam 2:55a) no longer clings to the two ends, light and dark, but ... .

aˈni hol(q), neg verb/adj prosp mod. ¶pwunˈpyel aˈni hol keˈs iˈl i (1518 Sohak-cho 8:13b) will not worry.

aˈni hoˈl i, neg v / adj prosp mod + postmod.

~ ˙ˈla (cop indic assert). ¶ˈPEP tutˈt ol a[ˈ]ni hoˈl i ˙ˈla (1459 Wel 2:36b) will not heed the Law.

~ ˙ˈleˈn i ˙ˈla (cop retr mod + postmod + copula indic assertive). ¶MYEY-˙HHWOYK ˙hoˈya koloˈchywoˈm ol patˈti aˈni hoˈl i ˙ˈleˈn i ˙ˈla (1463 Pep 1:208a) was too confused to get what was taught.

~ ˈsi.l i ˈl ˙s oy (cop hon prosp mod + postmod + cop prosp mod + postmod + pcl). ¶ ˙˙ta tasˈkwoˈm ol putˈti aˈni hoˈl i ˈsi.l i ˈl ˙s oy (1465 Wen 1:2:2:4a) since it may be that we cannot count on learning everything ... .

aˈni hol(q) s, neg v / adj prosp mod + postmod. ¶mozoˈm ay ˙senul hi neˈkiti aˈni hol s aˈni ˙honwoˈla (1475 Nay se:6a) it is not that I am not treating it coolly in my mind. ... ˙˙KEM-ˈPHAK ˙hwo.m oˈlwo puˈthe iˈle syeˈti aˈni hol s aˈni hoˈkwo (1475 Nay 1:34a) it is not that they do not rise into existence from ... and being frugal, nor ... . ˙ton swuˈl ul PPAY-ˈCI aˈni hol s aˈni ˙hwoˈtoy (1475 Nay 3:61a) it is not that one does not set out the sweet (= rice-and-barley) wine, nor ... . ˙˙mal-soˈm ol twutheˈi a[ˈ]ni hol s ˙˙epˈsi ˙ho.ya (1475 Nay 1:77a) making one's words not uncordial ... . YWEN ˙ol cwoˈcho.m ye ˙˙KAM ˙ay puthuˈsya.m i twulwu aˈni hol s aˈni ˙hosiˈna (1482 Kum-sam 5:10b) it is not that his seeking of pratyaya (secondary cause) and putting reliance on inspiration does not extend all around, but ... .

aˈni holq ˙s iˈm ye (postmod + cop substantive + copula infinitive) SEE holq ˙s iˈm ye

aˈni holq ˙s oy (postmodifier + particle). ¶ ˙nom koloˈchywoˈm ol aˈni hol ˙ss oy (1447 Sek 24:40a) as he did no teaching of it to others ... .

aˈni hoˈl ye SEE hoˈl ye

aˈni hom, negative v / adj substantive. SEE hom.

aˈni hon, neg v / adj mod. ¶ ˙ne y yeˈle ˙KEP ˙ey cephuˈti aˈni hon keˈkuy cephun mozoˈm ol ˙˙nayˈm ye ... (1459 Wel 7:48a) there where you were unafraid for many kalpas (eons) you show a fearful heart and ... . *kwut ti a ni hon key kwu tun ptu t ul meku sya* (1459 Wel 10:9a) harbors the feeling that it is firm in that place where is not firm.

a ni ho n i (postmod). ¶ *mwo m ol POYK-CHYEN ti Gwuy po lye two e lyep ti a ni ho n i* (1459 Wel 21:216ab) it is not at all (difficult =) uncommon to discard one's body hundreds of thousands of times.

a ni ho n i Ga SEE *ho n i Ga*

a ni hon toy SEE *hon toy*

a ni ho non, neg v / adj proc mod

a ni hono n i (postmod)

a ni honon ta (postmod). ¶ *kutoy non [SYE KHYENG] uy twu a to.l i na kocang [KUY- I] hwo.m ol pwo ti a ni honon ta* (1481 Twusi 8:24a) don't you see that Lord Xú's two sons are quite odd?

a ni hosin, neg v/adj hon mod. ¶ *PPYEN-QAN thi a ni hosin mo toy is kesi ton* (1475 Nay 1:40a) if [the king] has a stretch of being ill ... .

a ni hota < **a ni ho ta*, neg v/adj = **ani hata**. ¶ *nwo lwo.m ol a ni ho.ya is ta.n i* (1481 Twusi 7:23a) was not playing.

a ni hote tun, neg v / adj retr provisional

a ni hotwo ta, neg v / adj emotive indic assert. ¶ *[PPYENG] thi a ni hotwo ta* (1481 Twusi 7:12ab) is uneven. SEE *a ni thwo ta*

a ni ho.ywo m ol SEE *ho ywom*

a ni hwol(q), neg v / adj modulated prosp mod

a ni hwon, neg v / adj modulated prosp mod

a ni hwom, neg v / adj modulated subst. ¶ *is.non tos hwo toy is ti a ni hwo m i* (1459 Wel 1:36a) that it seems to exist yet does not exist.

a ni ka (= *a ni 'n ka* > **ani 'n ka**) is it not? ¶ *ta QWUY-NGWANG uy na mon KWONG a ni ka* (1463 Pep se:13a) is it not, all of it, the achievement left by the mighty king? *tye non hwo za salom a ni ka* (1475 Nay 2:1:16a) isn't he a person alone? SEE *a ni Ga*.

a ni kha.n i Gwa SEE *kha.n i Gwa*

a ni khan t i.n i 'la SEE *khan t i.n i 'la*

a ni khe tun SEE **khetun** < *khe tun*

a ni khey SEE **khey** < *khey*

a ni khwo n' SEE *khwo n'*

a ni khwan toy SEE *khwan toy*

a ni khways kwo = *a ni khwa 'ys kwo* (not wanting it to happen) SEE *khways kwo*

ani 'ko, neg cop ger. it is not and / but. ¶ *Kim sensayng i ani 'ko Pak sensayng ici yo* It isn't Mr Kim, it's Mr Pak. *Kulem cēng-mal ani 'ko [mālko]!* Yes, of course it's untrue! SYN **ani 'la, ani yo**.

ani 'l(q), abbr < **ani il(q)** (neg cop prosp mod). ¶ *Ayki ka ani 'l they 'n tey* After all, you are not (supposed to be) a baby!

a ni 'l(q) = *a ni '[y]l(q)*, abbr < *a ni il(q)* (neg cop prosp mod). ¶ *QILQ- TTI two stwo SAM-CHYEN pas k i a ni 'l s oy '.n i* (1482 Kum-sam 5:18a) it is because ... and the one Buddha-nature, moreover, is not other than everything in the chiliocosm (Buddha-world).

a n i l', mod < *a[l] ta* + postmod + pcl. ¶ *NGWEN- KAK SYENG a n i l' tel Gwo* (1465 Wen 1:1:2:134b) excepting those aware of the nature of complete enlightenment, ...

ani 'la, neg cop quotative < *a ni 'la* (neg cop indic assert). DIAL **a(y)i 'la(y)**.

1. = **ani 'ta** [used in quotations and quotative constructions] (says) it is not. ¶ *Ku kes i nay kes i ani 'la (hayss.ta)* It is not mine (they said). *Ney kes i ani 'la nay kes ita* It is not yours, it's mine = *Nay kes ici ney kes i ani 'ta* It is mine, it isn't yours.

2. [lit] = **ani 'ta**

3. = **ani 'ko**. SEE **(-ul) man ani 'la**.

NOTE: On marking subject and complement, see **ani 'ta** and *i*.

a ni 'la, neg cop indic assert. ¶ *... honwon ma l on sa la na ta honwon ma l i a ni 'la* (1447 Sek 6:36a) saying that ... is not to say they are born alive. *CIN- SSILQ S PPWO- SALQ oy TTYWU hwol kwo.t i a ni '.n i 'la* (1482 Kum-sam 3:34b) it is not a place where a real bodhisattva would dwell. ¶ *MA a ni 'la mu su ke s i l ywo* (1462 ¹Nung 9:101b) it is not a demon but what is it? *i MYENG uy MANG on nyenu a ni 'la KAK-MYENG i he mu l i towoy n i* (1462 ¹Nung 4:23b) the extravagance of this light is nothing but an error in the enlightenment.

a n i 'la, mod < *a[l] ta* + postmod + cop indic assert (1463 Pep 4:63b). knew.

ani 'la 'ci to, abbr < **ani 'la haci to**

a ni 'la ka, neg cop transferentive + pcl. ¶ *CIN- SSILQ lwo ZILQ- NGWELQ QWUY-KWANG oy NUNG hi pi chwuyywo m i a ni 'la ka SING- TI ye le pol kwo m ay mi che za CYWUNG-*

SOYNG ˙SYANG ˙i ¨cyokwo˙ma s so˙zi ˙lol CCYWONG ˙ho˙ya ... (1463 Pep 3:104b) to be sure, it is not really the full illumination of the mighty light of the son and the moon, yet just by managing to open up and shed light on the superior wisdom the characteristics of living things conform for a little while, and ... . (The reading note at the end of the Chinese clause is the affirmative *ila ka*, since the negation is included among the characters.)

ani 'la kko = **ani 'la ko**

ani 'la ko, neg cop quotative + pcl. (says) that it is not. ¶**Ku kes i nay kes i ani 'la ko hayss.ta** They said it is not mine.

ani 'la 'ko, abbr < **ani 'la (māl) hako** (neg cop quotative + vi ger). saying that it is not. ¶**Ku kes i nay kes i ani 'la 'ko cwuci anh.ess.ta** He said it wasn't mine and wouldn't give it to me.

ani 'la 'myen, abbr < **ani 'la hamyen**

ani 'la ('y) to. even if/though (you say) it is not.

a˙ni 'la ˙za, negative copula indic assert + pcl. ¶ ˙SYANG ˙i ˙kwot ˙SYANG *a˙ni 'la ˙za* CIN i towoyno˙n i 'la (1482 Kum-sam 3:12a) only when appearance is not appearance does it become reality.

ani 'lq ci ('la) to. even if it is not.

a˙ni 'len ˙t un SEE *˙ilen ˙t un*

a˙ni 'lol, neg + pcl. ¶ ¨twul˙h i ¨twul[h] *a˙ni ˙lol il˙hwum i* KHWONG-˙SYANG ˙i˙la ˙ho˙si.n i ''la (1464 Sim 38a) said the name for two-not-being-two is "unreality". ¨twul[h] *a˙ni ˙lol cwo˙cha* ˙SSYWUN ˙hosya˙m i ''la it is that he pursues the non-two [= the unique].

a˙ni 'l s, neg cop prosp mod + postmod. ¶*ye˙le* ˙KEP s QIN ˙i *a˙ni 'l s a˙ni '.m ye* (1496 ¹Yuk 1:47a) it is not that it is not the primary cause (hetu) of the kalpas, and ... .

ani 'lq swu, neg cop prosp mod + postmod. ~ **ēps.ta** cannot but be = is really (M 3:3:90).

a˙ni 'lwo˙la, neg var cop indic assert. ¶ *icey ˙na non kanan hwo.m i˙la* ˙PPYENG *a˙ni 'lwo˙la ˙ho.ya˙nol* ... (1482 Nam 1:30b) he said "now I am poor but I am not ill", ...

a˙ni ''lwom, neg var cop subst. ¶ ˙SSILQ *a˙ni 'lwo˙m i* MYENG-˙PPOYK ˙hotwo˙ta (1482 Kum-sam 2:27b) it is clear that it is not the truth. ˙TI ¨twul[h] *a˙ni ''lwo˙m on* ˙TI-˙HHYWEY 'lwo˙toy ... (1459 Wel 8:31b) that wisdom is not two things is [a matter of both] knowledge and discernment [together] and ... .

a˙ni ''lwo˙swo-ngi ''ta, neg alt copula emotive polite + cop indic assert. ¶CYE-˙PPWULQ ˙ul ˙pwo˙zowo˙m i ¨cye˙kun YWEN ˙i *a˙ni ''lwo˙swo-ngi ''ta* (1463 Pep 1:88b) seeing the Buddhas is no small contributing cause.

ani 'l ya, neg copula prosp modifier + postmod. ¶¹**Nak.hwa 'n tul kkoch i ani 'l ya, ssul.e musam halio** [obs = **mues hal i yo** = **mues haci yo**] "Fallen blossoms are blossoms still; do not sweep them away".

a˙ni˙lye = *a˙ni 'l ye* = *a˙ni '[y]l ye* ("would it not be ... ?!"). ¶*ku˙le a˙ni ''l ye ko˙cang e˙lye˙wu.n i ''la* (?1517- Pak 1:57b) it is just terribly hard.

ani 'm, abbr < **ani im** (cop subst).

a˙ni 'm = *a˙ni '[y]m*, abbr < *a˙ni im* (cop subst).

a˙ni ''m ye. ¶ ˙TI-¨THYEY ¨twul[h] *a˙ni ''m ye* (1459 Wel 8:31b) wisdom and substance are not two things, nor ... . ˙homol˙mye TUNG *a˙ni ''m ye* ¨pwom *a˙ni ''la* PWUN-˙PYELQ hwo˙m isto˙n ye (1462 ¹Nung 2:84a) with no light, with no sight, how can one distinguish?!

ani 'n, abbr < **ani in** (cop mod). ¶**yekan ani 'n nolyek ul hanta** makes great efforts.

a˙ni 'n = *a˙ni '[y]n*, abbr < *a˙ni in* (cop mod)

ani 'na talul ya (talulq ka). ('is not but is it different?' =) just as expected/suspected; to no one's great surprise.

a˙ni '.n i, neg cop mod + postmod. ¶ ˙TI-¨THYEY ¨twul[h] *a˙ni ''m ye* ¨KYENG ˙two ¨twul[h] *a˙ni '.n i* (1459 Wel 8:31b) wisdom and substance are not two things, nor is the object of wisdom two things.

~ ''la (cop indic assert). ¶ ¨won ˙kwo.t on *a˙zo.m ol* [˙WUY] ˙ho.ya 'y ˙Gwo ˙stwo [¨QUM-˙SSIK] ˙ul [˙WUY] ˙hwo.m i *a˙ni '.n i ''la* (1481 Twusi 8:33a) our coming is for our kinsmen and not for drink and food. ˙ile 'n ˙t o˙lwo ci˙zwul ˙tt i *a˙ni '.n i ''la* (1463 Pep se:12a) for this reason I will not create one.

ani 'n ka < *a˙ni 'n ˙ka*, neg cop mod + postmod. isn't it? ¶ ¨sa˙lo.m in ˙ka ¨sa˙lom *a˙ni 'n ˙ka ˙ho˙ya* NGUY-SIM toWoy˙n i (1459 Wel 1:15a) grew suspicious whether it was a human being or not. ˙ku ¨ha˙m ol ˙pwo˙sya ˙QILQ-˙SYEY ˙QILQ-˙PPWULQ s ˙HWA ˙hosya˙m i *a˙ni 'n ˙ka* NGUY-SIM ˙hosil ˙ss oy (1463 Pep 5:100a) for seeing the multitude he may doubt as to whether it is not the transforming [into

Buddhahood] of one Buddha each generation. ˙PEP-HHWA ˙ay s ¨KWA-˙KUY a˙ni ʼn ˙ka ˙honwo˙la (1462 ¹Nung 1:17b) I ask whether it is not the testimonial to phala ([cause and] effect) in the Lotus [sūtra].
ani ʼn key ani ʼla. ('it is not that it is not' =) sure enough, just as one thought, really; of course; to be sure. ¶ ~ kuleh.ta Certainly it is. ~ ku ⁿyeca ka miin iess.ta Sure enough, she was a beauty. SYN kwā.yen.
a˙ni ʼn ˙kwo, negative copula modifier + postmodifier. Are there examples of this structure? CF a˙ni ʼn ˙ka, a˙ni ˙Gwo.
a˙ni ˙non, ? adv + pcl; ? abbr < a˙ni ʼn [i n]on. ¶mwo˙ton ¨salom a˙ni ˙non elGwul is.no˙n i ˙Gwa elGwul ¨ep.su˙n i ˙Gwa ˙SYANG is.no˙n i ˙Gwa ¨ep.su˙n i ˙Gwa ˙lol kolo˙chisi˙n i (1462 ¹Nung 6:22-3) all those who are not human he taught, those with faces and those without, those with features and those without.
a˙ni ʼn ˙t ol, neg cop mod + postmod + pcl. ¶ ˙i CIN-˙SSILQ s ˙MYELQ-˙TTWO a˙ni ʼn ˙t ol ˙na y a˙lwo-ngi ʼ˙ta (1463 Pep 2:23a) I know that this is not true nirvāṇa. ko˙tok ʼ˙ti a˙ni ˙hwom a˙ni ʼn ˙t ol pan˙to˙ki a˙lwolq ˙t ilwo˙ta (1462 ¹Nung 1:67a) one must realize that it is not that it is not full.
ani ʼn ya, neg cop mod + postmod. isn't it?
a˙ni ʼn ye, neg copula modifier + postmod. ¶ ˙i ˙mwo.m i ˙khu˙n ye a˙ni ʼn ye (1464 Kumkang 61b) is this body big or isn't it?
a˙ni ʼsin, negative copula honorific modifier
a˙ni ˙si˙n i (postmod). ¶ ˙i ˙SYANG ˙on ˙YWOK-˙QOY ˙uy ¨na˙syan t i a˙ni ˙si˙n i (1462 ¹Nung 1:42a) this aspect is not what desire is born from.
a˙ni ʼsi˙ta[ʼ]s-ongi ʼ˙ta, negative copula honorific retr emotive polite + cop indicative assert). ¶ ˙i ˙non ˙wuli he˙mu.l i˙la ˙SYEY-CWON s ta˙s i a˙ni ˙si˙tas-ongi ʼ˙ta (1463 Pep 2:5b) this is our mistake; it is not the fault of the World-Honored.
a˙ni ʼ˙sya, inf < a˙ni ˙si˙ta. ¶pwuthye s a˙lom ˙ptu˙t i a˙ni ʼ˙sya he˙mu˙l i ˙SSILQ ˙lwo na ˙ykey is˙tas˙ta (1463 Pep 2:6a) it was not Buddha's idea, the fault is really mine.
a˙ni ˙syas˙ta, neg cop hon emotive indic assert. ¶HHUNG-SA ˙KKYEY ¨han ˙t i a˙ni ˙syas˙ta (1463 Pep 3:190a) they are not so numerous as the gāthās, which are in number like the sand of the Ganges.

an ita → ani ʼta

ani ʼta, (precop n + cop =) negative cop indic assertive. (it) is not. ¶Ku nun haksayng i ani ʼta He is not a student. Ku kes un kulen kes i ani ʼta It is not so. I kes i sīcheng iey yo? – Ani ʼta, sīmin-kwan ita Is this the City Hall? – No, it's not; it's the City Center.
NOTE 1: The complement, like the subject, is normally marked by the nominative particle i/ka, but that is sometimes omitted (see i). It is obligatorily suppressed when un/nun or to is attached to the complement, and it is usually omitted when man or ppun is attached.
NOTE 2: The negative copula has also been treated as a single stem ani-, as implied by the Hankul spelling, and as adverb an + copula ita, as in 1893 Scott 134, where the words are set apart by space in the Hankul as well as the Romanization: kecis mal an ita 'it is not a lie'.
a˙ni ˙ta, abbr < a˙ni ho˙ta (LCT 513b)
a˙ni ˙tha, abbr < a˙ni ho˙ta. ¶ ¨es˙tyey e˙lwo ˙TTYAK ho˙l i ˙Gwan˙toy ˙TTYAK ʼ˙ti a˙ni ˙tha nilo˙l ywo (1462 ¹Nung 1:75a) how can you say one is unattached when one IS attached?
a˙ni thwo˙ta, abbr < a˙ni ˙hotwo˙ta. ¶ ˙sol˙khwa kas ˙kwa y is˙ti a˙ni thwo˙ta (1481 Twusi 8:2a) = ˙solh ˙kwa kac ˙kwa ˙i is˙ti a˙ni ˙hotwo˙ta (both) flesh and skin are lacking. [SSIN-KUY] lowoy ˙ywo.m i ¨epti a˙ni thwo˙ta (1481 Twusi 16:22b) it does not lack in being miraculous!
a˙ni ˙two, adv + pcl. ¶ ˙tye ˙CYWUNG-SOYNG a˙ni ʼ˙m ye ˙CYWUNG-SOYNG a˙ni ˙two a˙ni ʼn i ¨es.tyey ˙Ge˙n ywo (?1464 Kumkang 128; cited from LCT 513a with inferred accents) what about those who are not creatures and those who are not even non-creatures?
ani ya, neg cop var inf. it is not. ~ yo → ani ye(y) yo = ani ʼey yo.
ani ye, negative copula infinitive
ani yess··· , negative copula past
ani ye(y) yo = ani ʼey yo, n + cop inf + pcl.
ani yo, 1. n + pcl. No(, sir).
  2. n + pcl. (= ani ʼko) is not and/but.
  3. (abbr < ani io) it is not [AUTH style].
  4. (= aney yo = anyey yo) = ani ʼey yo it is not [POLITE style].
a˙n[i] ʼywom = a˙nʼ ʼywom

-ˈan maˈlon = -ˈGan maˈlon = -ˈkan maˈlon = -ˈken maˈnon, effective mod + postmod. but, although. ¶ ¨aˈlay coˈcwo tutcoˈWan maˈlon ˈcukcaˈhi twolwo niˈce kos.pol ¨spwu.n iˈn i (1447 Sek 6:11a) I have often listened to it before and promptly forgotten it again, it is just so hard. ˈTTAY-SSIN ˈi ˈTHAY-¨CO ˈyn ˈkwoˈt ol aˈlan maˈlon (1447 Sek 24:52a) the minister was aware that he was the prince, but ... .

? -aˈnol = -kaˈnol = -keˈnul. SEE -yaˈnol.

¨aˈnon < *aˈ[lo]ˈnon, proc mod < ¨a[l]ˈta (knows). ¶ ¨aˈno.n i ˈˈla (1447 Sek 13:40b). CF ¨aˈnwon.

-ˈanˈta, effective mod + postmod. ¶ NUNG ˈhi aˈlanˈta ¨mwollanˈta (?1468- Mong 21b) do you know it well or do you not? aˈlan ta ... (1482 Kum-sam 2:13a) did you know? − ... . [ˈPPWULQ-¨CWO] uy heˈmul caˈpanˈta (1579 Kwikam 1:21a) would you pick fault with the ancestor of Buddha?

ˈanta = [h]anta. CF ˈnta = [ha]nta.

an t'ēy = an twēy / twāy = an toy(e) SEE toyta

anthey, particle = hanthey (to a person)

-ˈanˈti = -ˈanˈtˈi = -ˈkanˈtˈi, effective mod + postmod + pcl. ¶ ¨ne y poyˈhwanˈtˈi ¨enˈma woˈlaˈn ywo (?1517- ¹No 1:6a) How long have you been studying [Chinese]? mozomˈaˈlanˈtˈi yeˈleˈhoy ˈlwoˈtoy (?1517- Pak 1:71b) we have understood each other for many years now, and ... . ciˈp uy s ¨saˈloˈm iˈsyaˈchi ˈhwoˈm ol poyˈhwan (← poyhw[o-]an) ˈtˈi woˈla (1518 Sohak-cho 10:31a) our family has long been accustomed to luxury. cheem ulwo alhan t i holo n man uy nano.n i non (?1608+ Twu-hem 21a; che-e-m-u-lwo) when the first pain lasts a day. SEE -ˈyanˈti.

an toyta SEE toyta

-a nun SEE -e nun

ˈanun = [h]anun. CF ˈnun = [ha]nun.

ānun < ¨aˈnon < *aˈ[lo]ˈnon, proc modifier < ālta < ¨a[l]ˈta (knows)

¨aˈnwon < *aˈ[lo]ˈnwon, modulated proc mod < ¨a[l]ˈta (knows). ¶ ¨anwoˈn i (1463 Pep 3:178b, 1481 Twusi 8:24b).

anya = an' ˈya < aˈniˈhoˈya, negative auxiliary infinitive. ¶ wolayci an.ya (1887 Scott 69) 'in a short time'.

aˈnye = aˈn' ˈye

1. < *aˈniˈˈye, neg cop inf. ¶ ne aˈn' ˈye nwuˈyˈl ywu (1462 ¹Nung 2:30b) if not you who will it be? CF aˈniˈˈla, aˈniˈˈmye.

2. < aˈniˈhoˈye, neg aux inf. ¶ meˈmuˈti an' ˈye nwuˈe [= nwuˈwe] kwuulˈGwo (?1517- Pak 1:42b) [my sick horse] lies rolling ceaselessly about. ¨cˈaˈsiˈti aˈn' ˈye ¨kyeˈsikeˈtun (1586 Sohak 2:4b) if you have not eaten.

anyess- = ani yess- (copula past)

anyey yo = ani 'ey yo it is not [POLITE style].

-aˈn ywo, effective mod + postmod. ¶ ˈhyenˈma s CANG-NGEM ˈkwa ˈhyenˈma s KWONG-ˈYANG ˈi SSYANG-ˈSSYWUY ˈlol ˈphyeaˈn ywo (1459 Wel 17:23b) how much pomp and how much offering of food have unfolded favorable omens?

aˈn' ˈywom = aˈn[i] ˈywom (< *aˈni i-wo-m) that it is not (= aˈniˈˈlwom). ¶ is.nonˈtos ˈhwoˈtoy isˈti aˈniˈhwoˈm iˈsuchywom aˈn' ˈywoˈm i aˈniˈˈla (1459 Wel 1:36a) that it seems to exist yet does not exist is not a matter of thinking [about it]. TUNG aˈniˈm ye ¨pwom aˈn' ˈywoˈm i isˈta (1462 ¹Nung 2:83a) there is that which is not lamp and is not sight. ˈi non ¨pwoˈm iˈi ¨pwom aˈn' ˈywoˈm ol ˈKYELQ ˈhosiˈn i (1462 ¹Nung 2:92a) this entails that seeing is not really seeing (= the [heterodox] view is not the correct view) − The second ˈi translates an emphatic 'this' = 'really [is]' (= 'right not wrong'), which is the source of the modern Chinese copula shì.

-ap, [var] = -op(sose). please do. (Sometimes misspelled "-aph".)

aph, n. ANT twī; CF cen. 1. the front, the fore part; ... ~ ey in front of ... .

2. the head / lead, the foremost. ¶ aph ey suta is at the head, stands in front, takes the lead.

3. the presence of a person, before a person; addressed / directed to. ¶ Pak Sēycin aph To Pak Seycin.

4. (= mīlay) the future, what is to be. ~ ulo (n') in future, (ever) again.

5. (= moks) a share, portion, quota. ¶ Han salam aph i elma 'laˈn māl iya I mean, how much for each person?

6. the foregoing (part), the preceding part, the above. CF īsang, cen.

7. one's private parts. ¶ Aph i pointa You're showing (in front). Your (trouser) fly is open.

8. what is in front of one's eyes. ¶ ~ ul mōs ponta is blind.

9. the south.
10. (= **mangken** ~) the front of a horsehair headband.
aph-suta goes first, takes precedence. **aph-se (se)** previously, before, earlier; beforehand, in advance; ··· **pota aph-se se** ahead of, prior to.
-api, suffix; LIGHT ↔ **-epi**; VAR **-aypi**; CF **-ami**. (forms names of creatures). **ttakttakaypi** (a kind of grasshopper) < **ttak-ttak** snap snap. (But: **napi** butterfly < *na῾poy* < **napus napus** fluttering.)
-apta, bnd adj -W- (var < **-epta**). **pankapta** is glad < **pankita** rejoices. **potulapta** is soft < **potul (hata)**.
-a puthe SEE **-e puthe**
-῾*as*··· = -῾*a ῾s*- (= -῾*a ῾ys*-), abbr < -῾*a is*-, inf + aux. SEE ENTRIES, ···*yas*- = ···*ya ῾s*-. CF **-ess**-.
-a sa, [DIAL] 1. = **-a ya**. 2. = **-a se**.
-a se, inf + pcl. SEE **-e se**.
-a se ka SEE **-e se ka**
-a se man SEE **-e se man**
-a se n', **-a se nun** SEE **-e se n'**, **-e se nun**
-a se to SEE **-e se to**
-a se 'tun ci SEE **-e se 'tun ci**
-a se ya SEE **-e se ya**
-a sey ya [var] = **-a se ya**
-asi-/**-as-** [Phyengan DIAL (Kim Yengpay 1984: 104-5)] = **-ass-** (past).
Both **-asi-** and **-as-** occur before **-ta**, **-ti** (= **-ci**), and **-ko**; only **-as-** before **-uni**, **-umyen**, **-ul**, **-e**; **-asi ya** = **-ass.e ya**, **-ase yo** (in places **-esi yo**) = **-ess.e yo**.
-῾*asi*-, (···*y*, ···*i*) -῾*yasi*- = -῾*kasi*-, -῾*Gasi*- (effective hon) = -ᵁ/o῾*si῾ke*- (hon effective).
-῾*a ῾s(i)*··· , (···*y*, ···*i*) -῾*ya ῾s(i)*-, inf + abbr < *is(i)*··· (aux mod).
-῾*a ῾silq*, inf + abbr < *isilq* (aux prosp mod).
~ ῾*cey* (abbr < *ce῾k uy*). ¶ *na y ¨nyey CYE- ῾PPWULQ s kalo῾chisya῾m ol tut¨cop῾ti ¨mwot ῾hozo wa ῾silq ῾cey* (1462 ¹Nung 2:2b) when I was unable to hear the teachings of the Buddhas in the old days, ...
~ ῾*ta* (postmod). ¶ *῾TTAY-῾TUK ῾a ZYE-LOY nilu῾sinwon a῾hwop HHWOYNG-¨SO ῾lol ¨may ¨mwot tutco῾Wa ῾silq ῾ta* (1459 Wel 55-6; CF 1447 Sek 9:35b) Dà-dé, how come you have been unable to hear of the nine unnatural deaths told by the tathāgata?

-῾*a ῾si῾m ye*, inf + abbr < *isi῾m ye* (aux subst + cop inf). ¶··· ῾*KWEN-῾SSYWOK ῾kwa hon ῾toy ῾wa ῾si῾m ye* (1463 Pep 1:47b) they are here with all their ··· relatives, and ... . *CIN-῾SSILQ s ῾mwo.m on syang῾nyey mol῾ka ῾si῾m ye* (1482 Kum-sam 2:25a) the true body is always purified, and ... .
-῾*a ῾sin*, inf + abbr < *isin* (aux mod). ¶*sa῾la ῾sin ce῾k uy selu ma῾cwo ¨pwo῾m ay swul ῾ol me῾kwul ῾t i.n i ῾῾la* (1481 Twusi 15:38a) while alive what we should do is down some wine face to face (= in each other's company).
-῾*asi῾na* = -῾*a ῾si῾na*, inf + abbr < *isi῾na* (aux advers). ¶ ¨*twu ¨syewul s syel῾hun ¨salo῾m i pi῾lwok sa῾la ῾si῾na mwok-¨swu.m i ¨sil ῾kot ῾hwola* (1481 Twusi 8:36b) thirty people of the two capitals are alive, but their lives are like threads.
-῾*asi῾n i*, (···*y*, ···*i*) -῾*yasi῾n i* = -῾*kasi῾n i*, -῾*Gasi῾n i* (effective hon mod + postmodifier). ¶*pis῾kun nam῾k ol no῾la na῾masi῾n i* (1445 ¹Yong 86) he flew over the slanted tree [while his horse went under it].
-῾*a ῾si῾n i*, inf + abbr < *isi῾n i* (aux mod + postmodifier). ¶*wo῾lay an῾ca ῾si῾n i polo῾m i ko῾cang [¨NWO] ῾hono῾n i nacwo῾h oy [¨]mwoy.h i ka῾soy῾ye phu῾lutwo῾ta* (1481 Twusi 7:24ab) I have been seated a long while, and the wind rages fiercely; in the evening the mountains are all the greener! *as.ka non selu melli anca ῾si.n i* (1676 Sin.e 3:10a) a while ago they sat at a distance from each other.
-῾*asi῾nol* = -῾*kasi῾nol* (concessive honorific) = -(ᵁ/o)῾*sike῾nul* (hon concessive). ¶ ¨*wos ῾kwa ma῾li ῾lol ῾LWO-TYWUNG ey ῾phye῾asi῾nol* (1449 Kok 7 = 1459 Wel 1:4a) spread clothes and hair upon the roadside, whereupon ... . *ho῾ma ῾kol῾hwoy῾ya ma῾koy῾Gwasi῾nol* (1462 ¹Nung 2:96a) already discriminated and verified it, so that ... . ῾*TTOY mong῾kulasi[῾]nol* (1463 Pep 7:14a) built a tower and ... .
-῾*asi῾n ywo* = -῾*kasi῾n ywo* (effective hon mod + postmod) = -(ᵁ/o)῾*sike῾n ywo* (hon effective mod + postmod). ¶ *hyen ῾kwo῾t ol wol῾masi῾n ywo* (1445 ¹Yong 110) how many places did they move to?
-῾*asi῾tun* = -῾*kasi῾tun* (provisional honorific) = -(ᵁ/o)῾*sike῾tun*. ¶ ¨*salo῾m ol ῾pwo῾asi῾tun mwoncye ¨mal ῾hosi῾m ye* (1459 Wel 2:58b) when he sees people he speaks first and ... .

-ˊas.ken maˋlon = -ˊa 's.ken maˋlon, abbr < -ˊa is.ken maˋlon. ¶[ˋPWONG-ˋKAN] hol ¨malsoˋm i tap-saˋha 'sˋken maˋlon (1481 Twusi 8:4b) we have an accumulation of words to exhort by innuendo but ... .
-ˊas.keˋtun = -ˊa 'sˋketun, abbr < -ˊa is.keˋtun (also -ˊa 'ys.keˋtun). ¶saˋla 'sˋke tun i-patˋkwo (1481 Samkang hyo:32b) if I stay alive I will contribute [alms] and ... .
-ˊasˊno'-'i ''ta, abbr < -ˊa isˋno-ngi ''ta. ¶wang ˋwo wasˋno'-'i ''ta (?1517- Pak 1:59a) [the bowmaker] Wáng Wǔ is here, sir.
-ˊas.non = -ˊa 's.non, abbr < -ˊa is.non (also -ˊa 'ys.non). ¶ˋkil[h] maka 'sˋnon [= maˋka 'sˋnon] hon ˊpheˋki s ˋsaˋm i (?1517- Pak 1:40a) a hemp plant blocking the road. SEE -¨zow-.
-ˊas.noˋn i = -ˊa 's.noˋn i, abbr < -ˊa is.noˋn i. ¶ QILQ-ˋCHYEY S ˋZYEM-ˋCCYENG ¨CWONG-¨CO ˋlol me[ˋ]ke koˋchwoˋa 'sˋnoˋn i (1465 Wen 2:3:1:43a) it harbors all the pure-washed seeds [of wisdom]. selu naˋtha 'sˋnoˋn i (1482 Kumsam 3:53a) appear to each other.
-ˊas.non ˋta = ˊa 's.nonˋta, abbr < -ˊa is.non ˋta (also -ˊa 'ys.non ˋta). ¶ˋne y ¨aˋloy [SYEYHHWO] s ˋkyeng ˋey nyeˋle ˋwa 's.nonˋta (?1517- Pak 1:67a) have you been to the sights of West Lake [= Xī Hú in Hángzhōu]?
-ˊasoˋla, effective emotive indic assert. ¶ne-huy ˋtolˋh i aˋlasoˋla (1459 Wel 10:26a) you people know them. SEE -ˊesoˋla.
-ass- SEE -ess-
-ass.ci SEE -ess.ci
-ass.e SEE -ess.e
-ass.ess- SEE -ess.ess-
-ass.ess.keyss- SEE -ess.ess.keyss-
-ass.keyss- SEE -ess.keyss-
-ˊa ˋssye, inf + ? abbr < -ˋsywoˋsye. please do! ¶ˋna y ˊpwoa ˋcye ˋhonoˋta solˋWa ˋssye (1447 Sek 6:14b) please tell him I'd like to see him.
-ˊas.taˋka = -ˊa 's.taˋka, abbr < -ˊa 's.taˋka (also -ˊa 'ys.taˋka). ¶¨cams.kan ˋna 's.taˋka (1482 Nam 2:31a) was out a while and then ... .
-ˊasuˋla < -ˊasoˋla (effective emotive assertive)
-ˊasy... = -ˊa ˋsy..., abbr < -ˊa isy... (< isi-)
-ˊa ''sye, inf + abbr < i ˋsye. SEE -ˊe ''sye.
-ˊa ˋsye, inf + pcl. SEE -ˊe ˋsye.
-ˊaˋta = -kaˋta = -ˋkeˋta, effective indic assert. ¶kwoˋthiˋki moˋchaˋta (?1517- Pak 1:43a) got it all cured.

-a 'ta (ka) < -ˊa 'taˋka, inf + cop transferentive. ¶ ZILQ-ˋNGWELQ ˋul caˊpa 'taˋka kwuy ˋyey s kwuˋsul ˋhwo.l i ''laˋkhwo (1447 Sek 13:19-20) seeking to grab the sun and the moon and make them into earrings.
-atan, -atang, -ata(ng)kun(ey) [Ceycwu DIAL] = -aˋtan (etc) = -a ta (ka)
-ath = 'ath, abbr < path. phul-'ath [DIAL] = phul path grass field. ? pakkath outside < pakk-'ath. the 'ath = theq path field / garden adjacent to house. LHS lists the noun ath as a dialect version of path.
¨aˋti = ¨a[l]ˋti, suspective < ¨a[l]ˋta (knows): ¨aˋti ¨mwot (˚ho-) (1459 Wel 21:120b; 1462 ¹Nung 1:55a, 3:47b; 1463 Pep 2:60a, 3:180ab; ?1517- Pak 1:37b); accent-reduced as ¨ati ¨mwot ... (1463/4 Yeng 2:126a, 1475 Nay 3:58b, 1481 Twusi 8:29a, 1482 Nam 2:30b, 1518 Sohak-cho 10:18b).
-ˊa ˚tiˋta, inf + aux. ¶pesˋGa ˋtikeˋnul (1447 Sek 6:30-1) crumbles.
-a to, inf + pcl. SEE -e to.
-aˋton = -keˋtun if; when. ¶kilˋh ey KAN-NAN hon ¨salom ˊpwoaˋton ˋPWO-SI ˋhoteˋla (1447 Sek 6:15b) when he would see a poor man on the road he would give him alms.
-ˊa ˋtwo, inf + pcl. SEE -ˊe ˋtwo.
-a tul SEE -e tul
'atun = [h]atun. CF 'tun = [ha]tun.
-aˋtun = -aˋton = -keˋtun if; when. ¶alpˊph uy ˊpwoˋwaˋtun [conflated spelling of alˊph uy ˊpwoˋaˋtun] aˋlwon ¨yang hoˋkwo (?1517- Pak 1:25a) look to the front and pretend to know and ... . swon s paˋtaˋng ol tuˋle ˋhoy ˋtoˋl ol koˋliGwaˋton ˋZILQ-ˋNGWELQ-ˋSSIK ˋhoˋno.n i ''la (1459 Wel 2:2a) when he lifts his hand to hide the sun and the moon it is called an eclipse.
-a 'tun ci SEE -e 'tun ci
-a twu [var] = -e to
-aw- SEE -apta
awus, postn [OLD-FASHIONED]. (= kawus) and a half. ¶han toy ~ a cup and a half. twū pal ~ two and a half spans (= double yards).
ˋay, alt (after a, o, wo) of pcl ˋey = ey (in, at; ...). VAR ˋoy. ¶MA-YA s ˋskwum anˋh ay (1459 Wel 2:17b) in Maya's dream. paloˋl ay (1445 ¹Yong 2) into the sea. mwoˋm ay (1447 Sek 19:19b) on their bodies. SEE ˋey, ˋyey, ˋuy; ˋay ˋsye.
ay, adn. CF ches, say; a.yey.
   1. (? < ai child) the very young, a tiny (baby)

one. ¶ ~ **songaci** a newborn calf, a young calf. ~ **songi** stripling. ~ **swun** a fresh sprout. ~ **kkwāli** green ground-cherries. ~ **hō-pak** green pumpkin. ~ **thi** childlike ways.
  2. (? < **a.yey** from the first) the very first. ~ **pel** the first time. ¶ ~ **(tang)cho** the very beginning. ~ **(pel) ppallay** first laundering.
  3. (bnd) noun. ¶**ayq toyta** is childlike.
'ay = [h]ay = **hay**, inf < **hata**. ¶**Chwuk.ha 'ay** = **Chwuk.ha hay** Congratulations!
-ay, inf ← **-ah.ta**, ← **-eh.ta**.
-ay, suf; VAR **-ey**; CF **-kay, -i**. [Partly < - ˙*Gay*.]
  1. makes n from v (with minor irregularities). **casay** reel < **cās.ta** spins out (thread). **chay** whip, switch, swatter, drumstick < **chita** beats. **elkay** structure < **elk.ta** weaves, makes. **kalay** plow < **kālta** plows. **kallay** division, fork(ing) < **kaluta (kalle)** splits, cuts, divides. **makay** stopper, plug < **makta** obstructs, stops (up). **nolay** a song < **nōlta** plays. **patay** a reinforcement strip (…) < **pat.ta** receives. **ppallay** laundry < **ppalta** launders. **puchay** fan < **puchita** fans. **milay** leveller < **mīlta** pushes. **talay** coffin sideboards, mudguards < **talta** hangs. **tolay** bridle ring (etc.) < **tōlta** goes around.
  2. (? makes adv from adj or v). **killay** (for) long < **kīlta** (adj) is long. **mōllay** secretly, furtively, unbeknownst to others < **moluta** (v) knows not.
-ay-, pseudo-suf (makes vc). **ēps.ay-** exterminate < **ēps-** < ¨*eps-* 'not exist'. But this stem is probably a contraction of **ēps.i ha-** < ¨*ep˙si °ho-* (1465 Wen se:77a), as LHS has it.
-a ya, inf + pcl. SEE **-e ya**. VAR **-ay ya**.
-a ya 'ci SEE **-e ya 'ci**
-ayci [var] = **-aci**
a.yey, adv. from the start / beginning, in the first place, (not) by any means, (not) on any account, (not) at all. ¶**An cwulq kes ila 'myen a.yey poici 'na māltun ci** If you're not prepared to give it you shouldn't show it in the first place. **Kongpu lul halye 'myen yelqsim hi hatun ka, kuleh.ci anh.umyen a.yey kongpu lul māltun ka hay la** If you are going to study, then study hard, or else give up the idea of studying altogether. **A.yey kulenq yāyki mace puthe ka īsang hata 'n māl ia** To begin with, his story is very fishy in itself. **Na tele nun a.yey tōn tālla ko haci mal.ᵉ/a** Never ask ME for money! **A.yey kēcis mal haci mala** Never tell a lie.
a(y)i, adv [N Kyengsang DIAL] = **ani** not. SEE Choy Myengok 1979.
a(y)i 'la(y), [N Kyengsang DIAL] = **ani 'ta** (neg cop). ¶**Ku key cip i a(y)i 'la(y)** That is not a house. (Choy Myengok 1979:10. Presumably there are four variants **ayi 'lay, ayi 'la, ai 'lay,** and **ai 'la**, but that is unclear.)
-ayki, 1. var = **-aki**, suf (dimin). CF **-ak, -aci, -angi, -langi, -ali; -(u)laki, -(u)leki**.
  2. **solayki** = **soli** < *swo˙loy / swo˙li* sound, voice.
- ˙*a 'y˙la*, inf + abbr < ˙*i˙la* (cop). ¶*cyeki naa 'yla* (1795 ¹No-cwung [K]) = *cyek.i tywoha 'yla* (id. [P] 2:37a) = = ¨*cye˙ki ¨tywo˙ha 'y˙la* (?1517- ¹No 2:41a) I'm a little better! *mwol˙la ˙pwoa 'y˙la* (1459 Wel 23:86b) Dunno!
-aymi [var] = **-ami**
˙*ay n'*, pcl + pcl. ¶*yes˙us ka˙ci s ¨CCWOY ˙non hona˙h ay n' … ¨twul˙h ay n' … … ta˙so˙s ay n'* … (1447 Sek 24:2b) of the six sins, the first is … and the second … … and the fifth … .
˙*ay ˙na*, pcl + cop advers. *mwo˙m ay ˙'na mozo˙m ay ˙'na* (1463 Pep 1:106b) whether in the body or in the mind.
-ayngi [var] = **-angi. thokkayngi** < **thokki** a rabbit, a bunny. **kkochayngi** a spit / skewer < **kkochi** a skewer (der n < **kkoc.hi-** get thrust, be inserted). **kkomayngi** < **kkoma** midget.
- ˙*ay-ngi ˙'ta* (var) = - ˙*a-ngi ˙'ta*. ¶*na 'y ˙e˙mi ¨amwo ˙toy˙na 'ys.non ˙t i ¨mwol˙lay-ngi ˙'ta* (1459 Wel 21:53a) I do not know what place my mother has been reborn into.
˙*ay ˙non*, pcl + pcl. ¶*[¨SSI-KKYWOW] ˙ay non kuwuy s pe˙tu.l i ˙konol ˙Gwo* (1481 Twusi 7:6a) in Shìqiáo the willows of the government office are slender, and … . SEE ˙*ey ˙nun, ˙ay n'*.
-a yo SEE **-e yo**
-aypi [var] = **-api**
˙*ay s*, pcl + pcl. ¶*na 'y pa'l ay s hon the˙li ˙lol ¨mwot mwuu˙l i ˙'n i* (1447 Sek 6:27a) will not move one hair of my foot. *swon s pa˙tang ˙ay s ¨KWA-¨CO* (1482 Nam 1:25b) a cake in the palm of the hand. ˙*SYEY-KAN ˙ay s ˙MEN-¨PEP ˙i* (1482 Kum-sam 2:3b) the myriad laws of society. *te˙wun sa˙pal ˙ay s swo˙li non* (1482 Kum-sam 2:41a) the sound in the hot bowl. *pa˙hwoy s ¨koz ay s mwo˙ton kwo˙c i* (1482 Nam 1:3a) all the flowers at the edge of the

rock. ha˙nol.h ay s ˇsalom ˙two (1482 Nam 1:62b) the people in heaven, too. moy˙h ay s nul˙ku.n i ˙lwo (1482 Nam 1:4a) toward the old man on the moor. ˙mwoy.h ay s ˙kwulwum ˙kwa pa˙lo.l ay s ˙tol s ˙ptu.t ul ˇta niloko˙nul (1482 Kum-sam 3:36b) if we describe all the feelings of clouds on the mountain and moon on the sea. kozol s ha˙nol moy˙h ay s ˙mu.l ey SOM-LA y ˇce y na˙thwo.m i ˙kot ho˙n i (1482 Kum-sam 3:34b) it is like the spontaneous appearance of a dense forest by moorland streams under an autumn sky. ˙kwot-kwo˙t ay ˇmwoy˙h ay s kwo˙c i ˙phutwo˙ta (1482 Kum-sam 3:33a) everywhere the mountain flowers are in bloom. mwo˙m ay s KWANG-MYENG ˙i (1459 Wel 2:53b) the radiance of his body. HE-KHWONG ˙ay s kwo˙c i.l i ˙ˊla (1482 Kum-sam 2:73b) it will be a blossom in the void. cip ˇswo.p ay s ˇi.l ol ˇtos.ti ˇmalGwo, TTWO-TYWUNG ˙ey s ˙KHOYK towoy˙ywo.m ol ˙culki˙m ye (1482 Kum-sam 3:24a) instead of doting on the happenings within the home, delights to become a guest on the road. ˙QILQ-SOYNG ˙ay s CHAM-ˇHHAK ˙ho.ywol ˇi˙l i mo˙cho.l i ˙ˊla (1482 Kum-sam 2:1b) said the act of pursuing (Buddhist) learning for a lifetime would come to an end. SEE ˙ey s, ˙uy s, ˙oy s.
-˙a 'ys-, abbr < -˙a is-. SEE ˙ho˙ya 'ys-.
-˙a 'ys˙kasi˙n i, abbr < -˙a is˙kasi˙n i. ¶ye˙huy˙ya 'ys˙kasi˙n i (1462 ¹Nung 5:72b) he has kept them away.
-˙a 'ys.ke˙n i Gwa, abbr < -˙a is.ke˙n i Gwa. ¶ne 'y mwo˙m ay non ho˙ma pa˙thun ˙chwu.m i kwu˙sul towoy˙ywo˙m ol ˙pwo˙a 'ys.ke˙n i Gwa (1481 Twusi 8:31b) of your body you have already seen the drivel that was spat turn to jewels and in addition ... .
-˙a 'ys.ke˙tun, abbr < -˙a is.ke˙tun (also -˙a 's.ke˙tun). SEE ˙ho˙ya 'ys.ke˙tun.
-˙a 'ys˙kwo, abbr < -˙a is˙kwo. ¶kwo˙ki ˙mu.l ey ˙na 'ys˙kwo (1481 Twusi 7:7b) the fish are out in the water.
-˙a 'ys.non, abbr < -˙a is.non (also -˙a 's.non).
-˙a 'ys.no˙n i, abbr < -˙a is.no˙n i (also -˙a 's.no˙n i). ¶mwo˙ta 'ys.no˙n i ˙lol (1459 Wel 21:14a) those assembled. SEE -ˇzow-.
~ [ˊ]Gwo (postmod). ¶[NGWUN] un mu˙sum ˙ptu.t u˙lwo [KKUM-TTOY] ˙lol pa˙la 'ys.no˙n i Gwo (1481 Twusi 7:3b) I wonder what it means that clouds are arrayed on the harp stand.

-˙a 'ys.non ˙ta, abbr < -˙a is.non ˙ta (also -˙a 's.non ˙ta). ¶ TTAY-ˇTUK ˙a ZYE-LOY nilu˙sinwon a˙hwop HHOYNG-ˇSO ˙lol ˇmwot tutco˙Wa 'ys.non ˙ta (1447 Sek 9:35b; CF 1459 Wel 55-6) Dà-dé, have you been unable to hear of the nine unnatural deaths that are told by the tathāgata?
-˙a 'ys.non ˙t i, abbr < -˙a is.non ˙t i. ¶na 'y ˙e˙mi ˇamwo ˙toy ˙na 'ys.non ˙t i ˇmwol˙lay-ngi ˙ˊta (1459 Wel 21:53a; underlying object marked with nominative) I do not know what place my mother has been reborn into.
-˙a 'ys˙nwon, abbr < -˙a is˙nwon.
~ ˙t i. ¶ˇta ˙KHOYK-TTIN i towoy˙ya 'ys˙nwon ˙t i (1462 ¹Nung 1:113a) that it has all become useless dust ... .
-˙a 'ys.ta˙ka, abbr < -˙a is.ta˙ka (also -˙a 's.ta˙ka). ¶ˇa˙lay ce 'y ˙pe˙t i cwu˙ke ha˙nol˙h ay ˙ka 'ys.ta˙ka no˙lye ˙wa (1447 Sek 6:19b) his friend of former days who had died and gone to heaven descended and ... .
-˙a 'ys.tan, abbr < -˙a is.tan
-˙a 'ys.ta˙n i, abbr < -˙a is.ta˙n i. SEE -ˇzow-.
~ ˙ˊla. ¶na y ... ˙i SSYENG ˙ol moyng˙ko˙la 'ys.ta˙n i ˙ˊla (1463 Pep 3:196-7) I have built this castle ... .
-˙a 'ys.tan ˙t i˙m ye n', abbr < -˙a 'ys.tan ˙t i˙m ye n'. SEE -ˇzow-.
-˙a 'ys.te˙la, abbr < -˙a is.te˙la. SEE -ˇzow-.
-˙a 'ys.ten, abbr < -˙a 'ys.ten
-˙a 'ys.te˙n i, abbr < -˙a 'ys.te˙n i. ¶e˙ces.kuy ˙pwom s ˙pi lol si˙lum ˙hwo.m ay tato˙la 'ys.te˙n i (1481 Twusi 7:20b) yesterday I had reached the point of bemoaning the spring rain [hitting my leaky roof]. SEE ˙ho˙ya 'yste˙n i.
-˙a 'ys˙tesin, abbr < -˙a is˙tesin
-˙a 'ys˙tesi˙n i, abbr < -˙a is˙tesi˙n i. ¶na-˙ka 'ys˙tesi˙n i (1445 ¹Yong 49) [the king] had left.
-˙a 'ys˙tesi˙n i s˙ka, abbr < -˙a is˙tesi˙n i s˙ka. SEE -ˇzow-.
-˙a 'ys.two˙ta, abbr < -˙a is.two˙ta. ¶mozol˙h i ˇtwol[h] s ˙seli ˙yey mwo˙ta 'ys.two˙ta (1481 Twusi 7:10b) the village is clustered between rocks.
'ay se = [h]ay se = hay se, inf < hata + pcl.
˙ay ˙sye pcl + pcl. SEE ˙ey ˙sye, ˙yey ˙sye; ˙oy ˙sye, ˙uy ˙sye.
1. = ey se at, in; from. ¶ ˙cokya s na˙la.h ay ˙sye ke˙sul˙pcun ˇyang ˙honon ˙NAN (1447 Sek 9:33a) the difficulty of acting defiant in one's

own nation. *ne 'y kwo˙h ay ˙sye ¨nalq ˙t in ˙t ay n'* (1462 ¹Nung 3:24b) when this scent arises in your nose. *˙stwo sta˙h ay ˙sye ¨nan ˙t i a˙ni ˙'m ye* (1462 ¹Nung 8:123a) nor was he born on the earth, (nor) … . *sumul ˙hoy lol cwo˙cha ton˙nye hwen hi [TYANG-QAN] ˙ay ˙sye [˙CYWUY] ˙hotaswo˙la* (1481 Twusi 16:18a) for twenty years I have been getting drunk all over Cháng-ān.

2. (impersonal oblique subject). ¶*na˙la.h ay ˙sye mwo˙lwomay sa˙hwo.m ol [HHOYNG] ˙hwol ˙t iGe˙n i ˙Gwa* (1481 Twusi 20:4b) while the nation must conduct warfare … .

3. = **pota** than. ¶*a˙to˙l i a˙p[i] oy ˙na.h ay ˙sye kwop˙koy-˙kwom sa˙la* (1459 Wel 1:47b) the son lives to be fully double his father's age and … .

˙*ay ˙sye*, pcl + inf < °*sye˙ta* (vi 'stands'). Examples? SEE ˙*oy ˙sye*.

˙*ay ˙'sye*, abbr < ˙*ay i˙sye*. being at. Examples?

˙*ay ˙sye n'*, pcl + pcl + pcl. ¶*pwuthye s na˙la.h ay ˙sye n' pwuthye s na˙la˙h ol ha˙nol s ka˙won-˙toy ˙'la ho˙kwo TYWUNG-˙KWUYK ˙ul TWONG nyek ¨ko.z i˙la ˙ho˙ya TWONG-¨THWO ˙y˙la ˙hono˙n i* (1459 Wel 1:30ab) as for Buddha's land, they say Buddha's land to be in the sky and China to be its eastern border, so it is called the Land of the East.

˙*ay ˙ta ˙ka*, pcl + cop transferentive + pcl. ¶ ¨*es.tyey si˙le-kwom ¨na lol pwo˙nayya ne 'y ¨ko.z ay ˙ta ˙ka twu˙lye.n ywo* (1481 Twusi 25:27b) why must you send me off and keep me at your side?

'*ay to* = [h]*ay to* = *hay to*, infinitive < *hata* + particle.

˙*ay ˙two*, pcl + pcl. ¶*ZYE-LOY ˙i na˙la[h] ¨spwun a˙ni ˙'la nyenu na˙la.h ay ˙two ¨ta ¨kye˙sya* (1459 Wel 7:53a) the tathāgata was everywhere, not only in this land but also in other lands and … . SEE ˙*ey ˙two*, ˙*uy ˙two*.

-*ay ya* [var] = -*a ya*

'*ay ya* = [h]*ay ya* = *hay ya*, inf < *hata*.

-*ay yay 'ci* [var] = -*a ya 'ci*

'*ay yo* = [h]*ay yo* = *hay yo*, inf < *hata* + particle.

˙*ay ˙za*, pcl + pcl (alt of ˙*ey ˙za*). ¶ ˙*i ˙nal [˙]ay ˙za me˙li ¨cwos˙soWo˙n i* (1449 Kok 109) on this very day we bowed our heads.

-˙*a ˙za*, inf + pcl. SEE -˙*e ˙za*.

/···*c*/. By 1445 before pause (noun-final) the affricates ···*c* and ···*ch* had merged with the sibilant ···*s*, which then began merging with /···*t*/ in the early 1500s.

c. variant after vowel, *N, NG, N,* or *LQ* (before ˙*CCO* only, in 1465 Wen only) of *s* (adnominal pcl): *TI c ˙CCO* (2:2:1:39a) the character *TI*; *HHWANG c ˙CCO* (2:2:1:48a) the character *HHWANG*; *NGWEN c ˙CCO* (1:1:2:16a) the character *NGWEN*; ˙*PPWULQ c ˙CCO* (1:1:2:37a) the character ˙*PPWULQ*.

-*c'*, 1. abbr < -*ci*: ~ *anh.ta*, ~ *yo*.

2. abbr < -*cek*. **pipic' pipic'** = **pipi-cek** *pipi-cek* rubbing together [< *pipita*].

ca < ¨*CYA*, quasi-free n. person, one, thing.

1. ¶*i (ku, ce)* ~ this (that) person; he/him, she/her. **ilen** ~ such persons. ***Cwuk.un ca to iss.ta*** Some died.

2. when attached as suffix to a monosyllable ···*q ca* is usually spelled ···*cca* (< ···*q ca*); CF *swulanq-ca* egg poacher.

2a. **cēngcca** < **cēngq-ca**, **cincca** < **cinq-ca** a genuine (the real) thing. **cōcca** < **cōq-ca** a counterfeit. **kācca** < **kāq-ca** a false thing. **kongcca** < **kongq-ca** = **kongq kes** something free (had for nothing). **kōycca** < **kōyq-ca** a mystery man, an odd person. **malcca** < **malq-ca** the last (youngest) son. **mongcca** < **mongq-ca** a greedy person (= **mongni** < **mongq i**). **nalcca** < **nalq-ca**, **sayngcca** < **sayngq-ca** raw stuff; a greenhorn. **pyelcca** < **pyelq-ca** an eccentric, a nut. **tāycca** (< **tāyq-ca**) a big one. **thongcca** = **thongq-ca** the whole lump/mass. **māycca** = **māyp-ca** [DIAL] a fastidious person (usually woman). **twūncca** = **twūnq-ca** [DIAL] a dull person. Perhaps: **alcca** = **alccam** the best thing/part. But **thōyq-ca** 'rejection' has **ca** < ˙*CCO* 'written character', though the word has the prescribed spelling **thōycca**.

2b. **chalcca** (? < **chalq-ca**) a stickler. **ppengcca** (? < **ppengq-ca**) defective useless thing. **hāyngcca** ill will (= **hāyng-thi**).

ca, interj. come on/now, here (you/we are)! [inviting or urging] ¶***Ca, tulca*** (Come on,) let's drink. ***Ca, thayksi ka wass.ta, ppalli tha la*** Here's the taxi — get right in!

ca < ˙*ca*, inf < **cata** < °*ca˙ta* (sleeps).

-**ca**, subjunctive assertive (= propositive).

1. (PLAIN suggestion). CF -**ko ca (ce)**.

Let's eat. **Kaca** Let's go. **Wuli ku ke l' kkok kwūkyeng haca** Let's see that for sure.

1b. let me; let's; I want to, I will. ¶**Nay ka onul nāyca** Let me pay today. **Eti poca** Let's see now (Let's have a look at it) = Let me see. **Yēyki com tut.ca** Let me hear what you have to say = Tell me about it. **Na to com mekca** Let me eat some, too = I'll have some, too.

2. (temporal uses).

2a. as soon as, when (= ~ **māca**); and at once, instantly (1916 Gale 48). ¶**Kolye ttay ey tul.e oca** when we come to the Kolye period. **Phoun i cwukca māca** [1]**Yi Sengkyey ka hwanseng ul ollyess.ta** As soon as Phoun died [1]Yi Sengkyey raised a cry of joy. **Kaman iss.ca** Hold on; just a minute. *mekca thwo ho.yes.swo* (1916 Gale 48) I ate it and at once vomited. *pwul ey tule kaca nwok.as.swo* (ibid.) it went into the fire, and instantly melted. UNUSUAL with adj or adj-n: **Nal i ttattus haca** (= **hay cica**) **pi ka onta** As soon as the weather is (= gets) warm, it starts raining.

2b. when = as a result (of), where(upon). ¶**Swuto ka hām.lak toyca cēncayng un kkuth-nass.ta** With the fall of the capital the war came to an end. **Ku nun hak.kyo ka mun ul tat.key toyca kyōwen ul saim hayss.ta** When the school was closed he resigned his position as an instructor there. **Pap i nuc.ca** (= **nuc.uni-kka**) **an mek.ko kass.ta** The meal was late so he left without eating. **Ku** [1]**yeymun i ku ka wēn hanun kyengwu ey al-mac.ca ku nun kot ku kes ul chāythayk hayss.ta** The example sentence fit the situation he wanted, so he chose it immediately. **Āmuli pukkulepki lo se 'ni haca 'nun māl han mati cocha mōs hani?** However bashful you may be, can't you say even a word like 'let's do it'?

NOTE 1: The usual form is with **māca** rather than **mālca**, perhaps because it is a stereotyped structure created at an earlier period, when it was usual to drop the liquid of -L- stems before /t/ or /c/, as well as before /s/. Notice that an -l- in the first stem is sometimes dropped too: **kē(l)ca māca** as soon as one hangs it up.

NOTE 2: Honorific can be applied only to the first form: **na-kasica māca** as soon as you left (*na-kaca māsica, *na-kasica māsica).

3. (with past) even if it/one did (SEE -ess.ca). **hayss.ca** even if we said … = suppose, if (say);

if we were to say, if we make it the case that. SEE -ta 'yss.ca, -la 'yss.ca, -ca 'yss.ca.

4. (cop) at the same time (that it is): SEE **ica**.
'ca, abbr < haca, < ica.
c'ā, abbr < cwā < cōwa = cōh.a, inf < cōh.ta.
caca, subjunctive attentive < **cata**. let's sleep!
-ca 'ca, abbr < -ca (ko) haca.
caci, suspective < **cata**
-ca 'ci, abbr < -ca (ko) haci. (Also -cayci?)
caci l', abbr < caci lul, suspective + particle.
-ca cocha, subj assert + pcl [awkward]. ¶(Ūmsik ul) **mekca cocha an hani kekceng ita** It worries me that he shows no inclination even to eat.
-ca cwuuy, (cpd n). the doctrine of "let's … ": **haca cwuuy** activism. **nōlca cwuuy** hedonism. **mekca cwuuy** epicurism.
-(c)cak, suffix that derives adj-n (Xh), adv (XX), vni (XXh = Xk); LIGHT ↔ -(c)cek; PARAINTENSIVE -chak. ¶**alk-cak** pockmarked < **alk.ta**. **halccak** = **halth-cak** in little licks < **halth.ta**. **hopi-cak** scooping, gouging, grooving < **hopita**. **kalk-cak** scratching, scraping < **kalk.ta**. **(k)kam-cak** dotted < **(k)kām.ta** is black. **(k)kam-(c)cak** blinking, budging, quick, sudden, startled. **kantu'-cak** swaying gently < **kantul**. **kkol-ccak** (= **kkol-ttak**) gurgling < **kkol**. **(k)kom-(c)cak** budging, yielding, giving. **(k)kop-cak** bowing in awe < **kopta** is bent. **manci-cak** (? / -cek) **kelita** fumbles, twiddles < **mancita**. **nap-cak** = **nap-cwuk** flat (< **nelp.ta**). **waku'-cak** seething < **wakul**.
-ca k, [DIAL] abbr < -ca ko, subj assert + pcl: ~ hata.
-ca ka, subj assert + pcl [in neg cop phrases only]. ¶**Kaca ka ani 'la oca 'nun ttus ita** It does not mean let's go there, it means let's come here.
c'ākan (ey) = cwāwu-kan (ey)
cakceng < ˙CAK-˙TTYENG, 1. n. a decision, a determination; an intention, a plan, an idea, a thought, a notion; a purpose, a project, a goal: SEE -ulq ~ ita.

2. ~ hata, vnt. decides, determines, plans, proposes, intends (to do), makes up one's mind (to do), fixes one's mind (on doing).
-(c)cak-cikun hata, bnd cpd adj-n. LIGHT ↔ -(c)cek-; PARAINTENSIVE -chak-. is rather …ish. ¶**nok- ~** is rather languid. **talq- ~** is rather sweet.

-ca 'key, abbr < -ca (ko) hakey
(*)-ca khenyeng, subj assert + pcl [awkward]. ¶Ŭmsik ul mekca khenyeng [better: mekca haki (nun) khenyeng] tul.ye 'ta poci to anh.nunta He doesn't even look at his food, much less want to eat it.
caki < ˙CCO-ˇKUY, 1. n. (one's) self, oneself; he/himself, she/herself; you/yourself (p. 135). ¶ ~ sayngkak man hata thinks of oneself only. ~ maum tay lo hata does as one pleases. ~ lul pānseng hata reflects on oneself. Ku nun caki ka sinmun kica 'la ko sinpun ul palk.hyess.ta He identified himself as a reporter.
  2. adnoun. self-, auto-, ego-. ¶ ~ āmsi autosuggestion. ~ choymyen autohypnosis. ~ cwuuy egoism, egotism. ~ huysayng self-sacrifice. ~ kyengmyel self-contempt. ~ pōcon self-preservation. ~ pon.wi egoism, egoism. ~ swungpay self-worship.
  CF ce, cey.
-ca 'ki, abbr < -ca [ko] haki (? ey)
-ca kko [LIVELY] = -ca ko
-ca kkwuna (tul), subj assert + pcl (+ pcl). let's. ¶Kkuth kkaci ilk.e poca kkwuna (tul) Let's read to the end.
cako < ca˙kwo, ger < cata < °ca˙ta
-ca ko, subj assert + pcl.
  1. suggesting that we do.
  2. (sentence-final; usually pronounced -ca kwu) let's just [softens a suggestion]. ¶Ca kaca kwu Let's go, now.
cᵃ/ₑksimyen < cyaksimyen (1703), cyakimyen (1656), postmod. if (it is a case of): SEE -ulq ~ . ? abbr < cek 'time' + isimyen [obs] 'if it exist' (> iss.umyen); si (< ˙ssɪ 'time') + abbr cop conditional; CF ccak hamyen, -ulq seks ey, -ulla chimyen.
cakwu = cako, ger < cata.
-ca kwu, 1. = -ca ko.
  2. [northern DIAL] = -sey na [FAMILIAR suggestion].
  CF -la kwu.
cal, adv. 1. well, nicely, satisfactorily, favorably, fortunately.
  2. well, closely, thoroughly, intimately.
  3. well, excellently, expertly.
  4. well, carefully, with care; safely, without incident, in good health. ¶Cal ka (yo) 'Bye [to one who is going]. Cal iss.e (yo) 'Bye [to one who is staying].

  5. 5a. lots, a lot, in large number(s)/quantity, sufficiently, adequately.
   5b. lots, a lot, often, frequently.
  6. readily, easily.
  7. well, suitably, properly.
  8. well, at a good time, timely, opportunely, nicely (timed).
cal(q) < cal(q), prosp mod < cata < °ca˙ta. ¶QUM-˙YWOK ˙on namcin ˇkyeci˙p i hon-˙toy cal ˙ss i˙Gwo (1459 Wel 1:25b) [the word] "lust" refers to a man and a woman sleeping together. si˙hwok e˙tu˙wun ci˙p uy cal cey (1462 ¹Nung 9:88a) if you sleep in dark quarters.
-ca 'l(q), abbr < -ca (ko) hal(q). ¶Poca 'lq kes ēps.ta There is nothing worth looking at.
-ca 'la, abbr < -ca (ko) hala
ca la, inf + pcl = cake la sleep!
cala, subj attent < cata. ~ ko hanta tells one to sleep.
cam < ˙com, 1. subst < cata < °ca˙ta sleeps.
  2. n. sleep. ~ (i) tulta goes to sleep. ~ (ul) cata sleeps, has a sleep.
ˇcam, modulated subst < °ca˙ta. ¶˙skoy˙ywom ˙kwa ˇcam ˙kwa y syang˙nyey hona˙h i˙la (1462 ¹Nung 10:1b) being awake and being asleep are always just one and the same thing. ˙skoy˙m ye ˇca˙m ay mwuy˙Gwe ˙PYEN ˙hwo˙m ay ni˙lu˙le (1462 ¹Nung 10:81-2) one reaches the point where one changes in movements whether awake or asleep. ˇca.m ol [PPYEN-QAN] ˙hi ˙ho˙ya (1481 Twusi 8:27b) he slumbers peacefully. ˙com ˇca.m ol [TTYANG-SSYANG] ˙il honwo.n i [= ˙honwo˙n i] (1481 Twusi 23:15a) they always go to bed early.
-ca 'm, 1. abbr < -ca [ko] ham.
  2. [Hamkyeng DIAL] abbr < -ca 'm u'.
-ca māca SEE -ca
-ca man, subj assert + pcl. let's do it but. ~ un SAME. ¶Ne to kaca man (un) caymi nun pyel lo ēps.ulq kes ita I want you to go with me, but it won't be much fun for you.
-ca 'm u' [Hamkyeng DIAL] = -ca 'm una
-ca 'm una, abbr < -ca (ko) ham + pcl. let's just do it, OK? (similar to -ulye 'm una).
-ca 'myen, abbr < -ca (ko) hamyen. if one wants to do it, if one will / would do it; (in order) to do it. ¶Iyaki lul te casey hi tut.ca 'myen cip ey ka se ka cōh.keyss.ta (CM 2:95) If you want to hear more of the story it would be better to wait till we get home. Casey hi tā

poca 'myen yele sikan kellilq ke 'p.nita To see it all thoroughly would take several hours. Māl haca 'myen ... if you ask me; to put in plainly; so to speak, as it were, if anything.
can, mod < cata
-ca 'n('), abbr < -ca [ko] han (hanun)
cana, < cata: 1. advers. 2. FAMILIAR indic attent (= question).
-ca 'na, abbr < -ca (ko) hana
¨ca·nay, adv. by oneself, in person, personally, privately. ¶ ¨ca·nay ¨spwun ·e·ti-ti Wi ·nom kolo·chywo·m ol a·ni hol ·ss oy (1447 Sek 24:40a) as he was good just privately but he did no teaching of it to others. ¨ca·nay ZYE-LOY ·lol ma·ccop·kwo (1462 [1]Nung 1:31a) welcomed the tathāgata in person and ... .
caney < canay (1730) < canoy (1676), n. you [INTIMATE]. ¶Caney yeki anc.key na You sit here. CF ne, tangsin.
caney, FAMILIAR indic assert < cata
-ca 'ney, abbr < -ca (ko) haney. suggests we do.
-cang, -ccang (-q cang), suffix.
  1. = -cak (somewhat); HEAVY -ceng. ippu-cang hata / sulepta is lovely. mal-ccang (/mel-cceng) hata is intact, perfect (= malk-cang) — CF ceng hata is clean, pure (< ¨TTYENG). (k)kam-cang (= (k)kem-ceng) black.
  2. [? < 3 (place)]. aph ~ the lead, head, vanguard. kkuth ~ the end. ulumq ~ threat (subst < uluta menaces). elimq ~ '?' (CM 1:230) — mistake for elim-ca(y)ngi namby-pamby? CF talq-cang month (long), kot-cang at once, nuk-cang lingering.
  3. bnd postn (< ¨TTYANG). place. kyēngki ~ sports field. mūto ~ dance hall.
  4. bnd postn, usually -q cang (< *·CANG = ·SSANG). letter, document. hyep.pak ~ a threatening (intimidating) letter. [n]yenhaq ~ a New Year's card / note. phyochangq ~ a letter of commendation.
  5. (? < 6; ? < ¨TTYANG bnd n 'staff'; ? < TYANG bnd n. 'long [thing]'). "pis-cang" = (mun)piq cang a door bolt. "ttis-cang" = ttiq cang wooden piece across boarding. wulq cang a fence pale; [DIAL] a fence — CF tam cang [? DIAL] a wall.
  6. (< ·TYANG) stretch; sheet, layer.
  6a. el.umq cang layer / sheet / block of ice. kiwaq cang tile.
  6b. kwulumq cang a cloud sheet, overcast.

kwutulq cang thin flat stone for flooring over a hypocaust.
  7. phal-ccang = phalq cang folding one's arms. hwal-ccang = hwalq cang the body of a bow (to shoot arrows). CF (p)pet-cang tali a stiff leg.
cangi, cayngi, postn. [somewhat disrespectful] a professional / constant doer of ... , -er, -monger, a man who does ... ; a person characterized by, (or noted for) ... . CF -ce(y)ngi; -cha(y)ngi. [? < ·CCYANG bnd n 'artisan' + -i; ? < ca < ¨CYA 'person' or ci + -angi]
  ¶cwūceng ~ a drunken brawler. hayllo ~ a "hello" = an American; a westerner. hwān ~ a cheap artist. [1]ikan ~ a troublemaker. ip nay ~ a mimic(ker), an impersonator. iyaki ~ a story teller. kāsal ~ = kāsal kkwun, kāsal-i a hateful stuck-up person. kēcis mal ~ a liar. kep ~ a coward. kho ~ a "nose" = an Occidental, a westerner. khollok ~ a person with a hacking cough. kkomkkom ~ a stickler. kocip ~ a stubborn (pigheaded) person. kwansang ~ a physiognomist, a fortune-teller. kwūsik ~ an old-fashioned person, an old fogey. kwutwu ~ a shoe man (= a shoe dealer, a shoemaker, or a shoe repairer). manman ~ a pushover, a softy. mūtwu ~ a tanner. mes ~ a dandy. oip ~ an unfaithful husband, a philanderer. ōm ~ a person with the itch. pes ~ an unskilled artisan. pic ~ a moneylender. sācwu ~ a kind of fortune-teller. simswul ~ "a dog in the manger". sōmun ~ a scandalmonger. ssām ~ a quarrelsome person. swusen ~ a fussbudget; a chatterbox. tāycang ~ a blacksmith. ttaym ~ a tinker. ttotulak ~ a goldbeater. ttwu ~ a pimp. yangpok ~ a person in western clothes; a tailor. yāsal cangi = yāsal-i a peevish or crabby person, a crab, a curmudgeon. [1]yēm ~ a mortician, an undertaker. Yēyswu ~ a Bible thumper, a Christer.
'/-c' anh.ta, abbr < (ha)ci anh.ta. is not. kath.c' anh.ta, uyces 'c' anh.ta, eccanh.ta < enc.c' anh.ta, cemcanh.ta ? < cēlm.ci anh.ta, ? < cem(cik) haci anh.ta. CF -ch' anh.ta.
'c' anh- = ici anh-: SEE p. 323.
cani, < cata: 1. sequential. 2. indic attent.
-ca 'ni, abbr < -ca (ko) hani. ¶mekca 'ni pay ka puluko, nam cwuca 'ni akkapta is too full to eat it and too greedy to give it to others.

cwukca 'ni chengchwun i akkapta one is too young to die. SEE **kuleca 'ni**.
-ca 'no, abbr < **-ca (ko) hano** [< **hanun ko**]. [? DIAL] = **-ca 'y**?
canta, proc indic assert < **cata**
-ca 'nta, abbr < **-ca (ko) hanta**.
  1. suggests that we do.
  2. let's (do it [I urge]). ¶**Swūnphung ey toch ul talko payq nol.i kaca 'nta** Let's hoist sail in the favorable wind and go boating!
-ca 'nta 'yss.ca, abbr **-ca (ko) hanta (ko) hayss.ca**. ¶**Āmuli kaca 'nta 'yss.ca na n' mōs kakeyss.e** Urge me as you will, I won't go with you. SYN **-ca 'yss.ca**.
canun, proc mod < **cata**
-ca 'nun, abbr < **-ca (ko) hanun**. ¶**Ile 'ta ka tul ecci toyca 'nun kes in ya** What is to become of us if we let things go on like this? **Musunq īl lo na tele kkaci kaca 'nun ya** What on earth do you want me to go along for?
cao, AUTH < **cata**
-ca 'o, abbr < **-ca (ko) hao**
-caop- / **-cao(w)-** [< **-saop-**; CF - ̈**zop-**]. [obs] humbly does = I do. ¶**Tut.caopkentay** ... , **Tut.cao(wu)ni** ... From what I hear (I am told that) ... . **Mut.caopkentay** ... , **Mut.cao(wu)ni** ... (, ?**Mut.caopko** ...) May I inquire / ask ... . **Pat.caopko** ... I receive / accept / obey ... . **Anc.caop.naita** I seat myself. NOTE: Usually attached only to stems that end in **t**, **c**, or **ch**. Behaves like -W- stems. ABBR **-cap-** / **-caw-**.
cap < ˙**CCAP**.
  1. adnoun. mixed; poor; impure; vulgar. ~ **cōng.lyu** mixed kinds. ~ **kes** sundries. ~ **mas** adulterated (impure) flavor. ~ **phul** weeds. ~ **sayngkak** unworthy thoughts. ~ **soli** / **māl** foul language. ~ **son (cil)** busywork, unnecessary work. ~ **swuip** miscellaneous income.
  2. bnd n (pre-postnominal). ~ **toyta** = ~ **sulepta** is vulgar, low, dirty.
-cap-, abbr < **-caop-** (humble). NOTE: Behaves like -W- stems (inf **-cawe** or **-cawa**), conditional **-cawumyen**.
-capcap, bnd adj-n (~ **hata**); LIGHT ↔ **-cepcep**; after consonant **-ucapcap**. ···ish, slightly tinged or colored. SEE **-(u)sulum**.
ca 'p.nita, abbr < **-ca (ko) hap.nita**
-ca puthe, subj assert + pcl. ¶**Ku nun tāyhak ey tul.e kaca puthe ttwie nan caycwu lul natha-nāyki sīcak hayss.ta** He began showing outstanding talent right from when he entered college.
ca se, inf + pcl
casik < ¨**CO**-˙**SIK**, n. 1. one's children.
  2. [derogatory] a damn guy, a sonuvabitch, a bastard (of a fellow) [worse than **nom**]. CF **nyesek**.
˙**casi˙ta**, hon < ˚**ca˙ta** (sleeps). ¶**ku ˙casi˙m ye ¨kyesya˙m ol** (1475 Nay 1:44a) that he is there asleep. **wo˙nol hwangchwon i˙la ¨hwol sta˙h ay ˙ka ˙casi˙kwo** (?1517- Pak 1:64b) today we will go to a place called Hwangchwon (Yellow Village) and sleep there, and ... .
¨**c'a˙si˙ta** = ¨**cwasi˙ta** (? < **ca˙p-osi-** 'take'), hon verb = **capswusita** (eats). ¶**hon ti˙Gwuy ¨thang ¨c'a˙si˙ki mos˙kwo** (?1517- Pak 1:64b) finished a meal of soup and (then) ... . ¨**c'a˙si˙ti a˙n' 'ye ¨kye˙sike˙tun** (1586 Sohak 2:4b) if you have not eaten.
˙**casya**, inf < ˙**casi˙ta** (sleeps). ¶**holo s ˙pam ˙casya** (1482 Nam 2:76a) sleeps a night and ... .
˙**casya···** , modulated stem < ˙**casi˙ta** (sleeps). ¶¨**nim-kum ˙casya˙m ay ˙stwo ˙nwu y** [KWONG-PWONG] ˙**hozopnon ˙kwo** (1481 Twusi 10:9b) who will look after the king in his sleep?
¨**c'a˙sya···** (= ¨**cwa˙sya···**), modulated stem < ¨**c'a˙si˙ta** (eats).
¨**c'a˙sye**, infinitive < ¨**c'a˙si˙ta** (eats). ¶¨**man˙il i˙muy ¨c'a˙sye ¨kye˙sike˙tun** (1586 Sohak 2: 4b; sic ¨**man-˙il**) if you have already eaten.
cat-, ? pref (bnd adv / adn). fine, small. ~ **cwulum** fine creases / folds / pleats. ~ **kālta** grinds it up fine. ~ **talta** is small, petty. ~ **ta(la)h.ta** is extremely fine. [? < **ca'-q** < **ca-l-** be fine / small]
-ca 'ta (ka), abbr < **-ca (ko) hata (ka)**
cata < ˚**ca˙ta**, vi. sleeps. MK subst (and noun < subst) is ˙**com**, not *cam; modulated subst is ¨**cam**. MK infinitive ˙**ca**. ¶**wuli kuce tyey ˙tu˙le ca˙kwo ka˙cye** (?1517- ¹No 1:10b) let's go in over there and sleep before going on. ˙**na non ˙TTWO-TTWUW s mwol ˙Gay ˙yey ˙cata˙la** (1482 Kum-sam 4:5a) I slept on the sand at the ferry point. ˙**pul s pi˙ch ey ˙sye ˙cate˙la** (1481 Twusi 8:9b) they slept in the glow of the fire.
-ca 'tey, abbr < **-ca (ko) hatey**
-ca 'ti, abbr < **-ca (ko) hati**
ca to, 1. inf + pcl. even sleeping, sleeps but.
  2. noun + pcl. even / also a person who ··· . ¶**Cwuk.un ca to iss.ta** Some died.

¨ca˙toy, modulated accessive < °ca˙ta. ¶i˙thu˙l ul ¨ca˙toy (1481 Twusi 23a) slept for two days, and ... .
-ca 'toy, abbr < -ca (ko) hatoy
ca tul, infinitive + particle
-ca tul, 1. subj assert + pcl. ¶Ca kath.i swūhak kongpu haca tul Come on, let's get our math study done together.
2. abbr < -ca (ko) tul. ~ hanta suggests that we do.
-ca 'tula, abbr < -ca (ko) hatula
-ca 'tun, abbr < -ca (ko) hatun
cāy < ˙CCOY, adnoun. resident in. ~ Mi(kwuk) resident in America. ~ Il(pon) resident in Japan. ~ Sewul resident in Seoul.
cāy- < ˙CHOY, bnd adn. re-, second. ~ ip.hak readmission (to school). ~ sēnke reelection.
-ca 'y, abbr < -ca (ko) hay. suggests that we do.
ca ya, infinitive + particle
-ca ya, subj assert + pcl. ¶Kece mekca (ko) ya halq swu iss.na? How can we possibly propose to take it for nothing?
-cayca = -ca 'ca
-ca 'y la, abbr < -ca (ko) hay la
cāy ney, abbr < ce ay ney [DISRESPECTFUL] they / them. ~ tul SAME.
cayngi, var = cangi. ¶welkup ~ a "salaryman" (= salaried employee, white-collar worker).
ca yo, infinitive + particle
? -ca yo [Phyengyang DIAL] = -kulye
-ca 'y se, abbr < -ca (ko) hay se
-ca 'yss-, abbr < -ca (ko) hayss-
-ca 'yss.ca, abbr < -ca (ko) hayss.ca. ¶Āmuli kath.i kaca 'yss.ca na n' mōs kakeyss.e Urge me as you will, I won't go with you. SYN -ca 'nta 'yss.ca.
-ca 'y to, abbr < -ca (ko) hay to
-ca 'y tul, abbr < -ca (ko) hay tul (plural subject)
-ca 'y ya, abbr < -ca (ko) hay ya
-ca 'y yo, abbr < -ca (ko) hay yo
˙ca za, inf < °ca˙ta + pcl. ¶i˙thul s ˙pam ˙ca za (1481 Twusi 16:66a) only if one sleeps the next night.
-cca, suffix. SEE ca (quasi-free n).
ccak$_1$, 1. n. (= phyen-ccak, phyen) side. ¶i ~ ce ~ this side and that side, us and them. ~ salang one-sided (unrequited) love. Ccak ul cca kaciko nol.i lul sīcak hay ya 'ci Let's choose up sides before we start playing.
2. quasi-free n. (= ccok) direction; place. ¶Āmu ccak / ccok ey to mōs ssunta It is no good anywhere.
3. [? rare] quasi-free noun. (= kkol) shape, form, appearance. ¶Ku key musun ccak / kkol in ya What's this mess?!
4. ? bound noun. kwēy ~ a box. polki ~ buttocks. tōn ~ the circumference of a brass coin (yepcen).
ccak$_2$, n, counter. 1. a set, a pair. han-ccak a (full) set. ~ ul ilwuta forms (makes up) a pair.
2. one of a matched pair; a counterpart. kwutwu sēy ~ three odd / unmatched shoes. ~ (i) ēps.ta has no counterpart; is unmatched, unparalleled. SEE -ki ccaki i ēps.ta.
3. (= kalpi ~) a side (of ribs). kalpi han ~ a side of ribs.
-ccak SEE -(c)cak
cc^a/$_e$ksimyen SEE c^a/$_e$ksimyen
ccali, postnoun.
1. worth, value. ¶chen-wen ~ ciphyey (moca) a thousand-wen bill (hat). elma ~ wuphyo a stamp of what denomination / value?
2. amount. ¶samsip-kun ~ photay / pūtay a 30-pound bag (of rice). yel mal ~ (= tul.i) kamani a ten-mal bag.
3. [colloq] a person wearing ... . ¶yangpok ~ the fellow in the suit.
4. [impolite, except when used of one's own children] (a child of) the age of. ¶Yelq sal ccali ka hana iss.ta I have a ten-year-old.
-ccang, 1. (= -q cang < ˙CCANG entrails) pay ~, po ~ hidden thought, ulterior motive, mental reservation; boldness, nerve.
2. SEE (-q) cang.
ccay$_1$ < ˙cay (1465) < ˙ca˙hi (1459) < ˙ca (1459) — ¨twulch⋯ < ¨twulh c⋯, ¨seych⋯ < ¨seyh c⋯ ; ?< cha(y) < ˙CHO 'next'.
1. postn. a rank, a grade, -th. ¶ches (twūl, sēy) ~ first (second, third). ches (twūl, sēy) ~ lo firstly (secondly, thirdly). mal ~ [? DIAL], kkuth ~ (pen) last (= kkol-cci). twūl ~ lul chaci hata takes the second place, ranks second. sēy ~ lo ttel.e cita drops to third place. sēykyey ey se tases ~ lo khun san the fifth highest mountain in the world. twūl ~ hyeng the second oldest brother. ches ~ lo col.ep hata graduates at the head of one's class. Ku ka twūl ccay lo wass.ta He was the

second to come. **Yeki on kes un i kes ulo sēy ccay pen ita** This is the third time I have been here. VAR **cci**. CF **cēy**.

2. postmod = **chay** (just as it is).

ccay₂, postn. and all, together with, inclusive of, as it is. ¶**thong** ~ whole, intact, untouched, uncut. **sakwa lul kkepcil** ~ **mekta** eats an apple, rind and all. **sayngsen ul kasi** ~ **samkhye pelita** devours a fish, bones and all. **namu lul ppuli** ~ **ppopta** pulls up a tree by the roots. SYN **chay**. CF **tay**.

ccay₃, postmod. SEE **-ul ccay**.

-ccek SEE **-cek**

ccekta (= **-q cēkta**), postnom adj insep. feels gives/has a feeling of. **kyem.yen (kyeymyen)** ~ is abashed, shamefaced. **kōyi** ~ is queer, strange. **kōylan** ~ is disgusting (to see) [< blushing with shame]. **mian** ~ is regretful, apologetic, embarrassed. **misim** ~ is doubtful, suspicious. **uysim** ~ is doubtful, questionable (= **uysim sulepta**).

-cceng SEE **-(c)ceng**

-ccepta SEE **cepta**

ccey, postmod. SEE **-ul ccey**.

cci, postn [Seoul DIAL] = **ccay**. ¶**ches** ~, **twū** ~, **sēy** ~ first, second, third.

-ccik SEE **-(c)cik**

-ccimak SEE **-cimak**

ccok, quasi-free n. direction; side. ¶**palun/olun** ~ the right. **ōyn** ~ **ey** on the left. **i (ku, ce)** ~ this (that) direction/side. **tong/se** ~ **ey** to the east/west. **kanun (kan, katun)** ~ (CM 2:71) the direction one is going (has gone, was going). **Palam i pūlci anh.nun ccok ulo sālam tul un phī hay se tallye kass.ta** (CM 2:229) The people fled, running off in the direction that the wind was not blowing from. **Āmu ccok/ccak ey to mōs ssunta** It's no good anywhere. CF **phyen**; **cek** [obs]. NOTE: Instead of *nay ccok you say **nay ka iss.nun ccok** the side where I am. (Contrast **nay phyen**.) Yet CM 2:71 gives examples of **wuli casin ccok** and ("uncommon") **wuli casin uy ccok**; also **eti/enu** ~, **mōtun** ~, **ōn kac'** ~, **yele** ~ .

-ccok SEE **-(c)cok**

ccok-ccok, postmod. on every occasion (that), whatever time (that), whenever, every time, as often as ··· . ¶**māl hanun** ~ **ic.e mek.nunta** forgets every word that you say. **Ku twūl un mannanun ccok-ccok ssawum ita** Every time those two meet there is a quarrel. [? < **cek** time; ? < **ccok** direction; CF **kan tey cok-cok** (set phrase, ? rare) ? < ʽCYWOK bnd n 'foot']

-cco lo = **-q co lo**. SEE **co₂**, **co₃**.

-ccolok SEE **āmu** ~

··· ¨**ccop-** < **-c-** ¨**zop-**, < **-ch-**¨**zop-**

ccum, particle.

1. about (so much), approximately; (of a) caliber; so much of, of that extent. ¶**nēy sikan** ~ about four hours. **han-twū kun** ~ about two pounds. **Ku sālam ccum un mūncey ka ani ya** He's a pushover (= if he is all we have to worry about there's no problem). CF **yak** ··· .

2. at about, about (a certain time); SYN **kyēng**. ¶**nēy si** ~ about four o'clock. **meych si** ~ **hay se** about what time.

3. by (a certain time); SYN **kkaci ey**, **an ulo**. ¶¹**nayil** ~ by tomorrow.

4. (approximate) place. ¶**ku/i** ~ **ey** around there/here, in that/this vicinity. **Ce ccum kkaci ka-polq ka** Let's walk on as far as over there. **Sīcheng i eti ccum iss.ci yo** Just where is City Hall?

CF **theym**, **thek**; **cum** = **cuum**.

-ccum SEE **-(c)cum**

-ccumak SEE **-(c)cumak**

ccum chelem, pcl + pcl; ~ **iya**. ¶**Ku sālam ccum chelem (iya) mōs halq key mue iss.e** Is there any reason why you can't do as well as the likes of him?! SYN **chelem ccum**.

ccum cocha, pcl + pcl [? awkward]. ¶**Achim yelq si ccum cocha iluta 'ni sangtang hi cam-kkwuleki 'n ka pwā** He seems to be quite a sleepyhead to say even around ten o'clock in the morning is early!

~ **to**. ¶**I ccum cocha to mōs ttale omyen se musun khun soli ya** Why talk so big about following along when you can't even follow this far?

ccum ey, pcl + pcl. ¶**Twū si ccum ey osey yo** Come around two o'clock.

ccum eykey ya = **eykey ccum iya**. ¶**Ku sālam ccum eykey ya cici anh.ulq ke 'lq sey** I won't give in to the likes of him.

ccum ey 'na, pcl + pcl + pcl. at about ··· or so. ¶**Ku ka nēy si ccum ey 'na ol.nun ci** Perhaps he'll be here around four o'clock or so.

ccum ey se, pcl + pcl + pcl. ¶**I ccum ey se han cam capsita** Let's go to sleep (around) here somewhere.

ccum i, pcl + pcl. ¶**Sēy si ccum pota nēy si ccum i cōh.ci anh.ulq ka?** Wouldn't around four o'clock be better than around three? **Sēy si ccum i ani 'la nēy si ccum iess.ta** It wasn't around three o'clock, it was around four.

ccum ila to, (pcl + cop var inf) + pcl. ¶**Sēy si ccum ila to cōh.sup.nita** Around three o'clock will be OK.

ccum ina, pcl + copula adversative.

1. about (so much) or so. ¶**meych kun ~** about how many pounds. **meych sikan ~** about how many hours.

2. at about (a certain time) or so. ¶**nēy si ~** around four o'clock or so. **Ku ka nēy si ccum ina toymyen ol.nun ci** Perhaps he will be here around four or so.

3. by (a certain time) or around then.

ccum ina-ma, pcl + cop extended advers. ¶**Han ō-man wen ccum ina-ma iss.e pwass.umyen cōh.keyss.ta** I wish I had even fifty thousand wen.

ccum in tul, (pcl + cop mod) + postmod. ¶**Ku man han pūca ka sip-man wen ccum in tul mōs kkwue cwul lī ka iss.na?** Is there any reason why a rich man like him shouldn't lend one as much as a hundred thousand wen?

ccum iya, pcl + pcl. ¶**Ku man han pūca ka sip-man wen ccum iya mōs kkwue cwul lī ka iss.na?** Is there any reason why a rich man like him shouldn't lend one as much as a hundred thousand wen? **Kwacang cali ccum iya na to hakeyss.ci** I think I will get so I can handle the job of section chief, at least, one of these days.

ccum kkaci, pcl + pcl (**~ nun, ~ to, ~ ya**).

1. ¶**Sēy si ccum kkaci osey yo** Come by around three o'clock.

2. ¶**Sēy si ccum kkaci** [less commonly **kkaci ccum**] **nōlta ka kasey yo** Stay till at least around three o'clock.

3. ¶**Cong-lo ccum kkaci (nun) kel.e kass.ta ka keki se cha lul thalq ka hap.nita** I think I'll walk as far as Bell Street and then take a taxi. **I ccum kkaci ya ttale okeyss.ci** You will follow me this far at least (if not farther). **Ne nun nwun i cōh.a se mēn ku ccum kkaci to poci man, na nun yo ccum mace to mōs ponta** You've got good eyes so you can see all the way to over there but I can't see even this much.

ccum mace, pcl + pcl [? awkward]. ¶**Achim yelq si ccum mace iluta 'ni sangtang hi cam-kkwuleki 'n ka pwā** He seems to be quite a sleepyhead to say that even around ten in the morning is early!

~ to. SEE **ccum kkaci** for an example.

ccum man, pcl + pcl. ¶**Welkup i sip-man wen ccum man toye to kwaynchanh.ci yo** It is all right even if the salary is only around ten thousand wen.

~ ila to. ¶**I ccum man ila to hay noh.ko ya khun soli lul halq swu iss.ci** You have to do at least this much to have anything to brag about!

~ un. ¶**Ku ccum man un tul.ye 'ta pwā to toyci man te īsang un an toynta** It's all right to peer in that far, but nothing beyond.

ccum mankhum, particle + particle.

~ ina. ¶**Eti ccum mankhum ina kalq ka** I wonder how far we should go.

ccum mata, pcl + pcl. ¶**Ku nun nul cenyek ahop si ccum mata na-ka se cha lul han can masiko onta** He always goes out for a cup of tea around nine every evening.

ccum pota, pcl + pcl. ¶**Sēy si ccum pota nēy si ccum i cōh.ci anh.ulq ka** Wouldn't around four o'clock be better than around three?

~ nun. ¶**Ku ccum pota nun ce ccum i nās.keyss.ta** It would be better over there rather than there where you are.

~ to. ¶**Ku ccum (ey se) pota to i ccum ey se ponun phyen i te cal pointa** You can see better from here than from there where you are.

ccum puthe, pcl + pcl. ¶**Sēy si ccum puthe sīcak hapsita** Let's get started from around three o'clock.

~ ka. ¶**I ccum puthe ka elyewun kopi 'ta** From about here is the most difficult part.

~ nun. ¶**Kulena ce ccum puthe nun swiwun taymok ita** But from about there on is the easiest part.

~ se (less common than **ccum ey se puthe?**). ¶**Macimak kopi ccum puthe se** (= **ccum ey se puthe**) **talliki sīcak hay la** Start sprinting at the last critical moment.

ccum se, pcl + pcl (= **ccum ey se**). ¶**Ku ccum se wass.ta** I came from around there.

~ pota (nun / to); **~ puthe** (nun / ka).

ccum ssik, pcl + pcl (= **ssik ccum**). ¶**Han salam aph ey cwumek-pap twū-sene kay ccum**

ssik cwumyen cēmsim i toylq ke 'lq sey If each person is given two or three rice balls, that will do for lunch.

~ ila to. ¶I ccum ssik ila to cacwu man cwumyen cōh.keyss.ta I hope you'll often give at least this much to each one.

~ ina(-ma). ¶I ccum ssik ina-ma cacwu man cwumyen cōh.keyss.ta I hope you'll often give at least this much to each one.

~ man. ¶Han salam ey han-twū kay ccum ssik man kaciko kamyen toylq key 'p.nita You should give each only about two apiece.

~ man ila to. ¶Han salam aph ey han-twū kay ssik man ila to cacwu man cwumyen cōh.keyss.ta Even if it's just one or two per person I hope they are given often.

~ ulo (to). ¶Acwu elyewul ttay nun halwu ey ssal han hop ccum ssik ulo to sal.e wass.ess.ta At the most difficult times we managed to live on a hop of rice a day.

~ un. ¶Sakwa pāykup i cek.e to han salam aph ey ne-tāys kay ccum ssik un tol.a kal they 'ni kekceng mālkey Don't worry — the apples will be distributed so that each person gets around four or five at least.

ccum to, pcl + pcl. ¶Twū si ccum to cōh.ko, sēy si ccum to cōh.ta Around two o'clock is OK — or around three, either.

ccum ul, pcl + pcl. ¶I-kkacis chwuwi ccum ul ikye nāyci mōs hamyen etteh.key hay What is to be done if you can't take just this much cold?!

ccum ulo, pcl + pcl. ¶Ca i ccum ulo kkuth ul nāypsita Well, let's stop about here.

ccum un, pcl + pcl.
1. as for about (so much). ¶Nēy sikan ccum un kwaynchanh.ta I can maybe spend four hours on this (but no more).
2. as for about (a certain time). ¶Ilkop si ccum un nemu nuc.ci anh.ulq ka? Wouldn't seven o'clock be too late?
3. as for by (a certain time). ¶nēy si ~ by four o'clock. cikum ~ by now, by this time.

ccum uy, pcl + pcl. ¶Ku sālam ccum uy caysan un āmu kes to ani 'ta The property HE has is nothing.

ccwuk [= -q cwuk], bnd postmod. tul-ccwuk nal-ccwuk [= tulq cwuk nalq cwuk] uneven, jagged, serrated; CF tul lak nal lak.

-ccwuk SEE -cwuk
ccwung(-payki) SEE (-q) cwung(-payki)
ce₁ < ce (< ˙CCO 'self'), n.
1. [HUMBLE FORMAL] I, me. ¶Ce nun cal molukeyss.ˢup.nita I do not very well know, sir. ce ˙non inge ˙kuy ˙NGWEN ˙ho ˙nwon ˙ptu ˙t i ˙˙epta ˙n i ˙˙es ˙tyey 'Ge ˙n ywo (1459 Wel 13:35b) how come I have had no mind to want this [mahāyāna] part [of the doctrine]?
2. (= caki, casin, cachey) oneself; one (he, she). ¶ce ˙[G]wa ˙nom ˙kwa ˙lol ˙ecu ˙lye (1447 Sek 9:16b) dizzying self and others. ce ˙lul ˙HHAY ho ˙kwo (1462 ¹Nung 8:104b) harms one(self) and ... . a ˙pi ce ˙y a ˙to ˙l oy ˙ptu ˙t i sa ˙wonap ˙kwo ce ˙non HHWOW-˙KWUY ˙ho ˙ya (1447 Sek 13:19a) the heart of the father's own son is evil while he himself is gentle and noble.
3. [DIAL] you.

NOTE: The shape is cey (< ˙˙ce y) before pcl ka. Cey is also an abbreviation of cey ka and (< ce 'y) of ce uy < ce ˙uy; ce 'ykey is an abbreviation of ce eykey (< *ce ˙uy k[ung]ey). CF na, caki, casin, ˙cokya, ˙cokyay.

ce₂ < ˙tye. LIGHT co. CF i, ku.
1. adn. that (over there). ¶ ~ sālam / cip that person / house.
2. n. that (one), the more remote one, it.
3. (= ce i) that person over there, he / him (she / her) there, that one; (= ce kes) that thing, it, that.

ce₃, interj. well, by the way, say, if you please; er-r-r-r ··· , uh ··· . ¶Ce, ¹nayil tol.a osici yo? By the way, you're coming back tomorrow, aren't you? Ce, akka mwe 'la ko māl-ssum hasyess.ci yo Oh, what was it you said a while ago?

c'e 1. = cye = cyē, abbr < cie, infinitive < cita. SEE -ko ce.
2. = cwe = cwē, abbr < cwue, infinitive < cwuta.

ce (< ˙CCO), n. oneself; I / me, myself; he / him, himself; she / her, herself.
˙˙ce, adv = cel-˙lwo of itself, spontaneously. ¶˙spye ˙˙ce ˙na ˙no.n i ˙˙la (1466 Kup 1:52a) the bone emerges of its own accord.

ce-amuli = cey-amuli
ce ay, adn + n. that child; that person (over there), he / him (she / her) there. CF ce ca / chi / ēlun / i / kes / nom / pun / sālam / son; cyāy.

ce ca, adn + quasi-free n. that person (over there), he/him (she/her) there. CF **ce ay/chi/ ēlun/i/kes/nom/pun/sālam/son**.

ce ccok, adnoun + quasi-free noun.
1. that side or direction over there; the other side/direction. ¶ ~ **ey iss.nun cip** the house over there. **I ccok ey se to ce ccok ey se to pāntay ka tul.e wass.ta** Objections were heard on all sides.
2. the other party; they/them, he/him, she/her. ¶**Ce ccok i cengchi sēylyek i sēyta** The other party has stronger political power.

ce cek (ey), adn + n (+ pcl). (the) last time, previously. CF **ce pen**.

ce-cel lo, compound adverb (? < ¨ce + cel-'lwo). of/by itself, of its own accord, spontaneously, automatically, naturally. ¶**Choq pul i ce-cel lo kkē cyess.ta** The candle light went out all by itself. **I mun un ce-cel lo yellinta** This door opens automatically. **Ku kes un nācwung ey ce-cel lo al.e cinta** That will come to you in time; That will iron itself out. **Ku i aph ey se n' ce-cel lo kokay ka swukule cinta** I can't help bowing in respect for him. SYN **cey-cel lo, cel lo; cey mul ey/lo, cey phul ey/lo**.

ce chelem, n + pcl = **ce kath.i** (like that).

ce chi, adn + quasi-free n. [pejorative] that person (man/woman) over there, he/him (she/her) there. CF **ce ay/ca/ēlun/i/kes/nom/ pun/sālam/son**.

ce-cinan, cpd adn. before last time, the one before last. ¶ ~ **pam** night before last. ~ **pen** the time before last. ~ **tal** the month before last. ~ **hay** year before last. ~ **phyēnci** the letter before the last one. ? VAR < **ci-cinan** (< **cīnan cīnan** iterated vi mod); ? n 'that' + vt mod 'passed'; ? **cye** (< **cie** inf ← **cita**) + mod; ? abbr < **cen** 'before' + mod.

ce ēlun, adn + n ('that adult over there' =) he/him (she/her) there — still more honorific than **ce pun**. CF **ce ay/ca/chi/i/kes/nom/pun/ sālam/son**.

ce-huy < **ce-huy**, n. 1. [HUMBLE] we/us; I/me. ~ **tul** we/us; ourselves; themselves, they/ them. ¶**ce-huy 'ho'ya pulu'key ho'la** (?1517- Pak 1:6a) get them to sing. CF **wuli, na, ce**.
2. → **ce i tul** they/them.

ce-¨huy < **ce-huy 'i** (nominative). ¶**ce-¨huy selu 'culkye** (1481 Twusi 10:42b) to our mutual delight.

ce i, cpd n (adn + n). 1. that person over there; he/him (she/her) there. ~ **tul** those people over there; they/them there. CF **ce ay/ca/chi/ ēlun/kes/nom/pun/sālam/son**.
2. → **ce-huy** (we/us; I/me). 3. my husband.

ce i l', abbr < **ce i lul**

ce i n', abbr < **ce i nun**

cek, (quasi-free) n. 1. the time (when), (on) the occasion. ¶**yēys ~ ey** once upon a time, in the old days. **Yel ahop salq cek iess.ta** It was when I was nineteen. **Ku ka wass.ulq cek ey nay ka ēps.ess.ta** When he came to see me I was away. SEE **i/ku/ce** ~; **-un/-ulq/-nun** ~. CF **ttay; ccum, ccok-ccok; ci** (time since); ? **cik**.
2. [obs] = **ccok**

cek < **'TYEK**, 1. n. (= **mokcek**) a target, a mark, an object. ¶**pinan uy ~** the target of criticism. **coso uy ~ i toyta** becomes (gets to be) a laughing-stock.
2. bnd postn (SEE §5.3.1). quality, state, characteristic; -ic; -ical; -al; -like; -ive; a sort of. Followed by ··· (in) NOUN, ··· **ulo**, ··· **ita**, ··· **i ani 'ta**. CF **sāng**.

2a. (attached to one-syllable nouns as -q cek). **ciq ~** intellectual. **kuk ~** theatrical, dramatic. **miq ~** (= **sīmmi ~**) esthetic. **nāyq ~** inner, internal, mental. **ōyq ~** external, extrinsic. **pyēngq ~** pathological, morbid, diseased. **saq ~ = ¹yeksa ~** historical. **sēngq ~** sexual (CF **ⁿyeseng ~** feminine). **siq ~** poetic. **simq ~** mental, psychological. **tōngq ~** moving, active (CF **catong ~** automatic). **cenq ~ ulo** totally, completely. **kongq ~ ulo** publicly, openly. **saq ~ ulo** privately. **tanq ~ ulo** directly, frankly (CF **kuktan ~ ulo** extremely speaking). **swūq-cek ulo 'na sā.yong pinto ey iss.e se 'na** either by number or in frequency of use. **¹yāngq-cek ulo pota cilq-cek ulo** qualitatively rather than quantitatively (CF **tāylyang ~ ulo** in great quantity).

2b. **cik.ep ~** professional. **Cosen ~** Korean(-type/-style). **hyēnsilq ~** realistic. **ilpan ~ ulo** in general. **conghap ~ ulo** all combined, all in all, in general, in sum. **ilqsi ~** momentary. **kākup ~** (in)so far as possible. **kwuchey ~** (**ulo**) concrete(ly). **kyengcey ~** economic(al). **sayngsan ~** productive. **sēykyey ~** worldwide, international, all over the world. **tongyang ~** Oriental. **pi-hyēnsilq ~**

unrealistic. **sim.li-hak** ~ psychological. **i Hānkwuk uy pānto-cek sēngqkyek** this peninsular character of Korea. **min.yo-cek ka.yo** folksong-like songs. **kiswulq-cek en.e-hak** descriptive linguistics. **cito-cek pīphyeng-ka** a leading critic. **munhwa wa kwunsa uy kyolyang-cek yek.hal** the role of a sort of cultural and military bridge. **kwahak-cek ulo** scientifically. **kwahak-cek (in) thāyto a** scientific attitude. **thāyto ka kwahak-cek ita** has a scientific attitude. **thāyto ka kwahak-cek i ani 'ta** lacks a scientific attitude.

-(c)cek, suf deriving adj-n (Xh), adv (XX), vn (XXh = Xk); LIGHT **-(c)cak**; PARAINTENSIVE **-chek**; VAR **-(c)cik**; ABBR **-c'**. **amul-cek** barely glimpsed; squirming, swarming; equivocating. **elk-cek** lightly pockmarked. **elum-cek** vague; sloppy. **hwi-cek** swinging one's arms ? < **hwita** bends. **hwupi-cek** scooping, gouging < **hwupita**. **hepi-cek** scratching < **hepita**. **kentu'-cek** swaying gently < **kentul**. **(k)kem-cek** dotted < **(k)kēm.ta** is black. **(k)kwum-(c)cek** budging, moving. **kulk-cek** scratching, scraping < **kulk.ta**. **(k)kum-(c)cek** blinking, budging, startled, sudden. **(k)kwuki-cek** wrinkling, crumpling < **(k)kwukita**. **kkwul-ccek** = **kkwul-ttek** gurgling < **kkwul**. **(k)kwup-cek** bowing in awe < **kwupta** is bent. **memu-cek** hesitating < **memulta**. **mi-cek** procrastinating < **mīlta**. **pipi-cek** rubbing together < **pipita**. **ne(l)p-cek** is flat and broad (CF **nap-cak**). **ssu-cek** rubbing, sweeping < **ssulta**. **tetum-cek** groping, faltering, halting < **tetum.ta**. **ttut-cek** scratching < **ttut.ta**. **wumul(-ccek)** hesitantly, indecisively. [? < **cēkta** 'small']

ce ka, [DIAL] = **cey ka** I [formal]; oneself.

-(c)cek-cikun hata, bnd cpd adj-n. HEAVY ↔ **-(c)cak-**. is rather ...ish. **elq** ~ is tingling, smarting. **kelq** ~ omnivorous; foul-mouthed, abusive. **tulq** ~ (= **talq-ccak-cikun**) is rather sweet. CF **-chek-cikun**; **thucek-cikun** (belchy).

ce kes, adn + quasi-free n. 1. that thing (over there), that one there. 2. that person over there, he/him (she/her) there. CF **ce ay/ca/chi/ēlun/i/nom/pun/sālam/son**.

cekey, abbr. 1. (**cek' ey**) < **cēki ey**. 2. (**ce key**) < **ce kes i**.

cēki, n. that place, over there, yonder; uh ... . ¶**yeki** ~ here and there. **Ce ai ka cēki se mues ul han' ya** What's that boy doing over there? LIGHT **coki**. SYN **ce kos**. CF **yeki, keki; cek' ey**.

ce kkaci lo, n + pcl + pcl. to that trifling extent.

ce-kkacis, cpd adn (n + bnd n). that kind of, such (a ...), so trifling (a ...). LIGHT **co-kkacis**.

ceksimyen = $c^a/_e$**ksimyen**

cēkta, adj. 1. is small in quantity; is rare; are few. ANT **mānh.ta**.

2. [DIAL] = **cākta** (is small in size)

3. postnom adj. is small with respect to, is inadequate (disappointing) when it comes to; CF **ccekta** (< **-q cēkta**). **kayk** ~ (= **kayk sulepta**) is uncalled-for; is out of place (< 'guest; superfluous').

¶**hāyngmang** ~ is stupid, silly (bnd n ? < **hāyngmang** relying on luck). **kayngchwung** ~ / **mac.ta** is careless and stupid (bnd n < ?; CF **p^i/$_a$yng-chwung mac.ta** is clumsy / awkward). **k(w)aytali / k(w)aytalmeli** ~ is boorish, rude, crude; is impertinent, impudent, cheeky (bnd n < ?). **kwisal(meli)** ~ / **sulepta** is complicated, vexatious, troublesome (bnd n < ? 'ear' + 'flesh'; CF **kwiq-salmi** ? < *****kwiq-sal-meli** [DIAL] = **kwiq-sōk** inside of ear, inner ear). **mayk** ~ is bored, is ashamed (< 'pulse'). **mes** ~ is unbecoming (< 'taste'). **pyelmi** ~ is queer, weird, abnormal. **thwungeli** ~ is rash (bnd n < ?; CF **teythwung sulepta / mac.ta / hata** is clumsy). **yēl** ~ is ashamed (< [DIAL] 'gallbladder'). **yēlthwung** ~ is rude, coarse (< bnd cpd n 'gallbladder-crud').

cel [DIAL] = **kyel**

ce l', abbr < **ce lul**

c'e la = **c'ē la**, abbr < **c'e la** = **c'ē la**, abbr < **cie la**; < **cwue la**.

celay, inf < **celeta**, < **celeh.ta**.

cele < **'tye'le**, defective inf. LIGHT **cole**. CF **ile, kule, ette, āmule**.

1. vni. (~ **hanta** = **celenta**) does / says that way (there).

2. adj-n (~ **hata** = **celeh.ta**) is that way.

celeh.key, adj adverbative. like that; in that way, to that / such extent. ¶**Ce sayksi ka celeh.key sulphukey wūni wēyn kokcel io** That young woman is crying so bitterly; what has happened to her? **Cip ul celeh.key kkaykkus 'i chiwulye 'myen sikan i tunta** To keep a house so clean takes time. **Eccemyen celeh.key ppenppen halq ka!** What impudence!

~ **to** (pcl). ¶**Celeh.key to mōs nan sālam un cheum ponta** I've never seen anyone so stupid.
celeh.ta, adj -(H)- (inf **celay**), abbr < **cele hata**. is like that, is that way (there). ¶**celay pōy** (= **poye**) **to** in spite of (his) appearances. **ileh.ta celeh.ta māl i mānh.ta** says this and that, says things, criticizes, is critical (about), makes objections, raises a fuss. **ileni celeni māl haci mālko** setting aside all objections/criticisms, without any complaints. **Celay to mom un thunthun hata** He is sturdier than he looks. **Sālam i eccay celeh.ta 'm!** How can he do the things he does?!
celel(q), prospective modifier.
  1. < adj **celeh.ta**. (··· that is) to be like that.
  2. < vi. **celeta**. (··· that is) to do/say or to be done/said like that.
celel wu hata, adj prosp mod + postmod adj-n. it seems to be that way. [Usually spelled **celelwu···**.].
celem, 1. substantive < **celeta**, < **celeh.ta**.
  2. ? abbreviation < **celemyen**
celen₁ (< ˙**tyele** '**n**), adj mod < **celeh.ta**. like that, such, that sort of. ¶~ **chayk** a book of that sort. ~ **sālam** a man like him, the like of him. **Celenq īl pwass.na?!** What a (sorry) sight! **Ilenq īl celenq īl lo papputa** I am very busy what with one thing and another.
celen₂, vi mod < **celeta**. that has (or has been) done/said that way (like that)
celen₃, interjection (shows sudden realization or surprise). Oh dear! Goodness! Oh my! What a surprise! Indeed! Well well! My my! Gee whiz! ¶**Celen, cham kosayng hasyess.keyss.ˢup.nita** My goodness — you must had a hard time of it. CF **kulen₃, ilen₃**.
celeta, vi (infinitive **celay**); abbr < **cele hata**. does/says/thinks that way. CF **celi (ha)ta**.
celeta (ka), vi transferentive (+ pcl). you say (talk like) that but ... .
celi < ˙**tyeli**, adv. LIGHT **coli**. CF **kuli, ili**; **kuli** ~. (KEd "**cēli**" is a mistake.)
  1. (= **celeh.key, ce-taci**) to that extent or degree, in that way (there), so. SEE ~ **kkaci, ~ to**.
  2. (= ~ **lo**) that way there, that direction, over there. CF **cēki**. ¶**ili** ~ here and there. **Celi ka(ke) la!** Over there! Go away! **Celi kamyen eti yo** Where does that road over there lead to? **Celi com pīkhisio!** Step aside, please.

celi-khwung, adv + suffix. SEE **ili-khwung** ~.
celi kkaci, adv + pcl. ¶**Way celi kkaci yātan in ya** I wonder why there's all that fuss?
celi lo, adv + pcl = **celi** (that way, over there)
celi 'ta, abbr < **celi hata**. does/says/thinks that way. SYN **celeta**. CF **ili 'ta, kuli 'ta**.
celi to, adv + pcl. ¶**Celi to cal hana!** They do that so well!
celkhwuta, vi [DIAL] = **celeh.key (māl) hata** (Mkk 1960:3:34)
cel lo < **cel-˙lwo** = *****ce ˙lwo** (with conflated liquid), noun + pcl. of/by itself, spontaneously. ¶**pwu˙ph i cel-˙lwo ¨wu˙n i** (1449 Kok 80) the drums sounded of their own accord. **[¨]nyey s ˙wuy-an˙h ay kwo˙c i cel-˙lwo ˙phe 's.kwo ˙pwom na˙l ay say twolwo nolGe˙n i 'la** (1481 Twusi 8:34b) in the old garden the flowers are all abloom and on a spring day the birds have flown back. ˙**MANG hon ˙ptoy cel-˙lwo ¨ep˙non cyen˙cho ˙lwo** (1462 ¹Nung 1:77-8) because naturally there is no unseemly dirt. ALSO: 1459 Wel 2:45b. CF ¨**ce, ˙cey, ce(y)-cel lo**.
? **cel-lo**, abbr < **ce kes ulo**
cel' lo, abbr < **celi lo**
ce lul, noun + particle. 1. me [as object].
  2. that (one) over there [as object].
cemam-ttay, cpd n. about/around that time, (at) that time of day/night/year. SYN **comam-ttay**. CF **kumam-/imam-ttay**. [< **ce man + -pttay** that-extent time]
ce man hata, cpd adj-n. is that/so much, is to that extent. ¶**ce man han inmul** a man of that caliber/quality. **ce man han miin** so beautiful a woman, a woman of such great beauty. **ce man han caycwu ka iss.nun tey to** despite his talents, for all his gifts. **Ce man hamyen chwungpun hata** That much is good enough for me. **Ce man han hakca (i)myen se to kyoman haci anh.ess.ta** Yet with all of that scholarship, he was not proud. LIGHT **co man hata**. CF **ku/i man hata; (-ul) man hata**.
ce mankhum, noun + pcl. that/so much, to that extent. ¶**Na to ce mankhum halq swu iss.ta** I, too, can do that/as much. **Ce mankhum Yenge cal haki to him tulta** It is hard to speak English so well. **Ce mankhum ay lul ssess.nun tey to silphay hayss.ta** He failed in spite of all his efforts. CF **ku/i mankhum; ce-ta(k)ci**.
ce mata, cpd n (n + pcl 'each self' =) each one, everyone. ¶**Ce mata cey ka olh.ta ko hanta**

Every man claims that he himself is right. **Ce mata mence na-kanula ko selo ttēy mīnta** Everybody is pushing everybody else trying to get out first.

cen < *CCYEN*, n. 1. the front, the fore part. ¶ ~ **hwū ey se kōngkyek ul pat.ta** is beset from front and rear.

2. (as postn used to address a person in a letter) Dear ‥. ¶**Eme' nim cen sāngse** Dear Mother. CF **aph**.

3. (as adn) the former, the previous, the one-time / sometime. ¶ ~ **swusang** the ex-Prime Minister. ~ **cwūso** one's former (previous/old) residence / address. ~ **namphyen** her ex-husband. **Cen wuli kyōcang sensayng nim ip.nita** He is our former principal.

4. (in time) before, to (till), off, under. ¶**yelq si sip-o pun** ~ a quarter before ten. **selyek kiwen** ~ ‥ Before Christ (‥ B.C.). **ō-sip** ~ **namca** a man under fifty. **Phyo nun ilq-cwuil cen puthe phanta** They sell tickets a week in advance.

5. the last time, previous, ago, before, since. ¶**ithul** ~ **sinmun** a newspaper a couple of days old. ~ **nalq pam** the night before, the previous night. ~ **ey māl han pa wa kath.i** as previously stated. ~ **puthe** from way back (long ago); for some time now. **Cen ey ku kes ul tul.unq īl i iss.ta** I have heard it before. **Ku nun cen kwa talum i ēps.ess.ta** He hasn't changed since. **Ku kes un olay cenq īl** (= **olaynq īl**) **ita** It happened a long time ago. **Cen ey to ilenq īl i iss.ess.^{s}o?** Did anything like this ever happen before?

6. (often preceded by summative **-ki**) prior to, before, earlier than. ¶**Ku ka tōchak haki** ~ before his arrival. **Apeci nun nay ka naki cen ey tol.a-kasyess.ta** My father died before I was born. **col.ep (haki) cen ey** before graduating. **tāyhak ul col.ep haki cen ey** before graduating from college [better not to omit **haki**]. **yēyki (haki) cen ey** before talking (or telling it).

CF **aph**. ANT **hwū**.

ce n', abbr < **ce nun**

ce 'na, n + alt of **ina**

ce 'na-ma, n + abbr cop extended adversative. although it is (nothing more than) that. ¶ ~ **ku tay lo** (poor, worthless, trivial, etc.) as that is or may be. **Kwutwu ka hel.ess.ci man, ce 'na-ma sin.ulq swu pakk ey ēps.ta** I have to put on that pair of shoes, worn out though they are. CF **i / yo 'na-ma, ku 'na-ma**.

ceng, bnd postn. SEE **ceng kkey**.

-(c)ceng, suffix. 1. vulgarizes noun. **ip** ~ mouth. **? mith** ~ the number of times a baby has passed urine or feces. CF **-cheng**.

2. HEAVY ↔ **-(c)cang** (somewhat). **mel-cceng** (/ **mal-ccang**) **hata** is intact, perfect (< **melk-ceng**).

cengi, ceyngi, suffix. 1. stuff, one. **muk-** ~ used goods. **ssek-** ~ spoiled stuff. **kwup-** ~ a bent / curved thing. **nulk-** ~ [vulgar] an old one (person / animal). **ssek-** ~ something that is rotten / decayed; (= **sakcengi**) dead branches on a tree. Also perhaps **kkakcengi** acorn cup.

2. = **ca(y)ngi**. **kkakcengi** = **kkakcayngi** a shrewd / stingy person. CF **che(y)ngi**.

cēngkak < *TTYENG-'KAK*, n. the exact time; precisely, exactly (can precede or follow the specification). ¶**cēngkak ahop si ey** (M 1:1: 179) exactly at nine o'clock = **ahop si cēngkak ey** at the precise time of nine o'clock.

ceng kkey, bnd postn + postn. around the time of ‥, at that (vague) time. ¶**kwuwel** ~ around September. **āmu ceng kkey tanye kan Wensan acessi ālci?** (NKd 2837b) you know the fellow from Wensan who came to visit that time?

cengto < *TTYENG-'TTWO*, n.

1. degree, grade, extent, limit, measure, standard. ¶**saynghwal** ~ standard of living. ~ **mūncey** a matter of degree. **sōnhay uy** ~ the extent of the damage. **enu** ~ **kkaci** to some extent (or degree), up to a (certain) point. **Ku cengto lo hay twuci** Let's stop there (at that point). **Yo cengto mankhum ila to hay polyem** Why don't you just try it out to this extent, at least.

2. **-ulq cengto**:

2a. ~ **'ta** it is to the extent / point (of / that), is as much as to do / be, is even. ¶ **Kyewul ey etteh.key chwuwun ci pang an ey se to ōythwu lul ip.e ya halq cengto 'ta** It is so cold in winter that you have to wear your overcoat indoors, too. **Kēnkang i hoypok toye se icey n' swuyeng ul hay to cōh.ulq cengto 'ta** He has his health back to the point where he can even swim. **Etteh.key pappun ci phyēnci ssulq sikan khenyeng, pap mek.ulq sikan to ēps.ulq cengto 'ta** It's not merely that I'm too busy to write letters, I'm even too busy to eat!

2b. ~ **lo** to the extent that, as much as to (do/be), even. ¶**Com chelem āmu 'na manna cwuci to anh.ulq cengto lo kēman hata** He's so arrogant that he seldom sees anybody. **Phyēnci lul ssulq sikan to ēps.ulq cengto lo papputa** I'm so busy I have no time to write letters.

3. **-un cengto 'ta** it is (just) to the extent that (it was/did); no more than, merely. ¶**Cheum ey n' kāmki ey com kellin cengto yess.ta** In the beginning it was a mere cold (M 1:2:233).

ce nom, cpd n (adn + n). [pejorative] that damn guy ("S.O.B.") over there, he/him (there). CF **ce ay/ca/chi/ēlun/i/kes/pun/sālam/son**.

cenq pen, n + n. the other day, recently; the previous time. **ku ~** the time before that.

ce 'n tul, n + cop mod + postmod. though it be him. VAR **ceyntul**.

ce nun, n + pcl. 1. (< *ce 'non*) as for me, I. 2. (< *'tye non*) as for that (one) over there.

-cepcep, bnd adj-n (~ **hata**); after consonant **-ucepcep**. ...-ish, slightly colored/tinged. SEE **-(u)sulum**.

ce pen, adn + n ('that time' =) the last time, the other day, lately, previously; the last (or previous/earlier) one. ¶**~ il.yoil** last Sunday. **~ phyēnci** the previous letter. **~ ey māl-ssum tulin pa wa kath.i** as I let you know last time. **Ce pen ey tangsin i māl han kes kwa nun taluci anh.so?** Isn't this different from what you said the last time? CF **ku/i pen; cenq pen, ku cenq pen**.

ce phyen, cpd n = **ce ccok** (that side/direction).

cepta₁, vt. folds, furls; gives a handicap. VP **cep.hita**; INTENSIVE **cepchita**, VP **cepchi(i)ta**. CF **kyep; wu-cep-/-cip-** vi become superior, vt surpass < **wu/wi lul cep-**.

cepta₂, postnom adj insep -W-. is characterized by. **pich ~** is dignified. **swus ~** is simple-hearted, unaffected. CF **ilccepta** is annoying, irksome < **īlq cepta**. [? < **ci-** + **-ew-**; ? < **kyēw-** be extreme, CF **hūng kyēpta** is fun]

ce pun, adn + quasi-free n. that (honored) person over there; he/him (she/her) there. CF **ce ay/ca/chi/ēlun/i/kes/nom/sālam/son**.

ce sālam, adn + n. that person (over there), he/him (she/her) there; my husband. [NOTE: Unlike the Japanese ano⁻-hito, **ce sālam** does not mean 'you-know-who'.] CF **ce ay/ca/chi/ēlun/i/kes/nom/pun/son**.

c'e se = c'ē se, abbr:
1. = **cyē se**, abbr < **cie se**.
2. = **cwē se**, abbr < **cwue se**.

ce son, adn + quasi-free n. that person (over there), he/him (she/her) there. CF **i ay/ca/chi/ēlun/i/kes/nom/pun/sālam**.

c'ess-: 1. = **cyess-**, abbr < **ciess-**, past < **cita**.
2. = **cwess-**, past < **cwuta**.

ce-ta(k)ci, cpd adv. to that degree/extent, like that, so (very much), in that way. ¶**Ce-taci setwululq kes i mues iss.ta 'm!** What's the hurry?! **Ce-taci tōn ul moa se mues hana!** Why is he so eager to pile up money? LIGHT **co-ta(k)ci**.

ce tal, adn + n. last month. SYN **cīnan tal**.

ce tay lo, adn + n + pcl. like that, as it is/stands, intact, untouched. **~ twuta** leaves it just as it is, leaves it alone. CF **ku/i tay lo**.

ce to, n + pcl. 1. I (me) too/even.
2. that (one) over there too/even.

c'e to = c'ē to, abbr:
1. = **cyē to**, abbr < **cie to**.
2. = **cwē to**, abbr < **cwue to**.

ce ttawi, cpd n. [pejorative] a thing/person of that sort; that kind (of), that sort (of). SYN **co ttawi**. CF **ku/i ttawi**.

ce tul, n + postn. those people (over there); they/them. SYN **ce ney (tul)**. CF **ku/i tul**.

ce twu, n + var pcl = **na to**. 1. I (me) too/even.
2. that (one) over there too/even.

c'e twu = c'ē twu, abbr:
1. = **cyē twu** < **cie twu = cie to**.
2. = **cwē twu** < **cwue twu = cwue to**.

ce 'uy, n + pcl. one's (own). ¶*ce 'uy nul˙kwu˙m ul ¨wu˙zoWo˙n i* (1449 Kok 30) bewailed his own growing old. ABBR **ce 'y**.

cey₁, n. 1. < *¨ce y* < ***ce 'i*, n + pcl; CF **nay, ney**. VAR **ci**.

1a. [FORMAL, HUMBLE] I (alt of **ce** before the particle **ka**). ¶**Cey ka i hak.kyo kyōcang ip.nita** I am the principal of this school.

1b. abbr < **cey ka** I [as subject]. ¶**Kaptong-i tāysin ey cey (ka) kalq ka yo?** Shall I go in place of Kaptong-i?

1c. oneself, one; himself/herself, he/she; itself, it. ¶*¨ce y ne˙kywo˙toy* (1447 Sek 13:61a) in his (own) opinion ... *¨ce y il˙hu˙m ye* (1459 Wel 13:32a) one will lose it and ... *˙i CIN-˙CCYENG ˙TTAY-˙PEP ˙ul ¨ce y ˙TUK ˙'kwo ˙cye ˙ho˙ya* (1459 Wel 18:3a) we want to get the truly pure great law ourselves, and ... . ˙i ma˙thwo˙m i ˙ce y pan˙to˙ki twulu˙hye ne ʼy ˙kwo˙h ol ma˙tho.l [i] ʼye˙n i ʼˑston (1462 ¹Nung 3:8b) this scent would have to have come around itself to catch the attention of your nose. [ˑ]ce y woy[ˑ]ywo[ˑ]la ˙thwo˙ta (1463 Pep 2:7a) says he himself is at fault. ¨ce y twolo˙hye ˙HYANG khey ˙khwo cye ʼy.n i ʼˑla (1482 Nam 1:70b) he wanted to turn himself around. kozol s ha˙nol moy˙h ay s ˙mu.l ey SOM-LA y ¨ce y na˙thwo.m i ˙kot ho˙n i (1482 Kum-sam 3:34b) it is like the spontaneous appearance of a forest in the mountain streams under an autumn sky. ¨ce y ¨sywukwong ˙ul ¨en˙me ʼy˙na pat˙te˙n ywo (?1517⁻ Pak 1:19b) how much did he himself get for his labor?

2. abbr < **ce uy** (< ˙ce ʼy < *ce ˙uy), n + pcl.

3a. my, my own. ¶ ~ **moca** my hat.

3b. one's, his, her (own); its (own); proper, belonging, appropriate; fit(ting). ¶ ~ **tay lo** the proper way, properly; smoothly; as it should be; on time. ~ **mes tay lo** as one pleases, at will, ad libitum. ~ ¹**iik man sayngkak hata** looks to one's own interest. **Cey īl un cey ka hay ya hanta** One should look after one's own business.

¶ ˙ce ʼy mwo˙m ay s kwo˙ki ˙lol pa˙hye ¨naynun ˙to˙s ˙i ne˙kye ho˙m ye (1447 Sek 9:12a) it is regarded as like tearing the flesh off one's own body, and ... . ¨SYWOW-SSING ˙ey s ¨salo˙m i ce ʼy ˙mwom tas˙kol ¨spwun ho˙kwo ˙nom ˙CYEY-¨TTWO ¨mwot hol ˙ss oy (1447 Sek 13:36a) a person in hīnayāna just cultivates himself and does not save others, so ... . ku ¨say ku ke˙wulwu ˙ey s ce ʼy kulu˙mey ˙lol pwo˙kwo (1447 Sek 24:20b) the bird saw its image in the mirror and ... . ce ʼy ¨TTWOW-¨LI pwus˙ku˙lita ˙ka (1449 Kok 109) he [Kāśyapa] was ashamed of his own doctrine but ... . ce ʼy ˙mwom cwu˙kul ˙tt ol mwo˙lono˙n i ʼ-ngi ʼˑta (1459 Wel 7:18b) is unaware that his body will die. ce ʼy ˙emi ˙lol ˙KHWEN ˙ho˙ya ... (1459 Wel 21:20a) he exhorted his mother and ... . cyang˙cho ce ʼy ˙mwom.m o˙lwo ¨KWUY-SSIN ˙uy key pi˙le [ˑ]ci-ngi ʼˑta ¨CHYENG ˙hoke˙nul (1475 Nay 2:1:30a) when asked to pray in future to the spirits with one's own body ... . ce ʼy ˙pi.ch i [QUN] ˙kot ˙hwo.m i is˙twota (1481 Twusi 7:38b) at times it has a color like silver! ce ʼy tali ˙lol pe˙hoy¨twos.tela (1579 Kwikam 1:18b)

why, he had cut his own leg!

3c. (marking subject of an adnominalized sentence). ¶ce ʼy ˙hwol ¨yang o˙lwo ho˙key ho˙la (1447 Sek 6:27a) have them do as I do.

3d. SEE **cey-kkacis**.

CF **nay; caki; ce ʼykey, cey sikan; ceyntul**.

cey₂, n abbr < **cēki** (there)

cey₃ < ˙cey, abbr < ce˙k uy. (at) the time = **cek (ey)**. Dupont (314) says this is "elegant, little used in conversation". **i(n)-cey** now; from now on. **hwū-cey** sometime in the future. SEE **-ulq cey**.

cēy < ˙TTYEY, adn (makes Chinese numerals into ordinals). ---th. ~ **il** (ī, sam, sā, ō) the first (second, third, fourth, fifth). **cēy-il kwa** the first lesson, lesson one. CF **ccay**.

-cey, abbr < **-cei**, der adv < **-cepta**. **swus cey** (= **swus cepkey**) artlessly, naively.

ce ya, 1. n + cop var inf: it's me; it's that (one) over there.
2. n + pcl. only if it's me; only if it's that (one) over there.

cʼe ya = **cʼē ya**, 1. = **cyē ya**, abbr < **cie ya**.
2. = **cwē ya**, abbr < **cwue ya**.

cey-amuli, abbr < **cey ka āmuli** (···). however (···) oneself may be.

cey-cel lo = **ce-cel lo**

-ceyita [S Kyengsang DIAL (¹Na Cinsek 1977)] = **-p.nikka**

cey ka, n alt + pcl. I [formal]; oneself. VAR [often pejorative] **ci ka**; [DIAL] **ce ka**.

ce ʼykey, abbr < **ce eykey** (to me; to oneself)

cey-kkacis, cpd adn [n + bnd n]. such as him/her/them/oneself (but NOT "me/us"!).

cey˙kwom, abbr < **ceyye˙kwom** (individually), adv. ¶hon ¨sa˙lo˙m i˙na cey˙kwom sa˙lwol ˙chye˙swo ˙lol ¨et˙ti ¨mwot ˙ho˙ye ˑs.ke˙tun (1518 Sohak-cho 8:3a) if a person cannot find a separate home to live in.

cey mul ey / lo, phrasal adv. ("in/with its own juice" =) of its/one's own accord, of/by itself. SYN **cey phul ey / lo, ce(y)-cel lo**.

ce ʼyna (or **cey ʼna**), n + alt of **ina**

-ceyngi, var < **-cengi**, < **-cayngi**.

ceyntul, [nonstandard] var = **ce ʼn tul** though it be him. ¶**Ceyntul ppyocok han swu ka iss.na?** Him – he has no clever way out!

cey phul ey / lo, phrasal adv. ("in/with its own starch" =) of its/one's own accord, of/by itself. SYN **cey mul ey / lo, ce(y)-cel lo**.

ce yo, 1. n + AUTH cop (= **ce io**) it's me; it's that (one) over there.
2. n + polite pcl. (it's) me; (it's) that (one) over there.
c'e yo = **c'ē yo**, 1. = **cyē yo**, abbr < **cie yo**.
2. < **cwē yo**, abbr < **cwue yo**.
cēy se, abbr < **cēki se** (over there).
ceyye᾿kwom, n, adv (< ?; CF **cey**, ᾿**kwom**). ABBR **cey᾿kwom**.
1. n. each individual; separate(ly). ¶ *mwom ῾i e῾wulGwo ῾two me῾li ceyye῾kwo.m il ῾ss oy* (1449 Kok 134) since though the body is joined (to form a whole) the heads are separate … .
~ **s** (pcl). respective, (its / one's) own individual. ¶*ceyye᾿kwom s QIN-YWEN ῾u῾lwo* (1447 Sek 6:39b) by their respective causes and effects. ῾KAK-῾KAK *ceyye᾿kwom s yang῾co ῾lol ci῾zwo῾toy* (1459 Wel 8:19b) though each creates his individual style.
2. adv. respectively; separately, individually. ¶*pat ῾two ceyye᾿kwom non῾hwo῾m ye cip ῾two ceyye᾿kwom ῾῾cis.te῾n i* (1459 Wel 1:45a; each ῾*two* is loose reference to its clause as a whole) they both divided the fields individually and built separate houses.
/…ch/. In 1445 before pause (noun-final) the affricates …*c* and …*ch* had merged with the sibilant …*s*, which then began merging with /…t/ in the early 1500s. (It is unclear whether …*ch* had earlier merged with …*c*.)
cha, inf < **chata**
cha < ῾CHO, postmod, postnoun, prefix, suffix.
1. postmod (followed by cop or **ey**).
1a. -**ulye 'tun** ~ (on) the point / verge of (doing). ¶**Kalye 'tun cha 'ta** I was just about to leave. **Chac.ulye 'tun cha ey machim ku ka wass.ta** He's come at the very moment when I was going to see him.
1b. -**tun** ~ **ey** as an incidental consequence of; incidental (in addition) to, on the spur of. ¶**Sewul kass.tun cha** (= **kīm**) **ey tōngmul-wen kkaci poko wass.ta** I took advantage of the trip to Seoul to see the zoo, too. CF **chām**$_2$.
2. postn (followed by **lo**). for the purpose of, with the intention of, by way of. ¶**kwūkyeng ~ lo Sewul ey wass.ta** came to Seoul for sightseeing. **insa ~ lo wass.ta kanta** comes to pay one's respects.
3. prefix. next, the following, below, sub-. ¶ ~-**hoy** next time. **phyencip ~ -cang** a sub-editor. ~ -**phyen ulo / ey** by the next post.
4. suffix. order, rank, sequence; time; (math) degree. ¶**Cēy ī-~ sēykyey tāycen** World War Two. **cēy sam-~ nāykak** the third cabinet. **sam-~ ilk.ta** reads for the third time. **il-~ pangceng-sik** a simple (first-degree) equation.
5. suffix. material. **uy-~** material for clothes (= **os kām**).
cha [old-fashioned] = **chi**$_{11}$ (bad weather).
cha' < ῾*cho[l]*, adn, bnd n. glutinous, sticky.
1. adn. ¶ ~ **cenpyeng** a glutinous pancake. ~ **co** < *cho' cwo* (1748) glutinous millet. ~ **swuswu** < ῾*chol sywusywu* (?1660-) glutinous sorghum. ~ **tol** < ῾*cho' twol* (1542) calcite. **chapssal** = **cha'-pssal** < ῾*cho(l) ῾psol* (1489) (hulled) glutinous rice.
2. bnd n. ¶ ~ **cita** is glutinous.
cha- < ῾῾CHO, bnd adn [lit]. this (=i). CF **phi-**.
chak < ῾TTYAK, postnoun [semi-lit]. arrival, arriving. ¶**yelq si** ~ arriving (at) ten o'clock. **Sewul** ~ arriving (in) Seoul. CF **tōchak vni**.
-**chak**, suffix; PARAINTENSIVE < -**cak**; LIGHT ↔ -**chek**. (derives adj-n, adv, vni). ¶**ak-chak / ek-chek** stubborn(ly), unyielding.
-**chak-cikun**, bnd adj-n (~ **hata**); PARAINTENSIVE < -(c)**ak-cikun**. ¶**tal-~** sweetish.
chal < ῾*chol* (? < ῾*cholq* 'to attach'), adn, bnd n.
1. sticky, glutinous. ¶ ~ **hulk** clay. ~ **kes** glutinous foods. ~ **kicang** < ῾*chol kicang* (1527) glutinous millet. ~ **ok-swuswu** glutinous corn. ~ **pap** (cooked) glutinous rice. ~ **pye** < *chol pye* (1554) glutinous rice (plants). ~ **ttek** < ῾*chol ῾stek* a glutinous rice cake. ANT **mey**. ABBR **cha'**; CF **cha'-cita**. CF **chalkkak / chelkkek** sticking fast / tight.
2. sticky, persistent, unshakable, fanatic. ~ **kanan** dire poverty. ~ **kēmeli** a persistent leach. ~ **kyōin** a steadfast believer (of a religion). **chalcca** (? < **chalq ca**) a stickler.
chal(q), prosp mod < **chata**
cham$_1$, adv, interj, adn, adj-n, bnd n. [? < *****coh(.)am** irreg subst < **cōh-** adj, CF **chām**$_1$]
1. adv. truly, in truth, really, indeed, in fact; very, quite. SYN **cham-mal**, **cēng-mal**; CF **kwā.yen**, **tāytan hi**. ¶ ~ **cōh.ta** is quite good. **Cham nōllass.ta** I was surprised indeed. **Ku kes cham kuleh.kwun a** How true that is!
2. interj. oh, well (showing surprise); uh … , well now … , really now … (anticipating an emotional outburst); "and, oh yes, another

thing ...". CF **ce**. ¶**Cham onul i swuyoil ici** Oh — it's Wednesday, isn't it. **Cham pyel sālam to tā pokeyss.ta** Really now, I have never seen such a dreadful person! **Cham pyel māl tā tut.keyss.ta** Just what do you mean talking to me that way?!

3. adn. real, true, genuine; good. ¶ ~ **cwul a** rich vein of ore. ~ **kaykwuli** a green frog. ~ **kilum** sesame oil — also pronounced **chaym-/cha(y)ng-kilum**. ~ **kkay** sesame. ~ **kkoch** azalea (= **cin( )tallay**). ~ **māl** the truth, a true remark. ~ **mek** superior inkstick. ~ **nali** lily. ~ **namu** oak. ~ **oy** melon, cucumber — also pronounced **chaymey, chaymi**. ~ **pa** rope. ~ **pay** domestic pear. ~ **pis** fine-toothed comb. ~ **sal** healthy flesh. ~ **sālam** a genuine/good person. ~ **say** sparrow. ~ **swuch** oakwood charcoal. ~ **ttus** real meaning.

4. bnd n (pre-postnominal). **cham tapta** is true. **chamq toyta** is honest.

cham₂, subst < **chata**

chām₃, adj-n. ~ **hata** is nice, neat, pretty; is good, gentle, modest. [? < *coh(.)am irreg substantive < cōh.ta; CF **chak** adj-n 'good, virtuous' < *coh-ak]

chām₄ < *CHAM, 1. n. 1a. stage, a station.
1b. a stop, a resting place.
1c. a rest (period), a break, a recess; a time, a stretch, a sitting. SEE **han cham; -ul chām**.
2. vni [? lit] stops at a stage; stops, makes a stop; takes a rest, has a break.
3. **-nun/-tun** ~ **(ey)** (at) the point of doing, just as it is happening. ¶**Kalye 'tun chām ita/iess.ta** I was just on the verge of leaving. SEE **-nun chām, -tun chām, -ul chām; cha**.

chan, mod < **chata**

-chang, suf; LIGHT ↔ **-cheng**. **hoy-chang kelita** yields; is pliant.

chang, bnd postn. **kol(ang)** ~ ditch. **sikwung** ~ cesspool. **tolang** ~ gutter, drain.

changi, chayngi, postn, suf, postmod; ? PARA-INTENSIVE < **ca(y)ngi**. one, thing, stuff. ¶**selphi** ~ loose-woven stuff (cloth), gauze. **ol** ~ a tadpole. **can** ~ a small one; the littlest and poorest (thing/person) of the lot, the runt.

ch' anh.ta, abbr < **chi** (= **haci**) **anh.ta**. is not. **katang** ~, **kwayn** ~ [< **kwan-haci anh.ta**], **kwi** ~, **kin** ~, **siwen** ~, **ansim** ~; **ha-**~ [< **haci anh.ta**].

chata₁, adj. is cold (to the touch). CF **chwupta**.

chata₂, vi. gets full; gets filled with, fills; fulfills, gets fulfilled by. **swūm** ~ runs out of breath, pants, gasps. **ki** ~ is dumbfounded, flabbergasted, nonplussed. NOTE: **kēl-chata** 'is extremely fertile' and **sēy-chata** 'is powerful' are cpd adj < adj + vi.

chata₃, vt. kicks; clicks (the tongue); snatches away; puts it on, wears (on a string or around the waist).

chata₄, postnom adj insep (< **chata₂**). is full of. **an** ~ is bold. **alum** ~ is strenuous. **aph** ~ is self-confident. **cwulki** ~ (a downpour) is vigorous and steady. **ongkol** ~, **ong** ~, **ol** ~ is stout-hearted. **tām** ~ is brave. **wiem** ~ is stately. **wuleng** ~ is resounding, splendid.

chay₁, postmod, postn. just as it is, intact, as it stands, with no change. CF **ku chay lo; ku-nyang, tay (lo); ccay**.

1. postmod. ¶**sālam ul sān** ~ **mut.ta** buries a person alive. **sālam ul cwuk.un** ~ **nāy-pelye twuta** leaves a dead person unburied. **ōythwu lul ip.un** ~ **pang ey tul.e ota** comes into a room with one's overcoat on. **pul ul khin** ~ **cata** sleeps with the light on. **non ul pye ka sun** ~ **phalta** sells a paddy with the rice plants standing on it (rice plants and all).

2. [? DIAL] postn (= **ccay**). ¶**ttek tengi lul thong** ~ **lo samkhita** swallows a lump of rice cake (without chewing it). **ppuli** ~ **ppopta** pulls up by the roots. **talk ul ppye** ~ **tā mekta** eats a chicken, bones and all. **hōysa tōn ul thong** ~ **tul.e mekta** takes liberties with all the company's money.

chay₂, adv. 1. all, entirely, completely.
2. (not) yet; CF **chay-cen ey** long ago/before. ¶ ~ **...-ki cen ey** before (doing it) completely/fully. **Sakwa ka chay ikci anh.ess.ta** The apple is not fully ripe. **Yelq tal i chay toyci mōs hayss.ta** Not ten full months have passed (since then).

chay₃, n. 1. the length of a tall slender object; (= **meli** ~) long tresses of hair.
2. (bushclover) twigs, wicker.
3. (= **-ccik**) a whip, a switch; a drumstick, a pluck, a (piano-key) hammer.
5. uneven dye, streaky coloring. ~ **cita** gets dyed unevenly, gets/is streaky.
6. quasi-free n, count. a building, a section of a building; a wing; counter for houses and [Seoul colloquial] (= **tay**) for vehicles and

other machines. **an ~** the main building / wing of a house. **mom ~** the main wing (of a house/ building). **pakkath ~** an outbuilding, an annex, a side/back wing. **salang ~** a detached party / living room.

chayngi SEE **changi**

···chˑˑcop- (1445 ¹Yong 35) = ···ˑˑccop- < ···ch-ˑˑzop-

che-, verb prefix. abundantly, plentifully, thoroughly; extremely, excessively; severely; recklessly; without permission; without any cause. **~ mekta** eats greedily (immoderately). **~ ciluta** stuffs / shovels it in. [< chye = chyē < chie, inf < chita hits, ...]

chek, postmod vni = **chey** (pretense).

-chek, suf; PARAINTENSIVE < -cek (derives adj-n, adv, vni); HEAVY ↔ -chak. **ek-chek / ak-chak** stubbornly, unyielding.

-chek-cikun, cpd bnd adj-n (**~ hata**). quite ···ish. **swī-~** quite stale-smelling (musty, sourish). CF **-(c)cek-cikun**.

chek hata, postmod vni. SEE **chek = chey**.

chelem, pcl. like, (the same) as, as if. ¶**han cip-an sik.kwu chelem** like members of one family. **sāy chelem nalta** flies like a bird. **Na to ne chelem kuleh.key man ina(-ma) hay polq ka** Shall I try doing at least that much like you? **Ku īl un caney ka sayngkak hanun kes chelem kuleh.key swīpkey man to an toylq ke l'** That won't be quite as easy as you think! SYN **kath.i**, DIAL **manyang**. SEE **ce ~** , **i ~** , **ku ~** ; **com ~** ; **mo ~** .

?< ··· *chye lwo* (1730) < ··· *thye lwo* (1676) < ··· *thyey ˑlwo* (1586) < "THYEY 'body, form' + pcl. Attested *chelem* in 1898 Tayshin. The ···m is found also in **pota**(m) and **puthe**(m).

chelem ccum, pcl + pcl. **~ (iya)**. ¶**Ku sālam chelem ccum (iya) mōs halq key mue iss.e** Is there any reason why you can't do as well as the like of him?! SYN **ccum chelem**.

~ ina. ¶**Nay khi ka ce sālam chelem ccum ina toylq ka** Surely I am tall as he is.

~ ila to. ¶**Ku sālam eykey cwun kes chelem ccum ila to cōh.uni na 'ykey to cwusey yo** Give me one too, even if it's no more than like the one you gave him.

~ in tul. ¶**Ku mankhum kongpu lul yelqsim hi hanun tey Kaptong-i chelem ccum in tul mōs hakeyss.ni?** Studying so hard like that, surely you can do as well as Kaptong-i does.

~ kkaci ka. ¶**Sāsil un Kaptong-i chelem ccum kkaci ka mūncey 'ci** Actually it is a problem whether one can do even about as well as Kaptong-i.

~ kkaci ('la) to. ¶**Nolyek yeha ey ttala se nun Kaptong-i chelem ccum kkaci ('la) to kalq swu ya iss.ci** Depending on one's effort one can surely do even at least about as well as Kaptong-i.

~ kkaci man. ¶**Ney ka Poktong-i chelem ccum kkaci man hay to na nun māncok hakeyss.ta** If you do just about as well as Poktong-i I'll be satisfied.

~ kkaci 'n tul. ¶**Ku sālam i hanunq īl in tey Kaptong-i chelem ccum kkaci 'n tul mōs hal lī iss.keyss.na?!** Surely there's no reason he can't do (even) at least as well as Kaptong-i at the job.

~ kkaci ya. ¶**Poktong-i chelem ccum kkaci ya na to halq swu iss.e** I can do at least as well as Poktong-i.

~ man. ¶**Kaptong-i chelem ccum man kongpu hamyen Sewul tāy-hak.kyo tul.e kaki mūncey ēps.ulq ke ya** If you study just like Kaptong-i you'll have no problem getting into Seoul University.

~ man un. ¶**Poktong-i chelem ccum man un na to hay polq swu iss.ci man, Kaptong-i chelem ccum man un mōs michye kakeyss.ta** [awkward?] I can try doing as well as Poktong-i but I'll never get near the like of Kaptong-i.

chelem cocha, pcl + pcl. ¶**Caney chayk i ku sālam kes chelem cocha an phallinta 'ni wēynq īl ia** How come your book sells even worse than his?

chelem ila to, (pcl + cop var inf) + pcl. [a bit awkward] ¶**Encey 'na onul chelem ila to phallimyen kwaynchanh.keyss.e** It wouldn't be bad if I could always sell as much as today.

chelem ina, pcl + cop advers. ¶**Ku chelem ina sīn.loy hatun chinkwu lul pāypan hata 'ni!** How shameful of him to betray the friend who trusted him so much!

chelem ina-ma, pcl + cop extended adversative.

¶**Ne chelem ina-ma īl ul halq cwul al.e to cōh.keyss.nun tey (kuleh.ci mōs hata)** I'd be happy if I could do the job even as well as you.

chelem in tul, pcl + cop mod + postmodifier.

¶**Ku mankhum nolyek hanun tey Kaptong-i chelem in tul mōs hal lī iss.na?!** Surely there is no reason you can't do as well as Kaptong-i when you put in so much effort!

chelem iya, pcl + pcl. ¶Āmuli Yenge lul cal hanta hay to sensayng chelem iya hakeyss.e? However good he may be at English, surely he's no match for the teacher!

chelem khenyeng, pcl + pcl. ¶Ku sālam un tāyhak-sayng chelem khenyeng cwunghak-sayng mankhum to Yenge lul mōs hanta His English is no match for that of a middle school student, much less that of a college student.

chelem kkaci, pcl + pcl. ¶Ku chelem kkaci pūthak han kes ul ic.e pelita 'ni! How could you forget what I asked of you so earnestly!

~ **nun.** ¶Āmuli cal hanta 'y to Kaptong-i chelem kkaci nun mōs michici However well one does it won't be up to Kaptong-i's level.

~ **ya.** ¶Āmuli tōn ul cal ssunta hay to Choy pūca chelem kkaci nun mōs ssulq ke 'lq sey However much you spend you won't be able to match the rich Choys [of Kyengcwu].

chelem mace, pcl + pcl. [a bit awkward] ¶Ku chelem mace yok halq kes iya iss.na Is there any call for (even) such a scolding?! ~ **to.**

chelem man, pcl + pcl. ¶Onul chelem man tōn ul pēnta 'myen elma an ka payk.man-cāngca ka toykeyss.ta If I could make money the way I did today I'd soon be a millionaire. Wuli cip i tangsin cip chelem man khuta 'myen elma 'na cōh.keyss.e! How nice it would be if my house were as big as yours! ~ **(ila) to,** ~ **un.**

chelem mankhum, pcl + pcl [more common than **mankhum chelem**].

~ **ila to.** ¶Sewul lo muthek tāyko olla kan Kilqtong-i chelem mankhum ila to yōngki ka iss.e pwass.umyen cōh.keyss.ta I wish I were as brave as Kilqtong-i who daringly went up to Seoul. Ku sālam chelem mankhum ila to hay pwā la Try doing it at least somewhere near as much as he does.

~ **ina(-ma).** ¶Ku sālam chelem mankhum ina sinyung ul nāylq swu iss.ulq ka Can one do mimicry the way he can?

~ **in tul.** ¶Senguy man iss.umyen Kaptong-i chelem mankhum in tul mōs halq lī iss.na?! If you're just sincere there's surely no reason you can't be the equal of Kaptong-i.

~ **iya.** ¶Nay ka cal haki lo se 'ni ne chelem mankhum iya hakeyss.ni? I am doing well, to be sure, but I can hardly hope to equal you!

~ **man.** ¶Poktong-i chelem mankhum man hay to huymang un iss.e Doing just as much as Poktong-i means there's hope.

~ **to.** ¶Elin ay chelem mankhum to mōs hanun ēlun i musun khun soli ya What a lot of nonsense that a grown-up can't do as well as even a child!

~ **un.** ¶Ku sālam chelem mankhum un na to hanta I too can do as well / much as he does.

chelem pota, pcl + pcl. ~ **(nun).** ¶Nay ka han kes chelem pota (nun) cal hay ya 'ci You must do it better than the way I did.

?**chelem puthe,** pcl + pcl. ¶? Icey nay ka han kes chelem puthe sīcak hay yo Now first start off by doing it the way I did.

chelem to, pcl + pcl. ¶Ku chelem to mōs halq cwul un mōllass.e I never expected him to be so inept as all that! I chelem to hay poko ce chelem to hay pwā la Try (doing) it both this way and that.

chelem ya → **chelem iya.**

cheng, bnd n. a membrane. ¶kalq-tay ~ , tāy ~ the white membrane inside a reed. kho ~ the septum of the nose. kwi ~ the eardrum, the tympanum. mok ~ the vocal cords / bands. CF sim-cheng (= simswul a cross temper), ip-cheng (= ip-ceng mouth).

-chengi, -cheyngi, suffix; HEAVY ↔ **-cha(y)ngi.** But **enche(y)ngi** < *enchyengi* 'harelipped one' is from *[p]eh-tyengi* 'cut person' with nasal epenthesis (p.48) before the affricate.

cheng khentay, abbreviation < **cheng hakentay.** prithee, (if you) please, pray. ¶Cheng khentay nay anʰay ka toye cwusio Please be my wife. SYN **pala-kentay, wēn khentay.**

ches < *ches* (VAR *chez*), adnoun. the first, the beginning (one). ¶ ~ **ccay** first. ~ **insang** /chetinsang/ first impression. CF **cheum, cho.**

chey < "THYEY. 1. postnoun. body. ¶**cocik** ~ organized body. **yūki** ~ organism.

2. postnoun. a style (of writing). ¶**insway** ~ printed style (of characters). **philki** ~ handwritten style. **chose** ~ , **hullim** ~ cursive style of script. **sēsa** ~ narrative style. **kwūtwu** ~ colloquial style. **mun.e** ~ , **kūl** ~ literary style.

3. noun [lit] = **sechey** (style of script); = **munchey** (style of literature).

chey < *chyey* (1730, 1795) < *thyey*, postmod. pretense. ~ **hata,** vni. pretends to (do, have done, be): SEE **-un** ~ , **-nun** ~ . SYN **chek.**

ˈchez (m··· , n···), adn. = ˈches (first).
chi$_{1-9}$. 1. Korean inch (= swun)
2. [DIAL] = khi (winnow; rudder; height)
3. [DIAL] = chey (sieve)
4. [? DIAL, ? obs] a cherishing mind / attitude, concern; indignation (CF chi-ttuta).
5. [courtly] = sin (shoes)
6. whew! (what hard work!)
7. < ˝CHI [lit] = i (tooth)
8. < ˝TI the next to highest note of the Korean pentatonic scale.
9. [? < chay < ˝CHOY] (a kind of) vegetable: swuli ~ , sikum ~ , etc. CF kimchi (p. 47); ci.
chi$_{10}$ < chi, (quasi-free) n. CF achi, echi, eci; ci; chayngi. 1. stuff, thing(s); stuff for, a portion for (CF chi$_{12}$); goods. ¶alam / alum ~ one's own (thing), one's share. cwuk ~ goods that are sold by the tens = "by the dozen(s)". cwung(kan) ~ medium things (in size, price, ...). kilssam ~ (cotton) stuff for weaving. kol ~ [obs] = kol marrow; brain. mak ~ = hā ~ coarse (low-grade) stuff. nallim ~ shoddy goods. ol ~ this year's stuff. pēl ~ a wild cantaloupe. pelim ~ junk, rubbish; stuff to be discarded. phā ~ broken / damaged articles, defective / bad goods. pon ~ ('seen stuff' =) figure, appearance. sāng ~ top-grade stuff. sep ~ a useless / poor / worthless one (among many things). tangnyen ~ things produced that year. ? teng-chi = tengceli bulk [CF teng(el)i lump]. Thapkol ~ a kind of hempen sandal (mīthuli) made at Thapkol [outside East Gate in Seoul]. ¶pwoksyanghwa namwo ˙[G]wa pe˙tu' namwo s ˙kaci ˙lol TWONG nyek ˙kuy [= nye˙k uy] chi l' ˙KAK-˙KAK ˝sey nil˙kwup ˙CHWON ˙ol ka˙cye ˙ta ˙ka (1466 Kup 1:21-2) take a branch of peach tree and willow, the ones from the east, three and seven inches [long] respectively, and ...
2. animal; fish; [pejorative] person, thing, one (CF i). ¶al ~ a whitebait that has spawned. am ~ a dried (female) croaker (min.e). kal ~ a cutlass fish, hair-tail. kang ~ a sea lion. kkoli ~ Ateolopus japonicus (a fish). kkong ~ a mackerel pike. kom ~ a moray (eel). māy ~ game hunted by hawking. nep- [< nelp- ~] a flatfish, a sole. pul ~ game that is hunted by shooting. swu ~ a dried male croaker (min.e). twul ~ a barren female animal. ¶ i (ku/ce) ~ this (that) guy. Phyengyang ~ "Phyengyang trash". Sewul ~ "one of those Seoul bastards". Kim Pok.nam kath.un ~ "a jerk like Kim Pok.nam". Ce chi ka kuleh.key māl hayss.ta That guy told me so. ALSO: mongchi a club (= mongtwungi), mongchi / mungchi a lump; pal-chi where one's feet are when lying down, at the foot of, vicinity (CF 'chi$_{16}$); ? cangchi = canchayngi the littlest and poorest (thing / person) of the lot, the runt; c(h)wumchi [DIAL] = cwumeni bag, purse. kkochi (? < kkoc-chi) skewered stuff / food. [JOCULAR] kkal-~ his girlfriend / lover, teph-~ her boyfriend / lover.

chi$_{11}$, 1. postn. bad weather (around a certain day). ¶polum ~ bad weather in the middle of the month. cokum ~ bad weather on low-tide days. 2. ~ hata, postnominal vni. has / is bad weather. SYN cha.

chi$_{12}$, postnoun. a fixed quantity, a ration, a designated amount. ¶ i tal ~ the amount (charge, fee, dues, rent, income, ...) for this month. tas mal ~ the amount of five mal, a five-mal ration. NOTE: CM 1:224 says this can be preceded by any noun of time or place and gives these examples: kumnyen ~ , ¹naynyen ~ , ecey ~ , onul ~ , il-nyen ~ ; puekh ~ . CF chi$_{10}$, achi, echi, chi (< *˙CHI bnd n) 'value', chita$_5$.

chi$_{13}$, abbr < haci after voiced consonants and vowels other than a or e; CF 'ci. ¶Mulken toyn phūm i tuntun chi mōs hakeyss.ta It doesn't look very solid (substantial, strong).

chi(-)$_{14}$, quasi-prefix or bnd adv [< obsolete vi chita 'ascends']. up, upward.

chi$_{15}$, postn. a special sense, a sixth sense, a feel, a hunch. SEE nwun-chi (kho-chi).

'chi$_{16}$, abbr < pal-chi. sikwung (pal-)chi the vicinity of a cesspool.

-chi-, suffix. 1. derives causative verbs. kuluchita < kulu˙ch(u)- ruin ← kuluta < kulu- = kulh- be wrong. sos.chi- raise < sos- < swos- tower (up), rise. CF -i-, -y-, -hi-, -ki-, -ukhi-, -ikhi-, -li-, -iwu-, -ywu-; -wu-, -hwu-, -kwu-, -chwu-, -ay-; -˙Gi-, -˙Gwo-, -˙Gwu-, -o-, -u-.
2. makes intensive verbs: SEE -chita$_{22}$. CF -chwu-, -khi-, -li-, -lu-.

chica, subj assert < chita. SEE -ta ko chica.

-chik, suf; PARAINTENSIVE < -cik (derives adj-n, adv, vn). ᵉ/alyeng ~ dim, vague.

chiki, 1. summative < chita. ¶sāy ~ cutting in;

cuckoldry; snatching.
2. postnoun.
2a. (playing) a game. ¶ca ~ tossing/hitting sticks. ttakci ~ slap-match. kōng ~ a ball game; tennis. yes ~ a game of breaking taffy.
2b. (= chi) stuff, thing; one, person. ¶el-~ an in-between thing; a mongrel; a bastard; a dolt. tangnyen ~ goods lasting only one year, a year's wear. CF chwuki.
chiko, quasi-pcl [< vt ger 'considering as']. when it comes to, as for (= un/nun); every (= mata); as, in the capacity of, being (= ulo). ¶Tōn iss.nun sālam chiko (se) tōn akkici anh.nun sālam i tumulta Most rich people are careful about spending their money. Cosenq sālam chiko (se) nwu ka thōngil ul pāntay hakeyss.^{s}o What (= surely no) Korean will object to the unification of Korea! Haksayng chiko se Yenge mōsq ilk.nun i ka ēps.ta Every student can read English. Sālam chiko ku kes molulq sālam i iss.keyss.n' ya Is there anybody who doesn't know that?! Hak.kyo chiko cheyyuk-kwan ēps.nun hak.kyo ka eti iss.na Who ever heard of a school without a gymnasium?! Ce sālam un ūmsik chiko mōs mek.nun key ēps.ta 'nta I tell you, there is nothing he won't eat.
chiko 'la to, quasi-pcl + cop var inf + pcl. though it comes to; even if we assume that. ¶Ku sālam un pappe se mōs onta chiko 'la to talun sālam tul un etteh.key toyn ke yo Let's admit that he's too busy to come, but what happened to the others? Tases salam man onta chiko 'la to mān wen un tulq ke 'lq sey Even though we assume there will be only five guests, it will cost at least ten thousand wen. Han kay chen wen ssik chiko ('la) to yelq kay 'myen mān wen ita Even if they are only a thousand wen each, ten of them would be ten thousand wen. Tōn mounun ke n' twūl ccay chiko 'la to, wusen saynghwal ey kekceng ina ēps.ess.umyen cōh.keyss.^{s}o Even if one puts in second place the accumulation of money, it would be nice to have no worries about one's livelihood.
chiko n', abbr < chiko nun
chiko nun, quasi-pcl + pcl. when it comes to; as for every; as for being. ¶Cangsaq-kwun chiko nun pāpo 'ci As a businessman he's a fool.
chiko se, quasi-pcl + pcl (emphasized form of chiko). ¶Na nun wuli nala uy myengsung-ci chiko se an ka-pon tey ka ēps.ta I have been to every famous place in Korea.
chiko to, quasi-pcl + pcl. when it comes to ··· also/even/either; being also/even/either. SEE chiko 'la to.
chiko ya, quasi-pcl + pcl. only if it comes to; only (if it be) as; for. ¶Ku sālam chiko ya cal han sēym ici For him, it was rather well done, I'd say. Ām, ^{n}yeca chiko ya khi ka khuko mālko Yes, she sure is tall for a girl.
chil(q), prosp mod < chita
chim, subst < chita
chimyen, conditional < chita. ¶Hānkwuk uy ōymu-pu 'la 'n' kes un Mikwuk ulo chimyen kwuk.mu-seng ita Korea's Foreign Ministry (if we reckon it in terms of America) is the same as America's State Department. Mikwuk ulo chimyen cal han sēym ita From America's standpoint it can be regarded as well done. SEE -ta chimyen, -ulla chimyen.
chin, mod < chita
chita$_{1-15}$, v (1-13 vt) 1. (< 'thi'ta) hits; plays (ball); throws (at); beats, claps; makes, pounds into (rice cakes); sends (a telegram); strikes (the hour). CF cīs.ta.
2. attaches; defeats; denounces; (lightning) strikes; prunes, trims; slices into pieces; flays, skins (with knife).
3. (< chu'ta) removes; thins, weeds it out. VC, VP chiita < chuy(i)'ta (vc).
4. (< chu'ta) sifts, passes through (a sieve). DER N chey. CF path.(chi)ta.
5. counts, figures, computes (= sēyta); prices, values; admits, concedes; supposes, presumes. VP chiita. CF sēym chita. SEE chiko ('la to, nun, se, to, ya), -ta (son) chica, -ta chimyen, -ta (son) chitula to.
6. puts it (into), pours it (into); mixes with, covers with, seasons with.
7. wears, puts on, attaches, fastens (a belt-like thing); puts up, hangs, draws (the curtain), stretches; (kol ~) puts it on (a mold, a block, a last). VC chiita.
8. weaves (CF chiita); braids, plaits; hems, binds; draws, sketches, pictures; builds, throws up, constructs (a wall). VC chiita.
9. (< 'chi'ta) raises, rears, keeps (animals, roomers); breeds, reproduces, whelps; stores (honey); spreads, shoots out (branches).

10. shakes (rocks, swings, jogs) it. **kkoli** ~ wags / wiggles one's tail; acts seductive.
11. shouts (= **ciluta**). **koham** ~ screams, shrieks. **soli** ~ shouts.
12. does, makes, performs (playgame, swim, masturbation, walk); (**non** ~) creates (a rice paddy); (**mulq-kyel** ~) forms (waves); (**kwāng** ~) produces, emits (a glitter = scintillates; shows off, brags); (**kwup.i** ~) makes (bends, curves = meanders); (**¹nwūki** ~) acquires (dampness); **haksayng ul hāswuk** ~ boards students.
13. = **chiluta** pays off; undergoes; entertains, carries out.
14. (? = 9.) vi [obs] ascends, goes up, rises. VC **chikhita** (CF **chiwuta**): **Paci chikhye** 'Pull up your pants!'
15. *****chita** vi / vt. droops.
chīta$_{16-18}$.
16. vt = **chiwuta** removes, puts away, tidies.
17. vp = **chiita** gets hit, crushed, run over, trapped; loses its weave; is priced, valued.
18. vc = **chiita** (has it taken away, thinned; has it sifted; makes / lets wear; has it put up, hung; has it woven, hemmed, sketched, built).
chita$_{19}$, aux vt insep.
1. (follows inf to make intensive). does hard. **kām-tol.a** ~ keeps circling. **hwi-mol.a** ~ drives, urges. **kkamule** ~ faints dead away, swoons (defective inf). **mek.e** ~ devours. **wus.e** ~ guffaws, laughs uproariously. CF **tāyta**.
2. = **ttulita**. **ttel.e chita** / **ttulita** drops it.
chita$_{20}$, postnom adj insep; variant (? PARA-INTENSIVE) < **cita**. **is. yamyel** ~ is unkind, callous. CF **sulepta**.
chita$_{21}$, postnom vt insep. does.
1. **hap** ~ puts them together, unites. **cap** ~ spoils, ruins. **hāy** ~ spoils, mars, damages. **kyem** ~ combines, unites, puts together. **kyep** ~ puts one upon another.
2. CF **chita**$_{11}$.
3. CF **chita**$_{12}$.
4. **he(s)-thang** ~ does it in vain. **kotong** ~ pulses, pulsates. **thomak** ~ chops up (CF **chita**$_2$). **tōlyen** ~ trims; hems, irons in a hem. **tomang** ~ escapes. **yātan** ~ scolds.
5. **thaiphu** ~ type(write)s. **I selyu l' com thaiphu chie cwusey yo** Type this document for me, please.
-**chita**$_{22}$, 1. SEE -**chi**- (suffix; makes intensive verbs). **cep**- ~ , **cīna**- ~ , **eph**- ~ , **kēl**- ~ , **kkay(wu)**- ~ , **mīl**- ~ , **mulli**- ~ , **nēm**- ~ , **noh**- ~ , **pat**- ~ , **path**- ~ , **ppay**- ~ , **phul**- ~ , **ppet**- ~ , **sos**- ~ , **tat**- ~ , **teph**- ~ , **tot**- ~ , **ttwungki**- ~ , **twi**- ~ ; ? **kki**- ~ , ? **putic**- ~ ; **sosul**$^a/_e$ ~ ; **tacoc'-chi**- < **tacoci**- supervise closely; ? **hey**- ~ , ? **ttel**- ~ , ? **ttēy**- ~ . CF **kaykhi**- < **kāy**-fold up. [?< -**thi**-; CF -**the**- of **kelthe-anc.ta**]
2. SEE -**chi**- (suffix; derives causative verbs).
cho < ʾCHWO, postnoun, adnoun.
1. postn. the first, the beginning. ¶ **il-wel** ~ the beginning (days) of January. **hak.ki** ~ the beginning of the school term. **kongsa** ~ the beginning of construction work.
2. adn. early, the beginning, the first. ¶ ~ **kaul / yelum** early autumn / summer. ~ **cenyek** early evening. ~ **tacim** a snack to stay one's appetite. ~ **tāymyen** the first meeting. ~ **kongyen** the first performance. ~ **cepcen** first bout / encounter. ~ **ipsa** first entering the firm.
3. adn. of the first ten days of the month. ¶ ~ **halwu** ⋯ ~ **yelhul** the 1st ⋯ 10th of the month.
cho- < ʾTHYWOW, pref, bnd adn. ultra-, super-, sur-, trans-, transcendental. ¶ ~ **hyēnsil cwuuy** surrealism. ~ **hyēntay-cek** ultra-modern. ~ -**in** a superman. ~ **kāmkak-cek kāynyem** a transcendental concept.
choli, bnd postn (< **chwoli**, var < **kkoli** < **skwoˑli** 'tail'). a pointed / tapering end; [obs] a switch (= **hoy**-). ¶ **cēypi** ~ a swallowtail (shape). **hoy**- ~ (var **hwi-chwuli**, **hoy-chali** — also 'sprout') switch. **nwun** ~ the outer corner of the eye; a look askance. **sin** ~ a pluck fixed to the treadle shoe of a loom (**pey-thul sin**).
chongi, bnd postn. one, thing. ¶ **un**- ~ a horse with white testicles.
chuk < ʾCUK, quasi-free n. side. ¶ **kongsan** ~ the Communist side. **Yū-Eyn** ~ the U.N. side. ¹**yāng** ~ both (the two) sides. **Cal-mos un wuli (uy) chuk ita** The fault is on our side. **phyenghwa lul ōngho hanun** ~ the side that is defending peace. CM 2:67 gives examples of **yele chuk, enu chuk, mōtun chuk ey se; ōn kac' chuk uy; wuli nala chuk ulo puthe; pon / ponun / potun chuk ...** .
-**chwu**, alt of -**wu** (der adv). SEE **yath.chwu** < **yath.ta, kochwu** < **kot.chwu** < **kot.ta, kac.chwu** < **kac.ta; nuc.chwu** (Phyengyang DIAL = **nuc.key** late) < **nuc**-.
-**chwu**-, suffix. 1. derives causative verbs.

1a. **kot.chwu-** straighten it (out) < **kot-** be straight. **yath.chwu-** make it shallow (etc.) < **yath-** be shallow (low, light).
  1b. (< **-hwu-**): **nac.chwu-** = **nac.hwu-** < *noˑchwo-* makes it low ← **nac-** < *noc-* be low. **memchwu-** stop it < *memchwo-* (?1775) < *meˑc-hwu-* (1445) ← *mec-*. SEE **kac.chwuta, cac.chwuta, mac.chwuta, nuc.chwuta**.
  CF **-i-, -hi-, -ki-, -y-, -chi-, -hi-, -ki-, -ukhi-, -ikhi-, -li-, -iwu-, -ywu-; -wu-, -hwu-, -kwu-, -ay-; -ˑGi-, -ˑGwo-, -ˑGwu-, -o-, -u-**.
  2. makes intensive verbs (CF **-chi-, -khi-, -li-, -lu-**). **tulchwu-** rummages; reveals < **tu-l-** raises it, holds it up.
chwuk, n [colloq]. 1. free n as abbr < **sālam uy chwuk**. ¶**Chwuk ey to mōs tulci/kkici** He can't even be called a human being.
  2. quasi-free n. a group, a gang, a bunch (of people / things). ¶**Kulay po.ye to ku key ku cwung ey se nun kacang naun chwuk ila 'na** They may not look like much but they are the best of the lot, he says. **Ku sālam to ttokttok han chwuk ey tunta** He is one of the clever ones.
chwuki (? var < **chiki**), bnd postn. **pyēng** ~ a sickly person; an invalid.
-chwungchwung, bnd adj-n (~ **hata**); after consonant **-uchwungchwung**. ···ish, slightly colored / tinged. SEE **-(u)sulum**.
chwungi, postn (? var **-thwungi**). one, person, thing. **cam** ~ a sleepyhead. **ttek** ~ (= **ttek-po**) a rice-cake glutton. CF **-cwungi**.
chy palatalized affricate + palatal glide, usually pronounced just /ch/. This string is typically a reduction of the syllable **chi**, as in **kaluchye** < **kaluchie**. CF **thy**.
chye = **chyē**, abbr < **chie**, inf < **chita**.
chyey < ˑ**thyey** (type; like; pretend). SEE **chey**.
-ci < ˑ**ti** (< ˑ*t i*), suspective. [In the first three uses **-(ess.)ess.ci** and **-(ess.)keyss.ci** occur.]
  1. (sentence-final or followed by **yo**) CASUAL statement, question, suggestion, or command (often inviting confirmation or agreement): suppose, I suppose/guess/believe/think; if I am not mistaken; I venture to say, I daresay, I bet, I'd say, it seems to me; you know, you see, don't you know, wouldn't you say, n'est-ce pas. But sometimes **-ci** shows insistence ('I tell/warn you, mind you'), sometimes reassurance ('I assure you, of course'). This is not used in answering a question about oneself.
  Mekci (yo) [FALLING INTONATION] (1) I suppose he's eating. He's eating, you know. (2) Suppose we eat; let's eat. (3) Suppose you eat. (Go on and) eat!
  Mekci (yo)? [RISING INTONATION] He's eating, I suppose?
  Mekci (yo)?? [DIP-RISE INTONATION] (1) You know, he's eating! [lively statement]. (2) He is eating, I suppose? [lively question]. (3) He is eating, isn't he [rhetorical question]. (4) Are we eating? [a lively suggestion].
  Mekci (yo)! [A LOUD QUICK FALL ON THE LAST SYLLABLE] (1) He IS eating [an insistent statement]. (2) Suppose we eat = Let's eat! [insistent suggestion]. (3) Suppose you eat = Eat! [an insistent command].
  Mekci (yo)!! [WITH A DIP-FALL INTONATION] (1) I suppose he's eating? [a lively insistent question]. (2) He's eating, isn't he [a lively insistent rhetorical question]. (3) Suppose we eat! [a lively insistent suggestion]. (4) Suppose you eat! [a lively insistent command].
  ¶**Ne cikum yelq sal ici?** You are ten now, aren't you. **Incey caci!** Suppose we go to bed! (or: Now why don't you go to bed?!) **Ama ku i hanthey ai ka ēps.ci** He has, I believe, no children. **Sewul ey sālam i mānh.ci yo** There are quite a lot of people in Seoul, you know. **Ku ⁿyeca ka um.ak-hoy ka celpan ina cīna se wass.keyss.ci** She must have come when the concert was about half over, I guess.
  NOTE: It is unclear just when **-ci yo** came into use, but King finds examples (with the unaffricated *-ti* retained) in Starchevskiy 1890 and Khlynovskiy 1904. Another likely example: *nyek.yes.ciwo* (1894 Gale 113) = ⁿ**yekyess.ci yo** 'considered'. SEE **-e yo**.
  2. used within a complex sentence as a loose connective. SEE **-ki ey mangceng ici, -umyen ··· -ess.ci**.
  2a. is / does and + (SEMANTIC) NEGATIVE. ¶**Ku ka kulenq īl ul hanun ke n' caki lul wi hay se (i)ci nala lul salang hay se ka ani 'ta** His doing such a thing is for himself and not from loving his country. **Nay kes ici ney kes i ani 'ta** It is mine, it isn't yours (= **Ney kes i ani 'la nay kes ita** It is not yours, it's mine). **Cikum un kwaynchanh.ci cēncayng i kkuth-nako se ka mūncey 'ta** The present time is all

right, but (the period) right after the war is over is a problem. **Swun-i lang Poktong-i uy cip ey se tul yātan ici wuli cip ey se n' āmu kekceng anh.nunta** They are making a fuss at Swun-i's and at Poktong-i's but everything is quiet at my house. **Swun-i lang Poktong-i lang ku chayk ul sass.ci na nun saci anh.ess.ta** It is Swun-i and Poktong-i who bought that book, not I. **Poktong-i lang man kass.ci, Swun-i lang un kaci anh.ess.ey yo** I went there just with Poktong-i and not with Swun-i.

2b. ... **ina (ila ya, ila ya man)** ---**ci** + IMPOSSIBILITY or UNLIKELIHOOD. ¶**Ku sālam ina (ila ya, ila ya man) halq swu iss.ci talun sālam un elim ēps.ta** He can do it, but it would be out of the question for anyone else. **Ku sālam ina kamyen kass.ci talun sālam un mōs kanta** He might be able to go but no one else could. **Ku sālam ina tul.e kaci talun sālam un mōs tul.e kanta** He may get in but no one else will make it (in). **Kyōoy se 'na ppekkwuk sāy soli lul tul.ulq swu iss.ci sīnay se n' mōs tut.nunta** You may be able to hear a cuckoo in the suburbs, but you won't in town.

2c. [LIVELY] **X-ci X-e** (with verbs) go ahead and do it, let's go ahead and do it; (with adj, cop) it really is. The particle **la** cannot be added. ¶**Kuleh.key sulphumyen wūlci wul.e** If you're so sad, go ahead and cry. **Ku sālam ul kitalilq kes ēps.i wuli kkili mence mekci mek.e** Let's go ahead and eat without waiting for him. **Chinkwu ka cakkwu hala 'nun tey haci hay** Since your friend keeps telling you to do it, go ahead and do it. **Tōn ul mānh.i cwukeyss.ta 'nun tey ku catong-cha lul phalci phal.e** Go ahead and sell the car — they'll give you a lot of money for it. **Sikan i ēps.nun tey ku-nyang kaci ka** You have no time — just go on and go. **Kuleh.key poko siph.umyen ka se poci pwā** If you want to see it so much, go on and go see it. **Kuleh.key kwichanh.umyen cwukci cwuk.e** (or **cwuk.e pelici cwuk.e pelye**) If you are so bored, go on and drop dead. ¶**Cōh.ci cōh.a** It sure is nice. **Ku ⁿyeca ka ippuci ippe** She's real pretty.

¶**Yātan ici yātan ia / ie** It's a real uproar.

2d. -**ci kulay** why don't you. ¶**kath.i kalq sālam i ēps.umyen Kim sensayng kwa 'la to kaci kulay** If there is no one to go with (you), why don't you go with Mr Kim? **Kulem ese mekci tul kulay** Why don't you all start eating?

2e. **sāsil māl ici** in truth, to tell the truth. ¶**Cham-mal ici** (= **cham-mal**) **kulayss.ta** That's just what he said. That's just the way it was (just what happened).

3. 3a. -**ci man (un)**: does / is but. ¶**kuleh.ci man (un)** but, however, still, yet, nevertheless, notwithstanding (that). **Ku kes i ippuci man pissaci** That one is nice looking but I bet it's expensive.

3b. -**ci yo man (un)**. ¶**Ēps.keyss.ci yo man (un)** There probably aren't any(, but).

4. used with auxiliaries **anh.ta (ani hata)**, **mōs hata**, and **mālta** to negativize: does/is not. ¶**swīpci (lul / ka) anh.ta** is not easy. **mekci anh.nunta** does not eat. **mekci anh.ko iss.ta**, **mekci mōs hako iss.ta** is not eating. **Nay ka kako siph.ci anh.ta** I don't want to go. **Ku ka kako siph.e haci anh.nunta** He doesn't want to go. **Yenge lul an ssuci anh.nun ya** Isn't it true they use no English? **Kasici anh.sup.nikka** (**Kasici anh.usip.nikka, Kaci anh.usip.nikka** are less common) Aren't you going? ¶**Keki ey tāy hay se han mati to māl haci anh.ess.ta** He said not a single word about it. **Āmulye 'ni kuleh.ci anh.ci** Surely it can't be that way. **Khuci to anh.ko cākci to anh.ta** It isn't big and it isn't little, either. **Ney ka kaci anh.nun hān na to kaci anh.keyss.ta** Unless you go, I won't go either. **Kim sensayng i ani 'ko Pak sensayng ici yo** It isn't Mr Kim, it's Mr Pak. **Nemu elyewe se haci mōs hakeyss.ta** It is too hard for me to do. **Mul un saynghwal ey ēps.ci mōs hal mulken ita** Water is a thing without which there could be no life.

¶**Wūlci mala!** Don't cry! **Ic.ci mā** Don't forget! ⁿ**Yēm.lye [haci] māsey yo** Don't you worry. **Māl to haci māsipsio** Don't mention it; Of course; It goes without saying. **Cengke-cang ey se mannaci mālko tapang ey se mannaca** Let's not meet at the station, let's meet at the teahouse. **Nōlci mālko īl hapsita** Let's cut out the loafing and get to work. **Pakk ey na-kaci mālko cip ey iss.ke la** Don't go out, stay home. **Ic.ci mālko phyēnci lul sse la** Don't (you) forget to write the letter. **Sesum chi** (= *****sesum.ci**) **mālko cēnhwa hay cwusipsio** Do not hesitate to telephone me. **Onul kaci mālci yo** I won't go today (or: Let's not go today. or: You'd better not go today).

5. -ess.ci siph.ta SEE siph.ta.
SEE ~ ka, ~ to, ~ lul (-ci l'), ~ man (un); -e ya 'ci. CF ci; 'ci, chi (abbr < haci).
ci, postmod < ˙ti = ˙t i (postmod + nominative pcl). 1. the uncertain fact whether. SEE -un ci$_1$; -tun ci, -(ess.)ess.tun ci; -nun ci, -(ess.)ess.nun ci, -(ess.)keyss.nun ci; -ulq ci, -(ess.)ess.ulq ci. ¶ ~ ālta (moluta, ic.ta, kiek hata, sayngkak hata, māl hata) knows (knows not, forgets, remembers, recalls, tells) whether. 2. given the state of being: etteh.key ADJ-un ci it is so ... that (= nemu ADJ-e se). 3. (the time since) its happening. SEE -un ci$_2$. This is not a variant of -un cey 'time that ...' (despite the usage in Roth 457) but continues MK -un ˙t i; the time expression follows.
'ci, abbr. 1. < ici. 2. < ˙'ti, abbr < haci < ˙ho˙ti (after voiceless sounds, a, or e). ¶twok ci antha (1887 Scott 185 = 1893 Scott 229) is not poisonous, (wine) is not strong.
ci [var, often pejorative] = cey (I/me, etc.)
ci, bnd n. stuff, thing; pickles (= kimchi). ccan-ci pickled turnip slices. ces.kwuk-ci pickles soaked in a pickled fish soup; brine-soaked radishes. ci-ci cucumber pickles. kkal-cci (= kkalq-ci) = kkalkay a cushion (< kkalta spreads it out). than-ci embers of tobacco in a pipe. But kimchi 'pickled cabbage (etc)' is a variant from timchoy < TTIM-ˇCHOY 'soaked vegetables'; the k... is a hypercorrection of the palatalization in the expected cimchi, which occurs in dialects. CF chi; -eci / -aci; -echi, -achi; kkangchi dregs, cāngachi [DIAL] = cāngacci, cāchi = ca-thwuli (cloth) remnants.
-(c)ci, bnd n. kalak-ci ring. phal-cci bracelet; armband. (? < ccita [DIAL] = kkita vt).
ci < CI, adnoun, prefix. branch, subsidiary. ~ cem a branch store. ANT pon.
ci < CI [in Chinese clichés], 1. pcl = uy (of). ¶"sam-pun ci ī" two-thirds. "um.wu ci pi" preparation for a rainy day (against lurking dangers). "in ci sangceng" human nature. "uysik ci pang(ca)" a means of livelihood. "uysik ci wu" the worry / problem of making a living. "uysik ci hyang" a place where the living is easy. "īwang ci sā" bygones. "kumsulq ci lak" the pleasures of married life. 2. Chinese postverb (shows the Chinese verb is transitive). (does) it. ¶"il.en-i phyēy-ci" ('one utterance covers all' =) saying it in a single word. "yek-ci sa-ci" ('change it, think it' =) You should tailor your thinking to the circumstances.

-ci anh.ko < -˙ti a˙ni ho˙kwo, suspective + aux gerund. not being/doing; without being/doing; instead of being/doing. ¶Hana to namkici anh.ko tā kacye kass.ta They have taken it all away and left nothing. Āmu māl to anh.ko kuce kass.ta He went away without saying a word. Ku i nun an^{h}ay eykey cocha allici anh.ko cip ul na-kass.ta He left home without letting even his wife know. Pam itun ci nac itun ci kalici anh.ko nul īl ul hanta He works all the time (without discriminating between) night and day. khuna cak.una kalici anh.ko regardless of whether it is big or small. Ku ai nun talun ai tul hako sekk.ici anh.ko nul oy ttalo tōnta The boy does not mix with other boys but always keeps to himself. Wēn-swungi ka way khong ul kka se nun ce nun mekci anh.ko saykki eykey cwunun kwun a Why, the monkey shells the peanuts and then gives them to her baby instead of eating them herself! Ka (se) cwumusey yo — Na ttaymun ey caci anh.ko kitalici māsiko yo Go to bed — don't wait up for me. mekci anh.ko iss.ta is not eating. -ci anh.ko se nun an toylq kes ita it just wouldn't do not to = has just got to.
CF -ci mālko.

-ci anh.ta, suspective + aux (v, adj): SEE -ci.
-ci anh.e cita gets/becomes so it does/is not.
ci cocha, postmod + pcl. ¶punmyo ka eti (i)n ci cocha ālci mōs hanta does not even know where the grave is.
-ci cocha, suspective + pcl. ¶Ku sālam kwa yēyki lul haki khenyeng manna poci cocha mōs hayss.ta I didn't even get to see him, much less talk with him.
cie, 1. < ci˙ye, inf < cita < °ci˙ta carries on the back, bears; becomes.
2. < ti˙ye, inf < cita < °ti˙ta falls.
3. < ci˙ze, inf < cīs.ta < ˇcis˙ta makes.
ci enceng SEE -ulq ~
cieta, postmod. SEE -ulq cieta; cila (ko), ciita.
ciita, aux adj insep (follows inf -e). [obs, lit] wishes/desires that; may...! ¶Ttus i ilwue ciita our wish be realized! CF cieta, -ko ce.
cik < ˙cik, postsubst adj-n insep. SEE -um cik < -˙^{e}am ˙cik.

-(c)cik, suf (derives adj-n, adv); var < **-(c)cek**; PARAINTENSIVE **-chik**. **ilccik(-i)** early < **iluta**. **kacik** fairly near < **ka(kkaw)-**. **kaypcik** rather light < **kapy(ew)-**. **kiph-cik** rather deep. **k^i/$_y$al-ccik** rather long. **kwulk-cik** rather thick. **melccik** (NK spells **melcik**) fairly distant < **mē-l-**. **muk-cik** rather heavy < **muk(ew)-**. **na-cik** somewhat low < **nac.ta**. **nelccik** (< **nelp-cik**) somewhat broad. **noph-cik** rather tall / high. **nu-cik** rather late / slow / loose < **nuc.ta**. **toy-cik** somewhat thick, a bit too hard. **ttu-cik** rather slow. **yalccik** (< **yalp-cik**) rather shallow. CF **-um ci**, **-cimak**, **-cikun**, **-(c)cwuk**.

-ci ka, suspective + pcl (used to emphasize negative constructions, on stems of adjectives and certain processive verbs — see §11.7.2). ¶**Tolie kyelkwa ka cōh.ci (ka)** [= **cōh.ci lul**] **mōs hayss.ta** On the contrary, the results were no good at all. **coqken ey mac.ci ka anh.ko** without meeting the qualifications; lacking the least qualification. **Simsang chi ka anh.e se kulay yo** There's something amiss and that's why (I'm worried).

ci ka, postmod + pcl.
 1. (whether) ¶**Ku uy thāyto lul pomyen ku ka cham-mal ul hanun ci ka uysim sulepta** His attitude makes me suspicious whether he is telling the truth.
 2. (time since) ¶**Hayq pich ul pon ci ka olay 'ta** It has been a long time since we saw any sunshine. **Tongsayng i Mikwuk ey kan ci ka pelsse ō-nyen i toynta** My little brother has been in America five years already. **Yeki osin ci ka elma 'na toysip.nikka** How long have you been here?

ci ka, [var, often pejorative] = **cey ka** (I; self)
ci kan ey SEE **-tun** ~
cik hata < `cik °ho`ta. SEE **-um cik**.
ciki, postn. a guard, a keeper. **cheng** ~ [obs] steward. **kyō** ~ school custodian (janitor). **mun** ~ gatekeeper, goalie. **myō** ~ grave keeper. **san** ~ forest ranger; (= **nung** ~) tomb/grave keeper. **totwuk** ~ security guard. **tungtay** ~ lighthouse keeper. [? < bnd n **cik** < `TIK` upright (vigilant) + **i** person]
ciki, postn. an area of land (calling for a given amount of rice seed). ¶**tas mal** (**tas toy**, **twū sem**) ~ a plot of land that takes 5 **mal** (5 **toy**, 2 **sem**) of rice seeds.

ci kkaci, postn + pcl. SEE **-un** ~ .
-ci kkaci (nun), suspective + pcl (+ pcl). Often replaced by **-ki kkaci (nun)**. ¶**Ku sālam ul cikcep manna poci** (/ **poki**) **kkaci nun mōs hayss.una sosik un cal tut.ko wass.ta** I wasn't able actually to see him in person but I heard lots about him.
cik sulepta → **cik hata**
-cikun, bnd adj-n (~ **hata**). ···ish. **chwucep-** ~ filthy. **cwuk-** ~ droopy. **si-** ~ sourish. **nok-ci(ku)n hata** is droopy, tired. **swī-** ~ rather stale-smelling (musty, sourish). **thucek-** ~ belchy, burpy [< **thu-l-** + **-cek**]. CF **-chek** ~ , **-(c)cek** ~ , **-(c)cek-ci(ku)n**. [< **-cik** + **-un**]
cikyeng < `TTI-"KYENG`, n. 1. boundary, border. 2. (postmod after **-ulq**) situation, condition, circumstance. ¶**cwuk.ulq** ~ **ita** is in a bad fix. **Mulken kaps i nemu pissa se ki ka mak.hilq cikyeng iey yo** (Im Hopin 1987:34) Prices are so high it's enough to take your breath away! **Twū sālam i ^{1}ihon halq cikyeng ey ilun kes un ani 'ey yo** (ibid.) The two haven't reached the point of planning divorce. **Āmu soli chye to molulq cikyeng ulo cam tul.ess.e yo** (ibid.) I fell asleep dead to the world.
cil, postn. the act of (doing), ···ing [sometimes pejorative]. CF **cīs**, **cīs.ta**; **īl**; **kil**.
¶**celkwu** ~ pounding grain in a mortar. **hwuli** ~ fishing with a net. **hulk** ~ mud-plastering. **kawi** ~ cutting with scissors, scissoring. **khal** ~ wielding a knife. **kwayngi** ~ hoeing. **kyēycip** ~ womanizing. **no** ~ rowing, paddling. **nwupi** ~ quilting. **panu'** ~ sewing, needlework. **pangmangi** ~ paddling laundry. **sap** ~ shoveling. **sonq-kalak** ~ pointing (a finger). **sōngkos** ~ drilling. **tatum-** ~ finishing touches, finishing up. **tatum.i** ~ fulling (smoothing cloth). **tāyphay cil** planing. **tetum.i** ~ groping about; stammering. **thop** ~ sawing. **tocek** ~ stealing, pilfering, theft. **tōkki** ~ wielding an ax. **ttut-key** ~ unsewing old clothes. **yāngchi** ~ rinsing the mouth. (**ppallay** ~ 'laundering' is uncolloquial.)
¶**kkapum** ~ winnowing (< **kkapulm** = **kkapulum**). **pak.um** ~ backstitch(ing). **saykim** ~ carving; ruminating. **sumpak[kok]** ~ hide-and-seek. **tal.um(-pak)** ~ running. **ttwim(-pak)** ~ running; jumping. **ttāym** ~ tinkering, soldering, patching.
¶**katayk** ~ playing (a game like) tag. **mūtwu**

~ tanning, dressing skin. **salay** ~ winnowing, fanning. **thay** ~ threshing; thrashing. **yongtwu** ~ masturbating.
¶**katong** ~ kicking in the air. **ēlleng** ~ (a children's game). **haycak** ~ toying with food / drink. **petwung** ~ squirming; pawing the air. **pulā** ~ moving a baby's legs like a bellows. **ttalkkwuk** ~ hiccuping.

cil, n. potter's clay, unglazed clay. ~ **kulus / kiwa** unglazed earthenware / tile.

cil(q), prosp mod < **cita**, < **cilta**.

-ci l', abbr < **-ci lul**. ¶**Nōllaci l' māsey yo** (Im Hopin 1986:64) Don't be surprised, now. [1]**Yangsim sāng haci l' mōs hakeyss.ta** (Dupont 293) In conscience, I cannot do it.

ci 'la SEE **-un** ~ (**se**), **-nun** ~ (**se**), **-ess.nun** ~ (**se**); **-ulq** ~ **to**, **-(ess.)ulq ci 'la** = **-ulq ci 'n i 'la**. NOTE: There are no occurrences of *-**ul.nun ci 'la (se)**; but **-keyss.nun ci 'la (se)** and **-ulq ci 'la (se)** are possible in literary contexts.

cila (ko), indic attent ← **cita** aux vi sep (+ pcl); follows adj inf. that it may become, wanting it (saying for it) to become. ¶**Ese hwullyung hay cila ko pīnta** I pray that he may soon achieve fame. CF **-ko cita**.

ci'la, aux v indic assert (follows inf). wants to do. ¶*[SANG-ZYEN] 'hi 'i lol ['NGUY-'LWON] 'ho.ya ci'la ["CHYENG] 'ho.ya'nol* (1481 Twusi 22:34-5) precipitously asked to discuss this, whereupon ... .

ci lul, postmod + pcl. ¶**Nay ka ku lul etteh.key sayngkak hako iss.nun ci lul ku eykey māl hako siph.un chwungtong ul nukkyess.e yo** I felt the urge to tell him what I thought of him.

-ci lul, suspective + pcl (used to emphasize negative constructions — SEE §11.8.2). ¶**Tolie kyelkwa ka cōh.ci (ka/)lul mōs hayss.ta** On the contrary, the results were no good at all. **Cektang chi lul anh.e se mangsel iko iss.nun ke yo** I am hesitating because it is hardly appropriate. **Ku kes un poci lul anh.ess.ta** I didn't see it.

ciluta, bnd v, postnom v (? < vt 'thrusts'; CF **ttulita**). -LL-. (intensifies or vulgarizes). eph- ~ spills, slops. **kwuki-** ~ = **kwu(ki)-pak** ~ wrinkles it up. **kkwēy-** ~ [vulgar] puts on, wears (= **ipta** or **sin.ta**). **paswu- / puswu-** breaks / smashes it. **ssa-** ~ [vulgar] roams (= **ssa-tanita**); excretes (= **ssata**). ? **ce(-)ciluta** spoils / ruins it (< ?). ? **si(-)ciluta** dozes (< ?).

cim, subst < **cita**

-ci mā = **-ci mal.a** = **-ci mal.e** don't! SEE **mā**.

-(c)cimak, suf (derives adj-n, adv). **nacimak** rather low < **nac-**. **nucimak** fairly late < **nuc-**. **melccimak** (NK spells **melcimak**) fairly distant < **mē-l-**. CF **-(c)cik**, **-(c)cum(ak)**.

-ci mace, suspective + pcl. ~ **anh.ta**, ~ **mōs hata**. ¶**I pyēngsin mom i yōngki ka ēps.e cwukci mace mōs hako ileh.key kwukel ul hako tanip.nita** This frail body lacking the courage even to die, here I am going around begging like this. **Nwun i an poinun tey 'ta (ka) tut.ci mace mōs hani sal.e se mwes hakeyss.**[s]**o** Not only blind but unable to hear, as well, what good is there in living?

-ci mālta, suspective + aux v -L-. SEE **mālta**, **-ci mā**.

ci man SEE **-un ci man**

-ci man, suspective + particle.
1. though, although, notwithstanding the fact that, but. ¶**Kako nun siph.ess.ci man sikan i ēps.ess.ta** I wanted to come, but I lacked the time. **Sillyey 'ci man,** [n]**yensey ka elma 'na toysip.nikka** Excuse me for asking, but what is your age?
2. (with negative)
2a. ~ **anh-** just not (is / does): ¶**Cim i khutula to mukepci man anh.umyen tulko kakeyss.ta** I can bring the luggage even if it's bulky, just so it isn't heavy.
2b. ~ **mā-l-** don't (or let's not) just do. ¶**Ca, ttek ul mantulci man mālko mek.umyen se tul hasi yo** Don't just make rice cakes, people, eat some while making them. **Nōlci man mālko chayk ina com ilk.e yo** (Im Hopin 1986:76) Don't just loaf around, read a book or something.
2c. ~ **mōs ha-**. ¶**Hānq-ca lul ssuci man mōs haci, ilk.ulq cwul un āp.nita** I am able to read Chinese characters, I just can't write them.
3. ~ **se to** even though, despite the fact that. ¶**Mian haci man se to, kuleh.key nun mōs hakey toykess.**[s]**up.nita** Though I am very sorry, I won't be able to do that.
4. ~ **to** indeed but, though indeed, although quite / very. ¶**Komapki n' haci man to sa.yang hakeyss.**[s]**up.nita** I am grateful, indeed, but I will decline. **Mian haci man twu (= to) yo**

Excuse me, but ... .
5. ~ un (usually spelled -cimanun) but, yet. ¶nai ka elici man (un) young as one is, though young. Ku ka oki ya okeyss.ci man un nemu nuc.ci anh.umyen cōh.keyss.ta He's sure to come, all right, but I hope he won't be too late. SEE haci man, kuleh.ci man, ku'h.ci man.
-ciman un (= -cimanon 1896) → -ci man un.
cin < CIN, 1. adn. deep (in color). ~ pola deep purple. ~ punhong deep pink. ~ cwuhwang deep chrome.
2. adj-n. ~ hata is thick (rather than watery). ANT yēn.
cin < CIN, adn. true, genuine, real; [DIAL] on one's father's side (= tongseng).
cin, mod. 1. < cita.
2. < cilta is watery, muddy. ¶ ~ kwuleng a mire. ~ nwūn wet snow (cinnwun-kkaypi sleet). ~ cali soiled spot; spot where one was just born or has just died; the very spot.
-cin, suffix (makes impressionistic adverbs). ¶nokcin / nwukcin soft, supple, pliant < nwuk- adj (soft, limp). CF -sin; -cikun.
-ci n', abbr < -ci nun
ci 'na SEE -ulq ~
-ci 'na, suspective + cop advers. ~ anh.ta / mālta. ¶Sikan i te kellici 'na anh.umyen cōh.keyss.ta I certainly hope it won't take any longer [shows annoyance]. Yenghuy ka tto oci 'na anh.ulq ka hako na nun nal mata kitaliko iss.ta I wait every day thinking Yenghuy might come back to me [shows frustration]. (Ku ttawi sēthwulun Yenge pakk ey mōs halq pay ey ya chalali) Yenge lul paywess.ta ko calang ul haci 'na mālca! You shouldn't have bragged so much about your English (now that it's put to the test and it fails you). An cwulq kes ila 'myen a.yey poici 'na māltun ci If you're not prepared to give it you shouldn't show it in the first place. Kēcis mal haci 'na mala Don't tell me any lies, now!
cince, postmod [obs, poetic; < ?]. SEE -ulq ~ . CF cieta.
˙ci-ngi ˙ˈta, aux v polite + cop indic assert (follows inf, often the effective inf). ¶˙na y ˙nike ˙ci-ngi ˙ˈta ˙ka˙sya (1445 ¹Yong 58) saying "I must go" he went. ˙icey s ˙SYEY-CWON ˙kotka ˙ci-ngi ˙ˈta (1459 Wel 2:9b) I want to be like the present World-Honored. ¨TTYEY-¨CO hona˙h ol ˙cwu˙esi˙tun ¨mal tu˙le ilozo˙Wa ˙ci-

ngi ˙ˈta (1447 Sek 6:22b) if you let me have one of your disciples I want to build them [the monasteries] according to what he tells me.
-ci 'ni, [? DIAL] suspective + abbr cop indic attent [− or is this ni < ney < ne 'you', added as an afterthought?]. Makes a casual question. Cikum mekci 'ni? I suppose you are eating now? Mek.ess.ci 'ni? I suppose you ate? Mek.keyss.ci 'ni? I suppose you'll eat?
ci 'ni SEE -ulq ~
ci 'nila SEE -ulq ~
cintay, postmod [obs; lit; colloq]. SEE -ulq ~ . [? < ci + in cop mod + tay 'original stage']
-ci 'n tul, (suspective + cop mod) + postmod. ¶Selma ku sālam ul manna poci 'n tul (= manna poki ya) mōs hal ya Surely I should be able to SEE him at least.
ci nun SEE -ulq ci nun
-ci nun, suspective + pcl. ¶Kuleh.key elyepci nun anh.ta It's not so difficult. Yenge lul ssek cal haci nun mōs haci man, kulay to kkway hanta He may not speak English extremely well, still he speaks it fairly well. Ttal un cal sayngkici nun mōs hayss.una sēngqkyek un mopsi alum-tawess.ta The daughter was not at all pretty, but she had a very fine character.
-ci pakk ey, suspective + quasi-pcl. ¶Son cis ulo caki ttus ul cen haci pakk ey mōs hay yo He can only convey his thought by gestures. I eysukhulleythe nun olla kaci pakk ey anh.e yo This escalator only goes up [and not down].
ci puthe. SEE -ulq ~, -un ~ .
-ci puthe, suspective + pcl. ¶Ilk.ci puthe mōs hanun tey wēyn ke l' ssulq cwul ālkeyss.e yo When I can't read, even, how can I be expected to know how to write?
cīs < ¨cus, n [quasi-free; free in cīs (i) nanta frolics]. an act (of behavior), (one's) behavior, conduct; a motion, a gesture, a movement. ¶sonq ~ a motion of the hand; a wave; a hand signal. momq ~ a gesture, gesticulation. ip ~ making a mouth; moving one's lips; mouthing; eating. nwunq ~ a sign with the eyes, a look, an eye signal; eyeing, giving the eye to. kokayq ~ moving one's head. palq ~ moving one's foot / feet. nappun ~ bad conduct. I key musun cīs in ya Where are your manners?! Ne hanun cīs un pam-nac ku mo.yang ita Nothing you do ever amounts to much. SYN [vulgar] cīs keli, cīs-twungi.

cis-, bound adverb. hard, severely, roughly. ~ **ccih.ta**, ~ **chita**, ~ **ikita** (= **cisq-ikita**), ~ **kwukita**, ~ **māta**, ~ **mekta**, ~ **mucciluta**, ~ **nēlta**, ~ **palp.ta**, ~ **palp.hita**, ~ **ssipta**.

ci se puthe SEE **-un** ~

cita: Treat **cita** as vi (or vt) if **cinta** and **cinun** occur; as defective vi if only **cyess.ta** (**ciess.ta**) and **cin** occur; as adjective if only (N **i**/**ka**) **cita** occurs.

cita$_1$ < °**ci̇̄ta$_2$**, 1. vt. carries on the back, bears; owes (money), gets into debt; (**sinsey lul** ~) owes (gratitude), is indebted/obliged (to one); (**chayk.im ul** ~) assumes (the responsibility), takes it on, bears it. VC **ciwuta**; CF **cikey**, **cim**; **cinita**, **ita**.

2. vi. gets defeated, loses, is bested; gives in, yields (to). **mith** ~ takes a loss (in selling it).

cita$_2$ < °**ti̇̄ta$_1$**, vi. (a flower or a leaf) fades and falls, is shed, is gone, vanishes; (the sun/moon) sets, sinks, goes down; (**swūm i** ~) breathes one's last breath, gives up one's breath, dies, expires; (**pul i** ~) = **kkē cita** (fire) goes out, dies out; (dirt, a spot, paint) vanishes, fades away. CF **ciwuta**.

cita$_3$ < °**ti̇̄ta$_2$**, vi. it forms, sets in (→ **cita$_5$**). VC **ciwuta**.

1. ¶**kunul i** ~ it casts a shadow, gets shady.
2. ¶**Cangma ka ciess.ta** The rainy season has set in.

cita$_4$ < °**ti̇̄ta$_2$**, aux vi sep (follows inf; **nun**, **to**, **tul** may intervene).

1. gets to be, becomes, grows. Usually inf is adj but sometimes vi: **pel.e** → (**pēle**/) **pāla cita** it widens; **sul.e** → **sule**/**sala cita** vanishes. ¶**cōh.a** (**nappe**, **chwuwe**, **tewe**, **phikon hay**) ~ gets better (worse, colder, warmer, tired). **kiwul.e** ~ it tilts. **Nal i chacha kil.e cinta** The days are getting longer and longer. **Incey nun um.ak i cōh.a cyess.ta** Now I've come to like music.

2. gets/is done. Makes intransitives out of transitives — and some defective [bound] infinitives; intensifies intransitives. CF **ttulita**.

2a. (transitive infinitives). ¶**allye** ~ it gets known/told, it gets to someone's ears. **ccic.e** ~ it tears, gets torn. **engkhul.e** ~ it gets tangled. **hēy** ~ = **heye** ~ gets scattered, separates. **kalle** ~ it splits, forks, branches off. **kkāy** ~ it breaks, gets broken. **kkē** ~ is extinguished, vanishes, collapses. **kkulle** ~ it gets loose.

kkunh.e ~ it snaps, is snapped. **phul.e** ~ gets released/loose, comes untied/loose. **thē** ~ it splits. **ttel.e** ~ it drops/falls, is punctured. **ssot.a** ~ it pours out/down.

2b. (defective infinitives). ¶^{a}/$_u$**tungkule** ~ it warps. **icile** ~ it chips/wanes. **kk^a/$_e$kkwule** ~ falls head-first. **(k)kamule** ~ faints. **kasule** ~ grows stubborn; bristles. **p^a/$_u$sule** ~, **pule** ~ it breaks/crumbles. **(k)kopul^a/$_e$** ~ it bends. **mangkule** ~ is put out of shape, ruined. **okule** ~, **wukule** ~ it curls up, warps; it breaks. **pekule** ~ it splits, separates. **ppā** ~ falls (CF **ppāy-** extract it). **pulke** ~ it bulges out. **sakul^a/$_e$** ~ it collapses, withers. **ssule** ~ it topples/tumbles. **ekule** ~ gets dislocated; goes against. **thute** ~ it tears.

2c. (intransitive inf). ¶**nul.e** ~ it dangles.

cita$_5$ (< **cita$_4$**), 1. postnom adj insep. is, is characterized/marked by. **amphang** ~ is bold. **angkhal** ~ is persistent. **cha'** ~ is glutinous. **entek** ~ is hilly, sloping. **enthek** ~ is bumpy, uneven, rough. **kaphul-mak** ~ is precipitous. **kenpang** ~ is impertinent, overbearing. **kilum** ~ is fat(ty). **kkek** ~ is stout [<?]. **kkuntek** ~ is persistent. **kwusek** ~ is recessed; is sequestered, off to itself. **kaps** ~ is expensive, valuable. **kwuseng** ~ is in natural good taste. **mes** ~ is smart, tasteful. **mo** ~ is sharp, pointed, angular. **mey** ~ is nonglutinous. **newul** ~ (waves) are rough in the distance. **ō(tal)** ~ is replete [<?]. **ōy** ~, **pyek** ~, **hankas**/**-kyeth** ~ is remote, out-of-the-way. **ppye** ~ is "bony" = pithy. **telphek** ~ is buxom, portly. SEE **ēsayk** ~, **phutak** ~, **sal** ~, **salphak** ~, **swus** ~, **thul** ~; **y^e/$_a$mu** ~; **pala** ~ is short and fat; **chwu** ~ is wet (CF vi **chwuk-** get wet); **phu** ~ is abundant (CF **puphus hata**). NOTE: **k^a/$_e$ntule** ~ 'is coy; is lilting' < **k^a/$_e$ntul** 'swaying' is unusual (CF **cita$_4$** 2b). SYN [? PARAINTENSIVE] **chita**.

2. postnom vi sep (by **i**/**ka**). gets/becomes characterized by. ¶**along** ~, **ellek** ~, **ellwuk** ~, **elwuleki** ~ gets spotted, breaks out in a rash. **cangma** ~ it rains for days on end, turns into a long rain. **heki** ~ gets hungry. **hoth** ~ it gets simplified. **hwumi** ~ it forms an inlet. **kalangi** ~ it gets/is forked. **kkephul** ~ gets coated, has a skin form on it. **kunul (i)** ~ (shade) casts a shadow, (a shadow) shades, gets shady/shaded, forms shade, is shaded. **kwup.i**

~ (a river) makes a bend. ōy ~ gets isolated, sequestered. swumuk ~ gets blotted with ink. tengkwul ~, nengkhwul ~ (a vine) puts out runners. wumul ~ forms a dimple.

cita$_6$ < *˚ci˙ta$_1$ (lenited to ci˙la), aux adj insep [lit] = siph.ta (desires, wants). SEE -ko cita. CF -ko ce, ci˙la, ˙cye, -˙cye.

ci to, postmod + pcl. ¶Kulen ci to molunta Could be.

-ci to, suspective + pcl. SEE -un ~, -nun ~, -ulq ~. ¶Ilum ul ssuci to mōs hanta He can't even write his name. Talci to anh.ko sici to anh.ta It is neither sweet nor sour. (It is not sweet and it is not sour, either.) Musewe se chac.e kaci to mōs hanun tey yo He's too scared to even go visit! Poci to tut.ci to mōs hanta He can neither see nor hear. CF -' to ⋯ .

-ci tul, suspective + pcl. ¶Kulem ese mekci tul kulay Why don't you all start eating? Sōmun tut.nun kes pota ka-poni(-kka n') kuleh.ci tul anh.tun tey?! Instead of listening to rumors, you people should have gone to see.

cium, (quasi-free) n. [var] = ccum.

-ci ya, suspective + pcl. ¶Yeki kkaci oci ya mōs halq ka?! Can't he just get himself here (whether he does any work or not)?!

-ci yo, suspective + pcl. POLITE CASUAL STYLE statement, question, suggestion, or command (often inviting confirmation or assent). SEE -ci.

-ci yo man (un), suspective + pcl + pcl (+ pcl). is / does but [POLITE].

co$_1$, n, adn; LIGHT → ce (that over there).

co$_2$ < TTYWOW.
 1. n. (= kokco) an air, a tune; meter. cangq-co major key. tānq-co minor key.
 2. n. good conduct.
 3. quasi-free n (-q co after noun): ~ lo with an air of. ¶cangnan hanun co lo = cangnanq co lo jokingly, as a joke / prank. sīpiq co lo defiantly, with an air of defiance. pinanq co lo critically, in a critical vein. ^{1}nōngtamq co lo as a joke, in jest. sālam ul nollimq co lo ilunun māl a jocular term for a person. sihemq co lo = sihem sam.e as a test.

co$_3$ < TTYWOW.
 1. (? quasi-free) n. share, quota (= moks). ¶I pen ey ponay on sakwa nun wuli co lo on kes i punmyeng haney It is obvious that the apples sent this time are (for) our share (NKd).
 2. (after numerals) = comok article, clause, item. ¶cēy-sam ~ Article Three.
 3. postn (-q co): ~ lo with the stipulation of, as stipulated, as, per. ¶kyēyyak-kumq co lo as per contract, as the stipulated sum under the agreement. pangq-seyq co lo as rent. hakpiq co lo as school fees (tuition).
 4. postmod (after prosp mod < ālta only). basis, impetus. ¶ālq co a basis for knowing / realizing, enough to let you know, an adequate indication (= ālq kway "divination sign to know"): Kuleh.key elkwul i pulk.e cil ttay ey nun ālq co ka iss.ci yo When you blush like that it tells me everything I need to know (= I get the message). Etymology uncertain: CF cocim signs, indication, omen (= cohwu); cingco sign(s), indication, symptom; mangq-co = mang-cing phāy-co omens of ruin.

-c' 'o = -c' yo, abbr < -ci yo

? co ca = ce ca (that person)

cocha < cwo˙cha (< vt inf 'pursue'), particle.
 1. even; too; to boot, in addition, into the bargain. ¶punmyo ka eti (i)n ci cocha ālci mōs hata can't even tell where the grave is. Nay ka cēmsim to mōs mek.ko cenyek cocha kwulm.ess.ta I didn't eat any lunch and then skipped dinner as well. Ne cocha kulelq cwul un mōllass.ta I didn't know that (even) YOU would do that. Kutay ppun ani 'la ku sālam cocha kulen māl ul hatey As if it weren't enough for you to say it, he said it too. Non path to ppay-as.kiko, nācwung ey nun cip cocha ppay-as.kiko nun, hanun swu ēps.i, ōn sik.kwu ka Puk Kan-to lo tte-nass.ta Having our fields seized, and later our house taken to boot, there was nothing for it but for us to have the whole family leave for North Jiāndǎo [in Manchuria]. Pi ka onun tey palam cocha pūnta As if the rain weren't enough, there's a wind to boot.
 2. [DIAL] from (a distant place). ¶San ulo cocha (= puthe) palam i pul.e onta The wind blows from the mountains.

cocha ey, pcl + pcl [rare, CF ey cocha]. even (etc.) to, in, at, ⋯ . ¶Kulenq īl cocha ey kekceng ul hanta 'myen etteh.key sal.e kanta 'n māl io How can you get along in life if you're going to worry about even such trifles?

cocha ka, pcl + pcl. even (etc.) [as subject]. ¶Caney cocha ka kulen soli l' hana Even you talk like that! Pēl.i nun ēps.nun tey mulqka

cocha ka olla kani etteh.key sal.e kanta 'm! How can I get along with no income when even the price of rice is going up?!
cocha l', pcl + abbr pcl = cocha lul
cocha 'la to, pcl + cop var inf + pcl. though even (etc.). ¶**Kulen kes cocha 'la to iss.umyen cōh.keyss.e** I wish I just had one of that sort, even. **Ilum cocha 'la to ssulq cwul ālmyen cōh.keyss.e** I'd be happy if I could write my name, even.
cocha lo, pcl + pcl. ¶**Wēyn ke l' na cocha lo tol.a ol moks i iss.ess.ni** How come there was a share even for me, too?
cocha lul, pcl + pcl. even (etc.) [as direct object]. ¶**Ku nun caki ilum cocha lul mōs ssunta** He can't even write his name. **Ku nun tōn i mānh.umyen se to caki pumo eykey nun tan-ton han phun cocha lul an cwunta** Though he has lots of money he doesn't give a penny to his parents.
cocha mace, pcl + pcl. ¶**Nam tul i tā na lul pinan hanun tey caney cocha mace na l' silh.e hamyen musun mas ey sālkeyss.na** Everyone else criticizes me and if even you hate me, in addition, what kind of life can I enjoy?! CF **mace cocha**.
cocha n', pcl + abbr pcl = cocha nun
cocha 'na(-ma), pcl + (extended) cop advers. even (etc.) or the like, whether even (etc.); even (etc.) whatever. ¶**Kuleni caney cocha 'na(-ma) com towa cwukey** Then you too help out a little bit. **Kuleh.key nōlko man cīnayta ka n' poli cwuk cocha 'na(-ma) kwūkyeng hakeyss.ni?** You expect to loaf around all the time like that and then see barley porridge?! **Ileh.key ek.ap i sīm hani eti swūm cocha 'na swīkeyss.ni** Under such oppression we hardly breathe!
cocha nun, particle + particle. as for even (etc.). ¶**Talun sālam tul un motwu na lul yok hay to ku sālam cocha nun an kulekeyss.ci (= ku sālam cocha kuleci nun anh.keyss.e)** The others may all speak ill of me, but HE won't.
cocha puthe ka, pcl + pcl + pcl. (less common) = mace puthe ka.
cocha to, pcl + pcl. even also / either; even indeed. ¶**Il.yoil ila (se) sinmun cocha to salq swu ēps.ta** It being Sunday, you can't even buy a newspaper! **Na l' chac.e oki n' sāylo ey cēnhwa cocha to ēps.ess.ta** Far from (his) calling on me, there wasn't even a phone call.
cocha uy, pcl + pcl [? DIAL; awkward]. (the one that is) from even (etc.). ¶**Hyeng cocha uy sosik i ēps.ta** There's not a word from my brother, either.
cocha ya, pcl + pcl. only if (it be) even. ¶**Mom un nulk.e to maum cocha ya nulk.keyss.na?** Why should I let my spirit get old along with my body? **Ppesuq kaps iya ollass.ci man kichaq kaps cocha ya an ollikeyss.ci** The bus fares are up, but I don't think they'll raise the TRAIN fares, too.
co chi = ce chi (that guy)
cōchi → cōh.ci
co i = ce i (that person)
-(c)cok, suf = **-(c)cak**. **alk-cok = alk-cak** pockmarked. **halki-cok** looking displeased.
cok-cok, postmod [var] = **ccok-ccok**.
-cokcok, bound adj-n (~ hata); LIGHT ↔ **-cwukcwuk**; after consonant **-ucokcok**. ‥ish, slight colored / tinged. SEE **-(u)sulum**.
coki, n; LIGHT ↔ **cēki** (over there).
co kkaci lo, n + pcl + pcl. LIGHT → **ce kkaci lo** (to that extent).
co-kkacis, cpd adn. LIGHT → **ce-kkacis** (such as that).
˙**cokya** ?< ˙CCO-KA, n. [honorific] (one)self; him(self), he himself. VAR ˙**cokyay**. ¶˙**cokya pichwuy** ˙**Gwe** (1579 Kwikam 1:23b) made himself radiant and … . ˙**cokya** ˙**Gwa** ˙**nom** ˙**kwa** ˙KAK ˙i ˙chosil ˙ss oy (1463 Pep 1:93b) he (himself) and the others are full of spiritual enlightenment, so … . ˙**cokya s** ˙**kuy** (1445 ¹Yong 25) onto him [their leader]. ˙**cokya s na˙la.h ay** ˙**sye** (1447 Sek 9:33a) in one's own nation. ˙**cokya s mozo˙m i nik˙tesi˙n i** ˙˙**la** (1459 Wel 1:52b) his own mind had matured.
˙**cokyay**, 1. = ˙**cokya** (variant form, as LCT treats all cases). ¶˙**cokyay** ˙**two mwo˙lo˙sya** (1459 Wel 21:210b) he himself did not know, and … . HE-KHWONG ˙**ol mwolwoki** ˙**cokyay s** ˙**mwo.m ol** ˙˙**sa˙mosi˙m ye** (1482 Kum-sam 2:3b) he instantly creates his own form out of empty space, and … . ˙**cokyay s** ˙˙**KWA y** ˙˙**i˙ti** ˙˙**mwot** ˙**hwolq** ˙**t ila** ˙**two** (1462 ¹Nung 7:43a) even if no results come about for himself … . ˙**cokyay s mozo˙m i** (1465 Wen 1:1:2:37a) his (own) mind.
2. ?< ˙**cokya y** < *˙**cokya i** (nominative, as NKW 1979 treats the form). ¶˙˙**nyey LYWUN-**

NGWANG ˈi hon ˈpam ˈnas soˈzi ˈyey ˈcokyay taˈsoˈliˈsinwon ˈstaˈh ol ¨taˈ¨twoloˈsya ˈSSIP-¨SSYEN ˈoˈlwo ˈKYWOW-ˈHWA ˈhoˈsinoˈn i (1459 Wel 1:25b) between a night and a day the Wheel King goes all around the land he governs and converts the people to the ten virtues (= commandments). ˈcokyay ¨aˈlosyam ˈkwa ˈnom ¨aˈlosyam ˈkwa (1465 Wen 1:1:2:37a) that he knows and that others know.
cole, LIGHT [pejorative] → cele; CF yole, kole.
　1. vni (~ hanta = colenta) does / says that way (there).
　2. adj-n (~ hata = coleh.ta) is that way (there), is so.
coleh.ta, adj-n -(H)- (inf colay), abbr < cole hata.
coleta, vi (inf colay), abbr < cole hata.
coli, adv; LIGHT → celi. CF coki; koli, yoli.
　1. (= coleh.key, co-taci) in that way (there), like that (there), so, to that extent.
　2. (= ~ lo, col' lo) that way (there), that direction, over there.
co lo SEE co₁, co₂
col-lo, abbr < co kes ulo
col' lo, abbr < coli lo (that way)
com, n, adv, adn.
　1. abbr < cokum some, a little bit.
　2. please; just, some. CF ese. Often directly attached to a preceding noun (and optionally omitting the accusative or nominative marker) as if a particle. ¶Mul com cwusey yo Give me some water, please.
　3. (adn) petty, small. ¶~ totwuk a petty thief. ~ māl small talk.
cōm, adv. how, how very much [+ rhetorical question].
ˈcom, n < irregular subst < ˚caˈta. sleep(ing). ¶LYWONG ˈoy ˈco.m i PPYEN-QAN hoˈkwo (1482 Kum-sam 2:65a) the dragon's sleep is peaceful, and ... . ˈcom cal ˈcaˈkesiˈnol (1482 Nam 1:28b) he slept well, but ... . ˈcom ˈcasilq ˈcey (1449 Kok 118) when he sleeps ... . ˈcom ˈcasyam (1475 Nay 2:2:63a) sleeping.
comam-ttay = cemam-ttay
... ¨cop- < -¨zop-. SEE ... ¨ccop-, ...s¨cop-, ...ns¨cop-, ...¨nt¨cop-, ...n¨ccop-.
co ttawi = ce ttawi
cuk, postmod (follows -un, -ess.un) [somewhat lit]. if, when; as since, now that; so far as (it is) concerned, speaking of. ¶Sokum ul te chin cuk nemu cca cinta It gets too salty if you put in any more salt. Ney māl ul tul.un cuk cham an toyess.ta I am very sorry to hear that. Kyengchi (i)n cuk Kumkang san i Hānkwuk ey se cēy-il ita As far as scenic beauty goes, the Diamond Mountains are tops in Korea. Al.e pon cuk ku kes i hepo yess.ta On inquiry, the report proved false.
kulen ~ if so, then, if that is / be the case. ¶Kulen cuk etteh.key hamyen cōh.keyss.nun ya Well, then, what would you like me to do?
SEE -un ~, -ess.un ~, in ~. SYN cuk-sun. [< ˈCUK bnd n 'whereupon': MYENG ˈi ¨CYENG ˈthi aˈni hon ˈCUK EN ˈi ¨SYWUN ˈthi aˈni hoˈkwo (1588 ¹Non 3:36a) so long as the names go uncorrected, speech will be unruly, and ... .] ˈcuk ˚hoˈta = (-ᵉ⁄am) ˈcik ˚hoˈta. SEE -um cik.
cuk-sun, postmod [emphatic] = cuk. ? < cuk + un, ? < cuk-s[i n]un.
cum, abbr < cuum
-(c)cum, suf (makes adj-n, adv). kⁱ/yal-ccum rather long.
cumak = cuum. i / yo ~ about this time.
-(c)cumak, suffix (makes adj-n, adv). kⁱ/yal-ccumak rather long.
cuum, quasi-free n. approximate time, occasion. ¶i/yo ~ about this time. ku/ko ~ [rare] about that time. ilelq ~, kulelq ~ about such a time. kalq ~ when one goes. ... ey ~ ha.ye on the occasion of ... . SEE -ulq ~. VAR cium. ABBR cūm. CF cek, ttay; ccum; thum.
cwā, abbr < cōwa < cōa = cōh.a, inf < cōh.ta. ¶cwā 'nta = cōh.a hanta.
¨cwasiˈta (? < caˈp-osi- 'take'), hon verb (eats) = capswusita. VAR ¨c'asiˈta. ¶¨cwasiˈkwo (1449 Kok 64, 1459 Wel 2:25b); ¨cwasiˈm ye (1459 Wel 2:25b); ¨cwaˈsinonˈka (1449 Kok 122); ¨cwasywoˈsye (1449 Kok 100) please eat. ¨cwaˈsya, inf < ¨cwasiˈta (eats). 1449 Kok 62. ¨cwaˈsya..., modulated stem < ¨cwasiˈta (eats). ¨cwaˈsyalq kes (1449 Kok 63); ¨cwasyaˈm ol (1464 Kumkang 4b); ¨cwaˈsyan ¨il (1462 ¹Nung 6:99b).
cwāwu < ¨C[W]A-¨NGWUW, n.
　1. right and left, either side, both sides. ¶kang ~ ey on either side of the river.
　2. attendants, entourage, people around one.
　3. sway, influence, control; ~ hata, vnt. controls, sways, influences, affects.
cwāwu-kan (ey), adv. at any rate, anyhow, in any case (= ha.ye-kan).

cwe = **cwē**, abbr < **cwue**, inf < **cwuta**. (As aux usually has the short vowel.) ABBR **c'e**.
cwo⋅cha, pcl (< vt inf). SEE **cocha**.
cwū, abbr < **cwuwu** (= **cwuo**). (please) give. **Sālam sallye cwū!** Help!
cwucey, n. an (unseemly) appearance, looks. **~ kkol** SAME. **~ sānapta** looks seedy, has a shabby appearance; is cheeky, sassy, smart-alecky, impertinent. ¶**Ku cwucey ey yangpok ul tā ip.ess.ney!** Well, isn't HE all dressed up!
cwuk, ccwuk, bnd postmod. SEE **ccwuk**.
-(c)cwuk = **-(c)cek** suf. ¶**elk-cwuk** pockmarked. **i(ki)-/ya(ki)-cwuk** talking nonsense. **hulki-cwuk** looking displeased. **kalk-cwuk** = **kalk-cak, kulk-cwuk** = **kulk-cek** scraping, clawing, scratching. **k^a/$_e$l-ccwuk** rather rich/thick/full (< **kēlta** adj). **k^i/$_y$al-ccwuk** long and slender (< **kīlta**). **kk^a/$_e$l-cwuk** rough (to the touch). **kk^a/$_e$p-cwuk** frivolous. **kk^a/$_e$y-cwuk** chewing dryly; grumbling. **nap-cwuk** (= **nap-cak**) flat, **ne(l)p-cwuk** broad and long (= **nepcwuk**). **(s)s^i/$_a$ylki-cwuk** rickety. **s^i/$_a$yl-ccwuk** sullen.
-cwukcwuk, bnd adj-n (~ **hata**); HEAVY ↔ **-cwukcwuk**; after consonant **-ucwukcwuk**. ⋯ish, slightly colored/tinged. SEE **-(u)sulum**.
cwuk.ita, vc < **cwukta**. kills. SEE **-e cwuk.ita**.
cwukta, vi. dies. SEE **-e cwukta**.
cwul₁ < ⋅**cwul**, 1. n. string, cord, rope; line; row, file, queue; stripe, band, strip; (age) level; spider thread; ore vein.
   2. counter. (sheaf, tied bunch).
   3. → **cwūl** a file, a rasp.
   4. → **cwūl** the water oat (= **cwūl phul**).
cwul₂ < ⋅**cwul**, postmodifier, postnoun.
   1. postmod. the assumed fact; the likelihood, probability; the how, the way (how to). SEE **-un ~, -nun ~, -tun ~, -ulq ~**.
   ⋯ **cwul (lo) ālta** thinks (supposes, assumes, expects, believes) that ⋯; ⋯ **cwul (ul) ālta** knows (recognizes, acknowledges) that ⋯, **-ulq cwul (ul) ālta** knows how to (also: knows that it or one will be/do).
   ¶*alpho⋅ti a⋅ni ⋅hwon ⋅cwul[⋅]l i a⋅ni ⋅⋅Gen ma⋅non* (1475 Nay 2:2:7b) it is not that one is not ill but. *mwok molon ⋅cwul is⋅ta* (?1517- ¹No 1:62b) I feel thirsty.
   NOTE: The entry **cwul** of KEd (1507) should be revised to accord with what is said here.
   2. postn. a means, a way. **pap ~** a means of livelihood, a way to eat.

cwul(q) < *cwul(q)*, prospective modifier < **cwuta** < °**cwu⋅ta**
¨*cwul(q)*, modulated prosp mod < °**cwu⋅ta**. (1445 ¹Yong 20, 1447 Sek 9:12a, 1481 Twusi 7:40a, 1482 Nam 1:44-5)
cwum < *cwum*, substantive < **cwuta** < °**cwu⋅ta** ¨*cwum*, modulated substantive < °**cwu⋅ta**. (1481 Twusi 16:64ab)
cwun < *cwun*, modifier < **cwuta** < °**cwu⋅ta**
cwung < ⋅*TYWUNG*.
   1. n. the middle; medium. ¶**~ phūm** goods of medium quality. **~ khi uy sālam** a person of medium height. **Ku uy sengcek un cwung īsang ita** His school records are above average.
   2. (quasi-free n). midst. ¶**~ ey se** between, among, out of, in. **sip ~ phal-kwu** nine out of ten. **siksa ~ (ey)** in the middle of a meal. **kongpu (hanun) ~ (ey)** in the midst of one's study. **san ~ ey iss.nun cip** a house in the middle of the mountains. **wang ~ uy wang** the king of kings. **pinkon ~ ey se cala nata** grows up in poverty. **mōtun sālam ~ ey yūmyeng hata** (1881 Ridel 38) is the most famous of all men. **Yelq-twu pay cwung ey i pay ka te khuta** (1881 Ridel 38; odd?) This is the largest of the twelve boats = This is bigger than any other of the twelve boats. **Hyēntay Mikwuk cak.kok-ka cwung ey se na nun Khophullayntu ka cēy-il cōh.ta** I like Copland best of the contemporary American composers. **I twūlq cwung ey se enu kes i cōh.un ya** Which of these two things is better?
   3. postn, postmod (-nun ~): **~ ey** during, while, in, within. ¶**hyuka ~ (ey)** during the vacation. **kumcwu ~ ey** in the course of the week, within the week, before the week is out. ¹**nay-tal ~ ey** sometime during next month. **kēnchwuk ~ uy cip** a house that is under construction. **Thonghwa cwung ip.nita** The line is busy. **Wuli ka cako iss.nun cwung ey tocek i tul.ess.ta** A burglar broke into the house while we were sleeping. **Ku nun phyēnci lul ssunun cwung ita** He is writing a letter. **Ku sāqken un cikum cosa cwung ita** The matter is under investigation. **Sayngkak cwung ita** I am thinking (about it). **Ku i ka Mikwuk ul pāngmun (hanun) cwung ita** He is visiting America. **Cek un cikum kwunpi lul hwakcang cwung ila hanta** The enemy is increasing his

armaments [so we hear]. "**Catong wūntong cwung**" [elevator service] "(Temporarily) Self-operating" = "On Automatic". SEE **-un** ~. CF **tong-an, sai.**
  4. (grade, quality, etc.) "B" (= **cwungtung**). CF **sāng, hā; kawuntey, an, sōk.**
cwūng < ˝*TTYWUNG.*
  1. postnoun [-q cwung]. a weight of (so many ¹**nyang, tōn,** or **phūn**). ¶*han* ¹*nyangq* ~ the weight of one ¹**nyang** (tael); one-tael heavy.
  2. bound adnoun. heavy; important, weighty, serious. ~ **kikwan-chong** a heavy machine-gun. ~ **kongep** heavy industry. ~ **mūcang** heavy armor. ~ **phok.kyek-ki** a heavy bomber.
  3. adj-n. ~ **hata** is heavy, weighty, serious, grave, important.
-cwungi, ? suffix. one, person, thing. *yel-* ~ a chick out of its shell; a small weak person. CF **-chwungi; ecwungi-ttecwungi** ragtag and bobtail ? < **ette + -cwungi.**
-q cwung-payki, cpd postn (makes vulgar noun). *kho* ~ nose.
cwuta < ˚*cwuˑta*, vt (1–7), aux (8); ANT **pat.ta;** CF **tulita, pachita.**
  1. gives, bestows, furnishes, provides.
  2. gives, has to give, pays (an amount).
  3. gives, awards, confers, grants.
  4. gives, allots, assigns (homework).
  5. causes, inflicts, brings on / about; brings (influence) to bear.
  6. lets (a line) out, feeds / gives (line).
  7. puts (strength/force) into, puts forth (one's strength).
  8. aux v sep. does as a favor. SEE **-e cwuta.**
NOTE: Since **pilli-** means 'borrow', **pillye cwu-/tuli-** 'lend' is not the aux structure (*'does the favor of borrowing'); 'give' is the main verb, and the sense is 'gives as a borrowing'.
cy palatalized affricate + palatal glide, usually pronounced just /c/. This is most commonly a reduction of the syllable **ci,** as in the infinitive **kacye** < **kacie.** CF **sy.**
cyāy (= **cāy**), abbr < **ce ay.** that child over there; he / him, she / her. CF **kyāy, yāy.**
cye = **cyē,** abbr < **cie** inf < **cita;** as aux usually with short vowel; **cye** (= **c'e**) sounds just like **ce** 'that'. SEE **-ko ce.**
cye = ˑ*tye* (he). ~ *two* (1795 ¹No-cwung [P] 1:41a) he too.

˙*cye,* aux adj inf (abbr < *ciˑe*), after inf (often the effective inf) or gerund. SEE -˙*kaˑcye,* -˙*keˑcye,* -˙*aˑcye,* -˙*eˑcye;* -˙*kwoˑcye.*
-˙*cye,* incorporated auxiliary adj infinitive (desire or suggestion); perhaps to be treated as abbr < -[˙*kwo*] ˙*cye.* ¶*woˑnol* TTYWOW-˙CCIP *ul QIN ˑhoˑya ˑyetcopˑcye hoˑkwo* (1459 Wel 2:69a) today wishing to inform the court assemblage, ... *tutˑcye* (1447 Sek 19:6b) wanting to hear. *mekˑcye* (1481 Twusi 9:2_) wanting to eat. *peˑliti* ˝*ma[l]ˑcye* (1481 Twusi 16:18a) wanting not to throw it away. ˝*sa[l]ˑcye cwukˑcye* (1481 Twusi 23: 49b) life or death. SEE ~ ʼ*la, hoˑcye.*
˝*cyeˑki,* der adv < ˝*cyekˑta.* a little bit; somewhat. ¶˝*cyeˑki* ˝*tywoˑhaʼyˑla* (?1517-¹No 2:41a) I'm a little bit better! ALSO: 1481 Twusi 8:7a, ...
-˙*cyeʼʼla,* incorporated aux adj inf + cop indic assert. ¶*mwuˑte poˑliˑcyeʼʼla hoˑkwo* (1481 Samkang hyo:10; cited from LCT with inferred accents) wanting to finish the burial. SEE *hoˑcyeʼla.*
cye y = ˑ*tye y* (he). 1795 ¹No-cwung [K] 1:41b.
-c' yo, abbr < **-ci yo** (casual polite). Usually pronounced **-co.**
˝*cywokwom* (? abbr < ˝*cywokwoˑma;* ? var < ˝*cyaˑkwom* adj modulated subst), adv (also n?). a little (> **cokom, cokum, com**). ¶*cywokwom neh.e meku.m ye nʼ* (?1608+ Twu[-hem?] 1:56; cited from LCT because unfound in locus) if you ingest a little of it. *cywokwom two pahi nayci ani hokwo* (1703 Sam-yek 4:19; cited from LCT) does not put out the least bit.
˝*cywokwoˑma,* n, adv. a little, a (little) bit. ¶˝*cywokwoˑmaˑtwo keyGulˑGi aˑni theˑn i* (1514 Sok-Sam hyo:35; cited from LCT with inferred accents) was not the least bit lazy.
~ ˚*hoˑta,* adj-n. ¶*cham mata poy yey nolisiki elyepki non cywokwoma hokwo* (1676 Sin.e 6:21a) at each port it was a bit hard for them to get down to the boat, and ... .
˝*cywokwoˑm achi* (< ?), n, adv. a little (bit), some. ¶˙PPWULQ-˙PEP ˑ*iˑza naʼy ingeˑkuy ˑtwo* ˝*cywokwoˑm achi isˑta* (1482 Nam 1:14a; LCT 668a "˝*cywokwomˑmachi*") there is some of Buddha's law right here where I am, too.
˝*cywokwoˑmaʼn,* abbr < ˝*cywokwoˑma hon.* a little ... , some.

¨cywokwo˙ma s, n + pcl. a little ··· ; petty. ¶ ¨cywokwo˙ma s ˙poy ˙thokwo ˙cye s ˙ptu.t ul nis˙ti ¨mwot ho.l i 'lwota (1481 Twusi 15:55b) I will not forget my desire to ride in a little boat. ¨cywokwo˙ma s ¨LI ˙lol to˙thwoa ˙CI-CHIN ˙ol e˙kuyGey ma˙lwol ˙t iGe˙ta (1475 Nay 3:41a) one is not to turn against one's intimates in a struggle for petty profits.
¨cywokwo˙may (? abbr < * ¨cywokwo˙ma hi), adverb. ¶[KUM-NYEN] swul s [˙PPYENG] ˙ey ¨cywokwo˙may me˙kwu˙m ul ye˙le 'ys.nwo˙n i (1481 Twusi 8:42b) with my weakness for wine in recent years I have started to drink a little, and ... . ¨cywokwo˙may two me˙muti a˙ni ˙hotwo˙ta (1482 Nam 1:36a) doesn't stop a bit.
¨cywo˙kwo˙may s = ¨cywokwo˙ma s. ¶ ~ ˙il-˙kak ˙mwun (?1517⁻ Pak 1:58a) a small gate. [No other examples?]

E Not distinguished from **u** in many parts of Korea. If you cannot find a word you seek with the spelling **e**, try **u**.

-e < -˙e, infinitive. CF **-ko** < ˙kwo.

The shape is **-a** after a syllable containing /o/ or [DIAL, lit; the standard spelling] /a/. Some dialects, such as the N Kyengsang fishing village described in Choy Myengok 1979, use only **-a**, regardless of the preceding vowel. Compare the examples in early texts of -˙a where -˙e is expected (SEE **-a**, p. 415).

Irreg **hata** → **hay** or [lit] **ha.ye** < ˙ho˙ye / ˙ho˙ya. SEE ˚ho˙ta. In this book the vowel of **hay** is not marked long, but the pronunciation **hāy** may also be heard; see pp. 523-4.

Irreg **kuleta, kuleh.ta** → **kulay; ileta, ileh.ta** → **ilay; celeta, celeh.ta** → **celay; etteta, etteh.ta** → **ettay; āmuleh.ta** → **āmulay; ecceta** → **eccay;** ... .

Stem-final **u** is elided before **-e**, including that of **suta** (< **seta**) → **se** stand; there is no compensatory lengthening. A stem-final **wu** is optionally reduced to the semivowel (**cwuta** → **cwue** / **cwē**), but the unreduced forms of the polysyllabic stems are seldom heard (**nanwue** → **nanwe**). Stem-final **o** is similar (**pota** → **poa** / **pwā**), but for **ota** 'come' the dissyllabic full form **oa** is not normally used, only **wā**.

MK spellings usually treat these infinitives as unreduced (˙pwo˙a, non˙hwo˙a, ssa˙hwo˙a) but the infinitive of ˙wo˙ta 'comes' is always the reduced form ˙wa (and not *˙wo˙a). There is disagreement over which of the one-syllable compressions have compensatory vowel length; in this book they are usually written long when the form is not functioning as an auxiliary. According to the pronunciation rules prescribed by the Ministry of Education (Munkyo-pu kosi 1988:185) such contracted forms as **kyē** ← **kie**, **twē** ← **twue**, **twāy** (= **twēy** = **tōy**) ← **toye**, and **hāy** ← **ha.ye** are to be pronounced long, but **wa** ← (*)**oa**, **cye** ← **cie**, **ccye** ← **ccie**, and **chye** ← **chie** are short.

Stem-final **a** and **ay** attach zero: the ending is absorbed. Stem-final **ey** and **oy** either absorb the ending or attach [lit] **-e**, but ···**oye** is often spelled ¨**way**¨, as if from *wa.y-ᵉ/a, and **wie** is often spelled ¨**wey**¨; those versions are also sometimes heard. If the vowel of a one-syllable stem is short, it often gets lengthened in the versions that absorb the ending.

Stem-final **i** is optionally reduced to **y**: **cita** → **cie** (often spelled **ciye**, as was done in MK) → **cye**. But the unreduced forms of polysyllabic stems are seldom heard: **kitalye** ← **kitalie**. The copula infinitive is **i(y)e** < (*)˙i˙ye, but also **i(y)a** < *˙i˙ya. Although it is replaced by ˙i˙la before a particle, the Middle Korean infinitive ˙i˙ye surfaces as a quasi-particle ('or/and') and it is incorporated in the structure **-u˙m ye** (see those entries). The infinitive of honorific stems is **-ᵘ/o˙sya** (see below), and the copula honorific infinitive ˙i˙sya contrasts with **i˙sye**, which is the infinitive of **isi-** 'exist'.

The MK infinitive of a stem that ends ···**i**- is ···˙**ye**: **ka˙cye** (1459 Wel 2:13a, 1481 Twusi 8: 17b, 1482 Kum-sam 2:57a, ?1468⁻ Mong 5a) < **ka˙ci-** 'hold, have', **sol˙phye** (1463/4 Yeng se:3a) < **sol˙phi-** 'investigate', **ne˙kye** (1459 Wel 7:29b) < **neki-** 'regard as', ˙**ku˙lye** (1459 Wel 21:22a) < ˙**ku˙li-** 'long (yearn) for', **ki˙Gwulye** (1481 Twusi 15:52b) < **ki˙Gwuli-** 'lean/tend to', **kwo˙thye** (1447 Sek se:6a, 1459 Wel 1:21a) < **kwo˙thi-** 'correct', **ni˙kye** (1451 Hwun-en 3b) < **ni˙ki-** 'learn', **pskay˙hye** (1462 ¹Nung 2:50b) < **pskay˙hi-** 'dissect', ¨**hoy˙Gye** (1451 Hwun-en 3b) < ¨**hoy˙Gi-** 'let/make do'.

But sometimes the -*i*- retained its syllabicity: *twu˙li˙ye* (1447 Sek 6:29b, 1449 Kok 189, 1459 Wel 7:13b) = *twu˙lye* (1463 Pep 2:58b) < *twu˙li*- 'fear'; *pa˙m oy ˙ci˙ye to˙la˙ton* (1462 ¹Nung 1:16b) 'when night sets in' — CF *˙pep pat˙kwo ˙cye* (1586 Sohak 6:35b = 1518 Sohak-cho 9:39a) 'want to take it as a model'. The infinitive of the honorific -$^u\!/\!o$˙*si*- is always -$^u\!/\!o$˙*sya*; the earliest introduction of -$^u\!/\!o$˙*sye* is ¨*c'a˙sye* (1586 Sohak 2:4b) for ¨*cwa˙sya* (1449 Kok 62) 'eat'.

If a stem ends in ⋯*ay*-, ⋯*oy*-, or ⋯*woy*- the infinitive is ⋯*(y)a*: ¨*nay˙ya* (1447 Sek 6:9b, 1449 Kok 49) < ¨*nay*- 'put out, send', *moy˙ya* (1463 Pep 4:37b) < *moy*- 'attach, sew on', *towoy˙ya* (1447 Sek 6:5a, 6:20a, 6:34a; 1449 Kok 36; 1462 ¹Nung 1:19b) < *towoy*- 'become'. If a stem ends in ⋯*ey*- or ⋯*wuy*- the infinitive is ⋯*(y)e*: ¨*hyey˙ye* (1447 Sek 6:6a, 1459 Wel 7:31b) < ¨*hyey*- 'count, reckon', *ptwuy˙ye* (1462 ¹Nung 8:40a) < *ptwuy*- 'jump'. That is true also for the infinitives of stems that end in ⋯*uy*-, such as *i˙kuy˙ye* (1459 Wel se:9a) < *i˙kuy*- 'win', but *ye˙huy˙ye* (1462 ¹Nung 2:114b) is also found spelled as *ye˙huy[˙]ya* (1459 Wel 8:4-5, with the second dot omitted) = *ye˙huy˙ya* (1462 ¹Nung 1:90b, 5:72b) < *ye˙huy*- 'distance oneself'. NOTE: There are a few exceptional variants: ¨*hoy˙ye* (1482 Nam 2:5a); *towoy˙ye 'ys˙no˙n i ˙Gwo* (1481 Twusi 7:26b), *towoy˙ye 'ys.nwo˙n i* (1481 Twusi 8:5a); -˙*kwatoy˙ye* < *-˙kwa to[wo]y˙ye*.

1. (= ~ **se**) and so, and then; (attached to verb of movement) so as to, (goes) for/to. ¶ **Na-wā (se) nol.a (la)** Come out and play! **Na nun cikum talun tey yaksok i iss.e mōs kakeyss.ta** I have an engagement now somewhere else so I won't be able to go. **Hyengsik un chac.e mue l' hani** What good is there in going out of one's way (to look) for formality? **phīnan-min tul i mollye tul.e ota** refugees come pouring in. **kyēysok hay pyeng.lyek ul cungka hanta** they keep increasing their military strength.

2. (sentence-final) INTIMATE statement, question, command, or suggestion; ~ **yo** SAME [POLITE]; SEE -**ci**. ¶ **Sayngkak pakkwe** Change your mind! Reconsider!

3. (connecting with auxiliary verb) ~ **chita**, ~ **cita**, ~ **cwuta**, ~ **hata**, ~ **iss.ta**, ~ **kata**, ~ **nata**, ~ **nāyta**, ~ **noh.ta**, ~ **ota**, ~ **pachita**, ~ **(p)pelita**, ~ **poita**, ~ **pota**, ~ **ppā cita**, ~ **ssah.ta**, ~ **tālla (tao)**, ~ **tāyta**, ~ **ttulita**, ~ **tulita**, ~ **tul.ita**, ~ **tulta**, ~ **twuta**.

4. (pseudo-compounds < V₁-e V₂).

4a. ¶ **il.e nata** gets up. **al.e tut.ta** (hears and) understands. **twulle ssata** surrounds. **sa mekta** ("buys and eats" =) eats out (at a restaurant). **el.e puth.ta** gets ice-bound. **tongye māyta** ties up. **cikhye anc.ta** keeps one's seat. **il.e suta** rises from one's seat. **tul.e suta** steps / crowds in. We hyphenate the inseparable **tte nata** → **tte-nata** leaves, departs, **na kata** → **na-kata** goes out, leaves, **na ota** → **na-ota** comes out, **na suta** → **na-suta** steps / comes out, appears; and the separable **ka pota** → **ka-pota** goes to see, tries going.

4b. ¶ **chac.e kata / ota** visits (goes / comes to visit). **kkulh.e oluta** boils up. **ttwie naylita** jumps down.

4c. ¶ **kel.e / nal.e tanita** walks / flies about. ⁿ**yeca lul ccoch.a tanita** goes around chasing women. **ili ili tol.a tanita** wanders / ambles / roams about, loafs around. **Mus cimsung i ttey lul cie taninta** All sorts of animals move about in groups.

4d. ¶ **ka tah.ta** arrives (goes and gets there). **wā tah.ta** arrives (comes and gets here).

4e. ¶ **kal.e ipta** changes (clothes). **kal.e thata** changes (vehicles / mounts).

5. (followed by pcl) ~ **ka**; ~ **la**, ~ **lul**, ~ **man**, ~ **nun**, ~ **se**, ~ **to**, ~ **tul**, ~ **ya**.

NOTE: There are (past-)past infinitives **-(ess.)ess.e**, and also (past-)future infinitives **-(ess.)keyss.e**.

-e, suffix (makes approximate numbers) SEE **-es**

-˙**e**- 1. → -˙**Ge**- (after *l*, *y*, *i*) = -˙**ke**- (effective).

2. = -˙**ke**- (effective). This is usually treated as an unexplained variant, but Ko Yengkun (1980) has proposed that the vowel-initial version of the effective morpheme was used primarily with transitive verbs, while the velar-initial version was used with intransitives, including adjectives and copula. King (1988a) refines Ko's analysis by distinguishing "highly transitive" so that many of the exceptions that Ko found are explained as due to the "low" transitivity of the verb in question. They often involve an unmarked object (incorporated by the verb to make an intransitive expression) or

they refer to the lack of potential / ability, about which see the notes (p. 551) on the nominative marking of a substantive nominalization when it is the complement of a negative auxiliary, and (p. 815) on the source of the suspective -˙*ti* as the nominalizer *t* + nominative marker ˙*i*.

-˙*e* 1. → -˙*Ge* (after *l, y, i*) = -˙*ke* (effective inf).
  2. = -˙*ke* (effective inf).

eccay [ecc' 'ay], abbr < ecci hay. how is it (that); (~ se) why, for what reason. ¶**Ayki ka eccay wūnun ya** What makes the baby cry? **Ku ka eccay nuc.nun ci molukeyss.ta** I wonder why he is late. CF *way, ecci.*

eccayss- [ecc' 'ayss-], abbr < ecci hayss-: ~ -e, ~ -keyss.e; ~ -nun, ~ -tun.

eccayss.keyss.nun [ecc' 'ayss.keyss.nun], abbr < ecci hayss.keyss.nun. ¶**Nay ka ku ttay tōn i ēps.ess.tula 'myen eccayss.keyss.nun ci kasum i senul hata** I am afraid to think what I might have done that time if I had not had money.

eccayss.nun [ecc' 'ayss.nun], abbreviation < ecci hayss.nun. ¶**Ku ttay tōn i ēps.ess.tula 'myen eccayss.nun ci kasum i senul hata** I am afraid to think what I might have done at that time if I had not had money (right then).

eccayss.tun [ecc' 'ayss.tun], abbreviation < ecci hayss.tun. anyhow, in any case, at any rate. ~ ci SAME. ¶**Eccayss.tun ku lul han sikan te kitalipsita** At any rate, let's wait for him another hour. CF *āmu(le)h.tun, etteh.tun ci, ecci, ha.ye-thun,*

eccekeyss.nun [ecc' 'ekeyss.nun], abbr < ecci hekeyss.nun (= hakeyss.nun). ¶**Ku sālam i eccekeyss.nun** (= **eccel.nun**) **ci to molunta** I do not know what he may do.

eccel(q) [ecc' 'el(q)], abbr < ecci hel(q) [= hal(q)]. ¶**eccelq ci molunta** does not know how / why it will be. **Cōh.a se eccelq cwul ul mōlla yo** I like it so much I don't know what to do = I like it ever so much.

eccel.nun [ecc' 'el.nun], abbr < ecci hel.nun (= hal.nun): ~ ci.

eccemyen [ecc' 'emyen], abbr < ecci hemyen (= hamyen).
  1. now, what (I wonder), how; I wonder ... . ¶**Eccemyen ileh.key chwuwulq ka!** How cold it is! **Eccemyen celeh.key ppenppen halq ka!** What an impudence! **Eccemyen sālam i cele halq ka!** How can he be like that? **Eccemyen ...** I wonder!
  2. perhaps, possibly, by some/any possibility.

eccen [ecc' 'en], abbr < ecci hen (= han)

eccen ci [ecc' 'en ci], abbr < ecci hen (= han) ci. somehow (or other), without quite knowing why, for some reason or other. ¶**Eccen ci maum ey tul.e** Somehow he appeals to me.

eccenun [ecc' 'enun], abbr < ecci henun (= hanun): ~ ya why, how. ~ ci molunta does not know how / what one does.

ecceta [ecc' 'eta], abbr < ecci heta (= hata). does how / what. CF *etteh.ta < ette hata.* ¶**Kulem ecceni** Then what should we do? (CF **Kulem etteni** So what?)

ecceta (ka) [ecc' 'eta], abbr < ecci heta (= hata). 1. (= **wuyen hi**) by chance / accident, casually, unexpectedly. ¶ ~ **songkalak ul pēyta** cuts one's finger by accident. **Ecceta ka cam i kkāy se poni cip i thako iss.ess.ta** When I happened to wake up I found that my house was on fire. **Phyengyang ey se ecceta ka ku lul mannass.ta** I chanced to meet him in Phyengyang.
  2. (= **itta-kum**) once in a while, now and then, occasionally. ¶ ~ **swul ul masinta** I take a drink now and then. **Ku nun ecceta ka nōlle onta** He comes and sees us once in a while.

ecci (< ¨*es*˙*ti*), adverb. ~ **na**, ~ **to** SAME. CF *etteh.key, ette, ecce.*
  1. why, for what reason. ¶**Ecci nuc.ess.nun ya** Why were you late? **Ecci wass.nun ya** How is it that you are here? **Ecci kulenq īl ul hayss.nun ya** What did you do that for?
  2. how, in what way, by what means. ¶**Ecci ku wa ālkey toyess.nun ya** How did you come to know him? **Yo say ecci cīnaysip.nikka** How are you getting along these days? **Ecci sālam i kulen ya** How can he be like that? **Ku ka ecci toyess.ulq ka** What has happened to him? = (1) How can he be like that?, (2) What has become of him? **Ecci halq cwul molukeyss.ta** I don't know what to do. **Ku ka ecci halq ci molukeyss.ta** I don't know what measure he will take. **Ecci hay se īl i ileh.key toyess.nun ya** How have things come to such a pass?
  3. how, what; so (very). ¶**Ku ⁿyeca ka ecci ippun ci!** What a lovely girl she is! **Onul nal i ecci tewun ci!** It is so hot today!

ecci 'na, adv + cop advers. (~ ····-un ci ···) so (much), (ever) so. ¶**Ecci 'na musewess.tun ci soli to mōs cilless.ta** I was so afraid I couldn't utter a sound [/na/ is the cop advers (**ina**), not 'I', which is unexpressed]. **Nal-ssi ka ecci 'na chwuwun ci kalq swu ka ēps.ey yo** Because the weather is so cold I can't go (M 1:2:93). **Ecci 'na pappun ci phyēnci lul mōs hako iss.ta** I've been too busy to write letters. **Ecci 'na mek.ess.nun ci pay ka pulle cwuk.keyss.ta** I've eaten so much I could burst.

ecci to, adv + pcl. ¶**Ecci to cal hanun ci!** How well they do it!

-e ccum, infinitive + pcl. ¶**Ku os ul kacici nun anh.ul they 'ni mancye ccum ponun kes un kwaynchanh.keyss.ci?** That dress will not be mine, but may I just try touching it, at least?

-e ce = **-e c'e**, abbr < **-e cye**, < **-e cwe**.

echi < *`echi`, postn. worth. **kaps** ~ /**kapechi**/ SAME. ¶**payk-man wen** ~ **uy sangphum** a million **wen**'s worth of goods. **selthang ul sam-payk wen** ~ **sata** buys three hundred **wen**'s worth of sugar. **chel un han phun** ~ **to ēps.ta** hasn't got one penny's-worth of sense. **I sakwa lul chen wen** ~ **cwusipsio** Give me a thousand **wen**'s worth of these apples. VAR **achi** < `achi`. SEE **elma-chi** < **elma-achi**. CF **chi**; **myech**.

-e chita, inf + aux vt insep. does hard. SEE **chita**$_{19}$.

-eci, suf. stuff. **nameci** (< **nam-eci**) remainder, residue, excess. CF **echi, chi**.

-e ciita, inf + aux verb insep. [lit] I/we wish (desire) for it to happen. ¶**(Wen khentay) ttus i hanul ey se ilwun kes kath.i ttang ey se to ilwue ciita** (We ask that) thy will be done on earth as it is in heaven. SYN **-ko siph.ta**; CF **-ko ce**.

-`e ci`la, inf (or effective inf) + aux indic assert. ¶**`woy`lol me`ke ci`la `hoke`nul** (1481 Samkang hyo:30a) wants to eat melon, but ... .

-`e ci-ngi``ta**, inf (or effective inf) + aux polite + copula indic assert. wants to do. ¶**`cyang`cho ce `y `mwo.m o`lwo "KWUY-SSIN `uy key pi`le [`]ci-ngi ``ta "CHYENG `hoke`nul (1475 Nay 2:1:30a) when asked to pray in future to the spirits with one's own body ... .

-e cita, inf + aux vi separable (by **nun, to, tul**).

1. gets to be, becomes. ¶**hulye cita** it gets cloudy. **palkay cita** turns red, reddens. **miwe cita** comes to hate. **musewe cita** comes to fear. **mek.ko siph.e cita** gets so one wants to eat. **ēps.e cita** becomes nonexistent, disappears, vanishes. **talla to ciko pyēn hay to cici man ...** (Hong Kimun 1947:30-31) it becomes different, it undergoes changes, but ... . **Pinan i noph.a cyess.ta** Criticism mounted. **Kyengcey sangthay ka cōh.a cye kanta** Economic conditions are improving along.

cōh.a cinta, naa cinta it gets/grows better, it improves; **cōh.ci anh.e cinta** it gets so it isn't good, it deteriorates; **cōh.a cici anh.nunta** it doesn't improve (get better); **cōh.ci anh.e cici anh.nunta** it doesn't deteriorate (get so it isn't good).

Inf is usually adj but sometimes vi: **sul.e** → **sule/sala cita** vanishes; **naylye cita** comes gradually down [? sloppy usage].

2. (vt inf) gets/is done: makes vi out of vt and certain defective (bound) infinitives; intensifies vi. CF **-e ttulita**.

¶**kalye cita** it becomes hidden. **ccic.e cita** it tears, gets torn. **allye cita** it becomes known. **kitalye cita** one is awaited. **phul.e cita** it gets released, comes undone/loose. **ttel.e cita** it falls, drops; fails (in an exam); **sihem ey ttel.e nun cyess.ci man ...** flunked the test but ... . **kka cita** (flesh/fortune) dwindles. **kkwēy cita** gets torn, ripped; bursts. **nwun i tte cita** one's eyes come open. **ceng hay cyess.ta** it was determined/fixed.

NOTE: Although this makes a kind of passive structure, it can be applied (pleonastically and somewhat artificially) to a lexical passive: (**phyēnci ka**) **ssuye cye iss.ta** = **sse cye iss.ta** = **ssuye iss.ta** = **sse iss.ta** The letter is written. SEE **cita**; **ssot.a cita** (regular cpd).

-e cocha, inf + pcl. ¶**Nemu pappe se āy sse mantun ūmsik ul mek.e cocha mōs poko kass.kwun a** They were so pressed (for time) they left without even trying the food I had gone to the trouble of preparing!

-e cwuk.ita, inf + vc. does and kills, kills by doing. ¶**mok may(e) cwuk.ita** strangles one to death. **ttaylye cwuk.ita** beats one to death.

-e cwukta, inf + vi. does and dies, does to death [often used figuratively]. ¶**el.e cwukta** freezes to death. **kwulm.e cwukta** starves to death. **mall^e/a cwukta** dies for lack of water.

-e cwuk.keyss.ta (future). is mortified at doing / being; is so/such that one could just die. ¶nŏlla (se) cwuk.keyss.ta is scared to death. pay ka kopha cwuk.keyss.ta is (just) dying of hunger, is (nearly) starving to death. Ku kes i cōh.a cwuk.keyss.ta I (could) just love it to death!
-e cwuta, inf + aux v. does as a favor (for). ¶Kuleh.key hay cwusipsio Please do so. Seywe cwusey yo Stop [this taxi]!
-e cye, (abbr < -e cie =) inf < -e cita
-˙e ˙cye, inf (or effective inf) + aux inf. SEE -˙a ˙cye, -˙ke ˙cye.
-e hata, inf + aux vt sep (by nun, to, tul, lul). feels. SEE hata₅.
-eh.ta, bnd adj -(H)- (inf -ay), abbr < -e inf + hata; HEAVY ↔ -ah.ta. gives the impression of being, is, looks / feels.
  1. attaches to an adj stem, with irregularities. ¶hē.yeh.ta is pure / snow white, is quite pale. (k)kēmeh.ta is jet-black. mēlkeh.ta is dull (not quite clear), lusterless, pale. ppū.yeh.ta is grayish-white, smoky, cloudy. si-pheleh.ta is a deep blue. si-ppelkeh.ta is a deep red. si(s)-he.yeh.ta is the purest white. sis-nwuleh.ta is a saffron yellow. (t)twungkuleh.ta is round, is circular.
  2. attaches to an adverb, adj-n, or mimetic. ¶(s)senuleh.ta is chilly.
ei, adverb [poetic] = (abbr <) ecci how, why.
-e iss.ta, inf + qvi. is in a state resulting from; is done. ¶anc.e iss.ta is seated; is sitting. nwuwe iss.ta is lying down; is prone / supine. kēnne iss.ta is across, over, opposite, on the other side. allye cye iss.ta (iss.ci anh.ta) is known (unknown). cha iss.ta it has filled = it is full. ··· ulo toye iss.ta is made (up) of ··· , consists of ··· . sangca ey tul.e iss.ta is inside the box. sangca ey tul.e iss.nun kes, sangca ey tun kes what is inside the box. nay insang ey acik to nam.e iss.nun kes the thing that remains in my impressions yet. Mikwuk ey ka iss.ta is there in (= has gone off to) America. Hānkwuk ey wā iss.ta is here in (= has come to) Korea. Pul i khye (kkē cye) iss.ta The light is on (off).
-ek, suf, HEAVY ↔ -ak. somewhat (diminutive). ¶(k)kwumcilek = (k)kwumcil sluggish(ly). (k)kwumulek < (k)kwumul moving slowly. thelek (= theleki) < thel hair. pusek pusek hata is somewhat swollen < pū(s)- (vi) swell up. nulek nulek sluggishly < nuli- (adj) sluggish.
-˙e k, inf + emphatic pcl. ¶*kwot [KUN-˝KUY] lol wolm˙kye ˝wo.m ol ci˙ze k kozol s ˙poy s twos˙k ol [˝]nay ˝hen ci˙p ulwo ˙sye ˙na ka˙la* (1481 Twusi 20:52a) straightway convert a canvas [to use] as the sail for an autumn boat and set off from my shabby home [on your mission]. ˝*pem mun ˝salo˙m on wo˙cik swu˙l ul masye k tyangsyang ko˙cang ˝chywuy ˙khey ho˙m ye n' tangta.ng-i thele˙k ul ˝thwo ho˙l i ˙˙la* (1466 Kup 2:64a) for a person bitten by a tiger, if you get him very drunk just drinking wine for a long time then he will vomit up the hair as he should.
-e ka, inf < -e kata
? -e ka, infinitive + pcl (before auxiliary).
-e kaciko, inf + aux verb gerund. 1. with (the accomplishment of); doing (and keeping it) for oneself. ¶Tōn ul pēl.e kaciko wass.ta He came with all the money he had made. Chayk ul sa kaciko kongpu hay la Buy yourself a book and study it. Ūmsik un cey-kak.ki cwūnpi hay kaciko osio Everyone is to provide his own food. Ke, way tangsin i cal-mos hay kaciko na hanthey mīnta 'n [< mī-l- + han] māl io Just what do you mean by making a mistake yourself and then trying to put the blame on me? Kaci anh.e to cōh.ulq ke l' ka kaciko kongyen hi sikan man ēps.ayss.ta It was a pure waste of time for me to go when I didn't need to go. Ku nun paci ey hulk ul mut.hye kaciko tol.a wass.ta He came home with mud on his pants. Tali ka kuleh.key ccalp.e kaciko etteh.key ppalli kel.ulq swu iss.keyss.na You can't walk fast with your short legs! I sangca uy pīmil ul al.e kaciko wass.ta I have come here with a knowledge of the secret of this box. Petul kaci lul kkekk.e kaciko phili lul mantul.e pul.ess.ta He broke off a willow twig and made a whistle to blow.
  ~ nun. ¶Com chelem kongpu hay kaciko nun ku hak.kyo ey ip.hak mōs hanta You will hardly get into that school without a bit of studying. Pay ka kolh.a kaciko nun īl ul halq swu ka ēps.ta You can't work on a half-empty stomach!
  ~ ya. ¶Ku sālam i kulay kaciko ya etteh.key mit.ulq swu ka iss.keyss.ni How

can one trust him when he is the way he is?
2. [DIAL/COLLOQ] = -e se. SEE -a kacwuko.
-e kata, 1. inf + aux vi. gradually (goes off doing); keeps growing / becoming (getting to be), goes on, progressively; continues to do (from now on), keeps (on) doing. ¶Kyengcey sangthay ka cōh.a cye kanta Economic conditions are improving. cēmcem Yukyo uy kaluchim ey se mel.e kata is gradually getting away from the teachings of Confucianism. Mōtunq īl i cal toye kanta Everything is going off smoothly. Nala ka mōs toye kanta The nation is in decline. Toye kanun phūm i kulelq tus hata The way it is developing looks fine. Nal i chacha ccalp.e kanta The days keep getting shorter. Ku unhayng i ssule cye kanta 'nta The bank is on the verge of bankruptcy, I hear. Hyengsey ka kak.kak ulo pyēn hay kanta The situation keeps changing every minute. Na nun kansin hi sal.e kanta I barely manage to make a living. Kun.lo-ca tul un munhwa swucwun ul noph.ye kako iss.ta The toilers are raising their cultural level. Kulimca nun cēmcem kil.e kako sāpang un cēmcem etwuwe kass.ˢup.nita The shadows gradually lengthened and the surroundings gradually got dark. Phokphung-wu ka caki nun khenyeng te sīm hay kanta The storm, far from abating, increased in its fury. Sensayng nim kkey se nō hakeyss.nun ci 'la (se) swukcey lul tā hay kass.ta Apprehensive of the teacher's wrath, I went through all my homework. Ney-kkacis nom hanthey n' nem.e kaci anh.nunta I shall never be cheated by the likes of you. Sam-nyen pok.mu hakey toye iss.uni, icey keuy kkuth-na kap.nita (Pak Sengwen 271) He has to serve for three years, and now it is almost getting to the end. Cikum puthe (to) tōn ul moa kakeyss.ta ko hanta He says he will go on saving money from now on (too) (CF ¹Yi Kitong 1988:142). CF (1916 Gale 102) *cim i cemcem mukewe/mwukewe kamnoyta* the load is growing heavier and heavier; *cwuk.e kamneyta* he is dying — advancing toward death.
2. inf + vi (→ cpd v).
2a. ¶kel.e kata goes on foot, walks (there). na kata → na-kata goes out < nata; CF naa kata keeps improving < nās.ta, nah.a kata keeps giving birth < nah.ta. olla kata goes up. naylye kata goes down. kacye kata TAKES it away — emphasis on kacye (CF kaciko kata carries it AWAY — emphasis on kata). cīna kata/ota passes by (there/here). chwī-hay kan tōn money lent out. Īwang wass.uni tul.e kaca As long as we're here let's go in. Sāy tul i meli wi ey se cice kelinun ka hamyen talam-cwi tul i tali mith ul suchye kaki to hanta Not only are there birds chirping overhead but also there are squirrels darting (away) under foot. Ilum molulq sāy tul i nac.un hanul ul nal.e kako nal.e oko hayss.ˢup.nita Birds of unknown name flew back and forth low in the sky. Salang i ku eykey lo olm.kye kass.ta Her love shifted to him. Ku cen ey pillye kass.tun chayk ul tollye wass.ta He has returned the book he borrowed some time ago. Ku cek.un swuip (kkaci) ey se mace sēykum ul kulk.e kanta Even from such a small income they grab taxes.

2b. (errands) comes [and returns].
CF -e ota; nāy-kata.

-eki, suffix (? < -ek.i cpd suf); HEAVY ↔ -aki. diminutive. kempuleki < kempul dead leaves. ppuleki [DIAL] = ppuli root. theleki [DIAL] = thelek < thel hair. VAR -eyki. CF -ek, -eci, -engi, -lengi.

-e kkaci, inf + pcl. ¶Ku kes ul kuleh.key mancye kkaci posiko an sasip.nikka You mean you're not going to buy it, after handling it that way? Ileh.key elin ai tul ul tōl-poa kkaci cwusini cēng-mal komapsup.nita I am truly grateful for your going to all the trouble of looking after the children this way. Sālki elyewun sēysang ey ileh.key capswusye kkaci cwusini komapsup.nita We are grateful to you for troubling yourself to eat this way in such a difficult world [SARCASTIC]. CF -e mace.

? -ekw(un)i, suffix. ¶? echekwuni a whopper.
SEE -akwuni. CF -wuni, kwuni.

-e l', abbr < -e lul

-el, suf, HEAVY ↔ -al (dimin). ¶swuwel hata is easy < swiw-. ? nacel half the daylight hours < nac daytime. CF -eli; -ek, -eki.

-ˈel(q), effective prosp mod. SEE -eˈl i ··· , -elˈ(t)t i ··· .

-ˈeˈla, effective subj attentive (= command); = -keˈla. ¶meˈli heyˈhye elˈGey ˈpis woˈlwo piˈseˈla (?1517- Pak 1:44a) comb out my hair with a coarse-toothed comb. SEE -ˈaˈla.

-e la, inf + pcl (? < -e'la blended with **-e 'la** = -e 'y'la). 1. do! (plain-style imperative when not quoted; CF **-ula/-la**). ¶**I kes ul mek.e la** Eat this. **Yeki iss.e/iss.ke la** Stay here. **Cāmqkan man kitalye la** Wait a minute. SEE **-ke la**.
  NOTE: 1894 Gale 24 gives *ho.yela* (? = *hoyla* = *hay la*) as the spoken version of written *hola* (= *hala*).
  2. for unusual nonfinal examples of **pwā la** 'suppose = if', see **-e pota**.
  3. → **-e 'la**. **-e 'la**, inf + abbr < **ila** (cop indic assert); CF **-usye 'la, -'e 'y'la, -ᵘ/o 'la**. (with adj, iss-, ēps-) is indeed! (exclamatory). ¶**Cham ulo pulk.e 'la** How red it is! **Ai, koso hay 'la** Serves you right! **Komawe 'la** Heaven be praised! Thank goodness. **E, siwen hay 'la** My, it's refreshing! **Caymi iss.e 'la!** What fun! **Caymi ēps.e 'la** How dull!
  NOTE 1: CM 1:291 offers some exclamatory examples even for verbs "in poetic style".
  NOTE 2: Not used with the copula (*ie 'la, *ila 'la), nor with past (*-ess.e 'la) or future (*-keyss.e 'la).
  NOTE 3: The only MK examples of -'e ''la instead of -'e 'y'la seem to be 'ho'ye ''la and -'cye ''la. Unless these are due to the glide in the preceding syllable (here behaving as if the *ye* were *ey*), our explanation of the forms has a problem, somewhat like that posed by our claim that -'e 'ta 'ka contains the copula transferentive (otherwise unfound in MK).
-e lang, inf + pcl [rare; always followed by **pota** aux]. ¶**Mek.e lang poko se hanun māl iess.ˢup.nita** It was what he said after actually eating it. **Wusen manna lang poci** Well first let's meet him (and then decide).
-e 'la to, inf + cop var inf + pcl. ¶**Na l' com towa 'la to cwuess.umyen cōh.keyss.ta** I wish you'd just help me a little.
-e la tul, inf + pcl + pcl. ¶**Pang sōcey com hay la tul** You kids clean up your room, now!
-eli, suffix (< **-el.i**, cpd suf); HEAVY ↔ **-ali** (dimin). **tengeli** < *tengi* lump. **swungeli** < *swungi* bunch, cluster. **elkeli** outline < *elk.ta* ties up. **tungeli** [DIAL] = *tung* back. **thekeli** < *thek* chin. **kwi-mekeli** deaf person < *kwi mek-* (? var < *mak-*) grow deaf; **kho-mekeli** a person with a stopped-up (congested, stuffy) nose. **pengeli** a deaf-mute (< *peng-peng hata* is dumb/dumbfounded). CF **-eki, -ek**.

-'**e.l i 'Ga**, effective prosp mod + postmod + postmod (= *-'ke.l i 'Ga). ¶'*soyGwo 'cye hol cye'k uy [NUNG] 'hi ni'ce.l i 'Ga* (1481 Twusi 7:20b) [after yesterday's unpleasantness with the spring rains] could you forget when it is about to leak? SEE -'*ye.l i 'Ga*.
-'**e.l i 'ye**, effective prosp mod + postmod + postmod (= *-'ke.l i 'ye). ¶*e'lwu 'khukey masna'ta a'ni nil'Ge.l i 'ye* (1482 Kum-sam 3:5a) could we not say that we (meet =) have met with much [today]?
ellun, adv. (= **ese**) promptly, without delay/hesitation; quickly, fast (of an action not yet initiated; CF **ppalli**). ¶**Ellun tāytap hay la** Answer promptly. DIAL **e(l)ttun**.
elma < ''*en'ma* < **e'n[u] 'ma* (with the dissimilation of /nm/ > /lm/), n. DIAL (South Cenla) **emma**, (S Hamkyeng) **emmay**; (North/South Kyengsang) **elmay, welmay, [w]olmay, wulmay**; (S Chwungcheng) **welma**. (The ···y versions must have incorporated **-i**; the w··· versions remain unexplained.) Indeterminate quantity: INTERROGATIVE in questions with the falling intonation or questions that are quoted; INDEFINITE or GENERAL otherwise.
  1. what price, what sum of money, how much; a certain price, some amount, (not) much; any amount. ¶**Talkyalq kaps i elma 'n ya (elma in ya)** How much are eggs? **Ku kes i cēng-mal Kolye caki 'la 'myen, elma 'tun ci nāykeyss.ta** If it is a genuine piece of Kolye porcelain, I will pay any price for it. **Cip-sey ka elma 'n ya** How much is the rent? **Sakwa nun elma ey phap.nikka** How much do you sell your apples for? **Ku kes un elma ey sass.nun ya** How much did you pay for it? **Ku chayk un elma ka tul.ess.nun ya** How much did the book cost you?
  2. how long; a while; some/any length of time; (not) very long. ~ **ani ha.ye**, ~ **an hay se**, ~ **an(i) ka se** before very long; soon; in no time. ¶**Ku nun kyelhon han ci elma toyci anh.nunta** It is not long since he got married. **Ku nun elma iss.ta ka māl hayss.ta** He spoke after a while. **Elma an ka se ssalq kaps i ttel.e cikeyss.ta** It will not be long before the price of rice goes down. **Ku cengpu nun elma mōs kanta** That government won't last long. **Elmaq tong-an yeki iss.keyss.ni** How long will you be here? **Ku hanthey se elmaq tong-an sosik i**

ēps.ta I haven't heard from him for a while.
    3. what number / quantity, how much / many; some (quantity), a few, a bit; (not) many/much; any (quantity). ¶Selthang i elma sō.yong toyn' ya (= toynun ya) How much sugar do you take? Hōyuy ey sālam i elma wass.tun ya How many people were present at the meeting? Pay ka sangca ey elma nam.ess.nun ya (with FALLING intonation) How many pears are left in the box?; (with RISING intonation) Are there some pears left in the box?
    4. what weight/measure, how much; some weight/measure, (not) very much; any weight/ measure at all. ¶Ney mukey ka elma 'n ya What is your weight? Ku talk un elma tallin ya How much does the chicken weigh? Ku kes un elma an tallinta It doesn't weigh much. Ku uy khi ka elma 'n ya How tall is he?
    5. what distance, how far; some distance, (not) far; any distance at all. ¶Sewul se Inchen kkaci kēli ka elma 'n ya How far is it from Seoul to Inchen? Yeki (ey) se elma an ka se, cengke-cang i iss.ta Not far from here there is a station.
    6. what age, how old. ¶Ney nai ka elma 'n ya How old are you?
elma ccum (ina), n + pcl (+ cop advers). about how much. ¶Elma ccum ina tul.ess.ni What did it set you back? (= How much did it cost?)
elma-chi < elma [a]chi, n + postn. how much worth. ¶Elma-chi lul tulilq ka yo How much worth shall I give you? Elma-chi wuphyo ka phil.yo han ka yo What amount of stamps do you need? — Chen wen ccali wuphyo ka hana ey ī-sip wen ccali wuphyo ka sēys imyen cōh.keyss.ta One thousand-wen stamp and three twenty-wen stamps will do it.
elma 'myen, abbr < elma imyen. if it is how much. ¶Pang hana lul twūl i ssumyen elma 'myen toye yo How much would it be if two use one room? (M 3:3:208).
elma 'na, cpd adv (n + cop advers ina).
    1. (about) how much, (about) what price. ¶I swū-pak i elma 'na hap.nikka How much is this watermelon? Ku yangpok un elma 'na cwuess.nun ya How much did you pay for your suit?
    2. (about) how long. ¶Cwungkwuk-e lul kongpu han ci elma 'na toyp.nikka How long have you been studying Chinese?
    3. about what quantity, (about) how many/ much. ¶I tose-kwan ey chayk i elma 'na iss.nun ci molukeyss.^{s}up.nita I don't know how many books this library has.
    4. about what weight / measure, how ⋯ . ¶ ~ khun ya how big? ~ kiph.un ya how deep? ~ nelp.un ya how wide? ~ mukewun ya how heavy? ~ twukkewun ya how thick? ~ noph.un ya how high? Hān kang i elma 'na kīn ci ālkeyss.nun ya? Can you guess how long the Han River is?
    5. about what distance, (about) how far. ¶Yeki se elma 'na mēn ya What is the distance from here?
    6. about what age, (about) how old. ¶Ku uy nai ka elma 'na toyess.keyss.nun ya Do you have any idea how old he looked?
    7. about what degree / extent. ¶ ~ chwuwun ya how cold is it? ~ ssun ya how bitter is it? ~ ppalun ya how fast is it? Ney ka elma 'na ānta ko kulen māl ul hay What makes you think you know so much you can say that? Ku ka Tok.il-e lul elma 'na āni How good is his German? I kes ul tul.umyen ku ka elma 'na kippe halq ka! How glad he will be to hear it! Ku ka elma 'na kosayng hayss.ulq ka! What he has suffered! Ku yenghwa ey elma 'na kāmtong hayss.nun ci molukeyss.ta I can't tell you how impressed I was with the film. Na to Mikwuk ey kalq tōn i iss.ess.umyen elma 'na cōh.keyss.ey yo How nice it would be if I had the money to go to America, too.
    8. ~ hata, adj-n. SEE hata$_4$.
NOTE: Since 'na is the copula adversative, elma 'na cannot be predicated with the copula (*Elma 'na 'p.nikka). Use just elma + copula or substitute toyta 'become' for the copula: Elma 'p.nikka How much is it? = Elma 'na toyp.nikka How much does it amount / come to? In those few cases where a particle is permitted, it too follows elma rather than 'na; instead of *elma 'na ccum we hear elma ccum ina 'about how much'.
elme 'yna [Ceycwu DIAL (Seng ^{1}Nakswu 1984: 99)] = enme 'yna (id.:26) = elma 'na.
-˙el(q) ˙t ilwo˙ta, effective prospective modifier + postmod + var cop indic assert. ¶nil˙Gelq ˙t ilwo˙ta (1459 Wel 8:16b), nil˙Gel ˙t ilwo˙ta (1475 Nay se:7a), nil˙Gel ˙t ilwota (1579 Kwikam 1:5b) he said.

A Reference Grammar of Korean

-e lul, inf + pcl. SEE **ul** 14.

~ **iss.ta** (aux). ¶**Nal mata anc.e lul iss.ta** Day after day I'm sitting down.

~ **noh.ta** (aux). ¶ **Ku phyēnci lul sse lul noh.ass.ta** I got the letter all written.

~ **pota** (aux). ¶**I ke l' com mek.e lul poca** Let's trying eating a bit of this.

~ **twuta** (aux). ¶**Ku i ka ¹noymul ul pat.e lul twuess.ta** He took bribes.

ēlun, n. 1. a grown-up, an adult, a man.
2. one's elder(s); an older or elderly person.
3. an esteemed person [higher than **pun**]. ¶**i (ku/ce)** ~ this (that) person, he/him, she/her.
4. = **elusin(-ney)**

elusin(-ney), noun. 1. the esteemed father of someone else (CF **ape' nim**). ¶**Elusin-ney kkey se cip ey kyēysin i?** Is your father home?
2. an esteemed elder; sir (CF **sensayng nim**).
3. an esteemed person (usually male).

e῾lwo, e῾lwu, adv (lenited from *et-῾wᵘ/o, der adverb < ῾῾et- 'get'). possibly, can; (= ῾῾KA ῾hi) adequately (acceptably, well), may, might. ~ **si῾le** (1459 Wel 14:77a) can possibly. SYN **nilo, NUNG ῾hi, si῾le.**

-em/-am (derived substantive) < -῾ᵉ/am (effective subst). SEE **-um (cik hata),** -u῾l i 'Ge῾m ye.

-em, abbreviation < **-ewum.** ¶**kancilem** a tickling sensation < **kancilewum,** subst < **kancilepta** (< **kancil-ew-**) feels tickled, it tickles.

-e mace, inf + pcl. ¶(?) **Āmuli ku kes i kwī han kes iki lo se 'ni mancye mace mōs pokeyss.ni?** However valuable it may be, can't I just try touching it even? CF **-e kkaci.**

-e maci anh.nunta does it intently/continously (in certain clichés). ¶**Khetalan sengqkwa (ka) iss.ki lul pala maci anh.nunta** I earnestly hope that you have great results (Mkk 1960:3:29; it is more likely without **ka**). **Hoytap ul kitalye maci anh.nunta** I eagerly await a reply.

-῾e ῾mal῾la (inf + aux subj attent) = -e [῾ho῾ti] ῾῾mal῾la. ¶**kwu῾thuy῾ya ῾nwo῾ho῾ya [ho῾ti] ῾῾mal῾la** (?1517-¹No 2:19b) you need not worry necessarily.

-e man, infinitive + particle.

~ **iss.ta** (auxiliary). ¶**Ku ka nal mata anc.e/ nwuwe man iss.ta** He is just sitting/lying there day after day.

~ **noh.ta** (auxiliary). ¶**Phyēnci lul sse man noh.ass.ta** I got the letter just written (but not mailed yet).

~ **pota** (auxiliary). ¶**Ilk.e man poko ālq swu iss.ulq ka** How can one expect to know it just by reading it over?

~ **twuta** (auxiliary). ¶**Ku ka ¹noymul ul pat.e man twuess.ta** He just took bribes, that's all.

emci, 1. adn. principal, main. ¶ ~ **son(q-kalak)** thumb. ~ **pal(q-kalak)** big toe. ~ **kitwung** main pillar. ~ **po** main beam. ~ **chong** main sandal-wing.
2. noun, abbr < ~ **kalak** thumb or big toe.

-em cik < -῾em ῾cik (effective substantive + postsubstantive adj-n inseparable) SEE **-um cik.**

-e mekta, 1. inf + vt (= **-e se mekta**) does and eats, does to eat; [figurative] lives by doing, does habitually, makes a living at/by doing. ¶**pil.e mekta** begs for a living. **cap.ᵉ/a mekta** slaughters and eats; devours; needles a person. **ssip.e mekta** chews and eats it; chews it up. **ccic.e mekta** rips/tears and eats; rips/tears it up. **pes.kye mekta** skins/peels it and eats it.
2. inf + aux adj/verb insep (gives a strong vulgar and pejorative flavor to the preceding infinitive). SEE **mekta₃.**

-emi, suffix; HEAVY ↔ **-ami.** ¶**kesulemi** a hangnail, a splinter, a sticker < **kesuluta** goes against, opposes, bucks. **kkwulemi** package < **kkwulita** packs. **wulkemi** strap < *wulk.ta = **elk.ta** ties up. VAR **-eymi.**

-e n', abbr < **-e nun**

-en [Ceycwu DIAL (Seng ¹Nakswu 1984:79-80)] = **-e (se)** infinitive, = **-ko** gerund

-῾**en,** 1. → -῾Gen (after l, y, i) = -῾**ken.**
2. = -῾**ken** (effective modifier). ¶῾SYENG-ZIN pe῾ngulwo῾m i te῾wuk me῾len ῾῾salo῾m i wo῾cik ῾῾PI-῾LYANG ῾u῾lwo pu῾the a῾lwo῾m i ῾῾SSYANG ῾i῾n i (1463 Pep 2:41a) as for people more distanced from the sage, their knowledge, which stems from comparison and inference, is merely form.

-e῾na, 1. → -Ge῾na. ? 2. = -ke῾na.

-e 'na, inf + copula adversative. ¶**Wusen hana mek.e 'na poci** Eat one first and then see.

-e na, infinitive < **-e nata**

-e n'ā, abbr < **-e nwā** < **-e no(w)a** = **-e noh.a**

-e nata, 1. infinitive + auxiliary verb separable. 1a. keeps doing, does and does again. ¶**Him tunq īl to chacha hay na kamyen swiwe cinta** Even hard work becomes easier when you get used to it.

1b. (vi-e nata) does to the point of attaining results [ideal performance continued to the point where the implicit result comes about]. ¶cala nata grows up, matures. kkoch i phie nata flowers come into bloom.
2. inf + vi. does and exits, emerges doing. ¶kkāy nata recovers one's senses, comes to.
-e nāy, infinitive < -e nāyta
-e nāyta, 1. inf + aux v insep. does all the way (to the very end, thoroughly, through and through); does to the point of obtaining the result sought; manages to do (to get it done). ¶chac.e nāyta finds (searches/seeks/ferrets) it out, discovers. mak.e nāyta manages to check (stem, hold back, contain) it. sayngkak hay nāyta thinks up/out, devises. kac.un mo.yok ul kyentye nāyta stands up to insults of all sorts. ōn-kac' kōn.¹nan ul ikye nāyta fights it out alone to the bitter end. īl ul kiil ey tāy(e) hay nāyta finishes a job on time. cek ul mak.e nāyta holds the enemy off. pang ul ssul.e nāyta sweeps the room out. sangca an ey tun mulken ul al.e nāyta finds out what is in the box. kyēysan hay nāyta reads a deep meaning into it. Ku pēm.in i eti lo tomang kass.nun ci kkok al.a nāyko mālq ke 'ey yo (Im Hopin 1987:165) We will surely end up finding out for sure just where the culprit fled.
2. inf + vt (vc < nata). does and puts it out, ... ¶pha nāyta digs it up/out. kiph.un ttus ul ilk.e nāyta reads a deep meaning into it.
enceng, pcl (< [i]-enceng < ˙i-Gen ˙tyeng cop effective mod + bnd postmod). even if it be, even. Obsolete except in -ulq ci ~ < -ulq ˙ti ~ and in ⁿyengsa ~ 'even at the risk of one's life' (= cwuk.ulq ci enceng). [˙tyeng ? < Chinese; CF mangceng].
ēncey < ¨encey < e˙nu cey/cek, n. SYN enu ttay. Indeterminate time: INTERROGATIVE ('when') in questions with falling intonation or in quoted questions; otherwise INDEFINITE ('some time') or GENERAL ('any time').
1. (as INTERROGATIVE in a question with FALLING intonation, or in a quoted question) when, what time, how soon. ¶Ēncey ccum osikeyss.ˢup.nikka How soon can you come? Ēncey ka cōh.keyss.e What time would be good? (What time would you like/prefer?) Ēncey lul thayk halq ka What time shall we pick? ˙ne y ¨encey ˙kil[h] ˙na˙sil ˙kwo (?1517-

Pak 1:8b) when are you setting out on the road?
NOTE: Textbooks have ēncey ey 'at what time' but people do not say that; if an ey is called for, the structure usually gets conflated: ēncey 'n ya ey ttale se 'depending on [the answer to the question] when'.
2. (as INDEFINITE in a statement, or in a question with RISING intonation) some time (ago). ¶Ēncey nay ka cip ey onun kil ey ku lul mannass.ess.ta I met him on my way home some time ago.
3. (as GENERALIZED) any time (at all). ¶Ku ka ēncey enu ttay olq ci molukeyss.ta He may get here any minute now.
~ kkaci till when, how long. ¶Ēncey kkaci Sewul ey kyēysip.nikka How long are you staying in Seoul? Ku hanthey se tāytap ul ēncey kkaci 'na kitalilq swu ēps.ta I cannot wait indefinitely for an answer from him.
~ 'ko (= iko) some time or other, some day sooner or later, one of these days. ¶Ēncey 'ko ne hon nanta You will be sorry some day.
~ 'na just any time. ¶Kulenq īl un ēncey 'na iss.nunq īl i ani 'ta Such things do not happen every day.
~ 'n ka (= in ka) at one time, once, one day, some time ago. ¶Ēncey 'n ka ku māl ul tul.unq īl i iss.ta I have heard that before.
~ puthe since when, how long, from what time. ¶Ēncey puthe pyēng ul alh.sup.nikka How long have you been ill?
~ 'tun ci (= itun ci), ~ 'na (= ina) any time, at a moment's notice; all the time, always. ¶Ēncey 'tun ci nōlle osipsio Come and see me any time.
ēncey l', abbr < ēncey lul
ēncey 'l(q), n + cop prosp mod [= il(q)]
ēncey 'm, n + cop subst (= im)
ēncey n', abbr < ēncey nun
ēncey 'n, n + cop mod (= in). ~ ci, ~ ka, ~ ko, ~ tey, ~ tul, ~ ya.
ēncey nun, noun + particle. ¶Ēncey nun nuc.ci anh.ess.na? Were you ever on time?
-e neh.ta, inf + vt. does and puts it in. ¶cip.e neh.ta picks it up and puts it in(to a basket, pocket, ...). mol.a neh.ta crowds them in(to), pushes them in. pue neh.ta pours it in/down.
-eng, suffix; HEAVY ↔ -ang.
1. (dimin). kwuleng hollow, hole < kwūl hole, cave, cavity (< ¨kwul, CF ˙KWULQ).

2. (makes n from adj, v). **nwuleng** yellow < **nwuluta** is yellow. (p)**pelkeng** red < *pelk.ta, CF (p)pelkeh.ta/pulk.ta is red. **phuleng** blue < **phuluta** is blue. ī**eng** thatch < ī**s.ta** [ī(s)-] = ī**ta** roofs it. **sileng** shelf, rack < **sīt.ta** (sil.e) loads. **wuleng chata** is resounding < **wūlta** cries. **twuleng** levee ? < **twuluta** fences in, encircles.

3. (makes adv from adv, mimetic). **ssuleng ssuleng** chilly (relations) < **ssul-ssul** chilly. **i/kuleng(-seng) celeng(-seng)** like this and like that [< **ile (ha-), kule (ha-), cele (ha-)**]. **elmeng-(t)elmeng** bumpy [< ?].

-eng [Ceycwu DIAL (Seng ¹Nakswu 1984:79-80)] = **-e (se)** inf, = **-ko** ger

-engi, suffix; HEAVY ↔ **-angi**. CF **-eyngi**.

1. (dimin). **kkutengi** an end; a clue < **kkut** = **kkuth** or **kkus**. **kwutengi** a hollow, a pit < ˙**kwut** (> **kwus**). **ppulengi** [DIAL] = **ppuli** a root.

2. (makes n from adj or v). **twulengi** a kind of skirt worn by children < **twuluta** encircles. **kechilengi** a rough rice plant < **kechilta** is rough. **pū.yengi** pearly color, pearly-colored thing < **pū.yeh-/pō.yah-** be pearly/misty. But the constituency differs in: **(k)kwupuleng-i** a bent/crooked one, **nepuleng-i** bits (scraps, pieces), **nwuleng-i** a yellow one, **pulkeng-i** a red one. And also probably in: **ccwukuleng-i** crushed/withered one < (?)**ccwukuleng** < *ccwukul- (CF **ccwukule ci-/ttuli-, ccwukuli-**).

-˙**e-ngi** ˙**ta** = -˙**ke-ngi** ˙**ta**, effective polite + cop indic assert. ¶ ˙**e˙m[i] uy ¨kan ˙sta˙h ol mwu˙le a˙lwolq ˙toy ¨ep˙se-ngi** ˙**ta** (1459 Wel 21:21b) there is no way to ask what land your mother went to. **ha˙nol s HYANG ˙i ses-pe˙mule ˙kwot ˙kwot ¨ma˙ta ˙pwom s ˙pi˙ch i ˙nate˙la na ˙two me˙li l' ¨wulGwe˙le ¨syel˙We-ngi ˙ta ˙KWUW ˙hosywo˙sye ¨pi˙zoWwo˙n i** (1459 Wel 2:52a) mingled with the scent of heaven the colors of spring were out everywhere; I too lifted my head and begged "I entreat you, please redeem me!". (VAR -˙**ey-ngi** ˙**ta**.) SEE -˙**Ge-ngi** ˙**ta, -˙a-ngi** ˙**ta** (-˙**ay-ngi** ˙**ta**).

-eng-payngi, cpd suf. **pilengpayngi** a beggar < **pīlta** begs.

-eni [DIAL, lit, obs] = **-keni**; = **-uni**.

-˙**e˙n i**, 1. → -˙**Ge˙n i**. 2. = -**ke˙n i** (effective mod + postmod). ¶**kil[h] wu˙h uy [LYANG-˙SSIK] ni˙ce˙n i** (1445 ¹Yong 53) one could forget to carry food for the road [it was so thoroughly pacified]. **polo˙m i pule ˙mul s ¨ko˙z ay [˙]˙ken¨nay pu˙ch[y]e.n i ¨ku y ˙PPEM-MA-LA ˙KWUYK ˙sta.h ile˙la** (1459 Wel 8:99a) the wind blew and fanned across the water's edge; that was the land of the brahman nation.

~ ˙**Gwa**. ¶**NGUY-SIM ˙i ho˙ma ¨ep˙se.n i ˙Gwa** (1449 Kok 137) [they] already had no doubt, and moreover ... .

-eni, suf (makes adv from adv or adj-n) < **heni** < **hani** (= **hakey**). **ilccikeni** (< **ilccik-eni**) a bit earlier, **noph.cikeni** (< **noph.cik-eni**) a bit higher. **salkumeni / sulkumeni** (< **salkum-eni / sulkum-eni**). CF **-keni, -akseni**.

¨**en˙ma** (< *e˙nu˙ma) = **elma** (how much, ...). SYN ˙**hyenma**, ˙**myes.ma**; CF modern dialects: **emma** (S Cenla), **emmay** (S Hamkyeng). ¶**SIM-˙KWOK SIM-SAN ˙ay ¨en˙ma cephu˙kesi˙n ywo** (1449 Kok 123) in the deep valleys and the deep mountains how frightened will she be? **pi˙t i ¨en˙ma ˙y˙na ho˙n ywo** (1459 Wel 8:95a) about how much is the price?. ˙**HWA ˙hosyan ˙CYWUNG-SOYNG ˙i ku ˙SWU y ¨en˙ma ˙y-ngi s ˙kwo** (1463 Pep 4:167a) the creatures who have changed, how many are they in number?

~ **s**. ¶ ¨**en˙ma s swu˙l ul me˙ke˙n ywo** (?1517-¹No 2:39a) how much wine did we drink?

-˙**en ma˙lon** = -˙**Gen ma˙lon** = -˙**ken ma˙non** but, although. ¶ ˙**na y ¨a˙loy hon ¨twu ˙pen ton˙nyen ma˙lon** (?1517- ¹No 60b; **ton˙nyen** < **ton˙ni-˙Gen**) I have been there once or twice before, but ... .

This underlies the explanation for **-u˙lyen ma˙lon**, = -**u˙l i˙en** (< ˙**i-˙en**), which I have taken as **-u˙l [i]˙yen**.

-en man (obs var after -**i, -y**, or -**l**) = **-ken man** (semi-lit concessive)

¨**en˙me** [second vowel assimilated to first] < ¨**en˙ma** = **elma** (how much).

enme ˙yna [Ceycwu (Seng ¹Nakswu 1984:26)] = **elme ˙yna** (id.:99) = **elma ˙na** (how much)

e˙no, adverb = **e˙nu** = **es˙ti** (> **ecci**). how. ¶**[˙SYENG-ZIN SSIN-˙LUK] ˙i e˙no ˙ta sol˙Wo˙l i** (1445 ¹Yong 87) how can one tell all the divine power of this saintly man?

-e noh.a twuta, inf + cpd aux v. does it once and for all (in anticipation of later use/result), gets it all finished up now (so it will be ready later on and will not have to be done then). ¶**cēmsim ul mili mek.e noh.a twuta** gets lunch out of the way (so it won't interfere with later plans). **Phyo lul sa ('ta) noh.a twue cwusey yo** Buy the tickets and get that out of the way.

-e noh.ta, inf + aux v sep. CF **-e twuta**.

1. (v inf) 1a. does for later, does in advance, gets it done (so that it will be ready), does beforehand; completes, accomplishes, gets the doing off one's hands, frees oneself by doing. Not used with passives, awkward with verbs of wearing (→ **-ko iss.ta**) when they are not made causative; CF [1]Yi Kitong 1988:153. ¶ **mili kongpu hay noh.ta** prepares one's lessons in advance. **Mence tōn ul pēl.e noh.ko cip ul sa la** Make money first, and then buy a house. **Phyo lul sa ('ta) noh.a ('ta) cwusey yo** Buy the tickets (in advance). **I pang hako ce pang hako lul swuli hay noh.key** Have this room and that room remodeled (both). **Non un kal.e noh.ko pi lul kitalinta** We have finished with plowing the paddy field and are waiting for rain. **I īl un kkok hay noh.ko ya mālkeyss.ta** I will get this job done if it kills me! **Pay 'mye tāychwu 'mye sakwa 'mye yele kaci lul nul.e noh.ass.ta** They have on display pears, dates, apples, and so on. **I kwuk.hwa man un han kwungsil ey cīn.**[1]**yel hay noh.ass.ess.ta** These chrysanthemums alone have been put on exhibit in a certain room in the palace. **Nay ka hay noh.ko to way kulenun ya siph.ul ttay ka iss.ta 'ni-kka n'?!** There are times when, having done it, I wonder why I do it.

1b. does it and leaves it at that; does it for now / tentatively / anyway. ¶ **pang an ey sinmun ul nel.e noh.ta** litters a room with newspapers. **I ccum man ila to hay noh.ko ya khun soli lul halq swu iss.ci** You have to do at least this much to have something to brag about! **Nay kuce kulelq cwul al.ess.ta — Congsi chaq-can ul kkay ttulye noh.ass.kwun a** There — I told you so (I just knew you'd do it): you have ended up breaking the cup. **Ecey poni-kka āmu to ēps.tun tey nwu ka ilen kes ul hay noh.ass.ulq ka** I didn't see anybody around here yesterday, so who could have done this?

NOTE: For ··· **ul noh.a twuta** and **-e noh.a twuta** see **-e twuta**. Although **twue twuta** is used, ***noh.a noh.ta** is generally rejected in favor of **noh.a twuta**: **Phyēnci lul chayk-sang wi ey noh.a twuess.ta** I put the letter on the desk for the time being. **Ku kos ey cwi tech ul noh.a twuess.ta** I set a mousetrap in that spot. Accordingly, *-e **noh.a noh-** is replaced by **-e noh.a twuta**. Both ··· **ul twue noh.ta** and **-e twue noh.ta** occur.

2. (adj / cop inf) is in a state of being, is left being, remains (as an established situation), is already, is all ... . ¶ **Kil i cil.e noh.a se na-kaki ka silh.ta** The streets are all so muddy that I don't want to go out. **Nal i chwuwe noh.uni-kka kkomccak haci mōs hayss.ta** I found the weather so cold I couldn't budge. **Ku kes i nemu khe noh.uni-kka ecci halq swu ēps.ta** We've got such a big thing there I don't see what we can do with it. **Pap i nemu cil.e noh.a se mek.ki ka him tulta** (Dupont 89) The rice is so soft it is hard to eat [with chopsticks]. **Onul i machim il.yoil ila ('ta) noh.a se ku ka cip ey iss.ul.nun ci molukeyss.e** As today just happens to be a Sunday, I am not sure whether he will be at home or not.

-ˈeˈnol, 1. → **-ˈGeˈnol**. 2. = **-ˈkeˈnol** (lit concessive). ¶ **naˈla[h] nizu.l i ˈlol ˈchezeˈm uy kaˈcye** [CYE-MWU] **ˈey puˈthyeˈnol** [= **puthi-ˈeˈnol**] (1481 Twusi 8:17b) I put the continuity of the nation at first into the hands of the military, but ... . ¶ **seˈkenol** (1463 Pep 2:56b) it may rot, but ... .

eˈn' oy < ***eˈno oy**, n + pcl = **eˈnu** (adn). which. ¶ **eˈn' oy ˈTOY ˈyey ˈeˈtin ˈsaˈlom ˈi ˈepˈsuˈl i ˈGwo ˈhoteˈla** (1586 Sohak 5:48b) = **eˈno ˈtoy ˈyey ˈeˈtin ˈsaloˈm i ˈepsuˈl ywo ˈhoteˈla** (1518 Sohak-cho 7:15ab) asked in which age will there be no nice people. CF **enoy nala.h i** (1894 Gale 35) which country.

-ˈen ˈta, effective mod + postmod. ¶ **ˈQILQ-ˈTTYENG LYWUN-HHWOY ˈlol peˈsen ˈta** (1579 Kwikam 1:21a) have we cast off the fixed transmigration?

-ˈen ˈt i = **-ˈken ˈt i**, effective mod + postmod + pcl. ¶ **naˈkunay captuˈlen t i ˈna'-ˈto.l i ˈkilGeˈta** (1481 Twusi 15:23a) the days and months grow long since capturing the traveler. **pap mek.en t i cyekun tes ho.yatun** (1656 Naycwung 3:37, from LCT) when it has been a little while since eating. CF **-ˈyen ˈt i**; **-ˈan ˈt i**.

-ˈen ˈtyeng = **-ˈGen ˈtyeng** = **-ˈken ˈtyeng**, effective mod + bnd postmod. although.

enu < **eˈnu** (var **eˈnwu**, SEE **eˈn' oy**), adn. CF **musun**, **ette han** (**etten**), **en-**. Indeterminate adnominal: INTERROGATIVE in questions with a falling intonation, or in quoted questions; INDEFINITE or GENERAL otherwise.

1. (as INTERROGATIVE in a question with FALLING intonation or in a quoted question) which, what (one). ¶ ~ chayk/sālam/nal which book / person / day. ~ kes which one, which. **Enu kil lo kalq ka** Which way shall we go? **Enu Kim ssi 'n ya, khun Kim ssi 'n ya cak.un Kim ssi 'n ya** Which Mr Kim (is it), the older or the younger? **I cwung ey se enu kes ul kaciko siph.un ya** Which of these do you want? ¶ e᾿nu na῾la῾h ay no῾lisi῾key ho῾l [i] 'ye῾n ywo (1459 Wel 2:10b) what land should we have them descend to? nek῾s i e᾿nu CHYWU 'yey kan ῾twong "mwol῾la-ngi ῾῾ta (1459 Wel 21:27a) I do not know to which hell her spirit went. e᾿nu ῾psk uy (1481 Twusi 20:32a) at what time. e᾿nu ῾psk uy za (1481 Twusi 7:29a) at just what time. e᾿nu na῾l ay ῾za (1481 Twusi 10:27a) on just what day (at last). e᾿nu ῾kwo.t ol ῾HYANG ho῾ya (1482 Kum-sam 3:52a) heading toward what place?

2. (as INDEFINITE when in a statement, or when in a question with RISING intonation) some (··· or other), a certain. ¶ ~ nal some day, one day. ~ nal achim one morning. **Enu han kaci īl ey censim hay la** Devote yourself to some one subject. **Enu kyengwu ey nun ku kyuchik i tul.e mac.ci anh.nunta** That rule does not apply in some cases. **Enu ¹yekwan ey se ku lul mannass.ess.ulq kes ita** I must have seen him in some hotel or other.

3. (as GENERALIZED) whichever, any (one). ¶ ~ kes ina (itun ci, iko, ila to) whichever, any one. ~ cem ulo potun ci from every point of view, however you look at it, in every respect. **Enu pich ina tā cōh.ta** Either (any) of these colors will do.

4. e᾿nu (var e᾿no), adv = "es῾ti (> ecci) how; how come, why. ¶pwuthye s ῾PEP i CYENG-MI ῾ho῾ya cye῾mun a῾hoy e᾿nu tutco῾Wwo῾l i '-ngi s ῾kwo (1447 Sek 6:11a) Buddha's Law is so intricate, how can a young lad presume to take it in? MYEY-῾HHWOYK e᾿nu ῾phul῾l i (1449 Kok 74) how can we escape the confusion? cephun ῾ptu῾t i e᾿nu isi῾l i '-ngi s ῾kwo (1449 Kok 123) how will one have a feeling of fear / dread?! ha῾nol s [῾HEM] ῾un mo[῾]cho[῾]m ay [NAN] [῾]hi sye῾l i 'Gen malon sep [MWON] ῾ey e᾿nu ta῾si ῾῾ti-῾na ka῾l i Gwo (1481 Twusi 7:9b) one finally stands with difficulty at heaven's cliff but how is one to get past it to the twig gate again? e᾿nu kwu῾thuyye na῾l ywo (1481 Twusi 25:29a) why go to all the trouble of leaving? ye῾huyywo῾m i ῾mas.tang ho῾kwo n' ῾i ye῾huyywo῾m i ῾stwo e᾿nu isil ῾ppa 'y.l i ῾Gwo (1482 Kum-sam 2:37a) some separation is to be expected but why is there so much more of this separation?

5. e᾿nu, n = e᾿nu kes which/some one; what. ¶e᾿nu l' CCYWONG ῾ho῾si.l ye ῾'n ywo (1459 Wel 7:26a) which one will you follow? e᾿nu ῾lol nil῾Gwon ῾CYENG ῾PEP-"NGAN ῾kwo (1482 Kum-sam 2:69a) what does "the true Dharma Eye" mean? [epithematic identification with syntactic inversion of the Identified; the copula modifier is suppressed before ῾kwo]. e᾿nu ῾῾nwu ῾lul te῾pu῾lusi῾l [i] 'ye῾n ywo (1449 Kok 52) whom would you take with you?
e᾿nu y ῾i ῾pu.l i ῾'m ye e᾿nu y ci῾p i.m ye e᾿nu y ῾woyn ῾t ol ῾῾a῾ti ῾῾mwot ῾'kwo (1463 Pep 2:64-5) we cannot know which is this fire and which is the lodge and which is mistaken. e᾿nu y ῾i ῾TTYWU "ep.sun "TTWOW-"LI ῾Gwo (1482 Kum-sam 2:20a) which is the unstable logic?
e᾿nu y ῾za ῾mos "tywoho῾n i '-ngi s ῾ka (1447 Sek 6:35b) which one is best? ῾PWOK ῾TUK ῾i e᾿nu y ῾za ha῾l i '-ngi s ῾kwo (1447 Sek 23:5a) of happiness and virtue which is more plentiful?
enu ccok, adn + n. which one (of two), which alternative, either / neither one. ¶**Enu ccok i nās.ci yo** Which is better?
e᾿nu cek, adn + n. what time, when (= "encey). ¶[TWONG] nyek ῾moy῾h on e᾿nu ce῾k uy "yell [i] 'ye῾n ywo (1481 Twusi 7:25b) when will the eastern outlands open up? e᾿nu ce῾k uy za (1481 Twusi 21:19a) at just what time.
e᾿nu cey, adn + n. what time, when (= "encey). ¶e᾿nu cey [῾THOY PWU-ZIN] s [TTANG] wu῾h uy a῾zom ῾tol.h ol mwoy῾hwol ta (1481 Twusi 8:20a) when will you gather the clan up to the hall of the dowager?
enu cey [Ceycwu DIAL (Seng¹Nakswu 1984:25n)] = **ēncey**
enu kyelul ey, adn + n + pcl. ('in what spare moments' =) when with so little time to spare? ¶**Kongpu hamyen se enu kyelul ey kūlim ul kūlyess.nun ya** How did you ever find time to paint a picture in the midst of your school

work? **Enu kyelul ey Tok.il-e lul paywulq swu iss.e** Where can I find the time to learn German?
-ë‧nul, 1. → -‧Ge‧nul. 2. = -‧ke‧nul (lit concessive). ¶**ku LYWONG ‧ol ca‧pa ‧pcu‧ce me‧ke‧nul** (1447 Sek 6:32a) it grabs the dragon, tears it up and eats it, whereupon … . **HHAN-SAN ‧i wol SSI-‧CYELQ s ‧kil.h ul ni‧cenul** (1482 Kum-sam 3:23b) [the monk called] Cold Mountain had forgotten the way from when he had come, but … . **ku‧le ‧'na ‧YAK ‧ol ‧cwue‧nul mek‧t ol ‧sul‧hi ne‧ki‧n i** (1459 Wel 17:20a) but when we gave them medicine they did not want to take it. SEE -‧ye‧nul.
e‧nu l', n + pcl. which one. SEE e‧nu 5.
-e nun, infinitive + particle.
  ~ **cwuta** (auxiliary). ¶**Tōn ul ponay nun cwuess.una kece pīyong ina kyewu toytolok ponay cwuess.ta** They sent us the money all right, but (it was) scarcely enough to cover all the expense.
  ~ **iss.ta** (auxiliary). ¶**Nal mata anc.e nun iss.ess.una** (= anc.e iss.ki nun iss.ess.una) Day after day I was sitting down, but … .
  ~ **noh.ta** (auxiliary). ¶**Phyēnci lul sse nun noh.ass.ci man, puchici anh.ess.ta** I got the letter written but I didn't mail it.
  ~ **twuta** (auxiliary). ¶**Sēnmul ul pat.e nun twuess.ci man, acik yel.e poci anh.ess.ta** I got the present, but I still haven't opened it.
enu nwu(kwu) < e‧nu ‧nwu, cpd n [emphatic] = **nwu(kwu)** (who; someone). ¶**Enu nwu ka saykyess.nun ci, cham cal to saykyess.ta** Whoever carved it, he certainly carved it well. **[‧ZI-‧POYK ‧'HHWO] ‧lol e‧nu ‧nwu y [‧'CHYENG] ho‧n i** (1445 ¹Yong 18) who appealed to the two hundred households? **e‧nu ‧nwu ‧lul te‧pu‧lusi‧l [i] 'ye‧n ywo** (1449 Kok 52) whom would you take with you?
enu say, cpd adv (adn + n). in so little time, in no time (at all), so soon, quickly, already. ¶**Enu say kīn(q) yelum pānghak i tā kass.ta** The long summer vacation went all too soon. **Enu say Yenge lul kuleh.key cal paywess.nun ya** How did you ever learn English so well in such a short time? **Enu say sēngthan-il i wass.ta** Christmas has stolen upon us. **Enu say ku ka ka-pelyess.ta** He has slipped away.
enu-tes, cpd adv (adn + bnd n). in no time (at all), so soon; before one knows, unawares.

enu thum, cpd n (adn + n). so little time. ~ **ey** = **enu say**.
enu ttay, cpd n (adn + n). what time, when. ~ **(i)tun ci**, ~ **(i)na** any time, whenever, always. ~ **(i)ko** anytime, whenever; some time (or other), some day, one of these days, sooner or later. ¶**Enu ttay olq swu iss.nun ya** When can you come? **Kumkang san kwūkyeng haki ey enu ttay ka cēy-il cōh.sup.nikka** What season is it best to see the Diamond Mountains? **Enu ttay 'ko hwūhoy hal ttay ka iss.ta** You will be sorry for it sooner or later. SYN **ēncey**.
e‧nu y (‧za), n + pcl (+ pcl). SEE e‧nu 5.
-e nwā, abbr < **-e no(w)a** = **-e noh.a**
e‧nwu [var] = e‧nu, 1. adnoun. which. ¶**e‧nwu ‧CCANG s KUM ‧i ‧za** (1447 Sek 6:25b) just which vault's gold … . **e‧nwu na‧la‧h ay ‧ka‧sya ‧nasi‧l i '-ngi s ‧kwo** (1459 Wel 2:11b) which country are you going off to?
  2. adverb (= ¨es‧ti > **ecci**). how. ¶¨**es‧tyey ho‧ma taon mwok-¨swu‧m i e‧nwu teu‧l i '-ngi s ‧kwo** (1447 Sek 9:35a) how can a life already exhausted get any worse?
-‧e‧n ywo, 1. → -‧Ge‧n ywo. 2. = -‧ke‧n ywo (effective mod + postmod). ¶¨**es‧tyey a‧to‧l oy ‧YAK ‧ol me‧ke‧n ywo ‧hosi‧kwo** (1459 Wel 21:219a) he thought "why did I take my son's medicine?" ¨**en‧ma s swu‧l ul me‧ke‧n ywo – un ¨twu ‧lyang (‧)uy s swu‧l ul me‧ke‧ta** (?1517- ¹No 2:39a) how much wine did we drink? – we drank two silver taels worth of wine.
-e ota, 1. inf + aux vi. gradually (comes in doing); comes up (along); starts (has started) becoming / doing; has / had been doing. ¶**Incey n' na to cēmcem pay ka kopha oni ese ka se cēmsim mekci** Now I, too, am starting to get hungry so let's hurry up and go eat our lunch! **Tte-nal nal i cakkwu kakkwe onta** The day is coming up (drawing near, fast approaching) when we are (due) to leave. **Ku sālam kwa nun olayq tong-an sakwie on chinkwu 'ci yo** I have been friends with him for a long time. **Sewul kanq īlay lo Kim chemci nun caymi lul ponun mo.yang ulo tomuci cip ey nun sosik han cang to an ponay wass.ta** Since going to Seoul Mr Kim seems to having too much fun to write a single letter home. **Mit.ke la kille on oy atul i cha-sāko lo cwuk.ess.ta**

My only son, whom I was raising with every confidence (that he would have a long life), died in a car accident. **Sān.ep i kaypal toye onun han phyen wensi-cek in ssi-cok sāhoy ka mune cikey toyess.ta** As industry came to develop, the primitive clan society began to collapse. **Kūn sip-nyenq tong-an emeni nun na hako man sal.e wass.ˢup.nita** Mother has been living alone with me for nearly ten years. **Acwu elyewul ttay nun halwu ey ssal han hop ccum ssik ulo to sal.e wass.ess.ta** At the most difficult times we managed to live on a **hop** of rice a day. **Ecey puthe ku īl ul hay onun cwung iey yo** We have been in the midst of doing that job since yesterday. **Cak.nyen puthe tōn ul moa oko iss.ta** He has been saving up money since last year.

2. inf + vi. does toward here, comes doing.

2a. ¶**na-ota** comes out [the hyphenation is arbitrary]. **tul.e ota** comes in. **olla ota** comes up. **naylye ota** comes down. **kacye ota** brings (CF **kaciko ota** carries in, comes carrying). **chac.e ota** comes visiting, visits us. **chwī hay on tōn** money borrowed (by us). **Okey toyn kīm ey tangsin uy cim kkaci nalle wass.ey yo** I happened to be coming this way, so I brought your baggage. **Wuli tongmu tul ul pulle oca** Let's call our friends over. **Palamq kyel ey mulq kyel soli ka tullye onta** The wind brings with it the sound of the waves. **Ileh.key kakkawun tey kkaci lul mōs kel.e on sālam i tungsan un musun tungsan iya!** What kind of mountain climber is he, not to get this far?! **San ulo puthe palam i pul.e onta** The wind blows (down) from the mountains.

2b. (errands) goes [and returns]. ¶**Ese tanye osey yo** – **Ney tanye okeyss.ey yo** Please (don't let me detain you), be on your way (I'll see you later) – Yes, I'll be back. **Kulem, tanye olq key** Well, I'll go do it (and be back). CF **-e kata**.

-e p'ā, abbr < **-e pwā**

-e pachita, inf + aux v. does (as a favor) for a superior. SYN **-e tulita**.

-e (p)peliko mālta, inf + aux v insep ger + aux v sep. ends up doing (finally does) completely. ¶**Kkoch pyeng ul cip.e pangq patak ey tencye se kkay ttulye peliko mal.ess.ta** He finally threw the vase on the floor and smashed it.

-e (p)pelita, aux v insep. does completely, gets it (all) done, disposes of (the job); (does it) all/ up/down/away/off; does to my disappointment or regret; does it to my relief. ¶**ic.e pelita** (completely) forgets it. **ēps.ay pelita** gets rid of it. **cāngkap ul ilh.e pelita** loses one's gloves. **tha pelita** it burns up/down/away. **sayngsen ul kasi ccay samkhye pelita** devours a fish, bones and all. **Na nun ku chayk ul tā ilk.e pelyess.ta** I got (read all the way) through the book. **Ku tōn un tā sse pelin ke l'** (I'm sorry about it but) I have spent all the money. **Nalk.e pelyess.ta** It is quite antiquated. **Kuleh.key kwichanh.umyen cwuk.e pelici cwuk.e pelye** If you are so bored, go ahead and drop dead. CF **-e twuta**, **-e noh.ta**; **-ko nata**, **-ko mālta**.

-epi, suf, HEAVY ↔ **-api**. (forms animal names). **twukkepi** toad. VAR **-eypi**.

¨**ep˙non**, proc mod < ¨**ep˙ta**. ¶ MANG **hon ˙ptoy cel- ˙lwo ¨ep˙non cyen˙cho ˙lwo** (1462 ¹Nung 1:77-8) because naturally there is no unseemly dirt.

-e poita, (adj) inf + aux vi sep. looks like, appears to be. ¶**Ku nun cēngcik hay pointa** He looks like an honest person. **Namphyen pota puin i phek celm.e pointa** The wife looks much younger than the husband. **Pom ey pissa pointa** From its appearance, it looks expensive. **Ku nun poki ey to acwu yēng.li hay pointa** In appearance, too, he seems bright. **Nay ka poki ey (nun) cōh.a pointa** As I see it, it looks good. **Ney ka hanun kes ul poni-kka swiwe pointa** To see you doing it, it looks to be easy. **O-kanun sālam tul i motwu chwuwe pointa** The passers-by all look cold. **Kem.e tul pointa** They all look black. **Kulay po.ye to ku key ku cwung ey se nun kacang naun chwuk ila 'na** They may not look like much but they are the best of the lot, he says. **Kkaykkus hay pointa** It looks clean/nice. **Cōh.a to pointa** It looks good, too/indeed. NOTE: Normally the inf is of an adjective but also allowed is a verb with descriptive implication: **talm.e pointa** looks similar. ABBR **-e pōyta**. CF **-key poita**.

-e pota, inf + aux v sep (by man/nun/to/tul/ya)

1. (v inf) 1a. tries doing (to see how it will be); does it to see (how it is), tries out. CF **-ki ey him ssuta** tries (makes an effort) to do, **-ulye (ko) hata/tulta** tries (starts, sets out) to do. ¶**Hānkwuk ūmsik ul mek.e ponta** I try

Korean food. **Ilpon ey ka-ponq īl i iss.ey yo?** Have you been to Japan? **Hay popsita** Let's give it a try; Let's see (how it will turn out). **Hānkwuk sinmun ul pwā pwass.ey yo?** Have you tried reading a Korean newspaper? **Tto han pen cēnhwa lul hay posey yo** Try calling again. CF **-e lang (pota)**.

1b. do it and see; just do it please (softening a command). ¶**Cāmqkan kitalye posey yo** Just a moment, please(; I will check).

2. (v, adj, cop) inf + **pwā (la)** or **posey (yo)**: suppose, supposing, imagine, if (= **-umyen, -ess.tula 'myen**). ¶**Ēps.e posey (yo)!** (= **Ēps.ta ko hay posey yo**) Suppose you had none! **Ney ka nay māl ul an tul.e pwā (la) hon nako māl they 'n i** If you don't listen to me you'll be in trouble for sure. **Ku pang ey iss.e posey (yo) khunq īl nap.nita** You stay in that room and you'll be in trouble. **Pul i ēps.e posey kongpu to mōs haci** Without a light you won't (or wouldn't) be able to study. **Tōn i mānh.e posey yo eti ānun chey 'na hana** Suppose he had a lot of money, you think he'd pretend to know me?! **Kwun.in ie posey yo eti kulen tey l' kalq swu iss.na?** If you were a soldier, you would not be able to go to such places! **Mit.nun tey ka ēps.e posey yo pelsse Kunswun-i nun pelkum ul mul.ess.tun ci cingyek ul kass.tun ci hayss.keyss.ci yo** Unless there was something she could rely on (= someone whom she could turn to), by now Kunswun-i must have either paid a fine or gone to prison.

-e pōyta, abbr < **-e poita**

-e ppā cita, inf + cpd aux vi insep. gets to be (old/rotten/musty/...) through and through. ¶**kolh.a ppā cinta** grows thoroughly/utterly rotten, wallows in vice. **ssek.e ppā cyess.ta** is rotten/spoiled through and through. **keyulle ppā cin nom** a thoroughly lazy rascal. **yo yak.e ppā cin nom** this shrewd rascal.

ēps.i < ¨*ep˙si*, der adv < **ēps.ta**. without, not having, lacking. ¶**uysim** ~ without doubt. **thullim** ~ without fail; for sure. **(halq) swu** ~ unavoidably. **ttus** ~ /ttutēpssi/ senselessly. **cēngsin** ~ absentmindedly. **kuci** ~ endlessly, infinitely. **mayk** ~ listlessly, dejectedly. **moca (to) ēps.i ota** comes without (even) a hat. **capon ēps.i cangsa lul sīcak hata** starts up a business with no capital. **Ku ⁿyeca ēps.i nun** sālq swu ēps.ta I cannot live without her. **Cha ēps.i cīnaylq swu iss.ta** I can do without tea (or: without a car). **sokcel** ~ in vain, to no purpose < ˙*sywok˙cyel ¨ep˙si* (1459 Wel 9:7b, 1462 ¹Nung 1:3a, 1463 Pep 2:41a), accent-reduced as ˙*sywokcyel ¨ep.si* (1482 Nam 1:24a), *sywokcyel [¨]ep˙si* (?1517⁻ Pak 1:54a), *sywokcyel [¨]ep.si* (1481 Twusi 7:9a). **ma˙kon ˙toy ¨ep˙si** (1459 Wel se:8ab) without hindrance, unhindered. SEE **-ulq kes ēps.i**.

ēps.nun, proc mod < **ēps.ta**. 1. ... that is nonexistent; that (one) lacks. 2. (pseudo-adn) impoverished, needy, in want.

ēps.ta₁ < ¨*ep˙ta* = ¨*ep[s]˙ta*, qvi.

1. does not exist, there is not; does not have, has not (got); lacks. ¶**atul/sikan/tōn i** ~ has no sons/time/money. **Ku san ey namu ka ēps.ta** The mountain is bare of vegetation.

2. is gone, is missing, cannot be found, is lost, is absent. ¶**Ku nun palun phal i ēps.ta** He has lost his right arm. **Pangkum chayksang wi ey twun chayk i ēps.ta** I cannot find the book that I just put on the table. **Ēps.ta ko hay** Tell them I'm not here.

3. it is used up; runs/is out of, runs short of. ¶**Wumul ey mul i ēps.ta** The well has run dry. **Kaysollin i ēps.ta** We have run out of gas.

4. is wanting; is devoid of, lacks. ¶**caymi ka** ~ is devoid of interest, is uninteresting. **ttus i** ~ is meaningless. **cayswu ka** ~ is unlucky. **cēngsin i** ~ is absentminded, is absorbed; is at wit's end, is out of one's mind (frantic), (so busy one) doesn't know whether one is coming or going. **Na nun ku īl ey hūngmi ka ēps.ta** I am not interested in that business. **Ku nun ku kyēyhoyk ul silhayng hal him i ēps.ta** He lacks the power to carry out the plan. **Ku nun chayk ilk.ki ey cēngsin i ēps.ta** He is absorbed in a book he is reading.

5. is free from, is clear of, lacks. ¶**kyelqcem/sokpak i** ~ is free from faults/fetters. **Ku kan pyelko ēps.ess.ˢup.nikka?** Have things being going all right? **Thullim ēps.ˢup.nikka?** Is it true? (Are you sure?) **Aph kil ey kellilq kes i ēps.ta** There is nothing to stand in my way.

6. is deceased, defunct. ¶**apeci ka** ~ one's father is deceased/gone; has no father. **ēps.nun sālam** absent persons; poor people, a have-not; the deceased. ... **ēps.e se, ēps.ki ttaymun ey** for want of ... . ¶**I payk.hwa-cem ey ēps.nun**

kes i ēps.ˢup.nita This department store carries everything. Cikum Mikwuk ey kalq sayngkak un cokum to ēps.ta I haven't the slightest idea / intention of going to the States just now. Kulay to ku kes i ēps.nun kes pota nās.ta Still it is better than nothing. Kulen ⁿyephyenney nun tolie ēps.nun kes man mōs hata Such a wife is rather worse than no wife at all. Ku sōsel i caymi ēps.nun kes to ani 'ta The novel is not uninteresting. Na nun wus.ulq swu pakk ey ēps.ess.ta I could not help laughing. Ecci halq swu ēps.ta I just can't help it. Mul un saynghwal ey ēps.ci mōs hal mulken ita Water is something that there could be no life without. Ney towum i ēps.ess.tula 'myen, na nun silphay hayss.ulq kes ita If it had not been for your help, I should have failed. SEE -ulq kes ~. DER ADV ēps.i. VC ēps.ayta.

ēps.ta₂ < ēps.ta₁, postnom qvi sep; ? postnom adj insep. is lacking in; is deficient / bad with respect to.

1. postnom qvi sep. (This is just the regular structure of N V, since pcl i/ka can be inserted in most, though not all, examples.) ¶ha.yem ~ has no mind to do, is bored (irreg derived substantive < hata). chel ~, congcak ~, cikak ~ is senseless, stupid. yēl ~ is shy, soft ("lacking in gallbladder") mayk ~ is weak, tired. kuci (= kkuth i) ~ is endless.

2. ? postnom adj insep. sil ~ is unreliable; is silly (< sil substance, reality). ? sōk ~ is unsubstantial, empty (< sōk insides). phucep ~ is unfriendly, cold, aloof, distant (var < pūcep 'approachability, amiability').

NOTE: For certain words there is ambiguity or uncertainty whether the construction is to be treated as adj or as qvi. The expressions sokcel ~ 'is hopeless, futile' (bnd n < ?) and pucil ~ 'is futile, idle, trivial' (bnd n, CF pucilen [? pucil-en < *pucil hen / han]) seem to have both treatments. In doubt are cwūcha(y)k ~ 'is very silly', silum ~ 'is vacant-minded' (or 'has cares, is depressed'), both being qvi in the speech of ¹Yi Tongcay who treats the examples of (1) also as qvi [he is unfamiliar with phucep ēps-]. The form ēps.un is rare in the modern standard language, but it is incorporated in kā.yeps.un from the adjective kā.yeps.ta < kā i ēps- 'lacks limit'. The confusion may be because Phyengan uses ēps.un not ēps.nun, apparently in all cases (SEE ēps.un).

ADVICE: use ēps.nun for both 1 and 2 above.

ēps.ul(q), prosp modifier < ēps.ta. ¶Phyēnci lul ssulq sikan to ēps.ulq cengto lo papputa I am so busy I have no time to write letters. Ku ¹nōin i ppalli cwuk.ki nun khenyeng acik to sip-nyen un mūncey ēps.ulq kes ita You might think that old man would die soon, but he's got a good ten years to go.

῭ep῭sul(q), mod < ῭ep῭ta = ῭ep[s]῭ta.

(1) with an extruded epitheme. Example?

(2) with a transitional epitheme. Example?

(3a) with a summational epitheme (in various functions). ¶῭say ῭lwo pu῭the te al῭Gwoy῭ywol ῭cwu[῭]l i ῭ep.sul῭s oy (1482 Kum-sam 2:2a) since we are unable to reveal more from afresh. ῭SOYK-῭QWUN῭i ῭ep῭sul ῭spwun῭tyeng (1459 Wel 1:37b) they lack only the skandha of rūpa (= the attribute of form) but ... .

(3b) with the summational epitheme used to make a factual predication. ¶KWONG-῭KHYWOW ῭hosin PANG-῭PPYEN ῭un ta῭wo῭m i ῭ep῭su.l i ῭῭la (1447 Sek 9:29a) [Buddha's] ingenious expediencies [for promoting Buddhism] will never be exhausted. ῭es῭tyey ho῭l [i] ῭ye῭n ywo ῭hwo.m i ῭ep.su῭l i ῭lwo῭ta (1465 Wen se:13b) there will be no wondering how it would be. KWONG-῭TUK῭i ku῭c i ῭ep.su῭l i ῭Ge῭nul (1459 Wel 17:48-9) if one's achievement of virtue is boundless, ... ῭KAK-῭PPYELQ hi ka῭phwom ῭pola῭nwon mozom ῭ep.sul῭s i.n i (1482 Nam 2:63b) doesn't particularly expect repayment.

ēps.un, modifier < ēps.ta.

1. In Seoul rare, usually replaced by ēps.nun or ēps.tun '... that does (or did) not exist'.

2. [Phyengan DIAL; Kim Yengpay 1984:104-5] ¶tōn i ēps.un sālam a person without money; sālam i ēps.un pang a room with no one in it.

῭ep.sun, modifier < ῭ep῭ta = ῭ep[s]῭ta.

(1) with the epitheme extruded − from the [non-]possessor. ¶῭kaps ῭ep.sun kwu῭su.l un (1482 Nam 1:33a) the priceless jewel. mozom ῭ep.sun ῭kwulwu῭m i (1481 Twusi 7:23b) mindless clouds. ku῭ci ῭ep.sun ῭ptu.t ul (1482 Kum-sam 5:37b) boundless meaning. ῭TTYWU ῭ep.sun ῭TTWOW-῭LI (1482 Kum-sam 2:20a) the unstable logic. ῭i ῭TI-῭HHYWEY ῭ep.sun ῭PPI-KHWUW y (1447 Sek 19:30b) this witless almsman. QIN-YWEN ῭ep῭sun CCO ῭y῭la ho῭n i (1482 Kum-sam 2:2a) it is mercy without cause.

(2) with a transitional epitheme – of time. ¶ ˝ep.sun ˝HHWUW ˙ey ˙za (1463 Pep 1:55b) only after its absence.

(3a) with a summational epitheme (in various functions). ¶ ˙SWU ˝ep.sun ˙t ol a˙lwolq ˙t i.n i '˙la (1447 Sek 19:10b) it must be realized that they are innumerable. wo˙nol za a˙lwo˙n i ˙TI-˙HHYWEY ˝ep.su˙n i kot '˙tas-ongi '˙ta (1463 Pep 4:36a) that just today I found out is like having lacked wisdom.

(3b) with the summational epitheme, to make a factual predication. ¶ ne ˙[G]wa kol˙Wo˙l i ˝ep.su˙n i '˙la (1459 Wel 18:57b) there is no one to compare with you.

˝ep.su˙si˙ta, hon < ˝ep˙ta = ˝ep[s]˙ta. ¶ ˙LWUW ˝ep.su˙sya SO-˙NGUY hwo˙m i e˙lyewu˙syan ˙t i˙la (1463 Pep 2:22a) it is difficult to take everything into consideration.

ēps.utoy, concessive < ēps.ta. SEE -toy.

-epta₁, postnom adj -W-. = hepta. ¶ swung epta [DIAL] = hyung (h)epta is ugly.

-epta₂, bnd adj -W- (shape after vowel is -pta); VAR -upta, -apta. ¶ cingkulepta is weird, disgusting < cingkul-ew- < cingkul. ecilepta is dizzy < ecil-ew- < ecil. kᵃ/ᵤncilepta is ticklish < kᵃ/ᵤncil-ew- < kᵃ/ᵤncil tickly. kwutepta is gullible, quick to believe < kwut-ew- < kwut- firm (in belief). mikkulepta is slippery < mikkul-ew- < mikkul. mitepta (= mipputa) is trustworthy < mit-ew- < mit.ta trusts. mulepta is itchy < mul-ew- < multa bites. nekulepta is generous < nekul-ew- < nekul. nukkepta is felt; has a sensation < nukki- feel. pantulepta is smooth < pantul-ew- < pantul. putulepta is soft < putul-ew- < putul hata. sikkulepta is noisy < sikkul-ew- < sikkul. ttukepta is hot < ttuk-ew- < ttukta [obs] is hot. twulyepta is fearful < twuli-ew- < twulita [obs] fears. ¶ culkepta is delighted ? < culkita enjoys it. kalyepta is / feels itchy < kalk.ta scratches it. kke(l)kkulepta is rough, coarse ? < kkel kkel. kwīyepta is lovable ? < kwī (hata) precious, ? < var of kōyta [obs] loves. mukepta is heavy < muk-epta ? < mukta it remains. musepta is fearsome < mus-epta ? < mus crowd. patulepta is weak and dangerous ? < patul. pukkulepta is ashamed < pulk.ta gets red. singkepta is insipid ? < sita is sour.

˝ep˙ta = ˝ep[s]˙ta, qvi (= ēps.ta). SEE ˝ep˙non, ˝ep.sun. The predicate can be negativized as ˝ep˙ti a˙ni °ho-: ¶ [SSIN-KUY] lowoy˙ywo.m i ˝epti a˙ni thwo˙ta (1481 Twusi 16:22b) it does not lack in being miraculous! ˙na y ˙i ke˙s u˙lwo hon na˙la˙h ol ˝ta ˙cwue ˙two ˙wohi˙lye ˝ep˙ti a˙ni ˙khwo n' … (1463 Pep 2:77a) when I have no appreciable lack though I gave up a nation for this … '.

ēpus, adn = ūypus (step-)

-e puthe, inf + pcl. ¶ Kulem, wusen cāy puthe poca Well, let's measure it first, anyway.

-e pwā, inf < -e pota. Anc.e pwā Sit (back) down.

es(-), adn, bnd n, bnd adv. crooked, curved, diagonal, deviate, wrong; crosswise, mutual; almost, not quite, immature. CF pis, ekus.

1. adnoun. ¶ ~ kākey a slant-roof street stall. ~ kali a grain cover. ~ kulwu a slant-cut stump. ~ kwuttul, ~ kwuswu (hata) rather tasty. ~ kyel cross grain. ~ pittwulum (hata) somewhat oblique. ~-po a mutual guarantee. ~ pulwuki an immature bull. ~ sēym offsetting / cancelling each other. ~ sico a kind of sico poem with extra syllables in one of the nonfinal lines. ~ songaci a calf.

2. bound noun. ~ toyta (adj) is pert.

3. bound adverb. ¶ ~ kata goes astray; gets / grows perverse. ~ kkakk.ta cuts it slantwise. ~ kyēt.ta crosses, joins. ~ maykkita crosses, intertwines. ~ mekta deviates (in behavior) is spiteful. ~ mēyta carries it slung over one shoulder. ~ mullita interlocks. ~ na-kata splits slantwise; deflects, goes off at an angle. ~ pakkwuta interchanges, exchanges. ~ pēyta cuts slantwise (at an angle). ~ puth.ta sticks / attaches at an angle. ~ sekk.ta mixes. ~ suta stands there arrogant/insolent. ~ tāyta applies obliquely. ~ ttuta squints.

es- [Ceycwu DIAL] = ēps-. ¶ twon i es.uni cicwu mwos kap.neyta = Tōn ēps.uni Cēycwu mōs kap.nita (Seng ¹Nakswu 1984:13) I lack the money to go to Ceycwu.

-es, suf. makes approximate numerals; before noun / counter -e. twues, twue ⋯ about two < ˝twu-˙zeh two or three < ˝twulh + ˝sek / ˝seyh. yeles, yele ⋯ a number (of), numerous < ye˙leh ? < ˙yelh ten.

-˙es- = -˙e 's- (= -˙e 'ys-), abbr < -˙e is-. SEE ENTRIES. CF -ess-.

-e sa, inf + pcl. 1. [DIAL] = **-e ya**. 2. [? DIAL, mistake] = **-e se**.

ese, adv. 1. (= **ellun**) promptly, without delay / hesitation; quickly, fast (of an action not yet initiated; CF **ppalli**).
2. (please) go ahead and ... , right (away), without hesitation/reticence. ¶**Ese tul.e osey yo** Come right in. **Ese wā ese wā!** (It's) good to see you! **Ese mek.e la** Go ahead and eat. **Tul.e kasey yo! Ese!** Go to your room; now!

-e se < -'*e 'sye*, inf + pcl [emphasizes the inf].
1. and so; and then; (attached to motion verb) so as to, (goes) for / to. ¶**sangcem ey ka se mulken ul sata** goes to the store and buys (= to buy) goods. **i ka aphe se chiq-kwa ey kata** goes to the dentist's with a toothache. **kyēysok hay se īl hata** keeps (on) working. **cēmsim(q) sikan ul ¹īyong hay se sānqpo na-ota** makes use of lunch time to come out for a walk. **caki ka math.unq īl imyen cengseng ul tul.ye se hata** puts one's whole soul into anything one undertakes. **Kil i mikkulewe se catong-cha lul wūncen haki (ka) elyepta** The streets are slippery so it is hard to drive (a car). **Nal i nemu etwuwe se kōng ul polq swu iss.ey yo?** Won't it be too dark to see the ball? **Wā se sikyey (lul) pwā la** Come look at the watch! **Māl i thong haci anh.e se etteh.key īl ul hanun ya** How will you do your work, not being able to make yourself understood? **Na nun na se han pen to pyēng i an nass.ta** In all my life I have not been ill once. **Hyeng i kongcang ey ka se ēps.ta** My (older) brother is not home — he's gone off to the factory. **Ku ke l' mōs pwā se akkawun tey** It's a shame (I'm sorry) that we couldn't see that! **Ileh.key chac.e cwusye se tāytan hi kāmsa hap.nita** I appreciate your visiting me like this. **Mēlli osye se komapsup.nita** Thank you for coming such a distance. **Ileh.key nuc.e se mian hap.nita** I am sorry that I am so late. **Wuli ¹yehayng-sa ey ka se mul.e polq ka?** Shall we go to the travel agency to find out? **Pay ka kopha se mues com mek.ko siph.ta** I am hungry and want to get something to eat. **Yeki anc.e kitalisipsio** Please sit here and wait.
2. ~ **cōh.ta** it is good that, I am glad that. ¶**Ku i ka wā se (na nun) cōh.ta** It is good (I am glad) that he came. **Khe se cōh.ta** I'm glad it's big. **Na nun wuli chinkwu ka kongpu lul cal hay se cōh.a yo** I'm glad that our friend is studying hard (or: doing well at school).
3. (as for) doing. CF ~ **nun** (2). ¶**ilk.e se an toynun chayk** a book you shouldn't read.

NOTE: In the meaning 'and so, because' **-e se** is never followed by a command or by a proposition; **-uni-kka (n')** is used instead. CF 1894 Gale 41: "**[-uni-kka]** marks the cause with more definiteness".

-e se ka, inf + pcl + pcl. ¶**Tōn i ēps.e se ka ani 'p.nita** It is not that / because I haven't got the money. **Pay ka kopha se ka ani 'la pap mas i cōh.a se (iey) yo** It's not that I'm hungry, it's just that the food tastes so good. **Kim sensayng i moksa ye (= ie) se ka ani 'la swul i ēps.e se 'ta** It is not because Mr Kim is a preacher (that we are not drinking); it is because we don't have any liquor (to drink). **Iyaki lul te casey hi tut.ca 'myen cip ey ka se ka cōh.keyss.ta** (CM 2:95) If you want to hear more of the story it would be better to wait till we get home.

-e se 'la to, inf + pcl + cop var inf + pcl. ¶**Etteh.key hay se 'la to ai lul hak.kyo ey ponaysilye ko āy lul ssunta** They are striving to send their child to school somehow or other. CF **-e se 'tun ci**.

-e se man, inf + pcl + pcl [rare, ? awkward]. ¶**Ku ke n' kapyewun mulqcil ie se man cōh.un kes i ani 'la pich-kal to acwu alumtapta** (CM 1:196) It's not that it's a good thing just because it is a light substance, but the color too is quite beautiful.

-e se n', abbr < **-e se nun**

-e se 'na, inf + pcl + cop advers. ¶**Cikcep ka se 'na yēyki halq ka, cēnhwa lo ya etteh.key yēyki l' hay** We might talk to him directly, but how could we dare tell it to him on the phone?! **Cikcep manna se 'n tul yēyki mōs halq key iss.nun ya?** There's surely no reason you shouldn't talk directly with him.

-e se 'n tul, inf + pcl + cop mod + postmod. ¶**Saci nun mōs hal mangceng pillye se 'n tul mōs hal ya** True, we can't buy it, but why can't we manage by borrowing it? **Cha nun mōs thal mangceng kel.e se 'n tul mōs kal ya** So we can't go by car, can't we walk?!

-e se nun, inf + pcl + pcl.
1. does and THEN. ¶**Un.e lul cap.e se nun kangq ka ey se kwuwe mek.ki lo hayss.ney**

We've decided to catch the trout and then broil them and eat them on the river bank. **Wēnswungi ka way khong ul kka se nun ce nun mekci anh.ko saykki eykey cwunun kwun a** The monkey shells the peanuts and then gives them to her baby instead of eating them herself!
2. as for doing; ~ **an toynta** must not do. ¶**Nay chayk ul ilk.e se nun an toynta** You mustn't read my book. CF **-umyen an toynta**.

-e se puthe, inf + pcl + pcl. from when. ¶**elye se puthe** from when I was a child. **khe se puthe** from when I grew up. **na/nah.a se puthe** from birth, in all my life.

-e se to, inf + pcl + pcl. 1. = **-e to**.
~ **tul** (pcl). ¶**Achim ul nuc.key mek.ess.e to tul cēmsim ul mek.e ya hanta** You must eat some lunch even though you did all have breakfast late.
2. [? in clichés only] ¶**Mun.yey sāng ey iss.e se to say lowun cēnhwan ul hakey toyess.ta** In literary ideas, too, they began to turn over a new leaf.

-e se tul, inf + pcl + pcl. ¶**Cip ey ka se tul kongpu hay la** (You kids) go home and study.

-e se 'tun ci, inf + pcl + cop retr mod + postmod. ¶**Etteh.key hay se 'tun ci ku kes ul hay la** Do it somehow or other. CF **-e se 'la to**.

-e se ya, inf + pcl + pcl. if, even/only if; when even/only when; just because. ¶**incey nai ka tul.e se ya** only now that I have grown older. **hyēntay ey wā se ya** only when we come to the present age. **Tōn i ēps.e se ya sālq swu ēps.ˢup.nita** Without money we can't go on living. **Kongpu an hay se ya etteh.key cōh.un haksayng i toyp.nikka** If you don't study, how are you ever going to become a good student? **Cikum ileh.key nuc.e se ya etteh.key kana** How can we go when it's so late now? **Ku ka māl hay se ya piloso na nun kkaytal.ess.ta** I first realized it (only) when he told me. **Pam i nuc.e se ya piloso ku ka wass.ta** He didn't get here until late at night. **Yaksok han kes ul kuleh.key twī-nāyko hay se ya etteh.key kath.i īl ul halq swu ka iss.ˢo** Since you never even keep your promises, how can I do any business with you? **I phyo phanun chang aph uy cwul i ileh.key kil.e se ya eti sikan cen ey phyo lul sakeyss.ni** The line in front of this ticket window is so long, how will we ever get our tickets in time? **Ku sālam i onul olq ci an olq ci nun cēmsim ttay ka cīna se ya ālkey toylq ke ya** It won't be clear until lunch time has gone by whether he will come today or not. **Ileh.key to pap ey tōl i mānh.e se ya pap ul mek.um i ani 'la tōl ul ssip.nun kes kath.ta** With all these grits in the rice it is like chewing on grits rather than eating rice.
~ **hata** = **-e ya hata**. ¶**Kkuth ey ka se se ya (ha)ci** I suppose we have to go stand at the end?
SEE **-ta 'y se ya, ila 'y se ya**; **-ˈe ˈsye ˈza**.

-e sey ya, [var] = **-e se ya**

-esi-/-es- [Phyengan DIAL] (Kim Yengpay 1984: 104-5) = **-ess-** (past). Both **-esi-** and **-es-** are before **-e, -ul, -un, -umyen, -uni**; **-esi ya** = **-ess.e ya, -ese yo** (in places **-esi yo**) = **-ess.e yo**.

-ˈesi··· = **-ˈe ˈsi···**, abbr < **-ˈe isi···**

-ˈesi- (effective honorific) = **-(ᵘ/o)ˈsiˈke-** (honorific effective): **-ˈesin, -ˈesina, -ˈesiˈn i (ˈGwo/ˈGwa), -ˈesiˈnᵘ/ol, -ˈesiˈn ywo, -ˈesiˈta, -ˈesiˈtun**. SEE **-ˈyesi**.

-ˈesiˈn i = **-ˈkesiˈn i**, effective honorific + postmod. ¶**haˈnolˈh i ilˈGwesiˈn i** (1445 ¹Yong 21) heaven has ordained it.

-ˈesiˈnol, 1. → **-ˈGesiˈnol** 2. = **-ˈkesiˈnol** (= **-uˈsikeˈnol**, the honorific literary concessive). ¶**ˈCCYENG-ˈPPEN ˈi mwuˈlesiˈnol** (1449 Kok 15; for *ˈˈmwut.kesiˈnol** for *mwuˈlusikeˈnol**) upon [King] Śuddhodana's inquiring about it … .

-ˈesiˈton = **-ˈesiˈtun**. ¶**ˈnim-kum ˈi ˈpa.p ol ˈcwuˈesiˈton mwoˈlwoˈmay twosˈk ol ˈCYENG hi hoˈkwo mwoncyeˈmas ˈpwosiˈm ye** (1475 Nay 1:9-10) when the king gives rice, one adjusts one's seat without thinking about it and first tries the taste and … .

-ˈesiˈtun = **-ˈkesiˈtun** = **-uˈsikeˈtun**, honorific provisional. if/when one deigns. ¶**ˈˈTTYEY-ˈˈCO honaˈh ol ˈcwuˈesiˈtun ˈˈmal tuˈle ilozoˈWa ˈcingi ˈˈta** (1447 Sek 6:22b) if you let me have one of your disciples I want to build them [the monasteries] according to what he says.

-ˈe ˈs.keˈn i ˈla. ¶**[SYWUY-CCAN] honˈphu.l ul mutenˈhi neˈkye ˈs.keˈn i ˈla** (1481 Twusi 8:42a) I scorned what was left of the withered grass.

-ˈe ˈs.keˈnul, abbreviation < **-ˈe is.keˈnul**. ¶**chulk kwos.ka.l i kiˈGwuˈle ˈs.keˈnul** (1481 Twusi 23:54a) with ko-hemp hats aslant.

-ˈesketun = **-ˈe ˈs.keʃ]tun**, abbr < **-ˈe is.keˈtun**. ¶**TTAM ˈi maˈkhye ˈsketun** (1466 Kup 1:3b) if congested with phlegm.

-ˈesˈkwo = -ˈe ˈsˈkwo, abbr < -ˈe isˈkwo (also -ˈe ˈysˈkwo). ¶ kwuˈsul ˈlwo ˈmang moyˈca ˈskin kantaˈk ay tuˈliˈGwe ˈsˈkwo (?1517- Pak 1:29a) has sewn jewels into a net bag and run a string through it, and ... .
-ˈes.non = ˈe ˈs.non, abbr < -ˈe is.non (also -ˈe ˈys.non). ¶ ˊpeˈle ˈs.non ˈMEN-ˋSSYANG ˈi ˋta ˈkwot ˈSSILQ-ˈSYANG ˈiˈGwo (1463 Pep 1:227a) the myriad images that are arrayed are in fact the reality [of enlightenment].
-ˈes.noˈn i = ˈe ˈs.noˈn i, abbr < -ˈe is.noˈn i (also -ˈe ˈys.noˈn i). ¶ haˈnolˈh ay sˈmuˈl ey comˈkye ˈs.noˈn i (?1517- Pak 1:68a) it is soaked in the waters of heaven [it is so blue]. ~ ˈˈla. ¶ tas lyang kum ˈuˈlwo meyˈGwe ˈs.noˈn iˈˈla (?1517- Pak 1:19a) I have been shouldered with five taels of gold to pay.
-ˈesˈnwon = -ˈe ˈsˈnwon, abbr < -ˈe isˈnwon. ¶ puˈthe ˈsˈnwon mwoˈton ˈNGWUW ˈlul ˈTUK ˈˈti ˋmwot ˈhwolqˈt iˈla (1462 ¹Nung 6:53b) we cannot obtain all the existence we count on.
-ˈesoˈla, effective emotive indic assert. ¶ ne-huy ˈtolˈh iˈhimˈpsesola (1447 Sek 23:13a) you people must try hard. UM-AY yey iGwon phwul ul ta salGwa nayyesola (1747 Songkang [Kwansey] 3a, [Sengcwu] 4b) it revives the fading grass on the shady bank. SEE -ˈasoˈla.
-ess-, past. [< -e inf + iss- aux; CF anc.ess.ta sat down, anc.e iss.ta is seated]
1. was; did, has done.
2. Occasionally the meanings or translations are unexpected:
2a. (present) ¶ Sikan i acik to mel.ess.ta The time is still far off.
2b. (immediate future) ¶ Ne khunq īl nass.ta; incey apeci hanthey kekceng tut.key toyess.ta You are in for it now; you will catch it (= a scolding) from your father. Icey nun cwuk.ess.kwun a I'm (as good as) dead! NOTE: Pak Hwaca 1982 says that Korean does not use the past as a lively immediate future, so that Japanese Aˈa baˈsu ga kitaˈ 'Oh the bus is about to get here!' should be said as Ppesu ka onta. Also, that Korean does not use the past to confirm what is already known, so that Hoˈnˈya wa asoko daˈtta neˈ '(Let's see,) the bookshop was over there, wasn't it' translates as Chayk pang un cēki ˈci.
2c. cannot. ¶ Kuleh.ci man incey kongpu nun tā hayss.nun ke lˈ But I can't study now!

Occurs followed by -ess-, -keyss-, -sup-, -ta, -ney, -na?, -ˢo, -tula, -tey, -ti, -kwumen (-kwun (a), -kwulye), -e, -ko, -una(-ma), -uni(-kka), -ci, -ki, -um, -umye, -umyen (= -tula ˈmyen), -tumyen, -ul, -nun, -tun, -ketun; SEE -ess.ca.
Shapes are like those of the infinitive (-e). The shape is -ass- if the last vowel of the stem is o or a w that is reduced from a basic o, and in the literary language or in dialect also if the last vowel of the stem is a. The shape is -ss- (lit -ess-) if the stem ends ···ey, ···oy, or ···ay; it is -ss- (both colloq and lit) after ···a. But -oyess- is often spelled -wayss- and -wiess- is often spelled -weyss-; those pronunciations are sometimes heard, usually with a long vowel.
-e ssah.ta, inf + aux v insep. does to a great extent, extremely; does (? or is) to a sufficient extent, more than enough, ample; does (? or is) in throngs, in great / frequent numbers; does repeatedly, does (all too) often; does to excess (and much to my irritation). ¶ Twū ai ka ssawe ssah.nunta The two boys fight like cats and dogs. Mun pakk ey se nun ai tul i nol.a ssah.nunta The children are playing in throngs outside the door. Ai tul i ttē-tul.e ssah.nunta The kids are yelling and screaming. I man hamyen mek.e ssah.keyss.ta This will be plenty for me (to eat). NOTE: There is doubt whether this is acceptable with the descriptive stems (adj or cop): ? Ku ttawi nun yeki to hun hay ssah.ass.ta 'That sort of thing is all too common here, too'; ? Ku man hayss.umyen mānh.e ssah.keyss.ta 'That will be more than enough'. ¹Yi Kitong (1988:165-6) offers such examples as: Ku mul un ttukewe ssah.ass.ta 'The water is hotter than it need be'; Ku sālam un celm.e ssah.ass.ta 'The man is young enough'; Ku cip un cōh.a ssah.ass.ta 'The house is good enough'; but these are rejected by other speakers consulted. No examples are found for the copula.
-ess.ca, past subj assertive. SEE ALSO -ta ˈyss.ca, -la ˈyss.ca, -ca ˈyss.ca. ¶ Kicha ka āmuli ppallass.ca (= ppaluta ˈyss.ca) pihayng-ki lul ttalulq swu iss.keyss.nun ya? However fast a train might go, how could it keep up with an airplane?! Ku tul i pāntay lul ha.yess.ca āmulen yēnghyang ul cwuci mōs halq key ˈta Even if they should oppose it, that probably

would not exert any influence. **Cikum puthe āmuli kongpu lul hayss.ca sihem ey n' mōs puth.ulq ke l'** However hard he might study now, he won't be able to pass the test.

-ess.ci, past suspective. 1. ~ **yo**. CF **-umyen ··· -ess.ci**. 2. ¶**kaci anh.ess.ci man** didn't go but. 3. ~ **anh-** (in rhetorical question): §11.7.8.

-ess.e, past infinitive.
1. (sentence-final) did / was [INTIMATE]. ~ **yo**, ~ **-ess.ey yo** SAME [POLITE].
2. (before pcl) SEE ~ **to**, ~ **tul**, ~ **ya**, ~ **yo** (but *~ **la**, *~ **se**).

***-ess.e se**, past inf + pcl. Not used.

-ess.ess-, past-past: still more remote or more definitely completed than simple past. ¶**Ku i ka wass.ta** He has come (and is here) — **Ku i ka wass.ess.ta** He came (and was here but went away again). **Ku i ka kass.ta** He has gone (and is still away) — **Ku i ka kass.ess.ta** He went (and is now back). **Eti kasyess.ess.e(y) yo** Where have you been? **Nay atul i pyēng i nass.ess.ci man cikum un kkway naass.ta** My son got sick but he is quite recovered now.

NOTE: There are two uses. In one, something happened and / but then later the situation was reversed or changed. The other is more like the English pluperfect 'had done' (past with respect to a past frame of reference), as in: **Nay ka cwūmun han sukeyithu ka cīnan tal ey tōchak hayss.nun tey ku ttay Hān kang el.um un tā nok.ass.ess.ta** The skates that I ordered arrived last month, but by then the ice in the Han river had all melted (Pak Sengwen 224).

-ess.ess.e, past-past infinitive.
1. (sentence-final) did / was at an earlier time [INTIMATE]; **-ess.ess.e(y) yo** [POLITE].
2. (before pcl) did / was and so, etc.

-ess.ess.keyss.nun tey, past-past future proc mod + postmod. (given) the circumstance that someone will have done or probably had done (at some earlier time); had probably done and / but / so; [sentence-final] should have done (but). ¶**Ku ay ka na hanthey wass.ess.uni-kka ne hanthey to kass.ess.keyss.nun tey** He came to see me; he must have come to see you, too. **Kim kwun i ecey ccum un Sewul ey tōchak hayss.ess.keyss.nun tey manna pwass.nun ya** Kim must have arrived in Seoul yesterday; have you run into him? [Commonly replaced by **-ess.ess.ulq kes in tey** for 'probably'.]

-ess.ess.keyss.ta, past-past future indic assertive.
1. will have done (at some earlier time).
2. probably did: this is commonly replaced by **-ess.ess.ulq kes ita**.

-ess.ess.nun tey, past-past proc mod + postmod. (given) the circumstance that someone did (had done); did (had done) and / but / so. ¶**Sewul ey kass.ess.nun tey, sikan i ēps.e se Yensey tāyhak un mōs pwass.ta** I went to Seoul, but there wasn't time to see Yensey University. **Ku sālam cwūso lul al.ass.ess.nun tey cikum un ic.e pelyess.e yo** (Im Hopin 1987:191) I knew his address but now I have forgotten it.

-ess.ess.nun ya, past-past proc mod + postmod. (the question) whether it had been / happened.

-ess.ess.ta, past-past indic assertive. did (at an earlier time), had done. ¶**kass.ess.ta** went (and is back). **wass.ess.ta** came (and left again), was here (but isn't now). **mek.ess.ess.ta** ate (but is hungry again).

-ess.ess.tun, past-past retr mod. ¶**Kwulapha ey kasyess.ess.tun cek i iss.^{s}up.nikka** Have you ever been to Europe? **Path māyko iss.ess.tunq ^{n}yeca ka kokay lul tulko mēn san ul potula** The woman who had been weeding the field lifted her head up and looked at the distant mountain. CF **-ess.tun**.

-ess.ess.una, past-past advers. did (at an earlier time) but; ~ **-ma** did but anyway. ¶**Cheum ey nun sangtang hi mūnceyq-keli yess.ess.una cikum un swūnco loi cīnhayng toynta** At first it was quite a problem, but now it is going smoothly.

-ess.e to, past inf + pcl. even though (while) it happened; did but. ¶**Wihem han cwul un ālko iss.ess.e to 38-sen ul nēm.ki lo hayss.ta** Even though I knew the danger I decided to cross the 38th parallel. **Ku tangsi ku nun tāytan hi kanan hayss.e to nul culkepkey cīnayss.ta** In those days he led a happy life even though he was very poor. **Ilq-cwuil cen puthe man sīcak hayss.e to cikum ccum un tā tōyss.ul they 'n tey** If only we had started it a week ago we would be all done by now. **Ecey achim un pap ul mek.ess.e to nemu phikon hay se, wenki ka naci anh.ess.ess.^{s}up.nita** I was so tired yesterday morning that even after breakfast I just couldn't get my spirits up (= couldn't get going).

-ess.e tul, past inf + pcl (plural-subject). ¶Pap ul mek.ess.e tul They / We have eaten.

-ess.e ya, past inf + pcl. ¶Aycho (ey) puthe kulen sālam kwa nun sangcong ul mal.ess.e ya hanun ke ya You should have avoided associating with a man like him from the start. Mili māl-ssum tulyess.e ya hayss.(ess.)ulq kes ip.nita He probably should have told you beforehand.

-ess.e(y) yo SEE -ess.e. ? ~ man did but (CF -keyss.e yo man).

-ess.ken man, past semi-lit concessive. even though (although, while) one did. ~ un, ~ se to. Sometimes spelled -ess.kes-man as in Pam ey īl haci mālla ko kum ha.yess.kes-man se to yelq si kkaci īl halq swu pakk ey ēps.ˢo He forbade my working at night but I can't help working till ten o'clock.

-ess.kes.ta past tentative assertive. ¶Ne na tele silh.ta ko hayss.kes.ta – tasi nun an ol they 'ni You say you hate me, and I won't come again! Ne sensayng nim poko yok hayss.kes.ta – eti twuko poca You'd call the teacher names? – let's cut that out!

-ess.ketun, past provisional. SEE -ketun.

-ess.keyss.e, past-future inf. will have done; probably did [INTIMATE]. ~ (y) yo [POLITE].

-ess.keyss.nun tey, past-future processive mod + postmodifier. (given) the circumstance that someone will have done or probably has done; will have (probably has) done it and / but / so. ¶Wuli emeni ka onul mas-iss.nun ūmsik ul hasyess.keyss.nun tey kath.i ka se mek.ulq ka? I bet my mother has fixed some good food today – won't you come eat with us?

-ess.keyss.nun ya, past-future processive mod + postmodifier. (the question) whether it will have been (probably was) or whether someone will have done (probably did).

-ess.keyss.ta, past-future indic assert.
1. probably did. ¶Ku sālam uy nai sumul un nem.ess.keyss.ta I bet he will never see twenty again.
2. will have done.

-ess.keyss.tun, past-future retr mod

-ess.ki, past summative. SEE -ki.

-ess.ko, past gerund. did / was and. [Little used except in long sentences to anticipate a final past verb; or final in fragments, afterthoughts.]

-ess.na, 1. FAMILIAR past indic attent (= -ess.ni). ~ pota = -ess.nun ka pota.
2. = (used for) -ess.nun ka / ya.
~ ka (particle). ¶Ēncey natha-nass.na ka mūncey 'ta The question is when did it appear.
~ lul (pcl). ¶Ku ⁿyeca ka wass.na lul al.e pwā la Find out whether she came. Ecci palqtal tōyss.na lul poca Let's see how it has developed.

-ess.ney, FAMILIAR past indic assert (= -ess.ta).

-ess.ni, past indic attent. did / was it?

-ess.nola, [lit] = -ess.ta. CF (1916 Gale 2:60) -es.nwola "A book-form, having the force of -es.ta in the colloquial"; ··· ~ kwo says that he had himself ··· .

-ess.nun, past proc mod. Attaches to any stem (v, adj, cop) but is followed only by tey, ci, ka (question), ya (question), ke l' (exclamation), or by pep hata (– also tus hata / siph.ta?).

-ess.nun ci, past proc mod + postmod.
1. (the uncertain fact) whether it was / did. ¶Ku i ka sal.ess.nun ci cwuk.ess.nun ci āmu to molunta Nobody knows whether he is alive or dead. Ku i ka cēng-mal kulen māl ul hayss.nun ci kiek hasip.nikka? Do you recall whether he really said that? Nwukwu yess.nun ci āsip.nikka Do you know who it was?
2. ~ (to moluta, yo) maybe / perhaps it was or did. ¶Kass.nun ci (to molunta) Maybe he went. Maybe he's gone / there. Pi ka wass.nun ci (yo) Perhaps it rained.

-ess.nun ci 'la (se), past proc mod + postmod + cop var inf (+ pcl). as / since it did = -un ci 'la (se) 2. SEE -nun ci 'la (se).

-ess.nun ka, past proc mod + postmod. (the question) whether it was / did. ~ pota it seems to have been / done. ¶Ay ka eti tachyess.nun ka pota It seems the baby got hurt somewhere.
~ ka (pcl). ¶Ēncey natha-nass.nun ka ka mūncey 'ta The question is when did it appear.
~ lul (pcl). ¶Ku ⁿyeca ka wass.nun ka lul al.e pwā la Find out whether she came.

-ess.nun ke l' (= -un ke l'), past proc mod + postmod + pcl. did it so there! did it anyway! ¶Icey nun yēys nal(q iyaki) to mith-chen i ttel.e cyess.nun ke l' But, gee whiz, I've run out of (stories of) the old days.

-ess.nun tey past proc mod + postmod.
1. (given) the circumstance that one did; did and / or / but / so. ¶Wuli cip ey cheng hayss.nun tey acik to an onta We invited him to our

house, but he still hasn't come.
~ nun SEE -nun tey.
~ to (pulkwu hako) SEE -nun tey.
~ ya SEE tey ya.
2. ~ (yo)! (exclamation). ¶Cal hayss.nun tey (yo)! You did well!
-ess.nun ya, past proc modifier + postmodifier. (the question) whether it was or did. ¶Ne eti iss.ess.nun ya — halwu congil poici anh.uni Where have you been that I haven't seen you all day long?
-ess.n' ya, abbr < -ess.nun ya
-ess.ˢo, AUTH past indicative assertive
-ess.ta, 1. past indicative assertive
2. ~ (ka) past transferentive. ¶kass.ta osil ttay when you come back, on your way back. Eti kass.ta ka osey yo Where have you been?
-ess.ta ka nun, past transferentive + pcl [cannot be omitted] + pcl.
1. + nonpast: ¶Kulayss.ta ka nun may lul mac.key?! I do that and then I'll get whipped, won't I. (Ne) nay tongsayng ul ttaylyess.ta ka nun cwuk.nunta If you hit my young brother, you are a dead man (¹Yi Cenglo 1989).
2. + past: ¶Wass.ta ka nun ku tay lo kass.ta He came, but then he up and left right away.
-ess.ta ka se, past transferentive + pcl + pcl.
¶¹Noymul ul mek.ess.ta ka (se) hon nass.ta He took a bribe and got in(to) trouble.
-ess.ta ka to SEE -ta ka to
-ess.ta ka tul SEE -ta ka tul
-ess.ta ka ya SEE -ta ka ya
-ess.ta ka yo SEE -ta ka yo
-ess.ta ko/kko/kwu SEE -ta ko
-ess.ta 'myen, abbr < -ess.ta (ko) hamyen
-ess.ta 'y, abbr < -ess.ta (ko) hay
-ess.tey, FAMILIAR past retr assertive
-ess.ti, past retr attentive
-ess.tula, past retr assertive.
~ 'myen SEE -tula 'myen.
-ess.tumyen, past retrospective conditional. SEE -tumyen. Usually replaced by -ess.ta 'myen.
-ess.tun, past retr mod. 1. that had been/done; that was/did (at an earlier time). ¶Hulyess.tun hanul i malk.key kayess.ta The (previously) cloudy sky cleared up nicely. Yeki twuess.tun khal i eti kass.ni Where has the sword gone that I had put away here? Cwuk.ess.tun sālam i tasi sal.e nass.ta 'o A dead person came back to life, they say. 2. = -ess.tun ya (question).

-ess.tun ci 'la SEE -tun ci
-ess.tuni, past retr sequential. SEE -tuni.
-ess.tun mo.yang, past retr mod + n. ¶Pi ka wass.tun mo.yang ita It seems to have rained (to have been raining).
-ess.tun tey (yo), past retrospective + postmod (sentence-final exclamatory). ¶ka-poni(-kka n') pi ka mānh.i wass.tun tey when I went there I found it had rained a lot.
-ess.tun tul SEE -tun tul
-ess.u'q ka, abbr < -ess.ulq ka
-ess.ul(q), past prospective mod. Occurs + ka, kes, mangceng, pa, pep, ppun, they, tus, ya.
1. to have been. ¶elyess.ul ttay, elyess.ulq cek (the time) when one was young. haksayng iess.ul ttay when I was a student.
2. to have done — but the simple -ul(q) is often preferred, whenever that is unambiguous. ¶kihoy ka iss.ess.ul ttay when I got/had the chance. Nappun kes un an kaluchyess.ulq cwul lo āp.nita I presume (feel sure) that they didn't teach any bad things. Ku i ka kass.ul/kal ttay na to kass.ta When he went I went too. Nay ka kass.ess.ul ttay ku i to kass.ess.ta When I had been there he went by there, too.
3. -ess.ulq kes. SEE kes
3a. (with extruded subject for epitheme).
3b. (with extruded object for epitheme).
3c. (as summational epitheme): -ess.ulq kes ita probably did/was, would have done/been, must (surely) have done/been. ¶Enu ¹yekwan ey se ku lul mannass.ess.ulq kes ita I must have seen him in some hotel or other. Ppalli uysa eykey poyess.tun tul an cwuk.ess.ulq kes ita If he had seen the doctor right away, he wouldn't have died. Ney to wum i ēps.ess.tula 'myen, na nun silphay hayss.ulq kes ita If it had not been for your help, I should have failed. Ku ka selun sal kkaci man ila to sal.ess.tula 'myen ku cakphum ul wānseng hayss.ulq kes ita If only he had lived to the age of 30 he would have completed the work. Ku sālam iess.tula 'myen manna pwass.ulq kes ita If it had been that man I would have seen/noticed him. Mili māl-ssum tulyess.e ya hayss.(ess.)ulq kes ip.nita He probably should have told you beforehand. Tōn i ēps.ess.ki ey mangceng ici, (mān.il tōn i iss.ess.tula 'myen) totwuk eykey tā ppāys.kyess.ulq kes ita It is good that I had no money with me, otherwise

(if I HAD had some money with me) I would have been robbed of it all by the thief.

4. -ess.ulq ci 'la = -ess.ulq ci 'n i 'la [lit]. ¶Ku cimsung i swuph sōk ey swum.ess.ulq ci ('n i) 'la The beast must have hidden in the woods.

-ess.ulq kes kath.umyen (= -ess.tula 'myen) if one had done. ¶Ku i ka ku ttay hak.kyo lul ku man twuci anh.ess.ulq kes kath.umyen, cikum ccum un witay han hakca ka tōyss.ulq ke(y) ya If he hadn't quit school at that time he would have become a great scholar by now.

-ess.ulla, past prosp adjunctive. I fear that it happened. ¶Ku ka keki ey kass.ulla I'm afraid he may have gone there. SEE -ulla ko / kwu.

-ess.um, past substantive

-ess.umyen, past conditional. 1. ¶Kulssey yo, hak.kyo ey kaci anh.ess.umyen tose-kwan ey iss.ulq key yo Well, if he didn't go to school he must be at the library. Ku-kkacis kes ic.e pelyess.umyen ic.e pelyess.ci If you forgot such a thing, why, you forgot it.
CF -tu(la-)myen.

2. ~ siph.ess.ta SEE siph.ta.

3. ~ hanta. ¶Mannass.umyen hatun kil iyo (= mannass.umyen cōh.keyss.ta ko sayngkak hatun kil iyo) I was hoping we would meet. SEE -umyen 2b.

-ess.un, past mod = -un; occurs only in ~ cuk. According to CM 1:379 also in ~ tul, but we reject that usage in favor of -ess.tun tul.

-ess.una, past adversative. was / did but; ~ -ma was / did but anyway. ¶Kongchayk twū kwēn ssik un nona cwuess.una yenphil un acik an nona cwuess.ta I divided the notebooks up two apiece, but I haven't given out the pencils yet.

-ess.un cuk, past mod + postmod [somewhat lit]. ¶Ttek man mek.ess.un cuk sōk i cōh.ul lī ka iss.(ess.)keyss.na Why shouldn't you feel sick after stuffing yourself with rice cakes?!

-ess.uni, past sequential. ~ -kka (nun), ~ -kka n' SAME. ¶Īwang wass.uni tul.e kaca As long as we're here let's go in. Tōn i ēps.ess.uni-kka mōs sass.ci I didn't have the money to buy it. Mom i pulphyen hayss.uni-kka mōs kass.ci I wasn't feeling well so I couldn't go. Hānkwuk sālam iess.uni-kka mōs kass.ci He was Korean so he couldn't go.

-ess.utoy, past concessive. even though it was / did (= -ess.e to), although. SEE -toy.

-˙e ˙ssye, inf + ? abbr < -˙sywo˙sye. please do! ¶(¨es˙tyey pwu˙thye 'y˙la ˙hono.n i s ˙ka) ku ˙ptu˙t ul nil˙Ge ˙ssye (1447 Sek 6:16-7) (how come he is called Buddha?) please tell me what it means.

-˙es˙ta = -˙e 's˙ta, abbr < -˙e is˙ta (also -˙e 'ys˙ta). ¶ne˙pi ˙KWUYK-¨THWO ˙lol me˙ke 's˙ta (1462 ¹Nung 2:63a) has absorbed territory widely. ... ¨tung ˙un ˙kak-˙kak ilhwum twue 's˙ta (?1517- Pak 1:62a) they have all been given individual names. SEE ˙twu' 's˙ta = ˙twu' 'ys˙ta. CF -˙e ˙sye.

¨es(˙)te (> ette), defective inf. ~ ˚ho˙ta, adj-n. (is) how. ¶˙stwo nilo˙la mo˙cho˙m ay ¨es˙te ˙ho˙twoswo˙n ywo [˙thwoswo˙n ywo in the reading aid for the Chinese text] (?1468- Mong 52b) and also tell me, how will it be in the end? ¨es˙te khwan˙toy ¨twuy.h o˙lwo tol˙Gywo˙m ay ¨ce y il˙hu˙m ye pas[k] ˙MWULQ ˙ey ¨ce y mwo˙loke˙n ywo (1459 Wel 13:32a) how come because it depends on the future one will lose it and oneself be unaware of external objects? [¨LYANG-˙HAN ˙KWO-˙SSOJ ˙ay ¨es.te ho˙n i '-ngi s ˙kwo (1445 ¹Yong 28) how were they [in their roles] with respect to the history of the Two Hans? ta˙si ¨cwul ˙ptu.t i ¨es.te kho˙n i Gwo (1481 Twusi 7:40a) how about the thought of giving a second time? ne 'y key ¨es.te '˙l ywo (1482 Nam 1:63a) what is it to you?

¨es(˙)te 'n, abbr < ¨es˙te hon. what (kind of). ¶ku¨tuy ¨es.te 'n ¨sa˙lo.m in ˙ta (1459 Wel 10:29b) = ku¨tuy ¨es˙te 'n ¨salo˙m in ˙ta (1462 ¹Nung 7:62a) what kind of person are you? ¨es˙te 'n cyen˙cho ˙lwo (1459 Wel 9:35d) on what grounds. KWONG ˙oy nilku˙si˙nwon ke˙s un ¨es˙te 'n ¨ma˙l i-ngi s ˙kwo (1465 Wen se:68a) what words are you reading, my Lord? pan˙toki ¨TTYWOW-CYWUW y ¨es˙te 'n ˙MYEN-˙MWOK ˙in ˙t ol a˙lwo.l i '˙la (?1468- Mong 13a) we must recognize what countenance it is that the state of Zhào has. ¨es.te 'n cyen˙cho [G]wo (1482 Kum-sam 3:52a) what is the reason? ¨es.te 'n QIN-YWEN ˙u˙lwo (1447 Sek 24:9a) in what connection. ne 'y ¨es.te 'n salo˙m in ta ([1447→]1562 Sek 3:20a) ← *¨ne y ¨es˙te hon ˙salo.m in ˙ta what kind of person are you? ¨es.te 'n ¨salo˙m ol pwo˙l [i] 'ye.n i ˙Gwo (1481 Twusi 8:62a) what sort of person would he see? ¨ne y ¨es.te 'n a˙hoy ˙Gwan˙toy he˙thwuy ˙lol an˙a ¨wunun ˙ta (1459 Wel 8:

85b; sic *an-ˑa*) what kind of a child are you to cry, clinging to (the calf of) a person's leg? *es.ti* = ¨*esˑti*. ¶*[ˑ]i ˑaˑki es.ti ˑ'n i 'Gwanˑtoy nulˑkuˑn [i] uy heˑthwuy l' ¨*anˑkwo ˑiˑli- ˑtoˑlwok ¨*wunon ˑta* (1459 Wel 8:100-1) why does this child cling to (the calf of) the old man's leg and cry all this much?!
¨*es(ˑ)ti* (> *ecci*), adv. how; how come, why. ¶*cyecay s swuˑl ul [ˑ]hoˑya won ˑt ol ¨esˑti meˑkulˑkwo* (?1517- Pak 1:2b) we have got the market wine, but how will we drink it? *ˑstwo ¨esˑti i cuˑzuˑm ey ˑza kos won ˑta* (?1517- ¹No 2:3b) and how is it that you have only come at just this time? ¨*esˑti TANG WU cek ta[ˑ]sol[ˑ]lim ˑul ˑpep patˑkwo ˑcye ˑhosinoˑn i ˑ-'i s ˑkwo* (1586 Sohak 6:35b) = ¨*esˑtyey TANG WU siˑcel naˑla taˑsoˑliten ˑil ˑlul* [a miswriting (or a conflation?) of ¨*iˑl ul*] ˑ*pep* ⋯ (1518 Sohak-cho 9:39a) why do you want to take the governing of Táng and Wú as your model? *woˑnol selu ¨pwol ˑcwu.l ol ¨es.ti ¨all i ˑGwo hoˑn i* (1459 Twusi 15:47b) today we wonder how to find a way to look at each other.
¨*esˑtye* (? abbr < ¨*esˑtyey*; ? blend of ¨*esˑti* + ¨*esˑte*; ? abbr < ¨*esˑti ˑhoˑye* [= ˑ*hoˑya*]) = ¨*esˑti* how; why. ¶ˑ*ema ¨nim s yangˑco y ¨esˑtye kuˑli-tolwok yeˑwuysiˑn i ˑ-ngi s ˑkwo* (1459 Wel 23:87a) why does mother look so thin?
¨*es(ˑ)tyey* (?< *¨*esˑt[i] ˑyey*), adv = ¨*esˑti* how (come), why. ¶¨*esˑtyey ¨cywuˑng iˑla ˑhoˑno.n i s ˑka* (1447 Sek 6:18a) why are they called priests? ¨*esˑtyey ˑi naˑlaˑh ol [ˑ] e.yeˑspi neˑkye woˑti aˑni ˑkhesiˑn ywo* (1459 Wel 7:29b;) how can you love this land and never come to it? ¨*esˑtyey aˑtoˑl oy ˑYAK ˑol meˑkeˑn ywo* (1459 Wel 21:219a) why did I take my son's medicine? ¨*esˑtyey polˑki.l [i] ˑyeˑn ywo* (1463 Pep 1:13b) how would he have explained it? ALSO: 1447 Sek 6:29b, 9:26b; 9:35a, 19:13a; 1459 Wel 2:13a, 13:35b; 1462 ¹Nung 1:75a; 1463 Pep 1:140a, 2:250a; 1463/4 Yeng 1:90b, 2:62a; 1465 Wen se:13b; ?1468- Mong 62ab; 1482 Nam 1:63a; ... .
¶*pwusˑkulywoˑm i ¨es.tyey ¨epˑsusinˑka* (1449 Kok 120) how come he has no shame? ¨*es.tyey eˑli.n ywo* (1481 Twusi 8:2b) why are you being stupid? ¨*es.tyey hoˑl i ˑGwo* (1481 Twusi 8:29a) what am I to do? ALSO: 1459 Wel 14:65a; 1462 ¹Nung 5:72b; 1463/4 Yeng 2:62a; 1463 Pep 1:13b; 1481 Twusi 7:7b, 7:24b, 20:20a, 22:44b; 1463/4 Yeng 1:90b; 1464 Kumkang 11a; 1475 Nay 2:2:72a; 1482 Kum-sam 2:2a, 2:4a, 2:13b, 5:24b; 1482 Nam 1:17a.
¨*es[ˑ]tyeyˑla* (? < *¨*esˑt[i] ˑyey ˑ'la*), adv = ¨*esˑti* how (come). ¶¨*es.tyeyˑla ˑwos ˑkwa ˑpap [ˑ]kwa ˑay [KWUNG-ˑKHWON] ˑho.ya* (1481 Twusi 16:19a) how come we are needy for clothes and food, and ... .
-ˑ*esuˑla* < -ˑ*esoˑla*, emotive.
-ˑ*esy*⋯ = -ˑ*e ˑsy*⋯ , abbr < -ˑ*e isy*⋯ (< *isi*-)
-ˑ*e ˑsye*, inf + pcl. SEE -**e se**, ˑ*hoˑye ˑsye*, ˑ*ilaˑsye*. ¶ˑ*na y ywo soˑi mol-pwoˑki ¨eˑte ˑsye mol ˑthoˑti ¨mwot ˑhotaˑla* (?1517- Pak 1:37b) the last while I have been unable to ride a horse, having acquired an intestinal ailment. ¨*es.tyey sulˑhe twoˑla pwokwo ¨kenne ˑsye howol-lwo taptap ˑho.ya ˑkha.n ywo* (1481 Twusi 16:37b) why, after crossing over with a backward look of loathing, must I be so bored and lonesome? *iˑlul tikhuyye ˑsye ¨nwulˑul* [= ¨*nwuˑlul*] ¨*wuyˑkhwo ˑcye ˑhonoˑn ywo* (1586 Sohak 6:58a) = ˑ*i ˑptut kaˑcye ˑ¨sywuˑm un ¨nwuˑlul ¨wuyˑhoˑye ˑhonoˑn ywo* (1518 Sohak-cho 9:63a) [wanting it to be] for whose benefit do you go on maintaining this [thought]?
-ˑ*e ¨sye*, abbr < -ˑ*e iˑsye*, inf + aux infinitive.
~ *n'* (pcl). ¶*maˑzo.l ay saˑla ˑsye n' ˑptu.t ul [HHOYNG] ˑhwo.m ay is.noˑn i ˑ'la* (1481 Twusi 8:63b) living in office [in a barbarian land] lies in carrying out one's will. SEE ˑ*hoˑye ˑsye ˑnon*.
~ ˑ*za* (pcl). ¶*SYWU-PPWO-TTYEY paˑhwoy s ¨swoˑp ay PPYEN-QAN ˑhi anˑca ˑ'sye ˑza twoleˑhhye na ˑ'y ˑPEP-SIN ˑol ˑpwoˑno.n i ˑ'la* (1459 Wel 21:206a) Subhūti has to be seated safely inside the rock to view my dharmakāya (true Buddhahood).
-ˑ*eˑta*, effective indic assert. ¶*naˑlaˑh i QWUY-SSIN ˑul ilˑheˑta hoˑkwo* (1459 Wel 10:9b) said that the land has lost a mighty god, and ... . *un ¨twuˑlyang (ˑ)uy s swuˑl ul meˑkeˑta* (?1517- ¹No 2:39a) we drank two silver taels worth of wine. *i kwoki nik.eta* (1795 ¹No-cwung [P] 1:20a) this meat is well done = ˑ*i kwoˑki nik.keˑta* (?1517- ¹No 1:22a). *cim ta moyya sileta* (1795 ¹No-cwung [K] 1:42a) the bundles have all been tied and loaded (on the horses).

SEE ˈhoˑyaˑta, -ˑyeˑta, (-l [i]) ˈyeˑta.
-e 'ta (ka) < -ˑe 'taˑka, inf + cop transferentive (+ particle). with a shift of location, purpose, direction, benefit, etc. SEE ita 3b. ¶LA-ˑHHWUW-LA toˑlye 'taˑka SA-MI saˑmwo.l ye ˑhonoˑta (1447 Sek 6:2a) they intend to take Rāhula away and make him into a śrāmaṇera (a religious novice). ˑCCAP ˑCHWOW-ˑMWOK kesˑke 'taˑka noˑch ol kewuzoˑwonˑt ol (1449 Kok 62) though they cut sticks and challenged his face with them [would he flinch?!].
-e tāko [emphatic] = -e tao
-etakun(ey) [Ceycwu DIAL] = -e 'ta (ka)
-e tākwu [var] = -e tāko
-e tālla, inf + aux v. please do it (as a favor) for me. SEE tālla: Part I, §11.12.
-e tālla 'n ta, abbr < -e tālla ko hanta. wants (calls upon, requests, begs, asks) a person to do for oneself. SEE tālla 'nta; Part I, §11.12.
-etan [Ceycwu DIAL] → -eˑ'tan = -e 'ta (ka)
-e tanita, inf + vi. SEE -e.
-e tao, inf + aux v. please do it (as a favor) for me. ¶Chayk-sang wi ey iss.nun sacen com cip.e tao Hand me the dictionary on the desk.
-e tawu [var] = -e tao
-e tāyta, inf + aux verb. does terribly (awfully; a lot), does like mad/crazy/anything. SEE tāyta.
-e t'e, abbr < -e twe < -e twue
etey, 1. (et' ey) abbr < eti ey. 2. [DIAL] = eti
eti₁, n. Indeterminate place: INTERROGATIVE in questions with falling intonation or in quoted questions; INDEFINITE or GENERAL otherwise.
1. (as INTERROGATIVE in a question with FALLING intonation or in a quoted question). what place, where. ¶ ~ kkaci how far. ~ (ey) se from where, whence; where. Nay sin i eti iss.ni Where are my shoes? Eti kani Where are you going? Eti aphuni Where do you feel the pain? Yeki ka eti 'p.nikka Where are we now? What place is this? I kes kwa talun kes kwa eti ka talun ya Where(in) does this differ from the other? Kulen pelus i eti iss.e Where did you get such manners? Ku ⁿyeca uy eti ka ippun ci molukeyss.ta I don't see where she is so pretty; I see nothing pretty about her. Eti kkaci kani How far are you going? Etiq sālam in ya – Yekiq sālam ita Where are you from? – I'm from here.
2. (as INDEFINITE in a statement, or in a question with RISING intonation). somewhere, some place. ¶Ku nun eti 'n ka i kūnche ey se sāp.nita He lives somewhere around here. Ku sālam eykey eti 'n ka chēn han tey ka iss.ta There is something vulgar about him. Cāngkap ul eti ey 'n ka twuko wass.ta I have left my gloves somewhere. Ku ka eti ey na-kass.na pop.nita He seems to have gone somewhere else. Ku ka eti ey se 'n ka natha-nass.ta He appeared from (out of) nowhere.
3. (as GENERALIZED) any / every place; anywhere/everywhere; (+ NEG) nowhere, no place.
~ 'na, ~ 'tun ci anywhere at all, wherever.
~ kkaci 'na through and through, out and out, to the end/last, all the way. ¶Ku i nun eti kkaci 'na cey ūykyen ul kocip hayss.ta He stuck to his opinion to the bitter end. Eti kkaci 'na sinmun kica 'ta He is every inch/bit the newspaper reporter.
eti₂, interj [< eti₁]. well, well now, now, just, let me see (shows hesitation). ¶Eti, sānqpo 'na halq ka? Let's see, now, shall we take a walk? Eti, Yenge han pen hay pwā la! Now, let me hear you speak some English. Eti, sihem sam.e i yak ul mek.e poci! Well, I guess I might as well try this medicine. Wuli eti kuleh.key hay poca Let's just try it that way.
eti l', 1. abbr < eti lul. 2. ? abbr < eti lo. [Or lul substituting for lo?]
eti 'l(q), noun + copula prosp modifier [= il(q)]
eti 'm, noun + copula substantive [= im]
-ˑeˑ°tiˑta, inf + aux. ¶puˑzeˑtiˑye (1481 Twusi 15:44b); pteˑle tiˑti (1459 Wel 21:125b), pteˑle tiˑl [i] ˑyeˑn i (1464 Kumkang 64b), pteˑle tiˑm ye (1462 ¹Nung 8:87b), pteˑle tiˑm ye n' (1447 Sek 6:3b); mulˑGeˑtiˑtwos.teˑla (?1517⁻ Pak 1:9b), ˑsuˑle tiˑl i ˑ'la (?1517⁻ Pak 1:13b)
-e to < -eˑtwo, infinitive + particle.
1. though (although, even though) does / is; notwithstanding (the fact that); but, however. tōn i ēps.e to though I am poor. ¶ney ka olh.a to though you are right. ām' man mānh.e to at the very most. cek.e to at least. (ām' man) nuc.e to at the latest. (ām' man) ille to at the earliest. ām' man sayngkak hay to however hard I think. Nuc.e to tases si kkaci ey nun wā ya hanta You must be here by five at the latest. Ku kes i silh.e to hay ya hanta Though you do not like it, you must do it. Kwulm.e cwuk.e to, kulenq īl un an hanta Even though

I were starving I would not do such a thing. **Ām' man āy lul sse to ne nun sengkong mōs hanta** However hard you may work you will never succeed. **Ku kes un iss.e to cōh.ko, ēps.e to cōh.ta** It makes no difference whether I have it or not. **Etten ttay n' kel.e to kako, etten ttay n' thako to kanta** (or ⋯ **kel.e kaki to hako** ⋯ **thako kaki to hanta** or **kēt.ki to hako** ⋯ **thako to kanta**) Sometimes I walk and sometimes I ride.

2. does/is and indeed (does/is). ¶ **I sālam un nongsa lul cie to cal cīs.keyss.nun tey** This fellow must be quite a farmer! **Ku ay nun nolay lul pulle to chaṁ cal puluci yo** He sings — and sings very well, you know.

3. all it takes is ⋯ (for it to happen). ¶ **Ka.ya-kum soli (man) tul.e to nwun-mul i nanta** (Dupont 149) All it takes is hearing the sound of a Korean harp and tears well forth.

4. (in phrases used to ask/give permission). ¶ **Mek.e to cōh.un ya?** May I (Is it all right to) eat it? **Mek.e to cōh.ta** You may (It is all right to) eat it (CF **Mek.umyen an toynta** You must not eat it). **Mek.e ya hanun ya?** — **Mekci anh.e to kwaynchanh.ta** Must I eat it? — You need not (don't have to) eat it.

5. **X-umyen X-e to**. SEE **-umyen**. CF **-toy**.

6. (connecting with aux). SEE ~ **iss.ta**, ~ **noh.ta**, ~ **pota**, ~ **twuta**.

-e to iss.ta, inf + pcl + aux verb. ¶ **Nwuwe to iss.ess.ta** I was lying down, even.

-e˙ton = **-ke˙ton** (provisional). ¶ **¨twol.h o˙lwo ˙thye˙ton** (= **˙thi-e˙ton**) ˙PPI **˙ho˙ya to˙la** (1459 Wel 17:85a) ran away when they hit him with stones. SEE **-ye˙ton**.

-e to noh.ta, inf + pcl + aux v. ¶ **Phyēnci lul sse to noh.ass.ta** I got the letter written, even.

-e to pota, inf + pcl + aux v. ¶ **Anc.e to posey yo** Try sitting, too.

-e to toyta, inf + pcl + vi (= **e to cōh.ta**)

-e to tul, inf + pcl + pcl. ¶ **Sākwa lul hay to tul sō.yong ēps.ta** = **Sākwa lul tul hay to sō.yong ēps.ta** = **Sākwa lul hay to sō.yong tul ēps.ta** = **Sākwa lul hay to sō.yong ēps.ta tul** It does no good for them to apologize.

-e to twuta, inf + pcl + aux verb. ¶ **Ku nom i [1]noymul ul pat.e to twuess.ta** That bastard took bribes, even.

ette < **¨es˙te**, defective inf. ~ **hata**, adj-n = **etteh.ta** is what way (how), is some way. CF **ecci** < **¨es˙ti**, **eccay**; **ile**, **kule**, **cele**, **āmule**.

ette han, adj-n mod. ABBR **etten**. CF **kule/ile/cele/āmule han**. 1. what kind/sort of, like what. CF **musun**. ¶ **Ku ka ette han (etten) sālam in ya** What kind of a man is he? **Ette han chayk ul ilk.ko iss.nun ya** What book are you reading now? **Wenca-than ila 'n kes i ette han kes in ya** What is an atomic bomb like? **Ette hanq īl i iss.tun ci ney kyēyhoyk ul kochici mala** Whatever happens, don't change your plans. **Ette hanq īl i iss.e to ku kes un mōs hakeyss.ta** I won't do it, come what may.

2. a certain ⋯ , some (unnamed) ⋯ . CF **enu**. ¶ ~ **sālam** a certain person. ~ **nal achim** one morning.

ette hata, adj-n. ABBR **etteh.ta**. CF **ette han**, **ecci**. Indeterminate state: INTERROGATIVE in questions with falling intonation or in quoted questions; INDEFINITE or GENERAL otherwise.

1. is how, is like what (in a question with FALLING intonation). ¶ **I moca ka na hanthey ette hap.nikka (etteh.sup.nikka)** How does this hat look on me? **Yo say ette hasip.nikka (ettesip.nikka)** How ARE you, anyway? [1]**Nayil tte-nanun kes i ette han ya (etten ya)** How about starting tomorrow? **Kulay ku um.ak-hoy ka ette hayss.nun ya** (or **ettayss.n[un] ya**) So, how did you like the concert? **Onul ssalq kaps i ette han ya** How much is rice today? **Swul han can ette hap.nikka** How about having a drink? **Yo say Sewul i ette hap.nikka** How are things in Seoul these days? **Kanan hamyen ette hata 'n (etteh.ta 'n) māl in ya** What if you are poor?

2. is somehow, is a certain way; is any/every which way. ¶ **ette hata ko (etteh.ta ko) māl halq swu ēps.ta** nothing definite can be said on it; it cannot be described. **ette hata ko māl haki him tun īsang han um.ak** a weird and indescribable music.

3. is a bit dissatisfying (to me); (I) am not quite happy (about it), am not quite satisfied (with), am a bit uneasy. ¶ **Ku ka Mikwuk ey kanta 'nun tey nay maum ey ette hata** I am none too happy to hear that he is going to America.

etteh.ke' 'ta, abbr < **etteh.key heta** (= **hata**)

etteh.key, adj adverbative (abbr < **ette hakey**).

1. how (much), in what manner. ¶ **Etteh.key cīnaynun ya** How are you getting on? **Ku[n]yeca**

ka etteh.key os ul chalyess.tun ya How was she dressed? Tāychey ku īl i etteh.key il.e nass.n' ya How on earth did it happen? Ku ⁿyeca ka etteh.key ippun ci molukeyss.ta What a beautiful woman she is, indeed! Ku ka etteh.key komawun ci! He was so kind! Na nun etteh.key ku kes ul mantunun ci molunta I don't know how they make it. Etteh.key yeki wass.nun ya How is it that you are here?

2. somehow, in some way; anyhow, in any way. ¶etteh.key sayngkak hamyen if one starts thinking about it, if one goes into it (M 3:3:90). Etteh.key hay se 'tun ci ku kes ul hay la Do it no matter how. Etteh.key toyn ke yo [RISING intonation] Did something happen?; [FALLING intonation] What happened?

SEE etteh.key 'na, etteh.key to.

etteh.key hata, adj adverbative + vt.

1. does how / what. ¶Ku tōn ul etteh.key hayss.n' ya What did you do with the money? Etteh.key hay ya halq ci molukeyss.ta I don't know what to do. Etteh.key hay se kulen cīs ul hayss.n' ya How did you come to mess it up so? Kulen kes to mōlla se etteh.key han' ya You should have known a thing like that!

2. does / manages by some means or other, does somehow (at whatever risk/cost), manages to do. ¶Etteh.key hay se 'tun ci ku kes ul hay la Do it no matter how. Ku īl un cey ka etteh.key hakeyss.ˢup.nita I'll set the matter right somehow.

etteh.key 'na, adj adverbative + cop advers. ¶Etteh.key 'na pi ka onun ci aph i poici anh.nunta It's raining so hard that somehow I can't see in front of me at all. Ku ay ka etteh.key 'na wūnun ci cam ul mōs cass.e yo Because that child was crying so much, I could not sleep (M 1:2:93). CF āmuleh.key 'na.

etteh.key to, adj adverbative + pcl. ¶Ne nun etteh.key to kuleh.key cal kūlim ul kūlinun ya How do you ever manage to paint such fine pictures?

etteh.key toyta, adjective adverbative + vi.

1. how it becomes, how it turns out. ¶Ku i ka etteh.key tōyss.ulq ka I wonder what has become of him. Ku īl i etteh.key toylq ci molukeyss.ta I just don't know how things will turn out.

2. it turns / works out somehow or other, it is managed (one way or another), it takes care of itself. ¶¹Yepi nun etteh.key toylq kes kath.ta I think I can take care of my travel expenses somehow or other. Etteh.key toymyen ¹nayil tte-nalq swu iss.keyss.ta If things go well, I expect to get away tomorrow.

etteh.k' hata, abbr < etteh.key hata

etteh.ta, adj -(H)- (inf ettay); abbr < ette hata (is how). ¶Kulemyen etteh.ta 'n māl in ya So what? Kulem etteni So what? (CF Kulem ecceni Then what should we do?). CF celeh.ta, ileh.ta, kuleh.ta; āmuleh.ta; ecceta.

etteh.tun ci, cpd adv (adj retr mod + postmod); abbr < ette hatun ci. anyhow, anyway, in any case, at any rate, at all events, regardless, whether or not. ¶sīpi-kokcik un ~ whether it is true or not. pīyong mūncey nun ~ apart from the question of expense. Etteh.tun ci na nun pāym i ēncey 'na silh.ta I hate snakes at all times whatever the circumstances. Etteh.tun ci toylq swu iss.nun hān ku lul towa ya hanta In any case, I must help him all I can. Tōn un iss.ko ēps.ko, etteh.tun ci sālam i cinsil hay ya hanta A man should be sincere regardless whether he is rich or poor.

~ kan ey SAME

ettel(q), adj prosp mod = ette hal(q)

etten, adj mod = ette han (what kind of, ...)

etteng [Ceycwu DIAL (Seng ¹Nakswu 1984:25n)] = etteh.key, = etten (ette han)

etten-ssi, cpd noun. an adnoun (or a modifier). SYN kwanhyeng-sa.

-e ttulita, v inf + aux vt sep (by nun, to, tul). does it, makes it happen. This intensifies the transitivity of transitives and of some defective (bound) infinitives; it turns intransitive verbs into transitive verbs. ¶ttel.e nun ttulyess.ci man dropped it but ... . SEE ttulita. CF -e cita.

e˙tu (?= e˙tu[y]), n. what place, where; etu lwo is attested 1772. SEE e˙tu˙le, e˙tuy, e˙tu˙mey.

-e tul, infinitive + particle.

~ iss.ta (aux). ¶Nal mata anc.e tul iss.ta Day after day they are sitting down.

~ noh.ta (aux). ¶Ku phyēnci lul sse tul noh.ass.ni? Did you guys get your letters done?

~ pota (aux). ¶Ca incey mek.e tul poci Well, now, let's try the food!

~ twuta (aux). ¶Ku nom tul i ¹noymul ul pat.e tul twuess.ta Those bastards took bribes.

e˙tu˙le, adv ?< e˙tu[y] ˙le = e˙tu[y] ˙lwo n + pcl. where. ¶NGWANG ˙i e˙tu˙le ˙kasi˙n i '-ngi

s ˙kwo (1459 Wel 10:14-5) where did the king go? i˙cey e˙tu˙le ˙ka˙non ˙ta (ʔ1517- ¹No 1:1a) now where are you going?
~ ˙sye from where. ¶˙ne y ˙e˙tu˙le ˙sye won ˙ta (ʔ1517- ¹No 1:1a) where have you come from? ˙i ˙TI-˙HHYWEY ˙˙ep.sun ˙PPI-KHWUW y e˙tule ˙sye wo˙n ywo (1447 Sek 19:30b) where did this witless almsman (bhikṣu) come from?
etu ley [Ceycwu DIAL (Seng ¹Nakswu 1984:26)] = eti ley (Pak Yonghwu 1960:395) = eti lo where to / toward.
e˙tu˙li, adverb. how; where (to). ¶kungey CYENG- ˙SYA y ˙˙epke˙n i e˙tu˙li ka˙l ywo (1447 Sek 6:22a) how can I go there when there are no monasteries there? ˙ile ˙n ˙˙salom ˙tol˙h ol e˙tu˙li ˙CYEY-˙TTWO ho˙l [i] ˙ye˙n ywo ˙hota˙n i (1447 Sek 13:57b) [I] wondered how to save such people.
-e tulita, inf + aux v. 1. does as a favor for a superior. SYN -e pachita; CF -e cwuta.
2. → -e tul.ita.
-e tul.ita, inf + aux vt insep. does into (taking in). pat.e ~ takes in, accepts, adopts.
-e tulta, inf + aux v. does into / upon / at. tallye tulta goes at, attacks. tāy tulta defies; tackles. tempie tulta attacks, assaults, rushes. CF -e tul.ita.
e˙tu˙mey (ʔ< e˙tu ˙moy[h]), adv, ʔn. where, what (remote) place. ¶˙i ˙sta˙h i e˙tu˙mey ˙-ngi s ˙kwo (1459 Wel 8:94a; notice the copula) what place is this land? [˙CYEY-CYWUW] ˙non e˙tu˙mey is.no˙n i Gwo (1481 Twusi 8:37b) where is Ceycwu? e˙tu˙mey nilk˙ke ˙ka ˙s.non ˙ta (ʔ1517- Pak 1:49b) how far did you read?
-˙e˙tun, 1. = -Ge˙tun. 2. (= -˙[k]e˙tun) = -ke˙tun if; when. ¶˙PEP-˙LYWULQ ˙ey kulun ˙i˙l ol ci˙ze˙tun (1459 Wel 10:21a) if one commits a deed that is against the law. swuwul meke˙tun (ʔ1517- Pak 1:6a) when we've drunk the wine. ˙˙twol.h o˙lwo ˙thye˙tun (1447 Sek 19:31a) when they hit him with stones ... .
-e ˙tun ci = -e se ˙tun ci
e˙tuy, n, adv. what place, where. ¶e˙tuy pu˙thu.l i ˙Gwo (1459 Wel se:15a) where will one turn for support? icey e˙tuy is.no˙n i ˙-ngi s ˙kwo (1459 Wel 23:78a) where are they now? ˙˙nyey ye˙huyywo˙m on ˙i e˙tuy ˙le˙n ywo (1481 Twusi 21:30a) the separation of long ago, where was this? ˙˙ne y e˙tuy ˙ka is˙ten ˙ta (ʔ1517- Pak 1:37b) where have you been? ˙˙TTWOW ˙lol e˙tuy l' pu˙the il˙Gwu.l i ˙Gwo (1463/4 Yeng 1:4a) what can we rely upon to achieve the Way? ˙˙TTYWOW-CYWUW ˙non e˙tuy ˙lol QIN ˙ho.ya ˙˙ep˙ta nilo˙n ywo (ʔ1468- Mong 13b) what was the absence of the state of Zhào said due to?
e˙tuy ˙s˙ten, e˙tuy ˙˙sten, adv + vi retr mod. just where, (where) ever; how (ever), why (ever). ¶nyen˙k i e˙tuy ˙˙sten anco˙l i ˙-ngi s ˙kwo (1447 Sek 24:43b) where will the others ever sit? ZIN-SOYNG ˙i e˙tuy ˙s˙ten ˙i ˙kot ho˙n i isi˙l i ˙-ngi s ˙kwo (1447 Sek 6:5ab) how can there ever be a life as sad as this? e˙tuy ˙˙sten SAM- PWUN ˙i ˙˙mwot ko˙ca ˙PALQ-˙POYK sa˙wona˙Won ˙˙i˙l i isi˙l i ˙Gwo (1447 Sek 19:10b) without three divisions provided, where will there ever be eight hundred bad events?
e˙tuy ˙˙ston, var < e˙tuy ˙s˙ten. ¶e˙tuy ˙˙ston ˙syang˙kup ˙hosi˙ki ˙lul ˙po˙la˙l i s ˙ka (ʔ1517- Pak 1:60a) how could I ever hope you to tip me?
e˙tuy ˙˙stun, var < e˙tuy ˙s˙ten. ¶˙˙ne y e˙tuy ˙˙stun ˙˙na ˙lul i˙kuyl ˙ta (ʔ1517- Pak 1:22b) how will you ever beat me [at checkers]?
e˙tuy ˙za, adv + pcl. just where. ¶e˙tuy ˙za ˙˙tywohon ˙sto˙l i yang˙co ko˙co˙n i is.ke˙n ywo (1447 Sek 6:13b) just where is there a good daughter endowed with looks?
-e twe, abbr < -e twue
-˙e ˙two, inf (or effective inf) + pcl. ¶KKUY- ˙QYAK ˙ol ni˙ce ˙two (1449 Kok 78) though he forgot his engagements.
-e twu [var] = -e to
-e twuta < -˙e ˙˙twu˙ta, inf + aux v sep. CF -e noh.ta, -e noh.a twuta, -e pelita; -ko nata, -ko mālta. 1. does something to get it out of the way (perhaps as a precaution); gets it done, finishes it up (so it will be out of the way), does it once and for good, does thoroughly/ carefully now (so it will not have to be done again); does for later / future use or reference. ¶Kil tte-naki cen ey achim ul cal mek.e twue la Have a good breakfast before you set out on your trip. Ku kes ul cal kanswu hay twum sey I'll take good care of it for you. Encey chwuwi ka tul.nun ci moluni cikum kyewul os ul kkē-nāy twe ya hakeyss.ta Since you don't know when the cold weather will set in, I'd better get our winter clothes ready now. Ku os ul os cang ey 'na neh.e twusey yo Just put those clothes in the wardrobe, please. Cal kamchwe twuki n' hayss.ci man āmulay to

kamchwe twuki n' hayss.ci man āmulay to pokeyss.nun tey? Don't you think that perhaps somebody will find it even though we have nicely hidden it? **Ku ka oki cen ey īl ul hay twunun kes i cōh.keyss.ta** It would be better to finish the job (to get the work out of the way) before he comes. **Wusen poki ey 'na-ma cōh.key hay twuca** First let's make it nice to look at, say. **Mas un ēps.una ku-nyang mek.e twuca** It is not very tasty but let's eat it up anyway. **Nay nolay lul cal tul.e twe la** Listen carefully to my song (and keep it in mind). **Ku i ka etteh.key īl ul hanun ci cal pwā twue la** Watch carefully how he does the job (and don't forget it). **Na hanun kes ul cal pwā ('ta) twukey** Now look carefully at the way I am doing it (so I won't have to show you again). **I kes ul kiek hay twusio** Remember this. **Acik elin ai 'ni, weyn mankhum hay twusio** He is still just a child; go easy on him. **Cwūcha kūmci kwuyek ul Cong-lo kkaci lo hay twupsita** Let's have the no-parking zone all the way over to Bell Street. **Onul un ku man hay twuca** That is all for today, so much for today.

2. finishes it up tentatively / anyway; just lets it go at that (for the time being). ¶ **īl ul ku-man ce-man hay twuta** does one's work halfway, does a rough job (of it). **Nēy si kkaci lo ceng hay twupsita** Let's decide to have it by (or: have it last till) four o'clock. ¹**Imsi (lo) pyek ey 'la to kel.e twusipsio** Hang it on the wall for the time being. **Ku uy cal-mos ul i tay lo nāy-pelye twulq swu ēps.ta** We can't let his wrongdoings go unchallenged. **ku sālam ul cwuk.un chay nāy-pelye twuta** leaves the dead person unburied. **Nāy-pelye twue la; ssawuta (ka) mālci anh.ul i?!** Leave them alone – they won't fight long. **Chayk ul noh.in tay lo noh.a twuess.ta** I left the book just as it was. **Mek.nunta 'y ya elma 'na mek.keyss.ni – nāy-pelye twue la** Let him eat as much as he likes; he can't eat much, anyway.

NOTE: Both ⋯ **ul noh.a twuta** and **-e noh.a twuta** occur: **Chayk ul noh.in tay lo noh.a twuess.ta** I left the book as it was. **Swukcey lul mili mili hay noh.a twuess.ta** I got my homework all done way in advance. And **-e twue noh.ta** is also used: **Sikan iss.ul ttay swukcey lul tā hay twue noh.ca** When we have the time, let's get our homework all out of the way. The structure ⋯ **ul twue twuta** occurs (**I chayk ul cal twue twue la** Put this ook in a good safe place!) but *-e twue twuta is replaced by simple **-e twuta** or by **-e noh.ta**.
- ˙e ˙tye, inf + aux inf. ¶ ˙muyye ˙tye (1481 Twusi 16:29b)

-ew- SEE **-epta**

-e wā, inf < **-e ota**

EY When not initial, /ey/ is not distinguished from /yey/, and there are places such as Masan and Mokpho which fail to distinguish the two syllables in any position. If you cannot find a word you seek under **ey**, try **yey, yay**, or ¹**yey**.
- ˙ey = - ˙Gey = - ˙key (adverbative)
˙ey, pcl (alt ˙ay) = **ey** (in, at; ...). VAR ˙uy(/ ˙oy), (after ⋯i, ⋯y, or ⋯ywu) ˙yey. See the notes under ˙yey and ˙uy. SEE ˙ey ˙sye; ˙ey ˙key.

NOTE: The MK locative / allative particle has the two shapes ˙ey and ˙ay; about .55 of the examples use ˙ay. The vowel of the preceding syllable partly determines the shape preference. After *a(C), o(C),* or *woC* only ˙ay occurs; in *sep [MWON]* ˙ey (1481 Twusi 7:9b) 'to the twig gate' the writer was probably following the nativized word *mwun* that would have been the normal spoken version, as attested in Hankul somewhat later (?1517- Pak 1:12b). After *e(C), u(C),* and *wu(C)* only ˙ey occurs, but *y* is inserted after *ywu* (perhaps indicating a high front rounded allophone for that syllable): *e ˙nu* ˙CHYWU ˙yey (1459 Wel 21:27a) 'to which hell', ˙CING- ¨CHYWU ˙yey ˙za pi ˙luse (1465 Wen 2:3:1:25a) 'not until one attains truth through substantiation'. After *i(C)* only ˙ey appears, and *y* is inserted after syllable-final *i*: ˙konon ˙pi yey n' (1481 Twusi 7:7b) 'in a fine rain', ¨twu ha ˙nol s so ˙zi ˙yey (1447 Sek 6:45b) 'between the two heavens'. There are no examples found for *uy(C),* but after *wuyC* there is only ˙ey, as in ˙SYA- ˙NGWUY ˙KWUYK ˙ey (1447 Sek 6:14b) 'in the state of Śrāvastī' and ¨twuy.h ey ˙nun (1445 ¹Yong 30) 'behind him', and after *wuy* only ˙yey, as in *swul ˙Gwuy* ˙yey (1481 Twusi 7:34a) 'to a wagon' and ¨ku y kwuy ˙yey s ˙SSILQ- ˙SYANG ˙i ˙la (1447 Sek 19:16a) 'that is the ear's reality'. After *oyC* and *woyC* only ˙ay is found, as in *moy ˙h ay s ˙mu.l ey* (1482 Kum-sam 3:34b) 'in the moorland streams' and ¨mwoy ˙h ay s kwo ˙c i (1482 Kum-sam 3:33a) 'the mountain flowers'.

including the *oy* of ˙*poy* ˙*yey n'* (1449 Kok 70) 'in the belly', the *woy* of MWON ˙NGWOY ˙*yey* (?1468⁻ Mong 12b) 'outside the discipline', the *ay* of *nwol*˙*Gay yey* (1445 ¹Yong 16) 'in the ballad', and the *yey* of SYEY ˙*yey* (1462 ¹Nung 6:66a) 'in the world'. There is one example of *eyC*: ¨*ney*˙*h ey* (1462 ¹Nung 6:17b) '[divide] into four'.

ey < ˙*ey* (˙*ay*, ˙*uy*, ˙*yey*), pcl. SEE **ey uy**; **-eyq-** < ˙*ey s*; **-um ey**. NOTE: Examples are marked (where known) for insertibility of **'ta (ka)** as follows: [1] both **ey 'ta** and **ey 'ta ka** occur; [2] **ey 'ta** is awkward, **ey 'ta ka** is rejected; [3] probably only **ey** occurs; [?] uncertain.

1. (time) at, in, on (CF **ulo**). ¶**achim** (**ōcen, ōhwu, cenyek**) ~ in the morning (forenoon, afternoon, evening). **pam** ~ at night. **ku cen/hwū** ~ before/after that. **twū si (sip-o pun)** ~ at (a quarter after) two. **il.yoil (achim)** ~ on Sunday (morning). **sikan cen** ~ in time. **Cēmsim ey pap ul teywe mek.ess.ta** At lunch time I heated up some rice and ate it.

2. (age) at. ¶**ilkop sal** ~ **hak.kyo ey kata** goes to school at the age of seven.

3. (place, static location) at, in, on; among. CF **ey se**. ¶**mun** ~ at the gate. **pang** ~ in the room. **chayk-sang wi** ~ on the table. **namu mith** ~ under the tree. **chang pakk** ~ outside the window. **sip pheyici** ~ on page ten. **Sewul** ~ **tōchak hata** arrives in Seoul. **kongcwung** ~ **nalta** flies in the air. **Kil palun phyen ey payk.hwa-cem i iss.ta** There is a department store on the right side of the street. **Ku ney nwukwu** '**la** '**n māl yo, ha mānh.un sālam ey ālq swu iss.e?** How will you know who he is among so many people? **Payk-ka sēng kacin sālam ey cāngki cal twunun i ka iss.ˢo** There is one who plays chess well among those bearing the surname Payk.

NOTE: In some cases either **ey** or **ey se** is used: **I maul ey (se) sāsip.nikka** Do you live in this village? **Cēnthwu ey (se) sūng.li hanta** They are victorious at war. **Kosan sik.mul cwung ey (se) etten kes i yūmyeng han ya** Among alpine plants which ones are well known? But in the example **Ttul ey kkoch tul i alum-tapta** 'The flowers are pretty in the field' **ey se** is rejected, as it is in **Hānkwuk ey san i mānh.ta** 'There are many mountains in Korea'; on the other hand **ey** is rejected in **Kosan sik.mul ey se etten kes i yūmyeng han ya** 'Of Alpine plants which ones are well known?' (in contrast with acceptance in the example **Kosan sik.mul cwung ey** ··· given above), and **ey se** is preferred (though **ey** is not rejected) in **sēykyey ey se yūmyeng hata** 'is well known in the world'. CF **ey se** 1 NOTE.

4. (place as goal) onto, into. ¶ [1] **chilphan** ~ **kul ul ssuta** writes on the blackboard. [1] **ip** ~ **tāmpayq-tay lul multa** holds a pipe in one's mouth. [1] **ttang** ~ **ttel.e cita** falls to the ground.

5. (specific direction) to, in; CF **kkaci, ulo, eykey lo, ul, ey lul, ey 'ta (ka)**. ¶**hak.kyo** ~ **kata** goes to school. **cēncayng** ~ **na-kata** goes (off) to war. **Cekcin ey tolkyek ita** ~ **ese naa kaca!** It's a charge on enemy lines — let's go!

6. (impersonal indirect object; CF **eykey**).

6a. to, for. ¶ [1] **unhayng** ~ **ponayta** sends it to the bank. [1] **tose-kwan** ~ **chayk ul kicung hata** donates a book to the library. [1] **tāy-hak.kyo** ~ **phyēnci lul ssuta** writes a letter to the university. **I pi nun nongsa ey khunq ¹iik ita** This rain is of great benefit to the farming (CM 1:000 — better with ··· ¹iik i toynta).

6b. (in passive conversions) by, with. CF 7a. ¶ [1] **kāmceng** ~ **salo cap.hita** is swayed by one's emotions. [1] **kōngpho** ~ **salo cap.hita** is seized with fear. **cha ey tachyess.ta** was injured by a car.

6c. (in causative conversions that make an institution the causee: optionally **eykey** or **hanthey** for **ey**). ¶**Munkyo-pu ka ku hak.kyo ey/eykey tung.lok-kum ul naylikey hayss.ta** The Ministry of Education made that school lower its enrollment fee.

7. (agent) by, with.

7a. ¶**pi** ~ **cec.ta** gets wet with rain. **chong-al** ~ **mac.ta** is hit by a bullet.

7b. ¶ [1] **Ku uy pak.hak ey nōllass.ta** I am astounded by (I marvel at) his wide learning. [2] **Kwuncwung i hwanhuy ey nemchiko iss.ta** The crowds are overflowing with joy — CF [?] **Kang ey mul i nemchinta** The river is overflowing. **Yenki ey katuk chan pang-an** a room filled with smoke.

8. (cause) for, because, since, from (CF **ulo, -ki ey, -killey, -ki lo**). ¶**kule haki (ttaymun) ey** since it is like that. **Chwuwi ey cēngsin i ēps.ess.ta** I was numb from (with, because of)

the cold. **Eceyq pam palam ey kkoch i mānh.i ttel.e cyess.ta** Many blossoms fell in the wind last night. **Tempinun palam ey chayk ul kacye kalq kes ul ic.e pelyess.ta** In my hurry I forgot to take my book. **Cīnanun kīm ey tullyess.ta** I dropped in as I was passing by. **Pek-chan kāmkyek ey nwun-mul i kulqseng kulqseng hayss.ta** Tears welled up from deep emotion.

9. (provocation) in response to, provoked by. ¶ [1] **Pulunun soli ey cam i kkayyess.ta** I woke up at the call. [1] **Kath.ci anh.unq īl ey hwā lul nāyl phil.yo ka eti iss.ey yo** Why get mad over unlikely things? [1] **Kulenq īl ey mwe l' nōpal-tāypal ia** Why get so mad about it?

10. (defiance) despite, in (the face / brunt of). ¶ [1 awkward] **I pi ey eti kasip.nikka** Where are you going in all this rain?! **I kyenghwang ey um.ak i tā mwe yo** With circumstances as they are what is all this music for? **Chwuwi ey etteh.key cīnays[y]ey yo** How are you making out in the cold weather? — This example might better go under meaning 1 or 3.

11. (contrast) against, on, in contrast (with), with, and. ¶ [1] **huyn pathang ey kum munuy** a gold figure on / against a white background. [1] **Ku ⁿyeca nun nolan cekoli ey tahong chima lul ip.ess.ta** She wore a yellow coat and a pink skirt.

12. (selective enumeration) and, and all that, and whatnot, and the like (CF **kwa, hako, ina, ey 'ta**). ¶ [1] **Swul ey koki ey cal mek.ess.ta** I have had enough drinks, meat, and the like. **Hyeng nim ey, nwuna ey, kuliko tongsayng ey, ne nun cham yele hyengcey ka iss.e se cōh.keyss.kwun a** (Mkk 1961:4:10) My, but it must be nice having an older brother and sister and a younger brother, all those siblings.

13. (assignment) as, to be, for. ¶**Wiwen-cang ey nwu ka sēnchwul toyess.nun ya** Who was elected head of the committee? **Chwal.yeng ey Pak Chikwuk, yēnchwul ey Seng Ilkak, cōmyeng ey Pyen Kummyeng ip.nita; um.ak ey nwukwu lul pāytang halq ka yo** Camerawork is Pak Chikwuk, the director Seng Ilkak, and the lighting Pyeng Kummyeng; who will be assigned the music? **"kāy pal ey cwusek phyenca" "tin horseshoes for a dog's foot"** = something inappropriate.

14. (proportion) at, in for, by, per. ¶ [1] **payk wen ~ phalta** sells it at / for a hundred **wen**. [?] **Selthang un han kun ey elma (i)p.nikka** How much is sugar a pound? [?] **halwu ~ twū pen** twice a day. [?] **sip-nyen ~ han pen** once in ten years.

15. (reference, relation) for, to, in, of, with respect to. ¶ [1] **kēnkang ~ cōh.ta** is good for one's health. [1] **sālam uy chincel ~ kāmsa hata** is thankful for one's kindness. [1] **cilmun ~ tāytap hata** answers a question. [1] **enu īl ~ kwankyey hata** is connected with a certain matter. [1] **kongpu haki ~ papputa** is busy (with one's) studying. [?] **Ku chayk un ilk.ki ey elyepta** The book is too difficult for me to read. [1] **saynghwal ~ hūngmi lul kacita** takes an interest in life. [?] **sālam ~ / eykey hūngmi lul kacita** takes an interest in (other) people. [?] **chwīmi ~ mac.ta** is to one's taste. [1] **Yeksi ku api ey ku atul ikwun!** Like father like son. [2] **I yak un wiq-pyēng ey cēy-il ita** This medicine is the best thing for stomach trouble. **kāmki ~ kellita / tullita** catches a cold. **ku sālam ~ kwan hay se** concerning that person. **sālam ~ cōsim hata** is wary / chary / cautious of people. **Ku nun na ey mōs-'c(i) anh.key him i sēyta** He is just as strong as I am.

16. attached to adv, (bnd) n, or n phrase. ¶**cey mul ~** of its own accord, by itself. **īwang (~)** already, now that ... . **kattuk ~** on top of everything else. **paykcwu ~** in broad daylight. **pulqsi ~** out of season; unexpectedly. **tanpak (~)** at once, instantly.

17. (MK) = ˙**kwa** (similar) to, (the same) as; (different) from.

'ey = yey (= **ie it is**)

'ey = [h]ey = hay, inf < **hata**. ¶**Mian 'ey = Mian hay** I'm sorry.

-ey [var] = **-e** (infinitive). Usually only before **ya** or **yo**, but sometimes sentence-final after **-ess-, -keyss-, iss-, ēps-, kath-,** and honorific (**-usey**).

-ey, suffix [partly < -˙*Gey* = -˙*key*].

1. [var] = **-ay** (makes n from v, with minor irregularities). ¶**chey** sieve < **chita** sifts; CF **chay** drumstick < **chita** beats. **ssēley** harrow < **ssēlita** harrows (a field). **tekkey** scum < **tekk.ta** (dirt) accumulates, cakes. **tuley** dignity, weight of character, stability < **tulta** enters (etc.). **(soy) kho-ttwuley** (ox) nose ring < **ttwulh-** pierce.

2. irreg der n (= -i). ¶**ceciley** botching < **ceciluta** spoils. **ssuley** (**cil**) sweeping < **ssulta** sweeps. **tul-mēy** tying straw sandals to one's feet < **tul-mēyta** (suffix overlaps stem?).

CF **swus cey** (< **ce-i**) sincerely, der adv < **swus cew-** be pure, sincere; **suley** < **sule-i** = **suli** der adv < **sulew-**; **mukey** (< **muke-i**) weight, der n < **mukew-** be heavy.

-ey, bnd adj-n (~ **hata**). rather ⋯ , like ⋯ . ¶**kentuley** < **kentul-ey** < **kentul** a bit tipsy, somewhat intoxicated. **kwuciley** < **kwucil-ey** < **kwucil** squalid, filthy. **ssuley** < **ssul-ey** < **ssulta** aslant; tottering. **ssupssuley** < **ssupssul-ey** < **ssupssul** (< *psu-*) a bit bitter. CF **-uley**.

-eyq- (= **ey uy**) < *ey s*, pcl + pcl. ¶**mom-eyq-kes** = **momq kes** menstrual blood. **os-eyq-i** body lice (pronounced both as /oseynni/ and as /oteynni/). ALSO: **aph-eyq-kes**, **cip-eyq-tōn**, ? **payan-eyq-meli**, **puttumak-eyq-sokum**, **soth-eyq-mul**, **twī-eyq-kes**, **wi-eyq-kes**.

ey a = *ey [z]a*, pcl + pcl (> **ey ya**). ¶*stwo es.ti i cuum ey a kos won ta* (1795 ¹No-cwung [P] 2:3a) = *stwo ⸱es⸱ti i cu⸱zu⸱m ey ⸱za kos won ⸱ta* (?1517⁻ ¹No 2:3b) and how is it that you have only come at just this time?

-e ya < **-e (y)a** < *-⸱e ⸱za*, inf + pcl. VAR **-ey ya**. [There is no *-**keyss.e ya**; CF **-ess.e ya**.]

1. only to the extent that ⋯ **can/does one** (⋯); if you don't ⋯ you can't (⋯); it is by ⋯**ing that you** (⋯); you have to ⋯ in order to (⋯); only when/if you ⋯ do you (⋯).

1a. ¶**Hay ya hanta** One must (should, has got to) do it. **Hayss.e ya hayss.ta** One should (ought to) have done it. **Kuleh.key hasyess.e ya hayss.ey yo** That is what you should have done. **Cil iya etteh.tun (ci) kaps ila to ssa ya halq kes ani yo** Regardless of the quality, [isn't it the case that =] surely the price should be kept low. SEE (**-e ya**) **toyta**.

1b. ¶**Pēm uy kwul ey tul.e ka ya pēm ul cap.nunta** You have to enter the tiger's cave to catch the tiger. **Chen wen i iss.e ya tul.e kanta** You have to have a thousand **wen** to get in. **Tol.a ka ya 'keyss.ˢup.nita** I'll have to be getting on home now. **Ce mo-thwungi lul palun ccok ulo tol.a ya keki kalq swu iss.ta** You have to turn to the right at that corner to get there. **Tōn i iss.e ya Mikwuk ey kanta** It takes money to go to America. **Mili māl-ssum tulyess.e ya hayss.(ess.)ulq kes ip.nita** He probably should have told you beforehand. **Cikum ce uy maum ul etteh.key māl-ssum tulye ya cōh.ulq ci molukeyss.ˢup.nita** I don't know just how I ought to describe my feelings at this moment.

2. granted (presuming) that, even if; (~ ⋯ **elma 'na** ⋯) however (much) one may/might, to whatever extent. ¶**Ney ka mek.e ya elma 'na mek.keyss.ni** You can't possibly eat very much. **Ku i ka pūca 'la 'y ya** [or **pūca 'la (ko hay) ya**] **elma 'na tōn i iss.keyss.n' ya** However wealthy he may be, he surely cannot have all that much money. **Iyaki hay ya musun sō.yong i iss.na** What is the use of talking? **I yak ul mek.e pwā ya pyel sō.yong i ēps.e yo** (Im Hopin 1987:120) Taking this medicine does me no good. **Nal.e ya phali yo ttwie ya pyelwuk ita** You can fly no farther than a fly and jump no higher than a flea.

3. (connecting with aux). SEE ~ **iss.ta**, ~ **noh.ta**, ~ **pota**, ~ **twuta**.

4. SEE ~ **man**, ~ **tul**.

-e ya 'ci, inf + pcl + abbr < **haci**. must don't-you-see (often shows surprise, astonishment, or dismay). ¶**Ccak ul cca kaciko nol.i lul sīcak hay ya 'ci** Let's choose up sides before we start playing. **Nay ka han kes chelem pota (nun) cal hay ya 'ci** You must do it better than the way I did. **Him i iss.e ya 'ci** (I would have to have strength =) But I haven't got the strength! **Ūmsik ul ku man ce man mek.e ya 'ci** You have got to eat reasonably, you know (= How can I afford to feed such a glutton!). **Tōn i mue yekan tul.e ya 'ci** It costs so much money, you see, ⋯ (that I can't afford it). **Hay cwue ya (mue l' ha)ci** Why doesn't it ⋯ ? What can you do to make it (so that) ⋯ ? **Īl ul ku man twutun ci hay ya 'ci kuleh.key aphe se etteh.key hani** You may as well (or: You really ought to) leave off working where you are — how can you stay on in such agony? **Na nun mōlla yo mue sacin-ki hana sa cwue ya 'ci mue** I dunno, but you just have to buy me a camera (anyway). **Hal-ape' nim kkey lang to kac'ta tulye ya 'ci** I will have to take them to Grandfather and everyone, as well. **Pumo nim kkey puthe māl-ssum tulye ya 'ci** You should tell your parents first. **Hyeng nim kkey ya māl lo allye ya 'ci** It is my brother that I should inform. **Mue āmu 'na tā kulen cwul āna?** Do

you think I am just like (just as bad/mean/ dishonest) as the rest? **Oci mālla 'y to cakkwu onun tey ya na 'n tul etteh.k' 'elq tōli ka iss.e ya 'ci?!** What can I do when he keeps on coming here though I tell him not to?! **Ām, yenghwa pole ya ka ya 'ci!** Oh sure, by all means I simply must go see the movie!
~ **man hay / tōy** SAME
~ **yo.** ¶**Ppallay pich i huytolok ppal.e ya 'ci yo** You have to wash the clothes until they become clean and white.
VAR **-ey ya 'ci, -ey yey 'ci**; often **-e ya toyci**.
-e ya hata SEE **-e ya** 1a.
-e ya iss.ta, inf + pcl + aux. ¶**Nal mata anc.e ya iss.ess.ta** I was just seated day after day.
-e ya 'keyss.ta = -e ya hakeyss.ta will have to do.
-e ya man, inf + pcl + pcl. ¶**San i noph.a ya man kyengchi ka alum-tapta** For scenery to be beautiful you've got to have tall mountains. **Pantusi iss.e ya man hanun ka ka mūncey 'ta** (M 1:2:417) The problem is whether we really have to have it. **Ku tul un pamq cwung ey wā ya man hayss.ˢup.nita** They could only come in the middle of the night [loose reference].
-e ya mangceng ici [DIAL] = **-ki ey mangceng**.
-e ya 'nta = -e ya hanta has to do
-e ya noh.ta, inf + pcl + aux. ¶**Phyēnci lul sse ya noh.ass.ci** I did get the letter just written, you see.
-e ya pota, inf + pcl + aux. ¶(?) **Com mek.e ya pwā la** Try just eating a bit.
-e ya toyta SEE **toyta**
-e ya tul, inf + pcl + pcl. ¶**Kongpu hay ya tul hanta** (= **kongpu tul hay ya hanta = kongpu hay ya hanta tul**) You children must study.
-e ya twuta, inf + pcl + aux. ¶(?) **Ku nom i ¹noymul ul pat.e ya twuess.kwun** That bastard had to get his bribe, I see!
ey chelem, pcl + pcl. ¶**Ku tayk ey chelem son nim i mānh.i chac.e onun cip un ēps.ta** There is no (other) house that has as many callers as that one seems to.
-ey 'ci [var] = **-e ya haci**
ey cocha, pcl + pcl [CF **cocha ey**]. ¶**Cip ey cocha ēps.uni to-taychey et' ey l' kass.ulq ka** He isn't home, even; I wonder where on earth he could have gone. **Chayk pang ey cocha ēps.uni et' ey se i chayk ul kwu halq swu iss.ulq ka yo** I wonder where I can get hold of this book; it isn't even in the bookstores.

-ey hata SEE **-ey**
ey iss.e (se), particle + quasi-vi inf (+ particle). [FORMAL, bookish, or emphatic] = **ey** or **ey se**; CF **eykey iss.e se**. ¶**Haksik ey iss.e ku ey tāy halq sālam i ēps.ta** There is no one his equal in learning. **Na nun ku cem ey iss.e ne wa ūykyen ul talli hanta** I disagree with you there. **I kil ey iss.e se ku wi ey kalq sālam un ēps.ta** He is the best in this line.
ey iss.e se 'na (cop advers). ¶**swūq-cek ulo 'na sā.yong pinto ey iss.e se 'na** either by number or in frequency of use.
ey iss.e se nun (pcl). ¶**wuli ka ānun hān ey iss.e se nun** (NKd 5926b) to the best of our knowledge.
ey iss.e se uy (pcl). ¶**cinceng han ūymi ey iss.e se uy kwuk-munhak** a national literature in the true sense of the word.
ey ka, pcl + pcl [colloq].
1. to/at/in ⋯ [as complement] ¶**Nam Tāymun un Phyengyang ey ka ani 'la Sewul ey iss.ta** South Gate is not in Phyengyang, it's in Seoul.
2. emphatic locative / allative. ¶**Eti ey ka kulen key iss.nun ya** Where is there any such thing?! NOTE: The example give (as emphatic) at the top of CM 1:144 (**chilphan ey ka ⋯ nam.un kulq-ca ⋯**) is rejected.
eykey < ˙ᵘ⁄ₒy key (˙ᵘ⁄ₒy kungey, ˙ᵘ⁄ₒy ke˙kuy), pcl. (personal / animate indirect object) to, at, for, by (a living creature). ABBR **'key**. HON **kkey**. SYN **hanthey (henthey)**; CF **poko, tele,** ˙ᵘ⁄ₒy ¨swon-toy.
1. 1a. ['**ta** and '**ta ka** can be freely inserted] ¶**haksayng eykey** (⋯) **cwuta** gives the student some paper. **sacang eykey** (⋯) **kuleh.key māl hata** tells the boss that. ⁿ**yeca eykey** (⋯) **chwī hata** is intoxicated with a woman. **cek eykey** (⋯) **chong ul kyenwuta** aims a gun at the enemy. **atul eykey** (⋯) **tōn ul cwuta** gives money to one's son. **wuli eykey** (⋯) **phyēnci lul ssuta** writes us a letter. **nam eykey** (⋯) **īl ul hay cwuta** does the work for someone else. **Nay ka Payk kwun tāysin Mikwuk ey iss.nun chinkwu eykey** (⋯) **phyēnci lul Yenge lo sse cwess.ta** I wrote a letter in English for young Payk to his friend in America. **Son i tongsayng eykey** (⋯) **tah.ass.ta** His hand touched his little brother.
1b. [inserted '**ta ka** unlikely] ¶**emeni eykey tol.a ota** returns to his mother. **ku nom tul**

eykey sokta is deceived by those rascals. nam eykey cici anh.ta cannot stand losing to others. Hal-apeci eykey kamyen kwaynchanh.ta You may go to your grandfather (1936 Roth 548). Ku sālam eykey n' khun pyēn iess.ta He had a serious accident. Chengcwung tul eykey mian hanq īl ip.nita I am very sorry for the inconvenience to the audience.

2. (with causative conversions ['ta and 'ta ka can be freely inserted]) ¶haksayng eykey (…) chayk ul poita shows the book to the student. nam eykey (…) īl ul hakey hata has someone else do the job. ai eykey (…) pap ul mek.ita feeds the child. ku sālam eykey cing ul cap.hita has him take the gong. CF Sensayng i haksayng ul sikhye se pumo eykey (…) phyēnci lul ssukey hayss.ta The teacher had the student write a letter to his parents.

3. (with passive conversions).

3a. ¶nam eykey ('ta (ka)) tōn ul mek.hita gets one's money swindled away by others. [1]Nosea hāykwun i Ilpon hāykwun eykey (?*'ta (ka)) kyekpha lul tang hayss.ta The Russian navy suffered a defeat at the hands of the Japanese navy.

3b. ¶kwancwung tul eykey millita gets/is pushed by the spectators.

NOTE 1: In some cases either eykey or ey can be used: wēn-swungi ey/eykey hūngmi lul kacita takes an interest in monkeys; ōykwuk sālam ey/eykey hūngmi lul kacita takes an interest in foreigners; i yak un wiq-pyēng hwānca eykey/ey cēy-il ita This medicine is the best thing for stomach sufferers. Certain set phrases prefer ey even for people: uy hay se, ttal[e]/a se, kwan hay se, tāy hay se (in some of the meanings – see tāy hata); mōs-'ci anh.ta; cōsim hata. SEE ey iss.e (se), eykey iss.e (se).

NOTE 2: The example haksayng tul eykey [1]yohay ka kiph.ta (CM 1:156) is rejected in favor of haksayng tul ey tāy hanq [1]īhay ka kiph.ta 'has a deep understanding of students'.

eykey ccum, pcl + pcl [awkward, because eykey is not quite colloquial enough for the expression] = hanthey ccum. ~ iya (= ccum eykey ya). ¶Ku sālam eykey ccum iya cici anh.ulq ke 'lq sey I won't give in to the likes of him.

eykey chelem, pcl + pcl [a bit awkward]. ¶Na eykey chelem talun sālam eykey to tāy hanta 'myen motwu ku lul cōh.a hal they 'n tey If he would behave toward others the way he does toward me he would be loved by everyone.

eykey cocha, pcl + pcl. ¶Ku nun an[h]ay eykey cocha allici anh.ko cip ul na-kass.ta He left home without letting even his wife know.

eykey hako, pcl + pcl (= eykey wa). [a bit awkward] ¶Kim ssi eykey hako ku uy puin eykey man sosik ul allye cwuess.ta I told the news to Mr Kim and his wife only.

eykey iss.e (se), pcl + quasi-vi inf (+ pcl). [FORMAL, bookish, or emphatic] = eykey (se); CF ey iss.e (se). ¶Pōko lul pon-hōyuy ey se cīnswul hakey toyn kes un na eykey iss.e se kacang khunq yengkwang ip.nita It is a very great honor for me to have the opportunity to present a report to this conference. Haksayng tul eykey iss.e se kacang khun kwaep i mues ikeyss.[s]up.nikka What is the most important task for students?

eykey ka, pcl + pcl. ¶Kim sensayng eykey ka ani 'la Pak sensayng eykey cwuess.ta I gave it to Mr Pak, not to Mr Kim.

eykey khenyeng, pcl + pcl = hanthey khenyeng
eykey kkaci, pcl + pcl = hanthey kkaci
eykey 'ko (= eykey iko, pcl + cop ger) SEE iko.
eykey l', abbr < eykey lul
eykey lang, pcl + pcl = hanthey lang
eykey 'la to, pcl + cop var inf + pcl. ¶Kim sensayng eykey 'la to mul.e polq ka Shall I ask Mr Kim, maybe?

eykey lo, pcl + pcl. toward/to (a person). ¶atul ~ on phyēnci a letter that has come to/for my son. Ku hemul i nwukwu eykey lo tol.a kalq ka I wonder just who that mistake goes back to? Emeni eykey lo kake la Go to your mother. Salang i ku eykey lo olm.kye kass.ta Her love shifted to him.

eykey lo puthe, pcl + pcl + pcl. from (a person/creature). ¶Wel.nam ey ka iss.nun namphyen eykey/hanthey lo puthe (= … eykey/hanthey se) phyēnci lul pat.ess.ta I got a letter from my husband who is away in Vietnam.

eykey lo uy, pcl + pcl + pcl [awkward]. ¶Ku nun an[h]ay eykey lo uy salang i chacha sik.e kam ul nukkyess.ta He felt his affection for his wife gradually cooling.

eykey lul, pcl + pcl [emphatic]. to a person. ¶Hyeng nim eykey lul kanun tocwung ita I am on my way to my brother's.

eykey mace, particle + particle. ¶Ku eykey mace cyess.uni māl i ani 'ta You should be ashamed of yourself, getting beaten by him, too.

eykey man, pcl + pcl. just/only to (at/for/by) a person. ¶Na eykey man chayk.im i iss.nun ke n' ani 'ta I am not the only one who is responsible. I kes un kwahak-ca eykey man kwan.lyen toyn mūncey nun ani 'ta This is not a problem concerning scientists only.

~ **ila to**. ¶Yele salam eykey tā cwuci mōs han tāysin ey ku sālam eykey man ila to cwulq ke l' kulayss.e While I couldn't give to everybody, I should have given something at least to him.

eykey mankhum, pcl + pcl. ~ **man**. ~ **un**.

eykey mata, pcl + pcl. [replaces older mata eykey] ¶Āmu sālam eykey mata sinsey lul ciko iss.ta He owes an obligation to everyone he knows.

eykey n', abbr < **eykey nun**

eykey 'na, pcl + cop adversative. to/at/for/by a person (creature); whether to/at/for/by; to/at/ for/by whatever person (creature). ¶Nwukwu eykey 'na kkwum un iss.ta 'ney Everyone has his own dream, you know. Āmu eykey 'na mul.e pokey Ask just anybody.

eykey 'na-ma, pcl + cop extended advers. ¶Ku eykey 'na-ma allye cwulq ke l' kulayss.e I should have let HIM know at least.

eykey 'n tul, pcl + cop mod + postmod. even though (it be) to/at/for/by a person (creature); to/at/for/by a person (or creature) too. ¶Ku sālam i na eykey 'n tul kulen māl ul hal lī ka iss.keyss.na? Why should he confide in ME? Na eykey 'n tul casik ul salang hanun maum i ēps.keyss.ˢo? Why shouldn't I have affection for my own child?

eykey nun, particle + particle. as for to/at/for/ by a person (creature). ¶Wuli eykey nun mōs cwunun ya You are not giving US any? ABBR eykey n', 'key nun, 'key n'.

eykey pota, particle + pcl. ¶Emeni eykey pota apeci eykey mul.e posey yo You had better ask Father (about that) rather than Mother.

eykey puthe, particle + pcl. ¶Pumo nim eykey puthe māl-ssum tulye ya 'ci You ought to tell your parents first (and then other people).

eykey se, particle + particle.

1. from (a person). ¶atul ~ phyēnci ka ota gets a letter from one's son. I tōn i nwukwu eykey se na-wass.nun ya Who(m) did this money come from? Ku māl ul chinkwu eykey se tul.ess.ta I heard that from a friend.

? 2. (oblique subject). SEE kkey se, ey se.

eykey sekken, pcl + pcl. SEE hanthey lang.

eykey se mata, pcl + pcl + pcl. ¶Yele sensayng nim eykey se mata phyēnci lul pat.e sōngkwu sulepki hān i ēps.ˢup.nita I am overwhelmed beyond measure to receive letters from each of you gentlemen.

eykey se n', abbr < **eykey se nun**

eykey se 'n tul. Example under **eykey se to**.

eykey se nun, pcl + pcl + pcl. ¶Atul eykey se nun phyēnci ka wass.ci man ttal eykey se nun an wass.ta A letter came from my son, but not from my daughter.

eykey se puthe, pcl + pcl + pcl. ¶Aph ey sun sālam eykey se puthe tōn ul ketwusey yo Collect the money from the person(s) standing in front first.

eykey se to, particle + particle + particle.

1. from (a person) too/even/either. ¶Apeci eykey se to phyēnci ka an wass.ta I didn't get a letter from my father either. Elin eykey se to ku mankhum hyōqkwa lul ketwess.nun tey ēlun eykey se 'n tul an toyl lī ka iss.na? When you've got results like that even from children surely you will from grown-ups, too!

? 2. (oblique subject) too/even/either.

eykey se tul = **hanthey se tul**, pcl + pcl + pcl. ¶Sensayng nim eykey se tul yātan mac.ess.ta They got a scolding from their teacher.

eykey se ya, pcl + pcl + pcl. ~ **tul**. ¶Pumo eykey se ya tul saks(-ton) ul pat.ulq swu iss.na?! How can they possibly let their parents pay them for what they do?!

eykey 'ta (ka), pcl + cop transferentive (+ pcl): SEE eykey. ¶Nwukwu eykey 'ta ilen māl ul hay Just who do you think you're talking to? or: Just who(m) could I tell this to?

eykey to, particle + particle. to/at/for/by a person (creature) also/even. ¶Kim sensayng ~ Pak sensayng ~ phyēnci lul ssunta writes letters both to Mr Kim and to Mr Pak. atul ~ anʰay ~ tōn ul mōs cwunta he gives money neither to his son nor to his wife. pyēng nan sālam ~ īl ul hakey hanta works even the ill people.

eykey tul, pcl + pcl. ¶Ku i eykey tul kūlim ul kūlikey hasipsio Get them to draw pictures.

eykey uy, pcl + pcl. (the one) to, at for, by (a person / creature). **Kim sensayng ~ phyēnci** the letter to Mr Kim.

eykey wa, pcl + pcl [? awkward]. ¶**Apeci eykey wa emeni eykey n' māl-ssum tulyess.una talun sālam eykey nun ilchey māl haci anh.ess.ta** I told Father and Mother, but said nothing to anyone else.

eykey ya, particle + pcl. ¶**Ku sālam eykey ya cikcep mul.e polq swu iss.na yo?** How could we dare ask him directly? **Na eykey ya hal māl i ēps.keyss.ci yo** To ME he wouldn't have anything to say (by way of complaint / excuse). **~ māl lo.** ¶**Tangsin eykey ya māl lo i chayk i phil.yo hap.nita** It is YOU indeed who need this book. **Ku eykey ya māl lo i sāqken un khun thākyek iess.^{s}up.nita** It was for HIM that this incident was a great shock.

ey khenyeng, pcl + pcl. ¶**Hōysa ey khenyeng cip ey to phyēnci lul mōs nāyss.ta** I was unable to get a letter off home, much less to the office.

-eyki, diminutive suf (var < -eki; DIAL < -ayki). **ssuleyki** rubbish (**ssuley** < **ssulta** sweeps + **-eyki**).

ey kkaci, pcl + pcl. up to, to. ¶[1]**nōin ul catong-cha ey kkaci puchwuk hay cwuta** helps the old man to the car. **onul ey (iluki) kkaci cen ha.ye cyess.ta** has been handed down to the present day.

ey 'ko = ey iko, pcl + cop ger. SEE **iko**.

ey kwan han, ey kwan ha.ye (hay se) SEE **kwan hata**

ey l', abbr < **ey lul**

-'e 'y'la, inf + abbr < **i'la** (cop). makes an emotive exclamation (= **-e la**). ¶**'syeyn me'li yey 'pi.ch i ['ˉ]ep.se 'y'la** (1481 Twusi 8:70a) there is a lack of luster to white hair. **ˉwon 'kil'h ol ni'ce 'y'la** (1482 Nam 1:28b) why, I forget the road I came! **'na y syel'hun lyang un 'i i'sye 'yla** (?1517- Pak 1:62a) I have thirty taels of silver!

ey lang, pcl + pcl. 1. (= **ey sekken**) ¶**Hak.kyo (ey) lang tā tull(y)e okeyss.ta** I'll drop in at the school and so on.
2. = **ey hako** (= **ey wa**).

ey 'la to, pcl + cop var inf + pcl. even though (it be) to / at / in ··· ; just to / at / in ··· , to / at / i ··· some / any. ¶**Ku mutewun tey; et' ey pataq ka ey 'la to ka-pwass.umyen cōh.keyss.ta** Gee but it's hot (and humid); I wish I could just get out to the beach (at least). **Ānnay-so ey 'la to ka se al.e polq ka** Shall I try inquiring at the information desk, maybe? **Kalq tey ēps.umyen wuli cip ey 'la to wā iss.key** If you don't have any place to stay why don't you come and stay at my house? [1]**Imsi (lo) pyek ey 'la to kel.e twusipsio** Hang it on the wall for the time being. CF **ey to, ey 'n tul**.

ey llang, pcl + pcl [slang, obs] = **ey nun. ~ un** SAME. ¶**Ku kos ey llang kaci mal.e** Don't go to THAT place!

ey lo, pcl + pcl. to, toward (used instead of **ulo** to avoid possible confusion with the meaning 'by means of'). ¶**sāhoy cwuuy ~ kanun kil** the road leading to socialism.

ey lo uy, pcl + pcl + pcl. ¶**sāhoy cwuuy ~ kil** the road to socialism. **I kes i mincwu cwuuy ey lo uy ches tankyey 'ta** This is the first step toward democracy.

ey lul, pcl + pcl. [colloq] to (marks goal of motion). ¶**Sikol ey lul kani-kka n' piloso cham-mal Cosen ey on kes kath.tukwun yo** Going to the countryside I suddenly felt for the first time that I had truly come to Korea. ABBR **ey l'**. CF **ey, ul**.

ey mace, pcl + pcl. ¶**Kulen sāqken i sinmun ey mace naci anh.ess.uni wēynq īl ilq ka yo** How come such an incident isn't even in the papers? **Hak.kyo ey mace an wass.uni to-taychey et' ey l' kass.ulq ka** He didn't show up even at school; I wonder where on earth he could have gone.

ey man, pcl + pcl. just (only) to / at / in ··· . ¶**Tapang ey man tuna-tunta** He does nothing but visit teahouses. CF **man ey**.

-eymi, suf [var] = **-emi. kwulleymi** a wooden wheel < **kwuluta** rolls.

ey n', abbr < **ey nun**

'ey n', abbr < **'ey 'nun**. ¶**alph ˉtwuy'h ey n'** (1449 Kok 70) in front and behind. **yes'us ka'ci s ˉccwoy 'non ··· ˉsey'h ey n' ··· ˉney'h ey n' ··· ye'su's ey n' ···** (1447 Sek 24:2b) of the six sins, ··· and the third is ··· and the fourth ··· and the sixth ··· . **kolom s kil'h ey n'** (1481 Twusi 7:6a) along the river path.

ey 'na, pcl + cop advers. to / at / in ··· or the like (or something); whether to / at / in ··· ; to / at / in ··· whatever. ¶**Pam ey 'na onta 'ney** She (says that she) will be back around evening. **Sīcang**

ey 'na kass.ta oca Let's go to the market or something. **Yenghwa ey 'na kalq ka yo?** How about going to a movie? **Chen wen ey 'na sapsita** I'll buy it for a thousand **wen**. **Ku os ul os cang ey 'na neh.e twusey yo** Put those clothes in the closet, please.

'ey "na, pcl + cop advers. ¶ 'skwu.m ey "na ¨TTYWOW-CYWUW 'lol pwon 'ta (?1468⁻ Mong 58a) did you dream of the state of Zhào?

ey 'na-ma, pcl + copula extended adversative. ¶ **Ku kos ey 'na-ma apeci ka kyēysyess.umyen cōh.keyss.ta** I wish Father were THERE at least (if he can't be some place better). **Cip ey 'na-ma han pen ka-pwass.umyen cōh.keyss.ˢo** I wish I could at least have a visit home.

-eyngi, dimin suf, HEAVY ↔ **-angi**. **ppulyengi** < **ppuli** root.
- 'ey-ngi "ta = - 'e-ngi "ta. ¶ 'i syey-ngi '[']ta, kis 'key-ngi "ta (?1517⁻ ¹No 1:55b). CF - 'ay-ngi "ta; -u 'lyeyngi 'ta = -u 'l ye 'y-ngi "ta.

ey 'n ka = **ey in ka** (pcl + cop mod + postmod). ¶ **Cāngkap ul eti ey 'n ka twuko wass.ta** I've left my gloves somewhere.

ey 'n tul, particle + copula mod + postmodifier. even though (it be) to/at/in ⋯ ; even, also, too. ¶ **Ku-man han kes un wuli cip ey 'n tul ēps.ul ya** What makes you think we would not have such a thing at our house too? CF **ey ('la) to**.

ey nun, pcl + pcl. as for to/at/in ⋯ . ¶ **na poki** ~, **nay sayngkak** ~ in my opinion. **Yēnkuk ey nun twū kaci cōng.lyu ka iss.ta** There are two kinds of drama. **Kulay Mikwuk ey nun ēncey tte-nasilq yēyceng ip.nikka** So, when are you leaving for the States? ABBR **ey n'**.

'ey 'nun, pcl + pcl. ¶ ¨twuy.h ey 'nun ⋯ al 'ph oy 'non ⋯ (1445 ¹Yong 30) behind ⋯, ahead ⋯ .

ey nun khenyeng, pcl + pcl + pcl. ¶ **Hōysa ey nun khenyeng cip ey to phyēnci lul mōs nāyss.ta** I was unable to get a letter off home, much less to the office.

-e yo, inf + pcl. POLITE statement (= **-ta**), question (= **-ni?**, **-nun ya** etc.), command (= **-e la**, **-ula**), or suggestion (= **-ca**). CF **-ey yo**.

NOTE: We do not know just when **-e yo** came into use, but 1894 Gale 3 has *-e ywo* (including *ho.ye ywo* "pronounced *hoy ywo*") as "Respectful forms — in very common use", putting *-ciwo* (?= *-ci ywo*) with *howo* (= *hao*) as "forms used among friends, equals". SEE **-ci yo** (p. 453, **-ci** 1 NOTE).

-e yo man, inf + pcl + pcl. SEE **-keyss.e** (yo man).

-e yo tul, inf + pcl + pcl. ¶ **Mek.e yo tul** They're eating; Let's eat; You people eat!

-eypi [var] = **-epi**

ey pota, pcl + pcl. ¶ **I kūlim ul i ccok pyek ey pota ce ccok pyek ey kēnun key cōh.keyss.ney** We'd better hang this picture on the wall on that side rather than on the wall on this side.

ey puthe, pcl + pcl. ¶ **Sewul ey puthe kapsita** Let's go to Seoul first (and then go to the other places). **Aycho (ey) puthe kulen sālam kwa nun sangcong ul mal.ess.e ya hanun ke ya** You should have avoided associating with a man like him from the beginning.

-eys- = **-eyq-**

'ey s, pcl + pcl. ¶ ¨nwu 'n ey s 'tol (1482 Kum-sam 2:61b) moonlight on the snow. ¨SYWUY-TYWUNG 'ey 'pcon 'ma.s i 'm ye (1482 Kum-sam 3:39a) there is a salty taste to the water, and ⋯ . *moy 'h ay s kil 'h ey s 'noy lol* (1482 Nam 1:49b) the smoke that is on the path on the moor. *mulGuy s 'pwonwon elkwu 'l i 'skwu 'm ey s elkwul 'kot ho 'm ye* (1459 Wel 2:53a) all the faces one sees are like faces in a dream, and ⋯ . *pwuthye s wu[h] s ip-si Gwu 'l ey s the 'li hona 'h i na 'ma is 'kesi 'nol* (1447 Sek 23:56b) since there remained a single hair from Buddha's upper lip. ˢO-¨TTAY 'Gwa ¨NGWO-¨QWUN 'kwa y ke 'wulwu 'ey s ¨SSYANG 'i 'kot 'ho.ya ⋯ (1482 Kum-sam 3:31a) the mahābhūta (the four elements) and the pañca-skandha (the five components of an intelligent being) are like distinctive marks (lakṣana) in a mirror. ¨ta ˙SYENG-ZIN 'ey s ¨sa 'lo.m il 'ss oy (1447 Sek 6:45b) as they are all [among the] holy men ⋯ . SEE 'yey s, 'ay s, 'uy s, 'oy s.

- 'e 'ys-, abbr < - 'e is- (inf + aux).
- 'e 'ys.ke 'tun. SEE 'ho 'ya 'ys.ke 'tun.

ey se < 'ey 'sye, pcl + pcl.

1. (default / dynamic location) happening at / in (a place). ¶ **tāy-hak.kyo** ~ **kongpu hata** studies at the university. **cip** ~ **īl hata** works at home. **kongwen** ~ **sānqpo lul hata** takes a stroll in the park. **Ku pun i Pusan ey se Yenge lul kaluchinta** He teaches English in Pusan.

NOTE: For some verbs either **ey se** or **ey** can be used (CM 1:157): ¹**yekwan ey (se) memunun son nim** a guest staying at a hotel, ¹**yekwan ey (se) swīnun son nim** a guest resting at a hotel, san tul ey (se) phinun kkoch flowers blooming in the mountains, photay wi ey (se) nallinun kiq-pal the flag flying over the gun battery. But for some other verbs only one or the other occurs: aph ey nam.un / sun sālam the man left / standing in front, ttul ey se wūnun sāy tul the birds singing in the fields. Notice also Sewul ey se nun pec kkoch i han-chang ita In Seoul the cherry blossoms are in full bloom; Ilpon ey se yākwu ka tāy-inqki 'ta In Japan baseball is very popular. With iss.ta (and also ēps.ta, mānh.ta, hun hata, katuk hata, cēkta, tumulta) the choice depends on the meaning of the referent noun: kāngtang ey iss.tun phiano the piano (that was there) in the lecture room, kāngtang ey se iss.tunq īl the event (that was happening) in the lecture room. CF CM 1:154, Mkk 1961:4:8-11. Notice the contrast: Tāyhak ey se haksayng ulo iss.ta 'I am at the university as a student' ≠ Tāyhak ey iss.ta 'I am (or: It is) at the university'. In addition to sikol ey (se) sānta for 'lives in the country' there is also sikol sānta (CF Dupont 203).

2. from (a place, a position, a status, a group, a number); CF puthe. ¶Phyengyang ~ ota comes from Phyengyang. kicha ~ naylita gets off (down from) the train. pang ~ na-ota comes out of the room. Yel ey se twūl ul ppāymyen yetelp i nāmnunta When you take two from ten it leaves eight. Sengkong un sayngkak ham ey se pilos hanta Success begins with thinking (from the thought of it). Na nun wuli ilhayng ey se ttel.e cyess.ta I got lost from my group.

3. (impersonal oblique subject – groups, institutions; CF i/ka). ¶Sewul kyohyangak-tan ey se Pichang Kyohyangak ul hanta 'nta The Seoul Symphony Orchestra is playing the Symphonie Pathétique, you know. Hōysa ey se na hanthey sikyey lul cwuess.ta The company gave me a watch. Wuli hak.kyo ey se ikyess.ta Our school won (the game). Wuli kyōhoy ey se um.ak ¹yeypay lul hanun tey kkok osey yo Our church is having a musical service; please come. CF kkey se, (mata) puthe.

NOTE: Hak.kyo ey se ola 'nta (Dupont 203) can mean: (1) 'The school tells us to come', (2) 'Someone says the school wants us to come', or (3) 'Someone says for us to come [here / there] from school'.

4. [colloq] from a person (= eykey se); a person (as oblique subject – limited usage). ¶An ey se na-kass.ta My wife is out.

5. [lit] = pota than. ¶I ey se te khun salang i ēps.nani [= ēps.nun i] There is surely no greater love than this. CF 1881 Ridel 37 "in books, but not in conversation, pwota is often replaced by ey sye".

'ey se = [h]ey se = hay se (inf < hata + pcl).

ey se chelem, pcl + pcl + pcl. ¶Ku nun ēncey 'na musun māl ul hal ttay nun cayphan-kwan aph ey se chelem phyoceng i kwut.e cinta Whenever he talks he gets stiff as if he were before a judge.

ey se cocha, pcl + pcl + pcl. ¶Ōykwuk (ey) se cocha ku uy ilum ul molunun sālam i ēps.ta His name is known to everyone, even in other countries. Hak.kyo (ey) se cocha ccoch.kye nass.uni ku nom to incey n' tā tōyss.ci The rascal's had it now – he's been thrown out of school.

ey se hako, pcl + pcl + pcl. ¶Kyōhoy ey se hako cel ey se uy nukkim i etteh.key talun ka What difference do you feel between being in a chapel and being in a Buddhist temple?

ey se ka, pcl + pcl + pcl. at / in / from ··· [as complement]. ¶Kongwen ey se ka ani 'la cengke-cang ey se yess.ta It was not at the park, it was at the railroad station. Ku ka kulenq īl ul hanun kes un nala lul salang ham ey se ka ani 'la casin ul wi ham ey se 'ta His doing such a thing is not from loving his country but from promoting himself.

ey se khenyeng, pcl + pcl + pcl. ¶Cip ey se khenyeng hak.kyo ey ka se to kongpu lul an hanta 'p.nita He doesn't study even after he gets to school, much less at home!

ey se kkaci, pcl + pcl + pcl. ¶Hak.kyo (ey) se kkaci tung.lok-kum ollinta ko hani yātan ici yo They are talking of raising school tuition and it is making quite a stir.

ey se 'ko = ey se iko, pcl + pcl + copula ger. SEE iko.

ey sekken, pcl + pcl. SEE ey lang.

ey se lang, pcl + pcl + pcl. ¶Iwus cip ey se lang tā ne l' polye ko chac.e wass.ess.ta The folks next door all came to see you. SYN ey se sekken.

ey se ’la to, pcl + pcl + cop var inf + pcl. even though it (may) be in/at/from. ¶Pyel lo kalq tey ka ēps.uni kukcang ey se ’la to sikan ul ponay ya ’keyss.kwun Since I have no place in particular to go, I guess I'll just have to kill time at some theater. **Pi wā se sophung ul mōs kamyen cip ey se ’la to nōlki lo hapsita** If rain keeps us from going off for an outing let's have fun at home, even so. **Wuli nun āmuli elyewunq īl ey se ’la to twulyewe haci anh.nunta** We are not afraid in any situation, however difficult it may be.

ey se mace, pcl + pcl + pcl. ¶Ku nun cikcang ey se mace miwum ul pat.ko iss.ta He is disliked even at his workplace. **Ku kos ey se mace chwupang tang hayss.ˢup.nita** He was banished even from that place.

ey se mace puthe, pcl + pcl + pcl + pcl [perhaps a bit awkward]. ¶Hak.kyo ey se mace puthe thōyhak ul tang hayss.uni etteh.k' hamyen cōh.so Now that you've even been expelled from school, what will you do?!

ey se man, pcl + pcl + pcl. only (just) at/in/from …. ¶Sitan ey se man wuli nala uy kipayk ul polq swu iss.ta The spirit of Korea can be (truly) seen only in the field of poetry.

~ ila to. ¶Honam cipang ey se man ila to phungcak i toymyen cōh.keyss.nun tey I hope there will be good crops at least in the Honam area.

ey se mankhum, pcl + pcl + pcl. ¶Cip ey se nun tose-kwan ey se mankhum kongpu ka cal an toynta I can't study at home as well as I can in the library.

ey se mata, pcl + pcl + pcl [replaces older mata ey se] ¶Cip cip mata (ey) se nolay soli ka tullye onta The sound of singing comes from every house.

ey se n', abbr < ey se nun

ey se ’na, pcl + pcl + cop advers. at/in/from … or the like; whether at/in/from …, at/in/from … whatever. ¶Sāmu-sil ey se ’na ku lul mannalq swu iss.ulq ka, cip ey se nun mannaki him tunta You may be able to see him in the office but it would be difficult to see him at home. **Enu kos ey se ’na ¹yēyuy nun chikhye ya haney** You should be courteous everywhere.

ey se ’na-ma, pcl + pcl + cop extended advers. ¶O(twu-)mak cip ey se ’na-ma halwu pam muk.ulq swu iss.umyen cōh.keyss.ˢo I'd like to be able to stay overnight, in a shack if need be. **Hak.kyo lul mōs tanini cip ey se ’na-ma kongpu lul hay ya ’ci yo** Since I can't go to school I should study at home at least.

ey se nun, pcl + pcl + pcl. as for (happening) at/in (a place); as for (being) from; as for [an oblique subject]. ¶Na nun cimsung cwung ey se nun hōlang-i ka cēy-il cōh.ta I like the tiger best of the wild animals.

ey se nun khenyeng, pcl + pcl + pcl + pcl. ¶Cip ey se nun khenyeng hak.kyo ey se to kongpu lul an hanta ’p.nita He doesn't even study at school, much less at home.

ey se pota (to), pcl + pcl + pcl. (rather) than from/at (a place). ¶Cip ey se pota (to) hak.kyo ey se mannass.umyen cōh.keyss.ta I'd rather see you at school than at home.

ey se ppun man, pcl + pcl + pcl + pcl. ¶Wuli sēnswu nun nelp.i-ttwiki ey se ppun man ani ’la noph.i-ttwiki ey se to cōh.un kilok ul ollyess.ta Our athletes presented good records not only in the broad jump but also in the high jump.

ey se puthe, pcl + pcl + pcl. from (usually a place). ¶cip ~ cengke-cang kkaci from the house to the railroad station.

ey se puthe ka, pcl + pcl + pcl + pcl. ¶Kokay ey se puthe ka hēm hata From the mountain pass on is where it is dangerous.

ey se puthe nun, pcl + pcl + pcl + pcl. ¶Ku kos ey se puthe nun kil i phocang i toyess.ta From there on once again the road is paved.

ey se puthe uy, pcl + pcl + pcl + pcl. (that is) from. ¶hak.kyo ~ iyaki a story from school.

ey se sekken, pcl + pcl + pcl. = ey se lang.

ey se to, pcl + pcl + pcl. at/to/from … also/even/either. ¶I hōyuy ey nun Ilpon ey se to sālam i wass.ta People have come to this conference from Japan, too (or: even from Japan). **I ccok ey se to ce ccok ey se to pāntay ka tul.e wass.ta** Objections were heard on all sides. **Kyewul ey etteh.key chwuwun ci pang an ey se to ōythwu lul ip.e ya halq cengto ’ta** It is so cold in winter that you have to wear your overcoat indoors, too. **Cip ey se nun khenyeng hak.kyo ey se to kongpu lul an hanta ’p.nita** He doesn't even study at school, much less at home. **Payk.hwa-cem ey se to mōs santa** You can't buy it even in department stores. SEE **-ki ey se to.**

ey se tul, pcl + pcl + pcl. ¶**Cip ey se tul mues hayss.ey yo** What did you people do at home? **Swun-i lang Poktong-i lang uy cip ey se tul yātan ici wuli cip ey se n' āmu kekceng anh.nunta** They are making a fuss at Swun-i's and Poktong-i's but everything is quiet at my house.

ey se uy, pcl + pcl + pcl. (the one) at / in / from ... . ¶**cip ey se uy sosik** news from home. **Sewul ey se uy sīhap un cwungci toyess.ta** The game (scheduled to be held) in Seoul has been cancelled. **Kwuk.hoy ey se uy ku uy yēnsel un hwullyung han kes iess.ta** His speech in the National Assembly was an excellent one.

ey se wa, pcl + pcl + pcl. with (what is) at / in / from ... . ¶**wi uy kul ~ kath.i** just as in the above sentence. **Mikwuk ey se wa Ilpon ey se nun yākwu ka tāy-inqki 'ta** Baseball is very popular in America and Japan.

ey se ya, pcl + pcl + pcl. ¶**hak.kyo ey se ya swul ul mek.ulq swu iss.na yo?!** How could we possibly drink liquor at SCHOOL? **Ilen kos ey se ya cam ul calq swu iss.na yo?!** How can I get any sleep in a place like THIS?!

~ **māl lo**. ¶**Ku kos ey se ya māl lo na nun hāyngpok han saynghwal ul hayss.ta** It was right there that I lived a happy life.

-ey sey ya [var] = **-e se ya**

- ˙*e 'ysi˙n i*, abbr < - ˙*e isi˙n i*. ¶*SIM-˙CCYENG ˙kwa ˙SYWELQ-˙PEP ˙CCYENG ˙ey mas˙key ˙khwo ˙cye 'ysi˙n i* (1463 Pep 5:37-38) he wanted to have one conform to purity of heart and purity of doctrine.

- ˙*e 'ys.ke˙nul*, abbr < -˙*e is.ke˙nul*. ¶˙*ta-moyn hon ˙am˙h ol ¨e˙te 'ys.ke˙nul* (1459 Wel 7:17b) I have got just one female, but ... .

- ˙*e 'ys˙kwo*, abbr < -˙*e is˙kwo* (also -˙*e 's˙kwo*). ¶˙*swum.e 'ys˙kwo* (1482 Kum-sam 3:34a) is concealed.

- ˙*e 'ys.non*, abbr < -˙*e is.non* (also -˙*e 's.non*). ¶˙*hye 'ys.non ˙pul s pi˙ch ey 'sye ˙cate˙la* (1481 Twusi 8:9b) slept in the glow of the fire that was lit.

- ˙*e 'ys.no˙n i*, abbr < *is.no˙n i*. ¶*kozol s [¨CHOY-SWO] y se˙li ˙Gwa i˙sul ˙Gwa y psku˙lye 'ys.no˙n i* (1481 Twusi 16:73b) the winter vegetables are enveloped by frost and dew.

~ ˙'*la*. ¶˙*hoy [¨]e[˙]tuk [˙]ho[˙]ya nwu˙lu˙le 'ys.no˙n i ˙'la* (1481 Twusi 7:10a) the sun is dark and yellow; CF ˙*e˙tuk ˙ho˙ya* (1447 Sek 13:57a). *nul˙kun nam˙k un ko˙cang se˙li lol [¨]ti[¨]nay[˙]ye 'ys.no[˙]n i ˙'[˙]la* (1481 Twusi 7:10a) the old tree has been through much frost.

- ˙*e 'ys.nwo˙la*, abbr < -˙*e is.nwo˙la*. ¶*kwoki capo.m ye namwo ¨cywu.m ey ˙i [SOYNG] ˙ol pu˙thye 'ys.nwo˙la* (1481 Twusi 7:6b) for my livelihood I rely on catching fish and cutting wood.

- ˙*e 'ys.nwo˙n i*, abbr < -˙*e is.nwo˙n i*. ¶˙*na y nulk˙kwo [˙PPYENG] ˙ho.ya me˙mu˙le 'ys.nwo˙n i* (1481 Twusi 7:12a) I am staying here old and ailing.

- ˙*e 'ys.ta˙ka*, abbr < -˙*e is.ta˙ka*. ¶*mwulwu˙ph ul ˙phye 'ys.ta˙ka* (1481 Twusi 8:27b) [he was sleeping away and] had his knees spread out, and then ... .

- ˙*e 'ys.te˙la*, abbr < -˙*e is.te˙la*. ¶*[TWONG] nyek mwoy˙h ay ¨kin [KWA-˙KUK] ˙i e˙tu˙we 'ys.te˙la* (1481 Twusi 7:26-7) the eastern mountains are darkened with the long spears [of conflict].

- ˙*e 'ys˙ten*, abbr < -˙*e is˙ten*. ¶˙*phye˙e 'ys.ten pol˙h ol kwu˙phil sso˙zi ˙yey* (1447 Sek 6:2a) while bending the arm that one has stretched. ¨*a˙loy s ˙tule 'ys˙ten ¨HEM-¨TTWOW 'yn˙t ol ¨a˙ti ¨mwot ˙ho˙ya* (1459 Wel 21:120b; broken type on ¨TTWOW) not knowing that it was the dangerous path he had entered before.

- ˙*e 'ys.te˙n i*, abbr < -˙*e is.te˙n i*. ¶˙*QILQ-CHYEN CHYENG-LYEN ˙i two˙ta ˙phe 'ys.te˙n i* (1449 Kok 9) a thousand blue lotuses have sprung into bloom.

- ˙*e 'ys.two˙ta*, abbr < -˙*e is.two˙ta*. ¶*[KYENG-TWO] y ke˙chu˙le 'ys.two˙ta* (1481 Twusi 22:46a) the capital was unruly.

˙*ey ˙sye*, pcl + pcl. SEE ˙*ay / ˙oy ˙sye*, ˙*yey ˙sye*.

1. = **ey se** at, in; from. ¶˙*wolhi ˙Gwa kulyeki ˙Gwa y ˙hye 'ys.non ˙pul s pi˙ch ey ˙sye ˙cate˙la* (1481 Twusi 8:9b) the ducks and the wild geese slept in the glow of the fire that was lit. CF *tyengey ˙sye*.

2. (impersonal oblique subject). SEE ~ *n'*, ˙*ay ˙sye*.

3. = **pota** than. ¶*na˙h i ... syel˙hu.n in ˙hoy ˙yey ˙stwo ˙su˙mul˙h ey ˙sye SYWUY ˙ho˙ya* (1462 ¹Nung 2:6b) is weaker in the year that one's age is thirty than at twenty.

˙*ey ˙sye*, pcl + inf < ˚*sye˙ta* (vi 'stands'). Examples? SEE ˙*oy ˙sye*.

˙*ey ˙'sye*, abbr < ˙*ey i˙sye*, pcl + vi inf. being

at / in. Examples?
`ey `sye n', pcl + pcl + pcl. ¶*TYWUNG-`KWUYK `ey `sye n' TYWUNG-`KWUYK `ul ha`nol s ka`won-`toy `` la ho`kwo* (1459 Wel 1:30a) in China they think China to be the center of heaven and ... .

ey 'ta (ka), pcl + cop transferentive (+ pcl).

1. marks a SHIFT (of location/status) into/onto/upon; for. ¶**kōl-pang ~ kēlta** hangs it in the closet. **sang wi ~ noh.ta** puts it on the table. **congi ~ ssuta** writes it (down) on paper. **Nay cim ul Kim sensayng tayk ey 'ta ka math.kyess.ta** I left my bag at Mr Kim's house. **I pyek ey 'ta ka (or 'ta nun) kēlci mālko ce pyek ey 'ta kel.e la** Hang it on that wall, not this wall. **Pyek.hwa 'la 'n(un) kes un pyek ey 'ta kūlin kūlim ita** Murals are pictures painted on walls. **Mues ey 'ta ssunun ya** What is it used for? **Mues ey 'ta ka caymi lul puth.yess.nun ya** What did he get interested in? **Simcheng-i nun ssal sam-payk sek ey 'ta ka mom ul phal.ess.ta** Simcheng-i sold her body for 300 sek of rice.

2. emphasizes an indirect object. SEE **ey**.

3. (for emphatic and selective or accumulative enumeration) and, and the like. ¶**Chwum ey 'ta nolay ey 'ta yēnkuk kkaci iss.ess.ta** They had dancing and singing and even drama. **Nolang cekoli ey 'ta ka punhong chima ey 'ta ka kapsa tayngki kkaci sa osyess.ta** She went and bought a yellow jacket, and a pink skirt, and even a silk-gauze pigtail-ribbon. **Twūl ey 'ta ka yeses ul te hamyen yetel(p) i toyp.nita** Six added to two makes eight. **Ku ka Hānkwuk māl ey 'ta ka Ilpon māl ul sekk.e se yāyki hayss.ey yo** He talked in a mixture of Korean and Japanese.

NOTE: The sequence *ey 'na 'ta (ka) does not occur, but there are examples of **ey 'ta (ka) 'na: Ilen cangnanq-kam un cip ey 'ta ka 'na twue la** Leave this sort of plaything at home (don't bring it to school).

ey 'ta (ka) tul, pcl + cop transferentive (+ pcl) + pcl. ¶**Kwuk ey 'ta ka tul kilum ul chisey yo** Put some oil in your soup.

ey tāy han, ey tāy ha.ye (hay se) SEE **tāy hata**

ey to, pcl + pcl. to/at/in ··· also/even/either. ¶**Kwulapha ~ kata** goes to Europe too. **pam ~ mōs cata** can't/doesn't sleep (even) at night. **Sewul ey to Pusan ey to iss.ta** They have them both in Seoul and in Pusan. **Pusan ey to Sewul ey to ēps.ta** They have them neither in Pusan nor in Seoul. **Il.yoil ey to kukcang ey kanta** I go to the theater on Sundays too (as well as on other days). **Il.yoil ey to kukcang ey kanta** On Sunday I go to the theater too (as well as to other places).

'ey to = [h]ey to = hay to, inf < hata.

ey ttal^e/a (se), pcl + vi inf (+ pcl). depending on, according to. ¶**Siki ey ttal^e/a kaps i taluta** Prices vary with the season. **Kyuchik un ttay ey ttal^e/a pyēnkyeng halq swu iss.ta** The rule may be modified as the occasion demands.

NOTE: Always **ey**, even after an animate (not *eykey ttale). ¶**Sālam ey ttale se sēngqkyek i talup.nita** Character differs according to the person (M 1:2:194).

ey tul, pcl + pcl. ¶**Cip ey tul kass.ey yo** They (all) went home.

`ey `two, pcl + pcl = ey to. ¶*`syelWun `il s TYWUNG `ey `two LI-`PYELQ `ko.t ho`n i `ep.su`n i* (1447 Sek 6:6a) even among sad events there is nothing approaching separation.

ey uy, pcl + pcl. (the one) to/at/in···. ¶**sengkong ~ kil** the road to success.

ey uy han, ey uy ha.ye (hay se) SEE **uy hata**

ey wa, pcl + pcl [slightly awkward]. ¶**Cip ey wa hōysa ey nun cēnhwa lul hayss.ta** I phoned home and to the office.

ey ya, pcl + pcl. only if (it be) to/at/in ··· .
¶**Yo say S(s)olyen ey ya kalq swu iss.na yo?** You surely can't go to the Soviet Union these days?! **Wuli nala ey n' kulen kes ul kacin sālam i elma ēps.ci man, Mikwuk ey ya mānh.ci yo** There aren't very many who have such things in our country, but in America there are lots. **Hak.kyo ey ya kaci** If it's to school, then I'll go.

TIME **ey ya** TIME for the first time. ¶**Sāwel ey ya okeyss.ta** (1936 Roth 238) I will come first in April (or: I will not come before April).

-ey ya, var inf + pcl = -e ya

-ey yey 'ci = -e ya 'ci

'ey yo = yey yo (= ie yo it is)

'ey yo = [h]ey yo = hay yo, inf < hata.
¶**Mian 'ey yo = Mian hay yo** I'm sorry.

-ey yo, var inf + pcl.

1. = ···ye yo < ···ie yo, as in the honorific -usey yo = -usye yo < -usie yo. ¶**Kitaley yo = Kitalye yo** Wait!

2. = -e yo. Common after -ess-, -keyss-, iss-, ēps-, kath-.

˙ey ˙za, pcl + pcl (> ey a > ey ya). ¶ ku me ˙kun ¨HHWUW ˙ey ˙za (1459 Wel 1:43b) (only) after he had eaten. cwu ˙kun ¨HHWUW ˙ey ˙za (1447 Sek 24:28a) only after a person has died. ku ¨HHWUW ˙ey ˙za (1459 Wel 1:42b, 44b) only after that. ˙stwo ¨es ˙ti i cu ˙zu ˙m ey ˙za kos won ˙ta (?1517- ¹No 2:3b) And how is it that you have only come at just this time? ˙i ˙kot hon ¨sa ˙lom ey ˙za ˙WUY ˙ho ˙ya e ˙lwu nil ˙Gwol ˙tt i ˙m ye (1463 Pep 2:172ab; sic, ···lom-ey···) one can effectively tell it to just this kind of person, and ... .

- ˙ey ˙za → - ˙key ˙za: me ˙key ˙za (1518 Sohak-cho 7:18b) = me[k] ˙key ˙za.

- ˙e ˙za, 1. infinitive + pcl (= -e ya); SEE - ˙sa. ¶ WANG-¨CO ˙s ˙MYENG ˙i nil ˙Gwey ˙s ¨pwu.n i ˙lwoswo ˙n i ¨a ˙molyey ¨˙na mozom s ko ˙cang nwo ˙la ˙za ho ˙l i ʼ-ngi ¨˙ta (1447 Sek 24:28a) as the prince has only been alive for seven days he will somehow have to play to his heart's content. ˙wuli ˙tol ˙h i ¨PPWU-NGWANG s KWAN ˙ol ¨mey ˙zoWa ˙za ho ˙l i ʼ-ngi ¨˙ta (1459 Wel 10:12b) we must bear the coffin of the royal father. pan ˙to ˙ki MA-TUNG ˙i i ˙sye ˙za e ˙lwu hon ka ˙ci ʼ˙la nilo ˙l i ¨˙la (1462 ¹Nung 1:17a) Mātanga will necessarily have to be present before we can say it is the same. CYE- ˙PPWULQ ˙two ˙CHYWULQ-KA ˙hosya ˙za ¨TTWOW-¨LI ˙lol tas.ko ˙sino ˙n i (1447 Sek 6:12a) even the Buddhas must leave home in order to study the doctrine. ˙es ˙tyey ho.ya ˙za ˙e ˙mi ˙NGA-¨KWUY ˙lol ye ˙huy ˙l i ʼ-ngi s ˙kwo ( ) just what must I do to get rid of the hungry ghost of my mother? ˙co ˙syek na ˙ha ˙za kos ˙pwu ˙mwo ˙uy ˙un ˙hyey ˙lul ¨an ˙ta ˙ho ˙no.n i ¨˙la (?1517- Pak 1:58a) only when you have children of your own do you begin to wonder whether you have appreciated your debt to your parents. ALSO: 1447 Sek 24:28a, 52b; ... . SEE ˙ho.ya ˙za.

2. → - ˙Ge ˙za, effective inf + pcl.

/G/ lenited form of /k/ after y, i, l, and z (zG was often written sG). Probably pronounced as a voiced velar or laryngeal fricative, or as a glottal squeeze. Some cases of spelled G result from reducing W (lenited p): kol ˙Gwa (1482 Kum-sam 3:27a) = kol ˙Wa (1451 Hwun-en 12b) < *kolp- ˙a. And a few cases may result from reducing z (lenited s), but we will simply ignore the indications for G in the spelling of ˙ey ˙a = ˙ey ˙[z]a and of - ˙key ˙a = - ˙key ˙[z]a in 1586 Sohak and later texts. The lenition regularly took place in MK texts for the initial of a suffix attached to a stem. But later the unlenited k was restored either by analogy or under the influence of unwritten dialects which escaped the lenition that affected the central dialect represented in the texts. We also assume G between y and u or o, though there is no *···yyu or *···yyo to contrast with ···yGu, ···yGo.

-G- SEE -o-, -u-, - ˙Gwo-, - ˙Gwu-

˙Ga = ˙ka (question) after l (including LQ), y, and often i. ¶ ¨ne y ˙i ˙cey swo ˙li ˙Ga a ˙ni ˙Ga (1462 ¹Nung 4:126b) is it now your sound or isn't it? For more examples, see ˙ka, a ˙ni ˙Ga.

˙[G]a = ˙ka (question).

- ˙Ga- = - ˙Ge- = - ˙ke- effective (after l-, y-, cop ˙i-); a shorter version, simply - ˙a-, occurs after other sounds and in some of the formations after y and i (which add a y), and l (which in that case, like the other consonants, is linked to the following vowel).

- ˙Ga = - ˙Ge = - ˙ke, effective inf. CF - ˙a.

- ˙Ga ci ˙la, effective inf + aux indic assertive. wants to do. ¶ ˙na y ¨ku ˙ylwo ˙n i ingey ¨sal ˙Ga ci ˙la (1459 Wel 7:12a) therefore I want to live here.

- ˙Ga ˙la = - ˙ka ˙la = - ˙ke ˙la, effective subj attent (command). ¶ ˙i ˙non QON ˙ol ¨alGa ˙la ho ˙n i ˙ya QON ˙ol kap ˙ka ˙la ho ˙n i ˙ya (?1468- Mong 3lb) is this telling us to recognize the obligation or is it telling us to repay the obligation? CF -e ˙la, -Ge ˙la.

? - ˙Ga ˙l ya, ? - ˙Ga ˙l ye, ? - ˙Ga ˙l ywo

- ˙Gan = - ˙kan = - ˙ken, effective modifier. Are the examples limited to structures with bound postmodifiers (˙i, t, ˙man)?

? - ˙Ga ˙na SEE - ˙Ge ˙na

? - ˙Ga ˙n i; ? - ˙Ga.n i ˙Gwa, ? - ˙Ga.n i ˙Gwo, ? - Ga ˙n i ʼ˙la

? - ˙Gan ma ˙lon = - ˙kan ma ˙lon = - ˙ken ma ˙non but, although.

? - ˙Gan ma ˙non = - ˙kan ma ˙non = - ˙ken ma ˙non but, although.

? - ˙Ga ˙nol

? -ˈGan ˈta
? -ˈGan ˈti(⋯) = -ˈGan ˈt i(⋯) = -ˈkan ˈt i(⋯). CF -ˈan ˈti.
? -ˈGan ˈtyeng
? -ˈGaˈn ya, ? -ˈGaˈn ye. ? -ˈGaˈn ywo
 -ˈGaˈta = -ˈkaˈta, effective indic assertive
? -ˈGaˈton = -ˈkaˈton = -ˈkeˈtun. if; when.
 -ˈGay = -ˈkay, suf (makes v into n). nwolˈGay (1445 ¹Yong 13, 16) song. VAR -ˈGey.
 -ˈGe- = -ˈke- effective (after l, y, cop ˈi-); a shorter version, simply -ˈe-, occurs after other sounds and in some of the formations after y and i (which add a y), and l (which gets linked to the following vowel). CF -ˈe-.
 -ˈGe = -ˈke, effective inf. CF -ˈe. SEE -ˈGe cila, -ˈGeˈˈm ye, -ˈGeˈza.
 -ˈGe ciˈla, effective inf + auxiliary indic assert. wants to do. ¶woˈcik nilˈGwotoy [ˈKHWON-ˈKHWO] holˈs i ˈcywong towoyˈGe ciˈla ˈhonoˈta (1481 Twusi 8:1b) he will only say, "I am destitute and I want to become a slave".
 -ˈGeˈla = -ˈkeˈla. SEE -ˈGaˈla.
? -Geˈl ya, ? -Geˈl ye, ? -Geˈl ywo
 -ˈGeˈm ye = -ˈ[y]Geˈm ye, cop effective subst + cop inf. SEE -uˈl iˈGeˈm ye.
 -ˈGen = -ˈken (effective mod).
  1. (epitheme extruded from subject). ¶cwuktaˈka ˈˈsalGen [ˈPOYK-ˈSYENG] ˈi aˈto' ˈˈnim sˈkuy [QOY-ˈPPWOK] niˈphizoˈWoˈn i (1445 ¹Yong 25) the people saved from death dressed his son in royal robe.
  2. (epitheme extruded from the complement of the copula). ¶nyey s pe.t iGen [SWON ˈˈCOY] y (1632 Twusi-cwung 1:13a) Sūn Zǎi, a friend of days gone by, ...
  3. (epitheme extruded from object). ¶noˈm oyˈwos kwa ˈˈilˈGen kuˈluˈs ul naˈmolaˈti ˈˈmal.m ye (1475 Nay 1:9a) does not rebuke others for their attire or the mistakes they have made, ...
  4. (summational epitheme). SEE ~ ˈGeˈn i.
 -Geˈna = -keˈna (effective advers). ¶ ˈKUM-ˈKAYˈlul ˈˈhelGeˈna swoˈkye ˈˈkeˈcus ˈSYWELQ-ˈPEP ˈhokeˈna (1462 ¹Nung 8:77a) whether breaking the prohibitions or swindling people with false preaching ... . ˈˈtywohonˈmwom towoyGeˈna kwuˈcunˈmwom towoyGeˈna (1459 Wel 1:12a) whether one becomes a good body or becomes a bad body ... . ˈNGWENˈey eˈkuyGeˈna (1459 Wel 21:169b) if you oppose my wish. ˈˈaˈmwo 'yGeˈnaˈwa ⋯ ˈtwolaˈho.yaˈtwo (1459 Wel 1: 13a) whoever might come and ask you to give him ⋯ ; CF ˈˈamwo 'yˈna (1447 Sek 9:17a, 21a).
 'Geˈna = -ˈ[y]Geˈna, abbr < ˈiGeˈna (cop effective advers) after i or y. ¶piˈlwok LOY-ˈSYEY 'Geˈna siˈhwok ˈHYEN-ˈCCOY SOYNGˈay ˈSYENG-ˈPPWUN ˈul ˈˈeˈte (1459 Wel 21:105b) even if one gain holy status in a future age or, perhaps, in present-day life ... .
 -ˈGe-ngi ˈˈta, effective polite + cop indic assert. ¶ ˈTTI-ˈNGWOK ˈi ˈPYEN ˈhoˈya LYEN ˈmwoˈs i towoyˈGe-ngi ˈˈta (1550 ¹Yenghem 8b) hell turned into a lotus pond.
 -ˈGeˈn i = -ˈkeˈn i, effective mod + postmod ('fact') or quasi-free noun ('one who / that ⋯ ').
  1. (epitheme extruded). Examples?
  2. (summational epitheme). SEE -Geˈn i ˈˈla.
 'Geˈn i, 1. = ˈ[y]Geˈn i, abbreviation < ˈiGeˈn i (copula effective mod + postmod) after i or y. ¶ ˈˈpiˈnon ˈˈsaloˈm ol cwuˈl iˈGeˈn i ˈhomolˈmye ˈnye-naˈmon ˈˈchyenlyaˈng is.toˈn ye (1447 Sek 9:13a) ⋯ will give those to the begging people; are there still other provisions?
  2. abbr < (ˈ)hokeˈn i. SEE kuˈli 'Geˈn i.
 -ˈGeˈn iˈGwa = -ˈkeˈn iˈGwa, effective mod + postmod + pcl. ¶swoˈliˈGwa tulwum [G]wa y ˈˈtwulˈh i syeˈm ye n' ˈMWULQˈGwa na [G]wa y phyeˈn i ˈˈilˈGe.n iˈGwa swoˈliˈlul ˈMYELQ ˈhoˈya twuˈly₂ˈi tuluˈsiˈm ye n' ˈanˈkhwa [= ˈanhˈkwa] pas[k]ˈkwa y kiˈtulywoˈm i ˈepˈsusilˈss oy (1462 ¹Nung 6:29a) if both the sound and the hearing arise there occurs a spreading of the thing and the self, while if you extinguish the sound and listen all around you neither the internal or the external is to be expected.
? -ˈGeˈn iˈGwo = -ˈkeˈn iˈGwo, effective mod + postmod + ellipted cop mod + postmod
 -ˈGeˈn i ˈˈla = -ˈkeˈn i ˈˈla, effective mod + postmod + cop. ¶[ˈˈ]nyey sˈwuy-anˈh ay kwoˈc i cel-ˈlwoˈphe 's.kwoˈpwom naˈl ay say twolwo nolGeˈn i ˈˈla (1481 Twusi 8:34b) in the old garden the flowers are all abloom and on a spring day the birds have flown back.
 'Geˈn i ˈˈston = -ˈ[y]Geˈn i ˈˈston, abbr < ˈiGeˈn i ˈˈston (cop effective mod + postmod + pcl) after i or y. SEE aˈni 'Geˈn i ˈˈston. CF -keˈn i 'stoˈn ye.
 -Gen-kan man = -ˈGen maˈnon (with -kan- a rhythmic insert?). but. ¶[ˈCHILQ-ˈˈPWOW] ciye

salGen-kan man (?1530 Siyong 130-1) lives bearing the Seven Precious Things, but ....
- ˙Gen ma˙lon = -˙ken ma˙lon = -˙ken ma˙non but, although. ¶ ˝ep.sun ˙t ol al˙Gen ma˙lon (1465 Wen 1:1:1:42b) knew there was none, but ... . SEE ˙i˙Gen ma˙lon, a˙ni ˝˙Gen ma˙lon.
- ˙Gen ma˙non = -˙ken ma˙non but, although. SEE ˙i˙Gen ma˙non.
- ˙Ge˙nol = -˙ke˙nol (lit concessive). ¶ ... ci˙p i ˙ilGe˙nol ˙hoyn ˙ptwuy lwo ni˙ywu˙n i (1481 Twusi 7:1a) there was built a house but it was shaded by white cogan-grass thatching.
? - ˙Gen ˙ta = -˙ken ˙ta
- ˙Gen ˙t ay n' = -˙ken ˙t ay n'. ¶ ˙i e˙tewun an˙hay s ˝salom ˙kwa ˙tye mwo˙ton MOYNG-ZIN ˙kwa ˙twu ke˙mwu˙m ul ma˙chwo˙a ˝hyey˙Gen ˙t ay n' (1462 ¹Nung 1:101a) when one thinks of those in this darkness (of ignorance) and all those sightless together as the two blacknesses.
? - ˙Gen ˙ti(…) = ? -˙Gen ˙t i (…)
? -˙Gen ˙ti = -˙Gen ˙t i = -˙ken ˙t i. CF -˙en ˙ti.
? -˙Gen ˙t i˙n i, ? -˙Gen ˙t i.n i ˝la
? -˙Gen ˙t i˙la = -˙ken ˙t i˙la
- ˙Gen ˙t un = (?*)-˙ken ˙t un, effective mod + postmodifier + particle. ¶ ˙ne y ku˙li-two˙lwok chonchon hon ˝yang ul ˝hyey[˙]Gen ˙t un (?1517- Pak 1:64a; yang-ul) when you have figured it down such fine detail ... .
? -˙Gen ˙tyeng = -˙ken ˙tyeng, effective mod + bnd postmodifier. although.
-˙Ge˙nul = -˙ke˙nul (lit concessive). ¶ CYENG-˙SYA ci˙zwu˙l ye ˙the˙h ul kos ˝SI-˙CAK ˙ho˙ya ˙toyGe˙nul (1447 Sek 6:35ab) though you have just begun [measuring] the site to build the monastery. ta˙sos kwoc ˝twu kwo˙c i KHWONG-TYWUNG ˙ey me˙mulGe˙nul (1449 Kok 7) though two of the five flowers stayed in the air.
~ ˙za. ¶ pen˙tu˙ki ˙PEP-HHWA y a˙ni 'Ge˙nul ˙za ˙homol˙mye ˝TTWOW-˙KUY ˙Gwa ˝KWA-˙KUY ˙Gwa tal˙Gwo˙m i is.ke˙n i ˙sto˙n ye (1462 ¹Nung 1:17a) though they cannot be the Lotus sūtra exactly, just how much more would they differ from testimonials to marga (the way) and to phala ([cause and] effect)?!
- ˙Ge˙n ya = -˙ke˙n ya, effective mod + postmod. ¶ nil˙Gwo˙toy ˝KOYNG ˙ay ne 'y ˙swo˙n i ˝teyGe˙n ya ho˙n i (1518 Sohak-cho 10:3a; mistaken tone on KOYNG) said "did you burn your hand on the stove?".
- ˙Ge˙n ye = -˙ke˙n ye, effective modifier + postmod. ¶ QAN-SSYE ˙hi nil˙Gwotoy KOYNG ˙ay ne 'y ˙swo˙n i ˝teyGe˙n ye ho˙n i (1475 Nay 1:18a) calmly said "did you burn your hand on the stove?".
- ˙Ge˙n ywo, effective mod + postmod (question). ¶ ˝twu ˙salo˙m oy ˙PWOK ˙TUK ˝etwu˙m i hon ka˙ci ˝˙n i ˝es˙tyey 'Ge˙n ywo [< ˙hoke˙n ywo] (1447 Sek 23:4a) how did it happen that two people's obtaining happiness and virtue was the same? ˝CO-˝MWUW y QAN-˙LAK ˝˙ti ˝mwot ˙key ˙hono˙n i ˝es˙tyey 'Ge˙n ywo (1459 Wel 00:00) why has it been made such that son and mother cannot be at ease? CF -e˙n ywo.
- ˙Gesi- (effective honorific) = -(ᵁ/o)˙si˙ke- (hon effective): -˙Gesin, -˙Gesina, -˙Gesi˙n i (˙Gwo / ˙Gwa), -˙Gesi˙nᵁ/ol, -˙Gesi˙n ywo, -˙Gesi˙ta.
- ˙Gesi˙nol = -˙kesi˙nol (= -u˙sike˙nol, hon lit concessive). ¶ [˙TYEY-˙MYENG] ˙i no˙li˙Gesi˙nol (1445 ¹Yong 8) the emperor's command came down, and [in response] ... .
-˙Ge˙ta = -ke˙ta, effective indic assert. ¶ ˙TTAY-CCO-PI QWEN-QYANG ˝TYWOW ˙[G]wa KWONG-˙TUK tas.non na 'y ˙mwom ˙i ˙CYENG-˙KAK na˙l ay macwo ˝pwo˙l i 'Ge˙ta (1459 Wel 8:87a) the mandarin duck of vast compassion and my body which practices the achievement of virtue will be facing on the day of sambodhi (Buddha wisdom). ˙wolho˙m ye woy˙ywo˙m ol hon ti˙Gwuy ˙KYWO-˙CYENG (˙hwolttiGeta =) ˙hwolq ˙t iGe˙ta (1463 Pep 1:10b) it is a matter of checking what is right and wrong at the same time. na˙kunay captu˙len t i ˙na'-˙to.l i ˙kilGe˙ta (1481 Twusi 15:23a) the days and months grow long since capturing the traveler.
-˙Ge˙tun = -ke˙tun (> -ketun provisional). if; when. ¶ ˝nyey ˙SYWELQ-SAN ˙ay hon QOYNG-˝MWU y ˙i˙sywo˙toy e˙zi ˝ta ˙nwun ˝melGe˙tun ˝KWA-˙SSILQ ˙pta me˙kite˙n i (1459 Wel 2:12b) anciently, on the snowy mountain there was a parrot; when its parents both went blind it picked fruit and fed it to them. CF -˙e˙tun.
-˙Gey = -˙key, suffix (makes v into n). ¶ sil˙Gey (1481 Twusi 7:6a) shelf. ˙wul˙Gey (1447 Sek 6:32a) thunder. VAR -˙Gay.
-˙Gey = -˙key (> -key adverbative). ¶ KYWOW-˙HWA ˙non kolo˙chye ˙etil˙Gey towoy˙Gwol ˙ss i˙la (1459 Wel 1:19a) "culture" is [a word that

means] teaching one to be refined. ha˙nol˙h i tangtangi ˙i ˙phi˙lol ¨salom towoy˙Gey ˙ho˙si.l i ˙˙la (1459 Wel 1:7-8) heaven is to make this blood suitably into people. ˙CYENG-˙KYENG ˙ul ¨nay˙Gey ˙ho.ya ˙two (1459 Wel 21:20a) he got her to bring forth the correct view, but ... .

-˙Gey ˙s˙kwo, adverbative + ˙[y]s˙kwo, abbr < is˙kwo (vi ger). wanting or expecting it to be/do. ¶MYEY-˙HHWOYK hon kwo˙t ay na˙za ˙ka ¨al˙Gey ˙s˙kwo ˙ho˙si.n i ˙˙la (1462 ¹Nung 1:113a) wanted to proceed to the part where it was confusing and gain an understanding of it. ˙i nul˙ku˙n [i] uy ˙i ¨ma˙l on ¨salo¨m i ˙KEP-˙NGWOY ˙lol ˙HYANG ˙ho˙ya ¨alGey ˙s˙kwo ho˙n i (1482 Kum-sam 2:1b) these words of this old man people wanted to know on beyond this kalpa. SEE -˙kuy ˙s˙kwo.

˙˙Gey = ˙[y]˙Gey, abbreviation < ˙i˙Gey (cop adverbative) after i or y. so as to be, so that it is. ¶˙TI ˙Gwa PI ˙Gwa y hon ka˙ci ˙˙Gey hol˙ss oy (1459 Wel 2:61a) as it is arranged for wisdom and compassion to be (one and) the same. elkwu˙l i i˙Gwun nam˙k i˙Gwo mozo¨m i cwu˙kun ˙coy ˙˙Gey khe˙n i (1462 ¹Nung 9:61a) it was so arranged that the face be a withered tree and the soul be turned to dead ashes.

-˙Geys˙kwo = -˙Gey ˙s˙kwo. SEE -˙Gey.

-˙Ge ˙za, effective inf + pcl. just (if) do. ¶˙han ˙pi sa˙o˙l ilwo˙toy ¨pwuyGe ˙za ˙como˙n i ˙-ngi ˙˙ta (1445 ¹Yong 67) there was a heavy rain for three days, and just when they had cleared themselves away from that it [= the island] submerged. ko˙cang cyem˙kulGe ˙za ca˙s ay ˙tu˙le ˙wo˙si.l i ˙˙la (?1517- Pak 1:65a) we will come back into the (stronghold =) city only when the night is well upon us. SEE ˙iGe ˙za.

-˙Gi-, suffix. CF -i-, -y-, -hi-, -ki-, -chi-, -u-, -ukhi-, -ikhi-, -li-, -iwu-, -ywu-; -wu-, -hwu-, -kwu-, -chwu-, -ay-; -u-, -o-, -˙Gwu-, -˙Gwo-.

1. makes vc. nol˙Gi- (> nalli-) cause to fly ← nol- (> na-l-) fly. sal˙Gi- (> salli-) cause to live ← ¨sal- (> sā-l- live).

2. makes vp. mul˙Gi- (> mulli-) get bitten. skol˙Gi- (> kkalli- get spread) ← ˙skol- > kka-l-.

*-˙Gi. The summative -˙ki did not lenite.

-˙Goy = -˙koy = -˙key (> -key adverbative). ¶tuthu˙l i towoy˙Goy pes˙Ga ˙tike˙nul (1447 Sek 6:30-1) crumbles into dust.

-˙Guy = -˙kuy = -˙key (> -key adverbative). ¶¨HHWUW s ¨salo¨m ol ¨al˙Guy ˙honon ke˙s i˙la (1447 Sek se:1a) it is (written) so that later people may know. te˙Wun PPEN-¨NWOW ˙lol ye˙huy˙Guy hol nu˙c i˙n i (1459 Wel 1:18a) it is a sign that one will keep clear of heated vexations. ˙HWA-ZIN ˙on ˙SYEY-CWON s SSIN-˙LUK ˙u˙lwo towoy˙Guy ˙hosyan ¨sa˙lo.m i˙la (1447 Sek 6:7b) an incarnated Buddha is a person brought into existence by the divine power of the World-Honored.

˙Gwa, alt (> wa) after i or y, or (> kwa) after l, of ˙kwa (> kwa pcl). ¶˙ma˙li ˙Gwa swon-thwop ˙kwa ˙lol (1447 Sek 6:44b) the hair and the fingernails. a˙pa ¨nim s ˙kuy ˙Gwa a˙coma ¨nim s ˙kuy ˙Gwa (1447 Sek 6:1a) to father and to aunt. ¨KWA-˙SSILQ ˙Gwa ˙mul ˙Gwa (1459 Wel 1:5b) fruits and water. kozol ˙Gwa kyezul ˙Gwa s so˙zi (1481 Twusi 8:59a) between autumn and winter.

˙[G]wa, alt (> wa) of ˙kwa (> kwa pcl) after a vowel (other than i, which called for ˙Gwa). ¶pwuthye ˙[G]wa ¨cywung ˙kwa (1447 Sek 6:16b) Buddha and the priests. NOTE: If ˙kwa is a contraction from the infinitive kol˙Wa our notation may represent ˙[W]wa < [kol]˙Wa rather than the lenition of the initial of ˙kwa < k[ol]˙wa < kol˙Wa < *kol˙pa that the "[G]" is here assumed to represent. Unfortunately there is no attestation of *˙Wa or *Wwa for this morpheme. We find no pre-Hankul evidence for the existence of the particle in any form (nor of the verb kolp-), so we cannot say just when the contraction(s) occurred. The best evidence: the variant ko˙Wa in 1449 Kok 135.

-˙Gwa ˙˙la, (after l) exclamatory first-person statement. ¶[HHYEN] hon [¨CYWU-ZIN] ˙i ˙i lol ˙cwue si˙lu.m ul pwo˙nay˙Gey ˙hwo.m ol pi˙lwuswu ¨alGwa ˙˙la (1481 Twusi 7:23b) for the first time I learn of a wise master's giving this to dispatch the misery!

˙[G]wa ˙lol, pcl + pcl. ¶kwos ˙kwa ¨KWA-˙SSILQ ˙Gwa phul [˙]Gwa namwo ˙[G]wa [˙]lol me˙ku.l i ˙two isi[˙]m ye (1447 Sek 3:33b) there are also those that eat flowers and fruit and grass and wood, and ... .

˙Gwa ˙lwo, ˙[G]wa ˙lwo SEE ˙kwa ˙lwo

˙Gwa ˙lwo ˙sye, pcl + pcl + pcl. ¶˙SOYNG ˙kwa

˙MYELQ ˙Gwa lwo ˙sye i˙sywon ˙t i a˙ni ˙m ye (1462 ¹Nung 3:17a) ... nor is it in birth and extinction, ...

- ˙Gwa-ngi ˙˙ta, (after l) polite exclamatory first-person statement. ¶ ˙i ˙kot hon ˙PEP-QUM ˙ul tut¨cop˙kwo NGUY-¨HWOY ˙lol ¨ta ho˙ma ¨tel˙Gwa-ngi ˙˙ta (1463 Pep 2:24a) listening to the sounds of the Law I am already lessening my doubts and regrets. na ˙y mozo˙m i ˙SSILQ ˙lwo ˙mwom pas˙k uy i˙sywo˙m ol ¨al˙Gwa-ngi ˙˙ta (1462 ¹Nung 1:53a) I know that my mind really exists apart from my body

-Gwan˙toy = -kwan˙toy. since, as; such that, so that (followed by some question doubting the adequacy of the reason).

'Gwan˙toy = ˙[y]Gwan˙toy, abbr < ˙iGwan˙toy after i or y. ¶ ¨es˙tyey e˙lwo ˙TTYAK ho˙l i ˙Gwan˙toy ˙TTYAK ˙˙ti a˙ni ˙tha nilo˙l ywo (1462 ¹Nung 1:75a) how can you say that one is not attached when one IS attached? [˙]i ˙a˙ki es.ti ˙˙n i ˙Gwan˙toy nul˙ku˙n [i] uy he˙thwuy l˙ ¨an˙kwo ˙i˙li-˙to˙lwok ¨wunon ˙ta (1459 Wel 8:100-1) why does this child cling to [the calf of] the old man's leg and cry all this much?! ¨ne y ¨es.te ˙n a˙hoy ˙Gwan˙toy he˙thwuy ˙lol an˙a ¨wunun ˙ta (1459 Wel 8:85b; sic an-˙a) what kind of a child are you to cry, clinging to [the calf of] a leg?

˙[G]wa ˙oy, pcl + pcl (genitive). ¶ ˙say ˙Gwa ˙nyey ˙Gwa ˙oy KYWOW-˙CYEP ˙i˙la (1459 Wel 21:5a) it is the joining of new and old.

˙Gwa ˙two, pcl + pcl. ¶ZIN ˙kwa ˙TI ˙Gwa two ¨salo˙m oy key ˙stwo ku˙le ˙ho.ya (1482 Kum-sam 3:50b) benevolence and wisdom, too, are like that to people.

- ˙Gwa˙tye = -˙kwa˙tye. ¶ pen˙tu˙ki ¨swuy˙i ¨al˙Gwa˙tye ˙po˙lanwo˙n i (1462 ¹Nung 8:44b) they expect to learn it right away. na˙la[h] s ¨il si˙lum ˙ho.ya ˙hoy ka˙zomyel˙Gwa˙tye [˙NGWEN] ˙hono˙ta (1481 Twusi 8:52a) affairs of the nation being in sad shape, we are praying for a bountiful year.

˙Gwa y, pcl + pcl. ¶ kozol s [¨CHOY-SWO] y se˙li ˙Gwa i ˙sul ˙Gwa y psku˙lye ˙ys.no˙n i (1481 Twusi 16:73b) the winter vegetables are all enveloped by frost and dew. SEE ˙kwa y.

˙[G]wa y ˙za, pcl + pcl + pcl. ¶ ˙PWOW ˙[G]wa ˙HWA ˙[G]wa y ˙za pi˙luse ¨mal ¨kyesi˙n i (1482 Kum-sam 4:36b) only with (the start of) retribution and conversion does one (begin to) have words.

˙Gwo = ˙kwo (question) after l (including LQ), y, and often i. ¶ mu˙sum elkwul ˙Gwo (1462 ¹Nung 2:97a) what face is it? mu˙sus ¨CCWOY ˙Gwo (1459 Wel 1:7a) what sin is it? ¨es.tyey ˙Gwo (1459 Wel 14:65a) how is it?

˙[G]wo = ˙kwo (question). ¶ ˙PALQ-¨ZYA ˙[G]wo (1464 Kumkang se:8b) is it prajñā (wisdom)? ¨es.te ˙n cyen˙cho [G]wo (1482 Kum-sam 3:52a) what is the reason? — CF mu˙sum yang˙co ˙kwo ˙hota ˙ka (1462 ¹Nung 3:84a) inquired what are the looks, and then ... .

˙˙Gwo = ˙[y]˙Gwo, abbr < ˙i˙Gwo (cop ger) after i or y. ¶ HHWONG ˙on ˙swu[h] ˙muci˙key ˙˙Gwo i YEY ˙non ˙am ˙muci˙key ˙˙la (1462 ¹Nung 2:87b) [the Chinese word] HHWONG is the brighter of a double rainbow, and YEY is the paler.

˙[G]wo (= ˙y[G]wo), pcl (< cop ger). and. ¶ ne ˙[G]wo cye ˙[G]wo talu.l ya (1876 Kakok 13) = ne ˙y[G]wo no ˙y[G]wo talu.l ya (id. 122; no misspells na) would you and I be different?

- ˙Gwo = -˙kwo (> -ko ger): ~ ˙sye, ~ ˙two, ~ ˙za. ¶ ¨al˙Gwo (1463 Pep 2:138b, 1459 Wel 1:8b); ¨tel˙Gwo (1465 Wen 1:1:2:118b); ¨sal˙Gwo ˙cye ho˙m ye (1459 Wel 21:91a); e˙wul˙Gwo (1462 ¹Nung 3:38a). pwo˙nay˙Gwo (1464 Kumkang 21b); towoy˙Gwo (1459 Wel 9:22b). ˙MWULQ ˙uy ˙mos MI hon ke.s i˙Gwo (1482 Kum-sam 3:25b) they are the most delicate of objects and ... .

- ˙Gwo-, suf (? < -G- + modulator); CF -i-, -y-, -hi-, -ki-, -chi-, -u-, -ukhi-, -ikhi-, -li-, -iwu-, -ywu-; -wu-, -hwu-, -kwu-, -chwu-, -ay-; -u-, -o-, -˙Gwu-, -˙Gi-. makes vc. ˙skoy˙Gwo- (> kkaywu-) wake one up < ˙skoy- wake up. twol˙Gwo- = twolo-/twolG- < *twolo-G- (> tolu-/ toll-) cause to turn < ¨twol- turn.

- ˙Gwo k = -˙kwo k (gerund + emphatic pcl). ¨sal˙Gwo k (1459 Wel 23:78b). ye˙huy˙Gwo k (1462 ¹Nung 3:95a); ¨hyey˙Gwo k (1481 Twusi 15:4a).

- ˙Gwo ˙˙la, abbreviation < -˙kwo ˙ho˙la (= ˙ho˙l ya/ye). ¶ SO-¨CYA ˙pu˙lye pwo˙nay˙Gwo ˙˙la ˙ho.ya˙nol (1459 Wel 7:15b) said to send a messenger. mwo˙lwomay ˙NGWEN ˙i ¨i˙ti ˙mal˙Gwo ˙˙la ˙hote˙n i ([1447→]1562 Sek 11:30_, cited from LCT with accents inferred)

said the request must not be fulfilled.
ˊGwom, alt (after l, y, i) of ˊkwom, pcl. each. ¶ ˋPALQ-CHYEN ˮLI ˊGwom ˊnyenun ˋSSYANG ˊiˋla (1459 Wel 7:52b) it is an elephant that goes eight thousand leagues at a time. holo ˮNGWO-ˋPOYK ti ˊGwuy ˊGwom (1459 Wel 8:91b) five hundred times a day. kutuy ˊnay ˋKAK-ˋKAK hon aˋtol ˊGwom ˮnayˋya na ˋy SWON-ˮCO cwoˋcha kaˋkey hoˋla ˋhosiˋn i (1447 Sek 6:9b) he commands that each of you folks send a son to follow my grandson. yelˋhul ˊGwom (1481 Twusi 20:29a) ten days each time.
ˊ[G]wom, alt (after vowels other than i) of ˊkwom. ¶holo ˊ[G]wom (1459 Wel 1:37b) per day. SYWU-ˋTTALQ ˊi NGYANG-ˋSYA-SSYENG ˊulwo ˊsye ˋSYA-ˋNGWUY ˋKWUYK ˊey wol ssoˋzi (= wolq soˋzi) ˊyey hon TTYENG-ˋSYA ˊ[G]wom ˋˋcisˋkey ˊhoˋya ... (1447 Sek 6:23a) Sudatta had a monastery built every twenty leagues on the way while coming from Rāja-gṛha to the land of Śrāvastī, and ... .
- ˊGwom °ho- = - ˊkwom °ho- (do repeatedly). No examples?
- ˊGwo nˋ < - ˊkwo nˋ, ger + abbr pcl. and, but (much more / less ...). ¶ne ˋSA-ˋLI-ˋPWULQ ˊwohiˋlye ˊi KYENG ˊey ˋSIN ˊuˋlwo siˋle ˊtulˊGwo nˋ ˊhomolˋmye ˊnye-naˋmon SYENG-MWUN ˊistoˊ[Jn ye (1463 Pep 2:158b) when you yourself, Śāriputra, vest this sūtra with your faith, just how much more so do the śrāvakas (= first-stage hīnayāna disciples)! ˊmwo.m i na y iˋsywom aˋni ˋ ˊGwo nˋ ˊhomolˋmye meˋli ˋsto.nˋye (1482 Nam 1:53b) I have no body, much less a head! ilˋhwum ˊtwo tutˋti ˮmwot hoˋl i ˋˋGwo nˋ ˊhomolˋmye ˮpwoˋm istoˋn ye (1550 ¹Yenghem 5b) I have not even heard their names, much less seen them!
- ˊGwos < *- ˊkwos (? < - ˊkwo s). wanting it to happen. ¶ne-huy ˊtol.h on ˋKILQ hon ˮsaloˋm i ˊtowoyˊGwos hoˋn ye HYWUNG hon ˮsaloˋm i ˊtowoyˊGwos hon ˊye (1475 Nay 1:25b) do you want to become good people or bad people?
ˊGwos, alt (after l, LQ, y, i) of ˊkwos, pcl. just, precisely, indeed. ¶ ˋSYA-ˋLI-ˋPWULQ s alˋph oy ˊGwos (1447 Sek 6:33a) right in front of Śāriputra. ˋSYA-ˋLI-ˋPWULQ ˊGwos (1447 Sek 6:22b) just Śāriputra. aˋtol ˊGwos ˊnakeˋtun ... ˋstol ˊGwos ˊnakeˋtun (1459 Wel 8:96b) if it's a son that is born ... if it's a daughter that is born.

ˊ[G]wos, alt (after vowels other than i) of ˊkwos, pcl. just, precisely, indeed. ¶na ˊ[G]wos (1447 Sek 6:29a, 24:12b, 24:27a) I indeed.
- ˊGwu-, suf (? < -G- + modulator); CF -i-, -y-, -hi-, -ki-, -chi-, -u-, -ukhi-, -ikhi-, -li-, -iwu-, -ywu-; -wu-, -hwu-, -kwu-, -chwu-, -ay-; -o-, -u-, - ˊGwo-, -ˋGi-. makes vc. mey ˊGwu- (> meywu-) cause to shoulder < ˮmey- (> mēy- shoulder it).

/···h/. By 1445 before pause a noun-final ···h went unpronounced and was unwritten in Hankul. The ···h was retained before closely attached particles beginning with a vowel or a simple voiceless stop (such as ˊtwo and ˊkwa), with which it joined to produce the aspirated stops: ˊstah → ˊsta 'land', ˊstah ˮmaˋta → ˊsta ˮmaˋta; but ˊstahˋul → ˊstaˋhul, ˊstahˋkwa → staˋkhwa. The final aspirate of the strings ···lh, ···nh, ···mh behaved the same way: ˊkilh → ˊkil 'path'; but ˊkilhˋul → ˊkilˋhul, ˊkilhˋtwo → ˊkilˋthwo, ˊkilh ˊkwa → ˊkilˋkhwa. In this book we seek to reveal the underlying structures, yet permit conversion to the text orthography, through the judicious use of spaces and brackets, together with accent marks located before the syllable boundaries: ˊsta[h], ˊsta[h] ˮmaˋta, ˊstaˋh ul, ˊstaˋh two, ˊstaˋh kwa, ... From the late 1400s Korean began to restructure the h-final nouns so as to be just like those without the final aspirate (yielding modern kil, kil ul, kil to, kil kwa), and now only traces of the original ···h for a few of the nouns can be found surviving in compounds. Several nouns assimilated an initial stop to the final aspirate before it was dropped: ˊkwoh (kwoˋh ay 1447 Sek 13:38b) > ˊkhwoh (khwo.h ey 1677 Pak-cwung 2:47; cited from LCT) > khwo (ˊkhwo [ˊG]wa 1586 Sohak 3:7a) = kho 'nose'; polh 'arm' (polˋh ol 1447 Sek 6:2a) > pholh (pholˋh oy 1475 Nay 3:36a) > phol (phol ˊ[G]wa y 1489 Kup-kan 1:29; from LCT, accent inferred) = phal 'arm'; ˊkal/ ˊkalh (ˊkalˊGwa 1462 ¹Nung 6:28b), ˊkalh ˊkwa = ˊkalˋkhwa (1459 Wel 9:43b) > ˊkhalh (khal.h olwo 1617 Sin-sok chwung 3:2 [p.5]) > khal (khal ul ?1720+ Thayphyeng 1:11) = khal 'knife'. SEE ··· ˊthuˋl ey s. Noun-final ···lh elided that string when attaching the genitive

particle s; SEE ‑‑‑lh, s. CF ‑‑‑ng.
-h-, infix. makes paraintensives. SEE §12.3. CF kkelim c(h)ik hata is leery; hūyng hekhey [? < hekey = hakey] swiftly; kangphaluta < kaphaluta ? < ka paluta is steep / gaunt; yalphak [yalp-h-ak] rather thin; chom-chom fine, dense, delicate [? < cōm < cok^u/om, or directly from c(o)kom with k > h?].
ha < ˙ha, 1. inf < hata < °ha˙ta. CF ˙ha˙a.
   2. adv (< inf). much, many; extremely, very hard. ¶ ~ pissata is very expensive. ~ colla tāyta teases hard (for something). ~ cha-mukci anh.ta ("is not very cold and stale" =) isn't so bad, is fairly good. ¨mwo˙tin ˙PEP ˙ul ˙ha ci˙ze (1459 Wel 8:69b) much creating evil doctrine; creating many evil doctrines. SEE ha-chi ··· ; ha / hako mānh.ta, ha to. CF tāytan hi, mānh.i, phek, ssek, maywu, seywu, acwu, mopsi, cham, cēng-mal, kkway.
hā < ¨HHA.
   1. noun, adn. bottom, inferior, lower, lowest; (= alay) below. ¶ ~ -q kil bottom-quality goods. ~ chi low-grade stuff. ~ pokpu the lower abdomen. ~ chachey the under chassis. ~ sākwan a noncom(missioned officer). ~ wa kath.ta is as follows. ANT sāng.
   2. bnd adn. the last of two or three, later. ¶ ~ pānki the second semester / term. ~ pān-nyen the second half of the year. CF sāng, cwung.
   3. bnd postn. under. ¶ cengsey ~ under the situation. cocik ~ under the organization. coqken ~ under conditions. (··· uy) cihwi / cito ~ under the direction / guidance (of ···).
˙ha˙a, effective inf < °ha˙ta, adj. ¶ kunge˙kuy ˙sywo y ˙ha˙a (1459 Wel 1:24b) there are lots of cattle there. CF ¨hay (der adv).
haca, subj assert < hata. let's do/say/think/...; (= ~ māca) as soon as one does/says/thinks.
haca ko, subj assert + pcl. let's do it!
haca 'nta < haca (ko) hanta. suggests we do.
haca tul, subj assert + pcl (plural subject)
haca 'y, < haca (ko) hay
ha-ch' anh.ta, adj abbr < ha-chi anh.ta
ha-chi anh.ta, cpd adj, abbr < ha haci anh.ta.
   1. is none too good.
   2. is worthless, valueless, good-for-nothing, poor, trashy; is trivial, petty, insignificant; is of no account.
   3. mistake for ha cha-mukci anh.ta (is not so bad, is fairly good).

haci, suspective < hata.
   1. the questioned/denied fact of doing/saying /thinking; whether/that one does/says/thinks. ~ (lul) anh.ta does not do / say / think.
   2. the casual fact of doing / saying / thinking = a casual statement, question, command, or proposition. but, don't you know, suppose; I suppose/guess.
haci l', abbr < haci lul
haci man, 1. suspective + pcl. does/says/thinks but. 2. abbr < kule haci man = kuleh.ci man.
haita = ho˙i˙ta (vc) = sikhita (causes to do).
-hak (in yalphak adj-n) = -h-ak. SEE -h-.
hakey, 1. adverbative < hata; used as FAMILIAR command 'do!'.
   2. n. the familiar style of speech. ~ hata, vni. uses familiar speech.
haki, summative < hata. doing, saying/thinking, being, ...
haki l', abbr < haki lul
haki n', abbr < haki nun
haki nun, summative (< v or adj) + pcl.
   1. as for doing/being. ~ haci man does all right but, DOES do it but; is all right but, IS indeed but.
   2. in fact/truth, indeed. ¶ Haki nun kuleh.key tōy ya halq kes ia True, it's got to be that way.
haki ya, summative (< v or adj) + pcl.
   1. only doing / being.
   2. indeed, definitely. ¶ Haki ya tōn man iss.umyen cōh.un sāep ici It would definitely be a good business if one just had the money. Haki ya ku sālam māl to olh.ki n' hay Indeed what he says is quite true.
hako$_1$, ger < hata. ABBR -ko, -kho.
   1. (v) does and (also), doing, to do.
   2. (v) says and (also), saying, to say; thinks and (also), thinking, to think.
   3. (adj) is and (also); being, to be.
   4. (adj) [obs] being much, great, big (SEE ~ mānh.ta).
hako$_2$, quasi-pcl [< hako$_1$ (2)]. saying (quote) that [added at the end of something said or thought].
   ¶ Cōh.ta hako māl hayss.ta I said it was all right. Cōh.ta hako sayngkak hanta I think that it is all right. "Ne nun eti kass.ess.nun ya" hako ku nun na hanthey mul.ess.ta "Where have you been?" he asked me. "Swī tto nōlle osipsio" hako ku nun māl hayss.ta

He said, "Come visit me soon again". **Ku māl-thwu lo pwā "ku nun Phyengyangq sālam ikwun a" hako** (or: **ku nun Phyengyangq sālam ila ko) na nun sayngkak hayss.ta** From his accent I thought "Why, he is a Phyengyang man!" (I thought him to be ...).

NOTE: The report is direct, not paraphrased; it can be reported as SAID by anyone but as THOUGHT only by the speaker. CF **ko**.

hako₃, particle [< **hako₁**]. [colloq] = **kwa/wa** (with; and; like). Both options conjoined in a single phrase: *A hokwo B [k]wa ka* (1894 Gale 177, sentence 532) 'A and B'.

hako chelem, pcl + pcl (= **kwa chelem**). ¶**Tongkun-i hako chelem Kilqswu hako to ūy cōh.key nōlmyen cōh.ci anh.e?** Why don't you try to play with Kilqswu in as friendly a way as you do with Tongkun-i?

hako cocha, pcl + pcl (= **kwa cocha**). ¶**Ku sālam hako cocha mōs kakey hani to-taychey nwukwu hako kath.i kala 'n' māl ia** You won't let me go even with him, then just who in the world DO you want me to go with? **Emeni hako cocha sālki silh.ta 'ni nwukwu hako sālkeyss.ta 'n' māl ia** You (say you) don't want to live with your mother, even; just who WILL you live with?

hako ka, pcl + pcl (= **kwa ka**) [somewhat awkward]. ¶**Poktong-i hako ku uy chinkwu hako ka Hān kang ey se iksa hayss.ta 'y** They say Poktong-i and a friend of his drowned in the Han River. **I kes hako ce kes hako ka cēy-il mukepta** This one and that one over there are the heaviest.

hako khenyeng, pcl + pcl (= **kwa khenyeng**). ¶**I tōn kaciko n' caney hako khenyeng na honca to mōs kakeyss.ney** With this amount of money I won't be able to go even by myself, much less take you along.

hako kkaci, pcl + pcl. ¶**Ku sālam hako kkaci sai ka napputa 'ni** You are on bad terms even with him! **Ku sālam hako kkaci mōs kakey hani to-taychey musunq yengmun in ci molukeyss.e** I can't understand why in the world I am not allowed to go even with him.

NOTE: The expected synonym **kwa kkaci** is as unlikely to occur; **kwa** is less frequent than **hako**, and **hako kkaci** is infrequent itself.

hako l', abbr < **hako lul** (= **kwa lul**).
hako 'la to, pcl + cop var inf + pcl (= **kwa 'la to**). ¶**Kath.i kalq sālam i ēps.uni Pak kwun hako 'la to kath.i tte-nalq ka hap.nita** Since there is no one go with (me), I guess I'll leave with Mr Pak.

hako lul, pcl + pcl (= **kwa lul**). ¶**Swut-kal [swuq-kal] hako ceq-kal hako lul hap-chye se "swuce" 'la ko hanta** A set of spoon and chopsticks is called "swuce". **I pang hako ce pang hako lul swuli hay noh.key** Have this room and that room over there remodeled.

hako mace, pcl + pcl (= **kwa mace**). ¶**Ku sālam hako mace sai ka napputa 'n māl in ka?** You mean you are on bad terms even with him? **Emeni hako mace kath.i an kakeyss.ta 'ni to-taychey nwukwu hako kakeyss.ta 'nun ke ya** You won't go with your mother, even; who on earth WILL you go with?

hako man, pcl + pcl (= **kwa man**). ¶**Kūn sip-nyenq tong-an emeni nun na hako man sal.e wass.ˢup.nita** Mother has been living alone with me for nearly ten years. **Ku sālam hako man co'.yong hi yēyki hako siph.sup.nita** I'd like to have a quiet talk with him alone.

hako mānh.ta, ger < obs adj + adj. is plenty, plentiful, abundant, innumerable, numerous. ¶**Hako mānh.un caysan ul tangtay ey tā sse pelyess.ta** He squandered a tremendous fortune within his own lifetime. **Hako mānh.un sālam kawuntey way na poko ku īl ul hala 'nun ya** Why do you pick me of all people to do the work? VAR **hekwu mānh.ta**. SYN **ha mānh.ta**.

hako n' (= **hako nun**), 1. gerund + particle.

1a. after doing (/saying/...).

1b. doing/saying/... habitually. ~ **hayss.ta** used to do/say/... .

2. pcl + abbr pcl = **hako nun** (= **kwa nun**)
hako 'na, pcl + cop advers (= **kwa 'na**). ¶**Pak kwun hako 'na kath.i ka-polq ka yo** Shall I go with Mr Pak, maybe?

hako 'na-ma, pcl + cop extended advers (= **kwa 'na-ma**). ¶**Kath.i kalq sālam i ēps.uni Pak kwun hako 'na-ma kath.i kalq ka hay yo** Since there is no one to go with me, I think maybe I'll go with Mr Pak, anyway.

hako nun, pcl + pcl (= **kwa nun**). ¶**Pak sensayng hako nun sip-nyenq tong-an sakwie on sai 'p.nita** I have been associated with Mr Pak for ten years now. **Ney-kkān** (= **-kkās** = **-kkacis**) **nom hako nun ssawuki to silh.ta** I do not care to fight with the likes of you.

hako pota, pcl + pcl (= kwa pota). than with. ¶Kim sensayng hako pota Pak sensayng hako kanun key cōh.keyss.ˢo It would be better to go with Mr Pak rather than with Mr Kim.

hako puthe, pcl + pcl (= kwa puthe).

hako to, 1. pcl + pcl (= kwa to). ¶Ku sālam hako to kath.i mōs kalq pa ey ya chalali an kanun key cōh.keyss.ta I think I'd better not go at all if I can't go with him, even. Ku nun apeci hako to sai ka napputa 'y They say he is on bad terms with his father, too.
2. ger + pcl. even doing (/ saying / ...).

hako uy, pcl + pcl (= kwa uy). ¶Kim ssi hako uy yēyki nun phek hūngmi iss.ess.ta The talk with Mr Kim was quite interesting. Cēnca hako cwungseng-ca hako uy chaiq cem ul māl hasio State the differences between an electron and a neutron.

hako ya, pcl + pcl (= kwa ya). ¶Ku sālam hako ya kalq swu ēps.ci I don't think I can go with HIM.
~ **māl lo.** ¶Kim sensayng hako ya māl lo ttel.e cilq swu ēps.nun sai 'ci yo It is with Mr Kim that I can never break up.

hakwu [var] = hako (all meanings)

hakwun, APPERCEPTIVE < hata adj. oh it's ... .

hakwu n' [var] = hako n'

hal(q)₁ < *hol(q)*, prosp mod < hata < °*ho·ta*. to do / say / think / be / ... .

hal(q)₂ < *hal(q)*, 1. prosp mod < hata < °*ha·ta*, obs adj.
 1a. (epitheme extruded from the subject). ¶... ˙PWOK ˙TUK ˙i e˙nu y ˙za ha˙l i '-ngi s ˙kwo (1447 Sek 23:5a) of happiness and virtue, which is the more plentiful?
 1b. (summational epitheme). ¶hal ˙s i.n i (1482 Kum-sam 2:15b) it means they are many.
 2. adn = han great. **hal-apeci, -ape' nim** grandfather. **hal-'mi** a granny; an old woman. **hal-'meni, hal-'me' nim** grandmother.

hala < *ho·la*, 1. subj attent (= quoted / literary imperative) < hata < °*ho·ta*. (tells one) to do / say / think / be / ... ; do! CF hay la.
2. = hale (go) to do.

halai, postmod (? and verb-mood suf) [DIAL] = **kwulye** (apperceptive: Oh I see ...).

hala 'nta, abbr < hala (ko) hanta

hala 'y, abbr < hala (ko) hay. *holoy la* (1894 Gale 78) = *halayla* (1887 Scott 60) = hala 'y la tell him to do it!

halq ci, prosp mod < hata + postmod

hale, purposive < hata. (moves, goes) for the purpose of doing / saying / ... .

hal i, prosp mod + postmod / quasi-free n (often spelled **hali**)

halita₁ (hal i 'ta), prosp assert < hata

halita₂, vi. indulges in luxury, luxuriates, is extravagant (in).

halita₃, adj, LIGHT ↔ **hulita**. is indistinct, vague, hazy; is ambiguous, equivocal.

halq ka, prosp mod + postmod (often spelled **halkka**). the question whether to (whether one will) do / say / think / be / ... .

halla, 1. prosp adjunctive < hata. what with doing/saying/thinking/being and all ... ; let one do / say / think / be ... . 2. [VAR] = **halye**

halla 'y, abbr < halla hay = halye (ko) hay

hal.nun, prosp proc mod + < hata. ~ ci.

hal ya, prosp mod < hata + postmod (often spelled **halya**)

halya, 1. = hal ya, prosp mod + postmod. the question whether to (whether one will) do / say / think/be. SYN halq ka (often spelled **halkka**).
2. [VAR] = **halye**

halye, intentive < hata. with the intention of doing / saying / thinking / ... . ~ **(ko) hanta** intends / plans to (do), wants to (do), will (do).

halyem (una), cajolative < hata (+ pcl). do please do it now.

ham < *hom*, subst < hata < °*ho·ta*; CF **ha.yem** < ˙*ho·yem*, ˙*h(o·y)wom*. doing, saying, thinking, being, ... ; [DOCUMENTARY style] does, says, thinks, is, ...
~ **ulo** (often spelled **hamulo**) because one does / says / thinks / is / ... .
~ **ey** (often spelled **hamey, hamay**) at / upon doing / saying / thinking / being / ... .
~ **a** (often spelled **hama**) let me do it.

ham, subst < °*ha·ta*, adj.

¨**ham,** modulated subst < °*ha·ta*. ¶˙ku ¨ha˙m ol ˙pwo˙sya (1463 Pep 5:100a) sees the multitude. ˙PALQ-PWONG ˙oy ¨wo˙m i ¨ha˙m ol muten ˙hi ne˙kinwos˙ta (1482 Kum-sam 3:19a) treats casually the fact that the coming of the Eight Winds [which fan the passions] is frequent. [˙HHWAN-NAN] ¨ha.m ay [PPYEN-QAN] ˙hi ¨sati ¨mwot ˙hoswo˙la (1481 Twusi 8:43a) with so many misfortunes we cannot live at ease.

hama (= ham a), assumptive < hata. let me do it (for you).

ha mānh.ta (inf < obsolete adj + adj) = **hako mānh.ta** is plentiful, abundant, innumerable, numerous. ¶**Ku ney nwukwu 'la 'n māl yo, ha mānh.un sālam ey ālq swu iss.e?** How will you know who they are among so many people?
hamay, [lit] contingent < **hata**. at one's doing / saying / thinking / being (= **ham ey**).
hamey = **hamay**, **ham ey**
ham ey, subst < **hata** + pcl. SEE **ham**.
hamkkey, adv. together (with ⋯). < *hom-skuy* (?1517 Pak 1:21b) < *hon ˙psk uy* (1459 Wel 1:50a) at one (and the same) time.
hamye, conjunctive < **hata**. does / says / thinks / and (also).
hamyen, conditional < **hata**. if / when one does / says / thinks / is. **cachis** ~ (= **cachis hata ka nun**) at the slightest thing (slip / inadvertency or provocation). **kelphis** ~ for no reason, without provocation; quickly, at once, in a flash. **yecha** ~ if anything happens.
hamyen se, conditional < **hata** + pcl.
1. while one does / says / thinks / is / ...; ~ **to** (⋯ , yet). ¶**nolay lul hamyen se chwum ul chwuta** dances and sings at the same time.
2. SEE **'myen se (to)**.
han₁ < *hon*, mod < **hata** < °*ho˙ta*. that (someone) has done / said / thought / ... ; that is.
han₂ < *hon*, adn, num (alt of **hana** < *honah*).
  1. 1a. one, a(n). SYN **il**. ¶ ~ **salam** one man, a man. ~ **tal** one month, a month. ~ **cam₁** a spell of sleep, a nap.
  1b. a certain. ~ **sālam** a certain man.
  2. the same (CF **han kaci**). ¶ ~ **maum**, ~ **ttus** (of) the same mind, of one accord. ~ **pay** the same litter / brood. ~ **tongsayng** a blood sibling. **Twūl i han cip ey sānta** The two live in the same house.
  3. the whole / entire; full. CF **ōn**, **cen**. ¶ ~ **congil** the whole day long. ~ **koul ul chaci hata** possesses the whole county. ~ **yelum ul nakk.si cil lo ponayta** spends all the summer fishing.
  4. the peak, the extreme, the most, the very. ~ **cam₂** deepest sleep; the final long sleep of the silkworm. ~ **kawuntey** the very midst. ~ **kopi** the very climax/height. ~ **mul** ("the main stream"=) the height of the season (when fish / produce is at its best). ~ **nac** broad daylight. ~ **pamq-cwung** the midst of the night, the middle of the dark. ~ **patak** the busiest spot. ~ **pokphan** the very middle. ~ **tewi / chwuwi** the height of the heat / cold.
  5. about, approximately. ~ **yelhul** about ten days. ~ **ō-chen wen** about five thousand wen.
han₃ < *han*, adn [mod < **hata** < °*ha˙ta*, obs adj; CF **hal**]. big, large, great, main; proper. ¶ ~ **kekceng** a great worry. ~ **kunsim** great anxiety. ~ **kil** (> **hayngkil**) a vehicular road, a highway (CF **khun kil** a large road). ~ **swūm** a great sigh (of anxiety).
hān₄, adn [? < **han₃**; CF **hanul**]. outdoors, outside. ¶**hān tey** an outdoor (an open) place (CF **han tey** one place). **hān nwun** eyes looking away (averted). **hān twun** a bivouac, sleeping outdoors. **hān pap** food made after the regular mealtime is over.
hān₅ < ¨*HHAN*, n.
  1. (= **hānkyey**) a limit, limits; a bound, bounds. ¶ ~ **i iss.ta** is limited, restricted, finite, has a limit. ~ **i ēps.ta** is unlimited, boundless, endless, infinite, eternal. **musepki (ka) hān i ēps.ta** is frightened no end.
  2. (= **kihan**) a term, a period, a time limit, time. ¶ ~ **cen ey** before the time is up, before the fixed date. ~ **nāy ey** within the period of time. ~ **i ota** the time is at hand, the deadline comes up. ~ **i tā hata** the term expires (runs out), the time comes to an end (is up). **yelhul hān hako tōn ul chwī hay cwuta** lends money on condition that it be returned within ten days.
  3. (as postmod) as far as, to the limit that; (NEG +) unless. ¶**wuli ka ānun hān ey** (NKd 4926b) to the best of our knowledge. **Sāceng i he hanun hān ppalli tol.a okeyss.ta** I'll come back as soon as the situation permits. **Ney ka kaci anh.nun hān na to kaci anh.keyss.ta** Unless you go, I won't go either. **Toylq swu iss.nun hān tōn ul mānh.i chwī hay cwuo** Lend me as much money as possible. **Nay ka sal.e iss.nun hān ney maum tay lo haci mōs hanta** So long as I live, I won't let you have your way (= You'll have to do it over my dead body).
han, mod < °*ha˙ta*. much, many. SEE *ha˙n ye*. [Mistakenly written "*hyan*" in *hyan ˙TTAY-˙CYWUNG* (1465 Wen 2:1:1:11a) the many crowds.]
  1. epitheme extruded from the subject.
  1a. ¶*han ˙TTWOK ˙ol* (1459 Wel 21:118b) the many poisons. *han SOYNG ˙ol* (1462 ¹Nung

5:85b) for many lives. *han ka˙hi* (1463 Pep 2:113b) a horde of dogs. *nulkun han api* (1632 Twusi-cwung 14:17a) an old gaffer.

1b. (subject = the possessor). ¶ ˙*skwoy han twoco˙k ol* (1445 ¹Yong 19) the wileful thieves.

2. summational epitheme. ¶*co˙cwo ˙thye han SSI-˙CYELQ ey ˙za* (1465 Wen 2:3:1:52a) only when they were regularly striking in force (= in large numbers). *mu˙su.m u˙lye ¨mal han ¨yang ho˙l i ˙Gwo* (?1517‾ Pak 1:74a) why do you talk so much?

¨*han*, modulated mod < °*ha˙ta*. SEE ¨*ha˙n i*, ¨*hun ˙t i*.

hana < *honah* < *honnah* (?1517‾ Pak 1:42a; CF 1874 Putsillo *hanna / hanai*) ? < **hot[o]na* (1103 Kyeylim), numeral (**han** < *hon* before a noun or a counter).

1. one, one thing; the one ⋯ the other (one). ¶ ~ ~ one by one, piece by piece, separately. ~ **ssik** (also **hanak ssik**) one each. **catong-cha** ~ **twūl** (or **han twūl**) one or two cars. **Hana nun kēm.ko hana nun huyta** The one is black and the other is white. **Hana nun na 'ykey tōn i ēps.ta** For one thing, I have no money.

2. only one; the only one. ¶**I chayk ilk.un sālam un ne hana 'ta** You are the only one that has read this book.

3. the same, one and the same. ¶**I kil lo kana ce kil lo kana māy hana 'ta** It is the same whether you go this way or that way. **I moca 'na ce moca 'na kaps un hana 'ta** Both hats are the same price.

4. one body. ¶**Cen-kwuk.min i hana i toyta** [literary; = **hana ka toynta**] The entire nation is united. **hana i toye ssawuta, hana ka toye se ssawuta** fight as one body.

hana, 1. FAMILIAR indic attent < *hata*. does one do/say/think?; whether/or one does/says/thinks.

2. advers < *hata*. does/says/thinks/is/... but; whether it does/is (or whether ⋯).

3. adv (abbr < *kule hana*). however, but, yet.

hanak [var of **hana** before ssik]. ~ **ssik** = **hana ssik** one each. 1904 Razvedchiku has **hannak-si** for one 'each' (King 1990).

hana ka, 1. n + pcl. one [nominative].

2. (cop FAMILIAR indic attent + pcl) = **hanun ya/ka ka**. ¶**Kuleh.key hay ya hana ka mūncey 'ta** The question is whether we have to do that.

hana lul, 1. n + pcl. one [accusative].

2. (cop FAMILIAR indic attent + pcl) = **hanun ya/ka lul**. ¶**Kuleh.key hay ya hana lul al.e pwā la** Find out whether we have to do that.

hana twūl, cpd num = **han twūl** (one or two)

han cham, num + n. (for) a spell / time / while.

han ci, mod < *hata* + postmod. ~ **'la**. SEE -**un ci 'la,** *hon ci 'la*.

han cuk, cpd adv (adj mod + postmod). it is so (therefore), then (= **kule han cuk**). ¶**Han cuk incey etteh.key hanun kes i cōh.ulq ka** Then, what should we do now? **Han cuk tāytap haki lul caki nun ku kyēyhoyk ey chamka mōs hakeyss.ta ko hayss.ta** Then, he replied that he would not take part in the plan.

haney, FAMILIAR indic assert < *hata*. does / says / thinks / is / ... .**han han,** adn + (num + ⋯). about one (⋯).

ha-ngi˙'˙ta, adj polite + cop indic assert. is much; are many. ¶ ˙*SSIM ˙hi ha-ngi˙'˙ta* (1463 Pep 7:68b, 1464 Kumkang 62b) they are quite plentiful.

hani, adv (abbr < **kule hani**). so, therefore, then; ~ **-kka (nun / n')** SAME. ¶**Hani ka-pwā ya 'keyss.ta** So, I have to go. **Hani eccemyen cōh.ulq ka** Such being the case, what shall we do? **Hani eccayss.ta māl in ya** So what?

hani, sequential < *hata*. does / says / thinks / is and so. ~ **-kka (nun / n')** SAME.

hani, indic attent (= question) < *hata*. does one do / say / think / ... ?

¨*ha.n i,* modulated mod < °*ha˙ta* + postmod. ¶*kutuy ˙lul ¨pwon t oy n'* [¨*TTWOW-˙KHUY*] ¨*ha.n i* (1481 Twusi 7:21a) looking at you, [one sees that] the vital energy of the Way is great.

ha˙n i˙'˙la, mod < °*ha˙ta* + postmod + copula indicative assertive. is much, are many. ¶ ˙*hoyn ¨SSYANG ˙i ha˙n i˙'˙la* (1459 Wel 2:31b) there are many white elephants.

han ka, mod + postmod

han nath, 1. num + counter. one item.

2. adv/adn only, merely, nothing but. CF **tan**.

˙*hanon,* proc mod < °*ha˙ta*. ¶*ye˙lum˙hano˙n i* (1445 ¹Yong 2, the Manlyek text) its fruits are plentiful.

han phyen, cpd n, postmod, adv (num + n). CF **phyen, myēn, ilmyen, pānmyen; ilpang**.

1. one side; one way, one direction. ¶**kil uy** ~ one side of the street. **han phyenq kil (ey)** (for) one way.

2. ~ **ulo** somewhat, to some extent, in a way, a bit [NOT VERY COMMON]. ¶**Āmu to poici**

anh.ess.um ulo han phyen ulo nun kekceng to tōyss.ˢup.nita I was a bit worried that no one had shown up.

3. postmod. in addition to doing; on the one hand ⋯ on the other (hand); while (= -umyen se, tongsi ey); and, but (at the same time); while (on the one hand) ⋯ still. ¶cimsung ul kil-tul.inun ~ nongsa lul sīcak hata on the one hand domesticates animals and on the other begins farming. Sān.ep i kaypal toye onun han phyen wensi-cek in ssi-cok sāhoy ka mune cikey toyess.ta As industry came to develop, the primitive clan society started to collapse. Ku uy iyaki nun sulphun han phyen wusuwess.ta His tale was sad but at the same time amusing.

4. adv. ¶han phyen ⋯ tto han phyen ⋯ . on the one hand ⋯ and/but on the other hand ⋯ .

hanta < ˙hono˙ta, proc indic assert < hata. does / says / thinks / ⋯ . [colloq = lit hata v]

hanta 'l, abbr < hanta (ko) hal

hanta 'm, abbr < hanta (ko) ham. I wonder ⋯ .

hanta 'n, 1. abbr < hanta (ko) han.

2. = hanta '(nu)n

hanta '(nu)n, abbr < hanta (ko) ha(nu)n.

1. that says it does / says / thinks.

2. pseudo-adn. admitted to be capable/able or strong; mighty, influential, powerful, eminent, respectable. ¶Hanta 'nun cāngsa to i ke l' tul.e ollilq swu ka ēps.keyss.ci However mighty a strong man he might be, could anyone lift this?!

hanta 'y, abbr < hanta (ko) hay

hantey, pcl [DIAL] = hanthey

han tey, 1. mod + noun. one/same place; together (with).

2. mod + postmod. did (or is) and/but ⋯ .

hanthay, pcl [DIAL] = hanthey

hanthey, pcl [colloq] = eykey to, at, for, by (a person/creature).

hanthey ccum, pcl + pcl. ¶Ku ay tul hanthey ccum mōsq ikilq key mue iss.e What makes you think you can't get the best of boys no better than they are?!

hanthey ccum iya, pcl + pcl + pcl. ¶Ku ay tul hanthey ccum iya mōsq ikilq key mue iss.e What makes you think you can't win over boys no better than THEY are?!

hanthey chelem, pcl + pcl. ¶Ku i hanthey chelem tōn kkwue tālla 'ki him tun sālam un ēps.ta He is the hardest man in the world to borrow money from.

hanthey cocha, pcl + pcl. ¶Ku i hanthey cocha phyēnci lul nāyci mōs hayss.ta I haven't been able to write even to him.

hanthey hako, pcl + pcl. ¶Ku i hanthey hako ne hanthey mānh.un sinsey lul ciess.ta I owe a great deal to him and to you.

hanthey ka, pcl + pcl. ¶Kim kwun hanthey ka ani 'la Pak kwun hanthey tul.ess.ta It is not from Mr Kim but from Mr Pak that I heard it.

hanthey khenyeng, pcl + pcl. ¶Apeci hanthey khenyeng hyeng hanthey to mul.e poci anh.ko ku tōn ul ssess.ta He spent the money without asking even his brother, much less his father.

hanthey kkaci, pcl + pcl. ¶Ku i hanthey kkaci phyēy lul kkichyess.ta I troubled even him.

hanthey 'ko, pcl + cop ger. SEE iko.

hanthey l', abbr < hanthey lul

hanthey lang pcl + pcl. ¶Incey ku i hanthey lang (tā) insa kalye 'nta Now I am going to pay a (courtesy) call on him and the others. Hyeng hanthey lang tull(y)e se mul.e poko olye 'nta I'll drop by my brother's family and find out about it. Ney sā-chon hanthey lang tā allinun kes i cōh.keyss.ta I think it would be better to let your cousin and all (them) know. SYN hanthey sekken/lang; eykey sekken/lang.

hanthey 'la to, pcl + cop var inf + pcl. Ney hyeng hanthey to māl ul hako ku tōn ul sse la Talk to your older brother at least before you spend the money.

hanthey lo, pcl + pcl. toward/to (a person/creature) [colloq; = eykey lo].

hanthey lo puthe, pcl + pcl + pcl. from (a person/creature) [colloq; = eykey lo puthe].

hanthey lul, pcl + pcl. ¶Kim ssi hanthey lul mence tull(y)e se Pak ssi hanthey lo kalq cakceng ita I think I'll drop by at Mr Kim's first and then go to Mr Pak's.

hanthey mace, pcl + pcl. ¶Hyeng hanthey mace ku yāyki lul mōs hayss.ta I didn't get to tell the story even to my brother.

hanthey man, pcl + pcl. ¶Incey ku i hanthey man sungnak ul et.umyen toynta Now we only have to get consent from him.

hanthey mankhum, pcl + pcl. ¶Emeni hanthey mankhum apeci hanthey to cal hay tulye la Treat your father as nicely as you do your mother.

hanthey mankhum man, pcl + pcl + pcl.
¶ Emeni hanthey mankhum man apeci hanthey to cal hay tulye la (All I ask is that you) treat your father only as nicely as you treat your mother.
hanthey mata, pcl + pcl = eykey mata
hanthey n', abbr < hanthey nun
hanthey 'na, pcl + cop advers. ¶ Halq kes ēps.umyen tongmu hanthey 'na nōlle kalyem una If you have nothing to do why don't you go see some friends?
hanthey 'na-ma, pcl + cop extended advers. ¶ Ku i hanthey 'na-ma tōn ul kkwue tālla 'lq ka hanta I'm thinking of asking even him to lend me some money. Ney hyeng hanthey 'na-ma māl ul hako ku tōn ul sse ya 'ci You should talk to your brother at least before you spend the money.
hanthey nun, pcl + pcl. as for to / at / for / by (a person or a creature). ¶ Atul hanthey nun tōn ul ponayss.ci man, ttal hanthey nun an ponayss.ta I sent money to my son but not to my daughter. Ku i hanthey nun cēng-mal kulen māl mōs hakeyss.ta I really couldn't say a thing like that to HIM!
hanthey pota (to), pcl + pcl (+ pcl). ¶ Apeci hanthey pota (to) emeni hanthey māl hanun kes i naulq ka Would it be better to talk to Mother rather than Father?
hanthey puthe, pcl + pcl. ¶ Sensayng nim hanthey puthe insa hako hyeng hanthey insa hay la Greet your teacher first, then greet your brother.
hanthey se, pcl + pcl [colloq] = eykey se.
¶ Ittakum atul hanthey se phyēnci ka onta I receive occasional letters from my son. Ku sālam hanthey se tōn i elma 'na toyp.nikka How much are you supposed to get from him? Ku hanthey se tāytap ul ēncey kkaci 'na kitalilq swu ēps.ta I cannot wait for an answer from him indefinitely. Ku hanthey se elmaq tong-an sosik i ēps.ta I haven't heard from him for a while. Ku nun ileh.ta celeh.ta nam hanthey se māl ul tul.ulq īl i ēps.ta He is not open to criticism. Wēynq īl in ci ku hanthey se yo say sosik ēps.ta I don't know why (= for some reason or other) I don't hear from him any more. Wēyn kkatalk in ci, ku sālam hanthey se tapcang i ēps.ta I don't know why, but he doesn't answer my letters. Ape' nim hanthey se phyēnci lul pat.un hwū ey ne hanthey tāytap hakeyss.ta I'll give you an answer after I get the letter from Father.
hanthey se ka = eykey se ka
hanthey sekken, pcl + pcl = hanthey lang
hanthey se mata, pcl + pcl + pcl = eykey se mata.
hanthey se n', abbr < hanthey se nun
hanthey se puthe, pcl + pcl + pcl = eykey se puthe.
hanthey se to, pcl + pcl + pcl. from (a person) too / even / either. ¶ Apeci kkey se khenyeng hyeng nim hanthey se to phyēnci ka ēps.ta There has been no letter even from my brother, much less from my father.
hanthey se tul, pcl + pcl + pcl = eykey se tul
hanthey se ya, pcl + pcl + pcl = eykey se ya
hanthey 'ta (ka), pcl + cop transferentive (+ pcl): SEE eykey. ¶ Nwukwu hanthey 'ta ilen māl ul hay Just who do you think it is you are talking to (saying such things)?
hanthey to, pcl + pcl. ¶ Ku i hanthey to alliko na hanthey to allye cwuki palanta I hope you will let him know and me too.
hanthey tul, pcl + pcl = eykey tul
hanthey uy, pcl + pcl. ¶ Ku i hanthey uy pic i elma 'na toynun ya How much is your debt to him?
hanthey wa, pcl + pcl. ¶ Ku i hanthey wa na hanthey ne nun musun wēnhan i iss.e kulen māl ul hanun ya What (grudge) do you have against him and me that makes you say that?
hanthey ya, pcl + pcl. ¶ Talun sālam eykey n' allici mōs hay to ne hanthey ya allici I'll let YOU know for sure even if I inform no one else.
~ **māl lo**. ¶ Ne hanthey ya māl lo mānh.un sinsey lul ciess.ta It is to YOU that I owe a great deal.
hanthey ya tul, pcl + pcl + pcl = eykey ya tul
˝*han ˙t i*, modulated mod < ˚*ha˙ta* + postmod + pcl. ¶ HHUNG-SA ˙KKYEY ˝*han ˙t i a˙ni 'syas˙ta* (1463 Pep 3:190a) they are not so numerous as the gāthās which are like the sand of the Ganges in number.
hanula (ko), proc adjunct < hata (+ pcl). what with doing / saying / thinking / being and all.
hanun < ˙*ho˙non*, proc mod < hata < ˚*ho˙ta*. that is doing / saying / thinking / ... .
~ **ka**, ~ **ya** (often spelled **hanunya**) the question whether one is doing / saying / thinking.

~ i the one who is doing / ... ; (often spelled hanuni) the fact (or question) of doing / ... .
han ya, mod < **hata** + postmod
hanya, 1. **han' ya** [lit] abbr < **hanun ya** (the question whether one does / ...).
2. **hany a** [colloq] = **hani** does one do / say / think / ... ? [+ pcl a]
3. **han ya** the question whether one has done / said (or: whether one is). SYN **han ka**.
ha·n ye, adj mod + postmod. ¶*KWONG-'TUK i ha·n ye "cyeku·n ye* (1447 Sek 19:4a) are his meritorious achievements many or few?
hao, 1. AUTH statement or question < **hata**.
2. the authoritative (semiformal) style.
hapci yo, FORMAL CASUAL POLITE. does.
hapsey, FORMAL-FAMILIAR subj assertive (= proposition). let's do / say / think / ... .
hapsyo → **hapsio**
has, adn. 1. padded with cotton wadding. ~ **kes**, ~ **os** padded clothes. ~-**q ipul** padded quilt. ~ **paci** padded trousers. ~ **twulwu-maki** padded overcoat. ~ **cekoli** padded vest.
2. having a spouse (ANT **hol**). ~ **api** a man with a wife. ~ **emi** a woman with a husband.
hasa [lit] = **hasye, hasie**
hase = **hasye**
hasey, 1. FAMILIAR subj assert (proposition). let's do / say / think / ... .
2. [abbr < **hasyey yo**] = **hasye** (INTIMATE hon statement / question / command / proposition).
hasey yo, var < **hasye** (hon inf < **hata**) + pcl. deigns to do/say/think/be/... (POLITE statement / question / command / proposition).
hasie = **hasye**
hasil(q) < *'hosil(q)*, prosp mod < **hasita**.
hasim < *'hosim*, subst < **hasita**.
hasin < *'hosin*, mod < **hasita**. that (one) deigned to do/say/think, that one deigns to be.
'hasin, hon mod < °*ha·ta*, adj. ¶ "*PWON-LOY 'hasin 'KILQ-'KHYENG 'ey* (1449 Kok 18) to the happy events and the good omens which were plentiful from the start ... .
hasipsio, 1. please do (FORMAL hon command).
2. n. (= **contay**) the formal style of speech (**hap.nita, hap.nikka, hasipsio**, ...). ~ **hata** (vni) uses formal speech.
hasita, hon < **hata** v, adj. deigns to do / say / think / be / ... .
hasosey, inflectional ending (? and postmod) [obs] = **(-)kwulye** (apperceptive) Oh I see ... .

hasya [lit] = **hasye**
hasye, hon inf < **hata**. deigns to do / say / think / be; [often =] you do/say/think/are. ~ **to** even if one deign(s) to do/say/think/be. ~ **se (nun)** deigns to do/say/think/be and then; ~ **(se) ya** just/only by deigning to do / say / think / be, just deign to do/say/think/be and (then), only if one deigns to do/say/think/be. ~ **yo** (= **hasey yo**) deigns to do / say / think / be [POLITE statement / question/command/proposition]. CF **hay, ha.ye**.
hata$_{1-8}$ < °*ho·ta*; inf **hay** [colloq] or **ha.ye** [lit] < *'ho·ye* = *'ho·ya*. (The infinitive of **hata**$_9$ < °*ha·ta* is **ha** < *'ha*.) For an explanation of the irregular infinitive see °*ho·ta*.
hata$_1$, vt.
1. does, performs, makes, acts, conducts, practices. ¶**il ul** ~ does a job, works. **māl ul** ~ speaks, talks. **sēn ul** ~ does good, practices virtue. **yēnsel ul** ~ makes a speech. **cēncayng ul** ~ wages a war. **casal ul** ~ commits suicide. **halq swu iss.ta** is able to do it; it is doable, feasible, practicable. **halq swu ēps.ta** is unable to do it; it is undoable, unfeasible; there is no help for it, nothing can be done about it, it is inevitable.
2. makes (CF **sām.ta, cīs.ta**). ¶**ku ^{n}yeca lul an^{h}ay lo** ~ makes the woman one's wife.
3. experiences, goes through. ¶**kosayng ul** ~ undergoes hardship. **cingyek ul** ~ serves one's term.
4. acts (as), serves (as), works (as). ¶**uysa nolus ul** ~ practices medicine. **kongmu-wen nolus ul** ~ works as a civilian.
5. costs, is worth (CF **tulta**). ¶**sakwa han kay ey sam-payk wen** ~ the apples are three hundred wen each. **ō-payk man wen hanun cip** a house that costs five million wen.
6. [? DIAL, ? Japanese usage] passes, elapses (CF **cīnayta, kata**). ¶**elma an hay se** (= **ka se**) before long. **Sip-o pun hamyen** (= **kamyen**) **cong i chikeyss.ta** The bell will ring in ten minutes.
7. wears (CF **chata, ipta, kēlta, sin.ta, ssuta**). ¶**kwi teph.kay lul** ~ wears earmuffs.
8. (= **mekta**) eats; (= **masita**) drinks; (= **phiwuta**) smokes.
hata$_2$, vi.
1. says, tells, suggests, orders: preceded by the quotation, usually in indirect form and in the PLAIN-QUOTATIVE style, either directly or

with intervening particle **(ha)ko**. ¶**Ku nun na hanthey cwukeyss.ta (ko) hayss.ey yo** He said (that) he would give it to me = He told me that he would give it. **Ku nun na hanthey ku ka chinkwu hanthey cwukeyss.ta (ko) hayss.ey yo** He told me that he would give it to a friend. **Na hanthey ¹nayil ola (ko) hayss.ˢup.nita** They told me to come tomorrow. **Apeci ka san ulo kaca ko hayss.nun ya?** Did Father suggest going (suggest that we go) to the mountains? **Ney kes ila (ko) haci anh.ess.nun ya** Didn't you say it was yours? **Nay kes in ya (ko) hayss.e** He asked if it was mine.

NOTE: It is not always apparent how much of the preceding part is the quotation. Only the context can make it clear whether an initial **ku ka/nun** refers to the subject of "says" or to the subject of the quotation − or to both; whether **ku hanthey/eykey** refers to the person "to" whom spoken or "to/for" whom the quoted action is done − or to both.

2. thinks, intends, plans, wants. (After the intentive **-ulye** or intentive + **ko**, or after **-ko ce**.) ¶**Mikwuk ey kalye (ko) hanta** intends/plans/wants to go to America.

CF **-ess.umyen hanta** (SEE **-umyen**), **-ki lo hanta**.

hata₃, postnominal verb. does.

1. occurs after verbal nouns, both separable (virtually all vn of two or more syllables) and inseparable (most one-syllable vn). **cheng ~** invites, requests (vnt insep). **sok ~** belongs (vni insep). **kongpu ~** studies (vnt sep). **kyelhon ~** gets married (vni sep).

2. occurs after impressionistic adverbs (all inseparable) and means "gives the impression of doing"; here noted Xh, XXh = Xk.

3. occurs after postmodifier **(l)lak**. SEE **-(u)l ak/lak**.

4. **mulken ~** buys merchandise (for resale). This is limited to the purposive: **mulken hale kanta/onta (/taninta/...)** goes/comes to get goods to retail.

hata₄, postnominal adjective. is.

1. occurs after adjectival nouns: separable (some two-syllable, a few one-syllable), quasi-inseparable (most two-syllable and longer), and inseparable (most one-syllable). **sok ~** is speedy (adj-n insep). **puncwu ~** is busy (adj-n quasi-insep). **kwung ~** is destitute (adj-n sep).

2. occurs after impressionistic adverbs (all inseparable) and means "gives the impression of being"; here noted Xh, XXh.

3. uniquely occurs after **elma 'na** 'about how much' to make a complex adj-n construction, as in **elma 'na han sokto** 'what speed', **elma 'na han kothong** 'what anguish/agony'. The sentence is often rhetorical/exclamatory: **Ku uy kippum i elma 'na hayss.ul ya** What was not his joy?! = How great was his joy!

hata₅, aux vt. used after the infinitive of an adj or an adj-n construction that refers to human feelings (liking, fearing, reacting to, ...). The adj expression, which can take a nominative-marked adjunct expressing the cathectic object (what provokes the reaction, 'toward it/him') and/or a first-person subject ('I feel'), is converted by this auxiliary verb into a transitive expression that denotes a strong feeling on the part of any person, with the cathectic object marked by the accusative: **(nay ka) ku kes i cōh.ta** 'I like it' → **(nwu ka) ku kes ul cōh.a hanta** '(somebody) likes it'.

SEE **cōh.ta, komapta, mipta, musepta, ...** . Occasionally used after vi inf: **kamcil nata → kamcil na hanta** 'feels/acts insatiable.'.

hata₆, aux vi. it does/goes/passes (is all right), is possible, can happen.

1. **···-e ya ~** only if ··· will it do; it/one must (has got to) ···. **hay ya hanta** one has to do it. ¶**Phyēnci lul sse ya hakeyss.ta** I'll have to write a letter.

2. **-key ~** causes, makes, lets. ¶**kuli lo kakey hanta** makes/lets one go there. **kkoch ul kōpkey hanta** makes the flowers look pretty.

3. **A-tun ci B-tun ci ~** either does A or does B, does either A or B.

hata₇, aux adj (adj-**ki to hata**) is indeed. ¶**cōh.ki to hata** is really nice. **kup haki to hata** is real urgent. **kapcak sulepki to hata** is quite sudden.

hata₈, aux adj/v.

1. **-ki nun ~** is/does to be sure, but (still) ...: substitutes for a repeat of the adj/v, which can optionally take the tense of the repeat. ¶**swīpki nun swīpci/haci man** it is easy enough but. **pi ka oki nun oci/haci man** it rains all right but. **pi ka oki/wass.ki nun wass.ci/hayss.ci man** it rained all right, but ... . **Āl(keyss.)ki nun ālkeyss.ci/hakeyss.ci man** I understand, to be sure, but ... .

2. **-ki to** ~ is/does also (even); ? is/does [not] either. SEE **-ki lo**.
3. is/does one or the other: follows each of two contradictory expressions of modifier + **twung**. ¶**Pi ka on twung mān twung hayss.ta** It was hard to know whether it rained or not = We had no rain to speak of.
4. **-ko (nun)** ~ does regularly/sometimes, makes a habit of doing, DOES do. ¶**nōlko n(un) hanta** sometimes plays/relaxes. **nōlko n(un) hayss.ta** used to play/relax. **cēki iss.ko (nun) hanta** is always there.

hata₉ < °*ha˙ta*, adj [obsolete] is much, great, widespread; are many. Perhaps also vi 'gets to be plentiful' (SEE '*hanon*).
CF **ha (to)**, **ha/hako mānh.ta**, **han**, **hal**.
CF **khuta** < '*khu˙ta*.

hata (ka), transferentive < **hata** (+ pcl). does/says/thinks/is and/but then.

hata ka nun, transferentive < **hata** + pcl + pcl.
¶**cachis hata ka nun** = **cachis hamyen** at the slightest thing (slip or provocation).

hata mōs hata, vt transferentive + adv + vi. fails to do/make/finish, tries to do but does not. ¶**īl ul** ~ fails to complete one's work. **īl ul hata mōs hay se namkita** leaves a job unfinished. **hata mōs hay/ha.ye** goes so far as to (do); is driven by dire necessity to (do); faute-de-mieux, lacking alternatives; at (one's) wit's end, at the worst, at the least, at the extreme (end, limit); finally, at last. **Nappun cīs ul hata mōs hay nācwung ey nun totwuk cil kkaci hayss.ta** He went so far as to commit theft in the end. **Hata mōs hay il-nyenq tong-an un kwāngsan ey se īl hayss.ta** Left to my own resources, I had to work in a mine for a year. **Hata mōs hay tān payk-wen ul pat.e to ku mankhum** ¹**ī lowulq kes i ani 'n ya** At the worst, if you get only a hundred wen you are at least that much ahead. **Hata mōs hamyen sip-cen ey 'la to phal.e ya 'keyss.ta** I'll have to sell it − for ten cents if that is all I can get for it. **Māl ul hata mōs ha.ye pyel māl ul tā hanta** He has run the gamut of nasty things to say; He is going too far. **Īl ul hata mōs ha.ye him tul.e ku man twuess.ta** That was an endless job, and at last it got so tough that I gave up on it. **Īl ul hata mōs ha.ye nācwung ey nun mokwun kkaci hayss.ta** I have tried everything − finally even working as a coolie.

Hata mōs hay chen-wen ila to cwumyen cōh.keyss.ta At least you can let me have a thousand wen. **Uysa lul cheng halye 'myen, hata mōs hay, catong-chaq saks ila to iss.e ya toykeyss.ta** If you are going for the doctor, at least you'll have to have cab fare. **Hata mōs hay se chen-wen ul ku ay hanthey cwuess.ta** I had little choice but to give him the thousand wen. CF **-ta mōs hata**.

hatey, FAMILIAR retrospective assertive < **hata**. has been (doing/saying/thinking) it has been observed; was (doing) [I noticed].

hati, retrospective attentive (= question) < **hata**. has it been observed to be (to have been doing/saying/thinking)? was it (doing/...)?

ha to, adv + pcl. very much indeed, ever so (hard). ¶ ~ **papputa** is ever so busy. **kil ul** ~ **kel.e tali ka aphuta** walked so very hard that one's legs ache. **sēywel i** ~ **ppalli kata** time flies ever so fast.

hatoy, [lit] concessive of **hata** (= **hay to**)
¨*ha˙toy*, modulated accessive < °*ha˙ta*. 1445
¹Yong 13.

hatun < '*ho˙ten*, retrospective mod < **hata** < °*ho˙ta*. that (it/one) has been observed to be (to have been doing/saying/thinking/...).

~ **ka**, ~ **ya** [often spelled **hatenya**] the question whether (it/one) has been observed to be (to have been doing/saying/thinking/...).

~ **i** the one observed to be (to have been doing/saying/thinking); [often spelled **hateni**] the fact that it/one has been observed to be (to have been doing/saying/thinking/...).

ha twu [var] = **ha to**

hay, quasi-free n. possessed thing, one's. ¶**nay** ~ mine. **nwī** ~ whose? **ku i** ~ his/hers. **sensayng nim** ~ yours. CF **kes**.

hay, inf < **hata** (= **ha.ye**). does, says, thinks, is, ... SEE ~ **la**, ~ **se**, ~ **to**, ~ **ya**, ~ **yo**. CF **hasye**. This contraction of **ha.ye** is not attested till quite late; 1894 Gale 3 says *ho.ye ywo* is pronounced *hoy ywo* = **hay yo**. A short version is found in *holoyla* (1894 Gale 78) = *halayla* (1887 Scott 60) = **hala 'y la** 'tell him to do it!' It is unclear how the shape arose; was there an intermediate stage *hayye or *hoyye? 1902 Azbuka has the word long (**hāy**) after monosyllables, short after polysyllables (King 1989:39). Dictionaries list the abbreviation as **hāy** and that is the prescribed pronunciation of

the 1988 rules of the Ministry of Education (Munkyo-pu kosi 185). Since the form usually appears in a position where the distinction of vowel length is not maintained, here we write it as short in all positions.
῀hay, der adv < °ha˙ta. much; many. ¶ ῀hay MA ˙oy ˙HHWOYK ῀hoyGywo˙m ol ni˙pu.l i ˙l ῾ss oy (1462 ¹Nung 6:87b) since they much suffer from the vexations of devils … . ῀hay tu˙lwo˙m ol po˙lye (1447 Sek 9:13b) gave up listening a lot. … [˙CYANG-˙CHO] s ῀hay [˙COYK-˙PELQ] ˙hwo.l i ῾῾la (1481 Twusi 24:13a) … and you will pick up much future punishment.

ha.ya, 1. [obs] = **ha.ye** (lit inf < **hata**). 2. mistake for **hay ya**.

ha.yam < *ho.yam* = **ha.yem** < ˙*ho˙yem*. *ha.yam / ha.yem cuk ho-* (1887 Scott 62) be worth doing. CF *ho.yam*

ha.ye-kan (← *yeha-kan* < ZYE-HHA KAN), adv. anyway, anyhow, at any rate, in any case / event. CF **ha.ye-thun, cwāwu-kan (ey)**.

ha.ye-kum, adv (< lit inf + suf) [obs]. letting, making, forcing: **ulo ~ = eykey, ul sikhye**. ¶**ku lo ~ phyēnci lul ssukey hata** makes him write a letter. **Haksayng tul lo ha.ye-kum (= tul eykey) tose-kwan ul sā.yong hakey hanta** It gets the students to use the library. **Na lo ha.ye-kum hōy lul tāyphyo hakey hay la** Let me represent the association.

ha.yem < ˙*ho˙yem*, derived (= effective) subst < **hata** < °*ho˙ta*; CF **ham** < ˙*hom*, ˙*hwom*. **~ ēps.ta** (1) has no mind / inclination (to do); (2) is idle; is bored, has a dull time. **~ ēps.i** without doing anything, idly. **~ cuk / cik hata** is worth doing (or trying).

ha.yeng [Ceycwu DIAL (Seng ¹Nakswu 1984:9; LSN 1978:34-5)] = **mānh.i** (lots)

ha.yess.ta [lit] = **hayss.ta** (past < **hata**)

ha.ye-thun (← *yeha* [< ZYE-HHA] *hatun*), adv. anyway, anyhow, at any rate, in any case, in all events, somehow or other. ¶**ku kes un ~** be that as it may. **Ha.ye-thun na hako kath.i kaca** In any case, let's go together. **Ha.ye-thun nay tōn un chwī hay cwukeyss.ta** I will lend you the money in any event. **Ha.ye-thun oki nun haci?** You are coming anyway? **Ha.ye-thun pucilen han sālam ita** He is certainly a hardworking man after all. CF **ha.ye-kan**.

hay-(ke)lum, n. sunset, sundown, dusk; **~ ey** at day's end. [n + ? abbr < **kewulum** slanting]

hāyla, n. the plain style of speech (**hanta, hani, hay la**, …). **~ hata**, vni uses the plain style.

hay la, inf + pcl (= PLAIN-style command). do / say / think! CF **hala**.

hayng < ˙HHOYNG, postn [semi-lit]. bound for, dispatched to. ¶**Pusan hayng ¹yelcha** a train bound for Pusan, the Pusan train. **Tongkyeng pal Sewul hayng** (dispatched) from Tokyo to Seoul. **I kisen un Pusan hayng ita** This ship is bound for Pusan.

hay p'ā, abbr < **hay pwā**

hays (= NK **hayq**), adn [< **hay** n 'year; sun' + **-q** < *s*]. 1. new, of the year; spring. **~ kes** a new crop, the year's crop. **~ kok(sik)** the year's harvest. **~ mul₁** a spring that gushes forth only after the rainy season of the year. **~ khong** new beans. **~ phath** new red beans. **~ pye / poli / co** new rice / barley / millet. **~ pyengali** spring chickens.
2. sunny, of the sun. **~ kwi** the sun's rays, sunshine; the first rays of the sun. **~ muli**, **~ mul₂** the sun's halo. **~ pal / sal** sunbeams. **~ pyeth / pich** sunlight. **~ tes** a short autumn day.

hay se, inf + pcl.
1. does / says / thinks / is / … and so / then. **~ nun** SAME (with emphasis on what follows). **~ ya** just / only by doing / … , just do / … and (then); only if you do.
2. abbr < **motwu hay se** all (taken) together. **A hako B hako hay se** with both A and B together (Pak Sengwen 274).

hayss.ca, past subj assert < **hata**. SEE **-ta 'yss.ca, -la 'yss.ca, -ca 'yss.ca**.

hayss.ta, past < **hata**

hay to, inf + pcl. even though one does / says / thinks / … ; only if it is. **~ cōh.ta** may do.

hay tul, inf + pcl (plural subject)

hay ya, inf + pcl. **~ hanta** must do.

hay yo, inf + pcl = sentence-final POLITE-style statement / question / command / proposition. does, says, thinks; is.

he < ˙HE, postn. 1. [letterwriting] **Kim sayng he** (addressed) to Mr Kim.
2. about (5 to 10 lī away). **ō-li (sip-li) he** about 5 (10) lī away.

heko, hekwu [var] = **hako** (all meanings)

hel(q) = **hal(q)**, prosp mod < **heta** = **hata**

hel.nun = **hal.nun**, prosp proc mod < **heta** = **hata**. **~ ci**

hem = ham, subst < heta = hata
hen = han, mod < heta = hata
hēn, vi mod < hēlta (gets old). (··· that is) old, stale, lacking in newness; (··· that is) used, worn. ANT say.
henthey, pcl [colloq var; Phyengan DIAL (Kim Yengpay 1984:95)] = hanthey (to / at / by / for)
henun = hanun, proc mod < heta = hata
hepta, postnom adj -W- [< ho-W-]. hyung hepta is ugly, unseemly. VAR epta. CF hopta.
hes, adn, bnd n, bnd adv [< bnd n he < HE 'empty' + -q < s]. idle, vain, fruitless, empty; wrong, mistaken, mis-; open, open-air. CF hes-hes hata is hungry.
  1. adn. ¶ ~ akwungi fire-hole of an outdoor kitchen. ~ ay vain efforts. ~ cam feigned sleep; half-sleep. ~ cheng/kan barn. ~ chong blank shot. hesq īl /hennīl/ vain effort. ~ kākey a street stall. ~ kel.um wasted steps, going in vain. ~ kho kōlta pretends to snore. ~ kichim a dry cough. ~ kīm escaping steam. ~ kul useless booklearning. ~ kwuyek nausea without vomiting, dry heaves. ~ māl an untruth, a lie; empty talk. ~ mayngsey an empty oath. ~ mul khita makes vain efforts. ~ nolus vain efforts. ~ pang₁ a room empty of furniture. ~ pang₂ a miss (shot); pointless talk. ~ pay puluta is filling / satisfying but not substantial. ~ puekh an outdoor kitchen. ~ pul a random shot. ~ sim effort to no purpose. ~ soli nonsense; delirium. ~ sōmun false rumor. ~ son cil beating the air. ~ soth an iron pot used in an outdoor kitchen. ~ swu a useless move (in chess / checkers). ~ swūko vain efforts. ~ thang (chita) (engages in) lost labor. ~ thek tāyko with no aim, plan, or reason. ~ wus.um a feigned smile, smirk, simper; a silly laugh.
  2. bnd n. ~ toyta (adj) is vain; is useless; is unreliable; is short-lived, evanescent.
  3. bnd adv. ~ capta misgrabs. ~ titita missteps. ~ tut.ta mishears; pays little attention.
heta, v, adj [DIAL or HEAVY] = hata. ¶ swoloy lol khukey hekwo (1894 Gale 158) making a great noise.
hethun, pseudo-adn. silly. ¶ ~ swucak a silly trick. Kuleh.key hethun soli n' ku man twue Cut out such silly talk! [mod < heth- = huth- scatter]
hetun = hatun, retr mod < heta = hata

HEY The Hankul spelling distinguishes hey and hyey, but they are usually pronounced the same (as hey). If you cannot locate the word you are looking for under hey, look under hyey.
HI The Hankul spelling and our Romanization distinguish hi from huy but they are both pronounced the same (as hi). If you cannot locate the word you seek under hi, look under huy.
hi < ˙hi, der adv < hata < °ho˙ta (postnom adj 'is'). (in a way) so that it is, in a manner such that it is; ···ly. SYN hakey. ABBR 'i. CF -i.
  ¶ annyeng hi in good health, well, peacefully. casey hi < ˙cosyey hi (1482 Nam 1:24a) < ¨CO-˙SYEY ˙hi (1463/4 Yeng se:3a) in detail, (examining) closely; ˙CCO-˙SYEY (?1468- Mong 39b, 66b with "LETTER" instead of "DETAIL") is perhaps a play on words. ccayngccayng hi brightly shining. chin hi < CHIN ˙hi (1459 Wel 21:88-9, ?1468- Mong se:13a) intimately; personally, oneself (in person). chongchong hi in a hurry / rush. chwungpun hi adequately, fully, enough. cok hi < ˙CYWOK ˙hi (1463 Pep 2:111b) enough, sufficiently, adequately, fully. co'.yong hi quiet(ly), softly, calmly. hwaksil hi definitely, surely, assuredly, truly. hwū hi generously. ikswuk hi skillfully. kā hi < ¨KA ˙hi (1586 Sohak 4:9b) (can) well, (might) rightly; possibly. kakpyel hi < ˙KAK-˙PPYELQ ˙hi (1462 ¹Nung 1:89a, 1482 Kum-sam 4:30b) particularly, specially, remarkably. kaman hi quietly; secretly, furtively. kansin hi barely (managing), with difficulty. kantan hi simply. kinkup hi urgently. kongson hi respectfully. kongyen hi in vain, vainly, idly, wastefully. koyngcang hi impressively, quite (a lot). kup hi < [˙KUP] ˙hi (1481 Twusi 22:46a) hastily, quickly. mattang hi properly, appropriately, reasonably, as expected. mimyo hi < MI-˙MYWOW ˙hi (1462 ¹Nung 2:20b) subtly, delicately. musa hi safely, without mishap / incident. muten hi < muten ˙hi (1465 Wen 3:2:2:41ab, 1481 Twusi 8:42a, 1482 Kum-sam 3:19a) quite (nicely, satisfactorily), extremely; indifferently, casually. phyen.an hi < PPYEN-QAN ˙hi (1459 Wel 21:206a; 1463 Pep 2:138b; 1465 Wen se:5a; 1481 Twusi 8:27b, 8:43a) peacefully, safely, well, comfortably, at ease. punmyeng hi clearly, distinctly. pyēnpyen hi satisfactorily, well. sangtang hi adequately,

considerably, quite a lot. **sikup hi** < *SSI-ˈKUP ˈhi* (ʔ1468⁻ Mong 23a) urgently, rushing, at once. **sīm hi** < *ˈˈsim hi* (1481 Twusi 16:39b) < *ˈSSIM ˈhi* (1447 Sek 9:27a, 1459 Wel 7:14b, 1463 Pep 2:4b) severely, intensely, extremely, deeply. **sohol hi** indifferently, negligently, carelessly. **sohwal hi** negligently, sloppily. **tahayng hi** fortunately. **tantan hi** hard, solidly, tightly, severely. **tāytan hi** greatly, terribly, very, seriously, badly. **thukpyel hi** especially, in particular. **tōce hi** (not) at all, quite (impossible); thoroughly, perfectly. **tol.yen hi** suddenly, abruptly. **unkun hi** nicely, politely, attentively, courteously. **wenman hi** satisfactorily, happily. **wūyen hi** < *[NGWU-ZYEN] ˈhi* (1481 Twusi 24:59b) by chance / accident, unexpectedly, casually. **yelqsim hi** eagerly, fervently, with enthusiasm, hard.

¶ **cēng hi** < *ˈCYENG ˈhi* (1447 Sek 13:60b, 1465 Wen 2:3:1:38b, 1475 Nay 1:9-10, 1481 Twusi 8:6b) exactly; surely; just right. **chol hi** (1447 Sek 13:58a, 1463 Pep 2:28b, ...) = **cholhaˈli** (1465 Wen 2:3:1:82b, ...) > **chalali** rather, preferably. **chōng hi** all, entirely, wholly. *ˈcukca ˈhi* (1447 Sek 9:12b, 24:16a; 1459 Wel 2:6b) > *ˈcukcay* (1459 Wel 9:35f) immediately, suddenly. *ˈˈCYWONG-ˈˈCYWONG ˈhi* (1462 ¹Nung 2:61a) = **cong-cong** all sorts; often, frequently. **thuk hi** especially. *ˈtyele ˈhi* (1481 Twusi 15:23b) such(wise). *ˈˈYWENG ˈhi* (1462 ¹Nung 1:86b) long, for a long time.

¶ *CYWEN-CYENG ˈhi* (1463/4 Yeng 2:111a) so as to be totally devoted, concentrating. **hwen hi** (1459 Wel 2:22c, 1482 Nam 1:76b, 1481 Twusi 16:18a, [1447→]1562 Sek 3:20b) widely, broadly [penetrating], pervasively, all over. *KEN-C[Y]ENG hi* ʔ(1797 Olyun 3:11b) so as to be nice and tidy. *[ˈˈMAN-TTYWOW] ˈhi* (1445 ¹Yong 107) court-wide. *[ˈMEN-ˈKWUYK] ˈhi* (1445 ¹Yong 107) (throughout) all the land. *NAN ˈhi* (1463 Pep 5:148a) with hardship. *ˈpentuk ˈhi* (1462 ¹Nung 2:6-7) clearly. *QAN-SSYE ˈhi* (1475 Nay 1:18a) calmly. *[QIN-QIN] ˈhi* (1481 Twusi 7:24b) thunderously. *[SANG-ZYEN] ˈhi* (1481 Twusi 22:34-5) precipitously. *ˈsenul hi* (1475 Nay se:6a) coolly.

CF **kath.i** < *ˈkot ˈhi* like, as if; **mānh.i** < *ˈˈman [ˈ]hi* much / many, lots; **nung hi** < *NUNG ˈhi* ably, ...

-hi, der adv (= -i). *tol-hi* sweetly, indulgently.

-hi- < *-ˈhi-*, suffix. CF **-i-, -y-, -ki-, -chi-, -u-, -ukhi-, -ikhi-, -li-, -iwu-, -ywu-; -wu-, -hwu-, -kwu-,-chwu-,-ay-;** *-ˈGi-, -ˈGwᵘ/o-, -o-, -u-*.

1. derives vc. **anc.hi-** < *anˈchi-* seat ← **anc-** < *anc-* sit. **ip.hi-** < *niˈphi-* cause to wear (vc) ← **ip-** < *nip-* wear (vt).

2. derives vp. **mek.hi-** < *meˈkhi-* get eaten ← **mek-** < *mek-* eat. **pak.hi-** < *paˈkhi-, pakˈhi-* 'get stuck / printed' ← **pak-** < *pak-* 'stick in / on, print'.

ho < *HHWO*, adn. of foreign origin, especially from pre-modern China. ¶ ~ **khong** peanuts (= ttang/way khong). ~ **paychwu** Chinese cabbage. ~ **ttek** a kind of Chinese cake.

hoˈcye, v + incorporated aux inf (= *hoˈkwo ˈcye*). ¶ *ˈi ˈSYEY-ˈKAY ˈyey n' CHYEN-ˈPPWULQ ˈi ˈnasiˈl i ˈˈlwoswoˈn i ˈKEP ilˈhwu.m uˈlan HHYEN-ˈKEP ˈiˈla hoˈcye* (1459 Wel 1:40a) since into this world a thousand Buddhas will be born, I want the name of this kalpa to be the Wise Kalpa.

~ *ˈˈla* (cop indic assert). ¶ *mozoˈm ol hwen hi neˈkisiˈkey hoˈcye ˈˈla ˈhosiˈkwo* (1459 Wel 10:6a) I want us to [visit my ill father the king and] get him to treat his mind expansively. *mwoˈton hyengˈtyey ˈtolˈh i ˈˈuyˈlwon hoˈcye ˈˈla*, (ʔ1517⁻ Pak 1:1b) all the brothers want to discuss it.

hoˈiˈta = *ˈˈhoyˈta*, vc < *°hoˈta*. has (makes, lets) one do. ¶ *pyeˈsul hoˈinon ˈˈilˈtolˈh ol* (1518 Sohak-cho 8:21a) the matters of having government posts assigned.

ˈhoˈka-, effective < *°hoˈta*. See also *ˈhoˈke-, ˈhoˈye-, ˈho.ya-*.

ˈhokan, effective modifier < *°hoˈta*. ¶ *susung ˈhoˈkan maˈlon* (1481 Twusi 16:1a) I have made them my masters. SEE *ˈkhan = ˈho.yan*.

ˈhoka.n i ˈGwa SEE *ˈkha.n i ˈGwa*

ˈhokanˈt iGeˈn i ˈˈston (postmod + copula effective modifier + postmod + pcl). ¶ *ˈKAK-ˈPPYELQ ˈhi ˈˈwon ˈSYENG iˈsywuˈm i ˈmasˈtang ˈhokanˈt iGeˈn i ˈˈston* (1462 ¹Nung 1:89a) it is only natural that it would have a character that had specially come to it.

ˈhokanˈt iˈla (postmod + cop indic assert). ¶ *ˈi ˈˈsaloˈm on ZYE-LOY ˈlol ˈˈTYENG-ˈTOY ˈhokanˈt iˈla* (1459 Wel 17:36b) he carried the (body of the) tathāgata over his head.

ˈhokanˈtˈiˈn i ˈˈla SEE *(aˈni) khanˈtˈiˈn i ˈˈla*

ˈhokaˈn ywo SEE *ˈkha.n ywo*

`ho῾ke-, effective < °ho῾ta. See also `ho῾ka-, `ho῾ye-, `ho.ya-.
(?*)`ho῾ke, effective inf < °ho῾ta. SEE khe῾za.
`hoken = `hokan. SEE `khen.
`hoke῾na SEE khe῾na
`hoke῾n i, effective mod < °ho῾ta + postmod. SEE khe῾n i, ¨mwot 'ke῾n i.
`ho῾ke.n i ῾Gwa (pcl). ¶ ¨salo῾m oy wu῾h i towoy῾Gwo cye ho῾kwo ¨salo῾m oy a῾lay cye a῾ni `ho῾ke.n i ῾Gwa (1482 Kum-sam 3:55a) granted that he wants to become above other men and does not want to become below them.
  2. SEE ku῾li ῾Ge῾n i.
`ho῾ken ma῾lon SEE ¨mwot '῾ken ma῾lon
`hoke῾nol (= `hoke῾nul) SEE khe῾nol.
`hoke῾nol za SEE ¨mwot 'ke῾nol za
`hoken ῾tyeng, effective modifier < °ho῾ta + postmod. ¶so ῾thi a῾ni `hoken ῾tyeng (1588 ¹Non 2:50a) I had not thought of it, but … .
`hoke῾nul, literary concessive < °ho῾ta. ¶ … pi῾le [῾]ci-ngi '῾ta ¨CHYENG `hoke῾nul (1475 Nay 2:1:30a) when asked to pray. SEE khe῾nol.
`hoke῾n ywo SEE `khe῾n ywo
`hokesin ma῾lon SEE `khesin ma῾lon
`hokesi῾na SEE `khesi῾na
`ho῾kesi῾n i ῾Gwa SEE -`kesi῾n i ῾Gwa
`hokesi῾nol = `ho῾sike῾nul. SEE `khesi῾nol.
`hokesi῾n ywo SEE `khesi῾n ywo
*`ho῾kesi῾ta SEE -`kesi῾ta, ¨mwot '`kesi῾ta
`ho῾kesi῾tun. ¶NGWANG `i '῾pwo῾poy ῾lol ¨et῾kwo cye `ho῾kesi῾tun (1459 Wel 1:27a) when the king wanted to get the jewels. SEE '`kesi῾tun.
`hoke῾ta SEE khe῾ta.
`hoke῾tun, provisional < °ho῾ta. ¶ … ῾TTWO-῾THWALQ `hoke῾tun (1459 Wel 21:34ab) when one emancipates [them]. SEE 'ke῾tun, khe῾tun, ¨mwot '῾ke῾tun.
ho῾key, adverbative < °ho῾ta. ¶ `na y pwu῾le ne ῾lul esye ῾TUK-¨TTWOW ho῾key `hota῾n i (1447 Sek 24:3a) I have deliberately tried to get you to achieve the way [to enlightenment] quickly. SEE `khey, '῾key; ho῾kuy; ¨mwot '῾key.
*`hoke῾za SEE khe῾za
hok un, adv (`HWOK) + pcl. or (else) = tto nun.
ho῾kuy = ho῾key. ¶mozom cwo῾chwo ¨i῾l ol ho῾kuy `hwo.l i ῾῾la (1447 Sek 9:5a) I will let them work as they wish. ALSO: 1447 Sek se:6a, 24:2b, … . ABBR `khuy.
*`ho῾kwa (…) SEE `khwa
`ho῾kwa ῾῾la SEE '῾kwa ῾῾la, `khwa ῾῾la

`hokwa swo῾la SEE '`khwa swo῾la
`hokwan῾toy SEE khwan῾toy
`ho῾kwatoy῾ye SEE (¨mwot) '῾kwatoy῾ye
ho῾kwo₁, ger < °ho῾ta. ¶LYWONG ῾oy `co.m i PPYEN-QAN ho῾kwo (1482 Kum-sam 2:65a) the dragon's sleep is peaceful, and … . LOY-῾ZILQ `za pwo῾nay῾ywo.l i ῾῾la ho῾kwo (1459 Wel 7:16a) saying she would send him the very next day … . `khuy ¨cek[῾ti] ῾two `khu[῾ti] ῾two a῾ni ho῾kwo (1459 Wel 1:26b) was neither tall nor short. muce῾k ul cwos῾t ol a῾ni ho῾kwo (1482 Kum-sam 2:21a) will not peck at clumps of earth but … . un ῾kwa ¨pitan ῾tol[h] `syang῾kup ho῾kwo (?1517- Pak 1:57a) presented silver and silks, and … . ALSO: 1447 Sek 13:36a, 1459 Wel 1:30a. ABBR `khwo. SEE ¨mwot ῾kwo (`sye).
ho῾kwo₂ (= hako₃), pcl. and. ¶ `yel ῾tol ho῾kwo nil῾Gwey (1459 Wel 2:13a) ten months and seven days. ip hokwo khwo non (1728 Cheng-tay 108) his mouth and nose (were …).
ho῾kwo῾cye SEE `khwo῾cye
ho῾kwo k, ger + pcl. See example under -`a k.
ho῾kwo ῾῾la, v ger + abbr < ho῾la. ¶SOYNG-SOYNG `ay na 'y ῾NGWEN ῾ul il῾thi a῾ni `khey ho῾kwo ῾῾la (1459 Wel 1:13b) in life after life I do not want to let my desire be lost. ALSO: 1447 Sek 6:46a, … .
ho῾kwo n', ger + abbr pcl. ¶ye῾huyywo῾m i `mas.tang ho῾kwo n' `i ye῾huyywo῾m i `stwo e῾nu isil ῾ppa 'y.l i ῾Gwo (1482 Kum-sam 2:37a) separation is to be expected but why is there so much more of this separation? KWONG-῾TUK ῾two i῾le ho῾kwo n' `homol῾mye ῾TTWOK-῾SSYWONG `ho῾ya ῾TTAY-῾CYWUNG `uy key `nom `WUY `ho῾ya kol`hoy῾ya nilo῾m ye ¨mal ta῾Wi SYWUW-HHOYNG `hwo῾m isto῾n ye (1459 Wel 17:54a) with such achievement of virtue, how much more will one tell the people by chanting to teach others and by practicing asceticism according to the words?! ABBR `khwo n'.
ho῾kwo῾za SEE `khwo῾za
hol, bnd n, adn. lone. < hwol (1576 ¹Yuhap 2:44a) < howol (1481 Twusi 24:38a) < hon pol (1464 Kumkang 2:138; cited from LCT) 'one layer'. CF hoth, honca; ANT has.
  1. bnd n (preparticle). ~ lo alone.
  2. adn. 2a. ~ al an unfertilized egg, a wind egg. ~ mom a person who is single. ~-q swu an odd number (= ki-swu).
  2b. ~ api widower. ~ emi widow.

hol-, ? bnd adv. LIGHT ← **hwul-**.
¶ **hol-kapun hata** is very light. **hol-potul / hwul-putul hata** is very soft.
hol(q), prospective modifier < ˚ho˙ta.
 1. (epitheme extruded from subject). Example?
 2. (epitheme extruded from object). Example?
 3. (summational epitheme). ¶ ··· HHOYNG hol ¨spwu˙n iGen˙tyeng (1459 Wel 18:13b) even if you only practice ··· . mis˙ti ¨mwot hol kke˙s i (1464 Kumkang 87b) what we cannot attain. ¨nyey [˙LWOK-SAN] ˙oy [˙LWAN] hol kwo[˙]t ol ¨mwolla˙n i (1481 Twusi 15:47b) in the old days they did not know rebellion by the mountain feofdoms. twolo˙hye ˙TTYWU-˙TTYAK hol ˙kwo.t i isi˙l ye (1482 Kum-sam 2:20a) would there be any place [in the doctrine] I could get a firmer grasp? SEE a˙ni hol(q).
 4. (transitional epitheme). ¶ ˙MYENG-CYWUNG holq ce˙k uy (1459 Wel 8:69b) when they are about to die ... .
ho˙la, 1. subjunctive assertive < ˚ho˙ta.
 1a. (command) ¶ ˙i ¨i˙l ol ˙soyng˙kak ho˙la (1459 Wel 8:8b) think about this matter. ce-huy ˙ho˙ya pulu˙key ho˙la (?1517- Pak 1:6a) get them to sing. kutuy ˙nay ˙KAK-˙KAK hon a˙tol ˙Gwom ¨nay˙ya na ˙'y SWON-¨CO cwo˙cha ka˙key ho˙la ˙hosi˙n i (1447 Sek 6:9b) he commands that each of you folks send a son to follow my grandson. nyenu ke˙s u˙lan ¨ma˙wo ku˙lus ¨pwun cyang˙mang ho˙la (1459 Wel 7:42a) just get some dishes ready, not other things.
 1b. (exclamatory?) ¶ LWO-¨LWOW y kutuy s ¨wo˙m ol kitu˙li˙tela ho˙la (1482 Nam 1:50b) they have been long waiting for you to come, they say.
 2. purposive < ˚ho˙ta. (goes / comes) to do. ¶ KUM-LYWUN NGWANG a˙to˙l i ˙CHYWULQ-KA ho˙la ˙kano˙n i (1447 Sek 6:9b) the son of the Golden Wheel King goes off to become a monk.
 3. (var) = ho˙l ya / ye. SEE ho˙la ˙'n ˙t oy; -˙kwo ˙'la.
ho˙la ˙'n ˙t oy < ho˙la [ho]n˙t oy. ¶ ˙wu˙li ˙stwo ZYE-LOY s ˙TI-¨HHYWEY ˙lol QIN ˙ho˙ya PPWO-˙SALQ ˙tol[h] ˙WUY ˙ho˙ya ye˙le ¨pwoy˙ya pwul˙Ge ni˙l ˙Gwo˙toy ce ˙non inge˙kuy ˙NGWEN ˙ho˙nwon ˙ptu˙t i ¨epta˙n i ¨es˙tyey 'Ge˙n ywo ho˙la ˙'n ˙t oy (1459 Wel 13:35b) when we wonder, moreover, despite that a lot has been shown and enhanced in explanation by the bodhisattvas based on the wisdom of the tathāgata, "how come I have had no mind to want this [mahāyāna] part [of the doctrine]?" ... . QA-NAN a ˙hota ˙ka ˙stwo ˙i HYANG ˙i ne ˙'y kwo˙h ay ˙sye ˙nalq ˙t in ˙t ay n' nil˙Gwo˙toy ˙kwo˙h oy ¨nay˙ywon ke˙s i˙la ho˙la ˙'n ˙t oy pan˙to˙ki ˙kwo˙h ol pu˙the ¨nalq ˙t iGe˙nul ... (1462 ¹Nung 3:24b) say, Ānanda, perhaps again when this scent arises in your nose we say that it's something emitted by your nose ... . ˙SYEY-CWON ˙ha ZYE-LOY nilu˙syan KYENG ˙ey NGUY-SIM ˙ol a˙ni ˙ho˙zopnwo˙n l ¨es˙tyey 'Ge˙n ywo ho˙la ˙'n ˙t oy ˙QILQ-˙CHYEY ZYE-LOY s ˙mwom ˙kwa ¨mal-ssom ˙kwa ptu˙t ey s ˙NGEP ˙i ¨ta CHYENG-˙CCYENG ˙hosi˙n i (1447 Sek 9:26b) he said "O World-Honored! how is it that one has no doubts about the sūtra said by the tathāgata?", at which [the reply was that] all of the karma in the body and the words and the mind of the tathāgata is pure (= the tathāgata is pure in his act, in his word, and in his thought). ¨es.tyey QIN-YWEN ¨epke˙n ywo ho˙la ˙'n ˙t oy ˙CYWUNG-SOYNG ˙i ¨PWON-˙SYENG ˙i ˙KKWU-˙CYWOK ˙ho˙ya ˙say ˙lwo pu˙the te al˙Gwoy˙ywol ˙cwu.l i ¨ep.sul ˙s oy QIN-YWEN ¨ep˙sun CCO ˙'y˙la ho˙n i (1482 Kum-sam 2:2a) to the inquiry "how come there was no cause and effect?" there was the reply "living beings are endowed with their own natures and when there is no way further to inform them anew it is mercy without cause and effect". SEE ˙hosila ˙'n ˙t oy.
ho˙l i, verb prospective modifier + postmodifier.
 1. (˙i = epitheme from subject). Example?
 2. (˙i = (epitheme from object). Example?
 3. (˙i = summational epitheme). ¶ chol hi ˙tye kwo˙ma towoy˙Ga ci˙la ho˙l i ˙yel˙h ilwo˙toy (1463 Pep 2:28b) those preferring to become his concubine were more than ten [in number].
ho˙l i 'Ge˙nul (cop lit concessive). ¶ SAM-PPWO-TTYEY ˙lol il˙Gwu˙l i ˙'len ˙t ay n' pan˙toki ˙TTAY-SSING ˙u˙lwo ˙TTWO-˙THWALQ ˙ol ˙TUK ho˙l i ˙Ge˙nul (1463 Pep 2:6b) when you have achieved sambodhi (perfect enlightenment) you are then sure to obtain emancipation through the Greater Vehicle (mahāyāna), but ... .
ho˙l i 'Gwan˙toy (cop semi-literary sequential). ¶ ¨es˙tyey e˙lwo ˙TTYAK ho˙l i ˙Gwan˙toy ˙TTYAK ¨˙ti a˙ni ˙tha nilo˙l ywo (1462 ¹Nung 1:75a) how can you say one is unattached when one IS attached?

ho˙l i ˙Gwo (postmod). ¶ ¨es.tyey ho˙l i ˙Gwo (1481 Twusi 8:29a) so what am I to do? ˙na y ˙stwo mu˙sum si˙lum ho˙l i ˙Gwo (1459 Wel 21:49b) why am I still woeful? mu˙su.m u˙lye ¨mal han ¨yang ho˙l i ˙Gwo (?1517- Pak 1:74a) why do you talk so much? ALSO: 1481 Twusi 20:29a, ...

ho˙l i ˙'Gwo (copula gerund). ¶ ¨HHA-KON ˙on mwo˙lwo˙may ¨sey˙h ila ˙za ho˙l i ˙'Gwo ... (1459 Wel 14:31b) the lower roots must be three and ... . ALSO: 1481 Twusi 22:7b, ...

ho˙l i ˙Gwo n' (postmod + pcl). ¶ pilo me˙kun ye.s oy ¨mwom ˙two ˙et˙ti ˙mwot [= ˙mwom ˙two ¨et˙ti ˙mwot] ho.l i ˙Gwo n' ˙homol[˙]mye [CHYENG-˙CCYENG PPWO-TTYEY ¨KWA] ˙lol [¨KA] ˙hi ˙pola˙l ya (1579 Kwikam 1:36a) you may not get even the body of a mangy fox, so how can you possibly expect to see the fruit of pure bodhi (enlightenment)?

ho˙l i ˙'la (cop indic assert). ¶ ˙NYELQ-PPAN ˙TUK ˙hwo˙m ol na ˙kot ˙'key ho˙l i ˙'la (1447 Sek 6:1b) will let her achieve nirvāṇa like me. na ˙kot ho˙l i ˙'la (1459 Wel 1:17a) it is like me. ˙TWOY-˙TAP ˙ho.ya ˙za ho˙l i ˙'la (1462 ¹Nung 1:44b) will have to reply. ne-huy ˙tol˙h i SOYNG-¨SO pe˙swul ¨i˙l ol ˙him ˙pse KKWUW ˙ho.ya ˙za ho˙l i ˙'la (1459 Wel 10:14b) you people must endeavor to pursue the casting off of birth and death.
~ s SEE -u˙l i ˙'la s.

ho˙l i ˙'las˙ta (cop retr emotive indic assertive). ¶ tyey ˙ka ¨sek ˙to.l i˙na mwuk˙nwo˙la ˙ho˙ya cip sak[s] mwu˙le sywokcyel ¨ep˙si he˙pi ho˙l i ˙'las˙ta (?1517- Pak 1:54a) I uselessly wasted my money to pay the rent thinking I would go there and stay some three months.

ho˙l i ˙'le˙la (cop retr indic attent). ¶ mye˙chu˙l ul ˙syel˙Gwep ho˙l i ˙'le˙la (?1517- Pak 1:75a) how many days would he preach?

ho˙l i ˙'le.n i ˙'la (cop retr mod + postmod + cop indic assert). ¶ spol˙li ˙TUK ˙'ti ˙mwot ho˙l i ˙'le.n i ˙'la (1447 Sek 19:34ab) one cannot quickly obtain it [the wisdom of a Buddha]. MYEY-˙HHWOYK ˙ho˙ya kolo˙chywo˙m ol pat˙ti a˙ni ho˙l i ˙'le˙n i ˙'la (1463 Pep 1:208a) was too confused to get what was taught.

ho˙l i ˙'lq ˙s oy (cop prosp mod + postmod + pcl). ¶ hona˙h i ˙eti˙le ˙cu˙mun ¨salo˙m ol ˙tang ho˙l i ˙'l ˙ss oy (1459 Wel 1:28a) since one alone will easily be a match for a thousand people. CCO-PI s ¨hoyng˙tye˙k ul ˙ho.ya ˙za ho˙l i ˙'l ˙ss oy SA-MI ˙'la ho˙n i ˙'la (1447 Sek 6:2b) for they must perform their deeds of charity therefore they are called śrāmaṇera (religious novice). mwo˙lwo˙may ˙i kak˙si [˙]lwo ˙za ho˙l i ˙'l ˙ss oy (1459 Wel 7:15b) does it rather because of this woman. kil˙h ey [LIM] ˙ho.yas.ti ¨mwot ho˙l i ˙'l s oy ˙stwo [NGWANG-SWON ˙WUY] ˙ho.ya cyekun ˙te.t ul ˙sye ˙sywu˙la (1481 Twusi 8:2b) since he did not dare look to the way, he stood there for a little while for the sake of the king's grandson.

ho˙l i ˙'lwo˙swo-ngi ˙'ta (var cop modulated emotive polite + copula indic assert). ¶ KWONG-˙KYENG ˙ho˙ya KWONG-˙YANG ˙ho˙zoWa ˙za ho˙l i ˙'lwo˙swo-ngi ˙'ta (1459 Wel 9:52a) they must respect and nourish him.

ho˙l i ˙'lwoswo˙n i (var cop modulated emotive mod + postmod). ¶ ˙machi nul˙ke [˙PPYENG] ˙hwo.m ol i˙kuy˙ti ¨mwot ho˙l i ˙'lwoswo˙n i ¨es.tyey si˙le-˙kwom ˙ptut il˙hwu.m ul [SSWUNG-˙SSANG] ho˙l i Gwo (1481 Twusi 7:7b) it is as if I were too old to shake an illness; how can I possibly esteem losing my will? kwan-zin ˙tol˙h i ho˙ma ˙kak¨san ho˙l i ˙'lwoswo˙n i (?1517- Pak 1:7a) the officials are already about to disperse.

ho˙l i ˙'lwoswoy-ng' ˙'ta = ho˙l i ˙'lwo˙swo-ngi ˙'ta. ¶ nis˙ti ¨mwot ho˙l i ˙'lwoswoy-ng' ˙'ta (1475 Nay 2:2:37a) I cannot forget it.

ho˙l i ˙'lwo˙ta (var cop indic assert). ¶ ˙NYELQ-PPAN ay esye ˙tu-˙sa [= ˙tule ˙za] ho˙l i ˙'lwo˙ta (1447 Sek 13:58a) must enter nirvāṇa right away. ¨cywokwo˙ma s ˙poy ˙thokwo ˙cye s ˙ptu.t ul nis˙ti ¨mwot hol i ˙'lwota (1481 Twusi 15:55b) I will not forget my desire to ride in a little boat. ALSO: 1481 Twusi 7:4b, 7:10b; ... .

ho˙l i ˙'lwo˙toy (var cop accessive). ¶ ku˙le ˙'na ˙SYEY-KAN ˙ay tulu˙m ye ti˙ni˙l i ¨hyey˙ti ¨mwot ho˙l i ˙'lwo˙toy ¨KWA-ZYEN NUNG ˙hi ˙SSANG-˙HHYWEY nilowa˙to˙m ye (1459 Wel 17:34b) but we cannot reckon that they will hear it and will keep it in the human world; to be sure, it may bring about higher wisdom, and ... .

ho˙l i ˙'m ye (cop subst + cop inf). ¶ ¨nwu l' te˙pu˙le mwu˙le ˙za ho˙l i ˙'m ye (1447 Sek 13:15a) with whom should I inquire and ... . ˙QUK-CHYEN ˙ZILQ ˙i ˙kwot ˙ho˙ya ko˙chwo

¨pwo˙m *[o]l* ¨mwot ho˙l i ʾ˙m ye (1459 Wel 8:7a) it would take many more than a million thousand days to see it all, and ... . ˙MILQ-˙QIN ˙kwos a˙ni ʾ˙m ye n' na˙ta na˙ti a˙ni ho˙l i ʾ˙m ye (1462 ¹Nung 1:8b; *na˙ta na˙ti* is probably an error for *na˙tha na˙ti*) if they are not secret causes they will not appear, and ... . *CHAM-SSYEN* ˙un mwo˙lwo˙may ¨CWO-SO s KWAN ˙ol somo˙cha ˙za ho˙l i ʾ˙m ye (?1468- Mong 10b) the participant in dhyāna (meditation) must break through the barrier of the First Teacher (Bodhidarma), and ... .

ho˙l i ʾn (cop mod; summational epithemes). ¶ *mo˙chom-˙nay SSYENG-˙PPWULQ* ¨mwot ho˙l i ʾn cyen˙cho ˙lwo nilu˙ti ¨mwot ho˙l i ʾ˙la (1464 Kumkang 43a) one cannot tell it for the reason that in the end one will not be able to become a Buddha. [˙]CCYEK-˙MYELQ TTYANG ˙ay i˙sye SSYEN-˙YWELQ ˙ul ˙CHAN-¨CHOY ho˙l i ʾn [...] ˙ingey mozom ta˙wolq ˙t iGe˙ta (1462 ¹Nung 7:18a; broken by an interpolated note) now they will do their utmost in offering a banquet of dhyāna joy at the place where Buddha attained the truth of nirvāṇa.

ho˙l i ʾ-ngi s ˙kwo (cop polite + pcl + postmod). ¶ ¨es.tyey mozo˙m ol HHANG ¨hoy˙Gwa mozo˙m i ¨KAY-˙THWALQ ˙ol ˙TUK ho˙l i ʾ-ngi s ˙kwo (1482 Kum-sam 2:4ab) how is one to surrender one's mind and obtain the mind's emancipation? ¨es˙tyey ¨tele˙Wun ¨i˙l ol ˙cwohon ¨TTWOW ʾy˙la ho˙l i ʾ-ngi s ˙kwo (1459 Wel 9:24a) how can you say that an impure act is the pure Way? ... mwo˙lwo˙may ˙CHILQ-˙NGWELQ s ˙yel tas˙sway s ˙nal ˙za ho˙l i ʾ-ngi s ˙kwo (1459 Wel 23:91b) [why] must I do it precisely the fifteenth day of July?

ho˙l i ʾ-ngi ʾ˙ta (cop polite + cop indic assert). ¶ ˙wuli ˙tol˙h i ¨PPWU-NGWANG s KWAN ˙ol ¨mey˙zoWa ˙za ho˙l i ʾ-ngi ʾ˙ta (1459 Wel 10:12b) we must bear the coffin of the royal father. WANG-¨CO s ˙MYENG ˙i nil˙Gwey s ¨pwu.n i˙lwoswo˙n i ¨a˙molyey ʾ˙na mozom s ko˙cang nwo˙la ˙za ho˙l i ʾ-ngi ʾ˙ta (1447 Sek 24:28a) as the prince has only been alive for seven days he will somehow have to play to his heart's content. ... ˙NYELQ-PPAN ˙TUK ˙hwo˙m ol pwuthye ˙kothosi˙kuy ho˙l i ʾ-ngi ʾ˙ta (1447 Sek 6:4a) he will enable you to be like the Buddha ... and achieve nirvāṇa.

ho˙l i ʾ˙n i (cop mod + postmod). ¶ *ta˙si* ¨HWA-COY ye˙tulp pen cca˙hi ˙za ˙stwo ¨SYWUY-COY ho˙l i ʾ˙n i (1459 Wel 1:49b) and again as the eighth disaster there will be more floods. kan tay ˙lwo ¨salom sim˙kywu˙m i ¨mwot ho.l i ʾ˙n i (1463 Pep 4:86b; sic) cannot let people have it [= the sūtra] just at random. ALSO: 1462 ¹Nung 5:85b, 1465 Wen 1:2:3:6a, ...

ho˙l i ʾn [˙]t ay n' (cop mod + postmod + pcl + pcl). ¶ ˙CYWUNG-SOYNG ˙i ¨ta PPWO-TTYEY ˙lol ˙CING thi ¨mwot ho˙l i ʾn [˙]t ay n' ¨naycywong ¨nay ka˙poyya˙i PPEN-¨NWOW s ¨ko.z ay ye˙huyti a˙ni ˙hono˙n i ˙la (1482 Nam 2:6ab) since not all beings will witness bodhi, in the end one does do not easily keep oneself from the brink of agony.

ho˙l i ʾn ˙t ye (cop mod + postmod + postmod). ¶ ˙POYK-˙SYENG ˙ul PPYEN-QAN ˙khey ho˙l i ʾn ˙t ye (1475 Nay 1:7a) will we ease the lot of the people?

ho˙l i ʾsi.l i ʾl ˙s oy (cop hon prosp mod + postmod + cop prosp mod + postmod + pcl). ¶ ¨ta tas˙kwo˙m ol put˙ti a˙ni ho˙l i ʾsi.l i ʾl ˙s oy (1465 Wen 1:2:2:4a) since it may be that we cannot count on learning everything ... .

ho˙l i ˙za (pcl). ¶ ˙CI-¨TTWOW ˙lol CYWEN-CYENG ˙hi ho˙l i ˙za SSIN ˙ol mozo˙m ay mol˙ki˙ta nil˙Gwol tt i.n i˙la (1463/4 Yeng 2:111a) just concentrating on the true path (for man to take) clears the spirit in one's heart.

holq ˙ka s SEE *s* (particle) 15c

holq ˙kwo, v prosp mod + postmod. ¶ *musu.k iza hol kkwo* [= *holq kwo*] (?1464 Kumkang sasil 4; cited from LCT) just what shall we do?

hol lo, bnd n + pcl. alone. < *howol* ˙lwo (1463 Pep 1:167a) < *hon ˙pol ˙lwo* 'as one layer'.

ho˙l oy = ho˙l [i] ˙oy, v mod + ellipted postmod + pcl (SEE ˙uy). ¶ HHOYNG ho˙l [i] oy ˙PPYEN-NGUY (1463/4 Yeng 2:31a) the comfort of the traveler.

holq s, v/adj prosp mod + postmod: SEE a˙ni ~ .

holq ˙s i, v/adj prosp mod + postmod + pcl. ¶ ˙pu˙l i te˙wun [˙]PEP ˙in ˙t i ¨a˙ti ¨mwot hol ˙ss i il˙hwu˙m i ˙PWULQ-TTI ʾ˙Gwo (1463 Pep 2:60a) being unable to realize that it is the law for fire to be hot is called ignorance and ... .

holq ˙s (i...), v/adj prosp mod + postmod + cop. ~ i˙Gen ˙tyeng (cop effective mod + postmod). ¶ *na ʾy* ˙PPYENG ˙ul ¨tywo˙khey hol ˙ss iGen ˙tyeng (1447 Sek 24:50b) it means he will make my illness better, yet ... .

~ i ˈGwo (cop ger). ¶ ˙ney chaˑh in ˙puˑl ey sol ˙Gye HHWOYNG- ˙˙SO hol ˙ss i ˙Gwo (1447 Sek 9:37a) it is a matter of being burned to death in the fourth fire and ... . ˙HHOYNG on ˙HHAK-ZIN ˙oy HHOYNG hol ˙s iGwo (1482 Kum-sam 2:20b) [the word] ˙HHOYNG means that the scholar performs, and ... .

~ i ˙la (cop indic assert). ¶ ˙˙CHYENG hol ˙ss i ˙la (1447 Sek 6:46a) it means to request. ˙kuliˑ˙zopkeˑ˙na moyng ˙ko˙˙zopke˙na hol ˙ss i ˙la (1459 Wel 2:66b) it means to draw or make. HHYWEN-˙KUY ˙non miˑli ˙SSYWUW-˙KUY hol ˙s i ˙la (1465 Wen se:8b) [the word] HHYWEN-˙KUY means Buddha's giving his prophecies in advance to his disciples.

~ i ˑm ye (cop subst + cop inf). ¶ ˙SIN ˙on sesˑken kes ˙˙ep˙si CIN-˙SSILQ ˙ho˙ya ˙kechuˑti aˑni hol ˙ss i ˙m ye (1459 Wel 2:60a) trust means to be unadulteratedly genuine and not untruthful, and ... .

~ in (copula mod). ¶ ˙˙esˑti hol ˙s in [˙˙MYEN- ˙THYEP] ˙in ˙kwo (?1517- ¹No 1:3b) how is one excused from registering?

~ i.n i (copula mod + postmodifier). ¶ ˙na y pwuthye towoyˑywo.l ye hol ˙s i.n i (1482 Nam 2:6b) I want to become a Buddha. ˙˙SSYANG ˙on specus hol ˙ss i ˙n i pwuthye ˙˙kyeˑsin cek ˙kwa specus hol ˙ss i ˙la (1462 ¹Nung 1:2b) [the word] ˙˙SSYANG ("image") means to resemble; it means to be like when Buddha was present. teˑwuˑm ol ˙˙il ˙Gey hol ˙ss i ˙n i (1462 ¹Nung 3:12b) it makes the heat come into being.

holq ˙s ol SEE -ulq ˙s ol
holq ˙s on SEE -ulq ˙s on
holq ˙s oy, v prosp mod + postmod + pcl. ¶ NUNG ˙hi mwoˑm ay ˙CUK ˙hoˑya ˙kwot mozoˑm i ˙Gey ˙˙mwot hol ˙ss oy (1462 ¹Nung 10:18a) as one cannot approach the body and turn it at once into the mind. ˙CYWUNG-SOYNG ˙i ˙kwot kwoˑt ay ˙TTYAK hol [˙]ss oy ˙hhye naˑkey ˙hoˑta.n i ˙ˈla (1463 Pep 1:158b) people arrived everywhere and had him initiate them.
holq ˙s oy ˈ.n i ˈˈla (cop mod + postmod + cop indic assert). ¶ ˙khun CCO-SIM ˙PELQ ˙hwoˑm on ˙QILQ-˙CHYEY ˙SYEY-KAN ˙ol hon kaˑci ˙lwo twoˑWwoˑl ye hol ˙ss oy ˈ.n i ˈˈla (1459 Wel 9:22a) the origin of great compassion is in seeking to let all people become alike. ˙i ˙˙KWA- ˙PWOW y MWU-˙LYANG MWU-PYEN hol ˙ss oy ˈ.n

i ˈˈla (1459 Wel 21:142b) it is because this retribution (of karma) is immeasurable and unlimited. na y sile-kwom CYEY-SO thi mwot hol s oy ˈ.n i ˈla (1632 Kalyey 1:19b) it is because I cannot possibly do the ancestral rites. ALSO: 1447 Sek 13:36a, ...

holˑswongiˑta = holq ˙s ˈ[y]wo-ngi ˈˈta, v prosp mod + postmod + modulated cop polite + cop indic assert. ¶ SIM-CYE tay lwo non phyeti mwos hol swo-ngi ˈta (1676 Sin.e 8:31a; sic mwos) they are not revealing what their true intentions are.

holq ˙s ye, v prosp mod + postmod + postmod. ¶ ˙˙syel ˙Wun ˙˙il ˙two ˙iˑle hol ˙ss ye (1447 Sek 6:5b) oh sad indeed these events!

holˑsyentyeng = holq ˙s ˈyen tyeng = holq ˙t iGen ˙tyeng. ¶ woˑcik [CI-LAN] ˙olwo ˙˙hoyye ˙˙tywoˑkhey hol ˙s ˈyen tyeng ˙˙es.tyey kwuˑthuyˑye ciˑp ul i ˙Gwus ˙ho.ya ˙˙salla hoˑl i Gwo (1481 Twusi 20:29a) the iris and the orchid get along well together [as do I with my lord], but why go out of one's way to become neighbors?

holq ˙ta, v prosp mod + postmod. ¶ ˙˙esˑtyey ˙˙kyeciˑp uy ˙mwoˑm i spolˑli SSYENG-˙PPWULQ ˙ul ˙TUK hol ˙tta (1463 Pep 4:176b; broken type makes the first syllable look as if it were ˙es) how can a woman's body quickly gain Buddhahood? hon ˙phan ˙sik hol ˙ta (?1517- Pak 1:10a) how much (does it cost) per board? ˙˙ne y ˙culkye naˑˈy ˙emi ˑlul ˙˙hywo˙˙yang hol ˙ta (1586 Sohak 6:50b) = ˙˙ne y naˑˈy eˑmi ˑlul ˙hywo˙˙yang hol [˙]ta (1518 Sohak-cho 9: 55a) will you take care of my mother?

holq ˙t ol, v prosp mod + postmod + pcl. ¶ KHWONG ˙i eˑlwu eˑwulGwuˑti ˙˙mwot holq ˙t ol PYWOW ˙hoˑsya (1462 ¹Nung 3:68b) this represents the fact that the void cannot combine them. ˙˙SSYEN ˙ul ilˑhwu.m i ˙˙mwot hoˑl i ˈˑm ye ˙QAK ˙ol kil ˙Gwu.m i ˙˙mwot hol ˙tt ol (= holq ˙t ol) panˑtoki aˑlwol tt i ˑn i (1463/4 Yeng 1:5b) he must realize that it will not do to lose goodness and it will not do to cultivate evil.
hoˑl ya, (var) = hoˑl ye
hoˑl ye, prosp mod + postmod. CF hoˑla.
1. ¶ ˙kilˑh ul ilthi (= ilh-ˑti) aˑni hoˑl ye (1481 Twusi 21:38a) will he not lose his way?
2. ¶ ku ˙SWU ˑlul ˙˙alˑl ye ˙˙mwot hoˑl ye (1463 Pep 3:86a) can you tell me their number (or not)? eˑlwu SAM-˙SSIP ˙ZI ˙SYANG ˙oˑlwo ZYE-

LOY ˙lol pwo˙l ye ¨mwot ho˙l ye a˙ni '-ngi ' ˙ta (1464 Kumkang 69b) it is not whether one can see the tathāgata in his 32 aspects or not.
ho˙l 'ye˙n i = ho˙l [i] 'ye˙n i, prosp mod + (ellipted postmod +) cop effective mod + postmod. ~ ˙Gwa (pcl). ¶SYWU-MI SAN ˙two e˙lwu ki˙Gwul˙Guy ho˙l [i] 'ye.n i ˙Gwa CYE-˙PPWULQ s ¨ma.l on tal˙Gwolq ˙cwu˙l i ¨ep˙susi˙n i '-ngi ' ˙ta (1459 Wel 9:46b) even Mount Sumeru can be tilted, but there is no way the words of the Buddhas will vary.
ho˙l 'ye.n i 's˙ton SEE -u˙l 'ye.n i 's˙ton
ho˙l 'ye˙n ywo = ho˙l [i] 'ye˙n ywo, v prosp mod + ellipted postmod + cop effective mod + postmod. ¶ ˙ile 'n ¨salom ˙tol˙h ol e˙tu˙li ˙CYEY-˙TTWO ho˙l [i] 'ye˙n ywo ˙hota˙n i (1447 Sek 13:57b) [I] wondered how to save such people. e˙nu na˙la˙h ay no˙lisi˙key ho˙l [i] 'ye˙n ywo (1459 Wel 2:10b) what land should we have them descend to? ¨es˙tyey ho˙l [i] 'ye˙n ywo ˙hwo.m i ¨ep.su˙l i ˙lwo˙ta (1465 Wen se:13b) there will be no wondering how it would be.
ho˙l ywo, v prosp mod + postmod. ¶mu˙su ke˙s i ˙PWULQ-˙CYWOK ho˙l ywo (1447 Sek 6:24a) what is lacking? il˙hwu˙m ul mu˙su.k i˙la ho˙l ywo (1462 ¹Nung 2:81a) what does he call it?
hom, subst < °ho˙ta. SEE - ˙um, ˙hwom.
ho˙ma, adv. already; now.
ho˙m ye (cop inf). ¶ne-¨huy ¨salom ˙HHWO-TTI ho˙m ye (1447 Sek 21:68b) you people must protect the person and .... . tut˙kwo ˙two ¨mwot tulun ˙to˙s 'i ho˙m ye (1459 Wel 10:20b) they hear but act as if they do not hear, and ... . ˙swo˙n oy phye˙lak ¨cwuy˙lak ho˙m ye (1462 ¹Nung 1:113a) the hand opening and closing and ... . ˙hota˙ka is.no˙n i 'n˙t ay n' ¨es˙tyey ˙i ¨yang o˙lwo ˙tye ˙lol ˙CHA-¨TUNG ˙ho˙ya LWON-LYANG ho˙m ye (?1468- Mong 62ab) if it exists, how can we in this manner differentiate it for our consideration, and .... . ne ˙non kis˙ke ˙two ˙na non kis˙ti a˙ni ho˙m ye (1482 Kum-sam 2:5b) you may be happy but I am not, and .... . ALSO: 1447 Sek 9:12a, 24:28b; 1459 Wel 2:16a; 1475 Nay 1:76-7; 1482 Kum-sam 2:7b; 1586 Sohak 2:9b, ...
ho˙m ye n' (cop inf + pcl). ¶na 'y ˙NGWEN ˙ul a˙ni CCYWONG ho˙m ye n' (1459 Wel 1:12b) if you do not comply with my request. koma.n 'i is˙ti a˙ni ho˙m ye n' polk˙ti ¨mwot ˙ho˙non cyen˙cho ˙lwo (1462 ¹Nung 1:77b) because unless it is still it will not become clear. PPWO-TTYEY il˙Gwu.l i ˙Gwo n' ˙homol˙mye hon KYENG ˙ey ¨ta NUNG ˙hi ¨SSYWUW-TTI ho˙m ye n' ku YWEN ˙i te˙wuk ˙SING ho˙m ye ku ¨salo˙m i te˙wuk CWON ˙ho˙ya pwuthye towoy˙ywo˙m i ˙QILQ-˙TTYENG ˙thwo˙ta (1463 Pep 4:75a) as to the question of one's achieving enlightenment (bodhi), if one gets everything one can out of a single sūtra, its causality will all the more carry one and that person gets more respect and is assured of becoming a Buddha. ALSO: 1459 Wel 18:18b, 1462 ¹Nung 5:85b, 1463/4 Yeng 2:70a, 1464 Kumkang 64b, ...
ho˙m ye ˙sye (cop ger + pcl). ¶ ˙poy ˙thoki l' ¨ati ¨mwot ho˙m ye ˙sye (1463/4 Yeng 2:126a) not knowing to take the boat.
hon, mod < °ho˙ta. ALSO: 1481 Twusi 21:3b, ...
1. (epitheme extruded from the subject).
1a. ¶KAN-NAN hon ¨salom (1447 Sek 6:15b) a poor man. MI-˙MYWOW hon KWANG-MYENG ˙ul (1459 Wel 8:38b) a subtle aura. ˙SSILQ hon ¨THYEY (1462 ¹Nung 2:98a) real substance. ˙MANG hon ˙ptoy (1462 ¹Nung 1:77b) unseemly dirt. ce 'y ˙mwu˙l ey wuytwu hon ke˙s ul (1459 Wel 1:23b) the one who is the superior in his group. kotok hon kes (1586 Sohak 2:9b) a thing that is brimful.
1b. (subject = possessor). ¶ ˙NGWOK ˙kot hon mozo˙m ay s mye˙nuli ˙lol (1475 Nay se:8a) a girl with a heart like a jewel.
2. (epitheme extruded from object). ¶ku ˙TAL ˙hon ¨HYWOW (1586 Sohak 4:13a; = ˙TALQ hon) the filial piety that he attained.
3. (summational epitheme). ¶ ˙CHYWULQ-KA hon ¨HHWUW ˙lwo (1447 Sek 24:2a) after leaving home (to go to become a monk). kutuy [˙KWUY] hon ce˙k uy (1481 Twusi 16:61b) when you are so dear to me. ¨ne y ye˙le ˙KEP ˙ey cephu˙ti a˙ni hon ke˙kuy cephun mozo˙m ol ¨nay˙m ye ... (1459 Wel 7:48a) there where you were unafraid for many kalpas (eons) you show a fearful heart and ... .
hon ... , honah, numeral. one (> han ... , hana).
honca, n, adv. alone, by oneself. Hamkyeng DIAL hopun-ca, hapun-ca. < hwon˙ca (1518 Sohak-cho 10:6a) < howon˙za (1475 Nay 2:2:17b), howo˙za (1447 Sek 29b) < *hopo(n)˙za (CF hoWo˙za 1445 ¹Yong 35); ?< *ho[n] ¨pwun ˙sa 'just one only', ?< hon ˙po[l] ˙sa

'just one layer'. CF **hol (lo), hoth**.
hon ci 'la (1916 Gale 2:79) = **han ci 'la**: "A book form connective equal in force to [**hani**] when used with descriptive verbs. It frequently has the force of [**ham ulo**]."
`ho-ngi ˙'ta`, v polite + copula indic assertive.
`ho˙n i`, verb modifier + postmodifier.
  1. (epitheme extruded from subject). Example? SEE `ho˙n i ˙za`.
  2. (epitheme extruded from object). Example?
  3. (`˙i` = summational epitheme used in an extended predicate). ¶ `˙mas.tang ho˙n i` (1463 Pep 3:196b) it is fitting. NGUY-SIM `ho˙n i` (1462 ¹Nung 2:40b) doubted. `no˙m oy ¨cywong ˙i˙la ho˙n i ˙no˙m on ˙nwu ˙kwu` (?1468⁻ Mong 20b) you said he's the slave of another; who is the other? ALSO: 1462 ¹Nung 1:53a; 1475 Nay 1: 18a; 1481 Twusi 15:47b, 16:70b; 1518 Sohak-cho 6:102b, 10:3a, ...
`ho˙n i ˙Ga` (postmodifier). ¶ `sul˙hwu.m i inge˙kuy is˙ti a˙ni ho˙n i ˙Ga` (1481 Twusi 7:14a) is there no sorrow here? `te˙wun [˙KHUY-˙NGWUN] ˙i ¨wolwo [˙HELQ] ˙thi a˙ni ˙hono˙n i kye˙zul towoy˙ywo.m on ˙stwo e˙lyep˙ti a˙ni ho˙n i ˙Ga` (1481 Twusi 10:42a) the ailments due to the hot season are not fully abating; come winter won't things be even harder?
`ho˙n i ˙Gwo` (postmodifier). ¶ `ta˙si ¨cwul˙ptu.t i ¨es.te ho˙n i ˙Gwo` (1481 Twusi 7:40a) how about the idea of giving once again?
`ho˙n i ˙'la` (cop indic assertive). ¶ SA-MI `˙'la ho˙n i ˙'la` (1447 Sek 6:2b) is called a śrāmaṇera (religious novice). ALSO: 1482 Nam 2:5a, 1459 Wel 7:44b, 1463 Pep 2:113b, 1464 Kumkang 11a, ...
`ho˙n i ˙lol` SEE -`u˙n i ˙lol`
`ho˙n i '-ngi s ˙kwo` SEE -`u˙n i '-ngi s ˙kwo`
`ho.n i '-ngi ˙'ta` SEE -`u˙n i '-ngi ˙'ta`
`˙ho˙ni˙ta`, cpd verb (< `˙ho-˙ni-`). acts, moves. ¶ `˙na˙a ˙honi˙ti a˙ni ˙ho˙ya` (1447 Sek se:2b) does not move forward. ALSO: 1447 Sek se:1b; 1459 Wel 7:31b; 1462 ¹Nung 7:65b; ?1468⁻ Mong 27a.
`ho˙n i ˙uy` SEE -`u˙n i ˙uy`
`ho˙n i ˙ya` SEE -`u˙n i ˙ya`
`ho˙n i ˙za` (pcl; epitheme extruded from subject). ¶ `¨TTWOW ˙kot ho˙n i ˙za pi˙luse ¨a˙no.n i ˙'la` (1482 Kum-sam 2:3a) only those who have shared the same way come to know each other.

`˙ho(˙)non`, processive modifier < `˚ho˙ta`.
  1. (epitheme extruded from subject). ¶ CHIN-SIM `a˙ni ˙ho˙non ¨salo˙m oy` ... (1459 Wel 21: 215b) ... of a person who does not anger.
  2. (epitheme extruded from object). Example?
  3. (with summational epitheme). ¶ `ke˙sul˙pcun ¨yang ˙honon ˙NAN` (1447 Sek 9:33a) the difficulty of acting defiant. `koma.n ˙i is˙ti a˙ni ho˙m ye n' polk˙ti ¨mwot ˙ho˙non cyen˙cho ˙lwo` (1462 ¹Nung 1:77b) because unless it is still it will not become clear.
`˙hono˙n i (n')`, `˙ho˙no.n i ˙'la`, `˙hono˙n i '-ngi ˙'ta`, `˙ho.no.n i '-ng' ˙'ta`, `˙ho˙no.n i s ˙ka`, `˙hono˙n i '-ngi s ˙kwo`, `˙ho˙no˙n i '-'i s ˙kwo`. SEE -(˙)non (...).
`˙ho˙no.n i ˙non`. ¶ `pwus˙ku˙li˙ti a˙ni ˙ho˙no.n i ˙non` (1586 Sohak 4:43a) that they are unabashed.
`˙honon ˙kwo` (postmodifier). ¶ `mu˙sus ¨i˙l ol kyes˙kwowo˙l ye ˙honon ˙kwo` (1447 Sek 6:27a) whatever we are to compete at, ...
`˙honon ˙ta` (postmodifier). ¶ `¨ne y ˙SIN ˙honon ˙ta a˙ni ˙honon ˙ta` (1459 Wel 9:46a) do you believe it or don't you? `¨ne y ˙mye˙ch ul ¨hwo˙l ye ˙honon ˙ta` (?1517⁻ Pak 1:31b) how many do you want (to make it)?
`˙ho˙non t oy ˙lan`. ¶ `kos.ka ˙ho˙non t oy ˙lan mul me˙kiti malla` (?1517⁻ ¹No 1:35b) when one is trying hard let water not be drunk.
`˙hono˙ta`, v proc indic assert. ¶ LA-˙HHWUW-LA `to˙lye ˙ta ˙ka SA-MI sa˙mwo.l ye ˙hono˙ta hol ˙ss oy` (1447 Sek 6:2a) when she says the intention is to take Rāhula and make him into a śrāmaṇera (religious novice) ... . `˙na y ˙pwoa ˙cye ˙hono˙ta sol˙Wa˙ssye` (1447 Sek 6:14b) please tell him I would like to see him. `wo˙cik nil˙Gwotoy [˙KHWON-¨KHWO] hol ˙s i ¨cywong towoy˙Ge ci˙la ˙hono˙ta` (1481 Twusi 8:1b) he says only "I am destitute and want to become a slave". `˙como˙lak ˙ptu˙lak ˙hono˙ta` (1481 Twusi 7:2a) [the dragonflies] are sinking and floating.
`ho˙n oy` = `ho˙n [i] oy`, verb mod + ellipted postmod + pcl (SEE -`uy`). ¶ `˙PPYENG ho˙n [i] oy nek˙s i kwo˙t ay two˙la ˙wa` (1447 Sek 9:31a) the spirit of the ill one came back on the spot (= at once).
`hon ˙ta`, v mod + postmod. did it happen?
~ `¨ma˙ta` (every time it did) SEE -`˙un ˙ta`.
`hon [˙]ta ˙'sin ˙t ol`, abbr < `hon ˙ta ˙hosin ˙t ol`. ¶ `¨salo˙m i ¨twul˙h i˙Gey hon [˙]ta ˙'sin ˙t ol ka˙col˙pi˙si.n i ˙'la` (1462 ¹Nung 2:27b) [he]

wondered whether people had made them be two, but compared them anyway.

honta (1893 Scott 239) = **hanta** (1887 Scott 200 = 1893 Scott 157) = **hanta**

honˇt ay, v mod + postmod + pcl. SEE **-un ˇt ay**.

honˇt ol, v mod + postmod + pcl. SEE **-un ˇt ol**.

honˇt on, v mod + postmod + pcl. given that it happened; as for what one did. ¶ *[ˊNGWEN] honˇt on [KAN-*ˋQALQ] hwo.m ol ¨cyeki hoˇla* (1481 Twusi 8:7a) I would like you to provide a bit of information.

hon-ˇtoy, adv (< num + n 'one place'). together (with).

honˇt oy, v mod + postmod + pcl. ¶ *panˇtoˇki ¨nay cwoˇcha poˇlywolq ˇt iˇla honˇt oy* (1462 ¹Nung 7:54a) said we must excommunicate them [if they commit the four pārājika sins].

honˇtoy, v mod + n ('place'). ¶ *ˋCI-ˋKKUK ˊˋti aˋni honˇtoy ¨epˋkesiˋnol* (1462 ¹Nung 1:3a) while there is no place that is not extreme, ...

ˋhonwoˋla SEE **-ˋnwoˋla**

ho(ˋ)nwon, modulated proc mod < °hoˋta.

1. (epitheme extruded from subject). ?
2. (epitheme extruded from object). ¶ *pwoˋti aˋni hoˋnwon ˋSYANG ˋon* (1462 ¹Nung 2:37a) the signs that he does not see. *PWUN-ˋPYELQ ˋhoˋnwon kuliˋmey s* ... (1462 ¹Nung 1:90b) ... of the image that one distinguishes.
3. (summational epitheme). ¶ *polaˋkhwoˋcye ˋhoˋnwon mozoˋm i naˋm ye n'* (1462 ¹Nung 7:74b) if one gets in the mood to want to hope ... . *ˋNGWEN ˋhoˋnwon ptuˋt i ¨eptaˋn i* (1459 Wel 13:35b) I have had no mind to want it. *sulˋhe ˋhonwon yangˋco ˋy'la* (1459 Wel se: 16a) it means 'a sad look'. *pwuthye s ¨TTWOW-¨LI KKWUW ˋhonwon ¨yaˋng ol ¨pwonˇt oy n' ˋPWO-SI ˋlol ˋhwoˋtoy* (1447 Sek 13:18-9) seeing a manner to pursue the principles of Buddha, he gives alms and ... .

ˋhonwoˋn i (postmod; epitheme extruded from subject). ¶ *ˋil ¨epˋsun ¨TTWOW-¨LI ˋlol KKWUW ˋhonwoˋn i* (1459 Wel 1:11b) those seeking an uneventful doctrine.

ˋhoˋnwo.n i sˋka (postmod + postmod [+ ellipted cop polite] + pcl + postmod; summational epitheme). SEE **-ˋnwo.n i sˋka**.

ˋhoˋnwonˇt i.l i ˊˋla SEE **-ˋnwonˇt i.l i ˊˋla**

[ˊ]honwonˇt un SEE **-[ˊ]nwonˇt un**

ˋhonwonˇt ye SEE **-[ˊ]nwonˇt ye**

ˋhonwosˋta, proc effective < °hoˋta + emotive. ¶ *¨saloˋm on [KWA-YEN] ˋul kuˋchiˋsikwaˋtye solang ˋhonwosˋta* (1481 Twusi 20:4b) people would love to put an end to spears and lances.

ˋhonwoˋswo-ngi ˊˋta SEE **-ˋnwoˋswo-ngi ˊˋta**

ˋhoˋnwoswoˋn i SEE **-ˋnwoswoˋn i**

hopta < (1588) hwopta ? < °h[o]-ˋwo-W-, postnom adj insep -W- [obs] = **sulepta** (is etc.). ¶ **salang (h)opta** is attractive, lovable. **Cha hopta!** (bound noun cha < CHA 'sigh') Alas (oh how sad I am)! **O hopta!** (bound noun o < QWO 'exclamation' but often written as if QE 'at/in/to') How admirable! CF **hepta**.

ˋhopˋta, postnom adj insep -W- (> hwopta). ¶ *¨ta ˋCYWOK ˋhi solang ˋhopˋti aˋni kheˋnul* (1463 Pep 2:111b) everyone fails to love it adequately, but ... . *ku swoˋli CHYENG-HHWA ˋkhwo ¨KAM-¨TWONG ˋhopˋkwo kis.puˋn i* (1463 Pep 3:115b) the sounds are peaceful and moving and joyful. SEE ... ˋhoWon. CF **hepta**.

hoˋsa-ngi ˊˋta, v + ? bnd v polite + cop indic assert. ¶ *¨CO-ˋSIK ˋuy ilˋhwum ˋul aˋpi isiˋm ye [ˊ]eˋmi iˋsya ˋQILQ-ˋTTYENG hoˋsa-ngi ˊˋta* (1459 Wel 8:83a; il-ˋhwum-ˋul) I hope the name of the son will be decided in the presence of the father and the mother. *epeˋzi koˋca isin ceˋk uy ilˋhwu.m ul ˋQILQ-ˋTTYENG hoˋsa-ngi ˊˋta* (1459 Wel 8:96b) when the parents have got one [= a new child] they decide a name.

ˋhoˋsikeˋnul, honorific lit concessive < °hoˋta. ¶ *¨LYEY-ˋSWUW ˋhosikeˋnul* ([1447→]1562 Sekpo 11:13_; cited from LCT with inferred accents) showed proper manners.

ˋhoˋsikeˋtun, honorific provisional < °hoˋta. ¶ *CYE PPWO-ˋSALQ ˋtolˋkhwa [= ˋtolhˋkwa] ˋlwo ˋswoˋn ol simˋkye NGYENG-ˋCYEP ˋhoˋsikeˋtun* (1459 Wel 8:48b) offering his hand to the bodhisattvas and all he welcomed them.

(?ˋhoˋsiˋkey =) ˋhosiˋkuy, honorific adverbative < °hoˋta. ¶ *... kothosiˋkuy* (1447 Sek 6:4a) = ... *kot hosiˋkuy* so as to be like ... .

ˋhoˋsikwanˋtoy: ... ˋTTYWU ~ (1463 Pep 7:32-3) staying ... . SEE **-ˋkwanˋtoy**, ˋkhwanˋtoy.

ˋhosiˋkwo, hon ger < °hoˋta. said ... and (1447 Sek 13:15a), thought ... and (1459 Wel 21:219a).

ˋho(ˋ)silq, hon prosp mod < °hoˋta.

1. (epitheme extruded from subject). Example?
2. (epitheme extruded from object). Example?
3. (summational epitheme). ¶ *ˋCHYWULQ-KA ˋhosilq pstay ˊsilˋss oy* (1449 Kok 50) since it

is time to become a monk ... .
ˈhosila ˈn ˈt oy, v subj attent + abbr < hon ˈt oy (v mod + postmod + pcl) — SEE -uˈla ˈn ˈt oy. ¶kwoˈki capnon ˈpoy nwolˈGywo.m ol ˈpwonwoˈla ˈho.ya [ˈPPOYK-ˈZILQ] i wolˈma katolwok ˈhosila ˈn ˈt oy ˈˈman tyeng nulˈkun nyeˈlum ˈˈcis.non ˈnwoˈm on muˈsus keˈs i iˈsye selu ˈculkywoˈm ol ˈˈta hoˈl i Gwo (1481 Twusi 22:7b) not just have they spent much of the day's light enjoying the fishing boat, but with what [now] will the old farmers bring their mutual delight to its fullest?
ˈhoˈsi.l i, hon prosp mod < °hoˈta + postmod.
~ ˈˈla (cop indicative assertive). ¶haˈnolˈh i tangtangi ˈi ˈphi ˈlol ˈˈsalom towoyˈGey ˈhoˈsi.l i ˈˈla (1459 Wel 1:7-8) heaven is to make this blood suitably into people. pskayˈhye kolˈhoyˈti ˈˈmwot hoˈsi.l i ˈˈla (1462 ¹Nung 2:50b) cannot analyze them.
~ ˈleˈla (cop retr assert). ¶QA-ˈNWOK SAM-ˈMAK SAM-PPWO-TTYEY ˈlol ˈTUK ˈhosiˈl i ˈleˈla (1459 Wel 21:222a) he gained the unexcelled complete enlightenment of a Buddha's wisdom (anuttara-samyak-sambodhi).
ˈhosilq ˈs oy, honorific prosp mod < °hoˈta + postmod + pcl. ¶[ˈCI-ˈHYWOW] y ˈtyeˈle ˈhosil ˈss oy ... (1445 ¹Yong 92) his extreme filial devotion was such that ... . ce ˈy ˈˈnim-ˈkum [ˈWUY] ˈtha ˈhosil ˈss oy (1445 ¹Yong 121) saying they do it for their own king, he ... . woˈcik pwuˈˈthye y ˈza twuˈlyeˈi ˈCING ˈhosil ˈs oy (1465 Wen 1:2:1:16b) for only Buddha gives witness all around (—the Chinese version has "[ONLY BUDDHA] iza", with the Hankul as a reading note). ALSO: 1445 ¹Yong 34, 1459 Wel 2:62b, 1463 Pep 5:100a.
ˈhosil ˈˈspwun ˈtyeng, hon prosp mod < °hoˈta + postmod + bnd n. ¶ˈMYELQ-ˈTTWO ˈhosil ˈˈspwun ˈtyeng (1447 Sek 23:52b, 53a) only achieves nirvāṇa but ... .
ˈhosiˈl ye, hon prosp mod < °hoˈta + postmod.
ˈhoˈsi.l [i] ˈyeˈn ywo, hon prosp mod + ellipted pcl + cop effective mod + postmod. ¶eˈnu lˈ CCYWONG ˈhoˈsi.l [i] ˈyeˈn ywo (1459 Wel 7:26a) which one will you follow?
ˈhosim, hon subst < °hoˈta. Normally replaced by the modulated form ˈhosyam except in:
ˈhosiˈm ye (cop inf). ¶ˈˈsaloˈm ol ˈpwoˈasiˈtun mwoncye ˈˈmal ˈhosiˈm ye (1459 Wel 2:58b) when he sees a person he speaks first, and ... .

ˈhosiˈm ye nˈ (abbr cop inf + pcl). ~ ˈTHAY-ˈˈCO y ˈCHYWULQ-KA ˈhosiˈm ye ˈn (1449 Kok 36) when the prince becomes a monk ... .
ˈhosin, honorific modifier < °hoˈta. (1447 Sek 9:29a, 1447 Sek 13:35b, 1459 Wel 1:15a, 1459 Wel se:9a, 1475 Nay 1:40a).
ˈhosiˈn i (1445 ¹Yong 42, 64, 107; 1447 Sek 6:9b, 9:26b, 23:53b; 1449 Kok 43; 1459 Wel 1:52a, 10:15b; 1462 ¹Nung 2:92a, 10:42b; 1464 Kumkang 81b; 1482 Kum-sam 2:3b, 5:14a); hosiˈn i (1463 Pep 2:43b).
ˈhoˈsi.n i ˈˈla (1447 Sek 23:42a, 1463 Pep 4:193a, 1465 Wen se:6a, ?1468- Mong 49b).
ˈhosiˈna, hon adversative < °hoˈta. ¶aˈni ~ (example on p. 422). CF ˈhoˈsyaˈna.
ˈhosi-ngi ˈˈta, hon polite < °hoˈta + cop indic assert. ¶ˈMYENG ˈi ˈˈmeˈti aˈni ˈhoˈsi-ngi ˈˈta (1459 Wel 21:218b) [the end of] his life is not far off.
ˈhoˈsinon (/ ˈhosiˈnon), hon proc mod < °hoˈta. ¶CCO-PI ˈnon ˈCYWUNG-SOYNG ˈol PPYEN-QAN ˈkhey ˈhoˈsinon keˈs iGeˈnul (1447 Sek 6:5b) mercy is [in his] deigning to ease the lot of living creatures, yet ... . SYEY-PANG S ˈSYENG-ZIN ˈi ˈZIP-ˈMYELQ ˈhosiˈnon ˈSYANG (1447 Sek 23:22b) a scene of the holy man of the west achieving nirvāṇa.
ˈhoˈsinoˈn i, honorific processive modifier < °hoˈta + postmod. ¶ icey ˈstwo naˈy aˈtoˈl ol toˈlye ˈˈkaˈl ye ˈhoˈsinoˈn i (1447 Sek 6:5b) and now you want to take my son, in addition. pwuthye s ˈkuy patcoˈWa muˈsum ˈhwo.l ye ˈhoˈsinoˈn i (1459 Wel 1:10b) [he asks] what do you want to do in presenting them to Buddha? THYEN-ˈˈCO y ˈwuˈli ˈˈTTWOW-ˈˈLI ˈlan poˈlisiˈkwo ˈˈmen ˈtuy s HHWO-ˈKYWOW ˈlol KKWUW ˈhoˈsinoˈn i (1459 Wel 2:69a) the son of heaven rejects our doctrine and pursues alien teachings from distant places.
~ ˈˈla (cop indic assert). ¶CYE-ˈPPWULQ ˈi woˈcik hon ˈkhun ˈˈil s QIN-YWEN cyenˈcho ˈlu ˈSYEY-KAN ˈay ˈna ˈHHYEN ˈhoˈsinoˈn i ˈˈla ˈhoˈsi.n i ˈˈla (1465 Wen se:6a) he said that Buddhas appear in the world of people only as the result of cause by some major event.
~ ˈ-ngi s ˈkwo (cop polite + pcl + bnd n). SEE -uˈsinoˈn i ˈ-ngi s ˈkwo.
~ ˈsiˈn i ˈˈla. SEE -uˈsinoˈn i ˈsiˈn i ˈˈla.
~ ˈ-ˈ s ˈkwo = ~ ˈ-ngi s ˈkwo. SEE -uˈsinoˈn i ˈ-ˈ s ˈkwo.

`ho᐀sinon᐀ka`, hon proc mod + postmodifier.
¶ `[᐀]TUK᐀ho᐀syan᐀MYWOW-᐀PEP᐀ul nil᐀Gwo᐀l ye᐀ho᐀sinon᐀ka` (1447 Sek 13:25b) does he intend to tell the Wonderful Law that he has obtained?
`ho᐀sino᐀n ywo`, v hon proc mod + postmod. SEE -u᐀sino᐀n ywo.
`hosino᐀ta`, hon proc indic assert < °ho᐀ta.
`hosin᐀ta᐀᐀ma᐀ta` SEE -un᐀ta᐀᐀ma᐀ta
`hosi᐀nwon`, hon proc modulated mod < °ho᐀ta.
 1. (epitheme extruded from subject). Example?
 2. (epitheme extruded from object). ¶ `na᐀non pwuthye s solang᐀hosi᐀nwon az᐀G i᐀la` (1462 ¹Nung 1:86a) I am the younger brother whom the Buddha loves.
 3. (with summational epitheme). ¶ `᐀ta spol᐀li ᐀᐀ilGwa᐀tye᐀hosi᐀nwon cyen᐀cho᐀᐀y᐀la` (1463 Pep 5:169b) it is because everybody wants to become one [= a Buddha] fast.
 ~ `᐀t i` SEE -usi᐀nwon᐀t i
`ho᐀si᐀ta`, hon indic assert (or transferentive) < °ho᐀ta.
`ho᐀sita᐀ka`, hon transferentive < °ho᐀ta + pcl. ¶ `᐀᐀CCWA-SSYEN᐀ho᐀sita᐀ka na᐀la᐀h ay᐀᐀pil-me᐀ku᐀la᐀wosi᐀n i` (1459 Wel 1:5b) he [Gautama] did meditation (dhyāna) and then came to our land to beg alms. `cheze᐀m uy n'᐀᐀wo᐀lwo᐀TTWOK-᐀SSYWONG a᐀ni᐀ho᐀sita᐀ka᐀᐀naycywong᐀ay n'᐀NUNG᐀hi᐀KKYEY᐀lol tutco᐀wa ti᐀ni᐀sya` (1463 Pep 6:83a) at first he could not read the sūtras out perfectly but then in the end he listened to the gāthās (hymns) and remembered them, and ... .
`ho᐀sitan`, hon retr mod < °ho᐀ta. SEE -u᐀sitan.
`ho᐀si᐀ta[᐀]s-ongi᐀᐀ta`, honorific retrospective emotive polite + cop indic assert. ¶ `pwu᐀thye y᐀SSILQ᐀lwo᐀TTAY-SSING᐀u᐀lwo᐀KYWOW-᐀HWA᐀ho᐀si᐀tas-ongi᐀᐀ta` (1459 Wel 13:36b) Buddha truly educated us through the Greater Vehicle (mahāyāna). ¶ `han᐀salo᐀m o᐀lwo᐀᐀TTWOW-TTYANG᐀ay ni᐀lulGey᐀ho[᐀]si[᐀]tas-ongi᐀᐀ta` (1463 Pep 2:22a) he arranged for people to arrive at the seminary in large numbers.
`ho᐀sitas᐀ta`, hon retr emotive indic assertive < o᐀ta. SEE -u᐀sitas᐀ta.
`hosite᐀la` (= `ho᐀tesi᐀ta`). SEE -u᐀site᐀la.
`ho᐀siten`, hon retr mod < °ho᐀ta (= `ho᐀tesin`).
 ~ `ka` (postmod). ¶ `wuli epe᐀zi᐀ney᐀ta᐀mwo᐀m i phyen.an᐀ho᐀siten᐀ka` (?1517- Pak 1:51a) were my parents in good health?
 ~ `᐀t oy n'`. SEE -u᐀siten᐀t oy n'.

`ho᐀site-ngi᐀᐀ta` SEE -u᐀site-ngi᐀᐀ta
`hosi-ti᐀Wi` SEE -ti᐀Wi
`hosi᐀twos᐀te-ngi᐀᐀ta`, hon emotive retr polite < °ho᐀ta + cop indic assert. ¶ `nal᐀᐀ma᐀ta᐀᐀NGWO-᐀POYK SUNG-CAY᐀hosi᐀twos᐀te-ngi᐀᐀ta` (1459 Wel 23:74b) every day they held a service with five hundred priests.
`hosi᐀twoswo-ngi᐀᐀ta` SEE -u᐀si᐀twoswo-ngi᐀᐀ta
`ho᐀sitwo᐀ta`, hon emotive indic assert < °ho᐀ta. SEE -u᐀sitwo᐀ta.
`ho᐀sya`, honorific infinitive < °ho᐀ta (= hasye).
 ¶ `CYWUNG-SOYNG᐀o᐀lwo᐀QILQ-᐀CHYEY᐀SYEY-KAN᐀ay s᐀SIN᐀thi elye᐀Wun᐀PEP᐀ul᐀᐀ta tutco᐀Wa᐀᐀al᐀Gey᐀hwo.l i᐀᐀la᐀ho᐀sya` (1447 Sek 13:27a) he says "I will get all living beings to understand the Law that is so difficult for the world at large to believe". `᐀᐀mwot mi᐀chul᐀tu.s ᐀i᐀hosya` (1475 Nay 2:1:43a) acting as if he could not reach it. ALSO: 1447 Sek 6:9b, 6:12a, 6:17b, 13:27a; 1459 Wel 2:36b, 9:35e; 1462 ¹Nung 3:68b; 1463 Pep 2:231b, 6:144a; 1482 Kum-sam 2:2b, ...
`hosya᐀za`. ¶ `CYE-᐀PPWULQ᐀two᐀CHYWULQ-KA᐀hosya᐀za᐀᐀TTWOW-᐀LI᐀lol tas.ko᐀sino᐀n i` (1447 Sek 6:12a) to study the doctrine even the Buddhas must leave home.
... `kwa᐀ho᐀sya`. ¶ `PWU-ZIN᐀kwa᐀ho᐀sya᐀PPI-KHWUW cwocho᐀sya` (1459 Wel 8:93b) together with the lady he followed the almsman (bhikṣu) and ... .
`ho᐀syal(q)`, hon modulated prosp mod < °ho᐀ta.
`hosya᐀l i` (postmod; epitheme extruded from subject). ¶ `SILQ-᐀TTALQ᐀i᐀la᐀hosya᐀l i᐀na᐀sil na᐀l ay` (1447 Sek 6:17a) on the day that the one to be called Siddhārtha was born.
`ho᐀syal [᐀]t in᐀t ay n'`. SEE -u᐀syal(q).
`ho᐀syam`, hon modulated subst < °ho᐀ta.
`hosya᐀m ay` (1459 Wel 14:59a)
`hosya᐀m i` (1462 ¹Nung 10:42b, 1463 Pep 5:100a)
`ho᐀sya᐀m i᐀la` (1459 Wel 14:58a)
`hosya᐀m ol`. Example?
`hosya᐀m olwo`. ¶ `PI-᐀NGWEN s HWUN᐀hosya᐀m olwo pi᐀luse ingey ni᐀lu.n i` (1482 Nam 1:33b) with the emitting of fragrance by the great pitying vow [of Buddhas and bodhisattvas to save all beings], it has for the first time reached this place.
`hosya᐀m on`. ¶ `HHWUW s᐀PEP tuliGwu᐀m ila᐀hosya᐀m on` (1462 ¹Nung 1:17b) his saying that he will give down later laws.

`ho˙syan (< *`ho-si-`wo-n), hon modulated mod < °`ho˙ta. CF `hosin.
1. (with epitheme extruded from an embedded subject). ¶ `HWA-ZIN `on `SYEY-CWON s SSIN-`LUK `u˙lwo towoy `Guy `hosyan ¨sa˙lo.m i˙la (1447 Sek 6:7b) an incarnated Buddha is a person brought into being through the divine power of the World-Honored.
2. (epitheme extruded from object). ¶[`]TUK `ho˙syan `MYWOW-`PEP `ul (1447 Sek 13:25b) the Wonderful Law that he has obtained. SSIN-`LUK [`]uy `HWA `ho˙syan ke˙s un pas[k] ¨chyenlyang `ay ¨nam˙ti ho˙n i (1463 Pep 6:144a) what the supernatural power has brought into being is no more than external property.
3. (summational epitheme). Example?
ALSO: 1447 Sek 6:12a, 1463 Pep 4:169a, 1482 Kum-sam 2:2b, ...

`ho˙sya˙na, hon modulated adversative < °`ho˙ta. ¶ZYE-LOY hon `khun ¨i˙l ol `WUY `ho˙sya˙na (1465 Wen se:6a) the tathāgata devoted himself to a great work, but ... . CF `hosi˙na.

`hosya˙nol, hon lit concessive < °`ho˙ta. ¶PPWO-`SALQ i `phye ¨CHYENG `hosya˙nol ZYE-LOY y `cukcay SSIN-`LUK ¨nay˙sya (1463 Pep 6:97a) when the bodhisattva expressed his desire, the tathāgata at once displayed his supernatural power, and ... .

`hosyas˙ta, emotive indicative assertive < °`ho˙ta. ¶ `SYEY-CWON `i `SYEY-KAN `ay `na˙sya `SSIM `hi KKUY-`TTUK `hosyas˙ta (1459 Wel 7:14b) it was most commendable of the World-Honored to grace the human world with his birth.

`hosywo˙sye. please do it. ¶ ¨na l' `KWUW `hosywo˙sye (1449 Kok 98) please save me. ¨na `lol nil `Gwey `man NGWANG `i towoy `Gey `hosywo˙sye (1447 Sek 14:50b) let me become king for just seven days.

°`ho˙ta, v indic assert; inf `ho˙ya (later also `ho˙ye). ABBR `tha, `˙ta. SEE ¨mwot `˙ta, `kot `˙ta. On the accent, see ¶2.12.4 (pp. 71, 81-4).
NOTE: The irregularity of the infinitive form `ho˙ya and the effective `ho(˙)ya⋯ can be explained if we assume an original stem *`hyo-. The infinitive *`hy[o]-˙a = *`hya was conflated to `ho˙ya (and later `ho˙ye was created by analogy with ⋯i- stems reduced to ⋯y- before the infinitive), but in other forms *°`hyo- was reduced to °`ho-. The irregularity is evidence for the syllabic nucleus *yo, which we can reconstruct for a few other words on the basis of dialect forms. CF cen `hye; `hye = *`hya?

`hota˙ka, 1. indic assert + pcl. does / says and then; but. ¶ `nwun s ka˙won-toy s TTWONG-¨CO y nos [< noch] al˙ph oy s `salo˙m i.n i `˙la `hota˙ka (1482 Kum-sam 2:31b) the pupil in the middle of the eye is said to be a person in front of the face, but ... .
2. adv. sometimes; perhaps; if.

`hota˙la, retr indic assertive < °`ho˙ta. ¶ `na y ¨lwongtam `hota˙la (1447 Sek 6:24b) I was joking. `nyey `two `i˙le `hota˙la (1459 Wel 7:14b) in olden days too it was this way. `na y ywo so˙i mol-pwo˙ki ¨e˙te `sye mol `tho˙ti ¨mwot `hota˙la (?1517- Pak 1:37b) the last while I have been unable to ride a horse, having acquired an intestinal ailment.

`ho˙tan, retr modifier < °`ho˙ta (also `ho˙ten). ¶ ¨TTWOW-¨LI ma˙lwo˙l ye `ho˙tan cyen˙cho `lwo (1459 Wel 7:13b) because I have been unwilling to practice the doctrine.

`ho˙ta-ngi `˙ta, retr polite < °`ho˙ta + cop indic assert. ¶ `SSIM `hi `na y ¨KAM-SYANG `hwo˙toy ZYE-LOY s MWU-`LYANG TI-`KYEN `ul il˙hwo˙la `ho˙ta-ngi `˙ta (1463 Pep 2:4b) I was moved to such grief I was about to lose the tathāgata's immeasurable awareness.

`hota˙n i, retr mod < °`ho˙ta + postmod (also `hote˙n i). ¶ `na y pwu˙le ne `lul esye `TUK-¨TTWOW ho˙key `hota˙n i (1447 Sek 24:3a) I have deliberately tried to get you to achieve the way [to enlightenment] quickly. ¨es˙tyey ZYE-LOY y ¨SYWOW-SSING `PEP `u˙lwo `CYEY-`TTWO `khesi˙n ywo `hota˙n i (1463 Pep 2:5b) I wondered how the tathāgata had provided salvation through the dharma of the Lesser Vehicle (hīnayāna). [¨SYWOW-ZIN] `i ¨moy˙zil ci˙p uy is˙ti a˙ni `hota˙n i (?1517- Pak 1:58b) the commoner was not at home day after day.

`hotan˙t i˙m ye n' SEE -tan˙t i˙m ye n'
`ho˙ta[`]s-ongi `˙ta SEE -ta[`]s-ongi `˙ta
`hotaswo˙la SEE -taswo˙la
`ho˙taswo˙n i SEE -taswo˙n i
`hote˙la, retr indic assert < °`ho˙ta. ¶mwo˙ton ¨salom `kwa `LYWUK-SO [G]wa y pwo˙kwo koma.n `i ¨mwot i˙sye `CCO-ZYEN `hi ni˙le ¨LYEY-`SWUW `hote˙la (1447 Sek 6:30a) the assembled people and the Six Tīrthikas seeing (him) could not stay still but spontaneously

arose and bowed in courtesy. *chuki ne ki ti ¨mal la ˙hote la* (1447 Sek 24:3ab) "do not think ill of me", he said. *kil h ey KAN-NAN hon ¨salom ˙pwoa ton ˙PWO-SI ˙hote la* (1447 Sek 6:15b) when he would see a poor man on the road he would give him alms. ALSO: 1586 Sohak 5:48b, ... ABBR *thela*.

˙*ho ten*, retr modifier < °*ho ta* (also ˙*ho tan*). ¶ ˙*CYEY ˙hoten ˙sta h ol pwo kwo ˙cel ˙hota ka* (1447 Sek 6:19a) seeing a place where they were celebrating heaven with a festival, he [Sudatta] bowed and then ... .

˙*ho te-ngi ˙ta* SEE - *te-ngi ˙ta*

˙*hote n i*, retr mod < °*ho ta* + postmod (also ˙*hota n i*). ¶ *nwuyGus.pun mozo m ol a ni ˙hwo.l i ˙la ˙hote n i* (1447 Sek 6:8-9) you said you would not have a remorseful heart. ˙*icey pol h ol ˙solo sya ˙mwo m i kos ti ¨mwot ˙kesi ta ˙hote n i* (1459 Wel 2:42b) now he has burned off his arm and his body cannot be whole, (so) they said. ¨*es tyey ˙i na la h ol [˙] e.ye spi ne kye wo ti a ni ˙khesi n ywo ˙hote n i* (1459 Wel 7:29b) he said, "how can you love this land and never come to it?". ALSO: 1447 Sek 19:40b, 1459 Wel 2:42b.

˙*hote.n i ˙la* SEE - *te n i ˙la*

˙*ho tesin*, retr hon mod < °*ho ta* (= ˙*hosi ten*).

˙*ho tesi n i*, retr hon mod < °*ho ta* + postmod. ABBR ˙*thesi n i*. ¶ *sta h ay ˙sal i ¨pskeyye nul ¨LYEY-CCYWEN i swo sa ˙na a ˙CYWUNG-SOYNG ˙ol ˙KWUW ˙ho tesi n i* (1449 Kok 41) his arrow pierced the earth, but there a sweet spring gushed forth and saved the creatures.

˙*ho tesi ta* (= ˙*ho site la*). SEE - *tesi ta*.

˙*hote tun* SEE -*te tun*

hoth, n, adn. single, one-ply, single layer. ANT **kyep**. < *howoch* (1632 Twusi-cwung 1:19a) < *howoc* (1462 ¹Nung 8:15b) < *ho[nah]* + ?.

1. n (occurs only before **ulo**, **cita**, and **ita**). ¶ ~ **ulo toyta** is made of a single sheet. ~ **ita** /hochita/ is single-layered, is one-ply / -sheet.

2. adn. ¶ ~ **cip** a house without an annex. ~ **chima** a skirt worn without underpants. ~-**q ipul** /honnipul/ a single quilt. ~ **mom** alone; a woman who is not pregnant. ~ **moum** a simple vowel. ~ **os** /hotos/ an unlined garment. ~ **pel** single-fold (things). ~ **(-pel) sālam** a shallow-minded person. ~ **pyek** a thin wall. ~ **tam** a single-layer wall.

°*ho ti*, suspective < °*ho ta*. ABBR ˙*thi*, ˙*ti*.

˙*ho-ti Gwuy* does but. SEE ... *thi Gwuy*.

ho- tos SEE - *tos*

˙*ho twoswo n ywo*, v emotive-emotive mod + postmod. ABBR ˙*thwoswo n ywo*. ¶ ˙*stwo nilo la mo cho m ay ¨es te ˙ho twoswo n ywo* (?1468-Mong 52b) also tell: how will it be in the end?

˙*hotwo ta*, emotive < °*ho ta*. ABBR ˙*thwota*. ¶ ... MYENG- ˙PPOYK ˙*hotwo ta* (1482 Kum-sam 2:27b) it is clear (that ...). ... *pantok pantok ˙hotwo ta* (1482 Kum-sam 2:28b) it is quite clear that ... . *sa kwoynon ˙ptu.t un nul kul ˙solwok ˙stwo [CHIN] ˙hotwo ta* (1481 Twusi 21:15a) the older I get the more sociable I feel. SEE *a ni ˙hotwo ta*.

˙*hotwu ta* = ˙*hotwo ta*. SEE -*twu ta*.

... ˙*hoWon*, mod < ... *hopta*. ¶ *SIN ˙hoWon ˙ptu t ul ¨nay.n i ˙la* (1447 Sek 24:16b) showed a faithful mind.

˙*hoy*, n. 1. year(s). 2. (in cpds) sun. ¶ ˙*hoy s pich* sunlight.

˙*ho.ya-* (also ˙*ho ya-*), effective < °*ho-* 'do / be'. Also ˙*ho ye-*; ˙*ho ka-*, ˙*ho ke-*.

˙*ho ya*, inf < °*ho ta*. ¶ ˙*ecul khwo a tok ho ya* (1447 Sek 6:3b) disturbed and dazed, ... *SA-MWON kwa ˙ho ya coy cwo kyes kwu wo.l i ˙la* (1447 Sek 6:27b) we will pit our skills against those of the śramaṇa (ascetic). *pwuthye ˙lul NYEM ˙ho ya* (1447 Sek 9:24b) in thinking of Buddha. *cwu ku lak ¨sal lak ˙ho ya* (1447 Sek 24:29a, 1459 Wel 1:12b) [constantly] dying and living. *NAN-TTA y twu li ye ca pa nyehul kka ˙ho ya* (1459 Wel 7:13b) Nanda was afraid, thinking they might take him and put him in, and ... . ˙*PHEN- YEK ˙ho ya ˙wonan t i ko zuy ˙PALQ- POYK ˙hoy ˙n i* (1463 Pep se:21a) it is now almost 800 years since it was translated. ˙*PYEN ˙ho ya* (1462 ¹Nung 7:24a, 1550 ¹Yenghem 8b) changes / transforms (into). *cyem ku to lwok ˙acol ˙ho ya* (1485 Kwan 3a) gets more and more confused as the night darkens. *ce-huy ˙ho ya pulu key ho la* (?1517-Pak 1:6a) get them to sing. SEE ˙*kot* ~ , *(-) tos* ~ ; - *kwo cye* ~ ; ˙*HYANG* ~ , ˙*TANG* ~ , ˙*TWOY* ~ , ¨*wuy* / ˙*WUY* ~ ; *QIN* ~ (SEE in hata). VAR ˙*ho.ya*, ˙*ho ye*.

˙*ho.ya*, var = ˙*ho ya*. ¶ *KYWOW-KYWOW ˙ho.ya ¨pyel s kawon-toy s twu lyewun ˙to.l [˙]isyas ta* (1482 Kum-sam 2:24b) brightly shining it is a round moon in the midst of clouds. ¨*es.tyey la ˙wos kwa ˙pap [˙]kwa ˙ay [KWUNG- KHWON]* `ho.ya (1481 Twusi 16:19a) how come we are needy for clothes and food, and ... . `ke˙wulwu `ey s ¨SSYANG `i ˙kot `ho.ya (1482 Kum-sam 3:31a) they are like distinctive marks (lakṣana) in a mirror. ALSO: 1475 Nay 1:77b; 1481 Twusi 6:43a, 7:9b, 8:33b, 8:52a, 16:37b, 20: 29a, 22:7b, 22:34-5, 23:44a; 1482 Kum-sam 2: 10a, 2:57a, 2:65a, 3:27b, 5:35b, 5:40b; 1482 Nam 1:24a; ... .

`ho.ya ci˙la, inf < °ho˙ta + aux indic assert. wants to do. ¶*[CHANG-ZYEN]* `hi ¨i.l ol [˙NGUY-˙LWON] `ho.ya ci˙la [¨CHYENG] `ho.ya˙nol (1481 Twusi 22:35a) he asked to discuss the matter calmly, but ... .

`ho.ya ˙ci-ngi ˙˙ta, inf < °ho˙ta + aux polite + cop indic assert. ¶*TWONG-SAN kwu˙kyeng `ho.ya ˙ci-ngi ˙˙ta* (1459 Wel 2:27b) I want to see East Mountain.

`ho˙ya k, inf + pcl. ¶[¨HHOYNG] `hye [˙WUY] `ho˙ya k `etin [¨PWU-¨CYWU] ˙skuy na ʼy ˙kulGwe˙l ul [THWONG-˙TTALQ] ho˙la ko˙lo.m ay s kwo˙c i ti˙ti a˙ni `ho.ya ˙sye ko˙lom s [LWUW] `ey [˙SYANG-¨HHWOY] ¨hwo.l i la (1481 Twusi 25:56b) fortunately I managed to get my letter through to the wise governor and we will have a meeting at the river pavilion before the flowers in the river have faded.

`ho.ya˙l ye, effective prosp mod + postmod. ¶`e˙lwu `him ˙psuti a˙ni `ho.ya˙l ye (1475 Nay 2:1:16b) will she be unable to make the effort?

`ho˙yam (also `ho˙yem), effective subst < °ho˙ta. ho.ya/ₑm cok ho- be worth doing (1887 Scott 62, 1894 Gale 66). ¶¨KA `hi THYEN-¨HHA `ay [H]HOYNG `ho˙yam ˙cuk hon ¨HHWU[W] ˙ey [H]HOYNG `ho˙non ˙CYA [< ¨CYA] ʼy.n i ˙ʼla (1588 Mayng 13:13a) is one who went down to earth after it was possible to go there. *[PANG-˙CHWON]* ˙ma s mozo˙m ay ¨wuy˙kwoki [˙]ho.yam ˙cik ho˙n i (1481 Twusi 8:9a) in his heart of hearts is rather kind. SEE ha.yam.

`ho˙ya ¨mal˙la SEE -˙e ¨mal˙la

`ho.yan (also `ho˙yan), effective mod < °ho˙ta ʻdo/beʼ. CF `khan (< `ho-kan).

`ho.ya nʼ = `ho.ya non, inf + pcl. ¶*[PI-SYE]* ˙lol pwo˙ti ¨mwot `ho.ya nʼ mozo˙m ay il˙hun ˙tos `hote˙n i (1481 Twusi 7:29a) (when he was) unable to see the secret document it was as if he had lost his mind.

`ho.ya-ngi ˙˙ta, effective polite < °ho˙ta + cop indic assert. LCT 534a has two examples.

`ho˙yan ma˙lon, effective mod < °ho˙ta + bnd n. ¶*sol˙phywo.m i˙za ko˙cang `ho˙yan ma˙lon* ([1447→]1562 Sek 3:18a) I have investigated after my fashion but ... .

`ho.ya˙nol, lit concessive < °hota. ¶¨ne y na ʼy ¨ma˙l ol ¨ta tulul ˙tta `ho.ya˙nol ¨ne y MYENG-˙SSYEY ˙lol `hwo˙toy ... (1447 Sek 6:8b) I said "... will you heed my words?", whereupon you swore your oath ... . KUM-KWAN `ol tu¨zopta `ka ¨mwot `ho.ya˙nol (1447 Sek 23:23b) they tried to lift the chest of gold but were unable, whereupon ... . ˙icey `na non kanan hwo.m i˙la ˙PPYENG a˙ni ˙lwo˙la `ho.ya˙nol... (1482 Nam 1: 30b) he said "now I am poor but I am not ill", whereupon ... . ALSO: 1481 Twusi 22:34-5, ...

`ho.yan ˙ti = `ho.yan ˙t i (also `ho˙yan ˙ti), effective modifier < °ho˙ta + postmod + pcl. ¶SSYENG-˙˙PPWULQ `ho.yan ˙t i ... ˙KEP ˙i.n i (1459 Wel 17:22a) became a Buddha ... kalpas (eons) ago. MIN ˙i ¨SAN `ho˙yan ˙t i wo˙la˙n i (1588 ¹Non 4:62a; accent sic) it has been a long while that the people have strayed.

`ho.ya˙n ywo ma˙lon, effective mod < °ho˙ta + ? postmod + bnd n. ¶`me˙kwu.m ul ku-man ˙tye-man `ho.ya˙n ywo ma˙lon (1482 Kum-sam 3:52a) he was picky about his food, but ... .

NOTE: The ˙ywo is difficult to explain as ʻquestionʼ; the Chinese text has the assertive particle ¨YA followed by the Hankul reading note ¨wo malon and it is unclear why the wo (? = [G]wo) was chosen rather than ˙kwo if it was intended to be the question particle. In any event, the form would not be expected in front of ma˙lon; CF `ho˙yan ma˙lon.

`ho.yasi- (effective hon < °ho˙ta) = `ho˙sike- (honorific effective).

`ho˙ya ʼs(i)-, infinitive < °ho˙ta + abbreviation < is(i)- (auxiliary).

`ho.yasi˙la, effective hon subj attent < °ho˙ta (= `hosike˙la). ¶`hoy s ˙chiGwuy ˙yey ¨nyey s ˙kaci ˙lol [KYEN-¨SYWUW] `ho.yasi˙la (1481 Twusi 22:48b) secure the old branches against the year's cold weather.

`ho˙ya ʼsi˙la, inf < °ho˙ta + abbr < isi˙la (aux subj attent). ¶¨ne y ¨pangsim `ho˙ya ʼsi˙la (?1517- Pak 1:48a) rest easy, stop worrying.

`ho˙ya ʼsi˙m ye nʼ, inf < °ho˙ta + abbr < isi˙m ye nʼ (aux subst + cop inf + pcl). ¶¨man˙il [LYWUW ¨HHWOW] y ˙i sta˙h ay s ¨nimca˙h i towoy˙ti a˙ni `ho˙ya ʼsi˙m ye nʼ (1481 Twusi

15:45a) if Liú Hào had not become the owner of this land ... .

ho.ya῾si-ngi ῾῾ta, effective honorific < °ho῾ta + polite + copula indicative assertive. ¶ ῾῾na ῾lol si῾le ῾tulGey ῾ho.ya῾si-ngi ῾῾ta (1482 Nam 2:4b) [Buddha] made me able to lift it.

ho῾ya ῾si῾n i, inf < °ho῾ta + abbr < isi῾n i (aux modifier + postmodifier). ¶ [NGWANG SO] y [TWONG-῾KKWUN] a῾zwo῾m ol al῾Gwoy῾ti ῾῾mwot ῾ho῾ya ῾si῾n i (1481 Twusi 7:3b) we are unable to report that the king general has grasped the eastern counties.

ho῾ya ῾ ῾sin ma῾lon, inf < °ho῾ta + abbr < isin (aux modifier − accent is unexplained) + postmodifier. ¶ ho῾ma ῾῾wo῾lwo mas῾tikwo ῾cye ῾ho῾ya ῾ ῾sin ma῾lon (1463 Pep 2:232a) I was already wanting to entrust it rightly, but ... . NGWEN-῾KAK ῾ol na῾thwo῾l ye ῾ho.ya ῾ ῾sin ma῾lon (1465 Wen 1:1:2:74b) they were hoping to reveal the perfect enlightenment.

ho.yasi῾nol, effective lit concessive < °ho῾ta. ¶ ῾῾ne y ῾icey ῾two nowoy῾ya ῾nom muyWun ῾ptu῾t ul twul῾tta ῾ho.yasi῾nol (1459 Wel 2:64a) asked whether even now you still harbor hateful thoughts toward others, whereupon ... . ῾῾TYWOW-KHWA ῾i nilo῾sya῾toy PPWULQ ῾PEP ῾i ῾za na ῾y inge῾kuy [῾]two ῾῾cywokwo῾m achi is῾ta῾ ῾ho.yasi῾nol (1482 Nam 1:14a; LCT 668a has "῾῾cywokwom῾machi") Niǎo-kū ("Bird Nest") said "There is some of Buddha's law right here where I am, too", whereupon ... .

ho.yasi῾n ywo = ῾hosike῾n ywo, effective hon mod < °ho῾ta + postmod. ¶ mu῾sus ῾῾il lwo HHAN-SAN ῾on me῾li ῾῾nwo῾nywo῾m ol ῾culkye ῾icey ῾῾won ῾kil῾h ol ni῾ce ῾y῾la ῾ho.yasi῾n ywo (1482 Nam 1:28b) why did you, Hán-shān ("Cold Mountain"), enjoy yourself cavorting in far away places and then say now, "Why, I've forgotten the road I came!"?

ho῾ya ῾s.ke῾tun, inf < °ho῾ta + abbr < is.ke῾tun (aux provisional). ¶ ko῾lo῾m ay s kwo῾c i ti῾ti a῾ni ῾ho῾ya ῾s.ke῾tun [SYENG-TTWO] [῾]ay two῾la wo῾l i ῾lwo῾ta (1481 Twusi 8:23b) I will return to Chéngdū while the river flowers have not yet fallen.

ho.ya ῾s῾kwo, inf < °ho῾ta + abbr < is῾kwo. ¶ polom me῾kun phu῾lun ῾tay non [QYWEN-QYWEN] ῾ho.ya [῾CCYEK-῾CCYENG] ῾ho.ya ῾s῾kwo (1481 Twusi 7:2b) the green bamboo that has quieted the wind is graceful and calm, and ... .

~ cye (aux inf). ¶ [῾CYANG-῾CHO] s [SYWUY-῾῾LWOW] ῾hwo.m ay [῾TTAY-SSING] ῾ey [*SYE-῾῾CI] ῾ho.ya ῾s῾kwo cye [KAN-NAN] ῾ay ῾῾pe.t ul solang ῾honwo῾la (1481 Twusi 22:26a) as gradually age takes its toll, I want to lay aside the Greater Vehicle and give thought to my friends in need.

ho.ya ῾s.non, inf < °ho῾ta + abbr < is.non (aux proc mod). ¶ [῾῾CYWU-῾῾SYWUW] ῾ho.ya ῾s῾non [KA-SSIN] te῾pule mwu῾lwo.n i (1481 Twusi 7:37a) I inquired of the vassal in charge [of the fields].

ho.ya ῾s.no῾n i, inf < °ho῾ta + abbr < is.non + postmod. ¶ [PONG-TTIN] ῾i etuwe ῾῾yeti a῾ni ῾ho.ya ῾s.no῾n i ῾῾ne y ῾ka e῾nu ῾psk uy wol῾ta (1481 Twusi 8:37b) the dust storm is dark and unabating; when will you be back?

ho.ya ῾s.nwo῾la, infinitive < °ho῾ta + abbr < is.nwo῾la (aux proc modulated indic assert). ¶ mol῾kon swu῾l ol ῾culki῾kwo ῾etin ῾῾salo῾m ol [῾PPI] ῾ho.ya ῾s.nwo῾la nilo῾nwos.ta [→ nilo῾nwos.ta] (1481 Twusi 15:40b) he says that he enjoys clear wine and avoids wise men.

ho῾ya ῾s῾nwo-ngi ῾῾ta, inf < °ho῾ta + abbr < is῾nwo-ngi ῾῾ta (aux proc modulated polite + cop indic assert). ¶ ho῾ma ῾TUK ῾ho῾ya ῾s῾nwo-ngi ῾῾ta (1482 Nam 1:53b) I have already achieved it.

ho.yas῾ta, effective emotive indic assertive < °ho῾ta. ¶ ῾chon kwos ῾῾pwuli ῾Gwa sel῾phoyn ῾kaci [PAN] ῾man῾chi wu῾mul i῾kuyti ῾῾mwot ῾ho.yas῾ta (1481 Twusi 8:42a) the cold flower buds and the flimsy branches cannot half get the better of the well.

ho.ya ῾s.ta῾la, abbr < ῾ho῾ya (inf) + abbr < is.ta῾la (aux retr indic assert). ¶ wuli ... ZYE-LOY skey mwutcowo.m ul pwo῾ti ῾῾mwot ho῾m ye tut.ti mwot ῾ho.ya ῾s.tala (1463 Pep 5:95b — the missing accent dots not restored) we were unable to see or hear them pose their questions to the tathāgata.

ho῾ya ῾s.ta῾n i, inf < °ho῾ta + abbr < is.ta῾n i (aux retr mod + postmodifier). ¶ ῾῾na y ῾῾a῾loy ka῾ti a῾ni ῾ho῾ya ῾s.ta῾ni (?1517- Pak 1:67b) I have never been able to go.

ho῾ya ῾s῾ten, inf < °ho῾ta + abbr < is῾ten (aux retr modifier).

ho῾ya ῾s.te῾n i, inf < °ho῾ta + abbr < is.te῾n i (aux retr mod + postmodifier). ¶ ῾hat wo῾s ay ῾kwos ta῾won ῾phu.l ul [῾SYWUW] ῾ho῾ya ῾s.te῾n *i* (1481 Twusi 8:6b) on the single-layer garment was embroidered a flowery bush.

`ho.yas¨ti`, effective emotive suspective < °*ho¨ta*. ¶*kil¨h ey [LIM] `ho.yas.ti ¨mwot ho¨l i ¨l s oy* (1481 Twusi 8:2b) since he did not dare look to the way, ...

`ho.ya 's¨twoswo¨n i`, inf < °*ho¨ta* + abbr < *is¨twoswo¨n i* (aux emotive-emotive mod + postmod). ¶*[`MAK-¨PWU] `ey ¨tule [CCOY-`CILQ] `ul phye¨ti ¨mwot `ho.ya 's¨twoswo¨n i* (1481 Twusi 8:4b) having entered government service I am unable to spread my talents.

`ho¨ya 's¨two¨ta`, infinitive < °*ho¨ta* + abbr < *is.two¨ta* (auxiliary emotive indicative assertive). ¶*kama¨woti [SYEY] s nyek¨h oy pi¨chwuy¨ye 'ys.non ¨toy ¨nolkay mol `Gwoynwo¨la kwo¨ki capnon ¨twol.h ay kotok `ho¨ya 's.two¨ta* (1481 Twusi 7:5a) the cormorants crowd the fishing beams seeking to dry their wings in the western light.

`ho¨ya ¨sye`, inf < °*ho¨ta* + pcl. ¶*ko¨lo.m ay s kwo¨c i ti¨ti a¨ni `ho.ya ¨sye* (1481 Twusi 25:56b) before the flowers in the river have faded.

`ho.ya '¨sywo-`, abbreviation < `ho.ya i¨sywo-`.

`ho.ya '¨sywo¨toy` (accessive). ¶*[CCIN SAN] s nacwo¨h ol an¨ca sye [SYANG-TWOY] `ho.ya 'sywo¨toy* (1481 Twusi 15:10b) seated I face the evening of the mountains of Qín [or Mount Qín?], and ... .

`ho¨ya¨ta`, effective indic assert < °*ho¨ta*. ¶*cim si¨li ¨ta `ho¨ya¨ta* (?1517- ¹No 1:46a) = *cim sis.ki* [= *sit.ki*] *ho.yeta* (1795 ¹No-cwung [P] 1:41b) = *cim ta moyya sileta* (id. [K] 1:42a) the loading (of the horses) is all done.

`ho.ya¨ton`, provisional < °*ho¨ta*. ¶*a¨z i [`KHWEN] `ho.ya¨ton [HYWENG] `i ka¨pha selu me¨ku.m ye n'* (1481 Twusi 8:42b) if we drink urging each other on, first you and then I, ... . `na y ne ¨lul KUM ¨cwu¨l ywo `ho.ya¨ton* (1482 Nam 1:44-5) if I consider giving you money ... . *es.tyey ho.yaton pwuthye towoyno.n i '-ngi s kwo* (1569 Chiltay 21a) how does one become a Buddha?

`ho¨ya¨tun` = `ho.ya¨ton`. ¶*SYWU-¨HWA ¨lul KWU `ho¨ya¨tun* (1588 Mayng 13:19b; sic, ¨*lul* = ¨*lol*) if one seeks water and fire ... . *pap mek.en t i cyekun tes ho.yatun* (1656 Nay-cwung 3:37, quoted from LCT) when it has been a little while since eating.

`ho.ya ¨two`, inf + pcl (SEE **-e to** < *-e ¨two*). ¶*¨a¨mwo 'yGe¨na ¨wa ... ¨twola `ho.ya ¨two* (1459 Wel 1:13a) whoever might come and ask you to give him ... . ALSO: 1459 Wel 21:20a, 1481 Twusi 24:59b, ...

`ho.ya 'y¨Gwo`, inf + cop ger. ¶*a¨zo.m ol [`WUY] `ho.ya 'y¨Gwo* ... (1481 Twusi 8:33a) it is for our relatives and ... .

`ho¨ya 'ys.ke¨nul`, abbr < `ho¨ya is.ke¨nul`. ¶*CYENG-CWONG `i mos¨ti ¨mwot ho¨ya 'ys.ke¨nul* (1462 ¹Nung 8:57a) the original sect has by no means come to an end, but ... .

`ho¨ya 'ys¨kesi¨nol`, abbr < `ho¨ya is¨kesi¨nol`. ¶*CCWA ¨ay ¨ni¨ti a¨ni `ho¨ya 'ys¨kesi¨nol* (1463 Pep 1:106b) is unable to go to a seat, but ... .

`ho¨ya 'ys.ke¨tun`, abbr < `ho.ya is.ke¨tun`. ¶*TTAY-PPWO-¨SALQ `Gwa CYE SYENG-MWUN `CYWUNG `i `NGWUY-¨ZYWOW `ho¨ya 'ys.ke¨tun* (1459 Wel 17:35a) being surrounded by great bodhisattvas and crowds of śrāvakas.

`ho¨ya 'ys.non`, abbr < `ho¨ya 'ys.non`. ¶*[HE-KHWONG] ¨ay kotok `ho¨ya 'ys.non [SYENG-HHA] s ¨pi.ch i pu¨ze ¨ti¨ye 'ys.ke¨nol* (1481 Twusi 15:44b) the lights of the Milky Way that fill empty space are broken, yet ... .

`ho¨ya 'ys¨nwon`, abbr < `ho¨ya is¨nwon`. ¶*¨il mo¨chon nwu¨pi ¨cywung oy TWOY `ho¨ya 'ys¨nwon TI-QUM `i wo¨cik `i stolo¨m i¨la* (1482 Nam 1:58a) knowing the chant with respect to the quilt-robed priest who has finished his work is only just this.

`ho.ya 'ys¨ta`, abbr < `ho¨ya is¨ta`. ¶*twos¨k i kutoy s [`NGWA-SSANG] ¨ay [¨]tep[¨]ti a¨ni `ho.ya 'ys¨ta* (1481 Twusi 8:67b) the reed mat does not feel warm enough for you to use as a bed.

`ho¨ya 'ys.ta¨n i`, abbr < `ho¨ya is.ta¨n i`. ¶*¨cams.kan ¨two ¨HYEN `hi nilo¨ti a¨ni ho¨ya 'ys.ta¨n i* (1465 Wen 1:1:1:44b) it was not even for a moment clearly stated.

`ho.ya 'ys¨ta¨s-ongi ¨¨ta`, abbr < `ho¨ya is¨ta¨s-ongi ¨¨ta`. ¶*TI-`NGWEN ¨un son¨coy i¨sye il¨thi a¨ni `ho.ya 'ys¨ta¨s-ongi ¨¨ta* (1463 Pep 4:41a) we still have the will for wisdom and have not lost it.

`ho¨ya 'ys.te¨n i`, abbr < `ho¨ya is.te¨n i`. ¶*`i ¨mwoy¨h i ¨yelli¨la `ho¨ya 'ys.te¨n i* (1447 Sek 24:6b) this mountain will open up.

`ho.ya 'ys¨tesi¨n i`, abbr < `ho¨ya is¨te¨si¨n i`. ¶*CYE ¨TTAY SAM-¨MOY ¨lol ¨TUK `ho.ya 'ys¨tesi¨n*

i (1459 Wel 18:68b) had achieved the various great meditations (samādhi).
`ho´ya ´ys`twoswo·n i, abbreviation < `ho´ya is.twoswo·n i. ¶wo·na ka·na ¨ta ¨say ci·p i *[KYEM]* `ho.ya ´ys`twoswo·n i (1481 Twusi 7:16b) both coming and going, I take double advantage of the thatch hut.
`ho´ya ´ys.two·ta, abbr < `ho´ya is.two·ta. ¶ku·chun ping.ay ·non [`PPOYK-YEM] `ol *[TANG]* `ho´ya ´ys.two·ta (1481 Twusi 7:11a) the sheer cliff is assigned to White Salt Mountain.
`ho.ya·za, inf + pcl. ¶*CCO-PI* s ¨hoyng·tye·k ul `ho.ya·za ho·l i ´l ·ss oy *SA-MI* ´·la ho·n i ´·la (1447 Sek 6:2b) for they must perform deeds of charity therefore they are called śrāmaṇera (religious novice). ne-huy ·tol·h i *SOYNG-¨SO* pe·swul ¨i·l ol ·him ·pse *KKWUW* `ho.ya·za ho·l i ´·la (1459 Wel 10:14b) you people must endeavor to pursue the casting off of birth and death. `TWOY-`TAP `ho.ya·za ho·l i ´·la (1462 ¹Nung 1:44a) will have to reply. Also `ho´ya za (1586 Sohak 4:9b).
`ho´ye, var = `ho´ya; SEE ~ `la, ~ ·sye, ~ ·two. ABBR `hye. The 15th-century examples are all before ´ys-; see `ho´ye ´ys.te·n i, `ho´ye ´ys`tesi·n i. But the contracted form `hye is attested in a few phrases. SEE **hye**.
`ho´ye ´·la, var inf < °ho·ta + abbr < ´i·la (cop indic assert). ¶*[TTYWEN]* hol twong mal twong ho.ye ´la (1730 Chengkwu 104; cited from LCT) it is barely conveyed (?). phuyl stwong mal stwong ho.ye ´la (1763 Haytong 61) it is about to bloom.
`ho.ye·l ye, effective prosp mod < °ho·ta + postmod. ¶ku *[KWONG]* ·on *[SO-`NGUY]* `ho.ye·l ye (1464 Kumkang hwu-se 15; cited from LCT 561a with accent added [my copy has no hwu-se]) is that achievement conceivable?
`ho´yem = `ho´yam, effective subst < °ho·ta; CF ¨hom, ¨hwom.
~ [´]cuk[·cik ¨ho·ta is worth doing. ¶mu·su ¨i·l i cwuk·two·lwok `ho´yem [´]cuk ho·n i `Gwo (1518 Sohak-cho 10:24b) what matter is worth pursuing unto death? ¨KA `hi ·YWOK `ho.yem cuk ¨hwom ·ul nil `Gwon *SYEN* i `Gwo (1588 Mayng 14:16a) it is a goodness that is said to be desirable. ¨KA `hi ·pse *[NGJEN]* `ho.yem ·cik ´·ti a·ni ¨hwo·toy (1588 Mayng 14:21b) it is hardly worth saying (but ...).
ho.yen ti (?1660- Kyeychwuk 52) = `ho.yan·t i

`ho´ye ´s.no·n i, var inf + abbr < is[i].non (v proc modifier) + postmod. ¶epe·i ·lul pwo·ti ¨mwot `ho´ye ´s.no·n i inno·n ya [< is.no·n ya] ho·n i (1586 Sohak 6:7b) = epe·zi ·lol a·ni ·ka ¨pwoy·n i is.nu·n ya `ho´ya (1518 Sohak-cho 9:8a) asked if any of them had been unable to see their parents.
`ho´ye ·sye, var inf + particle (= **hay se**). ¶hon nye·k uy ta·sos ·sik pwun `ho´ye ·sye ·pswo·cye (?1517- Pak 1:54b) let's shoot after dividing [the arrows] into five for each side.
~ ·non. ¶ ·kul nilkta ·ka mos·ti ¨mwot `ho´ye ·sye ·non pi·lwok spolon ¨i·l i i·sye two (1518 Sohak-cho 8:38-9) though sometimes he cannot stop in the midst of reading so it is rapid.
`ho´ye·ta, effective indic assertive < °ho·ta. ¶ta imuy cyangman ho.ye *TYENG-TA WAN-PI* cim sis.ki [= sit.ki] ho.yeta (1795 ¹No-cwung [P] 1:41b) the loading (of the horses) is all done. SEE `ho´ya·ta.
`ho´ye ·two, var inf + pcl. ¶kotok `ho´ye ·two ¨nemsti·ti a·ni `ho·no.n i (1586 Sohak 2:30b) though full it does not overflow.
`ho´ye ´y.n i ´·la abbr < `ho´ye i.n i ´·la. ¶hoyng `ho´ywo·m ay ¨li khwa·tya `ho´ye ´y.n i ´·la (1518 Sohak-cho 8:25a) it is a matter of desiring to benefit from putting into practice [what one has learned].
`ho´ye ´ys.te·n i, abbr < `ho´ye ´ys.te·n i. ¶spol·li *MWON* ·ul ¨yel·la `ho´ye ´ys.te·n i (1459 Wel 10:25a) wanted to open the door quickly.
`ho´ye ´ys`tesi·n i, abbr < `ho´ye ´ys`tesi·n i. ¶*[SIN-SIM]* i *[PWULQ-TWONG]* ho.ye ´ys.tesi.n i (1463 Pep 1:54b) body and spirit are immobile. This is a reading aid to the Chinese text, the translation of which has `ho´ya ´ys`tesi·n i.
¨hoyGi·ta = ¨hoy·ta, vc < °ho·ta. Only forms attested: ¨hoy·Gye infinitive, ¨hoyGywom modulated subst. The entry " ¨hoyGywo·ta" in LCT is the result of a mistaken analysis. ¶ ¨salom ¨ma·ta ¨hoy·Gye ¨swu·Wuy ni·kye (1451 Hwun-en 3b) letting everyone learn it easily. ¨hay *MA* ·oy ·HHWOYK ¨hoyGywo·m ol ni·pu.l i ´l ·ss oy (1462 ¹Nung 6:87b) since they much suffer from the vexations of devils, ...
¨hoyGwo·ta = ¨hoy·ta, vc < °ho·ta. ¶ ¨es.tyey mozo·m ol *HHANG* ¨hoy·Gwa mozo·m i ¨KAY-·THWALQ ·ol ·TUK ho·l i ´-ngi s ·kwo (1482

Kum-sam 2:4ab) how is one to surrender one's mind and obtain the mind's emancipation?

ˮhoyl(q), prospective mod < ˮhoyˑta. ¶ ˮes.tyey HHANG-ˑPPWOK ˮhoyˑl i '-ngi s ˑkwo (1464 Kumkang 11a) how shall I subdue it [my mind]?

ˑhoyn, modifier < ˑhoyˑta, adj. white. ¶ ˑhoyn ˑptwuy lwo niˑywuˑn i (1481 Twusi 7:1a) it was shaded by white cogon-grass thatching.

ˑhoynon, processive mod < ˑhoyˑta. ¶ eˑtuwuˑlak twolwo ˑhoynoˑn i (1481 Twusi 7:14b) it is dark and then again it is [? gets] light again.

ˮhoysin, honorific modifier < ˮhoyˑta.
ˮhoysiˑn i '-ngi ''ta. ¶ ·· LYWONG-NGWANG ˑol HHANG-ˑPPWOK ˮhoysiˑn i '-ngi ''ta (1447 Sek 24:38a) made the dragon kings ··· surrender.

ˑhoyˑta, adj. is white; is light, bright. Also (ˑhoynon) vi 'gets white / light'?

ˮhoyˑta, vc < °hoˑta; inf ˮhoyˑye. has (makes, lets) one do. SYN ˮhoyGwoˑta, ˮhoyGiˑta.

NOTE: The uncontracted form hoˑiˑta was first attested 1518.

ˮhoy-tiˑGwuy. makes / lets one do but. ¶ MA ˑlol HHANG-ˑPPWOK ˮhoy-tiˑGwuy ... (1482 Nam 2:5a) he got the devil to surrender but ... .

ˮhoyˑye, inf < ˮhoyˑta. ¶ ˮce y ˑssukeˑna ˑnom ˑhoyˑye ˑssukeˑna (1447 Sek 9:41a = 1459 Wel 9:39a) whether writing it oneself or getting others to write it. Also (··· ˑolwo ˮhoyye): Twusi 7:16b, 20:29a.

ˑho.ywo- (< *ˑho.y[a]-wo-) = ˑhwo-, ˮhwo-, modulated stem of °hoˑta.

ˑho.ywolq (< *ˑho.y[a]-ˑwo-lq) = ˑhwolq, modulated prosp mod < °hoˑta. ¶ (summational epitheme) ˑQILQ-SOYNG ˑay s CHAM-ˮHHAK ˑho.ywol ˮiˑl i moˑcho.l i ''la (1482 Kum-sam 2:1b) said that the act of pursuing (Buddhist) learning for a lifetime would come to an end.

[ˑ]ho.ywoˑla (< *ˑho.y[a]-ˑwo-ˑla) = ˑhwoˑla, ˮhwo[ˑ]la, modulated indic assert < °hoˑta. ¶ ˑywo cwoˑzom puˑthe ˮwo.m ay hon ˑcwul s ˑkul ˑtwo patˑti ˮmwot ho.ywoˑla (1481 Twusi 21:25b) come the last little while I haven't had a line (of news) from him.

ˑhoˑywom = ˮhwom, modulated subst < °hoˑta. ¶ [SYE KWONG] ˑoy ˑwon kaˑci s ˮiˑl ol siˑlum aˑni ˑho.ywoˑm ol ˑna y ˮanwoˑn i (1481 Twusi 8:24b) I know that Lord Xú does not brood over all sorts of matters.

ˑhoyywoˑm, modulated subst < ˑhoyˑta (white). ¶ ˑile ˑn ˑt olwo keˑmu.m ye ˑhoyywoˑm ol nonˑhwo.n i 'ˑla (1481 Twusi 7:27a) hence distinguished [things] being black and being white. swowoˑm iˑlaˑwa hoyywoˑm ol koˑcang muyˑnwola (1481 Twusi 23:23a) I hate it that the willow branches are whiter than cotton. CF ˮhoyGywom < ˮhoyGiˑta.

ˮhoyywu-, vc (ˮhoy-) + modulator. ˮhoyywuˑla (1481 Twusi 16:66a) has him do it.

ˑhozop-, ˑhozo(W)-, humble < °hoˑta.
ˑhoˑzopkeˑna (1447 Sek 13:53a).
[ˑ]hozopˑkwo (1447 Sek 6:1b).
ˑhoˑzoptenˑt oy n' (1463 Pep 2:226a).
ˑhoˑzopnoˑn iˑGwa (1447 Sek 23:4a).
ˑhozopnon ˑkwo (1481 Twusi 10:9b).
ˑhoˑzoWaˑza (1459 Wel 9:52a).
ˑhoˑzoWwoˑl i (1459 Wel 23:65a).
ˑhozoˑwo.l i ''la (1482 Kum-sam 3:12a).
ˑhoˑzoWoˑm ye n' (1447 Sek 9:24b).

HUY The Hankul spelling and the Romanization distinguish **huy** from **hi** but they are both pronounced the same (as **hi**). If you cannot locate the word you seek under **huy**, look under **hi**.

-**huy**, suffix. Forms pronoun plural. SEE **ne-huy**, **ce-huy**. CF **ney**, **tul**.

-**huy** < HUY (bnd n 'princess'), suffix. Forms names or extended names for girls.

hwi-, bnd adverb. round and round, enveloping; thoroughly, completely; recklessly; briskly. ¶ ~ **cēs.ta** stirs (up); disturbs; waves (one's arms). ~ **ciluta** soils (one's clothes). ~ **cwumuluta** fumbles with. ~ **kam.ta** winds round and round. ~ **malta** rolls up, coils. ~ **mōlta** urges / drives on. ~ **nallita** (a flag) flaps in the breeze; distinguishes (one's name). ~ **nul.e cita** hangs loose, dangles, droops. ~ **salphita** watches all around. ~ **tallita** rushes around; rushes away. ~ **teph.ta** overspreads. ~ **tōlta** goes around. ~ **tollita** puts it around, revolves it. ~ **twuluta** brandishes; astonishes; takes command of (the situation). ~ **twungkuleh.ta** (HEAVY ↔ **hoy-tongkul^{e}ah.ta**) (eyes) are opened wide, is wide-eyed. **hwipssata** [< **hwi** + **pssata**] surrounds it; protects it; shelters it. **hwipssulta** [< **hwi** + **pssulta**] sweeps over, overwhelms. [CF **hwita** it bends; **hoy** round.]

ˑhwo-, ˮhwo- < *ˑho-ˑwo-, modulated stem of °hoˑta. VAR ˑho.ywo- < ˑho.y[a]-wo-.

`hwol(q)`, `¨hwol(q)`, modulated prosp mod < `°ho˙ta`.

1. (epitheme extruded from subject). Example?
2. (epitheme extruded from object). ¶ *ne-huy `uy elwu `NGWAN-`HWOW `hwolkke˙si* (= *`hwolq kes `i*) (1463 Pep 2:66-7) the things you folks are rather fond of. *QA-NYWUW-LWUW-TTA ʾy˙la `hwolq ¨salo˙m ol* (1447 Sek 24:13a) a person called Aniruddha.
3. (summational epitheme). ¶ *[12800] KWONG-`TUK ˙iˑza `NGUY-`LWON `hwolq ˙cwul ¨ep˙su.l i ʾʾla* (1447 Sek 19:10b) there is just no way to argue with 12,800 achievements of virtue. *wo˙lay ˙PPYENG `hwolq YWEN ˙ul ye˙huyˑya ˙ysˑkasiˑn i ¨es.tyey wo˙nol mun˙tuk mozom al˙phwo˙m i ˙nakeˑn ywo* (1462 ¹Nung 5:72b) for a long time he has kept the causes for falling ill away; why then is my heart suddenly seized with pain today? *CIN-˙SSILQ s PPWO-`SALQ ˑoy ˙TTYWU `hwol ˙kwo.t i aˑni ʾ.n i ʾʾla* (1482 Kum-sam 3:34b) it is not a place where a real bodhisattva would dwell. ˑe˙mi lʾ solang ˙hwo˙toy ˑe˙m[i] uy solang hwolq SSI-˙CYELQ (1462 ¹Nung 5:85b) when [the child] loves the mother and the mother loves [the child].

`hwo˙la`, `¨hwo[˙]la` < *`ho-˙wo-˙la`.

1. modulated indic assertive. ¶ *[˙MWU-CHWUN] ˙kwa ˙lwo taˑmos [KKI-˙YAK] ˙hwo.la* (1481 Twusi 7:14a) it will be limited just to late autumn. *˙na y il˙cuk ¨aˑti ¨mwot ¨hwola* (?1517⁻ Pak 1:37b) I didn't know earlier [of your illness] … . *ho˙ma MWU-˙HHAK ˑol ˙TUK ˙hwo˙la ˙hoke˙tun* (1447 Sek 24:3a) saying "I have already acquired aśaikṣa (the stage of being beyond learning)". VAR [ʾ]ho.ywo˙la.
2. = `hwo.l ye`. ¶ *hoˑma `KWUW-`KYENG `MYELQ-`TTWO ˙lol ˙TUK `hwo˙la `hoˑtaswoˑn i wo˙nol za aˑlwoˑn i ˙TI-`HHYWEY ¨ep.suˑn i kot ʾʾtas-ongi ʾʾta* (1463 Pep 4:36a) having earlier sought to acquire the ultimate nirvāṇa, that I just today found out is like having lacked wisdom.

`hwoˑl i`, modulated prosp mod + postmodifier. ¶ (epitheme extruded from object) `SYA-˙NGWUY `KWUYK ˑey hon `TTAY-SSIN SYWU-˙TTALQ ˙iˑla `hwoˑl i is.noˑn i (1447 Sek 6:14-5) there is a minister in the state of Śrāvastī who is named Sudatta.

`hwo.l i ʾʾla`, modulated prosp mod + postmod + cop indic assert. ¶ *nwuyGus.pun mozoˑm ol aˑni `hwo.l i ʾʾla `hoteˑn i* (1447 Sek 6:8-9) you said that you would not have a remorseful heart. `CYWUNG-SOYNG ˑoˑlwo `QILQ-˙CHYEY ˙SYEY-KAN ˑay s ˙SIN ˙thi elyeˑWun ˑPEP ˑul ¨ta tutcoˑWa ¨alˑGey `hwo.l i ʾʾla `hoˑsya (1447 Sek 13:27a) he says "I will get all living beings to understand the Law that is so difficult for the world at large to believe". `wuli ˑtolˑh i ileˑthus [= ileh-tus] hon `MANG-`LYANG ˑay s ˙SSYWUW-˙KUY ˑza `psuˑti aˑni `hwo.l i ʾʾla (1447 Sek 19:30b) we will not use this sort of prophecies of a future Buddhahood in false quantities. [¨CCWOY] ˑlol [¨CHYENG] hon ˑt ay [˙CYANG-˙CHO] s ¨hay [˙COYK-˙PELQ] `hwo.l i ʾʾla ˙thesiˑn i ʾ[˙]la (1481 Twusi 24:13a) he said, "Invite sin and you will pick up much future punishment".

`hwoˑl i ʾ-ngi ʾʾta`, modulated prosp mod + postmodifier + cop polite + cop indic assert. ¶ *niluˑsyan ¨yang ˑoˑlwo `hwoˑl i ʾ-ngi ʾʾta* (1447 Sek 6:24b) I will do as you say, sir. `NGWEN `honwon ˑiˑl ol ¨ta ¨ilˑGuy `hwoˑl i ʾ-ngi ʾʾta (1447 Sek 9:40b) I will make your every wish be accomplished.

`hwol(q) ˑt iGeˑn i ˑGwa`, modulated prosp mod + postmod + cop effective mod + postmod + pcl. ¶ *naˑla.h ay ˑsye mwoˑlwomay saˑhwo.m ol [HHOYNG] `hwol ˑt iGeˑn i ˑGwa ¨saloˑm on [KWA-YEN] ˑul kuˑchiˑsikwaˑtye solang `honwosˑta* (1481 Twusi 20:4b) while the nation must conduct warfare, the people would love to put an end to spears and lances.

`hwolq ˑt iGeˑnol`, modulated prosp mod + postmod + copula literary concessive. ¶ `khun [SSIN-¨HHA] non [˙MYWOW] ciˑze [HYENG-˙SIK] `hwol t iGeˑnol [¨HHWUW] ˑey s [˙CYEY-KKUY] y ¨es.tyey ˑtumulˑm ye keˑchu.n ywo (1481 Twusi 22:44b) the mighty courtier builds a shrine and offers a sacrificial meal, yet how come the later rituals are seldom and sparse?

`hwolq ˑt iGen ˑtyeng`, modulated prosp mod + postmod + cop effective mod + postmod. ¶ `¨CCWA ˑlol ˑPEP ˑuˑlwo `hwolq ˑt iGen ˑtyeng (?1468⁻ Mong 35a) one is to sit in meditation according to the Law, and yet … .

`hwolq ˑt iGeˑta`, modulated prospective modifier + postmod + cop effective indicative assertive. ¶ *wolhoˑm ye woyˑywoˑm ol hon tiˑGwuy `KYWO-˙CYENG (`hwolttiGeta =) `hwolq ˑt iGeˑta* (1463 Pep 1:10b) it is a matter of

checking what is right and wrong at the same time.
`hwolq ˙t i˙la`, modulated prosp mod + postmod + cop indic assert. ¶ `˙stwo e˙lwu ¨hyey˙ti ¨mwot ˙hwol tt i˙la` (1463 Pep 3:62b) they cannot reckon much, either. `˙CCO-ZYEN ˙hi QAN-˙LAK ˙HHOYNG-˙PEP ˙i ko˙ca SAM-˙TTWOK ˙TWO-˙MAN ˙uy NUNG ˙hi pwo˙cha˙ti ¨mwot ˙hwol ˙tt i˙la` (1463 Pep 7:182a) naturally the happy practice of the Law is enough so that there can be no torment from the jealousy and pride of the Three Poisons.
`hwolq ˙t ila` two (pcl). ¶ `cokyay s ¨KWA y ¨i˙ti ¨mwot ˙hwolq ˙t ila ˙two ˙stwo ˙SSIP-PANG ˙ay pwuthye s ˙SSYWUW-˙KUY ˙lol nipu˙si˙m ye` (1462 ¹Nung 7:43a) even if no results happen for himself, he bears to all places Buddha's prophecies (of future Buddhahood).
`hwolq ˙t i˙m ye n'`, modulated prosp mod + postmodifier + cop substantive + cop inf + pcl. ¶ `˙MWULQ ul ˙KYWOW-˙HWA hwolq ˙t i˙m ye n'` (?1468- Mong 65a) if brutes are to be enlightened.
`hwolq ˙t i˙n i`, modulated prosp mod + postmod + cop mod + postmod. ¶ `mwo˙lwo may ¨il moco il ˙Gwuzo ˙Wwo˙m ol mwoncye ˙hwolq ˙t i˙n i` (1459 Wel se:17a) I must first of all complete the task. `¨mwo˙toy ˙him ˙pswu˙m ol ˙khi SSI-˙KUP ˙hi a˙ni ˙hwolq ˙t i˙n i` (?1468- Mong 23a) must not greatly rush the use of one's strength. `ne˙pi ˙tye lol HYWUW ho˙m ye ˙HELQ ˙ho.ya ˙QILQ-˙NYEM ˙i ˙MEN-NYEN ˙i ˙Gey ˙hwol t i˙n i` (1482 Kum-sam 5:40b) it is so arranged that a moment's thought gives ten thousand years, letting them all relax at ease.
`hwolq ˙t i.n i ˙'la`, modulated prosp mod + postmod + cop mod + postmod + cop indic assertive. ¶ `pol˙kon TUNG ˙i towoy ˙Gwo SOYNG- ¨SO ˙mul s ˙kyel s ka˙won-˙toy ki˙li ˙poy towoy ˙ywo.l i ˙'la ˙hwolq ˙t i.n i ˙'la` (1459 Wel 9:22b) it is said that a bright light will come into being, and in the midst of the waves of life and death a lasting boat will appear. `poy˙hwo˙l i sol˙phye ¨CO-˙SYEY ˙hi ˙hwol ˙tt i.n i ˙'la` (1463/4 Yeng se:3a) the learner is to investigate in detail. `ku ¨CYENG ˙ul ¨SYWUN ˙hi ˙SYWU ¨hwol ˙tt i.n i ˙'la` (1588 Mayng 13:1b) one is to accept its correctness.
`hwolq ˙t in ˙t ay n'`, modulated prosp mod + postmod + cop mod + postmod + pcl + pcl.

¶ `¨TTWOW lol KKWUW ˙khwo cye ˙hwolq ˙t in ˙t ay n' ˙i po˙li˙kwo e˙tuy pu˙thu.l i ˙Gwo` (1459 Wel se:15a) if one desires to seek the Way, where will one turn for support, rejecting [all] this? `˙hota ˙ka CHAM-˙KWUW ey KAN-˙SSYEP ˙hwolq ˙t in ˙t ay n' ˙kwot KWONG-PWU ˙lul nil ˙Gwolq ˙t i.n i ˙'la` (?1468- Mong 33a) if there should arise any interference with the pilgrimage [to study the principles of dhyāna] one is to say the meditations [that have been learned]. `˙stwo nu˙lwum ˙kwa sa˙wona Wwom ˙kwa ˙lol ˙QILQ-˙TTYENG ˙hwolq ˙t in ˙t ay n' ˙nwu˙n un alp ˙kwa kyet ˙kwa ˙lol pwo˙kwo ¨twuy˙h ul ¨mwot pwo˙m ye` (1447 Sek 19:10a) given that ... and also (being) better and (being) worse are set, the eyes can see ahead and to the side but they cannot see what is behind, and ... . `KWONG-˙CCYANG paci y ˙i˙l ol i˙tay ˙khwo ˙cye ˙hwol t i.n ˙t ay n'` (1465 Wen se:80b; the "˙y" is a reminder of the ellipted nominative ˙i) if the artisan wants to do his work well.
`hwolq ˙t oy`, modulated prosp mod + postmod + particle. ¶ `pwu ¨thye y ˙i ˙MYWOW-˙PEP-HHWA KYENG ˙u˙lwo ˙pwu˙cywok ˙hwol ˙tt oy is˙key ˙khwo ˙cye ˙y.n i ˙'la` (1463 Pep 4:134b) Buddha wanted to have people keep relying on this Lotus sūtra.
`hwol(q) ˙tyen = ˙hwolq ˙t ye n'`, modulated prosp mod + postmod + postmod [question] + pcl. ¶ `˙CAK-˙PEP hwol ˙tyen ¨ne y ˙i.l i koca za ho˙l i ˙'.n i` (1496 ¹Yuk "se:12" = ¹yak-se:4b; there are 8 pages of se, 16 of ¹yak-se) if you would make laws you must do it with affairs all in hand.
`hwolq ˙tyeyn`, modulated prospective modifier + postmod. ¶ `QUM-˙SALQ ˙CYENG-˙SYENG ˙ul pwuy ˙Gwu˙l ye ˙hwolq ˙tyeyn` (1462 ¹Nung 8:7a) when you seek to lay bare the true nature of adultery and murder ... . `¨mwut ˙cowo ˙toy SYWUW-HHOYNG ˙hwo.l ye ˙hwol ˙ttyeyn ¨es.tyey HHANG-˙PPWOK ¨hoy˙l i ˙'-ngi s ˙kwo ho˙n i ˙'la` (1464 Kumkang 11a) he inquired, "If I seek to pursue the discipline, how shall I subdue it [my mind]?"
`˙hwo.l ye`, `¨hwo˙l ye`, modulated prosp mod + postmod. ¶ `pwuthye s ˙kuy patco Wa mu˙sum ˙hwo.l ye ˙ho˙sino˙n i` (1459 Wel 1:10b) what do you want to present to Buddha? `˙i ˙kot ho˙m ye n' ˙ZI-SSING ˙un mu˙sus he ¨mul ˙lwo tas˙ti a˙ni ˙hwo.l ye khe[˙]n ywo` (1463/4 Yeng 2:70a;

is *he῭mul* a carving mistake for *he῭mul*?) by what error are you reluctant to study the Two Vehicles? *῭ne y ῭mye῭ch ul ῭hwo῭l ye ῭honon῭ta* (?1517- Pak 1:31b) how many do you want? *῭hwolye῭ta* = *῭hwo.l [i] 'ye῭ta*, modulated prosp mod + (ellipted postmod +) cop effective indicative assertive. will likely do. ¶ *῭"il "ep῭sun "TTWOW-"LI ῭lol KKWUW ῭honwo῭n i cwuk-sa῭li s QIN-YWEN ῭un tut῭ti "mwot ῭hwo.l [i] 'ye῭ta* (1459 Wel 1:11b) those seeking an uneventful doctrine will hardly listen to the reasons for life and death.

῭hwom (also *"hwom*), modulated subst < °*ho῭ta*. ¶ *ha῭nol s "nim-῭ku῭m i῭la ῭hwom ῭ptu῭t i῭la* (1459 Wel 1:31b) it means he is the king of heaven. *SSILQ ῭hwom "ep.swu῭m un ...* (1464 Kumkang 87b) the lack of reality ... . *ko῭tok ' ῭ti a῭ni ῭hwom a῭ni῭n῭t ol pan῭to῭ki a῭lwolq῭t ilwo῭ta* (1462 ¹Nung 1:67a) one must realize that it is not that it is not full.

῭hwo.m a, modulated subst + pcl. ¶ *ho῭ma ku῭li ῭hwo.m a ῭hwon "i῭l i ...* (1475 Nay 3:21b) that I have already said I would do so.

῭hwo῭m ay, modulated subst + pcl. ¶ *MA ῭lol HHANG-῭PPWOK ῭hoy-ti῭Gwuy ῭PPWULQ-῭CO y CCO-PI a῭ni ῭hwo.m ay put῭ti a῭ni ho῭n i ῭la* (1482 Nam 2:5a) he got the devil to surrender but could not rely on the sons of Buddha (= his believers) not to show compassion.

῭hwo῭m i, modulated subst + pcl. ¶ *ney῭uy ῭e῭mi ῭ku῭lye ῭hwo῭m i* (1459 Wel 21:22a) that you are yearning for [your] mother. *CYE-῭PPWULQ ῭i CHYWULQ-῭SYEY ῭hwo῭m i NAN ῭hi ῭za mas-῭nano῭n i* (1463 Pep 5:148a) in renouncing the world the Buddhas confront much hardship. *"es῭tyey ho῭l [i] 'ye῭n ywo ῭hwo.m i "ep.su῭l i ῭lwo῭ta* (1465 Wen se:13b) there will be no wondering how it would be. ... *kalo῭chiti a῭ni ῭hwo.m i "mwot ho῭l i ῭la* (1475 Nay se:6a) cannot help but point out (that ...).

~ *῭za* (pcl). ¶ *phyen.an ῭hwo῭m i ῭za pit ῭swo῭m i ha῭n i ῭la* (?1517- ¹No 2:4a) just being in good health is of great value.

῭hwo῭m i῭Gwo (cop gerund). ¶ *"kyecip ῭tol῭h ol pwuthye s QUM-῭CCANG ῭SYANG ῭pwozop῭kuy ῭hwo῭m i῭Gwo* (1447 Sek 24:2b) is letting the womenfolk gaze upon the image of Buddha's retractable penis, and ... .

῭hwo.m i῭la (cop indicative assertive). ¶ *icey῭na non kanan hwo.m i῭la ῭PPYENG a῭ni ῭lwo῭la*

῭ho.ya῭nol ... (1482 Nam 1:30b) he said "now I am poor but I am not ill", whereupon ... .

῭hwo῭m ilwo῭ta (cop var indic assert). ¶ *῭i ῭i.l ol tut῭kwo cye ῭hwo῭m ilwo῭ta* (1482 Kum-sam 2:7a, *῭i* broken type) I want to hear about this.

῭hwo῭m isto῭n i-ngi s῭ka (pcl + cop polite + pcl + postmod). ¶ *KWONG-῭TUK ῭i ku῭ci "ep.su῭l i 'Ge῭nul ῭homol῭mye QA-LA-῭HAN "KWA ῭lol ῭TUK ' ῭key ῭hwo῭m isto῭n i-ngi s῭ka* (1459 Wel 17:48-9) if boundless virtue is achieved, is one ever allowed to get the karma of an arhan?

῭hwo῭m isto῭n ye (pcl + postmod). ¶ *῭homol῭mye TUNG a῭ni ' ῭m ye ῭pwom a῭ni ' ῭la PWUN-῭PYELQ ῭hwo῭m isto῭n ye* (1462 ¹Nung 2:84a) with no light, with no sight, how can one distinguish?! *῭homol῭mye CHIN ῭hi ye῭le ka῭ci s me῭cun "i῭l ol "SSYWU ῭hwo῭m isto῭n ye* (1459 Wel 21:88-9) just how much worse is the undergoing of evil deeds oneself?!

῭hwo῭m ol, modulated subst + pcl. ¶ *phye῭lak "cwuy῭lak ῭hwo῭m ol "ne y ῭pwono῭n i* (1462 ¹Nung 1:108b) you see it keep opening and closing. *῭machi nul῭ke [῭PPYENG] ῭hwo.m ol i῭kuy῭ti "mwot ho῭l i ' ῭lwoswo῭n i* (1481 Twusi 7:7b) it is as if I were too old to shake an illness. *tyele ῭hi ῭kot ῭hwo῭m ol [NGUY-SIM] ῭honwo῭la* (1481 Twusi 15:23b) I doubt that they are so alike.

῭hwo῭m o῭lwo, modulated substantive + particle. Example? CF *῭hosya῭m o῭lwo*.

῭hwo῭m on, modulated subst + pcl. ¶ *nay῭uy [SYWUY-"LWOW] ῭hwo.m on* (1481 Twusi 22:27b) that I am getting old and frail ... . *wo῭ywo.m i ῭stwo ῭wol῭hwo.m i῭la hwo.m on ...* (1482 Nam 1:39a) when we say that being wrong is also being right ... . *ka῭zomyel῭m ye [῭KWUY] ῭hwo.m on pan῭toki puculen ho[῭]m ye [SIN-"KHWO] ῭hwo.m ol pu῭the "etno῭n i* (1481 Twusi 7:31b) being rich and noble inevitably starts from hard work and hardship (before it is achieved).

῭hwon, modulated modifier < °*ho῭ta*.

1. (epitheme extruded from subject). ¶ *wo῭cik mozo῭m oy ῭HHYEN ῭hwon ke῭s ilwon῭t i ke῭wu῭lwu TYWUNG ῭ey s "SSYANG ῭i CCYWEN-῭"THYEY ῭i ke῭wu῭lwu ῭ylwon῭t i ῭kot ho῭n i* (1462 ¹Nung 2:17b) the fact that it is something that appears only in one's mind is like the fact that the image within a mirror is in its entire substance [just the] mirror.

2. (epitheme extruded from object). ¶ *na 'y*

˙TUK ˙hwon ˙TI-˙HHYWEY ˙non (1447 Sek 13: 57b) the wisdom that I have gained. *kasoy ˙lwo ˙hwon [MWON] ˙ulan sywokcyel [¨]ep.si [¨]ye[˙]ti [¨]mal[˙]la* (1481 Twusi 7:9b) do not to your regret open a door made of thorns.

3. (summational epitheme). ¶ ⋯ MYENG-˙SSYEY ˙PELQ-˙NGWEN ˙hwon ¨i˙l ol ¨hyeynon ˙ta mwo˙lonon ˙ta (1447 Sek 6:8a) are you taking into consideration that you uttered an oath -- or are you ignoring that? *kutuy s ˙hwon cwo˙chwo ˙ho˙ya* (1447 Sek 6:8b) I will do as you say, and ... . *alpho˙ti a˙ni ˙hwon ˙cwu[˙]l i a˙ni ˙˙Gen ma˙non* (1475 Nay 2:2:7b) it is not that one is not ill but ... .

˙hwo-ngi ˙˙ta, modulated polite < °*ho˙ta* + cop indic assert. ¶*pi˙lwok ¨salo˙m oy ˙mwu˙l ey ¨sa-˙nikwo ˙two cywungsoyng˙ma ˙two ¨mwot ˙hwo-ngi ˙˙ta* (1447 Sek 6:5a) even [my] living on in the society of human beings is inferior to [the life of] any living creature.

˙hwo˙n i, modulated modifier + postmodifier. ¶*mo˙cho.m ay ˙two˙wo.m i twowoy˙ti ¨mwot ˙hwo.n i* (1475 Nay 2:2:14a) in the end I couldn't be of help. *me˙li ˙thyey ˙lul ¨cye˙ki kiGwu.s ˙i ˙hwo˙n i* (1518 Sohak-cho 10:27a) the form of his head was small and lopsided.

˙hwon ˙t ay n', modulated mod + postmod + pcl + pcl. ¶*ki˙phi SO-LYANG ˙hwon t ay n'* (1482 Kum-sam 3:3b) on deeply considering it.

˙hwon ˙t i, modulated mod + postmod + pcl. ¶˙*i pwuthye KWONG-˙YANG ˙hwon ˙t i towoy˙ta ˙hosya˙m on* ... (1463 Pep 7:180b) [his] saying that this becomes the Buddha's offering of nourishment ... .

˙hwon ˙t i˙la, modulated mod + postmodifier + cop indicative assertive. ¶˙*SYANG ˙i ˙SYENG ˙uy nwo˙kywo˙m ol ˙TUK ˙hwon t i˙la* (1465 Wen se: 38b) the [manifested] form has gotten dissolved by the [inner] nature.

˙hwon ˙t i˙m ye n', modulated mod + postmod + cop subst + cop inf + pcl. if it is that one did. ¶*na ˙[G]wos MWU-˙SWU hon ˙KEP ˙ey ¨PPWU-¨MWUW ˙HYWOW-¨TTWOW ho˙kwo SA-MWON ˙kwa PPA-LA-MWON ˙kwa ˙lol KWONG-˙KYENG ˙hwon ˙t i˙m ye n'* (1447 Sek 6:29a) if it is [true] that for countless kalpas (eons) I have honored my parents and respected the śramaṇas and the brahmans, ...

hwopta SEE hopta

˙hwo˙toy, modulated accessive < °*ho˙ta*. ¶˙*na y solang ˙hwo˙toy* (1447 Sek 6:25b) I am thinking: ... . ˙*PWO-SI ˙lol ˙hwo˙toy* (1447 Sek 13:19a) he gives alms and ... . *is.non ˙tos ˙hwo˙toy is˙ti a˙ni ˙hwo˙m i ˙suchywom a˙n' ˙ywo˙m i a˙ni ˙˙la* (1459 Wel 1:36a) that it seems to exist yet does not exist is not a matter of thinking [about it]. ˙*SSIM ˙hi˙na y ¨KAM-SYANG ˙hwo˙toy* (1463 Pep 2:4b) I was moved to grief and ... . *NGWEN-˙KAK ˙ol ˙CING ˙khwo cye ˙hwo˙toy* (1465 Wen se:5a) wants to witness perfect enlightenment, and ... . *CYWUNG-˙ZILQ ˙tho˙lwok NGWEN-˙KAK ˙ol ˙hwo˙toy* (1465 Wen se:5b) enjoys perfect enlightenment all day long, and ... . ¨*THYEY ke˙pwu.p uy the˙li ˙kot ˙hwotoy* (1482 Kum-sam 2:66a) the body is like the hairs of a turtle, and ... . ALSO: 1447 Sek 13:19a, 23:5a, 24:1a, 24:3b; 1462 ¹Nung 5:85b; ... .

~ n' . ¶*SAM-˙NGWELQ QAN-KE ˙hwo˙toy n'* (1465 Wen 2:3:2:29b) staying quiet for three months, ...

hwū < ¨HHWUW, n. ANT cen. CF twī, taum.

1. afterwards, later (on), the future.

2. after (doing). 2a. -un ~ (ey). ¶Cĕmsim mek.un hwū ey tte-naki lo haca Let's set off after having lunch.

2b. abbr < VN [han] ~ . ¶swuep (han) hwū after class. siksa (han) hwū after eating. hōyuy (han) hwū after the meetings. tāyhak ul col.ep (han) hwū after graduating from college.

3. a descendant; an heir, a successor.

4. (as adn) later, latter-day, after, farther, further. ¶ ~ Into Farther India (= Indochina). ~ Paykcey later Paykcey. ~ techim medical complications from childbirth.

-hwu-, suffix [usually treated as -chwu-]. makes vc. cac.hwuta = cac.chwu-; kac.hwu- = kac.chwu-; mac.hwu- = mac.chwu-; nac.hwu- (so spelled in 1936 Roth 354) = nac.chwu-; nuc.hwu- = nuc.chwu-. CF -wu-, -kwu-, -chwu-; -iwu-, -ywu-; -˙Gwu-.

hwul-, ? bnd adv. HEAVY ↔ hol-. hwul-putul / hol-potul hata is very soft.

hyan, scribal mistake for *han* 'many' (1465 Wen 2:1:1:11a). Or, a variant / mistake for ˙hyen 'several, some; how many'; the Korean word is used to translate the Chinese pluralizer CYEY ⋯ .

hyang hata < ˙HYANG °*ho˙ta*, vnt.

1. faces, fronts, looks out on. ¶ ¨*salo˙m oy nos [← noch] al˙ph ol ˙HYANG ˙ho˙sya* (1482 Kum-sam 2:2b) deigns to turn to the front of

people's faces, and ... .
    2. heads for, starts / leaves for, is bound for, goes / proceeds to. ¶ *pas῾k ul ῾HYANG ῾ho.ya* (1482 Nam 1:24a) toward the outside. *e῾tuwun ka῾won-῾toy l' ῾HYANG ῾ho.ya* (1482 Kum-sam 2:65a).
    3. aims at, leans / tends towards.
hye < ῾*hye*, abbr < ῾*ho῾ye* = < ῾*ho῾ya*. **cen-hye** < *cyen ῾hye* (1447 Sek 6:24a, 1459 Wel 8:52a, ...) entire(ly), whole, complete < CYWEN 'entire' or CCYWEN 'exclusive' — both sources attested. **hāyng-ye** < **hāyng-hye** < ¨*hoyng ῾hye* < [¨*HHOYNG*] ῾*hye* (1481 Twusi 25:56b) fortunately. ῾*twok ῾hye* (1518 Sohak-cho 7:43b = 1586 Sohak 5:75a) uniquely, especially < ῾*TWOK* (id. 5:74b) ῾*hye* < ῾*TTWOK* (1447 Sek 6:40a) + *h[o῾]ye*.
hyēn < ῾*HHYEN*, adnoun. the present / existing / actual / real. ¶ ~ **wuli tul uy hyengphyen** our present situation. ~ **inphuley** the existing inflation. ~ **nāykak** the present cabinet. ~ **sēykyey** the contemporary world. ~ **swusang** the present prime minister.
῾*hyen*, noun. how many (= ῾*hyenma*, ¨*en῾ma*, ῾*myech*). ¶ ¨*cen mo῾l i ῾hyen pe῾n ul tin ῾t ol* (1445 ¹Yong 31) however many times the limping horse may fall. ῾*hyen ῾kwo῾t ol wol῾masi῾n ywo* (1445 ¹Yong 110) how many places have they moved to? ῾*hyen ῾nal in ῾t ol* (1449 Kok 74) however many days (it be).
hyēncang < ῾*HHYEN-*¨*TTYANG*, n. the spot, the scene (of action / labor), the field; (-nun ~) the very act / scene of doing.
῾*hyenma*, n. how many; how much (= ¨*en῾ma*, ῾*myes.ma*, ῾*hyen*, ῾*myech*). ¶ ¨*cywong ῾kwa mol ῾Gwa ῾lol ῾hyenma ῾yn ῾t ol* ¨*all i ῾Gwo* (1449 Kok 52) I wonder how many slaves and horses there are. CF **selma** < *hyelma* < ῾*hyenma*.
῾*hyen῾ma s*, n + pcl. ¶ ῾*hyen῾ma s PPWO-῾SALQ ῾[G]wa ῾hyen῾ma s ῾CYWUNG-SOYNG ῾i* (1459 Wel 17:23a) the many bodhisattvas and the many common creatures. ῾*hyen῾ma s CANG-NGEM ῾kwa ῾hyen῾ma s KWONG-῾YANG ῾i SSYANG-῾SSYWUY ῾lol ῾phyea῾n ywo* (1459 Wel 17:23b) how much pomp and how much offering of food have unfolded favorable omens?
hyengphyen < *HHYENG-PPYEN*, n.
    1. the situation, the state (of things), the aspect (of affairs), the development (of an affair). ¶ **hyēn wuli tul uy hyengphyen** our present situation. ... **selo uy hyengphyen ul cal ālko iss.ess.ta** they were well informed on how things were with each other. **Nala hyengphyen i mōs toyess.ta** The country is in an awful condition (in a mess); The nation is in sorry shape. ~ **ēps.ta** is terrible; is poor. ~ **ēps.i** terribly, mercilessly, completely, utterly.
    2. one's family circumstances (**cip** ~), one's financial situation. ¶ ... **ku hyengphyen ul cal ālko iss.ess.ta** I well understood his situation.
    3. the geographical aspect / features, the lay of the land, the topography.
    4. a condition, state (of affairs); convenience, circumstances.
    5. a kind, a shape.
    6. SEE **-nun** ~ (in) the process of doing.
CF **ccak, cengsey, hyengsik, kes, kkol, kyenghwang, kyengwu, pa, mo.yang, nolus, sāceng, sangthay, swu, tey**.
HYEY The Hankul spelling distinguishes **hey** and **hyey**, but they are usually pronounced the same (as **hey**). If you cannot locate the word you are looking for under **hey**, look under **hyey**.

i < ῾*i*, adn, n. LIGHT yo. ῾*i* + ῾*u῾lan* → ῾*il῾lan*, ῾*i* + ῾*u῾lwo* → ῾*il῾lwo*. CF **i ey, i eykey**; **ku** < *ku*, **ce** < ῾*tye*.
    1. adnoun. this / these ... ; present / current ... .
    2. noun. this (one), it. ¶ **Īl i i ey iluless.ta** Things have come to this!
    3. (= **i i**) this person, he / she, this one; this thing, it; the latter.
    4. SEE ῾*i ῾non*.
i < ῾*i*, quasi-free noun, postmodifier.
    1. a person, a man; one. ¶ **ilk.nun** ~ the reader, the person reading. **ciun** ~ the author, the writer / composer / creator / builder. **talun** ~ others, other people. **etten** ~ some people. **kan** ~ a person who has died, the deceased, a "goner". **Kim ila 'nun** ~ a man called Kim. **sīn.yong halq swu iss.nun** ~ a man one can trust. **cal nan** ~ a nice-looking one. **mōs nan** ~ an ugly one; (= **pāpo**) a fool. **Hōy ey on i ka mānh.ess.ta** There were many who came to the meeting. CF **i / ku / ce i**. SYN **sālam, pun, ca, nom**.
    2. a thing; one. ¶ **ik.un** ~ a well-boiled piece of meat. SYN **kes**.

3. (summational epitheme) the fact that ... . SEE -un i (pota / mankhum), -˙($^u/_o$)n i (...), -˙($^u/_o$)l i (...).

4. [DIAL] counter for people. SEE p. 187.

NOTE: The MK ˙i sometimes reduced to y and that was further reduced to zero when the genitive particle ˙$^u/_o$y was attached. SEE ˙uy.

i < ˙i, pcl (nominative). On the history of the nominative marker, see ka.

1. marks the subject of one or more following adjective or verb expressions.

1a. usually translated as the subject. ¶San i noph.ta The mountain is tall. San i noph.ko alum-tapta The mountain is tall and beautiful. San i noph.ko mul i malk.ta The mountains are tall and the waters are clear. San i noph.ko mul i malk.un nala 'ta It is a country where the mountains are tall and the waters are clear. tāythong.lyeng i yēnsel ul hasilq sikan the time when the President will make his address. Son nim i osyess.ta The guest has arrived. Ku sālam i pang an ey tul.e wā se uyca ey anc.ess.ta He came into the room and sat down on a chair. ku sālam i anc.ess.tun uyca the chair that he sat on. Tangsin i positun sinmun i ce kes i ani 'p.nikka Isn't that the newspaper you were looking at over there? Ku sōk ey mues i iss.nun ya What is inside it? Hyeng nim i cikum mues ul hasey yo What is your brother doing now? Ku kes i ippuci man pissaci That one is nice looking but I bet it's expensive. Ku haksayng i caki apeci hanthey phyēnci lul ssukeyss.ta ko hayss.^{s}up.nita The student said he would write a letter to his father (or: It is said that the student will ...).

1b. literally translatable as a subject, but freely translated as the object — of possession, ability, evaluation, or emotional affect. The person who possesses, is able, evaluates, or feels the emotion is also marked with the nominative particle. ¶tōn i ēps.ta there is no money, money is lacking / wanting = has no money, lacks / wants money. chayk i mānh.ta "books are many", there are lots of books = has lots of books. caynung i iss.ta there exists talent = has talent, is talented. mas i iss.ta there is flavor = has flavor, is flavorful / tasty / good, tastes good. son i aphuta one's hand is sore = one has a sore hand. pelus i napputa one's habits are bad = has bad habits.

kkoch i cōh.ta (1) flowers are good = (this plot / garden / place / ...) has nice flowers; (2) "flowers are liked" = I like flowers. maywun ūmsik i silh.ta "spicy food is disliked" = I dislike spicy food. Ku kes i poko siph.ta like to see that. Tal i poinun ya "Is the moon visible?" = Can you see the moon?

1c. marks the subject of a phrase as the possessor or as the person who is able, who evaluates, or who feels the emotion. The phrase can include a more immediate/direct subject for the verb or adj, expressing what is possessed or the target of the ability, the evaluation, or the emotion (1b). ¶Tangsin i tōn i iss.e yo? Have you got any money? I tose-kwan i chayk i mānh.ta This library has a lot of books. Namphyen i pelus i napputa The husband has bad habits. I kes i kaps i te ssata This one is cheaper (in price). Ku ilq-kwun i him i mānh.ta That workman is strong. Wuli ka pāym i musepta We are afraid of snakes. [NGWANG] ˙i ˙icey [˙SWUK-"PWU] y [CWON] ˙ho˙sitwo˙ta (1481 Twusi 8:10b) the king is now respectful of his uncle.

2. 2a. marks the subject of an affirmative copula phrase, which is often the Identified. The complement, often the Identifier, is marked only by the copula. ¶I kes i mues in ya What is this? Cikum i hak.kyo kalq sikan in ya? Is THIS any time to be going off to school?

2b. marks the complement (as well as the subject) of a negative copular phrase. ¶I kes i nay kes i ani 'n ya? Isn't this one mine? Ku sālam i haksayng i ani 'ko, chayk cangsa (i)ci He isn't a student, he's a bookseller.

But the particle may drop: Kulem cēng-mal ani 'ko [mālko]! Yes, of course it's untrue! cham in ci ani 'n ci ālta / mūt.ta knows / asks whether it is true or not. Onul ku sālam ani 'tumyen wuli phyen i cilq pen hayss.ci?! − Kuleki ey māl ici! I bet our team would nearly have lost today if it hadn't been for him. − You're absolutely right, I agree. On kes un talum ani 'la pūthak halq kes i hana iss.e wass.ta I have come for no other reason than just to ask a favor of you. Cil iya etteh.tun (ci) kaps ila to ssa ya halq kes ani yo Regardless of the quality, [isn't it the case that =] surely the price should be kept low. In some cases the noun is ellipted along with the particle: **Ku kes i cēng-mal in ci ani 'n ci ku ka mul.ess.ta** He asked if that was true or not.

Expressions with ⋯ **(-)cek** '-ic' (and other precopular nouns, which likewise normally do not function as a subject or an object) take the nominative marker: **kwahak-cek i ani 'ta** is not scientific (in attitude).

When the focus particles or delimiters are attached, the **i/ka** is normally suppressed: **Ku kes un kaykwuli to ani 'ko olchayngi to ani 'ta** That is neither a frog nor a tadpole. **Hak to pōng to ani 'ta = Cwuk to pap to ani 'ta** "is neither fish nor fowl" = **I man han sōnhay nun āmu kes to ani 'ta** Such a small loss is nothing to me. **Ku sālam ccum uy caysan un āmu kes to ani 'ta** The property HE has is nothing. **Twū sālam i ¹ihon halq cikyeng ey ilun kes un ani 'ey yo** (Im Hopin 1987:34) The two have not reached the point of planning to divorce. **I kes un kwahak-ca eykey man kwan.lyen toyn mūncey nun ani 'ta** This is not a problem that concerns scientists only. **Na eykey man chayk.im i iss.nun ke n' ani 'ta** I am not the only one who is responsible.

SEE ⋯ **kes (i) ani 'n ya, talum ani 'ko/'la, yekan ani 'ta**.

Middle Korean examples of copula negation:

With the particle ˙i: ⋯ ˙honwon ¨ma˙l on sa˙la na˙ta ˙honwon ¨ma˙l i a˙ni ˙'la (1447 Sek 6:36a) saying that ⋯ is not to say they are born alive. *KON ˙oy ¨nin ke˙s i a˙ni ˙'Gen ma˙lon* (1462 ¹Nung 2:81b) it is not that a root arose, but ... . ⋯ *QWUY-KWANG ˙oy NUNG ˙hi pi˙chwuyywo˙m i a˙ni 'la ˙ka* (1463 Pep 3:104b) it is not the full illumination of the mighty light ⋯, yet ... . *CIN-˙SSILQ S PPWO-˙SALQ ˙oy ˙TTYWU ˙hwol ˙kwo.t i a˙ni ˙.n i ˙'la* (1482 Kum-sam 3:34b) it is not a place where a real bodhisattva would dwell.

Without the particle ˙i: ¨sa˙lo.m in ˙ka ¨sa˙lom a˙ni 'n ˙ka ˙ho˙ya *NGUY-SIM toWoy˙n i* (1459 Wel 1:15a) grew suspicious whether it was a human being or not. ˙tye non hwo˙za ¨salom a˙ni ˙ka (1475 Nay 2:1:16a) isn't he a person alone? ˙*TI-¨THYEY ¨twul[h] a˙ni ˙'m ye ¨KYENG ˙two ¨twul[h] a˙ni ˙.n i; ˙TI ¨twul[h] a˙ni ˙'lwo˙m on ˙TI-˙HHYWEY 'lwo˙toy* ... (1459 Wel 8:31b) wisdom and substance are not two things, nor is the object of wisdom two; that wisdom is not two things is [a matter of] knowledge and discernment [together] and ... . ˙homol˙mye *TUNG* a˙ni ˙'m ye ¨pwom a˙ni ˙'la *PWUN-˙PYELQ* hwo˙m isto˙n ye (1462 ¹Nung 2:84a) with no light, with no sight, how can one distinguish?! ˙i *MYENG ˙uy ˙MANG ˙on nyenu a˙ni ˙la ˙KAK-MYENG ˙i he˙mu˙l i towoy˙n i* (1462 ¹Nung 4:23b) the extravagance of this light is nothing but an error in the enlightenment.

Omitting ˙i is particularly common after a Chinese word: ˙i ˙*SYWELQ-˙PEP ka,* ˙i ˙*SYWELQ-˙PEP a˙ni ˙Ga* (1482 Kum-sam 4:37b) is this preaching the law or isn't this preaching the law? ˙*PEP-HHWA ˙ay s ¨KWA-˙KUY a˙ni ˙'n ˙ka ˙honwo˙la* (1462 ¹Nung 1:17b) I ask whether it is not the testimonial to phala ([cause and] effect) that is in the Lotus [sūtra]. ˙*SYANG ˙i ˙kwot ˙SYANG a˙ni ˙la ˙za CIN i towoyno˙n i 'la* (1482 Kum-sam 3:12a) just when appearance is not appearance it becomes reality. ˙*TI-¨THYEY ¨twul[h] a˙ni ˙'m ye ¨KYENG ˙two ¨twul[h] a˙ni ˙.n i; ˙TI ¨twul[h] a˙ni ˙'lwo˙m on ˙TI-˙HHYWEY 'lwo˙toy* ... (1459 Wel 8:31b) wisdom and substance are not two things, nor is the object of wisdom two; that wisdom is not two things is [a matter of] knowledge and discernment [together] and ... . ˙homol˙mye *TUNG* a˙ni ˙'m ye ¨pwom a˙ni ˙'la *PWUN-˙PYELQ* hwo˙m isto˙n ye (1462 ¹Nung 2:84a) with no light, with no sight, how can one distinguish?! *MA* a˙ni ˙'la mu˙su ke˙s i˙l ywo (1462 ¹Nung 9:101b) it is not a demon but what is it?

But there are also examples of Chinese noun + ˙i (or its reduction y): *CYE-˙PPWULQ ˙ul ˙pwo˙zowo˙m i ¨cye˙kun YWEN ˙i a˙ni ˙'lwo˙swo-ngi˙'ta* (1463 Pep 1:88b) seeing the Buddhas is indeed no small contributing cause. pen˙tu˙ki ˙*PEP-HHWA y a˙ni ˙Ge˙nul ˙za* ... (1462 ¹Nung 1:17a) though they cannot be the Lotus sūtra exactly, ...

When a particle such as ˙kwos 'precisely, just' or ˙pwun 'only, just' is applied to the complement, the particle ˙i is obligatorily suppressed: ˙*MILQ-˙QIN* ˙kwos a˙ni ˙'m ye n' (1462 ¹Nung 1:8b) if they are not secret causes. wos.kwos hon kes ¨pwun a˙ni ˙'la (1447 Sek 13:39a) not just fragrant things, but ... .

In the normal MK negativizations V-˙ti a˙ni/ ¨mwot ˚ho-, the suspective ending derives from the postmodifier *t* + nominative ˙*i*; much less commonly there is found also V-˙*t ol a˙ni* / ¨*mwot* °*ho-*, with the accusative marker. The modern **V-ci anh- (mōs ha-)** comes from the MK V-˙*ti* but permits further marking by either the accusative (V-ci lul) or nominative (V-ci ka) to impart lively emphasis.

3. marks the complement of a change of state: into, into being) so as to be ··· (CF **ulo**). ¶**pam i toymyen** when it becomes (gets to be) evening; by evening. **Mul i ēlmyen el.um i toynta** When water freezes, it turns (in)to ice. **Sensayng i toye la** Become (Turn yourself into) a teacher!

But sometimes the particle drops: **Sālam toyko ani toynun kes un ney nolyek ey tallyess.ta** It depends upon your own endeavor whether you become a success or a failure. ¨*cywong towoy*˙*Ge ci*˙*la* ˙*hono*˙*ta* (1481 Twusi 8:1b) he says that he wants to become a slave. *no*˙*m oy* ¨*kye*˙*cip towoy*˙*nwo*˙*n i chol hi* ˙*tye kwo*˙*ma towoy*˙*Ga ci*˙*la* (1463 Pep 2:28b) I would rather become his concubine than another man's wife.

4. 4a. marks a phrase (ending mod + **kes**) that expresses the fact on which a following inference of likelihood is drawn: so (likely), and (probably). CF **-un** / **-nun tey**. ¶**Pal-mok i tāytan hi puun kes i ama pule cin mo.yang ita** His ankle is badly swollen; (and) I think it's broken. **Ay tul i cip an ey ēps.nun kes i ama pakkath ey se nōlko iss.na pota** The children aren't in the house; (so) they must be playing outdoors.

4b. (**kes i** = **kes ul**) but; although; yet. ¶**Ilenq īl i iss.ulq ka pwā se ilccik-i onta ko han kes i (nemu pappe se mōs wass.ta)** I was afraid that this kind of thing would happen, so I meant to come earlier, but ... . CF **-ta ka**.

5. In Middle Korean ˙*i* marks a substantive nominalization V-˙(ᵘ/ₒ)*m* as the complement of a negative auxiliary expression. (We would expect the accusative marker.) ¶*kan tay* ˙*lwo* ¨*salom sim*˙*kywu*˙*m i* ¨*mwot ho.l i* ˙'*n i* (1463 Pep 4:86b) cannot let people have it [= the sūtra] just at random. ··· *kalo*˙*chiti a*˙*ni* ˙*hwo.m i* ¨*mwot ho*˙*l i* ˙'*la* (1475 Nay se:6a) cannot help but point out (that) ··· . ¨*sa*˙*lo*˙*m uy a*˙*lomtye s* ˙*ywu*˙*mwu* ˙*lul ye*˙*ze pwo*˙*m i a*˙*ni* ˙*hwol* ˙*t i.n i* ˙'*la* (1518 Sohak-cho 8:22a) one is not to peek at other people's private letters.

6. MK ˙*i* sometimes marks the underlying object of a verb of knowing, whether negative (which could be treated as an extension of 5) or affirmative. SEE **-un** ˙*t i* 2 and compare **-un** ˙*t ol*. Structures with the postmodifier ˙*i* that occur as unmarked objects might (in some cases) have absorbed the nominative particle: *SSYA* ˙*two isi*˙*m ye* ˙*CYENG* ˙*two is.no*˙*n i a*˙*lwo*˙*m i NGUY khe*˙*ta* (?1468- Mong 39a) 'it is well to know that both wrong and right exist'; ˙*SYA-* ˙*NGWUY* ˙*KWUYK* ˙*ey hon* ˙*TTAY-SSIN SYWU-* ˙*TTALQ* ˙*i* ˙*la* ˙*hwo*˙*l i* ˙*is.no*˙*n i* ¨*alo*˙*sino*˙*n i* ˙'*-ngi s* ˙*ka* (1447 Sek 6:14-5) if that is taken as a postappositional epithematization 'do you know a minister by the name of Sudatta who is in the state of Śrāvastī?' rather than the more loosely knit 'there is a minister in the state of Śrāvastī who is named Sudatta; do you know him?' which is what I think was intended.

7. Middle Korean ˙*i* uncommonly marks the underlying subject of a causativized intransitive verb (which normally is converted to accusative or dative). ¶*pas*˙*k uy s* ¨*mal-so*˙*m i MWON an*˙*h ay* ˙*tuli*˙*ti* ¨*mal*˙*m ye* (1475 Nay 1:4b) letting no outside words enter the gate.

8. MK ˙*i* marks a complement of similarity, where modern Korean uses **kwa** (or **hako**). ¶ ˙*CHYWULQ-KA hon* ¨*salo*˙*m on sywo*˙*h i* ˙*kot.ti a*˙*ni ho*˙*n i* (1447 Sek 6:22a) the person who has become a monk is not like the common man. *CYE-* ˙*PPWULQ nilu*˙*sinwon* ¨*ma*˙*l on* ¨*NAY-CYWUNG* ¨*nay tal*˙*Gwolq* ˙*cwu*˙*l i* ¨*ep*˙*susi*˙*n i* ˙'*-ngi* ˙'*ta* (1447 Sek 9:27a) there is no way that the words said by the various Buddhas will differ in the end.

NOTE 1: In modern standard Korean this particle occurs only after a consonant; after a vowel it is replaced by **ka**. But in the literary language, and widely in dialects (especially of the north), **i** is not infrequent after a vowel, particularly in certain set phrases such as **ka i ēps.ta** (= **ka ka ēps.ta**) 'is without limit, is boundless' and **hana i toyta** = **hana ka toyta** 'becomes one, unites' (perhaps influenced by the elided consonant of earlier *honah*, CF 1936 Roth 40). SEE **key** (= **kes i, ke ka**), **nay (ka), ney (ka), cey (ka); pay** (< **pa i**).

NOTE 2: After a vowel other than *i* or *y*, the MK particle ˙*i* was reduced to *y* and attached to the preceding vowel to produce a diphthong:

˙na ˙i 'I' → ˙na y (1447 Sek 6:4a), ˙pye ˙i 'rice plant' → ˙pye y, ˙sywo ˙i 'ox' → ˙sywo y (1459 Wel 1:24b), e˙nu ˙i 'which one' → e˙nu y (1482 Nam 1:14a), ˙nwu ˙i 'who' → ˙nwu y (1445 ¹Yong 15, 99), ke˙wu(˙)lwu ˙i 'mirror' → ke˙wu˙lwu y (1481 Twusi 21:35b). If the preceding syllable was low-pitched the accent of the resulting diphthong was the blend of low + high = the rise that is marked by the double dot: ne ˙i → ¨ne y (1447 Sek 6:1a), pwuthye ˙i 'Buddha' → pwu¨thye y (1447 Sek 6:1a), ku 'that one' → ¨ku y (1447 Sek 19:16a). After ···i or ···y, the particle was further reduced to zero with no accentual trace when the last syllable of the noun was high-pitched: me˙li [˙i] (1447 Sek 13:7b) 'head', ˙poy [˙i] (1445 ¹Yong 20) 'boat'. After a low-pitched syllable the high pitch of the particle was retained and blended with the low pitch of the last syllable of the noun to make the rising accent: ···i ˙[i] = ¨···i, ···y ˙[i] = ¨···y: toli 'bridge' → to¨li (1481 Twusi 25:7a), poy 'pear' → ¨poy (1481 Twusi 20:9b), kwolay 'whale' → kwo¨lay (1481 Twusi 25:53a), motoy 'node' → mo¨toy (1481 Twusi 25:2b), nwuwuy 'older sister' → nwu¨wuy (1475 Nay 3:46a), ne-huy → ne-¨huy (1447 Sek 13:47b; 1459 Wel 2:26b, 21:68b) – CF the genitive-marked subject of ne-huy ˙uy elwu ˙NGWAN-˙HWOW ˙hwolkke˙si (= ˙hwolq kes ˙i) (1463 Pep 2:66-7) 'the things you folks are rather fond of'. But often the free-standing Hankul y was written after a Chinese character representing a syllable ···i or ···y (CF He Wung 338-9), just as it was written after syllables ending in other vowels where it was actually pronounced. And the subject could be left unmarked by ˙i to begin with, as in the obvious case of ˙mwom ˙khu˙kwo tali ˙khu˙kwo 'its head was large and its legs were large' and the less obvious ˙mwo˙m i ko˙cang ˙khu˙kwo tali ¨kwulk˙kwo (1447 Sek 6:32b) 'its head was extremely large and its legs were thick'; in both examples, we would expect ta¨li if a trace of the particle were present. When a high-pitched ˙···i or ˙···y is the subject, we have no way to know whether the particle was absorbed without a trace or was never attached in the first place.

NOTE 3: All of the remarks in Note 2 apply also to the copula ··· ˙i-, which reduces to ··· ˙y- in exactly the same way: ˙na 'I/me' → ˙na ˙y˙la (1459 Wel se:4b), ˙kye 'chaff' → ˙kye ˙y˙la (1463 Pep 1:195b), yang˙co 'appearance' → yang˙co ˙y˙n i (1459 Wel 1:16b), ˙nwu 'who' → ˙nwu ˙yGe˙n ywo (?1468- Mong 22b), ˙sywo 'ox' → ˙sywo ˙yn ˙t ol (1482 Kum-sam 2:3a); ku 'that one' → ¨ku ˙y˙Gwo (1447 Sek 13:36b), phunglywu 'music' → phwung¨lywu ˙y˙n i (1447 Sek 13:9a), ne 'you' → ¨ne ˙y˙m ye (1459 Wel 8:5b), mwoncye 'ahead' → mwon¨cye ˙ylwo˙ta (1481 Twusi 20:6b), pwuthye 'Buddha' → pwu¨thye ˙ysi˙n i ˙˙la (1447 Sek se:1a). Accent unexplained: ¨amwo 'anyone' → ¨amwo ˙y˙na (1447 Sek 9:17a, 21a) rather than the expected *¨a¨mwo ˙y˙na, and → ¨a˙mwo ˙yGe˙na (1459 Wel 1:13a) rather than *¨a¨mwo ˙yGe˙na.

Like the particle, the copula stem vanishes after ···i or ···y: ka˙hi 'dog' → ka˙hi ˙˙la (1459 Wel 21:42b), pwul˙hwuy 'root' → pwul˙hwuy ˙˙la (1459 Wel se:21a), kulu˙mey 'shadow' → kulu˙mey ˙˙la (1447 Sek 19:37a), HHWONG ˙on ˙swu[h] ˙muci˙key ˙˙Gwo i YEY ˙non ˙am ˙muci˙key ˙˙la (1462 ¹Nung 2:87b) [the Chinese word] HHWO is the brighter of a double rainbow, and YEY is the paler.

Like the particle, too, when attached to a low-pitched syllable, the copula stem leaves behind an accentual trace before vanishing: toli 'bridge' → to¨li ˙˙la (1459 Wel 21:77a); nwuuy 'big sister' → nwu¨uy ˙˙la (1459 Wel 21:162a); motoy 'node' → mo¨toy ˙˙n i (1459 Wel 10:118a), mo¨toy ˙.n i ˙˙la (?1468- Mong 43b).

These remarks also apply to ˙i + other particles such as ˙za: ˙nwu y ˙za NUNG ˙hi ˙TWOY-˙TAP ho˙l [i] ˙ye˙n ywo ˙hosi˙kwo (1447 Sek 13:15a) he said, "Just who will respond fully?", and ... .

i, particle [DIAL, obs] = ey to (a place).
1. [Ceycwu] cip i kaca = **cip ey kaca** (LSN 1978:3) let's go home.
2. [MK] ? (SEE LCT 607b.) ¶ *LUNG-NGEM kolo˙chywom tu˙li˙Gwusya˙m i KKWUN-SOYNG ˙ol ¨TTOY-˙CYEP ˙hosya˙m i ˙SSIM ˙hi twuthe˙wusi˙m ye HHOYNG-ZIN ˙ol ˙po˙lasya˙m i ka˙poyyap˙ti a˙ni ˙hosi˙n i ˙wuli ˙mwul on ˙him ˙pswu˙m i ˙mas.tang ho˙n i ˙˙la* (1462 ¹Nung 10:42b) he is very generous in letting the teaching of the Śurangama sūtra be heard and

in receiving the common people, and it is not easy for him to see a pilgrim; it behooves our group to bend every effort.

i, postmod. the question whether (= **ya**). SEE **-un** ~, **-nun** ~, **-ul** ~, **-tun** ~.

'i < ˈ'i, abbr < **hi** < ˈhi, der adv < **hata**. ¶**kkaykkus 'i** clean, neatly. **ttattus 'i** warmly, cordially. **khum-cik 'i** in a fairly big way. **ik' 'i** = **ik' hi** = **ikswuk hi** (knows it) well, expertly.

This form is usual after ···s, and often after ···k; colloquially — but not orthographically — after any voiced sound: **annyeng 'i** = **annyeng hi** in good health.

¶*koma.n 'i is ti a ni ho m ye n'* (1462 ¹Nung 1:77b) unless it is still. *me li thyey lul ¨cye ki kiGwu.s 'i ˙hwo n i* (1518 Sohak-cho 10:27a) the form presented by his head was small and lopsided.

SEE **namcis 'i, tus 'i; -i** (suffix) 6.

'i, abbr < **ii** (= **io**)

ī- < ¨*I*, (Chinese preposition). SEE **īcen, īha, īhwu, īkang, īlay, īnam, īnay, īoy, īpuk, īsang, īse, ītong**.

-i. Many nouns incorporated **-i** (after a vowel, reduced to **-y**) at various times in different dialects, including modern Seoul. The **-i** was either the noun **i** 'one = person/thing, fact' or the nominative particle; the resulting forms behave like any other noun and can be followed by the case particles **i**/**ka** and **ul**/**lul**. Often the shorter original form is found in other dialects or in MK texts.

Examples from Seoul: **nai** < ˙*nah-i* 'age' (SEE §4.2), **wi** < *wuy* < *wu[h]-i* 'above', ...

Examples from Ceycwu (LSN 1978:12-3): *kamay* < *kama* 'kiln', *cwokhay* < *cwokha* 'nephew', *kulq-cay* < *kulq-coy* < *kulq-co* 'letters', *swey* [swe:] = *sywoy* < *sywo* 'ox', *mwey* = *mwoy* < *mwo* 'seedling'; *kwongpi* < *kwongpwuy* (Seng ¹Nakswu 1948:13, 36, 47, 99, 100) < *kwongpwu*.

MK *ala-wuh* 'up and down' (= NK **alay-wu**, SK **alay-wi**) suggests that the MK *a ̇lay* 'below' may have attached **-i** or the locative marker *˙ay* (or both) to an original *ala* or even *al*, as found in modern **al lo** 'downward', usually taken as a shortening of **alay lo**.

-i, 1. [var] = **-o** (AUTH indic after vowel): **hai** = **hao** < **hata**, **khui** = **khuo** < **khuta**; **tui** = **tuo** < **tulta**; **pului** = **puluo** < **puluta**; CF **nwuwi (nwuw-ui)** = **nwupso** < **nwupta**.

2. = **-uy**, abbr < **-ui**

-i < -ˈ*i*, suffix. CF **-ey, -ay, -kay, -ki; -key**.

1. derives a noun from an adjective or a verb. the quality/act of; the one that (is/does).

1a. **anthakkapi** a jumpy person, worrywart ?< **anthakkapta**. **āy-pali** a skinflint < **āy-paluta**. **chwuwi** cold < **chwupta**. **khi** < *khu ̇i* stature (or < ˙*khi* [obs] greatly). **kil.i** < *ki ̇li* length (or < *ki ̇li* = *kil ̇li* ?< **kil ̇Gi* for a long time). **kiph.i** < *ki ̇ph ᵘ⁄oy* depth (or < *ki ̇phi* deeply). **kwup.i** a bend, a turn, a curve < **kwupta**. **nelp.i** width (= extent, area); **nepi** width (of cloth; Mkk 1960:3:25) ?< CF **nelli** widely < **neluta**. **noph.i** < *nwo ̇phoy* height (or < *nwo ̇phi* highly). **puphi** bulk < **puphuta**. **tewi** warmth, heat < **tēpta**. **yak-ppali** a shrewd person < **yak-ppaluta**.

1b. < v. **kel.um-kel.i** gait < **kēt.ta**. **kwui** roasted/baked meat or fish < **kwūpta**. **mek.i** food, feed < **mekta**. **mol.i** chasing, hunting, driving < **mōlta**. **muk.i** an old thing/person < **mukta**. **nol.i** amusement, game < **nōlta**. **phul.i** unfastening; exorcising; explaining < **phulta**. **pokk.i** something panbroiled/roasted < **pokk.ta**. **salm.i** harrowing < **sālm.ta**. **selkec.i** dishwashing < **selkec.ta**. **tat.i** /taci/ closing (bnd n) < **tat.ta**. **tatum.i** cloth to be fulled; fulling/smoothing (cloth) < **tatum.ta**. **ttel.i** what is knocked down/off; clearance goods < **ttēlta**. **tōnq pel.i** earning money < **pēlta**.

NOTE 1: The following derived nouns are the same as the stem, which ends in ···**i** or ···**y**: **kali** stack, **keli** act, **kalkhwi** rake, **kkochi** skewer (< **kkoc.hi-** get thrust in), **kkoy** wiles (< **kkōy-** seduce), **kkwumi** beef shreds (< **kkwumi-** decorate), **mungchi** lump, **nwupi** quilting, **olay** (for) a long time (< **olay-** be longlasting), **oli** cutting (strip), **sali** coil, **toy** measure, **tti** belt, ? **salphi** marker, divider (< **salphi-** inspect, consider). These cases could be considered as having absorbed the ending, or as formed with a zero (= with no) ending. We might also wish to consider the following cases as zero-ending derived nouns: **kamul** drought < **kamulta** goes without rain, ? **mak** the last < **mak-** put an end to (or perhaps an abbr < **macimak**), **phum** bosom (space between chest and clothes) < **phum.ta** carries in the bosom (CF §3.1); **pis** comb < **pis.ta** combs, **ppyēm** span < **ppyēm.ta** measures by the span, **sin** footwear < **sin.ta** wears on the feet. But we could instead derive the verbs from the nouns; there are few clues to the histories. See also the irregular derived nouns that end in **-y** and **-ey**.

NOTE 2: In set phrases V-**i** + (**lul**) **hata** = the verb: **mamuli hata** = **mamuluta** finishes up, **nah.i hata** = **nah.ta** weaves, **pun-phuli lul hata** = **pun-phulta** vents one's anger (CF **-um**), **sal cap.i hata** = **sal capta** props it up, **tacap.i hata** = **tacapta** supervises strictly.

NOTE 3: In the 1600s -˙*i* lost its productivity in favor of -˙*ki* (Katsuki 1968).

2. derives a noun from a mimetic adverb (or a bound element).

2a. a ··· one (thing / person / creature). **allok(-)i** / **ellwuk(-)i** mottled pattern. **a(l)long-i** / **e(l)lwung-i** a mottled one; mottling. **alulong-i** / **elwulwung-i** mottling, spots. **ccakcakkwung-i** clash, commotion; secret scheme. **ccolccol-i** a dogged follower, a hanger-on. **celttwuk-i** a lame person (= **celttwuk pal.i**). **chollang-i** a frivolous or careless person. **ellek-i** a spotted / dappled animal. **hapcwuk-i** a toothless person (with puckered lips). **helleng-i** an unstable person, a twit. **kenken-i** dried side-dishes. **khonapcak-i** a flat-nosed person. **khungkhung-i** a snorter. **kkaktwuk(-)i** chopped radish pickles. **kkalccwuk(-)i** a silver dime (coin, with milled edges). **kkapul-i** a flibbertigibbet, a flit, a twit. **kkelleng-i** a vile fellow, a no-good, a shiftless character. **kkengchwung-i** a lanky fickle man. **kkumc(c)ek-i** a person who blinks a lot (= **nwun ~**). **mengcheng-i** a dunce, a blockhead. **mulkheng-i** soft (or overripe) stuff; a softy, a milksop. **mungtheng-i** a lump/clump, a bundle. **nwutek(-)i** tatters, rags. **okulang-i** / **wukuleng-i** a thing that is pushed in or shriveled up; a crooked person. **ottok-i** a tumbler [person]. **pay-pulttwuk-i** a pot-bellied person. **phayng-i** a top. **phusek(-)i** a crumbly thing, a fragile thing, a frail person. **potuk(-)i** a dwarfed tree. **pulwuthwung-i** a protruding thing, a bulge. **salsal(-)i** a wily one. **tephel(-)i** a helter-skelter person. **thalthal(-)i** / **thelthel(-)i** one who is flat broke. **ttoktoki** = **ttokttok-i (capan)** a sliced-meat dish. **yamnyam-i** (< **yamq-yam i**) goodies, tasties, yummies, treats.

2b. a creature that goes ··· (that makes the sound ···). **kaykwul(-)i** a frog. **kilek(-)i** a wild goose. **kkoykkol(-)i** a bush warbler, a nightengale. **kwittwul(-)i** = **kwittwul(-)ami** a cricket. **māym(-)i** a cicada. **māyngkkong(-)i** a small round frog; an idiot. **peyccang(-)i** grasshopper. **ppekkwuk(-)i** a cuckoo. **pueng(-)i** a (hoot) owl. **ssululam(-)i**, **ssilulayki** (? < **ssilul^a/$_u$k(-)i**) a cicada. **ttaktakwul(-)i** a woodpecker. **ttaok(-)i** a crested ibis.

3. derives a noun from noun or bound noun. a ··· one (person / creature). CF **cangi**, **-swungi**.

3a. **kāsal-i** = **kāsal cangi** / **kkwun** a hateful and stuck-up person. **yāsal-i** = **yāsal cangi** a peevish person, a crab, a curmudgeon.

3b. **huyttuk-melwuk-i** a spendthrift, a show-off. **pīngchwung-i** / **pāyngchwung-i** (= **pīngchwung** / **pāyngchwung mac.i**) a clumsy and stupid person, an oaf, a dolt. **saythwung-i** a silly / flip person or act. **sisitek-i** a silly fool. **yamcen-i** a nice child.

3c. **kaksel-i** a storyteller. **mayngmun-i** a person completely in the dark (= ignorant) or lacking in sense. **pānphyen-i** a simpleton, a fool. **sikchwung-i** a glutton.

3d. **hōlang-i** a tiger. **patwuk-i** a spotted dog. **sengseng-i** a gorilla. **songchwung-i** pine-eating caterpillar. **Tongkyeng-i** a short-tailed dog.

4. derives adv from adj. in such a manner, ···ly, ···-wise. CF **-wu**, **-o**. SEE **hi**; **kath.i**, **siph.i**; **celi**, **ili**, **kuli**; **ecci**; **mōllay**; **suley**, **suli**. ¶ **cēkci anh.i** (= **anh.key**) in no small measure < **anh.ta** (aux adj). **cēk.i** slightly, somewhat. **ēps.i** without < **ēps.ta** (quasi-adj). **kakkai** near, nearby < **kakkapta**. **kappi** = **kappukey** uncomfortably hard < **kapputa**. **k^{e}ayulli** < *keyGul˙Gi* lazily, negligently < **k^{e}ayuluta**. **khi** < ˙*khi* [obs] = **khukey** greatly (or < ˙*khuy* stature). **kil.i** < *ki˙li* = *kil˙li* (1586 Sohak 4:53b) ?< *kil˙Gi* for a long time (or < *ki˙li* length). **kiph.i** deeply (< *ki˙phi*) or depth (< *ki˙ph^u/oy*). **koi** nicely < **kōpta**. **kwut.i** /kwuci/ firmly, strongly, solidly, hard. **kulli** < *kul˙Gi* wrongly < **kuluta**. **mānh.i** muchly, a lot (of), much < **mānh.ta**. **mēlli** < *me˙li* far away / off / back, distantly < **mēlta**. **noph.i** < *nwo˙phi* highly, aloft (or < *nwo˙phoy* height). **olh.i** rightly, correctly. **pappi** busily, briskly < **papputa**. **ppalli** < *spol˙li* fast, quickly < **ppaluta**. **talli** ?< *tal˙Gi* differently < **taluta**.

swii easily / soon < swīpta. hes-toyi uselessly, in vain. ik(.)i → ik' 'i SEE 'i.

NOTE 1: A few derived adverbs are the same as the stem: **nayli** 'down' < **naylita** 'descends', **teti** 'slowly' < **tetita** 'is slow'. And **olay** 'long, for a long time' is the same as both the stem and the infinitive of the adjective **olay-** 'long, longstanding'.

NOTE 2: The derived adverb often carries a more abstract meaning than the adverbative, so that **kiph.key phass.ta** 'I dug it deep' refers to the result of the action, while **kiph.i sayngkak hayss.ta** 'I thought about it deeply (in depth)' refers to manner or intensity.

5. vacuously attached to an adverb: **tewuk(-i)** all the more, particularly. **ilccik(-i)** early ? < ilta + -cek.

6. (= 'i) derives adverb from mimetic adverb (or bound element, defective adjectival noun).

6a. (p)pek(p)pek-i = (p)pek-(p)pek 'i without fail, for sure. **salkūm-i** / **sulkūm-i** = **salkūm** / **sulkūm** 'i furtively. **salmyes-i** = **salmyes** 'i softly; stealthily.

6b. **tok-i** alone, single-handed(ly) < bnd n **tok** < ˙*TTWOK*. **kie-i** without fail, by all means = **kie** 'i < **kie** [h]i < defective adj-n *KKUY-QE*.

7. derives adv from iterated n. ¶**aph.aph-i** /apaphi/ for each one. **ccokccok-i** in pieces. **chŏnchon-i** in every village. **cipcip-i** in every house. **kos.kos-i** in every place. **ilq.il-i** /illili/ one by one, in detail. **īlq.il-i** /īllili/ all things, everything. **kel.umkel.um-i** at each/every step. **moks.moks-i** /mongmokssi/ each / every share (portion), so as to be equal shares (portions). **na'-nal-i** day by / after day, daily. **namnam-i** between/among others, with unrelated persons. **ŏl.ol-i** every strand. **penpen-i** all the time, always, habitually. **ppulppul-i** (horn by horn =) separately, singly, severally. **sikansikan-i** hour by hour, every hour. **sīlsil-i** thread by thread, every thread (as in **os i ~ ttel.e/thut.e cyess.ta** the garment fell / tore apart thread by thread). **ssangssang-i** two by two, in pairs. **ta'tal-i** month by month, monthly, month after month. **yephq.yeph-i** /yemnyephi/ on this side and that side, on all sides. ALSO: **chungchung-i, cwulcwul-i, kkuth.kkuth-i, kyepkyep-i, myēnmyen-i, nath.nath-i, sath.sath-i, ssumssum-i, wen.wen-i**. CF **kilkil-i** high(ly) < kīlta long.

-i, suf. endearing diminutive added to personal names that end in a consonant. **Poktong-i** Little Poktong(-i) − CF **Poktong i** Poktong [as subject], **Poktong-i ka** Poktong-i [as subject]; **Poktong a** Hey, Poktong! **Poktong-i ya** Hey, Poktong-i!. **Yengswuk-i** Yengswuk-i, Little Yengswuk. **Kāyttong-i** Little Dog Dropping (said affectionately to babies). CF **-tongi**.

-˙i, vacuous suffix attached to names that end in a consonant. ¶*pwu*˙˙*thye y* ˙*MWOK-LYEN*-˙*i to*˙*lye nilo*˙*sya*˙*toy* (1447 Sek 6:1a) Buddha says to Maudgalyāyana. *KA*-˙*SYEP*-˙*i* ˙˙*spwun tut*˙*key* ˙*ho*˙*si.n i* '˙*la* (1447 Sek 23:42a) he let them hear only Kāśyapa. *CHA*-˙*NIK*-˙*i pulu*˙*sya* ··· *CHA*-˙*NIK*-˙*i* ˙*two* ˙˙*wulGenul* ... ([1447→]1562 Sek 3:29b) (the Prince) summoned Chandaka ··· Chandaka too wept, whereupon ... . ˙*PPALQ-TTYEY* '*la* ˙*sye QA-NA-*˙*LYWULQ-*˙*i to*˙*lye nil*˙*Gwo*˙*toy* (1459 Wel 7:1b) Bhadrika told Aniruddha as follows ... .

-i < ˙*ZI*, suffix (added to vn in Chinese clichés). and, while, but. ¶"**hak-i ci-ci**" "study and then know it" = acquiring knowledge by study. "**kyeng-i wēn-ci**" "respect but keep it distant" = keeping at a respectful distance.

-i- < -˙i-, suf. CF **-y-, -hi-, -ki-, -chi-, -ukhi-, -ikhi-, -li-, -iwu-, -ywu-; -wu-, -hwu-, -kwu-, -chwu-, -ay-;** -˙*Gi*-, -˙*Gwo*-, -˙*Gwu*-, -*o*-, -*u*-.

1. derives vc. **cwuk.i-** < *cwu*˙*ki-* kill ← **cwuk-** < *cwuk-* die. **kkulh.i-** < *kul*˙*hi-* make it boil, boil it ← **kkulh-** < *kulh-* boil, seethe. **hulli-** < *hul*˙*li-* make flow ← **hulu-** / **hull-** < *hulu-* / *hull-* flow.

2. derives vp. **nanw(u)i-** < *non*˙*hwoi-* get divided ← **nanwu-** < *non*˙*hwo-* divide. **moi-** < *mohwoi-* come together, gather ← **mo(u)-** < *moh(wo)-* gather it. **pulli-** < *pul*˙*li-* get called ← **pulu-** / **pull-** < *pulu-* / *pull-* call.

ia, cop var inf (= ie); abbr (after vowel) **ya**. The standard spelling is **iya** and that is probably well motivated historically, though we are treating the phonetic glide as nondistinctive. Before a particle **ia** is replaced by **ie** or **ila**.

1. it is ··· [used sentence-final in FAMILIAR style]. ¶**I kes i nay kes ia** This one is mine. **Kōngkal ia, cinq-ca ya** Are you bluffing / lying or telling the truth?

2. (rejected usage) and (= **iko, hako**).

i-amuli, abbr < **i ka āmuli** (···). however (···) this one may be.

i ay, cpd n (adn + n). ABBR **yay**. CF **i ca/chi/ elun/i/nom/pun/salam/son**.
 1. this child; he/him, she/her, it.
 2. this person/friend; he/him, she/her.
 3. you (there!)
 4. hey!, (hello) there. ¶**I ay i key musun cangnan in ya** Hey there — what's that you're doing there?!

ia(y) yo = ie(y) yo (polite copula). This is usually spelled **iya(y) yo**, but it is seldom seen.

ica, cop subj assert. (= **in tongsi ey**) at the same time that it is; as well as (being). ¶**Ku salam un hakca 'ca cengchi-ka 'ta** (= **haca 'n tongsi ey cengchi-ka 'ta**) He is a politician as well as a scholar. **Ku nun Mikwuk-in ica tongsi ey Hankwuk-in ila ko halq swu iss.ta** He is an American but we can say he is a Korean as well. **Ku ⁿyeca nun nay emeni 'ca sensayng iki to hata** She is my mother and she is also my teacher. **Ku ⁿyeca nun tongsayng ica, nay chinkwu uy puin ita** She is my sister and the wife of my friend.

i ca, adn + quasi-free n. [pejorative] this person (man/fellow/guy, woman), he/him, she/her. CF **i ay/chi/elun/i/nom/pun/salam/son**.

i ccak, adn + n.
 1. this member (of a pair), this one.
 2. = **i ccok**

i ccok, adn + n.
 1. (= **i phyen**) this side/direction; our side.
 2. our party; we/us. ¶**~ ce ccok** this way and that; we/us and they/them. **~ ulo kata** goes this way. **Unhayng un kil i ccok ey iss.ta** The bank is on this side of the street.

i ccok, cpd n (n + n). a broken piece of tooth, a chip from a tooth.

i ccum, n + pcl. CF **i cuum**.
 1. this much, this quantity/degree, (of) this caliber.
 2. somewhere (around here).

i cek (ey), adn + n (+ pcl). (at) this time, currently. CF **i cey, i pen**.

īcen < **ˉI-CCYEN**, n, postn. (time) previous/prior to, before, ago. **~ ey (nun)** formerly, before; in the old days. ¶**Īcen puthe ku i lul alko iss.ta** I have known him for a long time. **Īcen pota salki ka nas.ta** Living is easier than before. **haypang īcen** before the liberation. **taycenq īcen** before the (world) war.

i cey = i cek (ey). ¶**I cey 'na ku cey 'na machan-kaci 'ta** (Whether) this time or that time it's all the same.

icey, n [DIAL, lit] = **incey** (now)

˙**icey**, n. now, the present time. (1459 Wel 9:35f, 1481 Twusi 7:31b). ˙**i˙cey l'** (1462 ¹Nung 10:19a). **~ n'** (1463 Pep 2:41a). **~ s** (1459 Wel 2:9b, 9:35d). **~ ˙two** (1482 Kum-sam 2:59b). **~ ˙za** (1449 Kok 115). **~ ˙'la** (1459 Wel se:13b). **~ 'syas˙ta** (1482 Kum-sam 2:59b). **~ ˙stwo** (1447 Sek 6:5b, 1459 Wel 8:101a).

˙**i˙cey** (1462 ¹Nung 4:126b, ?1517- ¹No 1:1a) = ˙**icey**. ¶˙**i˙cey l'** (1462 ¹Nung 10:19a). ˙˙**ne y** ˙**i˙cey swo˙li** ˙**Ga a˙ni** ˙**Ga** (1462 ¹Nung 4:126b) is it now your sound or isn't it? ˙**i˙cey e˙tu˙le ˙ka˙non ˙ta** (?1517- ¹No 1:1a) now where are you going?

i chelem, n + pcl. like this, in this way/manner, this/so much. ¶**~ manh.i** so much, so many. **I chelem wa cwusye se komapsup.nita** Thank you for coming like this (as you have done). **I chelem achim ilccik eti kanun ya** Where ever are you going at this hour of the morning? SYN **i kath.i**.

i chi, cpd n. [pejorative] this person (man/woman), he/him, she/her. CF **i ay/ca/chi/elun/i/nom/pun/salam/son**.

ici, copula suspective. ¶**Nay kes ici ney kes i ani 'ta** It's mine, not yours = **Ney kes i ani 'la nay kes ita** It's not yours, it's mine. Modern uses of the copula suspective did not occur in Middle Korean, which has no examples of *__i˙ti__.

ici anh- (rhetorical question): §11.7.8 (p. 323).

ici man (un), copula suspective + pcl (+ pcl)

i cum = i cuum, cpd n. about this time.

ie, cop inf. it is ˙˙. VAR **iey** (abbr **yey, ey**), **ia**. ABBR after vowel **ye** (VAR **yey, ey, ya**). The usual spelling has been **iye** and that is probably well motivated historically, though here we are treating the phonetic glide as nondistinctive. NOTE: For the modern forms we write **ya, ye, yess-** (etc.) after a vowel, with no apostrophe, but for earlier Korean the apostrophe precedes the glide when it is reduced from **i** (including the cop infinitive used as a quasi-pcl ˙**i˙ye/ ˙˙ye**) except in the structure **-u˙m ye**.

ie la, cop inf + pcl. ¶**Alum-tawun salam ie la!** What a beautiful person he is!

i elun, adn + n. (this adult =) he/him (still more honorific than **i pun**).

ˈi ˈen = ˈi ˈGen (cop effective mod). SEE ˈyen.
ieng [Ceycwu DIAL] SEE iyeng
ieni [obs var] = ikeni (cop tent sequential)
ienul [obs var] = i-kenul (cop lit concessive)
*ie man (ya), cop inf + pcl (+ pcl). These forms do not occur.
ien man [obs var] = iken man (cop semi-lit concessive)
ˈien ˈtyeng = ˈiGen ˈtyeng (cop effective mod + postmod) though it is ‥ .
ˈi ˈen = ˈi ˈGen, cop effective mod. ABBR ˈˈyen.
ie se, cop inf + pcl. ¶ Pāpo ye se īl ul sikhilq swu ēps.ta He is so stupid you can't have him do the job.
iess-, copula past.
iess.ta ka, copula past transferentive + particle. ¶ Kim Yengsam un yātang iess.ta ka yētang i toyess.ta Kim Yengsam was in the opposition party and then he joined the party in power. Ku sālam i yātang iess.ta (ka) yētang iess.ta (ka) hanta He switches back and forth between the out party and the in party.
~ to (+ pcl). ¶ Pūca yess.ta ka to kapcaki kanan hay cinun swu nun elma ˈtun ci iss.ci There are ever so many cases of those who were rich suddenly turning poor.
ie to, cop inf + pcl even if it be. ¶ Pāpo ye to īl ul sikhilq swu iss.ta He may be stupid but you can get him to do the job. Usually replaced by ila to; CF ilotoy.
ietun [obs var] = i-ketun (cop provisional). ¶ Chencwu uy atul ietun ... (1936 Roth 536) if you are the son of God ‥ .
i ey < (?*) ˈi ˈyey, n + pcl. 1. to this (thing). ¶ Silhem ¹yusan i iss.ta; i / ku ey a.yen ul neh.usio There is some (laboratory) sulphuric acid; put zinc in this / it.
2. → iey₁. KEd was mistaken in treating this as an extension of (1).
iey₁ < ingey (abbr < ingeˈkuy), adverb.
1. hereupon, thereupon, whereupon; then; now; henceforth, thenceforth. ¶ Wang i pung.e hayss.ta; iey wang-sēyca ka tungkuk hayss.ta The King passed away; thereupon the Crown Prince ascended the throne. Ku ka mul.ess.ta; iey na nun ileh.key tāytap hayss.ta He asked me a question, whereupon I answered thusly.
2. at once, immediately. ¶ Ku māl ul tut.ko, iey cip ulo tol.a kass.ta On hearing that I went back home at once.

iey₂ [var] = ie (it is): ~ ya, ~ yo. ABBR yey, ey.
ie ya, cop inf + pcl. ¶ Pāpo ye ya īl ul sikhil swu iss.ta He would have to be stupid for you to be able to get him to do the job.
i ey se, noun + particle + particle.
1. from this. ¶ Kuliko i / ku ey se nanun swuso lul pat.usio Then take the hydrogen that is produced from this / it.
2. than this. ¶ I ey se te han pulhayng i ēps.ta There can be no greater misfortune than this.
i eykey, n + pcl. to this one / creature. ¶ Silhem thokki ka iss.ta; i / ku eykey cwūsa lul noh.a polq cakceng ita There is a laboratory rabbit; an injection is to be given to it.
ie yo, iey yo, cop inf + pcl (polite). ABBR ye yo, (y)ey yo. The usual spelling has been iye yo, iyey yo. SEE iya(y) yo = ia(y) yo.
ˈiGe, copula effective infinitive. SEE ˈiGe ˈza.
ˈiGeˈm ye, copula effective substantive + copula infinitive. SEE -uˈl i ˈGeˈm ye.
ˈi ˈGen, copula effective modifier. SEE ~ ˈywo.
ˈi[ˈ]Gen ˈ‥ SEE ˈiGeˈn i, ˈiGen ˈtyeng.
ˈiˈGen maˈlon it is ‥ but. ¶ naˈy ˈTUK ˈhwon ˈTI-ˈHHYWEY ˈnon MI-ˈMYWOW ˈhoˈya ˈTTYEY- ˈQILQ ˈiˈGen maˈlon (1447 Sek 13:57b) the wisdom that I have gained is subtle and most important, but ...
ˈi ˈGen maˈnon it is ‥ but. ¶ alphoˈti aˈni ˈhwon ˈcwu.l i aˈni ˈˈGen maˈnon (1475 Nay 2:2:7b) it is not that one is not ill, but ‥ .
ˈiGeˈna, cop effective advers. ¶ talon naˈlaˈh i pwoˈchanon ˈNAN ˈiGeˈna ˈcokya s naˈlaˈh ay ˈsye keˈsulˈpcun ˈyang ˈhonon ˈNAN ˈiGeˈna (1447 Sek 9:33a) whether it be the difficulty of supporting another nation or the difficulty of acting defiant in one's own nation ‥ .
ˈiGeˈn i, cop effective mod + postmodifier. SEE (-uˈl i) ˈGeˈn i; ˈyGeˈn i.
~ ˈˈston SEE ˈhokan ˈt iGeˈn i ˈˈston, -uˈl i ˈGeˈn i ˈˈston.
ˈiGeˈnol = ˈiGeˈnul, copula literary concessive. ¶ LUNG-NGEM ˈPEP cwozo lowoyˈywoˈm i ingey moˈchol stoloˈm iGeˈnol (1462 ¹Nung 1:22a) the importance of the Śurangama dharma just comes to an end here, but ‥ .
ˈiGen ˈtyeng, cop effective mod + bnd postmod. even if it be, even. ¶ ‥ HHOYNG hol ˈˈspwuˈn iGen ˈtyeng taˈsi ˈKAK-ˈPYELQ hon ˈPEP ˈi ˈˈep.suˈn i (1459 Wel 18:13b) there is no particular other dharma, even if you only

practice ‥ . SEE -ulq ˈs iGen ˙tyeng, -ulq ˈs ˈyen tyeng, -ulq ˙t iGen ˙tyeng.

˙iGeˈnul, copula lit concessive. ¶ CCYWEN-ˈˈTHYEY ˙non ˙i mozoˈm iGeˈnul (1462 ¹Nung 2:17b) the entire substance is in this mind, but ‥ . CCO-PI ˙non ˙CYWUNG-SOYNG ˙ol PPYEN-QAN ˙khey ˙hoˈsinon keˈs iGeˈnul (1447 Sek 6:5b) mercy is [his] deigning to ease the lot of living creatures, yet ‥ . SEE ˈyGeˈnul.

˙iGeˈn ywo, copula effective mod + postmod. ¶ ˙CYEY-ˈˈTTWO ˙CYWUNG-SOYNG ˙i ˈˈKUY CHYEN ˙MEN ˙iGeˈn ywo (1449 Kok 166) were the saved creatures several thousand myriad [in number]? ˙hyenˈma s ˙PPI-KHWUW ˈˈHWA-KWANG SAM-ˈMOY ˈGeˈn ywo (1449 Kok 193) how many almsmen are there who have done a samādhi (meditation) with emission of flames?

˙iˈGesin ˙tyeng, cop effective honorific modifier + postmod. ¶ ˈˈSYWUW ˙hosyan ˙MYENG ˙iˈGesin ˙tyeng (1463 Pep 5:126a; extruded object as the Identifier in an epithematic identification) he received an order ‥ , but ‥ .

˙iGeˈta, cop effective assert indic. SEE -Geˈta, -(wo)lq ˙t iGeˈta; ˈyeˈta.

˙iGeˈtun, cop provisional. ¶ TTYANG-SSYANG pam s TYWUNG ˙iGeˈtun ([1447→]1562 Sek 3:22b) always when it was in the middle of the night ‥ .

˙iˈGey, cop adverbative (= *ikey). so as to be, so that it is ‥ . ¶ ˈˈsaloˈm i ˈˈtwulˈh iˈGey hon ta ˈˈsin t ol kaˈcolˈpiˈsi.n i ˈˈla (1462 ¹Nung 2:27b) [he] wondered whether people had made them be two, but he compared them, anyway. NUNG ˙hi mwoˈm ay ˙CUK ˙hoˈya ˙kwot mozoˈm iˈGey ˈˈmwot holˈss oy (1462 ¹Nung 10:18a) as one cannot approach the body and turn it at once into the mind. twuˈthuy taˈsos ˙CHWON ˙iGey ˙khwo (1466 Kup 1:71b) makes it five inches in thickness and ‥ . neˈpi ˙tye lol HYWUW hoˈm ye ˙HELQ ˙ho.ya ˙QILQ-˙NYEM ˙i ˙MEN-NYEN ˙iˈGey ˙hwol t iˈn i (1482 Kum-sam 5:40b) it is so arranged that a single moment's thought gives ten thousand years, letting them all relax at ease. [THYEN-ˈˈHHA] ˙ay s ˙chiGwun ˈˈsaloˈm ol ˙khi ˙kunulˈGwe ˈˈta kis.pun noˈch iˈGey ˙ho.ya (1481 Twusi 6:43a) shelters the cold people of the earth and makes them all be happy faces, and ‥ . ˙sayˈswoˈ nam.kul ˙cumun ˙ca.h iˈGey nwopˈti ˈˈmwot hwo.m ol chuki neˈkinwoˈn i (1481 Twusi 21:5a) resents it that the new pine tree cannot be so tall as to be a thousand feet [in height]. SEE ˈˈGey; ˈˈilˈGey.

˙iGeˈza, copula effective inf + pcl. ¶ ˈˈiˈle hon [ˈˈ]MYWOW-ˈPEP ˙un CYE-ˈPPWULQ ZYE-LOY SSI-˙CYELQ ˙iGeˈza niluˈsinoˈn i (1447 Sek 13:47b) this sort of wondrous doctrine is told only in the time of a tathāgata. tyengey nan CHYEN-NYEN ˙iGeˈza (1463 Pep se:7b) not until it is a thousand years since it [the gathering] happened in that place ‥ . ABBR (after ‥y) ˈyGeˈza.

˙iˈGwa, n + pcl. with this. ¶ ˈˈYE ˙nun ˙iˈGwa ˙tye ˙[G]wa ˙honon ˙kye.ch ey ˙psunon ˙CCO ˈyˈla (1451 Hwun-en 1b) ˈˈYE (ˈˈand") is a character used as a particle that puts this and that together.

˙iˈGwo, copula gerund. ¶ hon THYEN ˙iˈGwo ˙SO-PANG ˙ay yeˈtulp ˙kwom peˈle is.keˈtun ‥ (1459 Wel 1:31a) as in each of the four directions there are spread eight [of the 33 Indra] heavens ‥ . tung ˈˈminˈt oy ˈˈtwu ˈˈnas ˈˈtwon ˙iˈGwo (?1517- Pak 1:52a) to get your back scrubbed is two coins, and ‥ . ALSO: ?1468- Mong 63b, ‥ . NOTE: Not used as conjunction 'and' until the late 19th century; see ˈ[G]wo, ˈy[G]wo.

i[G]wo SEE i(y)o

īha < ˈˈI-ˈˈHHA, n, postn. 1. less than, under, below. ¶ Sengcek i yēysang īha ita The result falls under what was expected. sam-manq īha less than thirty thousand. sip-chilq īha below seventeen. tases salam īha nun (1936 Roth 208) no more than five people.
2. under, below, beneath.
3. the following, the rest. ¶ ~ sayng.lyak (ham) the rest (is) omitted.

i hay, adn + n. this year, the current / present year. ¶ ~ yelum this summer. I hay nun phungnyen ita This is a bumper year.

i hwū, adn + n. after this, hereafter. ~ ey nun from now on.

īhwu < ˈˈI-ˈˈHHWUW, postnoun, postmodifier. after, from ‥ on. 1. postnoun [semi-colloq]. ¶ sip-chil-ilq īhwu after the seventeenth. Sēycong īhwu after [King] Seycong. Sēy si īhwu ˈmyen ēncey ˈtun ci cōh.sup.nita Any time from three o'clock on is all right.
2. postmod [semi-lit]. ¶ Hānkwuk ey sokay hanq īhwu since it was introduced into Korea. Ku i nun Sewul ey onq īhwu (= on hwū ey nun) wuli cip ey se sālko iss.ta He has been living at our house since he came to Seoul.

ii [var] = io (AUTH cop)

i i, adnoun + quasi-free n. this person (man/woman), he/him, she/her; this one. ABBR **i**. CF **i ay/ca/chi/ĕlun/i/nom/pun/sālam/son**.
i i l', abbr < **i i lul**
i i n', abbr < **i i nun**
i i tul, adnoun + noun + postnoun. these people; you people.
i ka, pcl + pcl. 1. [DIAL] = **i/ka** (nominative). CF **nay (ka), ney (ka), cey (ka)**.
2. [in hypostatic contexts only] "**Tōn i**" **ka ani 'la** "**tōn ul**" **ita** It is not [the phrase] "**tōn i**", it is "**tōn ul**".
3. SEE **ka** (question), NOTE.
īkang < "*I-'KANG*, n, postn. henceforth, and after (= **īhwu**).
i ke (ke n', ke l', kel-lo = ke lo), abbr < **i kes (un, ul, ulo)**
ikena, copula tentative assertive (= **ina**).
ikeni, cop tent sequential. **~ wa**. M 1:2:451 says that this form does not occur, but examples are possible: **Tōn i ēps.nun kes to khunq īl ikeni wa** (perhaps better with **ilye 'ni wa**) **sikan i ēps.nun kes i te mūncey 'ta** Not only am I without money, but even more of a problem is that I have no time.
iken man (un), cop semi-literary concessive
ikenul, cop literary concessive. VAR **ienul**.
i kes, adn + n. 1. this (thing/fact). ¶ **~ ulo sse pomyen** from what has been said, in view of these facts. **I kes un silh.ta** I don't like this one. **I kes un an toynta** This will never do.
2. = **i sālam** you (informal).
i kes ce kes. this and that; "this, that, and the other"; something or other. ¶ **~ sayngkak hata** thinks of this and that; gives consideration to various things, mulls things over, casts about. **~ hay pota** tries one thing or another. **~ halq kes ēps.i** with no further ado, without making a fuss; including everything, without (any) discrimination. **I kes ce kes sayngkak hamyen, āmu kyelqceng to ciulq swu ēps.ta** If you keep worrying about this and that, you will never make up your mind.
ikes.ta, copula tentative assertive. SEE **-kes.ta**.
iketun, cop provisional. VAR **ietun**. ¶**Ku kes i ney kes iketun ney ka kacye la** If it's yours, take it.
i key, abbr < **i kes i**
*****ikey**, copula adverbative. Does not occur; use **toykey** 'so as to become' or **ulo** 'as'. CF *i Gey*.

ikeyss.ta, cop fut indic assert. must be, probably is. ¶**Chelqswu ka cwuk.unq ¹īyu nun ku kes ikeyss.ta** That must be the reason Chelsswu died(, I tell you)! **Ku nun cik.kong ikeyss.ta** He is probably a factory worker.
~ ya (pcl) SEE **-keyss.ta ya**.
-ikhi-, suf. derives vc. **tol.ikhi-** turn (one's head) ← **tōl-** turn. CF **-i-, -y-, -hi, -chi-, -ukhi-, -li-, -iwu-, -ywu-; -wu-, -hwu-, -kwu-, -chwu-, -ay-; -'Gi-, -'Gwo-, -'Gwu-, -o-, -u-**.
ik' 'i = ik' hi = ikswuk hi (knows) well, expertly, with expertise.
iki, copula summative
iki ey, copula summative + particle
iki l', abbr < **iki lul**
ikilley, copula extended summative
iki lo, copula summative + particle
iki lul, copula summative + particle
iki man, cop summative + pcl. ¶**Haksayng i ani 'la ko hatuni e.yes han tāy-haksayng iki man haney** They say he is not a student, but he is a perfectly respectable undergraduate. **Cwuk in cwul al.ess.tuni pap iki man hatula** I thought it was gruel but I see it's rice.
iki n', abbr < **iki nun**
iki nun, copula summative + particle
iki to, cop summative + pcl. ¶**Ku i nun uysa (i)ki to hako um.ak-ka (i)ki to hata** He is both a doctor and a musician. **Wuli cip uysa iki to hako, iwus chinkwu iki to hata** He is both our doctor and a friendly neighbor.
i kkaci lo, n + pcl + pcl; LIGHT **yo kkaci lo**. to this trifling extent.
i-kkacis, cpd adn (n + bnd pcl); LIGHT **yo-kkacis**. this kind of ... , such a ... [usually pejorative]; ... so trifling/slight/little/small. ¶ **~ kes** such a trifle. **~ tōn** such a small sum of money. **I-kkacisq īl un kece mek.ki 'ta** A job like this is nothing to me.
iko, copula gerund.
1. (it is ...) and (also); and, or. VAR **iyo**; SYN **ulo**; CF **ila, imye, hako**; (*)**ikwo**. ¶**I kes un nay kes iko ku kes un ney kes ita** This is mine and that is yours. **Han pun un uysa (i)ko han pun un pyēnho-sa (i)ta** One is a doctor and the other is a lawyer. **Pap iko ttek iko kwukswu 'ko kwāca 'ko mak' mek.ney** We eat rice, rice cakes, noodles, fruit, anything. **Pyēngmyeng un mues iko pyēng un elma 'na cwūng-han ya ko mul.e pwass.ta** We asked what the name of

the disease was and how serious it was. NKd has examples of **ey** ~, **eykey** ~, **ey se** ~, **eykey se** ~.
2. (= **ina, itun ci**) any, ···ever. ¶**mues iko** whatever, whichever; anything. **ēncey 'ko on some/any occasion. Āmu congi 'ko tā cōh.ta** Any paper will do. **Pheyn iko yenphil iko tā kacye one la** Bring whatever you have, pen or pencil. **Mues iko hakeyss.ta** I'll do anything.
iko mālko, cop ger + aux v ger. of course it is.
i kos, adn + n. this place, here. LIGHT **yo kos**. SYN **yeki**.
i-kwantey, copula semi-lit sequential. ¶**Cey ka mues ikwantey sāngkam kkey se kule han hwūtay lul hasinaikka** What is it (= how does it come) that the king accords me such a warm reception?!
(*)*ikwo* SEE *'i ' Gwo*, *i[G]wo* > **i(y)o**; *'y ' Gwo*, *'y[G]wo*, *'[G]wo*.
ikwulye, cop apperceptive (FORMAL)
ikwumen, cop apperceptive (FAMILIAR); ~ **yo** (POLITE).
ikwun, cop intimate apperceptive; ~ **yo** (POLITE).
ikwuna = **ikwun a**, copula especially intimate apperceptive
īl < *"il*, n. Often pronounced **-q īl** = **nīl** when preceded by a consonant. ? < *"i[l]'ta* 'gets accomplished / achieved'.
1. a job, a task, a piece of work, business; a matter, a deal. ¶**swiwunq** ~ an easy job (piece of work). **kup hanq** ~ urgent business. **khunq** ~ **ul hata** achieves a great work / deed. ~ **i son ey puth.ci anh.nunta** is unable to bring oneself to work. **Ku mokswu nun yo say īl i ēps.ta** That carpenter has been out of work lately. **Na nun onul halq īl i mānh.ta** I have lots of things to do today. **Ku nun yo say swul masinun kes i īl ita** He does nothing but drink these days.
2. employment, occupation, vocation, line of work, job, business. ¶**Atu' nim un musunq īl ul hap.nikka − Ūmsikq īl ul hap.nita** What line of business is your son in? − He runs a restaurant.
~ **hata**, vni. works, does one's job. ¶**īl hale kata** goes to work.
3. a thing, a matter, an affair, a fact. ¶**ppan-hanq** ~ an obvious fact. **pul-yukhway hanq** ~ an unpleasant matter, something unpleasant, a nasty business. **cwūngyo hanq** ~ a matter of grave concern. **tōn ey kwan hanq** ~ a money matter. **Musunq īl in ya; eti aphun ya?** What's the matter with you; are you feeling ill? **Cham īsang hanq īl ita** It is a curious thing indeed. **Ku kes un ney ka ālq īl i ani 'ta** That is none of your business. **Musunq īl lo osyess.ey yo** What have you come for? = What can I do for you? **Musunq īl lo ileh.key kosayng hanun ci molukeyss.ta** I don't know what I have done to deserve this (such misery). **I key wēynq īl iyo!; etteh.key osyess.ᵇup.nikka** What a surprise; what brought you here?
4. a plan, a program, a project, a scheme, an idea. ¶~ **ul kkoy hata** makes a plan, forms a scheme. ~ **ul cīnhayng hata** carries a program forward. **Īl i swūnco lopkey cal toye kanta** The plan is on a fair way to success.
5. an incident, an event, a happening, an occurrence; an accident, a mishap; trouble. ¶**musunq** ~ **i iss.tula** to whatever happens, under any circumstances. **musunq** ~ **i iss.ul ttay ey nun** in case of emergency. **musunq** ~ **iss.ki lul palata** hopes that something happens. **Elin ai tul hanthey musunq īl i sayngkiketun kot na hanthey allye la** If anything should happen to the children let me know at once. **Puk Han ey se yo say khunq īl i il.e nass.ta** Trouble recently broke out in North Korea. **I kes i emeni hanthey allye cimyen khunq īl ita** If this gets to Mother's ears, there will be trouble.
6. [written style] a thing required / requested; it is requested that. SEE **īl ēps.ta**. ¶**Haksayng un kyōsil an ey se tāmpay phi(wu)ci mālq īl** Students are requested not to smoke in class.
7. postmod. experience. SEE **-unq (-nunq, -tunq) īl**.
il, adv, adn. early. ANT nuc. CF **ilccik(-i), ol**. [< **iluta** adj]
1. adv. ¶**il kkāyta** rises early. **il kkaywuta** wakes one early. **il tte-nata** starts early in the morning (CF **il-tte nata** springs up < **ilta** arises). **Il kake la** Come (there) early!
2. adn. ¶**ilq cam** going to bed early.
il(q) < *'il(q)*, cop prosp mod; ABBR **'l(q), 'yl(q)** but *'l(q)* after *i* or *y*. ··· that (it) is to be. ¶**koon ilq cey uy sangthay** (CM 2:66) conditions when it is high-temperature. **Ku khi khun i ka tāycang ilq pep hata** That tall one must be the general. **Khun san ilq swulok namu ka**

mānh.ta The bigger the mountains are, the more trees they have on them. **Ocwuk cōh.un chayk il i (yo)** Wouldn't it be a fine book, though?! SEE **il lī, ilq ka, ilq kes, ilq ko, ilq sey,** *ilq ̓s oy,* ... .
˝*il(q)* < **i ̓l[u]l(q),* prosp modifier < ˝*i[l] ̓ta* (become, ... ; summational epithemes). ¶*SSYENG ̓un ˝il ̓ss i ̓la* (1451 Hwun-en 13a) [the word] *SSYENG* means become something. ̓*chez MYENG- ̓SSYEY ˝ilq ̓t ol ˝alo ̓sya* (1449 Kok 114) he knows that the first oath will be accomplished. ˝*ilq ̓ka* (postmod). ¶*ses ̓ke ˝tele ̓wun ̓KYEN ̓i ˝ilq ̓ka cehu ̓sil ̓ss oy* (1462 ¹Nung 4:38b) because he was afraid that contaminated views might be formed.
i l', abbr < **i lul.** this (one) [as object].
ila < ̓*i ̓la* < ** ̓i- ̓ta,* cop indic assert (honorific: **isita** < ̓*isi ̓ta*). SEE *a ̓ni 'la, a ̓ni ̓la ̓ka.*

1. [QUOTED] cop indicative assertive (= **ita**). ¶**Ku sālam un kwun.in ila (ko) hayss.ta** He said he was a serviceman.
¶ ̓*SILQ- ̓TTALQ ̓i ̓la ̓hosya ̓l i ̓na ̓sil na ̓l ay* (1447 Sek 6:17a) on the day that the one to be called Siddhārtha was born. ˝*es ̓tyey ˝cywu ̓ng i ̓la ̓ho ̓no.n i s ̓ka* (1447 Sek 6:18a) why are they called priests?

2. [lit] cop var inf (= **ie** < ̓*i ̓ye*); CF **ila to** < ̓*ila ̓two,* **ila se** < ̓*ila ̓sye,* **ila ya** < ̓*ila ̓za,* **ci 'la; ila ('ta) noh.a se** (p. 476b).

2a. (= **ie se**) it is ... and (so). ¶**Onul i il.yoil ila (se) cēncha ey sālam i mānh.kwun yo** The train is crowded because it is (a) Sunday, I see.
¶*YA-SYWU ̓nun ˝kye ̓ci.p i ̓la ̓PEP ̓ul mwo ̓lol ̓ss oy* (1447 Sek 6:6b) Yaśodharā, being a woman, is ignorant of the Law, so ... .

2b. (= **iko**) SEE **ani 'la** < *a ̓ni ̓ ̓la* (= **ani 'ko** < ?**a ̓ni ̓ ̓Gwo,* **ani 'mye** < *a ̓ni ̓ ̓m ye*).

2c. [sentence-final, lit]. ¶**Hwūsayng i kāoy 'la** Young students should be treated with proper respect. (Often cites a Chinese saying.)
¶ ˝*TTWOW ̓non pwuthye s ̓PEP i ̓la* (1447 Sek se:4b) the Way is Buddha's Law. ̓*khun ̓po.yam s SSIN-LYENG ̓i ̓la* (1459 Wel 1:15a) it is the spirit of a large snake. ̓*PALQ-CHYEN ˝LI ̓Gwom ̓nyenun ̓SSYANG ̓i ̓la* (1459 Wel 7:52b) it is an elephant that goes eight thousand leagues at a time. *talon ˝pwo ̓m on SSYA- ̓KWAN ̓i ̓la* (1459 Wel 8:9b) other views are heresies. ̓*na ̓non pwuthye s solang ̓hosi ̓nwon az ̓G i ̓la* (1462 ¹Nung 1:86a) I am the younger brother whom the Buddha loves.

3. quasi-pcl (? abbr < **ilang**) and.

4. = ̓*ila ̓sye* (as subject marker). ¶*[KUM- ̋TYWOW] [G]wa [̓NGWOK- ̓THWO] tul a nwu 'yla ne lul scwos-nil kwantoy [̋KWUW- ̓MEN- ̋LI TTYANG-KHWONG] ul hewuy hewuy tan.ino.n i* (1876 Kakok p.9) oh bird of gold and hare of jade, in your pursuit who will go panting after you through the boundless sky?

5. [DIAL] = **ita.** SEE **ila(y).**

ila 'ca, abbr < **ila (ko) haca**

ila 'ci, abbr < **ila (ko) haci**

ila k, [DIAL] abbr < **ila ko:** ~ **hata.**

̓*ila ̓ka,* cop transferentive + pcl. SEE *a ̓ni 'la ̓ka,* **ita** (NOTE).

ila 'key, abbr < **ila (ko) hakey**

ila 'ki, abbr < **ila (ko) haki**

ila kko [LIVELY] = **ila ko**

ila ko, QUOTED cop indic assertive + particle.

1. (saying) that it is ... , calling it (by name); "quote" (= unquote). ¶**I kes ul mue 'la ko (mues ila ko) hanun ya** What do they call this? What is this called? **I kes i cintallay 'la ko hanun kkoch ita** This is a flower called the azalea. **Acessi 'la ko pulle** Call me "Uncle"! **Ku tangsi Cosen ul Kolye 'la ko pulless.ta** They called Korea "Kolye" at that time. **Caney kanun kos i eti 'la ko kulayss.na** Where did you say it was that you are going to?

2. grants (concedes, supposes, posits) that it is ... . ¶**Yūmyeng han hakca 'la ko hapsita; kulena tā ālkeyss.na yo?** I grant you he is a famous scholar; but does he know everything? (= **Yūmyeng han hakca 'la ko hay se tā ālkeyss.na yo?** So he is a famous scholar, does that mean he knows everything?!)

3. [IRONIC SURPRISE] ¶**I kes ul capci 'la ko sass.tuni ilk.ulq kes i hana to ēps.ta** I bought this "magazine" (as they pretend it to be) and can't find a thing in it to read. **Ku-kkacis kes ul īl ila ko hako iss.nun ya** Why are you (wasting time) on that so-called "job"? **I key Swun-i emeni 'la ko?** – **chen man ey!** This is Swun-i's "mother" you say? – no way! **Na nun ku key kāy 'la ko ko.yangi yess.kwun a** My "dog" turned out to be a cat, I see! **Ani i key Swun-i emeni ani 'la ko!** – **cham olay kan man ip.nita** Why, it can't be Swun-i's mother, what a surprise; my, how long it's been since I've seen you!

4. "... unquote" (marking the end of a direct quotation and followed by a verb of saying, typically hata). ¶Hongsek i "Hyosin i cip ey iss.ᵍup.nita" 'la ko (māl) hayss.ta Hongsek said "Hyosin is home" = Hongsek i "Hyosin i cip ey iss.ᵍup.nita" (hako) māl hayss.ta [the hako is optional] = Hongsek i "Hyosin i cip ey iss.ᵍup.nita" (–) hayss.ta [hako is not allowed] (King 1988b). Emeni ka ayki hanthey "Kongpu com halyem" ila ko hayss.ta The mother said to the child "How about doing a bit of homework, now". Namphyen i anʰay hanthey "Tōn ul" ila ko tāytap hayss.ta The husband answered his wife, "Money [that is what I want]".

NOTE: In this use if the verb of saying is just hata it must directly follow ila ko; but other verbs (including māl hata) will permit intervening constituents. Yengswu ka "Kulenq īl ccum mūncey ēps.ᵍup.nita" 'la ko casin manman hakey māl hatukwun [māl cannot be omitted] = Yengswu ka casin manman hakey "Kulenq īl ccum mūncey ēps.ᵍup.nita" 'la ko (māl) hatukwun [māl can be omitted] (Why,) Yengswu said confidently "Such a thing is no problem" (King 1988a).

4. [sentence-final] it is ... . SEE -ta ko (4).
ila 'ko, abbr < ila (ko) hako. saying that it is ... .
ila ko 'n('), abbr < ila ko han, < ila ko hanun.
ila 'ko n', abbr < ila 'ko nun.
ila ko 'nun, abbr. 1. < ila ko hanun. that is deemed to be ... ; called. ¶Ku san ey kōm ila ko 'nun kōm hana to ēps.ess.ta There was not a single bear (to speak of) on that mountain.
2. < ila (ko) hanun kes un as for (the one that is called); [lit] = un. ¶Ku i nun cakphum ila ko 'nun pyel lo ēps.ta He has nothing in particular (to show) in the nature of literary work. Hānkwuk ey hoswu 'la ko 'nun pyel lo ēps.ta Korea has no lakes to speak of.
ila 'ko nun, abbr < ila (ko) hako nun.
ila ko yo, QUOTED cop indic assert + pcl + pcl. [relaxed polite] it is ... . SEE -ta ko yo.
ila kwu = ila ko; ila kwu n' = ila ko n'
ila kwu yo = ila ko yo
ila 'l(q), abbr < ila (ko) hal(q). that is to be (said to be) ... , that is to be called ... . ¶Ku nun hakca 'la 'lq swu ka ēps.ta He can't be called a scholar.
*ila 'la, abbr < ila (ko) hala; *ila la!. Not used.

ila 'm, abbr.
1. < ila (ko) ham its being (said to be), ...
2. [SAME, or < ila 'n māl i(y)a?] do you mean to say that it is ... ? really? (shows incredulity, irritation, a complaint, or a reproach – often to oneself). ¶Kulen nom to sālam ila 'm? Can a guy like that be called a human being?
*ila man (ya). These forms do not occur.
ilamey = ila 'mye 2
ila 'mye, abbr < ila (ko) hamye.
1. says it is ... and.
2. = ila myen se (sentence-final rhetorical question, expressing surprise or disagreement with the implications of a remark just heard): SEE 'myen se. ALSO ilamey.
ila 'myen, abbr < ila (ko) hamyen. SEE ani 'la myen.
1. if it (be said to) be ... , if it were (the case) that ... . ¶Nay ka sāy 'la 'myen ne hanthey nal.e kalyen man If I were a bird I'd fly to you.
2. if it is (the case that) ... . ¶Ku kes i cēng-mal Kolye caki 'la 'myen, elma 'tun ci nāykeyss.ta If it is a genuine piece of Kolye porcelain, I will pay any price for it. Kup hako cwūng hanq īl ila 'myen pihayng-ki lul thako kkaci 'la to ka ya 'ci yo If it is urgent and important we will have to go by airplane, I guess. Na honca man uy mūncey 'la 'myen kantan haci yo It would be quite simple if it concerned only me. Ōlʰ-palun sayngkak ul kacin sālam ila 'myen nwukwu 'n tul ku puceng ey pūnkay haci anh.ul i?! Would any right-thinking person not be indignant at that injustice? Ceng i ne wa na wa ccum ila 'myen phyengsayng ssawulq īl i ēps.keyss.ken man If it is just between you and me, there will be nothing to quarrel about, but... . Caney hanthey 'la 'myen ilen māl to halq swu iss.ulq kes kath.kwun He may tell YOU such tales, too.
3. if (by that) you mean ... , if ... is (who/what is) meant. ¶Khun tosi ila 'myen kako siph.ci anh.e yo If it means a big city, I don't want to go. Ku haksayng ila 'myen kwaynchanh.e yo If it's that student you mean, he's OK. Onul ila 'myen, kaci mōs hap.nita If you mean today, I can't go.
ila 'myen se SEE 'myen se
ila 'n('), abbr.
1. < ila (ko) han / hanun that is (called) ... .
1a. ¶Kim ila 'n i / sālam a man called Kim.

Wenca-than ila 'n kes i ette han kes in ya What is an atomic bomb like? **I ilun-pa ca.yu 'la 'n kes un pāngcong ey cīnaci anh.nunta** This so-called liberty is mere license. **I penq īl un cal toye kanta 'tun i man tto silphay 'la 'n māl iya?!** You mean we've failed again, just when it was said to be going so nicely? **Ku ney nwukwu 'la 'n māl yo, ha mānh.un sālam ey ālq swu iss.e?** How will I know who they are (or: he is) is among so many people?

1b. $N_1 \sim N_1$. all the N, every N. ¶**Hawai ey se kwāil ila 'n kwāil un an mek.e pon kes i ēps.ta** There is no fruit in Hawaii that I have not eaten. **Wuli nala caypel tul un tōn ila 'n tōn ul tā mounta** The financial giants in our country rake in all the money.

2. < **ila ko han/hanun kes un** as for (the one that is called) ⋯ , [lit] = **un**. ¶**Tōngki 'la 'n kantan hata** As to motive, that is simple. **Wūnmyeng ila 'n cham yalus hata** Fate plays strange tricks. **Hānkwuk ila 'n kanan han nala 'ci man Ameylikha nun pū.yu han nala 'ta** Korea is a poor country, but America is a rich one. **Ku kyengchi uy alum-tawum ila 'n i-man ce-man han kes i ani 'ta** The scenery is lovely beyond all description. **Non ila 'n kong tul.in mankhum sōtuk i nani-kka yo** It's that you get out of a field according to the work you put into it. **Tōn ila 'n ēps.(ess.)ta ka to iss.ko iss.(ess.)ta ka to ēps.nun pep ita** The rich may get poor, the poor may get rich.

`ilan, cop retr mod (= `ilen). SEE `ila`n i.

ila 'na, abbr < **ila (ko) hana**.

1. (adversative) says that it is ⋯ but (anyway).

2. (? sentence-final adversative) it is ⋯ I guess [shows disinterest or distaste]. ¶**Kulay po.ye to ku key ku cwung ey se nun kacang naun chwuk ila 'na** They may not look like much but they're the best of the lot, I guess.

3. (FAMILIAR indic attent) do you (does one) say that it is ⋯ ?

ila 'ney, abbr < **ila (ko) haney**. 'I say it is' = I TELL you it is = it really is ⋯ ; it is ⋯ , you see. ¶**I ttang ey to incey n' pom ila 'ney; san kwa tūl ey n' kkoch i phiney** It is spring in this land, too, you know; flowers are blooming on the mountains and in the fields.

ilang, particle (after vowel **lang**).

1. [Seoul] = **sekken** and so on, and the like, and others. [Awkward for some speakers.]

2. = **hako** = **kwa/wa** (with, and). ¶**Na lang kath.i ka** (Dupont 213) Go with me. *melGwuy lang tolay lang mek.kwo* (?1544⁻ Akcang: Cheng san pyelkok) eating wild grapes and silvervine fruit. **Say moca lang kyōpok ilang sa wase** (= **wass.e**; Phyengan DIAL [Kim Yengpay 1984:94-5]) I went and bought a new hat and a school uniform.

3. SEE **-e lang**.

ilang ccum (iya), pcl + pcl (+ pcl).

1. [Seoul]= **sekken ccum**. ¶**Pok.nam-i lang ccum (iya) mūncey ka an toyci** The like of Pok.nam-i is no problem (= match)!

2. = **hako ccum** = **kwa/wa ccum**.

ilang cocha, pcl + pcl.

1. [Seoul] = **sekken cocha**. ¶**Hyeng nim ilang cocha kulen māl-ssum ul hasita 'ni** Even YOU talk like that!

2. = **hako cocha** = **kwa/wa cocha**. ¶**Poktong-i lang cocha sai ka napputa** is on bad terms even with Poktong-i. **Poktong-i lang cocha incey na hako nun nōlci anh.nunta** [awkward] Even Poktong-i and I have broken up.

ilang i, pcl + pcl = **hako ka** = **kwa/wa ka**. ¶**Swun-i lang Poktong-i lang i ku chayk ul sass.ci na nun saci anh.ess.ta** It is Swun-i and Poktong-i who bought that book, not I.

ilang ila to, pcl + cop var inf + pcl = **kwa/wa 'la to**. ¶**Poktong-i lang ila to nōlci kulay** You can play with Poktong-i at least, can't you?!

ilang iya, pcl + pcl.

1. [Seoul] = **sekken iya** [awkward].

2. = **kwa/wa ya**. ¶**Poktong-i lang iya sai ka cōh.ci yo** Surely he is on good terms with Poktong-i! **Swun-i lang Poktong-i lang iya ne lul yok hal lī ka iss.keyss.ni?** Swun-i and Poktong-i, of all people, wouldn't speak ill of you, would they?

~ **māl lo** [awkward]. (1) ¶**Poktong-i lang iya māl lo nappun ay tul ita** Poktong-i and his gang sure are bad kids. (2) ¶**Poktong-i lang iya māl lo ceng i thong hanta** It is with Poktong-i that I am in sympathy.

ilang khenyeng (pcl + pcl) = **sekken khenyeng**. ¶**Kwāil ilang (un) khenyeng ssal to sa oci mōs hayss.nun tey yo** I couldn't go buy any rice, even, to say nothing of fruit and all!

ilang kkaci, pcl + pcl.

1. [Seoul] = **sekken kkaci**. ¶**Na nun Swun-i lang Poktong-i lang kkaci koy lop.hiko siph.ci**

nun anh.ta I don't want to trouble even Swun-i and Poktong-i, too.
  2. = hako kkaci = kwa/wa kkaci.
ilang mace, pcl + pcl.
  1. = sekken mace. ¶Poktong-i lang mace tā teyliko kapsita Let's take along Poktong-i and all of them.
  2. = hako mace = kwa/wa mace. ¶Swun-i lang mace ne hako nōlci anh.umyen ne nun nōlq tongmu ka ēps.keyss.kwun a If even Swun-i won't play with you, why, you won't have any playmate! Swun-i lang mace sai ka nappe cyess.uni icey n' nwukwu hako nōllay Who you gonna play with now you broke up even with Swun-i?
ilang man, particle + particle.
  1. [Seoul] = sekken man. only ‥‥ and all (and others). ¶Poktong-i lang man mōllay hwumchye mek.ess.ci na nun an hwumchye mek.ess.ey yo It was just Poktong-i and them that robbed the cookie jar — I didn't.
  2. = hako man = kwa/wa man. ¶Swun-i lang Poktong-i lang man kass.ci wuli nun kaci anh.ess.ta Only Swun-i and Poktong-i went there, we didn't go. Poktong-i lang man kass.ess.ci Swun-i lang un an kass.ess.ta I went only with Poktong-i and not with Swun-i.
ilang pota (to), pcl + pcl (+ pcl).
  1. [Seoul] = sekken pota (to). ¶Kongchayk ilang pota (to) tōn ulo cwunun key nās.ci anh.ulq ka? Wouldn't it be better to give money rather than notebooks and so on?
  2. = hako pota = kwa/wa pota than with. ¶Poktong-i lang pota (to) Swun-i lang/hako nōnun key te caymi iss.ta It's more fun to play with Swun-i than with Poktong-i.
ilang puthe, particle + particle.
  1. [Seoul] = sekken puthe. ¶Kongchayk ilang puthe mence nona cwupsita Let's pass things out starting with the notebooks and so on.
  2. = hako puthe = kwa/wa puthe
ilang to, pcl + pcl = hako to = kwa/wa to. ¶Poktong-i lang to kath.i nōlmyen cōh.ci anh.un ya Wouldn't it be nice to play with Poktong-i and his friends, too? Swun-i lang Poktong-i lang to tā wass.ta Swun-i and Poktong-i, they are both here.
ilang tul, pcl + pcl. ¶Mo nāyki lang tul ppalli ppalli hay la You fellows hurry up with the transplanting of the rice seedlings and all.
ilang ul, particle + particle.
  1. [Seoul] = sekken ul. ¶I uyca lang chayk-sang ilang ul tā et' ey 'ta neh.e twulq ka Where do all these chairs and desks go? ¶Poktong-i lang ul et' ey teyliko kass.umyen cōh.ulq ka Where should I take Poktong-i and the other kids?
  2. = hako puthe = kwa/wa puthe
ilang un khenyeng, pcl + pcl + pcl. SEE ilang khenyeng.
ilang uy, pcl + pcl = hako uy = kwa/wa uy. ¶Swun-i lang Poktong-i lang uy cip ey se tul yātan ici wuli cip ey se n' āmu kekceng anh.nunta They are making a fuss at Swun-i's and Poktong-i's but all is quiet at my house.
ila 'ni, abbr < ila ko hani.
  1. (hani sequential). ¶Kim kwun ila 'ni enu Kim kwun māl in ya You said it was young Mr Kim but just which young Mr Kim do you mean? Pyek.hwa 'la 'ni musun pyek.hwa māl in ya By murals, what kind of murals do you mean? Ney wēn ila 'ni kulem um.ak-hoy ey kaca Since it is what you want to do, then, all right let's go to the concert. Ceng Mongcwu sensayng ila 'ni Phoun māl-ssum ici yo By Ceng Mongcwu I wonder if you are referring to Phoun. Sencwuk-kyo 'la 'ni musun ttus in ya What is the meaning of (calling it) "Noble-Bamboo Bridge"?
  2. (hani question) [LIVELY REALIZATION]. ¶A, pelsse ōceng ila 'ni? Can it be (time that it is) noon already? = Why, it is noon already! Pol man ila 'ni; ki ka mak.hin cāngkwan itun tey You say "worth a look" when it was a breathtaking sight! Kkweng ul cap.nun key māy 'la 'ni Why, it's a falcon that is catching the pheasants!
˙ila˙n i, cop retr mod + postmod. ¶˙na y ˙a˙lay s ne 'y ˙˙pe˙t ila˙n i (1447 Sek 6:19b) I was your friend in former days. ˙wuli ˙two SA-LA-SSYWU ˙TTAY-NGWANG s PWU-ZIN tol˙h ila˙n i (1459 Wel 8:100a) we too were wives of the king of the land of teak trees.
ila 'nta, abbr < ila (ko) hanta. 'I say that it is' = I TELL you it is = it really is ‥‥ ; it is ‥‥ , you see. ¶Ce palun phyen ey poinun ki nun Yengkwuk tāysa-kwan ki 'la 'nta The flag you can see over on the right is the flag of the British Embassy, you see. ALSO 'they say ‥‥ '.

ila 'nun [ABBR ila 'n(')].
1. abbr < ila (ko) hanun that is (called) ... .
1a. ¶**Kim ila 'nun i/sālam** a man named Kim. **Chwunhyang ila 'nun kīsayng uy ttal i iss.ess.ta** There was a kisayng's daughter called Spring Fragrance.
1b. ¶**Sang ila 'nun sang i tā ku sēnswu eykey kass.ta** The prizes all went to that player.
? 2. quasi-pcl, abbr < ila (ko) hanun kes un. as for (the one that is called) ... ; [lit] = un. ¶**Pyek.hwa 'la 'n(un) pyek ey 'ta kūlin kūlim ita** Murals are pictures painted on walls.
ila 'o, abbr < ila (ko) hao. 'I say it is' = I TELL you it is = it really is ...; it is ..., you see.
ila 'p.nita, abbr < ila (ko) hap.nita. 'I say it is' = I TELL you it is = it really is ... ; it is ... , you see.
ila 'psiko, abbr < ila (ko) haopsiko. [IRONICAL] saying/thinking/feeling that it is ... . ¶**Cey ka sacang ila 'psiko ppop-nāynta** He gets all puffed up about being boss of the company.
ila s, cop indic assert + particle. SEE *s* (15b).
ila se, cop var inf + pcl [lit] = ie se. CF *ila 'sye*.
1. it is ... and so. ¶**Hak.kyo sensayng ila (se) cemcanh.ta** He is well-mannered because he is a school teacher.
2. indeed, possibly, daring, audaciously, by any audacity. ¶**Nwukwu (i)la se (→ nwi 'la se) na lul ikil i yo** Who would dare to best me?!
ila siph.ta SEE siph.ta
i 'la[´]s-ongi 'ta. SEE -*u'l i 'la[´]s-ongi 'ta*.
i 'las ta, copula retr emotive indicative assertive. LCT cites 1677 Pak-cwung. SEE -*u'l i 'las ta*; -*tas ta*.
ila 'sye, cop var inf + pcl; replaces **iye 'sye*.
1. = ila se.
2. = ey se from. ¶*"amwo 'to 'la 'sye won 'twong mwo'lo'tesi'n i* (1459 Wel 2:25b) she didn't know just what place it had come from (*'la = [i]la*).
3. used as subject marker (substituting for *i*).
¶*'PPALQ-TTYEY 'la 'sye QA-NA-'LYWULQ-'i to 'lye nil'Gwo'toy* (1459 Wel 7:1b) Bhadrika told Aniruddha as follows ... . *tik.wel ila 'sye mwo[´]tol "salom 'oy 'swon-toy alGwoy 'la* (1518 ¹Ye-yak 37b = p.74) let the commissioner of traditional remedies inform those who gather. *azo 'la azo nwuuy 'la sye hyeng kwa mos nwuuy lul skwucicu.m ye n'* (1656 Kyengmin 11b) if the younger brother or sister reproves the older brother or sister. *sywul mekci macya the.n i sywul ila sye ce y stolwon ta* we urged ourselves not to drink, but did the wine of itself go along with that? (1876 Kakok 43, taken from 1728 Cheng-tay [LCT 614b with the Hankul spellings *swul-i-la-sye* and *sta-lwon-ta*]).
ila 'ta, abbr < ila (ko) hata
ila 'tey, abbr < ila (ko) hatey
ila 'ti, abbr < ila (ko) hati
ila to < *ila 'two*, cop var inf + pcl; usually replaces ie to.
1. even if (it be). ¶**Na nun mōs kakeyss.uni ne 'la to kass.ta** one la I can't go, but you had better go even without me. **Kkwum ey 'la to poko ciko** I wish I could see you if only in a dream. **Ne ani 'la to ku īl ul halq sālam i iss.ta** There are people besides you who can do the job. **Talun kes i ēps.umyen i kes ila to cōh.ta** This will do if you have no other.
¶*me'li '´m ye 'nwu.n i'm ye 'swon-'pa.l i'm ye mwo'm ay s kwo'ki 'la 'two "pi'non "salo'm ol cwu'l i 'Ge'n i* (1447 Sek 9:13a) to the person who is begging he will give his head, his eyes, his hands and feet, even the flesh on his body.
2. just, (or the) like (= ina); or even; any, some. ¶**Kulenq īl ila to hasimyen cōh.keyss.ey yo** I wish you'd just do that. **Mikwuk ey kalye 'myen Yenge 'la to paywe ya hao** If you're going to America you will have to learn some English. **Hapsung ila to thako kaca** Let's just take a jitney. **Nwukwu wa mannalq yaksok ila to iss.ˢup.nikka** Do you have some kind of appointment (to keep)? **Yenghwa 'la to polq ka yo?** Let's go see a movie or something, OK?. **Musun cōh.unq yenghwa 'la to iss.nun ka yo?** Are there any good movies (on/playing)? (M 1:2:131). **Cha 'la to masikeyss.ˢup.nikka?** How about some tea? − This shows "a lack of finality, forthrightness, or enthusiasm about one's choice" (M 1:1:250).
3. = ila ko to. ¶*"SYWOW KKWU-TTAM 'i KAM-'CYA NGWEN 'ey "sa'losil 'ss oy KAM-'CYA "SSI 'la 'two 'ho'te.n i ''la* (1459 Wel 1:8ab) Gautama the Lesser was also called Sugarcane Sire (Ikṣvāku) because he lived in a sugarcane garden. *QA-NYWUW-LWUW-TTWUW 'yla 'two 'ho'no.n i ''la* (1447 Sek 13:2a) [Anuruddha = Aniruddha] is also called ?Anuruddhu.
ila 'toy, abbr < ila (ko) hatoy

ila tul, cop + pcl. ¶**Tāyhak ul na-on sālam ila (se) tul māl hanun key eti 'n ka talle** There is something different about the way they talk since they got out of college.
ila 'tula, abbr < ila (ko) hatula
ila 'tun, abbr < ila (ko) hatun. ~ ka = ina (or)
ila 'tun ci, abbr < ila (ko) hatun ci. (the question) whether it be said to be. ¶**So 'la 'tun ci kāy 'la 'tun ci (kan ey) nun cip ey se kilunun cimsung ita** Animals such as cows and dogs are domestic animals. **Pang uy cangchi 'la 'tun ci pun.wiki 'la 'tun ci (kan ey), kokup ita** Whether (you speak of) the fixtures of the room, or the atmosphere, it is all very high-class. **Ku sāy ilum i mues ila 'tun ci ic.e pelyess.ta** I forgot what the bird is called.
˙**ila two**, cop var inf + pcl. This replaces *˙iye ˙two. SEE **ila to**.
˙**ila wa**, pcl (replacing earlier ᵁ/ola˙wa); yla˙wa after vowel, la˙wa (identical with earlier la˙wa from ᵁ/ola˙wa) after y or l. than (= **pota**). ¶**talon kowol˙h i ˙˙nyey s kowol˙h ilawa ˙˙tywothwo˙ta** (1481 Twusi 8:35a) the other towns are nicer than the [war-torn] home town of earlier days. **kutuy s cip s ˙hoyn [˙˙NGWAN] s pi.ch i se˙li ˙[G]wa ˙˙nwu˙n ila˙wa teu˙n i** (1481 Twusi 16:60a) the color of your family's bowl is whiter than the frost and the snow. ˙**pi.ch i ˙˙tywo˙ho˙n i ˙poy ˙˙salo˙m oy ˙spa.m ila˙wa teu˙kwo** (1481 Twusi 20:9b) they have such good color, the pears surpass the cheeks of a person. ˙**pwoksyeng s kwo˙c oy pul˙kwo.m i [˙˙KUM] ˙ila˙wa te˙wo.m ol na ˙y [PWUN] ˙ey s kes ˙˙sam˙ti ˙˙mwot ho˙kwo petul s kayya˙ci swowo˙m i˙la˙wa hoyywo˙m ol ko˙cang muy˙nwola** (1481 Twusi 23:23a) the red of the peach blossoms is deeper than that of brocade but I cannot make it my own, and I hate it that the willow branches are whiter than cotton.
NOTE: Perhaps = ˙i˙la ˙[G]wa < *˙i˙la kol˙Wa. But if so, what about the earlier form ˙ᵁ/ola˙wa?
ila(y), [N Kyengsang DIAL] = ita (cop indic assert). ¶**Ku key sālam ila(y)** That is a person. **Ku key cip i a(y)i 'la(y)** That is not a house. (Choy Myengok 1979:10.)
ilay, vi inf < ileta; adj inf < ileh.ta. LIGHT ↔ yolay.
1. doing this way, saying this; being this way.
2. does / says this; is this way [INTIMATE].
3. (= ilay se) does this way and (so), says this and (so); is this way and (so) = for this reason, on this account, (and) so.
īlay < ˙˙I-LOY, n, postn, postmod. (ever) since, after; during the past (time).
1. postnoun. ¶**Sēycong īlay lo** from (King) Seycong's time on. **I pen kyewul un ī-sip nyenq īlay uy chwuwi (i)ta** This winter is the coldest in twenty years.
2. postmodifier [semi-lit]. ¶**Ku i nun Sewul ey onq īlay** (= on hwū cwūk) **wuli cip ey se sālko iss.ta** He has been living at our house ever since he came to Seoul. **Ku nun sil.¹yen hanq īlay pam-nac cwuk.nun i sānun i yātan iey yo** Since his disappointment in love he is constantly talking about committing suicide. **Sewul kanq īlay lo Kim chemci nun caymi lul ponun mo.yang ulo tomuci cip ey nun sosik han cang to an ponay wass.ta** Since going to Seoul Mr Kim seems to be having too much fun to write a single letter home.
ila 'y, abbr < ila (ko) hay. ¶**Ku uy ilum un Tolq-soy 'la 'y** His name is said to be Tolssoy.
ila ya < ila (y)a (< *˙ila˙za), cop var inf + pcl. 1. [lit] = (ie) ya only if it be, unless it be. ~ **man** SAME.
1a. ¶**Ne 'la ya nung hi ku īl ul hakeyss.ta** It is YOU that can do the job. **Tal un pam ey 'la ya pich i nanta** The moon shines only at night (= It has to be night for the moon to shine). **Ney ka siin ila ya ku uy salang ul pat.ul i 'la** Unless you are a poet, how can you hope to win her love? **Nwukwu 'tun ci pyēngsin i ani 'la ya hapkyek i toynta** Anybody who is able-bodied (unhandicapped) will be qualified.
1b. SEE -ci 2b.
2. = **ila 'y ya** (< ila ko hay ya) only if it be (said to be).
ila 'y la, abbr < ila (ko) hay la
ila yo, cop var inf + pcl. [DIAL] = iey yo.
ila 'y se, abbr < ila (ko) hay se. ¶**Cal nan sālam ila 'y se nay ka ku lul salang hanun kes i ani 'ta** It is not because he is a handsome man that I love him.
~ **ya**. ¶**I kes i mān-wen echi 'la 'y se ya toyl māl ip.nikka?** Are you kidding to say that this is worth ten thousand wen?
ilayss-, 1. ilayss-, past < ileh.ta, < ileta.
2. **ila 'yss-**, abbr < ila (ko) hayss-.
ilay ya, [var] = ila ya (= ie ya). (if) only (it be).

ila 'y ya, abbr < ila (ko) hay ya. if only it be said (to be). ¶Ku lul āykwuk-ca 'la 'y ya olh.ci anh.un ka? Shouldn't one call him a patriot?
ila 'y yo, abbr < ila (ko) hay yo
`ila `za > ila (y)a > ila ya, cop var inf + pcl. ¶ ˙SYANG ˙i ˙kwot ˙SYANG a˙ni 'la ˙za CIN i towoyno˙n i 'la ˙hota ˙ka ... (1482 Kum-sam 3:12a) just when appearance is not appearance it becomes reality. mwo˙lwomay ˙i ˙LYANG ˙ay ne˙mun ¨salo˙m ila ˙za ˙woltha (1482 Kum-sam 3:14b) to be right they must be people who surpass in their capacity. ¨HHA-KON ˙on mwo˙lwo˙may ¨sey˙h ila ˙za ho˙l i ˙' ˙Gwo ... (1459 Wel 14:31b) the lower roots must be three in number and ... . SEE a˙ni 'la ˙za. ¹Itwu phonograms "i-la-sa".
ilq ci, cop prosp mod + postmod
ilq cwul, cop prosp mod + postmod
ile < ˙i˙le, defective infinitive. like this, so. LIGHT yole. CF kule, cele, ette, āmule.
  1. vni. ~ hanta = ilenta does/says this way.
  2. adj-n. ~ hata = ileh.ta is this way. ¶ile haci man is just so-so.
i˙le, inf < ¨i[l]˙ta becomes; is formed / made; is achieved. ¶ ¨nay˙h i i˙le palo˙l ay ˙kano˙n i (1445 ¹Yong 2) it becomes a stream and goes into the sea. KWONG-˙TUK ˙i i˙le tangtangi pwu¨thye y towoy˙l i 'le˙la (1447 Sek 19:34a) the virtue achievement was such that naturally he was to become a Buddha. i˙le isilq ce˙k un ˙TTYWU ˙KEP ˙i˙la (1459 Wel 1:47a) the time when it is all formed is the kalpa of existence (vivarta kalpa).
  ~ ˙za (pcl). ¶ ˙i ˙SYENG ˙i twu˙lye˙i i˙le ˙za e˙lwu SAM-HHYEN ˙ul ¨ken˙ney ptwuy˙ye ˙SSIP-˙SYENG ˙ey ˙tull i ˙'˙la (1462 ¹Nung 8:40a) only if there is accomplishment of this quality all around will one be able to jump past the three kinds of sage (bhadra) and enter the tenth rank of bodhisattva.
˙ile- cop retr (lenited from ˙i-te-). SEE ˙ile˙la, ˙ile˙n i, ˙ile˙n i ˙'˙la, ˙ilen˙t un, ˙ilesi-. CF ˙ila-.
ile cele SEE ile ile / cele
ileh.key, adj adverbative < ileh.ta. (so that it is) this way, like this, so; to this extent, this (so) much. ¶ileh.key sayngkak hay pomyen viewed / considered in this light. ileh.key toynq īsang ey nun since it has come to this. Īl i ileh.key toylq cwul nwu ka al.ess.na! Who would expect things to come to this! Ileh.key chwuwun nal-ssi nun cheum ita I have never seen such cold weather as this. Ileh.key hay la! Do it this way (like this). Ileh.key wā cwusye se, komapsup.nita Thank you for coming here like this (this way).
  ~ to (pcl). ¶Ileh.key to pap ey tōl i mānh.e se ya pap ul mek.um i ani 'la tōn ul ssip.nun kes kath.ta With all these grits in the rice it is like chewing on grits rather than eating rice.
  ~ ya (pcl). ¶Ileh.key ya hayss.keyss.na! You couldn't have done it this way!
˙i˙le hota, bnd adv + aux adj. is this way (like this). ABBR ˙i˙le tha. ¶ ¨nyey ˙two ˙i˙le ˙hota˙la (1459 Wel 7:14b) in olden days too it was this way. ˙ile ˙thu˙s ˙i [< ˙ho-˙tu˙s ˙i] kwo˙thye towoy˙sya˙m i ¨mwot nilo ¨hyey˙l i 'le˙la (1459 Wel 1:21a) thus it seemed one could not very well think he would become transformed. ˙ile ˙thus [< ˙ho-tus] hon ˙HWA ˙thi e˙lyeWun ˙KANG-˙KKANG hon ¨CCWOY-¨KWO ˙CYWUNG-SOYNG ol ˙TTWO-˙THWALQ ˙hoke˙tun (1459 Wel 21:34ab) when one emancipates this sort of hard-core sinners who are difficult to change ... . ˙ile ˙thi a˙ni tha ˙hwom ˙two (1482 Kum-sam 2:41b) to say that it is not this way, too, ...
ileh.ta, adj -(H)- (inf ilay), abbr < ile hata is this way.
ileh.ta celeh.ta, phrasal adv (adj transferentive iterated). (says) this or that. ¶ ~ māl hata says things, carps, complains, raises objection(s), citicizes. ~ māl halq kes ēps.i without saying a word, with no further ado, with good grace, without raising / voicing / offering objections, uncritically. Ku nun ileh.ta celeh.ta nam hanthey se māl ul tul.ulq īl i ēps.ta He is not open to criticism. Cikum wā se ileh.ta celeh.ta māl hanta 'yss.ca, sō.yong i ēps.ta It is too late now to make a(ny) fuss about it. Ileh.ta celeh.ta māl haci mālko, hala 'nun tay lo hay la Stop fussing and do what you are told.
ileh.tun (ci) celeh.tun (ci), cpd adv = adj retr mod (+ postmod) iterated. whether thus or so, at any rate, in any case/event, anyhow, anyway.
ileh-tus 'i, der adv. like this (= ilen tus 'i).
ile ile / cele hata, adj-n. is so and so, is such and such. ¶ile ile han sālam such and such a person. ile cele hanq ¹īyu lo for such and such reasons. CF ili ili.

ilek celek, cpd adverb [< ile + -k, cele + -k].
  1. somehow or other, one way or another.
¶ ~ **sal.e kata** ekes out a living, manages to keep the pot boiling. ~ **tāy-hak.kyo lul col.ep hata** somehow or other manages to get through college. **Ilek celek yelq si ka toyess.e(y) yo** It somehow got to be ten o'clock.
  2. nearly, about, almost, some. ¶ ~ **ī-nyenq tong-an** for about two years. **Ku ka Mikwuk kan ci ilek celek sip-nyen i toyess.ta** It has been some ten years or so since he went off to America. **Cipung ul kochinun tey ilek celek ō-man wen i tul.ess.ta** (What with one thing and another) it cost me some fifty thousand **wen** to repair the roof.
ile-khwung cele-khwung, cpd adverb. (like) this and (like) that.
ile kule, cpd adv. this way and that, somehow or other.
ilel(q), prospective modifier:
  1. < adj **ileh.ta** (… that is) to be like this.
  2. < vi **ileta** (… that is) to do/say (or be done/said) like this.
ilela [DIAL, lit] = **itula** (copula retr assertive) ˙ile˙la, cop retr assert. ¶ ˙LYWUK-SO ˙oy ˙mwu˙l i SAM-˙QUK ˙MEN ˙ile˙la (1447 Sek 6:28a) the hordes of the Six Tīrthikas were 300 million (in number). SEE ˙yle˙la, ˙le˙la.
ilelq swulok ey [colloq] = **ilelq swulok**
ilel wu hata, adj prosp mod + postmod adj-n. [Usually spelled **ilelwu.**] It seems to be this way, it is like this (one), it is similar to this.
ilen₁, adj mod < **ileh.ta.** like this, such, this sort of. ¶ ~ **ko lo** for this reason. ~ **ttay ey** at a time like this, at such a time. ~**q īl** such a thing, a thing of this sort. ~ **tay lo** (such) as it is; anyway. ~ **cuk** since it has come to this, such being the case. **Cek.un tōn ina, ilen tay lo pat.e cwusipsio** It is just a small amount of money, but please take what there is, anyway.
ilen₂, vi mod < **ileta.** which/who has done/said (or been done/said) this way (like this).
ilen₃, interj. Oh dear! Goodness! Oh my! What a surprise! Indeed! Well well! My my! (shows sudden realization, surprise). ¶**Ilen, wūsan ul an kaciko wass.kwun** Oh dear, I forgot to bring my umbrella with me. CF **kulen, celen.**
˙ilen, cop retr mod (= ˙ilan). SEE ˙ile˙n i, ˙ilen ˙t un, ˙ile.n ywo.
˙ile ˙n, abbr < ˙i˙le hon. such … , … of this sort.
¶ ˙ile ˙n ¨salom ˙tol˙h ol (1447 Sek 13:57b) such people. ˙ile ˙n KWANG-MYENG ˙ul (1447 Sek 13:25b) such light. ˙ile ˙n e˙lin ¨salo˙m i (1459 Wel 8:69b) stupid people of this sort. ˙ile ˙n ¨SSYWUW-¨KHWO ˙lol (1459 Wel 21:219b) such hardship.
~ ˙t o˙lwo for this reason. ¶ ˙i˙le ˙n ˙t olwo ˙PEP-HHWA-˙HHWOY ˙SSYANG ˙ay ta˙si ˙TTI-˙WUY s ¨ma˙l i ¨ep˙susi˙kwo (1462 ¹Nung 1:18b) there was thus no more talk of location for the Lotus doctrine study group. ˙ile ˙n ˙t o˙lwo ci˙zwul ˙tt i a˙ni ˙.n i ˙˙la (1463 Pep se:12a) for this reason I will not create one [here]. ˙ile ˙n ˙t olwo ke˙mu.m ye ˙hoyywo˙m ol non˙hwo.n i ˙˙la (1481 Twusi 7:27a) hence distinguished being black and (being) white. ˙ile ˙n ˙t olwo ˙TTAY-˙KAK SYEN ˙i˙la s il˙hwu.m i natho˙si.n i ˙˙la (1482 Kum-sam 2:15b) thus there appeared the name "Sage of the Great Awakening".
ilena celena, cpd adv (adj advers + adj advers). at any rate, in any case/event, anyhow, anyway. ¶**Ilena celena hay ponun key cōh.ta** At all events, you had better try.
ileng celeng, cpd adv = **ilek celek** somehow or other.
ileni, 1. sequential < **ileta** (abbr < **ile hani**).
  2. [DIAL, lit] = **ituni, itun i.** ¶**Īcen ey nun i uysa eykey wā se cīnchal pat.un i nun Cosenq sālam ppun ileni cuk.kum** [= **cikum**] **un se.yangq sālam to wā se cīnchal ul pat.nunta** (1936 Roth 497) Before it was only Koreans who came to consult this doctor but now westerners come, too.
˙ile˙n i, retr mod + postmod. ¶ ˙SYA-˙NGWUY ˙KWUYK ¨salo˙m i ˙SSIP-˙PALQ ˙QUK ˙ile˙n i (1447 Sek 6:28a) the people of the state of Śrāvastī were 1800 million (in number). KKWU-SO-LA ¨TYANG-¨CYA y ˙khuy ¨sek ˙ca˙h ile˙n i (1447 Sek 6:44a) Ghoṣira the rich man was three ˙cah tall. SEE ˙yle˙n i, ˙le˙n i.
ileni celeni, compound adverb (adj sequential + adj sequential). this or that; for some reason or other. ¶ ~ **māl halq kes ēps.i** without saying this or that, without much ado, without useless objection, with good grace. ¶ ~ **māl hata** says things, raises objection(s), makes complaints.
˙ile˙n i ˙˙la, cop retr mod + postmod + cop indic assertive. ¶ ¨KHWONG-¨CO s ¨TTYEY-¨CO mol˙ko˙n i ˙yel˙h ile˙n i ˙˙la (1463 Pep 1:32a) the bright disciples of Confucius were ten (in number).

˙ilen ˙t un, cop retr mod + postmod + pcl.
¶ ˙TTWONG-SAN i nil˙Gwo˙toy NGAM-TTWUW ˙[G]wos a˙ni ˙len ˙t un ˙TUK-SAN s ˙HALQ ˙ol ¨mwot ¨al˙l i ˙las˙ta ˙ho.ya˙nol (?1468⁻ Mong 32ab) Dòng Shān said "If it had not been for Yán Tóu I would not have known of the thirst of Dé Shān".
˙ile˙n ywo, cop retr modifier + postmod. ¶ ¨nyey ye˙huyywo˙m on ˙i e˙tuy ˙le˙n ywo (1481 Twusi 21:30a) the parting of long ago, where was this?
īl ēps.ta, cpd qvi (n + qvi). 1. there is no need for, has no use for, is unwanted.
2. [DIAL] OK, all right, no problem / sweat.
˙i˙lesi-, cop retr hon (= ˙isi˙le-)
˙i˙lesi˙n i, cop retr honorific mod + postmod.
¶pwuthye s ˙na˙hi syel˙hun ¨twul.h i˙lesi˙n i (1447 Sek 6:1a) Buddha's age was thirty-two.
˙i˙lesi˙ta, cop retr honorific indicative assertive.
¶SSYENG-˙PPWULQ ˙hosin il˙hwu˙m i ZYEN-TUNG ˙i˙lesi˙ta (1447 Sek 13:35b) the name under which he became a Buddha was the dīpamkara Buddha. KUM-˙SOYK mwo˙ya˙h i ˙to' ¨nim s KWANG ˙i˙lesi˙ta (1459 Wel 2:51b) the gold was the light of the moon. SEE -u˙l i ˙lesi˙ta.
ileta, vi (inf ilay), abbr < ile hata does / says / thinks this way. CF ili (ha)ta.
iley, 1. FAMILIAR copula retr assertive (= itey).
¶Wuli emeni ka kulesinun tey ¹Yongsan taum cengke-cang i palo Sewul iley My mother said Seoul was the station right after Yongsan.
2. [DIAL] = ilay, abbr < ila (ko) hay.
iley tul, FAMILIAR copula retr assertive + pcl.
¶Sewul se on sālam iley (tul) They are people who have come from Seoul.
¨ilGe˙nul (= *¨ilGe˙nol) = ¨ilGe˙nul. ¶ci˙p i ¨ilGe˙nol ˙hoyn ˙ptwuy lwo ni˙ywu˙n i (1481 Twusi 7:1a) there was built a house but it was shaded by white cogon-grass thatching.
¨ilGe˙nul, lit concessive < vi ¨i[l]˙ta (becomes).
¶[SYEY-CYENG] ˙ey [KWONG] ˙i ¨ilGe˙nul (1445 ¹Yong 41) in the western invasion good results were accomplished.
¨il˙Gesi˙nol, hon lit concessive < ¨i[l]˙ta.
¶[HYWENG] k ˙ptu˙t i ¨il˙Gesi˙nol (1445 ¹Yong 8) the older brother's will was accomplished.
¨ilGe˙tun, provisional < vi ¨i[l]˙ta (becomes).
¶ ˙i ¨SYANG ¨ilGe˙tun (1459 Wel 8:26a) if this thought is formed.
¨il˙Gey, adverbative < vi ¨i[l]˙ta (becomes).
¶te˙wu˙m ol ¨il˙Gey hol ˙ss i˙n i (1462 ¹Nung 3:12b) it makes the heat come into being.
¨il˙Guy, var of ¨il˙Gey, adverbative < ¨i[l]˙ta (becomes). ¶ NGWEN ˙honwon ¨i˙l ol ¨ta ¨il˙Guy ˙hwo˙l i '-ngi '˙ta (1447 Sek 9:40b) I will make all you desire come true.
¨ilGwa˙tye, vi ¨i[l]˙ta (becomes) + -˙kwa˙tye.
¶ ¨ta spol˙li ¨ilGwa˙tye ˙hosi˙nwon cyen˙cho ˙y˙la (1463 Pep 5:169b) it is because everybody wants to become one [= a Buddha] fast.
¨il˙Gwo, gerund < vi ¨i[l]˙ta (becomes). ¶ ··· ˙i ˙CHO-˙TTYEY ˙lwo ¨il˙Gwo (1459 Wel 1:39a) ··· becomes secondary and ... .
ili < ˙i˙li, adv. LIGHT yoli. CF yeki; kuli, celi.
1. (= ileh.key, i-taci) in this way, like this, so. ¶ ˙LYWUK-SO y ˙i˙li niluno˙n i (1447 Sek 6:26b) the Six Tīrthikas say this. SSIN-˙LUK ˙i ˙i[˙]li ¨seysil ˙ss oy (1449 Kok 40) since the divine power is this strong ... .
2. (= ~ lo) this way, this direction, here.
¶Ili osipsio This way, please (= Please come this way). Ili anc.e la Sit here. Pipimq-pap un ili cwusey yo − ¹nāyngmyen un celi tuli(si)ko yo The fried rice here, waiter − and the cold noodles there, please.
ili → il i
il i, 1. cop prosp modifier + noun. 2. = il ya
ili celi SEE ili ili (2)
ili hata, vni = ile hata does / says like this.
ili ili, cpd (iterated) adv. 1. so and so, such and such. ¶sālam eykey ~ hala ko māl hata tells a person to do such and such.
2. = ili celi, cpd adv. this way and that, here and there, all about. ¶ ~ tol.a tanita wanders / roams/rambles about, loafs around. ~ pang an ey sinmun ul nel.e noh.ta litters a room with newspapers. chayk ul ~ chac.ta looks high and low for a book.
ili-khwung celi-khwung, cpd adv = ile-khwung cele-khwung
ilikka, copula prospective attentive
˙ili-˙kwom, adv + suf. ¶ ˙ili-˙kwom ¨SYWUY-COY ˙hwo˙m ol ye˙tulp pen ho˙m ye n' (1459 Wel 1: 49b) when there were eight floods in this way.
˙i.l i '˙la, cop prosp mod + postmod + cop indic attent. (it's that) it will be; (it's that) it is.
¶HE-KHWONG ˙ay s kwo˙c i.l i '˙la (1482 Kumsam 2:73b) it will be a blossom in the void.
ili lo, adv + pcl = ili (this way, here). ¶Ku ka way ili lo olq ka Why is he coming this way? ABBR il' lo.

ilini, copula prospective sequential `i.l i ˙'n i`, cop prosp mod + postmodifier + cop mod + postmod. ¶ `˙hota ˙ka ZYE-LOY 'ysin ˙t ay n' ZYE-LOY y ho˙ma ˙i SSYANG ˙isil s oy ¨NGWO- ˙QUM ˙two ˙stwo pan˙toki SSYANG ˙i.l i ˙'n i` (1465 Wen 1:1:1:63a) if it is the tathāgata, the tathāgata is already constant, therefore the five constituents (pañca-skandha) must, moreover, be constant too.

ilinila, ilinita, cop prosp literary indic assertive

ilila, ilita, cop prospective indicative assertive

ili 'ta, abbr < ili hata does / says / thinks this way. SYN ileta. CF kuli 'ta, celi 'ta.

ili 'ta (ka), abbr < ili hata (ka) (transferentive). ~ tul. ¶ Ili 'ta ka tul ecci toyca 'nun kes in ya What is to become of us if we let things go on like this?

ili to, adv + pcl. ¶ Ili to cal hana! They do this so well!

`˙i˙li-˙to˙lwok`, adv (< `˙i˙li [˙ho]˙to˙lwok`). to this extent (1459 Wel 8:101a). CF `ku˙li-two˙lwok, tye˙li-˙two˙lwok`.

il i tul, 1. cop prosp mod + postmod + pcl = il ya tul. 2. cop prosp mod + quasi-free n + pcl.

? `i˙li-˙Wi`, adverb. like this, to this extent (LCT, NKW). But this is probably a mistaken reading due to worn type in an edition later than that reproduced by Sekang University in 1972, where the same passage (1459 Wel 2:36b) has `e˙lye˙Wi` 'with difficulty', making better sense in the context. (If the other reading were correct the accent should have been * `˙i˙li˙Wi`.) We can therefore disregard the connection LCT made between this word and the much later *istoypi* (?1855 ¹Nokyey; LCT 614a), which he takes as meaning 'up to this time'.

ilq ka, cop prosp mod + postmod. ¶ Ku ka oci anh.uni, wēyn sēym ilq ka I wonder why he doesn't come!

ilq ka tul, cop prosp mod + postmod

ilq ka yo, cop prospective mod + postmodifier + pcl. ¶ Kulen sāqken i sinmun ey mace naci anh.ess.uni wēynq īl ilq ka yo How come such an incident isn't even in the papers?

ilq ke l', abbr < ilq kes ul

ilq kes, copula prosp modifier + n (postmod). ¶ Cwūngyo hanq īl ilq kes kath.umyen kot ku sālam hanthey allisey yo If it seems to be an important matter, let him know right away. Ilchak un wuli Hānkwuk sēnswu ilq kes ulo pointa It appears that one of our Korean athletes will take first place.

ilq key, abbr.
1. < ilq kes ie / ia
2. < ilq kes i, ilq kes i-. ~ 'ci, ~ 'na, ~ 'ney, ~ 'ni, ~ 'ta, ~ 'la, ~ ya; yo (polite pcl; < io). Pullyang-ca 'lq key 'ta I think he's a bum.

ilkhwuta [DIAL] = ileh.key (māl) hata. Mkk 1960:3:34.

ilq ko, cop prosp mod + postmod. ¶ Ku kes i mues ilq ko What might that be?

`¨ill ¨ (+ ˙i` postmod) < *`i˙l[u]l(q)`, prosp mod < `¨i[l]˙ta` (becomes). ¶ `[CHAM-¨KHWUW] i ¨man ˙ho˙ya [¨CCWOY] ho˙ma ¨ill i ˙le˙n i` (1445 ¹Yong 123) there were many slanderous mouths and his guilt had been virtually decided.

`˙il˙lan (?= ˙i ˙lan` with conflated liquid), n + pcl. ¶ `˙il˙lan ¨ne y kwu˙thuy˙ye nilu˙ti ¨mal˙la` (?1517⁻ Pak 1:17a) this you don't have to say. `˙il˙lan ¨ne y kunsim ¨mal˙la` (?1517⁻ Pak 1: 47a) this, don't worry about it.

illang [colloq] = imyen

`˙illa˙wa (?= ˙i ˙lla˙wa` with conflated liquid) < `˙i + ˙ila˙wa.` than this (= i pota). ¶ `salo.m i illawa [¨SSIM] hwo.m i is.no.n i` (1632 Twusi-cwung 2:70a) people are sometimes more extreme than this.

illey [DIAL] = ikeyss.ta

il lī, cop prosp mod + postmod. SEE -ul lī. ¶ Ku māl i kēcis māl il lī ka ēps.ta That couldn't be a lie.

il' lo, abbr < ili lo.

`˙il˙lwo (?= ˙i ˙lwo` with conflated liquid) = i lo as / with / by this. ¶ `˙il˙lwo ¨hyey˙ye ˙pwoken ˙t ey n'` (1447 Sek 6:6a) when one considers it as this ... . `˙SYEK-KA ¨SSI ˙il[˙]lwo ˙nasi˙n i` (1449 Kok 10) with this, Lord Śakya(muni) was born. *illwo* (1887 Scott 29) = i llo by this. CF `kul˙lwo, ˙tyel˙lwo`. SEE llo.

`˙il˙lwo k (?= ˙i ˙lwo,` with conflated liquid, + emphatic particle *k*) = i lo puthe from this. ¶ `˙il˙lwo k ¨HHWUW ˙ey` (1459 Wel 2:13a) henceforth. `˙il˙lwo k ¨hwu ˙ey` (?1517⁻ Pak 1:72b) henceforth. `˙illwo k mwoncye` (1496 ¹Yuk 1:35a) prior to this.

`˙il˙lwo pu˙the = ˙i ˙lwo pu˙the`, n + pcl + pcl. ¶ `˙il˙lwo pu˙the ¨CO-SWON ˙i ¨ni˙zusi˙n i` (1459 Wel 1:8a) beginning with this there continued (a line of) sons and grandsons. `˙il˙lwo pu˙the`

THYEN ˙SSYANG ˙ay na˙l i ˙two isi˙l i ˙'n i (1447 Sek 9:19a) from this / here some will be born in heaven, too.
(?*) ¨ilm < *i˙l[u]m, subst < ¨i[l]˙ta becomes. No example of il˙m ye (n')? CF ¨nilm.
ilmyen < ˙QILQ-˙MYEN, noun, adverb.
1. one side / hand, one aspect, phase.
2. page one, the first / front page.
3. the whole surface; everywhere, all over.
4. a single meeting.
5. the whole myēn (township).
6. (= han phyen) but, on the other hand.
īlmyen, conditional < īlta
ilokwun, apperceptive < ilota; = ikwun. ~ a SAME, ~ yo SAME [POLITE]. ¶Ce key tāyhapsil ilokwun a Oh that's the lobby over there!
ilola [QUOTED or lit] = ilota (it is). ¶Naylola (na 'ylola = na ilola) hako ppop-nāynta He boasts "me! me! me!" as if he had the whole world in his hand. Nay ka sēysang uy pich ilola I am the light of the world (1936 Roth 537).
ilon < ˙ilwon, var cop mod. that is ··· .
ilona, advers < ilota; = ina.
iloni, sequential < ilota (= ini). ~-kka (n(un)).
ilosey = ilq sey (it is)
¨ilosil(q), hon prosp mod < ¨i[l]˙ta (becomes).
~ ˙i ˙lq ˙s oy. ¶[˙TTAY-HWUN] ˙i ¨ilosi˙l i ˙l ˙ss oy ... (1445 ¹Yong 66) since great merit would be achieved ... .
ilota < ˙ilwo˙ta [poetic or exclamatory] = ita (it is). ¶Ku nun kāwi kwunca (i)lota He can truly be said to be a gentleman. Ne cin pokca 'lo ta (1936 Roth 537) You are the truly blessed.
NOTE: Not all forms occur — apparently only those listed here. The suspective *iloci (= ici) does not occur, and tense markers cannot be inserted: *ilokeyss.ta, *ilwass.ta (CM 1:182-6).
ilotoy, concessive < ilota. it is ··· but; though it is ··· (= ila to). ¶I cip un namhyang ilotoy yak.kan tong ulo chiwuchin namhyang ita This house faces south but it is slightly tilted toward the east. Hōycang un hōycang ilotoy sillyek un ēps.ta It is true that he is chairman, but he has no power.
ilq pa, copula prosp modifier + postmodifier.
ilpang < ˙QILQ-PANG, postmod = han phyen. ¶Ku nun sengmyeng ul palphyo hanun ilpang puha tul eykey cochi lul chwī halq kes ul myēng.lyeng ha.yess.ta He issued a statement

and at the same time ordered his subordinates to take the necessary measures. Written style; perhaps influenced by Japanese ippoo, this is a rather awkward substitute for han phyen in most cases. Rejected examples: CM 2:36-7.
il s, copula prosp mod + postmod. SEE a˙ni 'l s.
ilq sey, cop prosp modifier + postmod = iney (FAMILIAR cop) it is ··· . ¶I kes i Yeyil tāyhak ilq sey This is Yale University. I chayk un nay kes ilq sey – caney kes i ani 'lq sey This book is mine, not yours. Payk kwun uy cacey 'lq sey (= cacey ilq sey) It is Payk's son. Ku kes un kutay uy cal-mos ilq sey You are to blame for it (or: You are wrong there). Ce san ul nēm.ki puthe ka palo ku elyewun kopi 'lq sey Beginning where you cross that mountain is right where the difficult pass is. CF ke 'lq sey, māl ilq sey.
˙ilq ˙s oy, cop prosp mod + postn + pcl. SEE -˙ᵘolq ˙s oy. ¶¨ta ˙SYENG-ZIN ˙ey s ¨sa˙lo.m il ˙ss oy ... (1447 Sek 6:45b) as they are all [among the] holy men ... .
ilsswu, quasi-free n. a constant bad habit/practice; ···-ki ka ~ 'ta is always doing ··· (something unpleasant). ¶Ku i nun nam pī-wus.ki ilsswu yo He is always sneering at others. Kēcis-mal haki ka (or hanun kes i) ilsswu 'ta He tells a lie every time he opens his mouth. Ce ay nun wūlki ka ilsswu 'ta She is a constant crybaby. [? < ilq-swu < ˙QILQ-¨SYWUW 'one hand']
NKd lists two other uses: (1) the best move or recourse; (2) quite often (= cal).
ilq swu, cop prosp mod + postmod. SEE -ulq swu.
ilta [DIAL, ?lit] = ita (cop); this must be a shortening of ilota. CF 1887 Scott 50: copula ilta / ila, ilteni / illeni, iltenya / illenya. sinsil hon salom ilta (1887 Scott 105) he is a trustworthy man; namwu 'lta (1887 Scott 51, 1893 Scott 136) it is wood; na 'y kes ilta (1889 Imbault-Huart 50) it is mine, ne y hol kes ani 'lta (54) it is not for you to do; nai kyes ilta (1890 Starchevskiy 668) it is mine; kum ilta (1894 Gale 2) it is gold. Ridel (1881:127) gives three versions of the copula, with the affirmative and negative forms: ilta, anilta; wolsita, ani wolsita; isilta, ani si(l)ta.
¨i[l]˙ta, vi. becomes (= towoy˙ta), comes into being, is formed, gets accomplished / achieved. SEE ¨il(q), i˙le (˙za), ¨il˙Gen, ¨ilGe˙nul, ¨il˙Gesi˙nol, ¨ilGe˙tun, ¨il˙Gey, ¨il˙Guy,

ˇilˇGwo, ˇill i 'leˇn i, ˇilosiˇl(q), ˇiluˇsya,
iˇlusyasˇta, ˇilq ˇt ol, ˇin, ˇinoˇn i, ˇiˇna,
ˇiˇta, ˇiˇta (s), ˇiˇti, ˇitwoˇta; (?*)ˇilm.

iltey, FAMILIAR retr assert < **i[l]ta** [DIAL cop]
= **itey**.

i lul, noun + particle. this (one) [as object].

ilul(q), prosp mod < **iluta** (adj, vt, vi)

*iˇ$l[u]l(q)$ = ˇ**ill**, prosp mod (before ˇi) < ˇ**i[l]**ˇ**ta**
(becomes). SEE ˇ**il(q)**, ˇ**ill** ··· . We presume the
ellipted vowel is u rather than o because the
-**ol(q)** version of the prospective modifier never
occurs after ···$i(C)$- (SEE -**ul(q)**).

ilula [DIAL, lit] = **itula** (cop)

ilun, mod < **iluta** (adj, vt, vi)

ilun-pa, cpd adv < vt mod + postnoun. what is
called, as it is called, so-called (= **sōwi** <
ˇ**SWO-**ˇ**NGWUY**). ¶**Ile han namca ka ilun-pa
sīnsa 'ta** Such a man is what is called (known
as a gentleman. **I ilun-pa ca.yu 'la 'n kes un
pāngcong ey cīnaci anh.nunta** This so-called
liberty is mere license.

ilunun, processive modifier < **iluta** (vt, vi)

ˇ**iluˇsya**, hon inf < ˇ**i[l]**ˇ**ta** (becomes). ¶SAM-
ˇMOY KWONG ˇi ˇ**iluˇsya** ... (1459 Wel 18:33b)
the merit of samādhi (meditation) is achieved.

ˇ**iˇlusyasˇta**, copula retr modulated hon emotive.
[ˇ**PWOW-**ˇ**WUY**] ˇ**thoˇsil nuˇc iˇlusyasˇta** (1445
¹Yong 100) it was an omen that he would
mount the throne. NOTE: The form has a
unique variant -**lu**- = -**le**- (lenited < -**te**-) for
the retrospective morpheme. LCT (280b and
1973:353), however, identifies -**lu**- with the
emotive -**two**- and treats the form as copula
emotive modulated honorific emotive. Both the
accent and the grammar (the linkage of ···c to
the vowel of the copula stem) keep us from
identifying the stem as ˇ**il**- 'become', unlike
ˇ**iluˇsya**. CF ˇ**isyasˇta**.

iluta₁ < il^u/o- / ilG- < *il^u/oG-, adj -LL- (inf
ille < **ilˇGe**). is early, is premature. ¶**ilun
sakwa / khong / kkoch** early apples / beans /
flowers. **ilun achim / pom** early morning /
spring. **Acik sikan i iluta** It is still early. **Ilulq
swulok cōh.ta** The earlier the better. **Ney ka
kyelhon haki nun acik iluta** You are too young
to get married. **Kumnyen un pye ka iluta** The
rice crop is early this year. ANT **nuc.ta**.
CF **ilccik(-i), il**.

iluta₂ < $niˇl^u/o$- / $nilG$- < *$niˇl^u/oG$-, vt -LL-
(inf **ille** < **nilˇGe**). 1. tells, reports. ¶**Nay ka
cenyek ey nuc.keyss.ta ko emeni hanthey ille
la** Tell mother that I will be late for dinner.
2. explains (it), teaches. ¶**kul ul ille cwuta**
teaches reading; explains a passage. **al.e tut.key
ille cwuta** explains ··· to make it clear.
3. tells/tattles on, informs/reports on. ¶**Apeci
hanthey ne lul ilukeyss.ta** I'm going to tell
Father on you.

iluta₃ < $niˇlul$-, vi (inf **ilule** < $niˇluˇle$).
1. arrives (at / in); reaches, attains, gets to.
¶**mokcek-ci ey** ~ arrives at the destination.
sengnyen ey ~ arrives at manhood. **kyellon ey**
~ reaches a conclusion. **ilunun kos mata** all
over, everywhere, throughout. **Pīyong i payk-
man wen ey iluless.ta** The expenditures came /
amounted to a million **wen**.
2. leads to. ¶**hāyngpok ey ilunun kil** the road
to happiness. **Sewul se Kyengcwu lul kechye
Pusan ey ilunun chelqto** a railway leading
from Seoul to Pusan by way of Kyengcwu. **I kil
lo kamyen kang ey ilunta** This road will take
you to the river.
3. ends up, results (in); comes to (the state
of), gets to (the point where), is brought to (the
brink/edge of). ¶**mit.ki ey** ~ comes to believe.
casal haki ey ~ goes so far as to commit
suicide (kill oneself). **Īl i yeki ey ilul i 'la ko,
nwu ka sayngkak hayss.ul ya** Who would have
dreamed that things would come to this (pass)!
**Kyelkwuk ku nun ku ⁿyeca wa kyelhon haki
ey iluless.ta** He finally ended up marrying her.
4. extends (to), reaches. **onul ey iluki kkaci**
until now, to this day, up to the present time.
¶**il-wel ey se sam-wel ey iluki kkaci** from
January to / till March. **casey han cem ey iluki
kkaci selmyeng hata** explains it right down to
the most minute details. **Ku san-mayk un
kwuk.kyeng ey kkaci ilunta** The mountain
range runs all the way to the frontier. **Wi lo
nun sacang ey se alay lo nun sāhwan ey iluki
kkaci cen-hōysa ka han maum ulo īl hanta**
The whole firm works hard, from the president
at the top to the office boy at the bottom.

ˇ**ilwoˇla**, var cop quoted indic assert. ¶**na 'y**
ˇ**TTYEY-**ˇ**CO y** ˇ**ce y neˇkywoˇtoy QA-LA-**ˇ**HAN**
ˇ**PYEK-CI** ˇ**PPWULQ** ˇ**ilwoˇla** ˇ**hoˇya** (1447 Sek
13:61a) my disciple said that in his opinion the
arhan is a pratyeka Buddha. ··· ˇ**iceyˇna non
kanan hwo.m iˇla** ˇ**PPYENG aˇni 'lwoˇla**
ˇ**ho.yaˇnol** ... (1482 Nam 1:30b) he said "··· now

I am poor but I am not ill", ... SEE ʾylwoˑla.
(?) ˑiˑlwom, var cop subst. SEE aˑni ʾlwom.
iˑlwom, modulated subst < ˮi[l]ˑta (becomes).
¶ ˑi ˑSYEY-ˑKAY iˑlwoˑm ay aˑni puˑthye (1459 Wel 1:38-9) not relying on this world's coming into being. VAR iˑlwum.
ˑilwon, var cop mod (epitheme extruded from copula complement). ¶ ˮta ZYE-LOY s QWUY-ˑLUK ˑilwon ˑkwoˑt ol aˑlala (1447 Sek 9:28a) know that all are parts of the tathāgata's authority. woˑcik mozoˑm oy ˑHHYEN ˑhwon keˑs ilwon ˑt i keˑwuˑlwu TYWUNG ˑey s ˮSSYANG ˑi CCYWEN-ˮTHYEY ˑi keˑwuˑlwu ʾylwon ˑt i ˑkot hoˑn i (1462 ¹Nung 2:17b) the fact that it is something that appears only in one's mind is like the fact that an image in a mirror is in its entire substance [just] the mirror.
ˑilwo-ngi ˮˑta, var cop polite + cop indic assert. ¶pwuthye s [ˮ]TTYEY-[ˮ]CO SA-MWON ˑilwo-ngi ˑˮta ([1447→]1562 Sek 3:20a) the disciple of Buddha is a śramaṇa (begging monk). ˑKILQ-SSYANG [ˑ]ilwo-ngi ˮˑta ([1447→]1562 Sek 3:43a) it is a good omen.
ˑilwoˑn i, variant copula modifier + postmodifier (summational epitheme in extended predicate). ¶ ˑna ˑnon ZYE-LOY s ˑmos cyeˑmun azˑG ilwoˑn i ... (1462 ¹Nung 1:76b) I am the tathāgata's youngest brother. naˑtwo ... ˑSYEY-KAN ˑay s aˑpi ʾlwoˑn i (1463 Pep 2:142a) I too am ... and a father in the human world. ku ˮPWON-LOY s ilˑhwuˑm un ˮamwoˑy ˑGwo naˑy ilˑhwuˑm un ˑaˑmwo ˑKAP ˑilwoˑn i (1463 Pep 2:222a) his original name is such-and-such and my name is something-or-other ˑKAP. SEE ʾylwoˑn i.
ˑilwon ˑt i, var cop mod + postmodifier + pcl. ¶SAM-SIN ˑon ˑi KKWEN ˑilwon ˑt i pantok pantok ˑhotwoˑta (1482 Kum-sam 2:28b) it is quite clear that the threefold body [of the Buddha] (trikāya) is this expedient power [of bodily transformation]. SEE ʾylwon ˑt i.
ˑilwon ˑt ol, var cop mod + postmod + pcl. ¶ ˑSYEY-KAN ˑi naˑkoˑnay ʾlwon ˑt ol aˑla (1462 ¹Nung 6:103b) knowing that the world of men is transient, ...
ˑiˑlwoˑswo-, var cop modulated emotive (= ˑilwo-s[o]-ˑwo-). LCT treats -ˑlwo- as lenited -ˑtwo- (modulated emotive): the normal copula modulated-emotive₁ modulated-emotive₂.
ˑiˑlwoˑswo-ngi ˮˑta, var cop modulated emotive polite + cop indic attent. SEE aˑni ˮˑlwoˑswo-

ngi ˮˑta, hoˑl i ˮˑlwoˑswo-ngi ˮˑta, -uˑl i ˮˑlwoˑswo-ngi ˮˑta.
ˑiˑlwoswoˑn i, var cop modulated emotive mod + postmod. ¶WANG-ˮCO s ˑMYENG ˑi nilˑGwey s ˮpwu.n iˑlwoswoˑn i ˮaˑmolyey ˮˑna mozom s koˑcang nwoˑla ˑzaˑhoˑl i ʾ-ngi ˮˑta (1447 Sek 24:28a) as the prince has only been alive for seven days he will somehow have to play to his heart's content. SSIN-LYENG ˑuy meˑli ˑˮm ye kwuy-s keˑs uy noˑch iˑlwoswoˑn i (1482 Kum-sam 2:7b) it is the head of a spirit and it is the face of a ghost. SEE -uˑl i ʾlwoswoˑn i, -wolq ˑt ilwoswoˑn i.
ˑilwoswoˑn ye, variant copula modulated emotive modifier + postmod. SEE -uˑl i ʾlwoswoˑn ye.
ˑilwoˑta, var cop. it is ... . ¶ icey ˑCYENG ˑhi ku SSI-ˑCYELQ ˑilwoˑta (1447 Sek 13:60b) now is exactly that time. ˑi ˑi.l ol tutˑkwo cye ˑhwoˑm ilwoˑta (1482 Kum-sam 2:7a) I want to hear about this matter. [ˮYA-ZIN] ˑin ˑt ol ˮalˑl i ʾlwoˑta (1481 Twusi 7:13b) we know that they are barbarians. SEE -uˑl i ʾlwoˑta, -wolq ˑt ilwoˑta; ʾylwoˑta.
ˑilwoˑtoy, var cop accessive. ¶ ˮmil ˑmuˑl i saˑoˑl ilwoˑtoy ˑnake ˑza ˑcomoˑn i ʾ-ngi ˮˑta (1445 ¹Yong 67) the water crested for three days and only when they left was the place inundated. chol hi ˑtye kwoˑma towoyˑGa ciˑla hoˑl i ˑyelˑh ilwoˑtoy ˑmaˑti aˑni thaˑn i (1463 Pep 2:28b) those [women] preferring to become his concubine were more than ten [in number] and they did not give up. TI ˮtwul[h] aˑni ˮˑlwoˑm on ˑTI-ˑHHYWEY ʾlwoˑtoy ... (1459 Wel 8:31b) that wisdom is not two things is [a matter of] knowledge and discernment [together] and ... . mozom aˑlan ˑt i yeˑle ˑhoy ʾlwoˑtoy (?1517-Pak 1:71b) we have understood each other for many years now, and ... . SEE -uˑl i ʾlwoˑtoy; ʾylwoˑtoy.
iˑlwum, modulated subst < ˮi[l]ˑta (becomes). ¶QUM-ˑNGWUN iˑlwuˑm ey kaˑcolˑpisiˑn i ˮˑla (1462 ¹Nung 9:85a) he compared it to the formation of rimes. VAR iˑlwom.
ilya → il ya
il ya, cop prosp mod + postmod
il ya tul, cop prosp mod + postmod + pcl
ilye, cop intentive. SEE FOLLOWING ENTRIES.
ilye ʾn i wa, cop intentive + abbr < han + bnd n + pcl. ¶Tōn to tōn ilye ʾn i wa kalq sikan i ēps.ta There's the money, for one thing, and

what's more I lack the time. The money is one thing, but a worse problem is the lack of time.

ilye ’n ka, copula intentive + abbr < han + postmod [lit, poetic]. might it be …? (= **ilq kes in ya**). ¶**Tanphung namu nun ku pich-kal i nemu to sen.yen hata; enu ¹yelqsa uy hullin phi ’lye ’n ka** The maples are dyed too deep a red; might it be the blood of some patriot?

ilyen man (un), copula frustrated intentive

ilyes.ta → **ilyetta**, copula intentive assertive. (NKd 1195.)

i˙l ywo, cop prosp mod + postmod. ¶*MA a˙ni ˙˙la mu˙su ke˙s i˙l ywo* (1462 ¹Nung 9:101b) it is not a demon but what is it? VAR ˙i˙l ywu.

im < **˙im**, copula substantive

imam-ttay, cpd n. about / around this time, (at) this time of the day / night / year. ¶**cak.nyen / ¹naynyen** ~ at this time last/next year. **¹nayil / ecey** ~ at this time tomorrow / yesterday. **Imam-ttay eti kan' ya** Where are going at this time (of night)? **¹Nayilq cenyek imam-ttay tto wā poypkeyss.ˢup.nita** Tomorrow evening at this time I'll come and see you again.

~ **ey nun** by this time, by now. ¶**Cak.nyen imam-ttay ey nun kokiq kaps i han kun ey chen wen iess.ta** Beef was selling at a thousand wen a pound a year ago at this time. **Imam-ttay ey nun pelsse Pusan ey tah.ass.ulq kes ita** He must have arrived in Pusan by this time. SYN **yomam-ttay**. CF **kumam-/cemam-ttay**. [? < **i man** + **pttay** 'this-extent time'; ? < **i ma(nkhu)m ttay**; CF **ipttay**.]

i man, cpd adv (n + pcl, or adn + n; SEE ~ **hata**). to this extent, this much, this far; now (with just this). ¶**Onul un i man haca** So much for today. **Ce nun i man ka ya ’keyss.ˢup.nita** I ought to go now (**¹Yi Kitong** 1988:61) = **Icey ku man ka ya ’keyss.ˢup.nita** (idem:62). SEE **˙i˙mas ··· = ˙i˙ma[n] s**. CF **ku man**.

i-man ce-man, cpd adv [used with negative constructions]. (not) to just this extent or that, (more than) so-so, (hardly) to any limited degree, (not) easy to dismiss, (not) in any offhand(ed) way. ¶**Onul tewe to, i-man ce-man tēpci anh.ta** It is hot today, and there are no two ways about it. **Ku ka Yenge lul hay to, i-man ce-man cal hanun kes i ani 'ta** He not only speaks English, he speaks it awfully well.

~ **hata**, adj-n. is (not) just so-so, is (hardly) describable. ¶**Ku ⁿyeca ka i-man ce-man han miin i ani ’ta** She is no everyday (run-of-the-mill) beauty. **Ku kyengchi uy alum-tawum ila ’n i-man ce-man han kes i ani ’ta** The scenery is lovely beyond all description.

i man hata, adj-n. is this much, is as much / big / many as this, is to this extent. ¶**I man han sōnhay nun āmu kes to ani 'ta** Such a small loss is nothing to me. **Ttwuk i i man hamyen chel.ong-seng ita** The dike is strong as can be now. **Nay chayk-sang un i man hata** My desk is this large. CF **(ku / ce / -ul) man hata**.

i mankhum, n + pcl. this much, so much, to this extent, "yea". ¶**Ecey cap.un sayngsen i i mankhum khess.ta** The fish I caught yesterday was this big (yea big). **Ī-chung ey chayk i i mankhum tto iss.ta** I have just as many books upstairs as down here. CF **ku / ce mankhum**.

··· **i mankhum** SEE **-un (-nun, -ul) i mankhum**

˙i˙mas ··· = ˙i˙ma[n] s, n + pcl + pcl. this much. ¶**˙i˙ma[n] s˙kam yang˙uy** (?1517- ¹No 2:22a) for no more sheep than this = **i man.skan yang ey** (1795 ¹No-cwung [P] 2:20a; by then /nkk/) = **i man yang ey** (id. [K] 2:21a).

i mo, adn + n; LIGHT **yo mo**. this corner / angle. ~ **ce mo** this angle and that, every facet / side / view: ~ **lo sayngkak hata** views the matter from every angle.

imye, cop conjunctive < ˙i˙m ye. CF **iko, iney, ina, in ka, itun ka, itun iye, ci**.

1. it is ··· and ··· . ¶**Ku nun kwun.in imye hakca ’ta** He is both a soldier and a scholar.

2. (used as a quasi-particle) and, or, and/or. ¶**Chayk imye tōn imye tā ilh.ess.ta** I have lost my books and my money, everything. **Pay ’mye tāychwu ’mye sakwa ’mye yele kaci lul nul.e noh.ass.ta** They have out (on display) pears, dates, apples, and so on.

˙i˙m ye, cop subst + abbr cop inf. ¶*SSING ˙i ˙˙twul.h i˙m ye ˙˙sey˙h i ˙˙ep˙su.n i ˙˙la* (1447 Sek 13:49b) there are no other two or three vehicles. *CYE-˙PEP ˙˙NGWUW-MWU ˙[G]wa ˙i ˙SSILQ ˙i˙m ye a˙ni ˙Gwa ˙i SOYNG ˙i˙m ye SOYNG a˙ni ˙lol kol˙hoyno.n i* (1463 Pep 5:30a) discriminates the existence (or lack) of the laws and [that] this is real or not real and [that] this is life or not life.

~ **n' ** (pcl). ¶*SYEY-PANG ˙ay ˙SYENG-ZIN ˙i ˙nasi˙nwoswo˙n i ˙˙i ˙˙HHWUW ˙lwo CHYEN-NYEN ˙i˙m ye n' ku ˙PEP ˙i ingey ˙na-wo˙l i ˙lwo˙swo-ngi ˙˙ta* (1459 Wel 2:49a) a sage has been born in the west; a thousand years from now his Law will appear here!

imyen, cop conditional (< ʾiˑm ye nʾ). if / when it is; as for (= **un**). ¶**pam mata ʾmyen** every night. **Phoun i chwul.ip hal ttay ʾmyen i tali wi lul cīnako nʾ hayss.ta** When Phoun came and went, he would pass over this bridge. **Yeki se han sam-pun imyen kanta** It is about three minutes (to get there) from here. **Nal mata nac imyen tewe ciko, pam imyen chwuwe cinta** Every day it warms up during the daytime and gets cold at night.

in < ZIN, bnd n, bnd postn. a person, a man.
 1. bound noun. ~q cek, "~ ci sangceng", ~q cwul, ~ kanan, ~q kichek, ~q kum, ~ nal, ~q pok, ~ pinul, ~ pusim, ~ twukep, ~ twullita, ...
 2. bnd postn. **munhwa** ~ a cultured man. **Hān(kwuk)** ~ a Korean.

in < ʾin, cop mod. ... that (it) is. After vowel ʾn and ʾyn, but ʾn = ʾ[y]n after i or y. CF **ani ʾn**, **aˑni ʾn**. SEE **ilon** < ʾilwon.
 1. (the epitheme is extruded from the copula complement). ¶**kwuk.hoy uywen in Kim Kiho paksa** Dr Kim Kiho, who is a member of the National Assembly. **wensi-cek in ssi-cok sāhoy** the primitive clan society. **ches kyōhwang in Peythulwu** 'Peter the first pope', **Pulucia uy wang iyo Tek.kwuk [= Tok.il] uy hwangcey in Wuilheylum** 'Wilhelm, King of Prussia and Emperor of Germany' (1936 Roth 81). ¶**ney chaˑh in ʾpuˑl ey** (1447 Sek 9:37a) in the fourth fire. ʾesˑti holˑs in [ʾMYEN-ˑTHYEP] ʾin ˑkwo (?1517- ¹No 1:3b) how is one excused from registering?
 2. (with a summational epitheme). ¶**Com pihyēnsilq-cek in kes kath.ey** It seems to be a bit impractical. **Ku sālam i nay chinkwu in kkatalk ip.nita** It is because he is my friend. **Sāpang i yātan in thong ey cēngsin ul chalilq swu ka ēps.ess.e** Things were in such uproar on all sides that I couldn't collect my thoughts. ¶**naˑh i ... syelˑhu.n in ˑhoy ˑyey** (1462 ¹Nung 2:6b) in the year one's age is thirty. ʾsumulˑh in SSI-ˑCYELQ ˑey ˑyelˑh in cey ˑlwo nʾ SYWUY hoˑm ye (1462 ¹Nung 2:8b) is weaker at twenty than when ten years old, and ... . ʾswuyˑn in SSI-ˑCYELQ ˑul ˑpwoken ˑt ay nʾ ˑpentuk ˑhi KKANG-ˑCANG ˑhoˑtaˑs-ongi ʾˑta (1462 ¹Nung 2:6-7) when one has seen fifty seasons one is clearly robust. ʾeˑtin namzin ˑin ˑyang ˑuˑlwo hoˑkwo is.keˑtun (?1517- ¹No 2:54b) he was pretending to be a good fellow, but ... .

ʾin < *iˑ[lu]n, modifier < ˑi[l]ˑta (becomes).
 1. (? the epitheme extruded from the subject = possessor). ¶ˑCYENG hon ˑyeluˑm un ˑTUK ˑin ˑsaloˑm ol kaˑcolˑpisiˑn i ˑʾla (1447 Sek 13:47a) he compared the true fruit to the person for whom virtue has come into being.
 2. (summational epitheme). ¶QIN ˑi hoˑma ˑin cyenˑcho ˑlwo (1462 ¹Nung 9:85a) for the reason that the primary cause (hetu) is already established.

i nʾ, abbr < **i nun** as for this (one).

ina, 1. cop FAMILIAR indic attent. is it ... ?
 2. cop advers. it is ... but. ¶**Māl un olh.un māl ina hayngtong i nappess.ta** He spoke the truth, but what he did was bad. SEE **ani ʾna talul ya (talulq ka)**.
 3. cop advers used as quasi-particle. NOTE: In view of the use of **in ka** and **itun ka** as similar quasi-particles perhaps these uses all properly belong with the indicative attentive of 1, of which 2 may be an extended meaning. Both are perhaps derived from ...n ˑ[k]a. CF **iney, im ye; itun ci**.
 3a. or the like, like, or something, or so; the likes of, any; at least, anyway, just (used in gently / vaguely urging, CF **una**), even if it is not of particular interest. ¶**Emeni ʾna mannan tus ʾi kippess.ta** He was happy as if he'd met his mother or something. **Cip ina swīpkey chac.ess.ˢup.nikka** Did you have any difficulty finding the house? **Kyewu ūysa ʾna cen hanta** I can barely express my ideas. **Pyesul ina han tus siph.ta** You act as if you had become a government official or something. **Talun kes un ku man twuko kongpu ʾna cal hay la** Put other things aside and just study hard. **Swul ina masipsita** Let's just drink some wine or something. **Kongpu lul / ʾna cal hanta ko ʾna halq ka yo** Let's just say he is (just) working hard at his studies. **Pap ina capswusipsio** Have something to eat. **Nay ka kass.ta olq / onun tong-an sinmun ina ilk.e pwā yo** Have a look at the newspaper while I am out. **Tōn ul ponay nun cwuess.una kece pīyong ina kyewu toytolok ponay cwuess.ta** They sent us the money all right, but scarcely enough to cover the expense. **Eti, sānqpo ʾna halq ka?** Let's

see, now, shall we take a walk? **Kuli 'na hay polq ka** I might do it that way. **Te 'na koy lop.hici mālkey** Please don't trouble me any more. SEE **kkway (kk'ay) 'na; una** (NOTE).

3b. about, around, approximately. ¶**twū pen ina** a time or two; two or three times. **twū sikan ssik ina** (about) two hours apiece. **(han) twū sikan ccum ina** (about) two hours. **Yel ina iss.ta** There are ten or so of them. **Pyesul hanun mulyep ey ttang maciki 'na cangman hayss.ta** He got himself a few pieces of land when he was an official in the government.

3c. as much / many as, to the (surprising) extent of, all of. ¶**Pelsse tases si 'na tōyss.ta** It is five o'clock already. **Tōn ul chen wen ina ilh.ess.ta 'n māl ya** I lost a good thousand wen, you see. **han cip-an ina talum ēps.ta** is almost (is as good as) one of the family. **Ku nom un cimsung ina pyel lo talum ēps.ta** He is little more than an animal. SEE **tholok ina**.

3d. (with indeterminates) wh--- it may be, ---ever, all, every. SEE ENTRIES OF: **nwukwu 'na** whoever (it may be), anyone, everyone. **mues ina** whatever (it may be), anything (at all), everything. **ēncey 'na** whenever (it may be), just any time, at all times, always; ever. **ecci 'na, etteh.key 'na** however it may be, in all sorts of ways; ever so much. **elma 'na** how / so very much; (3b) about how much. **meych (---) ina**; a (certain) number, several; (3b) about how many. **āmu ke 'na** anything at all; **āmu --- ina** any --- at all; **āmu 'na** (= **āmu sālam ina**) anyone at all, everyone (else). **āmuleh.key 'na** any which way, carelessly, in a slovenly/sloppy manner; **āmuli 'na** surely, ever (so).

3d. or, and, and/or; both --- and ---, either --- or --- (CF **tto nun** or in contrast, or again). ¶**kongchayk ina yenphil ina** notebooks and/or pencils. **I cip ina ce cip ina tā kath.ta** This house and that one are both alike. ¹**yeksa sāng ina cili sāng ulo pol man han kes** things worth looking at from the point of view of history or geography. **Ponun kes ina tut.nun kes ina tā say lowess.ta** Everything I saw or heard was new to me.

3e. SEE **-ci 'na (anh-/mā-l-)**
3f. SEE **-ci 2b**
3g. SEE **-ulq ci 'na**
3h. SEE **-ta (ka) 'na**
3i. SEE **kay 'na**

4. 4a. whether it is ---, is --- indifferently, (whatever) it is (= **itun ci, ikena**). ¶**enu phyen ina** either way. **nwukwu 'na tā** anyone and everyone. **I kes ina ce kes ina mues ina cōh.ta** Whether it's this or that or whatever it is, it's all right. **I moca 'na ce moca 'na kaps un hana 'ta** Both hats are the same price.

4b. (the question) whether it is --- (or is not / or is ---). SEE **ina lul**.

SEE **-e 'na, -e se 'na, -key 'na, -ko se 'na, -umye 'na; ccum ina, chelem ina, ey 'na, ey se 'na, hanthey 'na, kkaci 'na, kwa 'na, mata 'na, puthe 'na, tul ina, ssik ina; kkey 'na**. CF **una / na** (NOTE).

¨*i 'na*, cop advers. it is --- but. SEE ¨*isi 'na*.

¨*i 'na*, advers < ¨*i[l] 'ta* (becomes). ¶*[TWONG-CYENG]* ¨*ey* ¨*mwot* ¨*i 'na* (1445 ¹Yong 41) in the eastern invasion nothing was accomplished.

ina lul, cop advers + pcl. the question [as object] of whether it is --- (or whether ---). ¶**Hānkwuk-e 'na Hānqca-e 'na lul mullon hako** regardless whether it is a Korean word or a Sino-Korean (Chinese) word.

īnam < ¨*I-NAM*, n, postn. to the south (of ---); --- and south. **samphalq-senq īnam** south of the 38th parallel. ¶**Sewulq īnam** south of Seoul. **Hān kang īnam** south of the Han River. **Hungnam īnam** south of Hungnam. **Samchek īnam** Samchek and south.

ina-ma, cop extended advers. although it is --- ; at least, anyway; even. ¶**Hēn os ina-ma ip.e ya hakeyss.ta** I will just have to wear my old clothes. **Mas ēps.nun cīnci 'na-ma mānh.i capswusio** Please help yourself though it isn't a nice dinner. **Helum han cip ina-ma nay cip ul hana kacyess.umyen cōh.keyss.ta** I wish I had a house of my own however humble it might be. SEE **ulo 'na-ma**.

i 'na-ma, n + cop extended advers. although it is this; anyway, at least; even this (much). LIGHT **yo 'na-ma**. CF **ku 'na-ma, 'na-ma**.

i 'na-ma lul, n + cop extended advers + pcl [a bit awkward]. ¶**I 'na-ma lul** ¹**ihay mōs hata 'ni chenchi** ¹**lokwun** I see he's too stupid to understand even this much.

i 'na-ma to, n + cop extended advers + pcl. ¶**I 'na-ma to et.ki ka him tul.ess.ess.ta** It was hard to get even this (much).

i 'na-ma uy, cop extended adv + pcl. ¶**I 'na-ma uy ye.yu to ēps.e se etteh.key hay!** You ought

to have this much (time/money) to spare, at least.
ina to, cop advers + pcl. SEE **nemu 'na to**.
ina tul, cop advers + pcl. ¶**Mak' kelli 'na tul hasey** Let's have us some raw liquor, fellows.
īnay < ˙*I-˙NWOY*, n, postn. inside the limit, within, less than, not exceeding. ¶**ilq-cwuilq īnay** within a week. **sam-chen wenq īnay uy kum.ayk** a sum that does not exceed 3,000 wen. **tases salam īnay nun** (1936 Roth 208) no more than five people. **Wel.nam īnay** within Vietnam. **Cwungkwuk īnay** within China.
i(n)cey < *incoy* (1776 [n]Yempul 58) < *icoy* ([?]1720 Waye 2:34b) < ˙*icey* (< ˙*i cek*). now; starting now. (The form without the **n** is widely used, but **incey** is the usual form in the central area.) ~ **nun** from now on; any more.
in chek / chey, cop mod + postmod.
in ci, cop mod + postmod.
~ **ko** SEE (NKd 678b): SEE **-un ci ko**.
~ **'la (se)** (cop var inf) [lit] as/since it is ... (= **ie se**). ¶**Hak.kyo ey kanun kil in ci 'la cikum tullici mōs hakeyss.**[s]**o** I am on my way to school, so I can't stop in now.
in cuk(-sun), cop mod + postmod.
 1. to speak of, speaking of, as for [somewhat literary or lively, = **un/nun**]. ¶**sāsil in cuk** in fact (= **sāsil lo māl hamyen**); **cēng-mal in cuk** to tell the truth. **Māl in cuk olh.so** What he says is true. **Kul-ssi 'n cuk myengphil iyo** When it comes to the handwriting, that is excellent. **Kihoy 'n cuk cōh.un kihoy 'ta** As for the opportunity, it is a good one. **I twū māl un ttus i kath.ci man ku yōngqpep in cuk kath.ci anh.ta** These two words are identical in meaning, but differ in usage.
 2. since/as it is ... . SEE **-un cuk**.
in cwul, cop mod + postmod. ¶**Yeki ka eti 'n cwul molukeyss.nun tey** But I do not know what place this is! **Ku lul pāpo 'n cwul lo man al.ess.tuni kuleh.ci to anh.tukwun** I thought he was nothing but a fool, but I see he was not.
iney, copula FAMILIAR indicative assertive.
 1. it is ... .
 2. [somewhat odd] quasi-pcl = **hako, iko, kwa/wa** and. ¶**Hyeng iney awu 'ney cokha 'ney sonca 'ney ttey mol.a wass.ta** They all came in a group — brothers and nephews and grandchildren.
i ney, n + postn. these people. ~ **tul** SAME.

inge˙kuy (? < *˙i ngek ˙uy*), n. this place, here (> *iye˙kuy* > *ye˙kuy* > **yeki**); CF *yey, kunge˙kuy*. ¶˙*i* KYENG *ti˙nil ¨ssalo˙m i inge˙kuy i˙sye˙two* (1447 Sek 19:17b) even if there are people here who will preserve this sūtra ... . *ce˙non inge˙kuy˙*NGWEN *˙ho˙nwon˙ptu˙t i ¨epta˙n i ¨es˙tyey 'Ge˙n ywo* (1459 Wel 13:35b) how come I have had no mind to want this [mahāyāna] part [of the doctrine]? ˙PWULQ-˙PEP ˙*i˙za na 'y inge˙kuy two ¨cywoko˙m achi is˙ta* (1482 Nam 1:14a) there is some of Buddha's law right here where I am, too. *inge˙kuy n'* ¨NAY-CYWUNG ˙SSILQ ˙*hosya˙m ay mwo˙twosi˙n i˙'la* (1459 Wel 14:59a) here they are gathered for the ultimate reality.
ingey, abbr < *inge˙kuy*, adverb, noun. (in/to) this place, here; henceforth, (starting) now, hereafter. ¶... *ku˙*PEP ˙*i ingey˙na-wo˙l i˙'lwo˙swo-ngi˙'ta* (1459 Wel 2:49a) his Law will appear here! *ingey is.no˙n i* (1465 Wen 3:2:2:41ab) those who are here. *pi˙luse ingey ni˙lu.n i* (1482 Nam 1:33b) it has for the first time reached this place. *ingey ¨na˙m ol ¨a˙ti ¨mwot˙kwo˙sye* (1463 Pep 3:180ab) unaware (not knowing) that they will henceforth emerge ... . *ingey elwu mas-˙na˙*TUK ˙*ho˙ya ¨cams.kan˙two e˙lyewu˙m i ¨ep.su˙l i 'Ge˙nul* (1463 Pep 2:226a) henceforth we will not have the least moment of difficulty in getting to meet. ˙*ile 'n* ¨NGWUW-CCYENG ˙*tol.h on ingey˙sye cwu˙ku˙m ye n'* (1447 Sek 9:12b) if such sentient beings hereafter die ... . [˙]CCYEK-˙MYELQ TTYANG ˙*ay i˙sye* SSYEN-˙YWELQ ˙*ul˙*CHAN-¨CHOY *ho˙l i 'n [...] ingey mozom ta˙wolq˙t iGe˙ta* (1462 [1]Nung 7:18a; the accent may be the result of breaking the sentence for a note) now they will do their utmost in offering a banquet of dhyāna joy at the place where Buddha attained the truth of nirvāṇa.
˙*i-ngi s˙ka*, copula polite + pcl + postmodifier. ¶*a˙hwop* HHWOYNG-¨SO ˙*non mu˙su˙k i-ngi s ˙ka* (1447 Sek 9:35b) what are the nine unnatural deaths?
˙*i-ngi s˙kwo*, cop polite + pcl + postmodifier. ¶KWONG ˙*oy nilku˙si˙nwon ke˙s un ¨es˙te 'n ¨ma˙l i-ngi s˙kwo* (1465 Wen se:68a) what words are you reading, my Lord?
˙*i-ngi˙'ta*, cop polite + cop indic assert. ¶˙ZIN-˙ZYWOK˙THAY-¨CO ˙*uy il˙Gwu˙syan˙*YAK ˙*i-ngi ˙'ta* (1459 Wel 21:218b) it is a drug that Prince

Kṣānti concocted. ALSO: 1447 Sek 24:46b, ...
in hata < QIN °ho˙ta, vn [lit].
1. vnt. leaves it as it is.
2. vni (··· ey) ~ is in accord(ance with). ¶ **yēys phungsok ey in ha.ye** in accordance with olden customs.
3. vni (= **malmiam.ta**). (··· ulo) ~ is due (to), is caused (by), is attributable (to), comes (from), is a consequence (of). ¶ **pyēng ulo in hay se kyelqsek hata** is absent because of illness. **sāko lo in ha.ye cwukta** dies from (on account of) an accident.
4. (MK) vnt. ¶ ZYE-LOY S ˙TI-˙HHYWEY ˙lol QIN ˙ho˙ya (1459 Wel 13:35b) based on the wisdom of the tathāgata.
ini, 1. copula sequential.
1a. as/since it is ··· ; so. ¶ **Hwānca ka canun cwung ini han sam-sip pun kitalilq swu iss.keyss.ˢup.nikka?** As the patient is sleeping now, could you wait about thirty minutes? **Cenyek i tā cwūnpi toyn mo.yang ini siktang ulo kasipsita** As the dinner seems to be all prepared, let's go along to the dining room. **Īl ul math.kimyen cal hal they 'ni ⁿyēm.lye māsio** In undertaking the task, I intend to do a good job of it, so don't worry.
1b. it is ··· but / and.
1c. (= **iko**) it is ··· and also; also.
1d. (= *ikey, ulo) so as to be; as.
2. cop indic attent → **in i** = **in ya** is it ··· ?
3. whether it is ···; or, and, and/or (= **ina** 3b). ¶ **kongchayk ini yenphil ini hampu lo kanswu hata** does not take good care of notebooks and pencils and things like that. **Pēm ini kōm ini thokki 'ni nolwu 'ni tā pwass.ney** I've seen tigers, bears, rabbits, roe deer — everything.
in i, 1. copula modifier + noun / postmodifier.
1. the one (thing/person) that is ··· . ¶ **hak.kyo sensayng in i** the one who is (he / she who is) a schoolteacher.
2. the act / fact of being ··· :
~ **mankhum** inasmuch (insofar) as it is ··· , since it is ··· . ¶ **Ne nun pūca 'n** (= **in**) **i mankhum te kipu hay ya hanta** Inasmuch as you are richer, you ought to contribute more. SEE M 3:3:223.
~ **pota** rather than be ··· . ¶ **No.yey in i pota cwukem ul thayk hakeyss.ta** I will choose death rather than be a slave.
3. = **in ya** (question)

4. abbr < **in i 'la**. SEE **-un i ('la)**.
¨i˙n i (˙i.n i, i˙n i), cop mod + postmodifier. ¶ SSYENG-˙PPWULQ ˙ho.yan ˙t i ··· ˙KEP ˙i.n i (1459 Wel 17:22a) became a Buddha ··· kalpas (eons) ago. ˙swu˙l[i] uy me˙li SAN ˙i.n i (1463 Pep 1:20b) it is the mountain [called] Eagle's Head. ˙SYENG-ZIN pe˙ngulwo˙m i te˙wuk me˙len ¨salo˙m i wo˙cik ¨PI-˙LYANG ˙u˙lwo pu˙the a˙lwo˙m i ¨SSYANG ˙i˙n i (1463 Pep 2:41a) for people who are more distanced from the sage their knowledge, stemming from comparison and inference, is merely form. ˙MWOK-CCYEN ˙ey s ye˙le ˙PEP ˙i ke˙wulwu s ¨swop ay elkwul ¨pwo.m i˙n i (1482 Kum-sam 2:63a) the various laws that are before one's eyes are [just like] looking at one's face inside a mirror. SSYENG-˙PPWULQ ˙ho.yan ˙t i ··· ˙KEP ˙i.n i (1459 Wel 17:22a) became a Buddha ··· kalpas (eons) ago.
˙HHAP ˙kwa ˙HHAP a˙ni ˙Gwa s ¨LI ¨ta nilo˙syan ˙ptut tuthul s ˙HHWAN-˙SYANG ˙i.n i (1462 ¹Nung 2:107a) the meaning of all he has said about the principle of what is meet and what is not meet is [that it is but] the illusion of [floating] dust.
¨i˙n i, vi mod (< ¨i[l]˙ta) + postmodifier. ¶ ˙ili ˙ho.ya ˙za ˙SYEY-˙KAY ¨ta ¨i˙n i ¨ku y SSYENG ˙KEP ˙i˙Gwo (1459 Wel 1:47a) only thus did all the world get formed, so that it is the kalpa of formation, and ··· .
ini-kka (n'/nun), cop extended sequential (+ pcl). since it is; it is, you see. ¶ **Onul i tho.yoil ini-kka ōhwu ey nun kongpu ka ēps.ulq key 'ta** Today is Saturday so there probably won't be any classes in the afternoon. **Ku sālam ini-kka kkok ka yo** Him, he is sure to go.
init/ₗa = **in i 'ta / 'la**, cop lit indic assert (= **ita**)
in i 'la, cop mod + n + cop quotative indic assert. SEE **-un i ('la)**; **-ulq ci 'n i ('la)**.
˙i.n i ˙'la, cop mod + postmod + cop indic assert. ¶ ˙QIL[Q]-¨KAN ¨spwun ˙i.n i ˙'la (1588 Mayng 14:6a) and then [after killing all the relatives] does not kill himself, yet is just a short distance [from it].
in i tul, 1. cop mod + postmod + pcl = **in ya tul**.
2. cop mod + quasi-free n + pcl. the ones which / that are ··· .
in ka, copula modifier + postmodifier.
1. (= **in ya, ini?**) is it ··· ? ¶ **I kes i kimchi 'n ka yo?** Is this (the) kimchi?
2. (= **ina** as quasi-particle) **ēncey 'n ka** once

(upon a time). ¶ eti ey 'n ka somewhere or other. Eti ey se 'n ka natha-nass.ey yo He appeared from out of nowhere. Eti 'n ka taluta There's something different about it. Nwukwu 'n ka ka ku sālam ul kyēngchal ey pōko hayss.keyss.ˢup.nita Somebody must have reported him to the police.
  3. ~ pota it seems to be. ¶ Ku kes i ama tali 'n ka pota That seems to be a bridge.
in ka ka, cop mod + postmod + pcl = in ya ka. ¶ Cham māl in ka ka mūncey 'ta The question is whether it is true.
in ka lul, cop mod + postmod + pcl = in ya lul. ¶ Nwukwu uy kes in ka lul al.e pwā la Find out whose it is.
in ka tul, cop mod + postmod + pcl = in ya tul
in ke l', abbr < in kes ul
in kes, cop mod + postmod
in key, abbr < in kes i, in kes i-
in ko, cop mod + postmod. SEE ko³ < ˙kwo.
˙in ˙kwo, cop mod + postmod. ¶ mwo˙lwo˙l i 'lwo˙ta ˙myes noy˙zi.l in ˙kwo (?1517⁻ Pak 1:35a) I dunno just how many days from now it will be. ¨es˙ti hol˙s in [¨MYEN-˙THYEP] ˙in ˙kwo (?1517⁻ ¹No 1:3b) how is one excused from registering? poy˙hwo˙non ke˙s i mu˙su ¨i˙l in ˙kwo ˙ho˙ye (1518 Sohak-cho 8:33b) wondering what matters they study.
i nom, adnoun + n. [pejorative] this damn guy ("S.O.B."), he/him [not used of women]; this damn thing, it. CF i ay/ca/chi/ēlun/i/pun/sālam/son.
˙i˙non, n + pcl. 1. as for this; ... 2. it is (true) that ...; really, truly, indeed. This translates the Chinese adverb ˙SI (?1468⁻ Mong 31b, ...)
¨i˙non < *i˙l[o]˙non, processive modifier < ¨i[l]˙ta (becomes). ¶ ˙sso y pi˙luse ¨i˙non cyen˙cho 'y˙la (1465 Wen 1:2:2:140a) it is the reason events first arise
  ¨i[˙]no˙n i (postmodifier). ¶ mulGuy s ˙cco y mwo˙lwo˙may e˙wule ˙za swo˙li ¨i[˙]no˙n i (1451 Hwun-en 13a) every one of the letters must be combined [with others] for a sound [= a syllable] to result.
in pa, copula modifier + postmodifier.
˙in ˙ta, cop mod + postmodifier. ¶ ne y ¨es.te 'n salo˙m in ta ([1447→]1562 Sek 3:20a) [← *¨ne y ¨es˙te 'n ¨salo.m in ˙ta] what kind of person are you? ne y michin nwo.m in ta (1481 Samkang chwung:27a) are you a madman?
˙in ˙t ay n', cop mod + postmod + pcl + pcl. ¶ ˙hota ˙ka CIN-˙SSILQ s ne 'y mozo˙m in ˙t ay n' ¨ka˙m i ¨ep.su˙l i 'Ge˙nul (1462 ¹Nung 2:24b) while perhaps, it being your true intent, there may be no departing, yet ... . SEE ho˙l i 'n [˙]t ay n', -u.l i 'n ˙t ay n'.
in tey, copula modifier + postmodifier.
  1. it is ... and/but. ¶ I kes un nay chayk in tey poko cwukey This is my book; return it to me when you are through with it.
  2. (exclamatory) ¶ Cōh.un kos in tey Why, it's a very nice place!
˙in ˙t i, cop mod + postmod ('fact') + pcl. that it is ... . ¶ [SYANG-KWONG] oy [KWUN] ˙in t i ¨anwo.n i (1481 Twusi 7:25a) we know it is the troops of Duke Xiāng. SEE -un ˙t i.
˙in ˙t ol, cop mod + postmodifier ('fact') + pcl.
  1. that it is ... . ¶ wo˙cik mozo˙m oy na˙thwon ke˙s in ˙t ol ¨pwoy˙sya (1462 ¹Nung 2:17a) shows that it is manifest only in the mind. [¨YA-ZIN] ˙in ˙t ol ¨al˙l i 'lwo˙ta (1481 Twusi 7:13b) we know that they are barbarians. pan˙toki ¨TTYWOW-CYWUW y ¨es˙te 'n ˙MYEN-˙MWOK ˙in ˙t ol a˙lwo.l i ˙'la (?1468⁻ Mong 13a) we must recognize what countenance it is that the state of Zhào has. ˙stwo SSYEN ˙in t ol na˙thwosi˙n i (1482 Nam 1:52a) moreover, he revealed that it is dhyāna (meditation).
  2. though it be, even. ¶ ˙CYWUNG-˙LYWUY y ¨es.tyey ¨cams.kan ˙in t ol ˙NYELQ-PPAN ay ˙tull i ˙Gwo (1482 Kum-sam 2:13b) how will the monks possibly enter nirvāṇa even for a little while?
  SEE 'yn ˙t ol, -un ˙t ol.
˙in ˙t olwo, cop mod + postmod ('fact') + pcl. because it is. SEE -un ˙t olwo.
in tul, cop mod + postmod. granted that it be/is ..., even though it be/is ... . ¶ Kkwum ey 'n tul ic.keyss.nun ya? I shall never forget it even in my dreams. ¹Nak.hwa 'n tul kkoch i ani 'l ya, ssul.e musam halio [obs = mues hal i yo = mues haci yo] "Fallen blossoms are blossoms still — do not sweep them away". Nay ka an ic.ess.ketun ney 'n tul selma ic.ess.keyss.nun ya? Since I haven't forgotten it, how could you? SEE nwukwu 'n tul; ey 'n tul, eykey 'n tul, eykey se 'n tul, ey se 'n tul, kkaci 'n tul, kkey 'n tul, kkey se 'n tul, mace 'n tul, puthe 'n tul, se 'n tul, tele 'n tul; -ci 'n tul, -e se 'n tul, -key 'n tul, -ki 'n tul, -ki ey se 'n tul, -ko

'n tul, -ta ka 'n tul, -ulye 'n tul, -umye 'n tul, -umyen se 'n tul.
in tus, copula modifier + postmodifier
ın ˙t ye, copula modifier + postmod + postmod. SEE ˙isin ˙t ye, -un ˙t ye, -u˙n i 'n ˙t ye.
i nun, n + pcl. as for this (one).
inya → in ya
in ya, copula mod + postmod. ¶Poktong in ya Is it Poktong? Poktong-i 'n ya Is it Poktong-i? Nwukwu 'n ya Who is it? Yeki ka musunq yek in ya What station is this? Ku key musun soli 'n ya (= musun māl in ya) What do you mean by that?
~ ka (pcl). SEE nwukwu 'n ya ka; in ka ka.
~ lul (pcl). SEE in ka lul.
~ tul (pcl). ¶Tā haksayng in ya tul? Are they all students?
i-nyang, cpd adv. (in) this way, (in) the same way as this, as this is/was, with no change, still, with no letup. CF ku-/ce-nyang.
˙i˙n ye, cop mod + postmod. SEE a˙ni '˙n ye.
i-nyek, n. [vulgar] you. SYN kutay, i sālam, ...
inyo → in yo = in ya
io, 1. AUTH cop; abbr yo; var iwu. The standard spelling is iyo and that spelling is probably well motivated historically, though we are treating the phonetic glide as nondistinctive.
2. → i yo (it is this); → iyo (polite); → iyo = iko (cop ger).
-io → -i yo
iolssita [DEFERENTIAL] = ita (cop) it is ···. ¶Kim Poktong iolssita It is (or I am) Kim Poktong. After a vowel, olssita. Often spelled also iolsita/olsita. ?< iwolsywoita (1876 Kakok 80); < ? + -lq ˙s i-˙ta − we lack attestation of either *˙i˙ywolq or (var) *˙i˙lwolq for the modulated prospective modifier of the copula, finding only ˙ilq, the unmodulated prospective modifier.
iolsoita SEE isiolsoita
io man, AUTH cop + pcl. it is ··· but.
iong [Ceycwu DIAL (Pak Yonghwu 1960:397)] = iyeng < ieng = ileh.key like this, so.
īoy < ˙ı-˙NGWOY, n, postn, postmod. outside of (a limit), except for; ~ (ey) except(ing), save (for), outside (of), but, besides, in addition (to). CF pakk ey.
1. n. ¶Ioy(q) mūncey nun pyel kes i ani 'ta Other problems are unimportant (Dupont 253).
2. postnoun. ¶ī-welq talq īoy ey except for

February. Ku nun welkup īoy ey ttan swuip i com iss.ta He has a little separate income apart from (besides) his salary.
3. postmod. ¶Ku nun na hanthey i chayk ul cwunq īoy ey, tto kūlim to mānh.i cwuess.ta Besides giving me this book, he also gave me many pictures.
i p'ā = i pwā see here!
i pen, adnoun + noun (CF ku/ce pen).
1. this time, the present, the current one, this one; the recent/latest one. ¶~ sihem the recent/last examination. I pen man un yōngse hay cwusipsio Please forgive me just this time. I pen un ney ka chwum chwul chalyey 'ta Now it is your turn to dance. I pen cēncayng ey sālam i elma 'na cwuk.ess.^{s}up.nikka How many people were killed in the late war?
2. next time, the coming (one); presently, shortly, now, next. ¶i penq il.yoil next Sunday. i penq yelum pānghak the coming summer vacation. Ku nun i pen ey Mikwuk ey kanta He is going to America shortly.
i phyen, adnoun + noun.
1. this side/way. SYN i ccok. ¶Cengke-cang un kil i phyen ey iss.ta The station is on this/our side of the street.
2. this/our side, we/us, I/me. SYN i ccok; CF wuli. ¶Yākwu-cēn ey i phyen i ikyess.ta We won the baseball game.
3. your side, you (CF i sālam). ¶I phyen i mence ssawum ul kēlci anh.ess.^{s}o? You provoked the quarrel, didn't you?
ip.nikka, cop FORMAL indic attentive. is it ··· ?
ip.nita, cop FORMAL indic assertive. it is ··· .
ipsyo [Seoul DIAL; menial to superior] = iyo (polite). ····-nun ke l' ipsyo; ····-nun tey 'psyo.
iptikka, cop FORMAL retrospective attentive
iptita, copula FORMAL retrospective assertive
īpuk < ˙ı-˙PUK, n, postn. to the north (of ···); ··· and north. ¶samphalq-senq īpuk north of the 38th parallel. Sewulq īpuk to the north of Seoul. Hān kang īpuk north of the Han River. Samchek īpuk Samchek and north. īpuk sālam a northerner.
i pun, adn + quasi-free n. this esteemed person; he/him, she/her. CF i ay/ca/chi/ēlun/i/nom/ pun/sālam/son.
i pwā, n + vt inf. see here!
i( )sa = i( )za, pcl (+ pcl). CF isa, sa, za. ¶i mal isa tyeksil ho.m ye ... (1776 ^{n}Yempul 38)

these words are correct and ... . LCT takes this as is*[y]*a = ˙i˙sya cop hon inf.

isa, pcl [obs; DIAL (Kyengsang — Mkk 1960:3: 33)] = **iya**. After vowel sa (= **ya**).

i sai / say, adn + n. this interval; (as adv) these days, nowadays; lately, recently, of late. ¶ ~ **uy chengnyen tul** the young men of today. **I sai etteh.sup.nikka** How are you these days? **I sai pi ka mānh.i wass.ta** We have had much rain these days. LIGHT **yo sai / say**. CF **i cuum**.

i sālam, adnoun + noun.
1. this person; he / him, she / her. CF **i ay/ca/chi/ēlun/i/nom/pun/son**.
2. you (informal). ¶ **I sālam eti ka** Where do you think YOU are going? **I sālam wēynq īl ia** What's the matter with you? SYN **i kes**.

īsang < ˙I-˙SSYANG, n, postnoun, postmodifier.
1. more than, above, over, upward of. ¶ **sipchilq īsang** above / over seventeen. **sam-nyenq īsang i toyess.ta** it got to be more than three years (1936 Roth 208). **ī-payk īsang uy sālam i** more than two hundred people (1936 Roth 217). **Ku uy sengcek un cwung īsang ita** His school records are above average.
2. beyond, past, more than; further. ¶ **Ku ccum man un tul.ye ˙ta pwā to toyci man te īsang un an toynta** It's all right to peer in that far, but not beyond.
3. since, now that, seeing that. ¶ **ileh.key toynq īsang ey nun** since it has come to this.
4. that is all, that is the end. ¶ **Īsang ip.nita** That is all (I have to say) = Thank you (for listening / reading); Amen! (Dupont 249).

i say = **i sai**

ise = **isye** = **isie**

īse < ˙I-SYEY, n, postn [uncommon]. to the west (of ···); ··· and west.

isi···, verb stem 'exist'. SEE *is(i)˙ta*.

˙isi··· = ˙i-si-, copula honorific. SEE ˙isi˙na.

isici, copula honorific suspective

isie, 1. < ˙isi˙ye, cop hon inf (= **isye** < ˙i˙sye).
2. → **isiye** (pcl)

is(i)˙kwo, gerund < *is(i)˙ta* (vi). SEE *is˙kwo*.

˙isi˙kwo, copula hon gerund (1462 ¹Nung 1:18a).

isil(q) < ˙isilq, cop hon prosp mod. SEE *˙sil(q)*.

isil(q), prospective modifier < *is(i)˙ta* (exists; with summational epithemes). ¶ *na y ci˙p uy isilq ce˙k uy* (1447 Sek 6:7a) when I was at home. *ne-huy ˙non khe˙n i ˙Gwa ˙na ˙y ci˙p uy isilq ce˙k uy ¨SSYWUW-¨KHWO y ¨mantha˙la* (1459 Wel 10:23a) not so much you people but I am the one who had a lot of trouble when we were athome. *ye˙huyywo˙m i ˙mas.tang ho˙kwo n' ˙i ye˙huyywo˙m i ˙stwo e˙nu isil ˙ppa ˙y.l i ˙Gwo* (1482 Kum-sam 2:37a) separation is to be expected but why is there so much more of this separation?

isi˙la, subjunctive attentive < *is(i)˙ta*.

~ ˙'n ˙t oy. ¶ *ho˙ma hon ka˙ci lwo nwun-[˙]sep the˙li a˙lay isi˙la ˙'n t oy ˙QUNG-˙YWONG ˙i ˙stwo tangtangi ¨twu ka˙ci ¨ep˙su.n i ˙'la* (1482 Kum-sam 4:20b) since they [= Jāng Sān's two eyes] also are below the hairs of the eyebrow in the same way there are accordingly no two ways of putting them to use. SEE -˙ya ˙sila ˙'n ˙to y.

isilq ci, copula prosp modifier + postmodifier

isilq cwul, copula prosp modifier + postmodifier

isil i, 1. cop hon prosp mod + n. 2. = **isil ya**.

isi˙l i, prosp modifier ('exist') + postmodifier.

~ ˙Gwo (postmod). ¶ *e˙tuy ˙'sten SAM-PWUN ˙i ¨mwot ko˙ca ˙PALQ-˙POYK sa˙wona˙Won ¨i˙l i isi˙l i ˙Gwo* (1447 Sek 19:10b) without three divisions provided, where will there ever be eight hundred bad events? *MYENG-˙SWU TYWUNG ey ˙pte ˙tiye isi˙l i Gwo* (1482 Kum-sam 5:24b) why would you have ··· and fallen among the many people? *SAM-TTWO ˙ay pte˙le ti˙l [i] ˙ye˙n i mu˙sum ˙LI-˙QYEK isi˙l i ˙Gwo* (1464 Kumkang 64b) what profit is there if one falls into the three evil paths?

~ ˙'la (cop indic assert). ¶ *˙i ¨HHWUW ˙QILQ-˙QUK ˙SO-CHYEN na˙mon ˙hoy yey ˙za ˙stwo MI-˙LUK ˙PPWULQ ˙i isi˙l i ˙'la* (1447 Sek 23:13a) only a hundred million four thousand odd years from now will a maitreya Buddha exist again. *˙CYWUNG-SOYNG ˙CYEY-˙TTWO ˙honwo˙la s mozo˙m i isi[˙]m ye n' NUNG-¨SWO y isi˙l i 'la* (1482 Kum-sam 2:13a) if you have the mind to save living beings you will have the ability.

~ ˙'lwo swo-ngi ˙'ta (1462 ¹Nung 1:69a).

~ '-ngi s ˙kwo (cop polite + pcl + postmod). ¶ *cephun ˙ptu˙t i e˙nu isi˙l i '-ngi s ˙kwo* (1449 Kok 123) how will one have a feeling of dread?! *ZIN-SOYNG ˙i e˙tuy ˙'s˙ten ˙i ˙kot ho˙n i isi˙l i '-ngi s ˙kwo* (1447 Sek 6:5ab) how can there ever be a life as sad as this?

~ ˙'n i (cop mod + postmod). ¶ *il˙lwo pu˙the THYEN ˙SSYANG ˙ay na˙l i ˙two isi˙l i ˙'n i* (1447 Sek 9:19a) from this/here some will be

born in heaven, too.
ˈisiˈl i ˈˈm ye, cop hon prosp mod + postmod + cop subst + cop inf. ¶ZYE-LOY ˈtwo ˈstwo MWU-SSYANG ˈisiˈl i ˈˈm ye (1465 Wen 1:1:1:63a) the tathāgata is moreover impermanent, too.
isilq ka, cop hon prosp modifier + postmodifier
isilq kes, cop hon prosp mod + noun/postnoun
isilq key, abbr < isilq kes i/i…
isilq s, vi/aux prosp modifier + postmodifier.
  isilq ˈs iˈla (cop indic assert). ¶ ˈTTYWU-TTI ˈnon PPYEN-QAN ˈhi ˈTTYWU ˈho ya kaˈcye isil ˈs iˈla (1465 Wen se:5a) [the word] ˈTTYWU-TTI means having a peaceful life.
  isilq ˈs oy (pcl). ¶ZYE-LOY S CCYWEN-SIN i isil ˈss oy ˈ.n i ˈˈla (1463 Pep 4:89b) it is because it has the tathāgata's whole body (= strength).
isilq ˈt ol, prosp mod ('exist') + postmod + pcl. ¶twosˈk uy mululq ˈCYWUNG isil ˈtt ol miˈli ˈˈalosiˈm ye (1463 Pep 1:168a) he knew in advance that there would be a crowd who would retreat to their seat mats, and … .
isil ya, cop hon prosp modifier + postmodifier
isiˈl ye, prosp mod ('exist') + postmod. ¶ˈKEP ˈi ˈˈnaycywong taˈwoˈm i isiˈl ye (1463 Pep 4:53a) will it happen that the kalpa finally comes to an end? twoloˈhye ˈTTYWU-ˈTTYAK hol ˈkwo.t i isiˈl ye (1482 Kum-sam 2:20a) would there be any place [in the doctrine] where I could get a firmer grasp?
isim, (unmodulated) subst < is(i)ˈta (exists). CF iˈsywom.
  isiˈm ye (cop inf). ¶ ˈnwu y ˈza ˈTI-[ˈ]HHYWEY isiˈm ye ([1447→]1562 Sek 3:7a) just who has wisdom and … . ˈˈCO-ˈSIK uy ilˈhwum ˈul aˈpi isiˈm ye [ˈ]eˈmi iˈsya ˈQILQ-ˈTTYENG hoˈsa-ngi ˈˈta (1459 Wel 8:83a; il-ˈhwum-ˈul) I hope the name of the son will be decided in the presence of the father and the mother. SSYA ˈtwo isiˈm ye ˈCYENG ˈtwo is.noˈn i aˈlwoˈm i NGUY kheˈta (?1468- Mong 39a) it is well to know that both wrong and right exist.
  isiˈm ye nˈ (copula inf + pcl). ¶ ˈˈcyek.keˈna ˈˈeˈtwun keˈs i isiˈm ye nˈ ˈkwot ˈCYWOK ˈˈsamkeˈnul (1463 Pep 4:38a) if, when what is got is but little, one makes do with that … .
ˈisim, copula honorific substantive.
  ˈisiˈm ye (cop inf). ¶KUM s ˈpiˈch isiˈm ye (1447 Sek 6:17a) it is a golden color, and … . mozom polˈkin ˈˈsaloˈm isiˈm ye (1466 Mok 3; cited from LCT with inferred accents) he is a person of enlightened mind.
isim < ˈisim, copula honorific substantive
isin < ˈisin, copula honorific modifier
isin, modifier < is(i)ˈta (exists; summational epithemes). ¶epeˈzi koˈca isin ceˈk uy ilˈhwu.m ul ˈQILQ-ˈTTYENG hoˈsa-ngi ˈˈta (1459 Wel 8:96b) when the parents have got one [= a new child] they decide a name [transitional epitheme – of time].
ˈisiˈna, cop hon advers. ¶ ˈMEN-ˈLI ˈNGWOY s ˈˈil ˈisiˈna (1449 Kok 2) it [= Buddha's] is a work beyond the myriad leagues [of our land], but … .
isin ci, copula honorific modifier + postmodifier
isin cuk, copula hon modifier + postmodifier
isin cwul, copula hon modifier + postmodifier
isiney, cop FAMILIAR honorific indic assertive
isini, 1. copula honorific sequential. 2. → isin i.
isin i, 1. cop hon mod + postmod. 2. = isin ya.
ˈisiˈn i, cop hon mod + postmod. SEE aˈni ˈsiˈn i.
  ~ ˈˈla, (cop indic assert). ¶ ˈta ˈTTI wuˈh uy s PPWO-ˈSALQ s ˈTUK ˈisiˈn i ˈˈla (1459 Wel 17:26a) they all are the bodhisattva's virtue(s) on earth. ˈSSIP-ˈLYWUK ˈi ˈTI-ˈSING skey ˈkot hosiˈn i ˈisiˈn i ˈˈla (1463 Pep 2:43b) sixteen is (with reference to) the victories of his wisdom. SEE ˈysiˈn i ˈˈla.
isin ka, copula hon modifier + postmodifier
isin key, abbr < isin kes i/i…
ˈisin ˈkwo, copula honorific modifier + postmod. ¶muˈsum ˈpuˈlisyan iˈl isin ˈkwo (?1517- Pak 1:8a) what errand is it that you have? [= ˈˈil ˈisin ˈkwo]
isin pa, cop honorific mod + postmodifier
isin tey, cop honorific mod + postmodifier
ˈisin ˈt ol, cop hon mod + postmodifier + pcl. ¶[YWONG-KWUN] ˈisin ˈt ol [THYEN-ˈSYENG] ˈun polkoˈsiˈn i (1445 ¹Yong 71) he was a so-so monarch but heaven's intentions were clear.
isin tul, cop honorific modifier + postmodifier
ˈisin ˈt ye, cop hon mod + postmod + postmod. ¶woˈcik ˈSYENG-ZIN s ˈˈmaˈl isin ˈt ye (1463/4 Yeng 2:36b) are they solely the words of a saint? [taken as copula rather than 'exist']
isinya → isin ya, copula hon mod + postmod
isio (standard spelling isiyo), 1. AUTH cop hon indic assert. 2. (= isiko) cop hon gerund.
isiolsoita [obs] = isip.nita. ¶Onul nay maum ey ¹im hasin ca nun chencwu 'siolsoita (1936 Roth 537) God is present in my heart today.
isita, cop hon indic assertive (or transferentive)

`isi˙ta`, cop hon indic assertive (CF `˙i˙la`); INF `˙i˙sya`. (Indic assert example?) SEE `isi˙n i ˙'la`.
`is(i)˙ta = is˙ta` (> iss.ta), qvi (also aux). stays; exists, is; there is, has. The stem *isi-* regularly shortens to *is-* before an ending that starts with consonant + vowel, including -`˙ta` itself; both the shapes are preserved in modern Phyengan dialects. The modifiers and the substantive, and those forms that include them, do not shorten: `isil(q), isi˙l ye; isim, isi˙m ye.` ABBR `'s(i)˙ta` (after *y, i*), `'ys(i)˙ta`.

The predicates can be negativized as `is˙ti a˙ni °ho˙ta` (SEE `is˙ti`).

isita/is.ta [Phyengan DIAL (Kim Yengpay 1984: 104-5)] = **iss.ta**. Both *isi-* and *is-* are used before **-key, -ko, -ta, -ti** (= **-ci**); only *is-* before **-e, -ul, -un, -umyen, -uni; isi ya = iss.e ya, ise yo** (some places **isi yo**) = **iss.e yo**.
`˙isi˙ta[˙]s-ongi˙'ta` SEE `a˙ni 'si˙ta[˙]s-ongi˙'ta`
isi˙ton, provisional < *is(i)˙ta*. SEE *-˙ya 'si˙ton*.
isitun, copula honorific retrospective modifier
isiye, 1. pcl [lit honorific] = **a** (vocative); after vowels **siye**.
2. → **isie** (> **isye** > **ise**) cop honorific inf.
isi˙ye = i˙sye (v inf)
isiyo = isio, copula hon: (1) AUTH, (2) gerund.
¶ Kulisuto nun Chencwu isiyo sālam isiyo (1936 Roth 120) Christ is God and man.
is.ke˙n i, effective mod < *is˙ta = is(i)˙ta +* postmod. ¶ `˙TTAY-SSING ˙un ˙SYEY-˙KAY pas˙k uy ˙two ˙wohi˙lye ˙PEP-˙SYENG ˙SOYK ˙i is.ke˙n i ˙i ˙SO-THYEN ˙i hon-kas ¨ta ¨pwuy.l i ˙ye` (1459 Wel 1:37a) the Greater Vehicle (mahāyāna) has rather the character of lawfulness even beyond the world; will the four heavens all be empty alike? SEE *-˙a 'ys.ke˙n i Gwa*.
is˙kesi˙nol, aux hon lit concessive. ¶ *pwuthye s wu[h] s ip-si˙Gwu˙l ey s the˙li hona˙h i na˙ma is˙kesi˙nol* (1447 Sek 23:56b) since there remained a single hair from Buddha's upper lip.
is˙kesi˙ton, vi hon provisional. ¶ `PPYEN-QAN ˙thi a˙ni ˙hosin mo ¨toy is˙kesi˙ton` (1475 Nay 1:40a) if he [the king] has a stretch of being ill.
is.ke˙tun, provisional < *is˙ta = is(i)˙ta*. ¶ *e˙tin namzin ˙in ¨yang ˙u˙lwo ho˙kwo is.ke˙tun* (?1517- ¹No 2:54b) he was pretending to be a good fellow, but ... . SEE *˙ho˙ya 's.ke˙tun, ˙ho˙ya 'ys.ke˙tun*.
is˙key, adverbative < *is˙ta*. ¶ *pwu¨thye y ˙i ˙MYWOW-˙PEP-HHWA KYENG ˙u˙lwo ˙pwu˙cywok ˙hwol ˙tt oy is˙key ˙khwo ˙cye 'y.n i ˙'la* (1463 Pep 4:134b) Buddha wanted us to have people keep relying on this Lotus sūtra.
is˙kwo, ger < *is˙ta = is(i)˙ta*. ABBR *'s˙kwo*.
¶ `¨syeWul [˙CCUK SSIN] is˙kwo` (1445 ¹Yong 37) there was a traitorous minister in the capital, and ... . *wo˙cik [¨SYWUY] y is.kwo [˙TTI] y ¨ep.su˙m ye n' ki˙lum ˙ko.t hoy˙ya [= ˙ko.t hoy˙ya = ˙kot ho˙ya] hulle ti.l i ˙'m ye* (1579 Kwikam 1:21b) if you only have water and no land it flows down like oil, and ... . ALSO 1481 Twusi 7:23b, ... SEE *˙ho˙ya 's˙kwo*.
is.non, proc mod < *is˙ta = is(i)˙ta*. SEE *˙ho˙ya 's.non*. 1. (epitheme extruded from subject).
¶ *ingey is.no˙n i* (1465 Wen 3:2:2:42ab) those who are here. ¶ *TTANG pas[k] pwo˙l i is.no˙n ywo* (1462 ¹Nung 1:50b) are there any who watch [from] outside the hall?
2. (summational epitheme).
2a. ¶ *˙kwot is.non ˙t ol ¨a˙n i* (1482 Kumsam 2:2b) knew at once that they were there.
¶ *SSYA ˙two isi˙m ye ˙CYENG ˙two is.no˙n i a˙lwo˙m i NGUY khe˙ta* (?1468- Mong 39a) it is well to know that both wrong and right exist. *til˙Gwo˙m i pan˙to˙ki is.non ˙toy ¨ep˙su.l ye '˙n i 's˙ton* (1462 ¹Nung 1:67a) there need not be any stumbling blocks. *is.non ˙tos ˙hwo˙toy is˙ti a˙ni ˙hwo˙m i* (1459 Wel 1:36a) that it seems to exist yet does not exist.
2b. (summational epitheme used in extended predicate). ¶ *is.no˙n i ˙ya ¨ep˙su.n i ˙ya* (?1468- Mong 62a) is there or isn't there? *as.ka˙Won ˙ptu˙t i is.no˙n i ˙ye* (1447 Sek 6:25b) are you feeling stingy? *icey e˙tuy is.no˙n i '-ngi s ˙kwo* (1459 Wel 23:78a) where are they now? *e˙tuy ¨tywo˙hon mol ˙phol˙l i is.non ˙kwo* (?1517- Pak 1:62a) where is there a good horse dealer? *NAM THYEN-˙TYWUK pa˙lol s ¨ko˙z ay is.no˙n i* (1447 Sek 6:43b) it is on the shore of the sea of South India. *kutuy s a˙pa ¨ni˙m i is.no˙n i s ˙ka – is.no˙n i 'ngi ˙'ta* (1447 Sek 6:14b) Is your father here? – He is here, sir.
is.nwo˙la, proc modulated indic assert < *is˙ta = is(i)˙ta*. SEE *˙ho˙ya 's.nwo˙la*.
is˙nwon, modulated proc mod < *is˙ta = is(i)˙ta*.
~ ˙t i (postmod + pcl). ¶ *MWU-MYENG ˙i ˙SSILQ ˙lwo ¨THYEY is˙nwon ˙t i a˙ni ˙'la* (1459 Wel 2:22c) the primal darkness (avidyā = ignorance) does not really have form.
is˙nwo-ngi ˙'ta, proc modulated polite (< *is˙ta*

= is(i)·ta) + cop indic assertive. SEE 'ho·ya 's·nwo-ngi '·ta.
is'o = isyo, abbr < isio (AUTH cop honorific)
-iso(i) [Cincwu DIAL (Mkk 1960:3:34)] = -sipsio.
Kaiso(i) = Kasipsio Please go / come (there).
i son, adn + quasi-free n. this person; he / she; [IRONICAL] this "gentleman" / "lady". CF i ay/ ca/chi/i/nom/pun/sālam.
i·sopte·n i, aux v deferential retr modifier + postmod. SEE 'y·sopte·n i.
iss.ci anh.ta, negativized qvi. CF ēps.ci anh.ta.
iss.i, der adv < iss.ta; [DIAL] = iss.key. CF ēps.i. ¶Casin iss.i hayngtong hay la Act with confidence. Kunke iss.i māl ul halyem (CM 2:97) I'd like you to speak with some basis.
iss.ke la = iss.e la stay!
iss.nun, proc mod < iss.ta$_2$ ('stays'). In Seoul this normally replaces iss.un, the expected modifier of iss.ta$_1$ ('exists; is located; has').
iss.nunta, proc indic assert < iss.ta$_2$. stays; elapses. SEE p. 218, §11.7.3.
iss.nya, 1. iss.n' ya [lit] abbr < iss.nun ya
2. iss.ny a [colloq; < iss.ni a] = iss.ni?
iss.ta$_1$ < is(i)·ta, qvi. NEG (for all) ēps.ta, (for 1 and 2) iss.ci anh.ta. HON (meanings 1 and 2) kyēysita; (other meanings) iss.usita (– the exalting reference is to the possessor), but kyēysita is also possible for 3b, and for 3a if the possessed is animate. The paradigm of iss.ta$_1$ ('exists; is located; has') is hybrid, partly like an adjective (indic assert iss.ta), partly like a processive verb: the processive modifier iss.nun of iss.ta$_2$ replaces the modifier (*)iss.un. CF the remarks under ēps.ta. SEE isita/is.ta.
1. (existence). there is, it is (in existence), exists. Yēys nal ey ecinq īm-kum i iss.ess.ta Once there was (there lived) a wise king. Ilenq īl i eti iss.ta 'm! How can such things be?
2. (location).
2a. is (temporarily in / at a place). ¶Nay chayk i eti iss.n' ya – chayk-sang wi ey iss.ta Where's my book? – It's on the desk.
2b. is located / situated, is, lies, sits, stands. ¶kangq ka ey iss.nun cel a temple standing by the river bank. Cwungkwuk un Cosen se-ccok ey iss.ta China lies to the west of Korea. San twī ey sī'-nay ka iss.ta Behind the hill there runs a brook.
2c. is contained / included (in). ¶Ku chayk ey cēse mok.lok i iss.ta The book contains a bibliography.
2d. consists / lies / rests (in). ¶Cwuqkwen un uyhoy ey iss.ta Sovereignty resides in the Assembly. Hāyngpok un māncok ey iss.ta Happiness lies in contentment.
2e. is found / got / had (CF vt et.ta, chac.ta). ¶Cēnhwa chayk i eti iss.ess.nun ya Where did you find the phone book?
3. (possession)
3a. has, possesses, owns. [Both possessor and possessed can be marked by the nominative pcl i / ka, but the possessor is often thematized and subdued with un / nun and it may be marked by the dative hanthey or eykey.] ¶Ku uy ttal un um.ak caycwu ka iss.^{s}up.nita His daughter is endowed with musical talents. Na nun na hanthey iss.nun tōn ul tā ssess.ta I spent all the money I had. Tta' nim to kyēysip.nikka / iss.usip.nikka? Do you have a daughter, too? Nwu ka sikan i iss.na Who has time?
3b. has the occasion / experience, (does, has done) on occasion. ····-unq īl i iss.ta has (ever), once did. ····-nunq īl i iss.ta sometimes does, does do it. ¶Hak.kyo lul kaluchi(si)nq īl i iss.^{s}up.nikka (iss.usip.nikka, kyēysip.nikka)? Have you ever taught school?
3c. carries (in stock), keeps (for sale), sells, has (available). [Impersonal possessor marked by the dative ey or nominative i/ka]. ¶I kes un Hwasin ey man iss.ta This is (to be) had only at Hwasin [Dept Store]. Mikwuk tāmpay ka iss.^{s}up.nikka Do you sell American cigarettes?
4. (occurrence)
4a. (an event) is held, takes place, opens, comes off (CF yellita). ¶Taum hōyuy nun ēncey iss.nun ya When is the next meeting to be held? Ecey kiha sihem i iss.ess.ta We had an exam in geometry yesterday.
4b. it breaks out, arises, occurs, happens, takes place, there is (CF il.e nata). ¶musunq īl i iss.tun ci no matter what happens, come what may. Ku pupu sai ey musunq īl i iss.ess.nun ci na nun molukeyss.ta I don't know what has passed (gone on) between that couple. Il-nyen an ey yele kaci īl i iss.ess.ta In that one year many things happened.
iss.ta$_2$ = iss.nunta, vi. NEG iss.ci anh.ta = iss.ci anh.nunta; HON kyēysita = kyēysinta. Modern Seoul iss.ta$_2$ 'stays' has the paradigm

of a processive verb (^{1}Yi Tongcay 1989).

1. stays, stops; waits (around), pauses, waits (momentarily); is (temporarily) in a place. ¶**Ne yeki iss.e la** You stay here. **Kaman hi iss.ca** Just a second! (M 1:1:342). **Ne eti iss.ess.nun ya** Where have you been?

2. time elapses. ¶**com te iss.umyen** a little bit later on. **iss.ta ka** after a while.

iss.ta₃, aux vi. SEE **-ko ~ , -e ~** .

iss.ta₄ = **iss.ta (ka)**, transferentive of **iss.ta**₁,₂,₃

iss.ta ka, cpd adv (transferentive < **iss.ta** + pcl).

1. [often spelled **ittaka**] after a while, after a short time, a little later. ¶**Na nun com iss.ta ka cenyek ul mek.keyss.ta** I will have dinner a little later.

2. stays and / but then; elapses and / but then.

3. (other meanings of **iss.ta**?)

iss.ul(q), prosp mod < **iss.ta**. ¶**wūncen halq swu iss.ulq sālam** (^{1}Yi Tongcay 1989:352:n31) one who will be able to drive. **musunq īl i iss.ul ttay ey nun** in case of emergency. **Yo cuum un latio ka ecci 'na mānh.un ci pang mata hana ssik iss.ta ko halq swu iss.ulq cengto 'ci yo** Lately radios have become so common it's reached the point where you can say every room has one.

iss.un, mod < **iss.ta** [rare; usually replaced by **iss.nun** or **iss.tun**].

1. ... that existed / exists (etc). ¶**sēnke ka iss.un ithut-nal ey** on the day after the election was held. **wūncen halq swu iss.un sālam** (^{1}Yi Tongcay 1989:352:n31) one who could drive.

?2. ... who stayed. ¶**? cip ey iss.un na** (^{1}Yi Tongcay 1989:339) I who stayed at home.

iss.utoy, concessive < **iss.ta**. SEE **-toy**.

`is·ta` = `is(i)·ta` (exists). ¶`WUY ¨cyekwo·may is·ta` (1463/4 Yeng 2:62a) they have a small amount of position. `·PWULQ-·PEP ·i ·za na ·'y inge·kuy two ¨cywoko·m achi is·ta` (1482 Nam 1:14a) there is some of Buddha's law right here where I am. ALSO: 1462 ^{1}Nung 2:83a, 1482 Kum-sam 3:9b, ...

`is.ta·la`, retr indic assert < `is·ta = is(i)·ta`. SEE `·ho·ya ·'s.ta·la`.

`is·tan`, `is·ten`, retr mod < `is·ta = is(i)·ta`.

  `is·ta.n i` (postmod). ¶`nwo·lwo.m ol a·ni ho.ya is·ta.n i` (1481 Twusi 7:23a) was not playing. SEE `·ho·ya ·'s.ta·n i`.

  `is·te.n i` (postmod). SEE `·ho·ya ·'s.te·n i`.

  `is·ten ·ta` (postmod). ¶`¨ne y e·tuy ·ka is·ten ·ta` (?1517- Pak 1:37b) where have you been?

  `is·ten ·t ay n'` (postmod + pcl + pcl). ¶`·SYANG is·ten ·t ay n' pan·toki CIN-SIM ·ho·ya muy·ywu·m ul ¨nay.l i ·'le.n i ·'la` (1464 Kumkang 79b) when one had these distinctive marks (of ...) one would emit glaring hatred.

`is·tas·ta`, retr emotive indic assertive < `is·ta = is(i)·ta`. ¶`he·mu·l i ·SSILQ lwo na ·'ykey is·tas·ta` (1463 Pep 2:6a) the fault is really mine. ALSO: 1482 Kum-sam 4:22b.

`is·ten`, retr mod < `is·ta = is(i)·ta`. SEE `is·tan`; `·ho·ya ·'s·ten`.

`is·tesin`, retr hon mod < `is·ta = is(i)·ta`.

  ~ `·ka` (postmod). ¶`[CYA-YANG] k ¨sey ·cwuy ¨nyey ·two is·tesin ·ka` (1445 ^{1}Yong 88) were there [not] three rats on the eaves also in olden days?!

  `is·tesi·n i s ·ka` SEE `-·tesi·n i s ·ka`.

`is·ti`, suspective < `is·ta = is(i)·ta`. ¶`sul·hwu.m i inge·kuy is·ti a·ni ho·n i ·Ga` (1481 Twusi 7:14a) is there no sorrow here? `[¨SYWOW-ZIN] ·i ¨moy·zil ci·p uy is·ti a·ni hota·n i` (?1517- Pak 1:58b) the commoner was not at home day after day. `koma.n ·'i is·ti a·ni ho·m ye n'` (1462 ^{1}Nung 1:77b) unless it is still. `¨cams.kan ·ina mozom nwo·ha ·phyea·l ye ·mwom ·two ·wohi·lye is·ti a·ni khe·n i` (1475 Nay 2:1:2b) for just a little while I have wanted to set forth [what is in] my heart, and my body itself has been more or less absent. ALSO: 1481 Twusi 8:2a, ... CF `¨ep·ta`.

`·i ·ston`, `is·ton`, pcl < `·i s ·t on` ('as for the fact of [being] this'). just, precisely, only. ABBR (after y, i) `·'ston`. ¶` ... mozom ·is·ton mwuy ·Gwusi·l i ·ye` (1449 Kok 62) but would his mind waver?! `·homol·mye ... ·i ·sto·n ye` just how much more so?! ¶`·homol·mye CHIN ·hi ye·le ka·ci s me·cun ¨i·l ol ·SSYWU ·hwo·m isto·n ye` (1459 Wel 21:88-9) how much worse is it being subject to various evil deeds oneself?! `mozo·m i cwu·kun ·coy ·'Gey khe·n i ·homol·mye CIN-·SSILQ s ·TTYENG ·uy ·hi·m isto·n ye` (1462 ^{1}Nung 9:61a) when the soul was turned to ashes was the power of true samādhi (abstract meditation) just all the greater? `·homol·mye tey ·Gwun ce·k ul [TANG] ·hwo.m isto·n ye` (1481 Twusi 7:23a) just how much worse is it when faced with warming it [the food] up?!

  `·homol·mye ... ·isto·n i-ngi s ·ka` just how much more so?! ¶`·homol·mye QA-LA-·HAN ¨KWA

˙lol ˙TUK ˙˙kuy ˙hwo˙m isto˙n i-ngi s ˙ka (1447 Sek 19:4b) how much more so is being allowed to obtain the effect of an arhan?! ˙SWU ¨ep˙kwo n' ˙homol˙mye ku mwol˙Gay 'sto˙n i-ngi s ˙ka (1464 Kumkang 62b) they are innumerable, but how much more so is the sand?!

NOTE: It is not clear whether some instances would be better treated as *i 'sto˙n ye* with the nominative particle (and ellipted predicate), as we treat the parallel cases with *y 'sto˙n ye*.

SEE -*ke˙n i 'sto˙n ye*, -*Ge˙n i 'sto˙n ye*, -*no˙n i 'sto˙n ye*, -*u˙l [i] 'ye˙n i ˙˙ston*; *y 'sto˙n ye*. CF *is˙ten, e˙tuy 's˙ten* (˙˙sten, ˙˙ston, ˙˙stun).

is˙twoswo˙n i, emotive-emotive mod < *is˙ta = is(i)˙ta*. SEE ˙*ho˙ya 's˙twoswo˙n i*.

is˙twota, emotive indic assert < *is˙ta = is(i)˙ta*. ¶*ce 'y ˙pi.ch i [QUN] ˙kot ˙hwo.m i is˙twota* (1481 Twusi 7:38b) at times it has a color like silver! SEE -˙*a 'ys.two˙ta, ˙ho˙ya 's˙two˙ta*. ALSO: 1481 Twusi 25:47a.

*****isul(q)** → *isil(q)*, prosp mod < *is(i)˙ta* (exists)

*****isun** → *isin*, mod < *is(i)˙ta* (exists)

is'wu = **isyu**, abbr < **isiwu** = **isio** AUTH cop hon

˙isya⋯ , cop modulated honorific

˙i˙sya, cop hon inf. ¶*hon ka˙ci s ˙SYENG ˙i˙sya* (1447 Sek 13:29a) it is a kind of surname, and ⋯ . ˙*wuli susu˙ng i˙sya* (1459 Wel 18:42b) he is our teacher, and ⋯ . ALSO: 1459 Wel 8:83a, ⋯ . SEE ˙*isya˙two; a˙ni ˙˙sya*.

i˙sya = **i˙sye**, inf < *isi˙ta* (exists). ¶*hon me˙li ko[l]˙Wa i˙sya* ⋯ ¨*twu me˙li ko[l]˙Wa i˙sye* (1449 Kok 135) one head is engaged, ⋯ [when] two heads are engaged ⋯ . ALSO: *i˙sya* (1459 Wel 8:83a); *i˙sye* (1447 Sek 6:4ab). SEE *i˙sye*.

[˙]**isya-˙s-ongi ˙˙ta**, cop modulated hon + bnd v polite + cop indic assert. ¶*SYEY-PANG s ˙SYENG-ZIN ˙i ˙ZIP-˙MYELQ ˙hosi˙non ˙SYANG isya-˙s-ongi ˙˙ta* (1447 Sek 23:22b) it is a scene of the holy man of the west achieving nirvāṇa.

˙isyas˙ta, cop modulated hon emotive indic assert. ¶˙*i ˙skwu¨m un ZYE-LOY s ˙NYELQ-PPAN ˙SYANG ˙isyas˙ta* (1447 Sek 23:27b) this dream is a scene of the tathāgata's nirvāṇa. *SYEN-ZIN ˙tol˙h i hanolq* (= *hanol [s]*) *SSIN-LYENG ˙isyas[˙]ta* ([1447→]1562 Sek 3:33a) the immortals (ṛṣi) are spirits of heaven. *KYWOW-KYWOW ˙ho.ya ¨pyel s kawon-toy s twu˙lyewun ˙to.l [˙]isyas˙ta* (1482 Kum-sam 2:24b) brightly shining it is a round moon in the midst of clouds [epithematic identification]. CF *'syas˙ta, ˙i˙lusyas˙ta*.

˙isya˙two, cop hon inf + pcl. ¶*pi˙lwok ˙TTAY-˙SYENG ˙isya˙two NUNG ˙hi ˙MWULQ ˙ey na˙za ˙ka pskay˙hye kol˙hoy˙ti ¨mwot ho˙si.l i ˙˙la* (1462 ¹Nung 2:50b) even a great sage cannot approach objects and analyze them.

isye < ˙*i˙sye*, abbr < **isie** < ˙*isi˙ye*, cop hon inf *i˙sye*, inf < *isi˙ta* (exists). ¶*koma.n 'i ¨mwot i˙sye* (1447 Sek 6:30a) could not stay still but ⋯ . *SAM-NYEN ˙i ¨mwot ˙cha i˙sye* (1447 Sek 6:4ab) it is less than three years, and ⋯ . *SYENG-˙KAK ˙i ˙kus polk˙ta ˙hosya¨m on mol˙ka kwoyGwoy [˙]hi i˙sye pi˙chwuylq ˙s ol nil˙Gwo˙toy MI-˙MYWOW ˙hi pol˙kwo.m i˙Gwo* (1462 ¹Nung 4:13ab) his saying that the inherent knowledge is unmistakably bright means it shines in its calm clarity; it is a subtle radiance, and ⋯ . ALSO: 1481 Twusi 22:7a, ⋯ .

~ ˙*two*. ¶*mu˙zuyye˙Wun ¨i˙l i i˙sye ˙two* (1447 Sek 9:24b) though you have frightening experiences. ˙*i KYENG ti˙nil ¨ssalo¨m i inge˙kuy i˙sye ˙two* (1447 Sek 19:17b) even if there are people here who will preserve this sūtra ⋯ . ˙*kul nilkta ˙ka mos˙ti ¨mwot ˙ho˙ye ˙sye ˙non pi˙lwok spolon ¨i˙l i i˙sye two* (1518 Sohak-cho 8:38-9) though sometimes he cannot stop in the midst of reading, so it is rapid.

~ ˙*za*. ¶*pan˙to˙ki MA-TUNG ˙i i˙sye ˙za e˙lwu hon ka˙ci ˙˙la nilo˙l i ˙˙la* (1462 ¹Nung 1:17a) Mātanga will necessarily have to be present before we can say it is the same.

⋯ ˙*ay* / ˙*uy* / ˙*ey* ~ (being) in / at. ¶¨*mwoy.h ay i˙sye non* ⋯ (1481 Twusi 8:66a) in the mountains. *TUNG-KWANG ˙i cip pas˙k uy i˙sye* (1462 ¹Nung 1:53a) the lamplight is outside the house and (so) ⋯ . *ku TYWUNG ˙ey i˙sye* (1463 Pep 5:212b) is in their midst, and ⋯ . ALSO: 1459 Wel 17:35a; 1462 ¹Nung 1:50b, 7:18a; ⋯ .

i˙sye ˙˙la SEE *i˙sye ˙y˙la*

i˙syen < *i˙si-ye-n*, v effective mod. ¶˙*PEP ˙ey i˙syen il˙hwu¨m i* (1463 Pep 1:180a) the name that is in the Law. ˙*wa 's.te˙n i ˙i˙syen ˙t i* (1586 Sohak 6:32b) = ˙*wa ¨sate˙n i* (1518 Sohak-cho 9:36a) the time since being (= living) here.

i˙sye ˙y˙la, inf < *is(i)˙ta* + abbr < ˙*i˙la* (cop indic assert). SEE -˙*e ˙y˙la*.

isyo, abbr < **isio** (AUTH cop hon)

isyu, abbr < **isiwu** = **isio** (AUTH cop hon)
i·sywo- < **isi-·wo-*, v + modulator (= *i·sywu-*).
 i·sywo.l i ·'la (1459 Wel 7:26b), *i·sywol ·kwot* (1465 Wen 2:2:2:12a), *i·sywolq ·t in ·t ay n'* (1462 ¹Nung 1:55a)
 i·sywola (1481 Twusi 22:45a).
 i·sywo·m ay s (1447 Sek 13:17a); *i·sywo·m i* (1459 Wel 9:27b), *i·sywo.m i* (1481 Twusi 8:6b); *i·sywom ·kwa* (1459 Wel 7:31a); *i·sywo·m ol* (1462 ¹Nung 1:53a, 2:40a), *i·sywo.m ol* (1463/4 Yeng 2:31b), *isywo.m ol* (1481 Twusi 7:11b), *i·sywo.m ol* (1482 Kum-sam 2:11a); *i·sywo.m o·lwo* (1465 Wen 1:2:1:39b).
 i·sywo.n i (1481 Twusi 15:4b).
 i·sywo·toy (1447 Sek 9:2b, 1459 Wel 2:12b, 1462 ¹Nung 2:84b, ?1468⁻ Mong 63b).
i·sywu- < **isi-·wu-*, v + modulator (= *i·sywo-*).
 i·sywul ·tt in ·t ayn (1462 ¹Nung 1:51a).
 i·sywu·m i (1459 Wel 9:21b, 1462 ¹Nung 1:89a), *i·sywu·m on* (1463 Pep 3:71b). *·i ·i·sywum ·ka ·i ¨ep·swom ·ka* (1482 Kum-sam 3:39a) does this exist or does this not exist?
 i·sywu.n i (1481 Twusi 7:24b), *i·sywun ·t oy* (1462 ¹Nung 1:65b).
ita < **·i·ta* (→ *·i·la*), copula; after vowel **'ta** but MK **'y·ta* (→ *'y·la* but *·'la* after *i* or *y* only). VAR **ilota** < *·ilwo·ta*. SEE **iyo** (= **iko**), **ila** (= **ita, ie,** ...), **ia** (= **ie**). CF *¨i[l]'ta*, ? **ilta**.
 1. cop indic assert. it is / equals, it is a case (an instance) of, it is a matter of. **A ka X ita** A is X. **X ita** It is X; It is a matter of X. **A ka B ka ani 'ta** A is not B. **B ka ani 'ta** It is not B; It is not a matter of B.
 NOTE: Ordinarily the copula form must be preceded by something (typically a noun) to which it is attached without pause. After a vowel the stem **i-** is usually reduced to **y-** when an ending with a vowel is attached (**i-e → ye**) and omitted with a consonant is attached (**i-ta → 'ta**); the shortened forms are usual in speech and common in written sentences, too. (But monosyllabic forms such as **im, in, il(q)** often emerge intact.) That shortening makes many copula forms identical with forms abbreviated from **hata**, though the abbreviated forms were usually distinct in MK, where the copula was reduced no further than a glide *'y-* except after *i* and *y* where that would create an unacceptable string requiring further reduction of the glide to nothing. For clarity, it is often wise to write the unabbreviated forms of **hata** and **ita**. Many of the inflected forms of the copula are treated quite often as quasi-particles. For more on the negative copula, see **ani, i** (pcl) 3. On using or not using an apostrophe to mark the reduced forms of the copula, see **ie** (note).
 2. transferentive. it is ··· and then (something changes). ¶**Etten ttay pomyen nolan sayk ita (ka) etten ttay pomyen huyn sayk ita** Some times it looks to be yellow and other times it looks to be white. **Etten ttay n' waysik ita (ka) etten ttay n' yangsik ita (ka) kuleci yo** (What we do is) sometimes we have Japanese food and sometimes we have western food.
 3. (= **ita ka**) quasi-pcl (cop transferentive):
 3a. used after particles to show a shift of location or of purpose. ¶**Kōl-pang ey 'ta (ka) kel.ess.ta** He hung it in the closet. **Sang wi ey 'ta (ka) noh.ass.ta** He put it upon the table. **Congi ey 'ta (ka) ssusey yo** Write it on the paper. **Yeki 'ta tocang ul chisipsio** Stamp your seal here. **I kes ul tā mues ey 'ta ssun' ya** (= **ssunun ya**) What do you use all these things for?
 3b. inserted between infinitive (-e) and a verb of giving, to emphasize the shift in benefit of the favor reported. There is an interval of space involved between the "doing" and the "favoring", so that the one doing the favor has to "bring" the object that is involved. ¶**chayk ul pillye 'ta cwuta** does someone the favor of lending him some books. **Sinmun ul sa 'ta cwusey yo** Buy me a newspaper. **Sensayng nim kkey Hānkwuk ūmsik ul ma(y)ntul.e 'ta tulikeyss.ˢup.nita** I will make you some Korean food, sir. **Latio lul kochye 'ta tao** Get the radio fixed. CF **kac' 'ta** < **kacye 'ta**.
 3c. indicates a shift of direction after the infinitives **chyē** 'ascends', **kēnne** 'crosses', **nāy** 'puts out', **naylye** 'descends', **nemkye** 'puts over, transmits', **tol.a** 'returns', **tulye** 'puts in'. ¶**chyē 'ta pota** looks up. **kil ul kēnne 'ta pota** looks across the road. **chang pakk ul nāy 'ta pota** looks out the window. **naylye 'ta pota** looks down. **tam wi lo nemkye 'ta pota** looks over the wall. **pang ul tul.ye 'ta pota** looks into the room. **tol.a 'ta pota** looks back. **tol.a 'ta suta** turns around, turns one's back.
 3d. (miscellaneous, after inf) **tte 'ta mīlta**

pushes aside; shifts (blame) onto another. **phyo lul sa 'ta noh.ta** gets the tickets bought. **pat.e 'ta phalta** sells at retail.

3e. emphasizes the particles **ey, eykey, hanthey, ulo (sse)**. ¶**Nwukwu hanthey / eykey 'ta ilen māl ul hay** Just who do you think you're talking to? / Just who(m) can I tell this to? SEE **-ey 'ta, ulo 'ta**.

3f. (miscellaneous) **keki (ey) 'ta** on top of that, in addition, what's more.

NOTE: For a different interpretation of 3, as a shortening of **tak.a** inf of (*)**tak- = taku-** ('approach') see Choy Hyenpay, Hankul 127:7-27 (1960). I believe Ramstedt (1939:98, 156) was the first to treat **(-e) 'ta ka** as the copula transferentive. For a still different approach, taking both **ta** and **ka** as particles, see Hong Yunphyo 1975, who offers us examples of the precursor of **ey 'ta** from 1489 Kup-kan 6:8 [a text unavailable to me] and 1608 Thaysan 36b (*kasom ay ta thi.m ye n'* 'if one hits on the chest' *[ka-som-ay]*) and of **ey 'ta ka** from 1632 Twusi cwung-kan 25:27b (*na lol pwonayya ney ko[.z] ay ta ka twu.l 'ye.n ywo* 'would it send me to the shore where you are?'); also of **ulo 'ta ka** from 1677 Pak-cwung 1:20 (*kulkey lwo ta ka kulk-pis.ki lul* KEN-CENG *hi hwotwoy* 'tidied up the smoothing nicely by applying a carpenter's plane'), and later from 1797 Olyun 3:11b. But, for Hong's argument the telling examples are those of ˙*lol ta ˙ka*, twice used to translate the Chinese accusative preposition bǎ in ?1517⁻ Pak: (1:57a) *a˙ki ˙lul ta ˙ka ˙stwo meli kas˙kwo* (= *kask-˙kwo*) 'tonsures the child again and'; (1:56a) *a˙ki ˙lul ta ˙ka tol˙kwo˙ci ˙yey yes.no˙n i ˙'la* (= *ye[n]c.no˙n ˙i [i]˙la*) 'puts the child up onto the wagon'. A serious problem for our explanation of (3): why was the MK version -˙*e ˙'ta ˙ka* rather than *-˙*e ˙'yta ˙ka* or *-˙*e ˙'yla ˙ka*? There is a somewhat similar problem with explaining -˙*e ˙''la*. Also, there is an accentual anomaly (§2.12.4, p. 77).

ita, postnom v insep. does [usually = **hata**]. SEE **wumcik ~ , kkancak ~ , kkutek ~ , tulmek ~ , soksak ~ , (p)pantuk ~ , panttuk ~ . chwuk inta** wets, dampens (**chwuk-chwuk hata** is damp / wet). CF **kelita, hata**. NOTE: Since this is usually preceded by /k/ we are quite tempted to regard it as **k[el]ita**, but the preceding **k** generally belongs to the prior morpheme. And the few cases after /l/ might be taken to be **[ke]lita: soktal ~ = soktak ~** whispers; **cikkel / caykkal ~** clatters (but there is also **cikkel kelita**).

ita, vt. puts / carries on the head. VC **iwuta**.
īta, vt. roofs, puts a roof on. SYN **īs.ta**.
¨*i˙ta*, indic assert < ¨*i[l]˙ta*, vi. becomes (= *towoy˙ta*), comes into being, is accomplished / achieved. ¶ ··· ¨*hoyng˙tye˙k i ¨i˙ta ho˙n i ˙'la* (1459 Wel 7:44b) it is said that achievements (of ···) come into being. CF ˙*ilwo˙ta; towoy˙ta*.
~ s (pcl). ¶ ˙SSYWUK ˙*un ni˙kul ˙ss i˙n i ¨i˙ta s ˙ptu.t i˙la* (1462 ¹Nung 8:33b) [the word] ˙SSYWUK is "to ripen"; it has the meaning of "becomes something".

ita (ka), cop transferentive (+ pcl). it is ··· and then (something changes), SEE **ita 2-3; ey 'ta (ka), 'ta (ka), ulo 'ta (ka), tey 'ta (ka)**.

ita ka to, copula transferentive + pcl + pcl. ¶**Cōh.un nal-ssi 'ta ka to kapcaki pi ka ssot.a cikwu n' hayss.ta** It would be nice weather and then all of a sudden it would start pouring. SEE **iess.ta ka to**.

i-ta(k)ci, cpd adverb. to this extent / degree, like this, thus, in this way, so (much). ¶**Yenge ka i-taci him tul.e se ya, eti kongpu hakeyss.na!** With English as tough as all this, how can I ever learn it! **Kicha ka way i-taci nuc.ta 'm!** Why is the train so damn late?! LIGHT **yo-taci**.

i tay lo, adn + n + pcl. like this, as it is/stands, intact, untouched; as things now stand, thus. ¶**Hōy ey i tay lo ka to, cōh.un ya** May I go to the meeting as I am? **Kamul.um i i tay lo olay kamyen, khun hyungnyen i tulkeyss.ta** If the dry weather keeps on like this we will have a very bad year. **Chayk-sang wi ey chayk tul ul i tay lo twue la** Leave these books on the desk just as they are. **Ku uy cal-mos ul i tay lo nāy-pelye twulq swu ēps.ta** We can't let his wrongdoings go unchallenged. CF **ku/ce tay lo**.

itey, FAMILIAR cop retr assert. SYN **iley**. ¶**Ku haksayng i kkolcci 'tey** That student was at the bottom of the class.

iti, copula retrospective attentive

*****i˙ti**, copula suspective. Does not occur, because the cop negativizes only as *a˙ni ˙'ta* (= *a˙ni ˙[y]˙ta*). Modern uses of **ici** do not occur in MK.
¨*i˙ti*, suspective < ¨*i[l]˙ta* (become; be formed).

¶*mwo῾lo῾may* ·NGWEN *i ῎i῎ti ῎mal῎Gwo 'la ῎hote῎n i* ([1447→]1562 Sek 11:30_, cited from LCT 574b with inferred accents) wanted the request not to be fulfilled.

i to, n + pcl. this (one) too / even.

῾**ito῎lwok** = ῾*i῎two῎lwok*, cop projective. till it is (gets to be), for (a mounting quantity). ¶ *῾pam s tywung ῾ito῎lwok ca῎ti a῎ni ῎hosi῎m ye* (1475 Nay 2:2:38b) does not get to bed till midnight, and ... .

ītong < ῎I-TWONG, n, postn [uncommon]. to the east (of ...); ... and east.

(?*)**itoy**, copula concessive. although it is ... (= **ila to**). Usually replaced by **ilotoy**.

itta(ka) → **iss.ta (ka)** after a little while.

ittakum, adv < **iss.ta (ka)** + **-kum** or **(kak-)kum** (→ **kakkum**). from time to time, now and then, occasionally; frequently, often. ~ **ssik** every now and then, at intervals, from time to time, frequently. ¶**Ittakum atul hanthey se phyēnci ka onta** I receive occasional letters from my son. **Ku ka ittakum kongpu to hanta** Sometimes he studies, too.

i ttawi, cpd n. [pejorative]. a thing / person of this sort; such a one; this kind / sort (of) (**i ttawiq** when adnominal). ¶ ~ **chayk** this sort of book. **i ttawiq īl** a job of this kind. **I ttawiq īl un tangchey tasi an hakeyss.ta** I shall do nothing of this sort again. **I ttawi nun sa se mues hay** What do you buy such trash as this for? SYN **yo ttawi**. CF **ku / ce ttawi**.

i ttay, cpd n. (at) this time / moment / juncture / point. ~ **kkaci** until now, up to this day. **palo** ~ **(ey)** at this very moment. ¶**Palo i ttay, han namca ka pang ey tul.e wass.ta** At this point a man came into the room. **I ttay kkaci ileh.key hwullyung han sālam ul ponq īl i ēps.ta** I have never seen such a splendid man. **I ttay ey nun um.ak-hoy ka pelsse kkuth-nass.ess.ta** By this time the concert was over already. CF **ipttay**.

-i tul = **-o tul** (SEE **-ui / -i**)

i tul, pcl + pcl. ¶**Ku sensayng i tul cōh.uni?** Do you children like that teacher?

itula, copula retrospective assertive

itum, adnoun. next, the following, the ensuing. ¶ ~ **nal / tal / hay** the next day / month / year. CF **ithut-nal** < *i῎thu[l] s nal* second / next day; **ithul** < *i῎thul* (= *it-῎hul*) two days; **ithay** < ῾*i῎thoy* (= ῾*it-῎hoy*) two years; **īs.ta** < *i῎z[o]*-continue; **taum** next ?< **tah.um** touching.

itun, 1. cop retr mod. ¶**Payk.man-cāngca 'tun sālam i kēci ka toyess.ta 'n i!** I am shocked that a former millionaire has become a beggar! SEE ~**a**, ~ **cwul**, ~ **ci**, ~ **i**, ~**q īl**, ~ **ka**, ~ **kes**, ~ **ko**, ~ **pa**, ~ **tey**, ~ **tul**, ~ **ya**.

2. abbr < **itun ci**. 3. abbr < **itun ya**.

itun ci, cop retr mod + postmod; quasi-particle.

1. [? DIAL] whether it (has been observed to) be ..., regardless whether ... or ... . ¶**Ku i ka nwukwu yess.tun ci ic.ess.ta** I forget who he was. **Ku i ka nwukwu 'tun ci molukeyss.ta** I don't know who he was.

2. or, or the like, like, or something (= **ina**). ¶**Cangmi 'tun ci payk.hap itun ci sa la** Buy either roses or lilies. **Thayksi 'tun ci ppesu 'tun ci thako kaca** Let's go by taxi or bus.

3. (how)ever it (has been observed to) be. **mues itun ci** = **mues ina** whatever (it be), anything at all. **musun X itun ci** = **musun X ina** whatever X it be, any X at all. ¶**Caymi man iss.umyen āmu yenghwa 'tun ci cōh.ta** Any movie will do, just so it is interesting. **Nwukwu hanthey 'tun ci ku māl haci mala** Don't tell anybody. **Etteh.key hay se 'tun ci ku kes ul hay la** Do it somehow or other.

4. [? DIAL] ~ **(yo)** = ~ **to moluta** (I don't know whether =) maybe it was (observed) that ...). ¶**Yeki yess.tun ci to mōlla** Perhaps it was here (that it happened). **Sēnswu yess.tun ci (yo)** Maybe he used to be an athlete.

ituni, 1. cop retr sequential.

2. → **itun i**. ~ **la**, ~ **yo**, ~ **man (un)**.

itun ka, cop retr mod + postmod.

1. (the question of) whether it was (observed to be ...); was it ... ?.

2. (used as a quasi-particle) = **ina** (or / and). ¶**kwuntay 'tun ka kwunswu-phum itun ka** troops or supplies.

῾*i῎two῎lwok* (= ῾*ito῎lwok*), cop projective. ¶*samnyen ῾i῎two῎lwok* (?1517- Pak 1:37b, 1518 Sohak-cho 9:8a) for three years. ῾*il῎poyk ke῎lu῎m i῎two῎lwok ῎ey῎ti a῎ni ho῎m ye* (1518 Sohak-cho 8:2b) circling less than a hundred paces.

῎**itwo῎ta**, emotive indic assert < ῎*i[l] ta*. ¶*kutuy ῎ka ῎tul cci῎p i pol῎ssye ῎itwo῎ta* (1447 Sek 6:35b) a house for you to enter has already been built!

i twu, n + var pcl = **i to** this (one) too / even.

i twu, n + var pcl = **i to** this (one) too / even.
i wa < ˙*i* ˙*Gwa*, n + pcl. with this; this and, and this.
-iwu- (> **-ywu-**), suf. CF **-i-**, **-y-**, **-hi-**, **-ki-**, **-chi-**, **-ukhi-**, **-ikhi-**, **-li-**; **-wu-**, **-hwu-**, **-kwu-**, **-chwu-**, **-ay-**; -˙*Gi-*, -˙*Gwo-*, -˙*Gwu-*, *-o-*, *-u-*. derives vc. **ssuiwu-** = **ssuywu-** /ssiwu-/ (MK *su˙i-*) have one write ← ssu- < ˙*(s)su-* write. **caiwu-** = **caywu-** (MK ˙˙*cay-*) put to sleep ← ca- < °*ca-* sleep. **seiwu-** = **seywu-** < *syeyGwu-*, *syeyGwo-* (from 1576; earlier ˙˙*syey-*) set it up ← se- < °*sye-* stand (= su-).
iwu [var] = **io** (cop AUTH). The standard spelling is **iyu** and that is probably well motivated historically, though we are here treating the phonetic glide as nondistinctive.
iya₁ 1. = **ia** (cop var inf = **ie**) it is ⋯ . The standard spelling is **iya** and that is probably well motivated historically, though we are treating the phonetic glide as epenthetic. Does not occur before a particle (replaced by **ie** or **ila**). 2. = **i ya** (postmod + cop or pcl).
iya₂, pcl (after vowel **ya**); abbr **ya**; [DIAL, obs] **isa**. only if it be; if it is just (no more than), if it is nothing other / more than ⋯ ; if (it be), when it comes to; even, indeed; of course ⋯ , taking ⋯ for granted. (It marks a reinforced contingency / prerequisite for a main clause, one or the other of which is unlikely, unexpected, or anticipated to be difficult / unpleasant.) SEE **ccum iya, ey ya, eykey ya, ey se ya, kkaci ya, se ya, ulo ya; ila ya; -e ya, -e se ya, -ess.e ya, -key ya, -ki ya, -ko ya, -ta ka ya, -ullay ya, -ulye ya, -umye ya, -umyen iya, -umyen se ya; haki ya, ku cey ya, ku ya; iya māl lo**.
¶ **Ku kes iya kuleh.ci** THAT is certainly true! **Twīq īl iya nwu ka ālq swu iss.na** When it comes to the future, who can tell? **Ku os iya eti ip.ulq swu iss.nun ya** How on earth could I wear THAT dress?! **Ku sālam iya kulenq īl halq sālam i ani 'ta** HE would never do a thing like that! **Cil iya etteh.tun (ci) kaps ila to ssa ya halq kes ani yo** Regardless of the quality, [isn't it the case that =] surely the price should be kept low. **Sālam iya cōh.un sālam ici** He sure is a fine man! **Cal-mos han key ku sālam ppun ila ko man halq swu ya ēps.ci** You certainly can't say that he's the only one to blame. **Elkwul iya ette hatun ci maum man chak hamyen ssukeyss.ta** If only she's a woman of good nature, she is all right with me, regardless of what she looks like. **Nay sānun ke ya kuce kulel wu haci mwe** I'm just living along, that's all. **Incey ya māl lo wuli ka kwelki hal ttay 'ta** Now is the time for us to rouse ourselves to action. **Nam iya musun cīs ul hatun (ci), ne nun hangsang ponun twung mānun twung man hako tanimyen toynta** You should go your own way without paying attention to whatever others may be doing. **Ppesuq kaps iya ollass.ci man kichaq kaps cocha ya an ollikeyss.ci** The BUS fares are up, but I don't think they'll raise the TRAIN fares, too. **Nal-ssi ya chwupkena tēpkena kan ey yēyceng sikan ey tte-naca** Whether the weather is hot or cold, let's leave at the scheduled time. **Insa pyēn han tul sanchen iya kasilq son ya** Human affairs may change, but nature will surely never change. **Kil ul mul.mye 'n tul** (= **mul.umyen se 'n tul**) **ku cip iya mōs chac.e kakeyss.ni** I will surely be able to find the house, even if I have to ask. **Cal-mos han key ku sālam ppun ila ko man halq swu ya ēps.ci** You certainly can't say that he's the only one to blame. **I sālam iya palo nay ka māl han sālam ita** (1936 Roth 278) This is the very person I spoke of.

NOTE 1: The meaning of this particle is mutually exclusive with that of **un / nun** (as for) and usually that of **to** (also / even), but see pp. 817-8 (**to** NOTE) for examples of **un / nun iya** and **to ya**. Other particles (or strings of them) freely follow **iya**, but the nominative **i / ka** and the accusative **ul / lul** are usually omitted.

NOTE 2: Two lines of development may have occurred: ˙*i* ˙*za* > ˙*i* ˙*[z]a* > ˙*i* ˙*(y)a* = **iya**; *(⋯y)* ˙*za* > *(⋯y)* ˙*[z]a* > *(⋯y)* ˙*ya* > **iya** (by conflation) > **iya**. CF -˙*key* ˙*a*.
*****i ya**, pcl (nominative) + pcl → **[i] ya**. (Use just **ya**.) But most examples of MK ˙*i*˙*za* and *y*˙*za* are intended to be the nominative pcl ˙*i* + ˙*za*.
i ya, pcl + pcl. **i kes i ya** ≠ **i kes iya**; CF **pata ka ya** ≠ **pata ya**.
i ya, var < **(y)ey ya** < **ie / ye ya** (only if it be, only by being)
-i ya, var < **-ye(y)ya** < **-ie ya**. ¶ **kitali ya** < **kitalye ya** < **kitalie ya** only by waiting. **kaluchi ya** < **kaluch(y)e ya** < **kaluchie ya** only by teaching. **kasi ya** < **kas(y)e(y) ya** < **kasie ya** only by deigning to go.

iya māl lo, pcl + n + pcl. ('as what I am indeed saying' =) indeed, precisely, exactly, just, none other than. ¶**Kumkang san iya māl lo pol man han san ip.nita** The Diamond Mountains are just the thing for you to see. **I kes iya māl lo mayngcong ila hakeyss.ta** This indeed can be called blind obedience. **Cham iya māl lo hwullyung hakey toyess.ta** (1936 Roth 279) It turned out really splendid!

i ya māl lo, n + pcl + n + pcl. this very one/thing/person, this indeed (= **i kes iya māl lo**). ¶**I ya māl lo cēngtang han pīphyeng ila halq swu iss.ta** This indeed can be called just criticism. CF **iya māl lo; ku ya māl lo.**

i ¹**yāngpan**, adn + n. 1. [obsolete] this gentleman. 2. you − pejorative, but endearing when said between husband and wife (M 1:2:85 "used by women and men but usually only in reference to men" is misleading). ¶**I** ¹**yāngpan i meych si'n tey ileh.key yātan i(y)a** (M 1:2:81 − husband to wife) Why are you making such a fuss, what time is it anyway? CF **wuli cipq** ¹**yāngpan** my husband.

iya tul, pcl + pcl. ¶¹**Nayil iya tul etteh.key kakeyss.na** How can you folks leave tomorrow?

iya(y) yo = ia(y) yo = ie(y) yo copula POLITE. ¶**Enu nala sālam iya yo** (Pak Sengwen 1972: 92) What country is he from? − But younger speakers say ··· **iey yo.**

iye, pcl [after vowel ye]. HEAVY → **a** (vocative). ¶**kyōwu tul iye!** (1936 Roth 36) 'my fellow Christians!, brethren!'.

iye < (?*) ˙*i* ˙*ye* → **ie** (cop inf); often replaced by **ila** < ˙*i* ˙*la* before a particle. The common spelling **iye** is well motivated historically, though we are treating the phonetic glide as epenthetic.

~ **la**, ~ **se**, ~ **to** SEE **ie** ··· .

NOTE: In MK ˙*i* ˙*ye* (often after a vowel and reduced to ˙*ye*) was used as a quasi-particle 'whether, or; and; or/and the like': ˙*na.c i* ˙*ye* ˙*pa.m i* ˙*ye ki* ˙*li solang* ˙*ho.ya* (1475 Nay 2:2:17b) 'day and night ever yearning'. It was also used in exclamatory enumeration: *na* ˙*la[h] s* ¨*salo* ˙*m i* ¨*kwulku.n i* ˙*'ye hye* ˙*ku.n i* ˙*'ye* (1459 Wel 10:12b) people of the nation, [both] the big and the little ones. SEE ˙*'ye*, *-u* ˙*m ye.*

i yeksi, n + adv. this too/also/again. ¶**I yeksi kosik-cek cengchayk ey cīnaci anh.nunta** This again is but a temporizing policy.

iyeng < *ieng*, [Ceycwu DIAL]; after vowel *yeng*.

1. = **iko**, pcl < cop ger (LSN 1978:34-5); after a vowel the shape is *yeng*.

1a. with (= **kwa/wa** = **hako**). **na yeng kakey** = **na hako/wa kaca** go with me.

1b. and; both ··· and (= **kwa/wa** = **hako**). ¶*ku ttek iyeng i nungkum iyeng tā mek.ula* = **ku ttek kwa i nungkum kwa tā mek.e la** eat both that rice cake and this apple. *kai yeng na yeng iti se nwolass.cce* = **ku ai wa na wa yeki se nol.ass.ta** she and I amused ourselves here.

1c. also (= **to**). ¶*chayk iyeng kaceng wola* = **chayk to kaciko one la** bring your book(s), too. *ssol man malang kamcey yeng ta ciyeng kala* = **ssal man mālko kokwuma to tā ciko kala** don't just shoulder the rice, take the potatoes, too. *ku salum i ilpwon se wan, cip iyeng pas iyeng ha.yeng sass.cce* = **ku sālam i Ilpon ey se wā se, cip kwa path kwa lul mānh.i sass.ta** he came from Japan and bought a lot of houses and acreage.

2. = **ileh.key** like this, so (Seng ¹Nakswu 1984:32); also *iong*.

*iyo*₁ = **io** 1. < ˙*i* ˙*ywo* (AUTH cop). 2. = **i(y)o** < ˙*i* ˙*Gwo* = **iko** (copula gerund). The common spelling **iyo** is well motivated historically, but we treat the phonetic glide as nondistinctive.

i yo₂, 1. n + AUTH cop (= **i io**). it is this (one). 2. (= **i 'ko**, n + cop ger) it is this (one) and ... . 3. noun + polite particle. (it's) that (one).

iyo₃, particle (after vowel **yo**); POLITE.

1. makes a noun phrase into a polite sentence fragment. ¶"**Nwukwu yo**" − "**Swunkyeng iyo**" "Who is it?" − "The police." "**Cēnpo yo!**" − "**Ce hanthey yo?**" "Telegram!" − "For me?" **Kulem iyo ...** Well, now ... .

2. after the infinitive **-e/-a** makes a POLITE statement, question, command, or suggestion. And **-e yo** is often pronounced **-ey yo**, §9.4.(8). ¶**Kasey yo** (= **kasye yo**) (1) He goes. (2) Are you going? Will you go? (3) Go! (4) Let's go! **Kkok kath.e(y) yo** They are exactly the same. **Pelsse mek.ess.e(y) yo** I have already eaten. **Yeki iss.e(y) yo** It is here. **Kitalikeyss.e(y) yo?** Will you wait?

3. after suspective **-ci** makes a POLITE casual statement, question, command, or suggestion. ¶**Kaci yo** (1) I guess he goes (etc.). (2) I suppose he's going? (3) Suppose you go! = Go! (4) Suppose we go! = Let's go!

4. after -un ka (usually from adjective or copula) makes a POLITE question (= -e yo?). ¶Cip i khun ka yo? Is the house big? Hyeng nim isin ka yo? Is it your brother?
6. softens the strong insistence of -ta 'p.nita. ¶Kulayss.ta 'p.nita yo That really is what they said, you see.
NOTE: Similarly occurs after -ney and -tey (as first observed in 1937 by Choy Hyenpay [1959:539]), despite the rejection of -ney yo and -tey yo by some speakers and by KEd 1334b. CF -na yo, -un tey yo.
7. used freely as a polite pause particle ('you see, you know') after any part of a sentence. SYN ullang / llang. CF māl ia.
8. [var] = iko (cop ger) it is and.
9. → io (AUTH copula) it is.
10. → i yo = iey yo

i yo, var < (y)ey yo < ie(y) yo, < ye(y) yo (POLITE) it is. ¶Ku kes i yo = Ku kes ey yo = Ku kes ie(y) yo It is that one. I key mues i yo = I key mues ey yo = I key mues ie(y) yo What is this? Na i yo = Na (y)ey yo = Na ye yo It is me.

-i yo, var < -ye(y) yo < -ie yo. ¶kitali yo < kitalye yo < kitalie yo waits (POLITE). kaluchi yo < kaluch(y)e yo < kaluchie yo teaches (POLITE). kasi yo < kasey yo < kasye yo < kasie yo goes (POLITE). CF kasio₁ (AUTH honorific indicative assertive), kasio₂ (FORMAL subjunctive attentive).

¹īyu < ˙LI-YWUW, noun. reason, cause, motive, grounds, excuse. ¶ile ile hanq ¹īyu lo for such and such reasons. Nay ka ku lul mannam (or mannalye ko ham) ey nun yele kaci ¹īyu ka iss.ˢo There are various reasons for me to (want to) see him. Musunq ¹īyu? Is there some reason? SEE -nunq ~, -unq ~, -ulq.

˙i˙ywom, cop modulated subst. Examples? CF ˙i˙lwom.

˙i˙za, pcl; CF isa, sa, iya, ya, ˙za. It is not always clear which examples are intended to be the nominative pcl ˙i + ˙za, but most (if not all) are that.
1. Clearly can be treated as nominative ˙i ˙za. ¶wo˙cik ˙PPWULQ ˙i ˙za ˙a˙losi˙m ye ˙TTI ˙yey wolo.n i [i] ˙za pi˙lu˙se ˙SSYWUW ho˙l i ˙ˈn i (1465 Wen 1:2:3:6a) only Buddha alone knows [these three calamities] and only he who has risen upon earth will suffer them for the first time. THYEN-˙NYE ˙lul ˙pwoken ˙t ay n' na ˈy ˙kye˙ci.p i ˙za ˙nwun ˙men MI-HHWUW ˙kot ˙two˙swo-ngi ˈˈta (1459 Wel 7:12b) compared with the goddesses my [beautiful] wife is like a blind ape. e˙nwu ˙CCANG s KUM ˙i ˙za ˙ma˙chi skol˙Gi.l [i] ˈye˙n ywo (1447 Sek 6:25b) [I wonder] just which vault's gold will it take for it to be properly covered. ALSO: 1447 Sek 24:19a, 1449 Kok 121, 1463 Pep 3:177b, ...
2. ? Not to be treated as nominative.
2a. after ···k: musu.k iza hol kkwo [= holq kwo] (?1464 Kumkang sasil 4; cited from LCT) just what shall we do?
2b. after ···m: na ˈy ˙MYENG ku˙chwu.m i˙za mute˙ni ne˙ki˙ka.n i ˙Gwa ... (1459 Wel 10:4b) having treated lightly the very end of my life, ... sol˙phywo.m i˙za ko˙cang ˙ho˙yan ma˙lon ([1447→]1562 Sek 3:18a) I have investigated after my fashion but ... . etilwo.m iza etilGe.n i Gwa (1611 Nay-cwung 2:20) is wise indeed.
2c. after ···l: ˙ney cha s ha˙no.l iza (1447 Sek 6:36a; thematized locative?) precisely the fourth heaven, [that is where ...]. ˙tywo˙tha s ˙ma˙l i˙za nilo˙l ye (?1517- Pak 1:3a) can I say it's OK?
3. SEE -˙e y˙za (= -˙e ˙za)

˙i ˙za, n + pcl. precisely this. ¶ ˙i ˙za mozo˙m ay hwen hi ˙cul˙keptwo˙ta ([1447→]1562 Sek 3:20b) this very thing is a great delight to my heart.

˙izoW-, cop humble-deferential. ¶LA-˙HHWUW-LA ˙non ˙i pwuthye s a˙to˙l izo˙wo˙n i (1463 Pep 4:48b) Rāhula is the son of this Buddha.

-k, pseudo-suffix.
1. ? abbr < -ko. ¶ilek celek < ile cele somehow or other. kulek celek < kule cele such and such. CF (-)k hata, ··· khwuta; (-)lak.
2. ? abbr < -ki. ¶ilwuk hata undertakes, builds, < ilwuta achieves.
?3. diminutive. CF -ng, -ak, -ek, ...
4. (residue of an earlier cluster, as found in obsolete and dialect words). ¶? cilk = kil road. malk = malwu floor. tolk = tōl stone. kwumk = kwumeng hole. namk = namu tree (CF namak sin wooden clogs).

-k, abbr < ko, particle [DIAL]. SEE (-)k hata, ··· khwuta.

k, pcl. 1. (? < ˙k[a]) emphatic. SEE -˙a k, -˙e k, -˙kwo k, -kwo(k), -˙ta ˙ka k.
2. SEE ˙ᵘ/o˙lwo k starting from, with.
3. var < s (genitive particle) after -ng. SEE k ˙˙swon-˙toy.
¶ ˙˙CYWONG-˙˙CYWONG k kwos (1447 Sek 9:22b) all kinds of flowers.
¶ QA-SSYA-SYEY NGWANG k ˙˙CO-SWON (1447 Sek 24:23b) a descendant of King Ajātaśatru. CCYEN-SOYNG k ˙˙CCWOY-˙NGEP ˙ul ··· (1459 Wel 2:62b) ··· the karma of an earlier life. NGWANG k ˙CHWUY-˙LYENG ˙ul ··· (1459 Wel 1:9-10) ··· the king's command.
¶ [HYWENG] k ˙ptu˙t i (1445 ¹Yong 8) the elder brother's wish. NGWANG k ˙ptu˙t ul (1459 Wel se:16b) the king's will.
¶ ˙˙CYWONG-˙˙CYWONG k TTWANG-PHEN ˙u˙lwo (1447 Sek 9:22b) with all kinds of banners.
¶ [CHYA-YANG] k ˙˙sey ˙cwuy (1445 ¹Yong 88) three rats on the eaves. NGWANG k ˙˙swon-˙toy (1447 Sek 24:6a) to the king. SSYENG k SYEY-MWON (1459 Wel 2:67a) the west gate of the castle.
¶ NGWANG k ˙skwu˙m ey (1447 Sek 24:6a) in the king's dream.
¶ ˙˙CYWONG-˙˙CYWONG k HYANG (1447 Sek 9:22b) all kinds of incenses.
ka < ˙ka, infinitive < kata < °ka˙ta.
ka < ˙ka, bound noun. (MK lenites to ˙Ga after l, y, and often i.)
1. postmod = ya (question). SEE -un / -nun / -tun / -ulq ~. SYN ko, i, a. NOTE: In South Kyengsang attached directly to noun, omitting cop mod (Mkk 1960:3:35): N ka = N in ka. That is also a very common option for Middle Korean. In Phyengan (Kim Yengpay 1984:98) ka is attached directly to a vowel-final noun and a consonant-final noun attaches ika (? = i ka pcl + postmod, or ? = i-ka cop stem + postmod): I key ney chayk ika? 'Is this your book?'; Teki poinun key ne ney hak.kyo ka? 'Is what can be seen over there your school?'.
MK examples with omission of the copula modifier ˙in: hon ka˙ci ˙ka talo˙n i ˙ye (1459 Wel 8:31b) are they the same or different? — CF hon ka˙ci ˙Ga a˙ni ˙Ga (1462 ¹Nung 1:99a) is it the same or (is it) not? ˙i ˙non ˙˙SYANG ˙ka ˙PPELQ Ga (?1468- Mong 53b) is this a reward or a punishment? (The omission was not obligatory; see ˙in ˙ka, a˙ni ˙n ˙ka.)

MK examples with a genitive s substituting for the omitted copula modifier include -ngi s ˙ka (polite question), -˙n i s ˙ka (question), ... (see 4), and these are the source of the modern forms in 3.
2. postnoun. ki(ye)n ka mi(ye)n ka hata = kiyen miyen hata is uncertain (whether or not). CF 1 (NOTE).
3. SEE -(su)p.nikka, -ulikka.
4. MK ˙ka also occurs after the summational nominalization with ··· ˙i + adnominalizing s; SEE -ngi s ˙ka, -(ᵘ/o)˙n i '-ngi s ˙ka, -(-ᵘ/o)˙l i '-ngi s ˙ka. Before ˙ka and ˙kwo (perhaps also ˙ya and ˙ye) the copula modifier ˙in drops.

ka, pcl. Only after a vowel; i is used after a consonant and occasionally (earlier always) after a vowel, too — see note under i.
1. marks the subject of one or more following verb or adjective phrases.
1a. usually translated as the subject. ¶ Pata ka kiph.ta The sea is deep. Pata ka kiph.ko mulq koki ka mānh.ta The sea is deep and the fish are plentiful. pata ka kiph.ko mulq koki ka mānh.un kos a place where the sea is deep and the fish are plentiful. Nwu ka wass.nun ya Who has arrived? Eti ka cōh.un ya Where would be a good spot? Pi ka onta (Rain comes =) It rains (or is raining). Apeci ka osye se tōn ul cwusyess.ta Father came and gave me some money. apeci ka cwusin tōn the money that father gave me. An ey nwu ka iss.nun ya Who is inside? Ku catong-cha ka cōh.ci man pissaci That car is nice but I bet it costs a lot. Emeni ka cang pole kalye 'nta ko hayss.ta Mother said she was going to the store. (or: Someone said Mother was going to the store). ku kyōswu ka kānguy lul hasil ttay when the professor delivers / delivered his lecture.
1b. literally translatable as a subject, but freely translated as the object — of possession, of ability, of evaluation, or of emotional affect. The person who possesses, is able, evaluates, or feels the emotion is marked with the nominative particle, too (1c). ¶ phyo ka ēps.ta a ticket is lacking, there is no ticket = lacks a ticket, has no ticket. kyōswu ka cēkta the professors are few (in number), there are few professors = has few professors. ūymi ka iss.ta there is meaning, a meaning exists = has (a) meaning. meli ka aphuta one's head aches = has a

headache. **Yenghwa ka cōh.ta** (1) movies are good = has good movies; (2) movies are liked = I like the movies. **hak.kyo ka napputa** the schools are bad = has poor schools; the schools are at fault. **kongpu haki ka silh.ta** studying is displeasing = I dislike studying. **Capci ka poko siph.ta** I'd like to see the magazine. **Pata ka poinun ya** Is the sea to be seen (= visible)?; Can you see the sea?

1c. marks the subject of a phrase as the possessor or as the person who is able, who evaluates, or who feels the emotion. The phrase can include a more immediate/direct subject for the predicate (verb or adjective), expressing what is possessed or what is the target of the ability, of the evaluation, or of the emotion (1b). ¶ **Ce ai ka khi ka te khuta** That boy is taller. **Nay ka meli ka aphuta** I have got a headache. **Nay ka kāy ka musepta** I am afraid of dogs. **I hak.kyo ka kyōswu ka cēkta** This school has few professors.

2. 2a. marks the subject of an affirmative copula phrase, and that is often the Identified. The complement, which is often the Identifier, is unmarked except by the copula itself. ¶ **Ku i ka nwukwu (i)n ya** Who is he?

2b. marks the complement (as well as the subject) of a negative copular phrase. ¶ **Nay ka cak.ka ka ani 'la, hwāka (i)ta** I am not a writer, I'm a painter. **I moca ka nay moca ka ani 'lokwun** Why, this (hat) isn't my hat!

But sometimes the particle drops: **Ani i key Swun-i emeni ani 'la ko! – cham olay kan man ip.nita** Why, it can't be Swun-i's mother, what a surprise, how long it's been since I've seen you! **Ne ani 'la to ku īl ul halq sālam i iss.ta** There are people besides you who can do the job.

3. marks the complement of a change of state, into (being), so as to be. CF **ulo**; SEE **ita ka, ey 'ta ka**. ¶ **phyēy ka toymyen** if it's going to be any trouble. **Wuli chinkwu ka ku hwū cengchi-ka ka tōyss.ta** Our friend later turned into (became) a politician.

But sometimes the particle drops (SEE **i**): **pwuthye towoylq ˙t ol ¨all i ' ˙la** (1462 ¹Nung 7:26a) knows that he will become a Buddha.

4. and, but; emphasis. SEE **-ta ka; -ci ka, -ko ka, -key ka (toynta); ey ka** (NOTE). CF **i** 5a-b.

NOTE: The history of this case particle is controversial. In early texts there are very few examples that could be nominatives, and the earliest four are after ···y: ˙*QILQ-* ˙*CHYEY* ˙*ka* (1463 Pep 1:120b) 'all', ¨*ne y* ˙*ka* (1459 Wel 18:71b) 'you', *poy ka* (1572 letter) 'boat', *poy ka* ?(1676 Sin.e 1:8b) 'boat'; the first two cases are better explained (by He Wung 338:n49) as the infinitive ˙*ka* 'go and'. There are six examples after vowels other than *i* or ···y in a manuscript of 1700⁻ (Hong Yunphyo 1975:88). The clear examples of noun + nominative *i* (reduced to *y*) + *ka* date from the latter part of the 18th century (idem:69), one from 1783 Cahyul 8a (*ce y ka* 'I'), and two from royal edicts of about the same period (*nwu y ka* 'who' and *na y ka* 'I'). Of the same period, also, are these three examples from 1781 Sin.e-cwung: *wuli ka* (2:19a) 'we', *soyngswo ka* (1:7b – translating Japanese "fa" = wa, not "ka" = ga!) 'as for the inexperience', and *[SWONGSO] ka* (1:10a) 'envoy'. It appears that after a vowel the nominative marker *i*, having been reduced to *y*, was gradually strengthened by the addition of an emphatic particle *ka*, and then by the 1800s (except for traces of *i ka* surviving in dialects) it completely vanished in most areas, leaving the newly orphaned *ka* to fill the new role of a suppletive alternant of the nominative marker *i*. As was convincingly argued by Hong Yunphyo 1975, the emphatic particle ˙*ka* attached to the copula ˙*i* ˙*la* and ˙*i* ˙*ta*, just as did the "emphatic" (˙*i*)˙*za* (the source of modern (**i)ya**) and the "postposition" ˙*sye* (> modern **se**) deriving from *i* ˙*sye* < (*i*)*si-* ˙*e*, the infinitive of (*i*)*si-* 'exist' (> **iss-**). Hong's scenario: circa 1450 *··· ita ka → ··· ila ka →* 1600⁻ *··· i ka →* 1800⁻ *···V i / ···C [i] ka →* the present system, in which the earlier flux became systematized, i.e. standardized to the Seoul colloquial. See the note on **ita** for more on this. Because written forms of the language were deliberately kept "literary", therefore archaic, the particle **ka** (like the future **-keyss-** for written **-li-** and the processive **-nunta** for **-nota**) passed unnoticed before observation by foreign missionaries at the end of the 19th century (CF Kim Hyengkyu 1954), e.g. *i mwul i kipki ka elma na holis.ka* (1894 Gale 127) 'about how much is the depth of this water?'.

King 1990 reports a total absence of the nominative marker **ka** in the Korean dialects spoken in the USSR. The replacement of **i** by **ka** (after a vowel) was apparently quite late in the northernmost dialects, as also shown by the lack of attestation in 1902 Azbuka.

k'a, abbr < **kwa** pcl [S Kyengsang DIAL (Mkk 1960:3:31-2)]. In Soviet dialects (King 1990) used also after a vowel (= **wa** < ˙*[G]wa*).

kā < **ku ai**, n [Phyengan DIAL (Kim Yengpay 1984:95)] = **ku ai** he, she. CF **tā**, **yā**.

-˙*ka*- = -˙*ke*-, effective. SEE -˙*Ga*-; -˙*a*-; ˙*wona*-; ˙*ho.ya*-.

-˙*ka* = -˙*ke*, effective inf. ~ *ci˙la*, ~ ˙*ci-ngi* ˙'*ta* wants to do. SEE -˙*Ga*; -˙*a*; ˙*wo˙na*; ˙*ho˙ya*.

kac', 1. adv, abbr < **kaci**. [DIAL] = **kas** just (now). ~ **sumul** just twenty.
2. abbr < **kacwuk** (fur, leather, hide). ~ **os** fur garment. ~ **sin** leather shoes.
3. abbr < **kaci** (CF **ōn kac'**). **kac'-kac(i)** = **kaci-kaci** all kinds.

kaca, 1. subj attent < **kata** (let's go!). ~ (**ko**) **hanta** suggests we go. ~ **māca** as soon as one goes.
2. [DIAL] = **kalca**, subj attent < **kalta**.

kaca ko, subj assert + pcl. let's go!

kacang < *ko˙cang*, adv. most, ---est; extremely, very. ¶ ~ **cōh.un mulken** (1936 Roth 218) a very good product.

kaca 'nta, abbr < **kaca (ko) hanta**

kaca tul, subj assert + pcl (plural subject)

kaca 'y, abbr < **kaca (ko) hay**

kaci₁, n. 1. < ˙*kaci* branch; affix. 2. < *ka˙ci* kind, sort. 3. < *kaci* < *KA-"CO* eggplant.

kaci₂, adv [DIAL] = **kas** just (now).

kaci₃, suspective < **kata**; [DIAL] = **kalci** < **kalta**.

kaciko, gerund < **kacita**. ABBR **kac'ko**. SEE -**e kaciko**; ? -**a kacwuko**.

kaciko, quasi-particle (< vt gerund) [colloq].
1. (= **ul**) marks direct object. ¶**Ku sālam kaciko nemu kuleci māsio** Don't pick on him so! **Kattuk ina sēng-nan sālam kaciko way kulen ya** Are you trying to make him all the angrier?
2. (= **ulo**) with, by means of, ... ¶**kōng** ~ **nōlta** plays with a ball.
3. abbr < **ul kaciko** (taking). ¶**chayk (ul) kaciko hak.kyo ey kata** takes one's books (and goes) to school.

kaciko ya, quasi-pcl + pcl. only with. ¶**I tōn kaciko ya mānnyen-phil ul salq swu ēps.ci** You certainly can't buy a fountain pen with THIS amount of money!

-˙*ka* ˙*ci-ngi* ˙'*ta*, effective inf + aux polite + cop indic assert. ¶ ˙*icey s* ˙*SYEY-CWON* ˙*kotka* [< ˙*koth-*˙*ka*] ˙*ci-ngi* ˙'*ta* (1459 Wel 2:9b) I want to be like the present World-Honored.

kac'ko, abbr < **kaciko** (aux v ger)

kac.ta₁ < *koc˙ta*, adj. is complete/perfect, has everything, has all sorts. ¶**kac.un kes** all sorts of things, every thing; one (= a thing) with everything. **kac.un ttek** a well-made cake, a cake that has everything, all kinds of cakes. **kac.un yangnyem** proper seasoning, all sorts of spices. **kac.un kkoy lul tā ssuta** strains one's wits, taxes one's ingenuity. **kac.un ūmsik ul tā mantulta** makes all kinds of dishes. **kac.un sallim** a household that has everything. DER ADV **kac.chwu**. VC **kac.chwuta**. CF **ōn kac'**.

kac.ta₂, vt abbr < **kacita** (holds, has). 1. indic assert. 2. transferentive. (CF 1936 Roth 459.) ¶**Changko ey kac.ta twue la** Take it to storage and keep it there. **Changko ey kac.ta noh.a la** Take it to storage and place it there. **Tok ey kac.ta pue la** Take it to the jar and pour it in. **Pakk ey kac.ta pelye la** Take it outside and throw it away.

kac' 'ta, abbr < **kacye 'ta** (vt inf + copula transferentive). takes and ... (gives, does favor). ~ **cwuta** brings (as a favor). ¶**Maykcwu com kac' 'ta cwusio** Bring us some beer, please. [Do not confuse with **kass.ta** 'went', nor with **kass.ta (ka)** 'went and then'.]

kac.un, pseudo-adnoun (adj mod). SEE **kac.ta**.

kacwuko, [DIAL] ? = **kaciko**. SEE -**a kacwuko**.

? -˙*ka* ˙*cye*, effective inf + aux inf. SEE -˙*a* ˙*cye*.

˙*KA* ˙*hi*, der adv. adequately, acceptably, well; may, might (well). SYN *e˙lwo*, *e˙lwu*.

kai, *kain* [Ceycwu (Seng ¹*Nakswu* 1984:56)] < *ku ai*, *ku ai n(un)* = **ku i**, **ku i nun** he/she.

kak < ˙*KAK*, adn. each; every; all. ¶ ~ **chīmsil/cipang/hakca** every bedroom/area/scholar. ~ **sīnay (uy) hak.kyo ey se nun** in every school in town. **kak kaci** (≠ **kac' kaci**) all sorts/kinds, every sort/kind, various kinds of. **kak sālam ey hana ssik** one piece each. **kak yelq salam ssik** every ten people. **Kak pang ey twū salam ssik tul.e iss.ta** Two people are (living) in each room. SYN ··· **mata**.

? ka ka, infinitive + particle (for emphasis)
ka ka, postmod (question) + pcl. SEE -un ~,
 -nun ~; nwukwu 'n ka ka.
kake la, var inf + pcl = ka la Go!
kak.kak < ˙KAK-˙KAK, 1. adv. each (one), every
 (single) one; respectively, severally; separately,
 individually. ~-nayki a Dutch treat; unpaired
 "flower-card" game.
 2. ~ ulo, adv. from moment to moment, (at)
 every moment.
-kakkwun(a) → -kas.kwun(a) = -kes.kwun(a)
 = -keyss.kwun(a)
kal, postn. [< kalu- discriminate; CF kaluchi-
 teach, kalikhi- indicate]. CF kkal.
 1. discrimination, division, branch, kind.
 (sayk ~ =) pich ~ [also spelled pich.kkal]
 color. mas ~ [also spelled mas.kkal] taste.
 thāyq ~ [also spelled thaykkal] form and
 color; loveliness. 2. [NEOLOGISM] branch of
 study, -ology. Hankul ~ Koreanology.
-(k)kal SEE -kkal
ka l' = ka lul, inf + pcl (for emphasis)
kal(q), 1. < kal(q), prosp mod < kata (goes).
 2. < kol(q) < *ko[˙lo]l(q), prosp mod <
 kalta₁ < ko[l]˙ta (changes).
 3. < ˙kol(q) < *˙ko[˙lo]l(q), prosp mod <
 kalta₂ < ˙ko[l]˙ta (grinds).
¨kal(q)₁ (< *ka-˙wo-lq), modulated prosp mod
 < °ka˙ta (goes).
¨kalq ˙t i˙na. ¶mak¨tay ti˙phe [SSI] ˙lwo
 [NUNG] ˙hi˙na ¨kal t i˙na (1481 Twusi 8:13a)
 one is still able to get out now and then with
 the aid of a cane.
¨kalq ˙t i˙n i. ¶pol˙kon ka˙won-toy ca˙chwoy
 lol twu˙ti ¨ma[lG]wo twolo˙hye e˙tuwun
 ka˙won-˙toy l' ˙HYANG ˙ho.ya ¨kal t i˙n i (1482
 Kum-sam 2:65a) one is not to put the clues in
 the midst of where it is brightly lit but rather to
 go toward the midst of where it is dark.
¨ka˙l ye. ¶˙icey˙stwo na˙'y a˙to˙l ol to˙lye
 ¨ka˙l ye ˙ho˙sino˙n i (1447 Sek 6:5b) and now
 you want to take my son away, in addition.
 ci˙p ul ˙na˙a ¨ka.l ye ˙thesi˙n i (1449 Kok 45)
 he planned to leave home.
kāl(q) < ¨kal(q)₂ < *kal˙[o]lq, prosp modifier
 < kālta < ¨ka[l]˙ta (plows)
kāl, abbr < kaul, n. autumn. ~ kal.i autumn
 plowing.
-˙ka˙la, effective subj attent (command); = -ke˙la;
 CF -a˙la. ¶˙i ˙non QON ˙ol ¨alGa˙la ho˙n i ˙ya

QON ˙ol kap˙ka˙la ho˙n i ˙ya (?1468- Mong 31b)
 is this telling us to recognize the obligation or
 is it telling us to repay the obligation?
kala, subj attent < kata. ~ (ko) hanta says to go.
ka la, inf + pcl (plain style command) = kake
 la Go! ¶ ~ tul You guys leave!
kala 'nta, abbr < kala (ko) hanta
kala 'y, abbr < kala (ko) hay
kalang, adn. [? < kalak; CF kaluta (vt) divides]
 1. fine; tiny; shriveled. ¶ ~ pi drizzle. ~
 nwūn powdery snow. ~ ni (= kalangq i) nit,
 baby louse. kalangq iph dead leaf; (= ttek-
 kalq iph) oak leaf.
 2. (= kalangi) forked. ¶ ~ meli (a head of
 hair braided in two) pigtails. ~ muwu a
 forked radish. CF paciq-kalangi trouser leg.
kal.i, postnoun (der n < kalta). changing ….
 ¶kwutwu-chang ~ resoling shoes. thel ~
 changing skin / fur / wool; moulting.
kalm, subst. 1. < kolm < *ko˙l[o]m < kalta
 < ko[l]˙ta (changes). ¶kol˙m ye (1462 ¹Nung
 2:118a). 2. < ˙kolm < *˙ko˙l[o]m < kalta
 < ˙ko[l]˙ta (grinds). Example?
ka lul, inf + pcl (for emphasis)
? -ka˙l ya
kālyang < ˙KA-˙LYANG, postn (follows number).
 approximately (so many), about. ¶Yelq salam
 kālyang iss.ta There were about ten people.
 twue tal ~ about two months or so. elma ~
 about how much / many.
? -ka˙l ye, ?*-ka˙l ywo
ka 'm, abbr < ka (ko) ham, or < ka 'n māl
 ia?. SEE -nun ~, -tun ~; -un ~, in ~.
kam, 1. < kam, subst < kata < °ka˙ta (goes).
 2. = kalm, subst < kalta (changes).
kām = kālm < ¨kalm (example?) < *kal˙[o]m,
 subst < kālta < ¨ka[l]˙ta (plows).
¨kam (< *ka-˙wom), modulated subst < °ka˙ta
 (goes). ¶ ¨ka˙m i ¨ep.su˙l i 'Ge˙nul (1462
 ¹Nung 2:24b) there may be no departing, but ….
kām, 1. noun. a persimmon.
 2. noun. stuff, material, a suitable person.
 3. < ¨KAM₁, noun, vnt, vni. subtraction;
 drop, decrease, reduction, diminution.
 4. < ¨KAM₂, noun, postmodifier. a feeling
 (= kāmkak). SEE -nun / -un ~ (i iss.ta).
kamak, kkamak, adn [< (k)kām- adj + -ak].
 black; blind. kamak: ~ cokay corbicula; ~
 sali Bidens tripartita. kkamak: ~ ttaktakwuli
 (a kind of woodpecker); ~ nwun-i an illiterate;

~ **capki** blindman's buff; ~ **payca(/payci)** an illegal money levy (on a conscription card).
kāmali, postn. a person who is the butt of (**yok** ~) ridicule, (**mayq** ~) beatings, (**kekceng** ~) scoldings, or (**pinan** ~) criticism. [? < **kām** 'stuff' + **-al.i**]
ka n', abbr < **ka nun** (inf + pcl)
kan < ˙*KAN*, postn, bnd n. 1. (= **sai**, **tong-an**) interval, duration. ¶ **olay ~ man** (after) a long interval; **Olay kan man ip.nita** It has been a long time (since I last saw you). **Ku kan annyeng hasip.nikka** How have you been?
2. relationship; among, between, of (CF **sai**, **cwung**). ¶ **hyengcey ~** the relationship of brothers; "**hyengcey ci ~**" between / among brothers. **kā-pu ~** (whether) yes or no, right or wrong. **pu-ca ~** the relationship of father and son; **pu-ca kan hana** father or son (one or the other). CF **cwāwu-kan**, **ha.ye-kan**.
3. **kan ey**: SEE **-kena ~**, **-ko ~**, **-tun ci ~**, **-una ~**; **kulena-celena ~**.
kan, 1. < ˙*kan*, mod < **kata** < °**ka˙ta** (goes). ¶ **kan pam** = **cīnan pam** last night.
2. < ˙*kon* < *˙*ko[˙lo]n*, mod < **kalta** < **ko[l]˙ta** (changes).
3. < ˙*kon* < *˙*ko[˙lo]n*, mod < **kalta** < ˙**ko[l]˙ta** (grinds).
kān < ¨*kan*₁ < *˙**ka˙[lo]n**, mod < **kālta** < ¨**ka[l]˙ta** (plows)
¨*kan*₂ (< *˙**ka˙˙wo-n**), modulated mod < °**ka˙ta**. ¶ ˙*na y ˙icey ney ˙e˙m[i] uy ¨kan ˙sta˙h ol ¨pwoy˙ywo.l i ˙˙la* (1459 Wel 21:21b) I will now show you the land your mother went to.
-kān [Phyengan DIAL] = **-keyss.nun (ya)?**
-˙kan = **-˙ken**, effective mod. Examples limited to structures with bound postmodifiers (˙*i*, *t*, ˙*man*)? The form for °**ho-** is ˙**ho.yan**, after a verbal noun also ˙**khan** < ˙**ho-kan**. SEE **-˙Gan**.
? **-ka˙na** SEE **-ke˙na**
kana, advers < **kata**, < **kalta**.
kāna, advers < **kālta**.
kaney, 1. FAMILIAR indic assertive < **kata**, < **kalta**. ¶ **Olay kaney (yo)** It lasts a long time.
2. → **kan ey**, noun + particle.
kāney, FAMILIAR indic assert < **kālta**
kang(-) < ˙*KKANG*, adn, bnd adv. forced, harsh, severe, rough, unreasonable, trying; plain, unadulterated, unmitigated, unremitting, pure, straight; waterless, dry; forced, pretended.
1. adn. ¶ **~ cham-swuch** pure charcoal. **~ chwuwi** a spell of cold dry weather. **co- / poli-pap** boiled millet / barley with no rice in it. **~ cwūceng** feigned drunkenness. **~ hōlyeng** an undeserved scolding. **~ kotoli** dried baby mackerel. **~ kwul** dry oysters. **~ mo** young rice plants in a dry paddy. **~ palam** a dry wind. **~ pap** rice as it comes (with no soup). **~ phi** a red thornless variety of barnyard-grass. **~ phul** a thick paste. **~ sayam** unreasonable jealousy. **~ swul** liquor with no appetizers. **~ tacim** oppression; forced labor; eating rice as it comes (with no soup). **~ tam** a stone wall. **~ tewi** a spell of intense heat with no rain. **~ ttong** dry / hard feces. **kangq yes** [DIAL] = **kem.unq yes** dark (= unpulled) taffy.
2. bnd adverb. ¶ **~ maluta** is hard and dry.
CF **kang hata**₁ is strong, firm, violent; **kang hata**₂ is rigid, stiff, hard; **kkangkuli** wholly, **kkangkulita** finishes.
(-)kang < ˙*KKANG*, postnoun. ... strong, a little over / more, and a fraction. ¶ **ō-payk myeng ~** five hundred (persons) strong, a little over five hundred (people). **sam hop ~** three **hop** and a fraction. ANT **(-)yak**. SYN **(-)nek.nek**. CF **kang hata** is strong.
kang < *KANG*, noun. river.
kang < **ka-ang** [Ceycwu DIAL] = **ka˙se**, = **kako**.
kani < **kata**; = **kan i**, modifier + noun.
¨**ka˙n i**, vi modulated mod + postmod. ¶ ¨**ka˙cye ¨ka˙n i ¨es˙tyey capnon˙ta** (1459 Wel 2:13a) why do you take what I have brought there [with the thought to give it to someone else]?
-ka˙n i, effective mod + postmod. (summational epitheme used in extended predicate – here, in a loosely concatenated sentence) ¶ ˙*na y ˙nye ˙i ke˙s ul* [˙*KWAY-˙QI*] ˙*hi ne˙kika˙n i e˙nu kwu˙thuyye na˙l ywo* (1481 Twusi 25:29a) I go and think this odd, for why trouble to leave?
-˙ka.n i ˙Gwo. ¶ *etuy s nulkun han api wa sye ku lul cis.ka.n i Gwo* (1632 Twusi-cwung 14:17a) an old gaffer from what place arrived and composed that (poem)?
-˙ka.n i ˙Gwa. ¶ *na 'y ˙MYENG ku˙chwu.m i˙za mute˙ni ne˙ki˙ka.n i ˙Gwa* ... ˙*i ˙ney˙h ul ¨mwot ˙pwo˙a ˙honwo˙la* (1459 Wel 10:4b) having treated lightly the very end of my life, I find myself unable to look upon these four.
-˙kan ma˙lon = **-˙kan ma˙non** but, although.
? **-˙ka˙nol**, ? **-˙ka˙nol˙za**. SEE **-ya˙nol**.

kanta, proc indic assertive < **kata**, < **kalta**
kānta, proc indic assertive < **kālta**
? -ˈkanˈta
-ˈkanˈti(⋯) = -ˈkanˈti(⋯).
? -ˈkanˈti, effective mod + postmod + pcl. SEE -ˈGanˈti, -ˈkenˈti, -ˈanti, ˈho.yanˈti.
-kanˈtiˈla, effective mod + postmod + cop indic assertive. ¶ ˈi ˈˈsaloˈm on ZYE-LOY ˈlol ˈˈTYENG-ˈTOY ˈhokanˈtiˈla (1459 Wel 17:36b) he carried the tathāgata above his head.
-ˈkanˈtiˈnˈi, effective mod + postmod + cop mod + postmod. LCT has two examples.
-ˈkanˈti.n iˈˈla (cop indic assert). ¶ ne-huy ˈtolˈh i NUNG ˈhiˈiˈli hoˈm ye n' hoˈma CYE-ˈPPWULQ QON ˈol kapˈkanˈti.n i ˈˈla (1459 Wel 18:18b) when you people do this enough you have already repaid your indebtedness to the Buddhas. ˈi non piˈlwok kesangˈwo.s ol niˈpuna ku ˈSSILQ ˈun kesangˈul hoˈti aˈni khan [< ˈho-kan]ˈt i.n i ˈˈla (1475 Nay 1:70b) he wore mourning garb all right but the truth is he was not in mourning. [TTI-TYWUNG] cinˈsil lwo poˈlikanˈt i.n i ˈˈla (1481 Twusi 20:19b) the magistrate really abandoned it [the county].
? -kanˈtyeng
kanun, proc modifier. 1. < ˈkanon (1447 Sek 6:19a) < **kata** < °kaˈta (goes). 2. < koˈnon (example?) < *ko[ˈlo]ˈnon < **kalta** < ko[l]ˈta (changes). 3. < ˈkonon < *ˈko[ˈlo]non < **kalta** < ˈko[l]ˈta (grinds). ¶ ˈkonoˈn i (1482 Kum-sam 5:16a).
kānun < ˈkaˈnon < *kaˈ[lo]ˈnon, proc mod < **kālta** < ˈˈka[l]ˈta (plows). ¶ pat ˈˈkaˈˈ]non aˈpi (1481 Twusi 7:18b) a man plowing the field.
ka nun, 1. inf + pcl (as for going). 2. postmod (question) + pcl. SEE **-un ~**, **-nun ~**.
? -kaˈn ya; ? -kaˈn ye
-kaˈn ywo, effective mod + postmod. ¶ na lol oyˈGwoˈhyetaˈka pcaˈk ol ˈˈsamkey ˈhokaˈn ywo (1481 Twusi 16:1b) [you] have misled me and made me a match?
ka-p'ā = **ka-pwā** (inf < **ka-pota**)
ka-pota < ˈka-ˈpwota, vi inf + aux v. goes to see, tries going (to see). The auxiliary **pota** is separable (**ka nun / to / tul / ya po**⋯) but, just as a visual aid, we hyphenate the expression here.
ka p⁰/ᵤta SEE **pota**₂
kas, adverb. just (now). DIAL **kac(i)**.
kas, n. thing. ¶ kasˈmul (1527 Cahoy 3:1b=2b) the Chinese wordˈmul [= ˈMWULQ 'thing'].

phwunglywu s kaˈs i (1459 Wel 8:14b) musical instruments. CF *kes*.
ˈka s, pcl + pcl. SEE s_1 5a.
ka se, inf + pcl
ka se (se), 1. inf < **kata** + inf < **suta** (+ pcl). goes and stands and (then). 2. → **kasye (se)**.
-kasi- / -kas- [Phyengan DIAL (Kim Yengpay 1984:104-5)] = **-keyss-** (future). Both **-kasi-** and **-kas-** are used before **-key**, **-ko**, **-ta**, **-ti**, only **-kas-** before **-e**, **-ul**, **-un**, **-umyen**, **-uni**; **-kasi ya** = **-kass.e ya**; **-kase yo** (in some areas **-kasi yo**) = **-kass.e yo**.
-ˈkasiˈn i = -ˈkesiˈn i (effective hon mod + postmod) = -(ᵁ/o)ˈsikeˈn i (hon effective mod + postmod). ¶ woˈlay ˈPPYENGˈhwolq YWEN ˈul yeˈhuyˈya ˈysˈkasiˈn i (1462 ¹Nung 5:72b) he has long kept away the causes for falling ill.
ka siph.ta, (⋯ postmod) + aux adj. SEE **siph.ta**.
-kas.kwun(a) [Phyengan DIAL] = **-keyss.kwun(a)**
kass.ta, 1. past < **kata**.
2. ~ (**ka**) transferentive < **kata**. ¶ **Annyeng hi kass.ta wā yo** (Be on your way, I'll) see you back here later.
kasye (se), abbr < **kasie (se)**, hon inf < **kata** + pcl. (you / he) goes and (then).
ka siph.i, (⋯ postmod) + der adv. SEE **-nun ~**.
-kaˈta = **-keˈta**, effective indicative assertive. SEE **-Gaˈta**, **-ˈaˈta**; **ˈhoˈyaˈta**.
kata < °kaˈta, vi; inf **ka** < ˈka; plain command **kake la** or **ka la**. ANT **ota**. SEE **na-kata**.
1. 1a. goes, proceeds, travels (to ⋯ = ⋯ **ey / ul / ulo**; for ⋯ = ⋯ **ul**, ⋯**-ule**); frequents (a place); attends (school); (a road) leads to (the station), leaves for (a city), is bound for (a city). **kass.ta** is gone, is away. **kass.ess.ta** has been, went (and is back), was away.
1b. For figurative uses, see KEd.
2. (= **cwukta**) dies, passes away (= **kol' lo ~**). ¶ **Ku nun kako ēps.ta** He is dead and gone. He is no more.
3. (= **kkē cita**) (light) goes out, is out.
4. (= **ēps.e cita**) vanishes, disappears, goes away. ¶ os uy ttay ka ~ dirt comes off (out of) a garment. **mas i ~** loses its flavor; goes bad.
5. (= **cīnata**) (time) passes, elapses, goes by. ¶ **Kyewul i kass.ta** Winter is over / past / gone. **kan pam ey** last night. **elma an ka se** before (very) long.
6. (= **tulta**) is required / needed = it takes / requires / needs.

7. (= **tulta**) it costs; it is worth; it weighs.
8. it lasts, holds, keeps, endures, persists, wears. ¶**olay** ~ lasts a long time, wears well.
9. leans to one side.
10. goes to, is assigned (to you / them) = gets.
11. (= **toyta**) comes about. ¶**cimcak (phantan, naptuk) i** ~ comes to form an idea (to draw a conclusion, to reach an appreciation).
12. appears, comes (in an order, at a level).
13. (= **phāum hata**) has an orgasm (a sexual climax), "comes".
14. aux vi sep. SEE **-ko kata, -e kata**.
15. postnominal verb sep (with vn). goes to do. ¶**sānqpo (lul)** ~ goes for a walk. **yenghwa (lul) kwūkyeng** ~ goes to see a movie.
kata (ka), transferentive < **kata** (+ pcl).
1. goes and then (stops).
2. (pseudo-adv) sometimes; once in a while; at occasional intervals; on occasion(s), now and then. ¶ ~ **silqswu hata** sometimes makes a mistake. **Kata ka nun (Kata ka 'la to) han pen ssik tullisinun kes i etteh.ˢup.nikka** You might come and see me once in a while. How about dropping in now and then?
kata kata, iterated transferentive < **kata** = **kata (ka)** 2 (sometimes).
kath.i /kachi/ < ˙ko˙thi < ˙kot˙hi, der adv.
1. (= **kath.key, pisus 'i**) as, like, in the same way / manner, similarly, in a like / similar way, alike, likewise. ANT **talli**. ¶**Aph-se māl han pa wa kath.i ...** As said earlier ... .
2. (= **talum ēps.i, kongphyeng hi, tongil hakey**) equally, impartially, alike.
3. pseudo-pcl, abbr < **hako kath.i (chelem)** as if / though; like, as, as ··· as, (not) so ··· as.
4. (= **hamkkey**) together, with, together / along with, in company with.
5. (= **tongsi ey**) at the same time, together.
NOTE: Noun + **kath.i** is an abbreviation < noun + **hako** (or **kwa / wa**) + **kath.i**. But in meaning 4 the abbreviation is never used. The spoken form **na hako kath.i** can mean either 'with me' or 'like me', but **na kath.i** can mean only 'like me'. CF **poko**, *pu˙the*.
kath.ta₁ (< ˙kot[h]˙ta < ˙kot°ho˙ta), adj.
1. is like, is similar; (is) as. SYN **pisus hata**. ANT **taluta**. ¶**na kath.umyen** if it were me / I.
2. is equal (to), is the equivalent (of), is identical (with), is alike / like. SYN **tongil hata**. ¶**kath.un kaps ey** with no difference in price / distance / trouble / time, since they are the same [+ QUESTION]. **kath.un kaps imyen** the price / distance/trouble/time being equal, other things being equal.
3. (mod + **kes kath.ta**) it seems / looks like (as if / though). ¶**Pi ka olq (onun, on, otun, wass.tun) kes kath.ta** It looks as though it were going to rain (were raining, has rained, has been raining, had been raining).
CF **-ess.ulq kes kath.umyen**.
NOTE: Noun + **kath.ta** is an abbreviation < noun + **hako** (or **kwa / wa**) + **kath.ta**.
kath.ta₂, postnom adj insep. is ···like; is. ¶**cwippul** ~ is insignificant, piddling, trivial. **engtheli** ~ = **engtheli ēps.ta** is nonsense. **kamccok** ~ is as good as new, is perfectly mended; is complete, perfect. **kwul.wangsin** ~ (a thing) is old and dirty [< ?; CF **wāngsin** cantankerous person < ?]. **sayngttay** ~ is robust. **tuktol** ~ is satisfactory.
ka to, infinitive + particle
? **-ka˙ton** = **-ke˙tun**. if; when.
katta → **kass.ta**; → **kac.ta**, → **kac'ta**, → **kac' 'ta**; → **kath.ta**
ka tul, infinitive + particle (plural subject)
ka tul, pcl + pcl. ¶**Ku kāy ka tul musewuni?** Are you kids afraid of that dog?
ka uy, postmod + pcl. (the one) whether, ...
¶**mek.nun ka mek.hinun ka uy ssawum** a life-and-death struggle.
kawuntey < *ka˙won-˙toy* < *ka˙Won-˙toy* < adj mod (< *[kas]kap˙ta* 'near') + n 'place', noun.
1. the interior; the inside; within. CF **an, sōk**. ¶**cip kawuntey se na-ota** comes from within the house. **Cip kawuntey nun mōtun kes i twicwuk pakcwuk iess.ta** There was a great hubbub inside the house.
2. 2a. the middle, center, midst; the mean. CF **cwung, cwungang, cwungkan, pokphan**. ¶**cwung** ~ the very middle (= **han pokphan**). ~ **hyeng** the middle brother. ~ **sonq-kalak** the middle finger. ~ **lul puth-capta** holds the middle of (it), holds it in the middle. ~ **lul chwī hata** takes the mean; splits the difference.
2b. in, in the midst of, in the heart / center of; between, among, through; into; of, out of. CF **cwung (ey)**. ¶**sangca** ~ **neh.ta** puts it into a box. **twūl** ~ **hana lul thayk hata** chooses between the two; chooses one of the two. **mānh.un** ~ **se hana lul kacita** takes one of

many. **han pan ~ kacang wuswu han haksayng** the best student in the class. **kwuncwung ~ iss.ta** is in the midst of a crowd. **swuph ~ lul kel.e kata** goes through the woods. **Ikawuntey se etten kes itun ci sēys ul chwī hay la** Take any three of these.

3. **-nun ~ (se) = -nun cwung (ey)** while (in the process of) doing. ¶**Sensayng nim i posinun kawuntey (se)** while you are watching — CF **pappun kawuntey (*se)** in the midst of being busy [**se** cannot be inserted].

kawus < *kawos* (< ?), postn. and a half. ¶**sēk ca ~** three feet and a half, three and a half feet. **twū mal ~** two and a half pecks. **han toy ~ a "cup"** (= liter) and a half. VAR **awus**. CF **pān**.

kay₁, counter. a piece; a unit, an item. ¶**chayksang twū ~** two desks. **pokswunga sēy ~** three peaches. **pinwu sēy ~** three pieces/cakes of soap. CF **kay 'na**.

kay₂, bound noun (postmodifier, postnoun).

1. postmod. thing; place. **anc.ulq kay** the seat of a loom; a straddle seat; (= **mith sīt.kay**) the kickboard on a swing.

2. postmod, postn. **ssul kay** gall bladder (**ssul** prosp mod of **ssuta** 'bitter' — note lack of **-q**). **ttongq kay** ? gizzard (of a bird) (≠ 'stray dog' ≠ 'body weight').

[< ?; CF **kes, kos, -kay, hay**]

kay₃, bnd postn. SEE **āmu ~** anybody, so-and-so. ? < pcl **ka + i** person; ? < **kayk** guest; ? var < **kes** thing — CF Hamkyeng dialect **musⁱ/ᵤ kay = musun kes**.

(-)**kay₄**, bound postnoun (? < **kay** bnd n). thing. ¶(c)**coch.i-kay** an indispensable concomitant, a necessary [der n < **coch.ta** follows]. **cicim-kay cil = cicim cil** griddling, panfrying. **puchim-kay** a flat cake [**puchim** subst < **puchita** griddles].

-kay₅ < -`kay`, suf (makes v into n). instrument, gadget, device (for doing something); ···-er, one that does; result. VAR **-key**. CF **-ay** < -`Gay`.

¶**cci-~** a thin stew (< vt steam it). **ciwu-~** an eraser. **coli-~** a tightening thread; a lens iris. **kali-~** a twofold screen. **kam-~** [DIAL] = **kamki** (= **sinq kamki → sinq-kayngki**) side-windings on Korean sandals. (**yenphil**) **kkakk-~** a (pencil sharpener). **kkal-~** a cushion. **kkwumi-~** ornaments. **kwi hwupi-~** [DIAL] = **kwi i-~** (DIAL **kwi ci-~**) an ear pick. **mith sīt-~** the kickboard on a swing. **mith ssis-~** toilet paper. **nal-~** a wing. **nolikay < nol.i-~** a toy; a trinket; an accessory. **pey-~** a pillow. **pul ssosi~** tinder. **pyeng tta-~** a bottle opener. **ssa-~** a wrapper. **ssu-~** headgear, headwear. (i) **sswusi-~** a (tooth) pick. **teph-~** a lid. **thwi-~** a coil spring. **ci-~ → ci-key** an A-frame carrier (rack). **cip-~ → cip-key** tongs, tweezers. CF **tolikkay = toliq-kay** a flail (? < **tolita** gouges); **wusu-kay** jocularity, jest (? < **wusupta**).

kāy₆ < *ka·hi*, 1. n. dog.

2. adn. wild, stray, uncultivated; false, bogus, phony; poor, worthless, trashy. ¶**~ cwuk.um** death without honor. **~ kkoch** (a wild flower). **~ kkwum** a silly dream, a dream that does not come true. **~ melwu** wild grapes. **~ nali** the wild lily; CF **kāy nāl** [= **naul**] **i** a person's "betters" [SARCASTIC]. **~ phi** wild barnyardgrass. **~ salkwu** the wild apricot. **~ soli** unworthy talk. **~ swucak** trashy remarks. **~ sswuk** wild mugwort. **~ ttek** a cake made of some rough flour used instead of rice flour.

ka ya, 1. inf + pcl. **~ (ha)nta** must go.

2. postmodifier (question) + pcl. SEE **-un ~**, **-nun ~**.

*****ka ya**, pcl (nominative) + pcl → **[ka] ya**. (Use just **ya**.) But see also **-ta ka ya**.

kayk < `KHOYK`. 1. n (= son). a guest; a lodger, a roomer; a stranger, (in compounds) a person.

2. adn. extra, superfluous, uncalled-for (= **kwūn**). ¶**kayk sik.kwu** a temporary addition to a family. **kayk soli** an uncalled-for (gratuitous, impertinent) remark. **kaykq īl** unwanted work.

3. bnd n. **~ cekta / sulepta** is uncalled-for, unnecessary, impertinent, out of place.

kayna (= **kay 'na**), **kkayna** (= **kk'ay 'na**).

1. **kay 'na**, counter + copula adversative. just because of (a trifle). ¶**Cwumek kay 'na ssunta ko tempici māla** Don't come at me just because you can use your fists.

2. **kk'ay 'na**, abbr < (**ul**) **kkway 'na**, adv + cop advers. fairly well / much, to a fair extent (or so). ¶**Cip kk'ay 'na kacyess.ta ko kyoman hakey kwūlci māla** Don't be so stuck up just because you've got yourself a house. **Ku nun tōn kk'ay 'na iss.ta ko kkapul.e yo** He shows off just because he has a little money.

kāy ney, abbr < **ku ay ney** [DISRESPECTFUL] they / them. **~ tul** SAME.

-(k)kayngi, postn, suf (? dimin). ¶al kayngi a kernel, a grain; a berry. kol kayngi the core, the heart; the pith; the gist, the substance. tali kayngi [vulgar] leg. malla kkayngi a skinny / scraggly person [inf < maluta it dries up]. namu kkayngi splinter of wood (= namuq kaypi). CF kayngi [DIAL] = kaci branch.
ka yo, inf + pcl. goes; does ··· go?; go!; let's go!
-˙ke- = -˙ka-, effective. SEE -˙Ge-; -˙e-; ˙wona-; ˙ho.ya-.

The effective has a less common variant -˙ka- after aC-, o-, and i(C)-, but -˙ke- also occurs there, as well as after other stem final strings such as a-, e(C)-, oC-, u(C)-, wu(C)-, wo(C)-. The failure of -˙ka- to occur after ···a- may point to its source as the verb stem ˚ka-, since ˙na˙ka- will be taken as ˙na-˚ka- 'go out' and *˙ka-˙ka- suggests an unwanted iteration.

After ···l-, ···y-, copula i- and ¨ti- 'drop', the corresponding lenited forms -˙Ga- and -˙Ge- are used, with the same limitations, except that only -˙Ge- appears after y: ¨sayGe˙tun (1447 Sek 6:19a), ¨hyey˙Gen ˙t ay n' (1462 ¹Nung 1:101a), e˙kuyGe˙na (1459 Wel 21:169b), ˙twoyGe˙nul (1447 Sek 6:35b), towoy˙Ge-ngi ˙˙ta (1550 ¹Yenghem 8b). Exception: ye˙huy˙ya ˙ys˙kasi˙n i (1462 ¹Nung 5:72b), CF ˙co˙ma ˙ys.ke˙tun (1459 Wel 10:5b). The lenited -˙Ge- and -˙Ga- may further reduce to just -˙e- and -˙a-; those forms occasionally appear where we expect -˙ke- and -˙ka-. On choosing the vowel-initial forms (-˙e-, -˙a-) instead of those with a velar initial, see -˙e-.

Though we find no competing versions for a given phrase, the choice of the variants seems unmotivated: kap˙ka˙la (?1468- Mong 3lb), ¨samke˙nul (1463 Pep 4:38a); ˙hoka˙n ywo (1481 Twusi 16:1b), ˙hoke˙na (1462 ¹Nung 8:77a); ne˙ki˙ka.n i ˙Gwa (1459 Wel 10:4b), tinike˙na (1459 Wel 17:33b); cis.ka.n i Gwo (1632 Twusi-cwung 14:17a), is.ke˙n ywo (1447 Sek 6:13b).

NOTE: The stems made by the effective are sometimes called ¨intensive¨ or ¨emphatic¨.
-˙ke = -˙ka, effective inf. ~ ci˙la, ~ ˙ci-ngi ˙˙ta, ~ ˙za. SEE -˙Ge; -˙e; ˙wo˙na; ˙ho˙ya.
ke, abbr < kes. ~ l(ul), ~ n(un), ~ yo.
k'e, abbr < ku ke(s). ¶K'e p(w)ā (la)! See, I told you so.

kece, adverb. CF kuce.
 1. without doing anything (in particular); without bringing anything; with nothing (in hand / mind); without giving any reason, just like that, arbitrarily, just because (one wants to do it). ¶ ~ anc.e iss.ta is sitting down doing nothing. pyēngca wimun ey ~ kata visits a sick person without bringing him anything. ~ ttaylita beats one up for no good reason.
 2. (= kong ulo) without paying anything, gratis, free (of charge), gratuitously, for nothing. ¶nam uy kes ul ~ kacye kata takes away another's belongings without paying for them. ~ īl hata works for nothing. yenghwa lul ~ kwūkyeng hata sees the movie free.
 3. kece mek.ki an easy thing to do / achieve; a simple duty to perform, a job there is nothing to; a breeze, a snap, a cinch, something one can do without giving it a second thought.
ke 'ci, abbr < kes ici. ~ yo.
-˙ke ci˙la, effective inf + aux. ¶ku ˙a˙ki nil˙kwup ¨sel me˙ke a˙pi pwo˙la ˙ni˙ke ci˙la hon ˙t ay (1459 Wel 8:101b) at the age of eight the lad wanted to go see his father, and ... .
-[˙]ke ˙ci-ngi ˙˙ta, effective inf + aux polite + cop. ¶NGWUY-TTYEY-HUY ¨CHYENG ˙hozo[˙]Wa ˙CCYENG-¨THWO ˙ay ˙nike ˙ci-ngi ˙˙ta (1459 Wel 8:1a) Vaidehī wishes (= wished) to go to the Pure Land. mwo˙ton ¨nwollam ˙kwa ce˙hwom ¨epke ˙ci-ngi ˙˙ta (1463/4 Yeng 2:140b; LCT tacitly corrects the anomalous ce˙hwom to ce˙hwum) they want all surprise and fear to be gone.
?-˙ke ˙cye, effective inf + aux inf. SEE -˙a ˙cye.
keki < ke˙kuy, n, adv. LIGHT koki. SYN ku kos. CF yeki, cēki, eti.
 1. noun. that place, there.
 2. adverb (= keki ey). at that place, there; thereupon, then.
kēkum < ¨KKE-KUM, adnoun (or adv). (dating) back from today. ¶ ~ sampayk-nyen cen three hundred years ago.
ke˙kuy, adv, n. (to / at) that place, there. ¶KYENG ˙i ¨te˙leWun ke˙kuy MI-˙MYWOW hon ¨i˙l ol na˙thwowo˙m i (1447 Sek 13:33b) the sūtra reveals subtle things in that dirty place. ¨ne y ye˙le ˙KEP ˙ey cephu˙ti a˙ni hon ke˙kuy cephun mozo˙m ol ¨nay˙m ye ... (1459 Wel 7:48a) there where you were unafraid for many kalpas (eons) you show a fearful heart and ... .

··· s ~. to an esteemed person (> *skey*).
¶ ZYE-LOY s ke῾kuy me῾li kas῾ka (1459 Wel 9:35c) gave the tathāgata a tonsure, shaved Buddha's head.

ke l', abbr < **ke lul** = **kes ul**. SEE **-nun** ~, **-tun** ~, **-un** ~. Notice that **-ess.nun** and **-keyss.nun** occur before **ke l'** in its sentence-final exclamatory use.

ke 'l(q), abbr < **kes il(q)**

?-῾*kel(q)*, effective prosp modifier. SEE -῾*el(q)*.

ke 'la, abbr < **kes ila**

-ke la, var inf + pcl. SEE **ka-** ~, **na-** ~, **ca-** ~, **su-** ~, **toy-** ~; **iss-** ~, **tut-** ~, **cwuk-** ~, **anc-** ~, **mit-** ~. CF §8.3.6, §9.4.

NOTE 1: For some speakers all short verb stems ending in /a/ take this form: **sake la = sa la** 'buy!', **phake la = pha la** 'dig!'.

NOTE 2: In Cincwu (South Kyengsang) **-ke la** is optionally used for **-e la** with any verb: **cap-** ~, **yel-** ~, **noh-** ~, **wūs-** ~, **ciph-** ~ (Mkk 1960:3:35).

NOTE 3: CM 1:310 would derive **anc.kela** /ankkela/ 'sit!' from **anc.e iss.kela**, comparing it to **sess.kela** /sekkela/ from **se iss.kela** 'stand!'.

NOTE 4: The form probably derives from -῾*ke῾la*, despite the analysis in Note 3.

NOTE 5: Phyengan has **-ka la**, at least after syllables with **a** and **i** (Kim Yengpay 1984:102-3): **caka la = cake la** 'sleep!', **nika la** 'go!', **is.ka la** 'stay!'. CF Phyengan **ona la = one la** 'come!'.

-῾*ke῾la*, effective subj attent (command). ¶ ῾*icey ῾stwo ne ῾lul ye῾huy῾Gwo te῾wuk ῾῾wu-῾nino῾n i esye two῾la ῾nike῾la* (1459 Wel 8:101a) now I am letting you go again and I am all the more in tears; please go back. *tye cywung a key is.kela* (1747 Songkang 2:16a) yon monk stay where you are! SEE -῾*ka῾la*, -῾*a῾la*, -῾*e῾la*, -῾*Ga῾la*, -῾*Ge῾la*.

ke 'la to, abbr < **kes ila to**

(-q) keli₁, noun (usually quasi-free as postnoun or postmodifier). [? der n < **kēlta**; CF **kelita, kwūlta**]

1. material, matter, stuff, stock, makings; substance, basis, excuse, pretext. ¶ **kwuk** ~ soup stock, soup-makings. **wus.umq** ~ a laughing-stock, a butt of ridicule; a subject of laughter. **iyakiq** ~ a subject of talk, a topic. **īlq** ~ a place of work, a job. **sinmun kisaq keli lul kwu hanta** (1956 Dupont 297) seeks material for news articles. **Māl halq keli ka ēps.ta** I can't find any excuse (or pretext) to approach him. (or: I have no subject to talk on.) **Māl ul hallay to musun keli ka iss.e ya (ha)ci** I should like to approach him but I can't think of anything to say to him. SEE **thong**.

2. doings, action, stuff. SEE **cīs** ~. CF **tāy-keli** shift; replacement; talking back. ¶ **chitak-keli** management, arranging for, taking care of [? < **chita-q-keli**].

3. appearance. ¶ **os** ~ the appearance of one's clothing (CF **os kel.i**). **salq** ~ fleshiness, fattiness.

keli₂, n. a road, a street (CF **kil**). ¶ **khun** ~ a main street, a thoroughfare. **nēy** ~ a cross-street, a crossroads, four corners. **sam** ~ , **sēy** ~ an intersection of three streets, a place where three streets meet.

keli₃, noun, counter.

1. one of the (usually twelve) stages of an exorcism ceremony (= **kwus-keli**). CF **twīq-cēn**; **phutak-keli** exorcism [? < **phu(l)ta-q-keli**].

2. an act of a play.

keli₄, counter. a group of fifty (cucumbers / eggplants). ¶ **oy twū** ~ a hundred cucumbers.

keli₅, postn [der n < **keluta** skips, omits; CF **kēlchita**]. at intervals of; skipping, jumping. **ithul** ~ (lo) every other day. ¶ **sahul** ~ (lo) at three-day intervals, every three days. **yelhul** ~ every ten days. **han kān** ~ every other time / place. **kān keli hata = kān keluta** leaves an interval between. CF **kelle**; **kēnne**; **ssik, mata**.

keli₆ → **kel.i** (der n)

-keli, nd n. **to-keli (lo)** by the gross, in bulk. **thong-keli (lo)** as a lot, unbroken, in toto.

kel.i₁, postnoun (der n < **kēt.ta** walks). SEE **kel.um kel.i**.

kel.i₂, noun, postnoun (der n < **kēlta** hangs).

1. the act of hanging; a hanger (thing which hangs or on which something hangs). ¶ **os** ~ a clothes-hanger (CF **os keli**). **moca** ~ a hat rack. **tungkyeng** ~ a lamp pole, a lantern stand. **cing** ~ a shoemaker's jack. **phal** ~ an arm rest, an elbow rest. **pal kel.i₁** rung, pedal, footrest, stirrup. **palq-tung kel.i** forestalling; hanging by one's feet (CF **palq tungkeli** a small lantern).

2. [in wrestling] a foot-trip. **pal-kel.i₂** a footlock trip. **tes** ~ an armlock trip (CF **tes-**

keli an additional / extra thing). **anq ~** an inside foot-trip.
kel.i₃ → **keli₁** (stuff; doings)
?-ˈke.l i ˈGa, effective prosp mod + postmod + postmodifier. SEE -ˈe.l i ˈGa.
kelita, postnom verb insep. does repeatedly / continuously; does and does; keeps doing, does on (and on), does (keeps doing) it away; does again and again, does over and over again. SYN **tāyta**. X-**kelita** = XX-**hata**, but when X is a single syllable XX-**kelita** is common.
¶ **elis, hwuntul, kkungkkung, ppacici, paksin, pangkul, pesek, pepssek, swukun, ssikssik, twukun, twutel, ttwukttak, ttulssek ~** .
?-ˈke.l i ˈye, effective prosp mod + postmod + postmod. SEE -ˈe.l i ˈye.
-kellang (un) [DIAL] = **ketullang (un)** = **-ketun**
kelle, inf < **keluta**. skipping; at intervals; apart.
¶ **halwu ~** every other day. **ithul ~** every third day. **han cwul ~ ssuta** writes on every other line. **sip-o pun ~** at ten-minute intervals.
kel-lo, abbr < **kes ulo**; ?< **ku kes ulo**.
... **kellyo** SEE **ke l'q yo**
ke 'l.nun (ci), abbr < **kes il.nun (ci)**
ke 'lq sey, abbr < **kes ilq sey**. SEE **-ulq ~**.
ke lul = **kes ul**
kelum (ey), postmodifier [DIAL] = **kīm (ey)** impetus, influence. (< **kel.um** pace)
-kelum, bnd n, pseudo-postn. SEE **hay-(ke)lum**.
?-ˈke.l ye, ?-ˈke.l ywo
ke l'q yo /kellyo/ SEE **-ulq, -un, -nun, -tun ~**
ke 'm, abbr < **kes im**
-ˈkem, effective subst. SEE -u'l i 'Ge'm ye; -um cik hata (NOTE 2).
ken < **KKEN**, 1. adn. dry, dried. ¶ **~ taykwu a** dried cod. **~ photo** raisins. **~ ppang** hardtack.
2. bnd n (preparticle). **~ ulo** in vain.
3. adj-n. **~ hata** is dry.
ke n', abbr < **ke nun** = **kes un**
-ken', abbr < **-kena**. (Examples: NKd 163a.)
-ke'n, abbr < **-ketun**. (Examples: NKd 163a.)
-ˈken, effective modifier. CF -ˈGen, -ˈen; -ˈkan, -ˈGan, ˈkhan, ˈho.yan.
1. (the epitheme is extruded from the subject). **woˈlaken ˝men ˈKEP puˈthe ˈNYELQ-PPAN S ˈPEP ˈul ˈCAN-ˈTHAN ˈhoˈya** (1447 Sek 13:59a) has been praising the law of nirvāṇa for many long-ago kalpas (eons) and ... . ˝ti-ˈnaken ˝nyey ˝nwuy s SSI-ˈCYELQ ˈey (1447 Sek 6:8a) at a time in a long past ancient world.

2. (epitheme extruded from object). Example?
3. (summational epitheme). SEE -ˈkeˈn i.
ke 'na, abbr < **kes ina**
-kena, tentative adversative. ABBR **-ken'**. CF **-ulq ke 'na; -tun ci**. For **-kena lul** see p. 258.
1. what (when, where, how, ...) ever. ¶ **Ney ka mue 'la ko māl hakena, na n' kot.i tut.ci anh.keyss.ta** I won't believe you whatever you may say. **Ku sālam i etteh.key** (or **mue 'la ko**) **māl haken(a) sangkwan ēps.ta** It makes no difference what he says.
2. whether ... or ... (shows indifference toward the choice between two conflicting actions or states). ¶ **oken mālken = okena an okena** (= **ona an ona, otun ci an otun ci, wā to an wā to**) whether one comes or not. **Kakena okena ma(u)m tay lo hay la** Come or go – do as you please.
3. (linking two unrelated acts or states – followed by **hata**). ¶ **Sonq-pyek ul chikena khun soli lo wūs.kena haci māsio** Don't slap your hands or laugh loudly. **Mul i kiph.kena mulq-sal i sēykena hamyen, chalali pay lul thaca** If the water is deep or the current strong we had better get on the boat. **Wel.yoil ikena mok.yoil ikena hamyen mōlla to, talun nal un an toykeyss.ta 'y yo** If it is Monday or Thursday he doesn't know, but none of the other days will do, he says.
NOTE: The examples of **āmuli / etteh.key** ...**kena** in CM 1:346 are rejected.
-keˈna, effective adversative. ¶ **anskeˈna syekeˈna** (1447 Sek 19:5b) whether sitting or standing. ˝**cyek.keˈna ˝eˈtwun keˈs i isiˈm ye n' ˈkwot ˈCYWOK ˝samkeˈnul** (1463 Pep 4:38a) if, when what is got is but little, one makes do with that ... . ˈ**kuli ˝zopkeˈna moyngˈko˝zopkeˈna holˈss iˈla** (1459 Wel 2:66b) the images are the same and are either painted or sculpted to be like the features of Buddha. **nepkena nepun THYEN-HA** [sic] (1747 Songkang 1:4a) this wide, wide land beneath heaven.
ke 'na, abbr < **kes ina**
-kena kan ey. Equivalent to uses 1 and 2 of **-kena** (but not use 3).
1. ¶ **Musunq īl ikena kan ey cwunun kwaep un chwungsil hi hay ya hao** Whatever the task you are given, you must carry it out faithfully. **Nwu ka okena kan ey ppalli man wass.umyen cōh.keyss.ta** Whoever comes I hope it's soon.

2. ¶Nal-ssi ya chwupkena tēpkena kan ey yēyceng sikan ey tte-naca Whether the weather is hot or cold let's leave at the regular time.
*-ken ceng < -ken ˙tyeng. SEE (ci) enceng.
ke 'n ci, abbr < kes in ci
ke 'ney, abbr < kes iney
-˙ke-ngi ˙'ta, effective polite + copula indicative assertive. ¶˙na y ˙icey ˙SYEY-CWON ˙ol mocomak ˙pwo˙zoWwo˙n i chuk hon mozo˙m i ¨ep˙ke-ngi ˙'ta (1459 Wel 10:8b) now that at last I have seen the World-Honored, he does not have a bad soul.
˙'ke-ngi ˙'ta, abbr < ˙ho˙ke-ngi ˙'ta after voiceless sounds. ¶˙i the˙li ˙two ˙CYWOK ˙'ke-ngi ˙'ta (1447 Sek 23:58a) just this hair is enough.
ke 'n i, abbr < kes in i
ke 'ni, abbr < kes ini. 1. (question = kes in ya) ¶Ney kes kwa nay kes kwa (kkaci lul) hap-chin key kyewu i ke 'ni? Is this all that links your interests and mine?
2. (sequential) ~-kka (n').
˙'ke˙n i, abbr < ˙hoke˙n i after voiceless sounds; CF khe˙n i. SEE ¨mwot˙'ke˙n i.
-ke˙n i, effective modifier + postmodifier.
1. (epitheme from subject). Examples?
2. (epitheme from object). Examples?
3. (summational epitheme).

3a. (in a loosely concatenated sentence). ¶kungey CYENG-˙SYA y ¨epke˙n i e˙tu˙li ka˙l ywo (1447 Sek 6:22a) how can I go when there are no monasteries there?

3b. (SEE -keni 3). ¶wo˙lay nos¨kapke˙n i nwopke˙n i ho˙n i ˙'la (1481 Twusi 16:47b) for a long time they were first low then high (= sinking and rising).
-keni, tentative sequential (< -ke˙n i, effective mod + postmod). with the likely fact / reason that; for the likely reason that. CF -eni.
1. [literary — usually followed by rhetorical question] = -uni (sequential) since, as, so; but. ¶Na nun celm.ess.keni tōl in tul mukewul ya?! Since I am young, can any stone be heavy (for me)?! Sanchen i etwupkeni il-wel ul ecci pol ya?! The world is dark [and evil]; how can I hope to see [a man of virtue who will shine through like] the sun and the moon?!
CF ku il i chom kule hokeni (1916 Gale 69) 'that's so, it is true (after all)': "It is used when expressing one's conviction to oneself."

2. ~ hanun sayngkak (ey / ulo), ~ hamyen, ~ hako with the thought that probably / surely, with confidence / assurance that. ¶Cikum ccum un phyēnci ka wā iss.keni hanun sayngkak ey ppalli cip ulo wass.ta I have rushed home with the thought that the letter would surely be here by now. [1]Nayil imyen mannalq swu iss.keni hamyen mopsi kipputa Assured of seeing him tomorrow, I am very happy. Apeci ka cip ey kyēysikeni hako sōk ulo kippe hayss.ta He was happy at the thought that his father would be at home. NOTE: The example of -keni nun in CM 1:372 is rejected.

3. ~ siph.e cinta gets the feeling that … . ¶Cikum to salass.keni siph.e cinta I get the feeling he is still alive. CF -ulye 'n' i siph.e cinta.

4. (phrases in sequence) what with doing one thing and then another (in alternation); now … now … ; sometimes … (and) sometimes … ; by turns. ¶Cwukeni pat.keni yāyki ka kkuth i ēps.ess.ta What with my telling him and his telling me, there was no end to our talking. māl ul cwukeni pat.keni hata exchange words (with each other). Capkeni mīlkeni hay se san ey olla kanta We pull and push our way up the mountain. Masikeni mek.keni ha.ye tōn ul tā sse pelyess.ta Eating and drinking away, he has spent all his money. selwo cwukeni pas.keni homnoyta (1916 Gale 2:69) = selo cwukeni pat.keni hap.nita they keep throwing it and catching it.

-keni [Ceycwu DIAL (Seng [1]Nakswu 1984:58-9)] = -ca (māca) as soon as, right after. ¶Nu ka kakeni kai ka was.cye = Ney ka kaca māca ku ai ka wass.ci He / She came right after you left.

-˙ke.n i ˙Gwa, effective mod + postmod + pcl = -keni wa. ¶ha˙nol s ˙ptu.t un nwo˙pha ¨mwut.ti e˙lyepke.n i ˙Gwa ¨salo˙m oy ˙ptu.t un nul˙ku.n i ¨swuyi sulphu˙twota (1481 Twusi 23:9b) the will of heaven is lofty and hard to ask, but the will of a person is easy for an old man to sense! SEE ˙ho˙ke.n i˙Gwa.

-ke˙n i ˙Gwo, effective mod + postmod + postmod. ¶phu˙lun ˙tay yey ˙myes [¨]salo˙m i wol˙Ga ˙'s.ke˙n i [˙]Gwo (1481 Twusi 20:23b) how many people have ¨climbed into the green bamboo¨ (= failed achievement)?.

-keni 'ko, abbr < -keni hako. [Not in use?]

-ke᾽n i ᾽'la, effective mod + postmod + cop. ¶tyelun ᾽ta.m i ᾽hota ᾽ka isi᾽m ye n' [SYWUY-CCAN] hon ᾽phu.l ul muten ᾽hi ᾽kyes.ke᾽n i 'la (1481 Twusi 8:42a) let there be the tiniest wall and the straggling grass proliferates.

-keni lo, tentative sequential + pcl. Cwuk.keni sālkeni lo hamyen an toylq īl i ēps.ta When one is desperate anything is possible.

-keni 'myen, abbr < -keni hamyen. [Not in use?]

-keni 'nun, abbr -keni hanun. [Not in use?]

-ke᾽n i ᾽sto᾽n ye, effective mod + postmod + pcl + postmod. ¶pen᾽tu᾽ki ᾽PEP-HHWA y a᾽ni ᾽Ge᾽nul ᾽za ᾽homol᾽mye "TTWOW-᾽KUY ᾽Gwa "KWA-᾽KUY ᾽Gwa tal᾽Gwo᾽m i is.ke᾽n i ᾽sto᾽n ye (1462 ¹Nung 1:17a) though they cannot be the Lotus sūtra exactly, just how much more would they differ from testimonials to marga (the way) and to phala ([cause and] effect)?!

-keni wa, tent sequential + pcl (< -᾽ke.n i ᾽Gwa). "together with the likely fact that" = as well as, besides; admitting that; but (even so); not only ... but also; moreover, and what's more, plus; and even more (so). ¶Ku ke n' kuleh.keni wa Be that as it may. elkwul to kōpkeni wa maum-ssi to kōpta (she) has not only a pretty face but also a lovely disposition. Ku haksayng un wūntong to cal hakeni wa kongpu to cal hanta That student is a fine scholar as well as a good athlete. Ku sālam un Pusan ey hyeng i iss.e se kakeni wa tangsin un way kap.nikka He is going because he has a brother in Pusan, but why are you going? Ku sālam un Yenge lul cal hay se Hānkwuk māl chayk ul pen.yek hakeni wa Kim sensayng un Yenge to molunun tey etteh.key pen.yek ul hana yo That person can translate Korean books with a good knowledge of English, but how will Mr Kim translate when he does not know any English? Tōn to ēps.keni wa thum to ēps.ta Not only do I lack money, but also I haven't the time/opportunity. Pi to okeni wa mom to phikon hay se onul ōhwu ey n' nakaci mōs hanta It is raining and in addition I'm tired, so I won't go out this afternoon. San to noph.keni wa mul to malk.ta It has high mountains and the waters are clear, too. Kokco to cōh.keni wa kasa ka i tewuk cōh.ta The tune is nice, but the words are nicer.

-᾽ken ma᾽lon, effective mod + postmod. but, although. ¶᾽mul kiph᾽kwo ᾽poy "ep᾽ken ma᾽lon ha᾽nol᾽h i [MYENG] ᾽hosil ᾽ss oy mol ᾽thwon ca᾽hi "ken᾽nesi᾽n i-ngi ᾽'ta (1445 ¹Yong 34) the water was deep and he lacked a boat, but at heaven's command he crossed over it without dismounting. SEE -᾽en ma᾽lon.

-ken man < -᾽ken ma᾽non, semi-lit concessive. but, even though, although, while (= -ci man). ~ un, ~ se to. ¶Na nun ku lul salang haken man un ku nun na lul cōh.a haci anh.nunta Although I love him, he does not care for me. Nay hyeng un tōn i mānh.ken man na nun tōn i ēps.ta While my brother has lots of money, I have none. Ku nun kongpu nun cal haken man tāyseng un mōs halq key 'ta Even though he studies very hard, I doubt he can have any great success. CF -en man; -ess.ken man. Sometimes spelled -kes.man (as in 1936 Roth 468-9), -kes.ma.non (as in 1894 Gale 60). [Etymologies suggested in KEd are wrong.]

kēnne, 1. vt inf < kēnnuta.

2. n, postn. the other/opposite side (of). ~ phyen SAME. ¶kil ~ the other side of the road. kang ~ the opposite side of the river. kēnneq pang/cip a room/house on the opposite side. CF neme.

kēnneta, 1. kēnneta ~ kēnnuta crosses over.

2. kēnne ᾽ta, vt inf + abbr cop transferentive. so that it crosses, so that it is across/opposite. ~ pota looks across at; looks at covetously, covets, casts a jealous eye on (nam uy kes ul ~ covets another's possession).

-ke᾽nol, var of -᾽ke᾽nul (lit concessive). ¶"NGWO-᾽SOYK ᾽kwulwu᾽m i HE-KHWONG ᾽o᾽lwo "ti-᾽na ᾽kake᾽nol ku ka᾽won-᾽toy ᾽SSYWUY-᾽SSYANG ᾽i "kye᾽site᾽n i (1459 Wel 2:51b) five-colored clouds passed by in the air and among them there were propitious images (= good omens [personified and exalted]).

-ke᾽nol ᾽za, lit concessive + pcl. ¶cwukuf᾽]m ye sa᾽lwo.m ol "ati ᾽mwot ᾽ke᾽nol za ᾽homol᾽mye ᾽kil.h i ki᾽lwu.m ey ᾽es.tyey ho᾽l i ᾽Gwo (1481 Twusi 8:29a) ignorant of death and life as I am, my path is all the longer, so what am I to do?

᾽ke᾽nol za, abbr < ᾽hoke᾽nol za after voiceless sounds. SEE "mwot ᾽ke᾽nol za.

? -᾽ken ᾽ta SEE -᾽en ᾽ta

-kentay, literary conditional (< -᾽ken ᾽t ay).

1. when, if. ¶Sayngkak hakentay/khentay Come to think of it ... . Cāmsi tol.a pokentay (nun) If we just look back for a moment ... .

Pokentay On inspection ... . **Tut.kentay ku ka sāep ey silphay hayss.ta 'tun tey** As I hear it, he failed in business. **Pīyu hakentay insayng un ilqcang uy chwunmong ita** Figuratively speaking, life is a ("spring dream" =) passing dream. **Thong-thel.e māl hakentay wuli kyēyhoyk ey nun ōsan i mānh.ess.ta** There were a number of miscalculations in our plan, generally speaking. SEE **(cheng/wēn) khentay; pala-kentay**.

2. = **-kwantey** such / so that (followed by a question doubting the adequacy of the reason).

-kentay n', abbr < **-kentay nun**

-ˈken ˈt ay n', effective mod + postmod + pcl + pcl. ¶mwoˈtwoˈa nilukenˈt ay n' (1447 Sek 13:40a) he got them together and said ... . THYEN-ˇNYE ˈlul ˈpwokenˈt ay n' naˈy ˇkyeˈci.p iˈza ˈnwun ˇmen MI-HHWUW ˈkotˈtwo swo-ngi ˈˈta (1459 Wel 7:12b) compared with the goddesses my [beautiful] wife is like a blind ape.

ke 'n tey, abbr < **kes in tey**

-ˈkenˈt ey n', effective mod + postmod + pcl + pcl. ¶ˈil-ˈlwo ˇhyeyˈye ˈpwokenˈt ey n' muˈsum CCO-PI ˇkyeˈsikeˈn ywo hoˈkwo (1447 Sek 6:6a) "When one considers it as this, what mercy does he have?!" she said, and ... .

-ˈkenˈti(...) = -ˈkenˈt i(...).

-ˈkenˈti = -ˈkenˈt i, effective mod + postmod + pcl. (the time) since it happened (= **-un ci**). ¶ˇCCWOY-ˇNYE y haˈnolˈh ay ˈnakenˈt i woˈnol saˈoˈl i ˇti-naˈn i (1459 Wel 21:28b) today three days have passed since the sinful woman went to heaven. ˇsalo.m oy cip sˈnoy kus.kenˈt i woˈla.n i (1481 Twusi 8:34-5) it is a long time since the smoke ended from people's houses.

? -ˈkenˈt iˈla

? -ˈkenˈt iˈn i, ? -ˈkenˈt i.n iˈˈla

ke 'n tul, abbr < **kes in tul**

? -ˈkenˈt un, effective mod + postmod + pcl. SEE **-Genˈt un**.

-ˈkenˈtyeng, effective modifier + bnd postmod. ¶ˇcyeˈkusyaˈm i ˇkyeˈsikenˈtyeng (1463 Pep 3:189b) though there are those who have little. SEE **khenˈtyeng**.

-kenul (< -ˈkeˈnᵘ/ol), literary concessive [obs].

1. although, while (= **-ci man**). ¶**Sālam i tā hyengcey lul twuess.kenul nay hol lo ēps.tota** While all others have brothers, I alone have none.

2. as, since, when, upon (= **-um ey**). ¶**Sipi ey kāy cic.kenul im man yekye na-ka pon i** When the dog barked at the twig door I went out, expecting my beloved. **Maum-ssi ka cōh.kenul nay anʰay lo sām.ki lo hayss.ta** Her disposition being good, I decided to make her my wife. **Talk i palk.kenul sānqpo lul nawass.ta** As the moon was bright I came out for a stroll. SEE **khenul**.

-ˈkeˈnul (> **-kenul**), literary concessive. VAR -ˈkeˈnol, -ˈGeˈnul, -ˈGeˈnol, -ˈ[G]eˈnul, -ˈ[G]eˈnol, ˈwo-naˈnol / -naˈnul. From -ˈken [ ] ᵘ/ol, effective mod + zero postmod (i.e. direct nominalization of the adnominalized sentence) + pcl. For an example that can be taken as a direct object, see ˈwonaˈnol.

-ˈkeˈnulˈza, lit concessive + pcl. ¶ ˇaˈlay neˈy ˈeˈmi ˇnaˈlol yeˈhuyˈye siˈluˈm uˈlwo ˇsa-ˈnikeˈnul za, woˈnol neˈy ˈeˈmi neˈlul yeˈhuyˈyen ˈnwun sˈmulˈlwo ˇsaninoˈn i ˈˈla (1459 Wel 8:86a) while earlier your mother, freed of her ego, still lived on with worries, today your mother goes on living with her tears from having given you up. ¶ˈstwo ˈPWO-SI HHOYNG ˈhwo.m i CIN-ˈSSILQ lwo hoˈma ˈkhuˈkenulˈzaˈstwo ... (1482 Kum-sam 2:16a) and while indeed his practicing of almsgiving is already truly great, moreover ... .

ke nun = kes un

ke 'n ya, abbr < **kes in ya**

-ˈkeˈn ya, effective mod + postmod. ¶kwukˈi neˈy ˈswonˈol ˇteykeˈn ya ho.n i (1586 Sohak 6:102b) asked whether the soup burned your hand; CF neˈy ˈswoˈn i ˇteyGeˈn ya hoˈn i (1518 Sohak-cho 10:3a), neˈy ˈswoˈn i ˇteyGeˈn ye hoˈn i (1475 Nay 1:18a) asked, "Did you burn your hand?".

-ˈkeˈn ye, effective modifier + postmod. ¶ˈne y ˇcyekuˈna ˇtywokheˈn ye [← ˇtywoh-kenˈye] (?1517-¹No 2:41a) are you a little better?

-ˈkeˈn ywo, effective mod + postmod. ¶eˈtuyˈza ˈtywohon stoˈl i yangˈco koˈcoˈn i is.keˈn ywo (1447 Sek 6:13b) just where is there a good daughter endowed with looks? ˇes.tyey woˈnol munˈtuk mozom alˈphwoˈm i ˈnakeˈn ywo (1462 ¹Nung 5:72b) why today is my heart suddenly seized with pain? ˈPWULQ-PPYENGˈol kus.keˈn ywo (1482 Nam 2:70a) did it end the discontent? SEE ˈkheˈn ywo, -ˈeˈn ywo.

k'e p'ā (la) = ku ke pwā (la) See, I told you so!

kes₁ < *kes* (CF *kas*), quasi-free n — does not occur sentence-initial except as abbr < ku kes.
  1. 1a. a/the one (= person/thing). ¶i (ku/ce) ~ this (that). say ~ a new one. musun ~ which one. CF **tulq-kes** stretcher, **mulq-kes** (stinging) bugs.
  1b. abbr < ku kes.
  2. (preceded by modifier; see also kes₂) the one that. ¶pon ~ the one that saw it or the one that someone saw. ponun ~ the one that sees it or that someone sees. polq ~ the one to see. Cēki kanun kes i nwukwu 'n ya Who is that going by on the street over there? Elin kes twūl iss.ta I have two young ones (= children).
  3. (abbr < **uy kes**, often pronounced **-q kes**) the of, ···'s. ¶wuli ~ ours. sensayngq kes the teacher's; yours. ayki uy kes, aykiq kes the baby's; baby things.
  4. (= os) clothes, garment, things (to wear).
  5. (→ khes) the sex/gender. ¶am-khes (< amh kes) = am nom a female. swu-khes (< swuh kes) = swu nom a male.

kes₂, postmod (< kes₁).
  1. the fact that; the act of (doing); the doing/being. ¶pi ka onun kes ul ālta knows that it is raining. pi ka onun kes ul pota sees that it is raining, sees it raining, watches it rain. Achim ilccik il.e nanta 'nun kes un swiwunq īl i ani 'ta It's not easy to get up early in the morning. Nay māl tay lo hanun kes i cōh.ta You had better do just as I told you.
  2. the tentative/likely/probable fact, the real likelihood, the strong probability. SEE **-ulq kes**. ¶Kuleh.key māl hamyen sēng nāylq kes ita He is likely to get angry if you say that. ¹Yu'-wel i toymyen pi ka olq kes ita When June rolls around, it will rain (I'm sure).
  3. the thing to do; the thing one does, the obligation (or prohibition), the rule. ¶Hyeng hanthey nun an kulenun kes ita You shouldn't do that to your older brother. Yeki se an phiwunun kes ita (or phiwunun kes i ani 'ta) We don't smoke here = You're not supposed to (You shouldn't) smoke here.
  4. ··· kes (i) ani 'n ya (ani yo, ani 'p.nikka) isn't it the case that ··· [rhetorical question] = surely (it is true that) ··· . ¶Hata mōs hay tān payk-wen ul pat.e to ku mankhum ¹ī lowulq kes i ani 'n ya At the worst, if you get only a hundred wen you are at least that much ahead. Poktong-i kath.i nun haci mōs haci man Swupok-i pota 'la to cal hay ya toylq kes i ani 'n ya You may not be able to do as well as Poktong-i, but surely you ought to do better than Swupok-i. Ney ka īl ul cal hanun thas ulo sensayng nim i ne 'ykey cacwu sikhisinun key ani 'n ya I think Teacher calls on you all the time because you do so well. Cil iya etteh.tun (ci) kaps ila to ssa ya halq kes ani yo Regardless of the quality, [isn't it the case that =] surely the price should be kept low.
  5. 5a. ~ ul (= ke l'). SEE **-nun ke l'**, **-tun ke l'**, **-un ke l'**.
  5b. ~ i but. SEE **-nun (-un, -tun, -ulq, -ess.ulq) ~**. CF **nolus i**.

ke se, abbr < kes ey se

-ˈkeˈsi- (effective honorific) = -(ᵁ/o)ˈsiˈke- (honorific effective): -ˈkesin, -ˈkesina, -ˈkesiˈn i (ˈGwo/ˈGwa), -ˈkesiˈnᵁ/ol, -ˈkesiˈn ywo, -ˈkesiˈta, -ˈkesiˈton = -ˈkesiˈtun; -ˈkesiˈza.

-ˈkeˈsin = -(ᵁ/o)ˈsiˈken, honorific effective mod. ¶ˈˈti-ˈnaˈkesin MWU-ˈLYANG CYE-[ˈ]PPWULQˈskuy (1447 Sek 13:15a) to the immeasurable Buddhas who have passed by.
  ~ ˈt i. ¶ˈSYENG-ZIN ˈˈepˈkesin ˈt i woˈla.m ye n' (1459 Wel 9:7a) when the absence of a saint is long in duration ··· . See also -ˈkesiˈn i, -ˈkeˈsin maˈlon, -ˈkesiˈn ywo.

-ˈkesiˈna, effective hon adversative. ¶ZYE-LOY niloˈkesiˈna PPWO-ˈSALQ ˈi nilokeˈna SYENG-MWUN i nilokeˈna (1459 Wel 18:49b) whether the tathāgata tells it or the bodhisattva tells it or the śrāvaka tells it ··· . SEE ˈkhesiˈna.

-ˈkesiˈn i, effective honorific mod + postmod. ¶ˈˈaˈlay ˈkasin PALQˈˈCHOY-ˈNYE ˈtwo ˈniˈkesiˈn i muf·ˈ]su.k i ˈˈskelWuˈl i '-ngi s ˈkwo (1459 Wel 8:93ab) the eight comely maidens who have gone below (there), what difficulties must they too have had in going?.
  ~ ˈGwa (pcl). ¶ku ˈNGWEN ˈi ˈwohiˈlye moˈchwoˈm i ˈˈkyesiˈkesiˈn i ˈGwa (1459 Wel 21:149a) he had something of an excessive aspiration there, but ··· . cwuk-saˈli s ˈˈSSYWUW-ˈˈKHWO ˈlol aˈni ˈhoˈkesiˈn i ˈGwa (1459 Wel 1:12b) did not undergo the suffering of death and life, but ··· .
  ~ [ˈ]Gwo (postmod). ¶[*COM-ˈQUN] hon nwo.m ol kiˈtulˈGwoˈkesiˈn i Gwo (1481 Twusi 21:3b) was he waiting for the guy who had ducked into hiding?

-`ke`sin ma`lon, effective hon mod + postmod.
¶ MI-`MYWOW s us.tu`m i ho`ma kos`ke`sin ma`lon (1447 Sek 13:63a) it is already endowed with the utmost in subtlety. `nim-ku`m i si`lum `hosya[`TTWOW-`CCUK] ul [`KUP] `hi ne`ki`kesin ma`lon [KWUN-SO] y nul`ke [KYENG-TWO] y ke`chu`le 'ys.two`ta (1481 Twusi 22:46a) the king was troubled and quickly recognized the renegades, but his commanding general was old and the capital was unruly.
SEE `khe`sin ma`lon.

-`kesi`nol = -`kesi`nul, hon lit concessive (< effective honorific modifier + pcl). ¶pwuthye s wu[h] s ip-si`Gwu`l ey s the`li hona`h i na`ma is`kesi`nol (1447 Sek 23:56b) since there was left a single hair from Buddha's upper lip, … . NGWANG `i `mas `tule kas.ka`Wi `ho`kesi`nol (1459 Wel 2:5a) the king looked upon her with favor and kept her close to him. `CI-`KKUK ' `ti a`ni hon `toy ¨ep`kesi`nol (1462 ¹Nung 1:3a) while there is no place that is not extreme, … .
VAR -`Gesi`nol.

-`kesi`nul = -`sike`nul, hon lit concessive (< effective hon mod + pcl). ¶[THYEN-¨HHA] `ay [KWONG] `i `khusya`toy [`THAY-¨CO] z [`WUY] talo`kesi`nul ¨say ¨pye`l i na`c oy two`to`n i (1445 ¹Yong 101) his merits in the land were great but his rank was not that of crown prince; the evening star rose at noon.

-`kesi`n ywo, effective hon mod + postmod. ¶mu`sum ZYWOW-[`]QYEK `u`lwo `ile 'n KWANG-MYENG `ul `phye`kesi`n ywo (1447 Sek 13:25b) with what kindling has he spread such light?. SIM-`KWOK SIM-SAN `ay ¨en`ma cephu`kesi`n ywo (1449 Kok 123) in the deep valleys and the deep mountains how frightened will she be?
SEE `khesi`n ywo.

-`kesi`ta, effective honorific indicative assertive.
'`kesi`ta, abbr < *`ho`kesi`ta after voiceless consonant. ¶`icey pol`h ol `solo`sya `mwo`m i kos`ti ¨mwot ' `kesi`ta (< ho`kesi`ta) `hote`n i (1459 Wel 2:42b) now he has burned off his arm and his body cannot be whole, they said.

-`kesi`ton = -`kesi`tun, hon provisional. if/when one deign. ¶PPYEN-QAN `thi a`ni `hosin mo¨toy is`kesi`ton (1475 Nay 1:40a) if he [the king] has a stretch of being ill … .

-`kesi`tun = -u`sike`tun, honorific provisional. if/when one deigns to do it. ¶[TWONG] `oy `ni`kesi`tun (1445 ¹Yong 38) when he went to the east … . CYE-`PPWULQ s `SSIM `hi ki`phun ¨hoyng`tyek nilu`kesi`tun tut¨cop`kwo ne`kywo`toy (1447 Sek 9:27a) when the several Buddhas reach extremely deep conclusions he listens and considers them … . SEE `ho`kesi`tun.
'`kesi`tun, abbr < *`ho`kesi`tun. ¶ku cey lwo `wosin `t i son`coy wo`la`ti `mwot ' `kesi`tun (1463 Pep 5:119b) he had not been there for very long yet when … .

-`kesi `za < ?*-(ᵁo)si`ke `za, (inverted) hon effective inf + pcl. ¶¨PPWU-¨MWUW ¨ep`kesi `za pwuthye s `kuy `kazo`Wa (1459 Wel 23:85b) only when my father and mother were no longer alive did I go to Buddha, and … .

-kes.kwun(a) → -keyss.kwun(a).

-kes-man SEE -ken man

-kes.ta, tentative assertive. SEE -ess.kes.ta; CF -ulyetta. ?< -`ke `[i]s.ta, effective inf + aux; ?< -ke`ta, inserted s for emphasis; ?< -kes`ta.

1. is/does I assume/suppose/think. ¶Ne i tōngney sālkes.ta You must live in this village (I presume). Ku ka ¹naynyen imyen ō-sip i toykes.ta He will be fifty years old next year (won't he).

2. surely (certainly) is/does; you WILL do it (understand? − suggesting a threat). ¶Ku nun ēncey 'tun ci cikak hakes.ta He is always behind time! Kan pam ey pūltun palam (ey) mānceng tohwa (ka) tā cikes.ta The wind last night has certainly shed all the peach blossoms in the yard. Ne nun kakes.ta You ARE going!

3. given this and that (enumerates a series of reasons arguing a conclusion). ¶Tōn iss.kes.ta him iss.kes.ta musun kekceng iyo You've got money, you've got power, so what is your worry? I pen welmal ey nun chilulq cip-sey ka iss.kes.ta sēynap i iss.kes.ta kākey ōysang i iss.kes.ta welkup ul pat.e to han phun nām.ci anh.keyss.ta When I have paid the rent, the taxes, and the store bills at the end of the month, there won't be a single penny of my salary left.

4. → -keyss.ta.

-kes`ta, effective emotive indicative assertive. LCT has two examples from the 1600s and one of 1481: [NGWUW-¨TWUW SYENG] `pola wo`m ol hon-kas is`pi `hokes`ta [LYWONG-CCYWEN `KEM] `pha ¨nay`ywol ¨hyeyywu`m i ¨ep.se `y`la (1481 Twusi 21:42a) we have wearily gazed at the Ox star and the Pole star in vain; there is no scheme to dig out the Sword of Dragon Spring. See also ˚ho.yas˚ta.

-ke˚ta, effective indic assert. ¶si˚lum kiph.ke˚ta (1459 Wel 8:87b) I am deeply troubled. kwu˚cis˚ti ma˚lwo˚m i ¨HHOYNG khe˚ta [< ˚ho-ke˚ta] (1463 Pep 1:15b) fortunately it forgoes scolding. hon thelek ˚kut ˚ma 'y˚na isi˚m ye n' MWON ˚NGWOY ˚yey is.ke˚ta (?1468- Mong 12b) if there is but one hair end [unshaven on the head], one is outside the discipline. ˚i kwo˚ki nik.ke˚ta (?1517- ¹No 1:22a) this meat is well done = i kwoki nik.eta (1795 ¹No-cwung [P] 1:20a). SEE khe˚ta; -Ge˚ta, -e˚ta, ˚˚yeta; -ka˚ta, -Ga˚ta, -a˚ta; ˚wona˚ta.

ke 'ta, abbr < kes ita
ke to, abbr < kes to

-ke˚ton = -ke˚tun, provisional. if; when. ¶kwuy-s ke˚s uy nos ˚kwa SSIN-LYENG ˚uy me˚li no˚ch ol ˚TWOY ˚ho.ya ˚woke˚ton (1482 Kum-sam 3:27b) when you come to confront the face of a ghost or the face on the head of spirit.

-ketullang (un) [DIAL, lit] = -ketun

-ketumyen (un), tentative conditional [DIAL] = -umyen if/when. [Probably a blend of -ketun and -umyen.]

ke 'tun, abbr < kes itun

-ketun < -ke˚tun, provisional. There are past (-ess.ketun) and future (-keyss.ketun) forms.
   1. provided that, if, when (usually followed by a command, a suggestion, or a promise). ¶Ku sensayng ul mannaketun kuleh.key māl haca If we run into the teacher let's tell him so. Sewul kaketun kot phyēnci hay la Write to me as soon as you get to Seoul. Ku kes i ney kes iketun ney ka kacye la Take it if it is yours. Pom i toyketun īl ul sīcak hakeyss.ta I will begin the job when it gets to be spring. Noph.a se kkoktayki kkaci mōs kakeyss.ketun cwungkan kkey 'na-ma ka-polyem If it's too high to get to the peak why don't you go about half way up, at least. NOTE: More limited than -umyen (CF 1936 Roth 479).
   2. if, given that (+ a rhetorical question). ¶Ney ka kuleh.key kongpu hay ya haketun hamulmye nay ya? If you must work so hard, how much more must I! Nay ka an ic.ess.ketun ney 'n tul selma ic.ess.keyss.nun ya? Since I haven't forgotten it, how could you? Eceyq pam ey pi ka wass.ketun mul i ileh.key pūt.ci anh.keyss.ˢo? Isn't it natural that the river has risen like this since it rained last night? Ku sālam cip ey kass.ketun ne to cip ey kalyem If (= since) he has gone home why don't you go home, too.
NOTE: This is sometimes left dangling with a sentence-final yo: "Ne chinkwu poko yok hamyen mōs ssunta." – "Chinkwu tul to na poko yok haketun yo (kuleni-kka nay ka an halq swu iss.e ya ˚c' yo ?!)" "You mustn't speak ill of a friend." – "Well, what if my friends speak ill of me (how can I not do so)?"
   3. ~ (yo) sentence-final. 3a. (exclamatory) sure(ly), indeed, quite. ¶Kwā.yen cōh.ketun Yes, it sure is wonderful! Pi ka cham-mal mānh.i wass.ketun! It certainly did rain!
   3b. (explanatory) you see. ¶Ce nun kath.i kalq swu ēps.e yo; pappuketun yo (Im Hopin 1987:124) I can't go with you; I'm busy!

-ke˚tun, provisional (< -ke-˚t un). if; when. ¶KWONG-˚KYENG KWONG-˚YANG ˚hozo˚Wo.l i ˚Gwos is.ke˚tun ˚wuli ˚tol˚h i ˚i ¨salo˚m ol ˚NGWUY-˚HHWO ˚ho˚ya (1447 Sek 9:40a) if just there is one who will cherish and nourish [the scripture] we will guard this person. ¨man˚il i˚muy ¨c'a˚sye ¨kye˚sike˚tun (1586 Sohak 2:4b; sic ¨man-˚il) if you have already eaten ... . SEE ˚hoke˚tun, khe˚tun.

˚ke˚tun, abbreviation < ˚hoke˚tun after voiceless sounds; CF khe˚tun. ¨mwot ~ if one cannot.

-ketung, -kutung [S Kyengsang DIAL (Mkk 1960:3:35)] = -ketun

-ke˚tun ˚za, provisional + particle. ¶kwo˚ma ˚oy na˚hwon [¨CO-˚SIK] ˚ul ¨ne y i˚tay kil˚Ge ˚co˚lake˚tun ˚za ¨ne y talon namcin e˚lu˚la (1481 Samkang ¹yel:26a) provided only that you raise well the son by the concubine, you may consort with other men.

KEY The Hankul spelling distinguishes key and kyey, but both are usually pronounced the same (as key). If you cannot locate the word you seek under key, look under kyey.

-'q key (-u' kkey), abbr < -lq key. Alternant after vowel of -u(l)q key (-u' kkey). ¶Ka'q key I'll be right there.

key, n. 1. abbr < keki.   2. abbr < ku ay.
   3. [pejorative] you, you there. CF keyney.

key, abbr < kungey (or < ke˚kuy) < kunge˚kuy, noun, adverb. (in/at/to) that place, there. ¶key ˚ka ¨mwot ˚na˚si.l i ˚˚la hon ha˚nol (1459 Wel 2:11a) a heaven that they say you go there and you will never leave. *kwut ti a ni hon key kwu tun ptu t ul meku sya* (1459 Wel 10:9a) harbors the feeling that it is hard in that place that is not hard.

··· *s* ~ = ··· *skey* to an esteemed person (> *kkey*). ¶ *pwuthye s key na za ka* (1463 Pep 1:77a) went up to Buddha and ... . *KWONG i mwo ton SYENG-ZIN s key kocok ' key hosi n i* (1482 Kum-sam 4:45a) he had all the holy men filled with merit. *TUNG-MYENG skey wa* (1463 Pep 2:43b) comes to the [Buddha of the] lamp. *SSIP- LYWUK i TI- SING skey kot hosi n i isi n i ' la* (1463 Pep 2:43b) "sixteen" is referring to the victories of his wisdom. *ZYE-LOY skey* ... (1463 Pep 5:95b) to the tathāgata. SEE *s kuy, skuy*.

key, quasi-free n [colloq]. (my / your / his) place, home, part of the country, neck of the woods (follows nouns of humble or familiar reference — the only common cases are **wuli key** and **caney key**); CF **kkey**. ¶ **Wuli key nun kyewul ey mopsi chwupta** In winter it is very cold in our part of the country. **Caney nun nay key se cakey** You come sleep at my house! **Ku cim ul caney key lo ponay to kwaynchanh.keyss.e?** May I send the baggage to your place? **ku ay key** his/her place. **Poktong-i key** at Poktong-i's place. [? only after vowels; ? < '**key** = **eykey**; ? < (**uy**) **kos** (**ey**)]

key, abbr. 1. = **kes i, n + pcl**.
2. = **kes i···, n + cop**. ¶ **Ku key nwī key 'n ya** = **Ku kes i nwukwu uy kes in ya** Whose is it?
3. = **ku kes i**, adn + n + pcl.
4. = **ku kes i(ta)**, adn + n + cop.

'**key**, abbr < **hakey** (after voiceless sounds, **a**, or **e**); CF **khey**. NOTE: There is no *ikey (cop adverbative), but see ' *Gey* = *i Gey*.

' **key**, abbr < *ho key* (after voiceless sounds); CF *khey*. ¶ *QILQ- CHYEY CYWUNG-SOYNG ul LI- QYEK 'key khwo* [= *ho key ho kwo*] *cye ho ya* (1485 Kwan 1a) wanting to let all living beings benefit. *KWONG i mwo ton SYENG-ZIN s key kocok ' key hosi n i* (1482 Kum-sam 4:45a) he had all the holy men filled with merit. "*NGWUW- TUK hon salo m ol syey ye pat non hwoki lol KYWELQ 'key ho n i* (1447 Sek 9:19-20) had persons of virtue stand up and let them divide the fields.

'**key**, pcl abbr < **eykey** to, at, for by (a person / creature). ¶ **nay** ~ to/for me. **ney** ~ to/for you. **celm.un-i** ~ to/for young people. [Occurs only after a vowel, usually **i ey oy ay**.]

-key < - *key* / - *Gey*, adverbative. CF **-tolok, -i**; - *kuy* / - *Guy*, - *koy* / - *Goy*.

1. 1a. so as (to be / do), (in a way) so that, so that it is / does; so that one can; in a manner such that; -ly. ¶ **cīnachikey** excessively, overly, to excess, too (much / heavily); over-(doing). **khukey māl hata** speaks loud(er). **ppalukey kēt.ta** walks fast. **sikyey ka ttukey kata** a watch / clock runs slow. **ccalp.key selmyeng hata** explains it briefly. **cēkci anh.key** to no small extent, considerably, much. **swīpkey māl hamyen** to put it simply ... . **sālam hanthey chen hakey kwūlta** behaves despicably toward people. **caymi iss.key pota** looks at it with pleasure. **Mas i [i]ss.key tusipsio** Enjoy your meal [said by the waiter]. **Kāmki tulci anh.key cōsim hasio** Be careful not to catch cold, now. **Emeni ka īl ul hakey com co'.yong hi hay la** Be quiet so that Mother can work. **Son ul ssis.key mul com teywe cwusey yo** Please heat some water for me to wash my hands. **Kkoch i kōpkey phiess.ta** The flowers have come out beautifully. **Sip-o pun an ey kalq swu iss.key wūncen ul ppalli hasio** Drive fast so that we can get there within fifteen minutes. **Ku nun māl ul cal hakey sayngkyess.ta** His face says that he is quite eloquent. **Wais(y)assu hana nun onulq cenyek ey ip.ulq swu iss.key hay tālla ko hasio** Ask them to do one shirt so that I can wear it tonight. **Cal polq swu iss.key kakkai osey yo** Come closer so that you can see better. **Apeci ka atul hanthey chayk ul sakey tōn ul cwuess.ta** The father gave his son money so that he could buy books. **Swīpkey pēlko swīpkey ssunta** Easy come, easy go. **Nay sā-chwun** [= **sā-chon**] **un kongpu lul swīpkey cal hanta** My cousin studies well with no effort at all. **Ok.huy nun caki to molukey kokay ka swukule cyess.ta** Ok.huy's head bowed unawares (without her being aware of it) (CM 2:228). **na to molukey** without myself knowing, without my knowing it. **Eti se wass.nun ci to molukey, kapcaki ku sālam i wass.[s]up.nita** He suddenly showed up from I don't know where (1954 Lukoff 139).

1b. (considering it) to be; (looks / appears) to be. ¶ **īsang hakey sayngkak hata** thinks it strange. SEE **-key poita**.

2. shows change of state by SUBJECT of vi, by OBJECT of vt.

2a. (~ toyta / hata / mayntulta) into being / doing; becoming / making so that. ¶senul hakey hata / mayntulta makes it cool(er). wuli uy saynghwal ul nek.nek hakey hata enriches our lives. Ai ka khukey calass.ta The child grew big / bigger. Ku cip ul khukey hayss.ta They made the house large / larger. Caymi iss.key mayntulca Let's make it (so that it is) fun – or (usage 1): Let's make it in a fun way. Com sēlkey hay cwusey yo Make it [= the steak] a bit rare, please. Hak.kyo kyōyuk i ku lul ttokttok hakey mayntul.ess.ta Schooling made him bright. Sāwel i toymyen nongpu tul un puncwu hakey toynta When it comes to be April, the farmers get busy. Sewul-si nun Hān kang ey tali lul noh.a se kyothong ul phyen.li hakey hayss.ta The city of Seoul put a bridge over the Han River, making it easier for traffic. Pangsek ul kkal.e se cali lul phyen hakey haca Let's spread cushions to make the places we are sitting more comfortable.

2aa. ¶Acwu nolah.key mul ul tul.ye cwusey yo Dye it (so it is) good and yellow. (CF Acwu nolah.tolok mul ul tul.ye cwusey yo Be sure to dye it good and YELLOW.)

2b. (~ hata, ~ sikhita) causing / making / getting it to happen, letting it happen. ¶ayki eykey cam ul cakey hata gets the baby to go to sleep. Ai hanthey wuyu lul masikey hayss.se(y) yo I got the child to drink its milk. Haksayng hanthey anc.key hasio Have the student sit down. Wuli lul sayngkak hakey hanta It makes us think. Ku ay eykey ku kes ul selmyeng hakey hasey yo Have him explain it. Chwum chwukey mōs hanta They don't let you dance. Na nun sāmu-wen eykey sāhwan ul sikhye se congi lul cwūmun hakey hayss.ta I had the clerk get the office-boy to order some paper. Kalq swu iss.key hay poca Let's try to arrange it so that we can go. Ku sālam ul ¹nayil okey / otolok haci yo I'll see that he comes tomorrow.

2c. (~ toyta) turning out (getting to be, coming to pass, happening) so that; getting to be/do; being arranged so that. ¶um.ak ul cōh.a hakey toyta comes to like (be fond of) music. Hānkwuk ey tāy hay se kwansim ul kac.key toyta comes to have an interest in Korea. Mōs kakey tōyss.ta It's turned out we can't go. Chayk ul pokey toykeyss.ta We'll get to see the book. Kuleh.ta ko sayngkak toynta That's the way it seems to be. Ai ka payq nol.i lul cōh.a hakey tōyss.ta The child got so he liked taking boat rides. Tōn i ēps.e to kongpu hakey tōyss.ta Even though I had no money (it came about that) I got to study. Kim sensayng to māl hakey tōyss.ta Mr Kim happened / got to talk, also. Keki kasimyen caymi iss.nun phungsok ul te mānh.i ālkey toykeyss.⁵up.nita If you go there, you will discover more of these interesting customs. Halq swu ēps.i kath.i kakey tōyss.ta He had no choice but to go along. Musun cākyek ulo Mikwuk ey kasikey toyp.nikka In what capacity are you going to America? Sāhoy ey se acwu cel.yen toykey toyess.ta It got quite isolated from society. Say lowun munhak i na-okey tōyss.ta A new literature came to appear. Hak.kyo ka mun ul tat.key tōyss.ta The school got closed. Chacha āsikey toyp.nita You will gradually come to understand. Kikwan-ci lul kacikey tōyss.ta They acquired organs of publication. Caki hanthey n' ohilye cōh.key / cal tōyss.ci That turned out rather good for HIM.

3. (FAMILIAR command) do! (often followed by particle una/na). ¶Ili okey (na) Come here. Caney tul kkili kakey You guys go on. Ku īl ul caney ka math.key You take care of that.

4. (sentence-final question). 4a. ~ (toyci anh.keyss.nun ya) then won't it turn out that …?! [RHETORICAL]. ¶Kulayss.ta ka nun may lul mac.key?! I do that and I'll get whipped, won't I. Ku-man han tōn i iss.umyen cōh.key? Wouldn't it be grand to have so much money! Ku-kkacis nom i tā hamyen na to hakey?! If it's true that that so-and-so could do it all then wouldn't I be able to?!

4b. (in a riddle). ¶… : mwe 'key what is it? … : musun māl hayss.key what word did I say?

5. (sentence-final, similar to -ulye ko hanta; can be followed by yo, with the variant -ki yo).

5a. ¶"Ku ay nun way ponaysey yo" – "Hal-apeci to/lul osikey (halye ko ponaynta)" "Why do you send the child?" – "(I send her) to get (= bring) Grandfather."

5b. ¶"Mek.key yo?" – "Mek.key yo" "Wanna eat?" – "Sure." "Wuli to kakey yo?!" – "Nēy (wuli to kakey)!" "Aren't we going too?" – "Sure we are."

6. = **-k' ey**, abbr < **-ki ey**. ¶**Māl hak' ey tallyess.ta** (Dupont 199) That depends on how you say it.

-ˊ**key**, adverbative; -ˊ**Gey** after *i*, *y*. ¶ˊˊ**ip ˊkey towoyˊya** (1447 Sek 6:5a) get confused and ... . ˊ**NYELQ-PPAN ˊTUK ˊhwoˊm ol na ˊkot ˊˊkey hoˊl i ˊˊla** (1447 Sek 6:1b) will let her achieve nirvāṇa like me. ˊ**na y pwuˊle neˊlul esye ˊTUK-ˊˊTTWOW hoˊkey ˊhotaˊn i chuki neˊkiˊti ˊˊmalˊla ˊhoteˊla** (1447 Sek 24:3ab) "I have deliberately tried to get you to achieve the way [to enlightenment] quickly; do not think ill of me", he said.

-key < -ˊ**key**, suf (makes n from v). 1. [var] = **-kay**. **ci-key** an A-frame carrier (rack). **cip-key** tongs, tweezers.

2. (?) **ttut-key** (= **ttut-key os**) a worn-out garment that is to be unsewed. CF **ttut-key cil** unsewing old clothes.

ke ya, abbr < **kes iya**, < **kes ia**.

ˊ**keyˊa** = -ˊ**keyˊ[z]a** (> **-key ya**). ¶ˊˊ**neˊy aˊchomˊuyˊna-ˊka nus.keyˊa woˊm ye n'** ... (1586 Sohak 4:33a) if you go out in the morning and come [back] only late ... .

key ani ··· = **kes i ani** ··· . SEE **kes** (4).

-**key ccum**, adverbative + pcl. ¶¹**Naynyen imyen catong-cha lul hana sakey ccum toylq key 'ta** Next year I'll be in a position to buy a car.

key 'ci (= **ke yci**) = **kes ici**

-**key cocha**, adverbative + pcl. ¶**Pappuni-kka chinkwu (lul) mannakey cocha an toynta** I am so busy I don't even get to see my friends.

-**key hata** SEE **-key** (2a, 2b)

-**key ka**, adverbative + pcl. ¶**Pappuni-kka com chelem chinkwu tul mannakey ka an toynta** I am so busy I don't get the least chance to see my friends. **Icey n' cal kēt.key ka toyess.uni cham kippusikeyss.e yo** Now that you've got so you can walk well, you must be very happy.

-**key khenyeng**, adverbative + pcl. ¶**Pōthong sālam eykey n' ku kos ey tul.e kakey khenyeng kakkai to mōs kakey hanta** They won't let the average person go anywhere near the place, much less enter it.

-**key kkaci**, adverbative + pcl. even so that; until (the point that) it is or one does. ¶**nuc.key kkaci** till (it is) late. **Kuleh.key kkaci sāngsim halq kes un ēps.ta** There is no need to be so distressed.

-**key-kkum** [DIAL, colloq] = **-key-sili**

key 'l(q) (= **ke yl(q)**) = **kes il(q)**

-**key 'la to**, adverbative + cop var inf + pcl. ¶**Āmu'h.tun ku pun ul mannakey 'la to hay cwusey yo** Anyway let me at least see him.

'**key lo**, abbr pcl + pcl. toward/to (a person). ¶**na 'ykey lo on phyēnci** a letter that has come to/for me.

'**key lul**, adverbative + pcl. ¶**Cachwi lul hanikka cey ttay ey mek.key lul/ka an toynta** He does his own cooking, so he doesn't get to eat on time.

key 'm (= **ke ym**) = **kes im**

-**key mace**, adverbative + pcl. ¶**Ecci 'na pappun ci chinkwu lul mannakey mace an toynta** [this is better said as ··· **chinkwu mace mannakey an toynta**] I am just so busy I don't even get to see my friends.

~ **cocha**. ¶**Mēn tōngney lo isa lul (hako) oni chin han Poktong-i lul han tal ey han pen mannakey (mace) cocha an toynun kwun** Having moved here to this distant village I find I don't get to see my chum Poktong-i even once a month.

~ **to**. ¶**Silqcik ul hako nani poli pap ul mek.key mace to an toyney** With me having lost my job, matters are such that I can't even eat boiled barley.

-**key malyen ita**, [DIAL, colloq]. can't help doing/being; inevitably does/is.

-**key man**, adverbative + pcl. ¶**Nay ka hak.kyo ey tul.e kakey man toymyen elma 'na cōh.ulq ka** How nice it would be if only I could get to go to school!

~ **ila to**. ¶**Atul nom ul cwung-hak.kyo ey kakey man ila to ha(l)lye 'ni i kosayng ici yo** I am having a hard time trying just to let my son go to middle school.

~ **ina(-ma)**. ¶**Na to ne chelem kuleh.key man ina(-ma) hay polq ka** Shall I try doing at least that much like you?

~ **in tul**. ¶**Cwuci nun anh.keyss.ci man cāmqkan pokey man in tul mōs hakeyss.ni?** He won't give it to us but surely he will let us take a look at it.

~ **to**. ¶**Ku īl un caney ka sayngkak hanun kes chelem kuleh.key swīpkey man to an toylq ke l'** That won't be as easy as you think!

~ **un**. ¶**Pap i āmuli cil.e to cōh.uni tōykey man un haci mala** I don't care how soft the rice is, just don't cook it too hard.

'key man, abbr pcl + pcl. just / only at / for / by a person / creature. ¶Ne 'ykey man māl hay cwum a I'll tell it only to you.
-key ma(y)ntulta SEE -key
key 'n (= ke yn) = kes in
'key n', abbr pcl + abbr pcl. as for to / at / for / by a person / creature.
-key n', abbr < -key nun
/⋯keyna/ is to be treated as -key 'na in the absence of strong reasons to treat /na/ as the particle una / na: etteh.key 'na somehow, āmuleh.key 'na (CF āmu N ina), etc.
-key 'na, adverbative + cop advers. whether (or ⋯-ever) it be so that. ¶Āmuleh.key 'na mekci Let's eat any old way. ¶Āmu'h.tun ku sālam ul mannakey 'na toyess.umyen cōh.keyss.ta Anyway, I hope I will get to see him.
-key na, adverbative + pcl. do (now)! please do! [FAMILIAR]. ¶Anc.key na Have a seat, fella.
'key 'na, abbr pcl + cop advers. to/at/for/by a person/creature or the like; whether to/at/for/ by a person/creature; to/at/for/by whatever person. ¶Nay ttal un nwi 'key 'na (= nwukwu eykey 'na) cwulq swu nun ēps.ta I can't give my daughter to anyone.
keyney, n [DISRESPECTFUL; < keki ? + ne-huy, ? + ney]. 1. (hey) you, you all.
2. → -kay ney: āmu-kay ney certain persons.
3. → ku ay ney they / them.
'key 'n tul, abbr < eykey 'n tul
-key 'n tul, adverbative + cop mod + postmod. ¶Ney ka wēn hanta 'myen Mikwuk ey 'la to kakey 'n tul mōs hay cwukeyss.n' ya Won't they even let you go to America if you want to?
'key nun, abbr pcl + pcl. as for to / at / for / by a person / creature. ABBR 'key n'.
-key nun, adverbative + pcl. as for so that it is (or one does); indeed such that it is. ¶Kkoch i kōpkey n(un) phiess.e(y) yo The flowers HAVE come out lovely. Sosik ul cacwu tut.key nun toykeyss.ci We'll get regular news, all right.
ke yo, abbr < kes iyo (= kes iey yo); < kes io. SYN key yo.
(-)keypi, bnd n. tes ~ an extra thing / person, a burden, a nuisance.
[? < kaypi splint; CF tokkaypi hobgoblin.]
-key poita, (adj) adverbative + aux vi. looks, seems (like). ¶Alay sālam tul i cham cāk.key pointa The people down below seem so small! CF -e poita.

-key pota, adverbative + pcl. ¶Kuleh.key pota ileh.key hanun kes i te cōh.kess.ta It would be better to do it this way rather than that way. I os kām un cith.key pota yeth.key yēmsayk hanun kes i cōh.keyss.ta It would be better to dye this material light rather than dark.
-key puthe, adverbative + particle. ¶Ku tul uy yokwu nun wusen pap ul mek.key puthe hay tālla 'nun kes ita Their demand is that they be allowed to earn their bread first of all.
? -key se, abbr < -key hay se. ~ 'la to, ~ man, ~ 'n tul, ~ n(un), ~ to, ~ ya.
'key se, abbr pcl + pcl = eykey se. ~ chelem (man), ~ cocha, ~ ka, ~ 'la to, ~ mace, ~ man (un), ~ 'na, ~ 'n tul, ~ n(un), ~ pota, ~ puthe, ~ to, ~ ya.
-key sikhita SEE -key
-key-sili, extended adverbative [DIAL; < suli < suley < sule-i = sulepkey]. so that indeed. CF 1916 Gale 66. ¶Twīq īl i ēps.key-sili cal chēli hasio Manage the matter carefully so that there will be no trouble in the future. SYN -key-kkum. CF -tolok-i.
NOTE: Ramstedt (1939:132) describes -sili as "another form of the verb isita" (> iss.ta) "which is used in a specialized sense" — he presumably had in mind the form [i]si-'l i 'that it will be' (= iss.ulq kes).
*-ˈkeysˈkwo = *-ˈkey ˈsˈkwo SEE -ˈGey ˈsˈkwo, -ˈkuy ˈsˈkwo
-keyss-, future.
1. definite future: will (do / be).
2. probable nonfuture: probably does / is; -ess- ~ probably did / was. CF -ulq kes ita.
3. For other uses, see -keyss.ta.
This can be followed by -ˢup-, -ta, (-tay =) -ta 'y, -ney, -na, -ˢo, -tula, -tey, -ti, -kwumen (-kwun, -kwun a, -kwulye), -e, -ko, -una(-ma), -uni(-kka), -ci, -ki, -um, -umye, -umyen (= -tula 'myen), -tumyen, -nun, -tun.
NOTE: This marker (like the nominative particle ka for i after a consonant and -nunta for earlier -nota) was little noticed until it was observed by missionaries late in the nineteenth century; instead, archaic forms with -(u)li- (< -u.l i) were written. The only precursor cited by LCT is taken from ?1800 Hancwung 62: ani sikikeys.ta ho.n i '[he] said [that he] would not demand it'. Ramstedt (1939:93-4) would derive -keyss- from -key 'so that it will (do / be)'. The

source is probably the effective infinitive -῾ke + 'ys(i)῾ta abbr < is(i)῾ta; SEE -kasi-/-kas- [Phyengan] < -῾ka + 's(i)῾ta apheretic abbr.

-keyss.ci, future suspective. 1. ~ yo SEE -ci yo.

2. ¶kaci anh.keyss.ci man won't go but.

3. ~ anh- (rhetorical question): §11.7.8.

-keyss.e, future infinitive. 1. (sentence-final) will do be; probably does / is [INTIMATE]; ~ (y) yo [POLITE]. ¶Kitalikeyss.ey yo I'm willing to wait. (CF Kitalim a I'll be expecting you.) Ilkop si 'ni-kka pelsse cikcang ey se tol.a wass.keyss.e yo man, acik ¹yen.lak i ēps.e yo She must have come back from work by now but she hasn't been in touch with me.

2. (occasionally before particles to, se, ya in order to be more explicit or precise) = -e. Apparently not before man, despite -keyss.e yo man (example above); -e man without -keyss- (or -ess-) occurs in -e man AUX structures.

-keyss.ketun, future provisional. SEE -ketun.

-keyss.ki, future summative. ~ ey, ~ lo; (?*) ~ ttaymun ey. SEE -ki (esp 6-7).

-keyss.kwu(me)n, future apperceptive. I realize it will be or will do; why, it probably is / does! ¶Wūnpanq ¹yo ttaymun ey ssalq kaps i kkway pissakeyss.kwumen yo I realize that rice prices must be quite high because of transportation.

-keyss.na, 1. FAMILIAR future indic attentive.

2. = -keyss.nun ka / ya.

~ ka (pcl). ¶Pi ka ēncey okeyss.na ka mūncey 'ta The question is when it will rain.

~ lul (pcl). ¶Pi ka okeyss.na lul al.e pwā la Find out whether it is likely to rain.

~ man (pcl). ¶Enu sitay enu nala ka ani kuleh.keyss.na man un Any country at any period would be much the same, but ... .

-keyss.ney, FAMILIAR future indicative assertive

-keyss.ni, future indicative attentive

-keyss.nola [lit] = -keyss.ta

-keyss.nun, fut proc mod. Attaches to any stem (v, adj, cop) but occurs only before tey, ya, ci, ke l', ka (pota). Other uses reported (e.g. Ip mas i ēps.e se mōs mek.keyss.nun pap ul ···) are deviations from the standard -ulq.

'keyss.nun, 1. var (alt) of ikeyss.nun.

2. abbr < hakeyss.nun.

-keyss.nun ci, fut proc modifier + postmodifier.

1. (the uncertain fact) whether it / one will (do or be). ¶Ku kes ul phalkeyss.nun ci (phal.nun ci) mul.e polq ka Shall we ask them if they will sell it? Etteh.key kamyen cōh.keyss.nun ci (= cōh.ul.nun ci) mul.e poca Let's ask how to get there.

2. ~ (to moluta, yo) maybe, perhaps it / one will (do / be). ¶Kakeyss.nun ci (to molunta) Maybe he will go (= Kalq / Kal.nun ci). Pi ka okeyss.nun ci (yo) It may rain (= Pi ka olq / ol.nun ci).

-keyss.nun ci 'la (se), future processive modifier + postmod + cop var inf (+ pcl). [literary] as / since it will do or be. SEE -nun ci 'la (se).

-keyss.nun ka, 1. (nonstandard?) = -ulq ka; = -keyss.na. ~ pota = -ulq ka pota.

2. = -keyss.nun ka / ya.

~ ka (pcl). ¶Pi ka ēncey okeyss.nun ka ka mūncey 'ta The question is when will it rain.

~ lul (pcl). ¶Pi ka okeyss.nun ka lul al.e pwā la Find out whether it is likely to rain.

-keyss.nun ke l' (= -ulq ke l'). ¶Incey nun chwulpal cwūnpi lul hay ya 'keyss.nun ke l' But now we've got to get ready to leave!

-keyss.nun tey, future proc mod + postmod. CF -ulq tey. 1. (given) the circumstance that one / it will (do or be); will (do or be) and / but / so. ¶Onulq cenyek ey pataq ka ey kakeyss.nun tey kath.i kasikeyss.ˢup.nikka? This evening I'm going to the seashore; will you come along?

~ nun SEE -nun tey nun.

~ ya SEE tey ya.

2. exclamatory future. ¶Ileh.key olay alh.ta ka n' āmulay to cwuk.keyss.nun tey Having been sick so long surely I will die, anyway! ¹Nayil imyen nuc.keyss.nun tey But tomorrow will be too late!

-keyss.nun ya, fut proc mod + postmod. (the question) whether it / one will do/be or probably is/does. ¶Yō nun elma 'na pi ka okeyss.nun ya ka mūncey 'ta The point is, it's a question of how much it will rain.

-keyss.ˢo, AUTH future indicative assertive

-keyss.ta, future indicative assertive.

1. will do / be. The subject must be 1st person in a statement, 2d person in a question (CF M 1:1:98 — it should refer to this meaning only, since there is an example of 3d person + -e ya 'keyss.ey yo on the next page). ¶Na nun ku īl ul ¹nayil hakeyss.ta I will do it tomorrow. Ku tong-an ey tā nulk.keyss.ta I will get quite old in the meantime. Ku man mek.keyss.ˢup.nita That's all I'll eat. Khephi tulkeyss.e? Will you

drink a cup of coffee? **Kulem, kuleh.key hakeyss.ta** OK, I will do that [even though I may not want to] — Cf **Kuleh.key halla 'nta** I will do that [of my own accord], I have it in mind to do that. **Sālam i cwuk.keyss.ey yo** (Dupont 43) It's killing me = It's wearing me out = I'm exhausted.

2. 2a. probably is or does; I am afraid that (probably), really must / will. The subject is unrestricted, but most often it is third-person. ¶**Elkwul ul poni com keyulukeyss.ta** To judge from his appearance, he must be a bit lazy. **Caymi iss.keyss.ta** I bet it's fun. **Ku nun cik.kong ikeyss.ta** He is probably a factory worker. ¹**Nayil un swuyoil ikeyss.ta** Tomorrow must be Wednesday. **Nwu ka tut.keyss.ta** Someone may hear us (so lower your voice). **(Ku sālam i) kakeyss.ta** I'm afraid he's going = **kalq key 'ta** he is surely going; Cf **kalq kes kath.ta** apparently / likely he will go.

2b. N to ⋯-keyss.ta N to ...-keyss.ta both ⋯ and ... are true (I see, you tell me) so given all that — argues a conclusion or judgment, often left implied or stated as advice (M 3:3:211).

3. (often used for the present with verbs of knowledge, softening the statement by a faint suggestion of probability). ¶**Molukeyss.e yo** I wouldn't know (= **Mōlla yo** I don't know). **Āsikeyss.ˢup.nikka** Do you know it? / Do you understand (me)?

4. **-e ya (ha)keyss.ta** = **-e ya hanta**

5. (lively or deferential present). ¶**Cheum poypkeyss.ˢup.nita** (= **poypsup.nita**) How do you do. I am honored to meet you.

6. (lively past — for unexpected events). ¶**Cham pyel kkol tā pokeyss.ta** What a mess (you've presented for me) to look at!!

7. [rare, awkward] (used of third person). he ought to. See CM 1:323.

8. → **-kes.ta**

-keyss.ta ko / kko / kwu See -ta ko
-keyss.ta 'nun, abbr < -keyss.ta (ko) hanun
-keyss.ta 'y, abbr < -keyss.ta (ko) hay
-keyss.ta ya, future indic assertive + pcl. ¶**Pi ka okeyss.ta ya!** I'm afraid it's going to rain! **Nemu khukeyss.ta ya!** But it would be too big! **Chelqswu ka cwuk.unq ¹īyu nun ku kes ikeyss.ta ya!** Why, that must be the reason that Chelsswu died! **Mikwuk sālam ikeyss.ta ya!** Hey, I bet it's an American!

-keyss.ta 'yss-, abbr < -keyss.ta (ko) hayss-: ~-nun, -ta, -ulq.
-keyss.tey, 1. familiar future retr assertive.
   2. → -keyss.ta 'y
-keyss.ti, future retrospective attentive
-keyss.tu-kwumen/-kwun(a), abbr < -keyss.tun kwumen / kwun(a)
-keyss.tula, fut retr assertive. ¶**Aikwu ku sālam māl mā, ku sālam i kkok cwuk.keyss.tula** Oh dear, there is no question about it, (from what I observed of his condition) he's going to die. **Etteh.key mas nan ci, han cham ey yelq kay 'la to mek.keyss.tula** They were so good that I could have eaten ten of them at one sitting. **Sahul man iss.umyen, kkoch i hwalccak phikeyss.tula** In three days I think the flowers are sure to be in bloom.
-keyss.tun, fut retr mod. ¶**Keuy cwuk.keyss.tun sālam i sal.e nass.kwun a** A person about to die came back to life!
   (~ ya). **Kulay ku namca ka ku īl ul cal hakeyss.tun (ya)?** So, do you think that fellow will handle the job all right?
   ~ ka. ¶**Namca ēlun i ileh.key wūnun ke l' poni cēng-mal mōs chām.keyss.tun ka pwā** Apparently it must truly have been unbearable to see such tears from a grown man.
   ~ kwumen / kwun(a).
-keyss.tuni, future retr sequential. ~ man. ¶**Celm.ess.ul ttay nun cal ttwikeyss.tuni man icey nai tuni hanun swu ēps.kwun** When young I could surely jump quite well but now that I am this age there's no doing it!
-keyss.tun i, future retr modifier + quasi-free n
-keyss.tun ke l', fut retr modifier + postmod + particle. ¶**Kulay to īl un cal hay; hanta hanun cāngceng i wā to mōs ttalukeyss.tun ke l'** Nevertheless he works well; any other able-bodied young man wouldn't be able to keep up with him!
-keyss.tun tey, future retr mod + postmodifier. ¶**Namca ēlun i wūnun ke l' poni cham.ᵉ⁄a mōs pokeyss.tun tey** But surely I couldn't stand to see a grown man crying!
-keyss.um, future substantive. ~ ulo (particle): ¶**Ku pun i imi māl-ssum tulyess.keyss.um ulo cey ka tasi māl-ssum tulici anh.keyss.ˢup.nita** Since he must have told you about it already, I won't tell you over again.

-keyss.umyen, fut conditional: **Hasikeyss.umyen hasipsio** If you'd like to do it, please do so.

-keyss.una(-ma), (extended) future adversative. SEE **-una** for an example.

-keyss.uni, fut sequential; ~ **-kka**, ~ **-kka n(un)** SAME. SYN **-ulini**. ¶**Na nun mōs kakeyss.uni ne 'la to kass.ta one la** I can't go, but you had better go even without me.

Always followed by a command. Usually this is attached to v (CF M 2:2:366), but it can also attach to adj: **Nal-ssi ka nappukeyss.uni-kka wūsan ul kaciko ka la!** Take your umbrella, for the weather may be bad.

-keyss.utoy, future concessive. SEE **-toy**.

key 'ta (= **ke yta**) = **kes ita**

'key to, abbr pcl + pcl. also / even to/at/for/by a person / creature. ¶**nay ~ (ney ~) to / for me (you) also / even**.

-key to, adverbative + particle. even (indeed) so that; also / either so that. ¶**pulhayng hakey to** unfortunately (indeed); sad to say. **siwen hakey to** to one's relief. **Siwen hakey to tā cīnass.ta** It feels good to have it all over and done with.

-key toyta SEE **-key** (2a, 2c)

-key tul, adverbative + particle.
1. ¶**Motwu pappuni-kka cacwu mannakey tul an toynta** They are all so busy that we do not get to see them often.
2. ¶**Onulq pam wuli cip ey nōlle okey tul** You fellows come over to my house tonight.

-key ya < **-key (y)a** < **-key '[z]a**, adverbative + particle. ¶**(Kuleh.ta ko hay se) māl-sseng i sayngkikey ya an toykeyss.ci yo?** (In that case) it wouldn't give rise to any trouble, would it? **tyang-ci.ch i ta tikey ya nolGay lol kwothye tule** (1747 Songkang 2:8b) adjusts its wings just so that all the plumes fall. SEE **-'key 'a, -'key, 'za**.

key ya, var = **ke ya**; abbr < **kes iya**, < **kes ia**.

key yo, 1. = **ke yo** = **kes i yo** = **kes ie(y) yo**
2. = **ke yo** = **kes io**
? 3. [DIAL] = **ke ye** = **kes ie** = **kes i(y)a**

-key yo SEE **-key** 5. VAR **-ki yo**.

-'key 'za, adverbative + particle (= **-key ya**). ¶**mwo 'lwo 'may swul kwo 'ki 'lol me[k] 'key 'za ¨sal 'l i 'non** (1518 Sohak-cho 7:18b) those [frail elderly] who can live only if they partake of wine and meat … . **kamwun 'i ¨ep 'key za talon 'sa 'lom 'uy 'key ne 'chwul 's oy** (1542 Pun-on 1b) for want of family reaches out to other people. CF **-'key 'a**.

-ke 'za, effective inf + pcl. ¶**¨mil 'mu 'l i sa 'o 'l ilwo 'toy 'nake 'za 'como 'n i '-ngi ''ta** (1445 ¹Yong 67) the water crested for three days and only when they left was the place inundated. **'POYK-CHYEN 'hoy 'choke 'za twolwo 'SSYELQ- 'SYANG ol 'kato 'si 'kwo** (1447 Sek 6:39a [Taycey-kak repro]) he held his tongue back for a full hundred thousand years. **wo 'lake za** (1447 Sek 23:27b) only after a while. ALSO: 1447 Sek 24:19b, 1459 Wel 8:75b, 1463 Pep 3:114b, 1481 Twusi 16:3b, … .

? … **'kha** = …**h 'ka**, postn (question). LCT cites **honakha** [= **honah ka**] **yesus ka** (1462 ¹Nung 4:106) but it is not there; he probably misread **hona 'khwa yesus 'kwa** on the preceding page.

(')khan < **'hokan** = **'ho.yan**, effective mod < **°ho 'ta**. SEE **'khan ma 'lon, 'khan 't i.n i ''la, 'kha.n ywo**.

khang, pcl [South Kyengsang DIAL (Mkk 1960: 3:32)] = **kwa / wa, hako**.
¶**Ne khang na khang wuli kaca** Let's go as a pair, you and I. **Kkoch khang kath.ta** It is like a flower.

khani wa [obs] = **kheni wa**

'kha.n i 'Gwa < **'hoka.n i 'Gwa**. ¶**kutuy [´KWUY] hon ce 'k uy na 'y nul 'kwu.m ul chuki ne 'kiti a 'ni 'kha.n i 'Gwa** (1481 Twusi 16:61b) I do not resent it that I am getting old when you are so dear to me and moreover … .

'khan ma 'lon < **'hokan ma 'lon**. (1632 Twusi-cwung 22:52b, 23:4a, 24:17b)

khan 't i.n i ''la, abbr < **'hokan 't i.n i ''la**. ¶**kesang 'ul ho 'ti a 'ni khan 't i.n i ''la** (1475 Nay 1:70b) was not in mourning.

'kha.n ywo < **'hoka 'n ywo**. ¶**¨es.tyey sul 'he two 'la pwokwo ¨kenne 'sye howol-lwo taptap 'ho.ya 'kha.n ywo** (1481 Twusi 16:37b) why, after crossing over with a backward look of loathing, must I be so bored and lonely?

(-)k hata [DIAL] = … **ko hata**. CF … **khwuta**.

khen, pcl [DIAL (Mkk 1960:3:33)] = **khenyeng**

(')khen, abbr < **'hoken**. SEE **khe 'n i, 'khen ma 'lon, khen 't i, khen 'tyeng, khe 'n ywo**.

khena < **khe 'na**, abbr < **hakena** < **'hoke 'na**. ¶**talon ¨salo 'm i 'wona 'ton 'KHWEN 'ho 'ya an 'ca tut 'kuy khe 'na** (1447 Sek 19:6a) when other people came he asked they be allowed to sit and hear him, but … . **a 'lom-tapke 'na a 'lom-tap 'ti a 'ni khe 'na** (1447 Sek 19:20a) whether

they were beautiful or were not beautiful ... . ˙nom kolo˙chye tut˙key khe˙na ˙cey tinike˙na (1459 Wel 17:33b) whether letting others hear the teaching or observing it oneself ... .
-khe(y)ngi, suffix. one, person, thing. cicil ~ a scrubby/stunted one. CF mulkheng-i overripe thing; soft, weakling (< mulkheng/molkhang).
kheni, abbr < hakeni. oto/wutwu ~ vacantly, blankly, absentmindedly, idly.
 ~ wa [DIAL, obs] = khenyeng. ¶Ssal pap un kheni wa poli pap to mōs mek.nunta Rice? — we can't even eat barley! Kkoch un kheni wa iph to mōs pokeyss.ta We won't see a leaf, much less a blossom!
khe˙n i, abbr < ˙hoke˙n i after voiced sounds; CF ˙ke˙n i. ¶mozo˙m i cwu˙kun ˙coy ˙˙Gey khe˙n i ˙homol˙mye CIN-˙SSILQ S ˙TTYENG ˙uy ˙hi˙m i ˙sto˙n ye (1462 ¹Nung 9:61a) when the soul was turned to ashes was the power of true samādhi (abstract meditation) but all the greater?
 ~ ˙Gwa. to the contrary, just the opposite, hardly [the other] (= khenyeng). ¶kutuy s ˙˙ma˙l i CIN-˙SSILQ ˙lwo ˙wol˙tha khe˙n i ˙Gwa (= ˙wolh-˙ta [˙]hoke˙n i ˙Gwa) wo˙cik ˙SYEY-CWON ˙i ingey ˙wa ˙MYELQ-˙TTWO ˙hosi˙n i (1447 Sek 23:53b) what you say is hardly correct, for only the World-Honored has come here and achieved nirvāṇa. ne-huy ˙non khe˙n i ˙Gwa ˙na ˙y ci˙p uy isilq ce˙k uy ˙˙SSYWUW-˙˙KHWO y ˙˙mantha˙la [= ˙˙manh-ta-˙la] (1459 Wel 10:23a) not so much you people but I am the one who had a lot of trouble when we were at home.
 ~ ˙˙la. ¶tangtang-i ko˙lo˙m ay s [˙KYWULQ-˙YWUW] [˙]lol [TTIM] ˙ho˙no.n i ˙˙la [NGUY-SIM] khe˙n i ˙˙la (1481 Twusi 20:34b) we suspected that the oranges and limes at the lake must be sinking, and ... .
˙khen ma˙lon, abbr < ˙hoken ma˙lon after voiced sounds. ¶˙SYEY-KAN ˙CYWUNG-SOYNG ˙on ˙il-˙lwo kas˙kota ˙khen ma˙lon (1462 ¹Nung 2:12a) said that people are thus wrong, but ... . MWU-˙SWU ˙QAK-˙˙KWUY ˙Gwa ˙˙MANG-˙˙LYANG CYENG-˙MI pi˙lin ˙phi ˙lol mek˙kwo ˙cye ˙khen ma˙lon (1459 Wel 21:124-5) countless evil spirits and hobgoblins wanted to drink fresh blood, but ... .
khe˙nol, abbr < ˙hoke˙nol after voiced sounds. ¶mwo˙ta i˙sywo.m i [˙CYENG] hi ˙mas.tang khe˙nol (1481 Twusi 8:6b) all are properly gathered together, and yet ... . hol˙l on ˙˙pyeng ˙i ˙˙tywung khe˙nol (1586 Sohak 6:27a) one day when he fell gravely ill ... .
khentay, abbr < hakentay. ¶cheng, wēn, yo ~ .
khentay n' < khen˙t ay n', abbr < hakentay nun < ˙hoken˙t ay n' after voiced sounds. ¶KON-˙˙PWON ˙ol CHYWUY-SSIN khen˙t ay n' ˙˙ta ˙SOYK-˙SSYANG ˙ay mozom ˙TTYWU ˙hwo˙m ol pu˙thu.n i ˙˙la (1464 Kumkang 83a) all, in investigating the root, have relied upon keeping their minds on superficial form.
khen˙t i, abbr < ˙hoken˙t i after voiced sounds. ¶THYEN-˙˙TYEY S ˙MYENG ˙ul patco˙wa ˙wa ˙˙QWONG-˙HHWO khen˙t i wo˙lake˙ta (1462 ¹Nung 7:62a) having accepted the mandate of the king of heaven, I will long protect it.
khen˙tyeng, abbr < ˙hoken˙tyeng after voiced sounds. ¶˙˙nyey s ˙SYENG-ZIN ˙nay s ˙pwola˙m ol ˙˙pwo˙m i ˙mas.tang khen˙tyeng (?1468-Mong 20a) though it be proper to look at the indications of the saints of former days ... .
khenul, abbr < hakenul (literary concessive) = khe˙nul, abbr < ˙hoke˙nul after voiced sounds. ¶Tōngchen i malk.ta khenul wūcang ēps.i kil ul nan i We set out with no raingear, for 'tis said the winter sky is fair. Nulk.ki to sēl(w)e la khenul cim ul cocha cisilq ka?! How sad to age, they say, and yet you wish to carry your burden?! ˙no˙m on [KWU-SYWUW] ˙y˙la khe˙nul ... , ˙no˙m on cwu˙kywu˙l ye khe˙nul ... (1445 ¹Yong 77) people thought him an enemy but ... , people wanted to kill them, but ... . [˙˙MAN-TTYWOW] ˙hi ˙twu-˙sywo˙sye khe˙nul [˙CYENG-SSIN] ˙ul ˙wol˙tha ˙hosi˙n i (1445 ¹Yong 107) court-wide there was opposition, but he said the righteous minister was right.
khe˙nul˙za, abbr < ˙hoke˙nul˙za. ¶sa˙lwo˙m i ˙i˙le khe˙nul ˙za a˙to˙l ol ye˙huy˙l i˙'-ngi s˙ka (1449 Kok 143) with life the way it is, is one actually to give up a son?
khenyeng, particle [?< h(a)keni + ?]. far from (being), to say nothing of, let alone, on the contrary; not only; not only not; contrary to expectation, instead of (something desirable that one might expect). ¶Cāk.ki khenyeng khuta It isn't little; on the contrary it is quite big. Kongpu lul cal haki khenyeng kongpu lul cal mōs hanta ko pam-nac sensayng hanthey kkwucilam man tut.nunta Far from being a good student, he is always getting scolded by

his teacher for his poor marks. **Sam-payk wen khenyeng sam-sip wen to mōs pat.keyss.ta** Three hundred wen? — why, we won't even get thirty! **Ttek khenyeng pap to ēps.tula** Cake? — why, we didn't even have rice! **Sip-nyen khenyeng ō-nyen to an cīnass.ta** Not even five years passed by, much less ten. **Chen-nyen khenyeng payk-nyen to an tōyss.ta** Far from being a thousand years, it didn't amount to even a hundred years. **Sang khenyeng pel ul pat.ess.ta** Instead of a reward, we incurred punishment. **Hwan.yeng khenyeng paktay lul pat.ess.ta** Instead of open arms, we were given the cold shoulder. **Na n' chingchan khenyeng kkwucilam ul tul.ess.ta** Not praise did I hear, but scolding.

~ **to**. ¶ **Sip wen khenyeng (to) sip cen to mōs pat.keyss.ta** We won't get ten cen, much less ten **wen**.

~ **tul**. ¶ **Cōh.a haki (nun) khenyeng tul yok man hatula** Far from their liking it they had only bad to say about it.

~ **un** = **un** ~. ¶ **Cōh.a haki khenyeng un** (= **haki nun khenyeng**) **sayngkak man hay to keywuk cil i nanta** Far from liking it, the very thought of it makes me vomit.

~ **un tul**. ¶[1]**Nayil khenyeng (un) tul onul to tōn i ēps.ta** We have no money today, even, to say nothing of tomorrow.

CF **sāylo (ey)**, **kheniwa**; **(un) kosa hako**; **-nun tāysin ey**, **-nun pāntay lo**, **tolie**.

khe˙n ywo, abbr < *˙*hoke˙n ywo* after voiced sounds. ¶ *˙i ˙kot ho˙m ye n' ˙ZI-SSING ˙un mu˙sus he¨mul ˙lwo tas˙ti a˙ni ˙hwo.l ye khe[˙]n ywo* (1463/4 Yeng 2:70a; is *he¨mul* a carving mistake for *he˙mul*?) by what error are you reluctant to study the Two Vehicles?

khesin, abbr < *˙*hokesin* after voiced sounds, effective honorific modifier < °*ho˙ta*

khesi˙na, abbr < *˙*hokesi˙na* after voiced sounds. ¶ *MI-˙LUK ˙i ¨HHA-SOYNG ˙khesi˙na ho˙m ye n' ˙i ˙mwoy˙h i ˙yell i ˙'la ˙ho˙ya ˙ys.te˙n i* (1447 Sek 24:6b) he had said "when the maitreya is to be born this mountain will open up".

˙khe˙sin ma˙lon, abbr < *˙*hoke˙sin ma˙lon* after voiced sounds. ¶ *¨nim-˙ku˙m i [HHYEN] ˙khe˙sin ma˙lon [˙THAY-¨CO] ˙lol ¨mwot ¨etusil ˙ss oy* (1445 [1]Yong 84) the king was wise but he had no (crown prince =) son. *cip an˙h ay s ¨pwo˙poy s ˙CCANG ˙ul ¨pwoyGwo ˙cye ˙khesin ma˙lon* (1465 Wen se:43b) he wanted to show the treasure chest in his house, but ... .

˙khesi˙nol, abbr < *˙hokesi˙nol* after voiced sounds. ¶ *[KYENG-TWO] ˙ay twoco˙k i ˙tu˙le ¨nim-˙ku˙m i [˙PPI] ˙khesi˙nol* (1445 [1]Yong 33) the thieves entered the capital, and the king fled, but then ... .

˙khesi˙n ywo, abbr < *˙*hokesi˙n ywo*. ¶ *¨es˙tyey ˙i na˙la˙h ol [˙]˙e.ye˙spi ne˙kye wo˙ti a˙ni ˙khesi˙n ywo ˙hote˙n i* (1459 Wel 7:29b) "how can you love this land and never come to it?", he said. *¨es˙tyey ZYE-LOY y ¨SYWOW-SSING ˙PEP ˙u˙lwo ˙CYEY-˙TTWO ˙khesi˙n ywo ˙hota˙n i* (1463 Pep 2:5b) I wondered how the tathāgata had provided salvation through the dharma of the Lesser Vehicle (hīnayāna).

khe˙ta, abbr < *˙*hoke˙ta* after voiced sounds. ¶ *SSYA ˙two isi˙m ye ˙CYENG ˙two is.no˙n i a˙lwo˙m i NGUY khe˙ta* (?1468⁻ Mong 39a) it is well to know that both wrong and right exist.

khetun < *khe˙tun*, abbreviation < *haketun* < *˙hoke˙tun* after voiced sounds. ¶ *[KWONG-¨KHYWOW] hon ha˙l i [˙SSIM] ˙ho˙ya [˙PAY-¨KUM] ˙ul il˙Gwu˙l ye khe˙tun* (1445 [1]Yong 123) given that the clever slanderers are harsh and they will make elaborate embroideries (of the truth), ... *¨malsso˙m i THWONG-˙TTALQ khe˙tun ma˙lwol ˙tt iGe˙nol* (1463 Pep 1:9a) if the words are knowledgable they are not to be held back, but ... . *son˙coy ¨tywothi a˙ni khe˙tun* (1466 Kup 1:36a) if it is not better ... .

khey < *˙khey*, abbr < *hakey* < *ho˙key* (after MK voiced sounds. ¶ *yōng khey* cleverly, nicely, **Sayngkak khey hanta** It makes you think.

¶ *CCO-PI ˙non ˙CYWUNG-SOYNG ˙ol PPYEN-QAN ˙khey ˙ho˙sinon ke˙s iGe˙nul* (1447 Sek 6:5b) mercy is [his] deigning to ease the lot of living creatures, yet ... . *SOYNG-SOYNG ˙ay na ˙y ˙NGWEN ˙ul il˙thi a˙ni ˙khey ho˙kwo ˙'la* (1459 Wel 1:13b) in life after life I do not want to let my desire be lost. *¨TTWOW-˙LI ˙lol il˙thi a˙ni ˙khey ˙ho˙sino˙n i* (1459 Wel 9:11b) he is making it so that it does not lose its logic. *nowoy ˙tu˙ti a˙ni ˙khey ho˙m ye* (1459 Wel 21:120a) makes it so that he does not again enter [upon a wrong path], and ... . *syang˙nyey CIN-˙SSILQ ˙ul HHOYNG ˙khey ho˙m ye n'* (1464 Kumkang 64b) if you always have the truth practiced ... . ˙POYK-˙SYENG ˙ul PPYEN-QAN ˙khey ho˙l i 'n ˙t ye (1475 Nay 1:7a) will we ease the lot of the people? ALSO: 1459 Wel 2:38b, ...

~ ˙khwo [< ~ ho˙kwo]. ¶ chezem NUNG ˙hi pas˙k ol HE ˙khey ˙khwo [= ˙ho˙key ho˙kwo] (1462 ¹Nung 9:56b) for the first time he could make the outer world empty and ... . ˙na y ˙i ¨salo˙m ol ˙QAK-¨TTWOW ˙ay pte˙le ti˙ti a˙ni ˙khey ˙khwo [= a˙ni hokey ho˙kwo] ˙cye ˙honwo˙n i (1459 Wel 21:125b) I am afraid that I may be tending to let this man fall into the wrong path.

~ ˙tha [= ho˙ta]. Example? khe ˙za, abbr < [˙]hoke ˙za after voiced sounds. ¶ ko˙cang ˙PWULQ-˙TUK-¨I khe ˙za (= ˙hoke ˙za) pi˙luse kwu˙cicwu˙m ul te˙wul ˙t i.n i ''la (1475 Nay 2:1:16ab) only if it is absolutely necessary will the scolding be aggravated.

˙khe ˙za, inf < ˙khu˙ta + pcl. ¶ a˙to.l oy ptu˙t i ho˙ma ˙khe ˙za a˙pi a˙zom mwoy˙hwa (1463 Pep 2:224b) only when the son's aspirations were already great did the father and relatives gather and ... .

-khi-, suf. derives intensive verb. ¶ kay-khi- fold up < kāy-. CF -chi-, -chwu-, -li-, -lu-.

-kho = -h.ko (kuleh.ko, ileh.ko, celeh.ko)

kho, abbreviation < hako (aux ger) after voiced sounds. musim ~ unintentionally. kyel(qtan) ~ (not) ever, (not) under any circumstances, definitely (not). cengnyeng (~) definitely, for sure. phil.yen ~ for sure. kie ~ = kie 'i without fail, for sure. hānsa ~ at risk of life, desperately, relentlessly. camca' kho silently (< camcam hako).

-khom, var < -khum. tal-khom hata is rather sweet.

khulita, PARAINTENSIVE < kulita bnd postnom verb. does. SEE ong(song) ~ , wung(swung) ~ .

-khum, 1. = -kum. silkhum = silh.kum hata is dislikable.

2. PARAINTENSIVE < -kum. tᵃ/ᵤl-khum hata is rather sweet. sᵃʸ/ᵢ-khum hata is rather sour. kyalkhum [? Seoul DIAL] = kyalccum (long and slender).

-khun, suf (var < -khum). si-khun = si-khum; tul-khun = tul-khum.

˙khuy (abbr < ho˙kuy) = ˙khey (abbr < ho˙key). ¶ ˙nal ˙lwo ˙pswu˙m ey PPYEN-QAN ˙khuy ho˙kwo ˙cye holq stolo˙m i.n i ''la (1451 Hwun-en 3b) it is just that we want to make it easy [for people] to use every day. ALSO: 1447 Sek 9:19b, ...

···˙khwa = ···h ˙kwa. ¶ ha˙nol˙khwa [= ha˙nolh ˙kwa] (1459 Wel 1:14b) [like] heaven. ˙ip ˙kwa ˙nwun ˙kwa ˙kwuy ˙Gwa ˙kwo˙khwa [= ˙kwoh ˙kwa] (1462 ¹Nung 1:79b) the mouth and the eyes and the ears and the nose. MI-˙MYWOW ˙hi pol˙kon CIN-SIM ˙i ha˙nol˙khwa ˙sta˙khwa ˙lol ˙PPEM-NGWUY ho˙m ye (1462 ¹Nung 2:20b) a true heart that is delicately radiant envelops heaven and earth. hona˙khwa [= honah ˙kwa] ye˙sus ˙kwa s ˙ptu˙t i ˙na˙no.n i ''la (1462 ¹Nung 4:105b) there emerges the meaning of one and six.

~ ˙lol. ¶ MI-˙MYWOW ˙hi pol˙kon CIN-SIM ˙i ha˙nol˙khwa ˙sta˙khwa ˙lol ˙PPEM-NGWUY ho˙m ye (1462 ¹Nung 2:20b) a true heart that is wondrously radiant envelops heaven and earth.

~ ˙lwo. ¶ CYE PPWO-˙SALQ ˙tol˙khwa [= ˙tolh ˙kwa] ˙lwo ˙swo˙n ol sim˙kye NGYENG-˙CYEP ˙ho˙sike˙tun (1459 Wel 8:48b) offering his hand to the bodhisattvas he welcomed them.

~ ˙oy. ¶ ¨LI y ˙NGWOK ˙kwa ¨twolkhwa [= ¨twolh ˙kwa] ˙oy tal˙Gwo.m i ¨ep.swu˙toy (1475 Nay se:3a) reason does not have the differences of jade and stone.

~ ˙two. ¶ ha˙nol˙khwa ˙stakhwa ˙two [= ha˙nolh ˙kwa ˙stah ˙kwa ˙two] (1481 Twusi 21:12b) both heaven and earth.

~ y [< ˙i]. ¶ kas ˙kwa ˙sol˙khway [= ˙solh ˙kwa y] pwo˙tolap˙kwo (1459 Wel 2:40b) the skin and the flesh are soft and ... . MWON al˙ph oy hon ¨cywung ˙kwa hon sywo˙khway [= sywoh ˙kwa y] ¨kwoWon ¨kyeci˙p ul to˙lye ˙wa ˙y˙sye ˙pho˙no-ngi ''ta (1459 Wel 8:94b) in front of the gate a monk and a layman have come with a pretty girl whom they are selling.

˙khwa ''la, abbr < *˙ho˙kwa ''la after voiced sounds; CF ˙'-kwa ''la. ¶ a˙to˙l i ˙ile 'n ¨SSYWUW-¨KHWO ˙lol ho˙key ˙khwa ''la (1459 Wel 21:219b) I have made my son undergo such hardship!

˙khwan˙toy, abbr < *˙hokwan˙toy after voiced sounds. ¶ ¨es˙te khwan˙toy ¨twuy.h o˙lwo tol˙Gywo˙m ay ¨ce y il˙hu˙m ye pas[k] ˙MWULQ ˙ey ¨ce y mwo˙loke˙n ywo (1459 Wel 13:32a) how come because it depends on the future one will lose it and oneself be unaware of external objects?

˙khwa swo˙la, abbr < *˙ho˙kwa swo˙la after voiced sounds. ¶a˙tol ¨ep.swo˙m ol [¨MYEN] ˙khwa swo˙la (1481 Twusi 21:31b) it makes up for the lack of a son.

˙khways.kwo = ˙khwa ˙ys[˙]kwo < *˙ho˙kwa is˙kwo. wanting it to happen. ¶tal˙Gi ne˙ki˙ti a˙ni ˙khwa ˙ys.kwo ˙po˙lanwo˙la (1475 Nay 1:67a) I hope that it is not regarded differently.

˙khwo, abbr < ho˙kwo after voiced sounds; CF ˙¨kwo. ¶˙ecul ˙khwo ˙a˙tok ˙ho˙ya (1447 Sek 6:3b) disturbed and dazed, ... comcom ˙khwo (1447 Sek 24:2b) keeping silent. pi˙lwok ˙QILQ-˙CHYEY ˙KYEN-MWUN ˙KAK-˙TI ˙lol ¨ep˙key ˙khwo (1462 ¹Nung 1:89b) if one suppresses all seeing, hearing, realizing, and knowing, and ... . ne ˙lul pil˙Gye wol˙ma ¨salGey ˙khwo (1481 Twusi 7:20a) I shall borrow you and have you move and live [in my pavilion].

˙khwo ˙cye, abbr < ˙ho˙kwo ˙cye after voiced sounds. ¶wo˙lay ne ˙[G]wa ta˙mos ¨salGe˙na cwuk.ke˙na ˙khwo cye solang ˙honwo˙la (1481 Twusi 8:35a) for a long time I have been thinking I would like to live or die just with you. ˙QILQ-˙CHYEY ˙CYWUNG-SOYNG ˙ul ˙LI-˙QYEK˙key ˙khwo [= ho˙key ho˙kwo] cye ho˙ya (1485 Kwan 1a) wanting to let all living beings benefit. cyang˙cho CIN ˙ey two˙la ka˙kwo ˙cye ˙ho˙ya CIN ˙ol ˙khwo ˙cye ho˙m ye n' (1462 ¹Nung 7:73b) if in future one wants to go back to the truth and wants to do the true thing ... . NGWEN-˙KAK ˙ol ˙CING ˙khwo cye ˙hwo˙toy (1465 Wen se:5a) wants to witness perfect enlightenment, and ... . ˙pola ˙khwo ˙cye ˙ho˙nwon mozo˙m i na˙m ye n' (1462 ¹Nung 7:74b) if one gets in the mood to hope ... . ˙QILQ-˙CHYEY s SYWUW-HHOYNG hol ¨ssa˙lo.m o˙lwo ¨ZIN-˙ZYWOK PA-LA-˙MILQ ˙ul il˙Gwu˙key ˙khwo cye ˙hosi˙n i (1464 Kumkang 81b) he wanted to have kṣānti pāramitā (patience under insult) that is achieved by all people practicing asceticism. ¨ce y twolo˙hye ˙HYANG khey ˙khwo cye ˙y.n i ˙¨la (1482 Nam 1:70b) he wanted to turn himself around. ˙kwot ˙CYEY-˙TTWO ˙khwo ˙cye ˙khwo (1465 Wen 2:3:1:47a) wants to save them right away. pwu¨thye y ˙i ˙MYWOW-˙PEP-HHWA KYENG ˙u˙lwo ˙pwu˙cywok ˙hwol˙tt oy is˙key ˙khwo ˙cye ˙y.n i ˙¨la (1463 Pep 4:134b) Buddha wanted to have people keep relying on this Lotus sūtra. SIM-˙CCYENG ˙kwa ˙SYWELQ-˙PEP ˙CCYENG ˙ey mas˙key ˙khwo ˙cye ˙ysi˙n i (1463 Pep 5:37-8) he wanted to have people conform to purity of heart and of doctrine.

···khwom = ···h kwom. ¶hona˙khwom (1447 Sek 23:15a, 49a; 1462 ¹Nung 8:5a) = honah ˙kwom one each. ¨sey˙khwom (1449 Kok 153) = ¨seyh ˙kwom three each. ˙yel ˙ca˙khwom (1459 Wel 2:59b) = ˙yel ˙cah ˙kwom ten ˙cah (feet) each.

˙khwo n', abbreviation < ho˙kwo n' after voiced sounds. ¶˙SSYWOK ˙oy CAY-˙KAY ˙yey ˙two mek˙ti a˙ni ˙khwo n' ˙homol˙mye CIN-˙SSILQ s tas.no˙n i ˙sto˙n ye (1462 ¹Nung 8:4-5) when even in the fasts of commoners they refrain from eating them [the five forbidden roots], how much more so the true student (of the discipline)? ˙na y ˙i ke˙s u˙lwo hon na˙la˙h ol ¨ta ˙cwue ˙two ˙wohi˙lye ¨ep˙ti a˙ni ˙khwo n' ¨es˙tyey ˙homol˙mye CYE-¨CO y ˙sto˙n ye (1463 Pep 2:77a) when I have no appreciable lack though I gave up a nation for this, how much more so the masters!

˙khwo ˙za, abbr < ho˙kwo ˙za after voiced sounds. ¶SAM-˙SO ˙KWU ˙non ˙CYWUNG-SOYNG ˙ol ¨ta ˙CYEY-˙TTWO [˙]khwo ˙za ˙na y pwuthye towoy˙ywo.l ye hol˙s i.n i (1482 Nam 2:6b) with just three or four phrases saving all living beings, I want to become a Buddha.

khwu = kho = hako

-khwu = -h.kwu = -h.ko (kuleh.ko, ileh.ko, celeh.ko)

-khwum, suffix (var < -khum). ¶si-khwum = si-khum.

-khwung, suffix. SEE ile ~ cele ~, ili ~ celi ~.

··· khwuta [S Kyengsang DIAL (Mkk 1960:3:34)] = ··· ko hata (says that). ¶Cōh.ta khwunta He says it's good. Chayk ila khwunta He says it's a book. Kaca khwunta He suggests we go. CF (-)k hata.

khyen, noun [DIAL] = **phyen**

ki < ˙KHUY.

1. n. energy, strength, vitality; spirit, soul, mind; ... . ~ kkes SEE kkes. ¶Ki ka mak.hye ᾽la (M 1:2:62) I am surprised at you! CF kipun.

2. postnoun. (-q ki) a feeling of ···, ···ness. ¶kilumq ki oiliness. mulq ki (the) moisture, dampness, wetness. sicangq ki hunger.

᾽ki, 1. var (alt) < iki (copula summative).

2. abbr < haki (after vowel).

-ki < -˙ki, summative (CF -um, -i; kes). the act of ···, the fact that ···. [Past -ess.ki and future -keyss.ki occur.]

1. (as immediate subject) to do/be; that it does/is. SEE -ki ka.
¶ **paywuki (ka) swīpta** it's easy to learn. **Na tele pota nun ne tele māl haki ka swīpkeyss.ta** It would be easier for him to tell you than to tell me. **I 'na-ma to et.ki ka him tul.ess.ess.ta** It was hard to get even this (much). **ip.hak haki kacang elyewun hak.kyo** (1963 Wagner 53) the school that is the hardest to get into. **pal.um haki (ka) elyepta** is hard to pronounce.
¶ **Kul ilk.ki caymi iss.ta** Reading is fun. **na-kaki (ka) silh.ta** (I) hate to go out. **Na nun chwum chwuki (ka) cōh.ta** I like to dance — CF **I pang un chwum chwuki (ka) cōh.ta** This room is good for dancing. **Phyēnci lul pat.e sōngkwu sulepki (ka) hān i ēps.ˢup.nita** I am overwhelmed beyond measure to receive your letter. **Pang an ey man iss.ki ka taptap hay se cāmqkan na-kass.ta wass.ta** It was boring to stay inside, so I went out for a little while.
¶ **Ku haksayng uy thāyto to poki (ka) cōh.ci man elkwul to poki (ka) cōh.ta** Not only is his attitude pleasant, but he is good-looking, too.
¶ **i mwul i kipki ka elma na holis.ka** (1894 Gale 127) about how much is the depth of this water?
2. (as immediate object) to do/be; that it does/is. SEE -ki lul.
¶ **phyēnci lul ssuki (lul) sīcak** [= lit **pilos**] **hata** begins to write. **pay ka kophuki sīcak hata** (= **kopha cita**) starts to get hungry.
¶ **chamka haki lul kēcel hata** refuses to take part. **cwuki lul** (= **cwunun kes ul**) **cwuce hata** hesitates to give it.
¶ **īpuk ey kaki lul [better kanun kes ul] helak hata** permits one to go north. **nōlki lul [better nōnun kes ul] helak hata** allows a break/rest.
¶ **Tap.pyen haki lul him ul ssess.ta** I tried hard to find the answer; CF **Tap.pyen haki ey him ul ssess.ta = Tap.pyen haki ey chōng.lyek ul kiwul.yess.ta** I worked hard in giving/stating my answer.
¶ **Tose-kwan ey kaki lul yaksok hayss.ta** I did promise to go to the library [but perhaps not willingly] — CF **Tose-kwan ey kaki lo yaksok hayss.ta** I agreed to go to the library.
¶ **na-kaki (lul) silh.e hata** hates to go out. **Ne nun chwum chwuki (lul) cōh.a hanun ya** Do you like to dance? **Ku nun thuk hi si lul cīs.ki lul cōh.a hanta** He especially enjoys writing poems. **mit.ki lul wēn hata** wants to believe.

¶ **Swul ul (Tāmpay lul) mek.ki lul hana?** Surely he doesn't drink (smoke)? **Nul yok haki lul hayss.ta** He always made insults.
¶ **Nal-ssi ka ttattus haki lul kitalye se ssi lul ppulinta** We are waiting for warm weather to plant the seed.
¶ **Na nun ku i ka oki lul palanta** I am in hopes that he will come. **¹Nayil un nal i cōh.ki lul palanta** I hope that the weather will be nice tomorrow. **Mek.nun kes mata kkwul mas iki lul palanun ya?** Do you expect everything you eat to taste like honey? **Kuleh.key tōn ul hēyphi ssuko ya etteh.key tōn mouki lul palanta 'm!** The way you go throwing your money around, how can you expect ever to accumulate anything?! **Wuli pumo nim un nay sengcek i cōh.ki lul palasey yo** My parents expect me to get good grades.
NOTE: Many speakers reject **-ki lul chām.ta (ka) mōs hay se** 'unable to bear doing' (M 2:1: 125) in favor of **-ta ka chām.ta mōs hay se**.
2a. ~ (**ul**) **wi hay se** (**wi ha.ye**), ~ **wi han**: SEE **wi hata**. ¶ **ku sensayng ul hwan.yeng haki (lul) wi han hōy** a meeting (that is) for the purpose of welcoming the teacher. **tōpki (lul) wi hay se** in order to help. **Na nun nōlki wi hay se hak.kyo ey taninta** — **nay hak.kyo kongpu nun nōlki lul wi han kongpu 'ta** I just go to school for the sake of playing — my schoolwork is study for the sake of playing.
2b. (= -**toy**). ¶ **Ku i ka māl haki lul " ⋯ " hako māl hayss.ta** He said, " ⋯ ". **Han cuk tāytap haki lul caki nun ku kyēyhoyk ey chamka mōs hakeyss.ta ko hayss.ta** Then, he replied that he would not take part in the plan.
3. 3a. ~ **cen** before doing, before one does (did, will do). ~ **cikcen** right (immediately) before doing. ¶ **na-kaki cen ey pap ul mekta** (**mek.ess.ta, mek.keyss.ta**) eats (ate, will eat) before going out. **kongpu sikan i toyki cen ey** before (it gets to be time for) class. **Cēncayng i il.e naki (cik)cen iess.ta** It was (right) before the war broke out. **Ic.ki cen ey ese cwusey yo** Give it to me right away before you forget.
NOTE: Particle **to** can intervene: **Kēt.ki to cen ey ttwilye ko hanta** He tries to jump before he has learned to walk. Also: **cwuk.ki meych tal cen ey** some months before dying.
3b. ~ **ttaymun** because of doing/being, because it does/is; + cop, **ey**, or [? DIAL] **ulo**.

¶ Sikyey ka ēps.ki ttaymun ey nuc.key wass.ta I am late (getting here) because I have no watch. Tōn i ēps.ess.ki ttaymun ey ku chayk ul saci mōs hayss.ta I couldn't buy the book because I had no money with me. Swukcey lul an nāynun kes un mōs machyess.ki ttaymun ita The reason I can't hand in my homework is I didn't get it done. Pi ka okeyss.ki ttaymun ulo wūsan ul kaciko na-kanta I am going out with an umbrella because it may rain.

3c. ~ ccak i ēps.ta is unparalleled in ···ing = (is) ever so. ¶ Mian haki ccak i ēps.ess.e yo I am ever so sorry for what I did.

4. (followed by the copula – not common). ¶ Ileh.key haki 'ta Let's decided to do it this way (for the moment). ileh.key haki 'myen = ileh.key haki 'la hamyen if you say (for us) to do it this way, if you want to do it this way. Kuleh.key honca se caki / mek.ki 'ni? You want to sleep / eat alone like that? Ne cēng kuleki 'n ka / ya? You really intend to do it?

5. followed by particles. SEE ~ ka, lul, nun, to, lo, man, ya, ey, ey l', khenyeng, pota.

6. ? abbr < -ki ey/lo with/from the idea that. ¶ Namulamyen tasi nun an okeyss.ki (ey), kunyang twuess.ta Thinking not to come again if only to be scolded, I left them alone. ¹Naynyen imyen tasi phikeyss.ki (ey) cal ssa twuess.ta I wrapped them carefully, for they might bloom again next year.

7. (rarely, at the end of a sentence – ? abbr < -ki lo ...). ¶ Wēyn ke l' okeyss.ki? What makes you think he's coming? (= Wēyn ke l' okeyss.ki lo ney ka kitaliko iss.nun ya Why do you wait with the silly idea that he will show up?). Cf -ulla ko.

8. ~ kyem [STIFF] = ulq kyem.

9. derives n from v (or v phrase) – Cf -i (der n). Sewul naki a person born in Seoul, a Seoulite. sikol naki a country person, a rube, a rustic; a farmer. sinchwul nayki = phusna(y)ki / -kwun a newcomer, a green hand, a novice. swuwel nayki a pushover, an easy person to manage. tōn nayki gambling. ssuley pat.ki a dustpan. wen-pap sswuki soup with rice and rice cake in it. anq-cam caki a sleep-in maid. somay chiki a pickpocket; picking pockets. tot-poki long-distance spectacles. polum poki a one-eyed person. huk poki a squint-eyed person. māl cayki ('words fast' =) a gossip(monger). hay palaki a sunflower. Ramstedt (1938:177) has calaki 'a grown-up' but that is unknown to speakers I have asked, for whom the form only means 'growing up'.

NOTE 1: In KEd the ending -ki is called the "nominative", but that term is here used only for the nominative case particle i / ka.

NOTE 2: The MK ancestor -˙ki was little used, but there are such examples as "NGWUW-˙TUK hon ˙˙salo˙m ol ˙˙syey˙ye pat non˙hwoki ˙lol ˙KYWELQ ˙'key (= ho˙key) ho˙n i (1447 Sek 9:19-20) 'had persons of virtue stand up and let them divide the fields', ˙mul KWU ho˙ki ˙mwollwum ˙kot ha˙n i ˙'la (1463 Pep 4:91a) 'seem not to know to seek water', ˙kul ˙suki ˙Gwa kal[h] ˙psuki ˙[G]wa (1481 Twusi 7:15a) 'wielding pen and sword', and hon ti˙Gwuy ˙˙thang ˙˙c'a˙si˙ki mos˙kwo (?1517- Pak 1:64b) 'finished a meal of soup and (then) ... '. See also -˙ki l', -˙ki ˙lol, and -˙ki ˙yey. In ?1517-¹No we find as a gloss for Chinese bú yào 'you need not' both -˙ti and -˙ki + aux ˙˙mal-, as (both 2:7a) ka˙ti ˙˙mal˙la 'you need not go' and ˙ne y pwo˙nay˙ki ˙˙mal˙la 'you don't have to see me off'. ALSO: ˙˙ne y ko˙cang ˙il ˙ka˙ki mal˙la (1:26b) 'there's no need to go so early'; ˙na ˙non ˙˙twuy[h] ˙pwo˙ki ˙˙ma˙ta (1:37b) 'I don't need to go to the toilet'. Conjoining of two nominalizations is found: twocuk ho˙ki ˙Gwa ˙˙ke˙cu-˙˙mal nilo˙ki [˙] mal.m ye (2:43ab) 'avoid stealing and telling lies and ...'. SEE -˙ti.

By the 1650's are quite a few examples, including -ki lwo (1656 Kyengmin 21b, but with the meaning 'so as to be / do' and not 'because'). An example that shows the nuclear focus found in modern -ki nun ··· ha-: cham mata poy yey nolisiki elyepki non cywokwoma hokwo (1676 Sin.e 6:21a) 'at each port it WAS a bit hard for them to get down to the boat, and ... . The earlier examples were mostly after a vowel: none of the 26 -˙ki in ?1517- Pak follows a consonant (Katsuki 1986:59).

The ancestor of the suspective -ci, -˙ti (< ˙t i), was used more widely in Middle Korean, and in many cases it corresponds to modern -ki. Under Kim Wancin's interpretation the hyangka phonograms attest two examples of the precursor of -˙ki: mas-pwoki 1:6 (as theme) and tiniki 3:8 (as factual object of 'know'). Cf ¹Yi Congchel 1983:158.

A peculiarity of the ending **-ki** < -˙*ki* is that **haki** < *ho˙ki* does not abbreviate to ***khi** (*˙*khi*) after a voiced sound, unlike forms of **ha-** < °*ho-* with similar endings such as **-ko** < -˙*kwo* and **-ci** < -˙*ti*. The only abbreviation for **haki** is **'ki** after ···a or ···e, and this surely is part of the casual ellipsis of **ha-** after nonhigh back vowels that must be a modern innovation, though early precursors can be found in *i˙le [°ho]-* and *ku˙le [°ho]-*.

-ki-, suf. CF **-i-, -y-, -hi-, -chi-, -ukhi-, -ikhi-, -li-, -iwu-, -ywu-; -wu-, -hwu-, -kwu-, -chwu-, -ay-;** - ˙*Gi-*, - ˙*Gwo-*, - ˙*Gwu-*, *-o-*, *-u-*.

1. derives vc. **swumki-** < *swum˙ki-* conceal ← **swum-** < ˙*swum-* lie hidden. **pes.ki-** < *pes˙ki-* unclothe < **pes-** < *pes-* strip off.

2. derives vp. **ccic.ki-** be torn < **ccic-** tear it.

-ki ccum, summative + particle. ¶**Ēlun sok.iki ccum** [1]**yēysa lo hanun ay 'ta** He is a child of the sort ready to deceive grown-ups.

~ iya. ¶**Āmuli kwī han mulken iki lo (se) 'ni (ku ke l') mancye poki ccum iya mōs hakeyss.n' ya** However precious the article may be, couldn't I just touch it for a minute?

-ki chelem, summative + particle. ¶**Ku sālam mannaki chelem him tununq īl un ēps.ta** There is nothing so difficult as seeing him.

-ki cocha, summative + particle. ¶**Ku sālam un mannaki cocha him tunta** It is difficult even to get to see him. **Poki cōh.un ttek i mek.ki cocha phyen hata** A good-looking rice cake is easy enough to eat, too (− as well as look at).

kieng [Ceycwu DIAL] SEE *kiyeng*

-ki ey, summative + particle. CF *-um ey*.

1. for/in/by/from doing, to do. ¶**īl haki ey papputa** is busy working, is busy with one's work. **cwūnpi haki ey kantan hata** is simple to prepare. **swukcey lul machiki ey āy (lul) ssuta** tries to finish one's homework. **Na nun yo say cōh.un sengcek ul nāyki ey him (ul) ssunta** I have been trying to produce a good record lately. **Ku nun kūlim ul kūliki ey yenyem i ēps.ta** He is all absorbed in painting pictures. **mit.ki ey iluta** comes to believe/trust; **casal haki ey iluta** goes so far as to commit suicide. **Kumkang san kwūkyeng haki ey enu ttay ka cēy-il cōh.sup.nikka** What season of the year is best to see the Diamond Mountains? **Mues itun ci pelus haki ey tallinta** You can make a habit of anything (or: Anything can get to be a habit). CF **-nula ko**.

2. (= **-ki ttaymun ey, -killey**) as, because. ¶**Chayk i ssaki ey han kwēn ul sass.ta** As the book was cheap, I bought a copy. **Ku ka cheng haki ey ka-pwass.ta** Since he had invited me, I went to visit him. **Pi ka okeyss.ki ey wūsan ul kaciko wass.ta** I brought my umbrella along, expecting rain. **Nal i ha to cōh.ki ey sānqpo na-kass.ci yo** It was such a lovely day I went out for a stroll. **Nemu nuc.key il.e nass.ki ey kicha lul mōs thass.ta** I got up so late I missed the train. **Ku ka kul ul cal ssuki ey ilpule pūthak hanun key 'ta** He writes a good hand, so we should ask him to do it. **Kuleki ey sālam uy īl un molunta 'ni** So you never know what will happen to you in life.

NOTE: This expression for 'because' (like the Japanese ··· *no de*) can be used only in statements; in other sentences, use **-uni-kka** (similar to Japanese ··· *kara*). But it is possible to have a question that is made on an embedded statement: **Mues ul capswusyess.ki ey pay ka aphusip.nikka** What did you eat that gave you a stomachache? (M 1:2:319).

3. as, in accordance with. ¶**sayngkak haki ey** as I think, in my opinion. **Nay sayngkak haki ey (nun) ku-nye uy ūykyen i olh.un kes kath.ta** In my opinion her view seems correct. **Nay ka poki ey (nun) cōh.a pointa** As I see it, it looks good. **Ku kes i olh.ko kuluko nun sayngkak haki ey ttale se talle cilq swu iss.ta** Whether that is right or wrong can differ with how one thinks about it.

4. = **-kwantey** such that, so that (followed by a question doubting the adequacy of the reason). ¶**Tōn i mues iki ey kuli to sālam sōk ul thaywulq ka** What is it about money that gets people so upset?! **Ne ku sālam i nwukwu 'ki ey** (= **nwukwu 'n cwul ālko**) **kuleni?** Knowing who he is how can you act like that?! **I** [1]**nān.li thong ey keki ka eti 'ki ey** (= **eti 'la ko**) **kanta ko kuleni?** How can you think of going there, knowing what the place is like in the midst of this strife?!

5. SEE **-ta 'ki ey**

-ki ey chelem, summative + pcl + pcl. ¶**Kongpu haki lul nōlki ey chelem yelqcwung hanta 'myen musun kekceng ikeyss.ni** I'd have no complaint if you'd just study with the same enthusiasm you put into your play.

-ki ey cocha, summative + pcl + pcl. ¶Cēngsin ul et' 'ta phalko se pap mek.ki ey cocha tūnghan hani Where has your mind wandered that you so neglect to eat, even?

-ki ey kkaci, summative + pcl + pcl. ¶Ku uy emeni uy nolyek ulo ku nun tutie sengkong haki ey iluless.ta He finally achieved success through his mother's efforts.

-ki ey lang, summative + pcl + pcl. ¶Swukcey haki ey lang pappe se eti nōlle kalq swu to ēps.ta I am so busy with doing my homework and all that I can't go out anywhere.

-ki ey 'la to, summative + pcl + cop var inf + pcl. ¶Kongpu lul mōs halq pa ey nun chalali nōlki ey 'la to yelqcwung hay pwass.umyen cōh.keyss.kwun a Since you are not going to study you might at least put a bit of enthusiasm into your play.

-ki ey 'l mangceng, summative + pcl + copula prosp mod + postmod. ¶Mom kakkwuki ey 'l mangceng sohol hi halq swu ya ēps.ci One simply cannot be careless even about one's appearance/health.

-ki ey mace, summative + particle + particle. ¶Ha to keyulun kēci 'la (se) pēl.e mek.ki nun khenyeng ey et.e mek.ki ey mace silhq-cung na se cwuk.e pelyess.na puta (= pota) He was such a lazy beggar that he found it boring even to eat off others, much less work for a living, and so he let himself starve to death, it seems.

-ki ey man, summative + particle + particle. ¶Kongpu nun an hako nōlki ey man him ssuni kosayngq kil i hwēn hakeyss.kwun If you put all your effort into play, instead of studying, it's clear you've got a hard road ahead.

~ ila to. ¶Sīcho ey nun silphay lul hayss.ul mangceng macimak kkuth mayc.ki ey man ila to cal hamyen kwaynchanh.un hyōqkwa lul ketwulq ke 'lq sey Even if you fail at the beginning just so you finally do well at the end you are likely to get satisfactory results.

~ to (= -ki ey man hay to). ¶Nay ka tut.ki ey man (hay) to pelsse yelq pen ccay ya It is the tenth time I've heard it!

~ un. ¶Ilay pōy to chwum chwuki ey man un nwukwu eykey to an ppā cinta Seem this as it may, when it comes to dancing, at least, I take second place to none. Kōpkey nun mōs hatula to ppalli haki ey man un casin i iss.ta I may not be able to do it neatly but I have confidence that I can do it fast, at least. Talunq īl un tā ānun chek hamyen se tōn nāyki ey man un molun(un) chek hanta He pretends to know everything, except betting money!

-ki ey mangceng ici. it is fortunate that ⋯ ; fortunately ⋯ for otherwise; only owing to (because of). ¶Ku ka kaman hi iss.ess.ki ey mangceng ici mān.il tāyhang hayss.tula 'myen ssawum i toyl ppen hayss.ta If he had not kept quiet they would have quarreled. Ney ka elin ay 'ki ey mangceng ici khun sālam kath.umyen yōngse haci anh.keyss.ta It is a good thing you're a child; if you were a grown-up I would not forgive you. Tōn i ēps.ess.ki ey mangceng ici, (mān.il tōn i iss.ess.tula 'myen) totwuk eykey tā ppāys.kyess.ulq kes ita It was good that I had no money with me, otherwise (if, say, I HAD had money with me) I would have been robbed of it all by the thief.

-ki ey n', abbr < -ki ey nun. ¶cey ka tut.ki ey n' as I hear (understand it), from what I hear.

-ki ey 'na, summative + pcl + cop adversative. ¶Ku kes un wusen mek.ki ey 'na cōh.ci, twuko mek.ki ey nun cōh.ci anh.tula That was something good to eat first, not to be put aside for later eating.

~-ma. ¶Wusen poki ey 'na-ma cōh.key hay twuca First let's make it nice to look at, say.

-ki ey 'n tul, summative + pcl + copula mod + postmod. ¶Poki cōh.un ttek i mek.ki ey 'n tul nappul ya? How can a good-looking rice cake possibly be bad to eat?!

-ki ey nun, summative + pcl + pcl. for/in/by/from doing. ¶na poki ey nun the way I see it, in my opinion (= nay sayngkak ey nun). talun sālam poki ey nun the way others look at it. Ku ka um.ak ul kongpu haki ey nun com nuc.ess.^{s}up.nita It is a little late in life for him to study music.

-ki ey pota, summative + pcl + pcl. ¶Ku nun keth ulo poki ey pota acwu maum-ssi ka cōh.un sālam ita He is a much nicer person than he seems to be when you just look at him.

-ki ey se, summative + pcl + pcl. ¶Ku nun kul cīs.ki (ey) se ilqtung ul hayss.ta He won first prize in essay writing. Ku nun kūlim kūliki ey se ttwie nan caycwu lul po.yess.ta He showed outstanding talent in painting pictures. [The -ki phrase is lexicalized (no particle after object).]

~ chelem. ¶Māyil mek.nun siksa lul mek.ki nāyki ey se chelem mek.nunta 'myen wicang ey thāl i nako mālq key 'ta If you eat all your meals as if you were (trying to become the winner) in an eating contest, you will end up with stomach trouble.

~ kkaci to. ¶Kumnyen sīhap ey se wuli sēnswu nun yēyki an hayss.tun noph.i-ttwiki ey se kkaci to sūng.li lul ketwess.ta In this year's games our champions garnered victory even in the high jump, something which had been untalked-of (= was unanticipated).

~ 'la to. ¶Phohwan tenciki ey se 'la to cal man hayss.tula 'myen wusung halq kāmang i ēps.ci n' anh.ess.nun tey ... If we were just to do well in the shot put, at least, the possibility of winning wouldn't be completely out of the question(, but ...).

~ mace. ¶Phohwan tenciki ey se mace ilqtung ul hayss.tula 'myen kumnyen conghap wusung-ki nun wuli kes i tōyss.keyss.nun tey If we were to take first place even in the shot put, this year's grand pennant would be ours!

~ man. ¶Ku nun kul cīs.ki ey se man caki sālm uy culkewum ul chac.ess.ta He found joy for his life just in writing his works.

~ man un. ¶Na nun talunq īl un halq swu iss.e to thānkwang phaki ey se man un kyentye nalq swu ēps.ess.ta Though able to do other things, coal mining was the one thing I could not put up with. Ku nun ttwiki ey se man un chōyko kilok ul ollyess.ta He upped the record in the jump alone.

~ 'na-ma. ¶Na ya mwe talun caycwu nun ēps.ko hani mek.ki nāyki ey se 'na-ma han pen mayk ul sse pwā ya 'ci I have no talent for anything else, so an eating contest is one place I should really show my stuff!

~ nun. ¶Ku nun si lul cīs.ki ey se nun nam eykey ttel.e cici anh.una kūlim (ul) kūliki ey se nun pyel lo ttwie naci mōs han kes kath.ta = ··· cīs.nun tey (ey) nun ··· kūlinun tey (ey) nun He is no one's inferior when it comes to writing poems, but when it comes to painting pictures he is not at all outstanding, it appears.

~ 'n tul. ¶Kul cīs.ki ey se 'n tul ilqtung ul mōs hal ya? There is surely no reason I can't get first prize even in the essay writing.

~ puthe. ¶Ku nun cheum swuchay-hwa lul kūliki (ey) se puthe sīcak hayss.ta First he began with painting watercolors. Thānkwang phaki ey se puthe na uy cikcang saynghwal un sīcak tōyss.ta My working life began with coal mining.

~ to. ¶Wuli sēnswu nun nelp.i-ttwiki ey se ppun man ani 'la noph.i-ttwiki ey se to cōh.un kilok ul ollyess.ta Our champions made good records not only in the broad jump but also in the high jump.

~ 'tun ci. ¶Ku nun si lul cīs.ki ey se 'tun ci kūlim ul kūliki ey se 'tun ci nam eykey ttel.e cinunq īl i ēps.ta [slightly awkward — better with ··· cīs.nun tey 'na ··· kūlinun tey 'na ···] He is never inferior to others either in writing poems or in drawing pictures.

~ ya. ¶Tān-keli ttwiki ey nun casin i ēps.ci man, cang-keli ttwiki ey se ya nwukwu eykey to cic'anh.ci I have no confidence in my sprint but when it comes to long-distance running I concede to no one. Ku nun si lul cīs.ki ey se ya ilqtung ul hakeyss.ci hako sayngkak hayss.ta [? awkward] He thought "At least in writing poems I will be first".

-ki ey sekken, summative + pcl + pcl = -ki ey lang

-ki ey to, summative + pcl + pcl. also / even to do; also/even for/in/by/from doing. ¶Mantulki ey to kantan hako mek.ki ey to kantan hata It is both simple to prepare and simple to eat. Ku sālam un kul ssuki ey pāyl man ani 'la kūlim kūliki ey to yenyem i ēps.ta Not only is he skilled at writing but he is also devoted to painting. Ku nun poki ey to acwu yēng.li hay pointa In appearance too he seems bright.

-ki ey tul, summative + pcl + pcl. ¶Yeki kkaci osiki ey tul elma 'na swūko hasyess.^{s}o How kind of you people to have gone to the trouble to come all this way!

-ki ey ya, summative + pcl + pcl. ¶Keth ulo poki ey ya kulelq tus haci From the outside it looks great.

-ki ka, summative + pcl. SEE -ki.

~ swīpta is easy to do; it is easy for it to happen, is likely to; ~ elyepta is hard to do (*'is unlikely to do' — but OK with toy- 'become'). NOTE: With the honorific this only means 'easy / hard (for you / ···) to do'.

~ napputa it is difficult (hard/cumbersome/ unwieldy) to (do) ··· . ¶Ku thulek un wūncen haki ka nappe yo That truck is hard to drive.

~ **musepkey** no sooner ... than; hardly ... when. ¶**Māl i na-oki ka musepkey, Swunhuy nun kot nwun-chi lul chayss.ta** No sooner was the word out than Swunhuy got wind of it. **Say kil i naki ka musepkey sālam tul un motwu ku kil lo taniki sicak hayss.ta** The new road was hardly finished when all the people started using it. **Ku cip ulo tol.a oki ka musepkey tto pakk ulo na-kass.ta** (CM 1:384) Hardly had he returned home than he went out again.

~ **ilsswu 'ta** is always doing (something unpleasant). SEE **ilsswu**.

-**ki khenyeng**, summative + pcl. ¶**Kūlim ul kūliki khenyeng polq cwul to molunta** He does not know how to look at pictures, even, much less paint them! CF -**ki (nun) khenyeng**.

-**ki kkaci**, summative + pcl. until (even) it does. ¶**iluki kkaci** as far as it can reach/go, to the full(est) extent. **Cēncha ka tte-naki kkaci sippun iss.ta** We have ten minutes before the train leaves. **Ku os ul ip.e poki kkaci hasiko se an sasip.nikka?** Madam has tried actually wearing this dress and now won't buy it?! [salesperson]

ki kkes SEE **kkes**

-**ki kyem** = -**ulq kyem**

kil₁ < ˈ*kilh*, noun, adverb, postmodifier.

1. noun. 1a. a road, a way, a street; a route, a passage; (= **kēli**) distance. ¶**keliq** ~ a street, a thoroughfare. **payq** ~ a ship route. **chen-/mān-liq** ~ a long route, a great distance. **khun** ~, **han** ~ (→ **hayngkil**) a vehicular road, a highway. **cop.un** ~ a path, a lane, a narrow road. **kōl-mok** ~ a side road. **sanq** ~ a pass, a mountain road. **cilumq** ~ a short cut. **tolumq** ~ a roundabout way. ~ **ul kata** goes on one's way, journeys. ~ **kanun sālam** a wayfarer. ~ **chām hata** takes a rest on one's way. ~ **ul mūt.ta** asks one's way. ~ **ul ilh.ta** loses/misses one's way, gets lost. ~ **cal-mos tulta** takes a wrong turn, misses the way, goes astray. ~ **ul kalikhita** shows/tells the way, directs (one) to a place. ~ **ul pīkhita** makes way/room (for), gets out of the way. ~ **ul nāyta** makes a road, cuts a path. ~ **ul yēlta** opens up a road; pioneers. **hwūcin ul wi ha.ye** ~ **ul yēlta** gives the younger people a chance. **sungcin uy** ~ **ul yēlta** keeps the door to promotion open, gives one an opportunity for promotion. ~ **ul chiwuta** clears the way, keeps the passage open.

1b. a way (of behaving, of life); a path (of conduct), a duty; a moral principle/doctrine, teachings; truth, the true way. ¶**sēysok uy** ~ the way(s) of the world. **sālam uy** ~ one's path of duty, one's duty as a human being. **Kong-Mayng uy** ~ the teachings of Confucius and Mencius. **ani 'n** ~ **ul kata** errs/strays from the path of duty/righteousness. **Achim ey kil ul tul.umyen cenyek ey cwuk.e to cōh.ta** If I hear truth in the morning, I will gladly die in the evening.

1c. a line of business, vocation, profession, special(i)ty. ¶**Ku nun i kil uy tal.in ita** He is an expert in this line/trade. **I kil ey iss.e se ku wi ey kalq sālam un ēps.ta** He is the best in this line. (No one can touch/rival him in this profession.)

1d. **palq-kil** (the force of) a kick; one's steps, the path one's foot takes. **sonq-kil** an outstretched hand.

2. noun. a way, a means, a course, a step. ¶**sengkong hanun** ~ a road/way to success. **chwī halq** ~ the course to take (to be taken), the course of action to follow (to be followed). **ancen han** ~ a safe course. **sal.e na-kanun** ~ a means of livelihood. **Ālq kil i ēps.ta** There is no way to find out. There is no telling. **Sal.e na-kalq kil i mak.yen hata** I don't know how to make a living. **I pakk ey talli kil i ēps.ta** This is the only way/course open to me. There is no alternative left for me. I have no choice (but to do this). **kosayngq** ~ a hard row to hoe. **i-sungq** ~ the course of this life. **ce-sungq** ~ the course of the next life (of life beyond the grave).

3. noun, adverb, postmod. the midst of a way/course/process, incidental to a course of action; ~ **ey** on the/one's way, incidentally, en route, while, when, as, on the occasion (of), as a side event (to), in addition (to). ¶**hak.kyo ey kanun** ~ **ey** on one's way to school. **On kil ey halq iyaki ka iss.ta** I have something to talk about with you while I am here. **Iyaki hanun kil ey han-twū mati te hakeyss.ta** I will take this occasion/opportunity to add a few remarks. **Phyēnci ssunun kil ey nay phyēnci to com sse cwusey yo** Write a letter for me too while you are writing yours.

4. postmod [DIAL] = **īl** (experience, "ever").

kil₂, n. polish, gloss, brightness, domestication, training (of animals); (skill acquired through) experience. ¶**Malwu ka cal takk.e se kil i nass.ta** The floor shone from being polished. **Wuli cip kāy nun kil i cal tul.e se māl ul cal tut.nunta** Our dog is well trained and he minds what we say. **Icey n' kil i na se (tul.e se) cal hap.nita** Now that I've got the hang of it I am doing well.

kīl, noun. a grade, a class; (= **cil**) quality. (As second element in cpd usually **-q kil**.) ¶**kīl i cōh.ta** is (of) a good grade, has a good rating. **cwungq kil** medium quality. **hāq kil** lower quality. **sāngq kil** top quality. **wiq kil (wus kil)** the superior (better-grade) articles. **alayq kil** the inferior (lower-grade) articles.

kil(q), prospective modifier < **kita** (crawls) **kīl(q)** < ¨kil(q) < *ki·l[u]l(q), prosp mod < **kīlta** < ¨ki[l]·ta. ¶**kil** MAN (1576 ¹Yuhap 2:30b) [the Chinese word] MAN "to be prolonged".

-ki l', abbr < **-ki lul**

-·ki l', summative + pcl. ¶·poy ·thoki l' ¨ati ¨mwot ho·m ye ·sye (1463/4 Yeng 2:126a) not knowing to take the boat.

-ki 'la 'n' = **-ki 'la 'ni**

-ki 'la 'ni (or 'n' i?): **Kongpu man haki 'la 'ni cham him tun nolus ikwun** This business of studying all the time is really hard.

-ki 'la to, summative + cop var inf + particle. ¶**Ku i lul manna poki 'la to hayss.umyen cōh.keyss.ˢo** I wish I could just see him!

killay, adverb. long, for a long time, for ever. [< **kīlta** adj]

-killay = **-killey**. Roth 1936:306 ("entstanden aus **ki lo**"); Dupont 1965:199; LHS. Ramstedt (1939:105) has **-killay** = **-ki** + **-llay** "a regular case formation in North Korean dialects", labeled (124) as "instrumental-locative" and cited in "NK **aypi llay** 'for the father'", the only example given (but "in NK frequently used with many other kinds of nouns"). According to King 1990 the ¹Yuk-up dialect spoken in the USSR has **(i)llay** and **killay** 'because; since'; he gives the example **hyay illay watta** 'I came because she is my sister'.

Gale (1894:74) attests **-kil.noy** = /killay/ " = **-ki ey** (spoken for written **-ki lwo**)"; CF (1916 Gale 40) **hokil.nay** "An ordinary form of the connective **hokiey** in common use but never used of the 1st person", with these examples: **copwok hokil.nay ywongsye he.yes.swo** as he confessed, I forgave him. **cal mek.kil.nay te cwues.swo** he ate it so well that I gave him more. **silhye hokil.nay ku man twues.swo** he did not like it, so I gave it up. Gale wrote "-l.n-" regularly for /ll/, e.g. (1894:46) **kil.nwo** = **kil lo** 'by the road'.

-killey, extended summative [DIAL, colloq]. with the fact of doing; as, since, because. Myongdo (1:2:69) cites the form as **-killay** and says it is "used most frequently when the verb of the main clause is in the past tense" and is also used when one "asks the reason behind a certain fact, event, or occurrence", with the examples: **Yo say mues ul hakillay oci anh.e yo** What are you doing these days that you can't come visit? **Nwu ka wass.killay ileh.key yātan iey yo?** Who has come, I hear such a commotion! **Ku kes i mues ikillay swumkisey yo** What is it that you are hiding?

The etymology of **-killey** (**-killay**) is not entirely clear, but it appears to be a fairly late internal development to be explained along one of the following lines:

(1) < **-ki lo** < **-ki lwo** (1790 Chep.hay Monge 3:3 [LCT 113a]) 'as (being) ···ing' → 'because ··· ' with the second vowel fronted and unrounded in partial assimilation to the first vowel, or contaminated with **-ki ey** 'in ···ing → because ··· '; see below for the doubling of the liquid. But we lack an attestation of *-**kiley** or *-**ki(l)loy** as intermediate steps. And the variant **-killay** (if authentic) must be explained as a back formation due to the confusion of the mid and low front unrounded vowels. It is unclear whether the Ceycwu directional marker **ley** (also **teyley**, **leyley**) is a variant of **lwo** or a lenition of **tey** 'place' − or both; CF **etuley**, **etiley** = **eti lo** 'where to'. And perhaps related is the use of **ley** as a subject marker (Pak Yonghwu 1960:395), for which both **ley** and **lay** are reported from Phyengan (Kim Yengpay 1984:94). Notice that Ceycwu uses **-ki lwo** 'because' (Kang Cenghuy 1988:25n, 27-8).

(2) < **-ki [i]lay** < **-ki ila [ha]y** 'say it will be ···ing' or **-ki il ya** 'will it be ···ing' with metathesis of /lya/ > /lay/. That takes the variant **-killay** as basic; the standard **-killey** is explained as the usual raising of the low front unrounded vowel in noninitial position.

(3) < -ki lo + adverb-deriving -i (or 'i < hi < h[o]- 'do / be' + -i). Notice also lo-i < lo[w]-i (SEE lopta, suley < sule[w]-i, sulepta).
(4) < -ki l[o] ey with pcl ey.
(5) < -ki [ha]ll^a/_e [ha]y.

The double ll is a reinforcement that could be the result of emphasis, but it is probably just unmotivated, for similar cases can be found in (ce)cel-lo < (ce-)ce + lo, muel-lo < mue lo (= mues ulo), kel-lo < ke lo (= kes ulo) and perhaps /kellyo/ = ··· ke l'q yo, and as well as the variants -ull(y)e and -ull(y)a for -ulye. But the widespread dialect version ···llu- for the ···lu- stems is better explained as a reflex of the MK *lG*, as explained in Part I. From earlier sources we find 1887 Scott (28-30) *nallwo* 'by me', *nellwo* 'by you', *illwo* 'by this', as well as *muellwo* 'by what' – but *wuli lwo* 'by us', *nehuy lwo* 'by you', and *nwuy lwo* 'by whom'. There is at least one MK example of *llwo* for the particle *lwo* in the phrase ¨*nal'lwo* ¨*KAY-'THWALQ 'khey ho'n i* (1462 ¹Nung 7:27a) 'got released (emancipated) from his ego', and also for a variant *le* in the phrase *nalle nun es.ti salla hokwo* 'how will I live?' (?1544- Akcang kasili). See also *'il'lan* ?= *'i 'lan* (?1517- Pak 1:17a). An unusual example of liquid-doubling is seen in ¨*tyey-'il lon* (1518 Sohak-cho 8:22a) < *'TTYEY-'QILQ on* as for number one.

kīlm < ¨*kilm* < *ki'l[u]m*, substantive < kīlta < ¨*ki[l]'ta*. ¶ ¨*kil'm ye* (1482 Kum-sam 2:6b) is long and ... . CF *ki'lwom, ki'lwum*.

-ki lo, summative + pcl. CF -um ulo, -ki ey.
1. with / as / ... the doing. ¶Ku nun kul-ssi lul cal ssuki lo yūmyeng hata He is famous for his fine handwriting.
2. 2a. as, since, given that, it(s) being the case that, because. ¶Ku nun kul ul cal ssuki lo yēnsel wenko lul ku eykey pūthak hayss.ta I asked him to do the manuscript of the speech because he writes so well. Tal i palk.ki lo sānqpo haki lo hayss.ta Finding the moon bright, I decided to take a walk.
2b. thinking or supposing that; with the thought of its happening. ¶Pi ka okeyss.ki lo wūsan ul kaciko wass.ta Thinking it might rain, I have brought my umbrella. Wēyn ke l' ku ka okeyss.ki lo ney ka kitaliko iss.nun ya Why do you wait with the silly idea that he will show up? Yak mek.ki lo uywen eykey māl hayss.^so I spoke to the doctor about taking some medicine (1914 Underwood). Cip cīs.ki lo hyeng nim eykey kipyel hayss.^so I have sent word to my brother about building the house (1914 Underwood, who translates '[for him] to build the house', but 'to tell him that I will build the house' would be a more likely way to interpret the sentence).
3. (= ~ se 'ni, ~ se 'n tul) even though / if, even given / admitted that, it is true that ··· but. ¶Kel.um ul cal kēt.ki lo kicha lul ttalulq swu iss.na?! Even though he walks fast how can he (= can't) possibly beat a train. Ku i ka Yenge lul cal haki lo Kim sensayng mankhum halq ka?! He may speak English well, but surely not as well as Mr Kim. Cēntung i āmuli palk.ki lo hayq pich man halq ka?! No matter how bright a lamp may be how can it possibly rival the sun?!
4. 4a. ~ hata, ~ cakceng hata, ~ kyelqsim hata decides to do, makes up one's mind to do; arranges to do; fixes / arranges it so that; (~ yaksok ul hata) promises/agrees to do. ¶¹Nayil kaki lo haca Let's (decide / arrange to) go tomorrow = Let's put off going till tomorrow. Taum sikan un pēy(e) / ccalle mek.ki lo haca Let's cut the next class. Tōn ul cwusiki lo hasyess.ta He promised to give me money. Maum-ssi ka cōh.kenul nay an^hay lo sām.ki lo hayss.ta Her disposition being so good, I decided to make her my wife. Mikwuk ey se īl hanun kes potam Hānkwuk ulo ka se īl haki lo kyelqsim hayss.ci Rather than work in America, I made up my mind to go to Korea and work. ¹Nayil kaki lo yaksok ul hayss.ta He promised to go tomorrow.
4b. ~ hako iss.ta has it arranged so that; is so disposed as to do. Kakup-cek tōn ul pillye cwuci anh.ki lo hako iss.^sup.nita I do not lend money if I can help it.
4c. ~ toyta it gets so arranged / scheduled / decided / made that (so as to), gets to do, gets so one does, comes to do; ~ toye (tōy) iss.ta it is arranged / set that ··· , one is supposed to ··· . Examples: M 1:2:168-9.
5. ~ lo son = -ki lwo swon SEE (-)swon
-'ki 'lol, summative + pcl. ¶ '*PWO-SI ho'ki 'lol 'cul'kye* (1447 Sek 6:13a) delights in giving alms (and ...). ¨*kyecip 'CHWULQ-KA ho'ki 'lol*

ˈculkiˑti ˑˈmalˑla (1459 Wel 10:18b) do not allow yourself the pleasure of renouncing the world, woman. ALSO: 1447 Sek 9:19-20, 19:30a; 1459 Wel 2:71b, 23:3b. CF -ˈki lʼ.

-ki lo ʼni, summative + pcl + cop sequential (= -ki lo se ʼni). ¶Āmuli kwī han mulken iki lo (se) ʼni (ku ke lʼ) mancye poki ccum iya mōs hakeyss.nʼ ya However precious the article may be, couldnʼt I just touch it for a minute? Cey ka āmuli noph.i wass.ess.ki lo ʼni i sanq pongwuli kkaci ey nun mōs wass.ulq kes kath.ta However high he himself may have come I doubt he would have made it all the way up to this peak.

-ki lo nun, summative + pcl + pcl. ¶Nay ka ālki lo nun ku ka cēngcik han sālam ita As far as I know (From what I know of him) he is an honest man.

-ki lo se, summative + pcl + pcl. ¶Ku nun kongq kes man cal et.e mek.ki lo se yūmyeng hata He is famous for sponging off others.

~ ʼni (= ini), ~ ʼn tul (= in tul) even though indeed, it is true indeed that ⋯ but (SEE -ki lo 3). ¶Nay ka cal haki lo se ʼni ne chelem mankhum iya hakeyss.ni? I may do well, but surely I will never do as well as you! Āmuli pukkulepki lo se ʼni haca ʼnun māl han mati cocha mōs hani? However bashful you may be, canʼt you say even a word like haca ʻletʼs do itʼ? Āmuli kosayng sal.i lul haki lo se ʼni sumul sey sal ey nwu ka celeh.key nai ka tul.e pōynta ʼm! He is undergoing hardship, to be sure, but at only twenty-three years of age how could anyone look so old?! Āmuli ku kes i kwī han kes iki lo se ʼni mancye poki mace mōs pokeyss.ni? However valuable it may be, canʼt I just try touching it even?

-ki lo to, summative + pcl + pcl. ¶swul ul cōh.a haki lo to yūmyeng hata is famous for liking his liquor, too.

-ki lul, summative + pcl. 1. SEE -ki; -ˈki ˈlol. 2. (sentence-final) of course (= -ko mālko). ¶Ām, kuleh.ki lul Yes, of course! "Wuli to ¹nayil tūl-nol.i kana yo?" – "Ām, kaki lul!" "Are we going on the picnic tomorrow too?" – "Of course we are!".

-ki lwo (> -ki lo), summative + pcl. SEE -ki, -killey; (-)swon. Gale 1894:99 (ʻfor which reasonʼ) offers the earliest use of the causal meaning, and that (id.:74) was a written form.

kiˑlwom, kiˑlwum, modulated subst < ˑˈki[l]ˑta (long). ¶kiˑlwoˑm ol (1481 Twusi 8:11b); kiˑlwu.m ul (id. 15:12b).

kīm, postn, postmod. (on the) impetus (of); while (one is at / about it), when, as, since, as long as (⋯ anyway); incidental to the occasion of, in addition, as an incidental result of; on the spur of, by the force of, in an unplanned or unanticipated moment of ⋯ . CF palam, kyel, swūm, tun-son ey, kil, pūn-kim (ey), thōng (ey), pulq-kim (ey), tan-kim ey.

1. postn (usually -q kīm). ¶swulq kīm ey under the influence of alcohol. kolq kīm ey in a fit of anger. Hwāq / kolq kīm ey ppyam ul kalkyess.ta I boxed his ears in a moment of anger / rage.

2. postmod (-un ~, -nun ~). ¶Na nun hwā nan / nanun kīm ey kulus ul kkay ttulyess.ta I broke a plate in my anger. On kīm ey iyaki hako kakeyss.ta As long as I am here, I might as well have a talk with you before I go. Phyēnci puchinun kīm ey nay phyēnci to com puchye cwusey yo Please mail my letters too while you are at it. Hungpun toyn kīm ey eccelq cwul ul mōllass.ta I didnʼt know what to do in the excitement of the moment.

-ki mace, summative + pcl. ¶Icey nʼ kūlim ul kūliki mace silhq-cung i nass.ta Now Iʼve even gotten bored with painting pictures.

-ki malyen ita, [DIAL, colloq]. canʼt help doing / being; inevitably does / is.

-ki man, summative + pcl. just doing: ~ hata does nothing but; does / is after all (contrary to expectations). ¶Ēncey kkaci ku lul kitaliki man halq cakceng in ka How long do you intend to just keep waiting for him? Ayki ka caki / wūlki man hanta The baby does nothing but sleep/cry. Ku twū salam un mannaki man hamyen cik.epq yāyki lul hanta Whenever those two meet it is always shop talk. Ku ka nōlki man hatuni kkok ¹nakcey lul hanun kwun yo Heʼs done nothing but loaf so heʼs failing without a doubt! Māl hanun tāysin ey tut.ki man hasipsio Instead of talking, just listen. Na to haki man hamyen ku sālam mankhum hanta ʼp.nita If I devoted myself to it I could do as much / well as he. Alh.nunta ʼtuni melcceng hani tol.a taniki man cal hanta I heard heʼs sick, but look, he is going around sound as a bell. Nal i malk.ki man hata It is clear outside, after all. SEE **iki man**.

-ki mankhum, summative + pcl. ¶Sālam ul kitaliki mankhum him tununq īl un ēps.ta There is nothing so trying as waiting for people.

kīn < ¨kin < *ki˙[lu]n, mod < kīlta < ¨ki[l]˙ta. long. ¶ ¨kin [KWA-˙KUK] (1481 Twusi 7:26-7, 27b) long spears.

-ki n', abbr < **-ki nun**. ¶Ku-manq īl ey wūlki n' way wul.e Why all this crying over such a ittle thing?! Ēlun aph ey se wūs.ki n' (way wus.e) What do you mean laughing in front of a grown-up?!

-ki 'na, summative + cop advers. doing or the like. ~ **hanta** just does (nothing more than). ¶Na nun kaman hi anc.e se tut.ki 'na haci yo I'll just sit down and listen to you quietly.

-ki 'na-ma, summative + cop extended advers. ¶Poki silh.umyen tut.ki 'na-ma hay pwā la If you don't like to look, try listening, at least.

-ki 'ni, summative + cop indic attent. SEE **-ki**(4).

-ki 'n ka, summative + cop mod + postmod

-ki 'n tul, summative + cop mod + postmod. ¶Kul ul ssuki 'n tul kuli swiwun ka yo? Is it so easy to write?

-ki nun, summative + particle.

1. as for doing / being. ¶Ku i hako kath.i nōlki nun cōh.a to kath.i īl haki nun silh.ta To have fun with him is all right, but I don't like to work with him. Tangsin kwa 'na kanta 'myen molutoy honca kaki nun silh.e It's another question if you're accompanying me, but I hate to go alone. Ku īl ul nay ka haki nun com mues hata It is awkward for me to do that myself. Ku mūncey ey hap.uy lul poki nun elyewulq kes ulo pointa It seems it will be difficult to reach an agreement on that question. Ney ka kyelhon haki nun acik iluta You are too young to get married. ¹Yeksa ey kilok toyki nun han samchen-nyen cen puthe (i)ey yo It got recorded in history from about 3,000 years ago.

2. X-ki nun haci / hayss.ci / hakeyss.ci man = X-ki nun X-ci/-ess.ci/-keyss.ci man does all right (it is true) but; is indeed (I must admit) but. NOTE: **hanun tey** and X**-nun tey** can substitute for **haci man** and X**-ci man**; but past / future attaches only to the **-ki** forms. ¶I chayk ul ilk.ki nun ilk.ci / haci man ttus ul mōlla I DO read this book (all right) but I don't understand what it is talking about. Pi ka oki / wass.ki nun wass.ci / hayss.ci man It rained, all right (but ...). Ku kes ul mek.ki nun hayss.ci/mek.ess.ci man mas i ēps.ess.ta I did eat it, but it had no flavor. Phyēnci lul ssuki nun hayss.nun tey wuphyo ka ēps.kwun a I wrote the letter, all right, but now I find that I haven't got a stamp! SEE **haci man**.

Ne wūlki nun way wūni Why on earth are you crying? Wūs.ki nun to-taychey mue l' wūs.ni Just what the hell are you laughing at? Pappuki nun way pappuni What's the big rush (all about)?! (shows annoyance)

4. **-ki (nun) khenyeng** far from doing / being (on the contrary). ¶Pi ka oki (nun) khenyeng hay man ccayngccayng hi nanta Far from its raining, there is nothing but bright sunshine.

5. ~ **sāylo (ey)** [lit] = ~ **khenyeng** far from doing / being, instead of doing / being, on the contrary. CF **-ci nun anh.ko**, **-nun tāysin ey**, **-nun pāntay lo**, **tolie**.

6. ~ **kosa hako** far from (much less, not to mention) doing / being. SEE **kosa hako**.

7. **Ha.ye-thun oki nun haci?** You are coming anyway? SEE **haki nun**.

-ki 'n ya, summative + cop mod + postmod. SEE **-ki** (4).

-ki palata = **-ki lul palata** hopes that ... .

-ki pota, summative + pcl. ¶Na nun kūlim ul kūliki pota si lul ssuki lul te cōh.a hanta I prefer writing poems to drawing pictures.

~ **to**. ¶Ōykwuk sālam eykey n' Yenge lul ilk.ki pota (to) tut.ki ka te elyepta For the foreigner it is harder to hear English than to read it.

~ **nun**. ¶Na nun nolay lul puluki pota nun tut.ki lul cōh.a hanta I prefer listening to songs rather than singing them.

~ **ya**. ¶Āmuli sālki ka ko-toytula to cwuk.ki pota ya nās.keyss.ci However trying it may be to live, surely it is better than dying.

kipun < *kuy˙Gwun* < ˙*KHUY-PWUN*, n. feeling, mood, humor, frame/state of mind; atmosphere. ~ **i cōh.ta** feels good / well; is in good humor; is comfortable, pleasant. ¶I cuum kipun i etten ka − Kuce kule-kule halq sey How are you these days? − I only feel so-so. Say hay lul say kipun ulo (sse) mac.i haca Let us greet the New Year with a new state of mind. A, kipun cōh.a! Gee, I feel good!

-nun (-un) ~ what it feels like to do (to have done). CF M 2:1:10.

-ulq ~ ita is in a mood (in the frame of mind) to do. ¶chayk ilk.ulq kipun i ani 'ta is in not in the mood to read.

-ulq ~ i nata / naykhita (I) get in the mood to do. (First-person only.) CF M 2:1:11.

-ki puthe, summative + pcl. ¶Wusen pang ul chiwuki puthe hasey Let's start by getting the room cleaned up.

~ ka. ¶Ce san ul nēm.ki puthe ka palo ku elyewun kopi 'lq sey Beginning where you cross that mountain is right where the difficult pass is.

~ man. ¶Ta-cca ko-cca lo ppāys.ki puthe man ha(l)lye 'ni nwu ka cōh.a hay Starting off doing only such unexpected things how do you expect anyone to like it?!

~ se = -ki se puthe

-(k)kis, suffix (forms impressionistic adverbs). h^a/$_u$l-(k)kis glaring. CF -(k)kus.

-ki sa, summative + pcl. 1. [DIAL] = ki ya.

2. [? DIAL; mistake] = -ki se.

-ki se, summative + pcl = -ki ey se [but often awkward without the ey]. ¶Oy lowum i sēlepta hatoy pap kwūlm.ki (ey) se te halq ka It is sad to be lonely, but how much more so if you are starving as well.

-kita SEE -ki-

-ki 'ta, summative + cop. SEE -ki (4).

k' ita, abbr < ku kes ita it is that one.

-ki to, summative + pcl. doing/being also/even; -(ess)-ess/keyss-ki to.

1. ~ hata: 1a. (substitutes for repeat of the v / adj) does / is indeed (really). ¶chwupki to hata = chwupki to chwupta is really cold. wūlki to hanta = wūlki to wūnta really cries, cries hard. kongpu lul cal haki to hanta really / also studies hard. kongpu to cal haki to hanta really/also does even/also one's studying hard. Cham tanphung i alum-tapki to hata My, the autumn leaves are pretty! Kongpu man haki ka elyepki to hata It is pretty tough for one to do nothing but study all the time. Ku haksayng un pucilen haki to hata He is a truly hard-working student. Haksayng tul i mānh.i oki to hayss.kwun/wass.kwun Quite a lot of students have showed up, I see! Ney māl ul tul.e poni cham kuleh.ki to hay Hearing what you have to say I realize that you are quite right, indeed. SEE hata$_7$.

1b. Kako siph.ki to hay yo I sorta (sort of) want to go; I want to go and then again, I don't. Kako siph.e haki to ha(se)y yo He kinda (kind of) wants to go (but he is not sure he really wants to go).

1c. ¶Sāy tul i meli wi ey se cice-kelinun ka hamyen talam-cwi tul i tali mith ul suchye kaki to hanta Not only are there birds chirping overhead but also there are squirrels darting about under foot. Wuli ka tōn i ēps.ki to hay yo Also, (another reason is that) we don't have any money. Ku ka kulenq īl ul hanun kes un nala lul salang ham ey se man (i) ani 'la, casin ul wi ham ey se iki to hata His doing such a thing is not just from loving his country it's also for his own benefit. Hal-ape' nim un phyēnci ssuki lul cōh.a haki to hasey yo Grandfather enjoys writing letters, too.

1d. (a shortening of the double expression in 2c) does / is also [with negative: does / is not either]. ¶Achim ey pap ul an mek.ki to hanta Sometimes I don't have breakfast.

2. 2a. X-ki to X-ta = X-ki to hata (1a) really is / does (intensive).

2b. X-ki to hako Y-ki to hata does / is both A and B. ¶Cōh.ki to hako nappuki to hata It has its good points and its bad points. Ku ay nun mek.ki to cal hako nōlki to cal hanta He both eats well and plays hard. Na nun sihem ul cal ciluki to hako mōs chiluki to hanta Some exams I come through well, some I can't get through. Pay kophuki to hako mok maluki to hayss.ta I was both hungry and thirsty. Ku sālam un uysa (i)ki to hako um.ak-ka (i)ki to hata He is both a doctor and a musician.

2c. ¶Etten ttay n' kēt.ki to hako etten ttay n' thako to kanta = Etten ttay n' kel.e to kako etten ttay n' thako to kata = Etten ttay n' kel.e kaki to hako etten ttay n' thako kaki to hanta Sometimes I walk and sometimes I ride. Ku sālam ul silh.e haki to hako cōh.a haki to hanta Sometimes I like that person and sometimes I don't (NOTE: Not to be taken as 'I don't like him and yet again I do like him', showing indecision, nor as 'Some things about him I like and some things I don't').

3. ¶Cey tay lo cito lul poki to swiwunq īl i ani 'n tey It isn't so easy to look at a map the proper way. Ce mankhum Yenge cal haki to

him tulta It is hard to be able to speak English so well. **Nulk.ki to sēl(w)e la khenul cim ul cocha cisilq ka?!** How sad to age, they say, yet you wish to carry your burden?! **Kēt.ki to cen ey ttwilye ko hanta** He tries to jump before he has learned to walk. **Ney-kkān (= kkās = kkacis) nom hako nun ssawuki to silh.ta** I do not care to fight with the likes of you.

-ki ttaymun (ey) SEE -ki 3b

-ki tul, summative + pcl. ¶**Si lul cīs.ki tul cōh.a (tul) hasio?** Do you people like to write poems? **Mōs toyn cīs ul haki tul ttaymun ey** (and also: **haki ttaymun ey tul**, but not *haki ttaymun tul ey**) **yātan mac.ess.ta** They got bawled out for the bad things they did.

-ki wa, summative + pcl. ¶**Na nun thuk hi ilen kūlim ul kūliki wa ilen si lul cīs.ki lul cōh.a hap.nita** I especially enjoy drawing pictures of this sort and writing this sort of poems. **Na nun thuk hi kūlim ul kūliki wa poki (kāmsang haki) lul cōh.a hap.nita** I especially enjoy drawing and looking at (appreciating) pictures.

-ki ya, summative + pcl. only doing/being; if it is nothing more (or) other than; of course doing/being, to be sure. ¶**Ku (sālam) cengto lo kul ul ssuki ya him tunq īl i ani 'ta** It is not so hard to write up to HIS standards. **Ku i ka oki ya okeyss.ci man un nemu nuc.ci anh.umyen cōh.keyss.ta** Of course he'll get here, all right, but I hope he won't be too late. SEE **haki ya**. CF -ki nun.

kiyeng [Ceycwu DIAL, < *kieng*] = **kuleh.key** like that, so (Seng ¹Nakswu 1984:32, 34).

-ˈki ˈyey, summative + pcl. in doing. ¶*˝il hoˈki yey koˈlin keˈs i ˝cyektwoˈta* (1481 Twusi 25: 7b) has few hindrances in doing things.

-ki yo (var) = **-key yo** (SEE -**key** 5). ¶**(Nāyki ey) cin sālam un chwum ul chwuki yo? Nolay lul haki yo?** Shall we make the losers (in the game) do a dance? Sing a song? **Īl un an hako ileh.key anc.e man iss.ki yo?** Do you mean to just sit there doing nothing?!

-kka [S Kyengsang DIAL (¹Na Cinsek 1977)] = **-lq ka**

kkaci, pcl < *skoci* < **s koc(i)* < *s koˈc(ang)* < *s + *koˈco* (> *˝koz* 'brink').

1. (time) till, until; by; to; up to, down to. ¶**achim puthe cenyek ~ from morning to night. acik ~ up to now. yethay ~ till now; to date; up to the present. chilq-sip ~ sālta** lives to be seventy. **kōtay ey se hyēntay ~** from ancient times down to the present day. **Kicha ka tte-naki kkaci sip-pun iss.ta** We have ten minutes before the train will depart. **Ōychwulq sikan un pam yelq si kkaci ya** The hours (allowed out) are till ten at night. **I pen cēncayng i ēncey kkaci kal.nun ci nun āmu to molununq īl ita** No one knows how long this war is going to last.

2. (place) to; as far as, all the way to (CF **ey, ulo, ul**). ¶**yeki puthe cēki ~** from here to there. **Pusan ~ kanun cha phyo** a ticket to Pusan. **Sewul ~ kata** goes as far as Seoul. **muluph ~** up/down to one's knees. **Eti kkaci kasip.nikka** How far do you go?

3. (extent, emphasis) even; so far as; the very (CF **to, mace, cocha**). ¶**Ku uy hyeng kkaci ku lul cal-mos hayss.ta ko hanta** Even his big brother blames him. **Ku nun totwuk-cil kkaci hanta** He even steals. (He doesn't even stop at theft.) **Pi oko palam kkaci pūnta** It is raining and the wind is blowing as well. **Kuleh.key kkaci māl halq kes un ēps.ta** It is too much to say that. You go too far. **Way celi kkaci yātan in ya** I wonder why there's all that fuss.

4. [colloq] = **kkaci ey** (by)

kkaci ccum, particle + particle.

1. ¶**Sēy si kkaci ccum (= Sēy si ccum kkaci) kitalye pota (ka) an omyen kal they ya** I will wait till around three o'clock and then if you haven't come I'll leave.

2. ¶**Cong-lo kkaci ccum (un) kel.e kalq swu iss.ci yo** I guess I can walk as far as Bell Street.

kkaci ccum un, pcl + pcl + pcl. SEE **kkaci ccum**.

kkaci cocha, pcl + pcl. ¶**Ku mēlcˈanh.un kos kkaci cocha mōs kanta 'myen chalali tte-naci māsio** You'd better not set out if you think you won't even make it that far.

~ **to**. ¶**Kuleh.key swiwun kes kkaci cocha to mōs hani pap un mek.e se mwe l' hana** You can't even do something that easy, whatever will you do for your next bowl of rice?!

kkaci ey (nun), particle + particle (+ particle).

1. [colloq — from Japanese usage of **ma'de ni**] = **ccum (un)**, **an ulo (nun)** by (the time that ...), in the course of, before. ¶¹**nayil ~** by tomorrow; before tomorrow is over, sometime tomorrow. **sīcak haki ~** by the time it starts.

2. to (the place). ¶**Cey ka āmuli noph.i wass.ess.ki lo 'ni i sanq pongwuli kkaci ey**

nun mōs wass.ulq kes kath.ta However high he himself may have come I doubt he would have made it all the way up to this peak.
kkaci ey se, pcl + pcl + pcl. ¶Ku sālam kkaci ey se cwungci hala Stop counting when you get to him.
~ **mace.** ¶Ku cek.un swuip kkaci ey se mace sēykum ul kulk.e kanta Even from such a small income they grab taxes.
kkaci ka, pcl + pcl. till/to/even/... [as subject, complement]. ¶Yeki se keki kkaci ka meych macang ina toylq ka yo About how far (how many leagues) is it from here to where you are? Achim yetel(p)q si puthe ōhwu tases si kkaci ka yeki sāmu sikan ip.nita From 8 a.m. to 5 p.m. are our business hours. Yeses si kkaci ka ani 'p.nikka? Isn't it (Doesn't it last) till six o'clock? Sāsil un hak.wi lul pat.ki kkaci ka mūncey 'ta It really is a problem to get my (doctoral) degree.
kkaci khenyeng, particle + particle. ¶Onul kkaci khenyeng ¹nayil kkaci to tā mōs hakeyss.ta I won't be able to finish even by tomorrow, to say nothing of today. Pusan kkaci khenyeng Taykwu kkaci to mōs kakeyss.kwun yo I see we won't even be able to get to Taykwu, much less Pusan.
kkaci l', pcl + abbr pcl = kkaci lul
kkaci 'la to, pcl + cop var inf + pcl. ¶Ēncey kkaci 'la to kitalila 'n(') māl-ssum iyo? You mean I should wait forever? Sewul kkaci 'la to kalq swu iss.ta 'myen, elma 'na cōh.keyss.ˢo How nice it would be if I could get to Seoul, at least!
kkaci lo, pcl + pcl. ¶Nēy si kkaci lo ceng hay twupsita Let's decide to have it by (or: have it last till) four o'clock. Cwūcha kūmci kwuyek ul Cong-lo kkaci lo hay twupsita Let's have the no-parking zone all the way to Bell Street. SEE ku ~, ko ~.
kkaci lul, pcl + pcl. till/to/even/ ... [as direct object]. ¶Yēngtung-pho kkaci lul Sewul ila pulunta Yengtung-pho is included in the Seoul city limits. Sam-chon kkaci (lul) ttaylita 'ni kulen nappun nom i eti iss.na! What a wicked fellow he is to hit even his own uncle! Cey pumo kkaci (lul) musi hanun nom i musun khunq īl ul hakeyss.ta ko na-sess.na! What kind of a rascal is this who presents himself (as a candidate) when he has neglected even his own parents?! Ileh.key kakkawun tey kkaci lul mōs kel.e on sālam i tungsan un musun tungsan iya! What kind of mountain climber is he, not to get this far?!
kkaci mace SEE mace
kkaci man, pcl + pcl. just/only till/to/even/....
¶Twū si kkaci man okey Just get there by two (you need not come earlier). Sā-sip pheyici kkaci man ilk.usio Just read up to page 40.
~ **ila to.** ¶Nam Tāymun kkaci man ila to cha lul thako kapsita Let's ride all the way to South Gate (at least). Ku ka selun sal kkaci man ila to sal.ess.tula 'myen ku cakphum ul wānseng hayss.ulq kes ita If only he had lived to the age of thirty he would have completed the work.
kkaci n', abbr < kkaci nun. ¶Keki kkaci n' sayngkak ul mōs hayss.ta I've never thought of that.
-kkacin, [DIAL] = -kkacis
kkācin, [DIAL] = kkācis
kkaci 'na, pcl + cop advers. till/to/even/... or the like; whether till/to/even/...; till/to/even/... whatever. ¶eti ~ (= eti kkaci 'tun ci) to the utmost, in every possible way. Ēncey kkaci 'na kitalikeyss.ˢo I will wait forever. Kel.e kass.umyen Yēngtung-pho kkaci 'na kass.ulq ka I wonder if they could even have reached Yengtung-pho if they had walked.
kkaci 'na-ma, pcl + cop extended adversative. ¶¹Nayil kkaci 'na-ma ku kos ey kalq swu iss.ta 'myen elma 'na cōh.keyss.ˢo How nice it would be if I could get there by tomorrow, even. I kos kkaci 'na-ma olq swu iss.ta 'myen cōh.keyss.nun tey I wish he could manage to get at least as far as here. Te nun mōs palatula to hwānkap kkaci 'na-ma sāsyess.tula 'myen elma 'na cōh.ass.ulq ka All I wish is that he could have lived to see his sixtieth birthday.
kkaci nun, pcl + pcl.
1. as for (its being) till/to/even/.... ¶Yelq-sey sal kkaci nun sōin ulo chie to ku īsang un tā tāyin ia Up to thirteen years of age you are considered a "child" (for admission purposes), but above that age everyone is an "adult". Kaul ey se kyewul kkaci nun malk.un nal-ssi ka kyēysok toynta From autumn to winter, clear weather prevails. Nay ka haksil hi ālki kkaci nun ku sālam hanthey māl haci mal.e la Don't tell him until I know for sure.

2. = ccum un
-kkacis, bnd n [< kkaci + -q; DIAL -kkacin < kkaci + in]. such as … (makes adn, usually pejorative). ¶i/yo ~ this kind of. ku/ko ~, ce/co ~ that kind of. ney ~ such as you. cey ~ such as him/her/them; such as oneself (this does NOT mean "such as me/us"). ~ ccum/cocha = ~ (kes) ccum/cocha.
kkācis, abbr. 1. = ku-kkacis, adn.
2. = ku-kkacis kes, adn + n.
kkaci se, pcl + pcl. ¶Eti kkaci se poinun ya From how far away can it be seen?
kkaci to, pcl + pcl. till/to/… also/even; indeed even. ¶Tongmu ttale se Kangnam kkaci to kanta I will go even to Kangnam (= "to hell and back") with my comrades. Caki uy cēy-il kakkawun chinkwu kkaci to an chac.e poko tte-nass.ta 'nta You see, he didn't even say good-bye to his best friend! Nay chinkwu tul i na lul pinan hayss.ul ppun ani 'la nay anʰay kkaci to na lul pinan hayss.e Not only did my friends blame me, but my wife blamed me too. Ne wa kath.i 'la 'myen eti kkaci to kalq swu iss.ulq kes kath.ta I feel I could go anywhere if it were with you (I went). Nay ka ilay pōy to celm.ess.ul ttay nun Hān.la san kkoktayki kkaci to olla ka-poko, Kumkang san Pīlo-pong kkaci to olla ka-pwass.(ess.)ta 'nta Despite my appearance now, (I want you to know that) when I was young I managed to climb all the way to the top of Mt Hanla and also all the way up Pilo Peak in the Diamond Mountains.
kkaci tul, pcl + pcl. ¶Yele pun eti kkaci tul kasip.nikka How far are all you people going?
kkaci 'tun ci, pcl + cop retr mod + postmod. to the utmost, in every possible way (= eti kkaci 'na).
kkaci uy, pcl + pcl. (the one) till/to/even/… . ¶Onul kkaci uy na uy saynghwal un cham ulo hāyngpok ha.yess.ˢo My life has been a really happy one so far. Pusan ey se Sewul kkaci uy kichaq kaps i elma yo How much is the train fare from Pusan to Seoul?
kkaci ya, particle + particle. ¶¹Nayil kkaci ya tā toykeyss.ci yo It'll be all done by tomorrow at the latest. Āmuli kanan hay to kwukel kkaci ya hakeyss.ˢo? However poor he may be, would he actually go BEGGING? Ku kes kkaci ya nay ka māl halq swu ēps.ci I cannot go so far as to say THAT. ~ māl lo [? a bit awkward]. ¶Yeki se san mith kkaci ya māl lo cham ulo alum-tawun kyengchi ka kyēysok toyp.nita The beautiful scenery stretches from here all the way to the foot of the mountain. Ku ka sengkong han onul (ey iluki) kkaci ya māl lo pī halq tey ēps.nun kosayng uy kyēysok iess.ta Right up to this very day when he has succeeded it has been a stretch of unparalleled hardships.

-kkak, suf (makes impressionistic adv); LIGHT ↔ -kkek. kkolkkak kkolkkak gurgling < kkol kkol. (t)talkkak (XX) = (t)talkatak (XX) clattering, rattling < (t)tal-(t)tal. CF -ttak.

-kkal, postn (makes vulgar n from n). nwun ~ eye (CF nwun al eyeball). sēng ~ sharp temper. thāy ~ sulepta is haughty < thāy(to) attitude. pich kkal [also spelled pich kal] color. mas kkal [also spelled mas kal] flavor. CF kal. [? < -q kal]

kkamak, adn. SEE kamak.

kkamak', abbr < kkamakwi crow. ~ kkāchi crow and magpie.

kkan, 1. ~ (ey) quasi-free n (+ pcl). (by) one's own account/estimation/reckoning/view. ¶Cey kkan ey n' Yenge lul cal hanta ko sayngkak hanun mo.yang ita In his own eyes he seems to think he speaks English well. Cey ka han (māl hatun) kkan i iss.ta He knows what he did (said). nay (ney/tangsin/caney) ~ by my (your) account. caney/ne-huy tul ~ in you people's own estimation. caki (tul) ~ in one's (their) own eyes. ku i (tul) ~ his (their) own estimation. wuli (tul) ~ in our own eyes. SYN ttan. [? < -q kan ? < kan 'saltiness, seasoning', CF ttan; ? < KAN 'room', ? < ˙KHAN 'look, view']
2. bnd n. SEE kkan pota guesses, … .

kkān = kkās, abbr < kkacis (before nasal or -q i/y…). ¶Ney-kkān (= kkās = kkacis) nom hako nun ssawuki to silh.ta I do not care to fight with the likes of you. ku-kkānq īl = ku-kkacisq īl a trifle.

kkang, bnd n. ~ -kulita finishes it (= kkuth mayc.ta). ~-kuli all, utterly.

kkatalk, n; postmod (SEE -un/-nun/-tun/-ul ~). reason; cause; ground(s); account, occasion, score; a justification; an excuse; a motive. ¶ ~ ēps.i without reason; without good cause; without provocation; without rime or reason;

with no justification. ~ iss.nun reasonable; justifiable; with cause/reason; well-grounded. ~ **molulq īl** a strange/mysterious thing, an unexplainable thing; a mystery; a nonsensical thing; a thing without rime or reason. **Kkatalk cocha moluko se way ili tempinun ke yo** Why are you so hasty when you don't even know the score? **Kkatalk ccum (ina) ālko māl ul hasio** At least find out what the reasons may be before you speak.

~ **(ey/ulo)** because of; by reason of; on account of; for; on the grounds (that). ¶**musun ~ ey** why; for what reason; on what grounds. **Na nun musun kkatalk in ci lul molukeyss.ta** I don't know (the reason) why. **Kuleh.key hal kkatalk i iss.ess.ta** I had good reason to do so. **Musun kkatalk ey na lul chyess.nun ka** Why did you hit me?

SYN ¹**ī (li)**; ¹**īyu; yen.yu; thek.** CF **ttaymun.**

kkayna = **kkay 'na, kk'ay 'na.** SEE **kkway 'na; kay 'na.**

kke, inf < **kkuta.** ¶**Pul kke** Turn off the light!

kkeceng, kkecung pcl [S Kyengsang DIAL (Mkk 1960:3:33)] = **kkaci**

kkeci, particle [Phyengan DIAL] = **kkaci** (Kim Yengpay 1984:95)

-kkek, suf (makes impressionistic adv); HEAVY ↔ **-kkak. kkwulkkek kkwulkkek** gurgling < **kkwulkkek kkwulkkek** gurgling < **kkwul kkwul. (t)telkkek** (XX) = **(t)telketek** (XX) clattering, rattling < **(t)tel (t)tel.** CF **-ttek.**

kkes [< **kkec(i)** = **kkaci** < ...], postn, postmod.

1. to the full extent of, to the utmost of (capability/capacity).

1a. postn. ¶**īl ~** with much trouble, with great pain. **hān ~** to the limit/utmost. **sengsim /senguy/cengseng/ciseng ~** wholeheartedly, with utmost sincerity. **him ~ īl hata** works to the utmost of one's power, works as hard as one can. **hay ~ īl hata** works till dark, works all day long. **ki ~ kongpu hata** studies as hard as one can. **ki ~** to the utmost (of one's energy), **ki ~ hay ya** at most/best. **cengseng ~ tāycep hata** treats (a person) as well as one can. **pay ~ mekta/masita** eats/drinks one's belly full. ¹**yāng ~ mekta** eats one's fill, eats as much as one can. **yoksim ~ mekta** eats greedily, stuffs oneself. **maum ~ wūlta** cries one's heart out. **caykan/caycwu ~ hata** does/tries one's best. SEE **silkhes** 'to one's heart's content' < **silh-kes** (= *silh-kkes 'till one hates it'), but contrast **silh-cung** = **silhq-cung** /silccung/ 'aversion'.

1b. postmod. ¶**Elma 'na toynun ci iss.nun kkes kaciko wā pwā la** However much there may be, bring all there is.

2. (right) up to (now). SYN **kkaci. acik kkes** (not) yet. ¶**Yethay kkes han kes i i kes ppun ita** This is all I have done up to now. **Ku ay ka ipttay kkes wūlko iss.ta** The kid is still crying. **Ipttay kkes oci anh.ess.ta** He has not come as yet.

kkey, postn (< **key** = **ke˙kuy** 'there').

1. about/around, towards (a time). ¶**polum ~** about/towards the middle of the month. **kumum ~** about/towards the end of the month. **choswun/cwungswun/hāswun ~** around the first/second/last third of the month. **ōceng ~ ccum** around noontime, towards noon. **mence ~** the other day, some time ago. ? **kyewul key** two (1894 Gale 28) even in the winter time. CF **ecekkey, kucekkey, kelekkey; ceng kkey.**

2. around, in the vicinity/neighborhood of, near (a place). ¶**Nam Tāymun ~** near South Gate, in the vicinity of South Gate. **Cong-lo nēy-keli ~** around (in the neighborhood of) Bell Street Cross. **wumul ~** around the well.

kkey < **s˙kuy (˙s kuy)** < **s ke˙kuy/kungey,** pcl [hon for **eykey**]. to/at/for/by (one esteemed). ¶**Kim sensayng nim kkey ollim** presented to Mr Kim (with compliments). **Nay ka ape' nim kkey chayk ul tulyess.ta** I gave the book to Father. **Kim paksa ka Hankul lo ssun phyēnci lul moksa nim kkey pen.yek hay cwusinta** Dr Kim translates a Korean letter for the pastor.

-kkey, bnd adj-n (~ **hata**). dull and ugly (in color). **nolu-/nwulu-kkey** (a) dingy yellow. **phalu-/phulu-kkey** (a) dull and ugly blue.

-' **kkey** = -'**q key,** immediate future [abbr < -**lq key**]. Alternant after vowel of -**u' kkey** = -**u'q key.**

kkey chelem, pcl + pcl. ¶**Ku ay ka sensayng nim kkey chelem apeci eykey to** (or **ape' nim kkey to**) **tāy hanta 'myen elma 'na cōh.keyss.e yo** How nice it would be if he treated his father the way he treats you (or the teacher)! **Sensayng nim kkey chelem māl-ssum tuliki him tun pun un ēps.**ˢ**up.nita** You are the hardest person in the world for me to talk to.

kkey cocha, pcl + pcl. ¶Hyeng nim kkey cocha phyēnci lul mōs hako iss.ta I have been unable to write even to my brother.

kkey hako, pcl + pcl. ¶Kim sensayng kkey hako Son sensayng kkey nun alliko kake la Let Mr Kim and Mr Son know when you leave (= say good-bye to them).

-kkey hata SEE -kkey, bnd adj-n.

kkey ka, pcl + pcl. ¶Kim sensayng kkey ka ani 'la Pak sensayng kkey tulyess.ta I gave it to Mr Pak, not to Mr Kim.

kkey khenyeng, particle + particle. ¶Apeci kkey khenyeng hyeng kkey to phyēnci lul nāyci mōs hako iss.ta I haven't been able to get a letter off even to my brother, much less to my father.

kkey kkaci, particle + particle. ¶Apeci kkey kkaci kekceng ul kkichinun pulhyo casik ita He is such an unfilial son that he causes worry even to his father.

kkey lang, particle + particle. ¶Hyeng kkey lang tā allye la Let your brother and everyone (his family / group) know.

~ **to**. ¶Hal-ape' nim kkey lang to kac'ta tulye ya 'ci I'll have to take it to Grandfather and everyone, too.

~ **un**. ¶Olay kan man ey kōhyang ey l' kass.e to nemu 'na pappe se sā-chon hyeng kkey lang un tull(y)e poci to mōs hayss.ta Though I had not been to my home town for a long time, I was too short of time even to drop around to my cousin's place (where he and his family live).

kkey 'la to, pcl + cop var inf + pcl. ¶Ape' nim kkey se molusiketun hyeng nim kkey 'la to mul.e polyem If your father doesn't know, why don't you ask your older brother.

kkey lo, pcl + pcl. toward / to (an esteemed person). ¶Ce hanthey onun phyēnci nun tā cey hyeng nim kkey lo ponay cwusipsio Please forward to my older brother all the letters addressed to me.

kkey lo puthe, particle + pcl + pcl. from (an esteemed person). ¶Ape' nim kkey lo puthe (= ape nim kkey se) pheyn sēys ul pat.nunta (Wagner 8) I receive three pens from my father.

(?) kkey lul, pcl + pcl. ¶(?) Kim sensayng kkey lul mence tull(y)ess.ta ka Pak sensayng kkey lo kakeyss.ta I'll first drop by Mr Kim's and then I'll go to Mr Pak's.

kkey mace, pcl + pcl. ¶Ecci 'na pappun ci hyeng nim kkey mace phyēnci lul mōs hako iss.ta I have been so busy that I haven't been able to write even to my older brother.

kkey man, pcl + pcl. just / only to/at/for/by (an esteemed person). ¶I phyēnci nun ape' nim kkey man po.ye tulikey Show this letter to no one but your father. Sensayng nim kkey man māl-ssum in tey, ku pun uy pyēng i acwu cwūng han mo.yang ip.nita Just between you and me, his illness seems to be quite serious.

kkey mata, particle + particle. to/at/for/by each (esteemed person). ¶Sensayng nim kkey mata towa tālla 'nun phyēnci lul nāy pokeyss.ta I will send out letters asking each teacher (or: each of you gentlemen) to help.

kkey n', abbr < kkey nun

kkey 'na$_1$, postn + cop advers. ¶Cikum ccum eti kkey 'na kass.ulq ka Where could they have gone now?!

kkey 'na$_2$, pcl + cop adversative. to / at / for / by (an esteemed person) or the like; whether to/at/for/by (an esteemed person); to/at/for/by whatever (esteemed person). ¶Sensayng nim kkey 'na mul.e polq ka I might just ask the teacher (since no one else seems to know).

kkey 'na-ma$_1$, postnoun + copula extended adversative. ¶Kulem, noph.a se kkoktayki kkaci mōs kakeyss.ketun cwungkan kkey 'na-ma ka-polyem Well, if it's too high to get to the peak why don't you go about half way up, at least.

kkey 'na-ma$_2$, pcl + cop extended adversative. ¶Hyeng nim kkey 'na-ma mul.e poko cakceng halye 'p.nita I am going to consult Brother at least before making any decision.

kkey 'n tul, pcl + cop mod + postmod. to / at / for / by (an esteemed person). ¶Eme' nim kkey 'n tul ku māl-ssum ul tulilq swu iss.keyss.na How could we tell that to Mother?

kkey nun$_1$, postn + pcl. ¶Taykwu kkey nun ka-pwass.ci man Swūnchen kkey nun mōs ka-pwass.ta I have been to see Taykwu and its vicinity but not Swunchen.

kkey nun$_2$, pcl + pcl. as for to/at/for/by an esteemed person. ABBR kkey n'. ¶Ape' nim kkey nun phyēnci lul ssess.ci man, hal-ape' nim kkey nun an ssess.ta I wrote a letter to Father but not to Grandfather. Eme' nim kkey nun māl-ssum tulici mālkey Don't tell your

A Reference Grammar of Korean

mother.
kkey-op-se, cpd pcl (pcl + var of formal **-up-/ -sup-** + pcl) [lit, obs] = **kkey se** (but more highly honorific).
kkey pota, pcl + pcl. ¶**Apeci kkey pota hyeng nim kkey māl-ssum tulinun kes i cōh.ulq key yo** You would do better to talk to your brother rather than to your father. **Eme' nim kkey pota ape' nim kkey mul.e posey yo** You had better ask your father (about that) rather than your mother.
kkey puthe, pcl + pcl. ¶**Hak.kyo ey se tha on wutung-sayng ul apeci kkey puthe po.ye tulye la** Show the prize you won for being a good student at school to your father first (before you show it to the others). **Pumo nim kkey puthe māl-ssum tulye ya 'ci** You should tell your parents first.
~ **ka.** ¶**Apeci kkey (hanun cīs) puthe ka ku mo.yang ini** (or **kuleh.key pulqson hani**) **hyeng kkey ya ocik hakeyss.ni?** The way he treats his father, to begin with, how do you think he'll treat a mere older brother?!
kkey se, postn + pcl. ¶**Eti kkey se osyess.ci yo** Where did you come from?
kkey se, particle + particle.
1. from (an esteemed person). ¶**apeci ~ on phyēnci** (NKd 4234b) a letter that has come from Father. **apeci ~ pat.un tōn** the money that I got from Father. **Moksa nim kkey se ku māl ul tul.ess.ta** I heard that from the pastor.
2. marks a personal oblique (= honorific) subject. ¶**apeci ~ cwusin tōn** the money that Father gave me. **Moksa nim kkey se ku māl-ssum ul hasyess.^{s}up.nita** The pastor said that. **Sensayng nim kkey se cham mānh.un swūko lul hasyess.^{s}up.nita** You have gone to an awful lot of trouble for me. CF **ey se, (mata) puthe.** NOTE: Unlike the more usual subject marker (the nominative case particle **i/ka**), **kkey se** can be followed by focus particles (**un/nun, to, iya/ya**). The nominative particle has other functions, as in ··· **i toy-** 'become' (mutative complement) and ··· **i ani 'ta** 'is not ···' (negative-copula complement), for which **kkey se** is not used.
kkey se chelem, pcl + pcl + pcl. ¶**Emeni kkey se chelem na lul salang hanun sālam un ēps.ta** There is no one who loves me the way Mother does.

kkey se cocha, pcl + pcl + pcl. ¶**I cuum un hyeng nim kkey se cocha sosik i ēps.ta** Lately I haven't had a word even from my older brother.
kkey se ka, pcl + pcl + pcl. ¶**Onul un phyēnci nun apeci kkey se ka ani 'la acessi kkey se on kes ita** Today the mail was from Uncle, not Father. (?) **Hyeng nim kkey se ka** (or **kkey se puthe** or **kkey se puthe ka**) **kulen pōswu-cek in sayngkak ul kacisyess.nun tey apeci kkey se ya te māl hay mue l' hakeyss.^{s}up.nikka** Brother, YOU have such conservative opinions (to begin with), what point can there be in my talking to Father?
kkey se khenyeng, pcl + pcl + pcl. ¶**Apeci kkey se khenyeng hyeng nim hanthey se to phyēnci ka ēps.ta** There's been no letter even from my brother, much less from my father. **Wuli tam.im sensayng eykey apeci kkey se mōs kasimyen hyeng nim kkey se 'la to kaposye ya hakeyss.ey yo** If Father cannot go see my teacher then Brother at least will have to go.
kkey se kkaci, particle + particle + particle. ¶**Hyeng nim kkey se kkaci kuleh.key ce lul mit.ci anh.usip.nikka?** Even you distrust me so much, Brother?
kkey sekken, pcl + pcl = **kkey lang**
kkey se lang, pcl + pcl + pcl. ¶**Hyeng nim kkey se lang tā annyeng hasin ka?** How are your brother and his family?
kkey se 'la to, pcl + pcl + cop var inf + pcl. ¶**Hyeng nim kkey se 'la to phyēnci ka iss.umyen maum i noh.ikeyss.nun tey ...** I would feel relieved if there were a letter from Brother, at least, but (there isn't) ... .
kkey se mace, pcl + pcl + pcl. ¶**Hyeng nim kkey se mace ce lul tol.a posici anh.umyen nwukwu lul mit.ko sālkeyss.^{s}up.nikka** If even you won't take care of me, Brother, whom can I look to in this world?
kkey se man, pcl + pcl + pcl. ¶**Apeci kkey se man helak hasimyen na to Mikwuk kalq swu iss.ta** If only Father consents, I too will be able to go the States.
~ **to.** ¶**Kulenq īl ul tang hasin ke n' ape' nim kkey se man to ani 'p.nita** It wasn't just Father alone who underwent that.
~ **un.** ¶**Apeci kkey se man un helak ul an hasilq key 'ta** Father, at least, would not give you HIS permission.

kkey se mata, particle + particle + particle.
  1. (= **eykey se mata**). ¶**Yele sensayng nim kkey se mata phyēnci lul pat.e sōngkwu sulepki hān i ēps.ˢup.nita** I am overwhelmed beyond measure to receive letters from each of you gentlemen.
  2. (= **mata ka**). ¶**Yele sensayng nim kkey se mata phyēnci lul ssusye se sōngkwu sulepki hān i ēps.ˢup.nita** I am overwhelmed beyond measure that each of you gentlemen should write me a letter.

kkey se n', abbr < **kkey se nun**

kkey se 'na, pcl + pcl + cop advers. ¶**Hyeng nim kkey se 'na yōngq-ton ul cwusilq ka talun sālam un elim to ēps.ˢup.nita** Brother might sometimes give me spending money, but there's no way others will do so.

kkey se 'na-ma, pcl + pcl + cop extended adversative. ¶**Hyeng nim kkey se 'na-ma ce lul towa cwusye ya 'ci; kuleh.ci anh.umyen etteh.key salq swu ka iss.ˢup.nikka** You, at least, should help me, Brother, otherwise how can I get along? **Āmu to towa cwulq sālam i ēps.uni hyeng nim kkey se 'na-ma palalq swu pakk ey!** There's none who will help; what can I do but hope at least for something from you, Brother?

kkey se 'n tul, particle + particle + cop mod + postmod. ¶**Nam tul to ānunq īl ul hyeng nim kkey se 'n tul molusil lī ka iss.na?** Surely there is no good reason why my brother, of all people, should not know what others are well aware of.

kkey se nun, particle + particle + particle.
  1. as for from (an esteemed person). ¶**Eme' nim kkey se nun tōn ul pat.ess.ci man, ape' nim kkey se nun an pat.ess.ta** I got money from Mother but not from Father.
  2. as for (an esteemed person as subject). ¶**Hyeng nim kkey se nun etteh.key sayngkak hasip.nikka** What do YOU think, Brother?

kkey se pota, pcl + pcl + pcl. ¶**Emeni kkey se pota apeci kkey se te kippe hasilq kes ita** Father will be more delighted than Mother. **Eme' nim kkey se pota na lul te salang hay cwulq sālam un āmu to ēps.ˢup.nita** There is no one who loves me more than Mother does. **Hyeng nim kkey se pota apeci kkey se tōn ul pat.nun phyen i tēl mian hatula** I was less grateful receiving money from Father than from Big Brother.

kkey se puthe, pcl + pcl + pcl. ¶**Hyeng nim kkey se puthe kuleh.key sayngkak hasimyen toykeyss.ˢup.nikka** You, as my elder brother, shouldn't think that way, should you? **Hyeng nim kkey se puthe** (= **ulo puthe**) **on phyēnci 'ta** It is a letter come from Big Brother.
  ~ **ka** SEE **kkey se ka** for an example.

kkey se sekken, pcl + pcl + pcl = **kkey se lang**

kkey se to, particle + particle + particle.
  1. from (an esteemed person) also / even. ¶**Hyeng nim kkey se to phyēnci ka wass.e(y) yo** There was a letter from you, too.
  2. also / even (an esteemed person) [as the subject]. ¶**Hyeng nim kkey se to kath.i kasici yo** Why don't you come along with me? NOTE: When **to** follows a NON-honorific subject the particle **i/ka** is obligatorily suppressed, so that the phrase might be taken as object, since the accusative **ul/lul**, too, obligatorily drops before **to**. But **kkey se to** will not mark the object; there is no simple way to mark an object as honorific, other than choosing a specifically honorific noun as the object.

kkey se tul, pcl + pcl + pcl. ¶**Kath.un nal ey iptay hasin wuli tōngney apeci kkey se tul onul hyuka osinta 'nta** The fathers of our village who were conscripted on the same day will be back on holiday today.

kkey se wa, pcl + pcl + pcl. ¶**Hyeng nim kkey se wa apeci kkey se nun ēncey 'na ce lul mōs nan i lo sayngkak hasici yo** My brother and father always take me for a simpleton.

kkey se ya, pcl + pcl + pcl. ¶**Hyeng nim kkey se ya ce lul mit.usil they 'ci yo** I'm sure YOU trust me, Brother(, even if no others do).
  ~ **māl lo**. ¶**Hyeng nim kkey se ya māl lo cal-mos sayngkak hako kyēysip.nita** It is you who are wrong (in the way you think), Brother.

kkey to₁, postnoun + pcl. ¶**Cenkwuk ul tā tōlci nun mōs hayss.ci man Hamkyeng-to kkey to ka-poko Kyēngsang-to kkey to ka-pwass.ta** I was not able to tour the entire country, but I got to see the areas around Hamkyeng and Kyengsang provinces.

kkey to₂, particle + particle. also / even to (one esteemed).

kkey tul, pcl + pcl. ¶**Emeni kkey tul poyess.ta** They showed it to their mother(s). **Emeni tul kkey tul poyess.ta** They showed it to their mothers.

kkey uy, pcl + pcl. (the one) to / at / for / by (one esteemed). ¶**tāythong.lyeng ~ kongkayq-cang** an open letter to the President.

kkey ya, pcl + pcl. ¶**Apeci kkey nun mōlla to hyeng nim kkey ya māl-ssum ul tulye ya 'ci** You ought to talk to your brother at least, if not your father.

~ **māl lo.** ¶**Hyeng nim kkey ya māl lo allye ya 'ci** It is my brother that I should inform.

kkili, postn. ? < *kkuyli* < ˙*skuy˙l i* (1465 Wen 1:1:1:44b) 'those who shun / eschew it (= keep aloof)'.

1. the separate group of (like people); among (or between / by / to) ourselves / yourselves / themselves. ¶**Wuli nun wuli kkili kaca** Let's go separately (by ourselves). **Ce i tul kkili ssawunta** They quarrel among themselves. **Ai tul kkili (or ai kkili tul) nōnta** The children play among themselves. **Ai tul kkili (hako) nun cal nōnta** He plays nicely with the other children. **Pūca kkili cangsa hanta** Father and son are in business together (with no one else).

2. the separate group of (like-moving things); by themselves. ¶**So nun so kkili mointa** "Oxen keep to themselves" = Birds of a feather flock together. **pelley ~** the insects. **pakkuteyliya ~** the bacteria. **catong-cha (pihayng-ki) ~** the cars (planes).

3. [new?] with a separate group of like things. ¶**Cak.un namu nun cak.un namu kkili (lo) khun namu ka khun namu kkili sīm.ca** Let's plant the small trees with small trees and the big trees with big trees. **Chayk-sang un chayk-sang kkili han kwuntey noh.a la** Put the desks in one place together. CF CM 1:456: **tōl ~** stones, **molay ~** sand(s), ...

kkili kkili, adv (iterated postn). group by group, in separate groups, each group.

-kkis, suffix. SEE **-(k)kis.**

kko, pcl [LIVELY var] = **ko** (indirect quotation)

-kko [S Kyengsang DIAL (¹Na Cinsek 1977)] = **-lq ka**

kkol₁, n. 1. shape, form, appearance. ¶**Cham pyel kkol tā pokeyss.ta** What a mess (you've presented for me) to look at!! **Kkol com pwā la** Just look at you! SEE **cwucey ~** .

2. [pejorative] face, countenance, personal appearance. "mug", "pan". **kāy ~** a shameful face / appearance.

3. personal behavior, manner(ism), action, "business" (as with one's hands), "carrying on", the things one does. **māl hanun ~** one's manner of speaking.

kkol₂, n. pasture, forage; fodder.

kkol₃, postnoun. (priced) at the rate of ... each; per unit. ¶**Han kwēn ey chen wen kkol ita** The price is (at the rate of) a thousand wen per volume. CF **ssik, mata.**

-kkuley, suf (= **-kkey**). ¶**nolu-kk(ul)ey hata** is yellow-tinged.

-kkum, INTENSIVE < **-kum.** ¶**huy-kkum / hay-kkum hata** is rather white. ¶**hᵃ/ᵤl-(k)kum** leering (CF **hulkita** leers). SEE **-key-kkum.**

-kkun, suffix (makes adj-n, impressionistic adv). **cha-kkun** very cold, chilled. **tta-kkun** fairly hot. **may-/mi-kkun** smooth, slippery.

[< **-q kun;** CF **-kum, -kul, -kus.**]

kkus, n. marks, grade (= **~ swu, cemq-swu**).

-kkus, suffix. SEE **-(k)kus.**

kkuth, n. [VAR **kkuthu-** in **kkuthu-meli,** CF **kkuth(-)uleki.**]

1. an end, a tip, an extremity. CF **kkut-engi.**
2. the (tail) end, close, conclusion, finish.
3. the last, the tail end. CF **mak.**
4. a limit, a bound; limits, bounds. CF **hān.**
5. a bit, a touch, a dash: SEE **phul ~** .
6. (as postmod) the final consequence: SEE **-un ~ (ey).**

kkway, adverb. quite, fairly, pretty (much). ¶ **~ him tulta** is pretty hard. **~ khuta** is fairly large. **~ cal ilk.ta** reads quite well. [? < **kwā hi** < *[¨]kwa [˙]hi* < "*KWA ˙hi* excessively]

kkway 'na, kk'ay 'na, adv + cop adversative. fairly (well / much / many), to a fair extent (or so), rather. ¶**kongpu lul ~ hanta** studies fairly hard. **kwansang (ul) ~ ponta** reads one's face well. **khi ka ~ khuta ko ppekinta** boasts of one's height. **Pap swul kk'ay 'na "ttunta" ko myelqsi haci mala** Don't despise me for taking a goodly amount of food and wine (**ttunta** = **tulta** with expressive reinforcement). **Cengchi kk'ay 'na hanta ko yēnsel kk'ay na nul.ess.ta** He is doing quite a bit of politics, I understand, and his speeches have improved a lot.

(?*)**kkwu** = **kko** (LIVELY indirect quotation). This appears not to occur, probably because liveliness is associated with the light-isotope vowel /o/ as against the heavy-isotope vowel /wu/. But (**-ca**) **kkwuna** may have incorporated the form.

kkwulek → **(-q) kwulek**

kkwuleki, postn [? < -q kwulek + -i; ? < -q + kwū-l- + -ek.i; ? -q + abbr kwul.e tāyki]. a person who overdoes it; an overindulger; a glutton for ··· . ¶**yoksim** ~ a greedy person, a "hog". **cam** ~ a slugabed, a sleepyhead. **kep** ~ (= **kep-po**) a coward. **swul** ~ a tippler, a boozer, a heavy drinker. **na** ~ a person older than he looks (to be). **ttēy** ~ (= **ttēy cangi**) an insistent person, a nuisance. **māl-sseng** ~ (= **māl-ssengq kwun**) a troublemaker. **may** ~ a mischievous child. **simswul** ~ a cross / mean person. **akchak / ekchek** ~ a tough / hardheaded person; an unrelenting / indefatigable person. **āmsang** ~ a jealous person. **'yam-sim** ~ [< **sayam**] a mean and jealous person; a spiteful man / woman. **can-pyeng** ~ a hypochondriac. **chengsung** ~ a person with bad luck written on his face, a wretched-looking person, a sadsack. NOTE: Always spell with kk-. CF **kkwun = i-q kwun**.

kkwuleyki [var] = **kkwuleki**

kkwun (postn, postmod) SEE **-q kwun**

kkwuna, pcl. SEE **-ca** ~ . ? < **kwuna**; ? < -q + pcl kwu (CF -ca kwu) + pcl una / na.

kkwuna tul, pcl + pcl

ko₁, noun, adnoun. LIGHT [often pejorative] → **ku** (that). CF **yo, co**.

ko₂, pcl (? abbr < hako saying). VAR **kwu; kko**. SEE **-ta** ~ , **-la** ~ , **-ca** ~ ; **(-un) ya/ka** ~ .
1. (quote) that [added at the end of what is said / thought; optional if followed by a verb of saying / thinking]. ¶**Olh.ta ko sayngkak hanta** I think (that) it is right. **Ku nun na poko way wass.nun ya ko mul.ess.ta** He asked me why I had come. **Ku nun na poko ola ko hayss.ta** He told me to come. **Ku kes i mues in ya ko mul.ess.ta** He asked what it was. **Kath.i kaca ko hayss.ta** He suggested going (= that we go) together. **I kes ul mue 'la ko hasey yo** What do you call this? NOTE: The content may be said / thought by anyone, but it is reported as indirect (paraphrased). CF **hako, ila ko**.
2. (usually pronounced **kwu**). softens a plain suggestion / command. SEE **-ca ko, -la ko**.

ko₃ < ˙**kwo**, bnd n, postmod [colloq; poetic]. the (usually rhetorical, exclamatory, or quoted) question wh··· (BUT NOT whether ···). CF **ka**. SEE **-un / -nun / -tun / -ulq** ~ ; ˙**kwo**. SYN **yo**.

kō < ˙**KWO**, noun, adnoun, postmodifier.
1. noun, postmodifier. reason. SEE **ko lo**.
2. adnoun. ancient (= **yēys**).
3. adnoun. the late / deceased (= **cwuk.un**).

'ko, abbr < **iko,** < **hako**. CF ˙**'kwo,** ˙**khwo, kho**.

-ko < - ˙**kwo**, gerund. VAR **-kwu**.
1. 1a. (is or does) and also / too. CF **-umye**. ¶**pappuko phikon hata** is busy and tired. **pulk.ko khun kkoch** a huge red flower. **khuko talko kaps-ssan cham-oy** a melon that is big, sweet, and cheap. **kkaykkus hako ko.yo han kuliko palk.ko ttattus han cip** a house that is clean and quiet and that is bright and warm. **hel hako kkaykkus han hotheyl** a cheap clean hotel. **Pi ka oko palam i pūnta** It rains and the wind blows (too). **Hānkwuk un nam-puk i kīlko tong-se ka copta** Korea is long from north to south and narrow from east to west. **Atul nah.ko ttal nah.ko cal sal.ess.ta** And they lived happily ever after (giving birth to sons and daughters). **Mun tat.ko tul.e osipsio** Please close the door (as you come in). Please close the door behind you.

1aa. (is) and yet, and at the same time [often with opposites]. ¶**kiph.ko yath.un mul** waters that are both deep and shallow. **noph.ko nac.un pongwuli** peaks both high and low. **Kīlko ccalp.un kes un tāy(e) pwā ya ānta** You can't tell which is the longer unless you measure them. SEE **-ko kan ey**.

1b. [with negatives]. ¶**Na nun hak.kyo ey kaci anh.ko cip ey iss.keyss.ta** I am not going to school — I'm going to stay home(, instead).

1c. does or else (does). ¶**Īl i cal toyko calmos toyki nun tangsin uy nolyek yeha ey tallyess.ey yo** Whether the task is successful or not depends on the sort of efforts you put in. **Nal ul cal nāyko mōs nāynun tey se mikkun han cēyphum i na-onun ya kkechil kkechil han cēyphum i na-onun ya ka kyelqceng toynta** Proper exposure of the blade determines whether a smooth article or a rough article is produced.

1d. A is / does and (B is / does). ¶**Ku nun Mikwuk sālam iko na nun Hānkwuk sālam ita** He is an American and I am a Korean. **Ku nun khi ka khuko na nun khi ka cākta** He is tall and I am short. **Ku nun chayk ul ilk.ko na nun phyēnci lul ssunta** He is reading a book and I am writing a letter.

2. (= -ko se) (does) and then; doing and then. CF -umye. ¶mun ul yēlko son nim ul mac.ta opens the door and welcomes a visitor. mal ul thako kata goes (there) on horseback. ānkyeng ul ssuko pota looks at it with one's glasses on. os ul ipko meli lul pis.ta puts on one's clothes and combs one's hair. I chayk ul twuko ka yo I'll leave this book (and go). Yeki se halwuq-pam cako kalq swu iss.^{s}up.nikka? Can I stay here overnight (before going on)? Mek.ko wass.ta I ate before I came.

3. -ko iss.ta, ger + aux v sep (-ko [*ka/]lul/ man/nun/[*to/]tul/ya iss.ta); CF -e iss.ta.

3a. is doing. ¶kitaliko iss.ta is waiting. sayngkak hako iss.ta is thinking. Cikum ku kēnmul ul pak.mul-kwan ulo ssuko iss.ta They are using that building as a museum now. Ku hyengphyen ul cal ālko iss.ta I am well aware of his situation. Ecci 'na pappun ci phyēnci mōs hako iss.ta I've been so busy I haven't been able to write. NOTE: When the gerund is from a verb of carrying or wearing -ko iss.ta can be taken as either progressive ("is in the act of putting it on") or resultative-stative ("is wearing"): mulq tongi lul meli ey iko iss.ta is putting / carrying a water jug on her head, cim ul ciko iss.ta is putting / carrying a bundle on his back, cim ul mēyko iss.ta is shouldering a bundle / is carrying a bundle on her shoulders, moca lul ssuko iss.ta is putting on a hat / is wearing (has on) a hat. neykthai lul māyko iss.ta is putting on a necktie / is wearing (has on) a necktie, say os ul ipko iss.ess.ta was putting on / was wearing (had on) a new dress. Certain other verbs are similar: kāy lul capko iss.ta is catching the dog, has / keeps hold of the dog; nwun ul ttuko iss.ta is opening one's eyes, has/keeps one's eyes open; pul ul kkuko iss.ta is turning the lights off, has (or keeps) the lights off. With instantaneous actions the meaning is repetition of the action: kōng ul chiko/chako iss.ta is hitting/kicking a ball. (CF ^{1}Yi Kitong 1988:116-7.) The doffing of apparel is like the wearing of it: kwutwu lul pes.ko iss.ta will usually translate 'is taking off one's shoes' but it can also mean 'has one's shoes off; is (now) shoeless'.

3b. is / continues in a (changed) state; CF -e iss.ta. ¶pyēngwen ey ip.wen hako iss.ta is in the hospital. kako ēps.ta is gone.

3c. does it repeatedly (or habitually); they are doing it (separately).

3d. SEE -˙kuy 's˙kwo (wanting it to do/be), CF 5, 9; -ko ce < -˙kwo ˙cye, -ko cita.

NOTE 1: For the deictic verbs of motion the meaning can be either 3b or 3c, or it may be progressive (3a): Hānkwuk ey kako/oko iss.ta means 'is on one's way to Korea', 'visits Korea (repeatedly)', or 'they each go/come to Korea'.

NOTE 2: kyelhon hako iss.ta can only mean '(people) are getting married (every day)' or conceivably 'is in the midst of getting married (at this moment)', but (unlike the Japanese equivalent kekkon site iru) not 'is/are married', for which Korean uses the past form kyelhon hayss.ta.

NOTE 3: 'I am (in the midst of) staying at home' can be said as Cip ey iss.nun cwung ita but not as *Cip ey iss.ko iss.ta.

4. 4a. -ko nata just finishes doing – usually past (finished); CF nata. ¶pap ul mek.ko nass.ta has just finished eating / dinner. pāytal-pu ka ku tay lo cīna kako nan twī 'myen after the mailman has passed on by as usual [without leaving me anything]. Meychil cen ey alh.ko na se ip mas ul ilh.e pelyess.^{s}up.nita I just got over being sick a few days ago and I've completely lost my appetite. Kimchi lul mek.ko nani-kka n' ip an i ēl-ēl hata I've just eaten some kimchi and now my mouth is burning inside. Pic kaph.ko nan nameci lo cip ul sass.ta I have paid off the debt and bought a house with what was left. Silqcik ul hako nani poli pap ul mek.key mace to an toyney Having lost my job, matters are such that I can't even get boiled barley to eat. Mom i com kotan hay se swīko nass.tuni mom i kettun hata I was rather tired, but since I've had the nice rest I feel much better. Some reject this as final in a sentence: (?) Pap ul mek.ko nass.ta I have just finished eating; (?) Eti lul alh.ko nasyess.^{s}up.nikka Where were you ailing?

4aa. -ko namyen when / after one finishes. ¶Swuyong ul hako namyen pay ka kopha yo When I finish swimming, I feel hungry (M 1:2: 219).

4b. -ko mālta finishes up doing it, gets it done/completed; ends up doing, finally does it; does it anyway (despite reluctance, or after procrastination). SEE mālta. CF -ko ya mālta.

4c. = -ko [mālko] of course. ¶Kulem cēng-mal iko [mālko]! Yes, of course it's true!

5. -ko siph.ta, -ko siph.e hata wants to do(/be). ¶Kwūkyeng ul com te hako siph.ta I would like to do a bit more sightseeing. (Unusual with adjective: Alum-tapko siph.ta I want to be beautiful.) SEE -ko ka/lul/man/nun/to/tul/ya siph.ta.

NOTE 1: N ul/lul V-ko siph.ta can replace the accusative marker by the nominative (N i/ka V-ko siph.ta) but that is not possible for N ul/lul V-ko siphe hata. ¶Yenghwa lul/ka poko siph.ta I want to see a movie. Mues ul/i mek.ko siph.e? Do you want to eat something? Ku haksayng to yēyki lul com hay cwuko siphe haci anh.e yo? Doesn't that student (show indications that he might) want to tell us something, too?

NOTE 2: The negative is -ko siph.ci anh.ta (because siph.ta is an adjective) and -ko siph.e haci anh.nunta (because siph.e hanta is a verb). Kako siph.ci anh.ta for 'I don't want to go' is preferable to An kako siph.ta.

6. -ko tanita goes around doing, is always doing it. CF -e tanita (regular compounds). ¶ in.lyek-ke lul thako/mōlko tanita goes around in/pulling a ricksha. swul man mek.ko (tol.a) tanita goes around drinking all the time. cwumeni lul chako tanita goes around with/carrying a purse. kwūho mulqca lul ket(wu)ko tanita goes around collecting relief supplies. Ku nun sikol se chelem Sewul se to ciph sin ul sin.ko taninta He goes around in straw sandals in Seoul just as he did in the country. I pyēngsin mom i yōngki ka ēps.e cwukci mace mōs hako ileh.key kwukel ul hako tanip.nita This frail body lacking the courage even to die, here I am going around begging like this. Nam iya musun cīs ul hatun (ci), ne nun hangsang ponun twung mānun twung man hako tanimyen toynta You should go your way without paying attention to whatever others may be doing.

7. 7a. -ko (nun) hata does it sometimes/occasionally/habitually. ¶Yaksok han kes ul kuleh.key twī-nāyko hay se ya kath.i īl ul halq swu ka ēps.ta Since you seem to make a practice of never keeping your promises I can't do business with you at all. SEE -ko hani.

7b. -ko … -ko (… -ko) hanta does and does (and does). ¶Ilum molulq sāy tul i nac.un hanul ul nal.e kako nal.e oko hayss.ta Birds of unknown name flew back and forth low in the sky.

8. -ko pota (vt) does and then realizes (or considers the matter); CF -e pota. ¶Tut.ko poni … From what I heard(, I realize that …). Mek.ko poni kāy yess.ta After eating it I found out it was dog! (CF Mek.e poni mas i iss.tula When I tasted it, it was delicious.) Wusen mek.ko poca! Let's eat first and then worry about it (what it is; how to pay for it; …).

NOTE: Literal meanings also appear: ānkyeng ul ssuko pota looks at it with one's glasses on.

9. SEE -ko ce; -ko cita; -ko capta.

10. followed by the particles nun, to, se, ya; puthe; ka, lul; 'la to, … .

11. 11a. (with adj) X-ko X-un … which is ever so X. ¶kīlko kīn sēywel a long long time (CF kīna kīn iyaki a long long story).

11b. (with v) X-ko X-ta does further (still more). ¶kuliko kulin nay kōhyang my much-missed hometown. ilk.ko ilk.un ku phyēnci that letter which I read and read. Machim-nay … inmin uy ssah.iko ssah.in pulman kwa wēnhan un phokpal toyko ya mal.ess.ta The discontent and resentments of the people, which had kept accumulating (kept piling up and piling up) … finally burst out. Kitaliko kitalitun nal i wass.ta The long-awaited day has come. Sayngkak hako sayngkak halq swulok kōhyang un kako siph.un kos iess.ta The more I thought about it, the more (I knew) my hometown was the place I wanted to go.

12. (sentence-final or followed by yo). and … (in stating afterthoughts, and also sometimes in answering a question [Pak Sengwen 208-9]). ¶Phyo nun eti se sa yo — tto kaps un elma 'ko yo Where do we buy the tickets? And how much are they? Pipimq-pap un ili cwusey yo — [1]nāyngmyen un celi tuli(si)ko yo The fried rice here, waiter — and the cold noodles there, please. Ka (se) cwumusey yo — na ttaymun ey caci anh.ko kitalici māsiko yo Go to bed — don't wait up for me.

13. (as in 12, with emphatic intonation) does (you see)! ¶Tōn i iss.ko (yo)! I've got money! CF -ko mālko, -kwun (yo), -kwumen (yo).

? ko ay = ku ay (that person)

? ko ca = ku ca (that person)
 -ko ca, abbr. 1. [var] = -ko ce. ¶ ··· ila ko poko ca hanta We are inclined to regard them as ··· . 2. = -ko ce ha.ye (= -ulye). ¶Na to kongpu hako ca Sewul (ey) wass.ta I too have come to Seoul to study.
 ko˙cang (< *ko˙co 'edge' + -ang), n, adv. CF s ko˙cang. 1. end; extremity. 2. (= kacang) most; extremely.
 -ko capta [DIAL] = -ko siph.ta. ¶Poko cap.a se wass.ta I've come to see. Aikwu, mek.ko cap.a la Oh I'm so hungry!
 -ko cap.i [DIAL] one who wants (or is ready) to do. **mek.ko cap.i** one who is always hungry, a chow hound. **wūlko cap.i** a crybaby. **sālko cap.i** one obsessed with achieving a luxurious life. **poko cap.i** one who has to see everything. **hako cap.i** one who wants to do everything.
 ko ccum, n + pcl. SEE **ku ccum**.
 -ko ccum, ger + pcl. ¶Mek.ko ccum kanun ke ya kwaynchanh.ci man (ūmsik ul) kaciko kanun ke n' an toyp.nita It's all right just to eat and go but you shouldn't go taking food along with you (to eat).
 -ko ce (< -˙kwo ˙cye), ger + c(y)e abbr < cie (inf < cita). [lit] wanting to; ready/prepared/willing to; intending to, going to. ¶Sewul kako ce hanta I want to go to Seoul (or: I am going to Seoul). Tāyhak ey ip.hak hako ce hanta I am going to enter a university. "Pom minali sal-(c)cin mas ul nim eykey tuliko ce" I wish to offer my beloved the fat (= rich) taste of spring parsley. SYN -ulye; CF -ko siph.ta.
? ko chi = ku chi (that guy)
 -ko cita, ger + aux adj insep [lit = -ko siph.ta] wishes / wants / desires to. ¶Sālko ciko, sālko ciko, chen-nyen mān-nyen sālko ciko Long live, long live — live for thousands, for tens-of-thousands of years! Kako ciko kako cita, wuli cip ey kako cita I wanna go, I wanna go, I wanna go home! CF **-ko ce**, **-e ciita**, **-ulq cieta**.
 -ko cocha, ger + pcl [a bit awkward]. ¶Kicha lul thako cocha melmi lul hanta = Kicha ey se cocha melmi lul hanta I get motion-sick even on a train. Cha ey se nayliko (naylye kaciko) cocha melmi lul hanta Even after I have left the car I'm still sick.
 -ko hani, ger + sequential < hata. considering that. ¶Yo say nal-ssi to cōh.ko hani han pen nōlle osipsio Since the weather is fine these days and all, please come visit us. Icey col.ep to hako chwīcik to hako hayss.uni kyelhon hanun kes i etten ya Now that you've finished school and found a job, what about getting married? SEE **-ko 7a**; **-ko hay se**.
 -ko hata SEE **-ko 7a**
 ko hay se, pcl + inf + pcl. saying that ··· , on the ground(s) that ··· , with the excuse that ··· . ¶Ku i nun ¹noymul ul mek.ess.ta ko hay se silqcik ul tang hayss.ta He got fired on the ground that he had taken a bribe. Nay ka acik elita ko hay se ku kukcang ey mōs kakey hayss.ta He wouldn't let me go to the show, claiming that I was too young. Yaksok han kes ul kuleh.key twī-nāyko hay se ya etteh.key kath.i īl ul halq swu ka iss.⁵o Since you never even keep your promises, how can I do any business with you? (Kuleh.ta ko hay se) māl-sseng i sayngkikey ya an toykeyss.ci yo? (In that case) it wouldn't give rise to any trouble, would it? SEE **-ta ko hata**.
 -ko hay se, ger + v inf + pcl – preceded by (··· to) ··· to. ¶Kipun to cōh.ko nal-ssi to cōh.ko hay se sānqpo hayss.ta (M 3:3:196) Both mood and weather favored a walk. Kinkup hi māl-ssum tulilq īl to iss.ko hay se chac.e wass.ta I also came to talk to you about an urgent matter (M 3:3:205). SEE **-ko 7a**.
? ko i = ku i (that person)
 -ko iss.ta SEE **-ko 3**.
 -ko ka, gerund + particle. 1. (as subject). ¶Kako an kako ka wusen kyelqceng toye ya hap.nita It must first be decided whether we are going or not. 2. (as complement of negative cop). ¶Ōythwu lul ipko ka ani 'la kēlchiko kala 'n māl iyo Don't put your overcoat on, wear it over your shoulders! 3. (with auxiliary). ¶Mul i mek.ko ka siph.ta 'p.nita (Let me tell you) he has a powerful thirst for water! CF **-ko lul**.
 -ko kan ey, ger + n + pcl. ¶Pap iko ppang iko kan ey com cwusipsio Rice or bread, I don't care, just give me something to eat (M 3:3:81). mānh.ko cēk.ko kan ey neither many nor few.
 -ko kata, ger + vi. 1. goes (away) doing, does and goes (there). ¶I kes ul kaciko kasio Take this with you. Ne nun i taum ey teyliko kam a I will take you next time. Tulko katolok ssa cwusipsio Wrap them up so that I can carry

them. **Cacen-ke lul thako kalq ka yo, kel.e kalq ka yo** Shall we ride our bikes or walk? 2. does before going, does and then goes (away); (**an ~**) goes / leaves without doing; comes and does [an errand before returning there]. ¶**Na nun īwang on pa ey manna poko kakeyss.ta** As long as I am here, I might as well see him before I leave. **Pap i nuc.ca (= nuc.uni-kka) an mek.ko kass.ta** The meal was late so I left without eating.
CF **-ko ota, -e kata.**

ko kes SEE **ku kes**

-ko khenyeng, gerund + particle. ¶**Pihayng-ki lul thako khenyeng kicha lo to an olq key 'ta** Take a plane? – why, (he is such a miser) he probably won't even come by train.

koki, noun, adverb. LIGHT → **keki** (there).

-ko kkaci, gerund + pcl. ¶**Pihayng-ki lul thako kkaci ol lī ka ēps.ci** I see no reason for him (to be so extravagant as) to take a plane.

~ 'la to. ¶**Kup hako cwūng hanq īl ila 'myen pihayng-ki lul thako kkaci 'la to ka ya 'ci yo** If it's urgent and important we'll have to go by plane, I guess.

~ nun. ¶**Kup haci nun anh.uni pihayng-ki lul thako kkaci nun ol phil.yo ka ēps.ta** As it isn't urgent there is no need to come by plane.

ko kkaci lo, LIGHT → **ku kkaci lo**, n + pcl + pcl. to that trifling extent.

ko-kkacis, LIGHT → **ku-kkacis**, cpd adn (n + bound particle). that kind / sort of … , such a … [usually pejorative]; so trifling (trivial, slight, little, small, worthless, poor).

kol(q) < *ko[˙lo]l(q), prosp mod < *ko[l]˙ta*
˙*kol(q) < *˙ko[˙lo]l(q)*, prosp mod < *˙ko[l]˙ta*

-ko l', abbr < **-ko lul**

-ko 'la to, gerund + copula var inf + pcl. ¶**Tōn mounun ke n' twūl ccay chiko 'la to, wusen saynghwal ey kekceng ina ēps.ess.umyen cōh.keyss.ˢo** Even if accumulating money is put in second place, it would be nice to have no worries about livelihood.

kole, LIGHT [pejorative] → **kule**. CF **yole**, **cole**.
1. vni (**~ hanta = kolenta**) does/says that/so.
2. adj-n (**~ hata = koleh.ta**) is that way, is so.

koleh.ta, adj -(H)- (inf **kolay**), abbr < **kole hata**.
koleta, vi (inf **kolay**), abbr < **kole hata**.
kol˙Gwa < kol˙Wa, inf < *¨kolp˙ta* (line up).
SEE *-˙ᵘ⁄ol s ~*.
koli, adverb. LIGHT → **kuli**.

1. (**= koleh.key, ko-taci**) like that, so.
2. (**= ~ lo**) that way / direction, there.

kol-lo = ko kes ulo. CF **kel-lo**.
kol' lo, abbr < **koli lo** (to there). **~ kata** dies, passes on / away.

kolm < *ko˙l[o]m, subst < *ko[l]˙ta* (changes).
˙*kolm < *˙ko˙l[o]m*, subst < ˙*ko[l]˙ta* (grinds).

ko lo, noun + particle [literary].
1. (as adv) **= kulem ulo** (and so, therefore).
2. (as postmod) **= kkatalk ulo** (for the reason that). SEE **-nun ~ , -un ~**.

kolo, adv [var] **= kolwu** evenly **= kol(wu) kolwu**

-ko lul, ger + pcl. (Used to emphasize -ko + aux.) ¶**Āmu kes to peliko lul siph.ci anh.uni yātan ip.nita** The trouble is I don't want to get rid of anything.

(-)kolye → **(-)kwulye**

(-)kom < -˙kwom, particle, suffix.
1. particle [obs; Cenla DIAL] **= ssik** (each).
2. suffix [var, obs] **= -kum**. CF **-kkum**.

-ko mace, ger + pcl [awkward?]. ¶(?) **Icey pangkum mek.ko mace tto tālla 'ni?** Having just eaten you still are asking for more?! **Moca lul ssuko mace chac.nunta** He pays a call without taking his hat off. **Totwuk cil ul hako mace an hayss.ta ko hani?** You stole and yet you deny it?!

'ko mālko, abbr < **iko mālko**, < **hako mālko**.

-ko mālko, ger + ger < **mālta**. it is needless to say that … , there is no doubt about it that … , it is a matter of course that … . **~ yo** SAME [POLITE]. ¶**Kako mālko (yo)** Of course I will go. **Wiin iko mālko yēpu ka iss.na?** He is, without doubt, a great man. **Kiek hako mālko yo** Of course I remember. NOTE: The **mālko** is sometimes ellipted. SYN **-ta mālta**.

-ko mālta SEE **mālta**
komam-ttay = kumam-ttay
ko man₁, pcl + pcl. just / only (saying/thinking) that … . ¶**Chwupta ko man mālko com na-ka nol.a la** Don't keep on complaining about the cold, just go on out and play. **Cal-mos han key ku sālam ppun ila ko man halq swu ya ēps.ci** You certainly can't say that he's the only one to blame. **Ku nun caki ka olh.ta ko man hanta** He maintains that he is right.

ko man₂, cpd adv / n (< n + pcl) **= ku man**
-ko man, gerund + particle. only doing/being.
~ iss.ta (aux). ¶**Cam cako man iss.ta** He does nothing but sleep.

~ siph.ta (aux). ¶Kŏhyang ey tol.a kako man siph.ta All I want to do is return to my home town.
(-)koman → (-)kwumen
ko-man, adnoun. LIGHT ↔ ku-man.
ko-mas, bnd adn. LIGHT ↔ ku-mas (so much, such a, just, only).
(-)kom(y)en → (-)kwumen
(-)kon → (-)kwun (apperceptive)
kon < **ko[ˊlo]n*, mod < *ko[l]ˋta* (changes).
ˋ*kon* < *ˋ*ko[ˊlo]n*, mod < ˋ*ko[l]ˋta* (grinds).
ko n', pcl + abbr pcl = ko nun
ko 'n('), abbr < ko han(un)
-ko n', abbr < -ko nun. CF -ˋ*kwo n'*.
-ko 'n('), abbr < -ko han(un)
ko 'na, pcl + cop advers. (saying) just that ⋯ , or the like. ¶Kongpu lul /ˋna cal hanta ko 'na halq ka yo Let's just say he's working hard.
(-)kona → (-)kwuna
-ko 'na, ger + cop adversative. ¶Sicang han tey wusen mek.ko 'na polq īl ita We're hungry; let's just go ahead and eat, and then see.
-ko nata SEE -ko
kong < KWONG, postnoun. 1. (an honorific title that follows a surname, a penname, or a posthumous name). 2. Duke ⋯ .
? ko nom = ku nom (that guy)
-ko 'n tul, ger + cop mod + postmod. ¶Cēng kup hamyen pihayng-ki thako 'n tul mōs olq key mwe 'n ya If he is really in such a hurry is there any reason he can't come by plane?
ko nun, pcl + pcl. as for (saying / thinking) that ⋯ . ¶Hay pokeyss.ta ko nun māl hayss.ci man com kekceng i toynun ke l' I said I would try doing it, but now I feel a bit worried. Olh.ta ko nun halq swu ēps.ta I can't say he's right. Ku ka cēng-mal kulen cal-mos ul cecilless.ta ko nun mit.e cici anh.nun tey I find it difficult to believe he really committed such a blunder.
ko 'nun, abbr < -ko hanun
-ko 'nun, abbr < -ko hanun
-ko nun < (?)-ˋ*kwo* ˋ*non* (= -ˋ*kwo n'*), ger + pcl.
1. as for doing / being. ¶Ku kes i olh.ko kuluko nun sayngkak haki ey ttale se talle cilq swu iss.ta Whether that is right or wrong can well differ with how one thinks about it. Tāycep ul pat.ko mōs pat.ko nun cey ka hal nalum / thas ita The reception one gets depends on what one does.

2. when ⋯ , ⋯ then, upon doing (emphasizes the consequence). ¶Tut.ko nun kasum i senul hayss.ta When I heard that, I felt a cold fear pass through me. ⋯-ci anh.ko nun an toylq kes ita it wouldn't do not to = has (got) to. Na lul peliko nun kaci mōs hao I will not let you go leaving me behind.
3. ~ hata makes a habit / practice (a regular thing) of doing it; does it from time to time, sometimes does; DOES do, (+ NEG) never does.
~ hayss.ta used to do, did do, would do. ¶sānqpo kako nun hanta sometimes goes for walks, goes for walks now and then. Kongwen ey ka se nōlko nun hayss.ta We used to go to the park and play. Pata ey se heyem chiko nun hayss.ta We would swim in the ocean (from time to time).
4. (+ aux). ¶Kako nun siph.ci man (= kako siph.ki nun haci man) mōs kakeyss.ta I WANT to go, all right, but I can't. Hako nun iss.ci man ēncey kkuth nalq ci molukeyss.ta I am doing it, all right, but I don't know when I will get it finished. Poko nun ka to kaciko nun kaci māsey yo Look at it before you go but don't take it with you.
SEE chiko nun, hako nun, kaciko nun, -e kaciko nun.
ko-nyang, adv = ku-nyang
(-)konye, [? DIAL] = (-)kwumen. CF Dupont 78.
-ko ota, ger + vi. 1. comes (here) doing, does and comes (here). ¶I sangca uy pīmil ul al.e kaciko wass.ta I have come with a knowledge of the secret of this box. Elma 'na toynun ci iss.nun kkes kaciko wā pwā la However much there may be, bring all there is. Tōn ul pēl.e kaciko wass.ta He came with all the money he had made. Pi ka okeyss.ki ey / lo wūsan ul kaciko wass.ta Expecting rain, I brought my umbrella.
2. does before coming, does and then comes (here); (an ~) comes / leaves (for here) without doing; [errands] goes and does (before coming back here). ¶ Cāngkap ul eti ey 'n ka twuko wass.ˢup.nita I must have left my gloves somewhere. Cēmsim ul mek.una māna hako wass.tuni pay ka pelsse kophuta Having picked at my lunch (having eaten hardly any lunch) I am now very hungry. Sewul kass.tun cha (= kīm) ey tōngmul-wen kkaci poko wass.ta I took advantage of the trip to Seoul to

see the zoo, too. **Mues in ci sa kaciko wass.ta** She's gone and bought something or other. **Sangcem ey kass.tuni sakwa ka ēps.e kyul man sa kaciko wass.ta** When I went to the store they were out of apples so I just bought oranges. **Iss.na ēps.na lul poko wā la** Go see if he's in or not. **Ku sālam ul cikcep manna poci (/ poki) kkaci nun mōs hayss.una sosik un cal tut.ko wass.ta** I wasn't able actually to see him in person but I heard lots about him (while I was there).

-ko 'phe, abbr < -ko siph.e

-ko 'phuci, abbr < -ko siphuci = -ko siph.ci

-ko 'phul(q), abbr < -ko siph.ul(q)

-ko 'phum, abbr < -ko siph.um

-ko 'phun, abbr < -ko siph.un

-ko 'phuna, abbr < -ko siph.una; < -ko siphuna = -ko siph.na.

-ko 'phuney, abbr < -ko siphuney = -ko siph.ney

-ko 'phuni, abbr < -ko siph.uni; < -ko siphuni = -ko siph.ni.

-ko 'phuta, abbr < -ko siphuta = -ko siph.ta.

-ko poni SEE -ko (8.)

-ko pota₁, ger + pcl. ¶**Pihayng-ki lul thako pota kicha lul thako kanun key nās.ci** I guess we better to go by train rather than by plane.

-ko pota₂, gerund + verb. SEE -ko (8.)

-ko puthe, ger + pcl. (ever) since doing. ¶**Ku nun ku hak.kyo ey ip.hak hako puthe cwulkot wutung ul hayss.ta** He has been a straight honor student ever since he entered the school. **Na nun wūntong ul hako puthe pap mas i cōh.a cyess.ta** My appetite has improved since I started getting myself some exercise. **Ku lul mannako puthe cakkwu kōhyang sayngkak i nanta** Since meeting him I find myself getting homesick.

~ nun. ¶**Ku sālam i cāngkwan i toyko puthe nun tomuci mannalq swu ka ēps.ta** Ever since he became a cabinet minister it is impossible to see him.

~ se. ¶**Ile han sāhoy hyēnsang un ku hyek.myeng i il.e nako puthe se 'ta** Social phenomena of this sort started appearing with that revolution.

kos, 1. < ˙*kwot*, quasi-free n. a place, a spot, a point. ¶**i ~ this place (= yeki). i kos ce kos** here and there, this place and that. CF **kos kos, kos.kos-i** place after place; **tey.**

2. bnd n. a drill, an awl: **pa-~, song-~**.

3. → **kot**. 4. [mistake] → **kes**.

¨*kos* < *ko˙zo* < **ko˙co* (SEE *s ko˙cang*, **kkeci** = **kkaci**). brink, edge.

-ko sa, ger + pcl. 1. [DIAL] = -ko ya.

2. [? DIAL, mistake] = -ko se.

kosa hako < KWO-¨SA *ho˙kwo*, ger < defective vn (usually preceded by **N un** or **-ki nun**). apart from, let alone, setting aside, to say nothing of, not to speak of, not to mention; far from being / doing; much less. ¶**Chinkwu tul un kosa hako hyengcey tul to oci anh.ess.ta** Even his brothers did not come, to say nothing of his friends. **Nal-ssi nun kosa hako puncwu hay se kaci mōs hakeyss.ta** Aside from the weather, I am too busy to go, anyway. **Tōn ul pēlki nun kosa hako sōnhay man pwass.ta** Far from making money, he found himself with nothing but losses. **Sālam i oki nun kosa hako phyēnci cocha oci anh.ess.ta** Not even a letter came, much less a person. CF **khenyeng**.

ko sai / say. adn + n. LIGHT → **ku sai / say**.

-ko se < -˙*kwo ˙sye*, ger + pcl. (does) and then; doing and then. ¶**Tangsin ul mit.ko se wass.ˢo** I have come counting on your help. **Ciphayngi lul ciph.ko se kel.e taninta** He walks around leaning on a stick. According to M 2:2:12 the subject must be the same for the two clauses, though simple -ko is not so restricted. But when another particle follows (as in -ko se nun) the subjects sometimes differ.

The addition of se makes the relationship to the following predicate more immediate: -ko 'and (then)' could be used with a long interval between the two predicates, but -ko se 'and then (next)' could not.

-ko se ka, gerund + pcl + pcl. ¶**Cikum un kwaynchanh.ci man cēncayng i kkuth-nako se ka mūncey 'ta** The present doesn't matter, but (the period) right after the war is over is a problem. **Achimq pap ul mek.ko se ka ani 'la sikcen ey hala 'n māl ita** I mean do it before eating, not after you've had your breakfast.

-ko se 'la to, gerund + pcl + cop var inf + pcl. ¶**Kulen kosayng ul hako se 'la to sengkong man hamyen kwaynchanh.ta** If only I am successful, I will not mind having all that hardship. **Ne lul yeuyko se 'la to sālq swu man iss.ess.umyen cōh.keyss.ta man** I wish I could live without you (but I can't).

A Reference Grammar of Korean

-ko se man, ger + pcl + pcl. ¶**Kuleh.key (na lul) poko se man iss.ulq key ani 'la com kētul.e cwukey** Don't just stand there and look at me, give me a hand! **Ney ūymu lul tā hako se man (i) nam eykey to kwen.li lul cwucang halq swu iss.nun ke ya** Just fulfill all your obligations and you can demand your rights of others.

-ko se n', abbr < -ko se nun

-ko se 'na, ger + pcl + cop adversative. ¶**Īl uy kānungq-seng ul chwungpun hi poko se 'na māl halq ka, kulech'anh.umyen ip ul an ttēynun sālam ita** He is a person who will speak only after he has looked carefully at the possibility of a matter, otherwise he keeps his mouth shut. **Pay ka kophun tey wusen (pap ul) mek.ko se 'na polq īl ita** We're hungry — the thing to do is just go ahead and eat and then see (what happens).

-ko se nun, gerund + pcl + pcl. does and THEN (emphasizing the consequence).

   1. ¶**Ku ke l' kulay kaciko se nun āmu ccak ey to mōs ssukey toynta** If you treat it like that it will get so it's not worth a thing.

   2. ¶**Pap ul silkhes mek.ko se nun cikum an mek.ess.ta 'ney?** Having eaten till it's coming out your ears you now say you haven't eaten?!

   3. ¶**Hak.kyo ka sīcak toyko se nun yenghwa kwūkyeng han pen to mōs kass.ta** Since the beginning of school began I haven't been to a single movie.

   4. **-ci anh.ko se nun an toylq kes ita** it just wouldn't do not to = has just got to. ¶¹**Notong sayngsan nung.lyul ul ollici anh.ko se nun kwaep ul talqseng halq swu ēps.ˢup.nita** Unless we raise the productivity, we will be unable to fulfill our task.

-ko se puthe, gerund + pcl + pcl. ¶**Ku yak ul mek.ko se puthe acwu mom i cōh.a cyess.ta** From the time I started taking that medicine I have gotten much better.

-ko se to, ger + pcl + pcl. does and even then; even when. ¶**Yenphil ul hana ssik cwuko se to yepun i iss.ta** Even if you give each one a pencil, there will still be some left over. **Na lul poko (= pwā noh.ko) se to an pon chey hanta** He saw me, all right, but he pretends not to have seen me. **Cim ul ciko se to (= ciko iss.umyen se to) cal ttwinta** He jumps quite well even bearing a burden.

-ko se tul, ger + pcl + pcl. ¶**Son ul ssis.ko se tul pap ul mek.e la** You kids wash your hands before you eat.

-ko se 'tun ci, gerund + pcl + cop retr mod + postmod. ¶**Onulq pam cenyek ul mek.ko se 'tun ci kuleh.ci anh.umyen ¹nayil achim itun ci chac.e osio** Come and see us after dinner tonight, or else tomorrow morning.

-ko se ya, gerund + pcl + pcl. ¶**Kuleh.key īl ul mānh.i hako se ya etteh.key kyentye nāynta 'm** How can you (stand it to) do so damn many things?! **Ku uy kongcek un ku ka cwuk.ko se ya piloso ālkey toyess.ta** His achievements first became known only after he was dead. **Ku ka ku īl ul ālko se ya** (= ālko iss.umyen se ya) **ecci molunta ko hakeyss.na?** How can he say he doesn't even know that when he knows it perfectly well!

-ko siph.ta SEE **-ko**

kot₁, adv [? < **kot.ta**]. CF **kot-cal/-cang;** `kwos.

   1. (= **palo**) at once, straightway, straight off, immediately, directly, instantly, in an instant; in a moment, in no time (at all), right away, forthwith; before long, shortly; on the spot, then and there. ¶**Cip ulo kot kake la** Go home at once (Go right home). **Cikum kot kanta** I am coming in a moment; I'll be right there. **Ku cali ey se kot tāytap hayss.ta** I answered on the spot (without a moment's hesitation). **Sewul kaketun kot phyēnci hay la** Write to me as soon as you get to Seoul. **Incey kot tol.a olq kes ita** He will be right back. **Incey kot ōceng ita** It's almost noon.

   2. easily, readily, straight off, "right off the bat", "at the drop of a hat", at the least little thing, the least little thing and ... . ¶**Yuli kulus un kot kkāy cinta** Glassware breaks easily. **I kil lo kamyen kot ku cip ul chac.ulq swu iss.ta** Going this way, you will find the house right off. **Ku nun cokom hamyen kot sēng ul nāynta** He gets mad at the drop of a hat (He is readily offended). **Cokom hamyen kot kāmki ey kellinta** The least little thing and down I come with a cold.

NOTE: Sometimes attached directly to the preceding word, as if a particle (but perhaps this is kot₃): **hay kot cimyen** (?= **hay ka kot cimyen;** ?= **hay man cimyen**) as soon as the sun sets. **Ne kot pomyen** (?= **ne lul kot pomyen;** ?= **ne man pomyen**) **kipputula** I was happy as soon as I saw you.

kot₂, adv [? < kos]. (is) the same as, (is) no other than, (is) the very, (is) indeed, namely, by name, that is, to wit, viz., i.e., as it were. ¶**Sewul i kot Kyengseng ita** Seoul is (the same as) Kyengseng. **Twū atul i iss.ess.nun tey Yengsik-i Hyengsik-i kot ku tul ita** He had two sons, namely, Yengsik-i and Hyengsik-i. **I kos i kot kuy ka calan kos ita** This is the very place where he grew up. SYN **cuk**.

kot₃ < ˙kwos, pcl [? semi-lit; ? DIAL] = **man** (just): **kaki kot hamyen** = **kaki man hamyen** if one just go; **ālki kot hamyen** = **ālki man hamyen** if one just know.

⋯ ˙kot, pcl, adj-n (> ˙koth- adj). like.

1. pcl. ¶**ha˙nol s ˙˙pye˙l i ˙˙nwun ˙kot ti˙n i '-ngi ˙˙ta** (1445 ¹Yong 50) the stars of heaven fell like snow. CHYEY-˙KWEN towoyzo˙Wa ha˙nol ˙kot syem˙ki˙zopta˙n i (1449 Kok 140) having become a wife to him she looked after him like heaven. TTIN-SA ˙non hal ˙s i.n i TTIN ˙kot SA ˙kot ˙˙ta s ˙˙ma.l ila (1482 Kum-sam 2:15b) TTIN-SA is a word that means there are so many that it is like dust, like sand.

2. adj-n. ⋯ ˙kot °ho˙ta is like ⋯ .

¶ ˙kot ho˙kwo n' (1463 Pep 6:15b); ˙kot ho˙na (1462 ¹Nung 2:89b).

˙kot ˙ho˙ya (1447 Sek 9:4b, 23:11b; [1447 →]1562 Sek 3:17a; 1459 Wel 1:53a, 18:26b, 21:129b; 1462 ¹Nung 3:42b, 10:1b; ?1468- Mong 43a; 1485 Kwan 4b); ˙kot ˙ho.ya (1482 Nam 2:63a, 1482 Kum-sam 2:10a); ˙ko.t hoy˙ya (1579 Kwikam 1:21b) = ˙kot ho(y)˙ya.

˙ko˙t hi like, as if (1459 Wel 2:53a; 1462 ¹Nung 2:25a; 1465 Wen 2:3:1:37b, 2:3:2:7b) = ˙kot ˙hi (1465 Wen 2:3:1:38b); ˙ko.t hi (1463 Pep 4:117a, 1482 Nam 2:63b, 1482 Kum-sam 5:14a).

˙kot hon ⋯ (1459 Wel 17:12b, 21:129a); ˙kot ho˙n i (1445 ¹Yong 6, 1459 Wel se:11a), ~ ˙˙la (1462 ¹Nung 4:111a, 1482 Kum-sam 2:3a), ~ ˙la (1465 Wen 2:3:1:38b); ˙i ˙kot hon ˙t ol (1459 Wel 17:33b) though it was like this.

˙i ˙kot ho˙m ye n' (1463/4 Yeng 2:70a) if it is like this. HE-KHWONG ˙kot ˙hwom ˙two pwo˙m ye (1447 Sek 13:23b) sees indeed that it is like a void, and ⋯ .

3. ˙kot[h]˙ta, adj. ¶ ˙kot˙key (1447 Sek 6:1b) = ˙kot ˙˙key, ˙kot˙ta (1449 Kok 131) = ˙kot ˙˙ta, ˙kot.ta˙la (1481 Twusi 25:51a) = ˙kot ˙ta˙la,

˙kot˙te-ngi ˙˙ta (1459 Wel 9:36d) = ˙kot ˙˙te-ngi ˙˙ta, ˙kot˙ti (1459 Wel 17:12b) = ˙kot ˙˙ti, ˙kothosi˙kuy (1447 Sek 6:4a) = ˙kot hosi˙kuy.

NOTE: LCT's examples of ˙koth- (3) do not seem decisive; they could be taken as ˙ko.t [°ho]-, as we have treated them here. Only an example such as ?*˙ko˙tha (inf) = ˙kot ˙ho˙ya would be clearly an adjective rather than an adjectival noun. Even ˙kotco˙wo˙n i (1463 Pep 2:227a), ˙kot ˙copno˙n i ˙˙la (1462 ¹Nung 2: 45a), and ˙kotco˙wo.l i ˙l ˙˙ss oy (1463 Pep 5: 195b) could be explained as a result of surface assimilation after ˙ko.t [°ho]zo⋯ got contracted, and that appears to be historically correct, but our apostrophe notation would not be able to indicate that abbreviation and also preserve the surface consonants, so we write those as part of the stem ˙koth-. For the similar development of another adjective stem, see ˙˙man °ho˙ta > ˙˙man˙tha = mānh.ta.

-ko tanita SEE **-ko** (6)

ko to, pcl + pcl. (quote) that ⋯ also/even/either. ¶**Etten sālam tul un ku yenghwa ka cal tōyss.ta ko to hako etten sālam tul un cal an tōyss.ta ko to hanta** Some say that the movie is good, while others say that it is not. **Cōh.un sayngkak ila ko to halq swu iss.ci man com pi-hyēnsilq-cek in kes kath.ey** It may be a good idea but it seems to be a bit impractical.

-ko to < -˙kwo ˙two, ger + pcl.

1. 1a. both ⋯ and. ¶**Kang mul i malk.ko to kiph.ta** (CM 2:179) The river water is both clear and deep. **I kes i ssako to cōh.ta** This one is (both) cheaper and better.

1b. and yet, but, while/though. ¶**Ku nun kulenq īl ul hako to peces hayss.ta** He did it, and yet with a clear conscience. **Pap ul tā mek.ko to pap thwuceng ul hanta** You have finished all your rice and yet you are crying for more. **Ālko to molunun chey hap.nita** He pretends not to know though he does know. **Tut.ko to mōs tul.un chey hayss.ta** He heard perfectly well but pretended not to have heard.

2. sometimes ⋯ sometimes. ¶**Etten ttay n' kel.e to kako, etten ttay n' thako to kanta** (or: ⋯ **kēt.ki to hako** ⋯ **thako to kanta**) Sometimes I walk and sometimes I ride. **Na nun ku īl ul tōn ul pat.ko to hako an pat.ko to hanta** Sometimes I do that for money, and sometimes without taking money.

3. (with auxiliaries).
ko ttawi = ku ttawi
-ko tul, ger + pcl. ¶Kulem, caymi iss.key nōlko tul one la Well have a good time, all of you!
~ iss.ta (aux). ¶Cal nōlko tul iss.ta They are all enjoying themselves.
~ siph.ta (aux). ¶Kako tul siph.un ka Do you kids want to go?
ko tul, pcl + pcl. severally (saying/thinking) that … . ¶Tā kanta ko tul kulay yo They say that they are all going.
ko 'tun ci, particle + cop retr mod + postmod. ¶Cōh.ta ko 'tun ci kwuc.ta ko 'tun ci māl ul hay ya ālq key ani yo? You'll have to say one way or the other, or how will we know? ¶Ola ko 'tun ci hay ya oci, etteh.key nay ka mili ālko onta 'm! I'll come only if you tell me to; how can you expect me to know to come unless you tell me to come?!
-ko 'tun ci, gerund + cop retr mod + postmod. ¶Pihayng-ki lul thako 'tun ci kicha lul thako 'tun ci āmu'h.tun kakeyss.ta I'll get there somehow, whether on a plane or on a train.
-ˈkoy (uncommon variant) = -ˈkey, adverbative. ¶anco ˈsya ˈwo ˈs i como ˈkoy ¨wu ˈlusi ˈkwo nilu ˈsya ˈtoy … (1459 Wel 8:101a) he sat down and, letting his clothes settle, said in tears (as follows: …).
-ˈkoy-ˈkwom (suf). ¶a ˈto ˈl i a ˈp[i] oy ˈna.h ay ˈsye kwop ˈkoy-ˈkwom sa ˈla (1459 Wel 1:47b) the son lives to be double his father's age and … .
ko ya, abbr pcl + pcl. only if saying/thinking that … . ¶Palam i com pūlki n' haci man chwupta ko ya halq swu ēps.ci It IS a bit windy, all right, but still you can't say it is COLD.
'ko ya = iko ya (copula gerund + particle)
-ko ya < -ˈkwo ˈza, gerund + particle.
1. (usually followed by a rhetorical question) considering that … , when we just take into account … , with … . ¶Kuleh.key tōn ul hēyphi ssuko ya etteh.key tōn mouki lul palanta 'm! The way you throw your money around, how can you expect to accumulate money?! Cēngsin i kule hako ya toynunq īl i iss.keyss.na?! What can you get done in that frame of mind?! Ileh.key pi ka oko ya ecci kkoch i philq swu iss.keyss.na?! With such heavy rain, how ever will the flowers manage to bloom? Kuleko ya sengkong halq swu iss.na?! The way you act,
how can you expect to succeed?! Selma kaciko ya (= kaciko iss.umyen se ya) an kacyess.ta ko kulekeyss.ni? Surely he is not going to tell us he doesn't have it when he obviously does have it?! I ccum man ila to hay noh.ko ya khun soli lul halq swu iss.ci You have to do at least this much to have anything to brag about!
2. (followed by aux vi mālta). SEE mālta (3).
2a. does it all the way (= really does it); simply has (got) to do it. ¶hako ya mānun sālam a person who simply must do it (or who really goes at it). Ku i ka kongpu hanta ko hamyen kkok kkuth kkaci hako ya mānta When he studies he goes all out (at his work). Kkuth kkaci ssawuko ya mālkeyss.ta I've just got to (= I am determined to) fight it out. Kie-i hako ya mālkeyss.ta I will do it come what may. Kil.e to mokcek-ci kkaci nun kkok kako ya mālkeyss.ta I must get to my destination, however long the journey.
2b. ends in doing, finally does, ends/winds up by doing. ¶Ku i to machim-nay chong ulo casal hako ya mal.ess.ta He wound up by shooting himself, too. Machim-nay … inmin uy ssah.iko ssah.in pulman kwa wēnhan un phokpal toyko ya mal.ess.ta The discontent and resentments of the people, which had kept accumulating (piling up and piling up) … finally burst out. Pi ka kie-i oko ya mal.ess.ta It finally got around to raining. (CF Ku.yey pi ka oko mal.ess.ta It WOULD end up raining!)
3. (followed by aux vi paykita) must do it, can't stand not doing it, insists on doing it. ¶Chelqswu nun hako siph.un kes un hako ya paykinta What Chelsswu wants to do, he wants to do!
4. (with other auxiliaries). ¶Kako ya siph.ci man … cham pappe yo I do want to go, but … I am very busy (M 1:2:131).
SEE chiko ya, hako ya, kaciko ya, -e kaciko ya; -ˈkwo ˈza.
ko yo, pcl + pcl (polite quotation). -ta ~ .
'ko yo = iko yo (copula gerund + particle)
-ko yo, gerund + particle. SEE -ko 12.
-koy ya [var] = -ko ya
…k¨sop- < …k-¨zop-
k¨swon-ˈtoy < *s¨swon-ˈtoy (to a person)
ku < ku, adn, n. LIGHT ko. CF i, ce. ku + ˈu ˈlan → kul ˈlan, ku + ˈu ˈlwo → kul ˈlwo
1. adnoun. 1a. that, those; the former; the.

¶*ku swo`li* (1463 Pep 3:115b) those sounds. *ku ci[p]s `sto`l i* (1447 Sek 6:14a) the daughter of that house. *ku twoco`k i* (1459 Wel 1:6b) that thief. *`icey `CYENG `hi ku SSI-`CYELQ `ilwo`ta* (1447 Sek 13:60b) now is exactly that time. *`ku KUY-`PYELQ `ul* (1447 Sek 24:16a) that message. *ku `a`ki* (1459 Wel 8:101b) the lad. *ku namwo s pwul`hwuy `lol `spay`hhye* (1447 Sek 6:30b) uprooted the tree and .... *ku LYWONG `ol ca`pa `pcu`ce me`ke`nul* (1447 Sek 6:32a) it grabs the dragon, tears it up and eats it, whereupon ... . *ku mwol`Gay `sto`n i-ngi s `ka* (1464 Kumkang 62b) they are innumerable, but how much more so is the sand?! *`ku ¨ha`m ol* (1463 Pep 5:100a) [seeing] the multitude.

1b. of him/her/them; of it. ¶*ku `PEP `i* (1459 Wel 2:49a) his Law. *ku ¨PWON-LOY s il`hwu`m un* (1463 Pep 2:222b) his original name. *ku mozo[`]m ay mas`key thi`Gwuy* (1465 Wen 2:3:1:102a) it pleases him but ... . *ku `SWU `lul* (1463 Pep 3:86a) their number. *ku ¨CYENG `ul* (1588 Mayng 13:1b) its correctness. *ku YWEN `i* (1463 Pep 4:75a) its causality. *ku ¨HHWUW `ey `za* (1459 Wel 1:42b, 44b) only after that. *ku `psk uy mozo`m ay `na y ne`kywo`toy* (1463 Pep 2:23a) at that time my feeling was that ... . *ku TYWUNG `ey i`sye* (1463 Pep 5:212b) is in their midst and ... . *ku ka`won-`toy* (1459 Wel 2:51b) among them.

2. noun. 2a. that (one), it; (= ku i) that person, he/she, that one/thing, it. ¶*ku me`kun ¨HHWUW `ey `za* (1459 Wel 1:43b) (only) after he had eaten. *ku `casi`m ye ¨kyesya`m ol* (1475 Nay 1:44a) that he is sleeping.

2b. that amount or (order in) time. ¶**Tases ul tulilq ka yo?** – **Ku nun nemu mānh.so** Shall I give you five? – That's too many. **Sumul han pen ccay 'p.nita** – **Ku nun nemu nuc.un tey** It's the 21st (one). – That's too late! **Na nun ku pota hwelssin te olay tōy yo** It has been much longer than that for me.

ku-amuli, abbr < ku ka āmuli (···). however (···) it/he may be.

ku ay, adn + n. 1. that child.

2. [FRIENDLY] that person/fellow/guy/girl; he/him, she/her. CF **ku ca/chi/ēlun/i/kes/ nom/pun/sālam/son**.

ku ca, adn + quasi-free n. [pejorative] that person/fellow/guy/girl. CF **ku ay/chi/ēlun/ i/kes/nom/pun/sālam/son**.

ku ccok, cpd n (adnoun + quasi-free noun).
1. that side/direction; your side.
2. your party; you.

ku ccum, noun + particle.
1. that much, that quantity/degree; such a caliber. ¶ **Ku ccum un mūncey ka ani ya** To that extent (If that's all) there's no problem.
2. (somewhere) around there. ¶**I kes un ku ccum ey 'ta noh.a la** Leave that somewhere there (where you are).

kuce, adv. CF **kece**.
1. still, without ceasing/stopping, with no letup, with no halt; [+ v] keeps on doing. ¶**Kuce pi ka onta** It keeps on raining. **Kuce chayk ul ilk.ko iss.ta** He is still reading.
2. recklessly, immoderately, intemperately, heedlessly, throwing caution to the winds, wildly, blindly, at random. ¶**kuce mak' pic ul cita** goes into debt recklessly. **kuce cakkwu ttwutulita** hits wildly; beats a person blind.
3. so-so, all right (but not terribly good). ¶**Yenghwa ka caymi iss.ess.nun ka?** – **Kuce kuleh.tula** Was the movie interesting? – It was so-so.
4. please, I beg you. ¶**Kuce sallye cwusio** Please save me. **Kuce ney ka cham.e la** Won't you be patient, please.
5. there! (just as I expected); my my! ¶**Nay kuce kulelq cwul al.ess.ta** – **Congsi chaq-can ul kkay ttulye noh.ass.kwun a** There – I told you so (I just knew you'd do it): you have ended up breaking the cup. **Kuce** – **yo ke l'** My my, what's this [good or bad]. **Hey heyq** – **kuce!** Oh my (goodness)! [bad].
6. (= kece 1). without doing anything (in particular); without bringing anything; without giving any reason; with nothing (in hand/ mind); just because (one wants to), arbitrarily. ¶**Kuce anc.e iss.ta** He just sits there doing nothing. **Chayk ul heka ēps.i kuce kacye kass.ta** He took the book without permission. **Āmu māl to anh.ko kuce kass.ta** He went away without saying anything.
7. (= kece 2, kong ulo) without paying anything, gratis, free (of charge), gratuitously, for nothing. ¶**Kuce et.ess.ta** I got it free.

ku cen, adn + n. before that (time), previous/ prior to that time; former times/days; sometime before.

~ ey formerly, in former times, before, in days gone by; before that time, previous to that. ¶**Ku cen ey tol.a one la** Come back before that time. **Ku cen ey nun yeki cip i iss.ess.ta** Formerly a house stood here. **Ku cen ey pillye kass.tun chayk ul tollye wass.ta** He has returned a book he borrowed a while back.

~ **kath.i** as before, as of old, as usual, heretofore. ¶**Nulk.uni(-kka) him i ku cen kath.ci anh.kwun** Being old my strength isn't up to what it once was.

~ **kath.umyen** if it were (like). ¶**Ku cen (= yēys nal) kath.umyen ku-nyang an twuess.ulq key 'ta** If it were the old days I wouldn't have let you get away with it.

ku cenq pen, adnoun + noun + noun. the time before that / last.

kucey, noun, abbr < **kucekkey** (the day before yesterday).

ku cey = **ku cek ey** (at that time); = **ku cek** (that time).

ku cey 'na (= **ku cek ina**). ¶**Ney ka emeni ka toymyen ku cey 'na ālq swu iss.ulq key 'ta** You will know what it is to be a mother when you become one.

ku cey sa, ku cey se ya [DIAL] = **ku cey ya**

ku cey ya < *ku cey (y)a* < *ku cey ˙[z]a*, adn + n/adv (= **cek** time) + pcl. only then; not until; at that ... for the first time; only when / after. ¶**Sēy pen koham ul ciluni ku cey ya nāy 'ta pwass.ta** I called him three times and only then did he look out the window. **Nay māl ul tut.ko ku cey ya caki ka cal-mos han kes ul al.ess.ta** I had to point it out to him before he realized he had made a mistake.

ku'cey = **ku'h.cey**

ku cey ˙za, adn + adv / n + pcl. only then (1447 Sek 6:21a, 24:52b).

ku chay lo just as it is, with no change; without doing anything. CF **ku tay lo**.

ku chelem, n + pcl. like that (= **ku kath.i**).

kuchi = **ku'h.ci**, abbr < **kuleh.ci**

ku chi, adnoun + quasi-free n. [pejorative] that person (man / woman), he / him, she / her. CF **ku ay / ca / ēlun / i / kes / nom / pun / sālam / son**.

ku cuum / cum, adnoun + quasi-free n. about that time.

ku elma 'na. how very much. ¶**Ku elma 'na wēnthong hayss.ulq ka** How resentful he felt!

ku ēlun, adn + n ('that adult' =) that person, he / him, she / her (more honorific than **ku pun**). CF **ku ay / ca / chi / i / kes / nom / pun / sālam / son**.

ku ey < (?*)*ku ˙ey*, n + pcl. to that. SEE **i ey**.

ku eykey, n + pcl. to that (person). SEE **i eykey**.

ku ey se, n + pcl + pcl. from that. SEE **i ey se**.

ku'h.cey [DIAL] ? = **kuleh.key**, ? = **kuleh.ci** (yo)

ku'h.ci, abbr < **kuleh.ci**. ~ **man**.

ku'h.key, abbr < **kuleh.key**

ku'h.tolok SEE **ku'tholok**

ku i, adn + n. that person; he / him, she / her. ABBR **kuy, ku**. CF **ku ay / ca / chi / ēlun / kes / nom / pun / sālam / son**.

ku i l', abbr < **ku i lul**

ku i n', abbr < **ku i nun**

ku i tul, adn + n + postn. those people; they / them.

ku kath.i /kukachi/, cpd adv (n + der adv).
  1. like that, in that way, so. CF **kuleh.key**.
  2. (= **ku kath.i**) like that person (him / her).

ku ke ('n, n', ke l', kel-lo = ke lo), abbr < **ku kes (in, un, ul, ulo)**

ku kes < *ku kes*, adnoun + noun.
  1. that (thing), it. ¶**Ku kes un cōh.ta** That is good. **Ku kes ul kaciko kakeyss.ta** I will bring it with me. *ku kes ¨spwun* (1466 Kup 2:63a) that alone.
  2. [pejorative] that person, he / him, she / her.

ku key, abbr = **ku kes i**

kukha- [DIAL] abbr < **kuleh.key ha-** (say that)

kukhay(-) [DIAL] abbr < **kuleh.key hay(-)** say that (way), say so

kukhey = **ku'h.key**, abbr < **kuleh.key**

ku kkaci lo, noun + pcl + pcl. to that trifling extent. LIGHT **ko kkaci lo**.

ku-kkacis, cpd adn (n + bnd pcl). that kind of, such a [usually pejorative]; so trifling (trivial, slight, little, small, worthless, poor). ¶**Ku-kkacis kes un āmu 'la to halq swu iss.keyss.⁵o** Everyone can do that kind of thing. ABBR **kkācis, ku-kkās**. LIGHT **ko-kkacis**. CF **i- / ce-kkacis**.

ku-kkān (nom, -q īl, ...) = ku-kkās, abbr < **ku-kkacis**

ku kos, adn + n. that place, there. LIGHT **ko kos**.

-kul, suf (forms impressionistic adv). (s)sayng- / (p)payng-kul smiling. (t)tong- / (t)twung-kul round. CF **-(k)kus, -kuley** (= **-kul-ey**).

ku l', abbr < **ku lul**

kulay₁, inf < **kuleta** vni, < **kuleh.ta** adj.
  1. doing / saying / thinking that (way); being that way.
  2. [INTIMATE]:
    2a. does/says/thinks that (way); is that way. **kulay pōy / poye to** may not look it but; despite appearance(s). ¶**Simsang chi ka anh.e se kulay yo** There's something amiss and that's why (I'm worried). **Ku sālam i kulay kaciko ya etteh.key mit.ulq swu ka iss.keyss.ni** How can one trust him when he is the way he is? **I ¹nok.um-ki n' acwu mukepci man yenu kes un an kulay** This tape recorder is heavy, but most others aren't that way. **Chwupta 'nun i tēpta 'nun i hako pulphyeng hanun kes un kosayng ul mōs hay pwā se kulay** The way he keeps complaining about how cold it is, how hot it is, you can tell that he's never known hardships. **An kulay yo?** Don't you think so? (Don't you agree?)
    2b. (= **kulen ya**) does one do/say/think?, is it? ¶**Tōn ila 'n iss.ta ka to ēps.ta ka to hanun pep ici mwe l' kulay** Why worry about money; you can get by with or without it. **Way kulay** Why do you do / say that?; [rhetorical] Why do you ask (me)?! (= Of course!).
    2c. (= **kulay la**) do that! SEE **-ci** 2d. ¶**Kulem ese mekci tul kulay** Why don't you all start eating? **Poktong-i lang ila to nōlci kulay** You can play with Poktong-i at least, can't you?!
    2d. (= **kuleca**) let's do that!
    2e. **-un tey / kwun ~** and that's a fact; and that's all there is to it = it is for sure! **-nun tey / kwun ~** does it indeed!
  3. (= ~ **se**) does / says / thinks that and (so); is that way and (so) = for that reason, on that account, (and) so, therefore, accordingly. ¶**Cip ul na-sul ttay nun pi ka olq kes kath.ess.ta; kulay yangsan ul kaciko wass.ta** It looked like rain when I left home; so I brought an umbrella with me. **Eceyq cenyek un nuc.key kkaci caci anh.ess.ta; kulay cikum mopsi cōllinta** I stayed up late last night, and so I am now very sleepy.

kulay₂, interj (< **kulay₁**).
  1. yes, all right, OK (to equal or inferior).
  2. what?!; well!! (introduces a question with implications of sarcasm, blame, disgust, etc.). ¶**Kulay eccayss.ta 'n māl iyo** So what? What is it to you? **Kulay tangsin i eccel the iyo** Well, what are you going to do about it? **I key kulay musun kkol in ka** Well, what is THIS mess?! **I nom a, ku kes ul mōlla** What − you don't know THAT?!

kulay se, inf + pcl. does / says that and (so); is that way and (so) = for that reason, on that account, (and) so, therefore, accordingly, then.

kulay to, inf + pcl. even if one does / says that, does / says but; even if it is that way, is but = but, and yet, nonetheless, nevertheless, still, however. ¶**Kulay to ku kes i ēps.nun kes pota nās.ta** Still it is better than nothing. **Yenge lul ssek cal haci nun mōs haci man, kulay to kkway hanta** He is not able to speak English extremely well, still he speaks it fairly well. **Kulay to īl un cal hay; hanta hanun cāngceng i wā to mōs ttalukeyss.tun ke l'** Nevertheless he works well; any other able-bodied young man wouldn't be able to keep up with him!

kulay ya, inf + pcl. only if one does / says that; only if it is that way = only so, unless so. ¶**Pantusi kulay ya man toynta** It has to be that way.

kule < *ku'le*, defective infinitive. like that, so. LIGHT **kole**. CF **ile, cele, āmule, ette**.
  1. vni. ~ **hanta** = **kulenta** does that (way); does so.
  2. adj-n. ~ **hata** = **kuleh.ta** is that way; is so / such; is right, true. ¶**Kule hata − ney māl i mac.ess.ta** Yes, it is true − you are right. **Ku kes un kule hata** Yes, it is so.

kule, bnd inf. pulling, tugging; raking; holding, clutching. ~ **nāyta, neh.ta, tām.ta, tangkita, tul.ita, mouta, ān.ta, capta, cwīta**. [< var of **kkul.e** 'pull']

kuleca, indic attent < **kuleta**.
  1. let's do that. ¶**Kulem kuleca** Well / Yes, let's do it!
  2. then, thereupon, immediately, no sooner did that happen than … . ¶**Namphyen i kuleca anʰay ka tampak hwā lul nāyss.ta** No sooner did he do that than his wife flared up (= got angry).

kulec'anh.e to, abbr < **kuleci anh.e to**. even without this / that, even without one's doing / saying something, even without one's being so and so, nevertheless, in spite of this; already, even so, on top of (in addition to) everything else, as if this/that were not enough, moreover, in addition. ¶**Kulec'anh.e to han pen kakkai mannass.umyen hatun kil/chām iyo** (Quite independently of this encounter) I was hoping to see you once face to face. **Kulec'anh.e to phikon han tey tto han sikan īl ul te hala 'nta** I am already tired, and still he tells me to work an hour longer. **Kulec'anh.e to cēnhwa kellye hayss.nun tey** Actually, I was about to call you. **Kulec'anh.e to miwun tey tto tōn ul kkwue tālla ko hayss.ta** To be all the more hateful, he asked me to lend him some money.

kuleca 'ni, abbr < **kuleca (ko) hani**. ¶**Ileca 'ni ku nom i maum ey kkiiko, kuleca 'ni ce nom hanthey an tōyss.kwu** ... If I do this I offend the one guy and if I do that I offend the other (− I just can't please anyone)!

kulech'anh.e to → **kulec'anh.e to**

kulech'anh.umyen → **kuleh.c(i) anh.umyen**

kuleci, suspective < **kuleta**. ¶~ **anh.umyen** if one doesn't do/say that.

kuleh.ci, suspective < **kuleh.ta**. ABBR **kuh'ci**.

kuleh.c(i) anh.umyen or else, otherwise, if not

Kuleh.ci man (un), adj suspective + pcl. But ... ; However, ... ¶**Kuleh.ci man un ney kyēyhoyk ey chānseng halq swu ēps.ta** I cannot approve of your plan, however.

kuleh.k' 'a-, abbr < **kuleh.key ha-** (say that). INF **kuleh.k' 'ay**.

kuleh.key, adj adverbative < **kuleh.ta**. that way, like that, so; to that extent, that much.
 ~ **to** (pcl). ¶**Kuleh.key to cal hana!** He does it so very well!
 ~ **ya** (pcl). ¶**Kuleh.key ya hayss.keyss.na!** You couldn't have done it that way!

ku˙le ˚ho˙ta, adj-n. is like that, is so. ¶˙SYE-KUY ˙non ku˙le ho˙kuy s ˙kwo ˙po˙lanwo˙la ˙honwon ˙ptu.t i˙la (1447 Sek se:6a) [the word] ˙SYE-KUY ('almost') means we hope for it to be so. ˙KWU-LA ˙TYEY CIN-˙SSILQ ˙lwo ku˙le the˙n ye a˙ni the˙n ywo (1459 Wel 9:36d) was the emperor Kwula really as I said or wasn't he? SYWUY- ˙HUY KWONG ˙two ku˙le ho˙kwo n' NGWEN-TTI KWONG ˙ol a˙lalq t ilwo˙ta (1459 Wel 17:54a) achieving the sharing of the joy of others, how much more you will know of an all-embracing achievement of merit!
 ¶**pwu¨thye y ku˙le a˙ni ˙hosi˙n i ¨ep˙susi˙n i ˙˙la** (1465 Wen 1:1:2:125b) it never happens

that Buddha is not like that (= Buddha is always like that). **ku˙le a˙ni ˙˙l ye ko˙cang e˙lye˙wu.n i ˙˙la** (?1517⁻ Pak 1:57b) it is just terribly hard.

kuleh.ta, adj -(H)- (inf **kulay**) = **kule hata**. is that way; is so; is right, true.

kuleh-tus ('i). so very much. ¶**Kuleh-tus ('i) koptun elkwul i nulk.ess.ta** The once so very pretty face got old.

kulek celek, cpd adv. this way and that (way), one way or another, somehow (or other), by hook or by crook; in the meantime, meanwhile, already. ¶**Kulek celek sal.e kanta** I manage to get along, one way or another. **Kulek celek īl ul kkuth-nāyss.ta** Somehow I got the job done. **Kulek celek hanun kes ēps.i halwu ka cīna kass.ta** The day has been wasted on this and that (getting nothing accomplished). **Kulek celek cip ey tol.a kalq sikan i tōyss.ta** It is already time for me to go home.
 ~ **hata**, vnt. does it somehow (or other), manages (to do) in some way. ¶**Īl ul kulek celek hay kako iss.ta** I am managing to do the work somehow or other. **kulek celek hay se** = **kulek celek**.
SYN **kule kule** [? < **kuleko celeko**].

kulekey, adverbative < **kuleta**

kulekhey, 1. → **kuleh.key**.
 2. [DIAL] = **kulekhay** → **kuleh.k' 'ay**.

kuleki, abbr < **kule haki**. doing/saying that.
 ~ **ey**. ¶**Kuleki ey sālam uy īl un molunta 'ni** So you never know what will happen to you in life. **Kuleki ey sālam un sakwie pwā ya hanta 'ni!** I tell you you have to get to know him before you realize what he's really like!
 ~ **ey māl ici**. ¶**Onul ku sālam ani yess.tula 'myen wuli phyen i cilq pen hayss.ci?!** − **Kulek(i) ey māl ici!** I bet our team would nearly have lost today if it hadn't been for him. − You're absolutely right, I agree. **Māl [haci] anh.ulye 'ta ney ka kulek(i) ey māl ici onul cham asul asul hayss.ess.e** I didn't want to say anything, but now that you mention it today [the game] was really a cliffhanger.

kulekkey, n. year before last.

kule kule, adv. somehow (or other), in one way or another; bit by bit, little by little, gradually; in the meantime, meanwhile, already. ¶**Īl i kule kule tā tōyss.ta** Somehow or other the work got finished. SYN **kulek celek**.

kule kule hata, adj-n. is neither good nor bad, is middling, is so-so, is indifferent; is neither better nor worse, is about the same. ¶**Ku uy si to motwu ~** His poems are none too good, either. **I cuum kipun i etten ka ‒ Kuce kule kule halq sey** How are you these days? ‒ I feel only so-so.
kule kwule [DIAL] = **kule kule**
kulel(q), prospective modifier:
  1. < **kuleh.ta** adj: (which is) to be like that.
  2. < **kuleta** vi: (which is) to do / say or be done / said like that.
ku˙le 'l(q), abbr < *ku˙le hol(q)*. (to be) such ⋯ , ⋯ like that. ¶*ku˙le 'l 'ss oy* (1447 Sek 19:10b) therefore.
kulelq say SEE **-ulq say**
kulelq sey SEE **-ulq sey [῾la (ko)]**
kulelq si SEE **-ulq si**
kulel ssa hata, prosp mod + adj-n. [NK spells **kulel sa = kulelq sa**.] is plausible, is / seems likely (to be so), is OK (decent, acceptable, not bad). ¶**Ku ka ssata ῾ni na to kulel ssa hata** [or ⋯ **na eykey to kulel ssa hata** or ⋯ **na to kulel ssa hakey yekye cinta**] He says it is cheap and I think so too. **Nay ka ne lul miwe hanta ko sayngkak hanun kes un ney ka kuce kulel ssa hay se kulenun kes ita** It is just imagination that you should think I hate you.
kulel ssay = kulelq say [obs] therefore.
kulelssey = kulelq sey   **kulelssi = kulelq si**
kulelq swulok ey [colloq] = **kulelq swulok**
kulelq tus hata, adj-n. is plausible.
kulel wu hata, prosp mod + adj-n. (it) seems to be that way; is indifferent, so-so (CF **kule-kule hata**). ¶**Nay sānun ke ya kuce kulel wu haci mwe** I'm just living along, that's all.
kulem, 1. subst < **kuleh.ta**, < **kuleta**.
  2. adv (abbr < **kulemyen**). if that is so, if that is the case, if that is true / right, then, well (then). ¶**Kulem kaca** Then, let's go; OK, let's go. **Kulem ku ka cal-mos ita** If that is the case, he is to blame.
  3. interj (< subst). yes, indeed; that's true / right. ¶**Kulem, kuleh.ko mālko** Yes, of course that is true. **Kulem, ku nun cham-mal khun pūca ῾ta** Yes, indeed, he is a very rich man.
kulem ulo, subst + pcl. since it is so; since one does / says = therefore, so, for that reason.
kulemun [DIAL] = **kulemyen**; = **kulem**. ¶**~ kuleh.ci**. SEE **-umun**.

ku˙le 'm ye n', abbr < *ku˙le ho˙m ye n'*. then; if/when it is so (like that). (1588 Mayng 14:6a.)
kulemyen, conditional < **kuleh.ta**, < **kuleta**.
  1. (< **kuleh.ta**) if so, in that case, then, if / when it is like that; well then. ¶**Wuyu nun sohwa ka cal an toynun tey yo ... ‒ Kulemyen talun kel-lo sikhic' yo** (Im Hopin 1987:183). I have trouble digesting milk, you know ‒ In that case, order something else. **Son nim i osyess.^{s}up.nita ‒ Kulemyen tul.ye ponay cwusey yo** Guests have arrived ‒ Then, show them in.
  2. (< **kuleta**) if that happens, if you do that, if one does (or says) that / so, in that case, then. ¶**Kulemyen nwu ka musewe halq cwul ānun ya** Do you think I will be afraid if you do that?
kulemyen kuleh.ci, conditional + suspective < **kuleh.ta**. 1. Oh I see. Quite so. True enough. So that's it.
  3. Well, all RIGHT! Well, it's about time! THAT's the way! That-a-boy ('atta-boy)! That's what I mean! NOW you've / he's got it! (Shows satisfaction at the successful outcome of a temporarily frustrating situation.)
  4. I told you so! I thought so! See what I mean? (Said when a situation after all turns out the way a person had expected or intended, despite contrary indications along the way.) ¶**Kulemyen kuleh.ci ney ka nay māl ul tut.ci anh.e toykeyss.nun ya** THAT's a good boy ‒ it wouldn't do not to obey me now, would it. **Kulemyen kuleh.ci cip ey se onul to phyēnci ka ēps.ul lī ka iss.na** Well, it's about time! There just HAD to be a letter from home today.
kulemyen se, conditional < **kuleta** + pcl. in doing or saying so, when / while one is doing or saying that. ¶**I inhyeng ul ^{n}yeca chinkwu ka cwuess.^{s}up.nita. Kulemyen se sayngil ul chwuk.ha hanta ko hayss.^{s}up.nita** (Im Hopin 1987:185) A girl friend gave me this doll. In doing so, she congratulated me on my birthday.
kulen$_1$, adj mod < **kuleh.ta**. like that, such, that sort of. **~ ko lo** for that reason, therefore. **~ tus mān tus** barely, slightly, hardly. **~ yang ulo** in that manner; (= **~ chay lo**) in its own way, by / of itself. **~ cuk** therefore, so, accordingly; thereupon, then, consequently.
kulen$_2$, vi mod < **kuleta**. which / who has done / said or been done / said that way (like that).

kulen₃, interj. oh dear! goodness! oh my! what a surprise! indeed! well well! my my! (shows sudden realization, surprise). CF **ilen₃**, **celen₃**.

ku˙le 'n, abbr < **ku˙le hon**. such ..., ... of that sort. ~ ˙*t olwo* (1475 Nay 3:62a) therefore.

ku˙le ' ˙na, abbr < **ku˙le ho˙na**. but, even so, however. ¶*ku˙le ' ˙na ˙YAK ˙ol ˙cwue˙nul mek˙t ol ˙sul˙hi ne˙ki˙n i* (1459 Wel 17:20a) but when we gave them medicine they did not want to take it. ALSO: 1447 Sek 9:10b, 1459 Wel 17:34b, ...

kulena, adv, conjunction (advers < **kuleta**, < **kuleh.ta**). but, however. ¶**Kulena ce ccum puthe nun swiwun taymok ita** But from about there is the easiest part. **Yūmyeng han hakca 'la ko hapsita; kulena tā ālkeyss.na yo?** I grant you he is a famous scholar; but does he know everything? **Cōh.ta ko hapsita; kulena nemu cōh.a haci māsey yo** I grant you it is nice; but don't get too fond of it.

kulena celena, adv (< adversatives). ~ (**kan ey**) this way or that, anyway, at any rate.

kuleng celeng, adv, adj-n = **kulek celek**

kuleng-seng celeng-seng, adv. this and that, something of other; this way and that (way), somehow or other. ¶**Keki kwan hay se nun kuleng-seng celeng-seng māl i mānh.ta** There is a lot of talk about that. (People are saying this and that on that topic; you hear all sorts of things about that.) **Kuleng-seng celeng-seng ūykyen i mānh.ta** There are many different opinions. (Opinions are divided.)

~ **hata**, adj-n. (views) are divided/divergent. ¶**Kuleng-seng celeng-seng han ūykyen i mānh.ta** There are many different opinions. (Opinions are divided.)

? < *kulen-seng celen-seng; SEE **seng**.

kuleni(-kka), (extended) sequential < **kule(h.)ta**

1. therefore, then, so, consequently. ¶**Kuleni caney cocha 'na(-ma) com towa cwukey** Then you, too, help out a little bit. **Kuleni-kka tul kekceng ici yo** That is why we are bothered. **I kimchi nun maywe yo. Kuleni-kka cokum ssik capswusey yo** (Im Hopin 1987:184) This kimchi is quite hot, so eat it a little at a time.

2. [usually extended] what I mean is ... , I mean (to say) ... [to avoid a misunderstanding].

kulen tey, adj mod + postmod (ABBR **ku'n tey**).

1. such a place / situation; a place like that, a place where one did / said / is that. ¶**Kwun.in ie posey yo eti kulen tey l' kalq swu iss.na?** If you were a soldier, you wouldn't be able to go such places!

2. = ~ (**ey**) in such a situation; (is/does/says that) and / but; such being the case; by the way; ~ **to** despite that, nevertheless. ¶**Kulen tey eti ey kyēysey yo** By the way, where are you (are you calling from)?

Examples from Im Hopin 1987:183-4: **Pi ka op.nita. Kulen tey wūsan i ēps.kwun yo** It's raining. And I see I have no umbrella! **Sinmun ul sass.ˢup.nita. Kulen tey acik ilk.ci mōs hayss.ˢup.nita** I bought a newspaper. But I haven't had a chance to read it yet.

kulepsita, abbr < **kule hapsita**. OK, let's do so.

-kulepta, bnd adj -w-. ¶**tut-~** is noisy; CF **sikkulepta** is noisy [? < **sīt-kulew-** < **sīl-**]. **pukkulepta** is ashamed [? < **pulk-kulew-**]. **singkulepta** is fresh-smelling; (= **hwing hata**) is chilly. **cingkulepta** is crawly, creepy [? < **cingkul**]. **mikkulepta** is slippery [? < **mikkul** = **mikkun** ? < **mī-l-** plane, CF **mī-** get bald]. [? < **kule + (u)pta**; ? < **-ki koy lopta**; ? < **-kul (h)epta**].

kuleta, vi (inf **kulay**), abbr < **kule hata**. CF **kuli (ha)ta**.

-kuley (= **-kul-ey**), suf. (s)**sayng-** / (s)**sing-~**, (p)**payng-** / (p)**ping-~** smiling.

kuli < **ku˙li**, adverb. LIGHT **koli**. CF **ili**, **celi**.

1. (= **kuleh.key**, **ku-taci**) so, to that extent / degree; in that way. ¶**Kuli khuci anh.ta** It is not so big. **Kuli sayngkak hasio?** Do you think so? **Kuli sēng nāyci mao** Don't be so angry. **Son nim i i pang ul kuli cōh.a haci anh.usio** The guest does not much like this room.

~ **hata** < **ku˙li (˙)ho˙ta** = **kuleta** do so (that way), do that. ¶**Ney ka kuli halq cintay n' na 'n tul** (= **na in tul**) **ecci hal i** If you do that, what am I supposed to do? **Ku īl un ney māl tay lo kkok ney ka kuli halyetta** Now you will do that as you have promised, see / hear?

¶*na ˙two ku˙li ˙hwo.l i ˙'la* (1447 Sek 6:12a) I will do that, too. ˙*SYEY-KAN ye˙huyn ˙LAK ˙ol ˙NYEM ho˙kwo ku˙li ˙tha-ngi ˙'ta* (1459 Wel 7:5b; page numbers "5" and "6" are reversed) meditated on pleasure remote from the world of men and did like that.

2. (= ~ **lo**) that way / direction, there, to that

place. ¶**Kuli kal i 'ta** I'll come there. **Kuli kalye 'myen enu kil lo ka ya 'keyss.ˢo** Which way shall I take to get there (where you are)? ¹**Nāyngmyen ul mek.ulye 'myen motwu kuli kanta** Everybody goes there (who wants) to eat cold noodles. CF **keki**.
kuli, der adv < **kulita**. **kkang-~** all, without exception.
? *****kuli 'ca**, abbr < **kuli haca**. No examples. CF **kuleca**.
kulic(h)'anh.e to = **kulec(h)'anh.e to**
kuli celi, cpd adv. this way and that, such and so, in a hit-or-miss manner, by trial-and-error, feeling one's way (along). ¶ **~ māl ul twulle tāyta** prevaricates, makes random / temporary excuses. **~ yele swutan ul sse pota** tries various means at random, does something by trial and error.
~ hata, vni. tries this way and that, does it in a hit-or-miss manner, does it by trial-and-error, feels one's way along. ¶**Kuli celi hay se etteh.key sam-man wen ul mantul.ess.ta** He finally made thirty thousand wen in one way or another. **Kuli celi hanun tong-an ey sikan i tā kass.ta** Time has passed away while I have been fiddling around doing this and that.
ku ̇li ̇ Ge ̇n i, abbr < *ku ̇li ̇ [̇]ho ̇ke ̇n i*, adv + v effective mod + quasi-free n. one who did. ¶*ku ̇li ̇ Ge ̇n i ̈ywu ̇pwok ̇hotwu ̇ta* (?1517- Pak 1:46b) he who did so is fortunate indeed!
ku ̇li ̇ Gwos, adv + pcl. just / precisely that way. ¶*ku ̇li ̇ Gwos a ̇ni ho ̇m ye n' ̇CYENG- ̇KAK il ̇Gwu ̇ti a[̇]ni ̇hwo ̇l i '-ngi ̇'ta* (1459 Wel 8:62b) unless you do precisely that you will not achieve sambodhi (Buddha wisdom).
kuliko, kulikwu < **kuli 'ko**, abbr < **kuli hako** < (?*)*ku ̇li ho ̇kwo*, adverb, conjunction. and, and also / then; **tto ~** and also, (and) besides. ¶**kkaykkus hako ko.yo han kuliko palk.ko ttattus han cip** a house that is clean and quiet and that is bright and warm. **Wuli nala choki uy, kuliko chōyko uy munhak un hyangka lo puthe sīcak hanta** Korea's earliest and oldest literature begins with (the vernacular poems called) **hyangka**. **Na hanthey to mul com tao! Kuliko, i ay hanthey to mul com cwu(o)!** Give me some water — and give him some, too! **Pokswun-i ka tal ul chyē 'ta pwass.ta; kuliko ku ay nun sulphe cyess.ta** Pokswun-i looked up at the moon, and she fell sad. **Kuliko taum ey chinkwu tul ul chac.ess.ta** And then I called on my friends.
Examples taken from Im Hopin 1987:181-2: **Cey ilum un Swuk.huy 'ey yo. Kuliko cey chinkwu ilum un Yenghuy 'ey yo** My name is Swuk.huy and my friend's name is Yenghuy. **Kim sensayng nim un Yenge lul cal hap.nita. Kuliko swūhak to cal hap.nita** Mr Kim does well in English. And he's good in mathematics, too. **Sam-sip punq tong-an swīkeyss.ˢup.nita. Kuliko tasi kongpu hakeyss.ˢup.nita** We will take a break for ten minutes. And then we will resume studying. SEE ¹Yi Tongcay 1978.
kuliko, ger < **kulita** (vt). ¶**kuliko kulin nay kōhyang** my much-missed home town.
kūliko, ger < **kūlita** (vt). ¶**Kūlim ul kūliko pap ul mek.keyss.ta** I will draw a picture before I have lunch.
kuli-kwom (< *ku ̇li- ̇kwom*), adv + suf. ¶*kuli-kwom nekiti malosywosye* (1676 Sin.e 3:19b) please don't think of it that way.
kuli lo, adv + pcl = **kuli 2** (that way, there)
? **kuli 'myen**, abbr < **kuli hamyen**; **~ se**. Not used in Seoul (→ **kulemyen**).
ku ̇li ̇ 'mye n', abbr < *ku ̇li ho ̇m ye n'*. if / when one does that. ¶*ku ̇li ̇ 'mye n' ̇cuk ̇cay ̇su ̇le ti ̇l i ̇ ̇'la* (?1517- Pak 1:13b) if you do that, it will soon disappear. CF *ku ̇le ̇ ̇'m ye n'*.
kuli 'na, adv + cop advers. ¶**Kuli 'na hay polq ka** I might do it that way.
kuli sa, adv + pcl [DIAL = **kuli ya**] = **kuli to**
kuli 'ta, abbr < **kuli hata**. does/says/thinks that way. SYN **kuleta**. CF **ili 'ta, celi 'ta**. NOTE: Abbreviated forms of the copula (instead of hata) occur only as quasi-particles: **kuli 'na**, ...
kulita, bnd postnominal verb. does. ¶**kantong / kentwung ~** bundles it up neatly. **mongttong / mungttwung ~** bundles it up crudely. (**mom ul**) **ong(song) / wung(swung) ~, angtang / ungtung ~** shrinks (with one's body). **thwu ~** snarls. **kkang-~** finishes it. PARAINTENSIVE **khulita**. CF **kelita**.
kulita, vt. misses, yearns for/after, is lonely for, pines for.
kūlita, vt. draws, paints; pictures.
kuli to, adv + pcl. so much, to that extent (= **ku-taci to**). ¶**Kuli to mōs chām.keyss.tun ya?** Surely you could stand it that much?!

kuˑli-twoˑlwok, adv (< *kuˑli [ˑho]twoˑlwok*) to that extent. ¶ *¨ne y kuˑli-twoˑlwok chonchon hon ¨yang ul ¨hyey[ˑ]Gen ˑt un* (?1517⁻ Pak 1: 64a; *¨yang-ul*) when you have figured it down to such fine detail … . CF *iˑliˑˑtoˑlwok, tyeˑliˑtwoˑlwok.*

kulkhwuta [DIAL (Mkk 1960:3:34)] = **kuleh.key (māl) hata**

kulˑlan (?= *ku lˑlan* with conflated liquid). as for that/him (those/them). ¶*kulˑlan solang ˑthi aˑni ˑkhwo* (1459 Wel 7:17b) did not love them [his many consorts at home] but … . *kulˑlan ¨ne y mozop nwoˑhaˑsiˑla* (?1517⁻ ¹No 1:68a; *mozop* is a spelling error for *mozom*) as to that, let your mind be at ease about it. *kullan nyemnye malkwo* (?1608+ Twu-hem 45a) as to that, don't be concerned, … .

kullo, abbr. 1. (kul' lo) < kuli lo.
2. (ku 'l lo) < ku kel lo (= ku kes ulo).

kulˑlwo (?= *ku lˑlwo* with conflated liquid) = **ku lo** as/with/by that. ¶*kulˑlwo ilˑhwuˑm ul saˑmo.n iˑˑla* (1459 Wel 2:27b) made his name be that. *kulˑlwo ¨woˑm i MWU-ˑLYANG ˑKEPˑi.n iˑˑla* (1463 Pep 5:160b) since then there have been countless kalpas. CF *ilˑlwo, tyelˑlwo, ¨nalˑlwo, nellwo.*

ˑ**kulˑlwo**, n + pcl. as/with/by the writing(s). ¶*noˑm oy naˑla[h] sˑkuˑl ul ceˑy naˑla[h] sˑkulˑlwo kwoˑthyeˑssul ˑss iˑla* (1447 Sek se: 6a) it is a matter of translating the writing of another land into writing of one's own land.

kulssey, interj [? abbr < *kulelq sey*]. well, now, uh (shows some uncertainty, hesitation, doubt, reprimand): ~ 'ta, yo, olssita. ~ māl iya no kidding; I know what you mean; I agree.

ku lul, n. + pcl. that (one) [object]; him/her, it. ˑ*kuˑl ul*, n + pcl. ¶*pulˑkun ¨sayˑkuˑl ul muˑle* … (1445 ¹Yong 7) a red bird carrying in its beak an inscription … .

(-)kulye → **(-)kwulye**. Attested 1730.

-kum, suf. makes adv, adj-n. **malkkum** clean, completely, entirely [< malk-kum]. **tal-kum hata** is rather sweet. **si-/say-kum hata** is rather sour. **sulkum sulkum** stealthily [< sul sul softly]. SEE **silkhum** < **silh-kum, ittakum** < **iss.ta-kum, mankhum** < **manh-kum, ha.ye-kum**; CF **kakkum**; **kkaykkum** ?< **kkāyta + -q-kum**. VAR **-kom**. INTENSIVE **-kkum**; PARA-INTENSIVE **khum**.

NOTE: LHS 1955:281 says that this suffix intensifies adverbs, and he lists additional examples: **tasi-kum** again; **kata-kum** later on; **sile-kum** (= **sile-kom** [obs] < **sile**) = **nung hi** possibly; **ceykak-kum, se(y).ye-kom** [obs] = **cey-kak.ki** individually, respectively; **noph.i-kom** [obs] highly; **mēlli-kom** distantly. See also **-key-kkum**. CF **cokom** (> **com**), **cokum** (?< **cēkta**).

kumam-ttay, cpd n. about/around that time, (at) that time of day/night/year. ¶ **Ku nun ecey to palo kumam-ttay wass.ess.ta** He was here at just about that time yesterday too. **Sakwa nun kumam-ttay ka cēy-il mas na(n)ta** That is the time when apples taste best. **Kumam-ttay ka sanay lo sse han-chang kiwun nanun ttay 'ta** Men are at their strongest at that time of life. SYN **komam-ttay**. CF **imam-, cemam-**.

ku-man, bnd adn (? abbr < **ku-man han**). that little (amount of), so little (as that), to that (small) extent, such a; no more than, just, only. ¶**Ku-man swūko lul akkinun ya** Do you begrudge such a small favor? **Ku-man kes ul cici mōs halq ka** Who can't carry that much on his back? **Ku-manq īl ey ¹naksim in ya?** Don't feel disappointed about such a little thing. SYN **ku-man han, ku-mas**. CF **i-man, ce-man; man, pakk ey**. LIGHT **ko-man**.

ku man, cpd adv, n (< n + pcl). SYN **ko man**. SEE **ku man twuta (hata)**.

1. adv that much and no more, to that extent only, no more than that; [+ v] stops (doing). ¶**Ku man mek.e la** Eat no more than that = Stop eating. **Onul un ku man hay twuca** That is all for today, so much for today. **Kulemyen ku man ita** Well, that is all/enough; That's it; We'll leave it at that; Nothing more can be done. **Ku man hamyen tōyss.ta** (1) If you do that much you're done; (2) When you stop you're done.

2. adv. without doing anything further (more than that); just, right (then and there); with that, … ; … , just like that; … , that's all; [+ v] up and (does). ¶**Kulus i ku man malwu ey ttel.e cye se cokak-cokak kkāy cyess.ta** The dish just (up and) fell on the floor and broke to pieces(, that's all). **Ku soli lul tut.tuni ku man wul.um ul the ttulyess.ta** When he heard the news, he burst right out crying, just like that. **Ku man kaca** Let's just up and go. **Incey ku**

man cip ulo kake la Just go on home now! Icey n' ku man pi ka kuchilq pep hata The rain should be ending any time now. **Pyēng i kuce ku man hako iss.ta** There's no change in his condition (= illness).

3. n [colloq]. the best (in the world), the most, tops, "it", superb. ¶**I mas i ku man ita** This tastes superb. **Ku sālam i ku man ie** He is a peach (of a fellow). **Nal i cōh.ki nun ku man ikwun** I've never seen such a lovely day! (When it comes to weather this is really it!)

ku ˙man, n + pcl. just that. SEE *ku-man ˙tye-man*.

ku-man ce-man, cpd adv (cpd adv + cpd adv). to about that extent/degree, about so far/much, half way, reasonably (much), a reasonable amount; roughly; ever so (much), quite; greatly, extremely. ¶**īl ul ~ hay twuta** does one's work half-way, does a rough job (of it). **Ūmsik ul ku man ce man mek.e la** Eat reasonably (= a reasonable amount). **Īl i him tul.e to ku man ce man him tul.e ya 'ci** The job is ever so hard. (The work is more than difficult.)

~ **hata**, cpd adj-n. is so-so, is not too good and not too bad, is mediocre, is comme ci comme ça. ¶**Ku sālam pyēng i etteh.ˢup.nikka – Kuce ku-man ce-man hap.nita** How is he? – He's just so-so. **Ku-man ce-man han sālam i ani 'ta** He is no ordinary person (= He is an extraordinary man). **Ku īl un ku-man ce-man hay kaciko nun an toynta** You must not do a mediocre job of it.

ku man hata₁, cpd adj-n; HEAVY ↔ **ko man hata**. is about the same, is much the same, is as ... as ... ; lacks ups and downs, is in a lull. ¶**ku to khi ka kkok ~** he is just about the same height. **Ku ay nun khi ka ku man hay kaciko cokom to khuci anh.nunta** The boy remains just the same height and does not grow at all. **Pyēng i com ku man hata** His illness is a little bit better now. **Sāko ka ku man haki tahayng ita** It was fortunate for you that the accident wasn't so bad. CF **i/ce man hata; (-ul) man hata**.

ku man hata₂, cpd vnt. does just that (and then stops), does no more than that, stops at/with that; (= **ku man twuta**) stops, quits, ceases, discontinues.

ku mankhum, n + pcl. that/so much, to that extent. CF **i/ce mankhum**.

ku-man ku-man hata, adj-n; HEAVY ↔ **ko-man ko-man hata**. is neither more nor less (larger nor smaller, taller nor shorter, deeper nor shallower, better nor worse), is about/much the same, is so-so, is in between, is of a piece/sort. ¶**motwu ~** all of them are about the same (are so-so). **Haksayng tul uy Yenge sillyek i tā ku-man ku-man hata** All the students have about the same knowledge of English.

ku man twuta, cpd adv + vt. ABBR **kwān twuta**.

1. leaves it as it is, leaves it alone (at that). ¶**Latio lul kaciko kuleci mālko ku man twue la** Leave the radio as it is; Don't monkey with the radio. **Ku ay wūlla ku man twue la** Leave the child alone, or he will cry.

2. stops, ceases, gives up, quits, ends it; discontinues, breaks/leaves off, "knocks off". ¶**iyaki lul ~** stops talking (about it), drops the subject. **kongpu lul ~** gives up one's studies; stops studying, knocks off work (at one's studies). **īl ul ~** lays aside one's work; quits, knocks off (for the day). **kyēyhoyk ul ~** lays aside (drops) a plan, gives up a project (an idea, a scheme). **swul ul ~** gives up drinking, goes on the wagon. **hōysa lul ~** leaves (the service of) a company; quits, resigns from a company. **ssawum ul ~** gives up the fight, quits (fighting).

ku-man ˙tye-man, adv. ¶**me˙kwu.m ul ku-man ˙tye-man ˙ho.ya˙n ywo ma˙lon** (1482 Kum-sam 3:52a) he was picky about his food, but ... .

ku-mas, bnd adn; HEAVY ↔ **ko-mas**. that/so much of a, so much (as that), to that (small) extent, such a; no more than, just, only [more emphatic than **ku-man**]. ¶**~ kes** that much (stuff), such a quantity; no more than that, that little amount (of stuff/things). **~ tōn** that much money, such a (petty) sum. **ku-masq īl** such a (little) thing, a matter no more (important) than that. **~ māl** no more to say than that, just those words, nothing more (to say).

ku'n, abbr < **kulen** (such ···). **~ ke, ~ tey**.

ku n', abbr < **ku nun**

?**-(k)kun**, suffix. SEE **-kkun**.

ku nal, adn + n. that day; the very same day. ¶**Ku nal i ku nal ita** Every day is much the same; the days are much alike. **Ku nal ina i nal ina machan-kaci 'ta** It's the same these days as it was in those days. **~ ~** every day, daily; from day to day.

ku 'na-ma, cpd adv (n + cop extended advers). even so, even that much, at that, nevertheless, however. CF **i/yo 'na-ma, ce 'na-ma.**
ku ney, n + postn. those people, they/them; [DIAL] he/him. ~ **tul/kkili** they/them. SYN **ku tul, ku i ney, ku tul ney.**
kunge ̇kuy (? < *ku ngek ̇uy*), n. (to/at) that place, there (= *ke ̇kuy* > **keki**); CF *key*; *inge ̇kuy*. ¶*kunge ̇kuy ̇sywo y ̇ha ̇a* (1459 Wel 1:24b) there are lots of cattle there.
~ *s* (pcl). ¶*kunge ̇kuy s ̇CYWUNG-SOYNG THYEN-LYWONG YA-CHA ··· "TUNG ̇i ...* (1447 Sek 19:39b) the living beings, the devas, the yaksas, the ··· and all who were there ... .
kungey abbr < *kunge ̇kuy*, adv, n. (to/at) that place, there (= *ke ̇kuy*); CF *ingey, tyengey*. ¶*kungey CYENG- ̇SYA y ̈epke ̇n i* (1447 Sek 6:22a) there are no monasteries there. *kungey is ̇ten ̇PPI-KHWUW y ̈ta ni ̇le* (1447 Sek 24:44a) the almsmen who were there all arose.
··· '*u/oy* ~ (pcl). to (a person, where one is).
··· *s* ~ (pcl). to (an esteemed person), to where an esteemed person is.
~ *s* ··· (pcl). ··· of that place. ¶*kungey s KWUNG- ̇TTYEN ̇kwa CYE-THYEN ̇kwa y ...* (1459 Wel 1:50a) the palaces and heavens there. *kungey s ̈salo ̇m i* (1464 Amitha 13b) the people there.
~ *̇sye* (pcl). ¶*kungey ̇sye ̈sa ̇n i* (1459 Wel 2:7a) they lived there.
ku'n ke, abbr < **kulen kes** (such a thing/one)
ku nom, adn + n. [pejorative] that damn guy (S.O.B.), he/him [not used of women]; that damn thing, it. CF **ku ay/ca/chi/i/kes.**
ku'n tey, abbr < **kulen tey**
ku nun, n + pcl. as for that (one); he, she, it.
ku-nyang, adv. SYN **ko-nyang**; CF **i-/ce-nyang.**
1. (in) that way, (in) the same way as before, as it is/was, still, yet, with no change/letup; continuously. ¶ ~ **pi ka ota** it is still raining; the rain doesn't let up. ~ **twuta** leaves it as it is, leaves it/him alone. CF **acik to, kuce.**
2. (just) as one/it is, (just) without doing anything (CF **kuce**). ¶**Pap mekci anh.ko ku-nyang hak.kyo ey kass.ta** He went to school without his breakfast. **Kesulum un ku-nyang twusey yo** Keep the change.
3. just because, for no good reason. **Chayk ul ku-nyang kacye kass.ta** He just up and took the book (without paying or asking permission).
4. just as you are; empty-handed (with no gift). ¶**Ku-nyang osici kulay yo** (Don't bother with a gift or anything,) just come!
ku-nyang ce-nyang (= **ilek-celek**). ¶**Yo cum etteh.key cīnass.ey yo?** — **Ku-nyang ce-nyang cīnayci yo** How have you been getting along lately? — So-so.
ku-nye, n [semi-literary]. she/her, that woman.
kup [< ̇*KKUP*], pcl, adverb = **mich** (and)
ku pen, adn + n. that time; (= **cīnan pen**) the last time, the other day; the last/recent one. CF **ce pen, i pen.**
ku pyen, adnoun + noun. around there.
ku phyen, cpd n = **ku ccok** (that side/direction)
ku pun, adnoun + quasi-free n. that (esteemed) person; he/him, she/her. CF **ku ay/ca/chi/ ēlun/i/kes/nom/sālam/son.**
-(k)kus, suffix (derives impressionistic adverbs). ¶**h^a/u̯l-(k)kus** glancing to one side. **h^a/u̯y-kkus** (XX) spotted with white (< **huyta** is white). ? **kkaykkus hata** is clean (< **kāyta** becomes clear). **(s)sa(y)ng-/(p)pa(y)ng-kus** smiling. But **wulkus-pulkus** 'colorful' is from **pulk-us**. CF **-(k)kis, -(k)kul.**
ku sai/say, adn + n. the while, the interval, meantime; the time that has elapsed, this while (since ...), ~ **(ey)** in that time/interval, in the meantime; (= **enu thum ey pelsse**) all of a sudden, so soon. ¶**Ku sai ey cēmsim mek.ulq swu iss.ta** We can take our lunch in that time. **Ku say cēmsim(q) sikan in ya?** Is it lunch time so soon? **Ku sai ey ku nun tal.e nass.ta** He ran away in the meantime. **Ku sai ey ku nun cala se ēlun i toyess.ta** In the meantime, he grew up into manhood. **Ku sai annyeng hasip.nikka?** How have you been these days?
ku sālam < *ku ̈salom*, adn + n. that person; he/him, she/her. CF **ku ay/ca/chi/ēlun/i/kes/ nom/pun/son.** ¶*ku ̈salo ̇m oy ̈swon- ̇toy ̇wo ̇sya* (1459 Wel 8:55b) came to him and ... .
ku son, adn + quasi-free n. that person; he/him, she/her. CF **ku ay/ca/chi/ēlun/i/kes/nom/ pun/sālam.**
-kuss- [DIAL] = **-keyss-** (future)
ku-ta(k)ci, cpd adv. to that extent/degree, like that, in that way so (much). ~ **pissaci anh.ta** is not so expensive. ¶ ~ **cōh.ci anh.ta** is not so/that good. **Ku-taci sīm hakey kwūlci mal' la** Don't be so severe with me. LIGHT **ko-taci.**
~ **to**. ¶**Ku-ta(k)ci to mōs cham.ulq ke l' way wass.ni** Why did you come (Why are you

here) if you can't stand any more than that?! **Si-cip sal.i ka ku-taci to elyeptula** Life as a married woman was ever so hard (for me).

ku tal, adn + n. that month, the very same month.

kutay < *kutoy*, noun [old-fashioned, FAMILIAR]. you, thou; my beloved, you my love [male or female]. ¶**Ku kes un kutay uy cal-mos ilq sey** You are to blame for it (or: You are wrong there). **Kutay ēncey wass.nun ka** When did you get here? **Kutay ka osil ttay** ... When you come (to me), beloved, ... SYN **caney**.

ku tay lo, adn + n + pcl. CF **i / ce tay lo**.
1. like that, as it is / stands, intact; thus, that way, as things stand (there). ¶ ~ **twuta** leaves it just as it is, leaves it alone. CF **ku chay lo**.
2. thereupon, at once, immediately. ¶**Wass.ta ka nun ku tay lo kass.ta** He came and then left right away (without doing anything).

kutay tul, n + pcl. (all of) you, (you) people.

ku'tholok = **ku'h.tolok**, abbr < **kuleh.tolok** (< **kule hatolok**) to such an extent, so much. ¶**Ku'tholok cal hay cwusini komapsup.nita** Thank you for doing so much for me. **Āmu-ccolok ku'tholok man hay la** Do all that you possibly can. SEE **tholok**.

kuti (abbr < *kutuy*), n. you. ¶ ˙KWO-ZIN ˙on kuti ˙lol ¨alGe˙nol kuti ˙non ˙KWO-ZIN ˙ol ¨ati ¨mwot ˙hwo.m on ¨es.t[y]ey ˙Gwo (1475 Nay 3:58b) why is that the deceased recognizes you, yet you do not recognize the deceased? ˙na y SOYNG-SOYNG kuti s ka˙s i towoy˙Ga ci˙la (1459 Wel 1:11b) I want to become your wife in life after life.

ku¨ti, abbr < **kuti ˙i*, noun + particle. you [as subject]. ¶**ku¨ti ¨CO-˙SIK ¨epte˙n i mu˙sus ¨CCWOY ˙Gwo** (1459 Wel 1:7a) what was your sin that you had no son?

ku to, n + pcl. also / even that (one), he / him (she / her, it) too / even. ¶**Ku eykey mul.e pon pa ku to ālci mōs hakeyss.ta hatula** I asked him but he said he didn't know about it either.

ku tong-an, adn + n. this / that while, the while; recently.

kutoy = *kutuy*, n. you. ¶*kutoy ˙non [SYE KHYENG] ˙uy ¨twu a˙to.l i˙na kocang [KUY-˙I] ˙hwo.m ol pwo˙ti a˙ni ˙honon ˙ta* (1481 Twusi 8:24a) don't you see that Lord Xú's two sons are quite odd? *kutoy s [˙NGWA-SSANG] ay* (1481 Twusi 8:67a) in your bed. *kutoy ˙lol* (1481 Twusi 15:53a) you [as object].

ku ttawi, n [~ q when adnominal]. [pejorative] a thing / person of that sort; such a (one); that kind / sort (of ...). CF **ko ttawi**; **i / ce ttawi**.

ku ttay, cpd n. (at) that time / moment / juncture.

ku tul, n + postn. they / them. SYN **ku ney (tul)**.

kutuy < *kutoy* (< *ku ˙toy* 'that place' or *ku˙t ᵘ⁄oy* 'at that place'); *kutuy + ˙i → ku¨tuy*. you.

¶*kutuy ˙ka ˙tul cci˙p i pol˙ssye ¨itwo˙ta* (1447 Sek 6:35b) a house for you to enter has already been built!

¶*kutuy ˙Gwos na˙kunay ˙lul solang ˙thi a˙ni ˙hote˙tun* (1481 Twusi 15:31b) you failed to love the wayfarer, and ... .

¶*kutuy ˙lul ¨pwon t oy n' [¨TTWOW-˙KHUY] ¨ha.n i* (1481 Twusi 7:21a) looking at you, [one sees that] the vital energy of the Way is great.

¶*kutuy s a˙pa ¨ni˙m i is.no˙n i s ˙ka* (1447 Sek 6:14b) is your father here? *kutuy s ˙sto˙l ol mas˙kwo ˙cye ˙ho˙te-ngi ˙'ta* (1447 Sek 6:15a) he has been wanting to meet your daughter. *na 'y ˙mwo˙m i ¨ku 'y ˙Gwo ... kutuy s ˙mwo˙m i ¨ku 'y˙la* (1447 Sek 13:36b) my body is that one and ... your body is that one. *kutuy s ˙hwon cwo˙chwo ˙ho˙ya* (1447 Sek 6:8b) I will do as you say, and ... . ¶*LWO-¨LWOW y kutuy s ¨wo˙m ol kitu˙li˙tela ho˙la* (1482 Nam 1:50b) he has been long waiting for you to come.

¶*kutuy s ke˙kuy [˙NGUY] ˙lol ˙cye po˙lywo.n i sul˙he ˙hwo.n i me˙li ˙stwo ¨syeytwo˙ta* (1481 Twusi 7:28a) yielding to your righteousness there, I feel so sad my hair gets all the whiter. *kutuy s key ˙SSYWOK ˙ke˙tun* (1482 Nam 2:41a) if it belongs to you ... . Although the genitive is usually marked by the honorific ... *s*, there are a few examples of ... *uy*, too: *kutuy ˙uy ¨TAM ˙khukwo* (1482 Kum-sam 2:67a) your liver (= courage) is huge and ... . *kutuy ˙uy [QYWUW-SIM] hon ˙ptut ˙pswu.m ul ¨pwo.n i* (1481 Twusi 15:13a) [in a dream] I saw you effect your ulterior motive.

~ ˙*nay* you folks, you people. ¶*kutuy ˙nay kos˙pi ˙za ˙wotwo˙ta ma˙lon* (1447 Sek 23:53b) you people make haste to come but ... . *kutuy ˙nay ˙KAK-˙KAK hon a˙tol ˙Gwom ¨nay˙ya na 'y SWON-¨CO cwo˙cha ka˙key ho˙la ˙hosi˙n i* (1447 Sek 6:9b) he commands that each of you folks send a son to follow my grandson. *kutuy ˙nay ki˙Gwulye me˙kwu.m ul ˙pwonwo˙la* (1481 Twusi 15:52b) you fellows watch your tendency to drink [seeing what it has done to me].

~ ˙ney = ~ ˙nay. ¶*kutuy ˙ney khun il˙hwum il˙Gwu.m un* (1481 Twusi 8:55b) the achieving of fame by you people.

ku¨tuy < **kutuy ˙i*, n + pcl. you [as subject]. ¶*ku¨tuy ˙ka˙a a˙la tut˙key nilu˙la* (1447 Sek 6:6b) you go and tell her to understand. *ku¨tuy CYENG-˙SYA ci˙zwu˙l ye ...* (1447 Sek 6:35a) you, wanting to build a monastery, ... *ku¨tuy ¨es.te 'n ¨sa˙lo.m in˙ta* (1459 Wel 10:29b) = *ku¨tuy ¨es˙te 'n ¨salo˙m in˙ta* (1462 ¹Nung 7:62a) what kind of person are you?

ku twu, n + var pcl = **ku to** (he/she/it too/even).

kuy, spelling abbreviation for **ku** as abbr < **ku i** (he / him, she / her).

kuy, abbr < *ku ˙i*, adn + quasi-free n. that one. ¶*kuy ˙non ko˙cang ¨swuy˙Gwu.n i ''la* (?1517-Pak 1:47b) that is the easiest one.

¨*ku y*, abbr < *ku ˙i*, n + pcl. that [nominative]; he; it. ¶¨*ku y a˙ni e˙lisi˙n i* (1445 ¹Yong 39) is that not foolish of him?! ¨*ku y kwuy ˙yey s ˙SSILQ-˙SYANG ˙i˙la* (1447 Sek 19:16a) that is the ear's reality (the reality that is in the ear).

¨*ku 'y···*, abbr < *ku ˙i···*, n + cop. (it) is that. ¶*na˙y ˙mwo˙m i ¨ku 'y˙Gwo ··· kutuy s ˙mwo˙m i ¨ku 'y˙la* (1447 Sek 13:36b) my body is that one and ··· your body is that one. ¨*ku 'ylwo˙n i* (1459 Wel 7:12a) therefore.

-˙*kuy* [var] = -˙*key* (adverbative). SEE *ho˙kuy*, ˙*khuy*. ¶˙*mwo˙m i ˙khu˙kuy towoy˙ya HE-KHWONG ˙ay kotok ˙ho˙ya is.ta ka˙stwo ¨cyek˙kuy towoy˙m ye ...* (1447 Sek 6:34a) his body grows big and fills the void and then it because small again, and ... . ¨*kyecip ˙tol˙h ol pwuthye s QUM-˙CCANG ˙SYANG ˙pwozop˙kuy ˙hwo˙m i˙Gwo* (1447 Sek 24:2b) is letting the womenfolk gaze upon the image of Buddha's retractable penis, and ... – CF ˙*pwozop˙key* (1459 Wel 18:80b). *LYWONG ˙ol ce˙khuy* [< *ceh-˙kuy*] *ho˙n i* (1449 Kok 192) made the dragon take fright.

~ '*s˙kwo* (= *'[y]s˙kwo*, abbr < *is˙kwo*, vi ger). wanting it to be / do. ¶˙*SYE-KUY ˙non ku˙le ho˙kuy 's˙kwo ˙po˙lanwo˙la ˙honwon ˙ptu.t i˙la* (1447 Sek se:6a) [the word] ˙*SYE-KUY* ('almost') means we hope for it to be so. ¨*salom ¨ma˙ta ¨swu˙Wi a˙la SAM-¨PWOW ˙ay na˙za ˙ka put˙kuy 's˙kwo ˙po˙lanwo˙la* (1447 Sek se:6a) each of us is hoping to understand easily and advance to [where we] rely upon the Three Precious Things (= triratna: Buddha).

NOTE: This analysis is that of Kōnō Rokurō. CF ˙*khways˙kwo*; -˙*kwo ˙cye*.

··· ˙*kuy*, abbr < *ke˙kuy*. CF ˙*skuy* = *s ˙kuy*; ···*key*.

''*kuy*, abbr < *ho˙kuy* after voiceless sounds. ¶*syang˙nyey ˙ile ˙thu˙s 'i ˙QILQ-˙CHYEY ˙NGWUW-CCYENG ˙ul ˙LI-˙QYEK toWoy˙m ye QAN-˙LAK ''kuy ho˙la* (1447 Sek 9:41a; ˙*NGWUW-CCYENG* → ¨*NGWUW-CCYENG*) thus regularly comfort all sentient beings, becoming of benefit to them. ˙*homol˙mye QA-LA-˙HAN ¨KWA ˙lol ˙TUK ''kuy ˙hwo˙m isto˙n i-ngi s ˙ka* (1447 Sek 19:4b) how much more so is being allowed to obtain the effect of an arhan?!

ku ya, n + pcl. if it be that (thing / person); that, he / him, she / her, it. ¶**Ku ya kuleh.ci** Oh, that is true. **Āmulye 'ni ku ya kuleh.ci** Anyway, that's the way things are. **Ku ya kulelq swu iss.ci** That is quite possible. (Yes, that is all right. That can be done.) **Ku ya mullon ici yo** Of course. **Ku ya nwu ka moluna** Who would not know THAT? **Ku ya tōn i mānh.ci** Him – he has lots of money. **Ku ya pelsse yeki lul** [= **ey (lul)**] **meych tal iss.uni-kka yo** That's because I've been here a few months already (1954 Lukoff 111).

ku ya māl lo, n + pcl + n + pcl. CF **māl (iya)**.

1. he himself; she herself. ¶**Song Kiceng, ku ya māl lo malasong-kyey uy wangca yess.ta** Song Kiceng, in his day, was the king of the marathon.

2. really, indeed, certainly. ¶**Ku ya māl lo ney ka cal-mos ita** Certainly you are wrong; You are indeed / truly to blame. **Ku ya māl lo "kwusa-ilqsayng" ilokwun a** You really had a narrow escape.

3. that is ... indeed; all right, sure enough. ¶**Ku ya māl lo cham khuta** That is big indeed. **Ku ya māl lo him tunq īl ita** That is indeed a difficult job.

ku-yek, cpd adv (< n + adv). that / it also; [+ NEG] that / it either. ¶**Ku-yek sāsil ita** That also is true. **Ku-yek maum ey tulci anh.nunta** I don't like it, either. SYN **ku yeksi**. CF **yek**.

ku.yey, adv. at last / length, at long last, finally, ultimately, in the long run, in the last / final analysis. ¶**Ku.yey sihem ey hapkyek hayss.ta** He has passed the examinations at last. **Ku.yey pic ul pat.e nāyss.ta** I collected the debt at long last. **Ku.yey sengkong halq kes ita** In the long run he will succeed. CF **a.yey**. [? < **ku + ey**; ? < **ku ay ey**; ? < **kuye-i = kie-(h)i**]

kuy n' = ku (i) nun

ku yo, 1. n + AUTH cop (= **ku io**). it is that (one), it's him/her/it. 2. n + polite pcl. (it's) that (one), (it's) him/her/it.

-`kuys`kwo = -`kuy `'s`kwo (wanting it to be/do) SEE -`kuy. CF -`Gey `'s`kwo; `khways`kwo; -`kwo `cye.

kwa < `kwa, pcl; after vowel **wa** < `[G]wa but `Gwa after i, y, l (see the note below); probably < ko`Wa (1449 Kok 135) < kol`Wa < *kolp-`a 'lining them up, comparing them, competing' (SEE kol`Gwa, [G]wa, **ul kwa**). SYN **hako**; CF **iko, imye, ini, iney, ilang, sekken, ey 'ta, ina, hamkkey, tepul.e**. The MK pcl attached to the "free" form of such nouns as namwo / namk ··· 'tree', yezo / yezG 'fox', molo / moll ··· 'ridge', ... : namwo `[G]wa (1445 [1]Yong 89, 1447 Sek 3:33b), yezo `[G]wa (1463 Pep 2:110a), molo `[G]wa (1481 Twusi 9:28; cited from LCT).

1. (accompaniment) with, together with, in company with. ¶**wuli wa hamkkey/kath.i** with us. **tongmu wa cengkwu lul hata** plays tennis with a friend. **pumo wa kath.i cip ey iss.ta** stays with one's parents. **emeni wa** [1]**yehayng hata** travels with one's mother. **ayki wa nōlta** plays with the baby. [1]**Nayil Kim kwun kwa (hamkkey) osio** Come (together) with Mr Kim tomorrow. **Atul kwa sālkeyss.ta** I will live with my son.

2. and (links nouns in coordination; the last item is sometimes followed by the particle, too). ¶**swul kwa tāmpay lul sass.ta** bought liquor and tobacco. **kāy wa ko.yangi** a dog and a cat. **ne wa na** you and I. **hak.kyo wa tose-kwan uy sai** between the school and the library. **na wa nay chinkwu wa hamkkey** together with me and my friend. **Pēm kwa kōm un tā cimsung ita** The tiger and the bear are both animals. **Ku wa na wa nun kath.i kakeyss.ta** He and I will go together. **Tōn kwa ilum kwa kyēycip kwa sēy kaci nun sālam uy yok.mang uy kunponcek tāysang ila hanta** They say that three things — money, fame, and women — are the basic objects of men's ambition.

3. (harmony/agreement) with. ¶**ce sālam kwa sai ka cōh.ta** is on good terms with him/her. **chinkwu wa hyep.lyek hata** cooperates with a friend. **Cwungkwuk kwa son ul capta** goes hand in hand with China.

4. (association/relation) with. ¶**ōykwuk tāysa wa co.yak ul kyosep hata** negotiates with a foreign ambassador for a treaty. **unhayng kwa kēlay hata** has dealing (does business) with a bank, banks. **Na nun ne wa āmu kwankyey ka ēps.ta** I have nothing to do with you. **Ney ka ku i wa chinkwu 'ci?** Are you friends with him?

5. (mixing) with. ¶**Pap kwa namul kwa sekk.e se mek.e la** Mix your rice and greens.

6. (encounter/contact) with. ¶**chinkwu wa mannata** meets with a friend. **salyeng-pu wa** [1]**yen.lak hata** gets in touch with headquarters. **apeci wa iyaki hata** talks with one's father. **sitay wa pōco lul kath.i hata** keeps up with the times. **ce sālam kwa ālkey toyta** gets to know him, gets acquainted with him.

7. (= **hanthey, eykey**) to a person/creature. ¶**Ne ku sālam kwa nay māl hallay an hallay** Are you going to tell him what I said, or not?

8. (opposition) with, against. ¶**tongmu wa ssawuta** quarrels with a friend. **mulli-hak kwa ssilum hata** struggles with physics.

9. (separation/parting) with, from. ¶**chinkwu wa cakpyel hata** (**kwankyey lul kkunh.ta**) parts/breaks with a friend.

10. (comparison/contrast) with. ¶ ~ **pīkyo hay se** as compared with. ~ **tāyco hay se** in contrast with. **Ku nun seka lo se Chwusa wa (nun) pīkyo halq swu ēps.ta** He cannot compare with Chwusa as a calligrapher. **Ne wa na sai ka cwi wa ko.yangi kath.ta (pisus hata)** You and I are like cat and mouse.

11. 11a. (the same) as; like; (similar) to. CF **mankhum**; `kwa `lwo. ¶**ce sālam kwa kath.i** the same as him, like him (= **ce sālam kath.i**) or together with him (= **ce sālam kwa hamkkey**). **ce sālam kwa talli** in contrast with him, different from him. **pata wa pisus han hoswu** a lake like (similar to) the sea. **cen kwa machan-kaci lo tāytap hata** answers the same as before.

11b. (different) from. CF **pota**; `kwa `lwo. ¶**Nay chayk un Kim kwun kes kwa taluta** My book is different from Kim's. **Nay chayk kwa Kim kwun chayk kwa nun selo taluta** My book and Kim's book are different from each other. **Īl un sayngkak han kes kwa talli toyess.ta** (1936 Roth 424) The work went differently from what I thought it would. **Na nun ku cem ey iss.e ne wa ūykyen ul talli hanta** I disagree with you there.

12. (distinguishes) into. ¶**Kyelqcey selyu wa mīkyel selyu wa kwupyel hay la** Separate the completed documents from the uncompleted.
13. SEE **-ke-ni wa; -ulye 'n' i wa**.

NOTE 1: The MK pcl ˙kwa was weakened to ˙Gwa after *i*, *y*, and *l* (including *LQ*); with the loss of /*G*/ the form was further weakened to *[G]wa* = ˙wa after any vowel, but /˙kwa/ was restored after /*l*/. In 1902 Azbuka kwa occurs after vowels as well as consonants, as if the weakening had never taken place. Perhaps the velar was restored by analogy (as after /*l*/) or perhaps in certain dialects it never weakened to begin with. Many other cases of MK velar lenition do not surface in modern Seoul, where in everyday speech the particle **kwa/wa** itself is displaced by **hako** or **ilang**. In 1579 Kwikam ˙kwa is written after Chinese characters (given without Hankul readings) regardless of their pronunciation. The 17th century left several examples of ˙kwa after the final vowel of a Hankul word (Kim Sungkon 1978:117).

NOTE 2: When ˙kwa is attached to a noun with basic ˙˙*h* an automatic metathesis takes place: *nwo˙khwa* [= *nwoh ˙kwa*] ˙NGWOLQ ˙Gwa y ¨ta ¨ep˙sul ˙s oy (1465 Wen 1:1:1:61a) 'since both a cord and a stump are missing' [obscure Chinese metaphor translated literally].

-˙**kwa**, effective inf (exclamatory). SEE ~ ˙˙la, ~ swo˙la.

˙**kwa ˙ay**, pcl + pcl. ¶˙son-˙pal ˙Gwa ka˙som ˙kwa ˙ay (1463 Pep 2:19a) in the palm of the hand and in the chest. ¨es.tyey˙la ˙wos ˙kwa ˙pap [˙]kwa ˙ay [KWUNG-˙KHWON] ˙ho.ya (1481 Twusi 16:19a) how come we are needy for clothes and food, and ... . SEE **kwa ey**.

kwa ccum, pcl + pcl. ¶**Ku sālam hako uy ceng i ne wa na wa ccum ila 'myen phyengsang ssawulq īl i ēps.keyss.ken man** ... If the feelings with him were what they are between you and me, there'd be no quarreling, but ... .

kwa chelem (man), pcl + pcl (+ pcl). ¶**Talun sālam tul to ku wa na wa chelem (man) cīnaynta 'myen musun kekceng i iss.keyss.ni** If other people got along the way he and I do, surely there would be no trouble.

kwa cocha, pcl + pcl. even with. ¶**Kim kyōswu wa cocha an kakeyss.ta 'ni to-taychey nwukwu hako kakeyss.ta 'n māl iyo** You say you don't want to go even with Professor Kim; who on earth DO you want to go with?

kwa ey < ˙kwa ˙ay, pcl + pcl. to (or at/in/...) with/and/like. ¶**Ilpon ey tāy hay se nun cal ālci man Cwungkuk kwa Mikwuk kwa ey tāy hay se nun cal molup.nita** I am familiar with Japan but I know little about China and America.

˙**kwa ˙ho˙ya** (˙ho˙sya), pcl + inf. together with. ¶SA-MWON ˙kwa ˙ho˙ya coy˙cwo kyes˙kwu˙wo.l i ˙˙la (1447 Sek 6:27b) we will pit our skills against those of the śramaṇa (ascetic). NGWANG ˙kwa ˙ho˙ya ˙SYA-˙NGWUY ˙KWUYK KKI-HHAN CYENG-˙SYA ˙ay ˙ka (1447 Sek 24:37b) together with the king he goes to the Jetavana monastery in Śrāvastī – Kim Yengpay 1972:201 mistakes ˙kwa ˙ho˙ya for kwa ˙ho˙ya ([1447→]1562 Sek 3:11b) 'praising'. PWU-ZIN ˙kwa ˙ho˙sya ˙PPI-KHWUW cwocho˙sya (1459 Wel 8:93b) together with the lady he followed the almsman (bhikṣu) and ... .

kwa ka, pcl + pcl. with/and/like [as subject, complement]. ¶**Sensayng kwa ka ani 'ess.ta (anyess.ta)** It wasn't with the teacher.

kwa kkaci, pcl + pcl. ¶(?) **Ku sālam kwa kkaci kwankyey lul hal phil.yo nun ēps.ta** There is no need to have anything to do with him, either. SEE **hako kkaci** (NOTE).

kwa l', pcl + abbr pcl = **kwa lul**
˙**kwa l'**, pcl + abbr pcl. ¶˙a˙to˙l oy mozom ˙kwa ˙him ˙kwa l' ki˙lywo˙m on (1463 Pep 2:213b) the praising of the son's mind and strength.

-˙˙**kwa ˙˙la**, abbr < *˙ho˙kwa ˙˙la after voiced sounds. SEE -˙kwa ˙˙la. CF ˙khwa ˙˙la.

-˙**kwa ˙˙la**, exclamatory first-person statement. ¶¨ta ko˙cang HWAN-˙HUY ˙ho˙ya ¨nyey ¨ep˙ten ˙i˙l ol ˙TUK '-˙kwa ˙˙la ˙ho˙ya (1459 Wel 18:7b) = ¨ta ko˙cang kis˙ke ¨nyey ¨epten ˙i˙l ol ¨etkwa ˙˙la ˙hote˙n i (1447 Sek 19:40b) we are all very happy at getting an unprecedented event, they said. [MWU-SAN] ˙kwa [˙CHWO-¨SYWUY] s ˙pwo.m ol ¨twu pen pwo˙kwa 'la (1481 Twusi 7:13a) I have twice seen the spring of Wūshān and the waters of Chǔ! na ˙y ¨twu swang ˙say hwe˙l ul ta˙ka ¨ta ton˙nye ˙hoy˙ya po˙likwa ˙˙la (?1517- Pak 1:35a) I took my two pairs of new shoes and wore them both out getting about! ˙TI-˙TUK ˙uy ˙KKEN ˙hi ˙HWA ˙ho˙syan i˙l ol ho˙ma ˙pwo˙zopkwa ˙˙la (1463 Pep 4:169a; the Chinese text makes it clear that i˙lol = [¨]i˙l ol) I have now seen the event of wisdom and virtue strongly transforming!

ˈkwa ˈlan, pcl + pcl. ¶ pwuthye s ˈSYA-ˈLI ˈGwa KYENG ˈkwa ˈPPWULQ-ˈˈSSYANG ˈkwa ˈlan ˈkil[h] s SYEY s nyeˈk uy nwoˈˈsopˈkwo (1459 Wel 2:73b) as for Buddha's bones and sūtras and images, they were put to the west of the path ... .

kwa 'la to, pcl + cop var inf + pcl. ¶ Kath.i kalq sālam i ēps.umyen Pak sensayng kwa 'la to kaci kulay If there is no one to go with you, why don't you go with Mr Pak? I māl un pilok ney namphyen kwa 'la to māl hay se nun an toynta You mustn't tell this even to your husband.

kwa lo, pcl + pcl [rare]. as / with / by / being / ... with / and / like. ¶(?) I sacin kwa ku uy māl (kwa) lo mōtun kes ul cimcak halq swu iss.ta You can figure everything out from this picture and the way he talks. SEE ˈkwa ˈlwo.

~ nun. ¶ I sacin kwa ku uy māl kwa lo (= kwa man ulo) nun cinsang ul phaak halq swu ka ēps.ta From this picture and his tale it is impossible to grasp the truth.

ˈkwa ˈlol, pcl + pcl. ¶ ce ˈ[G]wa ˈnom ˈkwa ˈlol ˈecuˈlye (1447 Sek 9:16b) making oneself and others dizzy. haˈnolˈkhwa [= haˈnolh ˈkwa] ˈstaˈkhwa [= ˈstah ˈkwa] ˈlol ˈPPEM-NGWUY hoˈm ye (1462 ¹Nung 2:20b) encompass heaven and earth. SEE ˈkwa ˈl'.

kwa lul, pcl + pcl. with / and / like [as direct object, etc.]. ¶ A wa B wa lul kwupyel hay ya hanta A must be distinguished from B. I kūlim kwa ku kūlim kwa lul pīkyo hay posey yo Compare this picture with that one. Inchen kwa Sewul kwa lul wāng.lay hanun ppesu nun mānh.i iss.ta There are many buses running between Inchen and Seoul.

ˈkwa ˈlwo, pcl + pcl.

1. [ˈMWU-CHWUN] ˈkwa ˈlwo taˈmos [KKI-ˈYAK] ˈhwo.la (1481 Twusi 7:14a) it will be limited just to late autumn.

2. = ˈkwa (the same) as, like; (different) from. ¶ ne-huy ˈtolˈh i ... nay ˈoy tuˈliGwun ˈswon ˈkwa ˈlwo hon kaˈci ˈˈla CHA-ˈPPYELQ ˈˈep.suˈn i (1462 ¹Nung 2:19a) you people ... are the same as the hands I dangle, there is no difference. ˈˈsalom ˈkwa [ˈ]lwo hon ˈpsk uy ˈˈsal.m ye ˈstwo hon ˈpsk uy cwuˈku.l i ˈˈla (1481 Twusi 16:42a) we live together with people and we will die with people. NUNG ˈhi ˈMWULQ ˈGwa ˈlwo kolˈGwa (1482 Kum-sam 3:27a) it can well compete with material things. kwos tawo.m on [ˈSYEY-SSI] Gwalwo taonwos.ta (1481 Twusi 16:74a; accent dots obscured in repro?) when the blossoms come to an end they end with the season.

¶ ˈmwom ˈkwa mozom ˈkwa ˈlwo taloˈtwoˈta (1462 ¹Nung 2:46a) the body and the mind are different (from each other). SOYNG ˈkwa SOYNG ˈkwa y ˈˈes.tyey MWU-SOYNG ˈkwa ˈlwo taloˈl i (1482 Nam 1:17a) how will birth and [re]birth differ from birthlessness?

ˈkwa ˈlwo ˈsye. SEE ˈGwaˈ lwo ˈsye.

kwa mace, pcl + pcl. even with. ¶ Ku sālam kwa mace tathwess.uni icey n' māl puth.ye cwulq sālam to ēps.keyss.kwun Since you quarreled even with him, why now there won't be anybody who will talk to you.

~ to. ¶ Ce ay nun sensayng kwa mace to ssawu(l)lye ko tempini twulyewe hanun sālam i ēps.na pwā The way he rushes in to fight even with the teacher it appears there is no one he is afraid of.

kwa man, pcl + pcl. just/only with/and/like. ¶ Ku sālam un pam-nac chayk kwa man ssilum ul haci yo He is struggling with books night and day. Tangsin kwa man yēyki 'n tey ku pun pyēng i acwu cwūng han mo.yang iyo Just between you and me, he seems to be gravely ill.

~ ulo nun (example under kwa lo nun).

~ un. ¶ Tangsin kwa man un yēyki halq swu ka ēps.ˢo I can't tell it with just you here.

kwa n', abbr < kwa nun

ˈkwa n', abbr < ˈkwaˈnon. ¶ ˈNGWO-ˈCHALQ ˈGwa ˈˈNGA-SIN ˈkwa n' ˈˈta TTYANG ˈay ˈˈepˈkwo ˈKKYEY ˈyey is.noˈn i ˈˈla (1465 Wen 2:3:1:75a) the land of enlightenment (kṣetra) and the ego are both in the gāthās (hymns) and not part of the eternal.

kwān SEE kwān twuta

kwa 'na, pcl + cop advers. with / and / like or the like; whether with/and/like; with / and / like whatever. ¶ Tangsin kwa 'na kanta 'myen molutoy honca kaki nun silh.e It is another question if you're accompanying me, but I hate to go all alone. Ape' nim kwa nun an thong hani-kka hyeng nim kwa 'na māl hay pwā ya 'keyss.ta Since I can't communicate with Father I'll have to try talking to Brother, say.

-kwance (1876 Kakok p.9) < -kwanˈtye

-kwangi, suffix. a person. ¶ **michi-kwangi** a madman. **nuli-kwangi** a slowpoke (= **nulinpo**). [< **kwang** < KKWANG 'mania(c), fan' + **i** 'person'; CF **eli-kwang** playing the baby, **wusup-kwang sulepta** is ludicrous, **kwāngtay** clown]

-ˊkwa-ngi ˈˈta, polite exclamatory first-person polite statement. ¶ ˈna y NGWANG ¨mal-ssom tut¨copkwo ˈza na ˈy mozoˈm i ˈskoytotˈkwa-ngi ˈˈta (1447 Sek 24:29b) only after hearing Your Majesty's words is my mind awakened. ˈna y tut¨copˈkwo NGUY-SIM s ˈkumuˈl ul kusˈkwa-ngi ˈˈta (1463 Pep 2:24b) I listen and sever my net of doubts! woˈnol ˈi mwo[ˈ]ton ˈTTAY-¨HHWOY ˈGwa ˈstwo ˈna y ¨ta hoˈma ˈpwozopˈkwa-ngi ˈˈta (1463 Pep 4:169a) today this entire congregation and also I, we all have seen. woˈnol ˈza mas-ˈnaˈzopˈkwa-ngi ˈˈta (1463 Pep 3:120b) only today do I humbly meet them. SEE -ˈGwa-ngi ˈˈta; CF -ˈa-ngi ˈˈta.

kwangkyeng < KWANG-¨KYENG, n. spectacle, scene, sight; scenery, view. ¶ **Thayngkhu ka sīwi hanun haksayng tul ul kkal.e cwuk.inun kwangkyeng un cham.a polq swu ēps.ess.ta** I could not stand to look at the spectacle of tanks rolling over and killing the demonstrating students. **Ku sēnswu ka kwēnthwu sip-hoy cēn ul hako nan kwangkyeng ul poni kwēnthwu nun yāman-cek ita** The sight of the boxer emerging from a ten-round bout tells me that boxing is barbaric. **Atul i komun ul tang halq kwangkyeng ul sayngkak hamyen cam i an onta** When I think of (the scene of) my son about to undergo torture I cannot get to sleep. CF **mosup**.

kwan hata < KWAN ˚hoˈta, vni. The appropriate particle is **ey** for people or things.

1. (= **tāy hata**) refers (to), relates (to), is concerned (with), is about. ¶ **ku sālam ey kwan hay se māl hata** speaks concerning / about him. **cēncayng / kwun.in ey kwan han chayk** a book about war / soldiers.

2. (= **kwankyey hata**) has to do (with), has influence or bearing (on), affects, concerns. ¶ **kēnkang ey kwan han swutan** measures that bear on (affect) one's health. **mok-swum ey kwan han mūncey** a question of life (and death). **hung-mang ey kwan han kyelqceng** a decision that affects the destiny (of ⋯).

kwani, abbr < **ko hani**. SEE -**un** ~ .

kwankyey < KWAN-KYEY, n. 1. relation(ship), bearing, respect, connection. ¶ ~ **tāy-myengsa (pūsa)** a relative pronoun (adverb).

(-**un** / -**nun**) ~ **lo** in connection with; as a result of, because of. ¶ **Tāythong.lyeng un inchek kwankyey lo konan i mānh.ess.ta** The president got into a lot of trouble because of relatives. **Tōn i ēps.nun kwankyey lo cīn.hak haci mōs hanta** He cannot go on to higher schooling for financial reasons. **Ku ⁿyeca nun yeyppun kwankyey lo pak.myeng ita** She is ill-fated as a result of her beauty.

2. concern, interest; involvement, complicity; participation. ¶ **kwankyey-ca** the concerned party, the person(s) involved. **kwankyey-kwuk** the nation(s) concerned, a participant nation. ~ **kikwan / kwancheng** the agency / authorities concerned.

3. influence, effect.

4. sexual involvement, liaison, affair; sexual relations.

kwankyey hata, vni, vnt (CF **kwan hata**).

1. relates to, bears on, concerns, is connected.

2. takes part in, concerns oneself in, is a party to, has a hand in.

3. affects, has to do with, has influence / bearing on, matters.

4. has an affair (is sexually involved) with.

ˈkwa ˈnon, pcl + pcl. ¶ ˈkaci ˈGwa ˈnipˈkwa ˈnon saˈwonaˈWon ¨saloˈm ol kaˈcolˈpisiˈkwo ˈCYENG hon yeˈluˈm un TUK ¨in ¨saloˈm ol kaˈcolˈpisiˈn i ˈla (1447 Sek 13:47a) he compared the bad people with the branches and leaves and the people in whom virtue has formed with the true fruit. SEE ˈkwa nˈ.

-**kwantay** → -**kwantey**

-**kwantey** (< -**kwanˈtoy**), semi-lit sequential. such that, so that (followed by a question doubting the adequacy of the reason). ¶ **Yo say mues ul hakwantey han pen to oci anh.so** What in the world are you doing these days that you never come to see me? **Ney him i elma ˈna sēykwantey kuleh.key ppop-nāynun ya** Are you strong enough to be so proud? SYN -**kentey**. CF -**ki lo / ey**.

-**kwanˈtoy**. since, as; such that, so that (followed by a question doubting the adequacy of the reason). ¶ ˈSO-ˈTTYEY ˈstwo ¨es.tyey ˈkhuti aˈni khwanˈtoy (= h[o]kwanˈtoy) SYENG-MWUN ˈi KWAN ˈhoˈya WUY ¨cyekwoˈmay isˈta nileˈl i

ˈGwo (1463/4 Yeng 2:62a) how can the four dogmas be so lacking in greatness that the śrāvaka (= hīnayāna disciple in the first stage) would look at them and say "they have a small amount of position"? NOTE: The form appears as postmod in *scwos-nil kwantoy* (1876 Kakok p.9), said by LCT to have the apperceptive meaning of **kwumen**; see ˈiˈla (4), -ˈkwanˈtye.
? ˈkwanˈtoy, abbr < *ˈhokwanˈtoy. ? ¨mwot ~ .
kwān twuta, abbr < **ku man twuta**
-ˈkwanˈtye, apperceptive [= kwu(me)n]. ¶*woˈnol s ˈnal [ˈ]TTI-ˈNGWOK MWON alˈph oy ˈsye ˈaki ˈGwa selu pwoˈkwanˈtye* (1459 Wel 23:87a) today exchanges looks with the child before the gate of hell!
kwa nun, pcl + pcl. as for with / and / like. ¶**Ku sālam kwa nun chomyen ip.nita** This is my first meeting with him. **Ku sālam kwa nun olayq tong-an sakwie on chinkwu 'ci yo** I have been friends with him for a long time. **Talun sālam kwa nun yēyki hay to cōh.ci man, ku sālam kwa nun haci mala** You can tell it to the other people, but don't tell him. **I sālam kwa ku sālam kwa nun** (= **kwa uy twū salam un**) **Cwungkwuk māl ul kongpu hako iss.ey yo** This person and that person (= those two) are studying Chinese.
SEE ˈkwa ˈnon, ˈkwa nˈ.
ˈkwa ˈoy, pcl + pcl (genitive). ¶*yeˈle YWEN ˈun ˈkwot KUN ˈkwa ˈSIK ˈkwa ˈoy YWEN ˈhoˈnwon yeˈle kaˈci s ˈPEP ˈiˈla* (1462 ¹Nung 2:17a) the pratyayas (secondary causes) are the ways that source and awareness are caused.
¶*ˈsay ˈGwa ¨nyey ˈGwa ˈoy KYWOW-ˈCHEP ˈiˈla* (1459 Wel 21:5a) it is the joining of new and old.
kwa pota, pcl + pcl. ¶**I sālam kwa pota ce sālam kwa pīkyo hanun kes i cōh.keyss.ta** It would be better to draw a comparison with that person rather than with this person. **I sālam kwa pota ce sālam kwa kath.i kanun key cōh.keyss.ta** It would be better to go with that person rather than with this person.
SEE **hako pota**.
kwa puthe, pcl + pcl. ¶**Kim sensayng kwa puthe mence uy¹non hay ponun key cōh.ulq key 'ta** We should start the discussion with Mr Kim.
ˈkwa s, pcl + pcl. ¶*ˈTI ˈGwa ˈTTYENG ˈkwa s ˈhi.m i* (1463 Pep 2:153b) the powers of jñāna (wisdom) and samādhi (meditation). ¨*SYEN kwa*

ˈQAK ˈkwa s ˈNGEP ˈi.n i (1482 Nam 1:77a) is the karma of good and evil; ¨*KHWO [G]wa ˈLAK ˈkwa s ˈPWOW lul* (ibid.) the retribution of suffering and joy. ¨*es[ˈ]tyey ¨ta-mon ¨yelkhwa* [← ˈyelh ˈkwa] ˈ*QILQ-ˈPOYK ˈkwa s stoloˈm i.l i ˈ-ngi s ˈkwo* (1475 Nay 2:2:72a) how come it is only one hundred and ten? *haˈnolˈkhwa ˈstaˈkhwas* (= *haˈnolh ˈkwa ˈstah ˈkwa s) soˈzi ˈyey* (1481 Twusi 8:47b, 21:5b; 1482 Kum-sam 3:38b) between heaven and earth.
~ **kungey**. ¶*pwuthye ˈ[G]wa ¨cywung ˈkwa s kungey ˈPWO-SI hoˈm ye* (1447 Sek 13:23a) give alms to Buddha and the monks, and ... .
kwa se, pcl + pcl [rare]. from (or at / in / ...) ... with / and / like. ¶**Emeˈ nim kwa apeˈ nim kwa se sanguy hasin kyelkwa isa haki lo hayss.ta** As a result of discussions between mother and father, it was decided to move.
ˈkwa ¨spwun, pcl + postmod / postn. ¶*THYEN ˈkwa ˈNGWOK ˈkwa ¨spwun aˈni ˈˈGen maˈlon* (1465 Wen 2:1:2:43b) it is not just heaven and hell, but ... .
ˈkwa s [¨]spwun, pcl + pcl + postmod / postn. ¶¨*es[ˈ]tyey ¨ta-mon ¨yelkhwa* [← ˈyelh ˈkwa] ˈ*QILQ-ˈPOYK ˈkwa s stoloˈm i.l i ˈ-ngi s ˈkwo* (1475 Nay 2:2:72a) how come it is only one hundred and ten?
-**kwa swoˈla**, effective inf (exclamatory) + bnd v indic assert. SEE ˈ**khwa swoˈla**.
? ˈ**kwa swoˈla**, abbr < *ˈhoˈkwa swoˈla after a voiceless sound; CF ˈ**khwa swoˈla**.
No examples have been found.
kwa to < ˈkwa ˈtwo, pcl + pcl. with (and / like) also / even / either. ¶**Hyeng kwa to uy¹non hay pwā la** Talk it over with your older brother, too. **Nay maum un choq pul kwa to kath.ta** My heart is (just) like a flickering candle.
-ˈ**kwatoyˈye** < *-ˈkwa to[wo]yˈye. wanting to do. ¶*hoˈkwaˈtoyye* (1481 Twusi 20:34a; accent unexplained). ABBR -ˈkwaˈtye. CF -ˈkwoˈcye.
ˈˈ**kwatoyˈye**, abbreviation < *hoˈkwatoyˈye after a voiceless consonant. ¶*kwuyˈyey eˈlwu-siˈle tulul ¨spwu.n i ˈGen ˈtyeng iˈp ey eˈlwu-siˈle niloˈti ¨mwot ˈˈkwatoyˈye ˈhonwoˈla* (1475 Nay 1:37a) I can only hear it very well in my ears but I cannot possibly want to say it with my mouth.
kwa tul, particle + particle (plural subject)
ˈ**kwa ˈtwo**, particle + particle. SEE ˈ**Gwa ˈtwo**.
-ˈ**kwaˈtya** = ˈ**kwaˈtye**

-ˈkwa ˈtye, abbr < -ˈkwatoyˈye (< *-ˈkwa to[wo]yˈye). wanting to do. SEE -uˈsikwaˈtye.

kwa uy < ˈkwa ˈoy, pcl + pcl. (the one that is) with/and/like. ¶cip kwa path kwa uy sai between the house and the field. Yengkwuk kwa Cosen kwa uy talun cēm the differences (the points of difference) between England and Korea. kyēngchal kwa uy ¹yen.lak contact/ liaison with the police. Sewul kwa uy kēli ka elma 'na toyci yo How far is the distance to/ from Seoul?

ˈkwa y ← ˈkwa ˈi, pcl + pcl. ¶ˈsolˈkhwa kas ˈkwa y isˈti aˈni thwoˈta ← ˈsolh ˈkwa kac ˈkwa ˈi isˈti aˈni ˈhotwoˈta (1481 Twusi 8:2a) flesh and skin are lacking. SEE ˈGwa y.

ˈkwa 'yla ˈtwo, pcl + cop inf var + pcl. ¶kotok hon ˈKALQ ˈGwa TTUNG ˈkwa 'yla ˈtwo despite ample reeds and rattan (1482 Kum-sam 5:30-1).

kwa ya, pcl + pcl. only (if it be) with/and/like. ¶Ku sālam kwa ya cal ānun sai 'ci yo I know HIM very well. Ku īl kwa ya āmu kwankyey to ēps.ci It has nothing at all to do with THAT matter. Ku sālam kwa ya etteh.key tōn(q) yēyki lul halq swu iss.na yo How can I talk about money with HIM?

kwaynchanh.ta, adj (abbr < kwan[kyey] haci ani hata). CF cōh.ta.

1. is not (so) bad, is passably good, is OK, is all right, is tolerable, is acceptable, will do. ¶mas i ~ it tastes OK. kwaynchanh.un kaps a good price. Mom i kwaynchanh.ni? Are you feeling better?

2. it makes no difference, it is all right (for it to happen), it is permissible; one doesn't mind/ care (even if). ¶Incey ka to kwaynchanh.ta You may go now.

-ˈkway-ngi ˈˈta = -ˈkwa-ngi ˈˈta. ¶yeˈkuy nelˈGiˈkway-ngi ˈˈta (?1517- ¹No 1:59a) we've caused you a lot of trouble.

-kwaysˈkwo (< -kwa isˈkwo) SEE (aˈni) khwaysˈkwo

ˈkwa y ˈza, pcl + pcl + pcl. SEE ˈ[G]wa y ˈza.

-ˈkwo = -ko gerund. ~ k, ~ n', ~ ˈsye, ~ ˈtwo, ~ ˈza; ~ ˈcye, ~ ˈˈla, ~ ˈˈl ye.

ˈˈkwo, abbr < hoˈkwo after a voiceless sound; CF ˈkhwo; (cop) ˈˈGwo, 'yˈGwo. ¶ i CIN-ˈCCYENG ˈTTAY-ˈPEP ˈul ˈˈce y ˈTUK ˈˈkwoˈcyeˈhoˈya (1459 Wel 18:3a) we want ourselves to get the truly pure great law, and ... . SEE ˈˈmwot ~.

ˈkwo, postmod. the [often quoted, rhetorical, or exclamatory] question (whether); SEE -un (-nun/-tun/-ulq) ko. Lenited to ˈGwo after l, y, and often i. After other vowels the initial sometimes elides: ˈ[G]wo (Part I, §2.11.1). Before ˈkwo, as before ˈka, often (but not always) the copula modifier ˈin drops: N ˈkwo = N ˈin ˈkwo. ¶ i kwoˈc on muˈsum kwosˈkwo [← kwocˈkwo] (1447 Sek 23:40b) what flowers are these? ne 'y susuˈng i ˈnwuˈkwo (1447 Sek 23:41b) who is your master? ⋯ ˈi muˈsuˈkwo (1482 Kum-sam 2:41a) what is this? ˈˈes.te 'n cyenˈcho [G]wo (1482 Kum-sam 3:52a) what cause is it from?

NOTE: MK ˈkwo denotes only questions that contain a content-interrogative ('what' etc.) and it is not used for a yes-or-no question, while MK ˈka denotes either type of question.

-ˈkwoˈcya (1586 Sohak 6:18b) = -ˈkwoˈcye

-ˈkwoˈcye, ger + abbr < ciˈye (inf < ciˈta). wanting to do; ready/prepared/willing to do; intending to, going to. NOTE: Shibu 1975 says that -ˈkwoˈcye is a desire of the speaker for his own act but that -ˈkwaˈtye or -ˈkuy 'sˈkwo is a desire for others to act.

~ °hoˈta wants to do; intends to (do). ¶kutuy sˈstoˈl ol masˈkwoˈcyeˈhoˈte-ngi ˈˈta (1447 Sek 6:15a) he has been wanting to meet your daughter.

~ ˈhoˈya wanting/intending to (do). ¶ˈwuli ˈtolˈthwo [= ˈtolhˈtwo] ˈi CIN-ˈCCYENG ˈTTAY-ˈPEP ˈul ˈˈce y ˈTUK ˈˈkwoˈcyeˈhoˈya (1459 Wel 18:3a) we want ourselves to get the truly pure great law. ALSO: 1462 ¹Nung 7:73b, 1485 Kwan 1a.

~ s (pcl). SEE s (15c).

~ 'y.n i (abbr cop modifier + postmodifier). ¶NGEN ˈkwa [ˈ]KWAN ˈon PANG ˈol cwoˈcha wolˈmwom iˈsywo.m ol polˈkiˈkwo cye 'y'n i (1463/4 Yeng 2:31b) it wants to be clarified that speech and view sometimes change course.

-ˈkwo °hoˈta (= -ˈkwoˈcye °hoˈta) SEE -ˈkwo ˈˈla, -ˈkwo ˈˈl ye

-ˈkwo k, gerund + emphatic particle. ¶naˈla.h on [ˈPOYK-ˈSYENG] ˈulwo [KON-ˈˈPWON] ˈul ˈˈsamˈkwo k kwoˈki non ˈˈcwuliˈm ye n' ˈkwos-taˈwon naksˈpa.p ol [PI-ˈSSIK] ˈhono.n i ˈˈla (1481 Twusi 16:19b) the nation takes for its foundation the peasants and when the fish are

hungry they gobble up the gaudy bait. SEE -usi ˙kwo k.
-kwo(k) [Ceycwu DIAL] = -ko, gerund (Seng ¹Nakswu 1984:35, 51). ¶pang i tul.e kakwo(k) = pang ey tul.e kako entering the room. pap mek.kwok hok.kywo i kanta = pap mek.ko hak.kyo ey kanta I eat before I go off to my school. way-pay ka ka pwul.e sa na-wokwok holyes.swuta = way-pay ka ka pelye ya na-oko n' ha.yess.ˢup.nita They would not come out until the Japanese ship(s) had left.
NOTE: To this LSN 1978:104 compares the MK ho˙kwo k, ˙ho.ya k, etuwek (?), and also -u˙l ak. The final (-)k seems to be an emphatic particle, perhaps reduced from ˙ka, which was attached to the gerund -˙kwo or the infinitive -ᵉ⁄ₐ and perhaps to a few adverbs or particles. See k, -˙a k, -˙e k, -˙kwo k; -(u)˙l ak; -˙ta ˙ka.
-˙kwo ˙'la, abbreviation < -˙kwo ho˙la (= ho˙l ya/ye). ¶ ˙PWU-˙CYWOK ˙on ¨mal-ssom pu˙thye ¨amo˙lyey ho˙kwo ˙'la ¨CHYENG hol˙ss i˙la (1447 Sek 6:46a; sic, ¨amo˙lyey = ¨a˙molyey) [the term] ˙PWU-˙CYWOK means to request by (attaching) words wanting it to happen in a certain way. SOYNG-SOYNG ˙ay na ˙y ˙NGWEN ˙ul il˙thi a˙ni ˙khey ho˙kwo ˙'la (1459 Wel 1:13b) in life after life I do not want to let my desire be lost. SEE -˙Gwo ˙'la.
-˙kwo ˙'l ye, abbr < -˙kwo ho˙l ye. ¶na ˙y a˙ki ¨wuy ˙ho˙ya ¨e˙te pwo˙kwo ˙'l ye (1447 Sek 6:13b) I'd like you to seek her out [as a bride] for my boy.
˙kwom, pcl. each (= ssik). Alternant (after l, y, i) ˙Gwom, (after vowels other than i) ˙[G]wom. ¶hon KWANG-MYENG ˙kwom cwo˙cha ka (1447 Sek 24:24b) each following after a light. ¨sey pen ˙kwom (1475 Nay 1:39b) three times each. hon THYEN ˙i˙Gwo ˙SO-PANG ˙ay ye˙tulp ˙kwom pe˙le is.ke˙tun ... (1459 Wel 1:31a) as in each of the four directions there are spread eight [of the 33 Indra] heavens ... . ˙SYA-˙LI-˙PWULQ ˙uy kungey mwu˙la ¨twu cum˙key s ˙kil[h] ¨ma˙ta TTYENG-˙SYA ˙lol ¨sey˙khwom (= ¨seyh ˙kwom) ci˙zu˙n i (1449 Kok 153) he [Sudatta] asked Śāriputra [about the way to Śrāvastī] and in each path between two mighty trees he built three monasteries. NOTE: This particle fell into disuse in the written language by 1700 but it continues as part of the dialect of Cenla.

-˙kwom, suffix. intensifies adverb (CF -kum). ¶ta˙si-˙kwom (1447 Sek 6:6a) again. kwop˙koy-˙kwom (1459 Wel 1:47b) so as to double it. ¨es.tyey si˙le-˙kwom (1481 Twusi 7:7b) how possibly. SEE ˙ili-˙kwom, kuli-kwom.
-˙kwom ˚ho- do repeatedly; CF -ko n(un) ha-. ¶ ˙kwoti ˙aki ˙lol a˙na ˙ta ka ˙mul ey po˙likwom ˙hwo.m i ¨twu pen ˙ile˙n i (1485 Kwan 10b) there were a couple of occasions when they [the mothers] would hug the baby and then throw it in the water. ... a˙ni han te˙t ey ˙stwo wolo˙kwom hol˙ss oy (1463 Pep 1:164a) in a little while [the apes] starting climbing again.
-˙kwo n' (... ˙homol˙mye), ger + abbr pcl. and, but (much more/less ...). ¶ ˙SWU ¨ep˙kwo n' ˙homol˙mye ku mwol˙Gay ˙sto˙n i-ngi s ˙ka (1464 Kumkang 62b) they are innumerable, but how much more so is the sand?! SYWUY-¨HUY KWONG ˙two ku˙le ho˙kwo n' NGWEN-TTI KWONG ˙ol a˙lalq t ilwo˙ta (1459 Wel 17:54a) achieving the sharing of the joy of others, how much more you will know of an all-embracing achievement of merit! ˙tye hon SA-PPA ˙two ˙wohi˙lye ¨mwo˙tilwo˙m ol twu˙li˙kwo n' ˙SSIP-PANG on CIN-˙SSILQ ˙lwo e˙lyewul˙ss oy pwuthye s hi˙m ey KWONG ˙ol pwo[˙]nayzo˙wa ˙stwo ¨SYWUW-˙HHWO teu˙sya.m ol KKWUW ˙ho˙si.n i ˙'la (1463 Pep 4:192-3; sic, hi˙m ey ← ˙hi˙m ey; the smudge on ¨CIN¨ is not a tone mark) fearing the evil of that one world (of sahā), it is all the harder everywhere, so we consign our good works to Buddha's power as he seeks further to enhance our protection. SEE ˙Gwo n', two˙kwo n'.
(-)kwona (1894 Gale 38-9) = (-)kwun a
˙kwos, pcl. just, precisely, indeed. Alternant (after l, y, i) ˙Gwos, (after vowels other than i) ˙[G]wos. CF kot₃. ¶wo˙cik MA-NGWANG ˙kwos ce y ˙CCWA ˙ay PPYEN-QAN ˙hi ¨mwot an˙ca si˙lum ˙ho˙ya ˙hote˙la (1459 Wel 2:42b) only the king of māras was just too distressed to sit comfortably in his seat. QWUY-SSIN ˙kwos a˙ni ˙'m ye n' (1459 Wel 21:25a) in the absence of the supernatural. ¨pwo[˙]poy s ku˙lus kwos a˙ni ˙'m ye n' (1482 Nam 2:8a) unless it is a jewelled vessel. MI-˙MYWOW hon kalak ˙kwos ¨ep.su˙m ye n' (1463 Pep se:23a) lacking a fine and delicate tune. si˙lum s ˙kut ˙kwos ˙stwo [˙SYWEY-SSI] ˙lwo is.twota (1481 Twusi 8:36a)

the brink of sorrow comes with the times and seasons. SEE *aʾni ʾGwos, kuʾli ʾGwos, ʾoy ʾGwos, -ʾti ʾGwos.*
(*)-ʾkwo s, ger + pcl (? abbr < -ʾkwo ʾsye). SEE *twoʾkwo s.*
-ʾkwo ʾsye, ger + pcl. ¶ *aʾtok hon ¨saloʾm i ingey ¨naʾm ol ¨aʾti ¨mwot ʾkwo ʾsye ˙PPWULQ-¨TTWOW ʾay heʾmul ¨nilGwuyʾye keyGulʾGe mulʾlwul ʾptuʾt ul ¨naylʾss oy* (1463 Pep 3:180ab) dim-witted people, unaware that they will henceforth emerge, make errors in Buddhism and show a lazy disposition to withdraw.
ʾkwot, quasi-free n. place. SEE *kos.*
-ʾkwo ʾtwo, ger + pcl. ¶ *piʾlwok ¨saloʾm oy ʾmwuʾl ey ¨sa-ʾnikwo ʾtwo cwungsoyng ʾma ʾtwo ¨mwot ʾhwo-ngi ʾʾ ta* (1447 Sek 6:5a) even [my] living on in the society of human beings is inferior to the life of any living creature. *namʾk i nwophʾkwo ʾtwo pwulʾhwuy ʾlol paʾhiʾm ye nʾ yeʾlum ʾul ¨taʾpta meknoʾn i* (1449 Kok 99) though the tree be tall, if you cut its root you can pluck all its fruit and eat it. *tutʾkwo ʾtwo ¨mwot tulun ʾtoʾs ʾi hoʾm ye* (1459 Wel 10:20b) they hear but act as if they do not hear, and ... .
-ʾkwo ʾza, ger + pcl (> -ko ya). ¶ *i ¨mal tutʾkwo ʾza ¨HEM-¨TTWOW ʾlol aʾla* (1459 Wel 21:118b) only hearing these words did he realize the perilous path and ... . *˙PAN-ʾKEP ¨ti-¨nayGwo ʾza QA-LA-ʾHAN ʾol ilʾGwu.l iʾʾn i* (1459 Wel 8:58ab) only after half a kalpa had passed were the arhan (saints) created. *ʾileʾn ˙PYEN-ʾHWA ʾlol ¨pwoyGwo ʾza SSIN-ʾCYWOK ʾol kaʾta twolwo ¨PWON-ʾCCWA ʾay ʾtuʾle ancoʾn i ʾʾ la* (1447 Sek 6:34ab) only when he had demonstrated these transformations did he gather up his ṛddhipāda (deva-foot ubiquity) and go back to sit in his place. *ʾcoʾsyey ʾhi ¨mwut-cyeʾcwukwo ʾza* (?1517-¹No 1:51b) they insisted on inquiring of us in detail.
-kwu-, suf (derives vc). tot.kwu- make it higher, (= tot.wu-) raise it < tot- < twot- rise. sos.kwu- make it rise < sos- < swos- spring up. CF -i-, -hi-, -ki-, -chi-, -ukhi-, -ikhi-, -li-, -iwu-, -ywu-; -wu-, -hwu-, -ay-; -ʾGi-, -ʾGwo-, -ʾGwu-, -o-, -u-.
ʾ/-kwu [var] = ʾ/-ko
kwu, pcl [var] = ko. SEE -ula ~ , -ca ~ .
¶ *loynyen ey Cywungkwuk kanwola kwu hopteyta*
(1894 Gale 39) he says he is going to China next year.
kwuc.ta, 1. adj. is bad, nasty unpleasant.
2. postnom adj insep (rarely sep). is bad with respect to. ¶ simswul (i) ~ is ill-tempered. āmsang ~ is jealous. cīs ~ is bothersome, nagging. saysal / sisel ~ is dreadfully flippant. teysel ~ is light-headed, frivolous. yalmang ~ is difficult and despicable; CF yal-kwuc.ta is perverse or erratic. CF ay-kkwuc.ta is undeservedly mistreated, is to be pitied ?< ayk kwuc.ta (Ko Yengkun 1974:89).
(-q) kwulek, postn [?< kwū-l- + -ek] the act of. muliq kwulek (muli-kkwulek) paying off for another: ~ hata pays off [muli appears only in this structure; it is the derived noun < vt muluta 'returns it'].
-q kwuleki → kkwuleki
kwūlta, aux vi sep -L- [always preceded by an adverb or adverbative]. acts, behaves (toward a person), treats (a person). ¶ komapkey ~ acts kindly (toward a person), treats one kindly. mopsi ~ acts harshly (toward a person), treats a person severely. mōs kyentikey ~ behaves unbearably (toward a person). mipkey to ~ behaves most hatefully. CF kwulek.
(-)kwulya [Seoul female speech] = (-)kwulye. ¶ Atuʾ nim i tol.a wā se cōh.keyss.kwulya You must be glad that your son has come home.
(-)kwulye, FORMAL apperceptive.
1. ending and postmodifier = (-)kwumen.
2. particle following -sup.nita (formal indic assertive), attached to verb, adjective, or copula. ¶ Kuleh.key mānh.un phīnan-min tul i mollye tul.e wass.uni, sīnay uy sik.lyang pāykup i kōn.¹nan hakeyss.ˢup.nita kwulye With so many refugees pouring in, I realize it must be hard keeping the city supplied with food.
3. particle following -ney (the familiar indic assertive — attached to verb stems, to iss- and ēps-, to -ess- and -keyss-, and to ilq sey = iney); also retr -tey. ¶ Caney māl cal haney kwulye You are very eloquent, indeed. Payk kwun uy cacey ʾlq sey kwulye Why, it's Payk's son! Pap sang ul palq kil lo chatey kwulye He kicked the table with his foot!
4. [vulgar] particle following a formal or familiar statement (-upsita, -sey) or command (-usio, -key). ¶ Kapsita / Kasey kwulye Let's go. Kasio / Kakey kwulye Go on!

5. [DIAL] inflectional ending attached to verb stems as a kind of permissive command: go ahead and do it then. ¶**Cōh.tolok hakwulye** Do as you please. **Ol they 'myen okwulye** You may come if you want to.
NOTE: As a particle, usually pronounced **kulye** in Seoul. Attested both as *-kulye* and as *-kwule* in 1728.
(-)**kwulye tul**, FORMAL apperceptive + particle
(-)**kwulyo** → (-)**kwulye**
-**kwuma (yo)**, [Cincwu DIAL (Mkk 1960:3:34)] = -**e (yo)** attached to adj, cop, iss-, -ess-, -keyss-. CF -**nungkwuma (yo)**; -**kwumen (yo)**.
-**kwu mālkwu** [var] = -**ko mālko**
(-)**kwu man** = (-)**ko man**
(-)**kwuman** → (-)**kwumen**. ~ **se to** [DIAL].
(-)**kwumen**, FAMILIAR apperceptive. well I see ···, well so it is ···, so it is!, so it seems!, well I'll be (damned)!, hey look!, you see, don't you know, n'est-ce pas, isn't it, indeed (shows a sudden realization, confirmation, interest, delight, surprise, astonishment, or insistence). SYN (-)**kwun a** (much used by children and women), (-)**kwun** (often used among younger intimates), (-)**kwulye** (less familiar), (-)**kwun yo** (polite), (-)**kwumen yo** (more polite).
1. inflectional ending attached to the copula; to adj stems; to iss- and ēps-, to -ess- and -keyss- (attached to any stem); and to the retrospective -tu- attached to adjective stems or (replacing the retr modifier -tun) to verb stems. ¶**A kuleh.kwumen** Oh is that it! Indeed, that's right; I see what you mean; So it is; Well I'll be! **Pi ka wass.kwumen** Why it's rained! **Atu' nim i iss.ey yo?** − **Eti na-kass.kwumen yo** Is your son home? − Why, he seems to have gone out somewhere. **Tahayng hi phyo sanun sālam i mānh.ci anh.kwun a** Look, folks, luckily there aren't many buying tickets. **Ttok kath.kwun a** Why it looks just like it! **Kulem mūncey nun kantan hakwumen** Then the question is simple. **Hwalye han sayk-kal [= pich-(k)kal] i cōh.keyss.kwumen** I guess a fancy color would be nice! **Ku tōngney nun ōykwuk-chon kath.keyss.kwumen** That part of town must be line a kind of foreign colony! **Changtek-kwung i palo yeki 'kwun a** Why, Changtek Palace is right here! **Pom ey han pen te wā ya hakeyss.kwun** We'll have to come again sometime in the spring! **Wēn-swungi tul i cham mānh.kwun a** My, there are a lot of monkeys! **Palo ce pawi alay hōlang-i ka iss.kwun a** Look − there are tigers right under that rock! **Kulem cēngsik ul mek.ulq swu pakk ey ēps.kwun yo** Well, I see we have no choice but to eat the fixed meal. **Kulem ku kyelhon ey cwungmay-in i tāy-hwal.yak ul hayss.keyss.kwun yo** Well I'd say that in that marriage the go-between surely must have been extremely active! **Kulem ku mānh.un tōn un ku namphyen i tā kacyess.keyss.kwun a** Then the husband must have got all her money! **Ilponq sālam i(lo)kwun yo** He's a Japanese! **Mikwuk pihayng-ki '(lo)kwun yo** Why, that is an American airplane! **Cham cōh.un chayk ilokwun a** This is a nice book indeed. **Ce key tāyhap-sil ilokwun a** That's the lobby over there! **Pelsse ōceng ilokwun** Well, well, here it is noon already. **Kulay? Kulem swucay tul iess.kwun a** Really? Then they were a talented lot indeed!
2. postmodifier; follows processive (-nun) or retrospective (-tun) modifiers of verbs. But -**tun kwumen** (etc.) usually is shortened to -**tu-kwumen** (etc.). ¶**Pi ka onun kwumen** Well, I see it's raining! **Pi ka otun kwumen** (or **otu-kwumen**) Why, it's been raining! **Elin ay ka tāmpay lul phi(wu)nun kwun yo** Look, the young kids are smoking! **Ce alay sālam tul i cham cāk.key poinun kwun a** The people below look so small! **Ku sālam i kyelkwuk Hānkwuk ey kanun kwumen yo** I see he is finally going to Korea! **Ku ka nōlki man hatuni kkok ¹nakcey lul hanun kwun yo** He's done nothing but loaf so he's failng without a doubt! **Tases si ey nun mun ul tat.nun kwun a** Hey, (it says here) they close the gate at five o'clock! **Pelsse ce i tul un keki na-ka anc.e se cha lul masinun kwun a** Look, those other people have already gone out there to sit and drink their tea! **Sikol ey lul kani-kka n' chammal Hānkwuk ey on kes kath.tukwun yo** (= **kath.tun kwun yo**) Going to the country, I suddenly felt for the first time that I had truly come to Korea. **Sikol se nun acik to pumo tul i cacey tul uy hon.in ul cēng hako iss.tukwun yo** (= **iss.tun kwun yo**) In the country I found that the parents still arrange the marriages of

their children. **Thukpyel hi kimchi mas i yūmyeng hatukwun yo** I found the flavor of the kimchi in particular to be famous.
(-)kwumen (se) to [DIAL] = **(-)kwumen**
(-)kwumen tul, apperceptive + particle. ¶ **Tā osyess.kwumen tul** You are all here, I see!
(-)kwumen yo, more polite apperceptive. ~ **tul** = **(-)kwumen tul yo**.
(-)kwumyen [DIAL; written] = **(-)kwumen**
kwūn, adnoun. extra, excess, supernumerary, superfluous, unnecessary, uncalled-for, luxury: ~ **kes**, ~ **teteki** a superfluous / unnecessary thing. ¶ ~ **chim** slavver, drool. ~ **cīs** useless action. ~ **hoyk** an extra / unwanted stroke (in a character). ~ -**q īl** extra / needless / busy work. ~ -**q ip(-ceng)**, ~ -**q ip cil** eating between meals. ~ **kekceng** needless worry. ~ **kichim** a hack (cough). ~ **māl** needless (redundant or uncalled-for) words. ~ **mul** water drunk between meals; water added to boiling water; oozings. ~ **nay** an unnatural / unpleasant smell (≠ **kwuwun nay** a burnt smell). ~ **pap** extra food for an unexpected guest; leftover rice. ~ **pīyong** extra / unnecessary expenses. ~ **pul** extra fire made just for heating a room (not for cooking food). ~ **sālam** a supernumerary, an extra hand, a dispensable / temporary employee. ~ **sayngkak** useless thought(s). ~ **sik.kwu** a temporary extra member of the household, a guest (boarder). ~ **soli** nonsense; talking in one's sleep; ravings in a delirium; complaining. ~ **son cil** unnecessary touches (or handwork); "lifting things" (= stealing). ~ **son nim** an uninvited guest. ~ **thek** double chin. ~ **ūmsik** a (between-meals) snack.
kwun < *KWUN*, postnoun, noun.
  1. (a title after the surname or personal name of an equal or an inferior).
  2. you [to an equal or an inferior].
  3. [obsolete] Lord ... .
(-q) kwun < *KWUN*, postnoun, postmod. a man occupied with ... , a doer of ... , a person who is engaged in ... ; a person noted / notorious for ... . CF **kwuni**; **ca(y)ngi**.
  1. postnoun. **cangnanq** ~ a prankster, a practical joker, a mischief-maker, a naughty / mischievous child. **chongq** ~ a gunner; a hunter; a gunman. **cikeyq** ~ = **cimq** ~ a porter. **cwūcengq** ~ a drunken brawler. **iksalq** ~ a jokester, a wag. **in.lyek-keq** ~ a rickshaman. **īlq** ~ a laborer, a workman, a hand; an able man. **keycengq** ~ a grumbler. **kīlq** ~ a skilled gambler. **kwulwumaq** ~ a carter, a drayman. **kyeth** ~ an extra hand, a helper. **namuq** ~ a woodman, a woodcutter. **nōlumq** ~ a gambler. **nolyek** ~ = **nolyek-ka** a hard worker, a diligent person (CF [1]**nolyek-ca** toiler, a manual worker). **ssilumq** ~ a wrestler. **ssuleykiq** ~ a garbage collector.
  2. postmod. **pul ttaylq** ~ 'man to light fires' = a troublemaker.
[1] Yi Ungpayk (1961:501) seems to be alone in preferring the spelling **kkwun**; NKd even gives **kwun** as a free noun in the meaning 'personnel, member(s), participant(s)' — this seems to be a dialect equivalent of **ttey** or **muli** 'crowd'. And **kwun** also occurs free as abbr of **kīlq kwun** 'gambler'. The word was apparently borrowed from *KWUN* 'military troop(ers); army'.
(-)kwun, intimate apperceptive. SEE **(-)kwumen**.
kwu 'n('), abbr < **kwu han(un)** = **ko han(un)**
-kwu n', abbr < **-kwu nun** (= **-ko nun**)
(-)kwuna = **(-)kwun a**, 1. (inflectional ending, postmodifier) especially intimate apperceptive (much used by women and children). ~ **tul**, but there is no *(-)**kwun tul a**. SEE(-)**kwu(me)n**.
  2. SEE **kkwuna**
  3. CF **aikwu (na)** oh!; **elssikwu (na)** whoopee!
kwuni, postnoun [< -**q kwun** + **i**]. person. **cōpangq kwun(i)** a pimp. **pallok** ~ an idler, a playboy (**pallok** = **pallong** / **pellwung kelinta** gads about). CF -**ekw(un)i**, -**akw(un)i**, -**wuni**.
(-)kwun tul = **(-)kwumen tul**
-kwu 'n tul = **-ko [i]n tul**
kwu 'nun [var] = **ko 'nun**
-kwu nun [var] = **-ko nun**
(-)kwun yo, polite apperceptive. SEE **(-)kwumen**.
-kwu se [var] = **-ko se**
kwu twu, pcl + pcl [var] = **ko to**
-kwu twu [var] = **-ko to**
-kwu ya = **-ko ya**
kwu yo = **ko yo**
'kwu yo = **iko yo**
-kwu yo = **-ko yo**
kyāy, abbr < **ku ay**. that child; he / him, she / her. CF **cyāy**, **yāy**.
kyel$_1$, noun. 1. a wave. ¶ **mulq** ~ a wave (in the water). **swūmq** ~ waves of breath, breathing.

2. impetus, (on) the wave of. SEE kyel$_2$.

3. grain, texture. ¶namuq ~ grain of wood. tōlq ~ the grain of stone. ~ i kechilta is rough, is coarse(-grained). ~ i kōpta is fine(-grained). salq ~ i kōpta has a fine / delicate skin. pītanq ~ a silky / velvety texture.

4. = sēngq / maumq ~ disposition, temper, temperament.

5. = kyelq-ki impetuousness, vehemence.

6. anger. SEE ~ nata, ~ nāyta, ~ meli, ~ sakta; kyelq-cung. kyelq kīm ey = kolq kīm ey in a fit of anger. CF sēng, hwā, kol.

7. achimq kyel the forenoon. han-kyel much more; conspicuously; especially.

8. abbr < kyelul. enu ~ (= enu sai) in no time at all.

kyel$_2$, postnoun, postmodifier.

1. postn [usually -q kyel]. incidental (to), happening (to) in passing; "(on) the wave of". ¶nwunq ~ ey pota sees out of the corner of one's eye, catches a glimpse. kkwumq / camq ~ ey tut.ta listens half asleep. Kwiq kyel ey congq soli lul tul.ess.ta My ears happened to catch the sound of the bell. Palamq kyel ey mulq kyel soli ka tullye onta The wind brings with it the sound of the waves.

2. postmod [? abbr < kyelul; CF kyeth]. ¶tān ~ ey "while still hot (tālta)" = before the chance slips away.

-nun ~ (ey) = -nun kil (ey) (in) the course of; in passing while (doing); at the same time as; when, while, while one is at it. ¶cīna kanun kyel(ul) ey cāmqkan tullita drops in for a moment on one's way.

3. postmod. -un ~ (ey) = -un kīm (ey) (as) an incidental result of (having done). ¶Nōllan kyel ey kulus ul ttel.e ttulyess.ta I dropped the dish in my surprise.

4. postmod. SEE -ulq ~ (ey) = -nun ~ (ey). CF tun-son ey; palam, kīm, swūm.

kyelkwa < ˙KYELQ-˙KWA, noun. result, effect, consequence, outcome; issue, end, upshot; as a / the result. ¶sanguy han kyelkwa isa haki lo hayss.ta as a result of the discussions it was decided to move.

kyelkwuk < ˙KYELQ-˙KWUK, noun, adverb.

1. noun. the end, conclusion, finale. ~ ey n(un) in the final analysis, after all.

2. adverb = ~ ey ka se (nun) in the end, finally, after all. ¶Kyelkwuk ku nun ku ^{n}yeca wa kyelhon haki ey iluless.ta He finally ended up marrying her. Kyelkwuk kuleh.key toyn phok / sēym ita It seems that is the way it finally turned out to be. Ku sālam i kyelkwuk Hānkwuk ey kanun kwumen yo I see he is finally going to Korea!

kyelul, n. leisure, free time, time (to spare). ¶Phyēnci lul ssulq kyelul i ēps.ta I have no time to write letters. SEE enu kyelul ey. ABBR kyel. CF thum.

kyem < KYEM, n (occurs as postn -q kyem, as vn, and as postmod). and also, in addition, as well, plus, at the same time, combining (two functions).

1. as postnoun. ¶kwuk.mu chōng.liq kyem munkyo cāngkwan both Prime Minister and the Minister of Education (jointly). sāmu-silq kyem cwūthayk a combined (or combination) office and residence. Na nun nay pang ul chīmpangq kyem secayq kyem kayksil lo ssunta I use my room as a combined bedroom, study, and parlor. Chīmpangq kyem secayq kyem kayksil lo na nun pang hana lul ssunta I use one room as a bedroom-study-parlor.

2. as verbal noun. SEE ~ chita, ~ hata.

3. as postmodifier. SEE -ulq ~.

CF kyemtwu-kyemtwu, kyemsa(-kyemsa).

kyem chita, cpd vt (vn + postnominal vt insep). combines, unites (one thing with another); adds (one thing to another); (does them) together. ¶twū kaci īl ul kyem chie hata does two things at the same time. secay wa kayksil ul kyem chin pang a combination study and parlor, a room serving both as a study and as a parlor. Achim kwa cēmsim ul kyem chie/chye mek.ess.ta We combined breakfast with lunch. CF kyem hata.

kyem hata, vnt. holds more than one (post) at a time; combines two or more (jobs). ¶mun-mu lul ~ has accomplishments that are both civil and military. twū kwusil ul ~ has two roles (functions). Kwuk.mu chōng.li nun kwukpang cāngkwan ul kyem hako iss.ta The Prime Minister is also at the same time (serving as) the Minister of Defense. Ku pun un kyōcang, sensayng, hōykyey lul motwu kyem hako iss.ta He is principal, teacher, and treasurer, all in one. CF kyem chita.

kyēng < ˙*KHYWENG*, postn. about, around. ¶**sēy si ~ ey** (at) about three o'clock. CF **ccum, mulyep**.

kyengwu < ¨*KYENG-*¨*NGWU*, n. circumstance(s), a situation; an instance, an occasion, a time, a case. ¶**ku sālam uy ~ ey nun** in his case. **~ ey ttal^ea (se)** according to the circumstances. SEE **-nun / -ulq / -un ~**.

kyēpta, adj -**w**-. is too much for one; is extreme, excessive. DER ADV **kyewu**. CF **-cepta**.

¨*kyesi˙ta*, honorific verb. stays; is. CF ¨*kyey˙ta* passes, exceeds; **kyēysita**.

¨*kyesin ˙toy ˙lol* (1459 Wel 21:192a); ¨*kye˙sin cyek* (1462 ¹Nung 1:2b). ˙*SYENG-ZIN ˙i* ¨*kyesi.n i ˙'n i '-ngi s ˙ka* (1465 Wen se:68a) is there a holy man here?

¨*kye˙sike˙n ywo* (1447 Sek 6:6a); ¨*kye˙siken ˙tyeng* (1463 Pep 3:189b).

¨*kyesi˙kesi˙n i ˙Gwa* (1459 Wel 21:149a).

¨*kye˙sike˙tun* (1586 Sohak 2:4b).

¨*kye˙sim ˙ay* [probably broken type] (1586 Sohak 6:122a) = ¨*kye˙sil ˙cey ˙non* (1518 Sohak-cho 10:23b); CF ¨*kyesya˙m ay* ¨*kyesi˙m ye n'* ([1447→]1562 Sek 3:1a).

¨*kyesi˙ta ˙s-ongi ˙'ta* (1459 Wel 23:86b).

¨*kye˙site˙n i '-ngi s ˙ka* (1459 Wel 18:36b).

¨*kyesyas˙ta* (1459 Wel 2:13a).

¨*kyesywo˙sye* (1459 Wel 2:15b) please stay.

¨*kye˙sya*, infinitive < ¨*kyesi˙ta*. (1445 ¹Yong 110, 1447 Sek 6:4b, 1459 Wel 7:53a, 8:84a).

¨*kyesya ˙two* (1447 Sek 6:41b).

¨*kyesya⋯* , modulated stem of ¨*kyesi˙ta*.

¨*kyesya˙m ay* (1445 ¹Yong 26), ¨*kyesya˙m ol* (1475 Nay 1:44a), ¨*kyesya˙m on* (1463 Pep 3:189a).

¨*kyesyan* (1447 Sek 19:40a).

¨*kyesya˙toy* (1447 Sek 13:27b, 19:40b).

kyeth, n. side; neighborhood, vicinity. CF **yeph**.

KYEY The Hankul spelling distinguishes **key** and **kyey** but both are usually pronounced the same (as **key**). If you cannot locate the word you seek under **kyey**, look under **key**.

kyēyhoyk < ˙*KYEY-*¨*HWOYK*, noun, postmodifier. plan, project; intention.

-ulq ~ ita plans / intends to do. ¶**I pen ey mannamyen tantan hi ttacilq kyēyhoyk ita** I intend to give him a hard time when I see him.

~ hata, vnt. plans.

kyēy'psose, abbr < **kyēysipsose**
kyēy'psyo, abbr < **kyēysipsio**

kyēysita < ¨*kyesi˙ta* = **kyēysinta**, vi [hon] = **iss.ta** (see Part I, §11.2).

1. (one esteemed) is, there is, is located, stays; lives. ¶**Apeci kkey se nun salang ey kyēysinta** Father is in the living room. **yeki kyēysinun pun i** the lady / gentleman who is here.

2. stays, stops; waits (around / momentarily), pauses. ¶**Yeki kyēysipsio** Stay here. **Annyeng hi kyēysipsio (kyēysey yo)** Good-bye (to one staying). **Cāmqkan kyēysey yo** Wait a minute!

3. **-(usi-)ko kyēysita** (one esteemed) is doing. SEE **-ko iss.ta**.

⋯*l*. Before *s c t n* the final ⋯*l* generally elided in earlier Korean. This is still common in certain dialects, and Seoul retains a few traces, as in **-ca mā[l]ca**. Noun-final ⋯*lh* elided before the particle *s* but not before *t* (⋯*lh two* → /*lthwo*/), and stem-final ⋯*lh*- shows expected reflexes. SEE *s* (pcl), ⋯*lh*.

-**l**⋯ < -*l*⋯ SEE **-ul**⋯ , -*ul*⋯ .

'**l**⋯ < '*l*⋯ SEE **il**⋯ < ˙*il*⋯ , **i 'l**⋯ < ˙*i 'l*⋯ ; **hal**⋯ < *hol*⋯ .

'**l(q)**, 1. abbr < **il** (cop prosp mod).
  2. abbr < **hal(q)** (prosp mod < **hata**)

'*l(q)*, 1. abbr < *hol(q)* (v / aux prosp mod).
  2. = '*[y]l(q)*, abbr < ˙*il(q)* (cop prosp mod) after *i* or *y*. SEE *a˙ni 'l(q)*, '*l[q] ˙kwo*.

l', abbr pcl = **lul**

-**l(q)** < -*l(q)*, alt after a vowel of -**ul(q)** < -˙*^ul/ol(q)* (prosp mod). ¶*nal* (1527 Cahoy 1:17b =34a) < °*na-* 'emerge', *ta˙ol ˙kka* (1462 ¹Nung 1:62a) < *tao-* 'get exhausted', *hyel ˙ss i˙n i* (1462 ¹Nung 1:5a) < °*hye-* 'pull', *mwuu˙l i ˙'n i* (1447 Sek 6:27a) < *mwuu-* 'shake', *wolq* (1445 ¹Yong 25, 1447 Sek 6:23a) < °*wo-* 'come', *twul ˙tta* (1459 Wel 2:64a) < °*twu-* 'put away', ¨*nayl* (1463 Pep 3:180b) < ¨*nay-* 'put out', ¨*hyey˙l i ˙le˙la* (1459 Wel 1:21a) < ¨*hyey-* 'reckon, think', *i˙kuylq ˙ta* (1459 Wel 21:118b) < *i˙kuy-* 'win', *towoylq ˙t ol* (1462 ¹Nung 7:26a), ¨*mwuyl ˙ss oy* (1445 ¹Yong 2) < °°*mwuy-* 'move'.

la, particle. 1. follows v inf to make an unquoted plain-style command (CF **-ula / -la**): do! SEE **-e la**. NOTE: Some verbs have a special optional infinitive before **la**; see **-ke la**, **-ne la**.

2. follows adj inf to make an exclamation: is indeed, how ⋯ ! SEE -e la.
3. follows interj. ¶oho la alas! woe is me!
˙la, pcl (var < ˙lwo); alt of ˙ᵁ⁄ₒ˙la after a vowel, l, or LQ. ¶ ˙say la (1481 Twusi 8:35b) = ˙say ˙lwo newly. SEE ˙la n˙.
'la, 1. < ila < ˙i˙la (cop).
2. < hala < ho˙la.
˙˙la, 1. abbr < ho˙la.
2. = ˙[y]˙la, abbr < ˙i˙la (cop) after i or y. ¶pwul˙hwuy ˙˙la (1459 Wel se:21a) it is the root. to˙˙li ˙˙la (1459 Wel 21:77a) it means 'bridge'. nwu˙˙uy ˙˙la (1459 Wel 21:162a) it means 'older sister'.
3. SEE -˙e ˙˙la.
-la, alt of -ula after a vowel or the l-extension of an -L- stem. ¶Kala = Kake la Go! kala (ko) hata tells him to go. Ola = One la Come! ola (ko) hata tells him to come. Nōlla = Nol.a la Enjoy yourself! Nōlla (ko) hayss.ta I told him to enjoy himself.
-˙la SEE -u˙la
-˙la, lenited var < -˙ta (indic assert) with cop ˙i-˙la, var cop ˙ilwo-˙la; aux ci-˙la 'desire'; modulator -˙wᵁ⁄ₒ-˙la, modulated proc -˙nwo-˙la, modulated emotive (-)swo-˙la; retr -˙tᵉ˙la and cop retr ˙ile-˙la; but not after emotive -˙two- (-˙two˙ta) or effective -˙kᵉ˙a- (-ke˙ta, -Ge˙ta, -˙e˙ta), and not after honorific (-ᵁ⁄ₒ˙si-˙ta) or copula honorific (˙isi-˙ta).
-l a = -l ya
-˙la- = -˙ta- (retr). SEE -u˙si˙l i ˙˙la[˙]so-ngi ˙˙ta. CF -˙le- in ˙ile˙la.
'/-la 'ca, abbr < '/-la (ko) haca
'/-la 'ci, abbr < '/-la (ko) haci
lak, postmod = ak (alt after prosp mod from -L- stem; colloq var after prosp mod of any stem)
-l ak, alt after vowel stems (other than -L- stems) of -ul ak. CF -l lak.
-lak → -l ak. SEE -ul lak.
-˙lak SEE -u˙lak
˙la ka SEE ila ka
'/-la 'key, abbr < '/-la (ko) hakey
'/-la 'ki, abbr < '/-la (ko) haki
-laki, alt after a vowel of -ulaki (dimin suffix).
'/-la ko/kwu, 1. < ila ko. 2. < hala ko.
3. < -ula ko.
-la kwu, 1. = -la ko.
2. sentence-final [northern DIAL] = -key na (FAMILIAR command).

'/-la 'l, abbr < '/-la (ko) hal
'/-la 'la, abbr < '/-la (ko) hala
'/-la 'm, 1. < ilam.
2. alt of -ula 'm < -ula ko ham after a vowel or the l-extension of an -L- stem.
'/-la 'myen, abbr < '/-la (ko) hamyen. SEE ila 'myen, -ula 'myen.
'la 'myen se (< ila hamyen se) SEE 'myen se
'/-la 'n, abbr < '/-la (ko) han. SEE ila 'n(').
'/-la 'n', abbr < '/-la (ko) hanun. SEE ila 'n(').
˙la n', var pcl + abbr pcl (= ˙lwo ˙non). ¶ ˙say ˙la n' ˙PWO-SI KWONG-˙YANG ho˙m ye (1459 Wel 21:146a) give alms and make contributions anew, and ... .
˙lan, pcl; alt of ˙ᵁ⁄ₒ˙lan after a vowel, l or LQ.
'/-la 'na, abbr < '/-la (ko) hana
'/-la 'ney, abbr < '/-la (ko) haney
lang, alt after a vowel of ilang (particle)
-lang, [? var] = -llak
-langi, diminutive suffix. VAR -layngi. CF -angi, -aki, -aci.
'/-la 'ni, abbr < '/-la (ko) hani
-la 'no, abbr < -la (ko) hano [< hanun ko]. ? [DIAL] = -la 'y?
'/-la 'nta, abbr < '/-la (ko) hanta
-˙la 'n˙t oy SEE -u˙la 'n˙t oy
'/-la 'nun, abbr < '/-la (ko) hanun
'/-la 'o, abbr < '/-la (ko) hao
'/-la 'p.nita, 1. < ila 'p.nita < ila ko hap.nita.
2. < -ula 'p.nita < -ula ko hap.nita.
'la 'psiko, abbr < 'la (ko) hapsiko
˙la s = ˙ila s, cop indic assert + pcl. SEE s (15b).
'la se, abbr after a vowel of ila se
˙˙la[˙]s-ongi ˙˙ta SEE -u˙l i ˙˙la[˙]s-ongi ˙˙ta
'la siph.ta, abbr after a vowel of ila siph.ta
'la sye, abbr after a vowel of ila sye
'/-la 'ta, abbr < '/-la (ko) hata
'/-la 'tey, abbr < '/-la (ko) hatey
'/-la 'ti, abbr < '/-la (ko) hati
'la to, alternant after a vowel of ila to
'/-la 'toy, abbr < '/-la (ko) hatoy
'la tul, 1. (?) = ila tul. 2. = hala tul
la tul, particle + particle. SEE -e la tul.
-la tul, alternant after a vowel of -ula tul
'/-la 'tula, abbr < '/-la (ko) hatula
'/-la 'tun, abbr < '/-la (ko) hatun
'la 'tun ci, alt after a vowel of < ˙ila 'tun ci
˙la ˙two, alternant after ⋯i or ⋯y of < ˙ila ˙two. SEE ila to. CF 'yla ˙two.

la ˙wa, particle (after *l*, LQ, or *y*). than (= **pota**). SEE *illawa*, *nellawa*.
 1. = ˙*ola ˙wa*. ¶*THAM-˙YWOK ˙ay s ˙pu ˙l i ˙i ˙pul la ˙wa teu ˙n i ˙˙la* (1459 Wel 10:14b) the fire of greed is greater than this fire. ˙*pul s ˙pi.ch o ˙lwo CANG-NGEM ˙hwo ˙m i ˙ZILQ-˙NGWELQ la ˙wa nu ˙le* (1447 Sek 9:4b) its magnificence with the radiance of fire outdoes the sun and the moon.
 2. = ˙*ila ˙wa*. ¶*nyey lawa kwoysywosye* (?1530 Siyong hyangak po 138b) love him more than of old! [˙*KEN-CANG] hon [NAM-ZI] y sekun syenpoy lawa nutwota* (1632 Twusi-cwung 6: 40a) a sturdy lad is better than a putrid classicist.
'/-la 'y, abbr < **'/-la (ko) hay**
-lay (in **killay** 'for long') SEE **-ay**
lay, pcl [Phyengan DIAL] = **ley** = **ka** nominative (Kim Yengpay 1984:94:n13).
'/-la ya, 1. alt after a vowel of **ila ya**.
 2. = **'/-la 'y ya**
-layki, var < **-laki** (diminutive suffix)
'/-la 'y la, abbr < **'/-la (ko) hay la**
-layngi, dimin suf (var < **-langi**). ¶**kasi(-layngi)** a thorn.
'/-la 'y se, abbr < **'/-la (ko) hay se**; ~ **ya**.
'/-la 'yss-, abbr < **'/-la (ko) hayss-**
'/-la 'y to, abbr < **'/-la (ko) hay to**
'/-la 'y tul, abbr < **'/-la (ko) hay tul** (plural)
'/-la 'y ya, abbr < **'/-la (ko) hay ya**
'/-la 'y yo, abbr < **'/-la (ko) hay yo**
? **'la ˙za** (after ···*y*) = ˙*ila ˙za*
-le, alt of **-ule** after a vowel or the **l**-extension of an -L- stems ¶**hale** < **hata**, **tulle** < **tulta**, **ilule** < **iluta** reaches.
-le- < -˙*le-* [DIAL, obs] = **-tu-** (retrospective, with copula): ~ **-ni**, **-ni-la**, **(-ni)-ikka**, **(-ni)-ita**, **-la**. ¶*Cen ey nun cōh.un chinkwu* '*lenila* (= *itun i* '*la*) In the past he was a close friend of mine. **Yēys nal ey nun yeki ka pata** '*leniita* (= *ituniita* = **iptita**) In older days this was part of the sea. **Ku san un** ¹**yāngpan myōci** '*lenikka* (= *itunikka* = **iptikka**) Was the hill a burial ground for some nobleman's family? SEE ˙*ile ˙la*, ˙*i ˙lusyas ˙ta*, -˙*la-*.
-len [DIAL, obs] = **-tun** (retr mod): ~ **ka**, ~ **ko**, ~ **tul**.
len = [˙]*len*, var < ˙*lan*, pcl; alt of ˙*ᵁ⁄₀ ˙lan* after vowel, *l* or LQ. ¶˙*kul len mozom sul ˙then ˙sta.h ol solang ˙honwo ˙n i* (1481 Twusi 21: 13b) the poem recalls the land where I was sad.

'*le ˙n i* = ˙*ile ˙n i* (after ···*i* or ···*y*); CF '*yle ˙n i*. ¶*ye ˙le TTIN-˙LYWUY ˙lol ¨ket-˙nayno ˙n i ˙le ˙n i* (1462 ¹Nung 1:24b) carried one across many troubles.
-'*len ˙t ay n'* SEE -*u ˙l i* '*len ˙t ay n*'
'*len ˙t un* SEE ˙*ilen ˙t un*
'*le ˙n ywo* = ˙*ile ˙n ywo*. SEE -*usi ˙l i* '*le ˙n ywo*.
LEY The Hankul spelling distinguishes **ley** and **lyey** but within a word they are both usually pronounced the same way (as a reflex of **ley**); initially only ¹**yey** occurs (pronounced **yey**). If you cannot locate the word you are looking for with the spelling **ley**, look under **lyey** or **yey**.
'**ley**, abbr (alt) after a vowel of *iley* (cop retr)
ley, pcl [Phyengan DIAL] = **ka** nominative (Kim Yengpay 1984:94-5). ¶**Hak.kyo ley khuti yo** = **Hak.kyo ka khuci yo** The school is big. **Nay ley kulaysi yo** = **Nay ka kulayss.e yo** I did / said that. **Yā ley kulays.ti yo** = **I ai ka kulayss.ci yo** He did/said that. Perhaps < **(i)la** (cop) + **i**; in the 1930s both **ley** and **lay** were reported (Kim Yengpay 1984:94:n13).
ley, pcl [Ceycwu DIAL].
 1. = **ka** nominative (Pak Yonghwu 1960: 395). ¶*nwu ley wutung-seyng ka* = **nwu ka wutung-sayng in ya** who is the best student? [Are there other examples?]
 2. = **lo** to, toward (Pak Yonghwu 1960:396). ¶*hok.kywo ley kam ce* = **hak.kyo lo kanta** I head for the school. *samwu-swo ley kam ti* = **samu-so ey kanun ya**? (are you) going to the office? Is this a variant of **lo**, or a lenition of **tey** 'place'? Also *teyley*, *theyley*, *leyley*. CF *etu ley* = *eti ley*.
-ley [DIAL] 1. = **-lye**. 2. = **-la 'y**
-leyki, variant < **-leki** (diminutive suffix)
leyley, pcl [Ceycwu DIAL (Seng ¹Nakswu 1984: 25)] − after a vowel or *l*; CF *teyley*, *theyley*. assimilated or lenited form of *teyley* (toward / to). ¶*cel leyley kam ce* = **cel lo kanta** I go to the temple. *se leyley kam ce* = **se ulo kanta** I go west. *al leyley kala* = **alay lo kake la** go below.
? *l' ˙Gwa* SEE **ul kwa** (¨*nal ˙Gwa* = **na ˙lol kwa* and me)
···*lh* SEE ···*l*, ···*h*. There are a few doublets in MK, with competing forms in the texts: *ha ˙nol* or *ha ˙nolh* 'heaven', *kozol* or *kozolh* 'autumn', *sumul* or *sumulh* 'twenty', ˙*kal* or ˙*kalh* 'knife'. Noun-final ···*lh* reduces to ···*l* before particle *s*.

lī < ¨*LI*, postmod (follows prosp mod). (good) reason that / to ··· . ¶**Mōs ol lī ka ēps.ta** There is no reason he can't come. **Kulel lī ka iss.na** How can that be − I can't believe it. **Kulel lī ka ēps.ta** That can't be true. **Ku māl i kēcis māl il lī ka ēps.ta** That couldn't be a lie. **Kulemyen kuleh.ci cip ey se onul to phyēnci ka ēps.ul lī ka iss.na?** Well, it's about time! − There just HAD to be a letter from home today. **Yelqsim man iss.umyen īl hamye 'n tul kongpu mōs hal lī ka iss.nun ya?** Is there any (= Surely there cannot be any) reason you can't study even while working, if you are only earnest enough. CF ¹**īyu**. NOTE: We follow the usual orthography in writing -**ul lī** for what is in effect -**ulq** ¹**ī**.

-**l i**, alternant after a vowel of -**ul i**

-**li** → -**l i**

-**li**, suf (alt of -**i** after some l-extended stems and -LL- stems; derives adv from adj). in such a manner, ···ly, ···wise. ¶**mēlli** afar (< **mēlta**). **nelli** widely (< **neluta**; CF **nelp.i** width < **nelp.ta**). **talli** differently (< **taluta**). **kulli** wrongly (< **kuluta**).

-**li**-, suf. CF -**lu**-; -**i**-, -**y**-, -**hi**-, -**ki**-, -**chi**-, -**ukhi**-, -**ikhi**-, -**iwu**-, -**ywu**-; -**wu**-, -**hwu**-, -**ay**-; -˙*Gi*-, -˙*Gwo*-, -˙*Gwu*-, -**o**-, -**u**-.

1. derives vc. ¶**tulli**- < *tul˙Gi*- cause to hear ← **tut**-/**tul**- < *tut*-/*tul*- hear. **olli**- < *wol˙Gi* raise ← *wolo*-/*wolG*- rise. **tolli**- < *twol˙Gi*- turn it ← **tō-l**- < ¨*twol*- turn. **alli**- (MK *al˙Gwoy*-) inform ← **ā-l**- < ¨*al*- know.

2. derives vp. ¶**tulli**- < *tul˙Gi*- get heard ← **tut**-/**tul**- < *tut*-/*tul*- hear. **nwulli**- < ¨*nwul˙Gi* get pressed down ← **nwuluta** < *nwu˙lu*- press down.

3. derives intensive v. ¶(**tullu**- =) **tulli**- drop in < **tu-l**- enter. **cōlli**- get sleepy < **cō-l**- doze.

4. mistaken analysis of ···**lli**- as ···**l-li**- rather than ···**ll-i**-. SEE -**i**- (**hulli**- 'make flow', ...).

-˙*l i ˙Ga* SEE -*u˙l i ˙Ga*

-˙*l i ˙Gwo* SEE -*u˙l i ˙Gwo*

-**likka**, alt of -**ulikka** after a vowel or the l-extension of an -L- stem

-**lila**, alt of -**ulila** after a vowel or the l-extension of an -L- stem

-**lilo**ᵗ/ₗa, alt of -**ulilo**ᵗ/ₗa after a vowel or the l-extension of an -L- stem

-˙*l i '-ngi s˙ka*, alt of -ᵁ⁄ₒ˙*l i '-ngi s˙ka* after a vowel or ···l-

-˙*l i '-ngi '˙ta*, alt of -ᵁ⁄ₒ˙*l i '-ngi '˙ta* after a vowel or ···l-

-**lini**ᵗ/ₗa, alt of -**ulini**ᵗ/ₗa after a vowel or the l-extension of an -L- stem.

-**lio**, 1. = -**l i yo**. 2. → -˙*l i ˙Gwo*.

-**lita**, alt of -**ulita** after vowel or the l-extension of an -L- stem

-**l i tul** SEE -**ul i tul**

'**l i tul**, 1. = **il i tul**. 2. = **hal i tul**

-.*l i 'ye*, prosp mod + postmod + postmod. SEE -*u˙l ye*.

-**li yo** = -**l i yo** (rhetorical question, POLITE)

···*lk¨sop*- < ···*lk-¨zop*-

'**lq ka**, 1. = **ilq ka**. 2. = **halq ka**.

-**lq ka (tul)** SEE -**ul ka (tul)**

-**lq ke l'**, alt of -**ulq ke l'** after a vowel or the l-extension of an -L- stem

-**lq ke 'lq sey**, alt -**ulq ke 'lq sey** after a vowel or the l-extension of an -L- stem

-**lq key**, alt of -**ulq key** after a vowel or the l-extension of an -L- stem

-**lkhwuta** [S Kyengsang DIAL (Mkk 1960:3:34)] = ···**leh.key (māl) hata**; **ku** ~ , **i** ~ , **ce/cu** ~ .

? **l' kwa** = **lul kwa**, pcl + pcl. SEE **ul kwa**.

'*l[q] ˙kwo* = '*yl[q] ˙kwo* (cop prosp mod + postmod). ¶*e˙nu ¨hoy 'l˙kwo* (1481 Twusi 7:4b) what year was it?

···**ll**··· . Look also under ···**l**···, -**ul l**···, -**ul** ···, **il**···, -**u.l i 'l**··· for possible sources of a variant.

-**lla**, 1. alt of -**ulla** (prosp adjunctive) after a vowel or the l-extension of an -L- stem.

2. subjunctive attentive (command) of -L- stems. ¶**kēlla** < **kēlta**, **mulla** < **multa**, **mālla** < **mālta**.

3. [S Kyengsang DIAL] = -**lye** (purposive)

-**llak** = -**l lak** (shape of -**lak** after -L- stem)

-**lla 'mon**, -**lla 'myen** [DIAL] = -**lye 'myen**

-**lla 'ni** [DIAL] = -**lye 'ni**

l˙lan (?= ˙*lan* with conflated liquid), pcl. SEE *il˙lan*.

llang, alt of **ullang** (pcl) after a vowel

'**llang**, alt after a vowel of **illang** = **imyen**

-**llang**, [? var] = -**llak**. CF **tullang kelita** keeps coming and going (= **tullak nallak hata**) − or is this from **tullu**- = **tulli**- + -**ang**?

-**llangki yo**, [DIAL] SEE -**ullangki yo**

-**lla 'ni** [S Kyengsang DIAL (Mkk 1960:3:35)] = -**lye 'ni**

-**llay** = -**lye (ko) hay to**

-**llayta** = -**lye (ko) hata (ka)**

-lle, alt of **-ulle** after a vowel or the l-extension of an -L- stem
-llela, alt of **-ullela** after a vowel or the l-extension of an -L- stem. SEE **killey** for more.
-llen, 1. [DIAL] = **-keyss.tun** (fut retr mod): ~ **ka**.
    2. = **-len** (retr mod = **-tun**): ~ **ka**, ~ **ko**.
-lleni, alternant of **-ulleni** after a vowel or the l-extension of an -L- stem
-lley, alternant of **-ullela** after a vowel or the l-extension of an -L- stem
-lleyla = **-llela**
···*l ˙li(···)* < ···*l ˙[ᵘo]l i (···)*, prosp mod (of -L- verb) + postmodifier. the one that will ··· ; the fact that it / one will ··· .
llo < *l ˙lwo* = **lo** < *˙lwo*. **mue llo** → **muel-lo**. **ke llo** → **kel-lo**. SEE *˙il ˙lwo, kul ˙lwo, ¨nal ˙lwo, ˙tyel ˙lwo*; **nellwo** = **ne llo**.
l ˙lwo k = *˙lwo k*. SEE *˙il ˙lwo k, ¨nal ˙lwo k*.
-llya [DIAL] = **-(l)lye**
-llye, 1. [DIAL or emphatic] = **-lye**
    2. intentive of -L- stems. ¶**kēllye** < **kēlta**, **mullye** < **multa**, **nōllye** < **nōlta**.
-llye 'ni(-kka) SEE **-ulye 'ni(-kka)**
-l.nun, alt of **-ul.nun** (prosp proc mod) after a vowel or the l-extension of an -L- stem
lo, particle 1. alternant of **ulo** after a vowel or l.
    2. [S Kyengsang DIAL (Mkk 1960:3:31)] = **lul**. But **ulo** is not used for **ul**.
-lo [S Kyengsang DIAL] = **-le**. SEE **-ulo**.
loi, der adv < **lopta**. ¶**swūnco** ~ smoothly. **oy** ~ lonesomely. NOTE: The spelling "**lowi**" reflects a misanalysis; "**lohi**" is a mistake.
lo ˙i, derived adverb (< *lop ˙ta*) = **loi**
lo ka, particle + particle. SEE **ulo ka**.
'lokwun, abbr (alt) < **ilokwun**: ~ **a**, ~ **yo**.
lo l' = **(u)lo lul**
˙lol, particle (accusative). SEE **ul**.
lōl, abbr < **lowul**
'lola, abbr (alt) < **ilola**
lo lul, particle + particle. SEE **ulo lul**.
˙lol pu ˙the, particle + particle. SEE *˙ol pu ˙the*
˙lol ˙za, pcl + pcl. ¶"*CCYEM-˙KYWOW ˙lol ˙za ¨ta a ˙la tutco ˙Wo ˙n i* (1449 Kok 97) he fully understood the Gradual Teaching [that proceeds from the hīnayāna to the mahāyāna]. *˙i lol ˙za pwus ˙ku ˙lita ˙n i* (1449 Kok 121) I was ashamed of all this. SEE *˙ul ˙za*.
lōm, abbr < **lowum**
lo man, particle + particle. SEE **ulo man**.
lōn, abbr < **lowun**

lo n', particle + abbr particle = **(u)lo nun**
lo 'na, particle + cop adversative. SEE **ulo 'na**.
'lona, abbr (alt) < **ilona**
'loni, abbr (alt) < **iloni**. ~**-kka (nun / n')**.
lo nun, particle + particle. SEE **ulo nun**.
lop.hita, vc < **lopta**. causes it to be (or to be characterized by) ··· . ¶**hāy** ~ harms. ¹**ī** ~ benefits. **koy** ~ distresses, bothers.
lop ˙ta = **lopta**, postnominal adj inseparable -W-.
lopta, postnom adj insep -W- (inf **lowa**, var inf **lowe**). is (characterized) by. ¶**hāy** ~ is harmful. ¹**ī** ~ is profitable. **koy** ~ is distressed, is distressing (< ?). **oy** ~ is lonely / lonesome. **say** ~ is new. **ūy** ~ is rightful, is righteous. **ayche** ~ is pitiful / miserable. **ca.yu** ~ is free / unrestricted. **congyo** ~ is pivotal / essential, **cwuce** ~ is impoverished. **hanka** ~ is free / unbusy / inactive. **hohwa** ~ is brilliant / gaudy. **hyangki** ~ is fragrant. **kāso** ~ is ridiculous. **kkata** ~ is fastidious, fussy. **kongkyo** ~ is ingenious. ? **nalkha** ~ is sharp (?< *˙*nolh ˙ka[lh] l(w)op ˙ta*; ?< **nal-kha[l] opta**). **penke** ~ is annoying; is noisy. **phyenghwa** ~ is peaceful, is peaceable. **pōpay** ~ is precious. **sangse** ~ is auspicious. **sasa** ~ is personal. **say** ~ is new. **sulki** ~, **cihyey** ~ is wise. **swūko** ~ is troublesome. **swūnco** ~ is smooth, orderly. **tanco** ~ is monotonous. **(t)tasa** ~ is rather hot. **tāyswu** ~ is important, valuable (var < **tāysa** big fact). CF **sulepta, tapta; opta**.
lo se, particle + particle. SEE **ulo se**.
lo se mankhum, pcl + pcl + pcl. ¶**Ku nun hakca lo (se) nun cengchi-ka lo se mankhum allye cye iss.ci anh.ta** He is not so well known as a scholar as he is as a politician.
lo se n', abbr < **lo se nun**
lo se nun, pcl + pcl + pcl. SEE **ulo se nun**.
'losey, abbr (alt) < **ilosey**
lo so 'ni, [DIAL or mistake] = **lo se 'ni**
lo sse, alt (after a vowel or l) of **ulo sse**
lo sse n', abbr < **lo sse nun**
lo sse nun SEE **ulo sse nun**
'lota, abbr (alt) < **ilota**
lo 'ta ka SEE **ulo 'ta ka**
lo to, pcl + pcl. SEE **ulo to**.
'lotoy, abbr (alt) < **ilotoy**
lo uy, pcl + pcl. SEE **ulo uy**.
lowa, infinitive < **lopta**
lowe, variant infinitive < **lopta**
lowi → **loi**

lowoy˙i, der adv (< *loWoy˙ta*) = *lo˙i* = **loi**
lowoy˙ta < *loWoy˙ta* = *lop˙ta* = **lopta**, postnominal adjective inseparable.
lo˙Wi = *lo˙i*, der adv (< *lop˙ta*) = **loi**
lowul(q), prospective modifier < **lopta**
lowum, substantive < **lopta**
lowun, modifier < **lopta**
-˙l *oy* = -˙l *[y]oy*, abbr < -˙l *i* ˙*oy* of (etc.) that which ··· . SEE ˙*uy*.
···*lp¨sop-* < ···*lp-¨zop-* = ···*lW-¨zop-*
l' pu˙the SEE ˙*ol pu˙the*
-lq sa SEE **-ulq sa**
-lq salok [DIAL] = **-lq swulok**
-lq seng SEE **seng**
-lq sey, alt after a vowel of **-ulq sey**
'**/-lq sey**, 1. abbr < **halq sey**.
 2. abbr < **ilq sey** (it is). ¶**Payk kwun uy cacey '1q sey kwulye** Why, it's Payk's son!
 3. = **-ulq sey**.
-lq si, alt after a vowel of **-ulq si**
-lq son, alt after a vowel of **-ulq son**
···*l¨ssop-* < ···*lh-¨zop-*
-lq sun, alt after a vowel of **-ulq sun**
-lq swulok, alt after a vowel of **-ulq swulok**
-l(q)˙ta SEE -ᵘ*⁄ol(q)˙ta*
-l they, alt after a vowel of **-ul they**
-lq ˙ti··· = **-lq ˙t i(···)**, prosp mod + postmod ('fact') + pcl / cop. that it / one will ··· .
-lq ˙t ol, prosp mod + postmod ('fact') + pcl. that it / one will ··· . SEE -ᵘ⁄o**lq ˙t ol**.
?**-lq ˙t olwo**, prosp mod + postmod ('fact') + pcl. because it / one will ··· .
˙*lu*, var = ˙*lwo*, pcl. ¶CYE-¨PPWULQ ˙*i wo˙cik hon ˙khun ¨il s* QIN-YWEN *cyen˙cho ˙lu* ¨SYEY-KAN ˙*ay ˙na* ¨HHYEN ˙*ho˙sino˙n i ¨la ˙ho˙si.n i ¨la* (1465 Wen se:6a) he said that Buddhas appear in the world of people only as the result of cause by some major event. ˙*kaps ¨ep˙sun* ¨PWO-CYWU ˙*lu wos ¨swo˙p ay moy˙ya cwu˙kwo ˙nike˙nol* (1463 Pep 4:37b) lined his clothes with priceless jewels before setting off – unless ˙*lu* is a scribal error for ˙*lul*, perhaps influenced by the adjacent syllable *ku* in the line to the right.
-lu-, suf (bnd postverb). derives intensive verbs. ¶**cac.chwu-lu-** press, hurry, rush, urge on < **cac.chwu-**. **tullu-** / **tulli-** drop in < **tu-l-** enter. CF **-chi-**, **-khi-**, **-li-**.
-lu- [DIAL, obs] = **-tu-** (retrospective)

lul < ˙*lᵘ⁄ol*, pcl (accusative). alt shape of **ul** < ᵘ⁄o*l* after a vowel. ABBR **l'**.
*****lul iya** → **ya**. SEE ˙*ul ˙za*.
?**lul kwa**, pcl + pcl. SEE **ul kwa**.
?**lul lo**, pcl + pcl. SEE **ul lo**.
˙*lul pu˙the* SEE ˙*ol pu˙the*
*****lul ya** → **ya**. SEE ˙*ul ˙za*.
˙*lul ˙za*, pcl + pcl. SEE ˙*lol ˙za*, ˙*ul ˙za*.
-'**lum** = **-kelum**. SEE **hay-(ke)lum**.
-lum, bnd adj-n (~ **hata**), abbr < **-sulum**. ···-ish, slightly characterized by. SYN **-sum**.
-lun [DIAL, obs] = **-tun** (retr mod)
-˙*l uy* = -˙*l [y]uy*, abbr < -˙*l i ˙uy* 'of (etc.) that which ··· '. SEE ˙*uy*.
-*[˙]lwa* (1670) < -*[˙]lwo˙la* = -˙*nwo˙la*.
˙*lwo*, pcl (alt after a vowel or /l/ of ˙ᵘ⁄o˙*lwo*) = **lo**. VAR ˙*lu*. SEE ˙*u˙lwo*.
˙*lwo k*, pcl + pcl. SEE ¨*nal˙lwo k*, ˙*il˙lwo k*.
 1. from (= **lo se**, **lo puthe**). ¶¨*nyey ˙lwo k selu sa˙kwoynwo˙la* (1481 Twusi 20:44b) we two share companionship from way back. *ka.s oy heli lwo k wu.h uy* (1489 Kup-kan 6:21; cited from LCT) up above the narrow part of the traditional hat.
 ~ *pu˙the* from. ¶*[¨]nyey [˙]lwo k puf˙]the* ([1447→]1562 Sek 3:21b) from of old.
 2. than (= **pota**). ¶*ahoy lwo k mwoncye ka* (1632 Twusi-cwung 18:9a) goes ahead of the child.
-*[˙]lwo˙la* [variant] = -˙*nwo˙la*. ¶˙*ptonon ˙ma˙Gwa.m ol cwo˙cha ton˙nilwo˙la* (1481 Twusi 8:13b) I wander [drunkenly] with the floating water chestnuts.
'˙*lwom* = ˙*ilwom*, copula variant substantive.
˙*lwo n'*, pcl + pcl. SEE ˙ᵘ⁄o˙*lwo n'*.
'*lwon˙t i* SEE ˙*ilwon˙t i*
'*lwon˙t ol* = ˙*ilwon˙t ol*
lwop˙ta, postnom adj insep -W- (= **lopta**); CF *lap˙ta*, *loWoy˙ta*.
'˙*lwo˙swo-ngi¨ta* = ˙*i˙lwo˙swo-ngi¨ta*
˙*lwo˙sye*, pcl + pcl (alt of ˙ᵘ⁄o˙*lwo˙sye*) = **lo se**
˙*lwo˙ta* = ˙*ilwo˙ta*
˙*lwo˙toy* = ˙*ilwo˙toy*
˙*lwo˙two*, pcl + pcl = **lo to**. SEE ˙ᵘ⁄o˙*lwo˙two*.
˙*lwo˙za*, pcl + pcl = **lo ya**. SEE ˙ᵘ⁄o˙*lwo˙za*.
lwu, pcl [var] = **lo**
-lya → **-l ya**
-lya [DIAL] = **-lye**
'**/-l ya**, 1. abbr < **hal ya**.
 2. alt after a vowel of **-ul ya**.

-l ya 'myen, abbr < -l ya (ko) hamyen
-l ya tul SEE -ul ya tul
'l ya tul, 1. = il ya tul. 2. = hal ya tul
'/-lye, 1. abbr < halye.
    2. alt of -ulye (intentive) after a vowel or the l-extension of an -L- stem
-lye 'ci, abbr < -lye (ko) haci
-lye 'ki, abbr < -lye (ko) haki
-lye ko / kko / kwu: SEE -ulye ko / kko / kwu
-lye 'l, abbr < -lye (ko) hal
'lyem, abbr < halyem
-lyem, 1. alt after vowel of -ulyem (cajolative). ~ una SAME.
    2. abbr < -lye (ko) ham
'/-lye man, 1. < halye man. 2. -ulye man.
-lyemuna → -lyem una
-lye 'myen, abbr < -lye (ko) hamyen
-lye 'n('), 1. abbr < -lye (ko) han. 2. abbr < -lye (ko) hanun ya.
-lye 'na, abbr < -lye (ko) hana
-lye 'ney, abbr < -lye (ko) haney
-lye 'n' i SEE -ulye 'n' i: ~ wa.
-lye 'ni, abbr < -lye (ko) hani
-lyen man (un), alt after a vowel of -ulyen man
-lye 'nta, abbr < -lye (ko) hanta
-lye 'nun, abbr < -lye (ko) hanun
-lye 'nun ya, abbr < -lye (ko) hanun ya
-lye 'n ya, abbr < -lye (ko) han ya
-lye 'o, abbr < -lye (ko) hao
-lye 'p.nikka, abbr < -lye (ko) hap.nikka
-lye 'p.nita, abbr < -lye (ko) hap.nita
-lye 'ptikka, abbr < -lye (ko) haptikka
-lye 'ptita, abbr < -lye (ko) haptita
-lye se, intentive + particle = -lye (ko) ha.ye se: ~ nun, ~ ya.
-lyes-man → -lyen man
-lyes(s).ta → -lyetta; SEE -ulyetta, ilyetta.
-lye 'ta, abbr < -lye (ko) hata
-[˙]lye˙ta = -˙l [i] 'ye˙ta (will likely do / be): SEE ˙'ye˙ta.
-lye 'tey, abbr < -lye (ko) hatey
-lye to, intentive + particle = -lye (ko) ha.ye to
-lye 'tu-kwulye, abbr < -lye (ko) hatu-kwulye
-lye 'tu-kwu(me)n, abbr < -lye (ko) hatu-kwu(me)n
-lye 'tula, abbr < -lye (ko) hatula
-lye tul.e, infinitive < -lye tulta
-lyetta, alternant after a vowel of -ulyetta
-lye 'tun, abbr < -lye (ko) hatun

LYEY The Hankul spelling distinguishes **ley** and **lyey**, but within a word both are usually pronounced the same (as a reflex of **ley**); initially only ¹**yey** occurs (pronounced **yey**). If you cannot locate the word you seek with the spelling **lyey**, look under **ley** or **yey**.
-lye ya, intentive + particle.
    1. = -lye (ko) ha.ye ya
    2. = -lye to
-lyo (-ly' 'o), abbr < -lye 'o < -lye (ko) hao
-lyo, suffix, postnoun; noun.
    1. (= ¹**yōkum**) charge, fee (charged), rate, fare. **īmtay** ~ rental charge. **ipcang** ~ admission charge. **swuep** ~ tuition. **sā.yong** ~ use (user) fee. ¹**īpal** ~ charge for a haircut. **cēnhwa** ~ the charge for a telephone call.
    2. (= **pōswu**) remuneration, pay, fee (paid). **wenko** ~ payment (to the author) for copy, a contribution (or contributer) fee. **philqsa** ~ payment for copying, transcription fee.
    3. (= **caylyo**) material(s), ingredient(s). **comi** ~ seasonings, flavorings, condiments, spices. CF **hyang.lyo** aromatic essences / oils.
    NOTE: It is unclear when the SK orthography wants this to be spelled **(q)-¹yo**. Presumably it MUST be so spelled in **swusenq-¹yo** 'charges for repairs' because that is always pronounced as /swusennyo/ (not ···ll···!) and the word must be listed for NK as an irregularity — or treated as a two-word noun compound **swusenq ¹yo** (= **swusenq ¹yōkum**); likewise **wūnpanq ¹yo** = **wūnpanq ¹yōkum** 'transportation charge'. But what about /sēythangnyo/ 'laundry charges': should we follow the analogy of **swusenq ¹yo** and write **sēythakq ¹yo** or should we follow the analogy of **wenko-lyo** (etc.) and write **sēythak-lyo** (as is done by SK dictionaries for **ipcang-lyo**)? Notice that ¹**yō** can be a free noun as an abbreviation of ¹**yōkum**. Recommendation: treat it as a separate word (···q) ¹**yo** whenever that will not conflict with the pronunciation.

-m··· < -*m*··· SEE -um··· , -*um*··· .
'm··· < '*m*··· SEE im··· < ˙im··· , i 'm··· < ˙i '*m*··· ; ham··· < ˙hom··· .
'/-m, 1. < im. 2. < ham. 3. < -um.
-m' = -myen; SEE -um'.
-ma 1. [S Kyengsang DIAL (¹Na Cinsek 1977)] = -myen

2. suffix (? abbr < -umak). ¶**nulk-ma** = **nulkumak** one's old age.
'/-ma → **'/-m a**
'/-m a, 1. < **ham a**. 2. < **-um a**.
··· ˙**ma**, bnd n (quantity / number). SEE ¨**en˙ma**, ˙**hyenma**, ˙**myes.ma**; ˙**man**. CF ¨**cywokwo˙ma**.
2. pcl (= ˙**man**). SEE ··· ˙**ma ˙y˙na**, ··· ˙**ma s**, ··· ˙**ma˙two**.
mā, abbr < **mawu** < **mao** (but used as the equivalent of **mal.a** = **mal.e**). don't! [intimate style]. ¶**Ic.ci mā** Don't forget! **Wūs.ci mā** Don't laugh! **Kekceng [haci] mā** Don't worry!
mac'(-), adn, bnd adv [abbr < **macwu** der adv < **mac.ta**]. facing, before one's face, directly opposite, direct, straight, clear, in agreement; together, jointly; each other, mutually.
1. adnoun. ~ **cap.i** an equal (in strength). ~ **cekswu** a good match. ~ **cel** bowing to each other. ~ **hungceng** a direct deal / transaction. ~ **kwumeng** a hole on the opposite side. ~ **palam** a head wind. ~ **poki** plain-lense (unrefracting) eyeglasses. ~ **pyek** a double wall. ~ **pat.i** /**mappaci**/, ~ **palayki** opposing stone walls. ~ **thong** a tie (in gambling). ~ **tōn** cash payment.
2. adv. ~ **kēlta** wager each other; hang them opposite / facing. ~ **kellita** are hung opposite. ~ **mekta** (vi) are evenly matched, are quite comparable. ~ **nata** → **mannata** meets. ~ **pakkwuta** interchange. ~ **pota** face each other. ~ **puth.ta** stick together, grapple. ~ **putic.chita** dash against each other. ~ **ssōyta** compares them with each other. ~ **suta** face, stand opposite each other. ~ **tah.ta** comes in contact. ~ **takchita** approach one another. ~ **tak-tullita** come face to face. ~ **tangkita** tug at each other; is drawn from both sides. ~ **tāyta** face each other. ~ **tulta** lift it together.
mac, n = **maci** = **mat** (the first-born, eldest).
maca, pcl, adv [DIAL] = **mace**
māca [var] = **mālca**. **-ca** ~ SEE **-ca**.
mace < *moco*, adv, pcl. going to the extreme / limit of; (including) even; including (even the extreme case of); also (on top of everything / everyone else); above all, in particular; all the way; with everything else; with all the rest. CF **kkaci, to**; **cocha**; **macimak** < *mocomak*.
1. adv. ¶**Cip (ul) mace phal.ess.ta** He went so far as to sell his house. (He even had to sell his house — as the last of his misfortunes.)

Mace phal.ess.ta He went so far as to sell it. **I kes kkaci mace capswusio** Please eat this last one up, too. (Don't leave any.) **Pota mān chayk ul mace ilk.nunta** I am reading the rest of a book I had started (and then put aside).
2. pcl. ¶**Cip mace (lul) phal.ess.ta** He went so far as to sell his house. **Na mace teylye kasio** Take me with you too (since everyone else is going). **Hana mace capswusio** Please have (= eat) one more.
NOTE: It is often difficult to decide whether a given instance is adverb or particle; when in doubt, we treat it as a particle.
mace cocha, pcl + pcl (less common) = **cocha mace**
mace ka, pcl + pcl. [awkward] ¶**Tangsin mace (ka) kulen soli lul hamyen etteh.key hay** What am I to do if even you are saying such things?! **Ne mace (ka) na lul pelimyen na nun etteh.key sāni** If even you abandon me, how can I live?
mace 'la to, pcl + cop var inf + pcl. [awkward] ¶**Ilum mace 'la to sse noh.ass.tula 'mye n' chac.ulq swu iss.ess.ulq they 'n tey** If he [the owner] had just written his name [on it] we would have been able to find him.
mace lul, pcl + pcl. [awkward] ¶**Ku sālam mace (lul) totwuk nom chwīkup hata 'ni** What a shame they treat HIM as a thief! **Ne mace (lul) pelilq swu ēps.ta** I can't abandon YOU (of all people).
mace man, pcl + pcl. [awkward] ¶**I pen pūthak mace man tul.e cwusimyen tasi nun ilen pūthak ul an tulikeyss.^{s}up.nita** If you will just listen to this request I won't make any more of you again. CF ··· **man | mace** (in which **mace** is an adverb).
mace 'na-ma, pcl + cop extended adversative. [awkward]
mace 'n tul, pcl + copula mod + postmodifier [awkward]. ¶**Emeni mace 'n tul cōh.a hasil lī ka iss.keyss.^{s}o?** Is there any reason to think that even Mother will be happy about it?
mace nun, pcl + pcl. [awkward] ¶**Talun sālam un mōlla to sensayng nim mace nun kulesilq cwul mōllass.^{s}up.nita** I never thought that even YOU would do / say that, however others might act.
mace puthe, pcl + pcl [? awkward]. ¶**Tangsin mace puthe kulen soli l' hamyen etteh.k'**

hawu (= etteh.key hao) What's this, such talk coming even from YOU?
mace puthe ka, pcl + pcl + pcl. ¶(A.yey / Totaychey) kulenq yāyki mace puthe ka īsang hata 'n māl ia (To begin with / Indeed) his story is very fishy in itself. SYN (less common) **cocha puthe ka.**
mace to, pcl + pcl. even also / either; even indeed. ¶Onul un sinmun mace to salq swu ēps.ta Today you can't even buy a newspaper!
mace uy, pcl + pcl [rather awkward]. ¶Kotunghaksayng i ku cengto mace uy mūncey to mōs phul.e se etteh.key hay A high school boy ought to be able to solve problems of that level at least!
mace ya, pcl + pcl [awkward?]. ¶I pen pūthak mace ya mōs tul.e cwukeyss.na? Shouldn't I listen to your request this time at least?!
machi → **mankhum**
machim → **mankhum**
maci, noun = **mat** (the first-born, eldest).
māci [var] = **mālci**
macimak, noun. CF **mak, kkuth.**
  1. the last; the end, the conclusion. ¶ ~ swutan the last resort. ~ sālam the last man. ~ nal the last/final day, the closing/concluding day. ~ ssawum the final struggle, the last battle. ~ ey lastly, finally, at last, in the end. māyn ~ ey ota comes last (at the very end), brings up the rear (the tail-end). ~ ey khun sālam i toyta becomes a great man at last. ~ kkaci to the end / last. yenghwa lul ~ kkaci pota sits through a movie. ~ kkaci cēhang hata resists to the end. Ca, i kes i macimak ita Well, this is all I have (this is all that is left). Acwu cwūceng payngi ka tōyss.uni ku to macimak ita He's become such a drunkard it is the end of him. Ku hanthey tōn chwī hay cwumyen macimak ita If you lend him any money, that is the last you will ever see of it.
  2. ~ (ulo) lastly, (for) the last time. ¶māyn ~ ota comes last(ly), brings up the rear. Ilnyen cen ey pon kes i ku lul macimak pon kes iess.ta The last I saw of him was a year ago.
mac.ta₁, adj. is right, is correct.
mac.ta₂, vi (···ey ~); VC **mac.chwuta, mac.hita.**
  1. tallies / squares (with), fits together, meets, corresponds (to), matches.
  2. harmonizes, is in harmony / tune (with).
  3. fits, suits, is a good fit.
  4. matches, goes (with), compliments.
  5. agrees (with), is agreeable (to), suits; is in accord (with), conforms (with); **maum ey ~** is to one's liking, catches / strikes one's fancy.
  6. makes a good hit, hits (the mark), it tells, it hits; comes (turns out) true; (a plan) works.
mac.ta₃, vt; VC **mac.hita.**
  1. meets, goes out to meet, receives, greets, welcomes.
  2. takes, invites, engages, adopts (a person).
  3. is exposed to, is made to suffer from, has to face, confronts.
  4. is hit by/on/in ··· , receives a blow, gets / takes a punch, is struck / beaten / knocked.
mac.ta₄, postnom adj insep = **sulepta** (is, gives the impression of being). ¶**chaksal / chiksal ~** is stingy, mean, nasty, petty. **chengsung ~** is woebegone. **cicil ~** is tedious; is worthless. **iksal ~** is humorous, funny, droll, comical. **kwungsang ~** looks distressed / impoverished. **nungcheng ~** is deceitful. **nungkal / nungkul ~** is sly. **pangceng ~** is flighty, frivolous. **pīngchwung ~** is foolish, stupid. **umchwung ~** is sneaky, underhanded. ? **kēl ~** is well-matched — KEd treats this as < vt + adj, but it may be adj + adj (CF **kēl-ssata, -chata**); LHS has a short vowel, and no etymology.
mac.ta₅, aux adj [DIAL]. (intensifies adj inf). **pappa ~** , **kup hay ~** is in a great rush.
mak₁, adv. just, just / right at the moment. ¶Son i mak wass.ta A guest has just arrived. Incey mak na-kalye 'nun kil ey pi ka ssot.a cyess.ta I was just going out when it started pouring.
mak'₂, adv, adn. abbr < **makwu** (carelessly, at random, ... ; hard, much).
  1. adv. ¶ ~ toyta (adj) is ill-bred, wild. ~ māl a blunt remark (CF **'mak māl** the final remark, the last word). ~ pēlta earns wages as a day laborer. ~ pēy(e) mekta eats / cuts into. ~ sālta leads a rough (or wild) sort of life. ~ suta makes a stand (against), defies.
  2. adn. ¶ ~ chey a coarse sieve, a riddle. ~ chi a crude article, poor stuff. ~ hulk any old dirt. **mak'q īl** rough work.
'mak₃, adn, bnd n (abbr < **macimak**). the last. ¶ ~ cha the last train. ~ mul the last crop / catch. CF **'mak-nay** the last-born.
-mak, suffix (makes impressionistic adverbs). ¶kolmak kolmak all not yet full < **kolh-** (vi) not yet full. CF **-mek.**

'mak-nay, cpd n. the last born. ¶ ~ ai, ~ tongi the youngest child, the baby of the family. [abbr < macimak ?+ nāy- vc, ?+ abbr < nan ay born child]

makwu, adv [? der adv < mekta]. ABBR mak'.
1. carelessly, slapdash, sloppily, at random, desultorily, perfunctorily, haphazardly, in a disorderly way, without much discrimination/ discretion, hit-or-miss, blindly. ¶īl ul ~ hata does a half-baked (slapdash) job of it. kul-ssi lul ~ ssuta writes carelessly/sloppily. māl ul ~ hata talks at random; is rough-spoken. pang ul ~ nul.e noh.ta leaves a room in disorder. sālam ul ~ ssuta employs persons carelessly. sālam ul ~ talwuta handles a person roughly, manhandles. āmu kes ina ~ mekta eats just anything at all indiscriminately. chong ul ~ ssota fires blindly (at random). sālam ul ~ chita beats a person wildly.
2. hard, much. ¶pi ka ~ ota it rains hard. ~ yok hata much abuses, gives one a hard time. tōn i ~ tulta much money is needed.

mal < ˙MALQ, bnd n (postnoun, adnoun).
1. end. ¶hak.ki ~ end of term. kumnyen ~ at the end of this year.
2. ~ ccay last.
3. powder (= kalwu).

mal, 1. n. horse. 2. pseudo-adn. big, large-sized (animal/plant). ¶ ~ pēl a wasp. ~ pak a large gourd (≠ gourd used for mal measure). ~ pecim (pecum) psoriasis. ~ māymi a large cicada. ~ kēmeli a large leech.

māl, n. language, speech, words; what is said. ~ hata, vnt, vni. speaks; tells, says.

māl(q) < ¨mal(q) < *mal'[o]l(q), prosp mod < mālta < ¨ma[l]˙ta (desists). ¶ ¨malq ce˙k i ¨epno˙n i (1462 ¹Nung 8:125a) it never stops. CF ¨mall ⋯ ; ma˙lwol(q).

mala = mal.a (var inf < mālta) = mal.e does not; don't (do it)! (sentence-final command in INTIMATE style). ABBR mā.

māla, 1. var < mālla (subj attent < mālta) don't! (in quotation or literary passage).
2. → mala var < malla (= mal' la abbr < mal.e la) don't! (PLAIN style).
3. → mal.a (var inf < mālta) = mal.e don't! (sentence-final command in the INTIMATE style)

mal.a < ma˙la, [var] = mal.e inf < mālta
ma˙la k, inf < ¨ma[l]˙ta + emphatic pcl. ¶ne ˙[G]wa tamos ˙ho.ya [SAN-LIM] ˙ey sa˙lwo.m ol selu il˙thi [< ilh-˙ti] ma˙la k mwo˙m ay [˙YAK] ˙pson ke˙s ul kas.ka˙i ho˙kwo k swu˙l ul tyangsyang ka˙cywu.l i ˙˙la (1481 Twusi 8:33-4) neither of us will lose the life I had with you alone in the mountain woods, for I will keep close the elixir wrapped to my body and have the wine forever.

mālca, subj assert < mālta. -ca ~ SEE -ca.
mālci, suspective < mālta
mal.e, inf < mālta. ¶ ~ la (abbr malla, mala) don't!
māl ey yo = māl iey yo
māl ia, pseudo-interj (n + cop var inf) "it is to say" = I mean, you know, you see, uh, that is. ABBR māl ya. [Often spelled māl iya, māl ya.]
1. (inserted after any form) ¶Onul un pi ka oni-kka māl ia na-kalq swu ēps.ta māl ita It's raining today, uh, so we can't go out, you see. Cek.e to sam-nyen ul kellilq kes ila māl ia It will take — I mean — at least three years. Chac.e kani-kka cako iss.tula māl ia When I went to call on him, he was asleep, you know. Nwu ka kulen soli l' hatun ka māl ia Who told you that?!
2. (after un/nun as a sort of pcl) SEE māl ya.
3. (after mod as a sort of postmod) ¶Ku wa na wa kyelhon hanta 'n māl ia I mean she and I are getting married.

māl ie = māl ia
māl iey yo, pseudo-interj [POLITE] = māl ia
māl ilq sey, pseudo-interj [FAMILIAR] = māl ia
māl io, pseudo-interj. 1. [AUTH] = māl ia
2. = māl i yo
māl ita, pseudo-interj ("it is to say" =) I mean, you know, you see, uh, that is. SEE māl ia.
māl iya, 1. = māl ia. 2. n + pcl (only the words, ...).
māl i yo, [var] = māl ey yo = māl iey yo
malkan, adn [DIAL — Siberian?]. ordinary, usual, common. ¶ ~ mulken ppun just the usual things. ~ namu ppun only the common plants/trees. CF Kim Pyengha 1954:1:237. [? < malk.un < mol˙kon or mālkan < mālkah- 'clear']
mālko, 1. ger < mālta. 2. quasi-pcl [< ger]. not being. ¶I kes mālko to tto talun kes i iss.ci anh.sup.nikka? You would have another besides this, surely? I kes (un) mālko ce kes ul kacisio Take that and not this, please. Ne mālko ne pota khun sālam i wā ya hanta Not

you but a bigger boy is wanted! **I kes mālko com te kanun cwul un ēps.nun ya** Don't you have any thinner strings than this? CF **ani 'ko**.
¨mall i ··· = ¨mal[o]l i ··· < *ma'lo-l ['']i ··· , prosp mod (desists) + postmod.
~ 'Ga (1481 Twusi 8:47b).
~ ''lwoswo'n i (1481 Twusi 20:48a).
¨mal'l i ··· = ¨mal[o]'l i ··· < *mal'[o]l 'i ··· , prosp mod < ¨ma[l]'ta (desists) + postmod.
malla, abbr < **mal.e la** don't!
mālla, 1. subj attent < **mālta**. ¶**Ku sālam to sākwa ya mālla ko (haci) anh.keyss.ci** He won't tell me I don't have to apologize, either.
2. [var] = **mālle**, purposive < **mālta**.
3. [var] = **māla**.
mālm < ¨**malm** < *mal'[o]m, subst < **mālta** < ¨**ma[l]'ta**. ¶¨mal'm ye (1475 Nay 1:4b, 1586 Sohak 3:9b). CF **ma'lwom**.
malmiam.ta, vi [lit]. comes/arises from, is in consequence of, owes to, accords with. (··· **ulo**) **malmiam.**ᵉ/a owing to, in consequence of, on account of, because of; in accord(ance) with. ¶**sayngkak ulo malmiam.**ᵉ/a in accord with the thought/idea. **Pi lo malmiam.**ᵉ/a **oci mōs ha.yess.ta** I could not come on account of the rain. **Ku lo malmiam.**ᵉ/a **īl i thullyess.ta** The plan went wrong because of him. SYN **in hata**.
ma'lon, bnd n. but, however. SEE -'**ken ma'lon**, -'**en ma'lon**, ··· ; 'ho'**yan ma'lon**, 'ho'**ya'n ywo ma'lon**; -(ᵘ/e)'l i 'ye ma'lon. (? < ma'non)
māl-ssum, n. [DEFERENTIAL (honorific/humble)] = **māl**. what I say/said, my words; what you (or the teacher) say(s)/said; your (the teacher's) words. ~ **ip.nita** [FORMAL] = **māl ia**.
mālta, vt -L-. stops, ceases, drops, quits, gives up, desists, refrains from, avoids. ¶**māl ul ~** stops talking, shuts up, drops the subject; goes silent, refrains from talk. **ssawum ul ~** stops fighting, refrains from (avoids) wrangling. **īl ul mālko swie ya 'keyss.ta** I'll have to lay aside my work and take a rest. **Incey kongpu lul mālko cangsa lul halye 'nta** I am giving up my studies to go into business. NOTE: Perhaps all cases can be treated as VN **ul [haci] mālta**. See **mālta** 1 (NOTE 1); CF -u'l ye ¨mal'la, -'e ¨mal'la.
mālta < ¨**ma[l]'ta**, aux v sep -L-.
1. (follows the suspective -**ci** as a negative command or proposition) don't; be careful not to; please refrain from; avoid. For -**ci mal.e ya**

toyta 'must not' see **toyta**.
¶**Kaci mal(.e) la, Kaci mal.e/mā, Kaci māsey yo, Kaci māsipsio** Don't go. **Kaci mālca, Kaci māsey, Kaci māsey yo, Kaci māpsita** Let's not go. **Son ul tāyci māsey yo** Please do not touch (it). **Tul.e kaci māsey yo** Do not enter. **Maum ul noh.ci mālkey** Don't fall asleep at the switch, now (Keep your eyes open). **Kyōsil ey se nun tāmpay lul phiwuci māsio** Refrain from smoking in the classroom.
¶**Sesum chi** (= *sesum.ci) **mālko cēnhwa hay osipsio** Don't hesitate to telephone me. **Ic.ci mālko phyēnci lul sse la** Don't forget to write the letter. **Payk.hwa-cem ey se saci mālko cenmun-cem ey se sa la** Don't buy it at a department store; buy it at a specialty shop (at a place that specializes in them). **Nōlci mālko īl hapsita** Let's cut out the loafing and get to work. **ileni celeni māl haci mālko** setting aside all the objections and criticisms, without complaints. **Ileh.ta celeh.ta māl haci mālko, hala 'nun tay lo hay la** Stop fussing and do what you are told. **Nay ka hanun tay lo haci mālko tangsin maum tay lo hasipsio** Don't do just as I do, do as you like. **Pakk ey na-kaci mālko cip ey iss.ke la** Don't go out; stay home. **Latio lul kaciko kuleci mālko ku man twue la** Leave the radio as it is; Don't monkey with the radio. **Ca, ttek ul mantulci man mālko mek.umyen se tul hasi yo** Don't just MAKE the rice cakes, people, eat some while making them.
NOTE 1: The word **haci** can be omitted. ¶**Kekceng [haci] mala** Don't worry about it. **Elyewe [haci] māsey yo** Don't be embarrassed. ⁿ**Yēm.lye [haci] mal.e yo** Don't worry. **Māl-ssum [haci] māsipsio** Don't say anything. **Ku pun kwa kakkai [haci] māsey yo** Don't make friends with him (M 1:1:294). **Chwupta ko man mālko com na-ka nol.a la** Don't keep complaining it's cold, just go on out and play.
NOTE 2: All of the following occur: **Kaci mal.e cwusey yo, Kaci māsye cwusey yo, Kasici mal.e cwusey yo, Kasici māsye cwusey yo** Please favor me by not going (= staying a while longer); **Ka cwuci māsey yo, Ka cwusici māsey yo, Kasye cwuci māsey yo, Kasyei cwusici māsey yo** Please don't favor me (or him) by going = Please don't bother to go. Compare **Kaci māsey yo** (Please) don't go!

Also possible: **Kaci mal.e cwuci māsey yo, Kaci mal.e cwusici māsey yo, Kaci māsye cwuci māsey yo, Kaci māsye cwusici māsey yo, Kasici mal.e cwuci māsey yo, Kasici māsye cwuci māsey yo, Kasici mal.e cwusici māsey yo, Kasici māsye cwusici māsey yo** Please don't favor me (or him) by not going = Don't let me/him keep you from going.

This means you can make a negative request by negativizing the giving of the favor or the action that constitutes the favor, and you can mark as honorific (subject-exalting) any verb form and repeat the marking on any or all other verb forms in the structure. The final **māsey yo** could be said in the other styles (**māsye, māsikey**, and **māsio/māsiwu**) — or, without the honorific, as **mal.e yo, mālci yo, mal(.)e la, mālci, (mal.a =) mal.e = mā, mālkey, mao/mawu**.

NOTE 3: According to Roth (1936:436) if the subject is the same in both clauses, 'so as not to ···' is said as **-ci māllye ko, -ci ani halye ko,** or **-ci anh.key-sili**; if the subject is different, **-ci mālki lul wi ha.ye** or **-ci mālko lo** is used. But Seoul speakers reject the forms with **māl···** and for the last would say **-ci anh.key haki wi ha.ye**. The form **māltolok** is used only with a following propositive: **Kaci māltolok haca** Let's not go.

NOTE 4: Examples of **-ˊki ¨mal-** instead of **-ˊti (> ci)** are found in ⁷1517- ¹No; see -ˊki.

2. (follows a gerund -ko to show the eventual development of an action) ends up (by) doing, finally does it, gets around to doing it; does it anyway (despite reluctance or procrastination). ¶**Ku.yey pi ka oko mal.ess.ta** It WOULD end up raining! **Philkyeng ssawum i pel(.)e ciko mālkeyss.kwun a** I am afraid there will be a fight after all. **cwuk.ko mal.ess.ta** died, went and died, ended up dead. **Ku nun onul kako mānta** Finally, today at last, he gets around to leaving.

3. (follows a gerund -ko + pcl ya to show eventual resolution or completion of an action) finally gets around to doing, ends up doing. ¶**Pi ka kie-i oko ya mal.ess.ta** It finally got around to raining. **Ku ay tul i incey ssawuko ya mālkeyss.ta** Those children will end up quarreling yet. **I īl un kkok hay noh.ko ya mālkeyss.ta** I'll get this job done if it kills me!

4. (as gerund, follows a gerund and makes a strong affirmation) of course it is/does, there is no "either-or" about it, with no if's and's or but's. ¶**Kulem, kuleh.ko mālko** Yes, of course that is true. **Wass.ko mal.ess.ko (yo)** or **Wass.ko mālko (yo)** Of course he is here. **Chwupko mālko (yo)** There's no doubt about it, it's cold! **Ām, ⁿyeca chiko ya khi ka khuko mālko** Yes, she sure is tall for a girl.

5. (follows indic assertive, in indic assertive form, to make a strong affirmation) of course. ¶**Ām ā(l)ta mā(l)ta (yo)** Yes of course I know. **Ku sālam mannass.na? – Ām mannata mā(l)ta, cenyek kkaci kath.i mek.ess.nun tey!** Did you see him? – Of course I saw him, why I even had dinner with him!

6. (follows transferentive -ta [optionally + pcl ka] to show interruption) does a while and then stops. ¶**Pi ka ota (ka) ma!.ess.ta** It started to rain and then stopped. **Nāy pelye twue la; ssawuta (ka) mālci anh.keyss.ni?!** Leave them alone – they won't fight long.

7. [in paired phrases] (regardless whether) or not. SEE **-una māna, -kena māna, -tun ci māltun ci, -ulq ka mālq ka, -ulq ci mālq ci**.

8. **-ca mā(l)ca** as soon as ···, no sooner ··· than.

9. SEE **-e ¨mal'la**.

maˊlwol(q), modulated prosp mod < ¨**ma[l]ˊta**. ¶**maˊlwolq ˊt i ˊGeˊta** (1462 ¹Nung 6:42a; ⁷1468- Mong 18b, 30b; [**maˊlwol**] 1475 Nay 3:41a; 1482 Nam 1:24a); **maˊlwol ˊtt iGeˊnol** (1463 Pep 1:9a); **maˊlwol ˊt ilwoswoˊn i** (1481 Twusi 7:38b); **maˊlwol ˊt iˊn i** (1518 Sohak-cho 8:15a); **maˊlwolq ˊt i.n i ˊˊla** (⁷1468- Mong 5a, 36a; 1465 Wen 1:2:1:32a); **maˊlwo.l ye ˊysˊta** (1459 Wel 8:87b). ˊ**kwot maˊlwol ˊt iˊla ˊkhwo** (1465 Wen 1:2:2:4a) he says we will stop now and ... . ¨**TTWOW-¨LI maˊlwoˊl ye ˊhoˊtan cyenˊchoˊlwo** (1459 Wel 7:13b) because I have been unwilling to practice the doctrine.

maˊlwom, modulated substantive < ¨**ma[l]ˊta**. ¶**maˊlwoˊm i** (1463 Pep 1:15b).

māl ya, abbr < **māl ia**. ¶**Tōn ul chen wen ina ilh.ess.ta 'n māl ya** You see, I lost a whole thousand wen. **Ne oci anh.nunta ko māl ya ku ka hwā nāytula** He got mad, uh, that you weren't coming. **Kuleh.key hay se n' māl ya an toynta 'n māl ya** You shouldn't do as you are doing. **Ku sālam un māl ya ku-taci mit.ci mōs halq sālam ita** He is – uh – none too reliable a person. **Ku eykey n' māl ya cōh.un sanay ka iss.ta 'tula** They say she — uh — has a great guy. **¹Nayil māl ya wuli yenghwa kamyen ettelq ka** How about us — uh — taking in a movie tomorrow?

malyen < *MA-'LYEN*, n. 1. plan, makeshift; judgment. ¶ ~ **ēps.ta** is shiftless; has little judgment. ~ **ēps.i** without a plan (judgment); extremely, extraordinarily. **Icey n' mānh.un ke l' kikyey lo 'ta (ka) haki (lo) malyen iey yo** Now many things are supposed to be made by machine.

~ **hata**, vnt. plans, manages, handles, does; arranges; manages to get, gets; gets (it done).

2. [DIAL, colloq] **-ki, -key, -tolok ~ ita** can't help doing/being; inevitably does/is.

3. [DIAL] = **(-ki ey) mangceng**.

man < ˙*man*, pcl (and postn, adj-n [postnominal, postmodifier]). The nasal at the end may be an accretion; CF ¨*en˙ma*; ˙*hyenma*, ˙*hyen˙ma s*; ˙*myes.ma*; ˙*mas ··· = ˙ma[n]˙s*.

1. only, just (restrictive). ¶ **pap man mekta** only eats rice. **Kim sensayng man wass.ey yo** Only Mr Kim came. **Ku twū salam un selo mannaki man hamyen cangsa iyaki lul hanta** Whenever those two get together they just talk business. **Honca man ālko kyēysey yo** Keep it to yourself. **Hana man cwusio** Give me just one. **Ku nun kul ilk.ki man him ssunta** He devotes himself to his studies alone. **Na man cal-mos hayss.ˢup.nikka?** Am I the only one to blame? **Ku nun caykan i iss.ul ppun man ani 'la pucilen to hata** He is not only talented, but hard-working, as well. **Cal man hamyen toyci ppalli man hamyen cēy-il in ka?** The important thing is to do it well rather than fast.

2. 2a. just, to the extent of, as much as. ¶ **Sēk-ca man cwusio** Just give me three **ca** (feet) of it. 2b. = **pota** than: SEE **mōs hata** (adj-n).

3. [? postn, postmod] just (marks passage of time); for a period. ¶ **Ku ka on ci ka kkok twū hay man ita** It is just two years since he came. He has been here (for) two years. **olayn man (ey) = olay kan man (ey)** after a long time. **Olay kan man ip.nita** It has been a long time (since we saw each other last).

4. but, only — after indicative **-ta, -ney, -o**; suspective **-ci, -ci yo**; and rarely subj assert **-ca**; ? normally not after **-e yo**, but see **-keyss.e yo man**. Also after (rhetorical) **-keyss.na** and **-keyss.ˢup.nikka**. ¶ **Na to kako nun siph.ci man mōs kakeyss.ta** I want to go, too, only I cannot go. **Tōn un iss.ta man pillye cwuci anh.keyss.ta** I have the money but I will not loan it to you. **Ku kul ul ilk.ess.ˢup.nita man ¹īhay haci nun mōs hayss.ˢup.nita** I read the passage, but I didn't understand it. **Onul ¹nayil sāy lo nun etteh.keyss.ˢup.nikka man un thōywen hasici yo** He won't get any better between today and tomorrow, so how about taking him home.

SEE **ppun ~, -e ~, -ki ~, -ulye ~, -tuni ~, -ul ~; ku/ko ~, i/yo ~, ce ~**.

-man [S Kyengsang DIAL (¹Na Cinsek 1977)] = **-myen**

mān < ¨*man* (example?) < **ma˙[lo]n*, mod < **mālta** < ¨*ma[l]˙ta* (desists).

māna, adversative < **mālta**

manceng SEE ¨*man˙tyeng*

manchi, manchim → **mankhum**

man ey, pcl + pcl. to/at/for just/only. ¶ **Tte-nan ci sahul man ey tol.a wass.ta** He came back three days after he had left. **Olay kan man ey ku i lul mannass.ta** I saw him only after a long while (or: once in a great while). CF **ey man**.

mangceng, bnd n. SEE **-ki ey mangceng ici** (= DIAL **-uni mangceng ici, -e ya mangceng ici**), **-ul mangceng**.

mangi = mayngi

man hako, pcl + pcl. ¶ **Hyēnkum payk-man wen man hako cip han chay man iss.umyen āmu kekceng ēps.keyss.ta** If I just have a million wen in cash and a house there'll be no worries. NOTE: The expected synonym **man kwa** is unlikely to occur; **kwa** is less frequent than **hako**, and **man hako** is itself infrequent.

man hata, postnom adj-n, postmod adj-n.

1. postnom adj-n. is to the extent of, is as big/little as, is as much/little as, is the size of. ¶ **sāy al man hata** is the size of a bird's-egg, is as small as a bird's-egg. **hanul man hata** is vast as the sky, is "big as all outdoors". **kēy ttakci man han cip** a house no bigger than a crab's shell. **Ku khuki ka i man hata** Its size is this big. **Ku cwi ka kangaci man hata** The rat is the size of a puppy-dog. SEE **ku/ko ~, ce/co ~, i/yo ~**.

2. postmod adj-n (follows prosp mod). is sufficient (to do), is well worth (doing); is at the point (of doing), has reached the stage

(when one can do). ¶ pol ~ is worth seeing. mannal man han sālam a man worth meeting; the man to see. swīl man han kongwen a park that is a good place to relax in. pol man to hako tul.ul man to hata is both worth seeing and worth hearing. Atul ul tāyhak ey ponayl man han caysan i iss.ta He is rich enough to send his son to college. Ku i nun han-chang īl haki cōh.ul man han nai ey cwuk.ess.ta He died just at the age when he could lead an active life. Kkoch i phil man hani-kka palam i pūnun kwun a That old wind WOULD start to blow just when the flowers are so close to blooming! mit.ul ~ is trustworthy. mek.ul ~ is eatable. ilk.ul ~ is readable, is worth reading. kacil ~ is worth having (owning). sal ~ is (well) worth buying. ip.ul ~ is (well) worth wearing, is (quite) wearable.

mān hata, adj-n. [Hamkyeng DIAL (King 1990b)] = mānh.ta is much; are many.

man hay to, pcl + (vi inf + pcl 'even saying'). to mention only. SEE -ki ey man (hay) to.

mānh.i < ¨man [˙]hi (1482 Nam 1:36b), der adv < mānh.ta < ¨man ˚ho˙ta.

1. much / many, lots. ¶ Eceyq pam palam ey kkoch i mānh.i ttel.e cyess.ta Many blossoms fell in last night's wind. Siksa cwūnpi lul mānh.i nun mōs hay to ppalli mektolok ccum iya hay tulici yo I'll get you something to eat right away without going to a lot of trouble. Mānh.i to moass.ta We gathered a whole lot of them. Yo say saynghwal-nan ulo sālam tul i kwīcwung-phum ul mānh.i cap.hitula ko yo People have been hocking lots of their precious things because of the hardships of life these days. Nay ka tāyhak ey se kongpu hanun tong-an yele kaci cōh.un kyenghem ul mānh.i hayss.ta While studying at college, I had many valuable experiences.

2. muchly, mightily, very. ¶ Pi ka cēmcem mānh.i onun tey! The rain is coming down harder than ever! Nemu mānh.i kel.umyen phikon hay cinta If you walk too much, you get tired. Mānh.i aphe yo? Is she very ill?

3. often, lots = frequently. ¶ Elin ay ka i pyēng ey mānh.i kellinta Children often get this disease. Yo sai pi ka mānh.i wass.ta We have had much rain this last while.

¨man ˚ho˙ta (? < ˙MEN 'myriad' as sometimes written), adj n (> ¨man˙tha > mānh.ta, adj).

1. is much, are many; has much / many.
2. is frequent, prevalent, common, rife.

¶ ¨man ˙ho˙ya (1445 ¹Yong 123, 1459 Wel 1:16b) > manha (1765 Pak-sin 1:20b). ¨man ho˙kwo (1447 Sek 6:35b) = ¨man ˙khwo ("1586 Sohak cey:1" [but not there!]; cited from LCT with inferred accents).

mānh.ta, adj < mān ha- < ¨manh- (by 1765) ¨man ˚ho- (? < ˙MEN 'myriad'), adj-n. (But the usual MK equivalent was ˚ha˙ta.)

1. is much, are many; has much / many.
2. is frequent, prevalent, common, rife.

mānh.un, adj mod.

1. epitheme extruded from subject.

1a. ¶ ha mānh.un sālam ey among so many people. ileh.key mānh.un sakwa such a lot of apples. Kuleh.key mānh.un phīnan-min tul i mollye tul.e wass.uni ... With so many refugees pouring in, ... Cham mānh.un swūko lul hasyess.ˢup.nita You have gone to an awful lot of trouble for me.

1b. (subject = the possessor; or, epitheme extruded from genitive). ¶ swū mānh.un sālam tul a large number of people.

1c. epitheme extruded from the complement (the possessed). ¶ Kulem ku mānh.un tōn un ku namphyen i tā kacyess.keyss.kwun a Then the husband must have got all her money!

2. epitheme extruded from location. ¶ pata ka kiph.ko mulq koki ka mānh.un kos a place where the sea is deep and the fish are plentiful.

3. transitional epitheme. ¶ mānh.un kawuntey se hana lul kacita takes one of many.

4. summational epitheme.

4a. ¶ Haksayng tul i mānh.un ka ka mūncey 'ta The question is whether there are many students. mānh.un i mankhum inasmuch as they are many, as there is a lot.

4b. ¶ Ku nun tōn i mānh.un tus siph.ess.ta He seemed to be rich.

4c. (used as extended predicate). ¶ Yēy cen ey nun i san ey pēm i mānh.un i 'la At one time there used to be lots of tigers in these mountains.

man i, pcl + pcl. only just (etc.) [as subject].

¶ Pīwen un yēys nal wangpi wa kwungnye tul man i nōltun tongsan ita The Piwen (Secret Garden) is a garden grove that only the Queen and the ladies of the court visited in olden days. Ku i man i ānta He's the only one who knows. **Tānci na l' wi hay se man i, kelesil phil.yo nun ēps.e yo** I don't want you to do it just because of me.

man ila to, pcl + cop var inf + pcl. even only / just; only just. ¶**Ku i lul chac.e polq sikan man ila to iss.umyen cōh.keyss.ta** I wish I (only) had time enough to visit him. **Tangsin man ila to wā se towa cwusipsio** You alone could come and help me, please. **Sip-man wen i ēps.umyen ō-man wen man ila to pillye cwusipsio** Well, if you haven't got a hundred thousand **wen**, lend me fifty thousand at least.

man ina(-ma), pcl + cop extended adversative. ¶**Tōn un ēps.ta hay to salang man ina(-ma) iss.ess.umyen cōh.keyss.^{s}o** I wouldn't care if he has no money, just so he has affection. **Tā mōs kaph.tula to pān man ina(-ma) kaph.e cwusipsio** Even though you can't afford to pay back the total, at least pay back half.

man in tul, pcl + cop mod + postmod. even though (it be) only/just. ¶**Kāmsa uy ttus man in tul phyosi mōs hakeyss.^{s}up.nikka?** Could he not at least express a little appreciation? **Tōn un mōs puchitula to phyēnci man in tul mōs hakeyss.^{s}o?** Even though he can't afford to send the money, couldn't he at least write me a letter?

man iya. 1. pcl + pcl. only if (it be) just, only just. ¶**Ku sālam man iya mit.ulq swu iss.ci** You can surely trust HIM, I bet. **Onul man iya etteh.key toykeyss.ci** I guess we'll somehow manage to get by for TODAY, at least. **Ku i nun sikan man iya cal cikhici** He certainly is punctual, at least. **Swuep-lyo man iya elma an toyci** The tuition itself (alone) does not amount to much.

2. = **man ia** (postnoun + cop var infinitive). it is just / only (etc.).

mankhom → **mankhum**

mankhum. [VAR **machi, machim, manchi, manchim, mankhom;** ? < **mānh-** + **-kum**]

1. pcl. as much as, equal to.

1a. ¶**Ne to ku sālam mankhum halq swu iss.ta** You can do as well as he. **Nwukwu nun ne mankhum mōs hay se?** Do you think that someone (= I) can't do as well as you? **Na to haki man hamyen ku sālam mankhum hanta 'p.nita** If I devoted myself to it I could do as much / well as he. **I kes to ku kes mankhum cōh.ta** This one is as good as that one. **I kes un ku kes mankhum cōh.ci anh.ta** This one is not so / as good as that one.

1b. ¶**mānh.un i mankhum** inasmuch as they are many, as there is a lot. **Ne nun pūca 'n i mankhum te kipu hay ya hanta** Being richer you should donate more. **Na nun Kim sensayng eykey chwungko hal i mankhum chin haci anh.e** I'm not a good enough friend of Mr Kim to offer him advice.

2. postmod [abbr of noun **i** or **kes** + pcl]. so much that, enough to.

2a. (follows prosp mod). ¶**Khun cip ul ciul (i) mankhum tōn i ēps.ta** I don't have money enough to build a big house. **Silhq-cung i nal mankhum mek.ess.ta** I have eaten it so much / often that I am sick of it. **Pēm ila to cap.ul mankhum nallayta** He is fast enough to catch a tiger. **Na nun i kwamok ul kaluchil mankhum ānun kes i ēps.ta** I haven't the knowledge (= background) to teach this subject.

2b. (follows any mod). inasmuch as, since. ¶**Cikum i machim cengcho in (kes) mankhum wuli nala uy say hay lul selmyeng hay tulikeyss.ey yo** Inasmuch as New Year's is right at this time, I am going to explain the Korean New Year. **Tōn i sayngkin mankhum ku tong-an sako siph.ess.tun os ul sakeyss.ta** Now that I've got the money, I'm going to buy some clothes that I've been wanting to get.

mankhum chelem = **chelem mankhum**

mankhum cocha, pcl + pcl. ~ **to.** ¶**Elin ay mankhum cocha to mōs hamyen se mue l' khun soli ya** What are you making such a fuss about when you can do even less than a child?!

mankhum i, pcl + pcl. as much as [as subject]. ¶**Ku mankhum i** (or **ku manchi ka**) **te khun ya** Is it bigger by that much?

mankhum ila to, pcl + cop var inf + pcl. ¶**Yo cengto mankhum ila to hay polyem** Why don't you just try it out to this extent, at least.

mankhum ina(-ma), pcl + copula (extended) advers. ¶**Ku kes mankhum ina(-ma) hayss.ni?** Did you do at least as much as that?

mankhum iya, pcl + pcl. only if (it be) as much as. ¶**Āmuli khi ka khuta hay to na mankhum iya khulla kwu?** However tall he might be, surely he can't be as tall as I am.

mankhum man, pcl + pcl. ¶**Ku mankhum man iss.umyen toyess.ci** If there is (just) that much it will be all right.

~ ila to. ¶Ku mankhum man ila to cōh.uni cwusikeyss.ˢup.nikka Won't you give me just that little bit?

mankhum ssik, pcl + pcl. ¶halwu kēnne mankhum ssik every other day.

mankhum to, pcl + pcl. even / also / either as much as. ¶yo ~ even the least little bit. Ku mankhum to ūmsik ul mōs mek.ni? Can't you eat just that little bit of food? Ku sālam mankhum to cal mōs hani? Can't you do just as well as he can?

mankhum ul, pcl + pcl. ¶I mankhum ul hayss.e to acik mōs tā hayss.kwun Though we have done this much, I see we haven't yet done it all.

mankhum un, pcl + pcl. (as for) as much as. ¶Talun sālam un mōs mit.tula to ku sālam mankhum un mit.ulq swu iss.e Even though others may not be trusted you can trust him, at least. Na to wuli hyeng nim mankhum un mek.e I eat as much as my big brother does!

man kwa, pcl + pcl. SEE man hako (NOTE).

ma῾non, postmod (? bnd n − CF ma῾lon). but, however. SEE -῾ken ma῾non, -῾en ma῾non, ... (< man῾on or ma῾non?)

῾῾manon < *ma῾[lo῾]non, processive modifier < ῾῾ma[l]῾ta (desists). ¶῾῾mano῾n i (1481 Twusi 10:20a).

῾ma[n] s SEE ῾ma s

῾man s, pcl + pcl. ¶SO-HHWOW ῾man s ῾NYEM ῾two (1482 Kum-sam 2:15a) even the tiniest fraction of a kṣana (an instant).

man to < ῾man῾two (CF ῾ma῾two), 1. pcl + pcl. just (only) also / even / either. ¶Ne nun kāy man to mōs hata You are worse than a dog (= beast). NOTE: *man to ka / lul are rejected.
  2. SEE -ci man to
  3. SEE -ki ey man (hay) to
  4. adj-n + pcl. also / even / either worth. ¶pol man to hako tul.ul man to hata is both worth seeing and worth hearing.

mantulta, vt. -L-. VAR mayntulta.
  1. makes, manufactures, prepares, fixes up, concocts, cooks (up); makes it (into), turns it (into); makes out, draws up, frames, creates, writes; builds, erects, constructs; forms, sets up, organizes, establishes; cultivates, fosters, builds up, trains; invents, fabricates, makes up (a story); creates (from nothing).

  2. aux (follows adverbative -key to make a periphrastic causative that is more emphatic than -key hata). makes, causes, sets, forces, impels. ¶kakey ~ makes a person go, induces one to go. mit.key ~ makes one believe (in). kikyey ka tol.a kakey ~ sets a machine to work (in operation). myēng.lyeng ul pokcong hakey ~ forces one to obey an order. cacin hay se kipu hakey ~ induces a person to donate of his own accord.

῾man῾two, pcl + pcl. ¶῾῾a῾mwo ῾man῾two ῾῾mwot῾῾ti a῾ni ho῾kwo ce῾lol ῾῾cye῾ku῾na cwu῾m ye n'῾kwot ho῾l i῾῾la (?1517- Pak 1:43a) without its being very much if you give him just a little he will do it right away. ῾kul poyhwo῾ti a῾ni῾hwom῾man῾two῾kot῾῾ti ῾῾mwot ho῾n i῾῾la (1518 Sohak-cho 8:30ab; a smudge makes ῾kul look much like ῾kwol, but it is too far to the left) it is not as bad as being uneducated. CF ῾ma῾two.

῾῾man῾tyeng, bnd n (postn / postmod) + bnd n (postmod / postn). not just ... but. ¶῾pap me῾kulq ῾tet῾῾man῾tyeng TTYANG-SSYANG i῾῾i῾l ol ῾soyng῾kak ho῾la (1459 Wel 8:8b) think about this matter not just while you eat but all the time. kwo῾ki capnon῾poy nwol῾Gywo.m ol ῾pwonwo῾la῾ho.ya [῾PPOYK-῾ZILQ] i wol῾ma katolwok῾hosila 'n῾t oy ῾῾man tyeng nul῾kun nye῾lum῾῾cis.non῾nwo῾m on mu῾sus ke῾s i i῾sye selu῾culkywo῾m ol῾῾ta ho῾l i Gwo (1481 Twusi 22:7b) not just have they spent much of the day's light enjoying the fishing boat, but with what [now] will the old farmers bring their mutual delight to its fullest?

man ul, pcl + pcl. only / just (etc.) [as direct object]. ¶Hān-e man ul hanun sāhoy a society that talks only Korean.

man ulo, pcl + pcl. only / just as (with, etc.). ¶ ~ nun (as for) only / just as (with, etc.). Pap man ulo sānun kes i ani 'ta We do not live by bread alone. Sālam twūl man ulo uy wūncen ... (CM 2:130) Operation by just two persons ... . CF ulo man.

manun (pcl) = man un (pcl + pcl) but only.

mānun, 1. proc mod < mālta. 2. < mānh.un

man un, pcl + pcl. 1. as for only / just. ¶I kwuk.hwa man un han kwungsil ey cīn.¹yel hay noh.ass.ess.ta These chrysanthemums alone have been put on exhibit in a certain room in the palace.

2. (after indicative -ta or suspective -ci). but, only [often spelled -manun in this usage]. ¶Kako siph.ci man un pappe se kaci mōs hakeyss.ta I should like to go, only I'm too busy. Tōn un iss.ˢup.nita man un cikum kot pillye tulici nun mōs hakeyss.ˢup.nita I have the money but I can't lend it to you right now.
3. (sentence-initial adv / conjunction). But, ··· .
man uy, pcl + pcl. (the one that is) only / just (etc.). ¶Na honca man uy mūncey 'la 'myen kantan haci yo It would be quite simple if it concerned only me.
manyang, pcl [DIAL] = chelem (like).
˙ma˙s (?= ˙ma[n] s), pcl + pcl. ¶*[PANG-˙CHWON]* ˙ma˙s mozo˙m ay (1481 Twusi 8:9a) in his heart of hearts. SEE ˙i ˙ma[n] s; CF ¨cywokwo˙ma˙s.
māsica: Neither V-ci māsica nor V-usici mā(l)ca are used, because the honorific is incompatible with the plain hortative.
mas-¨nala, modulated indic assert < mas-na˙ta < mac-na˙ta (> mannata). (I) meet / face. ¶˙mwul˙s [˙TTWOW-¨CCUK] ˙ey two˙la kal ˙kil.h i ¨ep.su˙n i [SYWUY-¨LWOW] hon no˙ch oy [¨NGWEN-PANG] ˙ay mas-¨nala (1481 Twusi 8:13b) with no way to return to the band of brigands my aged face confronts a distant land.
(*)māsye la: Neither V-ci māsye la nor V-usici ma(l.e)la are used, because of the incongruity of the honorific with the plain command.
mat < ˙mot, n, adn. the first-born, first, eldest. ¶~ nwui the eldest sister. ~ ttal the eldest daughter, the first daughter. Ku i ka mat ita He/She is the eldest. ~ ulo nass.ta / nah.ass.ta was born first, is the eldest. NOTE: Many speakers replace the noun mat with maci, a new noun created from the pronunciation of mat i as /maci/: maci lul cwuk.yess.ta killed the first-born; maci lo nah.ass.ta was born the eldest; maci 'ta = mat ita is the first-born. Some speakers use a shortened version mac: mac ul pilos ha.ye beginning with the eldest (= maci lul = mat ul).
mata < ¨ma˙ta, particle. each (one), every, all (inclusive). ¶nal ~ every day < nal ˙ma˙ta (1459 Wel 23:74b) = māyil < ¨moy˙il (1586 Sohak 6:26b = 1518 Sohak-cho 9:30a) < ¨moy˙zil (?1517⁻ Pak 1:21a, 58b) < ¨MOY-˙ZILQ. cip cip ~ each and every house. kos kos ~ everywhere < ˙kwot ˙kwot ¨ma˙ta (1459 Wel 2:52a). kalq cek ~ every time one goes. Sālam mata ku lul chingchan hanta Everybody praises him. ¨salom pwo˙n i ¨ma˙ta (1447 Sek 24:13b; ˙i is functioning as a postappositional nominalization that semantically echoes the ¨salom) everyone he saw. ˙sta[h] ¨ma˙ta (1447 Sek 6:8b) each land. ¨em ¨ma˙ta ··· kwos wu[h] ¨ma˙ta (1447 Sek 6:31a) on each tusk ··· and on top of each blossom. namwo a˙lay ¨ma˙ta (1459 Wel 7:31a) under every tree. DIAL matang, matong, matwung. CF māy-, ssik; kkol. SEE -un ˙ta ¨ma˙ta.
NOTE 1: Redundant marking is possible (Im Hopin 1986:75): māyil ~ every day (= nal ~), māy cwuil mata every week, māy sikan mata every hour, māy sam-kaywel mata every three months. ALSO: māy sēt tal (mata) every December, māy sip-il wel(q tal) ~ every November. Awkward: (*)māy īl hanun nal (mata) every working day, māy chwuwun nal (mata) every cold day.
NOTE 2: The shape is identical with the unattested indic assert (and transferentive) of the negative auxiliary ¨ma[l]˙ta, from which the particle could have developed by way of an expression like "not stopping at just a / one ··· but [every] ··· ". Dialect forms with -ng may reflect the ˙ka of -˙ta ˙ka (transferentive).
māta [var] = mālta
mata ey, pcl + pcl. [a bit awkward; modern style omits ey] ¶Kolccaki mata (ey) colcol hulunun kaywul mul un cham ulo malk.ki to hata How clear the tiny streams are that bubble down each valley.
mata eykey (se), pcl + pcl. [older style] = eykey (se) mata
mata ey se, pcl + pcl + pcl. [older style] = ey se mata
mata ka, pcl + pcl. each, every, all [as neg cop complement]. ¶Ai mata ka ani 'la i ai hako ce ai man ici yo It's not every child, just this one and that one.
mata khenyeng, pcl + pcl. far from (its being) each / every / all. ¶Cēnchwuk un cip cip mata (nun) khenyeng hak.kyo ey to ēps.nun tey ka mānh.ta There are many schools that lack phonographs, to say nothing of their absence in every house!
mata kkaci, pcl + pcl. ¶Icey nun sanq-kol ey iss.nun cip cip mata kkaci cēnki ka tul.e

kakey toyess.ta Now electricity has come to every house in the mountain spots.
māta ko [var] = **mālta ko**
mata l' (pcl + abbr pcl) = **mata lul**
(*)mata lo, pcl + pcl [awkward]. ¶(?) Il.yoil nal sālam tul un kyōoy mata lo sophung ul kass.ta On Sunday people went out picnicking to every outskirt of town.
mata (*)lul, pcl + pcl. each, every, all [as direct object]. ¶cīna kanun sālam mata [lul] pota watches every person passing by.
mata man, pcl + pcl. ¶Cēnchwuk i hak.kyo mata man iss.e to kwaynchanh.ci yo It is all right for each school to have a phonograph.
mata n' (pcl + abbr pcl) = **mata nun**
mata 'na, pcl + cop advers. each/every/all or the like; whether each/every/all; each/every/all whatsoever. ¶Cip cip mata 'na na-wass.umyen īl i toylq ka There'd be no problem if people had come from each house.
matang, pcl [DIAL: Phyengan (Kim Yengpay 1984:95); Hamkyeng (Kim Thaykyun 1986: 191a)] = **mata** (each).
mata nun, pcl + pcl. as for each/every/all. ¶(Talun sālam un mōlla to) sensayng nim mata nun tā tulye ya 'ci (I don't know about giving the others but) we should give one to each teacher at least.
mata nun khenyeng, pcl + pcl + pcl. SEE **mata khenyeng**.
mata pota, pcl + pcl. ¶Yo cuum un latio ka ecci 'na mānh.un ci cip cip mata pota pang mata hana ssik iss.ta ko halq swu iss.ulq cengto 'ci yo Lately radios have become so common it has reached the point where you can say that every room has one, rather than every house.
mata puthe, pcl + pcl. ¶Kak kaceng mata puthe kyōyuk ey kwansim ul kacye ya hanta Each household must take an interest in education.
mata se, pcl + pcl. SEE **mata ey se**.
ˮmata ˙sye, pcl + pcl. ¶cip ˮmata ˙sye ˮsalo˙m ol ˙honwol˙Ginwos˙ta (1481 Twusi 15:6a) they are murdering people in every household.
mata to, pcl + pcl [awkward]. each/every/all also (either, even). ¶ⁿYeca ppun man ani 'la namca mata to ¹yuhayng ul ttaluko iss.ta Not only every woman but every man is following the fashion, too.
mata uy, pcl + pcl. (the one) of each/every/all. ¶sālam mata uy ūymu everybody's duty, the duty of every person.
mata wa, pcl + pcl. [a bit awkward] ¶Ku nun ponun sālam mata wa tathwunta He fights with everyone he sees.
mata ya, pcl + pcl. only if (it be) each/every/all. ¶Haksayng mata ya tā cwulq swu ēps.ci yo We can't let EACH student have one.
math, 1. n. [obs] = **matang** (a yard, a place). CF **meli-math** the head of the bed.
   2. postmod. [DIAL] = **kyel** (incidental to): -nun/-tun ~ ey/ulo.
ˮma˙ti, = **ˮma[l]˙ti**, suspective < **ˮma[l]˙ta**. ¶ˮma˙ti a˙ni tha˙n i (1463 Pep 2:28b) they did not give up.
matong, **matwung** [DIAL] = **mata**
mattana, quasi-pcl (always preceded by **māl**). [abbr < **mac.ta hana** 'says it fits but' =] according to (something said). ¶Caney māl mattana yēys nal ey nun yeki mos i iss.ess.ney As you say, there was a pond here in olden times. Yēys māl mattana am-thalk i wūlmyen cip-an mang hanun i 'la As the old saying goes, "when the hen crows [= when the woman wears the trousers] the family goes to ruin".
˙ma˙two (?= **˙ma[n]˙two**), pcl + pcl. ¶pi˙lwok ˮsalo˙m oy ˙mwu˙l ey ˮsa-˙nikwo ˙two cywungsoyng ˙ma˙two ˮmwot ˙hwo-ngi ˮta (1447 Sek 6:5a) even [my] living on in the society of human beings is inferior to [the life of] any living creature.
maum < *mozom*, noun.
   1. mind, soul, spirit, heart, idea, thought, mentality; disposition. ¶Mom un nulk.e to maum cocha ya nulk.keyss.na Why should I let my spirit get old along with my body? Him un yak halq ci 'la to maum un tantan hay ya hanta You should be firm in mind even though you are weak in body. Nay maum un choq pul kwa to kath.ta My heart is (just) like a flickering candle. Elkwul iya ette hatun ci maum man chak hamyen ssukeyss.ta If only she's a woman of good nature, she is all right with me, regardless of what she looks like.
   2. consideration, sympathy, tenderness, heart, kindness; concern. ¶Ku nun hak.kyo lul wi hanun maum ey se kuleh.key hayss.ta He did so out of concern for the school.

3. feeling, mood; worry, anxiety. ¶ Ileh.key maum i pul.an halq cwul al.ess.tula 'myen an ponaynun ke l' (kwayni ponayss.kwun a) If I had known I would feel so bad I wouldn't have sent him off (but I did). Ku ka Mikwuk ey kanta 'nun tey nay maum ey ette hata I am none too happy to hear that he is going to America. Na eykey 'n tul casik ul salang hanun maum i ēps.keyss.^{s}o? Why should I not have a feeling of love for my own child? ecci toyl.nun ci maum coita worries over what will happen. maum ul thek noh.ta puts one's mind at complete ease. Cikum ce uy maum ul etteh.key māl-ssum tulye ya cōh.ulq ci molukeyss.^{s}up.nita I do not know just how I ought to describe my feelings at this moment. Ku sosik ul tul.uni-kka maum i noh.inta Now that I hear the news, I feel better. Hyeng nim kkey se 'la to phyēnci ka iss.umyen maum i noh.ikeyss.nun tey ... I'd feel relieved if there were a letter even from my elder brother, but (there isn't any). Nam tul i na tele kongpu l' cal hanta 'nun i mankhum nay maum uy chayk.im un te mukewe cinta The more that people tell me how well I am doing in my studies, the heavier the burden on my soul.

4. fancy, taste, liking, mind, heart. ¶ caki maum tay lo hata does as one pleases. maum kkes wūlta cries one's heart out. Katun ci otun ci maum tay lo hakey Come or go, whichever you please. Nay ka hanun tay lo haci mālko tangsin maum tay lo hasipsio Don't do just as I do, do as you like. Ileca 'ni ku nom i maum ey kkiiko, kuleca 'ni ce nom hanthey an tōyss.kwu ... If I do this I offend the one guy and if I do that I offend the other guy (– I just can't please anyone)!

4a. ~ ey tulta is to one's liking, catches / strikes one's fancy, appeals to one; (?) is acceptable, satisfactory. ¶ Ney maum ey tun ya? (How) do you like it? Ku-yek maum ey tulci anh.nunta I don't like it, either. Eccen ci maum ey tul.e Somehow he appeals to me.

5. will, intention, inclination, plan, design, mind, heart. ¶ ttan ~ ulterior motive, secret purpose; duplicity, treachery. pon (ku uy) ~ un as for his real intention/nature. Nay ka sal.e iss.nun hān ney maum tay lo haci mōs hanta So long as I live, I won't let you have your way (= You'll have to do it over my dead body). han maum han ttus (of) the same mind, of one accord. Wi lo nun sacang ey se alay lo nun sāhwan ey iluki kkaci cen-hōysa ka han maum ulo īl hanta The entire company works hard, from the president at the top to the office boy at the bottom.

5a. SEE -ul ~ (i iss.ta / ēps.ta, ul mekta). CF ttus, cēngsin, ki, kipun, mes.

maumq cali, cpd n. temper(ament), disposition, nature, character. SYN maumq ssi, simci.

maumq kyel, cpd n. (= sēngq kyel) disposition, temper(ament).

maumq-po (= simq-po, simswul) will, temper, disposition (often bad). ¶ ~ ka sānapta is ill-willed / -disposed, bad-tempered, evil-minded.

maum-ssi a turn / kind of mind, a sort of person; nature, temper(ament), disposition. ¶ elkwul to kōpkeni wa maum-ssi to kōpta has not only a pretty face but also a lovely disposition. Ku nun keth ulo poki ey pota acwu maum-ssi ka cōh.un sālam ita He is a much nicer person than he seems to be when you just look at him. Ku ^{n}yeca uy maum-ssi ka etten ci nun moluci man (un) elkwul un yeypputula I do not know what her disposition is like but she had a pretty face (as I recall). Mom un yak hal mangceng maum un kwut.ta He may be weak physically but he has a strong will. Ku sayksi uy maum-ssi ka kowulq ci ettelq ci nun te kyekk.e pwā ya ālkeyss.e I will not know whether that girl has a nice disposition or not until I have seen more of her.

may$_1$, postn. shape, form, cast. ¶ mom ~ one's figure / shape, one's carriage / bearing. nwun ~ the expression / cast of one's eyes; one's eyes. heli s may the shape of one's waist. ip ~ a dab of food; a slapdash job; (the shape of) one's mouth. ?son ~ (CM 1:229) (the shape of) one's hands. CF maypsi < may-pssi) shapeliness; appearance. [< *moy* attire (?1660- Kyeychwuk) ? < *moy˙ta* > māyta ties, makes]

may$_2$, adn. quite, much (the same). ¶ ~ han kaci 'ta, ~ ilpan ita are much/about the same, come to the same thing after all. Eph.e cina cac.hye cina may machan-kaci 'ta It is six of one and half a dozen of the other. CF māy$_4$ (thoroughly), maywu, māyn.

māy$_3$ < ¨*moy* < ¨MOY, adnoun. each, every. ¶ ~ tal = māywel every / each month (= tal mata, but 'every two months' is only **twū tal mata**); **~ hay** = **māynyen** every/each year (= **hay mata**); but ***māy nal** is not said for **māyil** every day, each day (= **nal mata**). **~ haksayng** each student. **~ hak.ki** each school term (semester). **~ il.yoil** every Sunday. **~ myeng** every/each person. **~ cip mata** every house [rare without the **mata**]. **Māy math.un pa chayk.im ul kakca ka motwu wanswu haca** [a bit awkward] Let/May each of us fulfill every responsibility we have undertaken. CF **mata, ssik, kkol**. NOTE: Redundant marking with **māy ··· mata** occurs; see **mata**, NOTE 1.

¶ ¨*moy ˙hona˙h oy* (?1517⁻ Pak 1:32a; mistake for *hona˙h oy*?) for each one, apiece.

māy, adv. well, thoroughly; carefully (cooks). ¶ **~ ~** SAME. **~ ccih.ta** grinds it thoroughly. **~ pokk.ta** roasts it nicely. ? **may mancita** arranges, adjusts (clothes or hair). CF **maywu, maypta; māy** (quite).

¨*may*, adv. how come, why (= **way**).

'/-may [DIAL, lit] = **'/-m ey**

māyn, adnoun. 1. (pseudo-adn) LIGHT ↔ **mīn**.

1a. exclusively, nothing but, just, to the exclusion (or virtual exclusion) of everything else; lots, many; full of. ¶**Kwūkyengq keli nun ēps.ko māyn sālam tul ppun ita** There is nothing to see but lots of people. **Mos ey māyn koki 'ta** The pond is full of fish (swarms with fish). **Kākey ey māyn Ilpon mulken ita** The store is loaded with Japanese goods.

1b. unadulterated, nothing but, just unaided, unaccompanied, unprotected, bare, naked. ¶ **~ meli** a bare head; bareheaded (**māyn meli lo na-kata** goes out bareheaded, goes out without putting on a hat). **~ pal** bare feet; barefooted. **~ mom, ~ cwumek, ~ son** empty hands; empty-handed (**māyn son ulo sālam ul chac.ta** visits a person without bringing a gift). **~ pap** plain rice (with no side dishes). **māynq ip an** empty (unfed) mouth.

2. all the way, the very, the extreme/most. ¶ **~ cheum** at the very first; first of all, before anything else, before all others, foremost; at the very beginning, right at/from the start. **~ nācwung** at the very end/latest, last of all, behind all others, hindmost. **~ kkoktayki** (at) the very top; the highest, the uppermost. **~ alay** (at) the very bottom, the lowest, the nethermost. **~ ōyn phyen cip** a house at the very left; the house way at the left. **Pokto māyn kkuth ey iss.ˢup.nita** It's way down at the end of the hall.

-mayn [S Kyengsang DIAL (¹Na Cinsek 1977)] = **-myen**

··· ˙*ma 'y˙na*, pcl + cop advers. ¶*hon thelek ˙kut ˙ma 'y˙na isi˙m ye n' MWON ˙NGWOY ˙yey is.ke˙ta* (?1468⁻ Mong 12b) if there is but one hair end [unshaven on the head] one is outside the discipline.

-mayng [S Kyengsang DIAL] = **-myen se**

mayngi, postn, suf (? dimin). ¶**al ~** a kernel, a grain; substance, matter, content. **an.a ~** a hole in the back of a miner's lamp so that it can be attached to his pick [< vt var inf **an.a** = **an.e** embracing]. ? **kay ~ pep** [< **kāyta**].

VAR **mangi** (CF **pangmangi** club). CF **meyngi; kayngi, tayngi, layngi, payngi, ayngi, cayngi**.

mayntulta [var] = **mantulta**

me, abbr < **mwe** < **mue** < **mues** (what; ...)

-mek suffix (makes impressionistic adverbs; CF **-mak**). ¶**tulmek tulmek** exhilarated (< tu-l- vt lift up). **kwulmek kwulmek** all not yet full (< **kwulh-** adj not yet full).

me ka, abbr < **mwe ka** < **mue ka** = **mues i**

mekta₁, vt (VC **mek.ita**, VP **mek.hita**)

1. eats (HON **capswusita**).
2. lives (subsists, feeds) on.
3. smokes (= **phiwuta**); drinks (= **masita**).
4. takes, seizes, devours.
5. gets, receives, has.
6. gets, undergoes, suffers, catches.
7. (**sal ul ~**) gets, acquires (years of age). **twū sal mek.i** a two-year-old.
8. fixes, sets, makes up (one's mind).
9. harms, injures, slurs, slanders.

mekta₂, vi. 1. it bites, cuts (well).

2. it grinds (well).
3. it dyes (well), soaks in (well).
4. it gins (well).
5. (**ssi-nal ~**) it is all tied together; (warp and woof) are properly adjusted = is logical.
6. costs, is spent (consumed).
7. is worm-eaten, moth-eaten, decayed.
8. (an ear) loses its hearing, goes deaf.
9. **mac' ~** are well matched, comparable.
10. gets numbered (**chi ~** upward, **nayli ~** downward).

mekta₃, aux insep. (gives a strong vulgar and pejorative flavor to the preceding infinitive).

1. aux adj (follows adj inf). ¶keyulle ~ is a lazy bastard. CF ppā cita.

2. aux v (often limited to past or future). ¶phal.e ~ sells it away/off. ic.e ~ forgets. sok.ye ~ cheats, swindles, takes in. cip.e ~ swipes, filches.

hay ~ does (something bad / bothersome), does the damn thing; takes unjust possession of something, latches on to. ttwucayngi nolus ul hay ~ pimps, panders, is a damn pimp.

kaluchye ~ teaches (under some unpleasant circumstance), has to put up with teaching. Ay ka māl ul tut.ci anh.e kaluchye mek.ulq swu ēps.ta The boy won't listen to what I tell him, so I can't teach him a damn thing.

tōy (= toye) mek.ess.ta is, is shaped, is formed (in an unpleasant way). Kulus i cal twu (= to) tōy mek.ess.ta What a "nice" dish it is! [IRONICAL] = What an ugly dish! Casik cal twu tōy mek.ess.ta What a mess you are! (or ‥ he is!)

SEE puth-mekta.

mekwu˙li, n. frog. mekwu˙luy pap (?1517⁻ Pak 1:70b, 1527 Cahoy 1:5a=9b) water chestnut; duckweed < mekwu˙l[y] uy ˙pap < mekwu˙li ˙uy ˙pap frog food. CF ˙uy NOTE 2 (p. 923).

me˙kwu˙li = me˙kwu˙l i, vt modulated prosp mod + postmod. food. ¶sana˙ol me˙kwu˙l i l' ˙pwuy˙ye wo˙n i (1459 Wel 1:45a) for three or four days they kept cutting [grain for] food.

me l', abbr < mwe l(ul) < mue l(ul) = mues ul
me 'l, abbr < mwe 'l < mue 'l < mues il

mēl(q) < ¨mel(q) < *me˙l[u]l(q), prosp mod < mēlta < ¨me[l]˙ta (far). CF ¨mell ‥ .

me˙len, effective mod < ¨me[l]˙ta. ¶˙SYENG-ZIN pe˙ngulwo˙m i te˙wuk me˙len ¨salo˙m i (1463 Pep 2:41a) people more distanced from the sage.

meli, n. 1. the head; brains, intelligence.

2. the top (head, point, tip), an end (part). ¶peykay (chayk-sang) ~ the top of a pillow (a desk). alayq (wiq) ~ the bottom (top) end.

3. the beginning.

4. a chief, a boss, a top man.

5. (= ~ thel) the hair on one's head.

(-)meli, postnoun, suffix. (vulgarizes nouns); CF (-)taykali, (-)ttakci. ¶angtal ~ a person who is swollen with ambition. ciceng ~ inappropriate behavior. cincel ~ repugnance. cwūpyen ~ resourcefulness, flexibility. ēngteng ~ rump.

nentel ~ disgust. sēngceng ~ nature, stamp, temper(ament). ssak-swu ~ a good sign/omen, promise. sōkal ~ (perverse / stupid) mentality (< sōk al). ssi-al ~ a bad seed, a nasty fellow. taykal ~ the head. tōn ~ a sum of money. yamthong / yemthwung ~ (sense of) shame (< ¹yemchi < LYEM-¨CHI). NOTE: KEd put kkuthumeli here, but we will treat it as kkuth + -umeli, similar to kkuth(-)uleki.

¨mell ‥ (+ ˙i postmod) < *me˙l[u]l(q), prosp modifier < ¨me[l]˙ta (far). ¶¨mel˙l i '-ngi s˙ka (1459 Wel 8:1b) is it far?.

mel-lo = muel-lo = mues ulo (with what, ...)
me lo, abbr < mwel-lo = mues ulo (with what, ...)

mēlm < ¨melm < *me˙l[u]m, subst < mēlta < ¨me[l]˙ta (far). ¶¨mel˙m ya [= ye] kas.ka˙won toy (1586 Sohak 6:108a) places far and near.

me lul = mues ul (what / something)
me 'm, abbr < mwe 'm < mue 'm < mues im
me n', abbr < mwe n(un) < muenun = mues un
me 'n, abbr < mwe 'n < mue 'n < mues in

mēn < ¨men < *me˙[lu]n, modifier < mēlta < ¨me[l]˙ta (far). ¶¨men (1447 Sek 13:59a; 1449 Kok 139; 1459 Wel 2:69a, 7:12b). [¨]men ¨nwuy˙yey s (1459 Wel 23:93a) of a distant generation. it.ti ˙Gwos tewuk e˙kuy.m ye tot.ti [˙]Gwos tewuk ¨me.n i (1579 Kwikam 1:6a) the better it is the more one transgresses, and the more one runs the farther it is. CF me˙len.

-meng (se) [Ceycwu DIAL (Seng ¹Nakswu 1984: 45-6; LSN 1978:93, 101)] = -myen se, = -mye mengi, postn, suf [var] = meyngi.

'meni, an intensifier added to interjections [< emeni mother]. Aikwu 'meni! Good lord! Oh oh! Oh my! Alas!

me nun = mues un (noun + particle)

MEY South Korean spelling distinguishes mey and m^yey, but both sequences are usually pronounced the same (as mey). If you cannot locate the word you are looking for under mey, look under m^yey.

mey, adnoun, bnd n (? < ¨mwoy[h] 'mountain'). nonglutinous, not sticky.

1. adn. ¶ ~ co nonglutinous (regular) millet. meypssal = mey-pssal < ˙mwoy ˙psol (1527) hulled nonglutinous rice. ~ ttek nonglutinous cake. ~ pap (boiled) nonglutinous rice. ~ pye < mwoy pye (?1834⁻) nonglutinous rice plants. ANT chal (cha') < ˙chol (? < ˙cholq).

2. bnd n. ¶ ~ cita is nonglutinous.

mey, abbr < **mwey** < **muey** = **mue** what; what?!
me 'y, abbr < **mwe 'y** < **mwe ey** < **mue ey** < **mues ey**
me' y, abbr < **mwe' y** < **mue' y** = **mues i.**
'/-m ey. 1. = **ham ey.** 2. = **-um ey**

meych < ˙*myech*, noun [usually spelled **myech**]. how many; some, several, a few. ¶ ~ **ina** about how many; about so many, several (or so). ~ **ip.nikka** how old are you? ~ **sālam / kos** how people / places; several people / places. **Meych salam iss.ˢup.nikka** [falling intonation] How many people are there?; [rising intonation] Are there some people? ~ **hay** how many years; a few years, some/several years. VAR [lit] **myech.**

meych ey, n + pcl. to how many; to some. ¶**Meych ey tases ul ka hayss.nun ya** To how many were the five added?

meych eykey, n + pcl. to how many (to some) creatures. ¶**Thokki meych eykey** (= **meych mali eykey**) **punpay han sēym in ya** How many rabbits do you figure got their rations?

meych ey se, n + pcl + pcl. from how many (or how much); from some (several). ¶**Meych ey se tases ul cey hayss.nun ya** From how many were the five subtracted?

meychil < *mye˙chul*, noun [spelled **myechil**].
1. = **meychit nal** what day of the month.
2. how many days, how long; a few days. ¶**Ku īl hanun tey meychil kellikeyss.ˢo** How many days will it take to get the work done? **Meychil cen ey tte-nass.ta** He left here a few days ago. **Na nun meychil te iss.keyss.ta** I will stay for a few days longer.

meychit nal (*myechit nal* ? < *˙mye˙chu[l]s ˙nal*), cpd n [usually spelled **myechit-nal**]. what day of the month; the date; the something-(e)th. ¶**Onul i meychit nal in ka** What day of the month is it today? **Onul i sumu meychit nal ita** It is the 20-somethingth today.

meych meych, cpd noun [usually spelled **myech-myech**]. a (certain) number, several, some, a few; how many (all). ¶**Kim kwun hako tto meych meych chinkwu ka kath.i kanta** I am going with Kim and a few other friends [sic!]. **Ku chayk ōy ey meych meych kakwu ka iss.ess.ey yo** Besides the books there were a few pieces of furniture. **Incey chayk-sang ina meych meych iss.umyen toykeyss.ey yo** It will be all right now if we can get some tables.

meyngi, postn, suf (? dimin). **tōl** ~ a small stone, a pebble. VAR **mengi**; CF **mayngi** (etc.).

mich, pcl, adv [lit]. and. SYN **kup.** [< **mich(i)-** 'reach (to)']

mīl(q), 1. < **mīta.** 2. < ¨*mil(q)* < **mi˙l[u]l(q)* < **mīlta** < ¨*mi[l]˙ta* (pushes). ¶ ¨*mil ˙mu˙l i sa˙o˙l ilwo˙toy* (1445 ¹Yong 67) the water crested for three days and ... .

mīlm < ¨*milm* < **mi˙l[u]m* < **mīlta** < ¨*mi[l]˙ta* (pushes). ¶ ¨*cem¨cem ¨mil˙m ye n'* (1489 Kup-kan 3:10; cited from NKW 574a, accents inferred) when one gradually pushes.

mīn, 1. v mod. 1a. (< vi **mīta**$_1$) that is bald, that has grown bald. ~ **taykali** a bald head.
1b. (< vt **mīta**$_2$) having torn a hole; (< vp) with a hole torn in it.
1c. (< vt **mīta**$_3$) (having) ostracized.
1d. (< vt **mīlta**) < ¨*min* < **mi˙[lu]n* < ¨*mi[l]˙ta*. pushed; shaved. ¶*tung ¨min ˙t oy* (?1517- Pak 1:52a) to get your back scrubbed.
2. adnoun (< 1a). CF **māyn.**
2a. without trappings or appendages; pure, unadulterated. ¶ ~ **taykali** a bare (hatless, uncovered) head. ~ **mom** a bare body, having nothing on one('s body). ~ **mul** fresh water. ~ **nach** an unpainted (unadorned) face.
2b. bald, bare. ¶ ~ **nal** a naked / sharp edge, a bare dagger / sword. ? ~ **twungsan** a bald (treeless) mountain (NKd 1551b).

-min [Ceycwu DIAL (Seng ¹Nakswu 1984:30-2; LSN 1978:93)] = **-myen**

-minun [S Kyengsang DIAL (¹Na Cinsek 1977)] = **-myen**

mīnun, 1. processive modifier < **mīta.**
2. < ¨*mi˙non* < **mi˙[lu]non*, proc mod < **mīlta** < ¨*mi[l]˙ta*. ¶ ¨*nwo˙phi ¨mi˙no.n i ˙Gwa* (1465 Wen 1:1:1:89b) pushes them high.

mit.ke la [DIAL, lit] = **mit.e la** (believe it!) → adv. with every confidence, in complete trust. ¶**Mit.ke la kille on oy atul i cha sāko lo cwuk.ess.ta** My only son, whom I was raising with every confidence (that he would have a long life), died in a car accident.

-mma (after a vowel; ? after consonant **-umma**) [Hamkyeng DIAL (Kim Yengpay 1984:96)] = **-nun ka**

mō < ¨*MWUW*, adn. a certain. ¶ ~ **sīnay (uy) hak.kyo** = **sīnay (uy)** ~ **hak.kyo** a certain school in town. ~ **cipang /** ^{n}**yesa** a certain locality / lady.

-mo [DIAL] = -myen. SEE -umo.
mo chelem, bnd preparticle + pcl. ('like mo [?< āmu = āmo; ?< mues]' =) 1. at long last, finally; after much neglect or delay. 2. making a special effort, on purpose, taking great pains, with much trouble/effort, going out of one's way, showing consideration.
mōcilta, adj -L-. is wicked, harsh, cruel; is hard, tough. CF mōs, mo cita.
mo cita, noun + postnominal adjective. 1. is angular; is stiff, unsociable, sharp. 2. = mōcilta.
mok < ˙mwok, adn. 1. wood(en). ¶ ~ choq-tay a wooden candlestick. ~ tayya a wooden washbasin. ~ sangca a wooden box. ~ they a wooden frame. 2. (= mok.myen) cotton. ¶ mokq yangmal cotton socks.
moluta (< mwo˙lo˙ta < ¨mwot + ¨al-); inf mōlla (< ¨mwol˙la). does not know. This verb is often ellipted in expressing "I don't know whether = maybe" (1936 Roth 421): Ku sālam i sēy pen in ka nēy pen in ka [moluko] yeki wass.ess.ta He was here, I dunno, maybe three or four times. Onul onun ci = Onul olq ka = Onul okeyss.nun ci Maybe he'll come today. Ileh.key hamyen cōh.ul.nun ci (or cōh.ulq ka) Then maybe it will be all right. SEE -umyen 1b: ~ molulq ka (mōlla to).

NOTE: Molunta means 'I don't know'; Ālci anh.nunta 'I am not acquainted with it/him'; Ālci mōs hanta 'It is impossible (for me) to know'; Moluci anh.nunta 'It is not that I do not know'; Moluci mōs hanta 'I cannot not know'. SEE §11.7.3.

mon = monttak [Ceycwu DIAL (Seng ¹Nakswu 1984:60;21, 42, 51, 55, 93)] = motwu (all)
-mon [S Kyengsang DIAL (¹Na Cinsek 1977)] = -myen
-mong [Ceycwu DIAL (Seng ¹Nakswu 1984:45-6; LSN 1978:93, 101)] = -myen se, = -mye
monttak [Ceycwu DIAL (Seng ¹Nakswu 1984:60; 21, 42, 51, 55, 93)] = motwu (all)
mopsi < ¨mwo-˙psuy, adv. awfully, terribly, very; severely, harshly, badly. ¶ ~ kotan hata is awfully/very tired. ~ culkepta is terribly pleased. ~ chwupta is awfully cold. ~ papputa is horribly busy. ~ cōllinta is quite sleepy/drowsy. ~ kwūlta acts harshly, treats one ill (badly). Sēngqkyek un mopsi alum-tawess.ta She had a very fine character. ~ to (pcl). ¶ Mopsi to koy lowess.ta It was very painful. [< ¨mwot adv + *˙psuy der adv < ˙psu- 'use'; CF mopssul 'useless', ssi 'use']
mos [? misheard; ? DIAL] = mwes (what; ...)
mōs < ¨mwot, adv, adj-n, vn. [In phrases often short.] CF mopssul 'useless', mopsi 'awfully', mo-calata 'is insufficient', moluta 'not know'. On the modern spelling, with s instead of t: p. 102. SEE mōs hata, mōs toyta.

1. adv. not (possibly), definitely not, never, under no circumstances; can't, won't; no good (a strong denial or refusal; CF ani). ¶ Mōs kakeyss.^{s}o I can't go; I won't go; I refuse to go. Mōsq ilk.keyss.^{s}o I can't (won't, refuse to) read it. Ku chayk kacye kaci mōs hao You are not allowed to take the book; I will not let you take the book. Na lul peliko nun kaci mōs hao I will not let you go leaving me behind.

NOTE 1: A (processive) verb can make both the short form and the long form of the strong negative (mōs kanta and kaci mōs hanta 'cannot go') but adjectives take only the long form (cōh.ci mōs hata 'can't possibly be good, is not good at all' not *mōs cōh.ta) and the copula does not make a strong negative (the only negative: A ka B ka ani 'ta 'A is not B').

NOTE 2: For 'we can't begin' you may say either sīcak mōs hanta or mōs sīcak hanta, but it is uncommon to find mōs before other verbal nouns. For 'we can't try doing it' it is better to say mōs hay ponta rather than (*)hay mōs ponta. For 'it can't come to an end' you may hear either mōs kkuth nanta or kkuth mōs nanta. Similar remarks apply to an.

2. adj-n, vn. SEE mōs hata.
mōs-'c(i) anh.ta, abbr < mōs haci anh.ta (adj). is not inferior (to), is just as good (as), is no less (than). ¶ kap i ul ey ~ A is as good as B. Ku nun na ey mōs-'ci anh.un pūca 'ta He is quite as rich as I am. Ku nun na (ey) mōs-'c(i) anh.key him i sēyta He is as strong as I am. [Is mōs-'c(i) anh.key a new pseudo-particle?]
mōs hata₁, adj-n. ... man/pota ~ is lower (in degree/quality/quantity) than ..., is inferior to ..., is worse/less than ..., is not so good/strong/beautiful/much as ... . ¶ I kkoch i ce kkoch man mōs hata This flower is not up to that one (in beauty). Casik i nappun an^{h}ay man mōs hata Having a son is not as good as

having even a bad wife. **Onul sisey ka ecey sisey pota mōs hata** Prices today are lower than yesterday's. **Ney cheycwung i nay cheycwung man mōs hata** You weigh less than I do.

mōs hata₂, cpd vt (adv + vi) = [haci] mōs hata. cannot do, cannot possibly (do); will not do, refuses to do. ¶**Māl ul mōs hanta** He can't talk; He won't talk. **Īl ul mōs hanta** He can't work; He won't work. SEE **hata mōs hay/ha.ye**.

mōs hata₃, aux (follows suspective -ci).

1. aux adj-n (follows adj suspective). is not (at all, a bit). ¶**Mul i malk.ci mōs hata** The water is not (at all) clear. **Sālam i chak haci nun mōs haci man kwaynchanh.ta** He isn't a very good person, but that does not matter.

2. aux vn. does not; will not; never does. ¶**kaci ~** cannot go; will not go. **mekci ~** cannot eat; will not eat. **Ku lul mannaci mōs hayss.ta** I was unable to see him.

mōs toyta₁, cpd vi (adv + vi). SYN **an toyta**.

? 1. is not done / through / finished / over / ready, is uncompleted (= **an toyta**).

2. is short of, is not up to, does not reach / make. ¶**welkup i sam-man wen i ~** one's salary is under W30,000. ¹**yuk-sip i mōs toye cwukta** dies before sixty. **sēk tal i mōs toye tol.a ota** returns within three months.

3. gets in bad shape, looks poor; gets worse, declines. ¶**alh.ko na se elkwul i ~** looks poor after one's illness. **kēnkang i ~** one's health declines, suffers from poor health. **cip an i ~** a family goes downhill. **nala hyengphyen i ~** the country gets in a mess (an awful condition). **Nala ka mōs toye kanta** The nation is on the decline (the way down).

mōs toyta₂, cpd adj (adv + postnom adj). is bad, bad-natured, evil, wicked, wrong. ¶**mōs toyn nom** a bad egg, a rascal. **mōs toyn cīs** an evil deed, a misdeed, misbehavior, a wrongful / vicious act, a vice. **Mōs toyn songaci ēngtengi ey se ppul i nanta** "The bad calf has a horn on his rump" = A no-good person is acting up (putting on airs).

mosup < ˙*MWOW-˙SSIP*, n. the shape, figure, image, sight, appearance, look(s), features. **twīq ~** one's appearance from behind. ¶**nwun ~** the shape of one's eyes. **apeci ka kēt.nun ~** the image of one's father walking. **Atul i pam nuc.key kkaci kongpu hanun mosup ul pomyen emeni ka nwun-mul i na-onta** When she looks at the figure of her son studying deep into the night, the mother sheds tears. **Ku sēnswu ka kwēnthwu sip-hoy cēn ul hako nan mosup un checham hayss.ta** The image of the boxer emerging from the ten-round bout was appalling. **Atul i komun ul tang hal mosup ul sayngkak hamyen cam i an onta** When I picture my son about to undergo torture I cannot get to sleep. CF **mo.yang, kwangkyeng**.

mōtun < *mwo˙ton*, adn. [< vi mod **mot.un**]. all, every, each and every, every possible. ¶**~ sālam** all the people, everybody. **~ cōng.lyu uy mulken** all sorts of things. **~ swutan ul tā hata** tries / exhausts every possibility, tries out everything, goes to any lengths. **~ kyengwu lul sayngkak hata** considers all the situations imaginable. **~ cōy lul tā pēm hata** goes / runs through the catalog of crimes. **Mōtunq īl i cal toye kanta** Everything is going off smoothly. **mōtun sālam cwung ey yūmyeng hata** (1881 Ridel 38) is the most famous of all men.

motwu < *mwo˙two*, adverb (= **tā**), noun. all, everything, everyone. [der adv < vi **mot-** = **moi-** gather].

1. adv. ¶**motwu hay se** all (taken) together. **Cangma ka kuchim ey motwu kippe hayss.ta** Everyone was happy that the rainy season was over. **O-kanun sālam tul i motwu chwuwe pointa** The passers-by, they all look cold. **Māy math.un pa chayk.im ul kakca ka motwu wanswu haca** Let each one of us fulfill every responsibility we have undertaken.

2. noun (NKd 1411b). [Is this newish? No examples for *mwo˙two*.] ¶**motwu lul pulle kata** calls everyone out. **wuli motwu uy chayk.im** the responsibility of all / each of us. **motwu ka yelq-seys [ita]** altogether it is (or they are) thirteen. **chinkwu tul i motwu ka wass.ta** all my friends are here. **nay ka chinkwu tul ul motwu lul chotay hayss.ta** I invited all my friends.

mo.yang < ˙*MWOW-˙YANG*, n. 1. a shape, a form; a pattern, a design, a figure.

2. the appearance, a look, an air; signs, indications, symptoms; a way, a manner.

3. the state (situation, aspect, phase, position) of affairs, matters, things, progress, doings, movements, circumstances.

SEE **-un (-nun, -ess.tun, -ul) ~**.

˙*moyh*, n. moor, moorland; dry land; outland, a

remote place/terrain (1481 Twusi 7:1a, 7:25b).
¶ ˙moy.h on (1481 Twusi 7:25b); ˙moy.h ol (1481 Twusi 7:1a), ˙moy˙h ol (1482 Kum-sam 2:65b); ˙moy[h] s (1481 Twusi 7:28b); *˙moy˙hay → moy˙h ay (1463 Pep 6:154b), moy˙h ay s (?1468- Mong 27; 1482 Nam 1:4a, 1:49b; 1482 Kum-sam 3:34b), moy˙h ay sye (1481 Twusi 7:39a). CF e˙tu˙mey; ¨mwoyh.

-m say SEE say

-mq seng SEE seng

'/-m sey, 1. < ham sey. 2. < -um sey.

-mu [DIAL] = -myen. SEE -umu.

mu', pseudo-adnoun (< mul water, n). watery; thin. ¶ ~ cang unrefined soy sauce. ~ com athlete's foot. ~ sal morbid flesh. ~ sāmakwi wart. ~ seli first frost. CF mucikey < ˙mu'ci˙key rainbow. But not mutew- < ¨mwuteW- (1489) 'sultry' < ? + ¨teW- < *te˙pu-'hot'.

mue, noun, interjection. ABBR mwe, me.
  1. abbr < mues (what; something). ¶ I kes i mue yo What is this? I kes ul mue 'la ko hap.nikka What do you call this?
  2. interjection (shows disbelief). what?! huh?! ¶ Mue, ku sālam i cwuk.ess.e What! Is he dead? Mue, elma yo What! How much did you say it is?! Mue mue 'la ko What?! What did you say? Mue nay ka cal-mos hayss.e What? I am wrong?!
  3. but, but anyway, somehow or other, just. ¶ Na nun mōlla yo mue sacin-ki hana sa cwue ya 'ci mue I dunno, but you just have to buy me a camera (anyway). Tōn i mue yekan tul.e ya 'ci It is so expensive, you see, ... (I cannot afford it). Mue āmu 'na tā kulen cwul āna? Do you think I am just like (as bad/mean/dishonest) as the rest?
  4. mue 'ni mue 'ni hay to say what you will; let me tell you ... ; indeed ... ; my (oh my) ... .

mue l', abbr < mue lul = mues ul (what; ...)

mue 'l(q), abbr < mues il(q), n + cop prosp mod

mue 'la ko (yo), abbr < mues ila ko (yo)

mue 'la 'lq ka, abbr < mues ila (ko) halq ka. what's-it(-called), whatcha(ma)callit, what-do-you-call-it, whaddaya call it. ¶ Ku kes, mue 'la 'lq ka, ku "thānhwa-ki" 'la nun kes un mōs ssuci yo That uh, whaddaya call it, that uh "carburetor" is no good.

muel-lo = mue lo = mues ulo (with what, ...). mwuellwo (1887 Scott 30) = mue llo.

mue lo, abbr < mues ulo (with what, ...)

mue lul = mues ul (what/something)

mue 'm, abbr < mues im (n + cop subst)

mue n', abbr < mue nun = mues un

mue 'n, abbr < mues in, n + cop mod (... that is what/something): ~ ci, ~ ka, ~ ko, ~ tey, ~ tul, ~ ya.

mue nun, n + pcl. ¶ Mue nun ālko ... You know anything else? (= You know nothing!)

mues < mu˙(s)es (1586) < mu˙su kes (= mu˙suk, mu˙sum, mu˙su), n. Indeterminate thing: INTERROGATIVE in questions with falling intonation or in quoted questions; INDEFINITE or GENERAL otherwise. ABBR mwes, mue, mwe, me. ? VAR mo.
  what, which; something, anything. ¶ Mues ul mek.keyss.ˢo [falling intonation] What do you want to eat?; [rising intonation] Do you want something to eat? Mues i cōh.keyss.ˢo – cha ka cōh.keyss.ˢo, maykcwu ka cōh.keyss.ˢo Which would you prefer, tea or beer? Nay ka ne 'ykey mues ul kamchwukeyss.ni Would I hide anything from you? (= I am telling you the whole truth). Mues in ci sa kaciko wass.ta She's bought something or other. Mok ey mues in ci sayngkyess.ta I seem to have some sort of growth on my neck. Mues i ecc'ayss.ta ko? What? (What did you say? What are you talking about?) Ku mues hanun sālam in ya What is he? Ne mues hale wass.nun ya What did you come for? Mues com mek.e ya haci anh.so? Surely you have to eat something, don't you? mues ina (iko, itun ci) anything (at all). Mues iko hakeyss.ˢo I will do anything. talun mues what/something else (different).

mues ey, n + pcl. to (by) what/something. ¶ Mues ey a.yen ul noh.ass.nun ya What was the zinc put into?

mues eykey, n + pcl. to (by) what/some living creature. ¶ Mues eykey mullin cakwuk kath.ta It looks like a mark from having been bitten by something.

mues ey se, n + pcl + pcl. from what/something. ¶ Mues ey se swuso ka na-onun ya What was the hydrogen produced from?

mues ey 'ta, n + pcl + cop transferentive. ¶ Mues ey 'ta sse yo What is it used for?

mues hata, adj-n. is awkward, is hard to say/describe (to put into words); is embarrassing; is unsatisfactory. ¶ Ku īl ul nay ka haki nun com mues hata It is awkward for me to do that myself. **Mues haci man tōn ul chen wen man chwī hay cwuo** (I shouldn't but) may I ask you to lend me a thousand wen? **Ku sālam un com mues hata** He/She is not entirely satisfactory. **Kuleh.key kkaci māl hanun kes un com mues haci anh.sup.nikka?** Isn't it a bit much/harsh/embarrassing for you to say that? **I mulken un ku kes pota com mues hata** This one is a bit worse than that, I guess.

mues iko, mues ina, mues itun ci: SEE **mues**.

mues mues, iterated n. what and what, what all. ¶**Mues mues pwass.ni** What all did you see?

mues un, n + pcl. SEE **mue nun**.

muey = **mue** (what; what?!)

mue 'y, abbr < **mue ey** < **mues ey**

mue' y, abbr n + pcl = **mues i** what [subject]

mue' y-, abbr n + abbr cop (= **mues i-**). be what. ¶**mue' yna** (= **mues ina**), **mue' yko** (= **mues iko**) whatever it may be. **Mue' yn ya** What is it? **Mue' yla to mek.keyss.ta** I'll eat anything.

-muley [< **-(u)m-uley**], bnd adj-n (~ **hata**). ...ish. ¶**nolumuley** yellowish. **ph^a/_ulumuley** blu(e)ish.

-mulo = **-m ulo** (SEE **-um ulo**)

mulyep, quasi-free n. the time/occasion (when). ~ **ey** at the time, on the occasion, when, as. ¶**ku ~ ey** at that time. **Han-chang calanun mulyep ila mānh.i mek.nunta** As he is in that fast-growing stage, he eats a lot. **Pyesul hanun mulyep ey ttang maciki 'na cangman hayss.ta** He got himself a few pieces of land when he was an official in the government. **Cangma mulyep ey nāt al i mōs mek.key toyess.ta** The crop was damaged during (at the time of) the flood. **Hay ka ttul mulyep ey talk i wūnta** The rooster crows when the sun comes up.

NOTE: CM 2:62 suggests that **-nun/-tun mulyep ey** is rare, the common form being **-ul mulyep ey** (as in M 2:1:83). But the other modifiers are at least marginally acceptable: **Mikwuk ey tanye on/wass.tun mulyep ey cikum uy an^hay lul mannass.ta** I met my (present) wife when I was on a trip to America.

-mun, [Hamkyeng, Phyengan, S Kyengsang DIAL (Kim Yengpay 1984:96)] = **-myen**

mus··· SEE *mwus-*

mus < *mwus* (? < ˙*mwu[l] s*), adn. many all, all sorts of. ¶**~ may** a rain of blows, a drubbing. **~ palq-kil** a rain of kicks. **~ soli** many voices. **~ pyēl** myriad stars. **musq ip** /munnip/ public rebuke. **Mus sālam i tā ku lul chingchan hanta** All the people praise him. **Mus cimsung i ttey lul cie taninta** All sorts of animals move about in groups. **Mus nom i tallye tul.e ku lul ttaylye nwup.hyess.ta** A whole gang went at him and knocked him down. **Mus nyen i na eykey yoksel ul ph'e puess.ta** A number of the bitches cussed me out.

musepkey SEE **-ki ka musepkey**

mu˙su, 1. n. what. ¶*ku nil ˙Gwon ke˙s un mu˙su ˙kwo* (1465 Wen se:12a) what is it that he said? ˙*i mu˙su kwo* (1482 Nam 2:16b) = ˙*i mu˙su ˙kwo* (1482 Kum-sam 2:41a) what is this?

2. adn. what. ¶*mu˙su ke˙s i ˙PWULQ-˙CYWOK ho˙l ywo* (1447 Sek 6:24a) what is lacking? *mu˙su ke˙s u˙lwo ¨TTWOW ˙lol sa˙mo˙l ywo* (1459 Wel 9:22b) of what can we make the Way? ¨*et˙nwon* YAK ˙*i mu˙su kes ˙kwo* (1459 Wel 21:215b) what is the drug we are getting? *mu˙su ke˙s i cephu˙l i ˙Gwo* (?1517⁻ Pak 1:64a) what are you afraid of? ˙*mu˙su ¨il ho˙l i ˙Gwo* (?1517⁻ Pak 1:7b; the first dot is probably a scribal error) what shall we do? *poy˙hwo˙non ke˙s i mu˙su ¨i˙l in ˙kwo* (1518 Sohak-cho 8:33b) what is it we learn?

mu˙suk (?< *musu k[es]*), n. what. ¶*a˙hwop* HHWOYNG-¨*so ˙non mu˙su˙k i-ngi s ˙ka* (1447 Sek 9:35b) what are the nine unnatural deaths? *ne-huy ˙tol.h i mu˙su˙k ul ˙pwo˙noson ˙ta* (1459 Wel 10:28a) what do you people see? ¨*ne y mu˙su˙k ul ˙pwonon ˙ta* (1462 ¹Nung 1:83b) what do you see? *mu˙su.k i si˙lu.m i˙m ye mu˙su.k i kis˙pwu˙m i.l i ˙Gwo* (1463/4 Yeng 2:7a) what is grief and what is joy? *mu˙su.k ey ˙psusi˙l i* (1459 Wel 1:10b) what will you use them for? ¨*mwutnwo˙la ˙poy ptuy ˙Gwe ˙kanon ¨salo.m on mu˙su.k u˙la [QYEN-˙MWU] ˙lwo ˙tule ˙kano˙n ywo* (1481 Twusi 22:39b) I would like to ask why the man floating the boat away is going into the mist.

mu˙sum, 1. noun. (= *mu˙suk* = **mues**) what; something. ¶*mu˙sum ˙hwo.l ye ˙ho˙sino˙n i* (1459 Wel 1:10b) what do you propose to do? ˙*SYEY-KAN s tuthu˙l ul mu˙sum ˙man ne˙kisi˙l i* (1449 Kok 125) will you treat it as no more than the dust of the world?

2. adn. (= *mu˙sus* = **musun**) which, what.

A Reference Grammar of Korean

¶*mu ̇sum* CCO-PI ¨*kye ̇sike ̇n ywo* (1447 Sek 6:6a) what pity had he? *mu ̇sum te ̇wun sa ̇pa.l ay* (1482 Kum-sam 2:41a) in what hot bowl ... ?

3. adv (= *mu ̇su.m u ̇la*). why. ¶*na y ̇stwo mu ̇sum si ̇lum ho ̇l i ̇Gwo* (1459 Wel 21:49b) why am I still woeful?

mu ̇su.m u ̇la, n + pcl. for what reason, why. ¶*mu ̇su.m u ̇la ̇wosi ̇n i-ngi s ̇kwo* (1447 Sek 6:3a) why have you come?

mu ̇su.m u ̇lye = *mu ̇su.m u ̇la* (why). ¶*mu ̇su.m u ̇lye ¨mal han ¨yang ho ̇l i ̇Gwo* (?1517- Pak 1:74a) why do you talk so much?

musun, adn. what, what kind of; some, some kind / sort of. ¶**Musun mulken ul sale wass.ˢo** [falling intonation] What are you shopping for?; [rising intonation] Are you here to buy something? **Musunq īl i sayngkyess.ˢo** [falling intonation] What happened?; [rising intonation] Did something happen? **Musunq īl iko yelqsim hi hay ya hanta** Whatever (kind of) job it is, you should do it wholeheartedly. **Musun sālam i kuleh.key keyuluta ʼm?!** What a lazy man he is! **Musun ūmsik / kes ul ileh.key mānh.i mayntuless.ˢup.nikka?!** My, what a lot of nice food you have prepared for us! **Musunq īl ul kuleh.key tetikey hasio?!** Why are you so slow with the work?! **Musun soli ya** What are you saying? (What do you mean?). CF **enu, etten**.

mu ̇sus (< *mu ̇su s*), adn. what. ¶*mu ̇sus ¨i ̇l ol kyes ̇kwo wo ̇l ye ̇honon ̇kwo* (1447 Sek 6:27a) whatever we are to compete at ... . *ku ¨ti ¨CO- ̇SIK ¨epte ̇n i mu ̇sus ¨CCWOY ̇Gwo* (1459 Wel 1:7a) what was your sin that you had no son?

mwe, abbr < **mwes** < **mues** (what / something); sentence-final (exclamation). ¶**Nay sānun ke ya kuce kulel wu haci mwe** I'm just living along, and that's about all. **Cikum yetelp si ka nem.ess.nun tey yo, mwe** It is already past eight! (M 1:2:81). **Mikwukq ¹yuhak kass.ta (ka) sip-nyen man ey tol.a omyen se paksa hana to mōs hayss.ta ʼci mwe (yo)?!** Why, they say he spent ten years studying in America and yet he could not manage to get a doctorate, even!

mwe ka, n + pcl = **mues i** (what / something)
mwe lʼ, abbr < **mwe lul** < **mue l(ul)** = **mues ul**
mwe ʼl(q), abbr < **mue ʼl(q)** < **mues il(q)**, n + cop prosp mod
mwe ʼm, abbr < **mue ʼm** < **mues im**

?**mwe nʼ**, abbr < **mue nʼ** = **mues un**
mwe ʼn, abbr < **mue ʼn** < **mues in**, n + cop mod. ... that is what.
mwen [Ceycwu DIAL (Seng ¹Nakswu 1984:25)] = **musun** (which)
mwes, abbr < **mues** (what / something)
mwey, abbr < **muey** = **mue** (what; what?!)
mwe ʼy, abbr < **mwe ey** < **mwe ey** < **mues ey**
mweʼ y, abbr < **mueʼ y** = **mues i**
mwo ̇lo ̇ta (< ¨*mwot* + ¨*al-*), vi -LL-; infinitive ¨*mwol ̇la*. does not know.
mwollwo.l i ([1447→]1562 Sek 3:21b; aberrant form) = *mwo ̇lwo ̇l i*
mwos = ¨*mwot*. (1676 Sin.e 8:8b, 8:31a; 1748 Tongmun 2:59; ...).
¨*mwot*, adv. = *mōs*. ¶*ne-¨huy mek ̇kwo ¨mwot ¨tywoholq ̇ka* (1459 Wel 17:20b) won't you people surely be better taking it [= this good medicine]? *mol ̇tho ̇ti ¨mwot ̇hota ̇la* (?1517- Pak 1:37b) I have been unable to ride a horse. *ywo ̇kwoy- ̇lwo ̇wo ̇m ol ¨ati ¨mwot ̇ho ̇twu ̇ta* (1518 Sohak-cho 10:18b) is quite unaware that it is weird.

With abbreviation of aux °*ho-*:
¨*mwot ʼke ̇n i* (1447 Sek 24:28b) < ¨*mwot ̇hoke ̇n i*
¨*mwot ʼ ̇ke.n i ̇Gwa* (1459 Wel 9:11a) < ¨*mwot ̇ho ̇ke.n i ̇Gwa*
¨*mwot ʼ ̇ken ma ̇lon* (1463 Pep 6:31a) < ¨*mwot ̇ho ̇ken ma ̇lon*
¨*mwot ʼke ̇nol za* (1481 Twusi 8:29a) < ¨*mwot ̇hoke ̇nol za*
¨*mwot ʼ ̇kesi ̇ta* (1459 Wel 18:42b) < ¨*mwot ̇ho ̇kesi ̇ta*
¨*mwot ʼke ̇tun* (?1468- Mong 33a) = ¨*mwot ̇hoke ̇tun* (?1468- Mong 14a)
¨*mwot ʼ ̇key* (1449 Kok 155, 1465 Wen 1:2:3:9b) < ¨*mwot ho ̇key*
¨*mwot ʼ ̇kwo* (1462 ¹Nung 1:50b, 1464 Kumkang 64b, 1459 Wel 2:38b, 1481 Twusi 23:23a) < ¨*mwot ho ̇kwo* (1459 Wel 2:38b, 1481 Twusi 23:23a)
¨*mwot ʼkwo ̇sye* < ¨*mwot ho ̇kwo ̇sye*
¨*mwot ʼ ̇kwatoy ̇ye* < ¨*mwot ho ̇kwatoy ̇ye*
¨*mwot ʼ ̇ta* (1462 ¹Nung 2:43b) < ¨*mwot ho ̇ta*
mwo ̇ta, adv (inf < *mwot ̇ta*). ¶*wu ̇li mwo ̇ta coy ̇cwo ̇lol kyes ̇kwo ̇a* (1447 Sek 6:26b) all of us will pit our skills [against them] and ... .
¨*KWUW-LYWONG ̇i mwo ̇ta sis ̇kizo ̇Wo ̇n i* (1449 Kok 20) the nine dragons all bathed him.

mwo˙ton, adnoun (mod < *mwot˙ta*). all; each, every. ¶*hon ¨nath me˙li s thele˙k ul mwo˙ton ha˙nol˙h i ¨etco˙Wa* (1449 Kok 91) each of the heavens got a hair [from Buddha's head], and ... . *mwo˙ton ᴴᴴᴬᴷ-¨ᴄʏᴬ y ˙an[h] mozom s ᴋʏᴇɴɢ ˙ul ti˙nye* (1464 Kamkang se:6b) all the scholars preserved the sūtra in their [inmost] minds, and ... . *˙stwo ka˙omyel˙wom ˙un mwo˙ton [˙i] uy ¨wen¨mang ˙i˙n i* (1586 Sohak 6:83b) = *˙stwo ka˙zo˙mye˙lwo˙m on mwo˙ton ¨sa˙lom ˙uy ¨wen˙mang ˙ho˙non ke˙s isi˙n i* (1518 Sohak-cho 9:90a) and moreover being wealthy is something that all the other people resent. *mwo˙ton hyeng˙tyey ˙tol˙h i* (?1517- Pak 1:1b) all of the brothers.

mwo˙two, adverb (der adv < *mwot˙ta*). all; together. ¶*˙ꜱᴏʏᴋ ˙kwa ᴋʜᴡᴏɴɢ ˙kwa ᴄʏᴇ-˙ᴘᴇᴘ ˙ul mwo˙two tu˙le nilo˙sya ¨ᴄᴏ-˙ꜱʏᴇʏ ˙hi kol˙hoy˙Gey ˙ho˙si.n i ˙˙la* (1462 ¹Nung 2:49a) he mentioned them all, form and void and the laws, and enabled us to discriminate them in detail. *˙hay tut˙kwo ɴᴜɴɢ ˙hi mwo˙two ti˙ni.m ye* (1463 Pep 5:194a) [he who has a deep mind] listens much and can retain it all.

˙mwoyh = *¨mwoyh* (mountain). ¶*˙mwoy.h ay s* (1482 Kum-sam 3:36b) = *¨mwoy˙h ay s* (1482 Kum-sam 3:33a). *˙mwoy[h] s* (1481 Twusi 7:11a) = *¨mwoy[h] s* (1481 Twusi 8:28a).

¨mwoyh (> **mēy**), n. mountain (= san). ᴄꜰ *˙moyh* (moor = tul). ¶*¨mwoy˙h oy* (1482 Kum-sam 3:3b, 1481 Twusi 8:20a). *¨mwoy.h ay i˙sye non* ... (1481 Twusi 8:66a). Unmarked *mwoy.h i* (1481 Twusi 7:24b) may be an error for *¨mwoy˙h i* (1447 Sek 24:6b).

mwusa [Ceycwu ᴅɪᴀʟ (Seng ¹Nakswu 1984:21, 25n, 99, 100)] = **way** (why)

mwusom (1894 Gale 28) = **musun**

mwusin [Ceycwu ᴅɪᴀʟ (Seng ¹Nakswu 1984: 25n)] = **musun** (which)

mwusing ke [Ceycwu ᴅɪᴀʟ (Seng ¹Nakswu 1984: 26)] = **musun ke(s)** = **mues** (what)

mwusuke il ul [Ceycwu ᴅɪᴀʟ (Seng ¹Nakswu 1984:55:n27)] = **musunq īl ul**

'/**-mye**, 1. < **imye** it is and.
  2. < **hamye**
  2a. does / says / is and.
  2b. = '*myen se* (sentence-final: a question that seeks confirmation of a remark heard from a third party, or seeking confirmation). ¶**Isa kanun kil ey yēys chinkwu lul mannass.ta 'mye(n se)?** I hear you ran into an old friend while moving?! (− Well, well; I can hardly believe it.) ᴄꜰ Kim Cinswu 1987.
  3. < **-umye** (after a vowel or the l-extension of an -ʟ- stem).

'˙*m ye*, 1. abbr < ˙*ho˙m ye*. ꜱᴇᴇ - *˙ta ˙ka ˙'mye, pu˙the ˙'m ye*.
  2. (= '*[y]˙m ye*), abbr < ˙*i˙m ye* (cop) after *i* and *y*.

-˙*m ye* = -˙*(ᵁ/o)m ye* = **-umye**

myech < ˙*myech* (?< *m[u ˙u]y ˙ech[i]*), n [lit] = **meych** (how many, etc.). ¶*˙wu˙li ˙mye˙ch i ka˙l ywo* (?1517- Pak 1:54b) how many of us will go? *¨ne y ˙mye˙ch ul ¨hwo˙l ye ˙honon ˙ta* (?1517- Pak 1:31b) how many do you want (to make it)? *ne 'y ˙na˙h i ˙mye.ch in ˙psk uy ʜʜᴜɴɢ-ʜʜᴀ s ˙mu˙l ul pwon ˙ta* (1462 ¹Nung 2:8b) at what age did you see the waters of the Ganges? *icey n' ˙myes ˙kwo* (1463 Pep 5:178b) now how many [listeners] are there? *holo ˙myes ¨ʟɪ lol ˙nye˙sino˙n i '-ngi s ˙kwo* (1447 Sek 6: 23a) how many leagues does the tathāgata go in a day? *mol il˙hwum ˙kwa la˙kwuy il˙hwum ˙kwa y ˙myes ˙won ka˙ci ˙Gwo* (1482 Kum-sam 4:40a) how many (hundreds of) kinds of terms for horses and donkeys are there?

myechil ꜱᴇᴇ **meychil**

mye˙chul, 1. n. how many days. ¶*mye˙chu˙l ul ˙syel˙Gwep ho˙l i '˙le˙la* (?1517- Pak 1:75a) how many days would he preach?
  2. = ˙*mye˙ch ul* (?1517- Pak 1:31b), n + pcl. how much / many.

myēn < ˙*ᴍʏᴇɴ*, n. 1. surface, face; plane, level (= **phyengmyen**).
  2. dignity, honor, face.
  3. mask, face-guard.
  4. (= **phyen, ilmyen**) aspect, phase, side. ¶**Swun-i nun com eswulwuk han myēn i iss.ta** Swun-i is a bit on the gullible side. **Kongpu hanun myēn ey se pomyen Mikwuk i nās.ci man nōnun myēn ey se pomyen Hānkwuk i nās.ta** As a place to study, America is better, but Korea is better for having a good time.
  ? 5. = **ilmyen** = **han phyen** (but, on the other hand).

'/**-myen**, 1. < **imyen**. 2. < **hamye**. 3. < **-umyen** (after a vowel or the l-extension of an -ʟ- stem).

-˙*m ye n'* = -˙*(ᵁ/o)m ye n'* = **-umyen** (un)

'*myen se*, abbr < **hamyen se**.
  1. while doing / saying / thinking.

2. = **'mye** (sentence-final: a question that seeks confirmation of a remark heard from a third party). ¶ **Ku sālam i Mikwuk sālam ila 'mye(n se)?** Why, he's an American (– I can hardly believe it)! ¶**Nayil kanta 'mye(n se)?** But you are leaving tomorrow (– you won't have time to do all the things you talk of doing)! **Ani ku key chen-nyen muk.unq yumul ila 'mye(n se)?** That is a thousand-year old relic?!
~ **yo** (M 1:2:404-5). CF Kim Cinswu 1987.
ˇmyes = ˇmyech (how much)
ˇmyes.ma (< ˇmyech + ˇma), n. how much/many; (= ˇmyes pen) how many times. ¶ ˇmyes.ma CAY-KKWUW ˙ho.ya ¨men CHWON ˙ay ni˙lule˙n ywo (1482 Nam 2:2b) how many meals did I seek getting to the distant village? ˇmyes.ma HHOYNG-˙NGAK ol ¨twol˙m ye SYWOW-SYANG ˙ol ¨ket-˙naa˙n ywo (1482 Kum-sam 3:17a) how many times have I rounded Héng Peak and crossed the Xiāoxiāng [River]?

M^Y EY South Korean spelling distinguishes **mey** and "**myey**", but both are usually pronounced the same (as **mey**). If the word you seek is not under **m^y ey**, look under **mey**.

···m¨zop- < ···m-¨zop-

n, nasal-assimilated variant of *s* (pcl). ¶ *holo n man uy* (?1608+ Twu-hem 21a) for a day (= *holo s man ey*).

-n··· < -n··· SEE -un··· , -un··· .
'n··· < 'n··· SEE in··· < ˙in··· , i 'n··· < ˙i 'n··· ; han··· < ˚hon··· .
-n < -n, alternant after vowels of -un < -˙(ᵘ/ₒ)n (modifier). ¶ *nan* (1459 Wel 2:28b, ...) < ˚na- 'emerge', *hhyen* (1463 Pep 2:100b) < ˚hhye- 'drag', ˙*pson ke˙s ul* (1481 Twusi 8:33-4) < ˙pso- 'wrap', ˙*khun* (1445 ¹Yong 27; 1459 Wel 1:15a; 1463 Pep 2:231b, 2:232a, 7:141b; ?1468- Mong 47b; 1482 Kum-sam 3:25b, 4:2a) < ˙khu- 'big', *a˙ni cwun˙t ay* (1447 Sek 23:57b) < ˚cwu- 'give', *won* (1459 Wel 2:25b; ?1517- ¹No 1:1a, 2:3b; [1447→]1562 Sek 3:21b) < ˚wo- 'come', *e˙lin* (1459 Wel 8:69b) < *e˙li-* 'stupid', ¨*cayn* (?1517- Pak 1:30a) < ¨*cay-* 'swift', ¨*syeyn* (1445 ¹Yong 19) < ˚˚*syey-* 'get white', ˙*hoyn* (1445 ¹Yong 50, 1447 Sek 6:43b, 1481 Twusi 7:1a, 1527 Cahoy 2:14b=29b) < ˙*hoy-* 'white', ¨*woyn* (1447 Sek 9:36a) < ˚˚*woy-* 'wrong', *ye˙huyn* (1459 Wel 7:5b) < *ye˙huy-* 'get alienated / separated', ¨*mwuyn* (1482 Kum-sam 2:18a) < ˚˚*mwuy-* 'move'.

˙n-, bnd v (processive). SEE -˙n[o]-.
-**n'**, abbr < -ni, -(n)un ya (plain question). ¶**Mek.keyss.n'?** /mekkeyn/ = **Mek.keyss.ni?** Will you eat? **Mektun'?** = **Mektun ya?** Were they eating?

n', abbreviated particle = **nun**
'n, 1. abbr (alt) < in (copula mod). SEE **ani 'n**.
2. abbr < han (modifier < hata)
'n, 1. abbr < hon (v mod).
2. (= ˙[y]n) abbr < ˙in (cop mod) after *i* or *y*. ¶ *cel-˙lwo ka˙m ye cel-[˙]lwo [˙]wono[˙]n i 'n cip wu˙h uy s ¨cyepi ˙˙Gwo* (1481 Twusi 7:3b) swallows freely come and go atop the hall, and ... . ¨*mal-ssom ˙kwa ka˙col˙pywo.m o˙lwo mis˙ti ¨mwot hol kke˙s i ku* CIN-˙SSILQ *s TI 'n˙t ye* (1464 Kumkang 87b) is what we cannot attain by comparing it with what is said the true wisdom? SEE *a˙ni 'n*.

'**n'**, abbr < hanun; < hanun kes un.
na₁ < ˙na, n. ˙na + ˙i → ˙na y, ˙na + ˙uy → na ˙y. ˙na + ˙on → ˙na ˙non; ˙na + ˙ol → ¨na ˙lol, ¨na l'. ˙na + ˙kwa → ¨nal˙Gwa (but also *na ˙[G]wa*). ˙na + ˙o˙lwo → ¨nal˙lwo; ˙na + ˙o˙lan → *¨nal˙lan.
1. I, me.
2. oneself; self, ego. ¶ *i cen uy* ~ one's former self. **hyēncay uy** ~ one's present self. **cēy-i uy** ~ one's second self (alter ego). ~ **lul ic.ta** forgets oneself. **Na casin ālci mōs hanta** I don't know it myself. *na ¨al˙Gwo ˙nom cwo˙chye al˙Gwoyl˙ss i˙n i* (1459 Wel 1:8b) knowing it oneself one should let others know it, as well. *na ˙kot ho˙l i ˙˙la* (1459 Wel 1:17a) it is like me.
3. [DIAL] = **na uy my**. ¶ **[Ceycwu] *na kes*** = **nay kes** my thing, mine.

NOTE: The shape is **nay** before pcl **ka**. **Nay** is also an abbreviation of **nay ka** and of **na uy**; **nay key** (= **na 'ykey**) abbreviates **na eykey** and also **nay kes i**; *na + ˙o˙lwo* → ¨*nal˙lwo*.
SEE ¨*na l'*, ¨*na ˙lol*, ¨*na y*. CF **ce, cey; nay**.
na₂, particle. alt after vowel of **una** (softens commands; emphasizes conjunctions, adverbs). CF **-key na**; '**na** = **ina**.

na₃ < ˈna, inf < nata < °naˈta. NOTE: We hyphenate the inseparable compounds **na-kata, na-ota, na-suta**.

n'a = n'ā, abbr < nwā < nowa = noa < noh.a, inf < noh.ta; as aux usually short.

'na, 1. var (alt) < ina (cop).
 2. abbr < hana (< hata)

¨na = ˈ[y]ˈna, abbr < iˈna (cop advers) after *i* or *y*. ¶ ˈPPI-KHWUW ˈyˈna ˈPPI-KHWUW-NI ¨na (1447 Sek 19:29b) whether mendicant monk or nun. ¨aˈmolyey ¨na (1447 Sek 6:13b, 24:28a) anyhow, anyway; somehow.

-na-, effective (attached to °wo- 'come' only). SEE ˈwona-; CF ˈwoke-, ˈwa-.

ˈ/-n a = ˈ/-n ya
ˈ/-n' a = ˈ/-n' ya
-na → **-n a** (= -na ya), → **-n' a** (= -nun ya).

-na < -ˈna, 1. FAMILIAR indic attent (=question). is/does it? (= -ni?). ¶ **Chwup.na?** Is it cold? **Pissana?** Is it expensive? **Mek.ess.na?** Did you eat? **Kakeyss.na?** Will you go? **Cēki nwu ka iss.ta − mwe l' hako iss.na** Someone is over there − I wonder what he's up to. CF **-ulq ke 'na, -na siph.ta**.
 2. = (used for) **-nun ya, -nun ka**. ¶ **Ilpon ey ka-pwass.na mul.e poca** Let's ask him whether he's ever been to Japan. SEE ~ **ka**, ~ **lul**. CF Dupont 169: "for practical purposes **-na pota** < **-n[un k]a pota**".
SEE **-na pota, -na hata**; CF **-una** / **-na**.

-na (after vowel) alt of **-una** (adversative). but.

naa < naˈza, 1. inf < nās.ta < nasˈta (get/be better). 2. (= **na'a**) → **nah.a**, inf < **nah.ta**.

na ˈ[G]wa, n + pcl. with me. SEE ¨nalˈGwa.

nah.a se, vt inf + pcl. 1. bears (= gives birth to) and then/so. 2. (= **na se**) from/since birth, (in) all one's life, in all one's born days.

-na hata, FAMILIAR indic attent + vi. thinks/ believes that; wonders whether it doesn't (= **-nun ya hata**). ¶ **Pang an ey nwu ka iss.na hako tul.ye 'ta pwass.ta** I peeked in to see if there was anyone in the room. **Kim sensayng i pelsse cip ey tol.a kass.na hako tul.ye 'ta pwass.ta** I looked in to see if Mr Kim had gone home already. **Sāmu-sil i co'.yong hay se āmu to an kyēysina hayss.e yo** (Im Hopin 1987:173) The office was so quiet that I figured there wasn't anyone in it. **Ha to (an oki ey) cwuk.ess.na hayss.ta** I really wondered if he had died (− not coming [for so long]).

CF **-nun ka hata** (p. 726), **-na siph.ta** (p. 777).

-naikka [lit, obs] = -(su)p.nikka, -nun ya. (Does not attach to adjective or copula.)

-naita [lit, obs] = -(su)p.nita, -nunta. (Does not attach to adjective or copula.)

-na ka, 1. FAMILIAR indic attent + pcl = **-un ka ka**. ¶ **Ku ⁿyeca ka nemu khuna ka mūncey 'ta** The problem is whether she is too tall.
 2. = **-nun ka** / **ya ka**. ¶ **Ēncey natha-nana ka mūncey 'ta** The question is when it appears.

'na ka, abbr < hana ka = hanun ya. ¶ **Wuli ka kuleh.key hay ya 'na ka mūncey 'ta** The question is whether we have to do it (that way).

na ka, 1. n + pcl [DIAL] = nay ka (I).
 2. n + vi inf. (I go =) I'm leaving. G'bye.

na-ka < ˈna-ˈka, inf < na-kata < ˈna-°kaˈta

na-kata < ˈna-°kaˈta, cpd vi = vi (or vi inf) + vi. goes out; leaves. NOTE: While a case can be made for **na** as inf, the compound is not separable (*na nun/to/tul/ya ka···).

naki, 1. summative < nata vi.
 2. postn. a person born in ··· (= nāyki); a person from (just out of) ···; a person. phus ~ a greenhorn. pōthong ~ (= hayng nayki) a common person.

nal₁, n. day; (= nal-ssi) weather.

nal₂, 1. **nal(q)** prosp mod.
 1a. < nal(q), prosp mod < nata < °naˈta (emerges). CF ¨nal(q).
 1b. < nol(q) < *noˈloˈl(q), prosp mod < nalta < no[l]ˈta (flies).
 2. adn, n (preparticle). CF **sayng, sēn, phus**.
 2a. raw, uncooked; green, unripe; fresh, unpickled; unseasoned; crude, unprocessed. ¶ ~ **talkyal** / **kyēylan** a raw egg. ~ **koki** raw/uncooked meat or fish. ~ **kacwuk** raw hide, a pelt. ~ **kalwu** unrefined flour. ~ **kochi** raw cocoon. ~ **kiwa** unbaked tile. ~ **kimchi** unaged kimchi. ~ **congi** / **cāngphan** unoiled paper / floor. ~ **kām** / **pām** / **khong** green (unripe) persimmons / chestnuts / beans. ~ **lo mekta** eats it raw. **nalcca** [< nalq-ca] raw stuff; a crude fellow, a greenhorn; **nalcca lo mekta** eats it raw (uncooked); [colloq] "latches on to", appropriates, takes (without paying).
 2b. unreasonable, unjust, severe, harsh. ¶ ~ **pyelak** = sayng pyelak (unreasonable scolding, etc.). ~ **kāngto** barefaced robbery. ~ **totwuk nom** a barefaced robber.

na l', abbr < na lul. 1. n + pcl. 2. inf + pcl.

¨nal = ¨na l' = ¨na ˙lol me. ¶ ¨na l' kesulq twoco˙k ol (1445 ¹Yong 115) pirates who resist(ed) him. ¶ ¨na l' ˙KWUW ˙hosywo˙sye (1449 Kok 98) please save me. ¨na l' ˙WUY ˙ho˙ya nilo˙sywo˙sye (1459 Wel 1:17b) please tell me. ¨na l' ˙WUY ˙ho˙sya (1463 Pep 2:231b) [Buddha will] for my sake. ˙MEN-LYENG CYE-˙SYENG ˙i ˙ta ¨na l' to˙lye nilo˙sya˙toy (1459 Wel 2:52a) the spirits and sages all tell me [as follows]. ¨na l' te˙pule [¨KHWAN-˙KHWOK] ˙hi hon˙ta ¨ma˙ta yel˙hul ˙Gwom ¨ta ˙honwos˙ta (1481 Twusi 20:29a) every time they are so kind to me it takes a whole ten days.

na 'l(q) = na ilq, n + cop prosp mod. to be me. ¨nal(q) (< *na-˙wo-lq), modulated prosp mod < ˙na˙ta (emerges). ¶ ˙ma˙s i ¨nalq ˙toy ¨ep˙su.l i˙n i (1462 ¹Nung 3:50b) there is no way for the flavor to emerge. ¨na˙l i '-ngi ˙'ta. ¶ ˙i ˙tols ˙su˙mu ˙nal ˙pskuy ˙kil[h] ¨na˙l i '-ngi ˙'ta (?1517- Pak 1:8b) on the twentieth day of this month we will leave. ¨nalq˙t in˙t ay n'. ¶ ˙hota˙ka KHWONG˙ol pu˙the ¨nalq˙t in˙t ay n' ... (1462 ¹Nung 3:8b) if it emerged from empty space ... .

na 'la (= na ila), n + cop var indic assert. (that) it's me. ¶ ~ ko, ~ to, ~ 'myen, ~ 'n(un).

¨nal˙Gwa (?< ¨na l' ˙Gwa), n + pcl + pcl = na ˙[G]wa with me (= na wa / hako / 'lang). SEE ul kwa; CF nwul˙Gwa, ne ˙[G]wa. ¶ ¨nal˙Gwa TA-¨PWOW ZYE-LOY ˙Gwa ˙stwo CYE ˙HWA-˙PPWULQ ¨pwon t i towoy˙n i ˙'la (1463 Pep 4:140a) = na ˙[G]wa TA-¨PWOW ZYE-LOY ˙Gwa ˙HWA-˙PPWULQ ˙ul ¨pwo˙m i towoy˙n i ˙'la (1463 Pep 4:140b) they got to see him himself [the tathāgata] and the Ancient Buddha (Prabhūtaratna) and also the incarnate Buddhas (Nirmāṇabuddha). ALSO: 1447 Sek 13:25b, 1462 ¹Nung 5:56a.

nalle, var = ¨nal˙lwo. ¶ nalle nun es.ti salla hokwo how will I live? (?1544- Akcang kasili).

¨nal˙lwo (?= na ˙lwo with conflated liquid), n + pcl. ¶ ¨nal˙lwo ¨KAY-˙THWALQ ˙khey ho˙n i (1462 ¹Nung 7:27a) got released (emancipated) from his ego. ¨es˙tyey ˙wos ˙pa˙p ol ˙pse ¨nal˙lwo ingey ni˙lulGe˙n ywo (1463 Pep 2:240a) how come with food and clothing he has reached me here? nallwo (1887 Scott 28) = na llo by me.

¨nal˙lwo k (?= na ˙lwo k, with conflated liquid), n + pcl + pcl. than me. ¶ ... ¨ta ¨nal˙lwo k mwon¨cye 'ylwo˙ta (1481 Twusi 20:6b) [these writings] all are earlier than me (= before my time).

nalm < nolm < *no˙l[o]m, subst < nalta < no[l]˙ta (flies).

na lo, n + pcl. as / for / toward me.

¨na ˙lol, n + pcl. me. ¶ ZYE-LOY ˙THAY-¨CO s SSI-˙CYELQ ˙ey ¨na ˙lol ¨kyecip ¨sa˙mosi˙n i (1447 Sek 6:4a) when the tathāgata was prince he made me his wife. ¨es˙te 'n cyen˙cho ˙lwo ¨na ˙lol e˙li˙ta ˙ho˙sya ˙SYEK-¨CO 'ylwo˙la ˙hwo˙m ol ¨mwot ho˙l i ˙'la ˙ho˙sino˙n i '-ngi s ˙kwo (1459 Wel 9:35de) on what grounds do you say I am too young and refuse to call me a disciple of Buddha? ¨na ˙lol solang ˙ho.ya [NUNG] ˙hi ¨twu-[˙]ze [˙CCO] ˙lol ˙se ¨nilGwuylq ˙ta (1481 Twusi 23:44a) will you be able to achieve the writing of a few words [of poetry] with me in mind? ALSO: 1459 Wel 8:98a, ...

NOTE: Spelled nal.ul in ne y stwo nal.ul swokiti malla (1795 ¹No-cwung [P] 1:16b) = ¨ne y ˙stwo ¨na l' swo˙ki˙ti ¨mal˙Gwo˙l ye (?1517- ¹No 1:18b) now don't you go deceiving me! CF ¨nwu ˙lul.

na l' tele < ¨na l' to˙lye (1459 Wel 2:32a), ¨na l' te˙pu[˙]le (1481 Twusi 20:29a) = na tele to me.

nalul(q), prosp mod < naluta.

na lul, 1. n + pcl. me [as object]. 2. inf + pcl.

'na lul, 1. < ina lul. ¶ Hankul ina Hānq-ca 'na lul mak.lon hako Regardless whether it is Korean or Sino-Korean [Chinese].

2. < hana lul.

-na lul, 1. < -una lul (adversative + pcl).

2. (FAMILIAR indic attentive + pcl) = -nun ka / ya lul. ¶ Iss.na ēps.na lul poko wā la Go see whether he is in or not. SEE -na (2).

nalum, postn, postmod [< subst < vt naluta]. depending on ... .

1. postn. ¶ Ku kes un sālam nalum ita That depends on the person. Sālam nalum ici yo Everyone to his own taste. Yele kaps i iss.nun tey mulken nalum ita We have many prices and they depend upon the quality of the goods.

2. postmod (-ul ~). ¶ Ka.yong i cēk.key tulko mānh.i tunun kes un mek.ul nalum ila halq swu iss.ta Your living expenses might be said to be dependent upon the amount of food you eat. Tāycep ul pat.ko mōs pat.ko nun cey ka hal nalum / thas ita The reception one gets depends on what one does. CF thas.

nam < ˙*nam(⋯)*, substantive < **nata** < °*na˙ta* (emerges). CF ¨*nam*.

nam < ˙*nom*, noun. 1. a person other than you; another (person), other (people); the other fellow. ¶**Nam uy nappun māl ul haci mālla** Don't speak ill of others. **Nam ul salang hala** Love your neighbor.

2. an unrelated person, an outsider. ¶**Chŏnq-swu ka mēlci man acwu nam un ani 'ta** Though distant, he is still my relative. **Nam pota nun chinchek i nās.ta** Blood is thicker than water.

3. a stranger; an estranged person. ¶**Nam aph ey se nun ēncey 'na semek-semek hay cinta** I always get a bit ill at ease in front of strangers. **Ku tul un ¹ihon hayss.uni incey nam ita** Since they got their divorce they have nothing to do with each other.

4. I / me (CF **nwukwu**). ¶**Cey ka cal-mos hako nam poko cal-mos hayss.ta 'nta** It was your fault and you say it is my fault. **Ney ka way nam (= na) uy chayk ul kacye kanun ya** Why are you taking my book?

5. you. ¶**Ku sālam i way nam (= ne) uy chayk ul kacye kanun ya** Why is he taking your book?

6. he / him; she / her; they / them. ¶**Ku sālam i way nam (= ce sālam) uy chayk ul kacye kanun ya** Why is he taking the other fellow's (her, their) book?

ANT **ce (cey)**

nam, adnoun (abbr < **namca** < *NAM-*¨*CO*). man, male. ¶ ~ **tongsayng** a girl's younger brother. ~ **su' nim** (= **nam-sung**) a monk. ~ **swul a** man's spoon. ANT ⁿ**ye**.

-nam, 1. **-na 'm**, abbr < **(-n' a <) -nun ya (ko) ham**.

2. **-na 'm'**, abbr < **-nun ya 'n māl ia?**. ¶**Cēng-mal puth-cap.un cwul āna 'm?** (− **han pen kulay ponun kes ici**) Do you think I was really meaning to grab you? − why, I was just pretending. **Kulen māl nwu ka kot.i tut.na 'm** Who could believe such talk?! NOTE: Does not occur with adj or cop, or with past or future. Rejected by many speakers, in favor of **-ta'm**.

3. **-na m'**, abbr < **-na mwe**. ¶**Ne nun na poko māl ul hampu lo haci man nay ka ne 'ykey kulemyen cōh.keyss.na m'?** You say such awful things to me, but what if I talked to you that way?

¨*nam* (< *˙na-˙wo-m*), modulated subst < °*na˙ta*. ¶*ingey ˙na˙m ol ¨a˙ti ¨mwot 'kwo ˙sye* (1463 Pep 3:180ab) unaware that they will henceforth emerge ... . *pan˙to˙ki HE-KHWONG ˙oy ¨na˙m ol pwo˙l i 'Ge˙n i ˙¨ston* (1462 ¹Nung 2:122a) we are sure to see emergence into the void.

na 'm = **na im**, noun + cop subst. being me.

'/-na-ma, 1. alternant after vowel of **-una-ma** (extended adversative).

2. var (alt) < **ina-ma**

3. abbr < **hana-ma**

-na māna, alt after vowel of **-una māna**.

namcis, postn = ~ **'i**, der adv < ~ **hata** adj-n. fully, all of, at least, a bit over ⋯ (= **nek.nek**), ⋯ and then some. ¶**sam-sip namcis hanq** ⁿ**yeca** (Dupont 338) a woman a good thirty years old. [? < **nam(e)ci**.]

nameci, 1. noun. the remainder, the remnant(s), remainings, the rest, what is left, a leftover; what results; the surplus, the balance. ¶**Pic kaph.ko nan nameci lo cip ul sass.ta** I have paid off the debt and bought a house with what was left.

namecɨq ⋯ . ¶ ~ **kes** the remainder. ~ **pap** food left over, scraps of food; the rest of the food. ~ **caysan** what is left of (the residue of) one's property. ~ **īl** the remaining work, the rest of the job. ~ **pic** the balance owed. **Namecɨq tōn i elma 'na iss.nun ya** How much money have you got left? **Namecɨq sālam un eti iss.nun ya** Where are the rest of the people?

2. postmod. **-un** ~ **(ey)** as a result of, from an excess of, driven by. ¶**miwe han** ~ **(ey)** out of hatred. **cīnachin** ~ **(ey)** as a result of going too far (of overdoing it). **salang han** ~ **(ey)** from an excess of love. **Mikwuk un cēn.lyak phok.kyek-ki ey chīcwung han nameci misail uy yēnkwu lul sohol hi ha.yess.ta** As a result of overemphasizing the importance of strategic bombers, America neglected its research on missiles. **Cilthwu han nameci, namphyen ul cwuk.yess.ta** Driven by jealousy, she killed her husband. [< **nām**- vi + **-eci** suf; CF **namcis**]

-nami, bnd n (? < **nam** vi subst + **-i** suffix).

¶**ceng** ~ attachment, fondness, liking.

-nam.un / -nam.u (as adn), suf (< vi mod 'that remained'). Makes excess numerals out of decimal non-Chinese numerals; CF **-ye**. ¶**ye-nam.un** ten or so, ten odd, over ten. Usually

spelled **-namun**, but [1]Yi Ungpayk 1961 prefers **-nam.un**. Roth (1936:253) writes "**yen.am.un**" for **ye-nam.un** (< **ye[l] nam.un**).
namyen, conditional < **nata**.
na 'myen = **na imyen** if it's me
?-nan (seen in the 1920s) < -*non* = **-nun**
na n', abbr < **na nun**. 1. n + pcl. as for me.
  2. inf + pcl.
na 'n = **na in**, n + cop mod. ··· that is me.
nan, 1. < *nan*, mod < **nata** < °*na῾ta* (emerges). ¶ ¨*mwot na῾n i* (1445 [1]Yong 60). 2. < *non* < **no[῾lo]n*, mod < **nalta** < *no[l]῾ta* (flies).
-nan, **-naney** [Ceycwu DIAL (Seng [1]Nakswu 1984:8-10; does not attach to the copula)] = **-ni-kka (n')**.
na 'na, n ('I/me') or inf ('emerge') + alt of **ina**.
nana 1. < **nata**. 2. < **nalta**.
na 'ni, n (I/me) + alt < **ini**.
nani 1. < **nata**, 2. < **nalta**
-nani [obs, DIAL] < -*no῾n i*. CF 1936 Roth 532-3.
  1. = **-nuni** < **-nun i**; ~ **'la**.
  2. = **-uni(-kka)** [? with verbs only]
῾na ῾non, n + pcl. as for me, I. ¶ *῾na ῾non epe῾zi ye῾huy῾Gwo no῾m oy kungey pu῾the sa῾lwo῾toy* (1447 Sek 6:5a) I leave my parents and attach myself to another('s place) to live, and yet ... . *῾na ῾non ZYE-LOY s ῾mos cye῾mun a῾z ilwo῾n i* (1462 [1]Nung 1:76b) I am the youngest brother of the tathāgata. *ne ῾non kis῾ke two ῾na non kis῾ti a῾ni ho῾m ye* (1482 Kum-sam 2:5b) you may be happy but I am not, and ... .
na 'n tul, n + cop mod + postmod. though it be me. VAR **nayntul**.
na nun, 1. n + pcl. as for me. 2. inf + pcl.
nanun, 1. < *῾na῾non* (example?), proc mod < **nata** (emerges).
  2. < *nonon* < **no[῾lo]non*, proc mod < **nalta** < *no[l]῾ta* (flies).
-nanyo → **-nan yo** [lit, obs; DIAL] < -*no῾n ywo* = **-nun ya**, **-nun ka/ko**. CF 1936 Roth 533.
na-ota < *῾na-°wo῾ta*, cpd vi = vi (or vi inf) + vi. comes out, emerges. NOTE: While a case can be made for **na** as inf, the compound is not separable (***na nun/to/tul/ya o···**).
-na pº/ᵤta, FAMILIAR indic attent + aux adj. it seems that, I think that (= **-nun ka pota**). ¶**Nwu ka wass.na pota** I think someone is here. **Ku uy cip i i tali kūnche ey iss.ess.na pota** His house seems to have been in the vicinity of this bridge.

na se, inf + pcl. 1. emerges/exits/... and (then/so). 2. is born and then; (= **nah.a se**) from/since birth, (in) all one's life (one's born days).
n'a se = **n'ā se** < **nwa se** = **nwā se**, abbr < **nowa se** = **noa se** < **noh.a se**.
na-se < *῾na-῾sye*, inf < **na-suta** < **na-seta** < *῾na-sye῾ta*.
na-seta < *῾na-sye῾ta*, cpd vi. SEE **na-suta**.
-na siph.ta, FAMILIAR indic attent + aux adj.
nass-, past < **nata**
nāss-, 1. = **naass-**, past < **nās.ta**.
  2. = **nah.ass-**, past < **nah-**.
n'ass-, abbr < **nwass-**, abbr < **nowass-** = **noass-**, abbr < **noh.ass-**.
na-suta < **na-seta** < *῾na-sye῾ta*, cpd vi = vi (or vi inf) + vi. steps out, comes forth/out, appears; embarks upon; (··· **ey** ~) comes upon, runs into; it turns up, is found. NOTE: While a case can be made for **na** as inf, the compound is not separable (***na nun/to/tul/ya su···**).
nata$_{1-4}$ – NOTE: Treat **nata** as vi if **nanta** and **nanun** occur; as defective vi if only **nass.ta** and **nan** occur; as adj if only **nata** (and **nan**).
nata$_1$, vi. emerges: 1. comes into existence/being, is born, comes into the world.
  2. grows/comes out, sprouts, buds.
  3. (a smell / sound/ taste) comes out / forth; smells, sounds, tastes.
  4. becomes, grows to be, is (ill, interesting, fun brave, enthusiastic, efficient); acquires (a name, fame), develops/has (a cough, a wound).
  5. (emotion, a mood, anger) occurs; (**kiek / sayngkak i** ~) comes to mind, is recalled.
  6. breaks out, happens, takes place; has, we have, there is (fire, smoke, dust, flood, wind, disease, war, an accident, a breakdown, a hitch, trouble, fuss, a rupture).
  7. flows / runs / gushes out.
  8. is produced, raised, grown.
  9. (result). 9a. (a result) is forthcoming.
  9b. comes out as a result; results, turns out (to be), turns up (as). ¶**cal (to)** ~ is handsome. **mōs (to)** ~ is ugly; is stupid.
  9c. **kalak i** ~ hits one's stride / rhythm, gets into the swing (of things).
  10. leaves (= **tte-nata**), goes / gets out (= **na-kata**); (**nwun ey** ~) gets out of a person's favor / graces, is in bad with a person.
  11. (= **natha-nata**) appears (on the market, before the public).

12. (a hole, road, place = seat/job, apartment, school) opens up, is open, is available.
13. (a law, regulation, price) takes effect, goes into effect.
14. [quasi-transitive] passes (a season) = cīnayta.
15. [? DIAL] = toyta. ¶ palkak / thān.lo ~ gets discovered.
16. [DIAL] = kata. ¶ kulus ey kum i ~ a plate gets cracked.
17. [DIAL] = mekta. ¶ ahop sal (ey/i) nan ai = ahop sal (ul) mek.un ai a child of nine.

nata₂, aux v sep. SEE -e nata, -ko nata.

nata₃, postnominal adj insep. is. ¶ pyel nata is strange, peculiar. mas nata is tasty; CF mas (i) nanta flavor appears, it tastes:

    mas (i) nanta   mas nata
    mas (i) nanun   —
    mas (i) nass.ta   mas nass.ta
    mas (i) nan ···   mas nan ···

nata₄, postnominal vi insep. does, feels. ¶ kamcil nanta feels impatient. ? pyel nass.ta is strange, peculiar (defective vi).

na 'ta = na ita, n + cop (it's me)

na to, 1. < na ˙two (1463 Pep 2:142a), noun + pcl. I (me) too/even. 2. inf + pcl.

n'a to = n'ā to < nwa to = nwā to, abbr < nowa to = noa to < noh.a to.

'na to = ina to. SEE nemu 'na to.

na tul, 1. n + pcl (= na lul tul) they [do it to] me. 2. inf + pcl.

-na tul, FAMILIAR indic attent + pcl. ¶ Cikum ay tul ī-chung ey se kongpu hana tul? Are the children studying upstairs now?

na twu, noun + var pcl. I (me) too/even.

n'a twu = n'ā twu < nwa twu = nwā twu, abbr < nowa twu = noa twu < noh.a twu < noh.a to.

-na uy, abbr < -nun ka uy. ¶ na uy cwuk.na sāna uy kyelqceng my decision to live or die.

na ˙uy, n + pcl. of me, my; I. ¶ pwuthye ˙two ˙i ˙kot ˙ho˙sya na ˙uy ¨sywow ˙culkywo˙m ol ¨alo˙sya (1463 Pep 2:246b) Buddha knows that I take pleasure in the Lesser Vehicle.

na-wā < ˙na-˙wa, inf < na-ota < ˙na-˚wo˙ta.

nawi, postmod (preceded by prosp mod -ul and usually followed by a negative). (not) enough to; (hardly) worth ···ing; necessity. ¶ Sakwa al i cak.e mek.ul nawi ka ēps.ta The apple is too small to be worth eating. Pap i cek.e pay pullil nawi ka ēps.ta There is not enough rice to fill me up. Sacin i pol nawi ka ēps.ta The picture is not worth looking at.

māl hal ~ ēps.ta it is needless to say; it is not worth mentioning. ¶ māl hal ~ ēps.nun sallim a miserable living. māl hal ~ ēps.nun sālam an unmentionable person; (= te hal nawi ēps.nun sālam) the most wonderful person.

te hal ~ ēps.ta nothing is left to be desired; is the most satisfactory, is perfect, is the best, is first-rate, is matchless/superb/supreme. ¶ te hal ~ ēps.nun mulken a first-rate article. te hal ~ ēps.nun sālam the most wonderful person. te hal ~ ēps.i perfectly, thoroughly, all the way, with no room for improvement/deterioration. Ku tul un te hal nawi ēps.i cal nass.ta (mōs sayngkyess.ta) He is handsome (ugly) as can be. CF om-nawi < olm-nawi room to budge.

[CF nawu 'amply', der adv < nā(s)-]

˙na-˚wo˙ta SEE na-ota

nay₁, n. 1. = yenki (smoke).
    2. = nāymsay (smell).
    3. → nāy₆ = sī'-nay (stream)

nay₂, n. 1. [< ˙na y < *˙na ˙i; CF cey, ney].
1a. I (alt of na when followed by pcl ka). ¶ Nay ka kakeyss.ta I will go.
1b. abbr < nay ka I [as subject]. ¶ Nay kulen kes cheum pwass.ta I have never seen such a thing.
2. abbr < na uy (my) [< ˙na ˙y < ˙na ˙oy]. ¶ ~ chayk/ilum my book/name. ~ kes (often pronounced nayq kes) mine. nay kes ney kes mine and thine, meum and teum; nay kes ney kes ul hōntong hata confounds meum and teum, is confused over what is his and what is not; nay kes ney kes ul kalici anh.ta draws no line between what is one's own and what is not.

SEE na 'ykey; nayntul.

nay₃, interjection [LIVELY] = nēy (yes)

nāy₄, infinitive < nāyta

nāy₅ < ¨nay, postnoun. throughout, all through (a period of time). ¶ kau' nāy throughout the autumn. kyewu' nāy all winter long. Pom nāy pi ka onta It rains throughout the spring. Il-nyen nāy kkoch ul polq swu iss.ta You can see flowers all the year round. Palam i achim nāy pūp.nita The wind has been blowing all morning long. ¨naycywong ¨nay (1463 Pep 3: 41a, 1465 Wen 1:1:1:92a, 1475 Nay 3:29b)

= ¨NAY-CYWUNG ¨nay (1447 Sek 9:27a, 1459 Wel 21:51b) at/in the end, finally. CF kkuth-nāy, nāynay, nāyche, mōs-nay, machim-nay. ? < inf < nāyta; not nāy < ˙NWOY 'within' or lay < LOY 'come' because of the MK vowels.
nāy₆ = sī'-nay (stream)
nay, var of na = ˙na 'I' before ˙ᵘ⁄oy. SEE nay ˙uy.
na 'y, abbr < *na ˙ᵘ⁄oy.

1. my. ¶na 'y a˙to˙l ol (1447 Sek 6:5b) my son. na 'y ¨ma˙l ol (1447 Sek 6:8b) my words. na 'y SWON-¨CO (1447 Sek 6:9b) my grandson. na 'y pa˙l ay s hon the˙li ˙lol ¨mwot mwuu˙l i ˙'n i (1447 Sek 6:27a) will not move one hair of my foot. na 'y ˙mwo˙m i (1447 Sek 13:36b) my body. na 'y ¨TTYEY-¨CO y (1447 Sek 13:61a) my disciple. na 'y ˙PPYENG ˙ul (1447 Sek 24:50b) my illness. na 'y ˙NGWEN ˙ul a˙ni CCYWONG ho˙m ye n' (1459 Wel 1:12b) if you do not comply with my request. na 'y ¨mal ˙Gwos a˙ni tulu˙si˙m ye n' (1459 Wel 2:5b) if you do not listen to what I say. na 'y ¨kye˙ci.p i ˙za (1459 Wel 7:12b) my wife. na 'y ˙mwom ˙NGWOY ˙yey (1459 Wel 7:28b) aside from my own body (= my own self). na 'y cwume˙kwuy pi˙chwuyywo˙m ol (1462 ¹Nung 1:84a) the radiance of my fist. na 'y il˙hwu˙m un (1463 Pep 2:222b) my name. ˙PPWULQ-˙PEP ˙i ˙za na 'y inge˙kuy two ¨cywokwo˙m achi is˙ta (1482 Nam 1:14a) there is some of Buddha's law right here where I am, too. ˙pwoksyeng s kwo˙c oy pul˙kwo.m i [¨KUM] ˙ila ˙[G]wa te˙wo.m ol na 'y [PWUN] ˙ey s kes ¨sam˙ti ¨mwot ho˙kwo (1481 Twusi 23:23a) the red of the peach blossoms is deeper than that of brocade but I cannot make it my own, and ... . na 'y twu swang say hwel ul ta˙ka ¨ta ton˙nye ˙hoy˙ya po˙likwa ˙'la (?1517- Pak 1:35a; the Chinese has a genitive) I took my two pairs of new shoes and wore them both out getting about! na 'y ˙e˙mi ˙lul (1518 Sohak-cho 9:55a) my mother. na 'y sa˙wona˙won ¨il ˙lan (1518 Sohak-cho 8:15a) one's own bad deeds.

2. These examples are treated as genitive rather than nominative because of the accent; the subject is ellipted [˙na y]. ¶na 'y a˙ki ¨wuy ˙ho˙ya ¨e˙te pwo˙kwo ˙'l ye (1447 Sek 6:13b) I'd like you to seek her out [as a bride] for my boy. SOYNG-SOYNG ˙ay na 'y ˙NGWEN ˙ul il˙thi a˙ni ˙khey ho˙kwo ˙'la (1459 Wel 1:13b) in life after life I do not want to let my desire be lost.

na 'y ˙MYENG ku˙chwu.m i˙za mute˙ni ne˙ki˙ka.n i ˙Gwa ... (1459 Wel 10:4b) having treated lightly the very end of my life, ... na 'y mozo˙m i ˙SSILQ ˙lwo ˙mwom pas˙k uy i˙sywo˙m ol ¨al˙Gwa-ngi ˙'ta (1462 ¹Nung 1:53a) I know that my mind really exists apart from my body. na 'y ˙e˙mi ¨amwo ˙toy ˙na 'ys.non ˙t i ¨mwol˙lay-ngi ˙'ta (1459 Wel 21:53a; the underlying object is marked with the nominative particle) I do not know what place my mother has been reborn into.

3. I [as the genitive-marked subject of an adnominalized sentence]. ¶˙i kak˙si ˙za na 'y ¨et.ni˙nwon mozo˙m ay mas˙two˙ta (1447 Sek 6:14ab) precisely this girl matches the purpose I am pursuing. na 'y ˙TUK ˙hwon ˙TI-˙HHYWEY ˙non MI-˙MYWOW ˙ho˙ya ˙TTYEY-˙QILQ ˙i˙Gen ma˙lon (1447 Sek 13:57b) the wisdom I have gained is subtle and most important, but ... . pwu¨thye y nilo˙sya˙toy na 'y nilo˙ten ˙KWU-LA ˙TYEY CIN-˙SSILQ ˙lwo ku˙le the˙n ye a˙ni the˙n ywo (1459 Wel 9:36d) Buddha said "was the emperor Kwula really as I said or wasn't he?". kutuy [˙KWUY] hon ce˙k uy na 'y nul˙kwu.m ul chuki ne˙kiti a˙ni ˙kha.n i ˙Gwa (1481 Twusi 16:61b) I do not resent it that I am getting old when you are so dear to me and moreover ... ; CF nay ˙uy [SYWUY-¨LWOW] ˙hwo.m on (1481 Twusi 22:27b) 'that I am getting old and frail'.
na y [in texts without tone marks] = ˙na y, n + pcl. I [as subject]. ¶na y sile-kwom CYEY-SO thi mwot hol s oy ˙.n i ˙la (1632 Kalyey 1:19b) it's because I can't possibly do the ancestral rites.
˙na y, abbr < *˙na ˙i, n + pcl. I [as subject]. ¶˙na y ˙nike ˙ci-ngi ˙'ta ˙ka˙sya (1445 ¹Yong 58) saying "I must go" he went. ˙na y ˙pwoa ˙cye ˙hono˙ta sol˙Wa˙ssye (1447 Sek 6:14b) tell him I would like to see him. ˙na y ¨a˙lay s ney ¨pe˙t ila˙n i (1447 Sek 6:19b) I was your friend in former days. ˙na y NGWANG ¨mal-ssom tut¨copkwo ˙za na 'y mozo˙m i ˙skoytot˙kwa-ngi ˙'ta (1447 Sek 24:29b) only after hearing Your Majesty's words is my mind awakened. ˙na y ˙i ¨salo˙m ol ˙QAK-¨TTWOW ˙ay pte˙le ti˙ti a˙ni khey˙khwo [= a˙ni hokey ho˙kwo] ˙cye ˙honwo˙n i (1459 Wel 21:125b) I am afraid that I may be tending to let this man fall into the wrong path. ˙na y tut¨cop˙kwo NGUY-SIM s ˙kumu˙l ul kus˙kwa-ngi ˙'ta (1463 Pep 2:24b) I listen and sever my net of doubts!

ˈna y ˈi keˈs uˈlwo hon naˈlaˈh ol ¨taˈcwue ˈtwo ˈwohiˈlye ¨epˈti aˈni ˈkhwo n' ¨esˈtyey ˈhomolˈmye CYE-¨CO y ˈstoˈn ye (1463 Pep 2:77a) when I have no appreciable lack though I gave up a nation for this, how much more so the masters! woˈnolˈi mwoſ]ton ˙TTAY-¨HHWOY ˙Gwa ˈstwo ˈna y ¨ta hoˈma ˈpwozopˈkwa-ngi ˈˈta (1463 Pep 4:169a) today this whole entire congregation and also I, we all have seen. [SYE KWONG] ˈoy ˈwon kaˈci s ¨iˈl ol siˈlum aˈni ˈho.ywoˈm ol ˈna y ¨anwoˈn i (1481 Twusi 8:24b) I know that Lord Xú does not brood over all sorts of matters. ˈna y ne-huy ˈtolˈh ol koˈcang KWONG-ˈKYENG ˈhoˈya ¨epˈsi woˈt ol aˈni ˈhonwoˈn i (1447 Sek 19:29b) I do not come without the uttermost respect for you people. ˈna y ˈicey ney ˈeˈm[i] uy ¨kan ˈstaˈh ol ¨pwoyˈywo.l i ˈˈla (1459 Wel 21:21b) I will now show you the land where your mother went. ˙SSIM ˈhiˈna y ¨KAM-SYANG ˈhwoˈtoy ZYE-LOY s MWU-ˈLYANG TI-ˈKYEN ˈul ilˈhwoˈla ˈhoˈta-ngi ˈˈta (1463 Pep 2:4b) I was moved to such grief I wanted to lose the tathāgata's immeasurable awareness. ˈna y solang ˈhwoˈtoy (1447 Sek 6:25b) I am thinking [about it]. ˈna y ¨lwongtam ˈhotaˈla (1447 Sek 6:24b) I was joking. ˈna y pwuˈle ne ˈlul esye TUK-¨TTWOW hoˈkey ˈhotaˈn i (1447 Sek 24:3a) I have deliberately tried to get you to achieve the way [to enlightenment] quickly. ˈhotaˈkaˈna y ˈkhun ˙PEP ˈculˈkitenˈt ay n' (1463 Pep 2:232a) if I delighted in the great[er] dharma ... . ˈi CIN-˙SSILQ S ˈMYELQ-¨TTWO aˈni ˈnˈt ol ˈna y aˈlwo-ngi ˈˈta (1463 Pep 2:23a) I know that this is not true nirvāṇa. kuˈpsk uy mozoˈm ay ˈna y neˈkywoˈtoy (1463 Pep 2:23a) at that time my feeling was that ... . ˈna y panˈtoˈki CYWUNG-SIN ˈthoˈlwok KWONG-ˈKUP ˈhoˈya (1463 Pep 4:154b) without fail I will contribute until my death, and ... . ˈna y ˈnye (1481 Twusi 25:29a) I go and ... . ˈna y neˈlul KUM ¨cwuˈl ywo ˈho.yaˈton (1482 Nam 1:44-5) if I consider giving you money ... . ˈna y pwuthye towoyˈywo.l ye holˈs i.n i (1482 Nam 2:6b) I want to become a Buddha. ˈna y palo ¨alˈl i ˈlwoˈta (ˀ1517- Pak 1:14b) I understand it correctly. ˈna y ywo soˈi mol-pwoˈki ¨eˈte ˈsye mol ˈthoˈti ¨mwot ˈhotaˈla (ˀ1517 Pak 1:37b) the last while I have been unable to ride a horse, having acquired an intestinal ailment.

ˈna y ilˈcuk ¨aˈti ¨mwot ¨hwola (ˀ1517- Pak 1:37b) I didn't know earlier [of your illness] ... . ˈna y ˈstwo ˈsay tatay hwuyhwuy aˈni ˈGeˈn i ˈsto.n a (ˀ1517- Pak 1:73a) I am not a crude Tatar Muslim, after all!

The following examples are not to be mistaken for genitives: ˈna y ciˈp uy isilq ceˈkuy (1447 Sek 6:7a) when I was at [my] home; ne-huy ˈnon kheˈn i ˙Gwa ˈna y ciˈp uy isilq ceˈk uy ¨SSYWUW-¨KHWO y ¨manthaˈla (1459 Wel 10: 23a) not so much you people but I am the one who had much trouble when we were at home.

ˈna 'y··· , 1. abbr < * ˈna ˈi··· (n + cop). ˈna 'yˈla it means 'I' (1459 Wel se:4b). ··· ˈkazoˈWwon ˈna 'ylwoˈn i (1459 Wel 8:92b) I went ··· .

2. abbr < ˈna is··· (v inf + aux). na 'y ˈeˈmi ¨amwo ˈtoy ˈna 'ys.nonˈt i ¨mwolˈlay-ngi ˈˈta (1459 Wel 21:53a) I do not know what place my mother has been reborn into. ˈkononˈpi yey n' kwoˈki ˈmu.l ey ˈna 'ysˈkwo (1481 Twusi 7: 7b) in a fine rain the fish are out in the water.

··· ˈnay, var (after uy, i, iC) = ··· ˈney, postnoun. the group, all of ··· . ¶ ··· acaˈpa ¨nimˈnayˈskuy ¨ta QAN-¨PWUW ˈhozopˈkwo (1447 Sek 6:1b) greeted ··· and the uncles, everyone, and ... . ¨ney aˈtoˈl i ˙KAK-ˈKAK ˈema ¨nimˈnay ¨mwoyzopˈkwo nwuuy ¨nimˈnay teˈpuˈle ˈcukcaˈhi ˈna-kaˈn i (1459 Wel 2:6b) the four sons, accompanying their respective mothers and bringing along their sisters, immediately set out. nyenu PWU-ZIN ˈnay s aˈtol ¨neyˈh i (1459 Wel 2:4b) the four sons of his other wives. ZYE-LOY ¨mwoyzoˈWaˈkaˈsinon ˙SYENG-ZIN ˈnay ˈˈla (1459 Wel 2:52a) they are the holy men accompanying the tathāgata. kakˈsi ˈnay ˙ZI-˙POYK syelˈhun ¨saloˈm i (1459 Wel 2:76b) two hundred and thirty women. ¨nyey s ˙SYENG-ZIN ˈnay s ˈpwolaˈm ol ¨pwoˈm i ˈmas.tang khenˈtyeng (ˀ1468- Mong 20a) though it be proper to look at the indications of the saints of former days ... . SEE kutuy ˈnay.

-nay, pseudo-bnd n < vc stem (nāyta). ¶ip ~, hyung ~ mimicry.

na ya, 1. n + pcl. only if it is me. 2. n + cop var inf (= na ia) it's me. 3. inf + pcl.

n'a ya = n'ā ya < nwa ya = nwā ya, abbr < nowa ya = noa ya < noh.a ya.

nay-amuli, abbr < nay ka āmuli (···) however (···) I may be.

nāyci < ¨*NAY-*'*CI.*
1. postn [lit] (always attaches to a number and is always followed by a number). from ⋯ to. ¶**Sahul nāyci nahul kellikeyss.ta** It will take from three to four days. NOTE: Pause may occur after **nāyci**, but not before it.
2. pcl, adv [lit]. and, or, and/or (= **tto-nun, hok-un**). ~ **nun** SAME. ¶**Sewul nāyci Pusan ey se mānh.i polq swu iss.ta** They are a common sight in Seoul and Pusan. CF **mich, kup.**

nay ka, var n (< ˙*na y* < *˙*na ˙i* n + pcl) + pcl. I [as subject]. VAR **ney ka** (which is also 'you' = **ne/ni ka**); **na ka.**

na 'y ke˙kuy, abbr < *na ˙oy ke˙kuy.* to me. ¶*na 'y ke˙kuy he˙thwuy ˙Gwa pol˙khwa* [= *polh ˙kwa] ˙kot ho˙n i* (1475 Nay 2:1:30b) they are like legs and feet to me.

na 'ykey, abbr < **na eykey** (to me)

na 'y key, abbr < *na oy key* < *na ˙oy kungey.* to me. ¶¨*CCWOY-*¨*PWOK i* ¨*es˙tyey na 'y key pu˙thu.l i ˙Gwo* (1482 Nam 1:63a) how can sin or joy attach to me? ¨*tywohon* ¨*il ˙lan na 'y key pwo˙nay˙Gwo kwu˙cun* ¨*il ˙lan no˙m oy key ˙cwunu˙n i* (1464 Kumkang 21b) sends the good things to me and gives the bad things to others. *pwuthye s a˙lom ˙ptu˙t i a˙ni* ¨˙*sya he˙mu˙l i* ¨*SSILQ ˙lwo na 'ykey is˙tas˙ta* (1463 Pep 2:6a) it was not Buddha's idea, the fault is really mine. ALSO: 1462 [1]Nung 1:9b, 1465 Wen 2:3:1:54a, … .

nayki < **nāyki**, summative < **nāyta** vc.
1. noun. (= **tōn** ~) wagering, gambling.
2. postnoun. 2a. ¶**cen** ~ **(swul)** undiluted wine (**cen** < *CCYWEN* 'complete').
2b. product; display. ¶**cēn** ~ "shop" product; things made to display for sale.
2c. display; person displaying. ¶**simswul** ~ a person with a temper, a show of temper. **yekan** (adv) ~ [+ NEG] = **hayng** (bnd n) ~ [not] a common being.
2d. (= **naki**) a person born in. **Sewul** ~ a Seoulite. **sikol** ~ a country person. **Phyengan-to** ~ a person born in Phyengan province.
2e. **cōng** ~ a breed, stock, strain, variety, species.

na 'y kungey, n + pcl + n. to me, to where I am; to oneself (himself), to where he (himself) is. ¶*na 'y kungey* ¨*mwotil˙Gen ma˙lon ce 'y* ¨*nim-˙kum* ˙*WUY˙tha ˙hosil˙ss oy* (1445 [1]Yong

121) toward himself they had been rebellious but, saying they do it for their own king, he … .

na 'yna, [DIAL] = **na 'na**

nāyna, adv. eventually, finally (= **kyelkwuk**); after much effort, with great pains (= **īl kkes**). [? < **nāy** inf + **na** emphatic pcl or **ina**]

nāy-nay, adv. from start to finish, all the way through.

nayntul, [nonstandard] var = **na 'n tul** though it be me. ¶**Nayntul ecci hal i yo** (Dupont 149) Me — what can I do? CF **ceyntul.**

na yo, 1. noun + particle. (it's) me.
2. noun + cop [AUTH] (= **na io**) it is me.
2. inf + pcl (emerges, ⋯)

n'a yo = **n'ā yo** < **nwa yo** = **nwā yo,** abbr < **nowa yo** = **noa yo** < **noh.a yo.**

nay ˙oy = *nay ˙uy.* SEE **uy** 14.
¶*nay ˙oy ˙PWULQ-*¨*KHA SO-*˙*NGUY KWONG-*˙*TUK ˙ul ilkho˙la* (1459 Wel 7:67-7) citing my unusual achievements of virtue.

nāyta[1], vi. it smokes (emits smoke), gets smoky.
nāyta[2], vc < **nata.** 1. takes/brings (carries) out.
2. produces, turns out.
3. puts forth, displays it, shows (strength, ability, anger).
4. raises, elevates, distinguishes (one's name).
5. publishes, brings out.
6. mails (CF **ponayta** 'sends').
7. presents, sends in, submits, tenders.
8. sets forth, puts forward, starts.
9. takes out = gets, obtains (a license, a loan).
10. (puts out =) sets up, fixes, arranges (for), makes (time, room; a road, a gap, an opening, a window).
11. (**koksik ul** ~) sells (grain).
12. pays, gives, contributes (money, cost).
13. serves, offers, gives, treats a person to.
14. empties, clears (a bottle, a room).
15. puts forward, selects, appoints.
16. (**mal ul** ~) gets a marker round and off the **yuch** board.
17. transplants, sets out (rice plants).
18. applies (fertilizer, ashes) to a field.
19. (**cwū lul, cwūsek ul** ~) provides (a note).

nāyta[3], aux v insep. SEE **-e nāyta**.

nāy 'ta, vc inf + cop transferentive — SEE **ita (ka)**. ~ **pota** looks out, sees from within; looks forward to, foresees. ANT **tul.ye 'ta.**

nay ˙uy, n + pcl [also *nay ˙oy*]. 1. (= *na 'y*) my. ¶*nay ˙uy NGUY-SIM* (1462 [1]Nung 2:21b) my doubt. *nay ˙uy i˙Gwu˙c i a˙ni 'lwo˙ta* (1481 Twusi 7:13b) is not my neighbor.

2. I [as the subject of an adnominalized or nominalized sentence]. SEE **uy** 14. ¶*nay ˙uy ··· nil˙Gwo˙m ol tut˙kwo* (1463 Pep 5:197a) hear my telling of ··· , and ··· .

nay ya [? DIAL] = **na ya** only (if it be) I/me. ¶**Nay ya āna ce sālam i ālci** Do I know it?! — he's the one who knows it!

···**n¨ccop-** < ···**nc-¨zop-**

'/-n ci SEE **in ci, -un ci**

'/-n cuk SEE **in cuk, -un cuk**

'/-n cwul SEE **in cwul, -un cwul**

-ne SEE **-ne la** (**one la** < ˙*wona˙la*)

ne < *ne*, n. you (to a child or inferior). **ne** + ˙*i* → *ne y*, **ne** + ˙*uy* → *ne ˙y*. **ne** + ˙*on* → *ne ˙non*; **ne** + ˙*ul* → *ne ˙lul* (*¨*ne l*'). **ne** + ˙*kwa* → *ne ˙[G]wa* (*¨*nel˙Gwa*). **ne** + ˙*u˙lwo* → *¨*nel˙lwo* > *nellwo* (1887); **ne** + ˙*u˙lan* → *¨*nel˙lan*.

NOTE: The shape is usually **ney** before pcl **ka** and before **-kkacis**. **Ney** is also an abbreviation of **ney ka** and of **ne uy**; **ney key** = **ne 'ykey** is an abbreviation of **ne eykey**; CF **na, nay**.

ne [DIAL] = **ney** your. **ne kes** = **ney kes** your thing, yours. CF **nu**.

nē, numeral. four (= **nēys**).

n'ē, abbr < **nwē** < **nwuwe**, inf < **nwupta**; < **nwue**, inf < **nwuta**.

ne ˙[G]wa, n + pcl. with you (= **ne wa** / **hako** / **'lang**). ¶*ne ˙[G]wa kol˙Wo˙l i ¨ep.su˙n i ˙'la* (1459 Wel 18:57b) there is no one to compare with you. CF ¨*nal˙Gwa*.

ne-hoy = *ne-huy*. ¶*ne-hoy ˙WUY [˙]ho˙sya* (1463 Pep 7:17a; the text dot beside Hankul "*ne*" is not an accent mark) for you people.

ne-huy < *ne-huy*, n. you all, you people, you folks. ¶*ne-huy kos˙pwo˙m i ˙CI-˙KKUK ˙ho˙ya* (1463 Pep 3:196b) your drudgery is extreme. ALSO: 1482 Nam 1:32a, ··· .

ne-huy key (1459 Wel 18:15b) to you folks, to where you people are.

ne-huy lwo (1887 Scott 29) = **ne-huy lo** by you people.

ne-huy ˙non (1459 Wel 10:23a).

ne-huy ˙uy (1463 Pep 2:66b).

ne-¨huy, ne-˙huy < **ne-huy ˙i* (nominative). ¶*ne-¨huy pwuthye s ¨ma˙l ol kwo˙ti tulu˙la* (1447 Sek 13:47b) you people listen rightly to Buddha's words. *ne-¨huy spol˙li pa˙lol s ¨ko˙z ay ˙ka˙a* (1459 Wel 10:13ab) you people go to the seashore quickly. *ne-¨huy ¨salom ˙HHWO-TTI ho˙m ye* (1447 Sek 21:68b) you people must protect the person and ··· . *ne-¨huy na˙za ¨ka˙m i ˙mas.tang ho˙n i* (1463 Pep 3:196b) it is fitting that you people advance. *ne-˙huy ¨twul˙h i yey ˙wo˙nan ˙t i ¨en˙me wo˙la.n i ˙Gwo* (?1517- [1]No 1:68b) how long is it since you two came here? ALSO: 1447 Sek 13:62b, 1459 Wel 18:15b, ··· .

ne-huy tul < *ne-huy ˙tolh*. you all/people/folks.
ne-huy ˙tol˙h i (1447 Sek 9:40b, 13:62b, 23:13a; 1459 Wel 10:14b, 10:26a, 18:18b).
ne-huy ˙tol˙h ol (1447 Sek 19:29b).
ne-huy ˙tol.h on (1475 Nay 1:25b).

ne-i, 1. = **ne-huy** you all. 2. = **nē-i** four people.

nēk, numeral. four (= **nēys**).

ne ka, noun + pcl [DIAL] = **ney ka** (you)

nek.nek, 1. adverb (= **nek.nek hi**). enough. ~ **cap.e**, ~ **capko** at most (= **kocak**).

2. ~ **hata**, adj-n. is enough; is generous, ample; is rich.

3. postn. ···odd, ···strong; all of ···, at least ··· . ¶**nēk ca tases chi** ~ all of four and a half feet. **payk wen** ~ a hundred wen and then some. **sam-sip myeng** ~ some thirty (people) strong. ANT **ppa-tus**. SYN **kang, namcis**. CF **kocak, mānh.e to**.

ne l', abbr < **ne lul**. you [as object].

ne 'l(q) = **ne il(q)**, noun + cop prosp modifier

ne 'la (= **ne ila**), n + cop var indic assertive. (that) it's you. ~ **ko**, ~ **to**, ~ **'myen**, ~ **'n(un)**.

-ne la SEE **one la** < ˙*wona˙la* (come!)

nellawa (?= *ne llawa* with conflated liquid) < *ne* + ˙*ila˙wa*. than you. ¶*nellawa silum han na two* (?1544- Akcang: Chengsan) I who suffer even greater anguish than you.

nellwo (1887 Scott 30) = **ne lwo** (with conflated liquid), n + pcl. by you.

ne ˙lol = *ne ˙lul*. ¶*na y ne ˙lol ˙THIK ˙ho˙ya* (1462 [1]Nung 1:90b) I command you ··· .

ne l' tele = **ne tele** to you. CF **na l' tele**.

ne lul < *ne ˙lul*, n + pcl. you. ¶˙*icey ne ˙lul nwo˙ha pwo˙nay˙m ye n'* (1459 Wel 8:98a) now if I send you ··· . *˙na y ˙icey ne ˙lul nwot˙nwo˙n i ˙ptu˙t ul cwo˙cha ka˙la* (1459 Wel 13:19ab) I now send you off to follow your own mind.

neme [< **nem.e** inf < **nēm.ta** go beyond, exceed]; CF **kēnne**. 1. n, postnoun. beyond, over, the other side (of something tall / high); over = more than, in excess of. ¶**cay ~ maul** the village beyond the hill. **cipung neme (lo) poinun tal** the moon seen over the roof. **han tal ~ kellinta** it takes over a month. **Yo neme cengke-cang i iss.ta** There is a station just over on the other side (of / from here).
   2. adverb = **nemu** (overly, too).
nemeq cip, n + n. the house beyond. [DIAL VAR] **nemeyq cip** — CF **nem.eyq cip / san** (1936 Roth 318) the house/mountain beyond.
nemu < *nemwu*, derived adverb < **nēm.ta** < ¨*nem˙ta*. too (much), overly; ever so much. **~ 'na (to), ~ to** SAME. ¶**Nemu 'na to kuliwe** I yearn for you ever so much [from a popular song]. **Tanphung namu nun ku pich-kal i nemu to sen.yen hata; enu ¹yelqsa uy hullin phi 'lye 'n ka** The maples are dyed too deep a red; might it be the blood of some patriot? SYN **neme**; CF **nēmchikey** excessively.
ne 'myen = **ne imyen** if it's you
ne n', abbr < **ne nun**, noun + pcl. (as for) you.
-nen [DIAL] = **-nun** (processive modifier)
ne 'n tul, noun + copula mod + postmodifier.
ne nun < *no ˙non*, n + pcl. (as for) you. ¶*ne ˙non kis˙ke two ˙na non kis˙ti a˙ni ho˙m ye* (1482 Kum-sam 2:5b) you may be happy but I am not, and ... . [*˙NGWEN*] *hon ˙t on ne non [KAN-*˙QALQ] hwo.m ol ¨cyeki ho˙la* (1481 Twusi 8:7a) I would like you to provide a bit of information.
ne 'ta = **ne ita**, noun + copula. it's you.
ne to / twu, noun + particle. you too/even.
ne ˙uy, n + pcl. your; you. ¶*ne ˙uy ˙KAK-˙LYWOW NUNG-TI ˙ho˙nwon mozo˙m i* (1462 ¹Nung 1:66a) your mind that you have enlightened with knowledge. *pi˙lwok ku˙le˙na e˙nu y ne ˙uy ˙CCO-¨KUY ˙Gwo* (?1468- Mong 60a) But which is your [true] self?
ne ˙wa → **ne ˙[G]wa**
ney₁. 1. [< ¨*ne y* < *˙ne ˙i*; CF **nay, cey**].
   1a. you (alt of **ne** when followed by pcl **ka**). ¶**Ney ka hayss.ta** You did it.
   1b. abbr < **ney ka** you [as subject]. ¶**Ney meych sal in ya** How old are you?
   1c. SEE **ney-kkacis**.
   2. abbr < **ne uy** your [< (accent irreg) *ne 'y* = *ne ˙uy*, n + pcl]. ¶**Ney cip i eti 'n ya** Where is your home?
   3. [var] = **nay** (I; my). For such speakers 'you; your' is (**ney** →) **ni** or just **ne**.
   SEE **ney key** = **ne 'ykey; ney-kkacis, ney-nyen, ney-nom**; CF **cey**. Do not confuse with **nay** (despite the variant in 3).
nēy₂ < ¨*ney*, num (alt shape of **nēys** < ¨*neyh* as adnoun). ¶**~ sālam** four people. **chayk ~ kwēn** four books. CF **nē, nēk**.
   ¶¨*ney polo˙m ay* (1447 Sek 24:20b) on the four walls. ¨*ney ka˙ci s ¨SSYWUW-¨KHWO ˙lol ye˙huy˙ye* (1447 Sek 6:4a) escaping the Four Miseries (of birth, age, illness, death). ¨*ney cha˙h in ˙pu˙l ey* (1447 Sek 9:37a) in the fourth fire. ¨*ney cca s ˙KWU non* (1482 Nam 1:15a) the fourth phrase.
nēy₃, interj. yes. ¶**Nēy ālkeyss.ˢup.nita** Yes, I know. DIAL **yēy**. VAR SPELLING **nyey**. CF **nay**.
ney₄ < ˙*ney* (/ ˙*nay*), postnoun [FOLKSY].
   1. the group, all of ··· . This makes an explicit plural for nouns referring to people; it is also used in combination with the synonyms **tul** and **kkili**: **wuli, wuli ney, wuli tul, wuli ney tul, wuli tul ney** we/us. ¶**wuli ney, ce-huy ney we/us** all. **tangsin (ne-huy, caney, sensayng nim) ney** you all. **ku sālam / pun ney** they / them all. **yele pun ney** (ladies and) gentlemen. **ku ney** they / them; [DIAL] he / him. **caki ney kwuntay** one's / their / our own troops.
NOTE: Even explicit plurals sometimes have singular reference, especially as honorifics: **nulk.usin ney** old gentleman, **celm.usin ney** young gentleman, **elusin ney** the gentleman.
   2. (after a name) ··· and his/her relatives. **Poktong(-i) ney** Poktong(-i) and his family.
   3. abbr < ··· **ney (uy) cip** the family of ··· (all). ¶**wuli ney (cip)** our family; my family. **ku sālam ney (cip)** their family; his / her family. **ayki ney kes** (1) the thing(s) of the child's family, the thing(s) of the child and his family; (2) the children's thing(s).
   4. [Ceycwu DIAL] = **uy** 'of' (LSN 1978:2-3, 46); = **ney (uy)** '(of) the group' (Seng ¹Nakswu 184:33). ¶*nu ney emeng* = **ne uy emeni ka** your mother. *nu ney eme' nim* = **ne-huy ney (uy) eme' nim** the mother of you people. *samchwon ney tok* = **samchon uy talk i** my uncle's chicken. *kā ney cip i* = **ku ai uy cip ey** to his/her house.
   CF **tayk-ney, anak-ney**. Do not confuse this with **uy**, despite 3 (and 4).

··· ˙ney, postn. the group, all of ··· . Found after o, oy, aC, ay, uy and i. ¶ [˙PHAN-˙SSO] ney two (1676 Sin.e 1:2b) the judges, too. canoy ney alp.h un (1676 Sin.e 1:4b) ahead of you people. cyey-wang ˙ney ˙psu˙sil ¨pi˙tan ˙two a˙ni ˑ˙mye ˙stwo syang˙nyey ton˙ni˙non ¨pi˙tan a˙ni ˑ˙lwoswo˙n i (ʔ1517- Pak 1:14b) they are not silks for the kings. na˙ku˙nay ˙ney (ʔ1517-¹No 1:20a) travelers. kutuy ˙ney khun il˙hwum il˙Gwu.m un (1481 Twusi 8:55b) the achieving of fame by you people. ˙wuli epe˙zi ˙ney ¨ta ˙mwo˙m i phyen.an ˙ho˙siten ˙ka (ʔ1517- Pak 1:51a) were my parents in good health? VAR (after uy, i, iC) ··· ˙nay. SEE kutuy ˙ney.

ney, var of ne 'you' before ˙uy. SEE ney ˙uy.

ne y = ¨ne y (you [nominative]). ¶ ne 'y ¨es.te 'n salo˙m in ta ([1447→]1562 Sek 3:20a) ← *¨ne y ¨es˙te 'n ¨salo.m in ˙ta what kind of person are you?

ne 'y, abbr < *ne ˙uy. 1. your. ¶ ˙na y ¨a˙lay s ne 'y ¨pe˙t ila˙n i (1447 Sek 6:19b) I was your friend in former days. ne 'y ptu˙t ey n' (1447 Sek 19:34a) to your mind. CIN-˙SSILQ s ne 'y mozo˙m in ˙t ay n' (1462 ¹Nung 2:24b) it being your true intent. ne 'y susu˙ng uy ¨TTYEY-¨CO y (1447 Sek 6:29b) your master's disciple. ne 'y susu˙ng i ˙nwu ˙kwo (1447 Sek 23:41b) who is your master? ne 'y ˙e˙mi (1459 Wel 8:86a) your mother. ne 'y ˙e˙m[i] uy ¨kan ˙sta˙h ol (1459 Wel 21:21b) the land where your mother went. CIN-˙SSILQ s ne 'y mozo˙m in ˙t ay n' (1462 ¹Nung 2:24b) it being your true intent. ne 'y ˙kwo˙h ol (1462 ¹Nung 3:8b) your nose. ne 'y kwo˙h ay ˙sye (1462 ¹Nung 3:24b) in your nose. ne 'y ˙swo˙n i (1475 Nay 1:18ab), ne 'y ˙swon ˙ul (1586 Sohak 6:102b) your hand.

2. you [as subject of adnominalized sentence]. Examples?

˙ne 'y, 1. = ne 'y (your). ¶ ˙ne 'y ¨kyeci˙p i ¨kwo˙Wo.n i ˙ye (1459 Wel 7:10b) is your wife pretty?

2. = ¨ne y (you [nominative]). ¶ ˙ne y ¨cyeku˙na ¨tywokhe˙n ye [← ¨tywoh-ken ˙ye] (ʔ1517- ¹No 2:41a) are you a little better?

¨ne y, abbr < *ne ˙i, n + pcl. you [nominative]. ¶ ¨ne y KA-PPI-LA ˙KWUYK ˙ey ˙ka˙a (1447 Sek 6:1a) you go to the state of Kapila and ··· . ¨ne y na 'y ¨ma˙l ol ¨ta tulul ˙tta (1447 Sek 6:8b) will you then heed my words? ¨ne y ho˙ma mas-˙nazo˙Wa˙n i (1459 Wel 2:62b) you have already faced it. ¨ne y ˙icey ˙two nowoy˙ya ˙nom muyWun ˙ptu˙t ul twul ˙tta ˙ho.yasi˙nol (1459 Wel 2:64a) asked whether even now you still harbor hateful thoughts toward others, whereupon ··· . ¨ne y ye˙le ˙KEP ˙ey cephu˙ti a˙ni hon ke˙kuy cephun mozo˙m ol ¨nay˙m ye ··· (1459 Wel 7:48a) there where for many kalpas (eons) you were unafraid you show a fearful heart and ··· . ¨ne y ¨es.te 'n a˙hoy ˙Gwan˙toy he˙thwuy ˙lol an˙a ¨wunun ˙ta (1459 Wel 8:85b; sic an-˙a) what kind of a child are you to cry, clinging to [the calf of] a leg? ¨ne y ˙i ˙NYEM ˙ul twu-'ys.ten ˙ta a˙ni twu-'ys.ten ˙ta (1459 Wel 9:35c) do you hold this idea or don't you? ¨ne y ˙SIN ˙honon ˙ta a˙ni ˙honon ˙ta (1459 Wel 9:46a) do you believe it or don't you? ¨ne y ˙ka (1459 Wel 18:71b) you go and ··· . ˙CAK-˙PEP hwol ˙tyen ¨ne y ¨i.l i koca za ho˙l i ˑ.n i (1496 ¹Yuk "se:12" = ¹yak-se:4b; there are 8 pages of se, 16 of ¹yak-se) if you would make laws you must do it with affairs all in hand. ¨ne y ˙SWU ˙lol ¨all i ˑ˙lwoswo˙n ye (1459 Wel 21:14a) would you know the number? ¨ne y ˙ka [CHYEY-¨CO] ˙lol ma˙ca ˙woke˙nol (1481 Twusi 8:40a) you go to meet your wife (and come back), but ··· . ¨ne y ZYE-LOY ˙i ˙NYEM ˙ul cizwotoy (1482 Kum-sam 5:14a) you create this idea of the tathāgata. ¨ne y e˙tu˙le ˙lwo ˙sye pu˙the won ˙ta (ʔ1517- ¹No 1:1a) where have you come from? ¨ne y ˙stwo ¨na l' swo˙ki˙ti ¨mal˙Gwo˙l ye (ʔ1517- ¹No 1:18b) now don't you go deceiving me! ¨ne y ˙stwo tyele ˙lwo ˙wo˙na˙la (ʔ1517- ¹No 1:57b) you go there (and come back). ¨ne y ¨encey ˙kil[h] ˙na˙sil ˙kwo (ʔ1517- Pak 1:8b) when are you setting out on the road? ¨ne y palo ¨al˙l i ˑ˙lwoswo˙n ye (ʔ1517- Pak 1:14b) do you understand it correctly? ¨ne y e˙tuy ˙ka is˙ten ˙ta (ʔ1517- Pak 1:37b) where have you been? ¨ne y na 'y ˙e˙mi ˙lul ¨hywo¨yang hol [˙]ta (1518 Sohak-cho 9:55a) will you (be willing to) take care of my mother? ¨ne y a˙chom ˙uy ˙na-˙ka nus.key ˙a wo˙m ye n' ··· (1586 Sohak 4:33a) if you go out in the morning and come [back] only late ··· .

¨ne 'y = ne 'y, abbr < *ne ˙uy. ¶ ¨ne 'y a˙to˙l i (1459 Wel 2:6b) your son.

¨ne 'y···, abbr < *˙ne ˙i··· (n + cop). ¶wo˙cik ˙i ¨ne 'ylwo˙ta (1482 Kum-sam 4:56a) only this is you. ¨ne 'y˙m ye [˙]CYWUNG-SOYNG ˙tol˙h i (1459 Wel 8:5b) you and all living creatures.

A Reference Grammar of Korean

'ney, 1. alt < iney (cop). 2. abbr < haney
-ney, FAMILIAR indic assert [sometimes used in talking to oneself]. is/does (= -ta). ¶khuney it is big. chwup.ney it is cold. mek.ney eats. kaney goes. mek.ess.ney ate. kakeyss.ney will go; probably goes. Wuli sensayng i Kim sensayng isiney My teacher is Mr Kim. Na nun caney lul mit.ney I trust you. CF -ui (NOTE).
-ney (yo), ? abbr < -nun tey (yo). aha, now I see ··· (shows pleasant surprise); rather like -kwun (yo). CF Pak Sengwen 219.
-ney [Hamkyeng, S Kyengsang (Kim Yengpay 1984:96)] = -na (FAMILIAR indic attent)
ne ya, 1. noun + particle. only if it is you.
   2. noun + copula var infinitive. it's you.
ney-amuli, abbr < ney ka āmuli (···) however (···) you may be.
ney ka, 1. n alt [< ˉne y < *ne ˙i n + pcl] + pcl. you [as subject]. VAR ni ka; DIAL ne ka.
   2. [DIAL; Seoul] = nay ka I [as subject].
ne 'ykey, abbr < ne eykey (to you)
ney-kkacis, cpd adn [n + bnd n]. the likes of you, (a person) like you [pejorative]. ¶Ney-kkacis kes hanthey cikeyss.nun ya Never shall I be beaten by a guy like you. Ney-kkacis nom hanthey n' nem.e kaci anh.nunta I shall never be cheated by the likes of you.
ney kkan SEE kkan
ney-kkān SEE kkān
ney lang, postnoun + particle.
   1. = ney sekken and them (all); them and all. ¶Poktong-i ney lang tā manna pwass.ta I ran into Poktong-i and them (all).
   2. = ney hako/wa with them. SYN tul ney lang, ney tul ilang, tul lang.
-ney man, FAMILIAR indic assert + pcl. is/does but.
ne 'yna, [DIAL] = ne 'na (it's you but)
neyntul, [nonstandard] var = ne 'n tul though it be you. CF nayntul, ceyntul.
ne yo, 1. noun + particle. (it's) you.
   2. noun + copula [AUTH] (= ne io) it is you.
ney sekken, postnoun + particle. SEE ney lang.
ne 'y ˉswon-˙toy, n + pcl + pseudo-pcl. ¶ne 'y ˉswon-˙toy ˉNGWO-˙POYK NGUN ˉtwo.n o˙lwo ta˙sos cwul˙ki s LYEN-HWA ˙lol ˙sa˙a (1447 Sek 6:8a) he bought from you five lotus blossoms for five hundred pieces of silver money and ... .
-ney tul, FAMILIAR indic assertive + particle
ney tul lang, postn + postn + pcl = ney lang

ney ˙uy, noun + particle.
   1. (= ne 'y) of you, your. ¶ˉta ney ˙uy cwow-ˉpwu 'y.l i ˙'m ye (1462 ¹Nung 1:60a) all are your scorched entrails, and ... .
   2. you [as the subject of an adnominalized or nominalized sentence] SEE uy 14. ¶ney ˙uy ˙e˙mi ˙ku˙lye ˉhwo˙m i (1459 Wel 21:22a) that you long for [your] mother. ney ˙uy ˉPWON-LOY tet.tetun [= tet-tet hon] kes ul il˙hun cyen˙cho 'yl ˙ss oy (1462 ¹Nung 1:85a) as it is why you have lost your original honorableness. ney [˙]uy [˙NGWOK-SAN] ay s [ˉCHWOW-TTANG] ˙oy [˙CCYEK-˙CCYENG] ˉhwo˙m ol solang ˙honwo˙n i (1481 Twusi 7:32b) I love it that you are so quiet and tranquil in the grass pavilion on the jade mountain. ney ˙uy ˙KAK-˙LYWOW TI-˙KYEN ˙ho˙nwon mozo˙m i (1462 ¹Nung 1:54-5) your mind that you enlighten with knowledge.
-ney yo, 1. FAMILIAR indic assert + pcl (polite). (Occurs but is not accepted by some speakers.)
   2. SEE -ney (yo).
···ng. The velar nasal at the end of several nouns replaces an earlier final h, which usually just vanished. (CF LKM 1968:223:n30.) ttang < ˙stah (˙sta˙thwo = ˙stah ˙two 1447 Sek 6:23b) 'earth', (1459 Wel se:8a, 1:26b) 'a place'. patang (Ceycwu, South Cenla, Hamkyeng) < pa˙tah (pa˙ta˙h ay 1459 Wel 9:22a) 'sea', which also is reflected as patak (S Cenla, S Kyengsang). nalang (Hamkyeng) < na˙lah (na˙la˙h ay 1445 ¹Yong 24) 'land'. nong (Hamkyeng), nongi (northwest DIAL) < nwoh (nwo˙h o˙lwo 1447 Sek 9:10b) 'cord'. (meylq/cilq/kēlq) pang 'strap' < ?*pah = modern pa(q cwul) 'rope, tether', written with the phonogram "pak" in 1103 Kyeylim. Notice also matang 'yard, threshing ground' (from 1748) < *matah > math (ma˙th ol 1481 Twusi 7:18a) and congi 'paper' < cywonghuy (1690 Yek.e 1:25b) = cywonghoy (2:16b) < cywo˙hoy (1446 Hwun 28a) – the form tywohuy in 1894 Gale 168 is odd in more than one way. Hard to explain: mwo˙ya˙h(˙)i (1459 Wel 2:51b) = mwo˙yang < ˙MWOW-˙YANG 'appearance'. King suggests that the second element in words for 'rump' (kwung-/eng-/pang-twungi, kwung-/eng-tengi) may go back to ˉtwuyh 'behind'; but notice also tung 'back' (1445 ¹Yong 88).
-ng, suffix. 1. (a deverbative nominalizer). SEE -ang/-eng, -wung.

2. i/kuleng-celeng = i/kulek-celek somehow or other. SEE -ang, -eng; ˈtwong; -k.

-ng-, infix? (intensive). kangphaluta is very steep [? DIAL] < kaphaluta is steep (?< ka edge + paluta straight + -h-).

-ngi, bnd n. marker of polite style (= -sup- or yo). Only attached to a vowel; consonant-final stems add the modulator -ˑwᵘ/o- so as to have a vowel, or expand the stem to the modifier + the postmodifier ˈi ˈfact', predicated with the contracted copula, to which -ngi is added. But there is a single exceptional example of -ungi: talˑGwom ˑˑepˑs-ungi ˑˑta (1462 ¹Nung 2:9a) 'there is no difference' − CF ˑˑepˑse-ngi ˑˑta (1459 Wel 21:21b), ˑˑepˑke-ngi ˑˑta (1459 Wel 10:8b), ˑˑepˑswu-ngi ˑˑta (1462 ¹Nung 3:117a) ˑˑepta-ngi ˑˑta (1459 Wel 13:37a). In addition, if we treat the bound verb (emotive) -ˑs[o]- as -ˑs-, there are examples of -ongi in -ˑs-ongi ˑˑta, rather than "-ˑso-ngi ˑˑta". But while -no-ngi ˑˑta might be treated as -n-ongi ˑˑta the form with the vowel is preferred because in -no-ˑta the vowel seems to be intrinsic rather than merely epenthetic (see page 716, NOTE 1). [?< *-ngki < *-n ki; CF 'ngki yo]

1. attached to stem. SEE -ngi ˑˑta, -(u)ˑn i '-ngi ˑˑta, -noˑn i '-ngi ˑˑta, -(u)ˑl i '-ngi ˑˑta; -ngi s ˑka, -(u)ˑn i '-ngi s ˑka, -noˑn i '-ngi s ˑka, -(u)ˑl i '-ngi s ˑka; ˑci-ngi ˑˑta; ˑi-ngi s ˑka, ˑi-ngi s ˑkwo, ˑi-ngi ˑˑta.

2. attached to stem + effective, processive, retrospective, or retrospective emotive. SEE -ˑa-ngi ˑˑta, -ˑe-ngi ˑˑta, -ˑGwa-ngi ˑˑta, ˑho.ya-ngi ˑˑta, -ˑke-ngi ˑˑta, -ˑkwa-ngi ˑˑta, -ˑno-ngi ˑˑta, -ˑta-ngi ˑˑta, -ˑte-ngi ˑˑta, -ˑta-ˑso-ngi ˑˑta = -ta-ˑs-ongi ˑˑta.

3. attached to stem + honorific. SEE -uˑsi-ngi ˑˑta.

4. attached to stem + modulator. SEE -ˑwo-ngi ˑˑta, -ˑwu-ngi ˑˑta.

5. SEE -ˑsa-ngi ˑˑta.

6. ˑˑmwolˑlay-ngi ˑˑta (1459 Wel 21:53a) 'I do not know' is probably from ˑˑmwolˑla-ngi ˑˑta (1459 Wel 21:27a; the second vowel assimilated to the third) < *mwoˑl[o]l-ˑGa-ngi ˑˑta.

-ngi s ˑka, polite marker + pcl + postmodifier. ¶aˑhwop HHWOYNG-ˑˑsoˑnon muˑsuˑk i-ngi s ˑka (1447 Sek 9:35b) what are the nine unnatural deaths?

-ngi ˑˑta, polite marker + cop indic assert. ¶CIN-ˑSSILQ s ˑˑCYWU-ZINˑonˑˑce y ˑˑkalqˑkwotˑˑep-ˑtos ho-ngi ˑˑta (1462 ¹Nung 1:105b) it appears that the true master has no place to go himself. kwoˑc iˑphu-ˑtosˑho-ngi ˑˑta (1463 Pep 1:85b) the flowers seem in bloom. SEE -uˑsi-ngi ˑˑta.

-ngkkay [DIAL (Mkk 1960:3:35)] = -ni-kka

'ngki yo [DIAL] = 'nun ke(s) (i)yo.
SEE -ullangki yo.

-ng' ˑˑta, abbr < -ngi ˑˑta. SEE '-ng' ˑˑta, -uˑn i '-ng' ˑˑta.

'-ng' ˑˑta, 1. abbr < ˑho-ngi ˑˑta. ¶kuˑli aˑni '-ng' ˑˑta (1447 Sek 6:16a) No(, I am not doing that). 2. SEE -uˑn i '-ng' ˑˑta.

'ni, 1. abbr (alt) < ini (cop). 2. abbr < hani.
3. → -n i

ni [var] = ney (you/your)

'/-n i, 1. < in i < ˑiˑn i. SEE in i ('la).
2. < han i. 3. < -un i

ˑˑn i, 1. abbr < hoˑn i.

2. = '[y]ˑn i, abbr < ˑiˑn i (copula mod + postmod) after i or y. ¶ˑˑTYWUWˑnun pol[h] s moˑˑtoy ˑn i (1459 Wel 10:118a) the "elbow" is the joint of the arm. ˑkapsˑˑep.sun kwuˑsu.l unˑˑpwo[ˑ]poyˑyey sˑˑpwo[ˑ]poy ˑn i (1482 Nam 1:33a) the priceless jewel is a treasure among treasures. ˑPHEN-ˑYEKˑhoˑyaˑwonanˑt i koˑzuy ˑPALQ-ˑPOYKˑhoy ˑn i (1463 Pep se:21a) it is now almost 800 years since it was translated. SEE aˑni ˑˑn i.

-ni, indicative attentive. is it? does it? ¶mek.ni (mek.ess.ni, mek.keyss.ni)? does (did, will) one eat? kani (kass.ni, kakeyss.ni)? does (did, will) one go? nuc.ni? will you be late? cōh.ni? is it good? nappuni? is it bad? CF -un (-nun etc.) ya/i. [?< (1) -n i, (2) -nu'y < -nun i]

-ni, alt after vowel of -uni (sequential)

-ˑni- < °niˑta (goes). Attached to certain verb stems, with the meaning of a movement or a motion that is attenuated or extended. Some of the later versions have -nil-.

ˑˑetˑniˑta keeps looking for (seeking).

ˑhoˑniˑta (1447 Sek se:1b, se:2b; 1459 Wel 7:31b; 1462 ¹Nung 7:65b; ?1468- Mong 27a) acts, moves.

ˑˑketˑniˑta (1447 Sek 6:20b, 1449 Kok 16) > ˑˑkenniˑta (1481 Twusi 22:9ab, 22:38b) > kēnilta strolls.

kuwuˑniˑta (1447 Sek 9:27b, 1462 ¹Nung 9:47b, 1463 Pep 2:131a, ...) keeps rolling.

ˊna˙niˑta (1459 Wel 17:16b) gads about.
noˑniˑta (1459 Wel 2:33a, 1481 Twusi 21:14b) flies around.
¨nwo[ˑ]niˑta (1445 ¹Yong 52; 1447 Sek 6:24a, 19:19a; 1459 Wel 2:22a; 1462 ¹Nung 1:3b; ...) > nōnilta strolls.
¨saˑniˑta (1447 Sek 6:5a, 1459 Wel 8:86a) goes on living.
¨two[ˑ]niˑta (1447 Sek 9:1a, 1459 Wel 23:78b, 1482 Kum-sam 5:9b) > tōnilta walks around, circles.
totˑniˑta (1445 ¹Yong 113, 1447 Sek 6:16a, 1459 Wel 1:14b, 1462 ¹Nung 5:63b, ...) > tonˑniˑta (1459 Wel 9:61b, 1462 ¹Nung 1:86a, 1481 Twusi 7:24a, ...) > tanita goes around.
¨wuˑniˑta (1459 Wel 8:87b) > wunilta goes around crying, keeps weeping.
-ˑn i SEE -uˑn i
-ˑn i ˑGa SEE -uˑn i ˑGa
-ˑn i ˑGwo SEE -uˑn i ˑGwo
ni ka, [var] = ney ka (you).
ˑniˑke-, effective of °niˑta (goes).
ˑnikeˑla (effective subj attent). ¶ esye twoˑla ˑnikeˑla (1459 Wel 8:101a) please go back.
ˑniˑkesiˑn i (effective honorific modifier + postmod). ¶ ¨aˑlay ˑkasin ˑPALQ ¨CHOY-¨NYE ˑtwo ˑniˑkesiˑn i mu[ˑ]su.k i ¨skelWuˑl i '-ngi s ˑkwo (1459 Wel 8:93ab) the eight comely maidens who have gone below (there), what difficulties must they too have had in going?
ˑniˑkesiˑtun (hon provisional). ¶[TWONG] ˑoy ˑniˑkesiˑtun (1445 ¹Yong 38) when he went to the east ... .
ˑnikeˑnol (lit concessive). ¶ ˑkaps ¨epˑsun ¨PWO-CYWU ˑlu (?= ˑlwo, ?= ˑlul) wos ¨swoˑp ay moyˑya cwuˑkwo ˑnikeˑnol (1463 Pep 4:37b) lined his clothes with priceless jewels before setting off.
ˑniˑke, effective inf < °niˑta. ¶ na y ˑnikeˑci-ngi 'ˑta ˑkaˑsya (1445 ¹Yong 58) saying "I must go" he went. NGWUY-TTYEY-HUY ¨CHYENG ˑhozoˑWa ˑCCYENG-¨THWO ˑay ˑnikeˑci-ngi 'ˑta (1459 Wel 8:1a) Vaidehī wishes (= wished) to go to the Pure Land. ku ˑaˑki nilˑkwup ¨sel meˑke aˑpi pwoˑla ˑniˑke ciˑla honˑt ay (1459 Wel 8:101b) at the age of eight the lad said he wanted to go see his father, and ... .
niˑke, inf < nikˑta (gets ripe). 1459 Wel 2:12a, ?1468- Mong 10a.
-nikka SEE -sup.nikka

'/-ni-kka (n', nun), 1. alt after vowel of -uni-kka (n', nun) (extended adversative).
2. abbr (alt) < ini-kka (n', nun).
3. abbr < hani-kka (n', nun).
nik.keˑta, effective indic assert < nikta (gets ripe). ¶ i kwoˑki nik.keˑta (?1517- ¹No 1:22a) this meat is well done = i kwoki nik.eta (1795 ¹No-cwung [P] 1:20a).
niˑkye, inf < niˑkiˑta (ripens it; trains). ¶ ¨salom ¨maˑta ¨hoyˑGye ¨swuˑWuy niˑkye (1451 Hwun-en 3b) letting everyone learn it easily.
'n i ('la) SEE in i ('la)
-nila = -nita (= -ta)
-ˑn i ''la, mod + postmod + cop indic assert. SEE hoˑn i ''la, -uˑn i ''la, -uˑsi[ˑ]n i ''la.
'.n i ''la = 'i.n i ''la, cop mod + postmod + copula indic assert. ¶mo¨toy '.n i ''la (?1468- Mong 43b) it means 'node'. SEE aˑni '.n i ''la.
¨nilm < *niˑl[u]m, subst < ¨ni[l]ˑta (> ilta).
¶ ¨nilˑm ye (1449 Kok 172) arises and ... .
nilo, nilu (?< verb stem nilol- 'reach'), adverb. possibly, can. ¨mwot ~ (+ V), ~ (V-ˑti) ¨mwot °ho- cannot possibly do, can't very well do. SYN eˑlwu, eˑlwo, siˑle, nungˑhi.
(-)nilta, vi. -L-. 1. [obs] = ilta (arises). CF kwumnilta = kwupq-ilta.
2. bnd vi (< -ˑni-). kē-nilta strolls (< kēt-/kēl- walk). na-nilta hovers (< na-l- fly). nō-nilta ramble about (< nō-l- play); tō-nilta walks around (< tō-l- revolve). CF tanita (< tat-/tal- run + nita go).
nim (< ¨nim), 1. n = im [poetic] one's beloved; [obs] you; [obs] your majesty (CF īm-kum < ¨nim-kum king).
2. postn (makes titles, kin or role terms, and names honorific). esteemed ... .
2a. (titles) sensayng ~ respected teacher/maestro; you sir. cwuin ~ my honorable master; you sir. sinpu ~ Reverend Father. moksa ~ Reverend. su' (< sung) ~ Buddhist teacher/master priest. īm-kum ~ Your/His Majesty. paksa ~ esteemed doctor. samo ~ madam, lady; you ma'am; one's teacher's wife. hanu' ~, [Christian] hana' ~ God.
2b. (kinterms) hyeng ~ esteemed elder brother; you. pumo ~ esteemed parents. atu' ~ your son (atul). tta' ~ your daughter (ttal). ape' ~ esteemed father (apeci, api). eme' ~ esteemed mother (emeni, emi). hal-ape' ~ esteemed grandfather (hal-apeci). hal-

'me' ~ esteemed grandmother (hal-'meni, hal-'mi).

2c. (role terms) son ~ honored guest.

2d. (names) Kongca ~ Confucius, Mayngca ~ Mencius, Sek.ka Yelay ~ (Lord) Buddha. Yēyswu ~ (Lord) Jesus. Se Poki ~ Mr S. P.

NOTE: The dropping of l before n is no longer productive, and all newer formations restore the liquid: congtal nim a O skylark! (congtal say = congtali). posal nim /posallim/ 'venerable nun; bodhisattva'. tal nim /tallim/ 'the moon' — earlier also ta' nim (KEd) < ˙to[l] ˙˙nim (1459 Wel 2:51b). tal nala /tallala/ (the realm of) the moon. hanul nala /hanullala/ '(the realm of) heaven'. atul nom /atullom/ 'my (rascal of a) son', onul nal /onullal/ 'these days, nowadays'.

-˙n i ˙-ngi s ˙ka, alt after vowel of -ᵘ⁄ₒ˙n i ˙-ngi s ˙ka, mod + postmod + cop polite + pcl + postmod.

-˙n i ˙-ngi ˙˙ta, alt after vowel of -ᵘ⁄ₒ˙n i ˙-ngi ˙˙ta, mod + postmod + cop polite + cop indic assert.

°ni˙ta = °nye˙ta = ¨nyey˙ta, vi. goes (= °ka˙ta; it is unclear whether these four stems differ slightly in meaning). The verb °ni- is usually in an effective form (SEE °ni˙ke-), but ˙nye could be taken to be the convergence of its simple infinitive (as opposed to the effective infinitive ˙ni˙ke) with that of °nye˙ta (for which the effective infinitive is ˙nye˙a): SEE ˙nye.

NOTE: This stem survives in dialect forms, e.g. Phyengan nika la < ˙nika˙la 'go!' (Kim Yengpay 1984:102).

'n i tul, 1. = in i tul (1, 2). 2. = han i tul

-n i tul SEE -un i tul

-ni tul, subj attent + pcl. ¶Cikum ay tul ī-chung ey se kongpu hani tul? Are the children studying upstairs now?

-˙n i ˙n ˙t ye SEE -˙wo.n i ˙n ˙t ye

'/-n ka SEE in ka, -un ka. ~ pᵒ⁄ᵤta, ~ p(w)ā; ~ ka / lul / nun / to / ... .

'n ˙ka, abbr < ˙yn ˙ka, cop mod + postmod. SEE a˙ni ˙n ˙ka.

'n ka ka, cop modifier + postmodifier + pcl. ¶Nwukwu 'n ka ka ku lul kyēngchal ey pōko hayss.keyss.ci yo Someone must have reported him to the police.

'/-n ka 'm SEE in ka 'm, -un ka 'm

'n ka tul, 1. = in ka tul. 2. = han ka tul

-n ka tul SEE -un ka tul

'/-n ke l' SEE -n ke l', -un ke l'

'/-n kes SEE in kes, -un kes

'/-n key SEE in key, -un key

'/-n ko SEE in ko, -un ko

-n kwani, abbr < -n ko hani

-no [-n' 'o], abbr < -nun ko (question)

-(˙)n[o]- > -n(u)- / -nun-, processive aspect. LCT 1973:335 says that one use of this was to emphasize a fact and in that meaning it attached to adjective stems as well as verb stems. There are examples with is- 'exist' and ¨eps- 'lack', but each of these stems is uniquely classified as ambivalent with respect to processive versus descriptive. Other examples may involve a stem that functions both as adjective ('is ··· ') and as vi ('becomes'), like kwut- 'is/becomes hard' in the recognized case of kwutno˙n i (1465 Wen 2:2:105b, 1482 Kum-sam 2:29b) and kwutno˙n i ˙-'i ˙˙ta (1586 Sohak 4:53b). It is unclear whether this explanation can be extended to ye˙lum hano˙n i (1445 ¹Yong 2) 'its fruit is [? becomes] plentiful', polk˙ti ¨mwot ˙ho˙non cyen˙cho˙lwo (1462 ¹Nung 1:77b) 'because it is not [? does not become] clear', e˙tuwu˙lak twolwo ˙hoyno˙n i (1481 Twusi 7:14b) 'it is [? gets] dark and then again it is [? gets] light again', and ZYE-LOY ˙kot˙copno˙n i ˙˙la (1462 ¹Nung 2:45a) 'is [? becomes] like the tathāgata' — CF ˙kotco˙wo˙n i (1463 Pep 2:227a). Perhaps LCT's interpretation will help explain the coexistence of ¨ep˙sun / ¨ep˙non and isin / is.non and the development of the unique classes in the modern language with the survival of only some of the forms (ēps.ta but ēps.nun), and the emergence of iss.nunta 'stays' in contrast with iss.ta 'exists, is; has'.

NOTE 1: This probably came from a bound verb (˙)n-, to which the vowel was attached as epenthesis; CF the emotive (˙)s- and *(˙)t-. But the form -no-˙ta, which would not call for an epenthetic vowel, forces us to treat the MK basic form as (˙)no-. The modern -n(un)-ta < -no-˙ta, which makes a statement, is a new formation unconnected with the MK -non˙ta (proc mod + postmod) and -(o)n˙ta (mod + postmod), which ask a question.

NOTE 2: The processive is mutually exclusive with the effective -˙ke- and retrospective -˙te-.

noa = no[h.]a, inf < noh.ta. ABBR nwā.
noh.a twuta₁, cpd vt (vt inf + aux v sep).
   1. lays, puts, leaves (behind).
   2. leaves/lets alone, lets it be.
noh.a twuta₂, cpd aux v sep. SEE -e ~.
noh.ita, vp < noh.ta. ABBR nōyta.
noh.ta₁, vt [inf noh.a > noa, nowa, nwā]. CF neh.ta, twuta.
   1. puts, places, lays, sets; puts aside (for a moment). ¶swul ul ~ puts down one's spoon = finishes a meal; dies.
   2. lets go/off, releases. ¶māl ul ~ relaxes one's speech, talks plainly, dispenses with honorifics.
   3. frees, sets free, sets at large, lets/casts loose, unleashes, releases, liberates, sets at liberty; relieves oneself of (worry).
   4. (pul ul ~) sets (fire to), makes (a fire).
   5. fires, shoots, discharges (a gun, fireworks).
   6. puts in (as an intermediary); uses (a person as an agent).
   7. keeps, raises, rears (animals, silkworms).
   8. sows, plants, grows, cultivates (melons or cucumbers).
   9. (tech ul ~) sets (a trap).
   10. (chim ul ~) applies (a needle, acupuncture).
   11. (swū lul ~) does (embroidery).
   12. reckons, figures, calculates, computes; adds (a number); estimates
   13. (kaps ul ~) bids, names, offers (a price).
   14. (cēnpo lul ~) sends (a telegram).
   15. (tōn / pic ul ~) lends, loans (at interest).
   16. (sok.lyek ul ~) applies, puts on (speed).
   17. installs, puts in (a hypocaust, a telephone, a railroad, a bridge).
   18. puts / mixes in (food ingredients).
   19. = twuta: puts into, adds (to); stuffs/pads with. (os ey) ⋯ ul ~ pads (a garment) with ⋯.
   20. = twuta: (cāngki lul ~ / patwuk ul ~) plays (chess/checkers).
noh.ta₂, aux v sep. SEE -e noh.ta.
-noita < -ˊnwoˊ-iˊta < -ˊnwo-ngiˊˊta [obs] = -naita. Used of first person only (CM 1:285).
-ˊno-'iˊta, abbr < -ˊno-ngiˊˊta, proc polite + cop indic assert. ¶wang-ˊwoˊwaˊsˊnoˊ-iˊˊta (?1517- Pak 1:59a) I, Wáng Wǔ, am here.
nōl(q), 1. < ˙nwol(q) < *nwoˊ[lo]l(q), prosp modifier < nōlta < ˙nwo[l]ˊta.
   2. = nōˊl(q), abbr < noh.ul(q).

nol(q) < *nof'lo]l(q), prosp modifier < no[l]ˊta (flies). ¶nolq cywungsoyngˊiˊla (1459 Wel 21:113a) they are flying creatures. nolq tolaˊmiˊˊGwo (1462 Nung 8:119b) is a flying squirrel and ... .
-nola < -ˊnwoˊla, [lit]. Used for the first person only (1936 Roth 237; CF 1916 Gale 60).
   1. = -nula: ~ ko. ~ ˊmyen. ~ ˊni = -ulye hani(-kka).
   2. = -(nu)nta; -ta (after iss-, ēps-, -keyss-, -ess-). ¶mek.nola = mek.nunta. kanola = kanta. iss.nola = iss.ta. ēps.nola = ēps.ta.
   SEE -keyss.nola, -ess.nola. CF -tota, ilota.
-nola ˊney = -nola [ha]ney, [lit]. ¶San ey se sānun sāy nun kkoch i cōh.a san ey se sānola ˊney [= sānta ˊney] The birds living in the mountains live in the mountains because they like the flowers, they say — a poem.
nol.i, derived noun < nōlta. 1. noun.
   1a. (= nol.um nol.i) merrymaking. ¶pul ~ fireworks. nol.iq kwun a merrymaker.
   1b. an outing, an excursion, a junket, a picnic. ¶kkoch ~ kata goes out to view the blossoms. payq ~ kata goes boating.
   1c. a game. yuch ~ the Four Stick game.
   2. postn. (at) the approximate height (level) of ⋯. ¶kasum ~ (at) the level of one's chest, chest-deep/high. heliq ~ (at) the level of one's waist, waist-deep/high. kwanca ~ ("hat-string, ring level" =) the temples of the head. CF tol.i.
nolm < *noˊl[o]m, substantive < no[l]ˊta (flies). ¶nolˊm ye (1462 ¹Nung 4:26a). CF noˊlwom
nōlm < ˙˙nwolm < *nwoˊl[o]m, subst < nōlta < ˙˙nwo[l]ˊta. CF nwoˊlwom, nol.um.
nōlta < ˙˙nwo[l]ˊta, 1. vi. plays; enjoys oneself; visits; makes merry; relaxes; is idle, jobless, not in use; is loose, is unstable, wobbles.
   2. vt. plays (a game).
nol.um, noun [derived substantive < nōlta].
   1. (= ~ nol.i) merrymaking, play, a spree.
   2.→ nōl.um (usually spelled nōlum) gaming, gambling. 3. = nolus
nolus < nwoˊlos, 1. quasi-free n. a job, work, duty, function, an office, a place, a part, a role, a profession, an occupation. ¶kulen ~ a role of that sort. sensayng ~ a teaching job, teaching. sensayng ~ hata teaches, does teaching. kansa ~ hata acts as a manager, performs the duties of manager. uysa ~ ul

hata practices medicine. **kongmu-wen ~ ul hata** works as a civilian. **Chwunhyang-i ~ hata** takes/acts/plays/performs the part/role of Chwunhyang(-i). **ttwucayngi ~ ul hanta** pimps, panders. **ip ~ (ul) hata** has a bite to eat, eats, munches. **Talun māl uy tāysin nolus ul hanta** It functions as a substitute for some other word. **Ce nun cey nolus to mōs hay yo** (M 1:2:87) I am not worth my salt; I am not keeping up my end (of things). SYN **kwusil**. CF **cīs, nol.um**.

2. postmodifier. (= **hyengphyen**) situation, circumstance; a matter (of ...).

2a. ¶**Cham kwīsin i kok hal nolus in tey** How strange! ("it is like a ghost crying out"; M 1:2:82).

2b. **~ i** but (= **kes i**). ¶**Yele salam i kath.i onta 'tun nolus i na man okey toyess.ta** We were supposed to come together as a group, but as it turned out I came all alone.

no᾿lwom, modulated subst < **no[l]᾿ta** (flies). ¶**kulye᾿ki ᾿non ᾿SOYNG-᾿PUK ᾿ey no᾿lwo.m ol solang ho᾿kwo** (1482 Kum-sam 2:6b) the wild goose loves to fly to the cold north.

nom < ᾿nwom, noun.

1. [vulgar, pejorative] damn fellow, guy, wretch, trash, so-and-so, S.O.B.; damn thing. ¶**Nom tul i kulen ke(y) ᾿ci!** Those damn guys did that! **Nom-nyen** (or **Nyen-nom**) **tul i motwu pelus i ēps.ta ᾿n māl ia** The bastards and bitches (or bitches and bastards) have no manners, any/none of them. **i/yo ~** this damn guy. **ku/ko ~** that damn guy. **ce/co ~** that damn guy (there). Not used of women; var < NAM 'man'. CF **nyen**.

2. [DIAL] = **nam** (others; ...)

nom (before ᾿**oy**) ← ᾿**nom**. ¶**no᾿m oy na᾿la[h] s ᾿ku᾿l ul ce ᾿y na᾿la[h] s ᾿kul ᾿lwo kwo᾿thye ᾿ssul ᾿ss i᾿la** (1447 Sek se:6a) it is a matter of translating the writing of another nation into writing of one's own nation. **no᾿m oy ᾿kye᾿cip** (1463 Pep 2:28b) another man's wife. **no᾿m oy ci[p] s ᾿tam ᾿tol[h]** (?1517- Pak 1:9b) the walls of his house. KAN-NAN **ho᾿n i ᾿uy no᾿m oy ᾿pwo᾿poy ᾿hyey᾿ywom kot ᾿᾿ta** (1465 Wen 3:3: 1:62a) it is like a poor man's counting another man's treasures. **no᾿m oy sa᾿wona᾿won ᾿il ᾿lan** (1518 Sohak-cho 8:15a; **no᾿m oy** is smudged) the bad deeds of others. **no᾿m oy ᾿wos kwa ᾿il᾿Gen ku᾿lu᾿s ul na᾿mola᾿ti ᾿mal.m ye** (1475 Nay 1:9a) does not rebuke others for their attire or the mistakes they have made, ... **no᾿m oy kungey pu᾿the sa᾿lwo᾿toy** (1447 Sek 6:5a) I attach my life to another. **no᾿m oy key PWO-᾿SI hol ᾿s i᾿la** (1465 Wen se:77a; sic, PWO-᾿SI = ᾿PWO-SI) one should give alms to others. **no᾿m oy ci᾿zwun nye᾿lu᾿m ul** (1447 Sek 24:22a) fruits that others have grown. **no᾿m oy ᾿᾿cywong ᾿i᾿la ho᾿n i ᾿no᾿m on ᾿nwu᾿kwu** (?1468- Mong 20b) you said he is the slave of another; who is the other?

᾿**nom** (→ **nom** before ᾿**oy**) > **nam**, n. a person other than you; another (person), (other) people, others; the other fellow(s); he/him, ?she/her. ¶᾿**cokyay ᾿᾿a᾿losyam ᾿kwa ᾿nom ᾿᾿a᾿losyam ᾿kwa** (1465 Wen 1:1:2:37a) that he knows and that others know. ᾿**nom kolo᾿chye tut᾿key khe᾿na ᾿cey tinike᾿na** (1459 Wel 17:33b) whether letting others hear the teaching or observing it oneself ... . ᾿**nom ᾿᾿ep.si᾿Gwu᾿nun ᾿᾿sa᾿lo.m i᾿la** (1459 Wel 2:46a) is a person who scorns others. ᾿**nom muyWun ᾿ptu᾿t ul** (1459 Wel 2:64a) hateful thoughts toward others. ᾿**nom ᾿WUY ᾿ho᾿ya** (1459 Wel 17:54a) for the sake of others. ᾿**nom to᾿lye nilu᾿ti a᾿ni ᾿hote᾿tun** (1447 Sek 19:34ab) I did not tell the others but ... . ᾿**no᾿m i wolo᾿l i ᾿-ngi s ᾿ka** (1445 [1]Yong 48) could any other climb [such cliffs]? ᾿**nom ᾿i ᾿na᾿a kan ᾿t ol ᾿POYK-᾿SYENG ᾿tol᾿h i ᾿nom ᾿ol ᾿᾿ta cwo᾿cho᾿n i** (1449 Kok 11) though the others [the four sons of the second wife, who are good] go forth, yet the people follow the OTHER ones [the four sons of the first wife, who are bad].

᾿**nom ᾿kwa talo᾿sya** (1445 [1]Yong 51) it was different from others. **ce ᾿[G]wa ᾿nom ᾿kwa ᾿lol ᾿ecu᾿lye** (1447 Sek 9:16b) dizzying self and others.

᾿**no᾿m ol ᾿᾿ep᾿siGwul ᾿ss ol nil ᾿Gwo᾿toy** (1463 Pep 1:172b) it means that one scorns others.

᾿**no.m o᾿lan pwun᾿pyel a᾿ni ᾿khwo** (1447 Sek 13:36a) not thinking of others but ... .

᾿**no᾿m on** [KWU-SYWUW] ᾿**y᾿la khe᾿nul** ... , ᾿**no᾿m on cwu᾿kywu᾿l ye khe᾿nul** ... (1445 [1]Yong 77) people thought him an enemy but ... , people wanted to kill them but ... .

nōm, 1. → **nōlm**, substantive < **nōlta**.

2. = **nō'm**, abbr < **noh.um**, substantive < **noh.ta**.

-nomayla [obs] = **-nola**; = **-nun kwun a**.

non < **noˈ[ˈlo]n*, modifier < *no[l]ˈta* (flies). Example?
ˈ*non*, pcl (= **nun**). ¶ *na ˈnon epeˈzi yeˈhuyˈGwo* (1447 Sek 6:5a) I leave my parents and ... . ˈCYEY ˈ*non ˈkul ciˈzul ˈss iˈn i* (1451 Hwun-en 1a) the word ˈCYEY means to make letters. *kuliˈmey ˈnon ˈmuˈl ey s ˈtoˈl ol niloˈsi.n i ˈˈla* (1462 ¹Nung 2:84b) the image portrayed the moon on the water. VAR (after *e, u, wu, wuy*) ˈ*nun*. NOTE: The MK particle attached to the "free" forms of such nouns as *namwo / namk ...*, *pwulmwu / pwulmk ...*, *yezo / yezG ...*, *holo / holl ...* : *namwo ˈnon* (1481 Twusi 6:41a) 'the tree', *pwulmwu ˈnun* (1465 Wen 1:1:2:17b) 'the bellows', *yezo ˈnon* (1463 Pep 2:111b) 'the fox'. But also *namˈk on* (1445 ¹Yong 2) 'the tree', *holˈl on* (1459 Wel 2:51a) 'one day' with the "bound" forms.

-(ˈ)*non*, proc mod (= **-nun**). ¶*pwuthye s ˈkuy ˈlwo ˈkanon ceˈk uy* (1447 Sek 6:19a) when going to Buddha. ˈMANG *hon ˈptoy cel-ˈlwo ¨epˈnon cyenˈcho ˈlwo* (1462 ¹Nung 1:77-8) because naturally there is no unseemly dirt. ZIN-KAN ˈSYEY ˈ*yey s ˈkhi [ˈ]psunon keˈs i.m ye* (1482 Kum-sam 2:17b) is a thing greatly used in/by the human world, and ... . VAR (after *e, u, wu*) -(ˈ)*nun*. SEE ˈ*ho(ˈ)non*.

nōn, 1. < ¨*nwon* (example?) < **nwoˈ[lo]n*, mod < nōlta < ¨*nwo[l]ˈta*.
  2. nōˈn, abbr < noh.un.

-ˈ*no-ngi ˈˈta*, proc polite + cop indic assertive. ¶KKWU-TTAM ˈ*oy* ¨TTYEY-¨CO *y twuˈli ye* ¨*mwot woˈno-ngi ˈˈta* (1447 Sek 6:29b) the disciple of Gautama is afraid and won't come. SEE -*usiˈno-ngi ˈˈta*.

-**noni** < -ˈ*nwoˈn i*, [lit, DIAL] = **-uni(-kka)**, sequential [? with verbs only].
nōni, 1. sequential < nōlta.
  2. = nō'ni, abbreviation < noh.uni. ¶Kulay nō'ni(-kka) ecci an aphukeyss.ni When you do things like that how can you expect it not to hurt?!

-ˈ*noˈn i*, processive modifier + postmodifier.
  1. (epitheme extruded from the subject). the one that does ... . ¶*tay pehino.n i n' nwu 'y atol Gwo* (1632 Twusi-cwung 1:23a) whose boy is it that is cutting bamboo?
  2. (epitheme from the object). Examples?
  3. (summational epitheme). See next entries.
  4. (summational epitheme used in extended predicates). it is [the case] that it / one does. ¶*pwulˈhwuy kiˈphun namˈk on poloˈm ay aˈni* ¨*mwuylˈss oy kwoc* ¨*tywoˈkhwo* [= ¨*tywoh-ˈkwo*] *yeˈlum hanoˈn i* (1445 ¹Yong 2) the tree with deep roots, because it does not sway in the wind, bears good blossoms and much fruit. ˈ*icey ˈstwo naˈy aˈtoˈl ol toˈlye* ¨*kaˈl ye ˈhoˈsinoˈn i* (1447 Sek 6:5b) and now you want to take my son away, in addition. ... *pwuthye s ˈkuy patcoˈWa muˈsum ˈhwo.l ye ˈhoˈsinoˈn i* (1459 Wel 1:10b) [he asks] what do you want to do in presenting them [= the blossoms] to Buddha? ¨*man hi tutˈtolwok* ¨*etwuk* ˈSIN *thi aˈni ˈhonoˈn i* (1482 Nam 1:36b) the more I hear the less I believe.

~ ˈˈ*la*. ¶*cyangˈchos ˈpwoˈ[z]owol ˈtos ˈhoˈno.n i ˈˈla* (1586 Sohak 2:25a) we are likely to see him in the future. ˈCING-¨CHYWU ˈ*yey ˈza piˈluse* ¨NGA-¨THYEY ˈ*lol naˈthwoˈno.n i ˈˈla* (1465 Wen 2:3:1:25a) not until a person attains the truth through substantiation does he manifest the form of the ego.

-ˈ*noˈn i* ˈ*Ga*, proc mod + postmod + postmod (= ˈ*ka*). does it? is it doing? ¶*[HHYWEN-¨PHWO SAN] ˈi ˈmuyye ˈtye ˈwa ˈs.noˈn i [ˈ]Ga* (1481 Twusi 16:29b) has Mystery Garden Mountain become cracked?

-ˈ*noˈn i* ˈ*Gwa*, proc mod + postmod + pcl. does but/and (even more). ¶ZYE-LOY *s* ¨SSYANG ˈ*olˈi s yangˈco ˈlwo* KWONG-¨YANG ˈ*hoˈzopnoˈn i* ˈ*Gwa* (1447 Sek 23:4a) contribute an image of the tathāgata in the form of this, and ... . ˈ*kul lwo aˈlwom* ¨*samˈno.n i* ˈ*Gwa* (1465 Wen 1:1:1:89b) we turn knowledge into writings, and ... . ¨*nwoˈphi* ¨*miˈno.n i* ˈ*Gwa* (1465 Wen 1:1:1:89b) pushes them higher and ... .

-ˈ*noˈn i* ˈ*Gwo*, proc mod + postmod + postmod (= ˈ*kwo*). does it? ¶ ¨*es.tyey siˈle-kwom [HE-KHWONG] ˈswo.k ay s ˈwulGey non [QIN-QIN] ˈhi ˈsta[h] s [ˈMOYK] ˈol ˈchos.noˈn i Gwo* (1481 Twusi 7:24b) how can the thunder within the void seek out the vein of the earth?

-ˈ*noˈn i ˈ-ˈi ˈs ˈkwo* = -ˈ*noˈn i ˈ-ngi s ˈkwo*. ¶*muˈseˈs ol* ¨SO ˈ*hoˈnoˈn i ˈ-ˈi s ˈkwo* (1588 Mayng 13:26b) what is the matter?

-ˈ*noˈn i ˈ-ˈi ˈˈta* = -ˈ*noˈn i ˈ-ngi ˈˈta*. ¶*wuˈkhwa* [← *wuhˈkwa*] *aˈlay* NUNG ˈ*hi selu kwutnoˈn i ˈ-ˈi ˈˈta* (1586 Sohak 4:53b) the top and the bottom they both become fairly solid. *kuli niluˈopno.n i ˈ-ˈi ˈta* (1676 Sin.e 3:13a) says so.

-ˈno ˈn i ˈˈla, proc mod + postmod + cop indic assertive. ¶ˈcip ˈan[h] s ¨ˈsalo.m ol ¨ˈta ˈKWEN-ˈSSYWOK ˈiˈla ˈhoˈno.n i ˈˈla (1447 Sek 6:5b) all of the people of a household are called a family. nulˈkun namˈk un koˈcang seˈli lol [¨]ti[¨]nay[ˈ]ye ˈys.no.n i ˈla (1481 Twusi 7: 10a) the old tree has been through severe frost.
-ˈnoˈn i ˈ-ngi sˈka, proc mod + postmod + cop polite + pcl + postmod. SEE -uˈsinoˈn i ˈ-ngi sˈka, -ˈnoˈn i sˈka.
-ˈnoˈn i ˈ-ngi sˈkwo, proc mod + postmod + cop polite + pcl + postmod. ¶muˈsuˈk ul ¨TTWOW ˈyˈla ˈhonoˈn i ˈ-ngi sˈkwo (1459 Wel 9:23-4) what do you say is the Way? es.tyey ho.yaton pwuthye towoyno.n i ˈ-ngi s kwo (1569 Chiltay 21a) just how does one become a Buddha? SEE -uˈsinoˈn i ˈ-ngi sˈkwo.
-ˈnoˈn i ˈ-ngi ˈˈta, proc mod + postmod + cop polite + cop indic assert. ¶MWU-ˈQWUY ˈlol ˈSI ˈhoˈno.n i ˈˈla ˈhonoˈn i ˈ-ngi ˈˈta (1462 ¹Nung 6:43a) they say he dispenses abhaya (fearless confidence). ˈpam ˈkwa ˈnac ˈkwa ¨YEN-ˈTHYANG ˈhonoˈn i ˈ-ngi ˈˈta (1459 Wel 7:59b) they keep lecturing away night and day – the Hankul block for ˈnac has a superfluous stroke that is not to be taken as the vowel o; CF ˈpam ˈkwa ˈnac ˈkwa (1449 Kok 16). kuˈci ¨epˈsi kuwuˈninoˈn i ˈ-ngi ˈˈta (1447 Sek 9:27b) keeps on rolling without end.
-ˈnoˈn i ˈ-ngˈ iˈta = -ˈnoˈn i ˈ-ngi ˈˈta. ¶[ˈPAY-¨LYEY] lol hono.n i ˈ-ngˈ ita (1676 Sin.e 3:15b) they bow (in obeisance).
-ˈnoˈn i ˈ-ngˈ ˈta = -ˈnoˈn i ˈ-ngi ˈˈta. ¶SAM-ˈSYEY ˈyey s ˈiˈl ol ¨aˈlosil ˈss oy pwu¨thye ˈysiˈta ˈhoˈno.n i ˈ-ngˈ ˈta (1447 Sek 6:18a) he commanded knowledge of the three states of existence; therefore they say that he is Buddha.
-ˈnoˈn i ˈˈn i, proc mod + postmod + cop mod + postmod. ¶¨as.noˈn i ˈˈn i (1462 ¹Nung 9:40a) as (it is that) they plunder.
-ˈnoˈn i ˈn ˈt ay nˈ, proc mod + postmod + cop mod + postmod + pcl + pcl. ¶ˈhota ˈka is.noˈn i ˈn ˈt ay nˈ ¨esˈtyey ˈi ¨yang oˈlwo ˈtye ˈlol ¨CHA-¨TUNG ˈhoˈya LWON-LYANG hoˈm ye (?1468- Mong 62ab) if it exists, how can we in this manner differentiate it out for our consideration, and ...
-ˈnoˈn i s ˈka, proc mod + postmod [+ ellipted cop polite] + pcl + postmod. ¶kuˈstol toˈlye mwuˈlwoˈtoy kutuy s aˈpa ¨niˈm i is.noˈn i s ˈka – is.noˈn i ˈngi ˈˈta (1447 Sek 6:14b) he asks the daughter, "Is your father home?" – "He is, sir". SEE ˈhoˈno.n i s ˈka.
-ˈnoˈn i ˈstoˈn ye, proc mod + postmod + pcl + postmod. ¶ˈSSYWOK ˈoy CAY-ˈKAY ˈyey ˈtwo mekˈti aˈni ˈkhwo nˈ ˈhomolˈmye CIN-ˈSSILQ s tas.noˈn i ˈstoˈn ye (1462 ¹Nung 8:4-5) when even in the fasts of commoners they refrain from eating them [the five forbidden roots], how much more so the true student (of the discipline)? ˈna y ˈi keˈs uˈlwo hon naˈlaˈh ol ¨taˈcwue ˈtwo ˈwohiˈlye ¨epˈti aˈni ˈkhwo nˈ ¨esˈtyey ˈhomolˈmye CYE-¨CO y ˈstoˈn ye (1463 Pep 2:77a) when I have no appreciable lack though I gave up a nation for this, how much more so the masters!
-ˈnoˈn i ˈya, proc mod + postmod + postmod. ¶is.noˈn i ˈya ¨epˈsu.n i ˈya (?1468- Mong 62a) is there or isn't there?
-ˈnoˈn i ˈye, proc mod + postmod + postmod. ¶as.kaˈWon ˈptuˈt i is.noˈn i ˈye (1447 Sek 6: 25b) are you feeling stingy?
-ˈnon ˈka, proc mod + postmodifier. ¶¨THYEY ˈphyeˈm ye wums.non ˈka NGUY-SIM hoˈn i (1462 ¹Nung 2:40b) doubted that the form was expanding and shrinking. SEE -uˈsinonˈka, -ˈnwonˈka.
-ˈnon ˈkwo, proc mod + postmodifier. ¶ˈnwu y ciˈzuˈm ye ˈnwu y patnon ˈkwo ˈhwo.l i ˈˈla (1462 ¹Nung 4:91a) I wonder who will build it and who will get it. ¨nim-kum ˈcasyaˈm ay ˈstwo ˈnwu y [KWONG-PWONG] ˈhozopnon ˈkwo (1481 Twusi 10:9b) who will look after the king in his sleep? SEE ˈhononˈkwo.
nonon < nof ˈloɟnon, processive mod < no[l]ˈta (flies). ¶nonun keˈs iˈm ye (1459 Wel 1:11a) things that fly … . nonon pelGeˈci lˈ capˈnwola (1481 Twusi 10:7b) catches flying insects.
-ˈnon ˈta, proc mod + postmod. ¶[ˈ]i ˈaˈki es.ti ˈˈn i ˈGwanˈtoy nulˈkuˈn [i] uy heˈthwuy lˈ ¨anˈkwo ˈiˈli-ˈtoˈlwok ¨wunon ˈta (1459 Wel 8:100-1) why does this child cling to [the calf of] the old man's leg and cry all this much?! … MYENG-ˈSSYEY ˈPELQ-ˈNGWEN ˈhwon ¨iˈl ol ¨hyeynon ˈta mwoˈlonon ˈta (1447 Sek 6:8a) are you taking into consideration that you uttered an oath … or are you ignoring that? ˈiˈcey eˈtuˈle ˈkaˈnon ˈta (?1517- ¹No 1:1a) and now where are you going?
-nonta = -nunta. ¶ese meke la taypi skwucicu.n i selGwe ani meknonta (?1660- Kyeychwuk

196; cited from LCT) scolded to eat by the empress dowager, I am uneasy and do not eat.
-`non˙ti(···)` = -`non˙t i(···)`, processive modifier + postmodifier ('fact') + particle / copula. (the fact) that it / one does. ¶`na ’y˙e˙mi ¨amwo˙toy˙na˙’ys.non˙t i ¨mwol˙lay-ngi˙’˙ta` (1459 Wel 21:53a; object marked with the nominative) I do not know what place my mother has been reborn into.
-`non˙t ol`, proc mod + postmod ('fact') + pcl. the fact that it/one does. ¶`pwu¨thye y˙wuli˙uy mozo˙m ay ¨SYWOW-˙PEP˙cul˙kinon˙t ol ¨alo˙sya` (1463 Pep 2:231a) Buddha is aware that in our hearts we cherish the dharma of hīnayāna. `kwot is.non˙t ol ¨a˙n i` (1482 Kumsam 2:2b) knew at once that they were there.
-`non˙toy`, proc mod + noun. the place where (···). SEE `toy`.
-`non˙twong`, proc mod + postmod. whether (or not). ¶`is.non twong ep.sun twong ho.n i˙’la` (1481 Twusi 9:30; cited from LCT) asked whether there is or there is not. SEE `twong`, -`nun tong`.
-`non˙uy` = -`non˙[y]uy`, abbr < -`(˙)no˙n i˙uy` 'of (etc.) that which ···˙'. A single passage of 1586 Sohak 5:95b has two examples of the phrase ··· `twun˙non˙uy` (= `twu[e i]s.no˙n i˙uy) ¨mal˙i a˙ni˙’.n i` 'are not words vested with ···' (differently worded in 1518 Sohak-cho 8:15b).
-`no˙n ya`, processive mod + postmod (question). ¶`epe˙i˙lul pwo˙ti ¨mwot˙ho˙ye˙’s.no˙n i inno˙n ya` [< `is.no˙n ya`] `ho˙n i` (1586 Sohak 6:7b) = `epe˙zi˙lol a˙ni˙ka ¨pwoy˙n i is.nu˙n ya˙ho˙ya` (1518 Sohak-cho 9:8a) he asked whether any of them had been unable to see their parents.
-`no˙n ye`, proc mod + postmod (question). ¶`i TTANG TYWUNG˙ey i˙sye ZYE-LOY pwo˙ti ¨mwot˙’kwo TTANG pas[k] pwo˙l i is.no˙n ye` (1462 ¹Nung 1:50b) are there any who watch [from] outside, unable to be inside to watch?
-`no˙n ywo`, processive modifier + postmodifier (question). ¶`ne˙’y susu˙ng uy ¨TTYEY-¨CO y ¨es˙tyey a˙ni˙wono˙n ywo` (1447 Sek 6:29b) why is your teacher's disciple not arriving?
-`noson˙ta`, proc emotive mod + postmod. ¶`nehuy˙tol.h i mu˙su˙k ul˙pwo˙noson˙ta` (1459 Wel 10:28a) what do you people see?
-`nos.ta`, proc emotive indic assertive. ¶`atok hon konon pi wonos.ta` (1632 Twusi-cwung 12:25b)

a dim fine rain sets in.
-`no˙ta` > -`(nu)nta`, proc indic assert. ¶`pa˙m oy˙ci˙ye to˙la˙ton e˙li˙n i n’ mwo˙lono˙ta` (1462 ¹Nung 1:16b) when night sets in he is unaware that he is confused. SEE `hono˙ta`.
nowa = **no[h.]a**, inf < **noh.ta**. ABBR **nwā**.
-`noy` = -`n oy` = -`n [y]oy`, abbr < -`n i˙oy` 'of (etc.) that which ···˙'. SEE `oy, ho˙n oy`.
-**noyta** < -**nwoy’˙’ta** < -`nwo-ngi˙’˙ta` = -**noita nōyta**, 1. abbr < vp **noh.ita**
2. vt. resifts; reiterates, repeats.
’/-**n pa** SEE **in pa, -un pa**
···`ns¨cop-` (mistake?) → ···`nt¨cop-` = ···`n¨ccop-` < ···`nc-¨zop-`.
’**nta**, abbr < **hanta**. SEE -**ta ’nta; -ca ’nta, -la ’nta**.
-**nta**, alternant after vowels of -**nunta** (proc indic assert). does. ¶**kanta** goes. **onta** comes. **nōnta** enjoys oneself; plays, visits. **pulunta** calls.
-`n˙ta` (question) SEE -`un˙ta, in˙ta`.
-**nta ’l**, abbr < -**nta (ko) hal**
-**nta ’m**, alternant after vowels of -**nunta ’m**
-**nta ’n(’)**, abbr < -**nta (ko) han**, < -**nta (ko) hanun**.
-**nta ’ni**, alternant after vowels of -**nunta ’ni**
-**nta ’y**, abbr < -**nta (ko) hay**. ~ **to**.
···`nt¨cop-` < ···`nc-¨zop-`
’/-**n tey** SEE **in tey, -un tey**
-**ntey** < -**nta ’y**
-**n ti** [Ceycwu DIAL (Seng ¹Nakswu 1984:51-4)] = -**n tey**, = -**ss.nun tey**
-`n˙ti(···)` = -`n˙t i(···)`, mod + postmod ('fact') + pcl/cop. that it/one did (or is). SEE -`u˙syan˙t i`.
? ’`n˙t i`, 1. abbr < `hon˙t i`. 2. = ’`[y]n˙t i`, abbr < ˙`in˙t i` after *i* or *y*.
-`n˙t ol`, mod + postmod + pcl. (the fact) that it/one did (or is). SEE -`un˙t ol, -u˙sin˙t ol, ˙isin˙t ol`.
’`n˙t ol` = ’`[y]n˙t ol`, abbr < ˙`in˙t ol` (cop mod + postmod + pcl) after *i* or *y*. though it be, even. ¶`epe˙zi ’n˙t ol` (1447 Sek 9:12a) even (to) a parent. `konon˙pi˙’n [˙]t ol` (1481 Twusi 21:22b) even a drizzle. SEE `a˙ni˙’n˙t ol`.
-`n˙t olwo`, mod + postmod ('fact') + pcl. because it/one did (or is).
’`n˙t olwo`, abbr < `hon˙t olwo`. because it is. ¶`ku˙le˙’n˙t olwo` (1475 Nay 3:62a) therefore. `ile˙’n˙t o˙lwo ci˙zwul˙tt i a˙ni˙’.n i˙’˙la` (1463 Pep se:12a) for this reason I will not create one [here]. `ile˙’n˙t olwo ke˙mu.m ye˙hoyywo˙m ol`

non῾hwo.n i ῾῾la (1481 Twusi 7:27a) hence distinguished being black and being white.
-n῾t on, mod + postmod + pcl. given that it/one do (or be); if. SEE -un῾t on, hon῾t on.
'/-n tul SEE in tul, -un tul
'/-n tus SEE in tus, -un tus
'/-n῾t ye SEE -un῾t ye
nu [DIAL]. 1. = ne you.
2. = ney your. [Ceycwu] nu kes = ney kes your thing, yours.
nuc, adnoun, bound adverb. late, slow (< adj nuc.ta). ANT ol, il.
1. adnoun. ¶ ~ kaul late autumn. ~ tongi a child of one's later years. ~ tewi late heat (hot spell). ~ pye a kind of rice that ripens late. ~ palam a late evening breeze; dissipation late in life. ~ pucilen belated effort / diligence. ~ cam late sleeping. ~ seli a late frost.
2. bnd adv. ~ toynta grows/develops slowly.
-nuita [obs] = -naita
nu ka [Ceycwu DIAL] = ney ka (you [subject]).
-nu' 'men (yo), abbr < -nun kwumen (yo)
nul, adverb. always, all the time.
nu l' [Ceycwu DIAL] = ne l' = ne lul (you)
-nula, processive adjunctive.
1. what with doing, as a result of doing, because of (doing ···). ~ ko SAME. ¶kongpu hanula (phyēnci ssunula) cam calq say ka ēps.ta What with studying (and writing letters) I have no time to sleep. Cēmsim mek.nula (ko) nuc.ess.ta Lunch made me late.
2. with the idea to do, with the intention of doing, trying to do. SEE ~ ko.
-nula ko, processive adjunctive + particle.
1. = -nula (what with doing)
2. with the idea to do, with the intention of doing, trying to do. ¶ ~ (= -ulye ko, -ki ey) āy lul ssuta makes an effort to do. Panci-ppalukey Ilpon māl hanula ko kuleci mālko wuli māl lo hay la Say it in Korean instead of putting on airs trying to talk Japanese. Capci wenko ssunula ko pam nuc.key canta Stays up till late at night writing manuscripts for magazines. Cim ul kkwulinula ko yātan tul ita They are all in a bustle trying to get their bags packed. Alayq tōngney se lang chwusek nol.i cwūnpi hanula ko motwu yātan ita The people in the next village are all excited getting ready for the Harvest Festival. Ce mata mence na-kanula ko selo ttēy mīnta Everybody is pushing everybody else trying to get out first.
? 3. because frustratingly / onerously enough (Dupont 152).
-nula 'myen, processive adjunctive + abbr < hamyen. (while) in the process of doing, while doing; if. ¶kulenula 'myen meanwhile. Sānula 'myen pyelq īl ul tā tang hanun pep in i 'la You have to put with a lot of things to stay alive. Sikan i kanula 'myen tā ic.e pelikey toykeyss.ci yo As time goes by, that will all be forgotten (M 1:2:196). Ku pun ul kitalinula 'myen ēncey'n ka nun okeyss.ci yo If you wait for him, he'll come someday (¹Yi Kitong 348).
-nula 'ni(-kka), processive adjunctive + abbr < hani(-kka). ¶Honca iss.nula 'ni kapkap hata I feel quite lonesome all by myself.
-nu' 'men (yo), abbr < -nun kwumen (yo)
nun < ῾nun, pcl. alt shape of un after vowels.
'nun, abbr < hanun
-nun < -(῾)non, 1. processive modifier. ··· that (one) does, ··· which/who does; ··· that (one) is doing with, from, to, etc. ¶sinmun ul ponun (ku) sālam the person (who is) looking at the newspaper. ku sālam i ponun (ku) sinmun the newspaper (that/which) he is looking at. ku sālam i (ku) sinmun ul ponun cali the place (where) he is looking at the newspaper. nay ka yenphil man kkakk.nun khal the knife that I use only to sharpen pencils with. um.ak-ka tul i kanun tapang a teashop that musicians go to. Kwulunun tōl ey nun ikki ka kkici anh.nunta A rolling stone gathers no moss.
NOTE: The processive attaches only to verbs, iss-, and ēps-; but before postmodifiers ci, ka, ya, tey, and ke l' the past and future processive modifiers occur (-ess.nun, -keyss.nun), before ci the prospective processive modifier -ul.nun also occurs, and these complex forms can be attached to any stem (verb, adjective, copula).
2. As a sentence fragment; e.g., in an echo-question. "Tōn i iss.nun"? [Did you say he is a person who] "has money"?
-(῾)nun, var (after e, u, wu, y) < -(῾)non, proc modifier − uncommon before the merger of ···o with ···u was completed in the 1500s. ¶ ῾῾wu῾nun swo῾li (1447 Sek 19:14b) the sound of crying. SYWOW ῾non hywo῾kon ῾tay ῾lol yes῾ke ῾῾pwu῾nun ke῾s i῾la (1447 Sek 13:53a) a panpipe is a thing that you weave from a small stick of bamboo and blow on. ῾PALQ-CHYEN ῾῾LI ῾Gwom

˙nyenun ˙SSYANG ˙i˙la (1459 Wel 7:52b) it is an elephant that goes eight thousand leagues at a time. ˙nom ¨ep.si˙Gwu˙nun ¨sa˙lo.m i˙la (1459 Wel 2:46a) is one who scorns others. hulunun ¨soym (1459 Wel 7:30b) a flowing spring.

˙nun, var (after e, u, wu, y) < ˙non, particle – uncommon before the merger of ···o with ···u was completed in the 1500s. ¶ ¨NGE nun ¨mal-sso.m i˙la (1451 Hwun-en 1a) ¨NGE is [the same as] words. LWUW ˙nun tala˙k i˙la (1447 Sek 6:2b) a LWUW is a loft. ¨twuy.h ey ˙nun ¨mwotin twocok (1445 ¹Yong 30) behind him the evil renegades [were gathered].

nu n', [Ceycwu DIAL] = ne n' = ne nun (as for you).

-nun a = -nun ya

-nun ccok-ccok = -nun cok-cok. SEE ccok-ccok.

-nun cek, proc mod + n. the time(s)/occasion(s) that it happens; a present experience. ~ i iss.ta sometimes does, DOES do (on occasion); ~ i iss.ess.ta sometimes did, DID do (on occasion); ~ i ēps.ta never does, doesn't ever do; ~ i ēps.ess.ta never used to, didn't ever. ¶Kongwen ey sānqpo kanun cek i iss.ta We (do) sometimes go to the park for a walk. Yenghwa lul kwūkyeng kanun cek i ēps.ta We never have the occasion to go see a movie. Kim sensayng puin ul chac.e ponun cek i ēps.na yo? – Chac.e ponun cek i iss.kwu mālkwu yo Don't you ever go see Mrs Kim? – Of course I (sometimes) go see her. Achimq pap ul mek.nun cek to iss.ko an mek.nun cek to iss.ta Sometimes I eat breakfast and then sometimes I don't. SYN -nun ttay; CF -nunq īl.

-nunchamay → -nun chām ey

-nun cha ey = -nun chām ey.

-nun chal.na ey, proc mod + n + pcl. (at the) moment/instant that. ¶Nay ka tul.e onun chal.na ey pul i kkē cyess.ta The light went out the moment I came in.

-nun chām, proc mod + n. (~ ey) at the point of doing, just as (it is happening). ¶Komun ul hanun chām ey Mong.lyong i tol.yen hi natha-na se Chwunhyang ul kwū hayss.ta Just as they were on the point of torturing Chwunhyang, Mong.lyong suddenly appeared and saved her. SYN -nun cha ey. CF -tun chām; -ul chām; -nun the ey; -ulye ˙nun chal.na ey. SEE chām.

-nun chek hata = -nun chey hata. ¶Ku sālam i kwi-tam.e tut.nun chek un haci man sāsil un talun sayngkak hanun kes kath.sup.nita He is pretending to be all ears, but he seems to be really thinking about other things.

-nun chey hata, proc mod + postmod. pretends to do (to be doing). ¶Cam canun chey haca Let's pretend to be asleep. Katun ci an katun ci (kass.tun ci an kass.tun ci) nay ānun chey an hanta I don't care whether he goes (went) or not – CF katen ci an katen ci nay alwon thyey ani honta (1887 Scott 204).

-nun ci, proc mod + postmod. [-(ess.)ess.nun ci, -(ess.)keyss.nun ci, and -(ess.)ul.nun ci occur]

1. the uncertain fact of doing = whether it does. ¶Meych salam ina kanun ci āsey yo? Do you know how many people are going? Nwūn i onun ci an onun ci molunta I don't know whether it is snowing or not. Cikum īl hanun ci molukeyss.ta I don't know whether he is working right now or not. Iss.nun ci (ēps.nun ci) āsikeyss.ˢup.nikka Do you know whether there are any (or not)? Ku i ka musun sinmun ul ponun ci kiek hasey yo? Do you recall which newspaper he reads? Ku kes ul phal.nun ci mul.e polq ka Shall we ask them if they are going to sell it? Ku īl i etteh.key toynun ci ka kwungkum hata I am anxious about how that is coming along. Nay ka ku lul etteh.key sayngkak hako iss.nun ci lul ku eykey māl hako siph.un chwungtong ul nukkyess.e yo I felt the urge to tell him what I thought of him.

2. ~ (to moluta, yo) ('I don't know whether' =) maybe, perhaps it does. ¶Cam canun ci (to molunta) Maybe he's sleeping. Inchen ey to pi ka onun ci yo I wonder if it is raining in Inchen, too.

3. apparently, maybe. ¶Nay mūt.nun māl ul mōs tul.ess.nun ci ku nun iyaki lul kyēysok hako iss.ess.ta Apparently he didn't catch my question; he went on with what he was saying.

4. given the state of (its) doing: (etteh.key, etteh.key 'na, ecci 'na, elma 'na) ··· ~ , ···-e se 'n ci does it so much that (= nemu ···-e se). ¶Ku anawunse ka etteh.key/ecci 'na (elma 'na) ppalli māl hanun ci na nun ¹īhay haci mōs hay yo That announcer talks so fast I can't understand him.

5. ¶Enu nwu ka saykyess.nun ci cham cal saykyess.ta Whoever carved it, he certainly carved it well.

-nun ci 'la (se), proc mod + postmod + cop var inf (+ pcl). [lit] as/since it does (equivalent to colloquial -tuni, according to Roth). ¶Sal i poinun ci 'la kalye/kaliwe ya hakeyss.ta My skin is showing – I will have to cover it up. Tōn ul mānh.i cwuess.nun ci 'la mulken i nappul lī ka ēps.ta I have paid so much for it, it can't be poor in quality. Sensayng nim kkey se nō hakeyss.nun ci 'la (se) swukcey lul tā hay kass.ta Wary of the wrath of the teacher, I went through all my homework.

For sentence-final uses, see -un ci 'la (NOTE).

-nun cok-cok, proc mod + postmod (= -nun ccok-ccok). every occasion that it happens, whatever time (that), whenever, every time (that), as often as. ¶nah.nun cok-cok atul ita gives birth to sons every time. Mantunun cok-cok phallinta Every one that's made sells (is sold). Ponun cok-cok cap.e la Grab every one you see.

-nun cwul, proc mod + postmod. the assumed fact that it does: ~ (lo) ālta thinks (supposes, assumes, believes, expects) that — CF -nun kes (ul) ālta knows that ... , -nun ci ālta knows whether ... . ¶Yenge lul kongpu hanun cwul lo sayngkak hanta I expect that he is studying his English. Ku ai ka cikum cako iss.nun cwul āsey yo? Do you think the boy is in bed now? — CF Ku ai ka cikum cako iss.nun ci āsey yo? Do you know whether the boy is in bed now? Na nun ney ka an onun cwul al.ess.ta I thought you weren't coming. Mōs hanun cwul al.ess.tuni cal hanun kwun a I didn't think you could, but you're doing it nicely!

NOTE: The entry -nun cwul in KEd (371a) contains inaccurate information that should be corrected to accord with what is said here.

-nun cwung, proc mod + n. (in) the midst of doing: ~ ey in the midst of doing; ~ ita is in the midst of doing. ¶Cam canun cwung iess.ta It was in the middle of my sleep. It was while I was sleeping. Phyēnci lul ssunun cwung ey ku ilum i kiek nass.ta In the middle of writing the letter his name came back to me. Īl hanun cwung ita I am in the midst of work. I am working. SEE -un cwung.

nu-ney [Ceycwu DIAL] = ne-huy (ney) you people; = ne-huy ney (uy) of you people (Seng ¹Nakswu 1984:33).

nung hi < NUNG 'hi (1447 Sek 13:15a, ...), der adv. ably, competently, proficiently; fully, effectively; easily, freely, with no difficulty; can, could, may. ¶Īl ul ~ hata is able to do a job; does a job ably/well. ~ halq swu iss.ta is easily able to do it. Hāin i nung hi ney sikyey lul tocek cil ha.yess.ta The servant had no difficulty stealing your watch. SYN *e'lwu, e'lwo, si'le, nilo, "KA 'hi*.

-nungkate [S Kyengsang DIAL (Mkk 1960:3:34)] = -(su)p.nikka.

-nungkio, 1. [S Kyengsang DIAL (Mkk 1960:3:31)] = -(su)p.nikka. CF -nun ka yo.
2. ? abbr < -nun ke(s i)yo; CF -ullangki yo.

-nungkwuma (yo), [S Kyengsang DIAL (Mkk 1960:3:31,34)] = (Verb)-e (yo). CF -kwuma (yo), -nun kwumen (yo).

-nun hān, proc mod + n.
1. so long/far as, to the extent that (it does). ¶nay ka ānun hān as far as I know. toylq swu iss.nun hān so far as possible, to the best of one's abilities. sāceng i helak hanun hān so far as (the) circumstances permit. Nay ka sal.e iss.nun hān, kulenq īl un an hakeyss.ta As long as I may live I will never do such a thing. Solyen i wenca-than ul sā.yong haci anh.nun hān, Mikwuk to ku kes ul ssuci anh.ulq kes ita As long as the Soviet Union does not resort to the atom bomb, America won't use it either. Nay ka ānun hān ku pun un mit.ul man han pun ip.nita So far as I know, he is a reliable person.
2. ~ i iss.e to, ~ iss.tula to even if. ¶Nay ka cwuk.nun hān i iss.tula to i kes man un mōs cwukeyss.ta I'd die rather than hand this one over.

-nun hyēncang, proc mod + n. the very act/scene of doing. ¶Ku ay n' totwuk-cil ul hanun hyēncang ey se cap.hyess.ta The boy was caught red-handed (in the very act of) stealing.

-nun hyengphyen, proc mod + noun. (in) the process/circumstance of doing. ¶sangtang hi swuip hanun hyengphyen ita is importing quite a lot. CF -nun cwung.

'nun i, abbr < hanun i. SEE -ta 'nun i.

-' 'nun i, abbr < -ta hanun i. ¶Cikum ku-kkacis kkwum ul kaciko mwe l' musep' 'nun

i ecce' 'nun i (= musepta hanun i ecceta 'nun i) hanun ya ko phincan ici man kkāyn nal ey kulenq īl i tolpal hanta 'myen tangsin un etteh.keyss.e yo You are carrying on about what a frightening dream you just had and so on, but what would you do if such a thing happened when you were awake? Pap i ci' 'nun i tōy' 'nun i (man) haci mālko pay kophun sālam sayngkak to com hay pwā la Instead of complaining that the rice is too soft or too hard, give some thought to those who have no rice to eat at all.
-nuni = -nun i
-nun i_1 < -n^uo˙n i, proc mod + n (postmod). CF -nun kes; -ul i, -un i, -tun i.
   1. the one (thing / person) that (···) does.
    1a. (epitheme extruded from subject). ¶sang ponun i 'the one tending the table(s)' = the waiter. phanun i 'the one selling' = the seller, the vendor.
   ? 1b. (epitheme extruded from the object). one whom / that ··· . Example?
   2. (summational epitheme) the act / fact ··· .
    2a. ~ mankhum as much as the doing. ¶Āy lul ssunun i mankhum polam i nass.ta The results equalled the effort.
    2b. ~ man mōs hata is worse than doing, is not as good as doing. ¶Kkuth kkaci an kalq pay ey ya swus cey an kanun i man mōs hata Not going all the way is worse than not going at all. Kamcil i nanun ūmsik ul cokum pakk ey mekci malla 'ni an mek.nun i man mōs hakwun a You'd do better to tell me not to eat at all than to say I should eat only a little of this delicious food.
    2c. ~ pota rather than do. ¶Yok ul ponun i pota cwuk.nun key nās.ta It would be better to die than to face disgrace. Onul nal i cōh.uni pang an ey iss.nun i pota kongwen ey sānqpo kaca The weather is so nice, let's go to the park for a walk instead of staying indoors. Chenkwuk uy cong i toynun i pota chalali / ohilye ciok uy wang i toykeyss.ta I'd rather be a king in hell than a slave in heaven. Cam canun i pota ilccik il.e na (se) īl hanun key cōh.keyss.ta You ought to get up early and do your work rather than sleeping away. Kongpu lul hanun i pota tōnq pel.i hanun kes i cōh.ta It would be better to get out and earn some money rather than stick to your studies.

    3. abbr < -nun i 'la it is (the case) that. ¶Nal i mutewumyen pi ka onun i ('la) Sultry weather always brings rain. I kil lo han cham kamyen swulq cip i iss.nun i ('la) Follow this road for a while and you will find an alehouse. SEE -nun i 'la.
    4. abbr < -nun i pota rather than do (= 2c).
-nun i_2, (proc mod + postmod) = -nun ya (the question) whether it does. ¶Cip ey se nun ku lul hak.kyo ey ponaynun i mānun i māl i mānh.ta His family are arguing about whether they should send him to school or not. ¹Ihon ul hanun i mānun i ku cip ey se nun pam-nac ssawum ita They are always quarreling and talking about getting a divorce. Ku nun sil.¹yen hanq īlay pam-nac cwuk.nun i sānun i yātan ita Since his disappointment in love he is always talking about committing suicide.
-nu˙n i, proc mod + postmod. ¶kwos wu˙h uy ˙CHILQ-"PWOW ye˙lu˙m i ˙˙yenu˙n i (1459 Wel 8:12a) on the flowers the fruit of the seven precious things ripens. SEE -no˙n i.
-nu˙n i ˙Ga, proc mod + postmod + postmod. does it? is it doing?
-nu˙n i ˙Gwo, proc mod + postmod + postmod. does it? is it doing?
-nunq īl, proc mod + postmod. the experience of doing: ~ i iss.ta sometimes does, DOES do; ~ i iss.ess.ta sometimes did, used to do; ~ i ēps.ta never does; ~ i ēps.ess.ta never used to do. ¶Ai tul i selkec.i hanunq īl i iss.ta The children sometimes wash the dishes. Namca ka selkec.i hanunq īl i ēps.ni? Don't the men ever wash the dishes? Yo say Kim sensayng(q) tayk ey kanunq īl i ēps.ta Lately we never go to Mr Kim's house. CF -nun cek; -unq īl.
-nun i 'la, proc mod + n + cop quotative indic assertive. it is (a fact) that; one always / never does; it is sure to be/happen (said in instructing an inferior). ¶Ēlun eykey pelus ēps.nun māl un an hanun i 'la One does not say rude things to one's elders. Am-thalk i wūlmyen cip-an mang hanun i 'la "When the hen crows [= when the woman wears the trousers] the family goes to ruin". ABBR -nun i, -nu'y 'la. SYN -nun kes ita. CF -un (-tun) i 'la; -ni^t/ja.
-nu˙n i '-ngi s ˙ka SEE -no˙n i '-ngi s ˙ka
-nuni pota = -nun i pota (SEE -nun i_1). ~ tul.
-nun i tul, proc mod + postmod + pcl = -nun ya tul.

-nuni tul = -nun i tul, abbr < -nun i pota tul. ¶Onulq pam ey kanun i (pota) tul chalali ¹nayil achim ey kanun key ettay How about going tomorrow morning rather than tonight?
? nun iya, pcl + pcl. SEE p. 817-8 (to NOTE).
-nunq ¹īyu, proc mod + n. (for) the reason that it does. ¶Acik kkaci to ecey sinmun ul tul.ye 'ta ponunq ¹īyu ka eti ey iss.na Why are you still peering into yesterday's paper? Sencwuk-kyo lul kinyem hanunq ¹īyu nun olay cen ey i tali wi ey se il.e nan ¹yeksa-cek sāsil ey iss.ta The reason we remember Sencwuk Bridge lies in historical events that happened on this bridge a long time ago. I kes i palo ku tul i wuli cengpu lul cēnpok halye 'nunq ¹īyu ita This is the very reason why they intend to overthrow our government. SYN -nun kkatalk.
-nun ka, processive modifier + postmodifier.
  1. (the question) whether it does; does it/he?
  ~ yo does it/he? [POLITE]. ¶Mue l' hanun ka What are you doing? I sōsel ul ilk.nun ka yo? (or ilk.na yo? or ilk.e yo?) Are you reading this novel? Caney eti lul kass.ta onun ka Where have you been? Musa hi kass.nun ka molukeyss.ta I do not know whether he has arrived there safely.
  ~ ey. ¶Mūncey nun nwu ka te mānh.i te cal mantunun ka ey tallye iss.ta The question depends on who produces more and better (products).
  ~ lo. ¶Sālam tul uy sīsen un kikyey ka etteh.key cak.yong hanun ka lo cipcwung ha.yess.ta (CM 2:229) People's gaze focussed on how the machine works.
  2. [somewhat lit] (-ess-/-keyss-) ~ pota (adj) it seems as if it does (did / will do). CF -na pota. SYN -nun kes kath.ta, -nun mo.yang ita. ¶Pi ka onun (wass.nun, okeyss.nun or olq) ka pota It seems to be raining (to have rained, to be about to rain). Onul hak.kyo ey oci anh.un kes ul poni alh.nun ka pota I guess he is ill, for he is not in school today. Han pen kamyen tasi nun tol.a olq cwul molunun ka pota (moluna pota) Once you are gone, I won't know when you will ever return.
  3. -nun ka ha- (from Im Hopin 1987:173): Cwumusinun ka hay se cēnhwa lul pakkwe tulici anh.ess.ˢup.nita I had it that you might be sleeping so I did not put the call through. Kkāchi ka wūlki ey eti se cōh.un sosik i onun ka hayss.ey yo From the sound of the magpie I figured there was good news coming from somewhere. Tāyhak ey ip.hak hayss.nun ka hayss.tuni, enu say col.ep ikwun yo I was thinking you must have entered college and here you are graduating in no time! CF -na hata (p. 702), -na siph.ta (p. 777).
  4. -nun ka hamyen:
  4a. (= -nun ka pomyen). ¶Pi ka onun ka hamyen nwūn i oko, nwūn i onun ka hamyen pi ka oni, nal-ssi to cham īsang hata It can't make up its mind whether it wants to snow or wants to rain, it is such funny weather.
  4b. ¶Sāy tul i meli wi ey se cice-kelinun ka hamyen talam-cwi tul i tali mith ul suchye kaki to hanta Not only are there birds chirping overhead but also there are squirrels darting under foot.
  5. -nun ka siph.i/siph.key. ¶Sānun ka siph.i sal.e popsita Let's try living as if we were really living. CF siph.ta, -na siph.ta (p. 777).
-nunkaita ?< -nun ka ita, ?< -nun ka i 'ta [South Kyengsang DIAL (¹Na Cinsek 1977)] = -(su)p.nikka
-nun ka ka, proc mod + postmodifier + particle. ¶Mues ul mek.nun ka ka mūncey 'ta The question is what are we eating. Encey natha-nanun ka ka mūncey 'ta The question is when it is appearing.
-nun ka lul, proc mod + postmod + pcl. ¶Ku ⁿyeca ka onun ka lul al.e pwā la Find out whether she is coming.
-nun ka 'm, abbr < -nun ka (ko) ham or -nun ka 'n māl ia?. ¶Way kuleni, nwu ka kaci mālla 'nun ka 'm? What's your trouble — is anyone keeping you from going?! CF -tun ka 'm, -na 'm, -ta 'm.
-nun kām, proc mod + n. the feeling that it does. ~ i iss.ta, ~ i nata it gives the feeling that ···, it feels/seems like ··· . ¶I san tul ul poni Hānkwuk ey tol.a kan kām i nanta/iss.ta Seeing these mountains takes me back to Korea.
-nunkang [S Kyengsang DIAL (¹Na Cinsek 1977)] = -nun ka
-nun ka nun, proc mod + postmod + pcl. ¶Mues ul mek.nun ka nun kekceng mālla As for what to eat, don't worry about it.
-nunkata (?< -nun ka 'ta) [S Kyengsang DIAL (¹Na Cinsek 1977)] = -(su)p.nikka
-nun ka tul = -nun ya tul

-nun kawuntey (se), proc mod + n (+ pcl) [? rustic] = -nun cwung (ey)

-nunkay (? < -nun ka i) [S Kyengsang DIAL (¹Na Cinsek 1977)] = -(su)p.nikka

-nun ka ya, processive modifier + postmod + pcl. ¶Mues ul mek.nun ka ya kekceng mālla As for just what to eat, don't worry about it.

-nun ke, abbr < -nun kes

-nun ke 'ci, abbr < -nun kes ici

-nun ke l', abbr < -nun ke lul = -nun kes ul. When followed by the polite particle yo there is reinforcement: ke l'q yo /kellyo/. Past and future forms occur: -ess.nun / -keyss.nun ke l'.

1. although (in spite of the fact that) it does; but, anyway, so there! (= indeed, despite contrary anticipations or reservations). In this use -ess.nun and -keyss.nun can precede ke l'. ¶Kim sensayng uy thōlon un cheum tut.nun ke l'! Why, this is the first time I have heard Mr Kim take part in a discussion! Ileh.key maum i pul.an halq cwul al.ess.tula 'myen an ponaynun ke l' (kwayni ponayss.kwun a) If I had known I would feel so bad I would not have sent him off (but I did). Pi ka olq cwul al.ess.tula 'myen wūsan ul kaciko onun ke l' (kulayss.ta) If I'd known it was going to rain, I'd have brought my umbrella (but I didn't).

2. SEE -nun kes (1, 2, 3)

-nun ke 'l(q), abbr < -nun kes il(q). ~ sey.

-nun ke 'la, abbr < -nun kes ila

-nun ke l' ipsyo = -nun ke l'q yo

-nun ke l'q yo /kellyo/ SEE -nun ke l'

-nun ke n', abbr < -nun ke nun = -nun kes un

-nun ke 'n, abbr < -nun kes in.

~ tey. ¶Elyepci man anh.umyen na to ce kuney lul han pen tha ponun ke 'n tey If it isn't so difficult I should have tried riding that swing, too.

~ ya. ¶Nwukwu nun cāngkwan i toyko, nwukwu nun sacang i toynun tey, ne nun mwe l' hanun ke 'n ya ko emeni kkwucilam hasitula Mother was scolding "Some become cabinet ministers, some become the heads of companies, and what do YOU do?"

-nun ke 'na, abbr < -un kes ina

-nun kes, proc mod + n.

1. the thing / act that (someone) is doing. ¶Ney ka hanun kes ul poni-kka swiwe pointa To see you do it, it looks easy.

2. the thing / one that someone is doing; the one that is doing it. ¶Ponun kes ina tut.nun kes ina tā say lowess.ta Everything I saw or heard was new to me. Na nun i hak.kwa lul (i kwamok ul) kaluchil (i) mankhum ānun kes i ēps.ta I am without sufficient knowledge to teach this subject (course).

3. the doing, the fact or act of doing; the tentative fact that (someone) is doing. ¶Apeci hanthey pota (to) emeni hanthey māl hanun kes i naulq ka Would it be better to talk to Mother rather than Father? Pelus ēps.nun kes ul pomyen ku ai ka oy atul in ci (to molunta) Judging from his lack of manners, I would say maybe he is an only son. ¹Nayil tte-nanun kes i etten ya (ette han ya) How about starting tomorrow? Ku ttay na nun co'.yong han pam uy meych sikan ssik ul ¹yeypay-tang ey ka se myengsang ulo ponaynun kes i supkwan i toye iss.ess.ˢup.nita At that time I got in the habit of spending a number of hours every quiet evening meditating in the church. Ka.yong i cēk.key tulko mānh.i tunun kes un mek.ul nalum ila halq swu iss.ta Your living expenses might be said to be dependent upon the food you eat. Kuleh.key kkaci māl hanun kes un com mues haci anh.sup.nikka? Isn't it a bit much / harsh / embarrassing for you to say that? Payk pen tut.nun kes i han pen ponun kes pota mōs hata It is better to see a thing one time than to hear about it a hundred times. Tangmyen han cēy-il khun mūncey nun āmuli him i tultun (ci) cēyphum uy cil ul noph.inun kes iess.ta The biggest problem facing us was to raise the quality of the goods however hard that might be. Kulay to (ku kes i) ēps.nun kes pota nās.ta Still it is better than nothing.

~ ita it is (a / the fact) that ... . ¶Nwukwu l' māl hanun kes in ka Who is it that you are talking about? Nay ka ne lul miwe hanta ko sayngkak hanun kes un ney ka kuce kulel ssa hay se kulenun kes ita It is your imagination that you should think I hate you. Pap man ulo sānun kes i ani 'ta We do not live by bread alone. Ku i tele ka ani 'la ne tele kala 'nun kes ita It's not him but you they want to go to.

4. the proper thing to do (CF -nun pep);

~ ita ought. ¶Haksayng ulo se kulen nappun hayngtong un an hanun pep / kes ita As a student one ought not do such bad things. **Hyeng hanthey nun an kulenun kes ita** You shouldn't do that to your older brother. **Yeki se an phiwunun kes ita** (or **phiwunun kes i ani 'ta**) One does not smoke here = People are not supposed to (You shouldn't) smoke here. **Nay māl tay lo hanun kes i cōh.ta** You'd better do just as I told you. **Sensayng nim i māl hasin tay lo māyil kongpu hay ya paywunun kes ita** Just as the teacher said, to learn you have to study every day. **Ne nun na hako cengkwu haki silh.e se phingk^yey lul hanun kes ita** (= 3c); **wūntong haki silh.umyen kuleh.key palo māl hanun kes ita** (= 4) You don't like to play tennis with me, so you make excuses; if you dislike playing, you ought to come right out and say so.

~ **i cōh.ta** it would be better to (do). ¶**Cip ey kanun kes i cōh.keyss.ta** It would be well for us to go home. **Kongpu lul hanun i pota tōnq pel.i hanun kes i cōh.ta** It would be better to get out and earn some money rather than stick fast to your studies. **Ney sā-chon hanthey lang tā allinun kes i cōh.keyss.ta** I think it would be better to let your cousin and them know. **Apeci kkey pota hyeng nim kkey māl-ssum tulinun kes i cōh.ulq ke 'ey yo** You'd do better to talk to your brother rather than to your father. **Kuleh.key pota ileh.key hanun kes i te cōh.kess.ta** It would be better to do it this way rather than that. **Han cuk incey etteh.key hanun kes i cōh.ulq ka** Then, what should we do now? **Kulen cuk ¹nayil kanun kes i cōh.keyss.ta** That being the case, you had better leave here tomorrow.

5. ~ **ul** = **-nun ke l'**; also = 1, 2, 3 above as object: **kok.ka ka olunun kes ul pangci hako iss.ta** is preventing a rise in grain prices.

6. 6a. ~ **ulo pota** (**inceng hata, yekita, ālta, kancwu hata**) concludes (realizes, recognizes) that one does. ¶**Ney ka ōceng kkaci an omyen mōs onun kes ulo pokeyss.ta** If you don't show up by noon I'll take it that you are not coming at all. **Ku man hamyen cal hanun kes ulo (na nun) ponta** I feel you've done well to do that much.

6b. ~ **ulo poita** [written style] it appears / seems that one does. ¶**Cengpu nun i kyēyhoyk ey chānseng hanun kes ulo pointa** It appears that the government is favoring this plan.

7. ~ **i** but [CM 2:219; also other meanings]. NOTE: **Wumcik inun kes ita** (1) It's the thing that moves (or that someone moves); (2) It's the one that moves (or that someone moves); (3) It's a fact that someone moves it (or that it moves), you see; (4) One should move (or move it). **Wumcik inun kes i ani 'ta** (1) It's not the thing that moves (or that someone moves); (2) It's not the one that moves (or that someone moves); (3) It's not the fact that someone moves it (or that it moves); (4) One should not move (or move it).

-nun kes kath.ta, proc mod + postmod + adj.

1. it seems that it does. ¶**Ku sālam i kwitam.e tut.nun chek un haci man sāsil un talun sayngkak hanun kes kath.sup.nita** He is pretending to be all ears, but he seems to be really thinking about other things.

2. it is like the one/thing that (someone) does.

-nun ke 'ta, abbr < **-nun kes ita**. ¶**Tōn un ēps.ta ka to iss.nun ke 'ta** Money comes and goes (so don't let that bother you too much). **Kel.umye ka ani 'la tallimye ce phyocek ul mac.hila 'nun ke 'ta** They want us to hit that target running, not walking.

-nun key, 1. abbr < **-nun kes i**.

2. abbr < **-nun kes ie/ia**.

-nun ke ya, abbr < **-nun kes i(y)a**.

1. (cop inf = **ie/ia**) ¶**Ney ūymu lul tā hako se man (i) nam eykey to kwen.li lul cwucang halq swu iss.nun ke ya** Just fulfill all your obligations and you can demand your rights of others. **Emeni hako mace kath.i an kakeyss.ta 'ni to-taychey nwukwu hako kakeyss.ta 'nun ke ya** You won't go with your mother; so who on earth WILL you go with? **Aycho (ey) puthe kulen sālam kwa nun sangcong ul mal.ess.e ya hanun ke ya** From the start you should have avoided associating with a man like him.

2. (pcl **iya/ya**) ¶**Mek.ko ccum kanun ke ya kwaynchanh.ci man (ūmsik ul) kaciko kanun ke n' an toyp.nita** It's all right just to eat and go but you shouldn't go taking food along with you (to eat). **Nay sānun ke ya kuce kulel wu haci mwe** I'm just living along, that's about all.

-nun key 'ci = **-nun ke yci** < **-nun kes ici**
-nun key 'la = **-nun ke yla** < **-nun kes ila**
-nun key 'na = **-nun ke yna** < **-nun kes ina**
-nun key 'ney = **-nun ke yney** < **-nun kes iney**
-nun key 'ni = **-nun ke yni** < **-nun kes ini**

-nun ke yo = -nun key yo = -nun ke 'ey yo. ¶Kkatalk cocha moluko se way ili tempinun ke yo Why are you so hasty when you don't even know the score? An mek.ulye 'nun ke yo? You're not going to eat them? To-taychey tangsin un mue l' (halye ko) hanun ke yo Just what on earth do you think you're up to?

-nun ke yo man, abbr < -nun kes io man it's that ··· does but [AUTH].

-nun key, abbr. 1. < -nun kes i.
2. < -nun kes i- (cop).

-nun key 'ta = -nun ke yta, abbr < -nun kes ita (= -nun ke 'ta).

-nun key ya = -nun ke ya

-nun key yo, abbr. 1. < -nun ke 'ey yo < -nun kes ie(y) yo it's that ··· does [POLITE], ...
2. < -nun kes iyo [POLITE fragment].
3. < -nun kes io it's that ··· does [AUTH], ... ¶To-taychey tangsin un mue l' (halye ko) hanun ke yo Just what on earth do you think you're up to?

-nun kil, proc mod + n. 1. (in) the course of doing, while doing. ¶Hak.kyo kanun kil ey nul sīcheng ul cīna kanta On my way to school, I always pass the city hall. Cip ey tol.a kanun kil ey cāmqkan tullici yo I guess I'll stop in for a minute on my way back home.
2. [DIAL] = -nunq īl

-nun kīm, processive mod + postmod. (as) an incidental result of doing; while one is about it. SEE kīm.

-nun kkatalk, mod + n. (for) the reason that it does. ¶Na nun mul ul cōh.a hanun kkatalk ey nul pata ey kanta I always go to the sea, because I am fond of the water. Nay ka Kim sensayng ul cōh.a hanun kkatalk un ku inphum i kosang han kkatalk ita The reason I like Mr Kim is that he has a noble character.

-nun ko, proc mod + postmod. [colloq; poetic] the (usually rhetorical, exclamatory, or quoted) question wh··· does (BUT NOT whether ···). CF -nun ka; `kwo. ABBR -no [= -n' 'o].

-nun ko lo, mod + n + pcl [somewhat lit]. for the reason that it does. ¶Cwūuy haci anh.nun ko lo kulenq īl i sayngkinta Things like that happen through carelessness. Ku sālam un tōn i iss.nun ko lo caki ka hako siph.unq īl un mues ina tā halq swu iss.ˢup.nita He has got money so he can do anything he wants to. Na nun cikum īl ul hanun ko lo āmu tey to mōs kap.nita I can't go anywhere now because I am working. CF -nun kkatalk ey, -ki ttaymun ey.

-nunkong [South Kyengsang DIAL (¹Na Cinsek 1977)] = (-nun ko =) -nun ka

nun kosa hako SEE kosa hako

-nun kw'ani, abbr < -nun ko hani

-nun kwuly^e/a = -nun kwumen

-nun kwumen (yo), proc mod + postmod (+ pcl). SEE kwumen. ABBR -nu' 'men (yo).

-nun kyel(ul), processive mod + postmodifier. (in) the course of, in passing, while (doing); at the same time as; when, while. cīna kanun kyel(ul) ey passing by. CF -nun kīm/kil/palam.

-nun kwun (a), proc mod + postmod (+ pcl). SEE kwun. ABBR -n' 'wun (a).

-nun kyengwu, processive mod + n. the event/ circumstance of doing; if (and when). ¶mān.il sōnhay paysang ul haci anh.nun kyengwu ey nun in the event you do not make appropriate compensation for the damage ... . Ney ka chak han sālam i toynun kyengwu, ku ttay nun na to tasi sayngkak hay pom a When you become a nice person, then I will think about it again.

-nunkyo (?< -nun ka yo) [S Kyengsang DIAL (¹Na Cinsek 1977)] = -(su)p.nikka

-nun mankhum, abbr < -nun i mankhum

-nun mo.yang, proc mod + n. the looks of doing.
~ ita appears to be doing. ¶Ce phyen hanul i hulin kes ul poni ce phyen ey nun pi ka onun mo.yang ita I see that that part of the sky has clouded up; it appears to be raining over there. Palam to pūnun mo.yang ita The wind seems to be blowing, too.
~ ulo with the appearance of doing, appears to do and (so), (= -nun kes chelem) in the same way. ¶Sewul kanq īlay lo Kim chemci nun caymi lul ponun mo.yang ulo tomuci cip ey nun sosik han cang to an ponay wass.ta Since going to Seoul Mr Kim seems to having too much fun to write a single letter home. Paytuminthen to cengkwu hanun mo.yang ulo hamyen toynta You can play badminton just the way you play tennis. CF -nun yang.

-nun pa, mod + n [lit]. 1. = -nun kes.
2. ~ (ey) does and as a consequence (= -nun tey₂ = -uni); since, when.
~ ey ya if/since (as long as) one is doing it. ¶Hanun pa ey ya cal hay ya hanta Since we are doing it anyway, we ought to do it well.
3. that which does (which one does). SEE pa 3.

-nun palam (ey), proc mod + n (+ pcl). SEE palam₂.
-nun pep SEE pep
-nun phūm, proc mod + n. the appearance/looks/behavior of doing. SEE phūm.
-nun sai / say, proc mod + n. (in) the interval while it does. CF -nun tong-an. ¶Nay ka canun sai ey nay pangq tongmu ka kongpu lul cham mānh.i hayss.ta While I was sleeping my roommate did a whole lot of work. Nay ka ēps.nun say (ey) wuli cip ul cal pwā cwusey yo Please look after my house for me while I am away.
-nun seng siph.ta, proc mod + postmod + adj. seems, appears (to be doing). ¶Pi ka onun seng siph.ess.ta It sounded as if it were raining outside. ⁿYeca ka wūnun seng siph.ess.ta (or seng siph.un soli yess.ta) It was (a sound) like a woman's weeping.
-nun sesul, proc mod + postmod/n ('sharp edge; brunt'). ¶¹Non.li cēngyen hakey wuli chuk uy tāypho ka tul.[y]e tāynun sesul ey nom tul un māl mun i mak.hyess.ta (CM 1:135) The rascals were speechless at the sharp logic thrust at them by the representative of our side.
-nun sēym, processive modifier + postmodifier. ~ ita, ~ ulo SEE sēym.
-nun swu, processive modifier + postmodifier.
  1. an occasion (of doing ···); an event, a case, an instance, a happening, a circumstance. ¶Swul ul mek.umyen silqswu lul hanun swu ka mānh.ta I often make mistakes when I have been drinking. Sā.yong sāng chai ka iss.nun swu ka mānh.ta There are many cases of a difference in usage.
  2. = -nunq īl (experience): ~ iss.ta / ēps.ta sometimes/never does. ¶Il-welq tal ey nwūn i han pen to an onun swu to iss.ci It sometimes happens that January passes without a single snow. Sam-welq tal ey nwūn i onun swu to iss.ci It sometimes (occasionally) snows in March.
  3. a way or means of doing; a remedy, a resource, a help. ¶hanun swu ēps.i helplessly, reluctantly. Hanun swu ēps.ta There is no way out (no help for it). Nothing can be done.
-nunta, processive indicative assertive.
  1. (= statement). does. ¶mek.nunta (= lit mekta) eats. anc.nunta (= lit anc.ta) sits down. After vowels -nta. Occurs only directly attached to processive verb stems (including iss- 'stays') or to such stems + honorific -usi-. ~ wa. ¶(Nwukwu lul) cōh.a hanta wa (nwukwu lul) salang hanta wa nun ttus i ttok kath.ci anh.e yo Liking someone and loving someone are not exactly the same (in meaning). NOTE: This form for the processive indicative assertive (and its postvocalic shape -nta) went virtually unnoticed until it was observed by the missionaries at the end of the 19th century, for the written style preserved the literary version -n^{u}o-ta (Kim Hyengkyu 1954:106-7). But there are nine examples of -n˙ta from the early 1500s (He Wung 1989:361) and at least two examples of -non[˙]ta from the 1600s (LCT 123b, He Wung 1987:228). CF Ceycwu -unta.
  2. (= -nun ta) [lit, obs] = -nun ya / ko. CF -nun ci.
-˙nun˙ta = -˙non˙ta. ¶¨ne y ¨es.te 'n a˙hoy 'Gwan˙toy he˙thwuy˙lol an˙a ¨wunun˙ta (1459 Wel 8:85b; sic an-˙a) what kind of a child are you to cry, clinging to [the calf of] a leg?
-nunta 'l, abbr < -nunta (ko) hal
-nunta 'm, abbr < -nunta (ko) ham (? and of -nunta 'n māl ia). SEE -ta 'm.
-nun tām / taum, [? DIAL] processive mod + n. ~ ey ya if/since it happens (= -nun pa ey ya). ¶Nay ka han pen īl ul hanun tām ey ya ku ttawi lo haci nun anh.nunta If I do it at all, I won't do it that poorly.
-nunta 'myen, abbr < -nunta (ko) hamyen
-nunta 'n('), abbr. 1. < -nunta (ko) han.
  2. < -nunta (ko) hanun.
-nunta 'ni < -nunta (ko) hani. CF -ta ni, ila 'ni.
  1. says it does and (so) ... .
  2. I tell you; you mean to tell me? (shows surprise). ¶Kuleki ey sālam uy īl un molunta 'ni So you never know what will happen to you in this life. Il-nyenq tong-an ina hak.kyo ey taniko to ilum cocha mōs ssunta 'ni! You mean to tell me you've been going to school for a year and can't even write your name?! Kuleki ey sālam un sakwie pwā ya hanta 'ni! I tell you, you have to get to know him well before you see what he is like! Kim sensayng i cwuk.nunta 'ni?! − ku key wēyn māl ia! Mr Kim is dying? − I cannot believe it!
-nunta 'y, abbr < -nunta (ko) hay. says (feels, thinks) that it does. ¶Cikum kass.ta kot onta 'y He says he will be right back.

-nun tay lo, processive mod + noun + particle.

1. in accordance with, just as (it does), like; to the extent that; everything one does. ¶**toylq swu (halq swu) iss.nun tay lo** to the extent possible, as much/nearly as possible. **sikan i iss.nun tay lo** as much/far as time allows. **Nay ka hanun tay lo haci mālko tangsin maum tay lo hasipsio** Don't do just as I do, do as you like. **Sensayng i sikhinun tay lo swukcey lul kkok hay la** Be sure to do your homework just as the teacher told you to do. **Nay ka cwunun tay lo pat.usipsio** Please take what I have to give you. **C'āy (= Ce ay) nun ponun tay lo tā sa tālla 'nta** She wants me to buy everything she sees.

2. as soon as (it does), directly after; CF **-ca (māca)**. ¶**Ku i ka tol.a onun tay lo kot māl-ssum cen hakeyss.ˢup.nita** As soon as he comes back I will give him your message. ¹**yeqkwen i na-onun tay lo** as soon as my passport is issued. **Kot cali ka nanun tay lo allye tulikeyss.ˢup.nita** As soon as there is a place, I'll let you know right away. **Thum i nanun tay lo ku i lul chac.keyss.ta** I'll go see him just as soon as time permits. NOTE: For the past, use **-ca māca ··· -ess.ta**.

3. [DIAL] = **-nun tāysin ey/ulo** (instead of doing).

-nunta 'y se, abbr < **-nunta (ko) hay se**. ¶**Acik to molunta 'y se ya māl i toyna?!** It is absurd for you to say that you still don't know about it. **Cungki-sen un cungki lo kanta 'y se kuleh.key pulunta** A steamer is called that because it is run by steam.

-nun tāysin, proc mod + n: ~ (ey).

1. (as) a substitute for doing; instead of (in place of) doing. ¶**Māl hanun tāysin ey tut.ki man hasipsio** Instead of talking, just listen. **Hawai kanun tāysin ey i pen hyuka ey nun Kwulapha ey kako siph.ta** Instead of going to Hawaii this vacation, I want to go to Europe. **Tōn pēnun tāysin ey na nun tāyhak ey ka se kongpu hakeyss.ta** Instead of earning money, I'll go to college and study. **Totwuk i tāymun ulo na-kanun tāysin ey yuli-chang ulo na-kass.ta** Instead of leaving by the gate, the thief went out by the window. CF **-un tāysin; -ci anh.ko/mālko**.

2. as compensation for doing, to make up for doing, in return for doing. ¶**Tōn i iss.nun tāysin casik i ēps.ta** He has no children, but he has money, instead. **Ku i ka na hanthey Yenge lul kaluchye cwunun tāysin na nun ku i hanthey Tok.il-e lul kaluchye cwunta** I am teaching him German in return for his teaching me English.

-nunta 'y to, abbr < **-nunta (ko) hay to**. even if (one says). ¶**An mek.nunta 'y to cakkwu man kuleni?!** Why do you keep urging me to eat when I tell you I won't?!

-nunta 'y ya, abbr < **-nunta (ko) hay ya**. even if (it is said that). ¶**Cey ka āmuli cal kanta 'y ya han sikan ey payk-lī nun mōs kakeyss.ci** No matter how fast he walks he won't be able to walk a hundred li an hour. **Mek.nunta 'y ya elma 'na mek.keyss.ni − nāy-pelye twue la** Let him eat as much as he likes; he can't eat much anyway. **Cwuk.nunta 'y ya twulyewulq kes ēps.ta** I'm not afraid of his dying.

-nun tey₁, proc mod + n. the place where it does. **phanun tey** a selling place, a (vending) booth, a shop. **phyo phanun tey** a ticket-seller's; a ticket window. **os ul pes.nun tey** the place where one undresses; the (un)dressing room. **mek.nun tey** a place that one eats at. **kanun tey** a place that one goes to.

-nun tey₂, processive modifier + postmodifier.

1. the circumstance/process of doing. ¶**Ku nun kēnkang ul hoypok hanun tey il-nyen i kellyess.ta** It took a full year for him to get his health all back. **Ku kes un nōnun tey cīnaci anh.nunta** That is nothing but (nothing more than) playing! **Sēykyey yele nala tul i wenca-than ul silhem hanun tey pāntay hanta** We are opposed to the testing of atom bombs by the nations of the world.

~ **(ey)**. in/for (the process of) doing. ¶~ **ssuta** uses it for (doing). ~ **phil.yo hata** needs it for (doing), needs/requires it (so as) to do. ~ **phyen.li hata** is convenient for (doing). **Swukcey lul hanun tey elma 'na kellici yo** How long does it take you to do the homework?

~ **kkaci** as much/well/fully as one can. ¶**Kochinun tey kkaci kochyess.ta** I fixed it the best I could. **Kyēysinun tey kkaci kyēysey yo** Stay as long as you can. **Halq swu iss.nun tey kkaci īl hakeyss.ta** I will continue doing all (the most/best) I can. **Iss.ulq tey kkaci iss.e pokeyss.ta** I'll try to stick around (stay/wait) as long as I can. CF **-ulq tey kkaci**.

~ (ey) se. ¶Nal ul cal nāyko mōs nāynun tey se mikkun han cēyphum i na-onun ya kkechil kkechil han cēyphum i na-onun ya ka kyelqceng toynta Proper exposure of the blade determines whether a smooth or a rough article is produced. Ku ka māl hanun tey ey se īsang han cem ul palkyen hayss.ta I detected some odd things in what he was saying (M 3:3:203).
~ (ey) to = -nun tey to. SEE 3a.
~ nun. ¶Sok.inun tey nun halq swu ēps.ta There isn't very much you can do about their cheating.
2. (given) the circumstance that it does; does ··· and/but/so. ¶Kim sensayng eykey phyēnci lul ssunun tey musun pūthak hal māl-ssum i ēps.usip.nikka I am writing to Mr Kim — is there anything you would like me to tell him? Wuli tōngney han sālam i iss.nun tey caykan i pisang hata There is a man in our village who is (= and he is) extraordinarily talented. Saki nun sakeyss.nun tey cikum un tōn i ēps.ta I am going to buy it all right, but I have no money with me now. Kim sensayng puin i kulenun tey meychil cen ey cēntang-pho ey se sikyey hana lul sass.nun tey kkway cōh.tula 'ko yo Mrs Kim says she bought a watch at a pawnshop a few days ago and it has been quite good. Sikan i ēps.nun tey wuli tto talun tey lo kaci We haven't got much time, so let's go someplace else. Onulq cenyek ey chinkwu hako yenghwa kwūkyeng kaki lo hayss.nun tey tōn com cwusikeyss.ˢup.nikka I have made plans to go to a movie tonight with a friend; will you give me some money? Onul un yaksok i iss.nun tey — talun nal lo hapsita I have an engagement today — let's make it some other day. Sensayng nim ul cāmqkan poywess.umyen cōh.keyss.nun tey sikan i iss.usip.nikka I'd like to see you for a few minutes; do you have time? I pen si'-wel ey Hānkwuk ey kanun tey kath.i kasilq ka yo? I am going to Korea this October; why don't you come along? Pi ka onun tey com te kyēysita kasipsio Stay a little longer; it's raining.
3. 3a. ~ to even though it does, in spite of the fact that it does, despite that ··· . ¶Ku nun ō-sip i nem.ess.nun tey to ohilye hwang-so chelem īl ul hanta While past fifty, he works like an ox. Nwūn i onun tey to chwupci anh.e yo Despite the snow it is not cold (M 1:2:167).

3b. ~ to pulkwu hako regardless of (in spite of, disregarding) the fact that it does. ¶Ku nun nwūn i mopsi onun tey to pulkwu hako pakk ulo na-kass.ta He went out in spite of the heavy snow.
4. ~ (yo)! You see it's a case of doing ··· ! (sentence-final exclamatory — shows surprise, interest). ¶Cal hanun tey! You're doing well! Ku ai ka cal to sayngkyess.nun tey! What a handsome child! Pi ka cēmcem mānh.i onun tey! The rain is coming down harder than ever! Mas i 'ss.nun tey yo! How tasty it is! Cham olay kan man io; ca, tul.e owu; cip ul yōng khey chac.ess.nun tey! It's been a long time (since we've seen you), please come in; you found our house quite easily, I see. Cham, kkwum to īsang han kkwum ul kkwuess.nun tey! My what a weird dream I had! Cikum yetelp si ka nem.ess.nun tey yo, mwe It's already past eight (M 1:2:81). SEE (-nun tey) 'psiyo, ipsiyo.
5. marks a question in the INTIMATE or (~ yo) POLITE style that asks for the feelings or the opinion of the addressee ('you'), often rhetorically. ¶Poci mālla 'y to cakkwu (man) ponun tey? Why does he keep looking at it in spite of my telling him not to? Ne man pon key ani 'la, na to pwass.nun tey? Don't you know that I have seen it as well as you? Cal kamchwe twuki n' hayss.ci man āmulay to pokeyss.nun tey? Even though we have hidden it well don't you think somebody may find it?
NOTE: In Cincwu of South Kyengsang (Mkk 1960:3:35) this is said to attach [in all uses?] to adjective stems, as well as to processive verb stems: kath.nun tey = kath.un tey; cōh.nun tey = cōh.un tey; mānh.nun tey = mānh.un tey; tēp.nun tey = tewun tey.
SEE -ess(-ess/-keyss)-nun tey, -keyss.nun tey. DIAL -nun tay.
-nuntey₃ → -nunta 'y
-nun tey (ey) se SEE -nun tey (1)
-nun tey (ey) 'ta (ka). not only ··· but in addition (on top of that). ¶Sikan i ēps.nun tey 'ta (ka) tōn to ēps.ta I lack the time and, on top of that, I lack the money, too. Nwun i an poinun tey 'ta (ka) tut.ci mace mōs hani sal.e se mwes hakeyss.ˢo?! Not only blind but unable to hear, as well, what good is there in living?!
-nun tey to SEE -nun tey₂ (3)

-nun tey tul, proc mod + postmod + particle. ¶**Mollye onun tey tul = Mollye tul onun tey** They form a group and come.
-nun tey ya, proc mod + postmod + pcl. SEE **tey ya**.
-nun tey yo, proc mod + postmod + pcl. SEE **-nun tey₂** (4).
-nun the (ey) SEE **the 4**
-nun thong (ey) SEE **thong (ey)**
-nun ti [Ceycwu DIAL (Seng ¹Nakswu 1984: 51-4)] = **-nun tey**
-nunˑti(···) = -nun ˑt i(···), proc mod + postmod ('fact') + pcl/cop. that it/one does. ¶*na 'y ˑeˑmi ˑˑamwo ˑtoy ˑna 'ys.non ˑt i ˑˑmwolˑlay-ngi ˑˑta* (1459 Wel 21:53a; underlying object marked with nominative) I do not know what place my mother is being reborn into.
-nun ˑt ol, proc mod + postmod + pcl. (the fact) that it/one does. Examples? CF **-non ˑt ol**.
-nun ˑt olwo, proc mod + postmod + pcl. because it/one does.
-nun tong-an, processive mod + n. while doing. ¶**Wuli ka īl hanun tong-an ey āmu panghay ka ēps.ess.ta** There was no disturbance at all while we were working. **Nay ka tāyhak ey se kongpu hanun tong-an yele kaci cōh.un kyenghem ul mānh.i hayss.ta** While studying at college, I had many valuable experiences.
-nun tongsi ey SEE **tongsi**
-nuntota (= **-tota** = **-nola**) = **-(nu)nta**
-nun ttay, proc mod + n. the time(s)/occasion(s) that it happens; a present experience: ~ **ka iss.ta / mānh.ta (ēps.ta / tumulta)** sometimes / often (never / seldom) does. ¶**Ku i nun cēmsim ul kwūlm.nun ttay ka iss.ta** Now and then he skips lunch. SYN **-nun cek**; CF **-nunq īl**.
-nun ttaymun [DIAL] = **-nun kkatalk, -ki ttaymun**. CF CM 2:70.
(?*)**-nun tul**, proc mod + postmod. SEE **tul**.
-nun tūng, proc mod + postmod. (doing) and so on. ¶**Swuhay lul phī haki wi hay se nun twutwuk ul noph.i ssah.nunta 'tun ci namu lul sīmnun tūng yele kaci tāychayk i iss.e ya hanta** In order to prevent flood damage it is necessary to take all sort of measures, raising dikes and planting trees and so on. **Hak.nyen-mal ila chāyqcem, ip.hak sihem, col.ep-sik cwūnpi hanun tūng ulo mopsi pappup.nita** It being the end of the school year, I am terribly busy marking papers, preparing entrance exams and graduation ceremonies and so on.
-nun tus ('i), proc mod + postmod (+ der adv).
1. as if/though doing; as, like. ¶**ne-huy tul ponun tus 'i** as you people can see. **Mues ul sayngkak hanun tus ('i) camcakho iss.ta** He keeps silent as if thinking. CF **-ta siph.i**.
2. (with two contrastive expressions) you can't tell whether (it does) or whether ··· . ¶**Pap ul mek.nun tus ('i) mānun tus ('i) ceq-kalak cil ul hanta** From the way he is maneuvering his chopsticks you cannot tell whether he is eating or not.
3. (? sloppy for **-nun tus hatuni**). ¶**Kanun pi ka kuchinun tus kwulk.un pi ka sīcak ha.yess.ta** (CM 1:135) The fine rain seemed about to let up but then a heavy rain set in.
CF **-nun twung**.
-nun tus hata, proc mod + postmod adj-n. gives the idea/impression of doing; looks as if (like) it does. ¶**Ce haksayng un māl un an haci man kongpu lul cal hanun tus hata** That student doesn't say anything but he seems to study a lot. CF **-' tus hata**.
-nun tus siph.ta, proc mod + insep adj postmod + adj. gives the impression of doing; feels/looks as if it does; something tells one it does.
-nun twung < **-non ˑtwong**, processive modifier + postmodifier.
1. ~ **mānun twung** whether or not does, may or may not (with equal likelihood − CF **hanun ci mānun ci** very well may or perhaps may not). ¶**Ku ay nun kongpu hanun twung mānun twung yenphil kkuth man ssipko iss.ta** You can't tell, the way he's just chewing on his pencil, whether he is studying or not. **Nwūn i onun twung (to) mānun twung (to) hanta → hako iss.ta** You can't tell whether it is really snowing or not. **ku chayk ul ponun twung mānun twung hanta** gives the book a cursory reading, reads the book half-heartedly, **pap ul mek.nun twung mānun twung hayss.ta** just made a gesture of eating. **Nam iya musun cīs ul hatun (ci), ne nun hangsang ponun twung mānun twung man hako tanimyen toynta** You should go your way without paying attention to whatever others may be doing. CF **-nun tus**.
2. [DIAL] = **-nun ci** whether. ¶**Cip ul tte-nan ci ka olayn tey ku tong-an āmu thāl ina ēps.nun twung (= ci) molukeyss.ta** It has

been a long time since I left home and I don't know whether everything is all right or not.

'nun twung, abbr < (ko) hanun twung. ¶Kap i olh.ta 'nun twung ul i olh.ta 'nun twung ūykyen i kwukwu hata Opinions are divided whether A is right or B is right. I kes ul hala 'nun twung ce kes ul hala 'nun twung māl i mānh.ta All I hear is do this, do that.

-˙nu˙n uy = -˙nu˙n [y]uy, abbr < -˙nu˙n i ˙uy of (etc.) that which ··· .

? nun ya, abbr < nun iya. SEE p. 818 (to NOTE).
-nunya = -nun ya.
  ~ 'myen < -nun ya (ko) hamyen.

-nun ya, proc mod + postmod. (the question) whether it does ··· . This is a common way to state questions in the plain style, especially in quotations; CF -ni. SYN -nun (i), -nun ka.
NOTE: Used only for proc verbs (SEE -un ya); -ess.(ess.)nun ya and -(ess.)keyss.nun ya also attach to the stems of adjectives and the copula.
  ~ pota = -nun ka pota, -na pota.
  ~ (ha)nta asks/wonders (whether ···).

-nun ya ka, proc mod + mod + pcl. ¶Mues ul mek.nun ya ka mūncey 'ta The question is what we are eating. SEE -keyss.nun ya ka.

-nun ya ko [DIAL] = -nula ko

-nun yang, processive modifier + noun.
  1. ~ hata (vnt) makes a pretense of doing. ¶Khun chayk ul ssunun yang hanta He would have you think he's writing a mighty tome.
  2. (~ ita, ~ ulo) = -nun mo.yang.

-nun ya nun, proc mod + postmod + pcl. ¶Mues ul mek.nun ya nun kekceng mālla As for what to eat, don't worry about it.

-nun ya tul, proc mod + postmod + particle. ¶Cikum ay tul ī-chung ey se kongpu hanun ya tul Are the children studying upstairs now?

-nun ya 'y, abbr < -nun ya (ko) hay. ~ yo.

-nun ya ya, proc mod + postmod + pcl. ¶Mues ul mek.nun ya ya kekceng mālla As for just what to eat, don't worry about it.

-nunyo = -nun yo

-nun yo [obs] = -nun ya (question)

-nuta, alt of -nota, proc indic assert = -(nu)nta.

nuy [DIAL] = ney your. [Ceycwu] nuy sensing = ney sensayng your teacher.

-nu'y = /-ni/, abbr < -nun i. ~ 'la.

-˙n uy = -˙n [y]uy, abbr < -˙n i ˙uy 'of (etc.) that which ··· '. SEE ˙uy.

nwa = nwā, abbr < nowa = noh.a, inf < noh.ta; as aux usually short. ABBR n'a = n'ā.

nwē, abbr < nwuwe, inf < nwupta; < nwue, inf < nwuta.

nwi, [DIAL, obs]. 1. → nwī (< ¨nwu ˙y < *˙nwu ˙uy) = nwukwu uy whose.
  2. (< ˙nwu y < *˙nwu ˙i) = nwu ka who.
  3. (< ˙nwuy = ˙nwu) = nwukwu who. ¶nwuy lwo (1887 Scott 30) = nwi lo by whom.

nwi ka ? < *nwu i ka (n + pcl + pcl) [Taycen DIAL] = nwu ka who/someone. CF nwuy ka (Scott 1893:177)

nwi 'key [DIAL, obs] = nwukwu eykey

nwi 'la se, [DIAL, obs] = nwukwu 'la se. ¶Nwi 'la se nay hayngsayk kulye 'ta (n)im kyēysin tey tulilq ko If only there were someone to draw a picture of me to send you! Nwi 'la se ne poko kulen soli hatun? Did someone say that to you?

-˙nwo- < *-(˙)n[o]-˙wo-, modulated processive. Sometimes this is listed also as an emotive, but the emotive meaning seems to be carried by an attached morpheme (-s- or -˙swo-); perhaps the listing as emotive is in fact the same as LCT's treatment of -(˙)no- itself as also a way of emphasizing facts.

-˙nwo'-i ˙˙ta, abbr < -˙nwo-ngi ˙˙ta

¨nwol(q) < *nwo˙l[o]l(q), prospective modifier < ¨nwo[l]˙ta (plays). ¶nwol ㄹ [= ˙ㅇㅣㄹㅇ] (1576 ¹Yuhap 2:7a) to play.

-˙nwo˙la. SEE -nola.

  1. modulated proc indic attent. ¶˙i ¨ney˙h ul ¨mwot ˙pwo˙a ˙honwo˙la (1459 Wel 10:4b) I find myself unable to look upon these four [people]. mozo˙m ay ˙senul hi ne˙kiti a˙ni hol s a˙ni ˙honwo˙la (1475 Nay se:6a) it is not that I am not treating it coolly in my mind. wo˙lay ne ˙[G]wa ta˙mos ¨salGe˙na cwuk.ke˙na ˙khwo cye solang ˙honwo˙la (1481 Twusi 8:35a) for a long time I have been thinking I would like to live or die with you. tyey ˙ka ¨sek ˙to.l i˙na mwuk˙nwo˙la ˙ho˙ya cip sak[s] mwu˙le sywokcyel ¨ep˙si he˙pi ho˙l i ˙las˙ta (?1517-Pak 1:54a) I uselessly wasted my money to pay the rent thinking I would stay for some three months. ˙na-ka˙kwo cye tha ˙ka [¨HWO-LANG] ˙ol cen˙nwola [< ceh-no-wo-la] (1481 Twusi 8:29a) I want to go out but I fear the tigers.

  2. modulated processive purposive. ¶˙SYEK-KA ZYE-LOY ku ˙psk uy PPWO-˙SALQ s ¨TTWOW-¨LI

˙honwo˙la ˙ho˙ya (1447 Sek 6:8a) the tathāgata Śākya[muni], at that moment in time seeking to practice the bodhisattva's doctrine, ... ˙mul ¨ket-nanwo˙la ˙poy ˙tha ˙kata ˙ka (1482 Nam 1:36b) to cross the water they go by boat, but... .

3. ? modulated proc subj attent. ¶ kutuy ˙nay ki˙Gwulye me˙kwu.m ul ˙pwonwo˙la (1481 Twusi 15:52b) you fellows watch your tendency to drink [seeing what it has done to me].

¨nwolm < *nwo˙l[o]m, substantive < nōlta < ¨nwo[l]˙ta. Example?

nwo˙lwom, modulated subst < ¨nwo[l]˙ta (vi 'plays'). ¶ nwo˙lwo.m ol a˙ni ho.ya is˙ta.n i (1481 Twusi 7:23a) I was not being indolent.

˙nwom, 1. = nom (damn fellow; damn thing).

2. (ordinary) person. ¶ hon ˙nwo˙m i ˙khun ¨SSYANG ˙tho˙kwo ˙hwosi˙m ye (1459 Wel 10:28a; note the honorific) a fellow is riding a large elephant and ... . ¨mwo˙tin ˙nwo˙m oy ¨mal ˙on (1459 Wel 17:76b; sic ¨mal-˙on) what evil people say. nul˙kun ˙nwo.m oy ci˙p ilwo˙ta (1481 Twusi 7:6b) it is the house of an old man. nul˙kun nye˙lum ¨cis.non ˙nwo.m on (1481 Twusi 22:7b) the old peasant doing the farming.

¨nwon < *nwo˙[lo]n, modifier < ¨nwo[l]˙ta. ¶ ¨nwo˙n i (1447 Sek se:2b) it is uncommon.

-˙nwon, modulated processive modifier. ¶ ¨say ˙uy ˙culki˙nwon ˙ptu.t ul ˙pwonwola (1481 Twusi 7:11a) I see the joy that is felt by the birds. ˙i kak˙si ˙za na ˙y ¨et.ni˙nwon mozo˙m ay mas˙two˙ta (1447 Sek 6:14ab) precisely this girl matches the purpose I am pursuing. kwo˙ki ˙lol pa˙hye ¨nay[˙]nwon ˙to˙s ˙i (1447 Sek 9:12a [Taycey-kak repro looks like ¨¨naynun¨ but see LCT 142a, the ¹Yi Tonglim text]) like tearing off the flesh.

-˙nwo-ngi ˙˙ta, modulated proc polite + copula indic attent [1st person]. ¶ ˙na y solang ˙hwo˙toy e˙nwu ˙CCANG s KUM ˙i ˙za ˙ma˙chi skol˙Gi.l [i] 'ye˙n ywo ˙ho˙nwo-ngi ˙˙ta (1447 Sek 6:25b) I am thinking: just which vault's gold will it take for it be properly covered, so I am thinking. ABBR -nwoyng' ˙˙ta, -nwoy' ˙ta, -nwo'-i ˙ta.

-˙nwo˙n i, modulated proc mod + postmodifier.

1. the one (thing/person) that ... does.

1a. (epitheme extruded from the subject) one who/that does. ¶ ¨il ¨ep˙sun ¨TTWOW-¨LI ˙lol KKWUW ˙honwo˙n i cwuk-sa˙li s QIN-YWEN ˙un tut˙ti ¨mwot ˙hwo.l [i] 'ye˙ta (1459 Wel 1:11b) those who seek an uneventful doctrine hardly will listen to the reasons for life and death.

1b. (epitheme extruded from the object) one whom / that ... does. Example?

2. (summational epitheme used in extended predicate). it is [the case] that ... does. ¶ ha˙nol˙h ay ˙na˙a MWON-SSIN ˙i towoy˙ya is˙nwo˙n i (1447 Sek 6:20a) I have appeared in heaven and become a gate-guardian spirit. pen˙tu˙ki ¨swuy˙i ¨al˙Gwa˙tye ˙po˙lanwo˙n i (1462 ¹Nung 8:44b) they expect to learn it easily right away. no˙m oy ¨kye˙cip towoy˙nwo˙n i chol hi ˙tye kwo˙ma towoy˙Ga ci˙la (1463 Pep 2:28b) I would rather become his concubine than another man's wife. ˙na y ˙icey ne ˙lul nwot˙nwo˙n i ˙ptu˙t ul cwo˙cha ka˙la (1459 Wel 13:19ab) I will now send you off to follow your own mind.

-˙nwo.n i s ˙ka, modulated proc mod + postmod [+ ellipted cop polite] + pcl + bnd n. ¶ HWON-QIN ¨wuy ˙ho˙ya a˙zo˙m i ˙wona˙ton ipa˙two˙l ye ˙ho˙nwo.n i s ˙ka (1447 Sek 6:16ab) are you entertaining relatives come for a wedding?

-˙nwon ˙ka, processive modifier + postmodifier. ¶ ˙SYEY-CWON s ¨il sol˙Wwo.l i ˙'n i ˙MEN-¨LI ˙NGWOY s ¨il isi˙na nwun ˙ey ˙pwonwon ˙ka ne˙kizo˙Wosywo˙sye (1449 Kok 2) I will tell you of the World-Honored's work: it is a work beyond the myriad leagues [of our land] but please think of it as if (to wonder whether) you are seeing it in your eye. kwuy ˙yey tut˙nwon ka ne˙kizo˙Wosywo˙sye (1449 Kok 2; "tutnun" in Pak Pyenchay 1974:77 is a misprint) think of it as if perhaps hearing it in your ear.

-˙nwon ˙pa, modulated proc mod + postmod.

~ y (pcl). ¶ SIN ˙uy ¨NGWEN [= ˙NGWEN] ˙honwon ˙pa y a˙ni ˙'n i '-ng' ita [sic, "a-ni-ning-˙i-ta"] (1586 Sohak 6:44a) it is not that a subject is requesting it.

~ 'yl (copula prospective modifier). ¶ ¨nyey pu˙the sul˙nwon [= sulh-˙nwon] ˙pa 'yl ˙s oy (1481 Twusi 8:7b) because it is distressing from way back.

-˙nwon ˙t ... , modulated proc mod + postmod. the fact that it/one does.

~ i (pcl). ¶ MWU-MYENG ˙i ˙SSILQ ˙lwo ¨THYEY is˙nwon ˙t i a˙ni ˙˙la (1459 Wel 2:22c) primal darkness (avidyā = ignorance) does not really have form. na 'y ˙e˙mi ¨amwo˙toy ˙na 'ys.non ˙t i ¨mwol˙lay-ngi '˙ta (1459 Wel 21: 53a; the underlying object is marked with the nominative) I do not know what place it is that my mother is being reborn into. ¨ta ˙KHOYK-TTIN i towoy˙ya 'ys˙nwon ˙t i ˙swo˙n oy phye˙lak ¨cwuy˙lak ho˙m ye me˙li YWOW-¨TTWO ˙hwo˙m i ˙kot ho˙n i '˙la (1462 ¹Nung 1:113a) that it has all become useless dust is like the hand opening and closing and the head shaking [= is all too natural]. [QAN-¨TTWOW] ˙lol ˙chos.nwon ˙t i a˙ni ˙la (1481 Twusi 7:18a) one does not visit [the Bó Jū commentator] Dài Ān-dào.

- ˙nwon (˙)t i⋯ , modulated proc mod + postmod + copula.

 - ˙nwon t i˙la (copula indic assertive). ¶ ˙swoy oy ˙kuyGwun ˙on kozol s se˙nule˙wu.m i towoy˙nwon t i˙la (1482 Kum-sam 2:29b) the temper of the metal results from the autumn's being cool.

 - ˙nwon ˙t i.l i '˙la (copula prosp modifier + postmod + cop). ¶syang˙nyey ku TYWUNG ˙ey i˙sye KYENG-HHOYNG ho˙m ye ¨CCWA-˙NGWA ˙ho˙nwon ˙t i.l i '˙la (1463 Pep 5:212b) will always be in their midst, walking in meditation and sitting and lying down.

 -[˙]nwon ˙t ilq s oy (copula prosp modifier + postmod + particle). ¶MI-˙MYWOW hon KWANG-MYENG ˙ul ˙pwonwon ˙t il ss oy (= ilq s oy) ˙i PPWO-˙SALQ s il˙hwu˙m ul MWU-PYEN KWANG ˙ila ho˙kwo (1459 Wel 8:38b) because of seeing a subtle aura, they call this bodhisattva "Limitless Light" by name.

 -[˙]nwon ˙t i˙m ye (cop subst + cop inf). ¶pwu¨thye y syang˙nyey KKI-SSYA-˙KKWULQ SAN ˙ay i˙sye ˙TTAY-PPWO-˙SALQ ˙Gwa CYE SYENG-MWUN ˙CYWUNG ˙i ˙NGWUY-¨ZYWOW ˙ho˙ya 'ys.ke˙tun ˙SYWELQ-˙PEP ˙hwo˙m ol ˙pwonwon ˙t i˙m ye (1459 Wel 17:35a) Buddha is frequently on Mount Gṛdhrakūṭa (Vulture Peak), surrounded by great bodhisattvas and crowds of śrāvakas (= hīnayāna disciples in the first stage), and they are seen expounding the law, and ... .

 -[˙]nwon ˙t in ˙t ay n' (cop mod + postmod + pcl + pcl). ¶na 'y a˙tol ˙SILQ-˙TTALQ ˙i ˙wonwon ˙t in ˙t ay n' mwoncye KWANG-MYENG ¨pwoyywo˙m i syang˙nyey s SSYANG-˙SSYWUY '˙la (1459 Wel 10:7b) when my son Siddhārtha comes there is always a portent of first an illumination being seen.

 -[˙]nwon ˙t on, modulated proc mod + postmod + pcl. ¶ ˙CI ˙lol ca˙pa ˙pse selu ˙pwonwon ˙t on KWONG-˙KYENG ˙ho.ya ¨NGWUW-˙PPYELQ ˙hwo.m ol pol˙ki-kay '.n i ˙la (1475 Nay 1:77b) they caught a wild goose and the look they gave each other was enough to clarify the admirable rarity of the occasion [pol˙ki-kay = pol˙kinon kes].

 -[˙]nwon ˙t un < -nwon ˙t on. ¶[˙NGWEN] honwon ˙t un ... (1579 Kwikam 1:24b) what is requested is ... .

 -[˙]nwon ˙t ye, modulated proc mod + postmod + postmod [question]. ¶sulphu˙ta ¨nyey s salo˙m oy ¨ma.l ol ¨ati ¨mwot ˙honwon ˙t ye (1482 Nam 2:30b) 'Tis sad — are we quite unaware of what people of earlier days said? CF -un ˙t ye.

 -[˙]nwos˙ta < *-(˙)n[o]-˙wo-s-ta, modulated proc emotive indic assert. ¶ ˙i ¨salo˙m i ¨pwo˙poy ˙lol tye˙li-˙two˙lwok a˙ni as˙kinwos˙ta (1447 Sek 6:25-6) this person does not begrudge treasures to that extent! ¨salo˙m on [KWA-YEN] ˙ul ku˙chi˙sikwa˙tye solang ˙honwos˙ta (1481 Twusi 20:4b) the people would love to put an end to spears and lances. ˙PALQ-PWONG ˙oy ¨wo˙m i ¨ha˙m ol muten ˙hi ne˙kinwos˙ta (1482 Kum-sam 3:19a) treats casually the fact that the coming of the Eight Winds [which fan the passions] is frequent.

- ˙nwos.two˙ta, modulated proc emotive-emotive indic assert. ¶ ˙tol s ˙pi.ch i [HEN-¨HAM] ˙ay wo˙lo˙nwos.two˙ta (1481 Twusi 8:25b) the moon light rises to the balustrade.

- ˙nwoswo˙la < *-(˙)n[o]-˙wo-swo-˙la, modulated processive modulated emotive indicative assertive. ¶wuli ˙two ˙i ˙KKYEY ˙lol cwosco˙Wa woy˙Gwo˙nwoswo˙la (1459 Wel 8:100b) we too are memorizing this gāthā accordingly. [˙KALQ-HHWONG] ˙ul pwus˙kuli˙nwoswo˙la (1481 Twusi 21:34a) one feels embarrassed [at the slow journey] before Gĕ Hóng (a Confucianist of the Eastern Jīn).

- ˙nwo˙swo-ngi '˙ta, modulated proc modulated emotive polite + cop indic assert. ¶SYEY ˙yey ˙na SSYANG-˙TTYWU ˙lol ¨et˙key ˙honwo˙swo-ngi '˙ta (1462 ¹Nung 6:66a) lets one be born in the world and obtain permanent residence

[therein]. *twoco˙k i ˙THAY-¨CO ˙lwo pu˙the ˙na˙nwo˙swo-ngi ˙˙ta* (1475 Nay se:5b) the renegades come out, starting with the prince.
-˙*nwoswo˙n i*, modulated processive modulated emotive mod + postmodifier. ¶*[˙POYK-˙SYELQ] ˙un ¨ma˙l i ¨epkwo ˙cye ˙ho˙nwoswo˙n i ˙e˙cule˙wun kwo˙c on [NUNG] ˙hi ˙myes ˙ma s ˙psk i.n i ˙Gwo* (1481 Twusi 7:14a) the shrike is tending to be silent [as usual toward the end of spring]; how much time is there left for the kaleidoscope of flowers? SEE -*usi˙nwoswo˙n i*.
-*nwo˙ta*, modulated proc indic assert. ¶*achom mata mu.l ey ci[z]wun [LWUW] wu.h uy wolGa polanwota* (1632 Twusi-cwung 8:38b) every morning I climb the pavilion built on the water and gaze out.
-*nwoyng' ˙'ta*, abbr < -˙*nwo-ngi ˙˙ta*, modulated proc polite + cop. ¶*pwuthye ˙[G]wa ¨cywung ˙kwa ˙lol ¨CHYENG ˙ho˙zoWwo˙l ye ˙honwoyng' ˙˙ta* (1447 Sek 6:16b) I am planning to invite Buddha and his priests.
-*nwoy' ˙˙ta*, abbr < -*nwoyng' ˙˙ta* < -˙*nwo-ngi ˙˙ta*.
-**nwu** = -**no**
nwu < ˙*nwu*, n. ˙*nwu ˙i* → ˙*nwu y*, ˙*nwu ˙uy* → ¨*nwu 'y*. ˙*nwu* + ˙*kwa* → ¨*nwul˙Gwa*. ˙*nwu* + ˙*lul* → ¨*nwu ˙lul*, ¨*nwu l'*.
1. [obs] = **nwukwu** who / whom. SEE ˙*nwuy*.
2. alternant of **nwukwu** before pcl **ka**. NOTE: **nwukwu ka** is dialect, as is **nwi**.
nwu ka, n + pcl. who / someone [as subject].
nwukey [? < *nwu ka i*] [Ceycwu DIAL (Seng [1]Nakswu 1984:25n)] = **nwu ka**
˙*nwu ˙kwo*, n + postmod. who is it (= **nwukwu 'n ka**). ¶*pwu¨thye y ˙nwu ˙kwo* (1459 Wel 21:195a) who is Buddha? ¨*CYWONG-˙TI nay.l i nwu ˙kwo* (1463 Pep 5:196b; *nay.l i* = ¨*nay˙l i, nwu* = ˙*nwu*) who is to generate the seminal wisdom? ˙*i ˙nwu kwo* (1482 Kum-sam 4:6b) who is this? ¨*mwunnwo˙la mozo˙m ey ¨sim hi solang ˙hono˙n i n' ˙nwu kwo* (1481 Twusi 16: 39b) let me ask, who is it who at heart loves deeply? ˙*i ¨pe˙t un ˙nwu ˙kwo* (?1517- [1]No 2: 6a) = *i pe.s un nwukwo kwo* (1795 [1]No-cwung [P] 2:5a).
nwukwo = **nwukwu**, n. who. ¶*nwukwo kwo* (1795 [1]No-cwung [P] 2:5a) = ˙*nwu ˙kwo* (?1517- [1]No 2:6a) 'who is it?' but *nwukwu nun* (id. 1:14b) = ˙*nwu˙kwu non* (?1517- [1]No 1:16a), *nwukwu* (1583 Sek-chen 23b, 31a). LCT cites also *nwukwo 'm ye* (1763 Haytong 86). An odd and early example of this incorporation of the postmodifier ˙*kwo* by ˙*nwu* is seen in ˙*nwu˙kwo ˙[G]wo ¨mwu˙lusin ˙t ay* (1481 Samkang chwung:7b) 'when he inquired who it was' with a new version of ˙*kwo* attached.

nwukwu, noun. [alternant **nwu** before pcl **ka**]. An indeterminate person: INTERROGATIVE in a question with falling intonation or in a quoted question; INDEFINITE or GENERAL otherwise.

1. who; what person; (= āmu[-kay], etten i) a certain person, somebody, someone, so-and-so. ¶**Nwu ka kuletun ya** [WITH A FALLING INTONATION] Who said so?; [WITH A RISING INTONATION] Did someone say so? **Nwu ka kuletun tey ku nun pelsse tte-nass.ta 'tula** Somebody told me that he had left already. **Nwukwu nun cāngkwan i toyko, nwukwu nun sacang i toynun tey, ne nun mwe l' hanun ke 'n ya ko emeni kkwucilam hasitula** Mother was scolding "Some become cabinet ministers, some become company heads, and what do YOU do?" **nwukwu 'tun ci, nwukwu 'na (tā)** anyone, anybody, everyone.

2. (= **nwukwu uy**) whose. ¶**Ce [n]yeca ka nwukwu puin iyo** Whose wife is that woman [who is passing by over there]?

3. [IRONIC] I / me. CF **na**; **nam**. ¶**Nwu ka hal māl ul ney ka hanun kwun a** You are saying what I should say = You blame me, but I should be blaming you. It's me who should be saying that. **Kulemyen nwu ka musewe halq cwul ānun ya** Do you think I will be afraid if you do that?

4. [IRONIC, TEASING] you (said to a child), "someone I know" (= you). ¶**Nwukwu nun pam ey cata ka ocwum ssass.ta 'y yo** Someone I know wet his bed last night!

CF **nwī**, **nwī 'ykey**, **enu nwukwu**.
NOTE: The form was originally **nwu**; -**kwu** comes from the interrogative postmodifier **ko** < ˙*kwo*. SEE **nwukwo** just above.

nwu kwu = ˙*nwu ˙kwo* who is it (= **nwukwu 'n ka**). ¶˙*no˙m on ˙nwu ˙kwu* (?1468- Mong 20b) who is the other (person)?

nwukwu eykey, n + pcl. to whom; to someone.
NOTE: **nwī 'key** is dialect or obsolete.
nwukwu 'ko, n + cop ger. anybody, anyone;

whoever. ¶Nwukwu 'ko omyen i kes ul cwula If anyone comes, give this to him.
nwukwu l', n + abbr pcl (< nwukwu lul). who(m); someone [as direct object]. ¶Nwukwu l' māl hanun kes in ka Who(m) are you talking about? Nwukwu l' ponayss.nun ka [FALLING INTONATION] Who(m) did you send?; [RISING INTONATION] Did you send someone?
nwukwu 'l(q), n + cop prosp mod (= il).
nwukwu n', n + abbr pcl (< nwukwu nun). as for anyone / everyone. ¶Nwukwu n' moluna [FALLING or RISING INTONATION] Does anyone not know that? = Who doesn't know that?
nwukwu 'n, n + cop mod (= in). ⋯ that is who/someone. ~ ci, ~ ka, ~ tey, ~ tul, ~ ya.
nwukwu 'na, n + cop advers. ~ (tā) anyone, anybody, everyone.
~ V-e to = nwu ka V-e to whoever may V. ¶Nwukwu 'na ka to kwaynchanh.e = Nwu ka ka to kwaynchanh.e Anyone may go.
nwukwu 'n ci, n + abbr < in (cop mod) + postmod. 1. someone or other. ¶Nwukwu 'n ci wass.ess.ta Someone came (while you were away).
2. (the uncertain fact of) who it is. ¶Nwukwu 'n ci mōlla I don't know who it is.
nwukwu 'n ci n', abbr < nwukwu (i)n ci nun. ¶Ku kes i nwukwu 'n ci n' kot ālkey toylq ke 'ey yo That's something that anyone will get to know right away. Nwukwu 'n ci n' mōlla to cham cal ttwinun kwun a Whoever he is, he's sure a fine jumper!
nwukwu 'n ka, noun + copula mod + postmod.
1. who is it? 2. someone.
~ ka (pcl). ¶Ko.yangi ey pangwul ul talq sālam i nwukwu 'n ka ka mūncey 'ta The question is, who will bell the cat?
nwukwu 'n tul, noun + copula mod + postmod.
1. whoever it may be. ¶Ku key nwukwu 'n tul ne 'ykey musun sangkwan ia?! What does it matter to you who he is?
2. [in a rhetorical question] anyone, everyone. ¶Ōl^h-palun sayngkak ul kacin sālam ila 'myen nwukwu 'n tul ku puceng ey pūnkay haci anh.ul i?! Would any right-thinking soul not be indignant at that injustice?
3. (even) I/me. ¶Nwukwu 'n tul an kulen cwul āni? – tā machan-kaci 'la 'n' māl ia Do you think I'm different? – we are all alike, you see.
nwukwu 'tun ci, n + cop retr mod + postmod. anyone, anybody, everyone.
nwukwu nwukwu, iterated n. just who and who, who all. ¶Nwukwu nwukwu wass.na Who all are here? ~ halq kes ēps.i every last person (man / woman), every man Jack, without any distinction of person. Nwukwu nwukwu halq kes ēps.i tā napputa You are all to blame, every last one of you.
nwukwu 'n ya, n + cop mod + postmod. who is it?
~ ka (pcl). ¶Ko.yangi ey pangwul ul talq sālam i nwukwu 'n ya ka mūncey 'ta The question is, who will bell the cat?
¨*nwu l'* = ¨*nwu ˙lul*, n + pcl. whom. ¶¨*nwu l' te ˙pu ˙le mwu ˙le ˙za ho ˙l i ˙'m ye* (1447 Sek 13:15a) with whom should I inquire and … . ¨*nwu l' to ˙lye nilo ˙l i ˙Gwo* (1482 Kum-sam 2:45a) whom shall I say it to?
nwu ley, n + pcl [Ceycwu DIAL (Pak Yonghwu 1960:395)] = nwu ka who [as subject].
nwul ˙Gwa (1481 Twusi 8:46b) = ¨*nwul ˙Gwa* ?= ¨*nwu l' ˙Gwa* (1482 Nam 1:66b) with whom (= nwukwu wa / hako / 'lang). SEE ul kwa.
¨*nwu ˙lul*, n + pcl. whom. ¶*e ˙nu* ¨*nwu ˙lul te ˙pu ˙lusi ˙l [i] 'ye ˙n ywo* (1449 Kok 52) whom will you take along? ¨*nwu ˙lul ˙ho ˙ya ˙ka* ¨*etu ˙la ho ˙l ywo* (?1517- Pak 1:3a) whom will you get to go with you? ¨*nwu [˙]lol pu ˙thu.n ywo* (1482 Nam 1:80b) whom to rely on? NOTE: Spelled ¨*nwul ˙ul* in ˙*stwo namcin ˙uy kamwun ˙i ˙psu ˙le cwuk ˙e imuy* ¨*CIN ho.ye 'si ˙n i*, [˙]*ji ˙lul tikhuyye ˙sye* ¨*nwul ˙ul* ¨*wuy ˙khwo ˙cye ˙hono ˙n ywo* (1586 Sohak 6:58a) moreover your husband's family has died off and now is come to an end, so with whose benefit in mind do you go on guarding this? CF ¨*na ˙lol*.
-n' 'wumen, abbr < -nun kwumen
-n' 'wun (a / yo), [? DIAL], abbr < -nun kwun (a / yo). ¶Kkok olq cwul (lo) al.ess.nun tey an on' 'wun I thought he was coming for sure, but I see he isn't.
nwun-chi, n + postn. perceptiveness, an eye (for ⋯); attitude, design, intentions; revealing look. ¶ ~ pota probes, feels out (the situation). ~ chāyta senses, sniffs out, puts two and two together, has an inkling (catches wind) of. ~ kho-chi tā ālta is well aware of the situation;

~ **kho-chi to moluta** is blind to (is totally unaware of) the situation. **nwun-chiq pap** perfunctory hospitality. **nwun-chiq kwun** one quick to take his cue from others. **Kass.umyen cōh.keyss.ta 'nun nwun-chi yess.ta** (Dupont 275) He gave the impression he would like to see them leave.

nwun-i, cpd postn. (n + n). a person with eyes such that ··· . **sāphal** ~, [DIAL] **hilttuk** ~ a squint-eyed or cross-eyed person. **aykkwu** ~, **kwul-ces** ~ with a cataract blinding one eye. **wang** ~ a person with huge eyes. **ccalkkak** ~ a person with sore (or bleary) eyes. **cawung** ~ a person whose eyes are ill matched. **kkamak** ~ (a person with the eyes of) an ignoramus. CF **pal-i, son-i**; the immediate constituents of the compounds should be (n + -nwun) + i, but they are often treated as if n + (nwun + i).

nwuwe, inf < **nwupta** (lie down). ABBR **n(w)ē**.

˙**nwuy**, (var) = ˙**nwu** (who/whom). ¶ ¨*nim-kum syem˙kizo˙wo˙m ye namcin syem˙kywo.m i ˙nwuy yey ˙sye teu˙l i ˙Gwo* (1475 Nay se:3b) who could serve king and husband more?

˙**nwu y**, abbr < *˙**nwu ˙i**, noun + particle. who [as subject]. ¶ ˙*nwu y ma˙ko˙l i '-ngi s ˙ka* (1445 ¹Yong 15) who was to stop him? ˙*TWON-˙KYWOW ˙lol ˙nwu y a˙la tutco˙Wo˙l i* (1449 Kok 97) who will comprehend the doctrine of instant enlightenment? ˙*nwu y ˙MEN-˙HHOYNG ˙i towoy˙l i ˙Gwo* (1462 ¹Nung 1:8a) who can attain all modes of salvation? ˙*nwu y ci˙zu˙m ye ˙nwu y patnon ˙kwo ˙hwo.l i ˙'la* (1462 ¹Nung 4:9la) I wonder who will build it and who will get it. SEE *e˙nu ˙nwu y*, ˙*nwu y ˙za*. ALSO: 1482 Nam 1:59a, ··· .

˙**nwu 'y**···, abbr < ˙*nwu ˙i*···, n + cop. be who. ¶ ˙*no˙m on ˙nwu ˙'yGe˙n ywo ˙ho˙ya NGUY-SIM ˙hwo˙l i˙n i* (?1468⁻ Mong 22b) is suspicious who they might be. *ne a˙n' 'ye nwu 'y˙l ywu* (1462 ¹Nung 2:30b) if not you who will it be?

¨**nwu 'y** < *¨**nwu ˙uy**, noun + particle. of whom, whose. ¶ ¨*nwu 'y ˙stol ˙ol* (1449 Kok 36) whose daughter [as object]. *tay pehino.n i n' ¨nwu 'y atol Gwo* (1632 Twusi-cwung 1:23a) whose boy is it that is cutting bamboo? [The accent is irregular, as if from *¨*nwu ˙uy*.]

¨**nwuy** < **nwu˙li** (1527 Cahoy 2:1a) < *NWUli* (hyangka 13:8), noun. world; generation, time, era, age. ¶ ¨*ti-˙naken ¨nyey ¨nwuy s SSI-˙CYELQ ˙ey* (1447 Sek 6:8a) at a time in a long past ancient world. *[¨]men ¨nwuy ˙yey s* (1459 Wel 23:93a) of a distant generation.

nwuy lwo. SEE **nwi**.

˙**nwu y ˙za**, abbr < ˙*nwu ˙i ˙za*, n + pcl + pcl. just who [as subject]. ¶ ˙*nwu y ˙za NUNG ˙hi ˙TWOY-˙TAP ho˙l [i] 'ye˙n ywo ˙hosi˙kwo* (1447 Sek 13:15a) said "just who will respond fully?" and ··· . ˙*nwu y ˙za ˙TI-[˙]HHYWEY isi˙m ye* ([1447→]1562 Sek 3:7a) just who has wisdom and ··· .

-nya [southwestern DIAL (Song Sekcwung 1967: 144)] = **-ni** (indic attent)

-nya (ko) = **-n ya (ko)**

'/-n ya, 1. < **in ya**. 2. < **han ya**. 3. < **-un ya**.

-n' ya, abbr < **-nun ya**

-˙*n ya* (= -*u˙n ya*) SEE -*no˙n ya*

-nya 'myen = **-n ya 'myen**, abbr < **-n ya (ko) hamyen**

-nya 'n(') = **-n ya 'n(')**

-n ya 'n('), abbr. 1. < **-n ya (ko) han**. 2. < **-n ya (ko) hanun**.

-nyang, pseudo-postn [?< abbr cop mod **in** + **yang** 'appearance']. manner, way, like. SEE **i/ku/ce** ~ . CF **khenyeng** [?< **ku-nyang**, ?< **kulenq yang**]

-nya 'nta = **-n ya 'nta** < **-n ya (ko) hanta**

-nya 'nun = **-n ya 'nun** < **-n ya (ko) hanun**

'n ya tul, 1. = **in ya tul**. 2. = **han ya tul**

-n ya tul SEE **-un ya tul**

-nyay = **-n ya 'y**, abbr < **-n ya (ko) hay**.

-˙*n ye* SEE -*u˙n ye*

˙**nye**, inf < ˚*nye˙ta* (? and ˚*ni˙ta*). ¶ ˙*na y ˙nye* (1481 Twusi 25:29a) I go and ··· . *kol˙mye˙k[i] uy ˙nye ton˙nywo˙m on* (1481 Twusi 14:29b) the wandering of the seagulls. (But LCT seems to take that as the stem in a compound verb ˙*nye-ton˙ni-*.)

˙**nye˙a**, effective inf < ˚*nye˙ta*. ¶ ˙*kil˙h ul ¨mwot ˙nye˙a* (1449 Kok 86) cannot go the path. CF ˙*ni˙ke*.

˙**nye ˙ka**, vi inf + vi inf. ¶*[TWONG] nye.k ulwo [˙MEN-¨LI] ˙yey ˙nye ˙ka* (1481 Twusi 7:2a) I went east to Thousand League [Bridge] and ··· .

˙**nye ˚ka˙ta**, vi inf + vi. goes.

nyekh, quasi-free n. direction; towards, towards the time of, around, about. ~ **ccum (ey)**, ~ **ey** SAME. ¶**saypyek** ~ around dawn. **achim** ~ (= **achim ttay**) in the morning. **alayq** ~ [? DIAL] lower part; leeward; the south. **wiq/wuq** ~ [? DIAL] upper part; Seoul; the north. **nal(q) sayl** ~ toward dawn. **esul** ~ toward dusk (of evening / dawn). **hay cil** (? **ttul**) ~, **sek.yang** ~ toward sunset. **talk i wūl** ~ **ey** toward (the time of) cockcrow. **saileyn i wūl** ~ **ey** toward the time of the (curfew) siren. **nam (puk, tong)** ~ [old-fashioned] toward the south (north, east) [se 'west' has not been found]. **kaywul** ~ [poetic] near the stream. **wul** ~ [DIAL] rim (= ēncelí). **Saypyek nyekh ulo (n'), saypyek nyekh un**, and **saypyek nyekh ina** occur, but **ulo (n'), un**, and **ina** are rejected after **talk i wūl nyekh**. CF **inyek you < i nyekh, yeph < nyeph** (1617) = *nyekh* (1518), *nyeks* (?1800).

nyen, n. [vulgar and pejorative] damn woman, bitch, trashy female. ¶**Nyen tul i ku ke mōs ssukeyss.ta 'n māl ia** The bitches are just not worth a damn! **Nyen-nom** (or **nom-nyen**) **tul i motwu pelus i ēps.ta 'n' māl ia** The bitches and bastards (or: the bastards and bitches) have no manners, any / none of them. **i / yo** ~ this damn woman. **ku / ko** ~ that damn woman. **ce / co** ~ that damn woman there. *michin nyen* (1894 Gale 182) a mad woman. CF **nom, nyesek; kyēycip.** [var < **nye** < ¨*NYE* woman] (˙)*nyen*, adn (var) = *nyenu*. ¶*nowoy nyen ˙toy ka˙ti ¨mal˙la* (1463 Pep 2:211b) do not go anywhere else. *SSYANG-˙PWULQ-KHYENG ˙PPI-KHWUW y ˙nyen ˙PPWUN ˙isi˙l i ˙'-ngi s ˙ka wo˙nol s ˙nal˙ay ˙SYEY-CWON ˙isi˙n i* (1459 Wel 17:77b) the bhikṣu (almsman) Sadāparibhūta was none other than the World-Honored today.

nyen ᵘ/o, nyenk ··· (< **nyen ᵘ/ok*), noun; adnoun ~ also *nyen ···*, as if from *nyen[k] ···* .

1. other. ¶*nyenu PWU-ZIN ˙nay s a˙tol ¨ney˙h i* (1459 Wel 2:4b) the four sons of his other wives.

2. + NEG (or rhetorical question). no other than; what / who else but. ¶*nyenu ha˙no˙l ay s ci˙p un ¨ep˙kwo* (1447 Sek 6:36; ¹Yi Tonglim's text) there was a house in no other heaven. *˙i na˙la[h] ¨spwun a˙ni ˙'˙la nyenu na˙la.h ay ˙two* (1459 Wel 7:53a) not only in this land but also in other lands.

˙i MYENG˙uy ˙MANG˙on nyenu a˙ni˙la ˙KAK-MYENG˙i he˙mu˙l i towoy˙n i (1462 ¹Nung 4:23b) the extravagance of this light is nothing but an error in the enlightenment.

nyeno s ¨il ¨lan (1466 Kup 2:72a), *nyenu s ¨i.l ol* (1475 Nay 1:53a) the other matters.

nyen˙k i ¨ti-na˙l i ˙'-ngi s ˙ka (1445 ¹Yong 48) could another pass?! *nyen˙k i ka˙m ye n' ¨mwot i˙kuy.l i ˙'˙n i* (1447 Sek 6:22b) none other than one person could go and vanquish them.

[˙SO-¨HOY] ˙lol nyen˙k ul ¨cwu.l i ˙ye (1445 ¹Yong 20) would the four seas be given to anyone else?!

nyesek, n. [vulgar and pejorative] damn fellow, S.O.B. ¶**Nyesek tul a!** Bastards! CF **nom, nyen; casik.**

°*nye˙ta* = °*ni˙ta* = ¨*nyey˙ta*, vi. goes (= °*ka˙ta*; it is unclear whether these four stems differ slightly in meaning). ¶¨*TTWO y ku TYWUNG˙ey ˙nyeke˙tun* (1463 Pep 3:155b) the way, if one goes into the midst of it, ... *˙nasi˙ta ka˙'˙m ye TWONG-SYEY˙lwo nil˙kwup ke˙lum ˙nyesi˙n i* (1482 Kum-sam 4:54a) as soon as he was born he went seven steps to the east and the west. *e˙cey s pa˙m oy [˙]za˙to.l ay hon-˙toy ¨nyela* (1481 Twusi 23:6b) do not depart until you leave with the moon we had last night (= stay till the morning moon disappears).

¨*nyey˙ta* = °*nye˙ta* = °*ni˙ta*, vi. goes (= °*ka˙ta*; it is unclear whether these four stems differed slightly in meaning). ¶*kil.h oy nalhwoGye nyeyye cye lol* [= *tye lul*] *kitolye wonwola* (1795 ¹No-cwung [K] 1:1b) = *na y kil.h ol cwocha nalhwoGye nyeyye kitolye wonwola ho.n i* (1795 ¹No-cwung [P] 1:1b) *˙na y ˙kil[h] cwo˙cha nalhwoyye˙nye ki˙tul˙Gwe˙wo˙nwo˙la* (?1517- ¹No 1:1b) I walk [slowly] along the path and wait for him to catch up.

nyo, pcl (after a vowel **yo**) [DIAL] = **a** (vocative) **-nyo** = **-n yo** < -˙*n ywo* (question). CF Roth 533.

-˙*n ywo* SEE -*u˙n ywo*

···*n ̈zop-* < ···*n-¨zop-*

/o/ < /wo/, mid back rounded vowel (lower version of /wu/ < /wu/).

o, low back functionally unrounded vowel (lower version of /u/); an alternant or variant of epenthetic /u/ after low vowels, sometimes after other vowels.

-*o ···* SEE ALSO -*u···*

-*o-* < *-*G*-, suffix; CF -*u-*, -˙*Gwo-*, -˙*Gwu-*. makes vc. ¶*twolo-/twolG-* < **twolo-G-* < **twolGo-* (> **tolu-/toll-**) cause to turn < ¨*twol-* < **two˙lo-* (> tō-l-) turn.

'**o,** abbr < **hao.**

ō', abbr [before **t, c, s**] < **ōl,** adnoun. early (ripening). ¶ ~ **tomi** early bream (fish). ~ **co** early millet. ~ **sali** seafood (esp. shrimp) caught in early high tide.

# A Reference Grammar of Korean

-o, alt after vowel of -so, AUTH indic assertive / attentive; spelling var (= -ˢo) after -ss-, -ps-. ¶ **kao** goes. **pissao** is expensive. **mek.ess.ˢo** ate. **kakeyss.ˢo** will go. **iss.ˢo** exists, stays; has. **ēps.ˢo** does not exist; lacks. **Tangkio!** Pull! − CF **Mīsio!** Push! [to keep number of syllables identical?]. VAR **i**. SEE **-usio**. CF **-wu**.

-o, suffix (var of -wu; derives adv from adj and a few v or vn). 1. adj → adv. ¶ **ttalo** separately (< **taluta**). **caco** = **cacwu** (< **cac.ta**). **palo** = **palwu** (< **paluta**).
 2. vi → adv. ¶ **tolo** back, again (< **tōlta**). **salo** alive (< **sālta**).
 3. vn → adv. ¶ **piloso** < *piˈlwoˈswo*/*piˈluˈswo* for the first time < **pilos hata** < *piˈlwosˈta* < *piˈlusˈta* (? = *piˈlusˈˈta*) begins.

(?*)**oa** = **wā** < ˈ**wa**, inf < **ota**.
oca, subj attent < **ota**. ~ (**ko**) **hanta** suggests we come. ~ **māca** as soon as one comes.
oca 'nta, abbr < **oca (ko) hanta**
oca tul, subj assert + pcl (plural). let's go!
oca 'y, abbr < **oca (ko) hay**
ohilye < ˈ**wohiˈlye**, adv. rather, preferably, sooner; on the contrary, contrariwise, instead (of the expected). ABBR **ōylye**.
-oikka [obs] = **-(u)p.nikka**. ABBR **-oykka**.
-oita [obs] = **-(u)p.nita**. ABBR **-oyta**. CF **-soita**.
o-kata, cpd vi (vi + vi). comes and goes. ¶ **O-kanun sālam tul i motwu chwuwe pointa** The passers-by all look cold.
-ol- SEE ALSO *-ul-*
ˈ**ol**, particle (accusative). SEE ˈ**ul**.
ōl, adn, n. SEE **ōl-toyta**, **ōl-chata**. ANT **nuc**. CF **il**. ABBR **ō'**.
 1. adnoun. early (ripening). ¶ ~ **pye** early ripening rice (plants). ~ **khong** early ripening beans. ~ **pam** early chestnuts. ~ **phath** early ripening red beans. ~ **kamca** early potatoes.
 2. noun. vigor; early vigor; precociousness.
ol(q) < *wol(q)*, prosp mod < **ota** < ˚*woˈta*.
 1. ⋯ that is to come (etc.). ¶ **olq sālam** the people to come.
 2. this, the present; next, the coming. ¶ ~ **hay** this year. CF **onul** < *woˈnol* today ? < **wo[l]ˈnal*.
 3. (abbr < **ol hay**) this year.
-ol(q) = **-o(wu)l(q)**, FORMAL prosp mod [**-op-** + **-ul(q)**], [obs] = **-l(q)**. After a consonant **-saowul(q)**, **-saol(q)**.
-ˈ*ol(q)*, prospective modifier. SEE -ˈ*ulq*.

ola, subj assert < **ota**. ~ (**ko**) **hanta** tells one to come. CF **one la**
ˈ*oˈlan*, pcl; var of ˈ*uˈlan* (examples under that).
ola 'nta, abbr < **ola (ko) hanta**.
ˈ*olaˈwa*, particle (later > ˈ*ilaˈwa*); *laˈwa* after *l* or *y*. SEE *illawa*, *nellawa*. ¶ *kuˈˈmwoyˈh i ˈkwulwumˈkotˈhoˈya poloˈm olaˈwa spolˈli ˈˈKWO-SYEN SANˈay kaˈn iˈˈla* (1459 Wel 7:31-2) the mountain was like a cloud and it went faster than the wind to Old Wizard Mountain. ˈ*PALQ-MENˈSO-CHYEN PPWUW-TTWOˈˈPWO-ˈTHAPˈˈsyeyˈywoˈm olaˈwa teˈe* (1459 Wel 23:76b) it was more than building 84,000 stūpas and bejeweled pagodas. NOTE: This may have come from a contraction of ˈ*ᵘ⁄ₒla* = ˈ*ᵘ⁄ₒˈlwo* + a lenited form of ˈ*pwa* = ˈ*poˈa* (vt inf), 'looked at as'. CF later **pota**. Or perhaps it incorporates ˈ*[G]wa* 'with' = ˈ*kwa*, probably < *koˈWa* < *kolˈWa* < **kolp-ˈa* 'lining them up, comparing, competing'.
olay, 1. inf < **olayta**. 2. der adverb < **olayta**.
ola 'y, abbr < **ola (ko) hay**
ˈ*olˈGwa* SEE **ul kwa**
-oli, suffix; ? LIGHT ↔ **-wuli**. **pongoli** bud ? < **pong** peak. [? var < **-al.i**]
-ˈ*oˈl i*, prosp mod + postmodifier. ~ ˈ*Ga*, ~ ˈ*Gwom*, ~ ˈ*-ngi sˈka*, ~ ˈ*-ngiˈˈta*. SEE *-uˈl i*.
-olikka = **-o(wu)likka**, FORMAL prospective attentive [**-op-** + **-ulikka**]. [obs] = **-likka**.
-*oˈl iˈ-ngi sˈka*, prosp mod + postmod + cop polite + pcl + postmod.
-*oˈl iˈ-ngiˈˈta*, prosp mod + postmod + cop polite + cop indic assertive.
-olita = **-o(wu)lita**, FORMAL prospective assertive [**-op-** + **-ulita**]. [obs] = **-lita**.
-*o.l iˈye*, prosp mod + postmod + postmod (question). SEE -*.l iˈye*.
ˈ*ol puˈthe*, 1. pcl + pcl. (starting / coming) from. ¶ *[TTWONG-ˈˈLI]ˈlol puˈthe woˈn i* (1445 ¹Yong 97) came from the same town. *kaˈzomyelˈm ye [ˈKWUY]ˈhwo.m on panˈtoki puculen ho[ˈ]m ye [SIN-ˈˈKHWO]ˈhwo.m ol puˈtheˈˈetnoˈn i* (1481 Twusi 7:31b) being rich and noble inevitably starts from hard work and hardship (before it is achieved).
 2. pcl + vt inf. based on, stemming from, relying on. ¶ ˈ*iˈnon mozoˈm ol puˈtheˈˈKYENG ˈulˈˈnayywo.m iˈla* (1462 ¹Nung 4:27b) this sets boundaries based on the mind. *alˈph oy s*

ye˙le[h] al˙Gwoysya˙m ol pu˙the ˙i ˙lol pu˙the ne˙pi ti˙ni˙key ˙hosya ˙za mol˙lol il˙thi a˙ni ˙ho.ya ... (1463 Pep 1:16a) only if you get it to be widely preserved, relying upon informing those ahead, relying upon this, will we not lose the essence ... . ˙SYENG ¨ep˙sun ¨LI ˙lol pu˙the ˙za ˙sso y pi˙luse ¨i˙non cyen˙cho ˙y˙la (1465 Wen 1:2:2:140a) only from (= only on the basis of) the principle of lacking an intrinsic characteristic (− that) is the reason events arise. NOTE: The distinction between these two meanings is not clearcut; the particle probably developed from [˙ᵘ/ol] pu˙th-e.

olssita [after vowel] = **iolssita** [DEFERENTIAL copula]. it is. ¶**Capci olssita** It is a magazine. **Sinmun i ani olssita** It is not a newspaper. **Kim Hakswu olssita** It is (I am) Kim Hakswu.

-olq˙ti⋯ = **-olq˙t i(⋯)**, prosp mod + postmod ('fact') + pcl / cop. that it / one will.

-olq˙t ol, prosp mod + postmod ('fact') + pcl. that it / one will.

?-olq˙t olwo, prosp mod + postmod ('fact') + pcl. because it / one will.

olun, pseudo-adn = var adj mod < **olh.ta** (is right, etc.). (⋯ that is) right (= **palun**).

-ol˙uy = **-ol˙[y]uy**, abbr < **-ol˙i˙uy** 'of (etc.) that which ... '.

˙o˙lwo, alt of ˙u˙lwo. ~ k, ~ n', ~ ˙sye, ~ ˙za.

˙ol˙za, pcl + pcl. SEE ˙ul˙za, ˙lol˙za.

-om⋯ SEE **-um⋯**

-˙om, alt (after aC, oC, and woC) of -˙um, subst. - ˙o˙m ay; -˙o˙m i; -˙o˙m ol; -˙o˙m o˙lwo.

om < **wom(⋯)**, subst < **ota** < ˚o˙ta (comes). CF ¨wom.

omphak, bnd adn; LIGHT ↔ **wumphek**; var < **omphak** / **wumphuk** sunken hollow; ? **ōng** + **pha-** dig + **-k**. ¶~ **nwun** sunken eyes. NOTE: South Korean authorities inconsistently spell "wumpheng-nwun" but "omphak-nwun".

-o˙m ye = **-umye**; -o˙m ye n' = **-umyen (un)**

-on⋯ SEE ALSO **-un⋯**

˙on, particle. SEE ˙un; ˙non (NOTE).

on', abbr < **one la**. come! ¶**Ili on'** C'mere! (Come here!)

on < **won**, modifier < **ota** < ˚wo˙ta (comes).

on < ˙won, n, num. [obs] a hundred (= **payk**).

on, interj. Gee! Gosh! My goodness! (shows surprise, wonder, and usually disapproval). ¶**On, ku nwum** (= nom) **ppenppen to hata!** Gee, what a nerve he's got! CF **wēyn**.

ōn < wo˙won, mod < wo˙wol- (adj) < **wool-** < *wo[G]ol- < *wopol-, adnoun.
1. all, whole, entire, complete, perfect. ¶~ **paykseng** the whole nation, all the people. ~ **sēysang** all the world. ~ **kaci (lo)** (of) all kinds. ~ **ca.yu sēykyey** the entire free world. ~ **kil** the whole way, all the way. CF **ongkun**.
2. (= **ōn kac'**) all kinds/sorts of. ¶**Ōn soli tā hanta** You talk all sorts of rubbish / nonsense. **Ku moim ey ōn sālam tul i tā wass.ta** People of came to the meeting from all walks of life. CF **ōn-thong**.

-on = **-o(wu)n**, FORMAL mod [-op- + -un]. [obs] = **-n**. [After consonant -sao(wu)n.]

-˙on, modifier (SEE **-un** < -˙un).

-ona = **-o(wu)na**, FORMAL adversative [-op- + -una]. [obs] = **-na** (but etc.). [After consonant -sao(wu)na.]

ona⋯ SEE ˙wona-

one la, var inf < **ota** + pcl (plain command) = **wā la** Come! CF **ola**. NOTE: From ˙wona˙la (effective subj assert); SEE ˙wona-. Phyengan has the regular development into **ona la** (Kim Yengpay 1984:103).

ōng, adn. small and sunken. ¶~ **(ca)payki** small bowl. ~ **pāngkwuli** small jar. ~ **sayngwen** mean person. ~ **silwu** small steamer. ~ **soth** small kettle. ~ **tongi** small jar.

-ongi˙ta SEE **-ngi-**

ongkun, pseudo-adnoun (mod < **ongkulta**, adj). whole; intact, original; untouched. ¶~ **sakwa** a whole (undivided) apple. ~ **ūmsik** untouched food. ~ **sāym** a virgin spring. CF **ōn**.

ong-tal, adn. small and sunken. ¶~ **sāym** a small spring. ~ **silwu** a small steamer. ~ **soth** a small kettle. ~ **wumul** a small well. CF **-tal**.

-oni SEE **-owuni**

-˙o˙n i (⋯), modifier + postmodifier. SEE -˙u˙n i. ~ ˙Ga, ~ ˙Gwo, ~ ˙˙la, ~ ˙-ngi s˙ka, ~ ˙-ngi ˙˙ta.

-onikka [obs] = **-p.nikka**; **-up.nikka**.

ōn kac' < ˙won˙kas, adnoun; abbr < **ōn kaci** < ˙won ka˙ci. every kind of, all sorts of, all manner of. ¶~ **sālam** all sorts of people. ~ **swutan ul pulita** tries every means available. ~ **kosayng ul tā hata** goes through all kinds of hardship. CF **yele kaci**.

-on˙oy = **-on˙[y]uy**, abbr < **-on˙i˙oy**

ōn-thong, cpd adverb. all, altogether, entirely, wholly; ~ **ulo** SAME. ¶**Ku kes un ōn-thong**

kēcis māl ita That's just a story made out of whole cloth. **Cēy-il-kwa lul ōn-thong oywe pelyess.ta** I memorized the whole of Lesson One. **Ku ka ˈiik ul ōn-thong tā kacyess.ta** He took all the profits for himself. CF **ōn, thōng**.

-ˈon ˈti··· = -ˈon ˈt i(···), mod + postmod ('fact') + pcl / cop. that it / one did (or is).

-ˈon ˈt ol, mod + postmod ('fact') + pcl. that it/one did (or is). ¶ku ˈpsk uy CYE-ˈCO y api ˈuy PPYEN-QAN ˈhi ancon ˈt ol ˈˈal ˈGwo ˈˈta a ˈp[i] oy key ˈka a ˈp[i] oy key nil[ˈ]Gwo ˈtoy (1463 Pep 2:138b) at that time the masters, finding that the father was seated comfortably, all went to the father and said to the father as follows ··· . CF -ˈun ˈt ol.

-ˈon ˈt olwo, mod + postmod ('fact') + pcl. because it / one did (or is). SEE ˈn ˈt olwo.

-ˈon ˈt on, mod + postmod + pcl. SEE hon ˈt on, -ˈun ˈt on.

-ˈo ˈn uy = -ˈo ˈn [y]uy, abbr < -ˈo ˈn i ˈuy

ōnya, interj. yes (to an inferior).

-op- [obs; after a consonant -saop-] = -p-:
1. haop.naita, haop.nita = hap.nita.
2. haop.naikka, haop.nikka = hap.nikka.
3. haopteita, haoptita = haptita.
4. haopteikka, haoptikka = haptikka.

NOTE: Behaves like -W- stems; inf -(o)wa, mod -o(wu)n. ¶**Kaopko ca haop.naita** I am desirous of going. **Hyēncay cey ka yēnkwu ey molqtwu hako iss.op.naita** At present, I am deeply engaged in research.

-op, [lit] abbr (in documents / letters) < -opsose (please do). ¶**Allye cwusinun swūko lul hay cwuop** Please keep me informed. CF -(usi)ap.

-opsita, [obs] 1. = -psita (let's do). 2. = -sita (deigns to do).

-opsose, [lit] = -sio please do. SEE -saopsose.

opta, postnom adj insep -W-. [obs] = sulepta (is etc.). **nalkhalopta** is sharp (? < nal-kha[l] opta; ? < *ˈnolh ˈka[lh] l(w)op ˈta). **salang (h)opta** is attractive, lovable. CF hopta.

-ˈo ˈsi···, honorific. SEE -u ˈsi··· .
-ˈo ˈsya, hon inf. SEE -u ˈsya.
-ˈo ˈsya-··· , honorific + modulator. SEE -u ˈsya··· .

ota < ˈwo ˈta, vi; infinitive wā < ˈwa, plain command one la. ANT kata. SEE na-ota.

NOTE: The MK verb has two peculiarities: the effective is ˈwona- instead of *ˈwoka- (but in a few forms also ˈwoke- and ˈwa-); the infinitive is ˈwa instead of *ˈwo ˈa (CF ˈpwo ˈa).

1. comes, arrives. ¶**wass.ta** is here, is come / arrived, has come. **wass.ess.ta** was here (and left), came (and went), has been here.

2. comes, arrives, reaches, appears. ¶**Phyēnci ka wass.nun ya** Has the mail come yet? **Ne hanthey cēnhwa ka wass.ta** You are wanted on the phone. **Cēnthwu cwung wēnkwun i wass.ta** In the midst of battle, reinforcements arrived. **Sensayng i acik an wass.ta** The teacher hasn't shown up yet.

3. comes round, sets in, is due, draws near. ¶**onul nal ey wā se nun** today; nowadays. **Com iss.umyen yelum pānghak i onta** The summer vacation is just around the corner. **Sihem i kot onta** The examination is at hand.

4. comes (on us), falls, precipitates, rains, snows. ¶**pi ka ~** it rains. **nwūn i ~** it snows.

5. comes (from), is introduced (from), derives (from).

6. comes (of / from), is caused (by), is due (to), arises (from). ¶¹**yēnsup ey se onun soncaycwu** skill that comes from practice. **Kanan un cēncayng ey se onta** War breeds poverty.

7. aux vi sep. gradually (comes in doing), becomes, grows; does this way, comes doing. SEE -e ota. CF toyta.

8. postnom v sep (with vn). comes to do. ¶**sānqpo (lul) ~** comes for a walk. **yenghwa (lul) kwūkyeng ~** comes to see a movie.

ota (ka), transferentive < ota (+ pcl).
1. comes and then (stops).
2. **~ kata (ka)** occasionally, at times, now and then, once in a while, on rare occasions. ¶**Ce ay nun ota kata kēcis māl ul hanta** That child doesn't always tell the truth. **Pihayng-ki ka ancen haci man, ota kata ttel.e cinun swu to iss.ta** Planes are safe but once in a while they crash. CF **kata (ka), kata kata**.

-o tul, AUTH indic assert + pcl (plural)

-o(wu)l(q), FORMAL prosp mod [-op- + -ul(q)], [obs] = -l(q). After consonant -saowul(q), -saol(q).

-o(wu)likka, FORMAL prospective attentive [-op- + -ulikka]. [obs] = -likka.

-o(wu)lita, FORMAL prospective assertive [-op- + -ulita]. [obs] = -lita.

-o(wu)n, FORMAL modifier [-op- + -un]. [obs] = -n. [After consonant -sao(wu)n.]

-o(wu)na, FORMAL adversative [-op- + -una]. [obs] = -na but. [After consonant -sao(wu)na.]

-o(wu)ni, FORMAL sequential [-op- + -uni]. [obs] = **-ni**. [After consonant **-sao(wu)ni**.]

˙**oy**, pcl; var ˙**uy**.

1. (after animate noun) = **uy** (genitive); CF s. ¶ ˝salo˙m oy wu˙h i towoy˙Gwo cye ho˙kwo ˝salo˙m oy a˙lay cye a˙ni ˙ho˙ke.n i˙Gwa (1482 Kum-sam 3:55a) granted that he wants to become above other men and does not want to become below them … [ellipted gerund before second *cye*]. KWONG ˙oy nilku˙si˙nwon ke˙s un ˝es˙te˙'n ˝ma˙l i-ngi s˙kwo (1465 Wen se:68a) what words are you reading, my Lord? ˙LWOK-PPI ˙non sa˙so˙m oy ka˙ch i ˙˙la (1459 Wel 1:16a) ˙LWOK-PPI is (the Chinese word for) the skin of a deer. LYWONG ˙oy ˙co.m i PPYEN-QAN ho˙kwo (1482 Kum-sam 2:65a) the dragon's sleep is peaceful, and … . ˝salo˙m oy nos [← *noch*] al˙ph ol ˙HYANG ˙ho˙sya (1482 Kum-sam 2:2b) deigns to turn to the front of people's faces, and … . KHWONG-˙CYAK ˙oy skwo˙li s pis [← *pich*] ˙kot hon ˙phu˙l i na˙kwo (1459 Wel 1:46a) there springs up grass that is like the color of a peacock's tail. … LYWONG-NGWANG ˙oy ˙pi no˙liGwol ˙chezem ˙kwa ˙stwo ˙kot 'two˙ta (1482 Nam 1:34a) it is again like the beginning when the dragon king … made the rain come down. SYWU-˙TTALQ ˙oy CYENG-˙SYA ci˙zulq ce˙k i … (1447 Sek 6:40a) the time when Sudatta built the monastery (was when) … . ˙HHAK ˙oy ans.non toy 'la (1482 Kum-sam 2:61b) it is where the cranes sit. hwen hi somo˙chon KHWONG ˙on MA ˙oy tal˙Gayywon ˙pa 'y˙n i (1482 Nam 1:76b) the pervasive (˝widely penetrating˝) void (śūnya) is where the devils seduce. [SYE KWONG] ˙oy ˙won ka˙ci s ˝i˙l ol si˙lum a˙ni ˙ho.ywo˙m ol ˙na y ˝anwo˙n i (1481 Twusi 8:24b) I know that Lord Xú does not brood over all matters.

2. (after inanimate noun, typically a place) = ˙ay (/ ˙ey) = **ey** at, in (locative); to (allative). ¶ al˙ph oy ˙ka sye˙n i (1447 Sek 6:3a) went (and stood) in front. [QYENG-˝CYWU] z al˙ph oy ˝nay˝nay pwus˙kuli˙l i (1445 ¹Yong 16) he would be ever embarrassed before the Chief of Heroes. pa˙lo.l oy ki˙phwum ˙kot ho˙m ye, ˝mwoy˙h oy kwu˙twum ˙kot ho˙n i (1482 Kum-sam 3:3b) it is like the deepness of [= out at] sea and it is like the hardness of [= within] the mountain. ˙PALQ-PWONG ˙oy ˝wo˙m i ˝ha˙m ol muten ˙hi ne˙kinwos˙ta (1482 Kum-sam 3:19a) treats casually the fact that the Eight Winds [which fan the passions] arrive often. SEE ˙oy s.

NOTE 1: Choice of the variant forms depends in part on the preceding vowel. See p. 923 (˙uy NOTE 1) for details.

NOTE 2: In Middle Korean (CF LSN 1961: 112, He Wung 320-3) a preceding (˙˙˙)i had weakened to ˙˙y and then, once the syllables *yuy and *yoy had left the system, it simply vanished. Examples: p. 923-4 (˙uy NOTE 2).

oy < ˙**woy**, bound noun.

1. as adnoun. only, single, one, lone, sole, isolated. ¶ ~ **atul**, ~ **tongi** an only son. ~ **ccak** one of a pair; a single one. ~ **ekkay** one shoulder. ~ **katak**, ~ **ol** single-ply (thread). ~ **kil** a one-way road. ~ **kileki** a lone wild goose. ~ **kols** a single way / track / groove. ~ **mati** a single piece; an isolated syllable. ~ **namu tali** a log bridge. ~ **phal** one arm. ~ **sang** a table for one. ~ **son** one hand.

2. as noun (pre-postnominal). SEE ~ **lopta**.

3. as adverb. SEE ~ **ttalta**, ~ **tāyta**.

CF **hoth**; **ōyn** < **ōyta** is out of place, is off to one side, is wrong, is left; **ōylo** leftward, aslant; **ōy cita** is secluded.

ōy < ˙**NGWOY**, 1. n = **pakk** (outside). ~ **ey**, quasi-pcl = **pakk ey** except for.

2. adn. maternal. ¶ ~ **hal-'meni** (**hal-apeci**) maternal grandmother (grandfather).

-˙**oy** = -˙**Goy** = -˙**key** (adverbative)

˙**oy** ˙**Gwos**, pcl + pcl. precisely at/in/to. ¶ wo˙cik ˙SYA-˙LI-˙PWULQ a al˙ph oy ˙Gwos ˙pu˙l i ˝ep.sul ˝ss oy (1447 Sek 6:33a) only just in front of Śāriputra were there no flames, so … .

˙**oy ke˙kuy**, pcl + n. to a person (= ˙**oy kungey**). SEE **na 'y ke˙kuy**, ˙**uy ke˙kuy**.

˙**oy key**, quasi-particle (< pcl + n) > **eykey**.

1. to (a person), to where a person is (= ˙**oy kungey**). ¶ ku˙psk uy CYE-˝CO y api˙uy PPYEN-QAN ˙hi ancon˙t ol ˝al˙Gwo ˝ta a˙p[i] oy key ˙ka a˙p[i] oy key nil[˙]Gwo˙toy (1463 Pep 2: 138b) at that time the masters, finding that the father was seated comfortably, all went to the father and said to the father as follows … . ˝tywohon ˝il ˙lan na 'y key pwo˙nay˙Gwo kwu˙cun ˝il ˙lan no˙m oy key ˙cwunu˙n i (1464 Kumkang 21b) sends good things to me and gives bad things to others. no˙m oy key PWO-˙SI hol ˙s i˙la (1465 Wen se:77a; sic, PWO-˙SI = ˙PWO-SI) is to give alms to others.

2. than [= twuˑkwo, ᵘolla ˑwa, pwoˑta (ˑka)]. ¶ SYWU-PPWO-TTYEY ˑnon ˑnaˑkhwa [= ˑnahˑkwa] ˑTUK ˑkwa y han ¨saloˑm oy key nwoˑphol ˑss oy (1463 Pep 2:176b) as Subhūti in age and in virtue was superior to the multitude, ...

3. by / from [with passive]. ¶ ¨TTYWOW-CYWUW ˑuy ¨saloˑm oy key muyˑGin ˑkwoˑt ol ˑkus aˑla (?1468⁻ Mong 19b) well aware of where it was hated by the people of the state of Zhào, ...

ˑoy key ˑlwo n', pcl + n + pcl + pcl. ¶ pwu¨thye y ¨HWA-ˑHWA s ˑPEP moyngˑkoˑlosyaˑm on ˑcokya s ˑkuy ˑlwo n' SAM-ˑMOY ˑLUK ˑul naˑthwoˑsya ... ˑSYA-ˑLI swoˑsa ˑnasiˑkwo ¨saloˑm oy key ˑlwo n' ¨teleˑWun seˑkun ˑnay ˑlol koˑliWoˑm ye (1459 Wel 18:39ab) the way Buddha makes his cremation is to display the power of meditation (samadhi) to himself, and ... with the rising of the bones to conceal from people the dirty rancid smell, and ... .

-oykka abbr < -oikka [obs] = -(u)p.nikka

ˑoy kungey, quasi-particle (< pcl + n/adv). to (a person); to where a person is. ¶ noˑm oy kungey puˑthe saˑlwoˑtoy (1447 Sek 6:5a) I attach my life to another. QA-LAM-KA-LAN ˑoy kungey ˑPWULQ-ˑYWONG-ˑCHYE-ˑTTYENG ˑul SAM-NYEN ˑul niˑkisiˑn i (1449 Kok 58) [Siddhārtha] trained Ārāḍa-Kālāma [¨Ārāḍa and Kālāma¨, says Pak Pyengchay] in the contemplation of formlessness (akiñcanāyatana) for three years. NGWANG ˑi ¨CCWOY ciˑzun kakˑsi ˑlol ku ¨mwotin ˑnwoˑm oy kungey pwoˑnayˑya (1447 Sek 24:15ab) the king sent the woman who had sinned to that evil fellow and ... . CF s kungey.

~ n' (abbr pcl). ¶ LYWONG oy kungey n' iˑsywo.l i ˑˑla NGWANG s kungey n' ¨ka.l i ˑˑla (1459 Wel 7:26b) I will be where the dragon is, I will go where the king is.

oy lo-i, der adv < oy lopta. all alone, solitarily, lon●ly. ¶ ~ cīnayta leads a solitary life. ~ wūlta cries all alone. San wi ey nulk.un so' namu ka oy loi se iss.ta A lonely old pine tree stands on the hill.

oy lopta < ˑwoy l(w)opˑta, cpd adj -W- (n + postnom adj insep).

1. is all alone (having neither relatives nor friends), is solitary / lonely. ¶ oy lowun sālam a person who is left to himself, a lonely person.

2. is (or feels) lonely; is lonesome, solitary. ¶ Namphyen i cwuk.e se ku ⁿyeca nun oy lowess.ta She felt forlorn and helpless after her husband died.

ōyn < ¨woyn, pseudo-adn = adj mod < ōyta < °°woyˑta (is wrong, is to one side; is not right, is left). CF olun.

1. (... that is) left, to / on / at the left. ¶ ~ ccok (phyen) the left-hand side.

2. (... that is) wrong, out of place, off to one side. ¶ ~ kil the wrong way; an evil course. son i ~ kos a place located out of the way, a spot hard to reach.

ˑoy n', abbr < ˑoy ˑnon, pcl + pcl. ¶ nacwo[ˑ]h oy n' ˑmuˑl ey ˑkaˑcanoˑn i (1447 Sek 13:10b) in the evening goes to the water to sleep.

ˑoy ˑnon, pcl + pcl. ¶ ˑtwuy.h ey ˑnun ... alˑph oy ˑnon ... (1445 ¹Yong 30) behind him ... before him ... .

ˑoy s, pcl (locative) + pcl (genitive). ¶ iˑGwus mozolˑh oy s ¨salomˑtolˑh i (1459 Wel 23:74b) the people in the next village — CF mozol[h] s ¨salom (1459 Wel 23:66a) people of the village, village folk. pwuthye s noˑch oy s KUM ˑi (1482 Nam 1:1a) the gold on Buddha's face. alˑph oy s [ˑ]PWOK ˑTUK (1482 Kum-sam 2:72b) fortune and virtue in future. ˑnwun s kaˑwon-toy s TTWONG-¨CO y nos [< noch] alˑph oy s ¨saloˑm i.n i ˑˑlaˑhotaˑka (1482 Kum-sam 2:31b) the pupil of the middle of the eye is said to be a person in front of the face but ... .

NOTE: The locative function will not explain the example ˑyel-hon noˑch oy s KWAN-ˑCCO-ˑCCOY PPWO-ˑSALQ S ˑSYANG ˑol moyngˑkoˑla (1447 Sek 6:44a) make an image of the eleven-faced bodhisattva Avalokiteśvara and ... . SEE ˑuy s, ˑey s, ˑay s.

ˑoy ¨swon-ˑtoy (to a person) SEE ¨swon-ˑtoy

ˑoy ˑsye, pcl + pcl. SEE ˑuy ˑsye, ˑayˑsye, ˑey ˑsye, ˑyey ˑsye. ¶ [ˑ]TTI-ˑNGWOK MWON alˑph oy ˑsye ˑaki ˑGwa selu pwoˑkwanˑtye (1459 Wel 23:87a) exchanges looks with the child before the gate of hell!

ˑoy ˑsye, pcl + inf < °syeˑta (vi 'stands'). ¶ QA-NAN ˑkwa LA-NGWUN ˑun ˑpa[l]-ˑch[i] oy ˑsye ˑyˑsopteˑn i (1459 Wel 10:10a) Ānanda and Rāhula were standing at the foot.

-oyta, abbr < -oita [obs] = -(u)p.nita.

oy ttal, cpd n. an only daughter (= one's only child a girl; = the only girl among one's offspring).

oy ttal(q), prosp mod < oy ttalta.

oy ttalo < ˙*woy ˙pto˙lwo*, cpd adv. separated, isolated, solitarily, lonely, all alone. ¶ **tosi ey se mēlli ttel.e cye se ~ sālta** lives a lonely life far away from town, lives in seclusion. **Ku ai nun talun ai tul hako sekk.ici anh.ko nul oy ttalo tōnta** the boy does not mix with other boys but always keeps aloof.

oy ttalta, cpd adj -L- (adv + bnd adj). is alone, solitary, isolated, lone, lonely, sequestered, secluded. ¶ **oy ttan kos ey se sālta** lives in a secluded place.

oy ttan, 1. mod < **oy ttalta** is isolated. ¶ **~ cip** an isolated house.
 2. n. doing solitary (one-man) **thaykkyen** (the sport of kicking and tripping). ¶ **~ chita** engages in **thaykkyen** without a partner.

˙*oy ˙two*, pcl + pcl (var of ˙*ay ˙two* = **ey to**). ¶ *pa˙m oy ˙two ¨sey ˙psk ul ˙SYWELQ-˙PEP ˙ho˙tesi˙ta* (1459 Wel 2:26-7) in the evening, too, he would preach three times.

˙*oy tyengey* SEE ˙*uy tyengey*

˙*oy ˙za*, pcl + pcl (var of ˙*ay ˙za* = **ey ya**). ¶ *˙e˙cey s pa˙m oy [˙]za ˙to.l ay hon-˙toy ¨nyela* (1481 Twusi 23:6b) do not depart until you leave with the moon we had last night (= stay till the morning moon disappears).

-p- SEE **-p.nita, -ptita, -pci, -psiyo**

p = s (genitive particle), variant after ···*m* before voiceless obstruents. ¶ *¨salom p ˙ptu.t i˙l i '-ngi s ˙ka* (1445 ¹Yong 15) will it be (within) man's will? *¨salom p ˙seli ''la* (1459 Wel 1:19b) it is (in) the midst of people. *TTAM p ˙CCO* (1451 Hwun-en 4b, 10a) the character *TTAM*.

pa < [cham] **pa** < ¨*pa*, n. a rope (=**paq cwul**). ¶ *¨pa ˙tol[h] [¨]ta ¨tywo ˙ho˙ya is˙ta* (?1517-¹No 2:36a) the ropes are all OK (= secured).

pa < ˙*pa*, postmod. 1. way, means; a thing, that (which); SYN **kes**. ¶ **halq ~ lul moluta** doesn't know what to do. **wi ey māl han (wi ey pon) ~ wa kath.i** as has been said (seen) above. **Ne uy ālq pa ka ani 'ta** It is no concern of yours; It is nothing you would know anything about. SEE **-un (-nun, -ulq) pa ey**,
 2. [semi-lit] as a consequence (= **tey₂** and / but, **-uni** and so). ¶ **Wuli meych salam i ku hōy lul cwuchoy ha.yess.tun pa** (= **hayss.nun tey** or **hayss.tuni**) **ūyoy uy tāy-senghwang ul ilwess.ta** We few people sponsored the society and it has prospered beyond our expectations.
 3. [semi-lit]. that which is (= ZERO in more colloquial usage). ¶ **Wuli ka swucip han (pa) cengpo ey uy hamyen cek un cikum kwunpi lul hwakcang cwung ila hanta** According to the intelligence we have gathered, the enemy is increasing his armaments. **Māy math.un pa chayk.im ul kakca ka motwu wanswu haca** Let each of us fulfill every responsibility we have undertaken.

p'ā, abbr < **pwā**, inf < **pota**. **-e ~, -ulq ka ~, ...** . ¶ ˙*i ˙pa* (?1517- Pak 1:10a) Look here!.

pachi, postn. [pejorative] person with a vocation dating from the feudal period. ¶ **cangin ~** [DIAL] a repairman (= **cangsayk**). **cem ~** [DIAL] a fortune-teller (= **cem cangi**). **hosa ~** a fop, a dandy. **kac' ~** a maker of leather shoes/boots. **nol.um ~** a clown; an acrobat. **sengnyang ~** a blacksmith. CF **achi, cangi**.

pachita₁. 1. vt. presents, offers, dedicates, devotes, gives (to a superior).
 2. aux v sep. does for a superior.
 3. SEE **chi- ~** (rises up etc.)
 SYN **tulita, ollita**. CF **cwuta**.

pachita₂.
 1. → **pat.chita** (vc supplies; vp gets struck).
 2. → **pat.chita** (receives; props up).
 3. → **path.ita** (is strained, filtered).
 4. → **path.cita** (strains, filters).

pachita₃, ppachita, vt. is addicted to, is overly fond of (preoccupied with), is crazy (mad, wild) about. CF **ppā cita**.

-(p)pak, suffix (makes impressionistic adverb). ¶ **kam(p)pak** with a blink/flicker < (k)ke^am- adj 'black'. CF **-ppuk**.

-paki, 1. = **-pak.i**. 2. = **-payki**.

pak.i, postn, suffix [der n < **pakta**]. an inlaid/imprinted thing, one with something stuck/pressed in or attached (fixed on). ¶ **ssang•yel ~** a double-barreled gun. **na' ~** a person who looks older than his years. **tesq-i (tes-ni) ~** a spotted person/animal; an object of ridicule. **(pon)tho ~** an aborigine. **so ~** a dish with beef in it. **phan ~** a print, a printed book; a stereotype. **cha'-tōl ~** beef chuck gristle. **no-pak.i lo** fixedly. VAR **(-)payki**.

pakk < *pask*, 1. n (= **pakkath**) outside. ANT **an, sōk**. SYN **ōy**.
 2. **~ ey**, quasi-pcl. CF **Ku pakk uy sālam un ka to cōh.ta** (LHS) The others may go.

A Reference Grammar of Korean

2a. (as postn) outside of (a limit), (with the) exception (of). ... ~ ey ēps.ta there is nothing but/except, only, just. ttus ~ ey unexpectedly. ku ~ ey besides, in addition to that. ¶Ku pakk ey halq īl i ēps.ta I have nothing else to do. Ku sālam un ku pakk ey tōn to pat.ess.ta Besides that, he received a sum of money. Hanul hako pata pakk ey poici anh.ess.ta In sight there was nothing save sky and sea. Ku nun atul i hana pakk ey ēps.ta He has only one son.

2b. (as postmod; SEE -ulq ~). -ulq swu pakk ey ēps.ta has no choice but to (do), cannot help doing. ¶kalq swu pakk ey ēps.ta has no choice but to go. wūlq swu pakk ey ēps.ta cannot help crying. Na nun nōllalq swu pakk ey ēps.ess.ta I could not help being astonished.

NOTE: pakk ey + NEGATIVE = man + AFFIRMATIVE ('only'). SYN ōy ey.

(-)pal, bound noun. ¶iq ~ tooth.

pal, postn; often -q pal < s ˊpal (probably < ˊpal 'foot'). 1. lines, streaks, rays; impression. hayq ~ sun rays; a ray (of light) (CF hayq pich/pyeth sunshine) — or is this a calque of Chinese ilkak < ˊZILQ-ˊKAK 'feet of the sun'?. ¶inq ~ the impression/stamp of a seal. kulq ~ jottings, notes; a sentence — CF kul.wel [obs] < ˊkul-ˊGwel < ˊkul-ˊGwal < ˊkul-ˊWal < *ˊkul ˊpalq letters, a sentence; cek-pal notes jotted down (< cek- vi). nwūnq ~ < nwun s pal (1748 Tongmun 1:2; cited from LCT) streaks of snow, snow flakes. phiq ~ being bloodshot, congestion. piq ~ < pi s pal (?1775 Han-Cheng 13a) streaks of rain. salq ~ arrow streaks, streaking arrows. seliq ~ a layer of heavy frost.

2. sin pal a shoe.

3. cheyq pal [< ?] a stick placed across the already woven part of cloth on the loom to keep it in shape.

4. kiq pal < [KUY] s ˊpal (1481 Twusi 22:33a) flag, banner.

5. i-ppal (= iq pal) tooth. SEE (-)pal.

pal < ˊPELQ, postnoun, verbal noun

1. postn [semi-lit]. departure, dispatch (from a place or at a time). ¶ōcen ahop si pal kup.hayng the 9 a.m. express. (sam-wel sam-il) Inchen pal kisen the steamer leaving Inchen (on the third of March). sam-il pal a dispatch of the third. Wasingthon pal dispatch(ed) from Washington. Sewul pal Tongkyeng hayng dispatched from Seoul to Tokyo. ANT chak.

2. ~ hata: 2a. vnt. dispatches, sends it out; emanates, radiates; issues, publishes, puts out; utters, announces. 2b. vni. leaves, departs; bursts into bloom; springs from, originates. CF chwulpal (vni) departs.

p'ā la, abbr < pwā la inf + pcl. Look!.

palam₁, noun. 1. wind; air; a draught (draft).

2. palsy, paralysis. 3. dissipation, debauchery. ~ ca(y)ngi / twungi a playboy.

palam₂, 1. postnoun, postmod. (in) conjunction (with); (in) the process (of); (as a) consequence (of); (as a) result (of); impetus, momentum, influence. ¶swul ~ ulo ttē-tulta raves under the influence of alcohol. Catong-cha lul phī halye 'nun palam ey pal-mok ul ppiess.ta I sprained my ankle (in the process of) trying to dodge a car. tan palam ey [DIAL] = tan swum ey at a single breath/stretch/time. CF kyel, kīm, swūm, thong, sesul.

2. postn [usually pronounced -q palam] the state of not being properly dressed, with only (one's ... on). ¶māyn meliq palam ulo/ey bareheaded, without a hat on. s(y)assuq palam ulo in shirt-sleeves, without one's coat on. tong-cekoliq palam ulo na tanita goes around without wearing an outer coat. Ku nun māyn palq palam ulo pakk ey ttwie na-kass.ta He ran out into the street barefoot.

pal-chi, 1. cpd n. the foot of a bed; the dark side of the room. 2. bnd n. vicinity, place. ¶twuem ~ a muck bog. sikwung (pal-)chi a cesspool.

pali, postnoun, suffix.

1. a person. ¶ak ~ a harsh tough person; a hard and shrewd person. sayam ~ a jealous person. teythwung ~ a clumsy oaf. thuley ~ a crosspatch, a perverse person. twithum ~ a blunt rude person. ?yā(y) ~ a stingy person, a skinflint (or is this a variant < āy-pali der n < āy-paluta 'is keen on money'?).

2. ¶pēs ~ secret support, backing.

CF pal.i; ppali. [? < pal + i 'foot-person'; der n ? < paluta 'pastes, applies, etc.', CF kkom pali a tightwad/skinflint < kkom paluta is stingy, niggardly.]

pal-i, cpd postn (n + n 'foot person'). a person/thing with feet (or gait) such that ... . ¶ccok ~ a one-legged or fork-legged thing; "a Jap".

cachwum ~, **celttwuk** ~ a cripple. **cwiem** ~ a person with a withered foot. **mongtong** ~ a stump (leg-bereft thing). **sāmyen** ~ a crab-louse; a toady, a truckler. **ttwittwung** ~ a tottering person. ¹**yuk** ~ a person with six toes. CF **phal-i, son-i, nwun-i**.
   NOTE: The immediate constituents of the compounds ought to be (n + **pal**) + **i**, but they are often treated as if n + (**pal** + **i**).
? **pali**, postnoun. SEE **ppali**.
palita [DIAL] = **pelita** (throws it away)
palo < *pal(w)o*, der adv (< **paluta** < *palo˙ta*).
   1. right, directly, straight. ¶ ~ **cip ulo kata** goes right home. **kil ul** ~ **kata** goes straight down the road. ~ **capta** straightens, corrects.
   2. right, only, just, the very; just (as if). ¶ ~ **wi ey** right above. ~ **ku ttay ey** just at that moment. ~ **yeph ey** close at hand, right beside. ~ **i kūnche ey (se)** right in this neighborhood. ~ **ku sālam** the very person. **Palo O sensayng ita** It is Mr O himself. **Palo O sensayng i wass.ta** Mr O himself came.
   3. [uncommon, old-fashioned] used as quasi-free noun. right about this/that place. ¶ **Ku palo ka nay cip iss.nun kos ita** That area is where my house is. **Cong-lo palo ey iss.ta** It's in the vicinity of Bell Street.
(-)**palpang**, bnd n. ¶ **makwu** ~ sloppy behavior.
palun, adj mod < **paluta** (is to the right). (... that is) right, to/on/at the right. ~ **ccok/phyen** the right-hand side. CF **olun** (**olh.un**); **ōyn**.
paluta < *palo˙ta*, adj -LL-. is right; is to the right; is correct, is true; is upright, is honest; is direct, straight, immediate.
paluta, postnom adj insep -LL-. ¶ **mas** ~ tastes so good you wish there were more. **caycang** ~ is inauspicious. **panci-ppaluta** = **panciq** ~ is stuck-up, condescending. **seng** ~ [DIAL] = **seng siph.ta** appears/seems/looks (to be).
panciki, postn. adulterated with. ¶ **molay** (**tōl, kye, nwi, ek-say**) ~ **ssal** hulled rice with sand (stones, husks, bran, miscanthus) in it.
pang < *PANG*, postn. (in) care of, "c/o". ¶ **Kim Ilhwan ssi** ~ **Pak Hongsik ssi** (To) Mr Pak Hongsik c/o Mr Kim Ilhwan.
pang < *PPANG*, postnoun. shop, shopkeeper's, store. ¶ **unq** ~ a silversmith's. **kumq** ~ a goldsmith's. **yak** ~ a drugstore, a pharmacy. **ānkyengq** ~ an optician's. **poktek** ~ a real estate agency.

pangi, postn, suffix = **payngi**. ¶ **ancumpangi** (1894 Gale 183) = **anc.un payngi** a cripple.
pānmyen, noun.
   1. (< ˝*PEN-˙MYEN*) the other side/hand. ~ (**ey**) on the other hand = (**tto**) **han phyen**. ¶ **Asia ey nun kacang tewun cipang i iss.nun pānmyen ey kacang chwuwun cipang to iss.ta** (NKd 1627a) Asia has the hottest areas and on the other hand also the coldest areas.
   2. (< ˝*PAN-˙MYEN*) half the face, profile; one side, a half.
papputa, adj. [< *pas-po-* = *pach-po-* < *pach-* 'rush']; DER ADV **pappi** ('busily, briskly')
   1. is pressing, urgent, "rush", immediate(ly demanding); (**sikan i** ~) is short of time, is rushed. ¶ **Cēng sikan i pappumyen kel.umyen se 'n tul mōs mek.ul ya** If we are really so pressed for time, can't we eat while on our way? **Nemu pappe se āy sse mantun ūmsik ul mek.e cocha mōs poko kass.kwun a** They were so pressed (for time) they left without even trying the food I had gone to the trouble of preparing! **Olay kan man ey kōhyang ey l' kass.e to nemu 'na pappe se sā-chon hyeng kkey lang un tullile poci to mōs hayss.ta** Though I had not been to my home town for a long time, I was too short of time even to drop around to my cousin's place (where he and his family live). **Pappe se copan ul mek.nun tus mānun tus hako cip ul na-wass.ta** I was in such a hurry that I left home with hardly any breakfast. **Pappuki nun way pappuni** What's the big rush (all about)?!
   2. is busy. ¶ **pappuko phikon hata** is busy and tired. **Cikum un pappuni iss.ta (ka) 'na popsita** I am busy now but later on we'll see. **Caney pota nun nay ka te pappuney** I am busier than you. **Pappusin cwung ey i chelem īl ul towa cwusye se tāytan hi kāmsa hap.nita** I am very grateful to you for helping me in my work when you are busy. **Pappe se phyēnci lul ssulq sai ka ēps.ess.ta** I was so busy I didn't have time to write. **Nemu pappe se mōs wass.ta** I was too busy to come. **Kako siph.ci man un pappe se kaci mōs hakeyss.ta** I should like to go, only I'm too busy. **Ecci 'na pappun ci phyēnci mōs hako iss.ta** I've been so busy I haven't been able to write. **Motwu pappuni-kka cacwu mannakey tul an toynta** They are all so busy we never get to see them.

Sikol se nun yo cuum chwuswu ey han-chang pappulq key 'p.nita In the country they must be awfully busy these days gathering the harvest. Onul un com pappuni ku īl un ¹nayil hakeyss.ta I am rather busy today, so I'll take care of that matter tomorrow. **Pappun kkatalk ey kaci mōs hanta** I can't go because I'm busy. **Phyēnci lul ssulq sikan to ēps.ulq cengto lo papputa** I'm so busy I have no time to write letters.

  2a. ⋯ **ulo** is busy with ⋯ , is pressed/rushed owing to ⋯ . ¶**Ilenq īl celenq īl lo papputa** I am very busy what with this and that.

  2b. **-ki ey ~** is busy (do)ing. ¶**Na nun swukcey haki ey papputa** I am busy doing my homework. **Mek.ki ey tul papputa** They are all busy eating.

  3. [DIAL] is difficult.

˙*pa s*, postmod + pcl. SEE *s* 5e.

pa' s = ˙*pa[l] s*, n + pcl. of the foot.

p'ā se, abbr < **pwā se**, inf + pcl.

p'ass-, abbr < **pwass-**, past < **pota**.

pat.i /paci/, postn, suffix (der n < **pat.ta**).

  1. collecting, receiving, catching. ¶**pic ~** collecting debts.

  2. a thing/person/time for taking, collecting, receiving, or catching something; a catch (thing to catch it). ¶**palam ~** a windswept place, a wind tunnel. **ttam ~** a sweatshirt. **sal ~** the ground around a target. **isul ~** dew time; dew kilt; dew clearer. **chay ~** 'whip receiver' = beef shoulder. **thi ~** a dustpan.

  3. striking, hitting. ¶**ima ~** striking with the head, butting; catching on the forehead.

  CF **chang ~**, **chong ~**, **kelley ~**, **mac' ~**, **phalphung ~**, **tēm ~**, **un.e ~**, **'mak paci**.

p'ā to, abbr < **pwā to** (inf + pcl).

pat.ta₁, vt. VP **pat.hita**. INTENSIVE **pat.chita**; CF **pachita** gives (to a superior) < **pat.hita** vc.

  1. receives, gets, accepts, takes, is given.

  2. faces, has to put up with (CF **tang hata**).

  3. catches (a ball, etc.).

  4. holds (an open umbrella etc.), carries (over one's head). SYN **ssuta**.

  5. butts, gores, hits one's head against.

  6. inherits, succeeds, follows.

  7. buys (anything you can put in a container that you bring yourself). SYN **sata**.

  8. delivers (a baby).

  9. puts on (a patch), patches with. SYN **tāyta**.

pat.ta₂, vi. (food) agrees with a person, suits one's palate, sits (well).

pat.ta₃, postnom v sep. receives (an action), suffers, undergoes. (Functions as the passive for certain verbal nouns. CF **toyta**, **tang hata**, **ssuta**.)

  1. (**hata** → **pat.ta**) ¶**cwūmok ~** receives/enjoys attention. **hyep.pak ~** gets threatened.

  2. (**pulita** → **pat.ta**) ¶**ūngsek ~** lets a child get spoiled.

p'ā tul, abbr < **pwā tul**, inf + pcl (plural)

˙*pa y*, postmod + pcl (< ˙*i*) = **pa ka**. ¶*na y pan˙toki* ˙PEP *nil˙Gwon ˙pa y is.ta ne˙kiti ¨malla* (1482 Kum-sam 5:14a) do not think that dharma is necessarily what I have told.

p'āy = **pwāy** = **pwēy** = **pōy** < **poye**, inf < **pōyta** = **poita**.

p'ā ya, abbr < **pwā ya** (inf + pcl).

payk.i, var < **pak.i**. CF **payki**.

payki, **ppayki**, postn, suf [? < **pak.i**; ? dimin < **pa**]. 1. **payki**. ¶**ca-~** an unglazed earthenware bowl. **cwūceng ~** a drunken brawler. **kho ~** a big-nosed person. **kho-sa' ~** [< **kho-sal** nose skin], **khoq-cwung** (**kho-ccwung**) **~** [vulgar] nose. **no ~** (CM 1:221) ?= **no-pak.i** lo always; firmly. **nuli-~** a slowpoke. **okq-i** (**ok-ni**) **~** a person with inturned teeth. **ōng-(ca) ~** a tiny earthenware bowl. (**pon**)**tho ~** (CM 1: 221) = (**pon**)**tho-pak.i** aborigines.

  ¶**akchak** / **ekchek ~** a tough stubborn child. **elk-~** a pockmarked person. **elk.cek** / **alk.cak ~** a lightly pockmarked person. **elk.cwuk** / **alk.cok ~** a heavily pockmarked person. **entek ~** a hilltop. **kwānyek ~** the place directly opposite (< 'target'). **kop ~** double measure. **pap ~** a suddenly weaned baby who overstuffs on rice. **ttwuk ~** a deep round pottery bowl. ?**thak ~** a kind of coarse liquor (= **mak'-kelli**). **thwuk ~** [DIAL] = **ttwuk ~** a kind of earthenware bowl.

  2. **ppayki** = < **-q payki**. ¶**ay ~** the top of a ridge. **ima ~** [vulgar] forehead. **khi ~** (CM 2:231) ' ? '. **kho ~** [vulgar] (= **khoq-cwung payki**) nose. **kulwu ~** straw stubble. **meli ~** head of bed (= **meli ccok**). **sōkyen ~** (CM 1:231) 'narrow view'. **taykal ~** [vulgar] head.

  3. → **payk.i** (= **pak.i**).

  CF **ppak**, **pak.i**, **phayki**; **phayngi**, **ccwung-payki**; **thongi**. VAR **pe(y)ki**.

payngi, postn, suf, postmod. one, person, thing. ¶ **anc.un** ~ = *ancumpangi* (1894 Gale 183) a cripple, a wheelchair case. **antal** ~ a fretful person, a worrywart. **cang-tolq-** ~ = **cang-tollim** a peddler who makes the rounds of the markets. **capsal** ~ odds and ends, a jumble. **ccalla** ~ an undersized thing, a midget, a runt. **cwūceng** ~ a drunken brawler. **eᵃlk.um** ~ a badly pockmarked person. **kanan** ~ a pauper. **keyulum** ~ a lazybones, a lazy person. **nethel** ~ a fluttery thing. **pileng / paylang** ~ a beggar. **soktal** ~ lo (< ?) on a small scale. VAR **pe(y)ngi**. CF **payki** (pak.i), **phayngi, mayngi**, etc. [? < **pa** + -a(y)ngi]

p'ā yo, abbr < **pwā yo** inf + pcl.

'pci yo, abbr < **hapci yo**.

-pci yo, alt after a vowel of **-supci yo**.

-pc' (y)o, abbr < **-pci yo**.

peki, postn [var] = **payki**.

pel, bnd n (? < counter, ? < **pēlta**). **ay-~, cho-~, ches-~** the first time.

pel, counter. a suit (of clothes); a set (of dishes); a copy (of a set of documents). ¶ **os han** ~ a suit of clothes. **pansang(-ki) twū** ~ two sets of dishes. **chaq-can han** ~ a tea set / service. **munse han** ~ a copy of a set of documents. [? < **pēlta**]

pelita₁ < *po'li'ta*, vt. DIAL **palita**.
1. throws it away / out, wastes, disposes of, discards, gets rid of it. ¶ **ūmsik ul (ssuleyki lul, phyēymul ul ~)** throws away foodstuff (rubbish, waste). **tōn (sikan) ul ~** wastes money (time). **hēn sin ccak chelem ~** throws (something) away like an old shoe. **I kos ey hyuci lul pelici māsiap** Do not discard trash here. **Āmu kes to peliko lul siph.ci anh.uni yātan ip.nita** The trouble is I don't want to get rid of anything.
2. gives up, abandons, forsakes. ¶ **cip ul ~** leaves one's house. **namphyen ul (anʰay lul) ~** abandons one's husband (wife). **soksey lul (sēysang ul) ~** renounces the world; enters the priesthood. **ciwi lul (kyēyhoyk ul) ~** gives up a position (plan). **huymang ul ~** gives up hope. **pelus ul pelita (kochita)** breaks (gets rid of, gets over) a habit. **Nwu ka ai lul mun aph ey pelyess.ta** Someone has left a baby on the doorstep. **Na lul peliko nun kaci mōs hao I** will not let you go leaving me behind.
3. spoils, ruins; soils. ¶ **ai lul ~** spoils a child (or: abandons the child). **os ul ~** soils a garment (or: throws the garment out). **Na nun nay chayk ul pelyess.ta** I got my book dirty (or: I threw my book away).

pelita₂, ppelita, aux verb insep (follows the inf). finishes, gets through, does completely, gets it done, disposes of a job; does it to my regret / disappointment; does it to my relief. ¶ **ūmsik ul mek.e ~** eats the food up. **tōn ul sse ~** uses the money up. SEE **-e ~**. [**ppelita** is livelier and more emphatic than **pelita**.]

pelkay, inf < **pelkeh.ta**; HEAVY ↔ **palkay** (bright red).

pelus < *pe'lus*, noun. 1. a habit, an acquired tendency, a customary practice. ¶ **~ i sayngkita (puth.ta)** gets into a habit (of). **~ i iss.ta** has a habit (of). **~ ul pelita (kochita)** breaks (gets rid of, gets over) a habit. **~ ulo tāmpay lul phiwuta** smokes from force of habit. **māl ul toy-phul.i hanun ~ i iss.ta** has a propensity for repeating himself.
2. manners. ¶ **~ i napputa / ēps.ta** is ill-mannered, is badly brought up, is rude or uncouth. **~ ēps.i (ēps.key)** rudely. **pelus ēps.nun māl ul hanta** says rude things. **mālq ~ i napputa/ēps.ta, ip ~ i sānapta/napputa** is foul-tongued; talks vulgarly/rudely. **sonq ~ i napputa (ko.yak hata)** has a way of taking / swiping things, has sticky fingers, is light-fingered; is a kleptomaniac. **sonq ~ i sānapta (ko.yak hata)** is given to fisticuffs, is apt to hit ("slug") people. **swulq ~ i napputa (ko.yak hata)** is a mean drunk. **Sēy salq cek pelus i yetun kkaci kanta** "A habit acquired at three will persist to eighty" ("As the twig is bent, the tree will grow", "It is hard to teach an old dog new tricks".) **Cey pelus kāy mōs cwunta** "You cannot give your bad habits even to your dog" = Bad habits are hard to break.
3. **~ hata**, vni. forms a habit. ¶ **swul ul mek.e ~** takes to drink. **Mues itun ci pelus haki ey tallinta** "Everything depends on making it habit" = You can make a habit of anything; You can turn anything into a habit.

pēm < *PPEM*, adnoun. pan(-), all(-). ¶ **~ Asia (cwuuy)** Pan-Asia(nism). **~ Aphulikha** Pan-Africa. **~ Ameylikha, ~ Mi** Pan-America.

pengi [var] = **payngi**

-q pen hata, postmod adj-n — ? insep. [Follows prosp modifier; sometimes spelled **ppenhata.**] is / comes / goes near (doing); almost, nearly, well-nigh (does); just barely escapes (doing); "like(d) to", "the wonder is (it did not)", all but (does / did). ¶**cha ey chiil** ~ comes near being run over. **cwuk.ul** ~ is all but dead. **hon nal** ~ is frightened almost out of one's wits. **Kalq pen hayss.ta** The wonder is he didn't go; He almost went. **Mōs kal ppen hayss.ta** He nearly didn't go; The wonder is he went at all. **Ku ka sil-eps.i han māl i ku lul mangchilq pen hayss.ta** His casual remarks came near ruining him. **Na nun cwuk.ulq pen hayss.ta** I thought I'd die. **Kecin** [= **keuy**] **casal halq pen hayss.ta** He almost committed suicide. **Na nun ku i wa chin hay se kecin** [= **keuy**] **kyelhon halq pen hayss.ta** I was so friendly with him I came very near marrying him. **Kyewul nal i īsang sulepkey ttattus hay se kaynali ka philq pen hayss.ta** The winter weather was so unusually warm it wouldn't have been surprising to see the forsythia burst into bloom. **Hama-thumyen selo mannaci mōs halq pen hayss.ey yo** We almost missed each other. [? < **-q pen** < *pen* < PHAN 'order']

pep < ˙*PEP*, postmodifier. 1. (= **kes**) what is proper.

  -nun ~. ¶**Haksayng ulo se kulen nappun hayngtong un an hanun pep / kes ita** As a student one should not do such bad things. **Sānula 'myen pyelq īl ul tā tang hanun pep in i 'la** You have to put with a lot of things to stay alive. **Pap ul mekta ka 'la to son nim i osimyen il.e se ya hanun pep in i 'la** You should rise when guests appear, even in the middle of dinner.

  -un ~. ¶**Cey ttay ey pap ul mektolok mace an hay cwuta 'ni kulen pep i eti iss.na** What kind of deal is this — not even serving us on time?!

  2. (= **cek, swu, īl**) occasion, event.

  -nun ~. ¶**Thonghak hanun kil ey kakkum ssik tullinun pep to ēps.i n' anh.ci yo** (= **iss.ki n' iss.e yo**) I do drop in occasionally on my way to and from school.

pep hata, postmod adj-n sep. [Occurs after -(ess.)nun, -ulq.]

  1. has good reason (justification) to be / do.

  -ulq ~. ¶**Ku ka sēng nalq pep to hata** He has good reason (every right) to be angry; he SHOULD be angry.

  2. there is reason to expect; it is (or seems) reasonable that ⋯ ; it can be expected that ⋯ ; it ought (it is supposed) to be that ⋯ .

  -ulq ~. ¶**Ku khi khun i ka tāycang ilq pep hata** That tall one must be the general. **Ku i ka wass.ulq pep to hata** He surely must have arrived. **Pi ka olq pep to haken man un** It should rain but it doesn't.

  -nun ~. ¶**Mue palkwang hayss.ta 'n māl i iss.ess.nun pep han tey** ⋯ (It seems) he is supposed to have gone crazy or something ⋯ .

  3. (= **tus hata, tus siph.ta**) it seems likely that. ¶**Pi ka olq pep to hata** It looks like rain. **Ku sin i nay pal ey yak.kan cak.ulq pep hata** These shoes seem a little small for my feet. **Ku īl i toylq pep hata** That seems likely to happen.

pes-cangi, cpd postn. an unskilled person. ¶**mokswu** ~ a green carpenter. **hwallyang** ~ a poor archer.

p'ēy = **pwēy** = **pōy** < *poye*, inf < *pōyta* = *poita*.

peyki, postnoun [var] = **payki**

peyngi [var] = **payngi**. ¶**kwūm-peyngi** a white bug, a maggot; a sluggard. [< **kwūlm** subst < **kwūlm.ta** starves].

phaki, postnoun = **phayki**

phal(q) < ˙*phol(q)* < *˙*pho˙l[o]l(q)*, prosp mod < *phalta* < ˙*pho[l] ta* 'sells'. SEE ˙*pholl* ⋯ .

phal.i, postn. (der n < *phalta*). selling. ¶**phum** ~ hiring out for daily wages.

phal-i, cpd postn (n + n 'arm-person'). a person with an arm such that. ¶**kompay** ~ a person with a mutilated / deformed arm. CF **pal-i, son-i, nwun-i.** NOTE: The immediate constituents of the compounds should be (n + **phal**) + **i**, but they are often treated as if n + (**phal** + **i**).

phalm < ˙*pholm* < *˙*pho˙l[o]m*, subst < *phalta* < ˙*pho[l] ta* (sells)

phan, 1. n. scene, scene of action / competition; round, bout, match.

  2. postmod. situation (= **phan-kwuk**); ⋯ ~ **ey** in the situation where / that ⋯ . ¶**Ppalli ka to nuc.ul phan in tey (phan ini-kka) ppalli kaca** Even if we hurry we'll be late, but let's walk fast(er). **Tōn ul ttal phan ey pul i na-kass.ta** I was about to rake in the money [from the gambling table] when the lights went out. **Sinsey cinun phan ey han kaci te pūthak hapsita** Since am obliged to you anyway, let

me ask you one more favor. **Mok i khel-khel hatun phan ey han can cal hayss.ta** My throat was thirsty so I had a good drink. **Sicang han phan ey silkhes mek.ess.ta** I was hungry, so I ate my fill.
phan < ˙*phon* < **pho[˙lo]n*, mod < **phalta** < ˙*pho[l]˙ta* (sells)
phangi, postn, suffix = **phayngi**. ¶**kōm-phang(i)** = kōm mildew.
phayki, postn; var [? paraintensive] < **payki**. person, thing, one; child. ¶**simswul** ~ a crosspatch, a peevish person; a naughty child. **(a)twun** ~ a dim-wit(ted person). **kasum** ~ [vulgar] = **kasum** the chest, breast. **kol** ~ [vulgar] = **kol** = **meli** the head. VAR **phe(y)ki**.
phayngi, postnoun, suffix [? var < **payngi**; CF **phayki**]. person, thing, one. ¶**com** ~ a petty (narrow-minded) person. **nom** ~ a disreputable person; a girl's boyfriend. **okum** ~ the inner angle of a bend / curve.
'phe, abbr < **siph.e**. SEE **-ko 'phe**.
ph'e, abbr < **phye** < **phie**.
pheki, postnoun [var] = **phayki**
PHEY The South Korean spelling distinguishes **phey** and **ph**^{y}**ey**, but both these sequences are usually pronounced the same (as **phey**). If you cannot locate the word you seek under **phey**, look under **ph**^{y}**ey**.
pheyki, postnoun [var] = **phayki**
phi- < *PPI*, bnd adn [lit]. that. SYN **ce**. CF **cha-**.
phī- < ˝*PPI*, bnd adnoun. being subject to, ···ed. ¶**phī-senke(q kwen)** (the right) to be elected.
'phi, abbr < **puphi** 'bulk' (der n < **puphuta**). ¶**mom** ~ body build, physique; the size of a bowframe.
phie, 1. inf < **phiita**; < **phīta**. 2. = **phiye**, inf < **phiita**. 3. = **phiwe**, inf < **phiwuta**. ABBR **phye, ph'e**.
phiita$_1$, vt, vc [var] = **phi(wu)ta**
phiita$_2$, vp < **phita**$_2$; [= DIAL / lit **phyeita**].
1. = **phye cita** (gets unfolded, smoothed).
2. it gets better, mends, improves, is eased. ¶**cayceng kōn.**^{1}**nan i** ~ financial difficulties are eased, straightened circumstances improve. **sēym i** ~ becomes better off.
3. gets straightened out, is smoothed (down / over). ¶**īl i** ~ a matter gets straightened out, an affair is smoothed over.
4. vt, vc. mistake for **phi(wu)ta**.

phita$_1$, vi. [? < **phīta** < **phiita**].
1. [only in compounds?] it spreads (smooths, straightens) out. SEE **ph'ē ttulita /cita** [< **phyē** < **phie**]; **phita**$_2$, **phiwuta**.
2. it blooms, blossoms, flowers, comes out, comes into bloom (ANT **cita**). ¶**kkoch i** ~ a flower blooms (is in bloom); it (has) blossoms. **kkoch i phalah.key** ~ it blooms blue.
3. it eases (financially), it takes a turn for the better, it looks up. ¶**sim i** ~ one's financial condition eases (improves, looks up).
4. gets relieved, relaxed.
5. it burns, is kindled (ANT **kkē cita**). ¶**pul i** ~ a fire burns. **Cangcak i cal phici anh.nunta** The firewood burns poorly.
phita$_2$ < ˚*phyeta*, vt [= DIAL/lit **phyeta**]; [? < **phīta** = **phiwuta**]. VP **phiita**.
1. spreads it out, opens/unfolds it, stretches it out (ANT **cepta, kaykhita**); straightens it out; smooths it out. ¶**chayk ul** ~ opens a book. **son ul** ~ opens one's palm. **sinmun ul** ~ unfolds a newspaper. **ipul ul** ~ spreads bedding. **sōm ul** ~ spreads cotton out thin.
2. stretches (a part of the body). ¶**heli lul** ~ stretches one's back.
3. straightens / smooths it out. ¶**kwukimq-sal ul** ~ smooths (irons out) wrinkles. **kwup.un chelqsa lul** ~ straightens a crooked wire.
4. **ki lul** ~ eases one's mind, relieves one.
5. eases, alleviates, improves. ¶**ongsayk han sallim ul** ~ improves one's meager livelihood.
6. spreads, promulgates, propagates.
7. extends (power / influence), establishes.
phīta, abbr < **phiita**; < **phiwuta**.
phiwe, inf < **phiwuta**.
phiwuta, vt [vc < **phita**].
1. makes it burn, kindles. ¶**pul ul** ~ makes a fire. **cangcak ul** ~ burns firewood.
2. smokes / fumigates / burns it. ¶**hyang ul** ~ burns incense. **tāmpay lul** ~ smokes (tobacco), has a cigarette; smokes a pipe.
3. **nāymsay lul** ~ emits a scent, has an odor.
4. postnom v sep. does (= **hata**); displays, performs (= **pulita, ttēlta, ppāyta**). ¶**iksal** ~ plays the fool, jests. **kāsal** ~ behaves in a hateful (stuck-up) way. **eli-kwang** ~ plays the baby. **emsal** ~ pretends distress. **simswul** ~ acts cross. **k**^{e}/$_a$**tulum** ~ struts, swaggers. **palam** ~ fools around, cheats on one's spouse.
phiye, 1. inf < **phiita**. 2. → **phie**. 3. → **phiwe**.

pho, bnd n. quantity. ¶ **nal ~** a period of days, some days. **tal ~** a period of about a month. **hay ~** = *hoy phwo* (1894 Gale 137; ?1660 Kyeychwuk 11, cited from LCT) about a year. **pay ~** "belly quantity" = one's capacity, the scale / breadth of one's thinking. CF **pho-kayta, pho-cipta** heaps / piles them up, stacks; **pho-payki** doubling, folding. [? < phok]

phok₁, postnoun.
 1. of the same age group. ¶ **Elin tongsayng phok pakk ey an toyp.nita** They must be of the same age group as my little brother.
 2. **~ (ccum)** approximately, about. ¶ **Sip-li phok toynta** It is about ten li (leagues). **Yelq sikan phok ccum toynta** It is about ten hours. NOTE: CM 2:69 gives examples of N **uy phok un toynta** 'is as much as N'; is this phok < ˙*PWOK* 'strip of cloth; width'?

phok₂, postmodifier (= **sēym** 1). supposition; accounting (for); (to all) appearances; seeming. ¶ **Kyelkwuk kuleh.key toyn phok / sēym ita** It seems that is the way it finally turned out. **Kwīsin ul pon phok / sēym in ya?** You mean you saw a ghost?! **Cal toyki n' cal toyn phok ici** Still, it turned out all right. / It turned OUT all right (but) ... .

˙*phol(q)* < *˙*pho˙l[o]l(q)*, prospective modifier < ˙*pho[l]˙ta* (sells). CF ˙*pholl* ... .

˙*pholl* ... (+ ˙*i* postmod) < *˙*pho˙l[o]l(q)*, prosp mod < ˙*pho[l]˙ta* (sells). **mol ˙phol˙l i** (?1517-Pak 1:62a) a horse dealer.

˙*pholm* < *˙*pho˙l[o]m*, subst < ˙*pho[l]˙ta* (sells)

'**phuci, 'phuko, 'phul(q)** SEE -ko ~

phul(q) < ˙*phul(q)* < *˙*phu˙l[u]l(q)*, prosp mod < **phulta** < ˙*phu[l]˙ta* (loosens). CF ˙*phull* ... .

˙*phull* ... (+ ˙*i* postmod) < ˙*phul[u]l(q)*, prosp mod < ˙*phu[l]˙ta* (loosens; ...). ˙*phul˙l i* (1449 Kok 74). ˙*phul˙l i* ˙'*lesi˙ta* (1586 Sohak 4:9b).

phulm < ˙*phulm* < *˙*phu˙l[u]m*, subst < **phulta** < ˙*phu[l]˙ta* (loosens; ...). ¶ ˙*phul˙m ye* (1447 Sek 9:36b).

phum₁ < [˙]*phwum*, n. the bosom / breast, the space between one's chest and clothes; the width (of a coat). CF **phum.ta** < ˙*phwum˙ta* carries in one's bosom; **phulm**.

phum₂, n. labor, work. ¶ **halwu ~** a day's work. **~ ul phalta** sells one's labor, works for wages. **~ ul tulita** puts in work. **~ ul kaph.ta** works in return. **phumq kaps** wages, pay. **phum(-phal.i)q kwun** a day-laborer.

phūm₃, postmod. appearance, looks; behavior; the way (one looks/behaves). ¶ **sālam toyn ~** one's nature / character. **sālam sayngkin ~** one's looks / appearance. **nal-ttwinun ~** the way one gambols about; the wild / arrogant way one behaves. **Toye kanun phūm i kulelq tus hata** It seems to be developing fairly well. **Sayngkin phūm i māl i ani 'ta** The shape he was in is beyond description. **Mulken toyn phūm i tuntun chi mōs hakeyss.ta** It certainly does not look very solid / substantial / strong. [? < phūm₄ < ¨*PHUM*]

phūm₄ < ¨*PHUM*, n. 1. (= **phūmcil**) quality.
 2. grace, refinement, elegance; class.
 3. degree of official rank.
 4. (= **sangphum, phūmmul**) an article, merchandise, wares, goods.

'**phum, 'phun, 'phuna, 'phuney, 'phuni** → (siphu··· =) **siph-**

phun < ˙*phun* < ˙*phu[˙lu]n*, mod < **phulta** < ˙*phu[l]˙ta* (loosens).

phus, bnd n (? < *˙*phu[l] s*; CF **phuluta, phul**).
 1. adn. green, unripe, inexperienced; new, fresh. ¶ **~ kes** unripe produce; first produce of the season. **~ koksik** new crop. **~ na(y)ki** a greenhorn. **~ nay** the smell of new greens. **~ salang** puppy love. **~ som-ssi** a poor hand. **~ cang(cak)** brushwood used for fuel. **~ q yuch** /phunnyuch/ poor skill at playing yuch.
 2. SEE **elyem ~**

'**phuta**, abbr < (siphuta =) **siph.ta**

phye, abbr < **phie**

phyeita → **phiita**

phyel(q), prosp mod < ˚*phyeta* (1527 Cahoy 3:6a=12b). ¶ *pol[h] kwu phi˙la phyel sso˙zi ˙yey* (1459 Wel 21:4a) while bending and stretching the arm. *phye˙lak ¨cwuy˙lak* (1462 ¹Nung 1:108b, 1:113a) opening and closing it.

¨*phyel(q)*, modulated prosp mod < ˚*phyeta*. ¶ ˙*PEP-˙NGUY ˙lol ˙phye˙l ye ˙ho˙sino˙ta* (1447 Sek 13:26b) seeks to spread the sense of the Law.

phyen < *PYEN*, noun.
 1. (= **ccok, panghyang**) side, part, direction, way. ¶ **ōyn ~ (ulo)** (to) the left. **palun / olun ~ (ulo)** (to) the right. **kēnne ~ (ey)** (to/on) the opposite side. **nay ~** my side, my way. **enu ~ ina** either way. **Kil palun phyen ey payk.hwa-cem i iss.ta** There is a department store on the right side of the street. **nam phyen** the south side, a southern direction — CF **namphyen**

husband, man; ⁿyephyen-ney wife, woman.

2. (= kihoy) chance, opening, opportunity.

3. side(s), party, ally. ¶cey ~ one's own side, the friendly side. Onul un wuli phyen ita ka to ¹nayil un ce ccok phyen i toyl.nun ci nwu ka al.e Who knows whether he may be on our side today and on theirs tomorrow?

4. side, direction, inclination, preponderance; alternative. ¶com cek.un ~ ita is a little on the skimpy side. mānh.un ~ ita is rather much. cak.un ~ ita is on the small side. khun ~ ita is on the large side, is rather large / big. ippun ~ ita is on the pretty side. ippuci anh.un ~ ita is on the not-so-pretty side. Cak.un phyen i cōh.a yo I prefer it on the small side. Ku co'.yong han um.ak soli nun wass.ta kass.ta kel.umye pota anc.e swīmye tut.nun phyen i nāss.ta/cōh.ass.ta Rather than listen to that quiet music while walking to and from it would be better to sit down to relax and listen to it.

5. SEE han phyen (ulo nun)

6. SEE i phyen; ku / ce phyen

phyeta → phita

˚phyeta, vt = phita (stretches it; spreads it; expounds, tells; ...). ¶cwocco˙wa twulwu ˙phye (1462 ¹Nung 1:4a) following and spreading the word. ne ˙phye nil˙Gwol ˙tt in ˙t ay n' (1447 Sek 9:29a) as you say. ci˙p uy s ¨te˙lewu˙m ul ˙phyesi˙nwon cyen˙cho 'y˙n i (1482 Nam 1:5a) is the reason that he deigns to tidy up the mess of the house. ˙phye˙e 'ys.ten pol˙h ol kwu˙phil sso˙zi ˙yey (1447 Sek 6:2a) while bending the arm that one has stretched out. ˙phyesi˙m ye ˙phyesi˙kwo k (1462 ¹Nung 1:108b) stretching and stretching them. ˙SYEY-CWON ˙skuy na y ˙ptu˙t ul ˙phye˙a ¨sol˙Wosywosye (1447 Sek 6:6a) please tell the World-Honored my thoughts.

PHʸEY South Korean spelling distinguishes phey and phyey, but both these sequences are usually pronounced the same (as phey). If you cannot locate the word you seek under phʸey, look under phey.

pi(-), adn, bnd adv. twisted, askew, awry; mis-, wrongly, falsely, wrongfully, bad(ly). CF pis-.

1. adn. ~ kkus-, ~ suk, ~ sul, ~ sūs, ~ thucek, ~ thul, ~ thūm, ~ ttwu-, ~ ttwuk-, ~ ttwul-, ~ tūm (= pisutūm).

2. bnd adv. SEE ~ kkita, ~ kkōta, ~ kkule māyta, ~ thulta, ~ wūs.ta.

pi- < PI, bnd adn. non-, un, not, anti-. ¶~ cocik sālam tul nonorganization people. ~ Hānkwuk cek un-Korean. ~ Ameylikha cek un-American. ~ sāhoy cwuuy ¹nonca a non-socialist. ~ hyēnsilq cek impractical. ~ totek-cek amoral. CF pul-.

pī hata < ¨PI ˚ho˙ta, vnt = pīkyo hata compares it (with / to). ¶pī halq tey ēps.nun kosayng unparalleled hardships. ··· ey pī ha.ye (hay se) compared with / to ··· .

pīl(q) < ¨pil(q) < *pi˙l[o]l(q), prosp mod < pīlta < ¨pi[l]˙ta. ¶˙pil˙kel (1527 Cahoy 3:10a=22a) the Chinese word ˙kel [= ˙KHULQ] 'to beg'. ¨pil˙kuy (1527 Cahoy 3:14a=32b) the Chinese word kuy [= KKUY] 'to pray'.

¨pill ··· , ¨pil˙l ··· (+ i postmod) < *pi˙l[o]l, prospective mod < ¨pi[l]˙ta. ¶¨pil˙l i is.ke˙tun (1447 Sek 9:12a) if there be one who begs. e˙lwu kwo˙c ol ¨pill i '˙la (1481 Twusi 8:42a) can borrow blossoms.

pīlm < ¨pilm < *pi˙l[o]m, subst < ¨pi[l]˙ta.

pīlta < ¨pi[l]˙ta, vt -L-. 1. begs. 2. prays (for). 3. borrows.

pi˙lwol(q), modulated prosp mod < ¨pi[l]˙ta. ¶˙na y pi˙lwol ¨i˙l i i˙sye (?1517- Pak 1:59a) I have some borrowing [at a pawnshop] to do.

pi˙lwom, modulated subst < ¨pi[l]˙ta. ¶mozo˙m ay pi˙lwo.m o˙lwo (1462 ¹Nung 10:42a) by praying with one's heart. pi˙lwo.m i (1481 Twusi 21:13a) borrowing.

pi˙lwon, modulated mod < ¨pi[l]˙ta. ¶pi˙lwon ˙pa˙p ol (1449 Kok 122) the food [just now] begged.

pi˙lwum, modulated subst < ¨pi[l]˙ta. ¶˙pap pi˙lwu˙m ul (1465 Wen 1:2:2:117a) (the act of) begging one's food. pi˙lwum ˙kot ho˙n i '˙la (1459 Wel 7:70a) it is like begging.

pi˙lwun, modulated mod < ¨pi[l]˙ta. ¶na y ˙uy pi˙lwun ke˙s i˙la (1464 Kumkang hwu-se 6_; cited from LCT with inferred accents) it is what I have borrowed. pi˙lwun ilhwu˙m ul ca˙pa (1462 ¹Nung 6:100a) under an assumed name.

pīn < ¨pin < *pi˙[lo]n, modifier < pīlta < ¨pi[l]˙ta; CF pi˙lwun. ¨pi˙n i (1447 Sek 6:33b) prayed. ¶LYANG-˙SSIK ¨pin˙t ay (1447 Sek 6:14a) upon begging food. CF pi˙lwon, pi˙lwun.

pīnun < ¨pi˙non < pi˙[lo]˙non, proc modifier < ¨pi[l]˙ta. ¶¨pi˙non ¨salo˙m ol (1447 Sek 9:12b) people who are begging.

pis(-), ? adnoun, bnd adverb [= **piq(-)** < **pi(-)**]. crooked, sidewise, aslant, astray, wrong, mis-, mistaken. 1. adn. ¶ **~-cang** a crossbar. **~ kum** a deviant crease. **~ panca** an inclined ceiling.
  2. bound adverb. **~ (na-)kata**, **~ mac.ta**, **~ mekta**, **~ pota**, **~ tāyta**, **~ (te-)suta**, **~ titita**, **~ ttuta**.
-p.naykka = **-p.neykka** (→ **-p.nikka**)
-p.nayta = **-p.neyta** (→ **-p.nita**)
-p.ney, **-p.ni**, **-p.nuy** [DIAL; obsolescent] = **-e yo**
-p.neykka [DIAL] = **-p.nikka**
-p.neyta [DIAL] = **-p.nita**
-p.niikke [Kyengsang DIAL ([¹]Na Cinsek 1977)] = **-p.nikka**
'p.nikka, abbr < **ip.nikka**, < **hap.nikka**.
-p.nikka, alternant after a vowel of **-sup.nikka** (FORMAL indic attent). is / does it? (= **-ni?**). ¶**Pissap.nikka?** Is it expensive? **Kap.nikka?** Is he going? **Nwu ka nōp.nikka** Who is playing?
  ~ tul SEE **-sup.nikka tul**
  ~ yo SEE **-sup.nikka yo**
-p.nikk(y)e [Kyengsang DIALECT ([¹]Na Cinsek 1977)] = **-p.nikka**
-p.ninta = **-p.nunta**.
'p.nita, abbr < **ip.nita**, < **hap.nita**.
-p.nita, alt after a vowel of **-sup.nita** (FORMAL indic assertive). is; does. ¶ **pissap.nita** (it) is expensive. **kap.nita** goes. **nōp.nita** (< **nō-l-**) plays. **~ tul** SEE **-sup.nita tul**.
-p.nite [DIAL] = **-p.nita**
-p.nuy, alt after a vowel of **-sup.nuy**
-p.nuynta, alt after vowel of **-sup.nuynta** [DIAL; old-fashioned] = **-o** (AUTH statement/question).
-(˙)po- SEE **-puta** (bnd adj)
-(q)po, suffix (postmodifier, postnoun). one, thing, person (teasing / belittling).
  1. **-po**. ¶**ccay-po** a harelipped person; a half-wit. **ek-po** a strong-headed person; a bigot. **kōm-po** pockmarked person. **thēyng-po** (= **thēyng-soy**) a hollow shell of a person; an empty-headed person. **ttangttal-po** a stocky fellow. **yak-po** a shrewd person.
  1a. (postmod) ¶**nulin-po** (= **nuli-kwangi**) a slowpoke. ? **ttal-po** a narrow-minded person; (= **talaci**) a dwarf [? < **ttā-l-** be different].
  1b. (postn) ¶**kolim-po** an invalid; a mean person. **kep-po** = **kep-cangi** a coward. **kkoy-po** a shrewd person. **thāl-po** a penniless person. **thel-po** a hairy / shaggy person. **ttek-po** (= **ttek-chwungi**) a rice-cake glutton. **ttwung-po** a withdrawn / glum (an unresponsive) person; = **ttwungttwung-po** a fat person, a fatso.
  2. **-qpo**. ¶**cēnq-po** [? DIAL] bad manners; a person of low / base character. ¶**mālq-/eq-po** an uninhibited remark from a usually reticent person. **maumq-/simq-po** disposition (often bad), will, temper. **noyq-po** a low-down mean person. **nulq-po** a slowpoke. **tāmq-po** spirit, courage, pluck, grit, guts. **wungq-po** large-heartedness, magnanimity.
poa, inf < **pota**. Usually contracted to **pwā**.
poita$_{1-2}$ = **pōyta** < ¨**pwoy˙ta** [the modern form with /oi/ is analogical]. The infinitive **po.ye** is usually replaced by **poye** < ¨**pwoy˙ya** (< **pōyta** < ¨**pwoy˙ta**), normally contracted to **pōy** = **pwēy** (> **p'ēy**), often treated as **pwāy**.
poita$_1$ = **pōyta** < ¨**pwoyta**, vp < **pota** < °**pwo˙ta**). 1. is seen; is visible, one can see it; comes in sight; appears, shows up. ¶**Tal i (pata ka) poinun ya** "Is the moon (the sea) visible?" = Can you see the moon (the sea)? **Eti kkaci se poinun ya** From how far away can it be seen? **Hanul hako pata pakk ey poici anh.ess.ta** There was nothing in sight save sky and sea. **Etteh.key 'na pi ka onun ci aph i poici anh.nunta** It is raining so hard that somehow I can't see in front of me at all. **Nwun i an poinun tey 'ta (ka) tut.ci mace mōs hani sal.e se mwes hakeyss.**^{S}**o?!** Not only blind but unable to hear, as well, what good is there in living?! **Ku ccum (ey se) pota to i ccum ey se ponun phyen i te cal pointa** You can see better from here than from there where you are. **Ce palun phyen ey poinun ki nun Yengkwuk tāysa-kwan ki 'la 'nta** The flag you can see over on the right is the flag of the British Embassy, you see. **Ne eti iss.ess.nun ya − halwu congil poici anh.uni** Where have you been that I haven't seen you all day long?
  2. appears, shows up, arrives (at the door, on the stage, …). ¶**Āmu to poici anh.ess.um ulo han phyen ulo nun kekceng to tōyss.**^{S}**up.nita** I was a bit worried that nobody had showed up. **Akka ku i ka otun tey ecci i cali ey poici anh.nun ka** I saw him on his way here a little while ago − how come he isn't here?.
  3. looks; appears; seems. SEE **-un (-nun, -tun, -ulq) kes ulo ~**.
  4. aux v insep. it looks / seems like. SEE **-e ~**, **-key ~**.

poita₂ = **pōyta** < ¨*pwoyta*, vt (vc < **pota** < °*pwo ̇ta*). lets (one) see; shows. ¶**I phyēnci nun ape' nim kkey po.ye tulikey** Show this letter to your father. **Ku sālam i māl pota silqcey hayngtong ulo (sse) mopem ul po.ye cwunta** He gives an example in actual behavior rather than words.

poki, 1. vt summative. ¶**na poki ey** the way I see it, in my view / opinion.

2. n. (illustrative) example; adv. for example.

3. bnd n. ¶**pon-poki** example, model, pattern. **swus poki** a naive person. **eli-poki** a dimwit; a coward.

poko, particle [< vt gerund 'seeing'].

1. (asks / tells / shows) to (a person). ¶**swunsa ka wuli ~ sonq cis ul hata** the policeman motions to us. **na ~ yok ul hata** insults / scolds me. **Na poko kaluchila 'yss.ta** They asked me to teach. **Chinkwu poko way kulen māl hasey yo (way kulay yo)** Why do you speak to (behave toward) a friend that way? **Nwukwu poko 'na kongson hala 'y la** (= **hala ko hay la**) Tell him to be polite to everybody. CF **tele, eykey, hanthey**.

NOTE 1: The teller does not have to be face-to-face with the person told: **na poko cēnhwa lo kuleh.key hayss.ta** told me that by phone. The source can be sightless: **Cāng-nim i chinkwu poko kil ul kaluchilye tālla ko hayss.ta** A blind man asked a friend to tell him the way.

NOTE 2: The phrase **na poko** can mean either 'to me' or (= **na [lul] poko**) 'looking at me' but the honorific **na posiko** can only mean 'looking at me' (= **na [lul] posiko**).

NOTE 3: Sometimes also ··· **l(ul) poko**.

2. [DIAL] = **pota** than. Ramstedt (1939:99) says "Instead of poda, also pogo is used in comparisons". This has not been confirmed for standard speech, but a 1904 Russian work gives the form and King 1990 describes it as "typical Hamkyeng".

poko tul, pcl + pcl. ¶**Na poko tul kulayss.ta** That's what they said to me.

pole [blend of **poko** + **tele**], pcl. to (a person).

pom₁, noun. spring(time).

pom₂ < *pwom(···)*, subst < **pota** < °*pwo ̇ta*.

pon₁ < ¨*PWON*, adn. 1. this, the same / present.

2. the principal, the main, original.

3. real, genuine. ¶ **~ nay kyēyhoyk** my real / present / original plan. **~ (ku uy) maum un** his real intention / nature. **~ kaps** the cost / prime price. **~ kōhyang / kocang** one's old home town. **~ cip** one's principal residence. **~ pathang** the essence, true nature, substance. **~ sēngcil** basic personality. **~ sepang/puin** one's original husband / wife. **~ hōysa** main office.

pon₂ < *pwon*, mod < **pota** < °*pwo ̇ta*.

poni, sequential of **pota**. SEE **-ko, pota**.

pota₁₋₃ < °*pwo ̇ta*. The infinitive is **pwā** (< **poa** < ˙*pwo ̇a*), often contracted to **p'ā**; past **pwass-** (< **poass-**) often contracts to **p'ass-**.

pota₁, vt. 1. perceives; sees; looks (at / into).

2. (= **kwūkyeng hata**) sees (the sights); visits; views.

3. (= **hata**, postnominal verb sep) attends to (business); manages; conducts.

4. (= **math.ta**) takes charge of; looks after; watches; sets (the table); waits on (a table); tends (a child); keeps an eye on.

5. (= **ilk.ta**) reads; sees, looks at, peruses.

6. (= **sayngkak hata**) views, regards, sees. ¶**na / tangsin poki ey** in my / your opinion, as I / you see it. **enu cem ulo (enu mo lo) potun ci** from every point of view, in every respect.

7. encounters it personally; experiences it; undergoes, goes/passes through, suffers/enjoys. ¶**caymi lul ~** enjoys oneself, has a good time; enjoys prosperity. **Caymi posipsio** Good-bye [to someone going on a pleasure trip — Have fun!; to a shopkeeper — I hope you will have lots of business].

8. (= **chiluta**) takes (an examination).

9. (= **nwuta**) relieves nature. ¶**tāypyen ul ~** has a bowel movement. **sōpyen ul ~** urinates.

10. buys / sells in (a market). **cang ul ~** deals in a market; goes marketing, goes shopping. ¶**cang pole kata** goes off to do the shopping.

11. (= **kaps pota**) offers (a price); bids.

12. gets (a new relative). ¶**sawi / sonca lul ~** acquires a son-in-law / grandchild.

13. has a secret love affair with. ¶**kyēycip ul ~** keeps a mistress. **sanay lul ~** has a lover.

14. tells (fortunes); reads (one's fortune in); has one's fortune told by.

pota₂, aux adj. SEE **-un ka pota** (etc.), **-na pota**. VAR **puta**. NOTE: These expressions take all the styles, including **-ci (yo), -n tey (yo)**.

pota₃, aux v sep. SEE **-e pota, -ko pota, -ta (ka) pota** (NKd 1769). We arbitrarily hyphenate **ka-pota** 'goes to see, tries going'.

pota₄, pcl, adv [< vt transferentive 'when one looks at'; LHS lists a dialect equivalent **pota ka**]. SEE *pwota ̇ka*. CF **ey se**; **poko**.

1. pcl. than (used after the second member of a comparison, usually accompanied by **te**); rather than. ¶ ~ **te** more than. ~ **(te) napputa** is worse than; is inferior to. ~ **(te) nās.ta / cōh.ta** is better than; is superior to. **I kicha ka ce kicha pota ppaluta** This train is faster than that train. **Payk pen tut.nun kes i han pen ponun kes pota mōs hata** It is better to see a thing one time than to hear about it a hundred times. **Ku i nun nay ka sayngkak hayss.tun kes pota khi ka khess.ta** He was taller than I thought he would be. **Ku sakwa nun poki pota nun mek.e poni-kka mas i te cōh.ta** That apple tastes even better than it looks (M 3:3:141). SEE **-nun i pota**.
2. pcl. (other) than [an incorrect usage taken from the Japanese] = **hako** or **kwa/wa**.
3. pcl [+ neg] = **mankhum** [not] so much as.
4. pcl [Cenla DIAL] = **poko** (to).
5. adv [lit] = **te**. ¶ **pota khukey** = **te khukey** bigger / louder. **I kes i kaps pota ssata** (= **te ssata**) This (one) is cheaper.

pota khenyeng, pcl + pcl. ¶ **Ku nun Yenge nun Namsik-i pota khenyeng Tongkun-i mankhum to mōs hanta** In English he is no match for Tongkun-i, much less Namsik-i!

pota 'la to, pcl + cop var inf + pcl. ¶ **Poktong-i kath.i nun haci mōs haci man Swupok-i pota 'la to cal hay ya toylq kes i ani 'n ya** You may not be able to do as well as Poktong-i, but surely you ought to do better than Swupok-i.

potam, pcl [DIAL] = **pota** (than). ¶ **Mikwuk ey se īl hanun kes potam Hānkwuk ulo ka se īl haki lo kyelqsim hayss.ci** Rather than work in America, I made up my mind to go to Korea and work there. CF **puthem**; both **puthem** and **potam** are South Kyengsang (Mkk 1960:3:32) and Phyengan (Kim Yengpay 1984:95).

pota man, pcl + pcl. ¶ **Ney ka Swun-i pota man kongpu lul cal hay to āmu māl anh.keyss.ta** There wouldn't be any scoldings if you were only better at school work than Swun-i.

pota n', pcl + abbr pcl = **pota nun**.

pota 'na-ma, pcl + copula extended adversative [awkward]. ¶ **Ku ay pota 'na-ma kongpu lul cal hanta 'myen kwaynchanh.keyss.e** It would be a relief if you could at least do better at your school work than HE does.

pota nun, pcl + pcl. (rather) than. ¶ **kuleh.key haki** ~ rather than do that. **Hong-cha pota nun khephi ka nās.ci** Coffee would certainly be better than black tea. **Caney pota nun nay ka te pappuney** I am busier than you.

pota to, pcl + pcl. even than; than also / either. ¶ **san** ~ **noph.ko, pata** ~ **kiph.ta** is taller than the mountains and deeper than the sea. **Hong-cha pota to khephi ka te mek.ko siph.ta** I'd prefer to drink coffee rather than tea. **Kwulapha ey l' kalye 'ketun pihayng-ki pota to pay lo kakey** If you are planning to go to Europe, go by boat rather than plane.

pota uy, pcl + pcl. ¶ **kongkhulithu pota uy kyenko-seng** a strength greater than concrete.

pota ya, pcl + pcl. (only if it be) than, if (it's a case of being more etc.) than. ¶ **Him i yak han 'n tul ne pota ya yak hakeyss.nun ya** I may be weak, but I'm sure I'm no weaker than you.

-potwu, suffix. fellow, guy, person. ¶ **ekchek** ~ a stubborn person. [? **-po** + **twu** < *TTWUW* 'head']

pōy (= **pwēy**, "**pwāy**") < **poye**, inf < **pōyta** = **poita**. ¶ **kulay pōy / poye to**. may not look it but; despite appearance(s). **celay pōy** (= **poye**) **to** in spite of appearances; seem that as it may.

poye, inf < **pōyta** = **poita**, usually contracted to **pōy** = **pwēy** (standard spelling "**pwāy**").

po.ye, inf < **poita**, usually replaced by **poye**.

poypta < **poyopta** < *pwo-i-̇wo-p[o]*-, vt -w-. humbly sees or meets; is presented to; has an audience (an interview) with. ¶ **Ecey na nun tāython.lyeng ul poywess.ˢup.nita** I was seen (received) by the President yesterday. **Eti se poywusyess.ˢup.nikka** Where did he receive you? **Tto poypkeyss.ˢup.nita** Good-bye, I hope that we will see each other again. **Cheum poypsup.nita / poypkeyss.ˢup.nita** How do you do [on being introduced]. **A.yu, i key wēynq īl isey yo; yeki se poypta 'ni (yo)** Oh, what's this; what a surprise to see YOU!

NOTE: -w- may drop, so that **poy[w]e** = **poye**.

pōyta, abbr < **poita** (vp, vc); inf **poye** > **pōy**, often treated as **pwāy**.

ppachita SEE **pachita**

ppā cita. 1. cpd vi. falls, drops, sinks; indulges (in); falls out, comes out; is left out, omitted; gets thin, loses flesh; is removed, depleted; passes (all the way through), goes (by / out);

escapes, excuses oneself; leaves, quits, drops out; falls behind, is inferior; falls to one's lot.
2. 2a. cpd aux v insep (follows adj inf, or sometimes vi inf — mallᵉ⁄ₐ ~ shrivels up) — usually past or modifier. gets/becomes (old, rotten, musty, etc.) through and through; utterly, quite, thoroughly, to the core, all the way. ¶kᵉ⁄ₐyulle ppā cyess.ta is lazy through and through. nulk.e ppā cin ⁿyephyen-ney a withered old woman. ssek.e ppā cin cengchi politics which are rotten to the core. nalk.e ppā cin os well-worn clothes. Ku photo-cwu nun sie ppā cyess.ta The wine has all soured.
2b. postnom v (? adj). ¶saythwung ~ is terribly flippant, awfully silly (= saythwung sulepta).
ppak, 1. postnoun: vulgarizes a noun [? < -q pak(.)i]. meli ~ head. 2. → -(p)pak
ppal, quasi-free noun, postnoun.
1. [rare] manner (= sik); the way things are. ¶Ku ppal lo (= Kulen sik ulo) hata ka nun khunq īl nanta You keep on the way you are doing and there will be trouble. Ku ppal lo pelye twusio Leave it alone (as it is).
2. postn [var] = ppel (relationship, kinship standing/role).
3. SEE (-q) pal.
ppali = (p)payki, postn. ¶taykal ~ head.
ppalli, der adv < ppaluta. rapidly, quickly, fast, in haste. CF ellun, ese.
··· ppang < ···q pang, bnd n. ¶cil ~ = cilq pang a back-strap (for carrying things). mēyl ~ = mēylq pang a shoulder strap (for carrying things).
*ppāta, vi. falls, drops, drops out. SEE ppā cita, ppa ttulita, ppa-tus, ppāyta [? vc < ppa-i-], cappa cita/ttulita.
ppa-tus, postn [< adj-n 'tight, barely enough', abbr < *ppānun tus 'like falling'] a bit less than, just under, a little short of. ¶twū ca ~ just under two feet (long). SYN yak ··· , ANT nek.nek.
ppayki, postnoun, suffix. SEE payki.
ppāyta₁, vt [? vc < *ppāta].
1. extracts; (khal ul ~) draws (a sword); (pyeng-makay lul ~, mos ul ~) pulls out (a cork, a nail), takes out. CF ppopta.
2. (path uy mul ul ~) drains (water off a field).
3. (os uy ttay lul ~) removes, takes out (a stain).
4. (= ppāy noh.ta/mekta) leaves out, omits. ··· (ul) ppāy noh.ko (nun) omitting, leaving out; except (for), but (for), save, without.
ppāyta₂, postnominal verb sep. does (= hata); displays, performs. ¶kāsal ~ behaves in a hateful stuck-up way. kᵉ⁄ₐtulum ~ struts, swaggers.
ppel, postn. (kinship) standing, status, or role; (in) the relationship of, (in) the role of; as, as if, like. ¶hyeng ~ (lo) (in) the role of an older brother; as an older brother; like an older brother. Ku nun nay hyeng ppel i toynta (hyeng ppel ita) He is an older brother to me [in fact/role/age]. Na nun ku lul apeci ppel lo tāycep hayss.ta I treated him as a/my father. VAR ppal. [? < -q pel]
ppelita SEE pelita
ppen hata SEE -q pen hata
ppop.i, postn (der n < vt). an extractor (a pull, a pincer, a claw) for. mos ~ a nail claw. makay ~ a corkscrew.
-ppuk, suffix (makes impressionistic adverb). tamppuk chock-full < tām- (vt) fills, packs. CF -(p)pak.
ppun (< ˝spwun < ··· s ˝pwun), postnoun, postmodifier, particle. SEE ˝spwun.
1. postn. only; merely; just; alone. ¶Mit.ulq sālam un ne ppun ita I have no one but you to rely upon. Ku nun atul i tān hana ppun ita He has only one son. Ku kes ul halq swu iss.nun sālam un na ppun ita I am the only one who can do it. CF man, pakk ey (+ NEG).
2. postmod. [-(ess.)ul ~] nothing but; only, constantly. ¶Ayki ka halwu congil wūl ppun ita The baby does nothing but cry all day. Mulqka ka olul ppun ita Prices keep rising. Sinmun ul thong hay se āl ppun ita I just know it from the newspapers. Na nun nay ūymu lul tā hayss.ul ppun ita I have done nothing but my duty. Cēykwuk cwuuy nun cēncayng ul kacye ol ppun ita Imperialism will only bring war.
3. pcl (after indic assert, proc indic assert). SEE -ta ppun.
4. pcl (after N + pcl). ¶Nay ka ilen māl ul hanun kes un kyel kho kongmu lo se ka ani 'la, tā-man chinkwu uy cenguy phyosi lo se ppun ita My telling you this is not something official but just a friend expressing an opinion.

~ (man) ani 'la, ~ (man) tele not only ... but (also); moreover; furthermore; as well as; besides, in addition, on top of that. ¶**Cosen ey se ppun (man) ani 'la, Ilpon ey se to** not only from Korea, but also from Japan. **Ku nun hakca il ppun tele, siin iki to hata** He is a poet as well as a scholar. **Na nun phikon hayss.ul ppun tele, pay ka kophuki to hayss.ta** I was not only tired but also hungry. **Ku nun Cwungkwuk māl ul hal ppun ani 'la, Ilpon māl to hanta** He speaks Japanese as well as Chinese. **Khi ka khul ppun tele him to sēyta** He is not only big but also very strong. **Ppun tele ku twī nun ...** Not only that, but afterwards ... .

ps... sometimes represents *ss*- (or -*ss*- = -*q s*) instead of basic /*ps*/.

-**psayta** [DIAL] = -**psita**
-**psey**, alt after a vowel of -**upsey** (FORMAL-FAMILIAR subj assert).
'**psey**, abbr < **hapsey**
-**pseyta** [DIAL] = -**psita**
-**psie** [var] = -**psio**
-**psio**, 1. SEE -**usipsio**. 2. ? abbr < -**sipsio**. 3. [DIAL] = -**usio** (FORMAL subj attentive). VAR -**psie**, -**psye**. NOTE: **Hana sapsio!** 'Buy one!' — used by pleading peddlers — may be an abbreviation of **sa cwusipsio**.
-**psio tul** SEE -**usio tul**
'**psita**, abbr < **hapsita**
-**psita**, alt after a vowel of -**upsita** (FORMAL subj assert). ¶**Kapsita** Let's go. **Nōpsita** (< **nōlta**) Let's play.
-**psita tul** SEE -**supsita tul**
'**psiyo** = '**psyo** (= **ipsyo**). -**nun tey** -'**psiyo** = -**nun tey yo**.
psk, n. time. Usually cited as "'**psku**" but the epenthetic vowel cannot be part of the stem, since the nominative-marked form is '**psk i** and not *'**psku y**, as we would otherwise expect. The less common synonym '**pstay** probably originated as a variant *****pst** (the *k* assimilated to the *s* in its locus of articulation) which then incorporated the particle '**ay** 'at', but the form was frozen as a noun by the time of the Hankul texts, as shown by the accusative '**pstay [˙]lol** (1481 Twusi 8:66a). An attestation that would call for the nominative is lacking, and the marker '**i** would be absorbed by the ...**y** in any event, as is the copula stem '**i**... in '**pstay 'sil 'ss oy** (1449 Kok 50). In the 1600s the word is attested as **ptay** and later as **stay** = **ttay**, the modern form. The modern descendant of **psk** is **kki** = **kkini** (? < *'**psk i˙n i** 'it is the time'), with the meaning shifted to 'meal(time)'.
'**psk i** (1447 Sek 13:1a [cited by LCT as '**psk uy**], 1462 ¹Nung 1:22b, 1463 Pep 6:102a, 1464 Kumkang 83b, ?1468⁻ Mong 27a, 40b; 1482 Nam 1:54b).
'**psk i**... it is the time: '**psk i˙la** (1462 ¹Nung 1:23a, 3:26a), '**psk ilwo˙ta** (1481 Twusi 23:40a), '**psk i˙na** (1463 Pep 7:68b), '**psk i.n i ˙Gwo** (1481 Twusi 7:14a).
'**psk ul** (1459 Wel 9:52b, 1481 Twusi 8:6b, 1485 Kwan 11a).
'**psk u˙lwo** (1447 Sek 9:32a), '**psk u[˙]lwo** (1482 Kum-sam 3:45b).
¨**twu ˙psk un** (1462 ¹Nung 3:16a) the two occasions. ¨**twu ˙psk uy** (1462 ¹Nung 3:26a) on two occasions
ku ˙psk uy (1459 Wel 9:52a, 21:5a), '**tye ˙psk uy** (1482 Kum-sam 3:29a) at that time; '**tye cu˙zum psk uy** (1481 Twusi 8:3b) at about that time; **e˙nu ˙psk uy za** (1481 Twusi 7:29a) at just what time; '**psk uy n'** (?1468⁻ Mong 27a, 47a); **ku ˙psk uy s** ... (1447 Sek 19:35a, 1481 Twusi 16:41a).
...*p ¨sop*- < ...*p*-¨*zop*-, < ...*ph*-¨*zop*-, < ...*ps*-¨*zop*-, < ...*W*-¨*zop*-.
'**pstay** = **ttay** (time). SEE **psk**. CF -**un ˙ta ¨ma˙ta**.
-**psye**, abbr < -**psie**, var = -**psio**. ¶**A(n)nyē kapsye!** = **Annyeng hi kapsio!** Good-bye, sir — to departing restaurant guest.
'**psyo** = **ipsyo** [Seoul DIAL]. ¶**Cōysong hap.nita, tā phallyess.nun tey 'psyo** Sorry, we're all out of stock.
-**pta**, bnd adj -W- [after a consonant -**epta**, var -**upta** / -**apta**]. is characterized by.
¶**maypta** is peppery, stinging, hot, extreme < **may** whip; > HEAVY → **mipta** is hateful. **naypta** is smoky < **nay** smoke. (t)t^a/$_u$**supta** is nice and warm < (t)t^a/$_u$**su hata** is warm, mild.
¶**cōllipta** (?) is sleepy / drowsy < **cōllita** gets sleepy. **kulipta** is yearned-after < **kulita** yearns after. **nōllapta** is startling < **nōllata** gets startled. **swīpta** is easy < **swīta** rests.
'**ptikka**, abbr < **iptikka**, < **haptikka**.
-**ptikka**, alt after a vowel of -**suptikka** (FORMAL retr attent).
-**ptinta** [DIAL; old-fashioned] = -**ptita**

'ptita, abbr < iptita, < haptita.
-ptita, alt after a vowel of -suptita (FORMAL indic assert).
-(˙)pu- SEE -puta (bnd adj)
pu- = pul- before t··· or c··· (but pul before ch···).
¶ pu-totek immorality; (adj-n) immoral. pu-cwuuy carelessness; (adj-n) careless.
pul- < ˙PWULQ, bnd adn (neg prefix). [Shape is pu- before t··· or c··· (but not ch··· or s···).] not, un-, in-, non-, a(n)-. CF pi-, pulka(-).
¶ pul-kanung impossibility; (adj-n) impossible. pul-kyengki a business recession or slump; a depression. pul-myengyey dishonor, (adj-n) dishonorable. pulq-sengkong lack of success, failure; (vni.) fails.
¶ pul-chincel hata is unkind, is inconsiderate. pul-hwaksil hata is uncertain, is dubious. pul-punmyeng hata is indistinct; is inarticulate. pul-wancen hata is imperfect, is incomplete. pul-yukhway hata is unpleasant.
-puli, postn (der n < pulita). 1. one who works (something). ¶ māy ~ a falconer.
2. work(ing), doing, act(ion), trick. ¶ cwucen ~ snacking between meals.
pulita₁ < ˙pu˙li˙ta (1–4) but pu˙li˙ta (5), vt.
1. keeps (a person, a horse, etc.) at work; works; manages; uses.
2. works (a machine); operates.
3. wields, brandishes (a knife, a sword).
4. plays (a trick, a ruse, etc.); starts (trouble).
5. (cim ul ~) unloads, discharges (cargo).
pulita₂, postnom v sep. does (= hata); displays, performs. SYN ttēlta, phi(wu)ta, ppāyta.
¶ aykyo ~ acts charming. ekchek ~ acts stubborn. kocip ~ asserts oneself, persists in one's opinion, insists. māl-sseng ~ makes trouble. nekcang ~ dawdles. neksal ~ acts impudent. ¹nongkan ~ pulls tricks. yoksim ~ acts greedy.
¶ kāsal ~ (phita, ppāyta, ttēlta) behaves in a hateful stuck-up way.
¶ eli-kwang ~ (phita, ttēlta) plays the baby. emsal ~ (phita, ttēlta) pretends distress. iksal ~ (phita, ttēlta) plays the fool, jests.
¶ kē/ā tulum ~ (phita, ppāyta) swaggers.
¶ simswul ~ (phita) acts cross.
¶ a.yang ~ (ttēlta) plays the flirt. caylong ~ (ttēlta) acts sweet. kkoy ~ (ttēlta) pulls tricks. kukseng ~ (ttēlta) goes to extremes.
¶ ūngsek ~ (pat.ta) gets spoiled (as a child).

puluta < pulu˙ta, -LL-.
1. adj. 1a. is full; is satiated. VC pullita.
1b. is bulgy, bulges in the middle.
1c. is pregnant.
2. postnom adj insep [DIAL] = paluta. SEE seng ~.
3. vt. calls, summons; invites (VC pullita); bids, offers; sings.
pun₁ < ˙pwun < ˙PPWUN, quasi-free n, counter. [honorific] = sālam a person; counter for people. ¶ son nim twū ~ two customers; two guests. i (ku/ce) ~ this (that) gentleman/lady; he/him, she/her. yele ~ ladies and gentlemen; all of you; everybody. Onul meych pun ina osip.nikka How many people are you expecting today? SYN (more honorific) ēlun.
pun₂ < PWUN, counter, postn.
1. 1a. a part. ¶ sam ~ uy il a third part; one-third. phal ~ uy chil seven-eighths. Na nun phal (kwa) sā-pun uy il moca lul ssup.nita I wear a size eight-and-a-quarter hat.
1b. one of ten equal parts. ¶ sip ~ uy phal kwū eight or nine out of ten. chil ~ ina phal ~ uy (chil-pu 'na phal-pu) uy kāmang i iss.ta has seven or eight chances out of ten. Ku nun kwū pun uy sengkong halq kāmang i iss.ta He has a nine-to-one chance to make it.
1c. = phun ten taels (weight or coin).
2. a minute (of an hour/degree). ¶ sip ~ ten minutes. han sikan sam-sip ~ one hour and thirty minutes. twū si ī-sip ~ twenty minutes after two. puk-wi sam-sip to sip ~ 30 degrees 10 minutes north latitude. meych pun how many minutes (or, pun₁: how many people).
3. postn. a share; a part; a portion; amount; quantity; [counter +] enough for. ¶ sēy salam ~ uy cēmsim enough lunch for three persons. yelq salam ~ uy īl work sufficient for ten persons. Ku nun twū salam pun uy īl ul hanta He does the work of two.
4. (= pūnswu) one's lot (in life).
puta, aux adj [var] = pota. -un ka ~, -na ~.
-puta < -(˙)pu-, bnd adj. ¶ aphuta is painful < alpho˙ta = alh-po- < alh- ail. kapputa is uncomfortable/hard < kos.po˙ta = kosk-po- < kosk- toil (KEd wrong). kipputa is joyful < kis.pu˙ta = kisk-pu- < kisk- rejoice (KEd wrong). kophuta (stomach) is empty/hungry < kwolpho˙ta = kwolh-po- remain unfilled. (sōk i) kwupputa is hungry ? < *kwus.pu˙ta

= *kwuc-pu-* < *kwuc-* bad(-natured). **mipputa** is credible < *mit˙pu˙ta* = *mit-˙pu-* < *mit-* believe. **napputa** is bad ? < **nos.po˙ta* = *noc-po-* < *noc-* low. **nwiwupputa** is regretful / repentant < *˙nwuyGus˙pu˙ta* = *˙nwuyGuch-pu-* < *¨nwuyGuch(i)-* regret. **papputa** is busy < *pas.po-* = *pach-po-* < *pach-* rush (KEd is wrong). **sulphuta** is sad < *sulphu˙ta* = *sulh-pu-* < *sulh-* be sad. **ipputa** < **yepputa** is pretty < *¨e.yes.pu˙ta* = *e.yes-pu-* < ? (CF **e.yes hata** is respectable). Also **aytalphuta** 'is anguishing' < *ay˙tolp-* (< *˙ay˙tol-* 'fret' + *-p-*) perhaps blended with the adj *alpho˙ta* 'painful'; **kotalphuta** 'is weary' < *kwo˙tol˙pho-* < ?.

puthe < *pu˙the* (< v inf), particle.

1. from (a time), since. ¶**achim ~ cenyek kkaci** from morning till evening. **cheum ~ kkuth kkaci** from beginning to end. **ēncey ~** since when; for how long. **pelsse ~** for some time now. **Akka puthe kitalyess.ta** I had been waiting for some time. **Ilccik puthe al.ess.ta** I knew it before(hand). [1]**Yeksa ey kilok toyki nun han samchen-nyen cen puthe (i)ey yo** It got recorded in history from about 3000 years ago. **Taum puthe tewuk cōsim hay la** Be more careful from now on. **Ku nun elyess.ul ttay puthe Yenge lul paywuko iss.ta** He has been studying English since childhood. NOTE: 'from (a place)' is **ulo puthe, ey se puthe,** or just **ey se**; CF CM 2:161.

2. (order). 2a. beginning with; first, starting from. ¶ **~ sīcak hata** begins with / at / by / on. [1]**yeksa ~ kongpu hata** start one's studies with history; studies history first. **ēncey ~** starting when; from what date/time. **Sip-o pheyici tases ccay cwul puthe ilk.e la** Start reading from Line 5, Page 15. **Kim ssi tayk puthe pāngmun haca** Let's make some visits, starting at Mr Kim's. **··· Changtek kwung puthe kwūkyeng halq ka yo?** Shall we ··· see Changtek Palace first? (M 1:2:108).

2b. **N puthe V** does it first. Attached to the subject. ¶**Na puthe kuli lo kakeyss.e** I will go there myself first. **Son nim puthe capswe ya 'ci** Our guest should be the first to eat.

2c. **N puthe V** does it first. Attached to the direct object though the reference is to the entire verb phrase. (Examples from Im Hopin 1986:73.) **Son puthe ssis.ko capswusey yo** Wash your hands before you eat. **Etten siktang un tōn puthe nāy yo** In some restaurants you pay before you eat. **Nwun ttumyen tāmpay puthe phiwunun sālam i iss.e yo** Some people start the day with a cigarette.

2d. **N ey puthe V** does first to N; at N to start with. SEE **ey puthe**.

3. (oblique subject). SEE **mata puthe**. CF **ey se, kkey se**.

CF **ey se (puthe); -umyen se puthe**.

NOTE: In modern Korean the nominative and accusative markers are obligatorily suppressed before **puthe** (as before **un / nun, to, ya**). But there are examples of the accusative in earlier Korean; see *˙ol pu˙the*.

puthe cocha, pcl + pcl [uncommon]. ¶**Hyeng ney puthe cocha sosik i ēps.ta** There hasn't been word even from my brother's family.

puthe ka, pcl + pcl. from (etc.) [as subject, complement]. ¶**Ku i puthe ka cal-mos ip.nita** The mistake started with him. **Ilkop si puthe ka ani 'ta** It does not start at seven (o'clock). **Kulenq yāyki puthe ka īsang hata 'n māl ia** His story is very fishy in itself. CF **mace ~**.

puthe khenyeng, pcl + pcl. ¶[1]**Nayil puthe khenyeng moley puthe to sīcak haci mōs hakeyss.ta** We won't even be able to start day after tomorrow, let alone tomorrow.

puthe l', abbr < **puthe lul**.

puthe 'la to, pcl + cop var inf + pcl. ¶**Onul puthe 'la to sīcak hapsita** Let's begin TODAY!

puthe lul, pcl + pcl. from (etc.) [as direct object]. ¶**Um.lyek ulo n' onul puthe lul yelum ila ko hap.nita** Today is the beginning of summer, according to the lunar calendar. **I kos puthe lul Kyengki-to 'la ko hanta** You are now entering Kyengki province.

puthem, pcl [DIAL] = **puthe** (from). CF **potam** (both forms S Kyengsang — Mkk 1960:3:32, Phyengan — Kim Yengpay 1984:95).

puthe man, pcl + pcl. ¶**Ilq-cwuil cen puthe man sīcak hayss.e to cikum ccum un tā tōyss.ul they 'n tey** If we had only started a week ago we could be done by now!

pu˙the ˙'m ye, particle + abbreviation < *ho˙m ye*. ¶*QUY-˙PPWOK ¨QUM-˙SSIK pu˙the ˙'m ye ¨il capcwu˙ywom pu˙the ˙hwo.m ol ˙PPWU-¨MWUW y solang hosi˙nwon pa ˙lol ¨cams.kan ˙two kol˙Gwa [ho˙ti] ma˙la* (1475 Nay 1:55b; *˙PPWU = ¨PPWU* [broken type?]) do not equate for a moment the matter of your parents loving you with the providing of things, beginning with clothing and food and with the taking care of matters for you.

puthe n', abbr < puthe nun.

puthe 'na, pcl + cop advers. from (etc.) or the like; whether from (etc); from (etc) whatever. ¶¹Nayil puthe 'na hak.kyo ka sīcak toyl.nun ci I wonder if maybe tomorrow school will begin. Caki puthe 'na mence hay pola 'ci Tell him to try it himself first.

puthe 'na-ma, pcl + cop extended advers. ¶Icey puthe 'na-ma cal hay posio Try to do well from now on at least. ¹Nayil puthe 'na-ma sīcak halq swu iss.umyen cōh.keyss.e I wish I could get started (even) tomorrow.

puthe 'n tul, pcl + cpd mod + postmod. even though (it be) from (etc.). ¶Caki puthe 'n tul cōh.a hal lī ka iss.e? Even he himself would not like it! Cikum puthe 'n tul nuc.ci anh.uni yelqsim hi kongpu hasio It isn't too late to start studying hard even now.

puthe nun, pcl + pcl. as for (its being) from. ¶Onul puthe nun com te yelqsim hi kongpu halye 'nta I will study harder from today on. Ku sālam puthe nun āmu sosik i ēps.nun tey yo [? awkward] There's no word from him.

puthe pota, pcl + pcl. ¶I ccok puthe pota ce ccok puthe mence sīcak hapsita Let's begin from that side first, rather than from this side. Onul puthe pota ¹nayil puthe sīcak hanun kes i te cōh.ulq tus hap.nita I think we'd better begin tomorrow rather than today.

puthe se, pcl + pcl (less common than se puthe). ¶Onul un eti puthe se sīcak hap.nikka Today where shall we begin?

puˑthe ˑsye, particle + particle. ¶ˑSYA-ˑLI KWONG-ˑYANG puˑthe ˑsye ˑi s koˑcaˑng on ZIN-THYEN-ˑHHOYNG ˑol niluˑsi.n i ˑ'la (1447 Sek 13:54a; "ˑis-ko-ˑca-ˑngon") starting from the offering of food to Buddha's relics all of this is called the natural act of man with heaven.

puthe to, pcl + pcl. (starting) from ... also / even / either. ¶¹Nayil puthe to kayep i him tun kes kath.kwun yo It seems it will be hard to start doing business even tomorrow.

puthe tul, pcl + pcl. ¶Swukcey puthey tul hay la Do your homework first, children.

puthe uy, pcl + pcl. (the one) from (etc.). ¶Ku nal puthe uy ku uy saynghwal un cham ulo hāyngpok toyn kes iess.ta His life from that day on was a truly happy one.

puthe ya, pcl + pcl. only if (it be) from (etc.). ¶Cikum puthe ya saynghwal ey kekceng i ēps.keyss.ci From now on he won't have to worry about his life. Onul puthe ya kyewu īl i com phyen hay cyess.ey yo I can take it a little easier from today, at long last. Posuthon puthe ya tulaipu haki ka swīpci It's an easy drive (if you start) from Boston.

~ māl lo. ¶Icey puthe ya māl lo chamq toyn saynghwal i sīcak toylq kes io From now on, an upright life will begin for me.

puth.i /puchi/, postn. things of (a class / group); things of (the same kind); things made of ... ; things belonging to ... [when used of people, not too respectful]. ¶ilka ~ family relations; relatives. kalwu ~ bakery goods. kum ~ gold ware. kyeley ~ race; one's people. kyeth ~ distant relatives. sal ~ (1) kith and kind, lineage; (2) meats. soy ~ ironware, metalware.

pwā (< poa), inf < pota. ~ se, ~ to, ~ tul, ~ ya, ~ yo. ABBR p'ā.

pwā la, inf + pcl (command). Look! CF pola.

pwass- (< poass-), past < pota. ABBR p'ass-.

pwāy = pwēy = pōy < poye, inf < pōyta

pwēy = pōy < poye, inf < pōyta. ABBR p'ēy-.

pwol(q), prosp mod < ˚pwoˑta. ¶kwoˑc ol pwolq SSI-ˑCYELQ ˑey (1462 ¹Nung 2:111a) when one looks at blossoms.

ˑpwol(q) < *pwo-ˑwo-l(q), modulated prosp modifier < ˚pwoˑta (sees). ¶woˑnol selu ˑpwol ˑcwu.l ol ˑes.ti ˑall i ˑGwo hoˑn i (1481 Twusi 15:47b) today we wonder how to discover a way to look at each other.

¶macwo ˑpwoˑl i ˑGeˑta (1459 Wel 8:87a) they will meet.

¶ˑskwoy han twocoˑk ol mwoˑloˑsya ˑpwo.l i ˑ'la kiˑtuˑlisiˑn i (1445 ¹Yong 19) not knowing the [number of] wileful thieves (= renegades) he waited to see them.

¶ˑcosyey hi ˑpwol ˑt iGen ˑtyeng pasˑk ul ˑHYANG ˑho.ya ˑsywokcyel ˑep.si ˑetwoˑm ol mwoˑlwomay maˑlwol ˑt iGeˑta (1482 Nam 1:24a) even if you look closely you will have to give up vainly grasping toward the outside.

¶KWAN-ˑSYEY-QUM PPWO-ˑSALQ ˑol ˑpwol ˑtt iˑn i (1459 Wel 8:33b; with broken type on ˑpwol) one looks at the bodhisattva Avalokiteśvara (Kuān Yīn).

pwo ˙m(...), subst < °*pwo˙ta*. ¶*pwo ˙m ye* (1447 Sek 13:23b, 19:10a; 1465 Wen 1:2:1:39b).
¨*pwom* (< **pwo-˙wo-m*), modulated subst < °*pwo˙ta* (sees). ¶ ˙*homol˙mye TUNG a˙ni ˙'m ye* ¨*pwom a˙ni ˙'la PWUN-˙PYELQ hwo˙m isto˙n ye* (1462 ¹Nung 2:84a) with no light, with no sight, how can one distinguish?!
¨*pwo˙m ay*. ¶*SAN-HHA* ¨*pwo˙m ay TANG ˙ho˙ya LYWUW-LI ˙lol pwo˙l i ˙ye* (1462 ¹Nung 1:58a) facing the sight of mountains and rivers will one see emeralds?
¨*pwo˙m i*. ¶ ¨*THYEY* ¨*pwo˙m i e˙lyep˙twoswo˙n i* (1482 Kum-sam 2:7b) it is hard to see the form (body).
¨*pwo.m i˙n i*. ¶ ˙*MWOK-CCYEN ˙ey s ye˙le ˙PEP ˙i ke˙wulwu s* ¨*swo.p ay elkwul* ¨*pwo.m i˙n i* (1482 Kum-sam 2:63a) the laws before one's eyes are [like] seeing one's face in a mirror.
¨*pwo˙m ol*. ¶ ˙*tam˙kwa cip˙kwa ci˙ze NUNG ˙hi* ¨*pwo˙m ol˙pske ku˙chwulq˙t in˙t ay n'* (1462 ¹Nung 2:43b) if you build a wall and a house and (thereby) effectively destroy the view ... .
¨*pwo.m o˙lan*. ¶ ˙*tye* ¨*SOYNG hon* ¨*salo˙m oy twu˙lye˙wun kuli˙m ey* ¨*pwo.m o˙lan il˙hwu˙m ul mu˙su.k i˙la ho˙l ywo* (1462 ¹Nung 2:81a) when that person with cataracts sees a round figure what does he call it?
¨*pwo˙m on*. ¶ *talon* ¨*pwo˙m on SSYA-˙KWAN ˙i˙la* (1459 Wel 8:9b) other views are heresies.
pwon, mod < °*pwo˙ta*. ~ ˙*ta* (1462 ¹Nung 20:8b, ?1468 Mong 50a).
¨*pwon* (< **pwo-˙wo-n*), modulated modifier < °*pwo˙ta* (sees). ¶*CCYEN-SOYNG ˙ay s* ¨*i˙l i e˙cey* ¨*pwon ˙tos ˙ho˙ya* (1447 Sek 6:9a) events in my former life are as if I saw them yesterday.
¨*pwon˙t i*. ¶ ¨*nal˙Gwa TA-¨PWOW ZYE-LOY ˙Gwa ˙stwo CYE ˙HWA-˙PPWULQ* ¨*pwon˙t i towoy˙n i ˙'la* (1463 Pep 4:140a) they got to see him himself [the tathāgata] and the Ancient Buddha (Prabhūtaratna) and also the incarnate Buddhas (Nirmāṇabuddha).
¨*pwon˙t oy n'*. ¶*pwuthye s* ¨*TTWOW-˙LI KKWUW ˙honwon ˙ya˙ng ol* ¨*pwon˙t oy n' ˙PWO-SI ˙lol ˙hwo˙toy* (1447 Sek 13:18-9) seeing a way to pursue Buddha's principles he gives alms and ... . *kutuy ˙lul* ¨*pwon t oy n' [*¨*TTWOW-˙KHUY]* ¨*ha.n i* (1481 Twusi 7:21a) looking at you, [one sees that] the vital energy of the Way is great.
°*pwo˙ta*, vi = **pota** (see; ...). 1. indic assert. 2. (= ~ ˙*ka*) transferentive. ? 3. pcl (than) SEE *pwota˙ka, pwota n'*.

pwota˙ka, 1. vi transferentive + particle. sees (etc.) and then.
2. pcl. than. Examples in LCT 385b from 1783 Cahyul 2, ?1800 Hancwung 576, 1880 Kyengsin 84. Equivalent to the earlier *twu˙ko*, ˙*ᵘ⁄ola˙wa* or ˙*ila˙wa*, and ˙*ᵘ⁄olwo n'*.
pwota n', pcl + pcl. ¶*kalachisin mal-sam i nyey pwota n' thak.wel hosya* (1736 ⁿYe se:4; cited from LCT [not there in the Aseya munhwa-sa repro]) the words you have taught are superior to [those of] the past.
¨*pwo˙toy* (< ¨*pwo-˙wo-˙toy*), modulated accessive < °*pwo˙ta* (sees). ¶*PPWO-˙SALQ ˙i* ¨*ke˙cus ke˙s ul* ¨*pwo˙toy CCAY-LANG ce˙thos* [= *ceh-˙tos*] ˙*ho˙no.n i ˙'la* (1462 ¹Nung 8:86b) confronted by a falsehood the bodhisattva behaves as if in fear of a mountain wolf.
(... *s*) ¨*pwun*, bnd n. (? < ˙*PPWUN* 'portion'). just, only (= ˙*man*). ¶*NGWANG-¨CO S ˙MYENG ˙i nil˙Gwey s* ¨*pwu.n i˙lwoswo˙n i* (1447 Sek 24:28a) the life of the prince is only seven days old. *wos.kwos hon kes* ¨*pwun a˙ni ˙'la* (1447 Sek 13:39a) not just fragrant things, but ... . *phu˙lun ˙pis* ¨*pwun* ¨*pwo˙m i* (1465 Wen se:29b) seeing just the blue color. *nyenu ke˙s u˙lan* ¨*ma˙wo* (= ¨*mal˙Gwo*) *ku˙lus* ¨*pwun cyang˙mang ho˙la* (1459 Wel 7:41-2) just get some dishes ready, not other things. SEE *-uls* ~, ¨*spwun*.
pyel < ˙*(P)PYELQ*. extraordinary, uncommon, rare; unexpected, special.
1. preparticle. ~ **lo** specially, especially, in particular, particularly [+ NEGATIVE]. ¶**pyel lo cōh.ci anh.ta** is not particularly good; **pyel lo chwupci anh.ta** is not especially cold; **pyel lo halq īl i ēps.ta** has nothing in particular to do.
2. **pyel uy pyel** = **pyel-pyel**, adnoun. of various and unusual sorts. ¶**pyel-pyel sālam** all sorts of people. **pyel-pyelq īl** unusual things of all sorts. **pyel-pyel kaci uy ūmsik** all sorts of rare dishes. **Pyel-pyelq īl tā pwass.ta** I never saw such queer goings-on.
3. adnoun. ¶ ~ **kes** a rarity; an eccentric (person), an unexpected (a peculiar) incident. ~ **kkol** an "extraordinary" (= disgusting) spectacle = obnoxious thing / person, a mess. ~ **māl(-ssum)**, ~ **soli** an extraordinary (= preposterous / superfluous or unusually polite / gracious) remark. ~ **sālam** an eccentric, a queer bird, an odd duck. ~ **swu** special luck; (= ~ **swutan**) a special means, a secret key,

magic touch, proper technique. ~ **tōli** a better way / means / remedy; an alternative, a choice. **pyel tōli ēps.i** inevitably; helplessly, reluctantly.

4. bnd adv. ~ **taluta** is of a particular kind, is extraordinary. ~ **talli** differently.

5. adj-n. ~ **hata** = ~ **sulepta**, ~ **nata** (adj) is peculiar, eccentric, odd.

CF **thukpyel** (adnoun, adj-n) special, extraordinary.

···**q**(···). A morphophonemic symbol, used by the Yale Romanization to represent all instances of noninitial reinforcement (··· C → ···q C /···CC/, ···n $^i/_y$··· → ···nq i··· /···nn$^i/_y$···/, ···lq $^i/_y$··· /···ll$^i/_y$···/) regardless of the source and whether recognized by the Hankul spelling or not. In certain compounds that preserve a trace of the MK adnominal particle *s* the ···**q** is realized as /···t/ or (before **m** or **n**) as /···n/.

-**q**(-). 1. an adnominal marker that is largely unpredictable and in South Korea is written (with "**s**") after a vowel only, but is generally ignored in spelling words from Chinese; in North Korea it is written with an apostrophe after consonants as well as vowels, but is also widely ignored in spelling words from Chinese. An odd case: **yo** 'mattress' + **uy** 'clothing' → /yotī/ 'mattress cover', which is spelled "**yos-uy**" in South Korea but in the north is replaced by **yoq twi** /yottwi/, with a different etymology (**twī** 'behind'), it appears. SEE -**eyq**-, *q*, *s*.

2. as an infix, marks a derived intensive and is spelled with a doubled initial obstruent, as in **sseywuta** = **seywuta** 'stresses, emphasizes'.

q, *Q*. One of the Hankul symbols used in Middle Korean, this was intended to represent a glottal stop. It went unpronounced when initial (*Q*··· in Chinese words), but represented reinforcement when final (···*lq t*··· = /···*ltt*···/). See also ···*LQ*.

q = *s* (genitive pcl), written in a few texts after a vowel before the word ˙*CCO* 'character, letter'. ¶*NA q* ˙*CCO* (1451 Hwun-en 5b) the character *NA*. *MWU q* ˙*CCO* (?1468- Mong 11b, 12b, ...) the character *MWU*. In 1445 ¹*Yong* written after vowel or ···*l* with following ˙*pt*···: *[SYEN-¨KHWOW] q* ˙*ptut* (12) his father's will, **ha˙nol q** ˙**ptu˙t ul** (86) heaven's will.

/···*s*/ before pause (noun-final) began merging with /···*t*/ in the early 1500s; the merger was complete by 1700. The /···*s*/ had earlier (by 1450) absorbed /···*c*/ and /···*ch*/.

-**s**··· SEE ALSO -**usi**··· < -*usi*··· , -*osi*···

*s*₁, pcl (genitive); written separately or attached to the preceding or following syllable. Marks the preceding phrase as adnominal or as the subject of an adnominalized predicate. The preceding noun is either inanimate or honorific animate; for the nonhonorific animates MK used the genitive particle ˙$^u/oy$, the source of modern **uy**, which combines the functions of both MK particles. The particle *s* attached to the "free" form of such nouns as *holo* / *holl* ··· 'one day', *molo* / *moll* ··· 'ridge', *namwo* / *namk* ··· 'tree', *nyenu* / *nyenk* ··· 'other', ... : *holo s a˙cho.m oy* (1481 Twusi 8:17b) 'one morning', *molo s nam˙k ul* (1481 Twusi 24:10a) 'the ridgepole', *namwo s pul˙hwuy ˙lol* (1447 Sek 6:30b) 'the root of the tree', *nyenu s ¨i.l ol* (1475 Nay 1:53a) 'the other matters'. SEE ˙*ay s*, ˙*ey s*, ˙*yey s*; ˙*uy s*, ˙*oy s*, ˙*kwa s*; *t*, *z*.

1. (possession). of, ···'s; belonging to (= **i/ka kacin**); characteristic of. ¶ *KUM s ˙pi˙ch isi˙m ye* (1447 Sek 6:17a) it is a golden color. ˙*pwom s ˙pi.ch on* (1482 Kum-sam 2:12a) the colors of spring. *LYEN-HWA S HYANG* (1459 Wel 1:26b) the fragrance of the lotus blossom. *pwuthye s ˙na.h i syelhun ¨sey˙h i˙lesi˙n i* (1447 Sek 6:11b) Buddha's age was thirty-three.

2. (relationship). of; with respect to (in respect of / to), related / pertaining to, vis-à-vis, as regards (= **ey tāy han**). ¶*THYEN-¨CO ˙non ha˙nol s a˙to.l i˙n i* (1459 Wel 2:69a) (what is meant by) *THYEN-¨CO* is the son of heaven. *kutuy s cip s [HYWENG-¨TTYEY] uy [KWONG-MYENG] ˙i* (1481 Twusi 25:28a) the renown of the brothers of your household. *ha˙nol s ¨nim˙ku˙m i˙la ˙hwom ˙ptu˙t i˙la* (1459 Wel 1:31b) it means he is the king of heaven. *na˙la[h] s SSIN-¨HHA y ˙THAY-¨CO s nye˙k ul ˙tul˙m ye n'* (1447 Sek 6:25a) if the king's official takes the side of the prince. ˙*KAK-˙KAK ceyye˙kwom s yang˙co ˙lol ci˙zwo˙toy* (1459 Wel 8:19b) each creates his individual style, and ... .

2a. ¶ *ye˙le ˙mul s TYWUNG ˙ey pa˙lo˙l i ˙TTYEY-˙QILQ ˙kot ˙ho˙ya* (1459 Wel 18:26b) among the (several) bodies of water, the sea

seems the most important.
 2b. ¶ *cwuk-sa'li s QIN-YWEN 'un* (1459 Wel 1:11b) the reasons for life or death.
 3. (subject). of; done / felt / said by, on the part of (= ‥‥ **i / ka han**). CF 14.
 4. (goal / result). of; that was done / achieved / accomplished (= ‥‥ **ul han / ilwun**) or is to be done or achieved / accomplished (= ‥‥ **ul hal / ilwul**). ¶ *KYENG 'un pwuthye s 'ku.l i'la* (1447 Sek se:3b) sūtras are the scripture of Buddha. "*TTWOW 'non pwuthye s 'PEP 'i'la* (1447 Sek se:4b) the Way is Buddha's Law.
 5. 5a. (specification). of; that is (= **in**). ¶ *wo'nol s nal* (1482 Nam 1:40b) today. *SYEY s nye'k uy 'sye* (1447 Sek 6:33b) from (the direction of) the west. "*mwot il 'Gwuwolq 'ka s NGUY-SIM 'i "ep'susi'ta* (1449 Kok 53) has no doubt (as to) whether he cannot succeed. *kwuy-s kes* (1447 Sek 6:19b; 1482 Kum-sam 2:7b, 3:27b) ghost.
 5b. (designation). called, (by the name) of (= ‥‥ **ila hanun**); SEE 15b. ¶ *[KWANG SAN] s 'kul nilk'ten sta'h ay* (1481 Twusi 21:42b) in the land of Guāng Shān where I was studying.
 5c. (representation). of; that represents (= ‥‥ **uy phyosik in**). ¶ *'i mozol[h] s ca'chwoy 'Ge'tun* (1465 Wen 2:3:1:29b) if (it is =) there are traces of this village.
 5d. (characterized or described by). ¶ *CIN-'SSILQ s 'SOYK 'ol na'thwo'm ye* (1459 Wel 17:19a) displaying its true color.
 5e. mod + *pa s*. which / that ‥‥ [extruded object]. ¶ *pwuthye nilu'syan 'pa s 'PEP 'un* (1482 Kum-sam 2:40b) the Law that Buddha told. *nil 'Gwon 'pa s ZYE-LOY 'non* (1482 Kum-sam 5:14a) the so-called tathāgata. With the extruded object ellipted: *nilu'syan 'pa s [ ] "ne y ZYE-LOY 'i 'NYEM 'ul cizwotoy na y pan'toki 'PEP nil 'Gwon 'pa y is.ta ne'kiti "malla 'hosi'n i* (1482 Kum-sam 5:14a) what Buddha said is "you create this idea of the tathāgata and do not think that dharma is necessarily what I have told". "*HHA-MWUN 'ey nil 'Gwon pa s [ ] 'i 'ko.t hi "al'm ye* (1482 Kum-sam 5:14a) knows that what is said in the writings given down is like this, and ‥‥ .
 6. (pertinence). of, ‥‥'s; belonging to, attached to (= **ey puth.nun**). ¶ *kil[h] s "ney-ke'li 'yey* (1447 Sek 23:58b) at a road intersection.

 7. (origin / source) of, ‥‥'s; (coming) from, (produced) in / at (= **ey se nan**).
 8. 8a. (static location). of, in, at (= ‥‥ **ey iss.nun**). ¶ *"ta 'TTI wu'h uy s PPWO-'SALQ s 'TUK 'isi'n i ' 'la* (1459 Wel 17:26a) all are the bodhisattva's virtue(s) on earth. "*mwoy'h ay s kwo'c i* (1482 Kum-sam 3:33a) the mountain flowers.
 8b. to / on the ‥‥ of [the head is a noun of relative location]. ¶ *'SYA-'LI-'PWULQ s al'ph oy 'Gwos* (1447 Sek 6:33a) right there in front of Śariputra. *LUNG-KKYA SAN 'i NAM THYEN-'TYWUK pa'lol s "ko'z ay is.no'n i* (1447 Sek 6:43b) Lankā (Adam's Peak) is on the shore of the sea of southern India. *elkwul s tayka'li s "swo.p ay 'swum.e 'ys'kwo* (1482 Kum-sam 3:34a) is concealed within (= behind) the skin of the face. *'spye's "swo'k ay* (1459 Wel 1:13a) in the bone. "*THYEY wu'h uy s 'wo.s i'n i* (1482 Nam 1:68b) are garments on the body. "*twu ha'nol s so'zi 'yey 'ka'sya* (1447 Sek 6:45b) goes between the two heavens. "*twu 'THYELQ-NGWUY SAN s so'zi e'tuWun sta'h ay* (1459 Wel 1:28b) on the dark ground between the two iron-enclosing mountains (cakravāḍa). *KYWOW-KYWOW 'ho.ya "pyel s kawon-toy s twu'lyewun 'to.l isyas'ta* (1482 Kum-sam 2:24b) brightly shining it is a round moon in the midst of clouds.
 8c. (abstract location). ¶ *nil'kwup 'cha s ha'no.l i'la* (1459 Wel 1:20a) it is the seventh heaven. "*ney cha s ha'no.l iza* (1447 Sek 6:36a) precisely the fourth heaven.
 8d. (dynamic location). of, in, at, on, by, arising or happening at ‥‥ (= ‥‥ **ey se iss.nun**). ¶ *ingey s "mal 'lwo n'* (1459 Wel 18:68b) with the remarks made here.
 8e. (time). at, of. ¶ "*na y "a'lay s ne'y "pe't ila'n i* (1447 Sek 6:19b) I was your friend in earlier days. *alp s ku'l ey* (1465 Wen 1:2:1:4a; "*alps-ku-'ley*") in the earlier text. *SSI-'CYELQ s han "salo'm i* (1459 Wel 18:83a) the many people of the time. "*ma.l i kanan hon si'cyel s "i.l ey* (1475 Nay 2:2:47b) in the event that one is impoverished for words. *al'ph oy s KWONG-'TUK 'ey ka'col'piken 'ta y n'* (1459 Wel 17:32b) compared to the virtue achieved earlier. *'icey s HHWANG-'TYEY* (1447 Sek se:6b) the present emperor.
 8f. (quantity). of; to the extent of. ¶ *ta'sos cwul'ki s LYEN-HWA 'lol 'sa'a* (1447 Sek 6:8a)

bought five lotus blossoms, and ... . ˬney kaˈci s ˮSSYWUW-ˮKHWO ˈlol yeˈhuyˈye (1447 Sek 6:4a) escaping the Four Miseries (of birth, age, illness, death). hon ˬcwum s ˮsil (1482 Kumsam 3:46a) a handful of thread. ˈsuˈmul[h] hon ˈhoy s soˈzi ˈyey (1447 Sek 6:47a) for an interval of twenty-one years. pwuthye ˈtwo ˮsek ˈca[h] s ˈmwoˈm i towoyˈsya (1447 Sek 6:44a) Buddha too had a body three ˈcah (= 6 ft) tall.

9. (material). of; made of, made out of; made up (consisting) of. ¶ ˈphi s mwucek (1447 Sek 6:33a) a mass of blood.

10. (use). for; used for.

11. (similarity). like, of (= ··· kwa kath.un). ¶ ˈi s yangˈco ˈlwo (1447 Sek 23:4a) like this. ˈi s ˮyang oˈlwo (1459 Wel 18:15b) thus.

12. (object of reference, topic). of, about, depicting, referring to, directed at (= ··· ey tāy hay se ciun).

13. 13a. (as a part) of (= il-pupun ulo in). ¶ noyˈzil s aˈchoˈm ol (1482 Nam 1:40a) tomorrow morning. ˈSO-ˈNGWELQ S ˈPALQ-ˈZILQ ˈey (1459 Wel 2:48b) on the 8th day of April. koˈlom s ˮkoz (1445 ¹Yong 68) the sand banks of the rivers. ˈi peˈtul s niˈph i (1482 Nam 1:45a) this willow leaf; the leaf of this willow. pangha s ˈkwo ˈyˈn i (1447 Sek 6:31b) is the pestle of a mortar. ku namwo s pwulˈhwuy ˈlol ˈspayˈhhye (1447 Sek 6:30b) uprooted the tree and ... . pwuthye s elkwul (1482 Kum-sam 2:31b) Buddha's face. PPWO-ˈSALQ s kwoˈh ay (1459 Wel 1:36b) to the bodhisattva's nose. ˮTYWUW ˈnun pol[h] s moˮtoy ˈˈn i (1459 Wel 10:118a) the ˮelbow˝ is the joint of the arm. ˈkhun ˈpo.yam s SSIN-LYENG ˈiˈla (1459 Wel 1:15a) is the spirit of a large snake.

13b. (member) of (a group).

14. = ˈi = i/ka (marking the subject of an adnominalized predicate). CF 3.

14a. (epitheme extruded from the object). ¶ ˈna ˈnon pwuthye s solang ˈhosiˈnwon azˈG iˈla (1462 ¹Nung 1:86a) I am the younger brother whom the Buddha loves. ˈSYEY-CWON s ˮTTWOW ilˈGwusyan ˮiˈl oy yangˈco ˈlol ˈkuˈlye (1447 Sek se:5b) depicts aspects of the deed by which the World-Honored [Buddha] achieved the Way, and ... .

14b. (epitheme extruded from a genitive). ¶ hon ˈnwun s ˈPPYENG hon ˮsaloˈm i ... (1462 ¹Nung 2:92b) a person with one ailing eye.

14c. (summational epitheme that forms a nominalization). ¶ pwuthye s koloˈchisya[ˈ]m ol (1459 Wel 23:72a) Buddha's teaching. LWO-ˮLWOW y kutuy s ˬwoˈm ol kituˈliˈtela hoˈla (1482 Nam 1:50b) he has been long waiting for you to come. PI-ˈNGWEN S HWUN ˈhosyaˈm olwo piˈluse ingey niˈlu.n i (1482 Nam 1:33b) with the emitting of fragrance by the great pitying vow [of Buddhas and bodhisattvas to save all living beings], it has for the first time reached this place. ˈswoy oy ˈkuyGwun ˈon kozol s seˈnuleˈwu.m i towowoyˈnwon t iˈla (1482 Kum-sam 2:29b) the temper of the metal [personified – hence oy not s] results from the autumn's being cool.

15. that ··· : adnominalizes a sentence to a summational epitheme, stating its content. (The modern language will usually adnominalize a quotation of the content.)

15a. -ˈta s (= -ta ˈnun). ¶ TTIN-SA ˈnon hal ˈs i.n i, TTIN ˈkot SA ˈkotˈta s ˬma.l iˈla (1482 Kum-sam 2:15b) dust and sand are plentiful (things) so what it says is that it like dust and like sand. ˮKWANG-ˈCHI ˈnon neˈpi KWANG-MYENG ˈi piˈchwuyˈta s ˈptu.t iˈGwo (1459 Wel 2:9b) the expression ˮKWANG-ˈCHI (is =) has the meaning of light shining widely, and ... . ˈi ˈnon ZYE-LOY S QA-SUNG-KKI KWONG-ˈTUK ˈul nilˈGe ˈtwo NUNG ˈhi ˮta ˬmwot hoˈl i ˈˈla s ˈptuˈt ul ˈKYELQ ˈhoˈya naˈthwosiˈn i ˈˈla (1463 Pep 3:47a) this expresses the meaning that the tathāgata's asankhyeya (countless) achievements of virtue can never adequately all be told, tell as one will. ˬtywoˈtha s ˬmaˈl iˈza niloˈl ye (?1517- Pak 1:3a) can I say it's OK?

15b. ˈiˈla s (= ila ˈnun). ¶ ˈCYENG ˈPEP-ˮNGAN ˈon ˈCYENG hon ˈPEP-ˮNGAN ˈiˈla s ˬma.l iˈn i (1482 Kum-sam 2:68b) ˮˈCYENG ˈPEP-ˮNGAN˝ is a word that means the true Dharma Eye [one of the five cakṣuh: Physical Eye, Wise Eye, Divine Eye, Dharma Eye, Buddha Eye]. ˈile ˈn ˈt olwo ˈTTAY-ˈKAK SYEN ˈiˈla s ilˈhwu.m i nathoˈsi.n i ˈˈla (1482 Kum-sam 2:15b) thus there appeared the name ˮSage of the Great Awakening˝. ˮHHWUW-ˮTTWAN ˈay s ˮNAY-ˈCI ˈˈla s ˬmal ˈtwo ˈstwo ˈi ˈlol ˈLYEY ˈhoˈya aˈlwol ˈt iˈn i ˈˈla (1465 Wen 1:2:2:136a) and the word ˮNAY-ˈCI in the later column exemplifies this, also, so we know. SEE -uˈl i ˈˈla s.

15c. *-uˑlq ka s*. ¶ ˊsyeng-hhyen s ˈtti-ˈwuy ˈyey niˑluti ¨mwot hol ˈka s pwun-ˈppyelq ˈi ¨epˑsu.l i ʼˈla (1475 Nay 1:35b) it is bound to reach to the position of the sages.

15d. -ˈkwo ˈcye s (= -ko siph.ta ʼn). ¶ ¨cywokwoˑma s ˈpoy ˈthokwo ˈcye s ˈptu.t ul nisˑti ¨mwot ho.l i ʼlwota [← ¨mwot hoˑl i ilwoˑta] (1481 Twusi 15:55b) I will not forget my desire to ride in a little boat.

16. (adnominalizes an adverb). ¶ *ceyyeˑkwom s qin-ywen ˈuˑlwo* (1447 Sek 6:39b) by their respective causes and effects. *howoˑza s ¨mal* (1462 ¹Nung 9:118a) talking / saying to oneself. ˈhyenˑma s ppwo-ˈsalq ˈ[G]wa ˈhyenˑma s ˊcywung-soyng ˈi (1459 Wel 17:23a) the many bodhisattvas and the many common creatures / folk.

16a. (adnominalizes an adverbial phrase). ¶ ¨salom ¨maˑta s ˊmywow-ˈsyeng iˑn i (1463 Pep 2:162a) it is the wondrous nature of every man. See ˈkwa s.

17. See -ˈul s.

Note 1: Before the particle *s* the resonants /l/ and /n/ were often unwritten (Cf He Wung 285, 313-4), and they were probably elided in specific phrases except when the particle was set off by juncture, as in speech slowed down to capture the underlying structure.

¶ *yeˑle paˑlo[l] s kaˑwon-ˈtoy iˑsywoˑtoy* (1462 ¹Nung 2:84b) they are among the seas and ... ; *yeˑle aˑcomi ˈicey paˑlo[l] s ¨koˑz oy ˈkay ʼs[ˈ]kwo* (1481 Twusi 8:38a) the aunts are on the tidelands by the seaside, and ... – Cf *ne-¨huy paˑlol s ¨koˑz ay ˈkaˑa* (1459 Wel 10:13ab) you people go to the seaside and ... . ˈmu[l] s ˈkyeˑl ul ⋯ (1481 Twusi 18:11; cited from LCT) the waves – Cf ˈppi-ma-ˈcilq-ta ˈnon paˑlol s ˈmul s ˈkyel s swoˑli ʼˈla ˈhwon ¨ma.l iˑn i (1447 Sek 13:9b) [the name] Vimalacitra is a word that means the sound of the waves of the sea. *pa[l] s kalaˑk oˑlwo ˈstaˑh ol nwuˑlusiˑn i* (1447 Sek 6:39a [¹Yi Tonglim version]) he deigned to press the earth with his toes – Cf ˈpal s kalaˑk ol ˈchokwo (1482 Nam 1:50a) kicking his toes. ¨se[l] s toˑl ay (1466 Kup 2:58b) in December (> sēt tal ey) – Cf ¨sel s ˈnal (1481 Twusi 20:17a) New Year's day (> sēl nal). iˑthu[l] s naˑl ay (1459 Wel 1:6b) on the next day = iˑthu[l] s naˑl ay (1447 Sek 6:27a). *peˑtu[l] s ni.ph i* (1482 Kum-sam 4:42b), *peˑtul s ˈnip ˈkwa* (1459 Wel 23:91b) willow leaves. *mwu[l] s mwoy[h] s pwuli* (1632 Twusi-cwung 13:4b) all of the mountain peaks. *pskwu[l] s ¨pel* (1481 Twusi 18:4; cited from LCT) = *pskwul pel* (1632 Twusi-cwung 18:4a) honey bee. The elision could apply to final ⋯l < ⋯lh, as in *mozo[lh] s ˈnoy* (1481 Twusi 15:50b) the smoke of a village – Cf *mozol[h] s ¨salom* (1459 Wel 23:66a) people of the village, village folk. An unusual elision before *n*⋯ of the string *[l s]* occurs in ¨pwuyn swuˑphu[l s] nacwoy s ˈhoy s pi.ch i (1481 Twusi 7:4a) the evening sunlight of the empty forest.

¶ *swo[n] s twop naˑm ye* (1462 ¹Nung 1:51b) fingernails grew – Cf ¨twu swon s twop ˊsyang ˈol ¨chywu hoˑl ye (1462 ¹Nung 3:43b) ready to take the distinctive mark of double fingernails, *swon s paˑtang ˈay s ¨kwa-¨co* (1482 Nam 1:25b) a cake in the palm of the hand. ˊchwon ˈma[n] s ˈphu.l i (1482 Kum-sam 4:42b) an inch-high grass fife – Cf *so-hhwow ˈman s ˊnyem ˈtwo* (1482 Kum-sam 2:15a) even the tiniest fraction of an instant (kṣana). *nye[n] s kwoˑc iˑleˑla* (?1517- Pak 1:70b) it was a lotus blossom. The elision did not apply to final ⋯n < ⋯nh, to judge from *cip ˈan[h] s ¨salo.m ol* (1447 Sek 6:5b) the people of the household.

Many (perhaps most) of the ⋯*l* and ⋯*n* nouns are spelled with no evidence of the elision: ¨syelWun ¨il s tywung ˈey ˈtwo (1447 Sek 6:6a) 'even among sad events'; ˈnwun s ˈsal ˈtwo (1463 Pep 4:53a) 'even the furrow between the eyebrows'. There is no obvious explanation why some nouns have the elision, some do not. Not all of the examples can be dismissed as lexical compounds.

Other common elisions before the particle *s* are peculiar to individual words, such as *cip* 'house': *ku ci[p] s ˈstoˑl i* (1447 Sek 6:14a) the daughter of that house – Cf *cip s ¨iˑl ol* (1475 Nay 1:84a, 2:1:40b) events of the home; *cip s poloˑm ay* (1481 Twusi 25:2a) on the wall of the house; *kutuy s cip s [hyweng-¨ttyey] uy [kwong-myeng] ˈi* (1481 Twusi 25:48a) the renown of the brothers of your family.

NOTE 2: Between voiced sounds, 1445 ¹Yong often wrote the particle as *z*. The example *psol z CHWO ˙lol* (1466 Kup 2:21b) 'rice vinegar' probably has an unwanted baseline mistakenly added while carving the syllable block, for a couple of pages later we find the expected *psol s ˙CHWO ˙ay* (id. 2:24a). Several texts have a variant spelling *t* after ⋯*n* before *s*⋯ and *c*⋯. After a vowel or ⋯*l* the glottal stop ⋯*q* is written before ˙*ptut*. In 1451 Hwun-en and ?1468⁻ Mong the ⋯*q* is written after a vowel before the word ˙*CCO* 'character, letter'; 1465 Wen has examples of *c* before ˙*CCO* after a vowel, ⋯*N*, ⋯*NG*, or ⋯*LQ*, but after ⋯*M* it writes only *s* or *p*. In several texts before a voiceless obstruent the particle is written as *p* after ⋯*m*, as *k* after ⋯*ng*. After ⋯*l* the particle is attested at least once with *q* before *c*: ¨*swolq ¨ci˙n i* (1459 Wel 8:10b) = ˙*swol s ¨ci.n ol* (1466 Kup 2:63a). A free-standing *W* was written by 1451 Hwun-en after Chinese words ending in ⋯*w*. SEE *c*, *k*, *p*, *q*, *t*, *W*; **s ¨swon-˙toy* > *k ¨swon-˙toy*.

NOTE 3: Before the postmodifiers ˙*ka* and ˙*kwo* (question) the particle *s* functions as a substitute for the copula modifier after the postmodifier ˙*i* or the polite marker -*ngi*.

*s*₂, pcl (? abbr < ˙*sye*). SEE *u˙lwo ˙sye*; *two˙kwo s*. CF *cyang˙chos* in future (SEE -*s*).

*s*₃, postmod (follows only prosp mod -*ulq*). the fact that ⋯ . ˙*s ol*, ˙*s oy*, ˙*s i(*⋯*)*, ˙*s ye*, ˙*s 'yen ˙tyeng*.

s, postmod [obs] < *s*₃. the likely fact that ⋯ (= kes). SEE si, sun, son; -ulq say; ? sey; ˙*so*.

-˙s-, bnd v (emotive). SEE -˙*s[o]*-.

-s, suffix (CF -us). 1. derives impressionistic adv from adj, verb.

1a. < adj. ¶cilkis firm, unyielding < cilki-. mulus rather / quite soft < mulu-. pilis fishy-smelling < pili-. puphus bulky < puphu-. selphis rather loose-woven < selphi-. hulis dim < huli-. alis pungent < ali-.

1b. < vt. ¶kwukis/kokis wrinkled, crumpled < kwuki- / koki-.

1c. < vi. ¶mis-mis / mays-mays long and smooth < mīta, CF mīn / māyn.

1d. ? < vp. pois misty, pearly ? < poi- (CF pō.yah- adj).

2. other derivations: kulus by mistake (adv),

mistaking it (vnt) < kulu- be wrong (adj). *cyang˙chos* = *cyang˙cho* in future.

-s- (or the doubling of a following obstruent; n before m, n, l). SEE -q-.

-˙sa, particle = ˙*za* (directly attached to stem). ¶ ˙*NYELQ-PPAN ˙ay esye ˙tu-˙sa* [= ˙*tule ˙za*] *ho˙l i 'lwo˙ta* (1447 Sek 13:58a) has to enter nirvāṇa at once. ˙*na y cwuk-˙sa ho˙l i 'lwo˙ta* (1481 Samkang ¹yel:5a) I must die.

sa-, ? bnd v. SEE ˙*sa-ngi ''ta*.

sa, pcl [alt after vowel of isa; obs; DIAL − South Kyengsang (Mkk 1960:3:33), Ceycwu (Seng ¹Nakswu 1984:35), Hamkyeng] = ya (iya).

-sa < -˙*sya* [lit] = -sye, -sie (honorific inf)

(-)sa, bnd n. leftover (quantity), odd. twū nyang tōn-sa an odd two taels of money. han toy ~ an extra toy (to a measuring by mal = 10 toy).

(-q) sa hata SEE ssa hata

sai < *so˙zi*, noun, postmodifier. ABBR sāy.

1. a space between two points; an interval; a distance apart; a gap; between. CF thum.

2. an interval between two points of time; a while, a spell; between, during; a gap, a pause, a break; time, spare time. CF tong-an, sikan, thum. ¶Pappe se phyēnci lul ssulq sai ka ēps.ess.ta I was so busy I had no time to write.

3. (friendly / mutual) relations, terms; life / relationship together; interpersonal feelings. ¶ ~ ka cōh.ta is on good terms (with).

4. postmod. (-nun ~) while, during the time that; (-un ~) when, after. CF -ulq sāy.

-saita [obs] = -upsita (let's)

sakwi, bnd postn. ABBR -say. SEE iph ~ . [< ?; CF sakwita; -sayki; sai, say.]

-sal, bnd morpheme, suf. ? bad. ¶kan ~ , kepuk ~ , mip ~ , puncwu ~ , tok ~ , wuak ~ . anikkop-sal sulepta = anikkopta is disgusted. CF mom-sal general fatigue (from overwork); neks-sal (i) nata (NKd) loses one's temper, gets angry (? = neksal impudence) ? < neks + -sal. [? < ˙*SALQ* 'baleful'; ? < -sali = -suli.]

sāl(q) < ¨*sal(q)* < **sal˙[o]l(q)*, prosp mod < sālta < ¨*sa[l]˙ta* (lives).

sālam < ¨*salom*, n (< vi subst). person; people.

-sali, bnd var [DIAL] = suli -like, der adv < sulepta. ¶swīp-sali easily, readily.

sal.i, postnoun (der n < sālta vi).

1. living, life. ¶cingyek ~ serving one's term of imprisonment. si-cip ~ living with

one's husband's parents. **mesum** ~ working as a farmhand. **kosayng** ~ leading a hard life. **seysang** ~ way of living, mode of life. **cey** ~ self-support. **ko.yong** ~ **(lul) hata** leads the life of an employee. **Wen, casik i cheka sal.i lul hata 'ni!** How shameful for a man to be living in his wife's house! **Nul phīnan sal.i hatun ttay sayngkak hanta** I always think of the time when I was leading a refugee's life. **Si-cip sal.i ka ku-taci to elyeptula** Life as a married woman was ever so hard (for me).
    2. garb, clothes, wear. ¶ **yelum** ~ summer things / clothes, summerwear.
sālm < ¨*salm* < **sal˙[o]m*, subst < **sālta** < ¨*sa[l]˙ta* (lives). ¶ ¨*sal.m ye* (1481 Twusi 16:42a) = ¨*sal˙m ye* lives and ... . CF *sa˙lwom*, **sālam** < ¨*salom*.
salok [DIAL] = **swulok**
¨*salom*, n (< vi subst). person, people. ¶ ¨*salo˙m i* (1463 Pep 2:41a). *hon* ¨*sa˙lo˙m i˙na* (1518 Sohak-cho 8:3a) an individual.
sa˙lwom, modulated substantive < ¨*sa[l]˙ta*. life, living. ¶ *sa˙lwo˙m i* (1449 Kok 143). *sa˙lwo.m ol* (1481 Twusi 8:29a, 8:33-4).
sam.ᵉ/a, vt inf. by way of, for, for the sake of, as; ~ **se** SAME. ¶ **īl ul cangnan sam.e hata** does a job for fun (or half-heartedly). **sānqpo sam.e sīnay ey kata** goes downtown for the sake of a walk. **tongmu sam.e kath.i sālta** live together for companionship. **sihem sam.e** as a trial, on a trial basis.
sām.ta < ¨*sam˙ta*, vt.
    1. makes (something) of (a person or thing), makes one / it into (being). ¶ **koa lul yāngca lo** ~ adopts an orphan. **ku lul sawi lo** ~ makes him one's son-in-law. **chayk ul tongmu lo** ~ makes books one's companion.
¶ *mu˙su ke˙s u˙lwo* ¨*TTWOW˙lol sa˙mo˙l ywo* (1459 Wel 9:22b) of what (thing) can we make the Way? ˙*MYWOW-˙HHOYNG˙o˙lwo˙YWONG sa˙mwol˙tt i.n i* (1463 Pep 1:4b) through the profound act of faith [by which the good karma is produced] one will create function. ˙*i* ¨*say* ¨*wul˙Guy ho˙n i˙za PWU-ZIN˙ol sa˙mwo.l i˙'la* (1447 Sek 24:20b) precisely the one who has made this bird sing will I make my wife. *ZYE-LOY˙THAY-¨CO s SSI-˙CYELQ˙ey* ¨*na˙lol* ¨*kyecip* ¨*sa˙mosi˙n i* (1447 Sek 6:4a) when the tathāgata was prince he made me his wife.

kul˙lwo il˙hwu˙m ul sa˙mo.n i˙'la (1459 Wel 2:27b) made his name be that.
    2. makes (a sandal). ¶ **ciph sin ul** ~ makes straw sandals.
    3. spins. ¶ **myengcwu sīl ul** ~ spins silk.
sān < ˙*san* < **sa˙[lo]n*, modifier < **sālta** < ¨*sa[l]˙ta* (lives). alive.
sang < ˙*SYANG* (appearance): SEE ~ **paluta**, ~ **siph.ta**; CF **seng**, *syeng*.
sang < *SSYANG*, adn, bnd n. common, ordinary, everyday, vulgar, mundane, trivial, routine. ¶ ~ **nyen**, ~ **nom**, ~ **mal**, ~ **sulepta**, ~ **oli**, ~ **yong**, ~ **in**; ~ **sulepta**; ~**q talk**, ~**q sālam**, ~**q soli**, ~**q īl**, ~**q toyta**. CF **pisang**.
sāng < ˙*SSYANG*.
    1. n, adn. top, superior; above, preceding. ¶ ~ **chi** top-grade stuff. **sāngq kil** top quality. ~ **kitwung** top pillar. ~ **nulk.un-i** senior. ~ **welkup** top salary. ~ **tāycep** top treatment. ~ **tāyhwa** the above conversation. ANT **hā**.
    2. bnd adn. the first of two or three, earlier. ¶ ~ **pānki** first term. ~ **pān-nyen** the first half(-year). CF **hā, cwung**.
    3. bnd adn. going up to (the capital, etc.).
    4. bnd postn (see §5.3.1; usually pronounced with short a) with respect to, -wise; from the viewpoint / standpoint of. ¶ **mun.yey** ~ from the standpoint of literary arts. **sāhoy-hak** ~ with respect to sociology. **seykyey ¹yeksa** ~ from the standpoint of world history. **¹yeksa sāng ina cili sāng ulo pol man han kes** things well worth looking at from the perspectives of history or geography. **cili sāng (uy) kyēnci lo pwā se** seen from the standpoint of geography. **I ke n' kyengcey sāng uy** (less commonly **in**) **mūncey 'la ko polq swu iss.ta** This can be looked at as a question relevant to economics. **Ku mūncey nun cili sāng i ani 'la ¹yeksa sāng uy kyēnci lo pwā ya hanta** That problem must be viewed (looked at) not from the standpoint of geography, but that of history. **I mūncey nun cengchi sāng (ina) kwunsa sāng ul mak.lon hako sīmkak han mūncey 'ta** This is a very serious problem, and certainly with respect to either political or military affairs. **Kyengcey sāng kwa nun pāntay lo kwunsa sāng ulo nun tāytan hi cwūngyo han ciyek ita** In contrast with economic relevance, it is a very important area militarily. **Kyengcey sāng pota to kwunsa sāng ulo nun te cwūngyo han ciyek ita** It is an

area that is of greater importance militarily than it is economically.

-ˈsa-ngi ˈ ˈta, ? bnd v polite + cop indic assertive. I would like, I hope [speaking to a superior]. ¶ ˙ˈCO-·SIK ˙uy ilˈhwum ˙ul aˈpi isiˈm ye [ˈ]eˈmi iˈsya ˙QILQ-ˈTTYENG hoˈsa-ngi ˈ ˈta (1459 Wel 8:83a; il-ˈhwum-˙ul) I hope the name of the son will be decided in the presence of the father and the mother. ˙CCYENG-ˈˈTHWO ˙ay hon-ˈtoy ˈka nasa-ngi ˈ[ˈ]ta (1459 Wel 8:100b) I would like to go to the Pure Land and be reborn there together [with her].

sangpulu hata, postmod adj-n [DIAL; Siberian?]. SEE -ulq ~. CF seng pᵃ/ᵤluta.

sang paluta [Cenla DIAL (LHS 1512a)] = seng siph.ta

sang puluta [DIAL] = seng siph.ta. (LHS 3234a halq sang puluta = halq kes kath.ta).

sang siph.ta [obs] = seng siph.ta

sānun < ˙ˈsaˈnon < *saˈ[lo]ˈnon, proc mod < sālta < ˙ˈsa[l]ˈta (lives). living. ¶ ˙ˈsaˈnon ˙ˈsaˈlo.m iˈn i (1459 Wel 1:8b) is a living man. ˙ˈsanoˈn i (1447 Sek 13:10a, 1481 Twusi 25:23a) is living.

-saoita [obs] = -saop.nita, -sup.nita. VAR -uoita, -uoyta.

-sao(wu)l, formal prosp mod [-saop- + -ul; obs] = -ul. [After vowel -o(wu)l.]

-sao(wu)likka, formal prosp attentive [-saop- + -ulikka; obs] = -ulikka. ¶Ecci ic.saolikka How can I possibly forget!

-sao(wu)liᵗ/ₗa, formal prosp assertive.

-sao(wu)n, formal mod [-saop- + -un; obs] = -un. [After vowel -o(wu)n.]

-sao(wu)na, formal advers [-saop- + -una; obs] = -una (but etc.). [After vowel -o(wu)na.] ¶Ōylam han māl-ssum iona (or Ōylam haona) It is presumptuous of me to say, but … .

-sao(wu)ni, formal sequential [-saop- + -uni; obs] = -uni (so etc.). [After vowel -o(wu)ni.]

-saop- [obs -W-; after vowel -op-] = -sup-, -up-; inf -sa(o)wa, mod -sao(wu)n. VAR -uop-.

 1. -saop.n(a)ita = -sup.nita
 2. -saop.n(a)ikka = -sup.nikka
 3. -saopt(e)ita = -suptita
 4. -saopt(e)ikka = -suptikka
 5. -saopko = -ko
 6. iss.saop.naita = iss.ˢup.nita;
    ēps.saop.naikka = ēps.ˢup.nikka.

-saopsiko [obs] = -usiko (hon ger). ¶Onul-nal wuli eykey il.yong halq ¹yangsik ul cwuopsiko Give us this day our daily bread, and … .

-saopsita, [obs]. 1. = -upsita (let's do). ¶Cip ulo kaopsita Let us go home.

 2. = -usita (deigns to do). ¶Wang kkey se naopsita (or nasiopsita) A king is born.

-saopsose [lit, obs] = -usio. please do. ¶Ak ey se kwū haopsose Deliver us from evil.

-saoyta [obs] = -saop.nita, -sup.nita

-sap-, abbr < -saop-, [obs] = -sup-.

-sa(o)wa, formal inf [-saop-/-sap- + -ᵉ/a; obs] = -e. CF -u(o)wa.

say₁ < ˙say, 1. adnoun. new; ANT nalk.un, hēn, muk.un. ¶ ~ sin a new pair of shoes. ~ chayk a new book. ~ māl a new word. ~ cip a new house (CF sāy sip a bird house).

 2. preparticle, pre-postnominal. ¶ ~ lo newly, recently. ~ lopta is new. ~ loi newly.

 3. n. (MK) new thing/one (= say kes). ¶taˈsi ˙say ˈlol piˈhe (1463 Pep 3:94a) let it rain once more anew. nolˈkoˈn iˈl' ˈˈtelˈGwo ˙say ˈlol teˈuˈm ye (1465 Wen 1:1:2:118b) lessens the old and increases the new.

say₂, postsubst, postnoun. mode, manner, way.

 1. postsubst. ¶ccaim ~ the make, makeup, structure; the way something is put together. cha(y)lim ~ the set-up; one's manner of dressing. kkekk.im ~ the fold, the way it is folded back (turned down). kkim ~ secrets, inklings, hints ? < kkīta (fog / smoke / dust) hangs. mantulm ~ the make, workmanship. mek.um ~ cookery, appetite; table manners. nāym ~ smell, odor ? < nāyta emits. nel.um ~ the way things are spread out [irreg subst < nēlta]. nul.im ~ drawl, slowness in speech. pak.um ~ stitching, the stitches. pellim ~ arrangement, display. phallim ~ the (relative) sale, the demand (for things on sale) < phalli- (vp) is sold. sayngkim ~ looks, appearance.

 2. postn. ¶chwulyem ~ contributing jointly (< ˙CHWULQ-ˈˈLYEM). chung ~ ("layer" =) quality of gold. kan ~ saltiness, flavor. kum ~ price. kwumeng ~ the way a hole (or face) is shaped. meli ~ (the way one looks when) wearing a headpiece. myēn ~ surface, face. mo.yang ~ appearance, form. ōl ~ the weave. phu' say₁ starching. CF pon (adn) ~ original looks, nature; iph-say = iph-sakwi leaf.

say₃, postmodifier [< ˙s oy]. SEE -ulq ~.
say₄, counter. a 20-strand unit measuring the warp-thread density of cloth (SYN sung, CF sung-say). ¶sēk ~ 60-strand (cloth).
say-₅, prefix; LIGHT ↔ si-. vivid, deep, intense. ¶~ kkamah.ta is jet black. ~ ha.yah.ta is snow white. SYN says-. CF sayng-.
say₆ < *SOY, n. = kwuk-say the royal seal.
say₇, n. ore yield.
say₈, n. = sayq palam east wind [nautical].
say₉ < ¨say, n. sod, turf; (= ek-~) a kind of wild grass; (=ieng) straw thatch. CF phu' say₂ grasses, plants, pasturage; namu say firewood.
sāy₁₀ < ¨say, n. a bird.
sāy₁₁, abbr < sai (interval).
say lo < ˙say ˙lwo, n (preparticle) + pcl [? – or abbr < say loi]. newly, freshly; recently.
sāylo (ey), particle (+ particle) [literary; always preceded by -ki nun]. far from doing, instead of doing, on the contrary. ¶Na l' chac.e oki n' sāylo ey cēnhwa cocha to ēps.ess.ta Far from (his) calling on me, there wasn't even a phone call (from him). Phokphung-wu ka caki nun sāylo ey te sīm hay kanta The storm, far from abating, increased in its fury.
CF khenyeng; -nun tāysin ey, -ci anh.ko, -nun pāntay lo, tolie.
sāyloi → sāylo ey
say loi, der adv < say lopta. newly (= say lo).
sāylye, particle [DIAL] = sāylo ey.
sayng₁ < SOYNG, [lit]. 1. noun. life, living.
2. pronoun [in letters]. I / me (= na, ce).
3. postnoun (title). Young Mister ⋯ . ¶Kim ~ Young Mr Kim.
4. postnoun (after date or year name). born in ⋯ . ¶1920 ~ born in 1920. mū-cin ~ born in the 5th year of the 60-year cycle.
sayng₂ (< sayng₁), noun, adv. raw; reasonable.
1. n (preparticle). ~ ulo SEE sayng ulo.
2. adverb. ~ mekta "eats it raw" = feigns ignorance; ignores (one's words).
sayng₃ (< sayng₁), adn.
1. raw; unripe, uncooked, green; unhealed. ¶~ kes raw (things). ~ kwāsil unripe fruit. ~ kwul raw oysters. ~ ssal uncooked rice. ~ ttakci unhealed / raw scab.
2. crude, unprocessed, natural; wild; rough(-hewn); untrained, untutored; unassimilated. ¶~ kacwuk rawhide. ~ komu crude rubber.

~ mal an unbroken horse, a bronco. ~ muci = sayngq kwun a green hand, a novice. ~ myengcwu raw silk. ~ wuyu raw milk. ~ ⁿYecin an unassimilated Juchen.
3. live, living; healthy; not yet dry, undried, unseasoned, green. ¶~ cangcak unseasoned (green) firewood. ~ ciok a living hell. ~ coki undried corvina. ~ kwāpu a grass widow. ~ mok-swum life itself; an innocent person's life. ~ myengthay undried pollack. ~ namu a live tree; green wood; unseasoned wood. ~ sālam innocent / healthy / disinterested person. sayngq i (= sayng ni) a good / healthy tooth. sayngq ¹ipyel lifelong separation.
4. real, natural, original, untouched, pristine; raw; unprocessed; unsweetened, unflavored, unscented; unbottled. ¶~ apeci one's natural father. ~ cali an untouched place. ~ hulk virgin soil. ~ ttang virgin land. ~ maykcwu draft ("dry") beer.
5. unreasonable, irrational, arbitrary, forced, needless, uncalled-for, excess (CF sayngphan unreasonably). ¶~ cwuk.um an unnatural death. ~ hōlyeng an uncalled-for scolding. ~ kocip stubbornness. ~ kosayng needless suffering. ~ pyelak unreasonable scolding; undeserved misfortune; sudden calamity. ~ soli nonsense, unreasonable talk. ~ thucip a senseless dispute. ~ ttan-cēn evasive remarks or actions, beating around the bush, going off on a tangent. ~ ttey(-keli) obstinacy.
CF sayngsayng hata is fresh, lively; sayng-cayki undamaged part (? bnd n + suffix).
-sayngi, suf. ?stars. com ~ the Pleiades; small things. [? < bnd n seng < SYENG 'star' + -i]
sayngkak < ˙soyng˙kak, n. 1. thought, thinking, idea. ~ hata, vnt. thinks, thinks of, considers.
2. (= yēyceng) intention, idea, view, purpose. SEE -ulq ~.
sayng ulo, n + pcl. 1. raw (= nal lo). ¶talkyal ul ~ mekta eats an egg raw. CF sayng mekta.
2. unreasonably, irrationally, arbitrarily, wrongfully. ¶~ sālam ul ttaylita hits a person without reason.
says-, pref, LIGHT ↔ sis-. [LIVELY] vivid, deep, intense. ¶says-nolah.ta is a deep yellow. says-ha.yah.ta /saytha.yatha/ is extremely white.
⋯s¨cop-, 1. < ⋯s-¨zop-, ⋯sk-¨zop-, ⋯z-¨zop-.
2. (mistake) → ⋯t¨cop-, ⋯¨ccop-.

se < ˙*sye*, inf < **suta** < **seta** < °*sye˙ta* (stands).
se, pcl (< ˙*sye* < *[i]˙sye* = **iss.e** being). SEE **ey se**. CF **ulo (s)se**; **-so**, **swu**.

1. marks the location (dynamic or default): (happening) at / in (a place). ¶ **yeki ~ īl hata** works here (at this place). **Eti se sass.nun ya** Where did you buy it?

2. from (a place, a position, a status, a group, a number). ¶ **Mikwuk ~ wass.ta** came from America. **mēlli ~** from afar. **kakkai ~** from nearby. **Sewul se osin pun tul** people here from Seoul.

3. marks impersonal oblique subject. ¶ **Yen-Tay ey se ikyess.ta** Yensey University won.

4. ¶ **honca se** by oneself, alone. **twūl-i se** the two of them together, between themselves.

5. used for emphasis after INFINITIVE **-e**, GERUND **-ko**, and TRANSFERENTIVE **-ta (ka)**.

6. used after CONDITIONAL **-umyen** to change 'when / if' to 'while'. SEE **-umyen se**.

-se = **-sye**, abbr < **-sie** (honorific infinitive)
se chelem, pcl + pcl. ¶ **Ku nun sikol se chelem Sewul se to ciph sin ul sin.ko taninta** He goes around in straw sandals in Seoul just as he did in the country.
se cocha, pcl + pcl. SEE **ey se cocha**.
sē-i, n (num + count). three people.
-sek, suffix. SEE **-ssek**.
se hako, pcl + pcl (= **se wa**). SEE **ey se hako**.
se ka, pcl + pcl. at / from / ... [complement of neg cop]. ¶ **Sewul se ka ani 'la, Pusan se 'ta** It is not from Seoul, it is from Pusan. SEE **-e se ka**.
se khenyeng, pcl + pcl. ¶ **Yeki se khenyeng hak.kyo ey ka se to kongpu lul an hanta 'p.nita** I don't even go to school and study, much less study here!
se kkaci, pcl + pcl. SEE **ey se kkaci**.
sekken, pcl [colloq; < **sekk.e n'** inf 'mix' + abbr pcl]. and so on, and the like, and others, et cetera. ¶ **Kim sensayng sekken wass.ta** Mr Kim and various others came. **Swul sekken ttek sekken mānh.i mek.ess.ta** I had lots to eat and drink – cakes, wine, and so on. **Kāy sekken ōli sekken tā phal.ess.ta** He sold dogs and ducks and everything. ¹**Yi kwun sekken haksayng tul i tā eti iss.na** Where are ¹Yi and the other students?

NOTE: Many Seoul speakers use **ilang / lang** instead, but **sekken** is used in nearby areas of Kyengki and Hwanghay provinces. CF **ina**, **ini**.

sekken ccum (iya), pcl + pcl (+ pcl). SEE **ilang ccum (iya)**.
sekken cocha, pcl + pcl. SEE **ilang cocha**.
sekken iya, pcl + pcl [awkward]. ¶ **Poktong-i sekken iya etteh.key kath.i kakeyss.ni** How could Poktong-i and them possibly go with us?!
sekken khenyeng, pcl + pcl. SEE **ilang khenyeng**.
sekken kkaci, pcl + pcl. SEE **ilang kkaci**.
sekken mace, pcl + pcl. SEE **ilang mace**.
sekken man, pcl + pcl. SEE **ilang man**.
sekken pota (to), pcl + pcl (+ pcl). SEE **ilang pota (to)**.
sekken puthe, pcl + pcl. SEE **ilang puthe**.
sekken tul, pcl + pcl. SEE **ilang tul**.
sekken ul, pcl + pcl. SEE **ilang ul**.
sekken un, pcl + pcl. ¶ **Poktong-i sekken un cip ey iss.ke la** Poktong-i and the rest of you are to stay home (regardless of what others do).
sekken un khenyeng, pcl + pcl + pcl. SEE **ilang un khenyeng**.
sekken uy, pcl + pcl [rare]. ¶ **Poktong-i sekken uy os ul sa ya 'keyss.ta** We'll have to buy clothes for Poktong-i and the others.
seko (= **suko**), gerund of **seta** = **suta** (stands)
se 'ko = **se iko**, particle + copula gerund
seks, noun, postmod. 1. a fit of passion, a surge of emotion; sudden anger, pique. ¶ **Yengmun to moluko seks kīm ey ssawess.ta** They fought in a fit of anger, for no reason at all.

2. a mooring, a place to tie up a boat.

3. [? DIAL] postmod. SEE **-ulq seks ey**.

4. [DIAL] = **twukkey** (thickness); = **wuntwu** (brim height).

5. SEE *syeks*, ˙*syeks*.

sel(q) = **sulq**, prosp mod of **seta** = **suta** (stands)
se lang, particle + particle.

1. (= **se sekken**). ¶ **Alayq tōngney se lang chwusek nol.i cwūnpi hanula ko motwu yātan ita** The people in the next village are all agog making preparations for the Harvest Festival.

2. = **se wa** = **se hako**
se 'la to SEE **-e ~**, **ey ~**
seli₁ < *se˙li*, noun. frost.
seli₂, noun. 1. [obs] < ˙*seli* (= **sai** < *so˙zi*) space, interval. ¶ **cip the ~** the spare space around a house / building. **thum (~)** gap, interval, leisure.

2. place. ¶ **mo ~** corner, edge, angle (CF **ēnceli** edge < **ēn** + var of **seli** or **cali**). **phu' namu ~** a thicket, an overgrown place.

3. = **tūl** uncultivated field, moor.
seli₃, postnoun. mass, group. ¶**namu ~** a lot of wood. **sālam ~** a bunch of people.
seli₄, bnd n, suffix. ¶**myek (~)** a bag knitted of straw.
se llamuni [Kayseng DIAL] = **se nun. -ko ~**.
se llang (un), pcl + pcl (+ pcl), [obs; slang; Seoul DIAL] = **se nun. -ko ~**.
selma < *hyelma* < *'hyenma*, adv. hardly (+ NEG, rhetorical question).
sem = **sum**, subst < *seta* = *suta* (stands)
se mace, pcl + pcl. SEE **ey se mace**.
se man, pcl + pcl. only (just) at/in/from. ¶**I ke n' Mikwuk se man salq swu iss.ta** You can buy this only in America. **Na n' na se puthe Sewul se man ccwuk sal.ess.ey yo** Since birth I have lived only in Seoul. SEE **-e se man**.
se mankhum, pcl + pcl. ¶**Yeki se nun cēki se mankhum kongpu ka cal an toynta** I can't study here as well as I can over there.
se n', pcl + pcl = **se nun**
se 'n = **se in** (pcl + cop mod)
sen = **sun**, mod < *seta* = *suta* (stands)
sen < *SYEN*, noun, adnoun.
  1. noun. the first move (in chess/checkers).
  2. adnoun. first; prior. ¶**~ meli** beginning, onset. **~ son** the initiative, first blow. **~ polum** the first half of the month.
sēn, vi mod < *sēlta*. ('half-done' =) untrained, unskilled, immature, "green", new (novice). ¶**~ mūtang** a new shaman. **~ wus.um** a forced laugh. **~ cam** a cat nap. **~ haphum** a half-yawn; a slight indigestion. **~ mesum** a wild/mischievous boy. CF **nal**.
se 'na, pcl + cop advers. at/in/from ⋯ or the like (or such); whether at/in/from ⋯; at/in/ from whatever ⋯. ¶**Kulen mulken un Mikwuk se 'na salq swu iss.ci** You can buy that sort of stuff in the States. **Kyōoy se 'na ppekkwuk sāy soli lul tul.ulq swu iss.ci sīnay se n' mōs tut.nunta** You can hear a cuckoo in the suburbs, perhaps, but you won't hear one in town. (It is in the suburbs or the like that you will hear the cuckoo, not in town.)
se 'na-ma, pcl + cop extended advers. SEE **ey se 'na-ma**.
(-q) seng < *'SYENG*, postn, postsubst, postmod. quality, character(istic), temperament, -ness.
  1. postnoun. ¶**cōsimq ~** carefulness, caution. **cwūpyenq ~** resourcefulness; tact. **insaq ~** courtesy, courteousness. **kwīinq ~** nobility. **yungthongq ~** adaptability, flexibility.
  2. postsubst. ¶**coyimq ~** impatience, eager expectation. **kwīyemq ~** lovableness. **elyemq ~** social reserve. **mit.umq ~** reliability. **puth.imq ~** amiability. **twulumq ~** ingenuity, resourcefulness. **wukimq ~** stubbornness.
  3. postmodifier. ¶**cham.ulq ~** forbearance. CF **mek-seng** appetite.
seng < *syeng* < *'SYANG* (> *sang*), postmod.
  1. appearance, likelihood. ¶**polq seng** (usually spelled **polsseng**) outward appearance. SEE **~ siph.ta**, *-ulq syeng*.
  2. [DIAL] = **(-ulq) sēym** (ulo). SEE **-ulq ~**.
seng, ? suffix, ? bound n. ¶**ip-~** [DIAL, vulgar] clothes, garments, duds. CF **-seng(i)**.
-seng(i), suffix. ¶**tung-sengi, tung-seng malwu** the back; a ridge.
seng pᵃ/ᵤluta, (⋯ +) postmod + postnom adj insep -LL- [DIAL] = **seng siph.ta**. SEE *-ulq syeng pwuluta*.
seng siph.ta, (⋯ +) postmod + postnom adj insep. seems/appears (to be), I guess (that). ¶**nwūn i olq ~** it seems likely to snow, it looks as though it were going to snow. **ku lul han pen pon ~** it seems to me that I have met him before. VAR **sang siph.ta**.
se 'n tul, pcl + cop mod + postmod. ¶**Kulen kes ccum iya eti se 'n tul mōs kwu hal ya** A thing like that — couldn't you buy it just anywhere?
senun = **sunun**, proc mod < *seta* = *suta* (stands)
se nun, pcl + pcl. as for (happening) at/in (a place); as for (being) from; as for [oblique subject]. ¶**Sikol se nun yo cuum chwuswu ey han-chang pappulq key 'p.nita** In the country they must be awfully busy these days gathering the harvest. **Sewul se nun pec kkoch i han-chang ip.nita** The cherry blossoms are in full bloom in Seoul. SEE **-ko se nun, -e se nun, -ta (ka) se nun**.
se nun khenyeng, pcl + pcl + pcl. ¶**Yeki se nun khenyeng hak.kyo ey se to kongpu lul an hanta 'p.nita** I don't even study at school, much less here.
se pota, particle + particle. (rather) than from or (happening) at. ¶**Ilen mulken tul un Sewul (ey) se pota sikol (ey) se te cal phallip.nita** Such articles sell better in Seoul than they do in the country.

se puthe, pcl + pcl. from (usually a place). ¶**cēki se puthe yeki se kkaci** from there to here. **Sewul/Pusan se puthe** from Seoul/Pusan. **Na nun Cong-lo se puthe ccwuk kel.e wass.ta** I've walked all the way (here) from Bell Street. SEE -umyen ~ ; ey ~ .

se puthe nun, pcl + pcl + pcl. ¶**Keki se puthe nun kil i phocang i toyess.ta** From there on the road is paved.

-se se = -sye se, abbr < -sie se, hon inf + pcl. ~ ka, ~ nun, ~ to, ~ ya.

se sekken, pcl + pcl. SEE se lang.

se 'ss.ta, abbr < se iss.ta (is standing)

-sess- = -syess- abbr < -siess-, alt after vowel of -us(y)ess-. ~ -keyss-(ta), ~ -ess-(ta), ~ -ess.keyss-(ta).

sesul, 1. n. the edge / sharpness of a blade; one's mettle. 2. postmodifier. (by) the force of (= **palam**): **-nun ~ ey**. NOTE: We reject the examples in CM 2:63 (**chitun sesul ey**) and CM 2:229 (**chinun sesul ey**).

sesum, bnd n. hesitation. ¶ ~ **ēps.i** with no hesitation. **sesum chi** < *sesum haci replaces (?*)sesum.ci (though usually spelled as if that).

seta < *sye'ta*, vi. SEE suta (stands).

se to, pcl + pcl. at / from ... also / even / either. ¶**Mikwuk se to kulenq īl i iss.ta** That kind of thing happens in America, too (or: even in America). **Ku nun sikol se chelem Sewul se to ciph sin ul sin.ko taninta** He goes around in straw sandals in Seoul just as he did in the country. SEE ey se to, eykey se to, hanthey se to, kkey se to, ulo se to; -e se to, -ko se to, -umyen se to.

-se to (= -sye to), abbr < -sie to, hon inf + pcl.

se tul, pcl + pcl. SEE ey ~ , eykey ~ , kkey ~ , ulo ~ , -e ~ , -ko ~ ; -umyen ~ .

se 'tun ci, pcl + cop retr mod + post mod. ¶**Etteh.key hay se 'tun ci ku kes ul hay la** Do it somehow or other.

se uy, pcl + pcl. ¶**ku sālam uy Sewul (ey) se uy hwalqtong** his activities in Seoul.

se wa, pcl + pcl. with (what is) at / in / from ... . ¶**Sewul se wa sikol se nun saynghwal-pi ey sangtang han chai ka iss.ta** There is a big difference between living costs in Seoul and in the country.

sey, 1. postmodifier. SEE -ulq ~ .
2. postsubstantive. SEE -um sey; CF a.
[? < 's oy]

-sey, FAMILIAR subj assert. let's; let me (= -ca). ¶**Anc.sey** Let's sit. **Kasey** Let's go. **Nay ka onul nāysey** Let me pay today. CF -key (na).

-sey, 1. = -sye (hon inf). 2. = -sey yo please do.

se ya, pcl + pcl. SEE ey se ya, ulo se ya; -e se ya, -ta 'y se ya, ila 'y se ya.

-se ya (= -sye ya), hon inf + pcl (abbr < -sie ya).

sēym, postmod [< vt subst], followed by cop (or pcl **ulo**). 1. the calculation, conjecture, supposition; accounting (for); (judgment based on) appearances, to all appearances/indications, that one might call ... . ¶**Īl hako iss.nun sēym ita** We can say that he is working, sort of. **Kwacang in sēym ita** He is a sort of section head. **Caki ttan un apeci hanthey hyōto hanun sēym iess.ta** To hear him tell it, he was a filial son. **Kuleh.key hamyen ku sālam i sōnhay ponun sēym ikeyss.kwun** I bet it will turn out to his loss if we do that. **Ku sālam chiko ya cal han sēym ici** For him, it was rather well done, I would say. **Mikwuk ulo chimyen cal han sēym ita** From America's standpoint it can be regarded as well done. **Pi ka olq (onun) sēym in ka** I wonder if it will rain (if it is raining outside). **Īl hanun sēym in ka** Do you call THAT working?! **Kwīsin ul pon sēym iey yo?** You mean you saw a ghost?! **Thokki meych eykey** (= meych mali eykey) **punpay han sēym in ya** How many rabbits do you figure got their rations? **Chayk.im ul tā han sēym ulo haca** Let's consider it that you did all your duty. **Tō lul takk.nun sēym ulo san ey ka iss.ta** He's gone to the mountain as a way of seeking enlightenment. [1]**Nayil mek.ulq sēym ulo namkye noh.ass.ta** I saved it thinking to eat it tomorrow. SYN phok$_2$. CF wēyn sēym.
2. intention, intent, idea, expectation. ¶**I pen tho.yoil um.ak-hoy kalq sēym isey yo?** Will you be at the concert this Saturday? **Kantan hi ssun sēym ip.nita** I have tried (done my best) to write simply. **Kwuk.kyeng kkaci kalq sēym iess.nun ya** Did you intend to go all the way to the border? SEE sēym chita.

sēym chita, cpd vi (postmod + vt). supposes, assumes, grants (that). ¶**Kulenq īl i cēng-mal il.e nass.ta ko sēym chica** Let us suppose that it really happened. **Cenyek han kki mek.un sēym chiko, cek-sipca ey mān wen ul kipu hayss.ta** I donated ten thousand wen to the Red Cross, pretending to myself that I had eaten a nice dinner with the money. **Ceksēn hanun sēym chiko tōn ul an pat.keyss.ˢup.nita** I'll collect my payment in heaven [said in declining money for service]. **Cwuk.ulq sēym chiko sam-phalq sen ul nem.ess.ta** I crossed the 38th parallel at the risk of my life.

-sey na, FAMILIAR subj assert. let's just; let me just. ¶**Anc.sey na** Let's have a seat. **Nay ka onul nāysey na** Just let me pay today.

-se yo = **-sye yo**, abbr < **-sie yo**, hon inf + pcl.

-sey tul, FAMILIAR subj assert + pcl. ¶**Ese īl ul sīcak hasey tul** Let's get started on the job.

-sey yo, 1. = **-sie yo** (hon inf + pcl)
  2. (< 1.) please do. For nonfinal examples of **posey yo** 'suppose' = 'if' see **-e pota**.

'sey yo, abbr < **isey yo** = **isye yo** = **isie yo**. ¶**Nwukwu 'sey yo** Who is it [= Who are you]?

si, adnoun. one's husband's (relatives). ¶ ~ **apeci** a woman's father-in-law, the husband's father. ~ **hal-apeci** the husband's grandfather. ~ **acwupeni** the husband's older brother.

si, postmod + pcl (< ˙s i) [obs] = **kes i** the likely fact that ... [as subject]. SEE **-ulq si**. CF **iolssita**.

˙**si(…)** = ˙s i(…), postmod + pcl (cop). SEE **-ulq ˙s i(…)**.

'**si…**, abbr < ˙**isi…** (cop hon), < **isi-** (v hon), < ˙**hosi…** (v/adj hon).

si-, prefix; HEAVY ↔ **say-**. vivid, deep, intense. ¶ ~ **kkemeh.ta** is jet black. ~ **he.yeh.ta** is snow white. CF **sis-**.

-si, pseudo-suf (makes n from v). **nakk.si** a fish hook < **nakk.ta** (< *naksk-*) fishes. Historically this seems to be **naks** < ˙**naks** (n) + **-i** (suffix). It is unclear whether the Middle Korean verb is derived from the noun (with a formative *-k-*) or whether the noun is a reduced form of the verb stem, *naks[k]*.

-si- < -˙**si-**, alt (after vowel) of **-usi-** < -˙ᵘ⁄**osi-**.

-siap, [var] = **-siop(sose)**

-sica, abbr < **hasica**

'**/-sici**, 1. < **isici**. 2. < **hasici**. 3. = **-usici**.

'**/-sie**, 1. < **isie**. 2. < **hasie**. 3. = **-usie**.

sik < ˙**SIK**, noun, postnoun.
  1. style. ¶**Swun wuli sik ita** It is purely (our =) Korean style. **nallim** ~ coarse (rough-finish) style. **hulum** ~ = ¹**yuswu** ~ 'orderly-flow style' (NKd 4016a). CF **sinsik** new style, **kwūsik** old style.
  2. = **uysik** ceremony.
  3. = **pangsik** formula.
  4. = **hyengsik** form, shape.
  5. = **swūsik** mathematical expression.
  6. (philosophical) system.
  7. particle [lit] → **ssik**

˙**sik** < ˙**SIK**, particle. each, respectively, apiece (distributive). ¶ ˙**en˙me ˙uy hon ˙phan ˙sik hol ˙ta** (?1517⁻ Pak 1:10a) how much (does it cost) per board? **hon nye˙k uy ta˙sos ˙sik pwun ˙ho˙ye ˙sye ˙pswo˙cye** (?1517⁻ Pak 1:54b) let's shoot after dividing [the arrows] into five for each side.

'**/-sikeyss-**, 1. < **isikeyss-**. 2. < **hasikeyss-**. 3. = **-usikeyss-**.

sikhita < **si˙ki˙ta**, vt; postnom v sep. causes; makes, forces, lets; orders (it from him or him to do it). ¶**sālam eykey īl ul** ~ makes a person work, puts a person to work, uses a person. **ttal eykey nolay lul** ~ has one's daughter sing a song, asks one's daughter to sing. **capchay lul** ~ orders some **capchay**. **sālam ul sacik** ~ forces a person to resign, dismisses a person. **atul ul kongpu** ~ gives one's son an education. **sālam eykey Sewul kwūkyeng ul** ~ shows a person around Seoul. **ssawum** ~ gets a fight started, provokes a fight, gets someone to fight. **sālam eykey kukcang kwūkyeng ul** ~ treats a person to a show. **kupsa eykey siksa lul cwūnpi** ~ has the waiter prepare [the table for serving] the meal. **haksayng eykey ¹yuhak ul** ~ arranges for a student to study abroad. **sālam ul sikhye se uysa lul puluta** sends a person out for a doctor. **sikhinun tay lo hata** does as one is told (to do). **Apeci ka (na lul) col.ep sikhyess.ta** My father made me graduate. **Na nun sāmu-wen eykey kupsa lul sikhye se congi lul cwūmun hakey hayss.ta** I had the clerk get the office-boy to order some paper. **Ku ay eykey māl sikhye posey yo** Try to get the child to talk. **Ku kes un ilpan eykey kwūkyeng sikhici anh.nunta** They don't let the public look at it. **Ku īl un ce lul sikhye cwusipsio** Let me do it, please. CF **(-key) hata**; **toyta**. NOTE: The aspiration is attested in *sikhye* (?1660⁻ Kyeychwuk 193 [LCT]), but the older version *sikye* can be found in 1894 Gale 68. In 1904 Khlynovskiy the stem **siki-** means 'cause' but **sikhi-** means 'order': **i mal ul cel sikila ko sikhey la** [< **sikhye la**] 'Have this horse shoed!' (King 1991a).

'/-si-ki, 1. < isiki. 2. < hasiki. 3. = -usiki.
si‧ki‧ta = sikhita. ¶ ‧ce y ‧hoke‧na ‧no‧m ol si‧kye ‧ho.ya ‧two (1447 Sek 13:52a) whether one does it oneself or gets someone else to do it. cal hol ci cal mwos hol ci sikye pwoa ya al ci (1894 Gale 68) you will only find out whether he can do it well or not by trying him out [Gale mistranslates "you must try to let him know"].
'/-siko, 1. < isiko. 2. < hasiko. 3. = -usiko.
'/-sil(q), 1. < isil(q). 2. < hasil(q). 3. = -usil(q).
'sil(q), 1. abbr < ‧hosil(q).
   2. = '[y]sil(q), abbr < ‧isil(q) (cop hon prosp mod) after i or y. ¶ ‧CHYWULQ-KA ‧hosilq ‧pstay 'sil ‧ss oy (1449 Kok 50) since it is time to become a monk ... .
-sil, suffix. makes impressionistic adv. ¶ kamsil kamsil / kemsil kemsil sparsely dotted < kām-/kēm- (adj) black. keksil keksil cheerful, bouyant. (k)komsil w(r)iggling. (k)kopsil (k)kopsil / (k)kwupsil (k)kwupsil with bent body (inclined head) < kop-/kwup- (adj) bent. kunsil ... = kuncil tickling. kwunsil kwunsil itchy, crawly. namsil namsil / nemsil nemsil rubbernecking; overflowing. noksil noksil / nwuksil nwuksil elastic, pliant.
'/-sila, 1. < isila. 2. < hasila. 3. = -usila.
'/-silq ci, 1. < isilq ci. 2. < hasilq ci.
   3. = -usilq ci.
'/-silq cwul, 1. < isilq cwul. 2. < hasilq cwul.
   3. = -usilq cwul.
si‧le, adv. possibly, can (= e‧lwu, nilo, nung ‧hi, ‧KA ‧hi). ~-‧kwom SAME.
'siley, abbr (alt) < isiley. CF 'sitey.
'/-sil i, 1. < isil i. 2. < hasil i. 3. = -usil i.
-sili SEE -key-sili
'/-silq ka, 1. < isilq ka. 2. < hasilq ka.
   3. = -usilq ka.
'/-silq kes, 1. < isilq kes.
   2. < hasilq kes. ¶ Sensayng nim kkey se na tele 'tun ci ne tele 'tun ci kan ey īl ul towa tālla 'silq kes kath.tula The teacher may ask either you or me to help him.
   3. = -usilq kes.
'/-silq key, 1. < isilq key. 2. < hasilq key.
   3. = -usilq key.
'/-silq sey, 1. < isilq sey. 2. < hasilq sey.
   3. = -usilq sey.
'/-silq ya, 1. < isilq ya. 2. < hasilq ya.
   3. = -usilq ya.
'/-sim, 1. < isim. 2. < hasim. 3. = -usim.

-‧sim = -‧(^{u}/o)sim
'/-simyen, 1. < isimyen. 2. < hasimyen.
   3. = -usimyen.
'/-sin, 1. < isin. 2. < hasin. 3. = -usin.
'/-sin, 1. < ‧isin (cop hon mod). 2. < isin (v hon mod). 3. < ‧hosin (v hon mod). 4. < -^{u}/o‧sin
-sin, suffix. makes impressionistic adverbs. ¶ kkapsin kkapsin / kkepsin kkepsin giddily, frivolously. nwuksin nwuksin soft, supple, pliant < nwuk- (adj) soft, limp. CF -cin, -sil.
'/-sina, 1. < isina. 2. < hasina. 3. = -usina.
sinap ulo, bnd prepcl + pcl. at odd moments.
'/-sin ci, 1. < isin ci. 2. < hasin ci. 3. = -usin ci.
'/-sin cuk, 1. < isin cuk. 2. < hasin cuk.
   3. = -usin cuk.
'/-sin cwul, 1. < isin cwul. 2. < hasin cwul.
   3. = -usin cwul.
'/-siney, 1. < isiney. 2. < hasiney. 3. = -usiney.
'/-sini, 1. < isini. 2. < hasini. 3. = -usini.
'/-sin i, 1. < isin i. 2. < hasin i. 3. = -usin i.
'si‧n i, 1. < ‧isi‧n i (cop hon mod). 2. < isi‧n i (v hon mod). SEE -‧a ‧si‧n i. 3. < ‧hosi‧n i (v hon mod). 4. < -^{u}/o‧si‧n i.
'/-sin ka, 1. < isin ka. 2. < hasin ka.
'/-sin kes, 1. < isin kes. 2. < hasin kes.
   3. = -usin kes.
'/-sin key, 1. < isin key. 2. < hasin key.
   3. = -usin key.
-‧sino‧n i = -(^{u}/o)‧sino‧n i
'/-sin pa, 1. < isin pa. 2. < hasin pa.
   3. = -usin pa.
'/-sinta, 1. hasinta. 2. = -usinta.
'/-sin tey, 1. < isin tey. 2. < hasin tey.
   3. = -usin tey.
'/-sin tul, 1. < isin tul. 2. < hasin tul.
   3. = -usin tul.
'/-sinun, 1. < hasinun. 2. = -usinun.
-sinya → -sin ya
'/-sin ya, 1. < isin ya. 2. < hasin ya.
   3. = -usin ya.
sinyung, 1. noun, vnt. (= hyungnay) mimicry, imitating.
   2. postmodifier. showing signs, signalling, (= son cis) gesture. ¶ Ku ka mul ul tālla 'nun sinyung ul hap.nita He signals to give him water (M 2:2:324) = shows signs of wanting water. Kōm ul mannan namuq kwun i cwuk.un sinyung ul hayss.ta Encountering a bear, the woodman pretended to be dead.

'/-sio, 1. < isio. 2. < hasio. 3. = -usio.
  3a. ¶Kasio Go! Sesio = Susio Stop! Mīsio Push! (CF Tangkio Pull! — to keep number of syllables identical?)
  3b. ¶Musunq īl ul hasio What do you do?
  4. [var] = -sey yo
-siop, abbr < -siopsose (please do). CF -siap.
-sio tul SEE -usio tul
siph.e cita, cpd aux v (aux adj inf + aux v). SEE -ko ~; -keni ~, -ulye 'n' i ~.
siph.e hata, cpd aux v (aux adj inf + aux v). (··· -ko ~) wants / wishes (to do), is desirous of (doing), feels like (doing), would like (to do). ¶Ku i ka kako siph.e hanta He wants to go. Ku i ka kako siph.e haci anh.nunta He does not want to go.
siph.i, der adv < siph.ta. SEE -ta siph.i, (-nun) ka siph.i.
siph.ta, aux adj < sipwuta (1887 Scott 61) / siputa (1539, 1676) / siphuta (1632, 1676) < sikpu- (1449). CF siph.i.
  1. (···-ko ~) (I) want / wish (to), am desirous of (doing), feel like (doing), should / would like to. [In statements, usually first person only; in questions, also second person; embedded (etc.), any person. For other persons see siph.e hata.] ¶Kako siph.ta I want (would / should like) to go. Kako siph.ci anh.ta I do not want to go; I do not feel like going. Wūlko siph.umyen, wūlci wul.e If you feel like crying, go ahead and cry. Say catong-cha lul kaciko siph.ta I want a new car. Cha han can masiko siph.un ya Would you like a cup of tea? CF (···-ki) wēn hata, (···-ki) palata.
  2. looks, seems, appears; it feels like (as if maybe); is likely to. CF pota, hata; poita.
  2a. postnom adj insep: mod + ka, ya, sang, seng, tus + ~. ¶Com cak.un ka siph.ta It seems a bit small. ¹Nayil to nal i cōh.ulq ka siph.ta It promises to be another fine day tomorrow. Myengswu nun ileh.key māl ul hako se to Chengtek-i māl tay lo toyess.umyen elma 'na cōh.ulq ka siph.ess.ta Even though Myengswu talked that way, he still thought how nice it would be if only things turned out just the way Chengtek-i said. Onul nal sayngkak hamyen ku kes to cey casin uy sāsang kwanqcem i acik hwak.ko haci mōs ha.yess.tun thas i ani 'ess.tun ka siph.sup.nita As I look at it today, I have the feeling the fault for that may have been that my ideological viewpoint was not yet firm. Ku wa kath.un māl i ani 'n ka siph.ta It seems to be a word like that. Āmu īl itun com hay polq ka siph.ta I think I might be able to do any kind of work. swonaki ka wol ka siphwu (1894 Gale 98) I believe there is going to be a dash of rain.
  ¶Encey pi ka wass.tun ya siph.key hanul un ssis.un tus nwun pusikey kayess.ta The sky cleared up all washed and bright as if it hadn't been raining. Nay ka hay noh.ko to way kulenun ya siph.ul ttay ka iss.ta 'ni-kka n'?! There are times when, having done it, I wonder why I do it.
  ¶Ku ai nun khukey toylq sang siph.ta The boy gives promise of a great future.
  ¶Ku ka olq seng / ka siph.ci anh.ta He is not likely to come. Ku sālam i hwā ka nalq seng siph.e se ku māl ul haci anh.ass.e yo (Im Hopin 1987:169) I didn't say it, for he looked as if he might get angry.
  ¶Ku nun tōn i mānh.un tus siph.ess.ta He seemed to be rich. Pi ka ol tus siph.e se ku wūsan ul cwūnpi hayss.e yo (Im Hopin 1987:169) It looked as if it would rain, so I got my umbrella ready.
  2b. -na (FAMILIAR indic attent) ~. ¶Cip ey se nun ilen nāymak un moluko hāyng-ye 'na musun swu ka iss.na siph.e (se) unkun hi kitalyess.ta The family didn't know the inside story and hopefully waited, feeling that there might be some way out. Taykwu ey tōchak hayss.na siph.e se chachang pakk ul nāy 'ta poass.ˢup.nita (Im Hopin 1987:168) I looked out the window, for I thought we had reached Taykwu. CF -na hata, -nun ka ha- (p. 726).
  2c. -ess.ci ~. ¶Ama ku chinkwu nun hak.kyo ey kass.ci siph.e yo (Im Hopin 1987:169) My friend seems to have gone to school.
  2d. -kwuna siph.ess.ta. ¶Kulen yeyppun ⁿyeca to iss.kwuna siph.ess.ta (Im Hopin 1987:169) It seemed there was indeed such a pretty girl!
  2e. -ess.ta siph.(ess.)ta. ¶Ca.yu lowun mom i toye nay cip ulo na-wā nwuwess.uni incey nun sal.ess.ta siph.(ess.)ta Since I got my freedom and returned home to rest now I feel alive again.
  2f. ? ila ~ : CM 1:265 example is rejected.

2g. **-ullila** (= -ul i 'la) siph.ess.ta. ¶**I elin i tul i cangcha wuli nala lul tewuk hwullyung han nala lo mantul i 'la siph.ess.ta** These children have given the feeling that in the future they will build our country into a finer nation.

2h. **-ulq kes man siph.ess.ta** (= -ulq tus man siph.ess.ta). ¶**Ches nal puthe īl i toynun phūm i aph ulo yele kaci cal toylq kes man siph.ess.ta** From the way things went from the first day, it seemed there would be no doubt that everything would go on well.

2i. **-ess.umyen siph.ta** (examples from Im Hopin 1987:167). ¶**Onul un hak.kyo ey kaci anh.ess.umyen siph.ta** I don't feel like going to school today, somehow. **Ttay lo n' ¹yehayng kass.umyen siph.ul ttay ka iss.e yo** Every now and then there are times when I wish I were gone away on a trip. **Icey pi ka ku man wass.umyen siph.ta** It would be nice if it just stopped raining. **Kulen nappunq īl un ppalli ic.e pelyess.umyen siph.e** It would be best to forget quickly such unpleasant happenings.

2j. **-ess.umyen siph.ess.ta**. ¶**Ilen ttay n' ku sālam ila to wā cwuess.umyen siph.ess.ta** I wish that he, at least, were present at such times. **Yunpo nun wuphyen pāytal-pu ka i cak.ep-cang ey olq ttay mata caki cip ey se hoksi phyēnci 'la to wass.umyen siph.un sayngkak i pulsswuk sos.a oluta ka to pāytal-pu ka ku tay lo cīna kako nan twī 'myen kongyen han sayngkak ul hayss.ta ko hwūhoy hakwu n' hayss.ta** Every time the mailman would come to the shop, Yunpo would feel a sudden surge of hope that there might be a letter from home, but after the mailman has passed by as usual, he would regret having felt such a vain hope.

'/**-sip.nikka**, 1. < isip.nikka. 2. < hasip.nikka. 3. = -usip.nikka.
-sip.nikke [DIAL] = -sup.nikka
'/**-sip.nita**, 1. < isip.nita. 2. < hasip.nita. 3. = -usip.nita.
-sip.nite [DIAL] = -sup.nita
-sipsako SEE -usipsako
'/**-sipsio**, 1. hasipsio. 2. = -usipsio! please do! ¶**Kasipsio** Please go. **Kyēysipsio** Please stay.
'/**-sipsita**, 1. < hasipsita. 2. = -usipsita.
-sipsosako SEE -usipsosako

'/**-siptikka**, 1. < isiptikka. 2. < hasiptikka. 3. = -usiptikka.
'/**-siptita**, 1. < isiptita. 2. < hasiptita. 3. = -usiptita.
sis-, prefix; HEAVY ↔ **says-**; [LIVELY]. vivid, deep, intense. ¶**sis-nwuleh.ta** is a deep yellow. **sis-he.yeh.ta** /sithe.yetha/ is extremely white.
'/**-sita**, 1. < isita. 2. < hasita. 3. = -usita.
'**s(i)·ta**, abbr < is(i)·ta (exists). CF '**ys(i)·ta**.
-siten = -situn
-·site·n i = -(ᵘ⁄o)·site·n i
'/**-sitey**, 1. < hasitey. 2. = -usitey. CF '**siley**.
'/**-siti**, 1. < isiti. 2. < hasiti. 3. = -usiti.
'/**-sitoy**, 1. < isitoy. 2. < hasitoy. 3. = -usitoy.
'/**-situla**, 1. < isitula. 5 2. < hasitula. 3. = -usitula.
'/**-situn**, 1. < isitun. 2. < hasitun. 3. = -usitun.
'**si·tun**, abbreviation < is(i)·tun (if it be). SEE -·a 'si·tun.
siye, pcl. alt after vowel of **isiye** (hon vocative).
-siyo → **-sio**; → **-si yo** (< -sey yo < -sie yo).
'**s.ke·n i ·Gwo**, abbr < is.ke·n i ·Gwo. SEE -ke·ni ·Gwo.
s ke·kuy, pcl + n / adv. to an esteemed person. SEE ke·kuy.
skey = **s key**, pcl. to an esteemed person. SEE **key**.
s ko·cang, quasi-pcl (pcl + n). up to the limit, all the way to. ¶**mozom sko·cang** (1447 Sek 6: 11a) to my heart's content = **mozom s ko·cang** (1447 Sek 24:28a; "mo-zoms-ko-cang") to his heart's content. ·**SYA-·LI KWONG-·YANG pu·the ·sye·i s ko·ca·ng on ZIN-THYEN-·HHOYNG ·ol nilu·si.n i ·'la** (1447 Sek 13:54a; "is-ko-·ca-·ngon") starting from the offering of food to Buddha's relics all of this is called the natural act of man with heaven.
s kungey, quasi-pcl < pcl + n / adv. to (a person esteemed), to where an esteemed person is. ¶**pwuthye·[G]wa ¨cywung·kwa s kungey ·PWO-SI ho·m ye** (1447 Sek 13:22b) gives alms to Buddha and the monks … . CF ·**oy kungey**.
~ **n'** (pcl). ¶**LYWONG oy kungey n' i·sywo.l i·'la NGWANG s kungey n' ¨ka.l i·'la i ¨twu kwo·t ay e·tuy ¨kye·si.l [i] 'ye·n ywo** (1459 Wel 7:26b) will one be where the dragon is, will one go to where the king is, of these two places where will one be?
·**skuy** = **s ·kuy**, quasi-pcl (< pcl + n/adv). to an esteemed person. ¶·**CCYENG-[·]PPEN NGWANG ·skuy two·la ·ka** (1447 Sek 6:6ab) went back to

King Śuddhodana and ... . ˬti-ˊnaˈkesin MWU-ˈLYANG ZYE-LOY ˈskuy ˬTTWOW-ˬLI poyˈhwota ˈka ˊtwo SI-LA ˈlol ˬhelˈm ye (1447 Sek 9:13a) though he learned the doctrine from Buddha he broke the commandments (śila). CYE-[ˊ]PPWULQ ˈskuy (1447 Sek 13:15a) to the immeasurable Buddhas who have passed by. ˊcukca ˈhi ˈku KUY-ˈPYELQ ˈul NGWANG ˈskuy alˈGwoyn ˊt ay (1447 Sek 24:16a) as he immediately informed the king of that message, ... [ˊ]THAY-[ˬ]CO skuy kyeyˈGwuzoˈWo.n i ˊla ([1447→]1562 Sek 3: 13a) he was defeated by the prince. woˊcik ˊPWU-ˬMWO s ˈskuy ˬSYWUN ˊhoˈya za ˬKA ˈhi ˊpse kunsim ˈul ˈphulˈl i ˊlesiˊta (1586 Sohak 4:9b) only when you obey your parents will you be freed of your worries [conflated spelling of ˊskuy]; ˊPWU-ˬMWO = ˬPPWU-ˬMWUW, ˬSYWUN = ˈSYWUN.

¶ ˬtywohon ˬil ˊhoˊsitan ˊt in ˊt ay n' ˊema ˬnim s ˈkuy ˊtule ˈka ˊi ˬtwon ˊol KWONG-ˈYANG ˊhoˊzoWwoˈl i (1459 Wel 23:65a) when you have done good work I will go in to your mother and provide her with this money. ˬPPWU-ˬMWUW ˬepˊkesi ˊza pwuthye s ˈkuy ˊkazoˊWa (1459 Wel 23:85b) only when my father and mother were no longer alive did I go to Buddha, and ... .

~ ˊGwa (pcl). ¶aˊpa ˬnim s ˈkuy ˊGwa aˊcoma ˬnim s ˈkuy ˊGwa (1447 Sek 6:1a) to father and to aunt.

~ ˊlwo (pcl). ¶ˊkilˊh ul ˊchoˊca pwuthye s ˈkuy ˊlwo ˈkanon ceˊk uy (1447 Sek 6:19a) when, seeking the way, he was going toward Buddha ... . MA-YA ˈskuy ˊlwo ˈHYANG ˊhoˊya ˬsolˈWosyaˊtoy (1447 Sek 23:29a) said to Maya as follows.

~ ˊlwo n' (particle + particle). ¶pwuˬthye y ˬHWA-ˈHWA S ˈPEP moyngˊkoˊlosyaˊm on ˊcokya s ˈkuy ˊlwo n' SAM-ˈMOY ˈLUK ˈul naˊthwoˊsya ... ˈSYA-ˈLI swoˊsa ˊnasiˊkwo ˬsaloˊm oy key ˊlwo n' ˬteleˈWun seˈkun ˊnay ˊlol koˊliWoˈm ye (1459 Wel 18:39ab) the way Buddha makes his cremation is to display the power of meditation (samadhi) to himself, and ... with the rising of the bones conceal from people the dirty rancid smell, and ... .

ˊsˈkwo, abbr < isˈkwo, ger < is(i)ˊta (exists). ¶yeˈle aˊcomi ˊicey paˊlo[l] s ˬkoˊz oy ˈkay ˊs[ˬ]kwo (1481 Twusi 8:38a) the aunts are on the tidelands by the seaside and .... [ˬ]nyey s ˊwuy-anˊh ay kwoˊc i cel-ˊlwo ˊphe ˊs.kwo ˊpwom naˊl ay say twolwo nolGeˊn i ˊla (1481 Twusi 8:34b) in the old garden the flowers are all abloom and on a day of spring the birds have flown back. SEE ˈysˈkwo.

ˊso = s_3, postmod. the fact that (nominalizer): ... ˊs ol, ... ˊs oy, ... ˊs i(...), ... ˊs ye.

-ˊs[o]-, bnd v. emotive; modulated form -ˊswo-. SEE -(ˊta)ˊs-ongi ˊˊta, -(ˊta)swoˊn i, -(ˊta)swoˊla; -ˊasoˊla (-ˊasuˊla), -ˊesoˊla (-ˊesuˊla); ? -(ˊno)son ˊta. CF *-ˊt[o]-, -ˊtwo-. NOTE: The original shape was just ˊs- (as in the modulated form); the vowel is epenthetic. LCT 1973:349 associates this morpheme with the postmodifier s '(it's a) fact (that ...)'.

-so, AUTH indicative [-o after a vowel, -^{s}o after ...ss- or ...ps-]. VAR -ui (-uy, -i); -uo. CF -swu.
1. indic assert. is/does (= -ta). ¶Chwupso It is cold. Mekso He eats. Ēps.^{s}o There isn't any. Mek.ess.^{s}o He ate. Chwupkeyss.^{s}o It's probably cold.
2. indic attent. is/does it? (= -ni?, -nun ya?). ¶Chwupso? Is it cold? Mwes ul mekso What does he eat?

-sˊo = -syo, abbr < -sio. ¶Ese oso (= osio) Come right in! Pap mekso (= mek.usyo = mek.usio) Eat! (CF 1954 Lukoff 163.)

-so < -swo, bnd pcl = ulo (s)se. mom ~ < ˊmwom-swo/-zwo in person. CF son-swu. (KEd suggests "? var < se" but the earlier forms make this unlikely.)

-soita [obs] = -sup.nita. SEE -tosoita, ilosoita.

-soksok, bnd adj-n (~ hata); after a consonant -usoksok; LIGHT ↔ -swukswuk. ...ish, slightly colored/tinged. SEE -(u)sulum.

ˊs ol, postmodifier + particle. SEE -ulqˊs ol.

-sola [DIAL] = -sila. CF swoˊla.

-soˊla SEE -ˊasoˊla, -ˊesoˊla

ˊsolwok (< ˊsoˊlwo k) SEE -ul(q)ˊsolwok

-so man, AUTH + pcl. is/does but [UNUSUAL].

son, noun, quasi-free noun, counter.
1. n (< ˊswon) hand, ... ; (< swon) guest, ...
2. quasi-free n. man, fellow, guy (less polite than sālam). CF ce/i/ku ~. ¶ku nom uy son = ku (nom uy) casik that so-and-so, that son of a bitch.
3. counter. a pair, a brace. ¶taykwu han ~ a brace of (dried) cod.

son < ˊs on, postmod + pcl [obs var] = sun

son, pcl (follows **-ta**), postmod (follows **-ulq**). [lit] (supposing) that. ¶ ~ **chitula to** even if we suppose that …. ~ **chica** let us suppose that …. **Mikwuk ey kanta son chitula to** even if we suppose he goes to America. **ney ka cal-mos hayss.ta son chitula to** even supposing you to be in the wrong. **Ku i ka ōymu cāngkwan i toynta son chitula to Hān-Il kwankyey lul wenman hi hāykyel halq swu ēps.ulq kes ita** Even supposing that he does become Foreign Minister, I don't think he can solve Korean-Japanese differences satisfactorily. **Sam-cha tāycen i iss.ta son chica** Let us suppose there is a third world war. CF **sēym chita, -ulq son;** *swon*. NOTE: Pause, if any, is after **son**.

˙*s on*, postmodifier + particle. SEE *-ulq* ˙*s on*.

son ˙*coy*, adverb. 1. rather, preferably (= **ohilye**).
2. still, yet (= **acik to**).
?3. soon, immediately (= **inay**).

-songi, suffix. person. ¶**ay** ~ a novice, a young/ new person. ¶ **(p)palka-songi / (p)pelke-swungi, (p)palka-swungi** a naked body. CF **-soy**.

˙*so-ngi* ˙˙*ta* = ˙*s-ongi* ˙˙*ta*, emotive polite + cop indic assert. SEE *(-* ˙*ta)* ~ ; ˙*s[o]-* = ˙*s-* (bnd v).

son-i, cpd postnoun (n + n 'hand person').
1. a person with a hand such that …. ¶**comak** ~ a person with a withered hand. ¹**yuk** ~ a person with six fingers on a hand. CF **pal-i, nwun-i, phal-i**. The immediate constituents of the compounds should be (noun + **son**) + **i**, but they are often treated as if noun + (**son** + **i**).
2. a thing from a hand that is …. ¶**coli-pok** ~ a piece of hackwork.

-son ˙*ta*, emotive modifier + postmod. ¶*mu* ˙*sum* PANG-˙*PPYEN* ˙*ul pu* ˙*the* SAM-MA-˙TI ˙*yey* ˙*tuson* ˙*ta* (1462 ¹Nung 5:31b) what device does one rely on to enter samādhi [a trance-like state of unperturbable meditation]? SEE *-*˙*noson* ˙*ta*.

-˙*sop-* < -˙*zop-* = *-zoW-* < *-so* ˙*po-* or *-oso* ˙*po-*, deferential bound aux. After stems that end with basic *s, z, sk, h, lh, p, W, ph, ps, lp = lW, k, lk*. SEE -˙*zop-*.

-sose, [lit] = **-sio** please do. SEE **-usose**.

soswu, postn. plus some (extra), odd, a bit over. ¶**twū mal** ~ two mal and a bit over. **nēk nyang** ~ four nyang plus. **tases tal** ~ five months and some odd days. (Limited to those three counters?) [< sōswu < ˙˙SSYWOW-˙SWU 'a small number, a minority']

-so tul, AUTH indic assertive + particle

˙*s oy*, postmodifier + particle. SEE *-ulq* ˙*s oy*.

soy, noun. 1. metal; iron.
2. a compass (= **cinam-chim**).
3. [colloq] a key (= **yēlq soy**).
4. [colloq] a lock (= **camulq soy**).
5. a hinge or a flap (= leaf) of a hinge (CF swu ~, am ~).
6. = **nos soy** (brass)

soy, adnoun. a small one. ¶ ~ **kkweng-al** small pheasant egg(s). ~ **kolay** a small whale, a gray whale. ~ **muluph** Achyranthes japonica. ~ **phul** Andropogon brevifolius, sedge. ~ **pilum** purslane. ~ **tolphi** small Deccan grass. ~ **pyelwukci** a small flea. ~ **ttaktakwuli** pigmy woodpecker. Perhaps ~ **say** (a kingfisher). [? < **sō** < ˙˙*SYWOW* 'small' + **uy** < ˙*oy* pcl]

sōy < ˙˙*sywoy* (abbr < *sywo* ˙*oy*), adnoun. of cattle. ¶ ~ **koki** beef. ~ **phali** cattle flies. ˙˙*sywoy stwong* (1518 Sohak-cho 9:24b) ox dung.

-soy, suffix, postn. CF **-po; -tol, -tong(i), -huy; -songi**.
1. (informal names for boys). ¶**Tolq-soy** (?'Rock-metal'). **Pangwulq-soy** (?'Bell-metal').
2. guy, fellow, person. **allang-soy** a flatterer, a toady. ¶**kwutwu-soy** a miser, a tightwad [< **kwut-** stiff + **-wu** der adv]. **tallang-/telleng-soy** a flighty person, a flit, a fidget. **thēyng-soy** (= **thēyng-po**) a hollow shell of a person; an empty-headed person.
3. **molu-soy** (the principle of) playing dumb.

-soyta = **-soita** = **-sup.nita**

so ˙*zi* = **sai**, noun. the space / interval between; the time / interval while. ¶ ˙˙*twu* ˙*nolkay s so* ˙*zi* (1459 Wel 1:14b) between the two wings. ˙*mwom sso* ˙*zi* ˙*yey* (1462 ¹Nung 1:55a) between bodies. ˙˙*twu ha* ˙*nol s so* ˙*zi* ˙*yey* ˙*ka* ˙*sya* (1447 Sek 6:45b) goes between the two heavens. *ha* ˙*nol* ˙*khwa* ˙*sta* ˙*khwas* [= *ha* ˙*nolh* ˙*kwa* ˙*stah* ˙*kwa s*] *so* ˙*zi* ˙*yey* (1481 Twusi 8:47b, 21:5b; 1482 Kum-sam 3:38b) between heaven and earth. *kozol* ˙*Gwa kyezul* ˙*Gwa s so* ˙*zi* (1481 Twusi 8:59a) between autumn and winter. SEE *-ulq so* ˙*zi* ˙*yey*.

˙˙*spwun* (< … *s* ˙˙*pwun*), postn, postmod, pcl. only, just (> **ppun**). ¶ ˙*TTYEP* ˙*ul* ˙˙*es* ˙*tyey* ˙˙*sey[h]* ˙˙*spwun nil* ˙*Ge* ˙*n ywo* (1447 Sek 19:13a) why were only three folds lifted? *KA-* ˙*SYEP-* ˙*i* ˙˙*spwun tut* ˙*key* ˙*ho* ˙*si.n i* ˙*la* (1447 Sek 23:42a) he let them hear only Kāśyapa. ˙˙*ney*

¨em-˙ni ¨spwun kuce ¨kyesite˙la (1447 Sek 23:51a) he remained with just four molar teeth. ¨ca˙nay ¨spwun ˙e˙ti-ti˙Wi ˙nom kolo˙chywo˙m ol a˙ni hol ˙ss oy (1447 Sek 24:40a) he was good just privately but he did no teaching of it to others, so ... . hon ¨nath thelek ¨spwu˙n ul (1449 Kok 92) just a single hair. ku kes ¨spwun (1466 Kup 2:63a) that alone. hon-kas elkwul ˙Gwa kuli.m ey ¨spwu.n i˙lwoswo˙n i (1481 Twusi 16:41a) it was just in the face and the image only [that the rejuvenation worked].
-ul ~. ¶¨SYWOW-SSING ˙ey s ¨salo˙m i ce ˙y ˙mwom tas˙kol ¨spwun ho˙kwo ˙nom ˙CYEY-˙TTWO ¨mwot hol ˙ss oy (1447 Sek 13:36a) a person in hīnayāna just cultivates himself and does not save others, so ... . ˙mwom wu˙h uy n' ˙wo.s ol [KKWUW] ho˙kwo ˙poy lol pulu˙key hol ¨spwu˙n ilwo˙ta (1481 Twusi 8:27b) I just buy clothes for their bodies and see to it that their bellies are full.
-ul ~ ˙tyeng. only ... but. ¶CYE-THYEN ˙ul a˙ni ¨ta nilul ¨spwun ˙tyeng ˙SSILQ ˙ey n' ¨ta ˙wa ˙y˙ste.n i ˙'la (1447 Sek 13:7a) I will not say [the names of] all the heavens, but they all were present [among the angels]. ˙SOYK-˙QWUN ˙i ¨ep˙sul ¨spwun ˙tyeng ¨SSYWUW-¨SYANG HHOYNG-˙SIK ˙on is.no˙n i ˙'la (1459 Wel 1:37b) they lack only the skandha of rūpa (= the attribute of form) but they have the four immaterial skandhas (feeling, ideation, reaction, consciousness). ˙MYELQ-˙TTWO ˙hosil ¨spwun ˙tyeng (1447 Sek 23:52b, 53a) only achieves nirvāṇa, but ... .
-ss-, past. SEE -ess-.
ssa hata, postmod adj-n insep [NK spells sa (= q sa ···)]. it seems (to be). SEE kulel ~. CM 2:63 has examples with olq ~ and ttatus halq ~. KEd reported celel ~, ettel ~, and ilel ~, but these are unconfirmed and may be wrong, as is the assignment "vni". [? < -q sang < ˙SYANG appearance, CF sang siph.ta; ? < -q sa < ¨SSO resemble]
ssah.ta, 1. vt. piles/heaps/stacks it up; amasses, accumulates, stores up; builds, puts up.
2. aux v insep. SEE -e ssah.ta.
(-)ssa-tayki bnd cpd n (< ?). ¶kwi ~ the cheek (near the ear). myēn ~ the face (= nach).
sse < ˙pse, inf < ssuta < ˙psu˙ta. 1. uses; ... .
2. emphasizes the particle ulo. SEE ulo sse.

-(s)sek, suf (makes impressionistic adv). ¶tepsek suddenly < tempi- rush. tulssek tulssek bouncing up and down, fidgeting < tu-l- lift up. CF -(s)swuk.
-sseng SEE -q seng
-ss.ess.keyss.ta, past-past fut indic assertive.
-ss.ess.ta, past-past indic assertive.
ssi₁, postn < *˙psi, der n < ssuta < ˙psu˙ta. the use (state, conditions, quality, mode) of. ¶kel.um ~ a manner of walking, a gait, a walk. māl ~ a mode of expression, a way of speaking, use of words; accent. maum ~ a turn/kind of mind, a sort of person. nal ~ weather (conditions). nwun ~ the force of one's eyes, the power of one's stare. pal ~ familiarity to one's feet; skill with one's feet. palam ~ the state/favorableness of the wind, wind conditions. ALSO: kul-ssi, maypsi [< may-pssi], som-ssi [< son-pssi]. CF mopsi.
ssi₂, bnd n (< ssi₁). a part of speech. ¶ilum ~, im-~ a noun (= myengsa). wumcik-~, wum- ~ a verb (= tōngsa). etteh-~, et-~ an adjective (= hyengyong-sa). etten ~, en-~ an adnoun, a determiner (= kwanhyeng-sa). ecci ~, ec- ~ an adverb (= pūsa). is-~ a conjunction, a connective (= cepsok-sa). nukkim ~, nuk-~ an interjection (= kāmthan-sa). tho ~ a particle (= cōsa). ~ kkuth an (inflectional) ending, a verb ending (= ēmi). īmca ~ indeclinables (other than particles), nouns (= cheyen). phul.i ~ inflected words [verbs, adjectives, copula] (= yōngen), kkwumim ~ a modifier, a modifying word (= kwansa). SYN phūmsa. See Part I, §3.2.
ssi₃ < ?si (1576) < ¨SSI (1459 Wel 2:12b), postnoun.
1. Mr, Mrs, Miss. (a title of courtesy added to either surname or personal name; less formal than sensayng). ¶Pak ~ Mr (Mrs, Miss) Pak. Kim Kyengsik ~ Mr Kim Kyengsik.
2. a family, a clan, a lineage. ¶Antong Kim ~ the Kims of Antong.
ssik < ˙sik < ˙SIK, particle. each, respectively, apiece (distributive). ¶hana(k) ssik one by one. twūl ssik twūl ssik (1936 Roth 253) by twos. cokum ssik little by little. ai tul eykey payk wen ssik cwuta gives the children 100 wen each. nal mata yetel[p]q sikan ssik īl hata works eight hours every day. Nwukwu 'tun ci

ttok kath.i yelq kay ssik kacye la You each get exactly ten. **Meych pun ssik yēnsel ul hasip.nikka** How many minutes (1) do you each speak, or (2) do you speak each time, or (3) do you take for each speech? **Sālam i twūl ssik sēys ssik onta** People come by twos and threes. **Phyēnci lul halwu ey twū pen ssik pāytal hanta** Mail is delivered twice a day. **I kes tul un elma ssik ip.nikka** How much are these apiece? CF **kkol,** `**kwom**. NOTE: The reference of the distributive may be to the subject, the object, the frequency, or other semantic constituents of the sentence, and it is often ambiguous.

ssik chelem, particle + particle. ¶**Twū salam ssik chelem nēy salam ssik to halq swu iss.ta** We can do / play it with four people (each) just as we do with two.

ssik cocha, pcl + pcl. ¶**Han-kkepen ey twū salam ssik cocha an tul.ye ponaynun tey sēy salam ssik ina tul.ye ponaykeyss.nun ya** They are not even letting people in by twos; what makes you think they'll let them in by threes?!

ssik eykey, pcl + pcl. ¶**Sēy salam ssik eykey han kay ssik nona cwue la** Give one to every three people.

ssik hanthey, pcl + pcl = **ssik eykey**

ssik i, pcl + pcl. each one (respectively, apiece) [as subject]. ¶**Pihayng-ki nēy tay ssik i han phyentay ka toye se motwu yelq-twu phyentay ka nal.e kass.ta** All told twelve squadrons of four planes each flew.

ssik ila to, pcl + copula var inf + pcl. ¶**Han-kkepen ey twū salam ssik ila to cōh.sup.nita** Two people at a time is all right.

ssik ina, pcl + copula advers. about ··· apiece, approximately ··· each (respectively). ¶**Meych sikan ssik ina chayk ul ilk.usip.nikka** About how many hours (1) do each of you read, or (2) do you read each time, or (3) do you read each book? **I kwutwu tul un han khyelley ey elma ssik ina hap.nikka** About how much does a pair of these shoes cost?

ssik ina-ma, pcl + cop extended advers. ¶**Han salam ey han kay ssik ina-ma kolwu nona cwutolok hay la** Divide them up equally so that each one at least gets one (however small).

ssik in tul, pcl + cop mod + postmod. ¶**Han uyca ey nēy salam ssik in tul mōs anc.ul lī ka iss.keyss.^{s}o?** Is there any reason why even four people can't sit on each chair?

ssik iya, pcl + pcl. ¶**Han uyca ey nēy salam ssik iya mōs anc.keyss.^{s}o?** Can't four people, at least, sit on each chair? **Han salam ssik iya tul.e ka to kwaynchanh.keyss.ci** I guess it will be all right if you go in one at a time.

ssik khenyeng, pcl + pcl. ¶**Han uyca ey nēy salam ssik khenyeng sēy salam ssik to mōs anc.keyss.^{s}o** Three people can't sit on each chair, much less four.

ssik kkaci, pcl + pcl. ¶**Han salam i twū kay ssik kkaci kaciko kal phil.yo ka iss.ulq ka?** Is there any need for each one to take two?

~ **'la to**. ¶**I man hamyen payk salam ssik kkaci 'la to han-kkepen ey meyk.ilq swu iss.keyss.ta** With this much we'll be able to feed as many as a hundred people at a time.

~ **nun**. ¶**Han uyca ey nēy salam ssik kkaci nun anc.ulq swu iss.ta** Up to four people can sit on each chair.

ssik kwa, pcl + pcl. ¶**Ai tul un motwu yenphil han calwu ssik kwa kongchayk han kwēn ssik ul pat.ess.ta** The children each received a pencil and a notebook.

ssik mace, pcl + pcl. ¶**Han-kkepen ey twū salam ssik mace** (but **ssik cocha** is better) **an tul.ye ponaynun tey sēy salam ssik ina tul.ye ponaykeyss.nun ya** They are not even letting people in by twos; what makes you think they'll let them in by threes?!

ssik pota, pcl + pcl. ¶**Han salam ssik pota twū salam ssik kanun key naulq key 'ta** It would be better to go by twos (in pairs) rather than one at a time.

ssik puthe, pcl + pcl. ¶**Wusen han salam ssik puthe sīcak hapsita** Let's start off taking you one at a time.

ssik to, pcl + pcl. ¶**Twū salam ssik chelem nēy salam ssik to halq swu iss.ta** We can do / play it with four people (each) just as we do with two. **Han uyca ey nēy salam ssik khenyeng sēy salam ssik to mōs anc.keyss.^{s}o** Three people can't sit on each chair, much less four.

ssik ul, pcl + pcl. each (respectively, apiece) [as direct object]. ¶**kak.kak sakwa hana ssik ul sata** each buys one apple apiece. **Ai mata hana ssik ul cwue la** Give one apiece to each child (or: each child is to give one apiece). **Ai tul un motwu kongchayk han kwēn ssik kwa yenphil han calwu ssik ul pat.ess.ta** The children each received a notebook and a pencil. **Ku ttay na nun co'.yong han pam uy meych sikan ssik ul ku ¹yeypay-tang ey ka se myengsang ulo ponaynun kes i supkwan i toye iss.ess.ta** At that time I got in the habit of spending a few hours every quiet evening meditating in the church.

ssik ulo, particle + particle. as (with, etc.) each, respectively. ¶**Cek.kwun un sēys ssik ulo ccak ul cie sīnay lul swunsi hayss.ta** Enemy troops patrolled the streets in threes.

ssik un, pcl + pcl. ¶**Kongchayk twū kwēn ssik un nona cwuess.una yenphil un acik an nona cwuess.ta** I divided the notebooks up two apiece, but I haven't given out the pencils yet.

ssik un khenyeng, pcl + pcl + pcl. ¶**Sēy kay ssik un khenyeng twū kay ssik to an tul.e kakeyss.ta** There won't be room to get two apiece in, much less three!

ssik uy, pcl + pcl [artificial, English translation style]. ¶**Ai tul un tases calwu ssik uy yenphil kwa twū kwēn ssik uy kongchayk ul pat.ess.ta** The children received pencils, five each, and notebooks, two each.

-ss.keyss.ta, past-future indic assertive
... ¨ssop- < ...s-¨zop-, ...z-¨zop-, ...h-¨zop-.
...s¨sop- < ...s-¨zop-, ...z-¨zop-, ...h-¨zop-; <
...sk-¨zop-.

-ss.ta, past indic assertive; past transferentive

-ss.tun, past retrospective modifier

-sswuk, suffix; spelling variant -swuk.
 1. bound adj-n (~ **hata**). very. ¶**malsswuk** clean, comely (< **malk-**). **melsswuk** long and stringy, skinny and frail (< var of **mulk-**).
 2. suffix (makes impressionistic adverbs). ¶**pulsswuk** protruding abruptly < adj **pulu-** swollen. **calsswuk calsswuk / celsswuk celsswuk** limping (< **cēlta** limps); pinched in.

'ssye, 1. SEE -ᵉ⁄ₐ'ssye (please). CF -u'sywo'sye.
 2. SEE -(ᵁ⁄ₒ)l'ssye = -(ᵁ⁄ₒ)lq'sye.

's'ta = 's(i)'ta, abbreviation < is(i)'ta (exists). CF 'ys'ta.

's.tala = 's(i)tala, abbr < is(i)'tala. SEE 'ho.ya 's.tala.

's'ten = 's(i)'ten, abbr < is(i)'ten, vi retr mod. SEE e'tuy 's'ten, e'tuy ''sten. VAR ''ston, ''stun. CF 'ys'ten.

''ston(···), 's'ton(···), 1. abbr pcl. SEE 'i'ston, 'is'ton. 2. var < 's'ten. SEE e'tuy ''ston.

''stun, var < ''sten. SEE e'tuy ''sten.

'such, n. interval (= **sai**). ¶*ku'chun 'su.ch i ''epke'nul* (1482 Nam 1:13b) without a break. *ku'chul s 'sus ''ep.su'n i* (1459 Wel 7:58a) is without cessation.

-sul, suf (makes impressionistic adv). ¶**kopsul kopsul hata** is frizzly, curly < adj **kop-** bent.

sulel, abbr = **sulewul**, prosp mod < **sulepta**

sulem, abbr = **sulewum**, subst < **sulepta**

sulen, abbr = **sulewun**, mod < **sulepta**

sulepta, postnom adj insep -W-. is, is like, gives the impression of (being), seems, suggests, is suggestive of. DER ADV **suley, suli**. SYN [obs] **opta, hopta**. CF **hata, mac.ta, toyta, lopta, tapta, chita, kwuc.ta**.

¶**cap** ~ is wanton, dissolute. **comq** ~ is petty. **pok** ~ is prosperous-looking. **pyēn** ~ is strange, odd. **tham** ~ is charming.

¶**āmsang** ~ is jealous. **angkhum** ~ is excessive (in greedy cunning). **calang** ~ is proud. **chamtam** ~ is pitiful, is wretched. **changphi** ~ is shameful / ashamed. **chengsung** ~ (= **chengsung mac.ta**) is woebegone. **chik- /chak-sal** ~ is stingy, mean. **hāyngpok** ~ is happy. **iksal** ~ is droll, humorous. **ippu-cang** ~ (**yeppu-cang** ~) is lovely. **īsang** ~ is strange, odd. **kansa** ~ is wicked, cunning. **kanyen** ~ is shabby. **kapcak** ~ is sudden. **kepuk(-sal)** ~ is (quite) uncomfortable. **keykel** ~ is greedy. **keykem/kaykam** ~ is voracious. **kukseng** ~ is impetuous. **mayceng / muceng** ~ is callous. **nungcheng** ~ is sly, cunning, insidious. **pokseng** ~ is prosperous-looking, is sleek. **polthong / pulthwung** ~ is rough-mannered, blunt; is bumpy, bulgy. **pōpay** ~ is precious, valuable. **pu-ca.yen** ~ is artificial. **pucok** ~ is insufficient, wanting. **pyēntek** ~ is capricious. **salang** ~ is lovely. **sayngkup** ~ is abrupt. **saysal / sisel** ~ is flippant, shallow. **saysam** ~ is abrupt; is deliberate. **sinpi** ~ is mysterious. **siwen** ~ is refreshing. **sswuk** ~ is unseemly, inappropriate. **swusen** ~ is turbulent, noisy. **swūta** ~ is talkative. **taceng** ~ is compassionate. **tōsep** ~ is capricious, fickle. **twisulek** ~ is jumpy, restless, edgy. **wāngcheng** ~ is widely disparate. **yātan** ~ (a color) is loud, garish.

suley < **sule-i**, der adv < **sulepta**. like, as. ¶**kapcak** ~ sudden-like. **kongyen** ~ in vain, fruitlessly, to no avail. VAR **suli, -sali**.

suli = **suley**, der adv < **sulepta**. like, as.

kapcak ~ sudden-like.
-sulum, bnd adj-n (~ **hata**); after a consonant **-usulum**. [? < **sulem** < **sulepta**].
  1. ···ish, slightly colored / tinged. ¶**nwulu-**~ yellowish. **phulu-**~ bluish. SYN **-capcap** / **-cepcep, -chikchik, -cokcok** / **-cwukcwuk, -chwungchwung, -soksok**/**-swukswuk, -taytay**/ **-teytey, -tayngtayng**/**-teyngteyng, -thoythoy**/ **-thwithwi**.
  2. ···ish, slightly characterized by. ¶**kanu-**~ thinnish. **twungku-**~ roundish. **(k)kopu-** / **(k)kwupu-**~ somewhat bent.
  ABBR **-lum, -sum**. SYN **-ulum**. CF **-upsulum**.
-sum, bnd adj-n (~ **hata**), abbr < **-sulum**. ···ish, slightly characterized by. SYN **-lum**.
sun, postmod [obs] the unlikely fact that ... [as topic = **kes un**]. SEE **-ulq sun**. VAR **-ulq son**. [< **s** + **un** pcl]
-supci man, FORMAL suspective + pcl [Seoul colloq] = **-ci man**. Used by an older person to a younger person of higher status.
-supci yo, -supc' (y)o, FORMAL CASUAL POLITE [Seoul colloq] = **-ci yo**. Used by an older person to a younger person of higher status; sarcastic or ridiculing when used to an equal or an inferior (CF 1954 Lukoff 129). ¶**I käy nun āmu ke 'na cal meksupci yo** This dog eats anything at all. **Cey ka al.e popci yo** I will find out. **Iss.ˢupci yo** We have some. **Ēps.ˢupci yo** We haven't any. **Pwass.ˢupci yo** I saw it. **Pokeyss.ˢupci yo** I will look at it.
-sup.naykka = **-sup.neykka** (→ **-sup.nikka**)
-sup.nayta = **-sup.neyta** (→ **-sup.nita**)
-sup-ney/**-ni**/**-nuy** [DIAL, OLD-FASHIONED] = **-e yo**
-sup.neykka [DIAL] = **-sup.nikka**
-sup.neyta [DIAL] = **-sup.nita**
-sup.nikka, FORMAL indic attentive. is / does it? (= **-ni?, -nun ya?**). ¶**Chwupsup.nikka?** Is it cold? **Mues ul meksup.nikka** What will he eat? [After a vowel, **-p.nikka**; after ···ss- or ···ps-, -ˢ**up.nikka**.]
  ~ **tul**. ¶**Tā osyess.ˢup.nikka tul?** Are you all here? / Is everybody here? **Kongpu lul kkway hap.nikka tul?** Are they fairly good at their studies?
  ~ **yo** [DIAL, uneducated] = ~
-sup.ninta = **-sup.nunta**
-sup.nita, FORMAL indic assertive. is / does (= **-ta**). **Chwupsup.nita** It is cold. **Anc.sup.nita** He sits down. [After a vowel, **-p.nita**; after

...ss- or ···ps-, -ˢ**up.nita**.]
  ~ **man** is / does but (= **-ci man**).
  ~ **tul**. ¶**Acwu Yenge lul cal hasip.nita tul** You people speak English very well.
  ~ **yo** [DIAL, uneducated] = ~. (According to Song Sekcwung 1967 this is used in formal speech to younger people.)
-sup.nuynta [DIAL, OLD-FASHIONED] = **-so** / **-o** statement or question, AUTH style.
-supsayta, -supseyta [DIAL] = **-upsita**
-supsita [DIAL] = **-upsita**
-supsita tul, FORMAL subj assertive + pcl. ¶**Ese īl ul sīcak hasipsita tul** Let's get the job started.
-supteyta [DIAL] = **-suptita**. ¶**I kil i nemu hēm hako kkatalawe** [= **kkatalowᵉ/a**] **se taninun i ka cēksupteyta** (1936 Roth 432) This road is so dangerous and steep that there are few who travel it (I have noticed).
-suptikka, FORMAL retr attentive. has it been observed that ··· ?, is it known that ··· ?, did you hear (have you been told) that ··· ?, did you notice that ··· ?, have you found that ··· ? (CF **-ti**.) ¶**Ku sikyey ka cal kanta ko haptikka** Did they say that the watch runs all right? **I sikyey kath.un kes tto iss.ˢuptikka** Did you notice whether they have any more watches like this?
  ~ **yo** [DIAL, uneducated] = ~. [After a vowel, **-ptikka**; after ···ss- or ···ps-, -ˢ**uptikka**.]
-suptinta [DIAL, OLD-FASHIONED] = **-suptita**
-suptita, FORMAL retr assertive. it has been observed that ··· ; it is known that ··· ; as we all (or I) know ··· ; I hear (have been told) that ··· ; I noticed that ··· ; I've discovered (found out) that ··· (CF **-tey, -tule, iley**). ¶**Tangsin sikyey nun swusen hanun tey han han tal kellinta ko haptita** They said your watch would take about a month to repair. **Ku sikyey nun nemu hel.e se mōs ssukeyss.ˢuptita** That watch (I recall) is too old to be any good. [After a vowel, **-ptita**; after ···ss- or ···ps-, -ˢ**uptita**.]
-suptita yo [DIAL, uneducated] = **-suptita**.
suta < **seta** (as usually spelled) < ˙**sye˙ta**; inf **se** < ˙**sye**. stands (up); comes to a standstill, stops; ... . SEE **na-suta**.
(-)˙swo-, modulated emotive = bnd v -˙**s[o]-** (or -˙**s-**) + modulator **-wo-**.
(-)swo˙la, modulated emotive indic assert. SEE -˙**kwa** ~ ; -˙**nwoswo˙la**; -˙**taswo˙la**. ¶**˙na y nan** "HHWUW ˙**lwo** CHIN-SIM **hon cek** ¨**ep.swo˙la** (1459 Wel 21:216a) since my birth I have not

once been angry. *[˙HHWAN-NAN]* ¨*ha.m ay [PPYEN-QAN]* ˙*hi* ¨*sati* ¨*mwot* ˙*hoswo˙la* (1481 Twusi 8:43a) with so many misfortunes we cannot live at ease.

(-)swon, modulated emotive mod. *(amwoli ...)-ta swon*, *-ki lwo swon*; "spoken for" *(ho)-ten ci*, *(ho.y)-en ci* 'however much' (1894 Gale 69). SEE -˙*taswo˙n i*, *i˙lwoswo˙n i*; -*twoswo˙n i*, -*usi˙nwoswo˙n i*; -*u˙l i* ˙*'lwoswo˙n i*, -*u˙l i 'lwoswo˙n ye*.

-˙*swo-ngi* ˙*'ta*, 1. modulated emotive polite + cop indicative assertive. SEE -*two˙swo-ngi* ˙*'ta*, ˙*i˙lwo˙swo-ngi* ˙*'ta*; -(*u˙si)˙nwo˙swo-ngi* ˙*'ta*; -*u˙l i* ˙*'lwo˙swo-ngi* ˙*'ta*.

2. -*ul˙swongi˙ta* = -*ulq˙s ˙[y]wo-ngi* ˙*'ta*.

¨**swon-˙toy** (< *i˙sywon˙t oy* 'to the place where one is'), pseudo-pcl (bnd n usually preceded by a genitive). to (a person). ¶ *PPA-LA-MWON* ˙*i ˙kul˙Gwal˙ho˙ya SYWU-˙TTALQ˙oy* ¨*swon-˙toy pwo˙nayya˙nol* (1447 Sek 6:15b) the brahman wrote a letter and sent it to Sudatta, whereupon ... . *MWU-˙HHAK* ¨*swon-˙toy poy˙hwonon* ¨*sa˙lo.m i˙la* (1447 Sek 13:3a) is a person who is studying to become an arhat (who has cast off illusion and is beyond study). *QA-SYA-˙SYEY NGWANG k* ¨*swon-˙toy ka˙n i* (1447 Sek 24:6a) went to King Ajātaśatru. *SA-MWON˙uy* ¨*swon-˙toy* ¨*salom˙pulye nilun˙t ay* (1447 Sek 24:22a) as he had someone tell the śramaṇas, ... *ku* ¨*salo˙m oy* ¨*swon-˙toy˙wo˙sya* (1459 Wel 8:55b) came to that person. *tik.wel ila˙sye mwo[˙]tol* ¨*salom˙oy˙swon-toy al˙Gwoy˙la* (1518 ¹Ye-yak 37b [= p.74]) let him who is the commissioner of traditional Korean remedies inform those who gather.

-*swo˙wo-* < -*so[W]˙wo-*, modulated deferential emotive. ¶ ¨*twopswo˙wa* (1463 Pep 2:175a) = ¨*twopso[W]˙wa*. ¨*kipswo˙wo.m ol* (1481 Twusi 20:42b) = ¨*kipso[W]˙wo˙m ol*.

swu < ¨*SSYWUW*, noun.
1. long life, longevity. ¶ "*swu*"-*q ca lul swū noh.un os kolum* a coat-tie embroidered with the Chinese character for "long life".
2. (= *nai*) one's age. ¶*Swu ka meych ina toysinun ci yo* May I know your age?
3. one's (natural) life span. ¶*Ku nun swu ka ccalp.ess.ta* He had a short life. CF *swumyeng*.
4. *vni* ~ *hata* enjoys a long life, lives long. ¶*Ku ēlun un swu hasinta* He is enjoying a ripe old age. ⁿ*Yeca nun namca pota swu hanta* Women outlive men.

swu < ¨*SYWUW*, bnd noun, postmodifier, noun.
1. bound noun = son hand.
2. postmodifier. a way, a means, a remedy, a resource, help; CF *swutan*. ¶*hanun* ~ *ēps.i* helplessly, reluctantly. *halq* ~ *pakk ey ēps.ta* cannot help doing, has no choice but to do. *Mānh.ulq* ~ *pakk ey ēps.ta* There are bound to be a lot of them. *Hanun swu ēps.ta* There is no way out. (Nothing can be done.) *Na nun halq swu ēps.i wus.ess.ta* I could not help laughing. *halq swu helq swu ēps.nun sālam* a hopeless and helpless / hapless person.
3. postmod. an occasion, a possible occasion, a possibility, a likelihood; CF *īl*. ¶*Kulelq swu iss.ta (ēps.ta)* It may (cannot possibly) be so; Such things do (don't) happen. *Ilun pom ey seli ka naylilq swu to iss.ta* There is the possibility of frost in early spring.
4. postmodifier. ability, capability; CF *cwul*. ¶*halq swu iss.ta / ēps.ta* is able / unable to do, can/cannot do. *halq swu iss.nun hān* to the best of one's ability. *sānswul ul kaluchilq swu iss.nun sālam* a person capable of teaching arithmetic. *Ku si nun yele kaci lo hāysek halq swu iss.ta* The poem is susceptible to several interpretations. ¹*Nayil poylq swu iss.*ˢ*up.nikka* Can I see you tomorrow?
5. n. a move (in chess); a trick; ingenuity, resourcefulness. ¶*myō han swu lul noh.ta* makes a fine move (in chess). *pikimq swu a* tying move; a draw, a dead heat. *ikimq swu a* winning move. *wiq swu a* better player. *alayq swu a* poor player. *swu kiph.un sālam* a person of ingenuity, a resourceful man. *han swu ey cita* is beaten in one move. *Ku nun swu ka noph.ta* He is a better man at chess than I am. *Sēy swu ey ne lul ikilq swu iss.ta* I can beat you in three moves.

swū < ¨*SYWUW*, n. embroidery. ¶ ~ *noh.ta* embroiders. *pītan ey molan kkoch ul swū noh.ta* embroiders a peony on silk.

swū < ˙*SWU*, noun, numeral.
1. n. (= *wūnswu*) luck, fortune. ¶ ~ *ka cōh.ta (napputa)* has good (bad) fortune. ~ *ka nata* runs into a piece of good luck, hits the jackpot.
2. n. (= *swūhyo*) number, a figure. ¶ ~ *mānh.un sālam tul* a large number of people. ~ *ēps.nun pyēl tul* innumerable stars. *wūq-swu* an even number. *ki-swu*₁ an odd number. *ki-swu*₂ a cardinal number. *sē-swu* an ordinal

number. **uyca/kyōsil/haksayng uy swū** the number of chairs/classrooms/students. **Yo say sil.ep-ca uy swū ka tāytan hi cwul.ess.ta** The number of unemployed has fallen drastically.

3. (quasi-)num, adn. a few, several, a number (of). ¶ ~ **hak.kyo** a number of schools. ~ **pyengceng** a number of soldiers. ~ **hōykyey-nyen** several fiscal years.

4. (-q swū) postn, postcounter. the number of ··· . ¶**sālamq/myengq** ~ the number of people. **kwēnq** ~ the number of books. **hayq/talq/cwukanq** ~ the number of years/months/weeks. **punq/choq** ~ **lul ttacinta** counts (takes into account) the number of minutes/seconds.

swu < ˝*SYWUW*, counter. a poem, a piece, a selection. ¶**si han** ~ **lul ulph.ta** composes a poem, recites a poem.

swu < ˙*swuh*, adn, bnd n. [Basic shape in older compounds usually **swuh**.] ANT **am** < ˙*amh*.

1. male. ¶ ~ **khes** < **swuh kes** a male. ~ **khāy** < **swuh kāy** a male dog. ~ **khewi** < **swuh kewi** a gander. ~ **kho.yangi/khwāyngi** < **swuh ko.yangi/kwāyngi** a tomcat. ~ **khōm** < **swuh kōm** a male bear. ~ **thalk** < **swuh talk** a rooster, a cock. ~ **thot** < **swuh tot** = ~ **tho.yaci/thwāyci** < **swuh to.yaci/twāyci** a hog. ~ **phitwulki** < **swuh pitwulki** a he-dove. ~ **phēm** < **swuh pēm** a male tiger. ~ **phyengali** < **swuh pyengali** a rooster chick. ~ **khweng** < **swuh [k]kweng** a pheasant cock. ~ **saton** the father of one's son-in-law. ~ **nakwi** a jackass.

2. convex, external, protruding. ¶ ~ **chicil** external hemorrhoids. ~ **khiwa** < **swuh kiwa** a convex tile. ~ **tanchwu** (NOT /th/!) a snap, a button. ~ **thōlccekwi** < **swuh twōlccekwi** a hinge, a bolt.

's'wu = **'syu**, abbr < **'siwu** = **'sio** = **isio** (AUTH cop hon).

-**swu** [Seoul DIAL] var < -**so** (AUTH indicative). Used to seniors, including servants, within the family circle. To family juniors the intimate (-**e**) and the plain forms (-**ta** etc.) are used interchangeably, and to friends the familiar forms (-**ney** etc.) are used.

-**swu**, var < -**so** < -*swo*, bnd pcl = **ulo (s)se**. **son** ~ < *son-swo*, ˙*swon-zwo* (var ˙*swon-˙cwo*) with one's own hand. CF **mom-so**.

-**swuk** = -**sswuk**, suffix.

1. bnd adj-n (~ **hata**). very ··· . ¶**kiph-swuk** (= **kipsswuk**) quite deep, secluded. **nulk-swuk** (= **nuksswuk**) quite old. **malk-/melk-swuk** (= **mal-/mel-sswuk**) neat, clean.

2. (makes impressionistic adv). SEE -**sswuk**.

-**swukswuk**, bnd adj-n (~ **hata**); after consonant -**uswukswuk**; HEAVY ↔ -**soksok**. ···ish, slightly colored/tinged. SEE -(**u**)**sulum**.

-**swukuley** [< -**swuk-uley**], cpd bnd adj-n (~ **hata**). ···ish. ¶**nulk-**~ is oldish. **m^a/$_u$lk-**~ is watery, thin, juicy.

swulok (< *swolwok* < ˙*solwok* < ˙*s o˙lwo k*), postmod. (to the full) extent (that); increasingly with. SEE -**ulq** ~ . DIAL **salok**. NOTE: Optional ~ (**ey** [colloq]) only in **kulelq** ~ and **ilelq** ~ .

swun < *SSYWUN*, adn. pure; net. ¶**Swun wuli sik ita** It is purely Korean in style. ~ **hwang-sayk** pure yellow. ~ **munhak** pure literature. ~ ^{1}**īlon** pure theory. ~ ^{1}**īik** net profit. ~ **sōtuk** net income.

swung, postmod [DIAL] = **twung**. ¶**pon swung mān swung hata** glances/skims over, takes a cursory view of.

-**swung**, suffix (makes impressionistic adverb). ¶**k^{e}am-swung** sparsely dark: Xh, XX, XXh.

-**swungi**, suffix. one, thing. ¶**helup** ~ a sloppy fellow, a careless/reckless fellow. **palka** ~ = **palka-songi / pelke-swungi** a naked body. **thelpok** ~ a hairy/shaggy one. **wēn** ~ a monkey. CF -**songi**.

swus, adn, bnd n (pre-postnominal), adj-n. pure, unspoiled, spotless, undefiled, innocent. ¶ ~ **ki** (fresh) vigor. ~ **poki** unspoiled/simple person; virgin. ~ **sayksi/chēnye** a pure and innocent young girl, a virgin. ~ **kes/ūmsik** fresh food. ~ **chōngkak** an innocent boy, a male virgin. ~ **toyta**, ~ **cepta**, ~ **cita**, ~ **hata** is naive, artless, unaffected, unsophisticated, rustic, homely, simple, kind(hearted), unspoiled.

sy = palatalized s, but often pronounced just /s/. This is either a reduction of the syllable **si** or an attempt to pronounce the "sh" sound in English and other loanwords. CF **cy**.

-**sy**··· < -*sy*··· SEE -**usy**··· < -*usy*··· , -*osy*-

-**sya** [lit] < -˙*sya* = -**sye** < -˙*sye*, abbr < -**sie** < -*si˙ye*, hon inf. SEE -*u˙sya*; CF *i˙sya*.

-˙*sya*-···, hon + modulator (-˙*w^{u}o*-). SEE -*u˙sya*···.

syang (< ˙*SYANG*): SEE -**ulq sang siph.ta**; CF *syeng*.

˙*syas˙ta*, abbr < ˙*isyas˙ta*. SEE *a˙ni 'syas˙ta*, -˙*wo˙l i 'syas˙ta*.

-syas˙ta SEE -˙usyas˙ta

˙sye, inf < ˚sye˙ta, vi. stands. ¶cyekun ˙te.t ul ˙sye 'sywu˙la (1481 Twusi 8:2b) he stood there for a little while.

˙sye pcl (< [i]˙sye, vi inf). from; at (= se). ¶˙i TI-˙HHYWEY ¨ep.sun ˙PPI-KHWUW y e˙tule ˙sye wo˙n ywo (1447 Sek 19:30b) where did this witless almsman (bhikṣu) come from? ¨ne y ˙e˙tu˙le ˙sye won ˙ta (?1517- ¹No 1:1a) where have you come from? ¨amwo toy ˙sye won ˙t i ˙mwollwo.l i ([1447→]1562 Sek 3:21b; aberrant verb form) I don't know where they have come from. HYANG ˙ol ¨ta me˙li ˙sye ma˙tha (1447 Sek 19:19b) smelling from afar all the scents … . ¨sye˙wul ˙sye hoyng˙hoyng ˙i ¨encey ˙nasi˙l i 'le˙n ywo (?1517- Pak 1:53b) when is the imperial procession leaving the capital? ˙cukca ˙hi tyengey ˙sye ¨ep˙se twolwo ZIN-KAN ˙ay ˙na˙a (1447 Sek 9:12b) suddenly was absent from there and appeared again among human beings and … . ˙ile 'n ¨NGWUW-CCYENG ˙tol.h on ingey ˙sye cwu˙ku˙m ye n' (1447 Sek 9:12b) if such sentients hereafter die … . kungey ˙sye ¨sa˙n i (1459 Wel 2:7a) they lived there. SEE ˙ay ˙sye, ˙ey ˙sye, ˙uy ˙sye, ˙yey ˙sye; ˙u˙lwo ˙sye; tye ˙'y ˙sye = *˙tye ey ˙sye; -˙a ˙sye, -˙e ˙sye, -˙kwo ˙sye, -u˙m ye ˙sye. NOTE: Occurs only after vowel, y, or l.

˙s ye, postmod + postmod. SEE -ulq ˙s ye

-sye < (*)-˙sye, abbr < -sie < (*)-si˙ye.

1. honorific inf. SEE -usye < (*)-ᵁ⁄₀˙sye = -ᵁ⁄₀˙sya. ~ se, ~ to, ~ ya, ~ yo; ~ 'la.

2. inf < ⋯s- stem. masye < ma˙sye (1449 Kok 159) drink. (The honorific infinitive is masisye = unattested MK *masi˙sya.)

syeks (? < ˙syeks 'reins'), n. role, duty, position. ¶hon namcin hon ¨kyeci˙p un ˙SYE-ZIN ˙uy syek˙s ila (1475 Nay 1:80a) the role of the commoner means one woman to one man.

˙syeks, n. reins (= koppi).

syeng (? < ˙SYANG) appearance: SEE -ul syeng pwuluta, -ulq seng siph.ta

˙s 'yen ˙tyeng SEE -ulq ˙s 'yen ˙tyeng

sye˙ta SEE suta (stands)

⋯ ˙'sye ˙'y˙la = ˙isye ˙'la. SEE -˙twu˙syey˙la = -˙twu' ˙'sye˙'la.

-syo, abbr < -sio (hon AUTH)

-syu, abbr < -siwu = -sio (hon AUTH)

'syu, abbr < 'siwu = 'sio = isio (cop hon AUTH)

⋯ ˙sywo⋯ , abbr < ⋯si-˙wo-, verb stem (⋯si-) +

modulator. ¶swul ma˙sywom ˙kwa ¨NGWO-SIN me˙kwum ˙kwa (1462 ¹Nung 7:53b) the drinking of wine and the eating of the five forbidden pungent roots. ma˙sywo˙m on (1459 Wel 17:16b), ma˙sywo˙m ay n' (1481 Twusi 8:10a). SEE i˙sywo⋯ .

˙'sywo⋯ , abbr < isi-˙wo-. ¶na y mol ca˙pa ˙'sywo˙m a ¨ne y ¨twuy[h] ˙pwo˙la ka˙la (?1517- ¹No 1:37b) I'll take the horse, you go to the toilet.

-˙sywo˙sye SEE -u˙sywo˙sye. CF ˙ssye.

'sywo˙sye, abbr < (?*)isywo˙sye = isi-wo-si-˙(y)e, v modulated hon inf (CF i˙sya). ¶˙twu-'sywo˙sye khe˙nul (1445 ¹Yong 107) they said "please desist" (= there was opposition) but … .

-˙sywu⋯ , abbr < -si-˙wu- (hon + modulator). SEE -u˙sywu⋯ .

˙'sywu⋯ , abbr < isi-˙wu-. For an example of ˙'sywum see the entry ⋯˙ywum.

⋯˙sywu⋯ = ⋯˙sywo⋯ , abbr < ⋯si-˙wo-, verb stem (⋯si-) + modulator. ¶ma˙sywu˙toy (1586 Sohak 5:51a) drinks and … . cyekun ˙te.t ul ˙sye 'sywu˙la (1481 Twusi 8:2b) he stood there for a little while.

-t-, alt of -tu- (retrospective) before PLAIN attentive (-t-i), FAMILIAR assertive (-t-ey), modifier (-t-un), and sequential (-t-uni).

t_1, variant before s⋯ or c⋯ of s (genitive pcl). ¶nwun t si˙Gwu˙l ol (?1468- Mong 24b) the edge of the eyelid. nwun t co˙zo (1447 Sek 23:26b; 1459 Wel 21:215b) = ˙nwun s co˙zo ('y˙m ye) (1459 Wel 1:13a) the pupil of the eye. SYEY-THYEN t ¨CWO-SO (1447 Sek 24:4b) ancestral master of India. SYEY-THYEN t ˙CCO ˙ay s KYENG ˙i (1459 Wel se:23a) the sūtra in the script of India. KWUN t ˙CCO (1451 Hwunen 3b, 4a, 10b) the character KWUN. ˙ku˙l ey s ¨PWON t ˙CCO ˙non ˙MALQ t ˙CCO y ˙za ˙wol˙ho.n i ˙'la (1462 ¹Nung 10:9b) of original letters in the text only the characters at the end are correct.

t_2, postmod (summational). the fact that. SEE ˙t i(⋯), ˙t i, ˙t ol, ˙t olwo, ˙t oy (n'), ˙t ay (n'). CF -˙t ol, -˙t ul, -t ul; -˙t i > -˙ti > -ci.

*-t-, bnd v (emotive). SEE *-˙t[o]-, -˙two-.

-˙ta-, var = -˙te-, retrospective aspect. This variant is attested after o, a, e(C), and i(C): ˙hota˙la (1447 Sek 6:24b, ?1517- Pak 1:37b) and ˙hota˙n i (1447 Sek 13:57b, 1463 Pep 2:5b, ?1517- Pak 1:58b), ˙cata˙la (1482 Kumsam 4:5a), ˙ho.ya ˙s.tala (1463 Pep 5:95b), ˙phye˙ta˙la (1463 Pep 4:170a), ¨epta˙n i (1459 Wel 13:35ab), pwus˙ku˙lita˙n i (1449 Kok 121), a˙ni ho.ya is˙ta.n i (1481 Twusi 7:23a). The shape -˙te- also occurs after the same vowels, and after wo, wu, u, and Vy, where -˙ta- is not attested.

ta < ˙ta, postmod [obs, lit] = ya/ka (question).

 1. SEE -nun ~ ; -˙un ˙ta, ˙in ˙ta, -˙non ˙ta, -˙an ˙ta, -˙ten ˙ta, -ul(q) ˙ta; -(˙no)son ˙ta. CF ˙to. MK ˙ta may be from ˙t[o ˙G]a 'is it the fact that ... ?'

 2. SEE -˙un ˙ta ¨ma˙ta every time that .... It is unclear whether this may be merely a semantic extension of 'question'; CF ˙pstay time.

tā < ¨ta, adv (CF motwu).

 1. all, everything; everybody, everyone; (= twūlq tā) both. ¶Tā kath.i kaca Let's all go together. **Hana to namkici anh.ko tā kacye kass.ta** They have taken it all away and left nothing. **Tā wass.ta** (1) All (of us / you / them) have come = All are here; We / I have arrived all the way = Here we are (I am) [at last]; We're here / home. **Īl ul tā hayss.ta** I am all finished **Īl i tā thullyess.ta** All is over = Everything went wrong for us.

 2. [figurative] all, completely, quite, indeed; everything (else). ¶**Pyel kes tā pwass.ta!** Now I have seen everything! **Pyel pyel īl ul tā pwass.ta!** I never saw such queer goings-on! **Pyel māl-ssum tā hasip.nita** "You are being too kind to me (saying such nice things)" = Don't mention it; Not at all. **Pi ka tā onta!** And now it has to rain, on top of everything else! **Ha to ki ka mak.hye se pay-kkop i tā (= pay-kkop kkaci to) wūs.nunta** He is choked up with laughter all the way down to his bellybutton. **Ku cwucey ey yangpok ul tā ip.ess.ney!** Well, isn't HE all dressed up! **Tā naass.ey yo** I'm fully recovered.

tā < tye ay, n [Phyengan DIAL (Kim Yengpay 1984:95)] = ce ai he, she. CF kā, yā.

'ta, 1. abbr (alt) after vowel < ita. 2. abbr < hata after voiceless sounds, a, or e; CF tha, chi and 'ci.

'˙ta, 1. abbr < ho˙ta after voiceless sounds; CF ˙tha. SEE ¨mwot '˙ta, ˙kot '˙ta.

 2. = ˙[y]˙ta (cop) after i or y

-ta < -˙ta, inflectional ending; see also -˙la.

 1. indicative assertive (= statement). is, does. In the colloquial attached only to adj or adj + honorific (-usi-), and to the past (-ess-) and future (-keyss-) elements attached to any stem. In certain literary clichés attached also directly to verb stems (= -nun-ta < -no-˙ta); see -ta ppun, -ta siph.i. ¶**chwupta** it is cold. **mekta** [lit] = **mek.nunta** eats < *mekno˙ta* (1481 Twusi 25:18a). **kata** = **kanta** goes. SYN [lit] -nola, -tota. SEE i(lo)ta, i(lo)la, -tey, -ney, -so, -sup.nita; -ulita, -ulyes.ta, -kes.ta.

 2. transferentive (often followed by pcl ka, which cannot be omitted if a particle other than se or ka follows). SEE -ta ka. Because -ta ka can be followed by other particles — such as nun, se, to, tul, ya (as well as chelem, khenyeng, kkaci, mace, 'na, ...) and even another ka — a strong case can be made that -ta ka is the basic form, from which -ta is an abbreviation, and that is the conclusion of Song Sekcwung (1988:229). But historically the form probably developed from the indicative assertive + a particle, as we treat it here. The MK form was always accompanied by the ˙ka except when the particle ˙za was attached, and only then was ˙ka absent. SEE -˙ta ˙za.

 3. SEE -ta siph.i
 4. SEE -upsita
 5. SEE -ta mālta

-ta 'ca, abbr < -ta (ko) haca. ¶**Wuli lo se etten khulwusyokhu lul cocik hanta 'ca, kulena kiswulq-cek cito-ca ka ēps.ta 'myen, etteh.key sāep ul cīnhayng halq swu iss.keyss.nun ya** Even if, let's say, we ourselves were to form a "khruzhok" (= a circle), without a technical leader how could we possibly proceed with the undertaking?

-ta chelem, transferentive + pcl. SEE -ta ka chelem.

-ta chica. let's suppose, suppose / supposing ... .

-ta chimyen. if we suppose (that ...), suppose / supposing ... .

-ta chitula to. even though we (might) suppose that ... . ¶**Nay ka cal-mos hayss.ta (son) chitula to kuleh.key sīm hakey kulelq swu iss.nun ka?** Even though I did make a mistake, how can you say such hard things? SYN -tula to, -ta son chitula to.

taci, takci, postn. degree, extent. ¶ **i / yo ~** to this degree / extent, like this, so (much), in this way. SEE **ku / ko ~ , ce / co ~**.

-ta 'ci, abbr < **-ta (ko) haci**. says / thinks / feels that it is / does. ¶**Cham Tekswu-kwung ey to yūmyeng han pak.mul-kwan i iss.ta 'ci?!** By the way, didn't you say (or: don't they say) that there is a famous museum in Tekswu Palace, too?! **Mikwukq ¹yuhak kass.ta (ka) sip-nyen man ey tol.a omyen se paksa hana to mōs hayss.ta 'ci mwe yo?!** Why, they say he spent ten years studying in America and yet could not manage to get a doctorate, even!

-ta cocha, transferentive + pcl. SEE **-ta ka cocha**.

-ta hanun i SEE (abbr) **-ta 'nun i**

-ta ha(n)ta, abbr < **-ta ko ha(n)ta;** CF **-ta '(n)ta**.

-tah.ta (inf **-tay**), abbr < **-talah.ta** (is rather, quite, sort of, kind of; is ···ish).

-tak, 1. [Ceycwu DIAL] = **-lak** (= **-l ak**). ¶*ku salum un hotak matak tomuci senguy ka es.ta* he shilly-shallies around and is just terribly indifferent about it all. [? abbr < **-ta ka**]

-ta k, abbr < **-ta ko** [DIAL]: **~ hata**. CF **(-)k hata, khwuta**.

-(t)tak / -(t)tek SEE **-ttak / -ttek**

'ta ka, 1. abbr < **ita ka** (cop transferentive + pcl) after a vowel.
2. abbr < **hata ka** after voiceless sound, **a,** or **e**.

? **'ta ˙ka** < **˙hota ˙ka** (transferentive < **°ho˙ta** + pcl) after voiceless sounds. Examples?

-ta ka < **-˙ta ˙ka,** transferentive + pcl. The **˙ka** can be omitted in modern Korean provided no other particle follows, but it was present in MK unless **˙za** was attached; SEE **ita ka, a˙ni 'la ˙ka, -˙ta ˙za**.

does / did (is / was) and then; does / did (is / was) but; when. Shows a CHANGE or SHIFT of action or state. Attached to the stem, (1) this usually signals the interruption of an event before its completion; therefore the event must be durative not punctual. Attached to the past as **-ess.ta (ka),** (2) this represents a reversal, an undoing, a nullification, or an unanticipated, unrelated, and undesirable consequence; a series of two or more past transferentives represent intermittent or alternating events. The underlying subjects of clauses conjoined by the transferentive must be semantically harmonious (¹Yi Cenglo 1989) and are often identical. CF Gale (1916:49) "The same subject is seen in both clauses."

¶**Cang ey kata ka wuphyen-kwuk ey tullilq ka yo, cang ey kass.ta ka wuphyen-kwuk ey tullilq ka yo** Shall we (interrupt ourselves to) drop in at the post office when we go to market, or shall we go to market and then (shift our action to) drop in at the post office?

1. (nonpast). ¶**Kwutwu lul sin.ta (ka) kwutwu-kkun i kkunh.e cyess.ta** When I was putting on my shoe, the shoestring broke. **chām.ta mōs hay se wus.um ul the ttulita** is unable to control / keep oneself from bursting into laughter. **Yenphil ul kkakk.ta ka son ul pēy(e)ss.ta** I cut my finger (while I was) sharpening a pencil (Song Sekcwung 1988:237). **Yengswu nun cata ka kkāyss.ta** in the middle of his sleep Yengswu woke up (¹Yi Cenglo 1989). **Kitalita ka chām.ta (ka) mōs hay se tte-nass.ey yo** I couldn't put up with waiting, so I left. **Com te nōsita kasici yo** Stay (visit) a bit more before going. **Wuli i pūnswu aph ey anc.e se com swīta ka siktang ey ka se cēmsim mekci** Let's sit in front of this fountain and rest a bit before going ("and then go") to the restaurant for lunch.

¶ *˙kata ˙ka two˙la wolq [KWUN-¨sso y* (1445 ¹Yong 25) the troops who had returned from going [to battle]. *˙icey cye˙mun ce˙k u˙lan an˙cok mozom sko˙cang ¨nwota ˙ka ˙cola˙m ye n' e˙lwu ˙PEP ul poy˙hwozo˙Wwo˙l i '-ngi ˙'ta* (1447 Sek 6:11ab) now while I am young I will have fun to my heart's content for a while and then when I am grown I can duly learn the doctrine. *ce 'y ¨TTWOW-¨LI pwus˙ku˙lita ˙ka ˙QILQ-CHYEN ˙PPEM-˙CI te˙pul˙Gwo ˙i ˙na.l ay ˙za me˙li ¨cwos˙soWo˙n i* (1449 Kok 109) he [Kāśyapa] was ashamed of his own doctrine and, accompanied by a thousand brahmacārin (ascetics), on this day at last he bowed his head [to Buddha]. ALSO: 1447 Sek 6:19a, 23:57b; 1462 ¹Nung 3:84a; 1482 Kum-sam 2:13b, 2: 31b, 3:12a ... . SEE *(-˙ᵉ⁄ₐ) ˙'ta ka*.

NOTE: Song Sekcwung 1988:241 has proposed that this "interruptive" use of the transferentive represents an underlying **-ta ka mālko** 'does and then, desisting, ... '. The important thing is that the first action is incomplete, for if it were completed, the gerund **-ko** would be used.

2. (past). ¶**Ttwukkeng ul teph.e han sahul twuess.ta ka mek.nunta** You cover it with a lid and let it stand for about three days and then eat it. **Eti kass.ta wass.ey yo** Where have you been? **Cēki kass.ta (ka) wass.ta** I've been over there (= I went and then came back); I've been out [a noncommittal way to answer the preceding question]. **Pissan moca lul sass.ta (ka) ssan moca lo pakkwess.ta** I bought an expensive hat, but then I exchanged it for a cheap(er) one. **Phyēnci lul ssess.ta ka ccic.e pelyess.ta** I wrote a letter, and / but then I tore it up. **Congi lul ccic.ess.ta ka tasi phul lo puth.yess.ta** I tore up the paper and then glued it back together again. **Nay ka** [1]**yehayng ul hata ka tōn i ttel.e cyess.ta** (I ran out of money while traveling =) My money ran out in the midst of my trip (Song Sekcwung 1988:233). **Yengswu nun ttek ul mek.ess.ta ka tā thō hayss.ta** Yengswu ate the rice cake and then vomited it all up ([1]Yi Cenglo 1989). ¶*no˙la 's.ta ˙ka pte˙le ti˙m ye* (1462 [1]Nung 8:87b) flew but then fell, and ... . *mwulwu˙ph ul ˙phye 'ys.ta ˙ka* (1481 Twusi 8:27b) [he was sleeping away and] had his knees spread out, and then ... . KHWONG ˙ol a˙la is.ta ˙ka KHWONG ˙ol pte˙le po˙lil ˙s ila (1482 Kum-sam 2:13b) will be aware of the void and yet fall into the void.

3. When two (usually past) transferentives are followed by a form of the verb **hata**, the meaning is that of alternation; the particle **ka** may appear after either or both forms, but it is better to omit the first **ka** and still better to omit both. ¶**Sālam i kass.ta (ka) wass.ta (ka) hayss.ta** People kept going and coming. **Nay ka capci lul ilk.ess.ta (ka) latio lul tul.ess.ta (ka) hayss.ta** I was reading a magazine and listening to the radio off and on. **Kim sensayng i ssess.ta (ka) nay ka ssess.ta (ka) hanta** First Mr Kim writes and then I write, and so on, back and forth. **Na n' i hana ka nul aphess.ta kwaynchanh.ess.ta hanta** I have one tooth that always bothers me (that hurts) off and on. **Ku uysa nun etten ttay nun chincel hayss.ta (ka) etten ttay nun pul-chincel hayss.ta (ka) hanta** That doctor is gentle at times, but at other times he is rough. **Ilayss.ta celayss.ta pyēntek i mānh.ta** He is quite capricious. **Tal un han tal mata khe cita ka cak.e cita (ka)** (or, better: **khe cyess.ta ka cak.e cyess.ta ka**) **hanta** The moon waxes and wanes each month. **Pi ka ota mālta hanta** It rains off and on. **Nalssi ka tewess.ta ka chwuwess.ta ka hanta** The weather keeps changing from warm to cold and vice-versa (Song Sekcwung 1988:238).

4. For special use of the copula transferentive see **ita (ka), -e 'ta (ka), (-nun, -un) tey 'ta ka**. CF **et' 'ta = eti (ey) 'ta; kac' 'ta = kacye 'ta**.

5. SEE **iss.ta (ka)** (later on, after a while).

6. ? = **-ta (ka) ka [ani 'la ...]**. SEE **-ta ka ka**.

NOTE: For a different analysis, see Choy Hyenpay 1960, Hankul 127:7-27. For more on the syntax and semantics of **-ta ka**, see Song Sekcwung 1988:226-46 and [1]Yi Cenglo 1989. On the history, see Hong Yunphyo 1975 and our notes on **ita** (= **ita ka**) and **ka**. Ceycwu DIAL *-tak, -tan(ey), -tankuney, -tang(kuney)*.

-ta ka chelem, transferentive + pcl + pcl. ¶**Kata (ka) to ota (ka) chelem kulen caymi iss.nunq īl i iss.umyen cōh.keyss.ta** I hope we can run into as amusing an experience on our way back as we did on our way here.

-ta ka cocha, transferentive + pcl + pcl. ¶**Ku i nun pap ul mekta (ka) cocha musun sayngkak i tte olumyen silhem-sil lo ttwie tul.e kako n' hayss.ta** He would dart off into his laboratory when some thought occurred to him, even in the midst of a meal.

-ta ˙ka k, transferentive + pcl + emphatic pcl. ¶*makta ˙ka k ¨MYEN ˙thi ¨mwot ˙hono˙n i n* (1466 Kup 2:66a) obstructs it and then cannot relieve it [the final *n* is unexplained].

-ta ka ka, transferentive + pcl + pcl [limited to negative copula phrases]. ¶**Ku sayngkak i tte olun kes un chayk ul ilk.ta ka ka ani 'la swul ul masita (ka) yess.ta** That thought's occurring to me was not when I was reading, it was when I was drinking.

-ta ka khenyeng, transferentive + pcl + pcl. ¶**Ku nun chinkwu wa yāyki hata ka khenyeng kath.i swul ul masita (ka) to wūs.nunq īl i ēps.ta** He never even laughs when drinking with friends, much less when just chatting with them.

-ta ka kkaci, transferentive + pcl + pcl. ¶**Ku nun cam ul cata (ka) kkaci soli lul nāyko wūl**

ttay ka iss.ta He sometimes sobs even in the midst of his sleep.

-ta ka 'la 'myen, transferentive + pcl + cop var inf + abbr < (ko) hamyen. ¶Cikum un pappe se mōs towa tulici man, iss.ta ka 'la 'myen towa tulilq swu iss.^{s}up.nita I can't help you now but if you'll wait a bit I can.

-ta ka 'la to, transferentive + pcl + cop var inf + pcl. ¶Ku nun pap ul mekta (ka) 'la to musun sayngkak man tte olumyen silhem-sil lo ttwie tul.e kass.ta He darted off into his laboratory when some thought occurred to him, even in the midst of a meal. Pap ul mekta ka 'la to son nim i osimyen il.e se ya hanun pep in i 'la You should rise when guests appear, even in the middle of dinner.

-ta ka mace, transferentive + pcl + pcl. ¶Ku nun pap mekta (ka) mace musun sayngkak i tte olumyen silhem-sil lo ttwie tul.e kako n' hayss.ta He would dash into his laboratory when some thought occurred to him, even in the midst of a meal.

-ta ka mālta SEE mālta

-ta ka man, transferentive + pcl + pcl. ¶Pam-nac swul mekta (ka) man mālq cakceng in ya? Do you intend to go on doing nothing but drinking all the time?

-ta ka 'm ye, transferentive + pcl + abbr < ho'm ye. as soon as; (almost) simultaneously. ¶'na'ta ka·'m ye pu'the CHIN-SIM a'ni 'ho'non ··salo·m oy nwun t co·zo [G]wa ·KWOLQ-··SYWUY [G]wa 'y'n i '-ngi ''ta (1459 Wel 21: 215b) from the moment he was born he had the eyes and the marrow of a person who does not anger. a'tol na'hwo.m on sta'h ay 'tita 'ka 'm ye tunge'li 'yey s 'hi.m i cwozo lo'woy.n i (1481 Twusi 25:43a) when my son was born as soon as he fell to the ground he had formidable strength in his back. SEE -u'si'ta 'ka·'m ye.

-ta ka n', abbr < -ta ka nun

-ta ka 'na, transferentive + pcl + cop advers. ¶Kiwang on kīm ey com nōlta (ka) 'na kalq ka As long as I am here I may as well stay a while.

-ta ka 'n tul, transferentive + pcl + cop mod + postmod. ¶Hak.kyo tanita (ka) 'n tul si-cip mōs kal kkatalk i iss.nun ya? Is there any reason you can't get married (to some man) while in school?

-ta ka nun, transferentive + pcl + pcl.

1. does / did and THEN, does / did BUT. ¶kata ka nun suta goes and then STOPS; sometimes (every now and then) it stops. kakkum kata ka nun from time to time, every now and then.

2. sometimes (··· and sometimes). ¶Wūlta ka nun wūs.ko, wūs.ta ka nun wūlko hanta At times I laugh, at times I cry.

3. if one keeps on doing (then unfortunately). ¶Kuleta ka nun khunq īl nanta If you leave things like that [and do nothing about it] you'll be in a fix. Nōlki man hata ka nun nwiwuchil nal i iss.ulq kes ita One of these days you will be sorry for your idleness. Ileh.key sīm hanq īl ul hata ka nun ithul to mōs ka se ssule cikeyss.ta If I go on doing such heavy work I'll be worn out in a couple of days.

SEE -ess.ta ka nun.

-ta ka poni while ···ing (I find that) ··· happens. (Examples: M 1:2:455.)

-ta ka se (nun), transferentive + pcl + pcl (+ pcl). [emphatic] = -ta ka. ¶Ku ^{n}yeca nun hōysa ey tanita ka se si-cip ul kass.ci yo She got married while working in the office. SEE -ess.ta ka se.

-ta ka 'ta = -ta ka ita, transferentive + pcl + cop. (For an example, see -ta ka ka.)

-ta ka to < -'ta 'ka 'two, transferentive + pcl + pcl. ¶Ku nun pap ul mekta ka to musun sayngkak i tte olumyen silhem-sil lo ttwie tul.e kanta He darts into his laboratory when some thought occurs to him, even in the midst of a meal. Tōn un ēps.ta ka to iss.nun ke 'ta Money comes and goes (so don't let it bother you too much). Tōn ila 'n iss.ta ka to ēps.ta ka to hanun pep ici mwe l' kulay Why worry about money; you can get by with or without it. Onul un wuli phyen ita ka to ^{1}nayil un ce ccok phyen i toyl.nun ci nwu ka al.e Who knows whether he may be on our side today and on theirs tomorrow? Onul un pūca (i)ta ka to kapcaki ^{1}nayil un kanan-payngi ka toylq swu to iss.ci It may be that the rich man of today will suddenly become the poor man of tomorrow, you see. ¶Tōn ila 'n ēps.(ess.)ta ka to iss.ko iss.(ess.)ta ka to ēps.nun pep ita The rich may get poor, and the poor may get rich. Cata ka to ku sayngkak, anc.ess.ta ka to ku sayngkak, ic.ullay ya ic.ulq swu ēps.ta Asleep or awake I can't get that thought out of my

or awake I can't get that thought out of my mind. SEE **ita ka to, iess.ta ka to, -ˋta ˋka ˋtwo**. NOTE: In fast speech **ka** may elide.
-ta ka tul, transferentive + pcl + pcl.

1. (nonpast). ¶**Kulem, te nōlta (ka) tul okey** Well, stay there a little while longer (and then come). **Ili 'ta ka tul ecci toyca 'nun kes in ya** What is to become of us if we let things go on like this? **Haksayng tul i teymo lul hata ka tul cap.hyess.ta** The students got arrested in the midst of their demonstration.

2. (past). ¶**Haksayng tul i teymo lul hayss.ta ka tul hon nanta** The students are in trouble for putting on a demonstration.

-ta ka 'tun ci, transferentive + pcl + cop retr mod + postmod. ¶**Kata (ka) 'tun ci tol.a ota (ka) 'tun ci kkok wuli cip ey tullikey** Whether it's on your way there or back, be sure to stop in at our house.

-ˋta ˋka ˋtwo, transferentive + pcl + pcl. ¶**ZYE-LOY ˋskuy ¨TTWOW-¨LI poy ˋhwota ˋka ˋtwo SI-LA ˋlol ¨hel ˋm ye** (1447 Sek 9:13a) though he learned the doctrine from Buddha he broke the commandments (śīla). **ˋile 'n e ˋlin ¨salo ˋm i ¨mwo ˋtin ˈPEP ˋul ˋha ci ˋze pwus ˋku ˋlywum ¨ep ˋta ka ˋtwo ˈMYENG-CYWUNG holq ce ˋk uy ¨SSYEN TI-ˋSIK ˋol mas-ˋna** (1459 Wel 8:69b) stupid people of this sort are shameless in much creating evil doctrine, yet when they are about to die they face an awareness of the good, and ... .

-ta ka ya, transferentive + pcl + pcl.

1. and (only) THEN; only when. ¶**Na nun han cham iyaki hata ka ya piloso ku uy ilum i sayngkak nass.ta** It was only after I had listened to (= conversed with) him a good long while that I remembered his name. **Kil ul han tong-an kata ka ya kil ul cal-mos tun kes ul al.ess.ta** It was only after I had walked a good long distance that I realized I had taken the wrong way.

¶**"Las Vegas" ey wass.ta ka ya nōlum ul an halq swu iss.na?** Now that we are right here in Las Vegas, how can we not gamble?

2. of all times (while in the midst of doing). ¶**Īl ul hata ka ya ecci ku man twulq swu iss.na 'm** How can I leave in the middle of my work (of all times)?! **Swul masita ka ya etteh.key kongpu lul hakeyss.e yo** How do you expect to get any studying done in the midst of drinking?

-ta ka yo, transferentive + pcl + pcl. ¶**Kata (ka) yo?** On our way there(, do you mean)? **Kass.ta (ka) yo?** After we get there(, do you mean)?

takci SEE **taci**
-ta 'kena, abbr < **-ta (ko) hakena**
-ta 'keni, abbr < **-ta (ko) hakeni**
-ta 'key, abbr < **-ta (ko) hakey**
-ta k hata SEE **-ta k**
-ta khenyeng, transferentive + pcl. SEE **-ta ka khenyeng**.
-ta 'ki, abbr < **-ta ko haki**
-ta kkaci, transferentive + pcl. SEE **-ta ka kkaci**.
-ta 'ki ey, abbr < **-ta (ko) haki ey**. ¶**Sakwa lul cōh.a hanta 'ki ey com sa kaciko kass.ci yo** I heard that he liked apples so I bought some and took them to him. **Nal i chwupta 'ki ey ōpa lul ipkwu na-wass.ey yo** They said it was cold so I wore my overcoat (here).
-ta kko [lively] = **-ta ko**; ~ **yo**.
tāko < **¨ta ˋkwo (ˈla), ¨takwo ˈl ye**, ger < defective vt (**tā-l-**); [emphatic] = **tao** (give me). ¶**Ne i kes com hay tāko** Do it for ME, please. **sapal is.ketun hona[h] takwo** (1795 [1]No-cwung [P] 1:38a − **cwukwo ˈlye** [K] 1:38b) = **sapal is.ketun hona[h] ¨takwo ˈˈla** (?1517-[1]No 1:42a) if you have a bowl give me one. **¨ne y ¨na ˋlol na ˋzwo ˋwa tyelu ˋkey ˋho ˋya ¨takwo ˈˈl ye** (?1517- Pak 1:18b) I'd like you to make it a little smaller for me. VAR **tākwu**. NOTE: Both **tāko** and **tao** are becoming obsolescent as the semiformal (authoritative) style itself falls into disuse. The form **tāko** is not used as an ordinary gerund (for which either **tālla ko** or **cwuko** would be appropriate), but only as a shortening of some desiderative expression ('I want you to give me').

-ta ko, indicative assertive + particle.

1. (saying / thinking / feeling) that ... is / does. ¶**Cōh.ta ko hayss.ta** He said that he liked it. **Kongpu hanta ko hasey yo!** Tell him I am studying! **Sālam tul i tā wass.ta ko halq ka yo?** Shall I say that everyone is here? **Sikan i iss.keyss.ta ko sayngkak hay yo** I think we'll have time.

2. grants, concedes, supposes, posits (that ...). ¶**Cōh.ta ko hapsita; kulena nemu cōh.a haci māsey yo** I grant you it is nice, but don't get

cōh.a haci māsey yo Granted that it is nice, don't get too fond of it). Yelqsim hi kongpu hanta ko hapsita; kulena ilqtung ul hakeyss.ey yo? = Yelqsim hi kongpu hanta ko hay se ilqtung ul hakeyss.ey yo? Granted that you are studying hard, still how can you hope to take first place? (Examples from M 1:2:129.) SEE ko hay se, M 2:1:102-3.

3. "with the thought that" = and so. ¶Kulay "Cēngsik-i"; cengwel ey nah.ass.ta ko cey khun api ka Cēngsik ila ko ciess.ta 'nta That's right, (it's) "Cēngsik-i"; you see he was born in cengwel (January) so his uncle dubbed him Cēngsik. Ku tul un ¹nayil achim cha lo kwānkay kongsa-cang ey kanta ko pelsse puthe cim ul kkwulinula ko yātan tul ita They are going by car tomorrow morning to the irrigation-works site so for some time now they have been in a hustle getting their bags packed.

4. [Sentence-final colloq, usually pronounced -ta kwu.] I think/thought or hear/heard that ...! ¶Ei, nulk.un i ka chenha ey ... na n' cēngmal lo khong ul mānh.i na ttut.ess.ta 'kwu! Why you old rascal — I thought you'd picked lots of beans! Hapkyek i tōyss.ta 'kwu (1) I hear you passed the exams!; (2) Is it true that you passed the exams?; (3) I thought he passed the exams (but he didn't). CF -ta 'mye, -ta 'myen se (yo).

-ta ko 'na. ¶Kwi-chanh.uni na l' chac.e onun sālam eykey n' canta ko 'na tāytap hay cwusio Tell visitors that I am sleeping (or the like), to save me the bother of seeing them. I kes kkok mwe kath.ta ko 'na halq ka?! I wonder, just what is this like?

-ta ko tul. ¶Mattang hi olq sālam tul i an wass.ta ko tul yātan ita They are complaining that the expected people didn't come.

-ta ko yo, indic assertive + pcl + pcl [colloq; usually pronounced -ta kwu yo]. A neutral way of making a statement (by using a relaxed polite structure that avoids a decision between -sup.nita and -e yo styles). VAR -ta kko yo. CF -tula ko (yo).

¨ta ˙kwo ˙'la, ¨takwo ˙'l ye SEE tāko
tākwu [var] = tāko
-ta kwu [var] = -ta ko
(-)takwu, (-)takw(un)i, suffix, bound postnoun. [vulgarizes nouns]. a hard thing. ¶ak-takw(un)i a wrangle, a brawl. chel-ttakw(un)i < chelq takw(un)i sense. ppu'-takw(un)i a part or corner sticking up/out (< ppul horn). ppyamttakwi < ppyamq takwi cheek. ppye takwi bone. CF (-)ttakci, (-)ttakseni; ttak-ttak hata.

-ta kwu yo = -ta ko yo
tā-l-, defective vt [reflexive donatory verb]. give me; (a request for oneself). SEE tālla, tao, tāko (tākwu). CF ˙twola.

-tal, bnd n. place, spot. ¶yang ~ a sunny place, the sunnyside. ong ~ a hollow. san ~ hill country, a mountain area. ung ~ [< um-tal] a shaded place, the dark side. CF -thal. NOTE: From placenames LHS 1955:20 suggests that tal was a Kolye word meaning 'mountain'.

-ta 'l(q), abbr < -ta (ko) hal(q). ¶Ileh.ta 'lq ¹īyu ka ēps.ta There isn't any special reason (to speak of). Ne to cal hayss.ta 'lq kes i ēps.ta You yourself are not quite free from blame, either. CF -ca 'l(q).

-ta 'la, abbr < -ta (ko) hala
-˙ta˙la, retr indic assert. ¶˙na non ˙TTWO-TTWUW s mwol˙Gay˙yey˙cata˙la (1482 Kum-sam 4:5a) I slept on the sand [beach] at the ferry point. ˙phye˙ta˙la (1463 Pep 4:170ab) expounded [the sūtra]. SEE ˙hota˙la, ˙ho˙ya˙'s.ta˙la.

-talah.ta, bnd adj -(H)- (inf -talay). is rather, quite, sort of (sorta), kind of (kinda); is ···ish.

1. Attaches to adj stem, including unextended form of -L- stem. ¶ccalp-/ccalq-~ is quite short. cop-~ is rather narrow. kanu- is on the slender side (< kanulta). kīlq-talah.ta [DIAL] = kī-~ is sort of long (< kīlta). kiph-~ is deepish. kwulk-~ is rather thick. nelp-/nelq-~ is sort of wide. noph-~ is quite high/tall. yalp-~ /yalttalatha/ is rather thin.

2. [DIAL] Attaches to adjectival n. ¶chamq ta(la)h.key gently (< cham hata).

ABBR -tah.ta. CF -tamah.ta, -ah.ta/-eh.ta.

-ta 'la to, transferentive + cop var inf + pcl. SEE -ta ka 'la to. ¶Com swīta (ka) 'la to kasilq ke l' It's too bad you can't rest a little before leaving. Iss.ta (ka) 'la to osiketun kuleh.key māl-ssum cen hay cwusey yo If he comes later on, please tell him that.

-talay, inf < -talah.ta

tal.i < to˙li, der n < talta < to[l]˙ta (hangs); hanging/attached thing (> toli > tali bridge; ladder). ¶po-ttali (= poq-tal.i) bundle. ko tal.i an attached finger-loop. sil-kwup tal.i a an attached finger-loop. **sil-kwup tal.i** a porcelain dish with a base attached. **kā-ttali** (< **kāq-tal.i**) [DIAL] an outsider, a would-be: ~ **sik.kwu** an unwanted member of the family, ~ **sēnswu** a would-be athlete, ~ **kīsayng** an extra-service girl, ~ **swunkyeng** a fake cop.

(-)tali, postnoun, suffix.

1. one, fellow, guy [pejorative]. ¶**khi** ~ a tall fellow, "a beanpole". **cak-** ~ a little guy, "a shrimp", "a (little) squirt". **nulk-** ~ an old animal/person, an old gaffer/geezer. CF **(p)pet-cang** ~ a stiff leg; a rigid thing.

2. **mo.yang** ~ = **mo.yang say** (form, shape).

3. **so.yong** ~ (CM 1:231) ?= **so.yong-tol.i** whirlpool. **ssulcak** ~ (CM 1:231) ?= **solcang-tali** Salsola collina.

tālla < ˉtal˙la, subj attent (= PLAIN command) < defective vt **tā-l-**.

1. give (to) me; do me the favor — replaces expected **cwue la** (though that is sometimes heard); obligatorily replaces an expected **cwula** 'give me' in quoted sentence (SEE **tālla ko**). ¶**Mul com tālla** Give me some water. (CF **Hwānca hanthey cwue la** Give it to the patient.) **(Ne) i kes com hay tālla** Do this for me, please. *swuˉl ul ˉtalla ˙ho.ya mekno˙ta* (1481 Twusi 25:18a) asks for wine to drink. SYN ˙*twola*.

NOTE: When not quoted, the reflexive request may well be in a style that offers only a form of **cwu-**: **Na hanthey cwukey (cwusey yo, cwusipsio)**. The substitute verb has forms only for the plain and the semiformal (authoritative) styles. Forms of **cwu-** must be also used for the various adverbializations: **na hanthey cwuko (cwue se, cwuni-kka, cwumyen, ...)**.

2. SEE **tālla 'nta**.

tālla ko, subj attent + pcl. ~ **hanta** (ABBR **tālla 'nta**). ¶**Poksa tele khal ul na 'ykey tolwu tālla ko hay la** Tell the fortune-teller he is to return the knife to me (give me back the knife); CF **Cey tongsayng eykey nungkum han ccok ul cwula ko hay la** Tell him he should give his brother half the apple (1936 Roth 341).

tālla 'ko, abbr < **tālla (ko) hako**

tālla 'nta, abbr < **tālla (ko) hanta**. asks one to give (or do it for) oneself; wants one to give (or do it for) oneself. ¶**Ku sālam i na poko ku kes com tālla 'nta** (**tālla 'p.nita, tālla 'y, tālla 'y yo, tālla 'o, tālla 'sey yo,** ...) He asks me to do that for him; CF **Ku sālam i na poko ku kes com hay cwula 'nta** He asks me to do that for someone (other than himself). **Mul com tālla 'nta** He wants water (from me, you, or someone else); CF **Mul com cwula 'nta** He wants me (or you or someone) to give water to someone (other than himself). **Kongchayk ul sa 'ta (ka) tālla 'nta** He wants someone (you, me, her, ...) to buy him a notebook. CF **-ulye 'nta** wants/intends to do.

tālla 'y, abbr < **tālla ko hay**. ~ **yo**, ~ **se**, ~ **to**, ~ **ya**, ~ **la**.

tāllaynta → **tālla 'nta**. A back formation from **tālla 'y**, perhaps contaminated with the verb **tallay-** 'coax, wheedle' < *tal˙Gay-* (probably from a causative of **tal-** 'be sweet'), or with **-ullay** = **-ulye (ko hay)**.

tālla 'yss.ta, abbr < **tālla ko hayss.ta**

talta, adj -L- (different). SEE **taluta**.

*****tālta** SEE **tā-l-**

talum, 1. subst < **taluta**. 2. n. (being) other, different.

~ **ani 'ko/'la** ··· (for) no other reason than ··· . ¶**On kes un talum ani 'la pūthak halq kes i hana iss.e wass.ta** I have come for no other reason than just to ask a favor of you. **Talum i ani 'la** ··· I am just writing to say/ask ··· [introduces the subject of a letter].

(··· **kwa**) ~ (i) **ēps.ta** is no different (from ···), is the same (as ···); is constant, unchanging, steady. ¶**Ku nun cen kwa talum i ēps.ess.ta** He hasn't changed since. **cen kwa talum i ēps.nun wūceng (salang)** a steady friendship (a constant love).

··· **ina** ~ (i) **ēps.ta** is the same as (being/doing), is like. ¶**han cip-an ina talum ēps.ta** is almost/like (is as good as) one of the family.

~ **ēps.i** equally, in the same way. ¶**Twūl i talum ēps.i sēngmi ka ko.yak hata** They are both equally ill-tempered.

talun, mod < adj **taluta**. (··· that is) other, different, dissimilar, separate.

taluta, adj -LL- [attested 1586 Sohak]. is different. [var **talta** < *talo-/talG-* < **talok-*]

tam, ttam, postn. latent power, ability; impact, "wallop", what something is "loaded" with. ¶**ip tam, mālq tam** word power; the impact of one's words; skill at talking. **pul ttam** (= **pulq tam**) the (potential) heat in a log. **pis tam** ease of combing. [< **tām.ta** packs in]

-ta 'm, abbr.

2. [usually to oneself] do you mean to say that ... ?!; don't tell me that ... !; really?! (shows incredulity, irritation, complaint, or reproach — often of oneself). ¶**I-kkacis sēnmul un mues halye hanta 'm** (or **halye 'nta 'm**) Why do they bother to give me such a (shabby) gift? **Kulen māl nwu ka kot.i tut.nunta 'm** Who could believe such talk! **Sālam i eccay celeh.ta 'm** How can he be that way; How can he do the things he does?! **Ecci sālam i ileh.ta 'm** How can he do/treat me this way! **Ku kicha ka way i-taci nuc.ta 'm** Why is that train so damn late?! **Acik cho-cenyek in tey pelsse canta 'm** Why, here the evening has just begun, and you mean to tell me you're already going to bed? **Musun pi ka kuleh.key onta 'm** What a (heavy/lengthy) rain! **Wēyn cip i kuleh.key khuta 'm** Well, is that house really so large (I wonder)? **Kulay ku īl ul mōs hanta 'm** So he can't do the job — really! **Āni, nwu ka na lul chac.e wass.ta 'm?!** Why, what makes you think that anyone came to see me?! **I key eti phuluta 'm** THIS isn't blue!

NOTE: This is more common with verbs than with adjectives or the copula. With the copula the form is **ila 'm**. CF **ka 'm, -na 'm**.

-ta mace, transferentive + pcl: SEE **-ta ka mace**. ¶**Ku nun cam cata (ka) mace soli lul nāyko wūnta** He sobs even in his sleep.

-tama hata, bnd adj-n; ABBR **-tamah.ta**. looks to be about so much; is rather, quite, sort of (sorta), kind of (kinda). (Used of physical size only; **-talah.ta** is used of all appearances.) ¶**khe-~** is biggish (**khe-** = **khu-**). **kwulk-~** is on the bulky side. **kī-~** is longish (< **kī-l-**). [? < **man** pcl, CF **i-man, i-mas**]

-tamah.ta, bnd adj -(H)- (inf **-tamay**), abbr < **-tama hata** (looks to be about so much). CF **-talah.ta**.

-ta mā(l)ta$_1$, transferentive + aux v indic assert. SEE **mālta**.

-ta mā(l)ta$_2$, indic assert + aux v indic assert. of course (= **-ko mālko**). **~ yo** SAME [POLITE]. **Ām ā(l)ta mā(l)ta (yo)** Yes, of course I know.

-tama 'n, abbr < **-tama han**, mod < **-tama hata**.

tā-man < ˝**ta-ˊmon** < ˝**ta-ˊmoyn**, adv. only, just; but, however. (The etymology in KEd is probably wrong.)

-ta man, ending + particle.

1. indic assert + pcl. is/does but. **~ un** SAME. ¶**Cōh.ki n' cōh.ta man (un) nemu pissata** It's nice, all right, but too expensive. **Yenghwa kwūkyeng ul cōh.a haki n' hanta man (un) onul nemu kotan hay se mōs kakeyss.ta** I like seeing movies, all right, but I'm too tired to go today. **I ke n' pissan kes ita man hana sa cwuci** This is an expensive thing but I will buy you one. **I pen ey nun chāmnunta man (...)** I'll put up with it this time (but ...).

2. transferentive + pcl. SEE **-ta ka man**.

-ta mān = **-ta (ka) mān** (< **mālta**). ¶**mekta mān pap** food one had not finished eating, leftover (food). **Pota mān chayk ul mace ilk.nunta** I am reading the rest of a book I had started (and then put aside).

-tamay, inf < **-tamah.ta**

-tamey (yo), (var) = **-ta 'mye** 2

˝**ta-mon** (1475 Nay 2:2:72a) = ˝**ta-ˊmon**.

˝**ta-ˊmon** (1447 Sek 13:49b, 13:59a) < ˝**ta-ˊmoyn**, adv. just, only; but, however.

-ta mōs hata, transferentive + adv + vt. fails to (do), tries to but does not.

-ta mōs hay (se), -ta mōs ha.ye at the extreme, in the extreme case (of doing), (even) driven by necessity (to do), (even) at the worst. ¶**chām.ta mōs hay** impatient, unable to hold back. **Mekta mōs hay ku ttawiq kes ul mek.e!** I wouldn't eat such stuff if I starved to death! CF **hata mōs hay**. NOTE: The transferentive is seldom followed by **ka** in these expressions.

˝**ta-moyn** = ˝**ta-ˊmoyn**, adv. ¶ ˝**ta-moyn ˝tey-ˊptun neˊki.m iˊn i** (1462 ¹Nung 1:65a) it is that one just floats.

˝**ta-ˊmoyn**, adv. just, only; but, however. ¶ ˝**ta-ˊmoyn ˊHHAP-**˝**CYANG kheˊna** (1463 Pep 1:221b) just join the hands, but ... .

-ta 'mye. 1. SEE **'mye**

2. abbr < **-ta (ko) hamyen se** (sentence-final: a question that seeks confirmation of a report heard from a third party). ¶**Ne-huy ney apeci kkey se cāngkwan i toynta 'mye?!** Can it be true that your father is becoming a cabinet minister? CF Kim Cinswu 1987. ALSO **-tamey**.

-ta 'myen, abbr < **-ta (ko) hamyen**. if, when; if/when(, say, ...); if only. CF **ila 'myen**.

¶**Wuli cip i tangsin cip chelem man khuta 'myen elma 'na cōh.keyss.e!** How nice it would be if my house were as big as yours! ¹Nayil kkaci 'na-ma ku kos ey kalq swu iss.ta 'myen elma 'na cōh.keyss.ˢo How nice it would be if somehow I could get there even by tomorrow. I kos kkaci 'na-ma olq swu iss.ta 'myen cōh.keyss.nun tey I wish he could manage to get as far as here, at least.

¶Ūmsik ul mek.nunta 'myen (i)ya mek.nun ka siph.i/siph.key mek.e ya 'ci In eating, you should do it with appetite. Tangsin kwa 'na kanta 'myen molutoy honca kaki nun silh.e It's another question if you are accompanying me, but I hate to go alone. Onul chelem man tōn ul pēnta 'myen elma an ka payk.man-cāngca ka toykeyss.ta If I could make money the way I did today I'd soon be a millionaire. Sihem chie se ttel.e cinta 'myen chalali sihem ul an chim man to mōs haci You would be better off not to take the examination than to fail it. Ku kes ulo sse to an toynta 'myen, tōce hi pul-kanung hanq īl ici If it cannot be done with that either/even, then it is quite impossible. Ku mēlc'anh.un kos kkaci cocha mōs kanta 'myen chalali tte-naci māsio You'd better not set out if you think you won't even make it that far. Ku ay ka sensayng nim kkey chelem apeci eykey to (ape' nim kkey to) tāy hanta 'myen elma 'na cōh.keyss.e yo How nice it would be if he treated his father the way he treats you (or the teacher)! Kongpu haki lul nōlki ey chelem yelqcwung hanta 'myen musun kekceng ikeyss.ni I'd have no complaint if you'd just study with the same enthusiasm you put into your play.

¶Ku īl hayss.ta 'myen yekcek ita If he did that, then he is a traitor.

-ta 'myen se, abbr < -ta (ko) hamyen se.

1. while doing/saying/thinking that ... .

2. ~ (yo) = -ta 'mye (sentence-final: a question that and seeks confirmation of a report heard from a third party): SEE 'myen se (yo). CF Kim Cinswu 1987.

tan < TAN, adn. only (one), single. ¶ ~ han salam only one man. yenphil ~ twū kay only two pencils. ~ pel os the only suit one has, one's one-and-only suit. ~ swum ey, [DIAL] ~ palam ey at a single breath/stretch/time. CF tān kyel ey at a stretch/heat (mod < tā-l- 'get hot', misidentified in KEd).

-tan, 1. -ta 'n, abbr < -ta (ko) han. ¶Mue palkwang hayss.ta 'n māl i iss.ess.nun pep han tey ... (It seems) he is supposed to have gone crazy or something and ... . Kulen yāyki puthe ka īsang hata 'n māl ia His story is very fishy in itself. Kulay eccayss.ta 'n māl iyo So what? What is it to you? Kulemyen etteh.ta 'n māl in ya So what? Kanan hamyen ette hata 'n (etteh.ta 'n) māl in ya What if you are poor?

2. -ta 'n', abbr < -ta (ko) hanun. ¶Ku wa na wa kyelhon hanta 'n māl ia I mean she and I are getting married. Nyen tul i ku ke mōs ssukeyss.ta 'n māl ia The bitches are just not worth a damn! Yenghwa pole to an kakeyss.ta 'n māl in ya? You mean you're not going even to see the movies (or: going to see the movies, either)? Cip ulo mace an kakeyss.ta 'n māl in ka Do you mean you won't even go home?

3. -ta n', abbr < -ta (ka) nun

-tan (?= *-ta nun) [Ceycwu DIAL] = -ta ka

-ˈtan, retrospective modifier (= -ˈten). ¶haˈnol s KWANG-MYENG TYWUNG ˈey ˈtuˈle ˈˈaˈlay s ˈˈKWA-ˈPWOW kyes-ˈniˈtan ˈcwuˈl ul solˈWwoˈn i (1459 Wel 2:62-3) I report that I have entered the radiance of heaven and experienced the rewards for the merits of the past. SEE ˈhotan.

'tan (?= *itan = *ita nun), [Ceycwu DIAL (Seng ¹Nakswu 1984:68)] = 'ta ka. ¶cengsi lul cheng ho.ye 'tan san the l' pwass.swuta = cikwan ul cheng ha.ye 'ta ka sanso the lul pwass.ˢup.nita I had a geomancer examine the site for the tomb.

-ta 'na, 1. abbr < -ta (ko) hana. ~ p(w)ā. ¶Ama ku i to kanta 'na p(w)ā It seems there is talk he may go, too.

2. = -ta (ka) 'na (< ina). ¶Cikum un pappuni iss.ta (ka) 'na popsita I am busy now but later on we'll see. Com nōlta (ka) 'na kasilq ke l' Too bad you can't stay here a bit longer. Com swiess.ta (ka) 'na kasilq ke l' Too bad you can't relax a while and then go.

-ta 'ney, abbr < -ta (ko) haney. ("I say it is/does" = I TELL you ... = (really) is/does, you see. ¶Wuli manwula ka cwuk.ess.ta 'ney My old lady died, ya see. SEE -ta 'nta (NOTE).

-taney [Ceycwu DIAL] = -ta ka

-tang [Ceycwu DIAL] = -ta ka

Tang < TTANG, noun, adnoun.

1. n. the T(')ang (dynasty of ancient China).

2. adnoun. of Chinese origin. ¶ ~ hō-pak a small red pumpkin used for decoration. ~ mek Chinese ink. ~ nakwi a donkey. ~ sengnyang Chinese matches. ~ mosi ramie cloth. ~ twulwu-mali, ~ cwuci rolled Chinese paper. ~q talk (a kind of chicken); a squat fat man.

tang < *TANG*, adnoun, postnoun.

1. adnoun. the said; that; the concerned; the appropriate; (age) at the time. ¶ ~ hōysa / hak.kyo / putay the concerned firm / school / outfit. ~ Mikwuk cwūcay (uy) cicem ulo se nun as the concerned branch office in America. ~ ī-sip sey 20 years old at the time.

2. postnoun. (for) each, per. ¶il-in ~ = han salam ~ per person.

tang hata < ˙tang °ho˙ta < *TANG* °ho˙ta.

1. vnt (CF **pat.ta, kamtang hata**). suffers, undergoes, sustains, has to put up with, is afflicted with, faces, has to face, has something unpleasant happen to one. (The object is a noun expression, a verb substantive, or a verbal noun. With pre-separable verbal nouns **tang hata** can function as a separable postnominal verb like **hata**.) ¶**puchin sang ul ~** suffers the loss of one's father. **changphi han kkol ul ~** is put to shame. **atul i apeci sayngsin ul ~** the son has his father's birthday to face. **kēcel (ul) ~** is refused, gets turned down. **tōn ul kēcel tang hata** is refused the money. **paychek (ham) ul ~** gets boycotted. **ki ham ul ~** gets shunned, is disliked, suffers ostracism (taboo). **hwānnan ul ~** suffers misfortune. **supkyek (ul) ~** is raided. **kyelpak ~** is tied up.

2. vni. faces, confronts; stands up to. ¶**Ku cāngsa eykey nun nay him man ulo n' tang haci (tang hay nāyci) mōs halq kes kath.ta** I am no match for a strong man like him. ¶**hona˙h i ˙eti˙le ˙cu˙mun ˙salo˙m ol ˙tang ho˙l i ˙l ˙ss oy** (1459 Wel 1:28a) since one alone will easily be a match for a thousand people. **mu˙su.k u˙lwo mozom sa˙ma na 'y cwume˙kwuy pi˙chwuyywo˙m ol** *TANG* ˙honon ˙ta (1462 ¹Nung 1:84a) what will you make your heart be that it face the radiance of my fist? *SAN-HHA* ¨pwo˙m ay *TANG* ˙ho˙ya *LYWUW-LI* ˙lol pwo˙l i ˙ye (1462 ¹Nung 1:58a) facing the sight of mountains and rivers will one see emeralds?

3. adj-n = **haptang hata** = **mattang hata** (< ˙mas.tang °ho˙ta) is suitable, fitting. ¶I kyengwu ey kkok tang han māl ita That's just the word for this situation.

-˙ta-ngi ˙'ta, retr polite + cop indic assert (= -˙te-ngi ˙'ta). ¶˙*SSIM* ˙hi ˙na y ¨*KAM-SYANG* ˙hwo˙toy *ZYE-LOY S MWU-˙LYANG TI-˙KYEN* ˙ul il˙hwo˙la ˙ho˙ta-ngi ˙'ta (1463 Pep 2:4b) I was moved to such grief I was about to lose the tathāgata's immeasurable awareness. ˙wuli nil˙Gwo˙toy ¨*PWON-LOY KKWUW* ˙ho˙nwon mozom ¨epta-ngi ˙'ta ˙honwo˙n i (1459 Wel 13:37a) we say that originally there was no mind seeking it.

-*tangkuney* [Ceycwu DIAL] = -ta ka

tangsin < *TANG-SIN*, noun.

1. you (to equal / inferior; between husband and wife). ¶**Tangsin eti se wass.ˢo** Where are you from? **Tangsin i com towa cwuo** = **Tangsin son com pillipsita** You help me with the work.

2. [old-fashioned, hon (= **caki**)] he, himself (referring to an elder, especially a man's father or grandfather); oneself, Him(self) (= God). ¶**Hal-apeci tangsin kkey se son-swu ciusin cip ita** This is the house which my grandfather built himself. **Tangsin kkey se ku ttay nai sam-sip isyess.ta** He was thirty years old at that time. **Chencwu nim kkey se tangsin ul wi hanun sālam tul ul tōl-pwa cwusinta** God helps those who honor Him.

3. [Christian] thee / thou (to God).

4. [DIAL, JOCULAR] = **sālam**. ¶**i ~** this person; I; you. **ku ~** that person; you **ce ~** that person; he / him, she / her.

-ta 'ni, abbr < -ta (ko) hani. CF -(nu)nta 'ni.

1. says that it is/does and so (etc.). ¶**Ku nom i cip ulo cocha an kakeyss.ta 'ni etteh.key hamyen cōh.keyss.e** He even refuses to go home; (so) what should I do? **Kim sensayng kwa cocha an kakeyss.ta 'ni to-taychey nwukwu hako kakeyss.ta 'n māl yo** You say you don't want to go even with Mr Kim, then who on earth do you want to go with?!

2. (= -nun kes ul poni) judging from the way / fact that it does. ¶**Kulen cīs ul hata 'ni ne to pāpo 'ta** It's very silly for you to do such a thing.

3. (sentence-final — can be followed by **yo**) [? abbr < -nun kes ul poni ...].

3a. what a shame (how disgusting) that ... ! ¶**Wen, casik i cheka sal.i lul hata 'ni!** How shameful for a man to be living in his wife's house! **Tut.ki silh.e; pāpo chelem mac.ko man tanita 'ni; ese tul.e ka se kul tul ina ilk.e la** I don't want to hear any more; how disgusting to go around getting beaten up; go on in and read your books. **Ilum to mōs ssuta 'ni!** How shameful; you can't even write your name! **Swul man mek.ko tol.a tanyess.ta 'ni!** How shameful that he went around drinking all the time! **Nwūn i okeyss.ta 'ni!** What a shame, it's going to snow! **Ku sālam i kkang-phay yess.ta 'ni!** I never thought that HE would be a hoodlum! **Sewul kkaci ka se Changkyeng-wen kwūkyeng to mōs hata 'ni?!** You mean you went all the way to Seoul and didn't even visit Changkyeng Park? **Ku chelem ina sīn.loy hatun chinkwu lul pāypan hata 'ni!** How shameful of him to betray the friend who had trusted him so much! **Ku sālam mace lul totwuk nom chiko hata 'ni** What a shame they treat HIM as a thief! **Sam-chon kkaci lul ttaylita 'ni kulen nappun nom i eti iss.na!** What a wicked fellow he is to hit even his own uncle! **Ku tholok ina āy lul ssuko to an tōyss.ta 'ni?!** What a shame, to work so hard and not be successful! **Twū tal theym ina kellinta 'ni?** You say that it takes two whole months?!

3b. how surprising that ... ! ¶**A.yu, i key wēynq īl isey yo; yeki se poypta 'ni (yo)** Oh, what's this; what a surprise to see YOU!

3c. **Kuleki ey sālam uy īl un molunta 'ni** So you never know what will happen to you in life. **Kattuk ina elyewun the ey pyēng kkaci nata 'ni!** Not only is it terribly difficult, but on top of that I've fallen ill. **Ku chelem kkaci pūthak han kes ul ic.e pelita 'ni!** How could you forget what I asked of you so earnestly!

-ˈta·n i, retrospective modifier + postmodifier.

1. (extruded epitheme). Not used?

2. (summational epitheme used in extended predicate) it is [the fact] that ... was/did. ALSO -ˈte·n i. ¶**ile 'n ˈsalom ˈtol·h ol e·tu·li ˈCYEY-ˈTTWO ho·l [i] 'ye·n ywo ˈhota·n i** (1447 Sek 13:57b) [I] wondered how to save such people. **ˈi lol ˈza pwusˈku·lita·n i** (1449 Kok 121) I was ashamed of all this. **nwoˈlwo.m ol aˈni ho.ya isˈta.n i** (1481 Twusi 7:23a) was not playing. **cyangˈcho na·p i ˈhoyta neˈkita·n i** (1482 Kum-sam 4:22b) it has been deemed that

in the future monkeys will be white. **ˈnayˈye po·lita·n i** (1518 Sohak-cho 10:34b) threw them out. SEE ˈhota·n i.

~ ˈ'la (cop indic assert). ¶**ˈCYWUNG-SOYNG ˈi ˈkot kwo·t ay ˈTTYAK hol ss oy ˈhhye na·key ˈho·ta.n i ˈ'la** (1463 Pep 1:158b) people arrived everywhere and had him initiate them. SEE -ˈa ˈy.sta·n i ˈ'la.

-ta 'ni-kka (n'), abbr < -ta (ko) hani-kka (n'). ¶**Nay ka hay noh.ko to way kulenun ya siph.ul ttay ka iss.ta 'ni-kka n'?!** But I just told you, there are times when, having done it, I wonder why I do it. **Hanta 'ni-kka** (Dupont 127) I (have already) told you it does!

-ta 'ni yo SEE -ta 'ni (3). ABBR -ta 'n' yo.

-tankuney [Ceycwu DIAL] = -ta ka

-ta 'no, abbr < -ta (ko) hano [< hanun ko]. [? DIAL] = -ta 'y?.

-ta 'nta, abbr < -ta (ko) hanta. "I say that it is/does" = I TELL you it is/does; it really is/does; it is/does, you see (mind you). ¶**Ku i ka na hanthey tōn ul cwukeyss.ta 'nta** He really will give me money; He'll give me some money, I tellya. **I tōng.li ey nun kak.kwuk tāysa-kwan i mānh.ta 'nta** There are many embassies of different countries in this district, you see. NOTE: Only the shortened form has this meaning; for the meaning "says/thinks/feels it is/does" standard speakers use only the unabbreviated form. Similar are -ta 'ney, -ta 'o, -ta 'p.nita; contrast -ta 'y, -ta 'ci, etc.

-ˈtan·t ay n' = -ˈten·t ay n'. Unattested?

-ˈtan·t i·m ye n', retr mod + postn + cop subst + cop inf + pcl. ¶**ˈi ˈTTWOW-ˈSSO y CYENG-SSYENG ˈi ˈCI-ˈKKUK ˈhotan·t i·m ye n' ha·nol·h i tangtangi ˈi ˈphi ˈlol ˈsalom towoyˈGey ˈho·si.l i ˈ'la** (1459 Wel 1:7-8) when these students of the Way (= bodhisattvas) have shown extreme devotion, heaven is to make this blood suitably into people.

-ˈtan·t in·t ay n' SEE -u·sitan·t in t ay n'

-ta 'n tul, abbr < -ta ko han tul. ¶**Him i yak hata 'n tul ne pota ya yak hakeyss.nun ya** I may be (said to be) weak, but I am sure that I am no weaker than you.

-ta nun, transferentive + pcl (= -ta ka nun). and then (suddenly). ¶**Ku tay lo kata nun ōn caysan ul tā kka mek.key toylq kes ita** You keep on at that rate and you will find yourself eaten out of house and home! **Ileta nun khunq** īl nakeyss.ta If this goes on you'll get in trouble.

-ta 'nun, abbr < -ta (ko) hanun. ¶Swī Mikwuk ulo tte-nanta 'nun sōmun tul.ess.ci I hear (rumors) that you are soon leaving for America.

-ta 'nun i, abbr < -ta (ko) hanun i. ¶Chwupta 'nun i tēpta 'nun i hako pulphyeng hanun kes un kosayng ul mōs hay pwā se kulay The way he keeps complaining about how cold it is, how hot it is, you can tell he has never known hardships. ABBR -' 'nun i.

~ mankhum. ¶Nam tul i na tele kongpu l' cal hanta 'nun i mankhum nay maum uy chayk.im un te mukewe cinta The more people tell me just how well I am doing in my studies the heavier the burden on my soul.

~ pota (nun). ¶Tōp.nunta 'nun i pota chalali panghay 'ta He is more hindrance than help. Napputa 'nun i pota nun cōh.ta 'nun key tut.ki ey ya cōh.keyss.ci It would be nice to hear something good about it, for a change.

-ta 'nun kes, abbr < -ta ko hanun kes. ¶Achim ilccik il.e nanta 'nun kes un swiwunq īl i ani 'ta It is not an easy thing for me to get up in the morning. Yelqsim hi hay ya hanta 'nun kes ul kkaytal.ess.ta I realized that I must do it with enthusiasm.

-ta 'n' 'wumen (yo), abbr < -ta (ko) hanun kwumen (yo)

-ta 'n' 'wun (a), abbr < -ta (ko) hanun kwun (a)

-ta 'n' yo, abbr < -ta 'ni yo. ¶Kim sensayng nim i osita 'n' yo What an unexpected pleasure to have you come, Mr Kim.

tao < tawo (1730), AUTH command < defective vt tā-l-. give me, do it for me. ¶Na hanthey to mul com tao! Kuliko, i ay hanthey to mul com cwu(o)! Give me some water — and give him some, too! (Ne) i kes com hay tao Do this for me, please. VAR tawu. CF tāko (tākwu).

-ta 'o, abbr < -ta (ko) hao. "I say it is/does" = I TELL you it is/does = it really is/does; it is/does, you see (mind you). SEE -ta 'nta (NOTE).

-ta 'p.nita, abbr < -ta (ko) hap.nita. "I say it is/does" = I TELL you it is/does = it really is/does; it is/does, you see (mind you). SEE -ta 'nta (NOTE).

-ta poni = -ta (ka) poni

-ta ppun, indic assert + pcl. [followed by rhetorical question with (usually future) copula]

it is merely that ··· ?! ¶Kala 'myen kata ppun ikeyss.nun ya?! Do you think I won't go if you tell me to go?! Atta ota ppun ikeyss.e? [rarely ... onta ppun ...] Of course he will come! M 1:2:219 says that this pattern can be used when a hearer wishes to recapitulate a statement more forcefully: Ku pun i mānh.i mek.nunta ppun ikeyss.^{s}up.nikka? He eats much? — I say he eats too much. Olh.ta ppun in ka! (CM 2:201) Not just right, totally right!

-ta 'psiko, abbreviation < -ta (ko) haopsiko. [IRONICAL] saying/thinking/feeling that it is/does. ¶Hak.kyo ey kanta 'psiko na-sess.ta He left home claiming that he was going to school. Na nun cal hanta 'psiko han kes i ileh.key toyess.ta It turned out this way, but I thought I was doing the right thing. Cyāy (= ce ay) ka acwu cal hanta 'psiko ppop-nāynta He puffs himself up thinking/saying that he is doing very well.

tapta, postnom adj insep -w- [inf tawe, lit inf tawa]. is like, is worth being, is worthy of the name, is a compliment to ··· , is every bit a ··· . ¶kkoch ~ is flower-like, is lovely as a flower. kwīcok ~ is aristocratic. sālam ~ is as becomes a human being. yengwung ~ is heroic. namca/sanay ~ is manly, is every inch a man. ^{n}yeca ~ is womanly. ^{n}yewang ~ is queenly. wang ~ is kingly. cham ~ is true. ceng ~ is intimate, close, familiar. sil ~ is dependable, trustworthy, faithful. hakca ~ is scholarly. cito-ca ~ is a real leader. kkol ~ is ugly, unseemly (= kkol sānapta). sīnsa tapkey hayngtong hata behaves like a gentleman. Tāyhan uy ^{n}yeca tapkey in a manner worthy of a daughter of Korea. kul tawun kul an essay worthy of the name. Ku eykey nun yĕyswul-ka tawun tey ka iss.ta He has something of the artist in him. Ku eykey nun hakca tawun tey ka cokum to ēps.ta There is nothing of the scholar about him. Ku nun siin tawun siin ita He is a poet worthy of the name. Tāyhak tawun tāyhak i cēkta Few of the universities are worthy of the name. (There are hardly any universities as we understand the word.) Kuleh.key hayngtong hanun kes un āykwuk-ca tapci anh.ta It doesn't become a patriot to act like that. Kuleh.key māl hanun kes un kutay tapci anh.ta It doesn't become you (is not like you) to say so. Kwā.yen sulki lopko pucilen hamye tay kot.un Cosenq ⁿyeca tapta She is a worthy woman of Korea, wise and hard-working, and straight as a stick. ¹notong-ca sitay uy pulk.un kwahak-ca tapta is an exemplary Red scientist of the age of the workers' party. (?) ssang-twu chen.li-ma lo tallinun onul uy chengnyen tapta is one of today's fine young men who run like a pair of thousand-league horses. CF alittapta, alumtapta (SEE §5.2.8); lopta, sulepta. NOTE: 1916 Gale 101 glosses tapta as 'conformable to, in line with' and gives an example with no noun preceding (tapci mwos hon mal 'unreasonable word') as well as with a noun: es.tekhey cal mantules.non ci cham mwulken tapswo 'so well made, it is really a thing worth seeing'.

-ta 'ptita, abbr < -ta (ko) haptita. "I say it was (or has been doing)" = I TELL you it was (or has been doing) = it really was (or has been doing), you see (mind you). SEE -ta 'nta.

tas (also thas) = thas (fault; reason)

-˙ta˙s, cop indic assertive + pcl. SEE s (15a).

-ta se, transferentive + pcl [fast speech only] = -ta (ka) se. ¶Yeki se com swīta (ka) se kakey na Relax here a while before going. Sikan i ēps.nun tey wuli kata (ka) se sa mekci We have no time, so let's eat on our way there.

~ nun. Example?

-ta siph.i, indicative assertive + derived adverb. [Usually treated by Korean grammarians as an unanalyzed ending -tasiphi.] in a way that tends to do, in a way inclined toward doing, in a way such that it is possible/likely; in a way that is virtually in accordance with, practically, virtually, as much as to do, almost, as if to, "like-to". ¶posita siph.i as you (can) see. āsita siph.i as you know, as you must realize. Tangsin i pota siph.i na nun tōn i ēps.ta As you can see, I have no money. Ku chayk ul ōyta siph.i ilk.ess.ta I have read that book to the point where I have the book practically memorized. Yeki se sālta siph.i hanta They like-to (= practically) live here, they are here so much. Ku tul i (Wuli ka) kwūlm.ta siph.i hanta They (We) are almost starved. Ce nun cenyek mata kukcang ey kata siph.i hayss.ey yo I went to the theater practically every evening.

NOTE: This is a literary cliché and may be attached to the unextended alternant of l- extending stems as well as to the extended alternant: āta/ālta siph.i.

-ta siph.ta, indic assert + aux adj. SEE siph.ta.

-ta son chitula to. even though (we suppose that) ... . ¶Tōn un ēps.ta son chitula to ki mace kkekk.il ya I may be penniless, but is that any reason to lose heart?! SYN -ta chitula to. CF -tula son chila to.

-˙ta˙s-ongi ˙'ta, retr emotive polite + cop indic assert. ¶ "swuy˙n in SSI-˙CYELQ ˙ul ˙pwoken ˙t ay n' ˙pentuk ˙hi KKANG-˙CANG ˙ho˙ta˙s-ongi ˙'ta (1462 ¹Nung 2:6-7) when one has seen fifty whole seasons one is clearly robust. SEE -u˙si˙ta˙s-ongi ˙'ta, a˙ni˙'si˙ta[˙]s-ongi ˙'ta.

-˙tas˙ta, retrospective emotive indic assertive. ¶pwuthye s a˙lom ˙ptu˙t i a˙ni ˙'sya he˙mu˙l i ˙SSILQ ˙lwo na ˙'ykey is˙tas˙ta (1463 Pep 2:6a) it was not Buddha's idea, the fault is really mine. ˙i [PPWO-SYENG] ˙ey [˙KWUY-SSIN] i ˙tu˙tas˙ta (1481 Twusi 16:30a) a ghost has entered Púchéng. cyang˙cho na˙p i ˙hoyta ne˙kita˙n i ˙stwo na˙p i ke˙mu.n i is˙tas.ta (1482 Kum-sam 4:22b) in future they will have said that monkeys are white;or again there will have been some monkeys that are black. SEE ˙i˙las˙ta, -u˙sitas˙ta, ˙ho˙sitas˙ta.

-˙taswo˙la, retr modulated emotive indic assert. ¶˙sumul ˙hoy lol cwo˙cha ton˙nye hwen hi [TYANG-QAN] ˙ay ˙sye [˙CYWUY] ˙hotaswo˙la (1481 Twusi 16:18a) for twenty years I have been getting drunk all over Cháng-ān. [˙TUK-CIN] ˙oy ˙pis ˙na˙m ol tol-hi nye˙kiti a˙ni ˙hotaswo˙la (1481 Twusi 24:30ab) one has not looked kindly on the luster of the special promotion.

-˙taswo˙n i, retrospective modulated emotive modifier + postmod. ¶ho˙ma ˙KWUW-˙KYENG ˙MYELQ-˙TTWO ˙lol ˙TUK ˙hwo˙la ˙ho˙taswo˙n i wo˙nol za a˙lwo˙n i ˙TI-˙HHYWEY ˙ep.su˙n i kot ˙'tas-ongi ˙'ta (1463 Pep 4:36a) having earlier sought to acquire the ultimate nirvāṇa, that I just today understand it is like I had lacked wisdom. pwuthye nilu˙sinwon "HHAY-˙THWALQ ˙ol ˙wuli ˙two ˙TUK ˙ho˙ya ˙NYELQ-PPAN ˙ay tato˙lwon ˙ka ˙ho˙taswo˙n i wo˙nol s ˙nal ˙i ˙ptu˙t ul ˙mwot ˙azo˙Wo˙l i ˙'lwo˙ta (1447 Sek 13:43b) we, too, getting the emancipation that Buddha tells us of, wonder whether we have reached nirvāṇa, but today we cannot know (this =) its meaning.

-ta 'ta, 1. abbr < -ta (ko) hata. ~ ka.
2. ? = -ta (ka) [i]ta
-ta 'tey, abbr < -ta (ko) hatey
-ta 'ti, abbr < -ta (ko) hati
-ta to, transferentive + particle. SEE **-ta ka to**.
-ta 'toy, abbr < -ta (ko) hatoy
tā tul, adv + pcl. everybody, everyone, all of them / you / us. ¶ Tā tul eti kass.ey yo Where is everybody? (Where have they all gone?)
-ta tul, transferentive + particle. SEE **-ta ka tul**.
-ta 'tula, abbr < -ta (ko) hatula.
~ **'ni** < (ko) hani. ¶ Kwī hasin caney ka wuli cip ey l' onta 'tula 'ni ku key cēng-mal in ka? I have been hearing that you, dear soul, will come to our house; is it true?
~ **'tuni** < (ko) hatuni. ¶ Swun-i ka ne hak.kyo kanta 'tula 'tuni yethay an kass.kwun Swun-i said that you were going to school but you still haven't gone, I see.
-ta 'tula 'ci, abbr < -ta (ko) hatula (ko) haci
-ta 'tula 'y, abbr < -ta (ko) hatula (ko) hay
-ta 'tun, abbr < -ta (ko) hatun.
1. ¶ Onta 'tun sālam i wass.ta The man they said would come is here. Yele salam i kath.i onta 'tun nolus i na man okey toyess.ta Our plan was to (= We were supposed to) come together as a group but it turned out that I came all alone.
2. ¶ Ku sālam ēncey onta 'tun? When did he say he would get here?
-ta 'tun ci, 1. (transferentive + ...) SEE **-ta ka 'tun ci**.
2. abbr < -ta (ko) hatun ci. ¶ Chayk ul ilk.e ponta 'tun ci kūlim ul kulye ponta 'tun ci mwe l' com hay pwā la Try doing something, maybe read a book or draw a picture. Swuhay lul phī haki wi hay se nun twutwuk ul noph.i ssah.nunta 'tun ci namu lul sīmnun tūng yele kaci tāychayk i iss.e ya hanta In order to prevent flood damage it is necessary to take all sort of measures, raising dikes and planting trees and so on.
-ta 'tuni, abbr < -ta (ko) hatuni. ¶ Alh.nunta 'tuni melcceng hani tol.a taniki man cal hanta I heard he's sick, but look, he is going around sound as a bell.
~ **man (un)**. ¶ I penq īl un cal toye kanta 'tuni man tto silphay 'la 'n māl iya?! You mean we've failed again, when I heard it was going so nicely?!

-ta 'tun ka, abbr < -ta (ko) hatun ka
-ta 'tun kes i, abbr < -ta (ko) hatun kes i. ¶ Pi ka onta 'tun kes i nwūn i onun kwun a (CM 2:219) They predicted rain, but it's snowing!
-ta 'tun tey, abbr < -ta (ko) hatun tey. ¶ Tut.kentay ku ka sāep ey silphay hayss.ta 'tun tey As I hear tell, he failed in business. SEE **-tun tey** for more examples.
-ta 'tun ya, abbr < -ta (ko) hatun ya. ¶ Ku sālam kanta 'tun ya onta 'tun ya (ttok-ttok hakey māl com hay pwā la) Tell me clearly — did you say he's going, or coming? Na 'la ko pam-nac nappunq īl man iss.ta 'tun ya?! Do you think I have hard luck ALL the time?!
taum, n. next, second; following, coming, ensuing, adjoining, adjacent; (-un ~) next after (doing). ¶ ~ nal the next / following day, the day after. ~q pang the next / adjoining room. ~q sālam the next / following person. ~q pen the next time / occasion. ~q tal (KBC) the next month. ~ puthe (nun) from now on. taum taum (the one) after the next
~ **ey** next, secondly, in the second place; then, after (that); next / another time / occasion; in the following. ¶ Taum ey cwūuy halq kes un tōn ul akkye ssulq kes ita Secondly, you must be frugal with your money. Ne nun i taum ey teyliko kam a I will take you next time. Ku kisa nun taum kwa kath.ta The article is as follows. Kuliko taum ey chinkwu tul ul chac.ess.ta And then I visited friends.
tawo SEE **tao**
tawu [var] = **tao**
tawul(q), prospective modifier < **tapta**
tawum, substantive < **tapta**
tawun, modifier < **tapta**
t'āy = twāy = twēy = tōy < **toye**, inf < **toyta**.
tay < *tay*, noun, postmod, postnoun. SEE ~ lo. ches ~ / ccay (lo) first(ly). CF **ccay, chay**.
tay, postmod. [DIAL] = **tey** (circumstance; and, but). CF Roth 481.
tay [var] = *toy* place. SEE -*wolq tay*.
t ay, postmod + pcl. SEE -*'ken 't ay n', -'un 'tay (n'), -u'sin 't ay (n'), (-ulq) 't in t ay n'*.
-tay = -*toy*
-tay, inf < **-tah.ta**.
-ta 'y, abbr < -ta (ko) hay. says / thinks / feels that it is / does. ¶ Tōn i ēps.ta 'y He says (or: they say / I hear) that he has no money.
~ **to**. ¶ An mek.nunta 'y to cakkwu man

mek.ula 'y?! Must you keep urging me to eat when I tell you I won't?!

-ta ya, 1. transferentive + pcl. SEE **-ta ka ya**, which sounds better; - ˈta ˈza.

2. indic assertive + pcl. SEE **-keyss.ta ya**.

tāy hata < ˈTWOY°hoˈta, vni, vnt (insep).

1. vnt. faces, fronts, confronts, is opposed to, is over against. ¶**Cel i san ul tāy hako sunta** A temple stands facing a hill. **elkwul ul macwu tāy hako anc.ta** sit facing each other, sit face to face. **cek ul ~** confronts an enemy; engages (deals with) an enemy.

2. vnt. sees, faces; addresses, receives, treats. ¶**sālam ul tāy haki silh.e hata** doesn't like to see people. **sālam ul ttattus 'i ~** receives a person warmly / cordially. **sālam ul hwū hi ~** treats a person generously.

3. vni. refers (to), concerns, is concerned (with), is about; toward, to, against. CF **kwan hata**. ¶**congkyo ey tāy han secek** books on religion. **sisa mūncey ey tāy han kāngyen** a lecture on current affairs. **kwuk.ka ey tāy han ūymu** one's duty to(ward) the nation. **sensayng ey tāy han thāyto** one's attitude toward one's teacher. **munhak ey tāy han hūngmi** one's interest in literature. **cilmun ey tāy han tāytap** an answer to a question. **kyel.uy ey tāy han hānguy** a protest against a decision. **ap.lyek ey tāy han cēhang** resistance against pressure.

4. vni. compares; against, to. ¶**Yeki tāy hamyen ku kaps un pissata** Compared with this, the price of that is too high. **Ku uy payk phyo ey tāy hay se na nun ī-payk phyo lul et.ess.ta** I got two hundred votes to / against his one hundred.

5. vni. matches, equals, rivals. ¶**Haksik ey iss.e ku ey tāy halq sālam i ēps.ta** There is no one his equal in learning.

NOTE: In 4 and 5, the appropriate particle for people / creatures is **eykey** or **hanthey**, for things **ey**; in 3 the appropriate particle is **ey** for both. Under 1 there are expressions such as **Sensayng nim eykey tāy hanun thāyto ka acwu ¹yeycel i iss.ta** (Mkk 1961:4:10) He has a very polite attitude toward his teacher.

(-)taykali, 1. n [vulgar] head (= **meli**). **wus ~** chief. 2. postnoun, suffix (vulgarizes nouns). **mas ~**, **mes ~** taste, flavor. CF **(-)ttakci**.

-taykangi = **-taykali** 2. **mas ~**, **mes ~** taste, flavor.

tāykay, 1. noun. outline, summary, gist.

2. adverb. in general, by and large, mainly, for the most part; nearly, almost; probably, most likely. VAR **tēykey**.

(-)(t)tayki, postnoun, suffix. thing, one; body part; piece (= **cokak, tongkang**).

1. **ttayki** < **-q tayki**.

1a. **hye ~** tongue. **kwi ~** ear. **pay ~** stomach, belly, "tummy". **phal ~** arm. **pol ~** [DIAL] = **ppyam ~** cheek. **tung ~** back.

1b. **chel ~** good sense, discretion. **col ~** petty job / person; Korean chess pawn. **congi ~** a piece of paper. **kamani ~** a shabby / dirty straw bag. **kecek ~** a straw mat. **namu ~** a small piece of wood, a stick, a board. **non ~** a small rice paddy. **path ~** a small field (CF **path han ttwayki** a strip of field). **yo ~** shabby / dirty / flimsy bedding.

2. **tayki**.

2a. **kwi-mith ~** the roots of one's ears. **kwi ssa ~** the area where the cheek meets the ear. **(myēn)ssa ~** face (= **nach**); CF **nach-patayki** [< **patak + i**] face.

2b. **pan ~** a flattened dumpling, (= **pan**) sheet; a saucer. ¶**phan ~** a wide board, a plank. **pho ~** a baby's quilt.

? < **tay stick + -ayki**; CF **mak-tayki** (dimin < obs **mak-tay**) a stick, a staff, a cane

-ta 'y 'la, abbr < **-ta (ko) hay la**

tay lo < ˈtay ˈlwo, n + pcl (used as postmod, postnoun). as, just as, just as it is / was, with something still (as it was); in accordance with; (~-nun ~) as soon as.

1. postmodifier. ¶**Halq tay lo hay la** Do as you like. (Have your own way.) **Na hanun tay lo hay la** Do as I do. **Chayk ul noh.in tay lo noh.a twuess.ta** I left the book as it was. **Kwutwu lul sin.un tay lo pang ey tul.e kass.ta** He went into the room with his shoes (still) on. **Mek.ulq tay lo mek.ess.ta** I have eaten as much as I can. (I have eaten my fill.) **Palun tay lo māl hay la** Tell the truth! **Toylq tay lo toye la** I don't care what happens. SEE **-nun tay lo, -un tay lo, -wulq ˈtay ˈlwo**.

2. postn. ¶**kulq-ca ~** to the letter, literally. **maum ~** as one likes / wants / wishes. **ttus ~** as one expected. **pep ~** according to law. **ney māl ~** as you say/said. **cey ~** the proper way, properly; smoothly; as it should be; on time. **Cey mes tay lo hanta** He does as he pleases.

Ku tay lo twue la Leave it as it is. Na / Wuli tay lo man hay la Do it my / our way.

3. → tāy lo, abbr < tāysin. ¶Ne tāy lo nay ka kam a I'll go in your place.

-ta(y) 'myen → -ta 'myen (< -ta ko hamyen). The ···y version is probably from analogy with -ta 'y yo < -ta ko hay yo.

˙t ay n' SEE - ᵘ/on ˙t ay n', (-ᵘ/olq) ˙t in t ay n'

-tayngi, suffix.

1. person [? DIAL var < -ca(y)ngi]. chong ~ a gunner; a hunter, a gun(s)man.

2. place [? var < tey place + -angi; ? var < -tayki]. yeph ~ (the place) right beside.

-tayngtayng, bound adjectival noun (~ hata); after a consonant -utayngtayng; LIGHT ↔ -teyngteyng. ···ish, slightly colored / tinged; slightly characterized by. SEE -(u)sulum.

-ta yo, 1. transferentive + pcl. SEE -ta ka yo.

2. [Phyengan DIAL] = -kwulye 3.

3. SEE -sup.nita yo. There is no *hanta yo (→ hap.nita), nor is there a *mek.nunta yo (→ meksup.nita). CF -ta ko / kwu yo.

-ta 'y se (ya), abbr < -ta (ko) hay se (ya). ¶Sonq-kum ponta 'y se sonq-kum ca(y)ngi 'la ko hanta A "palmist" is so called because he reads (the lines of one's) palms. Caney ka an onta 'y se ya toyl māl in ka Don't tell me you won't BE here! Acik to molunta 'y se ya māl i toyna?! It is absurd for you to say that you do not know about it yet. SEE ila 'y se (ya).

tāysin < ˙TTOY-SIN, n. 1. a substitute; ··· uy ~ (ey) instead of ··· , in place/lieu of ··· ; ~ ulo as a substitute. ¶ku tāysin ey instead. Talun māl uy tāysin nolus ul hanta It functions as a substitute for some other word. Kaptong-i tāysin ey cey (ka) kalq ka yo? Shall I go instead of Kaptong-i? Nay ka Payk kwun tāysin Mikwuk ey iss.nun chinkwu eykey phyēnci lul Yenge lo sse cwess.ta I wrote a letter in English for young Payk to his friend in America.

~ i toyta serves as, does duty for.

~ hata (vnt) takes the place of, substitutes for, replaces. ¶Ku i lul tāysin halq sālam i ēps.ta There is no one who can take his place. Ape' nim ul tāysin hay se cey ka poywulye ko wass.ˢup.nita I have come to see you in place of my father.

2. compensation, return; ··· uy ~ (ey / ulo) in return / compensation for ··· , to make up for ··· .

3. (as postmodifier) SEE -un / -nun ~ (ey).

-ta 'yss-, abbr < -ta (ko) hayss-

-ta 'yss.ca, abbr < -ta (ko) hayss.ca. (let's say it is =) suppose, if.

-ta 'yss.ta, abbr < -ta (ko) hayss.ta

tāyta$_{1-6}$, vt. 1. brings into contact, connects, links; touches, puts (one's hand to); lays, places, holds (one's hand on); fixes, puts, attaches; compares (it) with.

2. draws (water) into, irrigates; supplies, provides, furnishes.

3. depends upon for (supplies), get one's (supplies) from, draws a supply of.

4. tells, indicates, shows, informs of; tells (the truth), speaks up / out, confesses, "spits it out".

5. pulls up, stops (a vehicle).

6. bets, takes.

7. ekci lul tāyta / ssuta behaves stubbornly.

tāyta$_7$, aux v insep. (does) terribly, awfully, a lot, like mad / crazy / anything — gives emphatic force to a preceding verb infinitive. ¶kēcis māl ul kkwumye ~ fabricates a downright lie. mol.a ~ runs (a person) down like anything, denounces severely. wul.e ~ cries a lot, wails to high heaven. mek.e ~ stuffs oneself with food. wus.e ~ laughs one's head off, laughs to beat the band. masye ~ drinks like a fish. ssawe ~ is always quarreling. mul.e ~ scolds at, questions closely. wukye ~ stubbornly clings to. ttē-tul.e ~ is terribly noisy.

tāyta$_8$, postnom v insep [colloq] = kelita (does repeatedly, etc.). SEE ppi-tayta, puph-tayta.

-taytay, bnd adj-n (~ hata); after a consonant -utaytay; LIGHT ↔ -teytey. ···ish, slightly colored / tinged; slightly characterized by. SEE -(u)sulum.

-ta 'y to, abbr < -ta (ko) hay to. SEE -ta 'y.

-ta 'y ya, abbr < -ta (ko) hay ya. ¶Ney nwun ulo pwass.ta 'y ya ku ka kot.i tul.ulq kes ita He will be convinced only if you tell him you have seen it with your own eyes. El.um i mul pota chata 'y ya māl i toyci To make sense you have to say that ice is colder than water.

-ta 'y yo, abbr < -ta (ko) hay yo. SEE -ta 'y.

-˙ta za, transferentive + pcl (= -ta ya). ¶˙NGUY lol pu˙the ˙KWAN ol niluwoy˙ta ˙za pi˙luse CIN-˙CYENG hon SYWUW-HHOYNG i towoy.l i ˙l ˙s oy (1465 Wen 2:3:2:68a) for only when one raises one's consciousness relying upon righteousness

does proper ascetic practice come into being.
⋯t ̈cop- < ⋯t- ̈zop- (including -T/L-), < ⋯th- ̈zop-; = ⋯ ̈ccop- < ⋯c- ̈zop-, < ⋯ch- ̈zop-.
-te- [DIAL] = -tu- (retrospective)
- ̇te-, retrospective. Attested (like its variant - ̇ta-) after o, a(C), eC, i(C): ̇hote ̇la (1447 Sek 6:30a), ̇cate ̇la (1481 Twusi 8:9b), ̇katen ̇t ey n' (1445 ¹Yong 51), pat ̇te ̇n ywo (?1517- Pak 1:19b), ̈epte ̇n ye (1459 Wel 8:91b), ̈he ̇ten (1463 Pep 2:166a; < ̈hel-), nilu ̇site ̇n i (1447 Sek 13:27a), nik ̇tesi ̇n i ̇ ̇la (1459 Wel 1:52b). Also occurs (unlike - ̇ta-) after wo(C), wu(C), u, and Vy: na ̇za ̇woten ̇t ey n' (1445 ¹Yong 51), mwot ̇te ̇n i (1445 ¹Yong 9), ̇twuten ̇t ay n' (1463 Pep 2:231b), ̈mwut ̇tesi ̇tun (1482 Kum-sam 3:12a), nilu ̇te ̇si-ngi ̇ ̇ta (1459 Wel 7:53a), ̇na- ̇ka ̇ys ̇tesi ̇n i (1445 ¹Yong 49), ̇twu-ys.ten ̇ta (1459 Wel 9:35c).
t'e = t'ē, abbr < twe = twē, abbr < twue, inf < twuta.
te, adverb. 1. more (quantity); longer (time), on longer; farther (distance), on farther; further, on further; any more. ¶Te tusici yo Have some more (to eat / drink); Have a second helping. Com te kel.e kake la Walk a little bit farther. Com te iss.ta ka kasey yo Stay a little longer. Te iss.na yo? Is there any more?
2. more (than), still more; more than any other, most (of all). ¶Ku nun na pota khi ka (te) khuta He is taller than I am. Yelq-twu pay cwung ey i pay ka te khuta (1881 Ridel 38; odd?) This is the largest of the twelve boats (= bigger than any other of the twelve boats).
CF tewuk(-i), tekwu(nta)na; tēl.
te hata, 1. adj-n. is more (so), is greater, is worse. 2. vni. gets more (so), is aggravated / worsened, it worsens; it grows (in intensity), gets intensified. 3. vnt. adds it; increases it.
-tei(-kka, -ta) [obs] = -ti- (retrospective)
-tek / -tak SEE -ttek / -ttak
(-)teki, postn, suffix. one, guy, thing. ¶chēn ~ a despised person, a child of scorn. ken ~ solid ingredients (in soup etc.). CF nwuteki (< nwutek + i) shabby clothes, tatters; muteki (?< mut- = mot- + -eki) heap; kwuteki maggot (< ?). VAR (-)teyki; (-)tek.kwungi. CF (-)ttuki.
(-)tek.kwungi, suffix = (-)teki (one, guy, thing).
t'e la = t'ē la, abbr < twe la = twē la, abbr < twue la.

- ̇te ̇la, retrospective indicative assertive. ¶ ̇wolhi ̇Gwa kulyeki ̇Gwa y ̇hye 'ys.non ̇pul s pi ̇ch ey ̇sye ̇cate ̇la (1481 Twusi 8:9b) the ducks and the wild geese slept in the glow of the fire that was lit. mek ̇te ̇la (?1517- ¹No 2:53b) ate. SEE ̇hote ̇la.
tele, pcl < to ̇lye inf < to ̇li ̇ta (> teylita take a person along) — 1893 Scott 19 tolye / tele animate 'to'; 154, 216 just tolye. CF te ̇pu ̇le.
1. (orders / tells / instructs / shows) to (usually an inferior); CF poko, eykey, hanthey. ¶Apeci kkey se na tele sim-pulum kala ko hasinta Father tells me to go on an errand. Nwu ka ne tele cal-mos hayss.ta 'nun ya Who's blaming you? (= I'm not blaming you). Ku nulk.un-i ka ai tele kil ul mul.ess.ta The old man asked his way of a child. Ku i tele to ola ko māl hayss.ni? Did you tell him to come too? CF §10.8.11. SEE na l' tele (= na tele), ne l' tele (= ne tele); but no *na lul tele, *ne lul tele.
2. SEE ppun ~
tele chelem, pcl + pcl. ¶Ku i tele chelem tōn nāyla ko haki him tun sālam un ēps.ta He is the hardest man on earth to get money out of.
tele cocha, pcl + pcl. ¶Ku i tele cocha ola 'n māl i ēps.ess.ta They didn't invite even him.
tele ka, pcl + pcl. ¶Ku i tele ka ani 'la ne tele kala 'nun kes ita It is not him but you that they want to go.
tele khenyeng, pcl + pcl. ¶Ku i tele khenyeng na tele to ola 'n māl i ēps.tula They didn't invite even me, much less him.
tele kkaci, pcl + pcl. ¶Musunq īl lo na tele kkaci kaca 'nun ya What on earth do you want me to go along for?
tele 'la 'myen. ¶Na tele 'la 'myen ku sālam i iss.ci malla ko hayss.keyss.ci If it were (to) me he would tell me not to stay.
tele lang, pcl + pcl. ¶Poktong-i tele lang kath.i kētul.e cwula ko hayss.nun tey cal hako iss.nun ci molukeyss.ta I told Poktong-i (and them) to help him; I wonder if they are getting along all right.
~ to. ¶ Ku i ka ne tele lang to kulen māl ul hatun? Was he telling you the same thing?
~ un. ¶Ku i tele lang un kulenq iyaki haci mal.e Don't tell that story to HIM.
tele 'la to, pcl + cop var inf. ¶Ku i tele 'la to com wā se towa tālla ya ̇keyss.ta I think I'll have to ask even him to come help me.

tele 'la ya, pcl + cop var inf + pcl. ¶Kkok caney tele 'la ya māl haci, talun sālam tele nun mōs hakeyss.ta 'y He says he will tell it only to you and to nobody else.

tele man, pcl + pcl. ¶Ne tele man kacila ko hatula He wanted only you to keep them.

tele 'na, pcl + cop advers. ¶Ku i tele 'na towa tālla ko halq ka I wonder if I should ask HIM for help.

tele 'na-ma, pcl + extended copula adversative. ¶Ku i tele 'na-ma com towa tālla ko hay ya 'keyss.ta I think I'll have to ask even him to help me.

teleng, pcl → tul ilang

tele 'n tul, pcl + cop mod + postmod. ¶Hyeng hanthey halq swu iss.nun māl ila 'myen na tele 'n tul mōs halq key mue 'n ka What is it that you can tell my brother and not tell me?

tele nun, pcl + pcl. Na tele nun a.yey tōn tālla ko haci mal.e Never ask ME for money!

tele pota, pcl + pcl. ¶Na tele pota ne tele hala 'nun kes ita He wants you to do it rather than me.

~ **nun**. ¶Na tele pota nun ne tele māl haki ka swīpkeyss.ta 'y (He says that) it would be easier for him to tell you than to tell me.

~ **to**. ¶I nolay nun opheyla kaswu tele pota to ccaycu-singke tele pulle tālla 'nun key cōh.keyss.e It would be better to have a jazz singer sing this song rather than an opera singer.

tele puthe, pcl + pcl. ¶Ku i tele puthe kac'ta cwusey yo Bring his (order) first. Na tele puthe mōs hanun māl ul ne tele 'n tul hakeyss.ni? Would they tell you something they wouldn't be able to tell me first? Ku i tele puthe mence hala ko hasio Tell HIM to do it first.

tele to, pcl + pcl. ¶Ne tele to ola ko hatula They (said they) want YOU to come, too.

tele 'tun ci. ¶Sensayng nim kkey se ne tele 'tun ci na tele 'tun ci kan ey īl ul towa tālla 'silq kes kath.tula The teacher may ask either you or me to help.

tele wa, pcl + pcl [awkward]. ¶Ne tele wa na tele ku īl ul hay ya hanta ko sensayng nim kkey se māl-ssum hasyess.ta The teacher told you and me to do the work.

tele ya, pcl + pcl. ¶Ku i tele ya etteh.key tōn ul nāyla 'lq swu ka iss.na How could we ask HIM to put out the money?

~ **māl lo**. ¶Ku i tele ya māl lo kipu lul hala ko hay ya 'ci HE is the one you should ask for a donation.

'/-ten [DIAL, lit] = **'/-tun**

-'*ten*, retr mod. ¶ "*epten ¨pen¨key ¨lul ha¨nol¨h i pol¨kisi¨n i* (1445 ¹Yong 30) heaven shone with lightning that had not existed (before). "*nyey ¨epten ¨i¨l ol* (1447 Sek 19:40b) = "*nyey ¨ep¨ten ¨i¨l ol* (1459 Wel 18:7b) an event that is unprecedented. KYENG "*ho¨ten cyen¨cho¨lwo* (1463 Pep 2:166a) for the reason that they had spoken ill of the sūtra. SEE '*hoten, 's¨ten*; CF -'*t on*. VAR -'*tan*.

-'*te-ngi¨'ta*, retr + polite marker + cop indic assertive. ¶*kutuy s¨sto¨l ol mas¨kwo¨cye¨ho¨te-ngi¨'ta* (1447 Sek 6:15a) he has been wanting to meet your daughter.

'*te-ngi¨'ta*, abbreviation < '*ho¨te-ngi¨'ta* after voiceless sounds. ¶ 'SSILQ¨*lwo* 'SYEY-CWON ¨*mal¨kot*¨'*te-ngi¨'ta* (1459 Wel 9:36d) it really was like what the World-Honored said.

-teni [DIAL, lit] = **-tuni**

-'*te¨n i*, retr mod + postmod. ALSO -'*ta¨n i*.

1. (extruded epitheme). Not used?
2. (summational epitheme used in an extended predicate). it is [the fact] that ··· was/did. ¶*[¨PPWONG-THYEN THWOW-¨CCWOY] 'sil¨ss oy [SYEY-PANG CYE-HHWUW] y mwot¨te¨n i* (1445 ¹Yong 9) since he served heaven and avenged evil, the western lords gathered [round him]. SEE '*hote¨n i*.

~ '*'la* (copula indic assertive). ¶ "SYWOW KKWU-TTAM¨*i* KAM-¨CYA NGWEN¨*ey* "*sa¨losil¨ss oy* KAM-¨CYA ¨SSI '*la¨'two¨'ho¨te.n i¨'la* (1459 Wel 1:8ab) Gautama the Lesser was also called Sugarcane Sire (Ikṣvāku) because he lived in a sugarcane garden.

~ '*-ngi s¨ka* (copula polite + pcl + postmodifier). SEE -*u¨site¨n i¨'-ngi s¨ka*.

~ '*-ngi¨'ta* (cop polite + cop indic assert). ¶KKEN-¨THALQ-PPA¨*oy a¨tol¨i nwol* Gay¨*lol pul¨la ¨CHILQ-¨PWOW KKUM¨ul ¨nwote¨n i¨'-ngi¨'ta* (1459 Wel 21:190a) the son of the gandharvas [Indra's musicians] was singing and playing the harp of the seven precious things.

-'*ten¨ka*, retr mod + postmod. SEE '*ho¨si¨ten ka*.

-ten ko [DIAL, obs] = **-tun ka**

-'*ten¨'ta*, retr mod + postmod. ¶ "*ne y¨i* 'NYEM¨*ul¨twu-'ys.ten¨'ta a¨ni¨twu-'ys.ten¨'ta* (1459

Wel 9:35c) do you hold this idea or don't you? ˝ne y e˙tuy ˙ka is˙ten ˙ta (?1517- Pak 1:37b) where have you been?

-˙ten ˙t ay n', retr mod + postmod + pcl + pcl. ¶˙hota˙ka˙wuli˙khun ˙PEP ˙cul˙kil mozo˙m ol ˙twuten ˙t ay n' pwu˝thye y ˝na l' ˙WUY ˙ho˙sya ˙TTAY-SSING ˙PEP ˙ul nilo˙si˙l i ˙'las-ongi˙'˙ta (1463 Pep 2:231b) if we have kept minds that rejoice in the greater dharma, Buddha will for my sake tell the law of the greater vehicle (mahāyāna). ··· ˙SYANG is˙ten˙t ay n' pan˙toki CIN-SIM ˙ho˙ya muy˙ywu˙m ul ˝nay.l i ˙'˙le.n i ˙'la (1464 Kumkang 79b) when one had these distinctive marks (of ...) one would emit glaring hatred (I recall).

-˙ten˙t ey n', retr mod + postmod + pcl + pcl. ¶˝a˙zoWwo˙toy na˙za wo˙n i mul˙le˙katen˙t ey n' mwok-˝swum mo˙cho˙l i '-ngi s˙ka (1445 ¹Yong 51) knowing this he advanced; if he had withdrawn would he have ended (= lost) his life?

-˙ten˙t ol, retr mod + postmod + pcl. ¶ cis.ki lol il hoten t ol cyeki mak.ki tywohulle.n i (1677 Pak-cwung 3:45; cited from LCT) it was good that there was little to hinder work on the construction.

-˙ten˙t oy n', retr mod + postmod + pcl + pcl. ¶˙hota˙ka NUNG˙hi mozo˙m ay selu ˝THYEY-˙SIN ˙ho˙zopten˙t oy n' ingey elwu mas-˙na ˙TUK ˙ho˙ya ˝cams.kan˙two e˙lyewu˙m i ˝ep.su˙l i ˙Ge˙nul (1463 Pep 2:226a) perhaps if we can trust each others' bodies to our minds, henceforth we will not have the least moment of difficulty in getting to meet.

-tenya [DIAL, obs] = -tunya = -tun ya

-˙te˙n ye, retrospective modifier + postmodifier. ¶as.ka˙Wun ˙ptu˙t i ˝epte˙n ye (1459 Wel 8:91b) did he feel no regret? pwu˝thye y nilo˙sya˙toy na˙'y nilo˙ten ˙KWU-LA ˙TYEY CIN-˙SSILQ ˙lwo ku˙le the˙n ye a˙ni the˙n ywo (1459 Wel 9:36d) Buddha said "Was the emperor Kwula really as I said or wasn't he?"

-˙te˙n ywo, retrospective mod + postmodifier. ¶ ˝ce y ˙sywukwong ˙ul ˝en˙me˙'y˙na pat˙te˙n ywo (?1517- Pak 1:19b) how much did he get for his labor himself?

tepeki, postnoun. lots / heaps of. ¶(cīn) hulk ~ paychwu a muddy cabbage. os i mek ~ ka toyta gets ink all over one's clothes. menci ~ (all) covered with dust. nwūn ~ covered with snow. kalwu ~ caked with flour. CF tepulwuk hata; pempek, thwusengi.

te˙pu˙le, 1. inf < ˙te˙pu[l]˙ta. 2. (quasi-pcl) = (ul) to˙lye to (an inferior). ¶ SYWU-˙TTALQ ˙i ˙SYA-˙LI-˙PWULQ te˙pu˙le mwu˙lwo˙toy ... (1447 Sek 6:23a) Sudatta asks Śāriputra [as follows].

tepulta < te˙pu[l]˙ta, vt -L- (now normally defective: gerund and infinitive only).

1. vt. takes / brings (a person) along; escorts, is accompanied by. ¶kacok ul tepulko kata flees with one's family. ˙QILQ-CHYEN ˙PPEM-˙CI te˙pul˙Gwo (1449 Kok 109) accompanied by a thousand brahmacārin (ascetics).

2. vi. is entailed. ¶Ku mūncey ey yele kaci kōn.¹nan i tepulko iss.ta The problem entails many difficulties.

3. vi. ··· ulo / kwa tepul.e (together) with (= ··· kwa hamkkey / kath.i). ¶chenci lo tepul.e mukwung hata is everlasting with heaven and earth. Ku i wa tepul.e tathwul phil.yo ka ēps.ta You need not quarrel with him.

tes(-), adnoun, bound adverb [< te + s]. added, additional, put-on, affixed.

1. adnoun. SEE ~ cangphan, ~ cekoli, ~ keli, ~ keypi, ~ kwutwu, ~ mun, ~ mul, ~ nal, ~ nēl, ~ pesen, ~ sin, ~ twuli; tesq yangmal, tesq i = tes-ni /tenni/.

2. bnd adverb. SEE ~ nata, ~ nāyta, ~ puth.ta, ~ puth.ita, ~ tulta, ~ tullita.

3. ip-tes morning sickness < ip [mas i] tes [nam]. ¶ ~ (i) nata gets morning sickness.

tes < ˙tet, bnd n. interval of time (= tong-an). enu-tes before one knows it, unawares, in no time at all. ku-tes [obs] = ku tong-an (ey) meanwhile. tes-ēps.ta /tetēptta/ (most often as modifier tes-ēps.nun) is transient, ephemeral; tes-ēps.i /tetēpssi/ ephemerally [No particle can intervene]. hayq-tes a short autumn day. cēk(.)un-tes [? DIAL; obs (SEE ˙tet)] in a little while, in just a minute.

t'e se = t'ē se, abbr < twe se = twē se, abbr < twue se.

-˙te˙sin, retr hon mod (= -u˙siten). ¶˙hota˙ka ta˙si ˝a˙lay s pwuthye ˙hote˙sin PANG-˙PPYEN ˙LUK ˙ul ˙NYEM ˙ho˙ya (1447 Sek 13:58a) perhaps again bearing in mind the force of the expedient methods (upāya) employed by some earlier Buddha ... .

-˙te˙si-ngi˙'˙ta, retr hon polite + cop indic assert (= -u˙site-ngi˙'˙ta). ¶ZYE-LOY ˙i na˙la[h]

˝spwun a˙ni ˙˙la nyenu na˙la.h ay ˙two ˝ta ˝kye˙sya ˝KHWO-KHWONG MWU-SSYANG MWU-˝NGA [G]wa ˙LYWUK PA-LA-˙MILQ ˙ul nilu˙te˙si-ngi ˙˙ta (1459 Wel 7:53a) the tathāgata was not only in this land but also in other lands and he told of the emptiness of suffering, the lack of permanence, the irreality of the ego, and the six paramitās.

-˙tesi˙n i, retr hon mod + postmod (= -u˙site˙n i). ¶ ˝˝nim-˙ku˙m i ˙na-˙ka ˙ys˙tesi˙n i (1445 ¹Yong 49) the emperor had fled away. MWON ˙tol˙h ol ˝ta kwu˙ti com˙kye ˙twu-˙ys˙tesi˙n i (1447 Sek 6:2b) locked up all the doors firmly and stayed there. SEE ˙ho˙tesi˙n i.

-˙tesi˙n i ˙˙la, retr hon mod + postmod + cop. ¶ ˙cokya s mozo˙m i nik˙tesi˙n i ˙˙la (1459 Wel 1:52b) his own mind had matured.

-˙tesi˙n i s ˙ka, retr hon mod + postmod [+ ellipted cop polite] + pcl + postmod. ¶ kutuy ˙non a˙ni tutco˙Wa˙ys˙tesi˙n i s ˙ka (1447 Sek 6:17a) you have not heard [about Buddha's name]?

-˙tesin ˙ka, retr hon mod + postmod (= -u˙siten ˙ka). ¶ [CHYA-YANG k ˝sey ˙cwuy ˝nyey ˙two is˙tesin ˙ka (1445 ¹Yong 88) were there [not] three rats on the eaves also in the olden days?! ˙thwu˙kwu ˝sey ˙sa˙l i ˝nyey ˙two ˙stwo is˙tesin ˙ka (1445 ¹Yong 89) were there [not] moreover three arrows [shot] at the helmet also in the olden days?!

-˙tesi˙ta, retr hon indic assert (= -u˙site˙la). ¶ ˙KYWOW-˝HWA ˙ho˙tesi˙ta (1447 Sek 6:44a) he converted him. LYWONG ˙kwa ˝KWUY-SSIN ˙kwa ˝wuy ˙ho˙ya ˙SYWELQ-˙PEP ˙ho˙tesi˙ta (1447 Sek 6:1a) (he) preached the doctrine for the sake of the nāga (serpents) and the ghosts-and-spirits. ˝SSYEN-˙HHYWEY tut˝cop˙kwo kis˙ke ˙ho˙tesi˙ta (1459 Wel 1:18ab) [the bhikṣu (almsman)] Shànhuì heard [this] and rejoiced.

-˙tesi˙tun, retr hon provisional (?= *-u˙site˙tun, CF -te˙tun). if, when. ¶ ˙hota ˙ka pwu˝thye y ˙SYANG ˙ol ˝mwut˙tesi˙tun ˙stwo NUNG ˙hi ˙SYANG ˙olwo ˙TWOY-˙TAP ˙hozo˙wo.l i ˙˙la (1482 Kum-sam 3:12a) if one asks Buddha about a phenomenon he will respond with a phenomenon.

t'ess.ta, abbr < twess.ta, abbr < twuess.ta.

˙tet, n. a time (interval), a while. ¶ ˙CHALQ-NA ˙non a˙ni han ˙te.t i˙la (1462 ¹Nung 2:7a) a kṣetra (= an instant) is a brief moment. ˙pap me˙kulq ˙tet ˝man ˙tyeng TTYANG-SSYANG ˙i ˝i˙l ol ˙soyng˙kak ho˙la (1459 Wel 8:8b) think about this matter not just while you eat but all the time. cyekun ˙te.t ul ˙sye ˙sywu˙la (1481 Twusi 8:2b) they stand a little while.

t'e to = t'ē to, abbr < twe to = twē to, abbr < twue to.

-˙te˙tun, retr provisional (?< -te-˙t un retr + 'fact' + pcl). but, and; if, when. ¶ ˙nom to˙lye nilu˙ti a˙ni ˙hote˙tun QA-˙NWOK TA-LA SAM-˙MAK SAM-PPWO-TTYEY ˙lol spol˙li ˙TUK ˙˙ti ˝mwot ho˙l i ˙˙le.n i ˙˙la (1447 Sek 19:34ab) I did not tell the others but one cannot quickly obtain unexcelled complete enlightenment (anuttara-samyak-sambodhi). kutuy ˙Gwos na˙kunay ˙lul solang ˙thi a˙ni ˙hote˙tun ˙kumwom na˙l ay ˙stwo si˙lu.m ul teu˙l i ˙las˙ta (1481 Twusi 15:31b) you failed to love the wayfarer, and at the end of the month that will add more to your sorrow. ˙hay ˙na y il˙cuk ˝a˙ti ˝mwot ˝hwola ˝pol˙sye ˝a˙te˙tun pwo˙la ˝ka.m i ˝tywo˙thas˙ta [= ˝tywoh-˙ta-s-˙ta] (?1517- Pak 1:37b; accent of ˝pol˙sye a scribal error?) oh, I didn't know earlier [of your illness], if I had but known I should have gone to see [how you were]. CF -˙tesi˙tun, -ke˙tun.

tewuk, adverb. more, still more / less, much more / less, all the more. ~ te still more. ~ ~ more and more, increasingly.

tewuk-i, adverb [usually spelled te-wu-ki]. 1. = tewuk. 2. particularly, especially; into the bargain; on top of that, what's more. ¶ Pi onun tey tewuk-i palam kkaci pūnta It is raining and on top of that the wind is blowing, too.

tewuk ina, adverb + copula adversative [usually spelled te-wu-ki-na; CF una]. still more.

tekwu(nta)na, adv. in addition, into the bargain, to boot, what's more, moreover; more, still more, all the more.

tey, quasi-free n. a place; a case, a circumstance. ¶ wihem han ~ a dangerous spot (place). phyo phanun ~ a ticket-seller's, a ticket window, a box office. āmu ~ any place. Kanun tey ka eti 'n ya Where / What is the place you are going to? I kes un meli aphun tey mek.nun yak ita This is the medicine you take when you have a headache. CF kos, kyengwu.

tey, postmod. (given the) circumstance; and, but. SEE -nun ~, -tun ~, -un ~. DIAL tay.

⋯ ~ ey cīnaci anh.nunta is nothing more

than a case of ... .
tey-, bound adverb. incompletely, partially, unsatisfactorily. ¶ ~ **ālta** knows halfway, has a partial knowledge of. ~ **ikta** is half-cooked. **(cam i)** ~ **kkāyta** comes half awake. ~ **sālm.ta** parboils. ~ **sayngkita** is immature. ~ **toyta** (vi) falls short. [? < **tēl**]
'tey, abbr < **hatey**; < **itey**.
-tey, FAMILIAR retrospective assertive. it has been observed that, it is known that, as we all (or as I) know, I hear (have been told) that, I've discovered (found out) that. ¶**Kwūkyengq kwun i mānh.i otey** (We noticed that) lots of people were coming to see the sight. **Kyengchi ka kwā.yen cōh.tey** The scenery sure was grand! **Yo say un.e ka cal cap.hinta ko hatey** I understand (= I recall hearing) that lots of trout are being caught lately.
t'ēy = **twēy** = **tōy** < **toye**, inf < **toyta**.
t'e ya = **t'ē ya**, abbr < **twe ya** = **twē ya**, abbr < **twue ya**.
tēykey, adverb. 1. < /tweykey/ = **tōykey** very, terribly. 2. < /tāykay/ < **tāykay** in general, by and large.
(-)teyki, postn, suf; var < **-teki**. [pejorative] one guy, thing. ¶**sopak** ~ a mistreated / deserted wife. **'yam-sim** ~ a jealous person. **yangpok** ~ [vulgar] (foreign-style) clothes, "duds". **saychimq** ~ a person who feigns modesty. **puekh** ~ a kitchen-maid.
-teykka [obs] = **-tikka** (retrospective)
teyley, pcl [Ceycwu DIAL (Seng ¹Nakswu 1984: 25); ? < **tey lo**]. to / toward. Apparently after a consonant only; CF **theyley**, **leyley**. **yek teyley ka-pwola** = **yek ulo ka-pwā la** Go check at the station. **san teyley kanta** = **san ulo kanta** I am headed for the mountains.
-teyngteyng, bound adjectival noun (~ **hata**); after a consonant **-utayngtayng**; HEAVY ↔ **-tayngtayng**. ...ish, slightly colored / tinged; slightly characterized by. SEE **-(u)sulum**.
tey nun, postmodifier + particle. ¶**Kwansang cal ponun tey nun cham ulo nōllaci anh.ulq swu ēps.ess.ta** I couldn't help being surprised at his ability to read faces (and tell fortunes).
t'e yo = **t'ē yo**, abbr < **twe yo** = **twē yo**, abbr < **twue yo**.
-teyta [obs] = **-tita** (retrospective)
tey 'ta (ka), postmod + cop transferentive (+ pcl). SEE **-nun** ~ , **-un** ~ .

-teytey, bnd adj-n (after a consonant **-uteytey**); HEAVY ↔ **-taytay**. ...ish, being slightly tinged / colored; being slightly characterized by. SEE **-(u)sulum**.
tey to, postmod + pcl. despite the circumstance that ... ; even though. ¶**ce man han caycwu ka iss.nun tey to** despite his talents, for all his gifts. **Ce mankhum ay lul ssess.nun tey to silphay hayss.ta** He failed in spite of all his efforts.
-tey tul, FAMILIAR retr assertive + particle
tey ya, postmodifier + pcl. ¶**Oci mālla 'y to cakkwu onun tey ya na 'n tul etteh.k' 'elq tōli ka iss.e ya 'ci?!** What can I do when he keeps coming here though I tell him not to?! **Mek.ess.nun tey ya halq swu ēps.ci!** If they have eaten, that is that! **Hon nakeyss.nun tey ya halq swu ēps.ci!** If I get into trouble, that's it (for me)!
-tey yo, FAMILIAR retr assertive + pcl (polite). (Occurs, but not accepted by some speakers.) CF **-ney yo**.
tha₁ < ˙**tha**, inf < **thata** < ˙**thota**. mount; ride. ¶ ˙**mul ˙˙ket-nanwo˙la ˙poy ˙tha ˙kata ˙ka** (1482 Nam 1:36b) to cross the water they go by boat, but ... .
tha₂ < ˙**tha**, abbr < **hata** < **ho˙ta** after voiced consonants and vowels other than **a** or **e**. CF **'ta** < ˙**'ta**; **chi** < ˙**thi**, **'ci** < ˙**'ti**.
··· ˙**tha**, abbr < **ho˙ta** after voiced sounds; CF ˙**'ta**. ¶ ˙**es˙tyey e˙lwo ˙TTYAK ho˙l i 'Gwan˙toy ˙TTYAK ˙'ti a˙ni ˙tha nilo˙l ywo ˙hota ˙ka** (1462 ¹Nung 1:75a) said "How can you say one is unattached when one IS attached?" and then ... . **SYWU-PPWO-TTYEY mu˙sum ˙˙TTWOW-˙˙LI ˙lol pwo˙kwo ˙kwot HUY-˙˙NGWUW ˙tha nilo˙n i ˙Gwo** (1482 Kum-sam 2:1b) seeing what logic did Subhūti forthwith declare that it is rare? **la˙kwuy me˙ki.m ye mol me˙kywom ˙kot hi ˙tha ˙hwo.m on ˙KAK-˙PPYELQ hi ka˙phwom ˙pola˙nwon mozom ˙ep.sul ˙s i.n i** (1482 Nam 2:63b) when we say that it [= taking care of one's basic needs] is like feeding a donkey and feeding a horse we mean there is no particular expectation of repayment. SEE **a˙ni ˙tha**.
··· ˙**tha** = ···**-h-˙ta**. ¶ ˙**wol˙tha** = ˙**wolh-˙ta** (1445 ¹Yong 107) is correct.
··· **tha ˙ka**, abbr < ˙**hota ˙ka** after voiced sounds. ¶ ˙**na-ka˙kwo cye tha ˙ka [˙˙HWO-LANG] ˙ol cen˙nwola [< ceh-no-wo-la]** (1481 Twusi 8:

29a) I want to go out but I fear the tigers.

-thaki, bound postnoun (< summative of **thata** 'splits / divides it'). ¶ **hom** ~ a crotch.

-thali, bound postnoun. ¶ **wul** ~ fence, hedge enclosure; outer rim of shoes (= **sin wul**). < **thal** 'place, edge' (CF **pithal** 'cliff') + **i** 'one, thing'; CF **-tal**.

-thang, suffix. LIGHT ↔ **-theng**. ¶ **kopul** ~ a bit bent.

··· ˈtha-ngi ˈˈta, abbr < ˈhota-ngi [i]ˈta. ¶ ˈSYEY-KAN yeˈhuyn ˈLAK ˈol ˈNYEM hoˈkwo kuˈli ˈtha-ngi ˈˈta (1459 Wel 7:5b; the page numbers "5" and "6" are reversed) meditated on pleasure remote from the world of men and did such as that. ˈi ˈko.t hi solang ˈkhwo kisˈke ˈculkywoˈm ol ˈˈnayˈti aˈni ˈtha-ngi ˈˈta (1463 Pep 2:249b) thinking like this has created no joyous delight.

··· ˈthaˈn i, abbreviation < ˈhotaˈn i. ¶ ˈku ˈpsk uy mozoˈm ay ˈna y neˈkywoˈtoy ˈMYELQ-ˈTTWO ˈay siˈle niˈlulGwa ˈˈla ˈthaˈn i (1463 Pep 2:23a) at that time my feeling was that I had managed to reach nirvāṇa.

thas < **tas** (also **thas**), quasi-free noun, vnt.

1. quasi-free noun. 1a. fault (CF **cal-mos, ttaymun**). ¶ **nwukwu** ~ whose fault. **caki (ku sālam)** ~ one's own (his) fault. **nay / cey** ~ my fault. **ney** ~ your fault. **Musun thas in ya** Where lies the fault? What's the trouble?

1b. reason, ground(s). ¶ **Tāycep ul pat.ko mōs pat.ko nun cey ka hal thas** (or **nalum**) **ita** The reception one gets depends on what one does. **Way thas ēps.i sālam ul chinun ya** Why do you hit me unprovoked?

-nun thas / kkatalk ulo because: **Ney ka īl ul cal hanun thas ulo sensayng nim i ne 'ykey cacwu sikhisinun key ani 'n ya** I think that the teacher calls on you all the time because you do so well.

2. vnt. ~ **hata** blames. ¶ **Thas halq key ēps.uni pyel ke l' kaciko tā thucip ul cap.ney** He will pick on the least little thing to blame people for. CF **cītawi**.

··· ˈtha s (ˈˈma.l iˈla), abbr < hoˈta s (ˈˈma.l iˈla). ¶ ˈˈney cca s ˈKWU non ˈˈPWON-LOY ˈtwu-ˈys.nwon KWANG-MYENG ˈi woˈnol s ˈnal ˈHHYEN ˈtha s ˈˈma.l iˈla (1482 Nam 1:15a) it means that the light originally put in the fourth phrase is manifest today.

thay, der n < **thata** (vt 'splits / divides it'). a crack, a fissure.

-thay(ki), bnd n. ¶ **mang** (~) a net (mesh) bag. **sam-thay** [DIAL] = **sam-thayki** a basket for carrying dirt / rubbish (< ?). SEE **-thaki**.

-thayki, var < **-thaki**

-thayngi, suffix (? dimin). ¶ **okum** ~ the inner angle of a bend / curve. **kwu** ~ [Chwungcheng DIAL] corner (= **kwusek**).

the, noun, postmodifier.

1. a site, a place; building land, a building lot / site, the foundation of a building.

2. the foundation, the ground; a footing, a foothold, groundwork, spadework.

3. (= **the-swu**) one's status, lot, financial / social standing.

4. postmod (= **the-swu, sai**) relationship, friendship, terms, a footing; (= **kyengwu**) circumstance, ~ **ey** in addition to, moreover. ¶ **Cal ānun the ey kulen soli lul halq swu nun ēps.ci** I know him too well to say such things to him. **Kath.un cangsa lul hanun the ey kulen soli lul halq swu nun ēps.ci** We are in the same business; I couldn't say a thing like that to him. **Kulech'anh.e to sai ka nappun the ey, ku īl i iss.kwu na se puthe nun acwu māl to an hakey tōyss.ta** We were on such a bad footing anyway that after that happened we stopped speaking altogether. **Nwūn i onun the ey palam kkaci pūnta** Not only is it snowing but to make matters worse the wind is blowing. **Kattuk ina elyewun the ey pyēng kkaci nata ˈni!** Not only is it terribly difficult, but on top of that I have fallen ill.

5. postmodifier [lit] = **they** (plan, schedule; expectation, anticipation).

··· (ˈ)**the-**, abbr < ˈ**hote-**

thek$_1$, n. 1. jaw; chin. ~ **sal** SAME [vulgar]. DIAL **thak**.

1a. jaw. ¶ **alay / wi** ~ the lower / upper jaw.

1b. chin. ¶ **swuyem** ~ chinwhiskers, beard. ~ **cīs** a movement of (gesture with) the chin. ~ **mith** (right) under one's chin, very near (= "right under one's chin"). ~ **pat.ki** a bib, a pinafore. **cwukek** ~ a wide flat chin like a rice paddle.

2. a rise, a swell, a bump, a hillock, a hill, a promontory. ¶ ~ (**i**) **cita** it swells, forms a rise. **mun** ~ a threshold, a door sill. **cwung** ~ the middle part (of a rise?). **malwu** ~(-**i**) a rise at the top of a hill. CF **enthek** (1) the rise (of a hill etc.), (2) [DIAL] = **entek** hill [< obs **en**

'dike, embankment' = twuk]; tek(i) a plateau.
thek₂, n. a treat (an entertainment provided for others, especially to celebrate one's own good fortune or happiness). ¶Han thek nāy ya 'ci You must give/stand us a treat (to celebrate your good fortune).
thek₃, quasi-free noun, postmodifier, postnoun [? dimin < the].
  1. reason, ground. ¶Kuleh.key kyēyhoyk i chimil han tey an toyl thek i iss.nun ya? With such detailed plans is there any reason for it to fail? Musun thek in ci molukeyss.ta I don't know what the reason is.
  2. (limited) extent, only, just; moderation, limitation. ¶Acik ku thek ici yo That's all that is left.
  3. a footing, a foothold; a basis; resources, backing, the means, wherewithal. ¶⋯ cam i ol thek i ēps.ess.ta (Dupont 305) could not get to sleep.
  4. postnoun = theym (as much as, all of).
  NOTE: Though it is normally only quasi-free, thek does not require a modifier in ~ ēps.ta 'is groundless, immoderate, helpless' or ~ ēps.i 'groundlessly, immoderately, helplessly'.
thek₄, adverb. completely secure. ¶maum ul ~ noh.ta puts one's mind at complete ease. ~ na-ota, ~ natha-nata appears with complete composure. son ul ~ capta holds one's hand passionately. son ul ~ nāy mīlta asks for something without hesitation.
-theki, bnd postn (< thek₁ + i). ¶kulwu ~ a stump; stubble. malwu-thek(i) a ridge.
⋯ thela, abbr < ˙hote˙la. ¶ho.ya cila thela (1514 Sok-sam hyo:2; cited from LCT) was wanting to do it.
thelita [DIAL; 1936 Roth 366] = ttulita
them, postnoun = theym (as much as, all of)
-theng, suffix; HEAVY ↔ -thang. ¶kwupul ~ a bit bent.
(-)thengi, postnoun, suffix (? augmentative). ¶kwuleng ~ a chasm, an abyss.
⋯ the˙n i, abbr < ˙hote˙n i. ¶˙say cip ci˙zi l' ˙˙mwot '˙key ˙hwo˙l ye the˙n i (1449 Kok 155) they wanted to make the construction of the new building impossible.
⋯ ˙thesi˙n i, abbr < ˙hotesi˙n i. ¶[˙MEN-˙KWUYK] ˙hi ˙cul ˙kike˙nul [˙SYENG-CCYENG] ˙ey ˙˙woyta ˙thesi˙n i (1445 ¹Yong 107) though all the land opposed he said "they are contrary to what is sacred" [and removed a thousand temples]. ci˙p ul ˙na˙a ˙˙ka.l ye ˙thesi˙n i (1449 Kok 45) he planned to leave home.
~ ˙'la. ¶[˙˙CCWOY] ˙lol [˙˙CHYENG] hon˙t ay [˙CYANG-˙CHO] s ˙˙hay [˙COYK-˙PELQ] ˙hwo.l i ˙˙'la ˙thesi˙n i ˙'[˙]la (1481 Twusi 24:13a) he said, "Invite sin and you will pick up much future punishment".
they, postmodifier. plan, schedule; what one has in mind; intention; expectation, anticipation; impression. SEE -ul ~ ('ta); -un ~, -nun ~, -tun ~. SYN the.
they 'ci yo SEE -ul they 'ci yo
-theyki, var < -tha(y)ki, < -theki.
they 'l = they [i]l, postmod + cop prosp mod.
theyley, particle [Ceycwu DIAL (Seng ¹Nakswu 1984:26)]. to/toward (= teyley, leyley). All examples seem to be after a noun that had final ⋯h in Middle Korean. ¶wu theyley polay pwola = wi lo pala pwā la look up above (MK wuh). twuy theyley polay pwola = twī lo pala pwā la look behind (MK ˙˙twuyh). tulu theyley kanta = tūl lo kanta I go to the moors (MK tu˙luh). palu theyley kanta = pata lo kanta I head for the sea (MK pa˙tah = pa˙lol < *pa˙tolh).
theym, postnoun. as much as, all of (usually followed by ina). ¶han sēm theym ina mekta eats a whole bag of rice. Twū tal theym ina kellinta 'ni? You say that it takes two whole months?! VAR them, theymi. CF thek; ssum.
they 'm = they [i]m, postmodifier + cop subst.
they 'n = they [i]n, postmod + cop mod. ~ tey.
(-)theyngi, [var] = (-)thengi
they 'ta SEE -ul they 'ta
they yo SEE -ul they yo
⋯ ˙thi, abbr < ho˙ti after voiced sounds; CF ˙'ti.
  1. ¶CWON-˙˙TTYWUNG ˙thi ˙˙mwot ˙ho˙si.l i ˙'l ˙ss oy (1459 Wel 9:11b) since he cannot esteem it. ko˙lo.m i hullwu.m i [˙KHUY-˙NGWUN] ˙i [PPYENG] ˙thi a˙ni ˙hotwo˙ta (1481 Twusi 7:12ab) the way the clouds are flowing is uneven. ˙mwo.m ol ˙WUY khwo ˙˙salo˙m ol ˙WUY thi a˙ni ho˙m ye n' (1482 Kum-sam 5:48-9) when it is for my own body and not for (other) people … . CHYENG-˙CCYENG ˙thi ˙˙mwot ˙'˙kwo (1464 Kumkang 64b) is definitely not pure, and … . ku˙le ˙thi ˙˙mwot ˙ke˙tun (?1468- Mong 33a) if it is not that way at all … .
  2. ¶˙CYWUNG-SOYNG ˙o˙lwo ˙QILQ-˙CHYEY ˙SYEY-KAN ˙ay s ˙˙SIN ˙thi elye ˙Wun ˙PEP ˙ul ˙˙ta

tutco᷄Wa ῀al῀Gey ῀hwo.l i ῀῀la ῀ho῀sya (1447 Sek 13:27a) he says "I will get all living beings to understand the doctrine that is so difficult for the world at large to believe". *῀ile ῀thus hon ῀HWA ῀thi e῀lyeWun ῀KANG-῀KKANG hon ῀῀CCWOY-῀῀KWO ῀CYWUNG-SOYNG ol ῀TTWO-῀THWALQ ῀hoke῀tun* (1459 Wel 21:34ab) when one emancipates this sort of hard-core sinners who are difficult to change … .

thi₁ < *῀thuy*, n. 1. a mote, particle, grit, foreign element. 2. a flaw, speck, spot. 3. a small wad of cotton put in a falcon's mouth. 4. looks, appearance, feel, signs, indication (?= **thi₂**).

thi₂ (? < **thi₁**), postn. a spot (touch / smack / taste / air) of … . ¶**sikol** ~ a bit of the rustic (in him). ¹**yāngpan** ~ something of the gentleman (about him).

(-)thi₃, bnd n. road. ¶**kokay** ~ a precipitous road over a mountain ridge.

··· *thi῀Gwuy*, abbr < *῀ho-ti῀Gwuy* after voiced sounds. does but. *ku mozof῀]m ay mas῀key thi῀Gwuy* (1465 Wen 2:3:1:102a) it pleases him but … .

῀thi῀ta, vt. strikes, hits (= **chita**). SEE *῀thye*.

··· *῀th ol*, abbreviation (after voiced sounds) < *ho῀t ol* = **haci l(ul)**. ¶*PPEM ῀kwa SYENG ῀kwa ῀lol THWONG ῀th ol a῀ni ῀hosi῀n i* (1482 Kumsam 2:3b) he does not communicate through sinners and saints.

··· *῀thol* = ···*h-῀t ol* (= ···**h-ci l[ul]**). ¶*il῀thol ma῀la* (1459 Wel 8:8b) = *ilh-῀t ol ma῀la* don't lose it!

··· *῀tholh* = ···*h ῀tolh* (plural). ¶*῀nyena῀mon ha῀nol῀thol῀h oy* [= *ha῀nolh ῀tol῀h oy*] *namcin ῀kyecip mwo῀m ay HYANG ῀ol ῀῀ta me῀li ῀sye ma῀tha* (1447 Sek 19:19b) smelling from afar all the scents of the men and women in the other heavens. *SYEY-THYEN na῀la῀thol῀h ay* [= *na῀lah ῀tolh ῀ay*] *῀hoyn ῀῀SSYANG ῀i ha῀n i ῀῀la* (1459 Wel 2:31b) in the lands of the western heaven (India) there are many white elephants.

tholok, quasi-pcl (abbr < **hatolok**) < *thwolwok* < *῀tho῀lwok* < *῀ho-to῀lwok*. to the extent of. ¶**i / yo** ~ to this extent. **ku / ko** ~, **ce / co** ~ to that extent. **congil** ~ all day long, the whole day. **congsin** ~ all one's life, one's whole life (long). **kwānyen** ~ till past the marriageable age (for females; CF **kwānyen hata**). **yēngwen** ~ unto eternity (CF **yēngwen hata**). **mukwung** ~ into perpetuity (CF **mukwung hata**).

NOTE: The following proposed examples are tentatively rejected: **ithul** ~ two whole days; **han tal** ~ one whole month; **twū hay** ~, **ī-nyen** ~ two whole years; **elma** ~ to what extent; **chen wen** ~ a whole thousand **wen**; **payk-lī** ~ a whole hundred leagues; **yelq kun** ~ ten whole **kun** (pounds); **sumu kay** ~ a whole twenty of them.

῀tho῀lwok. ¶*CYWUNG-῀ZILQ ῀tho῀lwok NGWEN-῀KAK ῀ol ῀hwo῀toy* (1465 Wen se:5a) enjoys perfect enlightenment all day long, and … . *῀na y pan῀to῀ki CYWUNG-SIN ῀tho῀lwok KWONG-῀KUP ῀ho῀ya* (1463 Pep 4:154b) without fail I will contribute until my death, and … .

῀thwo῀lwok. ¶*SIN ῀i CYWONG ῀thwo῀lwok* (1588 Mayng 13:29a; sic CYWONG < CYWUNG) until one's body dies.

tholok ina, quasi-pcl + cop advers. ¶**Congil tholok ina ayki lul pokey hako se tōn han phun to an cwutun?** You watched the baby all day long and they didn't give you one penny? **Ku tholok ina āy lul ssuko to an tōyss.ta 'ni?!** What a shame, to work so hard!

thong, counter. a (head of) cabbage, a gourd; (= **phil**) a roll of cloth.

thong, 1. adverb (= **ōn-thong**). entirely, all, completely; (not) at all.

2. adnoun. whole, intact, untouched. ¶ ~ **keli (lo)** everything, in all, in toto. ~-**q kum** the total account / price. ~ **namu** a whole log. ~ **kimchi** uncut kimchi. ~ **talk** chicken cooked whole. ~ **cangcak** unchopped firewood. ~ **phath** unground red beans.

3. bound noun. ¶ ~ **ccay (lo)** whole, intact; untouched, uncut. ~ **ulo samkhita** swallows it whole.

[? < ῀῀THWONG (of ῀῀THWONG-῀QILQ > thōngil 'unification'); ? < **tong(-)** 'round']

thong, postn, suffix. thing; part of body. ¶**mok** ~ a throat; a screw. **mom** ~ body. **āy** ~ guts, bowels [figurative]. **pay** ~ belly. **ekkay** ~ the girth of one's shoulders. **sang** ~ [vulgar] face. **tali** ~ thick legs. ? **cok** ~ a hoof, a foot. **pol** ~ [DIAL] = **ppyam ttayki** cheek. ? **yem-** ~ the heart (= **simcang**). **sim(swul)** ~ meanness.

[? < **thong** < *῀TTWONG* 'tube; caliber']

thong ey, postn, postmod (after -**nun**, -**un**). as a consequence / result of, under the influence of (something disturbing). SYN (**-q) palam**.

1. postnoun. ¶¹**Nān.li thong ey** (= ¹**Nān.liq**

palam ey) chayk ul cōy ilh.e pelyess.ta We lost all the books during the war.
2. postmod (after -nun, adj -un, cop in). ¶Son nim i mānh.i chac.e onun thong ey kongpu lul cokum to mōs hayss.e So many guests dropped in I didn't get a bit of studying done. Sāpang i yātan in thong ey cēngsin ul chalilq swu ka ēps.ess.e Things were in such an uproar on all sides that I couldn't collect my thoughts. Nal i (nemu) chwuwun thong ey āmu kes to mōs hayss.e The weather has been too cold to get anything done. Nemu musewun thong ey soli to mōs cilless.ta I was too scared to let out a sound.

thong hata < THWONG °ho·ta, vni (1-13), vnt (14-16).
1. runs, is open for traffic. ¶achim ilkop si puthe cēncha ka ~ the streetcars run / operate from 7 a.m. kicha ka say lo Pusan kkaci ~ the railway was recently opened as far as Pusan. Ahyen kokay ey thenneyl i ~ a tunnel is open at Ahyen Hill.
2. runs, reaches, leads to. ¶kicha ka Māsan kkaci ~ a train runs to Masan. kil i puekh ulo ~ a path leads to the kitchen / cookhouse.
3. (electricity) flows, is charged; is on / live. ¶cēnki ka ~ is charged with electricity. cēnki ka thong han soy cwul an electrified wire; a live wire.
4. (a telephone call) goes through, is put through; (a line) is on = is on the line; a line / telephone is working. ¶cēnhwa ka ~ a phone call is put (goes / gets) through, is on the line; the phone is working. cēnhwa ka thong haci anh.ta a call fails to go / get through; the phone is out of order (is dead); a line is interrupted.
5. excrement (urine / feces) is passed / voided. ¶tāypyen i ~ has regular bowel movements, is regular (in bowel movements). sōpyen i ~ has regular urination, has no difficulty urinating. tāy-sōpyen i ~ has regular passage, has no excretory difficulties. tāypyen i thong haci anh.ta is constipated. sōpyen i thong haci anh.ta has difficulty in urinating, suffers from anuria / anuresis. tāy-sōpyen i thong haci anh.ta has trouble getting rid of body wastes, has excretory difficulties.
6. goes/passes through, is circulated. ¶kongki ka cal ~ has good ventilation. tāmpayq-tay ey yenki ka cal ~ a pipe draws well.
7. (a language) is understood, is spoken, is the medium of communication. ¶Yenge ka ~ is able to speak (in) English; can get by (make oneself understood) with English. selo māl i thong haci anh.ta are unable to communicate with each other because of the language barrier (problem). Hānkwuk ey nun Yenge ka thong haci anh.nunta English isn't spoken in Korea.
8. enjoys (mutual) understanding; understand (each other). ¶selo ūysa ka ~ understand each other's sentiments. minceng i wi ey ~ the conditions of the people are appreciated by those above (= the government).
9. makes sense. ¶kul ttus i thong haci anh.ta a sentence doesn't make sense.
10. is well versed (in), is proficient (in), is an expert (in / on), is a master (of), is familiar / conversant (with), is well up / informed (on). ¶chenmun ey ~ knows a lot about astronomy. Yenge ey ~ is proficient in English, knows one's English. nāymak ey ~ is well up on the inside story.
11. passes (for / as), is known (as). ¶kwen.wi lo ~ is acknowledged as an authority. A 'la 'n ilum ulo ~ passes under the name of A, goes by the name of A.
12. passes, circulates, holds good, is good / valid. ¶hwāphyey ka ~ a currency is valid (can be used). kyuchik i ~ a regulation holds (good). cha phyo ka thong haci anh.ta a train ticket isn't valid (is no good).
13. passes, gets by, serves its purpose, is admitted / accepted. ¶Kulen kwusil un thong haci anh.nunta That sort of excuse won't do / serve. Ney ūykyen un thong haci anh.nunta Your opinion is not acceptable.
14. goes / passes / gets through. ¶puekh ul ~ goes through the kitchen. cenkwuk ul thong hay se throughout the whole country. sīnay lul thong hay kata goes through the city. sālam ul thong hay se (thong ha.ye) through a person, by the agency / medium (good offices) of a person. sālam ul thong hay se sosik ul cen hata sends news through a person. sālam ul thong hay se chwīcik wūntong ul hata tries to get a job through the good offices of a person. il-nyen ul thong hay se phyēnci han cang ponayci anh.ta lets the whole year go by without writing a single letter.

15. informs a person of, lets (it) be known, tells. ¶**sēngmyeng ul** ~ introduces oneself, gives / tells one's name. **ūykyen ul** ~ lets (a person) know one's opinion. **cek eykey pīmil ul** ~ lets the enemy in on a secret, betrays a secret to the enemy. **selo ki-mayk ul** ~ have a tacit understanding with each other.

16. shares (intimacy with) = becomes intimate (with), commits adultery (with), has an illicit affair / contact (with). ¶**ceng ul** ~ has illicit intercourse (with); CF **ceng i** ~ is in sympathy with (= 8).

thongi, postn. person, thing, one. ¶**simswul** ~ a crosspatch, a peevish person. **mo** ~ (= mo-thwungi) a corner. **pol** ~ [DIAL] = **ppyam ttayki** cheek. VAR **thwungi**; CF **thong, tongi**. CF **payki**.

··· ˙thos ˚ho˙ta = ···h-˙tos ˚ho˙ta. ¶*PPWO-˙SALQ* ˙i ¨ke˙s ke˙s ul ˙pwo˙toy *CCAY-LANG* ce˙thos [= ceh-˙tos] ˙ho˙no.n i ˙'la (1462 ¹Nung 8:86b) confronted by a falsehood the bodhisattva behaves as if in fear of a mountain wolf.

··· ˙tho˙s ˚ho˙ta = ··· ˙thus ˚ho˙ta, abbr < ho-˙tus ˚ho˙ta. ¶*PPWOLQ-˙PPWOLQ* ˙'i tao˙n i ˙'la ˙thos ho˙n i (1462 ¹Nung 2:19a) it seems that it has been quickly exhausted.

··· ˙tho˙s ˙'i = ··· ˙thu˙s ˙'i, abbr < ho-˙tu˙s ˙'i. like. ¶¨*NGAN-[˙]MWOK* kansywu ˙tho[˙]s ˙'i ho[˙]m ye (1465 Wen 2:3:2:88b) it was like the eye was on guard, and ... .

-thoythoy, bnd adj-n (~ **hata**); after a consonant **-uthoythoy**; LIGHT ↔ **-thwithwi**. ···ish, slightly colored / tinged. SEE **-(u)sulum**.

··· ˙thu˙l ey s < ˙tul˙h ey s. ¶¨mwo˙tin ¨*SSYANG* ˙kwa *SO-*¨*CO* [G]wa ¨pem ˙kwa ˙ilhi ˙Gwa ¨kwom ˙kwa ¨mwo˙tin ˙po.yam ˙kwa mulq ˙pel ˙Gey ˙thu˙l ey s mu˙zuyye ˙Wun ¨i˙l i i ˙sye ˙two (1447 Sek 9:24b) even though you have frightening experiences with evil elephants and lions and tigers and wolves and bears and evil snakes and biting insects and all ... . ˙*QAK* ˙on nwol˙Gay ˙chwum ˙thu˙l ey s coy˙cwo ˙'la (1447 Sek 13:9a; CF 1463 Pep 1:49b) music is the talents of singing and dancing and the like, and ... . sama˙kwoy ˙huk ˙thu˙l ey s he˙mu.l i ¨ep˙susya˙m i ˙*ZI-*˙*SSIP* ¨*NGWOW* ˙ysi˙kwo (1463 Pep 2:15-6) number 25 (of Buddha's distinctive marks) is that he has no blemishes such as moles or (black) spots or the like, and ... . *KKUY-NGWAN* ˙un ˙kulim ˙thu.l ey s coycwo ˙y˙la (1475 Nay 1:28b; coycwo = coy˙cwo) *KKUY-NGWAN* is (= means) talents like painting and so on. twot ˙kwa ka˙hi ˙Gwa yezo ˙[G]wa nap ˙kwa ˙poyyam ˙kwa kama˙kwoy ˙Gwa soylwo˙ki ˙thu˙l ey s ˙mwo˙m ilwo˙ta (1550 ¹Yenghem 15b) they are bodies such as the pig and the dog and the fox and the monkey and the snake and the crow and the eagle. ˙i ˙thu˙l ey s ˙*PEP* ˙ul (1459 Wel 7:66b) the laws of these.

*··· ˙thulh. The expected *··· ˙tulh < ···h ˙tulh is unattested (unlike ··· ˙tholh < ···h ˙tolh): *kulu ˙thulh < *kuluh ˙tulh 'roots'.

thulita [var] = **ttulita**

thum < ˙thum, n (< subst < **thuta** < *˙thu˙ta).
1. gap, chink, opening, crevice; crack, break.
2. room, space; interval; time. ¶**enu** ~ **ey pelsse** so soon, all of a sudden. CF **sai**.
3. spare time, leisure. CF **kyelul**.
4. opening, opportunity, chance. ¶ ~ **ul thata** takes advantage of (seizes) an opportunity, makes the most of a chance. **Tōn to ēps.keni wa thum to ēps.ta** Not only do I lack money, but I haven't the time / opportunity.

··· ˙thus ˚ho˙ta, abbr < ˙ho-tus ˚ho˙ta. ¶˙ile ˙thus hon ˙*HWA* ˙thi e˙lyeWun ˙*KANG-*˙*KKANG* hon ¨*CCWOY-*¨*KWO* ˙*CYWUNG-SOYNG* ol ˙*TTWO-*˙*THWALQ* ˙hoke˙tun (1459 Wel 21:34ab) when one emancipates this sort of hard-core sinners who are difficult to change ... .

··· ˙thu˙s ˙'i, abbr < ho-˙tu˙s ˙'i. like. ¶syang˙nyey ˙ile ˙thu˙s ˙'i ˙*QILQ-*˙*CHYEY* ˙*NGWUW-CCYENG* ˙ul ˙*LI-*˙*QYEK* toWoy˙m ye *QAN-*˙*LAK* ˙'kuy ho˙la (1447 Sek 9:41a; *NGWUW-CCYENG* → ¨*NGWUW-CCYENG*) thus regularly comfort all sentient beings, becoming of benefit to them. ˙ile ˙thu˙s ˙'i kwo˙thye towoy˙sya˙m i ¨mwot nilo ¨hyey˙l i ˙le˙la (1459 Wel 1:21a) thus it seemed one could not very well think he would become transformed.

···˙thwo = ···h ˙two. ¶hona˙thwo [= honah ˙two] ˙*SSILQ* hon ¨*THYEY* ¨ep˙se (1462 ¹Nung 2:98a) not one of them has any real substance, and ... . ˙wuli ˙tol˙thwo [= ˙tolh ˙two] ˙i *CIN-*˙*CCYENG* ˙*TTAY-*˙*PEP* ˙ul ¨ce y ˙*TUK* ˙'kwo ˙cye ˙ho˙ya (1459 Wel 18:3a) we want ourselves to get the truly pure great law, and ... . ˙*CHALQ-*˙*TYEY-*˙*LI* ˙*KWAN-*¨*TYENG NGWANG* ˙tol˙thwo [= ˙tolh ˙two] *TTYANG-*¨*SSYWUW* ho˙kwo ˙*PPYENG* ˙ep˙se [mistake for ¨ep˙se?] (1459 Wel 9:55ab) King

Abhiṣecana / Abhiṣeka of the kṣatriya caste and all were long-lived and illness-free, and ... .

··· ˙thwo, abbr < ho-˙two after voiced sounds. ¶ SYWUN thwo ani hon KYENG ey (1466 Mok 37; cited from LCT) in circumstances less than felicitous. ili thwo cyeli thwo mwos hota (1748 Tongmun 2:59; cited from LCT) can do neither this nor that.

˙thwoswo˙n ywo, abbr < ˙ho˙twoswo˙n ywo after voiced sounds.

··· ˙thwo˙swo-ngi ˙˙ta, abbr < ˙hotwo˙swo-ngi ˙˙ta after voiced sounds. ¶ mozo˙m i PPYENG-"TUNG ˙ho˙ya Q[O]N-˙TUK ˙i talo˙ti a˙ni thwo˙swo-ngi ˙˙ta (1459 Wel 10:31b) their hearts are equal and they do not differ in grace and virtue.

··· ˙thwo˙ta, abbr < ˙hotwo˙ta after voiced sounds. ¶ [˙]ce y woy[˙]ywo[˙]la ˙thwo˙ta (1463 Pep 2:7a) says that he himself is at fault. SEE a˙ni thwo˙ta.

thwu (?< *¨TTWOW), n. 1. habit(ual way). ¶ ~ ka pak.ita is stereotyped. māl hanun thwu ka sēthwuluta expresses oneself poorly (Dupont 277). māl ~ one's way of talking.
  2. form, style. ¶ phyēnci ~ the forms of letter writing, epistolary style.

-thwuli < -thwo˙li, suffix. remnant. ¶ ca ~ odd ends of yardage < cathwoli (1690 Yek.e 2:5a) ?< *cah twol-i. kkothwuli a pod, a shell; cigarette butt; origin, cause < kwo˙thwo˙li (1527 Cahoy 3:3b=6a, [1517→]1614 Saseng 1:52a) ?< *kwoh twol-i.

thwungi, postn (var < thongi). person, thing, one. ¶ cam ~ a sleepyhead. cayng-~ a person who has let poverty make him mean and cross [< cayng- mutter]. cec ~ [vulgar] a woman's breast. has ~ padded clothes (esp. worn out of season). kkoy ~ a person with a lot of petty guile / wiles. kocip ~ a hardheaded (stubborn) person. kwi ~ the base of the ear; (= mo-thwungi) a corner, an angle. kwul ~ a gimcrack, a gewgaw (bnd n ?< 'hollow', ?< 'oyster'). milyen / maylyen ~ a stupid fool. mo-thwungi a corner, an angle. mul ~ a thing all water-soaked and swollen; a small annual plant (Pilea peploides). nolang ~ a person with an unusually yellow complexion. nwun ~ bags under the eyes. po ~ a bundle, a package. pol ~ [DIAL] = ppyam ttayki cheek. CF twungi, ttwungi, chwungi.

thwuse(y)ngi, postn. covered / smeared all over with, full of. ¶ menci ~ covered with dust. phi ~ all blood-smeared, all covered with blood. ppye ~ being all bones. os i hulk ~ toyta one's clothes get all covered with mud; gets one's clothes splattered with mud. chayk i ōsik ~ 'ta the book is full of (is riddled with) misprints. VAR thwuke(y)pi, thwukwuli.

thy, pronounced /ch/. Usually an abbreviation of the syllable thi, as in pethye < pethie.

˙thye (abbr < ˙thiye), inf < ˙thi˙ta (strikes). ¶ ¨HHWUW ˙ey THYEN PYENG ˙i co˙cwo ˙thye han SSI-˙CYELQ ey ˙za pi˙luse HHANG khe˙tun (1465 Wen 2:3:1:52a) only later on when the heavenly troops would regularly strike in great force did they submit.

thye lwo, postn + pcl [< ˙thyey ˙lwo]. like (= chelem). ¶ cun stek thye lwo montola (?1608+ Twu-hem 60a) make it like sticky rice cake.

˙thyey ?< ¨THYEY (form, body).
  1. n, postn. type, kind; pattern, shape. ¶ me˙li ˙thyey ˙lul ¨cye˙ki kiGwu.s ˙i ˙hwo.n i (1518 Sohak-cho 10:27a) the form presented by his head was small and lopsided. sywupak i.m ye poy 'm ye kywul thyey yey s ke.s ul meki.m i mas.tang thi ani ho.n i (1608 Twu-cip 2:4b) it is not suitable to feed them things such as watermelon or pear or orange.
  ~ ˙lwo like (= chelem). ¶ ancum ˙ul ˙khi ˙thyey ˙lwo ¨mal˙m ye (1586 Sohak 3:9b) don't sit like a winnow, and ... .
  2. ~ °ho˙ta, postmod vni. pretends, feigns. ¶ [¨HWO-˙HAN] in chyey ho.m ye n' (1795 ¹No-cwung [K] 2:51a) = etin namco 'yn thyey hoketun (id. [P] 2:49a) = ˙e˙tin namzin ˙in ¨yang ˙u˙lwo ho˙kwo is.ke˙tun (?1517- ¹No 2:54b) he was pretending to be a good fellow, but ... . CF 1887 Scott 204 "thyey = chey (pretense)".

˙ti(···) = ˙t i(···), bnd postmod + pcl / cop. SEE -(ᵁ/o)n ˙t i; -nun ˙t i, -nwon ˙t i; -(ᵁ/o)l ˙tt i = -(ᵁ/o)lq ˙t i; -wᵁ/olq ˙t i; -kan ˙t i, -tan ˙t i.
  1. the fact that [as subject].
  2. the time since [as subject].
  3. (know) that [as nominative-marked object of verb of knowing]
  4. + negative copula. CF -˙ti + neg cop.
  5. ˙t i··· (affirmative copula stem + further structures). SEE (wᵁ/olq +) ˙t iGe˙n i, ˙t iGe˙n i ˙Gwa(tye), ˙t iGen ˙tyeng, ˙t iGe˙ta, ˙t i˙la

('two), ·t ilwo·ta, ·t ilwoswo·n i, ·t ilq ·s oy, ·t i·m ye, ·t i·m ye n', ·t i·na, ·t i·n i, ·t in ·t ay n', ·t ye, ·t ye n', ...
-·ti, suspective (> -ci). This is the bound noun t + nominative pcl ·i, attached directly to the stem. Sometime between 1459⁻ and 1518 the form took on the new status of a paradigmatic ending; CF -·ti ·Gwos and -·ti ·non. In the 1400s modern -ci l(ul) was -·t ol (surviving as -t ul in S Chwungcheng) and modern -ci n(un) was -·t on. The MK copula does not take the suspective (*·i·ti).
Under the interpretation of the phonograms by Kim Wancin 1980 there is no example of the suspective in the hyangka. He takes *anti* (2:3) and *antin* (19:4) as simply equivalent to *a·ni* and *a·ni ·n*, and dismisses *antol* (19:8, 21:10, 22:10, 23:4; 13:2) in the same disturbing way, though these strings would appear to contain the nominative and accusative markers. Kim has two examples each of the precursor of -lq ·t i (*hosilti* 3:4, *holti* 3:8) and of -lq ·t on (*alosilton* 7:9, *taolton* 25:1), but not of -lq ·t ol.
1. + negative auxiliary (a·ni °ho·ta, ¨mwot °ho·ta, ¨ma[l]·ta).
2. -·ti ·non (= -·t on) + negative auxiliary. ¶ ¨naycywong ¨nay psu·ti ·non a·ni ·hwo·la (1518 Sohak-cho 10:1b) in the end I do not actually use it.
3. SEE -·ti Gwos.
4. (= modern -ki ka) as the complement of e·lyep·ta 'is hard to do', ·sul °ho·ta 'hates to do', ¨tywo·tha = ¨tywoh-·ta 'likes to do', and pwus·kuli·ta 'is embarrassed / ashamed to do'. ¶ SIN ·thi e·lyeWun ·PEP ·ul (1447 Sek 13:27a) a doctrine that is difficult to believe. ·HWA ·thi e·lyeWun ... (1459 Wel 21:34a) ... that are difficult to change. hye·ti e·lyep·ta (?1517⁻ ¹No 2:31a) = *toloyki elyepta* (1795 ¹No-cwung [P] 2:28a) = *toloyki cywochi ani hokwo* (id. [K] 2:29b) (the bow) is hard to draw. ko·cang pwo·ti ¨tywo·ho.n i ·´la (?1517⁻ Pak 1:5b) they are a joy to see.
-ti, [DIAL] = -ci
'ti, 1. < iti. 2. < hati.
'·ti, abbr < ho·ti (suspective) after voiceless sounds; CF ·thi. ¶ ko·tok ·´ti a·ni ·hwom a·ni ·n ·t ol pan·to·ki a·lwolq ·t ilwo·ta (1462 ¹Nung 1:67a) one must realize that it is not that it is not full. ¨HHA[Y]-·THWALQ ·ol ·TUK ·´ti

¨mwot ho·l i ·´m ye (1464 Kumkang 28a) is unable to obtain emancipation and ... . ¨es·tyey e·lwo ·TTYAK ho·l i 'Gwan·toy ·TTYAK ·´ti a·ni ·tha nilo·l ywo (1462 ¹Nung 1:75a) how can you say that one is unattached when one IS attached? NOTE: There is no '·ti = *'/[y]·ti, abbr < *·i·ti (cop suspective).
t'i(-), [? DIAL] abbreviation < tul.i adv (hard, relentlessly). ¶ ~ ttwita = tul.i ttwita.
-ti, retrospective attentive [? < -tey, ? < -tun i / ya]. 1. (= -tun ya) has it been observed that ... ?; is it known that ... ?; did you hear (have you been told) that ... ?; did you notice that ... ?; have you found that ... ?. ¶ Ssan kes i iss.ti? Did you notice if they had any cheap ones? Elma 'na khuti How big was it? Mues iti What was it?
2. X-ti X-ta really is, is ever so, is ever/quite (CF X-una X-un). ¶ kēm.ti kēm.ta is real black. khuti khuta is ever so big.
NOTE: This construction occurs for many one-syllable adj stems (chata 'cold', cōh.ta 'good', copta 'narrow', huyta 'white', kōpta 'pretty', mēlta 'far', mipta 'hateful', pulk.ta 'red', sita 'sour', ssuta 'bitter', talta 'sweet', yalp.ta 'thin', yath.ta 'shallow', ...) but not for all: there are no such forms for cākta 'little', cēkta 'few', ... It is unusual for two-syllable stems, and apparently most speakers reject forms such as (?*)ppaluti ppaluta 'is ever so fast' and (?*)kakkapti kakkapta 'is ever so near' and (?*)ttukepti ttukepta 'is ever so hot'. The adjectival noun yak 'weak' occurs (yak hati yak hata 'is ever so weak'), but the form is rejected for longer adjectival nouns such as co'.yong hata 'is quiet'. It seems to be fairly common to drop the liquid of -L- stems in this structure: ta(l)ti talta 'it is ever so sweet', mē(l)ti mēn kos ey 'to a place that is awfully far away'. If a speaker feels uncomfortable with one of these structures, he can turn to a highlighted form (kīlki to kīlta / hata is ever so long) or, in the adnominal form only, a gerund-linked iteration: kīlko kīn kyewulq pam = kīlti kīn kyewulq pam a long winter night.
-ti [Phyengan DIAL (Kim Yengpay 1984:100)] = -ci (suspective)
-ti-, alt of -tu- (retrospective) after formal (-sup-ti-); followed by the assertive (-sup-ti-ta) and by the attentive (-sup-ti-kka).

ti-); followed by the assertive (-sup-ti-ta) and by the attentive (-sup-ti-kka).

-ti ˙Gwey (?< -˙ti ˙Gwoy ?< -ti ˙Gwuy, ?< -ti ˙Gwuy yey) + NEG. but; and (yet). ¶wo˙cik nwo˙phon nwol˙Gay ˙ˊye [˙˙KWUY-SSIN] is.non ˙tos ˙hwo.m ol ˙˙a-ti ˙Gwey mu˙su.m u[˙]la ˙˙cwulye cwu˙ke kwul˙he.ng ey myes.kwuy˙ywol ˙˙i.l ol ˙˙all i ˙Gwo (1481 Twusi 15:37b) we just may know that lofty songs seem to be spiritual, but how can we know the experience of starving to death and plugging up a hole [in the gutter]?

-˙ti ˙Gwos, suspective + pcl. the more … . ¶˙i ha˙nol tol˙h i nwop˙ti ˙Gwos mwok-˙˙swu˙m i wo˙lano˙n i (1459 Wel 1:37b) the higher these heavens the longer life gets [wo˙la-, usually descriptive (= adjective) is here functioning as processive (= vi)]. ˙QILQ-˙POYK pen pwul˙Gi˙ti ˙Gwos te˙wuk CYENG ˙ho˙ya (1462 ¹Nung 7:13a) a hundred times the more it flashed the finer it was, and … . ˙˙wulGwe˙ti ˙Gwos te nwopho˙si˙kwo pi˙puy˙ti ˙Gwos te kwutu˙si˙ta ho˙n i ˙ˊla (1463 Pep 2:173a) said the more that you raise your head the higher they [?= pimples] are, and the more you rub the harder they are. it.ti ˙Gwos tewuk e˙kuy.m ye tot.ti [˙]Gwos tewuk ˙˙me.n i (1579 Kwikam 1:6a) the better it is the more one transgresses, and the more one runs the farther it is.

-˙ti ˙Gwoy (?< -ti ˙Gwuy, ?< -ti ˙Gwuy oy) + NEG. but; and (yet). ¶hon-kas ˙˙ti-˙na ˙kanon nakunay ˙nwun s ˙mu.l ul pwo-˙ti ˙Gwoy [˙˙CYWU-ZIN] ˙uy [QON-˙HHYWEY] ˙non ˙˙et.ti ˙˙mwot ho˙l i ˊlwo˙ta (1481 Twusi 7:10b) one looks upon the passing wayfarer's tears in vain, but [= for] he will not receive the master's grace and favor.

ti ˙Gwuy < ˙˙TTI-˙WUY, noun, counter, bnd noun.

1. noun. position. ¶˙˙syenghyen ti ˙Gwuy ˙yey ˙˙mwot kal ˙ka pwun˙pyel a˙ni hol ke˙s i˙l i (1518 Sohak-cho 8:13b) will not worry whether one might be unable to go to the position of a sage.

2. counter. time(s), occasion(s) = pen, pol. ¶˙i KYENG ˙ul ma˙zon a˙hwop ti ˙Gwuy nilk˙kwo (1447 Sek 9:32b) reads this sūtra forty-nine times, and … .

3. bnd noun. SEE -ti ˙Gwuy, -ti ˙Wi; thi ˙Gwuy.

ˊ-ti ˙Gwuy + NEG, abbr < ˙i-ti ˙Gwuy (cop). is but; is and (yet). ¶il˙hwu.m i ˙HHWAN-˙TI ˊ-ti ˙Gwuy ˙TI-˙˙THYEY ˙non ˙i ˙HHWAN a˙ni ˙ˊla (1465 Wen 2:2:1:31ab) it is called obscure wisdom but as far as the form of the wisdom goes this is not obscure.

-ti ˙Gwuy + NEGATIVE. but; and (yet). ¶MA ˙lol HHANG-˙PPWOK ˙˙hoy-ti ˙Gwuy ˙PPWULQ-˙˙CO y CCO-PI a˙ni ˙hwo.m ay put˙ti a˙ni ho˙n i ˊla (1482 Nam 2:5a) he got the devil to surrender but could not rely on the sons (= believers) of Buddha not to show compassion.

SEE -u˙si-ti ˙Gwuy.

-tikka SEE -suptita

-ti lwok (1747 Songkang 1:1a) the more … .

˙ti˙myen = ˙t i˙m ye n'. SEE -tan ~, -wolq ~, -wulq ~ .

˙tin˙tayn = ˙t in ˙t ay n', postmod + cop mod + postmod + pcl + pcl. SEE -ulq, -wolq, -un, -nwon ~. LCT has two examples of ˙t in ˙t ay non: chyeng khen t ay non (1539 Ilon-cwung 12a) 'prithee; I pray'; kwuntywung ey kal ˙t in ˙t ay non (1542 Pun-on 11b) 'when one goes to the army'. In the reading aids of the Chinese text of 1588 Mayng 9:5b there is an unusual form ˊyntan, which corresponds to iltintayn = ˙ilq ˙t in ˙t ay n' in the translation.

-˙ti's ˊi = -tu˙s ˊi. like. ¶ke˙wulwu ˙ey nos pwo-˙ti˙s ˊi ˙hwolq ˙t i˙n i (1459 Wel 8:20b) it is like looking at one's face in a mirror.

… ˙ti˙s ˊi = … tu˙s ˊi. like. ¶˙pwosi˙kwo ˙za ˙˙an [˙]ti˙s ˊi ˙hosi˙n i (1449 Kok 43) just looking he seemed as if he knew. SUNG-CAY ˙lol ˙hotan ˙ti˙s ˊi ho˙n i (1459 Wel 23:65b) it was as if they had provided food for the monks.

ti˙ta > cita. SEE cita. INF ti˙ye, ˙tye.

-ti tul, retrospective attentive + particle

-ti ˙Wi (= -ti ˙Gwuy) + NEGATIVE. but; and (yet). ¶ZYE-LOY ˙˙ta-˙mon hon ˙PPWULQ-SSING ˙o˙lwo ˙CYWUNG-SOYNG ˙˙wuy ˙ho˙ya ˙SYWELQ-˙PEP ˙hosi-ti ˙Wi ˙nye-na˙mon SSING ˙i ˙˙twul.h i˙m ye ˙˙sey˙h i ˙˙ep˙su.n i ˙ˊla (1447 Sek 13:49b) the tathāgata preaches the Law to the people as just the one Buddha vehicle, but there are no other two or three vehicles. wo˙cik ˙i [˙]mwom nahon ˙emi ˙lol [˙]KWUW ho-niWi [= -˙˙tiWi] [˙]tye [˙˙]men ˙˙nwuy ˙yey s CHYENG-TTYEY ˙lol ˙KWUW ˙hwo.m i af˙]ni ˊ[˙]la (1459 Wel 23:93a – the syllable "ti" lacks a top line; several accent dots are missing) I save only the mother who gave birth to my body, I am not saving (?)Nīladi [the earlier and mean-spirited

˙CYENG-˙PEP ˙ul poy˙hwo-˙ti˙Wi ¨ep˙siGwu˙m ul ¨mal ˙ss i˙Gwo (1459 Wel 10:20b) the nun is to go study the true dharma and not to lose it (let it vanish).

˙to = t₂, postmod. 1. the fact that (nominalizer): ˙t ol, ˙t on, ˙t olwo; ˙t i(···), ˙tin˙tayn. NOTE: ··· ˙ti = ··· ˙t i; perhaps -˙toy = -˙to y < ˙to + ˙i (pcl) or -˙i (suffix).

2. = ˙toy place. ¶ ¨amwo ˙to 'la ˙sye won ˙twong mwo˙lo˙tesi˙n i (1459 Wel 2:25b) she didn't know just what place it had come from (˙la = [i]la).

*-˙t[o]- or *-t-, bnd v (emotive). SEE -˙two- (< modulated emotive). Postulated on the basis of that (*modulated) form and the parallelism of the synonymous emotive -˙s[o]- : -˙swo- and the processive -(˙)n[o]- : -˙nwo-.

···' to, abbr < -ci/-ki to (in set expressions). ¶Tut' to po' to mōs han sālam a person that I neither heard nor saw. NOTE: In earlier Korean the particle ˙two freely attached directly to the stem without the help of the nominalizing -˙ti that corresponds to most instances of modern -ci/-ki. SEE ˙two.

to < ˙two, pcl of highlighting focus (reinforced emphasis). Ramstedt 1939:166 calls this the "augmentative particle", taking the term from Chamberlain's treatment of the corresponding Japanese particle mo.

1. 1a. also/too (or even) + AFFIRMATIVE; (n)either, (n)or even + NEGATIVE. ¶Na to kakeyss.ta I will go, too. Na to an kakeyss.ta I won't go, either. Ku i tul ttek to mek.ess.ta They ate the rice cake, even/too. Ttek to mekci anh.ess.ta They didn't eat any rice cake even/either. ¹Nayil to cōh.ta Tomorrow will be all right, too. ¹Nayil to cōh.ci anh.ta Tomorrow won't do, either. Ku nun īl ul cal hal ppun ani 'la ppalli to hanta Not only does he work well, he works fast, too. Ku kes to kaciko osey yo Bring that, too.

1b. both ... and + AFFIRMATIVE; (n)either ··· (n)or ··· + NEGATIVE (and also occasionally elsewhere — see last example). ¶Na to awu to kakeyss.ta Both I and my little brother will go. Na to awu to an kakeyss.ta Neither I nor my little brother will go. Ttek to yes to mek.ess.ta They ate both the rice cake(s) and the taffy. Ttek to yes to an mek.ess.ta They didn't eat either the rice cake(s) or the taffy. Pol man to hako tul.ul man to hata It is both worth seeing and it is worth hearing. Palam to pūlko pi to onta The wind is blowing and it is raining, as well, both. Kkoch to phiko iph to phinta The flowers are blooming and the leaves are coming out, both. Kim sensayng to Pak sensayng to Cang sensayng to pwass.ta I saw Mr Kim and Mr Pak and Mr Cang, all three (or: ... all three saw it/me). Kim sensayng to Pak sensayng to Cang sensayng to an wass.ta Mr Kim, Mr Pak, Mr Cang — none of them came. Talci to anh.ko sici to anh.ta It is neither sweet nor (is it) sour; It isn't sweet but it isn't sour, either. Kalq swu to ēps.ko, an kalq swu to ēps.ey yo I can't go, and yet I cannot get out of going. Palam i pūlq tus to hako pi ka olq tus to hata It looks as though the wind might blow or it might rain.

2. even, yet, still, even though/if; at all; indeed (CF kkaci, cocha, mace). ¶Han pen to cal han nal i ēps.ta There wasn't even one day when he did it well. Acik to cēlm.ta They are still young. Cikum to canta He is still asleep. Enu nwu ka sakyess.nun ci, cham cal to saykyess.ta Whoever carved it, he certainly carved it well. Payk.hwa-cem ey se to mōs santa It cannot be bought even in department stores (either). Āmu kes to ēps.ta There is nothing; We have nothing. Āmu sālam to an wass.ta Nobody came at all. Ppalli to kaney It really goes fast! Mānh.i to moass.ta We have gathered a lot of them, indeed. Tal to palk.ta The moon is so bright. Elkwul i mōs to nass.ta (= mōs naki to hayss.ta) He has a real(ly) ugly face. Hanul ey nun pyēl to mānh.ta What a lot of stars are in the sky! SEE celeh.key to, etteh.key to, ha to, ileh.key to, kuli to, celi to, ku-ta(k)ci to, nemu ('na) to.

3. loosely refers to the predicate or to the sentence as a whole, though attached to a noun phrase. CF Dupont 210-1: Cip to khe 'What a big house!' (in other contexts: 'The house is big, too' or 'Even the house is big'); Sālam to mānh.ta 'What a lot of people!'.

4. (attached directly to stem). SEE ···' to, ˙two.

NOTE: Except for occasional loose reference (as in 3), the Korean particle always refers to the immediately preceding word or phrase; English translations are frequently ambiguous. The meaning of to is mutually exclusive with that of un/nun ('as for') and usually with that of ya/iya ('only if it be'), but Pak ¹Yongchel (1904-34) began a poem with the string **to ya** (**Na to ya kanta** 'I go, too') and at least one speaker today finds nothing objectionable about (?) **Na nun iya kanta** 'I, at least, am going'. The sentence **Na nun ya silh.ta** (LHS 1961: 1942a) 'I, at least, dislike it (or: don't want to do it)' uses an abbreviation of **iya**. The particle **to** freely follows other particles and sequences of particles, but **i/ka** (nominative) and **ul/lul** (accusative) drop in standard colloquial usage.

SEE **-ci to, -e to, -e se to, -ess.e to, -key to, -ki to, -ko to, -ko se to, -ule to, -ulye to, -ullay to, -umyen se to, -umye to; -tula to, ila to; (-un/-nun/-tun) tey to.**

to-, 1. bnd adv (?< TWO). **to-math.ta** assumes (takes on) all responsibility; undertakes in toto.
2. ? bnd noun. **to-keli** by the gross, in bulk.

CF **tomay** wholesale buying; **thong-keli (lo)** as a lot, unbroken, in toto; **thongcca** = **thongqca** the whole lump/mass; **(ōn-)thong** all.

to ani 'ko, pcl + neg cop gerund. ¶ **Ku kes un kaykwuli to ani 'ko olchayngi to ani 'ta** That is neither a frog nor a tadpole.

to ani 'ta, pcl + neg cop indic assert. ¶ **X to Y to ani 'ta** is neither X nor Y. **Hak to pōng to ani 'ta** = **Cwuk to pap to ani 'ta** "is neither fish nor fowl" (= does not make sense).

tōcwung, n. 1. (< ¨TTWOW-TYWUNG) on the way, en route; while traveling, while on the road; before arrival.
2. (< TTWO-TYWUNG, accent borrowed from 1) in the midst, before finishing; **(-nun ~)** (in) the midst of doing, while doing.

tok < ¨TTWOK, adnoun. by oneself, alone. ¶ **~ chaci** monopoly. **~ mutay** (having) the stage all to oneself. **~ pang** a room to oneself; a solitary cell. **~ sallim** self-support. **~ thang** a bath/bathroom to oneself.

tokon = two ˙kwo n', pcl + pcl [obs] = **pota** than.
tokos = two ˙kwo s, pcl + pcl [obs] = **pota** than.
tol, adn. 1. wild; rough, untutored; inferior. ¶ **~ kam** a wild persimmon. **~ pay** a wild pear. **~ nom** a boor. **~ nungkum** a crabapple. **~ phath** wild red beans. **~ minali** wild parsley. **~ sam** wild hemp. **~ phi** wild barnyard grass. CF **tul** < tu˙luh moor; wild.
2. = **twul** (barren). ¶ **~ chi, ~ kyēycip.** [< tōl < ¨twolh stone]

-tol, bnd n. (a popular second element in boys' names). CF **tol-i**. [?< tōl stone; ?< tō-l-]

˙t ol, postmod + pcl. SEE -un ˙t ol, in ˙t ol, 'yn ˙t ol, ˙ilwon ˙t ol; -non ˙t ol; -ten t ol; -ulq ˙t ol.

-˙t ol, suspective + particle (= **-ci lul**). CF -˙t ul.

1. (+ negative auxiliary). ¶ ˙na y ne-huy ˙tol˙h ol ko˙cang KWONG-˙KYENG ˙ho˙ya ¨ep˙si wo˙t ol a˙ni ˙honwo˙n i (1447 Sek 19:29b) I do not come without the utmost respect for you people. ˙PEP tut˙t ol a[˙]ni ho˙l i ˙'la (1459 Wel 2:36b) will not heed the Law. ˙wohi˙lye po˙lki˙t ol ¨mwot ˙ho˙ya (1462 ¹Nung 2:67a) being unable to make it clear. [˙SYWUN] ˙ul nis˙t ol ¨mwot ˙ho.ya (1481 Twusi 7:9b) being unable to forget Shùn. muce˙k ul cwos˙t ol a˙ni ho˙kwo (1482 Kum-sam 2:21a) they will not peck at clumps of earth but ... .

2. (+ vt). ¶ku˙le ˙'na YAK ˙ol ˙cwue˙nul mek˙t ol ˙sul˙hi ne˙ki˙n i (1459 Wel 17:20a) but when we gave them medicine they did not want to take it.

tol(q) < *to˙l[o]l(q) < to[l]˙ta is sweet. (1527 Cahoy 3:6b=14a.)

˙tol(q) < *˙to˙l[o]l(q) < ˙to[l]˙ta hangs.

˙tolh, postnoun, postmodifier. the group (of ···), the several (···); ··· and others. SEE ˙tholh (< ···h ˙tolh); VAR ˙tulh, ˙thul (ey s).

1. postn. ¶un ˙kwa ¨pitan ˙tol[h] ˙syang˙kup ho˙kwo (?1517- Pak 1:57a) presented silver and silks, and ... . PPWO-˙SALQ ˙tol[h] ˙WUY ˙ho˙ya (1459 Wel 13:35ab) for the bodhisattvas. ¨salom ˙tol˙h ol (1447 Sek 13:57b), ¨salom ˙tol˙h i (1459 Wel 23:74b) people. ¨kyecip ˙tol˙h ol (1447 Sek 24:2b) the womenfolk. MWON ˙tol˙h ol ... (1447 Sek 6:2b) doors. a˙zom ˙tol.h ol (1481 Twusi 8:20a) the relatives, the clan. ˙ile ˙'n ¨NGWUW-CCYENG ˙tol.h on (1447 Sek 9:12b) such sentients. ˙POYK-˙SYENG ˙tol˙h i (1449 Kok 11) the people. a˙pi ¨CO-˙SIK ˙tol˙h i (1459 Wel 17:17b) fathers and sons. ˙wos ˙tol˙h i (1459 Wel 2:33a) fancy raiments. ˙i ha˙nol ˙tol˙h i (1459 Wel 1:37b) these heavens. PWU-ZIN ˙tol˙h ila˙n i (1459 Wel 8:100a) they were wives. CYE PPWO-˙SALQ ˙tol˙khwa [= ˙tolh ˙kwa] ˙lwo ˙swo˙n ol sim˙kye NGYENG-˙CYEP ˙ho˙sike˙tun (1459 Wel 8:48b) offering his hand to the bodhisattvas and all he welcomed them.

¶ ˙wuli ˙tol˙h (we): SEE ˙wu˙li. ne-huy ˙tol˙h (you people): SEE ne-huy.

2. postmodifier. ¶stwo kal˙h ay ¨hel.m ye

¨twochoy ˙yey pehun ˙tol˙h ay s CHANG ul kwo˙thywotoy (1466 Kup 1:82a) moreover it will cure wounds such as those of boils arising from a knife or those from cutting on an ax.
tol.i₁, postnoun (der noun < tōlta). CF **twuli**.
  1. [spelled **toli**]. a general area of the body (CF **nol.i**). ¶**alayq** ~ from the waist down; the lower half of the body. **wus** ~ from the waist up; the upper part of the body; jacket; a coolie foreman. **heliq** ~ the general area of the waist, around the middle of the body.
  2. that which wraps around, a wrap. ¶**mok** ~ a neckpiece, a scarf. **kwup** ~ paper used as base molding around a room.
  3. a circle, a ring. ¶**sin** ~ the decorative ridge running round the top of a Korean sandal. **so.yong** ~ a whirlpool, a swirl.
  4. SEE **cap-toli** supervision (CF **cap-coyta** supervises).
tol-i₂, cpd postn. 1. a person, fellow, guy. ¶**sam** ~ the three (kind of) impossible people: **kām** ~ those who will cooperate when there is something in it for them, **pey** ~ those who stand aloof when it is not to their interest, **ak** ~ those who are ugly to work with. **kkan** ~ [Kyengsang DIAL] a frivolous person.
  2. (second element of boy's name + dimin suffix). SEE **-tol, -i**.
tōli < ¨*TTWOW-¨LI*, noun.
  1. reason. ¶ ~ **ey mac.ta** it stands to reason, is reasonable.
  2. duty. ¶**casik ulo uy** ~ one's duty as a son.
  3. a way, a means. 3a. ¶**pyel** ~ a better way/means/remedy, an alternative; a choice. **pyel** ~ **ēps.i** inevitably, helplessly, reluctantly.
  3b. **-ulq** ~. ¶**Ku kes un ecci halq tōli ka ēps.ta** There's nothing to be done about it. **Ku sālam ulo se to ecci halq tōli ka ēps.ess.ci yo** Even for him there was no way out. **Oci mālla ˙y to cakkwu onun tey ya na ˙n tul etteh.k' ˙elq tōli ka iss.e ya ˙ci?!** What can I do when he keeps coming here though I tell him not to?! **Tōn i ēps.uni pic ul nāylq pakk ey tōli ka ēps.ta** Since I am broke, I've got to get a loan. **Ku sālam i an oni honca calq tōli pakk ey ēps.ta** He didn't come, so I must sleep alone.
tolm < *˙to˙l[o]m*, subst < *to[l]˙ta* (sweet).
˙**tolm** < *˙to˙l[o]m*, subst < *to[l]˙ta* (hangs).
˙**tolok**, abbr < **hatolok**. (There is no *i-tolok.)

-tolok < *-to˙lwok*, projective [attaches to v, adj; cop *i-tolok is lacking despite MK ˙i˙two˙lwok and ˙ito˙lwok]. CF **-key, -key-kkum, -key-sili**.
  1. 1a. to the point where, until (a result); (arranges/tries to do it) so that. ¶**kulenq īl i ēps.tolok caki lul kyēngkyey hata** is on one's guard so that such a thing will not happen. **Acwu nolah.tolok mul ul tul.ye cwusey yo** Be sure to dye it good and YELLOW. (CF **Acwu nolah.key** ··· Be sure to dye it quite yellow.) **Cōh.(usi)tolok hasipsio** Do as you please. (CF **Com te cōh.key halq swu ēps.na yo?** Can't you make it a little better? **Com te cal halq swu ēps.na yo?** Can't you do it in a little nicer way?) **Yelq si ey copan ul mektolok hay cwusio** Please have your breakfast by ten (or: Please prepare my breakfast so that I may have it at ten). ¹**Nayil achim ey ilccik il.e natolok hasey yo** (Im Hopin 1987:173) Please arrange/try to get up early tomorrow morning. **Ppallay pich i huytolok ppal.e ya ˙ci yo** You have to wash the clothes until they become clean and white. **Kulen tōn un pat.ci anh.tolok hasipsio** See to it that you do not ever take that kind of money. **Tulko katolok ssa cwusipsio** Wrap them up so that I can carry them. **Nwun-mul i na-otolok wus.ess.ta** I laughed till the tears ran down my face. **Tōn ul ponay nun cwuess.una kece pīyong ina kyewu toytolok ponay cwuess.ta** They sent us the money all right, but scarcely enough to cover the expenses. **Ic.e pelici anh.tolok hasipsio** Try not to forget (it). **I kulus i kkāy cici anh.key cōsim hatolok hakeyss.ˢup.nita** (Im Hopin 1987:173) I will try to take care (so) that this plate does not get broken. NOTE: Though usually followed by a verb, the **-tolok** phrase sometimes shows the extent of an adjective: **Ttang ey kkullitolok kīn chima lul hay ip.ul phil.yo ka ēps.ta** (CM 2:55) There is no need to wear a skirt that is so long it drags on the ground.
  1b. (indirect requests). ¶**Ce pun i hak.kyo ey ositolok ku ai eykey māl hayss.ta** I told that boy to ask him to come to school [osikey would be inappropriate here].
  1c. ¶**Ku sālam ul ¹nayil otolok (= okey) haci yo** I will see that he comes (or: Let him come) tomorrow. **Ku pun ul yeki ey ositolok (= osikey) hako siph.ta** I'd like to get him to come here.

2. **toytolok (imyen)** ... as ... as possible; if (at all) possible. ¶¹**Nayil un toytolok ilccik il.e nakeyss.ta** Tomorrow morning I will get up as early as possible. **Toytolok imyen ilccik osipsio** Come early if you can. CF **Il.yoil i toytolok ku i nun tol.a oci anh.ess.ta** He didn't come back till Sunday.

3. ¶**olaytolok** for a long time. **nuc.tolok = nuc.key toytolok** till (it gets) late.

SEE **tholok, ku'tholok;** ˙*i˙li-˙to˙lwok*.

-tolok ccum (un / iya), projective + pcl (+ pcl). ¶**Siksa cwūnpi lul mānh.i nun mōs hay to ppalli mektolok ccum iya hay tulici yo** I'll get you something simple to eat right away without going to a lot of trouble. **Nay him ulo ku īl i ppalli toytolok ccum (un) halq swu iss.ci** I guess I can see that that gets done fast without help from others.

-tolok cocha, projective + particle. ¶**Cey ttay ey pap ul mektolok cocha an hay cwuta 'ni kulen pep i eti iss.na** What kind of deal is this — not even serving us on time?!

-tolok i, projective + pcl [with neg cop only]. ¶**I pen os un menceq kes pota khutolok i ani 'la cāktolok hay cwusey yo** Please make this garment small from the start, and not big.

-tolok-i, extended projective. [? DIAL] so that (to the point that) indeed. ¶**Ili otolok-i māl-ssum ul tulyess.ˢup.nita** I told him to come this way. CF **-key-sili/-kkum.** [? < -˙*to˙lwo˙k ay*]

-tolok ila to, projective + cop var inf + pcl. ¶**Mannaci nun mōs hal mangceng sesin ¹yen.lak ul hatolok ila to hay cwusipsio** Let me get in touch with him by letter, anyway, even if I can't see him.

-tolok ina, projective + cop advers. ¶**Panchan un ēps.e to cey ttay ey pap ul mektolok ina hay cwuess.umyen cōh.keyss.ta** With no side dishes, you'd think they could feed us on time, at least.

~ **-ma** (extended). ¶**Wāng.lay nun mōs halq mangceng phyēnci ¹yen.lak ul hatolok ina-ma tōyss.umyen cōh.keyss.ta** I can't go back and forth, but I'd like to keep in touch by letter, at least, anyway.

-tolok in tul, projective + cop mod + postmod. ¶**Nay ka tōn man pēlmyen ne lul tāyhak ey katolok in tul mōs halq ka pon ya** Doesn't it look as though I can send you to college if I just earn (enough) money?

-tolok itun ci, projective + cop retr modifier + postmodifier. ¶**Āmu'h.tun ne lul Mikwuk ey katolok itun ci Yengkwuk ey katolok itun ci kkok hay cwum a** Anyway, (I promise) I will send you either to America or to England.

-tolok iya, projective + pcl. ¶**Kotung hak.kyo lul machitolok iya mōs hay cwukeyss.n' ya** I think I can at least see you through school!

-tolok khenyeng, projective + pcl. ¶**Ileh.key cip hyengphyen i elyewe se ya atul ul tāyhak ul kakey hatolok khenyeng cwunghak to mōs machikey halq ka pwā kekceng ita** Family circumstances are so tough that I worry about even seeing my boy through middle school, much less send him to college. **Īl i i ccum khukey pel(.)e cyess.uni toytolok khenyeng āmu ccak ey to mōs ssukey toyess.ta** The job had grown so big that far from being a success, it has turned out worthless. **Toytolok khenyeng an toytolok to mōs hanta** Far from merely being possible, it is sure to happen.

-tolok kkaci, projective + particle. ¶**Hak.kyo ey tanitolok kkaci hay cwusini cēng-mal komapsup.nita** I am truly grateful to you for actually letting me attend school.

-tolok mace, projective + pcl. ¶**Cey ttay ey pap ul mektolok mace an hay cwuta 'ni kulen pep i eti iss.na** What kind of deal is this — not even serving us on time?!

-tolok malyen ita [DIAL, colloq]. SEE **malyen**.

-tolok man, projective + pcl. ¶**ip ey pap i cel-lo tul.e otolok man palanun keyulum-pangi** an idler who seeks nothing more than a way to get food to fall in his mouth of itself.

~ **ila to**. ¶**Han pen mancye potolok man ila to hay cwusio** Just let me touch it once.

~ **ina-ma**. Are there examples?.

-tolok mankhum (un), projective + pcl (+ pcl). ¶**Etteh.key hay se 'tun ci ney ka tāyhak ey katolok mankhum un hay cwukeyss.ta** One way or another I will at least see to it that you get to college.

-tolok man un, projective + pcl + pcl. ¶**Chān un ēps.e to cey ttay ey mektolok man un hay tulikeyss.ˢup.nita** I will be feeding you in due course, even though we have no side dishes.

-tolok pota, projective + pcl. ¶**Wutung-sayng i toytolok pota sengsil han sālam toytolok nolyek hala** Endeavor to become a true person rather than a ranking student.

-tolok puthe, projective + particle. ¶**Ai tul i hak.kyo lul tanitolok puthe hay ya toylq key ani yo?** Shouldn't we start off by putting the children in school?

-tolok to, projective + particle. ¶**Hak.kyo lul machitolok to mōs hay cwusikeyss.ta 'n māl-ssum ip.nikka?** You mean you won't even let me finish school?

-tolok tul, projective + pcl. ¶**Toylq swu iss.nun tay lo hak.kyo nun machitolok tul hakey** You kids try to finish school if possible.

-tolok un, projective + pcl. ¶**Toylq swu iss.nun tay lo hak.kyo lul machitolok un hay ya 'ci** You'd better get through school if possible.

't o᾽lwo, postmodifier + particle. because, since. SEE -*(ᵁ/o)n ~* , -*nᵁ/on ~* ; ? -*(ᵁ/o)lq ~* .

-*'to᾽lwok*, projective (> **-tolok**). ? < *'t o᾽lwo* + *k* (emphatic particle) or *[᾽ho]᾽k[ey]*.

 1. to the point that, until, so that. ¶*hon ᾽KEP ᾽i ¨nam᾽to᾽lwok nil᾽Ge two* (1447 Sek 9:10b) even if I told it until there was only one kalpa (eon) remaining. *i᾽Gwus ci[p] s ᾽pu.l un ᾽pa.m i kipto᾽lwok pol᾽ka ᾽ys.two᾽ta* (1481 Twusi 7:6b) the fire in the neighboring house was bright deep into the night. *kwo᾽ki capnon ᾽poy nwol᾽Gywo.m ol ᾽pwonwo᾽la ᾽ho.ya [᾽PPOYK-᾽ZILQ] i wol᾽ma katolwok ᾽hosila ᾽n ᾽t oy ¨man tyeng nul᾽kun nye᾽lum ¨cis.non ᾽nwo᾽m on mu᾽sus ke᾽s i i᾽sye selu ᾽culkywo᾽m ol ¨ta ho᾽l i Gwo* (1481 Twusi 22:7b) not just have they spent much of the day's light enjoying the fishing boat, but with what [now] will the old farmers bring their mutual delight to its fullest?

 -*᾽tolwo᾽k ay* (+ pcl) SAME. ¶*cwuk᾽tolwo᾽k ay cwo᾽cha tot-᾽nye* (1447 Sek 19:21-2) I will follow after them until they die. *¨say᾽to᾽lwok cye᾽mu᾽tolwo᾽k ay kos᾽pi ᾽NGEP ᾽ul ¨cis.no᾽n i* (1463/4 Yeng 1:41b) we busily create karma night and day.

 2. (all) the more, more and more, increasingly (= **-ulq swulok**). ¶*¨man hi tut᾽tolwok ¨etwuk ᾽SIN thi a᾽ni ᾽hono᾽n i* (1482 Nam 1:36b) the more I hear the less I believe. *cyem᾽ku᾽to᾽lwok ᾽acol ᾽ho᾽ya* (1485 Kwan 3a) gets more and more confused as the night darkens.

 NOTE: *᾽i᾽li-᾽to᾽lwok* 'to this extent' (1459 Wel 8:101a) is an adverb lexicalized from the phrase *᾽i᾽li ᾽ho᾽to᾽lwok*; CF *᾽tho᾽lwok*.

to᾽lye, 1. vt inf < *to᾽li᾽ta* (take / bring a person). ¶*᾽icey ᾽stwo na ᾽y a᾽to᾽l ol to᾽lye ¨ka᾽l ye ᾽ho᾽sino᾽n i* (1447 Sek 6:5b) and now you want to take my son, in addition.

 2. = *ᵁ/ol to᾽lye*, quasi-particle (> **tele**) to [an inferior]; CF *te᾽pu᾽lta*. ¶*pwu¨thye y ᾽MWOK-LYEN-᾽i to᾽lye nilo᾽sya᾽toy* (1447 Sek 6:1a) Buddha says to [his disciple] Maudgalyāyana [as follows] ... . *SYWU-᾽TTALQ-i l᾽ to᾽lye nil᾽Gwo᾽toy* (1447 Sek 6:19b) says to Sudatta [as follows] ... . *᾽MEN-LYENG CYE-᾽SYENG ᾽i ¨ta ¨na l᾽ to᾽lye nilo᾽sya᾽toy* (1459 Wel 2:52a) the spirits and sages all tell me [as follows] ... . *ney ka na l᾽ tolye ywok honon kwona* (1894 Gale 38) you insult me, do you?

-' **to mōs hata** (vi), abbr < **-ci to mōs hata** (in a few expressions). ¶**Po' to tut' to mōs hanta** He can neither see nor hear. **O' to ka' to mōs hanta** We are stuck (− we can neither come nor go). **Olu' to nayli' to mōs hanta** It (the elevator) is stuck — it won't go up or down.

-*ton* (probably < *'t on* 'given the fact').

 1. if, when. SEE **-ketun**, **-te᾽tun**, **is᾽ton**; -*᾽t on*.

 2. = (? var of) -**ten**, retr mod. SEE *᾽ston*.

-*᾽t on* suspective + pcl (= **-ci nun**). ¶*kwoti tulpt on ani howoy* (1676 Sin.e 1:19a) is not sincere. (Probably < *᾽t on*; CF -*᾽ton*.)

᾽t on, postmod + particle. SEE **-nwon᾽t on**, **-un᾽t on**, **hon᾽t on**.

ton < **to[᾽lo]n*, mod < *to[l]᾽ta* (sweet). ¶*to᾽n ye ᾽psu᾽n ye* (1462 ¹Nung 3:49b) is it sweet or is it bitter?

᾽ton < **᾽to[᾽lo]n*, modifier < *᾽to[l]᾽ta* (hangs). ¶*᾽ton᾽t ay* (1447 Sek 24:20b).

tōn < *¨twon*, 1. n. money. 2. < **two᾽[lo]n*, modifier < **tōlta** < *¨two[l]᾽ta* (goes around).

tong$_1$, 1-7 n, 8-9 counter. [probably < "round", CF **tong-kulta**; perhaps < **tō-l-** + **-ng**].

 1. reason, logic, coherence, consistency. ¶**~ i tah.ta** squares with logic, stands to reason, is consistent.

 2. a period, a term, an interval, a time limit (CF **tong-an**). ¶**~ i ttuta** has an interval or gap (between), is spaced.

 3. a cuff. ¶**somayq ~**, **kkuth ~** sleeve cuff.

 4. (**sangchi ~**) a lettuce stalk.

 5. **cwung ~** the middle part / cut, the waist.

 6. (= **tongkang**) a piece, a part. ¶**~ nata** it breaks into pieces − also (2) "interval occurs" = it runs out, it is out of stock.

7. (= **mal**) a **yuch** marker.

8. counter: one of the four rounds necessary to complete a game of **yuch**.

9. counter. a bundle (bunch, load).

tong₂ < TTWONG, adn. the same; the said. ¶ ~ **pēnci** the same / said address. ~ **cemq-swu** the same / said score. ~ **panghyang** the same / said direction.

tong₃ → ˙twong (postmodifier)

tong-, ? bnd adv (CF **tong**₁ 6). ¶ ~ **caluta** cuts in long pieces. CF **t(h)omak** piece, **tong-kulta** is round.

-tong, suffix. 1. (forms boys' names). child, boy. ¶**Kilqtong** Kilqtong, "Lucky Boy". **Poktong** Poktong, "Happy Boy". CF **-i, tongi**. [? < bnd noun TTWONG 'child'; ? < 'round']

2. mith ~ root, base, bottom. [< ?]

tong-an, noun. [< 'period of time' + 'inside']

1. an interval, a while, a space of time, a period. After quantifier often **-q tong-an**. ¶**yele hayq tong-an** (for) a period of several years. **cāmqkanq tong-an** for a little while. **elmaq tong-an** (for) how long. **sip-nyenq tong-an** ten years. **han talq tong-an** for a month. **meych talq tong-an** how many months (of time)? But: **ku tong-an** (= **ku kan**) that interval; since the last time.

2. (**-nun** ~, **-ulq** ~, **-un** ~) while (doing).

-tong-i, cpd suffix. child, one. (forms endearing names for children). **Poktong-i** (or **Pok-tongi**) Little Poktong. **ccollay** ~ a frivolous urchin. **'mak(-nay)** ~ the youngest son. **yak** ~ a clever boy. **cheng meli** ~ a blue-top kite. CF **-twungi, tengi**.

tongsi < TTWONG-˙SSI, n. the same time / period. ~ **uy** simultaneous, concurrent, synchronous, contemporaneous. ~ **ey** concurrently (with), at the same time, simultaneously, coincidentally; at a time, at once; while; both … and; not only … but also. ¶**caykan iss.nun tongsi ey pucilen hata** is both talented and industrious. **Tungsan un yukhway hana tongsi ey wihem hata** Mountain climbing is a pleasant sport, but it is dangerous, too. **tongsi-seng** simultaneity.

-˙tos, adverb, adj-n attached directly to the stem (= **-'tus** = **-' tus 'i**). (is) as if, like, giving the appearance of. ¶˙POYK-˙SYENG ˙i ˙cye˙cay ka-˙tos mwo˙ta ˙ka (1459 Wel 2:7a) the farmers are starting to gather as if to go to market.

~ °ho˙ta. ¶kwo˙c i ˙phu-˙tos ˙ho-ngi ˙'ta (1463 Pep 1:85b) the flowers appear to be in bloom. TUNG-KWANG ˙i cip pas˙k uy i˙sye NUNG ˙hi ci˙p ul pi˙chwuy˙ti ¨mwot ho-˙tos ho˙n i (1462 ¹Nung 1:53a) it is like being unable to light up a house with lamplight that is outside the house. **kotok hon kes pat-tu-˙tos ˙ho˙ya** (1586 Sohak 2:9b) it is as if one held up something brimful. **syem˙ki˙zop-˙tos ˙ho˙ya** (1447 Sek 6:4a) as if serving. **ilkhot¨cop-˙tos ˙ho˙ya** (1447 Sek 9:26a) as if saying.

SEE ⋯-˙thos °ho˙ta = ⋯h-˙tos °ho˙ta.

˙tos, adverb, postmod adj-n. (is) as if, like, as, giving the appearance of; no sooner ⋯ than.

-(ᵁ/o)n ˙tos °ho˙ta. ¶[PI-SYE] ˙lol pwo˙ti ¨mwot ˙ho.ya n' mozo˙m ay il˙hun ˙tos ˙hote˙n i (1481 Twusi 7:29a) (When he was) unable to see the secret document, it was as if he had lost his mind.

-wᵁ/on ˙tos °ho˙ta. ¶CCYEN-SOYNG ˙ay s ¨i˙l i e˙cey ¨pwon ˙tos ˙ho˙ya (1447 Sek 6:9a) events in my former life are as if I had seen them yesterday.

-(˙)non ˙tos °ho˙ta. ¶is.non ˙tos ˙hwo˙toy is˙ti a˙ni ˙hwo˙m i ˙suchywom a˙n' 'ywo˙m i a˙ni ''la (1459 Wel 1:36a) that it seems to exist yet does not exist is not a matter of thinking [it].

-(ᵁ/o)l(q) ˙tos °ho˙ta. ¶ ⋯ cyang˙chos ˙pwo˙[z]owol ˙tos ˙ho˙no.n i ''la (1586 Sohak 2:25a) we are likely to see him in the future.

-(ᵁ/o)l(q) ˙tus °ho˙ta. ¶nal tus mal tus ho.ya (?1608⁺ Twu-hem 25b) when they are about to emerge (= appear).

-˙ᵉ/as ˙tos °ho˙ta. ¶[NG]WOK ˙ol ca˙pa s tos ho˙m ye (1586 Sohak 2:9b) it is like grasping a jewel.

-˙to˙s 'i. as if, like. ¶**syang˙nyey mek-˙to˙s 'i** (1542 Pun-on 24a) as if always eating.

⋯ ˙to˙s 'i (< ˙hi, der adv). as if, like.

-(ᵁ/o)n ˙to˙s 'i. ¶tut˙kwo ˙two ¨mwot tulun ˙to˙s 'i ho˙m ye (1459 Wel 10:20b) they hear but act as if they do not hear, and ⋯ .

-(˙)non ˙to˙s 'i. ¶no˙la totnon ˙to.s 'i (1481 Twusi 8:57a) as if flying along.

-(˙)nun ˙to˙s 'i. ¶ce 'y mwo˙m ay s kwo˙ki ˙lol pa˙hye ¨naynun ˙to˙s 'i ne˙kye ho˙m ye (1447 Sek 9:12a) it is regarded as like tearing the flesh off one's own body.

-(ᵁ/o)l(q) ˙to.s 'i. ¶i˙kuy˙ti ¨mwot hol ˙to.s 'i ho˙m ye cyang˙chos il˙hol ˙to.s 'i ho˙m ye

(1586 Sohak 2:9b) it is as if one cannot win, and it is as if in future one will lose it, and ... .
-tosoita, [lit] formal indic assert (= -sup.nita). ¶Chencwu ye ne nun inca hasitosoita (1936 Roth 537) O Lord, thou art merciful.
-tota, [lit] indic assert (= colloq -ta). CF -tula. SEE -twoˑta.
  1. (attaches to adjective stems). ¶chwuptota = chwupta is cold. khutota = khuta is big.
  2. = -nola. ¶katota = kanola (= kanta, kata) goes. kass.tota = kass.nola (= kass.ta) went. kakeyss.tota = kakeyss.nola will go (= kakeyss.ta).
  ?3. (attached to processive modifier — mistake or hybrid form?) ¶hanun-tota, pat.nun-tota (1936 Roth 537).
to-taychey < TWO-ˈTTAY-ˈTHYEY, adverb. (what, who, ...) in the world (on earth), the devil / deuce / dickens, the hell / heck; (not) at all, from the start.
  1. anticipates a content interrogative. ¶Ku sālam hako kkaci mōs kakey hani to-taychey musunq yengmun in ci molukeyss.e I can't understand why in the world I'm not allowed to go even with him. Kim sensayng kwa cocha an kakeyss.ta 'ni to-taychey nwukwu hako kakeyss.ta 'n māl iyo You say you don't want to go even with Mr Kim, then who on earth DO you want to go with? To-taychey eti l' kani Where the hell / blazes do you think you are going? To-taychey etteh.key hay tālla 'n māl ip.nikka What on earth do you expect me to do? (M 1:2:210).
  2. (with a negative or a negative implication). ¶To-taychey (or: A.yey) kulenq yāyki mace puthe ka īsang hata 'n māl ia To begin with (or: Indeed) his story is very fishy in itself.
to tul, pcl + pcl. ¶¹Nayil to tul kakeyss.ey yo They will (all) go tomorrow, too, I think.
towoyˑta < toWoyˑta = toyta (becomes). VAR twowoyˑta.
  ¶ˈTTI-ˈNGWOK ˈi ˈPYEN ˈhoˑya LYEN ˈmwoˑs i towoyˑGe-ngi ˈˈta (1550 ¹Yenghem 8b) hell turned into a lotus pond. tuthuˑl i towoyˑGoy posˑGa ˈtikeˑnul (1447 Sek 6:30-1) crumbles into dust. ˈˈna ˈlol nilˑGwey ˈman NGWANG ˈi towoyˑGey ˈhosywoˑsye (1447 Sek 14:50b) let me become king for just seven days. ˈsaloˑm i towoyˑlak pelˑGey cywungsoyngˑi towoyˑlak ˈhoˑya (1459 Wel 1:12b) sometimes becoming a person and sometimes becoming a bug or an animal. pwuthye ˈtwo ˈˈsekˑca[h] sˑmwoˑm i towoyˑsya (1447 Sek 6:44a) Buddha too had a body three ˈcah (c. 6 ft) tall. KWONG-ˈTUK ˈi iˑle tangtangi pwuˈˈthye y towoyˑl i ˈleˑla (1447 Sek 19:34a) the virtue achievement was such that naturally he was to become a Buddha.
  ¶ˈna y pwuthye towoyˑywo.l ye holˑs i.n i (1482 Nam 2:6b) I want to become a Buddha. ˈˈtywohonˑmwom towoyGeˑna kwuˑcunˑmwom towoyGeˑna (1459 Wel 1:12a) whether one becomes a good body or becomes a bad body ... . wuˑli eˑzi aˑtoˑl iˑwoy lopˑkwo ˈˈipˈkey towoyˑya (1447 Sek 6:5a) parent (= mother) and son we are left lonely and bewildered.
tōy (= twēy = twāy) < toye, inf < toyta.
ˈtoy, 1. < itoy. 2. < hatoy.
toy(-), (? bound) adverb. back, again, in reverse.
  ¶ ~ chac.ta, chita, kelkita, mut.ta, nemkita, pat.ta, sata, sālta, saykita, sīt.ta, ssipta, ssuywuta, thwita, tol.a kata, tulta.
  SYN toylo. CF tolo, tolie; twī lo; twi(-).
-toy, concessive (= -e to) < -ˈtoy (accessive). After iss-, ēps-, -ess-, -keyss- (and in dialects after all consonant stems) the shape is -utoy. CM 2:235 says -(u)toy "hardly ever attaches to adjectives, nor to certain verbs". The copula form is usually ilotoy. The ending probably derives from -ˈtwoy < -ˈwo-ˈtoy, modulated accessive.
  1. although (even though) it does / is. ¶Pi nun otoy palam i an pūnta It rains but the wind is not blowing. Tōn un mānh.toy ssulq cwul ul molunta He has lots of money but he doesn't know how to spend it. Cip i namhyang ilotoy tong ulo com chiwuchyess.ta The house faces south but it leans slightly to the east.
  2. does / is and indeed (does / is). ¶Palam i pūltoy mopsi pūnta The wind is blowing and blowing very hard, too. Khi ka khutoy yekan khun khi ka ani 'ta He is tall, even unusually tall. Pi ka otoy cham mānh.i onta It is raining and really raining hard.
  3. [DIAL, lit] and. ¶Nay ka ne lul ssis.ki-toy sēngpu wa sēngca wa sēngsin uy ilum ul in ha.ye hanola (1965 Dupont 151) = syengpu wa syengco wa syengsin uy ilhwom ulwo syeylyey lul cwunwola (1916 Gale 33) I baptise

thee in the name of the Father, the Son, and the Holy Spirit.

4. Ku i ka māl hatoy " ⋯ " ('la ko) hayss.ta He said " ⋯ ". SYN -ki lul.

5. X-umyen X-toy SEE -umyen

˙toy, quasi-free noun. place (where ⋯). ¶ ˙TTAY-NGWANG ˙ha, na ˙two ZYE-LOY ¨kyesin ˙toy ˙lol mwo˙lozo˙Wa-ngi ʼ˙ta (1459 Wel 21:192a) oh mighty king, I do not myself know where the tathāgata is! ˙hota ˙ka ¨ta aˑlwol ˙tt in ˙t ay nʼ til˙Gwoˑm i pan˙toˑki is.non ˙toy ¨ep˙su.l ye ʼˑn i ʼsˑton (1462 ¹Nung 1:67a) perhaps, since all know, there will not necessarily have to be any stumbling blocks. mozom ˙kwa ˙pep ˙kwa e˙Wun ˑtoy kwot mozom isˑnwon ˑtoy ʼlwoˑta (1462 ¹Nung 1:64a) where mind and Law are joined is the place where the mind is. ˙HHAK ˑoy ans.non toy ʼla (1482 Kum-sam 2:61b) is where the cranes sit. SEE -ul(q) ˑtoy, ¨amwo ˑtoy. CF hon-ˑtoy, ka˙won-ˑtoy, ¨swon-ˑtoy.

-ˑtoy (? < ʻplaceʼ; ? < ˑt oy), accessive. Usually modulated: -ˑwᵘ⁄o-ˑtoy, honorific -(˙ᵘ⁄o)sya-ˑtoy; copula ˑilwo-ˑtoy. The modern concessive -toy is from -ˑtwoy < -ˑwo-ˑtoy (the modulated accessive). CF -kwanˑtoy. NOTE: Sometimes called the "evidential", but that is misleading.

1. and; and yet, yet, but. ¶ye˙le paˑlo[l] s ka˙won-ˑtoy i˙sywoˑtoy (1462 ¹Nung 2:84b) they are among the seas and ⋯ . is.non ˑtos ˑhwo toy isˑti aˑni ˑhwoˑm i ˑsuchywom aˑnʼ ʼywoˑm i aˑni ʼˑla (1459 Wel 1:36a) that it seems to exist yet does not exist is not a matter of thinking [about it]. ˙SSIM ˑhi ˑna y ¨KAM-SYANG ˑhwoˑtoy ZYE-LOY s MWU-˙LYANG TI-˙KYEN ˑul ilˑhwoˑla ˑhoˑta-ngi ʼˑta (1463 Pep 2:4b) I was moved to such grief I was about to lose the tathāgata's immeasurable awareness. NGWANG ˑi ˑmas ˑtule kas.ka˙Wi ˑhoˑkesiˑnol ⋯ (1459 Wel 2:5a) the king looked upon her with favor and kept her close to him. ¨aˑzoWwoˑtoy naˑza woˑn i mulˑle ˑkaten ˑteynʼ mwok-¨swum moˑchoˑl i ʼ-ngi s ˑka (1445 ¹Yong 51) knowing this he advanced; had he withdrawn would he have ended (= lost) his life?

2. [introducing a quotation] and what follows is what was said; [said/thought] as follows ⋯ . ¶ˑna y solang ˑhwoˑtoy eˑnwu ˙CCANG s KUM ˑi ˑza ˑmaˑchi skol˙Gi.l [i] ˑyeˑn ywo ˑhoˑnwo-ngi ʼˑta (1447 Sek 6:25b) I am thinking: just which

vault's gold will it take for [that] to be properly covered, so am I thinking. ku ˑpwup swoˑli [ˑ]yey ˑsye ¨maˑl ol nil˙Gwoˑtoy ⋯ (1447 Sek 24:1b) what the drum said was this: ⋯ . ku ˑstol toˑlye mwuˑlwoˑtoy kutuy s aˑpa ¨niˑm i is.noˑn i s ˑka (1447 Sek 6:14b) he asks the girl, "Is your father home?". ¨mwuˑlusyaˑtoy ˑne ʼy ¨kyeciˑp i ¨kwoˑWo.n i ˑye (1459 Wel 7:10b) he inquired, "Is your wife beautiful?". ¨mwutˑcowoˑtoy SYWUW-HHOYNG ˑhwo.l ye ˑhwol ˑttyeyn ¨es.tyey HHANG-ˑPPWOK ¨hoyˑl i ʼ-ngi s ˑkwo hoˑn i ʼˑla (1464 Kumkang 11a) he inquired, "If I seek to pursue the discipline, how shall I subdue it [= my mind]?". SYWU-˙TTALQ ˑi nil˙Gwoˑtoy niluˑsyan ¨yang ˑoˑlwo ˑhwoˑl i ʼ-ngi ʼˑta ˙THAY-¨COy nil˙Gwoˑtoy ˑna y ¨lwongtam ˑhotaˑla (1447 Sek 6:24b) Sudatta says "I will do as you say, sir"; the prince says "I was joking". pwu¨thye y niloˑsyaˑtoy naˑy niloˑten ˙KWU-LA ˙TYEY CIN-˙SSILQ ˑlwo kuˑle theˑn ye aˑni theˑn ywo (1459 Wel 9:36d) Buddha said "was the emperor Kwula really as I said or wasn't he?".

? to ya, pcl + pcl. SEE to (NOTE).

toye, infinitive < toyta, usually > tōy = twēy.

tōykey, adverb (adverbative < tōyta). terribly, very. VAR tēykey.

toylo, adverb. back, again, contrariwise, in reverse. Is this a preparticle toy(-) + ulo? Or var < tolo, der adv < tōlta? CF twī lo, twi(-).

toyn, mod < toyta₁₋₃.

tōyn, mod < tōyta₄. ¶ ~ soli "hard" sounds = reinforced obstruents, geminates (pp tt cc ss kk).

toyta < twoy- (1518) < towoy- < toWoy-: inf toye, usually contracted to tōy = twēy (and further to tʼēy), often treated as twāy. The past is toyess- > tōyss- = twēyss- (> tʼēyss-), often treated as twāyss-. SEE §9.4.

toyta₁, vi. 1. becomes, gets to be, turns into, grows to be, is. (The complement is a noun, an adverb, or an adverbialization. The noun is marked by i/ka or ulo/lo; in MK it is either marked by ˑi/y or left unmarked.) ¶ēlun i ~ becomes an adult, grows up, attains adulthood. cāngkwan i ~ becomes a cabinet minister. sam hak.nyen i ~ becomes a junior (a third-year student). Ku sālam i pūca ka toyess.ta He became a rich man = He got rich. Khun hakca lo toyess.ta He turned into (became) an eminent scholar.

2. becomes, turns, reaches, attains. ¶Pelsse sikan i tā tōyss.ta Time is up already. yelqtases sal i ~ turns / becomes fifteen, attains / reaches the age of fifteen. sengnyen i ~ comes of age. sēl nal i toymyen when it gets to be New Year's.

3. turns / changes / passes into, resolves / fades into, develops into. ¶mul i swu-cungki ka ~ water turns / changes into vapor. phulun pich i cholok i ~ blue changes / passes / fades into green. mul i sānso wa swuso ka ~ water resolves into oxygen and hydrogen = water is composed of oxygen and hydrogen. kāmki ka ph^{y}ēy^{1}yem i ~ a cold develops into (leads to) pneumonia.

4. comes, sets in, becomes. ¶pom i ~ spring has come; spring is with us. cho sahul i ~ the third of the month has come around.

5. passes, elapses, is (since). ¶Mikwuk kan ci sam-nyen toynta It is three years since he went off to America. Ce namu sim.un ci ō-nyen i toynta It is five years since we planted that tree. Elma 'na olay toyp.nikka How long has it been?

6. amounts / comes to, runs up to, makes / is. ¶meych chen chek ina toynun kiph.un mul water that is several thousand feet deep. Twūl ey sēys ul ka hamyen tases i toynta Two and three makes five. Pūchay ka ō-man wen i toynta I have run up a debt of 50,000 wen. Chōngayk i sam-chen wen i toynta The total comes / amounts to 3,000 wen.

7. it turns out, proves (to be), results in. ¶kēcis māl i ~ turns out false. ilq-cang uy kkwum i ~ turns out (to be) just a dream. sōnhay ka ~ results in (proves to be) a loss. chimyeng-sang i ~ proves (to be) fatal. pap i cal an ~ the food does not turn out very well. Ku kyelkwa ka etteh.key toylq ka What will be the result? How will it turn out? Where will it lead to? Sēnke ka ecci toylq ka How will the election turn out? Toylq tay lo tōy la (toyke la) Go to the devil! Devil take him! I don't care a damn about it. I tām ul tol.a se han sip-o pun kamyen Changkyeng-wen i tōy yo Go around this wall and you'll get to Changkyeng Park in about fifteen minutes.

8. consists (of); is composed (formed, made, made up) of; forms (is in the form of). ¶cip i pyek tōl lo ~ the house is made of bricks. chayk i sēy kwēn ulo ~ the book consists of (is published in) three volumes. Kwuk.hoy ka sāng-ha ^{1}yāng-wen ulo toynta The Assembly consists of two Houses, upper and lower. Ku hālyu ka samkak-cwu lo toye iss.ta Its lower reaches form a delta.

9. is made; is finished, completed; is attained, accomplished; succeeds. ¶chayk i ~ a book is completed. īl i ~ one's work is done; succeeds in one's attempt, a plan is effected, a project materializes. tōn i ~ succeeds in getting money. sālam i ~ becomes / is a fine man. Ēncey toynun ya When will it be done / ready? Sālam toyko ani toynun kes un ney nolyek ey tallyess.ta It depends upon your own endeavor whether you become a success or failure. Īl i toyko ani toynun kes un wūn ey tallinun swu to iss.ta The success or failure of a plan sometimes depends upon luck. Tā toyess.ey yo It is (We are) all done / finished.

10. grows, thrives, prospers. ¶cip an i cal ~ a family is prosperous, thrives. cip an i cal an toye kata a family is going downhill. cangsa ka cal ~ does (a) good business, business is good. I ttang ey nun chāyso ka cal toynta Vegetables grow well in this soil.

11. serves the purpose, will do, works, is all right, is OK (acceptable); (toyci anh.nunta = an toynta) is unacceptable, is no good, won't do. ¶I kes un an toynun tey! This one's no good! Ku kes un māl i toyci anh.nunta That is nonsense / absurd. toyci anh.nun māl absurd remarks, nonsense, bosh. toyci anh.un casik a worthless fellow / son, a good-for-nothing. An tōyss.^{s}up.nita That's too bad; That's a shame. Tōyss.e yo (1) OK; All right. (2) That's OK = No, thank you.

-ci anh.ko se nun an toylq kes ita = an ····-ko se nun an toylq kes ita it just wouldn't do not to do it = has just got to do it.

-ci anh.umyen an ~ = an ····-umyen an ~ ought to (should) do it.

-ci mal.e ya ~ must not do it. With the honorific (Dupont 33): osici mal.a ya toyp.nita = oci malusye ya toyp.nita = osici malusye ya toyp.nita you must not come.

-e se (nun) an ~ must not do it. ¶ilk.e se an toynun chayk a book that you mustn't read. Nay chayk ul ilk.e se nun an toynta You must not read my book.

-e se ya ~. ¶Kuleh.key hay se ya toykeyss-ni?! That won't do. (You shouldn't do that.)

-e to ~. ¶Hay to toyp.nikka? = Hay to cōh.sup.nikka? May I (do it)? **I thayksi tha to tōy yo?** Is it all right for me to take this taxi?

-e ya ~ has (or is) to do/be; must, should, ought. ¶Tā tul co'.yong hi hay ya toykeyss.ta Everyone should be quiet (Wagner 47). SEE **-ci mal.e ya ~** [above].

-e ya man ~ just has to do/be. ¶Pantusi kulay ya man toynta It just has to be that way.

-nun kes un an ~ shouldn't (mustn't) do.

-ulye se nun an ~ shouldn't try/seek to do.

-umyen ~. ¶Ku tōn imyen toykeyss.ta That amount of money will do.

-umyen an ~ shouldn't (mustn't) do. SEE **-umyen**.

12. acts as, plays the role of, serves as/for. ¶Haymullithu ka ~ plays the role (takes the part) of Hamlet. **Alkhol un sotok-yak i toynta** Alcohol acts as a disinfectant. **I kulus un cay-ttel.i ka toykeyss.ta** This dish will serve as/for an ashtray.

toyta$_2$, aux v sep (follows the adverbative **-key**). it turns out, gets to be, comes to pass, happens (so that); gets (to); it is arranged (so that); comes (to). SEE **-key ~**.

toyta$_3$, postnominal verb/adjective.

1. 1a. v sep (replaces **hata** to make a kind of passive for certain verbal nouns). gets to be, becomes, is. NOTE: Often **i/ka** can be inserted. ¶sīcak ~ begins, has a beginning. **kekceng (i) ~** is worried/anxious (about). **sōnhay (ka) ~** results in a loss, proves (turns out to be) a loss. ^{1}**nwū (ka) ~** is troublesome, is vexing [KEd mistakenly put this with 2]. **hāykyel ~** gets solved/resolved. **cali ka cwūnpi ~** a table is ready. **phok.kyek ey uy ha.ye phākoy toyn kēnchwuk-mul** buildings (that got) destroyed in the bombings. **Pāykup un swūnco loi cīnhayng toynta** The rationing is going nicely/smoothly. **Selyu nun kilok i toye iss.ta** The documents have been recorded. **Wēnco mulqca ka ō.yong toylq ^{n}yēm.lye ka iss.ta** There is a fear that aid goods may get misused. **Kēnkang un wancen hi hoypok toysyess.^{s}up.nikka** Is your health completely recovered?

1b. adj-n + **toynta** = abbr < adj-n + hakey toynta. ¶hōn.lan ~ gets disordered.

2. [often **-q toyta**] adj insep. forms adjectives from nouns, bound nouns, adverbs, and bound adverbs; CF **sulepta, lopta, tapta**. ¶**ayq ~** looks young/new. **cap ~** is vulgar. **chamq ~** is genuine, pure, truthful, sincere. **ecwungq ~** is excessive, undue. **hes ~** is false; is in vain, is futile. **ip ~** has fancy tastes, is a gourmet. **mak' ~** is rough, rude. **māng.lyeng ~** is silly (in one's dotage); is unreasonable/preposterous. **saq ~** is private, is to one's private advantage. **(s)sang ~** is quite (utterly) vulgar. **sayng ~** is immature, green. **sok ~** is vulgar, common. **swunq ~** is simple-hearted, sincere. **tēl ~** is not ripe, is unfinished, is deficient, is no good. **wāngchengq ~** is widely disparate.

? **ko(-)toyta** is trying, tough, hard.

SEE **mōs ~, es ~**; CF **ilq toyta** (adv + vi) ripens early.

tōyta, adj. 1. (gruel/paste) is thick, (rice) is hard.

2. is severe, intense, heavy; is hard, trying, bitter, tough. CF **tōykey**.

'tt ... : -('^{u}/o)l 't t ... = -('^{u}/o)lq 't (...)

-ttak, suffix (makes impressionistic adv); LIGHT ↔ **-ttek**. **kkol-ttak kkol-ttak** gurgling < **kkol kkol**. CF **-(c)cak, -kkak**.

(-)ttakci, postnoun, suffix. "crud" [vulgarizes nouns]. ¶**akam ~** gill plates. **aph ~** the vamp of a shoe. **kkol ~** an unpleasant face, a "mug", a "pan". **kōm-po ~** a pockmarked person. **kyel ~, kol ~** (a fit of) anger. **simswul ~** ill temper. **wuphyo ~** a postage stamp. CF **kho ttakci** snot, **nwun ttakci** eye matter (scum).

(-)ttakseni, postn, suffix. ¶**chel ~** (good) sense. SYN **(-)ttakw(un)i**.

ttalta < *'**ptol 'ta**, bnd adj **-L-: oy ~**; **ttalo, tan**.

ttalo < 'pto'l(w)o, adverb. separately, apart. [der adv < *ttalta = *ttaluta < taluta]

ttalum, 1. subst < **ttaluta** v (follows etc.).

2. postmod (subst < *ttaluta adj). just, only (= **ppun**). SEE **-ul ~ (ita)**.

*ttaluta, ? reinforced variant < **talu-**, adjective (different). SEE **ttalum (2), ttalo, ttan** (adn).

ttan, quasi-free n (... ~ ey nun, ... ~ un; rare except for **cey ~** and **ney ~**). one's own kind judgment. ¶**ney/tangsin ~ ey nun** in your own eyes. **cey/caki ~ ey nun** by one's own kind judgment. **nay ~ ey nun** in my own eyes. **caki tul ~ ey nun** in their own eyes. **caney atul ~ ey nun** in your son's own eyes. [< **-q- tan** ? < directly nominalized adnominal **tān** < **to'lon** 'sweet(ness)', CF kkan; ?< *TWAN* 'decision, judgment' or 'edge', *TTAN* 'platform']

ttan, adn. another, different, separate, irrelevant. ¶ ~ sālam quite another (a different) person; a new being, a changed person. **Ku nun incey acwu ttan sālam i toyess.ta** He has become a new man. ~ **phay** another (a separate) group. ~ **swucak** irrelevant remarks. ~ **tōn** money set aside for another purpose. ~ **ttay** (at) another time, (on) a separate occasion. ~ **tey** another place, somewhere else. **Ttan sayngkak ul hamyen mōs ssunta** You should not let yourself get distracted (by other thoughts). ALSO: ~ **maum, māl, mas, soli.** CF **pyel, taluta.** [attested ?1800 Hancwung; abbr < ttalun mod < *ttalu- reinforced var of adj talu-, CF ttalo]

ttan un, adv (? abbr < nay ttan un). now that I come to think of it, as for that, to be sure.

ttawi, postnoun. (and) the like, (of) the sort, (and) such, et cetera (etc.). ¶ **nongcak-mul ~** agricultural products and the like. **i (ku/ce) ~** [pejorative] a thing / person of this (that) sort; such a one; this kind / sort (of).

NOTE: ⋯ **ttawiq** when adnominal.

[< -q tawi < taw-i, der n < tapta]

ttay₁ < ˙*pstay* ?< *˙psk ay* (SEE *psk*), n. The earlier *p* survives in compounds with -pttay: **ipttay** < **i pttay, cepttay** < **ce pttay, imam-ttay** < **i man pttay.**

1. time (= sikan). ¶ ~ **ka kata** time passes (goes by, elapses). ~ **ka kanun tey ttal^e̯a** as time goes by, in the course of time. ~ **kanun cwul moluta** is unconscious of (ignores) the passage of time, takes no note of time. ~ **lul akkita** watches (is careful of) the time, is sparing of time, begrudges the time. ~ **lul ponayta** passes one's time, spends time (in). ~ **lul kath.i hata** agrees in time; is contemporary with. ~ **lul kath.i ha.ye** at the same time / moment. ~ **lul ekita** is behind time, is not punctual, is late. ~ **lul ekici anh.ta** is on time, is punctual.

2. occasion, (con)juncture, moment, time, season; case, instance; (⋯ ~ **ka ēps.ta**) never, (⋯ ~ **ka iss.ta**) sometimes. CF **cek, īl.**

2a. N ~ ; -un, -nun, -tun, -ul ~. ¶ **cenyek ~** evening (time). **cēncayng ~** wartime. **wihem han ~** a time of danger. **chwuswu ~** the harvest time. **kkoch phil ~** the flower season. **han ttay** (at) one time, sometime. **etten ttay n(un)** on some occasions, sometimes. **Ilen ttay n' ku sālam ila to wā cwuess.umyen siph.ess.ta** I wish that he were present at such times. **Ku ttay nun uysa lul ponun kes i cōh.ta** In that case, you had better consult your doctor. **Palo ku ttay kwūho-cha ka tataless.ta** The ambulance car arrived at just that moment. **Kkok cōh.un ttay wass.ta** You have come at just the right moment. **Kyuchik un ttay ey ttale pyēnkyeng halq swu iss.ta** The rule may be modified as the occasion demands. **musunq īl i iss.ul ttay ey nun** in case of emergency. **Incey ya māl lo wuli ka kwelki hal ttay 'ta** Now is the time for us to rouse ourselves to action. **Phoun i chwul.ip hal ttay 'myen i tali wi lul cīnako n' hayss.ta** When Phoun came and went, he would pass over this bridge. **Ku nun ēncey 'na musun māl ul hal ttay nun cayphan-kwan aph ey se chelem phyoceng i kwut.e cinta** Whenever he talks he gets stiff as if he were before a judge. **Ku nun cam ul cata (ka) kkaci soli lul nāyko wūl ttay ka iss.ta** He sometimes sobs even in the midst of his sleep. **Acwu elyewul ttay nun halwu ey ssal han hop ccum ssik ulo to sal.e wass.ess.ta** At the most difficult times we managed to live on a hop of rice a day.

2b. -ul ~ (the time) when. ¶ **celm.ess.ul ~** in one's youth, when young. **Mannass.ul ttay ku iyaki lul hayss.ta** I told him about it when I saw him. SEE -**ul ttay.**

4. opportunity, chance, time. ¶ **talun ~** (at) another time, some other time. ~ **lul mannata** has a favorable opportunity; the time is in one's favor; has one's day (time of prosperity), had luck. ~ **lul noh.chita** misses (passes up) an opportunity / chance. ~ **lul kitalita** waits (bides) one's time, waits for a favorable opportunity. ~ **lul yes-pota** watches for an opening / opportunity, watches and waits. ~ **et.un** ⋯ timely, opportune, seasonable, well-timed. ~ **lul et.ci mōs han sālam** a person who is out of tune / touch with the times. ~ **lul thata** avails oneself of an opportunity. **Ca, ttay ka wass.ta** Now the time / chance has come. Now is the time / hour. **Incey han pen him sse pol ttay 'ta** It is high time for us to try our best. **Ttay ka ¹ī lopci mōs hata** It is not a favorable moment / time. **Mōtun kes ey tā cey**

ttay ka iss.ta There is a time for everything.

2. a meal time; a meal — CF **kki(ni)**. ¶**Ttay lul kelless.tuni sicang hata** Having skipped a meal, I am hungry. **Halwu han ttay pakk ey mōs mek.ess.ta** I had only one meal a day. **Onul un twū ttay lul kkulh.yess.ta** We made/had two meals today.

ttay₂ < *ptoy*, n. 1. dirt, grime, filth. 2. a mean streak, meanness. 3. a false charge, a stain/blot (on one's honor).

(-)ttayki SEE **(-)tayki**

ttāym, 1. vt subst. mending, soldering (= ~ **cil**).
2. postn. warding off, stopping, staying (evil fate). ¶**wūnswu/phalqca** ~ holding off fate.

ttaymun, postn; [DIAL] quasi-free n, postmod.
1. postn. (follows n or -ki) reason; because (of). ¶**Na ttaymun ita** It's because of me. **Ku ttaymun iess.ta** It was for that reason.
~ **ey**. ¶**mues** ~ **ey** for what reason. **ku ttaymun ey** for that reason, because of that. **(kuleh.ki) ttaymun ey** therefore. **Ka (se) cwumusey yo** — **Na ttaymun ey caci anh.ko kitalici māsiko yo** Go to bed — don't wait up for me. **Pi ka oki ttaymun ey hōy ka yenki toyess.ta** Because of the rain the meeting was postponed. **Chwupki ttaymun ey mos i el.ess.ta** The pond is frozen from the cold. **Tōn i ēps.ess.ki ttaymun ey ku chayk ul saci mōs hayss.ta** I couldn't buy the book because I had no money with me.

SEE **-ki** ~, **kkatalk**. NOTE: Instead of (?*)-**keyss.ki ttaymun ey**, use -**keyss.ki ey**.

2. quasi-free n [DIAL]. (for) the sake of; on account (because) of. ¶**Nay ttaymun ita** It is for my sake. **Nwukwu uy ttaymun in ya** For whose sake is it? **Musun ttaymun ey na lul yok hanun ka** Why do you slander me? NOTE: These examples (taken from KEd) are rejected by Seoul speakers, but they are said to be used in southern dialects.

3. postmod [DIAL]. -**nun**/-**un** ~ = -**nun**/-**un kkatalk**, -**ki ttaymun** (CF CM 2:70). ¶**Namuq iph tul i pulk.key toyn ttaymun iess.ta** It was because the leaves had turned red (Wagner 39).

-ttek, suffix (makes impressionistic adv); HEAVY ↔ **-ttak**. **kkwul-ttek kkwul-ttek** < **kkwul kkwul**. CF **-(c)cek**, **-kkek**.

ttekhwi, bnd n. luck. ¶**nal** ~ the day's luck. **pal** ~ the luck of the road (in consequence of one's destination). **son** ~ a touch for (good/bad) luck. [? < -**q tek hoy** = **tek** < ˙*TUK* 'virtue' + **hoy** < *(˙)HHWOY* 'a time/round']

ttel.e, defective infinitive. ~ **ttulita** drops it. ~ **cita** it drops.

tteli, postnoun. thing [vulgar]. ¶**tung tteli** back. [Is this the only example?]

ttēlta₁, vt. -L-. VP **ttelita**; INTENSIVE **ttelchita**; DER N **ttel.i**.

1. trembles (quivers, shivers, quakes, shakes) with (one's body, hands, limbs, ...).
2. shakes it, beats it.
3. takes it off/away, deducts it.
4. clears out (gets rid of) stock, closes it out.
5. strips/robs of, empties; loses the contents of (one's purse).
6. drops it. SEE **ttel.e** (**cita**, **ttulita**).

ttelta₂, postnominal verb sep -L-. does (= **hata**); displays, performs. SYN **pulita**, **phi(wu)ta**, **ppāyta**. ¶**iksal** ~ (**pulita**) plays the fool, jests. **kāsal** ~ (**pulita**/**phiwuta**/**ppāyta**) behaves in a hateful stuck-up way. **eli-kwang** ~ (**pulita**/**phita**) plays the baby. **emsal** ~ (**pulita**/**phita**) pretends distress. **a.yang** ~ (**pulita**) plays the flirt. **kukseng** ~ (**pulita**) goes to extremes. **caylong** ~ (**pulita**) acts sweet. **kkoy** ~ (**pulita**) pulls tricks.

tto < ˙*stwo*, adv. 1. and, also, too, (not only) ... but also, (both ...) and, again, besides, what is more, moreover. ¶**tto kuliko** and also/besides.
2. once/one more, again. ¶**tto tasi** yet again; once more, over again; (for) a second time.
3. while, on the other hand, contrary (to expectations etc.).

tto-han, adv. also, too, again, likewise; either, neither. Often preceded by **N to**. ¶**Ku kes to tto-han mūncey 'ta** That, too, is a problem. **I kes to tto-han swīpci anh.ta** This one is not easy, either.

-ttok(ay), bnd n. ¶**kām** ~ a windfall persimmon.

ttolay, quasi-free n. of the age/size. ¶**Ko ttolay meych i chac.e wass.ess.ta** A group (of boys) of that age had been here to call. **Ku ttolay lul meych kay te sa 'ta cwuo** Buy a few more of that size. **Motwu ku ttolay 'ta** All are of the same age/size. Examples from NKd: **atul kwa kath.un** ~ **uy** ... of the same age as my son; **Tongsik-i** ~ **ka sip-ye myeng i mo.ye** over ten of Tongsik-i's age got together; **Wuli ttolay cwung ey se ku ka kacang ttok-ttok hata** He is the brightest of our age group.

tto nun, adv + pcl. or (else). ¶¹**nayil ~ moley** tomorrow or the day after. SYN **hok un**.

-ttuk, suffix (makes impressionistic adverb). ¶**huy-ttuk huy-ttuk** splotchy white < adj **huyta** is white.

(-)ttuki, postnoun, suffix. [pejorative] one, guy, thing. ¶**sāphal ~** a cross-eyed (or squint-eyed) person. **sikol ~**, **chōn ~** a hick, a country bumpkin. **Sewul ~** a Seoulite, a city slicker. **chil ~** a person born prematurely (in the 7th month of pregnancy); a moron, an idiot. CF **-teki, -teyki, -ttayki**; **chi**. [? < **ttuta**, CF **el ttuki** a half-wit < **ēl ttuta** is slow-witted]

ttulita, auxiliary vt sep. VAR **thulita**; CF **chita, ciluta**. 1. follows an infinitive — intensifies the transitivity of vt (1a) and of certain defective [bound] infinitives (1b); makes vi transitive (1c). CF **cita**.

1a. ¶**hey ~** scatters, disperses. **kkay ~** breaks/smashes it. **kke ~** lets a fire/light go out. **kkwēy ~** punctures it. **naylye ~** drops it, throws it down. **nem.e ~** topples it. **okule/ wukule ~** curls/warps/breaks it. **the ~** bursts (explodes/collapses) it. **ttel.e ~** drops it.

1b. ¶**kkamule ~** causes to faint — also used as an intensive vi (= **kkamule cita**). ¶**k^e/akkwule ~** throws it down. **(k)kopul^e/a/ (k)kwupule ~** bends/curves it. **(k)kyawul.e/ (k)kiwul.e ~** tilts it. **mangkule ~** puts it out of shape, ruins it. **p^a/$_u$sule ~**, **pule ~** breaks it. **pekule ~** splits/separates it. **sakul^e/a ~** collapses it, withers it. **sosul^e/a ~** frightens, startles. **ssule ~** topples/tumbles it.

1c. ¶**kiwul.e ~** tilts it. **nul.e ~** dangles it.

2. attached directly to vt stem [? as abbr of **-e ttulita**]. ¶**ccic- ~** tears it apart. **kamu- ~** = **kamulita** steals it. **putic- ~** smashes it into something. **ssot- ~** spills/slops it. **ttēl-** acts haughty. **tul.i- ~** tosses it in.

NOTE: The following are cited by CM 1:408 as lacking a corresponding **cita** (vi) form: **nāy- ~**, **tatak- ~**, **tak- ~**, **mangku- ~**, **putic- ~**, **cac- ~**, **cec- ~**, **chi- ~**, **kki- ~**. But all the pre-**cita** forms are infinitive (or defective infinitive) in **-e** or **-a**, so this finding is surprising only for **nāy(-)**, if that is the infinitive rather than just the stem.

ttut.i /ttuci/, postn (der n < **ttut-**). ¶**ppye ~** meat off the bone. **al ~** late-autumn crab that has spawned.

tu-, bnd adv (emphatic adj prefix). very. ¶**~ malk.ta** is very clear. **~ nelp.ta** is very wide. **~ noph.ta** is very high. **~ sēyta** is very strong. [? < vt **tulta**; ? var < **te**; ? < **to** < ʼTTWO 'degree'; CF **to-**]

-tu-, retrospective. Occurs after honorific (**-usi-tu-**), past (**-ess-tu-**), future (**-keyss-tu-**); before assertive (**-tu-la**), conditional (**-(ess-)tu-myen**), and apperceptives (**-tu-kwumen, -tu-kwun, -tu-kwulye**). Alternants **-ti-** after formal (**-sup-ti-**); **-t-** before plain attentive (**-t-i**), familiar assertive (**-t-ey**), the modifier (**-t-un**), and the sequential (**-t-uni**). SEE **itey, iley**.

NOTE: According to Cang Sekcin 1973:74 "the subject of discourse, direct or indirect, cannot be coreferential with the speaker (in direct discourse) or the reporter (in indirect discourse)". The recollection by the speaker (in a statement) or the hearer (in a question) is based on his own observation of the event or state described in the discourse, and not on his own participation in it. SEE p. 325.

-tuikka [var] = **-tunikka** (= **-ptikka**)

-tuita [var] = **-tuniita** (= **-ptita**)

-tukwulye, retr apperceptive. SEE **(-)kwumen**. SYN **-tun kwulye**.

-tukwuma (yo) [DIAL] = **-(su)ptita**. (Mkk 1960: 3:34.) VAR **-twukwuma**.

-tukwuman (yo) = **-tukwumen (yo)**

-tukwumen (yo), retrospective apperceptive. SEE **(-)kwumen**. SYN **-tun kwumen (yo)**.

-tukwumun [DIAL] = **-tukwumen**

-tukwun (yo), retrospective apperceptive. SEE **(-)kwumen**. SYN **-tun kwun (yo)**.

-tukwun a, retr apperceptive. SEE **(-)kwumen**. SYN **-tun kwun a**.

tūl < *tuʼluh*, n. 1. a plain, a moor (SYN **pel, pel phan**); uncultivated field (CF **path**). ¶**mu.yen han ~** a vast field. SYN **tūl phan**, [obs] **seli**.

2. (adnoun). field-grown, wild (CF **san, kāy**).

tul < ʼ*tolh*, postn, pcl, adv. (acting as) a group, all, all together, and others, together with others, etc. CF **ney, kkili**.

1. postn. ¶**wuli ~** we/us. **sālam ~** people, other people. **elin ay ~** children. **Yāy tul a** Hey you people/folks/guys/all! **Sewul Pusan Phyengyang tul khun tosi ey nun cēncha ka iss.ta** There are streetcars in the large cities such as Seoul, Pusan, Phyengyang, and so on. **Haksayng tul i mānh.i onun kwun a** The

students are coming in droves, I see. NOTE: **namu hako phul tul** (1) trees and grasses/plants (those things), (2) a/the tree and some grass — CF **phul tul hako namu** some grasses/plants and (the) tree(s).

2. pcl. (acting) severally. (Follows almost any word in a sentence to indicate that the subject, stated or implied, is specifically plural.) ¶**Cal tul hayss.ˢup.nita** You all did nicely. **Ppalli tul kass.ta** We all went quickly. **Ese tul tanye osey yo** Please be on your way, people, I'll see you all later. **Cal tul kongpu hasey yo** Study hard, people. **Mānh.i tul mek.ess.ta** They/We ate lots. **Caymi iss.key tul nōsipsio** Have a good time, everybody. **Nōlle tul kapsita** or **Nōlle kapsita tul** Let's all go out and have some fun. **Tā tul kass.nun ya** Has everybody gone? **Mōs tul mek.nun ya?** Aren't you folks eating? **Mek.ki ey tul papputa** They are all busy eating. **Ili tul osey yo** Come this way, you people. **Pi ka oki ttaymun ey tul kyelqsek i mānh.kwun a** We have quite a lot of absences because of the rain, I see. **Mek.ko tul nōnta** They eat and play. **Mek.umyen se tul nōnta** They play while eating. **Mekci tul māsio** Don't eat it, anybody! **Mek.e tul poca** Let's (us) try it (and see how it tastes). **Tul.e tul osio** Come in, you people. **Kem.e tul pointa** They look black. **Motwu ipputa tul** They are all pretty. **Wuli nun mom i thunthun tul hata** We have strong bodies. (Our bodies are strong.) **Yeki anc.usio tul** Sit here, (you) folks. **Ttek ina mek.e la tul** Have a rice cake or something, children. **Cikum kongpu lul halq ka tul** Shall we study now? **Cikum yeki se nōp.nikka tul** Are they playing here now? **Kkaykkus tul hata** They are all clean. **Hānkwuk ey se nun Ilpon māl ul hay se nun an toynta ko tul haci anh.e?** Don't they all say you shouldn't speak Japanese in Korea? **Kuleh.key tul ttē-tulci māsio** Don't make so much noise, you people!

¶**Mek.key tul haca** Let's get them to eat (or let them eat) — reference is to the underlying subject ("they will eat"). **Kuleni-kka tul kekceng ici yo** That is why we are bothered. **Ili 'ta ka tul ecci toyca 'nun kes in ya** What is to become of us if we let things go on like this?

SEE **(-)kwumen tul (yo), (-)kwumen yo tul**.

3. [colloq, rare] adv. **Tul nōpsita** Let's go (= play), you all! (On with the game!) **Tul anc.usey yo** Sit down, folks. **Tul onta** "They" (= the police) are coming.

NOTE 1: The frequent use of **tul** seems to be spreading, perhaps as a result of equating it with foreign plurals. It is not unusual to find such pleonastic uses as **Chayk tul i mānh.i iss.ta** 'There are lots of books' and even **Mānh.i tul wass.ta** 'Lots of them have come' — **mānh.i tul** seems to be used only of people.

NOTE 2: There are several possible ways to say 'You all hurry up and get your studying done and then play (with us)':
(1) **Ne-huy tul ese kongpu hako nol.a la**.
(2) **Ne-huy tul ese tul kongpu hako nol.a la**.
(3) **Ne-huy tul ese kongpu tul hako nol.a la**.
(4) **Ne-huy tul ese tul kongpu tul hako nol.a la**.
(5) **Ne-huy tul ese tul kongpu hako tul nol.a la**.
(6) **Ne-huy tul ese tul kongpu tul hako nol.a la tul**.

NOTE 3: As a particle, the reference is to the "actor", who is usually the subject. But when the sentence is causative or it is passive, the reference can be to the indirect (underlying) subject, whether stated or implied: **Kūlim ul kūlikey tul hasipsio** Get them to draw pictures = **Ku i tul eykey** (or **Ku i eykey tul**) **kūlim ul** ··· . In an adnominalized sentence, the plural reference is to the UNDERLYING subject (now the epitheme): **san ey tul iss.tun namu** must be taken as 'the trees on the mountain'. But when the nature of the underlying subject does not permit a plural interpretation, the reference will be to some other noun: **san ey tul iss.tun nwūn** 'the snow which was on the mountains' (1954 Lukoff 201). This represents a kind of loose reference; some speakers will prefer the rephrasing **san tul ey iss.tun nwūn**. Notice that **Cōsim tul hasey yo** means 'Everyone be careful!' and not *'Take every precaution!' CF LHS 1955:282; [1]Yi Seklin 1955.

NOTE 4: There are variable constraints on the acceptability of structures that contain this particle. It is most comfortable after an adverb, but that phrase should not be placed before an overtly stated subject: **Cal tul hanta** 'They do well' and **Haksayng tul i cal tul hanta** 'The students do well' are both fine, but (?)**Cal tul haksayng tul i hanta** seems awkward, at best. **I kes ul tul hanta** 'They do this thing' is found acceptable by many speakers; (?)**I kes i tul** cōh.un ya? 'Do you folks like this?' perhaps by fewer speakers; and (?*)Haksayng i tul cal hanta or (*)Haksayng tul i tul cal hanta 'The students, they do well' perhaps by none. Since I kes tul ul hanta 'They do (or: He does) these things' (the postnoun pluralizes kes) is quite normal, we expect to find also (?)I kes tul ul tul hanta 'They do these things' and even (??)I kes tul i tul cōh.un ya? 'Do you like these things?' but many speakers will find the two appearances of the morpheme tul uncomfortably close in those sentences, to say nothing of such sentences with the particle ellipted: (?*)I kes tul tul hanta and (?*)I kes tul tul cōh.un ya?

NOTE 5: Use 2 (as the ubiquitous particle) seems to be a recent addition to the spoken language, unnoticed till 1937 (Choy Hyenpay).

tul, postmodifier (< ˙t ol postmod + pcl). the conceded fact (that ···); granted that ··· . SEE -un ~, -(ess.)tun ~. NOTE: A problem arises for (-ko) iss-, ēps-, -ess-, and -keyss-, which would normally replace the -un form with -nun. It is unclear whether (?*)-nun tul is acceptable in these cases. CF MK -non ˙t ol.

*˙t ul seems to be unattested; see ˙t ol. (Does this argue for ˙to as the underlying or earlier shape of t? But notice the following entry.)

-˙t ul, suspective + pcl (= -ci lul). ¶mwok-˙˙swu˙m ul me˙mulGwu˙t ul ˙˙mwot ˙hosi˙n i (1459 Wel 10:15b) he could not let his life stop. selu ki˙tulGwu˙t ul a˙ni ho˙n i (1481 Twusi 16:70b) they did not wait for each other. CF -˙t ol.

-t ul [S Chwungcheng DIAL]: ~ anh- not do/be. Na-ot ul anh.ass.ta (Dupont 288) He did not come out. Is this emphatic (= -ci lul anh-), as implied in Dupont?

tul(q) prosp mod < tulta < tu[l]˙ta, ˙tu[l]˙ta. SEE tull ··· , ˙tull ··· .

1. < tul(q) < tu[˙lu]l(q) < tu[l]˙ta (lifts). ¶tul toy (1527 Cahoy 3:10b=23b) the Chinese word toy [= TTOY] 'to lift'.

2. < ˙tul(q) < ˙tu[˙lu]l(q) < ˙tu[l]˙ta (enters). ¶˙tul cci˙p i (1447 Sek 6:35b) a house to enter. ˙tul ˙tt ol (1463 Pep 1:55b) that you can enter.

tul-, bound adverb. hard, violently, thoroughly: ~ engkita, kkapulita, kkapulta, kkunh.ta, nallita, nollita, pokk.ta, putic.(chi)ta, pusita, sswusita, ssuta, twutulita. But tul-ttetulta '(people) make noise' (KEd 535b, NKd 1045b) must be just tul (plural subject) + ttē-tulta (vi): Kuleh.key tul ttē-tulci (tul) māsio (*Kuleh.key tul tul-ttetulci māsio) Don't make so much noise, you people. CF tul.i, tul-ipta; tūl-tul, tule-. [? < tulta].

'tula, 1. < itula. 2. < hatula.

-tula, retrospective assertive.

1. it has been observed that ··· , it is known that ··· , as we all (or I) know, I hear (have been told) that ··· , I noticed that ··· , I've discovered (found out) that ··· . ¶Ku i ka akka celi katula He was (noticed to be) going that way just a little while ago. Ecey nun phek chwuptula It was indeed quite cold yesterday (as I noticed). Kumkang san ul ka-poni-kka kwā.yen myengsan itula I went there and found that the Diamond Mountains really are magnificent mountains.

2. ~ sam.e to, ~ (son) chitula to even if we/one (should) suppose that ··· ; CF -ta son chi(tu)la to. ¶Cey āmuli cal ttwitula son chitula to cik.ep sēnswu ey tang hal ya No matter how fast he may run how can he match a professional trackman?

-tula 'ci, abbr < -tula (ko) haci

-tula 'ki, abbr < -tula (ko) haki

-tula ko (yo), retr indic assert + pcl (+ pcl) = -tula (as an afterthought). ¶Yo say sayngḥwal-nan ulo sālam tul i kwīcwung-phum ul mānh.i cap.hitula ko yo People have been hocking lots of their precious things because of the hardships of life these days.

-tula man, retr assertive + particle. ¶Chac.e kani cōh.a (haki n') hatula man, nemu sinsey kkichinun key mian hay se ... They were glad to see me (all right), but I hated to cause them so much trouble.

-tula 'myen, abbr < -tula (ko) hamyen [always preceded by past]. if (we said it had been observed that) one had done; if only; if it had been. ¶Com te khess.tula 'myen nay pal ey mac.ulq kes ul kulayss.ta It the shoes had been a little bigger they would have fit my feet. Ku sālam iess.tula 'myen manna pwass.ulq kes ita If it had been that man I would have seen/noticed him. Ku pun i twū si ey wass.tula 'myen mannass.ulq ke l' If he had come at two o'clock I could have seen/met him. Ku īl ul hayss.tula 'myen cōh.ass.ulq kes ul I wish he had done it (but he didn't) − counterfactual; CF **Ku īl hayss.ta 'myen yekcek ita** If he did that, then he is a traitor. CF **-tumyen; -ess.ulq kes kath.umyen; -e pota.**

-tula 'n', abbr. 1. < **-tula (ko) han.** 2. < **-tula (ko) hanun.**

-tula to, retr assert + pcl [? abbr < **-tula (ko) hay to**]. even though (it has been observed that ...). ¶ **musunq īl i iss.tula to** whatever may happen, under any circumstances (whatsoever). **Pi lul mac.tula to ka ya hakeyss.ta** I have to go even if I get drenched in the rain. **Sellyeng cal-mos toyn kes i iss.tula to yōngse hasipsio** Even if (you have discovered that) there is a mistake, please forgive him for it. CF **(-ta son) chitula to.**

-tula tul, retr assert + pcl. ¶ **Poli pap ila to cal man mektula tul** They eat heartily, even when it is nothing but barley rice.

-tula 'tun ci, abbr < **-tula (ko) hatun ci.** ¶ **Ku tul i i kil lo katula 'tun ci ce kil lo katula 'tun ci yēyki com hay cwusye ya toylq key ani yo?** Whether they take this path or that, surely you should tell us.

-tula 'y, abbr < **-tula (ko) hay** (says it has been observed that ...). ~ **yo.**

-tula 'y to, abbr < **-tula (ko) hay to**. even if (it is said that it has been observed that ...). even though. ¶ **Kel.e katula 'y to han sip-pun pakk ey an kellinta** It takes no more than ten minutes even by foot. **Na n' talun kos un mōs potula 'y to Yensey Tāyhak ul kkok poko siph.ta** Even if it means skipping other places, I want to be sure we see Yensey University.

tul.e, 1. inf < vi **tulta** enter, ...
2. inf. < vt **tulta** hold, take, ... ; < vt **tut.ta** listen, hear.
3. intensive quasi-prefix [< vt inf] takes and does. CF **tul-**.

tuleng, pcl → **tul ilang**

tul eykey, postn + pcl. to/by/for the group of ... . CF **eykey tul.**

ˈ**tulh** [var] = ˈ**tolh**, postn (group). ¶ **wo¨lan kye¨ley ˈtul ˈh i** (1586 Sohak 6:75a) = **wo ˈlan kamwun ˈtol ˈh i** (1518 Sohak-cho 9:81a) the ancient clansmen. **poy tulthwo** [< **tulh two**] (1676 Sin.e 5:17b) the boats too. SEE ˈ**thulh.**

tul hanthey = **tul eykey**

tul.i-, 1. bnd adv. hard, extremely, recklessly,

suddenly: ~ **ciluta, khita, pat.ta, ph'e pūs.ta, pusita, ssah.ta, sswusita, takchita, tempita.**
2. vc stem or bound adverb. into, inward: ~ **khita, kkiwuta, kus.ta, mac.chwuta, masita, seywuta, ttulita.**

tul.i$_1$, postn (der n < vt **tulta** holds). holding ... (the unit of holding capacity). ¶ **sē mal ~ calwu** a sack holding three **mal**, a three-**mal** bag. **maykcwu twū thasu ~ sangca** a box holding two dozen bottles of beer.

tul.i$_1$, postn (der n < vi **tulta** enters). ¶ **cip ~ (hata)** (has) a housewarming party.

tul ilang, postn + pcl. SYN **tul ney lang, ney tul ilang, ney lang.**
1. = **tul sekken** all of them and so on. ¶ **Hak.kyo sensayng tul ilang tā na wass.tula** All the teachers (and so on) were out (here).
2. = **tul hako/kwa** with them.

tulita$_1$, vt [? < **tul.ita** vc < vt **tulta** holds]. SYN **pachita**. 1. (humbly) gives, offers, presents.
2. aux v sep. does as a favor (for a superior). SEE **-e tulita**. For **pillye tuli-** see **cwuta** NOTE.

tulita$_2$, vt. winnows (the grain from the chaff by fanning). [? < **tul.ita** vc < vi **tulta** enters]

tulita$_3$, vt. twists (in several plies), entwists, throws. [? < **tul.ita** vc < vi **tulta** enters]

tulita$_4$, vt. makes, arranges, installs, puts in (a floor, a room). [? < **tul.ita** vc < vi **tulta** enters]

tulita$_5$, vt. shuts up, closes (a shop for the day).

tulita$_6$, vt = **tuliwuta** (lets hang down, ...).

tul.ita$_7$, vt (vc < vi **tulta** enters).
1. lets/allows in, admits.
2. lets join/participate, admits, lets in.
3. employs (a live-in servant); adopts, takes into the family.
4. takes/brings/carries in, gets (in).
5. acquires (a taste for), takes to.
6. induces, invites (sleep). ¶ **elin ay eykey cam ul ~** puts a child to sleep.
7. dyes, soaks (a dye into). ¶ **os ey kemceng mul ul ~** dyes one's clothes black.
8. (**kil ul ~**) imparts (training to); tames, domesticates, trains, breaks in; teaches.
9. (**kil ul ~**) gives (a polish to); polishes/ shines (up), puts (a sheen/luster on).
10. puts in, spends (money, time, effort).
11. (**ttam ul ~**) causes (sweat) to subside, lets (sweat) cool off; rests, cools off.
12. aux v insep. SEE **-e tul.ita.**

tul iyo, pcl + pcl. ¶**Nwukwu tul iyo** (1) = **Nwukwu tul io** Who all are they / you? [AUTH], (2) = **Nwukwu tul yo** Who all? [POLITE sentence fragment].

tull ··· (+ ˙*i* postmod) < *tul[u]l(q)*, prosp mod < *tu[l]˙ta*. Example?

˙*tull* ··· (+ ˙*i* postmod) < ˙*tul[u]l(q)*, prosp mod < ˙*tu[l]˙ta*. ¶˙*tull i˙'la* (1462 ¹Nung 8:40a). ˙*tull i˙Gwo* (1482 Kum-sam 2:13b).

tulm < ˙*tulm* < *tu˙l[o]m* (lift), < ˙*tulm* < ˙*tu˙l[o]m* (enter), subst < **tulta** < *tu[l]˙ta* (lifts), < ˙*tu[l]˙ta* (enters). ¶˙*tul˙m ye n'* (1447 Sek 6:25a) entering. CF *tu˙lwum*, ˙*tu˙lwum*.

tul ney lang, postn + postn + pcl = **ney lang**

tul sekken, postn + pcl. SEE **tul ilang**.

tulta₁ < ˙*tu[l]˙ta*, vi -L-. VC **tul.ita**; CF **tulita**, **tullita**, **tul.ikhita**. Infinitive **tul.e** < ˙*tu˙le* (1449 Kok 101) but also ˙*tu˙la* (id. 157); CF ˙*tu˙lwulq* = ?*˙*tu˙lwolq*.

1. enters, comes / goes in.
2. puts up (at), stops (at). ¶**Enu ¹yekwan ey tul.ess.nun ya** What inn did you stay at?
3. visits, attacks, afflicts, breaks into.
4. (a season, etc.) comes round, sets in.
5. it dyes, it takes color, is dyed; is stained, tainted, tinged.
6. joins (a society), goes into.
7. enters (a school); passes (an examination).
8. it is included / inserted / contained = holds it, accommodates (an amount).
9. it is contained = has it in it; is in it.
10. it is needed/required/spent = takes/costs it.
11. **maum ey** ~ is acceptable, satisfactory; is to one's taste / liking.
12. **mas i** ~ a taste sets in; gets a taste to it; gets ripe; becomes stale, gets to tasting (stale).
13. (a knife, ...) cuts (well).
14. **nai (ka)** ~ puts on years, grows older.
15. (rain / weather / it) clears up.
16. (sweating) subsides, stops.

tulta₂ < *tu[l]˙ta*, vt -L-. VP **tullita**, **tulkhita**; VC **tullita**; CF **tulita**.

1. raises, lifts (up), puts / holds up.
2. holds, has, carries.
3. partakes, drinks, eats. SEE **tusita**.
4. cites, mentions, offers, gives (an example), produces / raises (evidence).
5. SEE **tu-** (emphatic adj prefix), **tul.e**, **tul.i**.

tulta₃, aux v [< vi **tulta**₁ enters]. into, upon, at. SEE **-e tulta**, **-ulye (ko) tulta**.

tul tul, 1. pcl + pcl. ¶**Ku i tul tul com posey yo** (= **Ku i tul com posey yo tul**) You people take a look at them!

2. **tul tul(q)** pcl + vt prosp mod. ¶**Han can tul tul they 'n ya** You people want a drink?

tulum, subst < *tut˙ta* (hears). ¶*tulu˙m ye* (1459 Wel 17:34b) will hear and ... .

˙*tu˙lwol(q)* = ?*˙*tu˙lwul(q)*, modulated prosp modifier < ˙*tu[l]˙ta* (enters). ¶˙*tu˙lwolq˙t i ˙'n i* (1462 ¹Nung 2:111a).

tu˙lwul(q), modulated prosp modifier < *tu[l]˙ta* (lifts). Example?

tu˙lwum, modulated subst < *tu[l]˙ta* (lifts). ¶*tu˙lwu˙m i* (1482 Kum-sam 3:22a).

˙*tu˙lwum*, modulated subst < ˙*tu[l]˙ta* (enters). Example?

tul yo, pcl + pcl. ¶**Nwukwu yo – Ku i tul yo** Who? – Them.

CF **(-)kwumen tul yo** = **(-)kwumen yo tul**.

tum → **tulm**

-tuman [DIAL] = **-tukwumen**

-tumen [DIAL] 1. = **-tukwumen**. 2. = **-tumyen**

-tumyen, retr conditional [always preceded by past]. if one had done ··· ; if it were (or had been) ··· . NOTE: This is obsolescent or dialect usage; replaced by **-tula 'myen** in the standard language. ¶**Hak.kyo ey kass.ess.tu(la ')myen sensayng ul pwass.ulq kes ita** If I had gone to the schoolhouse I would have seen the teacher. **Ama i chayk i ssass.tu(la ')myen cikum ccum un tā ēps.e cyess.ulq kes ita** If this book were cheap(er), by now all the copies would have disappeared. **I chayk i ssass.tu(la ')myen na to han kwēn sass.keyss.ta** If this book had been cheap(er), I would have been sure to buy a copy myself. **Te kel.ess.tu(la ')myen pyēng i nass.ulq ci to molunta** If I had walked any more, I might have come down sick. CF **-tula 'myen**.

tun, mod < **tulta**.

1. < *tun* < *tu[˙lu]n* < *tu[l]˙ta* (lifts). ¶*tu˙n i* (1481 Twusi 8:35a).
2. < ˙*tun* < ˙*tu[˙lu]n* < ˙*tu[l]˙ta* (enters). ¶˙*tu˙n i* (1447 Sek 13:10a). **sangca ey tun kes** what (= the thing that) is inside the box (= **sangca ey tul.e iss.nun kes**).

-tun, retrospective modifier.

1. ... that has been observed to (be/do); ... that has been doing, that used to do; ... that was, that used to be. ¶**hak.kyo sensayng itun Kim**

sensayng the Mr Kim who was (or used to be) a schoolteacher. tōn i ēps.tun / ēps.ess.tun sālam the person who had no money. alh.tunq i (ka) ppā cin kes kath.ta "is like having a sore tooth fall out" = feels sudden relief. Yeki ka yūmyeng han Kyengki Konye ka iss.tun cali ya This is (the place) right where the famous Kyengki Girls' High School used to be. Ecey kiph.tun mul i onul un yath.ta The water which was (noticed to be) deep yesterday is shallow today. Haksayng iess.tun yēys nal ul sayngkak hanta I think back to the old days when I was a schoolboy. Kath.i kul paywutun yēys tongmu ka kulipta I miss my old class mates. Cham ku cen ey ssutun nay hēn sikyey acik to iss.ey yo? Oh, is the old watch that I was using before still around? Olayq tong-an chām.ko iss.tun nwun mul i ku man ttel.e-ciki sīcak hayss.ᔆo The tears that had been long suppressed began to fall.

2. SEE -tun kes

3. abbr < -tun ci. ¶cwuktun (ci) sāltun (ci) ssawuta engages in a life-and-death struggle. Cwuktun (ci) sāltun (ci) na molunta I don't care whether he lives or dies. Ecci tōyss.tun (ci) na nun kanta I am going, in any event. Tangmyen han cēy-il khun mūncey nun āmuli him i tultun (ci) cēyphum uy cil ul noph.inun kes iess.ta The biggest problem facing us was to raise the quality of the goods, however hard that might be.

NOTE: With paired phrases, if either ci is expressed, both must be present.

4. = -tun ya

5. [DIAL] = -ci nun

'tun, 1. < itun. 2. < itun ci. 3. < hatun.

-˙tun = -˙ton. SEE ˙'ston.

˙t un < ˙t on, postmodifier + pcl. SEE -[˙]nwon ˙t un, ˙ilen ˙t un.

-tun a = -tun ya

?-tun ccok-ccok SEE ccok-ccok

-tun cek, retr mod + n. the time / occasion that it has (been observed to have) happened:

-(ess.)ess.tun cek i iss.ta has ever done/been, once happened

-(ess.)ess.tun cek i iss.ess.ta had ever done / been, once had happened

-(ess)ess.tun cek i ēps.ta has never done/been

-(ess)ess.tun cek i ēps.ess.ta had never done / been

-tun cha, retr mod + noun. (in) the course of something (that was observed to be) happening. ¶Cēncha lul thatun cha ey hak.kyo sensayng nim ul mannass.ta When I was getting on the streetcar, I saw the schoolteacher. Nay ka cip ey katun cha yess.ta It was on my way home. Kalye 'tun cha 'ta I was just about to leave. SYN -tun kil.

-tun cha ey = -tun cha. SEE cha.

-tunchamay → -tun chām ey

-tun chām, retr mod + n. on the point of, just when it was (has been) happening. ¶Kalye 'tun chām ita / iess.ta I was on the verge of leaving; I was just about to leave. Mak ōychwul halye 'tun chām ey son nim tul i osyess.ᔆup.nita (Im Hopin 1987:35) I was just about to go out when guests arrived. Tol.a katun chām ey sensayng ul mannass.ta Just when I had got back I ran into the teacher. CF -nun chām ey. SEE chām.

-tun ci, retr mod + postmod. ('the uncertain fact that it has been observed that' =) whether it was (observed to be / happen).

1. (= -tun ya / ka). ¶Kaps i elma yess.tun ci kiek i an nanta I don't remember how much it was. Ku kes i mues iess.tun (= iess.nun) ci sayngkak i an nanta I can't recall what it was. Nay ka way cōllyess.tun ci āsey yo? Do you know why I was sleepy?

2. used with an indeterminate (interrogative-indefinite word): any at all, regardless of which, --(so)ever. ¶mues ul hatun ci whatever (it be found that) one does. ēncey wass.tun ci whenever (it be observed that) he is here. nwu ka eti lul kass.ess.tun ci regardless of who went where. musun haksayng itun ci whatever student (it may be), any student at all. ēncey 'tun ci any time at all, whatever time it may be. eti kass.ess.tun ci wherever he had been (to). eti kkaci 'tun ci to the utmost, in every possible way. meych si ey wass.ess.tun ci whatever hour it was that he had been here. Elkwul iya ette hatun ci maum man chak hamyen ssukeyss.ta If only she's a woman of good nature, she is all right with me, and it doesn't matter what she looks like.

3. ~ kan ey no matter (what, who, when, ...). ¶Musunq īl i iss.tun ci kan ey onulq pam ey na-kaci mala Don't go out today no matter what happens. Eti 'tun ci kan ey cēnci

hasipsio Take a change of climate, no matter where. **Ku i ka musun māl ul hatun ci kan ey na nun ku ⁿyeca wa kyelhon hal they 'ta** No matter what he says, I'm going to marry her.

4. in paired phrases of contrastive meaning: (regardless) whether ... or ... ; ~ **kan ey** SAME. SYN **-una, -kena, -tun**. ¶**otun ci an otun ci** or **otun ci māltun ci** whether it comes or not = **o(ke)na an o(ke)na** = **wā to an wā to**. **Pam itun ci nac itun ci kalici anh.ko nul īl ul hanta** He keeps working all the time, whether it be night or it be day. **Ku sālam i wass.tun ci an wass.tun ci sangkwan i ēps.ta** It makes no difference whether he is here or not. **Ku sālam i wass.ess.tun ci an wass.ess.tun ci sangkwan i ēps.ta** It makes no difference whether he was here (= had come and left) or not. **I kes itun (ci) ku kes itun (ci) twūlq cwung uy hana kacisey yo** Take one of the two, either this one or that one (= **i kes ina ku kes ina** ...). **Katun ci otun ci maum tay lo hakey** Come or go, whichever way you please. **Pi ka onun tey com te kyēysita kasitun ci, i wūsan ul kaciko kasitun ci hasipsio** It is raining; either stay a little longer or take this umbrella along with you. **Ku-nyang iss.ki ka silh.umyen katun ci, kaki ka silh.umyen na hanun tay lo nāy-pelitun ci (– way kuleh.key yātan in ci molukeyss.e)** If he doesn't like being here in this situation, he can go; and if he doesn't want to go, why doesn't he let me (alone to) do things my way?

5. [? DIAL] ~ **(to moluta)**, ~ **(yo)** (I don't know whether) maybe/perhaps it has happened/been. ¶**Cosen se kaluchyess.tun ci to mōlla** Perhaps he had been teaching in Korea. **Ku sālam i pelsse wass.ess.tun ci** Maybe he has already been here (for all I know). **Cam catun ci yo** Maybe he was asleep. [2d verb ellipted:] **Īl ul ku man twutun ci hay ya 'ci kuleh.key aphe se etteh.key hani** You may as well (or really ought to) leave off working where you are – how can you go on in such agony?

6. given the state of having been (doing): **etteh.key** ... ~ has been (doing) to such an extent/degree/amount that. ¶**Etteh.key kichim ul hatun ci kumsey swūm mak.hye cwuk.ulq kes kath.ess.ta** He coughed so hard that I was afraid he might choke to death right there.

7. ~ **lul** SEE **-tun ul**.

-tun ci 'la (se), retr mod + postmod + cop var inf (+ pcl). [lit – with v only]. as/since (it has been observed that) it was/did. ¶**Ku tul un nul phyēnci wāng.lay ka iss.ess.tun ci 'la selo uy hyengphyen ul cal ālko iss.ess.ta** Since there had been a steady stream of letters between them, they were well informed on how things were with each other.

-tun ci tul, retr mod + postmod + pcl. ¶**Pang ul com chiwutun ci tul** (= **chiwuna tul**) **i key musun kkol in ya** You kids better clean up this messy room!

-tun (c)cok-(c)cok, [SUBSTANDARD, ? DIAL] = **-nun (c)cok-(c)cok**. CF CM 2:71.

-tun cwul, retr mod + postmod. the assumed fact of having been (observed to be) happening. ¶**Ku i ka Hānkwuk se Yenge lul kaluchinq īl i iss.ess.tun cwul lo ānta (kiek hanta)** I think (recall) that he had taught English in Korea.

tūng < "*TUNG*, 1. postn [semi-lit]. etc., and the like, and so on; the above several. ¶**moca 'mye cāngkap imye kwutwu tūng** hats and gloves and shoes, etc. **tāythong.lyeng, cāngkwan, kwuk.hoy uywen tūng(-tung)** the President, the ministers, and the members of the National Assembly. NOTE: Always attached without a pause; at least two items must be mentioned.

2. postmod. SEE **-nun** ~. (There is no *-un/-ulq/-tun ~.)

tūngci < "*TUNG-'TTI*, postnoun, ? quasi-free n. 1. postn. (after two or more placenames) and such places, the above several places; (after only one placename) and its vicinity. ¶**Sewul Pusan (Taykwu) ~ ey se nun** Seoul, Pusan, (Taykwu,) and such places; the cities of Seoul and Pusan (and Taykwu). **Pusan ~** Pusan and (its) vicinity.

2. ? quasi-free noun = **kūnpang** (vicinity). ¶**I tūngci ey se nun ssal kaps i etteh.so** ([¹Yi Ungpayk 1961:387) What is the price of rice like around here?

tūng-tung < "*TUNG "TUNG*, quasi-free n [semi-lit]. ¶**ssal, poli, tūng-tung** = **ssal imye poli 'mye tūng-tung** rice and barley and so forth. NOTE: May be preceded by pause; at least two items must be mentioned.

'tuni, abbr < **hatuni**. SEE **-ta 'tuni**. ¶**Swun-i ka ne hak.kyo kanta 'tula 'tuni yethay an kass.kwun a** Swun-i said you were going to school but you still haven't gone, I see.

-tuni₁, retrospective sequential. NOTE: -tuni-kka (n') does not occur.

1. as now it has been observed that ... ; when (now / then) ... , since (now / then) ... ; ... and now / then; ... but now / then.

1a. (attached directly to verb or adj stem, second-person or third-person subject). ¶**Palam pūltuni pi ka onta** First the wind, and now the rain. **Pi ka otuni nal i ttattus hay cyess.ta** It has been raining and now it has turned warm. **Cheum ey nun huytuni nācwung ey nun kkāmah.key tōyss.ta** It was white at first, but later it turned black. **Ecey nun chwuptuni onul un tēpta** It was cold yesterday but it's warm today. **Kim kwun un yelqsim hi kongpu lul hatuni i pen hak.ki ey ches ccay lul hayss.ta** Mr Kim studied so hard that he placed first this term. **Ku ka nōlki man hatuni kkok ¹nakcey lul hanun kwun yo** He's done nothing but loaf so he's failing without a doubt! **Phalq tus siph.i māl hatuni phalci anh.nunta ko hanta** He hinted that he would sell it but now he says he won't. **Ku soli lul tut.tuni ku man wul.um ul the ttulyess.ta** When he heard the news, he burst right out crying, just like that.

1b. (attached to verb past -ess-, usually with first-person subject). ¶**Han cham swiess.tuni mom i kattun hata** I have had a bit of rest and now I feel wonderfully refreshed. **Han can hayss.tuni kentuley han kes i cōh.ta** I've had a drink or two and now I feel wonderfully high. **Kulus ul takk.ess.tuni kwāng i acwu cal nanta** I've polished the dishes and now they are really shining. **Kongpu lul hayss.tuni meli ka aphuta** I have been studying and now I've got a headache. **Sangcem ey kass.tuni sakwa ka ēps.e kyul man sa kaciko wass.ta** When I went to the store they were out of apples so I just bought oranges. **Nay ka Kim senayng(q) tayk ey kass.tuni Kim sensayng i ēps.e se kunyang wass.ta** I went to Mr Kim's house but he was out so I just left (and came back) — CF **Cikum Kim sensayng i tayk ey kass.uni ppalli ka se posipsio** Mr Kim just went home, so hurry to go see him. **Ttay lul kelless.tuni sicang hata** Having skipped a meal, I am hungry. **I kes ul capci 'la ko sass.tuni ilk.ulq kes i hana to ēps.ta** I bought this "magazine" (as they pretend it to be) and can't find a thing in it to read.

Mom i com kotan hay se swīko nass.tuni mom i kattun hata I was rather tired, but since I've had the nice rest I feel much better. **Hal māl ul tā hako nass.tuni kasum i tā siwen hata** Now that I have had my say ("have got that off my chest") I feel much relieved. **Chayk ul ilk.ulye ko hayss.tuni cēnki ka kkunh.e cyess.ta** I was about to read a book when the lights went out. **Sānqpo na-kalye ko hayss.tuni, wēyn ke l' sonak-pi ka ssot.a cyess.ta** I was going out for a walk but then, by George, it started to shower. **Cēmsim ul mek.una māna hako wass.tuni pay ka pelsse kophuta** Having picked at my lunch (having eaten hardly any lunch) I'm now very hungry. **Cam ul cana māna hayss.tuni mopsi kotan hata** Having slept but fitfully I am very tired.

Mukewun cwul al.ess.tuni kapyewun tey yo I thought it was heavy but it's light! **Ku lul pāpo 'n cwul lo man al.ess.tuni kuleh.ci to anh.tukwun** I thought he was nothing but a fool, but I see he wasn't. **Mōs hanun cwul al.ess.tuni cal hanun kwun a** I didn't think you could, but you're doing it nicely! **Cwuk in cwul al.ess.tuni pap iki man hatula** I thought it was gruel but I see it's rice. **Al.e pwass.tuni ku nun ī-nyen cen ey cwuk.ess.ta** I found out that he has been dead for two years.

1c. [uncommon] (attached to verb future -keyss-, usually with first-person subject). SEE -keyss.tuni.

2. (sentence-fragment; is this just a case of -tun i₁ 3?) it used to be that ... but / and now ... . ¶**Yēys nal ey n' kaul imyen sasum i naylye otun( )i** In days gone by the deer used to come down in autumn (but not any more). **Ku ttay nun sanyangq kwun i tumultuni** (At that time) there used to be very few hunters (but now ...). **Ku cen ey nun i kos i ¹yen-mos itun( )i** This used to be a pond.

-tuni₂ → -tun i

-tun i₁, retrospective modifier + noun.

1. the one / thing / person that has been (or has been doing it); the one that it has been doing.

2. the act / fact of having been (or having been doing it).

3. abbr < -tun i 'la.

CF -tun kes; -ul i, -nun i, -un i.

-tun i₂ = -tun ya

-tuniikka [lit, obs] = -ptikka. ¶Nim i kkoch ul salang hatuniikka? Is my lord pleased with the flowers?

-tuniita [lit, obs] = -ptita. ¶Ku maul uy mus sālam i ku uy tek ul chingsong hatuniita Everyone in the village extols his goodness. SYN -tuita.

-tunq īl, retr mod + postmod. the experience of having (been observed to have) been doing:

-(ess.)ess.tunq īl i iss.ta has ever done/been, once happened

-(ess.)ess.tunq īl i iss.ess.ta had ever done/been, had once happened

-(ess.)ess.tunq īl i ēps.ta has never done/been/happened

-(ess.)ess.tunq īl i ēps.ess.ta had never done/been/happened

¶Nay ka elyess.ul ttay kiph.un swuph sōk ey se kil ul ilh.ess.tunq īl i iss.ess.ta Once when I was young I lost my way in a deep forest. Nal i mopsi tewe se pataq ka ey kass.ess.tunq īl i iss.ta Once it was so hot I went to the seashore. Ku cen ey nun keki ey kako siph.ess.tunq īl i ēps.ess.ta I'd never had the desire to go there before. Yeki nal i cōh.ass.tunq īl i ēps.ta We have never had good weather around here.

-tunila = -tun i 'la

-tun i 'la, retr mod + postmod + cop quotative indic assert. (I tell you) it used to be that ··· [semi-literary, didactic flavor]. ¶Cak.nyen ey iss.tun seki nun kul-ssi lul cal ssutun i 'la The clerk we had last year used to write a good hand. Yēy cen ey nun i san ey pēm i mānh.un i 'la At one time there used to be lots of tigers in these mountains. Ku cen ey nun i kos i khun ¹yen-mos itun i 'la This used to be a huge pond. ABBR -tun i. SYN -tun kes ita. CF -nun i 'la, -un i 'la; -nit/ₗa.

-tuni man (un), retr sequential + pcl (+ pcl). ··· and NOW/THEN; ··· but NOW/THEN. ¶Palam i yele nal pūltuni man (un) khun pi ka onta The wind has been blowing for several days and NOW we get a heavy rain. Han pen katuni man (un) sosik i ēps.ta We've had no word from at all since he left.

-tun i tul, 1. retr mod + postmod + pcl = -tun ya tul.

2. retr mod + quasi-free n + pcl. the ones which were (observed to be/do).

-tun i yo, retrospective modifier + noun + pcl (polite) [? awkward]. it used to be that ··· . ¶Ku cen ey nun i kos i khunq ¹yen-mos itun i yo (cikum un path i toyess.ey yo) This used to be a huge pond (and now it has become field).

-tun ka, retrospective modifier + postmodifier.

1. (the question) whether it was (observed to be/happen); (did you notice) was it?; (did you hear/find) was it? ~ yo SAME [POLITE]. ¶Eti iss.tun ka Where was it? Cham, nay ka tangsin hanthey i sikyeyq kaps ul tulyess.tun ka yo Oh, did I give you the money for the watch? Ku kes i khutun ka cāktun ka Was it large, or small (I wonder)? Elma 'na khutun ka How big was it? Ku ka eti lo katun ka Where was he going (I wonder)? Ku kes i eti iss.tun ka Where was it? Where did I leave it? Elma 'na mānh.ess.tun ka kiek i an toyp.nita I fail to remember just how many of them there were. Nay ka way kuli hayss.tun ka hwūhoy toyp.nita I have come to worry why I did that. Ku ka nwukwu yess.tun ka ic.e pelyess.ta I have forgotten who he was. Cip ey iss.ess.tun ka ēps.ess.tun ka mul.e pwā la Find out whether he was home or not (CF ··· iss.ess.tun ya ko mul.ess.ta I asked whether he was ···). Sinpu pang ey kyēysitun ka (1936 Roth 236) Is the Father in the room [you just left]?

2. 2a. (either ···) or else. ¶Ku nun pam imyen yenghwa kwūkyeng ul katun ka cip ey se sōsel ul ilk.ess.ta Of an evening he would either go to a movie or read a book at home. Kongpu lul halye 'myen yelqsim hi hatun ka, kuleh.ci anh.umyen a.yey kongpu lul māltun ka hay la If you are going to study, then study hard, or else give up the idea of studying altogether. Hal-'meni ka ositun ka emeni ka osikeyss.ci (CM 2:242) Either Grandmother will come, or else Mother will come. Kwul-tay ka te kwulk.tun ka, pakhwi kwumeng i cek.e ya 'keyss.ˢo (CM 2:242) Either the axle will have to be bigger, or else the wheel hole will have to be smaller.

2b. V₁-tun ka V₂-tun ka hay se by either V₁-ing or V₂-ing. ¶Keki ey sālam ul ponaytun ka phyēnci lul hatun ka hay se ppalli i mūncey lul hāykyel hay ya 'keyss.ˢup.nita We will have to settle the problem either by sending a person there or (else) by writing a letter.

3. **-tun ka pota** (adj) 'it seems there is a question of its having been observed to do / be' = maybe it has been (has been happening). ¶**Ku ttay Pak sensayng i cip ey se kongpu lul hako iss.ess.tun ka pota** Maybe Mr Pak was doing some studying at home.

4. **ila 'tun ka** [colloq] = **ina** or.

-tun ka ka, retr modifier + postmodifier + pcl. ¶**Ku ttay pi ka otun ka ka mūncey 'ta** The question is whether (it was noticed that) it was raining at that time.

-tun ka lul, retr modifier + postmodifier + pcl. ¶**Pi ka otun ka lul al.e pwā la** Find out if it was (noticed to be) raining.

-tun ka 'm, abbr < **-tun ka (ko) ham**. ¶**Wēyn yakcwu lul nwu ka kuleh.key capswusila 'yss.tun ka 'm**? What's your complaint, did someone order you to drink all that whiskey?!

-tun kan ey = **-tun ci kan ey**

-tun ka tul, retr modifier + postmodifier + pcl

-tun ke, abbr < **-tun kes**

-tun ke 'ci, abbr < **-tun kes ici**

-tun ke l', abbr < **-tun ke lul** = **-tun kes ul**. CF **-ess.tun ke l'**, **-keyss.tun ke l'**.

NOTE: When followed by the polite particle **yo** there is reinforcement: **ke l'q yo /kellyo/**.

1. the thing / one that has been doing (or that someone has been doing) [as the direct object]. ¶**Nay ka ssutun ke l' ku ka kacye kass.ta** He took away the thing / one that I had been using.

2. despite the fact that it has been doing (or being done); anyway, despite reservations, after all, indeed, so there! ~ **iyo**, ~ **yo** → **-tun ke l'q yo /-tunkellyo/** SAME [POLITE]. ¶**Sikyey ka cal katun ke l' kongyen hi kochile ponayss.ta** You needn't have sent the watch to be repaired — it was working all right. **Ku nun māl ul cal hatun ke l'** He spoke well, after all! **Kumkang san ul ka-poni cōh.tun ke l'** I have been to see the Diamond Mountains and found them very nice, indeed.

-tun ke 'l(q), abbr < **-tun kes il(q)**

-tun ke 'la, abbr < **-tun kes ila**

-tun ke l'q yo (kellyo) SEE **-tun ke l'**

-tun ke n', abbr < **-tun ke nun** = **-tun kes un**

-tun ke 'n, abbr < **-tun kes in**

-tun ke 'na, abbr < **-tun kes ina**

-tun kes, retrospective modifier + noun.

1. the thing / act that (it has been observed) someone was doing.

2. the thing / one that (it has been observed) someone was doing; the one that was doing it. ¶**Ku i nun nay ka sayngkak hayss.tun kes pota khi ka khess.ta** He was taller than I had thought he would be.

3. the tentative fact that (it has been observed that) one has done: ~ **ita** has been doing (according to observations at that time); ~ **iess.ta** was doing. ¶**Kyōswu ka yēnkwu hatun kes ita** It's the one/thing the professor has been doing research on — or: The professor has been doing research, you see. **Ku ttay Kim yang un tāmpay lul phitun** (or **phiko iss.tun** or **phiko iss.ess.tun**) **kes iess.ta** Miss Kim was smoking at the time. **Ku i nun chongchong hi hak.kyo ey katun kes iess.ta** He was in a hurry on his way to school.

4. 4a. ~ **ul** but: SEE **-tun ke l'**. SYN **-tun pa**.

4b. ~ **i** but: SEE **-tun kes i**, **-tun key**.

5. ~ **ulo poita** [written style] it appears / seems that one has / had been (doing). ¶**Cengpu nun i kyēyhoyk ul chānseng hayss.tun kes ulo pointa** It seems that the government had already agreed to this plan. **I kyēyhoyk ul silqsi haki nun elyewess.tun kes ulo pointa** It must have been hard to put this plan into effect. **Ku sālam han ttay sinmun kica yess.tun kes ulo pointa** He seems to have once been a newspaperman.

-tun kes i, retr mod + postmod + pcl. ¶**Akka pi ka otun kes i** (= **otun key**, **otuni**) **nwūn i onta** It was raining a while ago, but now it is snowing. **Pi ka onta 'tun kes i nwūn i onun kwun a** (CM 2:219) They predicted rain, but it's snowing!

-tun kes kath.ta, 1. (**kes** is summational). it seems that it has been (doing) or that someone has been doing it.

2. (**kes** is an extruded epitheme). it is like the one/thing that has been (doing) or that someone has been doing.

-tun key, 1. abbr < **-tun kes i**

2. abbr < **-tun kes ie / ia**

-tun ke 'ta, abbr < **-tun kes ita**

-tun ke ya, abbr < **-tun kes i(y)a**

-tun key 'ci = **-tun ke yci**, abbr < **-tun kes ici**

-tun key 'la = **-tun ke yla**, abbr < **-tun kes ila**

-tun key 'na = **-tun ke yna**, abbr < **-tun kes ina**

-tun key 'ney = -tun ke yney, abbr < -tun kes iney
-tun key 'ni = -tun ke yni, abbr < -tun kes ini
-tun ke yo = -tun key yo (1, 2, 3)
-tun ke yo man, abbr < -tun kes io man it's that ··· did / is but [AUTH].
-tun key ya = -tun ke ya
-tun key yo, abbr. 1. < -tun kes ie(y) yo it's that ··· did / was [POLITE], etc.
 2. < -tun kes iyo [POLITE fragment].
 3. < -tun kes io it's that ··· did / was [AUTH]
-tun kil, retrospective modifier + noun.
 1. (while on) the way (one has been observed to be doing); the way from doing. ¶kass.tun kil ey while (I was) out, while (I was) there, on my way. Sānqpo lul hatun kil iess.ta It was while I was taking my walk. Hak.kyo ey katun kil ey sensayng ul mannass.ta I met the teacher on my way to school.
 2. [DIAL] = -tunq īl
-tun kkatalk, retr mod + noun. (for) the reason that (it has been observed that ···). ¶Nay ka ku chinkwu lul ilh.un kes un phyēnci lul an hayss.tun kkatalk ita My losing that friend was because I didn't write him letters. Nay ka sikan i nuc.un kes un kicha lul noh.chyess.tun kkatalk ita The reason I was late is that I had missed the train.
-tun ko, retr mod + postmod. [colloq; poetic] the (usually rhetorical, exclamatory, or quoted) question whether it has been (doing).
-tun kwulye, kwumen, kwun (a) SEE (-)kwumen
-tun mo.yang, retrospective modifier + noun. the appearance of having been doing.
 ~ ita. appears to have been doing. Examples limited to -ess.tun ~ ?
 (?*) ~ ulo. No examples.
tu'non, 'tunon SEE tunun
-tun pa, retrospective modifier + noun [lit].
 1. = -tun kes.
 2. ~ (ey) did and as a consequence (= -tun tey₂ = -tuni); since, when.
 ~ ey ya if / since (as long as) one has been doing. ¶Hatun pa ey ya kyēysok hay ya hanta Since we have been doing it we should stay with it.
 3. that which did (which one did). SEE pa 3.
-tun sesul ey [? DIAL] → -nun sesul ey
-tun tey₁, retr mod + n (= -tun kos). the place where (it has been observed that) it has been or (someone) has been doing. ¶ai ka nōltun tey the place where the child has been playing.
-tun tey₂, retrospective modifier + postmodifier.
 1. = -tun tey (ey) (given) the circumstance of its having been observed that ··· ; under the circumstance that it has been; has been ··· and / but / so. ¶Phulangsu māl to kongpu hatun tey pen.yek-ka ka toylq kes kath.tukwun yo He has (is known to have) been studying French also — (that being the circumstance) maybe he's going to become a translator! Akka ku i ka otun tey ecci i cali ey poici anh.nun ka I saw him on his way here a little while ago — how come he hasn't shown up? Ecey poni-kka āmu to ēps.tun tey nwu ka ilen kes ul hay noh.ass.ulq ka I didn't see anybody around here yesterday, so who could have done this? Ku ttay poni-kka wungpyen itun tey way ileh.key sa.yang hasey yo I know you are a good speaker from that other time, so why do you hesitate to make the speech? Sang ul thass.ta 'tun tey han thek nāysici yo You got an award, I hear; you should treat me (to celebrate that).
 2. ~ (yo) You see it's a case of (being found that) ··· ! (sentence-final exclamatory). ¶Yenge lul kongpu hatun tey yo Well, what do you know — I found that he's (been) studying English! Caney atul i kongpu lul cal hatun tey But I have found your son doing quite well in school (why do you worry?)
 3. rhetorical question [INTIMATE]. ¶Sōmun tut.nun kes pota ka-poni(-kka n') kuleh.ci tul anh.tun tey?! Different from what I had heard, when I went there (whaddaya know but) I found out they weren't like that.
'tun tey, abbr < hatun + postmod. SEE -ta ~.
-tun tey (ey) SEE -tun tey
-tun tey (ey) se. from the situation / place of having been (doing). ¶Cwuk.ulq swu pakk ey ēps.tun tey (ey) se ekci lo hey(e) na-wass.ta With much effort I managed to get myself out of a situation / place where I was sure to die.
-tun tey 'ta ka. not only did but moreover (in addition, what's more, on top of that). ¶Son nim tul i wass.tun tey 'ta ka īlq son i mo-cala se cēngsin ēps.ess.ta I had all those guests come and then there wasn't enough help (to clean up after), so I was beside myself!

-tun tey to. ¶Sihem ul cal chiess.ta 'tun tey to mit.e cici anh.nunta I can't believe my ears that he did well on the exam!

-tun tey tul, retr mod + postmod + pcl. ¶Ai tul i pay kopha hatun tey tul mek.ulq ke l' sa kaciko kapsita The children have been showing signs of hunger so let's buy them something to eat before we leave.

-tun ttay, retrospective modifier + noun. the time that (it is known that) it was happening. ¶wang ul ēps.ayko caki ka wang i toylye ko kacun kkoy lul ssutun ttay (at) the time when he was employing all his wiles with the idea of getting rid of the king and becoming the king himself. Nay ka simsim hamyen elin ai tul hako kath.i nōltun ttay ka mānh.ess.ta Many were the times that (I recall) I used to play with the children when I was weary of myself. Nul phīnan sal.i hatun ttay sayngkak hanta I always think of the days when I was leading a refugee life.

NOTE: The preferred usage is -(ess.)ul ttay.

-tun tul, retr mod + postmod [lit (always after past?)]. granted that, even if (it had been known to happen that); if it had happened that. ¶Ku nun ppalli uysa eykey poyess.tun tul an cwuk.ess.ulq kes ita If he had seen the doctor right away, he would not have died. ¹Yī Swunsin i ēps.ess.tun tul sēykyey uy ¹yeksa nun pyēn hayss.ulq kes ita If we had not had [Admiral] ¹Yi Swunsin the history of the world would have changed. CF -tula 'myen, -e to.

-tun tus hata, retr modifier + adj-n. gives the impression of having (been observed to have) done. ¶Nay ka elyess.ul ttay ku sālam ul cōh.a hayss.tun tus hata It seems to me that I liked him when I was young.

-tun tus 'i, retr modifier + der adv. as if having (been observed to have) done. ¶Ce nulk.un i nun han ttay cāngkwan ina cīnayss.tun tus 'i kēman hata The old man is as conceited as if he had sometime been a cabinet minister or something.

-tun ul = -tun ci lul. ¶Se.yangq sālam itun (ci) tongyangq sālam itun (ci l)ul mak.lon hako, tā ai tul un cōh.a hanta It matters not whether one is Occidental or Oriental, everyone likes children.

tunun, processive modifier < tulta.

1. < tunon < tu[ˈlu]non < tu[l]ˈta (lifts).

¶tunoˈn i (1463 Pep 4:19a).

2. < ˈtunon < ˈtu[ˈlu]non < ˈtu[l]ˈta (enters). ¶ˈtunoˈn ye (1462 ¹Nung 1:64b). ˈtunoˈn i ˈˈla (1459 Wel 9:35d).

tuˈnwon, modulated processive modifier < tu[l]ˈta (lifts). Example?

ˈtuˈnwon, modulated processive modifier < ˈtu[l]ˈta (enters). Example?

-tunya = -tun ya

-tun ya, retrospective modifier + postmodifier.

1. is it (known) that ··· ? was it observed that ··· ? did you notice that ··· ? ¶Ney hyeng i cikum il.e natun ya Is your brother getting up now? Ney hyeng i il.e nass.tun ya Has your brother got(ten) up? Se sensayng i cīnan cwumal ey eti lul kass.ess.tun ya Where did Mr Se go this past weekend? Ku i ka eti lo katun ya Did you notice where he was going? Ku sālam i khutun ya cāktun ya Was he tall or short? Ku kes i mues itun ya What was that?

2. (in quotative constructions) whether it has been observed that ··· . ¶Nwu ka wass.tun ya ko mūt.nunta He wants to know who was here.

tun ya, mod < tulta + pcl (did it enter?, ··· , ···). ¶Ney maum ey tun ya Do you like it?

-tun yang, 1. abbr < -tun mo.yang

2. ~ hata vni. pretends to have been doing.

-tun ya tul, retr mod + postmodifier + particle.

tus, postmod used as adv (= tus 'i der adv < tus hata). appearing (to be), looking (like); seeming as if; as if/though. ¶khunq īl ina hanun tus (ˈi) yātan pepsek hata fusses about as if one were doing some important job. khun pyesul han tus (ˈi) ppekita swaggers as if one had become a high official. pic ul cwulq tus (ˈi) iyaki hata talks as if one would give a loan. sālam ul chilq tus (ˈi) tempye tulta goes at a person as if he is going to hit him.

SEE tus hata, tus siph.ta, tus siph.i.

···' tus = ···' tus 'i. (is) as if, like, as, giving the appearance of.

1. abbr < -nun (? - or -ulq?) + tus (ˈi). ¶so mek' tus (ˈi) mekta eats like a horse. Ney hyeng i ha' tus (ˈi) hay la Do as your brother does. Myōmok i wūhwu ey cwukswun na-o' tus (ˈi) na-onta The young trees spring up like bamboo shoots after the rain. Nwun-mul i pi o' tus (ˈi) ssot.a cinta Tears pour down like rain. Sēywel i mul hulu' tus (ˈi) kanta Time

flies. **Cōy pēm haki lul mul masi' tus 'i hanta** (1936 Roth 423) He commits sin as if it were water to drink.

2. Occasionally attached directly to adj stem. ¶**kuleh-tus ('i)** /kulethusi/ seeming to be that way. **Apeci ka khi ka khu-tus ('i) atul to khi ka khuta** Just as the father is tall, so is the son.
tus hata, adj postmod insep (= postmod + postnom adj insep), seems (to be), looks like; seems as if, looks as though; gives every appearance of (being). ¶**Pom i on tus hata** Spring seems to have come. **Cwi cwuk.un tus hata** "It seems as if all rats have died away" = not a sound is to be heard, is very quiet. **Pi ka onun tus hata** It seems to be raining — CF **Pi ka o' tus hata** It is as if it were raining [This distinction is possible in the processive present only]. **Pi ka olq tus hata** It looks like rain. **Congi ka com nam.ulq tus hata** It looks as though we will have more than enough paper. **Huyn tus hata** It looks white. **Haksayng in tus hata** He looks like a student. DER ADV **tus 'i**. CF **tus, tus ⋯ tus hata, tus siph.ta, kes kath.ta, mo.yang**.
-' **tus hata**. is like, is as (if).
  1. abbr < **-nun tus hata**.
  1a. ¶**kalangq iph ey pul puth' tus hata** flares up like tinder = gets mad at the drop of a hat. **kul-ssi lul kēy-pal kūli' tus hata** writes like a crab's claws = henscratches, scrawls. **kwulengi tām nem.e ka' tus hata** is like a serpent going over a wall = (succeeds) in an unnoticed way. **kanan han cip ey cēysa tol.a o' tus hata** seems to come round as often as the anniversary of a poor man's ancestors (= "comes around as often as the bill collectors"). **Nwūn i o' tus hata** It is as if it were snowing — CF **Nwūn i onun tus hata** It seems to be snowing [This distinction is possible in the processive present only].
  1b. [? attached directly to v stem] **kaymi cheyq pakhwi tol' tus hata** goes round and round like ants on the frame of a sieve.
  2. abbr < adj-**un tus hata** [uncommon]. ¶**Machi hwang-so him sēy' tus hata** He is strong as an ox. **Caki apeci pucilen ha' tus hata** He is diligent like his father.
˙**tus °ho˙ta** = ˙**tos °ho˙ta** (is like). ¶**nal tus mal tus ho.ya** (?1608+ Twu-hem 25b) when they are about to emerge (= appear).

-˙**tu˙s 'i** = -˙**to˙s 'i** (like). ¶¨**say cip ˙kwa ˙sal pca˙ki** [MWON] **'i ¨pyel ˙hut-tu˙s 'i ¨sano˙n i** (1481 Twusi 25:23a) with a thatched cottage and a twig door we live like scattered stars.
⋯ ˙**tu˙s 'i** = ⋯ ˙**to˙s 'i** (like). ¶¨**mwot mi˙chul ˙tu.s 'i ˙hosya** (1475 Nay 2:1:43a) acting as if he could not reach it.
tusita, hon < **tulta**. [EUPHEMISM] has = eats / drinks / partakes. ¶**Mues ul tusikeyss.ey yo** What will you have, sir? [said by the waiter]. **Han can tusipsita!** Let's have a drink!
tus siph.i, der adv < **tus siph.ta**. as if, looking like, seeming as if. ¶**sālam ul ssolq tus siph.i chong ul kyenwuta** aims a gun at a person as if he were going to shoot him. **Phalq tus siph.i māl hatuni phalci anh.nunta ko hanta** He hinted he would sell it but now says he won't.
tus siph.ta, postmodifier + postnom adj insep. looks / feels like, seems as if; "something tells one that … ". ¶**Ku nun haksayng in tus siph.ta** He looks like a student. **Com khulq tus siph.ta** Something tells me it will be a bit too big. **Pēm ila to cap.ulq tus siph.ta** I feel strong enough to catch a tiger. **Pi ka olq tus siph.ta** It looks like rain; Something tells me that we are in for a rain. **Ceypep īl hanun tus siph.ta** You look as if you were working nicely. **An mek.e to mek.un tus siph.ta** Though I haven't eaten anything, I feel as if I had eaten. **Pyesul ina han tus siph.ta** You act as if you had become a government official or something.
tus ⋯ tus hata, postmod ⋯ postmod + postnom adj insep. it hardly seems one way or the other; it hardly feels as if; one hardly knows whether. [The second modifier is always from **mālta**.] ¶**pon tus mān tus han sālam** a person one is not quite sure whether one has met or not, a person one is not well acquainted with. **Pap i cek.e mek.un tus mān tus hata** There was so little rice I hardly feel as if I have eaten any at all. **Pappe se copan ul mek.nun tus mānun tus hako cip ul na-wass.ta** I was in such a hurry that I left home with hardly any breakfast. **Eceyq pam un moki ka mul.e canun tus mānun tus hayss.ta** I was bitten by mosquitos so badly that I got hardly any sleep last night. **Na nun kalq tus mālq tus hata** I am not sure whether I will be going or not. **Kāy ka ku ppye nun mek.ulq tus mālq tus hata** It is hard to tell whether the dog will eat the bone or not.

twā, abbr < towa, inf < tōpta.
twāy = twēy = tōy < toye, inf < toyta.
twe = twē, abbr < twue, inf < twuta; as aux usually short. ABBR t'e = t'ē.
twēy = tōy < toye, infinitive < toyta. Usually spelled twāy.
twī < ˘twuyh, noun. ANT aph; CF hwū, taum.
1. the back, the rear (end), behind.
2. the future, later (on); afterwards; (-un ~) after doing.
3. the end, the conclusion, the latter part; consequences, results, aftermath.
4. a descendant, offspring, descent, posterity.
5. what is left behind by a predecessor; the footsteps of.
6. what is wanted, one's needs.
7. [EUPHEMISM] feces, excrement, stools; a bowel movement.
8. the tenth place around the outer circle of a yuch board, diagonal from the starting point.
9. the north.
10. (= mangken ~) a net worn under a horsehair headband.
twi-, bound adverb [< twī]. CF toy-; twita vt.
1. back(wards), opposing: ~ huntulta, kkapulta, nēm.ta, (noh.ta), nōlta, pyēntek sulepta, ttuta.
2. extremely; recklessly, rashly; randomly: ~ eph.ta, kkulh.ta, pakkwuta, paluta, pat.ta, pemulita, pota, sekk.ta, thulta; twi-ttelta (< ttēlta); twi-ttetulta (< ttē-tulta); twi-pempek.
3. thoroughly, completely: ~ teph.ta (and some of the verbs under 2?).
-˙two-, emotive (< bnd v *-˙t[o]- + modulator). SEE -˙twos-, -˙two˙swo-, -two˙ta.
˙two, particle = to (also, even, ...).
NOTE 1: The MK pcl could freely attach to a stem before a negative auxiliary. Whether or not it is the correct historical explanation, we can (following Ramstedt 1939:104) treat the structure as the result of an optional ellipsis of the suspective ending -˙ti (= -ki / -ci): ˙khuy ˘cek[˙ti] ˙two ˙khu[˙ti] ˙two a˙ni ho˙kwo (1459 Wel 1:26b) was neither tall nor short; pwo[˙ti] ˙two ˘mwot ho˙m ye tut[˙ti] ˙two ˘mwot ˙ke˙n i (1447 Sek 24:28b) (you say) you were unable to see and unable to hear; ˙CCYEK-˙MYELQ ˙un ˘sa[˙ti] ˙two a˙ni ho˙m ye cwuk[˙ti] ˙two a˙ni hol˙ss i˙n i (1459 Wel 2:16a) the (state of)

nirvāṇa means neither living nor dying. CF He Wung 375. Notice, however, that swo˙n i ˙wona two (1481 Twusi 25:23a) 'though a guest comes' is the effective infinitive + particle.
NOTE 2: The MK particle attached to the "free" form of such nouns as namwo / namk ... : namwo ˙two (1447 Sek 23:22a) the trees too.
two˙i (?< *towo[y]-i), der adv < towoy˙ta. so that it becomes. ¶˙PHYEY ˙lol mwo˙lwomay CYENG-SSYENG two˙i ho˙m ye (1475 Nay 1:76-7) ought to turn one's vice into sincerity, and ... . [˙PPYENG] twoi ne˙kinwo˙la (1481 Twusi 16:9a) I regard it [the local capital] as plagued.
two˙kwo [var] = twu˙kwo, particle. than.
~ n' (abbr pcl). ¶pulun cey hon mal etum twokwo n' nau.n i (1795 ¹No-cwung [K] 1:40a = ... nau.n i 'la [P] 39b) = pulun ˙cey hon mal ˙e˙twum twu˙kwo n' ˙te˙u.n i (?1517- ¹No 1:43b; ˙e˙twum = ˘e˙twum) it surpasses getting a peck [of rice] when you are full.
~ s (pcl). ¶pwom kwos twokwo s cywohay 'la (1763 Haytong 103; cited from LCT) are nicer than spring flowers.
˘twol(q) < *two˙[lo]l(q), prospective modifier < ˘two[l]˙ta (goes around).
˙twola = ˘tal˙la (reflexive request). ¶˘a˙mwo 'yGe˙na˙wa ... ˙twola ˙ho.ya ˙two (1459 Wel 1:13a) whoever might come and ask you to give him ... . [?< twolo˙la (1481 Twusi 8:5a) < twolo- / twolG- 'make it go (pass it) around'.]
˘twolm < *two˙l[o]m, substantive < ˘two[l]˙ta
-˙two˙lwok, variant < -˙to˙lwok. ¶hon ˙pstay ˘kyeytwo˙lwok (1459 Wel 7:9b) to the point that/where a certain amount of time had passed.
˘twon, 1. n. money. 2. < *two˙[lo]n, modifier < ˘two[l]˙ta (goes around).
˙twong, postmod. [knows / asks] wh... (whether). SEE -non˙twong, -un˙twong, -ulq˙twong.
-˙twos-, emotive-emotive.
-˙twos˙ta (indic assert). ¶cheem pwotwos.ta (1632 Twusi-cwung 13:30a) we see it [a red sun] for the first time.
-˙twos.te˙la (retr indic assertive). ¶[˙CHYEK-LYENG] ˙ul ˙pwoy˙twos.te˙la (1481 Twusi 8:38b) you have shown me a wagtail! pwo˙n i no˙m oy ci[p] s ˙tam ˙tol[h] ˘ta mul˙Ge ˙ti˙twos.te˙la (?1517- Pak 1:9b) I see the walls of his house have all fallen down! ce 'y tali ˙lol pe˙hoy˘twos.tela (1579 Kwikam 1:18ab) why, he had cut his own leg!

-῾twosʾte-ngi ῾ʾta (retr polite + copula indic assertive). SEE ῾hosiʾtwosʾte-ngi ῾ʾta.

-twos.ten kwo (retr mod + postmod). ¶ nwu ʾyla sye kamakwuy lul kemko hywung tha hotwos.ten kwo (1876 Kakok p.59) who has declared the raven black and [therefore] evil?!

-twos.ten t i (retr mod + postmod + pcl). ¶ CHYWUN-PHUNG WOK-TYEK SYENG uy ches-com ul skoytwos.ten t i (1747 Songkang 1:2b) from having just fallen asleep I awoke to the sound of a jade flute in the spring breeze.

-῾twoʾswo-, modulated emotive-emotive:

-῾twoʾswo-ngi ῾ʾta (polite + cop indic assert). ¶ SYEY-CWON ῾i ῾SSILQ hon ῾ʾTTWOW ῾lol niloʾsi-ti ʾGwuy PA-SSYWUN ῾un ῾i ῾ʾiʾl i ῾ʾepʾtwoʾswo-ngi ῾ʾta (1463 Pep 2:26a) the World-Honored preaches the true Way, but [the devil] Pāpīyān never does this.

῾twoʾswo-ngi ῾ʾta, abbr < ῾hotwoʾswo-ngi ῾ʾta. SEE ··· thwoʾswo-ngi ῾ʾta.

-῾twoswoʾn i (modifier + postmodifier). ¶ kwuy-s kes ῾kwa ῾ʾmwoʾtin cywungsoyng ῾i muʾzuyyepʾtwoswoʾn i (1447 Sek 6:19b) there are ghosts and evil creatures to be afraid of! ciʾp i [SYYOW-῾SIK] mwuʾlwol toy ῾ʾepʾtwoswoʾn i (1481 Twusi 7:39b; the nominative particle is loose reference) there is no place to ask news of home.

-῾twoswoʾn i ῾ya (modifier + postmodifier + postmodifier). ¶ kuʾle ῾hoʾtwoswoʾn i ῾ya aʾni ῾hoʾtwoswoʾn i ῾ya (?1468- Mong 57a) is it so or is it not?

-῾twoswoʾn ywo, (mod + postmod). ¶ ῾stwo niloʾla moʾchoʾm ay ῾ʾesʾte ῾hoʾtwoswoʾn ywo [῾thwoswoʾn ywo in the reading aid to the Chinese text] (?1468- Mong 52b) also tell me, how it will be in the end?

-῾twoʾta, emotive indic assertive. ¶ ῾i ʾza mozoʾm ay hwen hi ῾culʾkeptwoʾta ([1447→]1562 Sek 3:20b) this very thing is a great delight to my heart. ῾i kakʾsi ʾza naʾy ῾ʾet.niʾnwon mozoʾm ay masʾtwoʾta (1447 Sek 6:14ab) precisely this very girl matches the purpose I am pursuing. kutuy ῾ka ῾tul cciʾp i polʾssye ῾ʾitwoʾta (1447 Sek 6:35b) a house for you to go enter has already been built! ῾il hoʾki yey koʾlin keʾs i ῾ʾcyektwoʾta (1481 Twusi 25:7b) has but few hindrances in doing things. ῾kwot-kwoʾt ay ῾ʾmwoyʾh ay s kwoʾc i ῾phutwoʾta (1482 Kum-sam 3:33a) everywhere mountain flowers are in bloom. ῾ʾTHYEY ῾ʾpwoʾm i eʾlyepʾtwoswoʾn i mwuyʾGwu.m ul ῾ʾmwot hoʾm ye kwuʾte heʾlwo.m i eʾlyeptwoʾta (1482 Kum-sam 2:7b) it is hard to see the form (body); there is no movement and it is so firm that demolishing it is difficult. ῾SSILQ aʾni ʾlwoʾm i MYENG-῾ʾPPOYK ῾hotwoʾta (1482 Kum-sam 2:27b) it is clear that it is not the truth. ῾solʾkhwa kas ῾kwa y isʾti aʾni thwoʾta (1481 Twusi 8:2a) ← ῾solh ῾kwa kac ῾kwa ῾i isʾti aʾni ῾hotwoʾta flesh and skin are (both) lacking. kutuy ῾nay kosʾpi ʾza ῾wotwoʾta maʾlon (1447 Sek 23:53b) you people make haste to come but ... . talon kowolʾh i ῾ʾnyey s kowolʾh ilaʾwa ῾ʾtywothwoʾta (1481 Twusi 8:35a) the other towns are better than the [war-torn] home town of earlier days. kuʾli ʾGeʾn i ῾ʾywuʾpwok ῾hotwuʾta (?1517- Pak 1:46b) he who did so is fortunate indeed!

SEE ῾twoʾta, ··· thwoʾta; -῾two-swo-.

-῾twoʾta, abbr < ῾hotwoʾta after voiceless sounds. ¶ ῾thwos.k[i] uy spul ῾kot ῾[ ]twoʾta (1482 Kum-sam 2:66b) is like a rabbit's horns. CF ··· ῾thwoʾta.

twowoyʾta, variant < towoyʾta (becomes). ¶ moʾcho.m ay ῾twoʾwo.m i twowoyʾti ῾ʾmwot ῾hwo.n i (1475 Nay 2:2:14a) in the end I could not be of help.

-῾twoy < -῾woʾtoy. ¶ ῾ʾcyekʾun aʾhoy ῾lol kolGoʾchiʾtwoy (1586 Sohak 5:2b; sic ῾ʾcyekʾun = ῾ʾcyeʾkun) = hyeʾkun aʾhoy lol koloʾchywoʾtoy (1518 Sohak-cho 6:2b) in teaching a small child ... .

῾TWOY °hoʾta, vnt = tāy hata. ¶ ῾i ʾta YWEN ῾ul ῾TWOY ῾ho.ya ῾phyesyan ʾt ila (1482 Kum-sam 5:35b) this all developed with respect to pratyaya (secondary causation). kwuy-s-keʾs uy nos ῾kwa SSIN-LYENG ῾uy meʾli noʾch ol ῾TWOY ῾ho.ya ῾wokeʾton (1482 Kum-sam 3:27b) when you come to confront the face of a ghost or the face on the head of spirit.

twu, particle [variant] = to

twū, alt (before noun or counter) of twūl 'two'

-῾twu- = -῾two- (emotive). SEE -twuʾta = -twoʾta.

-(t)twuk, suf (makes impressionistic adv). ¶ cel-ttwuk cel-ttwuk limping < cē-l-. elk-twuk elk-twuk all pockmarked < ēlk-. kkᵉ⁄ak-twuk kkᵉ⁄ak-twuk chopping < kkakk-. CF (c)cwuk.

? twuki, postmod. person. ¶ ? ippun ~ a good-looking person (CF ippu-tongi a pretty child). ? miwun ~ a hateful person.

twuko (n') < *twuˈkwo (n')* (? < *ˈtwuˈkwo* ger < *twuˈta*), pcl [obs] = **pota** (than). VAR **toko** < *twoˈkwo (n')*. ¶*wu[h] s ¨salom twuˈkwo teun ¨yang ˈhoˈya* (1447 Sek 9:14a) in a manner greater than the superiors. *paˈlol twuˈkwo kiˈphuˈm ye* (1459 Wel 21:78b) is deeper than the sea, and … . *ˈhiˈm i SSYANG-ˈLYEY s ˈQILQ-ˈPOYK ¨SSYANG twuˈkwo te ¨seyˈm ye* (1459 Wel 1:28a) has a strength that is greater than a hundred ordinary elephants, and … . *coyˈcwo ˈhol ¨syeng ˈi ˈnom twuˈkwo n' teuˈn i non* (1518 Sohak-cho 8:37b) those who have talent greater than others.

-twukwuma, var of **-tukwuma**. ¶*-twukwuma* (1916 Gale 83) "a low form of *ho-pteyta*" [*ta* is misprinted as "*ma*"].

twul, adn. sterile, barren (of a female). ¶ ~ **amthalk** a sterile hen. ~ **amso** a sterile cow. ~ **amthoth** a sterile sow. ~ **amkhay** a barren bitch. [< **tōl** < *¨twolh* 'stone'; CF meanings of Chinese **sek** < *ˈSYEK*]

twūl < *¨twulh*, num. two. ALT **twū** … < *¨twu* … .

twuli, 1. bnd n [? var < **tol.i**; ? irreg der n < **twuluta**]. round: ~ **kitwung**, ~ **-pan**, ~ **-pen**; **kā** ~, **they** ~. 2. → **twūl-i** (two people).

twung, postmod. you can't tell whether; may or may not: one of two contradictory but equally likely appearances, of which the second is usually, but not always, some form of **mālta** 'desists'. Either or both may be followed by the particle **to** and the entire expression is usually concluded by **hanta** (aux v) or **hata** (aux adj) as appropriate, but **hata** (or **kuleh.ta**) may be preferred when the V-nun is viewed as static. SEE **-un** ~, **-nun** ~, **-ulq** ~. DIAL **swung**.

-(t)twung-eli: mom-ttwungeli = mom-ttwungi.

-(t)twungi, suf, postn, postmod. thing, one, guy. ¶**mom-ttwungi** a body, a frame. **ēlpalam-twungi** a crazy person, a crackpot, a nut. **wuk-twungi** a hothead, a rash person < **wulk-**. **kem-/kkam-twungi** a Negro, a black. **cem-twungi** a brindled dog; "spotty"; a person with a birthmark. **cilki-twungi** tough stuff, a tough fellow. **cīs-twungi** [vulgar] = **cīs** (act, …). **tēyn twungi** [pejorative] a person burned or scalded. **kwīyem-twungi** (= **-tongi**) a lovable child. ? **pangtwungi** the rump; ? **mongtwungi** a stick. CF **-tongi**; **-thwungi**; **-tengi**; **-swungi**.

ˈtwunˈnonˈuy = *ˈtwu[e i]s.noˈn i ˈuy* (1586 Sohak 5:95b). SEE *ˈtwusˈta*.

ˈtwusˈta = *ˈtwu' 'sˈta*, abbr < *ˈtwue is(i)ˈta* (also *ˈtwuysˈta* = *ˈtwu' 'ysˈta*). has put it away, … ; (*-e* ~) did it for good, got it all done. ¶… *ˈtwunˈnonˈuy* (= *ˈtwu[e i]s.noˈn i ˈuy*) *¨malˈi aˈni '.n i* (1586 Sohak 5:95b) are not words vested with … .

… *ˈtwuˈsyeyˈla* = *ˈtwu' ˈsye 'yˈla*, abbr < *ˈtwu[e i]ˈsye 'yˈla* (< ?). ¶*¨tye y na 'y un tas lyang ˈul ˈpte-ˈtiGwe ˈtwu' ˈsye 'yˈla* (?1517-Pak 1:34a) that guy short-changed me five taels of silver [= money]!

twuta₁ < *°twuˈta*, vt. CF **noh.ta**.

1. 1a. puts, places, lays; puts away, puts up. ¶**Pangkum chayk-sang wi ey twun chayk i ēps.ta** I cannot find the book that I just put on the table.

1b. leaves it intact (as it is), leaves it alone; stops, does no more. ¶**Ku tay lo twue la** Leave it as it is. **Chayk-sang wi ey chayk tul ul i tay lo twue la** Leave these books on the desk just the way they are. **Īl ul hata ka ya ecci ku man twulq swu iss.na 'm** How can I leave in the middle of my work (of all times)?! **Ku man twula 'ki ka com mian hata** I feel sorry to tell him to give it up. **Kuleh.key hethun soli n' ku man twue** Cut out such silly talk! **Īl ul hata mōs ha.ye him tul.e ku man twuess.ta** That was an endless job, and at last it got so tough that I gave up on it. **Ku cen** (= **yēys nal**) **kath.umyen ku-nyang an twuess.ulq key 'ta** If it were the old days I wouldn't have let you get away with it. **Namulamyen tasi nun an okeyss.ki (ey), ku-nyang twuess.ta** Thinking not to come again if only to be scolded, I left them alone. **Ku ay wūlla kaman twue la** Leave the child alone or he will cry. **Ne sensayng nim poko yok hayss.kes.ta** — **eti twuko poca** You would call the teacher names? — (let's) cut that stuff out!

2. leaves (behind). ¶**Cāngkap ul eti ey 'n ka twuko wass.ey yo** I have left my gloves behind somewhere. **I chayk ul twuko ka yo** I'll leave this book (and go).

3. keeps, stores, holds. ¶**I sōk ey twun kes i chayk ilyetta** It must be books that are in it. **Ttwukkeng ul teph.e han sahul twuess.ta ka mek.nunta** You cover it with a lid and let it stand for about three days and then eat it.

4. posts, stations, puts (in a post).

5. keeps, employs, engages; has (in one's household). ¶ kāy lul ~ has a dog. chep ul ~ keeps a concubine. Sālam i tā hyengcey lul twuess.kenul nay hol lo ēps.tota While all others have brothers, I alone have none.
6. sets up, establishes.
7. places, puts, appoints.
8. leaves (an interval); puts (time/distance between). ¶ sēy sikan ul twuko for three hours.
9. bears, entertains, cherishes, sets (one's mind) on, has, holds (feelings). ¶ ··· ey maum ul twuko iss.ta has one's mind set on ··· ; CF ··· ey maum ul noh.ko iss.ta has one's mind (taken) off ··· .
10. gives (a pledge).
11. (··· ey swukyel ul ~) signs (a document), puts one's signature to.
12. = noh.ta: puts into, adds (to); stuffs / pads with. ¶ (os ey) ··· ul ~ pads (a garment) with ··· .
13. = noh.ta: (cāngki lul ~ / patwuk ul ~) plays (chess, checkers), moves (a chessman, a checker / marker)
twuta₂, aux v. SEE -e twuta.
-twuˑta = -twoˑta (emotive indicative assertive). ¶ ¨ayGwaˑthye asˑkyem ˑcik ˑhotwuˑta (1462 ¹Nung 3:116b) is inclined to be anxious and possessive. ywoˑkwoy-ˑlwo woˑm ol ¨ati ¨mwot ˑhoˑtwuˑta (1518 Sohak-cho 10:18b) is quite unaware that it is weird.
ˑtwuysˑta = ˑtwu' ˑysˑta, abbr < ˑtwue is(i)ˑta (also ˑtwusˑta = ˑtwu' ˑsˑta). has put it away, ··· ; (-e ~) did it for good, got it all done.
ty dental stop + palatal glide; this is usually a reduction of the syllable ti, as in titye < titie.
ˑtye (> ce), adn, n. ˑtye + ˑi → ˑtye y (also ¨tye y), ˑtye + ˑuˑlwo → tyelˑlwo; ˑtye + ˑuˑlan → *ˑtyelˑlan. CF ˑtyelˑlwo; tyengey.
1. adnoun. 1a. that, those; the. ¶ ˑi ˑkwot ˑtye ˑkwoˑt ay (1445 ¹Yong 26) in this place or that place. ˑtye pwuthye s ˑstaˑh i (1447 Sek 9:10b) that land of Buddha's, Buddha's land. ˑtye pwuthye s ˑHHOYNG ˑkwa ˑNGWEN ˑkwa KWONG-¨KHYWOW ˑhosin PANG-ˑPPYEN ˑun (1447 Sek 9:29a) those deeds and words of Buddha and his ingenious expediencies.
1b. of him (her, it); his, her, its. ¶ noˑm oy ¨kyeˑcip towoyˑnwoˑn i chol hi ˑtye kwoˑma towoyˑGa ciˑla (1463 Pep 2:28b) I would rather become his concubine than another man's wife. [¨]LI lol nilˑGwol [¨]ttyeyn ˑtye KAY-CHA y ¨epˑkwo [¨]HHOYNG ˑol nil[¨]Gwol [¨]ttyeyn KWONG ˑol ssa[¨]ha [¨]za somo[¨]cho.l i ˑ[¨]n i (1463/4 Yeng 1:22a) when we speak of the principle, there are no differences of level, and when we speak of practice, for it to sink in we must accumulate merits.
2. noun. that (one), those; he/him, she/her, it. them. ¶ ˑtye ˑuy mwok-¨swuˑm ul kusˑkuy [= kuch-ˑkuy] ˑhokeˑtun (1447 Sek 9:17a) given that they brought his life to an end ··· . ˑtye ˑuy ˑhiˑm ul kapkeˑn i ˑGwa (1462 ¹Nung 8:124a) not only rewarding his strength but also ··· . taˑsi ˑtye ˑoy wolmˑkywoˑm i towoyˑya (1462 ¹Nung 1:19b) it came about that he moved it again. ˑtye non hwoˑza ¨salom aˑniˑka (1475 Nay 2:1:16a) isn't he a single person all alone? ˑNGWEN honˑt on ˑwuˑli ¨CCWOY ˑlol ˑzywo ˑhoˑsya ˑtye ˑ[G]wa kyesˑkwuˑa ˑmas-pwoˑkey ˑhosywoˑsye (1459 Wel 2:70b) we beg of you, please forgive our transgressions and allow us to confront him in competition. ¨esˑtyey ˑi ¨yang oˑlwo ˑtye ˑlol ¨CHA-¨TUNG ˑhoˑya LWON-LYANG hoˑm ye (?1468- Mong 62ab) how come in your consideration you grade him this way?
··· ˑtye, 1. -ˑeˑtye (< tiˑe), infinitive < -ˑe tiˑta (infinitive + auxiliary).
2. (postmod) = ˑt ye, postmod + postmod. SEE -unˑt ye, -u.n iˑnˑt ye, -nwonˑt ye.
3. SEE -ˑkwaˑtye, -ˑGwaˑtye.
ˑtye < tiˑye, inf < tiˑta
tyeˑkuy (abbr < *tyengeˑkuy), adv, n. that place, there.
ˑtyeˑle (> cele), defective inf. like that, so. CF ˑiˑle, kuˑle, ¨esˑte, ¨aˑmoˑla.
ˑtyeˑle °hoˑta, adj-n. is that way, is such. ¶ [ˑCI-ˑHYWOW] y ˑtyeˑle ˑhosil ˑss oy ··· (1445 ¹Yong 92) his extreme filial devotion was such that ··· .
ˑtyele ˑhi, der adv. ¶ ˑtyele ˑhi ˑkot ˑhwoˑm ol [NGUY-SIM] ˑhonwoˑla (1481 Twusi 15:23b) I am suspicious of such resemblance.
tyeleˑlwo woˑnaˑla (?1517- ¹No 1:57b) you go there (and come back). CF ˑtyelˑlwo.
ˑtyele ˑn, abbr < ˑtye[ˑ]le hon. such. ¶ ˑtyele 'n ¨mwoˑtin ¨iˑl i ˑHHAY ˑthi ¨mwot hoˑm ye (1447 Sek 9:17b) such evil things can do no harm and ··· .
ˑtyeli (?< ˑtyel[e ˑh]i), adv. like that, so. ¶ cey ˑkan ˑol ˑtyeli mwoˑlol ˑss oy (1449 Kok 40)

since they did not know their own rating to be such ... .

tye ̇li-̇two ̇lwok, adverb (abbr < *tyel[e] ̇[h]i [̇ho] ̇two ̇lwok*). to that extent/degree/amount. ¶ *i ¨salo ̇m i ¨pwo ̇poy ̇lol tye ̇li-̇two ̇lwok a ̇ni as ̇kinwos ̇ta* (1447 Sek 6:25-6) this man does not begrudge treasures to that extent!

̇*tyel ̇lwo* (?= ̇*tye ̇lwo* with conflated liquid) = **ce lo** as/with/by that. ¶ ̇*hye ̇non SOYNG-̇MYENG ̇ul me ̇ke ̇tyel ̇lwo pa ̇to ̇m ye ̇chom ̇key ̇ho ̇non cyen ̇cho ̇lwo ̇mas ¨pwo ̇m ay ¨ti- ̇na ¨SSYWUW-¨KHWO ̇lol PELQ ̇ho ̇ya* (1462 ¹Nung 8:104b) because the tongue puts up with letting him eat (all) his life it initiates suffering through taste. CF *il ̇lwo, kul ̇lwo, ¨nal ̇lwo; nellwo;* **muel-lo.**

̇*tye ̇man*, n + pcl. just that. SEE *ku-man ̇tye-man.*

... ̇*tyen* = ̇*t ye n'*, postmodifier + postmodifier [question] + pcl. SEE *-wolq ~ .*

̇*tyeng*, bnd n (postmodifier/postnoun). but. SEE *-ken ̇tyeng, -ul ¨spwun ̇tyeng, ¨man ̇tyeng;* **mangceng, enceng.**

tyengey, abbr < **tyenge ̇kuy* (CF *tye ̇kuy, ingey, kungey*), adverb, noun. (at/to) that place, there. ¶*tyengey YWEN-̇QUNG ̇ho ̇sya.m i ̇la* (1459 Wel 14:58a) it is placing the cause right there. *tyengey nan CHYEN-NYEN ̇iGe ̇za* (1463 Pep se:7b) not until it is a thousand years since it [the gathering] happened in that place ... .

... ̇*uy ~* (to that person) SEE ̇*uy tyengey.*

~ ̇sye. ¶*cukca ̇hi tyengey ̇sye ¨ep ̇se twolwo ZIN-KAN ay ̇na ̇a* (1447 Sek 9:12b) suddenly was absent from there and appeared again among human beings and ... .

tyey, 1. abbr < *tyengey* (or < *tye ̇kuy*), n, adv. (in/at/to) that place, there. ¶*tyey ̇two HE-KHWONG ̇i.n i* (1482 Nam 1:50a) that place too is a void. *wuli kuce tyey ̇tu ̇le ca ̇kwo ka ̇cye* (?1517- ¹No 1:10b) let's go in over there and sleep before going on. *tyey ka ¨sek ̇to.l i ̇na mwuk ̇nwo ̇la ̇ho ̇ya cip sak[s] mwu ̇le sywokcyel ¨ep ̇si he ̇pi ho ̇l i ̇las ̇ta* (?1517- Pak 1:54a) I went there and uselessly wasted my money to pay the rent thinking I would stay for some three months.

2. = *tye 'y,* abbr < ** ̇tye ey,* n + pcl. SEE *tye 'y ̇sye.*

̇*tye 'y...* , n + cop. ¶*¨PI ̇non ̇tye 'y ̇Gwo* (1459 Wel 26a) [the word] *¨PI* means 'that', and ... . ̇*kwot ̇tye 'y ̇la ̇hosya ̇m on* (1462 ¹Nung 3:2a) that one says straightway it is him ... .

̇*tyey* = ̇*tye y,* noun + particle. that one, he [nominative]. ¶ ̇*tye y ̇him isi ̇m ye* (1462 ¹Nung 8:124a) he has strength and ... .

¨*tyey* = ¨*tye y* = ̇*tye y,* n + pcl. ¶ ¨*tye y an ̇cok [̇]cul ̇kye sul ̇hi ne ̇ki ̇ti a[̇]ni ho[̇]m ye* (1463 Pep 2:85b) still rejoicing he does not find it displeasing, and ... .

... ̇*tyeyn,* postmod (< ̇*t ye n'*). SEE *-wolq ~ .*

... ̇*tyeyn ̇tye* = ... ̇*tyeyn ̇tye,* postmodifier + postmodifier (< ̇*t ye 'yn ̇t ye*). SEE *-wolq ~ .*

tye 'y ̇sye = ** ̇tye ey ̇sye,* n + pcl + pcl. ¶*ku ¨CCWOY y ̇stwo tye 'y ̇sye ne ̇mu.l i ̇'la* (1463 Pep 4:83a) such sin is greater than that.

U Not distinguished from **e** in many parts of Korea. Usually not distinguished from **uy** when initial (both are pronounced **u**); often dropped or absorbed when following a vowel. If you cannot find a word you seek with the spelling **u**, try **uy** or **e**.

/u/ < *u,* a high nonfront (= central or back) unrounded vowel; the high counterpart of /o/ (> **a**..., ...**u,** sometimes **o** or **e**); the unrounded counterpart of /wu/ < *wu;* often epenthetic, with MK alternant /o/ (> **u**) after /o/ or /a/.

-u... SEE ALSO *-o*...

u, pcl [S Kyengsang DIAL (Mkk 1960:3:31)] = **uy**

-u- < *-^{u}/o-* < **-G-,* suffix; CF **-i-, -ki-, -chi-, -ukhi-, -ikhi-, -li-, -iwu-, -ywu-; -wu-, -hwu-, -kwu-, -chwu-, -ay-;** *-o-, - ̇Gi-, - ̇Gwu-, - ̇Gwo-.* makes vc. ¶*kilu-* < *kil^u/o-/kilG-* < **kil^u/o-G-* raise, rear, nurture ← **kī-l-** < *¨kil-* < **ki ̇lu*-long; [obs] be/get big, grow. **tolu-** < *twolo-/twolG-* < **twolo-G-* distribute, deal out/around, cause to turn around ← **tō-l-** < *¨twol-* < **two ̇lo-* revolve, turn.

-ucapcap, bnd adj-n (~ **hata**); after a vowel **-capcap;** LIGHT ↔ **-ucepcep.** ...ish, slightly colored/tinged. SEE **-(u)sulum.**

-ucepcep, bnd adj-n (~ **hata**); after a vowel **-cepcep;** HEAVY ↔ **-ucapcap.** ...ish, slightly colored/tinged. SEE **-(u)sulum.**

-uchikchik, bnd adj-n (~ **hata**); after a vowel **-chikchik.** ...ish, slightly colored/tinged. SEE **-(u)sulum.**

-uchwungchwung, bnd adj-n (~ hata); after a vowel **-chwungchwung.** ···ish, slightly colored / tinged. SEE **-(u)sulum.**

-ucokcok, bound adj-n (~ hata); after a vowel **-cokcok;** LIGHT ↔ **-ucwukcwuk.** ···ish, slightly colored / tinged. SEE **-(u)sulum.**

-ucwukcwuk, bnd adj-n (~ hata); after a vowel **-cwukcwuk;** HEAVY ↔ **-ucokcok.** ···ish, slightly colored / tinged. SEE **-(u)sulum.**

-ui, [var, with adj only] = **-so** (AUTH indicative after a consonant): **cek.ui** = **cēkso** < **cēkta** are few; but **chwuwui** = **chwupso** < **chwupta** is cold, **naui** = **nās.so** < **nās.ta** is/gets better. ¶**Caney māl i olh.ui** You are right. ABBR **-uy** = **-i.** NOTE: A grammatical tradition says that this is the adjective assert indic in the FAMILIAR style; that tradition would limit **-ney** to verbs. But present-day usage is in conflict with the traditional prescription.

-uiso(i) [DIAL] = **-usipsio.** ¶**Anc.uisoi** = **Anc.usipsio** Please sit down (Mkk 1960:3:34). CF **-iso(i).**

-ui tul = **-so tul** (SEE **-ui)**

-ukhi-, suffix. derives vc. ¶**il.ukhi-** raise < **īlta** rise. **al.ukhi-** inform < **ā-l-** know. CF **-i-, -ki-, -chi-, -u-, -ikhi-, -li-, -iwu-, -ywu-; -wu-, -hwu-, -kwu-, -chwu-, -ay-;** -˙*Gi*-, -˙*Gwo*-, -˙*Gwu*-, -*o*-, -*u*-.

-u' kkey, immediate future (abbr < **-ulq key;** after a vowel **-' kkey).** I will do right away (I promise); ~ **yo** SAME [POLITE]. ¶**Cāmqkan tanye o' kkey − kitaliko iss.ke la** Please wait here − I'll be right back. **Nay ellun poko cwu' kkey − cāmqkan man poye cwue yo** Please show it to me for a moment − I'll give it right back to you. **Nay ka cip.u' kkey** I've got it! (when reaching for something dropped). **Nay ka itta** (= **iss.ta**) **mun ul tat.u' kkey yo** I'll shut the door a little later.

-*ul*··· SEE ALSO -*ol*···

ul < ˙*ᵘ/ol*, particle (after a vowel **lul,** abbr **l'**), accusative case marker.

1. marks the direct object of a transitive verb; translates as English object of verb or of verb + preposition. ¶**sinmun ul pota** reads (or looks at) the newspaper. **sālam ul chac.ta** visits (or looks for, or finds) a person. **mal ul thata** mounts / rides a horse. **thum ul thata** seizes (takes advantage of) an opportunity. **ttay lul kitalita** bides one's time; waits for (awaits) the time. **sihem cwūnpi lul hata** prepares for the exams. **pap ul mekta** eats one's food / rice, eats (has a meal). **sālam uy meli lul ttaylita** hits a person's head = hits a person on the head. **pata lul poki lul wēn hata (palata)** wants (hopes) to see the sea. **cal haki lul palata** hopes that one will do well. **kuleh.key haki lul cōh.a / silh.e hata** likes / hates to do so (do that). **Hāyngpok / Kēnkang / Sengkong ul pīp.nita** We pray for your happiness / health / success. **Ku kes ul / i poko siph.ta** I'd like to see that. **I kes ul kaciko kasio** Take this with you. **I māl ul ku i hanthey cen hasio** Give this message to him.

2. marks the direct object of a transitive passive verb with the meaning "suffers it", and often gets translated as an English preposition. ¶**cengkayngi lul kkayita** gets hit in the shin. **sonq-kalak ul khal ey peyita** gets one's finger cut on a knife. **kasum ul chayita** gets kicked in the chest. **yakcem ul cap.hita** has one's weak spot seized / played upon. **pal ul cap.hita** gets caught by the leg. **mok ul ccallita** gets one's throat cut; "gets fired". **Kongsan-kwun eykey Sānghay lul ppay-as.kyess.ta** suffered the loss of Shanghai to the Communist troops.

3. marks the goal or direction of a verb of movement, with or without a preceding pcl **ey** (CF **ey, ulo**). ¶**hak.kyo (ey) lul kata** goes to school. **eti lul kana** wherever one goes (one may go). **Ēncey Sewul ul wass.n' ya** When did you come to Seoul? **Pang ul tul.e kanta** (1936 Roth 278) I go into the room.

4. marks the path of a verb of movement. ¶**keli lul kēt.ta** walks (down) the street. **hanul ul nalta** files (in) the sky. **kang ul kēnne kata** crosses a river.

5. marks the purpose of a verb of movement (CF **hale**). ¶¹**yehayng ul tte-nata** sets out on a trip. **yenghwa kwūkyeng ul kata** (or **yenghwa lul kwūkyeng kata**) goes to see a movie. **isa lul ota / kata** moves (house) here / there.

6. marks the duration of a verb (CF **tong-an ey**). ¶**sahul ul ota** comes for three days. **sam-il ul aphess.ta** was ill for three days. **Sā-nyen ul haksayng ulo ku hak.kyo ey iss.ess.ta** I was in / at that school four years as a student. **Pi ka halo** [= **halwu**] **lul wass.ta** It rained for a day. **Han sikan ul kitalikey** (1936 Roth 278) Wait an hour. **twū sikan ul cam cata** sleeps (for)

two hours. **i mun i ō-payk nyen ul se iss.nun tong-an** during the 500 years that this gate has been standing. *QA-NAN ʾi ʿCHYWULQ-KA hon ¨HHWUW ʾlwo ʾsuʾmu naʾmon ʾhoy ʾlol pwuthye cwotcoʿWa* [← *cwoch-cop-(ʿa)*] *iʿsye* (1447 Sek 24:2a) Ānanda has followed the Buddha for over twenty years after leaving home (to become a monk).

7. 7a. marks the frequency ('for ··· times'). ¶**Sēy pen ul wass.ta** (1936 Roth 278) They came three times. *¨cen moʾl i ʾhyen peʾn ul tin ʾt ol* (1445 ¹Yong 31) however many times the limping horse may fall.

7b. marks the sequence order of a verb (CF **ulo**). ¶**ches ccay lul kata** goes / ranks first.

8. marks the cognate complement of a verb. ¶**cam ul cata** sleeps (a sleep). **chwum ul chwuta** dances (a dance). **swūm ul swīta** breathes (a breath).

9. [colloq] as a paraphrase of other particles (often **ey**), **ul** marks various kinds of indirect objects, etc. In sloppy speech that occasionally leads to two objects both marked with the same particle. This usage can be treated as adding emphasis to a specific marker, which need not be (but often is) omitted. See §10.6. CF **N ul pel / sang cwuta** (1936 Roth 277) 'gives a reward / punishment to N, punishes / rewards N'. In most of these structures, the "sloppy object" is best put right before the verb, with a normal object placed earlier: **Chayk ul ku ⁿyeca (eykey / hanthey) lul cwuess.ta** 'I gave her the book' sounds better than (?*)**Ku ⁿyeca (eykey / hanthey) lul chayk ul cwuess.ta**.

9a. = **ey** to, in, on, with. ¶**aph-cang ul suta** stands in the van / lead. **Ku ya pelsse yeki lul** [= **ey (lul)**] **meych tal iss.uni-kka yo** That's because I've been here a few months already (1954 Lukoff 111).

9b. = **eykey** = **hanthey** to / for (an animate indirect object). ¶**Na l' cwe** (= **Na lul cwue** = **Na hanthey tālla**) Gimme! (= Give it to me!) **Nwui ka elin awu lul / eykey os (ul) ip.hinta** The sister dresses her little brother. **Sakwa nun emeni lul tulilye 'nta** I intend to give the apple to Mother. **Chayk un sensayng ul poye tulinta** He shows the book to the teacher. **Na lul ola 'l** (= **na eykey ola ko hal**) **kkatalk i iss.na?!** I see no reason he should ask me to come. *[ʿSO-¨HOY] ʾlol nyenʿk ul ¨cwu.l i ʾye* (1445 ¹Yong 20) would the four seas be given to anyone else?! With particle ellipted: *laʾkwuy meʾki.m ye mol meʿkywom ʾkot hi* (1482 Nam 2: 63b) like feeding a donkey and feeding a horse.

9c. (= **ulo**) as, for, so as to be. ¶**Ku ssal ul / ulo pap ul cīs.nunta** They use that rice for cooking. **Yengswuk-i lul caki uy myenuli lul sam.ess.ta** He made Yengswuk his daughter-in-law. **Mikwuk ulo yāngca lul kass.ta** They went to America as adopted children.

9d. (= **uy** when it is marking a whole-part relationship, in which either could separately be treated as the object). ¶**Poli lul ssi lul ppulinta** I sow the barley seed. SEE §10.6.

10. 10a. marks the direct object of an omitted verb expression. ¶**Way ku īl ul [māl haci anh.ko] camcakho iss.ess.ni** Why did you keep the matter to yourself (keep quiet on the matter)? **Ku-kkacisq īl ul [kaciko] mwe kuleh.key yātan in ya (kekceng in ya, sīpi 'n ya, chamkyen in ya)** Why are you raising so much fuss (worrying so much, arguing so much, meddling so much), when it is such a trivial thing?! **Kulenq īl ey mwe l' (hako) nōpal-tāypal ia** Why get so mad about it?

10b. ¶**Tek.kwuk inmin i Cosen inmin pota sam-pay lul te manh.a yo** (Roth 1936:278) The German people are three times as numerous as the Korean people.

11. marks a transitive relationship between two noun expressions when no verb is expressed. The second phrase is usually marked by the particle **ulo** 'as, so as to be', and the gerund **hako** 'making it' can often be added at the end. **X ul sangtay lo** with X for a counterpart (and opposite number). ¶**X ul kipan ulo** with X for / as a basis. **ku kes ul kwūsil lo** with / using that for an excuse. **Sewul ul cwungsim ulo** with Seoul as the center / focus. **munqpep ul cwungsim ulo kongpu lul hata** is working mainly on grammar; is studying with the main emphasis on grammar. **pānto lul mūtay lo (hako)** with the peninsula for a stage. **putong-san ul cētang ulo unhayng ey se pic ul nāyta** gets a loan from the bank with one's real estate as / for collateral. **Sewul ul cipan ulo chwulma hata** runs for election with Seoul for one's constituency.

12. emphasizes a negative expression when it is attached to **-ci** and followed by the negative

auxiliary. ¶kaci lul anh.ta (or mōs hata) just won't go. SEE -ci lul; CF -ci ka.

13. 13a. emphasizes a desiderative expression when attached to -ko and followed by the auxiliary adjective siph.ta. SEE -ko lul.

13b. emphasizes the purposive. SEE -ulye lul.

13c. emphasizes the adverbative, apparently only in the structure -key lul / ka an toynta. SEE -key lul.

NOTE: Although some of the expressions that can be emphasized by attaching ul may be regarded as adverbial, the adverbs in general cannot be so treated. We reject *ppalli lul kako siph.ta 'wants to get there fast' (HSIKL 3:384) as well as *Ku ka cha lul etteh.key lul kochyess.ni 'How did he fix the car?' (HSIKL 3:390).

14. [JOCULAR] attaches to an infinitive with a following verb or auxiliary — for a humorous effect. ¶mek.e lul pota takes a bite of it (just to sample it). tol.a lul kata trots off home.

15. marks an antithetical clause that ends in a modifier + kes. although, but; (it's) too bad (that / yet ...), in spite of the fact that ... ; anyway, so there! (used to end a sentence with the meaning 'indeed', or 'despite contrary anticipations / reservations', or 'I guess'.) CF -ulq ke l', -un ke l', -nun ke l', -tun ke l'; -kenul. ¶Silh.ta ko hanun kes ul pumo ka cāngka lul tulkey hayss.ta His parents made him get married over his protests (in spite of his refusal). Keki n' cham pissalq ke l' (= Keki nun cham pissalq kes ul) But that place would be very expensive! Hayss.tula 'myen cōh.ass.ulq kes ul I wish he'd done it anyway (but he did not do it). Ama molusilq ke l'q yo (kellyo) But you probably wouldn't know, in any event. Ku yenghwa nun cangcha wuli Inchen ey to olq ke l' After all, that movie will come to us in Inchen one of these days. Ku nun māl ul cal hatun ke l' He spoke well, after all!

16. ¶Hānkwuk-e 'na Hānqca-e 'na lul mullon hako regardless whether it is Korean or Sino-Korean (Chinese). Ecci palqtal toyess.na lul poca Let's see how it has developed.

17. marks an object raised from the subject of a putativized sentence: (na nun) ku namca ka maum-ssi ka cōh.ta ko mit.ess.ta 'I believed that he was of good nature' → ku namca lul maum-ssi ka cōh.ta ko mit.ess.ta 'I believed him to be of good nature', but not *ku namca lul maum-ssi lul ⋯ for only one nominative phrase can be raised to serve as the object of a putative sentence (as was observed by Choy Yengsek 1988:178:n8): ku namca uy maum-ssi ka cōh.ta ko mit.ess.ta 'I believed that his nature was good' → ku namca uy maum-ssi lul cōh.ta ko mit.ess.ta 'I believed his nature to be good'.

18. in MK marks the underlying subject of a causativized verb (where we expect a dative): ¨HHWUW s ¨salo˙m ol ¨al˙Guy ˙honon ke˙s i˙la (1447 Sek se:1a) it is (written) so that later people may know. CF 9.

NOTE 1: Sequences of ul / lul followed by another particle (ul man, ul cocha, ...) are just literary or formal variants of colloquial expressions in which the ul / lul is omitted. But the particle obligatorily drops before the focus particles un / nun, to, and ya / iya. SEE ey lul, ey l'; eykey lul, hanthey lul.

NOTE 2: The MK particle has two versions, ˙ul / ˙lul and ˙ol / ˙lol. The shapes ˙ul / ˙lul are usually picked when the vowel of the preceding syllable is u or wu, as in mu˙su˙k ul (1459 Wel 7:28b, 9:23b), ˙ptu˙t ul (1447 Sek 13:43b, 1459 Wel 2:64a, 1463 Pep 3:47a, 3:180b), e˙nu ¨nwu ˙lul (1449 Kok 52), and ˙i ¨twul˙h ul (1449 Kok 52). But there are a few examples of the other shapes: e˙nu ˙lol (1482 Kum-sam 2:69a); SSYANG-˙TTYWU ˙lol (1462 ¹Nung 6:66a), [˙KYWULQ-˙YWUW] [˙]lol (1481 Twusi 20:34b), ˙cwu.l ol (1481 Twusi 15:47b), ˙LYWULQ ˙ol (1462 ¹Nung 1:19a), ˙SWU ˙lol (1459 Wel 21:14a) — CF ˙SWU ˙lul (1463 Pep 3:86a). After a syllable with uy or wuy both versions occur, but ˙ol / ˙lol seems to be more common: e˙tuy ˙lol (?1468- Mong 13b), ˙PEP-˙NGUY ˙lol (1447 Sek 13:26b), ˙NGUY lol (1465 Wen 2:3:2:68a), [˙LWOK-˙KUY] ˙lol (1481 Twusi 8:3b), [KUN-¨KUY] lol (1481 Twusi 20:52a); pwul˙hwuy ˙lol (1447 Sek 6:30b, 1449 Kok 99), MWU-˙QWUY ˙lol (1462 ¹Nung 6:43a), TTIN-˙LYWUY ˙lol (1462 ¹Nung 1:24b), [QAN-NGWUY] ˙lol (1481 Twusi 10:12a), SSYANG-˙SSYWUY ˙lol (1459 Wel 17:23b) — but ˙KWOLQ-¨SYWUY lul (?1468- Mong 32b), ¨twuy˙h ul (1447 Sek 19:10a), TYWUNG-˙KWUYK ˙ul (1459 Wel 1:30a).

The higher-vowel shapes are common when the syllable of the preceding syllable is e or ey, as in *ne ˙lul* (1447 Sek 23:24b, 24:3a; 1459 Wel 8:101a, 8:86a; 1462 ¹Nung 1:90b; 1481 Twusi 7:20a; 1482 Nam 1:44b; ...) and *ke˙s ul* (1462 ¹Nung 8:86b, 1481 Twusi 8:34a, 25:29a; ...), ¨*ney˙h ul* (1459 Wel 10:4b) and ˙*thyey ˙lul* (1518 Sohak-cho 10:27a). Only a few examples are found of the lower-vowel shapes, as in *pwuthye ˙lol* (1463 Pep 5:121b) – CF *pwuthye ˙lul* (1447 Sek 6:19a, 9:24b), *mu˙se˙s ol* (1588 Mayng 13:26b), and *kulu˙mey ˙lol* (1447 Sek 24:20b). But after ⋯*YEY* the only examples are of ˙*lol*: *MYENG-*˙*SSYEY ˙lol* (1447 Sek 6:8b), ˙*SYEY lol* (1463 Pep 4:148b), ˙*KKYEY ˙lol* (1447 Sek 19:31b, 1463 Pep 6:83a), *SAM-PPWO-TTYEY ˙lol* (1447 Sek 19:34b, 1459 Wel 21:222a, 1463 Pep 2:6b), *CHYENG-TTYEY ˙lol* (1459 Wel 23:93a), ˙*SYEY lol* (1463 Pep 4:148b), ˙*PHYEY ˙lol* (1475 Nay 1:77a).

After *wo* or *woy* the lower-vowel shapes are usual, as in *coy˙cwo ˙lol* (1463 Pep 1:49b), *PPEN-*¨*NWOW ˙lol* (1459 Wel 1:18a), ˙*mwo.m ol* (1482 Kum-sam 5:48b), ˙*swon ˙ol* (1586 Sohak 6:102b), *LYWONG ˙ol* (1447 Sek 6:32a, 1449 Kok 192); *ca˙chwoy ˙lol* (1462 ¹Nung 2:114b), *NGUY-*¨*HWOY ˙lol* (1463 Pep 2:24a), [¨*CCWOY*] ˙*lol* (1481 Twusi 24:13a). The other shapes are not attested after *woy* and I have found only two examples after *wo*, *SSYWUN-PWONG ˙ul* (1463 Pep 4:148b) and [˙*KALQ-HHWONG*] ˙*ul* (1481 Twusi 21:34a). After *a, ay, o*, or *oy*, the shapes ˙*ol* / ˙*lol* are overwhelmingly favored, as in ¨*na ˙lol* (1447 Sek 6:4a; 1459 Wel 8:98a, 9:35d; 1481 Twusi 23:44a), *na˙la˙h ol* (1459 Wel 7:29b, 1463 Pep 2:77a), *nwol˙Gay ˙lol* (1459 Wel 21:190a), *yang˙co ˙lol* (1447 Sek se:5a, 1459 Wel 8:19b), ˙*hoy ˙lol* (1447 Sek 24:2a), *ZYE-LOY ˙lol* (1459 Wel 17:36b, 1464 Kumkang 69b), ˙*CYWUNG-SOYNG ˙ol* (1447 Sek 6:5b, 1482 Nam 2:6b). But there are rare examples of the higher-vowel shapes: ˙*SYWU-*¨*HWA ˙lul* (1588 Mayng 13:19b), *kesang ˙ul* (1475 Nay 1:70b), ˙*KUM-*˙*KAY ˙lul* (1462 ¹Nung 8:77a), *na˙kunay ˙lul* (1481 Twusi 15:31b).

After syllables containing the vowel *i* both versions occur, but the low-vowel shapes are more common. For a given word I have not found competing versions: only ¨*i˙l ol* (1447 Sek 6:18a, 6:27a, 19:40b; 1459 Wel 8:8b, 10:21a, 18:7b; 1481 Twusi 8:24b; ...) 'affair' and ˙*i lol* (1449 Kok 121, 1482 Kum-sam 5:

14a, 1481 Twusi 7:23b) 'this'; only *ci˙p ul* (1449 Kok 45, 1462 ¹Nung 1:53a) 'house'.

-ul(q) < -⋅ᵘ*⁄ol(q)*, prospective modifier [after a vowel **-l(q)**]. Initial **p t c s k** of a following word are regularly reinforced to **pp tt cc ss kk**, unless a pause is inserted, so we write **-ulq p**⋯ etc. Most of the cases of word-initial **y** and **i** (including ¹y ⁿy ¹i ⁿi) are treated as **ny** and **ni** when directly preceded by a consonant, so what we write as **-ulq y**⋯ (**i**⋯) is pronounced /ully⋯/ (/ulli⋯/). The modern Hankul spelling usually ignores all these reinforcements. The earlier texts sometimes did the same, but quite often they wrote ⋯*q* or geminated the following obstruent. On a possible source of the ⋯*q* see -˙*ul s*.

1. ⋯ that is to be/do; ⋯ that will be/do; ⋯ that one will do (at/to/from/with). ¶ **catong-cha lul phalq sālam** the man who will (is to, wants to) sell the car; the man with the car for sale. **ku sālam i phalq catong-cha** the car that the man will sell; the car that the man has for sale. **ku sālam i catong-cha lul phalq kos (sikan)** the place where (time when) the man will sell the car. **ssul phyēnci** letters to write. **phyēnci lul ssulq sālam tul** persons to write the letters; persons to write letters to. **na hanthey phyēnci lul ssulq sālam tul** persons to write letters to me. **nay ka phyēnci lul ssulq sālam tul** persons for me to write letters to. **tte-nal nal** the day that one is to leave. **Na hako kath.i wūntong halq sālam ul chac.nun cwung ita** I am looking for someone to play (the sport) with me. **Kulelq casin i ēps.ta** I lack the confidence to do that. **Ku kes un ecci halq tōli ka ēps.ta** There's nothing to be done about it. **Halq īl i mānh.ta** There is lots to do (to be done). **Na nun yēnkuk-cang ey kal heka lul (helak ul) et.ess.ta** (1936 Roth 548) I have (obtained) permission to go to the theater.

¶ ˙*kata ˙ka two˙la wolq [KWUN-*¨*SSO] y* (1445 ¹Yong 25) the troops who had returned from going [off to battle]. ¨*nyey [*˙*LWOK-SAN] oy [*˙*LWAN] hol kwo[*˙*]t ol* ¨*mwolla˙n i* ... (1481 Twusi 15:47b) (?) in the old days they did not know rebellion by the mountain feofdoms ... .

2. (with time words). SEE ~ **ttay**, ~ **cek**, ~ **mulyep**, ~ **tong-an**, ~ **sai**.

3. SEE ~ **cwul**, ~ **kyem**, ~ **lī**, ~ **man**, ~ **ppun**, ~ **swu**, ~ **the(y)**.

NOTE 1: -(ess.)ess.ul and -ul.nun also occur.

NOTE 2: After a consonant-final stem the MK ending has the two shapes -˙ul(q) and -˙ol(q). Choice of the shape is determined by the vowel of the preceding syllable. After aC, oC, or woC only -˙ol(q) occurs, as in tas˙kol (1447 Sek 13:36a), mo˙chol (1447 Sek 6:3b), and two˙tolq (1449 Kok 14). After e, uC, wuC, or iC only -˙ul(q) occurs, as in me˙kulq (1459 Wel 8:8b), sul˙hul (1459 Wel 2:22b), cwu˙kul (1459 Wel 7:18b), and mi˙tulq (1447 Sek 6:11b).

Stems ending in ⋯l- reduce the expected strings l-ul and l-ol to just l, as in ¨ilq ˙ka (1462 ¹Nung 4:38b) < ¨il- 'be formed' and ˙tul (1463 Pep 1:55b) = ˙tulq (1462 ¹Nung 2:114b) from ˙tul- 'enter' — compare tulul (1447 Sek 6:8b, 1462 ¹Nung 2:107a) < tut- 'listen'. But before the postmodifiers ˙i 'fact' or 'one' and ˙ye (also ˙ya ?) 'question', only the epenthetic vowel is suppressed, leaving /lll/: ˙tull i ˙˙la (1462 ¹Nung 8:40a), ¨ill i ˙le˙n i (1445 ¹Yong 123), ¨mel˙l i ˙'-ngi s˙ka (1459 Wel 8:1b), ¨all i ˙Gwo (1459 Wel 21:14a; 1481 Twusi 15:37b, 47b). The postmodifier itself sometimes vanishes: ¨yell [i] ˙ye˙n ywo (1481 Twusi 7:25b). Notice that the basic forms (such as *˙tululq, *a˙lolq, …) never surface except in one of the two reductions: as ˙tulq or ˙tull (i), as ¨alq or al˙l (i), … . When the contractions were made, those stems which begin with the low (unmarked) pitch kept the high accent of the ending and blended it with the low pitch to produce the rising tone marked with the double dot (¨); that is why the dictionary form (= the indicative assertive) of an -L- verb begins either ˙⋯ or ¨⋯. The modulated prospective modifier is formed as expected, with the ⋯l- of the stem (and its high or low basic accent) intact, simply appending the modulator and the ending of the prospective modifier (-˙wᵘ/olq), as in mu˙sum ˙pho˙lwol ¨il (?1517-¹No 2:3a) 'the business of what to sell' and sa˙lwol ¨chye˙swo ˙lol (1518 Sohak-cho 8:3a) a home to live in … .

-ul a = -ul ya

-ula < -˙ᵘ/o˙la (?< -˙ᵘ/o˙l [y]a or -˙ᵘ/o˙l [G]a 'willya'; ?< -˙ᵉ/ᵃ˙l a 'you will!') subjunctive attentive; -la < -˙la after a vowel or l-extension of -L- stems. SEE ho˙la.

1. (command, literary or in quotations) do it! may / let it happen! ¶ Anc.ula = Anc.e la Sit down! Iss.ula = Iss.(k)e la Stay! anc.ula (ko) hata tells one to sit down. iss.ula (ko) hata tells one to stay. Sinpu nim i ilccik cwumusila ko hay yo (Dupont 123) Tell the Father to get to bed early. Hānkwuk ey thōngil i iss.ula Let there be unification in Korea! ilcye˙muli ˙ho.ya he˙mu.l i ¨ep.su˙la ho˙kwo (1475 Nay 1:84a) let there be no blunders in the early evening, it says, and … . ˙QILQ-SIM ˙u˙lwo kwoyGwoy ho˙la (1464 Kumkang 12a) be utterly quiet [and listen to what I say]!

2. 2a. = -ule [going] for the purpose of doing, to do. ¶ KUM-LYWUN NGWANG a˙to˙l i ˙CHYWULQ-KA ho˙la ˙kano˙n i (1447 Sek 6:9b) the son of the Golden Wheel King is leaving to become a monk. ˙ema ¨nim˙i PPI-LAM NGWEN ˙ul pwo˙la ˙kasi˙n i (1449 Kok 17) the mother went there to see Lumbinī Park. ¨TTWOW-¨LI poy˙hwo˙la ˙na˙a ˙ka˙sya (1459 Wel 1:5a) goes out to study the doctrine.

2b. [DIAL] = -ulye. CF -˙ᵘ/o˙la ˙'n˙t oy.

3. = -ta (ka) < -˙ta˙ka (transferentive); CF -ul ak, -˙ᵘ/o˙lak.

3a. doing in alternation. ¶ pol[h] kwu˙phi˙la phyel sso˙zi ˙yey (1459 Wel 21:4a) in the interval between bending and spreading one's arm.

3b. and then; then; whereupon. ¶ ¨cams.kan anco˙la nonon kama˙kwoy ˙non (1481 Twusi 7:1b) the crow who perches for a moment and then flies on.

˙u˙la = ˙u˙lwo, pcl (after a vowel ˙la = ˙lwo). mu˙su.k u˙la (1481 Twusi 22:39b) = mu˙su.m u˙la (1447 Sek 6:3a) for what reason, why. VAR u˙lye. NOTE: There is no attestation of *˙o˙la, unlike ˙o˙lan. But see ˙ola˙wa.

-ula ˙ca, abbr < -ula (ko) haca

-ula ˙ci, abbr < -ula (ko) haci

-ulak → -ul ak

-ul ak, prosp mod + postmod; the shape is -l lak after -L- stems (and colloquially that is optional after all vowel stems), -l ak after other vowel stems. one of two alternating conditions: ~ māl lak (hanta) [auxiliary vi] (is) on the point / verge of doing, almost does, (hesitates) whether to do (or not).

¶ Ol ak kal ak coming and going, milling about. olul ak naylil ak rising and falling, fluctuating. phulul ak nwulul ak now green now yellow. **mīlchil ak tālchil ak** pushing and pulling. **Kwulum i ol ak kal ak hanta** The clouds come and go. **Pi ka ol ak kal ak hanta** It rains off and on. **Cēngsin i ol ak kal ak hanta** I don't know whether I am going or coming (I am so terribly busy / tired / drugged). **Elkwul i pulk.ul ak phalul ak hanta** His face gets red and blue (with anger).

¶ **Cikum wus.ul (l)ak māl lak hanta** He is on the verge of laughing. **Soli ka tullil (l)ak māl lak mēlli sala cinta** Hardly to be heard, the sound fades away in the distance. **Ku uy ilum i sayngkak nal (l)ak māl lak hamyen se sayngkak naci anh.nunta** His name is on the tip of my tongue, but I just can't think of it. **Satali ka ssule cil (l)ak māl lak hani tah.chici mal.e la** Don't touch the ladder — it is so delicately balanced that it may fall at any moment. **Onul un kwulum i mānh.e se hay ka nal (l)ak māl lak hanta** The sun can't make up its mind whether to come out or not, it's so cloudy today. **Māl ul hal (l)ak māl lak hanta** He is hesitating whether to say anything or not. **Welkup i ō-chen wen toyl (l)ak māl lak hanta** He has a salary a bit short of 5,000 wen. **Mak cam i tul ak māl lak hanun tey cēnhwa ka wass.ta** Just when I was on the point of falling asleep, the telephone rang. NOTE: (1916 Gale 81) "*hol.nak mal.nak howo* [= hal lak māl lak hao] expresses indifference, inattention to the work on hand or interruption of the same".

This structure might be a contraction of **-u(l)la k[o]** = **-ulye ko**, as suggested by M 3: 3:103. If so, the postmodifier **ak** is a new entity and perhaps just an artifact of the analysis. The dialect variant form **-tak** suggests that /lak/ may, instead, be a lenition from /tak/, which looks like a shortening of **-ta ka**; but some kind of restructuring would have to be posited to account for the epenthetic **u** after a consonant stem. Neither of these two histories, however, seems likely in view of the examples from early Hankul texts which show a structure identical to the modern one. Yet, since -$(^u/o)$ `lak` also had the meaning of -`ta `ka`, perhaps it was a lenited variant from early on (CF `ila `ka`). SEE **-u`lak**.

-$^u/o$`lak, nonfinite ending (? < -$^u/ol$ `ak, ? < -ta k[a]).

1. doing alternatively/sometimes. ¶ *cwu`ku`lak `sal`lak `ho`ya* (1447 Sek 24:29a, 1459 Wel 1:12b) [constantly] dying and living. "*salo`m i towoy`lak pelGey cywungsoyng `i towoy`lak `ho`ya* (1459 Wel 1:12b) sometimes becoming a person and sometimes becoming a bug or an animal. *phye`lak "cwuy`lak `hwo`m ol "ne y `pwono`n i* (1462 ¹Nung 1:108b) you see it keep opening and closing. *`como`lak `ptu`lak `hono`ta* (1481 Twusi 7:2a) [the dragonflies ...] are sinking and floating. *"twul[h] `cay s hyeng `un wo`lak ka`lak ho`kwo* (?1517- Pak 1:39b) Number Two Brother keeps coming and going.

2. and / but then (at once). ¶ *e`tuwu`lak twolwo `hoyno`n i* (1481 Twusi 7:14b) it gets dark and then it gets light again. *"soym swo`li lol `tulu`lak `stwo kus.no`n i* (1481 Twusi 7:23b) one hears the sound of the spring and then it ceases. *`CANG-"SSO `uy pol[h] kwu`phi`lak phyel so`zi `kot `ho`ya* (1485 Kwan 4b) it is like the interval between a strong man bending his arm and stretching it out, and ... . *[SYEY] lwo kalak stwo [TWONG] olwo wonwos.ta* (1632 Twusi-cwung 17:19a) goes to the west and then comes to the east.

NOTE: The ...`l`lak version for -L- stems may contain ...`l[o]l(q)` prosp mod < ...`l`-. SEE **-ul(q)**.

-ula k, [DIAL] abbr < **-ula ko**, subj attentive + particle: ~ **hata**.

-ulaki, suffix; LIGHT ↔ **-uleki**. diminutive. ¶ **ciphulaki** a piece of straw < **ciph** straw. **kkakkulaki** < awns and bits of rice or barley husk < **kkakk.ta** cuts. **pasulaki** < crumbs, shreds, bits < **pās.ta** = **paswuta** smashes, breaks. VAR **-ulayki**.

-ula 'ki, abbr < **-ula (ko) haki**. ¶ **Ku man twula 'ki ka com mian hata** I feel sorry to tell him to give it up.

-ula kko [LIVELY] = **-ula ko**

-ula ko, subj attentive + pcl. ¶ **Kot kala ko ille la** Tell him to go / get there at once. **Ese ola ko yātan i nass.ta** They are really raising the roof for you to come at once. **I kes ul pola ko hasio** Tell him to take a look at this. **Mas i cōh.ula ko kuleh.key kkulh.yess.ta** I boiled it that way to make it to taste good. **Maypci mālla ko kochwuq kalwu lul neh.ci anh.ess.e** I left out the red pepper to keep it from being spicy.

~ **(yo)** [sentence-final] do it (I tell you); (fragment of quoted command).

-ula kwu, 1. = **-ula ko**. 2. [sentence-final, northern DIAL] = **-key na** (FAMILIAR command).

A Reference Grammar of Korean

-ula 'l, abbr < -ula (ko) hal. ¶Na lul ola 'l kkatalk i iss.na?! I see no reason for him to ask me to come.

-ula 'la, abbr < -ula (ko) hala

-ula 'm, abbr < -ula (ko) ham. ¶Cēng-mal ku man twula 'm? Do you really mean for me to give it up?

-ula 'myen, abbr < -ula (ko) hamyen. if/when told to (do), if I tell you to do, if you tell me to do. ¶Kala 'myen kasey yo If I tell you to go, you go!; Kala 'myen kakeyss.ey yo If you tell me to go, then I will go (M 1:2:165). But some speakers reject examples of the past, such as (?*)Kala 'myen kass.ey yo (ibid.) When I told him to go he went.

ˑuˑlan, pcl < ˑuˑla n' = ˑuˑlwo n'; ˑlan after a vowel or *l* or *LQ* (VAR [ˑ]lan); ku + ˑuˑlan → kulˑlan. as for — marks a theme, normally not one extruded from the underlying subject, for in that case the particle ᵘ⁄ₒn is preferred (Kim Sungkon 1978:66). VAR (after ⸺oC or ⸺woC) ˑoˑlan; no examples of ⸺oC ˑuˑlan, and only one of ⸺woC ˑuˑlan.

¶ˑicey cyeˑmun ceˑk uˑlan anˑcok mozom skoˑcang ¨nwotaˑkaˑcolaˑm ye n' eˑlwu ˑPEP ul poyˑhwozoˑWwoˑl iˑ'-ngiˑ'ta (1447 Sek 6:11ab) now while I am young, you see, I will have fun to my heart's content for a while and then when I am grown I can duly learn the Law. kasoyˑlwoˑhwon [MWON] ˑulan sywokcyel [¨]ep.si [¨]ye[ˑ]ti [¨]malˑla (1481 Twusi 7:9b) do not to your regret open a door that is made of thorns. nyeˑlum ciˑzwul ¨ilˑlan ¨saloˑm oy [¨]ma[ˑ]l ol tutˑkwoˑmwoy[h] sˑpi.ch uˑlan ¨sayˑuyˑculkiˑnwonˑptu.t ulˑpwonwola (1481 Twusi 7:11a) harvest work — I hear the people talking; the radiance of the mountains — I see the joy of the birds.

¶THYEN-¨CO yˑwuˑli ¨TTWOW-¨LIˑlan poˑlisiˑkwo ¨menˑtuy s HHWO-ˑKYWOW ˑlol KKWUWˑhoˑsinoˑn i (1459 Wel 2:69a) the son of heaven rejects our doctrine and pursues alien teachings from distant places. kos.kaˑhoˑnon t oyˑlan mul meˑkiti malla (?1517-¹No 1:35b) when one is trying hard let water not be drunk. naˑ'y saˑwonaˑwon ¨ilˑlan kwoˑthiˑkwo noˑm oy saˑwonaˑwon ¨ilˑlan kwoˑthiˑti maˑlwolˑt iˑn i (1518 Sohak-cho 8:15a; noˑm is smudged) one should correct one's own bad deeds and not correct the bad deeds of others. ¨tywohon

¨ilˑlan naˑ'y key pwoˑnayˑGwo kwuˑcun ¨ilˑlan noˑm oy keyˑcwunuˑn i (1464 Kumkang 21b) sends good things to me and gives bad things to others. swulˑlan homa maop.swo (1676 Sin.e 1:19b) give up drinking now.

¶mozomˑoˑlan aˑni tasˑkwo (1449 Kok 121) not cultivating one's mind. ˑtye ¨SOYNG hon ¨saloˑm oy twuˑlyeˑwun kuliˑmeyˑpwo.m oˑlan ilˑhwuˑm ul muˑsu.k iˑla hoˑl ywo (1462 ¹Nung 2:81a) when the man who has cataracts sees a round image what does he call it? KHWONG-CWONGˑon ¨NGWUWˑlan QUYˑGwaˑKYEY ˑGwaˑ'yˑla niloˑkwo KHWONGˑoˑlan NGWEN-SSYENGˑiˑla nilokeˑtun (1465 Wen 1:1:1:60b) when the Śūnya sects say that reality for us is dependence (on others) and counting everything as real ([PYEN-]ˑKYEY = parikalpita) and they say that unreality is complete perfection, ...

-ulan, 1. → -ulaˑ'n, abbreviation < -ula (ko) han. ¶Ku i tele khenyeng na tele to olaˑ'n māl i ēps.tula They didn't invite even me, much less him.

2. → -ulaˑ'n', abbr < -ula (ko) hanun.

-ˑᵘ⁄ₒˑlaˑ'n SEE - ˑᵘ⁄ₒˑlaˑ'nˑt oy

-ula 'na, abbr < -ula (ko) hana

-ula 'ney, abbr < -ula (ko) haney

-ula 'ni, abbr < -ula (ko) hani. CF ilaˑ'ni, ˑilaˑn i.

-ula 'ni-kka, abbr < -ula (ko) hani-kka. ¶Na kala 'ni-kka (Dupont 127) [I thought I] told you to go!

-ula 'nta, abbr < -ula (ko) hanta. says/tells one to do. ¶Meli lul etteh.key kkakk.ulaˑ'p.nikka How does he want me to cut his hair? — Nemu ccalpci anh.ulq cengto lo kkakk.e cwusipsio Not too short, please.

-ula 'nta 'yss.ca, abbr < -ula (ko) hanta (ko) hayss.ca. ¶Āmuli na poko i īl ul halaˑ'nta ˑyss.ca naˑn' mōs hakeyss.e Tell me to do this as you will, I won't do it. SYN -ula 'yss.ca.

-ˑᵘ⁄ₒˑlaˑ'nˑt oy, abbr < -ˑᵘ⁄ₒˑla [ˑho]nˑt oy, subj assert + abbr v mod + postmod + pcl. if, when; since (= -ulq kes kath.umyen, -lq cintay). ¶⸺ CYENG-¨SYA ciˑzulaˑ'nˑt oy ilhwuˑm ul ⸺ ˑKUP-KWO-ˑTTWOK NGWENˑiˑla hoˑla (1447 Sek 6:40a) [the two together] set to build the monastery, so call it Anāthapiṇḍada's Garden [With Prince Jeta's Trees]. ˑileˑ'n ¨saloˑm i QAN-ˑLAKˑol pwoˑlaˑ'nˑt oyˑPWOK moyngˑkoˑla ¨THWO-ˑTIˑlol kaˑphwolqˑt i

'Ge ˙nul (1459 Wel 21:125a) if such people enjoy peace and joy they create happiness and make up for the earth [that is needed to build a monastery], and so ... . [KWANG SAN] s ˙kul nilk˙ten sta˙h ay me˙li ¨syeyla 'n ˙t oy ¨tywohi two˙la ¨wol ˙t i.n i ˙'la (1481 Twusi 21:42b) in the land of Guāng Shān where I was studying my hair was turning white; I have well come back. SEE ho˙la 'n ˙t oy, ˙hosila 'n ˙t oy.

-ula 'nun, abbr < -ula (ko) hanun. ¶Ku mul un kwāil capswusin hwū ey son ul ssis.ula 'nun kes ip.nita The water is to wash your hands in after you have eaten the fruit. Kisa lul ssula 'nun pūthak ul pat.ess.ta I received a request to write a newspaper article. Chinkwu ka cakkwu hala 'nun tey haci kulay Since your friend keeps telling you to do it, go ahead and do it. Ku tul uy yokwu nun wusen pap ul mek.key hay tālla 'nun kes ita Their demand is that they be allowed to earn their bread first of all. I kes ul hala 'nun twung ce kes ul hala 'nun twung māl i mānh.ta All I hear is do this, do that. Hako mānh.un sālam kawuntey way na poko ku īl ul hala 'nun ya Why do you pick me among all the people to do the work? Kel.umye ka ani 'la tallimye ce phyocek ul mac.hila 'nun ke 'ta They want us to hit that target running, not walking. Ileh.ta celeh.ta māl haci mālko, hala 'nun tay lo hay la Stop fussing and do what you are told. Way kuleni, nwu ka kaci mālla 'nun ka 'm? What is your trouble — is anyone keeping you from going?!

-ula 'o, abbr < -ula (ko) hao

-ula 'p.nita, abbr < -ula (ko) hap.nita tells one to do.

-ula 'ta, abbr < -ula (ko) hata

-ula 'tey, abbr < -ula (ko) hatey

-ula 'ti, abbr < -ula (ko) hati

-ula 'toy, abbr < -ula (ko) hatoy

-ula tul, subj attent + pcl. ¶Pang sōcey com hala tul You kids clean up your room a little!

-ula 'tula, abbr < -ula (ko) hatula

-ula 'tun, abbr < -ula (ko) hatun

˙ula˙wa, pcl. SEE ˙ola˙wa, la˙wa, ˙ila˙wa.

-ula 'y, abbr < -ula (ko) hay: ~ to, ~ la, ~ se, ~ ya, ~ yo.

1. says / tells one to do. ¶Ku lul ola 'y se kath.i nōlca Let's ask him to come play with us. Ku lul kot ola 'y ya toykeyss.ta I must tell him to come at once.

2. [? DIAL] ¶Na com pola 'y Look at me (I tell you)!

-ulayki, [var] = -ulaki

-ula 'yss.ca, abbr < -ula (ko) hayss.ca. ¶Āmuli na poko i īl ul hala 'yss.ca na n' mōs hakeyss.e Tell me to do this as you will, I won't do it. SYN **-ula 'nta 'yss.ca**.

-ulq cakceng, prosp mod + n. the intention / resolve / decision to do, being decided to do.

~ **ita** is decided / resolved / determined to do, plans / intends to do. ¶Ku tong-an yelqsim hi paywulq cakceng ita I have decided to study real hard during that time.

~ **ulo** with the intention of doing; decides to do and. ¶Uysa ka toylq cakceng ulo Sewul ey wā se tāyhak ey ip.hak hayss.ta Resolved to become a doctor, I came to Seoul to enter the university.

CF **-ulq yēyceng, -ulq sayngkak, -ul they; -ulye, -ule; -ki lo cakceng / cēng hata**.

-ul ccay = -ul ccey → -ulq cey (when). Not from -ul ttay.

-ulq cᵃ/ₑksimyen, prosp mod + bnd postmod. if it is a case of doing, if you like to do, if one does, if it comes to doing, if (it becomes a matter of doing) [LIVELY, JOCULAR, or LIT for -umyen]. ¶Polq cᵃ/ₑksimyen ··· (1) If you ask me ··· , it seems to me that ··· ; (2) In appearance ··· [said in introducing a description]. Tul.ulq cᵃ/ₑksimyen ··· (1) From what I hear ··· ; (2) If you will listen; Just wait till you hear ··· . Ālq cᵃ/ₑksimyen ··· If you know (then tell).

-ulq cek, prosp mod + n. the time when it is / does (or is about to do). ¶Pap ul mek.ulq cek ey son nim i wass.ta A guest came when we were eating. Na nun Sewul kalq cek mata tōngmul-wen ul kwūkyeng hanta I visit the zoo whenever I go to Seoul. ABBR **-ulq cey**. CF **-ul ttay**.

-ᵘ/ₒlq ce˙k uy, prosp mod + n + pcl. ¶pwu¨thye y ˙na˙silq ce˙k uy (1459 Wel 1:8b) at the time when Buddha was born.

-ᵘ/ₒlq ˙cey, abbr < -ᵘ/ₒlq ce˙k uy (when). ¶ ··· tut¨cop˙ti ¨mwot ˙hozo˙wa 'silq ˙cey (1462 ¹Nung 2:2b) when I was unable to hear ··· .

-ulq cey, abbr < -ulq cek (ey) when. ¶kalq cey when one goes. pulk.ulq cey when it is red. koon ilq cey uy sangthay (CM 2:66) conditions when it is high-temperature. celm.es.sul ccey

(1894 Gale 31) = celm.ess.ulq cey when (I was) young.

-ul chām, prosp mod + n. the time / turn to do; when it is about to happen, when one is going (set) to do. ¶**Icey nun Ok.huy ka kuney lul ttwil chām ita** And now it is Ok.huy's turn to swing. **Ney ka kal chām ita** It is your turn to go. CF **-nun / -tun chām**.

-ulq ci, prosp mod + postmod.

1. 1a. (= **-keyss.nun ci, -ul.nun ci**) the uncertain fact that it will be / do, whether it will be / do. ¶**Ku ka olq ci an olq ci molukeyss.ta** There is no knowing / telling whether he will show up or not. **Nwukwu uy khi ka te khulq ci tāy(e) pwā ya ālkeyss.ta** We will have to measure ourselves against each other to see who is taller. **Cangcha musunq īl i sayngkilq ci cimcak ul mōs hakeyss.ta** There is no guessing what will happen in the future.

1b. ~ **mālq ci** whether to do or not. ¶**Mek.ulq ci mālq ci sayngkak cwung ita** I am considering whether to eat or not. **Nal-ssi ka nappe se kalq ci mālq ci hako iss.ta** The weather is so bad I'm uncertain about going. CF **-ulq twung mālq twung, -ulq ka mālq ka**.

2. 2a. ~ **(yo)** I wonder whether it will be/do. ¶**Kulssey kalq ci (yo)** I wonder if he will go. **Kuleh.key sikan i mānh.ulq ci** I wonder if I'll have that much time to spare.

2b. ~ **(to moluta, yo)** maybe / perhaps it will be / do. ¶**Kalq ci (yo), Kalq ci to molunta** Perhaps he will go.

3. ~ **'na** (< **ina**) it is proper / right to do it but. ¶**Cōy lul pwā se nun empel ey chē halq ci 'na** In view of the crime, it is only proper to inflict a severe punishment, but ... . **Sinkan ul ilk.ulq ci 'na kwu hay ya ilk.ci** I ought to read the new books but that means buying them.

4. ~ **'n i** (< **in i**) it is proper/right to do and (so). ¶**Nay ka ilk.ulq ci 'n i co'.yong hi tul.e la** I am to read, so listen quietly (= carefully).

5. ~ **'n i 'la** (< **in i 'la**), ~ **'la** it is proper / right to do; surely will, must. ¶**Haksayng un kongpu ey him ssulq ci 'n i 'la (ssulq ci 'la)** It is proper for students to devote themselves to their studies.

-ulq ci enceng, prosp mod + postmod + pcl (< **-'ulq't iGen'tyeng**). even if; CF **-ul mangceng**. ¶**Kwulm.e cwuk.ulq ci enceng ku hanthey sinsey nun an cikeyss.ta** Even if I starve to death, I won't ask a favor of him. **Cwuk.ulq ci enceng kwusok un pat.ci mōs hakeyss.ta** I'd rather die than be confined. [1]**Nakcey lul halq ci enceng khening un an hanta** I'd rather fail than cheat. [-(ess.)ess.ulq ci enceng occurs.]

-ulq cieta, prosp mod + postmod < -'^{u}olq't iGe'ta]. [lit] = **-e la** (command). ¶**Polq cieta!** Behold! CF **-e cila (ko), -e ciita**.

-ulq ci 'la SEE **-ulq ci** 5

-ulq ci 'la to, [lit]. even though, although, notwithstanding that ... , regardless of (= **-e to**). ¶**Samswu kapsan ul kalq ci 'la to hal māl un hay ya 'keyss.ta** I have to speak my mind now, no matter how far I may be sent in exile for doing so. **Him un yak halq ci 'la to maum un tantan hay ya hanta** You should be firm in mind even though you are weak in body.

-ulq ci 'na SEE **-ulq ci** 3

-ulq cince, prosp mod + postmod < -'^{u}olq't in't ye (1588 Secen 1:8a, 8b). it behooves one to do (= **kkok hay ya hanta**). ¶**Hakto nun Sāse lul ilk.ulq cince** It behooves students to read the Four Books. **Khun mul i naci anh.key halye 'myen san ey namu lul mānh.i sim.ulq cince** To prevent floods we should reforest the mountains. [Past forms occur: -(ess.)ess.ulq cince it behooves one to have done.]

-ulq ci 'n i SEE **-ulq ci** 4

-ulq ci 'n i 'la SEE **-ulq ci** 5

-ulq cintay, prosp mod + postmod (< 't in't oy). [obs] = **-umyen** (if, when). ~ **n(un)** SAME. ¶**Ney ka kuli halq cintay n' na 'n tul** (= **na in tul**) **ecci hal i?** If you do that, what am I supposed to do? [Past -(ess.)ess.ulq cintay occurs.]

-ulq ci nun, prosp mod + postmod + pcl. ¶**Ku sayksi uy maum-ssi ka kowulq ci ettelq ci nun te kyekk.e pwā ya ālkeyss.e** I will not know whether that girl has a nice disposition or not until I have seen more of her. **Ku sālam i onul olq ci an olq ci nun cēmsim ttay ka cīna se ya ālkey toylq ke ya** It won't be clear until lunchtime is over whether he is coming today or not.

-ulq ci puthe, prosp mod + postmod + pcl. ¶**Elma 'na mek.ulq ci puthe al.e kaciko ūmsik ul mantul.e la** Find out how much people will eat before you prepare the food.

-ulq cium [var] = **-ulq cuum**

-ulq ci to SEE **-ulq ci** 2b.

-ulq cuum, prosp mod + noun. about the time when. ¶**Hak.kyo lul kalq cuum ey pi ka oki sīcak hayss.ta** About the time I went to school it started to rain. **Pyēl i pich naki sīcak hako mēn san ey se n' pueng sāy soli ka tullye wass.ta; ilelq/kulelq cuum imyen u^ylyey ku nun cenyek hwū uy sānqpo lul na-kanun kes iess.ta** The stars began to shine and from the faraway mountain came the hoot of an owl; at such an hour it was his wont to go out for an after-dinner stroll.

-ulq cwul, prospective modifier + postmodifier. [-(ess.)ess.ulq cwul occurs.]
  1. the assumed fact that it is to be/do or that one will be/do. 2. the way (how) to do.
  ~ **(lo) ālta** thinks (supposes, assumes, expects, believes) that it or one will be/do. ~ **(ul) ālta** (1) knows (realizes, senses, is aware, recognizes, acknowledges) that it or one will be/do, (2) knows how to do − CF **-ulq swu (ka) iss.ta** is able to do. ¶**Kot tol.a olq cwul lo sayngkak hanta** I think he will be right back. **Ku ka na hanthey phyēnci lul ssulq cwul un mōllass.ta** I didn't know that he was going to write me a letter. **Musunq īl itun ci cengseng ul tā hamyen pōthong sālam imyen sengkong halq cwul ānta** I believe the ordinary person will succeed at anything if he throws himself into it wholeheartedly. **Yenge lul halq cwul āsey yo?** Do you know (how to speak) English? Can you speak English? **Cēncha lul thako keki kalq cwul un moluci man kel.e se kalq cwul un ānta** I don't know how to get there by streetcar, but I can get there on foot. **Nappun kes un an kaluchyess.u!q cwul lo āp.nita** I feel sure they didn't teach any bad things.
  NOTE: Correct the entry **-ulq cwul** in KEd (1301b) to accord with what is said here.

-ule, purposive (**-le** after a vowel or l-extension of -L- stems). (moves) for the purpose of, in order to: **mek.ule** to eat < **mekta, ciule** to build < **cīs.ta, tul.ule** to hear < **tut.ta** (CF **tulle** to enter/lift < **tulta**). Must be followed by a verb of going/coming (except in use 3).
  1. ¶**Na nun īl hale kanta** I am going to work. **Ne lul pole wass.ta** I have come to look at (or after) you. **sālki cōh.un kos ul chac.ule tanita** goes looking for a suitable place to live (in). **hak.kyo ey kongpu hale tanita** goes to school to study.
  2. ¶**tanphung kwūkyeng hale Kumkang san ul chac.ta** visits the Diamond Mountains to see the autumn leaves. **Ku lul pulule ponayss.ta** I sent for him. **Nay ka sik.mo lul sēythak hale ponayss.ta** I sent the maid to do the laundry. **Sikyey lul kochile ponayp.nita** I will send the watch (out) to be repaired.
  3. (in questions, often rhetorical) ¶**Mwe hale cwuk.ni** Why did he (have to) die? [present used for vivid past]. **Mwe hale (= halye ko) īl hay** Why do you work (when you need not)?
  DIAL **-ula, -ulo.** ?< -'u⁄o'l [y]e; CF **-ulye.**

-uleki, suffix; HEAVY ↔ **-ulaki.** diminutive. ¶**kkuthuleki** chips, shaving scraps < **kkuth** end. **cisuleki** remnants, refuse ?< **cīs.ta** aborts. **pusuleki** crumbs, shreds, bits < **pūs.ta** = **puswuta** smashes, breaks. VAR **-uleyki.**

-ule lul, purposive + pcl. ¶**Kakkum nōlle lul kakeyss.^sup.nita** We'll go play sometimes.

-ule nun, purposive + pcl. ¶**Swul mek.ule nun ka to yenghwa pole nun an kakeyss.ta** I might go for a drink but I don't want to go to any movie.

-ule to, purposive + pcl. ¶**Yenghwa pole to an kakeyss.ta 'n māl in ya?** You mean you're not going even to see the movies (or: to see the movies, either)?

-ule tul, purposive + pcl. ¶**Yenghwa pole tul kasey** Let's go see the movie. **Nōlle tul kapsita** (= **Nōlle kapsita tul**) Let's all go have fun.

-uley [DIAL] 1. = **-ulye.** 2. = **-ula 'y.**

-uley, bnd adj-n (~ **hata**). somewhat ... , ...ish. ¶**huy-/hay-kkumuley** < **huy-kkum-uley** whitish. **pulk-uley** reddish. CF **-swukuley** < **-swuk-uley; -(u)muley** < **-(u)m-uley; -ey hata.**

-ule ya, purposive + pcl. ¶**Ām, yenghwa pole ya ka ya 'ci!** Oh sure, by all means I simply must go see the movie!

-uleyki [var] = **-uleki**

'u⁄ol 'Gwa SEE **ul kwa**

ul ha.ye-kum, pcl + adverb [lit] = **eykey** (in causative sentences), **ul sikhye.** SEE **ha.ye-kum, ulo ha.ye-kum.**

-uli → **-ul i**

-ul i < -'u⁄o'l i, prosp mod + postmod.
  1. the one (thing/person) that is to be/do; one who(m)/that ... .
  1a. (epitheme extruded from the subject) one who ... . ¶**kwos 'kwa "KWA-'SSILQ 'Gwa phul [']Gwa namwo '[G]wa [']lol me'ku.l i**

˙two isi[˙]m ye (1447 Sek 3:33b) there are also those that eat flowers and fruit and grass and wood, and ... .

1b. (epitheme extruded from the object) one whom/that ... . ¶ne ˙[G]wa kol˙Wo˙l i ¨ep.su˙n i ˙'la (1459 Wel 18:57b) there is no one to compare with you.

2. the act/fact that it is to be/do. SEE ~ mankhum, ho˙l i ˙za.

2a. (= ~ ˙'la) it is (the fact) that it will do/be [an explicit statement]. ¶[QYENG-¨CYWU] z al˙ph oy ¨nay¨nay pwus˙kuli˙l i (1445 ¹Yong 16) he would be ever embarrassed before the Chief of Heroes. ˙NGWOY-¨TTWOW ˙yn ˙t ol a˙ni cwocco˙Wo˙l i (1449 Kok 99) will not follow any false doctrines.

2b. is it (the fact) that it will do/be? [an explicit question]. ¶[˙SYENG-ZIN SSIN-˙LUK] ˙i e˙no ¨ta sol˙Wo˙l i (1445 ¹Yong 87) how can one tell all the divine power of this saintly man? MYEY-˙HHWOYK e˙nu ˙phul˙l i (1449 Kok 74) how is one to escape confusion?

3. [poetic, lit] = -ulita/-ulila

4. ~ (yo) = -ul ya (rhetorical question). ¶Kongca (i)n tul hūmcel i ēps.ul i (yo) Would Confucius himself lack faults? Ocwuk cōh.un chayk il i (yo) Wouldn't it be a fine book, though?! SEE -ul i yo.

-˙ᵘ⁄o˙l i ˙Ga, prosp mod + postmod + postmod (= ˙ka). will it (do/be)? ¶[˙LWOK-˙KUY] ˙lol ¨salo˙m i si˙le-˙kwom twu˙l i ˙Ga (1481 Twusi 8:3b) [with no coral for the market] will the man be able to maintain his thoroughbreds?

-˙ᵘ⁄o˙l i ˙Ge˙m ye = -ᵘ⁄o˙l i ˙[y]Ge˙m ye, prosp mod + postmod + cop effective subst + cop inf. ¶pwuthye ˙lul ˙NYEM ˙ho˙ya KWONG-˙KYENG ˙ho˙zoWo˙m ye n' ¨ta pe˙se na˙l i ˙Ge˙m ye ... ¨ta pe˙se na˙l i ˙'la (1447 Sek 9:24b) when you show respect in thinking of Buddha all will be shed, and [if ...] they will all be shed. CHYENG-˙CCYENG hon ˙PEP ˙ul e˙lwu poy˙hwo˙l i ˙Ge˙m ye (1459 Wel 2:12a) you can well learn the pure dharma, and ... . ku˙ci ¨ep.sun ˙ptu.t ul ¨ta ¨al˙l i ˙Ge˙m ye (1482 Kum-sam 5:37b) you will be aware of all the boundless meaning, and ... .

-˙ᵘ⁄o˙l i ˙Ge˙n i, prosp mod + postmod + cop effective mod + postmod. ¶¨pi˙non ¨salo˙m ol cwu˙l i ˙Ge˙n i ˙homol˙mye ˙nye-na˙mon ¨chyenlya˙ng is.to˙n ye (1447 Sek 9:13a) will give those to the begging people; are there still other provisions? SAM-˙KAY yey na˙l i ˙Ge˙n i ¨CCWOY-˙PWOK i ¨es˙tyey na ˙ykey pu˙thu.l i ˙Gwo (1482 Nam 1:63a) born (as I am) into the Three Worlds, how can sin or joy attach to me? ˙MYWOW-˙HHAY ˙lol ¨etu˙l i ˙Ge˙n i ¨es.tyey e˙lwu NGEN-˙KYWOW ˙ay pu˙thye ˙KWUW-˙KYENG ˙ol sa˙ma MYENG-˙SWU TYWUNG ˙ey ˙pte ˙tiye isi˙l i Gwo (1482 Kum-sam 5:24b) about to get the wondrous understanding, why would you have adhered to verbal teachings, created limits, and fallen among the many people?

-˙ᵘ⁄o˙l i ˙Ge˙n i ˙Gwa, prosp mod + postmod + cop effective mod + postmod + pcl. ¶hon ˙KEP ˙i ¨nam˙to˙lwok nil˙Ge ˙two ¨mwot ¨ta nilu˙l i ˙Ge˙n i ˙Gwa ku˙le ˙'na ˙tye pwuthye s ˙sta˙h i ˙CCAP ¨mal ¨ep˙si CHYENG-˙CCYENG ho˙kwo (1447 Sek 9:10b) I could not tell it all, to be sure, even if I spoke for over a kalpa (eon), but Buddha's land, to put it briefly, is pure and ... . ne ˙y ˙nwu˙n un pwo˙l i ˙Ge˙n i ˙Gwa mu˙su.k u˙lwo mozom sa˙ma na ˙y cwume˙kwuy pi˙chwuyywo˙m ol TANG ˙honon ˙ta (1462 ¹Nung 1:84a) your eyes may see, but what will you make your heart be that it face the radiance of my fist?

-˙ᵘ⁄o˙l i ˙Ge˙n i ˙'ston, prosp mod + postmod + cop effective modifier + postmod + particle. ¶˙hota˙ka˙i PANG ˙ay ˙tu˙lwolq ˙t in ˙t ay n' ˙kwum˙k ul ye˙le PPYENG ˙ul ka˙hwolGwo˙m ay pan˙to˙ki HE-KHWONG ˙oy ¨na˙m ol pwo˙l i ˙Ge˙n i ˙'ston (1462 ¹Nung 2:122a) perhaps if one enters in this direction it will open holes and tilt the bottle so that we are sure to see emergence into the void. e˙wu˙le swon s patang ˙i ˙ano˙ta ˙hwolq ˙t in ˙t ay n' ye˙huy˙ye ˙CHYWOK ˙i ˙tulwo˙m ay pol˙khwa [= polh ˙kwa] KWOLQ-˙SYWUY y pan˙to˙ki ˙stwo ˙tulq SSI-˙CYELQ s ca˙chwoy ˙lol ¨al˙l i ˙Ge˙n i ˙'ston (1462 ¹Nung 2:114b) when joined, the palms of the hands are said to know, but separate them and at the entering of a feeling the arm and the marrow, too, must be aware of a trace from when it entered.

-˙ᵘ⁄o˙l i ˙Gen ma˙lon, prosp mod + postmod + cop effective modifier + postmodifier. ¶ha˙nol s [¨HEM] ˙un mo[˙]cho[˙]m ay [NAN] [˙]hi sye˙l i ˙Gen malon sep [MWON] ˙ey e˙nu ta˙si ¨ti-˙na ka˙l i Gwo (1481 Twusi 7:9b) at last one finally

stands with difficulty at heaven's cliff but how is one to get past it to the twig gate again?
- ᵘ⁄₀ˑl i ˈGeˑnol = -ᵘ⁄₀ˑl i ˈGeˑnul. ¶ SIM ˑQUY-ˑSIK ˑul yeˑhuyˑl i ˈGeˑnol (1462 ¹Nung 10:14a) when you stand back from the consciousness of your heart ... .
- ᵘ⁄₀ˑl i ˈGeˑnul, prosp mod + postmod + cop lit concessive. ¶ KWONG-ˑTUK ˑi kuˑc i ˈˈep.suˑl i ˈGeˑnul ˑhomolˑmye QA-LA-ˑHAN ˈˈKWA ˑlol ˑTUK ˑˈkey ˑhwoˑm istoˑn i-ngi s ˑka (1459 Wel 17:48-9) if the virtue achievement is boundless does it happen that one is allowed to get the karma of an arhan? SEE hoˑl i ˈGeˑnul.
- uˑl i ˈGeˑta, prosp modifier + postmod + cop effective indic assertive. ¶ ˑTTAY-CCO-PI QWEN-QYANG ˈˈTYWOW ˑ[G]wa KWONG-ˑTUK tas.non na ˈy ˑmwom ˑi ˑCYENG-ˑKAK naˑl ay macwo ˈˈpwoˑl i ˈGeˑta (1459 Wel 8:87a) the mandarin duck of vast compassion and my body which practices the achievement of virtue will meet on the day of sambodhi (Buddha wisdom).
- ᵘ⁄₀ˑl i ˈGwanˑtoy, prosp mod + postmod + cop semi-lit sequential. SEE hoˑl i ˈGwanˑtoy.
- ᵘ⁄₀ˑl i ˈGwo, prosp mod + postmod + postmod (= ˑkwo). will it (do/be)? ¶ eˑlwu niˑcu.l i ˈGwo (1463 Pep 3:56a) can one ever possibly forget? SAM-ˑKAY yey naˑl i ˈGeˑn i ˈˈCCWOY-ˑPWOK i ˈˈesˑtyey na ˈy key puˑthu.l i ˈGwo (1482 Nam 1:63a) born into the Three Worlds, how can sin or joy attach to me? eˑnˈ oy ˈˈTOY ˑyey ˑeˑtin ˈˈsaˑlom ˑi ˈepˑsuˑl i ˈGwo ˈhoteˑla (1586 Sohak 5:48b) asked in which age will there be no nice people. ˈˈcywong ˑkwa mol ˑGwa ˑlol ˑhyenma ˈyn ˑt ol ˈˈall i ˈGwo (1449 Kok 52) I wonder how many slaves and horses there are. haˑnol s [ˈˈHEM] ˑun mo[ˑ]cho[ˑ]m ay [NAN] [ˑ]hi syeˑl i ˈGen malon sep [MWON] ˑey eˑnu taˑsi ˈˈti-ˑna kaˑl i ˈGwo (1481 Twusi 7: 9b) one finally stands with difficulty at heaven's cliff but how is one to get past it to the twig gate again? SYENG-MWUN ˑi KWAN ˑhoˑya WUY ˈˈcyekwoˑmay isˑta nileˑl i ˈGwo (1463/4 Yeng 2:62a) how can the four dogmas be so lacking in greatness that the śrāvaka (hīnayāna disciple in the first stage) would look at them and say "they have a small degree of position"? eˑtuy ˑsten SAM-PWUN ˑi ˈˈmwot koˑca ˑPALQ-ˑPOYK saˑwonaˑWon ˈˈiˑl i isiˑl i ˈGwo (1447 Sek 19: 10b) without three divisions provided, where will there ever be eight hundred bad events?

ˑMYWOW-ˑHHAY ˑlol ˈˈetuˑl i ˈGeˑn i ˈˈes.tyey eˑlwu NGEN-ˑKYWOW ˑay puˑthye ˑKWUW-ˑKYENG ˑol saˑma MYENG-ˑSWU TYWUNG ˑey ˑpte ˑtiye isiˑl i Gwo (1482 Kum-sam 5:24b) about to get the wondrous understanding why would you have adhered to verbal teachings, created limits, and fallen among the many people? SEE hoˑl i ˈGwo.
~ n' (ˑhomolˑmye). ¶ PPWO-TTYEY ilˈGwu.l i ˈGwo n' ˑhomolˑmye hon KYENG ˑey ˈˈta NUNG ˑhi ˈˈSSYWUW-TTI hoˑm ye n' ku YWEN ˑi teˑwuk ˑSING hoˑm ye ku ˈˈsaloˑm i teˑwuk CWON ˑhoˑya pwuthye towoyˑywoˑm i ˑQILQ-ˑTTYENG ˑthwoˑta (1463 Pep 4:75a) as to the question of achieving bodhi (enlightenment), if one obtains everything that one can out of a single sūtra, its causality will all the more carry one and that person gets more respect and is assured of becoming a Buddha. pilo meˑkun ye.s oy ˈˈmwom ˑtwo ˑetˑti ˑmwot ho.l i ˈGwo n' ˑhomol[ˑ]mye [CHYENG-ˑCCYENG PPWO-TTYEY ˈˈKWA] ˑlol [ˈˈKA] ˑhi ˑpolaˑl ya (1579 Kwikam 1:36a; ˈˈmwom = ˑmwom) (the question being that) you may not get even the body of a mangy fox, so how can you expect to see the fruit of pure bodhi (enlightenment)? SEE hoˑl i ˈGwo n'.
- ᵘ⁄₀ˑl i ˈˈGwo, prosp mod + postmod + cop ger: ~ k (pcl). ¶ ˑmwom sswoˑp ol pwo[ˑ]l i ˈ[ˑ]Gwo k (1462 ¹Nung 1:64b) on looking into oneself.
-ulikka, prospective attentive (-likka after a vowel or l-extension of -L- stem). will it do/be? (= -keyss.ni). ¶ Nwu ka halikka (ilk.ulikka) Who will do (read) it? Cikum kot ka olikka Shall I go (and come back) right now? [< -ˑuˑl i ˈ-ngi s ˑka]
-ulikko = -ulikka
-ulila (-lila after a vowel or l-extension of -L- stem) < -ˑuˑl i ˈˑla.
1. (in quotations) = -ulita. SEE ~ siph.ess.ta (under siph.ta).
2. = -ulla 2 (lest, etc.)
3. (it is that) it will do/be; is to do/be; is. ¶ [12800] KWONG-ˑTUK ˑiˑza ˑNGUY-ˑLWON ˑhwolq ˑcwul ˈˈepˑsu.l i ˈˑla (1447 Sek 19:10b) there is just no way one can argue with 12,800 individual achievements of virtue. ˈˈne y hoˑma mas-ˑnazoˑWaˑn i CCYEN-SOYNG ˈˈCCWOY-ˑNGEP ˑul eˑlwu peˑsu.l i ˈˑla ˈhosilˑss oy (1459 Wel 2:62b) you have already faced it; because he

says you are to rid yourself well of the sinful deeds of an earlier life ... . ˙*QILQ-SOYNG* ˙*ay s CHAM-˙HHAK* ˙*ho.ywol* ¨*i˙l i mo˙cho.l i* ʼʼ*la* (1482 Kum-sam 2:1b) declared that the act of pursuing the study of Buddhism for a lifetime would come to an end. *pan˙to˙ki MA-TUNG* ˙*i i˙sye* ˙*za e˙lwu hon ka˙ci* ʼʼ*la nilo˙l i* ʼʼ*la* (1462 ¹Nung 1:17a) Mātanga will necessarily have to be present before we can say that it is the same. *pwuthye towoylq* ˙*t ol* ¨*all i* ʼʼ*la* (1462 ¹Nung 7:26a) knows that he will become a Buddha. SEE *ho˙l i* ʼʼ*la*; -˙*wo.l i* ʼʼ*la*; -*u˙si.l i* ʼʼ*la*.
-ulila ʼci, abbr < -ulila (ko) haci
-ulila ʼki, abbr < -ulila (ko) haki
-ulila ʼko, abbr < -ulila (ko) hako
*-ulila ʼl, abbr < -ulila (ko) hal. Not used (CM 1:403).
-ulila ʼm, abbr < -ulila (ko) ham
-ulila ʼn, abbr < -ulila (ko) han. ~ cuk.
  *~ tul. Not used (CM 1:403).
-ulila ʼna, abbr < -ulila (ko) hana
-ulila ʼney, abbr < -ulila (ko) haney
-ulila ʼni, abbr < -ulila (ko) hani
-ulila ʼnta, abbr < -ulila (ko) hanta
-ulila ʼnun, abbr < -ulila (ko) hanun
-ulila ʼo, abbr < -ulila (ko) hao
- ᵘ/ₒ˙*l i* ʼʼ*la s*, prosp mod + postmod + cop indic assert + pcl. ¶ ˙*i* ˙*non ZYE-LOY s QA-SUNG-KKI KWONG-˙TUK ˙ul nil˙Ge* ˙*two NUNG* ˙*hi* ¨*ta* ¨*mwot ho˙l i* ʼʼ*la s* ˙*ptu˙t ul* ˙*KYELQ* ˙*ho˙ya na˙thwosi˙n i* ʼʼ*la* (1463 Pep 3:47a) this expresses the clear meaning that the tathāgata's asankhyeya (countless) achievements of virtue can never all be told, tell as one will.
- ᵘ/ₒ˙*l i* ʼʼ*la*[ ]*s-ongi* ʼʼ*ta*, prosp mod + postmod + cop indic assert + bnd v polite + cop indic assert. SEE -*u˙si˙l i* ʼʼ*la*[ ]*s-ongi* ʼʼ*ta*.
- ᵘ/ₒ˙*l i* ʼʼ*las˙ta*, prosp mod + postmod + cop retr emotive indic assert. ¶*kutuy* ˙*Gwos na˙kunay* ˙*lul solang* ˙*thi a˙ni* ˙*hote˙tun* ˙*kumwom na˙l ay* ˙*stwo si˙lu.m ul teu˙l i* ʼ*las˙ta* (1481 Twusi 15:31b) if you, indeed, have not cherished the traveler, by the end of the month you will be all the lonelier. ˙*TTWONG-SAN i nil˙Gwo˙toy NGAM-TTWUW* ˙[*G*]*wos a˙ni* ˙*len˙t un* ˙*TUK-SAN s* ˙*HALQ* ˙*ol* ¨*mwot* ¨*al˙l i* ʼ*las˙ta* ˙*ho.ya˙nol* (?1468- Mong 32ab) Dòng Shān said if it had not been for Yán Tóu I would not have known of the thirst of Dé Shān. SEE *ho˙l i* ʼ*las˙ta*.
-ulila ʼtey, abbr < -ulila (ko) hatey

-ulila ʼtun, abbr < -ulila (ko) hatun
-ulila ʼy, abbr < -ulila (ko) hay
- ᵘ/ₒ˙*l i* ʼ*le˙la*, prosp mod + postmod + cop retr assert. ¶*KWONG-˙TUK* ˙*i i˙le tangtangi pwu*¨*thye y towoy˙l i* ʼ*le˙la* (1447 Sek 19:34a) the virtue achievement was such that naturally he was to become a Buddha. ˙*ile* ˙*thu˙s* ʼ*i* [< *ho-˙tu˙s* ʼ*i*] *kwo˙thye towoy˙sya˙m i* ¨*mwot nilo* ¨*hyey˙l i* ʼ*le˙la* (1459 Wel 1:21a) thus it seemed that one could not very well think that he would become transformed. SEE *ho˙l i* ʼ*le˙la*.
- ᵘ/ₒ˙*l i* ʼ*le˙n i*, prosp mod + postmod + cop retr modifier + postmod. ¶ ¨*KWA-ZYEN* ˙*QAK* ˙*u˙lwo THYEN-*¨*HHA* ˙*lol* ¨*nwol˙lay˙l i* ʼ*le˙n i* (1463 Pep 2:28b) indeed would shock the world with evildoing. ¨*nyey s* ¨*hay* ˙*non kas.ka˙wa* ¨*swuy* ¨*all i* ʼ*le˙n i* (1518 Sohak-cho 8:41a) the harm of the old days is readily recognized from up close.
- ᵘ/ₒ˙*l i* ʼ*le˙n i* ʼʼ*la*, prosp mod + postmod + cop retr modifier + postmod + cop indic assertive. ¶[*HHYEN-LYANG*] ˙*ul pilwok phye˙ti* ¨*mwot* ˙*ho.ya* ˙*two* [*LANG-˙MYWOW*] ˙*ay n*ʼ [*NGWU-ZYEN*] ˙*hi ton˙ni˙l i* ʼ*le˙n i* ʼ*la* (1481 Twusi 24:59b) even though wisdom and virtue have failed to develop, one would visit the government offices occasionally. SEE *ho˙l i* ʼ*le.n i* ʼʼ*la*.
- ᵘ/ₒ˙*l i* ʼ*len* ˙*t ay n*ʼ, prosp mod + postmod + cop retr mod + postmod + pcl + pcl. ¶*SAM-PPWO-TTYEY* ˙*lol il˙Gwu˙l i* ʼ*len* ˙*t ay n*ʼ *pan˙toki* ˙*TTAY-SSING* ˙*u˙lwo TTWO-˙THWALQ* ˙*ul* ˙*TUK ho˙l i* ʼ*Ge˙nul* (1463 Pep 2:6b) when you have achieved sambodhi (perfect enlightenment) you are sure to obtain emancipation through the Greater Vehicle (mahāyāna), but ... .
- ᵘ/ₒ˙*l i* ʼ*le˙n ywo*, prosp mod + postmod + cop retr mod + postmod. SEE -*usi˙l i* ʼ*le˙n ywo*.
- ᵘ/ₒ˙*l i* ʼ*lesi˙ta*, prosp mod + postmod + cop retr hon indic assert. ¶*wo˙cik* ˙*PWU-*¨*MWO s* ˙*skuy* ¨*SYWUN* ˙*ho˙ya za* ¨*KA* ˙*hi* ˙*pse kunsim* ˙*ul phul˙l i* ʼ*lesi˙ta* (1586 Sohak 4:9b) only when you obey your parents will you be freed of your worries [conflated spelling of ˙*skuy*; ˙*PWU-*¨*MWO* = ¨*PPWU-*¨*MWUW*, ¨*SYWUN* = ˙*SYWUN*].
- ᵘ/ₒ*l i* ʼ*lota* = -*ulita*; SEE - ᵘ/ₒ˙*l i* ʼ*lwo˙ta*.
- ᵘ/ₒ˙*l i* ʼ*lq* ˙*s oy*, prosp mod + postmod + cop prosp mod + postmod + particle. ¶*THYEN-ZIN* ˙*i mwo˙to.l i* ʼ*l* ˙*ss oy CYE-THYEN* ˙*i* ¨*ta kis.so˙Wo˙n i* (1449 Kok 13) the heavens all

are joyful that the angels will assemble. *MI-ˉMYWOW hon ˝TTWOW ˙ay na˙za ka˙l i ʼl ˙ss oy ˙i˙le ʼn ˙t olwo ˙PEP-HHWA-ˉHHWOY ˙SSYANG ˙ay ta˙si ˙TTI-ˉWUY s ˝ma˙l i ˝ep˙susi˙kwo* (1462 ¹Nung 1:18b) with their progress into the subtle teachings there was thus no more talk of location for the Lotus doctrine study group. *˙NGUY lol pu˙the ˙KWAN ol niluwoy˙ta ˙za pi˙luse CIN-˙CYENG hon SYWUW-HHOYNG i towoy.l i ʼl ˙s oy* (1465 Wen 2:3:2:68a) for only when one raises one's consciousness by relying upon righteousness does proper ascetic practice come into being. SEE *ho˙l i ʼlq ˙s oy*.

- ˙ᵘ⁄ₒ˙l i ʼ˙lwo˙swo-ngi ˙˙ta, prospective modifier + postmod + var cop modulated emotive polite + cop indic assert. ¶*SYEY-PANG ˙ay ˙SYENG-ZIN ˙i ˙nasi˙nwoswo˙n i ˙i ˝HHWUW ˙lwo CHYEN-NYEN ˙i˙m ye nʼ ku ˙PEP ˙i ingey ˙na-wo˙l i ʼlwo˙swo-ngi ˙˙ta* (1459 Wel 2:49a) a sage has been born in the west; a thousand years from now his Law will appear here! *SSIN-˙LUK ˙u˙lwo ˙cu˙mun ˙KEP ˙ey ˝hyeyGa˙l ye two ˝mwot ˝all i ʼ˙lwo˙swo-ngi ˙˙ta* (1459 Wel 21:14a) even if, with supernatural power, I were to reckon for a thousand kalpas (eons) I could not know it. *pan˙toki pwu˝thye y towoy˙l i ʼ˙lwo[ʼ]swo-ngi ˙˙ta ho˙n i* (1463 Pep 1:249a) said he is sure to become a Buddha. SEE *ho˙l i ʼ˙lwo˙swo-ngi ˙˙ta*.

- ˙ᵘ⁄ₒ˙l i ʼ˙lwoswo˙n i, prosp modifier + var cop modulated emotive mod + postmod. ¶*moy˙h ay sye ˝wunon swoli ˙yey ˙chozom sa˙hwo.m ol tulu˙l i ʼ˙lwoswo˙n i namwo ˙ci˙non nwol˙Gay non ˝cyeki mozol˙h olwo ˙na ˙wonwos˙ta* (1481 Twusi 7:39a) with the sound of wailing from the moor I first hear the warfare, then a few wood-chopping songs emerge from the village. *pan˙toki cwu˙ki˙l i ʼ˙lwoswo˙n i* (1463 Pep 2:240a) since he will inevitably kill me. SEE *ho˙l i ʼ˙lwoswo˙n i*.

- ˙ᵘ⁄ₒ˙l i ʼlwoswo˙n ye, prosp mod + postmod + var cop emotive mod + postmod. ¶*TWOW-˙LI THYEN ˙ey mwo˙ta ˙ys.no˙n i ˙lol ˝ne y ˙SWU ˙lol ˝all i ʼ˙lwoswo˙n ye* (1459 Wel 21:14a) those who are assembled in the Indra heaven (Trāyastriṁśa), would you know their number? *˝ne y palo ˝al˙l i ʼ˙lwoswo˙n ye* (⁇1517⁻ Pak 1:14b) do you understand it correctly? *LYENG KWONG ˙i PWU-IN to˙lye mwu˙le kol˙Gwo˙toy ˝al˙l i ʼlwo˙swon ˙ye ˙i ˙nwu kwo* (1586 Sohak 4:29b; *PWU-IN* < *PWU-[Z]IN*) Lord Líng asked his wife "Do you know? Who is this?"

- ˙ᵘ⁄ₒ˙l i ʼlwoswoy-ngʼ ˙ta: SEE *ho˙l i ⋯*

- ˙ᵘ⁄ₒ˙l i ʼlwo˙ta, prosp mod + postmod + var cop indic assert. ¶*˝ywu˙yey ˙psu˙l i ʼlwo˙ta* (⁇1517⁻ Pak 1:2a) I will spend amply. *˙na y palo ˝al˙l i ʼlwo˙ta* (⁇1517⁻ Pak 1:14b) I understand it correctly. SEE *ho˙l i ʼlwo˙ta*.

- ˙ᵘ⁄ₒ˙l i ʼlwo˙toy, prosp mod + postmod + var cop accessive. SEE *ho˙l i ʼlwo˙toy*.

-ul i mankhum, prosp modifier + noun + pcl [ABBR -ul mankhum]. enough to do, as much as necessary for doing. ¶**Na nun cip ul ciul (i) mankhum tōn i ēps.ta** I haven't got money enough to build a house. **Na nun sip-li lul te kel.ul (i) mankhum him i ēps.ta** I lack the strength to walk another ten leagues. **Na nun i hak.kwa lul (i kwamok ul) kaluchil (i) mankhum ānun kes i ēps.ta** I am without sufficient knowledge to teach this subject (this course). **Na nun ku eykey chwungko hal i mankhum ku i hako chin haci anh.ta** I'm not a good enough friend of his to give him advice. **Pay ka an kophul i mankhum mek.ess.ta** I have eaten enough not to feel hungry. **Silhq-cung i nal mankhum can-soli lul hako iss.ta** He complains so much that I get sick of it.

- ˙ᵘ⁄ₒ˙l i ʼ˙m ye, prosp mod + postmod + cop subst + cop inf. ¶*pas˙k on QWUY-NGUY na˙thwo.l i ʼ˙m ye* (1463/4 Yeng 2:19a) on the outside displays a dignified mien, and … . *˙PPWULQ TI-˙KYEN ˙ol ˝yell i ʼ˙m ye* (1463/4 Yeng 2:20a) it opens Buddha's [penetrating power of] wisdom and vision, and … . *wo˙cik [˝SYWUY] y is.kwo [˙TTI] y ˝ep.su˙m ye nʼ ki˙lum ˙ko.t hoy˙ya [= ˙ko.t ho˙ya = ˙kot ho˙ya] hulle ti.l i ʼ˙m ye* (1579 Kwikam 1:21b) if you only have water and have no land it flows down like oil, and … . SEE *ho˙l i ʼ˙m ye*.

- ˙ᵘ⁄ₒ˙l i ʼn, prosp mod + postmod + cop mod. SEE *ho˙l i ʼn*.

- ˙ᵘ⁄ₒ˙l i ʼ-ngi s ˙ka, prosp mod + postmodifier + cop polite + pcl + postmod. ¶*sa˙lwo˙m i ˙i˙le khe˙nul ˙za a˙to˙l ol ye˙huy˙l i ʼ-ngi s ˙ka* (1449 Kok 143; *khe˙nul ˙za* < ˙*ho-˙kenul ˙za*) with life the way it is, is one actually to give up a son? *[˙SO-˝CYA] ˙lol pwo˙naysin ˙t ol [˙CHILQ-˙TTOY CI NGWANG] ˙ol ˙nwu y ma˙ko˙l i ʼ-ngi s ˙ka* (1445 ¹Yong 15) he sent his commissioners, but who was to stop the kings of the seven dynasties? [> -ulikka]

-ʔúo'l i '-ngi s ˈkwo, prosp mod + postmod + copula polite + particle + postmod. ¶ *pwuthye s* ˈ*PEP i* CYENG-MI ˈho ˈya cye ˈmun aˈhoy eˈnu tutcoˈWwoˈl i '-ngi s ˈkwo (1447 Sek 6:11a) Buddha's Law is so intricate, how can a young lad presume to take it in? ˈesˈtyey ho.ya ˈza ˈeˈmi NGA-ˈKWUY ˈlol yeˈhuyˈl i '-ngi s ˈkwo ([source?]) just what must I do to get rid of the hungry ghost of my mother? ˈesˈtyey hoˈma taon mwok-ˈswuˈm i eˈnwu teuˈl i '-ngi s ˈkwo (1447 Sek 9:35a) how can a life that is already exhausted get any worse? *cephun* ˈptuˈt i eˈnu isiˈl i '-ngi s ˈkwo (1449 Kok 123) how will one have a feeling of dread?! ˈes.tyey ˈta-mon ˈyelkhwa [= ˈyelhˈkwa] ˈQILQ-ˈPOYK ˈkwa s stoloˈm i.l i '-ngi s ˈkwo (1475 Nay 2:2:72a) how come it is only a hundred and ten? SEE hoˈl i '-ngi s ˈkwo.
-ʔúo'l i '-ngi ˈˈta, prosp mod + postmod + cop polite + copula indicative assertive. ¶ ˈCO-SWON ˈi kuˈchuˈl i '-ngi ˈˈta (1449 Kok 36) [if Buddha's son renounces the world] there will be no more descendants. ˈi tol s ˈsuˈmu ˈnal ˈpsk uy ˈkil[h] ˈnaˈl i '-ngi ˈˈta (?1517- Pak 1:8b) on the twentieth day of this month we will leave. SEE hoˈl i '-ngi ˈˈta. [> = ulita]
-ulini (< -ʔúo'l i 'ˈn i), prospective sequential (-lini after vowel or l-extension of -L- stem). as / since it will happen (= -keyss.uni); this is usually followed by a command, proposition, or statement of volition. ¶ Nay ka si lul ulph.ulini ne nun nolay lul pulle la As I will be reciting a poem, you sing a song.
-ʔúo'l i 'ˈn i, prosp mod + postmod + cop mod + postmod. ¶ na ˈy paˈl ay s hon theˈli ˈlol ˈmwot mwuuˈl i 'ˈn i (1447 Sek 6:27a) will not move a single hair of my foot. ˈPAN-ˈKEP ˈti-ˈnayGwo ˈza QA-LA-ˈHAN ˈol il ˈGwu.l i 'ˈn i (1459 Wel 8:58ab) only after half a kalpa had passed were the arhan (saints) created. ˈSO-ˈPPYENG yeˈhuy.n i ˈza CHYENG-ˈCCYENG ˈul ˈall i 'ˈn i (1465 Wen 2:3:1:110a) only he who has distanced himself from the Four Ailments (mistaken ways of seeking perfection) will know pariśuddhi (perfect purity). ˈilˈlwo puˈthe THYEN ˈSSYANG ˈay naˈl i ˈtwo isiˈl i 'ˈn i (1447 Sek 9:19a) from this / here some will be born in heaven, too. SEE hoˈl i 'ˈn i, -ˈwo.l i 'ˈn i.
-ʔúo'l i '.n i 'la, prosp mod + postmod + cop mod + postmod + cop indic assert. ¶ hon ˈkut ˈtwo ilˈhwuˈm i ˈˈepˈsuˈl i '.n i 'ˈla (1518 Sohak-cho 8:2b) there will be no loss of even an end of it.
-ulinit/ɟa, prospective lit indic assert (-linit/ɟa after a vowel or l-extension of -L- stem). is sure to do, will surely be [old-fashioned – used by old people talking to the young]. ¶ Ku cip un payk-man wen un halinila I tell you the house will certainly cost a million wen. Kulelq pep to iss.ulinila That may well be.
NOTE: The usual form is -ulinila [< -ul i 'n i 'la "it is a fact that it is a fact that one will"].
-ʔúo'l i 'n ˈt ay n', prosp mod + postmod + cop mod + postmod + pcl + pcl. ¶ QIN-ˈKWA ˈlol ˈpsuˈle poˈli.l i 'n ˈt ay n' ˈCI-ˈKKUK hon ˈkhun ˈHHAY '.n i 'ˈla (?1468- Mong 47b) if you sweep away the cause and effect it is harmful to the extreme. SEE hoˈl i 'n [ˈ]t ay n'.
-ˈuˈl i 'n ˈt ye, prosp mod + postmod + cop mod + postmod + postmod. SEE hoˈl in ˈt ye.
-ulio 1. = -ul i yo. 2. → -uˈl i ˈGwo.
-ʔúo'l i 'si.l i 'l ˈs oy SEE hoˈl i 'si.l i 'l ˈs oy
-ulita, prospective assertive (-lita after a vowel or l-extension of -L- stems). SEE -ulila.
1. I (or we) will gladly do it. ¶ Nay ka halita (ilk.ulita) I'll be glad to do (read) it. Ku īl un nay ka math.e polita I'll take care of that.
2. will probably be / do (= -ulq kes ita). ¶ Ku pāym ul kēntulimyen mullilita If you touch the snake you'll get bitten. Ku pyēngsey nun palam ul ssōymyen te halita If you expose yourself to the outside air, your condition (= illness) will get worse.
[< -ʔúo'l i '-ngi ˈˈta]
-ul i tul, prosp mod + postmod + pcl = -ul ya tul
*ul iya (pcl + pcl) → iya. SEE ˈulˈza.
-ʔúo'l i ˈya, prosp mod + postmod + pcl. ¶ ˈnwu ˈy ˈstol ˈol kolˈhoy.ya ˈza myeˈnol ˈi towoyˈya woˈl i ˈya (1449 Kok 36) whose daughter is the one we are to pick as a wife for my son?
-ʔúo'l i ˈye, prosp mod + postmod + postmod (question). ¶ ˈTTAY-SSING ˈun ˈSYEY-ˈKAY pasˈk uy ˈtwo ˈwohiˈlye ˈPEP-ˈSYENG ˈSOYK ˈi is.keˈn i ˈi ˈSO-THYEN ˈi hon-kas ˈˈta ˈˈpwuy.l i ˈye (1459 Wel 1:37a) the Greater Vehicle (mahāyāna) has rather the character of lawfulness even beyond the world; will the four heavens all be empty alike? SAN-HHA ˈˈpwoˈm ay TANG ˈho ˈya LYWUW-

LI ˙lol pwo˙l i ˙ye (1462 [1]Nung 1:58a) facing the sight of mountains and rivers will one see emeralds?

-ʷo˙l i ˙'ye' ma˙lon, abbr < -ʷo˙l i ˙'yen ma˙lon, prosp mod + postmod + cop effective mod + postmod. ¶QON-[˙]HHYWEY ˙za mwo˙lo.l i ˙'ye ma˙lon ¨ney ka˙ci s ¨SSYWUW-¨KHWO ˙lol ¨wuy ˙ho˙ya ˙honwo˙la ([1447→]1562 Sek 3:35a) perhaps I know nothing of my obligation, but I work on behalf of [relieving] the Four Miseries.

-ul i yo [POLITE] = -ul ya (rhetorical question). ¶Na 'n tul (= Na in tul) ecci hal i yo What can I do about that? (= Nobody can do anything.)

-ulq [1]īyu, prosp mod + n. the reason that it is to be/do. ¶Nay ka keki ka ya halq [1]īyu ka eti iss.n' ya Where do you find any reason for me to have to go there? Way kongpu lul an hanun ci molulq [1]īyu 'p.nita I fail to understand why he doesn't study. Way say os ul ipki silh.e hanun ci molulq [1]īyu 'ta I don't see why he doesn't want to wear his new suit. Ileh.ta 'lq [1]īyu ka ēps.ta There isn't any special reason (to speak of).

-˙u˙l i ˙za, prosp mod + postmod + pcl. ¶¨sey˙h ila ˙za ho˙l i ˙'Gwo (1459 Wel 14:31b) they must be three in number. SEE ho˙l i ˙za.

-ulq ka < -ʷolq ˙ka, prosp mod + postmod (-lq ka after a vowel); usually spelled ⋯(u)lkka in South Korea.

1. (the question) whether it is to be/do; will it be/do?; ~ yo SAME [POLITE]; -(ess.)ess.ulq ka occurs.

1a. ¶[1]Nayil to nal i hulilq ka Will it be cloudy again tomorrow? Ku ka way ili lo olq ka Why is he coming this way? Ilk.e man poko ālq swu iss.ulq ka How can one expect to know it just by reading it over? Ku-man kes ul cici mōs halq ka Who can't carry that much on his back? [1]Nayil māl ya wuli yenghwa kamyen ettelq ka How about us, uh, taking in a movie tomorrow? Sēnke ka ecci toylq ka How will the election turn out? Ku kes i elma 'na toylq ka cimcak hay pwā la Guess how much it amounts to. [1]Nayil kwā.yen nal i malk.ulq ka mūncey 'ta It is doubtful whether the weather will be clear tomorrow after all. Na nun i tal welkup ulo sikyey lul hana salq ka mangsel iko iss.ta I am toying with the idea of buying a watch with this month's pay. Ku ka ecci toyess.ulq ka What happened to him? = (1) How can he be like that?, (2) What has become of him?

1b. [rhetorical] ¶Nay khi ka ce sālam chelem ccum ina toylq ka Surely I am tall as he is. Cip cip mata 'na na-wass.umyen īl i toylq ka There'd be no problem if people had come from each house. Nay ka hak.kyo ey tul.e kakey man toymyen elma 'na cōh.ulq ka How nice it would be if only I could get to go to school!

2. 2a. shall we do? = let's do. [Usually with fall-rise intonation.] ¶Kalq ka (yo) Shall we go? Let's go. Ce ccum kkaci ka-polq ka Let's walk on as far as over there. Cacen-ke lul thako kalq ka yo, kel.e kalq ka yo Shall we ride our bikes, or walk? Enu kil lo kalq ka Which way shall we go?

2b. shall I do? = I might as well do; let me just (do). ¶Sensayng nim kkey 'na mul.e polq ka I might just ask the teacher Kiwang on kīm ey com nōlta (ka) 'na kalq ka As long as I am here I may as well stay a while. Kuli 'na hay polq ka I might do it that way.

3. ~ hanta: 3a. is thinking of doing. (CF -ulq ka pota 5b.) ¶Cenyek hwū ey cengkwu lul halq ka hanta I am thinking of playing tennis after supper. Cenyek cen ey hak.kyo ey ka se sensayng nim ul mannalq ka hanta Before supper I think I'll go to school to see the teacher. Ku taum ey nun tose-kwan ey ka se chayk ul pillilq ka hanta Then after that I think I'll go to the library and borrow a book.

3b. thinks it/one might. ¶Hāyng-ye 'na ku ka olq ka hako kitalyess.ta I waited thinking he might just happen along. Pi ka olq ka hay se wūsan ul kacye wass.ta (Im Hopin 1987: 173). I brought an umbrella, for I thought it might rain. Hyeng nim kkey se 'na yōngq-ton ul cwusilq ka hay se chac.e wass.[s]up.nita I came to see you hoping that YOU at least might give me some pocket money, Brother. Tapang ey kamyen sensayng nim ul mannalq ka hayss.e yo (Im Hopin 1987:173) I thought I might see you if I went to the teahouse.

4. ~ mālq ka (hanta) (is) on the point of doing, is just about to do; is hesitating/deciding whether to do or not. ¶Cikum mak kalq ka mālq ka hanun/hatun cwung ita I am just on

the point of going (or: deciding whether to go).
5. ~ **pota** (adj).
   5a. it seems that (it is a question of) its going to be/do; it might, might as well. CF **-ulye 'nun ka pota**. ¶**Pi ka olq ka pota** It seems as though it might rain. **I kes i ku kes pota khulq ka pota** This looks larger than that. **Talun sālam tul i kani na to ka-polq ka pota** Since the others are going, I might as well go, too.
   5b. I think I will, I may. (This seems to be limited to the forms **pota** and **pwā**.) CF **-ulq ka hanta**. ¶**Swul com masye polq ka pwā** I think I'll have some wine. **Īl ul sīcak halq ka pota** I guess I'll get down to work. [1]**Nayil achim ilccik il.e nalq ka pota** Tomorrow morning I may get up early.
   5c. **-ulq ka pon ya** what makes you think I will?! ¶**Ne hanthey cwulq ka pon ya** I would not dream of giving it to you!
   6. perhaps (one may) but. ¶**Sāmu-sil ey se 'na ku lul mannalq swu iss.ulq ka, cip ey se nun mannaki him tunta** You may be able to see him in the office, but it would be difficult to see him at home. **Cikcep ka se 'na yēyki halq ka, cēnhwa lo ya etteh.key yēyki l' hay** We might talk to him directly but how could we dare tell him on the phone?!
- *ᵘlolq ˙ka*, prosp mod + postmodifier (usually spelled *-ulkka* or *-ulka*). ¶ *″nwu ˙lul ka˙colpilq ˙ka* (1449 Kok 143) whom would one compare [with him]? ... *˙kulye ˙za ″a˙zoWol ˙kka* (1445 [1]Yong 43) would we have to record it [his achievement] to know it?! *NAN-TTA y twu˙li˙ye ca˙pa nyehul ˙kka ˙ho˙ya* (1459 Wel 7:13b) Nanda was afraid, thinking they might take him and put him in, and ... . *NGWANG ˙i nil˙Gwo˙toy ″e˙te ˙pwo˙zoWal ˙kka* (1447 Sek 24:43b) the king said "can I see it?".
-ulq ka p'ā = **-ulq ka pwā (se)**. ¶**Pumo tul un pyēng tun atul i cwuk.ulq ka p'ā ⁿyēm.lye hay yo** (1936 Roth 410) The parents are worried that their ill son may die.
-ulq kaps ey, prosp mod + n + pcl. [DIAL] = **-ul mangceng** (even though)
- *ᵘlolq ˙ka s* SEE *s* (pcl) 15c.
-ulq ka tul, prosp mod + postmod + pcl
-ulq ke, abbr < **-ulq kes**
-ulq ke 'ci, abbr < **-ulq kes ici**

-ulq ke l', abbr < **-ulq ke lul** = **-ulq kes ul**. CF **-kenul**. NOTE: **-(ess.)ess.ul ke l'** occurs; in meaning 2 **-ess.nun ke l'** and **-keyss.nun ke l'** occur. When followed by the polite particle **yo** there is reinforcement: **ke l'q yo** /kellyo/.
   1. the thing/one/likelihood to do/be [as direct object].
   2. although, but, in spite of the fact that; anyway; so there! indeed! (despite contrary anticipations or reservations); I guess, maybe. ~ **iyo**, ~ **yo** → **-ulq ke l'q yo** /···ulkkellyo/ SAME [POLITE]. ¶**Ama molusilq ke l'q yo** But you probably wouldn't know, anyway. **Keki n' cham pissalq ke l'** But that place will be very expensive! **Ku nun cikum cip ey se kongpu halq ke l'** I guess he is studying at home now. **Ku moca nun na hanthey com khulq ke l'** I guess the hat is a bit too big for me. **Kil ul mul.umye 'na kamyen molulq ka ku cip chac.ki ka com elyewulq ke l'** The house will be difficult to find unless perhaps you ask along the way. **Ku yenghwa nun cangcha wuli Inchen ey to olq ke l'** After all, that movie will come to us in Inchen in the future.
   3. (I wish I had) but ... (I didn't) — regretting lost opportunities; I should have (but I didn't).
   3a. ¶**Māl ul halq ke l'** I should have said something. **Ku chayk ul salq ke l'** I wish I had bought that book. **Oki cen ey cēnhwa hay polq ke l'** I should have phoned before coming.
   3b. ¶**Ku ka hayss.tula 'myen cōh.ass.ulq ke l'** I wish he had done it, anyway(, but he didn't do it). **Hak.kyo ka ileh.key mēn cwul al.ess.tula 'myen cēncha lul thass.ulq ke l'** If I had known the school was this far I would have taken a streetcar! **Ku kes ul mekci anh.ess.tula 'myen aphuci anh.ess.ulq ke l'** If I hadn't eaten that, I wouldn't have gotten sick (M 1:2:142).
   4. (with question intonation) but I wonder if ... , but do you think ... . ¶**Kel.e naylye kanun key ōylye ppalulq ke l'?** But I wonder if it would be (still) quicker to go down on foot? [1]**Yī wangpi kkey se kuce sāsiko kyēysilq ke l'?** But do you think the Yi queens are still living there as before?
-ulq ke 'l(q), abbr < **-ulq kes il(q)**. ~ **sey**.
-ulq ke l' ipsyo = **-ulq ke l'q yo**
-ulq ke 'la, abbr < **-ulq kes ila**

-ulq ke 'lq sey, abbr < -ulq kes ilq sey. probably will. ¶Mikwuk ey kamyen ku sālam ul mannakey toylq ke 'lq sey When you go to America you will probably meet him. Ku sālam eykey ccum iya cici anh.ulq ke 'lq sey I won't give in to the likes of him. Han salam aph ey cwumek-pap twū-sene kay ccum ssik cwumyen cēmsim i toylq ke 'lq sey If each person is given two or three rice balls, that will do for lunch. Tases salam man onta chiko 'la to mān wen un tulq ke 'lq sey Even though we assume there will be only five guests, it will cost at least ten thousand wen. Āmuli tōn ul cal ssunta hay to Choy pūca chelem kkaci nun mōs ssulq ke 'lq sey However much money you spend you won't be able to match the rich Choy family [of Kyengcwu]. Sīcho ey nun silphay lul hayss.ul mangceng macimak kkuth mayc.ki ey man ila to cal hamyen kwaynchanh.un hyōqkwa lul ketwulq ke 'lq sey Even if you fail at the beginning just so you finally do well at the end at least, you will probably get satisfactory results.

-ulq ke l'q yo (kellyo). SEE -ul ke l'.

-ulq ke n', abbr < -ulq ke nun = -ulq kes un

-ulq ke 'n, abbr < -ul kes in

-ulq ke 'na, abbr < -ulq kes ina (= in ya). [lit, poetic] will / shall I?; (= -ulq ka) shall we, let's. ¶Hwiyengcheng palk.un tal ey nim mac.ulye kalq ke 'na With the moon lit so brightly, shall I go out to welcome my beloved?

-ulq kes < -^{u}/olq kes, prosp modifier + noun / postmod. The most common meaning is 3.

1. a / the matter that is to be / do or that one is to do. ¶Na nun ^{1}nayil kalq kes ita I am to go tomorrow. Tangsin i sangkwan halq kes i ani 'p.nita That is none of your business (M 1:2: 262). Tempinun palam ey chayk ul kacye kalq kes ul ic.e pelyess.ta In my hurry I forgot to bring the book. Ku nun puha tul eykey cochi lul chwī halq kes ul myēng.lyeng ha.yess.ta He ordered his subordinates to take the necessary measures.

2. the one that is to be / do or that one is to do. ¶Ilk.ulq kes i hana to ēps.ta There isn't a thing to read. Aph kil ey kellilq kes i ēps.ta There is nothing standing in my way. Pūthak halq kes i hana iss.e wass.ta I have come to ask a favor of you. An cwulq kes ila 'myen a.yey poici 'na māltun ci If you're not prepared to give it then you shouldn't show it in the first place.

3. the tentative fact or likelihood that it is (to be / do) or that one is to do; probably, likely.

~ ita it is probable (a probable fact) that it will, I think that it will, probably will (do / be). ¶Incey kot tol.a olq kes ita He will be right back. Pissalq kes ita It must be (I bet it is) expensive. Ku kes i elma 'na halq ko hani han chen wen un halq kes ita If I were to say how much it costs, I would say maybe about a thousand wen. Ney nwun ulo pwass.ta 'y ya ku ka kot.i tul.ulq kes ita He will really be convinced only if you tell him that you have seen it with your own eyes. Ku tay lo kata nun ōn caysan ul tā kka mek.key toylq kes ita You keep on at that rate and you will find yourself eaten out of house and home! Emeni kkey se pota apeci kkey se te kippe hasilq kes ita Father will be more delighted than Mother. Ku i ka ōymu cāngkwan i toynta son chitula to Hān-Il kwankyey lul wenman hi hāykyel halq swu ēps.ulq kes ita Even suppose he does become Foreign Minister, I don't think he can resolve Korea-Japan relations in a satisfactory manner. Haki nun kuleh.key toye ya halq kes ia Indeed it has got to be that way. Hata mōs hay tān payk-wen ul pat.e to ku mankhum ^{1}ī lowulq kes i ani 'n ya At the worst, if you get only 100 wen you are at least that much ahead.

¶ ˙mwo˙m ol ¨mwot mi˙tulq ke˙s i˙n i (1447 Sek 6:11b) the body is not to be trusted.

4. reason, point, need, call. SEE -ulq kes ēps.ta.

5. ~ ulo poita [written style] it appears / seems that one will do/be. ¶Cengpu nun ^{1}nayil hōyuy lul kacilq kes ulo poip.nita It appears that the government will hold a conference tomorrow. Ku mūncey ey hap.uy lul poki nun elyewulq kes ulo pointa It seems that it will be difficult to reach an agreement on that question. Ilchak un wuli Hānkwuk sēnswu ilq kes ulo pointa It looks as though one of our Korean athletes will take first place.

6. ~ i = ~ ul but: SEE -ulq kes i, -ulq kes ul.

NOTE: Salq kes ita (1) It's a thing that one will / would buy; (2) It's the one that one will / would buy; (3) One will / would probably / likely buy it. Wumcik ilq kes ita (1) It's the thing that will move (or that one will move); (2) It's the one that is to move (or that one will or is to move), It's the one to move; (3) It is likely to move (or one is likely to move it), it probably moves.

-ulq kes ēps.i, prosp mod + n + adv. without doing (CF **-ci anh.ko, -ci mālko**). ¶**Wuli talun kes kwūkyeng halq kes ēps.i kot siktang ulo olla ka se cēmsim mekci** Let's break off our sightseeing and go right up to the restaurant to have lunch. **Ku sālam ul kitalilq kes ēps.i wuli kkili mence mekci mek.e** Let's go ahead and eat without waiting for him. **i kes ce kes halq kes ēps.i** with no further ado, without making a fuss; including everything, without discrimination. **ileni celeni māl halq kes ēps.i** without saying this or that, without further ado, without any useless objection, with good grace. **Nwukwu nwukwu halq kes ēps.i tā napputa** You are all to blame, every last one of you. NOTE: The particle **i** cannot be inserted. [More examples: Pak Sengwen 297.]

-ulq kes ēps.ta, prosp modifier + noun + qvi.

1. = **-ulq kes i ēps.ta** there is nothing to (do). ¶**Polq kes (i) ēps.ey yo** There is nothing to see/read. **Mek.ulq kes ēps.na yo?** Isn't there anything to eat?

2. [pcl **i** cannot be inserted] there is no need to (do), one need not (do); there is no point in doing; there is no reason/call to do it. ¶**Kalq kes ēps.ta** There is no need to go. **Kongyen hi tto salq kes ēps.ta** There isn't any point in buying another for no good reason. SEE **-ulq kes ēps.i**.

-ulq kes i, prosp modifier + noun + particle.

1. will/would but; although; yet. ¶**Ilenq īl i iss.ulq ka pwā se ilccik-i onta ko han kes i ... (nemu pappe se mōs wass.ta)** I was afraid that this kind of thing would happen, so I meant to come earlier but ... (I was too busy to make it). **Yelum kath.umyen acik hay ka noph.i iss.ulq kes i pelsse hay ka ciko etwuwe onta** (CM 2:219) If it were summer the sun would still be high but the sun is already setting and it is growing dark. CF **-ta ka**.

2. (expected meanings) SEE **-ulq kes**.

-ulq kes kath.ta, prospective modifier + noun + adj. [-(ess.)ess.ulq kes kath.ta occurs.]

1. it seems that it will be/do. CF 1936 Roth 479-80. 2. [less common] it is like the one/thing that will be or that (one) will do (= **-ulq kes kwa kath.ta**). ¶**Olq kes kath.ta** It seems to be coming. (Less common: It is like the one that is to come.) **Ku catong-cha ka ssalq kes kath.ci anh.ta** It is hardly likely that the car will be cheap. **Ōhwu ey pi ka olq kes kath.ta** It is likely to rain in the afternoon. **Etteh.key kichim ul hatun ci kumsey swūm mak.hye cwuk.ulq kes kath.ess.ta** He coughed so hard that I was afraid he might choke to death at any moment. **Ku yenghwa ka caymi iss.ulq kes kath.ta** The movie is likely to be interesting.

3. **-ulq kes kath.umyen** if it seems/happens to be; if it is. ¶**Cwūngyo hanq īl ilq kes kath.umyen kot ku sālam hanthey allisey yo** If it seems to be an important matter, inform him right away. SEE **-ess.ulq kes kath.umyen**.

-ulq kes man siph.ess.ta = **-ulq tus man siph.ess.ta**. SEE **siph.ta**.

-ulq kes ul, prosp mod + n + pcl: SEE **-ulq ke l'**.

1. ¶**Com te khess.tula 'myen nay pal ey mac.ulq kes ul (kulayss.ta)** If the shoes had been a little bigger they would have fit my feet. **Ku īl ul hayss.tula 'myen cōh.ass.ulq kes ul** I wish I had done it (but I didn't). **Ese cip ulo ka ya halq kes ul ney ka way puth-tulko noh.ci anh.nun ya** (CM 2:225) Why are you detaining me when I have to hurry home?

2. (expected meanings) SEE **-ulq kes**.

-ulq ke 'ta, abbr < **-ulq kes ita**

-ulq key, abbreviation. 1. < **-ulq kes i**. ¶**Mues ponaysilq key iss.**ˢ**up.nikka?** Do you have something to send?

2. < **-ulq kes ie/ia**. probably does or is.

3. = **-u' kkey** (immediate future).

-ulq ke ya, abbr < **-ulq kes iya**, < **-ulq kes ia**. ¶**Ku sālam i onul olq ci an olq ci nun cēmsim ttay ka cīna se ya ālkey toylq ke ya** It won't be clear until lunchtime is over whether he is coming today or not. **Kaptong-i chelem ccum man kongpu hamyen Sewul tāy-hak.kyo tul.e kaki mūncey ēps.ulq ke ya** If you study just like Kaptong-i you'll have no problem getting into Seoul University.

-ulq key 'ci = **-ulq ke yci**, abbr < **-ulq kes ici**

-ulq key 'la = **-ulq ke yla**, abbr < **-ulq kes ila**

-ulq key 'na = **-ulq ke yna**, abbr < **-ulq kes ina**

-ulq key 'ney = **-ulq ke yney**, abbr < **-ulq kes iney**

-ulq key 'ni = **-ulq ke yni**, abbr < **-ulq kes ini**

-ulq ke yo = **-ulq key yo**, abbr (1, 2, 3). ¶**Ku**

kes i nwukwu 'n ci n' kot ālkey toylq ke yo You will soon get to know who that is. / That's something anyone will get to know right away.
-ulq ke yo man, abbr < -ul kes io man it probably is but [AUTH].
-ulq key 'ta = -ulq ke yta, abbr < -ulq kes ita. ¶Ne honca man ulo se nun com him tulq ke 'yta It will be a bit hard for you all by yourself.
-ulq key ya = -ulq ke ya, abbr < -ulq kes iya, < -ulq kes ia.
-ulq key yo, abbreviation. 1. < -ulq kes ie(y) yo: now largely replaced by -ulq ke 'ey yo. 2. < -ulq kes iyo [POLITE fragment]. 3. < -ulq kes io probably does / is [AUTH].
-ulq kil, processive modifier + noun. 1. a way to do. ¶halq kil i ēps.ta there is no way to do it. 2. [DIAL] = -ulq īl
-ulq ko < -^{u}olq ˙kwo, prosp mod + postmod (-lq ko after a vowel), often spelled -ulkko; [colloquial; poetic]. the (usually rhetorical, exclamatory, or quoted) question wh-- will (BUT NOT whether ...). CF -ulq ka; ˙kwo. ¶I pi ka ēncey 'na kāylq ko Will this rain (n)ever get around to clearing?! Ku kes i mues ilq ko What might that be? Ku kes i elma 'na halq ko hani han chen wen un halq kes ita If I were to say how much it costs, I'd say maybe about a thousand wen.
? ul kwa, particle + particle. No examples from the modern language; instead, we find kwa lul. The few MK examples of /¨nal˙Gwa/ 'and me / ego' are objects, so that they may be representing *˙na˙lol˙kwa = ¨na l'˙Gwa: ZIN ˙kwa ¨na l'˙Gwa˙pwono˙n i (1447 Sek 13:25ab) 'see the Benevolent (= Mañjuśri) and the ego', ... ¨twu ¨salo˙m i˙Gwo ¨na l'˙Gwa kol˙Gwo.n i nil˙kwu.p i˙n i (1475 Nay 2:1:22b) 'together with two people and me it is seven'. But both the internal structure and a nearby paraphrase cast doubt on that interpretation for ¨nal˙Gwa TA-¨PWOW ZYE-LOY ˙Gwa ˙stwo CYE ˙HWA-˙PPWULQ ¨pwon t i towoy˙n i ˙'la (1463 Pep 4:140a) = na ˙[G]wa TA-¨PWOW ZYE-LOY ˙Gwa ˙HWA-˙PPWULQ ˙ul ¨pwo˙m i towoy˙n i ˙'la (1463 Pep 4:140b) they got to see him himself [the tathāgata] and the Ancient Buddha (Prabhūtaratna) and also the incarnate Buddhas (Nirmāṇabuddha). And that explanation cannot account for /nwul˙Gwa/ (1481 Twusi 8:46b) = ¨nwul˙Gwa (1482 Nam 1:66b) 'with whom', where it may well be a relic of the source of the particle ˙kwa, which I think was contracted from the infinitive form of a transitive verb, probably *(... ul) kol˙Wa < *kolp-˙a 'lining them up, comparing, competing'. NOTE: King 1991a reports that /nalkwa/ 'with me' is found in 1904 Khlynovskiy.

-˙^{u}olq ˙kwo, prosp modifier + postmod (usually spelled -ulkkwo or -ulkwo). ¶cwozo lowoyn kil˙h ey e˙nu na˙l ay ˙za ¨kin [KWA-˙KUK] ˙ul ¨mal kkwo (1481 Twusi 10:27b) just what day (at last) will they give up long spears on the major roadways?
-ulq kyem, prosp mod + noun. combining (one thing); (doing it) with something else; (doing) along the way. SEE kyem. ¶Insa tulilq kyem meych mati cek.ess.^{s}up.nita Please excuse my brevity; this was just a short note to say hello. $V_1 \sim V_2 = V_1 \sim V_2$-ko = V_1-ko $V_2 \sim$ both to do V_1 and to do V_2. ¶Sewul kwūkyeng to halq kyem hōy ey to kalq kyem (or ... halq kyem ... kako or ... hako ... kalq kyem) taum cwuil ey nun Sewul ey kakeyss.ta I am going to Seoul next week both to sightsee and to go to a meeting. Palam to ssōyko chinkwu to mannalq kyem, pataq ka ey osipsio Come to the seaside to enjoy the breeze and see your friends, too. Cha to masiko cōh.un um.ak to tul.ulq kyem Kumkang Tapang ey kaca Let's go to the Diamond Tearoom where we can listen to nice music while we have our tea.
-ulq kyengwu, prosp mod + noun [rare?]. the event / circumstance to do. ¶Pi ka olq kyengwu ey nun hōy lul ¹naycwu lo yenki hanta In case of rain the meeting will be postponed a week.
-ulla [DIAL] = -ulye (Mkk 1960:3:35); = -ula.
-ulla, prospective adjunctive (-lla after a vowel). 1. (= -nula) what with doing. ¶Kongpu halla (phyēnci lul ssulla) cam calq say ka ēps.ta What with studying (and writing letters) I have no time to sleep. 2. [? abbr < -ulila] lest, for fear that it will (introduces a command after a warning). ¶Pi ka olla wūsan kaciko kake la Take your umbrella, for it may rain. Kekceng tul.ulla ese cip ey kake la Go home at once, or you will catch it. Pyēng nalla ku man mek.e la Stop

eating before you get sick. **Ku ay wūlla kaman twue la** If you don't leave the child alone he'll cry. **Kkok cap.e la − noh.chilla** or **Noh.chilla kkok cap.e la** Hold it tight or it will get away. NOTE: M 2:2:434 says that -ulla is essentially sentence-final and that it makes an exclamation with a meaning something like "it is about to happen unless steps are taken to prevent it (or at least cope with it)", those steps often getting expressed in a following advisory command (as in the examples above). CF 1916 Gale 84 *hol.na* [= **halla**] "This form is used as a warning or caution. Be careful."

3. "Used sometimes as a simple future. *loyil kal.na* [= **nayil kalla**] I'll go tomorrow" (1916 Gale 84).

4. [DIAL] -ula = -ulye. ¶**Chayk ul ilk.ulla kwu** [= **ilk.ulye ko**] **hayss.tuni cēnki ka kkunh.e cyess.ta** I was about to read a book when the lights went out. CF -*u'la*.

5. SEE -ess.ulla, -ulla ko/kwu.

-ulla chimyen, prospective adjunctive + vt conditional. [DIAL] ("if you consider what with doing" =) whenever, if (= -umyen). ¶**Pom i toylla chimyen i san ey kkoch i mānh.i phinta** When spring comes, many flowers bloom on this mountain. **Il.yoil kath.un ttay tōngmulwen ey ka-polla chimyen sālam i koyngcang hi mānh.ta** If you visit the zoo of a Sunday, you will find an awful lot of people there.

-ul lak SEE **-ul ak**. Usual before ⋯ **māl lak**.

-ulla kko [LIVELY] = **-ulla ko**

-ulla ko, prospective adjunctive + particle.

1. ¶**Wēyn ke l' olla ko?** What makes you think he's coming? CF -ki (6).

2. = -ulye ko [S Kyengsang DIAL (Mkk 1960:3:35)].

3. For more on this form, see NKd 1137a (-llakwu).

-ulla kwu = **-ulla ko**. ¶**Āmulye 'ni ku ay ka kulen cīs ul hayss.ulla kwu** Surely he would not have done such a thing?! **Āmuli khi ka khuta hay to na mankhum iya khulla kwu?** However tall he might be, surely he can't be as tall as I am. **Kukcang ey kal lī ka iss.ulla kwu** You can be sure he will not go to the theater (M 3:3:119; more: M 3:3:123).

-ulla 'mon, -ulla 'myen [DIAL] = -ulye 'myen [S Kyengsang DIAL (Mkk 1960:3:35)].

ullang, particle (llang after a vowel); BABYISH or RUSTIC. 1. (= **un**) as for (marking the topic). ¶**Ne llang celi kako ce ai llang ili ola ko hay la** You go over (there) and tell that boy to come here.

2. (= **iyo**) uh, and-uh, don't you know, you see (a kind of pause particle that is similar to Japanese *ne*). ¶**Keki se llang pi lul manna se llang cako se llang ecey wass.ˢo** We were, uh, caught in the rain, and uh, we stayed there overnight, and uh returned home yesterday.

-ullangki yo [DIAL] = **-ulye 'nun ke(s i)yo**. ¶**An mek.ullangki yo?** = An mek.ulye 'nun ke yo? You're not going to eat them?

ullang un, pcl + pcl = ullang

-ulla 'ni [DIAL] = **-ulye 'ni** [S Kyengsang DIAL (Mkk 1960:3:35)].

-ullawi → **-ul nawi**

-ulla 'y (< DIAL abbr of -ulla hay).

1. = **-ulye (ko) hay to** even if wanting/trying to do. ~ **to** SAME. ¶**Kkunh.ulla 'y kkunh.ulq swu ēps.nun sai ka toyess.ta** They are quite inseparably bound up with each other. **Kath.i kalla 'y kwaynchanh.e?** I want to go with you, OK? (or: May I go too? or: Shall we go together [or: with them])?

2. = **-ulye (ko) hay** I will; will you? ~ **yo** (Examples: M 2:2:273). ¶**Poktong-i lang mace sai ka nappe cyess.uni icey n' nwukwu hako nōlla 'y** Who (are) you gonna play with now that you have broken up even with Poktong-i? **Ne ku sālam kwa nay māl halla 'y an halla 'y** Are you going to tell him about me, or not? **Mul com kac' 'ta cwulla 'y?** You wanna bring me some water?

-ulla 'y 'ki = **-ulye (ko) haki (ey)**

-ulla 'y 'ta = **-ulye (ko) hata (ka)**

-ulla 'y ya = **-ulye (ko) hay ya**

-ulla 'y yo [POLITE] = **-ulla 'y**

-ulle, [var] = **-ulla, -ullay**; = **-ulye**; = **-ule**

-ullela (-llela after a vowel) [DIAL] = **-keyss.tula** (future retrospective assertive)

-ullen ka [lit] = **-keyss.tun ya**; = **-ul.nun ci** I wonder if it will. ¶**Kkwum ila to kkwumyen un − cam tulmyen mannallen ka** If I but dream, when I fall asleep I wonder if we will meet?

-ullen ko = **-ullen ka**

-ulleni (-lleni after a vowel) [DIAL] = **-keyss.tuni** (future retrospective sequential)

-ullen ya = **-ullen ka**

-ulley (-lley after a vowel), 1. [var] = -ulla 'y 2. [DIAL] = -keyss.tey (FAMILIAR future retrospective assertive)
-ulleyla = -ullela = -keyss.tula
-ul lī, prosp modifier + postmod. a reason to do. ~ ka iss.na? surely there is no good reason to do or be. ~ ka ēps.ta there is no reason to do or be. SEE lī.
? **ul lo**, particle + particle. Marginally occurs in hypostatic contexts only: "nay ka" lul "na lul" lo kochyess.ta corrected "I" to "me".
? **ullo**, var < ulo, particle. SEE llo.
-ullya [DIAL] = -ulye
-ullye [DIAL] = -ulye
-ullye 'ni [DIAL or emphatic] = -ulye 'ni
-ullyen man (un) [DIAL or emphatic] = -ulyen man (un)
-ul māl, prosp mod + n. the word that one is to do/be: ~ lo nun/ya [lit] speaking of ... . ¶Pūn ham ul cham.ul māl lo nun na to nwukwu mōs-'ci anh.ta When it comes to keeping temper under control, I yield to no man. Ku yak i cōh.ul māl lo ya mues ey 'ta pikil ya?! There is nothing to compare with that medicine for effectiveness.
? **-ul man (ani 'la)**, abbr < -ul i man (ani 'la)
-ul mangceng, prosp mod + bnd n [-(ess.)ess.ul mangceng occurs]. even though, it's true that ... , but (of course); CF -ulq ci enceng, -ki ey mangceng ici. ¶Mom un yak hal mangceng maum un kwut.ta He may be weakly of body but he has a strong will. Kwulm.e cwuk.ul mangceng totwuk-cil un an hanta I'd rather starve than steal. Ney tāysin Sewul ey nun mōs kal mangceng tose-kwan ey ya mōs ka cwukeyss.ni?! While I can't go to Seoul for you, it's true, I CAN go to the library for you, can't I? Pil.e mek.ul mangceng ku hanthey sinsey nun an cikeyss.ta Even if I were brought to begging, I would never ask a favor of him. Pat.un kyōyuk un ēps.ul mangceng ānun kes i mānh.ta He has had but little in the way of education, it's true, but he knows a lot of things. El.e cwuk.ul mangceng kyeq pul un an ccōynta "I will not stoop to warm myself with fire made from rice hulls even if I freeze" = I maintain my pride even at the price of discomfort/distress.
-ul man hata, prosp modifier + adj postmod. SEE man hata.

-ul mankhum, abbr < -ul i mankhum
-ul maum, prosp mod + noun. a mind to (do), the intention of (doing), a desire to (do). ¶Kulel maum i ēps.e I have no intention of doing so; I have no desire to do so. Tāyhak-wen ey ip.hak ul hal maum i iss.ta I have it in mind to go to graduate school; I would like to go to graduate school. ¹Yehayng hal maum iss.ta (maum ul mek.ess.ta) (1936 Roth 206) I have it in mind to take a trip.
-ul mo.yang, prosp mod + n. the appearance of going to do/be.
    ~ ita appears about to do, seems/looks as if it will do, shows signs of becoming/being. ¶Nwūn i ol mo.yang ita It looks like it's going to snow.
    ? *~ ulo No examples.
-ul nalum, prosp mod + postmod. depending on ... . ~ ita it depends upon ... . SEE nalum.
-ul.nun, prosp proc mod. Attaches to any stem (v, adj, cop) but occurs only before postmod ci; CF -ulq (ci), -keyss.nun (ci). ~ ci:
    1. (the uncertain fact) whether it will do/be. ¶ecci toyl.nun ci maum coita worries about what will happen. Ku kes ul phal.nun ci mul.e polq ka Shall we ask them if they are going to sell it? Pi ka ol.nun ci ka mūncey 'ta (CM 2:225) The problem is whether it will rain.
    2. ~ ci (to moluta, yo) ("I wonder whether" =) maybe/perhaps it will do/be. ¶Pi ka ol.nun ci (yo) I wonder if it's going to rain. Ku ka kal.nun ci (to molunta) Maybe he will go. Ku ka kass.ul.nun ci (to molunta) Maybe he's left/gone. Tōn i mānh.ess.ul.nun ci to mōlla There may/might have been lots of money.
-ul nyekh SEE nyekh
-ulo [S Kyengsang DIAL (Mkk 1960:3:35)] = -ule
ulo < ᵘ⁄ₒ ˙lwo, pcl (lo < ˙lwo after vowel or l).
    1. (manner) as, in, with; ? SYN ulo sse. ¶hol lo alone, by itself/oneself. hoth ulo singly, in a single sheet. sengsim ulo sincerely, with sincerity, in good faith. sil/cinsil/sāsil lo, cham ulo in fact/truth, as a matter of fact. keth ulo outwardly. sōk ulo inwardly. cikcep ulo directly. kāncep ulo indirectly. haptong ulo jointly. pyel lo (not) especially. say lo newly. sēy ai lul chalyey lo anc.hita seats the

three children in order. **pōthong (ulo)** [better without the particle] as a (as the) usual thing, usually, commonly.

2. 2a. (function) as, for, to be, in the capacity of; SYN **ulo se**. ¶**tāyphyo lo** as representative. **kwun.in ulo Hānkwuk ey kata** goes to Korea as a serviceman. **Mikwuk sālam ulo khi ka cākta** is short for an American. **Ppang un etten kes ulo tulilq ka yo** What shall I bring you in the way of bread? **Nay ka mues ulo ne hanthey kaph.ulq ka** What shall I pay you with? **Mues ulo kāmsa uy phyo lul hal.nun ci yo** What shall we present / give as a token of our appreciation? **Hānkwuk uy ōymu-pu nun Mikwuk ulo chimyen kwuk.mu-seng ita** Korea's Foreign Ministry (if we reckon it in terms of America) is the same as America's State Department. **Mikwuk ulo chimyen cal han sēym ita** From America's standpoint it can be regarded as well done. **Wuli tāyphyo-tan ilum ulo tangsin eykey chwuk.ha lul tulip.nita** I greet you in the name of our delegation. **"Hankul mūn-tap" ila 'n ilum ulo yekk.e nāyta** compiles them under the name / title "Questions and Answers about Korean".

2b. (as a substitute for **ul** when the direct object is the result of a choice). ¶**cōh.un kes ulo koluta** chooses the good ones. **Kanswumey lo kac' 'ta cwusio** Bring us consommé (for the first course). **Wuli Phulangsu ppang ulo haca – ku kes ulo cwusio** Let's make it French bread (rather than some other kind) – bring us that. **Phyoci ka tun-tun han kes ulo kolla cwusipsio** Pick out a well-bound one for me.

3. 3a. (state, status) is and, being as; ? SYN **ulo sse**; CF **iko, iyo, ila, ica**. ¶**Ku ⁿyeca nun Kim sensayng ttal lo Pusan ey sālko iss.ta** She is Mr Kim's daughter and lives in Pusan. **¹yāng ulo 'na cil lo 'na** whether (it be) in quantity or in quality. **mat ulo nata** is born eldest. **cōng ulo nass.ta** was born a slave.

3b. (state or status recognized, known, or thought) to be, as that, knowing it as, in view of; SYN **ulo se**. ¶**Pi lul nwūn ulo al.ess.ta** I took the rain for snow. **Kāq-ca lul cinq-ca lo inceng hayss.ta** I considered the fake to be genuine. **Onul puthe caney lul nay chinkwu lo sayngkak haci anh.keyss.ta** From this day on I shall not think of you as my friend. **Ku i nun sālam ul kāy lo ānun ka pota** He acts as if he thought people were dogs. **Nay kes in cwul lo al.ess.ta** I took it to be (I thought it was) mine. **Sālam uy casik ulo ecci ney ka kulelq swu iss.n' ya** As a human being, how can you do such a thing? **¹Yangsim iss.nun kyōyuk-ca lo kulen māl iya halq swu iss.na?** As an educator with a conscience, how can you say such a thing? **Yelq-sey sal kkaci sōin ulo chinta** Up to thirteen you are considered to be (you are counted as) a minor. **Elin ay ka yang cayq-mul ul sathang ulo ālko mek.ulye tul.ess.ta** The baby was about to eat the caustic soda, thinking it was candy. SEE **(ulo) cwul**.

3c. ~ **poita** it seems to be. [Of limited occurrence.] ¶**Hānkwuk sālam ulo poinun ⁿyeca ka han pen chac.e wass.ta** A woman who seemed to be a Korean once came to call. **Cito lo pointa** It appears to be a map. CF **-un / -ulq / -nun / -tun kes ulo poita**.

4. 4a. (change of state) into; CF **i / ka**. ¶**Khun hakca lo toyess.ta** He turned into (became) a great scholar. **Penhwa hatun sewul i ku man sswuk path ulo pyēn hayss.ta** The once-flourishing capital had been reduced to a mere field of sagebrush. **san i pata lo pyēn hako, pata ka san ulo pyēn hatula to** though the mountains turn to seas, the seas to mountains.

4b. (exchange) for; (purchase / sale) at, for. ¶**hēn kes ul say kes ulo pakkwuta** exchanges an old one for a new one. **chen wen ccali lul can tōn ulo pakkwuta** breaks a thousand wen bill (into small change). **mān wen ulo sata / phalta** buys / sells it for a thousand wen.

4c. (making / arranging it) so that. ¶**haki lo hata** decides / arranges / plans / agrees to do it. **haki lo toyta** gets to, gets so one does, has it arranged so that it / one does; comes to do. **Kakup-cek tōn ul pillye cwuci anh.ki lo hako iss.ˢup.nita** (I have it fixed / decided so that) I don't lend money if I can help it.

5. (means) with, by (means of), using; SYN **ulo sse**. ¶**pihayng-ki lo ota** comes by plane. **pus ulo ssuta** writes with a brush. **inkhu / yenphil lo ssuta** writes in ink / pencil. **khun / cak.un soli lo māl hata** speaks in a loud / soft voice (loudly / softly). **Say hay lul say kipun ulo (sse) mac.i haca** Let us greet the New Year with a new state of mind. **ciph ulo cipung ul īs.nunta** thatches a roof with straw, **kiwa lo cipung ul teph.nunta** tiles a roof. **Um.lyek ulo n' onul puthe lul yelum ila ko hap.nita**

Summer begins today by (according to) the lunar calendar. **Māl pota silqcey hayngtong ulo (sse) mopem ul po.ye cwunta** He gives an example in actual behavior rather than words. **Ku sayngsayng han nāyyong un iyaki lo (sse) phyohyen hanun kes pota chalali yenghwa lo (sse) pōy cwunun key nās.keyss.ey yo** Rather than express that lively content in a story it would be better to show it as a film.

6. (SYN **ulo sse**):

6a. (consistency, constituency) of: ⋯ **ulo toyta** gets / is composed of ⋯ , consists of ⋯ , is made (up) of ⋯ , forms ⋯ . ¶**Ku hālyu ka samkak-cwu lo toye iss.ta** Its lower reaches form a delta. **hoth ulo toyess.ta** is made of (forms) a single sheet.

6b. (content) (full) of, with. ¶**mul lo chata (katuk hata)** is full of water. **I kos un ikkal namu lo katuk chass.ta** This place is full of larch trees.

7. (material) with, of (made) out of; SYN **ulo sse**. ¶**namu / tōl lo ciun cip** a house made of wood / stone.

8. 8a. (the general direction) toward(s), to, (heading) for; CF **ey, ey lul, ul**. ¶**ili lo** this way. **pang an ulo tul.e ota** comes into the room. **Ōyn / palun phyen ulo kasey yo** Go to the left / right. **San ulo (pata lo) kaca** Let's go to (or: head for) the mountains (the sea). **Eti lo na-kanun ya** Where are you off for? **I kil lo kamyen Uycwu lo kako, ce kil lo kamyen Wensan ulo kanta** This road will take you to Uycwu, and that one to Wensan. **thōyq malwu cen ulo anc.ta** sits toward the front of the porch. **Tūl phan ey se sanq kisulk ulo ōn-thong pay namu 'ta** There is nothing but pear trees in the field all the way up to the foot of the mountain. **Tūl phan ey se sanq kisulk ulo ōn-thong pay kkoch i hā.yah.ta** The fields are white with pear blossoms all the way up to the foot of the mountain. **San mith ulo iss.nun cip tul man ku-nyang twunta** They are leaving alone only the houses that are up toward the bottom of the mountain.

8b. = **ey se** (at / from): SEE **ulo puthe**.

9. 9a. (general time) at, in. ¶**Aph ulo tto mannapsita** See you again (in the days ahead). **Sēycong īlay lo** from Seycong's time on.

9b. (timing of a gradual increase) gradually more by (a unit of time). ¶**nal lo** by the day, day by day. **tal lo** by the month, month by month. **Achim cenyek ulo senul hay cinta** It is getting cooler of a morning and of an evening. **Hānkwuk uy kongep un nal lo yakcin hanta** Korea's industry leaps forward by the day.

10. (cause) for, as, with, from, because of, due / owing to; (result) as a consequence of, (in accordance) with. SYN **ulo sse**; SEE **-ki lo, -um ulo**. ¶**Phungnyen ulo in hay se ssalq kaps i ttel.e cyess.ta** With (= because of, as a result of) the good harvest year, the price of rice has fallen. **Phyēyq-pyeng ulo cwuk.ess.ta** He died of / from / with TB. **kāmki lo nwuwe iss.ta** is in bed with a cold. **ku kkatalk ulo** for that reason. **musun tōngki lo** with what motive. **i kes ulo malmiam.^{e}/a, i kes ulo in hay se (in ha.ye)** as a consequence of (or: due to) this. **ttal uy mūncey lo pyēng nakey toyta** gets ill because (as a consequence) of one's daughter's affairs. **yelqsim hi kongpu han tek ulo onul uy sengkong ul hayss.ta** achieved the success of today as a result of (thanks to) one's hard work. **silphay lo ūyki ka cēsang hata** one's spirits drop with (= because of) the failure. **welkan-ci uy yocheng ulo ssuta** writes it at (in response to) the request of a monthly journal.

11. (agent) by. A somewhat literary substitute for **ey(key)** in certain passive sentences.

12. [S Kyengsang DIAL (Mkk 1960:3:31)] = **ul / lul** (accusative marker)

SEE **eykey / hanthey / kkey lo; chiko (se); ulo ha.ye(-kum), ulo in ha.ye, ulo malmiam.^{e}/a**.

NOTE: Occurs with bound preparticles as follows: **sinap ulo** at odd moments, **kakkas ulo** barely, **pa.yah ulo** nearly, **kekkwu lo** upside down, **no-pak.i lo** fixedly (= **puth-pak.i lo**), **ken ulo** in vain, **sayng ulo** raw / unreasonably, **nal lo** raw; ? **ka( )lo** horizontally, ? **sēy( )lo** vertically, ? **se( )lo** mutually.

ulo cocha, pcl + pcl.

1. ¶**Ku nom i cip ulo cocha an kakeyss.ta 'ni etteh.key hamyen cōh.keyss.e** He even refuses to go home; what should I do?

2. [DIAL] = **ulo puthe** from (a distant place). SEE **cocha** 2.

ulo ha.ye, pcl + v literary inf. due/owing to, on account of. ¶**I pen ey palphyo toyn Cengchi Cēnghwaq-pep ulo hay se kwāke uy cengchi-in tul i cengkyey ey na-oci mōs hakey tōyss.ta**

On account of the recently published Political Purge Law politicians of the past have become unable to appear in the political world.

ulo ha.ye-kum, pcl + adv (< v literary inf). ¶Sensayng ulo ha.ye-kum hyāngsang sikhilye 'myen pōswu mānh.i cwue ya hanta If you want to improve teachers, give them rewards.

ulo ka, pcl + pcl. as, with, ... [as subject or as complement of negative copula]. ¶Wuli uy saynghwal un ku tay lo ka nolay 'ta (CM 2:126) Our life is a veritable song. Na nun tangsin uy tong.lyo lo (se) ka ani 'la ... It is not as your colleague (that I speak, but) ... . Cip ulo ka ani 'la kongcang ulo kanun kil ita It's the way to the factory, not home.

ulo kkaci, pcl + pcl. ¶Ku pun un wuli nala lo kkaci wass.^{s}up.nita That gentleman came all the way to Korea. Ce sālam i tāyhak kyōswu lo kkaci toyess.^{s}up.nita He even became a university professor. Pesu lul Ceng-^{1}nung ulo kkaci yencang hanta 'y I hear that they are extending the bus line all the way out to Ceng-^{1}nung. CF kkaci lo.

ulo l' = ulo lul

ulo lang, pcl + pcl. ¶Cenyek imyen wiq cip ulo lang iwus ul kako n' hayss.ta Of an evening I would go visit neighbors up the street.

ulo 'la to, pcl + cop var inf + pcl. ¶Sikan i nuc.ess.uni wuli cip ulo 'la to kapsita The hour is late, so let's go to MY house. Pheyn i ēps.umyen yenphil lo 'la to ssukey If you don't have a pen, write with a PENCIL.

ulo lul, particle + particle (accusative used for emphasis). ¶Caki atul ul cwuk.in nom ul atul lo lul sam.ess.ta He actually adopted the rascal who murdered his son.

ulo mace, particle + particle. ¶Cip ulo mace an kakeyss.ta 'n māl in ka Do you mean you won't even go home?

ulo man, particle + particle. only / just with (as, by, ...). ¶pheyn ulo man ssuta writes only with a pen. I kes ulo man pwā to ku i ka cēngcik han kes ul ālkeyss.ta This fact alone shows how honest he is. CF man ulo.

ulo n', abbreviation < ulo nun. ¶Ku hwū lo n' hyēntay sōsel to mānh.i sse cyess.ta From that time on (= after that) many modern novels got written. Kongep citay lo n' eti ka cēy-il cwūngyo han kos in ya As an industrial region what is the most important place?

ulo 'na, pcl + cop advers. as/with/... or the like; whether as/with/...; as/with/... whatever. ¶^{1}Yang ulo 'na cil lo 'na sitan ey se man hāypang toyn wuli nala uy kipayk kwa ūyki lul polq swu iss.ta Whether it be in quantity or in quality, the spirit and will of liberated Korea can be (fully) seen only in the field of poetry.

ulo 'na-ma, pcl + copula extended adversative. ¶Kōhyang ulo 'na-ma kalq swu iss.umyen elma 'na cōh.keyss.^{s}o How nice it would be if I could go to my old hometown at least. Ppang han ccokak ulo 'na-ma kkini lul ttaywe ya 'keyss.ta For lunch I'll have to make do with a piece of bread at least (if there is no rice).

ulo nun, pcl + pcl. as for (its being) as/with/... . ¶Pōthong ulo nun kuleh.key an hanta We usually don't do that. Cosenq sālam ulo nun khi ka phek khun sālam ip.nita He is awfully tall for a Korean. ^{1}yāngpan ulo nun thāy-naci anh.ess.ci man though he was not born of a noble family. Chinkwu lo (se) nun haci mōs halq īl ul hayss.ta He did something that as a friend he should not have done. Tōn ulo nun nay kyelqsim ul pyēn haci mōs hanta Money cannot induce me to abandon my resolve. I kes ulo nun an toynta We can't do it with this. (This won't do.) Yo say kwunham ul namu lo nun mantulci anh.nunta Nowadays men-of-war are not made of wood. San ulo nun kaci māsey yo Don't go to the mountains. Kwukca cēyceng hwū lo nun yūmyeng han siin i na-wass.ta (With the period) after establishment of the national script, famous poets appeared.

ulo pota, pcl + pcl. ¶I ccok ulo pota ce ccok ulo kanun kes i cōh.keyss.kwun I see it would be better to go that direction rather than this. Hyēnkum ulo pota swuphyo lo cwusipsio I'd prefer to have it as a check rather than in cash.

ulo puthe, pcl + pcl. ¶Hak.kyo lo puthe tol.a olq kes ip.nita He'll be coming back from school (1954 Lukoff 109). Wuli cip ulo puthe hak.kyo kkaci nun yak payk mīthe kālyang toyp.nita [better: Wuli cip ey se (puthe) ...] It is about a hundred meters from my house to school. Ku sālam ulo puthe pat.ulq tōn i elma 'na toyp.nikka [more colloquially: Ku sālam hanthey se ...] How much are you due (supposed to get) from him?

~ ka. ¶San kwa tūl lo puthe ka ani 'la,

palo pata lo puthe pul.e onun palam i kuleh.key hyangki lowa yo The wind that blows not from the mountains or the fields but straight from the sea smells so good.

ulo se < ˙*u̯*o˙lwo ˙sye, particle + particle.

1. an emphatic synonym of **ulo** in some of its meanings, including these:

1a. (function) as, for, to be, in the capacity of. ¶**tāyphyo lo se** as a representative.

1b. (state or status that is thought/known/recognized) to be, as; that, knowing it is, in view of. ¶**Icey nun caney lul nay chinkwu lo se sayngkak haci anh.keyss.ta** I will not think of you as my friend any more.

2. from, from the direction of (= **ulo puthe**). ¶**palam i pata lo se pul.e ota** a wind blows in from the sea.

NOTE: Followed by various other particles:

~ **ka**. ¶**Nay ka hanun kes un kyel kho kongmu lo se ka ani 'la, tā-man chinkwu uy cenguy phyosi lo se ppun ita** My telling you this is not as something official but just as an expression of concern by a friend.

~ **uy**. ¶**kyōsa lo se uy chayk.im** one's duty as a teacher.

~ **to**. ¶**Na lo se to kaman hi iss.ulq swu ka ēps.e** Me being the way I am, I just can't stay quiet.

~ **ya**. ¶**Na lo se ya ku īsang etteh.key hakeyss.nun ka** Me being just myself, what more can I do?

~ **nun**. ¶**Sālam ulo se nun mōs halq kes ita** It is something that one cannot do as a human being.

~ **man**. ¶**Ku i nun yele pangmyen ey se hwal.yak hayss.ess.una, cikum un cwu lo Hān-hakca lo se man ku ilum i nam.e iss.ta** He was active in many fields, but now his name is preserved mainly just as a scholar of Chinese classics.

~ **pota (to)**. ¶**Ku nun cengchi-ka lo se pota to, siin ulo se cal allye cyess.ta** He is better known as a poet than as a statesman.

~ **ppun**. ¶**Nay ka hanun kes un kyel kho kongmu lo se ka ani 'la, tā-man chinkwu uy cenguy phyosi lo se ppun ita** My telling you this is not as something official but just as an expression of concern by a friend.

~ **puthe**. ¶**Wuli nala choki uy, kuliko chōyko uy munhak un hyangka lo puthe sīcak hanta** Korea's earliest and oldest literature begins with the (poems called) **hyangka**.

ulo sekken, particle + particle = **ulo lang**

ulo se 'ni SEE **-ki lo se 'ni**

ulo se nun, pcl + pcl + pcl. ¶**Tōn man ulo se nun ku īl i hāykyel toyci anh.nunta** You can't settle the matter with money alone. **Ne honca man ulo se nun com him tulq ke 'yta** It will be rather hard for you all by yourself.

ulo se to, pcl + pcl + pcl. ¶**Ku sālam ulo se to ecci halq tōli ka ēps.ess.ci yo** Even for him there was no way out.

ulo so 'ni, [DIAL or mistake] = **ulo se 'ni**

ulo sse, particle + vt inf ('using'). An emphatic synonym of **ulo** in certain of its meanings: (means) with, by, by means of, through, using; (constituency, content) made of, formed from, full of/with, (made) out of; (cause) for, as, with, from, because of, due to; (result) as a consequence of, with, in accord(ance) with; ? (state, status) as, being; ? (manner) as, in, with. ¶**sselmay lo sse kata** goes by sled. **mānnyen-phil lo sse ssuta** writes it with a fountain pen. **namu/tōl lo sse cīs.ta** builds it of wood/stone. **Ku nun hakca lo sse Kim paksa wa pīkyo halq swu ēps.ta** He cannot compare with Dr Kim as a scholar. **I lo sse ku uy cin.uy lul cimcak halq swu iss.ta** His true intentions can be surmised from this. **Ku tāyhwa lo sse motwu mūncey ka hāykyel toyki sīcak hayss.ta** As a result of that talk the problems all started to get solved.

~ **to**. ¶**Ku kes ulo sse to an toynta 'myen, tōce hi pul-kanung hanq īl ici** If it cannot be done with that either/even, it must be quite impossible.

~ **nun**. ¶**Han nala tāykwel lo sse nun com cak.un kām i iss.ci** It gives one the feeling that it is rather small for the royal palace of a country, I'd say.

CF **ulo 'ta (ka)**; **-um ulo (se)**.

ulo 'ta (ka), pcl + cop transferentive (+ pcl) [emphatic] = **ulo sse**. ¶**Icey n' mānh.un ke l' kikyey lo 'ta (ka) haki (lo) malyen iey yo** We are arranging to do many things by machine from now on. **Conghap-cek ulo 'ta ka cal tōyss.ta ko polq swu pakk ey ēps.ta** We have to regard it as well done in general.

ulo to, pcl + pcl. as / with / ... also / even / either. ¶**Ku i nun siin ulo to ilum i iss.ta** He is noted also as a poet. **Ku i nun sensayng ulo to sinmun kica lo to silphay hayss.ta** He was a failure both as a teacher and as a newspaper reporter. **Ku cāngkwan un māl lo to pus ulo to hyengyong swu halq ēps.ta** The grandeur of the country is beyond description by speech or ny pen. **Keki nun catong-cha lo to kicha lo to kalq swu iss.ta** You can get there either by car or by train.

ulo tul, pcl + pcl. ¶**Eti lo tul kasip.nikka** Where are you (two / all) going?

ulo uy, pcl + pcl. (the one) as, with, to, ... ¶**san ulo uy kil** the road to the mountains. **cip ulo uy sosik** news (intended) for home.

ulo ya, pcl + pcl. ¶**Cikcep ka se 'na yēyki halq ka, cēnhwa lo ya etteh.key yēyki l' hay** We might talk to him directly but how could we dare tell him on the phone?! **Tasi kōhyang ulo ya tol.a kalq swu iss.na yo?!** How could I dare go back home?! **Pihayng-ki lo ya halwu man ey kalq swu iss.ci** By plane you can get there in a single day.

~ **māl lo** [somewhat awkward]. ¶**Wi lo ya māl lo kaci mōs hanta** It just won't go UP!

-ulq pa, prosp mod + n [lit; -(ess.)ess.ulq pa occurs]. 1. = **-ulq kes**

2. 2a. = ~ **ey (nun)** if / since one is to do; if it is arranged that; if one is obliged to do; if it's a matter of doing (= **-ulye 'myen**). ¶**Īwang tte-nalq pa ey cwuce halq kes i mues iss.na** Since we are leaving, why shilly-shally? **Tōn ul cwulq pa ey nun toytolok ppalli cwusio** If you are going to let me have the money, please do so (give it to me) as soon as possible.

2b. ~ **ey ya** if / since (as long as) one is to do. ¶**Echaphi kkwucwung ul tul.ulq pa ey ya solqcik hakey māl-ssum ina yeccwulq kes ul** As long as I was going to get scolded anyway, I might as well have let him know just what I thought. **Ku kes ul salq pa ey ya cōh.un kes ul sapsita** If we are (supposed) to buy it, let's buy a good one (M 1:2:118).

3. that which is to do (which one is to do).

-ulq pakk, prosp mod + noun [-ess.ulq pakk occurs]. outside of (other than, alternative to) doing: ~ **ey (ēps.ta)** = **-ulq swu pakk ey (ēps.ta).** ¶**Halq īl ēps.uni chayk ul ilk.ulq pakk ey** I have nothing to do but read. **Tōn i ēps.uni pic ul nāylq pakk ey tōli ka ēps.ta** Since I am broke, I've got to get a loan. **Ha to ei ēps.nun swucak ul hani wus.ulq pakk ey (ēps.ta)** His remark is so absurd that I can't do anything but laugh (I can't help laughing).

-ulq pen, prospective modifier + postmod adj-n (? insep). SEE **pen hata**.

-ulq pep SEE **pep (hata)**

-ul ppen → **-ulq pen**

-ul ppun, prosp mod + postmod (SEE **ppun**). ~ **tele**.

'ul pu'the SEE **'ol pu'the**

-'ᵘˡol s, 1. prosp mod (as direct nominalization) + adnominal pcl. ¶*'HHAP 'kwa 'HHAP a'ni 'Gwa s "LI "ta nilo'syan 'ptut tuthul s 'HHWAN-'SYANG 'i.n i* (1462 ¹Nung 2:107a) the meaning of all he has said about the principle of what is meet and what is not meet is [that it is] the illusion of [floating] dust. *ku'chul s 'sus* (1459 Wel 7:58b) = *ku'chul 'sus* (1462 ¹Nung 7:23a) a period of cessation. *"se 'twoy 'tu'lil s HHWA-PPYENG 'ul nwo'khwo* (1459 Wel 10:119a) placing a vase with a capacity of three cupfuls. *pes'kil s kap's ol* (?1517- ¹No 2:17b; *pes-kils-kap-sol*) (contract) copying fee. NOTE: This is probably the source of the ⸺*q* of -'ᵘˡolq.

2. prosp modifier + postmod. ¶*ta'ol s "ep'si* (1462 ¹Nung 1:4b) without ever running out, inexhaustibly; *ta'ol s "ep'se* (1463 Pep se:18a) is inexhaustible; CF *ta'ol "ep.swu'm ul* (1463 Pep 2:131a, incorrectly cited ["*taols*"] by LCT 1973:205 and ["1:131"] 392) with the prosp modifier directly nominalized. *sulphul s "ep.si* (1481 Twusi 25:53a) with no sadness. SEE *(a'ni) hol s; a'ni 'ls; -'ul .s kol'Gwa*.

-ulq sa [poetic, lit] — attaches to v or adj as exclamatory. SEE NKd. [? < -'ᵘˡolq 's ye]

-ulq sa hata SEE **ssa hata**

-ulq salok [DIAL] = **-ulq swulok**

-ulq sang paluta SEE **sang paluta**

-ulq sangpulu hata prosp mod + postmod adj-n [DIAL — Siberian?]. it looks to be. ¶**Nal-ssi ka cōh.ulq sangpulu hata** (1954 Kim Pyengha 231) It looks to be nice weather.

-ulq sang puluta SEE **sang puluta**

-ulq sang siph.ta [var] = **-ulq seng siph.ta.** ¶**I citay nun san.lim pota mokcang i cōh.ulq sang siph.sup.nita** This area would seem to be better for ranches than for forests.

-ulq say, 1. prosp modifier + postmod < *-ulq ˙s oy*. [obs] since, as; while.
   2. = -ulq sai, prosp mod + noun. the time (opportunity) to do.
   3. [? DIAL] = -ul ttay, prosp mod + noun. (the time) when. CF Roth.
   4. → -ulq sey

-ulq sayngkak, prosp mod + n. the thought / idea / plan / intention / hope to do.
   ~ ita is thinking of doing, has the idea to do, plans / intends to do. ¶**I penq ¹yu'-wel ey ttenalq sayngkak ita** I am thinking of leaving (planning/hoping to leave) this June. **¹Yehayng ul mānh.i halq sayngkak ita** I hope to do lots of travelling.
   ~ ulo with the thought / idea / intention of doing. ¶**Cheypho toylq sayngkak ulo teymo lul hayss.ta** They demonstrated with the idea of getting arrested.
   CF -ulq cakceng, -ulq yēyceng, -ul they; -ulye, -ule, -ki lo.

-ulq seks ey, prosp mod + n (+ pcl) [? Cenla DIAL]. despite the fact that one ought / should, although expected (to), while anticipated that. ¶**Kaciko olq seks ey tolie tālla 'nta** He really should have brought it with him, but instead he is asking us for one!

-ulq seng SEE seng (quality)

-ulq seng puluta = -ulq seng siph.ta

-ulq seng siph.ta, prosp modifier + postmod + postnom adj insep. seems (it will), looks like (it would), gives the appearance (of going to do / be). ¶**Nwūn i olq seng siph.ta** It looks as though it were going to snow. **Mul i kiph.ulq seng siph.ta** The water looks (looks as if it would be, looks to be) deep. CF -ulq tus hata.

-ulq seng ulo [? DIAL] = -ulq sēym / sayngkak ulo with the expectation that; with the idea of; with an eye to. NOTE: The example at the bottom of CM 1:135 is rejected.

-ulq sey, prospective modifier + postmodifier.
   1. [? DIAL] = -ney (FAMILIAR indic assertive − with adj and cop). ¶**Cham cōh.ulq sey** That's fine. **I cuum kipun i etten ka − Kuce kule kule halq sey** How are you these days? − I feel only so-so. SEE ilq sey. CF kulssey; -um sey; -ulq si ko.
   2. ~ 'la (< ila) [obs] (there is a fear) lest, there is a danger of; it will, it might / could (= -keyss.ta); in a way so as to avoid / forestall (= -ci anh.key, -ci anh.tolok). ¶**aphulq sey 'la** it might hurt you; lest you feel pain, so there won't be any pain. **Canq ¹yen khaylye 'ta ka kwulk.unq ¹yenq iph tachilq sey 'la** I am afraid you will hurt the large leaves of the lotus in trying to take the small lotuses.
   3. ~ **māl ici** "what fear is there that" = there is no risk / danger of, there is hardly any chance / likelihood that; I ask you now (what chance is there?! etc.); I tell you there's no likelihood. ¶**Pi ka olq sey māl ici** (1) It will be all right if it rains, but it won't; (2) Will it rain? − believe me, it won't. **Namuq kaci lul hana kkekk.ess.ta ko yātan hana namuq kaci ka elma 'na khulq sey māl ici** He is making such a fuss over the branch I broke, but I ask you, how big a branch is it anyway?! **Ku nom i sālam ilq sey māl ici** He isn't even a human being (= You should have nothing to do with him; Never mind what he says).
   4. ~ 'ta → -ul syeyta (1894 Gale 65) = -ulq seng siph.ta (seems).
   5. → -ulq say = -ulq sai, = *-ulq ˙s oy*.

-ulq sēym, prosp mod + postmod. ~ ita, ~ ulo SEE sēym.

-ulq s-i, prosp mod + (postmod s + pcl i) [obs]. the likely fact that it will be / do. ¶**Cēki onun sālam i Pak sayngwen ilq s-i punmyeng hata** There is no doubt that that is old Pak coming from over there.

-ᵘ*olq ˙s i,* prosp mod + postmodifier + pcl. ¶¨*salom mute˙ni ne˙kil ˙ss i* CUNG-˙SSYANG-˙MAN *i˙la* (1447 Sek 9:14a) [the word] CUNG-˙SSYANG-˙MAN means treating people nicely.

-ᵘ*olq ˙s i ˙Gen ˙tyeng,* prosp mod + postmod + cop effective mod + postmod. ¶*wo˙cik a˙pa ¨nim s ˙*PPYENG ˙*i ¨tywo˙hosil ˙s i ˙Gen ˙tyeng ˙mwo˙m ol ˙*POYK-CHYEN *ti ˙Gwuy po˙lye ˙two e˙lyep˙ti a˙ni ho˙n i* (1459 Wel 21:216ab) but even if your father's illness improves, it is not (difficult =) uncommon to discard one's body hundreds of thousands of times. SEE *holq ˙s i ˙Gen ˙tyeng*.

-ᵘ*olq ˙s i ˙Gwo,* prosp mod + postmod + cop gerund. ¶*CWONG ˙on palol ˙ss i ˙Gwo* HHWOYNG ˙*on pis˙kul ˙ss i˙la* (1462 ¹Nung 1:113b) [the word] CWONG means to be upright (= vertical) and [the word] HHWOYNG means to be sideways (= horizontal). SEE *holq ˙s i ˙Gwo*.

-ʷolq ˙s i˙la, prosp mod + postmod + cop indic assertive. ¶ ˙MYENG-CYWUNG ˙un mwok-˙˙swum mo˙chol ˙ss i˙la (1447 Sek 6:3b) [the word] ˙MYENG-CYWUNG means life coming to an end. (Similar examples: 1447 Sek 23:3a, 14a, 14b, 15b; 24:2a, 10b.) ˙TTYWU-TTI ˙non PPYEN-QAN ˙hi ˙TTYWU ˙ho˙ya ka˙cye isil ˙s i˙la (1465 Wen se:5a) [the word] ˙TTYWU-TTI means having a peaceful life. woy˙ywo.m i ˙stwo ˙wol˙hwo.m i˙la hwo.m on ˙˙SSI ˙Gwa PI ˙Gwa y hon ˙˙THYEY ˙l ˙s ila (1482 Nam 1:39a) when we say that being wrong is also being right we mean that yes and no are a single entity. SEE hol ˙s i˙la.
-˙ʷolq ˙s i˙m ye, prosp mod + postmod + cop subst + cop inf. SEE holq ˙s i˙m ye.
-˙ʷolq ˙s i˙n i, prosp mod + postmod + cop mod + postmod. ¶ ˙˙CYEY ˙non ˙kul ci˙zul ˙ss i˙n i (1451 Hwun-en 1a) [the word] ˙˙CCYEY means to create a written composition. (Similar: 1447 Sek 23:3a, 24:2a.) SEE holq ˙s i.n i.

ul sikhye (se) SEE sikhinta. CF ulo ha.ye-kum, eykey.

-ulq si ko [colloq; poetic] = -un tey exclamatory (after certain adjectives only): **Kowulq si ko** = **Kōpkwun** How lovely! **Cōh.ulq si ko** = **Cōh.kwun** How nice!

-˙ʷol ˙s kol˙Gwa (< kol˙Wa), prosp modifier + postmod + vt inf ('lining up the doing').

1. by the time it has happened − translates the Chinese bì-jí … shí (= Japanese … ni na˙tte kara). ¶ tyey ˙ka ˙˙tyem ˙˙e˙tul ˙s kol˙Gwa ˙tye ˙˙twul˙thwo (= ˙˙twulh ˙two) wo˙l i ˙'la (?1517- ¹No 1:66b) = tyey ka tyem etu.m ay micho.m ye n' tye twul[h] two wo.l i ˙la (1795 ¹No-cwung [P] 1:60a) = cyey ka [˙˙TYEM] ul choco.m ay micho.m ye n' (id. [K] 1:61a) by the time I get there and find the shop those two will be getting here, also. ˙cim si˙lwo˙m ul mo˙chol ˙s kol˙Gwa ˙tye ˙two ˙pap-e˙ki mo˙cho˙l i ˙'lwo˙ta (?1517- ¹No 1:45b) = cim sis.ki moschom ay micho.m ye n' cye two pap mek.ki mocho.l i ˙lwota (1795 ¹No-cwung [P] 1:41a) = cim sis.ki moscho.m ay tatolu.m ye n' cye y pap ul stwo mek.e moschol ske.s i.n i (id. [K] 1:41b) by the time we are done getting the packs loaded he will finish eating, too.

2. while; and meantime − translates Chinese bìjí … qíjiān. ¶ ˙ne y pwoy ˙phol ˙s kol˙Gwa ku so˙[z]i ˙yey ˙na y yang ˙sa (?1517- ¹No 2:21a) while you are getting the cloth sold I'll buy some sheep.

-˙ʷolq ˙s ol, prosp modifier + postmodifier + pcl. ¶ SYENG-˙KAK ˙i ˙kus polk˙ta ˙hosya˙m on mol˙ka kwoyGwoy [˙]hi i˙sye pi˙chwuylq ˙s ol nil˙Gwo˙toy MI-˙MYWOW ˙hi pol˙kwo.m i˙Gwo (1462 ¹Nung 4:13ab) his saying that the inherent knowledge is unmistakably bright means it shines in its calm clarity; it is a subtle radiance, and … . ˙˙cyey te nwo˙pha ˙PEP ˙ul ˙˙ep˙siGwu˙m ye ˙no˙m ol ˙˙ep˙siGwul ˙ss ol nil˙Gwo˙toy CUNG-˙˙SSYANG-˙MAN ˙i˙la (1463 Pep 1:172b) [the word] CUNG-˙˙SSYANG-˙MAN [hīnayāna arrogance] means that one, being being superior himself, scorns (the law of) the Lotus sūtra and scorns others.

With a dangling accusative, in valence with whatever verb the copula is propredicating: ˙˙CYWONG-˙˙CYWONG ˙hi ˙PELQ-MYENG holq ˙s ol il˙hwu˙m i ˙MANG-˙˙SYANG ˙i˙n i (1462 ¹Nung 2:61a) the name is "Wild Thought" which means to discover all sorts of things. ˙YWOK ˙ay i˙sywo˙toy ˙YWOK ˙˙ep.su˙m ye TTIN ˙ey i˙sywo˙toy TTIN ˙ol ye˙huyl ˙ss ol ˙SSYEN ˙i˙Gwo (?1468- Mong 63b) and dhyāna means to have no desire in the midst of desire and in the midst of dust to keep one's distance from the dust.

With epithematic identification (a stylistic inversion of the underlying subject = the Identified): cyens˙kos ˙˙cywung i tu˙le ˙˙nay˙Gey hol ˙ss ol nil˙Gwon ˙CCO-˙CO ˙yla (1462 ¹Nung 1:29a) [the word] ˙CCO-˙CO (pravāraṇa = end of restraint) means letting the monks express themselves as they will.

-˙ʷol(q) ˙solwok, prosp modifier + postmod (< ˙s o˙lwo k). the more … the more. ¶ sa˙kwoynon ˙ptu.t un nul˙kul ˙solwok ˙stwo [CHIN] ˙hotwo˙ta (1481 Twusi 21:15a) the older I get the more sociable I feel.

-ulq son, 1. prosp mod + n. the hand / guest / … that will be / do.

2. [obs] prosp mod + postmod s + pcl [var of un]. the likely fact that it will be / do = **-ulq kes (un)**.

3. [obs] prosp mod + postmod s + ? **[i]on** (< ˙i˙ywon, modulated copula modifier). ~ ya, ~ ka, ~ ko will / would it? how can/could it? (rhetorical question). ¶ **Sēysang i n tul kiin sanswu cocha na l' kiilq son ya** People may play tricks on me, but nature will never (do

so). **Insa pyēn han tul sanchen iya kasilq son ya** Human affairs may change, but nature will never change.

-ˈᵘ⁄₀lq ˈs on, prosp mod + postmod + pcl. ¶ *es.ti hol s on i [¨MYEN-ˈTHYEP] kwo* (1795 ¹No-cwung [K] 1:3b; *i* 'this'?) = *es.ti hol s on [¨MYEN-ˈTHYEP] in kwo* (id. [P] 1:3b) = ¨es ˈti hol ˈs i [¨MYEN-ˈTHYEP] ˈin ˈkwo (?1517- ¹No 1:3b) how is one excused from registering?

-ulq sonya → -ulq son ya

-ˈᵘ⁄₀lq ˈs oy, prosp mod + postn + pcl. SEE *holq ˈs oy.*

~ ˈ'la (cop indic assert). ¶ *wu ˈle cwo ˈchwo ˈm on ˈQOY mun ˈtuk po ˈlywo ˈm i e ˈlyewul ˈss oy ˈ ˈla* (1463 Pep 3:97b) that she (the mother) follows them in tears is because it is hard to give up (her) love all at once.

~ ˈ'm ye (cop subst + cop inf). ¶ ˈTTAY-SSING ˈey si ˈhwok tu ˈle ¨HE ˈhosya ˈm on ˈTTAY-SSING ˈay s ¨salo ˈm on ˈHHOYNG ˈi ko ˈcol ˈss oy ˈ ˈm ye (1463 Pep 6:145b) that he sometimes allows [those in] the Greater Vehicle (mahāyāna) to listen is because the people in the Greater Vehicle are perfect in their performance (of the discipline), and ... .

~ ˈ'n i (cop mod + postmod). ¶ ˈQILQ-ˈTTI ˈtwo ˈstwo SAM-CHYEN pas ˈk i a ˈni ˈl ˈs oy ˈ.n i (1482 Kum-sam 5:18a) it is because ... and the one Buddha-nature, moreover, is not other than everything in the chiliocosm (Buddha-world). ˈSSILQ ˈhwom ¨ep.swu ˈm un ˈPEP-¨THYEY KHWONG-ˈCCYEK ˈho ˈya ˈSYANG ˈi e ˈlwu ˈTUK ˈhwol ˈkkes ¨ep.sul ˈss oy ˈ ˈn i (1464 Kumkang 87b) the lack of reality is because the body of the law is beyond materiality and form cannot acquire it (? — or: it cannot acquire form).

~ ˈ.n i ˈ'la (cop mod + postmod + cop indic assert). ¶ ZYE-LOY S CCYWEN-SIN i isil ˈss oy ˈ.n i ˈ'la (1463 Pep 4:89b) it is because it has the tathāgata's whole body (= strength). SEE *holq ˈs oy ˈ.n i ˈ'la.*

-ˈᵘ⁄₀lq so ˈzi, prosp mod + n. (the time / interval) while one does. ¶ *a ˈcik na ˈy ˈpap me ˈkul sso ˈzi l' ki ˈtuli ˈla* (1447 Sek 24:22b) wait a bit while I eat. *pol[h] kwu ˈphi ˈla phyel sso ˈzi ˈyey* (1459 Wel 21:4a) in the interval between bending and spreading one's arm. ˈCANG-¨SSO ˈuy pol[h] kwu ˈphi ˈlak phyel so ˈzi ˈkot ˈho ˈya (1485 Kwan 4b) it is like the interval between a strong man bending his arm and stretching it out ... .

-ˈᵘ⁄₀ls ¨pwun ˈtyeng = ˈᵘ⁄₀l ¨spwun ˈtyeng, prosp mod + postmod + bnd n (postmod / postnoun). ¶ ˈCYWUNG-SOYNG ˈi ˈchozom ¨NAY-CYWUNG ˈul ˈpwozoWols ¨pwun ˈtyeng ˈPEP-SIN ˈon na ˈm ye ˈtu ˈlusya ˈm i ¨ep ˈsusi ˈn i ˈ ˈla (1447 Sek 23:44a) the living beings have only seen the beginning and the end, but the essence of being (dharmakāya) fails to get into them. SEE ¨spwun.

-ul ssa hata, prosp mod + postmod vni. seems. SEE ssa hata.

-ul ssa 'la = -ulq sey 'la (lest, etc.)

-ˈᵘ⁄₀l ˈssoy = -ˈᵘ⁄₀lq ˈs oy

-ulq s-un, prosp mod + (postmod s + pcl un) [obs]. the likely fact that it will be / do = **-ulq kes (un)**. VAR **-ulq son**.

-ulq ˈs un = -ulq ˈs on

-ulq swon(···) = -ulq son (···)

-ul ˈswongi ˈta = -ulq ˈs ˈ[y]wo-ngi ˈ ˈta. SEE *hol ˈswongi ˈta.*

-ulq swu, prospective modifier + noun.

1. an occasion to do / be; a possible / likely occasion (event, happening, instance, situation, case, circumstance); a possibility, a likelihood. ¶**Kulelq swu iss.ta** It may be so; (It) could be; That's possible.

2. a way / means to do; a remedy, a resource, a help; the possibility of doing / being. ¶**Halq swu pakk ey ēps.ta** I just can't help doing it. **Kyengthan haci anh.ulq swu ēps.ta** You can't help admiring them. **Kel.ulq swu pakk ey ēps.ˢup.nita** (1936 Roth 207) We will have to walk. **Mānh.ulq swu pakk ey ēps.ta** There are bound to be a lot of them. **Ku kes i cōh.ci anh.ulq swu** (= **an cōh.ulq swu**) **ēps.e yo** (M 1:2:221) It has to (must) be good; it can't help but be good.

3. the ability / capability / capacity to do; CF **-ulq cwul**. ¶**halq swu iss.ta / ēps.ta** is able / unable to do; can/cannot do. **Na lul towa cwulq swu iss.ˢup.nikka** (1936 Roth 206) Can you help me?

NOTE: The copula form **ilq swu** is little used, despite an example like ··· **sōpak han kes ilq swu pakk ey ēps.ta** 'are nothing if not naive' (Kang Henkyu 1988:288). Where **ilq swu** is wanted, ··· **i / ka toylq swu** can be used instead. But the negative form occurs: SEE **ani ˈ'lq swu**.

-ulq swulok, prosp mod + postmod (< *swolwok* < ˈs o ˈlwo k). increasingly with (being/doing); the more (better, bigger, etc.) ··· the more.

1. ¶**Kalq swulok san ila** The farther we go, the more mountains we encounter (run into). **Khulq / cak.ulq swulok cōh.ta** The bigger / littler the better. **Khun san ilq swulok namu ka mānh.ta** The bigger the mountains are, the more trees they have on them. **Ūmsik un tewulq swulok cōh.ta** The warmer the food is, the better. **Tōn un ssulq swulok sayngkinta** "The more money you spend, the more you'll get" = Don't worry about money; there's more where that came from. **Ku hwacho nun nal i cīnalq swulok khe cinta** That plant gets bigger by the day. **I chayk ul ilk.ulq swulok caymi iss.ta** The more I read this book, the more interesting it is.

2. **(X-umyen) X-ulq swulok.** ¶**Sālam tul un (mānh.umyen) mānh.ulq swulok (te) cōh.ta** The more the merrier. In these expressions **X-umyen** is optional and **te** 'more' is optional before the final predicate. Cf Pak Sengwen 241.

-ᵘ⁄olq ˙s ye, prosp mod + postmod + postmod. (rhetorical question used as exclamation; much like the modern apperceptive). ¶ *YEM-PPWUW-TTYEY ˙yey me˙li ˙sye ˙wosil ˙ss ye* (1447 Sek 23:29a) why, he has come to us in Jambudvīpa from far away! ¨*KHWO lop-˙two* ¨*KHWO lowoyl ˙ss ye* (1447 Sek 24:15b) oh, it is hard, hard! See *holq ˙s ye*.

-ᵘ⁄ol˙ssyᵉ⁄a = -ᵘ⁄olq ˙s yᵉ⁄a = -ᵘ⁄olq ˙s ye. ¶*machi tywohi ne y wol s ya* (1795 ¹No-cwung [P] 2:59b) = *maschi cywohi ney wonata* (id. [K] 2:61b) = ˙*ma˙chi* ¨*tywo˙hi wol ˙s [y]e* (?1517- ¹No 2:66a) how very nice of you to come! = welcome! See *holq ˙s ye*.

-ᵘ⁄ol˙syentyeng = -ᵘ⁄olq ˙s ˙yen tyeng = -ᵘ⁄olq ˙t iGen ˙tyeng. See *hol˙syentyeng*.

-ul syeyta (1894 Gale 65) = -ulq syeng pwuluta = -ulq seng siph.ta

-ᵘ⁄ol(q) ˙ta, prosp mod + postmod. ¶ ¨*ne y na ˙y* ¨*ma˙l ol* ¨*ta tulul ˙tta* [= *tululq ˙ta*] ˙*ho.ya˙nol* (1447 Sek 6:8b) when I asked whether you would heed all of my words, ... ¨*ne y ˙icey ˙two nowoy˙ya ˙nom muyWun ˙ptu˙t ul twul ˙tta ˙ho.yasi˙nol* (1459 Wel 2:64a) asked whether even now you still harbor hateful thoughts toward others, whereupon ... . NUNG ˙*hi han ˙TTWOK ˙ol i˙kuylq ˙ta* (1459 Wel 21:118b) will you be able to conquer the many poisons? *e˙nu cey [˙THOY PWU-ZIN] S [TTANG] wu˙h uy a˙zom ˙tol.h ol mwoy˙hwol ta* (1481 Twusi 8:20a) when will you gather the clan up to the hall of the dowager? ¨*na ˙lol solang ˙ho.ya [NUNG] ˙hi* ¨*twu-[˙]ze [˙CCO] ˙lol ˙se* ¨*nilGwuylq ˙ta* (1481 Twusi 23:44a) will you be able to achieve the writing of a few words [of poetry] with me in mind? ¨*en˙me ˙uy hon ˙phan ˙sik hol ˙ta* (?1517- Pak 1:10a) how much (does it cost) per board? *twolwo pwonayl il i mwos twoyl ta nilusi.m ye n'* [sic] (1676 Sin.e 8:8b; sic *mwos*) when / if he asks whether it will be impossible to send them back, ... See *holq ˙ta*.

~ ¨*malq ˙ta* whether or not. ¶*[NUNG] ˙hi me˙mul ta ˙mal ta* (1481 Twusi 15:42b; LCT 266a has ¨*mal ˙ta*) can I stay [for this year's festival] or not?

-ulq tay lo See **tay lo**

-ulq tey, prosp mod + n. Cf -keyss.nun tey.

1. a place / circumstance to be / do. ¶**salq tey** (= *salq kos*) a place to live. **ssulq tey ēps.ta** is useless, worthless, unnecessary; lacks a place to use it. **kaps i pissalq tey lul mulqsayk hanta** looks for places that will rise in value (bring higher prices in the future).

2. ~ kkaci. ¶**Kitalilq tey kkaci kitalica** Let's wait as long as we can. **Iss.ulq tey kkaci iss.e pokeyss.ta** I'll try to stick around (stay / wait) as long as I can. Cf -nun / -un tey kkaci.

3. → -ul ttay '(time) when'.

-ul the, 1. prosp mod + n. the site / place to do it. ¶**Cip ul ciul the 'ta** It is the place to build the house (= the site to build the house on).

2. prosp mod + postmod = -ul they. ¶**cip ul ciul the ita** = **cip ul ciul they 'ta** is going to build a house.

-ul they, prosp mod + postmod. the intention / expectation to be / do; -(ess.)ess.ul they occurs. See ~ 'ci (yo), ~ yo, ~ ya; ~ 'n ya, ~ 'n i, ~ 'n tey, ~ 'ni; ~ 'm ulo, ~ 'myen.

~ 'ta (= copula ita) intends / expects to, is going to, will (likely); is expected / supposed to. ¶**Phyēnci lul ssess.ni? – Ani, nācwung ey ssul they 'ta** Have you written the letter? – No, I'm going to write it later. **Ku i ka musun māl ul! hatun ci kan ey na nun ku ⁿyeca wa kyelhon hal they 'ta** No matter what he says, I am going to marry that girl.

M 1:2:143 says that this meaning is limited to statements with a first-person subject and questions with a second-person subject. When used with a third-person subject the meaning is one of "supposition or anticipation", with the translations 'I think he / she / it ⋯ ' rather than 'going to ⋯ '. A general translation of **they** is 'what one has in mind (to / that ⋯)', so that 'I have the impression that it will / would ⋯ ' covers many of the 'I think' situations.

CF -ulq cakceng, -ulq sayngkak, -ulq yēyceng; -ulye, -ule, -ki lo.

-ul they 'ci (yo), prosp mod + postmod + cop suspective. ¶**Ku kes un kwaynchanh.ul they 'ci yo** I think it will be OK (M 1:2:143). **Onul kanun kes i cōh.ul they 'ci yo** It will be better to go today, you know.

-ul they 'm, prosp modifier + postmod + cop subst; ~ ulo. ¶**yenghwa lul pokey toyl they 'm ulo** since we are planning to see a movie; since we expect to get to see a film.

-ul they 'myen, prosp mod + postmod + cop conditional. ¶**Sacin ul ccik.ul they 'myen ppalli ccik.usipsio** (M 1:2:404) If you are going to take a picture, hurry up and take it. See also M 1:2:403-4.

-ul they 'na, prospective modifier + postmod + copula adversative or FAMILIAR indic attentive.

-ul they 'ney, prospective modifier + postmod + FAMILIAR copula indicative assertive

-ul they 'n i, prosp mod + postmod + cop mod + postmod. ¶**Ney ka nay māl ul an tul.e pwā (la) hon nako māl they 'n i** If you don't listen to me you'll be in trouble for sure. **Ne na tele silh.ta ko hayss.kes.ta − tasi nun an ol they 'n i** You say you hate me, I won't come again!

-ul they 'ni (PLAIN question) = -ul they 'n ya.

-ul they 'ni, prospective modifier + postmod + copula sequential.

¶**Ku os ul kacici nun anh.ul they 'ni mancye ccum ponun kes un kwaynchanh.keyss.ci?** That dress will not be mine, but may I just try touching it, at least? **Īl ul math.kimyen cal hal they 'ni ⁿyēm.lye māsio** In undertaking the task, I intend to do a good job of it, so don't worry. M 2:2:384 says the subject is usually 1st or 3rd person with verb, always 3d person with adj as in: **Ku ka cikum puncwu hal they 'ni kaci mā** I think he is busy now, so don't go (M 2:2:385). See also M 1:2:372-3, 2:2:384.

~ **(-kka)**. ¶**Ecey ccum Mikwuk ey tōchak hayss.ul they 'ni-kka kot sosik i iss.keyss.ta** He is supposed to have arrived in America yesterday, so we'll be hearing from him soon.

-ul they 'n tey, prosp mod + postmod + cop modifier + postmod. CF Pak Sengwen 135-6.

1. ¶**Kanan han sallim ey kwī han mulken to ēps.ul they 'n tey** (= **the in tey**) One wouldn't expect a poor man's house to have valuables in it. **Ayki ka ani 'l they 'n tey** You are not (supposed to be) a baby, after all! **Cikum ccum un ku i ka pyēngwen ey se na-wass.ul they 'n tey** He must have been discharged from the hospital by now (but I haven't seen him).

2. Preceded by -ess.e to, -ta 'myen, or -tula 'myen: if it had happened ⋯ would have done / been. 2a. ¶**Ilq-cwuil cen puthe man sīcak hayss.e to cikum ccum un tā tōyss.ul they 'n tey** If we had only started a week ago we could be done by now!

2b. With ⋯ cōh.ass.ul they 'n tey: I wish that it had happened. ¶**Kim sensayng i yeki ey wass.tula 'myen cōh.ass.ulq they 'n tey** I wish Mr Kim had come (M 1:2:140).

-ul they 'n ya, prosp modifier + postmod + cop modifier + postmod. ¶**Mek.ul they 'n ya an mek.ul they 'n ya** (= **the in ya**) Do you expect to eat or not? **Han can tul they 'n ya** You want a drink? − here **tul** is prosp mod < tu-l- 'lift'; CF **Han can tul tul they 'n ya** 'You people want a drink?' where the first **tul** can only be the particle marking an explicitly plural subject, the second can only be the prosp mod.

-ul they ya (< ia). ¶**Sēy si kkaci ccum** (= **Sēy si ccum kkaci**) **kitalye pota (ka) an omyen kal they ya** I'll wait till around three o'clock and then if you haven't come I'll leave.

-ul they yo, 1. abbreviation < -ul they 'ey yo < -ul they ie yo. I or you have it in mind (to / that), I / you intend to do; I think (I'm under the impression) that ⋯ . ¶**Ce nun ¹nayil un pappul they 'n tey yo** I think I will be busy tomorrow (M 1:2:144). **Onulq cenyek ey eti kasil they yo** Where are you going to go tonight?

2. prosp mod + postmod + AUTH cop (io).

-ᵘ⁄olq ˙ti⋯ = -ᵘ⁄olq ˙t i(⋯), prosp modifier + postmod + pcl (cop). that it / one will.

SEE -˙wolq ˙t(⋯): ~ iGe˙n i, ~ iGe˙nol, ~ iGe˙nul, ~ iGen ˙tyeng, ~ iGe˙ta, ~ i˙la, ~ ila ˙two, ~ ilwoswo˙n i, ~ ilwo˙ta, ~ i˙m ye, ~ i˙na, ~ i˙n i, ~ i.n i ˙'la, ~ i˙n i ˙'-ngi ˙'ta, ~ in ˙t ay n', ~ ye n'.

SEE -˙wolq ˙tyeyn, -˙wolq ˙tyeyn ˙tye.

-ˈᵘˡolq ˈt iGen ˈtyeng, modulated prosp mod + postmod + cop effective mod + postmod. ¶ ··· kuˈle ˈ'm ye n' suˈsu-lwo ˈSAL [= ˈSALQ] ˈthi aˈnilˈttiGenˈtyeng [= aˈni ˈlq ˈt iGen ˈtyeng] ˈQIL[Q]-"KAN "spwun ˈi.n i ˈ'la (1588 Mayng 14:6a) and then [after killing the relatives] does not kill himself, and yet is just a short distance [from it].

-ˈᵘˡolq ˈt ol, prosp mod + postmod('fact') + pcl. that it/one will. ¶pwuthye towoylq ˈt ol ¨all i ˈ'la (1462 ¹Nung 7:26a) knows that he will become a Buddha. ˈSYEY-CWON ˈi SYWU-ˈTTALQ ˈi wol ˈtt ol ¨aˈlosiˈkwo (1447 Sek 6:20b) the World-Honored, knowing Sudatta was coming ... . ce ˈy ˈmwom cwuˈkul ˈtt ol mwoˈlonoˈn i ˈ-ngi ˈ'ta (1459 Wel 7:18b) is unaware that his body will die. ¨ep.sun ¨HHWUW ˈey ˈza eˈlwu ˈMYWOW-ˈPEP ˈey ˈtul ˈtt ol ¨pwoyˈsi.n i ˈ'la (1463 Pep 1:55b) only after its absence was it possible to show that you can enter saddharma (the wonderful truth of the Lotus sūtra). ˈi ¨saloˈm on ˈTTYEY-ˈQILQ HUY-¨NGWUW hon KWONG-ˈTUK ilˈGwul tt ol ¨all i ˈ'lwo[ˈ]swongi ˈ'ta (1464 Kumkang 72b) this person knows that he will succeed in the rarest kind of virtue achievement. twosˈk uy mululq ˈCYWUNG isil ˈtt ol miˈli ¨alosiˈm ye (1463 Pep 1:168a) knew in advance that there would be a crowd who would retreat to their seat mats, and ... . SEE holq ˈt ol.

?-ˈᵘˡolq ˈt olwo, prosp modifier + postmodifier ('fact') + particle. because it/one will.

-ulq tong-an, prospective modifier + noun. during the interval while (one does). ¶Nay ka kass.ta olq/onun tong-an sinmun ina ilk.e pwā yo Have a look at the newspaper while I am out. Nay īl ul halq/hanun tong-an, caney n' um.ak ina tut.ko iss.key You listen to some music while I am working.

-ˈᵘˡolq ˈtoy, prosp mod + n (place). ¶caˈchwoy eˈlwu puˈthwul ˈtoy ˈep.swun ˈt iˈla (1465 Wen 1:1:1:15b; ˈep.swun = ¨ep.swun) there is nothing one can rely upon in the way of a clue.

-ˈᵘˡol tt··· SEE -ˈᵘˡol(q) t···

-ul ttalum, prosp modifier + postmodifier. just, only: ~ ita it is just/only that ··· . ¶Ku i nun tāmpay man phiwul (phiwuko iss.ul) ttalum iess.ta He was just (sitting there) smoking. Kwittwulami ka wūl ttalum iess.ta The only sound was the chirping of crickets. Nam eykey cōh.unq īl man hal ttalum ita I'm just doing good things for others. Āy man ssul ttalum ita I'm just trying, that's all.

-ul ttay, prosp modifier + noun. the time when (it is/does, was/did, will be/do) — CF -un ttay; -(ess.)ess.ul ttay occurs. SEE ttay.

¶cenyek hal ttay time to make dinner. Sewul ey ol ttay mata every time I come to Seoul. Ku i ka kal ttay na to kakeyss.ta When he leaves, I'll go too. Elyess.ul ttay lul sayngkak hay posio Think of the time when you were a child. kihoy ka iss.ess.ul ttay when I had the chance. ney ka keki kass.ess.ul ttay when you were there.

NOTE 1: Both kapkap hal ttay and kapkap han ttay have the meaning 'when it is boring; when I am bored'. Some do not like the -un ttay version, but it is freely used in Seoul.

NOTE 2: The string -ul ttay '(time) when' is often pronounced the same as -ulq tey.

ul tul, pcl + pcl. ¶Mues ul tul chac.ni What are you people looking for? Sahul ul tul mōs cham.e se kuleh.key yātan tul iyo They are raising a fuss, unable to wait three days for it!

-ulq tus ('i), prosp mod + postmod (+ der adv). as if/though to do/be; tending to. ¶kumpang ttaylilq tus 'i nolye pota glares at you as if he were going to strike you at that very moment. cwuk.ulq tus 'i sin.um hata groans as if he were going to die.

-ulq tus hata, prosp mod + adj postmod. gives the idea/impression that it will; looks as if it would/will. ¶Palam i pūlq tus to hako pi ka olq tus to hata It looks as though there might be wind or rain. CF -ulq seng siph.ta, -ul syeng pwuluta, -ul syeyta.

-ulq tus siph.ta, prosp modifier + adj postmod insep + adj. gives the impression of going to be/do ··· ; feels/looks as if it will/would ··· ; "something tells one it will". ¶Nwūn i olq tus siph.ta It feels like snow. Ku i ka imi ttenass.ulq tus siph.ta I had the feeling he must have already left. Ku i ka keki kass.ess.ulq tus siph.ess.ta Something tells me he has been there (and left). Ku i ka ku īl ul halq tus siph.un ya Is he likely to do that?

-ˈᵘˡolq ˈtwong, prosp modifier + postmodifier. ¶[TTYWEN] hol twong mal twong ho.ye 'la (1730 Chengkwu 104; cited from LCT) it is barely conveyed (?). phuyl stwong mal stwong ho.ye la (1763 Haytong 61) it is about to bloom.

-ulq twung, prosp mod + postmod (< *-ulq ˙twong*). whether or not will/may … (with equal likelihood). ¶ **Ku nun kalq twung mālq twung hanta** He is not sure whether he will go or not; He hesitates to go. **Ku nun cip.ulq twung mālq twung hanta** He is uncertain whether to pick it up or not. **Nwūn i olq twung mālq twung ha(n)ta** It may snow, and then again it may not [v/adj: see twung]. **Ku kkoch pongoli pich i pulk.ulq twung mālq twung hata** The buds of that flower look somewhat reddish.

-ulu, suffix (makes adv); CF **-wulwu**. ¶ **(c)cilulu** slimy < **cilta** be damp. **(c)colulu / (c)cwululu** trickling, dripping (CF **cwul**); **(c)cwalulu** splashing, rushing down. **itululu = itul itul** lustrous (CF **ikul ikul** glowing). **okululu = okul okul** in swarms. **palulu, polulu** boiling, flaring up. **pa/encilulu = pa/encil pa/encil** sleekly (CF **pancilew-** < **pancil** + **-ew-**). **pa/entululu = pa/entul pa/entul** smoothly (CF **pantulew-** < **pantul** + **-ew-**). **payngkululu / pingkululu** smiling. **(p)pe-/(p)pa-/(p)pu-/ (p)po-kululu = (p)pek (p)pek** boiling, seething. **sululu = sul sul** gently. **wa/e(ku)lulu = wakul wakul** in swarms. **waktakululu / wektekululu = waktal wak- / tak-takul** rattling. **waykululu = waykul waykul** in scattered bits / grains.

-ululuk = -ululu-k, cpd suffix (makes adv). ¶ **(c)coluluk / (c)cwululuk** trickling, dripping; **(c)cwaluluk** splashing, rushing down.

-ulum, bnd adj-n (~ **hata**), abbr < **-usulum**. …ish, characterized by. ¶ **petulum** slightly protruding < **pet-ulum** < **pet.ta** it spreads out. ABBR **-um**.

˙ᵘ/ₒ˙lwo (˙lwo after vowel or *l* or *LQ*), pcl = **ulo**. After a consonant (other than *l* or *LQ*) the MK particle has two shapes, ˙u˙lwo and ˙o˙lwo, and there is a less common variant ˙wo˙lwo. After *oC* the shape is always ˙o˙lwo, as seen in *han˙salo˙m o˙lwo* (1463 Pep 2:22a) 'for people in large numbers' and *mozol˙h olwo* (1481 Twusi 7:39a) 'to the village'. After *aC* the shape is usually ˙o˙lwo, as in *nilu˙syan ˙˙yang ˙o˙lwo* (1447 Sek 6:24b) 'as you say' and ˙kal.h olwo (1462 ¹Nung 6:109b) 'with a knife', but there at least two examples of ˙u˙lwo: ˙˙PI-˙LYANG ˙u˙lwo pu˙the (1463 Pep 2:41a) 'stemming from comparison and inference', ˙e˙tin namzin ˙in ˙˙yang ˙u˙lwo (?1517- ¹No 2:54b) like a good fellow. Only the shape ˙u˙lwo is used after *uC*

and *wuC*, as in SSIN-˙LUK ˙u˙lwo (1447 Sek 6:7b) 'by the divine power' and *mu˙su.k u˙lwo* (1462 ¹Nung 1:84a) '(making it) into what', ˙skwu.m u˙lwo (1445 ¹Yong 13) 'in a dream' and *wu˙h u˙lwo* (1447 Sek 13:13b) 'up(wards)'. And ˙u˙lwo is usual after *eC*, as in ˙i ke˙s u˙lwo (1463 Pep 2:77a) 'for this' and ˙PEP ˙u˙lwo (?1468- Mong 35a) 'according to the Law', but we also find *hon nye.k o˙lwo n'* … *hon nye˙k o˙lwo n'* (1446 Sek 6:3a) 'on the one hand … on the other hand' and ˙SSIP-˙˙SSYEN ˙o˙lwo (1459 Wel 1:25b) 'to the ten virtues'; notice too ˙i˙le ˙n ˙t olwo (1462 ¹Nung 1:18b, 1463 Pep 7:140a, 1481 Twusi 7:27a, 1482 Kum-sam 2:15b) 'hence, thus'. After *iC* both versions occur: ˙pul s ˙pi.ch o˙lwo (1447 Sek 9:4b) 'with the radiance of fire', ˙him ˙olwo (1482 Nam 1:50b) 'with one's strength'; *na ˙y ˙˙hen ci˙p ulwo ˙sye* (1481 Twusi 20:52a) 'from my shabby home', ˙TTAY-SSING ˙u˙lwo (1459 Wel 13:36b, 1463 Pep 2:6b) 'through the Greater Vehicle'. The only two examples I have found with *VyC* take ˙o˙lwo: ˙CYWUNG-SOYNG ˙o˙lwo (1447 Sek 13:27a) 'by all living beings', ˙˙twuy.h o˙lwo tol˙Gywo˙m ay (1459 Wel 13:32a) 'because it depends on the future'. For the variant, see ˙wo˙lwo. See also ˙il˙lwo, kul˙lwo, ˙tyel˙lwo; ˙˙nal˙lwo, nellwo; ˙u˙la, ˙u˙lan; ˙lu.

NOTE: The MK particle attached to the "free" form of such nouns as *pwulmwu / pwulmk*… and *kolo / kolG*…: *pwulmwu ˙lwo* (1465 Wen 1:1:2: 17b) 'with bellows' (and not **pwulm˙k u˙lwo*), *kolo lwo* (1677 Pak-cwung 2:1; cited from NKW) 'with flour' (not **kol˙Go ˙lwo*).

˙ᵘ/ₒ˙lwo k, pcl + pcl. SEE ˙lwo k, ˙il˙lwo k.
˙ᵘ/ₒ˙lwo n', pcl + pcl. SEE ˙ᵘ/ₒ˙lwo, ˙ᵘ/ₒ˙lan.

1. ¶ *hon nye.k o˙lwo n'* … *hon nye˙k o˙lwo n'* (1446 Sek 6:3a) on the one hand … on the other hand. TANG-SSI ˙lwo n' ZYE-LOY S ˙PEP LYWUW-˙˙SYWUY ˙yey put˙ti ˙˙mwot hol˙ss oy (1459 Wel 2:60a) at that time the tathāgata's law cannot rely on flowing water, so … . ˙an.h o˙lwo n' ˙SYANG ˙ol cwo˙cha i˙Ge˙kwo pas˙k o˙lwo n' ˙˙KYENG ˙ul cwo˙cha totno˙n i (1462 ¹Nung 2:20ab) inwardly moves in pursuit of form and outwardly goes about in pursuit of bounds.

2. than (= ˙ᵘ/ₒla˙wa, twu˙ko). ¶ ˙sumul˙h in SSI-˙CYELQ ˙ey ˙yel˙h in cey ˙lwo n' SYWUY ho˙m ye (1462 ¹Nung 2:8b) is weaker at twenty than when ten years old, and … . ˙KAK-˙PPYELQ

ʼhi LWOW-SIM ʼhwo.m oʼlwo nʼ teuʼn i ʼla (1482 Kum-sam 4:30b) surpasses even extraordinary mental exertion.

·ᵘ⁄₀ʼlwo puʼthe, particle + particle. ¶naʼkunay [NAM-HHYWEN] ʼulwo puthe ʼwa (1481 Twusi 7: 23a) a traveler came from the southern counties. ʼsay ʼlwo puʼthe te alʼGwoyʼywol ʼcwu.l i ˵ep.sul ʼs oy (1482 Kum-sam 2:2a) since we are unable to reveal more from afresh, ... SEE ʼilʼlwo puʼthe.

·ᵘ⁄₀ʼlwo s, pcl + pcl (? abbr < ·ᵘ⁄₀ʼlwo ʼsye).

1. from. ¶˵SSYANG-·KWUY ʼlwo s ˵woʼm ay (1462 ¹Nung 1:2b) upon returning from the second (the formal / image) period of teaching Buddhism.

2. than. ¶ʼkhun ˵TTWOW-˵LI ʼnon haʼnol ʼlwo s mwoncye naʼn i (1459 Wel 2:70a) the great doctrine came into being prior to the heavens. ʼTTI ʼyey woloʼsiʼn i ʼlwo s wuʼh iʼla (1465 Wen 1:1:2:63a) it is higher than he who has climbed to the land. ·PPOYK-·PPWULQ ʼlwo s aʼlay nʼ ˵SYWOW-SSING ʼul ʼil ʼculʼkita ʼka (1463 Pep 2:178b) below the step of addressing Buddha one first takes delight in the hīnayāna (lesser vehicle) and then ... .

·ᵘ⁄₀ʼlwo ʼsye, particle + particle = ulo se. from. ¶NGYANG-·SYA-SSYENG ʼulwo ʼsye ·SYA-·NGWUY ·KWUYK ʼey wol ssoʼzi (= wolq soʼzi) ʼyey (1447 Sek 6:23a) on the way while coming from Rāja-gr̥ha to the land of Śrāvastī. MYEY ʼlwo ʼsye twoʼla ʼwonaʼn i (1463/4 Yeng 1:90b) those who have returned from confusion. na ʼy ˵hen ciʼp ulwo ʼsye ʼna-kaʼla (1481 Twusi 20: 52a) set out from my shabby home.

~ puʼthe. ¶˵ne y eʼtuʼle ʼlwo ʼsye puʼthe won ʼta (?1517- ¹No 1:1a) = ne y etule lwo sye cwocha won ta (1795 ¹No-cwung [P, K] 1:1a) where have you come from?

·ᵘ⁄₀ʼlwo ʼtwo, pcl + pcl = ulo to. ¶˵NGWUW-SIM ʼulwo ʼtwo somosʼti ˵mwot hoʼm ye MWU-SIM ʼulwo ʼtwo somosʼti ˵mwot hoʼl iʼla (?1468- Mong 12a) you cannot penetrate it consciously nor can you penetrate it unconsciously.

·ᵘ⁄₀ʼlwo ʼza, pcl + pcl = ulo ya. ¶QWUY-SSIN ʼkwos aʼni ʼm ye nʼ mwoʼlwoʼmay ·NGEP-·LUK ʼulwo ʼza kaʼl iʼn i (1459 Wel 21:25a) in the absence of the supernatural I must go by the very power of karma itself. mwoʼlwoʼmay ʼi kakʼsi [ʼ]lwo ʼza hoʼl i ʼl ʼss oy (1459 Wel 7: 15b) he does it rather because of this woman.

PHI-YWU ʼlwo ʼza piʼluʼse ˵a.n i ʼʼla (1463 Pep 1:131a) it has been understood only through parables. mwoʼlwoʼmay ʼpoy ʼlwo ʼza ˵sitʼno.n i ʼla (?1517- ¹No 2:44a) = mwolwom.i poy lwo ya sis.no.n i ʼla (1795 ¹No-cwung [P] 2:39b) we have to carry them by boat.

ulwu, particle [variant] = ulo

-ul wu, prosp mod + postmod adj-n − ? insep. general appearance. SEE celel / ilel / kulel wu.

-ul ya < -·ᵘ⁄₀ʼl ya (= -·ᵘ⁄₀ʼl ye), prospective modifier + postmodifier. CF -uʼla.

1. will it do / be? (This is usually rhetorical − CF -keyss.nun ya, -keyss.ni.) ¶Kkamakwu (= kkamakwi) chil ha.ye kem.umye hayoli nulk.e huyl ya Is the crow black because he was painted, the heron white because he is old? ¶piʼlwok mool.h ina tonʼniʼl ya (1586 Sohak 3:5a) can we keep going to the village even so? ʼhomol[ʼ]mye [CHYENG-·CCYENG PPWO-TTYEY ˵KWA] ʼlol KA ʼhi ʼpolaʼl ya (1579 Kwikam 1:36a) can one all the more look toward the fruit of pure bodhi (perfect enlightenment)?

2. shall / should I? do you want me to? ¶Khal ul sa cwul ya yenphil ul sa cwul ya Shall I buy you a knife, or a pencil? CF (1916 Gale 81) holya "interrogative form used by the first person only".

*ul ya (pcl + pcl) → iya. SEE ᵘ⁄₀l za.

-ulya (ko) = -ul ya (ko)

-ul ya man (un) SEE ya man

-ulya ʼmyen = -ul ya ʼmyen, abbr < -ul ya (ko) hamyen

-ulyan = -ul ya ʼn(ʼ)

-ulq yang, prosp mod + n. 1. (= -ul mo.yang) the appearance of going to do / be.

2. the intention / idea to do, the prospect of doing. 2a. ~ ulo (= -ulq yēyceng ulo) with the expectation of doing, with a view to doing, in order to do it, with the intention of doing. ¶Chinkwu lul chac.e polq yang ulo Sewul ey wass.ta He came to Seoul with the idea of seeing a friend. Ne lul manna polq yang ulo sāpang ulo chac.e tanyess.ta I've been looking all over for you. Sacen ul han kwēn mantulq yang ulo caylyo lul mouko iss.ta I'm gathering data with a view to compiling a dictionary.

2b. ~ imyen (= -ulye hamyen) if it is the intention/idea to do, if one is going to do; hol yang imyen (1916 Gale 82) 'if it were so'. ¶Hānkwuk ey kalq yang imyen han tal un kellikeyss.ta It will take one month to get to Korea. **Cang ey kalq yang imyen ppalli chaliko na-se la** Dress up quickly if you want to go to the market. **Kangsan kwūkyeng ul tā halq yang imyen meych nal i toylq ci molukeyss.kwun a** There is no telling how many days it will take if we see all the sights.

-ulya 'nun = **-ul ya 'nun,** abbr < **-ul ya (ko) hanun**

-ul ya tul, prosp modifier + postmod + pcl

u˙lye = *u˙la* = *˙ᵘ⁄₀˙lwo*, pcl. SEE *mu˙su.m u˙lye* = *mu˙su.m u˙la* (why).

-*˙ᵘ⁄₀˙l ye*, prosp mod + postmod. SEE *ho˙l ye*. CF -*˙ᵘ⁄₀˙l ya*, -*˙ᵘ⁄₀˙la*.

1. ¶*twolo˙hye ˙TTYWU-˙TTYAK hol ˙kwo.t i isi˙l ye* (1482 Kum-sam 2:20a) would there be any place [in the doctrine] where I could get a firmer grasp? *˙tywo˙tha s ˙˙ma˙l i˙za nilo˙l ye* (?1517- Pak 1:3a) can I say it's OK?

2. ¶*NUNG ˙hi nilo˙l ye ˙˙mwot nilo˙l ye* (1459 Wel 17:22a) will he be able to tell or won't he?

3. ¶·*CYEY-˙TTWO ˙hosin KWONG-˙TUK ˙ul e˙lwu i˙kuy˙ye ki˙lizo˙Wo˙l ye* (1459 Wel se:9a) shall I praise being able to conquer the virtue achievement which has delivered me?

4. ¶*e˙lwu ˙him ˙olwo to˙thwo.l ye* (1482 Nam 1:50b) wanting to pit one's strength effectively.

5. ¶*ku˙le a˙ni ?˙l ye ko˙cang e˙lye˙wu.n i ?˙la* (?1517- Pak 1:57b) it is just terribly hard.

6. ~ ˙˙*mal˙la* (= -*u˙l ye [ho˙ti] ˙˙mal˙la*). ¶˙˙*ne y ˙i˙li kan-˙˙tay˙lwo ˙kap˙s ul pa˙two˙l ye ˙˙mal˙la* (?1517- ¹No 2:10b) don't ask for such an outrageous price! ˙˙*ne y ko˙cang nemu pa˙two[˙]l ye ˙˙mal˙la* (?1517- ¹No 2:11a) don't try to get the most exorbitant price!

-ulye < -*˙ᵘ⁄₀˙l ye* (-**lye** after a vowel or the l-extension of -L- stems); DIAL variants **-ullye, -ull(y)a**.

1. (intentive). with the thought in mind to do, with the intention of doing, with the desire to do; ready / prepared / willing to do; about to do. ~ **ko** SAME. Must have the same subject as the following verb phrase. ¶**Kkoch i philye ko pongoli lul mayc.ess.ta** The flower has formed a bud and will soon come out. **Cip ul salye ko unhayng ey se pic ul nāyss.ta** I took out a loan from the bank in order to buy a house.

1a. ~ **(ko/kko/kwu) hanta** intends / plans / wants to do; is going to do, will do, is ready / prepared / willing to do, has it in mind to do, is out to do; tries to do, sets out / about to do. ¶**Kyelhon halye ko hanta** I plan / intend to get married; I am about to get married. **Kyelhon halye ko haci anh.nunta** I am not about to (= don't intend to) get married. **Kyelhon haci anh.ulye ko hanta** I want to avoid (get out of) getting married; I am trying not to get married. **Kyelhon haci anh.ulye ko haci anh.nunta** I am not trying to get out of getting married. ¶**Han sēk tal te iss.ulye ko hanta** I intend (am prepared) to stay another three months. **Pi ka olye ko hanta** It is going to rain. **Pul i kalye ko hanta** The electricity is about to go off. **Yenghwa ka sīcak halye (kkuth-nalye) ko hanun tey!** The movie is about to start (end)! **Palam i pul.e se mun i cakkwu tat.hilye / yellilye hanta** The door keeps wanting to close / open because of the wind. **Choq pul i kkē cilye ko hanta** The candle is about to go out.

1b. ~ **(ko) tulta** gets / is on the verge of doing, is about to do, threatens to do, aims at doing, tries to do. ¶**Māl ul tut.ko kot ttaylilye ko tul.ess.ta** He was going / set to hit me the moment he heard me speak. **Yātan ul hani-kka n' ku nun na lul ttaylilye tul.ess.ta** When I scolded him, he threatened to hit me. **Elin ay ka yang cayq-mul ul sathang ulo ālko mek.ulye tul.ess.ta** The baby was about to eat the caustic soda, thinking it was candy.

2. [obs] = **-ulya** = **-ul ya.**

-ulye 'ci, abbr < **-ulye (ko) haci.** ~ **man.**

-ulye cocha, intentive + pcl. ¶**Na lul chyē 'ta polye cocha haci anh.ess.ta** He wouldn't even look up at me.

-ulye 'kena, abbr < **-ulye (ko) hakena**

-ulye 'keni, abbr < **-ulye (ko) hani**

-ulye 'ketun, abbr < **-ulye (ko) haketun**

-ulye khenyeng, intentive + particle. ¶**Pap ul mek.ulye ('ki nun) khenyeng tol.a 'ta poci to anh.nunta** He won't even turn to look around, much less think about eating.

-ulye 'ki, abbr < **-ulye (ko) haki**

-ulye kkaci, intentive + particle.
¶**(Ecci kothong i sīm hayss.tun ci) ip.wen halye kkaci hayss.ess.ci yo** (He was in such pain) he finally decided to go to the hospital.

-ulye ko / kko / kwu, intentive + pcl: SEE **-ulye.** ~ **lul** SEE **-ulye lul.**

-ulye 'l(q), abbr < **-ulye (ko) hal(q)**

-ulye l', abbr < **-ulye (ko) lul**

-ulye 'la to, intentive + copula var infinitive + pcl. ¶Ūmsik ul mek.ulye 'la to tulmyen com kwaynchanh.keyss.ta I would worry less if he would just try to eat.

-ulye lul, intentive + particle. ¶Thong yak ul mek.ulye (ko) lul an hani etteh.key hamyen cōh.so He flatly refuses to take his medicine; what can we do? Ne nun tangcho'y [= tangcho ey] mek.ulye lul tulci anh.ni? Aren't you about ready to eat now?

-ulyem (-lyem after a vowel or l-extension of -L- stem). 1. (cajolative). do please, come now (an endearing command). ~ una SAME (softer). ¶Ppalli kalyem una Why don't you (I hope you will) go there right away. Cāmqkan man kitalilyem una Why don't you wait for just a wee bit? Attested: -(u)lyem and -(u)lye.m un 1730, as -(u)lye.m una 1703.

2. (= -ulye 'm) abbr < -ulye (ko) ham.

-ulye mace, intentive + pcl. ¶Yak ul mek.ulye mace an hani cham sōk i sang hanta I am distressed that he won't even take any medicine [Somewhat better said Yak mace mek.ulye an hani ··· or Yak mace an mek.ulye hani ···].

-^{u}/olyemalon = -^{u}/o'lye' ma'lon < -^{u}/o'l [i] 'yen ma'lon. ¶["KAM] hi cwu'kwu.m ul as'ki.l [i] 'ye' ma'lon (1481 Twusi 10:47a) he would bravely hold death dear, but ... .

-ulye man, intentive + particle. just with the intention/idea of doing. ¶Ne nun hak.kyo ey kkok mues ul paywulye man kanun cwul āni?! Do you think we're going to school just to learn things?!

-ulyemuna → -ulyem una

-ulye 'myen, abbr < -ulye (ko) hamyen. ¶Cip ul celeh.key kkaykkus 'i chiwulye 'myen sikan i tunta It takes time to keep a house so clean. ¹Nāyngmyen ul mek.ulye 'myen motwu kuli kanta Everybody goes there (who wants) to eat cold noodles. Olh.key kwūkyeng halye 'myen halwu congil kellilq key 'ta To see it properly would take a whole day.

-ulye 'n('), 1. abbr < -ulye (ko) han

2. abbr < -ulye (ko) hanun (ya). ¶May mas ul polye 'n'? Looking for a taste of the whip?

-ulye 'na$_1$, abbr < -ulye (ko) hana. ¶Nal i kāylye 'na? I wonder if it will clear up? Pap i tto nuc.ulye 'na pwā It looks as though the meal is going to be late again. Kulay caney an olye 'na? Well you won't come, then? I ¹yēy ka ku kyengwu ey al-mac.ulye 'na? Wouldn't this example fit that case?

-ulye 'na$_2$ (= -ulye ina), intentive + cop adversative. ¶Yak ul mek.ulye 'na tulmyen cōh.keyss.ta I wish you'd just be willing to take some medicine.

-ulye 'n cuk, abbr < -ulye (ko) han cuk

-ulye 'ney, abbr < -ulyo (ko) haney

-ulye 'n' i, abbr < -ulye (ko) hanun i; CF -ta 'nun i. [We reject the ~ nun ··· of CM 1:371.]

1. ~ hanta. ¶Ku ka na lul towa cwulye 'n' i hako unkun hi mit.ess.ta I secretly expected him to help me. Acik to ilulye 'n' i hako sikyey lul poni pelsse caceng ul hwelssin nem.ess.ess.ta I thought it was still early but when I looked at my watch it was way past noon. Nay ka wūnun kes ul poko emeni ka na lul wilo hay cwulye 'n' i hayss.ta I figured that Mother would see me crying and comfort me. Yenghwa kwūkyeng ul ka-polye 'n' i hako cip ul na sess.nun tey tōcwung ey se pi ka oki sīcak hayss.ta He stepped out of the house with the idea of taking in a movie but it started to rain before he got there.

2. ~ siph.e cinta gets the feeling that it will happen. ¶Kot tol.a olye 'n' i siph.e cinta I get the feeling that he will come right back. CF -keni siph.e cinta.

3. ~ wa but; and anyway (what's more), moreover. ¶Ku nun kalye 'n' i wa ne kkaci kalq kes i mues in ya He may leave, but why should you leave too? Sangcen i pyēn ha.ye pyek.hay nun toylye 'n' i wa im hyāng han ilphyen tansim iya kasilq cwul iss.ul ya Mulberry fields may change into a sea, but my devoted heart toward my beloved will never change. Nay mom kkēm.ta, wūs.ci mālla, kecwuk un kem.ulye 'n' i wa sōk cocha kem.ulq son ya?! My body is black, but do not laugh; the hide may be black, but what makes you think the inside is black too? For more examples, see M 1:2:452-3.

-ulye 'ni, abbr < -ulye (ko) hani [DIAL var -ulla 'ni]. ¶Atul nom ul cwung-hak.kyo ey kakey man ila to ha(l)lye 'ni i kosayng ici yo I am having a hard time trying just to let my son go to middle school. Ta-cca ko-cca lo ppāys.ki puthe man ha(l)lye 'ni nwu ka cōh.a hay Starting off doing only such unexpected things how do you expect anyone to like it?!

-ᵘ/oˑl 'yeˑn i = -ᵘ/oˑl [i] 'yeˑn i, prosp mod + (ellipted postmod +) cop effective mod + postmod. ¶ tuˑluˑh ey [LYWONG] ˑi ssaˑhwoˑa [ˑSO-ˑCHILQ ˑCYANG] ˑi ilˑGwu.l [i] 'yeˑn i (1445 ¹Yong 69) on the field [of battle] the dragons fought and four-times-seven (= 28) generals were to prevail. SAM-TTWO ˑay pteˑle tiˑl [i] 'yeˑn i muˑsum ˑLI-ˑQYEK isiˑl i ˑGwo (1464 Kumkang 64b) what profit is there if one falls into the three evil paths?

~ ˑGwa (pcl). ¶ ˑKEP ˑun spolˑli taoˑl [i] 'ye.n i ˑGwa ˑtye pwuthye s ˑHHOYNG ˑkwa ˑNGWEN ˑkwa KWONG-ˑKHYWOW ˑhosin PANG-ˑPPYEN ˑun taˑwoˑm i ˑepˑsu.l i ˑˑla (1447 Sek 9:29a) the kalpa will quickly come to an end, to be sure, but the deeds and desires of Buddha and his ingenious expediencies, those will have no end. SEE hoˑl 'yeˑn i ˑGwa.

~ ˑGwo (pcl). ¶ ˑes.te 'n ˑsaloˑm ol pwoˑl [i] 'ye.n i ˑGwo (1481 Twusi 8:62a) what sort of person would he see?

~ ˑ'ston (pcl). ¶ ˑhotaˑka pasˑk ol puˑthe ˑwolˑt inˑt ay n' mwoncye tangtangi noˑch ol pwoˑl [i] 'ye.n i ˑˑston (1462 ¹Nung 1:64b) if we rely on the outward appearance (coming to us) first we must just look at the face. ˑhotaˑka KHWONG ˑol puˑthe ˑnalqˑt inˑt ay n'ˑi maˑthwoˑm iˑce y panˑtoˑki twuluˑhye neˑ'y kwoˑh ol maˑtho.l [i] 'yeˑn i ˑˑston (1462 ¹Nung 3:8b) if it emerged from empty space this scent would have to have come around itself to catch the attention of your nose.

~ 'sˑton SAME (spelling variant). ¶ aˑlwoˑm iˑmwom ssoˑziˑyey iˑsywolqˑt inˑt ay n' mozoˑm i NUNG ˑhi ˑˑaˑti ˑmwot hoˑl [i] 'yeˑn i 'sˑton (1462 ¹Nung 1:55a) if knowledge is between bodies then the mind would not be able to know [things].

-ulye 'ni-kka, abbr < -ulye (ko) hani-kka. now that I am going to (do), now that I want to (am ready / set / about to); (just) when I was about to (do). ¶ Calye 'ni-kka cam i oci anh.e yo Now that I am ready to sleep, I can't get to sleep. Pap ul mek.ulye 'ni-kka meli ka aphe yo Here I am all ready to eat and I get a headache! Il ul halye 'ni-kka pay ka koph.ass.e yo There I was all set to work when I felt hungry. Cenyek ul cwūnpi halye 'ni-kka ku man twula ko hayss.e yo Just as I was going to prepare dinner he told me not to do so. (The examples: M 1:2:141, with new translations).

-ulye 'n ka, abbr < -ulye (ko) han ka. [lit] = -ulq kes in ya. SEE ilye 'n ka.

-uˑlyenmaˑlon = -uˑl 'yen maˑlon = -uˑl [i] 'yen maˑlon, prosp mod (+ ellipted postmod) + cop effective mod + bnd n. ¶ ˑSO-THYEN ˑˑHHA ˑlol kozom ˑˑaˑlosi.l [i] 'yen maˑlon nulˑku.n i ˑPPYENG hoˑn i cwuˑkun ˑˑsalom ˑpwosiˑkwo ˑSYEY-KAN ˑsulˑhi neˑkiˑsya ˑCHYWULQ-KA ˑhoˑsya (1447 Sek 6:17b) he governed all the world below the four heavens but when he saw the old, the ill, and the dead, he found the world sad and left home to become a monk, and … . ˑCYENG-ˑKAK ˑol ilˑGwuˑl [i] 'yen maˑlon ⋯ ˑPEP tutˑt ol af ˑ]ni hoˑl i ˑˑla ˑhoˑsya (1459 Wel 2:36b) said "they have achieved sambodhi (Buddha wisdom) but ⋯ they will not listen to the Law", and … .

-ulyen man (un) < -ul [i] 'yen manon < -uˑl [i] 'yen maˑlon. I had hoped that … but; it should have … but; I wish that … but. ¶ Ku ka kamyen na to kalyen man un If only he would go, I'd go too. Tōn i iss.umyen ku chayk ul salyen man un I would buy the book if I had the money. Nay ka sāy 'la 'myen ne hanthey nal.e kalyen man If I were a bird I'd fly to you. Apeci ka ppalli osimyen cōh.ulyen man un I wish Father would hurry back (but …), Pom i wā im to olyen man un acik to sosik to ēps.ta Now that spring has come, my beloved should be here, too, but I have no word yet.

NOTE: In KEd and KM this was called the "frustrated intentive" and assumed to contain the intentive -ulye < -ᵘ/oˑl ye.

-ulyenmanon = -ᵘ/oˑl 'yen maˑnon = -ᵘ/oˑl 'yen [i] maˑnon. ¶ kocang mekem cuk 'i cal talhwo.l [i] 'yen manon (1676 Sin.e 2:8b) they have worked it so that it is quite edible but … .

-ᵘ/oˑlyeˑnol = -ᵘ/oˑl 'yeˑnol = -ᵘ/oˑl [i] 'yeˑnol, prosp mod + (ellipted postmod +) cop lit concessive. SEE -ᵘ/oˑsiˑl [i] 'yeˑnol.

-ulye 'nta, abbr < -ulye (ko) hanta. ¶ Na nun ¹nayil kalye 'nta I'm going to go tomorrow.

-ulye 'n tul, 1. abbr < -ulye (ko) han tul ? 2. abbr < -ulye in tul, intent + cop mod + postmod. ¶ ? Celeh.key yēmsey-cek ini yak ul mek.ulye 'n tul tulkeyss.na? Is he so jaded he would even indulge in drugs? (SEE -ulye tu-l-.)

-ulye 'nun, abbr < -ulye (ko) hanun. ¶ mok-swum to pachilye 'nun āykwuk cēngsin a

patriotic spirit willing to sacrifice life itself.
-ulye nun, intentive + pcl. ¶**Mwes itun ci hay polye nun yelqsim i iss.e ya hanta** You have to put enthusiasm into whatever you try to do.
-ulye 'nun chal.na ey at the moment when (one is) on the point/verge of doing. ¶**Ka(l)lye 'nun chal.na ey ku ka wass.ta** He arrived just when we were on the point of leaving.
-ulye 'nun ka pota (adj). (he/she/it/they) may/might do, seems to be thinking of doing. ¶**Pi ka olye 'nun ka poci (pota, pwā, pop.nita)** It may rain. CF -ulq ka pota, -ulq ka hanta.
-ulye 'nun tey, abbr < -ulye (ko) hanun tey. ¶**Nay ka cip ul mak na-kalye 'nun tey ku ka chac.e wass.ta** Just as I was about to leave the house, he came see me.
-ulye 'nunya = -ulye 'nun ya, abbr < -ulye (ko) hanun ya
-ulyenya = -ulye 'n ya, abbr < -ulye (ko) han ya
-ulyenywo = -ˈᵘ/ol ˈyeˑn ywo = -ˈᵘ/ol [ˈi] ˈyeˑn ywo, prosp mod + (ellipted postmodifier) + cop effective mod + postmod. ¶**eˑnwu ˈCCANG s KUM ˈi ˑza ˑmaˑchi skolˈGi.l [i] ˈyeˑn ywo** (1447 Sek 6:25b) [I wonder] just which vault's gold will it take for it to be properly covered. **ˈesˑtyey polˈki.l [i] ˈyeˑn ywo** (1463 Pep 1:13b) how would he have explained it? [TWONG] nyek **ˑmoyˑh on eˑnu ceˑk uy ˈˈyell [i] ˈyeˑn ywo** (1481 Twusi 7:25b) when will the outlands of the east open up? **kilˑh ey ˑpsul keˑs i kumun-ˑtyeˑmun moˑto.l [i] ˈyeˑn ye** (?1517- Pak 1:54a) how long would you figure your travel funds to last? SEE holˈyeˑn ywo.
-ulye 'o, abbr < -ulye (ko) hao. ABBR -ulyo.
-ulye 'p.nikka, abbr < -ulye (ko) hap.nikka
-ulye 'ptita, abbr < -ulye (kɔ) haptita
-ulye puthe, intent + pcl [a bit awkward]. ¶**Yak ul mek.ulye puthe an hani etteh.key hamyen cōh.so** If he starts right off with refusing to take any medicine, what shall we do?
-ulye se (nun/ya), intent + pcl (+ pcl) = -ulye (ko) ha.ye se. ¶**Kulen kes ul phī halye se nun an toynta** You shouldn't try to get out of (evade) that sort of thing. **Caney ka an halye se ya toyna?** Is it in any way reasonable for you not to be unwilling to do it?
-ulyes-man → -ulyen man
-ulyes(s).ta → -ulyetta
-u[ˈ]lyeˑta = -ˈᵘ/oˑl ˈyeˑta = -ˈᵘ/oˑl [i] ˈyeˑta, prosp mod + (ellipted postmod +) cop effective

indic assert. will likely. ¶*SYEY-KAN ay s nwu.n i ep.su.l [i] ˈyeta* ([1447→]1562 Sek 11:11_); cited from LCT) will lack the eyes of the world of men. SEE ˈhwolyeˑta.
-ulye 'ta (ka), abbr < -ulye (ko) hata (ka). is going to (wants to, sets out to, tries to) do but. ¶**Cha lul thalye 'ta ka ttel.e cyess.ˢup.nita** (M 1:2:400) I fell getting into the car. **Canq ¹yen khaylye 'ta ka kwulk.unq ¹yenq iph tachilq sey 'la** I am afraid you will harm the large leaves of the lotus in trying to take the small lotuses. **Māl anh.ulye 'ta ney ka kuleki ey māl ici onul cham asul asul hayss.ess.e** I did not want to say anything, but now that you mention it, today that [the game] was really a cliffhanger.
-ulye 'tey, abbr < -ulye (ko) hatey
-ulye to, intent + pcl = -ulye (ko) ha.ye to. VAR -ullay (to).
-ulyetta, intentive assertive [old-fashioned]. In Hankul usually spelled -ulyes.ta but sometimes -ulyess.ta; ?< -ulye + iss.ta, ?< -ulye(q) + -ta. CF -kes.ta.
  1. it is sure/bound/agreed to happen, surely it will happen; you WILL do it (understand? – suggesting a threat). ¶**Pi ka wā to ku i nun olyetta** He is bound to come even if it rains. **Ku īl un ney māl tay lo kkok ney ka kuli halyetta** Now, you will do that as you have promised, see/hear? **Tasi nun twū māl mōs halyetta** (1) You will never break your word again, understand? (2) This will certainly put him to silence. **Ku ka onun kes man un sāsil ilyetta** I am sure he is coming – there's no question about that.
  2. will likely/probably happen; probably is. ¶**¹Nayil ccum un pi ka olyetta** I expect that it will rain by tomorrow. **I os i ku eykey nun com khulyetta** This garment must be a bit too big for him. **I sōk ey twun kes i chayk ilyetta** It must be books that are in it.
-ulye 'tu-kwulye, abbr < -ulye (ko) hatu-kwulye
-ulye 'tu-kwu(me)n, abbr < -ulye (ko) hatu-kwu(me)n
-ulye tul, intent + pcl. ¶**Motwu tōn ul pēllye tul tunta** They are all bent on making money.
-ulye tul(q), prosp mod < -ulye tulta
-ulye 'tula, abbr < -ulye (ko) hatula
-ulye tul.e, infinitive < -ulye tulta
-ulye tulta, intentive + aux v. SEE -ulye.

-ulye tun, mod < -ulye tulta
-ulye 'tun, abbr < -ulye (ko) hatun. ~ ka, ~ ya. ¶Nay ka palo ku yāyki lul halye 'tun kil ita I was just going to talk about that.
-ulye 'tun cha SEE cha
-ulye 'tun ci, intent + cop retr mod + postmod [a bit awkward]. ¶Yak ul mek.ulye 'tun ci pap ul mek.ulye 'tun ci tulmyen cōh.keyss.ᶳo How nice it would be if he would try either to take some food or to take some medicine.
-ulye ya, intentive + particle. VAR -ullay ya.
   1. = -ulye (ko) ha.ye ya. ¶Kongpu lul halye ya chayk ul sa cwuci I won't buy you the book unless you (intend to) study.
   2. = -ulye to. ¶Chayk ul salye ya salq kil i ēps.ta There is no way to buy the book at all.
-ulq yēyceng, prosp mod + n. the plan (project, schedule, intention, anticipation) to do.
   ~ ita plans / intends to do, anticipates (looks forward to) doing; is scheduled to do. ¶Kulay Mikwuk ey nun ēncey tte-nasilq yēyceng ip.nikka Well, so when are you leaving for the States? Ēncey ccum tte-nalq yēyceng in ya When are you scheduled to leave?
   ~ ulo with the plan / project / schedule / aim / intention to do. ¶Ceypho toylq yēyceng ulo teymo lul hayss.ta They demonstrated with the intention of getting arrested.
   CF -ulq cakceng, -ulq sayngkak, -ul they; -ulye, -ule, -ki lo.
-ᵘ⁄₀ˈlyeyngiˈta = -ᵘ⁄₀ˈl yeˈy-ngiˈˈta, prosp mod + postmod + cop polite + cop indic assert. ¶naˈy ˈˈmalˈGwosaˈni tuluˈsiˈm ye nˈnowoyˈculkeˈWun mozoˈm iˈˈep.suˈl yeˈy-ngiˈˈta (1459 Wel 2:5b) if you do not listen to what I say you will not have a happy heart again.
-ᵘ⁄₀ˈlyey.niˈla = -ᵘ⁄₀ˈl yeˈy.n iˈˈla, prosp mod + postmod + cop mod + postmod + cop indic assertive. ¶cyangˈcho twuluˈhhye cwozo lowoyˈywoˈm ol nilˈGwoˈl yeˈy.n iˈˈla (1463 Pep 1:123a) turning to them in the future it is expected that they will be said to be essential. cyangˈchoˈpse taˈsi naˈzwoˈl yeˈy.n iˈˈla (1475 Nay 1:43a) in the future we expect to improve it still more.
-ᵘ⁄₀ˈlyeysˈta = -ᵘ⁄₀ˈl yeˈysˈta, prosp mod + postmodifier + abbr < isˈta. ¶ˈkwoWonˈˈnimˈˈmwotˈpwozoˈWaˈsolˈGusˈˈwuˈnitaˈn i woˈnol sˈnalˈay nekˈs iˈla maˈlwo.l yeˈysˈta (1459 Wel 8:87b) unable to see my beautiful beloved, I have been sobbing with my sadness; today I am at the point where I am about to lose my mind.
-ulyo, 1. (= -uly' 'o) abbr < -ulye 'o < -ulye (ko) hao. 2. abbr < -ul i yo
-ulq ¹yolyang, prosp mod + n. the plan / idea / intention / mind to do. ¶kalq ¹yolyang ita has a mind to go, thinks of going, plans / aims to go. phyēnci ssulq ¹yolyang ulo with the intention / idea of writing a letter.
-ᵘ⁄₀ˈl ywo, prosp modifier + postmod. ¶ˈˈesˈtyey eˈlwoˈTTYAK hoˈl iˈGwanˈtoyˈTTYAKˈˈti aˈniˈtha niloˈl ywo (1462 ¹Nung 1:75a) how can you say one is unattached when one IS attached? ¶naˈyˈnyeˈi keˈs ul [ˈKWAY-ˈQI]ˈhi neˈkikaˈn i eˈnu kwuˈthuyye naˈl ywo (1481 Twusi 25:29a) I go and think this odd, for why go to the trouble of leaving? SEE hoˈl ywo. CF iˈl ywo, -ˈwoˈl ywo. VAR -ᵘ⁄₀ˈl ywu (SEE ˈyˈl ywu).
ᵘ⁄₀l ˈza, pcl + pcl. ¶ˈiˈˈtwulˈhulˈza teˈpuˈlusiˈn i (1449 Kok 52) he combined these very two. ˈˈesˈtyey CCYENG-MYENG hon HE-KHWONGˈol ˈza ilˈhwuˈm ul CHYENG-MYENG honˈnwu.n iˈlaˈhonoˈn ywo (1462 ¹Nung 2:111a) why is the clear void itself called the bright eye?
NOTE: This structure did not survive to become modern *ul (i)ya.
-um < -ᵘ⁄₀m, substantive (-m after a vowel or l-extension of -L- stem). SEE ALSO -uˈm ye.
   1. the act / fact of doing / being (= modifier + kes). ¶māl hanun tey elyewum i ēps.ta has no difficulty in talking. Yelq pen tul.um i han pen pom man kath.ci mōs hata Seeing once is better than hearing ten times. (There is nothing like seeing for oneself.) Mom i kēnkang ham ul ttala cēngsin to kēncen ha.ye cinta Sound mind comes from sound body. ("Sound mind in sound body.") Kuleh.key pal.um haci ani ham i sāsil ita It is a fact that it [the word] is not pronounced that way. Ileh.key to pap ey tōl i mānh.e se ya pap ul mek.um i ani 'la tōl ul ssip.nun kes kath.ta With all these grits in the rice it is like chewing on grits rather than eating rice. sayngkak i kot māl i ani 'm kwa kath.i just as thought is not language. Meych nyen hwū ey ku kes i sāsil im ul ālkey toyess.ta (Im Hongpin 1987:127) Several years later I came to realize that it was true. Ne uy sinpun i haksayng im ul ic.ci mal.e la Don't forget that you are (in the status of) a student.

ekus nam i ēps.ta nothing is amiss, all is well, is exactly right, is in order. **Tāmpay ēps.um ita** No tobacco (to sell today).

2. 2a. the process or result of doing. ¶**cam** sleep(ing). **chwum** dance, dancing. **kel.um** step, walk, gait.

2b. (complementary object of some other form of the same verb). ¶**chwum (ul) chwuta** dances. **cam (ul) cata** sleeps. **Eswusen han kkwum ul nemu kkwum un kēnkang ey hāy lopta** (CM 2:384) Having too many nightmares is harmful to one's health.

3. with various particles (SEE ~ **ulo**, ~ **ey**) and the copula (e.g. **-ulq sēym ita**).

4. SEE ~ **cik hata**

5. (as sentence-final) [DOCUMENTARY style] does, is. ¶**Kwuk.lyen un Kwukcey ¹Yenhap uy cwūn-mal im** "U.N." is the abbreviation of "United Nations". **Wūchen in kyengwu ey nun swūn.yen ham** In case of rain, to be postponed till the next fair day. **Aph ciluci mōs ham** No Passing [roadsign]. **Muyong-ca uy chwul.ip ul emkum ham** Unauthorized entry (is) strictly forbidden. **Onul un swuep i ēps.um** No class today. **Kim kyōswu kkey tulim** To Professor Kim [with the author's compliments]. **Pak Hongki ka ollim** From Pak Hongki [with best regards].

6. X-**um hata** = X-**ta**. ¶**ayk-ttaywum hata** = **ayk-ttaywuta** forestalls a major misfortune by accepting a minor one. **kalum hata** = **kaluta** divides / discriminates. **pal-tot.wum hata** = **pal ul tot.wuta** stands on tiptoes. **ssawum hata** = **ssawuta** quarrels. **tathwum hata** = **tathwuta** fights. ¶ˈsta.h i [QYWUW-ˈPYEK] hol ˈs oy ˈwos-kowoy nipwu ˈm ul keyGulˈGi ˈhonwoˈla (1481 Twusi 7:5a) the land is remote so people dress casually (are careless about what they wear).

7. 7a. X-**um** X-**um**. ¶**cakum-cakum** = **cak.um cak.um** all small alike. **hullim hullim** in little driblets. **kkekk.im kkekk.im** folded back here and there. **puth.im puth.im** amiably, warmly. **sayngkim-sayngkim** appearance. **tul.um tul.um** hearing it little by little.

7b. X-**um** X-**i**. ¶**kel.um-kel.i** gait, **mek.um-mek.i** way of eating, appetite.

7c. X-**um** X-**um-i**. ¶**kel.umkel.um-i** at every step. **pompom-i** appearance(s). **toymtoym-i** makeup, character. **ccamccami** < **ccamccam-i**

a secret promise, undercover negotiations.

NOTE 1: Certain of the -**w**- stems have variant shortened substantives in -**m** as well as the expected form -**wum**; e.g., **musem** = **musewum**, **etwum** = **etwuwum**, **kwiyem** = **kwiyewum**, **pukkwulem** = **pukkwulewum**, **pulem** = **pulewum**.

NOTE 2: There are also a few irregularly formed DERIVED SUBSTANTIVES. These are lexicalizations that carry specialized meanings. ¶**kuul.um** soot (CF **kuulm**), **capam** a pinch of ··· (CF **cap.um**), **cokom** a little (CF **cek.um**), **cōl.um** drowsiness (CF **cōlm**), **cwukem** corpse (CF **cwuk.um**), **el.um** ice (CF **ēlm**), **wul.um** weeping (CF **wūlm**), **heyem** swimming (CF **hēym**), **ha.yem** (···) doings, doing (CF **ham**), **makam** conclusion (CF **mak.um**), **mokum** a gulp (CF **mek.um**), **mutem** tomb (CF **mut.um**), **nōlum / nol.um** gambling (CF **nōlm**), **sālam** (CF **sālm**), **swūm** breath (CF **swīm**), **wumkhum** a handful (CF **wumkhim**); **sayam** jealousy < **saywuta** is jealous of (CF **saywum**; **sāym** < **sāyta** = **saywuta**); **kiem-kiem** crawling < **kita**; **ttutem ttutem** faltering (= reading / speaking falteringly) < **ttut-**; **kkoyum kkoyum** beguilingly < **kkōy-**; **palpam palpam** treading aimlessly < **palp-** (CF **palp.um**); **ttuyem ttuyem** sparsely < **ttūyta** = **ttuywuta** (CF **ttuy[wu]m**); **cipem cipem** picking them up one by one (CF **cip.um**); **cwusem cwusem** picking them up one by one < **cwū(s)-** [DIAL] = **cwūw-** pick up; **cepchem cepchem** with fold after fold < **cep-chi-** fold / furl it; **son ccikem** striking, beating < **ccik-** punch; **poam poam** to all appearances, **poam cik hata** is eye-catching, appealing < **po-** (CF **pom**); etc. SEE ALSO **cham** ? < **cōh.am** (CF **cōh.um**).

The derived substantives that end ···**em** or ···**am** go back to the effective substantive -ᵉ⁄ₐ**m**. SEE -**um cik hata** (NOTE 2), -uˈl i ˈˈGeˈm ye.

NOTE 3: After a consonant, the MK ending has two shapes, -ˈum and -ˈom. The choice of shape depends on the vowel preceding the stem-final consonant. After a, o, or wo the shape is -ˈom, as in capo.m ye (1481 Twusi 7:6b), toˈzom ˈye n' (1465 Wen 2:3:1:46a), and ˈwolhoˈm ye (1463 Pep 1:10b). After other vowels + consonant the shape is -ˈum, as in keˈmu.m ye (1481 Twusi 7:27a), tuluˈm ye (1459 Wel 17:34b) < tut- 'hear', cwuku[ˈ]m ye

(1481 Twusi 8:29a), il˙hu˙m ye (1459 Wel 13:32a). The Middle Korean substantive marks a nominalization (like modern modifier + kes). Except when followed by ye (from the copula infinitive), the ending is usually attached (as -m) to the modulated stem, which ends in -˙wo- or -˙wu-, according to the rules for attaching the modulator, so that the forms end -˙wom or -˙wum. But there are several examples of unmodulated substantives before the particles ˙ᵘ⁄ol, ˙i, and ᵉ⁄ay: ta[˙]so[˙]lim ˙ul (1586 Sohak 6:35b), sa˙hwo.m ol (1481 Twusi 7:39a, 20: 4b); mo[˙]cho[˙]m ay (1463 Pep 1:84a, 1481 Twusi 7:9b), mo˙cho.m ay (1475 Nay 2:2:14a, 1482 Kum-sam 2:12b, 1482 Nam 1:43b), mo˙cho˙m ay (1459 Wel 10:16a, 1462 ¹Nung 1:4a, ?1468- Mong 52b); ˙co.m i (1482 Kum-sam 2:65a); ˙skwu˙m ey s elkwu˙l (1459 Wel 2: 53a). While these examples are lexical nouns, not sentential nominalizations, such is not true of ¨kye˙sim ˙ay (1586 Sohak 6:122a) – but that is probably broken type for ¨kyesya˙m ay 'in his staying', nor of ¨sa˙lo˙m uy a˙lomtye s ¨ywu˙mwu ˙lul ye˙ze pwo˙m i a˙ni ˙hwol˙t i.n i˙˙la (1518 Sohak-cho 8:22a) 'one is not to peek into other people's private letters', or [sywupak i.m ye poy ˙m ye kywul thyey yey s] ke.s ul meki.m i mas.tang thi ani ho.n i (1608 Twu-cip 2:4b) 'it is unsuitable to feed them things [such as watermelon or pear or orange]'. In ˙pis ˙na˙m ol (1481 Twusi 24:30ab) 'the (shining =) glory' ˙nam is accentually reduced from ¨nam, the modulated substantive; CF mas-¨na.m i (1462 ¹Nung 5:85a) 'meeting'.

-um, bnd adj-n (~ hata), abbr < -u(su)lum. ···ish, characterized by. ¶kilum longish < kīlta [or is this kī- + -lum?]. mulum rather soft < muluta. pelum slightly ajar < pēlta. pittwulum aslant < pittulta. ttelum rather astringent < ttēlp.ta. ttuum < ttuta. yathum a bit shallow < yath.ta. CF -umuley.

-um, abbr < -umyen [rapid colloq]. ¶Ikim' allikwu mālkwu Of course I'll let you know if I win. Cōh.um' cōh.ta kwu hay If you like it say so! CF S Kyengsang (Cincwu) forms listed in Mkk 1960:3:35. SEE kulem.

-uma, 1. → -um a. 2. [S Kyengsang DIAL (¹Na Cinsek 1977)] = -umyen

-um a < -˙wᵘ⁄o˙m a, assumptive (subst + post-subst). I will gladly (do it for you); let me, (I promise that) I will ··· . ¶I os i na 'ykey cak.e cimyen ne 'ykey cwum a When I outgrow these clothes I'll give them to you. Ku īl un nay ka math.e pom a I'll take care of that matter. Ku kes un kutay lo hay cwum a I'll do it just as you wish. ¹Nayil kam a I'll come tomorrow. Kitalim a I'll be expecting you. (CF Kitalikeyss.ey yo I am willing to wait.) Ney ¹yepi nun nay ka pūtam ham a I'll provide your travel expenses. Ney ka āmulay twu silh.ta(y) 'myen nay ka ssom a I'll shoot it, if you refuse to do so [SEE -tay 'myen]. Chayk ul sa cwum a ko hayss.ta He promised to buy me a book. cey ka wo.m a hanta (1887 Scott 200 = 1893 Scott 157) = cey ka wo.m a kwo honta (1893 Scott 239) he says he will come. ··· wo.m a ho.yas.swo (1894 Gale 188) he said he would go ··· and return. SYN -um sey. NOTE: (1916 Gale 72) "This ending is a low form of the future tense of the active verb, equal in force to hokeys.ta." All of his examples have a first-person subject, e.g. yelq-twu si ey ka.m a (7) 'I will go at twelve o'clock'. SEE ˙wᵘ⁄o.m a.

-umak, cpd suffix (= -um-ak). ¶nucumak → nucimak (bnd adj-n) rather late. nulkumak = nulk-ma one's old age.

-um a 'ni-kka, [DIAL] = -um a ko hani-kka

-umay, [DIAL, lit; spelling] = -um ey (1)

-˙ᵘ⁄o˙m ᵉ⁄ay, subst + pcl. The MK substantive form is usually modulated (-˙wo-m or -˙wu-m, honorific -u˙sya-m), but for certain stems the modulator appears only as a change in the accent that results in the rising tone that is marked with the double dot. Without the tone markings it is not obvious that the substantive is modulated for monosyllabic stems that end in e, a, o, or wo, such as that found in SAN-HHA ¨pwo˙m ay TANG ˙ho˙ya LYWUW-LI ˙lol pwo˙l i ˙ye (1462 ¹Nung 1:58a) 'facing the sight of mountains and rivers will one see emeralds?'. And the marking is optionally suppressed with stems of two or more syllables ending in e, a, o, or wo: me˙li ˙sye ˙pola˙m ay (= ˙pola˙wo˙m ay) nwo˙phi ha˙nol˙h ay ta˙has.kwo (?1517- Pak 1:68a) seen from afar it touches the sky on high. SEE -˙wo˙m ay, ··· ˙ywo˙m ay, -˙wu˙m ey, ···ywu˙m ey, ˙hwo˙m ay, ¨pwo˙m ay.

-umayn [S Kyengsang DIAL (¹Na Cinsek 1977)] = -umyen; -umayng [S Kyengsang DIAL (Mkk 1960:3:35)] = -umyen se

A Reference Grammar of Korean

-um chita, abbr < -um ul chita (does)
-um cik hata < -⁽ᵉ⁾am ˙cik ˚ho˙ta, subst + postsubst adj-n insep. it is / seems likely (to be / do); it is possible / acceptable to (do), it is all right to (do); it is acceptably (rather/somewhat/ quite) ··· ; it is worth doing (= -ul man hata). ¶ mit.um cik han sālam a man you can trust. sālam i ham cik hanq īl things a person is likely to do (or can do). toym cik hanq īl a thing that may happen (that is possible). ttum cik hata is slow, grave, solemn, dignified. Chalim-chalim ul poni ku ay ka ku īl ul ham cik hayss.ta From his appearance he surely must have done it. Na lul chac.e ol i 'la to ham cik han tey ... You'd think he would come to see me at least, but ... . khum cik hata is quite big. caymi iss.um cik hata it looks like fun. Ku swū-pak i mek.um cik hata That watermelon looks like good eating.

NOTE 1: Instead of the expected form pom cik hata 'is worth noticing' the irregular derived substantive poam is used: poam cik hata is attractive, appealing, eye-catching. CF tul.um cik hata is worth listening to.

NOTE 2: The MK forms used the effective substantive -˙⁽ᵉ⁾am. ¶ ˙PEP pa˙tam cik hol˙ss oy (1447 Sek 19:25b) is worthy of receiving the doctrine, so ... . [HUNG] ˙ul ˙tham cik ho˙n i (1481 Twusi 7:2a) it is worth availing oneself of the pleasure (˙tham = ˙th[o]-a-). [THYEN-˙CO] ˙s kuy patco˙wam ˙cik ho˙n i (1481 Twusi 7:13b) is worthy of presenting to the emperor. "HEM-˙NAN TTYANG-˙NGWEN ˙ey ˙kam ˙cik ho˙m ye "ken˙nem ˙cik ˙hwo˙m ol ˙anwo˙n i (1463 Pep 3:178b) I know that you are fit to go and make the crossing to perilous places far away. ˙kwot "ma˙ta ˙LWOK-YANG ˙i mol moy ˙Gyam cik ho˙kwo (1482 Kum-sam 4:48b) the green-leafed willows all about make good mainbeam ties, and ... . "ayGwa˙thye as˙kyem ˙cik ˙hotwu˙ta (1462 ¹Nung 3:116b) is apt to be anxious and possessive. ˙TUK ˙i ko˙ca pwuthye s ˙i˙l ol mas˙tyem ˙cik ˙hwo˙m i (1459 Wel 2:64b) that he has virtues worthy of undertaking Buddha's work ... '. Later cik was also cuk: ˙i˙p ey me˙kem ˙cuk ho˙n i ˙lwo "kwol ˙Gwa mek˙te˙la (?1517- ¹No 2:53b) = ip ey mek.em cuk hon ke.s ul kolho.ye mektela (1795 ¹No-cwung [P] 2:48a) chose to eat those foods that appealed to the mouth. SEE ˙ho˙yam ˙cik, ˙ho˙yem ˙cik.

-um cil, substantive + postnoun. SEE cil.
-um cocha, substantive + pcl. ¶ Kūlim ul kūlim cocha silhq-cung i nass.ta He got bored even with painting pictures. Hak.kyo ey tanim cocha him tunta It is difficult even to attend school. Twī lul tol.a pom cocha haci anh.ess.ta He didn't even look back. Ku-nye nun elma 'na keyulless.tun ci kkoch han phoki kakkwum cocha mōllass.ta She was too lazy even to know how to raise a flower.
-umeli, suffix. ¶ kkuthumeli end, tip < kkuth end. (KEd treated this as kkuthu + meli; unique shapes are involved either way.)
-umeng (se) [Ceycwu DIAL (Seng ¹Nakswu 1984: 45-6; LSN 1978:93,101)] = -umyen se, -umye
-um ey < -˙wᵘ⁄ₒ˙m ⁽ᵉ⁾ay, subst + pcl [More common in writing than speech; CF -um ulo, -ki ey, -uni-kka.] SEE -˙wo˙m ay, -˙wu˙m ey.

1. (= -umay) upon doing, as/when it is/does; since, because, given the fact that ··· . ¶ Pom ey pissa pointa From its appearance, it looks as if it were expensive. Nay ka māl ul ham ey ku i ka nōllass.ta When I spoke, he was startled. Cwuin ul chac.um ey han ¹nōin i na-wass.ta Upon our seeking out the owner, an old man appeared. Ape' nim pyēnghwan i cwūng hasim ey cip ul pānsi tte-nalq swu ēps.ta As my father is seriously ill, I can't leave the house even for a short while. Swunkyeng i ccoch.a kam ey totwuk nom un ttwiess.ta upon the policeman giving chase, the thief ran. Ku sēnmul ul pat.um ey mopsi culkewess.ta I was delighted to receive the gift. Cangma ka kuchim ey motwu kippe hayss.ta Everyone was happy that the rainy season was over. Kim kwun i ku chayk ul ilk.um ey na nun twīq nal ilk.ki ko hayss.ta Since Kim is reading the book, I decided to read it some other day. Ku lul pom ey yele kaci sayngkak i tte olunta When I see him, all sorts of thoughts occur to me. En-ttus ku lul pom ey acwu yēng.li han kes kath.ta At first glance he seems quite bright.

2. in the doing, in / for doing (or being). ¶ Ku nun icey ku lul kitalim ey cichin tus hata He seems to have grown tired of waiting for him any longer.

3. ~ iss.e se in the doing / being. ¶ Caki tul uy kwaep tul ul silhyen ham ey iss.e se

kacang cwūngyo han kes uy hana nun sāsang kwanqcem ul olh.key kac.nun mūncey 'ta (CM 2:385) One of the most important things in carrying out our own undertakings is to have a proper ideological viewpoint.

  4. ~ kwan ha.ye (hay se) with respect to the doing / being.

  5. ~ pān ha.ye (hay se) contrary to (as opposed to) the doing / being.

  6. ~ pī ha.ye (hay se) as compared (or in comparison) with the doing / being.

  7. ~ tāy ha.ye (hay se) with reference to the doing / being.

  8. ~ thullim ēps.ta there's no mistaking it, ...; unmistakably, definitely.

  9. ~ ttal^e/a (se) in accordance with (true to, in conformity to) the doing/being. ¶Munhwa ka palqtal ham ey ttala (se) as civilization progresses, with the progress of civilization. Swuip i nul.e kam ey ttala se cichwul to nul.e kanta As one's income increases one's outlay increases also.

-um ey 'l ya, substantive + pcl + cop prosp mod + postmod. [? DIAL] ¶Com ilun tul ettel i, echaphi kakey toylq kos im ey 'l ya! (NKd 1288b) If we have to go there anyway, surely it doesn't matter if we are early!

-um ey nun, substantive + particle + particle.

  1. (= -umay nun). ¶Pom ey nun acwu yēng.li han tey He looks quite bright.

  2. ¶Nay ka ku lul kitalim ey nun pyēn ham i ēps.^sup.nita I have not given up waiting for him. Nay ka ku lul mannam (or mannalye ko ham) ey nun yele kaci ^līyu ka iss.^so There are all sorts of reasons for me to (want to go) see him.

-um ey se, subst + pcl + pcl. ¶Ilen māl ul hanun kes un motwu nala lul salang ham ey se ita Saying such things is all from my love of the nation.

  ~ ka ... ~ 'ta. ¶Ku ka kulenq īl ul hanun kes un nala lul salang ham ey se ka ani 'la casin ul wi ham ey se 'ta His doing such a thing is not from loving his country but from promoting himself.

  ~ 'la to [awkward]. ¶Casin ul wi ham ey se 'la to [= wi hay se 'la to] kulenq īl un mōs halq key 'ta He couldn't do such a thing even for promoting himself.

  ~ man. ¶Nala lul salang ham ey se man ani 'la casin ul wi ham ey se iki to hata It is not just from loving his country, it's also from promoting himself.

  ~ 'na [a bit awkward]. ¶Phapel un kāyin uy ^līik ul sayngkak ham ey se 'na sayngkye nalq swu iss.ulq ka, nala lul salang ham ey se nun kyel kho sayngkye nalq swu ēps.ta Factions may arise from thinking of individual interests and the like but they can never arise from loving the nation.

  ~ nun [awkward]. ¶Ku ka kulenq īl ul hanun kes un caki lul wi ham ey se ici nala lul salang ham ey se 'nun ani 'ta [= ... caki lul wi hay se (i)ci nala lul salang hay se ka ani 'ta] His doing such a thing is for himself and not from loving his country.

  ~ ppun (man) [a bit awkward]. ¶Ilen ūykyen chwungtol un (kāyin uy ^līik ul sayngkak ham ey se ppun man ani 'la) nala lul salang ham ey se to sayngkye nalq swu iss.ta A conflict of opinion like this can arise (not only from thinking of individual interests but) also from loving one's country.

  ~ puthe [a bit awkward]. ¶Twū nala sai uy ^līhay nun selo munhwa lul kyolyu ham ey se puthe sīcak toynta Understanding between two nations begins with exchanging culture.

  ~ to [a bit awkward]. ¶Ilen ūykyen chwungtol un (kāyin uy ^līik ul sayngkak ham ey se ppun man ani 'la) nala lul salang ham ey se to sayngkye nalq swu iss.ta A conflict of opinion like this can arise (not only from thinking of individual interests but) also from loving one's country.

  ~ 'tun ci. ¶Ku wen.in i nala lul salang ham ey se (i)tun ci kāyin uy ^līik man ul wi ham ey se (i)tun ci kan ey yeha-thun phapel i sayngkinta 'nun kes un cōh.unq īl i ani 'ta Regardless whether the reason is from loving the nation or from individual interests, the emerging of factions is not a good thing.

  ~ ya [a bit awkward]. ¶Nala lul salang ham ey (iss.e) se ya tangsin ina na 'na talum i ēps.ci yo You and I are the same in loving the nation.

-um ey to, subst + pcl + pcl [more common in writing than in speech].

  1. even though, although. ¶Welkup ul te

cwum ey to an toynta 'y She says it is no good even though we give her more salary. **Na nun chayk i ēps.um ey to kongpu halq swu iss.ta** I can study even though I have no books. **Cip ey chac.e kass.um ey to ku lul mannaci mōs hayss.ta** Although I went to his house looking for him, I was unable to see him.

~ **pulkwu hako** despite (in spite / disregard of) the doing / being. ¶**Pi ka om ey to pulkwu hako ¹notong-ca tul un kyēysok pangcwuk ul ssah.ass.ta** (CM 2:385) Despite its raining the workers kept on building up the embankment.

2. even / also / indeed in (the doing). ¶**Ku nun icey ku lul kitalim ey to cichin tus hata** He seems to have grown tired of waiting for him any longer.

-**um ey ya**, subst + pcl + pcl. ¶**Ku lul kitalim ey ya pyēnhwa ka ēps.ci yo** The monotonous thing is waiting for him.

-**um hata** SEE -**um**, bnd adj-n

-**um i** < -ˈwᵘoˈm i, substantive + pcl. ¶**Ku lul manna pom i yeha hao?** How about seeing him? [Old-fashioned (or sarcastic?).] For more examples see -**um**, -ˈwum.

-**um ila to**, substantive + cop + pcl. ¶**(Nay ka Mikwuk kanta 'nun kes ul ālmyen) na lul chac.e om ila to ham cik han tey ... (ama molunun mo.yang ici)** (If he knows I am going to America) you'd think he would come to see me at least, but ... (maybe he doesn't know).

-*umin* [Ceycwu DIAL (Seng ¹Nakswu 1984:30-2; LSN 1978:93)] = -**umyen**

-**um in tul**, subst + cop mod + postmod. ¶**Nim (= Im) ul wi ham in tul ecci kuli cengseng sulewulq swu ka iss.⁵o** Granted that it is for one's king, how can one be that devoted / loyal?

-**uminun** [S Kyengsang DIAL (¹Na Cinsek 1977)] = -**umyen**

-**um iya**, substantive + pcl. ¶**Nim (= Im) ul kitalim iya tangyen hanq īl ici** It is but natural that I should wait for my beloved.

-**um iyo**, substantive + pcl (var = **iko**). ¶**Ku ka conkyeng ul pat.nun kkatalk un ku ka nul ūy lul hayng ham iyo, ku ka pū.yu ham i ani 'ta** The reason he is respected is that he always does the right thing, and not that he is wealthy.

-**um khenyeng**, subst + pcl [a bit awkward] = -**ki khenyeng**. ¶**(Phok.kyek i iss.ess.ci man) sālam i cwuk.um khenyeng cwi saykki han mali to an cwuk.ess.ta** (Despite the bombing) not a single mouse died, much less any people.

-**um kwa**, subst + pcl [? limited to ~ **tongsi ey**]. ¶**Wuli nun sēykyey phyenghwa lul wi hay se nolyek ham kwa tongsi ey munhwa hyāngsang ul wi hay se to chōysen ul tā hay ya toynta** Together with working for world peace we must do our best for the improvement of culture.

-**um man (to)**, subst + pcl (+ pcl). ¶**Sihem chie se ttel.e cinta 'myen chalali sihem ul an chim man to mōs haci** You would be better off not to take the examination than to fail it.

-**um mankhum (to)**, subst + pcl (+ pcl). ¶**Wānhayng-cha lul tham un ppesu lul tham mankhum to mōs hanun i 'la** [old-fashioned] Taking a bus would be better than taking a slow train, you know.

-**umo** [DIAL: S Kyengsang (¹Na Cinsek 1977), N Kyengsang (Choy Myengok 1979)] = -**umyen**

-**umon** [S Kyengsang DIAL (¹Na Cinsek 1977)] = -**umyen**

-*umong* [Ceycwu DIAL (Seng ¹Nakswu 1984:45-6; LSN 1978:93, 101)] = -**umyen se**, = -**umye**

-**um puthe**, subst + pcl [a bit awkward]. from (= since, because of) the doing. ¶**Emeni payq sōk ey se na-om puthe kosayng ita** It has been a bitter life from my mother's womb on.

-**um say**, subst + postsubstantive. the mode / manner / way of. SEE **say**.

-**umq seng**, subst + postsubstantive. SEE **seng**.

-**um sey**, FAMILIAR assumptive (substantive + postsubst). I will gladly (do it for you); let me [to close friends, often as a promise]; CF -**um a**. ¶**Nay twī lo kam sey** I'll be along later. **Ku kes ul cal kanswu hay twum sey** I'll take good care of it for you. **Kot kaph.um sey** I'll pay you back right away. **Ku chayk un nay ka ilk.um sey** I'll be glad to read the book.

-**um to**, substantive + pcl. ¶**Ku ka kuleh.key chwulqsey lul ham to tā pumo uy tek in i 'la** [old-fashioned] His succeeding in the world that way is all due to his parents.

-**umu** [S Kyengsang DIAL (Mkk 1960:3:35)] = -**umyen**

-**um ul** < -ˈwᵘoˈm ᵘol, subst + pcl. ¶**I kes un (n)im i kuliwum ul aycel hakey natha-nāyn si 'ta** This is a poem expressing with pathos his yearning for his beloved. **Na nun kutay tul i om ul polye ko myech pen ina tōngkwu pakk ey na-kass.tun ko** (CM 2:385) I don't know how many times I went out to the entrance to the village hoping to see you folks arrive! More examples: SEE -um; -ˇwoˑm ol.

-umuley [< -um-uley], bnd adj-n (~ hata). ...-ish. ¶ pᵃ/ᵤlkumuley reddish. CF -muley.

-umulo = -um ulo

-um ulo < -ˇwᵘ/ₒˑm ᵘ/ₒˑlwo, subst + pcl [more often written than spoken]. with / as / by the doing or being; since (because of) the doing or being. ~ se, ~ malmiam.ᵉ/ₐ SAME. ¶ Nal i ccalp.um ulo īl ul mānh.i halq swu ka ēps.ta Because the day is short I can't do much work. Khi ka cak.um ulo ku lul Kkoma 'la ko pulless.ta We called him Shorty because he is small. Mom i he.yak ham ulo cwūng-¹notong un mōs sikhikeyss.ta As his health is weak, he cannot be put to heavy work. Na lul cakkwu chyē 'ta pom ulo musunq īl in ya ko mul.e pwass.ta He kept looking up at me, so I asked him what was the matter. SEE -keyss.um ulo, -ess.um ulo. CF -um ey, -ki ey / lo, -killey.

NOTE 1: Used in statements only; for other contexts -(u)ni-kka is appropriate.

NOTE 2: In the 1400s -ˇᵘ/ₒˑm ᵉ/ₐy was used for 'because', so there are only a few examples of -ˇwᵘ/ₒm + the particle ˑᵘ/ₒˑlwo (SEE -ˇwoˑm oˑlwo, ˇhosyaˑm oˑlwo). The first 'because' example is ˇepˑswu.m woˑlwo (?1517- ¹No 2: 2b) with an assimilated variant of the particle.

-um un, subst + pcl. ¶ Kutay lul pom un (n)im ul ponun ke wa kath.so Seeing you is like seeing my beloved (in person).

-umun, [Hamkyeng, Phyengan, S Kyengsang DIAL (Kim Yengpay 1984:96)] = -umyen

-ˇᵘ/ₒˑm ye, subst + cop inf (> -umye). NOTE: Although otherwise the copula after a vowel is written with an apostrophe ʼy... (including the other use of the infinitive, as a quasi-particle ˑiˑye / ˑʼye 'and'), this string was in transition to an integrated ending, just as we write it for modern Korean. In other uses the substantive was normally modulated (-ˇwo-m, -ˇwu-m), but when it was followed by ˑye or by ˑye nˑʼ the unmodulated form was usual. In this formation only, the substantive of -L- verbs, basically ...ˑlum or ...ˑl-om, was reduced a syllable by omitting the epenthetic vowel: ˑkwotˑiˑsywo ˑynˑtol ˇˑalˑm ye (1482 Kum-sam 2:3a) 'knew at once that it was this ox, and ... '. The expected (*)aˑlom 'knowing' was normally replaced by aˑlwom with the modulator -ˇwo-, as in ˑSSILQˑlwoˑptut aˑlwoˑm ol puˑthwulˑtt i.n i ˑʼla (1463 Pep 4:148b) '... one will have to rely on really knowing the meaning', but it appears unmodulated in specialized meanings 'one's purview, private matter / thing' (whence the adverb aˑlom-tye < *aˑlom tiˑye 'privately, personally') and is probably incorporated in the adjective stem aˑlom-taW- 'beautiful'. When the unmodulated form occurs, it is often to be taken as a substantive-derived noun: ˇˑsa(ˑ)lom means 'person', while saˑlwom means 'living, life' (1449 Kok 143; 1481 Twusi 8:29a) despite LCT's (1682) example of salwom 'person'; cwuˑkem (1459 Wel 9:36a, 1463 Pep 2:108b, 1481 Twusi 20:16a), with the effective -ˑ[k]e-, means 'corpse, dead person' while cwuˑkwum (1449 Kok 123) means 'dying, death' — in contrast with the unmodulated cwukuˑ[ˑ]m ye (1481 Twusi 8:29a). CF -uˑl ye > -ulye, where ˑye is the postmodifier 'question' (= ˑya).

¶ [TWO-MANG] ˑay [MYENG] ˑul miˑtu.m ye nwolˇGay yey ilˑhwum miˑtu.n i (1445 ¹Yong 16) he trusted the Will of Heaven for his escape and he trusted the name [like his] in the ballad. ˑemiˑtwo atoˑl ol mwoˑloˑm ye aˑtolˑtwo ˑemiˑlul mwoˑlo.l iˑʼn i (1447 Sek 6:3b) the mother neither knows the son nor does the son know the mother. ˇTTI-ˑNGWOK ˑtwoˑˑpwuyˑm ye ... (1449 Kok 18) the hells too are empty and ... . ˇhoma polˑko.m ye eˑtuwun ˇtwu kuˑth ey putˑti ani hoˑkwo (1482 Kum-sam 2:55a) no longer clings to the two ends, light and dark, but ... . ˑnaˑta ka ˑˑm ye puˑthe (1459 Wel 21:215b) from the time one is born.

SEE hoˑm ye, -ˑuˑm ye nˑʼ, -ˑuˑm ye ˑsye.

-umye < -ˇᵘ/ₒˑm ye, conjunctive (-mye after a vowel or l-extension of -L- stem); ?< -um + ie cop inf. 1. does / is and [semi-literary variant for gerund -ko, often marking a larger break]. ¶ Wuli nun selo towa cwumye kaluchye cwue ya hanta We should help each other and teach each other. Wuli nun thokki ʼmye sasum imye kkweng ul sanyang hayss.ta We hunted rabbits, deer, and pheasants. Nal un cemulko pay nun kophumye kalq kil un mel.ess.ta The night was falling, I was hungry, and I had a long way to go. Namphyen un hakca ʼko puin un siin imye, atul un uysa ʼko ttal un hwāka ʼta The husband is a scholar, the wife a poet; the son is a doctor, the daughter an artist.

2. = ~ **puthe** beginning with, from the time that. ¶**tongciq tal ey cep.e tulmye puthe nalssi nun mopsi chwuwe cyess.ta** As soon as November set in the weather got quite cold.

3. ~ **mālmye hata** does off and on. ¶**Pi ka omye mālmye hanta** It rains off and on.

4. [lit] = **-umyen se** (while). ¶**Īl hamye paywuca!** Let us work while we learn and learn while we work! **Kil ul mul.umye 'na kamyen molulq ka ku cip chac.ki ka com elyewulq ke l'** The house will be difficult to find unless perhaps you ask along the way.

5. SEE **(-ta) 'mye, (-ta) 'myen se**

-umye cocha, conjunctive + particle. ¶**Ne nun mek.umye cocha kwūn soli ka mānh.kwun a** You complain even though you are eating!

-umye ka, conjunctive + pcl [? limited to neg cop]. ¶**Kel.umye ka ani 'la tallimye ce phyocek ul mac.hila 'nun ke 'ta** They want us to hit that target running, not walking.

-umye khenyeng, conjunctive + pcl. ¶**Ku nun swul masimye khenyeng cha masimye to chayk ul mōsq ilk.nun sēngcil ita** He is of such a nature that he can't read while drinking tea, much less while drinking liquor.

-umye kkaci, conjunctive + pcl. ¶**Kakseng-cey lul mek.umye kkaci kongpu hal phil.yo ka iss.na?** Is there any need to study to the point of taking stay-awake pills?

-umye 'la to, conjunctive + cop var infinitive + particle. ¶**Kīlmye 'la to** (better: **Kīlmyen se 'la to**, best: **Kil.e to**) **mokcek-ci kkaci nun kkok kako ya mālkeyss.ta** I must get to my destination, however long the journey.

-umye mace, conjunctive + pcl. ¶**Ce sālam un kil kel.umye mace chayk ul ilk.nunta** He has his nose in a book even walking the street.

-umye man, conjunctive + particle [awkward]. ¶**Cenyek ul mek.umye man latio lul tut.nunta** We listen to the radio only during dinner. **Na nun āmuli sikkulewun sōk ey se 'la to chayk ul ilk.ulq swu iss.ci man um.ak ul tul.umye man (un) mōsq ilk.keyss.e** However noisy it is I can read, but the one thing I can't do is listen to music and read.

-umye mata, conjunctive + pcl [awkward]. ¶**Na nun cenyek ul mek.umye mata** (= **mek.ul ttay mata**) **nul phīnan sal.i hatun ttay sayngkak hanta** Every time I eat dinner I think of the days when I was leading a refugee life.

-ˈuˈm ye nˈ, substantive + cop inf + abbr pcl (> **-umyen (un)**). if; when. ¶**ˈˈmwoˈtin kilˈh ey pteˈle tiˈm ye nˈ** (1447 Sek 6:3b) if one falls into an evil path … . **ˈˈcolaˈm ye nˈ eˈlwu ˈPEP ul pwoyˈhwozoˈWwoˈl i ˈ-ngi ˈˈta** (1447 Sek 6:11ab) when I am grown I can duly learn the Law. **ˈSYENG-ZIN ˈˈepˈkesin ˈt i woˈla.m ye nˈ** (1459 Wel 9:7a) when the absence of a saint is long in duration … . SEE **hoˈm ye nˈ**.

-umyen, conditional (**-myen** after a vowel or l-extension of -L- stem). ABBR **-umˈ/-mˈ**; DIAL **-umon, -umo, -umu**. This had emerged as an ending by 1728 (SEE **-umyen se**), from earlier **-ˈᵘ⁄oˈm ye nˈ**. CF **-umyen un; -ko nun**. The ending can be preceded by **-ess-, -keyss-,** and **-ess.tu-** (CF **-ess.tulaˈmyen**).

1. 1a. if, provided; when, whenever. ¶**sikan i iss.usimyen** if/when you have (the) time. **com te iss.umyen** in/after a little while. **cēnsel ey uy hamyen** according to tradition, as legend has it. **wēn hasimyen** if you like. **tasi māl hamyen** (to put it in) in other words. **kuleh.ci anh.umyen** ("if it is not that way" =) otherwise, else, or else. **Nemu mānh.i kel.umyen phikon hay cinta** If you walk too much, you get tired. ¹**Nayil omyen na hanthey māl hay la** Speak to me about it when you come tomorrow. **Ku i wa sakwimyen sakwilq swulok cōh.ta** The more I get to know him the more I like him. **Mān.il i kes i com te ssamyen sālam tul i mānh.i sakeyss.ta** If this item were cheaper people would buy lots of them. **Pom i omyen kkoch i phinta** When spring comes the flowers bloom. **Sewul un elma 'na te kamyen toylq ka** How much longer before we get to Seoul? **Pi ka omyen kaci mōs hakeyss.ta** I won't go if it rains. **Khi ka khumyen sōk i ēps.ta** If a man is (too) tall he lacks "depth" (= sense). **Ney kes i ani ('la) 'myen, nwukwu uy kes ici** If it isn't yours, I wonder whose it is?

1b. ~ **molulq ka,** ~ **mōlla to** provided that (as long as) it does not happen; unless … . ¶**Kil ul mul.umye 'na kamyen molulq ka ku cip chac.ki com elyewulq ke l'** The house will be hard to find unless perhaps you ask someone the way. **Son nim i omyen mōlla to ku yaksok un cikhikeyss.ta** I will keep the appointment unless I should have a visitor. **Kim Ilqseng i cwuk.umyen mōlla to Hānkwuk un thōngil** haki elyepta It will be difficult for Korea to unite as long as Kim Ilqseng is alive.

2. 2a. (cēypal) ~ cōh.keyss.ta (1) I hope it will, I wish it would, it would be nice if it did, it will be nice if it does; (2) It would be better to do. ¶Kaul i kaci anh.umyen cōh.keyss.ta It would be nice if autumn would not leave us. Hānkwuk māl ul cal hamyen cōh.keyss.ey yo I hope I speak Korean well (or: I wish I spoke Korean well). Incey wuli ka cip ey kamyen cōh.keyss.ta We better go home now.

2b. -ess.umyen hanta, abbr < -ess.umyen cōh.keyss.ta ko sayngkak hanta. I wish that, I hope that. ¶Catong-cha lul kacyess.umyen hanun tey yo I sure wish I had a car. Nal i cōh.ass.umyen hanta I hope the day is nice.

2bb. -ess.umyen! = -ess.umyen hanta. Tōn i iss.ess.umyen! If only I had the money!

2c. ~ komapkeyss.ta I would like someone / you to do it; ~ komawe hakeyss.ta he would like someone/you to do it. ¶Ilccik com osimyen komapkeyss.ey yo I'd appreciate your coming a little early.

2d. ~ toynta has only got to do it (that's all); it works out (if one does it). ¶Nay ka chwīcik man hamyen toynta I only have to get a job. Cito man kūlimyen toynta You've only (got) to draw a map, that's all. Cikum kamyen toynta If you go now, you'll make it.

2e. ~ an toynta, ~ mōs ssunta it won't (will not) do to do it, one must / ought / should not do it; -ci anh.umyen an toynta ought to (should) do it. ¶Cip ey iss.ci anh.umyen an toynta We ought to stay at home. Mun an ey kamyen an toynta We shouldn't go to town. CF -e se nun an toynta.

2f. -ess.umyen siph.ess.ta SEE siph.ta

3. SEE ~ se (to); ~ un.

4. X-umyen ⋯ X-ess.ci. ¶Kwulm.umyen kwulm.ess.ci ku sālam hanthey kwukel un haki silh.e I'd rather starve than beg from him. Ku sālam ina kamyen kass.ci talun sālam un mōs kanta HE might be able to go, but no one else could go. Cwuk.umyen cwuk.ess.ci ku ke n' cēng-mal mōs hakeyss.e I'd rather die than do that!

5. X-umyen ⋯ X-e to (or X-toy) + NEGATIVE. cwuk.umyen cwuk.e to desperately, strongly, obstinately, under any/whatever circumstances. molumyen mōlla to, molumyen molutoy if my guess is right, perhaps, maybe.

6. X-umyen X-ulq swulok SEE -ulq swulok

-umye 'na, conjunctive + cop adversative. ¶Kil ul mul.umye 'na kamyen molulq ka ku cip chac.ki ka com elyewulq ke l' The house will be a bit hard to find unless perhaps you ask along the way.

-ˑᵘ⁄ₒˑm yeng [var] = -ˑᵘ⁄ₒˑm ye. ¶teuˑm yeng teˑle (1466 Kup 1:70b) increasing it and decreasing it.

-umyen i, conditional + particle [limited to neg cop]. ¶Sālam i nemu mānh.i omyen i mūncey ka ani 'la, hana to an omyen etteh.k' 'enun ya ka mūncey 'ta It isn't a question of (what we do) if too many people come, it's a question of what (we do) if not even one shows up.

-umyen ina, conditional + cop adversative. ¶Ku sālam i twū si kkaci omyen ina molulq ka i īl un onul kkaci kkuth nāyki nun him tulq ke l' Unless he is here by, say, two o'clock, it will be hard to get this job finished today.

-umyen in tul, conditional + copula modifier + postmod. ¶Kil ul mul.umyen in tul cip iya mōs chac.e kakeyss.ˢo? Will I be unable to find the house even if I ask?

-umyen iya, conditional + particle. ¶Ku yak man mek.umyen iya tangcang ey nās.ci If you just take this medicine I think you'll get better in no time at all. Swul han thek ul cal et.e mek.umyen iya nācwung ey ka se khun soli mōs haci You would not complain later on if only you were given a good treat of wine to drink. ABBR -umyen ya.

-umyen khenyeng, conditional + pcl [cute?]. ¶Ku ¹nōin i ppalli cwuk.umyen khenyeng acik to sip-nyen un mūncey ēps.ulq kes ita You might think that old man would die soon, but he's got a good ten years to go.

-umyen se, conditional + particle. Attested from 1728 as -umyen sye. 1. while ⋯ at the same time. ¶nolay lul hamyen se chwum ul chwuta dances and sings at the same time. wūlmyen se māl hata tells it in tears. um.ak ul tul.umyen se kōhyang ul sayngkak hata thinks of home while listening to the music. achim(q pap) ul mek.umyen se sinmun ul ilk.ta reads the newspaper over the breakfast table. pul tha olumyen se kala-anc.ess.ta sank in flames. wūlmyen se kyeca lul mekta "eats mustard while shedding tears"= swallows a bitter pill".

Huymyen se melken kes ul huy-melkeh.ta hanta A coloring that is white and clean is described as "nice and fair". CF (1916 Gale 53) chocho ho.ye kamyen sye pwopsyeyta let's see as time goes [on/by]; salom i sal.a kamyen sye yele kaci hwannan ul tang homnoyta as one lives one's life, one meets all sorts of troubles. NOTE: V-umyen se is the main or continuing activity.

2. = ~ to while ··· yet; although ··· also; at the very same time that. [CF -e to, which can have different subjects for the two clauses; -umyen se (to) usually has the same subject for both.] ¶Tōn un ēps.umyen se (to) cal ssunta While you have no money, yet you spend a lot.

3. for a special sentence-final use of the abbreviated form of hamyen se SEE 'myen se.

-umyen se ka, conditional + particle + particle. ¶Kel.umyen se ka ani 'la co'.yong hi anc.e se yēyki hayss.ta We didn't talk while walking, we sat down and talked quietly. Kil i yeki lul cīnamyen se ka te hēm hata (CM 2:120) The road is steeper when passing by this place. Ku nun um.ak ul tul.umyen se ka ani 'la swul ul masimyen se si lul ssunta He writes his poetry not when listening to music but when drinking.

-umyen se kkaci, conditional + pcl + pcl. ¶Ku ka cwuk.umyen se kkaci han pūthak in tey an tul.e cwulq swu ēps.ci We could not fail to heed the request he made on his deathbed.

-umyen se 'la to, conditional + pcl + copula var inf + pcl. ¶Yāhak ey tanimyen se 'la to kongpu nun hay ya 'ci! You ought to get some education, even if it is just night school!

-umyen se man, conditional + pcl + pcl. ¶Ku nun swul ul masimyen se man si lul ssunta He writes poetry only when drinking.

-umyen se n' = -umyen se nun

-umyen se 'na, conditional + pcl + cop advers. ¶Ku īl un ha to elyewe se pōswu lul cal pat.umyen se 'na halq īl ici kece nun mōs halq īl ita That is such a terribly difficult job that it is something I will do for some sort of remuneration but not for free.

-umyen se 'n tul, conditional + pcl + cop mod + postmodifier. ¶Cēng sikan i pappumyen kel.umyen se 'n tul mōs mek.ul ya If we are really so pressed for time, can't we eat while on our way?

-umyen se nun, conditional + particle + pcl. ¶Cwūngyo hanq yēyki 'ni-kka n' kel.umyen se nun mōs hakeyss.ta It is too important for me to tell it while walking (= on the street). Na nun um.ak ul tul.umyen se nun chayk ul mōsq ilk.nunta I can't read (books) while I am listening to music.

-umyen se puthe, conditional + pcl + pcl. from the moment that ···, starting when ··· . ¶Tāy-hak.kyo kongpu lul haki sīcak hamyen se puthe tāmpay lul phiwukey tōyss.ta I took up smoking from the time that I began my college work. Emeni uy mok-soli lul tul.umyen se puthe pyēng i nās.nun kes kath.ess.ta My illness seemed to get better from the moment I heard Mother's voice. Hak.kyo ey kamyen se puthe acwu co'.yong hay cyess.ta He quieted down tremendously when he began going to school. Namyen se puthe yeki sālko iss.ta I have been living here ever since I was born. Ku cip un kacang i cwuk.umyen se puthe mang haki sīcak hayss.ta From the day the patriarch died the family began going downhill.

-umyen se to, conditional + particle + pcl (SEE -umyen se 2). ¶Ne nun pap ul cal mek.umyen se to pulphyeng in ya You complain even when well fed? Ku man han yēyki 'la 'myen kel.umyen se to halq swu iss.ko han cali ey anc.e se to halq swu iss.nun key 'ci If that is all that's to be said it can be said walking or seated.

-umyen se tul, conditional + pcl + pcl. ¶Ca, ttek ul mantulci man mālko mek.umyen se tul hasi yo Don't just make rice cakes, people, eat some while making them. TV lul pomyen se tul kongpu (tul) hamyen (tul) an toynta You kids mustn't study in front of the TV.

-umyen se 'tun ci, conditional + pcl + cop retr mod + postmod. ¶Chayk ul pomyen se 'tun ci kūlim ul kūlimyen se 'tun ci ttan sayngkak ul hamyen mōs ssunta Regardless of whether you are reading a book or painting a picture, you should not let yourself get distracted by other thoughts.

-umyen se ya, conditional + pcl + pcl. ¶Pap ul ssip.umyen se ya etteh.key māl ul hani How can I talk while I'm chewing on rice this way?! Kongcang ey tanimyen se ya kongpu lul halq swu iss.na? How can one study while going to and from the factory?!

-umyen tul, conditional + pcl. ¶Sicang hamyen tul wusen chan pap ila to mekci If you (all) are hungry, eat the leftover (cold) rice first. Hak.kyo ey kamyen tul cōh.un chinkwu lul sakwie ya hanta When you go to school, children, you must make good friends.
-umye 'n tul, conjunctive + copula modifier + postmodifier. ¶Kil ul mul.mye 'n tul (= mul.umyen se 'n tul) ku cip iya mōs chac.e kakeyss.ni I will surely be able to find the house, even if I have to ask. Yelqsim man iss.umyen īl hamye 'n tul kongpu mōs hal lī ka iss.nun ya? Is there any (= Surely there isn't any) reason you can't study even while working, if you are only earnest enough.
-umye nun < -ʼuo ̇m ye ˙nun, conjunctive + pcl. ¶Tallimye nun (= tallimyen se nun) mōs mac.hye to kel.umye nun (= kel.umyen se nun) ce phyocek ul mac.hil swu iss.ta Even if I can't hit the target running, walking I can.
-umyen un, conditional + pcl [< -umye nun]. ¶I yak ul mek.umyen un (= mek.umyen) palo nās.nunta When you take this medicine you will get better right away. Attested from 1730 as ⋯myen un vs. ⋯mye.n un, but often spelled as an unanalyzed ending, no different from -umye nun. It is unclear whether there is a real difference in meaning between the two modern sources of the same phonemic string.
-umyen ya, abbr < -umyen iya
-umye pota, conjunctive + pcl [a bit awkward]. ¶Ku co'.yong han um.ak soli nun wass.ta kass.ta kel.umye pota anc.e swīmye tut.nun phyen i nāss.ta / cōh.ass.ta Rather than listen to that quiet music while walking to and fro, it would be better to sit down and relax and listen to it. Cha lul masimye pota swul ul masimye yāyki hanun key te ceng i thong haci It is easier to get one's feelings across chatting over liquor than it is over tea.
-umye puthe, conjunctive + pcl. SEE -umye 2.
-umye' se, [SLOPPY] abbr < -myen se
-ʼuo ̇m ye ˙sye, subst + cop inf + pcl. SEE ho ̇m ye ˙sye.
-umye to, conjunctive + pcl [? a bit awkward]. ¶Ku īl un kotoynq īl ini mek.umye to hako swīmye to hay la That is a tough job so take breaks to eat and to rest while doing it. Ku tōngsang un keli han pokphan ey iss.ki ttaymun ey omye to poko kamye to polq swu iss.ta That statue is right in the middle of the street so you can see it both coming and going.
-umye tul, conjunctive + pcl. ¶Kulem, kwāca 'la to mek.umye tul anc.e iss.key Well, sit and have some pastries, you fellows.
-umye 'tun ci, conjunctive + cop retr mod + postmod. ¶Kel.umye 'tun ci tallimye 'tun ci āmu'h.tun ce phyocek man mac.hye pwā la Try hitting the target either while walking or while running, whatever way.
-umye ya, conjunctive + pcl. ¶Swul masimye ya chayk ul ilk.ulq swu iss.na? Can you possibly read when you're drinking (liquor)?
-un⋯ SEE ALSO -on⋯
un < ˙ uon, particle (after vowel nun < ˙nuon, abbr n' < ˙n'). "as for": marks the theme, subdues the focus on the preceding word or phrase in order to foreground the rest of the sentence for various reasons, including these:

1. Because the sentence is long you choose some part or parts as the least novel, the most easily omitted. ¶Na nun cīnan tho.yoilq pam ey kongwen ey se chinkwu lul mannass.ta (Me — what I did was this:) I met a friend last Saturday night in the park. Cīnan tho.yoilq pam ey nun nay ka kongwen ey se chinkwu lul mannass.ta Last Saturday night I met a friend in the park. Kongwen ey se nun cīnan tho.yoilq pam ey nay ka ku chinkwu lul mannass.ta In the park last Saturday night I met that friend. Ku chinkwu nun cīnan tho.yoilq pam ey i kongwen ey se nay ka mannass.ta (That friend —) I met him last Saturday night in this park. Cīnan tho.yoilq pam ey nun na nun kongwen ey se (nun) chinkwu lul mannass.ta I met a friend and it was in the park, last Saturday night. Tal un han hay ey yelq-twu pen tōnta The moon rotates twelve times (in) a year. Nala nun cwuqkwen kwa ¹yengtho wa kwuk.min ulo toye iss.ta A nation is made up of sovereignty, territory, and people.

2. Because the item has been mentioned before, it is OLD information, so you subdue the emphasis when you repeat it. ¶Pokswun-i ka tal ul chyē 'ta pwass.ta; tal un maywu palk.ess.ta Pokswun-i looked up at the moon; it was very bright. Pokswun-i ka tal ul chyē 'ta pwass.ta; kuliko ku ay nun sulphe cyess.ta Pokswun-i looked up at the moon; she fell sad.

3. Some other part of the sentence demands foregrounding because it is a focus of inquiry or denial. ¶Ne nun mues ul hanun ya What are you doing? Ttek un nwu ka mek.ess.nun ya Who ate the rice cake? Kim sensayng un ēncey tte-nasinun ya When is Mr Kim leaving? Kwūkyeng un mōs hayss.e yo? Didn't you do any sightseeing?

4. Two items in contrast are backgrounded so as to play up the points of contrast. (Notice that English puts stress on the items, not the contrasts.) ¶Na nun Pusan se oko, chinkwu nun Māsan se wass.ta I come from Pusan, and my friend comes from Masan. I kes un cōh.ci man ku kes un nappe yo THIS one is good, while THAT one is bad. Pokswun-i nun pucilen haci man, awu nun com keyuluta Pokswun-i is hard-working, but her little brother is a bit lazy. Cal un hatoy olay nun mōs hanta He does it well but not for long.

NOTE 1: The meaning of this focus particle is mutually exclusive with those of ya / iya (only if it be) and to (also, even). The particle freely follows other particles and sequences, but i / ka and ul / lul obligatorily drop. SEE -ko nun, -ki nun, -e nun, -ci nun.

NOTE 2: The MK particle has two versions, ˙un / ˙nun and ˙on / ˙non. The more common version is the latter. The shapes ˙un / ˙nun are usual when the vowel of the preceding syllable is u or wu, as in ˙ptu.t un (1481 Twusi 23:9b), il˙hwu˙m un (1463 Pep 2:222b), and LWUW ˙nun (1447 Sek 6:2b); but even so there is an occasional example of the version ˙on / ˙non, as in ˙kuyGwun ˙on (1482 Kum-sam 2:29b). The higher-vowel shapes are also found when the syllable of the preceding syllable is e or ey, as in ke˙s un (1463 Pep 6:144a), ¨NGE nun (1451 Hwun-en 1a), and ¨twuy.h ey ˙nun (1445 ¹Yong 30); but the lower-vowel shapes also occur and seem to be more common, as in ce ˙non (1459 Wel 13:35ab), ne ˙non (1481 Twusi 8:7a, 1482 Kum-sam 2:5b), and ¨THYEY ˙non (1447 Sek 19:10b). Only the lower-vowel version occurs after a syllable with the vowels uy and wuy, as in ˙SYE-KUY ˙non (1447 Sek se:6a) and NGWUY-NGWUY ˙non (1459 Wel 1:1b); likewise for oy, woy, ay: kutoy ˙non (1481 Twusi 8:24a), SYEN-SOYNG ˙on (1482 Nam 1:30b), kama˙kwoy ˙non (1481 Twusi 22:39b), ¨NAY ˙non (1459 Wel se:

13a). When the preceding vowel is o or wo or a only the lower-vowel version occurs: ˙CHO ˙non (1447 Sek5a), ˙no˙m on (1445 ¹Yong 24), ¨salo˙m on (1447 Sek 6:22a, 1466 Kup 2:64a, ...), kwo˙c on (1447 Sek 23:40b), SYWOW ˙non (1447 Sek 13:53a), ˙na ˙non (1447 Sek 6:5a, 1462 ¹Nung 1:86a, ...), ¨ma˙l on (1447 Sek 6:36a, 9:27a). An exceptional case: KKUY-NGWAN ˙un (1475 Nay 1:28b). After a syllable with i there are examples of the higher-vowel version, as in ˙TTAY-SSING ˙un (1459 Wel 1:37a), but ˙on / ˙non is the norm: ˙i ˙non (1462 ¹Nung 4:27b), a˙coma ¨ni˙m on (1447 Sek 6:1a), NGUY-SIM ˙on (1447 Sek 24:3b), ...

NOTE 3: SEE ˙non (NOTE).

-un < -ᵘ⁄₀n, modifier (-n after a vowel); SEE -ess.un (past modifier).

1. (with adj, cop) ... that (which) is, ... who is. ¶cak.un namu a tree that is little, a little tree — CF cāktun namu a tree that used to be little, a once small tree. kwuk.hoy uywen in Kim paksa Dr Kim, who is a member of the National Assembly — CF kwuk.hoy uywen i(ess.)tun Kim paksa Dr Kim, who was (had been) a member of the National Assembly. malk.ko ko.yo han pam a night that is clear and calm.

2. (with v) ... that/who has done, ... that/which one has done; ... that (one) did; ... that (one) did to / from / with / for / ... . ¶(phyēnci lul) pat.un sālam the man who received it (the letter). (ku sālam i) pat.un phyēnci the letter that was received (by the man). wuli ka selo mannan cali the place where we met each other. ku sālam i pap ul mek.un cip the house that he ate his meal at. Ku ka tte-nan ithut-nal the day after he left. SEE X-una X-un.

NOTE 1: For some of the -L- stems, there are variant modifier forms as if made from -LL- stems. Besides regular ecin < ecilta 'is kind' there is the variant ecilun, and besides regular situn < situlta 'withers, wilts' there is the variant situlun. Compare some of the irregular substantives (like el.um 'ice', differing from ēlm 'freezing').

NOTE 2: After a consonant-final stem the MK ending has the shapes -˙un and -˙on. Choice of the shape is determined by the vowel of the preceding syllable. After aC, oC, or woC only -˙on occurs, as in na˙mon (1447 Sek 23:13a,

1459 Wel 8:91b), koˑcon (1459 Wel 8:97a, 1463 Pep 2:176b), and ῭tywohon (1459 Wel 8:90a); the exception nwoˑphun (?1517- Pak 1:5a) for nwoˑphon (1481 Twusi 15:37b) is unusual. After e, uC, wuC, or iC only -ˑun occurs, as seen in meˑkun (1459 Wel 1:43b), nulˑkun (1481 Twusi 7:10a, 22:7b), cwuˑkun (1447 Sek 24:28a), and kiˑphun (1445 ¹Yong 2, 1447 Sek 9:27a). Stems ending in l reduce the expected strings l-un and l-on to just n, as in ῭mwoˑtin (1447 Sek 9:24b; 1459 Wel 8:69b, 9:24b) < ῭mwoˑtil- 'bad', ῭men (1447 Sek 13:59a, 1459 Wel 7:12b) < ῭mel- 'distant', ˑsun (1462 ¹Nung 9:86a) < ˑsul- 'vanish', ῭wuˑnˑi (1447 Sek 24:20b, 1449 Kok 80) < ῭wul- 'cry', ῭cwon (1463 Pep 1:190a) < ῭cwol- 'shrink', ˑskon (1482 Kum-sam 3:59a) < ˑskol- 'spread it', ῭an (1462 ¹Nung 9:13a) < ῭al- 'know'. Another way to describe that: the final l drops so that the ending is attached without the epenthetic vowel, as expected after a stem that now ends in a vowel. The basic shape of the -L- stems is ⋯l^{u} /o- but in the surface forms this is reduced by dropping the vowel or the whole syllable; for stems which begin with a basic low (unmarked) pitch, the high accent of an ending is kept and blended with the low to produce the rising tone marked with the double dot (῭); that is why the dictionary form (the indicative assertive) of an -L- verb begins either ῾⋯ or ῭⋯. The modulated modifier is formed as expected, with the ⋯l- of the stem (as well as its high or low basic accent) retained, by simply appending the modulator before the modifier ending (-ˑw^{u}/o-n): ˑpiˑlwon ˑpaˑp ol (1449 Kok 122) the food [just now] begged; woˑnol za aˑlwoˑnˑi (1463 Pep 4:36a) that I just today found out … .

una, particle (na after a vowel)

1. please (softens a command). SEE -ulyem una, -key na, -sey na, -ca 'm una.

2. indeed (emphasizes interjections, adverbs).

2a. (interjections). ¶eme na, ikhi na, ikki na, elssikwu na, eykku / eykhu na.

2b. (adverbs). ¶phek una really quite. yepuk una (not) to any small degree, indeed. cak-hi na not much.

NOTE: After a vowel it is not always easy to tell whether /na/ represents 'na (= ina) or na (= una). When in doubt, we treat it as ina: āmuli 'na 'surely', hāyng-ye 'na 'fortunately', kuli 'na 'that way', nemu 'na 'ever so much', kkway (kk'ay) 'na '(fairly) well / much', te 'na '(any) more'. The word that is usually spelled tewukina 'still more' could be treated either as tewuk-i na (as in KEd) or as tewuk ina, but kattukina 'on top of that / everything, still (more)' is probably best viewed as kattuk ina rather than kattuk 'i 'na (< ? kattuk hi ina), so we will treat them both the same (as ina). After indeterminates na represents ina (= itun ci): elma 'na, ecci 'na, etteh.key 'na; CF enu kes ina.

-una < -ˑ^{u}/oˑna, adversative (-na after a vowel); -(ess.)ess.una and -(ess.)keyss.una occur.

1. does / is but; though it is / does; admittedly ⋯ but. ¶Nac un tewuna cenyek un senul hata The days are hot but the nights are cool. Khi nun khuna him un cēkta Though tall, he has little in the way of strength. Tōn un mānh.una pulhayng hata Although he is rich, he is unhappy. Kako siph.una sikan i ēps.ta I'd like to come but I haven't got the time. Ku nun yelqsim un iss.una caycwu ka ēps.ta He has enthusiasm but he lacks talent. Ku pun un hwullyung han hakca (i)sina sangsik i ēps.usita He is a splendid scholar, but he lacks common sense. Āy nun mānh.i ssess.una polam i ēps.ess.ta I tried very hard, but all in vain. Ku kos ey kaki nun kass.ess.una nwū' nim hanthey tullici nun anh.ess.ess.ta I was there, to be sure, but I did not stop by my older sister's. Hwaksil hi nun molukeyss.una Hangkali ey pān.lan i il.e nass.ta ko hanta I don't know for sure, but I heard that a revolt has broken out in Hungary. Ku ay nun keki ey hyeng i iss.e se kass.ess.keyss.una ne nun way keki kass.ess.nun ya He must have gone there because he has a brother living there, but what was the reason you went there?

2. 2a. ~ (kan ey) (whether ⋯) or, or the like, or whatnot. ¶ilena celena (kan ey) ⋯ whether doing this or doing that. iss.(ess.)una ēps.(ess.)una whether there is / was or not. Nay ka ponun kes ina tut.nun kes ina tā say lowess.ta Everything I saw or heard was new to me. ona an ona (= otun ci an otun ci) whether he comes here or not. khuna cak.una kalici anh.ko regardless of whether it is big or small. mues ina (= mues itun ci) anything (at

A Reference Grammar of Korean

all), everything. **Mikwuk sālam ina Yengkwuk sālam ina sangkwan i ēps.ta** It doesn't matter whether it is an American or an Englishman. **Cōh.una silh.una** (= **cōh.tun ci silh.tun ci**) **hay ya hanta** You must do it whether you like it or not. **Onul kana ¹nayil kana machan-kaci 'ta** It makes no difference whether you go there today or tomorrow.

2b. (however it might be) still, nonetheless, yet. ¶**Āmuli puluna tāytap hanun sālam un ēps.ess.ta** However hard I shouted there was no one who answered.

3. ~ **talum ēps.ta** is no different from, is just (all) the same as (= **hako kath.ta**). ¶**han cip-an ina talum ēps.ta** is almost (is as good as) one of the family. **Ku nun cimsung ina pyel lo talum ēps.ta** He is little more than an animal. **Payk-nyen hacheng ul kitalina talum ēps.ta** "it is just like waiting a hundred years for the muddy river to clear up" = "is like waiting for pigs to fly".

4. **X-una X-un** that is very / quite X, that is really (ever so) X — said of impressive things. ¶**khuna khun cip** a really big house. **nelp.una nelp.un pata** a sea that is just ever so wide. **noph.una noph.un san** such a high mountain, ever so high a mountain. **kiph.una kiph.un mul** water ever so deep. **mēna mēn kil** a road / journey ever so long. **cōh.una cōh.un** ever so nice. **kīna kīn** ever so long (usually of time, CF **kīlko kīn, kīn kīn**). NOTE: 1894 Gale 221 spells *khun.akhun* for *khuna khun*, apparently regarding the *-a-* as a kind of infix lodged in a structure iterating an adjective modifier (like "big-Oh!-big"?).

5. **tuna-tulta** comes and goes, frequents. [Or is this **tu-l-** + **na-**?]

? 6. (sentence-final) SEE **ila 'na**

7. SEE **-una māna**

-una → **-un a** = **-un ya**

-una lul, advers + pcl. ¶**Hankul ina Hānq-ca 'na lul mak.lon hako** Regardless whether it is Korean or Sino-Korean [Chinese]. CF **-na lul**.

-una-ma, extended adversative. (is / does) but anyway; however; despite (the value-detracting fact that). ¶**Mas un cōh.ci mōs hana-ma hana tusio** They are not very tasty, but please have one anyway. **Cip un cek.una-ma cali ka cōh.ta** The house may be small, but it's nicely located.

-una māna, advers + advers < **mālta**. there is no need to, one might as well not, it is useless / unnecessary to. ¶**Māl hana māna, Hānkwuk kyengcey palqcen i kup-senmu 'ta** Needless to say, the development of Korea's economy is of utmost urgency. **Kulen kwamok un paywuna māna 'ta** It is useless to study a subject like that. **Ku i hanthey mul.e popsita — Mul.e pona māna** Let's ask him — There's no point in asking him (he wouldn't know).

~ **'ci (yo)** [< **ici (yo)**] it does not matter (makes no difference) whether ... or not; it will do no good whether ... or not. ¶**Ku yenghwa lul ka-poca — Ka-pona māna 'ci** Let's go see that movie — What's the point in seeing it?! **Yak ul mek.una māna 'ci yo** (M 2:1:113) It doesn't help whether I take the medicine or not.

~ **hata**, vni. does off and on, does fitfully, does halfheartedly / hesitantly, hesitates. (CF **-un twung mān twung**). ¶**Cam ul cana māna hayss.tuni mopsi kotan hata** Having slept but fitfully I am very tired. **Cēmsim ul mek.una māna hako wass.tuni pay ka pelsse kophuta** Having just picked at my lunch (having eaten hardly any lunch) I am now hungry. **Cikum ku cip ey l' kana māna** (= **kalq ka mālq ka**) **hako iss.ta** I am hesitating now (trying to decide) whether to go to his house or not.

-una-ma to, extended adversative + pcl [a bit awkward]. ¶**Tōn un ēps.una-ma (to) toylq swu iss.nun tay lo towa tulikeyss.ˢup.nita** I have no money; even so, I'll help you all I can.

-una-ma yo, extended adversative + pcl. ¶**Toylq swu iss.nun tay lo towa tulikeyss.ˢup.nita — tōn un mānh.i ēps.una-ma yo** I will help you all I can — but I haven't much money.

-(u)nan, -(u)naney [Ceycwu DIAL (Seng ¹Nakswu 1984:8-10); does not occur with copula] = **-(u)ni-kka (n')**.

-una tul, advers + pcl [? rare]. ¶**Pang ul com chiwuna tul** (= **chiwutun ci tul**) **i key musun kkol in ya** You kids better clean up this messy room!

? **-un ccok-ccok** SEE **ccok-ccok**

-un cek, mod + n. the time (= occasion) that it happened; a past experience; CF **-unq īl, -un swu**. ~ **i iss.ta** has ever / once happened; ~ **iss.ess.ta** had ever / once happened. ~ **i ēps.ta** has never happened; ~ **i ēps.ess.ta** had never happened. ¶**Na to kulen māl ul tul.un cek i iss.ta** I have heard such talk, too. **Pihayng-ki**

lul tha pon cek i ēps.ta I have never traveled by plane. Hānkwuk ey se (han pen to) phyēnci pat.usin cek i ēps.ˢup.nikka? You haven't ever (even once) received a letter from Korea? Ku cen ey Ilpon ey ka-pon cek i iss.ess.nun ya Had you ever been to Japan before? Ku i eykey se han pen phyēnci lul pat.un cek i iss.ta I once received a letter from him.

-un cengto, modifier + noun. SEE cengto.

-un chay, mod + postmod. just as it is/did, (in) the original state of ⋯ , as is/was. ¶nwun ul kam.un ~ with eyes closed, without opening one's eyes. ip ul tamun ~ with mouth shut, without opening one's mouth. os ul ip.un ~ with clothes on, without undressing. Kwutwu lul sin.un chay lo tul.e wā to cōh.ta You may/can come right in with your shoes on. Uyca ey anc.un chay ku nun wuli lul mac.ess.ta He greeted us from (= seated in) his chair (without getting up). Pēm ul sān chay lo cap.ess.ta We caught a tiger alive. CF -un tay lo.

-un chek/chey hata, mod + postmod vn insep. pretends to be (to have done). ¶Ku nun poko to mōs pon chey hako cīna kass.ta He passed by, pretending not to see me. Cal nan chey haci mala Don't pretend you're somebody (= Don't be conceited). Pāpo 'n (= in) chey hako sālam ul sok.inta He fools/deceives people by pretending to be a fool.

-un ci₁, modifier + postmodifier (< -ᵘ⁄ₒₙ ˙t i, mod + postmod + pcl).

1. (with adj, cop) the uncertain fact of being = whether it is (for "whether it did" see -ess.nun ci); CF -un ya/ka. ¶meych in ci (mues in ci, nwukwu 'n ci, ēncey 'n ci) ālta knows how many they are (what it is, who it is, what place it is, when it is). pissan ci ssan ci (khun ci, cak.un ci, kem.un ci huyn ci) moluta (ālta, mūt.ta, ic.e pelita) doesn't know (knows, asks, forgets) whether it is costly or cheap (big or small, black or white). cham in ci ani 'n ci ālta/mūt.ta knows/asks whether it is true or not. Ku kes i elma 'n ci (= elma in ci) ic.e pelyess.ta I've forgotten how much it is. Ku kes i cēng-mal in ci ani 'n ci ku ka mul.ess.ta He asked if it were true.

2. 2a. ~ (yo) I wonder whether (how, what, ⋯). ¶Elma 'na khun ci (yo) I wonder how big it is. Ku ka Mikwuk ey se osin pun in ci (yo) I wonder if that is the person who came from America (or: Perhaps he came from America [3]). Wēynq īl in ci ku hanthey se yo say sosik ēps.ta I don't know why (= for some reason or other) I don't hear from him any more. Ku ai ka oy atul in ci pelus i ēps.ta Maybe the boy is an only son, the way he lacks manners. Nailon i ssan ci yo say nwukwu 'na nailon os ul ip.ess.ta I wonder if nylon is cheap; these days everybody wears nylon clothes.

2b. ~ yo (as a diffident question). ¶Keki nwukwu 'sin ci yo May I ask who is speaking (who you are)? Cen hal māl-ssum i iss.usin ci yo? Would there be any message (you would like to leave)? (Examples from M 2:1:283).

3. ~ (to moluta, yo) (I don't know whether =) maybe, perhaps it is. (NOTE: With adj and cop only; for "perhaps it did" see -ess.nun ci.) ¶Ku i ka Mikwuk ey se osin pun in ci to molunta Perhaps he (is the one who) came from America. Pelus ēps.nun kes ul pomyen ku ai ka oy atul in ci (to molunta) Judging from his lack of manners, I'd say maybe he is an only son. Nulk.e se kulen ci It must be my age (be because I am old).

4. given the state of being ⋯ : (etteh.key, etteh.key 'na, ecci 'na, elma 'na) ⋯ ~, ⋯-e se 'n ci it is so ⋯ that (= nemu ⋯-e se). ¶Nal i etteh.key chwuwun ci nwun ey se nwun-mul i na-onta The weather is so cold it brings tears to my eyes. Kēli ka mel.e se kulen ci yeki se poni-kka n', ku tali ka phek cāk.key pōynta The distance is so far the bridge appears quite small, when you look at it from here. Chwuwe se 'n ci keli ey sālam i ēps.ta It is so cold there is no one on the street.

-un ci₂, verb mod + postmod (< -un ˙t i mod + postmod + pcl). (the long time) since, from the time when: + TIME WORD + ita or i/ka toyta. ¶Sensayng nim ul poywun ci ka olay 'p.nita It has been a long time since we've seen you. Phyēnci lul pat.un ci (ka) sēk tal i toynta It's been three (long) months since I got a letter [NOTE: sahul 'three days' would sound funny because that seems too short a period]. Yeki on ci ō-nyen i toyess.ta It is five years since I was here. Ku i wa cakpyel han ci elma 'na toyn ya How long is it since you saw him last? Wui Tong pec kkoch ul mōs pon ci ka pelsse sā-nyen i tōy yo It has been four years now since I've been able [that I have not been able] to see the cherry blossoms at Wui Tong.

NOTE: The verb before -un ci can be affirmative ("it has been ⋯ since it happened") or negative ("it has been ⋯ that it has not happened") with the same truth value. The negative is usually strong (mōs rather than an).

-un ci kkaci, modifier + postmod + pcl. ¶**I os i elma 'n ci kkaci nun āl phil.yo ka ēps.ta** There is no need to know how much the dress costs.

-un ci ko, mod + postmod + pcl. [adj/cop only; lit] = -un tey! (exclamatory). ¶**Ā kippun ci ko** Oh such delight! **Hyung han ci ko** O woe! O evil day! (SEE NKd 678b.) CF -ulq si ko.

-un ci 'la (se), modifier + postmodifier + cop var inf (+ pcl). [lit] as, since (= -e se).

1. (with adj, cop) as/since it is. ¶**Ku nun wen.lay him i sēyn ci 'la tanpak ey penccek tul.ess.ta** Naturally strong as he is, he lifted it with the greatest of ease. **Ku nun kiek i cōh.un ci 'la se Sāse lul tā ōynta** As he has a good memory, he knows all the Four Books by heart. **Nemu 'na kippun ci 'la chwum chwumye nolay pulunta** They are so happy they dance and sing. **Ppioneyl(u) ka ppioneyl(u) in ci 'la, mōtun sāep ey se pi-cocik atong tul eykey mopem ul pointa** The "Pioneer", as a Pioneer, shows a good example to the nonorganization children in all undertakings. SEE hon ci 'la.

2. (with v) as/since it did; SYN -ess.nun ci 'la (se). ¶**Tongsayng eykey se phyēnci lul imi pat.un (= pat.ess.nun) ci 'la ku hyengphyen ul cal ālko iss.ess.ta** Since I had already received a letter from my little brother, I well understood his situation. CF Gale (1916:60) "A book form having the force of [-es.sunikka] in the colloquial. It has the force of <u>as, since</u> or a comma."

NOTE: Richard Rutt tells me that in early 19th-century writings (and infrequently in the 1937 translation of the Bible), there are found sentence-final examples of -un/-nun ci 'la. Perhaps these can be regarded as analogous to some of the uses of -un/-nun i 'la or -un/nun kes ita 'it is a fact that ... '. Are there examples of -un/-nun ci 'n i 'la, like -ulq ci 'n i 'la?

-un ci man, mod + postmod + pcl. ¶**Na nun ku īl i tānci kulen ci man al.ess.nun tey** I knew that (matter/job) would be just like that.

-un ci nun, mod + postmod + pcl. ¶**Ku ⁿyeca uy maum-ssi ka etten ci nun moluci man (un) elkwul un yeypputula** I do not know what her disposition is like but she had a pretty face (as I recall).

-un ci (se) puthe, mod + postmod (+ pcl) + pcl. ¶**Na nun ke ⁿyeca uy elkwul pota maum-ssi ka etten ci (se) puthe ālko siph.ta** I want to know first what her disposition is like, rather than her face.

-un ci to, mod + postmod + pcl. SEE -un ci (3).

-un (c)cok-(c)cok [substandard, ? DIAL] = -nun (c)cok-(c)cok. CF CM 2:71.

-un cuk(-sun), mod + postmod [somewhat lit; CF -umay = -um ey; -umyen un]. SEE in cuk; cuk (< ˙CUK).

1. since, as, when. ¶**Nay ka kuleh.key māl han cuk ku nun pelkhek sēng ul nāyss.ta** When I said that he flared up in anger. **Ttek man mek.un cuk sōk i cōh.c'anh.ta** Since I had nothing but rice cake my insides don't feel so good. **Nay ka ka-pon cuk pelsse mulken i tā na-kass.tula** When I went to see, the goods had already all run out. **Tol.a pon cuk ippun ⁿyeca ka iss.ess.ey yo** When I looked around, there was a pretty woman there. **Ku uy cip ey ka-pon cuk āmu to ēps.ess.ta** I tried going to his house but there was no one there. **Māl ul tut.ko pon cuk kulelq tus hata** As I heard him tell it, it seems quite plausible. **Kulen cuk ¹nayil kanun kes i cōh.keyss.ta** That being the case, you had better leave here tomorrow. **Ku chayk un nay kes in cuk tollye cwusio** As the book is mine, give it back to me. **Sicang han cuk sōk i ssulita** Since I am hungry I have a pain in my stomach.

2. if, then. ¶**Mul i malk.un cuk khun koki ka tulci anh.nunta** When the water is clear there are no big fish in it. **Ip ul pellin cuk māl i "cheng-sanq ¹yu-swu" 'ta** Once he opens his mouth he is all ("green mountains and flowing water" =) eloquence. **San ey namu ka ēps.un cuk hongswu uy wihem i iss.ta** If there are no trees in the mountains there is a danger of floods.

-un cwul, mod + postmod. the assumed fact that it is/did. ¶**Ku i ka kulen cwul (ul) mōllass.ta** I had no idea he would be that way. **Cey ttong kwulin cwul ul molunta** People do not realize that their own excrement stinks = People are blind to their own defects = "The pot calls the kettle black". **Ku ka kānchep in cwul nwu ka al.ess.ul ya** Who ever suspected that he was a spy? ··· ~ **(lo) ālta** thinks (supposes, assumes, expects, believes) that ··· ; CF **-un kes ul ālta** knows that ···, **-ul(.nun) ci ālta** knows whether ···. **Ku sacen i tul.e on cwul ānta** I think/believe that the dictionary has come in; CF **Ku chayk i tul.e wass.ta ko sayngkak hanta** I think that the book has come in.

-un cwung, mod + n. (in) the midst of being. ¶**Pappusin cwung ey i chelem īl ul towa cwusye se tāytan hi kāmsa hap.nita** I am very grateful to you for helping me in my work when you are busy.

-ʰ⁄ongi ˮta SEE *-ngi ˮta*

-ungkkay [DIAL (Mkk 1960:3:35)] = **-uni-kka**

-un hwū < ⁻ ʰ⁄on ¨HHWUW, modifier + noun. after going; after it happens (happened, will happen). ¶**Apeci hanthey se phyēnci lul pat.un hwū ey ne hanthey tāytap hakeyss.ta** I will give you an answer after I get the letter from my father. **Ku kes i Mikwuk ey osin hwū iess.ˢup.nikka?** Was that after you had already come to America? ANT **-ki cen ey**. SYN **-un twī**; CF **-un taum**.

-uni₁ (< ⁻ ʰ⁄oˈn i), sequential (-ni after a vowel); -(ess.)ess.uni, -(ess.)tuni, -(ess.)keyss.uni all occur.

1. (= **-uni-kka n'**): 1a. since it is/does; so. ¶**Nemu khuni pakkwuca** It is too big, so let's exchange it. **Onul un com pappuni ku īl un ¹nayil hakeyss.ta** I am rather busy today, so I'll take care of that matter tomorrow. **Halq īl i ēps.uni sānqpo ˈna halq ka yo?** Since we have nothing to do, shall we take a walk? **Na nun cal molu(keyss.u)ni sensayng hanthey mul.e pwā la** I don't really know, so ask the teacher. **Cēki sungkang-ki ka naylye oni ellun ka se thaca** There's an elevator over there, so let's go right over and take it. **Sikan i nuc.ess.uni wuli catong-cha thako kapsita** As it is late, let's go in a taxi.

1b. when (in the past), then (I found that), as. ¶**Ku ka nwukwu ˈn ka hani palo Pak kwun uy hyeng nim ila ˈney** When I wondered who he was they told me he was Pak's brother.

2. but, and; but/and now; but/and here; but as it turns out (to one's surprise, contrary to expectations), when. ¶**sayngkak hani** when I (stop to) think about it. **I chayk tul ul tā ilk.ulq sayngkak ul hani aph i kkāmah.ta** I have little hope of getting all these books read.

3. [DIAL, semi-lit] = **-key** in a way such that, so that it is/does. ¶**khetalani** (= **khetalah.key**) **hata** makes it a little bigger. **kkamatuk hani** (= **hakey**) **mēlli** darkly distant. **meng hani se iss.ta** stands around with a blank face (on one). **Alh.nunta ˈtuni** (= 1) **melcceng hani** (= 3) **tol.a taniki man cal hanta** I heard he's sick, but look, he is going around sound as a bell.

4. in accordance with, as; mod + **kes ul poni** to judge (judging) from the fact that ···, in view of the fact that ···. ¶**Kūnca ey say cip san kes ul poni tōn ul mānh.i pēl.ess.nun ka pota** Look at the way he bought a new house not long ago; he must have made a lot of money.

5. (= **-ko**) and also (giving further details). ¶**Ku ka pyesul ey oluni ku ttay nai ka sumul iess.ta** He was appointed to a government post at the age of twenty (= "and he was twenty at that time").

-uni₂ → **-un i₁**, **-un i₂**

-un i₁ < ⁻ ʰ⁄oˈn i, mod + n (postmod). CF **-un kes**; **-ul/-nun/-tun i**.

1. the one (thing/person) that is/did; one who(m)/that ··· (was/did).

1a. (epitheme extruded from subject) one who ···. **ciun i** "the one who composed it", the writer, the author; the creator, the builder. **nulk.un i** an old person.

1b. (epitheme extruded from object) one whom ···. Example?

2. (summational epitheme) the act/fact of being or of having done:

2a. ~ **mankhum**. ¶**mānh.un i mankhum** as much as there is, as many as there are. **Ne nun pūca ˈn** (= in) **i mankhum te kipu hay ya hanta** Inasmuch as you are richer, you should contribute more. **Wuli ttattus han pang ey se āmu kekceng ēps.i cīnayn i mankhum, tewuk kanan han sālam tul sayngkak ul hay ya toynta** We are living in a warm room with no worries, and that is all the more reason we should give thought to the poor people.

2b. ~ **pota**. ¶**Tōn i mānh.un i pota kēnkang han kes i nās.ta** Health is preferable to wealth.

3. abbr < -un i 'la it is (the case) that. ¶Sipi ey kāy cic.kenul im man yekye na-ka pon i When the dog barked at the twig door, I went out expecting my beloved. CF -ulq ci 'n i, -ul they 'n i.

-un i$_2$ = -un ya. ¶nay kes in i ney kes in i tathwuta "fights over whether it is mine or yours" = struggles for possession. Nulin i keyulun i hyung man ponta He is always finding fault with me, saying how slow I am, how lazy I am, and whatnot.

-˙^{u}/o˙n i, mod + postmod. SEE -o˙n i, ho˙n i; -(^{u}/o)˙si˙n i; -˙nu˙n i, -˙no˙n i, -(^{u}/o)˙sino˙n i; -˙ta˙n i, -˙te˙n i, -(^{u}/o)˙site˙n i, -˙tesi˙n i; -˙ke˙n i, -˙Ge˙n i, -˙e˙n i, -˙ka˙n i, -˙Ga˙n i, -˙a˙n i.

-˙^{u}/o˙n i ˙Ga, mod + postmod + postmod (= ˙ka). did/is it? SEE ho˙n i ˙Ga.

-˙^{u}/o˙n i ˙Gwo, mod + postmod + postmod (= ˙kwo). did/is it? ¶SYWU-PPWO-TTYEY mu˙sum ˙˙TTWOW-˙˙LI ˙lol pwo˙kwo ˙kwot HUY-˙˙NGWUW ˙tha nilo˙n i ˙Gwo (1482 Kum-sam 2:1b) seeing what logic did Subhūti forthwith say that it is rare? SEE ho˙n i ˙Gwo.

-unq īhwu, modifier + postmodifier. SEE īhwu.

-uni-kka, extended sequential. NOTE: *-nuni-kka and *-(ess.)tuni-kka do not occur.

1. since/as it is/does, so, and so. ¶Han sene tal te iss.uni-kka chēnchen hi īl hay to cōh.ta As there are about three more months, we can take our time on the job. Ney ka hanun kes ul poni-kka swiwe pointa To see you do it, it looks easy. Ku sosik ul tul.uni-kka maum i noh.inta Now that I hear the news, I feel better. Kuleni-kka kuleh.ci That's why, you see.

2. when (in the past), then, as, and/but then. ¶Nai lul mul.uni-kka ku ^{n}yeca nun acik samsip mīman ila ko māl hayss.ta When I asked her age, she said that she was still under thirty. Casey hi poni-kka ku kes un kācca cincwu yess.ta When I looked it over closely, I found that it was an imitation pearl. Cēnhwa lul hani-kka āmu to pat.ci anh.ess.ta When I phoned, nobody answered. Nay ka kani-kka ku ka sinmun ul poko iss.ess.ta When I called on him, he was reading a newspaper.

~ n(un) SAME (subdued to emphasize the clause that follows). ¶Mēlli se poni-kka n' chen.yen sān sālam kath.ta When you look at it from a distance it's just like a living person.

~ tul SAME (with plural subject). ¶Kuleni-kka tul kekceng ici That is why we are bothered.

~ yo SAME [POLITE]. ¶Non ila 'n kong tul.in mankhum sōtuk i nani-kka yo It's that/because you get out of a field according to the work you put into it. Ku ya pelsse yeki lul [= ey (lul)] meych tal iss.uni-kka yo That's because I've been here a few months already (1954 Lukoff 111). CF M 3:3:59-60.

-uni-kka 'n tulwo (1893 Scott 97) = -uni-kka 'n tulwu [Chwungcheng DIAL (LHS)], -uni-kka 'n ulwu [DIAL]. because, since, as. ¶meniskantulwo kal swu ep.so (1894 Gale 72) as it is a long distance I cannot go. palam i puwuni-kka 'n tulwo silkwa ttele cyes.swo (1887 Scott 63) the wind having risen the fruit fell off. CF -˙^{u}/on˙t olwo.

-unq īl, modifier + postmod. the experience of having done. ~ i iss.ta has ever done, once did. ~ i iss.ess.ta had ever/once done. ~ i ēps.ta has never done. ~ i ēps.ess.ta had never done. ¶Ilpon ey ka-ponq īl i iss.n' ya? Have you ever been to Japan? Ku i eykey se han pen phyēnci lul pat.unq īl i iss.ta I once got a letter from him. Pihayng-ki lul tha ponq īl i ēps.ta I have never traveled by airplane. Hānkwuk ey se phyēnci lul pat.usinq īl i han pen to ēps.^{s}up.nikka (ēps.usip.nikka) You have never received any letters from Korea? Hak.kyo lul kaluchi(si)nq īl i iss.^{s}up.nikka/iss.usip.nikka/kyēysip.nikka? Have you ever taught school? CF -un cek.

-un i 'la < -˙^{u}/o˙n i ˙'la, mod + postmod + cop indic assert. it is (the case) that. ¶Ney ka nay māl ul an tul.e pwā la hon nako māl they 'n i 'la If you don't listen to me you'll be in trouble. Sānula 'myen pyelq īl ul tā tang hanun pep in i 'la You have to put up with a lot of things to stay alive. Pap ul mekta ka 'la to son nim i osimyen il.e se ya hanun pep in i 'la You should rise when guests appear, even in the middle of dinner. ABBR -un i. SYN -tun kes ita. CF -ulq ci 'n i 'la, -nun/-tun i 'la, -ul i 'la; -nit/$_l$a.

¶˙ile 'n ˙PYEN-˙HWA ˙lol ˙˙pwoyGwo ˙za SSIN-˙CYWOK ˙ol ka˙ta twolwo ˙˙PWON-˙CCWA ˙ay ˙tu˙le anco˙n i ˙˙'la (1447 Sek 6:34ab) only when he had demonstrated these transformations did he gather up his ṛddhipāda (deva-foot ubiquity) and go back to sit in his place. *ne ˙[G]wa kol˙Wo˙l i ˙˙ep.su˙n i ˙'˙la* (1459 Wel 18:57b) there is no one to compare with you. *˙ile 'n ˙t olwo ke˙mu.m ye ˙hoyywo˙m ol non˙hwo.n i ˙'˙la* (1481 Twusi 7:27a) hence distinguished being black and (being) white.

-unq īlay, mod + postmod. SEE *īlay*.

-*˙ᵁo˙n i ˙lol*, modifier + postmodifier + particle. ¶*mwo˙lwomay [PWONG-˙HWA] ˙ay s wuytwu ho˙n i lol a˙lal ˙t ilwo˙ta* (1481 Twusi 15:42b) it is by all means to recognize those who lead in moral reform by example.

-uni mangceng ici [DIAL] = **-ki ey mangceng ici**. CF **-uni 3**.

-un i mankhum / pota SEE **-un i₁**.

-*˙ᵁou˙n i '-ngi s ˙ka*, mod + postmod + cop polite + pcl + postmod. ¶*˙SYENG-ZIN ˙i ˙˙kyesi.n i ˙'˙n i '-ngi s ˙ka* (1465 Wen se:68a) is there a holy man here? *ye˙sus ha˙no˙l i e˙nu y ˙za ˙mos ˙˙tywoho˙n i '-ngi s ˙ka* (1447 Sek 6:35b) of the six heavens just which is best?

-*˙ᵁo˙n i '-ngi s ˙kwo*, mod + postmod + cop polite + pcl + postmod. ¶*[˙˙LYANG-˙HAN ˙KWO-˙˙SSO] ˙ay ˙˙es.te ho˙n i '-ngi s ˙kwo* (1445 ¹Yong 28) how were they [in their roles] with respect to the history of the Two Hans?

-*˙ᵁo˙n i '-ngi ˙'˙ta*, mod + postmod + cop polite + cop indic assert. ¶*pwuthye s the˙li ˙lol a˙za ka˙n i '-ngi ˙'˙ta* (1447 Sek 24:30a) had to grab Buddha's hair. *˙TTAY-KKWU-TTAM ˙i ˙il˙Gwu˙n i '-ngi ˙'˙ta* (1449 Kok 5) Gautama (the Greater) achieved it.

-*˙ᵁo˙n i '-ng' ita* = -*˙ᵁo˙n i '-ngi ˙'˙ta*, mod + postmod + cop polite + cop indic assert. ¶*SIN ˙uy ˙˙NGWEN [= ˙NGWEN] ˙honwon ˙pa y a˙ni ˙'˙n i '-ng' ita* [sic *a-˙ni-ning-˙i-ta*] (1586 Sohak 6:44a) it is not that a subject is requesting it. *[MWU-˙˙SSO] ho.n i '-ng' ita* (1676 Sin.e 2:3b) was safe (without incident).

-*˙ᵁo˙n i '-ng' ˙'˙ta*, abbr < -*˙ᵁo˙n i '-ngi ˙'˙ta*. ¶*SAM-˙SYEY ˙yey s ˙˙i˙l ol ˙˙a˙losil ˙ss oy pwu˙˙thye 'ysi˙ta ˙ho˙no.n i '-ng' ˙'˙ta* (1447 Sek 6:18a) ⋯ and he commanded knowledge of the three states of existence; therefore they say that he is Buddha.

-*˙ᵁo˙n i ˙'˙n ˙t ay n'*, mod + postmod + cop mod + postmod + pcl + pcl. ¶*˙˙twu nul˙ku˙n [i] uy ˙KWOLQ-˙˙SYWUY lul somos pwo˙n i ˙'˙n ˙t ay n' ˙kwot ˙˙tywo˙hi hon ti˙Gwuy ˙˙mal ˙ho˙ya ye˙le pang ˙ay s ˙˙ma˙l ol kus.nwu˙lu.l i ˙'˙n i* (?1468-

Mong 32b) since he saw the two old men's true essence he immediately spoke with them on good occasion and would have a discussion on various subjects.

-*u.n i 'n ˙t ye* SEE -*wo.n i 'n ˙t ye*

-un i tul, 1. mod + postmod + pcl = **-un ya tul**. 2. mod + quasi-free n + pcl. the ones which are / did. ¶*celm.un i tul* the young people.

-*˙ᵁo˙n i ˙uy* (pcl). ¶*KAN-NAN ho˙n i ˙uy no˙m oy ˙˙pwo˙poy ˙˙hyey˙ywom kot ˙'˙ta* (1465 Wen 3:3: 1:62a) it is like a poor man reckoning another's treasures.

-*˙ᵁo˙n i ˙ya*, mod + postmod + postmod. ¶*˙i ˙non QON ˙ol ˙˙alGa˙la ho˙n i ˙ya QON ˙ol kap˙ka˙la ho˙n i ˙ya* (?1468- Mong 31b) is it that we are to recognize obligation or are we to repay obligation? *˙i non ˙POYK ˙˙TTYANG s ˙hi˙m ol ˙TUK ho˙n i ˙ya* (?1468- Mong 31a) has he really got the strength of a hundred men?

-*˙ᵁo˙n i ˙ye*, mod + postmodifier + postmodifier. ¶*˙˙mwu˙lusya˙toy ˙ne 'y ˙˙kyeci˙p i ˙˙kwo˙Wo.n i ˙ye* (1459 Wel 7:10b) he inquired "is your wife pretty?". *a[˙]ni nemwu spolo˙n i ˙ye* (1481 Twusi 8:67a) isn't it too hasty?

-*˙ᵁo˙n i ˙za*, mod + postmod + pcl. ¶*kwos ˙ni˙ph i ˙˙cye˙ku.n i ˙za ⋯* (1459 Wel 8:18a) precisely because they have few blossoms and leaves. SEE *ho˙n i ˙za*.

-unq ¹īyu, mod + n. the reason that (it is / did). ¶*Ku sāep ey silphay han kes i ku ka sacik hanq ¹īyu (i)ta* He failed in the job and that is the reason he resigned. *Chelqswu ka cwuk.unq ¹īyu nun ku kes ikeyss.ta (ya!)* That must be the reason Chelsswu died(, I tell you)! CF **-ulq ¹īyu**.

-un ka < -*˙ᵁon ˙ka*, modifier + postmodifier.
1. (the question) whether it is / did; is / did it? ~ **yo** SAME [POLITE]. ¶*Kath.un ka?* Are they the same? *Nwukwu 'n ka yo* (= *Nwukwu in ka yo*) Who is it? NOTE: This is a common way to form INTIMATE and (with **yo**) POLITE questions for adjective or copula; for verbs **-na (yo)** is more common. CF **-tun / -nun / -ulq ka**.
2. **-un ka ha-**. ¶*Ku ka nwukwu 'n ka hani palo Pak kwun uy hyeng nim ila 'ney* When I wondered who he was they told me he was Pak's brother.
3. (adj or cop +) **-un ka pº/ᵤta** it seems that ("it is a question of"); SYN **-na pº/ᵤta**. [For verbs, *iss-*, *ēps-*, *-keyss-* the proc modifier is

used: -nun ka pᵒ/ᵤta.] ¶Kim sensayng in ka pota It seems to be Mr Kim. Pakk i chwuwun ka pota It seems cold outside.

-un ka ka, mod + postmod + pcl. ¶Haksayng tul i mānh.un ka ka mūncey 'ta The question is whether there are too many students.

-un ka ko [Hamkyeng DIAL] = quoted -un ka

-un ka lul, mod + postmod + pcl. ¶Cengto uy pūsa ka etten cengto in ka lul natha-nāynta Adverbs of degree show (to) what degree it is. Ku ⁿyeca ka khun ka lul al.e pwā la Find out whether she's tall.

-un ka 'm, 1. abbr < -un ka (ko) ham
2. abbr < -un ka (ko) han māl ia?. ¶Ku key eti kwuksan in ka 'm – Mi-cey 'ci! What do you mean that's a Korean product – why, it's American made! Ku key eti sayk i huyn ka 'm – nolah.ci! That's not white – it's yellow. NOTE: Many speakers reject this use with adj, some reject it with the copula, too; none use it with verbs. CF -ta 'm, -na 'm.

-un kām, mod + n. the feeling that it is / did; ~ i iss.ta / nata it feels / seems like, it gives the feeling of. ¶Ku kes i com cak.un kām i iss.ta It gives the feeling that it is rather small, I'd say. Onul nal i cham malk.kwun – kaul i on kām i nanta These days are very clear, I notice – it feels as if autumn were here.

-un ka nun, mod + postmod + pcl. ¶Nwu ka khun ka nun mūncey ka toyci man ... It is a question who is taller, but ... .

-un ka tul, mod + postmod + pcl = -un ya tul

-un ke, abbr < -un kes; ~ 'ey yo (= iey yo)

-un ke 'ci, abbr < -un kes ici

-un ke l', abbr < -un ke lul = -un kes ul. When followed by the polite particle yo there is reinforcement: ke l'q yo /kellyo/.
1. although (in spite of the fact that) it is or (= -ess.nun ke l') did; indeed, despite contrary anticipations / reservations; but, anyway; so there!; (it's) too bad that ⋯ , too bad but ⋯ . ~ iyo, ~ yo = -un ke l'q yo (kellyo) SAME [POLITE]. ¶Ku sālam i him i kkway sēyn ke l' But he is terribly strong! Ku tōn un tā sse pelin ke l' (I'm sorry but) I have spent all the money. Na n' akka wuli apeci ka pām sa 'ta cwun ke l', acwu ... My daddy bought ME some chestnuts a while ago!
2. SEE -un kes (1,2,3)

-un ke 'l(q), abbr < -un kes il(q)

-un ke l'q yo (kellyo) SEE -un ke l'

-un ke 'la, abbr < -un kes ila

-un ke n', abbr < -un ke nun = -un kes un

-un ke 'n, abbr < -un kes in

-un ke 'na, abbr < -un kes ina

-un kes < -ᵘ/ₒn kes, modifier + n (postmod).
1. a thing that is or that (one) did. ¶Nay kulen kes cheum pwass.ta I have never seen such a thing. I payk.hwa-cem ey ēps.nun kes i ēps.ˢup.nita This department store carries everything.
2. one that is or that (one) did. ¶I kes mālko to tto talun kes i iss.ci anh.sup.nikka? You have another besides this, surely? Sellyeng cal-mos toyn kes i iss.tula to yōngse hasipsio Even if (you have discovered that) there is a mistake, please forgive him.
3. the (tentative) fact that it is or that (one) did. ¶Tōn i mānh.un i pota kēnkang han kes i nās.ta Health is preferable to wealth. I pen ey ponay on sakwa nun wuli co lo on kes i punmyeng haney It is obvious that the apples sent this time are (for) our share (NKd). Il-nyen cen ey pon kes i ku lul macimak pon kes iess.ta The last I saw of him was a year ago. Onul hak.kyo ey oci anh.un kes ul poni alh.nun ka pota I guess he is ill, since he is absent from school today.
4. 4a. ~ ul = -un ke l'.
4b. ~ i = -un key but. SEE i 5b. ¶Na nun cal hanta 'psiko han kes i ileh.key toyess.ta It turned out this way, but I thought I was doing the right thing.
5. ~ ulo poita [written style] it appears/seems that it or one is / did. ¶Cengpu nun i kyēyhoyk ey chānseng han kes ulo pointa It seems that the government has agreed on this plan. Ilchak un wuli Hānkwuk sēnswu in kes ulo pointa In first place seems to be one of our Korean athletes.
NOTE: Pulk.un kes ita (1) It's a red thing; (2) It's the red one; (3) (It's a fact that) it's red = It's red, you see. Nay kes i pulk.un kes ita Mine is the red one; Mine is red, you see.

-un kes kath.ta, mod + n + adj. 1. it seems that it is / did; 2. it is like the one / thing that is or that (one) did. ¶Cōh.un kes kath.ta (1) It seems to be good; (2) It's like the good one. Mikwuk ey se say lo osin pun in kes kath.ta He seems to be the gentleman newly arrived from America. **Ku nun cĕmsim ul kwūlm.un kes kath.ta** It seems he skipped lunch. CF **-un ka pota, -un mo.yang ita, -un seng siph.ta, -un tus hata, -un yang hata.**

-un key, 1. abbr < **-un kes i**

2. abbr < **-un kes ie/ia**

-un ke ya, abbr < **-un kes i(y)a**

-un key 'ci = **-un ke yci,** abbr < **-un kes ici**

-un key 'la = **-un ke yla,** abbr < **-un kes ila**

-un key 'na = **-un ke yna,** abbr < **-un kes ina**

-un key 'ney = **-un ke yney** < **-un kes iney**

-un key 'ni = **-un ke yni,** abbr < **-un kes ini**

-un ke yo = **-un key yo** (1, 2, 3.). ¶**Talun sālam un etteh.key toyn ke yo** What happened to the other people?

-un ke yo man, abbr < **-un kes io man** it's that ··· is/did but [AUTH]

-un key 'ta = **-un ke yta,** abbr **-un kes ita**

-un key ya = **-un ke ya**

-un key yo, abbr. 1. < **-un kes ie(y) yo;** now largely replaced by **-un ke 'ey yo.**

2. < **-un kes iyo** [POLITE fragment].

3. < **-un kes io** it's that ··· did/is [AUTH], etc.

un khen [S Kyengsang DIAL (Mkk 1960:3:33)] = **un khenyeng**

un khenyeng (un), pcl + pcl (+ pcl). ¶**Ku nun ilum un khenyeng nai to moluney** He doesn't know how old he is, much less his name. **I tōn ulo n' mānnyen-phil un khenyeng (un) yenphil to mōs sakeyss.ta** With this amount of money you won't even be able to buy a pencil, much less a fountain pen.

-un kīm, modifier + postmod. (as) an incidental result of (being or having done) = **-un kyel.** ¶**Okey toyn kīm ey tangsin uy cim kkaci nalle wass.ey yo** I happened to be coming this way, so I brought your baggage.

-un kkatalk, modifier + n. (for) the reason that it is/did [the strongest way to state a cause and effect]. ¶**Kanan han kkatalk ey kulenq īl ul hay ya hanta** He has to do such work because he's poor. **Pappun kkatalk ey kaci mōs hanta** I can't go because I am busy. **Mun kwa chang ul cal tat.ci anh.un kkatalk ey totwuk i tul.e wass.ta** The burglar got in because we didn't close the doors and windows properly. **Ku ka nay chinkwu in kkatalk ita** It's because he is my friend. **Meli ka aphun kes un ama wūn kkatalk in ka pwā** Your headache is likely the result of crying, it appears.

-un kkuth (ey), mod + n (+ pcl). (as) the final consequence of doing; in the end, after doing. ¶**Twū sikan kyekcen han kkuth ey cek ul mullichyess.ta** After two hours of fierce battle we drove the enemy back.

-un ko < -*ᵘ⁄ₒn ˙kwo,* mod + postmod. [colloq; poetic] the (usually rhetorical, exclamatory, or quoted) question wh··· (BUT NOT whether ···) it is/did. SEE **-un ka;** *˙kwo.* ¶**Elma 'na khun ko** How big is it (I wonder)?

-un ko lo, modifier + noun + particle [bookish]. for the reason that it is/did. ¶**Ku nun ōykwuk sālam in ko lo ku kes un an hay to cōh.ta** Being a foreigner, he does not have do that. **Ku phyēnci lul mōs pat.un ko lo na nun molukeyss.ta** I don't know because I never received the letter. **Kanan han ko lo ¹yuhak ul mōs hakeyss.ta** Because I have no money I will be unable to study abroad. CF **-uni(-kka, -kka n'), -ki ey, -ki lo, -killey, -ki ttaymun ey, -un kkatalk ey, -um ulo, -nula ko, -e (se).**

un kosa hako SEE **kosa hako**

-un kwani, abbr < **-un ko hani**

-*ᵘ⁄ₒn ˙kwo,* modifier + postmodifier (= **-un ko**).

-un kyel, modifier + postmod. (as) an incidental result of (having done). ¶**Nōllan kyel ey kulus ul ttel.e ttulyess.ta** In my surprise I dropped the dish. SYN **-um kīm.**

-un kyengwu, mod + n. in the case/event of its being. ¶**kulen kyengwu ey nun** in such event.

-*ᵘ⁄ₒn ma˙lon,* modifier + postmodifier. but. SEE -*˙an ma˙lon;* -*ᵘ⁄ₒ˙sin ma˙lon.*

-un mankhum, abbr < **-un i mankhum**

-un mo.yang, mod + n. the appearance of being or of having done.

~ **ita** appears to be or to have done. ¶**Kim sensayng isin mo.yang ita** It appears to be Mr Kim. **Swun-i to na-kan mo.yang ita** Swun-i appears to have gone out, too.

(?*) ~ **ulo** No examples.

-un nameci SEE **nameci**

-*ᵘ⁄ₒ˙n oy* = -*ᵘ⁄ₒ˙n [y]oy,* abbr < -*ᵘ⁄ₒ˙n i ˙oy* 'of (etc.) that which ··· '. SEE *˙uy.*

-un pa < -*ᵘ⁄ₒn ˙pa,* modifier + noun [lit].

1. = **-un kes.** ¶**īsang māl han pa wa kath.i** as has been stated above. **Cwungkwuk ey se palmyeng han pa (i)ta** (1) It is something that was invented in China; (2) It is the one that was invented in China; (3) It was invented in China, you see.

2. ~ (ey) since, when. ¶**Ku uy māl ul tul.e pon pa (ey) sāsil kwa thullim ēps.ta** According to what he says, it is true to the fact. (or: What he says is true to the fact.) **Īwang on pa ey manna poko kakeyss.ta** As long as I am here, I might as well see him before I leave. **Ku eykey mul.e pon pa ku to ālci mōs hakeyss.ta hatula** I asked him, but he said he didn't know about it either.
  ~ **ey ya** if/since (as long as) one did. ¶**Yeki kkaci on pa ey ya, kwūkyeng hay ya 'ci yo** Since we are here, we have to see it (M 1:2:108).
  3. SEE **pa**
-**un pep**, mod + adj-n. SEE **pep hata**.
-**un phūm**, modifier + n. the appearance / looks / behavior of having done or of being. SEE **phūm**.
-**un sai/say**, modifier + noun. while (in the state resulting from having done), during the interval following. ¶**on sai (ey)** while here, following (one's) arrival. **kan sai (ey)** while gone / away, following (one's) departure.
-**un seng siph.ta**, mod + postmod + adj. seems, looks like, gives the appearance of.
  1. (with adj, cop). ¶ **Chwuwun seng siph.ta** It looks cold outside. **Say lo mantun sacin in seng siph.ta** It looks like a new photograph.
  2. (with v; siph.ta usually past). ¶**Pi ka on seng siph.ess.ta** It seems to have rained.
-**un sēym**, mod + postmod. ~ **ita**, ~ **ulo** SEE **sēym**.
-**un swu**, modifier + noun.
  1. an occasion of having done or of being; a past event (happening, instance, doing); a state, condition, instance (of being), circumstance, case. ¶**Celm.un sālam to yūmyeng han hakca in swu ka iss.ta** There are instances of young men (too) who are famous scholars. **Machan-kaci 'n swu ka iss.ta** Sometimes they are alike (or: Some of them are alike). **Ō-wel cangma chel ey to nal i cōh.un swu ka iss.ci yo** There are nice days even in the May rainy season.
  2. [? awkward] = -**unq īl** (experience): ~ **ka iss.ta** / **ēps.ta** has ever / never (once) done it. ¶**Ku cwūsa lul mac.ko cōh.a cin swu to iss.e?** Has anybody ever benefited from having that shot?
- -ᵘ⁄ₒ**n ta**, modifier + postmodifier. ¶ "**ne y ˙e˙tu˙le ˙sye won˙ta** (?1517- ¹No 1:1a) where have you come from? **˙stwo ¨es˙ti i cu˙zu˙m ey ˙za kos won˙ta** (?1517- ¹No 2:3b) and how is it that you have only come at just this time? SEE ˙**in˙ta, hon˙ta;** -˙**an˙ta,** -˙**non˙ta,** -˙**nun˙ta,** -˙**ten˙ta**.
- -ᵘ⁄ₒ**n ta ¨ma˙ta** every time that ... . ¶**pwuthye ˙SYWELQ-˙PEP ˙hosin˙ta ¨ma˙ta ¨ta NUNG ˙hi nwol˙Gay ˙lwo pulu¨zopno˙n i ˙'˙la** (1459 Wel 1:15a) every time that Buddha has preached everyone sings with song. ¨**mwuyn˙ta ¨mata ˙PEP ˙ey e˙kuy.m ye n'** (1482 Kum-sam 2:18a) if every time you move you violate the Law ... . ¨**na l' te˙pule [¨KHWAN-˙KHWOK] ˙hi hon˙ta ¨ma˙ta yel˙hul ˙Gwom ¨ta ˙honwos˙ta** (1481 Twusi 20:29a) every time they are so kind to me it takes a whole ten days.
-*unta* [Ceycwu DIAL (Seng ¹Nakswu 1984:65)] = -**nunta**. ¶*mek.unta* (?< 1677 *meknota*) eats.
-**un tām**, abbr < -**un taum**.
-**un taum**, mod + n. next (right) after doing. ¶**Phyēnci lul pat.un taum ey hyeng nim hanthey cēnhwa lul hayss.ta** Right after I got the letter I phoned my brother. **Cēnhwa lul han taum iess.ta** It was (the next thing) right after making the phone call.
- -ᵘ⁄ₒ**n˙t ay**, mod + postmod + pcl. ¶˙*MWOK-LYEN ˙i ˙CCYENG-˙PPEN NGWANG ˙skuy two˙la ˙ka ˙i SSO-YWEN ˙ul sol˙Won˙t ay NGWANG ˙i ˙TTAY-˙QOY-˙TTWOW ˙lol pul˙le nilo˙sya˙toy* (1447 Sek 6:6ab) Maudgalyāyana went back to King Śuddhodana and told him the gist of this, so the king summoned Mahāprajāpati and said to her [as follows]. **a˙ni cwun˙t ay** (1447 Sek 23:57b) since he did not give it, ... ˙**cukca˙hi ˙ku KUY-˙PYELQ ˙ul NGWANG ˙skuy al˙Gwoyn ˙t ay** (1447 Sek 24:16a) as he immediately informed the king of that message, ... **ku kak˙si ke˙wulwu l' ka˙cye˙ta ˙ka ¨ney polo˙m ay ˙ton˙t ay ku ¨say ku ke˙wulwu˙ey s ce˙'y kulu˙mey ˙lol pwo˙kwo wu˙lwu˙m ul ¨wu˙n i** (1447 Sek 24:20b) that lady got some mirrors and hung them on the four walls, so that the bird saw its image in the mirror and chirped its song. *SA-MWON ˙oy ¨swon-˙toy ¨salom ˙pulye nilun˙t ay* (1447 Sek 24:22a) as he had a man tell the śramaṇas, ... *CCYWONG ˙thi a˙ni hon˙t ay* (1447 Sek 24:49b) since he did not obey. SEE -ᵘ⁄ₒ˙**sin˙t ay**.
-**un tay lo**, modifier + n + pcl. just as it is/did; according to the original state. ¶**Sensayng nim i māl hasin tay lo māyil kongpu hay ya paywunun kes i iss.ta** Just as the teacher said,

to learn you have to study every day. For more examples see tay lo. CF -un chay; -nun tay lo.
-ᵘ⁄ₒn ᐟt ay n', mod + postmod + pcl + pcl. SEE -ᵘ⁄ₒ ˙sin ᐟt ay n', ˙in ᐟt ay n'.

-un tey₁, mod + n (= -un kos). 1. a place that is ⋯ ; the place where it is or (one) did. ¶chwuwun tey (= chwuwun kos) a cold place. mēn tey ey iss.ta is in a distant place, is far away. Ney ka os ul san tey ka eti 'n ya (= eti in ya) Where did you buy your suit?
2. as much / well as one has done. ¶Sensayng nim i hasin tey kkaci ce to hakeyss.ˢup.nita I will do as much / well as you have done. CF -nun / -ulq tey kkaci.

-un tey₂, mod + postmod [adj and cop only; verbs use proc mod -nun tey, -ess.nun tey].
  1. the circumstance that it is.
  -un tey (ey) SEE ALSO 2; -un tey 'ta ka.
  -un tey (ey) se. ¶Ku ka keyulun tey se mōtun sāko ka sayngkyess.ta All the mishaps occurred because of his laziness (M 3:3:203).
  -un tey (ey) to = -un tey to: SEE 3a.
  2. (given) the circumstance of its being; is ⋯ and / but / so. ¶Nal i chwuwun tey ōythwu lul ip.nun kes i cōh.keyss.ta It's so cold that you better wear an overcoat. Totwuk nom in tey nun thullim i ēps.una ... There's no doubt he is a thief, but ... . Ku cham-oy nun kaps un ssan tey mas i ēps.ta The melon is cheap but lacks flavor. I chayk i kkok phil.yo han tey salq ka yo? I really need this book; shall I buy it? Na to ilen kūlim ul sako siph.un tey tto iss.ulq ka yo? I'd like to buy a picture like this myself; do you think they'd have any more? Son ul ssis.ko siph.un tey cāmqkan yōngse hasipsio Excuse me a minute, I want to wash my hands. Ku ⁿyeca ka cōh.un tey way kyelhon ul an hasip.nikka If you like that girl why don't you marry her? (or: She's a nice girl, why don't you marry her?). Phyēnci ssuki silh.un tey sse ya hay se hwā ka nap.nita I dislike writing letters; it makes me mad to have to write one.
  3. 3a. ~ to even though it is, in spite of the fact that it is, despite that ⋯ . ¶Hānkwuk māl i elyewun tey to ku pun un cham cal hay yo Although Korean is difficult, he speaks it quite well (M 1:2:167).
  3b. ~ to pulkwu hako in spite of (regardless of, disregarding) the fact that it is. ¶Nal-ssi ka mopsi chwuwun tey to pulkwu hako ōythwu lul ipci anh.ko na-kass.ta He went out without wearing an overcoat in spite of the bitter cold. Kulen sangthay (i)n tey to pulkwu hako ku nun cokum to kāyuy halye tulci anh.ess.ta He made no attempt to concern himself in spite of the condition things were in.
  4. ~ (yo)! you see (it's a case of its being) ⋯ ! (sentence-final exclamatory). ¶Nal i com sensen han tey It's a bit cold, I'd say! Ku kul-ssi myengphil in tey yo What a fine piece of handwriting it is!
  5. marks a question in the INTIMATE or (~ yo) POLITE style that asks for the feelings or the opinion of the addressee ('you'), often rhetorically. eh (what), don't you think, you see, n'est-ce pas, hein (Dupont 190).
  ¶Chelqswu to haksayng in tey? Well, isn't Chelsswu a student, too? Ku tongsayng to ttokttok han tey? Don't you realize his little brother is bright, too? CF -nun / -tun tey.

-un tey₃ → -unta ᐟy.
-un tey₄ → -un tay. ~ lo.
-ᵘ⁄ₒn ᐟt ey n' SEE -˙ken ᐟt ey n', -˙ten ᐟt ey n'
-un tey nun, mod + postmod + pcl. ¶Pay ka kophun tey nun halq swu ēps.ta When one is hungry what else can one do?
-un tey se = -un tey (ey) se: SEE -un tey (1).
-un tey 'ta (ka). not only ⋯ but in addition (on top of that). ¶I congi nun yalp.un tey 'ta ka nemu pissap.nita In addition to this paper being thin, it is too expensive (M 1:2:454). Kulen tey 'ta ka tto tachyess.ta (Dupont 141) And on top of that, what did he do but injure himself!
-un tey to, mod + postmod + pcl. SEE -un tey₂ 3.
-un tey tul, mod + postmod + pcl. ¶Chwuwun tey tul ppalli tul.e wā la Everybody hurry in out of the cold!
-un tey ya, modifier + postmodifier + particle. ¶Pay kophun tey ya halq swu ēps.ta When one is HUNGRY what else can one do?
-un tey yo, mod + postmod + pcl. SEE -un tey₂ 4.
-un ti [Ceycwu DIAL (Seng ¹Nakswu 1984:51-4)] = -un tey, = -ess.nun tey
-ᵘ⁄ₒn ˙ti⋯ = -ᵘ⁄ₒn ᐟt i(⋯), mod + postmodifier ('fact') + pcl / cop. that it / one did (or is).
-ᵘ⁄ₒn ᐟt i, modifier + postmodifier + particle.
  1. (knowing) that – with the underlying object marked nominative (CF -ᵘ⁄ₒn ᐟt ol). ¶[SYANG-

KWONG] oy [KWUN] ˙in t i ˝anwo.n i (1481 Twusi 7:25a) we know it is the troops of Duke Xiāng. *˙pu˙l i te˙wun [˙]PEP ˙in ˙t i ˝a˙ti ˝mwot hol ˝ss i il˙hwu˙m i ˙PWULQ-TTI ˙˝Gwo* (1463 Pep 2:60a) being unable to realize that it is the law for fire to be hot is called ignorance, and ... . *˝amwo toy ˙sye won ˙t i ˙mwollwo.l i* ([1447→]1562 Sek 3:18a) I don't know where they have come from − CF *˝amwo ˙to ˙la ˙sye won ˙twong mwo˙lo˙tesi˙n i* (1459 Wel 2:25b) was not aware where they came from.

2. (the time) since it happened. SEE *-ᵁ⁄o˙sin ˙t i; -˙an ˙t i, ˙ho.yan ˙t i, -˙yan ˙t i.*

-˙ᵁ⁄on ˙t ol, modifier + postmodifier + particle.

1. that it / one did (or is). ¶*ku˙le ˙l ˝ss oy ˙i ˝THYEY ˙non ˝PWON-LOY ˙SWU ˝ep.sun ˙t ol a˙lwolq ˙t i.n i ˙˝la* (1447 Sek 19:10b) therefore it must be realized that these bodies basically are without number (= are innumerable). *a˙pi ˝CO-˙SIK ˙tol˙h i ˝KHWO-˝NWOW y ˙i ˙kot hon ˙t ol pwo˙kwo* (1459 Wel 17:17b) seeing that the worries of the fathers and sons are like this, ...

2. despite the fact that it / one is or did; is / did but. ¶*wo˙la hon ˙t ol ˙wosi˙l i ˙-ngi s ˙ka* (1445 ¹Yong 69) though told to come would he come? *˙nom ˙i ˙na˙a kan ˙t ol ˙POYK-˙SYENG ˙tol˙h i ˙nom ˙ol ˝ta cwo˙cho˙n i* (1449 Kok 11) though the others [the four sons of the second wife, who are good] go forth, the people follow the OTHER ones [the four sons of the first wife, who are bad]. *cyecay s swu˙l ul [˙]ho˙ya won ˙t ol ˝es˙ti me˙kul ˙kwo* (?1517- Pak 1:2b) we have got the market wine, but how shall we drink it? *[LAN-MAN] hi phun t ol musu.k i [˝NGWUW-˙QOYK] ho.l i Gwo* (1481 Twusi 18:1; cited from LCT 122a) they may sell profusely, but what profit will there be?

SEE *-ᵁ⁄o˙sin ˙t ol, ˙isin ˙t ol, ˙in ˙t ol, ˙yn ˙t ol, (a˙ni) ˙n ˙t ol*. CF *-ᵁ⁄on ˙t ol.*

-˙ᵁ⁄on ˙t olwo, modifier + postmodifier + pcl. because it / one is or does. SEE *˙n ˙t olwo.*

-˙ᵁ⁄on ˙t on, modifier + postmodifier + particle. given that one is / did; as for what one did. ¶*˙NGWEN hon ˙t on nilu˙sywo˙sye* (1447 Sek 13:44b) we beseech you to tell us. *˙NGWEN hon ˙t on ...* (1447 Sek 24:18a) what I want [to happen] is ... . CF *hon ˙t on, -˙nwon ˙t on.*

-un tong-an, mod + n. (during) the interval that (it has happened). ¶**Na-kan tong-an ey totwuk i tul.e wass.ta** A burglar broke in while we were out.

-ᵁ⁄on ˙toy, mod + n. 1. the place where. SEE *˙toy.*

2. → *-ᵁ⁄on ˙t oy*, mod + postmod + pcl.

2a. in the doing of ... , to do. ¶*tung ˝min ˙t oy ˝twu ˝nas ˝twon ˙i ˙Gwo* (?1517- Pak 1:52a) to get your back scrubbed is two coins, and ... .

2b. despite the fact that ... . ¶*ewa ewa kiluki mehon t oy amu il ep.si kennesi.n i* (1676 Sin.e 1:10b) despite the cries of the imperiled wild geese [in the storm] he crossed over without incident. SEE *hon ˙t oy, ho˙la ˙n ˙t oy.*

-˙ᵁ⁄on ˙t oy n' SEE *-˙won ˙t oy n'; -˙ten ˙t oy n'.*

-un ttay, modifier + noun.

1. a time when it is; a time that is [with adj and copula only; verbs use the proc mod: -nun ttay]. ~ **ka iss.ta** there are times when it is, it sometimes is. ¶**kulen ttay nun** in that case. **wihem han ttay** a time of danger. **cōh.un ttay** the right moment. **Nampang ey to chwuwun ttay ka iss.ta** In the south, too, it is sometimes cold. **Kumam-ttay ka sanay lo sse han-chang kiwun nanun ttay 'ta** At that time of life men are at their strongest. **Il.yoil kath.un ttay tōngmul-wen ey ka-polla chimyen sālam i koyngcang hi mānh.ta** If you visit the zoo of a Sunday, you'll find an awful lot of people there. NOTE: Both **kapkap hal ttay** and **kapkap han ttay** have the meaning 'when it is boring' or 'when I am bored'; some seem to dislike the ... **han ttay** version, but it is freely used in Seoul.

2. (= **-unq īl**) the experience of ever / once having done. ~ **ka iss.ta / ēps.ta** has ever / never (once) done.

un tul, particle + particle. ¶¹**Nayil un tul mwe hakeyss.ey yo** What are you people going to do tomorrow?

-un tul, mod + postmod [lit]. granted that, even though it is/does [often followed by a rhetorical question]. ¶**Kanta han tul acwu kal ya** Even though (we say) he leaves, surely he will not be going away for good. **Him i yak hata han tul ne pota ya yak hakeyss.nun ya** I may be weak, but I am sure I am no weaker than you. **Pūca 'n (= in) tul etteh.key kuleh.key hwalye hakey sālq swu iss.ul ya** Even though he is a wealthy man how can he live so extravagantly? **Chingchan ul mānh.i pat.un tul musun sō.yong i iss.ul ya** So he received much praise − what good is it? SEE **in tul** (M 1:2:452 is inaccurate in saying the copula does not take this pattern). CF **-e to**, **-tula 'myen**.

-un tus ('i), modifier + postmod (+ der adv).

1. as if, though, -like. ¶**Ce sāy tul un kippun tus ('i) cicekwinta** Those birds are chattering away as if they were happy (or: happily).

2. ~ **mān tus ('i)** you can't tell whether ··· or not. ¶**Ku sālam un na lul pon tus ('i) mān tus ('i) cīna kass.ta** He passed by without paying me any attention; He snubbed me. CF **-un twung**.

-un tus hata, mod + adj postmod. gives the idea/impression of being (or of having done); looks as if, looks like. ¶**Ku kos i co'.yong han (kos in) tus hata** That place seems to be quiet (to be a quiet one). **Kaul i on tus hayss.ta** It looked as though autumn had come.

-un tus siph.ta, mod + adj postmod insep + adj. gives the impression of being (or of having done); feels/looks as if it is/did. ¶**Nal i hulin tus siph.ta** It looks as if the weather were cloudy. **Chinkwu ka na-kan tus siph.ess.ta** Something told him his friend had gone out.

-un twī, modifier + noun. after doing. ¶**Na nun sensayng ul manna pon twī ey kongwen ey sānqpo kass.ta** After seeing the teacher I went to the park for a walk. **Yenghwa ka sīcak han twī yess.ta** It was after the movie had started. SYN **-un hwū**; CF **-un taum**.

-ᵘ⁄ₒn ˙twong, mod + postmod. ¶*nek˙s i e˙nu ˙CHYWU ˙yey kan ˙twong ¨mwol˙la-ngi ˙'ta* (1459 Wel 21:27a) I do not know to which hell her spirit went. *¨amo˙lan ¨hen tuy 'n ˙twong ¨mwolla 'y˙la* (?1517- Pak 1:13a) I don't know just what injury it is. *¨amwo ˙to 'la ˙sye won ˙twong mwo˙lo˙tesi˙n i* (1459 Wel 2:25b) did not know where they came from — CF *¨amwo toy ˙sye won ˙t i ˙mwollwo.l i* ([1447→]1562 Sek 3:21b) I don't know where they came from.

-un twung, modifier + postmodifier (< -ᵘ⁄ₒn ˙twong). whether or not is/did (with equal likelihood), may or not be; appears (not) to have done (or to be). SEE **twung**. ¶**Pi ka on twung mān twung ha(n)ta** It is hard to tell whether it rained or not = We have had no rain to speak of [v/adj: SEE **twung**]. **Ku sālam un na lul pon twung mān twung cīna kass.ta** He passed by in such a hurry that I don't know whether he saw me or not.

-ᵘ⁄ₒn ˙t ye, modifier + postmod + postmod.

··· ˙isin ˙t ye. ¶*wo˙cik ˙SYENG-ZIN s ¨ma˙l isin ˙t ye* (1463/4 Yeng 2:36b) are they solely the words of a saint? [the accent shows this is the copula rather than 'exist']

··· 'ysin ˙t ye. ¶ ··· *ku ˙TAL [= ˙TALQ] ˙hon ¨HYWO [= ¨HYWOW] 'ysin ˙t ye* (1586 Sohak 4:13a) is it the [level of] filial piety that he attained?

··· 'n ˙t ye = ··· ˙in ˙t ye. ¶ ¨*mal-ssom ˙kwa ka˙col˙pywo.m o˙lwo mis˙ti ¨mwot hol kke˙s i ku CIN-˙SSILQ s TI 'n ˙t ye* (1464 Kumkang 87b) is what we cannot attain by comparing it with what is said the true wisdom?

··· 'yn ˙t ye. ¶*pwus˙ku˙li˙ti a˙ni ˙ho˙no.n i ˙non ku YWU 'yn [˙]t ye* [sic] (1586 Sohak 4:43a) is it for that reason they are not ashamed?

CF -ᵘ⁄ₒ˙n i 'n ˙t ye, -˙nwon ˙t ye.

-ᵘ⁄ₒ˙n uy = -ᵘ⁄ₒn [y]uy, abbr < -ᵘ⁄ₒ˙n i ˙uy 'of (etc.) that which ··· '. SEE ˙*uy*.

? un ya, particle + particle. SEE **to** (NOTE).

-un ya, mod + postmod. (the question) whether it is [with adj and cop only; CF **-nun**/**-tun ya**]. ¶**Way yūmyeng han ya** Why is it famous? **Sikan un nek.nek han ya** Have we got enough time? **Kath.i kanun kes i etten ya ko hayss.ta** He asked me if you would like to go with him. **Ku kes i mues in ya ko mul.e pwā la** Ask him what it is. **Kath.i kanun kes i etten ya 'nun māl iyo** I am asking if you would like to go with him. **Ku kes i mues in ya 'nun cilmun i iss.ess.ta** There was a question (asking) what it was.

-ᵘ⁄ₒ˙n ya (modifier + postmod) SEE -˙no˙n ya

-unya (ko) → **-un ya (ko)**

-unya 'myen = **-un ya 'myen**, abbr < **-un ya (ko) hamyen**

-unyan = **-un ya 'n(')**

-un ya 'n('), 1. abbr < **-un ya (ko) han**.

2. abbr < **-un ya (ko) hanun**. ¶**Ku sālam tul i nwukwu 'n ya 'n' māl ici** I mean, who are they?

-unq yang, modifier + noun.

1. ~ **hanta** makes a pretense of being or of having done. ¶**Pankawunq yang hayss.ta** She made a pretense of being glad. **Sensayng inq yang hayss.ta** He pretended to be a teacher. **Ku nun tomoci an ponq yang hayss.ta** He pretended not to see me at all. **Ku nun kuce pay ka pulunq yang hako iss.ta** He is just pretending "to have a full belly" (= to be rich).

2. ~ ita, ~ ulo = -un mo.yang. ¶Kwun.in inq yang ulo māl hanta He talks as if he were a serviceman.

-unya 'nun = -un ya 'nun, abbr < -un ya (ko) hanun

-un ya nun, mod + postmod + pcl. ¶Nwu ka khun ya nun mūncey ka toyci man ... It is a question who is taller but ... .

-un ya tul, modifier + postmodifier + particle. ¶Tā kwaynchanh.un ya tul? Is everybody all right? Tā kippun ya tul? Is everybody happy?

-un yay = -un ya 'y, abbr < -un ya (ko) hay

-ᵘ/oˑn ye, mod + postmod (question). ¶KWONG-ˑTUK i haˑn ye ¨cyekuˑn ye (1447 Sek 19:4a) are his meritorious achievements many or few? CIN-ˑSSILQ ˑlwo kuˑle theˑn ye aˑni theˑn ye (1459 Wel 9:36d) was it really so or wasn't it? eˑliˑn ye solkaˑwoˑn ye (1462 ¹Nung 4:36a) is he stupid or smart? SEE aˑniˑ'n ye.

-unyo = -un yo

-un yo [obs] = -un ya (question)

-ᵘ/oˑn ywo, mod + postmod [question]. ¶ˑi ˑTI-ˑHHYWEY ¨ep.sun ˑPPI-KHWUW y eˑtule ˑsye woˑn ywo (1447 Sek 19:30b) where did this witless almsman (bhiksu) come from? ¨es.tyey eˑli.n ywo (1481 Twusi 8:2b) why are you being stupid? ¨nwu [ˑ]lol puˑthu.n ywo (1482 Nam 1:80b) whom to rely on.

-uo [DIAL] = -so (AUTH). According to Roth (1936:138), this is mostly used as a command: Pat.uo! Take it! Tat.uo! Close it!

-uoita [obs] = -saop.nita, -sup.nita

-uop- [obs] = -saop-, -sup-

-u(o)wa formal inf [-uop-/-op- + -e; obs] = -e. CF -saowa, -sawa.

-uoyta = -uoita

-upci yo = -supci yo

-up.nikka, 1. = -ˢup.nikka, spelling alt/var of -sup.nikka (FORMAL indic attentive) after ···ss- and ···ps-. ¶Iss.ˢup.nikka? Does it exist? Does he stay? Is he there? Have we got one/any? Ēps.ˢup.nikka? Doesn't it exist? Is it lacking? Haven't we got one/any? Ancess.ˢup.nikka? Did he sit down? Mek.keyss.ˢup.nikka Will he eat?

2. [DIAL] = -sup.nikka. ¶mek.up.nikka → meksup.nikka.

-up.ninta = -up.nuynta

-up.nita, 1. = -ˢup.nita, spelling alt/var of -sup.nita (FORMAL indic assertive) after ···ss and ···ps. ¶iss.ˢup.nita exists; stays; has. chwupkeyss.ˢup.nita it will be cold; it must be cold. anc.ess.ˢup.nita sat down. ēps.ˢup.nita does not exist; lacks.

2. [DIAL] = -sup.nita. ¶mek.up.nita → meksup.nita.

-up.naykka = -up.neykka (→ -up.nikka)

-up.nayta = -up.neyta (→ -up.nita)

-up.ney, -up.ni, -up.nuy [DIAL; old-fashioned] = -e yo

-up.neykka [DIAL] = -up.nikka

-up.neyta [DIAL] = -up.nita

-up.nuynta [DIAL; old-fashioned] = -so/-o, statement or question in AUTHORITATIVE style. After a vowel -p.nuynta.

-upsayta [DIAL] = -upsita

-upsey, FORMAL-FAMILIAR subjunctive assertive = proposition (-psey after a vowel). let's; let me. ¶Kapsey Let's go. Com popsey Let me just have a look at it.

-upseyta [DIAL] = -upsita

-upsio [DIAL] (-psio after a vowel); VAR -upsie, -upsye. 1. = -usio (FORMAL command). SEE ye-popsio. 2. ?= -(su)p.nita.

-upsita, FORMAL subj assertive = proposition (-psita after a vowel).

1. let's (= -ca). ¶Anc.upsita Let's sit down.

2. let me, let's; I want to, I will. ¶Naylipsita Let me off, please [said in leaving a bus, etc.]. Chen wen ey sapsita I'll pay a thousand wen for it [bargaining]. Kil com mul.upsita (= Kil com mūt.keyss.ˢup.nita) May I ask you for directions, please? Māl-ssum com mul.upsita Let me (May I) ask you a question.

-upsulum, bnd adj-n (~ hata). ···ish, slightly colored/tinged. ¶hay-/huy-upsulum whitish, CF -usulum.

-upsye, abbr < -upsie, var = -upsio

-upsyo = -upsio

-upta, bnd adj -W- [var < -epta]. is characterized by. ¶wusupta is comical < wūs.ta laughs.

-uptikka, 1. = -ˢuptikka, spelling alt/var of -suptikka (FORMAL indic attent) after ···ss and ···ps. ¶Iss.ˢuptikka? Was there any (when you looked)? Chwupkeyss.ˢuptikka? Was it going to be cold? Ēps.ˢuptikka? Didn't you find it/any? Was it lacking? Wasn't it there?

2. [DIAL] = -suptikka. ¶mek.uptikka → meksuptikka.

-uptita, 1. = -ˢuptita, a spelling alt/var of -suptita (FORMAL indic assertive) after ⋯ss and ⋯ps. ¶Iss.ˢuptita There was some; They had some. Kass.ˢuptita (When I got there) he was gone. Chwupkeyss.ˢuptita It was going to be cold. Ēps.ˢuptita I found they hadn't any.
   2. [DIAL] = -suptita.
-us, suf; derives impressionistic adv, adj-n. CF -s
   1. from adjective. ¶copus hata is a bit narrow < copta is narrow. (k)kamus (k)kamus / (k)kemus (k)kemus dotted/specked with black; (k)kamus / (k)kemus hata is blackish. malkus malkus rather thin/watery < malk.ta. nolus nolus / nwulus nwulus spotty/splotchy yellow < noluta / nwuluta is yellow. phulus phulus spotty blue < phuluta is blue. (p)palkus (p)palkus / (p)pulkus (p)pulkus spotty red < pulk.ta is red.
   2. from vi. ¶memus memus = memulus memulus hesitating < memulta = memuluta stops, stays. okus okus irregularly curved < okta bends in, is bent.
   3. from vt. ¶hal(k)kis hal(k)kis / hul(k)kis hul(k)kis glaring, leering < (nwun ul) hulkita glares, leers. (k)kokis (k)kokis / (k)kwukis (k)kwukis < (k)kwukita crumples it.
   4. from bound stem. ¶kephus kephus flapping (= kephul kephul). napus napus / nepus nepus fluttering (CF napi butterfly). nukus nukus nauseated.
-usa [lit] = -usye = -usie (hon inf)
-use = -usye = -usie (hon inf)
-usey [var] = -usye (hon inf). ~ ya, ~ yo.
-usey yo ([var] = -usye yo), POLITE honorific statement, question, command, or proposition. ¶Ese anc.usey yo Please sit down. Kath.i kasey yo Let's go together. Tōn i iss.usey yo? Have you got any money?
-usi- < -ᵘoˑsi-, honorific (-si- after a vowel).
-uˑsi⋯, honorific. SEE ALSO -oˑsi⋯.
-usiap [var] = -usiop(sose). ¶Motwu osiap All are invited to come. I kos ey hyuci lul pelici māsiap Do not discard trash here. NOTE: Not to be spelled -aph!
-usica, hon subj attentive. This cannot be used as a suggestion, for the honorific is incongruous with the plain-style hortative, except when that is quoted: Han can tusica ko hayss.ta I suggested we have a drink; I said "Let's have a drink!" (= tusipsita or tusisey). And it can be used in the structure -usica māca 'as soon as an esteemed person does'.
-usici, hon suspective (-sici after a vowel)
-usie, hon inf (-sie after a vowel); ABBR -us(y)e
-uˑsikeˑn i, honorific effective mod + postmod. ¶hoˑma ˑMYWOW ˑkhwo ˑNGWEN ˑhoˑsikeˑn i (1463 Pep 7:106b) is already wondrous and perfect. SEE - kᵉasiˑn i.
-ᵘoˑsiken ˑtyeng, honorific effective modifier + bound postmodifier. ¶ˑˑcyeˑkusyaˑm i ˑˑkyeˑsiken ˑtyeng (1463 Pep 3:189b) though there are those who have little, ⋯ .
-ᵘoˑsikeˑnul, hon lit concessive (< hon effective mod + pcl). SEE ˑhoˑsikeˑnul; CF -ˑkesiˑnol.
-ᵘoˑsikeˑn ywo, hon effective mod + postmod. ¶ˑil-ˑlwo ˑˑhyeyye ˑpwokenˑt ey n' muˑsum CCO-PI ˑˑkyeˑsikeˑn ywo hoˑkwo (1447 Sek 6:6a) "When one considers it as this, what mercy does he have?!" she said, and ⋯ .
-ᵘoˑsikeˑtun, hon provisional. ¶ˑˑmanˑil iˑmuy ˑˑcˑaˑsye ˑˑkyeˑsikeˑtun (1586 Sohak 2:4b; sic ˑˑman-ˑil) if you have already eaten.
-usikey, honorific adverbative. This can be used as a FAMILIAR command or question: Ilccik com osikey (Arrange to) come a little early! Kasikey yo? You're gonna (fix it to) go?
-ᵘoˑsiˑkey, hon adverbative. ¶eˑnu naˑlaˑh ay noˑlisiˑkey hoˑl [i] ˑyeˑn ywo (1459 Wel 2:10b) what land should we have them descend to?
-usikeyss-, hon future: ~ -ta, ~ -ni?, ~ ⋯ .
-usiko, honorific gerund
-ᵘoˑsiˑkuy, honorific adverbative. ¶⋯ ˑNYELQ-PPAN ˑTUK ˑhwoˑm ol pwuthye ˑkot( )hosiˑkuy hoˑl i ˑ-ngi ˑˑta (1447 Sek 6:4a) he will enable you to be like the Buddha and achieve nirvāṇa.
-ᵘoˑsikwanˑtoy: SEE ˑhoˑsikwanˑtoy
-ᵘoˑsikwaˑtye, honorific + -kwaˑtye (desiderative structure). wanting to do. ¶naˑlaˑh ay ˑsye mwoˑlwomay saˑhwo.m ol [HHOYNG] ˑhwol ˑt iGeˑn i ˑGwa ˑˑsaloˑm on [KWA-YEN] ˑul kuˑchiˑsikwaˑtye solang ˑhonwosˑta (1481 Twusi 20:4b) while the nation must conduct warfare, the people would love to put an end to spears and lances.
-ᵘoˑsiˑkwo, hon ger. ¶tuluˑsiˑkwo (1447 Sek 13:30b) hears and. te nwophoˑsiˑkwo (1463 Pep 2:137a) the higher they are, and. ˑSYEY-CWON ˑi SYWU-ˑTTALQ ˑi wolˑtt ol ˑˑaˑlosiˑkwo (1447 6:20b) the World-Honored, knowing that

Sudatta was coming, ... THYEN-ˑCO y ˈwuˑli ˈˑTTWOW-ˑˑLI ˈlan poˑlisiˑkwo ˈˑmen ˈtuy s HHWO-ˑKYWOW ˈlol KKWUW ˈhoˑsinoˑn i (1459 Wel 2:69a) the son of heaven rejects our doctrine and pursues alien teachings from distant places. *anco sya ˈwoˑs i comoˑkoy ˈwuˑlusiˑkwo niluˑsyaˑtoy* (1459 Wel 8:101a) sat down and, letting his clothes settle, said in tears (as follows: ...). MI-ˑMYWOW hon ˈˑTTWOW ˈay naˑza kaˑl i ˈl ˈss oy ˈiˑle ˈnˑt olwo ˑPEP-HHWA-ˑHHWOY ˑSSYANG ˈay taˑsi ˑTTI-ˑWUY s ˑˑmaˑl i ˈˑepˑsusiˑkwo (1462 ¹Nung 1:18b) with their progress into the subtle teachings there was thus no more talk of location for the Lotus doctrine study group.

-ᵘ/o ˈsiˑkwo k, honorific gerund + emphatic pcl. ¶ ˑCUK-SSI ˈyey ZYE-LOY y ˑTTAY-ˑCYWUNG TYWUNG ˈey taˑsos LYWUN-ˑˑCI ˈlol kwuˑphiˑsya kwuˑphisiˑkwo k ˈstwo ˈphyesiˑm ye ˈphyesiˑkwo k (1462 ¹Nung 1:108b) at that time, the tathāgata in the midst of all the priests curved his [wheel-like] Buddha fingers repeatedly and then opened them repeatedly.

-usil(q) < -ᵘ/o ˈsil(q), honorific prospective modifier (-sil(q) after a vowel)

-ᵘ/o ˈsil(q), hon prosp mod. ¶ *iˑkiˑsilq [ˑSWAN] ˈol cimˑcus ˈˑepˑkey ˈhosiˑn i* (1445 ¹Yong 64) he deliberately fixed the score [against an inferior opponent] so that he would not win. *[ˑPWOW-ˑWUY] ˈthoˑsil nuˑc iˑlusyasˑta* (1445 ¹Yong 100) it was an omen that he would mount the throne.

-usila < -ᵘ/o ˈsiˑla, hon subj assertive (-sila after a vowel). Used only in quoting a command: **sensayng nim kkey kitalisila ko hayss.ta** told the teacher to wait. SEE **-usica**.

-ᵘ/o ˈsiˑla ˈnˑt oy SEE ˈhosila ˈnˑt oy, - ~ ˈla ˈnˑt oy

-ᵘ/o ˈsiˑl i, honorific prosp modifier + postmod.

-ᵘ/o ˈsi.l i ˈˑla, hon prosp mod + postmod + cop indic assert. ¶ *haˑnolˑh i tangtangi ˈi ˈphi ˈlol ˈˑsalom towoy ˈGey ˈhoˑsi.l i ˈˑla* (1459 Wel 1:7-8) heaven is to make this blood suitably into people.

-ᵘ/o ˈsi.l i ˈˑla[ˈ]s-ongi ˈˑta (bnd v polite + cop indic assert). ¶ *pwuˑˑthye y ˈwuˑli ˑWUY ˈhoˑya ˑTTAY-SSING ˑPEP ˈul niloˑsiˑl i ˈˑlas-ongi ˈˑta* (1459 Wel 13:36a) Buddha will tell us the law of the Greater Vehicle (mahāyāna). *ˈhota ˈka ˈwuli ˈkhun ˑPEP ˈculˑkil mozoˑm ol ˈtwutenˑt ay nˈ pwuˑˑthye y ˈˑna lˈ ˑWUY ˈhoˑsya ˑTTAY-SSING ˑPEP ˈul niloˑsiˑl i ˈˑlas-ongi ˈˑta* (1463 Pep 2:231b) if we keep minds to enjoy the greater dharma perhaps Buddha will tell the dharma of the Greater Vehicle (mahāyāna) for my sake.

-ᵘ/o ˈsiˑl i ˈˑlasˑta, hon prosp mod + postmod + cop retrospective emotive indicative assertive. ¶ *ˈhota ˈka ˈna y ˈkhun ˑPEP ˈculˑkitenˑt ay nˈ ˈˑwoˑlwo masˑtisyaˑm i woˑlasiˑl i ˈˑlasˑta* (1463 Pep 2:232a) if I delighted in the great[er] dharma, he would leave me completely in charge for long periods.

-ᵘ/o ˈsiˈl i ˈˑleˑla, hon prosp modifier + postmod + cop retr assert. ¶ *ˈcukˑcay mol ˈthoˑsiˑl i ˈleˑla* (?1517- Pak 1:64b; *ˈcukˑcay = ˈcukcay = ˈcukcaˑhi*) will straightway get on their horses. SEE *ˈhosiˑl i ˈleˑla*.

-ᵘ/o ˈsiˈl i ˈleˑn ywo, hon prosp mod + postmod + copula retr modifier + postmod. ¶ *ˈsyeˈwul ˈsye hoyngˈhoyng ˈi ˈˑencey ˈnasiˑl i ˈleˑn ywo* (?1517- Pak 1:53b) when is it that the imperial procession will leave the capital?

-ᵘ/o ˈsi.l i ˈlq ˈs oy, hon prosp mod + postmod + cop prosp mod + postmod + pcl. ¶ *[THYEN-ˑˑHHA] ˈlol mas.tosi.l i ˈl ˈss oy* (1445 ¹Yong 6) will take charge of the land, so ... . *YEM-PPWUW-TTYEY ˈnaˑsi.l i ˈl ˈss oy* (1449 Kok 13) will be born in Jambudvīpa, ... SEE *hoˑl i ˈsi.l i ˈl s oy*.

-ᵘ/o ˈsiˈl i ˈˑlwoswoˑn i, hon prosp mod + var cop emotive mod + postmod. ¶ *ˈi ˑSYEY-ˑKAY ˈyey nˈˈ CHYEN-ˑPPWULQ ˈi ˈnasiˑl i ˈˑlwoswoˑn i ˑKEP ilˈhwu.m uˈlan HHYEN-ˑKEP ˈiˑla hoˑcye* (1459 Wel 1:40a) since into this world a thousand Buddhas will be born, I want the name of this kalpa to be the Wise Kalpa.

-ᵘ/o ˈsiˑl i ˈ-ngi s ˈka, hon prosp mod + postmod + cop polite + pcl + postmod. ¶ *woˑla honˈt ol ˈwosiˑl i ˈ-ngi s ˈka* (1445 ¹Yong 69) though told to come would he come?

-ᵘ/o ˈsiˈl i ˈ-ngi s ˈkwo, hon prosp mod + postmod + cop polite + pcl + postmod. ¶ *muˑsu.m uˈla ˈwosiˑn i ˈ-ngi s ˈkwo* (1447 Sek 6:3a) for what reason have you come here? *eˈnwu naˈlaˑh ay ˈkaˑsya ˈnasiˑl i ˈ-ngi s ˈkwo* (1459 Wel 2:11b) which country are you going off to?

-ᵘ/o ˈsiˈl i ˈ-ngi ˈˑta, hon prosp mod + postmod + cop polite + cop indic assert. ¶ *ˈˑkuˈy ˈzaˈi ˑCCWA ˈay ancoˑsiˑl i ˈ-ngi ˈˑta* (1447 Sek 24:43b) just he will sit in this seat.

-ᵘ⁄ₒˑsiˑl i ˑye, honorific prospective modifier + postmodifier + postmodifier. ¶ ˑCCAP ˝CHWOW-˙MWOK kesˑke ˑta ˑka noˑch ol kewuzoˑWon ˑt ol mozom ˑisˑton mwuyˑGwusiˑl i ˑye (1449 Kok 62) [the mischievous boys] they cut sticks and went at his face [piercing each ear], but would his mind waver?!

-ᵘ⁄ₒˑsilq ˑka, hon prosp mod + postmodifier (usually spelled -usilkka or -usilka). ¶ ˑna-ˑkasilq ˑka cehoˑsya (1449 Kok 46) fearing that he would leave ... .

-ᵘ⁄ₒˑsilq ˑkwo, hon prosp mod + postmodifier (usually spelled -usilkkwo or -usilkwo). ¶ ˝ne y ˝enceyˑkil[h] ˑnaˑsil ˑkwo (?1517- Pak 1:8b) when are you setting out on the road?

-ᵘ⁄ₒˑsilq ˑs iGen ˑtyeng, honorific prosp modifier + postmod + cop effective mod + postmod. ¶woˑcik aˑpa ˝nim s ˑPPYENG ˑi ˝tywoˑhosil ˑs iGen ˑtyeng mwoˑm ol ˑPOYK-CHYEN tiˑGwuy poˑlye ˑtwo eˑlyepˑti aˑni hoˑn i (1459 Wel 21:216ab) but even if your father's illness improves, it is not (difficult =) uncommon to discard one's body hundreds of thousands of times. [Accent: p. 85.]

-ᵘ⁄ₒˑsilq ˑs iˑla, hon prosp mod + postmod + cop indic assert. ¶kaˑcolˑpizoWˑwol ˑttoy ˝epˑsusil ˑss iˑla (1447 Sek 6:41a [¹Yi Tonglim version]) there is nothing to compare with it. [SEE p. 85.]

-ᵘ⁄ₒˑsilq ˑs ol, hon prosp mod + postmod + pcl. ¶PPEN-˝NWOW paˑloˑl ay ˝ket-˝nayˑya ˝naysil ˑss ol ˑCYEY-˙TTWO ˑyˑla ˑhoˑno.n i ˑˑla (1459 Wel 1:11a) carrying one over a sea of troubles (and putting one out of it) is called salvation.

-ᵘ⁄ₒˑsilˑssoy = -ᵘ⁄ₒˑsilq ˑs oy, hon prosp mod + postmodifier + particle. ¶SAM-˙SYEY ˑyey s ˝iˑl ol ˝aˑlosil ˑss oy pwu˝thye ˑysiˑta ˑhoˑno.n i ˑ-ngˑˑta (1447 Sek 6:18a) he commanded the knowledge of the three states of existence; so therefore they say that he is Buddha. ˝SYWOW KKWU-TTAM ˑi KAM-ˑCYA NGWEN ˑey ˝saˑlosil ˑss oy KAM-ˑCYA ˝SSI ˑla ˑtwo ˑhoˑte.n i ˑˑla (1459 Wel 1:8ab) Gautama the Lesser was also called Sugarcane Sire (Ikṣvāku) because he lived in a sugarcane garden. sesˑke ˝teleˑwun ˑKYEN ˑi ˝ilq ˑka cehuˑsil ˑss oy (1462 ¹Nung 4:38b) because he feared that contaminated views might be formed.

-ᵘ⁄ₒˑsilˑssye = -ᵘ⁄ₒˑsilq ˑs ye, hon prosp mod + postmod + postmod. (rhetorical question used as an exclamation that is much like the modern apperceptive). ¶ ˝syelˑWun ˝il ˑtwo ˑTTAY-NGWANG i ˑileˑ'n ˑKWUY hon mozoˑm ol ˝naysil ˑss ye (1447 Sek 24:37ab) such a noble heart the great king has shown us!

-ᵘ⁄ₒˑsilq ˑt ol, hon prosp mod + postmod + pcl. that it / one will. ¶ ˑSYEK-KA ˑPPWULQ towoyˑsilq ˑt ol ˝PHWO-KWANG ˑPPWULQ ˑi niloˑsiˑn i ˑ-ngi ˑˑta (1459 Wel 1:3a) the Buddha of universal light (dīpamkara) said that Śākya will become a Buddha.

-ᵘ⁄ₒˑsiˑl ye, hon prosp modifier + postmodifier. ¶ ˑHHWUW ˑey ˑstwo ˑLYWULQ ˑol ˝twoˑosiˑl ye (1462 ¹Nung 1:19a) later, seeking to further the discipline (vinaya, monastic rules) ... .

-ᵘ⁄ₒˑsiˑlyenmaˑlon = -ᵘ⁄ₒˑsiˑl ˑyen maˑlon = -ᵘ⁄ₒˑsiˑl ˑyen [i] maˑlon, hon prosp mod + cop effective mod (+ ellipted postmod) + bnd n. ¶ ˑSO-THYEN ˝HHA ˑlol kozom ˝aˑlosi.l [i] ˑyen maˑlon nulˑku.n i ˑPPYENG hoˑn i cwuˑkun ˝salom ˑpwosiˑkwo ˑSYEY-KAN ˑsulˑhi neˑkiˑsya ˑCHYWULQ-KA ˑhoˑsya (1447 Sek 6:17b) he governed the world below the four heavens but when he saw the old, the ill, and the dead he found the world sad and left home to become a monk, and ... . pwuˑthye y ˑwuˑli ˑWUY ˑhoˑya ˑTTAY-SSING ˑPEP ˑul niloˑsiˑl i ˑˑlas-ongi ˑˑta (1459 Wel 13:36a) Buddha will tell us the law of the Greater Vehicle (mahāyāna). ˑhotaˑka ˑwuliˑkhun ˑPEP ˑculˑkil mozoˑm ol ˑtwuten ˑt ay n' pwu˝thye y ˝naˑl' ˑWUY ˑhoˑsya ˑTTAY-SSING ˑPEP ˑul niloˑsiˑl i ˑˑlas-ongi ˑˑta (1463 Pep 2:231b) if we keep minds to enjoy the greater dharma perhaps Buddha will tell the dharma of the Greater Vehicle (mahāyāna) for my sake.

-ᵘ⁄ₒsilyenywo = -ᵘ⁄ₒˑsiˑl ˑyeˑn ywo = -ᵘ⁄ₒˑsiˑl [i] ˑyeˑn ywo, honorific prosp modifier (+ ellipted postmod) + cop effective mod + postmod. ¶eˑnu ˝nwuˑlul teˑpuˑlusiˑl [i] ˑyeˑn ywo (1449 Kok 52) whom would you take with you?

-usim, honorific substantive (-sim after a vowel)

-ᵘ⁄ₒˑsiˑm ye, hon subst + abbr copula inf. ¶CYE-ˑPPWULQ ˑtwo piˑchwuysiˑm ye ... (1449 Kok 18) the Buddhas emit radiance and ... . twosˑk uy mululq ˑCYWUNG isil ˑtt ol miˑli ˝alosiˑm ye (1463 Pep 1:168a) knew in advance that there would be a crowd who would retreat to their seat mats, and ... .

~ n' (pcl). ¶na ˑy ˝malˑGwos aˑni tuluˑsiˑm ye n' nowoyˑculkeˑWun mozoˑm i ˝ep.suˑl ye 'y-ngi ''ta (1459 Wel 2:5b) if you do not listen to what I say you will not have a happy heart again. twolwo pwonayl il i mwos twoyl ta nilusi.m ye n' [sic] (1676 Sin.e 8:8b) when/if he asks whether it will be impossible to send them back, ...

-usin < -^{u}/o˙sin, hon mod (**-sin** after a vowel)

-^{u}/o˙sin, honorific modifier. ¶ ˙PWON-LOY ˙hasin ˙KILQ-˙KHYENG ˙ey (1449 Kok 18) to the happy events and good omens which were plentiful from the start ... . SEE ˙hosin.

-usina < -^{u}/o˙si˙na, hon adversative. (1459 Kok 26; 1482 Kum-sam 5:10b). SEE ˙hosi˙na.

-usiney, FAMILIAR hon indic assert

-^{u}/o˙si-ngi ''ta, hon polite + cop indic assertive. ¶eyng ˙wolho˙si-ngi ''ta (1447 Sek 13:47a) sure enough, he is right. SEE ˙ho˙si-ngi ''ta.

-^{u}/o˙si˙n i, hon mod + postmod. ¶ ˙skwoy han twoco˙k ol mwo˙lo˙sya ¨pwo.l i ''la ki˙tu˙lisi˙n i (1445 ^{1}Yong 19) not knowing the [number of] wileful thieves (= renegades) he waited to see them. ¨epten ˙pen˙key ˙lul ha˙nol˙h i pol˙kisi˙n i (1445 ^{1}Yong 30) heaven shone with lightning that had not existed (before). [THYEN-˙SYENG] ˙un polko˙si˙n i (1445 ^{1}Yong 71) the intentions of heaven were clear. ˙PWULQ-SYENG two˙tolq ˙cey ˙PPOYK ¨SSYANG ˙ol ˙thosi˙n i (1449 Kok 14) when the auspicious stars of the asterism puṣya rose, they were on a white elephant. ˙ema ¨nim ˙i PPI-LAM NGWEN ˙ul pwo˙la ˙kasi˙n i (1449 Kok 17) the mother went to see Lumbinī Park. ˙i ¨twul˙h ul ˙za te˙pu˙lusi˙n i (1449 Kok 52) he combined these very two. ZYE-LOY ˙THAY-¨CO s SSI-˙CYELQ ˙ey ¨na ˙lol ¨kyecip ¨sa˙mosi˙n i (1447 Sek 6:4a) when the tathāgata was the prince he made me his wife. wo˙cik pwu¨thye y ˙za NUNG ˙hi ¨a˙losi˙n i (1463 Pep 4:63a) only Buddha fully knows. ALSO: 1447 Sek 6:39a [^{1}Yi Tonglim version], 1459 Wel 10:15b, 1482 Kum-sam 4:54a, ... SEE ˙isi˙n i, a˙ni 'ysi˙n i; -˙esi˙n i, -˙kesi˙n i, ˙ilesi˙n i.

~ ''la (cop indic assert). ¶pe˙kun PWU-ZIN ˙i towoy˙si.n i ''la (1447 Sek 6:1b) she became his second wife. kuli˙mey ˙non ˙mu˙l ey s ˙to˙l ol nilo˙si.n i ''la (1462 ^{1}Nung 2:84b) the image portrayed the moon on the water. ¨ep.sun ¨HHWUW ˙ey ˙za e˙lwu ˙MYWOW-˙PEP ˙ey ˙tul ˙tt ol ¨pwoy˙si.n i ''la (1463 Pep 1:55b) only after its absence was it possible to show you that you can enter saddharma (the Lotus sūtra's wonderful truth). ALSO: 1447 Sek 23:42a, 44a; 1463 Pep 3:47a; 1482 Kum-sam 2:15b; ... .

~ '-ngi ''ta. ¶[SYENG-SWON] ˙ol ¨naysi˙n i '-ngi ''ta (1445 ^{1}Yong 8) the august grandson was born. mol ˙thwon ca˙hi ¨ken˙nesi˙n i '-ngi ''ta (1445 ^{1}Yong 34) he crossed over on horseback. ¨PHWO-KWANG ˙PPWULQ ˙i nilo˙si˙n i '-ngi ''ta (1449 Kok 5) the Buddha of universal light (dīpamkara) had foretold it. CYE-˙PPWULQ nilu˙sinwon ¨ma˙l on ¨NAY-CYWUNG ¨nay tal˙Gwolq ˙cwu˙l i ¨ep˙susi˙n i '-ngi ''ta (1447 Sek 9:27a) there is no way that the words said by the various Buddhas will differ in the end.

~ s ˙ka SEE -˙tesi˙n i s ˙ka

-^{u}/o˙sin ˙ka, hon mod + postmod. ¶hon NGUY-SIM ˙on pwu¨thye y a˙ni ta˙si ˙nasin ka ho˙kwo (1447 Sek 24:3b) one doubt: whether Buddha has not been born again ... . pwus˙kulywo˙m i ¨es.tyey ¨ep˙susin ˙ka (1449 Kok 120) how come he has no shame? [Accent: see p. 85.]

-^{u}/o˙sin ˙kwo, hon modifier + postmod. ¶mu˙sum ˙pu˙lisyan i˙l isin ˙kwo (?1517- Pak 1:8a) what errand is it that you have? [cop hon mod ˙isin]

-^{u}/o˙sin ma˙lon SEE -˙ke˙sin ma˙lon

-^{u}/osi˙no-ngi ''ta, hon proc polite + copula indic assert. ¶HE-KHWONG ˙o˙lwo ho˙ma ˙wosi˙no-ngi ''ta (1459 Wel 10:8a) is already coming to the void.

-^{u}/o˙sino˙n i, honorific proc mod + postmodifier. ¶CYE-˙PPWULQ ˙two ˙CHYWULQ-KA ˙hosya ˙za ¨TTWOW-¨LI ˙lol tas.ko˙sino˙n i (1447 Sek 6:12a) even the Buddhas must leave home in order to study the doctrine. ˙PEP ul nilu˙sino˙n i (1462 ^{1}Nung 1:38a) he is telling the Law (= preaching the doctrine).

~ '-i s ˙kwo = '-ngi s ˙kwo (= ˙i-ngi s ˙kwo). ¶ ¨es˙ti TANG WU cek ta[˙]so[˙]lim ˙ul ˙pep pat˙kwo ˙cye ˙hosino˙n i '-''i s ˙kwo (1586 Sohak 6:35b) why do you want to take the governing of Táng and Wú as your model?

~ ˙si˙n i ''la [with two nominalizations and two honorifications]. ¶mu˙l ey s ˙tol ˙kot hi ˙MWULQ-˙QUNG ˙ho˙sino˙n i ˙si˙n i ''la (1463 Pep 4:117a) they are reflecting on things as if moonlight on the water.

~ '-ngi s ˙ka. ¶ ˙SYA-˙NGWUY ˙KWUYK ˙ey hon ˙TTAY-SSIN SYWU-˙TTALQ ˙i˙la ˙hwo˙l i is.no˙n i ¨alo˙sino˙n i '-ngi s ˙ka (1447 Sek 6:14-5) there is a minister in the state of Śrāvastī who is named Sudatta; do you know him? ¨e˙styey hon QUM-˙NYE ˙WUY ˙ho˙ya ¨ta po˙li˙kwo ˙ka˙sino˙n i '-ngi s ˙ka (1459 Wel 7:17b) how can you throw everything away for the sake of a lewd woman? ~ '-ngi s ˙kwo. ¶ ¨es.te 'n QIN-YWEN ˙u˙lwo wuzyen ˙ho˙sino˙n i '-ngi s ˙kwo (1447 Sek 24:9a) in what connection are you smiling [in relief]? [the "smiling" is from Kim Yengpay's interpretation]. ¨es˙te 'n cyen˙cho˙lwo ¨na˙lol e˙li˙ta ˙ho˙sya ˙SYEK-¨CO 'ylwo˙la ˙hwo˙m ol ¨mwot ho˙l i ˙'la ˙ho˙sino˙n i '-ngi s ˙kwo (1459 Wel 9:35de) on what grounds do you say I am too young and refuse to call me a disciple of Buddha?

-ᵘ/o˙sinon ˙ka, hon proc mod + postmodifier. ¶ mu˙sum ˙mul ˙lwo ˙ptoy sisu˙sinon ˙ka (1449 Kok 124) with what water does he wash off his dirt? SEE ˙ho˙sinon ˙ka.

-ᵘ/o˙sinon ˙kwo, hon proc mod + postmodifier. ¶ e˙tuy ˙kasinon ˙kwo (?1517- Pak 1:7b) where are you going?

-ᵘ/o˙sino˙n ywo, hon proc modifier + postmod. ¶ mu˙sus ¨i˙l ol nil˙Gwo˙l ye ˙ho˙sino˙n ywo (1447 Sek 13:26a) what do you want to tell?

-ᵘ/o˙sino˙ta, hon proc indic assert. ¶ ˙PEP-¨NGUY ˙lol ¨phye˙l ye ˙ho˙sino˙ta (1447 Sek 13:26b) he seeks to spread the meaning of the Law.

-usinta, honorific processive indicative assertive (-sinta after a vowel)

-ᵘ/o˙sin ˙t ay, hon mod + postmodifier + pcl. ¶ ˙nwun spal˙Ga ˙pwosin ˙t ay ˙MALQ-˙LI HWA-MAN ˙ol twolwo ¨nay˙ya po˙li˙n i (1449 Kok 49) when his eyes peered too closely [at the girl], she took back the bejeweled garland of jasmine blossoms [that she had put around the prince's neck] and threw it away.

-ᵘ/o˙sin ˙t ay n', hon mod + postmod + pcl + pcl. ¶ ˙hota ˙ka ZYE-LOY 'ysin ˙t ay n' ZYE-LOY y ho˙ma ˙i SSYANG ˙isil s oy ¨NGWO-˙QUM ˙two ˙stwo pan˙toki SSYANG ˙i.l i ˙'n i (1465 Wen 1:1:1:63a) if it is the tathāgata, the tathāgata is already constant, therefore the five constituents (pañca-skandha) must be constant, as well.

-ᵘ/o˙sin ˙t i, hon modifier + postmod + pcl. ¶ ku cey lwo ˙wosin ˙t i son˙coy wo˙la˙ti ˙mwot ˙'kesi˙tun (1463 Pep 5:119b) he had not been there for very long yet when ... .

-ᵘ/o˙sin ˙t ol, honorific mod + postmodifier + pcl. ¶ [NGWANG] ˙i ku ˙i ˙lul ˙choco˙sya [˙LWOK-¨MWUW PWU-ZIN] ˙oy naho˙sin ˙t ol ¨alo˙si˙kwo ([1447→]1562 Sek 11:32_; here cited from He Wung 1975:683 with inferred accents) the king visited him and learned that the lady Mr̥gamāta (Deermother = Viśākha, wife of Sudatta = Anāthapiṇḍada) had given birth, and ... . [˙SO-¨CYA] ˙lol pwo˙naysin ˙t ol [˙CHILQ-˙TTOY CI NGWANG] ˙ol ˙nwu y ma˙ko˙l i '-ngi s ˙ka (1445 ¹Yong 15) he sent his commissioners, but who was to stop the kings of the seven dynasties? SEE ˙isin ˙t ol.

-usinun, hon proc mod. ¶ Tayk ey se ilk.usinun sinmun i musun sinmun ip.nikka At your house what newspaper do you read? Swu ka meych ina toysinun ci yo May I ask your age?

-ᵘ/o˙si˙nwon, honorific modulated proc modifier. ¶ pwuthye nilu˙sinwon ¨HHAY-˙THWALQ ˙ol (1447 Sek 13:43b) the emancipation that Buddha is telling of. KWONG ˙oy nilku˙si˙nwon ke˙s un ¨es˙te 'n ¨ma˙l i-ngi s ˙kwo (1465 Wen se:68a) what words are you reading, my Lord? ci˙p uy s ¨te˙lewu˙m ul ˙phyesi˙nwon cyen˙cho ˙'y˙n i (1482 Nam 1:5a) is the reason that he deigns to tidy up the mess of the house. SEE ˙hosi˙nwon.

-ᵘ/o˙si˙nwon ˙t i, hon proc mod + postmod + pcl. ¶ HHOYNG ˙ol ˙PHYEY ˙ho˙sinwon ˙t i a˙ni ˙'la (1459 Wel 17:42a) it is not that he is giving up the practice [of the five pāramitā disciplines].

-ᵘ/o˙si˙nwon ˙t i˙la, hon proc mod + postmod + cop indic assertive. ¶ CYE-˙PPWULQ ˙i hon ˙khun ¨il s QIN-YWEN ˙u˙lwo ˙SYEY-KAN ay ˙nasi˙nwon ˙t i˙la (1447 Sek 13:49a) the Buddhas are born into the human world as a consequence of some great event.

-ᵘ/o˙sinwos˙ta, hon emotive. ¶ [KUY-˙I] hon the˙li lol si˙hwok ¨may lol ˙cwu˙sinwos˙ta (1481 Twusi 8:8a) presents a rare fur or a falcon.

-ᵘ/o˙si˙nwo˙swo-ngi ˙'ta, hon modulated proc modulated emotive polite + cop indic assertive. ¶ wo˙nol ˙stwo wu[h] ¨ep˙sun ˙mos ˙khun ˙PEP-LYWUN ˙ul wolm˙ki˙si˙nwo˙swo-ngi ˙'ta (1463 Pep 2:47a) today we again move the peerless great wheel of dharma.

-ᵘ/o˙si˙nwoswo˙n i, hon modulated processive modulated emotive mod + postmod. ¶ SYEY-PANG ˙ay ˙SYENG-ZIN ˙i ˙nasi˙nwoswo˙n i ˙i ¨HHWUW ˙lwo CHYEN-NYEN ˙i˙m ye n' ku ˙PEP ˙i ingey ˙na-wo˙l i ˙'lwo˙swo-ngi ˙'ta (1459 Wel 2:49a) a sage has been born in the west; a thousand years from now his Law will appear here!

-ᵘ/o˙si˙n ywo SEE -˙kesi˙n ywo

-usio₁, 1. AUTH hon indic assertive (-sio after a vowel). ¶Son nim i i pang ul kuli cōh.a haci anh.usio The guest does not much like this room. 2. [var] = -usey yo
-usio₂, FORMAL subj attentive (-sio after a vowel; -psio after hon -usi-). do! ¶Anc.usio Sit down.
-usiop, [lit] abbr < -usiopsose (please do)
-usiopsose, [lit] = -usipsio please do.
-usio tul, FORMAL subj attentive + pcl. ¶Kulem ese yāyki hasio tul Well come on, people, talk!
-usip.nita, FORMAL hon indic assert (-sip.nita after a vowel). is (= deigns to be); does (= deigns to do). ¶Kim sensayng isip.nita It is Mr Kim. Hal-ape' nim i ku phyēnci lul ilk.usip.nita Grandfather reads the letter.
-usipsako, -usipsosako [? abbr] = -usipsio hako saying "please do it". ¶Sinpu nun cwukyo eykey hōncap kyelhon kwanmyen ul nāy cwusipsosako kāncheng ha.yess.ta The priests requested the bishop to issue a dispensation for a mixed marriage. Sawen i sacang eykey caki atul kyōyuk-pi lul pothay cwusipsako pūthak hayss.ta The employee asked the boss to help him with his son's school fees. Sensayng nim kkey towa cwusipsako māl-ssum tulilye ko wass.ˢup.nita I have come to ask for your help. [The form and the examples were brought to my attention by Richard Rutt.]
-usipseysa, honorific formal + ?. ¶poyksyeng ul phyengan hokey hosipseysa (1916 Gale 13) Give peace to thy people.
-usipsio, FORMAL hon subj attentive (-sipsio after a vowel). please do! ¶Anc.usipsio Please have a seat.
-usipsita, FORMAL hon subj assert (-sipsita after a vowel). please let's, let's just. ¶Anc.usipsita Let's please sit down.
-usipsosako SEE -usipsako
-usiptikka, FORMAL hon retr attentive (-siptikka after a vowel)
-usiptita, FORMAL hon retr assertive (-siptita after a vowel)
usisey, FAMILIAR hon subj assertive. let's do it.
-usita, hon indic assertive (or transferentive)
-ᵘ/oˑsiˑta, hon indic assert. ¶QA-ˑNWOK SAM-ˑMAK SAM-PPWO-TTYEY ˑlol ˑTUK ˑhosiˑta tuluˑsiˑkwo (1447 Sek 13:30b) hears tell that he obtains anuttara-samyak-sambodhi (unexcelled complete enlightenment), and ... . ˑmwot ilˑGwuwolqˑka s NGUY-SIM ˑi ˑˑepˑsusiˑta (1449 Kok 53) has no doubts (as to) whether he will fail to succeed. ˑwulGweˑti ˑGwos te nwophoˑsiˑkwo piˑpuyˑti ˑGwos te kwutuˑsiˑta hoˑn i ˑˑla (1463 Pep 2: 173a) said the more you raise your head the higher they [?= pimples] are and the more you rub the harder they are.
-ᵘ/oˑsiˑtaˑka, honorific indic assertive + pcl. SEE ˑhositaˑka.
~ ˑˑm ye (abbr < hoˑm ye). ¶ˑnasiˑta kaˑˑm ye TWONG-SYEY ˑlwo nilˑkwup keˑlum ˑnyesiˑn i (1482 Kum-sam 4:54a) as soon as he was born he went seven steps to the east and the west. SEE -ˑtaˑkaˑˑm ye.
-ᵘ/oˑsitan, honorific retrospective modifier.
~ ˑt inˑtˑay nˑ. ¶ˑtywohonˑˑilˑhoˑsitanˑtˑin ˑtˑay nˑˑ ema ˑˑnim sˑkuyˑtuleˑkaˑiˑˑtwonˑol KWONG-ˑYANG ˑhoˑzoWwoˑl i (1459 Wel 23: 65a) when you have done good work I will go in to your mother and provide her with this money.
-ᵘ/oˑsiˑtaˑs-ongiˑˑta, hon retrospective emotive polite + cop indic assert. ¶cwuˑke ˑHWA-ˑLAK THYEN-KWUNG ˑey nasi.l i ˑGeˑnul THYEN-KWUNG ˑey ˑˑmwotˑpwoˑzoˑWwoˑn i twoloˑhhye ˑTTI-[ˑ]NGWOK ˑay ˑˑkyesiˑtaˑs-ongiˑˑta (1459 of Nirmāṇarati ("joy-born heaven") but cannot see her for she is instead in purgatory. SEE ˑhoˑsiˑta[ˑ]s-ongiˑˑta, aˑniˑsiˑta[ˑ]s-ongiˑˑta.
-ᵘ/oˑsitasˑta, hon retr emotive indic assertive. ¶... MWU-ˑLYANG QA-SUNG-KKIˑKEPˑey ˑˑPPWU-ˑˑMWUWˑHYWOW-ˑYANG ˑhoˑsitasˑta (1459 Wel 21:208a) for countless jillions of kalpas (eons) has kindly ... and provided parental nurture.
-ᵘ/oˑsiteˑla, hon retr indic assertive (= -ˑtesiˑta). ¶iˑlwok SAM-SSING ˑol nilˑGeˑtwoˑˑta-ˑmon PPWO-ˑSALQ koloˑchywo.m iˑlaˑhositeˑla (1447 Sek 13:59a) he said, even telling of the Three Vehicles it is just the bodhisattva teaching.
-ᵘ/oˑsiten, hon retr modifier (= -ˑteˑsin). ¶ˑalay niluˑsitenˑPEP-HHWA KYENGˑey sˑZI-ˑSSIP CHYEN-ˑMENˑQUKˑKKYEYˑlolˑˑta tutˑˑcopˑkwo (1447 Sek 19:31b) I listened to every one of the twenty-thousand billion gāthās in the Lotus sūtra that he uttered earlier. ku kaˑwon-ˑtoy ˑSSYWUY-ˑSSYANGˑiˑkyeˑsiteˑn i (1459 Wel 2: 51b) among them there were propitious images (= good omens [personified and exalted]). CF -ᵘ/oˑsitan.

-ᵘ/ₒ˙site-ngi ˈ˙ta, hon retr polite + cop indic assertive (= -˙teˈsi-ngi ˈ˙ta). ¶*poy tulthwo* [= *tulh two*] *twolwosikwatya [MWON-QAN] hositengi ˙ta* (1676 Sin.e 5:17b) the boats themselves tending to whirl, they questioned their safety.

-ᵘ/ₒ˙siteˈn i, hon retro modifier + postmodifier (= -˙tesiˈn i). ¶ˈPEP ˙ul niluˈsiteˈn i (1447 Sek 13:27a) he told the Law (= preached the doctrine).

~ ˈ-ngi s ˙ka. ¶ˈSYEY-CWON ˙ha ˈSYEY-CWON ˙ha sonˈcoy ˈSYEY-KAN ˙ay ˈˈkyeˈsiteˈn i ˈ-ngi s ˙ka (1459 Wel 18:36b) oh honored one, oh honored one, are you still among the mortals?

-ᵘ/ₒ˙sitenˈka, hon retr mod + postmod (= -˙tesinˈka). SEE ˈhoˈsitenˈka.

-ᵘ/ₒ˙sitenˈt oy nˈ, hon retr mod + postmod + pcl + pcl. ¶*tal*ˈ*Gay*ˈ*ti a*ˈ*ni* ˈ*hositen*ˈ*t oy n*ˈ (1463 Pep 2:226a) since he had not appeased them.

-ᵘ/ₒ˙si-tiˈGwuy + NEG. but; and (yet). ¶ˈSYEY-CWON ˈi ˈSSILQ hon ˈˈTTWOW ˈlol niloˈsi-ti˙Gwuy PA-SSYWUN ˈunˈiˈˈiˈl iˈˈepˈtwoˈswo-ngi ˈ˙ta (1463 Pep 2:26a) the World-Honored preaches the real dharma, but Pāpīyān [the devil] never does this.

(*)-ᵘ/ₒ˙siˈtun SEE -ˈkesiˈtun = -ᵘ/ₒ˙sikeˈtun

-usitun, honorific retrospective modifier

-ᵘ/ₒ˙siˈtwoswo-ngi ˈ˙ta, hon emotive modulated emotive polite + copula indicative assertive. ¶ˈˈnyey s ˈPEP ˙ul cwochoˈsyaˈm iˈmas.tang ˙hosiˈtwoswo-ngi ˈ˙ta (1475 Nay 2:1:49a) it is proper for you to follow the old law!

-ᵘ/ₒ˙sitwoˈta, honorific emotive. ¶[*NGWANG*] ˈi ˈicey [ˈSWUK-ˈˈPWU] y [CWON] ˈhoˈsitwoˈta (1481 Twusi 8:10b) the king is now respectful of his uncle.

-usiyo → -usio; → -usi yo < -usey yo < -usie yo

-usoksok, bound adj-n (~ hata); after a vowel -soksok; LIGHT ↔ -uswukswuk. ⋯ish, slightly colored/tinged. SEE -(u)sulum.

-usola, [? DIAL, ? old-fashioned] = -usila

-usose < -usywoˈsye (-sose < -sywoˈsye after a vowel) [lit; = -usio]. please (I beg you to) do. ¶**Payk-sey chen-sey nwulisose** Long may you live! **Yōngse hasose** I beg you to forgive me. **Ce uy kānkwu lul tul.usose** Pray listen to my plea. **¹Yangchal ha.ye cwusose** Please consider carefully. **Say hay ey pok mānh.i pat.usose** May you receive much joy in the New Year.

-usulum (after a vowel -sulum; ABBR -ulum, -usum, -um). 1. bnd adj-n (~ hata).

1a. ⋯ish, slightly (a bit) colored/tinged. ¶**kemusulum** < kem- blackish. **pᵃ/ᵤlkusum** < pᵃ/ᵤlk- reddish. SYN -ucepcep, -ucokcok, -uchwungchwung, -ucwukcwuk, -usoksok, -uswukswuk, -utᵉ/ₐy(ng)tᵉ/ₐy(ng), -uthwithwi.

1b. ⋯ish, slightly characterized by. ¶**nepcek-sulum** < nelp-cek flattish. **twungku-sulum** < twungku-l- roundish. **yalpusulum** < yalp- rather thin.

2. suffix. ¶**cenyek-usulumq kil ey** on the dusky road.

-usum, bnd adj-n (~ hata), abbr < -usulum.

-uswukswuk, bnd adj-n (~ hata); after a vowel -swukswuk; HEAVY → -usoksok. ⋯ish, being slightly colored/tinged. SEE -(u)sulum.

-usy⋯ SEE ALSO -osy⋯

-usya < -ᵘ/ₒ˙sya = -usye < (*)-ᵘ/ₒ˙sye [SEE -e], hon inf. ¶*mwoˈloˈsya* (1445 ¹Yong 19). ˈna y ˈnikeˈci-ngi ˈˈtaˈkaˈsya (1445 ¹Yong 58) saying "I must go" he went. *pwuthyeˈtwoˈˈsekˈca[h] sˈmwoˈm i towoyˈsya* (1447 Sek 6:44a) Buddha too had a body three ˙cah (6 feet) tall. ˈˈtwu haˈnol s soˈzi ˈyeyˈkaˈsya (1447 Sek 6:45b) goes between the two heavens and ⋯ . ˙na-ˈkasilqˈka cehoˈsya (1449 Kok 46) fearing that he would leave ⋯ . ˈˈTTWOW-ˈˈLI poyˈhwoˈla ˙naˈaˈkaˈsya (1459 Wel 1:5a) goes out to study the doctrine. *PWU-ZINˈkwaˈhoˈsya ˈPPI-KHWUW cwochoˈsya* (1459 Wel 8:93b) together with the lady he followed the almsman (bhikṣu) and ⋯ . ˈkuˈˈhaˈm olˈpwoˈsya ⋯ (1463 Pep 5:100a) seeing the multitude ⋯ . *pwuˈˈthye y ˈwuliˈuy mozoˈm ay ˈˈSYWOW-ˈPEPˈculˈkinonˈt olˈˈaloˈsya* (1463 Pep 2:231a) Buddha is aware that in our hearts we cherish the dharma of hīnayāna and ⋯ . CF -ˈsya-⋯ , ⋯ˈsye.

-ᵘ/ₒ˙syaˈtwo (pcl). ¶*naˈlaˈh ay twoˈlaˈwosyaˈtwo cowolGaˈWi aˈniˈhoˈsya* (1447 Sek 6:4b) even though he comes back to his homeland [from all that] he is not affectionate, ⋯ .

-ᵘ/ₒ˙syaˈza (pcl). ¶ˈwosyaˈza saloˈsi.l iˈˈl ˈss oy ⋯ ˈkasyaˈza iˈkisiˈl iˈˈl ˈss oy (1445 ¹Yong 38) only if he came would they live ⋯ only if he went would they win.

-ᵘ/ₒ˙sya-⋯ , 1. (?= 2; p.271) hon + modulator.

-ᵘ/ₒ˙syal(q) (prosp mod). ¶ˈSILQ-ˈTTALQ ˈi ˈla hosyaˈl iˈnaˈsil naˈl ay (1447 Sek 6:17a) on the day that the one to be called Siddhārtha was born. *cyangˈcho CYENG-TTI ˈlol naˈthwoˈsya.l iˈˈla* (1459 Wel 17:78b) in future will give evidence of his possession of fine qualities.

~ ˙t in ˙t ay n' (postmod + copula mod + postmodifier + pcl + pcl). ¶ ˙SYENG-ˮKWA ˙ay ˙pek˙key ˙khwo ˙cye ˙ho˙syal [˙]t in ˙t ay n' (1465 Wen 1:1:2:75b) when one wants to make it secondary to the fruit of the saintly life.
~ ˙tyeyn (postmod). ¶tas.ko˙syal ˙ttyeyn (1463 Pep 5:21b) when one studies it.
-$^u\!/\!o$˙syam (subst): note that ⋯˙sywom is from ⋯si-˙wo-m (for which the honorific would be ⋯si-˙syam), as in ma˙sywom (1462 ^{1}Nung 7:53b) < ma˙si-'drink' and i˙sywom (1459 Wel 7:31a) < isi- 'exist'. ¶ [˙TUK-NGWEN] ˮwol˙mosyam ˙two (1445 ^{1}Yong 4) that he moved to Tek.wen. pwuthye s kolo˙chisya[˙]m ol (1459 Wel 23:72a) Buddha's teaching. SEE ˙ho.syam.
-$^u\!/\!o$˙syan (mod). ¶pwuthye nilu˙syan ˙pa s ˙PEP ˙un (1482 Kum-sam 2:40b) the Law that Buddha told. nilu˙syan ˮyang ˙o˙lwo ˙hwo˙l i ˙-ngi ˙ˑta (1447 Sek 6:24b) I will do as you say, sir. ˙SYEY-CWON s ˮTTWOW il˙Gwusyan ˮi˙l oy yang˙co ˙lol ˙ku˙lye (1447 Sek se:5b) depicts aspects of the deed by which the Way was achieved by the World-Honored [Buddha], and ⋯ . SEE ˙ho˙syan.
~ ˙t i (postmod + pcl). ¶ ˙i ˙SYANG ˙on ˙YWOK-˙QOY ˙uy ˮna˙syan ˙t i a˙ni ˙si˙n i (1462 ^{1}Nung 1:42a) this aspect is not what desire is born from.
~ ˙t i ˙la (postmodifier + copula indicative assertive). ¶ ˙LWUW ˮep.su˙sya SO-˙NGUY hwo˙m i e˙lyewu˙syan ˙t i ˙la (1463 Pep 2:22a) it is difficult to take everything into consideration. ˙i ˮta YWEN ˙ul ˙TWOY ˙ho.ya ˙phyesyan ˙t ila (1482 Kum-sam 5:35b) this all developed with respect to pratyaya (secondary causation).
~ ˙t ol (postmod + pcl). ¶pi˙luse ˙QILQ-˙CHYEY CYE-˙PPWULQ ˙i ˙i KYENG pu˙the ˙nasyan ˙t ol ˮall i ˙'n i (1464 Kumkang se:6b) only then do we realize that all the Buddhas first came into being out of this sūtra.
-$^u\!/\!o$˙sya˙na$_1$ (adversative). SEE ˙ho˙sya˙na.
-$^u\!/\!o$˙sya˙toy (accessive). ¶ ˮmwu˙lusya˙toy (1459 Wel 7:10b) made inquiry as follows: ⋯ . [THYEN-ˮHHA] ˙ay [KWONG] ˙i ˙khusya˙toy [˙THAY-ˮCO] z [˙WUY] talo˙kesi˙nul (1445 ^{1}Yong 101) throughout the land his deeds were great, yet in the rank of crown prince was someone else. nilu˙sya˙toy (1459 Wel 2:52a, 7:14b, 8:101a, 9:36d) = nilo˙sya˙toy (1447 Sek 6:1a; 1459 Wel 2:52a, 9:36d) said as follows: ⋯ . Notice that ⋯˙sywu˙toy (?< *⋯˙sywo˙toy) is not honorific in ma˙sywu˙toy (1586 Sohak 5:51a) 'drinks and ⋯ '; the honorific form would be (?*)ma˙sisya˙toy.
2. abbr < -$^u\!/\!o$˙si-˙(G)a-, hon effective (etc).
-$^u\!/\!o$˙sya˙na$_2$ (adversative). Example?
-$^u\!/\!o$sya˙nol (lit concessive). SEE ˙hosya˙nol.
-$^u\!/\!o$sya-˙s-ongi ˙ˑta (bnd v polite + cop indic assertive). SEE ˙isya-˙s-ongi ˙ˑta.
-$^u\!/\!o$˙syas˙ta (emotive indicative assertive). ¶ ˙QILQ-˙CHYEY pwuthye ˙kot ˙hosi˙n i ˮep˙susyas˙ta ˙hosi˙n i (1459 Wel 1:52a) they all said there is just no one like Buddha. PWU-ZIN ˙two mwok-ˮswu˙m i ˙yel ˙tol nil˙Gwey ki˙the ˮkyesyas˙ta (1459 Wel 2:13a) the lady [Māya] herself had ten months and seven days of life left. KYENG ˙ul e˙lwu ˙ta tutco˙wosyas˙ta (1463 Pep 6:83ab) got to hear the entire sūtra. [Accent: p. 85.] SEE ˙hosyas˙ta, ˙i˙lusyas˙ta, ˙isyas˙ta.
⋯usye < (?)⋯$^u\!/\!o$˙sye abbr < ⋯usie < ⋯$^u\!/\!o$si˙ye, hon inf. Often pronounced /-use/. CF ⋯sye. There are no early examples, and it is unclear when (?)-$^u\!/\!o$˙sye came to replace -$^u\!/\!o$˙sya, but the ˮcwa˙sya of 1449 Kok 62 corresponds to ˮc'a˙sye of 1586 Sohak 2:4b for the infinitive of ˮc'asi-, a variant of ˮcwasi- 'deign to eat'.
*-usye la, honorific infinitive + particle.
1. Not used as a verb command because the honorific is incongruent with the plain-style command. An honorific command is quoted as -usila (ko hanta). 2. → -usye ˈla.
-usye ˈla, hon infinitive + abbr < ila (cop indic assert). Attached to adjective, iss-, and ēps- as an exclamation referring to an exalted person. ¶Chinkwu to mānh.usye ˈla! My, you have a lot of friends! Sensayng un khi ka khusye ˈla! Gee, you're tall! Son nim i caymi to iss.usye ˈla! What an interesting customer/guest you are!
-usye se, honorific infinitive + particle
-usyess-, hon past [abbr < -usiess-]. ~-keyss-, ~-ta, ⋯ . Often pronounced /-usess-/ and so spelled in 1936 Roth 393 (cwusess.e).
-usye to, honorific infinitive + particle
-usye ya, honorific infinitive + particle. ¶Cikum kasye ya hap.nikka? Have you got to go now? VAR -usey ya.
-usye yo, honorific inf + pcl (POLITE statement/question/command/suggestion). VAR -usey yo.

-⁽ᵘ⁾o῾sywo῾sye, polite command. ¶anco῾sywo῾sye (1447 Sek 6:3a) please sit down (have a seat)! ῁ma῾losywo῾sye (1447 Sek 24:52b) please don't do it! ῁cwasywo῾sye (1449 Kok 100) eat! wonol nal wuli uykey il.ywong hol lyangsik ul cwusywosye (1916 Gale 14) Give us this day our daily bread. SEE ῾hosywo῾sye. CF -῾ᵉ⁄ₐ῾ssye.

-utayngtayng, bnd adj-n (~ hata); after a vowel -tayngtayng; LIGHT ↔ -uteyngteyng. ···ish, slightly colored/tinged; slightly characterized by. SEE -(u)sulum.

-uteyngteyng, bnd adj-n (~ hata); after a vowel -teyngteyng; HEAVY ↔ -utayngtayng. ···ish, slightly colored/tinged; slightly characterized by. SEE -(u)sulum.

-utaytay, bnd adj-n (~ hata); after a vowel -taytay; LIGHT ↔ -uteytey. ···ish, slightly colored/tinged; slightly characterized by. SEE -(u)sulum.

-uteytey, bnd adj-n (~ hata); after a vowel -teytey; HEAVY ↔ -utaytay. ···ish, slightly colored/tinged; slightly characterized by. SEE -(u)sulum. ¶palkuteytey < palk-uteytey reddish. kemuteytey < kem-uteytey blackish. neputeytey flattish (< nelp- + -uteytey). CF nepcek-sulum.

-uthoythoy, bnd adj-n (~ hata); after a vowel -thoythoy; LIGHT ↔ -uthwithwi. ···ish, slightly colored/tinged; slightly characterized by. SEE -(u)sulum.

-uthwithwi, bnd adj-n (~ hata); after a vowel -thwithwi; LIGHT ↔ -uthoythoy. ···ish, slightly colored/tinged; slightly characterized by. SEE -(u)sulum.

-utoy [after a consonant] = -toy (concessive); [DIAL − except after ···ss and ···ps].

-uw-, bnd adj. SEE -upta.

-uwa SEE -u(o)wa

UY Usually pronounced u when initial and i elsewhere, but the particle uy is pronounced ey. The reading pronunciation ui (as two syllables) is increasingly popular in certain words. If you cannot find a word you seek with the spelling uy, try u or i.

uy (/ey/ < ⁽ᵘ⁾oy), pcl (genitive). (the one) of ··· (marks modification or subordination, usually adnominal; the exact reference often remains ambiguous). LIT SYN ci (in Chinese clichés). SEE ey uy, eykey uy, kkaci uy, man uy, kwa uy, se uy, ulo uy, ey lo uy, (ey se) puthe uy, pota uy; ... (-nun) ka uy. CF quasi-adnouns with uy (§5.3.1).

1. (possession) of, ···'s; belonging to ··· (= ··· ka kacin). ¶tangsin uy kwutwu your shoes. molunun sālam uy cip the house of a stranger, a stranger's house. uysa uy ilum the doctor's name. hyangswu uy nāymsay the smell of a perfume. sangphum uy kakyek the price of commodities. kum uy mukey the weight of gold. Kim sensayng uy kūlim Mr Kim's picture (= the picture that belongs to Mr Kim).

2. (relationship) of; with respect to (in respect of/to), related/pertaining to, vis-à-vis, as regards (= ··· ey tāy han). ¶na uy (= nay) enni my older brother. ne uy (= ney) awu your younger brother. nwukwu uy atul whose son; somebody's son. wuli hōy uy hōywen tul the members of our society. na uy (= nay) chinkwu hana one of my friends, a friend of mine. Ku hak.kyo uy haksayng a student of that school. i kongcang uy ¹notong-ca tul the workers of this factory. ne 'y susu῾ng uy ῁TTYEY-῁CO y ῁es῾tyey a῾ni῾wono῾n ywo (1447 Sek 6:29b) how come your master's disciple is not coming?

3. (subject) of; done/felt/said by, on the part of (= ··· ka han). CF 14.

3a. ¶hakca tul uy thwucayng the struggle of/by the scholars. inmin uy hāyngpok the happiness of (enjoyed by) the people. nulk.un-i uy kippum the joys of the aged. tangsin uy ūykyen your opinion. sensayng uy māl-ssum the teacher's words (= what the teacher said). Pok.nam-i uy iyaki what Pok.nam-i had to tell (= told). emeni uy sayngkak/nukkim the mother's thought/feeling.

3b. (authorship/creation) of, by, from; created/made (written, composed, drawn/painted, concocted, built) by (= i/ka ciun). ¶Kim Pūsik uy Samkwuk Saki Kim Pusik's Historical Record of the Three Kingdoms. Solke uy kūlim a painting by Solke, one of Solke's paintings. ōyin uy pīphyeng criticism by (from, on the part of) a stranger. Kim sensayng uy kūlim Mr Kim's picture (= the picture that Mr Kim drew).

3c. (source/author of an achievement) of; achieved (accomplished, attained, reached) by (= ··· ka ilwun). ¶Sin.la uy thōngil the Sinla unification. kōtay uy munhwa the culture of ancient times. **Paykcey uy pūhung** the Paykcey restoration.

4. (the goal / result) of; that was achieved / accomplished (= ··· **ul han / ilwun**) or is to be achieved / accomplished (= ··· **ul hal / ilwul**). ¶**cilqse uy hwak.lip** the establishment of order. **Nam-puk uy thōngil** the unification of North and South. **nongtho uy pun.ye** the distribution of farmland. **Sewul uy phok.kyek** the bombing of Seoul.

5. 5a. (specification) of; that is (= ··· **in**). ¶**chōytay uy kyem.yang** the greatest humility, humility of the greatest sort. **thōngil uy wiep** the great task of (= which is) unification.

5b. (designation) called, (by the name) of (= ··· **ila hanun**). ¶**chāmswu uy hyeng** the punishment of (that is known as) decapitation. **Kumkang (san) uy sūngci** that beauty spot [that is] the Diamond Mountains. **Kimhay uy koul** the county of Kimhay.

5c. (representation) of; that represents (= ··· **uy phyosik in**). ¶**ca.yu uy kil** the road of freedom. **cēncayng uy wihem** the danger of war. **chwulpal uy nal** the day of departure. **saynghwal uy cachwi** traces of life.

6. (pertinence) of, ...'s; belonging to, attached to (= ··· **ey puth.nun**). ¶**Hān kang uy kun.wen** the source of the Han River. **Yengkwuk kwa Cosen kwa uy talun cēm** differences (points of difference) between England and Korea.

7. (origin / source) of, ...'s; (coming) from, (produced) in / at (= ··· **ey se nan**). ¶**Anseng uy yuki** brassware from Anseng. **Cēycwu uy mal** a Ceycwu horse. **Kayseng uy insam** ginseng from Kayseng. **Hwangcwu uy sakwa** the apples of Hwangcwu. **Kolye uy caki** Kolye pottery.

8. 8a. (static location) of, in, at (= ··· **ey iss.nun**). ¶**Tong.lay uy onchen** the hot spring at Tong.lay. **Kangwen-to uy Kumkang san** the Diamond Mountains in Kangwen Province. **i chōn uy inkwu** the population of this village. **puekh uy an**ʰ**ay** the wife in the kitchen. **sikyey uy menci** the dust on / in the clock. **hanul uy kwulum** a cloud in the sky.

8b. (the head is a noun of relative location) to / on the ··· (of). Example?

8c. (abstract location) ¶**cinceng han ūymi (ey iss.e se) uy kwuk-munhak** a national literature in the true sense of the word.

8d. (dynamic location) of, in, on, arising /

happening at (= ··· **ey se iss.nun**). ¶**mulq sōk (ey se) uy cak.ep** underwater operations. **Kwucwu (se) uy tāycen** the European War, the war in Europe. Perhaps: **inkan uy sangsa** the affairs of men, the everyday things that happen to one.

8e. (time) at, in, of. ¶**achim uy sānqpo** a morning stroll. **pom uy kkoch tul** the flowers of spring. **ku ttay uy Sewul** Seoul at that time.

8f. (quantity) of; to the extent of. ¶**sahul uy ¹yangsik** three days provisions. **yel mali uy kāy** ten dogs. **thāypan uy haksayng tul** the majority of the students. **kapcel uy pīyong** double costs.

9. (material) of; made of, made out of. ¶**mu'-soy uy mangchi** a hammer of pig iron. **thokki-thel uy moca** a rabbit-fur hat. **tāyli-sek uy kitwung** a marble column, a column of marble.

10. (use) for; used for. ¶**caypong-chim uy kilum** sewing-machine oil. **mūtay uy sō-tokwu** stage properties. **ok-swuswu uy pīlyo** fertilizer for corn.

11. (similarity) like, of (= ··· **kwa kath.un**). ¶**Sesi uy mi** a beauty like Sesi's, the beauty of Sesi = Xīshī (a famous beauty of olden China). **mek.nun ka mek.hinun ka uy ssawum** a life-and-death struggle. **hwangkum uy mulq-kyel** golden waves.

12. (object of reference, topic) of, about, depicting, referring to, directed at (= ··· **ey tāy hay se ciun**). ¶**kaul uy nolay** a song of (celebrating) autumn. **inmul uy phyēng.lon** criticism of the characters. **emeni uy sacin** a photograph of my mother. **Kim sensayng uy kūlim** Mr Kim's picture (= the picture that portrays Mr Kim).

13. 13a. (part) of (= **il-pupun ulo in**). ¶**elin i uy son** the child's hand. **haksayng tul uy tāy-pupun** the majority of the students. **catong-cha uy pakhwi** the wheel of an automobile. **so'-namu uy iph** the leaves of a pine tree. *kutuy ˙uy ˝TAM ˙khukwo* (1482 Kum-sam 2:67a) your liver (= courage) is great and ... . *˝THYEY ke˙pwu.p uy the˙li ˙kot ˙hwotoy* (1482 Kum-sam 2:66a) the body is like the hairs of a turtle, and ... . *SSIN-LYENG ˙uy me˙li ˙ʼm ye kwuy-s-ke˙s uy no˙ch i˙lwoswo˙n i* (1482 Kum-sam 2:7b) it is the head of a spirit and it is the face of a ghost.

13b. (member) of (a group). ¶*˙MWULQ ˙uy ˙mos MI hon ke.s i ˙Gwo* ··· *˙MWULQ ˙uy ˙mos* the most delicate of objects and ··· are the largest of objects.

14. = **i / ka** (marking subject of an adnominal modifying phrase). ¶ **Na uy (= Nay ka) wēn hanun kes i i kes ita** The one (that) I want is this one. **Ney ka sālam uy sānun mokcek ul ānun ya** Do you know the goal that men live for? CF 3. There may be MK evidence for a sequence of two markers ˙i ˙uy (reduced to ···y ˙uy), in that when they are the subject of a nominalization (or an adnominalization) *na* 'I' and *ne* 'you' appear as *nay* ˙ᵘ⁄ₒy and *ney* ˙uy (CF He Wung 356), as in *nay* ˙*uy [SYWUY-* ˙*LWOW]* ˙*hwo.m on* (1481 Twusi 22:27b) 'that I am getting old and frail', *ney* ˙*uy* ˙*e* ˙*mi* ˙*ku* ˙*lye* ¨*hwo* ˙*m i* (1459 Wel 21:22a) 'that you long for [your] mother'. But in *nay uy [CHA-THA] hon mozo.m ol* (1632 Twusi-cwung 21:23b) He Wung prefers the construal 'my faltered heart' with a genitive modifying the phrase 'the heart that has faltered' over one that might mean something more like 'the heart with/in which I faltered'; he is perhaps wrong, as he may be when he seems to take *nay* ˙*oy tu* ˙*liGwun* ˙*swon* (1462 ¹Nung 2:19a) as 'my hands which [I] have let dangle' rather than 'the hands which I have let dangle', both to be translated 'my dangling hands'. A stronger example for the genitive: *nay* ˙*oy mozom* ˙*kwa* ˙*nwu* ˙*n ol* ˙*pswu* ˙*n i* '*-ngi* '˙*ta* (1462 ¹Nung 1:45a) 'it used my heart and eyes'. SEE ˙*nay* ˙*uy,* ˙*ney* ˙*uy.*

The most common source of the epitheme (= the head of the adnominalization) is an extruded object: *SA-MWON* ˙*on no* ˙*m oy ci* ˙*zwun nye* ˙*lu* ˙*m ul mekno* ˙*n i* '*-ngi* '˙*ta* (1447 Sek 24:22a) the begging monk (śramaṇa) eats fruits that others have grown; *SYWU-* ˙*TTALQ* ˙*oy ci* ˙*zwun TTYENG-* ˙*SYA* ¨*ma* ˙*ta* ˙*tu* ˙*lusi* ˙*m ye* (1447 Sek 6:38 [¹Yi Tonglim version]) deigned to enter each hostel that Sudatta had built, and ··· ; *SYWU-* ˙*TTALQ* ˙*oy moyng* ˙*ko* ˙*lwon* ˙*CCWA* ˙*ay* (1447 Sek 6:30a) to the seat that Sudatta had made; ¨*ZIN-* ˙*ZYWOK* ˙*THAY-* ¨*CO* ˙*uy il* ˙*Gwu* ˙*syan* ˙*YAK* ˙*i-ngi* '˙*ta* (1459 Wel 21:218b) it is a drug, sir, that Prince Kṣānti has concocted. But sometimes the epitheme is extruded from some other role, such as locative V N ← N ˙*ey (˙sye)* V: *PA-SO-* ˙*NIK NGWANG* ˙*uy* ¨*sa* ˙*non SSYENG* (1464 Kumkang 4b) the castle where Prasenajit is/was living. Or even a mutative complement V N ← N ˙ᵘ⁄ₒ˙*lwo* V: *SSIN-* ˙*LUK [* ˙*]uy* ˙*HWA* ˙*ho* ˙*syan ke* ˙*s un pas[k]* ¨*chyenlyang* ˙*ay* ¨*nam* ˙*ti* ¨*mwot ho* ˙*n i* (1463 Pep 6:144a) what the supernatural power has brought into being is nothing more than external property. And in at least one example, from an accusative: ˙*na y* ¨*nyey KA-* ˙*LI* ˙*uy pe* ˙*hywo.m i towoy* ˙*ywom* ˙*kot* ˙*ho.ya* (1482 Kum-sam 3:29a; the ˙*uy* translates *CI*) it is like the way I got to cut down (= vanquish) [King] Kali[ṅga] in bygone days.

There are also summational epithemes, such as nominalizations with the substantive: *KAN-NAN ho* ˙*n i* ˙*uy no* ˙*m oy* ¨*pwo* ˙*poy* ¨*hyey* ˙*ywom kot* '˙*ta* (1465 Wen 3:3:1:62a) it is like a poor man's counting another's treasures. *kunge* ˙*kuy* ¨*SSWUW-* ¨*KHWO hol* ¨*ssalo* ˙*m i* ˙*KAK-* ˙*KAK* ¨*CCWOY* ˙*oy* ¨*cyeku* ˙*m ye* ˙*khwu.m u* ˙*lwo* ˙*KEP-* ˙*SWU* ˙*lul ti-* ¨*nayno* ˙*n i* (1459 Wel 1:29b) the people who anguish there pass the appropriate number of kalpas (eons) in accordance with their individual sins being small or great. *KA-* ˙*LI* ˙*uy e* ˙*lywu.m o* ˙*lwo* (1482 Kum-sam 3:30a; ˙*uy* translates *CI*) with the stupidity of [King] Kali[ṅga] = because Kali[ṅga] is stupid.

NOTE: In a few kinds of phrases people are uncertain whether to treat /ey/ as the adnominal particle **uy** or the adverbial particle **ey**. We would expect **chen mān uy māl-ssum (ip.nita)** for '(It is) a word among the myriad [of words]' = 'Not at all; Don't mention it', but the expression is often written as **chen mān ey māl-ssum**, perhaps because of the common relaxed version **chen mān ey yo = chen mān [uy māl-ssum i]ey yo**. The Koreanized version of the Chinese expression **sam-pun ci il** 'one third' we expect to be **sēy pun uy han pun** but 1936 Roth 257 has **sēy pun ey han pun**.

˙*uy*, particle; variant ˙*oy*.

1. (after animate noun) = **uy** (genitive). CF *s*. ¶ ˙*tye* ˙*uy mwok-* ¨*swu* ˙*m ul kus* ˙*kuy [= kuch-* ˙*kuy] ˙hoke* ˙*tun* (1447 Sek 9:17a) given that they brought his life to an end … . ··· *KKI-TTA* ˙*oy* ˙*twu-* '*ys.non ke.s i* ˙*n i* (1447 Sek 6:40a) are things that Jeta put aside. *kwuy-s-ke* ˙*s uy* [˙]*KHWOLQ* ˙*ey* ˙*toma* (1482 Kum-sam 3:34b) holes up in the cave of a ghost and … . SEE **uy** for more examples.

for more examples.

2. (after inanimate noun, typically a place or time) = ˙ey(/ ˙ay) = ey at, in (locative); to (allative). ¶ho˙ma [SYENG-˙KWAK] s pas˙k uy ˙na tuthu˙l ey s ¨i.l i ¨cyekwo˙m ol ˙anwo˙n i ... [= ¨anwo˙n i] (1481 Twusi 7:2a) he already knew that going outside the castle wall there were few problems from dust (and that) ... . YA-SYWU s KWUNG ˙uy ˙ka-pwo˙n i (1447 Sek 6: 2b) went to the palace of Yaśodharā [Buddha's wife]. ¨ne y a˙chom ˙uy ˙na-˙ka ... (1586 Sohak 4:33a) you go out early and ... .

NOTE 1: The MK genitive particle, as an adnominal or as marking the subject of an adnominalized verb, had the variant shapes ˙uy and ˙oy; about .56 of the examples use ˙oy. The vowel of the preceding syllable partly determines the shape preference. After e(C) the shape is always ˙uy except for ye.s oy (1579 Kwikam 1:36a) = yez˙G oy (1462 ¹Nung 8: 120a) 'of the fox' < *yez[o]G ˙oy, reflecting the elided o, which surfaces in yezo. After a(C) the choice is usually ˙oy but there are a few exceptions: QWUY-NGWANG ˙uy (1463 Pep se:17a), ˙TWO-˙MAN ˙uy (1463 Pep 7:182a), PA-SO-˙NIK NGWANG ˙uy (1464 Kumkang 4b), [¨HHYEN-SAN] al˙ph oy (1481 Twusi 7:4b). After o(C) and wo(C) the choice is ˙oy with at least two exceptions each: ˙THAY-¨CO ˙uy (1459 Wel 21:218b), ˙CANG-¨SSO ˙uy (1485 Kwan 4b); ˙pwu˙mwo ˙uy (?1517- Pak 1:58a), [˙PPWULQ-¨CWO] ˙uy (1579 Kwikam 1:21a). After u(C) and wu there are only examples of ˙uy: susu˙ng uy (1447 Sek 6:29b), ˙TI-˙TUK ˙uy (1463 Pep 4:169a), SSIN-˙LUK [˙]uy (1463 Pep 6:144a); TA-SYWU ˙uy (1447 Sek 6:9b) ke˙pwu.p uy (1482 Kum-sam 2:66a), ˙MWULQ ˙uy (1482 Kum-sam 3:25b). After uy, ey, oy, and ay the shape is always ˙uy, as in kutuy ˙uy (1481 Twusi 15:13a, 1482 Kum-sam 2:67a), ney ˙uy (1459 Wel 21:22a, 1463 Pep 1:60a), ˙YWOK-˙QOY ˙uy (1462 ¹Nung 1:42a), and nay ˙uy (1481 Twusi 22:27b), with the exception of nay ˙oy (1462 ¹Nung 1:45a, 2:19a). But the one example of woy is ˙swoy oy (1482 Kum-sam 2:29b) and the particle seems to be unattested after wuy(C). After i(C) both ˙uy and ˙oy occur: ¨CO-˙SIK ˙uy (1459 Wel 8:83a), ¨kyeci˙p uy (1463 Pep 4:176b), a[˙]pi ˙uy (1463 Pep 2:138b; but a˙p[i] oy in the next line); ¨i˙l oy (1447 Sek se:5b), [˙TUK-CIN] ˙oy (1481 Twusi 24:30ab). But both ···i ˙uy and ···i ˙oy often elide the i, as described in Note 2.

As a substitute for the locative or allative ˙ᵉ/ₐy, the variants enjoy the same preferences, but there seem to be no examples of i(C) oy and only the one case of [i] oy in ˙pa[l]-˙ch[i] oy (1459 Wel 10:10a) but none of [i] uy. The exceptions with a(C) uy instead of a(C) oy are alp˙ph uy [conflated spelling of al˙ph uy] (?1517- Pak 1:25a) 'in front' and holo n man uy (?1608+ Twu-hem 21a) 'for a whole day'; with o(C) uy instead of o(C) oy only a˙chom ˙uy (1586 Sohak 4:33a) for a˙cho˙m oy (1447 Sek 6:3b) 'in the morning'. The only cases of wo(C) uy for wo(C) oy are twos˙k uy (1463 Pep 1:168a) 'to their seat mats' and SA-MWON ˙uy (1447 Sek 24:22a). There are no exceptional cases of *e(C) oy or *wu(C) oy. Regardless of the vowel that precedes it, the noun psk 'time' takes only ˙uy: ku ˙psk uy (1459 Wel 9:52a, 21:5a; 1463 Pep 2:23a, 2:138b) 'at that time', ¨twu ˙psk uy (1462 ¹Nung 3:26a) 'on two occasions', ˙su˙mu ˙nal ˙psk uy (?1517- Pak 1:8b) 'on the twentieth day'. And the bound nouns s and t 'the fact that' take only oy: -ulq ˙s oy, -un ˙t oy, -non ˙t oy. We treat ˙tuy in ¨men ˙tuy s HHWO-˙KYWOW ˙lol (1459 Wel 2:69a) 'alien teachings from distant places' as a variant of ˙toy 'place' rather than t (or ˙to) 'place' + pcl. Notice also e˙n' oy < *e˙no oy = e˙nu.

NOTE 2: In Middle Korean (CF LSN 1961: 112, He Wung 320-3) a preceding (···)i had weakened to ···y and then, once the syllables *yuy and *yoy were no longer part of the system, it completely vanished: ˙a˙ki baby → ˙a˙k[i] oy pi˙t i (1459 Wel 8:81b) the debt for the baby, a.k[i] uy i.p ey susu.m ye n' (1608 Thaysan 76b) if you rinse in the baby's mouth. ˙e˙mi → na y ˙e˙m[i] uy ¨kan˙sta˙h ol spol˙li nilo˙sywo˙sye (1459 Wel 21:21b) quickly tell me the land where my mother went. a˙pi father → a˙p[i] oy ¨chyenlyang (1447 Sek 13:18b) the father's fortune, a˙p[i] oy MWON-TTYENG ˙i nwopke˙nul (1482 Kum-sam 3:25a) though the father's gateyard is high. ˙ilh[i] uy skwo˙li (?1517- Pak 1:30b) a fox tail. kwo˙ki meat → LYWONG ˙on kwo˙k[i] oy TYWUNG ˙ey wuytwu hon ke˙s i˙n i (1459 Wel 1:14ab) dragon is the best of meats [personified, thus ˙oy not s]. kol˙mye˙k[i] uy ˙nye ton˙nywo˙m on (1481 Twusi 14:29b) the wandering of the seagulls. ˙thwos.k[i] uy spul ˙kot 'two˙ta (1482 Kum-sam 2:66b) is like a rabbit's horns. The pronoun ˙wu˙li did not undergo weakening, according to He Wung 323, and that accounts for pwu¨thye y˙wuli ˙uy mozo˙m ay ¨SYWOW-˙PEP ˙cul˙kinon ˙t ol ¨alo˙sya (1463 Pep 2:231a) Buddha is aware that in our hearts we cherish the laws of hīnayāna and ... – CF ˙swu˙l[i] uy me˙li SAN ˙i.n i (1463 Pep 1:20b) it is the mountain [called] Eagle's Head. The weakening totally ellipted the postmodifier ˙i in the structures -˙n [i] $^u\!/oy$, -n$^u\!/o$˙n [i] $^u\!/oy$, and -($^u\!/o$)˙l [i] $^u\!/oy$.

The locative ˙$^u\!/oy$ and the dative/allative ˙$^u\!/oy$ k[ung]ey occasion the same weakening: CYE-¨CO y ci˙p uy ˙na a˙p[i] oy key na˙za ˙ka (1463 Pep 2:70b) the masters went out to the house and went up to the father. ˙a˙ki na˙hi˙ten ˙e˙m[i] uy key un˙kwa ¨pitan˙tol[h] ˙syang˙kup ho˙kwo (?1517- Pak 1:57a) presented silver and silks to the mother who had born the child. QA-NAN ˙kwa LA-NGWUN ˙un ˙pa[l]-˙ch[i] oy ˙sye ˙y˙sopte˙n i (1459 Wel 10:10a) Ānanda and Rāhula were standing at the foot.

When the particle marks the subject of an adnominalized predicate, the final ···i of the noun often stays intact: ka˙h[i] oy ˙SYENG ˙un ··· han ka˙hi ˙uy cwu˙kem to˙thwa ca˙pwo˙m ay talo˙ti a˙ni ho˙n i ˙'la (1463 Pep 2:113b) the nature of the dog is nothing other than the fighting to death of a horde of dogs. ku ˙psk uy CYE-¨CO y api ˙uy PPYEN-QAN ˙hi ancon˙t ol ¨al˙Gwo ¨ta a˙p[i] oy key ˙ka a˙p[i] oy key nil[˙]Gwo˙toy (1463 Pep 2:138b) at that time the masters, finding that the father was seated comfortably, all went to the father and said to the father as follows ··· . Therefore we might conclude that a˙p[i] oy cwu˙kwu˙m ul tut˙kwo (1463 Pep 5:158a) is better taken as 'hearing of the father's death' rather than 'hearing that the father dies'. But there are also examples that show the weakened version: ˙na y ˙icey ne ˙'y ˙e˙m[i] uy ¨kan ˙sta˙h ol ¨pwoy˙ywo.l i ˙'la (1459 Wel 21:21b) I will now show you the land where your mother went; ˙e˙mi l' solang ˙hwo˙toy ˙e˙m[i] uy solang hwolq SSI-˙CYELQ ˙ko˙thi ho˙m ye n' ˙emi ˙Gwa ¨CO-˙SIK ˙kwa y

han SOYNG ˙ol selu e˙kuy˙ye ¨me˙ti a˙ni ho˙l i ˙'n i (1462 ¹Nung 5:85b) if it is the same when [the child] loves the mother and the mother loves [the child], mother and child will not be estranged by conflict throughout many lives together.

The weakening and vanishing of ···i before the adnominal particle explains examples of ···˙n $^u\!/oy$ and ···˙l $^u\!/oy$, for they are sentences adnominalized to the postmodifier ˙i 'one (the person) who ··· ': ˙PPYENG ho˙n [i] oy nek˙s i kwo˙t ay two˙la ˙wa (1447 Sek 9:31b) the spirit of the ill one came back on the spot (= at once). HHOYNG ho˙l [i] oy ˙PPYEN-NGUY (1463/4 Yeng 2:31a) the comfort of the traveler.

Examples of the modern usage whereby uy is attached to the unweakened ···i, just like any other vowel, began appearing in the early part of the 16th century (He Wung 322): [¨NGE ˙PPOYK-ZI] kwo[˙]ki uy ilwu (([1517→]1614 Saseng 2:59b) 'the milt of fish'.

-˙uy = -˙Guy = -˙key (adverbative)

-uy, abbr < -ui

uy hata, vni insep (N ey ~ people or things).

1. follows, accords (with/to), is according/pursuant (to). ¶Uy halq cen.lyey ka ēps.ta There is no precedent to follow. cēnsel ey uy hamyen in accordance with tradition.

2. is based (on/upon), is founded on, depends (on/upon). ¶sōmun ey uy hamyen according to rumor, as gossip has it, judging from reports. ku uy māl ey uy hamyen according to him (to what he has to say). hyengphyen ey uy hay se according to the circumstance(s). Wuphyo kaps un phyēnci cwūng.lyang ey uy hanta The postage depends on the weight of the letter.

3. is due/owing (to), is because of; is (done) by. ¶phok.kyek ey uy ha.ye phākoy toyn kēnchwuk-mul buildings (that got) destroyed in the bombings.

˙uy ke˙kuy, quasi-particle (< pcl + n/adv). to a person (= ˙uy kungey). ¶˙TTAY-˙CYWUNG ˙uy ke˙kuy ˙nom ¨wuy ˙ho˙ya kol˙hoy-¨nay nilu˙m ye (1447 Sek 19:8a) tells it to the multitude selectively for the sake of others, and ... .

~ n' (pcl). ¶[KWONG-HHWUW] ˙uy ke˙kuy n' [KUY-˙I] hon ˙salo˙m i ˙na˙no.n i ˙'la (1481 Twusi 21:20a) to the nobility emerge strange people.

uykey → eykey

`uy key`, quasi-particle (< pcl + noun / adv). to (a person), to where a person is. ¶ *KWONG-˙TUK ˙two i˙le ho˙kwo n' ˙homol˙mye TTWOK-˙SSYWONG ˙ho˙ya TTAY-˙CYWUNG ˙uy key ˙nom ˙WUY ˙ho˙ya kol˙hoy˙ya nilo˙m ye ¨mal ta˙Wi SYWUW-HHOYNG ˙hwo˙m isto˙n ye* (1459 Wel 17:54a) with such achievement of virtue as this, how much more will one tell the people by chanting [the sūtras] to teach others and practicing asceticism according to the words?! *cyang˙cho ce ˙y ˙mwo.m o˙lwo ¨KWUY-SSIN ˙uy key pi˙le [˙]ci-ngi ˙˙ta ¨CHYENG ˙hoke˙nul* (1475 Nay 2:1:30a) when asked to pray in the future to the spirits with one's own body ... .
~ ˙sye (pcl). ¶ *cumsoyng uy key sye taloki non* (1656 Kyengmin 28; cited from LCT [not at the cited locus in the edition available to me]) differing from animals.
`uy kungey`, quasi-particle (< pcl + noun / adv). to (a person), to where a person is. ¶ ˙*SYA-˙LI-˙PWULQ ˙uy kungey mwu˙la* (1449 Kok 153) he [Sudatta] asked Śāriputra ... .
~ ˙sye (pcl). ¶ ˙*CYWUNG-SOYNG ˙oy ˙PWOK ˙i ¨cywu˙ng uy kungey ˙sye ¨nam ˙kwa ¨na˙t i pa˙th oy ˙sye ¨nam ˙kwa ˙kothol ˙ss oy* (1447 Sek 6:19a) the bliss of all the living creatures springs from the priests, just as the grain springs from the field.
~ ˙za (pcl). ¶ *MWU-˙LYANG ˙PPI-KHWUW ˙uy kungey ˙za hona[h] ¨twul[h] ˙man ˙CYENG-¨SSYWUW ˙lul solang ho˙m ye* (1447 Sek 23:34b) of the countless almsmen (bhikṣu) only one or two enjoy samādhi (abstract meditation), and ... .
`uy n'`, abbr < ˙*uy ˙non*, pcl + pcl. Examples?
`uy ˙non`, pcl + pcl. ¶ *mi˙th uy ˙non ...* (1449 Kok 70) in the nether regions of her body ... . *wu˙h uy nun mozom ¨ep.sun ˙kwulwu˙m i is˙kwo* (1481 Twusi 7:23b) up above, there are mindless clouds and ... .
ūypus, adnoun. step-(relative). ¶ ~ **ttal** a stepdaughter. ~ **atul** /ūputatul/ a stepson. ~ **api** /ūputapi/ a stepfather. ~ **emi** /ūputemi/ a stepmother. ~ **casik** a stepchild. VAR **ēpus**. [? < **ūypu** < ˙*NGUY-¨PPWU* stepfather + *s* pcl]
`uy s`, pcl (locative) + pcl (genitive). ¶ *ku ¨tuy ˙i kwum˙k uy s kayya˙mi pwo˙la* (1447 Sek 6:35 [¹Yi Tonglim version]) you just look at the ant in this corner (or: this ant in the corner). ˙*mos wu˙h uy s ¨twu ha˙no˙l on* (1447 Sek 6:35-6) the two highest heavens. *ci˙p uy s ¨te˙lewu˙m ul ˙phyesi˙nwon cyen˙cho ˙y˙n i* (1482 Nam 1:5a) is the reason that he deigns to tidy up the mess of the house. *nwun-[˙]sep mi˙th uy s ¨twu ˙nwu.n i ko˙cang PWUN-MYENG ho˙n i* (1482 Kum-sam 3:19b) the two eyes below the brows are very distinct. SEE ˙*oy s*, ˙*ay s*, ˙*ey s*.
`uy ¨swon-˙toy` (to a person) SEE ¨*swon-˙toy*
`uy ˙sye`, pcl + pcl. SEE ˙*ay ˙sye*, ˙*ey ˙sye*, ˙*oy ˙sye*, ˙*yey ˙sye*. ¶ *ku ci˙p uy ˙sye ˙cha˙pan moyng˙kol sswo˙li wuyculen ˙hoke˙nul* (1447 Sek 6:16a) in the house it is all noisy with the sound of people preparing food. *SYEY s nye˙k uy ˙sye* (1447 Sek 6:33b) from (the direction of) the west. *twos˙k ol kye˙th uy ˙sye ¨pwo˙m ay* (1462 ¹Nung 2:81b) when you look at the mat from the side.
`uy ˙sye`, pcl + inf < ˙*sye˙ta* (vi 'stand'). Examples? SEE ˙*oy ˙sye*.
`uy ˙˙sye`, abbr < ˙*uy i˙sye*, pcl + vi inf. being at. Examples?
`uy ˙two`, pcl + pcl. ¶ ˙*SYEY-˙KAY pas˙k uy ˙two* (1459 Wel 1:37a) even beyond the world. SEE ˙*ay ˙two*, ˙*ey ˙two*.
`uy tyengey`, pcl + n. to that person (him / her), over there where he / she is. ¶ ˙*PPWULQ SSIN-˙LUK ˙uy tyengey THWONG-˙LUK pil˙Gisya˙m ol QIN ho˙n i* (1459 Wel 18:7b) by the virtue of borrowing an all-pervasive power from the divine power of the Buddha ... .
`uy ˙za`, pcl + pcl (var of ˙*ey ˙za* = **ey ya**). ¶ *nil˙kwup SAN pas˙k uy ˙za HHAM-¨SYWUY pa˙ta˙h i is.ke˙tun* (1459 Wel 1:23b) only outside the [realm of] the seven mountains is there salt-water sea ... . CF ˙*oy ˙za*.

···W is used to represent a final labial semivowel in Chinese loanwords, but it was probably ignored in pronunciation. This was written either as a subcircled "light *p*" (**kapyewun piup**) or "light *m*" (**kapyewun mium**).
···W···, a lenited version of *p*, pronounced as a voiced bilabial fricative [β] or as a labial semivowel (= *w*).
W (**ttan kapyewun piup**), variant of *s* (genitive pcl) written by 1451 Hwun-en after Chinese words ending in ···W before ˙*CCO*. ¶ ¨*TWUW W ˙CCO* (5a) the character ¨*TWUW*. *KYWUW W ˙CCO* (3b) the character *KYWUW*. *PHYWOW W ˙CCO* (6a) the character *PHYWOW*.

-w- < -W-, bound adjective. SEE -pta.
ˈwa- < *ˈwoˈa-, vi ('come') + effective (= ˈwoˈke-, ˈwoˈna-). SEE ˈwaˈton.
wa (< ˈwa = ˈ[G]wa), pcl (after a vowel) = kwa (with / and / like)
wā < ˈwa, infinitive < ota < °woˈta.
wa cocha, pcl + pcl (after vowel) = kwa cocha
wa ey, pcl + pcl (after a vowel) = kwa ey
wa ka, pcl + pcl (after a vowel) = kwa ka
wa lʼ, pcl + abbr pcl = wa lul
wā la, infinitive + pcl (plain command) = one la come! CF ola.
wā la ʼnta, abbr < wā la (ko) hanta
wā ʼla to, pcl + cop var inf + pcl (after a vowel) = kwa ʼla to
wā la tul, inf + pcl + pcl (plural subject). you people come!
wā ʼla ʼy, abbr < wa la (ko) hay
wa lo, pcl + pcl (after a vowel) = kwa lo
wa lul, pcl + pcl (after a vowel) = kwa lul
wa mace, pcl + pcl (after a vowel) = kwa mace
wa man, pcl + pcl (after a vowel) = kwa man
wa nʼ, pcl + abbr pcl = wa nun = kwa nun
wā nʼ, infinitive + abbr pcl = wā nun
wa ʼna, pcl + cop advers = kwa ʼna
wang < NGWANG, 1. noun. king (= tāywang, īm-kum).
  2. pseudo-adn. large, king-size. ¶ ~ kām big persimmon. ~ kāymi Hercules ant. ~ kemi giant spider. ~ kye chaff. ~ mati largest node (on bamboo). ~ molay grit. ~ pām large chestnut. ~ pēl giant hornet. ~ pha large Welsh onion. ~ phali horsefly. ~ tay long-jointed bamboo. ~ pangwul a huge bell (? or large drop). ~ ciney a giant centipede.
wang, alt after a vowel of kwang, pcl [Ceycwu DIAL] = kwa / wa (in comparison) with. ¶ku salum kwang kothun ya? = ku sālam kwa kath.ten ya? was he / she like that person? pap kwang ttek kwang enu key cwoni = pap kwa ttek kwa enu kes i cōh.un ya which do you prefer, rice or rice cake? keyki wang pey wang enu ke mekhwukkang = koki wa pay wa enu kes ul mek.keyss.nun ya which will you eat, the meat or the pears?
wang < wo-ang [Ceycwu DIAL] = wā se, = oko (come).
-wantey [obs] = -kwantey (such / so that)
-wanˈtoy = -Gwanˈtoy

wa nun, pcl + pcl (after a vowel) = kwa nun
wā nun, infinitive + pcl
wa se, pcl + pcl (after a vowel) = kwa se
wā se, infinitive + pcl. comes and (then / so).
wass- (< o-ass- < o-a iss-), past < ota
wa to, pcl + pcl (after a vowel) = kwa to
wā to, infinitive + pcl. even if one comes.
ˈwaˈton < (?*)ˈwoaˈton, vi provisional (= ˈwokeˈton, ˈwonaˈton). ¶ ˈQILQ-ˈCHYEY ˈyey ˈpi ˈwaˈton (1463 Pep 3:2b) if rain comes to all.
wa tul, pcl + pcl (plural subject) = kwa tul
wā tul, infinitive + pcl (plural subject)
wa uy, pcl + pcl (after a vowel) = kwa uy
way < ˝may, 1. adverb. why, for what reason, with what purpose (CF etteh.key). ¶ ~ kulen ci for some reason (or other). Way nuc.ess.nun ya Why were you late? Way nuc.ess.nun ci molukeyss.ta I wonder why you were late. Way kuleh.key wūs.nun ya What makes you laugh so? Way kulay Why do you do / say that?; [rhetorical] Why do you ask (me)?! (= Of course!).
  2. interj. why. ¶ "Ecey on sālam i nwukwu ʼn ya." – "Way, ku ka Kim uysa uy tongsayng icʼ anh.e?!" Who was it that came to see you yesterday? – Why, it was Dr Kimʼs brother!
wa ya, pcl + pcl (after a vowel) = kwa ya
wā ya, infinitive + pcl. only if one comes.
waynya = way ʼn ya why is it: ~ ʼmyen ("if you ask why" =) the reason is.
wa yo, pcl + pcl (after a vowel) = kwa yo
wā yo, infinitive + pcl. comes [POLITE].
ˈwa ʼyˈsye, vi inf + aux inf (abbr < iˈsye). ¶MWON alˈph oy hon ˝cywung ˈkwa hon sywoˈkhway [= sywoh ˈkwa y] ˝kwoWon ˈkyeciˈp ul toˈlye ˈwa ʼyˈsye ˈphoˈno-ngi ˈˈta (1459 Wel 8:94b) in front of the gate a monk and a layman have come bringing a pretty girl and they are selling her.
ˈwa ʼyˈste.n i ˈˈla, vi inf + aux retr mod (abbr < is(i)ˈten) + postmod + cop indic attent. ¶ ˝ta ~ (1447 Sek 13:7a) they were all present.
wen < NGWEN, adnoun. the original. ¶ ~ nay kyēyhoyk my original plan.
wēyn, adnoun. what sort / manner / kind of. SYN musun. [? < way + in ʼ ⋯ that is howʼ]
wēynq īl, adn + noun [or (> wēynq il) cpd n?]. what matter, what cause, what reason. ¶ ~ in ci for some reason (or other). Wēynq īl in ya What is all this? What is the matter? Whatʼs got

into you? **Wēynq īl lo wass.nun ya** What has brought you here?

wēyn ke l', interjection. (expresses surprise or disappointment at an unexpected result) Oh my! Why (no)! Goodness (no)! Gee (whiz)! Gosh (darn)! ¶**Sānqpo na-kalye ko hayss.tuni, wēyn ke l' sonak-pi ka ssot.a cyess.ta** I was going out for a walk; but, by George, it started to shower. **Wēyn ke l', ku ka onul hōy ey olla ko** Gee, I wonder if he isn't coming to today's meeting now, after all. **Wēyn ke l' ileh.key mānh.un sakwa lul kacye osyess.^{s}up.nikka** My goodness gracious — what a lot of apples you have brought for me! "**Kulay, ōymu cāngkwan ul manna pwass.ni?**" — "**Wēyn ke l'!**" Well, did you see the Foreign Minister? — Gosh, no! **Wēyn ke l' okeyss.ki** (or **Wēyn ke l' olla ko**) What makes you think he is coming? **Ilk.ci puthe mōs hanun tey wēyn ke l' ssulq cwul ālkeyss.e yo** When I can't read, even, how can I be expected to know how to write?

wēyn kkatalk, adn + noun. why, what cause, what reason. ¶**Wēyn kkatalk ulo ku ka casal hayss.nun ya** Why did he kill himself? **Wēyn kkatalk in ci, ku hanthey se tapcang i ēps.ta** I don't know why, but he doesn't answer my letter.

wēyn kokcel, adn + noun. what circumstances, what kind of trouble, what cause (or reason). ¶**Ce sayksi ka celeh.key sulphukey wūni wēyn kokcel io** That young woman is crying so bitterly; what could have happened to her? **Wēyn kokcel lo ku pupu ka nul ssawunun ci molukeyss.ta** I don't know what leads the couple to fight with each other all the time. **Wēyn kokcel lo wūsio** Why are you crying? What makes you cry?

weyn-man hata, adj-n. is fairly good, tolerable, passable, satisfactory, all right, pretty close to it; [ironically] is terrific, tremendous, splendid. [Awkward when sentence-final?] ¶**?sayngkim-sayngkim i ~ is** quite good-looking. **?swuip i ~ has** a handsome income. **weyn-man hamyen** if you please, if you like, if you don't mind, how about (doing ···). **?Ku uy yoksim i weyn-man hakwun!** What greed he has! **Ku ^{n}yeca uy khi ka weyn-man hata** She is such a huge woman. **?Onul chwuwi ka weyn-man hata** It's pretty cold today. **Ku nun weyn-man han hakca ka ani 'ta** He is no mean scholar. **Weyn-man hamyen, cey ka kath.i kaci yo** I'll go with you, if you don't mind. **Weyn-man hamyen, cha han can masipsita** How about having a cup of tea? SYN [? abbr <] **wuyen-man hata**.

weyn mankhum / manchi, cpd adverb [abbr < weyn-man hal mankhum]. to a certain degree, fairly, passably, considerably; moderately, appropriately, properly. ¶**Yenge lul ~ hata** speaks English fairly well. **swul ey ~ chwī hata** is rather tipsy. **Koki ka weyn mankhum ik.ess.ta** The meat is done to a turn. [1]**Nōngtam to weyn mankhum hay la** Don't go too far with your jokes; Enough of your jokes. **Ku ^{n}yeca nun phiano lul weyn mankhum cal chinta** She is not half bad at the piano. **Weyn mankhum masye / mek.e la** (Take it) easy on the liquor / food. **Acik elin ai 'ni, weyn mankhum hay twusio** He is still just a child; go easy on him. **Kongpu lul weyn mankhum hay la** You study too hard — take it easy.

wēyn sēym, adn + noun. what circumstances / matter / reason / cause, (the) why. ¶**Ku ka oci anh.uni, wēyn sēym ilq ka** I wonder why he doesn't come! **Ku ka sacik hayss.nun tey, wēyn sēym in ci molukeyss.ta** I don't quite see what made him resign.

wēynq yengmun, cpd n = **wēyn sēym**

wi, n. NK **wu**; CF **wus**. In compounds mostly **wi** ··· except for lexicalizations of **wus** (adn < n + obsolete pcl **s**) and **wis** (= **wiq**, in spelling modeled after **wus**). The earlier form was **wu** < **wuh**; the modern Seoul form incorporates **-i** (**wu[h]-i** > **wuy** > **wi**).

1. the upside, the top(side), the upper part, the above. ¶**~ lul chyē 'ta pota** looks upward. **kang wi lul olla kata** follows a river upstream.

2. the top, the summit. ¶**entek ~ lul olla kata** climbs to the top of the hill.

3. the (upper) surface, the top (side), on. ¶**chayk-sang wi uy chayk** the books on the desk. **pyek ~ ey ('ta) kūlim ul kēlta** hangs a picture on the wall. **Hāy-phali ka pata wi ey tte iss.ta** A jellyfish is floating on the sea.

4. senior(ity), superior(ity); above, higher, (nai ka ~ 'ta) older. ¶**Ku nun na pota han sal wi 'ta** He is a year older than I am.

5. ~ ey in addition, on top of. ¶**ku wi ey** moreover, what's more, besides, to boot.

? -Wi [probably a ghost form] SEE **i'li-'Wi**

wi hata < ¨*wuy* °*ho˙ta* < ˙*WUY* °*ho˙ta*, vnt.
1. serves, honors, respects, reveres, looks up to, esteems, venerates, worships. ¶ **pumo lul ~** honors (takes good care of, is devoted to) one's parents. **elin ai tul ul ~** is kind to children, loves children. **cosang ul ~** worships one's ancestors. **sin-pul ul ~** worships Taoist and Buddhist deities.
2. makes much of, values, esteems, has regard for, treats with care, takes good care of. ¶ **mom ul ~** takes care of oneself. **myengyey lul mok-swum pota te ~** puts honor above life. **myengyey pota to tōn ul te ~** is more interested in money than in glory.
3. does for the good / sake / benefit of, does in favor / behalf of (in the interest of). ¶ **cey aph man ul ~** looks after one's own interest only. **hōysa lul ~** looks to the interests of the firm. **yēyswul ul wi han yēyswul** art for art's sake. ¹**noncayng ul wi han** ¹**noncayng** argument for the sake of argument. **Ku nun hak.kyo lul wi hanun maum ey se kuleh.key hayss.ta** He did so out of concern for the school. **Ne lul wi haki ttaymun ey ku ka kuleh.key māl han kes ita** He told you that for your own good.
3a. (⋯-ki) **wi hay se** (**wi ha.ye**) in order to, to the end that, so as to, so that, for the purpose, with the intention of, with a view to. ¶ **sang ul thaki wi hay se yelqsim hi kongpu hata** studies hard in order to get a prize. **canye lul kongpu sikhiki wi hay se cēkum hata** saves money toward the education of one's children. **Ku nun cip ul cīs.ki wi hay se ttang ul sass.ta** He has bought land with a view to building a house.
3b. (⋯-ki) **wi han ... for the purpose of ...** . ¶ **sensayng ul hwan.yeng haki (lul) wi han hōy** a meeting for the purpose of welcoming the teacher.
3c. **Wi ha.ye!** Cheers! Skoal! Bottoms up!
wis, adn (= **wiq**), var **wus**; ANT **alayq**. the upper, the above, the outer. ¶ **~ kaci, ~ kil, ~ mak.i, ~ mok, ~ mul, ~ pay, ~ pyen, ~ salang, ~ tong(ali)**.
~ salam = wus salam seniors, superiors.
wisq (n)i the upper teeth, an upper tooth.
˙*wo*; -˙*wo*, '-˙*wo* = ˙*Gwo*, ˙*[G]wo*; -˙*Gwo*, '˙*Gwo* → ˙*kwo*; -˙*kwo*, '*kwo*
-˙*wo-* = -˙*w*ᵘ*/o-*, modulator. SEE §9.9.10; -*u*˙*sya-*; -˙*yw*ᵘ*/o-*.

*˙*wo˙a* → ˙*wa* (infinitive < °*wo˙ta*)
˙*wohi˙lye* (> *ohilye*), adverb. rather, sooner, preferably; on / to the contrary, contrariwise, instead (of the expected). Examples: 1459 Wel 1:37a, 21:149a; 1462 ¹Nung 2:67a; 1463 Pep 2:77a, 4:192-3; 1475 Nay 2:1:2b; ... .
-*wo k* → -˙*Gwo k* (gerund + emphatic particle)
˙*wo˙ke-*, vi ('come') + effective. But see also ˙*wo˙na-*, ˙*wa-*.
˙*woke˙na*, vi effective adversative. ¶ ¨*salo˙m i* ¨*mwo˙tin* ˙*skwu˙m ul* ¨*e˙te kwu˙cun* ˙*SYANG* ˙*ol* ˙*pwoke˙na QYWOW-* ˙*KWAY lo* ˙*Woyn* ¨*say* ˙*woke˙na* (1459 Wel 9:43a) whether a person has a bad dream and sees dire omens or an uncanny bird turns up.
˙*woke˙nol*, vi lit concessive. ¶ ¨*ne y* ˙*ka [CHYEY-* ¨*CO] ˙lol ma˙ca* ˙*woke˙nol* (1481 Twusi 8:40a) you go to meet your wife (and return), but ... .
˙*wo˙kesi˙nol = ˙wo˙nasi˙nol*, vi lit concessive. ¶ *ku* ˙*kil.h u˙lwo* ˙*wo˙kesi˙nol* (1459 Wel 7:10a) when you come by that path ... .
(?*) ˙*wo˙kesi˙ton* SEE ˙*wo˙nasi˙tun*
˙*woke˙tun*, ˙*woke˙ton = ˙wona˙ton*, provisional < °*wo˙ta* vi. ¶ ˙*hota* ˙*ka pcwo˙chye* ˙*woke˙tun* (1459 Wel 10:25a) if one starts to get pursued. *kwuy-s-ke˙s uy nos* ˙*kwa SSIN-LYENG* ˙*uy me˙li no˙ch ol* ˙*TWOY* ˙*ho.ya* ˙*woke˙ton* (1482 Kumsam 3:27b) when you come to confront the face of a ghost or the face on the head of a spirit.
wol(q), vi prosp mod. ¶ *wolq* ˙*t ol* (1449 Kok 147) that he would come.
¨*wol(q)* (< **wo-˙wo-lq*), vi modulated prosp mod. ¶ ˙*pi* ¨*wol* ˙*tt i* ¨*m ye n'* (1463 Pep 3:35a) when it is about to rain. ¨*tywohi two˙la* ¨*wol˙t i.n i* '˙*la* (1481 Twusi 21:42b) I have well come back. ˙*hota* ˙*ka pas˙k ol pu˙the* ¨*wol˙t in˙t ay n'* (1462 ¹Nung 1:64b) if we rely on outward appearance (coming to us).
-˙*wol(q)*, modulated prospective modifier.
1. (the epitheme extruded from the subject). Example?
2. (epitheme extruded from the object). ¶ *CYE-* ˙*PPWULQ nilu˙sinwon* ¨*ma˙l on* ¨*NAY-CYWUNG* ¨*na y tal˙Gwolq* ˙*cwu˙l i* ¨*ep˙susi˙n i '-ngi* ¨*ta* (1447 Sek 9:27a) there is no way that all the words said by the various Buddhas are different from me.
3. (summational epitheme). ¶ *ci˙p i [SYWOW-* ˙*SIK] mwu˙lwol toy* ¨*ep˙twoswo˙n i* (1481 Twusi 7:39b; the nominative particle is a loose

reference) there is no place to ask news of home. kwo˙c ol pwolq SSI-˙CYELQ ˙ey (1462 ¹Nung 2:111a) when one looks at blossoms ... . LYWONG-NGWANG ˙oy ˙pi no˙liGwol ˙chezem ˙kwa ˙stwo ˙kot ˙two˙ta (1482 Nam 1:34a) it is again like the beginning when the dragon king ... made the rain come down. SEE ... ˙ywol(q), ˙ho.ywolq = ˙hwolq, ¨hwolq; ¨wolq, ˙pwolq, ˙kal, ¨nalq; -usyalq. CF -˙ywol(q).
- ˙wo˙la, modulated indic assertive. ¶ye˙lwo˙la (1481 Twusi 7:3a) I open it. ˙kwulwu˙m ey na˙kunay ˙lwo ˙pap me˙kwola (1481 Twusi 7:14b) we eat as travelers in the clouds. SEE ˙hwo˙la.
wo˙la, vi subj assert. ¶wo˙la hon ˙t ol (1445 ¹Yong 69) though told to come. CF ˙wona˙la.
wo˙la˙ta, adjective. is a long time, is long.
- ˙wo˙l i, modulated prosp mod + postmodifier. ¶ce˙hwo.l i ¨ep.sul ˙ss oy (1459 Wel 2:38a) there is none he [the lion] fears. SEE ˙hwo˙l i.
- ˙wo.l i ʼ˙la, modulated prosp mod + postmod + cop indic assert. SEE -˙ywo.l i ʼ˙la, ˙hwo.l i ʼ˙la, ¨pwo.l i ʼ˙la.
- ˙wo˙l i ʼ-ngi ʼ˙ta, modulated prosp mod + postmod + cop polite + cop indic assert. SEE ˙hwo˙l i ʼ-ngi ʼ˙ta.
- ˙wo.l i ʼ˙n i, modulated prosp mod + postmod + cop modifier + postmod. ¶ ˙SYEY-CWON s ¨il sol˙Wwo.l i ʼ˙n i ˙MEN-¨LI ˙NGWOY s ¨il ˙isi˙na ˙nwun ˙ey ˙pwonwon ˙ka ne˙kizo˙Wosywo˙sye (1449 Kok 2) I will tell you of the World-Honored's work: it is a work beyond the myriad leagues [of our land] but please think of it as if seeing it in your eye.
- ˙wo˙l i ʼsyas˙ta, modulated prosp modifier + postmod + cop modulated hon emotive indic assert. ¶e˙lwu sol˙[W]wo˙l i ʼsyas˙ta (1463 Pep 4:70-1) it will be possible to tell them.
- ˙wol(q) ˙ta, modulated prosp mod + postmod. ¶e˙nu cey [˙THOY PWU-ZIN] s [TTANG] wu˙h uy a˙zom ˙tol.h ol mwoy˙hwol˙ta (1481 Twusi 8:20a) when will you gather the clan up to the hall of the dowager?
- ˙wolq˙tay, modulated prosp mod + quasi-free n. ¶pwu¨thye y ˙KAK-˙KAK ˙hwolq˙tay ˙lol cwo˙cha (1459 Wel 13:51a) Buddha pursued each individual place. pwu¨thye y ˙KAK-˙KAK i˙kuy˙ywol ˙ttay lʼ cwocho˙sya (1463 Pep 3:19b) Buddha pursued each place where he might prevail. ˙PEP tulu˙l i hi˙m uy pa˙twol

˙ttay lʼ cwo˙cha (1463 Pep 3:41b) those who would hear the Law followed where their strength would bear.
- ˙wol ˙(t)tiGe˙ni = -˙wolq ˙t iGe˙n i, modulated prosp mod + postmod + cop effective mod + postmod. SEE ... ˙ywol(q) ˙t iGe˙n i.
~ ˙Gwa (+ pcl). SEE ˙hwol(q) ˙t iGe˙n i ˙Gwa.
- ˙wol ˙(t)tiGe˙nol = -˙wolq ˙t iGe˙nol, modulated prosp mod + postmod + copula lit concessive. ¶¨mal-sso˙m i THWONG-˙TTALQ khe˙tun ma˙lwol ˙tt iGe˙nol (1463 Pep 1:9a) if the words are knowledgable they are not to be held back, but ... . SEE ˙hwolq ˙t iGe˙nol.
- ˙wol ˙(t)tiGen˙tyeng = -˙wolq ˙t iGen˙tyeng, modulated prosp mod + postmod + cop effective mod + postmod. SEE ˙hwolq ˙t iGen˙tyeng, ¨pwolq ˙t iGen˙tyeng.
- ˙wol ˙(t)tiGe˙nul = -˙wolq ˙t iGe˙nul (= ˙iGe˙nul), modulated prosp mod + postmod + cop lit concessive. ¶kwo˙c ol pwolq SSI-˙CYELQ ˙ey ˙nwu˙n i pan˙to˙ki ko˙lywo˙m i ¨ep˙swul ˙tt iGe˙nul (1462 ¹Nung 2:111a) when one looks at blossoms one's eyes must necessarily not cloud over, yet ... . pan˙to˙ki ˙kwo˙h ol pu˙the ¨nalq ˙t iGe˙nul (1462 ¹Nung 3:24b) it must be that it [= the scent] emerges from your nose.
- ˙wol ˙(t)tiGe˙ta = -˙wolq ˙t iGe˙ta, modulated prosp mod + postmod + copula effective indic assert. ¶¨cywokwo˙ma s ¨LI ˙lol to˙thwoa ˙CI-CHIN ˙ol e˙kuyGey ma˙lwol ˙t iGe˙ta (1475 Nay 3:41a) one is not to turn against one's intimates in a struggle for petty profits. ˙stwo kis.pun mozom ¨nayti ma˙lwolq ˙t iGe˙ta (?1468- Mong 18b) one is not to put forth a happy heart. ¨mwo˙toy ¨cye˙ki a˙lwo˙m ol ma˙lwolq ˙t iGe˙ta (?1468- Mong 30b) by no means should one learn merely a little. [ˊ]CCYEK-˙MYELQ TTYANG ˙ay i˙sye SSYEN-˙YWELQ ˙ul ˙CHAN-¨CHOY ho˙l i ˙n ... ˙ingey mozom ta˙wolq ˙t iGe˙ta (1462 ¹Nung 7:18a) now they will do their utmost in offering a banquet of dhyāna joy at the place where Buddha attained the truth of nirvāṇa. SEE -˙ywol(q) ˙t iGe˙ta, ˙hwolq ˙t iGe˙ta.
- ˙wol ˙(t)ti˙la = -˙wolq ˙t i˙la, modulated prosp mod + postn + cop indic assert. ¶˙SYANG a˙ni ˙la nil˙Gwolq t i˙la (1462 ¹Nung 6:59a) will say that it is not a sign. ˙kwot ma˙lwol ˙t i˙la

ˊkhwoˋta tasˋkwoˑm ol putˋti aˋni hoˋl i ˏsi.l i ˏl ˋs oy (1465 Wen 1:2:2:4a) he says we will stop now and since it may be that we cannot count on learning everything ... . SEE ··· ˏywolq ˋt iˋla, ˋhwolq ˋt iˋla.

- ˏwolq ˋt ila ˋtwo (+ pcl). ¶ ˝SSYEN-KUN ˋul ˝YWENG ˋhi mulˋlwolq ˋt ila ˋtwo (1462 ¹Nung 1:86b) even though one may long retreat from one's good roots (kuśala-mūla). SEE ˋhwolq ˋt ila ˋtwo.

- ˏwolq ˋ(t)tilwoswoˋni = - ˏwolq ˋt ilwoswoˋn i, modulated prosp mod + postmod + cop + bnd v mod + postmod. ¶ [ˋCHA-KE ˝NGWAN] ˋay pi ˋchwuyywoˑm ol isˋpi maˋlwol ˋt ilwoswoˋn i ce ˋy ˋpi.ch i [QUN] ˋkot ˋhwo.m i isˋtwota (1481 Twusi 7:38b) the clamshell bowl is unflaggingly resplendent; at times it has a color like silver!

- ˋwol ˋ(t)tilwoˋta = - ˏwolq ˋt ilwoˋta, modulated prosp modifier + postmod + cop indic assert. ¶ koˋtok ˏˋti (< hoˋti) aˋni ˋhwom aˋni ˏnˋtol pan ˋtoˋki aˋlwolq ˋt ilwoˋta (1462 ¹Nung 1:67a) one must realize that it is not that it is not full. SEE ··· ˏywol(q) ˋt ilwoˋta.

- ˋwol ˋ(t)tiˋmye = - ˏwolq ˋt iˋm ye, modulated prosp mod + postmod + cop inf. SEE ˋhwolq ˋt iˋm ye.

~ n' (+ pcl). if; when. ¶ [˝SO-SSIN] ˋuy ˋpu.t un [ˋTTAY-˝YWU ˝LYENG] ˋey kuˋchye poˋliˋti maˋlwol t iGeˋta (1481 Twusi 24:43b; the second syllable of poˋliˋti miswritten as ˋla) the writing brush of the chronicler, smooth as a wave, will not come to an end at Dàyŭ Ridge [in the capital district]. ˋkhun ˋkwulwuˑm i cyang ˋcho ˋpi ˝wol ˋtt iˋm ye n' ˋpenˋkey ˋpis-na ˋkwo ˋwulˋGey ˝mwuynoˋn i (1463 Pep 3:35a) when a big cloud is about to rain it flashes with lightning and rumbles with thunder [the first nominative phrase is thematized]. SEE ˋhwolq ˋt iˋm ye n'.

- ˋwol ˋ(t)tiˋna = - ˏwolq ˋt iˋna, modulated prosp mod + postn + cop adversative. ¶ ˋmal-soˑm i eˋlwu ˝peyphwuˑm i isˋta eˋlwu nilˋGwol t iˋna (1482 Kum-sam 3:9b) it can well be said that your message is well spread but ···. ˋi ˋnon ˋSOYK ˋi piˋlwok eˋlwu pskay ˝hyelq ˋt iˋna KHWONG ˋi eˋlwu eˋwulGwuˋti ˝mwot holq ˋt ol PYWOW ˋhoˋsya (1462 ¹Nung 3:68b [˝hyelq = hye-ˋwo-lq; the first nominative phrase is thematized]) this represents the fact that, though with colors it may break them [into many], the void cannot combine them. SEE ˝kalq ˋt iˋna.

- ˋwol ˋ(t)tiˋni = - ˏwolq ˋt iˋn i, modulated prosp mod + postn + cop mod + postmod. ¶ molˋka ˋza CIN-SSYANG ˋiˋla nilˋGwolq ˋt iˋn i (1462 ¹Nung 2:108a) only when it is clear do we say it is true and eternal. ˋMYWOW-˝HHOYNG ˋoˋlwo ˋYWONG saˋmwol ˋtt i.n i (1463 Pep 1:4b) with the profound act of faith [by which good karma is produced] one will create function. ˋHWAN ˋol teˋlwol t iˋn i (1465 Wen 1:1:1:7b) it lessens the illusion. polˋkon kaˋwon-toy caˋchwoy lol twuˋti ˝ma[lG]wo twoloˋhye eˋtuwun kaˋwon-ˋtoy l' ˋHYANG ˋho.ya ˝kal t iˋn i (1482 Kum-sam 2:65a) one is not to put the clues in the midst of where it is brightly lit but rather to go toward the midst of where it is dark.

SEE ··· ˏywol(q) ˋt iˋn i, ˋhwolq ˋt iˋn i, ˝kalq ˋt iˋn i, ˝pwolq ˋt iˋn i.

- ˋwol ˋ(t)tiniˋla = - ˏwolq ˋt i.n i ˊˋla, modulated prosp mod + postn + cop mod + postmod + cop indic attent. ¶ ˋswu ˝ep.sun ˋt ol aˋlwolq ˋt i.n i ˊˋla (1447 Sek 19:10b) it must be realized that they are innumerable. ˋCI-˝TTWOW ˋlol CYWEN-CYENG ˋhi hoˋl iˋza SSIN ˋol mozoˑm ay molˋkiˋta nilˋGwol tt i.n iˋla (1463/4 Yeng 2:111a) just concentrating on the true path (for man to take) clears the spirit in one's heart. ··· koˋchwo NGUY-SIM maˋlwol ˋt i.n i ˊ[ˋ]la (1465 Wen 1:2:1:32a) will put an end to all the doubt. ˋhotaˋka CHAM-˝KWUW ey KAN-ˋSSYEP ˋhwolq ˋt in ˋt ay n' ˋkwot KWONG-PWU ˋlul nilˋGwolq ˋt i.n i ˊˋla (?1468- Mong 33a) if there should be interference with the pilgrimage [to study the principles of dhyāna] the pilgrim is to recite the meditations [that have been learned]. SIN-SIM ˋkwa ˝KYENG-ˋKAY ˋGwa ˋlol panˋtoki twoˋla pwoˋti maˋlwolq ˋt i.n i ˊˋla (?1468- Mong 36a) one is to ··· and is not necessarily to look back on one's body and mind and [their] realm of the phenomenal. ˋstwo mozoˑm ol kaˋcye aˋlwoˑm ol kiˋtulGwuˋti maˋlwolq ˋt i.n i ˊˋla (?1468- Mong 5a) moreover, having a mind one must not delay recognition (of the truth).

SEE - ˏywol(q) ˋt i.n i ˊˋla, - ˏywol(q) ˋt i.n i ˊˋla, ˋhwol(q) ˋt i.n i ˊˋla.

- ˋwol ˋ(t)tiˋningiˋta = - ˏwolq ˋt iˋn i ˊ-ngi ˊˋta, modulated prospective modifier + postnoun + cop modifier + postmod + cop polite + cop indicative attentive. ¶ ··· CYE ZYE-LOY y ˋswo.n *o˙lwo me˙li mon˙cisya˙m i towoyn˙t ol pan˙toki a˙lwol˙tt i˙n i '-ngi ' ˙ta* (1463 Pep 7:175a; the smudge on "ZYE" is not a tone mark) surely knows that ... and that the tathāgatas (incarnate Buddhas) patted him on the head.

-˙wol˙(t)tin˙tayn = -˙wolq˙t in˙t ay n', modulated prosp mod + postn + cop mod + postn + pcl + pcl. ¶*ne˙phye nil˙Gwol˙tt in˙t ay n'˙KEP˙un spol˙li tao˙l ye '.n i˙Gwa˙tye pwuthye s˙HHOYNG˙kwa˙NGWEN˙kwa KWONG-˙˙KHYWOW˙hosin PANG-˙PPYEN˙un ta˙wo˙m i ˙˙ep˙su.l i ' ˙la* (1447 Sek 9:29a) as you say, the kalpa will quickly come to an end, but the deeds and desires and ingenious expediencies [for promoting Buddhism] of Buddha, those will have no end; CF *ne˙phye nil˙Gwol˙tt in˙tay n'˙KEP˙un spol˙li tao˙l ye '.n i˙Gwa* (1459 Wel 9:49a). *˙hota˙ka˙˙ta a˙lwol˙tt in˙t ay n' til˙Gwo˙m i pan˙to˙ki is.non˙toy˙˙ep˙su.l ye ' ˙n i˙'s˙ton* (1462 ¹Nung 1:67a) if all are aware, there need not be any stumbling blocks. *˙CCO-˙SYEY˙hi nil˙Gwolq˙t in˙t ay n'* (?1468- Mong 66b) when we tell it in detail. SEE *˙hwolq˙t in˙t ay n', -u˙syal(q)˙t in˙t ay n'*.

-˙wol˙(t)toy = -˙wolq˙t oy, modulated prosp mod + postmod + pcl. SEE *˙hwolq˙t oy*.

-˙wol˙tyen = -˙wolq˙t ye n', modulated prosp mod + postmod + postmod [question] + pcl. SEE *˙hwol(q)˙t ye n'*.

-˙wol˙(t)tyeyn = -˙wolq˙tyeyn, modulated prosp mod + postmod. ¶*˙ches mozo˙m ay SAM-˙MOY˙yey˙tulwolq˙tyeyn te˙tuy˙m ye spol˙lwo˙m i˙LYWUY hon ka˙ci a˙ni '-ngi ' ˙ta* (1462 ¹Nung 6:54a) when one's mind initially enters into samādhi (perfect absorption), the tardiness or promptness is not of a single type. *ko˙chwo nil˙Gwol˙tyeyn˙PALQ-˙SIK s mozo˙m i ZYE-LOY˙CCANG˙ay THWONG ho˙n i* (1465 Wen 1:1:1: 45b) if one is to tell it completely, the spirit of the eight kinds of consciousness (parijñāna) pervades the storehouse of Buddha's teaching (the tathāgatagarbha). *yel˙Gwun˙SYEY lol˙HWA hwol˙ttyeyn mwo˙lwo˙may SSYWUN-PWONG˙ul pu˙thwul˙tt i˙m ye ZIN THYEN-˙˙NGAN˙ol ye˙lwol˙ttyeyn˙SSILQ˙lwo˙ptut a˙lwo˙m ol pu˙thwul˙tt i.n i ' ˙la* (1463 Pep 4:148b) if one is to transform the open world, it will be necessary to rely on guileless ways and if one is to open people's deva-eye (unlimited vision) one will have to rely on really knowing the meaning. SEE *˙hwolq˙tyeyn, -ᵘ⁄ₒ˙syalq˙tyeyn*.

-˙wol˙(t)tyeyn˙tye = -wolq˙tyeyn˙tye, modulated prosp mod + postmod + postmod. ¶*[˙˙]LI lol nil˙Gwol [˙]ttyeyn˙tye KAY-CHA y˙˙ep˙kwo [˙]HHOYNG˙ol nil[˙]Gwol [˙]ttyeyn KWONG˙ol ssa[˙]ha [˙]za somo[˙]cho.l i '[˙]n i* (1463/4 Yeng 1:22a) when we speak of the principle, there are no differences of level, and when we speak of practice, for it to sink in we must accumulate merits.

˙wo˙lwo, variant < ˙ᵘ⁄ₒ˙lwo (the first vowel assimilated to the second). ¶*sathang˙wo˙lwo* (?1517- Pak 1:4b) with sugar. *˙pis wo˙lwo* (?1517- Pak 1:44a) with a comb. *˙˙pet˙uy˙key cwuk˙u.m wolwo˙pse* (1586 Sohak 2:11a; sic *cwuk-˙u-mwo-lwo*) letting one's friends die. *ho[n] nye˙k wo˙lwo* (1466 Kup 2:77b) on the other hand. *˙˙CA s nye˙k wolwo ... ˙˙NGWUW s nye˙k wolwo* (1482 Kum-sam 3:3b) to the left ... to the right.

~ n' (pcl). ¶*˙hon nye˙k wo˙lwo n' ... hon nye˙k wo˙lwo n'* (1459 Wel 2:43-4) on the one hand ... on the other hand.

~ ˙two (pcl). ¶*pas˙k wolwo˙two ... ˙an˙h olwo˙two* (?1468- Mong 64a) both outside ... and inside.

~ 'yGe˙na (cop effective advers). ¶*˙pwu˙t iGe˙na swon thwo˙p wo˙lwo 'yGe˙na* (1447 Sek 13:52b) either by brush or by fingernail.

-˙wo.l ye, modulated prosp mod + postmod. SEE *˙hwo.l ye*.

-wolyenywo = -˙wo.l˙'ye˙n ywo = -˙wol [i]˙'ye˙n ywo, modulated prosp modifier (+ ellipted postmodifier) + copula effective modifier + postmodifier. ¶*˙˙encey˙˙sayGe˙tun pwuthye˙lul˙ka-˙pwozo˙Wwo.l [i]˙'ye˙n ywo˙hote˙n i* (1447 Sek 6:19a) "should I wait for dawn to go see Buddha?" he wondered.

-˙wolye˙ta = -˙wo.l [i]˙'ye˙ta. SEE *˙hwolye˙ta = ˙hwo.l [i]˙'ye˙ta*.

-˙wo˙l ywo, modulated prosp mod + postmod. ¶*˙˙na y ne˙lul KUM˙˙cwu˙l ywo˙ho.ya˙ton* (1482 Nam 1:44-5) if I consider giving you money ... .

-˙wom, modulated substantive. ¶*poy kwol˙phwom˙kwa mwok mol˙lwom˙kwa* (1459 Wel 2:42a) having an empty stomach and a dry throat (= hunger and thirst). *˙i mwo˙m ol ka˙cye˙na y˙˙te˙lewu˙m ye˙kwo˙lwom hul˙le* (1465 Wen 1:2:2:25a) with this body I am dirty and fester with pus. SEE *˙hwom; ˙˙wom, ˙pwom, ˙˙kam, ˙˙nam; -u˙syam*.

˙wom = ˙Gwom, ˙[G]wom, alt of ˙kwom (pcl)
wom(⋯), subst < °wo˙ta. Example?
¨wom (< *wo-˙wo-m), modulated substantive < °wo˙ta. SEE ¨wo˙m ay, ¨wo˙m i, ¨wo˙m ol.
-˙wo˙m a, modulated subst + pcl. I promise, I will. ¶ ˙na y ne to˙lye nil˙Gwo˙m a (?1517- Pak 1:32b) I will tell you. nonhwa ¨cwu.m a ˙hwo.m i (1481 Twusi 7:39a) that one promises to share it. CF He Wung 1989:139.
-˙wo˙m ay, modulated substantive + particle. ¶ ˙CHYWOK ˙i ˙tulwo˙m ay (1462 ¹Nung 2:114b) at the entering (= onset) of a feeling ... . SEE ˙hwo˙m ay, ¨pwo˙m ay, ¨wo˙m ay, -˙ywo˙m ay; ˙hosya˙m ay.
¨wo[˙]m ay, vi modulated subst + pcl. ¶ ˙ywo cwo˙zom pu˙the ¨wo.m ay (1481 Twusi 21:25b) come the last little while ... .
-˙wom °ho- = -˙Gwom °ho- = -˙kwom °ho-
¨wo˙m i, vi modulated substantive + particle. ¶ ˙PALQ-PWONG ˙oy ¨wo˙m i ¨ha˙m ol muten ˙hi ne˙kinwos˙ta (1482 Kum-sam 3:19a) one treats casually the fact that the coming of the Eight Winds [which fan the passions] is frequent.
-˙wo˙m i, modulated substantive + particle. ¶ ˙homol˙mye ¨TTWOW-˙KUY ˙Gwa ¨KWA-˙KUY ˙Gwa tal˙Gwo˙m i is.ke˙n i ˙sto˙n ye (1462 ¹Nung 1:17a) just how much more would they differ from testimonials to marga (the way) and to phala ([cause and] effect)?! kozol s ha˙nol moy˙h ay s ˙mu.l ey SOM-LA y ¨ce y na˙thwo.m i ˙kot ho˙n i (1482 Kum-sam 3:34b) it is like the spontaneous appearance of a dense forest by moorland streams under an autumn sky. SEE ˙hwo˙m i, ˙hosya˙m i.
~ ˙za (pcl). SEE hwo˙m i ˙za.
-˙wo˙m i ˙Gwo, modulated subst + cop ger. SEE ˙hwo˙m i ˙Gwo.
-˙wo.m i ˙la, modulated subst + cop indic assert. SEE ˙hwo.m i ˙la.
-˙wo˙m ilwo˙ta, modulated subst + var cop indic assert. SEE ˙hwo˙m ilwo˙ta.
-˙wo˙m i ˙sto˙n ⋯ , modulated subst + pcl + ⋯ . SEE ˙hwo˙m i ˙sto˙n ⋯ .
¨wo˙m ol, vi modulated subst + particle. ¶ LWO-¨LWOW y kutuy s ¨wo˙m ol kitu˙li˙tela ho˙la (1482 Nam 1:50b) he has been long waiting for you to come. kwot [KUN-¨KUY] lol wolm˙kye ¨wo.m ol ci˙ze k kozol s ˙poy s twos˙k ol [¨]nay ¨hen ci˙p ulwo ˙sye ˙na-ka˙la (1481 Twusi 20:52a) straightway convert a canvas [to use] as the sail for an autumn boat and set off from my shabby home [on your mission].
-˙wo˙m ol, modulated substantive + pcl. ¶ ˙ho˙ma [SYENG-˙KWAK] s pas˙k uy ˙na tuthu˙l ey s ¨i.l i ¨cyekwo˙m ol ˙anwo˙n i ... [= ¨anwo˙n i] (1481 Twusi 7:2a) he already knew that going outside the castle wall there were few problems from dust (and that) ... . ¨hay tu˙lwo˙m ol po˙lye (1447 Sek 9:13b) gave up listening a lot.
-˙wo˙m o˙lwo, modulated subst + pcl. ¶ ¨mal-ssom ˙kwa ka˙col˙pywo.m o˙lwo mis˙ti ¨mwot hol kke˙s i ku CIN-˙SSILQ s TI ˙n ˙t ye (1464 Kumkang 87b) is what we cannot attain by comparing it with what is said the true wisdom? ¨tywo˙hwom i˙sywo.m o˙lwo SOYNG ˙ol pwo˙m ye ˙MYELQ ˙ol ˙pwo˙no.n i ˙ˊla (1465 Wen 1:2:1:39b) sometimes sees birth and sees extinction as being good. SEE ˙hosya˙m o˙lwo.
-˙wo˙m on, modulated substantive + pcl. ¶ a˙tol na˙hwo.m on sta˙h ay ˙tita˙ka˙m ye tunge˙li ˙yey s ˙hi.m i cwozo lo˙woy.n i (1481 Twusi 25:43a) when my son was born as soon as he fell to the ground he had formidable strength in his back. SEE ˙hwo˙m on; ˙hosya˙m on.
˙won, 1. num. a hundred. 2. adn. all (= ¨won); ~ ka˙ci all sorts.
won, mod < °wo˙ta. Examples: 1485 Kwan 9a; ?1517- ¹No 1:33a, 1:54a, 1:65b.
¨won, adnoun. all; total, complete.
¨won (< *wo-˙wo-n), vi modulated modifier. ¶ ˙KAK-˙PPYELQ ˙hi ¨won ˙SYENG i˙sywu˙m i ˙mas˙tang ˙hokan˙t iGe˙n i ˙ˊston (1462 ¹Nung 1:89a) it is only natural that it would have a character that had specially come to it. ¨won ˙kil˙h ol (1482 Nam 1:28b) the road (that one has) come.
-˙won = -˙Gwon = -kwon and, but (much more / less ⋯)
-˙won, modulated modifier.
1. (epitheme extruded from subject). ¶ wo˙cik mozo˙m oy na˙thwon ke˙s in˙t ol ¨pwoy˙sya (1462 ¹Nung 2:17a) shows that it is (a thing) manifest only in the mind.
2. (epitheme extruded from object). ¶ SYWU-˙TTALQ ˙oy moyng˙ko˙lwon ˙CCWA ˙ay (1447 Sek 6:30a) to the seat that Sudatta had made.
3. (summational epitheme). ¶ mol ˙thwon ca˙hi ¨ken˙nesi˙n i ˙'-ngi ˙ˊta (1445 ¹Yong 34) he crossed over on horseback. ¨won ˙kwo.t on a˙zo.m ol [˙WUY] ˙ho.ya ˙'y ˙Gwo ˙stwo [¨QUM-˙SSIK] ˙ul [˙WUY] ˙hwo.m i a˙ni ˙'.n i ˙ˊla (1481 Twusi 8:33a) our coming is for our kinsmen

and not for drink and food. SEE ˈhwon; ˇwon, ˇpwon, ˇkan, ˇnan; -uˈsyan.

woˈna-, vi 'come' + effective; CF woˈke-, ˈwa-.

woˈna, vi effective inf. ¶ ˈwoˈna ciˈla (1481 Samkang hyo:29a) wants to come. SEE ~ ˈtwo.

woˈnaˈla, vi effective subj attent (= command). ¶ twolwo ˈwonaˈla (1459 Wel 7:7b) come back! ˇne y ˈstwo tyele ˈlwo ˈwoˈnaˈla (?1517- ¹No 1:57b = 1795 ¹No-cwung 1:52a) you go there (and come back).

woˈnan, vi effective mod. ¶ ˊPHEN-ˈYEK ˈhoˈya ˈwonan ˈt i koˈzuy ˊPALQ-ˊPOYK ˈhoy ˈˈn i (1463 Pep se:21a) it is now almost 800 years since it was translated. ne-ˈhuy ˈtwulˈh i yey ˈwoˈnan ˈt i ˈenˈme woˈla.n i ˊGwo (?1517- ¹No 1:68b) how long is it since you two came here? ALSO: 1463 Pep 2:245b, 1586 Sohak 5:49a.

ˈwonaˈn i, vi effective mod + postmod. ¶ MYEY ˈlwo ˈsye twoˈla ˈwonaˈn i ˈˈes.tyey ˇCHYEN ˈi aˈni ˈˈm ye (1463/4 Yeng 1:90b) how are those not shallow who are back from confusion ... .

~ ˊGwa. ¶ chezem puˈthe maˈchwo-ˈpce ˊCING ˈho.ya kaˈcye ˈwonaˈn i ˊGwa (1482 Kum-sam 2:57a) not only have they witnessed it from the beginning, ...

ˈwoˈnan maˈlon, vi effective mod + postmod. ¶ kutuy ˈnay meˈli ˈsye kosˈpi ˈwoˈnan maˈlon (1447 Sek 23:54a) you folks have rushed here from afar, but ... .

ˈwonaˈnol, vi lit concessive. ¶ ku ci[p] s ˈstoˈl i ˈpsol kaˈcye ˈna ˈwonaˈnol PPA-LA-MWON ˈi pwoˈkwo kisˈke (1447 Sek 6:14a) when the daughter of the house brought out the rice the brahman saw and rejoiced (or: the brahman saw the daughter of that house bring out the rice and he rejoiced). ALSO: 1445 ¹Yong 109, 1449 Kok 34. CF ˈwokeˈnol.

ˈwonaˈn ywo, vi effective modifier + postmod. ¶ muˈsu.m uˈla paˈm oy ˈna ˈwonaˈn ywo (1447 Sek 6:19b) why have I come out at night? ALSO: 1459 Wel 18:2a.

ˈwoˈnasiˈnol = ˈwoˈkesiˈnol, honorific literary concessive of vi. ¶ pwuˈthye y ˈwoˈnasiˈnol ˈpwozoˈWa solWˈwoˈtoy (1447 Sek 6:44b) when Buddha comes he looks upon him and says ... .

ˈwoˈnasiˈtun = (?*)ˈwoˈkesiˈton, vi honorific provisional. ¶ [SYEY] ˈyey ˈwoˈnasiˈtun [TWONG-*ˇˇPI] ˈpoˈlazoˈWoˈn i (1445 ¹Yong 38) when he came west people in the east wished for him.

ˈwonaˈta, vi effective indic assertive. ¶ swuwul ˇeˈtuˈla ˈkateˈn i ˈˈta twoˈla ˈwonaˈta (?1517- Pak 1:3a) those who went to get wine have all come back. ALSO: 1795 ¹No-cwung [K] 2:61b.

ˈwonaˈton = ˈwokeˈtun, ˈwokeˈton, ˈwaˈton, vi provisional. ¶ HWON-QIN ˇwuy ˈhoˈya aˈzoˈm i ˈwonaˈton ipaˈtwoˈl ye ˈhoˈnwo.n i sˈka (1447 Sek 6:16b) are you entertaining relatives come for a wedding? talon ˇsaloˈm i ˈwonaˈton ˊKHWEN ˈhoˈya anˈca tutˈkuy kheˈna (1447 Sek 19:6a) when other people came he asked they be allowed to sit and hear him, but ... . ALSO: 1459 Wel 2:25b, 1463 Pep 6:12a, ?1468- Mong 2b, 1586 Sohak 6:95a; ˈwonaˈtun (?1517- Pak 1:40a), ˈwoˈnaˈtun (?1517- ¹No 1:44b).

ˈwonaˈtwo, vi effective inf + pcl. ¶ swoˈn i ˈwonaˈtwo muyˈywo.m ol muten ˈhi neˈkikwo [NGYENG-PPWONG] aˈni ˈhonwoˈla (1481 Twusi 25:23a) though the guest arrives I treat him with disdain and do not go out to greet him.

-ˈwo-ngi ˈˈta, modulated polite + cop indicative assertive. ¶ ˈi CIN-ˈSSILQ s ˊMYELQ-ˈTTWO aˈni ˈnˈt ol ˈnay aˈlwo-ngi ˈˈta (1463 Pep 2:23a) I know this is not true nirvāṇa. SEE ˈhwo-ngiˈˈta.

ˇwo-ngi ˈˈta, modulated polite < ˚wo- (come) + copula indicative assertive. ¶ ˊTTAY-NGWANG ˈol ˈpwoˈzoWwoˈla ˇwo-ngi ˈˈta (1459 Wel 8:90b) I come to see the (great) king.

woˈn i, vi mod + postmod. Examples: 1445 ¹Yong 51; ?1517- ¹No 1:30b, 1:45a.

-ˈwoˈn i, modulated modifier + postmod. ¶ na y naˈhwo.n iˈn i (1463 Pep 2:222b) I was born and ... . ˈcye.c uˈlwo moyngkˈkolwoˈn i ˊLAK ˈiGwo (1482 Kum-sam 3:39b) what is made from milk is cheese, and ... . SEE ˈhwoˈn i.

-ˈwo.n i ˈnˈt ye, modulated mod + postmod + cop mod + postmod + postmod. ¶ ˊSIN-ˈHHAY hoˈla ˈhosyaˈm i ˈi lol nilˈGwo.n iˈnˈt ye (1482 Kum-sam 5:14a) did his saying that we should believe and understand [the doctrine] refer to this?

-ˈwonˈka, modulated modifier + postmodifier. ¶ ˊNYELQ-PPAN ˈay tatoˈlwon ˈka ˈhoˈtaswoˈn i (1446 Sek 13:43b) we wonder whether we have reached nirvāṇa, but ... .

*-ˈwo-(ˈ)no- (modulated proc) does not exist; SEE -ˈnwo- < *-(ˈ)n[o]-ˈwo- (proc modulated).

ˈwonon, vi processive modifier. ¶ neˈy susuˈng uy ˇTTYEY-ˇCO y ˈˈes.tyey aˈni ˈwonoˈn ywo (1447 Sek 6:29b) why is your teacher's disciple not arriving?

˙wo ˙no-ngi ˈˈta, vi proc polite. ¶ ˜mwot ˙wo ˙no-ngi ˈˈta (1447 Sek 6:29b) he will not come.

- ˙won t ay n, modulated mod + postmod + pcl + pcl. SEE ˙hwon t ay nˈ.
- ˙won ˙t i, modulated mod + postmod + pcl. SEE ˙hwon ˙t i, ˜pwon ˙t i.
- ˙won ˙t i ˙la, modulated mod + postmod + cop indic assert. SEE ˙hwon ˙t i ˙la.
- ˙won ˙t i ˈm ye nˈ, modulated mod + postmod + cop subst + cop inf + pcl. SEE ˙hwon ˙t i ˈm ye nˈ.
- ˙won ˙t in ˙tay nˈ SEE -ˈnwon ˙t in ˙t ay nˈ
- ˙won ˙t oy nˈ, mod + postmod + pcl + pcl. SEE ˜pwon ˙t oy nˈ.

˙wonwon, vi proc modulated mod. ¶ ˙wonwon ˙t in ˙t ay nˈ (1459 Wel 10:7b) when he comes.

˙wonwos ˙ta, emotive < °wo ˙ta vi. ¶ -- namwo ˙ci ˈnon nwol ˙Gay non ˜cyeki mozol ˈh olwo ˙na ˙wonwos ˙ta (1481 Twusi 7:39a) -- then a few wood-chopping songs emerge from the village.

˙wos = ˙Gwos or ˙[G]wos (= ˙kwos, pcl)

˙wosil(q), vi honorific prosp modifier. ¶ ˙wosi ˙l i ˈ-ngi s ˙ka (1445 ¹Yong 69) would he come? ko ˙cang cyem ˙kul Ge ˙za ca ˙s ay ˙tu ˙le ˙wo ˙si.l i ˈˈla (?1517- Pak 1:65a) we will come back into the (stronghold =) city only when the night is well upon us. --- ˙wosil ˙ss ye (1447 Sek 23:29a) he has come [from far away]!

˙wosin, vi modifier. ¶ na ˙la ˙h ay ˜pil-me ˙ku ˙la ˙wosi ˙n i (1459 Wel 1:5b) he came to our land to beg. mu ˙su.m u ˙la ˙wosi ˙n i ˈ-ngi s ˙kwo (1447 Sek 6:3a) for what reason have you come here? ku cey lwo ˙wosin ˙t i son ˙coy wo ˙la ˙ti ˙mwot ˈˈkesi ˙tun (1463 Pep 5:119b) he had not been there for very long yet when ... .

˙wosi ˙no-ngi ˈˈta, vi polite honorific processive. ¶ HE-KHWONG ˙o ˙lwo ho ˙ma ˙wosi ˙no-ngi ˈˈta (1459 Wel 10:8a) is already coming to the void.

˙wosi ˙ta, vi honorific indic assertive. comes.

˙wo ˙sya, vi hon inf. ¶ ku ˜salo ˈm oy ˜swon- ˙toy ˙wo ˙sya (1459 Wel 8:55b) came to that person. na ˙la ˙h ay two ˙la ˙wosya ˙two (1447 Sek 6:4b) though he comes back to his homeland ... .

- ˙wo ˙sye, - ˙wo ˙two, - ˙wo ˙za = - ˙Gwo ˙sye, - ˙Gwo ˙two, - ˙Gwo ˙za

°wo ˙ta, vi (comes). SEE ota; ˜wo-, ˜wol(q), ˜wom, ˜won, ˙wona-.

˙woten, vi retr modifier. ¶ na ˙za ˙woten ˙t ey nˈ (1445 ¹Yong 51) if he had come forward.

- ˙wo ˙toy, modulated accessive. SEE - ˙toy. ¶ --

nil ˙Gwo ˙toy (1462 ¹Nung 3:24b) --- we say (as follows:) ... . SEE ˙hwo ˙toy (nˈ), ˜pwo ˙toy.

~ nˈ. ¶ QUM- HYANG tu ˙lwo ˙toy nˈ (1462 ¹Nung 6:68a) hearing the sound, ...

wu, n [NK] = wi (above)

wu, postmod adj-n insep. general appearance. SEE -ul ~ .

-wu, [Seoul] var < -o (AUTH indic). SEE -swu.

-wu, suffix. VAR -o; ALT -chwu. CF -i / -li.

1. derives adverbs. 1a. from adjectives. ¶ caywu promptly, briskly < cāyta. kolwu equally, evenly < koluta. toywu severely, hard < tōyta. cacwu often < cac.ta. maywu very < maypta pungent. seywu [DIAL, obs] often, very < sēyta strong. ttalwu / ttalo separately, apart < ttaluta different. palwu / palo right, directly < paluta. CF kwutwu-soy miser < kwut.ta stiff + -wu.

1b. from verbs. ¶ nemu overly < nēm.ta. macwu (= macˈ) facing, opposite < mac.ta. pathwu closely, densely < path.ta. motwu all < motuta = mouta gathers. ilwu hardly, (not) possibly < iluta reaches. nulwu over a long period < nulta advances, increases. makwu (= makˈ) indiscriminately, wildly < makta obstructs. tolwu / tolo again, back < tōlta turns around, circles. kochwu straight < kot.chwuta corrects.

2. derives noun from verb. ¶ nalwu ferry < naluta transports.

-wu-, suffix. 1. derives vc from adj and vi. ¶ kkaywu- < ˙skoy ˙Gwo- wake someone up < kkāy- < ˙skoy- wake up. palwu- < pa ˙lo- right it ← palu- < pa ˙lo- be right. ilwu- < il ˙Gwu-, il ˙Gwo- accomplish, achieve < ī-l- < ˜˜il- come into being, happen. CF -i-, -hi-, -ki-, -chi-, -ukhi-, -ikhi-, -li-, -iwu-, -ywu-; -hwu-, -kwu-, -chwu-, -ay-; - ˙Gi-, - ˙Gwo-, - ˙Gwu-, -o-, -u-.

2. derives vt from vt. ¶ milwu- shift, delay, infer < mī-l- < ˜mil- push, shove. ketwu- < ke ˙twu- reap; ... < ket- < ket- roll / gather up.

- ˙wu- = - ˙wᵘ/o-, modulator. SEE Part I, §9.9.10.

wu hata, postmod adj-n insep. it seems to be. SEE -ul ~ .

-wul, ? suffix. CF yewul, kaywul. [? < mul]

- ˙wul(q) modulated prospective modifier.

1. (with epitheme extruded from the subject). Example?

2. (epitheme extruded from object). Example?

3. (summational epitheme). ¶ *ne-huy ˙tolˑh i* SOYNG-ˈˈSO peˑswul ˈˈiˑl ol ˑhim ˑpse KKWUW ˑho.ya ˑza hoˑl i ˑˈla (1459 Wel 10:14b) you people must endeavor to pursue the casting off of birth and death. *aˑtok hon ˈˈsaloˑm i ingey ˈˈnaˑm ol ˈˈaˑti ˈˈmwot ˑkwo ˑsye* PPWULQ-ˈˈTTWOW ˑay heˑmul ˈˈnilGwuyˑye keyGulˑGe mulˑlwul ˑptuˑt ul ˈˈnaylˑss oy* (1463 Pep 3:180ab) dim-witted people, not knowing that they will henceforth emerge, make errors in their Buddhism and show a lazy disposition to withdraw. *caˑchwoy eˑlwu puˑthwul ˑtoy ˑep.swun ˑt iˑla* (1465 Wen 1:1:1:15b; ˑep.swun = ˈˈep.swun) there is nothing one can rely upon in the way of a clue. ... *keyGulˑGe [ˈˈHHAY-CYWO] ciˑzwul mozoˑm i ˑep.swoˑla* (1481 Twusi 7:1b) he is too lazy to want to plot a scam.

wūl(q) < ˈˈ*wul(q)* < *wuˑl[u]l(q)*, prosp mod < **wūlta** < ˈˈ*wu[l]ˑta* (cries).

- ˑ*wuˑla*, modulated indic assert. ¶ ˑ*kwulwum ˑskin swuˑphuˑl ey ne-huy ˑmwu.l ul ˑetwuˑla* (1481 Twusi 7:30b) in the woods between the clouds I will get to have the lot of you.

wuli < ˑ*wuˑli*, n. we/us; I/me; our(s), my/mine. ~ **ney**, ~ **tul**, ~ **kkili** SAME. ¶ ~ **cip** / **apeci** / **kāy** my house / father / dog. ~ **cwuin** my husband, ~ **manwula (an sik.kwu)** my wife (Dupont 321). ~ **nala** our / my country; Korea. ~ **māl** our language; the vernacular; Korean. ~ **Hānkwuk-in we** Koreans. **Ku sensayng un wuli hanthey em hata** That teacher is severe with us. **Wuli nun hyengcey (i)p.nita** We are brothers. CF **ce-huy, na, ce**.

¶ ˑ*wuˑli eˑzi aˑtoˑl i ˑwoy lopˑkwo ˈˈipˑkey towoyˑya* (1447 Sek 6:5a) parent (= mother) and son we are left lonely and bewildered. *wuˑli* ˈˈTTWOW-ˈˈLI ˑlan poˑlisiˑkwo (1459 Wel 2:69a) rejects our doctrine and ... . *wuli Gwos kyeyˑGwuˑm ye n'* (1459 Wel 2:72a) if we are the ones defeated. *wuli n' tuˑlwoˑn i* (1459 Wel 2:69b) as we heard it ... . *wuli ˑtwo* (1459 Wel 8:100a) we too. *wuˑli* ˈˈWUY ˑhoˑya (1459 Wel 13:36a) for / to us. *iˑnon ˑwuli heˑmu.l iˑla* (1463 Pep 2:5b) this is our mistake. *wuli ˑuy mozoˑm ay* (1463 Pep 2:231a) in our hearts.

¶ *ˑwuli ˑtolˑh i* ... (1447 Sek 9:40a, 19:30b; 1459 Wel 10:12b, 10:31a, 18:18b) we.

-**wuli**, suffix; ? HEAVY ↔ -**oli**. **pongwuli** peak < **pong** peak. [? var < -**el.i**]

wūlm < ˈˈ*wulm* < *wuˑl[u]m*, subst < **wūlta** < ˈˈ*wu[l]ˑta* (cries). CF *wuˑlwum*.

- ˑ*wulqˑtayˑlwo*, modulated prospective modifier + postmodifier + pcl. ¶ ... *holo hon penˑpap meˑkwumˑkwa ˑpaˑp ol meˑkwulqˑtayˑlwo* ˈˈ*hyeyˑye meˑkwumˑkwa* ... (1459 Wel 7:31b) ... and eating once a day, and eating (counting just as one eats =) as often as one feels like, and ... .

- ˑ*wulˑ(t)ti(...)* = -ˑ*wulqˑt i(...)*, modulated prosp modifier + postmodifier + particle/copula.

ˑ*wulqˑt i* (pcl). ¶ ˑ*ile 'nˑt oˑlwo ciˑzwulˑtt i aˑni '.n i ˑˈla* (1463 Pep se:12a) for this reason I will not create one [here].

- ˑ*wulqˑt iˑla* (cop) = -*wolqˑt iˑla*. ¶ ... *ilˑhwuˑm ul [ˈˈ]CWO ˑyˑla nilˑGwulqˑt iˑla ˑhoˑsi.n i ˑˈla* (?1468- Mong 49b) he said that the name will be called "Patriarch" [when ...].

- ˑ*wulˑ(t)tiˑmye* = -ˑ*wulqˑt iˑm ye*, modulated prosp modifier + postmodifier + cop subst + cop inf. ¶ *yelˑGwun* ˑSYEY lol ˑHWA hwolˑttyeyn mwoˑlwoˑmay SSYWUN-PWONGˑul puˑthwulˑtt iˑm ye ZIN THYEN-ˈˈNGAN ˑol yeˑlwolˑttyeyn ˑSSILQ ˑlwo ˑptut aˑlwoˑm ol puˑthwulˑtt i.n i ˑˈla* (1463 Pep 4:148b) if one is to transform the open world, it will be necessary to rely on guileless ways and if one is to open people's deva-eye (unlimited vision) one will have to rely on really knowing the meaning.

~ **n'** (+ pcl). ¶ *ches swoˑli ˑlol eˑwulˑGwe ˑpswulqˑt iˑm ye n' kolˑWa ˑssuˑla* (1451 Hwun-en 12b) when you combine initial sounds write them in a row.

- ˑ*wulˑ(t)tiˑni* = -ˑ*wulqˑt iˑn i*, modulated prosp modifier + postnoun + cop mod + postmod. ¶ *mwoˑton ˑkhun* MANG-ˈˈNGE ˑlul kuˑche teˑlwulq t iˑn i* (1462 ¹Nung 6:111b) it is to end and remove all great untruths. *[ˑLWOK-CWON] ˑulwo mwoˑlwomay ˑnaˑl ol taoˑtolwok meˑkwul t iˑn i ˈˈsyen meˑli ˑpwo.m ol ˈˈtywohi iˑkuynoˑta* (1481 Twusi 15:6a) we drink from a leaking vat, till we unwittingly use up the days; whitened hair defeats the spring with ease.

- ˑ*wulqˑt i.n i ˑˈla* (cop indicative assertive). ¶ *mwoˑlwoˑmay* ˑSYENG-ˈˈKYENG ˑul puˑthwulˑt i.n i ˑˈla* (1465 Wen 2:3:2:44a) will have to cross the sacred boundary. *stwo panˑtoki* ˑCCO-ˑSYEY ˑhi mozoˑm ol ˑpswulqˑt i.n i ˑˈla* (?1468- Mong 39b) and moreover one must use great care.

-ˈwul ˈ(t)tinˈtayn = -wulq ˈt in ˈt ay ˈn',
modulated prosp modifier + postnoun + cop
modifier + postnoun + pcl + pcl. ¶ˈtam ˈkwa
cip ˈkwa ciˈze NUNG ˈhi ¨pwoˈm ol ˈpske
kuˈchwulq ˈt in ˈt ay n' (1462 ¹Nung 2:43b) if
you build a wall and a house and (in doing so)
effectively destroy the view … .

-**wulwu**, suffix (makes adv). ¶(t)**teykwulwulwu**
= (t)**teykwul** (t)**teykwul** rolling. **hwulwulwu**
whistling (< ?).

wuˈlwom, wuˈlwum, modulated substantive <
¨wu[l]ˈta (cries). ¶wuˈlwoˈm ol (1462 ¹Nung
9:69a). wuˈlwuˈm ul (1445 ¹Yong 96). wuˈlwum
ssoˈloy (1459 Wel 1:27b). CF ¨wulm.

wumphek, bnd adn; HEAVY ↔ **omphak**. ¶ ~
nwun sunken eyes. [var < **wumphuk/omphok**
sunken, hollow; ?< ōng + pha- dig + -k]
NOTE: Linguists in S Korea inconsistently spell
¨wumpheng-nwun¨ but ¨omphak-nwun¨.

-ˈ**wum**, modulated substantive (= -ˈ**wom**).
 -ˈwuˈm a. ¶meˈkywuˈm a (?1517- ¹No 1:55b)
I will feed them.
 -ˈwuˈm ey. ¶cwuku[ˈ]m ye saˈlwo.m ol ¨ati
¨mwot ˈkeˈnol za ˈhomolˈmye ˈkil.h i kiˈlwu.m
ey ¨es.tyey hoˈl i ˈGwo (1481 Twusi 8:29a)
ignorant of death and life as I am, my path is
all the longer, so what am I to do?
 -ˈwuˈm i. ¶seˈnuleˈwu.m i towoyˈnwon t[o]
iˈla (1482 Kum-sam 2:29b) … results from its
[the autumn's] being cool.
 -ˈwuˈm ul. ¶aˈp[i] oy cwuˈkwuˈm ul tutˈkwo
(1463 Pep 5:158a) hearing of the father's
death. ciˈp uy s ¨teˈlewuˈm ul ˈphyesiˈnwon
cyenˈchoˈyˈn i (1482 Nam 1:5a) is the reason
that he deigns to tidy up the mess of the house.
 -ˈwuˈm uˈlwo. ¶khwu.m uˈlwo (1459 Wel
1:29b) by its size.

-ˈ**wun**, modulated mod. ¶SA-MWON ˈon noˈm oy
ciˈzwun nyeˈluˈm ul meknoˈn i '-ngi ''ta (1447
Sek 24:22a) the begging monk (śramaṇa) eats
fruits that others have grown. SEE -ˈ**won**.

wūn < ¨wun < *wuˈl[u]n, modifier < **wūlta**
< ¨wu[l]ˈta (cries).

-**wung**, suffix. ¶**macwung** meeting, reception <
mac-wung < **mac.ta** meets. **kitwung** pillar <
kit-wung = **kit** [obs]. ? **cipung** roof < **cip-
wung** < **cip** house – but LKM 1968:223:n30
says this is from *cip wuh* 'house top' as in *cel-
ˈlwo kaˈm ye cel-[ˈ]lwo [ˈ]wono[ˈ]n i 'n cip
wuˈh uy s ¨cyepi ''Gwo* (1481 Twusi 7:3b)
'swallows freely come and go atop the hall, and
… '; see ⋯**h**, ⋯**ng**.

-ˈ**wu-ngiˈ'ta**, modulated polite + copula indic
assertive. ¶¨naycywong ¨nay mwuyˈye wol
ˈmwoˈm i ¨epˈswu-ngiˈ'ta (1462 ¹Nung 3:117a)
in the end there is no body to move.

-**wuni**, suffix [DIAL]. ¶**kolccakwuni** [DIAL] ravine
< **kolccak(i)** valley. CF **echekwuni** a whopper.

-ˈ**wuˈn i**, modulated mod + postmod. ¶i ˈsaloˈm
on ZYE-LOY ˈpuˈlywu.n i ''m ye (1463 Pep
4:76b) this person served the tathāgata and … .

-ˈ**wun ˈt iˈla**, modulated mod + postmod + cop
indic assertive. ¶caˈchwoy eˈlwu puˈthwul ˈtoy
ˈep.swun ˈt iˈla (1465 Wen 1:1:1:15b; ˈep.swun
= ¨ep.swun) there is nothing one can rely
upon in the way of a clue.

wūnun < ¨wuˈnun < *wuˈ[lu]ˈnun, proc mod
< **wūlta** < ¨wu[l]ˈta (cries). ¶¨wuˈnun swoˈli
(1447 Sek 19:14b) the sound of crying.

wus, adn (= **wis**). the upper, the above, the
outer [< **wu** + obsolete adnominal particle **s**].
 ¶ ~ **akwi**, ~ **al**, ~ **cali**, ~ **cekoli**, ~ **cim**,
~ **ēlun**, ~ **kan**, ~ **kel(k)i** = ~ **os**, ~ **nal**,
~ **nyekh**, ~ **os**, ~ **pang**, ~ **pi**, ~ **salam**, ~
salang, ~ **tekkengi**, ~ **toli**, ~ **tōn**.
 ¶ ~ **kil** = **wis kil**, ~ **mok** = **wis mok**, ~
mul = **wis mul**, ~ **pay** = **wis pay**, ~ **pyen**
= **wis pyen**, ~ **tong(ali)** = **wis tong(ali)**.
 ¶**wusq (n)i** = **wisq (n)i** upper teeth / tooth.
 ¶**wus ccak** = **wi ccak**, **wus ccok** = **wi ccok**;
wus chay = **wu chay**, **wus cheng** = **wu
cheng**, **wus chung** = **wi chung**, **wus thek** =
wi thek, **wus thong** = **wi thong**.

-ˈ**wu-ˈtoy**, modulated accessive. SEE -ˈ**ywuˈtoy**.

¨**wuy / ˈWUY** ˚**hoˈta**, vnt = **wi hata**. ¶ceˈy ¨nim-
ˈkum [ˈWUY] ˈthaˈhosilˈss oy (1445 ¹Yong 121)
saying that they do it for their own king, he … .
ˈmwo.m ol ˈWUY khwo ¨saloˈm ol ˈWUY thi aˈni
hoˈm ye n' (1482 Kum-sam 5:48-9) when it is
for my own body and not for (other) people … .

¨**wuy / ˈWUY ˈhoˈya** (hon ˈhoˈsya), inf. for
(the sake of); to (a person). ¶naˈy aˈki ¨wuy
ˈhoˈya ¨eˈte pwoˈkwo ''l ye (1447 Sek 6:13b)
I'd like you to seek her out [as a bride] for my
boy. ¨ney kaˈci s ¨SSYWUW-¨KHWO ˈlol ¨wuy
ˈhoˈya ˈhonwoˈla ([1447→]1562 Sek 3:35a) I
endeavour on behalf of [relieving] the Four
Miseries. HWON-QIN ¨wuy ˈhoˈya aˈzoˈm i
ˈwonaˈton ipaˈtwoˈl ye ˈhoˈnwo.n i s ˈka (1447
Sek 6:16ab) are you entertaining relatives come

Sek 6:16ab) are you entertaining relatives come for a wedding? ALSO: 1447 Sek 6:1a, 13:49b.

¶ `wu˙li ˙wUY ˙ho˙ya` (1459 Wel 13:36a) for / to us. `nom ˙wUY ˙ho˙ya` (1459 Wel 17:54a) for the sake of others. `¨na l' ˙wUY ˙ho˙ya nilo˙sywo˙sye` (1459 Wel 1:17b) please tell it to me. `¨na l' ˙wUY ˙ho˙sya` (1463 Pep 2:231b) [Buddha will] for my sake. *ne-hoy ˙wUY [˙]ho˙sya* (1463 Pep 7:17a; the text dot beside Hankul "*ne*" is not an accent mark) for you people. *i˙kot hon ¨sa˙lom ey ˙za ˙wUY ˙ho˙ya e˙lwu nil˙Gwol ˙tt i˙m ye* (1463 Pep 2:172ab; sic, *…lom-ey…*) one can effectively tell it to just this kind of person, and ... . ALSO: 1459 Wel 7:17b, 13:35ab; ... .

y, abbr pcl. 1. [obs] = **i** (nominative pcl). But the modern Seoul **nay** (< `˙na y` < *`˙na˙i`) can be treated as an abbreviation of **nay ka** 'I'; similarly **ney** and **cey**.

2. = **uy** (genitive pcl). **nay** (< *na˙'y* < **na˙oy*) = **na uy** 'my, of me / mine', **ney** (< ¨*ne y* < **ne˙uy*) = **ne uy** 'your, of you / yours', **cey** (< *ce˙'y* < *ce˙uy*) = **ce uy** '(of) one's own; my; I [as subject of an adnominalization]'.

(**'**)**y-**, abbr < **i-** (cop). SEE **key 'ta = ke yta**, etc.
'y-, abbr < *˙i-* (cop) after a vowel. After *i* or *y* written '- (= *'[y]*-). NOTE: It is unclear just when the preconsonantal abbreviation of the copula stem after vowels other than *i* came to suppress its palatal glide: we are not sure when `˙na˙'y˙la` (1459 Wel se:4b) became **na 'la** '(says) it's me'. The full stem is still heard in explicit speech and especially for the short forms **in, ilq, im**, but the *'y* version persists only in a few expressions such as ··· **key 'ta** (< **ke[s] ita**) = ··· **ke 'ta** and ···**nun pay 'ta** (< *-n^{u}on pa˙'y*···) = **-nun pa 'ta**. Notice also dialect forms such as **nayntul** for **na 'n tul** 'though be me'. The shortening must have taken place before 1730, for otherwise the form *ho.ye 'la* found in *[TTYWEN] hol twong mal twong ho.ye 'la* (1730 Chengkwu 104; cited from LCT) 'it is barely conveyed' should be *ho.ye 'yla*. Two examples from somewhat later: *phuyl stwong mal stwong ho.ye 'la* (1763 Haytong 61) 'it is about to bloom', *kuy nwukwo 'm ye* (1763 Haytong 86) '(and) who is he?'.

-y. The reduced form (after a vowel) of **-i**, incorporated from **i** 'one = person / thing, fact' (or from the nominative particle) by attachment to many nouns in different dialects, including modern Seoul. SEE **-i**.

-y, suffix (makes irreg der n; SEE **-i**). ¶ **mukey** weight < **mukepta** is heavy; **thay** fissure < **thata** (= **thuta**) splits. But **ttey** < *˙ptey* 'raft' < *˙ptu-* 'float' must be **pt[u-G]ey* and **ttey** < *ptey* 'group' (?1517⁻ ¹No 2:24b) < *ptu-* 'separate' must be **pt[u-G]ey*; SEE **-ey**.

-y- < **-y-** (< *-˙i-*), suffix. 1. derives vc. ¶ **kēnney-** < ¨*ken˙ney-* carry it over ← **kēnne-** (= **kēnnu-**) < ¨*ken˙ne-* < ¨*ket-°na-* cross over. **pōyta** < ¨*pwoy-* show ← **pota** < °*pwo-* see.

2. derives vp. **pōyta** < ¨*pwoy-* get seen ← **pota** < °*pwo-* see.

-ya- (after *y, i* but not *l*) < **-a-** = **-ka-** (var) = **-ke-** (effective). SEE *˙ho.ya-*.

ya, postmod (question).

1. (? abbr < ··· *i˙[G]a*). SEE *-ke˙n ya, -no˙n ya, -te˙n ya, -u˙l ya, -u˙n ya*.

2. (? conflated form of 1). SEE *-u˙l i˙ya, -u˙n i˙ya, -˙twoswo˙n i˙ya; -ulq˙s ya = -ulq˙s ye*. Also: *˙na˙c ya˙pa˙m ya* (?1517⁻ Pak 1:68a) whether day or night. But see *˙ye*.

ya < *˙ya*, postmodifier. the question (whether). SEE **-un ~, -(ess./keyss.)nun ~, -ul ~, -tun ~; ~ ka, ~ man, ~ nun, ~ siph.ta, ~ ya**. SYN **ka, i, a, ya, ko**.

ya, pcl, alternant (after a vowel) of **a** (vocative / exclamatory). hey! say! o(h)! 1. (vocative). ¶ **Chelqswu ya!** Hey Chelsswu! **Sāy ya sāy ya phalang sāy ya!** Oh birdie, birdie, blue birdie!

2. (exclamatory). SEE **-keyss.ta ya**.

ya, pcl: (after vowel) alternant of **iya** − CF *yya*; (after consonant) abbr < **iya** (SEE **-umyen ya**); [DIAL, obs] *sa* < *˙za*. only if it be; if (it be), when it comes to; even, indeed. (Marks a reinforced contingency or prerequisite for the main clause. One of the two clauses expresses something unlikely, unexpected, or anticipated to be difficult or unpleasant.)

1. (after n or n + pcl). ¶ **ku cey ya** (= **ku cey ey ya**) only then. **Twī ya toylq tay lo toyla 'ci** (So long as it is later on) I don't give a damn what becomes of it! **Onul ey ya wass.e** TODAY you finally came (after promising to so often). **Onul ey ya ssess.kwumen** You got it written TODAY (at last)! **Incey ya sayngkak i nanta** NOW I remember.

2. SEE **ya māl lo**.

3. SEE **-e ya**. 4. SEE **-e ya 'ci**.

5. SEE -e se ya
6. SEE -ko ya, -ko ya mālta
7. SEE -ulq pa ey ya
8. SEE (ya) mālta ko

NOTE 1: The meaning of this focus particle is mutually exclusive with that of un / nun (as for) and usually that of to (also / even), but see the note on to for possible cases of un / nun iya and to ya. The particle freely follows other particles and sequences, but i / ka (nominative) and ul / lul (accusative) are usually omitted. Yet in Middle Korean ˙(l)ul / (l)ol ˙za occurs, and most examples of ˙i˙za and of its reduction y˙za represent the nominative pcl ˙i + ˙za. SEE -ta ka ya.

NOTE 2: The particle ya is not very common in the modern language, except for structures such as -e ya (hanta, ...). A study by Andrew Dillon of about 40,000 syllables of fiction in a monthly magazine turned up only 32 examples and of those only ten followed a noun or particle. But MK ˙za is quite common in many early texts.

NOTE 3: The shape ya is attested from 1747.

ya (after a vowel) = ia (cop); (after a consonant) abbreviation < ia. ¶Cinq-ca ya It's the truth! Kōngkal ya (= ia) It's a lie! Na ya or Ce ya (Hello,) it's me [on the telephone].

ya, abbr pcl = iya (only if it be, ...)

yā < ˙i ai, n [Phyengan DIAL (Kim Yengpay 1984:95)] = i ai he; she. CF kā, tā.

-˙ya, variant of -˙ye (inf after ···i- or ···y-), irregular inf of ˚ho- 'do'.

-˙ya ˙ci-ngi ˙˙ta, (after ···i- or ···y-) = -˙a ˙ci-ngi ˙˙ta, inf (or effective inf) + aux polite + cop indic assert. ¶SA-PPA ˙SYEY-˙KAY ˙lol ye˙huyya ˙ci-ngi ˙˙ta (1459 Wel 8:4-5) we want to distance ourselves from this present world (of sāha).

yak < ˙QYAK, adnoun. about, more or less, approximately (= ··· ccum). ¶~ ī-sip pun around / about twenty minutes. ~ payk myeng a hundred persons or so. CF keuy, tāykang (adverb); han (adnoun); ··· ina.

(-)yak < ˙ZYAK, postn. a bit less than, just under, a little short / weak of. ANT (-)kang. SYN (-)ppa-tus.

ya ka, postmod (question) + pcl. SEE -un ~ , -nun ~ , -keyss.nun ~ .

yāl- bound adverb (adj prefix). ¶yāl-mipta is detestable. ? yal-kwuc.ta is strange, queer [vowel shortening unexplained]. CF yālus hata is queer. [? DIAL abbr of yāsal peevishness]

? *-ya˙l ya

? -ya˙l ye, effective prosp mod + postmod. SEE ˙ho.ya˙l ye.

? *-ya˙l ywo

ya māl lo (after a vowel), pcl + n + pcl. ('as what I am indeed saying' =) indeed, precisely, exactly, just, really, none other than. ¶Ku ya māl lo ... Indeed ... . Ku ya māl lo cinceng han hakca 'ta He is indeed a true scholar. Yenge ya māl lo sēykyey ey se kacang elyewun māl ita English is really the most difficult language in the world. Incey ya māl lo wuli ka kwelki hal ttay 'ta Now is the time for us to rouse ourselves (in)to action. Ce ya māl lo cal-mos hayss.ˢup.nita I am the one at fault. SEE iya māl lo.

ya man, particle + particle. SEE -e ya man.

ya man (un), postmod + pcl (+ pcl). ¶Onul kath.un nal ey pi ka ol ya man (un) wūsan ul tulko na-kass.ta It's unlikely to rain on a day like this, but I brought my umbrella anyway.

ya 'myen, abbr < ya (ko) hamyen

-yan (after y, i; but l links without y) < -an = -kan (var) = -ken (effective mod). SEE -˙yan ˙t i, -˙yan ma˙lon; ˙ho.yan.

? *-ya˙na

yang, n; postmod (-unq/-nunq/-tunq/-ulq ~).
1. abbr < mo.yang < ˙MWOW-˙YANG. ¶Ku uy yang ul chyē 'ta pwass.ta I looked up at his figure.
2. (< ¨yang < ˙YANG), postmodifier vni. ~ hata pretends to.
4. (? abbr < yēyceng < YE-˙TTYENG; ?< ūyhyang < ˙QUY-˙HYANG) expectation, plan, intention.

yang < YANG, adn (abbr < se.yang Occident). Occidental; foreign(-style). ¶ ~ kalpo prostitute catering to foreigners. ~ ttalki strawberries. ~ meli western hairstyle. ~ ssal Formosan or Annamese rice. ~ pha onion. ~ kho a big nose.

¹yāng < ¨LYANG, num, adn. both. ¶ ~ cipang both places. ~ kuktan both poles. ~ tangpha both parties. ~ ekkay both shoulders. ~ son both hands. ~ ccok both sides.

¹yāngpan < ¨LYANG-PAN, n. 1. [obs] gentleman, nobleman. 2. [pejorative] "gentleman", so-and-so. CF i ~ . ¶wuli cipq ¹yāngpan my husband.

? *-ya˙n i (˙´la), ? *-˙ya.n i ˙Gwa/ ˙Gwo
- ˙yan ma˙lon, effective modifier + postmodifier. ¶ pay˙yan ma˙lon (1445 ¹Yong 90) capsized. SEE ˙ho˙yan ma˙lon
? *-˙yan ma˙non
-ya˙nol (after y, i) = ? *-a˙nol = -ke˙nol. ¶ pwo˙nayya˙nol (1459 Wel 7:15b) though he sent her back. SEE ˙ho.ya˙nol
? *-ya˙nol ˙za
ya 'nta, abbr < ya (ko) hanta
? *-˙yan ˙ta
? -˙yan ˙ti(···) = -˙yan ˙t i(···)
? *-˙yan ˙t i˙la (˙t i˙n i, ˙t i.n i ˙´la)
-˙yan ˙ti = -˙yan ˙t i (after y, i) = -˙an ˙t i, effective mod + postmod + pcl. ¶ CHYE-˙KWEN towoy˙yan˙ ˙t i SAM-NYEN ˙i ¨mwot ˙cha i˙sye (1447 Sek 6:4ab) it is less than three years since he acquired a family, and ... . SEE ˙ho˙yan ˙t i.
? *-yan ˙tyeng
ya nun, postmod (question) + pcl. SEE -un ~ , -nun ~ .
? *-ya˙n ya, ? *-ya˙n ye, ? *-ya˙n ywo
-˙yasi- (after ···y, ···i) = -˙asi- = -˙kasi-, -˙Gasi- (effective hon) = -ᵁ⁄ₒ˙si˙ke- (hon effective). SEE ˙ho˙yasi-.
-˙ya 'sil, (after ···y, ···i) inf + abbr < isil(q) (aux prospective mod). ¶ [HHWA-LYWUW] ˙non sas˙ki towoy˙ya ˙'sil ce[˙]k uy ho[˙]ma ˙phi ˙sto.m ol ¨nay˙Gwo (1481 Twusi 8:30ab) a worthy horse exudes a greasy sweat when it has become with colt.
-˙ya ˙'sila 'n ˙t oy, (after ···y, ···i) inf + abbr < isi˙la 'n ˙t oy (aux subj attent + abbr < hon ˙t oy, verb mod + postmodifier + pcl). ¶ [˙]na y [˙]CYWUNG-SOYNG oy a[˙]pi towoy[˙]ya ˙'sila 'n ˙t oy (1463 Pep 2:86b) since I have become the father of all beings ... .
-˙yasi˙ton, (after ···y, ···i) provisional honorific. ¶ ZYE-LOY ¨CYWONG-¨CYWONG SSIN-˙LUK ˙ul ˙pwoy˙yasi˙ton (1459 Wel 8:43b; ˙pwoy··· = ¨pwoy··· [broken type?]) when the tathāgata has displayed all sorts of supernatural powers ... .
ya siph.ta, (··· postmod) + aux adj. SEE siph.ta.
-˙ya ˙sye, (after ···y, ···i) inf + pcl. ¶ [˙]na [˙]two [˙]stwo ˙i ˙kot ˙ho˙ya ˙QILQ-˙CHYEY ˙TTWOW-SO y towoy˙ya ˙sye (1463 Pep 3:197a) I am become the leader of all, and ... .
-˙ya ˙¨sywo-, (after ···y, ···i) infinitive + abbr < ˙i˙sywo- (aux + modulator).
-˙ya ˙¨sywo˙la (indic assertive). ¶ swo˙n on ho˙ma [˙CYWUY] khe˙nol ˙na y howo˙za skoyya ˙sywola (1481 Twusi 8:31b) the guests are already drunk and I alone am sober.
-˙ya ˙¨sywom (substantive). ¶ wo˙lay na˙kunay towoyya ˙¨sywo.m i tangtang ˙i ˙wuli [¨TTWOW] ˙y.n i (1481 Twusi 7:9a) it is our natural way to have become a longtime traveler.
-˙ya˙ta (after y, i) = -˙a˙ta, effective indic assertive. SEE ˙ho˙ya˙ta.
-˙ya˙ton, -˙ya˙tun (after y, i) = -˙a˙ton. SEE ˙ho˙ya˙ton, ˙ho˙ya˙tun.
yāy, abbr < i ay. this child; he/him, she/her; you; you there, hey there! CF kyāy, yāy.
ya ya, postmod (question) + pcl. SEE -un ~ , -nun ~ .
···˙ya ˙ys-, infinitive + auxiliary. SEE ˙ho˙ya ˙ys-.
···˙ya ˙ys˙kasi˙n i. ¶ ye˙huy˙ya ˙ys˙kasi˙n i (1462 ¹Nung 5:72b).
···˙ya ˙ys˙nwon ˙t i. ¶ towoy˙ya ˙ys˙nwon ˙t i (1462 ¹Nung 1:113a).
···˙ya ˙ys.te˙n i ˙´la. ¶ ¨TTWOW-TTYANG ˙ay ˙wa ˙SSYANG-¨SYWUW y towoy˙ya ˙ys˙te.n i ˙´la (1465 Wen 2:3:2:91b) had come to the seminary and become its head.
···˙ya ˙ys˙tesi˙ta. ¶ MWUN-SSYWU-SO-˙LI ˙SSYANG-¨SYWUW y towoy˙ya ˙ys˙tesi˙ta (1462 ¹Nung 1:30b) Mañjuśri had become the head (seminarian).
ya 'yss.ta, abbr < ya (ko) hayss.ta
ya(y) yo = ye(y) yo, abbr < ie(y) yo (polite copula). Younger speakers say (y)ey yo.
-ya˙za, inf (after ···y, ···i) + pcl. ¶ ˙nwu 'y ˙stol ˙ol kol˙hoy.ya˙za mye˙nol ˙i towoy˙ya wo˙l i ˙ya (1449 Kok 36) whose daughter is the one we are to pick as a wife for my son? SEE ˙ho.ya˙za.
ye, pcl; HEAVY → ya (vocative − after a vowel).
ye < ˙'ye, abbr (after vowel) = ie < (?*)˙i˙ye, cop inf; CF ila < ˙i˙la. VAR yey, ey. CF -u˙m ye > -umye, -u˙m ye n' > -umye n(un).
NOTE: In MK ˙i˙ye (most often after a vowel and reduced to ˙'ye) was used as a quasi-particle 'whether, or; and', 'or/and the like': wo˙cik nwo˙phon nwol˙Gay ˙'ye [¨KWUY-SSIN] is.non ˙tos ˙hwo.m ol ¨a-ti˙Gwey (1481 Twusi 15:37b) we just may know that lofty songs and the like seem to be spiritual, but ... . SEE ˙i˙ye.
ye··· (this) SEE yeki, yethay; CF yo, i.
-ye < YE, suffix. Makes excess numerals out of decimal and higher-unit Chinese numerals.

¶**sip-ye** ten or so, ten odd, over ten. **payk-ye** 100 odd. **payk īsip-ye** some 120. **chen-ye** over a thousand. **mān-ye** over ten thousand.
ˑye (? var < ˑya), postmod (question). SEE -uˑn ye, -keˑn ye, -teˑn ye, -uˑl ye; -ulq ˑs ye, -un ˑt ye. The form -uˑl i ˑye may be a conflation of -uˑl ye, which is a variant of -uˑl ya < -uˑl i ˑ[G]a. SEE ˑya.

Perhaps an example: ˑna.c ye ˑpa.m ye (1481 Twusi 8:29a), ˑnaˑc ye ˑpaˑm ye (?1517⁻ Pak 1:13b, 1518 Sohak-cho 8:15a) 'whether day or night'. But that could be taken as ˑnac ˑˑye ˑpam ˑˑye, a contraction of ˑna.c i ˑye ˑpa.m i ˑye (1475 Nay 2:2:17b), here treated as a usage of the copula infinitive.

ˑˑye < (?*) ˑi ˑye (cop inf → ˑi ˑla), after vowel or consonant: ˑkil[h] maka ˑs ˑnon [= maˑka ˑs ˑnon] hon ˑpheˑki s ˑsaˑm i ˑpi ˑwonaˑtun kwos ˑphwuyˑGwo polom ˑkolˑkyeˑtun yeˑlum moys.non keˑs ˑye (?1517⁻ Pak 1:40a; moys.non ← moyc-non) a hemp plant blocking the road blossoms when it rains and bears fruit when the wind strikes. SEE **ye** (NOTE), **iye** < (?*) ˑi ˑye.

-ˑye, 1. orthographic variant of -ˑe (inf) after ···y- and ···i but not ···l-; irregular alt after (ˑ)ho- 'do' − (ˑ)hoˑye = (ˑ)hoˑya. ¶iˑkuyˑye (1459 Wel se:9a) win, conquer. ¨hyeyˑye (1447 Sek 6:6a, 1459 Wel 7:31b) count, consider. twuˑliˑye (1447 Sek 6:29b, 1459 Wel 7:13b) fear. SEE -ˑye ˑtwo, ˑho.ya ˑtwo.

2. abbr < ···i ˑye = ···i ˑGe (effective inf).
-ye-, 1. orthographic variant (after ···y-, ···i- but not ···l-) of -e- = -ke- (effective).

2. abbr < ···i ˑye- = ···i ˑGe- (effective inf).
ⁿye < ¨NYE, adn (abbr < ⁿyeca < NYE-¨CO). woman, female. ¶~ **tongsayng** a male's younger sister. ~ **su' nim** (= ⁿye-sung) a nun. ~ **hak.kyo** a girls' school. ~ **paywu** an actress. ~ **uysa** a woman doctor. ANT **nam**.
yek < ˑYEK, adverb = **yeksi** (likewise)
yekan < ZYE-KAN, adverb, adnoun, bound noun.

1. trifling, petty, mediocre [+ neg predicate]. ¶**Ku nun yekanq īl ey nun sēng nāyci anh.nunta** He never gets angry over trifles. **Yekan nayki ka ani 'ta** He is no ordinary (mediocre) person; he is an uncommon person.

2. (+ neg or implied neg) not a little, to no small extent / degree; quite, extremely, terribly. ¶**Ku lul keki se poko na nun yekan nōllaci anh.ess.ta** I was not a little surprised to see him there. **Khi ka khutoy yekan khun khi ka ani 'ta** He is tall and even unusually tall. **Tōn i mue yekan tul.e ya 'ci** It is so expensive, you see, ... (I can't afford it). **Yekan caymi iss.ci anh.ta** It is a lot of fun (or: quite interesting).

3. ~ **ani 'ta** is uncommon, unusual, rare, extraordinary, remarkable. ¶**yekan ani 'n nolyek ul hanta** makes great efforts. **yekan ani 'n miin** a woman of extraordinary beauty, a rare beauty. **Onul chwuwi ka yekan ani 'ta** It is awfully cold today. **Ku uy caycwu ka yekan ani 'ta** He has a remarkable talent.
yeki (< yeˑkuy < ingeˑkuy), n. this place, here, this point / spot. LIGHT → **yoki**. SYN **i kos**. CF **cēki**, **keki**.
yeksi < ˑYEK-¨SSI, adverb (= **yek**). likewise, as well, also; indeed, after all, as expected, all the same. ¶**Yeksi ku api ey ku atul ikwun!** Like father, like son. CF **i yeksi**, **ku yeksi** = **ku-yek**.
yeˑkuy (< ingeˑkuy), n, adv. (at / to) this place, here. ABBR **yey**. ¶**yeˑkuy ˑtwo** HE-KHWONG ˑiGwo (1482 Nam 1:50a) this place, too, is a void. ˑna y yeˑkuy ˑkal ilˑhwo.n i ¨HHWUW ˑey yey ˑwa ¨eˑtwu.l i ˑˑla (1482 Nam 1:36b) = ˑna y yeˑkuy ˑkal.h ol ilˑhwo.n i ¨HHWUW ˑey yey ˑwa ¨eˑtwu.l i ˑˑla (1482 Kum-sam 4:28a) I have lost a knife here; later I will come back here to get it.
yel-, bnd adn (prefix). young, new. ¶~ **mu(wu)** new turnips. ~**-cwungi** a chick out of its shell; a small weak person. [? < **yēlta**, ? < **yēn** < ¨ZYWEN soft, ? < **elita**]
yēl(q) < ¨yel(q) < *yeˑl[o]l(q), prosp mod < **yēlta** < ¨ye[l]ˑta (opens it). CF ¨**yell** ··· .
ye la, abbr cop inf + pcl. SEE **ie la**.
yele < yeˑle, num (alt of **yeles** as adn). several, many; various, diverse, manifold. ¶~ **salam** several people, all sorts of people. ~ **hak.kyo** many schools, various schools. ~ **mo** many angles; polyangular, many-angled. ~ **tay** many generations. ~ **nal / tal** a number of days / months. ~ **hay** many years, several years; perennial.

yele kaci all sorts (of), various kinds (of); several varieties, many varieties. ¶**yele kaci uy mulken** all sorts of things. **yele kaci lo wilo hata** consoles a person in every way. **Cangmi**

kkoch ey nun yele kaci ka iss.ta There are many varieties of roses.
 yele pen several (or many) times, frequently, often. ¶Yele pen Ilpon ey ka-ponq īl i iss.ta I have been to Japan a number of times. Ku hanthey yele pen māl hayss.ta I told him over and over again.
 yele pun many esteemed people; all of you, everybody, ladies and gentlemen. ¶Yele pun, annyeng hasip.nikka Good morning, (all you) people. Good afternoon, ladies and gentlemen. Yele pun i ku kyēyhoyk ey pāntay hayss.ta Many people were against the plan.
yeles < ye˙leh, noun, numeral (as adnoun yele). a large number, many; many (lots of) people. ¶Kuleh.key sayngkak hanun sālam i yeles ita There are many who think that way. Yeles i ku sihem ey ¹nakcey hayss.ta Many failed in that examination. Talkyal yeles i [better: yele kay ka] ssek.ess.ta Many of the eggs have gone bad. [yel 'ten' + -es 'approximate numeral']
-˙ye.l i ˙Ga (after y, i) = -˙e.l i ˙Ga, effective prosp mod + postmod + postmod. ¶['KWUYK-"THYEY] ˙uy [QAN-NGWUY] ˙lol kwu˙thuyye "hyeyye.l i ˙Ga (1481 Twusi 10:12a) will we think in particular about the safety of the national polity?
˙yell ··· (+ ˙i postmod) < *ye˙l[o]l(q), prosp mod < "ye[l]˙ta (opens it). ¶"yell [i] ˙ye˙n ywo (1481 Twusi 7:25b).
yēlm < "yelm (example?) < *ye˙l[o]m, subst < yēlta < "ye[l]˙ta (opens it). Cf "ye˙lwum.
"ye˙lwum, modulated subst < "ye[l]˙ta (opens it)
? *-ye˙l ya / ye / ywo, effective prospective modifier + postmod. See ˙ho.ye˙l ye.
ⁿyēm < ˙NYEM, quasi-free n. intention, plan, idea; mind, spirit. ¶caysan ul moulq ⁿyēm un tangcho ey thulliko his original plan to save up money was thwarted, and ··· . kāmsa uy ~ ulo in a spirit of gratitude, with grateful heart. Cf NKd 741a.
? -yen (after y, i; but l links without y) < -en = -ken (effective modifier). ¶? cyemiyen ([1493 ?→]1610 Ak.hak kweypem Tongtong, so says LCT 655b, but the Taycey-kak edition has no Hankul there). Cf -˙ye.n i ˙Gwa.
'˙yen, abbr < ˙i˙en = ˙i˙Gen, copula effective modifier. See '˙ye˙n i.
yēn < "yen < *ye˙[lu]n, mod < yēlta < "ye[l]˙ta (opens it). ¶ ··· "yen ˙tos ho˙n i (1481 Twusi 22:50a) seems to open ··· .
yēn < "ZYWEN, 1. adnoun. light (in hue). ¶~ pola light purple. ~ punhong light pink. ~ cwuhwang light chrome. 2. adj-n. ~ hata is light, soft. Ant cin (hata).
¹yen < LYEN, 1. n. continuation. ~ hata, vnt. connects, continues.
 2. adnoun (prenumeral). continuing through, running. ¶ ~ sahul three days running. ~ ithul two consecutive days, two days in a row. ~ sam-nyen three full years, three years through.
? *-ye˙na
yeng, alt of ieng (> iyeng) [Ceycwu DIAL] = iko: See iyeng.
yengmun [< ?], noun. 1. the situation, the circumstances. 2. reason, cause, the matter. ¶musunq ~ ulo for what reason, why; for some reason.
yeni = yenu
'˙ye˙n i, effective mod + postmod. See -u˙l [i] '˙ye˙n i.
-˙ye.n i ˙Gwa = -˙e.n i ˙Gwa = -˙ke.n i ˙Gwa, (effective mod + postmod) + pcl. ¶˙chay s kuli˙mey muy˙ye.n i ˙Gwa (1465 Wen se:58b) [the horses] moreover are afraid of the shadow of a whip.
? *-˙ye.n i ˙Gwo; ? *-˙ye˙n i '˙la
? *-˙yen ma˙lon, ?*-˙yen ma˙non
? *-ye˙nol. Cf -˙e˙nol. See -ya˙nol.
? *-˙yen˙ta
-˙yen˙ti(···) = -˙yen˙t i(···)
-˙yen˙ti = -˙yen˙ti (after y, i) = -˙en˙t i, (effective mod + postmod) + pcl. ¶wol cek uy pisun meli elkhuyyen t i SAM-NYEN ila (1747 Songkang 1:11b; cek-uy) it is three years now that my hair, combed upon arriving, has been tangled. Cf -˙yan˙t i.
? *-˙yen˙t i˙la (˙t˙i˙n i, ˙t i.n i '˙la)
? *-yen˙tyeng
yenu [Seoul usually pronounces it yeni], adnoun.
 1. ordinary, usual. ¶Yenu sālam un kulenq īl ul mōs haci! An ordinary person wouldn't be able to do that, you know.
 2. the other (ones), most (the usual) other. ¶I ¹nok.um-ki n' acwu mukepci man yenu kes un an kulay This tape recorder is heavy, but most others aren't that way. Hwāhak un yeni kongpu hekwu talle se silhem ul mānh.i hay ya toynta Chemistry, unlike (the usual) other studies, requires many experiments.

-`ye´nul` (after ···y, ···i) = -`e´nul` (= -`ke´nul`, lit concessive). ¶ `kwulwu´m i pi´chwuyye´nul [´ZILQ-KWAN] ´ol [CCYWONG] ´hosi´n i` (1445 ¹Yong 42) a cloud shone [red], whereupon he [Thaycwo] took his astrologer's advice. `sta´h ay ´sal ´i ¨pskeyye´nul ¨LYEY-CCYWEN i swo´sa ´na´a ´CYWUNG-SOYNG ´ol ´KWUW ´ho´tesi´n i` (1449 Kok 41) his arrow pierced the earth, but there a sweet spring gushed forth and saved the living creatures.
? *-`ye´nul ´za`
yēnun < ¨`ye´nun` (example?) < *`ye´[lu]´nun`, proc mod < ¨`ye[l]´ta` (opens it).
? *-`ye´n ya`, ? *-`ye´n ye`
? *-`ye´n ywo` (CF -`e´n ywo`)
ye-po (< `yeki poo` 'look here'), interjection.
  1. Also **ye-pwā (la), ye-posio, ye-posey yo, ye-posipsio** — hey!; hello! (said to gain one's attention). A telephone is usually answered **Ye-posey yo!** 'Hello!'. This expression (in any style) "is sometimes used to show contempt when one gets angry, irritated, annoyed, or when fighting" (M 1:1:420). Also heard (often showing annoyance): **I p(w)ā / po(o)!** See here!
  2. (wife speaking to husband) you, dear.
-**yepta**, bound adj-n -w-. ¶ `nō-~` is offensive, displeasing (< bound noun 'anger' < ¨`NWO`).
ye se, abbr copula infinitive + pcl. SEE **ie se**.
-`ye-si-` (after y, i) = -(ᵁ⁄o)`si-´ke-` (honorific effective): -`yesi´na`, -`yesi´nol`.
-`yesi´na`. ¶ `swokwom si´lwon swul´Gwuy ´yey pi´lwok [´KUY-¨MA] ´lol moy´yesi´na` (1481 Twusi 7:34a) though they have tied the saddle horse to a wagon loaded with salt.
-`yesi´nol`. ¶ `SAM-CHYEN ´KAY lol pichwuyyesi´nol` (1465 Wen se:43a) he illuminated the three thousand worlds, whereupon ... .
yess.nun, abbr / alt < **iess.nun** (that it was)
yess.ta, abbr / alt < **iess.ta**. was; ~ (ka) was and then. ¶ **Yātang cengchi-ka yess.ta (ka) yētang cengchi-ka ka toyess.ta** He was an out-party politician but then he became an in-party politician. **Yātang cengchi-ka yess.ta (ka) yētang cengchi-ka ka toyess.ta (ka) hanta** He changes back and forth between being an out-party politician and an in-party politician.
-`yesy···` = -`ye ´sy···`, abbr < -`ye isy···` (< `isi-`)
-`ye ´sye` SEE `ho´ye ´sye`
-`ye´ta` (after y, i) = -`e´ta`, effective indic assertive. ¶ ´`SYA-´LI-´PWULQ i i´kuyye´ta` (1447 Sek 6:31b [etc.]) Sāriputra has won!
-`´ye´ta`, abbr copula effective indicative assertive (= ´`iGe´ta`). SEE -`u´l ´ye´ta` = -`u´l [i] ´ye´ta`.
yethay, adverb. up to now, till now. ~ **kkaci**, ~ **kkes** SAME. SYN **ipttay**.
-`ye´ton` (after y, i) = -`e´ton` (provisional). ¶ ¨`salo´m i ´swo.n o´lwo ´to´l ol kolo´chye ¨salom ¨pwoyye´ton` (1462 ¹Nung 2:23a) if a person shows the moon to people by pointing at it with his hand ... . ¨`sa´lo´m i ¨ywu´mwu ´lul mas´tye pwo´nayye´ton` ... (1518 Sohak-cho 8:22a) if a person has entrusted a letter to be sent, ...
-`ye´tun` (after y, i) = -`e´tun` (provisional). ¶ ¨`camskan twolwo pwo´nayyetun [´]CYEY ho´kwo twolwo pwo´nay´ywo.l i ´´la` (1459 Wel 7:15b) if you send her back for a while we will return her after the festival.
-`´ye ´two`, inf + pcl. `hyey´ye ´two` (?1517- Pak 1:61b) even figuring. SEE `ho.ye ´two`.
YEY When not initial **yey** is not distinguished from /ey/. But after pause (thus often initially in a word) the two syllables are kept distinct, though not in certain areas (such as Masan or Mokpho) which have only /yey/. The syllable /yey/ itself may come from ¹**yey** (with the liquid suppressed) or from **yay** (with the vowel raised). If you cannot find a word you seek under **yey**, try ¹**yey** or **yay** or **ey**. SEE **LYEY**.
´**yey** (orthographic variant after ···i, ···y, or ···ywu) = **ey** pcl. ¶ ¨`twu ha´nol s so´zi ´yey ´ka´sya` (1447 Sek 6:45b) goes between the two heavens. `kwuy ´yey tut´nwon ka` (1449 Kok 2) as if (to wonder whether) you are hearing it in your ear. ´`QAK-´CHYWU ´yey` (1459 Wel 21:120b) = ´`QAK-´CHYWU ´ey` (id.:117a) to [one of the] hells for incarnations of the evil; `e´nu ´CHYWU ´yey` (1459 Wel 21:27a) to which hell. SEE -`ki ´yey`.
  NOTE 1: The stem ´`kaci` 'branch' is truncated before attaching the locative / allative particle, which then takes the shape `[´]ay`: `cum´key s ´kac´ ay yenco´n i` (1445 ¹Yong 7) placed it on the branch of an oak — CF `namwo s ´kaci ´yey` (1481 Twusi 15:4a) on the branch of a tree. A similar truncation for ´`hway` 'torch' takes place in `sel´k uy s ´wos ´tol´h i ´hwa' ´yey ´na´a kel´Gi´m ye` (1459 Wel 2:33a) fancy raiments in wicker trunks emerged to be hung on the torches. SEE ¨`es´tyey`; ´`uy` (NOTE).

NOTE 2: Occasionally `yey is found after ··-e or ···a (He Wung 344): `spye `yey ni`lu.n i (1481 Twusi 7:22b) reached the bones; chima `yey s `aki `lol (1459 Wel 10:24b) the child in the skirt — CF two`ma [`Jay `sye ti`n i (1481 Twusi 16:16a) it fell from the chopping board, twoma ey s [TYE-`ZYWUK] ul sala kala (1795 ¹No-cwung [K] 1:18b) buy the pork (that is) on the chopping board. Apparently this occurs only when there is a y before the vowel or the preceding syllable contains i. There are a few examples that simplify ···y `yey as in `hwa' `yey (1459 Wel 2:33a) 'to the torches' where we expect `hway `yey. CF He Wung 323.

yey, abbr < ingey (or < ye`kuy) < inge`kuy, adv, noun. this place, here; CF. key, tyey. ¶ `i KYENG ti`nilq ¨salo`m i pi`lwok yey i`sye `two (1447 Sek 19:18a) even if there are people here who will preserve this sūtra .... ne-`huy ¨twul`h i yey `wo`nan `t i ¨en`me wo`la.n i `Gwo (?1517- ¹No 1:68b) how long is it since you two came here?

yey, 1. abbr < iey (= ie) it is. ¶Mues yey yo /mueseyyo/ = Mues iey yo = Mues ie yo What is it? Chayk yey yo /chaykeyyo/ It is a book.
2. var < ye it is. ¶Mue yey yo /mueeyyo/ = Mue ye yo = Mue ie yo What is it? Catong-cha yey yo /catongchaeyyo/ = Catong-cha ye yo = Catong-cha ie yo It is an automobile.
VAR ey, i.

yēy, adv (CF nēy). 1. yes; I see; I understand. 2. eh? oh? really?

yēy, noun. (= yēys cek) olden times, yore. SEE yēys.

ye ya, abbr cop inf + pcl. SEE ie ya.

yēyceng < YE-`TTYENG, noun. prearrangement; a plan, a schedule. ~ phyo a schedule, a prospectus. ~-il a prearranged date, the scheduled date. ····ulq ~ ita plans / expects to (do); ABBR -ulq yang ita. SEE -ulq ~ .
~ hata, vnt. arranges beforehand, plans, prearranges, schedules; expects, intends.

`yey n', abbr < `yey `non, pcl + pcl. ¶ `poy `yey n' ··· `KWOLQ-¨SYWUY `yey n' ··· es`key `yey n' (1449 Kok 70) in her belly ··· and in her bone marrow ··· and on her shoulders .... `konon `pi yey n' kwo`ki `mu.l ey `na `ys`kwo (1481 Twusi 7:7b) in a fine rain the fish are out in the water.

`yey `non, pcl + pcl. ¶KYENG-¨UY COY `yey `non SWO-THWONG ho`kwo (1586 Sohak 6:9b) = KYENG-¨UY COY `yey `non ikoy myeng ho`kwo (1518 Sohak-cho 9:10b) is well-informed on scriptural rituals and ... .

`yey s, pcl + pcl (= `ey s). ¶ `chiwuy `yey s kwo`ki non (1481 Twusi 7:7a) fish in the cold. ¨PPEM un ¨swoy ¨tiki `yey s `swo.h i `Gwo (1462 ¹Nung 2:20b) ¨PPEM is [a Chinese word that means] a mold in the casting of metal. SAM-`SYEY `yey s ¨i`l ol (1447 Sek 6:18a) events (matters) of the three states of existence. ZIN-KAN `SYEY `yey s `khi [`]psunon ke`s i.m ye (1482 Kum-sam 2:17b) it is something that is greatly used in / by the human world, and ... . `kaps ¨ep.sun kwu`su.l un ¨pwo[`]poy `yey s ¨pwo[`]poy '`n i (1482 Nam 1:33a) the priceless jewel is a treasure among treasures.

yēys, adn, bnd n. (var < yēy yore). old, olden, ancient. ¶ ~ nal / cek olden times (= yēy). ~ puthe = yēy lo puthe from (of) old. ~ nay chinkwu my old friend.

··· `ye `ys-, abbr < ··· ye is- (infinitive + aux).
··· `ye `ys`kwo. ¶ `ciye `ys`kwo (1481 Twusi 7:11a).
··· `ye `ys.non. ¶ `cye `ys.non (1481 Twusi 7:1a).
··· `ye `ys.no`n i. ¶psku`lye `ys.no`n i (1481 Twusi 16:73b).
··· `ye `ys.no`n i `Gwo. ¶ `myes `hoy `lol [¨TTYANG-SA] `ay s na`kunay towoy `ye `ys.no`n i `Gwo (1481 Twusi 7:26b) for how many years have you been a traveler to Chángshā?.
··· `ye `ys.no`n i '`la. ¶nul`kun nam`k un ko`cang se`li lol [¨]ti[¨]nay[`]ye `ys.no[`]n i '[`]la (1481 Twusi 7:10a) the old tree has been through much frost.
··· `ye `ys.no`n ywo. ¶kozol`h i ¨ka`m ay ¨nwu `y ci`p i towoy `ye `ys`no`n ywo (1481 Twusi 8:42a) at the departure of autumn whose house has it become?
··· `ye `ys.nwo`la. ¶ ··· ey `i [SOYNG] `ol pu`thye `ys.nwo`la (1481 Twusi 7:6b) has staked this life (upon ···).
··· `ye `ys.nwo`n i. ¶ ··· towoy `ye `ys.nwo`n i (1481 Twusi 8:5a) it has become ··· .
··· `ye `ys.ta`ka. ¶mwulwu`ph ul phye `ys.ta`ka (1481 Twusi 8:27b) [he was sleeping away and] had his knees spread out, and then ... .
··· `ye `ys.two`ta. ¶ ¨pwuyn swu`phu[l s] nacwoy s `hoy s pi.ch i tol`Gye `ys.two`ta (1481 Twusi 7:4a) the evening sunlight of the empty forest lingers suspended (in the air).

˙yey ˙sye, pcl + pcl (after *i*, *y*) = ˙ey ˙sye. ¶ KUM-KANG ˙on ˙swoy [ˉ]yey ˙sye nan ˙mos kwu˙tun ke˙s i˙n i (1459 Wel 2:28b) diamond is the hardest of the metals. ku ˙pwup swo˙li [ˉ]yey ˙sye ¨ma˙l ol nil˙Gwo˙toy ··· (1447 Sek 24:1b) what the drum said was this: ··· . ˙PYEN ˙un SSYANG-˙LYEY yey ˙sye talol ˙ss i˙Gwo (1459 Wel 1:15a) ˙PYEN ("queer") means that it is different from the usual, and ... .

˙yey ˙sye, pcl + inf < °sye˙ta (vi 'stands'). Examples? SEE ˙oy ˙sye.

˙yey ˙ʼsye, abbr < ˙yey i˙sye, pcl + vi inf. being at. Examples?

˙yey ˙two, pcl + pcl. ¶ ˙SSYWOK ˙oy CAY-˙KAY ˙yey ˙two (1462 ¹Nung 8:4-5) even for popular religious fasts. SEE ˙ey ˙two.

yey yo (also ey yo) it is: 1. abbr < iey yo (= ie yo). 2. var < ye yo (= ie yo).

˙yey ˙za, pcl + pcl (= ˙ey ˙za = ey ya). ¶ ˙i ¨HHWUW ˙QILQ-˙QUK ˙SO-CHYEN na˙mon ˙hoy [ˉ]yey ˙za ˙stwo MI-˙LUK ˙PPWULQ ˙i isi˙l i ˙ʼla (1447 Sek 23:13a) only a hundred million four thousand some years from now will a maitreya Buddha exist again. ˙CING-¨CHYWU ˙yey ˙za pi˙luse ¨NGA-¨THYEY ˙lol na˙thwo˙no.n i ˙ʼla (1465 Wen 2:3:1:25a) not until one attains truth through substantiation does one manifest the form of the ego. na y ˙mwom ˙NGWOY ˙yey ˙za mu˙su˙k ul as˙ki˙l ywo (1459 Wel 7:28b) what will be taken aside from my body/self?

ʼ[y]Ge˙m ye, cop effective subst + cop inf. SEE -u˙l i ˙Ge˙m ye.

ʼy˙Gen, abbr < ˙i˙Gen (cop effective mod)

ʼyGe˙na, abbr < ˙iGe˙na (cop effective advers). ¨a˙mwo ʼyGe˙na (1459 Wel 1:13a). ¶ CHYENG-˙CCYENG hon ˙PPI-KHWUW ʼyGena ˙PPI-KHWUW-NI ʼyGe˙na (1462 ¹Nung 7:7b) whether it be a pure mendicant monk or a nun. SEE ¨amwo (ʼyGe˙na).

ʼyGe˙n i, abbr < ˙iGe˙n i, copula effective mod + postmodifier.

~ ˙Gwa (pcl). ¶ ˙cas an˙h ay n' [ˉSSIP-˙MEN ¨HHWO] ʼyGe˙n i ˙Gwa ˙i sta˙h ay n' ¨twu-˙ze ci˙p ilwo˙ta (1481 Twusi 7:7b) inside the fortress are a hundred thousand households, while on this land there are [just] two or three houses.

ʼyGe˙nul, abbr < ˙iGe˙nul, cop lit concessive. ¶ [*CCOY-LANG] ˙i [¨KANG-¨HWA] ʼyGe˙nul (1445 ¹Yong 111) the jackals and wolves [= invaders] made havoc.

ʼyGe˙n ywo, abbr < ˙iGe˙n ywo, cop effective inf + postmodifier. ¶ ˙nwu ʼyGe˙n ywo (?1468-Mong 22b) who was it?

ʼy˙Gey, abbr < ˙i˙key (copula adverbative) after vowel. After *i* and *y* written ˙ʼGey = ʼ[y]˙Gey. Examples after other vowels?

ʼyGe˙za, abbr < ˙iGe˙za, cop effective inf + pcl. ¶ CYE-˙PPWULQ ˙i SSI ʼyGe˙za nilo˙kesi˙tun ˙CYWUNG-SOYNG ˙two SSI ʼyGe˙za si˙le tut¨cop˙no.n i ˙ʼla (1482 Kum-sam 4:50b) if the Buddhas tell [the doctrine] only when it is time, the people can hear it only when it is time.

··· ʼy[G]wo, pcl < cop ger. and. ¶ ne ʼy[G]wo no ʼy[G]wo talu.l ya (1876 Kakok 122; noy = /nay/) = ne ʼ[G]wo cye ʼ[G]wo talu.l ya (id. 13) would you and I be different?

ʼy˙Gwo, abbr < ˙i˙Gwo, cop ger. After *i* and *y* written ˙ʼGwo = ʼ[y]˙Gwo. ¶ ¨won ˙kwo.t on a˙zo.m ol [ˉWUY] ˙ho.ya ʼy˙Gwo ˙stwo [¨QUM-˙SSIK] ˙ul [ˉWUY] ˙hwo.m i a˙ni ˙.n i ˙ʼla (1481 Twusi 8:33a) our coming is for our kinsmen and not for drink and food. ku ¨PWON-LOY s il˙hwu˙m un ¨amwo ʼy˙Gwo na ʼy il˙hwu˙m un ¨a˙mwo ˙KAP ˙ilwo˙n i (1463 Pep 2:222b) his original name is such-and-such and my name is something-or-other "kap". ¨TTWOW ʼy˙Gwo (1459 Wel 9:24a) it is the Way and ... .

ʼy˙key, abbr < ˙oy˙key < ˙oy˙kungey. to (a person). SEE na ~ .

(ʼ)yl(q), abbr < il(q). SEE key ʼl(q) = ke yl(q) = kes il(q).

ʼyl(q), abbr < ˙il(q) (cop prospective mod) after a vowel. After *i* or *y* written ʼl(q) = ʼ[y]lq. ¶ nim-kum kwa [SSIN-¨HHA] ʼyl s oy (1632 Twusi-cwung 6:32a) it being a matter of king and court ... .

ʼy˙la, abbr < ˙i˙la (cop) after vowel. After *i* and *y* written ˙ʼla = -[y]˙la. ¶ ··· wo˙nol ˙za CIN-˙SSILQ s ˙i ˙PPWULQ-¨CO y ˙ʼla (1463 Pep 2:8a) ··· today at last is this true disciple of Buddha. ˙kye ʼy˙la (1463 Pep 1:195b) it means 'chaff'. ˙na ʼy˙la it means 'I' (1459 Wel se:4b), sul˙he ˙ho.nwon yang˙co ʼy˙la (1459 Wel se:16a) it means 'a sad look'. ¨TTWOW ʼy˙la (1459 Wel 9:23b) it is the Way.

ʼyla˙two SEE ila˙to

yla˙wa = ˙ila˙wa (after a vowel). than. ¶ ptele tywu.m i [PPWO-¨LYWUW] ylawa mwoncye ʼylwota (1481 Twusi 18:18_; cited from He Wung) its fall was earlier than that of Púlĭu.

'yla ˙za SEE ˙ila ˙za

'yle˙la, abbr < ˙ile˙la, cop retr indic assert. ¶ *ku twoco˙k i PPWO-˙SALQ S CCYEN-˙SYEY SOYNG S QWEN-SSYWU 'yle˙la* (1459 Wel 1:6b) that thief was an enemy from the bodhisattva's life in an earlier world.

'yle˙n i, abbr < ˙ile˙n i, cop retrospective mod + postmod. ¶ *hon NGWANG ˙i il˙hwu˙m i PPIN-TTWUW-PPA-LA 'yle˙n i* (1447 Sek 24:11a) (there was) a king whose name was Bimbisāra – the first nominative is a thematized genitive.

'y˙lesi˙n i, abbr < ˙i˙lesi˙n i, cop retr hon mod + postmodifier. Example?

'ylwo˙la, abbr < ˙ilwo˙la, alt cop indic assert. ¶ ˙˙*es˙te 'n cyen˙cho ˙lwo ˙˙na ˙lol e˙li˙ta ˙ho˙sya ˙SYEK-˙˙CO 'ylwo˙la ˙hwo˙m ol ˙˙mwot ho˙l i '˙la ˙ho˙sino˙n i '-ngi s ˙kwo* (1459 Wel 9:35de) on what grounds do you say that I am too young and refuse to call me a disciple of Buddha?

'ylwo˙n i, abbr < ˙lwo˙n i, alt cop mod + postmod. ¶ ˙˙*alay ˙PALQ ˙˙CHOY-˙˙NYE matco˙Wa ˙PPEM-MA-LA ˙KWUYK LIM ˙CCYENG ˙SSO ˙lwo ˙kazo˙Wwon ˙na 'ylwo˙n i* (1459 Wel 8:92b) I met the eight comely maidens and went [with them] to Woods-Calm Temple in the land of the brahmans – with epithematic identification (stylistic inversion of the underlying subject = the Identified).

'ylwon˙t i, abbr < ˙ilwon˙t i, alt cop mod + postmod + pcl. ¶ *wo˙cik mozo˙m oy ˙HHYEN ˙hwon ke˙s ilwon˙t i ke˙wu˙lwu TYWUNG˙ey s ˙˙SSYANG ˙i CCYWEN-˙˙THYEY ˙i ke˙wu˙lwu 'ylwon˙t i ˙kot ho˙n i* (1462 ¹Nung 2:17b) the fact that it is something that appears only in one's mind is like the fact that an image in a mirror is in its entire substance [just] the mirror.

'ylwo˙ta, abbr < ˙ilwo˙ta, alt cop indic assert. ¶ *mwon˙˙cye 'ylwo˙ta* (1481 Twusi 20:6b) it is the first time.

'ylwo˙toy, abbr < ˙ilwo˙toy, alt cop accessive. ¶ *nil˙kwu˙p i ˙PYEN ˙ho˙ya a˙hwo˙p i towoy˙n i ˙˙ta YANG-˙SWU 'ylwo˙toy* (1462 ¹Nung 7:24a) seven turns into nine; both are odd numbers ... .

'y˙l ywu, abbr < ˙i˙l ywu, cop prosp mod + postmod (= ˙ywo). ¶ *ne a˙n' 'ye nwu 'y˙l ywu* (1462 ¹Nung 2:30b) if not you who will it be?

(')ym, abbr < im. SEE key 'm = ke ym = kes im.

'ym, abbr < ˙im (cop subst) after a vowel. After *i* or *y* written 'm = ˙[y]m.

'y˙m ye, abbr < ˙i˙m ye (cop subst + cop inf) after a vowel. After *i* or *y* written '˙m ye = ˙[y]˙m ye. ¶ *SWON˙on a˙to.l i˙m ye SWON-˙˙CO 'y˙m ye* (1459 Wel 7:1a) descendants are sons and (are) grandsons, and ... . ˙˙*ne 'y˙m ye [˙]CYWUNG-SOYNG ˙tol˙h i* (1459 Wel 8:5b) you and all living creatures.

(')yn, abbr < in. SEE key 'n = ke yn = kes in; **nayntul = na 'n tul, neyntul = ne 'n tul, ceyntul = ce 'n tul.**

'yn, abbr < ˙in (cop mod) after a vowel. After *i* or *y* written 'n = ˙[y]n. ¶ *CIN-ZYE 'yn cyen˙cho 'y˙la* (1465 Wen 1:1:1:47a) is the reason it is true. ˙*TTAY-SSIN ˙i ˙THAY-˙˙CO 'yn ˙kwo˙t ol a˙lan ma˙lon* (1447 Sek 24:52a) the minister was aware that he was the prince, but ... . SEE 'yn˙t ol.

'y˙na, abbr < i˙na, cop advers. ¶ ˙˙*amwo 'y˙na* (1447 Sek 9:17a, 21a) anyone. ˙*PPI-KHWUW 'y˙na ˙PPI-KHWUW-NI '˙na* (1447 Sek 19:29b) whether mendicant monk or nun.

'y˙n i, abbr < ˙i˙n i, cop mod + postmodifier. ¶ *phwung˙˙lywu 'y˙n i* (1447 Sek 13:9a) it means 'music'. CF '˙n i.

'y˙n ka, abbr < ˙in ka, cop mod + postmod. SEE a˙ni˙n˙ka.

? 'yn˙t i, abbr < ˙in˙t i, cop mod + postmod + particle.

'yn˙t ol abbr < ˙in˙t ol, cop mod + postmod + pcl. 1. that it is. ¶ ˙*cywong˙kwa mol˙Gwa ˙lol˙hyenma 'yn˙t ol ˙˙al[o].l i˙Gwo* (1449 Kok 52) I wonder know how many slaves and horses there are. ˙˙*a˙loy s˙tule 'ys˙ten ˙˙HEM-˙˙TTWOW 'yn˙t ol ˙˙a˙ti ˙˙mwot˙ho˙ya* (1459 Wel 21:120b; broken type on ˙˙TTWOW) not knowing that it was the dangerous path he had entered before. ˙*kwot ˙i˙sywo 'yn˙t ol ˙˙al˙m ye* (1482 Kum-sam 2:3a, spelled ˙˙*sywoyn-tol*˙) knew at once that it was this ox, and ... .

2. despite the fact that it is; though it is. ¶ ˙*NGWOY-˙˙TTWOW 'yn˙t ol a˙ni cwocco˙Wo˙l i* (1449 Kok 99) though they are heretics will they not follow [the dragon they worship in its defeat]?

'yn˙t olwo, abbr < ˙in˙t olwo, copula modifier + postmodifier + particle. because it is.

'yn˙t ye, abbr < ˙in˙tye, cop mod + postmod + postmod. SEE -*un˙t ye*. ¶ *pwus˙ku˙li˙ti a˙ni*

ˈhoˈno.n i ˈnon ku YWU ˈyn [ˈ]t ye [sic] (1586 Sohak 4:43a) is it for that reason that they are not ashamed?

(*)/yo/. Hankul symbols were invented to write both /yu/ and /yo/; though these did not exist in 1445 Seoul speech, they were said to be found in dialects. From forms in modern dialects it is possible to reconstruct several words that must have had *yo in pre-Hankul Korean (LKM 1978, 1979). For internal evidence of *yo see the explanation of ˈhoˈya under the entry of °hoˈta. The dialect of Ceycwu island retains a reflex of yo but it is unclear how well that is now distinguished from ye. No evidence has been found to encourage reconstructing *yu.

yo, n, adn; LIGHT → i. CF ko, co; yoki; ye··· .

1. [pejorative] this little (one). ¶ ~ kath.i like this. ~ nom you little thing, you squirt; you despicable / nasty / mean fellow.

2. right near at hand (in time or space). ¶ ~ say, ~ cimak these days, nowadays, lately, recently. ~ kūnche (ey) (in) this neighborhood, near / around here. Yo neme cengke-cang i iss.ta There is a station just over on the other side (of here).

yo < ˈywo, postmod 1. [obs] = ya (question). SEE -un ~ , -nun ~ .

2. [colloq, poetic; SYN ko]. SEE -un ~ , -nun ~ , -tun ~ , -ul ~ .

yo, 1. alternant or abbr of iyo, polite particle.

1a. (after a vowel) alternant of iyo. SEE -e yo, -ci yo, -un ka yo, -na yo, -sup.nita yo. ¶Nwukwu yo Who (is it)? — CF Nwukwu yo (< io) Who is it? [AUTH style (2b)].

1b. (after a consonant) abbreviation < iyo. ¶Kim sensayng yo (= iyo) (It is) Mr Kim. SEE (-ulq, -nun, -un, -tun) ke l'q yo (kellyo).

2. alternant or abbr of io (AUTH cop).

2a. (after a vowel) alternant of io. ¶Kim Paksa yo It's Dr Kim.

2b. (after a consonant) abbr < io. ¶Kim sensayng yo (= io) It's Mr Kim.

3. < iyo < ˈiGwo = iko is and

yo cuum, yo cum(ak) < ˈywo cwoˈzom (LIGHT → i cuum) = yo say

yoki, n. LIGHT → yeki. right here, this place. SYN yo kos.

yo kkaci lo, n + pcl + pcl. LIGHT → i kkaci lo (to this trifling extent).

yo-kkacis, cpd adn. LIGHT → i-kkacis. this kind of, such a ··· [usually pejorative]; so trifling / small / slight / little / small.

yole, LIGHT [pejorative] → ile; CF kole, cole.

1. vni. ~ hanta = yolenta does / says this way. 2. adj-n. ~ hata = yoleh.ta is this way.

yoleh.ta, adj -(H)- (inf yolay), abbr < yole hata

yoleta, vi (inf yolay), abbr < yole hata

yoli, adv. LIGHT → ili. CF koli, coli; yoki.

1. (= yoleh.key, yo-taci) in this way, like this, so. 2. (= ~ lo) this way/direction, here.

yomam-ttay, noun. LIGHT → imam-ttay

yo man = io man (AUTH cop + pcl)

yo-man, adnoun. LIGHT → i-man

? yo-mas, adnoun. LIGHT → i-mas

yo mo, cpd n; LIGHT → i mo (this corner / angle)

yo ˈna-ma, n + copula extended adversative (LIGHT → i ˈna-ma). although it is this; anyway, at least; even this much.

yo sai = yo say

yo say adnoun + noun; LIGHT → i sai. these days; nowadays, recently, lately.

yo ttawi = i ttawi

ˈysiˈkwo, abbr < ˈisiˈkwo, copula honorific gerund. ¶samaˈkwoy ˈhuk ˈthuˈl ey s heˈmu.l i ˈepˈsusyaˈm i ˈZI-ˈSSIP ˈNGWOW ˈysiˈkwo (1463 Pep 2:15-6) number 25 (of Buddha's distinctive marks) is that he has no blemishes such as moles or (black) spots or the like, and ... .

ˈysil(q), abbr < ˈisil(q), copula prosp modifier. Examples? SEE ˈsil(q).

ˈysin, abbr < ˈisin, cop hon mod. ~ ˈt ay nˈ SEE -un ˈtay nˈ. ~ ˈt ye SEE -un ˈt ye.

ˈsiˈn i (postmod). ¶ ˈSSILQ ˈol naˈthwosiˈn i ˈkwot ˈPEP-HHWA ˈysiˈn i (1462 ¹Nung 1:18a) that which expresses the truth is namely the Lotus sūtra.

ˈysiˈn i ˈˈla (postmod + cop indic assertive). ¶pwuˈˈthye ˈysiˈn i ˈˈla (1447 Sek se:1a) it is Buddha.

ˈys(i)ˈta, abbr < ˈis(i)ˈta (exists). CF ˈs(i)ˈta.

ˈysiˈta, abbr < ˈisiˈta, cop hon indic assertive. ¶SAM-ˈSYEY ˈyey s ˈiˈl ol ˈˈaˈlosil ˈss oy pwuˈˈthye ˈysiˈta ˈhoˈno.n i ˈ-ngˈ ˈˈta (1447 Sek 6:18a) ... and he commanded knowledge of the three states of existence; so therefore they say that he is Buddha.

ˈys.keˈnul, abbr < is.keˈnul. SEE -ˈe ˈys.keˈnul.

ˈys.keˈtun, abbr < is.keˈtun. SEE -ˈe ˈys.keˈtun, ˈhoˈya ˈys.keˈtun.

ʼys ˙kwo, abbreviation < is ˙kwo. SEE -˙a ʼys ˙kwo, -˙e ʼys ˙kwo, -˙Gey ʼs ˙kwo, -˙kuy ʼs ˙kwo, -kwa ʼys ˙kwo.

ʼys.non, abbr < is.non. SEE -˙a ʼys.non, -˙e ʼys.non.

ʼys.no ˙n i (ˈ ˙la), abbr < is.no ˙n i (ˈ ˙la). SEE -˙e ʼys.no ˙n i (ˈ ˙la).

ʼys.non ˙ta, abbr < is.non ˙ta. SEE -˙a ʼys.non ˙ta.

ʼys.non ˙t i, abbr < is ˙non ˙t i. SEE -˙a ʼys.non ˙t i.

ʼys ˙nwon ˙t i, abbr < is ˙nwon ˙t i. SEE -˙a ʼys ˙nwon ˙t i.

ʼy ˙sopte ˙n i, abbr < i ˙sopte ˙n i, auxiliary verb deferential retr mod + postmod. ¶ QA-NAN ˙kwa LA-NGWUN ˙un ˙pa[l]-˙ch[i] oy ˙sye ʼy ˙sopte ˙n i (1459 Wel 10:10a) Ānanda and Rāhula were standing at the foot.

ʼys ˙ta = ʼys(i) ˙ta, abbr < is(i) ˙ta (exists); CF ʼs ˙ta. SEE -u ˙l ye ʼys ˙ta.

ʼys.ta ˙ka, abbr < is.ta ˙ka. SEE -˙e ʼys.ta ˙ka.

ʼys.ta ˙n i, abbr < is.ta ˙n i. SEE -˙a ʼys.ta ˙n i.

ʼys.tan ˙t i ˙m ye n', abbr < -˙a ʼys.tan ˙t i ˙m ye n'. SEE -˙a ʼys.tan ˙t i ˙m ye n'.

ʼys.te ˙la, abbr < is.te ˙la. SEE -˙a ʼys.te ˙la.

ʼys ˙ten, abbr < is ˙ten. SEE -˙e ʼys ˙ten.

ʼys ˙tesi ˙n i s ˙ka, abbr < is ˙tesi ˙n i s ˙ka. SEE -˙a ʼys ˙tesi ˙n i s ˙ka.

y ʼsto ˙n ye, abbr pcl + abbr pcl + postmodifier. ¶ ˙homol ˙mye CYE-˙˙CO y ʼsto ˙n ye (1463 Pep 2:77a) how much more so the [great] masters! ˙homol ˙mye MWUN-˙CCO y ʼsto ˙n ye (1465 Wen se:11a) how much more so the letters!

ʼys.two ˙ta, abbr < is.two ˙ta, aux verb emotive indic assertive. SEE -˙e ʼys.two ˙ta.

ʼy ˙sye, 1. abbr < i ˙sye, aux verb honorific inf. SEE wa ʼy ˙sye.

2. abbr < i ˙sye < isi ˙ye, cop honorific inf.

(ʼ)yta, abbr < ita. SEE key ʼta = ke yta.

*ʼy ˙ta, abbr < *˙i ˙ta, copula indic assertive. Replaced by ʼy ˙la, after i and y written ˙ ˙la = ˈ[y] ˙la.

*ʼy ˙ti, abbr < *˙i ˙ti, cop suspective. Does not occur.

YU for Middle Korean is here written ywu even though then as now there was no *yu. In the Yale Romanization as we adapt it for Middle Korean, the high back rounded vowel is always written wu, though for modern Korean we omit the "w" after p ph pp m y. Similarly, the mid back rounded vowel of earlier Korean is always written wo, even after y.

*/yu/. Hankul symbols were invented to write both /yu/ and /yo/; though these did not exist in 1445 Seoul speech, they were said to be found in dialects. From forms in modern dialects it is possible to reconstruct several words that must have had *yo in pre-Hankul Korean (LKM 1978, 1979), but no evidence has been found to encourage reconstructing *yu. One dialect of Kanglung distinguishes a syllable yu: (with long unrounded high central vowel) from ye: (with long unrounded mid central vowel), according to [1]Yi Iksep 1972, who cites yu:l 'gallbladder', yu:pwu 'yes or no', yu:ngkam 'an elderly gentleman', and yu:n hata 'is soft' as opposed to ye:n 'kite' and ye:n kkwoch 'lotus blossom'. Since etymologically these should all be /ye/, it is unclear how the differentiation came about.

···yu, abbr ···wu = ···i-o

yu, abbr < iwu = io (AUTH copula)

···y.wo SEE ʼy[G]wo

ʼywo (> yo), adn, n. this. ¶ ʼywo [˙QILQ-˙HALQ] [˙]i (1579 Kwikam 2:63b) this cry. SEE ˙ywo so ˙zi.

ʼywo (abbr < ··· ˙i ˙[G]wo), postmod (question). SEE -u ˙n ywo, -no ˙n ywo; -(ᵘ/o) ˙l ywo = -(u)lq ka. As the etymology suggests, this does not occur after a noun, unlike ˙kwo and ˙ka: there are no examples of *N ʼywo or *N i ˙n ywo. VAR ˙ywu (SEE ʼy ˙l ywu). CF ˙ya.

-˙ywo- (after y, i) = -˙wo- (modulator): -ywo ˙la, -ywo ˙l i, -˙ywo.l i ˈ ˙la, -ʼywo ˙l ye, -˙ywom, -˙ywo.m o ˙lwo, -ywo ˙m (ay / ey, i, ol, on), -˙ywo ˙m i ˙Gwo, -˙ywon, -ywo ˙n i, -ʼywon t i ˙la, -˙ywo-ngi ˈ ˙ta, -˙ywol(q) (˙t i ˙m ye, ˙t iGe ˙n i ˙Gwa), -˙ywol(q) ˙tyeyn, -˙toy. SEE ˙ho ˙ywo- = ˙˙hwo-.

··· ˙ywo- < ···i-˙wo-: ··· ˙ywom, ··· ˙ywo ˙m i, ··· ˙ywo ˙m i ˙la, ··· ˙ywo ˙m i ˙za, ··· ˙ywo ˙m ol, ··· ˙ywo ˙toy.

˙ywo cwo ˙zom (cwo ˙zwom, cwo ˙zwum, cwu ˙zum), noun + pcl. lately. ¶ ˙ywo cwo ˙zwom aca ˙pi ma ˙zon ˙˙salo ˙m ol ˙˙pwo.n i (1481 Twusi 8:16b) recently I saw forty uncles. ˙ywo cwo ˙zwum nwu ˙n ey ˙˙pwo.n i [CIN-ˈSSILQ] ˙lwo [CING-˙˙HEM] hwom i is ˙twota (1481 Twusi 25:47a) recently seeing it with my own eyes I have substantiated my faith. ˙ywo cwu ˙zwum nwu ˙n ey s ka ˙soy a ˙za po ˙li-˙to ˙s ˈi ku ˙˙sya ˙wong ˙ol peng˙uliGwa˙to.n i (1481 Twusi 25:9b) lately she has spurned her husband as if he were a thorn in the eye.

-˙ywol(q) (after y, i), modulated prosp modifier. ¶ (with summational epitheme) ˙say ˙lwo pu˙the te al˙Gwoy˙ywol ˙cwu.l i ˙˙ep.sul ˙s oy (1482 Kum-sam 2:2a) since we are unable to reveal more from afresh ... .

... ˙ywolq < ...i-˙wolq: ~ ˙t iGe˙n i, ~ ˙t in ˙tayn'.

-˙ywo˙la, 1. (after y, i) modulated indic assert. ¶ [˙]ce y woy[˙]ywo[˙]la ˙thwo˙ta (1463 Pep 2:7a) says he himself is at fault. 2. SEE ho.ywo˙la.

-˙ywo.l i ˙˙la (after y, i), modulated prosp mod + postmod + cop indic assertive. ¶ ... twolwo pwo˙nay˙ywo.l i ˙˙la (1459 Wel 7:15b) ... we will return her after the festival. LOY-˙ZILQ ˙za pwo˙nay˙ywo.l i ˙˙la ho˙kwo ... (1459 Wel 7:16a) saying she would send him the very next day ... . SOYNG-˙˙SO ˙mul s ˙kyel s ka˙won-˙toy ki˙li ˙poy towoy˙ywo.l i ˙˙la ˙hwolq ˙t i.n i ˙˙la (1459 Wel 9:22b) it is (to be) said that ... and in the midst of the waves of life and death a lasting boat will appear. ˙na y ˙icey ne ˙y ˙e˙m[i] uy ˙˙kan ˙sta˙h ol ˙˙pwoy˙ywo.l i ˙˙la (1459 Wel 21:21b) I will now show you the land where your mother went. ˙mu˙su.m ula ˙˙cwulye cwu˙ke kwul˙he.ng ey myes.kwuy˙ywol ˙˙i.l ol ˙˙all i ˙Gwo (1481 Twusi 15:37b) ... how can we know the experience of starving to death and plugging up a hole [in the gutter]?

... ˙ywol(q) ˙t iGe˙n i < ...i-˙wol(q) ˙t iGe˙n i (cop effective modifier + postmodifier). ¶ ˙PEP ˙two ˙wohi˙lye pan˙toki po˙lywol ˙t iGe˙n i (1465 Wen 1:1:1:67a) the law itself would preferably have to be abandoned.

-˙ywolq ˙t iGen ˙tyeng (after y, i), modulated prosp mod + postmod + cop effective mod + postmodifier. ¶ ˙khun ˙PEP-˙KHUY towoy˙ywolq ˙t iGen ˙tyeng (?1468- Mong 44b) though it become a great vessel for the law, ...

-ywolq ˙t i˙la < ...i-˙wolq ˙t i˙la. ¶ pan˙to˙ki ˙˙nay cwo˙cha po˙lywolq ˙t i˙la hon ˙t oy (1462 ¹Nung 7:54a) said we must excommunicate them [if they commit the four pārājika sins].

... ˙ywol(q) ˙t i˙n i < ...i-˙wol(q) ˙t i˙n i. ¶ ˙culke˙wun ˙˙il is.ke˙tun hon ka˙ci ˙lwo ˙cul˙kywol ˙t i˙n i (?1517- Pak 1:72b) if he [my younger brother] has the occasion to rejoice, I rejoice the same way (= with him).

-˙ywol(q) ˙t i.n i ˙˙la (after y, i), modulated prosp mod + postmod + cop mod + postmod + cop indic assertive. ¶ pan˙toki ˙˙pwoyywol ˙t i.n i ˙˙la (1465 Wen 1:1:2:82a) it is bound to be shown.

-˙ywolq ˙t in ˙t ay n' (after y, i), modulated prosp modifier + postmod + copula modifier + postmod + pcl + pcl. ¶ ˙hota ˙ka ka˙won-˙toy ye˙huy˙ywolq ˙t in ˙t ay n' ˙PAN ˙on KON ˙ey e˙wul Gwo ˙PAN ˙on ˙˙KYENG ˙ey e˙wul ˙ss kot ˙˙tabeing so far away, half joins the root and half joins the mirror.

... ˙ywolq ˙t in ˙t ay n' < ...i-˙wolq ˙t in ˙t ay n'. ¶ a˙lwo˙m i ˙mwom sso˙zi ˙yey i˙sywolq ˙t in ˙t ay n' (1462 ¹Nung 1:55a) if knowledge is between bodies, then ... .

-˙ywo˙l ye, modulated prosp mod + postmod. ¶ ˙na y pwuthye towoy˙ywo.l ye hol ˙s i.n i (1482 Nam 2:6b) I want to become a Buddha.

-˙ywom (after ...y-, ...y- < ...i-), modulated subst. ¶ KAN-NAN ho˙n i ˙uy no˙m oy ˙˙pwo˙poy ˙˙hyey˙ywom kot ˙˙ta (1465 Wen 3:3:1:62a) it is like a poor man's counting another's treasures. mol me˙kywom ˙kot hi ... (1482 Nam 2:63b) like feeding a horse ... . syem˙kywo.m i (1475 Nay se:3b) serving one. ˙culkywo˙m ol (1463 Pep 2:249b, 1481 Twusi 22:7b) joy, delight. swul ma˙sywom (1462 ¹Nung 7:53b) drinking wine. LUNG-NGEM kolo˙chywom tu˙li˙Gwusya˙m i (1462 ¹Nung 10:42b) his letting the teaching of the Śurangama sūtra be heard ... . is.non ˙tos ˙hwo˙toy is˙ti a˙ni ˙hwo˙m i ˙suchywom a˙n' ˙ywo˙m i a˙ni ˙˙la (1459 Wel 1:36a) that it seems to exist yet does not exist is not a matter of thinking [about it].

˙˙ywom, abbr < ˙i˙ywom, cop modulated subst (CF ˙i˙lwom). SEE ˙˙ywo˙m ol. CF a˙n' ˙ywom = a˙n[i] ˙ywom (< *a˙ni i-wo-m) is not (= a˙ni ˙˙lwom).

... ywo˙m ay < ...i-˙wom ˙ay. ¶ ˙˙twuy.h o˙lwo tol˙Gywo˙m ay (1459 Wel 13:32a) because it depends on the future.

-˙ywo˙m i (after y, i), modulated subst + pcl. ¶ ... pwuthye towoy˙ywo˙m i ˙QILQ-˙TTYENG ˙thwo˙ta (1463 Pep 4:75a) is sure to become a Buddha. woy˙ywo.m i ˙stwo ˙wol˙hwo.m i˙la hwo.m on ... (1482 Nam 1:39a) when we say that being wrong is also being right ... . QWUY-KWANG ˙oy NUNG ˙hi pi˙chwuyywo˙m i

a˙ni ’la ˙ka (1463 Pep 3:104b) it is not the full illumination of the mighty light ··· , yet, ... ye˙huyywo˙m i ˙mas.tang ho˙kwo n' (1482 Kum-sam 2:37a) separation is to be expected. ···˙ywo˙m i < ···i-˙wom ˙i. ¶pwus˙kulywo˙m i ˙˙es.tyey ˙˙ep˙susin ˙ka (1449 Kok 120) how come he has no shame? ˙nwu˙n i pan˙to˙ki ko˙lywo˙m i ˙˙ep˙swul ˙tt iGe˙nul (1462 ¹Nung 2:111a) one's eyes must necessarily not cloud over, yet ... . ki˙tulywo˙m i ˙˙ep˙susil ˙ss oy (1462 ¹Nung 6:29a) ··· it is not to be expected, so ... . ˙QOY mun˙tuk po˙lywo˙m i e˙lyewul ˙ss oy ˙'la (1463 Pep 3:97b) it is because it is hard to give up (her) love all at once. mwo˙ta i˙sywo.m i [˙CYENG] hi ˙mas.tang khe˙nol (1481 Twusi 8:6b) all are properly gathered together, and yet ... . [SSIN-KUY] lowoy˙ywo.m i ˙˙epti a˙ni thwo˙ta (1481 Twusi 16:22b) it does not lack in being miraculous!
- ˙ywo˙m i˙la (after y, i), modulated subst + cop indic assert. ¶˙i ˙non mozo˙m ol pu˙the ˙˙KYENG ˙ul ˙˙nayywo.m i˙la (1462 ¹Nung 4:27b) this sets boundaries based on the mind.
···˙ywo˙m i˙la < ···i-˙wom ˙i˙la. ¶˙˙ta-˙mon PPWO-˙SALQ kolo˙chywo.m i˙la (1447 Sek 13:59a) it is just the bodhisattva teaching.
···˙ywo˙m i˙za < ···i-˙wo˙m i˙la. ¶sol˙phywo.m i˙za ko˙cang ˙ho˙yan ma˙lon ([1447→]1562 Sek 3:18a) I have investigated after my fashion.
- ˙ywo˙m ol (after y, i), modulated substantive + particle. ¶mu˙su.k u˙lwo mozom sa˙ma na ’y cwume˙kwuy pi˙chwuyywo˙m ol TANG ˙honon ˙ta (1462 ¹Nung 1:84a) what will you make your heart be that it face the radiance of my fist? ˙wolho˙m ye woy˙ywo˙m ol hon ti˙Gwuy ˙KYWO-˙CYENG (˙hwolttiGeta=) ˙hwolq˙t iGe˙ta (1463 Pep 1:10b) it is a matter of checking what is right and wrong at the same time. TTWO-TYWUNG ˙ey s ˙KHOYK towoy˙ywo.m ol ˙culki˙m ye (1482 Kum-sam 3:24a) delights to become a guest on the road, and ... .
···˙ywo˙m ol < -˙i-˙wo-m ˙ol. ¶na ’y mozo˙m i ˙SSILQ ˙lwo ˙mwom pas˙k uy i˙sywo˙m ol ˙˙al˙Gwa-ngi ˙'ta (1462 ¹Nung 1:53a) I know that my mind really exists apart from my body. kis˙ke ˙culkywo˙m ol ˙˙nay˙ti a˙ni ˙tha-ngi ˙'ta (1463 Pep 2:249b) it has not created joyous delight. MYEY-˙HHWOYK ˙ho˙ya kolo˙chywo˙m ol pat˙ti a˙ni ho˙l i ˙'le˙n i ˙'la (1463 Pep 1:208a) was too confused to get what was taught. ˙˙mal-ssom ˙kwa ka˙col˙pywo.m o˙lwo (1464 Kumkang 87b) by comparing it with what is said. NGEN ˙kwa KWAN ˙on PANG ˙ol cwo˙cha wol˙mwom i˙sywo.m ol pol˙ki˙kwo cye ’y˙n i (1463/4 Yeng 2:31b) it wants to be clarified that speech and view sometimes change course.
˙'ywo˙m ol = [i]˙ywo˙m ol, cop subst + pcl. ¶TTWONG-˙NGEP ˙on ˙MANG ˙ol hon kac' ˙'ywo˙m ol nilo˙si.n i (1462 ¹Nung 2:79b) as for those in the same trade, he said that their sense of disorder is the same.
- ˙ywo˙m on (after y, i), modulated subst + pcl. ¶˙ile ’n ˙t olwo ke˙mu.m ye ˙hoyywo˙m ol non˙hwo.n i ˙'la (1481 Twusi 7:27a) hence distinguished being black and (being) white. ˙nyey ye˙huyywo˙m on ˙i e˙tuy ˙le˙n ywo (1481 Twusi 21:30a) that separation of long ago, where was this?
···˙ywo˙m on < ···i-˙wom ˙on. ¶a˙to˙l oy mozom ˙kwa ˙him ˙kwa l’ ki˙lywo˙m on (1463 Pep 2:213b) the praising of the son's mind and strength. kol˙mye˙k[i] uy ˙nye ton˙nywo˙m on (1481 Twusi 14:29b) the wandering of seagulls.
- ˙ywon (after y, i), modulated modifier.
1. (with epitheme extruded from the subject). Example?
2. (epitheme extruded from object). ¶QA-NAN a˙hota˙ka˙stwo˙i HYANG˙i ne ’y kwo˙h ay ˙sye ˙nalq˙t in˙t ay n' nil˙Gwo˙toy˙kwo˙h oy ˙˙nay˙ywon ke˙s i˙la ho˙la ’n˙t oy pan˙to˙ki ˙kwo˙h ol pu˙the ˙˙nalq˙t iGe˙nul ... (1462 ¹Nung 3:24b) say, Ānanda, perhaps again when this scent arises in your nose we say that it is something emitted by your nose ... .
3. (with a summational epitheme). ¶hwen hi somo˙chon KHWONG ˙on MA ˙oy tal˙Gayywon ˙pa ’y˙n i (1482 Nam 1:76b) the (widely penetrating =) pervasive void (śūnya) is where the devils seduce.

˙ywo so˙zi (> ˙ywo so˙[z]i > yo sai), adn + n. ¶˙HYANG ˙on a˙ni wo˙lan ˙ywo so˙zi ˙'la (1459 Wel se:26a) ˙HYANG is [a Chinese word that] means it is not long (in time). ˙ywo so˙i ˙yey (= ˙ywo so˙[z]i ˙yey) lately. ˙na y ywo so˙i mol-pwo˙ki ˙˙e˙te ˙sye mol ˙tho˙ti ˙˙mwot ˙hota˙la (?1517- Pak 1:37b) the last while I have been unable to ride a horse, having picked up an intestinal ailment.
- ˙ywo˙toy (after y, i), modulated accessive. ¶˙˙ce y ne˙kywo˙toy (1447 Sek 13:61a) in his own opinion ... . mozo˙m ay ˙na y ne˙kywo˙toy (1463 Pep 2:23a) my feeling was that ... .

tut˙cop˙kwo ne˙kywo˙toy (1447 Sek 9:27a) he listens and considers them and ... .
··· ˙*ywo˙toy* < ···*i-˙wo˙toy*. ¶*ye˙le pa˙lo[l] s ka˙won-˙toy i˙sywo˙toy* (1462 ¹Nung 2:84b) they are among the seas and ... . ˙*YWOK ˙ay i˙sywo˙toy ˙YWOK ¨ep.su˙m ye TTIN ˙ey i˙sywo˙toy TTIN ˙ol ye˙huyl ˙ss ol ˙SSYEN ˙i˙Gwo* (?1468⁻ Mong 63b) and dhyāna means to have no desire in the midst of desire and in the midst of dust to keep one's distance from the dust. *stwo kal˙h ay ¨hel.m ye ¨twochoy ˙yey pehun ˙tol˙h ay s CHANG ˙ul kwo˙thywotoy* (1466 Kup 1:82a) moreover it will cure wounds such as those of boils arising from a knife or those from cutting on an ax. ¨*nyey ˙SYWELQ-SAN ˙ay hon QOYNG-¨MWU y ˙i˙sywo˙toy e˙zi ¨ta ˙nwun ¨melGe˙tun ¨KWA-˙SSILQ ˙pta me˙kite˙n i* (1459 Wel 2:12b) anciently there was a parrot on the snowy mountain; when its parents both went blind it picked fruit and fed it to them.
˙*ywu*, var = ˙*ywo*, postmodifier. SEE ʼ*y˙l ywu*.
- ˙*ywu-* (after *y, i*) = - ˙*wu-* (modulator): - ˙*ywu˙toy*, - ˙*ywu˙m ul*, - ˙*ywu˙n i*.
···*ywu-* < ···*i-wu-*: -*ywu˙la*, -*ywu˙l i ʼ˙la*, - ˙*ywum*, - ˙*ywun*. SEE ¨*hoyywu-*.
-*ywu-* (= -*y.wu* = -*y-wu*, not -*yu*): SEE -*iwu-*.
···*ywu˙la* < ···*i-wu˙la*. ¶*cyekun ˙te.t ul ˙sye ˙sywula* (1481 Twusi 8:2b) he stood there for a little while.
···*ywu˙l i ʼ˙la* < ···*i-wul ˙i ʼ˙la*. ¶··· *swu˙l ul tyangsyang ka˙cywu.l i ʼ˙la* (1481 Twusi 8:34a) I will ··· and have the wine forever. ˙*CCYENG-˙PPEN NGWANG ˙i TA-SYWU ˙uy ˙ptu˙t ul nwu˙kywu.l i ʼ˙la ˙ho˙sya* (1447 Sek 6:9b) Śuddhodana sought to ease Yaśodharā's mind.
···*ywu˙l ye* < ···*i-wu˙l ye*. ¶˙*no˙m on cwu˙kywu˙l ye khe˙nul* ... (1445 ¹Yong 77) people wanted to kill them, but ... .
··· ˙*ywum* < ···*i-˙wu.m*. ¶*p[w]us˙ku˙lywum ¨ep˙ta ka ˙two* (1459 Wel 8:69b; *pus* seems to be a graphic mistake for *pwus*) they are shameless, yet ... . *[NGWANG ˙CHAN] ˙uy ci˙p i [¨HHYEN-SAN] al˙ph oy wu˙mu˙l ul me˙mul˙Gwe ʼ˙sywum ˙kwa tangtangi ˙kot ho˙l i ˙lwo˙ta* (1481 Twusi 7:4b) the royal banquet hall should be similar to the keeping of a well in front of Mount Xiǎn. *[LYWONG-CCYWEN ˙KEM] ˙pha ¨nay˙ywol ¨hyeyywu˙m i ¨ep.se ʼy˙la* (1481 Twusi 21:42a) there is no scheme to dig out the Sword of Dragon Spring.

- ˙*ywum*, (after *y, i*) modulated substantive.
··· ˙*ywu˙m ey* < ···*i-˙wu-m ˙ey*. ¶*kwoki capo.m ye namwo ¨cywu.m ey ˙i [SOYNG] ˙ol pu˙thye ˙ys.nwo˙la* (1481 Twusi 7:6b) I rely on catching fish and cutting wood for my livelihood.
··· ˙*ywu˙m i* < ···*i-wu-m ˙i*. ¶*kan tay ˙lwo ¨salom sim˙kywu˙m i ¨mwot ho.l i ʼ˙n i* (1463 Pep 4: 86b) cannot let people have it [= the sūtra] just at random.
- ˙*ywu˙m ul*, modulated subst + pcl. ¶*muy˙ywu˙m ul ¨nay.l i ʼ˙le.n i ʼ˙la* (1464 Kumkang 79b) ··· one would emit glaring hatred (I recall).
··· ˙*ywun* < ···*i-˙wu-n*. ¶¨*CHOY-¨NYE ˙nun ˙skwu˙mywun kak˙si ʼ˙la* (1459 Wel 2:28a) a ¨*CHOY-¨NYE* is a prettified girl.
- ˙*ywu˙n i* (after *y, i*), modulated modifier + postmod. ¶··· *ci˙p i ˙ilGe˙nol ˙hoyn ˙ptwuy lwo ni˙ywu˙n i* (1481 Twusi 7:1a) there was built a house but it was shaded by white cogon-grass thatching.
- ˙*ywu˙toy*, (after *y, i*) modulated accessive. ¶˙*QILQ-˙CHYEY ¨ta pwuy˙ywu˙toy* (1462 ¹Nung 5:59b) all are empty.
yya = *ya* (after Chinese words). ¶*[MYENG-˙SSYEY] yya ho.ya* (1876 Kakok 95) making indeed a pledge.
y˙za, y ˙za, abbr < ˙*i˙za, ˙i ˙za*, pcl. Usually only after Chinese characters for syllables ending in a vowel; for Hankul words ending in a vowel just ˙*za* was used, but there are a few examples with nativized Chinese words and with indeterminates. It is not always clear in a given case whether what is intended is the nominative particle ˙*i* + ˙*za*, but that seems likely, so we write most examples as *y ˙za*.
1. ¶˙*TTAY-˙QOY-¨TTWOW y ˙za CIN-˙SSILQ ˙lwo ¨SSYEN hon ˙ptu˙t i ha˙m ye* (1459 Wel 10:19a) Mahāprajāpati [Buddha's foster mother (and aunt)] truly had many good intentions and ... . ˙*TTAY-˙QOY-¨TTWOW y ˙za kilozoWo[˙]l i ʼ-ngi ʼ˙ta* ([1447→]1562 Sek 3:3ab) Mahāprajāpati will raise him herself. *PPI-SYA-PA MILQ-TA-LA y za mos eti.n i ʼ-ngi ˙ta* ([1447→]1562 Sek 3:7a; missing accents not restored) Viśvāmitra is the very wisest one.
2. ¶*wo˙cik pwu¨thye y ˙za NUNG ˙hi ¨a˙losi˙n i* (1463 Pep 4:63a) only Buddha fully knows it. *ye˙sus ha˙no˙l i e˙nu y ˙za ˙mos*

῀tywoho῀n i '-ngi s ῾ka (1447 Sek 6:35b) of the six heavens just which is best? ῾nwu y ῾za ῾TI-[῾]HHYWEY isi῾m ye ([1447→]1562 Sek 3:7a) just who has wisdom and ... . SEE ῾hosilq ῾s oy.

z variant of the particle s between voiced sounds, explicitly so noted in the spellings of 1445 ¹Yong: ῀ko῾z ay z ῾wum῾h ul (5) a cave on the shore. QYENG-῀CYWU z al῾ph oy (16) before the Chief of Heroes. wo῾nol z na῾l ay (16, 56, 76) today. [῀HHWUW] z ῾nal (26) later days. [῾SWU-῀MEN ῀LI] z ῀ni῾m i῾Gesi῾n i (31) the lord of myriads of leagues. [῾POYK-῾PPWO] ῾ay z ye῾lum ῾sswo῾sya (63) at a hundred paces his shot hit the fruit. pa῾lol z wu῾h uy (83) upon the sea. ha῾nol z mozo῾m ol ··· na῾la[h] z il῾hwum ··· [THYEN-῀CO] z mozo῾m ol ··· (85) the will of heaven ··· the nation's name ··· the will of the son of heaven. ῾nwun z ῾mu῾l ul (91) tears. ῀nim-῾kum z ῀mal (98) the king's words. ῾mul wu῾h uy z [LYWONG] ῾i (100) the dragon atop the water. [῾THAY-῀CO] z [῾WUY] ··· [῾SYEY-῀CO] z [῾WUY] (101) the position of crown prince ··· the position of heir-apparent.

῾za, pcl = ya. Attaches to final n (see -ketun za), l, or vowel (including ···y). After k the form is ῾i῾za; there are also attestations of ῾i῾za after m and of isa after l. Attached as ῾sa directly to the verb stem (= -῾e ῾za) in a few examples. CF (l)ol za, (l)ul za, isa, sa.

1. After unmarked direct object. ¶ ῾wuli ῾tol῾h i ile῾thus [= ileh-tus] hon ῾MANG-῾LYANG ῾ay s ῾SSYWUW-῾KUY ῾za ῾psu῾ti a῾ni ῾hwo.l i ῾῾la (1447 Sek 19:30b) we will not use this sort of prophecies of future Buddhahood in false quantities. ῾i ῀say ῀wul῾Guy ho῾n i ῾za PWU-ZIN ῾ol sa῾mwo.l i ῾῾la (1447 Sek 24:20b) precisely the one who has made this bird sing will I make my wife. QON-[῾]HHYWEY ῾za mwo῾lo.l i ῾ye ma῾lon ῀ney ka῾ci s ῀SSYWUW-῾KHWO ῾lol ῀wuy ῾ho῾ya ῾honwo῾la ([1447→]1562 Sek 3:35a) perhaps I know nothing of my obligation, but I work on behalf of [relieving] the Four Miseries. Perhaps: [12800] KWONG-῾TUK ῾i῾za ῾NGUY-῾LWON ῾hwolq ῾cwul ῀ep῾su.l i ῾῾la (1447 Sek 19:10b) there is just no way to argue with 12,800 individual achievements of virtue.

2. After an unmarked subject ending in /i/ or /y/; could be treated as ellipsis of nominative particle: [῾i] ῾za. ¶ ῾wuli ῾za pwuthye ῾lol cwosco῾Wa tut῀cop῾kwo (1463 Pep 5:121b) we humbly listen to Buddha with our heads bowed. ῾i kak῾si ῾za na ῾y ῀et.ni῾nwon mozo῾m ay mas῾two῾ta (1447 Sek 6:14ab) precisely this girl matches the purpose I am pursuing. ῾SO-῾PPYENG ye῾huy.n i ῾za CHYENG-῾CCYENG ῾ul ῀all i ῾῾n i (1465 Wen 2:3:1:110a) only the one who has well distanced himself from the Four Ailments [mistaken ways of seeking perfection] will know parisuddhi (perfect purity). ῀TTWOW ῾kot ho῾n i ῾za pi῾luse ῀a῾no.n i ῾῾la (1482 Kum-sam 2:3a) only those who have shared the same way come to know each other. ῀ku y ῾za ῾i ῾CCWA ῾ay anco῾si῾l i ῾-ngi ῾῾ta (1447 Sek 24:43b) just he will sit in this seat.

3. After an adverb. ¶ kutuy ῾nay kos῾pi ῾za ῾wotwo῾ta ma῾lon (1447 Sek 23:53b) you people make great haste to come, but ... . CYE-῾PPWULQ ῾i ῾CHYWULQ-῾SYEY ῾hwo῾m i NAN ῾hi ῾zo mas-῾nano῾n i (1463 Pep 5:148a) in renouncing the world the Buddhas confront much hardship. ta῾si ῀HWA-COY ye῾tulp pen cca῾hi ῾za ῾stwo ῀SYWUY-COY ho῾l i ῾῾n i (1459 Wel 1:49b) and as the eighth disaster there will be more floods.

4. After a time or place noun ending in /y/; could be regarded as ellipsis of the locative/allative particle: [῾yey] ῾za. ¶ ῾i cey ῾za (1459 Wel 1:41b) only now. ku cey ῾za (1447 Sek 6:21a, 24:52b) only then.

5. After a time noun ending in /l/ (= ῾ey ῾za). ¶ LOY-῾ZILQ ῾za pwo῾nay῾ywo.l i ῾῾la ho῾kwo ... (1459 Wel 7:16a) saying she would send him the very next day ... . ··· mwo῾lwo῾may ῾CHILQ-῾NGWELQ s ῾yel tas῾sway s ῾nal ῾za ho῾l i ῾-ngi s ῾kwo (1459 Wel 23:91b) [why] must I do it precisely (on) the fifteenth day of July? ··· wo῾nol ῾za CIN-῾SSILQ s ῾i ῾PPWULQ-῀CO y ῾῾la (1463 Pep 2:8a) ··· today at last is this true disciple of Buddha − the Chinese text has ῀[NOW DAY] ey za῀.

NOTE 1: This particle is explicitly mentioned in 1459 (Wel se:13a): ῀NAY ῾non ῾za ῾ho῾nwon ῾kye.ch i῾la Chinese ῀NAY ('at last') is a particle that means ῾za.

NOTE 2: In 1465 Wen ῾za is often followed by pi῾lu῾se 'for the first time' or its synonyms.

SEE ῾i῾za; (ᵘ⁄ₒ)῾lwo ῾za, ῾(y)ey ῾za, -ke῾nul ῾za, -ke῾tun ῾za, -῾kwo ῾za, -ᵉ⁄ₐ ῾za, -ke ῾za, ῾ila ῾za.

˙*[z]a*, particle. SEE -˙*key* ˙*a*.
⋯¨*zop-* < ⋯*l-*¨*zop-* (-L- stems)
-¨*zop-* < *-*so*˙*po-* < *-*oso*˙*po-*, deferential bound aux. Alternant shapes: -¨*sop-*, ⋯¨*ssop-*, -¨*cop-*, ⋯¨*ccop-*. SEE -*swo*˙*wo-* < -*so[W]*˙*wo-*. In general, strings like -*zowo*⋯ are treated as being modulated (= -*zoWwo-*), while strings like -*zoWo-* are treated as unmodulated. But for those endings that do not permit the modulator to intrude, strings like -*zowo-* are equivalent to the unmodulated -*zoWo-*. The relevant cases are -¨*zowo*˙*m ye* = -¨*zoWo*˙*m ye*, -¨*zowo*˙*m ye n'* = -¨*zoWo*˙*m ye n'*, and the infinitive -¨*zo*˙*wa* = -¨*zo*˙*Wa*. Before the honorific -*(*^{U}*o)si-* and the modulated honorific -*(*^{U}*o)sya-* strings like -*zowo-* are also equivalent to -*zoWo-*. There is only one modulation in -¨*zo*˙*wosya*˙*m ol*.

+ -˙*a*, infinitive. ¶ ˙*hozo*˙*wa* (1465 Wen se: 77a) = ˙*hozo*˙*Wa* (1447 Sek 24:5b), ˙*hozo[*˙*]Wa* (1459 Wel 8:1a) < °*ho-* do; ˙*kazo*˙*wa* (1463 Pep 3:121ab) = ˙*kazo*˙*Wa* (1459 Wel 23:85b) < °*ka-* go, *pwo[*˙*]nayzo*˙*wa* (1463 Pep 4:193a) < *pwo*˙*nay-* send, ¨*mey*˙*zoWa*˙*ci-ngi*˙'˙*ta* (1459 Wel 10:10b) wants to shoulder/bear it, ¨*mwoyzo*˙*Wa* (1447 Sek 23:31b) < °°*mwoy-* escort, *towoyzo*˙*Wa* (1447 Sek 6:5b, 1449 Kok 140, 1463 Pep 4:48b) < *towoy-* become, ˙*pwozo*˙*Wa* (1447 Sek 6:44b, 1459 Wel 8:87b) < °*pwo-*, *ku*˙*lizo*˙*Wa* (1447 Sek 23:37a) < *ku*˙*li-* depict; ˙*hozo*˙*Wa ci*˙*la* (1447 Sek 24:8a, 9b); ˙*hozo*˙*Wa*˙*ci-ngi*˙'˙*ta* (1447 Sek 24:8b) < °*ho-* do, *ilozo*˙*Wa*˙*ci-ngi*˙'˙*ta* (1447 Sek 6:22b) I want to build them < *il*^{U}*o- / ilG-*; ˙*sozo*˙*Wa* (1459 Wel 21:212a) < ˙*sol-* burn; ¨*tamzo*˙*Wa* (1459 Wel 10:14b) < ¨*tam-* pack, ¨*anzo*˙*Wa* (1459 Wel 2:43b = 1449 Kok 23) < ¨*an-* embrace.
kapso˙*Wa* (1447 Sek 23:29b) < *kaph-* repay, *kas*¨*kapso*˙*wa* (1463 Pep 4:49a) < *kaskaW-* be near, *sis.so*˙*Wa* (1447 Sek 23:37b) < *sis-* wash, *kis.so*˙*Wa* (1447 Sek 6:21b, 24:8b, 24:51a) < *kisk-* rejoice, *cesso*˙*Wa* (1445 [1]*Yong* 75) < *ceh-* fear, *sul*˙*sso*˙*Wa* (1445 [1]*Yong* 91, 1447 Sek 23:37a) < *sulh-* grieve, ¨*cwosso*˙*wa* (1462 [1]*Nung* 1:52b) < ¨*cwoz-* kowtow.
patco˙*Wa* (1459 Wel 1:10b, 1462 [1]*Nung* 7:62a) < *pat-* get, *putco*˙*Wa*˙*za* (1459 Wel 18:80b) < *puth-* rely on, *tutco*˙*wa* (1463 Pep 6:83a) = *tutco*˙*Wa* (1447 Sek 13:27a, 13:54b, 23:31b)

< *tut-/tul-* hear, *cwosco*˙*Wa* (1447 Sek 13:60a; 1459 Wel 10:31b, 1463 Pep 2:48b) = *cwotco*˙*Wa* (1447 Sek 24:2a) = *cwocco*˙*Wa* (1447 Sek 24: 45b, 1459 Wel 23:76b), *cwocco*˙*wa* (1462 [1]*Nung* 1:4a) < *cwoch-* follow.
-˙*asilq* = -˙*a*˙'*silq* (= *isilq* effective hon prosp mod). ¶*tut*¨*cop*˙*ti*¨*mwot*˙*hozo*˙*wa*˙'*silq*˙*cey* (1462 [1]*Nung* 2:2b) when I was unable to hear it; ⋯¨*may*¨*mwot tutco*˙*Wa*˙'*silq*˙*ta* (1459 Wel 56b) how come you have been unable to hear of them?
-˙*as.non* = -˙*a*˙'*s.non*. ¶¨*mwoyzo*˙*wa*˙'*s.non hyekon* SSIN-¨HHA˙'*y*˙*la* (1475 Nay 1:39b) it is a gathering of minor subjects.
-˙*a*˙*sye*. ¶*toWoyzo*˙*Wa*˙*sye* (1447 Sek 6:5b) < *toWoy-* become.
-˙*a*˙*two*. ¶˙*pwo*˙*zowa*˙*two* (1462 [1]*Nung* 1: 47a) < °*pwo-* see; *puluzo*˙*Wa*˙*two* (1459 Wel 8:16b) < *pulu-/pulG-* call.
-˙*a*˙'*ys.non*. ¶[¨]*mwutco*˙*wa*˙'*ys.non sta.h i* 1481 Twusi 8:62a) < [¨]*mwut-/mwul-* visit.
-˙*a*˙'*ys.non*˙*ta*. ¶*tutco*˙*Wa*˙'*ys.non*˙'˙*ta* (1447 Sek 9:35b) < *tut-/tul-* hear.
-˙*a*˙'*ys.ta*˙*n i*, ¶˙*hozo*˙*wa*˙'*ys.ta*˙*n i* (1464 Kumkang 72b) < °*ho-* do.
-˙*a*˙'*ys.tan*˙*t i*˙*m ye n'*. ¶*tutco*˙*Wa*˙'*ys.tan*˙*t i*˙*m ye n'* (1459 Wel 9:34a) < *tut-/tul-* hear.
-˙*a*˙'*ys.te*˙*la*. ¶˙*pwozo*˙*Wa*˙'*ys te*˙*la* (1447 Sek 24:19a) < °*pwo-* see.
-˙*a*˙'*ys*˙*tesi*˙*n i s*˙*ka*. ¶*tutco*˙*Wa*˙'*ys*˙*tesi*˙*n i s*˙*ka* (1447 Sek 6:17a) < *tut-/tul-* hear.
-˙*a*˙*za*. ¶˙*pwo*˙*zoWa*˙*za* (1459 Wel 8:26a) < °*pwo-* see, ˙*ho*˙*zoWa*˙*za* (1459 Wel 9:52a) < °*ho-* do, ˙*ka*˙*zoWa*˙*za* (1447 Sek 23:40a) < °*ka-* go, ¨*mey*˙*zoWa*˙*za* (1459 Wel 10:12b) bear it; ¨*pi*˙*zoWa*˙*za* (1449 Kok 106) < ¨*pil-* pray, beg; *kapso*˙*Wa*˙*za* (1447 Sek 23:21b) < *kaph-* repay; *ilkhotco*˙*Wa*˙*za* (1459 Wel 10: 75b) < *ilkhot-/ilkhol-* say.
+ -˙*al(q)*, effective prospective modifier.
-*alq*˙*ka*. ¶˙*pwo*˙*zoWal*˙*kka* (1447 Sek 24:43b, 1447 Sek 24:43b) < °*pwo-* see.
+ -˙*an*, effective modifier.
-˙*a.n i*. ¶¨*nwol*˙*lazo*˙*Wa*˙*n i* (1445 [1]*Yong* 47) they took sudden fright. ¨*twu* PPWO-˙SALQ ˙*ol*˙*pwozo*˙*Wa.n i*˙*Gwa* (1459 Wel 8:17b) saw two bodhisattvas. ¨*ne y ho*˙*ma mas-*˙*nazo*˙*Wa*˙*n i* (1459 Wel 2:62b) you have already faced it.
-˙*a.n i*˙*Gwa*. ¶˙*pwozo*˙*Wa.n i*˙*Gwa* (1459 Wel 8:17b) < °*pwo-* see, ˙*hozo*˙*wa.n i*

˙Gwa (1463 Pep 2:50a) < °ho- do.
 -˙an ma˙lon. ¶tutco˙Wan ma˙lon (1447 Sek 6:11a) < tut- / tul- hear.
 -an ˙t i. ¶˙pwo˙zoWan ˙t i (1459 Wel 21: 191ab) < °pwo- see.
 -an tye. ¶˙pwo˙zoWan tye (1459 Wel 23: 82b) < °pwo- see.
 -a˙n ywo. ¶¨cwos˙soWa˙n ywo (1449 Kok 28, 109) did he bow his head (kowtow)?
 + -˙a-ngi ˙˙ta, effective polite + cop indic assertive. ¶mwo˙lozo˙Wa-ngi ˙˙ta (1459 Wel 21:192a) I do not know.
 + -˙a˙nol, concessive. ¶¨nwol˙lazo˙Wa˙nol (1445 ¹Yong 61) < ¨nwol˙la- get terrified at; cesso˙Wa˙nol (1445 ¹Yong 61) < ceh- fear; patco˙Wa˙n ol (1447 Sek 24:45b) < pat- get, ¨mwut˙cowa˙nol (1482 Kum-sam 3:12b) < ¨mwut- / mwul- ask.
 + -˙a ˙silq, effective honorific prospective modifier. ¶˙hozo˙wasilq ˙cey (1462 ¹Nung 2:2b) < °ho- do; tutco˙Wasilq ˙ta (1459 Wel 9:56b) < tut- / tul- hear.
 + -˙asi˙nol, honorific literary concessive. ¶¨pwoyzo˙Wasi˙nol (1459 Wel 8:84a) < ¨pwoy- show; ¨mwutco˙wasi˙nol (1463 Pep 1:67b) < ¨mwut- / mwul-.
 + -˙a˙ta, effective transferentive. ¶niluWa˙ta ˙wa (1447 Sek 23:53a) < nilu- / nilG- rouse; ¨etco˙Wata ˙ka (1447 Sek 23:53b) < ¨et- get.
 + -˙cye, suggestion / desire. ¶¨etcop˙cye ho˙kwo (1459 Wel 2:69a) < ¨et- get.
 + -ke˙na, effective adversative. ¶˙ho˙zopke˙na (1447 Sek 13:53a) < °ho- do, hon˙swo˙n ol tu¨zopke˙na (1447 Sek 13:53b) or raising a hand or ... < tul- raise, lift. ˙kuli¨zopke˙na moyng˙ko¨zopke˙na hol ˙ss i˙la (1459 Wel 2:66b) it means to draw or make.
 + -ke˙n i, effective mod + postmod. ¶kil[h] cap¨sopke˙n i micwo¨ccopke˙n i (1459 Wel 21:203a) whether taking the road or following after (< cap- take, micwoch- follow right after).
 + -ke˙nul, concessive. ¶¨wu˙zopke˙nul (1459 Wel 10:1b) < ¨wul- cry; mak¨sopke˙nul (1449 Kok 100) obstruct; cwoch¨copke˙nul (1445 ¹Yong 36) = cwo¨ccopke˙nul (1449 Kok 187) < cwoch- follow.
 + -ken ˙t ay n', effective mod + postmod + pcl + pcl. ¶kyen˙cwu˙zopken ˙t ay n' (1462 ¹Nung 1:99b) < kyen˙cwu- compare.

 + -ke˙tun, provisional. ¶˙ho˙zopke˙tun (1459 Wel 7:55; cited from LCT [page missing in Yensey repro]) < °ho- do.
 + -˙key, -˙kuy, adverbative. ¶¨na˙lol ˙pwozop˙key ˙hosywo˙sye (1459 Wel 18:80b; the smudge at the left of ˙pwo is not a second dot) please let them gaze on me. ˙pwozop˙kuy ˙hwo˙m i˙Gwo (1447 Sek 24:2b) is letting them gaze. ¨sitcop˙key (1447 Sek 24:10b) < ¨sit- / sil- load, tut¨cop˙kuy (1459 Wel 8:1b) < tut- / tul- hear.
 + -[˙]kwa ˙˙la, exclamatory statement. ¶˙pwo˙zopkwa ˙˙la (1463 Pep 4:169a) I have seen it.
 + -˙kwa-ngi ˙˙ta, exclamatory polite statement. ¶¨etcop˙kwa-ngi ˙˙ta (1459 Wel 13:6b) < ¨et- get. mas˙na˙zop˙kwa-ngi ˙˙ta (1463 Pep 3: 120b) < mac- meet. ¨ta ho˙ma ˙pwozop˙kwa-ngi ˙˙ta (1463 Pep 4:169a) we have all now seen.
 + -˙kwo, gerund. ¶˙hozop˙kwo (1447 Sek 6:1b, 24:5b) < °ho- do; ˙pwozop˙kwo (1445 ¹Yong 59, 1447 Sek 6:40a) < °pwo- see; ka˙cizop˙kwo (1447 Sek 24:5b) < ka˙ci- have; ¨samzop˙kwo (1475 Nay 2:2:17a) < ¨sam- make; ¨azop˙kwo (1449 Kok 109) < ¨al- know; ¨twozop˙kwo (1447 Sek 23:43b) < ¨twol- turn around; kuzu¨zop˙kwo (1459 Wel 2:35b) < kuzu- / kuzG- drag; nip¨sop˙kwo (1459 Wel 2:72a) < nip- wear; pus¨sop˙kwo (1447 Sek 23:23a, 1449 Kok 34) < ¨puz- pour, ¨cwo.ssop˙kwo (1447 Sek 6:45a) < ¨cwoz- kowtow, nwo¨ssop˙kwo (1447 Sek 9:22b, 1449 Kok 191, 1462 ¹Nung 1:31a) < nwoh- put, nye¨ssop˙kwo (1447 Sek 23:23a, 23:58b; 1459 Wel 1:7b) < nyeh- put it in; ma¨ccop˙kwo (1462 ¹Nung 1:31a) < mac- meet, cwo¨ccop˙kwo (1459 Wel 2:17a) < cwoch- follow, yen¨ccop˙kwo (1447 Sek 23: 38a; 1459 Wel 2:39a, 10:13b) = yent¨cop˙kwo (1447 Sek 23:49a; 1459 Wel 10:10a) < yenc- put on top, tut¨cop˙kwo (1445 ¹Yong 59) < tut- / tul- hear, ilkhot¨cop˙kwo (1447 Sek 13: 59a) < ilkhot- / ilkhol- praise.
 -kwo ˙cye. ¶tut¨copkwo ˙cye (1462 ¹Nung 1:38a) < tut- / tul- hear.
 -kwo ˙za. ¶tut¨copkwo ˙za (1449 Kok 106) < tut- / tul- hear.
 + -˙non, proc mod. ¶poy˙hwo¨zopnon (1463 Pep 5:43b) < poy˙hwo- learn; cwo¨ccop˙non (1463 Pep 1:24b) < cwoch- follow.

-no˙n i. ¶ pwo˙zopno˙n i (1445 ¹Yong 5) < °pwo- see; ˙ho˙zopno˙n i (1463 Pep 5:186a) < °ho- do; pat¨copno˙n i (1449 Kok 117) < pat- offer.

-no˙n i ˙Gwa. ¶ ˙ho˙zopno˙n i ˙Gwa (1447 Sek 23:4a) < °ho- do.

-˙no.n i ˙'la. ¶ ki˙tuli¨zop˙no.n i ˙'la (1447 Sek 24:5b) < ki˙tu˙li- wait; ˙kot˙copno˙n i ˙'la (1462 ¹Nung 2:45a) < ˙koth- = ˙kot°ho- be like.

-no˙n i n'. ¶ ˙hozopno˙n i n' (1463 Pep se:17a) < °ho- do.

-no˙n i ˙-ngi s ˙kwo. ¶ pwo˙zopno˙n i -ngi s ˙kwo (1463 Pep 1:67a) < °pwo- see.

-no˙n i ˙-ngi ˙'ta. ¶ nip¨sopno˙n i ˙-ngi ˙'ta (1463 Pep 3:109b) < nip- wear.

-non ˙kwo. ¶ ˙hozopnon ˙kwo (1481 Twusi 10:9b) < °ho- do.

+ -no-ngi ˙'ta, processive polite + cop indic assert. ¶ ˙ho˙zopno-ngi ˙'ta (1463 Pep 1:165b) < °ho- do.

+ -no˙ta, proc indic assert. ¶ pwo˙zopno˙ta (1459 Wel 18:55b) < °pwo- see.

+ -nwo˙la, modulated proc indic assertive. ¶ tut¨copnwo˙la (1459 Wel 10:26a) < tut-/tul- hear.

+ -nwon, modulated processive modifier. ¶ pwozop˙nwon cyen˙cho ˙lwo (1459 Wel 8:28a) < °pwo- see; ilkhot¨copnwon ¨ma.l i˙n i (1482 Kum-sam 4:11b) < ilkhot-/ilkhol-.

-nwo˙n i. ¶ ˙ho˙zopnwo˙n i (1447 Sek 9:26b = 1459 Wel 9:46b) < °ho- do.

+ -˙nwo-ngi ˙'ta, proc polite + copula indic attentive. ¶ ˙hozop˙nwo-ngi ˙'ta (1463 Pep 2:49a, 1464 Kumkang 13b) < °ho- do.

+ -nwos.ta, processive exclamatory statement. ¶ ki˙lizopnwos˙ta (1481 Twusi 20:5b) < ki˙li- praise.

+ -˙ol(q), (unmodulated) prosp modifier. ¶ tutco˙Wolq ¨salo˙m oy (1447 Sek 9:2a) < tut-/tul- hear.

-o˙l i. ¶ ˙hozo˙Wo.l i ˙Gwos (1447 Sek 9:40a) < °ho- do, mwo˙lozo˙Wo˙l i (1445 ¹Yong 86); cesso˙wo˙l i (1449 Kok 190) < ceh- fear, ¨kolp˙sowo˙l i (1463 Pep 2:17a) < ¨kolW- line up; tutco˙Wo˙l i (1449 Kok 97) < tut-/tul- hear, cwocco˙Wo˙l i (1449 Kok 99) < cwoch- follow.

-o˙l i ˙Ge˙na. ¶ tuzo˙Wo˙l i ˙Ge˙na (1447 Sek 23:2b) < tul- lift.

-˙o.l i ˙Gwo. ¶ kap.so˙wo.l i ˙Gwo (1482 Nam 1:41b) < kaph- repay.

-o˙l i 'le˙la. ¶ pwo˙zoWo˙l i 'le˙la (1459 Wel 7:55; cited from LCT [page missing in the Yensey repro]).

-o˙l i 'le˙n i. ¶ pwo˙zoWo˙l i 'le˙n i (1459 Wel 8:17a).

-o.l i '˙lq ˙'s oy. ¶ kotco˙wo.l i '˙l ˙'ss oy (1463 Pep 5:195b) < ˙koth- be alike.

-o˙l i ˙'lwo˙ta. ¶ pwozo˙Wo˙l i ˙'lwo˙ta (1459 Wel 17:19b) < °pwo- see, ¨mwot ¨azo˙Wo˙l i ˙'lwo˙ta (1447 Sek 13:43b) < ¨al- know.

-o˙l i ˙'-ngi ˙'ta. ¶ kilozoWo[˙]l i ˙'-ngi ˙'ta ([1447→]1562 Sek 3:3ab) < kil^Uo-/kilG- raise.

-o˙l i ˙'-ngi s ˙kwo. ¶ iluzo˙Wo˙l i ˙'-ngi s ˙kwo (1447 Sek 24:9b-10a) < ilu-/ilG- create.

-˙o.l [i] 'ye˙n ywo. ¶ pwozo˙Wo.l [i] 'ye˙n ywo (1459 Wel 8:17b) < °pwo- see.

-olq ˙ka. ¶ ¨a˙zoWol ˙kka (1445 ¹Yong 43) < ¨al- know.

-olq ˙'s oy. ¶ pwo˙zoWol ˙'ss oy (1459 Wel 8:28a) < °pwo- see.

-o˙l ye. ¶ ki˙lizo˙Wo˙l ye (1459 Wel se:9a) < kili- praise.

+ -o˙la. ¶ ˙ho˙zoWo˙la (1447 Sek 19:41b), ˙pwo˙zoWo˙la (1459 Wel 8:92a).

+ -˙om, (unmodulated) substantive. Only in:

-o˙m ye. ¶ ˙ho˙zowo˙m ye (1462 ¹Nung 1:39a) = ˙ho˙zoWo˙m ye (1447 Sek 6:17a) < °ho- do; patco˙Wo˙m ye (1459 Wel 18:62b) < pat- get, ¨mwut˙cowo˙m ye (1462 ¹Nung 2:11b) < ¨mwut-/mwul- ask.

-o˙m ye n'. ¶ ˙ho˙zoWo˙m ye n' (1447 Sek 9:24b) < °ho- do; ¨a˙zowo˙m ye n' (1463 Pep 5:187b) < ¨al- know.

+ -˙on, (unmodulated) mod. ¶ pwo˙zoWon ˙salo˙m on (1459 Wel 8:28a) < °pwo- see; tutco˙Won ¨salo˙m i (1447 Sek 13:54a) < tut-/tul- hear.

-o˙n i. ¶ po˙lazo˙Wo˙n i (1445 ¹Yong 38) < po˙la- wish, ¨pwoyzo˙Wo˙n i (1445 ¹Yong 7) = ˙pwoy˙zoWo˙n i (1449 Kok 29) < ¨pwoy- show, ni˙phizo˙Wo˙n i (1445 ¹Yong 25) < ni˙phi- dress someone, a˙to˙l izo˙wo˙n i (1463 Pep 4:48b) < ˙i- (cop); mekso˙Wo˙n i (1459 Wel 7:26a) < mek- eat, ¨twop˙soWo˙n i (1445 ¹Yong 29) < ¨twoW- help; ¨cwos˙soWo˙n i (1449 Kok 109) < ¨cwoz- kowtow, kis.so˙Wo˙n i (1449 Kok 13) < kisk-

rejoice, cessoˇWoˇn i (1445 ¹Yong 62) < ceh- fear; kwutcoˇWoˇn i (1445 ¹Yong 66) < kwut- hard, ˇkotcoˇwoˇn i (1463 Pep 2:227a) < ˇkoth- be alike, tutcoˇWoˇn i (1449 Kok 97) < tut-/tul- hear, cwotcoˇWon (1447 Sek 24:33b) = cwoccoˇWoˇn i (1449 Kok 14) < cwoch- follow.
 -ˇo.n i ''la. ¶kyeyˇGwuzoˇWo.n i 'la ([1447→]1562 Sek 3:13a) he was defeated; patcoˇWo.n i ''la (1459 Wel 1:9a) < pat- get.
 -ˇo.n i '-ngi ''ta. ¶patcoˇWoˇn i '-ngi ''ta (1445 ¹Yong 63) < pat- offer.
 -onˇtˇay. ¶ˇhoˇzoWonˇtˇay (1447 Sek 6: 9-10) < °ho- do.
 -onˇtˇiˇn i. ¶ˇpwoˇzoWonˇtˇiˇn i (1459 Wel 8:28a) < °pwo- see.
 -ˇonˇtˇol. ¶kewuzoˇWonˇtˇol (1449 Kok 62) < kewu- oppose.
 -oˇn ywo. ¶¨etcoWoˇn ywo (1447 Sek 13:16b) < ¨et- get.
 + -ˇoˇna, adversative. ¶mwotcoˇWoˇna (1445 ¹Yong 11) < mwot- gather.
 + -ˇosiˇkwo, hon gerund. ¶ˇcwuzoˇwosiˇkwo (1459 Wel se:13a).
 + -ˇosilq, hon prosp (unmodulated) mod. ¶¨pwoyˇzoˇWosilqˇcey (1445 ¹Yong 91) < ¨pwoy- show.
 + -oˇsin, honorific (unmodulated) modifier. -osiˇn i. ¶¨syeyzoˇWosiˇn i (1449 Kok 34) < ¨syey- make stand; patcoˇWosiˇn i (1449 Kok 6) < pat- offer, anccoˇWosiˇn i (1449 Kok 46) < anc- sit.
 -osiˇn i '-ngi ''ta. ¶kiluzoˇWosiˇn i '-ngi ''ta (1459 Wel 10:19a) < kil ᵁ⁄ₒ- / kilG- raise.
 -ˇosinˇtˇay. ¶ˇpwoyzoˇWosinˇtˇay (1449 Kok 128) < ¨pwoy- show.
 + -ˇoˇsiten, hon retr mod. ¶ˇpwozoˇwoˇsiteˇn i (1463 Pep 5:87a) < °pwo- see.
 + -ˇosyam, honorific modulated substantive. ¶ˇpwozoˇwosyaˇm ol (1482 Kum-sam 4:6a) < °pwo- see; patcoˇwosyaˇm ol (1459 Wel 18:62b) < pat- get.
 + -ˇosyasˇta, honorific exclamatory statement. ¶tutcoˇwosyasˇta (1463 Pep 6:83b) < tut-/tul- hear.
 + -ˇosyaˇtoy, honorific modulated accessive. ¶¨mwutcoˇWosyaˇtoy (1459 Wel 1:10b) < ¨mwut-/mwul- ask.

 + -osywoˇsye, polite command. ¶neˇkizoˇWosywoˇsye (1449 Kok 2) < neˇki- think.
 + -ˇta, indicative assertive. ¶ˇpwozopˇta (1459 Wel 8:28a, 18:81a) < °pwo- see.
 + -taˇka, transferentive + pcl. ¶THAPˇay nyeˇheˇtwu-'ys¨soptaˇka (1447 Sek 24:31b) were kept in the stūpa. KUM-KWANˇol tu¨zoptaˇka ¨mwotˇho.yaˇnol (1447 Sek 23:23b) they tried to lift the chest of gold but were unable.
 + -taˇn i, retrospective mod + postmodifier. ¶syemˇkiˇzoptaˇn i (1449 Kok 140) < syemˇki- serve.
 + -teˇla, retr assert. ¶pat¨copteˇla (1459 Wel 2:37b) < pat- get; ˇhoˇzopteˇla (1447 Sek 23:58b, 1459 Wel 2:33b) < °ho- do.
 + -ˇten, retr modifier. ¶ˇhozopˇten (1447 Sek 13:51a) < °ho- do; ¨ep.sopˇten (1449 Kok 75) < ¨eps- lack.
 -teˇn i. ¶ˇwoˇzopteˇn i (1449 Kok 23) < °wo- come, ˇsyeˇy¨sopteˇn i (1459 Wel 10:10a) were standing (< is[i-s]op-).
 -tenˇtoy n'. ¶ˇhoˇzoptenˇtˇoy n' (1463 Pep 2:226a) < °ho- do.
 + -ˇti, suspective. ¶¨as.sopˇti aˇniˇhwo-ngi ''ta (1447 Sek 24:31b) < ¨az- seize.
 + -wol(q), modulated prospective modifier. ¶ˇhozoˇWo.l iˇGwos (1447 Sek 9:40a), ˇhoˇzoWwoˇl i (1459 Wel 23:65a) < °ho- do; ˇpwozoˇWwo.l [i] 'yeˇn ywo (1447 Sek 6:19a) < °pwo- see, poyˇhwozoˇWwoˇl i '-ngi ''ta (1447 Sek 6:11b) < poyˇhwo- learn / study, kap.soˇWwol ¨iˇl ol (1459 Wel 9:62b) < kaph- repay, tutcoˇWwoˇl i '-ngi sˇkwo (1447 Sek 6:11a) < tut-/tul- hear.
 + -wom, modulated subst. ¶ilˇGwuzoˇWwoˇm ol (1459 Wel se:17a) < ilˇGwu- achieve; sulˇssoˇWwoˇm ay (1459 Wel se:10b) < sulh- grieve.
 + -won, modulated modifier. ¶ˇkazoˇWwonˇna 'ylwoˇn i (1459 Wel 8:92b) < °ka- go, ˇpwoˇzoWwoˇn i (1459 Wel 10:8b, 23:86b) < °pwo- see, ¨piˇzoWwoˇn i (1459 Wel 2:52a) < ¨pil- beg; pis.soˇwoˇn i (1463 Pep 3:108a) < pih- sprinkle, sow.
 + -woˇtoy, modulated accessive. ¶¨aˇzoWwoˇtoy (1445 ¹Yong 51) < ¨al- know; ¨mwutˇcoWwoˇtoy (1447 Sek 6:20b, 1459 Wel 9:23b) < ¨mwut-/mwul- ask.

INDEX

INDEX

INDEX

This is primarily an index to Part I, but included are Part II references to entries taken from the earlier pages. In seeking information on a subject or form not entered below, the reader should consult the alphabetical list in Part II, which contains many Middle Korean words, as well as more detailed information on the modern forms.

Note: English plural references are often listed with the singular: "stem" = "stem" or "stems", "verb" = "verb" or "verbs". References to centuries are regularized to numerical notation: for "fifteenth century" see "15th century". For the most part, verbs are entered in the stem shape.

7th century (Chinese) 1, 46, 50, 61
12th century (language) 196
1400s 50, 431, 815; late 1400s 513; 1490s 49
15th century (language/text) 1, 4, 22, 42, 43, 44, 45, 46, 47, 49, 53, 54; (lenition) 56, 59; 60; (accent) 69; (short variants of °ho- forms) 92; (text) 96; 108, 196, 134, 232, 233, 235, 237, 238, 255, 267
1500s 35; early ~ 49, 81, 431, 764; 1540s 56
16th century 15, 42, 44, 45, 46, 49, 53, 56, 59; (dictionary Cahoy) 65; (text) 71; 238
1600s 52, 52, 554, 608, 759; early ~ 269; 1650s 622
17th century: (texts) 56; 267; 663
1700s 26, 35, 51
18th century 17, 47, 56
1800s 28, 52, 594; late ~ 419
19th century 26, 27, (texts) 56, 122; (late) 594, 613
1920s 234; early ~ 28
1930s 675; early ~ 13
20th century 1, 17, 18, 42, 56, 60, 112; 332
" " 197
-a < -˙a (inf) 231, 251; (vs -e for inf after ···aC- stem) 343; 415, 465
-a 'child' 165
···a- stems: (all high-low) 71; (absorb inf) 252, 267; (lists) 349, 350
a = ya 'question' (postmodifier) 160, 306
a / ya (vocative / exclamatory particle) 196, 415
˙···a-˙a (effective inf) 267
abbreviated form/shape 40, 232, 258, 259
abbreviated quotative constructions 244, 332
abbreviation 5; (of wu to u and ywu to yu in notation) 8; 13, 18; (of copula to 'y-) 55; 87, 89, 92, 130, 133, 150, 193, 217, 220, 235, 243, 245, 260, 265, 299, 300, 331, 339, 679; (table of abbreviations used in this book) 414
aberrant etymology 219

ability 315
ablaut 341
abrupt end 142
absolute case 286
absolute constructions 130; numeral in ~ 174
absolute position 140; (of adverb) 135
absolute use of nouns 280
absorbed h 35
absorbed infinitive ending 38
abstract: events 324; meaning 344; noun 131, 279
accent 6; ~ and spelling in MK texts 85; ~ of earlier forms 60; change (to rising) 271; 274
accent classes 66
accent dots (positioning) 85
accent evidence for -taka analysis 214
accent groups by stem shape 72
accent-marked attestations 68
accent marks of Middle Korean 35
accent patterns 35
accent suppression before particles 68
accent types of stems 70
accentual anomaly 71, 72, 588
accentual distinctions (lost in modern Seoul) 60
accentual doublets 84
accentual motivation (for lenitions) 53
accentual patterns (not from China) 61, 64
accentual patterns of nouns and adverbs 62
accentual residue (of a lost vowel) 268, (from contraction) 270
accentual variants 64
accentuation (confirming derivation ¨ti- from *ti-˙[G]i- 55
accentuation of verb forms 69
acceptability of noun compounds 296
accessive -˙toy → -˙w^{u}o˙toy 266, 271, 329, (of verb of saying) 332
accidental gaps 30
accreted noun / suffix -i (early examples) 65

accretion of the suffix -i 43
accretion of y after ‑y or ‑i 54
accusative 130, 282; (not marking direct object) 284; 286; 847-50
accusative(-marked) phrase 216
accusative-marked noun/phrase 216, 284, 326
accusative-marked object 130; (of vi) 216
accusative marker/particle (ul/lul) 12, 99, 100; (omitted) 111; 173, 195, 216, 268, 274
achi 145, 156, 415
-aci 145, 415
āci = ālci 242
acik 48, 137
acoustic impressions 23
active: (verb) 218; (adjective) 289; (voice) 297; (sentence) 315
addressee 245, 268, 299, 312
adjacent elements 274
adjectival exclamations 300
adjectival noun 33, 89, 140, 162, 189, 190; (that is from a bound adverb) 256; (+ an ellipted hakey) 277; (+ derived adverb ← postnominal adjective; + postnominal adjective) 345
adjectival postadjectivals 191
adjectival postnoun/postmodifier 160
adjectival sentence 296, 300
adjective (= descriptive verb) 89, 189, 220, 226; (takes two subjects in possessive meaning) 287; 289, 290, 298, 305, 307, 315, 316, 332, 340
adjective: adverb from ~ 163, 164
adjective: noun from ~ 164
adjective infinitive + la 243
adjective sentence 295
adjective stem 191; (ending in w) 233; 309, 310
adjectives (prefer long negative) 316; (and double negative) 322
adjectives of: evaluation and emotion 291; frequency, quantity 294; size 288
adjunct 272, 274, 277, 286; (expansions) 287; (within a nominalized sentence) 323; 326, 330, 335
adjunctive 258
adnominal 134, 282
adnominal conversion of copula 151
adnominal endings 245
adnominal extended pcl phrase 194
adnominal function 324
adnominal modification 171, 286, 335

adnominalization 248, 297, 300, 302, 323, 324; (of retrospective) 326; (based on quotation) 328; 338
adnominalized copula 332
adnominalized phrase 131; (adverbial) 135
adnominalized quotation (as a substitute for the adnominalized copula) 332
adnominalized sentence 272, 290, 324, 326, 327; (plural reference in ~) 830
adnominalized verb: subject of ~ 69
adnominalizer 259; (English ~) 328
adnominal particle 172, 235, 261, 284
adnominal phrase 19, 280, 297
adnominal relationship (of pcl to noun) 280
adnominal sentence 281
adnominal treatment of object of vnt 188
adnoun: 26, 45, 88, 146; (+ noun, + quasi-free noun) 19; 26, 45, 88, 146; (+ noun, + noun phrase, + postnoun) 276; 277
adnouns: list 1 (exclusive) 147
adnouns: list 2 (non-exclusive) 147
adnouns: list 3 (pseudo-adnouns) 149
adnoun title 133
adverb: (+ verb) 19, 277; (ending in ‑i triggers velar lenition) 55; 88, 135; (modifying other adverb) 135; (conjunctional ~) 135; (+ **tul** but not + focus partcle) 136; (as if noun with dropped particle) 136; (+ number) 138, 276; 145, 162; (movable ~) 174; (between VN **ul/lul** and **ha-**) 189; (in reciprocal valence) 194; (+ noun) 276; (+ copula) 277; (limited in use) 296; 340, 345
adverbative 3; (-ˋkey) 54, 70; (~ forms) 140; (adj lacks) 217; (-**key**) 226; 247, (~ mood) 255; 308, 330, 339
adverb-deriving suffix -i 234, 347
adverbial 3; (~ role) 130, 282; (~ conversions) 151; (~ extended pcl phrase) 194, 281, 282; (~ phrase) 19, 88, 135, (adnominalized) 135, (numeral as) 174, 272, 280, 281, 282, 297; (treatment of the object of a vnt) 188; 255; (~ sentence) 280, 281, 300; (~ relationship) 286; (~ modification) 335
adverbialization 247, 297, 300, 303, 329, 339
adverbialized number 172
adverbialized phrase: (extruded) 326; 329
adverbialized quantifier (new?) 172
adverb-intensifying suffix 55
adverbs of: assertion, contingency, degree 138; manner 139; place 140; time 136, 282

adversative -una / -na 100, 243, 249 266, 329
affirmative 297; (sentence) 315; (copula) 316; 327
affix 275
affricate 28, 46, 49, 57; (nasal before ~) 48
affricate-initial phonograms 45
affrication (~ of palatalized stops) 46; (dating the ~ of t(h)i and t(h)y) 47, 111; 48; (~ and nasality) 48
afterthought 300, 303, 304, 331
agent 315; 496
···ah- (stems) 231, 251; (list) 349
···a(h)- stems (list) 104-5, 365
-ah- / -eh- 220; 415
ahistorical elision 54
ahop-i, ahopq-i 187
ahuley; ahuleyq nal 185
- ˙a k 416
-ak / -ek 163; 347; 416
ak / lak (postmodifier) 161, 416, 852
akka 137
-akw(un)i 163
···a-l- stems (list) 360
-al = -al / -el 163, 416
al (adnoun) 147, 416
al (counter) 180, 416
ā-l- 'know' 224, 240, 242, 255, 271, 318, 332, 336; 417
alay 196
alay(q), alays (pseudo-adnoun) 150
alay a (= a˙lay o) 25
a˙lay o = alay a 42
ālci mōs ha- 318
al.e tut- 251
alh.i (postnoun < der n) 158, 416
-al.i 163, 416
alittaw- 144; 361
'all' 173
alli- (vc) 224, 240
allomorph 98, 99; ("altered" ~) 110; 274
allophones (of /l/) 28; (of l) 51
allophonic level: assimilations at ~ 51
allye ci- 315; allye cye iss.ta 291
/allyeng/ 122
ālm 255, 417; ¨al˙m ye > ālmye 255
alo- 141
alphabet 95; Korean ~ 106
alphabetization 21
alphabetizing lists 5

alternant shapes (of stems and endings) 230
alternation 99, 100; (of w) 233
···alu- stems 361
alum: (in alum tapta) 144; (counter) 184
āl.um = ālm 'knowledge' 242
al.un for ān 242
al.up.nita = āp.nita 242
alveolar 17; (~ affricates) 24; (~ ridge) 28
always-high stems 70
-am = -em (derived substantive) 255, 887, 889
ama (to) 138; 304, 334; 418
ambiguity 20, 133, 278, (inherent) 280, 282, 283, 286, 314
ambiguous sentence 283; (adnominal / adverbial) 280; 336
ambivalent stems = -(H)- stems 231, 242, 251; (list) 365
-amchi 163, 418
Americans 300
am(h) (adnoun, bound noun) < ˙amh 'female' 109, 149; 417
-ami 164, 418
ām' man 138, 418
āmo = āmu 145, 148, 418
*¨am˙o-l- (defective stem) 256, 418
¨a˙mo˙la 219, 256, 418
¨amo˙lan 256, 418
¨a˙moli > āmuli (der adv < defective adj) 256, 418, 419
āmu 296, 418
āmu-ccolok 139, 145, 164, 418
āmulay 243, 252, 418
āmule-, āmule(h)- 134, 219, 251, 252, 418-9
āmule ha- < āmuleh- 256, 418
āmuley for āmulay 252
āmuli 134, 138, 419
āmu tey 134
an (neg adv) 189, 419; anq (y···, i···) 111
an < ˙anh 'inside' 197
-an 'shore' 165
ān- (vt) 231, 232; 364
analogical innovations 240
analogy (restoring lenited velar?) 663
analytic phrases (abbreviations of ~) 265
analytic structures 267
anaphora 135
anaphoric designator 135
anaphoric use of deictics 134
a(n)c- (vi) 48, 108; 364
anc- 216, 223, 231, 232, 243, 288, 319

anc.e iss.ta: (vs anc.ess.ta) 244; 291
anc.e la and anc.ke la 243
ancestral forms 61
an cha- 229
anc.hi- 313
anc.key ha- 313
anc.ko iss- 294
"and" forms 329
-ang / -eng 163, 347, 420
ʾanh > an 'inside' 109
anh-, ani ha- < aˑni ˚ho- (aux): -ci ~ 228, 339; 364; 420
anh.i (der adv) 146, 420
anh.nunta 339
ani < aˑni 59; (+ copula) 136; (as interj) 136; (as precopular noun) 146; (an(i)) 139, 146; 420-1
aˑni (optional triggering of lenition) 55; ~ ˑGa, ~ ˑGwo = *~ ˑkwo, ~ ˑka, ~ ʾn ˑka, ~ ʾn ˑkwo 55; (+ accusative, locative, comitative) 135
ani 'ci (negative copula suspective) 273, 421
*aˑni ˙ʾeps- 218
/anietta/ = ani 'ess.ta 316
(?*)aˑni is- 218
anq iss- /anniss-/ 111
ani 'la (neg cop) 151, 423
aˑni ˙'la (? < *aˑni 'ta) 273, 423
aˑni ˙lol 135, 424
aˑni ˙'lwo ˙la (?*aˑni ˙lwo ˙ta) 273, 424
animate (noun) 131, 287, 288, 291; (honorific) 764; 744
animate-inanimate distinction 292; 744, 764
animate direct-object verbs 289
animate indirect-object verbs 289, 292
animate-subject verbs 288
animation 289, 291
aˑni ˙non 135, 425
aninya = ani ʾn ya 316, 425
ani 'ta (negative copula) 146, 195, 286, 289; (as unanalyzed anita) 316, 425
aˑni ˙˙ta = aˑni [ho]ˑta 273
aˑni ˙tha = aˑni h[o]ˑta 273, 425
ani to 135; aˑni (···) ˙two 135, 425
aˑni ˙yey 136
anoˑ-hito (Japanese) 444
anomalous forms 256
anomalous vowel length in infinitives 38
anomaly (accentual: transferentive) 71, 72, 588

Anpyen 41
An Pyenghuy 112
anq (y···, i···) 111
An Sangchel 33, 240
anticipation (of consonants that are reinforced or aspirated) 52
anticipatory 226
antithetical clause 849
antonym 146, 162
Antong 34, 60
an tul V 135
anxiety 323
an' 'ya (neg cop inf) 273, 426
aˑnʾ 'ye = (?*)aˑni ˙ʾye (neg cop inf) 273, 426
/anyetta/ = an' yess.ta 316
-ap- / -p- = -aw- / -w-: SEE -ep-.
apeci, ape' nim 299
aph 197, 426-7
-api 164
apical 17, 46, 48, 58, 93
apical elision 242, 265
apical lenition 57, 234
apostrophe 4, 5, 13, 28, 40, 54; (to note elision) 58; 87; (location) 89; 150, 235
apperception 297, 300, 305, 338
apperceptive: (mood) 245; 246; (element) 259; (sentence) 260, 302; 264; (··· kwun) 281; (ending, postmodifier) 307
apposition 286, 335
approximate numerals 166, 174
approximate cardinal numerals: list 178
approximate ordinal numerals: list 179
a[r]-, aˑr- (Japanese) 70, 218
arguments taken by the predicate 283
arithmetic 177
articles 88, 192
articulation 27, 46, 57, 93
articulatory process 261
artificial distinction 249
artificial pause 100
artificial readings 44, 61, 95
artificial spelling distinction 41
as- 'seize' 236; 363
asking (verb of ~) 295
aspect 84; (~ marker) 70, 72, 214, 304; (~ morphemes) 244; 246; (~ formative) 258; 261; (~ marking of sentence types) 265; 290, 296
aspirate 24, 27, 49; (that is from assimilation to an aspirate) 116

aspirated (consonants / obstruents) 27; (the final velar) 60
aspiration 29, 232
-ass- 244, 246
assertion: adverbs of ~ 138
assertive: (mood) 245, 304; 246, 248; (ending) 257, 300
assertive and attentive endings: list 248
-ass.ess.keyss.nun 250
-ass.ess.tun 250
-ass.ess.ulq 250
assibilation 31
assigning particles to roles 297
assimilated variants of genitive s 23
assimilation 23, 26; (of apicals) 31; 32, 39; (of u to a labial) 43; 51; (of vowel to prior vowel) 238, 348; 268
assimilatory: adjustments 51; voicing 59
-ass.keyss.nun, -ass.keyss.tun, -ass.nun 250
association of borrowed word with character 95
-ass.tun 249
-ass.ulq 250
assumptive 247
asterisk 4
asup 187
āta (= ālta) siph.i 242
attachment rules unique to -῭zoW- 268
attentive: (mood) 245, 246, 304; (ending -kka) 257, 258
attitude (marked by particle) 192
attributive terms (treated as nouns or adnouns) 216
atul, atu' nim 299
"augmentative particle" 817
-aunsu (counter) 184
authoritative: 3; (style) 248, 254, 297
automatic alternation (of pitches) 61, 99; 109, 116, 231
automatic compression 102
automatically predictable phonetic entity 29
automatic lengthening of final vowel in one-syllable phrase 33
automatic metathesis 663
automatic morphophonemic rules 8
automatic reinforcement 13, 27, 31, 44, 130
automatic suppression of y after i or y 232, 274
auxiliary 38, 218; ~ (processive) verb 89, 93, 219, (list) 226; ~ adjective 94, 219, 226, 227; 252; 251, 259; (~ constructions) 290; 291, 315, 330, 333

auxiliary conversions: recursiveness 229
auxiliary preemphasis 291, 318
available undergoing (of an action) 222
awkward examples 214
awu < azo / azG··· < *asok 239
awulle: ··· kwa ~ 195
awus (postnoun) 156, 428
ay 25, 43
/ay/ and /ey/ (merger) 252, 257
-ay (makes noun or adv) 164, 257, 429
-ay- (formative for vc) 220, 224, 429
···ay- stems: (absorb inf ending) 252; (lists) 349, 350
···ay- stems 466
····ay (inf of ambivalent stem) 231, 251
ay (adnoun, noun, bound noun) 148, 428-9
-a(y)ci 163, 429
···ay(h)- stems 365
···ay-l- stem 360
a.yey 148
āykel ha- 'appeal' 295
-a(y)ki / -e(y)ki 163, 429
āymen (pseudo-adnoun) 150
-aymi 164, 429
-a(y)ngi / -e(y)ngi 163, 429
-aypi 164, 429
ayq toyta 148
···ay῭ya (inf) 466
Azbuka 28, 47, 93, 595
back formation 25, 27, 39, 47, 112, 237
back low rounded version (of e in Seoul) 43
back rounded vowels 4
back-shift of initial accent (of copula ῭i- and of particle ῭o῭lwo) 65
back unrounded vowel 4; (high) 18
back vowels: earlier articulation of modern ~ 43
bar (written for repeat vowel) 34
base = stem 87
basic accent 34, 69, 84, 241
basic dots in endings (not shown) 61
basic finals 30
basic form 29, 48, 55; (with impermissible coda) 100; 238; (of -L- verbs) 241; 297
basic ···h 56
basic phonemes 6
basic rising accent of deferential -῭zoW- 85
basic sentence types 296
basic shape 15, 31, 50, 52, 95, 245
basic t (nouns ending in ~) 101
basic vocabulary 94

basic vowel length 33
'because' 330, 623
behavioral 227
Beijing 97, 98
beneficiary 298
Biblical names 132
bibliography 407-3
bilabial fricative [F] 27, 36
binoms 113
blending of low and high pitch/tone (> rise) 232, 237, 241
Bloch, B. 3
body part 285
bookish style 132
book titles 133
borrowed words 95
borrowing 45, 95, 46; (early) 95
boundary 8, 32, 53, 220
bound adjectival noun = postadjectival 144, 191, 257
bound adjective 219, 220
bound adjective -p- 57, 60
bound adnoun 88, 141, 144, 151
bound adverb 131, 140
bound auxiliary (honorific) 268
bound Chinese morpheme 146, 275
bound compound noun 144; (+ postnoun) 276
bound counter -es 174
bound element 12, 54; (of core numerals) 176; 220, 278
bound infinitive 220
bound morpheme 17, 152
bound noun 88, 109, 131, 144, 220
bound particle la (origins) 217
bound postnoun 88, 131, 151, 144, 156, 162, 164, 278
bound postnouns (Chinese): list 165
bound postverb 88, 144, 219, 220, 243
bound prenumeral 156
bound preparticle 106, 131, 144, 145-6, 870
bound preverb (bound adverb or prefix) 88, 131
bound shortening 278
bound stem 70, 71, 72, 53, 84, 214, 263, 268, 269
bound verb 88, 219
boys' names 164, 818, 819
brackets 4, 5, 55, 58, 61
breathy release (of nasal or liquid) 28
broken type 61, 68, 267

Brown, R. 344
brusqueness 287
Buddhism 4; Buddhist terms 98
"but" forms 329
···c(-) examples 103; ···c- stems (list) 363
c (noun-final ~) treated as if s 102
c for ty (in 1632) 112
···c ≠ ···ch (phonogram evidence for) 49, 58; (merger of both with ···s) 431
-ca (subj assert): (+ pcl ko) 213; 245, 246, 248, 306, 307; 431-2
-ca = -ca (māca) 'as soon as' 58, 329; 432
-ca 'person' 165
··· ca < ˬCYA 'person' 97, 131, 134, 165, 288, 290, 431
ca- < °ca- 'sleep' 243, 271; 431, 435
ca (auxiliary): -ko ~ 227
ca (counter) 180, 183
cachey 'oneself; itself' 134
cacwu 137
Cahoy 51
cajolative -ulyem / -lyem (una) 247, 258, 308
-cak = -(c)cak 164, 191, 432
-cak (counter) 183
cāk- (adj) 288, 344; 364
cakceng 161, 432
cake la 243
cak-hi 257
caki 'oneself' 134, 135, 433; ~ tul 134
-ca kkwuna 213, 433
caksimyen = c^e/aksimyen (postmodifier): -ulq ~ 'if' 160, 433
-ca kwu 305, 433
cal (adv) 139, 141, 189, 433
calmos (adv or noun) 102, 136
calque (= loan translation) 98
calwu$_1$ < calo / calG··· < *calok 'sack' 239
calwu$_2$ < colo / colG··· < *colok 'handle' 239; (as counter) 180
cam (subst < ca-): ~ (ul) ca- 254, 279, 433
-ca (māca) 'as soon as' 58. SEE -ca.
/camcakho/ = cam-ca' kho < cam-cam hako 343
cāmqkan 137
'can', 'cannot' 315
can (counter) 181
can (pseudo-adnoun) 150
caney 'you' 133, 296, 434; ~ tul / kkili 133
-cang = -(c)cang = -(c)cak 164, 434

-cang₁ 'chief' 165
-cang₂ 'place' 165, 434
-cang₃ = (q)-cang 'document' 165, 434
-cang (counter) 184
cang (counter) 180
cangi = ca(y)ngi (postnoun) 157, 434
Cang Kyenghuy 326
Cang Sekcin 2, 134, 326, 829
Cang Sengen 1, 294
Cang Yengswuk 1
-c' anh- 323; 'c' anh- = ici anh- 434
canonical shapes 61
-ca 'nta 332, 435
Canton (Guǎngdōng) 50; Cantonese 61, 95
-caow- / -cao- 299, 435
cap < ˙CCAP (adnoun, bound noun) 148, 435
capam (counter) 181
cap.hi- (vpt) 221, (vp / vc) 222
cap.i (postnoun < der n) 158
capitalized letters 5
capswusi- 226, (capswus-) 298
cardinal numerals: list 176
cas (NK adnoun) = cat- 150
case 286
case marker 88; (casual dropping) 89; 230, 286; (lost when extruding epitheme) 326
case-marking: function 3; particles 282
casin 'oneself' 134
casual: (construction) 38, (statement) 42, 301; (form) 259; (sentence) 273, 300, 301, 302
cat- 140, 435
categories of sentence relationship 304
categorizers 144
category designator 133; 372
catheticizer 227
cathectic object 522
causal assertion 330
causative 22, 39, 107, 173; (conversion for vn) 192; (verb/stem) 218, 312; (used like transitive passive) 222; 227, 262; (voice) 297; 312; (conversions) 330, 337; 496
causative and passive stems that are derived from monosyllabic vowel stems 73
causative formative (bound postverb): (- ˙i-) 70; 218, 220; (shapes shared with passive) 222
causative made on a causative 314
causative sentence: (with two **ul** phrases) 314; 315; (plural reference in ~) 830
causativization 173
causativized negative 335

causativized negativized causative 335
-caw- 299; 361
cāylay 295
ca(y)ngi (postnoun) 156, 436
cc (tends to suppress sibilant) 29
-ccak- = -(c)cak 164, ~-cikun 191, 432
··· ccak 'direction; appearance' 131; 436
ccak (counter) 181, 185, 436
ccali (postnoun) 156, 436
ccalp- / ccelp- (< *cyelp*- < ...) 105, 238; 363
-ccang = -(c)cang = -(c)cak 164
ccay 'and all, as it is' (postmod, postn) 160, 437
ccay '-th' (postnoun [postnumeral]) 156; 436-7
-ccek = -(c)cek 164, 292, 441
ccek- (postnom adj sep) 229; 364; 437
-ccek-cikun = -(c)cek-cikun 191, 441
···cci- stems (list) 353
ccic- (vt) 363; ccic.e ci- 315
···ccie → ···ccye = / ···cce/ 93
-ccik = -(c)cik 164, 456
-ccimak = -(c)cimak 164, 457
-ccok = -(c)cok 164, 461
··· ccok 'direction' 131, 437
ccok-ccok, cok-cok (postmodifier) 160, 437
-ccolok 164. SEE āmu ~ .
-ccum = -(c)cum 164, 462
ccum (pcl) 196, 198; 437-9
-ccumak = -(c)cumak 164, 462
ccum eykey 198m 437
ccum mata (older usage) 198, 438
-ccwuk = -(c)cwuk 164, 463
-ce 'authored by ···' 165
ce (as pronoun) 135, 439
ce 'I / me' 133, 193, 296; 'oneself' 134, 146; 'you' 134; 439
ce < ˙*tye* 'that (yonder)' 131; (/ co) 134, 148; 345; 439
ce (= c'e) = cye < cie 259, 439
ce (auxiliary): -ko ~ 227
ce-cel lo = ce(y)-cel lo 146; 440
cē-huy 133, 134; (never *~ uy) 295; 440
-cek = -(c)cek 164, 441; ~-cikun 191, 441
··· cek < ˙*TYEK* '···ic' (bound postnoun) 151, 162; (-cek) 165; 440-1
cek < *cek* 'time' (etymology) 98; 131, 161; 440
cēk- (adj) 255, 288, 294, 345; 364; 441
ce ka = cey ka 'I' 196
ce (kes) 'it' 134, 439, 441; ~ tul 'they/them' 134
cēki (/ coki) 134; 140, 344, 441
cēk-i (= cēk.i) vs cak-hi 257
ce-kkacis (/ co-kkacis) 147, 441

ceksimyen = c^eaksimyen (postmodifier):
  -ulq ~ 'if' 160, 441
··· cek ulo 140; 440
-cel 'festival' 165
celay / colay 237, 243, 252
cele / cole < ˈtyeˈle 134, 219, 237, 243, 252, 441
celey said for celay 252
celi (/ coli) < ˈtyeli 134; 140, 256; (never *~ uy, *~ ey, *~ 'ta) 295; 442
cel lo < cel-ˈlwo 146, 442
celpan 174
-cem = (q)-cem 165, 188
cem 'o'clock' (counter) 183
ce man 140; 442
cēmsim 47
(-)cen (category designator) 133
-cen (counter) 182
cen(-) 'entire' (bound adnoun) 147, 152
cen(-) 'former' (bound adnoun) 152; 443
cen 'before' (postn, n, adn) 148, 158, 197; 443
cen < cen-hye < cen-ha.ye 141
Cen Cayho 22
Cen Cenglyey 272
-ceng (counter) 183
-ceng 'one' [vulgar], -cengi 'stuff' [vulgar] 163
Ceng Insung 175, 218, 223, 260
Ceng Yenchan 61, 62, 69
ceng kkey (bound postnoun + postnoun) 156, 443
ceng-wel 187
cēnha (title) 132
cen-hye 138
Cenla 233, 238, 668
central area 150, 231
central articulation of u 43
central dialect 42, 43
cep (counter) 181
-cepcep (bnd adj-n) 191; 444
cepsi (counter) 180
cēpttay 134
ce-taci = ce-ta(k)ci 140, 444
*ce ttay 134
ce tul / kkili 'you all' 134, 444
cew- (postnom adj insep) 229; 361; 444
-cey₁ (bound noun) 'remedy' 165, 193
-cey₂ (bound noun) 'system' 165
cey- 'several' (bound adnoun) 152
cēy- (bnd prenumeral 157; = cēy '...th' 147, 445

cey (counter) 181
cey 'I [formal]' 92, 133, 193; 'you' 134; 444-5
cey < ce uy 92; 'one's own' (as pseudo-adnoun) 149; 444-5
ce(y)-cel lo 146
Ceycwu 4, 5, 25, 42, 48, 58, 59, 60, 93, 171, 239, 553, 627, 675, 711, 789, 796, 808, 810, 907, 926
cēy ha.ye: ··· ey ~ 194
cēy-il (as pseudo-adnoun) 149, 175; 178
cēy-ī (as pseudo-adnoun) 149
cey ka 'I' 196
ceyˈkwom 55, 445
cey-kkacis 147, 445
cēypal 139
cēy payk 175
ceyyeˈkwom 55, 446
(C)h and (C)s intrinsically voiceless 51
···ch(-) examples 104; ···ch- stems (list) 363
ch for thy in 1632 112
ch (noun-final ~) treated as if s 102, 446
··· cha < ˈCHO 97; (-tun ~) 161; 446
cha- (postnom adj insep) 229, 447
cha- (adj) 'cold' 316, 447
chac- 231, 288, 290; 363
cha iss.ta 291
-chak 164, 446
cha(l) (adnoun, bound noun) 'sticky' 149, 446
cham (adverb) 138, 149; 446-7
cham < chām (counter) 'spell' 182
chām 'verge' 161
Chamberlain, B.H. 817
chamq ta(la)h- → chamq ta(la)h.key 220
-changi = -cha(y)ngi 163, 447
character readings 61; (artificial) 95; (not used in loanwords) 112; (assigned phonetically) 132
··· chay 175, 447
chay (counter for buildings) 171, 180, 447-8
chay 'intact' (postmodifier, postnoun) 160, 447
-chayk 'policy' 165
chayk 'book' 275
-chayngi = -cha(y)ngi 165, 447
-che 'place' 165
che- 141, 448
chēci 163
-chek 164, 444; ~-cikun 191, 444
-chek (counter) 183
chek (counter) 180
Chelqcaq-pep period 4

chelem 145, 193, 196; 448-9
-cheng 'govt office' 165
cheng ha- 'request; invite' 295, 313; cheng khentay 449
-chengi = -che(y)ngi 165, 449
chēn ha- (adj-n insep) 313
chen-ye ccay 179
chep (counter) 181
ches ⋯ 'first' (spelling) 102; 147, 156, 449
ches ccay 175, 178, 449; ~ lo 334
cheum (ulo) 137
chey (chek) < ˙thyey 'pretense' (postmod vni insep) 161, 449
chey < ″THYEY (postnoun; noun) 158, 449
-che(y)ngi 163, 449
-chi- (intensive; vc formative) 220, 224; 450, 452
⋯chi- stems (list) 354
chi- (auxiliary) 224, 226, 230, 290, 452
chi- (postnom v sep) 228, 229, 452; (postnom adj insep) 452
chi- < ˙chi- 'raise' 224, 451
chi- < ˙thi- 141, 145, 158; 451-2
chi 'bad weather' postn (postnom vni) 160, 450
chi 'fixed quantity'; 'feel' (postn) 157, 450
chi (counter) 183, 450
chi = haci after voiced sound 92, 450
⋯ chi 'stuff, thing; guy, one' 131, 450
⋯chie → ⋯chye = /⋯che/ 93
chiki (postnoun < summative) 158, 452
chiko (as quasi-pcl) 194, 451
children: (names) 164; 343
⋯chie → ⋯chye = /⋯che/ 93
Chiltay 57
chilu- 242; 361
chin- (bound adnoun) 152
chin < CHIN (adnoun, adj-n) 152
China 4, 46, 94, 132
Chinese 1, 4, 13, 14, 18, 45, 47, 50; (~ passage) 56, (~ text) 57; (classical ~) 60, 95, 96; 85, 86, 132, 274
Chinese binoms 50, 278
Chinese borrowings: prehistoric ~ 98
Chinese bound adnouns 151, (list) 152
Chinese calques (= loan translations) of Indic 98
Chinese characters 1, 4, 6, 22, 33, 42, 44, 45, 50, 96, 112, 113, 132; 372
Chinese characters (phonological representations of Korean) 42, 96

Chinese clichés 555
Chinese components: words with ~ 5
Chinese dialects 50; (words borrowed from ~) 97
Chinese elements (treated as if Korean) 14; 32
Chinese etymology 113
Chinese l⋯ 4
Chinese loans (loanmorphs, loanwords) 14, 16, 17, 30, 31, 33, 43, 45,61, 95, 109; (false?) 98; 107, 109, 121, 132; (with ⋯w, the final labial semivowel) 925
Chinese loanwords naturalized early 16
Chinese morpheme 162, 280
Chinese names 4
Chinese numerals 147, 174
Chinese origin 16, 33, 45; (forgotten) 97; 275
Chinese particle YA 56
Chinese philologists 95
Chinese philosophical concept 344
Chinese phonologists 60, 61
Chinese readings 46, 49
Chinese suffixes 156; (list) 165
Chinese tones 35
Chinese transcriptions of Indic words 98
Chinese verb-object phrase 14
Chinese vocabulary 94; (basic shapes) 95, 112; 113, 151; (verbal nouns) 189; 275, 295, 344
Chinese words 6, 23, 35, 45, 50, 61, 95; (not associated with characters) 98; 110, 267, 270
-cho 'plant' 166
-cho 'seconds (of time)' (counter) 182
cho(-) < ˙CHWO (adnoun for the first ten days of the month) 148, 186; 452
cho- < ˙THYWOW 'super' (bnd adnoun) 153, 452
-chon (counter) 183
chōng- 'total' (bound adnoun) 153
-chongi 165, 452
chōy- 'most' (bound adnoun) 153
Choy Hak.kun 2, 48, 109, 187, 238, 239
Choy Hyenpay 2, 142, 175, 220, 224, 233, 243, 259, 260, 325, 588, 592, 790
Choy Iceng 17
Choy Myengok 58, 59, 415, 465
Choy Seycin 22
Choy Sungca 2
Choy Tongcwu 326
Choy Yengsek 283, 333, 849
⋯ chuk < ˙CUK 'side' 131, 452
-chung 'floor' (counter) 182

chwī ha- 288
-chwu- 220; (= -chi- intensive bnd postverb) 224; (formative for vc) 224, 256, 288, 452-3
··· chwuk 'group' 131, 453
chwuk (counter) 181, 182
chwum (ul) chwu- 279
Chwungcheng 240
-chwungi 163, 453
chwuw- (adj) 288, 289, 316; 362
chy = /ch/ 453
"chye" (spelling) 46, 48
chye (= /che/) 93; (= chie) 252, 453, 465
···chye 252
c(h)ye > c(h)ey with [ts-] 48
-ci$_{1-4}$ (bnd n) 'place, land'; 'paper'; (newspaper title); 'periodical' 166; 455
-ci < -˙ti (suspective ending) 31, 42, 227, 230, 232, 236, 247, 306; (~ style) 296, (statement) 302; 306, 324; 453-5
···ci- stems (list) 353-4
°ci-$_1$ 'want to do' (auxiliary) 79
ci- < °ti- (postnom v / adj insep) 146, 228, 229, 459
ci- < °ti- (aux sep) 218, 219, 227, 228, 230, 252, 259, 288, 290, 291
ci- verbs 289; 317
ci = haci after voiceless sound 92
ci < ˙ti = ˙t i '(uncertain) fact, ... ' (postmod) 160, 166, 250, 251, 300, 324, (forming an oblique question) 332; 455
ci < ˙ti = ˙t i '(the time) since' (postmod) 160, 455
ci 'stuff, thing' 145
ci < CI (Chinese pcl = uy) 188, 196, 455
···cie → ···cye = /···ce/ 93
cie as /ciye/ 237
cie (auxiliary): -ko ~ 227
cii-: -e ~ 227
-cik = -(c)cik 166, 456
cik < ˙cik (adjectival postsubst insep) 254, 455, 889
-ci ka anh-, -ci lul anh- 316; 456, 457
cikey (noun) 257
˙cik °ho˙ta 255, 263
ciki (postnoun) 157, 456
cikum 282
cil (postnoun) 157, 343, 456-7
cilmun ha- 'inquire' 295
cilu- (auxiliary): -e ~ 227; 361; 456-7

cim (counter) 181; cim ul ci- 279
-cimak = -(c)cimak 166, 457
-ci man (un) 244, 257, 259, 329; 457-8
-ci man anh- 318, 457
-ci man mōs ha- 318, 322, 457
-ci mōs hala, -ci mōs hay la 321
-cin (in mimetics) 164, 458
cin < CIN (adnoun, adj-n) 148; 458
cīna- 34, 47, 288
-ci 'na mālci 322
cīnay- 34
cince (postmodifier) 160, 458
Cincwu 27, 196, 233, 234, 237, 196, 233, 234, 237, 584, 602, 670, 732, 888
Cin.en kwenkong 45
-ci 'ni 306, 458
··· cin(i) 'falcon' 144
cintay (postmodifier) 160, 458
-ci nun anh-, -ci nun mōs ha- 322, 458
cip- 'pick up' 234; 362
-ci pakk ey mōs ha- 318, 458
cip-cip-i 255, 257
cip cip mata 347
cipkey (noun) 257
circle 18, 22, 49; (that is used to mark peculiar phonemes) 51
circumstantial sentences 260, 300
cis- (preverb) 140, 145, 459
cī(s)- 145, 157; (postnom v sep) 228; 231, 237; 363
cīs < ¨cus (? < *ci˙z-us) 'act, motion' 131, 157, 343; 458
citation form (of high/low stem) 71, 221
citations 18; (of forms) 20; 61
-ci to anh-, mōs ha- 318, 322, 460
··· ci to molunta 'maybe' 300, 303
-ci ya mōs hal ya 322, 460
-ci (yo) 42, 453, 460
-ci yo (~ style) 296; 306, 309
-ci yo → -c[y]o (-c' yo) 38, 464
-ci yo man (un) 214, 460
classes (of adjectives, nouns, verbs) 297
classical Chinese 60, 95, 97
clause 265
cliché 259, 300; 555; 800
closed o 25
closed syllable 51, 236, 341
close juncture 50, 192, 196
close-knit idioms 284

cluster 18, 22; (restrictions) 30; (reduction, reinforcement) 31; 43; (table) 99; (permitted) 100; 255
CM (= Cosen-e munqpep) 4, 141, 150, 175, 177, 195, 197, 217, 221, 222, 223, 229, 251, 291, 292, 294, 295, 296, 305, 322, 329, 335, 345, 500, 571, 602, 603, 604, 615, 717, 753, 761, 774, 777, 781, 794, 829, 874, 883
co (deictic) 'that' 148, 344, 460
coarticulation 46
coch- 231; 363
cocha (pcl) 194, 196, 460-1
coda 28, 29, 42, 49, 51, 341
codification of character readings 95
coexistence of two or more forms 8
cognate: ~ pitch and length in dialects 34; ~ borrowings (Japanese) 98; putative Japanese ~ 98; ~ complement 848
cognate object 216, 280, 848
cognate subject 216
cōh- 229; (shortened forms) 237; 288, 291
cōh.a = /cōa/ or /cōwa/ 237; cōh.a ha- 323
-cok = -(c)cok 166, 461
-cok 'tribe' 166
cok-cok, ccok-ccok (postmodifier) 162, 461
cok hi 257
coki (deictic) 344, 461
co-kkacis 147, 461
cokom 255, 344
cokomah- 243
cokum 150, 255, 344
*¨Col (not word-initial) but ¨ColC 241
coli 340, 462
collapsing constituents (IC's) 278
collapsing syllables 61
collective 347
collocation of particles 88
colloquial: (~ usage) 108; (~ Korean) 130; (~ speech) 231, 314; (~ contraction) 253; (~ language) 251; (~ variant) 251; (~ usage) 284; (~ form) 305
colloquialisms 284
combinatorial: (~ restrictions) 130, (of -usi-) 298; (~ factors for word boundaries) 261
colon 20, 32
com (adnoun; noun) 150; 255, 344, 462
comitative 287
comma 20; (~ intonation) 41, 42
command (~ form) 38; 41, 87, 217; (~ pcl la) 243; 245, 249, 251, 253, 257, 264, 297, 300, 305, 307, 318, 321, (cannot follow causal -e se) 330, 338
command-like instructions 305
compensatory lengthening 34, 36, 37, 38; 465
competing order (of particles in sequence) 198
competing phrases 109
competing reductions of syllable excess 102
competing variants 23, 243
competing version 57, 239
complement 130, 286, (a ~ noun) 318; (of the copula) 327; (~ proposition) 323; (of change of state) 551; (of neg aux) 551; (of similarity) 551
complementary distribution 46; (of symbols) 49
complementary object 254
completive 226
complex adnominalization 328
complex conversion 298
complex forms of the processive modifier 250
complex moods/endings: (built on effective) 54, (incorporating the gerund) 54; 245; (built on substantive) 247, 257, 258; 261
complex negative 315
complex -nun modifiers 324
complex sentence 296; (adnominalization applied to ~) 328
complex "tentative" forms 258
complex vowel nuclei 24
component (the palatal ~ of a front vowel) 254; (~ of a Chinese character) 372
component letters (of digraphs) 21
components 23
compound 31, 32; (~ verb) 38, 466; 44; (~ stem) 58; 65, 95; (~ adjective) 102; 107, 140; (~ verb stem) 141, 271; (~ noun) 233, (with lenition of -p-) 57, 261, 278; 270, 274; (~ adnoun + noun) 276
compounds: (borrowed from Chinese dialects) 97; (Chinese ~ made up in Korea and then nativized) 98; (spelled phonemically) 107; (list) 278
compressed 27, 36
compression 27; (of syllables) 36; 51, 52, 53, 68, 73; (automatic ~) 102; 260, 265
com-te = com te 140
concessive: (-toy, -utoy) 247, 823; (MK -´ke´nul etc.) 265, 268; (~ conversions) 329. See literary ~.
concrete events 324
condensation 297

conditional (**-umyen**/**-myen**): (of defective vn) 189; 259, 266, 329; 893-6
conflated forms: (misleading ~) 52; 53
conflation 27, 51, 52, 53, 86
conflation of ⋯*s* + vowel-initial particle 53
confusing **hi** or **[h]i** with **-i** 256
-cong 'variety' 166
conjoined objects, conjoined subjects 284
conjoining 249; (~ sentences) 284, 285, (with **-ko**) 316
conjugations 130, 230, 231
conjunctional (connective) adverbs 135; (list) 139
conjunctive 247, 329; 892
connecting form 251, 259
connotation: (of personal pronouns) 135; 343
connotational (meaning, relationship, variant) 340, 340, 343; (feeling) 344
conservative spellings 42
consonant 5, 8, 9, 12, 24, 25, 26; (descriptions) 27; 29, 31; (word ending in ~) 130
consonant clusters: (in foreign words) 18; (no special names for ~) 22; (final ~) 86, 99
consonant liaison 28, 29
consonant(-final) stem 40, 231; (~ vs vowel-final stems) 234; 236, 243; (adj) 306; (lists) 363-4
consonant-stem conjugation 130
consonant strings between vowels 52
constituency 19, 27; (~ cut) 197; 275, 278, 280, (~ analysis) 317, 336
constituent 274, 275, 277, 282, 284, 326
constraints 88; (on recursive aux conversions) 229; 287, 289; (between pronouns and styles) 295; 297; (with negative preemphasis) 315; 337, 339
construal: (of sentence) 282; 328
construction 274, 275; (~ with quantification) 284; 315, 321, 324, 328, 330, 344
cōntay style 300
content-interrogative 302, 303, 667
content words 2
context 222, 274, 296
contextual particles 88
contiguous elements 18
contingency: adverbs of ~ 138
contingent 247, 329
continuative: (~ stem) 3; 226
contracted forms 331, (of **ha**-) 332
contracted infinitives 237
contraction 29, 36, 38, 40, 45; (of °*ho*-) 50; 59,
85, 72, 92, 221, 235, 237, 244, 256, 263, 268, 296, 311, 330
contrast (of tense and lax stops) 44
contrasting order (of particles in sequence) 198
controlled acts 315
convergence: (of morpheme shapes) 99; (of forms) 196; 222; (in shape of vc and vp) 317
conversion 3; (~ of the nominative to the dative in causative) 173; (~ constraints on vn) 191; (of vn sentence) 192; 218, 230, 296, 305, 325, 326; (~ to make request reflexive) 333; (order of applying ~ processes) 335
coordinate clause 265
-¨*cop*- 268, 462
copula 89; (**i-**) 130; (forms used as if pcl) 194, 197; 217, 226, 235, (ellipted) 264, (no aux) 273; 287; (affirmative vs neg) 288; 290; (form unexpressed) 296; 298, 305, 307, 310, 323; (~ adnominalizations) 328; (adverbializations built on quotation) 331
copula: MK ~ (´*i*⋯) 54, 78, 88, 89, 262, 273
copula adversative (**ina** / **'na**) 472, 575-6
copula gerund 55
copula indicative assertive 248, 309
copula infinitive 93, 247, 252, (absorbed or unexpressed) 254, 308
copula modifier ´*in* suppressed 55, 593, 667
copula negative construction ⋯ **i / ka ani 'ta** 197, 288
copula phrase 19; copula-predicated noun 332
copular sentence = copula sentence
copula sentence: (modified by adverbial phrase) 135; 294, 296, 297, 298, 300, 305, 307, 310, 322
copula stem: 23; (abbreviation of ~) 55; (basic form) 55; 257, 307
copula transferentive 260, 292, (as quasi-pcl) 296; (inf + ~) 491, 507; 587-8
copying a nominative or accusative marker 173
core: (~ vocabulary) 95; (~ suffix) 162; (~ numerals) 174; (~ element) 275
core vocabulary 94, 95; (vn) 189; 190
corporation names 133
correlations of accent and canonical shape 61
correlatives 134
Co Sek.yen 217, 221, 292, 309, 318
Cosen chelqcaq-pep 4
Cosen-kwan 49, 54, 57
Cosen mal kyupem cip 4
countable noun 171

counter + noun 276
counter phrase: (+ pcl) 276; (+ verb, + copula) 277
counters: (selection) 131; 171; (two sets) 174; (list) 179
count nouns 131
cōy (ta) 'all' 138; cōy-ta = cōy ta 140
crasis (low + high > long rise) 61
crisp release 44
cross references 21
(C)s and (C)h are intrinsically voiceless 51
cuk (postmodifier) 135, 139, 251, 462
cuk(-sun) 'when' (postmodifier) 160, 462
*¨*Cul* (not word-initial) but ¨*CulC* 241
culkew- 291
cultural language 4
-cum = -(c)cum 166, 462
-cumak = -(c)cumak 166, 462
cumun < ˙*cu˙mun* 177
-cung = (q)-cung₁ 'certificate' 166
-cung = (q)-cung₂ 'ailment' 166
⋯ cuum (cium) 'approximate time' 131, 462
cuum ha.ye: ⋯ ey 194
(-)cwa 133
cwe = cwue 252
-cwu 'boss' 166
-cwu (counter) 180
cwu- < ˚*cwu-* 'give' (vt/aux) 230, 233, 237, 243, 252, 270, 288, 289; (as aux) 291, 312; 333; 464, 465
cwucang hanta 331
cwuce- 219
-cwuil, cwuil 'week' (counter) 182
-cwuk = -(c)cwuk 164, 463
cwuk- (vi) 'die' 216, 223, 243, 255, 262, 288, 289, 291, 315, 317; 364
cwuk (counter) 180
cwukan (as counter) 182
cwuk.e la and cwuk.ke la 243
cwuk.i- (vc) 223, 288, 289
cwuk.keyss.ta (auxiliary): -e (se) 227, 230
cwul (counter) 181
cwul < ˙*cwul* (postmod) 160; (as summational epitheme) 272; 463
cwula (ko ha-) 333
cwumusi- 226, 298
cwung(-) 'middle' (bound adnoun) 153
cwung < ˙*TYWUNG* 'midst, middle of' (postn, postmod) 160, 197; (-nun ~ ey, -un ~ ey) 289; 463-4

cwūng- < 'heavy' (bound adnoun) 153, 464
cwūng < ¨*TTYWUNG* 'weight' (postnoun, noun, adnoun, adj-n) 159, 464
-cwungi 163, 464
cwungkan (quasi-pcl) 193
cwung(-payki) (postnoun) 157, 464
cwup.i (sīpiq ~) 158
cwusa 'director; petty officer' (titles) 132
cwusiap, cwusiop, cwusiopsose 299
Cwu Sikyeng 6, 18
cwuuy 'ism', cwuuy-ca '-ist' 158
cwūw- 233, 234; 362
cwuwi 197
"cye" (spelling) 46
cye = /ce/ 93
cye = cyē < cie (inf < ci- aux) 252, 464, 465
⋯cye 252
-cyo /co/ = -c[y]o < -ci yo 38, 302, 309
Cyrillic spellings 28
dangling: (-ketun) 609; ~ accusative 875
"dark l" 28
dash (−) to mark long vowel 34
dating (of forms) 239
dative 282, 286, 287, 292
dative marker/particle 173; **(ey)** 195; **(hanthey)** 295
dative phrase (optionally marked by accusative particle) 173
days: counting ~ 185
days of the month (naming ~) 185; (first ten ~) 186
days of the week 186
de (Japanese pcl) 295
decimal and higher-unit Chinese numerals 171
decimal numerals 163, 164
declarative 245, 246, 248
deep transitivity 280
default: (~ Hankul spelling) 31; (~ category) 130; 249; (~ locative marker) 295
defective adjectival noun 150
defective infinitive 219
defective paradigm 336
defective verb 89, 220
defective verbal noun 89, 189
deference (toward subject) 244, 298, 299
deferential infinitive 232
deferential -¨*zop*- 70, 72, 85; (inf) 232; 261, 268
definite: (versus indefinite) 130; (the ~ article in English) 192; (~ future) 244; (~ past) 258;

(~ assertion) 259; (~ expectation) 305
degree: adverb of ~ 135, 138
deictic: (~ verbs and adjectives) 132; 133; (~ adverbs of manner and direction, place nouns) 140; 296, 332, 340; (~ verbs of motion) 641
"deictic center" 132
deletion 283, (of particle) 286, 287. SEE elision, ellipsis, omission, suppression; dropped.
delimiter 88, 316, 550
demarcation of particles 86
denial 193
dental 17; ~ affricate [ts] 29; ~ stops 24
dependent nouns 131
depersonification 291
derivationally related noun and verb stem 87
derivative bound postverb 223
derivatives of a stem (reduce excess) 107
derivative suffix 342, 347
derived adverb 140; (of a defective adj-n) 189, 193; 243, 256, 330
derived adverb/noun ending (-i, -li; -o, -wu) 233, 247, 255
derived causative verb 313
derived form 18
derived noun 3, 276, 324
derived nouns used only as postnouns: list 158
derived stems: (preserve excess) 107; (vc, vp) 315
derived substantive 87, 255, 344, 887
descriptive auxiliary (= auxiliary adjective) 219
descriptive verb (= adjective) 141, 189, 216-217; (stem) 218; 249
descriptive vs processive (intransitive verb) 216; (stems that are either) 217
desiderative 227
desiderativized negative 336
desire 264
destination (marked by accusative) 216
desyllabification of **i**, **wu**, and **o** 37
detailing apposition 335
determined 110
devices to exalt status 299
devices to write *G* 23, 50, 54
devoiced syllable 36
devoicing of vowel nuclei 26
diacritic marks 4
dialect 4, 8, 13, 17, 25, 26, 27, 35, 36, 42, 43, 45, 46, 51, 53, 54, 56, 57, 58, 59, 60, 66, 93, 106, 132, 175, 231, 234, 236, 237, 239, 251, 253, 305, 311, 321, 595

dialect: doublets 17; evidence 57; influences 57; mixture 59; pronunciation 16; variants 37, 42, 94, 110, 145; variation 1; versions of stems 238
dialects that never underwent lenition 234
diaries 320
dictionary 21, 22, 32, 36, 94, 111, 112, 121, 141, 162, 189, 194, 196, 218, 219, 221, 234, 242, 274, 280, 291, 333; 372
dictionary entries 58, 73
dictionary form (= indicative assertive) 851, 898
dictionary of character readings 95
dieresis (raised double-dot) 35
digraph 8, 21, 43, 44; (**w** + **u**) 233
digraph "ng" 5, 9
Dillon, A. 938
diminutive 145, 162
diminutive suffixes 94; (list) 163; (-˙*zo* = ˙˙*co*) 240; 347
dip (in pitch) 41, 42
diphthong 12, 26, 29, 43
direction: (deictic adverbs of ~) 140; (shift of ~) 260
directional adverbs 295
directly adverbialized pure nouns 136
direct nominalization: (~ of a noun predication) 135; 259
direct object 140, 188, 216, 297, 312, 326; (that is raised subject of putativized sentence) 332
direct quotation 213, 331, 332
direct subject 298
disanimation 289, 291
disappearing **h** 35, 37
discourse 193
disinterest 282
dispalatalization 46; (of *hy*... to **h**...) 48; (of **m**ʸ**ey** and **ph**ʸ**ey**) 48; (of *sye*) 46, 48, 111; (now weakening) 112
displacement of native words by Chinese 95
dissyllabic stems: originally ~ 232
dissyllable 43
distal (correlatives / deictics) 134, 135
distance traversed (marked by accusative) 216
distinction: (unrealistic ~) 96; (unpronounced) ~ 109
distinctive pitch 6
documentary style 254, 300, 321, 323
dot 8, 35
dot (center ~ inserted before particle in KEd) 20
dot (= period) in Romanized forms 8, 13, 16,

52, 232
dotted syllables 61
dot misplaced by scribe? 70
double-consonant **pat.chim** 107
double consonants 21
double dot (¨) 35, 38, 60, 61, 232
double emotive 263
double exclamation-point (intonation) 42, 301
double flap 28
double infinitive-auxiliary conversions: chart 230
double negative (= negativized negative) 318, 321, 336
double objects 286
double question-mark (intonation) 41, 42, 301
double-subject adjectives 288
doublet 27, 47, 48, 58; (forms) 60; (compounds) 97; (Chinese ~ differing only by accent) 97; 108, 109; 238, 239; 675
double zero (symbol) 22
doubt 323
dropped ⋯h⋯ 33, 35
dropped k 92
dropped p 92
dropped ⋯u⋯ 33
dropped w 35
dummy (verb / adjective) 227, 340
Dupont, R. 51, 627, 908
duration (marked by accusative) 216, 847-8
dyads of like verbal nouns 192
e (Seoul allophones) 24; (raised to u) 25; (vs ē, vowel quality) 33; (for a in common words) 41
-e (as abbr of -e se?) 214
-e (inf ending) 3; 231; (shape after ⋯aC- in Seoul) 236, 252; 251; (~ style) 296; 306; 465
-e 'language' 166
⋯e- stems 237, 252
⋯e- stems: (all high) 71; (no monosyllabic ~ without preceding y) 72
⋯´e < ⋯u-´e 267
-ᵉ⁄ₐ = -e / -a (inf) 230, 233, 235, 236
-´ᵉ⁄ₐ (inf): (cognate with Japanese a[r]-?) 70; (and -´ke) 244; 271. See **-e (se)**.
-´ᵉ⁄ₐ- (effective aspect marker) 84, 262, 415, 466-7; and (-´kᵉ⁄ₐ-) 263
earlier: (Korean) 4, 95, 323; (diphthongs) 25; 41; (vowels) 42; (initials) 43; (finals) 49
early: (spellings) 49; (loanwords/borrowings) 94, 95; (texts) 4, 13, 42, 52, 53, 108, 238, 256, 284, 316, 327
east 34

/eccay/ = ecc' 'ay abbr < **ecci hay** 134, 243
ecce 243
ecci < ¨es´ti 134, 139, 243, 256, 467
ec(ekk)ey 136; ecey 134
echi 'worth' (postnoun) 156, 468
echoed consonant 22
echo questions 193
-eci 163
-e ci- 315, 468
eci-l- 'be kind, good' 242
ēcwup-, ēcwuw- (adj) 362
-e cye = -e cie 93
⋯´e- ´e (effective inf) 267
effective 3; (forms) 72; 84; (aspect) 214, (stem) 258, 260, 261, 262, 268; (infinitive -´ke) 244, 267; (substantive) 255, 418, 473, 509, 603, 889; (modifier) 258; (formative -´ke-) 259; (adversative, conditional) 266; (modifier) 268; 466-7, 508-10, 511, 716
effective (as source of -k- and -n-) 244
effective honorific = honorific effective 268
⋯eh- stems (list) 104-5, 349; ⋯e(h)- stems 365
-eh- / -ah- 220; 469
-e hanta (transitivizes emotive adj) 221, 291
-e iss- 319; (uncontracted / contracted) 325
-´e k 469
-ek / -ak 163; 347; 469
ek- 141
⋯e-l- stems (list) 360
-e la 213; (-´(k)e-´la) 214; (exclamatory) 217; 244, 251, 263, 306, 307, 471
elements: prosodic ~ 88
elevating the object rather than the subject 299
elevating the status of the subject 337
-el.i 163, 471
elicitation 4
elided 4; (velar) 56; (consonant) 58; (forms of velar-initial morphemes) 261
elided-initial version (-´ᵉ⁄ₐ⋯) of the effective 241
elided W (lenition of p) 56
elided -z- 234
elision 6; (variable ~ of nasal) 48; 53, 54, 61; (apical ~) 242, 265; (before pcl s) 767
elision of final ⋯i from the first member of a compound 94
elision of -h- 236
elision of initial vowel of copula 273
elision of l 57, 58, 238; (before s) 241, 767
elision of n 57, 58; (before s) 767
elision of noun-final ⋯p 57

elision of stem-final *... ᵘ⁄o- 231, 232, 234; 240
elision of -z- 54
ellipsis: (of **ha-**) 256; (of forms of **ha-**) 277, 283; (of uncertainty sentence) 332
ellipted copula substantive 135
ellipted extruded object 765
ellipted modulator leaving accentual trace 70
ellipted noun 328
ellipted postmodifier *[ˇi]* 264, 924
ellipted subject 707
ellipted syllable 61
ellipted words (demarcated by brackets) 5
elliptical versions of extended predicate 264
ellun 137, 471
elma < ¨*enˇma* 134, 174, 471, 475
...**elu-** stems 361
eˇlum 'ice' < ¨*el-* 'freeze' 255, 272
elwu (pseudo-preverb) < *eˇlwu* 'possibly' 141; 473
elyei (der adv) 256
elyew- 256; 361
el[y]ey = elyei (der adv) 256
-em or **-am** (der subst) 255, 473, 887
-ᵉ⁄am (effective substantive) 263, 473, 887, 889
embedded adnominalizations 328
embedded sentence 323, 327
emci (adnoun 'main', noun 'thumb') 149, 473
emeni, eme' nim 299
emerging tense (reinforced) obstruents 96
-emi 164, 473
emotional: connotation 44; meanings 192
emotion transitivizer 227
emotive: (bound verb *s-*) 259; (structures) 260; 261; (bound stems, questions) 263; (morpheme *-ˇtwo-*) 273; (adjectives) 291
emotive-emotive (= double emotive) 261
emphasis 35, 192, 233, 241, 265, 266, 283, 286, 332, 347, 551, 848-9
emphasized object 286
emphatic (= effective) 601
emphatic particle *ˇka* 594
emphatic prefix 44
emphatic synonym 333
emphatic version of doublet preserved as modern stem 44
enceng (pcl): **-ulq ci** ~ 196; 474
ēncey 134, 136, 474
endearing command 258; endearing names 164, 555
ending + particle: sequences of ~ 213

ending morphemes 245
endings: (calling for velar lenition) 54; (standing as if free when stem is ellipted) 87, 89; (less colloq) 213; (+ particles and quasi-particles) 213, (table) 215; 220, 230, 238; (table) 246
endo-developmental 226
-e neh- 226
-eng / -ang 163, 347, 420; 475
English 1, 5, 7, 18, 20, 21, 23, 27, 33, 34, 37, 39, 44, 51, 99, 102, 130, 131, 132, 144, 192, 216, 222, 261, 274, 301, 302, 305, 312, 328, 340
English gloss 62
English loans: verbal nouns 189
English speaker 28, 251, 283
English sentence 283
English translation 136, 249; (of modifier) 249
English vocabulary (borrowed into Korean) 94
engmang 295
-eng-payngi 163, 475
engtheli kath- 229
-eni 163, 475
Enmun-ci 112
ēnmun 6
"entering tone" 50, 60
enu 134, 148, 476-7; ~ **hay** 186; ~ **tey** 134
eˇnuˇma 134
environment 98, 99; (of noun) 130
-ep- (**-up-, -ap-**) / **-p- = -ew-** (**-uw-, -aw-**) / **-w-** 220, 482
epenthesis: (of palatal glide) 254; (source of vowel in processive) 716
epenthetic glide 254
epenthetic **-l-** 16
epenthetic ...ᵘ⁄o... 268
epenthetic vowel 54; 779
epenthetic **w** 35, 237
epenthetic **y** in **iya** < *ia* < *ˇiˇza* 54
ephemeral lenition: **-s-** > **-z-** > **-(s)-** 59, 237
-epi 164, 479
epithematic identification 327, 420, 477, 558, 586, 875, 945
epithematization: See postappositional ~.
epithematized Identified (as Identified in matrix sentence) 327, 477, 558, 875, 945
epitheme: (extruded from object) 272; 324, 326. See extruded, summational, transitional.
¨*epˇnon* 218, 479
-e posey (yo) 330, 335
-e ppeli- = -e peli- 343

ēps- 218; (postnom v/adj insep) 228; 231; (two subjects) 287, 288, 294, 298, 305, 306, 307, 308, 310, 319, 326; 480-1
ēps.ey yo 253
ēps.i 'without' 218, 480
ēpsin-yeki- = ēpsi(-)nyeki- 141
ēps.nun: (as pseudo-adnoun) 150; 218; 480
*ēps.nunta 218
ēps.ta (ka) 296
¨ep˙sun 218, 481-2
ēps.un 218, (usually → ēps.nun or ēps.tun) 326; 481
ēps.usi- 319
-e pwā (la) 330, 335
errands 470, 479
-es / -e (approximate numerals) 164, 482
es(-) (adnoun, bound adverb) 140, 149, 482
-e (se) < -˙e ˙sye 214, 244, 251, 329, 330; 483-4
ese 137, 139, 483
-ess- 40, 218, 220, 230, (-e iss- 244) ; (~ and -keyss-) 246; 304, 305, 306, 307, 308, 310, 325; 363; 485
-ess.ci anh- (in rhetorical question) 323
*-ess.e se → -e se 330
-ess-ess- 244, 486
-ess.ess.keyss.nun 250, 486
-ess.ess.nun, -ess.ess.tun 250, 486
-ess.ess.ulq 250
-ess.ess.un (acceptable?) 251
-ess.keyss.nun 250, 487
-ess.keyss.tun 250, 325, 487
-ess.ki 324, 487
-ess.nun 250, 324, 487-8
-ess.tun 249, 488
-ess.ey (yo) = -ess.e (yo) 253
-ess.ulq: (~ kes ita) 244, 250, 325; 488-9
-ess.um 324, 489
-ess.un 249, 489; ~ tul (rejected) 251
-ess-uni(-kka) 330, 489
* ¨est- (defective stem) 256
¨es˙te (bnd adv < defective inf) 219, 256, 489
et- 'get' 288; 363
-e ('ta) cwu- / tuli- 260
-e 'ta (ka) 491
etey 134, 491
eti 134, 140, 491
-e to < -˙e ˙two (inf + pcl) 244, 251; (~ cōh.ta / kwaynchanh.ta) 316; 329; 491-2, 494
ettay 237, 243, 252
ette, ette- 219, 237, 243, 252; 492-3

ette ha-, etteh- 134, 492-3
ette han ···, etten ··· 134, 492-3
ettey said for ettay 252
etwuw- 344; 362
etymological: accent 84; analysis 37; meaning 280; sets 46; speculations 343; ties between words 340; writing 58
etymological examples of lenited $t \to l$ 57, 92, 235
etymological n pronounced as /l/ 16
etymological "object" (incorporated in Chinese vn) 189
etymology 39, 52, 53, (with elided l) 58; 90, 98, 100, 107; (obscure) 141, 144, 145; (unclear) 151; 220, 260, 278, 347
etymon 55, 62; (serving as both Chinese and non-Chinese) 275, 340
euphemisms 298
European languages 94
"even" tone 60, 61
exaltation: (MK) 268; 342
exceptions to excess reduction 100
excess: syllable ~ 95; (replacement of ~) 100; (reduction of ~) 102
excess at beginning of syllable: relics of ~ 101
excess mk 101
excess numeral 163, 164, 174
excess reduced even before vowel 100
exclamation 249, 250, 264, 307, 321; (emotive ~) 502; 609, 674, 699, 867, 877, 911, 914, 919
exclamation point 20
exclamation-point intonation 41, 42, 142, 301, 302
exclamatory: (meaning) 217; (use of adj-^{e}/a la) 243; (sentence/statement) 260, 263, 265, 300, 302; 488, 522, 528, 571, 579, 602, 614, 640, 663, 666, 667, 729, 732, 839, 866, 873, 875, 906, 908
exclamatory enumeration 591
exclamatory first-person statement 511, 512, 663, 665
exclamatory particle 415, 422, 471, 937
exhaustive 226
exo-developmental 226
expanded: quotation 332; sentence 297; variant 145
expanding: (~ adnominalized sentence) 326; (~ noun/expansion with adnominals) 336, 337; (~ sentence with adverbial adjuncts) 337

expansion: (as adverbial) 286; 287, 335
"expansive notation" 4
expectation 245
experimental elements in early orthography 45
explicit: (marking of roles) 282, (particles) 283
exploratory 227
expository 3; (~ prose) 194
expressive length(ening) 33, 34, 142, 421
expressive reinforcement 639
extended adverbative 247
extended adversative 246, 318, 329
extended apperceptive 246
extended conjunctive = conditional 247
extended particle phrases: defective verbal noun in ~ 190, 194, 197, 214, 292
extended predicate 232, 264, 266, 267, 273
extended predication 327
extended projective 247
extended sequential 247, 330
extended shape of l-extending stem 256
extended stem 41, 234, 240, 241
extended structures (based on substantive) 267
extended summative 247
extent (as object) 280
external punctuation 20
extrasyllabic element 49
extrasyllabic finals: (list of examples) 103; 108
extrasyllabic morpheme shapes 95
extruded complement (of copula) 509, 575
extruded complement (of mutative) 922
extruded complement (the possessed) 686
extruded destination 326
extruded epitheme (´i 'the one that ··· ') 264; 326
extruded genitive 686, 765
extruded Identified 327
extruded instrument 326
extruded location 326, 686, 922
extruded object 272, 324, 326, 481, 509, 532, 534, 536, 537, 544, 546-7, 558, 765, 857, 922, 928, 932, 949
extruded possessor 481, 518, 532, 575, 686
extruded subject 326, 509, 516, 517, 532, 533, 534, 536, 537, 546, 583, 603, 686, 719, 725, 735, 856, 902, 932
extruded time 326
extrusion: (of epitheme) 264; (and thematization of implied subject) 298
ey (MK diphthong) 25, 43
ey (raised to **i**) 25, 253; (replaced by **i**) 38

/ey/ = uy (genitive pcl) 43
/ey/ and /yey/ for basic yēy 110
/ey/ replacing /yey/ 109
-ey (noun from v) 164, 497-8
-ey = -e 308, 497
-ey- (formative for vc) 224
···ey- stems: (absorb inf) 252; (lists) 349, 350
···*ey*- stems 466
ēy- (pseudo-preverb) 141
ey (locative/allative particle) 136, 140, 144, 193, 195, 216, 282, 284; (locative) 285; (impersonal indirect object) 287, 288, 291, 292, 294, 295, 299; (in voice conversions) 314; 496-7
-˙*e*⁄*ay* (locative / allative pcl) 68, 239, 259; (~ **uy ha.ye**) 315; 330; 495-6
-e ya < -˙*e* ˙*za* (inf + pcl) 244, 251; 329; 498-9
···eye (lit var inf) = ···ey 253
ey iss.e se: ~ 'na, ~ nun, ~ uy 198; 499
ey kelchye: ··· ey ~ 195
eykey (particle) 193, 195, 197, 213, 282, 284; (personal indirect object) 287; 288, 291, 292, 295, 299; (in voice conversions) 312, 314, 315; 499-502
eykey mata 501
eykey se 195, 214, 282, 299, (with periphrastic passive) 313; 501
eykey se mata 198, 501
eykey 'ta (ka) 293, 501
-˙*e*⁄*a ˙y˙la* 263, 502
-eymi 164, 502
-e yo: (~ tul) 213; (~ style) 296, 301; 310, 503
-e(y)pi 164
ey se: (as a collocation) 88; 195; (with optional ey) 214; 275, 282; (locative) 285; 294, 299, 503-6
eyse (as a single particle) 214
(ey) se mata 198, 505
ey se ppun man 198, 505
ey 'ta (ka) 195, 260, 292, 507
···*ey ˙ye* (inf) 466
-e (yo): (~ tul) 213; 329
-ey yo ← -e yo 253, 306, 507-8
[F] 27, 36
"fa" = wa (Japanese pcl) 594
factual: (statement) 265; (nominalizer) 258; (predication) 267, 327
fall 41, 42
falling intonation 21, 134
falling tone (of Middle Chinese) 112

false analogy 47, 262
familiar indicative assertive **-ney** 307
familiar indicative attentive **-na** 249, 307, 310
familiar retrospective assertive **-tey** 307, 308
familiar style 248, 297, 300, 307
familiar subjunctive assertive **-sey** 308
family name: SEE surname.
fast speech 32
favor 222, 227, 252, 260, 333
fear 323
female names 132, 164
fictive form 109
Figulla, H.H. 29
figurative meaning 344
filter: morphophonemic ~ 30
final: consonant / cluster 6, 8, 18, 49, 86; double consonant 21; 29, 42
"final" as component of an orthographic syllable (= **pat.chim**) 100
final geminates 21
final *h* 49; (no way to write) 86
final ⋯**m** ⋯**n** ⋯**ng** ⋯**l**: devoicing spread to ~ 51
final **-ng** 29; final ⋯**ng** dropped 32
final ⋯*ng* vs zero (circle symbol) 49
final postmodifier 280
final punctuation 21
final vowel in a one-syllable phrase 33
final zero 29, 49
finite-mood shift 297
finite moods 305
finite verb forms 331
first person 244; 717
first-person statement: (exclamatory) 263
first-person subject (expressed by the modulator) 272
first syllable (of a word) 32
fish names 95
fixed word order 283, 284, 286
flap allophone of *l* 57
flap [r] 4, 28, 102, 111; ~ for coda /*ll*/ 51
"float" (of numbers) 173
focus 192, 285, 286; (settings) 297; (of emphasis) 302; (on nominalization) 330; 340; (nuclear ~) 622
focus and emphasis (in Japanese) 328
focus highlighting 318
focus particle 22, 88; (**to**) 160, 161; 193, 283, 316; 550, 637, 849
focus subdual (avoided in modifying phrase) 327

foreign borrowing 46
foreigner 132
foreign loanword 94
foreign missionaries 594
foreign names 133; ~ of Koreans 132
foreign order (of full personal name) 132
foreign spelling of names when Romanizing 132
foreign words 18, 46
form 1, 2, 3, 4, 8, 13, 22, 23, 27, 33, 34, 39, 242
formal: (style) 246, 248, 253, 280, 297, 300; 311-2; (~ question ending) 318; 339
"formal lateral style" 301
formal writing 243
formative: (*-Gi-*) 22; 218, 219, 220; (MK vc and vp) 225
fortition 233
four tones (of Chinese) 60
fractions 188
fragment: (inserted from presumed echo) 193; (sentence) 213; 303, 331
free adnoun 151
freedom of combination 274
freedom or bondage of Chinese morphemes 151-2, 162
free element 12; free form 19
free form / shape of a noun (used before certain particles) 49, 101; 108; 239; 764, 842, 880
free noun 44, 88, 152, 165, 188, 190, 278
free postnoun 162, 165
free-standing *W* 23, 768, 925
free-standing *y* (= **ttan i**) 23; 552
free two-syllable Chinese nouns 152
free variation of accent patterns 62
free verbs 88
free word order 283
free words vs bound words / forms 88, 152
French 27; "French transcription" 27
frequency (marked by accusative) 848
frequent combinations 20
fricative 27, 36, 51. SEE spirant.
front (as vowel component / feature) 37
frontal articulation vs frontal coarticulation 46
fronting 36; (of vowel) 39, 47, (before **y** or **i**) 59, 344
front of mouth 43
front rounded glide 26
front rounded vowel 25
front unrounded vowel 25
front-/fronted-vowel honorific stems (lists) 355-8

frustrated intentive 247, 257, 329
fully automatic alteration 99
function: (change of ~ for mod + postmodifier) 272; (adverbial vs predicative ~) 273
functional load 28
functional semivowel 43
future: (marker) 220, 244, 249; 246; (~ proc and retrospective modifier) 250; 297, 304, 310; (nominalization) 324; 335, 338
future modifier -keyss.un (rejected form) 251
future perfect 244
future processive modifier 332
future prospective modifier -keyss-ul (as rejected form) 251
future tentative 304
/G/ 508; (indirect notation) 262
[G] notation 54
-G-: (distinctive only after l z y i) 50; (loss of phonetic effect) 51; (as juncture phenomenon) 54; (as neutralization) 54, 57; 508
-G- (formative for vc) 225, 508
ga (Japanese) 327; (more emphatic than no) 328
-`Ga ('la, swo 'la) 263
Gale, J.S. 47, 51, 52, 53, 108, 109, 483, 571, 605, 627, 629, 713, 717, 775, 785, 789, 800, 852, 867, 899
-`G^ea- (effective) 84; 508-10, 511
-`[G]^ea- as source of -·^ea- 262
geminate 21; (letters) 22; (vowels) 34; (MK spellings) 44; (clusters, initials) 50, 95
gemination of l in ···l- stems 238
general (vs specific) 130
general auxiliary 227
generalization of lenited forms of -T/L- verbs 234
generalizing epitheme 324
generation reference (in personal names) 132
generic (correlatives / deictics) 134
genetic relationships 1
genitive 173, 282
genitive-marked subject of adnominalized v 69
genitive marker 259
genitive particle s 23, 43, 44; (attached to the modifier ending) 50; (strings created by ~) 51; (free shape used before ~) 101; 764-8
genitive relationship (of juxtaposed nouns) 282
genitivization 283, 284
genuineness 302
Gerdts, D.B. 173, 174
"German transcription" 27
gerund -ko 3, 41; 47; (-`kwo) 54, 70; (+ aux)

19, 219; (of defective verbal nouns) 189; (in phrasal postpositions) 194; 226, 232, 243, 247, 259, 266, 295, 300, 303, 329, 339, 640-2
gerund-related pseudo-moods 259
-`Gey = -`key (adverbative; suffix) 510-1
'`Gey = '[y]`Gey < `i`Gey (cop adverbative) 511
ghost form 121
-`Gi- (formative for vc, vp) 225, 511
given name 132
glide 23, 36, 46, 47, 111; glide y 23, 259
gloss (translation) 6, 113
glossaries: (Manchu and Mongol) 51; 240
glottal catch 142
glottal h 27
glottalized consonants 27
glottal squeeze 54
glottal stop 13, 22; (initial = onset) 44, 45, 46; 49, 50, 96
"going" tone 60, 61
-`Goy = -`koy = -`key (adverbative) 511
grammar (awareness of ~) 100
grammarian 21, 110, 243, 247, 336
grammatical analysis 21
grammatical categories 3
grammatical device 245, 331
grammatical function 86
grammatical information 261
grammatical juncture 86
grammatically conditioned alternant 32
grammatical relationship 192; ~ of a phrase to the sentence 193
grammatical specification 297, 326
grammatical terms 3; (list of Korean ~) 380-8, (English index) 389-6
grammatical ties 20
graphic components / elements 46; 372
graphic convention 54
graphic syllable s 51
graphic syllables and morphemes 261
Great Vowel Shift 43
Greek 286
-`Guy = -`kuy = -`key (adverbative) 271, 511
`Gwa = `kwa (pcl) 511; `[G]wa 511
-`Gwa (of -`Gwa '`la / swo'la) 262, 263, 271
-`Gwo 271
'`Gwo = '[y]`Gwo < `i`Gwo 274
`Gwom, `[G]wom = `kwom (pcl) 513
-`Gwo n' = -`kwo n' 513
`Gwos, `[G]wos 513
-`Gw^uo- (formative for vc) 225, 512

A Reference Grammar of Korean

Gwu˙the < **Wu˙the* < *pu˙the* 57
-˙*Gwᵘ/oy-* (formative for vc) 225
/h/ between voiced sounds 27; (murmured and dropped) 51
h of hwey (< hoy) 36
h⋯ syllable (dropped) 35
h⋯ 49, 51; ⋯*h* 513-4
⋯h- (examples) 104; (stem list) 349
⋯h(-) 101
-h- (paraintensive infix) 343, 514
-ha (bound postnoun) 'under' 166, 514
hā(-) (bound adnoun) 153, 514
ha- < °*ho-* (v/adj) 21, 87, 89, (shortened variant forms) 92, 95, 188, 189, 258; (postnom v/adj) 189, 190, 219, 228, 229, 256; (forms used as if pcl) 194; (aux v/adj) 217, 218, 227, 228, 230; 242, 243, 251, 252; ('say') 288, 290, 343; 521-3. SEE -e hanta.
ha- < °*ha-* 'big, much, many' 70, 79; 147, 243, 271, 344; 523
ha 514. SEE ha (to).
habitual (-ko nun / n' hanta) 259
hachi anh.ta 344, 514
haci 'does' (suspective): (shortened var optional in neg) 92; (optionally dropped before neg aux) 321, 683; 514
haci (counter) 182
-hak 'science' 166
hakey 'so as to do' 88; (after defective vn) 190; (dropped / ellipted) 191, 277; (~ style) 301; 514
haki 'doing' 88; 514
hako (ger): 3, 189; (ellipted / dropped / omitted) 188, 192, 283, 321; ('saying') 331; 514, 515-6
hako (pcl) 194, 196, 197, 295; 515
hako (direct-quotation quasi-pcl) 331, 332; 514-5
hako (mānh.ta) 344, 515
-hal (counter) 182
hal = hal(q) (prosp mod) 343, 516
hal (adnoun) 'great; proper' 147, 334, 335, 344
hal-apeci 344
half-assimilated Chinese loans 64
halth- 231, 232; 363
halwu < *holol < *holo / holl⋯ < *holol 'one day' 239
halwu; halwuq nal 185
halye (intentive) 259
ham: (dropped / omitted) 188, 258, 300, 321, 343; 516
Hamhung 34, 60

hamkkey 137, 194, 195, 517
Hamkyeng 17, 28, 29, 34, 45, 47, 49, 53, 54; (earlier speech) 59; 69, 92; (dictionary) 109, 233; 234, 321, 336; 690, 694, 892
hamye (ellipted) 283
hamyen 189, 190, 517
-han 'guy' 166
⋯ han < *hon* (mod) 189, 190; (as aux adj mod) 218; 343; 517
han < *han* (adnoun) 'great; proper' 147, 343, 344, 517
han < *hon* (adnoun) 'one; whole; most; about' 147
hān (adnoun) 'outdoors, outside' 147
hān < ″*HHAN* (postnoun) 'extent, limit' 161
Hana ⋯ 334
hana / han < *honah* / *hon* 174, 518
hana ccay / chay 175
han(a)-i, hanq-i /hanni/ 187
hanak ssik = hana ssik 177, 518
han(a)-twul, han-twu 178, 518
Hānqca = Hānmunq-ca 113; ~ sacen 113
han-ccak 185
(-)hāng 'port' (category designator) 133
hāng = hāngkwu 'port' 159
hang.lyelq ca 132
hān ha.ye: ⋯ ey ~ 194
Hani ⋯ 333; 518
han kaci 140
han kay ccay / chay 175
Hankul 1, 4, 5, 6, 8, 9, 12, 18, 20, 23, 26, 30, 38, 94, 113, 132, 242, 254, 256, 258
Hankul h 13
Hankul orthographic prescription 236
Hankul orthography 5, 34, 220, 231, 235, 236, 243, 248
Hankul readings of Chinese characters 60
Hankul spelling 5, 7, 9; (~ of u after labials) 18; 18, 30, 42, 43, 50, 94; (disregards automatic alternations) 99; 231, 232, 237, 238; (of MK accent) 241; 243, 244; (usually ignores q) 250, 764; 252, 254, 316
Hankul spelling rule (for -L- and -T/L-) 242
Hankul syllables 4; (number of different ~) 7
Hankul symbols 6, 43; (for the Middle Chinese distinctions) 95; 764
Hankul texts 1, 13, 18, 20, 22, 29, 42, 196, 238, 242, 261; (chronological list) 397-401, (alphabetized) 401-6
Hankul writing system 13, 18, 53; 233, 238

Hankul-written words 45
ha῾nolh / ha῾nol 'heaven' 109
han phyen (postmod, n, adv) 160; 333; 518-9
han salam vs **han | salam** 172
hansup 187
hanta < ῾*hono῾ta*: (as aux v) 218, (transitivizes adj inf) 221, 259; (after transferentives) 260; ('says') 331; 519. See **ha-**.
hanta 'nun (pseudo-adnoun) 150, 519
hanthey (pcl) 195, 197; (personal indirect object) 287; 288, 291, 292, 299; (in vc conversions) 314; 315; 519-20
hanthey se 195, 214; (with periphrastic passive) 313; 520
hanthey 'ta (ka) 293, 520
han-twues / -twue 178
hanun < ῾*ho῾non* (as aux v proc mod) 218
hanq yeph = /hannyeph/ 'one side' 110
hao style 300, 521
hara⌐ (Japanese) 95
hara⌐mu (Japanese) 95
has (adnoun) 147; 521
hasipsio style 300, 521
hata < °*ho῾ta*: See **ha-**.
ha (to) ⋯ 344, 514, 523
hay (quasi-free n) 'one's (thing)' 131, 156, 523
hay 'year' (as counter) 182; 186
hay, hays (= **hayq** < ῾*hoy s*) 149, 524
hay = **ha.ye** < ῾*ho῾ye* (inf < **ha-** < °*ho-*) 21, 40, 88, 95, 237, 242, 243, 251, 465, 523-4
hāy = **hay** (inf < **ha-**) 253, 465
(-)**hāy** 'sea' (category designator) 133
ha.ya 243, 252
⋯ **ha.ye** 190
ha.ye < ῾*ho῾ye* 194; (⋯ **ulo** ~) 195; 243, 252, 523
ha.ye-kan 138, 524
ha.ye-kum: ⋯ **ulo** ~ 195, 524
ha.yess- 243, 524
ha.ye-thun 139, 524
hāy-la style 300, 524
hay mata 137
hayng < ῾*HHOYNG* (postnoun) 157
-h-ayngi 144
hayngkil < **han kil** 344
hays: See **hay**.
⋯ **hay se** 190
hay se 194, 524
hayss- 242, 243; 331
hay to and **nāy to** 252

⋯ **hay ya** 189, 524
h-dropping stem 231, 236
he- 'false' (bound adnoun) 153
he- = **ha-** 'do / be' 41, 344, 525
he < ¨*HE* 'approximately' (postnoun) 157, 524
'he / him' 135
headlines 188
head noun (of adnominalization) = epitheme 327
head of adverbial (nominal, verbal) phrase: verb form serving as ~ 88
head of structure 326
hearer 282
heavy aspiration 27, 49
heavy *l* 51
heavy vowel 343
hekwu for **hakwu** for **hako** (pcl) 41
heli (counter) 184
h-elision 27, 28, 29, 35, 37, 38, 256, 257
Hena ⋯ 334
h-final nouns 49, 56, 101; (as doublets) 109; (list) 109; 513-4
h-final stem 35, 104, 232, 236, 237
hēn (pseudo-adnoun) 'old' 146, 150, 525
he(n)ta: See **he-**.
Hendon, R.S. 2
⋯ **henthey** = ⋯ **hanthey** 41, 525
hes(-) (adnoun; bound noun) < **heq** ⋯ < *HE s* 140, 149, 525
hesitation 42
He Wung 2, 33, 34, 58, 60, 61, 68, 69, 72, 235, 253, 267, 268, 271, 272, 384, 392, 552, 553, 668, 711, 730, 744, 767, 842, 922, 923, 924
hey said for **hay** 252
hēy- 'swim' 255
hh 23; **hh**⋯ 49
H(H)H → H(H)L before particle or copula 62
hhi, hhye 46
°*(h)hye-* 'pull' 80, 270
hi 46; **hi**⋯ > **si** 46
hi and **huy** 525
-hi- (formative for vc, vp) 220, 223, 225, 526
⋯ **hi** < ῾*hi* 136, 140, 189, 190, 243, 256; (and ⋯'**i**) 257; 525-6
high (as vowel feature) 6, 26, 35, 60
high back unrounded *u* 42
high back vowel after a labial 18
high component of the rising pitch (automatically lost in C^uoC syllables) 236
high front rounded vowel [ü] 43
high front vowel 36

highlighting: (focus) 297; (copula) 316
high/low stems 70, 71; (high when compounded) 72; 79
high pitch 34; (of an elided syllable retained) 61; (as distinctive only in first syllable) 68; 232; (retained ~ of elided vowel) 234, 237
high(-pitched) stems 71, 75
high tone 60
high vowel 36
high-vowel nuclei 26
hiragana newspapers 18
historical arguments (against -ta ka as ending + particle) 214
historic(al) change 68, 253
historical considerations 275
historical contraction 244
historical development 235
historical explanation 58, 234
historically correct y··· and i··· 111
historical ny-, ly-, and li- 110
historical origin of -keyss- 244
historical present 305
historical reasons for spellings 109
historical shape 15
historical spelling 40, 236
history: (of sounds and forms) 1; (of words) 7; (additional information from ~) 16; (of vowel length in stems) 33; 60
hiuh (treated as hius) 106
°ho- 'do; be; say' (only ··· ᵘ/o- stem) 71; 81; (incorporated in ···h- stems) 108; (postnom adj) 256, 267; 332; 537
°ho-/ho.y- < *hyo- 270
hō- 'broad-stitch' ? < *°hwo- 71
-ho (counter) 180
-ho 'number; issue; name' 166
°ho-kᵉ/a- > ˙khᵉ/a··· 40, 72
ho˙kwo 527
hol(q)N 528
hol-/hwul- 141
hol lo 146, 527
holli- (vp) 224
hollow dot 71
hom 532
ho˙ma 532
homonym 33, 39; (clash) 59; 89, 133, 152; 218; 355
homonymous causative and passive verbs 222; (no difference of accent or vowel length) 223
homonymous stems/verbs 298, 319

homonymy 25
homophone 188; homophonous phrase 20, 100; homophonous string 99; homophony 37, 41
ho˙m ye 532
hon (mod < °ho˙ta) 532
honah 'one' 109, 532
honca 48, 60, 140, 532-3
hon ka˙ci (optional triggering of lenition) 55
Hong Kimun 286
Hong Wungsen 221
Hong Yunphyo 588, 594, 790
hon-nass.ta (auxiliary): -e (se) ~ 227
honor 268
honorific (= subject-exaltation) 241, 246, 249, 261, 267, 282, 288, (status) 297, 312, 320; (~ stem lists) 355-8; (-usica māca) 432
honorificated negative 335
honorificated negativized honorific 335
honorification pleonastically repeated 319
honorific command 333
honorific favor 227
honorific marker -usi- 220, 226; (as basically vowel-initial) 241; 244, 248, 298, 299, 312
honorific marker -(ᵘ/o)˙si- 70, 72; (accent) 85; 94, 133; 232
honorific modifier 232
honorific ··· nim 135
honorific particle kkey 133, 299
honorific terms 299
hop (counter) 183
(h)opinta 344
Horne, E.C. 1, 3, 237
horses: counting ages 187
hortative 217, 245
hortative -˙cye 70
˙ho˙si- (honorific < °ho-) 536
˙ho˙syam (hon modulated substantive < °ho-) 267, 536
˙hote··· > ˙the··· 72
hoth (adnoun; ~ ulo) 146, 149, 538
(h)ow- (postnom adj insep) 229, 534
-hoy 'meeting' 166
-hōy 'time' (counter) 182
¨hoy- 'makes/lets do' 74, 543
˙ho.ya- (effective < °ho-) 262, 538
˙ho˙ya (MK optional quotation marker) 332
˙ho˙ya, ˙hoya (infinitive < °ho-) 267, 538-9
Hoylyeng 17, 34
˙ho˙ye = ˙ho˙ya 542
"h-pat.chim" 49

huk (huk) 141
hulli- < *hul˙l-i-* 223
hulu- 'flow' 239, 271; 361
humble (form, stem, terms) 261, 299; 435
humility (referring to object) 299
hun ha- 290, 294
hu-nukki- 'sob' 141
hupsa hata 195
huy and hi 543
-huy (in female names) 132, 164
-huy (pronoun plural) 164
hw (articulation) 27, 36; (dropped) 36
-hwa₁,₂ (bnd n) '…ize, …ization'; 'flower' 166
-hwan (counter) 182
Hwanghay 26, 43, 233, 234, 772
hway (counter) 184
hwi- (bnd adv) 140, 543
°*hwo-* (vt) 'broad-stitch' 76
˙*hwo-*, ¨*hwo-* (modulated stem < °*ho-*) 544
˙*hwom*, ¨*hwom* = ˙*ho˙ywom* (modulated subst < °*ho-*) 267, 270, 546
hwu (pronunciation) 27; (reduced to hw) 36
-hwu- (spelled -chwu-) 220, 547
hwū < ¨ʜʜᴡᴜᴡ 161, 197, 547
hwū(-) < ¨ʜʜᴡᴜᴡ (bound adnoun) 153, 546
Hwun 49, 50, 51
Hwun-en 23, 768
Hwunmin cengum enhay 22
Hwunmong cahoy 22
(h)wupinta 344
hy… (> s(y)…)46; (> h…)48
hyangka: (orthography) 196; 622, 815
Hyang-kup 49
hyang ha.ye: … ul ~ 194; 547-8
Hyangyak 49
hybrid (form) 109; (paradigm) 584
hye (assumed to be palatalized) 46
°*hye-* 'pull' 267; 'draw [a needle]' 270
hye < ˙*hye* < ˙*ho˙ye* = ˙*ho˙ya* 548
hyēncang 161, 548
˙*hyenma*, ˙*hyen˙ma s* 68, 548
hyeng (nim) 299
hyengphyen 161, 548
Hyen Phyenghyo 239
hyey vs hey 48, 109, 548
¨*hyey-* 'reckon' 267
*hyo- (unique shape) 71
hypercoristic suffix 132
hypercorrection 47; hyperurbanism 25

hyphen 5, 6, 8, 9, 13, 20, 52, 152, 241, 245, 261
hyphenation (of Chinese compounds) 162
hypostatic contexts 193
hypothetical final: ~ consonant 23; ~ *h* 60
*/i/ < ˙*uy* (genitive) 43
…*ı̄* (Chinese word ending ~) 267
…*i* (nouns and adverbs ending in ~) 55
…*i* triggering lenition 55
-i- < -˙*i-* (formative for vc, vp) 220, 223, 225, 555
-i < -˙*i* (hypercoristic suffix for names ending in a consonant) 132, 164; 555
-i < -˙*i* (adv < iterated noun, der adv / n < adj) 140, 164, 255, 330, 553-5
…i adverb with no … **hata** partner 257
(-)i, *(-)i* (incorporated by noun) 108, 109, 121, 187, 553
-i (suffix) accretion 43
i… (and y…) 17; (for ni… or li…) 110; (stems beginning ~ reinforced after prefix or neg adv) 111
i… < MK *i*… and i… < MK *ni*… 110
…i- stems: (of more than one syllable) 252, 256, 267; (longer ~) 348, (lists) 350-60; (one-syllable ~, list) 349; 465
…i- or …y-: stem with final ~ (and coinciding noun / adverb) 87
ī- < ¨*ı̄* (Chinese preposition) 553
… i- (postnom v insep) 228; (… **inta**) 345; (… **ita**) 588
i- copula stem: 12; (ellipted / suppressed after vowel) 55, 87, 89; (reduced to **y-**) 89, 465; (following an overstuffed morpheme) 95, 217
˙*i-* (copula stem) 55, 273
˙*i-* 'cover' 262
-i form (of Japanese) 3
…*i / y* + particle ˙*ey* spelled "…*i /* y ˙*yey*" 37
˙*i* (postmodifier) 55, 232, 258, 259, 263, 267; (as summational epitheme) 264, 272; ('one that …') 324; (not epithematized?) 327
˙*i* (nominative particle) 54, 239; in adnominalized sentence 327
i = i / ka (nominative pcl) 3; (shortened to **y**) 92; 130, 140, 188, 193, 195, 196; (~ **tul**) 197; 229, 282; (omitted) 287; 291, 316, 330; 425, 459, 481; 549-53; 559, 584, 587, 590, 593-5, 622, 637, 638, 642, 766, 865, 869; (drops before **to**) 818, (before **ya**) 938; 922

i < ˙i 'this': (/ yo) 134; (as pronoun) 135; 148, 171, 344; 548, 826
i < ˙i 'person, one; fact, act' 12, 131, 134, 145, 161, 257; 548-9
i 'one, person' (bound noun) used as counter 187
i = ya 'question' (postmodifier) 160, 306, 553
i < ˙ni 'tooth': (spelled ni) 13; 110
··· 'i and ··· hi 257, 553
¹i··· 15, 25, 37
···i- stems: leniting ~ 54; (both high/low and high types) 72
*/i/ < ˙uy (genitive) 43
'I / me' 133, 135
ia / ya = ie / ye (cop inf) 251, 254, 555
IC (= immediate constituent) 3; (~ cut) 274, 277, 336
ic- (vt) 290, 332; 363
ica (cop subj assert) 556
i ccok 135, 556
icey, incey 136, 556
ici (copula suspective) 273, 556; ~ anh- (in rhetorical question) 323
identical obstruents 44
identificational sentence 327
Identified: (not epithematized) 327; SEE epithematized ~.
Identifier 327, 558
idiom 284
idiomatic: (expression) 131, 286, 298; (flavor) 274,
ie inf < i- or < ī(s)- 252
ie → yē 252
ie / ye (cop inf) 254; (often ia / ya) 308; 556
···ie infinitives 37; (···ie → ···ye) 93
iey < ingey (adv) 557
iey / yey (··· yey = /ey/) = ie / ye (cop inf) 254
iey / [y]ey yo (polite cop) 4; (shortened to (y)ey yo) 254; (? < iya(y) yo) 273; 557
˙i ˙Gem (cop effective subst) → ··· ˙[y] ˙Gem 263
˙i ˙Gey (cop adverbative) 54, 273, 558
*˙i ˙Gi (no cop summative) 273
˙i ˙Gwo (cop ger) 54, 273, 558
···ih- 104-5, 349
īhwu < ¨ɪ-¨HHWUW (postn, postmod) 159, 558
ii (der n) ← ī(s)- 256
i(-i): ~ tul / kkili 'you all' 133
i ka [DIAL] = i (nominative) 92, 559
i (kes) 'it' 134, 559; ~ tul 'they / them' 134
*ikey 'so that it is ··· ' 217, 274, 559
-ikhi- (formative for vc) 220, 224, 243, 559

iki- 290
iki (cop summative) 273, 316, 559
(-)ikka (occurs only in -(u)likka 257
i-kkacis / yo-kkacis 559
iko (cop ger) 559-60
-il 'day' 167
···i-l- stems (list) 360
i-l- → il.e 'rises' 253
*˙i-l- (defective stem) 256
¨il- 'become, come into being' 273, 571-2
˙il(q) ≠ ¨il(q) / ¨ill(q) 274
il 'early' (pseudo-preverb, adverb, adnoun) 141, 148, 560
il(q) (cop prosp mod) 217, 328, 560
īl < ¨il (? < ¨il-) 87, 110; (as postmodifier) 160; ('work', only separable monosyllabic vni) 190, (as free vn) 313; 321; 560
ila < ˙i ˙la (lenited from ita < ˙i ˙ta?) 54, 58; (˙i ˙la) 65, 71, 232; 235; (~ / 'la) 248; (functioning as cop inf) 254, 273, 274, 306, 308, 465; 561
˙i ˙la replaces (?) ˙i ˙ta except for -ngi ˙˙ta and ··· 'ta ˙ka 273
˙i ˙la °ho- (NAME ~) 332
ila ko (direct-quotation pseudo-pcl) 331, 332; 561-2
ila 'myen 330, 562
ilang / lang 196, 197, 198, 563
··· ila 'ni 330, 564
ila 'nun ← ila hanun 244, 565
··· ila 'nun ···, ··· ila 'n ··· 328
ila (se) = ie se 254, 565
ila to = ··· ie to 197, 198, 254, 565
··· ila 'y = ··· ila hay 308, 566
ilay / yolay 237, 243, 252, 566
īlay < ¨ɪ-LOY (postnoun, postmodifier) 159
ilayss- 243, 566
il-ccik (adv) 141; ilcciki 257
il-chen = chen 177
ilq-co = co 177
ile (/ yole), ileh- 134, 219; (~ hay) 243; 253; 567
˙i ˙le (bnd adv < defective inf) 219, 237, 243, 256; 567
i ˙le (inf < ¨i[l] ˙ta) 273, (vs ˙i ˙la) 274; 567
il-ek = ek 177
il.e na- 251
˙i ˙lesi ˙ta (cop retr hon indic assert) 273; 569
iley (cop retr) lenited from itey? 54, 58, 248, 306, 307; 569

iley said for ilay 252
iley '7 days' 177; 185; 240
ilG- / il ᵁ⁄₀- < *il ᵁ⁄₀G- (vc < ¨il- for which the modulated stem is il˙Gw ᵁ⁄₀- 274
¨il˙Gey, ¨il˙Guy 274, 569
ilh- 108; ilh- 231, 232; 363
il(q)-ī 111, (ilq-ī) 174, (/il-ī, il-lī/) 178
ili (/ yoli) < ˙i˙li 134, 140, 256; (never *~ uy, *~ ey, *~ 'ta) 295; 569
ilk- 231, 290; 364
īlqkena mālkena 231
ilkop-i, ilkopq-i 187
il(ko)-yetel(p) 178
ille 242
il-man = mān 177
ilo- (defective var cop stem) 217, 221, 307; 571
ilop 187
ilpan 195
il-payk = payk '100' 177
··· ilsswu 'constant (bad) habit' 131, 571
···ilu- stems
ilu- → ille < il ᵁ⁄₀- / ilG- < *il ᵁ⁄₀G- (adj) 'early'; < ni˙l ᵁ⁄₀- / nilG- < *ni˙l ᵁ⁄₀G- (v) 'say' 141, 231, 242; 361; 572
ilu- → ilule < ni˙lul- 'reach' 242, 253; 361; 572-3
¨ilu˙sya 273, 572
˙i˙lusyas˙ta (cop retr hon emotive) 273, 274, 572
˙i˙lwo- (var cop) 270, 273; (?< *˙i-˙t(e)-˙wo-) 274, 572-3
?˙i˙lwom / ˙(y)˙lwom = ?˙i˙ywom / ¨˙(y)wom (cop modulated subst) 135, 267, 573
˙ilwo-ngi ˙˙ta 273, 573
˙i˙lwo˙swo-ngi ˙˙ta (*˙i-˙swo-ngi ˙˙ta) 273, 573
˙i˙lwoswo˙n i (*˙iswo˙n i) 273, 573
?*˙i˙lwo˙syam / ˙(y)˙lwo˙syam 267
˙ilwo˙ta 65, 263, 273, 573
*˙ilwo-˙two˙swo- (unfound) 273
im < ˙im (cop subst) 217, 574
im 'beloved' < nim (same etymon as ··· nim < MK ¨nim 'esteemed ··· ') 111
i man 140, 574
Imbault-Huart, M.C. 17, 571
¹im ha.ye: ··· ey ~ 194
Im Hopin 656, 689, 761, 778
immediate constituent 3, 20, 193
immediate future -ukkey / -kkey 247, 259
immediate history 260
immediate sequence 245
immediate sources of forms with elision 54

imperative ending -ula / -la 217; (attached to MK bound stem) 214; 245, 246, 248
imperfect: (= unrealized) 261; 265
imperfect adnominal (= prospective modifier) 87, 263
"imperfect nouns" 131
impersonal: (indirect object, object, subject) 282, 314; (writing) 300
implied: agent 315; conclusion 303; nominal 328; subject 244, 298, 830
impressionistic adverb 140, 162, 164, 189, 340, 344
imye < ˙i˙m ye 267, 574
imyen 330 < ˙i˙m ye n' 267, 330, 574
(-)in < ZIN 'person' (bnd n) 162, 167, 574; (counter) 187
in < ˙in (copula modifier) 151, 217, 328, 575
˙in (cop mod) 55; (≠ ¨in) 274, 575; (dropped) 539, 667
ina / 'na (cop adversative) 151, 198, 291, 296, 575-6
inalienable possession 285
ina lul 198, 576
ina(-ma) 197, 213, 576
inanimate: (~ noun) 131, 744; 287; (~ subject verbs) 288; (~ object verbs) 289; 291
ina tul 198
i-nay 'this my ···; my' (as pseudo-adnoun) 149
inceptive 227
i(n)cey 134, 577
inchi (counter) 184
inclusive proposition 245
inconsistencies in spelling practices 15
incorporation by noun of -i 108, 109. SEE (-)i.
indefinite article (in English) 192
indefinite meaning 21
independent form (= free form) 57
independent variables 188
indeterminate (correlatives / deictics) 21; (accent peculiarities) 68; 132, 134, 303
Indic 98
indicative (aspect) 244, 246, 304
indicative assertive -ta < -˙ta 70, 71, 216, 234; 248, 305
indicative attentive 248, 305
indirect evidence for usual reading of Chinese character 97
in-directive 226
indirect object: (+ verb) 19; (multiple) 285; 287; (inherent) 288; (intensification) 292; (socially

inferior to subject) 295; (exalted) 299; 314; (extruded) 326
indirect-object particle 173, 299, 314
indirect quotation: (marker **ko**) 213, 248; (three kinds) 332
indirect quoting of intentive 331
indirect subject 244, 298, 299, 830
infinitive 3, 19, 35, 37; (of stems that end in unrounded ···**u**-) 38; (as adverb) 40; (the zero alternant of the ~) 87; (alternant shape **-y** in **hay** < **ha-**) 95; 100; (+ aux) 19, 219, 226, 231, 232, 235, 238, 240, 241, 242; (special ~ used only before **la**) 243; 246, 251; (at the end of a sentence) 253; 263, 265, 267, 291, 300, 308, 329; 465-6
infinitive-adverbialization 318
infinitive-auxiliary conversion 325
infinitive ending -˚e/a: (accent often suppressed when pcl follows) 61; (a bound stem?) 70; 71, 93, 232
infinitive (of defective vn) + pcl 189
infinitive (+ **se**) in phrasal postposition 194
infinitive + verb (with inserted **'ta**) 260
infix 262, 268; 343; 514, 899
inflected form 30, 40; (used as adverb) 140; (postnoun taken from ~) 156; 230, (+ pcl) 244; 324, 329
inflected and uninflected words 86, 88
inflected stems 233
inflection 340
inflectional ending 88, 99; (vowel that begins an ~) 100; 130
inflectional paradigm 255
inflectional system 231, 232
informal names 164
˙**i-ngi** ˙**'ta** 273, 577
in ha.ye: ··· **ey** ~ 194; ··· **ulo** ~ 195; 578
inherent indirect object 288
ini / **'ni** (cop indic attent) 257, 309, 330; (cop sequential) 578; (= **in i**) 578
initial 6, 29, 42, 49
initial alternation in mimetics 346
initial clusters 44
initial consonant 6
initial flap 15
initial geminates 21, 43
initial high (pitch) 48; in ···**l**- stems 241
initial [1] and [n] 15
initial nasal of **nye** and **ni** dropped 16
initial n and l 8

initial **ng**··· vs zero (merger in writing) 49
initial reinforcement that results from truncation 112
initial sibilant in clusters 44
initial syllable 257
initial zero 9, 29
˙**in** ˙**kwo** 55, 579
¨**i** ˙**non** (mod < ¨**il**- 'become') 274, 579
innovation 331
inseparable adjectival noun 190
inseparable adjectival postmodifier 161
inseparable adnoun 147
inseparable auxiliary verb 89, 219
inseparable postnominal verb 188
inseparable verbal noun 89, 188; (vnt) 19
inseparable verbal postmodifier 161
insertions 333
insistence 42, 332
instructing 295
instrumental: (more than one ~ phrase) 285, 286, 287
instrumentality: (kinds of ~) 285; 297
··· **inta** (postnom v insep): SEE ··· **i-**.
intensity 302
intensive: (form) 23; (stem) 57; (formative) 220; (bound postverb) 224; 226; (mimetic) 341, 343, 346; (= effective) 601
intentive (**-ulye** / **-lye**) 213, 217, 247, 257, 258, 259; (as proposition) 308; 330
intentive assertive **-ulyetta** / **-lyetta** 247, 258
intercalated palatal semivowel 37, 40; (always written in MK) 252
interjection 142, 146, 345
interludes 42, 44, 51
internal development of accent patterns 61
internal punctuation 18, 20
internal reconstruction 42
internal rounding 24
internal structure 20, 86
International Phonetic Alphabet 33
interrogation: unmarked except by intonation 21
interrogative: (ending, meaning) 21; 245, 246, 248
interrogative-indefinites 132
interrogativization 336
interrogativized negative 336
interruptive use of transferentive 789
intersyllabic strings 23, 42, 51
intervocalic **-h-** dropped 34
intimate style 87, 251, 253, 254, 297, 300

intonation 21, (patterns) 23, 41, 308, 309, 323
intransitive 287; (preferred to passive) 315
intransitive passive verb (vpi) 221
intransitive verb (vi) 89; (stem) 218; (mistaken for adj) 221; 288, 315, 332
intransitive verbal noun (vni) 89, 190
intrinsically plural or singular words 130
intrinsically voiced sounds 51
intrinsic ambiguity of adnominal relationship 326
intrinsic meaning 130
intrinsic vowel (rather than epenthetic) 714
intrinsic ⋯z⋯ 45
intruded epitheme 272
intruded palatal glide 39
in tul < ˙in ˙t ol 197
invariant LH words 64
inversion (stylistic / syntactic) 172, 304, 327, 477, 875, 945
inverted apostrophe 28
invitation 144
"io" and "iyo" 249, 580
iolssi- (defective var cop stem) 217, 221, 580
ionized parts of speech 88
ip- (vt) 223, 231, 233, 289, 290, 319; 362
ip.hi- (vc) 223
i phyen 135, 580
ip.nikka (cop formal indic attent) 257, 580
ip-seng 60
ipttay 134
irregular adjective ha- 'be' 242
irregular pronunciation 40
irregular stems 237
"irregular T" stems 231, 234
irregular vowel stems 242
is- > modern iss- 59, 218
ī(s)- 252, 255; 363
(i)sa [DIAL] = (i)ya (particle) 54, 581
i sālam 'you' 133, 135; 581
ī-sam 174
isi- 59, 581
˙isi- (cop hon) 273, 581
˙isi ˙m ye (n') 267, 582
*is ˙non (accentual exceptions implying ~) 84
is.non ⋯ (unaccented) 84; 218; 583
is ˙nwon 218, 583
isolated letters / symbols 23
*i ˙son 218, 584
isotopes 340, 343
isotopic vowels 344
iss- < is(i)- 40, 111, 216, 218; (aux) 227, 230,

319; 231, 243, 244, 259; (two subjects) 287; 288; (-e ~) 290, 291; (-ko ~) 290; 294; (honorific forms) 298; 305, 306, 307, 308, 310, 318, 326; 584-5
iss.ci ka / lul anh- 318
iss.e la 214, 243, 584
iss.e (se): ⋯ ey ~ 194
iss.ey (yo) = iss.e (yo) 253
(*)iss.i 'with' 218, 584
iss.ke la 214, 243, 584
iss.nun 218, 584
iss.nunta vs iss.ta 218, 584
iss.ta (ka) 137, 296
iss.un (usually → iss.nun or iss.tun) 218, 326, 584, 585
iss.usi- 319
is ˙ti a ˙ni °ho- 218, 585
˙i ˙sya (copula honorific infinitive) 273, 465
?* ˙i ˙syam / '(y) ˙syam 267
˙i ˙sye (infinitive < is(i)-) 465
˙i ˙syw ᵘ⁄om / '(y) ˙syw ᵘ⁄om (modulated substantive < is(i)-) 267
ita (postnominal verb inseparable): SEE ⋯ i-.
ita / 'ta (copula indicative assertive) 151, 257; (→ ila / 'la) 305, 316; 587
ita / 'ta (ka) (copula transferentive) 197, 198, 260, 291; 587-8
i-taci 140
item (and arrangement / process) 3
iterated adjectival noun + postnominal adj 345
iterated adjective 347; 899
iterated adverb / interjection 345
iterated modifier 150; 899
iterated noun: (+ adv-deriving -i) 100; (adverb from ~) 140, 162, 164, 347, 555
iterated particle 193, 196
iterated postnoun → adverb 276
iterated processive verbs 347
iterated verbal noun + postnominal verb 345
iteration 347; (unwanted) 601; (gerund-linked) 815
itey 307, 588
ithul, ithut nal 185; 235
¨i ˙ti < ¨il- occurs but not * ˙i ˙ti (cop suspective) 273, 588
*itolok 217; ˙ito ˙lwok = ˙i ˙two ˙lwok 589
ittakum 164, 589
i ttay 134, 589
itum (adnoun) 147, 589

itun / 'tun ci 197, 198, 296, 589
* ˈi- ˈtwo ˈswo- (unfound) 273
-(i)wu- 220, 590
...l y 23
ˈiy- as basic form of copula stem 55, 70, 78, 262
iya / ya < (i) ˈza (pcl): 12; (vs ia = ie cop inf) 40; 88, 130, 193, 195; (~ mal lo) 198; 291, 590
i(y)a (in Seoul sentence-final only) = i(y)e (cop inf) 273, 465; (~ se / to / ya [DIAL]) = i(y)e ··· 273; 590
* ˈi ˈ(y)a (cop inf if stem is ˈi-) 273
iyaki > yāyki > yēyki 34, 41, 47
iya yo 4, 591
(*) ˈi ˈye (cop inf if stem is ˈiy-) 273
ˈi ˈye / ˈ ˈye (as quasi-pcl < cop inf) 273, 591
iye older spelling of ie (cop inf) 40, 252, 591
...i yo = ...ey yo = -e yo 253
iyo (pcl) and io (cop) 40
iyo / yo (polite pcl) 12, 130, 196, 334, 591
iyo / yo (var = iko) < ··· ˈi ˈGwo (cop ger) 254, 591
iyo tul (*NOUN ~) 213
ˡīyu < "LI-YWUW 'reason' 161, 592
ˈi ˈywo- / ˈ ˈywo- (modulated copula stem) 270
? ˈi ˈywom (unabbreviated modulated cop subst) 135, 267, 270
ˈi ˈza (pcl) 592; 594
ˈizoW- (cop deferential; * ˈilwozoW-) 273, 592
(?) * ˈizow ˈo ˈsi- (cop deferential hon, unfound) 273
Japan: (word spacing in ~) 18; 132, 304
Japanese 1, 3, 4, 18, 20, 29, 31, 34, 35, 70; (pronunciation of English loanwords) 94; 95, 98, 132, 134, 135, 151, 157, 172, 173, 192, 218, 251, 274, 283, 284, 287, 290, 295, 305, 324, 327, 328, 330, 332, 444, 485, 594, 623, 632, 641, 817
Japanese pitch accent 60
Japanese placenames 133; (list) 371
Japanese r 28
judgment 295
juncture 12, 19, 20, 28, 31, 44, 51, 52, 56, 108; (dropped after accusative pcl); 172, 192, 196; (resolving ambiguity) 278; 331; 767
juxtaposed morphemes 52
juxtaposing locatives 285
juxtaposition: (of two hanthey phrases) 314; (of nominalization and noun) 324; 335

[k] > [tš] 47
k (lenited to G) 262
···k for s (pcl) 768
···k- stems 262; ···k- stems (list) 364
-k 163, 341, 592
k (emphatic pcl) 416, 469, 593, 667-8, 790, 821
-ka₁₋₄ (bnd n) 'professional'; 'song'; (quasi-title for surname); 'street' 167
-ˈka- = -ˈke- (effective): (first-person?) 263; 595
ka- < °ka- 'go' 79; (default motion verb) 132; ('go to do') 188; (as postnominal verb) 219; (aux) 226, 230; 243, 252, 257, 263, 271; 288, 289; (-e ~) 291; 294; 598-9
(k)a- words (of Japanese) 134
ka < ˈka (inf < ka-) 252, 267, 593, 594. SEE ka iss-.
ka (suppletive alt of nominative pcl i) 92, 193; (in -ta ka) 260; 292, 306, 310, 324; 593-5
ka < ˈka 'question' (postmodifier) 55, 160, 195, 248, 250; (ellipted) 281; 318
"ka" = ga (Japanese particle) 594
kac' ··· = kacwuk 146, 595
kacang < ko ˈcang 'most; very' 60, 138, 595
kaci (counter) 180
kaci- (vt) 'hold, have' 296, 595
kaciko 194, 595; (-e ~) 227, 230, 469
kācis mal 344
kac'ta < kacye 'ta 296, 595
kac.un (pseudo-adnoun) 150, 595
ka iss- 291
kak < ˈKAK (adnoun) 'each, every' 147
kake la 214, 243, 596
kak.ha (title) 132
kakkai (der adv / n) 140, 233, 256
kakkas ulo 145, 870
kakkaw- 231
kākwan 295
kal '-ology' (postnoun) 157, 596
ka la for kake la 214, 244, 596
kala-(anc-) 141, 219, 288
kalasitay < ko ˈlo ˈsya ˈtoy 379
kal.i (postnoun < der n) 158, 596
kalikhi- 'point out' 295
kalma- 219
kalo- (< kolo- / koll··· < *kolok-) 'say' → kalotoy < kol ˈGwo ˈtoy 220; 379
ka( )lo 146, 180
kalo-ssuki 'horizontal writing' 6
kaluchi- < kolo ˈchi- 288, 289, 290, 295, 332; 379

kalwu < *kolo/kolG…*, */koll…* < **kolok*, **kolol*
'powder' 239
kālyang 'approximately' (postnoun) 157, 596
kām- 231; 364
kām < ¨*KAM* 'feeling' 161; -kam 167
kama (counter) 181
kāmali (postnoun) 157, 597
kāmang 295
kaman ha- 340
kamcil na- 228, 291
kāmki (ey) tulli- 'catches a cold' 289, 317
(kām)-phalu- 'be (dark) blue' 242; 361
kan (counter) 183
kan < *KAN* 'interval; between' (postnoun) 157, 186
-kān = -keyss.nun (ya) 306, 597
(-)kang < ˙*KKANG* 'a little over … ' (postn; adv) 159
kang(-) < ˙*KKANG* (adn; bnd adv) 'forced; plain; dry' 149; (bnd adn) 'tough, hard, strong' 154
kang < *KANG* 'river': (as category designator) 133; 159; 697
Kang Cenghuy 627
Kanglung 234
Kangwen (Tokyey) 239
ka⁷no-zyo (Japanese) 135
kap (counter) 181
kapcaki 257
kapcel 185
ka-preemphasizable 289
kapyewun liul 51
kapyewun mium, kapyewun piup 925
… kara vs … no de (Japanese) 330, 623
Karlgren, B. 46, 95
kas (adverb, adnoun) 136, 150; 598
ka(-)tah- 226
katakana words 34
kath- (adj) < ˙*kot °ho-* 193; (postnom adj insep) 229; 231, 253, 308; 363; 599
kath.ey (yo) = kath.e (y)o 253
kath.i 137, 193, 195, 526, 599
kath.ta 195, 599
Katsuki Hatsumi 622
katuk hata 294
ka ulo and kalo 146
kawuntey (as quasi-pcl) 193; 197; 599-600
(k)awus 'and a half' (postnoun) 157, 176, 177, 428, 600
-kay (suffix; bound postnoun) 257, 600

kay (counter) 179, 181, 182, 600
kāy 'wild' (adnoun < noun 'dog') 148, 600
kayk < ˙*KHOYK* (adnoun, bnd n; noun) 149, 167
… ka yo 310
-kayso (counter) 180
-kaywel (counter for months) 182, 186
KBC (= Korean Basic Course) 25, 29
-˙k^e/a- (effective) 70, 72; (basic accent) 84; 258; (2d/3d-person?) 263; 601
-ke version of inf -e (+ la) 243; 253
ke (shortened variant of kes) 244
kēcis mal 344
KEd (= A Korean-English dictionary) 16, 20, 30, 34, 38, 108, 122, 135, 145, 221, 233, 235, 343, 345, 463, 566, 622, 681, 761, 781, 796, 831, 856, 884, 898
keki (/ koki) < *ke˙kuy* 134; 140, 344, 601
kekkwu lo = (k)k^e/akkwu(-)lo 146, 870
ke l' 250, 281, 329, 330, 602
kē-l- < ¨*kel-/ke˙lo-* < **ke˙lo-* 'hang' 235, 240
keli- (postnom v insep) 219, 228, 345, 603
keli (counter) 181
keli (postnoun 'skipping') 158, 602
keli = …q keli (postn < der n) 'material' 131, 158, 602
kel.i (postnoun < der n) 158, 603-4
k-ellipsis 92
kelme- 219; kelthe- 219
kelum 'fertilizer' 239
kel.um < *kelum* 'gait, pace' < ¨*ket-/kel-* < **ke˙lu-* 'walk' 272; 279
-˙*kem* (effective subst) 263, 603
ken < *KKEN* (adn, preparticle, adj-n) 149, 603
-kena < -˙*ke˙na* 329, 603
-keni < -˙*ke˙n i* 329, 604
-˙*ke˙n i ˙Gwo* 55, 604
-keni wa 213, 605
-ken man < -˙*ken ma˙non/ma˙lon* 329, 605
kēnne- pronounced kēnnu- 41; 350; 605
kēnne (inf < kēnnu-) 605; ~ iss- 291
kēnney- (vc) 238
kēnnu- spelled kēnne- < ¨*ken˙ne-* < ¨*ket-°na-* 224, 238, 270, 288; 350
-kentay (literary conditional) 247, 329, 605-6
-˙*ken ˙t ^{e}/ay n'* 259, 606
-kenul < -˙*ke˙n^u/ol* 329, 606
ken ulo = kenseng (ulo) 146, 870
kernel (phrase, sentence) 297
ke = ke(s) (postmodifier) 258, 601

kes (postmodifier) 'thing; one; fact' 131, 134, 160, 161, 263, 267, 324, 329, 330, 607
kes (modifier + ~) 'the fact that ...' = Middle Korean ‥‥·$(^{u}/o)m$ 328
kes as a generalized replacement for an extruded epitheme 328
keseyn māl 341
⋯ kes i 329, 330
-ˈke-ˈsi- = -ˈ$(^{u}/o)$ˈsi-ˈGe- 261, 607
-kes.ta 249, 259, 608
⋯ kes ul 281, 329, 330
⋯ kes ulo 330
ket- (vt) 'gather up' 235; 363
kēt-/kel- 'walk': (kel.um (ul) ~) 279; 288; 363
-keˈta (effective indicative assertive) 259, 609
ket.i /keci/ (postnoun < der n) 158
¨ket-°na- 270
-ketumyen 329, 609
-ketun < -ˈkeˈtun (-ˈkeˈton) 258, 259, 329, 609
keuy, kecin 138
key vs kyey 609
ʾˈkey < hoˈkey after voiceless sound 92, 610
-key < -ˈkey (adverbative ending) 3, 136, 140, 247, 255, 306, 330, 610-2
-key (suffix, makes noun from v) 164, 257, 612
key < kes i 322, 610
⋯ key 'one's place, home' 131, 610
key ani 'ta 322
-key an toynta 291
-key hanta 218, 312, 611
-key-kkum 247, 612
-key mantu-l- (periphrastic causative) 313, 611
-key na 213, 306, 613
keyney 'you all' 134, 613
-keypi (in tes-keypi) 163, 613
-key-sili 247, 613
-keyss- 40, 218, 220, 230, (and -ess-) 244, 246, 304, 305, 306, 307, 308, 310; 363; 594, 613-4
-keyss.ci anh- (in rhetorical question) 323
-keyss.ey (yo) = -keyss.e (yo) 253, 614
-keyss.ki 324, 614
-keyss.nun 250, 251, 614
-keyss.ta (future) 259, 614-5
-keyss.tun 250, 615
-keyss.ul, -keyss.un (rejected forms) 251
-keyss.um 324, 615
-keyss.uni 257, 616
/-keytta/ = -kes.ta (var) or -keyss.ta 259
-key to 247, 616
-key toy- 315, 317, 611

keyulu- 290; 361
⋯-kh (examples) 104
ˈkh^e/a⋯ < °ho-k^e/a- 40
-khengi 163, 617
khenyeng 195; (~ tul, ~ un) 198; 617-8
khey- = khi- (khye-) 238
ˈkhey < hoˈkey after MK voiced sound 92, 618
-khe(y)ngi 163, 617
-khi- 220, 619
khi- < khye- 238
khi (der n < khu-) 256
khi cil ha- 242
khillo (counter) 184
Khlynovski, M. 775, 866
⋯ kho 189
khu- < ˈkhu- 'be/get big' (adj/vi) 217, 220; 267, 288, 344, 349
k(h)uli- (postnom v insep) 228
ˈkhuy < hoˈkuy after voiced sound 92
khway (counter) 182
ˈkhwo < hoˈkwo after voiced sound 92, 620
-khwung 164, 620
khye- > khi- 41, 237, 349
khye ← khie 237; khye ci- 317
khyel(l)ey (counter) 180
-ki- < -ˈki- (formative for vc, vp) 220, 223, 225, 623
-ki < -ˈki (summative) 144, 247; 267, 277, 323, 324; 620-3
-ki$_{1-3}$ (bnd n) 'device'; 'machine; airplane'; 'period' 167
kiˈchwum = kiˈchum < kich- 'sneeze' 272
kiek na- 332
-ki ey 214, 244, 247, 330, 623; ~ him ssu- 227, 299; ~ mangceng 144, 623
ki ha.ye: ⋯ ul ~ 195
kiil 167
kī-l- 'long' 240, 256, 257
kil (counter) 184
kil < ˈkilh 'path' 161; 240; 626
kil.i (der adv/n) 256
kilk- (Phyengan DIAL) = kī-l- 240
killay (adv) 'long' 257, 627
-killay = -killey 'because' 247, 330, 627
-ki lo 214, 244, 330, 627
ˈkilqˈh ol 240
kīlung for kīnung 111; kilyem for kinyem 111
kīm (postmod, postn, n) 'impetus' 159, 160, 629
-ki mangceng 160, 685
-ki man ha- 340, 629

Kim Chakyun 69
kimchi (etymology) 47
Kim Cin.wu 54
Kimhay 25, 34, 60
Kim Hyengkyu 54, 59, 594, 730
Kim Hyenglyong 7, 100
Kim Minswu 2, 4, 15, 34, 38, 221, 379
Kim Payklyen 285
Kim Pyengha 142, 333, 682
Kim-Renaud, Y. [Kim Yengki] 2, 44, 233, 240
Kim Sek.yen 1
Kim Senhuy 2
Kim Sungkon 332, 663, 853
Kim Thaykyun 2, 17, 28, 54, 103, 690
Kim Tongsik 323
Kim Wancin 2, 43, 48, 59, 61, 69, 72, 96, 98, 196, 622, 815
Kim Yengcwu 323
Kim Yengpay 26, 33, 41, 42, 46, 48, 53, 234, 239, 240, 593, 627, 690, 742, 757, 761, 775, 815, 892
kin, kinship roles, kin terms 299
King, J.R.P. 2, 17, 27, 28, 42, 47, 49, 59, 234, 235, 263, 331, 332, 466, 595, 627, 713, 756, 866
kīn-kin 150
k-inserting stem 243, 253
-ki nun: V₁-ki nun ha- = V₁-ki nun V₁- 218, 630
-ki nun (ha-) 324, 630
kiph- 'be / get deep' (adj / v) 217; 363
kiph.i < ki˙phi (der adv) 255
-kis = -(k)kis 164
-ki to (ha-) 227, 324, 340, 631
-ki ttaymun ey 330, 621-2
-ki wa 214, 632
kk < sk examples 104
···kk- stems (list) 364
-kka 230, 246
kkaci (pcl) 60, 136, 195, 632
-kkak / -kkek 164, 347
kkal (postnoun) 157
··· kkan (ey) 'by one's own account' 131, 634
kkatalk 'reason' 161; (~ ulo) 330; 634-5
kkaykkus hi 256; kkaykkus 'i /kkaykkusi/ 257
(-)(k)kayngi 147, 163
kkē ci- 317
-kkek 164
(k)kᵉ/akkwu(-)lo 146, 870
kkes 140, 157, 635

-kkey (bnd adj-n) 191, 635
kkey (postnoun) 157, 635
kkey (pcl) 133, 299, 635
kkey se 195, 198, 282, 299, 637
kki (counter) 184
kki = kkini 'meal(time)' 759
kkik 'ingest' 112
kkiko: ··· ul ~ 195
kkili 131, 140, 157, 639
-(k)kis 164, 631
kkokci (counter) 181
kkol (postnoun) 157, 631
(k)kol chen pen 177
-(k)kul 164, 651
kkul.e 'pulling' 219
-(k)kulum (bnd adj-n) 191
-(k)kum 'rather' (bnd adj-n) 191, 657, 639
kkunh- 231, 232; 364
-(k)kus 164, 659
kku(s)- < kuzu- / kuzG- < *kusuk- 'pull' 239
kkuth (postmod, n) 160, 639; Kkuth ulo ... 334
kkway 135, 138, 639
kkwuleki (postnoun) 157, 640
kkwulek = ···q kwulek (postnoun) 157, 669
kkwule(y)mi (counter) 181
kkwum (ul) kkwu- 279
kkwun = ···q kwun (postnoun) 157, 671
kkwuna 213; (as pcl) 214; -ca ~ 196, 433; 640
k lenited to G 54
k-lenition 50
KM (= Korean Morphophonemics) 22, 41, 42, 235, 259, 884
knowhow 315
-ko < ˙kwo (gerund) 3, 247, 280, 329, 640-2. SEE gerund.
ko (deictic) 'that' 148, 230, 232, 233, 236, 640
ko < ˙kwo (postmod) 'question' 160, 640, 667
ko (quotation / quotative particle) 196, 213; (optionally follows -nula) 258; 331, 640
kō < ᴋwo (adn 'deceased'; n, postmod 'reason') 148, 640
koc 'the Cape of ··· ' (postnoun) 157
-ko ca, -ko ce 227, 259, 643
ko˙cang 60, 643
-ko cie 227
"kohi" = koi (der adv) < kōw- 256
-ko iss- 319, 641; -ko iss.usi- 320
-kok (counter) 183
Kok (Wel.in chenkang ci kok = 1449 Kok) 45, 49, 56, 85

koki (deictic) 344, 644
-ko kyēysi- 320
[¨]kol- 'change' < *ko˙lo- 241
˙kol- 'grind' < ˙ko˙lo- 241
koli 340, 644
ko lo 135, 139, 161
¨kolp- 57, 241
kol payk pen 177
kols 'course' generally treated as kol 108
¨kolW- 57, 241
-kom (ha-) 164, 644
-ko mālko (yo)! 'of course ···!' 304, 644
komaw- 291
-ko na- (gerund + auxiliary) 226, 641
-kong 'artisan' 167
kong 'zero' 174
kongpu (vn, free n) 188
kōn.¹nan 41, 111
ko nom 344, 645
Kōno Rokuro 2, 46, 661
-ko nun 244; ~ ha- 340; 645
kop 185
kop-cayngi 185
kopcel (counter) 184
kopha, kophu- 252
-ko 'phuta = -ko siph.ta 94, 646
Korea 46, 132, 186, 304
Korean 40; (unlike tone language) 60; (syllables) 95; (vocabulary) 95; (plain obstruents) 96; (sentence) 222, 283, 286, 315; 234; (syntax) 274, 286; (word) 275; (speaker) 283; 284; (nominals) 286; 287, 295, 300, 305, 322
Korean grammarians 21, 39, 40, 41, 145, 146, 214, 220, 234, 238, 244, 274, 284, 292, 299, 316
Korean Language Society 37, 94, 251
Korean linguists 344
Korean provinces 133
Korean readings of Japanese placenames 133
Korean-Russian dictionary 27
Koreans 252, 294
··· kos < ˙kwot 'place' 131, 646
-ko se 214, 330, 646
-ko siph-: SEE siph-.
kos.kos-i 257
kot- (adj) 256, 348; 363
kot (adv) 136, 137, 139, 647-8
kot-cang 137
kot.chwu (spelled kochwu) 256
-˙koy / -˙Goy 267

Ko Yengkun 2, 187, 263, 466
-ko (yo) 329
koz- ? < *ko˙s[o]- 'cut' 237
···ks (examples) 104; (obsolete stem) 364
ku (/ko) 'that' 131, 134; (as 3d-person pronoun) 135; 148, 171; (as n) 193; 344, 649-50
ku ··· (i, sālam, pun, nom, ca, ...) 'he/him, she/her' 134
kuc(ekk)ey 134, 136
ku (kes) 'it' 134, 651; ~ tul 'they/them' 134
kuk hi 257
ku-kkacis / ko-kkacis 147, 651
-kul = -(k)kul 164, 651
*ku-l- (defective stem) 256
kulam (counter) 184
kulay (/ kolay) 237, 243, 252, 652; **Kulay se** ··· 333, 652; **Kulay to** ··· 334, 652; kulayss- 243
kule 'dragging, pulling' 219, 652
kule (/ kole) < ku˙le (bnd adv < defective inf) 134; 219, 237, 243, 252, 256, 652
kule- 'do/say that way' 132, 141, 231, 243; (~ ha.yess-, hayss-) 243; 655
Kuleca ··· 333, 652
kulech'anh.e to = kulec'anh.e to 343, 652-3
kule(h)- 'be that way' 132, 134, 243, 653
Kuleh.ci man ··· 334, 653
Kuleh.ta (ha)tula 'y to ··· 334
kulek celek 140, 653
Kuleki ey ···, **Kuleki ttaymun ey** ··· 333, 653
Kulelq ci 'la to ··· 334
kulem 243; (**Kulem** ···, **Kulem ulo** ···) 333; 654
kulemyen 139; (**Kulemyen** ···) 333; 654
kulemyen se: (**Kulemyen se** ···) 333; 654
kulen 'such' 171, 654
kulena 243; (**Kulena** ···) 334; 655
Kulen cuk ··· 333
Kuleni ···, **Kuleni-kka (n')** ··· 333; 655
Kuleta ka ··· 334
kuley said for kulay 252
kuli (/ koli) < ku˙li 134, 140, 256; (never *~ uy, *~ ey, *~ 'ta) 295; 655-6
kuliko 139; (**Kuliko** ···) 333; 656
kūlim ul kūli- 279
kulssey 138, 657
kulus (counter) 181
kulwu (counter) 180
(-)kulye 305, 311, 657
-kum (suffix) 107, 137, 657
-kum = (k)kum (ha-) 164, 657
ku man 'just that' (n + pcl) 140, 193, 657-8

ku-man / ko-man 147, 657
kʷo-man ha- 340, 658
ku-mas / ko-mas 147, 658
kumum (nal) 185
kun (counter) 183
kūn < ˊKKUN (adnoun; ? bound noun) 149
ku (ney) tul 'you all' 133, 659
ku ⋯ ney (tul) 'they / them' 134, 659
kung ha.ye: ⋯ ey ~ 194
ku nom 344, 659
kunul (i) ci- 317
ku-nye 135
kup hi 257
*kupttay 134
Kuroda Shige-Yuki 324
-kus = -(k)kus 164, 659
ku-taci 140, 659
kutay < *kutoy* 'you' 133, 296, 660
ku ttay 134, 660
ku ⋯ tul 'they / them' 134, 660
-ˋkᵘoy (= -ˋkᵉay) 54; (never modulated) 271, 661
ˊˋkuy < hoˋkuy after voiceless sound 92, 661
kuz- < *kuzGu- < kusuk- 'pull' 237
-kwa = (q)-kwa 'course; taxonomic family; section' 167
-ˋkwa (of -ˋkwa ˊˋla / swoˋla) 262, 263, 271, 663, 666
ˋkwa (pcl) 55, 56, 233, 239, 663
kwa / wa, (k)wa (pcl) 130, 196, 197, 214, 295, 662-3
kwa kkaci (→ hako kkaci) 197, 663
-kwan₁,₂ (bnd n) 'govt official', 'building' 167
kwan (counter) 183
kwan ha.ye: ⋯ ey ~ 194
Kwan-yek = Cosen-kwan yek.e 48, 60
-ˋkwaˋtye < -ˋkwatoyˋye < *-ˋkwa to[wo]yˋye 263, 667
-kwangi 163
/kwēllyen/ 'cigarette' spelled phonemically but etymologically kwēn.yen 111
-kwen = (q)-kwen 'power' 167
kwēn₁ (counter) 179, 181
kwēy-ccak (counter) 181
-ˋkwo (never modulated) 271; 667
ˊˋkwo < hoˋkwo after voiceless sound 92, 274, 667
ˋkwo 'question' (postmodifier) 55, 56, 667
-ˋkwom (adverb-intensifying suffix) 55, 668
ˋkwom 'each' (pcl) 55, 56, 668

¨kwom (< *kwoˋma) 'bear' (etymology) 98
ˋkwos 'precisely' (pcl) 55, 56, 668-9
¨kwoW- 234
-kwu- (formative for vc) 220, 224, 669
-kwu = -ko (ger) 41, 259, 303
-kwu₁,₂ (bnd n) 'wicket; opening'; 'tool' 168
(-)kwu 'ward (of city)' 133
kwū- 'old' (Chinese bound adnoun) 154, 146
kwuc-: (postnom adj usually insep) 229; 363; 669
-kwuk (bnd n) 'nation', 'agency, office' 168
Kwuk Ungto 234
kwū-l- (aux vi sep): -key ~ 227; 669
kwulup 187
(-)kwulye (postmod, ending, ? pcl) 160, 196, 213, 214, 246, 259, 305, 307, 311, 669
(-)kwumen (postmod, ending, ? pcl) 160; (~ yo) 310, 670-1
kwumeng (< *kwumwu / kwumk*⋯ < *kwumwuk) 'hole' 238
-kwun (bound noun) 'army' 168
(-)kwun (postmod, ending, ? pcl) 160, 246, 306, 307
(-q) kwun 671
kwun (title) 132
kwūn (adnoun) 147
kwūn 'county (prefecture)' (category designator) 133
(-)kwun a (postmod, ending, ? pcl) 160, 213, 246, 307, 671
(-)kwung 'palace' 133
kwuni (postnoun): pallok ~ 157, 671
Kwunsan 34
(-)kwun yo 306, 310. SEE (-)kwumen.
kwut- 'get / be hard' (v / adj) 217; (adj) 340; 363
kyek ha.ye (hako): ⋯ ul ~ 194
kyel 'impetus' (postmod, postnoun, noun) 159, 160, 672
kyelqceng cī(s)- / ha- 229
kyel-kho 139
kyem (postmod, noun [postn, vn]) 139, 160, 672
kyeng- 'light' (bound adnoun) 154
kyēng (postnoun) 157, 673
Kyengki 24; 772
Kyengsang 47, 53, 57, 69, 92, 106, 136, 144, 233, 238, 253, 300; 870
kyenti- 290
¨kyeˋsi- 267
kyeth 197, 673
kyewu 138

kyey vs key 48; (both /key/) 109; 673
-kyēy 'world' (bound?) 152
-kyey$_{1-4}$ (bound noun) 'world, realm'; 'system'; 'ga(u)ge; scheme'; 'report' 168
Kyeylim (Kyeylim ^{1}yusa = 1103 Kyeyilom) 48, 49, 59, 713
kyēysi- 109, 217, 226, 319, 673
-kyo 'religion' 168
kyōswu (title) 132
-kyun (counter) 183
Kyupem-cip period 4
^{1}⋯ before **i, y** 124
l (elided before apical) 93, 673; (l + n → /ll/) 99; (reduced from **lp, lph, lm, lth, lk**) 100; (not after pause) 110; (lenited from *t*) 234
l⋯ (initial) 45; (of *L*⋯ (not distinguished from *n*⋯?) 45
-*l*- as unique variant of -*te*- (retr) 273, 274
l⋯ (→ **n**⋯ (in older loanwords) 110; (Chinese morphemes with basic ~) 124; (~ morphemes standardized to **n**⋯) 124
⋯**l** 341, 343
⋯*l* (as lenition of *t*) 50; (made onset of next syllable) 54; (triggering lenition) 55; (unlinked to following vowel) 56; (MK nouns ending in ~) 58, 673, 767
⋯*l(q)* ← ⋯l[^{u}/o]-l(q) (except before *i* or *y*) 241
⋯*l*- stem: (substantive uncontracted) 255, 265; (prospective modifier contracted) 851
"⋯*l*.-" = /⋯*lG*-/ 238
⋯*[l]*⋯ 58
⋯*LQ* < Middle Chinese ⋯t 50, 55, 61; (treated as voiceless) 92
⋯*lq* 50; (~ cluster) 44; (~ *C*⋯) 45
⋯**l**- (stem-final) 58, 231, (lenited from pre-MK **t*) 241
⋯**-l-** (basic to stem but here treated as vowel extension) 130, 240
-L- stem 58, 61; (with related noun) 87; 233; (confused with regular or l-doubling stem) 242; 851; (mod) 897-8
⋯**lq-** stem (< ⋯**lu-**) 363
'*l(q)* 23
'**l(q)** = **hal(q)**; = **il(q)** 89, 673
l' abbr of **lul** (pcl) 89, 196, 235, 673
l and **n** (alternation of ~) 100, 110
-**la**: (+ pcl **ko**) 213; 240, 246, 263, 674
la (pcl after inf) 196, 213, 214, 243, 251, 253, 673-4
labial 8, 18, 31, 39, 42; (~ semivowel) 23; (~ stop) 24, 43, 233; (dropped ~) 36; (~ elision) 56, 57, 92; (~ lenition) 57, 60, 233; 239
labialized velar fricative 57
labial-onset syllables with **u** vs **wu** 18
lag in phase of phoneme feature 37
lag in voicing vowel after **s** 28
lak: SEE **ak** / **lak**.
'**la ko** (as pseudo-particle) 331, 674
-**la kwu** 305, 674
-**la 'nta** 332, 674
"laryngealized" vowel 27
laryngeal tension 27
last member of a phrase 88
Late Middle Korean 42
lateral: allophone 28; articulation 51; release 52
lateral for coda /*l*/ 51
lateral + flap 28
late(r) text 55, 56
Latin: (infinitive) 251; 286
lax allophone 44
lax apical stop 44
lax consonant 24, 27
lax obstruent 27; (+ reinforced obstruent) 31
layers of vocabulary 95
⋯**lc**⋯ vs ⋯**lqc**⋯ 31
⋯*l C*⋯ written for ⋯*lq C*⋯ 50
⋯*l CC* 45; ⋯*l CC*⋯ = ⋯*lq C*⋯ 50
⋯*lC* clusters 50
-**lC**- clusters 28
LCT (= ^{1}Yu Changton) 23, 38, 44, 47, 52, 54, 55, 56, 58, 65, 73, 96, 105, 221, 239, 261, 263, 269, 271, 273, 274, 570, 572, 613, 627, 648, 666, 716, 730, 779
Ledyard, G. 43
l doubling 528
l-doubling vowel stems 41, 231, 238, 252, 253, 256; 361
l-dropping vowel stems 234. SEE l-extending.
league = Korean mile 110
l-elision (before apical) 58; (before *n*) 716
length (alternations) 33, 34; 37
lengthening of vowel for emphasis 35
lenited forms of velar-initial morphemes 261
lenited-initial version (-˙$G^e a$⋯) of effective 241
lenited *k* 54
lenited labials 56; lenited *p* 54, 57; lenited **p** 130
lenited *s* (= *z*) 54; lenited sibilant 48
lenited shape 273
lenited *t* 57
lenited velar 54, 56, 254

leniting ⋯i- stems 54
leniting t 33
"leniting T" stems 57
lenition 33, 53; (lasting effects in v stem) 53; (exceptions) 55; 60; 234, 237, 274, 307
lenition after ⋯li- stems 262
lenition of k 50
lenition of -p⋯ in compound nouns 57
lenition of velar-initial particles (dating) 56
lenition phenomena of earlier Korean 51
less direct subject (= indirect subject) 298
letters 6
ley (particle [Phyengan]) 627, 675
ley (particle [Ceycwu]) 675
/ley/ and /yey/ for lyey 110
lexical derivations 18
lexical accent 35
lexical causatives 218, 219
lexical compounds 291
lexical derivation 18, 324
lexical items 274
lexicalization 56, 60, 66, 144, 277
lexicalized exceptions (to the rules of particle demarcation) 86
lexicalized phrase 144, 176
lexical lenition 56
lexical marking (of vowel length) 33
lexical nominalization 888
lexical passive verb 219
lexicon 131
l-extending vowel stem 31, 33, 231, 234, 235, 240, 253; (list) 360
l-extension (of vowel stem) 231
l-final stems = -T/L- stems 33
⋯lG⋯ > ⋯ll⋯ 238, 239
⋯lh- 39; 101; (examples) 105; 233; (stem list) 363
⋯lh nouns 109, 673; 675
LHL and LHH (no distinction?) 68
⋯lh.n⋯ spellings 52
LHS (= ¹Yi Hisung) 15, 34, 38, 122, 141, 157, 221, 238, 275, 657, 757
li⋯ 15; (pronounced as ni⋯) 46
⋯'l i '- 262; ("-li-") 594
-li- 220, 676
-li (suffix making der adverb-noun) 164, 255
-li (counter) 183
⋯li- stems 55; (list) 359-60
(-)lī 'village' (category designator) 133; 159

lī 'reason' (postmodifier) 160, 676
liaison 28, 29, 50, 51, 54
light isotope 340, 343
light l 51; light p, light m 925
lightly aspirated release 28
light vowel 343
-lila (counter) 183
linear measure 183
linkage (conflicts) 19
l-inserting vowel stems 231, 242, 253; 361
lip rounding 24; (throughout syllable) 18
liquid 24, 27, 28, 50, 51; (dominating the nasal) 52; 359; (doubling) 628
liquid elision 48; (before genitive particle s) 58; (in modern dialects) 58; (before apical) 93; 235, 238; (before n) 716
liquid nasalization 31
liquid reduced from a cluster (endings reinforced after ~) 102
liquid suppressed (⋯[l]m) 255
listener 268, 321, 326
literal meaning 344; literal question 336
literary 8; (form/var) 21, 243; 38; (cliché) 251, 800
literary concessive -kenul 247, 259, 329
literary conditional -kentay 259, 329
literary contexts 296
literary desiderative -ko ca / ce hanta 259
literary idioms 323
literary Korean 216; literary language 251
literary style 320
liul 110
lively (intonation) 42
lk (reduction of ~) 102
⋯lk(-) (examples) 105; (stem list) 364
LKM (= ¹Yi Kimun) 42, 43, 44, 47, 48, 49, 51, 55, 58, 60, 61, 713, 936, 946, 947
/ll/ 28; ll < l 628; ll for nn 41
⋯ll- perforce written ⋯l-l⋯ 238
⋯ll⋯ 676
⋯ll (before i or y) ← ⋯l[ᵘ/o]-l(q) 240, 677
-LL- stems (⋯lu-/⋯ll-) 53, 101
⋯lli- stems (lists) 359-60
⋯l-li- < -Gi- (formative for vc, vp) 224
lm (reduction of ~) 102
⋯lm (contracted unmodulated subst) 255
⋯lm(-) examples 105
⋯lm- stems: (reanalyzed as ⋯mu-) 58; (list) 364
"l.n" written for /ll/ 52
⋯l.n⋯ or ⋯l.nn⋯ ← ⋯lh- + -n⋯ 52

-lo 'street' 168
lo = ulo after vowel or ···l 130, 677
lo [DIAL] = lul 196, 677
loan = loanword 31, 94, 95; loanmorph 116
loan translation 98
local breath 27
location: (nouns of relative ~) 196; (shift in ~) 260; 297
locative-allative particle ‵*e*/*ay* 68, 495-6
locative constraints 294
locative marker / particle 43, 69
logographic characters 95
logotypes 6
loi (der adv) < low- 256
*···lok, *···lol 239
long and short vowels (quality differences) 24
long constructions 19
longer infinitives in ···wue 38
longer predicates 315
longer strings 261
longer vowel stems 350
long form: (broken by space) 19; (of negative) 315, 316
long lateral 52
long mark 32
long negative 315, 316
long noun phrases; (constituency) 277
long phrases 61
long string of high syllables (avoidance of ~) 62
long syllable 61
long vowel: 6, 32; (length shown by a macron) 9; (from vowel + h + u) 37
long vowels from contraction 34; 237
long vowels in modern loanwords 34
long vowels: new ~ 33
long vowels shortened in certain verb forms 237
long vs short low-pitch nuclei (Antong) 34
loosely attached particles 52
loosely concatenated sentence 597, 605
loose reference 446, 499, 817, 830, 928-9
lop.hi- 229, 677
loss of consonants between vowels 53
loss of *p*··· and *s*··· in clusters 50
lost MK vowel *o* (sounded like Seoul **e**) 42, 43
lost vowel with high tone 33
'lots' 173
low- (postnom adj insep) 219, 229, 251, 256; 361, 677
··· *lo*W- 234
low: (pitch / tone) 6, 26, 34, 35, 60, 232; (low +

high > rise) 61, 237, (reduction to just low) 241; (···*l*- stems beginning ~) 241
low back (and functionally unrounded) vowel *o* 4, 42
low front rounded vowel [ɶ] 43
low-initial dissyllables 234, 237
low(-pitched) stems 7, 74
low vowel 36
lp (reduction of ~) 102
···lp- examples 105; (stem list) 363
lph (reduction of ~) 102
···*lph*, ···*lph*(-) (examples) 105
···lph- verb stems (truncated from ···lphu-) 106; (list) 363
···lphu- 106
"lq" (look under just "l" above)
/ls/ 31; ls 102; ls vs lss 233
···ls- examples 105
···ls··· vs ···lqs··· 31
···*ls C*··· 50
···*l se* 233
LSN (= ¹Yi Swungnyeng) 59, 93, 271, 553, 668, 711, 744, 923
-*lq ˙s oy* 264
-L/T- stem: SEE -T/L- stem.
···lt- (underlying form of -T/L- stems?) 234
···lt··· vs ···lqt··· 31
···l-t···, ···l-c···, ···l-s··· in Chinese binoms 50
lth (reduction of ~) 102
···lth- (examples) 105; (stem list) 363
···*l ˙tta = -lq ˙ta* 44
···*[l]- ˙two* treated as ···*[-ti] ˙two* 58
-lu- 220
lu [DIAL] = lul (pcl) 196
˙*lu* = ˙*lwo* (pcl)
···*l*ᵘ/*o*- (basic form) reduced to ···*l*- or ···- 241
*···*l*ᵘ/*oG*- stem as lenited from *···*l*ᵘ/*ok*- 238
*···*l*ᵘ/*ok*(-), *···*l*ᵘ/*ol*(-) 101, 239
Lukoff, F. 1, 2, 28, 29, 286, 298, 330, 784
···*l*ᵘ/*om* (uncontracted subst of ···*l*- verbs) 255
*···*l*ᵘ/*op*- > ···*lp*- / ···*l*ᵘ/*o*- 238
···*lW*- stem 5; ···lw- stem 231, 361
˙*lwo* (instrumental) 239, 678
··· *lwo*W- 234, 678
-lwupul (counter) 183
ly··· pronounced as *ny*··· 46
-lye 240, 679
lyel 16, 125
lyey 109; (=/ley/ and /yey/) 110, 679
-lyo 'fee; materials' 168, 679

···lyo > ···lo (Phyengan) 46
-lyu 'species' 168
···lyu > ···lwu (Phyengan) 46
lyul 16, 125
m (dropped after p) 92
m reduced to w 32
-m (+ vowel-initial pcl) 240; 343
-m < -wum 254
'm abbr < ham, im 258, 679
-m a 240
˙ma (and ˙man) 58, 680
¨ma- 'dislikable, disliked' 221
mā (counter) 184
mac-: (postnom adj insep) 229; 363; 681
mac' (adnoun, bound adverb) 149, 680
māca ← mālca 329, 680
macang (counter) 184
mace (adverb, particle) 194, 196, 680
machan-kaci 295
machi 138
ma'-ciki (counter) 184
macimak 681; Macimak ulo ··· 334
macron 6, 9, 32
ma˺de ni (Japanese) 632
mahun 176
-mail (counter) 184
'mak ··· = macimak 146, 681
mak- (vt) 255, 290, 340; 364
-mak / -mek 164, 340, 347, 681, 692
mak.lon hako: ··· ul ~ 195
'mak-nay 148
mak-talu- 242; 361
mal- 'end, last' (bound adnoun) 154
mal 'last' (adnoun): ~ ccay 156
mal (counter) 177, 183
māl 'words, ... ' 161; (māl) ha- 'tell' 295, (as free vn) 313; māl ha- 331, māl haki lul ··· 331
mā-l- (aux): -kwo (ya) ~ 226; -ci ~ 227; 320; 683-4; -ta (ka) ~ 226, 684; 689; 789
male colleague 299
mali (counter) 179
··· māl ia (iya), iey yo, iney, ita 335, 682; māl ya 684-5
mālko (as quasi-pcl) 194; (-kwo ~) 226; 682-3
malmiam.ᵉa (se): ··· ulo 195, 220; 683
¨ma[l]˙ta 'desists' 221, 683-4, 689
malu- / mall- < molo- / moll- < *molol- 'dry up' 239
-malukhu (counter) 183
malwu < molo / moll··· < *molol 'ridge' 239

(-)man 'bay' 133
man- 'full' (bound adnoun) 154
man 'worth ···ing' (postmod adj-n insep; pcl, postnoun) 161, 688
man (pcl) 136, 160, 188; (also adj-n) 193; 195, 257, 259, 291, 297, 316; 525, 615, 685, 695
˙man (final n a separate morpheme?) 58
manchi 195
Manchu 49, 51, 95
-mang 'network' 168
mang- (bound adnoun) 'deceased' 154
mangceng (postmod, bound noun) 144, 160, 685
man ha- (N ~, -ul ~) 160, 685-6
mān ha- < ¨man ˚ho- = mānh- < ¨manh- 108; 288, 290, 294; 686
mānh.i 526
mānh.un 173, 686
mān.il < ¨man˙il < ˙MEN-˙QILQ 'if' 138
mankhum 164, 194, 195, 198, 687
mankhum chelem 198, 687
mankhum eykey 198
mankhum kkaci 198
man kwa (→ man hako) 197, 688
manna- 289; 350; 689
manner: adverbs of 139
man to, man un (ending + ~) 214, 688
··· man to hata 160, 688
mantu-l- 286, 688
˙ma[n]˙two ? = ˙ma + ˙two 58
mān-ye ccay 179
marked case 286
marking: special ~ (for plurality) 130
Martin, S.E. 4, 27, 28, 33, 41, 44, 49, 51, 53, 57, 59, 196, 231, 233, 234, 235, 237, 238, 286, 324, 327, 328, 330
masculine orientation 135
masi- 290
mas i 'ss- vs mas iss- 92, 100
mas-˚na- 'meet' 271
mass nouns 131
mat < ˙mot 146, 148, 689
māta- 'reject, abhor' 221
mata < ¨ma˙ta (particle) 196, 689
mata ey (older usage) → mata 198, 689
mata kkey se (older usage) → kkey se mata 198
matang 'instance, case' 161
matang (particle [DIAL]) = mata 690
matrix (sentence) 323, 324, 327
mattana 194, 690
Matveev, N.P. 28, 47

maximal system of vowels 24
may (postnoun) 157, 691
may (counter) 180
māy- 'wear (necktie)' 290; 349
māy < ¨moy < ¨MOY (adnoun) 'each' 147
mayc.ki (postnoun < summative) 158
māyn (/ mīn) (adnoun) 146, 150, 692
maynani lo 146
ma(y)ngi 163, 692
māynyen 137
māywel 137
maywu 'very' 138
McCune-Reischauer (Romanization) 5
meaning 41, 113, 269, (of modulator) 271, 287; (of isotopes) 343
measurable noun 171
measure counter 171
medial 6, 11, 29
Meiji period 18
*···m^{e}ak 101
-mek 164, 692
mek- (vt) 223, 231, 243; (aux, -e ~) 226, 290, 692-3; 230, 255, 262, 288, 340; 364; 692
mek.hi- (vpt) 222
mek.i- (vc) 223, 288
mekum- 255
mē-l- 256
-meli 163
(-)meli (postnoun, noun) 158, 693
mēlli 140, 256
melwu 'mulberry' 240
men 343; men's speech 344
mence 48, 137; (+ nominative pcl) 140
merger of abbr cop with abbr of °ho- 274
merger of accent patterns 62; (timing) 66
merger of /ay/ and /ey/ 252
merger of ···c ≠ ···ch 49
merger of ···c ···ch ···s 49
merger of c(h)e with c(h)ye 46
merger of labialized velar fricative and velarized labial fricative 57
merger of ···ln··· and ···nl··· with ···ll··· 52
merger of low rising accent with high 68
merger of lye with le > ne 46
merger of morphophonemic strings 51
merger of ni··· with i··· [word-initial] 46
merger of ny··· with y··· [word-initial] 46
merger of nye with ne > ne 46
merger of o with u 42
merger of ···p ···t ···k in Chinese dialects 50

merger of ···s with ···t 44, 53
merger of sye with se 46
merger of ···t with ···s [noun-final] 108
merger of ···th, ···ch, and ···c with ···s [noun-final] 108
merger of t(h)y with c(h)y (in south) 111
merger of ti with ci 46
merger of ty with c 58
merger of tye with ce 46
merger of u and e 43
merger of uy with u or i 27
merger of vowels in Kimhay 25
merger of (w)oy with wey 26
mesial (correlatives / deictics) 134
metaphoric use of distal deictic 135
metathesis: (of glide y) 39; (of h + C) 49, 56, 92, 232, 663; (of noun-final ···h) 57, 233
metathesis: Cye(···) > Cey(···) 39, 47
-m ey 240
mey vs m^{y}ey 48, 693
mey (adnoun, bound noun) 149, 693
meych < myech (numeral) 134, 173, 174; ~ ccay 175
meychil < mye˙chul 185, 235, 694
meychit nal 185, 694
meych hay, meych-kaywel 186
meych nal 185
meych nyen, meych tal, meych wel 186
···mh 101; (noun list) 109
mī- (bound adnoun) 'not yet' 154
mich 135, 139, 694
mid 60
"middle" [of Korea] 59
"middle" (= middlingly respectful) form 301
Middle Chinese 22, 23; (distinctions) 44; 45, 92, (sounds) 95; (readings reconstructed) 98
Middle Korean 1, 3, 4, 5, 16, 17, 22, 23, 25, 35, 38; (pronunciations of Chinese characters) 42; (allomorph) 43; (lenition) 51; (voicing of stops and affricate) 51; (spelling) 51, 56, 52; 93, 111, 135; 217, 225, 233, 234, 240, 252, 258, 268, 324, 325, 327, 332
Middle Korean adnominal particle s 5
Middle Korean examples of multiple objects 285
Middle Korean finite forms (basic scheme) 261
Middle Korean low tone 33
Middle Korean particles 327
Middle Korean stem alternants 238
Middle Korean texts 23, 327. SEE Hankul texts.
Middle Korean verb forms 260

Middle Korean vowels 43
mid front monophthong (vowel) **ey** 47
mid front rounded vowel [ö] 43
mid pitch 34
mid vowel 36
Mikami Akira 330
mi˙lu 'dragon' 240
mimetic: (word) 30, 33, 45, 95, 107; (constituents) 144; (adverb) 189, 144, 344; 340; (construction, effects, phenomena) 344
minimal pairs 28
minimal system of vowels 25
minimal vowel (^{u}/o) 22, 54; (quality) 61; 71; (elision) 108; 235, 236, 237, 241, 252, 259
Ministry of Education (Munkyo-pu) 5, 40, 252, 465, 524
minor constraints 295
minor sentence 142, 296
misinterpretations 52
missing consonant (suspected) 54
missing tone marks 61
missionaries 594, 613, 730
misspelling: (from morphophonemic confusion) 31; 32, 242, 248
mistake 252; mistaken forms 256
Misu 'Miss', **Misuthe** 'Mr' (adnoun title) 133
mith 197
[mi]-ti (Japanese) 144
miw- 291; 362
MK: SEE Middle Korean.
Mkk (= Mal kwa kul) 16, 20, 27, 40, 92, 109, 112, 140, 196, 217, 233, 234, 237, 295, 584, 602, 732, 757, 866, 867, 868, 870, 888, 906
···mm··· (multiple spellings for ~) 99
mo (Japanese particle) 817
mo (counter) 181, 183
mō-cala- 'be insufficient' 141, 316
mō-ccolok 145, 164
mo chelem 137, 145, 695
model (and shortening) 8; (for abbr) 243
modern dialects 48
modern Hankul 29
modern Korean 4, 44, 45, 49, 273
modern loanwords 94
modified verbal noun (takes no object; usually + accusative particle) 189
modifier -(˙^{u}/o)n 70
modifier: (+ noun, quasi-free noun) 19, 99; (of defective vn) 189; (in phrasal postposition) 194; 242, 245, 246, 247; (+ postmod) 247, 249; 267, 274, (mood) 280; (constraints) 290; 324; (+ postnoun) 328; 329
modifier form: (of copula) 23; 134, 221, 233; (of MK) 240; 277, 303
modifier phrase 297
modifying noun phrase 131
modifying position 175
modulated: (~ stem) 72; (~ form) 241; (~ inf) 263; (~ honorific) 263, 268, 270, 271; (~ substantive) 272; (~ modifier of -L- stem) 898
modulator -˙w^u/o- 70, 72, 84, 232; (obligatory in MK subst) 255; (rules for attaching ~) 269; (suppressed but assumed) 270; (sentence adnominalized to object-extruded epitheme) 271; (marking first-person subject) 271, 272
*···mok- 238
mokcek 'aim, purpose' 161
moks 'portion' generally treated as **mok** 108
moksa 132
mokum (counter) 181
[˙]mol- 'roll it up' < *mo˙lo- 241
mol 'horse' (etymology) 98
molay 'sand' 240
mōlla (irreg vowel length) 238, 252
mōllay 257
molo- 'get dry' 271
molu- < *˙mwolol- 238, 252, 257, 318, 332, 695
Molumciki ··· 334
mōmo han 150
mom-so 145
money: units of ~ 171
Mongolian 45, 49, 51; Mongol 95, 98
monophthongization of diphthongs 26, 43
monophthongization of **nuy** to **ni** 46
monophthongization of **oy wi wey way** 24, 25
monophthongization of *tuy* 46
monophthongization of *way* > **way** [ɟ̈e] to [ö] 43
monophthongization of *wey* > **wey** to [ö] 43
monophthongization of **wi** to [ü] 43
monophthong vowel (*wo*) 36
monosyllabic adverbs 141
monosyllabic infinitives: vowel length of ~ 38
monosyllabic noun: accent loss before genitive particle *s* 69
monosyllabic nouns that retain accent before the locative particle 69
monosyllabic stem: (accent groups for vowel ~) 71; 270
monosyllabic tonic nouns (accentual cleavage) 69

A Reference Grammar of Korean

monosyllabic verbal nouns 190
monosyllabic vowel stems: causative and passive stems derived from ~ 73
monosyllabic word (attached to adjacent words) 133
monosyllabification 240
monosyllable of Chinese 275
months: counting or naming ~ 186
mood: (endings / morphemes) 220, 245; 245, 246, 261; (conversions) 304, 305
mood shift table 306
mopsi 40, 138, 695
morph 32, 98
morpheme 7, 3, 16, 25, 31, 52, 61, 98; (~ level) 261; 304; (of emphasis) 319; 347
morpheme boundary 16, 27, 30; (within word) 95; 102
morpheme divisions: (etymologically motivated ~, misguided ~) 53
morpheme identification 33, 55; (that overrides phonetic considerations) 85
morpheme shapes (number of syllables) 5
morpheme with final resonant 86
morpheme with syllable excess 100
morphemic marking (of vowel length) 33
morphemic structure 52, 176
morphemic ties between words 340
morphemic writing system of Chinese 95
morph-final strings 100; (list) 101
morph-final w 233
morphological identity 248
"morphological" passives and causatives 312
morphology 278
morphophonemic criterion 316
morphophonemic decisions 31
morphophonemic dissyllables 7
morphophonemic finals 49
morphophonemic grounds to write G as W 56
morphophonemic orthography / spelling 7, 35
morphophonemic phenomenon 50
morphophonemic relics (left by etyma) 101
morphophonemic rules 99
morphophonemic spelling: (of 1449 Kok) 45; (of variant copula infinitive **ia / ya**) 254
morphophonemic strings 52
morphophonemic writing: (of syllable excess) 49; 51, 58
morphs (in ending of verb form) 41
mōs < ¨mwot (adv): (basis for modern spelling) 102; 135, 138, 139, 141, 145, 189, 289, 315, 695-6
mōs 'be inferior' (adj-n) 190, 313, 695-6
mōsq (y···, i···) 111
mōs ā-l- 318
mōs ha- (····ci ~) 289, 317, 696
····' mōs ha- = -ci mōs ha- 94
mōs(q) iss- /mōnniss-/ 111
mōs negative 316
mōs sālkeyss.ta (auxiliary): -e (se) ~ 227
mōs to 135
mōs tul 136
mōs VN ha- and VN mōs ha- 321
moswum (counter) 181
motion verbs (as deictic) 132
motivated epenthesis 48
motivated semivowel 37
motivation 59
motivation for lenitions (probably accentual) 53
motivation of liquid elision 48
mot' ta 138
mōtun < mwo·ton 150, 173, 696
motwu as noun (new?) 173
motwu (ta) < mwo·two 'all' 138, 696
motwu-ta = **motwu ta** 140
movable adverbs 174
movable string 51
mo.yang 'appearance' 161
mozom > **maum** 60
mucin-cang 295
mue(s) 134, 302, 697
mu- (bound adnoun) 'without' 154
mukew- 344; 361
-mul (bound postnoun) 'stuff, matter' 168
mul- / mūt- 'ask': SEE mūt- / mul-.
/mullyak/ = mulq yak 111
-m ulo 240
"multiparous" 283
multiple adjunct (kinds of ~) 285
multiple ambiguities 286
multiple-case marking 173
multiple locatives 285
multiple nouns 284
multiple objects 283, 284
multiple readings (Chinese characters given ~) 97, 116; (index) 123
multiple subjects 283, 284
multiple-subject sentences 283
multivalent word **tul** 'plurally' (as particle) 190
muluph 'knees' > **mulup** or **muluphak** 108
··· **mulyep** 'time' 131, 161

-mun (counter) 180, 182, 184
(-)mun 'gate' (category designator) 133
mūncey 'ta 195
munhwa-e 4
murmured h 28
-mu (counter) 183
... ˙m`ᵘ/o- (stems) 232
[¨]mul- 'bite' < *mu˙lu- 241
mus ... (adnoun) 'many, all sorts of' (< mwu[l] s) 146, 147, 235, 698
mus (counter) 181, 182
musew- 291; 361; 698
musum / musam < mu˙sum 134, 698
musun (adnoun) 134, 147; (~ hay, nal, tal, wel) 186; 699
musunq yoil 186
mut- 'bury' 255; 363
mūt- / mul- 'ask' 295, 299; 331; 363
muth ulo 146
mutually exclusive aspects 261
mutually exclusive particles 193
*...mwok 238
¨mwol˙la 267
mwo˙lo- / ¨mwoll- 'not know' 267, 271, 699
¨mwot 50, 141, 699; (> mōs) 695
¨mwoy˙si- < ¨mwoy˙ye isi- 268
*-mwuk 238
mwu˙lwo˙toy 332
mwun nativized version of MWON 'gate' 97
mwuwu < muzu / muzG... < musuk 239
myech (→ meych) 39; 48; 700
myech-i 187
myechil 185
-myen 240. SEE -umyen.
(-)myēn 'township' (as category designator) 133
myeng (counter for people) 180, 187
myēng.lyeng hanta 331
'myen se 281
myey for /mey/ (= mʸey) 109
n and l (alternations) 110
n (weakened to nasality before i or y) 59
...n 343; ...n nouns 767
n... for etymological l... 16
¹n... 15, 23, 124
-n = -(u)n (mod) 95, 232, 701; (← ...l[ᵘ/o]-n) 240
-n- (processive morpheme) 251
'n = han (mod < ha-); = in (cop mod) 89, 701
n' (abbr of nun pcl) 89, 196, 701
na- < °na- 'emerge' 80; (postnom v insep) 228;

229; (auxiliary) 226, 230; 236, 237, 243; (as effective after °wo-) 263, 271; 705-6
-na 248; (used for -nun ka / ya) 249; 306; 702
na 'I / me' 130, 133, 193, 296, 701
na [DIAL] = nai (age) 108
nacel 'half-day' (bound noun?) 144
nah- 'give birth to' 236; 702
nah.i (postnoun < der n) 158
nai 'age' < ˙nah 108
nahul; nahut nal 185
(na-)ka- (postnom v sep) 228
nake la 243
naki (postnoun < summative) 158, 702
nakk-si 164
nal (adnoun, ~ lo) 'raw' 146, 149, 702, 870
nalk- 340; 364
nalu- 'transport' 255; 361
nalum (postnoun, postmodifier) 159, 160, 703
nalup 187
nalwu < nolo / nolG... < *nolok 'ferry' 239; 255
nām- < ¨nam- (vi) 232; (nam.e iss-) 291; 294, 328, 340, 364
nam < ˙nom 'another person' 69, 718
namcis (postnoun, adverb) 159, 178, 179, 704
name (as pronominal substitute) 133
name form of verb 251
name + title (as 2d-person pronoun) 135
names 5, 132, 164, 299, 328, 819
names of fish 95
names of Hankul letters 22, 106
naming construction 332
"naming" form of high/low verb 71
Nam Kisim 2, 330
Nam Kwangwu 2. SEE NKW.
nam-nam-i 255
namu < namwo / namwok... < *namwok 'tree' 238
-nam(.)un 158, 164, 174, 704
na'-nal-i 255
nan cil 328
na o- → na-o- 251
na-o- < ˙na-°wo-: ('come out to do') 188; (postnom v sep) 228; 705
nappu- 291
narrowing of specification 284
nā(s)- 'get / be better' (v / adj) 217, 236, 288; 363
nasal 12, 27, 28, 31; (before affricate) 48; (of ny... (dropped in south) 111
nasal assimilation 31; (rules) 52
nasal consonants 24

nasal dispalatalization 17
nasal elision 48
nasal epenthesis 12, 48, 499
nasal-initial particles 52
nasality 48
nasal lateralization 31
nasal velar 22; (initial *ng*⋯) 49
nasal vowel 28
natāl 185
nath (counter) 179
native Korean: (compounds, sequences) 12; (words) 44, 49; (vocabulary) 94; (elements) 162; (speaker) 336
native oddities (with initial ny⋯ and ni⋯) 110
native speaker 33, 275, 336
nativized borrowings 44, 45, 60, 95
nativized Chinese (noun/word): (velar elision in ~) 56; (unaccompanied by characters) 96; 240
nativized fish names 46
natural readings of Chinese characters 45
nawi (postmodifier) 160, 706
Nay = Nayhwun = 1475 Nay 86
¹nay- 'coming' (bound adnoun) 155
nay ('I', 'my') 92, 133; (pseudo-adnoun) 149; 193; 706
nāy- (adnoun) 'internal; female' 155
nāy- (vc): (heard as lāy-) 99; (aux) 226, 230, 290; ('put out') 237; ('pay') 243; 252, 709
nāy (inf) 252, 706
nāy (postnoun) 'throughout' 157, 706-7
nāyci < ˇNAY-ˋCI 196, 709
nayki (postnoun < summative) 158, 709
nay-kkacis 147
nayli- 294
naylye ('ta) 260
-na yo 306, 310
⋯nc- (examples) 106; (stem list) 364
⋯(n)c- stems reduced to ⋯s 108
nc ? > c (example) 48
-n-e in one la 253
ne 'you' 133, 193, 296, 710
nē 'four' 175, 710
near-doublets 84
n-elision 59
negating 337; negation 297
negative 227; (constraints, constructions) 289; 297; (with verbal noun) 321; 327
negative adverb: (mōs and an) 111; 315
negative auxiliary 315
negative command 320

negative conversions 315
negative/negativized copula 146, 151, 214, 283; (with nominatives otherwise unpermitted) 288; 316
negative expressions 322
negative preemphasis 291, 316; (with commands and propositions) 321
negative proposition 320
negative question 264; (used rhetorically) 322; 336
negative sentences 315
negativization: (rhetorical ~) 144; 291, 336
negativized causativized negative 335
negativized copula: SEE negative copula.
negativized desiderative 335
negativized honorific 335
negativized interrogation 336
negativized periphrastic causative 335
neh- (Seoul, attested 1466) for expected yeh- < neh- = nyeh- 'put in' 47, 112; 243
ne-huy 'you all' 133; (never *~ uy) 295; 710
nē-i 'four people' 187, 710
nēk 'four' 175, 710
nek.nek (hi) 257, 710
nelli (der adv < nelu-) 255
nelp-, nelu- < nel^U/o-, nep- ? < *nelup- 105; 238; 363
nelp.i (der n < nelp-) 255
nēm- < ˇnem- 340; 364; 711
nemu 138, 711
neologisms 22, 110
n-epenthesis 5, 12; (pervasive) 111
netes/nete 178
nete-tays 178
neutral deictics 344
neutral form (neither light nor heavy) 343
neutralization: (of syllable-final consonants) 49; (represented by G) 54, 57; (of accent toward/ at the end of a word) 61, 64
newspaper headlines 300
next-to-last vowel 36
ney > ni 46
-ney: (+ pcl) 213; 248, 306; (style) 296; 713
ney 'group (of people)' (postnoun) 157, 711
ney ('you', 'your') 92, 133; 149; 711
nēy vs yēy 'yes' 47; (< *nyēy) 110, 711
ˇneyh 'four' 109
ney-kkacis 147, 713
-ney k(w)ulye 306, 307
nēys ccay (SK) = nēy ccay (NK) 175

-ney yo 713,
NG··· (illegitimate examples) 46
ng··· 45, 46; (not pronounced) 49
···ng 22, 341
ng (dropping between vowels) 32; (reduced to nasality) 59; (beginning a morpheme shape) 95
-ng' (reduction of -ngi) 268
-ngaci 'offspring of' 95
NGA-TWO for A-TWO 46
···nge (in fish names) 46; -nge 'fish' 95
ngek 46
···ngh (two examples) 109
-ngi (polite marker) 46; (like the bound stems in accent behavior) 70; (never accented) 85; 261, 268; 714
··· '-ngi = [i]-ngi (cop polite) sometimes ellipted 268
-ngi ''ta (inaccurate analysis?) 273
NGW···, NGYW··· 46
n[h] 35
···nh(-) 101
···nh- (examples) 105; (stem list) 364
···nh (nouns) 109
- ˙n i 272, 714
-ni (indic attent) 248; 305, 306, 307, 714
ni··· 15, 17, 46
°ni-₁ 'roof, thatch (a roof)' 70, 79
°ni-₂ 'go': (accent) 72; 714, 716
ni: (pronunciation for ¹Yi) 15; (word-initial) 46; (not occurring after pause) 110
ni··· cases treated as reinforcement ···q i··· 110
ni (Japanese particle) 295
nickname 299
nik- 262, 715
˙ni-ke- forms 72, 715
nim (counter) 180
nim (postnoun) 132, 134, 299, 715-6
n-inserting stems 243, 253
niph (counter) 182
-niᵗ/ₗa (literary indic assert) 248
niun 110
NK (= North Korean): dialect 28; spelling / orthography 16, 48, 456, 524, 553, 627, 654, 679, 781, 927, 934
NKd (= the North Korean dictionary, Cosen mal sacen) 4, 13, 14, 15, 16, 34, 38, 107, 109, 122, 150, 221, 222, 344, 560, 571, 671, 831, 867, 873
NKW (= Nam Kwangwu) 2, 58, 73, 196, 570
···n.l··· < ···nn··· 40

···n.¹n··· 40, 41
nn··· ← ···h- + -n··· 52
···nn··· words pronounced ···ll··· 40; 111
- ˙no-, -(˙)no- 70, 72; (accent) 84; 716
'no' 142
no (Japanese) 327, 328
··· no de vs ··· kara (Japanese) 330, 623
noh- 'put' (vt) 223; (aux) 226, 230; 230, 231, 232, 243, 290, 716-7
noh.i- (vp) 223
nŏ-l- 243, 256, 288, 290, 717
*[¨]nol- 'fly' < *no˙lo- 241
-nola 258, 717
nol.i (der n) 256, 717
nŏlsey and nŏsey 240
nolus (postnoun) 131, 158, 717-8
nolus (~ i 'but') 161, 718
nolwu < nwolo / nwolG··· < *nwolok 'roe deer' 239
nom < ˙nwom 'person' 131, 134, 328, 718
˙nom > nam 'another person' 69, 718
nominal: (~ phrase) 19, 88, 272, 280, 323; (~ sentence) 280, 300; (without marker) 286; 324
nominalization 217, 254, 263, 264, 267; (MK ~ with t) 273; 297, 300, 323; (with substantive ··· ˙(ᵁ/o)m) 327, 888
nominalized sentence 323
nominalizer 267
nominalizing: (~ moods) 280; 339
nominals: particles that appear only after ~ 88
nominative 130, 282, 286; (particle i / ka) 287
"nominative" = summative 3
nominative-marked phrase (extruded) 326
nominative-marked quantifier (floated from an underlying subject converted to dative) 173
nominative-marked subject 130
nominative marker / particle (i / ka) 23, 99, 100, 132, 151, 172, 193, 316, 327
- ˙non, -(˙)non (proc mod): (usually unaccented) 84; 272, 719
···non ← ···l[ᵁ/o]-no-n 240
˙non (subdued focus particle) 239, 719
non-affricate > affricate 48
non-Chinese bound adnoun 151
non-Chinese elements 151
non-Chinese etymology 95
non-Chinese expressions 50
non-Chinese morpheme 33, 86, 280
non-Chinese origin: (of 3-syllable given names) 132; (nouns of ~) 151

non-Chinese suffix 162
non-Chinese vocabulary 16
non-Chinese words 22; (with /lc/ and /lt/) 31
nondistinctive feature 51
nonfinal: (clause) 251, (suffix) 262, (ending) 265; (infinitive) 280
-ˈno-ngi ‧‧‧ 85
-ˈno-ngi ˈta (optionally modulated) 272; 719
nonhigh vowels 36
nonhonorific stems 298
-(ˈ)no-ˈn i (proc mod + postmod, 'you / he ...') 272; 719
noninitial syllables 42, 252
non-Korean words (brought in as nouns) 94
nonlabial sounds 36
nonoccurring sentences 336
nonoccurring syllable types 29
nonpalatalized affricate 29, 46
nonpast negative (of Japanese) 305
nonrhetorical negative questions 323
nonsense words 99
non-Seoul speech 237
nonstandard: (variant) 249, (dialect form) 259, (variant of intentive) 331
nonstandard treatments of -L- verbs 240
-(no)n ˈtoy 265, 721
no-pak.i lo 146, 870
noph- (adj) 223, 231
normal spoken version of Chinese words 97
normal status 297
normal word order 297
north 13, 16, 17, 29, 34, 39, 46, 109, 111, 196
North America 27
North Cenla 34
northeast 59, 60, 92
northern dialect 28, 196, 308
northerners 15, 111
northern Hamkyeng dialects 17
northern Mandarin 50
northern speakers 238
northern spelling 16
North Hamkyeng dialect 28
North Korea 4, 5, 8, 15, 16, 21, 22, 27, 40, 41, 107, 124, 133
North Korean: (data) 4; (rule) 13; 20; (spelling / orthography / system) 13, 34, 40, 110, 124, 125, 141, 259
North Korean dictionary (NKd) 33, 116, 150
North Koreans 15, 16
North Kyengsang 34, 54, 58, 59

northwest 59
-ˈno-s-on (proc emotive mod) 263; ~ ˈta 721
-noˈta (proc indic assert) 84, 594, 721
notation 58, 235, 241, 249, 261
noun 3; (ending in ‧‧‧*i* triggers velar lenition) 55; (ending in ‧‧‧*ng*) 85; 156, 280; (classes of ~) 287; (of relative location) 290; 323, 324, 325; (alone in adnominal position) 328
noun arguments (epithematized) 327
noun compound 19, 58
noun + copula 19; (left unanalyzed in Hankul spelling) 85; 277
noun + counter 276
noun + derived noun 276
noun + noun 12, 19, 275
noun + noun phrase 275
noun + particle 19; (subject to velar lenition) 54; (syllabification) 86; 276; (strings) 283
noun + postnoun 276
noun + pseudo-compound noun 275
noun + subject marker 297
noun + vi substantive 275
noun-final h (in modern compounds) 108
noun-final *h*: (19th-century evidence) 108; 233
noun-final lk (reduces to k) 102
noun phrase: (grammatical function marked by pcl) 86; 130; noun phrase (+ noun) 275; (+ pcl, + postn) 276; (+ cop, + verb) 277; 324; (as head of adnominalization) 328
noun predication (directly nominalized) 135
noun-predicator 54, 89. SEE copula.
noun prefix 88
noun roles 283
noun specified as adnominal with pcl **uy** 328
noun suffix 88
noun unmarked for number (categorizes) 130
nouns vs verb stems 130
nouns with alternants like those of v stems 238
nouns without vowels 108
-ˈno-ˈwo- → -ˈnwo- (modulated processive) 272
no¹yey /no(.y)ey/ 'slave' (spelled **no.yey** even in north) 124
novel information 281, 282; novelty 302
N_1 *s* N_2: (variant phrasing junctures) 44; 51; (→ compound noun) 69
‧‧‧*n t c*‧‧‧/*s*‧‧‧ for ‧‧‧*n s c*‧‧‧/*s*‧‧‧ 768
‧‧‧ ˈ*n*ᵘ/ₒ- (stems) 232
nuc- 'get / be late' (v / adj) 216, 217; 363
nuc (adnoun; ? adverb) 149, 722
nuclear focus 340; 622

nuclear sentence: (type) 296; 299, 324, 335, 336
nucleus 6
*-n^u/ok 239
[¨]nul- 'be better' < *nuˋlu- 241
-nula (ko) 258, 331, 722
nulk- 'get old; be old' 217, 340; 364
number: (~ phrase, ~ construction/expression) 156, 171; (adverbialized ~) 172; (~ word) 173; ("floating" of ~) 173; (+ particle, + postnoun) 276
number of times (marked by accusative) 216
numeral 19, 130, 148, 156, 164, 171, 174; (variant forms) 187
numeral counter (= counter for numeral) 171
numeral + counter 19; 172, 173; (numeral substituting for ~) 174; 276
numeral + noun 276
numerals: list of subclasses 174
*-n^u/ok 101
n(ᵘ/on) (focus pcl) 259
-nun (proc mod) 230, 232, 233, 235, 236, 250, 277, 280, 306; -(ˋ)nun 722-3
nun (particle) 89
'nun = hanun 89
····nun ci (to molunta) 332, 723
nung hi 526, 724
-nun ka 306
-nun ke l' (yo) 329
-nun kwumen yo 310
-nun kwun (yo) 306, 310
-nunta/-nta 230, 306, 730
-(nun)ta + particle ko 213
-nun tey 244, 306, 731-3; (= -nun [ya]) 306, 308; ~ (yo) 329
-nun ya 213, 244, 280, 734; -nun ya 'nta 332
nuy > ni 46
nwi ka [DIAL] = nwu ka 196, 734
-ˋnwo- (modulated processive) 84, 261, 734
-ˋnwo-ˋla (modulated proc indic assert 'I/we ...') 258, 272, (also purposive) 734-5
ˋnwom 'lowly person' 69, 735
-ˋnwon (modulated proc mod) 272, 735
-ˋnwo-ngi ˋˋta (vacuously modulated proc polite) 272, 735
-ˋnwo-ˋn i (modulated proc mod + postmodifier 'I/we ...') 272, 735
-ˋnwo-s-ˋtwo- 261, 736
-ˋnwo-ˋswo- 261, 736-7
-ˋnwu- 84
nwu ka, nwukwu 134, 737

nwuleh-/nolah- 288
nwūlle (inf) < nwūlu- < nwuˋlu-/nwull- < *nwuˋlul- 'press down' 242; 361
nwulu-/nolu-, nwulule 'be yellow' 242; 361
nwun-i (postnoun) 158, 739
nwuwe iss- 291
ny···: (modern words with initial ~) 17, (cases treated as reinforcement ···q y···) 110; ny··· 46
-n' ya? < -nun ya 306, 739
nyang (counter) 177, 182
°nye- 'go': (accent) 72; 80, 270, 716, 739, 740
nyeh- 'put in' 17, 47, 112
nyekh 'direction; toward' 161, 739-40
nyen 131, 740
-nyen 'year' (counter) 182
···nyen-to as a binom ···nyento 170
nyesek 131, 740
¨nyey- 'go' 72, 74, 716, 740
*nyēy 'yes' 110
o replaced by wo in dialects 42; (> e) 42; 740
o 25; (reduced to w or nothing) 38; 740
-o (ending) 240, 741; (style) 296. SEE -ˢo 249.
-o (suffix making der adv) 255, 741
···o- stems (only °ho-) 267
···o- stems: (lists) 349, 350
o- < °wo- 'come' (semantically marked motion verb) 132; (as aux) 226, 230, 243, 257, 288, 289, 294, 743
ō' = ōl (adnoun) 148, 740
object: (+ verb) 19; (marked, unmarked) 99; 136, 138, 172; (numeral as) 173; (complement) 216; (with vp) 221; (of adnominalized sentence, extruded) 264; (role) 274; 277; (of extent) 280; (special types) 280; 282; (put before subject for emphasis) 286; (role) 326. SEE accusative, direct/indirect object.
object-exaltation 261; (and subject-exaltation) 268; 277, 282, 297
objective versus subjective reason 330
object marker/particle 89; (on separable vn) 188; 286
obligation 245
obligatory categories: English ~ 130
obligatory processive marker 248, 251
obligatory reduction 324
obligatory reinforcement 12
obligatory suppression of i/ka 316
obligatory velar lenition 55
oblique: (forms, subject) 282, 501, 504, 637; (object) 297

oblique-case phrase (extruded) 326
oblique questions 331, 332
obscure: (elements) 141, 144; (etymology) 219
obsolete: (symbols) 22; (noun) 145; (element, ending, imperative, honorific) 299; (pcl) 327
obstruent 27; (~ clusters) 44; (voicing of ~) 51
O Changhwan 235
odd forms of numerals (regularized) 175
···oh- stems (list) 104-5, 349
ohilye < ˙wohi˙lye 139, 741
o-ka- 279, 741
okphyen "Jewel Book" (= character dictionary) 113
˙ol (pcl) = ˙^{u}/ol
ŏl (adnoun) 'early-ripening' (n 'vigor') 148, 741
···o-l- stems (list) 360
olay 137, 741
Old Chinese 46, 98
Old Japanese future ending ···(a)-mu 248
older loanwords 110
older Seoul: speakers 37, 306; speech 60
older varieties (of Korean) 51
olh- (adj) 146; 363
ol[h] ulo 146
-oli 163, 741
olli- < wol˙G-i- 223
olm- (vi), olm.ki- (vc) 223; 364
···olu- stems 361
olun (≠ olh.un) 41, 146, 150, 742
˙o˙lwo (as adverbialization of cop) 65; 742
ŏ-^{1}yuk /ŏ.yuk, ŏlyuk, ŏnyuk/ 178
omission of i / ka after complement of ani˙ta and toynta 316
omitted case markers 287
on < ˙won 'hundred' 177, 742
ŏn (adnoun) 147, 742
ona la [DIAL] = one la 262
one la < ˙wo˙na˙la 214, 243, 251, 742
one-shape (particle / element / ending) 130, 230, 240, 258, 305
one-syllable adjectival noun 313
one-syllable adjective stem 815
one-syllable elements 18; (Chinese) 162, 275
one-syllable phrases (automatically long) 252
one-syllable stem 37, 38; (···m- or ···n-) 232; (···a-) 244; (···w-i) 254; (···V- or ···h- stem) 349
one-syllable verbal noun 188, 313, 321
ong 'the Venerable Mister ··· ' (postnoun) 157
ongkun 150, 742
ŏn kac' (adnoun) 147, 742

onomatopes 30
onset 12, 27, 29, 42, 44, 49, 51
ŏn-thong 146, 742-3
opaque lexical item 57
open o 25
open syllable 51
optional abbreviation 315
optional contraction 235
optional lenition 55
optional order of honorific 268
optional reinforcement 111
optional retreat (or spread?) of high pitch 66
oral obstruent 43
oral release of nasals 27
order (marked by accusative) 216, 848
order (of adjuncts / expansions) 281, 283, 297. SEE word order.
order (of applying conversions) 317, 321, 335
order (of the 214 Radicals) 113
ordering (verb of ~) 295
ordinal numerals: list 178
orthographic 24
orthographic strings 52
orthographic syllables 29, 30, 100
orthographic tradition: the failure to establish or maintain an ~ 59
orthography 242, 679
out-directive 226
overanalysis 86
overcorrected pronunciations 253
overlap of vowels 37
overlength 42
overloudness 41
"overstuffed" morphemes 49, 95, 100
"overstuffing" = syllable excess 100
overt genitive structure 286
overt pause or slowdown between words 86
overtly stated subject 830
oxen: (counting ages of) 187
oy (diphthong) 43
···oy- stems: (absorb inf) 252, 465; (lists) 349, 350
···oy- stems 466
ōy- (vt) 'memorize' 26, 243
ōy- (adj) 146
oy = wey → [w]ey = ey 36
oy vs wey 24, 253
oy 'only, single' 148, 744
ōy < ˙NGWOY (bnd adnoun) 'external', (adnoun) 'maternal' 149; (n = pakk) 'outside' 155; 744

ʼoy (particle) 744. SEE ʼuy.
···oye → ···ōy 38, 253, 465
ōy ey (quasi-particle) 193, 744
ōy lo 146
ōyn (pseudo-adnoun) 150, 745
···oyʼya (infinitive) 466
···p ···l ···k < ···p ···t ···k of Middle Chinese 95
···p + nasal → ···m 99
···p for s (particle) 768
p··· (no endings begin with ~) 57
···p··· retained in dialects 56
-p- (bound adjective) 57
···p- stems 234; (list) 361-2
pa < ʼpa (postmodifier) 160, 746
pachi- (auxiliary) 230, 746
pachi (postnoun) 157, 746
ppā ci- 317
packaging multiple nouns 284
-pak = -(p)pak 164, 347, 746; 758
pak- (vt) 'embed' 262; 364
Pak Changhay 2
Pak Hwaca 135, 485
(-)pak.i 158, 164, 746
p(h)a(y)ki, p(h)e(y)ki (postnoun) 157, 752
pakk (postnoun, postmodifier, noun) 108, 149, 159, 161, 746-7
pakk ey (as quasi-particle) 193, 746-7
Pak Pongnam 2, 29
paksa (title) 132; ~ nim 299
Pak Sengwen 303, 321, 642, 713
Pak Wensik 233, 234
Pak Yonghwu 627, 675
-pal (bound noun) 163, 747
-pal 'shot' (counter) 182
pal = (···q) pal (postnoun) 157, 747
pal < ʼPELQ (postn, vnt, vni) 'dispatch(ed)' 159, 747
pāl (counter) 177, 184
palam = (···q) palam (postnoun) 157, 159, 747
pala po- 291
palatal 17, 26
palatal affricate 29
palatal denasalization 17
palatal feature (= front component) as alternant shape of infinitive ending 95
palatal glide 254
palatalization 28, 46; (spreading north) 112; 344
palatalization of affricates before back unrounded vowels 29
palatalization of velars 47

palatalized affricates 28
palatalized articulations of the apicals 46
palatalized l and ll 28
palatalized s 28
palatalized ss 28
palatalized version of suspective (-ci) 46
palatal quality: (erosion of ~) 46; (shifted from consonant to vowel) 47
palatal s (sibilant) 28, 94
palatal stop 29, 46
pali (counter) 181, 182
pal-i (postnoun) 158, 747-8
palo < ʼpal(w)o, palwu (der adv) 131, 136, 139, 146; (usage as quasi-noun) 194; 256; 748
palp- 231
palun (pseudo-adnoun) 150, 748
pam (as counter) 182]
pān- 'anti-' (bound adnoun) 155
pān 'half ··· ; ··· and a half' < ʼPAN 106, 149, 174, 175
panciki (postnoun) 157, 748
pang < PANG (postnoun) 'in care of' 157
pang < PPANG (postnoun) 'shop' 159, 748
pāng (counter) 182, 183
-pangi, -pe(y)ngi 163, 748
pān ha.ye: ··· ey ~ 194
pankai (der adv) 256
pankaw- 256
pān-mal (= intimate or polite) style 301
pān sios 22
pāntay (lo, ʼta) 195
panth [DIAL] 106
pantusi 257
pappi (der adv) 256, 748
pappu- 289, 748-9
paradigm 53, 56, 57, 59, 217, 235, 319
paradigmatic endings (number) 244
paradigmatic form 54, 58, 70, 89, 189; (lacked by adj) 216; 218, 235, 268
paradigmatic gaps 134
paradigmatic sets 341
paraintensive 341, 343, (~ mimetic) 346
paraphrase 216, 253, 285, 848
parasitic final stop 30
parentheses 6, 20
partial assimilation 36
participle 245
particle: (writing ~ with noun or verb) 18; (~ + particle) 19; 51; (treated as word) 56; (origin of ~) 88; (vowel-initial ~ after over-

stuffed morpheme) 95; 130; (ending + ~) 213; (criteria for defining ~) 214; 219, 275, 280, 281, 282, 286, 292, 295, 311, 323
particle: noun + ~ (vs noun + noun) 193; ~ vs postnoun 198
particle after nominalization (often ellipted) 323
particle-colored sentences 281
particle distribution: consequences of ~ 214
particle phrase: (+ particle) 276; (+ copula) 277
particles 28; (after numeral) 174; (inserted before postnominal verb) 188; 192; (~ proper: list) 195; (in sequence) 197; (not preceded by a verb form) 213; (of location) 260; 261; (in an adnominalized sentence after extrusion of epitheme) 327
particle sequence 193, 197; (in contrasting or competing order) 198; (listed by prior member) 199; (listed by latter member) 206; 275, 299; (allowed only with neg cop) 318
parts of speech 86, 88; (chart) 90-1; 130
pa(s)- (= paswu-) < *pozo-/pozG- < *posok- 'crush' 239
passive (voice) 22, 39, 107, 220, 288, 289, 297, 312; (and negative preemphasis) 317; 337
passive/passivizing conversions: 189; (for verbal nouns) 191; 315; 496
passive sentences 315; (plural marking in ~) 830
passive transitive: SEE transitive passive.
passive verb (vp) 218, (typically vpi) 312
past (form/element/marker/tense) 38, 220, 221, 233, 235, 240, 242, 244, 246, 249, 251, 252, 259, 260, 289, 297, 304, 310, 324, 325, 330, 335, 338; (English ~) 249
past adversative 489
past conditional 489
past future 244, 487; ~ modifiers (processive or retrospective) 250, 325, 487; 304
past gerund 487
past infinitive 466, 486
past modifiers 249, 250
past negative copula 316
past nominalization 324
past-past 244, 289, 486; ~ modifiers 250; 304
past-past future 244, 486; ~ processive modifier 250, 486; 304
past-past infinitive 466, 486
past-past modifier -ess.ess.un (acceptable?) 251
past-past retrospective 305
past-past tentative 305
past processive modifier 487

past prospective modifier 488-9
past retrospective modifier 488
past sequential 489
past transferentive 260
pat- (postnom v sep) 228; (vnt ~) 288; 363
pat- 57
pat.chim 6, 49
path traveled (marked by accusative) 216, 847
(-)pat.i /paci/ (postnoun < der n) 158, 164, 749
pat.ki (postnoun < summative) 158
patterns of: pitch and vowel length 60; accent 62; shapes of Chinese morphemes 95
pause 19, 20, 24, 28, 31, 38, 86, 99, 109, 100, 113, 130, 192, 217, 261, 274, 780, 835, 850
-pay 'group' 168
pāy- < poy- 'conceive (a child)' (etymology) 95
pa.yah ulo (spelled pa-ya-hu-lo) 106, 145, 870
payk ccay 175; payk-ye ccay 179
paymi (counter) 180
(-)payngi (postmodifier, postnoun) 159, 160, 163, 749-50
paywu- 288
pC⋯ 43
pc⋯ 44
PDRK 8
'pedestal' 6
pejorative connotation 343
p(h)e(y)ki = p(h)a(y)ki (postnoun) 157, 752
pel (counter) 180, 750
peleci 'worm' 240
(p)peli- (auxiliary): -e ~ 226, 230; 750
p-elision 92
pᵉ/alke- 219, 750
pelsse (adverb) 136
pemulli- (vc, vp) < pe˙muli- (vc) 224
pen 'time' (quasi-free noun) 171, (counter) 182
pen = ⋯q pen ("ppen") 161, 750-1
... pen ccay 175
Pen.yek Sohak enhay = 1518 Sohak-cho 86
pep < ˙PEP (postmod adj-n sep) 161, 250, 751
people: counting ~ 187
People's Democratic Republic of Korea 8
perceptual experience/observation 325
perfect (= realized) 261; (English) 249; 265
perfect adnominal form (= modifier) 263
perfective particle ⁻NGUY 46
perfect-resultative structure 325
period 20, 21; (~ intonation) 41, 42, 301, 302
peripheral: (utterances) 214; (particles) 239
periphrastic: (causative) 218, 219; (passive) 219;

(expression) 244; (construction / conversion / structure) 245, 248, 312, 313, 315; (negativization) 315; (passive) 315, 317
permission 315
permutability (of sentence underlying fixed word order) 286
perseverative 226
personal 288; (names) 132, 133; (pronouns) 135; (indirect object, subject) 282; 288; (subject) 298, (exalted) 299; (title honorific with ··· **nim**) 299
personalizers 162; personification 291, 297
perspective (of word and sentence) 193; 283
pes- (vt), **pes.ki-** (vc) 223; **peyi-** (vpt) 222
p(h)e(y)ki = p(h)a(y)ki (postnoun) 157, 752
···**ph(-)** (examples) 104
···**p(h)-** stems 262; (list) 363
-pha 'faction' 168
pha- (vt) 290, 340
phā'-il 186
pha-l- (vt) 224, 288, 751
phal-i (postnoun) 158, 751
phal.i (postnoun < der n) 158, 751
phal-il 186
phalli- (vp) 224
-phauntu (counter) 183, 184
p(h)a(y)ki, p(h)e(y)ki (postnoun) 157, 752
pha(y)ngi (postnoun) 144, 157, 752
phe (inf < **phu-**) 252
phenomime 140, 141, 144, 340
phey- [DIAL] = **phi-** (< **phye-**) 23**ph**ʸ**ey** 48; 752
phʸ**ēy** 'lungs' 109
phʸ**ēyha** (title) 132
phʸ**ēy¹yem** 'pneumonia' 16, 171
p(h)e(y)ki = p(h)a(y)ki, (postnoun) 157, 752
phi- < ˙**phye-** 238, 289, 317, 349
phi(wu)- (postnom v sep) 228
phī- 'undergoing' (bound adnoun) 155
phil (counter) 180, 181
phīthu (counter) 184
phok (counter) 180, 753
phok (postnoun) 157, 753
phok (postmodifier) 160, 753
˙**phol-** 'sell' < *˙**pho˙lo-** 241, 753
phone 98
phoneme 6, 23; (~ component y) 256
phonemic 30
phonemically determined alternation (replacement of excess) 100; 233

phonemic form 31, 49; phonemic norm 27
phonemic notations 5
phonemic orthography 7; (even when the syllable excess is pronounced) 107
phonemic shape 7, 13
phonemic spelling 296; phonemic writing 41
phonetic: the ~ of a character 113; 372
phonetically equivalent consonant strings 52
phonetic articulations 23
phonetic assimilations 51
phonetic cues 32
phonetic distinctions of Middle Chinese 95
phonetic features (of intonation) 42
phonetic notations 5; phonetic realizations 27
phonetic syllabification 56, 86
phonetic syllable 45
phonetic symbolism 340, 341
phonetic values of characters: traditional Chinese ~ 95
phonogram 1, 4, 46, 48, 49, 54, 57, 59, 60
phonological bond(age) 20, 89
phonological criterion (for writing spaces) 86
phonological cues (to word boundaries) 274
phonological juncture 192
phonology 42
phonomime 140, 144, 340
phrasal postposition 194
phrase 32, 41, 42, 64; (word accentually treated as ~) 66; (boundaries, level) 261; (structure) 274; 280; (as adjunct) 286; (in expansion) 299
phrase-internal strings 44
phrase order 297
phu- spelled **ph** + **wu** 252
···**phu-** stems (list) 351
-phulang (counter) 183
phulmu < *pwulmwu / pwulmk*··· < ***pwulmwuk** 'bellows' 238
phulu- 'be blue' 242; 361
-phum 'goods' 169
phūm (postmodifier) 160, 753
phun (counter) 183
-phung 'manner(s), style 169
phus (adnoun, bnd noun) ?< ˙**phu[l]˙s** 148, 753
*···**phu˙the** 57
phye- > **phi-** 237, 349, 753
phye ← **phie** 237, 753
-phyen 'compiled by ···' 169
phyeng (counter) 183
Phyengan 26, 33, 42, 47, 112, 218, 233, 234, 239, 240, 253, 306, 307, 593, 598, 675, 690,

716, 742, 757, 761, 803, 815, 892
phyeng-seng 60
Phyengyang 15, 94
phye- pronounced phi- 41
phyey (SK spelling) for /phey/ (= ph^{y}ey) 109; 754
-pi 'expenditures' 169
pi- < PI 'non-, un-' (bound adnoun) 140, 152, 155, 754
pi(-), pis(-) = piq(-) (adn, bnd adv) 149, 754, 755
pich cew- 229
pichwe: ⋯ ey ~ 194
pī ha.ye: ⋯ ey ~ 194
pilok < pi˙lwok 138
pilos ha.ye: ⋯ ul ~ 194
piloso 137
Pīnyīn Romanization 4
pis(-): SEE pi(-).
pis- = pi- 140; (vt stem) 363
pitch 34; (and vowel length) 34, 35; (not distinctive in ancestral language?) 61
pitch accent (area where lost) 59
pitch levels 34, 60; pitch sandhi 34
*pk⋯ 44
place: adverbs of ~ 140; 297
placement of syllable boundary 52
placenames (free nouns) 133
place nouns: deictic ~ (used as adverbs) 140
place postnouns 159
place traversed (marked by accusative) 216
place words 130
plain command 217, 243
plain mimetic 346
plain present 218
plain quotation forms 213
plain series of Korean obstruents (in the modern readings of Chinese characters) 96
plain style 280, 281, 297, (as basic) 300, 305
plateaus [of pitch] 62
p-leniting stems 33, 53, 57; 233-4
pleonastic compound / phrase 280
pleonastic ka (nominative) in i ka 92
pleonastic use (of plural marker) 830
pluperfect (English) 244
plural: (intrinsically ~ words) 130; (used as singular) 130; 347; (foreign ~) 830; (interpretation of subject not permitted) 830
plural marking (individuates) 130
plural particle tul 174; plural-subject marker 174
-po = -(q-)po 'one, thing, person' 163, 755

po- < °pwo- (verb) 57; ('see to it, do') 188; (aux) 227, 230; (postnom v sep) 228; 237, 288; (-e ~) 291; 295; 756-7
poetic: (statement) 263; (context) 296
poetry 304
poi-: (vp) 283, 294; (vc) 288, 295; (vc and vp converge) 317; 755-6. SEE pōy-
point of contact between morphemes or words 99
poko (particle) 57, 195, 197, 295, 756
polite copula 4
polite marker -ngi ⋯ (bound stem) 70, 72, 85, 261, 268, 714
politeness 287
polite style / stylization 130, 251, 253, 254, 280, 297, 300, 310
polite ⋯ yo 281
pol˙sye = pol˙ssye 241
polum (nal) 185
polysyllabic stems ending ⋯i- (inf of ~) 93, 465
polysyllabic stems ending ⋯li- 55
polysyllabic ⋯w- stems 254
pon < ˝PWON (adnoun) 147, 756
ponay- 288
pong (counter) 181
popular usage of Chinese words 61
posi- 299
positive force (negative sentences with ~) 322
possessed 287, 298
possessor 282, 287, 288, 298
postappositional epithematicization 551
postappositional nominalization 324
postconsonantal shape 130, 197, 214
postconsonantal w 36
postcounter 156, 171, 174
postmodifier 131, 161, 261, 272, 281, 290, 295, 300, 302, 303, 306, 310, 325, 329
postmodifiers: list 160
postmodifier adjectival noun 161
postmodifier verbal noun intransitive 161
postnominal adjective: (toy-) 140; 189; (ha-) 190; (list) 229
postnominal verb 89; (ci-) 146, 188, 219; (list) 228
postnoun 88, 131, 156; (tul) 174; 194; (versus particle) 198; 295, 299
postnoun phrase + postnoun 276
postnoun / postmodifier adjectival noun man 160
postnouns also used as free nouns: list 158
postnouns (exclusive): list 156
postnouns that are also postmodifiers: list 159

postnouns that are inflected forms: list 158
postnumeral 175
postposition 192; phrasal ~ 194
postpositional particle 86
postsubstantive 160
postsubstantive adjectival noun cik 160
postverb 88
postvocalic: (~ "-s") 13; (~ shape) 22, 89 (~ final -h) 109; (~ form) 130; (~ u) 37, 237; (~ h) 237
pota (particle; adverb) 57, 194, 196, 695, 757
pota: (aux adj ⋯ ka ~) 249; (verb) SEE po-
potential pause 19
potential undergoing (of an action) 222
-potwu 163
pōy- (vp/vc) 222, 223; (aux) 230; *pōysi- 358; 757
pōyw- 233, 299; *pōywusi- 358; 361, 757
pozG- < *posok- 'crush' 237
pp tt kk 44; (as one device to write reinforced consonants) 53
ppā ci- (auxiliary): -e ~ 226, 230; 757-8
-(p)pak 164, 347; 758
ppak (postnoun) 157, 758
⋯ ppal 131; 758
ppalli (der adv) 136, 137, 256
ppa-tus (postnoun, adverb) 159, 758
ppāy- (postnom v sep) 228; 294, 758
ppāy-as- 236; > ppāys- 363; ppay(a)s.ki- 222
ppel (postnoun) 157, 758
(p)pet-: (as bound adv) 141; (stem) 363
ppop.i (postnoun < der n) 158, 758
⋯ ppu- stems (list) 351
-ppuk 164, 347, 758
ppun < "spwun 'only' (postmod, postn) 159, 160; (pcl) 196, 213, 214, 316; 425; 758-9
ppun (man) 198, 759
(p)puye(h)- 251
ppyem (counter) 184
pre-1933 spellings 4
precision variants 32
preconsonantal forms of the low -L- stems (rising accent) 61
precopular noun 146, 316
predicate 274
predicate complement 151, (of copula) 316
predicated adjective 216
predicating a noun 217, 296
predication (structures) 263; 264
predicator of nouns 54

preemphasizing negation 338
prefix 26, 88; (to verb stem) 111; 131, 151
"pre-flapped [l]" 28
pre-Hankul 4; (~ Korean) 43; (~ lenition) 231; 238; (~ distinction) 263; (~ *yo) 947
prehistoric borrowings from Chinese 98
prehistory 1
pre-inseparable inseparable verbal noun 89
pre-inseparable postmodifier 161
pre-inseparable verbal noun 188
"pre-la" shape (of infinitive) 214
pre-MK (= pre-Hankul): (~ forms) 238, (~ dissyllable) 240
pre-modern spellings 4
prenoun = adnoun 88, 131, 146
preparticle: SEE bound preparticle.
preposed adverbial [of quantity]: in Japanese but not in Korean 172
prepositions 192
pre-postnominals 144; (+ na-) 146
prescribed readings/pronunciations 4, 23
prescriptive orthographers 96
prescriptive readings: coexisting with nativized versions 96
present tense: (by default) 249; (or timeless) 297; 304
present "resultative" meaning shown by past 221
pre-separable inseparable verbal noun 89
pre-separable verbal noun 188
presumed future 258
preverb 88, 131, 140, 141
primary articulation 28
primary particles 239
prior conversions 328
probable future 244, 258
probable past 244; probable present (or past) 244
process of derivation 297
process of phonetic realization 331
processive: (stems that are ~ or descriptive) 217; (aspect) 245; 246, 261, 265, 304
processive adjunctive -nula 258, 330, 722
processive assertive -(nu)nta 216, 218, 260, 305
processive auxiliaries 219
processive forms 189; (adj lacks) 216
processive morpheme -n- 251, 258
processive modifier -nun 216, 250, 251; (cop lacks) 274; 306
processive morpheme -no-: (attached tightly to the verb stem) 52; (unaccented after deferential, accented before polite -ngi) 85

processive verb/stem: (noun from ~) 163, 164; 218; (aux) 226; 249; (+ transferentive) 260; 306
processive verbal nouns (= vn proper) 92, 189
progressive 227
prohibitive 227
projective 3; (adj lacks) 217; 249, 330
prologs 333
promise 264
pronominal reference 135
pronominal substitutes 133
pronoun: (accent peculiarities) 68; 130, 132, 133, 295, 332
pronunciation: (before the 15th century) 42; 113
proper nouns 130, 132
proposition 217, 245, 257, 297, 300, 305; (cannot follow causal -e se) 330
propositive 217, 245, 246
prosodic adjustment 62, 72
prosodic conditions for lenition 59
prosodic displacement 85
prosodic evidence (for word boundaries) 261
prosodic morphophonemics 70
prospective (aspect) 244, 246, 304
prospective adjunctive -ulla/-lla 258
prospective assertive -ulita/-lita 257, 258
prospective attentive -ulikka/-likka 247, 257
prospective literary indicative assertive -ulini^t/la /-linit^t/la 247, 257
prospective modifier 12; 50; (-(˙^{u}/o)lq) 44, 70, 247, 250, 257, 258, 271, 325, 331
prospective morpheme -ul-/-l- 258
prospective processive modifier -ul.nun 250, 251, 332
prospective sequential -ulini/-lini 247, 257, 329
pro-verb °ho- > ha- 'do/be' 108
provinces 233; (list) 370
provisional -ketun 247, 258, (= effective conditional) 266, 268, 329
proximal (correlatives/deictics) 134
ps not distinguished from pss 100
⋯ps (noun-final) simplified to ⋯p 107
⋯ps(-) (examples) 104; 363
ps⋯ 44, 759
pseudo-adnouns 146, 149
pseudo-boundaries 30
pseudo-command form (of adj sentence) 321
pseudo-compound 274; (~ noun + noun) 275, 276
pseudo-constructions 275

pseudo-diminutives 162
pseudo-float 173
pseudo-intransitive verb 216, 288
pseudo-moods 259
pseudo-particle 331, 695
pseudo-preverbs 141
pseudo-suffix -si 163, 164
pseudo-vowel uy 26
pseudo-word 99
-psio 249, 312, 759
-psita 249, 759
psk 'time' 108, 759
pst⋯ psk⋯ 44
˙pstay 'time' 759
˙psu- 'use' 267
psychological: involvement 132; subject 298
pt⋯ pth⋯ 44
˙ptu- 'float' 267
*pu 8; pu (as abbr of pwu) 18
-pu- 220
-pu$_{1,2}$ (bnd n) 'ministry; office'; 'menial' 169
⋯˙p[^{u}/o]- 234
⋯˙p^u/o- stems 232
puekh 60; (as obsolescent for puek) 108
puin, samo (nim) (title) 132, 134
[¨]pul- 'envy' < *pu˙lu- 241
pul-/pu- 'not' < ˙PWULQ (bound adnoun) 120, 155, 760
-pul (counter) 183
puli- (postnom v sep) 228, 760
(-)puli (postnoun < der n) 158, 760
pul i nakhey = pul i nakey 343
pulk- 288; 364
pulko/pulkwu hako: (⋯ ul ~, ⋯ey to ~) 195
pulkwa (? adnoun, ? adverb; adj-n) 149
pulli- 221
pulu- < *pulul- 238, 252; 361; 760
pul-wancen myengsa 131
⋯ pun < ¨pwun < ˙PPWUN 'esteemed person' 131, 134, 760
pun < PWUN (postn 'portion'; counter 'minute') 159, 180; (-pun) 182; -pun uy/ci ⋯ , (-)punci (fractions) 188
punctuation 9, 18, 20
puphi (der n) 256
pure adverb 130; pure noun 130, 136, 138, 140
purpose: (marked by accusative) 216, 257, 847
purposive (mood) -ule/-le 3; (+ pcl) 213; 217, 247, 257, 330, 856
putative structure 331, 332

putativized sentence 332, 849
puthe < pu͏̇the (pcl) 57, 136, 194, 195; 761
puth.i /puchi/ (postnoun < der n) 158, 762
puth-pak.i lo 146
Putsillo, M. 22, 29, 47, 48, 59
puzG- < **pusuk*- 237
pwā < po- 230, 762
°*pwo-* 'see' 80, 270, 762-3
pwu spelled pu 8
¨*pwul-* 'blow' 241
"P'yang" 39
P'yankov, V.G. 22
pye⋯ > -*Wye*⋯ 57
˙PYELQ and ˙PPYELQ (doublet) 97
-pyel 'division' 169
pyel < ˙(P)PYELQ (adnoun, bnd n) 'special' 149, 763-4
pyel lo 138, 146, 763; pyel na- 221, 229, 764
pyel-pyel, pyel-uy pyel 149, 763
pyeng (counter) 181
pyēng 'illness' (as free or bound noun) 162; (= (q)-pyēng) 169
q (morphophonemic symbol for reinforcement) 8; (surfacing of ~) 250; 764
Q (dating disuse) 45
Q⋯ omitted when Chinese words got nativized 46
q⋯ (to write Chinese glottal-stop initial) 44; (not pronounced) 49; 764
⋯q for s⋯ (particle) 768
-q- (intensive infix) 343, 764
"-q" phenomena 110
⋯(q) ⋯ (optional reinforcement) 111
⋯q, -q 4, 5, 8, 9, 13, 17, 21, 22; (for final glottal catch) 142
⋯q i⋯ = /⋯nni⋯/, ⋯q y⋯ = /⋯nny⋯/ 110
quantification 171, 284
quantified period of time 186
quantifier: (adverbialized ~) 172; (nominative-marked ~) 173
"quantifier forward floating" 172
"quantifier float" 173, 174
quantifying adjectives 294
quantity: (adverbs of ~) 138; 288
quasi-adnoun: (always followed by noun or noun phrase) 131; 144; (with and without uy) 151; (defective adj-n + ⋯ han as a ~) 190
quasi-adverb 190
quasi-compound 278, 328
quasi-free (noun) 19, 26, 88, 131, 272, 295
quasi-homonym 37

quasi-inseparable adjectival noun 190
quasi-numeral 174
quasi-particle 193, 213, 214, 296, 575
quasi-processive verb 218, 287, 326
quasi-verb intransitive (qvi) 218
question 20, 21, 41, 42, 55, 245, 249, 251, 264, 265, 297, 300, 305, 320, 338
question conversions 324, 328
question forms 281
question mark 21, 41
question-mark intonation 42, 302
quick fall 41
quotation: (unquotable sentences) 213; 235, 297, 300, 308, 320, 321; (direct and indirect ~ the same in MK) 332; (unmarked in MK when the saying verb was °*ho-*) 332; 339
quotation conversion 330
quotation marks 4; (single ~) 6; 20
quotative constructions 243, (abbreviated) 244; 248, 305
quotative plain style 300
quotative structure -ta (ha)- 221; 254
quoted: command 307; content 331; favor request 333; sentence 297, 331
*r as well as l? 234
radical: the ~ (number) of a character 113; (list of ~ names) 372-9
raised dot 35
raised vowels 25
raising of adverbial elements (rejected) 333
raising of mid vowels 25
raising of ney to ni 46
raising of subject 332, 849
raising of tey to ti 46
Ramsey, S.R. 2, 33, 44, 45, 48, 53, 59, 60, 61, 62, 65, 66, 68, 69, 72, 233, 234, 237, 239
Ramstedt, G.J. 22, 28, 588, 613, 622, 627, 756, 817, 842
rapid pronunciation 132
rapid speech 24, 27, 28, 29, 31, 32, 33, 36, 38, 52, 253
rasp 33
reading: (of the Chinese characters) 44, 45; 50; (artificial ~) 95; (character with more than one ~) 97
reading pronunciation 26, 35, 100
reaffirmation 322; realization 302
reappearance of dropped liquid 102
'reason': ¹ī = /ī/ but -ul lī (?= ulq ¹ī) 110
recent loanwords 28, 29, 110

recent past 245, 325
recipes 305
reciprocal valence 194
reconstructed dots in endings (not shown) 61
reconstructing pre-Hankul forms of stems 238
reconstruction of Middle Chinese phonology 95
recurrence of conversions 335; recursion 339
reduced forms of the copula 23
reduction: (of the syllable-excess) 13; (of basic forms) 29; 32; (of strings) 36, 37, 39; (of ⋯nc-) 48; (= contraction) 87
reduction of double dot to single before locative particle 69
reduction of i to y 223
reduction of ⋯lh and ⋯lth- 233
reduction or elision of initial vowel of MK copula 273
reduplication 64; (of particle) 196; 239, 347
redundant marking 689, 692. SEE pleonastic.
reference 335, 830. SEE loose reference.
reference of particle tul (to subject only) 174
reference tag (to identify character) 113
reflex appropriate to t 102
reflex of ⋯h (phonemic spelling of ~) 101
reflexive request 227, 333
"regular compound" (of infinitive-linked verbs) 251
regular (= unextended) stem 241
regularized forms 21
reinforced (murmured) breathiness 49
reinforced consonants 14, 27; (emergence of ~ as phonemes) 53
reinforced forms 13
reinforced obstruent 50, 96; reinforced stop 44
reinforcement 5, 8, 12, 13, 14, 15, 31; (in obstruent clusters) 44; (with sonant-final stem) 100; 107; 232, 237; 346; (in ke l'q yo) 628, 727, 838, 863, 905; (after prosp mod) 850
reinforcement: ignored in Chinese loanwords 13
reinforcement: optional 32, 111
reinforcement types: table 13
relational location 285
relationship between adnominalized sentence and the nominal it modifies 326
relationships of initial consonants 343
relative adverb (= adnominalizer or adverbializer of English) 328
relative location: nouns of ~ 196
relative pronoun (= English adnominalizer) 328

relaxed speech 99, 253
release of coda consonants (foreclosed) 51
release of lax obstruents 27
release of reinforced consonant 27
reminder notation 55
repeated (sentences, phrases, words) 347
repetition 286
rephrasing 314, 316, 830
replacement of excess: subject to further replacements 100
reply to negative question 144
reported speech 332
request 312; requested favor 333
required specification 287
residual locative marker 295
residual-stroke count 113; 372
resonant-ending noun (detached from particle) 85
respect 84, 268
restoration of missing dots (to show structure) 61
restored h 35
restriction 297
restrictions that require or preclude the modulator 271
restructuring 55, (by analogy) 59, (of syllable-excess nouns) 107
resultative 227; (~ verbs) 289; (~ epitheme) 326
retained coda 51
retreat of pitch 66
retrospective (aspect) 84, 244, 245, 246, 258, 261, 265, 297, 304, 305; (subject of modern predicative form cannot be 'I') 325; (broader use in MK) 325; 716; 829
retrospective apperceptive 245, 307
retrospective assertive 248, 307
retrospective attentive 248
retrospective conditional form -te˙tun (= -te-˙t un) 258, 266
retrospective emotive forms 71
retrospective endings 21
retrospective formative -˙te- 258
retrospective modifier 245, 249, 307
retrospective question 307
retrospective statement 307
rhetorical (question) 42, 296, 318, 336; 453, 462, 486, 522, 528, 556, 562, 604, 609, 614, 640, 649, 667, 676, 701, 729, 740, 773, 795, 796, 799, 839, 856, 857, 862, 866, 875, 877, 881, 906, 908, 909, 914

rhythmically misanalyzed compound nouns (as postnouns): list 158
Ridel, F.-C. 15, 22, 27, 28, 29, 53, 287, 571
rime lists 95; riming guides 61
rise: (from low to high pitch) 35; (gradual nondistinctive ~) 41; 42, 61; (~ patterns in verb forms) 64; (words with more than one ~) 64
rising accent / pitch / tone (ʹ) 48, 232, 234, 235, 237; (of vowel-final monosyllabic stem with modulator suppressed) 270; 851
rising intonation 21, 134
rising stems 71
"rising" tone (of Middle Chinese) 60, 112
"r"-like sound of /l/ before /h/ 28
role 130; (player) 282; 284, 326; (of epitheme) 327, 328
role-specifying particle 274
Romanization 4, 5, 8, 9, 15, 16, 20, 27, 30, 36, 43, 52, 54, 89, 94, 124, 125; (of names) 132; 220, 231, 252
Romanized: (~ form) 1, 252; (~ Korean) 5; (~ names) 133
Roman letters 9
Ross, J. 35, 37
Roth, L. 27, 39, 47, 53, 108, 132, 234, 240, 243, 301, 335, 605, 627, 684, 705, 717, 911
ROUNDED component / feature 37
rounded front vowels 24
rounded vowel 35, 42, 43
rounding of **e** to [ɔ] 43
rules 9; (for writing *G*) 57; (stem + ending) 95
rules to convert morphophonemic / orthographic strings to phonemic strings 30, 31
Russian: [r] 22; (transcription) 28; 286
Rutt, R. 901, 917
Ryūkyūs 33
ˢ... 21
[s] retained for MK *z* in dialects 59
s: (etymologically final ~) 22, (vs ss) 28; (from **c*) 45; (voiceless when not lenited) 51
···s treated as ···t 256
···s + hi 256
···s > ···t 44; (dating) 49, 764
··· s ··· (written as separate syllable) 13; 44
···s (as t even before vowel) 106; (as ···q) 141
s- irreg alt of ha- < ˙ho-? 243
···s- stem: (list) 363
···(s)- verb (stem) 59, 236; (< ···z-) 237; (list) 363

s (postmodifier) 'fact' 108; (as summational epitheme) 264, 272, 327; (mod + *s* + cop as extended predicate) 273; (marking subject of adnominalized sentence) 327; 768, 779
s (particle): (liquid elision before ~) 58; 145; (*N *s* Num) 173; 239; 764-8. SEE N₁ *s* N₂.
-sa₁,₂ (bnd n) 'master'; 'scholar, person' 169
(-)sa₃ 'company' 169, (category designator) 133
(-)sa₄ 'temple' (category designator) 133
(-)sā 'history' 169, (category designator) 133
sa- 'buy' 237, 243
˙sa inf < ˚sa- 'buy' 267
˙sa = ˙za (particle) 88; = -˙e ˙za 265
sahul, sahut nal 185; 235
sai, say < so˙zi 'midst' 161; (as quasi-pcl) 193; 197; (-nun / -un ~ (ey)) 289; 768
sai phyo 4, 13, 22; sai sios 8, 13, 22
-sakwi, -say (in iph-sakwi/-say) 163, 768
sakwi- < sa˙koy- 38
sal (counter) 182
sā-l- (vi) 224, 255, 288, 294, 768
sala / sule ci- 317
salam (counter) 180, 187
sālam < ¨salom 134, 171, 255, 768
salang 'love' 113
sal.i (postnoun < der n) 158, 768-9
salli- (vc) 224
sālm 'life' 255, 769
salo (pseudo-preverb) 141
salu- 'winnow' 242, 361; 'set afire' 361
salup 187
sām- < ¨sam- < sa˙m[o]- 232; 286; 364; 769
samkak hyeng 22
samo (nim) (title) 132, 299
san (Japanese title) 157
san 'mountain': (as category designator) 133; 159; 275
sanāl 185
sānaw- 229
sang < SSYANG (adnoun, bound noun) 'common' 149, 769
sang (postnoun for Japanese names) 157
sāng- < ˙SSYANG 'first of 2 or 3; earlier' (bnd adnoun) 155, 769
··· sāng = ··· sang < ˙SSYANG '···-wise' (bound postnoun) 151, 162, 769
sangca (counter) 181
sāng-seng 60
sangwu- 'harm' 95; 351

Sanskrit 4
-sa(o)w- / -ow- 299, 770
Sapir, E. 344
say (postmod: -ulq ~) < ˙s oy 160, 771
say (postsubstantive, postnoun) 770
say (counter) 185, 771
say < ˙say 'new' 146, 148, 770, 771
sayq- / siq- 141; 365. SEE say(s)- / si(s)-.
sāylo (ey) / sāylye (pcl): -ki nun ~ 196
-sayng 'student; birth' 169
sayng < SOYNG (adnoun; ~ ulo; ~ mek-) 146, 149, 771, 870
sayngkak < ˙soyng˙kak 113; (~ ha-) 331; (~ na-) 332; 771
sayngwen (title) 132
say(s)- / si(s)- 141, 771. SEE sayq- / siq.
···sC(C)··· > ···tC(C) 44
"sC···" clusters 44
(s)C··· (in early verb doublets) 44
···s C··· 44
schoolroom pronunciation 236
scope: (of negative) 316; (of epitheme) 328
Scott, J.S. 6, 15, 39, 60, 251, 571, 628, 814
scrambled order 287
scrambling (of adjuncts) 283, 286
scribal error / mistake 55, 71, 72, 241, 269
scribe 43, 44, 50
s-dropping stem 33, 231, 236, 256
se- < ˙sye- 'stand' pronounced su- 41, 349
-se < -sye < -si-e 37
-se 'writing' 169
se < ˙sye (pcl) 195; (as abbr < ey se) 214, 233; 226; (after inf) 251; 288, 291, 294; 772
sē 'three' 175
secek 275
second and third person 244
secondary doubling (of n) 241
secondary loss of the accent 72
secondary source 61
sē-i 'three people' 173, 187, 772
-sek = -(s)sek 164, 347, 781
-sek (counter) 183
sek- 'rot' 262; 364
Sek = Sekpo sangcel = 1447 Sek 85, 316
sēk 'three' 175
Seki 186
sekken 196, 197, 198, 213, 772
-sel 'theory, view' 170
sel- (as bound adverb) 141
sela = sula (subj attent < su- 'stand') 243

se la and suke la 'stand!' 243
selection of counters 131
sel(h)un 176, 177
sēl (nal) 235
se( )lo 146, 870
sēlw- < sēlew- 231, 234; 361
sēlwum 234
sem (counter) 183
semantically empty use of processive morpheme 251
semantic categories 142, 244
semantic constraints 287
semantic direct object 216
semantic echo of subject / object in adnominalized sentence 324
semantic extension 130, 217, 221, 295, 788
semantic predication 196
semantic relations 286
semantic types of adverbialization 329
semantograms 4
semblative 227
semicolons 20
semiformal 3; (~ style) 297, 300, 339. SEE authoritative.
semiformal indicative assertive -so / -o 309
semi-literary clichés 194
semi-literary concessive -ken man (un) (= -kes man) 247, 259, 329
semi-literary sequential -kwantey 247, 259
semivowel 6, 26, 27, 36; (within morpheme) 37; 71; 267
-sen₁ 'selected by ···' 170
(-)sen₂ 'line' (category designator) 133; 170
sen < SYEN (adnoun; noun) 'prior' 149
sen (adnoun, from vi modifier > sun) 237
sēn 'half-done = immature' (pseudo-adnoun) 146, 150
sene-netes / -nete 178
senes / sene 178
seng = s^{e}ang 'appearance' 161, 773
sēng = (-q) sēng < ˙SYENG 'quality' (postnoun, postsubst, postmod) 159, 160, 170, 773
Sēng ··· < ˙SYENG 'Saint ··· ' (adn title) 133, 149
sēngha (title) 132
Seng ¹Nakswu 58, 711, 796, 808, 810, 907
sēng p^a/$_u$lu- 229, 773
sēngsang (title) 132
s^{e}ang siph- 229, 773
sensayng nim 299
sentence: (adverbial) ~ 19; 42; 261;(~ types)

263; 264, 281, 296; (~ expansion) 297; (~ fragment) 331; (~ generation, ~ paradigms) 336
sentence connectors 139, 333
sentence-final adnominalization 328
sentence-final adverbialization 329
sentence-final default intonation 42
sentence-final forms indirectly quoted (except for apperceptive) 331
sentence-final gerund 303
sentence-final ko (quotative particle) 331
sentence-final mood 280
sentence-final substantive 254, 323
"sentence phrases" 280
sentence stress (in English) 192
sentential negation / negativization 315, 316
sentential nominalization 324, 888
sentential nucleus (focus on ~) 324
Seoul 4, 24, 25, 26, 27, 28, 33, 34, 36, 39, 41, 42, 43, 46, 48, 51, 58, 59, 60, 94, 102, 107, 111, 112, 175, 177, 187, 197, 198, 218, 233, 234, 236, 237, 238, 240, 241, 243, 251, 252, 253, 259, 301, 300, 311, 344; 437, 447, 481, 553, 563, 580, 584, 585, 594, 619, 656, 663, 669, 670, 673, 713, 759, 772, 773, 784, 786, 828, 879, 909, 927, 934, 937, 941, 947
sepang (title) 132
separability constraints 291
separable (vs inseparable) 88
separable adjectival postmodifier 161
separable adnoun 147
separable auxiliary verb 89, 219
separable postnominal adjective 189
separable postnominal verb 89, 188
separable verbal noun 190
separable verb **ha-** 190
separable vni + **ul/lul** or **i/ka** 189
sepsep hi 257
sequence: (writing a ~ as separate words) 18; (~ variants) 23, 32; (~ of particles) 193, 197; (~ of ending + particle) 213, 214; (~ of like-marked phrases) 323
sequence positions (of morphemes in endings) 244, 245, 261
sequential **-uni** 3; (never + a particle) 213; (< adverbialization of modifier + postmod) 247; 329, 340
sesul 'force' 161, 774
set: phrase / expression 175, 177, 216; greeting 300; exclamation 328

sēt tal 187, 235
se ulo and selo 146
-sey (ending) 213, 230, 248, 306, 774
-sēy (counter) 182, 184
sēy- 'count' 237, 243
sey (postmod): -ulq ~ 160, 774
Seycong 6
¨seyh 'three' 109
sēy( )lo 146, 870
sēym 254, 774
sēyn māl 341
sēys / sēy / sēk / sē < ¨seyh / ¨sek / ¨se 174
sēys ccay (SK) = sēy ccay (NK) 175
sēysup [DIAL] 187
seywu- (vc) 224, 237
s-final stem 59, 236
sG written for zG 54
shape: (~ alternation) 53; 98; (~ types, noun with more than one ~) 99, (Chinese ~ types) 112; (representing either v or adj) 218
'she / her' 135; (consonant-final vs vowel-final) 249; (of mimetic adverbs) 346; (stem ~) 348
shared predicate 285
shifting: (voice) 337; (mood, tense-aspect) 338; (style) 339
Shinran (in 1272 used word spacing) 18
short combinations 20
short elements 18
shortened: (form / word / variant) 89, 93; (shapes of core numerals) 175; (forms of cōh-) 237; (form of mōs) 316
shortened stem 240, 241
shortened substantive 254
shortened vowel in forms of one-syllable l-extending stem 240
shortening: (of longer infinitives in ···ie) 37; 46, 54, 57, 94; (to zero = dropping) 217; 257, 278
shorter stems 231, 348
short forms for personal names 132
short object 19
short predicates 315
short sequence 19
short vowel 38
short-vowel morphs 32
short-vowel variants of long-vowel morphs 32
short word 86
showing (verb of ~) 295
si (as palatal syllable) 46

···si- stems (lists of longer ~) 355-8
···si- NOT representing honorific 268
'si- 267; 775
si (counter) 'o'clock' 182
si 'city' (as category designator) 133
sibilant 5, 28; (~ release of the affricate) 29; (articulation) 44; 49, 53; 355
sibilant clusters 44
sibilant directly after a MK ···l- stem 241
sibilant elision 59
sibilant lenition: (exceptions to) 59; (morpheme-initial) 60
sīcak (vnt, vni) 188, 323
···sie → ···sye = /···se/ 93
siin 'poet' 167
sik- 'get cool' 262; 364
sikan (as counter) 182
sikhi- < si ki- 188; 192; (as postnom v sep) 219, 228; 223, 243, 312, (vn ~) 313; 775, 776
sikhye se (in causative conversion) 312
-sil (suffix) 164, 347, 776
-sil (bnd noun) 'room, lab' 170
sil- / sīt- 'load': SEE sīt- / sil-.
sil 'valley' (in Omey-sil) 159
sileng 'shelf' 240
silh-: (front vowel late) 47; 291; 363
sil ha- (adj-n insep) 313
silhq-cung /silccung/ 107, 166
silh.e hanta 'dislikes' 221
sil.i (cim ~) 158
silwu < silu / silG··· < *siluk 'steamer' 239
/silye/ = silh.e 39
sil¹yen 'disappointment in love' 124
sim pseudo-postnoun (payq ~, ip ~) 159
sīm(q)- < simo- / simk- < *simok- 'plant' 238
simple negative 315
simple obstruents but not h: reinforcing ~ 50
simple quotation (vs expanded and abbreviated) 331
simple vowel nuclei 24
simplex noun from a substantive (modulated or unmodulated) 271
simplex sentence 3, 283; simplex verb 286
simplification: (of MK Chinese readings) 45; (of syllable excess [relatively late]) 108
simswul kwuc- 229
simu- = sim- 231
-sin (suffix) 164, 347, 776
sin- (bound adnoun) 'new' 152, 155

sinap ulo 145, 776, 870
"since / therefore" forms 330
single dot (˙) 38, 60, 61; (for earlier double) 68; 232
single-word: (~ synonym, ~ translation) 274
"sing-song" tune (at end of phrase) 61
singular / plural (intrinsic) 130
Sin Kichel 177
Sinla language 59
Sino-Japanese 46; Sino-Korean 94, 98
sinpu 132
sin-sēykyey vs say sēykyey 152
siph-: (as postnom adj insep) 161, 189, 229; (as aux, -ko ~) 227, 291, 642; (siph.e hanta) 259; 777-8
siph.i (der n): SEE -ta ~.
siphu- 94, 231, 777
sip-ye ccay 179
sīt- / sil- 'load' 234; 363
si-tha = si-thay 121
situ-l- 'wither, wilt' 242
situlun = situn 242
si(y)e > sye 46
'six': Chinese word for ~ 110
size 288
SK = South Korea(n)
···sk- (> ···kk-) 108
···sk- stems reduced to ···s- 108
˙s ka = s ˙ka 768
˙skol- 'spread it out' < *˙sko˙lo- 241
˙s kwo = s ˙kwo 768
˙skwu-: (< dissyllabic stem) 71; 76
slant bar 249; slash 5, 6
sloppy speech 32, 36, 314, 848
slowdowns 261; slow speech 27, 52, 767
slow pronunciations 31
sna˙hoy, sona˙hoy > sanay 43
's.non 84
(-)˙s[o]- (emotive bnd v) 71, 263
-ˢo 40, 249
-so (-uo) / -o: (+ pcl) 213; 230, 246, 248, 306, 779
-so (bnd n) 'place, facility' 170
sō-₁,₂ (bnd adn) 'small, little'; 'few, scanty' 155
Sohak = Sohak enhay = 1586 Sohak 86
Sohak-cho = Pen.yek Sohak 86
sōk '(deep) inside' 197
sok ha- (adj-n insep) 313
˙sol- 'burn it' < *˙so˙lo- 241
solang hwo˙toy 332

s-leniting stem 237
¨solp- 241
-s-on (emotive modifier) 263
son (as particle) 196, 213, 214, 780
son (counter) 182
sonant 12, 100, 231; sonant-final stems 231
-songi 164, 780
Song Sekcwung 2, 130, 222, 784, 789, 790
Son Homin 2
son-i 158, 780
Soothill, W.E. 96
-¨sop- 268, 780. SEE -¨zop-.
-sose 299, 780
soswu < sōswu (postnoun) 157, 780
"so that, so as to" forms 330
sound-alikes distinguished by vowel length 33
sound changes between two consonants 8
sounds 23; (perceptibly different ~) 98
source sentence 323, 327
sources of G 53, 54
south 13, 16, 17, 22, 28, 34, 39, 40, 43, 46, 47, 59, 60, 109
South Cenla 48, 106
South Chwungcheng 815
southerners 25
southern Mandarin 50
southern speakers 46, 102
South Hamkyeng 41, 47, 48, 59, 108
South Korea 5, 15, 16, 21, 25, 40, 41, 48, 109, 124, 157
South Korean 107, 249
South Korean dictionaries 33, 679
South Korean grammarians 40
South Korean orthography/spelling 13, 16, 40, 109, 679
South Koreans 15, 125, 248
South Kyengsang 27, 34, 196, 233, 234, 237, 584, 602, 732, 757, 761, 867, 868, 870, 888, 892, 906
Soviet: (materials) 234; (Korean dialects) 595
-soy (informal names for boys) 164, 780
soy-koki < ˙sywoy-kwo˙ki 39
"sp··· st··· sk···" 44
sp st sc sk written for reinforced consonants 53
space 6, 8, 9, 13, 20, 52; 86; 197, 261; +25
spacing 18, 19, 86
Spanish r 28
speaker 245, 282, 296, 299, 321, 323, 325, 332, 325, 331
speaker and hearer: relative position/location/

involvement of ~ 132
specification 282, 284, 287, 297, 335, 337; (of the agent) 315
specification-narrowing structures 285
specific counters 171
"specific reference" nouns (obligatory marking of plural) 130
specified expansion (with focus subdued/highlighted) 335
specifying apposition 335
speech 21, 33, 37; (~ situation) 193
speeds of articulation 52
spellers 52
spelling 5; (problems) 7; (devices, systems) 8; 13, 21, 26, 37, 38, 40, 41; (tradition) 43; (contrasts) 44; 51, 52, 53, 58; (conventions) 109; 237, 261; (variant) 311
spellings: (at variance with the prescriptions) 21; (knowable only from the etymology or reading pronunciations) 100
spirants 24
˙spol- < *˙spo˙lo- 241
spontaneous acts 315
sporadic epenthesis 48
spread (of voiceless stretch) 51; (of pitch) 66
¨spwun 780-1
ss 44
···ss- stems (examples) 103; (list) 363
-ss- (past) 95; 246. SEE -ess-.
ssa 'appearance' (postmod vni insep) 161, 781
ssah- (auxilary): -e ~ 226, 230, 290, 485; 781
ssam (counter) 181
ssang 'pair' 112; (as counter) 185
ssāyss- < ssah.ye iss- 363
-(s)sek 164, 347, 781
-ss.ess.keyss.nun, -ss.ess.tun 250
-ss.ess.ulq, -ss.ulq 250
···ssi- stems (list) 355
ssi 'clan; Mr' (postnoun) 112, 132, 157, 781
ssi < (p)ssi (postnoun < der n) 158, 781
ssik < ˙sik < ˙SIK (pcl) 196, 198, 213, 781-2
-ss.keyss.nun, -ss.keyss.tun 250
-ss.nun 250; -ss.tun 249
ssu- (postnom v sep) 228; 237, 243, 289, 290
-(s)swuk 164, 347, 783, 786
sswuki (postnoun < summative) 158
···st- (> ···th-) stems reduced to ···s- 108
stage directions 305
standard 13, 25, 34, 35, 37, 38, 39, 57, 60
standard form 8

standardization 4, 23, 41
standardization of vowel-fronted forms 39
standardization variants 39
standardized 14
standardized spellings 40
standardizing prescriptions 251
standard language 34, 42
standard Japanese 132
standard Korean 34
standard orthography 46, 106
standard relaxed speech 25
standard speakers 41
standard speech 218, 223
standard spelling 48; (iya / ya for pcl only) 254
standard treatment 41, 350
standard usage 40, 132
standard version 41
standard written form 39
standard written language 25, 95
Starchevskiy, A.V. 27, 88, 453, 571
statement 21, 41, 243, 245, 249, 251, 264, 265, 297, 300, (treated as basic) 305, 321, 323
statement of volition 257
stative verbs 295
status 84, (morpheme) 244, 246; (elevation) 297; (conversions) 298
stem 19, 39, 41, 54, 58, 86; (⋯C-, ⋯V-) 130; 243
stem + ending 86
stem alternants (in Hankul texts) 238
stem-final a, ay, ey 465
stem-final ⋯h-(→ t or n) 52; h 233
stem-final ⋯l 58, 231
stem-final m, n 231
stem-final o, oy 465
stem-final u 465; *^{u}/o- 231
stem-final w 233
stem-final wu 465
stems ending in i 37
stems ending in ⋯l- = -T/L- stems 234
stems ending in t c ch nc 299
stems ending in wu 38
stem shapes 348
stranded: consonant 217, high tone 232.
 SEE dangling
stretches of tones 60
string: (of morphemes) 7; (of phonemes) 6, 29, 340; (of consonants) 30; (of lax obstruents) 31; (of three dotted syllables) 61; (of endings) 244
string of particles: constituents of a ~ 88

stripped-down copular sentence 284
strong negative 289, 297, 315, 316, 318, 321
strong positive 321
style 244, 246; (paradigm) 248; (shift) 297; (conversions) 299
stylistic device 304
stylistic dropping of copula 328
stylistic inversion: SEE inversion.
stylistic variant 327
stylization 299
su- 'stand' written as se- < ˙sye- 224, 237, 243, 288, 294, 349; 465
⋯˙s[^{u}/o]- 237
⋯˙s^u/o- stems 232
*⋯s^u/ok(-) 239
subcategories 130
subdued: (focus) 130, 297, 318; (adjunct) 327
subduing / highlighting focus: of expansion 337; on negation 338; on the sentence itself 340
subject: (~ + verb) 19; (unmarked ~) 99; 136, 138, 140, 172; (numeral as a ~) 173; (not required) 222; (of an adnominalized sentence) 327, (extruded) 264; 268, 277, 282; (+ verb forming an idiom) 284; (marker) 286; 287, 297, 316; (role) 326; 327, 330; (raising) 332
subject-exaltation 272
subject-exalting -(^{u}/o)˙sya- 272
subject-extruded epitheme (the modifier is not modulated) 272
subjective adjective: (⋯W-) 57; 291
subjective judgment 273
subjective statement 263
subjunctive (aspect) 244, 245, 246, 304
subjunctive assertive (= hortative or propositive) -ca 217, 227, 248, 307, 329
subjunctive attentive (= imperative) -ula / -la < -(^{u}/o)˙la 70, 217, 243, 248, 307
subjunctive forms (adj lacks) 217
subordinate clause 265
subordinating particle uy 'of' 295
subphonemic shape 254
substandard: (pronunciations) 25; (speech) 240
substantive (-um / -m < -(˙^{u}/o)m) 3; 70; (not detached from particle even in Kok) 85; (earlier uncontracted form) 87; (+ postsubstantive) 160; (+ pcl) 214; 216, 243, 247, (mood) 254, (= literary summative) 267; (vc ~ + (noun + noun)) 275; (vt ~ + postn) 276; 280, 300, 323, 324, 330, 339
substitute: (noun ~) 171

substitution 296, 335, 336
substyles 300; subtleties of reference 298
sudden perception / realization 245, 302; 307
suffix 43, 86, 88, 131, 132, 144; (= bound postnoun) 162; 220, 261, 268, 278
suggestion 41, 245, 251, 264, 318, 338
-sul 164, 347, 783
˙sul- 'vanish' < *˙su˙lu- 241
sulew- (postnom adj insep) 188; 219; 229, 256; 361, 783
suley = suli (der adv < sulew-) 256, 783
-sulum 342, 784
summarizing apposition 335
summational epitheme 261, 263; (mod optionally modulated) 272; 327; (in a factual predication) 481, 482; 488, 516, 518, 528, 530, 532, 533, 534, 536, 543, 544, 561, 575, 582, 583, 604, 686, 766
summational epitheme used in extended predicate 533, 573, 583, 597, 686, 719, 735, 798, 805, 902, 922
summational nominalization 267
summative -ki < -˙ki 3; (no lenition to *-˙Gi) 54; (bound stem?) 70; 144; (+ pcl ey) 214; 247; (little used in MK) 273; 280, 324, 323, 330, 339
sumu ccay 175, 178; sumul-i 187
sumu-nam(.)un / -nam(.)u 178
sumu-nam(.)u ccay 179; sumu nal 185
-sung (counter) 183
-sup- (formal) < -¨zoW- (deferential) 53
-(su)pci yo 249, 305, 784
superscript letters 21, 40
superscript [1]··· and [n]··· 8, 40, 87, 110
-(su)p-ni- 268
-sup.nikka / -p.nikka 248, 306, 311, 318, 784
-sup.nita / -p.nita 102, 230, 232, 233, 235, 236, 248; (style) 296; 306, 311; (~ kulye) 306; 784
suppletive alternant (of nominative marker) 92, 173, 594
suppletive form of MK effective aspect marker 214
suppletive ka (nominative particle) 196
suppletive negative 318, 336
suppressed ha- (treated as shortened variant) 89
suppressed i- (treated as copula alternant) 89
suppressed juncture 28
suppression of accent (inf + pcl) 61
suppression of initial s in clusters 44
suppression of new vowel length 37

suppression of postvocalic h and u 237
suppression of second of three dots 61
suppression of stem-final l before t n c s 48
suppression of velar initial (of particles) 55
suppression of vowel or resonant after ···h 6, 38
-supsita 249, 311, 784
-suptikka / -ptikka 248, 306, 784
-suptita / -ptita 248, (~ kulye) 306, 311, 784
surface: (process) 61; (reduction) 71; (adhesion) 260; (strings) 260, 261; (junctures) 261; (transitivity) 280; (sentence) 284
surnames 5, 15, 132, 167; (list) 366-7, (alphabetical) 368-9
suru (Japanese auxiliary verb) 218
suspective -ci < -˙ti: (Phyengan -ti) 46; 70; 226, 243, 247, 300, 308, 315, 329, 339; 453-5; 815
suspended sentence 300, 303
suspensive or triple-dot intonation 302, 303
susu lo 145
*···sVk 101
swī- 'rest' 237, 255
swii (der adv < swīw-) 256
swīn 'fifty' 176
switching emphasis 297
swīw- (adj) 256; 362
(-)˙swo- 261, 263, 784; (-)swo˙la 263
swu (counter) 180, 182, 786
-swu / -wu ← -so / -o 301, 786
-swu (of son-swu) 145, 786
-swu 'hand, person' 170
(···q) swū < ˙swu 'number of ··· ' (postcounter) 156, 162, 171; 785-6
swū ··· 174; swū-chen 179; swū-ek 179
swu(h) < ˙swuh 'male' (adnoun, bnd noun) 109, 149, 786
-swuk = -(s)swuk 164, 347, 786
-swuk, -swuk(-)uley (bnd adj-n) 191, 786
-swul 'technique, art' 170
swul 'spoon' 235
swuley 'wagon' 240
swulok (postmod) 160, 786
swūm (i) ci- 317
swun (adnoun) < SSYWUN 147
swun (counter) 182
swūnco low- 256
-swung 164, 347, 786; -swungi 163, 786
swū-payk 179
swus (adnoun) 147
swus cew- 229; swus cey (der adv) 256
swū-sip 179

swut kalak 235
sy [š] ≠ *s* 47
syassu / syaccu 'shirt' 94
···sye pronounced /sye/ 94; 252
sye = /se/ 93
sye > *se* 46; *sye* > *sey* 48; *sye* < *si(y)e* 46
˚*sye*- 237
˙*sye* (particle): (after ˙*i ˙la*) 273; 787
syem (substantive < ˚*sye*- 'stand') 267
¨syem = sye˙wum (modulated subst < ˚*sye*- 'stand') 267
syllabicity 23, 34; (of high vowel) 36
syllabic nuclei (vowels) 51
syllabification: (phonetic ~) 56; 85, 86
syllable 4, 6; (morphophonemic ~) 7; 8, 23, 24, 26, 29, 33, 36, 39, 41; (~ nuclei) 42; (15th century ~) 49; (~ types in Chinese) 95
syllable block 6, 238
syllable boundary 30, 52
syllable division 8, 244, 261
syllable excess 49, (types) 100, 232. SEE excess.
syllable-excess nouns 6; (restructuring) 107
syllable-final consonant + onset h- 28
syllable-final n 12, 28
syllable-final ···*s* as sibilant in transcriptions 49
syllable-final symbolism 341
syllable-final ···t phoneme 49
syllable-final ···*t* ? < ···*t[V]* 50
syllable-initial clusters 28
syllable-initial l 28
syllable-initial y 54
syllable onset 28
syllable structure 23, 29
syllables: (orthographic ~) 7; (not in spoken words) 29; (number of distinct ~) 29, 30; (permissible ~) 95
synchronic description 220
synonym 146, 162, 197, 275, 282, 287, 295, 299, 314
synonymous: (~ morpheme) 280; (~ expression) 340
syntactic ambiguity 282
syntactic components 274
syntactic constraints 287
syntactic criteria (for word boundaries) 86
syntactic inversion: SEE inversion.
syntactic object 284
syntactic properties (of underlying adj) 330
syntactic subject 284
systematic alternation in medial vowels 341

systematic process 296
¨˙*syw*ᵘ/*om* 267
t → *l* 57
t 57; (reflex appropriate to ~) 102
t + hi → chi, t + i → /ci/ 102
···*t* = ···*s* (> ···q)? 141; 787
-t: no Chinese syllables ending in ~ (→ **-l**) 22
···**t(-)** (examples) 103; (···t lacking examples) 108
···*t*- stems 57; (nonleniting) 234; (list) 363
t 'fact' (postmod) 108, 274, (as summational epitheme) 327; 787
-˙*ta*- (retrospective): (first-person?) 263; 787-8
-˙*ta* (indic assert, 'you / he ...'; → -˙*la* after modulator) 272
-ta (indicative assertive ending) 31, 102, 230, 232, 234, 236, 246, 248, 251; (style) 296; 306; 788. SEE -ta (ka).
'ta < ita (cop transferentive) 227, 587-8; 788, 789
¨˙*ta* < *ho˙ta* after voiceless sound 92; 788, 789
˙*ta* (postmod) 'question' 263, 788
tā < ¨*ta* 'all' 138, 173, 788
ta˙a inf < *tao*- 267
ta-cca ko-cca lo 146
taci = ta(k)ci 789
tachi- < 221
tag game: counting in ~ 187
tag translations 265
tah- 243; tāh.a and tāh.e 251
tahayng 'fortunate' (defective adj-n) 146, 190
*tak- (> tah- 'touch, arrive, ... ') 220
'ta (ka): SEE ita (ka).
-ta (ka) < -˙*ta* ˙*ka* (transferentive) 198, 220, 247, 260, 292, 296, 329; 789-90; 852
-ta ka ka (pcl + pcl?) 197, 790
-ta (ka) ka 198, 214
-ta (ka) mōs ha- 226, 795
-ta (ka) nun 198, 791, 798
-ta (ka) to 198, 791-2, 801
-ta (ka) ya 198, 792, 802
-taka (as unanalyzed ending) 214
-*ta˙ka* as bound infinitive 71
'*ta ˙ka* (inaccurate analysis?) 273
taka '(drawing) near' 220
tak.a (inf < tak- = taku-) 260
'ta ka tul 198
ta(k)ci (postnoun) 157, 789
takk- 231; 364
tāko (tākwu) 220, 230, 333, 792
-ta ko (tul) hanta 213; 792-3

-takwu, -takw(un)i 163, 793
-ta kwulye 213
tal 'month' (as counter) 182; 186; (~ mata) 137
tā-l- (reflexive donatory verb) 220, 793
-ta(la)h- 220; 365; 793
talh- [Taycen DIAL] = talu- (adj) 238
(-)tali (postnoun, bound postnoun) 159, 163, 794
tal.i: (sil-kwup ~) 158; 793
talk → /tak/ 102; widely treated as tak 108
talkyal < tol'k oy al 39
tālla 230, 333, 794
tāllanta = tālla 'nta = tālla (ko) hanta 220, 333, 794
talli 195
tālm- 231, 232
talp- (Kyengsang), talpu- (Cenla) = talu- 238
talu- < talo- / talG- < *taloG- < *talok- (or *talop-?) 195, 238, 239, 256, 794
taluh- / talu- [Phyengan DIAL] = talu- 240
talun (pseudo-adnoun) 150, 794
-tam$_{1,2}$ (bnd n) 'talk(s), tale' 170; 'lake' 171
-tama, -tala → -tamah-, -talah- (bnd adj-n) 191
-tamah-, -tama ha- 220
tamku- < tomk- / tomo- < *tomok- 'soak' 238
-ta mōs ha- 260, 340, 795
tam(p)ul 187
-tan (counter) 183
tan (counter for bunches) 181, 182
tan < TAN (adverb, adnoun) 147, 150, 796
-ta 'ney 332, 796
tang < TANG (adn; postn; vnt; vni) 149, 797
tangcho'y = tangcho (ey) 137
tang hanta 313
tang ha.ye: ⋯ ul ~ 194
tangible noun 279
tangmyen 'confront' (defective vn) 190
tangsin (tul / kkili) 'you (all)' 133, 296, 797
tani-: -ko ~ 226
Tanki 186
-ta 'nta ← -ta hanta 244, 332, 798
tantan hi 257
tao 220, 333, 799
-ta 'o 332, 799
tapal (counter) 181
-ta 'p.nita 332, 799
-ta ppun 213, 799
target of adnominalization 326
tases-i, tasesq-i 187
-ta ppun 213
-ta siph.i 800

-ta son 213, 800
tassay; tassayq nal 185
tasup 187
tat- 231; 363
tatat- / tatal- 242; 363
ta'-tal-i 255
tatalu- 242; 361
*-ta tul hako (ila ko) hanta 213
taum 'next' 161, 801; taum-taum 149
taw- (postnom adj insep) 219, 229; 361; 799
tawu 333, 801
-ta 'y = -ta hay 308, 801-2
-tay$_{1,2}$ (bnd n) 'group, outfit'; 'belt; zone' 170
-tay (counter for machines) 180
tāy- (postnom v insep) 219, 228, 345; (aux) 226, 230, 290; 803
tay (counter for cigarettes, slaps) 180
tāy-$_1$ 'great, big' (bound adnoun) 155
tāy-$_2$ against, toward' (bound adnoun) 155
tāy < 'TWOY 'face, relate to' (vn insep) 190; 802
Taycen 238, 240, 242
tāy ha.ye: ⋯ ey ~ 194; 802
tāy(-)ka- 226
(-)taykali 159, 163, 802
-tayki = -(t)tayki 158, 163, 802
Taykwu 25
tay (lo) (postn, postmod) 159, 160, 290, 802-3
tāymo han (pseudo-adnoun) 150
-tayngi (in yeph-tayngi) 163, 803
tāy(-)o- 226
tāys 178
Tayshin, A.I. 26, 27, 28, 47, 108, 112, 239
tāysin < 'TOY-SIN 161, 803
tāy-yeses 178
-tcc- 31
-'t^{e}a- 70, 72; (basic accent) 84; (second-/third-person?) 263; 804
-te- and -tu-: distinction between ~ 21
te 'more' 138, 141, 804
techniques for highlighting or subduing focus 324
te'e (inf < teu-) 267
te ha- 229, 804
(-)teki = (-)te(y)ki 158, 163, 808
(-)tek.kwungi (bound postnoun) 158, 163, 804
Tek.wen 41
tēl (adv) 'less' 138, 141
tele (dative particle) 195, 197, 295, 804, 821
tele (adverb) 'somewhat' 138

telling (verb of ~) 295
tempo 30, 52
tempo-controlled articulations 27
temporal-locative particle 140
"temporary counters" 171
tengeli (counter) 181
tengke-tang = cengke-cang 94
tense: (markers) 220; 244, 246, 290
tense: (unaspirated stops) 27, 44; (allophones of stops) 44; (apical stop) 44; (component) 50; (obstruents) 96
tense-aspect conversions 304
tense-aspect shift 297; (recurrent?) 335
tense markers 304, 305
tenseness as feature of clustering 44
tentative 297, 304
tentative adversative **-kena** 247, 258, 329
tentative assertive **-kes.ta** 247, 259
tentative conditional **-ketumyen** 247, 259, 329
tentative modifier 259
tentative sequential **-keni** 247, 258, 329
tentative suspective **-kes.ci** 247, 259
tepeki (postnoun) 157, 806
tepu-l- < te˙pul- 'accompany' 220, 806
tepul.e (se): ··· kwa ~ 195; 220; 806
tepulko 220, 806
terminative 226
terminology 3, 286
tes(-) (adnoun, bnd adv) = teq ··· < te 149, 806
tes < ˙tet 'interval of time' 144, 806, 807
-˙t^{e}a-˙si- = -(^{u}/o)˙si-˙t^{e}a- 261, 806-7
tēw- 289, 316
tewi (der n < tēw-) 233, 256
tewuk te 140, 807
textbooks 474
texts 17, 26; (that treat particles as words) 56; (15th-century) 60; (16th-century) 71; 261, 263, 271; (chronological list of texts) 397-401, (alphabetized) 401-6
textual spellings 44
tey > ti 46
-tey 248, 808
tey- (bnd adv) 141, 808
··· tey 'circumstance, event' (postmod) 160, 250, 300, 302, 303, 324, 329, 330, 807
··· tey 'place' (quasi-free n) 131, 161, (= kos) 303, 807
(-)te(y)ki 158, 163, 808
··· tey to 329
teywu- 288

t-final consonant stems 234
···t(h)- stems 262
···th(-) (examples) 103
th (noun-final ~) treated as if s 102
th + i → chi 102
tha- 219, 808
˙tha < ho˙ta after voiced sound 92, 808
thā (counter) 185
Thak Huyswu 112
thāl < ¨thal 'karma' (unknown origin) 112
thāl 'mishap, ... ' (unknown origin) 112
··· thas 'fault' (also vnt 'blame') 131, 809
thaykuk 'the great ultimate' 344
-thayngi 163, 809
thaywu- 222
the (noun, postmod) 160, 161; 809
˙the··· < ˙hote··· 72, 809
··· thek 'reason, grounds' (quasi-free n) 131, 161
thek, them (postnoun) = theym 157, 810
thematization 286, 298
they (counter) 180; they (postmodifier) 160, 810
theym, theymi (postnoun) 157
(-)the(y)ngi 163, 810
/thi/ within a morpheme: no cases of ~ [except in foreignisms] 102
˙thi < ho˙ti after voiced sound 92, 810
thi (postn) 157, 811; -thi in kokay-thi 144, 811
thing vs event (as subject) 294
third-person pronoun 135
˙tho- 'ride' 262
tholok (< hatolok) 194, 811
thon (counter) 184
-thong 'thing; part of body' 163
-thong 'pain' 170
thong (counter) 181, 811
thong (adnoun, adv, bnd noun) 'whole' 149, 811
thong (postn, postmod) 'impetus' 159, 160, 811-2
thong ha.ye (hay se): ··· ul ~ 194, 812
thonghwa (counter) 181
Thongil-an (period) 4
thong ulo 146
three contiguous dots 61
"throat" sounds 49
thuli- = ttuli- 343, 813
thwungi / thongi (postnoun) 157
thwuse(y)ngi 157, 814
thy 94, 814
···t.hye ← ···t.hi-e 252
···th.ye from ···th.ie 252
ti (modern Seoul syllable) 46

-ti (retrospective attentive) 248, 306, 815
-ti (Phyengan) < MK -˙ti suspective 46, 815
-˙ti (suspective < ˙t i): (triggers lenition) 55; 265, 622; 815
ʼ˙ti < ho˙ti after voiceless sound 92, 815
°ti- (vi) 'fall' 262
¨ti- vc < °ti- vi 55; (= ¨tiy- < *ti-˙i-) 262
tikut 101
ti-mata (Japanese) 144
time: (~ words) 130; (adverbs of ~ + ablative and/or allative) 136; (units of ~) 171; 297
timeless (verb form) 249
title 132; (as pronominal substitute) 133; ('you') 135, 296
-ti˙Wi 265, 816
¨tiy-₁, ¨tiy-₂ 55, 70, 74
-tk- → -tkko → -kko 236
t lenited to l 234
-T/L- stem (from lenited t) 57, 102, 233, 242, 268; (list) 363
*-˙t[o]- 263, 817
to- (in to-math-) 141
-to 'degree' (counter) 182
-to₁ '(year) period' 170
-to₂ 'painting, drawing, view' 170
-to₃ 'ferry' (category designator) 133
(-)to₄ 'island' (category designator) 133
(-)tō 'province' (as category designator) 133
to < ˙two (particle): (adverb + ~) 135; (focus particle) 136; 189, 190, 193, 196, 197, 228, 229; (inf + to) 251; 283, 291, 292, 296, 297, 316, 324, 335, 340; 816-7
(to)cwung 'midst' 161
... to iu / itta ... (Japanese) 332
... (to iu) waˈke desu (Japanese) 332
Toklip sinmun 18
˙t ol 265, 818
[¨]tol- 'be sweet'; 'weigh it' 241
˙tol- 'hang' < *˙to˙lo- 241
tō-l- 290
tolaci 'bellflower' 240
tol.a ka- 291
tol.a kasi- 'die' 226, 298
˙tolh 'group' (plural) 109, 818
-tol(-i) (boys' names) 164, 819
tolie < twolihye < twolo-˙(h)hye 38
tol.ikhi- 243
tolk 'chicken' (etymology) 98
tollimq ca 132

-tolok < -˙to˙lwok (projective) 3, 164, 247, 330; 819
-tolok-i 247, 820
-˙to˙lwok 265, 271, 819, 821
to˙lye (> tele) 821
ton (counter) 183
tonal residue of ellipted syllable 61
tone: (Chinese ~) 50; (~ language) 60; 61
tone dots / marks: (words without ~) 60, 61; unexplained ~ 95
tone-marked text 60
tong- (in tong-calu-) 141, 822
-tong(-i) 164, 822
tong-an 'while' 161; (···q ~) 186; (-nun / -un ~ (ey)) 289; 822
tongci 'comrade' (postnoun title) 133
Tongkwuk cengwun 4
Tongkwuk readings 95, 96, 97, 126
tongsi ey: ··· kwa / wa ~ 197; 822
tongue tip 28; tongue position 24
tōp- = tōw- 233, 234; 361
topic: (+ verb) 19; (particle) 89
topographical feature 285
˙tos (bnd adj-n) 265, 822-3
-˙tos 'like' (attached to stem) 72, 822
To Swuhuy 54
tot.i /toci/ (postnoun < der n) 158
to tul 198, 823
towoy-, toWoy- 54, 273, 823
-toy < -˙toy (accessive): 265; (always modulated) 271; 329; (~ " ··· " (°ho-)) 332; 823-4
toy- 'become' (vi) 54, 237, 243; (postnom adj insep) 140, 229; ('get done') 188, 189; (postnom v sep) 219, 228; (aux, -key ~) 227; 283, 286, 289, 290; (··· ulo) toy.e iss-) 291; (vn ~) 313; 316, 317; (inf) 465; 824-6
toy (counter) 177, 183
tōy (inf < toy-) 252
toy-ciki (counter) 184
toylq tay lo toy(ke) la 244
-toy.ye 265
toz- < *to˙s[o]- 'love' 237
traditional Chinese distinctions 44
traditional Chinese readings 22, 44
traditional initial 46
transcription 29; (of tone dots) 61; 98
transferentive 57; (accent as if bound stem) 71; (-ta as abbr of unanalyzed -taka) 214; 226, 247, 260, 266, 329, 789-90, 795

A Reference Grammar of Korean

transforming expansions 297
transitional 226; ~ epitheme (of time / place / circumstance) 326; 482, 582; 686
transitive: (vs intransitive) 216; 287
transitive passive verb (= vpt) 221, 288, 312; (with expressed object) 317, 847
transitive relationship between two nouns 848
transitive verb (vt) 89; (stem) 218, 315
transitive verbal noun (vnt) 89, 188, 190
transitivity: (deciding ~ of Chinese verbal noun) 189; 227, 280, 314; (high vs low ~) 466-7
translation 4; (of Korean particle) 192; 221, 222, 263, 282, 328
traversal object 216, 280, 288
triangle 22; (~ symbol for MK /z/) 59, 237
triphthongs 43
triple-dot intonation 42
triplet reading (of Chinese character) 97
truncation 103, 104, 108, 112, 231, 241, 263, 329
truth value 283, 322, 323, 901
-tss- 31
Tsukamoto Hideki 172, 173
"…tt…" foreign interlude spelled s.tt or s.th 53
-ttak = -ttak / -ttek 164, 347, 826
(-)ttakci (postnoun) 159, 163, 826
-ttakseni 163, 826
ttal 299
ttal^e/a (se): … ey ~ 194
ttalu- 242; 361
ttalum 'only, just' (postmodifier) 160; 826
(t)tam 158
ttan … 23
… ttan (ey) '(by) one's own kind judgment' 131, 826
ttan i 23, (552)
tta' nim 299
ttan kapyewun piup 23, 925
ttan kiyek 23
ttan liul 23
ttan niun 23
ttan pān sios 23
… ttawi 'of the sort, and the like' 131, 158, 827
ttay < ˙pstay 'time (when …)' 161, 325, 827-8
-(t)tayki 158, 163, 802
ttāym (postnoun < substantive) 158, 828
ttaymun 131, 159; (noun vs postnoun) 193; 828
-ttek 164, 828
ttē-l- (postnom v sep) 228, 828

INDEX 1023

ttel.e ci- 317, 828
tteli (postnoun): tung ~ 158, 828
tto < ˙stwo, tto tasi 140, 828
… ttolay 'of (that) age or size' 131, 828
-ttuk 164, 347
(-)ttuki (postnoun) 158, 163
ttuli- (auxiliary): -e ~ 227
ttut.i /ttuci/ post (der n): ppye ~, al ~ 158, 829
ttwayki (counter) 180
ttwāyki (vowel development) 253
ttwi- 288; ttwim ul ttwi- 279
-(t)twuk 164, 347, 843
ttwulyes 'i 257
-(t)twungi 163, 844
/tty/ 94
… ˙t^u/o- stems 232
tu- 141, 829
-tukwu(me)n yo 245, 311, 829
-tukwun (yo) 306, 829
tul- (preverb, bnd adv) 141, 831
tu-l- < ˙tul- < *˙tu˙lu- 'enter' 102, 240, 241; 360
[¨]tul- 'lift' < *tu˙lu- 241
tu-l-, tul.i- (aux): -e ~ 219, 227, 230, 832, 833
tul- / tut- 'hear': SEE tut- / tul-.
tul < ˙tolh (plural) '(as a) group': 118, 134, 130; (adv + ~) 135; 159; (postnoun vs pcl) 174; 196, 139, 188, 213, 226, 228, 291, 320; 829-31
tul (postmod 'conceded fact') < ˙t ol 160, 831
tūl 'wild' (adnoun < noun 'moor') 148
-tula (retr assertive): (+ pcl ko) 213; 248; 306, 307, 325, 831
tul.e (inf of 'hear' or 'enter') 102, 242; (~ ka-, ~ o-) 289; (~ iss-) 291; 832
tul.e la and tut.ke la 243
tulem (counter) 182
tuli- 'give to a superior' 223, (aux) 230
tul.i- (bnd adv) 141, 832; (aux) SEE tu-l-
tul iyo (NOUN ~ not *NOUN iyo tul) 213, 833
tulkhi- 224
tulli- 'be heard' 288
tulli-: ('catch a cold') 221; (= tullu- 'drop in') 223; (vp / vc) 223
tullu- / tulli- 'drop in' 288, 350
¨tulp- 241
tul.ye ('ta) 260
tumu-l- 288

-tun 249, 306, 833-4
-tun < -tun [ya] 307
-ˈtun (-ˈton) < t (postmod) + ᵘ⁄on 258, 834
-tun ci 244, 296, 834-5
... tūng < ¨TUNG (postnoun) 158
... tūngci < ¨TUNG-TTI (postnoun; ? quasi-free n) 131, 158
tungsan 'mountain climbing' 275
... tūngtung < ¨TUNG ¨TUNG 'et cetera' 131
Tung T'ung-Ho 46
Tungusic 45
-tuni: (vs -teni) 40; 836
-tun ka (yo) 306, 311, 837-8
-tun kwulye 307
-tun kwumen 245, 307, (~ yo) 311
-tun kwun (a) 307
-tun kwun yo 306
-tun tey (yo) 310, 311; 839
-tun ya 213, 840
ˈtus 88
tus (postmod adj-n sep) 161; (~ hata / siph.ta) 250; 840-1
...-' tus ha- = -nun tus ha- 94, 841
... tus 'i 'as if' 257
tus siph- (postnom adj insep) 229, 841
tut- / tul- 'hear': (accentual exception) 33; 102, 231; (Phyengan treatment) 234; (unique vowel and MK accent) 235; 242, 288, 299
Tut.kentay ... 334
tuy > ti 46
twāy = tōy (inf) 253, 465, 842
twāyci 'pig' < to.yaci (vowel development) 253
twi- (bound adverb) 140, 842
twī < ¨twuyh 197, 842
'two': Chinese word for ~ 110
ˈtwo (pcl) 88, 233, 239; (ˈiˈla ~) 273; 842
-ˈtwo = -ˈti ˈtwo 72, 265, 842
-ˈtwo- (modulated emotive) 263, 273; (?< -ˈt[o]-ˈwo-) 274; 842
two hanthey phrases 314
two-morpheme words 113
two nominative phrases in putative sentence 332
two-shape (element / particle) 100, 130; (ending) 230, 237, 240, 242, 258, 305
-ˈtwo-ˈs(wo)- 261, 263, 843-3
two-syllable: (~ strings) 7; (~ nouns optionally HL/LH) 65; (~ words that are only attested HH) 66; (~ verbal nouns) 300
two syllables (run together) 99
two ul phrases 314

¨twoW- (often spelled ¨two[W]-) 234; (irregularities) 252
twoˈwo- (modulated stem) 234
two-word units 197
twu- < ˚ˈtwu- 'put away' 81, 270, 844-5
twu- (auxiliary): -e ~ 226, 230; 465
-twu (counter) 180, 183
twu ← to (pcl) 41
Twū ccay lo ... 334
twue ccay 179
twues / twue < ¨twuˈzeh / ¨twuˈze 174, 178
-twuk = -(t)twuk 164, 347, 843
twuko-twuko 137
¨twulh 'two' 109
twūl-i, twū-i 187
twū(l)-seys / -sey / -sek / -se 178
twūl / twū 174
twūl ccay 175, 178
twung (postmodifier) 160, 844
-twungi = -(t)twungi 163, 844
twungkuleh- 243
twū-senes / -sene 178; twū-sene ccay 179
twū-sey ccay 179
Twusi = Twusi enhay = 1481 Twusi 4, 44, 45, 61, 86
twūsup 187
ty (as reduction of ti) 845
ty- > c- (south), t- (north) 58, 94; 235
tyalo- / tyel ᵘ⁄o- 238
tye < ti(y)e < tuy(y)e 46
*ˈtye-l- (defective stem) 256
ˈtyeˈle (bnd adv < defective inf) 219, 256
types of sentence 263
typically voiced sound 27, 92
typically voiceless sound 92
typical shape 244
typology 35
u ≠ wu even after labials 43
"u": notational abbreviation of /wu/ 43, 252
"u" after labial: morphophonemic behavior 18
u after labial in derived forms 18, 29
u and wu 18
u (particle) [DIAL] = uy, = ul 27, 196
u/e vowel (of Kimhay): quality of ~ 25
*ᵘ⁄o (undecided) ?< *yo... 239
... ᵘ⁄o- stems (all high except for ˚ho-) 71
...u- stems 252, 256, 267
...u- stems: (lists) 349, 350
-u- < *-Gᵘ⁄o- (formative for vc) 220, 224, 225
-ui / -i 246, 248, 309, 553, 847

-(u)k 164
-ukhi- (formative for vc) 220, 224, 847
-(u)l- (verb formative) 219
···u-l- stems (list) 360
-ul (in mimetics) 342
-ulq / -lq < -˙(ᵘ/o)lq (prosp mod) 164, 230, 250, 251, 272, 277, 280, 850, (shape selection) 851
ul / lul (accusative pcl) 130, 140, 188, 193, 195, 197; (substituting for some other pcl) 216; 282; (replacing ulo, ey, eykey 285; (omitted) 287; (= ey 'to', = tong-an) 288; 291, 316, 329; 553, 590, 638, 642, 818, 840; 847-50; 870, 897, 938
˙ul = ˙ᵘ/ol / ˙lᵘ/ol (accusative pcl) 239; (shape selection) 849-50
-ula / -la < -˙ᵘ/o˙la (subjunctive attentive) 245, 246, 248, 306, 851
-ula / -la 'y 308, 854
-ulq cwul 315, 856
-ule / -le 3, 330, 856. SEE purposive.
-uley / -ley = -(u)lye 308
-ulᵉa(y)ki / -lᵉa(y)ki 163, 856
-ulᵉa(y)ngi / -lᵉa(y)ngi 163
-˙ᵘ/o˙l i '··· 55
-˙ᵘ/o˙l i ˙Ga 55, 857
-˙ᵘ/o˙l i ˙˙Ge˙m ye 263, 857
-˙ᵘ/ol i ˙Gwo 55, 858
-ulikka / -likka (prospective attentive) 249, 858
-ᵘ/o˙l i ˙˙la 272, 858-9
-ᵘ/o˙l i '-ngi ˙˙ta 272, 861
-ulini < -˙ᵘ/o˙l i ˙'n i 272, 329, 861
-ulita / -lita (prospective assertive) 247, 249, 861
-ulq ka < -˙ᵘ/olq ˙ka 244; (~ hanta) 257, 331; 306, 308, 862-3
"-ulka" or "-ulkka" for -ulq ka 41
-ulq ka yo 306, 311
-ulq ke l' 329, 863
-ulq kes ēps.i 321, 865
-ulq kes ita 244, 258
-ulq kes man siph- 228
-ulq key (probable future) 259
-ulq ke y··· or -ulq ke ··· (probable future) 254
-ulq ke yo 254, 865-6
-ulla / -lla (var of -ulye / -lye) 258, 331, 866-7
ullang / llang (var) = un / nun (pcl) 196, 258, 334, 866-7
-ulla 'nta 331; -ulla 'y 331, 867
-ullya / -llya, -ullye / -llye 41, 868
-ul.nun / -l.nun 250, 251, (always + ci) 332, 868

ulo / lo < (˙ᵘ/o)˙lwo (pcl) 130, 136; (noun + ~ as adv) 140; (after bnd preparticle) 145; 193, 195; (after subst) 254; 282, 284, 295; (replaced by ul / lul) 314; 315; (~ toy-) 317, 330; 868-70
··· (ulo) (optional pcl) 136
ulo ha.ye(-kum) 195, 315, 870-1
ulo in ha- 'be due to' 190; ulo in ha.ye 315
ulo malmiam.ᵉ/a 315
ulo se / lo se < ˙ᵘ/o˙lwo ˙sye (pcl) 195, 872
ulo se ppun 198
ulo sse / lo sse (pcl) 195, 872
ulo sse (nun) 198, 872
ulph- 231, 363
-ulq say 160, 874
-ul(q) sey 307, 874
-ul˙swongi˙ta = -ulq ˙s ˙[y]wo-ngi ˙ta 270, 876
-ulq swu iss.ta / ēps.ta 315, 876
-ulq ttay (ey) 330, 879
ul tul (pcl + pcl) 197, 879
-ulu 164, 347, 880
···ulu- stems 361
ulu [DIAL] = ulo 196
ulwu [DIAL] = ulo 196
-ulya / -lya hanta 331
-ulye / -lye < -(˙ᵘ/o)˙l ye 41, 280, 306, 330; (~ ha-) 332; 882
-ulye ko: 213 (~ ha-) 227, 257, 331, 332; (~ tu-l-) 227; 882
-ulyem / -lyem (una) 213, 247, 883
-ulyenman / -lyenman 329, 884
-ulye 'nta ← -ulye hanta 244, 332, 884
-ulyes.ta, -ulyetta / -lyetta 247, 249, 258, 885
um 'the dark side' 344
-um (in mimetics) 342
-(u)m = -um / -m < -(˙ᵘ/o)m 164, 230, 247, 254, 277; (V-um ul V- = V-) 288; (vn ~ ul pat.nunta, tang hanta) 313; (vs -ki) 323; 886-7
-(˙ᵘ/o)m → -˙wᵘ/om, always modulated except in the structure -(˙ᵘ/o)˙m ye (n') 271
-um a 160, 248, 254, 888. SEE -˙wᵘ/o.m a.
-umay / -may 247
-um cik ha- < -˙ᵉ/am ˙cik °ho- 254, 889
-um / -m ey (-umay / -may) < -˙(w)ᵘ/o˙m ᵉ/ay 21; 214, 215, 247, 254, 259, 323, 329
umlaut 36; umlauting rule 49
-um say 160; -um sey 160, 891
-umq seng 160, 773
-um ulo < -˙(w)ᵘ/o˙m ᵘ/o˙lwo 21; (as unanalyzed ending) 214; 244

-(ᵘ/o)ˈm ye (conjoins predicates) 70, 267, 273, 892
-(ᵘ/o)ˈm ye (n') (never modulated) 271
-umye / -mye < -(ᵘ/o)ˈm ye 214, 247, 329, 892
-umyen / -myen < -(ᵘ/o)ˈm ye n' 329, 230, 247, 259, 280; (~ an toy-) 316; 893-4
-umyen / -myen se 214, (~ kkaci, ~ tul) 215, (~ to) 329
-un (in mimetics) 342
-un / -n < -ˈ(ᵘ/o)n (modifier) 164, 246, 249, 258, 272, 277, 280, 324, 897
un / nun (focus pcl) 130; (adv + ~) 135, 136, 190, 193, 196, 197, 226, 228, 257, 283, 291, 297; (subduing suspective in double negative) 322; 324; (subduing focus on theme of matrix) 328; 329, 330; 425, 451, 577, 584, 590, 637, 682, 761, 818, 849; 896-7; 938
ˈᵘ/on (subdued focus) 239
-una / -na < -(ᵘ/o)ˈna: (+ pcl) 146, 213; 230, 236, 296; 329, 898-9
una / na (emphasis particle): (-key ~, -ulyem ~, interj ~, adv ~) 142, 196; 213, 214, 258, 308; (and ina / 'na) 898
unanalyzable ending 41, 214
unanalyzed: (ending) 21, 214, 243, 244; (unit) 257; (entity) 260; (element) 275; (adverb) 296
-una-ma / -na-ma: (+ pcl) 213, 246; 329; 899
unaspirated obstruent after sibilant 44
unaspirated voiceless initials of Middle Chinese 96
unassimilated information 307
uncertainty sentence 300, 303, (as elliptical) 332
uncontracted forms 237; (preserved from earlier language) 240
underarticulation (of stop as flap) 234
underlying accent 85
underlying adnominal (genitive) relationship 283
underlying forms 6
underlying h 35
underlying morphophonemic strings 30
underlying object (marked by nominative) 551, 707
underlying role (more than one extruded) 328
underlying subject 173, 327, 328; 551; (plural reference to) 830; (marked by accusative) 849
Underwood, H.G. 27, 135
unelided velar 56
unextended -L- stem 41, (in compounds) 235
unheralded epitheme 328

-uni / -ni < -(ᵘ/o)ˈn i 3, 247; 272, 306, 902-3
-un i 306
unified spelling system 4; Unified System 8
*-ˈᵘ/oˈn i 'G… (no examples) 55
-ˈᵘ/oˈn i ˈGa, -ˈᵘ/oˈn i ˈGwo 55
…unikka < …-ˈᵘ/oˈn i s ˈka 318
-uni-kka / -ni-kka 247, 318, 623; ~ (yo) 329; ~ (n') 330
-uni(-kka) vs -e (se) 330
-(ᵘ/o)ˈn i ˈ'la 272, 903
-un i mankhum 213, 902
uninflected words 88
-un i pota 213, 902
unique compound of adnoun + postnoun 175
unique string …l.nn… 52
unique syllable-initial geminate nn… 52
unit counter 171
-un ka (yo) 306, 307, 310, 904-5
unlenited consonants 53; unlenited velars 56
unlenited p 234
… un / nun kheneng un (pcl + pcl + pcl) 198, 906
unmarked case 286
unmarked category 130
unmarked indirect object + verb 19
unmarked low tone (of MK) 61
unmarked object + verb 19
unmarked subject + verb 19
unmarked tone 241
unmodulated substantive: (contracted for …-l- verbs) 255; (surviving in contracted version) 255, 272; (before pcl) 888; 892
unmotivated ll for l (as dialect variant) 111
unmotivated semivowel 37
unmotivated variants 62
unordered strings 3
unpronounced distinction 109
unpronounced h (restored) 233
unquoted: (plain style) 251; (~ verbal sentence) 307
unrealistic distinctions 96
unreleased voiceless stops (= …p, …t, and …k) of Chinese 61
unshortened forms (of inf) 252
unstated rule 53
-un tey (as question) 308, 908
-unula / -nula (substandard) = -nula 258, 910
unusual syllables 30
unwritten reinforcement 50
-un ya (for Hankul -unya) 21; 213; 910

-uo vs -so 40; 249
-uo/-o 309, 910
-up.nikka 311, 911
-up.nita: (for -sup.nita) 40; 311, 911
-ˢup.nita 249
-(u)psey 249, 305, 911
-upsio = -usio 249, 911
-upsita/-psita 248, 306, 311, 911
-upsulum (bnd adj-n) 191, 912
-ˢuptikka 249; -uptikka 911; -uptita 912
-(u)s (adj-n) 33, 164, 191, 342, 912
-use < -usye < -usi-e 37, 912
-usey yo = -us[y]ey yo ← -usye yo 253; 912
-usi-/-si- 226, 230, 308
-˙ᵘ/osi- ← -ᵘ/o˙si- 85
-usiap-/-siap-, -usia-/-sia- 299, 912
-ᵘ/o˙silq 272, 913
-ᵘ/o˙sin 272, 913
-ᵘ/o˙si˙non 272, -(ᵘ/o)˙sino˙n i 915
-ᵘ/o˙si˙nwon (modulated hon proc mod) 272, 916
-usio/-sio/-psio 248, 306, 312, 917
-usio/-usipsio → -us(y)o/-usips(y)o 38
-usiop-/-siop-, -usio-/-sio- 299
-usiopsose/-siopsose 299, 917
-(u)sipsita 312, 917
-usi yo = -usey yo ← -usye yo 249, 918
USSR 28, 595
-ᵘ/o˙sya (honorific infinitive) 465, 466, 918
-ᵘ/o˙sya- (modulated honorific) 270, 271, 272, 918
-ᵘ/o˙syalq (modulated hon prosp mod) 272, 918
-ᵘ/o˙syam (hon modulated subst) 267, 919
-ᵘ/o˙syan (modulated hon modifier) 272, 919
-(u)tay-tay, -(u)tey-tey, -(u)tayng-tayng, -(u)teyng-teyng; -(u)thoy-thoy, -(u)thwi-thwi (bound adj-n) 191, 920
utterance 41
uttum 178
uy (the syllable) 43; (> i when not initial, > u when initial; partially restored as ui) 43
uy (digraph) 8; (in Hamkyeng) 17; (syllable) 25; 920
···uy- stems: (lists) 349, 350; ···uy- stems 466
uy < ˙ᵘ/oy (particle) 151, 196, 197, 214, (*N uy Num) 173; (makes nominal phrase adnominal) 280; 282, 295; (not used to adnominalize a nominalization with -um or -ki) 324; (used for i/ka) 327, (as deemphasis) 328; (˙ᵘ/oy for ˙i in adnominalized sentence) 327; 920-2, 922-4

˙ᵘ/oy (var of locative-allative particle ˙ᵉ/ay) 68; (genitive particle) 69; 239
uy ha.ye: ··· ey ~ 194, 924
uynon 'discussion' and uylon 'argument' (?= uy¹non) 122
ūypus, ēpus (adnoun) 147, 925
uysa 132
uyseng-e, uythay-e 340
···uy˙ye (inf) 466
vacuous use of modulator 271
Vandesande, A.V. 2
variable long vowel 32; variable vowels 261
variant 8, 27, 39, 47; (spellings) 44, 52; (forms) 56; (accent patterns attested) 62; (accents in verb forms) 68; (reductions of syllable excess) 102; 240
variant infinitive 251
variant names for letters 22
variants in conjugation (of -L- stems) 240
variant treatments of -T/L- verbs 234
variation in spacing and punctuation 18
variations of /l/ with /t/ 235
velar 31, 239, 240
velar elision 54; (in nativized Chinese words) 56; 92, 254
velar elision or lenition (optional) 56
velar friction 27; velar h 27
velar initial (elided) 54
velarization: (of aspirates) 27; 28; 57
velarized glottal h 27
velarized labial fricative 57
velar lenition 50, 54, 70; (MK ~ that fails to surface in modern Seoul) 663
velar nasal 5; (syllable-initial ~) 22; (ng as onset of noninitial syllable) 28; 45; (merger of letter shape with that of zero initial) 46; (initial ~) 96
velar nasal fronted and weakened (or vanishing) 28
velar palatalization 47
velar stops 24
verb: (~ form) 5, 12, 58; (vowel length in ~) 61; (= stem + ending) 88; (~ form as source of pcl) 88; (~ form never + pcl) 213; (~ stem) 275; (~ form) 277, 280; (classes of ~) 287; (constraint classes) 288; 290, 297, 332, 340
verb + ending: (with velar lenition) 54; (left unanalyzed in the Hankul spelling) 85

verb + verb (vs adverb + verb) 141
verbal: (~ phrase) 19, 88; (particles which appear only after ~) 88; (~ meaning) 94; (~ origin of several particles) 194; (~ phrase, ~ sentence) 280; 281, 296, 307
verbal noun 89, 94; (native-Korean) 95; 161, 188; (conversion constraints) 191; 219; (+ ellipted **hako** or **ham** = **ha(n)ta**) 277; (+ postnominal verb) 277, 321, 345; (+ verbal noun) 277; (vn **ul** = vn **halye**) 294; (+ (**ul**) **pat-**, **tang ha-**) 317
verb doublet 44
verb / verbal ending 57, 220, 244, 261, 273, 332
verb gerund + verb 277
verb infinitive 57, (+ aux) 277. SEE **-e**.
verb of: activity 294; becoming 318; beginning 323; continuing 323; departure / arrival 305; discovery 323; giving 260; going / coming 304; helping 323; motion 257; perception 323; stopping 323; saying (telling, inquiring) 331, 332; thinking (opinion, intention) 331
verb paradigm 336
verb phrase (with **tul** inserted) 213; (negated by the short negative) 316
verb prefix 88, 140
verb stem 5, 17, 19, 41, 44, 48; (of Chinese origin?) 95; 230, 310
verb suffix 88
verb unaccompanied by adjuncts 328
vertical line of writing 18
Vietnamese 60, 132
vocabulary 30, 94; (layers) 95; (structure) 275
vocal tract 27
vocative (particle) 196, 287, 415
voice: causative / passive (vs active) 221, 312
voice conversions 219, 312, 314
voice-derived verbs 39, 312
voiced: typically ~ phonemes 35
voiced fricative 5; (Old Chinese velar ~) 46; (W) 50; (velar or laryngeal) 54; 233; (velar) 238
voiced **h**: (~ initial) 23; 28
voiced sound 35, 36; voiced stop 51
voiced sibilant [z] as allophone of ···c··· 108
voicelessness 51
voiceless obstruent: (initial) 44; (after voiceless stop) 130
voiceless oral + nasal (→ nasal + nasal) 51
voice qualifier 33, 41, 42, 142
voice-related pairs of verbs 223

voice shift 297
voicing: of /h/ 27; of lax obstruents between voiced sounds 27; of **s** to [z] 51
volitive (original meaning of modulator?) 271
voluntary acts 315
vowel 5, 6, 9, 12, 17, 18, 22, 23, (chart) 24, 25, 26, 27, 29, 33, 34, 36, (component) 37, 39; (nouns with no ~) 108; (word ending in ~) 130
vowel + **h** + **u** reduced to a long vowel 37
vowel + *w* (treated as a vowel) 55
vowel + **y** (as a string rather than a digraph) 16
vowel alternation patterns in word isotopes 346
vowel assimilation 38, 348. SEE assimilation.
vowel beginning of a syllable 8
vowel descriptions 24
vowel distinctions 4
vowel elision 53, 61
vowel features = components 37
vowel-final monosyllabic stems: accent 73, 75, 76, 79
vowel-final polysyllabic stems 270
vowel-final syllables 22
vowel fronting 47
vowel-initial ending 237; vowel-initial word 22
vowel length 21; (variants) 32; (lexical versus morphemic marking) 33; (distinctions) 33, 34; 60; (in Chinese morphemes) 112; (suppressed) 151; (from elision of a consonant between like vowels) 237
vowel lengthening (compensatory) 37, 38
vowel nucleus 6, 8
vowel onset 49
vowel phonemes (of Kimhay) 25
vowel quality 343
vowel raising 12, 273, 344
vowel reduction 38
vowel shift: timing of ~ 43
vowel stem 231, 236, 237, 243; (lists) 349-63
vowel-stem conjugation 130, 242
vowel strings shortened after dropping **h** or **ng** 94
vowel system 42
vulgar 4; (and pejorative) 226
vulgarizers 144, 162
/W/ 233. SEE free-standing W.
W (as the lenited form of *p*) 50; (voiced bilabial fricative) 234; 925
W = ···w (labial glide coda in Chinese readings, not pronounced) 50, 925

A Reference Grammar of Korean

w (dating the disuse) 45
-*W*- < *p* (in all cases) 268
-*w*- ("*p*-leniting") stems (···*w*-/···*p*-) 33, 53, 57; (= -W/P- stems) 233; 234
···*W*- (subjective adjectives) 57
/w/ (pronunciation) 24; (stems ending in ~) 231
w reduced from **o** 251
-w- 101
···w- < lenited **p** 130
···w- stems 254, 256; (list) 361-2
···*wa*- < ···*wo*-˙*a* 267
wa (syllable) 43
"*wa*" = ˙*[G]wa* (elided form of ˙*kwa*) 56, 926
wa = **wā** (inf) 465
wā (inf < **o**-) 'come' 38, 251; **wā iss**- 291; 926
Wagner, E.W. 2, 3
wā la 214, 244, 926
-˙*Wat*- > -˙*Gwat*- > -wat- 57
wa(-)tah- 226
way (syllable) 24; *way* (syllable) 43
way < ˙˙*may* 'why' 134, 136, 139, 926
wāykwuk = **ōykwuk** 253
we: Hankul symbol for ~ 12; *we* 43
···*we* < ···*wu*-˙*e* 267
"we" (English): royal or editorial ~ 130
'we/us' 133, 135
weakening (of consonants between vowels) 53; (of labial) 57
weather (condition/statement) 289, 298, 316
Wel = Wel.in Sekpo = 1459 Wel
Wel.in chen-kang ci kok = 1449 Kok 85
w-elision 36
-wel(q tal) 187
-wen₁₋₃ (bnd n) 'institution', 'garden; park' 170; 'clerk, member' 171
(-)wen (counter, money unit) 182
west 34
western: Japan 33; languages 192; names for Chinese radicals 372
wey (syllable) 24, 43
···**wey**- stems: (absorb inf) 252; (list) 349
···**wēy** = ···**wie** (inf) 253, 465
wēyn 926
"when/if" forms 329
Whitman, J. 332
whole-part: (adnominal relationship) 222, 284; (genitivization) 285, (with accusative marking) 848
wi (monophthong vs diphthong) 24
wi 'atop, above' 149, 196, 290, 927

[w]i- (Japanese) 218
···**wi**- stems: (lists) 349, 350
···**wie** 253; 465
wi ha.ye: ··· **ul** ~ 194
wie → **ōy** → **wey** 38, 253, 465
wi(q), wis (pseudo-adnoun) 'upper' 149, 928
wish 245
wo (syllable) 36
°*wo*- 'come' 80, 263, 270, 743, 934
˙*wohi˙lye* 38
˙*wo˙ke*- = ˙*wo˙na*- (effective < °*wo*-) 262, 743
-˙*wo.m a* 932
women 253, 308, 343. SEE female names.
˙*wo˙na*- (effective stem of °*wo*-) 262, 743, 933
˙*wo˙na˙la* 251, 742, 933
[w]oˀr- (Japanese) 218
word 32; (assigned to part of speech) 86; 275
word boundaries (based on syntax) 86, 261
word division 18, 20, 21, 274
word families 343
word isotopes 341, 343
word order 88; (in English) 192
word spaces 18
word-structure information in Hankul spelling 8
word types 88; word variants 110
woy (syllable) 43; ···*woy*- stems 466
(w)oy treated as **way** 26
writing 278
writing system 29; (morphemic ~ of Chinese) 95
written Korean 37, 38, 217, 254
written standard 93
written syllables 6; written texts 190
[w]u (Romanized abbreviation) 18
wu abbreviated to **u** after a labial 29
wu (NK) = **wi** 'atop, above' 14, 149, 927, 934
wu reduced to **w** or nothing 38
wu substituted for **o** 25
wu written as **u** after **p ph pp m** 18
-wu (suffix making der adv) 255, 934
-wu- (formative for vc) 220, 224, 934
wu (postmod adj-n insep) 161, 934
-˙*w*ᵘ⁄*o*- attached to processive 84
···*w*ᵘ⁄*o*- stems all high/low except ˙*skwu*- 71
···**wu**- stems 267; (lists) 349, 351
wue (as mistaken spelling for **wuwe**) 252
wuh 'above' > NK **wu**, SK **wi** < *wu[h]* + *-i* 108, 109
wu[h] s 150
···(w)ul 341

-˙wᵘol(q) (modulated prosp mod) 272, 851
···wu-l- stems (list) 360
wū-l- 255, 290
-wᵘo-˙la 272
wulelu- 242; 361
˙wu˙li (suppression of second accent before a particle or as 'our') 68
wuli 'we/us' 130, 133, 935
wuli (counter) 182
-wulwu 164, 347
¨wul˙m ye n' > wūlmyen 255
···wulu- stems 361
wu˙lum 'crying' < ¨wul- 'cry' 255, 272, 935
wu˙lwum = wulwum (···) 272, 936
-˙wᵘom (modulated subst) 267, 931, 932, 936
-˙wu.m a 936
wumcik i- 228
-˙wᵘon 272, 898, 936
-wung 164, 936
-˙wᵘo˙n i ('I/we ...') 272; 936
-wuni [DIAL] 163, 936
wuq (pseudo-adnoun) spelled wus 150, 936
wus (adnoun) < wu[h] s 149, 150, 936
wūs- 'laugh' 59, 231, 237, 288, 290; 363
wus.um (ul) wūs- 279
wuthi [DIAL] 'above' 109
···wuw- 252
···wuwe as mistaken spelling for ···wue 252
wuy (syllable) 25, 43; wuy > wi 43
wuy > wu (in Phyengan polysyllables) 26
···wuy- stems, ···wuy˙ye (inf) 466
Ww 234
-Wye··· < pye··· 57
···Y 267
/y/ (pronunciation) 24
y reduced from i: (unpronounced but retained) 252; 937
···y (triggering lenition) 55
y··· after ···y or ···i (if not added, then G) 23
'y··· 54; 'y- abbr < ˙i- (copula) 274, 937
'[y]- (suppressed abbreviated copula written '-) 274, (before 1730) 937
y··· for ny··· or ly··· 110
y··· stems reinforced after prefix or neg adv 111
···y- stems 256
-y- (formative for vc, vp) 220, 224, 225, 937
y- (reduction of cop stem before vowel) 217, 937; (as var, even after consonant) 254
¹y··· 15, 16; -¹y··· 16; ···¹y··· 125

ya = ye (cop inf) 308, 465
ya (particle): (after inf) 251; 937; (abbreviation of iya) 818; 937. SEE iya, ˙za
ya < ˙ya 'question' (postmod) 160, 195; (+ pcl ko) 213; 228, 248, 250, 257, 324, 331, 937
yak- 290; 364
yak < ˙QYAK (adnoun) 'about' 147
yak < ˙ZYAK (postnoun, adv) 'just under' 159
yāl- (preverb) 141, 938
Yale dictionary (KEd) 33
Yale Romanization 2, 4, 5, 8, 9, 13, 18, 35, 99, 100, 764
yamchi = ¹yemchi (ēps.ta) 344
yang 'the bright side' 344
(-)yang 'ocean' 133, 159, 938
yang 'Miss' (title) 132, 158
yang 'pretense; appearance; intention' 161, 938
¹yāng < ¨LYANG 'both' 148, 174, 938
¹Yang Insek 2, 330
-yass- 246
yath- 256, 363; yath.chwu 256
yātu (counter) 184
ye → ey 39
ye > yey > ey rather than metathesis? 47
ye (var of postmod ya) 257, 258
ye (cop inf) 308, 465, 939
ye··· < MK ye··· and ye··· < MK nye··· 110
···˙ye < ···i-˙e 267, 465
···ye- stems 237, 252
-ye (excess Chinese numeral) 171, 174, 940
years: counting or naming 186
yeh- [DIAL] 'put in' 112
(-)yek 'station' (category designator) 133
yekcen = yek 280
yeki (/ yoki) 134, 140, 344, 940
yeki- 283
yel- 'young, new' 151
yē-l- 315 yel.e ci- 315
yel, yelq 'ten' 175
yelamu(n) 174, 178
yele ··· 135, 149, 174, 941
ye˙leh 'several' 109, 941
yele pun 'you all' 134, 941
yeles / yele < ye˙leh/ye˙le 174, 178, 941
yeles-i 187; yelesi [DIAL] 187
yele(s) ccay as abbr of yele pen ccay 179
yel han ccay 175
yelhul; yelhul nal 185
yel-i, yelq-i 187
y-elision before ᵘo 259

yelli- 222, 315
yellup 187
yēlp-pulk- /yēlpulk-/ 102
yelq tal 186
[1]yelqto 'archipelago' (category designator) 133
yelq-twul / -twu 175
yem = (q)-yem '...itis' 171
... ˙ye (n') (substantive ~) 255
[1]yen < LYEN (pre-numeral adn; n, vnt) 149, 941
[1]yen (counter) 181
[n]yen (word) vs nyen (morpheme) 'year' 111
yēn < ¨ZYWEN (adj-n) 148
-yen hi 140
ye-nam(.)un / -nam(.)u 174, 177, 178
ye-nam(.)u ccay 179
ye(n)c- 48
[1]yeng 'zero' 174
[n]yento 'year period' 170
yenu < nyen^u/o / nyenk··· < *nyen^u/ok 239, 941
yenu(y), yeni 147, 941
y-epenthesis 237
yeph 196, 290
yes- 141, 142
yes 'six' 177
yes-or-no question 302, 667
yeses-i, yesesq-i 187
-yess- 246
yessay; yessayq nal 185
-yess.ess.keyss.nun 250
-yess.ess.tun 250
-yess.ess.ulq 250
-yess.keyss.nun 250
-yess.keyss.tun 250
-yess.nun 150
-yess.tun 249
-yess.ulq 250
yesup 187
yet-ahop 178
yetelq = yetel[p]q 175
yetel-i, yetelp-i 187
yetelp: reduced to /yetel/ 102; (> yetel(q) for most speakers) 107; 175
yetelp hay 177
yetelp-i 177
yetel[p]q tal 186
yethay 134
yetuley, yetuleyq nal 185
yetup 187
yewu < yez^u/o / yezG··· < *yes^u/ok ? < *yosok 239
/yey/ 12; (automatically replaced by ey) 109

yey (alternation of ~ [with ey]) 100; 942
/yey/ and /ley/ for lyey 110
yēy < ¨nyey 'ancient' 147, 943
yēy and nēy 'yes' < *nyēy 47, 110, 943
ye(y) ca 183
yēyceng 'intention' 161, 943
yey-niley 177, 185; yey-nilkop 177, 178
···ye yo → ···ey yo 253
yēys < yēyq ··· < ¨nyey s 147, 943
yeyswun 176
ye(y) yo (= ey yo) 310
··· '[y]˙Gem 263, 944
yGi vs y.i (= /yyi/), yGy vs yy 22
yGo, yGu 54
[1]Yi = [1]Yī < ¨LI (surname) 15
[1]Yi Cenglo 2, 132, 330, 789, 790
[1]Yi Cengmin 330
[1]Yi Congchel 108
[1]Yi Huysung 2. SEE LHS.
[1]Yi Hyosang 301, 302, 307, 326
[1]Yi Iksep 234
[1]Yi Kimun 2. SEE LKM.
[1]Yi Kitong 2, 132, 315, 321, 641
[1]Yi Mayngseng 2
[1]Yi Namtek 2
[1]Yi Pongmun 18
[1]Yi Sangek 68, 69, 72
[1]Yi Swungnyeng 2. SEE LSN.
[1]Yi Tongcay 2, 31, 218, 229, 240, 306, 656
[1]Yi Unceng 273
[1]Yi Ungpayk 13, 40, 107, 121, 122, 240, 249, 257, 671, 705
[1]Yi Yangha 1
[1]Yi Yuncay 105, 106
˙y˙la 232, 944
···y ˙'m ye (< ˙i˙m ye or ho˙m ye) 274, 945
*yo 43, 344, 946
yo pronounced as yu 25
yo (polite particle) 251, 253, 273, 280, 946
yo 'question' (postmod) 160, 946
yo (deictic) 'this' 148, 946, 947
Yō khentay ··· 334
yoki (deictic) 344, 946
yōkwu ha- 295
yoli (deictic adv) 340, 946
yolyang 'plan, intention' 161
-yōng 'use' 171
[1]Yong = [1]Yongpi echen ka = 1445 [1]Yong 61, 86; 768
Yō nun ··· 334

'you' 133, 135
younger speakers 1, 21, 25, 26, 33, 37, 43, 175
*yoy 8, 744
Yōyak hamyen ⋯ 334
'ys.non 84, 947
-yss.ess.keyss.nun 250
-yss.ess.tun, -yss.ess.ulq 250
-yss.keyss.nun, -yss.keyss.tun 250
-yss.nun 250; -yss.tun 249; -yss.ulq 250
'y˙syw^u/om 267
⋯y˙'ta < ⋯y ho˙ta 274, 947
*yu 43, 946, 947
"yu" = y + wu 29; yu for yo 25
yuch 145
^{1}Yu Changton 2. SEE LCT.
^{1}Yu Huy 7, 42, 112
yuil (~ han, ~ uy, ~ mui ⋯) 150
^{1}yuk 'six' 110
Yun Cengmi 333
*yuy 744
-ywu- < -i-wu- (formative for vc) 224, 950
⋯Y y 23; yy vs yGy 22; */yyo/, */yyu/ 54
[z] (as allophone of /s/) 29, 59; (as weakening of /c/) 29; (> -(s)-) 237
/z/ 237
z (no motivation for devoicing) 59; (immediate ancestor always s) 268; (for pcl s) 768, 951

z- and z⋯ (pronunciation unclear) 45
-z- (area where lost) 59
⋯z⋯ < lenition of s 45; < *c 45, 60; (words surviving with affricate) 60
z⋯ in nativized Chinese words 45
⋯z made onset of next syllable 54
⋯z- verb stems < *⋯z^u/o- 45; (lenited from ⋯s-, reduced to ⋯s-) 108
˙za (particle) 54, 60; (~ ˙i˙la) 273; 951
zero 6, 22, 29
zero abbreviation of copula stem 55
zero allomorphs 286
zero beginning of a syllable 8
zero circle 51
zero ending (for infinitive) 252
zero final 22
zero form of derived noun suffix 256
zero initial 22, 34, 49, 262
zero onset, zero-onset syllables 18
zG written sG 54
-˙zo (= ¨co) 240
-¨zop- (bound stem) =-¨zoW- (deferential) > -sup- (formal style) 53, 60; (< *-zo˙po- < *-oso˙po-) 85; 268-9; 952-5. SEE deferential.
-zowo- (as modulated) = -zoWwo- 271, 952
⋯ zyoo (Japanese) 151
zywoh 'mattress' 109